Interlinear Greek-English New Testament

Interlinear Greek-English New Testament

WITH A GREEK-ENGLISH LEXICON AND NEW TESTAMENT SYNONYMS

by
George Ricker Berry

KING JAMES VERSION

BAKER BOOK HOUSE
Grand Rapids, Michigan

Reprinted by Baker Book House
from the original edition issued by
Handy Book Company, Reading, Pennsylvania

Tenth printing, December 1987

Formerly published as two volumes in one binding:
The Interlinear Literal Translation of the Greek New Testament, etc.
and *A New Greek-English Lexicon to the New Testament, etc.*

ISBN: 0-8010-0700-3

Printed in the United States of America

The Value of HEBREW and GREEK to Clergymen.

---

1. Without *some* knowledge of Hebrew and Greek, you cannot understand the critical commentaries on the Scriptures, and a commentary that is *not* critical is of doubtful value.

2. Without *some* knowledge of Hebrew and Greek, you cannot satisfy yourself or those who look to you for help as to the changes which you will find in the Revised Old and New Testaments.

3. Without *some* knowledge of Hebrew and Greek, you cannot appreciate the critical discussions, now so frequent, relating to the books of the Old and New Testaments.

4. Without *some* knowledge of Hebrew and Greek, you cannot be certain, in a single instance, that in your sermon based on a Scripture text, you are presenting the correct teaching of that text.

5. Without *some* knowledge of Hebrew and Greek, you cannot be an independent student, or a reliable interpreter of the word of God.

6. As much knowledge of Hebrew can be secured, with the same method, under the same circumstances, by the same pupil, in *one* year, with the aid of the Interlinear Old Testament, as can be gained of Latin in three years. Greek, though somewhat more difficult, may be readily acquired within a brief period with the aid of the Interlinear New Testament (which contains a lexicon) and an elementary Greek grammar.

7. The Hebrew language has, in all, about 7,000 words, and of these 1,000 occur in the Old Testament over 25 times each.

8. The Hebrew grammar has but *one* form for the Relative pronoun in all cases, numbers and genders; but *three* forms for the Demonstrative pronoun. The possible verbal forms are about 300 as compared with the 1,200 found in Greek. It has practically no declension.

9. Within ten years the average man wastes more time in fruitless reading and indifferent talk, than would be used in acquiring a good working knowledge of Hebrew and Greek that in turn would impart to his teaching that quality of independence and of reliability which so greatly enhances one's power as a teacher.

10. There is not *one* minister in *ten* who might not if he but *would*, find time and opportunity for such study of Hebrew and Greek as would enable him to make a thoroughly practical use of it in his work as a Bible-preacher and Bible-teacher.

INTRODUCTION.

THERE are many ways scarcely needing mention in which the Interlinear New Testament may prove its value, not the least of which is the facility with which it enables one, even if rusty in his Greek, to put his finger on the original Greek word or phrase, and at the same instant upon a literal rendering. To many it will repay its cost in the time saved from turning to a Greek dictionary. Of course it becomes a necessary adjunct to every complete working library.

The ever-growing interest in New Testament study makes it desirable that the general reader, who would be well informed on current topics, should have some acquaintance with the relation of the standard English version to the original text, while a still more intimate knowledge on the part of the clergyman and the Bible Class teacher would seem almost imperative. Toward this end no aid is likely to be more helpful than the Interlinear New Testament.

This work is intended therefore to help the English reader of the New Testament, who may desire to refer to the actual words used in the Greek text. It has not been framed to teach people Greek, though it may be used to good advantage for that purpose.

The Interlinear Translation brings to view certain points of interest that no other translation has ever pretended to give. Take for instance the word 'master.' This word 'master' is used in the Authorized Version to translate *six* different Greek words, all bearing different shades of meaning. The word 'judgment' in the Authorized Version stands for *eight* different Greek words in the original; and so of many others. Of particles, 'but' represents *twelve* different words; 'by,' *eleven;* 'for,' *eighteen;* 'in,' *fifteen;* 'of,' *thirteen;* and 'on,' *nine.*

We do not intend to imply that a given Greek word can be, or that it is desirable that it should be, translated in all places by the same English word. On the other hand, one should be able to ascertain, on occasion, just what the facts are; and it is an interesting feature of the Interlinear New Testament that in the margin appears the English word of the Authorized Version; in the text appears the Greek original of that particular word; and immediately under it, the English word that is its nearest literal equivalent.

We give the Greek Text, with an interlinear translation as literal as may be to be useful; and in the margin the Authorized Version, divided into paragraphs to correspond to the Greek text.

This work also gives in its notes not only the various readings of six different editors of the Greek Testament, but also these variations *in English* whenever the sense is affected thereby, but without attempting to present in every case all the minute shades of meaning which a Greek scholar will attach to them. Many of these variations may be thought to be of no great importance, descending even to the different spelling of the same word ; but from this they rise to variations of the greatest importance. All are of interest, because they concern the word of God, and are here made available to the English reader, to whom we furnish in this volume all he may require both as to the *text* of the New Testament, and for its word-for-word *translation.*

THE GREEK TEXT.

The Greek Text is that of Stephens, 1550, which has long been in common use ; but as the edition of Elzevir, 1624, is the one often called the Received Text, or Textus Receptus, because of the words, "Textum . . . . ab omnibus receptum," occurring in the preface, we give the readings of this Elzevir edition in the notes, and mark them E. It is the text commonly reprinted on the Continent. In the main they are one and the same ; and either of them may be referred to as the Textus Receptus.

There are a number of minute variations between the editors which we do not attempt to present. In all these cases we have followed the majority of modern editors. With them we have also added the final ν to the third person singular and plural in σι ; third singular in ε ; in datives plural in σι, &c. For οὑτω we have given οὑτως, and αὑτοῦ where some have αὐτοῦ.

As to the *form* of the Greek text a few words are needed.

1. PARAGRAPHS.—We were disappointed in finding nothing like *authority* for where a paragraph ought to be. Ancient manuscripts were no help : they have few or no paragraphs. The editors all differed, each making paragraphs according to his own judgment. We were therefore obliged, after referring to the best examples, to form paragraphs for ourselves. We are anxious that our readers should remember that the paragraphs have *no authority*, which they might have had if the ancient manuscripts had agreed in the placing of them.

2. PARENTHESES.—Most of the editors have placed here and there parentheses in their Greek texts. These we have disregarded, seeing that there are no such things in the early Greek copies. We have placed them in the English where we deemed them necessary to preserve the sense, but not being in the Greek they also have no authority.

3. INVERTED COMMAS.—Some editors mark with inverted commas the words that are spoken, and others in a similar way mark the quotations from the Old Testament. But in some places it is doubtful where these quotations close, and it was thought best to omit them. These also, being absent from the ancient Greek copies, have no authority.

4. POINTS.—There is no authority anywhere for the punctuation. There are few or no points in the ancient copies, and editors naturally differ in their system of pointing. We have been obliged to punctuate for ourselves as we judged

best. We have not attempted to note the difference in the punctuation of the various editors, except in places where it materially alters the sense.

5. CAPITALS.—The only remark needed here is in reference to the names of God, of Christ, and of the Holy Spirit. The greatest difficulty is touching the word 'Spirit.' In some places it is very difficult to say whether the Holy Spirit as a person or the spirit of the Christian is referred to (see Rom. viii. 9); and if sometimes a small letter and sometimes a capital had been placed to the word πνεῦμα, in the Greek, persons would naturally have concluded that the question was thus indisputably settled. It was therefore judged best to put a small π everywhere. In the English we have been obliged to put a capital S when the Holy Spirit was referred to and so have retained it wherever we thought this was the case; but in some places it is really doubtful, and becomes a question for the spiritual judgment of the reader. The Greek will not help in the difficulty, because in the earliest copies every letter was a capital. In the other names we have followed the usage of modern editors; putting in the Greek a capital to Jesus but a small letter for Christ, and a small letter for Lord and for God.

6. VERSES.—In a few places it is doubtful where the verses should commence. In these cases we have followed Bruder's "Greek Concordance," though that work does not in all cases agree with itself.

THE INTERLINEAR TRANSLATION.

1. The plan. The Greek words have always been kept in their right order, and where the interlinear English would not make sense in the same order, the words have been numbered to show how they must be read. Thus, "And [7]related [8]to [9]them [2]also [1]those [3]who [4]had [5]seen [[6]it]" (Luke viii. 36) are numbered so as to read "And those also who had seen [it] related to them."

To prevent this numbering, and transposition in reading, being increased unnecessarily, a few words are often made into a phrase. This has been done at the commencement of each sentence, where needed, two or more words being joined with a *low* hyphen. Thus, instead of

Ἐγένετο δὲ		Ἐγένετο-δὲ.
[2]it [3]came [4]to [5]pass [1]and	we have printed	And it came to pass.

The words in brackets [ ] are what have been added in the English to complete the sense where there is no word in the Greek to correspond to the words added.

Where a Greek word occurs which the English idiom requires should *not* be translated, the word stands alone with no English word under it: as ὅτι, 'that,' in Mark xii. 7; and οὐ in verse 14, where there are *two* negatives, which, if both were translated, would in English destroy one another; and so of μή, where it simply marks the sentence as a question.

In a few places we have been obliged to put a double translation, mostly because of the double negatives used in the Greek, where they do not immediately follow one another, and so could not be translated by such strengthened expressions as 'not at all,' 'in no wise,' &c. In such cases we have placed a literal translation below the one required in English. Thus—

οὐδὲν.
anything.
(*lit.* nothing.)

2. Points of grammar. *The Aorist.* This tense of the Greek verb has been at all times the most difficult to deal with, being translated, in the Authorized version (and by others), sometimes by the *present*, sometimes by the *past*, sometimes by the *future*, and sometimes by the *perfect.* Grammarians say that, in the main, it is the *indefinite past*, and we have endeavored, as far as may be, to keep it to this, avoiding, except in a few places, the translation of it as a perfect. We all know what stress is often laid—and rightly so—upon the word 'have.' If I say, 'he *has* cleansed me,' it is more than saying 'he cleansed me.' The former expression indicates the *perfect*, and implies a continuance of the act, or its effects, to the present time; whereas the latter speaks of an act at some time in the past, without anything being implied as to its continuance.

For this reason it appeared unadvisable to translate the aorist as the perfect, except in a few places where the true sense would otherwise have been destroyed. It is true that the English idiom requires it elsewhere, but it was thought best to preserve the above distinction. An extreme case will illustrate this point. In 1 Corinthians v. 9 occurs the word ἔγραψα, 'I wrote;' and in verse 11 the same word precisely—'I wrote;' but the Authorized Version (and others) put for the *latter* 'I have written.' It is there accompanied with the word 'now'—'now I have written.' This is needed for good English; we have put 'I wrote' in both places, but have placed a comma after the word 'now' to make it read more smoothly. We preserve this uniformity for the sake of literalness, always remembering the fact of the Authorized Version being in proximity, which will make all plain in such instances.

In a few places we have translated the aorist as a *present* where the sense demanded it. As, for instance, ἔγνω, in 2 Timothy ii. 19: "The Lord *knows* those that are his," instead of "the Lord knew," &c.

The Imperfect. This is mostly translated as 'I was writing,' or 'I wrote.' But there are a few places where this tense is said to have a different meaning. This will be best illustrated by the much-disputed passage in Romans ix. 3: "For *I could wish* that myself were accursed from Christ for my brethren." Here the word for 'I could wish' is in the imperfect. If the learned were agreed as to a translation we should have kept to the same, but while some translate 'I could wish,' as a *conditional present*, others give 'I could have wished' as a *conditional past.* We have thought it best to keep the sense of the simple imperfect as referred by Winer to this passage. "*I felt a wish*, and should do so still, could it be gratified . . . . (a conditional clause being understood)." We have put "I was wishing."

The Perfect. This we have kept as uniform as we could, implying an act perfected, but continuing to the present in itself or its consequences. In a few places we have translated it as a *present:* as in Matthew xii. 47, in the sense of 'they have stood and still *are standing.*'

The Subjunctive. In this mood perhaps we have deviated further from ordinary practice than in any other, but we have endeavored, as far as practicable, to keep it distinct from both the English *imperative* and the Greek *future.* Thus in Romans xiii. 9 for *οὐ φονεύσεις* (future indicative) we have, 'thou shalt not commit murder;' but in James ii. 11, for *μὴ φονεύσῃς* (aorist subjunctive) 'thou mayest not commit murder.'

THE PRONOUNS. At times it is important to know whether the pronouns are emphatic or not. *ἐγὼ γράφω* and *γράφω* are both 'I write;' but where the *ἐγώ* is put in the Greek, it makes the pronoun emphatic. This however is somewhat due to the writer's style, and in John's Gospel and Epistles, it has been judged that, from his peculiar style of composition, he puts in the pronouns where emphasis is not always intended. John ix. 27 gives a good example of the same verb with and without the pronoun in the Greek: "Why again do ye wish to hear? do *ye* also wish to become his disciples?"

COMPOUND WORDS. It was found impracticable to translate these uniformly throughout. For instance, if *γνῶσις* be translated 'knowledge,' it might be thought that *ἐπίγνωσις* should be 'full knowledge,' &c.: but on referring to a Concordance it will be seen that the latter word cannot be intensified in all places, and then to translate it by 'knowledge' in some places, and 'full knowledge' in others looks too much like interpretation. We have therefore translated both words by 'knowledge.' In the few places however where one of each of such words occurs in the same sentence, some distinction was imperative.

THE NOTES.

The references to the notes are marked thus in the text [a]*αὐτοῦ*[a]: the mark[a] showing how far the variation extends. In a few places a note occurs *within* a note. If words are to be omitted or transposed by some editors but not by others, these latter may want to alter a word in the sentence. In such cases *one tick* shows the termination of the *inner* note. Thus [a] . . . . [b] . . . [b'] . . . . [a] See notes [v] and [w] Matthew v. 44.

This mark — stands for *omit;* and + for *add;* but in some places all the editors do *not* actually omit, some putting the word in brackets as *doubtful.* In that case it is put thus, "—*αὐτοῦ* [L] TTr"; which means that Lachmann marks the word as *doubtful*, and Tischendorf and Tregelles *omit* it. In some cases, *all* mark a word as doubtful, and then it could be put either thus, *δὲ* [LTTr], or [*δὲ*] LTTr; we have adopted the latter plan. In some places the editors mark *part* of a word as doubtful, mostly in compound words. See for instance [*ἐκ*]*διώξουσιν* read by TrA in Luke xi. 49.

It will be seen by this that the marks [ ] *applied to the Greek or the editors* in the notes always refer to readings which the editors point out as doubtful. They must not be confounded with the same marks *in the English* text and notes, which always point out that there is *no* corresponding word in the Greek.

INTRODUCTION.

In some places where a word is added by the editors, another English word is added in the note to show the *connection* of the new word. Thus in Luke xv. 2, the word 'both' is added; but it falls between the words 'the' and 'Pharisees,' therefore it is put thus in the note "+ τε both (the) LTTrA" to show that it must be read 'both the Pharisees.' Slight variations in the use of the parenthesis occur in the course of the work, but we trust the meaning intended will in all cases be plain to the student.

Where long pieces are to be omitted they are marked in the text where they commence and where they end, but in the notes the first word or two only and the last are named with . . . between. Thus in Luke ix. 55, note [s] stands, [s]—καὶ εἶπεν (*verse* 55) . . . . σῶσαι (verse 56) LTTrA;—ὁ γὰρ . . . . σῶσαι G. The four editors omit the whole twenty words; but G omits only the last twelve. In Luke xxiv. 10, note [r] is thus, [r] + ἡ the [. . .], implying that *some* word must be added.

We have endeavored to make the notes as plain as possible for the English reader. One point still needs to be explained. For instance, in Luke vii. 22 occur the words "and [2]answering [1]Jesus said;" but a note omits the word 'Jesus,' and then it must be read (as stated in the note) "and answering he said." This is because the word εἶπεν (as already explained) stands for both 'he said,' and 'said.' Also in verse 27 occur the words ἐγὼ ἀποστέλλω, 'I send,' but a note omits the word ἐγὼ, 'I,' and then ἀποστέλλω is to be read 'I send,' but without emphasis on the 'I.'

The Money and Measures of the New Testament.

1. Money. It was deemed better not to attempt to *translate* the sums of money named in the New Testament, as we have no corresponding pieces to those then in use. We have therefore used the Greek words untranslated, and give a list of them here. It is not without interest and instruction to know the approximate value of money and the extent of the measures used. For instance, in Revelation vi. 6 we read of "a measure of wheat for a penny" in the Authorized Version; but this leaves the reader in doubt as to how far it speaks of scarcity and dearness. We want at least to know the value of the 'penny,' and the capacity of the 'measure.'

The following lists, it is hoped, will be useful; but approximate values only can now be arrived at.

GREEK.	AUTHORIZED VERSION.	IN THIS WORK.	APPROXIMATE VALUE. $
λεπτόν	mite	lepton	0.001875
κοδράντης	farthing	kodrantes	0.00375
ἀσσάριον	farthing	assarion	0.015
δηνάριον	penny	denarius	0.16
δραχμή	piece of silver	drachma	0.16
δίδραχμον	tribute money	didrachma	0.32

INTRODUCTION.

GREEK.	AUTHORIZED VERSION.	IN THIS WORK.	APPROXIMATE VALUE.
			$
στατήρ	piece of money	stater	00.64
μνάα	pound	mina	15.75
τάλαντον	talent	talent	943.66

ἀργύριον piece of silver. This is the common word for silver and money, as *l'argent* in French. In different places it would represent wholly different coins.

2. Measures of Capacity.

GREEK.	AUTHORIZED VERSION.	IN THIS WORK.	APPROXIMATE. Gallon.	Pint.
ξέστης	pot (liquid measure)	vessels*	0	1
χοῖνιξ	measure (dry ")	chœnix	0	2
μόδιος	bushel (dry ")	corn measure*	2	0
σάτον	measure (dry ")	seah	2	1
βάτος	measure (liquid ")	bath	7	4
μετρητής	firkin (liquid ")	metretes	8	4
κόρος	measure (dry ")	cor	64	1

It is judged that those marked * are referréd to as measures independent of their capacity: such as "washing of vessels," &c.

3. Long Measure. Here the names already in use were near enough to be retained.

			Feet.	Inches.
πῆχυς	cubit	cubit	1	6 to 9
ὀργυιά	fathom	fathom	6	0
στάδιον	furlong	furlong	606	9
μίλιον	mile	mile	4854	0
ὁδὸς σαββάτου	sabbath day's journey	6 furlongs		

LIST OF SIGNS AND EDITIONS USED.

E Elzevir, 1624.
G Griesbach, 1805.
L Lachmann, 1842–1850.
T Tischendorf, Eighth Edition, 1865–1872.
Tr Tregelles, 1857–1872.
A Alford, vol. i. 1868; vol. ii. 1871; vol. iii. 1865; vol. iv. 1862, 1870.
W Wordsworth, 1870.
+ signifies *an addition.*
— ,, *an omission.*
[ ] ,, in the interlinear translation, that there is *no Greek word* corresponding to the English.
[ ] signifies in the notes that an editor marks the reading as *doubtful.*
ǁ ,, how far the variation in the Greek text extends.
Text. Rec. refers to *both* Stephens 1550 and E.

[a]ΤΟ ΚΑΤΑ ΜΑΤΘΑΙΟΝ ΑΓΙΟΝ ΕΥΑΓΓΕΛΙΟΝ.‖
THE [4]ACCORDING [5]TO [6]MATTHEW [1]HOLY [2]GLAD [3]TIDINGS

ΒΙΒΛΟΣ γενέσεως Ἰησοῦ χριστοῦ, υἱοῦ [b]Δαβίδ,‖ υἱοῦ
BOOK of [the] generation of Jesus Christ, son of David, son
Ἀβραάμ.
of Abraham.
2 Ἀβραὰμ ἐγέννησεν τὸν Ἰσαάκ· Ἰσαὰκ.δὲ ἐγέννησεν τὸν
Abraham begat Isaac; and Isaac begat
Ἰακώβ· Ἰακὼβ.δὲ ἐγέννησεν τὸν Ἰούδαν καὶ τοὺς ἀδελφοὺς
Jacob; and Jacob begat Judas and [2]brethren
αὐτοῦ· 3 Ἰούδας.δὲ ἐγέννησεν τὸν Φαρὲς καὶ τὸν Ζαρὰ ἐκ
[1]his; and Judas begat Phares and Zara of
τῆς Θαμάρ· Φαρὲς.δὲ ἐγέννησεν τὸν Ἐσρώμ· Ἐσρὼμ.δὲ
Thamar; and Phares begat Esrom; and Esrom
ἐγέννησεν τὸν Ἀράμ· 4 Ἀρὰμ.δὲ ἐγέννησεν τὸν [c]Ἀμιναδάβ·‖
begat Aram; and Aram begat Aminadab;
[c]Ἀμιναδὰβ‖.δὲ ἐγέννησεν τὸν Ναασσών· Ναασσὼν.δὲ ἐγέννη-
and Aminadab begat Naasson; and Naasson be-
σεν τὸν Σαλμών· 5 Σαλμὼν.δὲ ἐγέννησεν τὸν [d]Βοὸζ‖ ἐκ τῆς
gat Salmon; and Salmon begat Booz of
Ῥαχάβ· [d]Βοὸζ‖.δὲ ἐγέννησεν τὸν [e]Ὠβὴδ‖ ἐκ τῆς Ῥούθ· [e]Ὠβὴδ‖
Rachab; and Booz begat Obed of Ruth; [2]Obed
δὲ ἐγέννησεν τὸν Ἰεσσαί· 6 Ἰεσσαὶ.δὲ ἐγέννησεν τὸν [b]Δαβὶδ‖
[1]and begat Jesse; and Jesse begat David
τὸν βασιλέα. [b]Δαβὶδ‖.δὲ [f]ὁ βασιλεὺς‖ ἐγέννησεν τὸν [g]Σολο-
the king. And David the king begat Solo-
μῶντα‖ ἐκ τῆς τοῦ Οὐρίου· 7 Σολομὼν.δὲ ἐγέν-
mon of the [one who had been wife] of Urias; and Solomon be-
νησεν τὸν Ῥοβοάμ· Ῥοβοὰμ.δὲ ἐγέννησεν τὸν Ἀβιά· Ἀβιὰ
gat Roboam; and Roboam begat Abia; [2]Abia
δὲ ἐγέννησεν τὸν [h]Ἀσά·‖ 8 [h]Ἀσὰ‖.δὲ ἐγέννησεν τὸν Ἰωσαφάτ·
[1]and begat Asa; and Asa begat Josaphat;
Ἰωσαφὰτ.δὲ ἐγέννησεν τὸν Ἰωράμ· Ἰωρὰμ δὲ ἐγέννησεν τὸν
and Josaphat begat Joram; and Joram begat
[i]Ὀζίαν· 9 [j]Ὀζίας‖.δὲ ἐγέννησεν τὸν Ἰωάθαμ· Ἰωάθαμ.δὲ
Ozias; and Ozias begat Joatham; and Joatham
ἐγέννησεν τὸν Ἄχαζ· Ἄχαζ.δὲ ἐγέννησεν τὸν [k]Ἐζεκίαν·‖
begat Achaz; and Achaz begat Ezekias;
10 [l]Ἐζεκίας‖.δὲ ἐγέννησεν τὸν Μανασσῆ· Μανασσῆς.δὲ ἐγέν-
and Ezekias begat Manasses; and Manasses be-
νησεν τὸν [m]Ἀμών‖· [m]Ἀμὼν‖.δὲ ἐγέννησεν τὸν [n]Ἰωσίαν·‖
gat Amon; and Amon begat Josias;
11 [o]Ἰωσίας‖.δὲ ἐγέννησεν τὸν Ἰεχονίαν καὶ τοὺς ἀδελφοὺς
and Josias begat Jechonias and [2]brethren
αὐτοῦ, ἐπὶ τῆς μετοικεσίας Βαβυλῶνος. 12 Μετὰ.δὲ
[1]his, at [the time] of the carrying away of Babylon. And after

**THE book of the gen-
eration of Jesus Christ,
the son of David, the
son of Abraham.**

**2 Abraham begat
Isaac; and Isaac be-
gat Jacob; and Jacob
begat Judas and his
brethren; 3 and Judas
begat Phares and Zara
of Thamar; and Pha-
res begat Esrom; and
Esrom begat Aram;
4 and Aram begat A-
minadab; and Ami-
nadab begat Naasson;
and Naasson begat
Salmon; 5 and Salmon
begat Booz of Rachab;
and Booz begat Obed
of Ruth; and Obed
begat Jesse; 6 and
Jesse begat David the
king; and David the
king begat Solomon
of her *that had been
the wife* of Urias;
7 and Solomon begat
Roboam; and Roboam
begat Abia; and Abia
begat Asa; 8 and Asa
begat Josaphat; and
Josaphat begat Jo-
ram; and Joram begat
Ozias; 9 and Ozias
begat Joatham; and
Joatham begat A-
chaz; and Achaz be-
gat Ezekias; 10 and
Ezekias begat Manas-
ses; and Manasses be-
gat Amon; and Amon
begat Josias; 11 and
Josias begat Jechonias
and his brethren, about
the time they were
carried away to Ba-
bylon: 12 and after**

---

[a] Εὐαγγέλιον κατὰ Μαθθαῖον (Ματθ. GW) GLTrW; [Εὐαγ.] κατὰ Μαθθ. A; κατὰ Μαθθ. T.
[b] Δαυῒδ GW; Δαυεὶδ LTTrA. [c] Ἀμειναδάβ A. [d] Βοὸς LTr; Βοὲς TA. [e] Ἰωβὴδ LTTrA.
[f] — ὁ βασιλεὺς LTTrA. [g] Σολομῶνα GTTrAW. [h] Ἀσάφ LTTrA. [i] Ὀζείαν LTTrA.
[j] Ὀζείας LTTrA. [k] Ἐζεκείαν L. [l] Ἐζεκείας L. [m] Ἀμώς LTTrA. [n] Ἰωσείαν LTTrA.
[o] Ἰωσείας LTTrA.

they were brought to Babylon, Jechonias begat Salathiel; and Salathiel begat Zorobabel; 13 and Zorobabel begat Abiud; and Abiud begat Eliakim; and Eliakim begat Azor; 14 and Azor begat Sadoc; and Sadoc begat Achim; and Achim begat Eliud; 15 and Eliud begat Eleazar; and Eleazar begat Matthan; and Matthan begat Jacob; 16 and Jacob begat Joseph the husband of Mary, of whom was born Jesus, who is called Christ.

17 So all the generations from Abraham to David *are* fourteen generations; and from David until the carrying away into Babylon *are* fourteen generations; and from the carrying away into Babylon unto Christ *are* fourteen generations.

18 Now the birth of Jesus Christ was on this wise: When as his mother Mary was espoused to Joseph, before they came together, she was found with child of the Holy Ghost. 19 Then Joseph her husband, being a just *man*, and not willing to make her a public example, was minded to put her away privily. 20 But while he thought on these things, behold, the angel of the Lord appeared unto him in a dream, saying, Joseph, thou son of David, fear not to take unto thee Mary thy wife: for that which is conceived in her is of the Holy Ghost. 21 And she shall bring forth a son, and thou shalt call his name JESUS: for he shall save his people from their sins. 22 Now all this was done, that it might be fulfilled which was spoken of the Lord by the prophet, saying, 23 Behold, a virgin shall be with child, and shall bring forth a son, and they shall

την μετοικεσίαν Βαβυλῶνος, Ἰεχονίας [q]ἐγέννησεν[||] τὸν Σαλα-
the carrying away of Babylon, Jechonias begat Sala-
θιήλ· Σαλαθιὴλ.δὲ [q]ἐγέννησεν[||] τὸν Ζοροβάβελ· 13 Ζοροβά-
thiel; and Salathiel begat Zorobabel; [2]Zoroba-
βελ δὲ [q]ἐγέννησεν[||] τὸν Ἀβιούδ· Ἀβιοὺδ.δὲ ἐγέννησεν τὸν
bel [1]and begat Abiud; and Abiud begat
Ἐλιακείμ· Ἐλιακεὶμ.δὲ ἐγέννησεν τὸν Ἀζώρ· 14 Ἀζὼρ.δὲ
Eliakim; and Eliakim begat Azor; and Azor
ἐγέννησεν τὸν Σαδώκ· Σαδὼκ.δὲ ἐγέννησεν τὸν Ἀχείμ· Ἀχεὶμ
begat Sadoc; and Sadoc begat Achim; [2]Achim
δὲ ἐγέννησεν τὸν Ἐλιούδ· 15 Ἐλιοὺδ.δὲ ἐγέννησεν τὸν Ἐλεά-
[1]and begat Eliud; and Eliud begat Elea-
ζαρ· Ἐλεάζαρ.δὲ ἐγέννησεν τὸν [r]Ματθάν·[||] [r]Ματθὰν[||].δὲ ἐγέν-
zar; and Eleazar begat Matthan; and Matthan be-
νησεν τὸν Ἰακώβ· 16 Ἰακὼβ.δὲ ἐγέννησεν τὸν Ἰωσὴφ τὸν
gat Jacob; and Jacob begat Joseph the
ἄνδρα Μαρίας, ἐξ ἧς ἐγεννήθη Ἰησοῦς ὁ λεγόμενος χριστός.
husband of Mary, of whom was born Jesus, who is called Christ.
17 Πᾶσαι.οὖν αἱ γενεαὶ ἀπὸ Ἀβραὰμ ἕως [s]Δαβὶδ[||]
So all the generations from Abraham to David [were]
γενεαὶ δεκατέσσαρες· καὶ ἀπὸ [s]Δαβὶδ[||] ἕως τῆς μετοικεσίας
[2]generations [1]fourteen; and from David until the carrying away
Βαβυλῶνος, γενεαὶ δεκατέσσαρες· καὶ ἀπὸ τῆς μετοικεσίας
of Babylon, [2]generations [1]fourteen; and from the carrying away
Βαβυλῶνος ἕως τοῦ χριστοῦ, γενεαὶ δεκατέσσαρες.
of Babylon to the Christ, [2]generations [1]fourteen.
18 Τοῦ.δὲ.[t]Ἰησοῦ[||] χριστοῦ ἡ [v]γέννησις[||] οὕτως ἦν. Μνη-
Now of Jesus Christ the birth thus was. [5]Having
στευθείσης [w]γὰρ[||] τῆς.μητρὸς.αὐτοῦ Μαρίας τῷ Ἰωσήφ, πρὶν.ἢ
[6]been [7]betrothed [1]for [3]his [4]mother [2]Mary to Joseph, before
συνελθεῖν αὐτοὺς εὑρέθη ἐν.γαστρὶ.ἔχουσα ἐκ πνεύματος
[2]came [3]together [1]they she was found to be with child of [the] [2]Spirit
ἁγίου. 19 Ἰωσὴφ.δὲ ὁ.ἀνὴρ.αὐτῆς, δίκαιος ὤν, καὶ μὴ θέλων
[1]Holy. But Joseph her husband, [2]righteous [1]being, and not willing
αὐτὴν [x]παραδειγματίσαι,[||] ἐβουλήθη [y]λάθρα[||] ἀπολῦσαι αὐτήν.
her to expose publicly, purposed secretly to put [2]away [1]her.
20 ταῦτα.δὲ αὐτοῦ.ἐνθυμηθέντος, ἰδού, ἄγγελος κυρίου
And [5]these [6]things [1]when [2]he [3]had [4]pondered, behold, an angel of [the] Lord
κατ' ὄναρ ἐφάνη αὐτῷ, λέγων, Ἰωσήφ, υἱὸς [s]Δαβίδ,[||] μὴ
in a dream appeared to him, saying, Joseph, son of David, [2]not
φοβηθῇς παραλαβεῖν Μαριὰμ τὴν.γυναῖκά.σου· τὸ.γὰρ ἐν
[1]fear to take to [thee] Mary thy wife, for that which in
αὐτῇ γεννηθὲν ἐκ πνεύματός ἐστιν ἁγίου. 21 τέξεται.δὲ υἱόν,
her is begotten [2]of [[3]the] [5]Spirit [1]is [4]Holy. And she shall bring forth a son,
καὶ καλέσεις τὸ.ὄνομα.αὐτοῦ Ἰησοῦν· αὐτὸς.γὰρ σώσει τὸν
and thou shalt call his name Jesus; for he shall save
λαὸν αὐτοῦ ἀπὸ τῶν.ἁμαρτιῶν.αὐτῶν. 22 Τοῦτο.δὲ ὅλον
[2]people [1]his from their sins. Now this all
γέγονεν, ἵνα πληρωθῇ τὸ ῥηθὲν ὑπὸ [z]τοῦ[||] κυρίου
came to pass, that might be fulfilled that which was spoken by the Lord
διὰ τοῦ προφήτου, λέγοντος, 23 Ἰδοὺ ἡ παρθένος ἐν
through the prophet, saying, Behold, the virgin [3]with
γαστρὶ.ἕξει καὶ τέξεται υἱόν, καὶ καλέσουσιν τὸ ὄνομα
[4]child [1]shall [2]be, and shall bring forth a son, and they shall call [2]name

[q] γεννᾷ begets A. [r] Μαθθάν LTTrA. [s] Δαυίδ GW; Δαυείδ LTTrA. [t] — Ἰησοῦ Tr. [v] γένεσις GLTTrAW. [w] — γὰρ for LTTr[A]. [x] δειγματίσαι LTTrA. [y] λάθρᾳ L. [z] — τοῦ (read | the |) LTTrAW.

αὐτοῦ Ἐμμανουήλ, ὅ ἐστιν μεθερμηνευόμενον, Μεθ' ἡμῶν
[1]his Emmanuel, which is, being interpreted, [2]With [3]us
[a]ὁ‖ θεός. 24 [b]Διεγερθεὶς‖.δὲ [c]ὁ‖ Ἰωσὴφ ἀπὸ τοῦ ὕπνου, ἐποί-
[1]God. And [2]having [3]been [4]aroused [1]Joseph from the sleep, did
ησεν ὡς προσέταξεν αὐτῷ ὁ ἄγγελος κυρίου· καὶ παρέλαβεν
as had ordered him the angel of [the] Lord, and took to [him]
τὴν.γυναῖκα.αὐτοῦ, 25 καὶ οὐκ.ἐγίνωσκεν αὐτὴν ἕως οὗ
his wife, and knew not her until
ἔτεκεν [d]τὸν‖ υἱὸν [e]αὐτῆς τὸν πρωτότοκον‖ καὶ ἐκάλεσεν
she brought forth [2]son [1]her the firstborn; and he called
τὸ.ὄνομα.αὐτοῦ Ἰησοῦν.
his name Jesus.

2 Τοῦ.δὲ.Ἰησοῦ γεννηθέντος ἐν Βηθλεὲμ τῆς Ἰουδαίας,
Now Jesus having been born in Bethlehem of Judæa,
ἐν ἡμέραις Ἡρῴδου τοῦ βασιλέως, ἰδού, μάγοι ἀπὸ ἀνατολῶν
in [the] days of Herod the king, behold, magi from [the] east
παρεγένοντο εἰς Ἱεροσόλυμα, 2 λέγοντες, Ποῦ ἐστιν ὁ τεχ-
arrived at Jerusalem, saying, Where is he who has
θεὶς βασιλεὺς τῶν Ἰουδαίων; εἴδομεν γὰρ αὐτοῦ τὸν ἀστέρα
been born King of the Jews? for we saw his star
ἐν τῇ ἀνατολῇ, καὶ ἤλθομεν προσκυνῆσαι αὐτῷ. 3 Ἀκούσας
in the east, and are come to do homage to him. [5]Having [6]heard
δὲ [f]Ἡρῴδης ὁ βασιλεὺς‖ ἐταράχθη, καὶ πᾶσα Ἱεροσόλυμα
[1]but [2]Herod [3]the [4]king he was troubled, and all Jerusalem
μετ' αὐτοῦ· 4 καὶ συναγαγὼν πάντας τοὺς ἀρχιερεῖς καὶ
with him. And having gathered together all the chief priests and
γραμματεῖς τοῦ λαοῦ, ἐπυνθάνετο παρ' αὐτῶν, ποῦ ὁ χριστὸς
scribes of the people, he inquired of them where the Christ
γεννᾶται. 5 Οἱ.δὲ [g]εἶπον‖ αὐτῷ, Ἐν Βηθλεὲμ τῆς Ἰουδαίας·
should be born. And they said to him, In Bethlehem of Judæa:
οὕτως.γὰρ γέγραπται διὰ τοῦ προφήτου, 6 Καὶ σὺ Βηθλεέμ,
for thus it has been written by the prophet, And thou, Bethlehem,
γῆ Ἰούδα, οὐδαμῶς ἐλαχίστη εἶ ἐν τοῖς ἡγεμόσιν Ἰούδα· ἐκ
land of Juda, in no wise least art among the governors of Juda, [2]out
σοῦ γὰρ ἐξελεύσεται ἡγούμενος, ὅστις ποιμανεῖ τὸν.λαόν.μου
[3]of [4]thee [1]for shall go forth a leader, who shall shepherd my people
τὸν Ἰσραήλ. 7 Τότε Ἡρῴδης [h]λάθρα‖ καλέσας τοὺς μάγους,
Israel. Then Herod, [2]secretly [1]having called the magi,
ἠκρίβωσεν παρ' αὐτῶν τὸν χρόνον τοῦ φαινομένου ἀστέρος·
inquired accurately of them the time of the [2]appearing [1]star.
8 καὶ πέμψας αὐτοὺς εἰς Βηθλεὲμ εἶπεν, Πορευθέντες [i]ἀκρι-
And having sent them to Bethlehem, he said, Having gone, accu-
βῶς ἐξετάσατε‖ περὶ τοῦ παιδίου· ἐπὰν.δὲ εὕρητε,
rately inquire for the little child; and when ye shall have found [him]
ἀπαγγείλατέ μοι, ὅπως κἀγὼ ἐλθὼν προσκυνήσω αὐτῷ.
bring word back to me, that I also having come may do homage to him.
9 Οἱ.δὲ ἀκούσαντες τοῦ βασιλέως ἐπορεύθησαν· καὶ ἰδού, ὁ
And they having heard the king, went away; and behold, the
ἀστήρ, ὃν εἶδον ἐν τῇ ἀνατολῇ, προῆγεν αὐτοὺς ἕως ἐλθὼν
star, which they saw in the east, went before them, until having come
[k]ἔστη‖ ἐπάνω οὗ ἦν τὸ παιδίον. 10 ἰδόντες.δὲ τὸν ἀστέρα,
it stood over where was the little child. And having seen the star,
ἐχάρησαν χαρὰν μεγάλην σφόδρα· 11 καὶ ἐλθόντες εἰς
they rejoiced [with] joy [2]great [1]exceedingly. And having come into

call his name Emmanuel, which being interpreted is, God with us. 24 Then Joseph being raised from sleep did as the angel of the Lord had bidden him, and took unto him his wife: 25 and knew her not till she had brought forth her firstborn son: and he called his name JESUS.

II. Now when Jesus was born in Bethlehem of Judæa in the days of Herod the king, behold, there came wise men from the east to Jerusalem, 2 saying, Where is he that is born King of the Jews? for we have seen his star in the east, and are come to worship him. 3 When Herod the king had heard *these things*, he was troubled, and all Jerusalem with him. 4 And when he had gathered all the chief priests and scribes of the people together, he demanded of them where Christ should be born. 5 And they said unto him, In Bethlehem of Judæa: for thus it is written by the prophet, 6 And thou Bethlehem, *in* the land of Juda, art not the least among the princes of Juda: for out of thee shall come a Governor, that shall rule my people Israel. 7 Then Herod, when he had privily called the wise men, inquired of them diligently what time the star appeared. 8 And he sent them to Bethlehem, and said, Go and search diligently for the young child; and when ye have found *him*, bring me word again, that I may come and worship him also. 9 When they had heard the king, they departed; and, lo, the star, which they saw in the east, went before them, till it came and stood over where the young child was. 10 When they saw the star, they rejoiced with exceeding great joy. 11 And when they

[a] — ὁ L. [b] ἐγερθεὶς having risen LTTrA. [c] — ὁ T. [d] — τὸν (*read* a son) LTTrA. [e] — αὐτῆς τὸν πρωτότοκον LTTrA. [f] ὁ βασιλεὺς Ἡρῴδης LTTrA. [g] εἶπαν T. [h] λάθρᾳ L. [i] ἐξετάσατε ἀκριβῶς LTTrA. [k] ἐστάθη LTTrA.

were come into the
house, they saw the
young child with Mary
his mother, and fell
down, and worshipped
him: and when they
had opened their trea-
sures, they presented
unto him gifts; gold,
and frankincense, and
myrrh. 12 And being
warned of God in a
dream that they
should not return to
Herod, they departed
into their own coun-
try another way.

13 And when they
were departed, behold,
the angel of the Lord
appeareth to Joseph in
a dream, saying, Arise,
and take the young
child and his mother,
and flee into Egypt,
and be thou there until
I bring thee word: for
Herod will seek the
young child to destroy
him. 14 When he arose,
he took the young
child and his mother
by night, and departed
into Egypt: 15 and was
there until the death
of Herod: that it might
be fulfilled which was
spoken of the Lord by
the prophet, saying,
Out of Egypt have I
called my son. 16 Then
Herod, when he saw
that he was mocked of
the wise men, was ex-
ceeding wroth, and
sent forth, and slew
all the children that
were in Bethlehem,
and in all the coasts
thereof, from two
years old and under,
according to the time
which he had diligent-
ly inquired of the wise
men. 17 Then was ful-
filled that which was
spoken by Jeremy the
prophet, saying, 18 In
Rama was there a voice
heard, lamentation,
and weeping, and great
mourning, Rachel
weeping *for* her chil-
dren, and would not
be comforted, because
they are not.

19 But when Herod
was dead, behold, an
angel of the Lord ap-
peareth in a dream
to Joseph in Egypt,
20 saying, Arise, and
take the young child
and his mother, and go

τὴν οἰκίαν, [l]εὗρον‖ τὸ παιδίον μετὰ Μαρίας τῆς-μητρὸς-αὐτοῦ,
the house, they found the little child with Mary his mother,
καὶ πεσόντες προσεκύνησαν αὐτῷ καὶ ἀνοίξαντες τοὺς
and having fallen down did homage to him: and having opened
θησαυροὺς αὐτῶν προσήνεγκαν αὐτῷ δῶρα, χρυσὸν καὶ
[2]treasures [1]their they offered to him gifts; gold and
λίβανον καὶ σμύρναν. 12 καὶ χρηματισθέντες κατ'
frankincense and myrrh. And having been divinely instructed in
ὄναρ μὴ ἀνακάμψαι πρὸς Ἡρώδην, δι' ἄλλης ὁδοῦ
a dream not to return to Herod, by another way
ἀνεχώρησαν εἰς τὴν-χώραν-αὐτῶν.
they withdrew into their own country.

13 Ἀναχωρησάντων-δὲ αὐτῶν, ἰδού, ἄγγελος κυρίου
Now [2]having [3]withdrawn [1]they, behold, an angel of [the] Lord
[m]φαίνεται κατ' ὄναρ‖ τῷ Ἰωσήφ, λέγων, Ἐγερθεὶς παράλαβε
appears in a dream to Joseph, saying, Having risen take with [thee]
τὸ παιδίον καὶ τὴν-μητέρα-αὐτοῦ, καὶ φεῦγε εἰς Αἴγυπτον,
the little child and his mother, and flee into Egypt,
καὶ ἴσθι ἐκεῖ ἕως ἂν εἴπω σοί· μέλλει γὰρ Ἡρώδης ζητεῖν τὸ
and be there until I shall tell thee; [3]is [4]about [1]for [2]Herod to seek the
παιδίον, τοῦ ἀπολέσαι αὐτό. 14 Ὁ-δὲ ἐγερθεὶς παρέλαβεν
little child, to destroy him. And he having risen took with [him]
τὸ παιδίον καὶ τὴν-μητέρα-αὐτοῦ νυκτός, καὶ ἀνεχώρησεν εἰς
the little child and his mother by night, and withdrew into
Αἴγυπτον, 15 καὶ ἦν ἐκεῖ ἕως τῆς τελευτῆς Ἡρώδου· ἵνα
Egypt, and was there until the death of Herod: that
πληρωθῇ τὸ ῥηθὲν ὑπὸ [n]τοῦ‖ κυρίου διὰ τοῦ
might be fulfilled that which was spoken by the Lord through the
προφήτου, λέγοντος, Ἐξ Αἰγύπτου ἐκάλεσα τὸν-υἱόν-μου.
prophet, saying, Out of Egypt have I called my son.
16 Τότε Ἡρώδης, ἰδὼν ὅτι ἐνεπαίχθη ὑπὸ τῶν μάγων,
Then Herod, having seen that he was mocked by the magi,
ἐθυμώθη λίαν, καὶ ἀποστείλας ἀνεῖλεν πάντας τοὺς
was enraged greatly, and having sent he put to death all the
παῖδας τοὺς ἐν Βηθλεὲμ καὶ ἐν πᾶσιν τοῖς-ὁρίοις-αὐτῆς, ἀπὸ
boys that [were] in Bethlehem and in all its borders, from
διετοῦς καὶ κατωτέρω, κατὰ τὸν χρόνον ὃν ἠκρίβω-
two years old and under, according to the time which he had accurately
σεν παρὰ τῶν μάγων. 17 Τότε ἐπληρώθη τὸ ῥηθὲν
inquired from the magi. Then was fulfilled that which was spoken
[o]ὑπὸ‖ Ἱερεμίου τοῦ προφήτου, λέγοντος, 18 Φωνὴ ἐν Ῥαμᾶ
by Jeremias the prophet, saying, A voice in Rama
ἠκούσθη, [p]θρῆνος καὶ‖ κλαυθμὸς καὶ ὀδυρμὸς πολύς, Ῥαχὴλ
was heard, lamentation and weeping and [2]mourning [1]great, Rachel
κλαίουσα τὰ-τέκνα-αὐτῆς, καὶ οὐκ [q]ἤθελεν‖ παρακληθῆναι,
weeping [for] her children, and [2]not [1]would be comforted,
ὅτι οὐκ-εἰσίν.
because they are not.

19 Τελευτήσαντος-δὲ τοῦ Ἡρώδου, ἰδού, ἄγγελος κυρίου
But [2]having [3]died [1]Herod, behold, an angel of [the] Lord
[r]κατ' ὄναρ φαίνεται‖ τῷ Ἰωσὴφ ἐν Αἰγύπτῳ, 20 λέγων, Ἐγερ-
in a dream appears to Joseph in Egypt, saying, Having
θεὶς παράλαβε τὸ παιδίον καὶ τὴν-μητέρα-αὐτοῦ, καὶ πορεύου
risen take with [thee] the little child and his mother, and go

---

[l] εἶδον they saw GLTTrAW. [m] κατ' ὄναρ ἐφάνη in a dream appeared L; κατ' ὄναρ φαίνεται Tr. [n] — τοῦ (*read* [the]) LTTrAW. [o] διὰ through LTTrAW. [p] — θρῆνος καὶ LTTrA. [q] ἠθέλησεν L. [r] φαίνεται κατ' ὄναρ LTTrA.

εἰς γῆν Ἰσραήλ· τεθνήκασιν.γὰρ οἱ ζητοῦντες τὴν ψυχὴν
into [the] land of Israel: for they have died who were seeking the life
τοῦ παιδίου. 21 Ὁ.δὲ ἐγερθεὶς παρέλαβεν τὸ παιδίον καὶ
of the little child. And he having risen took with [him] the little child and
τὴν.μητέρα.αὐτοῦ, καὶ [s]ἦλθεν[‖] εἰς γῆν Ἰσραήλ. 22 ἀκούσας
his mother, and came into [the] land of Israel. [2]Having [3]heard
δὲ ὅτι Ἀρχέλαος βασιλεύει [t]ἐπὶ[‖] τῆς Ἰουδαίας ἀντὶ [v]Ἡρώδου
[1]but that Archelaus reigns over Judæa instead of Herod
τοῦ.πατρὸς.αὐτοῦ,[‖] ἐφοβήθη ἐκεῖ ἀπελθεῖν· χρηματισ-
his father, he was afraid there to go; [2]having [3]been [4]divinely
θεὶς δὲ κατ' ὄναρ, ἀνεχώρησεν εἰς τὰ μέρη τῆς Γαλιλαίας,
[5]instructed [1]and in a dream, he withdrew into the parts of Galilee:
23 καὶ ἐλθὼν κατῴκησεν εἰς πόλιν λεγομένην [w]Ναζαρέτ·[‖]
and having come he dwelt in a city called Nazareth;
ὅπως πληρωθῇ τὸ ῥηθὲν διὰ τῶν προφητῶν, ὅτι
so that should be fulfilled that which was spoken by the prophets, that
Ναζωραῖος κληθήσεται.
a Nazaræan shall he be called.

3 Ἐν.δὲ ταῖς.ἡμέραις.ἐκείναις παραγίνεται Ἰωάννης ὁ
Now in those days comes John the
βαπτιστής, κηρύσσων ἐν τῇ ἐρήμῳ τῆς Ἰουδαίας, 2 [x]καὶ[‖] λέγων,
Baptist, proclaiming in the wilderness of Judæa, and saying,
Μετανοεῖτε· ἤγγικεν.γὰρ ἡ βασιλεία τῶν οὐρανῶν. 3 Οὗτος.γάρ
Repent, for has drawn near the kingdom of the heavens. For this
ἐστιν ὁ ῥηθεὶς [y]ὑπὸ[‖] Ἡσαΐου τοῦ προφήτου, λέγοντος,
is he who was spoken of by Esaias the prophet, saying,
Φωνὴ βοῶντος ἐν τῇ ἐρήμῳ, Ἑτοιμάσατε τὴν ὁδὸν κυ-
[The] voice of one crying in the wilderness, Prepare the way of [the]
ρίου· εὐθείας ποιεῖτε τὰς.τρίβους.αὐτοῦ. 4 Αὐτὸς.δὲ ὁ Ἰωάννης
Lord, straight make his paths. And [2]himself [1]John
εἶχεν τὸ.ἔνδυμα.αὐτοῦ ἀπὸ τριχῶν καμήλου, καὶ ζώνην δερ-
had his raiment of hair of a camel, and a girdle of
ματίνην περὶ τὴν.ὀσφὺν.αὐτοῦ· ἡ.δὲ τροφὴ [z]αὐτοῦ ἦν[‖] ἀκρίδες
leather about his loins, and the food of him was locusts
καὶ μέλι ἄγριον.
and [2]honey [1]wild.

5 Τότε ἐξεπορεύετο πρὸς αὐτὸν Ἱεροσόλυμα καὶ πᾶσα ἡ
Then went out to him Jerusalem, and all
Ἰουδαία καὶ πᾶσα ἡ περίχωρος τοῦ Ἰορδάνου· 6 καὶ ἐβαπτί-
Judæa, and all the country around the Jordan, and were bap-
ζοντο[a] ἐν τῷ Ἰορδάνῃ[b] ὑπ' αὐτοῦ, ἐξομολογούμενοι τὰς ἁμαρ-
tized in the Jordan by him, confessing [2]sins
τίας αὐτῶν. 7 Ἰδὼν.δὲ πολλοὺς τῶν Φαρισαίων καὶ Σαδδου-
[1]their But having seen many of the Pharisees and Saddu-
καίων ἐρχομένους ἐπὶ τὸ.βάπτισμα.[c]αὐτοῦ,[‖] εἶπεν αὐτοῖς,
cees coming to his baptism, he said to them,
Γεννήματα ἐχιδνῶν, τίς ὑπέδειξεν ὑμῖν φυγεῖν ἀπὸ τῆς μελ-
Offspring of vipers, who forewarned you to flee from the com-
λούσης ὀργῆς; 8 ποιήσατε οὖν [d]καρποὺς ἀξίους[‖] τῆς μετα-
ing wrath? Produce therefore fruits worthy of repent-
νοίας· 9 καὶ μὴ.δόξητε λέγειν ἐν ἑαυτοῖς, Πατέρα ἔχομεν
ance: and think not to say within yourselves [4For] [5]father [1]we [2]have

into the land of Israel: for they are dead which sought the young child's life.
21 And he arose, and took the young child and his mother, and came into the land of Israel.
22 But when he heard that Archelaus did reign in Judæa in the room of his father Herod, he was afraid to go thither: notwithstanding, being warned of God in a dream, he turned aside into the parts of Galilee:
23 and he came and dwelt in a city called Nazareth: that it might be fulfilled which was spoken by the prophets, He shall be called a Nazarene.

III. In those days came John the Baptist, preaching in the wilderness of Judæa,
2 and saying, Repent ye: for the kingdom of heaven is at hand.
3 For this is he that was spoken of by the prophet Esaias, saying, The voice of one crying in the wilderness, Prepare ye the way of the Lord, make his paths straight.
4 And the same John had his raiment of camel's hair, and a leathern girdle about his loins; and his meat was locusts and wild honey.

5 Then went out to him Jerusalem, and all Judæa, and all the region round about Jordan,
6 and were baptized of him in Jordan, confessing their sins.
7 But when he saw many of the Pharisees and Sadducees come to his baptism, he said unto them, O generation of vipers, who hath warned you to flee from the wrath to come?
8 Bring forth therefore fruits meet for repentance:
9 and think not to say within yourselves, We have Abraham to *our* fa-

---

[s] εἰσῆλθεν entered LTTrA. [t] — ἐπὶ (*read* τῆς Ἰου. over Judæa) LT[TrA]. [v] τοῦ πατρὸς αὐτοῦ Ἡρώδου LTTrA. [w] Ναζαρέθ LTT W. [x] — καὶ LT[T]A. [y] διὰ through LTT AW. [z] ἦν αὐτοῦ LTTrA. [a] + [πάντες] all L. [b] + ποταμῷ river LTTrA. [c] — αὐτοῦ (*read* the baptism) LT[TrA]. [d] καρπὸν ἄξιον fruit worthy GLTTrAW.

ther: for I say unto
you, that God is able
of these stones to raise
up children unto Abra-
ham. 10 And now also
the axe is laid unto
the root of the trees:
therefore every tree
which bringeth not
forth good fruit is
hewn down, and cast
into the fire. 11 I in-
deed baptize you with
water unto repent-
ance: but he that
cometh after me is
mightier than I, whose
shoes I am not worthy
to bear: he shall bap-
tize you with the Holy
Ghost, and *with* fire:
12 whose fan *is* in
his hand, and he will
throughly purge his
floor, and gather his
wheat into the garner;
but he will burn up
the chaff with un-
quenchable fire.

τὸν Ἀβραάμ· λέγω.γὰρ ὑμῖν, ὅτι δύναται ὁ θεὸς ἐκ τῶν λίθων
Abraham: for I say to you, that able is God from ²stones
τούτων ἐγεῖραι τέκνα τῷ Ἀβραάμ. 10 ἤδη.δὲ [e]καὶ‖ ἡ ἀξίνη
¹these to raise up children to Abraham. But already also the axe
πρὸς τὴν ῥίζαν τῶν δένδρων κεῖται· πᾶν οὖν δένδρον μὴ
to the root of the trees is applied: ²every ¹therefore tree not
ποιοῦν καρπὸν καλὸν ἐκκόπτεται καὶ εἰς πῦρ βάλλεται.
producing ²fruit ¹good is cut down and into [the] fire is cast.
11 Ἐγὼ μὲν [f]βαπτίζω ὑμᾶς‖ ἐν ὕδατι εἰς μετάνοιαν· ὁ.δὲ
I indeed baptize you with water to repentance; but he who
ὀπίσω μου ἐρχόμενος ἰσχυρότερός μου ἐστίν, οὗ οὐκ.εἰμὶ
after me [is] coming mightier than I is, of whom I am not
ἱκανὸς τὰ ὑποδήματα βαστάσαι· αὐτὸς ὑμᾶς βαπτίσει ἐν
fit the sandals to bear: he ³you ¹will ²baptize with [the]
πνεύματι ἁγίῳ καὶ πυρί. 12 οὗ τὸ πτύον ἐν τῇ χειρὶ
²Spirit ¹Holy and with fire. Of whom the winnowing fan [is] in ²hand
αὐτοῦ, καὶ διακαθαριεῖ τὴν.ἅλωνα.αὐτοῦ, καὶ συνάξει
¹his, and he will thoroughly purge his floor, and will gather
τὸν.σῖτον.αὐτοῦ εἰς τὴν ἀποθήκην,[g] τὸ.δὲ ἄχυρον κατακαύσει
his wheat into the granary, but the chaff he will burn up
πυρὶ ἀσβέστῳ.
with fire unquenchable.

13 Then cometh Je-
sus from Galilee to
Jordan unto John, to
be baptized of him.
14 But John forbad
him, saying, I have
need to be baptized of
thee, and comest thou
to me? 15 And Jesus
answering said unto
him, Suffer *it to be so*
now: for thus it be-
cometh us to fulfil all
righteousness. Then
he suffered him. 16 And
Jesus, when he was
baptized, went up
straightway out of the
water: and, lo, the
heavens were opened
unto him, and he saw
the Spirit of God de-
scending like a dove,
and lighting upon him:
17 and lo a voice from
heaven, saying, This
is my beloved Son, in
whom I am well
pleased.

13 Τότε παραγίνεται ὁ Ἰησοῦς ἀπὸ τῆς Γαλιλαίας ἐπὶ τὸν
Then comes Jesus from Galilee to the
Ἰορδάνην πρὸς τὸν Ἰωάννην, τοῦ βαπτισθῆναι ὑπ' αὐτοῦ.
Jordan to John, to be baptized by him.
14 ὁ.δὲ.[h]Ἰωάννης‖ διεκώλυεν αὐτόν, λέγων, Ἐγὼ χρείαν ἔχω
But John was hindering him, saying, I ²need ¹have
ὑπὸ σοῦ βαπτισθῆναι, καὶ σὺ ἔρχῃ πρός με; 15 Ἀποκριθεὶς
by thee to be baptized, and ²thou ¹comest to me? ³Answering
δὲ ὁ Ἰησοῦς εἶπεν [i]πρὸς αὐτόν,‖ Ἄφες ἄρτι· οὕτως.γὰρ
¹but ²Jesus said to him, Suffer [it] now; for thus
πρέπον ἐστὶν ἡμῖν πληρῶσαι πᾶσαν δικαιοσύνην. Τότε
becoming it is to us to fulfil all righteousness. Then
ἀφίησιν αὐτόν. 16 [j]Καὶ βαπτισθεὶς‖ ὁ Ἰησοῦς [k]ἀνέβη
he suffers him. And having been baptized Jesus went up
εὐθὺς‖ ἀπὸ τοῦ ὕδατος, καὶ ἰδού, [l]ἀνεῴχθησαν‖ [m]αὐτῷ‖ οἱ
immediately from the water: and behold, were opened to him the
οὐρανοί, καὶ εἶδεν [n]τὸ‖ πνεῦμα [o]τοῦ‖ θεοῦ καταβαῖνον ὡσεὶ
heavens, and he saw the Spirit of God descending as
περιστεράν, [p]καὶ‖ ἐρχόμενον ἐπ' αὐτόν. 17 καὶ ἰδού, φωνὴ
a dove, and coming upon him: and lo, a voice
ἐκ τῶν οὐρανῶν, λέγουσα, Οὗτός ἐστιν ὁ.υἱός.μου ὁ ἀγα-
out of the heavens, saying, This is my Son the be-
πητός, ἐν ᾧ [q]εὐδόκησα‖.
loved, in whom I have found delight.

IV. Then was Jesus
led up of the Spirit in-
to the wilderness to be
tempted of the devil.
2 And when he had
fasted forty days and
forty nights, he was af-
terward an hungred.

4 Τότε [r]ὁ‖ Ἰησοῦς ἀνήχθη εἰς τὴν ἔρημον ὑπὸ τοῦ πνεύ-
Then Jesus was led up into the wilderness by the Spi-
ματος, πειρασθῆναι ὑπὸ τοῦ διαβόλου. 2 καὶ νηστεύσας
rit to be tempted by the devil. And having fasted
ἡμέρας [s]τεσσαράκοντα‖ καὶ [t]νύκτας τεσσαράκοντα,‖ ὕστερον
²days ¹forty and ²nights ¹forty, afterwards

---

[e] — καὶ LTTrAW. [f] ὑμᾶς βαπτίζω LTTrW. [g] + αὐτοῦ (*read* his granary) LTrW. [h] — Ἰωάννης (*read* he was hindering) LT[TrA]W. [i] αὐτῷ L. [j] βαπτισθεὶς δὲ LTTrAW. [k] εὐθὺς ἀνέβη LTTrW. [l] ἠνεῴχθησαν L. [m] — αὐτῷ [L]T. [n] — τὸ (*read* [the]) T[A]. [o] — τοῦ T[A]. [p] — καὶ LT [TrA]. [q] ηὐδόκησα T. [r] — ὁ A. [s] τεσσεράκοντα TTrA. [t] τεσσεράκοντα νύκτας T; νύκτας τεσσερ. TrA.

ἐπείνασεν. 3 καὶ προσελθὼν [v]αὐτῷ‖ ὁ πειράζων εἶπεν[w], Εἰ
he hungered. And having come to him the tempter said, If
υἱὸς εἶ τοῦ θεοῦ, εἰπὲ ἵνα οἱ.λίθοι.οὗτοι ἄρτοι γένωνται.
[3]Son [1]thou [2]art of God, speak that these stones [3]loaves [1]may [2]become.
4 Ὁ.δὲ ἀποκριθεὶς εἶπεν, Γέγραπται, Οὐκ ἐπ' ἄρτῳ μόνῳ
But he answering said, It has been written, Not by bread alone
ζήσεται [x]ἄνθρωπος, ἀλλ' [y]ἐπὶ‖ παντὶ ῥήματι ἐκπορευομένῳ διὰ
shall [2]live [1]man, but by every word going out through
στόματος θεοῦ. 5 Τότε παραλαμβάνει αὐτὸν ὁ διάβολος εἰς
[the] mouth of God. Then [3]takes [4]him [1]the [2]devil to
τὴν ἁγίαν πόλιν, καὶ [z]ἵστησιν‖ αὐτὸν ἐπὶ τὸ πτερύγιον τοῦ
the holy city, and sets him upon the edge of the
ἱεροῦ, 6 καὶ [a]λέγει‖ αὐτῷ, Εἰ υἱὸς εἶ τοῦ θεοῦ, βάλε σεαυ-
temple, and says to him, If [3]Son [1]thou [2]art of God, cast thy-
τὸν κάτω· γέγραπται.γάρ, Ὅτι τοῖς.ἀγγέλοις.αὐτοῦ ἐν-
self down: for it has been written, To his angels he
τελεῖται περὶ σοῦ, καὶ ἐπὶ χειρῶν ἀροῦσίν σε,
will give charge concerning thee, and in [their] hands shall they bear thee,
μήποτε προσκόψῃς πρὸς λίθον τὸν.πόδα.σου. 7 Ἔφη αὐτῷ
lest thou strike against a stone thy foot. [2]Said [3]to [4]him
ὁ Ἰησοῦς, Πάλιν γέγραπται, Οὐκ.ἐκπειράσεις κύριον τὸν
[1]Jesus, Again it has been written, Thou shalt not tempt [the] Lord
θεόν σου. 8 Πάλιν παραλαμβάνει αὐτὸν ὁ διάβολος εἰς
[2]God [1]thy. Again [3]takes him [1]the [2]devil to
ὄρος ὑψηλὸν λίαν, καὶ δείκνυσιν αὐτῷ πάσας τὰς βασι-
a mountain [2]high [1]exceedingly, and shews to him all the king-
λείας τοῦ κόσμου καὶ τὴν.δόξαν.αὐτῶν, 9 καὶ [b]λέγει‖ αὐτῷ,
doms of the world and their glory, and says to him,
[c]Ταῦτα πάντα σοι‖ δώσω, ἐὰν πεσὼν προσκυνήσῃς
[2]These [3]things [1]all to thee will I give if falling down thou wilt worship
μοι. 10 Τότε λέγει αὐτῷ ὁ Ἰησοῦς, Ὕπαγε[d], σατανᾶ·
me. Then [2]says [3]to [4]him [1]Jesus, Get thee away, Satan;
γέγραπται.γάρ, Κύριον τὸν.θεόν.σου προσκυνήσεις, καὶ
for it has been written, [The] Lord thy God shalt thou worship, and
αὐτῷ μόνῳ λατρεύσεις. 11 Τότε ἀφίησιν αὐτὸν ὁ διάβολος·
him alone shalt thou serve. Then [3]leaves [4]him [1]the [2]devil,
καὶ ἰδού, ἄγγελοι προσῆλθον καὶ διηκόνουν αὐτῷ.
and behold, angels came and ministered to him.

12 Ἀκούσας.δὲ [e]ὁ Ἰησοῦς‖ ὅτι Ἰωάννης παρεδόθη, ἀν-
But [2]having [3]heard [1]Jesus that John was delivered up, he
εχώρησεν εἰς τὴν Γαλιλαίαν. 13 καὶ καταλιπὼν τὴν [f]Ναζαρέτ,‖
withdrew into Galilee: and having left Nazareth,
ἐλθὼν κατῴκησεν εἰς [g]Καπερναοὺμ‖ τὴν παραθαλασσίαν,
having come he dwelt at Capernaum, which [is] on the sea-side,
ἐν ὁρίοις Ζαβουλὼν καὶ Νεφθαλείμ, 14 ἵνα πληρωθῇ
in [the] borders of Zabulon and Nephthalim, that might be fulfilled
τὸ ῥηθὲν διὰ Ἡσαΐου τοῦ προφήτου, λέγοντος, 15 Γῆ
that which was spoken by Esaias the prophet, saying, Land
Ζαβουλὼν καὶ γῆ Νεφθαλείμ, ὁδὸν θαλάσσης πέραν τοῦ
of Zabulon, and land of Nephthalim, way of [the] sea, beyond the
Ἰορδάνου, Γαλιλαία τῶν ἐθνῶν, 16 ὁ λαὸς ὁ καθήμενος
Jordan, Galilee of the nations, the people which was sitting

3 And when the tempt-
er came to him, he
said, If thou be the
Son of God, command
that these stones be
made bread. 4 But he
answered and said, It
is written, Man shall
not live by bread alone,
but by every word that
proceedeth out of the
mouth of God. 5 Then
the devil taketh him
up into the holy city,
and setteth him on a
pinnacle of the temple,
6 and saith unto him,
If thou be the Son
of God, cast thyself
down: for it is written,
He shall give his
angels charge con-
cerning thee: and in
their hands they shall
bear thee up, lest at
any time thou dash
thy foot against a
stone. 7 Jesus said
unto him, It is written
again, Thou shalt not
tempt the Lord thy
God. 8 Again, the devil
taketh him up into an
exceeding high moun-
tain, and sheweth him
all the kingdoms of
the world, and the
glory of them; 9 and
saith unto him, All
these things will I give
thee, if thou wilt fall
down and worship me.
10 Then saith Jesus
unto him, Get thee
hence, Satan: for it is
written, Thou shalt
worship the Lord thy
God, and him only
shalt thou serve.
11 Then the devil
leaveth him, and, be-
hold, angels came and
ministered unto him.

12 Now when Jesus
had heard that John
was cast into prison,
he departed into Gali-
lee; 13 and leaving
Nazareth, he came and
dwelt in Capernaum,
which is upon the sea
coast, in the borders
of Zabulon and Neph-
thalim: 14 that it
might be fulfilled
which was spoken by
Esaias the prophet,
saying, 15 The land of
Zabulon, and the land
of Nephthalim, *by* the
way of the sea, beyond
Jordan, Galilee of the
Gentiles; 16 the peo-
ple which sat in dark-

---

[v] — αὐτῷ TTrA. [w] + αὐτῷ to him LTTrAW. [x] + ὁ LTTrAW. [y] ἐν LTrA. [z] ἔστησεν set LTTrA. [a] εἶπεν said L. [b] εἶπεν said LTTrA. [c] ταῦτά σοι πάντα TTrA. [d] + ὀπίσω μου behind me G[L]W. [e] — ὁ Ἰησοῦς TTrAW [f] Ναζαρὰθ Nazarath L; Ναζαρὲθ W; Ναζαρὰ Nazara TTrA. [g] Καφαρναοὺμ LTTrAW.

ἐν [h]σκότει εἶδε φῶς‖ μέγα, καὶ τοῖς καθημένοις ἐν
in darkness has seen a [2]light [1]great, and to those which were sitting in [the]
χώρᾳ καὶ σκιᾷ θανάτου, φῶς ἀνέτειλεν αὐτοῖς. 17 Ἀπὸ
country and shadow of death, light has sprung up to them. From
τότε ἤρξατο ὁ Ἰησοῦς κηρύσσειν καὶ λέγειν, Μετανοεῖτε·
that time began Jesus to proclaim and to say, Repent;
ἤγγικεν.γὰρ ἡ βασιλεία τῶν οὐρανῶν.
for has drawn near the kingdom of the heavens.

18 Περιπατῶν.δὲ [i]ὁ Ἰησοῦς‖ παρὰ τὴν θάλασσαν τῆς Γαλι-
And [2]walking [1]Jesus by the sea of Gali-
λαίας εἶδεν δύο ἀδελφούς, Σίμωνα τὸν λεγόμενον Πέτρον, καὶ
lee he saw two brothers, Simon who is called Peter, and
Ἀνδρέαν τὸν.ἀδελφὸν.αὐτοῦ, βάλλοντας ἀμφίβληστρον εἰς
Andrew his brother, casting a large net into
τὴν θάλασσαν· ἦσαν.γὰρ ἁλιεῖς. 19 καὶ λέγει αὐτοῖς,[k] Δεῦτε
the sea, for they were fishers: and he says to them, Come
ὀπίσω μου, καὶ ποιήσω ὑμᾶς ἁλιεῖς ἀνθρώπων. 20 Οἱ.δὲ
after me, and I will make you fishers of men. And they
εὐθέως ἀφέντες τὰ δίκτυα ἠκολούθησαν αὐτῷ. 21 Καὶ
immediately having left the nets, followed him. And
προβὰς ἐκεῖθεν, εἶδεν ἄλλους δύο ἀδελφούς, Ἰάκωβον τὸν
having gone on thence, he saw other two brothers, James the [son]
τοῦ Ζεβεδαίου καὶ Ἰωάννην τὸν.ἀδελφὸν.αὐτοῦ, ἐν τῷ πλοίῳ
of Zebedee, and John his brother, in the ship
μετὰ Ζεβεδαίου τοῦ.πατρὸς.αὐτῶν, καταρτίζοντας τὰ δίκτυα
with Zebedee their father, mending [2]nets
αὐτῶν· καὶ ἐκάλεσεν αὐτούς. 22 οἱ.δὲ εὐθέως ἀφέντες τὸ
[1]their, and he called them; and they immediately having left the
πλοῖον καὶ τὸν.πατέρα.αὐτῶν ἠκολούθησαν αὐτῷ.
ship and their father followed him.

23 Καὶ περιῆγεν [l]ὅλην τὴν Γαλιλαίαν ὁ Ἰησοῦς,‖ διδάσκων
And [2]went [3]about [4]all [5]Galilee [1]Jesus, teaching
ἐν ταῖς.συναγωγαῖς.αὐτῶν, καὶ κηρύσσων τὸ εὐαγγέλιον τῆς
in their synagogues, and proclaiming the glad tidings of the
βασιλείας, καὶ θεραπεύων πᾶσαν νόσον καὶ πᾶσαν μαλακίαν
kingdom, and healing every disease and every bodily weakness
ἐν τῷ λαῷ. 24 καὶ ἀπῆλθεν ἡ ἀκοὴ αὐτοῦ εἰς ὅλην τὴν Συ-
among the people. And went out the fame of him into all Sy-
ρίαν· καὶ προσήνεγκαν αὐτῷ πάντας τοὺς.κακῶς.ἔχοντας,
ria. And they brought to him all who were ill,
ποικίλαις νόσοις καὶ βασάνοις συνεχομένους, [m]καὶ‖ δαιμονιζο-
by various diseases and torments oppressed, and possessed by
μένους, καὶ σεληνιαζομένους, καὶ παραλυτικούς· καὶ ἐθερά-
demons, and lunatics, and paralytics; and he
πευσεν αὐτούς. 25 καὶ ἠκολούθησαν αὐτῷ ὄχλοι πολλοὶ ἀπὸ
healed them. And [3]followed [4]him [2]crowds [1]great from
τῆς Γαλιλαίας καὶ Δεκαπόλεως καὶ Ἱεροσολύμων καὶ Ἰουδαίας
Galilee and Decapolis and Jerusalem and Judea
καὶ πέραν τοῦ Ἰορδάνου.
and beyond the Jordan.

5 Ἰδὼν.δὲ τοὺς ὄχλους, ἀνέβη εἰς τὸ ὄρος· καὶ καθίσαν-
But seeing the crowds, he went up into the mountain; and [2]having [3]sat
τος αὐτοῦ, [n]προσῆλθον‖ [o]αὐτῷ‖ οἱ.μαθηταὶ.αὐτοῦ. 2 καὶ ἀνοί-
[4]down [1]he, came to him his disciples. And having

ness saw great light; and to them which sat in the region and shadow of death, light is sprung up. 17 From that time Jesus began to preach, and to say, Repent: for the kingdom of heaven is at hand.

18 And Jesus, walking by the sea of Galilee, saw two brethren, Simon called Peter, and Andrew his brother, casting a net into the sea: for they were fishers. 19 And he saith unto them, Follow me, and I will make you fishers of men. 20 And they straightway left *their* nets, and followed him. 21 And going on from thence, he saw other two brethren, James *the son* of Zebedee, and John his brother, in a ship with Zebedee their father, mending their nets; and he called them. 22 And they immediately left the ship and their father, and followed him.

23 And Jesus went about all Galilee, teaching in their synagogues, and preaching the gospel of the kingdom, and healing all manner of sickness and all manner of disease among the people. 24 And his fame went throughout all Syria: and they brought unto him all sick people that were taken with divers diseases and torments, and those which were possessed with devils, and those which were lunatic, and those that had the palsy; and he healed them. 25 And there followed him great multitudes of people from Galilee, and *from* Decapolis, and *from* Jerusalem, and *from* Judæa, and *from* beyond Jordan.

V. And seeing the multitudes, he went up into a mountain: and when he was set, his disciples came unto him: 2 and he

[h] σκοτίᾳ φῶς εἶδεν LTrA; σκότει φῶς εἶδεν TW. [i] — ὁ Ἰησοῦς GLTTrAW. [k] + [ὁ Ἰησοῦς] Jesus L. [l] ὁ Ἰησοῦς ὅλῃ τῇ Γαλιλαίᾳ L; [ὁ Ἰησοῦς] Tr (— ὁ Ἰησοῦς TA) ἐν ὅλῃ τῇ Γαλιλαίᾳ TTrA; ὁ Ἰησοῦς ὅλην τὴν Γαλιλαίαν W. [m] — καὶ LTrA. [n] προσῆλθαν TTr. [o] — αὐτῷ L.

ξας τὸ.στόμα.αὐτοῦ ἐδίδασκεν αὐτούς, λέγων, 3 Μακάριοι οἱ
opened his mouth he taught them, saying, Blessed [are] the
πτωχοὶ τῷ πνεύματι· ὅτι αὐτῶν ἐστιν ἡ βασιλεία τῶν οὐρανῶν.
poor in spirit; for theirs is the kingdom of the heavens.
4 [p]μακάριοι οἱ πενθοῦντες· ὅτι αὐτοὶ παρακληθήσονται.
Blessed they who mourn; for they shall be comforted.
5 μακάριοι οἱ πραεῖς· ὅτι αὐτοὶ κληρονομήσουσιν τὴν γῆν.‖
Blessed the meek; for they shall inherit the earth.
6 μακάριοι οἱ πεινῶντες καὶ διψῶντες τὴν δικαιοσύνην· ὅτι
Blessed they who hunger and thirst after righteousness; for
αὐτοὶ χορτασθήσονται. 7 μακάριοι οἱ ἐλεήμονες· ὅτι αὐτοὶ
they shall be filled. Blessed the merciful; for they
ἐλεηθήσονται. 8 μακάριοι οἱ καθαροὶ τῇ καρδίᾳ· ὅτι αὐτοὶ τὸν
shall find mercy. Blessed the pure in heart; for they
θεὸν ὄψονται. 9 μακάριοι οἱ εἰρηνοποιοί· ὅτι [q]αὐτοὶ‖ υἱοὶ θεοῦ
³God ¹shall ²see. Blessed the peacemakers; for they sons of God
κληθήσονται. 10 μακάριοι οἱ δεδιωγμένοι ἕνεκεν δικαιο-
shall be called. Blessed they who have been persecuted on account of right-
σύνης· ὅτι αὐτῶν ἐστιν ἡ βασιλεία τῶν οὐρανῶν. 11 μακάριοί
eousness; for theirs is the kingdom of the heavens. Blessed
ἐστε, ὅταν ὀνειδίσωσιν ὑμᾶς καὶ διώξωσιν, καὶ εἴπωσιν πᾶν
are ye when they shall reproach you, and shall persecute, and shall say every
πονηρὸν [r]ῥῆμα‖ καθ' ὑμῶν [s]ψευδόμενοι,‖ ἕνεκεν ἐμοῦ. 12 χαί-
wicked word against you, lying, on account of me. Re-
ρετε καὶ ἀγαλλιᾶσθε, ὅτι ὁ.μισθὸς.ὑμῶν πολὺς ἐν τοῖς οὐρανοῖς·
joice and exult, for your reward [is] great in the heavens;
οὕτως.γὰρ ἐδίωξαν τοὺς προφήτας τοὺς πρὸ ὑμῶν.
for thus they persecuted the prophets who [were] before you.
13 Ὑμεῖς ἐστε τὸ ἅλας τῆς γῆς· ἐὰν.δὲ τὸ ἅλας μωρανθῇ,
Ye are the salt of the earth: but if the salt become tasteless,
ἐν τίνι ἁλισθήσεται; εἰς οὐδὲν ἰσχύει ἔτι, εἰ.μὴ [t]βλη-
with what shall it be salted? for nothing has it strength any longer, but to be
θῆναι‖ ἔξω, [v]καὶ‖ καταπατεῖσθαι ὑπὸ τῶν ἀνθρώπων. 14 Ὑμεῖς
cast out, and to be trampled upon by men. Ye
ἐστε τὸ φῶς τοῦ κόσμου· οὐ.δύναται πόλις κρυβῆναι ἐπάνω
are the light of the world, ³cannot ¹a ²city be hid on
ὄρους κειμένη· 15 οὐδὲ καίουσιν λύχνον καὶ τιθέασιν αὐτὸν
a mountain situated. Nor do they light a lamp and put it
ὑπὸ τὸν μόδιον, ἀλλ' ἐπὶ τὴν λυχνίαν, καὶ λάμπει πᾶσιν τοῖς
under the corn measure, but upon the lampstand; and it shines for all who
ἐν τῇ οἰκίᾳ. 16 οὕτως λαμψάτω τὸ.φῶς.ὑμῶν ἔμπροσθεν
[are] in the house. Thus let shine your light before
τῶν ἀνθρώπων, ὅπως ἴδωσιν ὑμῶν τὰ καλὰ ἔργα, καὶ δοξά-
men, so that they may see your good works, and may
σωσιν τὸν.πατέρα.ὑμῶν τὸν ἐν τοῖς οὐρανοῖς.
glorify your Father who [is] in the heavens.
17 Μὴ.νομίσητε ὅτι ἦλθον καταλῦσαι τὸν νόμον ἢ τοὺς προ-
Think not that I came to abolish the law or the pro-
φήτας· οὐκ.ἦλθον καταλῦσαι, ἀλλὰ πληρῶσαι. 18 ἀμὴν.γὰρ
phets: I came not to abolish, but to fulfil. For verily
λέγω ὑμῖν, ἕως.ἂν παρέλθῃ ὁ οὐρανὸς καὶ ἡ γῆ, ἰῶτα ἓν ἢ
I say to you, Until shall pass away the heaven and the earth, ²iota ¹one or
μία κεραία οὐ.μὴ παρέλθῃ ἀπὸ τοῦ νόμου, ἕως.ἂν πάντα
one tittle in no wise shall pass away from the law until all

opened his mouth, and
taught them, saying,
3 Blessed *are* the poor
in spirit: for theirs is
the kingdom of hea-
ven. 4 Blessed *are*
they that mourn: for
they shall be comfort-
ed. 5 Blessed *are* the
meek: for they shall
inherit the earth.
6 Blessed *are* they
which do hunger and
thirst after righteous-
ness: for they shall
be filled. 7 Blessed *are*
the merciful: for they
shall obtain mercy.
8 Blessed *are* the pure
in heart: for they
shall see God. 9 Bless-
ed *are* the peace-
makers: for they shall
be called the children
of God. 10 Blessed *are*
they which are per-
secuted for righteous-
ness' sake: for theirs
is the kingdom of
heaven. 11 Blessed are
ye, when *men* shall
revile you, and perse-
cute *you*, and shall say
all manner of evil
against you falsely,
for my sake. 12 Re-
joice, and be exceeding
glad: for great *is* your
reward in heaven: for
so persecuted they the
prophets which were
before you.
13 Ye are the salt of
the earth: but if the
salt have lost his sa-
vour, wherewith shall
it be salted? it is
thenceforth good for
nothing, but to be cast
out, and to be trodden
under foot of men.
14 Ye are the light of
the world. A city that
is set on an hill cannot
be hid. 15 Neither do
men light a candle,
and put it under a
bushel, but on a can-
dlestick; and it giveth
light unto all that are
in the house. 16 Let
your light so shine be-
fore men, that they
may see your good
works, and glorify
your Father which is
in heaven.
17 Think not that I
am come to destroy
the law, or the pro-
phets: I am not come
to destroy, but to ful-
fil. 18 For verily I say
unto you, Till heaven
and earth pass, one jot
or one tittle shall in
no wise pass from the
law, till all be fulfilled.
19 Whosoever there-

[p] Verses 4, 5, *transposed* LTTr. [q] — αὐτοὶ (*read* κληθ. they shall be called) [L]T[TrA]. [r] — ῥῆμα (*read* [thing]) LTTrA. [s] — ψευδόμενοι L. [t] βληθὲν having been cast LTTrA. [v] — καὶ LTTrA.

fore shall break one
of these least com-
mandments, and shall
teach men so, he shall
be called the least in
the kingdom of hea-
ven: but whosoever
shall do and teach
them, the same shall
be called great in the
kingdom of heaven.
20 For I say unto you,
That except your
righteousness shall
exceed *the righteous-
ness* of the scribes and
Pharisees, ye shall in
no case enter into the
kingdom of heaven.
21 Ye have heard
that it was said by
them of old time,
Thou shalt not kill;
and whosoever shall
kill shall be in dan-
ger of the judgment:
22 but I say unto you,
That whosoever is
angry with his brother
without a cause shall
be in danger of the
judgment: and who-
soever shall say to his
brother, Raca, shall be
in danger of the coun-
cil: but whosoever
shall say, Thou fool,
shall be in danger of
hell fire. 23 Therefore
if thou bring thy gift
to the altar, and there
rememberest that thy
brother hath ought
against thee; 24 leave
there thy gift before
the altar, and go thy
way; first be recon-
ciled to thy brother,
and then come and
offer thy gift. 25 Agree
with thine adversary
quickly, whiles thou
art in the way with
him; lest at any time
the adversary deliver
thee to the judge, and
the judge deliver thee
to the officer, and thou
be cast into prison.
26 Verily I say unto
thee, Thou shalt by
no means come out
thence, till thou hast
paid the uttermost
farthing.
27 Ye have heard
that it was said by
them of old time, Thou
shalt not commit adul-
tery: 28 but I say
unto you, That whoso-
ever looketh on a
woman to lust after
her hath committed
adultery with her al-
ready in his heart.
29 And if thy right eye
offend thee, pluck it
out, and cast *it* from

γένηται. 19 ὃς.ἐὰν οὖν λύσῃ μίαν τῶν.ἐντολῶν.τούτων τῶν
come to pass. Whoever then shall break one of these commandments the
ἐλαχίστων, καὶ διδάξῃ οὕτως τοὺς ἀνθρώπους, ἐλάχιστος κλη-
least, and shall teach [2]so [1]men, least shall
θήσεται ἐν τῇ βασιλείᾳ τῶν οὐρανῶν· ὃς.δ'.ἂν ποιήσῃ καὶ
be called in the kingdom of the heavens; but whoever shall practise and
διδάξῃ, οὗτος μέγας κληθήσεται ἐν τῇ βασιλείᾳ τῶν
shall teach [them], this [one] great shall be called in the kingdom of the
οὐρανῶν. 20 λέγω.γὰρ ὑμῖν, ὅτι ἐὰν.μὴ περισσεύσῃ [w]ἡ δικαιο-
heavens. For I say to you, That unless shall abound [2]right-
σύνη ὑμῶν‖ πλεῖον τῶν γραμματέων καὶ Φαρισαίων, οὐ.μὴ
eousness [1]your above [that] of the scribes and Pharisees, in no wise
εἰσέλθητε εἰς τὴν βασιλείαν τῶν οὐρανῶν.
shall ye enter into the kingdom of the heavens.
21 Ἠκούσατε ὅτι [x]ἐῤῥέθη‖ τοῖς ἀρχαίοις, Οὐ.φονεύσεις·
Ye have heard that it was said to the ancients, Thou shalt not commit murder;
ὃς.δ'.ἂν φονεύσῃ, ἔνοχος ἔσται τῇ κρίσει. 22 ἐγὼ.δὲ
but whoever shall commit murder, liable shall be to the judgment. But I
λέγω ὑμῖν, ὅτι πᾶς ὁ ὀργιζόμενος τῷ.ἀδελφῷ.αὐτοῦ [y]εἰκῇ‖
say to you, That every one who is angry with his brother lightly,
ἔνοχος ἔσται τῇ κρίσει· ὃς.δ'.ἂν εἴπῃ τῷ.ἀδελφῷ.αὐτοῦ,
liable shall be to the judgment: but whoever shall say to his brother,
[z]Ῥακά,‖ ἔνοχος ἔσται τῷ συνεδρίῳ· ὃς.δ'.ἂν εἴπῃ, Μωρέ,
Raca, liable shall be to the Sanhedrim: but whoever shall say, Fool,
ἔνοχος ἔσται εἰς τὴν γέενναν τοῦ πυρός. 23 Ἐὰν οὖν προσ-
liable shall be to the Gehenna of fire. If therefore thou
φέρῃς τὸ.δῶρόν.σου ἐπὶ τὸ θυσιαστήριον, κἀκεῖ μνησθῇς
shalt offer thy gift at the altar, and there shalt remember
ὅτι ὁ.ἀδελφός.σου ἔχει τὶ κατὰ σοῦ, 24 ἄφες ἐκεῖ τὸ δῶρόν
that thy brother has something against thee, leave there [2]gift
σου ἔμπροσθεν τοῦ θυσιαστηρίου, καὶ ὕπαγε, πρῶτον διαλ-
[1]thy before the altar, and go away, first be
λάγηθι τῷ.ἀδελφῷ.σου, καὶ τότε ἐλθὼν πρόσφερε τὸ δῶρόν
reconciled to thy brother, and then having come offer [2]gift
σου. 25 Ἴσθι εὐνοῶν τῷ.ἀντιδίκῳ.σου ταχύ, ἕως.ὅτου εἶ
[1]thy. Be agreeing with thine adverse party quickly, whilst thou art
[a]ἐν τῇ ὁδῷ μετ' αὐτοῦ,‖ μήποτέ σε παραδῷ ὁ ἀντίδικος τῷ
in the way with him, lest [5]thee [4]deliver [1]the [2]adverse [3]party to the
κριτῇ, καὶ ὁ κριτής [b]σε παραδῷ‖ τῷ ὑπηρέτῃ, καὶ εἰς φυλακὴν
judge, and the judge thee deliver to the officer, and into prison
βληθήσῃ. 26 ἀμὴν λέγω σοι, οὐ.μὴ ἐξέλθῃς ἐκεῖθεν,
thou be cast. Verily I say to thee, In no wise shalt thou come out thence,
ἕως.ἂν ἀποδῷς τὸν ἔσχατον κοδράντην.
until thou pay the last kodrantes.
27 Ἠκούσατε ὅτι [x]ἐῤῥέθη‖ [c]τοῖς ἀρχαίοις.‖ Οὐ.μοιχεύ-
Ye have heard that it was said to the ancients, Thou shalt not commit
σεις· 28 ἐγὼ.δὲ λέγω ὑμῖν, ὅτι πᾶς ὁ βλέπων γυναῖκα πρὸς
adultery: but I say to you, that every one that looks upon a woman to
τὸ ἐπιθυμῆσαι [d]αὐτῆς,‖ ἤδη ἐμοίχευσεν αὐτὴν ἐν τῇ
lust after her, already has committed adultery with her in
καρδίᾳ [e]αὐτοῦ.‖ 29 εἰ.δὲ ὁ.ὀφθαλμός.σου ὁ δεξιὸς σκανδαλίζει
[2]heart [1]his. But if thine eye, the right, cause [2]to [3]offend
σε, ἔξελε αὐτὸν καὶ βάλε ἀπὸ σοῦ· συμφέρει.γάρ σοι ἵνα
[1]thee, pluck out it and cast [it] from thee: for it is profitable for thee that

[w] ὑμῶν ἡ δικαιοσύνη TA. [x] ἐρρήθη LTTrAW. [y] — εἰκῇ LT[TrA]. [z] ῥαχά T. [a] μετ' αὐτοῦ ἐν τῇ ὁδῷ LTTrAW. [b] — σε παραδῷ LT[Tr]. [c] — τοῖς ἀρχαίοις GLTTrAW. [d] αὐτὴν LTrAW; — αὐτῆς T. [e] ἑαυτοῦ L.

ἀπόληται ἓν τῶν.μελῶν.σου, καὶ μὴ ὅλον τὸ.σῶμά.σου βληθῇ
should perish one of thy members, and not ²whole ¹thy ³body be cast
εἰς γέενναν. 30 καὶ εἰ ἡ.δεξιά.σου χεὶρ σκανδαλίζει σε, ἔκκοψον
into Gehenna. And if thy right hand cause ²to ³offend ¹thee, cut off
αὐτὴν καὶ βάλε ἀπὸ σοῦ· συμφέρει.γάρ σοι ἵνα ἀπόληται
it and cast [it] from thee: for it is profitable for thee that should perish
ἐν τῶν.μελῶν.σου, καὶ μὴ ὅλον τὸ.σῶμά.σου [f]βληθῇ εἰς γέενναν.‖
one of thy members, and not ²whole ¹thy ³body be cast into Gehenna.
31 [g]Ἐρρέθη‖ δέ, [h]ὅτι‖ ὃς.ἂν ἀπολύσῃ τὴν.γυναῖκα.αὐτοῦ,
It was said also that whoever shall put away his wife,
δότω αὐτῇ ἀποστάσιον. 32 ἐγὼ.δὲ λέγω ὑμῖν, ὅτι [i]ὃς.ἂν
let him give to her a letter of divorce: but I say to you, that whoever
ἀπολύσῃ‖ τὴν.γυναῖκα.αὐτοῦ, παρεκτὸς λόγου πορνείας, ποιεῖ
shall put away his wife, except on account of fornication, causes
αὐτὴν [k]μοιχᾶσθαι‖ καὶ [l]ὃς.ἐὰν‖ ἀπολελυμένην [m]γαμήσῃ,‖
her to commit adultery; and whoever her who has been put away shall marry,
μοιχᾶται.
commits adultery.

33 Πάλιν ἠκούσατε, ὅτι [g]ἐρρέθη‖ τοῖς ἀρχαίοις, Οὐκ.ἐπιορ-
Again, ye have heard that it was said to the ancients, Thou shalt not
κήσεις, ἀποδώσεις.δὲ τῷ κυρίῳ τοὺς.ὅρκους.σου· 34 ἐγὼ
forswear thyself, but thou shalt render to the Lord thine oaths. ²I
δὲ λέγω ὑμῖν μὴ ὀμόσαι ὅλως, μήτε ἐν τῷ οὐρανῷ, ὅτι θρόνος
¹but say to you not to swear at all, neither by the heaven, because [the] throne
ἐστὶν τοῦ θεοῦ· 35 μήτε ἐν τῇ γῇ, ὅτι ὑποπόδιόν ἐστιν τῶν
it is of God; nor by the earth, because [the] footstool it is
ποδῶν.αὐτοῦ· μήτε εἰς Ἱεροσόλυμα, ὅτι πόλις ἐστὶν τοῦ
of his feet: nor by Jerusalem, because [the] city it is of the
μεγάλου βασιλέως· 36 μήτε ἐν τῇ.κεφαλῇ.σου ὀμόσῃς, ὅτι
great King. Neither by thy head shalt thou swear, because
οὐ.δύνασαι μίαν τρίχα λευκὴν [n]ἢ μέλαιναν ποιῆσαι.‖ 37 [o]ἔστω‖
thou art not able one hair white or black to make. ²Let ⁵be
δὲ ὁ.λόγος.ὑμῶν, ναὶ ναί, οὒ οὔ· τὸ.δὲ περισσὸν τούτων ἐκ
¹but ³your ⁴word, Yea, yea; Nay, nay: but what [is] more than these from
τοῦ πονηροῦ ἐστιν.
evil is.

38 Ἠκούσατε ὅτι [g]ἐρρέθη,‖ Ὀφθαλμὸν ἀντὶ ὀφθαλμοῦ, καὶ
Ye have heard that it was said, Eye for eye, and
ὀδόντα ἀντὶ ὀδόντος· 39 ἐγὼ.δὲ λέγω ὑμῖν μὴ ἀντιστῆναι τῷ
tooth for tooth; but I say to you not to resist
πονηρῷ· ἀλλ᾽ ὅστις σε [p]ῥαπίσει ἐπὶ‖ τὴν.δεξιάν.[q]σου σιαγόνα,‖
evil; but whosoever thee shall strike on thy right cheek,
στρέψον αὐτῷ καὶ τὴν ἄλλην· 40 καὶ τῷ θέλοντί σοι κρι-
turn to him also the other; and to him who would with thee go
θῆναι καὶ τὸν.χιτῶνά.σου λαβεῖν, ἄφες αὐτῷ καὶ τὸ ἱμάτιον·
to law and thy tunic take, yield to him also [thy] cloak;
41 καὶ ὅστις σε ἀγγαρεύσει μίλιον ἕν, ὕπαγε μετ᾽ αὐτοῦ δύο.
and whosoever thee will compel to go ²mile ¹one, go with him two.
42 τῷ αἰτοῦντί σε [r]δίδου‖ καὶ τὸν.θέλοντα ἀπὸ σοῦ [s]δανεί-
To him who asks of thee give; and him that wishes from thee to bor-
σασθαι‖ μὴ.ἀποστραφῇς.
row thou shalt not turn away from.

thee: for it is profitable for thee that one of thy members should perish, and not *that* thy whole body should be cast into hell.
30 And if thy right hand offend thee, cut it off, and cast *it* from thee: for it is profitable for thee that one of thy members should perish, and not *that* thy whole body should be cast into hell.
31 It hath been said, Whosoever shall put away his wife, let him give her a writing of divorcement: 32 but I say unto you, That whosoever shall put away his wife, saving for the cause of fornication, causeth her to commit adultery: and whosoever shall marry her that is divorced committeth adultery.

33 Again, ye have heard that it hath been said by them of old time, Thou shalt not forswear thyself, but shalt perform unto the Lord thine oaths: 34 but I say unto you, Swear not at all; neither by heaven; for it is God's throne: 35 nor by the earth; for it is his footstool: neither by Jerusalem; for it is the city of the great King. 36 Neither shalt thou swear by thy head, because thou canst not make one hair white or black. 37 But let your communication be, Yea, yea; Nay, nay: for whatsoever is more than these cometh of evil.

38 Ye have heard that it hath been said, An eye for an eye, and a tooth for a tooth: 39 but I say unto you, That ye resist not evil: but whosoever shall smite thee on thy right cheek, turn to him the other also. 40 And if any man will sue thee at the law, and take away thy coat, let him have *thy* cloke also. 41 And whosoever shall compel thee to go a mile, go with him twain. 42 Give to him that asketh thee, and from him that would bor-

---

[f] εἰς γέενναν ἀπέλθῃ into Gehenna go away LTTrA. [g] ἐρρήθη LTrAW. [h] — ὅτι LTTrA. [i] πᾶς ὁ ἀπολύων every one that puts away LTTrA. [k] μοιχευθῆναι LTTrA. [l] ὁ he who L. [m] γαμήσας has married L. [n] ποιῆσαι ἢ μέλαιναν LTTrA. [o] ἔσται shall be LA. [p] ῥαπίζει εἰς strikes upon LTTrA. [q] σιαγόνα σου LTrA; — σου (*read* the right cheek) T. [r] δός LTTrA. [s] δανίσασθαι T.

row of thee turn not
thou away.
43 Ye have heard
that it hath been said,
Thou shalt love thy
neighbour, and hate
thine enemy. 44 But
I say unto you, Love
your enemies, bless
them that curse you,
do good to them that
hate you, and pray for
them which despite-
fully use you, and per-
secute you; 45 that ye
may be the children of
your Father which is
in heaven: for he mak-
eth his sun to rise on
the evil and on the
good, and sendeth rain
on the just and on the
unjust. 46 For if ye
love them which love
you, what reward have
ye? do not even the
publicans the same?
47 And if ye salute
your brethren only,
what do ye more *than
others?* do not even the
publicans so? 48 Be ye
therefore perfect, even
as your Father which
is in heaven is perfect.

VI. Take heed that
ye do not your alms be-
fore men, to be seen of
them: otherwise ye
have no reward of your
Father which is in hea-
ven. 2 Therefore when
thou doest *thine* alms,
do not sound a trum-
pet before thee, as the
hypocrites do in the
synagogues and in the
streets, that they may
have glory of men.
Verily I say unto you,
They have their re-
ward. 3 But when
thou doest alms, let
not thy left hand know
what thy right hand
doeth: 4 that thine
alms may be in secret:
and thy Father which
seeth in secret him-
self shall reward thee
openly.

5 And when thou
prayest, thou shalt not
be as the hypocrites
are: for they love to
pray standing in the
synagogues and in the
corners of the streets,

43 Ἠκούσατε ὅτι [t]ἐῤῥέθη,‖ Ἀγαπήσεις τὸν.πλησίον.σου καὶ
Ye have heard that it was said, Thou shalt love thy neighbour and
μισήσεις τὸν.ἐχθρόν.σου· 44 ἐγὼ.δὲ λέγω ὑμῖν, Ἀγαπᾶτε τοὺς
hate thine enemy. But I say to you, Love
ἐχθροὺς ὑμῶν, [v]εὐλογεῖτε τοὺς καταρωμένους ὑμᾶς, καλῶς
[2]enemies [1]your, bless those who curse you, [2]well
ποιεῖτε [w]τοὺς μισοῦντας ὑμᾶς,‖ καὶ προσεύχεσθε ὑπὲρ τῶν
[1]do to those who hate you, and pray for those who
[x]ἐπηρεαζόντων ὑμᾶς καὶ‖ διωκόντων ὑμᾶς· 45 ὅπως γένησθε
despitefully use you and persecute you; so that ye may be
υἱοὶ τοῦ.πατρὸς.ὑμῶν τοῦ ἐν οὐρανοῖς· ὅτι τὸν.ἥλιον.αὐτοῦ
sons of your Father who [is] in [the] heavens: for his sun
ἀνατέλλει ἐπὶ πονηροὺς καὶ ἀγαθούς, καὶ βρέχει ἐπὶ δικαίους
he causes to rise on evil and good, and sends rain on just
καὶ ἀδίκους. 46 ἐὰν.γὰρ ἀγαπήσητε τοὺς ἀγαπῶντας ὑμᾶς,
and unjust. For if ye love those who love you,
τίνα μισθὸν ἔχετε; οὐχὶ καὶ οἱ τελῶναι [y]τὸ αὐτὸ‖ ποιοῦσιν;
what reward have ye? [2]not [3]also [4]the [5]tax [6]gatherers [7]the [8]same [1]do?
47 καὶ ἐὰν ἀσπάσησθε τοὺς.ἀδελφοὺς.ὑμῶν μόνον, τί περισ-
and if ye salute your brethren only, what extraordi-
σὸν ποιεῖτε; οὐχὶ καὶ οἱ [z]τελῶναι‖ [a]οὕτως‖ ποιοῦσιν; 48 ἔσεσθε
nary do ye? [2]Not [3]also [4]the [5]tax [6]gatherers [7]so [1]do? [3]shall [4]be
οὖν ὑμεῖς τέλειοι, [b]ὥσπερ‖ ὁ.πατὴρ.ὑμῶν [c]ὁ ἐν τοῖς οὐρανοῖς‖
[2]therefore [1]ye perfect, even as your Father who [is] in the heavens
τέλειός ἐστιν.
perfect is.

6 Προσέχετε[d] τὴν.[e]ἐλεημοσύνην‖.ὑμῶν μὴ ποιεῖν ἔμπροσθεν
Beware your alms not to do before
τῶν ἀνθρώπων, πρὸς.τὸ.θεαθῆναι αὐτοῖς· εἰ.δὲ.μήγε, μισθὸν
men, in order to be seen by them: otherwise reward
οὐκ.ἔχετε παρὰ τῷ.πατρὶ.ὑμῶν τῷ ἐν [f]τοῖς‖ οὐρανοῖς. 2 ὅταν
ye have not with your Father who [is] in the heavens. When
οὖν ποιῇς ἐλεημοσύνην, μὴ.σαλπίσῃς ἔμπροσθέν σου,
therefore thou doest alms, do not sound a trumpet before thee,
ὥσπερ οἱ ὑποκριταὶ ποιοῦσιν ἐν ταῖς συναγωγαῖς καὶ ἐν ταῖς
as the hypocrites do in the synagogues and in the
ῥύμαις, ὅπως δοξασθῶσιν ὑπὸ τῶν ἀνθρώπων· ἀμὴν λέγω
streets, that they may have glory from men. Verily I say
ὑμῖν, ἀπέχουσιν τὸν.μισθὸν.αὐτῶν. 3 σοῦ.δὲ ποιοῦντος ἐλεη-
to you, they have their reward. But thou doing
μοσύνην, μὴ.γνώτω ἡ.ἀριστερά.σου τί ποιεῖ ἡ.δεξιά.σου,
alms, let not [4]know [1]thy [2]left [3]hand what does thy right hand,
4 ὅπως [g]ᾖ σου ἡ.ἐλεημοσύνη‖ ἐν τῷ κρυπτῷ· καὶ ὁ.πατήρ.σου
so that [3]may [4]be [1]thine [2]alms in secret: and thy Father
ὁ βλέπων ἐν τῷ κρυπτῷ [h]αὐτὸς‖ ἀποδώσει σοι [i]ἐν.τῷ.φανερῷ.‖
who sees in secret himself shall render to thee openly.
5 Καὶ ὅταν [k]προσεύχῃ, οὐκ.ἔσῃ ὥσπερ‖ οἱ ὑποκριταί,
And when thou prayest, thou shalt not be as the hypocrites,
ὅτι φιλοῦσιν ἐν ταῖς συναγωγαῖς καὶ ἐν ταῖς γωνίαις τῶν
for they love in the synagogues and in the corners of the

[t] ἐρρήθη LT AW. [v] — εὐλογεῖτε . . . μισοῦντας ὑμᾶς LTTrA. [w] τοῖς μισοῦσιν ὑμᾶς GW. [x] — ἐπηρεαζόντων ὑμᾶς καὶ LTTrA. [y] οὕτως so LTrA. [z] ἐθνικοὶ heathen GLTTrAW [a] τὸ αὐτὸ, the same LTTrAW. [b] ὡς as LTTrA. [c] ὁ οὐράνιος the heavenly LTTrA. [d] + δὲ but T[ ]. [e] δικαιοσύνην righteousness GLTTrAW. [f] — τοῖς T. [g] ἡ σου ἐλεημοσυνη ᾖ T. [h] — αὐτὸς LTTrA. [i] — ἐν τῷ φανερῷ LTTrAW. [k] προσεύχησθε, οὐκ ἔσεσθε ὡς ye pray, ye shall not be as LTTrA.

πλατειῶν ἑστῶτες προσεύχεσθαι, ὅπως [l]ἄν‖.φανῶσιν τοῖς
streets standing to pray, so that they may appear
ἀνθρώποις· ἀμὴν λέγω ὑμῖν, [m]ὅτι‖ ἀπέχουσιν τὸν μισθὸν
to men. Verily I say to you, that they have [2]reward
αὐτῶν. 6 σὺ.δέ, ὅταν προσεύχῃ, εἴσελθε εἰς τὸ.[n]ταμιεῖόν‖.σου,
[1]their. But thou, when thou prayest, enter into thy chamber,
καὶ κλείσας τὴν.θύραν.σου, πρόσευξαι τῷ.πατρί.σου τῷ ἐν
and having shut thy door, pray to thy Father who [is] in
τῷ κρυπτῷ· καὶ ὁ.πατήρ.σου ὁ βλέπων ἐν τῷ κρυπτῷ ἀπο-
secret; and thy Father who sees in secret will
δώσει σοι [o]ἐν.τῷ.φανερῷ‖. 7 Προσευχόμενοι.δὲ μὴ.[p]βαττολο-
render to thee openly. But when ye pray do not use vain
γήσητε,‖ ὥσπερ οἱ ἐθνικοί· δοκοῦσιν.γὰρ ὅτι ἐν τῇ πολυλογίᾳ
repetitions, as the heathens: for they think that in [2]much [3]speaking
αὐτῶν εἰσακουσθήσονται. 8 μὴ οὖν ὁμοιωθῆτε αὐτοῖς·
[1]their they shall be heard. [2]Not [3]therefore [1]be like to them:
οἶδεν.γὰρ ὁ.πατὴρ.ὑμῶν ὧν χρείαν ἔχετε πρὸ τοῦ ὑμᾶς
for [3]knows [1]your [2]Father of what things [3]need [1]ye [2]have before ye
αἰτῆσαι αὐτόν. 9 οὕτως οὖν προσεύχεσθε ὑμεῖς· Πάτερ.ἡμῶν
ask him. Thus therefore pray ye: Our Father
ὁ ἐν τοῖς οὐρανοῖς, ἁγιασθήτω τὸ.ὄνομά.σου· 10 [q]ἐλθέτω‖
who [art] in the heavens, sanctified be thy name; let come
ἡ.βασιλεία.σου· γενηθήτω τὸ.θέλημά.σου, ὡς ἐν οὐρανῷ, καὶ
thy kingdom; let be done thy will as in heaven, [so] also
ἐπὶ [r]τῆς‖ γῆς· 11 τὸν.ἄρτον.ἡμῶν τὸν ἐπιούσιον δὸς ἡμῖν σή-
upon the earth; our bread the needed give us to-
μερον· 12 καὶ ἄφες ἡμῖν τὰ.ὀφειλήματα.ἡμῶν, ὡς καὶ ἡμεῖς
day; and forgive us our debts, as also we
[s]ἀφίεμεν‖ τοῖς.ὀφειλέταις.ἡμῶν· 13 καὶ μὴ.εἰσενέγκῃς ἡμᾶς εἰς
forgive our debtors; And lead not us into
πειρασμόν, ἀλλὰ ῥῦσαι ἡμᾶς ἀπὸ τοῦ πονηροῦ. [t]ὅτι σοῦ ἐστιν
temptation, but deliver us from evil. For thine is
ἡ βασιλεία καὶ ἡ δύναμις καὶ ἡ δόξα εἰς τοὺς αἰῶνας. ἀμήν.‖
the kingdom and the power and the glory to the ages. Amen.
14 Ἐὰν.γὰρ ἀφῆτε τοῖς ἀνθρώποις τὰ.παραπτώματα.αὐτῶν,
For if ye forgive men their offences,
ἀφήσει καὶ ὑμῖν ὁ.πατὴρ.ὑμῶν ὁ οὐράνιος· 15 ἐὰν.δὲ μὴ
[5]will [6]forgive [8]also [7]you [1]your [2]Father [3]the [4]heavenly. but if [2]not
ἀφῆτε τοῖς ἀνθρώποις [u]τὰ.παραπτώματα.αὐτῶν,‖ οὐδὲ ὁ
[1]ye [3]forgive men their offences, neither
πατὴρ ὑμῶν ἀφήσει τὰ.παραπτώματα.ὑμῶν.
[3]Father [2]your [1]will forgive your offences.

16 Ὅταν.δὲ νηστεύητε, μὴ.γίνεσθε [v]ὥσπερ‖ οἱ ὑποκριταὶ
And when ye fast, be not as the hypocrites,
σκυθρωποί· ἀφανίζουσιν.γὰρ τὰ.πρόσωπα.[w]αὐτῶν,‖
downcast in countenance; for they disfigure their faces,
ὅπως φανῶσιν τοῖς ἀνθρώποις νηστεύοντες· ἀμὴν λέγω
so that they may appear to men fasting. Verily I say
ὑμῖν, [x]ὅτι‖ ἀπέχουσιν τὸν.μισθὸν.αὐτῶν. 17 σὺ.δὲ νηστεύων
to you, that they have their reward. But thou, fasting,
ἄλειψαί σου τὴν κεφαλήν, καὶ τὸ.πρόσωπόν.σου νίψαι· 18 ὅπως
anoint thy head, and [2]thy [3]face [1]wash, so that
μὴ.φανῇς [y]τοῖς ἀνθρώποις νηστεύων,‖ ἀλλὰ τῷ πατρί
thou mayest not appear to men fasting, but to [2]Father

that they may be seen of men. Verily I say unto you, They have their reward. 6 But thou, when thou prayest, enter into thy closet, and when thou hast shut thy door, pray to thy Father which is in secret; and thy Father which seeth in secret shall reward thee openly. 7 But when ye pray, use not vain repetitions, as the heathen *do*: for they think that they shall be heard for their much speaking. 8 Be not ye therefore like unto them: for your Father knoweth what things ye have need of, before ye ask him. 9 After this manner therefore pray ye: Our Father which art in heaven, Hallowed be thy name. 10 Thy kingdom come. Thy will be done in earth, as *it is* in heaven. 11 Give us this day our daily bread. 12 And forgive us our debts, as we forgive our debtors. 13 And lead us not into temptation, but deliver us from evil: For thine is the kingdom, and the power, and the glory, for ever. Amen. 14 For if ye forgive men their trespasses, your heavenly Father will also forgive you: 15 but if ye forgive not men their trespasses, neither will your Father forgive your trespasses.

16 Moreover when ye fast, be not, as the hypocrites, of a sad countenance: for they disfigure their faces, that they may appear unto men to fast. Verily I say unto you, They have their reward. 17 But thou, when thou fastest, anoint thine head, and wash thy face; 18 that thou appear not unto men to fast, but unto thy Fa-

[l] — ἂν LTTrAW. [m] — ὅτι LTTrA. [n] ταμεῖόν TA. [o] — ἐν τῷ φανερῷ LTTrA. [p] βατταλογήσητε TA. [q] ἐλθάτω T. [r] — τῆς LTTrAW. [s] ἀφήκαμεν have forgiven LTTrA. [t] — ὅτι σοῦ *to end of verse* GLTTrAW. [u] — τὰ παραπ. αὐτῶν T. [v] ὡς LTTrA. [w] ἑαυτῶν L. [x] — ὅτι LTTrA. [y] νηστ. τοῖς ἀνθρώ. L.

ther which is in secret: and thy Father, which seeth in secret, shall reward thee openly.

19 Lay not up for yourselves treasures upon earth, where moth and rust doth corrupt, and where thieves break through and steal: 20 but lay up for yourselves treasures in heaven, where neither moth nor rust doth corrupt, and where thieves do not break through nor steal: 21 for where your treasure is, there will your heart be also. 22 The light of the body is the eye: if therefore thine eye be single, thy whole body shall be full of light. 23 But if thine eye be evil, thy whole body shall be full of darkness. If therefore the light that is in thee be darkness, how great *is* that darkness!

24 No man can serve two masters: for either he will hate the one, and love the other; or else he will hold to the one, and despise the other. Ye cannot serve God and mammon. 25 Therefore I say unto you, Take no thought for your life, what ye shall eat, or what ye shall drink; nor yet for your body, what ye shall put on. Is not the life more than meat, and the body than raiment? 26 Behold the fowls of the air: for they sow not, neither do they reap, nor gather into barns; yet your heavenly Father feedeth them. Are ye not much better than they? 27 Which of you by taking thought can add one cubit unto his stature? 28 And why take ye thought for raiment? Consider the lilies of the field, how they grow; they toil not, neither do they spin: 29 and yet I say unto you, That even Solomon in all his glory was not arrayed like one of these. 30 Wherefore, if God so clothe the grass of the field, which to day

σου τῷ ἐν τῷ [z]κρυπτῷ·‖ καὶ ὁ.πατήρ.σου ὁ βλέπων ἐν τῷ
1thy who [is] in secret; and thy Father who sees in
[z]κρυπτῷ‖ ἀποδώσει σοι [a]ἐν.τῷ.φανερῷ.‖
secret will render to thee openly.

19 Μὴ.θησαυρίζετε ὑμῖν θησαυροὺς ἐπὶ τῆς γῆς, ὅπου
Treasure not up for yourselves treasures upon the earth, where
σὴς καὶ βρῶσις ἀφανίζει, καὶ ὅπου κλέπται διορύσσουσιν καὶ
moth and rust spoil, and where thieves dig through and
κλέπτουσιν· 20 θησαυρίζετε.δὲ ὑμῖν θησαυροὺς ἐν οὐρανῷ,
steal: but treasure up for yourselves treasures in heaven,
ὅπου οὔτε σὴς οὔτε βρῶσις ἀφανίζει, καὶ ὅπου κλέπται οὐ.δι-
where neither moth nor rust spoils and where thieves do not
ορύσσουσιν οὐδὲ κλέπτουσιν. 21 ὅπου.γάρ ἐστιν ὁ θησαυρὸς
dig through nor steal: for where 3is 2treasure
[b]ὑμῶν,‖ ἐκεῖ ἔσται [c]καὶ‖ ἡ καρδία [b]ὑμῶν.‖ 22 Ὁ λύχνος τοῦ
1your, there will be also 2heart 1your. The lamp of the
σώματός ἐστιν ὁ ὀφθαλμός[d]· ἐὰν [e]οὖν‖ [f]ὁ.ὀφθαλμός.σου
body is the eye; if therefore thine eye
ἁπλοῦς ᾖ,‖ ὅλον τὸ.σῶμά.σου φωτεινὸν ἔσται· 23 ἐὰν.δὲ ὁ
single be, 2whole 1thy body light will be. But if
ὀφθαλμός.σου πονηρὸς ᾖ, ὅλον τὸ.σῶμά.σου σκοτεινὸν ἔσται.
thine eye evil be, 2whole 1thy body dark will be.
εἰ οὖν τὸ φῶς τὸ ἐν σοὶ σκότος ἐστίν, τὸ σκότος πόσον;
If therefore the light that [is] in thee darkness is, the darkness how great

24 Οὐδεὶς δύναται δυσὶ κυρίοις δουλεύειν· ἢ.γὰρ τὸν ἕνα
No one is able two lords to serve; for either the one
μισήσει, καὶ τὸν ἕτερον ἀγαπήσει· ἢ ἑνὸς ἀνθέξεται, καὶ
he will hate, and the other he will love; or [the] one he will hold to, and
τοῦ ἑτέρου καταφρονήσει. οὐ.δύνασθε θεῷ δουλεύειν καὶ [g]μαμ-
the other he will despise. Ye are not able 3God 1to 2serve and mam-
μωνᾷ.‖ 25 διὰ τοῦτο λέγω ὑμῖν, μὴ.μεριμνᾶτε τῇ.ψυχῇ.ὑμῶν,
mon. Because of this I say to you, be not careful as to your life,
τί φάγητε [h]καὶ‖ [i]τί πίητε·‖ μηδὲ τῷ.σώματι.ὑμῶν,
what ye should eat and what ye should drink; nor as to your body
τί ἐνδύσησθε. οὐχὶ ἡ ψυχὴ πλεῖόν ἐστιν τῆς τροφῆς καὶ
what ye should put on. 2Not 3the 4life 5more 1is than the food and
τὸ σῶμα τοῦ ἐνδύματος; 26 ἐμβλέψατε εἰς τὰ πετεινὰ τοῦ
the body than the raiment? Look at the birds of the
οὐρανοῦ, ὅτι οὐ.σπείρουσιν, οὐδὲ θερίζουσιν, οὐδὲ συνάγουσιν
heaven, that they sow not, nor do they reap, nor do they gather
εἰς ἀποθήκας, καὶ ὁ.πατὴρ.ὑμῶν ὁ οὐράνιος τρέφει αὐτά· οὐχ
into granaries, and your Father the heavenly feeds them: 2not
ὑμεῖς μᾶλλον διαφέρετε αὐτῶν; 27 τίς.δὲ ἐξ ὑμῶν μερι-
3ye 4much 1are better than they? But which out of you by being
μνῶν δύναται προσθεῖναι ἐπὶ τὴν.ἡλικίαν.αὐτοῦ πῆχυν ἕνα;
careful is able to add to his stature 2cubit 1one?
28 καὶ περὶ ἐνδύματος τί μεριμνᾶτε; καταμάθετε τὰ κρινα
and about raiment why are ye careful? observe the lilies
τοῦ ἀγροῦ, πῶς [k]αὐξάνει·‖ οὐ.[l]κοπιᾷ‖ οὐδὲ [m]νήθει·‖ 29 λέ-
of the field, how they grow: they labour not nor do they spin: 2I
γω δὲ ὑμῖν, ὅτι οὐδὲ Σολομὼν ἐν πάσῃ τῇ.δόξῃ.αὐτοῦ περιε-
3say 1but to you that not even Solomon in all his glory was
βάλετο ὡς ἓν τούτων. 30 εἰ.δὲ τὸν χόρτον τοῦ ἀγροῦ, σήμερον
clothed as one of these. But if the grass of the field, to-day

[z] κρυφαίῳ LTTrA. [a] — ἐν τῷ φανερῷ GLTTrAW. [b] σου thy LTTrA. [c] — καὶ L. [d] + σου thy L. [e] — οὖν T. [f] ᾖ ὁ ὀφθαλμός σου ἁπλοῦς LTA. [g] μαμωνᾷ GLTTrAW. [h] ἢ or LTr; — καὶ T. [i] — τί πίητε T. [k] αὐξάνουσιν LTTrA. [l] κοπιῶσιν LT; κοπιοῦσιν TrA. [m] νήθουσιν LTTrA.

ὄντα, καὶ αὔριον εἰς κλίβανον βαλλόμενον, ὁ θεὸς οὕτως
[1]which is and to-morrow into an oven is cast, God thus
ἀμφιέννυσιν, οὐ πολλῷ μᾶλλον ὑμᾶς, ὀλιγόπιστοι; 31 μὴ
arrays, [will he] not much rather you, O [ye] of little faith? [2]not
οὖν μεριμνήσητε, λέγοντες, Τί φάγωμεν. ἢ τί πίωμεν,
[3]therefore [1]be careful, saying, What shall we eat? or what shall we drink?
ἢ τί περιβαλώμεθα; 32 πάντα.γὰρ ταῦτα τὰ ἔθνη [u]ἐπι-
or with what shall we be clothed? For all these things the nations seek
ζητεῖ·‖ οἶδεν.γὰρ ὁ.πατὴρ.ὑμῶν ὁ οὐράνιος ὅτι χρῄζετε
after. For knows your Father the heavenly that ye have need
τούτων ἁπάντων· 33 ζητεῖτε.δὲ πρῶτον [o]τὴν βασιλείαν τοῦ
of [2]these [3]things [1]all. But seek ye first the kingdom
θεοῦ καὶ τὴν.δικαιοσύνην‖.αὐτοῦ, καὶ ταῦτα πάντα προσ-
of God and his righteousness, and [2]these [3]things [1]all shall
τεθήσεται ὑμῖν. 34 μὴ οὖν [p]μεριμνήσητε‖ εἰς τὴν αὔριον·
be added to you. [2]Not [3]therefore [1]be careful for the morrow:
ἡ.γὰρ αὔριον μεριμνήσει [q]τὰ‖ [r]ἑαυτῆς.‖ ἀρκετὸν τῇ
for the morrow shall be careful about the [things] of itself. Sufficient to the
ἡμέρᾳ ἡ κακία αὐτῆς.
day [is] the evil of it.

7 Μὴ.κρίνετε, ἵνα μὴ.κριθῆτε· 2 ἐν ᾧ γὰρ κρίματι κρίνετε,
Judge not, that ye be not judged: [2]with [3]what [1]for judgment ye judge,
κριθήσεσθε· καὶ ἐν ᾧ μέτρῳ μετρεῖτε, [s]ἀντιμετρηθήσεται‖
ye shall be judged; and with what measure ye mete, it shall be measured again
ὑμῖν. 3 Τί.δὲ βλέπεις τὸ κάρφος τὸ ἐν τῷ ὀφθαλμῷ τοῦ
to you. But why lookest thou on the mote that [is] in the eye
ἀδελφοῦ.σου, τὴν.δὲ ἐν τῷ.σῷ ὀφθαλμῷ δοκὸν οὐ.κατανοεῖς;
of thy brother, but the [2]in [3]thine [[4]own] [5]eye [1]beam perceivest not?
4 ἢ πῶς ἐρεῖς τῷ.ἀδελφῷ.σου, Ἄφες ἐκβάλω τὸ
Or how wilt thou say to thy brother, Suffer [that] I may cast out the
κάρφος [t]ἀπὸ‖ τοῦ.ὀφθαλμοῦ.σου· καὶ ἰδού, ἡ δοκὸς ἐν τῷ
mote from thine eye: and behold, the beam [is] in
ὀφθαλμῷ.σου; 5 ὑποκριτά, ἔκβαλε πρῶτον [v]τὴν δοκὸν ἐκ
thine [own] eye! hypocrite, cast out first the beam out of
τοῦ.ὀφθαλμοῦ.σου,‖ καὶ τότε διαβλέψεις ἐκβαλεῖν τὸ κάρφος
thine [own] eye, and then thou wilt see clearly to cast out the mote
ἐκ τοῦ ὀφθαλμοῦ τοῦ.ἀδελφοῦ.σου.
out of the eye of thy brother.
6 Μὴ.δῶτε τὸ ἅγιον τοῖς κυσίν· μηδὲ βάλητε τοὺς
Give not that which [is] holy to the dogs, nor cast
μαργαρίτας ὑμῶν ἔμπροσθεν τῶν χοίρων, μήποτε [w]κατα-
[2]pearls [1]your before the swine, lest they should
πατήσωσιν‖ αὐτοὺς ἐν τοῖς.ποσὶν.αὐτῶν, καὶ στραφέντες
trample upon them with their feet, and having turned
ῥήξωσιν ὑμᾶς.
they rend you.
7 Αἰτεῖτε, καὶ δοθήσεται ὑμῖν· ζητεῖτε, καὶ εὑρήσετε·
Ask, and it shall be given to you: seek, and ye shall find:
κρούετε, καὶ ἀνοιγήσεται ὑμῖν. 8 πᾶς.γὰρ ὁ αἰτῶν λαμβάνει,
knock, and it shall be opened to you. For everyone that asks receives,
καὶ ὁ ζητῶν εὑρίσκει, καὶ τῷ κρούοντι [x]ἀνοιγήσεται.‖
and he that seeks finds, and to him that knocks it shall be opened.

is, and to morrow is cast into the oven, *shall he* not much more *clothe* you, O ye of little faith? 31 Therefore take no thought, saying, What shall we eat? or, What shall we drink? or, Wherewithal shall we be clothed? 32 (For after all these things do the Gentiles seek:) for your heavenly Father knoweth that ye have need of all these things. 33 But seek ye first the kingdom of God, and his righteousness; and all these things shall be added unto you. 34 Take therefore no thought for the morrow: for the morrow shall take thought for the things of itself. Sufficient unto the day *is* the evil thereof.

VII. Judge not, that ye be not judged. 2 For with what judgment ye judge, ye shall be judged: and with what measure ye mete, it shall be measured to you again. 3 And why beholdest thou the mote that is in thy brother's eye, but considerest not the beam that is in thine own eye? 4 Or how wilt thou say to thy brother, Let me pull out the mote out of thine eye; and, behold, a beam *is* in thine own eye? 5 Thou hypocrite, first cast out the beam out of thine own eye; and then shalt thou see clearly to cast out the mote out of thy brother's eye.

6 Give not that which is holy unto the dogs, neither cast ye your pearls before swine, lest they trample them under their feet, and turn again and rend you.

7 Ask, and it shall be given you; seek, and ye shall find; knock, and it shall be opened unto you: 8 for every one that asketh receiveth; and he that seeketh findeth; and to him that knocketh it shall be opened. 9 Or

---

[u] ἐπιζητοῦσιν LTTrA. [o] τὴν δικαιοσύνην καὶ τὴν βασιλειαν L; — τοῦ θεοῦ (*read* its righteousness) LT[A] [p] μεριμνήσετε E. [q] — τὰ (*omit* the [things] of) LTTrAW. [r] αὐτῆς A. [s] μετρηθήσεται it shall be measured GLTTrAW. [t] ἐκ out of LTTr. [v] ἐκ τοῦ ὀφθαλμοῦ σου τὴν δοκὸν LTTrA. [w] καταπατήσουσιν they shall trample upon LTTrA. [x] ἀνοίγεται it is opened LTr.

what man is there of
you, whom if his son
ask bread, will he give
him a stone? 10 Or if
he ask a fish, will he
give him a serpent?
11 If ye then, being
evil, know how to give
good gifts unto your
children, how much
more shall your Father
which is in heaven give
good things to them
that ask him?

12 Therefore all
things whatsoever ye
would that men should
do to you, do ye even
so to them: for this
is the law and the prophets.

13 Enter ye in at
the strait gate: for
wide *is* the gate, and
broad *is* the way, that
leadeth to destruction,
and many there be
which go in thereat:
14 because strait *is* the
gate, and narrow *is* the
way, which leadeth unto
life, and few there
be that find it.
15 Beware of false
prophets, which come
to you in sheep's clothing,
but inwardly they
are ravening wolves.
16 Ye shall know them
by their fruits. Do
men gather grapes of
thorns, or figs of
thistles? 17 Even so
every good tree bringeth
forth good fruit;
but a corrupt tree
bringeth forth evil
fruit. 18 A good tree
cannot bring forth evil
fruit, neither *can* a corrupt
tree bring forth
good fruit. 19 Every
tree that bringeth not
forth good fruit is
hewn down, and cast
into the fire. 20 Wherefore
by their fruits ye
shall know them.

21 Not every one
that saith unto me,
Lord, Lord, shall enter
into the kingdom of
heaven; but he that
doeth the will of my

9 ἢ τίς [y]ἐστιν‖ ἐξ ὑμῶν ἄνθρωπος, ὃν [z]ἐὰν‖ [a]αἰτήσῃ‖ ὁ υἱὸς
Or what [2]is [3]there [4]of [5]you [1]man who if [3]should [4]ask [2]son
αὐτοῦ ἄρτον, μὴ λίθον ἐπιδώσει αὐτῷ; 10 [b]καὶ ἐὰν ἰχθὺν
[1]his bread, a stone will he give him? and if a fish
αἰτήσῃ,‖ μὴ ὄφιν ἐπιδώσει αὐτῷ; 11 εἰ οὖν ὑμεῖς πονηροὶ
he should ask, a serpent will he give him? If therefore ye, [2]evil
ὄντες οἴδατε δόματα ἀγαθὰ διδόναι τοῖς.τέκνοις.ὑμῶν, πόσῳ
[1]being, know [how] [2]gifts [1]good to give to your children, how much
μᾶλλον ὁ.πατὴρ.ὑμῶν ὁ ἐν τοῖς οὐρανοῖς δώσει ἀγαθὰ
more your Father who [is] in the heavens will give good things
τοῖς αἰτοῦσιν αὐτόν;
to them that ask him?

12 Πάντα οὖν ὅσα.[c]ἂν‖ θέλητε ἵνα ποιῶσιν ὑμῖν οἱ
All things therefore whatever ye desire that [2]should [3]do [4]to [5]you
ἄνθρωποι, οὕτως καὶ ὑμεῖς ποιεῖτε αὐτοῖς· οὗτος.γάρ ἐστιν ὁ
[1]men, so also [2]ye [1]do to them: for this is the
νόμος καὶ οἱ προφῆται.
law and the prophets.

13 [d]Εἰσέλθετε‖ διὰ τῆς στενῆς πύλης· ὅτι πλατεῖα [e]ἡ πύλη‖
Enter in through the narrow gate; for wide the gate
καὶ εὐρύχωρος ἡ ὁδὸς ἡ ἀπάγουσα εἰς τὴν ἀπώλειαν, καὶ
and broad the way that leads to destruction, and
πολλοί εἰσιν οἱ εἰσερχόμενοι δι' αὐτῆς· 14 [f]ὅτι‖ στενὴ [g]ἡ
many are they who enter through it: for narrow the
πύλη‖ καὶ τεθλιμμένη ἡ ὁδὸς ἡ ἀπάγουσα εἰς τὴν ζωήν, καὶ
gate and straitened the way that leads to life, and
ὀλίγοι εἰσὶν οἱ εὑρίσκοντες αὐτήν.
few are they who find it.

15 Προσέχετε.[h]δὲ‖ ἀπὸ τῶν ψευδοπροφητῶν, οἵτινες ἔρχονται
But beware of the false prophets, who come
πρὸς ὑμᾶς ἐν ἐνδύμασιν προβάτων, ἔσωθεν.δέ εἰσιν λύκοι ἅρ-
to you in raiment of sheep, but within are [2]wolves [1]ra-
παγες. 16 ἀπὸ τῶν.καρπῶν.αὐτῶν ἐπιγνώσεσθε αὐτούς· μήτι
pacious. By their fruits ye shall know them.
συλλέγουσιν ἀπὸ ἀκανθῶν [i]σταφυλὴν‖ ἢ ἀπὸ τριβόλων σῦκα;
Do they gather from thorns a bunch of grapes, or from thistles figs?
17 οὕτως πᾶν δένδρον ἀγαθὸν καρποὺς καλοὺς ποιεῖ· τὸ.δὲ
So every [2]tree [1]good [4]fruits [3]good produces, but the
σαπρὸν δένδρον καρποὺς πονηροὺς ποιεῖ. 18 οὐ.δύναται
corrupt tree [2]fruits [1]bad produces. [4]Cannot
δένδρον ἀγαθὸν καρποὺς πονηροὺς [j]ποιεῖν,‖ οὐδὲ δένδρον σα-
[1]a [3]tree [2]good [6]fruits [5]evil produce, nor a [2]tree [1]cor-
πρὸν καρποὺς καλοὺς [j]ποιεῖν.‖ 19 πᾶν[k] δένδρον μὴ ποιοῦν
rupt [5]fruits [4]good [3]produce. Every tree not producing
καρπὸν καλὸν ἐκκόπτεται καὶ εἰς πῦρ βάλλεται. 20 [l]ἄραγε‖
[2]fruit [1]good is cut down and into fire is cast. Then surely
[m]ἀπὸ‖ τῶν.καρπῶν.αὐτῶν ἐπιγνώσεσθε αὐτούς.
by their fruits ye shall know them.

21 Οὐ πᾶς ὁ λέγων μοι, Κύριε, κύριε, εἰσελεύσεται εἰς
Not every one who says to me, Lord, Lord, shall enter into
τὴν βασιλείαν τῶν οὐρανῶν· ἀλλ' ὁ ποιῶν τὸ θέλημα τοῦ
the kingdom of the heavens, but he who does the will

---

[y] — ἐστιν LTr [A]. [z] — ἐὰν LTTrA. [a] αἰτήσει shall ask LTTrA. [b] ἢ καὶ ἰχθὺν αἰτήσει or also a fish shall ask LTTrA. [c] ἐὰν T. [d] εἰσέλθατε LTTrA. [e] — ἡ πύλη L[T]. [f] τί how GLTTr. [g] [ἡ πύλη] LT. [h] — δὲ but LT [TrA]. [i] σταφυλὰς grapes LTTrA. [j] ἐνεγκεῖν bear T. [k] + [οὖν] now L. [l] ἄρα γε LTrA. [m] ἐκ L.

πατρός-μου τοῦ ἐν [n] οὐρανοῖς. 22 πολλοὶ ἐροῦσίν μοι ἐν
of my Father who [is] in [the] heavens. Many will say to me in
ἐκείνῃ τῇ ἡμέρᾳ, Κύριε, κύριε, οὐ τῷ.σῷ ὀνόματι [o]προεφη-
that day, Lord, Lord, [3]not [5]through [6]thy [7]name [1]did [2]we
τεύσαμεν,‖ καὶ τῷ.σῷ ὀνόματι δαιμόνια ἐξεβάλομεν, καὶ
[4]prophesy, and through thy name demons cast out, and
τῷ.σῷ ὀνόματι δυνάμεις πολλὰς ἐποιήσαμεν; 23 καὶ
through thy name [2]works [3]of [4]power [1]many perform? And
τότε ὁμολογήσω αὐτοῖς, ὅτι οὐδέποτε ἔγνων ὑμᾶς· ἀποχωρεῖτε
then will I confess to them, Never knew I you: depart ye
ἀπ' ἐμοῦ, οἱ ἐργαζόμενοι τὴν ἀνομίαν.
from me, who work lawlessness.

24 Πᾶς οὖν ὅστις ἀκούει μου τοὺς λόγους [p]τούτους,‖
Every one therefore whosoever hears [2]my [3]words [1]these,
καὶ ποιεῖ αὐτούς, [q]ὁμοιώσω αὐτὸν‖ ἀνδρὶ φρονίμῳ, ὅστις ᾠκοδό-
and does them, I will liken him to a [2]man [1]prudent, who built
μησεν [r]τὴν.οἰκίαν.αὐτοῦ‖ ἐπὶ τὴν πέτραν· 25 καὶ κατέβη ἡ
his house upon the rock: and came down the
βροχὴ καὶ [s]ἦλθον‖ οἱ ποταμοὶ καὶ ἔπνευσαν οἱ ἄνεμοι, καὶ
rain, and came the streams, and blew the winds, and
[t]προσέπεσον‖ τῇ.οἰκίᾳ.ἐκείνῃ, καὶ οὐκ.ἔπεσεν· τεθεμελίωτο.γὰρ
fell upon that house, and it fell not; for it had been founded
ἐπὶ τὴν πέτραν. 26 καὶ πᾶς ὁ ἀκούων μου τοὺς λόγους
upon the rock. and everyone who hears [2]my [3]words
τούτους καὶ μὴ.ποιῶν αὐτούς, ὁμοιωθήσεται ἀνδρὶ μωρῷ,
[1]these and does not do them, he shall be likened to a [2]man [1]foolish,
ὅστις ᾠκοδόμησεν [v]τὴν.οἰκίαν.αὐτοῦ‖ ἐπὶ τὴν ἄμμον· 27 καὶ
who built his house upon the sand: and
κατέβη ἡ βροχὴ καὶ ἦλθον οἱ ποταμοὶ καὶ ἔπνευσαν οἱ
came down the rain, and came the streams, and blew the
ἄνεμοι, καὶ προσέκοψαν τῇ.οἰκίᾳ.ἐκείνῃ, καὶ ἔπεσεν, καὶ ἦν
winds, and beat upon that house, and it fell, and [5]was
ἡ πτῶσις αὐτῆς μεγάλη.
[1]the [2]fall [3]of [4]it great.

28 Καὶ ἐγένετο ὅτε [w]συνετέλεσεν‖ ὁ Ἰησοῦς τοὺς λόγους
And it came to pass when [2]had [3]finished [1]Jesus [5]words
τούτους ἐξεπλήσσοντο οἱ ὄχλοι ἐπὶ τῇ.διδαχῇ.αὐτοῦ· 29 ἦν
[4]these astonished were the crowds at his teaching: [2]he [3]was
γὰρ διδάσκων αὐτοὺς ὡς ἐξουσίαν ἔχων, καὶ οὐχ ὡς οἱ
[1]for teaching them as [2]authority [1]having, and not as the
γραμματεῖς[x].
scribes.

8 [y]Καταβάντι.δὲ αὐτῷ‖ ἀπὸ τοῦ ὄρους, ἠκολούθησαν αὐτῷ
And when [2]had [3]come [4]down [1]he from the mountain, [3]followed [4]him
ὄχλοι πολλοί· 2 καὶ ἰδού, λεπρὸς [z]ἐλθὼν‖ προσεκύνει αὐτῷ,
[2]crowds [1]great. And behold, a leper having come did homage to him,
λέγων, Κύριε, ἐὰν θέλῃς, δύνασαί με καθαρίσαι. 3 Καὶ
saying, Lord, if thou wilt thou art able me to cleanse. And
ἐκτείνας τὴν.χεῖρα ἥψατο αὐτοῦ [a]ὁ Ἰησοῦς,‖ λέγων,
having stretched out [his] hand [2]touched [3]him [1]Jesus, saying,
Θέλω, καθαρίσθητι. Καὶ εὐθέως [b]ἐκαθαρίσθη‖ αὐτοῦ ἡ λέπρα.
I will, be thou cleansed. And immediately was cleansed his leprosy.

Father which is in heaven. 22 Many will say to me in that day, Lord, Lord, have we not prophesied in thy name? and in thy name have cast out devils? and in thy name done many wonderful works? 23 And then will I profess unto them, I never knew you: depart from me, ye that work iniquity.

24 Therefore whosoever heareth these sayings of mine, and doeth them, I will liken him unto a wise man, which built his house upon a rock: 25 and the rain descended, and the floods came, and the winds blew, and beat upon that house; and it fell not: for it was founded upon a rock. 26 And every one that heareth these sayings of mine, and doeth them not, shall be likened unto a foolish man, which built his house upon the sand: 27 and the rain descended, and the floods came, and the winds blew, and beat upon that house; and it fell: and great was the fall of it.

28 And it came to pass, when Jesus had ended these sayings, the people were astonished at his doctrine: 29 for he taught them as *one* having authority, and not as the scribes.

VIII. When he was come down from the mountain, great multitudes followed him. 2 And, behold, there came a leper and worshipped him, saying, Lord, if thou wilt, thou canst make me clean. 3 And Jesus put forth *his* hand, and touched him, saying, I will; be thou clean. And immediately his leprosy was cleansed. 4 And

[n] + τοῖς the LTTrA. [o] ἐπροφητεύσαμεν LTTrA. [p] [τούτους] LTr. [q] ὁμοιωθήσεται he shall be likened LTTr. [r] αὐτοῦ τὴν οἰκίαν LTTrA. [s] ἦλθαν Tr. [t] προσέπαισαν struck against L; προσέπεσαν TTrA. [v] αὐτοῦ τὴν οἰκίαν LTTrA. [w] ἐτέλεσεν LTTrA. [x] + αὐτῶν (*read* their scribes) LTTrA; + καὶ οἱ Φαρισαῖοι and the Pharisees L. [y] καὶ καταβάντος αὐτοῦ L; καταβάντος δὲ αὐτοῦ Tr. [z] προσελθὼν having come to [him] LTTrAW. [a] — ὁ Ἰησοῦς (*read* he touched) LTTrA. [b] ἐκαθερίσθη T.

Jesus saith unto him, See thou tell no man; but go thy way, shew thyself to the priest, and offer the gift that Moses commanded, for a testimony unto them.

4 Καὶ λέγει αὐτῷ ὁ Ἰησοῦς, Ὅρα μηδενὶ εἴπῃς· [c]ἀλλ'[‖] ὕπαγε,
And [2]says [3]to [4]him [1]Jesus, See no one thou tell; but go
σεαυτὸν δεῖξον τῷ ἱερεῖ, καὶ [d]προσένεγκε[‖] τὸ δῶρον ὃ προσ-
thyself show to the priest, and offer the gift which [2]or-
έταξεν [e]Μωσῆς,[‖] εἰς μαρτύριον αὐτοῖς.
dered [1]Moses for a testimony to them.

5 And when Jesus was entered into Capernaum, there came unto him a centurion, beseeching him, 6 and saying, Lord, my servant lieth at home sick of the palsy, grievously tormented. 7 And Jesus saith unto him, I will come and heal him. 8 The centurion answered and said, Lord, I am not worthy that thou shouldest come under my roof: but speak the word only, and my servant shall be healed. 9 For I am a man under authority, having soldiers under me: and I say to this *man*, Go, and he goeth; and to another, Come, and he cometh; and to my servant, Do this, and he doeth *it*. 10 When Jesus heard *it*, he marvelled, and said to them that followed, Verily I say unto you, I have not found so great faith, no, not in Israel. 11 And I say unto you, That many shall come from the east and west, and shall sit down with Abraham, and Isaac, and Jacob, in the kingdom of heaven. 12 But the children of the kingdom shall be cast out into outer darkness: there shall be weeping and gnashing of teeth. 13 And Jesus said unto the centurion, Go thy way; and as thou hast believed, so be it done unto thee. And his servant was healed in the selfsame hour.

5 [f]Εἰσελθόντι[‖].δὲ [g]τῷ Ἰησοῦ[‖] εἰς [h]Καπερναούμ,[‖] προσῆλθεν
And [2]having [3]entered [1]Jesus into Capernaum, [3]came
αὐτῷ [i]ἑκατόνταρχος[‖] παρακαλῶν αὐτὸν 6 καὶ λέγων, Κύριε,
[4]to [5]him [1]a [2]centurion, beseeching him and saying, Lord,
ὁ.παῖς.μου βέβληται ἐν τῇ οἰκίᾳ παραλυτικός, δεινῶς βασα-
my servant is laid in the house paralytic, grievously tor-
νιζόμενος. 7 [k]Καὶ[‖] λέγει αὐτῷ [l]ὁ Ἰησοῦς,[‖] Ἐγὼ ἐλθὼν θερα-
mented. And [2]says [3]to [4]him [1]Jesus, I having come will
πεύσω αὐτόν. 8 [m]Καὶ ἀποκριθεὶς[‖] ὁ [i]ἑκατόνταρχος[‖] ἔφη, Κύριε,
heal him. And [3]answering [1]the [2]centurion said, Lord,
οὐκ.εἰμὶ ἱκανὸς ἵνα μου ὑπὸ τὴν στέγην εἰσέλθῃς· ἀλλὰ μόνον
I am not worthy that [2]my [1]under roof thou shouldest come, but only
εἰπὲ [n]λόγον,[‖] καὶ ἰαθήσεται ὁ.παῖς.μου. 9 καὶ.γὰρ ἐγὼ ἄν-
speak a word, and shall be healed my servant. For also I a
θρωπός εἰμι ὑπὸ ἐξουσίαν[o], ἔχων ὑπ' ἐμαυτὸν στρατιώτας·
man am under authority, having under myself soldiers;
καὶ λέγω τούτῳ, Πορεύθητι, καὶ πορεύεται· καὶ ἄλλῳ, Ἔρχου,
and I say to this [one], Go, and he goes; and to another, Come,
καὶ ἔρχεται· καὶ τῷ.δούλῳ.μου, Ποίησον τοῦτο, καὶ ποιεῖ.
and he comes; and to my bondman, Do this, and he does [it].
10 Ἀκούσας.δὲ ὁ Ἰησοῦς ἐθαύμασεν, καὶ εἶπεν τοῖς ἀκολου-
And [2]having [3]heard [1]Jesus wondered, and said to those follow-
θοῦσιν[p], Ἀμὴν λέγω ὑμῖν, [q]οὐδὲ ἐν τῷ Ἰσραὴλ τοσαύτην
ing, Verily I say to you, Not even in Israel so great
πίστιν[‖] εὗρον. 11 λέγω.δὲ ὑμῖν, ὅτι πολλοὶ ἀπὸ ἀνατολῶν
faith have I found. But I say to you, that many from east
καὶ δυσμῶν ἥξουσιν, καὶ ἀνακλιθήσονται μετὰ Ἀβραὰμ καὶ
and west shall come, and shall recline [at table] with Abraham and
Ἰσαὰκ καὶ Ἰακὼβ ἐν τῇ βασιλείᾳ τῶν οὐρανῶν· 12 οἱ.δὲ υἱοὶ
Isaac and Jacob in the kingdom of the heavens; but the sons
τῆς βασιλείας [r]ἐκβληθήσονται[‖] εἰς τὸ σκότος τὸ ἐξώτερον· ἐκεῖ
of the kingdom shall be cast out into the darkness the outer: there
ἔσται ὁ κλαυθμὸς καὶ ὁ βρυγμὸς τῶν ὀδόντων. 13 Καὶ εἶπεν
shall be the weeping and the gnashing of the teeth. And [2]said
ὁ Ἰησοῦς τῷ [s]ἑκατοντάρχῳ,[‖] Ὕπαγε, [t]καὶ[‖] ὡς ἐπίστευσας
[1]Jesus to the centurion, Go, and as thou hast believed
γενηθήτω σοι. Καὶ ἰάθη ὁ.παῖς.[v]αὐτοῦ[‖] [w]ἐν τῇ ὥρᾳ
be it to thee. And was healed his servant in [2]hour
ἐκείνῃ.[‖]
[1]that.

14 And when Jesus was come into Peter's house, he saw his wife's mother laid, and sick of a fever. 15 And he

14 Καὶ ἐλθὼν ὁ Ἰησοῦς εἰς τὴν οἰκίαν Πέτρου, εἶδεν
And [2]having [3]come [1]Jesus to the house of Peter, saw
τὴν.πενθερὰν.αὐτοῦ βεβλημένην καὶ πυρέσσουσαν, 15 καὶ
his wife's mother laid and in a fever; and

---

[c] ἀλλὰ EGLTTrA. [d] προσένεγκον LTTrAW. [e] Μωϋσῆς LTTrAW. [f] εἰσελθόντος LTTrA. [g] αὐτῷ he GW; αὐτοῦ he LTTrA. [h] Καφαρναοὺμ LTTrAW. [i] ἑκατοντάρχης T. [k] — καὶ LT[Tr]A. [l] — ὁ Ἰησοῦς (*read* he says) LT[Tr]A. [m] ἀποκριθεὶς δὲ LTTr. [n] λόγῳ by a word GLTTrAW. [o] + τασσόμενος placed L. [p] + αὐτῷ him L [q] παρ' οὐδενὶ τοσαύτην πίστιν ἐν τῷ Ἰσραὴλ with no one so great faith in Israel LTrA. [r] ἐξελεύσονται shall go forth T. [s] ἑκατοντάρχῃ GLTTrAW. [t] — καὶ LT[Tr]A. [v] — αὐτοῦ (*read* the servant) LTT[A]. [w] ἀπὸ τῆς ὥρας ἐκείνης from that hour L.

ἥψατο τῆς χειρὸς.αὐτῆς, καὶ ἀφῆκεν αὐτὴν ὁ πυρετός· καὶ
he touched her hand, and [3]left [4]her [1]the [2]fever; and
ἠγέρθη καὶ διηκόνει [x]αὐτοῖς.
she arose and ministered to them.

16 Ὀψίας.δὲ γενομένης προσήνεγκαν αὐτῷ δαιμονιζομένους
And evening being come, they brought to him [2]possessed [3]with [4]demons
πολλούς· καὶ ἐξέβαλεν τὰ πνεύματα λόγῳ καὶ πάντας τοὺς
[1]many, and he cast out the spirits by a word, and all who
κακῶς ἔχοντας ἐθεράπευσεν· 17 ὅπως πληρωθῇ τὸ
[2]ill [1]were he healed: So that might be fulfilled that which
ῥηθὲν διὰ Ἡσαΐου τοῦ προφήτου, λέγοντος, Αὐτὸς τὰς
was spoken by Esaias the prophet, saying, Himself the
ἀσθενείας ἡμῶν ἔλαβεν, καὶ τὰς νόσους ἐβάστασεν.
infirmities of us took, and the diseases bore.

18 Ἰδὼν.δὲ ὁ Ἰησοῦς [y]πολλοὺς ὄχλους περὶ αὐτόν, ἐκέ-
And [2]seeing [1]Jesus great crowds around him, he com-
λευσεν ἀπελθεῖν εἰς τὸ πέραν. 19 καὶ προσελθὼν εἷς
manded to depart to the other side. And having come to [him] one
γραμματεὺς εἶπεν αὐτῷ, Διδάσκαλε, ἀκολουθήσω σοι ὅπου.ἐὰν
a scribe said to him, Teacher, I will follow thee whithersoever
ἀπέρχῃ. 20 Καὶ λέγει αὐτῷ ὁ Ἰησοῦς, Αἱ ἀλώπεκες φωλεοὺς
thou mayest go. And [2]says [3]to [4]him [1]Jesus, The foxes [2]holes
ἔχουσιν καὶ τὰ πετεινὰ τοῦ οὐρανοῦ κατασκηνώσεις, ὁ.δὲ υἱὸς
[1]have, and the birds of the heaven nests, but the Son
τοῦ ἀνθρώπου οὐκ.ἔχει ποῦ τὴν κεφαλὴν κλίνῃ. 21 Ἕτερος
of man has not where the head he may lay. [2]Another
δὲ τῶν.μαθητῶν.[z]αὐτοῦ εἶπεν αὐτῷ, Κύριε, ἐπίτρεψόν μοι
[1]and of his disciples said to him, Lord, allow me
πρῶτον ἀπελθεῖν καὶ θάψαι τὸν.πατέρα.μου. 22 Ὁ.δὲ.[a]Ἰησοῦς
first to go and bury my father. But Jesus
[b]εἶπεν αὐτῷ, Ἀκολούθει μοι, καὶ ἄφες τοὺς νεκροὺς θάψαι
said to him, Follow me, and leave the dead to bury
τοὺς.ἑαυτῶν νεκρούς.
their own dead.

23 Καὶ ἐμβάντι αὐτῷ εἰς [c]τὸ πλοῖον, ἠκολούθησαν αὐτῷ
And [2]having [3]entered [1]he into the ship, [3]followed [4]him
οἱ.μαθηταὶ αὐτοῦ. 24 καὶ ἰδού, σεισμὸς μέγας ἐγένετο ἐν τῇ
[1]his [2]disciples. And lo, a [2]tempest [1]great arose in the
θαλάσσῃ, ὥστε τὸ πλοῖον καλύπτεσθαι ὑπὸ τῶν κυμάτων·
sea, so that the ship was covered by the waves;
αὐτὸς.δὲ ἐκάθευδεν. 25 καὶ προσελθόντες [d]οἱ μαθηταὶ [e]αὐτοῦ
but he was sleeping. And having come to [him] the disciples of him
ἤγειραν αὐτόν, λέγοντες, Κύριε, σῶσον [f]ἡμᾶς, ἀπολλύμεθα.
awoke him, saying, Lord, save us; we perish.
26 Καὶ λέγει αὐτοῖς, Τί δειλοί ἐστε, ὀλιγόπιστοι; Τότε
And he says to them, Why fearful are ye, O [ye] of little faith? Then,
ἐγερθεὶς ἐπετίμησεν τοῖς ἀνέμοις καὶ τῇ θαλάσσῃ, καὶ ἐγένετο
having arisen he rebuked the winds and the sea, and there was
γαλήνη μεγάλη. 27 οἱ.δὲ ἄνθρωποι ἐθαύμασαν, λέγοντες,
a [2]calm [1]great. And the men wondered, saying,
Ποταπός ἐστιν οὗτος, ὅτι [g]καὶ οἱ ἄνεμοι καὶ ἡ θάλασσα
What kind [of man] is this, that even the winds and the sea
[h]ὑπακούουσιν αὐτῷ;
obey him?

touched her hand, and the fever left her: and she arose, and ministered unto them.

16 When the even was come, they brought unto him many that were possessed with devils: and he cast out the spirits with *his* word, and healed all that were sick: 17 that it might be fulfilled which was spoken by Esaias the prophet, saying, Himself took our infirmities, and bare *our* sicknesses.

18 Now when Jesus saw great multitudes about him, he gave commandment to depart unto the other side. 19 And a certain scribe came, and said unto him, Master, I will follow thee whithersoever thou goest. 20 And Jesus saith unto him, The foxes have holes, and the birds of the air *have* nests; but the Son of man hath not where to lay *his* head. 21 And another of his disciples said unto him, Lord, suffer me first to go and bury my father. 22 But Jesus said unto him, Follow me; and let the dead bury their dead.

23 And when he was entered into a ship, his disciples followed him. 24 And, behold, there arose a great tempest in the sea, insomuch that the ship was covered with the waves: but he was asleep. 25 And his disciples came to *him*, and awoke him, saying, Lord, save us: we perish. 26 And he saith unto them, Why are ye fearful, O ye of little faith? Then he arose, and rebuked the winds and the sea; and there was a great calm. 27 But the men marvelled, saying, What manner of man is this, that even the winds and the sea obey him!

[x] αὐτῷ to him LTTrAW. [y] ὄχλον a crowd L. [z] — αὐτοῦ (*read* the disciples) LTTr. [a] — Ἰησοῦς (*read* he said) T. [b] λέγει says LTTrAW. [c] — τὸ (*read* a ship) LTrA. [d] — οἱ μαθηταὶ [L]TTr. [e] — αὐτοῦ GLTTrAW. [f] — ἡμᾶς LTTrAW. [g] — καὶ L. [h] αὐτῷ ὑπακούουσιν LTTrA.

28 And when he was
come to the other side
into the country of the
Gergesenes, there met
him two possessed with
devils, coming out of
the tombs, exceeding
fierce, so that no man
might pass by that
way. 29 And, behold,
they cried out, saying,
What have we to do
with thee, Jesus, thou
Son of God? art thou
come hither to torment
us before the time?
30 And there was a
good way off from
them an herd of many
swine feeding. 31 So
the devils besought
him, saying, If thou
cast us out, suffer us
to go away into the
herd of swine. 32 And
he said unto them, Go.
And when they were
come out, they went
into the herd of swine:
and, behold, the whole
herd of swine ran
violently down a steep
place into the sea, and
perished in the waters.
33 And they that kept
them fled, and went
their ways into the
city, and told every
thing, and what was
befallen to the possessed of the devils.
34 And, behold, the
whole city came out
to meet Jesus: and
when they saw him,
they besought *him* that
he would depart out of
their coasts.

IX. And he entered
into a ship, and passed
over, and came into his
own city. 2 And, behold, they brought to
him a man sick of the
palsy, lying on a bed:
and Jesus seeing their
faith said unto the
sick of the palsy, Son,
be of good cheer; thy
sins be forgiven thee.
3 And, behold, certain
of the scribes said
within themselves,
This *man* blasphemeth. 4 And Jesus knowing their thoughts
said, Wherefore think
ye evil in your hearts?
5 For whether is easier,
to say, *Thy* sins be for-

28 Καὶ [i]ἐλθόντι αὐτῷ‖ εἰς τὸ πέραν εἰς τὴν χώραν τῶν
And when [2]had [3]come [1]he to the other side to the country of the
[k]Γεργεσηνῶν‖ ὑπήντησαν αὐτῷ δύο δαιμονιζόμενοι ἐκ τῶν
Gergesenes, [5]met [6]him [1]two [2]possessed [3]by [4]demons out of the
μνημείων ἐξερχόμενοι, χαλεποὶ λίαν, ὥστε μὴ ἰσχύειν τινὰ
tombs coming, [2]violent [1]very, so that not [3]was [4]able [1]any [2]one
παρελθεῖν διὰ τῆς ὁδοῦ ἐκείνης· 29 καὶ ἰδού, ἔκραξαν λέγοντες,
to pass by that way. And lo, they cried out, saying,
Τί ἡμῖν καὶ σοί, [l]Ἰησοῦ,‖ υἱὲ τοῦ θεοῦ; ἦλθες ὧδε πρὸ
What to us and to thee, Jesus, Son of God? art thou come here before [the]
καιροῦ βασανίσαι ἡμᾶς; 30 Ἦν δὲ μακρὰν ἀπ' αὐτῶν ἀγέλη
time to torment us? Now there was far off from them a herd
χοίρων πολλῶν βοσκομένη. 31 οἱ δὲ δαίμονες παρεκάλουν
of [2]swine [1]many feeding; And the demons besought
αὐτόν, λέγοντες, Εἰ ἐκβάλλεις ἡμᾶς, [m]ἐπίτρεψον ἡμῖν ἀπελθεῖν‖
him, saying, If thou cast out us, allow us to go away
εἰς τὴν ἀγέλην τῶν χοίρων. 32 Καὶ εἶπεν αὐτοῖς[n], Ὑπάγετε.
into the herd of the swine. And he said to them, Go.
Οἱ δὲ ἐξελθόντες [o]ἀπῆλθον‖ εἰς [p]τὴν ἀγέλην τῶν χοίρων·‖
And they having gone out went away into the herd of the swine:
καὶ ἰδού, ὥρμησεν πᾶσα ἡ ἀγέλη [q]τῶν χοίρων‖ κατὰ τοῦ
and behold, [7]rushed [1]all [2]the [3]herd [4]of [5]the [6]swine down the
κρημνοῦ εἰς τὴν θάλασσαν, καὶ ἀπέθανον ἐν τοῖς ὕδασιν.
steep into the sea, and died in the waters.
33 οἱ δὲ βόσκοντες ἔφυγον, καὶ ἀπελθόντες εἰς τὴν πόλιν
But those who fed [them] fled, and having gone away into the city
ἀπήγγειλαν πάντα, καὶ τὰ τῶν δαιμονιζομένων.
related everything, and the [events] concerning those possessed by demons.
34 καὶ ἰδού, πᾶσα ἡ πόλις ἐξῆλθεν εἰς [r]συνάντησιν‖ [s]τῷ‖ Ἰησοῦ·
And behold, all the city went out to meet Jesus;
καὶ ἰδόντες αὐτόν, παρεκάλεσαν [t]ὅπως‖ μεταβῇ ἀπὸ
and seeing him, they besought [him] that he would depart from
τῶν ὁρίων αὐτῶν.
their borders.

9 Καὶ ἐμβὰς εἰς [v]τὸ‖ πλοῖον διεπέρασεν καὶ ἦλθεν εἰς
And having entered into the ship he passed over and came to
τὴν ἰδίαν πόλιν. 2 καὶ ἰδού, [w]προσέφερον‖ αὐτῷ παραλυτικὸν
his own city. And behold, they brought to him a paralytic
ἐπὶ κλίνης βεβλημένον· καὶ ἰδὼν ὁ Ἰησοῦς τὴν πίστιν αὐτῶν
on a bed lying; and [2]seeing [1]Jesus their faith
εἶπεν τῷ παραλυτικῷ, Θάρσει, τέκνον, [x]ἀφέωνταί‖
said to the paralytic, Be of good courage, child; [3]have [4]been [5]forgiven
[y]σοι αἱ ἁμαρτίαι σου.‖ 3 Καὶ ἰδού, τινὲς τῶν γραμματέων [z]εἶπον‖
[6]thee [1]thy [2]sins. And lo, some of the scribes said
ἐν ἑαυτοῖς, Οὗτος βλασφημεῖ. 4 Καὶ [a]ἰδὼν‖ ὁ Ἰησοῦς τὰς
in themselves, This [man] blasphemes. And [2]perceiving [1]Jesus
ἐνθυμήσεις αὐτῶν, εἶπεν, [b]Ἵνα τί‖ [c]ὑμεῖς‖ ἐνθυμεῖσθε πονηρὰ
their thoughts, said, Why [2]ye [1]think evil
ἐν ταῖς καρδίαις ὑμῶν; 5 τί γάρ ἐστιν εὐκοπώτερον, εἰπεῖν,
in your hearts? For which is easier, to say,

---

[i] ἐλθόντος αὐτοῦ LTTr. [k] Γερασηνῶν L; Γαδαρηνῶν Gadarenes TTrA. [l] — Ἰησοῦ GLTTrA. [m] ἀπόστειλον ἡμᾶς send us GLTTrA. [n] + [ὁ Ἰησοῦς] Jesus L. [o] ἀπῆλθαν LTr. [p] τοὺς χοίρους the swine GLTTr. [q] — τῶν χοίρων GLTT[A]. [r] ὑπάντησιν LTTr. [s] τοῦ T. [t] ἵνα L. [v] — τὸ (*read* a ship) LTTr[A]. [w] προσφέρουσιν they bring L. [x] ἀφίενταί are forgiven LTTr. [y] σου αἱ ἁμαρτίαι LTTrA. [z] εἶπαν LT. [a] εἰδὼς knowing LTr. [b] Ἱνατί GTW. [c] — ὑμεῖς LTTrA.

[d]'Αφέωνταί‖ [e]σοι‖ αἱ ἁμαρτίαι· ἢ εἰπεῖν, [f]"Εγειραι‖ καὶ
[3]Have [4]been [5]forgiven [6]thee [[1]thy] [2]sins, or to say, Arise and
περιπάτει; 6 ἵνα.δὲ εἰδῆτε ὅτι ἐξουσίαν ἔχει ὁ υἱὸς τοῦ ἀν-
walk? But that ye may know that authority has the Son of
θρώπου ἐπὶ τῆς γῆς ἀφιέναι ἁμαρτίας· τότε λέγει τῷ παρα-
man on the earth to forgive sins: then he says to the para-
λυτικῷ, [g]'Εγερθεὶς‖ ἆρόν σου τὴν κλίνην, καὶ ὕπαγε εἰς τὸν
lytic, Having arisen, take up thy bed, and go to
οἶκόν σου 7 Καὶ ἐγερθεὶς ἀπῆλθεν εἰς τὸν.οἶκον.αὐτοῦ.
[2]house [1]thy. And having arisen he went away to his house.
8 ἰδόντες.δὲ οἱ ὄχλοι [h]ἐθαύμασαν,‖ καὶ ἐδόξασαν τὸν θεόν,
And [3]having [4]seen [1]the [2]crowds wondered, and glorified God,
τὸν δόντα ἐξουσίαν τοιαύτην τοῖς ἀνθρώποις.
who gave [2]authority [1]such to men.

9 Καὶ παράγων ὁ 'Ιησοῦς ἐκεῖθεν εἶδεν ἄνθρωπον καθήμενον
And [2]passing [1]Jesus thence saw a man sitting
ἐπὶ τὸ τελώνιον, [i]Ματθαῖον‖ λεγόμενον, καὶ λέγει αὐτῷ, 'Ακο-
at the tax-office, [2]Matthew [1]called, and says to him, Fol-
λούθει μοι. Καὶ ἀναστὰς [k]ἠκολούθησεν‖ αὐτῷ. 10 Καὶ ἐγένετο
low me. And having arisen he followed him. And it came to pass
[l]αὐτοῦ ἀνακειμένου‖ ἐν τῇ οἰκίᾳ, [m]καὶ‖ ἰδού, πολλοὶ τελῶναι
at his reclining [at table] in the house, that behold, many tax-gatherers
καὶ ἁμαρτωλοὶ ἐλθόντες συνανέκειντο τῷ 'Ιησοῦ καὶ
and sinners having come were reclining [at table] with Jesus and
τοῖς.μαθηταῖς.αὐτοῦ. 11 καὶ ἰδόντες οἱ Φαρισαῖοι [n]εἶπον‖
his disciples. And having seen [it] the Pharisees said
τοῖς.μαθηταῖς.αὐτοῦ, [o]Διατί‖ μετὰ τῶν τελωνῶν καὶ ἁμαρ-
to his disciples, Why with the tax-gatherers and sin-
τωλῶν ἐσθίει ὁ.διδάσκαλος.ὑμῶν; 12 'Ο.δὲ.[p]'Ιησοῦς‖ ἀκούσας
ners eats your teacher? But Jesus having heard
εἶπεν [q]αὐτοῖς,‖ Οὐ χρείαν ἔχουσιν οἱ ἰσχύοντες ἰατροῦ,
he said to them, [6]Not [7]need [5]have [1]they [2]who [3]are [4]strong of a physician,
[r]ἀλλ'‖ οἱ κακῶς ἔχοντες. 13 πορευθέντες δὲ μάθετε τί ἐστιν,
but they who ill are. But having gone learn what is,
[s]"Ελεον‖ θέλω, καὶ οὐ θυσίαν· οὐ γὰρ ἦλθον καλέσαι δικαίους,
Mercy I desire, and not sacrifice: [4]not [1]for [2]I [3]came to call righteous
[t]ἀλλ'‖ ἁμαρτωλοὺς [v]εἰς μετάνοιαν.‖
[ones], but sinners to repentance.

14 Τότε προσέρχονται αὐτῷ οἱ μαθηταὶ 'Ιωάννου, λέγοντες,
Then come near to him the disciples of John, saying,
[w]Διατί‖ ἡμεῖς καὶ οἱ Φαρισαῖοι νηστεύομεν [x]πολλά,‖ οἱ.δὲ.μαθη-
Why [2]we [3]and [4]the [5]Pharisees [1]do fast much, but [2]disci-
ταί.σου οὐ.νηστεύουσιν; 15 Καὶ εἶπεν αὐτοῖς ὁ 'Ιησοῦς, Μὴ
ples [1]thy fast not? And [2]said [3]to [4]them [1]Jesus,
δύνανται οἱ υἱοὶ τοῦ νυμφῶνος πενθεῖν ἐφ'.ὅσον μετ' αὐτῶν
Can the sons of the bridechamber mourn while with them
ἐστιν ὁ νυμφίος; ἐλεύσονται δὲ ἡμέραι ὅταν ἀπαρθῇ
is the bridegroom? [3]will [4]come [1]but [2]days when will have been taken away
ἀπ' αὐτῶν ὁ νυμφίος, καὶ τότε νηστεύσουσιν. 16 οὐδεὶς.δὲ
from them the bridegroom, and then they will fast. But no one
ἐπιβάλλει ἐπίβλημα ῥάκους ἀγνάφου ἐπὶ ἱματίῳ.παλαιῷ·
puts a piece of [2]cloth [1]unfulled on an old garment:

given thee; or to say,
Arise, and walk? 6 But
that ye may know that
the Son of man hath
power on earth to for-
give sins, (then saith
he to the sick of the
palsy,) Arise, take up
thy bed, and go unto
thine house. 7 And he
arose, and departed to
his house. 8 But when
the multitudes saw *it*,
they marvelled, and
glorified God, which
had given such power
unto men.

9 And as Jesus passed
forth from thence, he
saw a man, named
Matthew, sitting at
the receipt of custom:
and he saith unto him,
Follow me. And he
arose, and followed
him. 10 And it came
to pass, as Jesus sat at
meat in the house, be-
hold, many publicans
and sinners came and
sat down with him and
his disciples. 11 And
when the Pharisees
saw *it*, they said unto
his disciples, Why eat-
eth your Master with
publicans and sinners?
12 But when Jesus
heard *that*, he said un-
to them, They that be
whole need not a phy-
sician, but they that
are sick. 13 But go ye
and learn what *that*
meaneth, I will have
mercy, and not sacri-
fice: for I am not come
to call the righteous,
but sinners to repent-
ance.

14 Then came to him
the disciples of John,
saying, Why do we and
the Pharisees fast oft,
but thy disciples fast
not? 15 And Jesus said
unto them, Can the
children of the bride-
chamber mourn, as
long as the bridegroom
is with them? but the
days will come, when
the bridegroom shall
be taken from them,
and then shall they
fast. 16 No man put-
teth a piece of new
cloth unto an old gar-
ment, for that which

---

[d] ἀφίενταί are forgiven LTTr. [e] σου (*read* thy sins) GLTTrAW. [f] ἔγειρε LTTrAW. [g] ἔγειρε arise LTr. [h] ἐφοβήθησαν were afraid LTTrA. [i] Μαθθαῖον LTTrA. [k] ἠκολούθει T. [l] ἀνακειμένου αὐτοῦ L. [m] — καὶ T. [n] ἔλεγον LTTr. [o] διὰ τί LTrA. [p] — 'Ιησοῦς LT[Tr]A. [q] — αὐτοῖς LTTrA. [r] ἀλλὰ LTr. [s] 'Ελεος LTTrA. [t] ἀλλὰ TTrAW. [v] — εἰς μετάνοιαν GLTTrAW. [w] Διὰ τί LTrA. [x] — πολλά LT.

is put in to fill it up taketh from the garment, and the rent is made worse. 17 Neither do men put new wine into old bottles: else the bottles break, and the wine runneth out, and the bottles perish: but they put new wine into new bottles, and both are preserved.

18 While he spake these things unto them, behold, there came a certain ruler, and worshipped him, saying, My daughter is even now dead: but come and lay thy hand upon her, and she shall live. 19 And Jesus arose, and followed him, and *so did* his disciples.

20 And, behold, a woman, which was diseased with an issue of blood twelve years, came behind *him*, and touched the hem of his garment: 21 for she said within herself, If I may but touch his garment, I shall be whole. 22 But Jesus turned him about, and when he saw her, he said, Daughter, be of good comfort; thy faith hath made thee whole. And the woman was made whole from that hour.

23 And when Jesus came into the ruler's house, and saw the minstrels and the people making a noise, 24 he said unto them, Give place: for the maid is not dead, but sleepeth. And they laughed him to scorn. 25 But when the people were put forth, he went in, and took her by the hand, and the maid arose. 26 And the fame hereof went abroad into all that land.

27 And when Jesus departed thence, two blind men followed him, crying, and saying, *Thou* Son of David, have mercy on us. 28 And when he was come into the house, the blind men came to him: and Jesus saith

αἴρει γὰρ τὸ.πλήρωμα.αὐτοῦ ἀπὸ τοῦ ἱματίου, καὶ χεῖρον
[5]takes [6]away [1]for [2]its [3]filling [4]up from the garment, and a worse
σχίσμα γίνεται. 17 οὐδὲ βάλλουσιν οἶνον νέον εἰς ἀσκοὺς
rent takes place. Nor put they [2]wine [1]new into [2]skins
παλαιούς· εἰ.δὲ.μήγε ῥήγνυνται οἱ ἀσκοί, καὶ ὁ οἶνος ἐκχεῖται,
[1]old, otherwise [3]are [4]burst [1]the [2]skins, and the wine is poured out,
καὶ οἱ ἀσκοὶ [y]ἀπολοῦνται·‖ ἀλλὰ [z]βάλλουσιν οἶνον νέον εἰς
and the skins will be destroyed; but they put [2]wine [1]new into
ἀσκοὺς‖ καινούς, καὶ [a]ἀμφότερα‖ συντηροῦνται.
[2]skins [1]new, and both are preserved together.
18 Ταῦτα αὐτοῦ.λαλοῦντος αὐτοῖς, ἰδού, ἄρχων[b] [c]ἐλθὼν‖
[5]These [6]things [1]as [2]he [3]is [4]speaking to them, behold, a ruler having come
προσεκύνει αὐτῷ, λέγων, [d]"Οτι‖ ἡ.θυγάτηρ.μου ἄρτι ἐτελεύ-
did homage to him, saying, My daughter just now has
τησεν· ἀλλὰ ἐλθὼν ἐπίθες τὴν.χεῖρά.σου ἐπ' αὐτήν, καὶ
died; but having come lay thy hand upon her, and
ζήσεται. 19 καὶ ἐγερθεὶς ὁ Ἰησοῦς [e]ἠκολούθησεν‖ αὐτῷ
she shall live. And having arisen Jesus followed him,
καὶ οἱ.μαθηταὶ.αὐτοῦ.
and his disciples.
20 Καὶ ἰδού, γυνὴ αἱμοῤῥοοῦσα δώδεκα ἔτη, προσελ-
And behold, a woman having had a flux of blood twelve years, having
θοῦσα ὄπισθεν ἥψατο τοῦ κρασπέδου τοῦ.ἱματίου.αὐτοῦ.
come behind touched the border of his garment.
21 ἔλεγεν.γὰρ ἐν ἑαυτῇ, Ἐὰν μόνον ἅψωμαι τοῦ ἱματίου
For she said within herself, If only I shall touch [2]garment
αὐτοῦ σωθήσομαι. 22 Ὁ.δὲ.[f]Ἰησοῦς‖ [g]ἐπιστραφεὶς‖ καὶ ἰδὼν
[1]his I shall be cured. But Jesus having turned and having seen
αὐτὴν εἶπεν, Θάρσει, θύγατερ· ἡ.πίστις.σου σέσωκέν σε.
her he said, Be of good courage, daughter; thy faith hath cured thee.
καὶ ἐσώθη ἡ γυνὴ ἀπὸ τῆς.ὥρας.ἐκείνης.
And [3]was [4]cured [1]the [2]woman from that hour.
23 Καὶ ἐλθὼν ὁ Ἰησοῦς εἰς τὴν οἰκίαν τοῦ ἄρχοντος,
And [2]having [3]come [1]Jesus into the house of the ruler,
καὶ ἰδὼν τοὺς αὐλητὰς καὶ τὸν ὄχλον θορυβούμενον,
and having seen the flute-players and the crowd making a tumult,
24 [h]λέγει αὐτοῖς,‖ Ἀναχωρεῖτε· οὐ γὰρ ἀπέθανεν τὸ κοράσιον,
says to them, Withdraw, [5]not [1]for [4]is [6]dead [2]the [3]damsel,
ἀλλὰ καθεύδει. καὶ κατεγέλων αὐτοῦ. 25 ὅτε.δὲ ἐξεβλήθη
but sleeps. And they laughed at him. But when [3]had [4]been [5]put [6]out
ὁ ὄχλος, εἰσελθὼν ἐκράτησεν τῆς.χειρὸς.αὐτῆς, καὶ ἠγέρθη
[1]the [2]crowd, having entered he took hold of her hand, and [3]arose
τὸ κοράσιον. 26 καὶ ἐξῆλθεν ἡ.φήμη.αὕτη εἰς ὅλην τὴν
[1]the [2]damsel. And [3]went [4]out [1]this [2]report into all
γῆν ἐκείνην.
[2]land [1]that.
27 Καὶ παράγοντι ἐκεῖθεν τῷ Ἰησοῦ, ἠκολούθησαν [i]αὐτῷ‖
And [2]passing [3]on [4]thence [1]Jesus, [8]followed [9]him
δύο τυφλοί, κράζοντες καὶ λέγοντες, Ἐλέησον ἡμᾶς, [k]υἱὲ
[5]two [6]blind [[7]men], crying and saying, Have pity on us, Son
Δαβίδ.‖ 28 ἐλθόντι.δὲ εἰς τὴν οἰκίαν, [l]προσῆλθον‖ αὐτῷ οἱ
of David. And having come into the house, came to him the

---

[y] ἀπόλλυνται are destroyed LTTr. [z] οἶνον νέον εἰς ἀσκοὺς βάλλουσιν L. [a] ἀμφότεροι GLTTrAW. [b] + εἷς (*read* a certain ruler) GLTr. [c] προσελθὼν having come to [him] L; εἰσελθὼν having entered TAW. [d] — ὅτι T. [e] ἠκολούθει LTTrA. [f] — Ἰησοῦς T. [g] στραφεὶς LTTrA. [h] ἔλεγεν said LTTrA. [i] — αὐτῷ L[Tr]. [k] υἱὸς Δαυείδ LTTrA; υἱὲ Δαυίδ GW. [l] προσῆλθαν LTr.

τυφλοί, καὶ λέγει αὐτοῖς ὁ Ἰησοῦς, Πιστεύετε ὅτι δύναμαι
blind [men], and [2]says [3]to [4]them [1]Jesus, Believe ye that I am able
[m]τοῦτο ποιῆσαι;‖ Λέγουσιν αὐτῷ, Ναί, κύριε. 29 Τότε ἥψατο
this to do? They say to him, Yea, Lord. Then he touched
τῶν.ὀφθαλμῶν.αὐτῶν, λέγων, Κατὰ τὴν.πίστιν.ὑμῶν γενη-
their eyes, saying, According to your faith be
θήτω ὑμῖν. 30 Καὶ [n]ἀνεῴχθησαν‖ αὐτῶν οἱ ὀφθαλμοί· καὶ
it to you. And were opened their eyes; and
[o]ἐνεβριμήσατο‖ αὐτοῖς ὁ Ἰησοῦς, λέγων, Ὁρᾶτε μηδεὶς γινω-
[2]strictly [3]charged [4]them [1]Jesus, saying, See [2]no [3]one [1]let
σκέτω. 31 Οἱ.δὲ ἐξελθόντες διεφήμισαν αὐτὸν ἐν ὅλῃ τῇ
know [it]. But they having gone out made [2]known [1]him in all
γῇ ἐκείνῃ.
[2]land [1]that.

unto them, Believe ye that I am able to do this? They said unto him, Yea, Lord. 29 Then touched he their eyes, saying, According to your faith be it unto you. 30 And their eyes were opened; and Jesus straitly charged them, saying, See *that* no man know *it*. 31 But they, when they were departed, spread abroad his fame in all that country.

32 Αὐτῶν.δὲ ἐξερχομένων, ἰδού, προσήνεγκαν αὐτῷ [p]ἄν-
And as they were going out, behold, they brought to him a
θρωπον‖ κωφὸν δαιμονιζόμενον. 33 καὶ ἐκβληθέντος
man dumb, possessed by a demon. And [3]having [4]been [5]cast [6]out
τοῦ δαιμονίου, ἐλάλησεν ὁ κωφός· καὶ ἐθαύμασαν οἱ ὄχλοι,
[1]the [2]demon, [9]spake [7]the [8]dumb. And [3]wondered [1]the [2]crowds,
λέγοντες, [q]Ὅτι‖ οὐδέποτε ἐφάνη οὕτως ἐν τῷ Ἰσραήλ. 34 Οἱ.δὲ
saying, Never was it seen thus in Israel. But the
Φαρισαῖοι ἔλεγον, Ἐν τῷ ἄρχοντι τῶν δαιμονίων ἐκβάλλει
Pharisees said, By the prince of the demons he casts out
τὰ δαιμόνια.
the demons.

32 As they went out, behold, they brought to him a dumb man possessed with a devil. 33 And when the devil was cast out, the dumb spake: and the multitudes marvelled, saying, It was never so seen in Israel. 34 But the Pharisees said, He casteth out devils through the prince of the devils.

35 Καὶ περιῆγεν ὁ Ἰησοῦς τὰς πόλεις πάσας καὶ τὰς κώμας,
And [2]went [3]about [1]Jesus [5]the [6]cities [4]all and the villages,
διδάσκων ἐν ταῖς.συναγωγαῖς.αὐτῶν, καὶ κηρύσσων τὸ εὐαγ-
teaching in their synagogues, and proclaiming the glad
γέλιον τῆς βασιλείας, καὶ θεραπεύων πᾶσαν νόσον καὶ πᾶσαν
tidings of the kingdom, and healing every disease and every
μαλακίαν [r]ἐν τῷ λαῷ.‖ 36 ἰδὼν.δὲ τοὺς ὄχλους ἐ-
bodily weakness among the people. And having seen the crowds he was
σπλαγχνίσθη περὶ αὐτῶν, ὅτι ἦσαν [s]ἐκλελυμένοι‖ καὶ
moved with compassion for them, because they were wearied and
[t]ἐρριμμένοι‖ [v]ὡσεὶ‖ πρόβατα μὴ ἔχοντα ποιμένα. 37 τότε λέγει
cast away as sheep not having a shepherd. Then he says
τοῖς.μαθηταῖς.αὐτοῦ, Ὁ μὲν θερισμὸς πολύς, οἱ.δὲ ἐργάται
to his disciples, The [2]indeed [1]harvest [is] great, but the workmen
ὀλίγοι· 38 δεήθητε οὖν τοῦ κυρίου τοῦ θερισμοῦ, ὅπως
[are] few; supplicate therefore the Lord of the harvest, that
ἐκβάλῃ ἐργάτας εἰς τὸν.θερισμὸν.αὐτοῦ.
he may send out workmen into his harvest.

35 And Jesus went about all the cities and villages, teaching in their synagogues, and preaching the gospel of the kingdom, and healing every sickness and every disease among the people. 36 But when he saw the multitudes, he was moved with compassion on them, because they fainted, and were scattered abroad, as sheep having no shepherd. 37 Then saith he unto his disciples, The harvest truly *is* plenteous, but the labourers *are* few: 38 pray ye therefore the Lord of the harvest, that he will send forth labourers into his harvest.

10 Καὶ προσκαλεσάμενος τοὺς δώδεκα μαθητὰς αὐτοῦ,
And having called to [him] [2]twelve [3]disciples [1]his
ἔδωκεν αὐτοῖς ἐξουσίαν πνευμάτων ἀκαθάρτων, ὥστε
he gave to them authority over [2]spirits [1]unclean, so as
ἐκβάλλειν αὐτά, καὶ θεραπεύειν πᾶσαν νόσον καὶ πᾶσαν
to cast out them, and to heal every disease and every
μαλακίαν.
bodily weakness.

2 Τῶν.δὲ δώδεκα ἀποστόλων τὰ ὀνόματά ἐστιν ταῦτα·
Now of the twelve apostles the names are these:

X. And when he had called unto *him* his twelve disciples, he gave them power *against* unclean spirits, to cast them out, and to heal all manner of sickness and all manner of disease. 2 Now the names of the twelve apostles are these; The

[m] ποιῆσαι τοῦτο L. [n] ἠνεῴχθησαν LTTrA. [o] ἐνεβριμήθη LTTrA. [p] — ἄνθρωπον (*read* [one]) [TrA]. [q] — ὅτι GLTTrAW. [r] — ἐν τῷ λαῷ GLTTrAW. [s] ἐσκυλμένοι harassed GLTTrAW. [t] ῥεριμμένοι L; ἐριμμένοι TTrA. [v] ὡς Tr.

πρῶτος Σίμων, ὁ λεγόμενος Πέτρος, καὶ Ἀνδρέας ὁ ἀδελφὸς
first Simon who is called Peter, and Andrew ²brother

αὐτοῦ· [w]Ἰάκωβος ὁ τοῦ Ζεβεδαίου, καὶ Ἰωάννης ὁ ἀδελφὸς
¹his; James the [son] of Zebedee, and John ²brother

αὐτοῦ· 3 Φίλιππος, καὶ Βαρθολομαῖος· Θωμᾶς, καὶ [x]Ματθαῖος‖
¹his; Philip, and Bartholomew; Thomas, and Matthew

ὁ τελώνης· Ἰάκωβος ὁ τοῦ Ἀλφαίου, καὶ [y]Λεββαῖος ὁ
the tax-gatherer; James the [son] of Alphæus, and Lebbæus who

ἐπικληθεὶς Θαδδαῖος·‖ 4 Σίμων ὁ [z]Κανανίτης,‖ καὶ Ἰούδας
was surnamed Thaddæus; Simon the Canaanite, and Judas

[a] [b]Ἰσκαριώτης,‖ ὁ καὶ παραδοὺς αὐτόν.
Iscariote, who also delivered up him.

5 Τούτους τοὺς δώδεκα ἀπέστειλεν ὁ Ἰησοῦς, παραγγείλας
These twelve ²sent ³forth ¹Jesus, having charged

αὐτοῖς, λέγων, Εἰς ὁδὸν ἐθνῶν μὴ.ἀπέλθητε, καὶ εἰς
them, saying, Into [the] way of the Gentiles go not off, and into

πόλιν [c]Σαμαρειτῶν‖ μὴ.εἰσέλθητε· 6 πορεύεσθε.δὲ μᾶλλον
a city of [the] Samaritans enter not; but go rather

πρὸς τὰ πρόβατα τὰ ἀπολωλότα οἴκου Ἰσραήλ. 7 πο-
to the sheep the lost of [the] house of Israel. ²Go-

ρευόμενοι δὲ κηρύσσετε, λέγοντες, Ὅτι ἤγγικεν ἡ βασιλεία
ing ¹and proclaim, saying, Has drawn near the kingdom

τῶν οὐρανῶν. 8 ἀσθενοῦντας θεραπεύετε, [d]λεπροὺς καθαρί-
of the heavens. Sick heal, lepers cleanse,

ζετε, νεκροὺς ἐγείρετε,‖ δαιμόνια ἐκβάλλετε. δωρεὰν ἐλάβετε,
dead raise, demons cast out: gratuitously ye received,

δωρεὰν δότε. 9 Μὴ-κτήσησθε χρυσόν, μηδὲ ἄργυρον, μηδὲ
gratuitously impart. Provide not gold, nor silver, nor

χαλκὸν εἰς τὰς.ζώνας.ὑμῶν, 10 μὴ πήραν εἰς ὁδόν, μηδὲ
money in your belts, nor provision-bag for [the] way, nor

δύο χιτῶνας, μηδὲ ὑποδήματα, μηδὲ [e]ῥάβδον·‖ ἄξιος.γὰρ ὁ
two tunics, nor sandals, nor a staff: for worthy the

ἐργάτης τῆς.τροφῆς.αὐτοῦ [f]ἐστιν.‖ 11 Εἰς.ἣν.δ᾽.ἂν πόλιν ἢ
workman of his food is. And into whatever city or

κώμην εἰσέλθητε, ἐξετάσατε τίς ἐν αὐτῇ ἄξιός ἐστιν· κἀκεῖ
village ye enter, inquire who in it worthy is, and there

μείνατε, ἕως.ἂν ἐξέλθητε. 12 εἰσερχόμενοι.δὲ εἰς τὴν οἰκίαν,
remain until ye go forth. But entering into the house,

ἀσπάσασθε αὐτήν. 13 καὶ ἐὰν μὲν ᾖ ἡ οἰκία ἀξία, [g]ἐλθέτω‖
salute it: and if indeed ³be ¹the ²house worthy, let come

ἡ.εἰρήνη.ὑμῶν ἐπ᾽ αὐτήν· ἐὰν.δὲ μὴ.ᾖ ἀξία, ἡ.εἰρήνη.ὑμῶν
your peace upon it; but if it be not worthy, ²your ³peace

πρὸς ὑμᾶς ἐπιστραφήτω. 14 καὶ ὃς.[h]ἐὰν‖ μὴ.δέξηται ὑμᾶς,
⁵to ⁶you ¹let ⁴return. And whoever will not receive you,

μηδὲ ἀκούσῃ τοὺς.λόγους.ὑμῶν, ἐξερχόμενοι [i]τῆς οἰκίας ἢ τῆς
nor will hear your words, going forth of [that] house or

πόλεως ἐκείνης, ἐκτινάξατε τὸν κονιορτὸν [k]τῶν.ποδῶν.ὑμῶν.
²city ¹that, shake off the dust of your feet.

15 ἀμὴν λέγω ὑμῖν, ἀνεκτότερον ἔσται γῇ Σοδόμων
Verily I say to you, More tolerable it shall be for [the] land of Sodom

καὶ [l]Γομόρρων‖ ἐν ἡμέρᾳ κρίσεως, ἢ τῇ.πόλει.ἐκείνῃ. 16 Ἰδού,
and of Gomorrha in day of judgment, than for that city. Lo,

first, Simon, who is called Peter, and Andrew his brother; James *the son* of Zebedee, and John his brother; 3 Philip, and Bartholomew; Thomas, and Matthew the publican; James *the son* of Alphæus, and Lebbæus, whose surname was Thaddæus; 4 Simon the Canaanite, and Judas Iscariot, who also betrayed him.

5 These twelve Jesus sent forth, and commanded them, saying, Go not into the way of the Gentiles, and into *any* city of the Samaritans enter ye not: 6 but go rather to the lost sheep of the house of Israel. 7 And as ye go, preach, saying, The kingdom of heaven is at hand. 8 Heal the sick, cleanse the lepers, raise the dead, cast out devils: freely ye have received, freely give. 9 Provide neither gold, nor silver, nor brass in your purses, 10 nor scrip for *your* journey, neither two coats, neither shoes, nor yet staves: for the workman is worthy of his meat. 11 And into whatsoever city or town ye shall enter, inquire who in it is worthy; and there abide till ye go thence. 12 And when ye come into an house, salute it. 13 And if the house be worthy, let your peace come upon it: but if it be not worthy, let your peace return to you. 14 And whosoever shall not receive you, nor hear your words, when ye depart out of that house or city, shake off the dust of your feet. 15 Verily I say unto you, It shall be more tolerable for the land of Sodom and Gomorrha in the day of judgment, than for that city. 16 Behold, I send you forth

[w] + καὶ and LT. [x] Μαθθαῖος LTTrA. [y] — Λεββαῖος ὁ ἐπικληθεὶς LTr; — ὁ ἐπικληθεὶς Θαδδαῖος TA. [z] Καναναῖος Cananæan LTTrA. [a] + ὁ the EGLTAW. [b] Ἰσκαριὼθ L. [c] Σαμαριτῶν T. [d] νεκροὺς ἐγείρετε, λεπροὺς καθαρίζετε GLTTrAW. [e] ῥάβδους staves W. [f] — ἐστιν (read [is]) LTTrA. [g] ἐλθάτω TTr. [h] ἂν LTTrA. [i] + ἔξω out LTTrA. [k] + ἐκ (read from your feet) LT. [l] Γομόρρας TrA.

ἐγὼ ἀποστέλλω ὑμᾶς ὡς πρόβατα ἐν μέσῳ λύκων· γίνεσθε
I send forth you as sheep in [the] midst of wolves: be ye
οὖν φρόνιμοι ὡς οἱ ὄφεις, καὶ ἀκέραιοι ὡς αἱ περιστεραί.
therefore prudent as the serpents, and harmless as the doves.
17 προσέχετε.δὲ ἀπὸ τῶν ἀνθρώπων· παραδώσουσιν.γὰρ ὑμᾶς
But beware of men; for they will deliver you
εἰς συνέδρια, καὶ ἐν ταῖς.συναγωγαῖς.αὐτῶν μαστιγώσουσιν
to sanhedrims, and in their synagogues they will scourge
ὑμᾶς· 18 καὶ ἐπὶ ἡγεμόνας δὲ καὶ βασιλεῖς ἀχθήσεσθε
you: and before governors also and kings ye shall be brought
ἕνεκεν ἐμοῦ, εἰς μαρτύριον αὐτοῖς καὶ τοῖς ἔθνεσιν.
on account of me, for a testimony to them and to the nations.
19 ὅταν.δὲ [l]παραδιδῶσιν‖ ὑμᾶς, μὴ.μεριμνήσητε πῶς ἢ τί
But when they deliver up you, be not careful how or what
λαλήσητε· [m]δοθήσεται.γὰρ ὑμῖν ἐν ἐκείνῃ τῇ ὥρᾳ τί [n]λαλή-
ye should speak: for it shall be given you in that hour what ye shall
σετε·‖ ‖ 20 οὐ.γὰρ ὑμεῖς ἐστε οἱ λαλοῦντες, ἀλλὰ τὸ πνεῦμα
speak: for [1]not [3]ye [2]are they who speak, but the Spirit
τοῦ.πατρὸς.ὑμῶν τὸ λαλοῦν ἐν ὑμῖν. 21 Παραδώσει.δὲ
of your Father which speaks in you. But [3]will [4]deliver [5]up
ἀδελφὸς ἀδελφὸν εἰς θάνατον, καὶ πατὴρ τέκνον· καὶ ἐπανα-
[1]brother brother to death; and father child: and [2]will
στήσονται τέκνα ἐπὶ γονεῖς, καὶ θανατώσουσιν αὐτούς.
[3]rise [4]up [1]children against parents, and will put to death them.
22 καὶ ἔσεσθε μισούμενοι ὑπὸ πάντων διὰ τὸ.ὄνομά.μου·
And ye will be hated by all on account of my name;
ὁ.δὲ ὑπομείνας εἰς τέλος, οὗτος σωθήσεται. 23 ὅταν.δὲ
but he that endures to [the] end, he shall be saved. But when
διώκωσιν ὑμᾶς ἐν τῇ.πόλει.ταύτῃ, φεύγετε εἰς [o]τὴν.ἄλλην·‖ [p]
they persecute you in this city, flee to another:
ἀμὴν.γὰρ λέγω ὑμῖν, οὐ.μὴ τελέσητε τὰς πόλεις
for verily I say to you, In no wise will ye have completed the cities
[q]τοῦ‖ Ἰσραὴλ ἕως.[r]ἂν‖ ἔλθῃ ὁ υἱὸς τοῦ ἀνθρώπου. 24 Οὐκ
of Israel until be come the Son of man. [4]Not
ἔστιν μαθητὴς ὑπὲρ τὸν διδάσκαλον, οὐδὲ δοῦλος ὑπὲρ
[3]is [1]a [2]disciple above the teacher, nor a bondman above
τὸν.κύριον.αὐτοῦ. 25 ἀρκετὸν τῷ μαθητῇ ἵνα γένηται ὡς
his lord. Sufficient for the disciple that he become as
ὁ.διδάσκαλος.αὐτοῦ, καὶ ὁ δοῦλος ὡς ὁ.κύριος.αὐτοῦ. εἰ [s]τὸν
his teacher, and the bondman as his lord. If [3]the
οἰκοδεσπότην‖ Βεελζεβοὺλ [t]ἐκάλεσαν,‖ πόσῳ μᾶλλον
[4]master [5]of [6]the [7]house [3]Beelzebul [1]they [2]called, how much more
[v]τοὺς οἰκιακοὺς‖.αὐτοῦ; 26 Μὴ οὖν φοβηθῆτε αὐτούς
those of his household? [3]Not [4]therefore [1]ye [2]should fear them;
οὐδὲν.γάρ ἐστιν κεκαλυμμένον ὃ οὐκ.ἀποκαλυφθήσεται·
for nothing is covered which shall not be uncovered,
καὶ κρυπτὸν ὃ οὐ.γνωσθήσεται. 27 ὃ λέγω ὑμῖν ἐν τῇ
and hidden which shall not be known. What I tell you in the
σκοτίᾳ εἴπατε ἐν τῷ φωτί· καὶ ὃ εἰς τὸ οὖς ἀκούετε κη-
darkness speak in the light; and what in the ear ye hear pro-
ρύξατε ἐπὶ τῶν δωμάτων. 28 καὶ [w]μὴ.φοβηθῆτε‖ ἀπὸ
claim upon the housetops. And ye should not fear because of

as sheep in the midst
of wolves: be ye there-
fore wise as serpents,
and harmless as doves.
17 But beware of men:
for they will deliver
you up to the councils,
and they will scourge
you in their syna-
gogues; 18 and ye shall
be brought before go-
vernors and kings for
my sake, for a testi-
mony against them
and the Gentiles.
19 But when they de-
liver you up, take no
thought how or what
ye shall speak: for it
shall be given you in
that same hour what
ye shall speak. 20 For
it is not ye that speak,
but the Spirit of your
Father which speaketh
in you. 21 And the
brother shall deliver
up the brother to death,
and the father the
child: and the chil-
dren shall rise up a-
gainst *their* parents,
and cause them to be
put to death. 22 And
ye shall be hated of all
men for my name's
sake: but he that en-
dureth to the end shall
be saved. 23 But when
they persecute you in
this city, flee ye into
another: for verily I
say unto you, Ye shall
not have gone over the
cities of Israel, till the
Son of man be come.
24 The disciple is not
above *his* master, nor
the servant above his
lord. 25 It is enough
for the disciple that he
be as his master, and
the servant as his lord.
If they have called the
master of the house
Beelzebub, how much
more *shall they call*
them of his household?
26 Fear them not there-
fore: for there is no-
thing covered, that
shall not be revealed;
and hid, that shall not
be known. 27 What I
tell you in darkness,
that speak ye in light:
and what ye hear in
the ear, *that* preach
ye upon the housetops.
28 And fear not them

[l] παραδῶσιν they shall have delivered LTTr. [m] [δοθή. γὰρ ὑμῖν ἐν ἐκείνῃ τῇ ὥρᾳ τί λαλή.] L. [n] λαλήσητε ye should speak TTrA. [o] τὴν ἑτέραν the next GLTTr. [p] + κἂν ἐν τῇ ἑτέρᾳ (κἂν ἐκ ταύτης G) διώκωσιν ὑμᾶς, φεύγετε εἰς τὴν ἄλλην and if in the next (and if from this) they persecute you, flee to another G[L]. [q] — τοῦ LTrA. [r] — ἂν TA. [s] τῷ οἰκοδεσπότῃ L. [t] ἐπεκάλεσαν they have surnamed GLTTrAW. [v] τοῖς οἰκιακοῖς L. [w] μὴ φοβεῖσθε fear ye not GLTTrW.

which kill the body, but are not able to kill the soul: but rather fear him which is able to destroy both soul and body in hell. 29 Are not two sparrows sold for a farthing? and one of them shall not fall on the ground without your Father. 30 But the very hairs of your head are all numbered. 31 Fear ye not therefore, ye are of more value than many sparrows. 32 Whosoever therefore shall confess me before men, him will I confess also before my Father which is in heaven. 33 But whosoever shall deny me before men, him will I also deny before my Father which is in heaven. 34 Think not that I am come to send peace on earth: I came not to send peace, but a sword. 35 For I am come to set a man at variance against his father, and the daughter against her mother, and the daughter in law against her mother in law. 36 And a man's foes *shall be* they of his own household. 37 He that loveth father or mother more than me is not worthy of me: and he that loveth son or daughter more than me is not worthy of me. 38 And he that taketh not his cross, and followeth after me, is not worthy of me. 39 He that findeth his life shall lose it: and he that loseth his life for my sake shall find it. 40 He that receiveth you receiveth me, and he that receiveth me receiveth him that sent me. 41 He that receiveth a prophet in the name of a prophet shall receive a prophet's reward; and he that receiveth a righteous man in the name of a righteous man shall receive a righteous man's reward. 42 And whosoever shall give to drink unto one of these little ones a cup of cold

τῶν [x]ἀποκτεινόντων‖ τὸ σῶμα, τὴν.δὲ ψυχὴν μὴ.δυναμένων
those who kill the body, but the soul are not able

ἀποκτεῖναι· [y]φοβήθητε.‖δὲ μᾶλλον τὸν δυνάμενον [z]καὶ‖
to kill; but ye should fear rather him who is able both

ψυχὴν καὶ σῶμα ἀπολέσαι ἐν γεέννῃ. 29 οὐχὶ δύο στρουθία
soul and body to destroy in Gehenna. [2]Not [3]two [4]sparrows

ἀσσαρίου πωλεῖται; καὶ ἓν ἐξ αὐτῶν οὐ.πεσεῖται ἐπὶ τὴν
[6]for [7]an [8]assarion [1]are [5]sold? and one of them shall not fall to the

γῆν ἄνευ τοῦ.πατρὸς.ὑμῶν· 30 ὑμῶν.δὲ καὶ αἱ τρίχες τῆς
ground without your Father. But of you even the hairs of the

κεφαλῆς πᾶσαι ἠριθμημέναι εἰσίν. 31 μὴ οὖν [a]φοβηθῆτε·‖
head all numbered are. [3]Not [5]therefore [1]ye [2]should [4]fear;

πολλῶν στρουθίων διαφέρετε ὑμεῖς. 32 Πᾶς οὖν ὅσ-
than many sparrows better are ye. Every one therefore whoso-

τις ὁμολογήσει ἐν ἐμοὶ ἔμπροσθεν τῶν ἀνθρώπων, ὁμολογήσω
ever shall confess me before men, [3]will [4]confess

κἀγὼ ἐν αὐτῷ ἔμπροσθεν τοῦ.πατρός.μου τοῦ ἐν [b] οὐρανοῖς
[2]also [1]I him before my Father who [is] in [the] heavens.

33 ὅστις.[c]δ' ἂν‖ ἀρνήσηταί με ἔμπροσθεν τῶν ἀνθρώπων,
But whosoever shall deny me before men,

ἀρνήσομαι [d]αὐτὸν κἀγὼ‖ ἔμπροσθεν τοῦ.πατρός.μου τοῦ ἐν
[3]will [4]deny [5]him [2]also [1]I before my Father who [is] in

[e] οὐρανοῖς. 34 Μὴ.νομίσητε ὅτι ἦλθον βαλεῖν εἰρήνην ἐπὶ
[the] heavens. Think not that I came to place peace on

τὴν γῆν· οὐκ.ἦλθον βαλεῖν εἰρήνην, ἀλλὰ μάχαιραν. 35 ἦλθον
the earth: I came not to place peace, but a sword. [2]I [3]came

γὰρ διχάσαι ἄνθρωπον κατὰ τοῦ.πατρὸς.αὐτοῦ, καὶ θυγα-
[1]for to set at variance a man against his father, and a daugh-

τέρα κατὰ τῆς.μητρὸς.αὐτῆς, καὶ νύμφην κατὰ τῆς πεν-
ter against her mother, and a daughter-in-law against [2]mother-

θερᾶς αὐτῆς· 36 καὶ ἐχθροὶ τοῦ.ἀνθρώπου οἱ οἰκιακοὶ
in-law [1]her. And enemies of the man [shall be] [2]household

αὐτοῦ. 37 Ὁ φιλῶν πατέρα ἢ μητέρα ὑπὲρ ἐμὲ οὐκ.ἔστιν
[1]his. He that loves father or mother above me is not

μου ἄξιος· καὶ ὁ φιλῶν υἱὸν ἢ θυγατέρα ὑπὲρ ἐμὲ οὐκ
of me worthy; and he that loves son or daughter above me [2]not

ἔστιν μου ἄξιος· 38 καὶ ὃς οὐ.λαμβάνει τὸν.σταυρὸν.αὐτοῦ
[1]is of me worthy. And he that takes not his cross

καὶ ἀκολουθεῖ ὀπίσω μου οὐκ ἔστιν μου ἄξιος. 39 ὁ εὑρὼν
and follows after me [2]not [1]is of me worthy. He that has found

τὴν.ψυχὴν.αὐτοῦ ἀπολέσει αὐτήν· καὶ ὁ ἀπολέσας τὴν
his life shall lose it; and he that has lost

ψυχὴν αὐτοῦ ἕνεκεν ἐμοῦ εὑρήσει αὐτήν. 40 Ὁ δεχόμενος
[2]life [1]his on account of me shall find it. He that receives

ὑμᾶς ἐμὲ δέχεται· καὶ ὁ ἐμὲ δεχόμενος δέχεται τὸν ἀπο-
you me receives; and he that me receives receives him who sent

στείλαντά με. 41 ὁ δεχόμενος προφήτην εἰς ὄνομα προ-
me. He that receives a prophet in [the] name of a

φήτου μισθὸν προφήτου [f]λήψεται·‖ καὶ ὁ δεχόμενος
prophet [the] reward of a prophet shall receive; and he that receives

δίκαιον εἰς ὄνομα δικαίου μισθὸν δικαίου
a righteous [man] in [the] name of a righteous [man] the reward of a righteous

[f]λήψεται.‖ 42 καὶ ὃς.[g]ἐὰν‖ ποτίσῃ ἕνα τῶν μικρῶν
[man] shall receive. And whoever shall give to drink to one [3]little [4]ones

---

[x] ἀποκτενόντων G; ἀποκτεννόντων LTTrA. [y] φοβεῖσθε fear ye TA. [z] [καὶ] L. [a] φοβεῖσθε fear ye LTTrA. [b] + τοῖς the L[Tr]A. [c] δὲ LTTrA. [d] κἀγὼ αὐτὸν LTTrA. [e] + τοῖς the L[Tr]A. [f] λήμψεται LTTrA. [g] ἂν LTr.

τούτων ποτήριον ψυχροῦ μόνον εἰς ὄνομα μαθητοῦ,
of [2]these a cup of cold [water] only in [the] name of a disciple,
ἀμὴν λέγω ὑμῖν, οὐ.μὴ ἀπολέσῃ τὸν.μισθὸν.αὐτοῦ.
verily I say to you, in nowise shall he lose his reward.

11 Καὶ ἐγένετο ὅτε ἐτέλεσεν ὁ Ἰησοῦς διατάσσων τοῖς
And it came to pass when [2]had [3]finished [1]Jesus commanding
δώδεκα μαθηταῖς αὐτοῦ, μετέβη ἐκεῖθεν τοῦ διδάσκειν καὶ
[2]twelve [3]disciples [1]his, he departed thence to teach and
κηρύσσειν ἐν ταῖς.πόλεσιν.αὐτῶν.
to preach in their cities.

2 Ὁ.δὲ.Ἰωάννης ἀκούσας ἐν τῷ δεσμωτηρίῳ τὰ ἔργα τοῦ
Now John having heard in the prison the works of the
χριστοῦ, πέμψας [h]δύο[‖] τῶν.μαθητῶν.αὐτοῦ, 3 εἶπεν αὐτῷ,
Christ, having sent two of his disciples, said to him,
Σὺ.εἶ ὁ ἐρχόμενος, ἢ ἕτερον προσδοκῶμεν; 4 Καὶ ἀποκρι-
Art thou the coming [one], or another are we to look for? And [2]answer-
θεὶς ὁ Ἰησοῦς εἶπεν αὐτοῖς, Πορευθέντες ἀπαγγείλατε Ἰωάννῃ
ing [1]Jesus said to them, Having gone relate to John
ἃ ἀκούετε καὶ βλέπετε· 5 τυφλοὶ ἀναβλέπουσιν, [i]καὶ[‖]
what ye hear and see: blind receive sight, and
χωλοὶ περιπατοῦσιν· λεπροὶ καθαρίζονται, [k]καὶ[‖] κωφοὶ
lame walk; lepers are cleansed, and deaf
ἀκούουσιν· [l]νεκροὶ ἐγείρονται, [k]καὶ[‖] πτωχοὶ εὐαγγελίζονται·
hear; dead are raised, and poor are evangelized.
6 καὶ μακάριός ἐστιν, ὃς.[m]ἐὰν[‖] μὴ.σκανδαλισθῇ ἐν ἐμοί.
And blessed is, whoever shall not be offended in me.

7 Τούτων.δὲ πορευομένων ἤρξατο ὁ Ἰησοῦς λέγειν τοῖς
But as these were going [2]began [1]Jesus to say to the
ὄχλοις περὶ Ἰωάννου, Τί [n]ἐξήλθετε[‖] εἰς τὴν ἔρημον
crowds concerning John, What went ye out into the wilderness
θεάσασθαι; κάλαμον ὑπὸ ἀνέμου σαλευόμενον; 8 ἀλλὰ
to look at? a reed by [the] wind shaken? But
τί [n]ἐξήλθετε[‖] ἰδεῖν; ἄνθρωπον ἐν μαλακοῖς [o]ἱματίοις[‖] ἠμφιεσ-
what went ye out to see? a man in soft garments ar-
μένον; ἰδού, οἱ τὰ μαλακὰ φοροῦντες ἐν τοῖς οἴκοις
rayed? Behold, those who the soft [garments] wear in the houses
τῶν βασιλέων [p]εἰσίν.[‖] 9 ἀλλὰ τί [n]ἐξήλθετε[‖] [q]ἰδεῖν; προ-
of kings are. But what went ye out to see? a pro-
φήτην;[‖] ναί, λέγω ὑμῖν, καὶ περισσότερον προφήτου·
phet? Yea, I say to you, and [one] more excellent than a prophet.
10 οὗτος.[r]γάρ[‖] ἐστιν περὶ οὗ γέγραπται, Ἰδού, [s]ἐγὼ[‖]
For this is [he] concerning whom it has been written, Behold, I
ἀποστέλλω τὸν.ἄγγελόν.μου πρὸ προσώπου.σου, [t]ὃς[‖] κατα-
send my messenger before thy face, who shall
σκευάσει τὴν.ὁδόν.σου ἔμπροσθέν σου· 11 Ἀμὴν λέγω ὑμῖν,
prepare thy way before thee. Verily I say to you,
οὐκ.ἐγήγερται ἐν γεννητοῖς γυναικῶν μείζων Ἰωάννου
there has not risen among [those] born of women a greater than John
τοῦ βαπτιστοῦ· ὁ.δὲ μικρότερος ἐν τῇ βασιλείᾳ τῶν
the Baptist. But he that [is] less in the kingdom of the
οὐρανῶν μείζων [v]αὐτοῦ ἐστιν.[‖] 12 ἀπὸ.δὲ τῶν ἡμερῶν Ἰωάννου
heavens greater than he is. But from the days of John

water only in the name of a disciple, verily I say unto you, he shall in no wise lose his reward.

XI. And it came to pass, when Jesus had made an end of commanding his twelve disciples, he departed thence to teach and to preach in their cities.

2 Now when John had heard in the prison the works of Christ, he sent two of his disciples, 3 and said unto him, Art thou he that should come, or do we look for another? 4 Jesus answered and said unto them, Go and shew John again those things which ye do hear and see: 5 the blind receive their sight, and the lame walk, the lepers are cleansed, and the deaf hear, the dead are raised up, and the poor have the gospel preached to them. 6 And blessed is *he*, whosoever shall not be offended in me.

7 And as they departed, Jesus began to say unto the multitudes concerning John, What went ye out into the wilderness to see? A reed shaken with the wind? 8 But what went ye out for to see? A man clothed in soft raiment? behold, they that wear soft *clothing* are in kings' houses. 9 But what went ye out for to see? A prophet? yea, I say unto you, and more than a prophet. 10 For this is *he*, of whom it is written, Behold, I send my messenger before thy face, which shall prepare thy way before thee. 11 Verily I say unto you, Among them that are born of women there hath not risen a greater than John the Baptist: notwithstanding he that is least in the kingdom of heaven is greater than he. 12 And from the days of John the

---

[h] διὰ by (his disciples) LTTrAW. [i] [καὶ] LTr. [k] [καὶ] L. [l] + καὶ and [L]TTrA. [m] ἂν LTr. [n] ἐξήλθατε LTTrA. [o] — ἱματίοις (*read* [garments]) [L]TTrA. [p] — εἰσίν (*read* [are]) T[A]. [q] προφήτην ἰδεῖν; (*read* But why went ye out? to see a prophet? TA. [r] — γάρ for T[LTrA]. [s] [ἐγὼ] L. [t] καὶ (*read* and he shall prepare) L. [v] ἐστὶν αὐτοῦ A.

Baptist until now the
kingdom of heaven
suffereth violence, and
the violent take it by
force. 13 For all the
prophets and the law
prophesied until John.
14 And if ye will re-
ceive *it*, this is Elias,
which was for to come.
15 He that hath ears to
hear, let him hear.
16 But whereunto shall
I liken this generation?
It is like unto children
sitting in the markets,
and calling unto their
fellows, 17 and saying,
We have piped unto
you, and ye have not
danced; we have
mourned unto you,
and ye have not la-
mented. 18 For John
came neither eating
nor drinking, and they
say, He hath a devil.
19 The Son of man
came eating and drink-
ing, and they say, Be-
hold a man glutton-
ous, and a winebibber,
a friend of publicans
and sinners. But wis-
dom is justified of her
children.

20 Then began he to
upbraid the cities
wherein most of his
mighty works were
done, because they re-
pented not: 21 Woe
unto thee, Chorazin!
woe unto thee, Beth-
saida! for if the mighty
works, which were
done in you, had been
done in Tyre and Si-
don, they would have
repented long ago in
sackcloth and ashes.
22 But I say unto you,
It shall be more toler-
able for Tyre and Sidon
at the day of judg-
ment, than for you.
23 And thou, Caper-
naum, which art ex-
alted unto heaven,
shalt be brought down
to hell: for if the
mighty works, which
have been done in
thee, had been done in
Sodom, it would have
remained until this
day. 24 But I say unto
you, That it shall be
more tolerable for the
land of Sodom in the
day of judgment, than
for thee.

τοῦ βαπτιστοῦ ἕως ἄρτι, ἡ βασιλεία τῶν οὐρανῶν βιά-
the Baptist until now, the kingdom of the heavens is taken by
ζεται, καὶ βιασταὶ ἁρπάζουσιν αὐτήν. 13 πάντες.γὰρ οἱ
violence, and [the] violent seize it. For all the
προφῆται καὶ ὁ νόμος ἕως Ἰωάννου [w]προεφήτευσαν· 14 καὶ
prophets and the law [2]until [3]John [1]prophesied. And
εἰ θέλετε δέξασθαι, αὐτός ἐστιν [x]Ἠλίας ὁ μέλλων ἔρχεσθαι.
if ye are willing to receive [it], he is Elias who is about to come.
15 ὁ ἔχων ὦτα [y]ἀκούειν, ἀκουέτω. 16 Τίνι.δὲ ὁμοιώσω
He that has ears to hear, let him hear. But to what shall I liken
τὴν.γενεὰν.ταύτην; ὁμοία ἐστὶν [z]παιδαρίοις [a]ἐν ἀγοραῖς
this generation? [3]like [1]it [2]is to little children in [the] markets
καθημένοις, [b]καὶ προσφωνοῦσιν τοῖς.ἑταίροις.αὐτῶν, 17 καὶ
sitting, and calling to their companions, and
λέγουσιν, Ηὐλήσαμεν ὑμῖν, καὶ οὐκ.ὠρχήσασθε· ἐθρηνήσαμεν
saying, We piped to you, and ye did not dance; we mourned
[c]ὑμῖν, καὶ οὐκ.ἐκόψασθε. 18 Ἦλθεν.γὰρ Ἰωάννης μήτε ἐσθίων
to you, and ye did not wail. For [2]came [1]John neither eating
μήτε πίνων, καὶ λέγουσιν, Δαιμόνιον ἔχει. 19 ἦλθεν ὁ υἱὸς
nor drinking, and they say, A demon he has. [5]Came [1]the [2]Son
τοῦ ἀνθρώπου ἐσθίων καὶ πίνων, καὶ λέγουσιν, Ἰδού,
[3]of [4]man eating and drinking, and they say, Behold,
ἄνθρωπος φάγος καὶ οἰνοπότης, τελωνῶν φίλος καὶ
a man a glutton and a wine bibber, of tax-gatherers a friend and
ἁμαρτωλῶν. καὶ ἐδικαιώθη ἡ σοφία ἀπὸ τῶν.[d]τέκνων αὐτῆς.
of sinners. And [2]was [3]justified [1]wisdom by [2]children [1]her.

20 Τότε ἤρξατο ὀνειδίζειν τὰς πόλεις ἐν αἷς ἐγένοντο
Then he began to reproach the cities in which had taken place
αἱ πλεῖσται δυνάμεις.αὐτοῦ, ὅτι οὐ.μετενόησαν. 21 Οὐαί
the most of his works of power, because they repented not. Woe
σοι, [e]Χοραζίν· οὐαί σοι, [f]Βηθσαϊδάν· ὅτι εἰ ἐν Τύρῳ καὶ
to thee, Chorazin! woe to thee, Bethsaida! for if in Tyre and
Σιδῶνι ἐγένοντο αἱ δυνάμεις αἱ γενόμεναι ἐν ὑμῖν,
Sidon had taken place the works of power which have taken place in you,
πάλαι ἂν ἐν σάκκῳ καὶ σποδῷ μετενόησαν. 22 πλὴν λέγω
long ago in sackcloth and ashes they had repented. But I say
ὑμῖν, Τύρῳ καὶ Σιδῶνι ἀνεκτότερον ἔσται ἐν ἡμέρᾳ κρίσεως
to you, For Tyre and Sidon more tolerable shall it be in day of judgment
ἢ ὑμῖν. 23 Καὶ σύ, [g]Καπερναούμ, [h]ἡ [i]ἕως τοῦ οὐρανοῦ
than for you. And thou, Capernaum, who to the heaven
[k]ὑψωθεῖσα, ἕως ᾅδου [l]καταβιβασθήσῃ· ὅτι εἰ ἐν Σοδό-
hast been lifted up, to hades shalt be brought down: for if in Sod-
μοις [m]ἐγένοντο αἱ δυνάμεις αἱ.[n]γενόμεναι ἐν σοί,
om had taken place the works of power which have taken place in thee,
[o]ἔμειναν.ἂν μέχρι τῆς.σήμερον. 24 πλὴν λέγω ὑμῖν, ὅτι
it had remained until to-day. But I say to you, that
γῇ Σοδόμων ἀνεκτότερον ἔσται ἐν ἡμέρᾳ κρίσεως
for [the] land of Sodom more tolerable shall it be in day of judgment
ἢ σοί.
than for thee.

---

[w] ἐπροφήτευσαν LTTrA. [x] Ἠλείας T. [y] — ἀκούειν T[Tr]A. [z] παιδίοις GLTTrAW. [a] καθημένοις ἐν ἀγορᾷ (market) L; καθημένοις ἐν ταῖς ἀγοραῖς TTrA. [b] ἃ προσφωνοῦντα τοῖς ἑταίροις who calling to the companions (ἑτέροις *read* calling to the others TTr) (+ [αὐτῶν] their A) λέγουσιν say LTTrA. [c] — ὑμῖν LTTrA. [d] ἔργων works TTr. [e] Χοραζείν TTrA. [f] Βηθσαϊδά LTr. [g] Καφαρναούμ LTTrAW. [h] μὴ LTTrA, ἢ W. [i] — τοῦ LTTrA. [k] ὑψωθήσῃ; shalt thou be lifted up? LTTrA; ὑψώθης W. [l] καταβήσῃ thou shalt descend LTrA. [m] ἐγενήθησαν LTTrA. [n] ἐν σοὶ γενόμεναι L. [o] ἔμεινεν LTTrA.

25 Ἐν ἐκείνῳ τῷ καιρῷ ἀποκριθεὶς ὁ Ἰησοῦς εἶπεν, Ἐξομο-
At that time answering Jesus said, I
λογοῦμαί σοι, πάτερ, κύριε τοῦ οὐρανοῦ καὶ τῆς γῆς, ὅτι
praise thee, O Father, Lord of the heaven and the earth, that
[p]ἀπέκρυψας‖ ταῦτα ἀπὸ σοφῶν καὶ συνετῶν, καὶ ἀπεκάλυψας
thou didst hide these things from wise and prudent, and didst reveal
αὐτὰ νηπίοις. 26 ναί, ὁ πατήρ, ὅτι οὕτως [q]ἐγένετο εὐδοκία‖
them to babes. Yea, Father, for thus it was well-pleasing
ἔμπροσθέν σου. 27 Πάντα μοι παρεδόθη ὑπὸ τοῦ.πατρός.μου·
before thee. All things to me were delivered by my Father.
καὶ οὐδεὶς ἐπιγινώσκει τὸν υἱὸν εἰ.μὴ ὁ πατήρ· οὐδὲ τὸν
And no one knows the Son except the Father; nor the
πατέρα τις ἐπιγινώσκει εἰ.μὴ ὁ υἱός, καὶ ᾧ.ἐὰν
Father [2]any [3]one [1]does know except the Son, and he to whomsoever
βούληται ὁ υἱὸς ἀποκαλύψαι. 28 Δεῦτε πρός με, πάντες
[3]may [4]will [1]the [2]Son to reveal [him]. Come to me, all
οἱ κοπιῶντες καὶ πεφορτισμένοι, κἀγὼ ἀναπαύσω ὑμᾶς.
ye that labour and are burdened, and I will give [2]rest [1]you.
29 ἄρατε τὸν.ζυγόν.μου ἐφ' ὑμᾶς, καὶ μάθετε ἀπ' ἐμοῦ, ὅτι
Take my yoke upon you, and learn from me, for
[r]πρᾷός‖ εἰμι καὶ ταπεινὸς τῇ.καρδίᾳ· καὶ εὑρήσετε ἀνάπαυσιν
meek I am and lowly in heart; and ye shall find rest
ταῖς.ψυχαῖς.ὑμῶν. 30 ὁ.γὰρ.ζυγός.μου χρηστὸς καὶ τὸ φορτίον
to your souls. For my yoke easy and [1]burden
μου ἐλαφρόν ἐστιν.
[2]my light is.

12 Ἐν ἐκείνῳ τῷ καιρῷ ἐπορεύθη ὁ Ἰησοῦς τοῖς [s]σάββασιν‖
At that time went Jesus on the Sabbath
διὰ τῶν σπορίμων· οἱ.δὲ.μαθηταὶ.αὐτοῦ ἐπείνασαν, καὶ
through the corn-fields; and his disciples were hungry, and
ἤρξαντο τίλλειν στάχυας καὶ ἐσθίειν. 2 οἱ.δὲ Φαρισαῖοι
began to pluck [the] ears and to eat. But the Pharisees
ἰδόντες [t]εἶπον‖ αὐτῷ, Ἰδού, οἱ.μαθηταί.σου ποιοῦσιν ὃ
having seen said to him, Behold, thy disciples are doing what
οὐκ.ἔξεστιν ποιεῖν ἐν σαββάτῳ. 3 Ὁ.δὲ εἶπεν αὐτοῖς, Οὐκ
it is not lawful to do on sabbath. But he said to them, [3]Not
ἀνέγνωτε τί ἐποίησεν [v]Δαβίδ,‖ ὅτε ἐπείνασεν [w]αὐτὸς‖ καὶ
[2]ye [1]have read what [2]did [1]David, when he hungered himself and
οἱ μετ' αὐτοῦ; 4 πῶς εἰσῆλθεν εἰς τὸν οἶκον τοῦ θεοῦ, καὶ
those with him? How he entered into the house of God, and
τοὺς ἄρτους τῆς προθέσεως [x]ἔφαγεν,‖ [y]οὓς‖ οὐκ ἐξὸν ἦν
the loaves of the presentation he ate, which [3]not [4]lawful [1]it [2]was
αὐτῷ φαγεῖν, οὐδὲ τοῖς μετ' αὐτοῦ, εἰ.μὴ τοῖς ἱερεῦσιν μόνοις;
for him to eat, nor for those with him, but for the priests only?
5 Ἢ οὐκ.ἀνέγνωτε ἐν τῷ νόμῳ, ὅτι τοῖς σάββασιν οἱ ἱερεῖς
Or have ye not read in the law, that on the sabbaths the priests
ἐν τῷ ἱερῷ τὸ σάββατον βεβηλοῦσιν, καὶ ἀναίτιοί εἰσιν;
in the temple the sabbath profane, and guiltless are?
6 λέγω.δὲ ὑμῖν, ὅτι τοῦ.ἱεροῦ [z]μείζων‖ ἐστὶν ὧδε. 7 εἰ.δὲ
But I say to you, that [3]than [4]the [5]temple [1]a [2]greater is here. But if
ἐγνώκειτε τί ἐστιν, [a]Ἔλεον‖ θέλω καὶ οὐ θυσίαν, οὐκ ἂν
ye had known what is, Mercy I desire and not sacrifice, [2]not

25 At that time Jesus answered and said, I thank thee. O Father, Lord of heaven and earth, because thou hast hid these things from the wise and prudent, and hast revealed them unto babes. 26 Even so, Father: for so it seemed good in thy sight. 27 All things are delivered unto me of my Father: and no man knoweth the Son, but the Father; neither knoweth any man the Father, save the Son, and *he* to whomsoever the Son will reveal *him*. 28 Come unto me, all *ye* that labour and are heavy laden, and I will give you rest. 29 Take my yoke upon you, and learn of me; for I am meek and lowly in heart: and ye shall find rest unto your souls. 30 For my yoke *is* easy, and my burden is light.

XII. At that time Jesus went on the sabbath day through the corn; and his disciples were an hungred, and began to pluck the ears of corn, and to eat. 2 But when the Pharisees saw *it*, they said unto him, Behold, thy disciples do that which is not lawful to do upon the sabbath day. 3 But he said unto them, Have ye not read what David did, when he was an hungred, and they that were with him; 4 how he entered into the house of God, and did eat the shewbread, which was not lawful for him to eat, neither for them which were with him, but only for the priests? 5 Or have ye not read in the law, how that on the sabbath days the priests in the temple profane the sabbath, and are blameless? 6 But I say unto you, That in this place is *one* greater than the temple. 7 But if ye had known what *this* meaneth, I will have mercy, and not sacrifice, ye would not

---

[p] ἔκρυψας LTTrA. [q] εὐδοκία ἐγένετο LT. [r] πραΰς LTTrA. [s] σαββάτοις L. [t] εἶπαν LTTrA. [v] Δαυείδ LTTrA; Δαυὶδ GW. [w] — αὐτὸς GLTTrAW. [x] ἔφαγον LT. [y] ὃ LTTrA. [z] μεῖζόν LTTrAW [a] Ἔλεος LTTrA.

have condemned the
guiltless. 8 For the
Son of man is Lord
even of the sabbath
day.

9 And when he was
departed thence, he
went into their syna-
gogue: 10 and, behold,
there was a man which
had *his* hand withered.
And they asked him,
saying, Is it lawful to
heal on the sabbath
days? that they might
accuse him. 11 And he
said unto them, What
man shall there be
among you, that shall
have one sheep, and if
it fall into a pit on
the sabbath day, will
he not lay hold on it,
and lift *it* out? 12 How
much then is a man
better than a sheep?
Wherefore it is lawful
to do well on the sab-
bath days. 13 Then
saith he to the man,
Stretch forth thine
hand. And he stretch-
ed *it* forth; and it was
restored whole, like as
the other.

14 Then the Pharisees
went out, and held a
council against him,
how they might de-
stroy him. 15 But
when Jesus knew *it*,
he withdrew himself
from thence: and
great multitudes fol-
lowed him, and he
healed them all; 16 and
charged them that
they should not make
him known: 17 that
it might be fulfilled
which was spoken by
Esaias the prophet,
saying, 18 Behold my
servant, whom I have
chosen; my beloved, in
whom my soul is well
pleased: I will put my
spirit upon him, and
he shall shew judg-
ment to the Gentiles.
19 He shall not strive,
nor cry; neither shall
any man hear his voice
in the streets. 20 A
bruised reed shall he
not break, and smok-
ing flax shall he not
quench, till he send
forth judgment unto
victory. 21 And in his
name shall the Gen-
tiles trust.

κατεδικάσατε τοὺς ἀναιτίους· 8 κύριος.γάρ ἐστιν [b]καὶ‖ τοῦ
[1]ye [2]had condemned the guiltless. For Lord [5]is [1]also [2]of [3]the
σαββάτου ὁ υἱὸς τοῦ.ἀνθρώπου.
[4]sabbath the son of man.

9 Καὶ μεταβὰς ἐκεῖθεν, ἦλθεν εἰς τὴν.συναγωγὴν.αὐτῶν.
And having departed thence, he went into their synagogue.
10 καὶ ἰδού, ἄνθρωπος [c]ἦν τὴν‖ χεῖρα ἔχων ξηράν· καὶ
And behold, a man there was [2]the [3]hand [1]having withered. And
ἐπηρώτησαν αὐτόν, λέγοντες, Εἰ.ἔξεστιν τοῖς σάββασιν
they asked him, saying, Is it lawful on the sabbaths
[d]θεραπεύειν;‖ ἵνα κατηγορήσωσιν αὐτοῦ. 11 Ὁ.δὲ εἶπεν αὐτοῖς,
to heal? that they might accuse him. But he said to them,
Τίς [e]ἔσται‖ ἐξ ὑμῶν ἄνθρωπος, ὃς ἕξει πρόβατον ἕν,
What [2]shall [3]there [4]be [5]of [6]you [1]man, who shall have [2]sheep [1]one,
καὶ ἐὰν ἐμπέσῃ τοῦτο τοῖς σάββασιν εἰς βόθυνον, οὐχὶ
and if [2]fall [1]this on the sabbaths into a pit, will not
κρατήσει αὐτὸ καὶ [f]ἐγερεῖ;‖ 12 πόσῳ οὖν διαφέρει ἄν-
lay hold of it and will raise [it] up? How much then is [3]better [1]a
θρωπος προβάτου; ὥστε ἔξεστιν τοῖς.[g]σάββασιν‖ καλῶς
[2]man than a sheep? So that it is lawful on the sabbaths [3]well
ποιεῖν. 13 Τότε λέγει τῷ.ἀνθρώπῳ, Ἔκτεινον [h]τὴν χεῖρά
[1]to [2]do. Then he says to the man, Stretch out [2]hand
σου.‖ Καὶ ἐξέτεινεν, καὶ [i]ἀποκατεστάθη‖ ὑγιὴς ὡς ἡ
[1]thy. And he stretched [it] out, and it was restored sound as the
ἄλλη.
other.

14 [k]Οἱ.δὲ Φαρισαῖοι συμβούλιον ἔλαβον κατ' αὐτοῦ ἐξελ-
But the Pharisees [5]a [6]council [4]held [7]against [8]him [1]having
θόντες,‖ ὅπως αὐτὸν ἀπολέσωσιν. 15 Ὁ.δὲ.Ἰησοῦς γνοὺς
[2]gone [3]out how him they might destroy. But Jesus having known
ἀνεχώρησεν ἐκεῖθεν· καὶ ἠκολούθησαν αὐτῷ [l]ὄχλοι‖ πολλοί,
withdrew thence, and followed him [2]crowds [1]great,
καὶ ἐθεράπευσεν αὐτοὺς πάντας· 16 καὶ ἐπετίμησεν αὐτοῖς
and he healed them all, and strictly charged them
ἵνα μὴ φανερὸν αὐτὸν ποιήσωσιν· 17 [m]ὅπως‖ πλη-
that [3]not [6]publicly [7]known [5]him [1]they [2]should [4]make. So that might
ρωθῇ τὸ ῥηθὲν διὰ Ἡσαΐου τοῦ προφήτου, λέγοντος,
be fulfilled that which was spoken by Esaias the prophet, saying,
18 Ἰδοὺ ὁ.παῖς.μου ὃν [n]ᾑρέτισα,‖ ὁ.ἀγαπητός.μου [o]εἰς
Behold my servant whom I have chosen, my beloved in
ὃν‖ [p]εὐδόκησεν‖ ἡ.ψυχή.μου· θήσω τὸ.πνεῦμά.μου ἐπ'
whom [3]has [4]found [5]delight [1]my [2]soul. I will put my Spirit upon
αὐτόν, καὶ κρίσιν τοῖς ἔθνεσιν ἀπαγγελεῖ· 19 οὐκ.ἐρίσει
him, and judgment to the nations he shall declare. He shall not strive
οὐδὲ κραυγάσει, οὐδὲ ἀκούσει τις ἐν ταῖς πλατείαις τὴν
nor cry out, nor shall [3]hear [1]any [2]one in the streets
φωνὴν.αὐτοῦ. 20 κάλαμον συντετριμμένον οὐ.κατεάξει, καὶ
his voice. A [2]reed [1]bruised he shall not break, and
λίνον τυφόμενον οὐ.σβέσει, ἕως.ἂν ἐκβάλῃ εἰς νῖκος τὴν
[2]flax [1]smoking he shall not quench, until he bring forth [3]unto [4]victory [1]the
κρίσιν. 21 καὶ [q]ἐν‖ τῷ.ὀνόματι.αὐτοῦ ἔθνη ἐλπιοῦσιν.
[2]judgment. And in his name [the] nations shall hope.

---

[b] — καὶ GLTTrAW. [c] — ἦν τὴν LTTrA. [d] θεραπεῦσαι; T. [e] — ἔσται TrA. [f] ἐγείρει he raises [it] up L. [g] σαββάτοις L. [h] σου τὴν χεῖρα LTTrA. [i] ἀπεκατεστάθη LTTrAW. [k] ἐξελθόντες δὲ οἱ Φαρισαῖοι συμβούλιον ἔλαβον κατ' αὐτοῦ LTTrW. [l] — ὄχλοι (read πολλοί many) LT[TrA]. [m] ἵνα that LTTrA. [n] ᾑρέτισα Tr. [o] ἐν ᾧ Tr; — εἰς LA. [p] ηὐδόκησεν TTr. [q] — ἐν (read [on]) GLTTrAW.

22 Τότε [r]προσηνέχθη‖ αὐτῷ [s]δαιμονιζόμενος, τυφλὸς
Then was brought to him one possessed by a demon, blind
καὶ κωφός·‖ καὶ ἐθεράπευσεν αὐτόν, ὥστε τὸν [t]τυφλὸν καὶ‖
and dumb, and he healed him, so that the blind and
κωφὸν [v]καὶ‖ λαλεῖν καὶ βλέπειν. 23 καὶ ἐξίσταντο πάντες
dumb both spake and saw. And [4]were [5]amazed [1]all
οἱ ὄχλοι καὶ ἔλεγον, Μήτι οὗτός ἐστιν ὁ υἱὸς [w]Δαβίδ;‖
[2]the [3]crowds and said, [2]This [1]is the son of David?
24 Οἱ.δὲ Φαρισαῖοι ἀκούσαντες εἶπον, Οὗτος οὐκ.ἐκβάλλει
But the Pharisees having heard said, This [man] casts not out
τὰ δαιμόνια εἰ.μὴ ἐν τῷ Βεελζεβοὺλ ἄρχοντι τῶν δαιμονίων.
the demons except by Beelzebul prince of the demons.
25 Εἰδὼς.δὲ [x]ὁ Ἰησοῦς‖ τὰς.ἐνθυμήσεις.αὐτῶν εἶπεν αὐτοῖς,
But [2]knowing [1]Jesus their thoughts he said to them,
Πᾶσα βασιλεία μερισθεῖσα καθ' ἑαυτῆς ἐρημοῦται· καὶ
Every kingdom divided against itself is brought to desolation, and
πᾶσα πόλις ἢ.οἰκία μερισθεῖσα καθ' ἑαυτῆς οὐ.σταθήσεται.
every city or house divided against itself will not stand.
26 καὶ εἰ ὁ σατανᾶς τὸν σατανᾶν ἐκβάλλει, ἐφ' ἑαυτὸν ἐμε-
And if Satan [3]Satan [1]casts [2]out, against himself he was
ρίσθη· πῶς οὖν σταθήσεται ἡ.βασιλεία.αὐτοῦ; 27 καὶ εἰ ἐγὼ
divided. How then will stand his kingdom? And if I
ἐν Βεελζεβοὺλ ἐκβάλλω τὰ δαιμόνια οἱ.υἱοὶ.ὑμῶν ἐν τίνι
by Beelzebul cast out the demons, your sons by whom
ἐκβάλλουσιν; διὰ τοῦτο αὐτοὶ [y]ὑμῶν ἔσονται κριταί.‖
do they cast out? on account of this they of you shall be judges.
28 εἰ.δὲ [z]ἐγὼ ἐν πνεύματι θεοῦ‖ ἐκβάλλω τὰ δαιμόνια, ἄρα
But if I by [the] Spirit of God cast out the demons, then
ἔφθασεν ἐφ' ὑμᾶς ἡ βασιλεία τοῦ θεοῦ. 29 ἢ πῶς δύναταί
has come upon you the kingdom of God. Or how is able
τις εἰσελθεῖν εἰς τὴν οἰκίαν τοῦ ἰσχυροῦ καὶ τὰ σκεύη
anyone to enter into the house of the strong [man] and [2]goods
αὐτοῦ [a]διαρπάσαι,‖ ἐὰν.μὴ πρῶτον δήσῃ τὸν ἰσχυρόν;
[1]his to plunder, unless first he bind the strong [man]?
καὶ τότε τὴν.οἰκίαν.αὐτοῦ [b]διαρπάσει.‖ 30 ὁ μὴ.ὢν μετ' ἐμοῦ
and then his house he will plunder. He who is not with me
κατ' ἐμοῦ ἐστιν· καὶ ὁ μὴ.συνάγων μετ' ἐμοῦ σκορπίζει.
against me is; and he who gathers not with me scatters.
31 Διὰ τοῦτο λέγω ὑμῖν, Πᾶσα ἁμαρτία καὶ βλασφημία
Because of this I say to you, Every sin and blasphemy
ἀφεθήσεται [c]τοῖς ἀνθρώποις· ἡ.δὲ τοῦ.πνεύματος βλασ-
shall be forgiven to men; but the [2]concerning [3]the [4]Spirit [1]blas-
φημία οὐκ.ἀφεθήσεται [d]τοῖς ἀνθρώποις.‖ 32 καὶ ὃς.[e]ἂν‖ εἴπῃ
phemy shall not be forgiven to men. And whoever speaks
λόγον κατὰ τοῦ υἱοῦ τοῦ ἀνθρώπου, ἀφεθήσεται αὐτῷ·
a word against the Son of man, it shall be forgiven him;
ὃς.δ'.ἂν εἴπῃ κατὰ τοῦ πνεύματος τοῦ ἁγίου, [f]οὐκ.ἀφε-
but whoever speaks against the Spirit the Holy, it shall not
θήσεται‖ αὐτῷ, οὔτε ἐν τούτῳ τῷ αἰῶνι οὔτε ἐν τῷ μέλλον-
be forgiven him, neither in this age nor in the coming
τι. 33 Ἢ ποιήσατε τὸ δένδρον καλὸν καὶ τὸν καρπὸν
[one]. Either make the tree good and [2]fruit

22 Then was brought
unto him one possessed
with a devil, blind,
and dumb: and he
healed him, insomuch
that the blind and
dumb both spake and
saw. 23 And all the
people were amazed,
and said, Is not this
the Son of David?
24 But when the Phari-
sees heard *it*, they said,
This *fellow* doth not
cast out devils, but by
Beelzebub the prince
of the devils. 25 And
Jesus knew their
thoughts, and said
unto them, Every
kingdom divided a-
gainst itself is brought
to desolation; and
every city or house
divided against itself
shall not stand: 26 and
if Satan cast out Satan,
he is divided against
himself; how shall
then his kingdom
stand? 27 And if I by
Beelzebub cast out
devils, by whom do
your children cast
them out? therefore
they shall be your
judges. 28 But if I cast
out devils by the Spirit
of God, then the king-
dom of God is come
unto you. 29 Or else
how can one enter into
a strong man's house
and spoil his goods,
except he first bind the
strong man? and then
he will spoil his house.
30 He that is not with
me is against me; and
he that gathereth not
with me scattereth
abroad. 31 Wherefore
I say unto you, All
manner of sin and
blasphemy shall be
forgiven unto men:
but the blasphemy
against the Holy Ghost
shall not be forgiven
unto men. 32 And
whosoever speaketh
a word against the
Son of man, it shall
be forgiven him: but
whosoever speaketh a-
gainst the Holy Ghost,
it shall not be for-
given him, neither in
this world, neither in
the *world* to come.
33 Either make the
tree good, and his fruit

[r] προσήνεγκαν they brought L. [s] δαιμονιζόμενον τυφλὸν καὶ κωφόν L. [t] — τυφλὸν καὶ LTTrA. [v] — καὶ LTTrA. [w] Δαυίδ GW; Δαυείδ LTTrA. [x] — ὁ Ἰησοῦς LTTrA. [y] κριταὶ ἔσονται ὑμῶν LTTrA. [z] ἐν πνεύματι θεοῦ ἐγὼ GLTTrAW. [a] ἁρπάσαι to seize upon LTTrA. [b] ἁρπάσει he will seize upon L; διαρπάσῃ he might plunder T. [c] + [ὑμῖν] to you A. [d] — τοῖς ἀνθρώποις LTTr[A]. [e] ἐὰν LTTrAW. [f] οὐ μὴ ἀφεθῇ in nowise shall it be forgiven L.

good; or else make
the tree corrupt, and
his fruit corrupt: for
the tree is known by
his fruit. 34 O gene-
ration of vipers, how
can ye, being evil,
speak good things?
for out of the abun-
dance of the heart the
mouth speaketh. 35 A
good man out of the
good treasure of the
heart bringeth forth
good things: and an
evil man out of the
evil treasure bringeth
forth evil things.
36 But I say unto you,
That every idle word
that men shall speak,
they shall give account
thereof in the day of
judgment. 37 For by
thy words thou shalt
be justified, and by
thy words thou shalt
be condemned.

αὐτοῦ καλόν, ἢ ποιήσατε τὸ δένδρον σαπρὸν καὶ τὸν καρπὸν
[1]its good, or make the tree corrupt and [2]fruit
αὐτοῦ σαπρόν· ἐκ.γὰρ τοῦ καρποῦ τὸ δένδρον γινώσκεται.
[1]its corrupt: for from the fruit the tree is known.
34 Γεννήματα ἐχιδνῶν, πῶς δύνασθε ἀγαθὰ λαλεῖν, πονηροὶ
Offspring of vipers, how are ye able good things to speak, [2]wicked
ὄντες; ἐκ.γὰρ τοῦ περισσεύματος τῆς καρδίας τὸ στόμα
[1]being? for out of the abundance of the heart the mouth
λαλεῖ. 35 ὁ ἀγαθὸς ἄνθρωπος ἐκ τοῦ ἀγαθοῦ θησαυροῦ
speaks. The good man out of the good treasure
[g]τῆς καρδίας‖ ἐκβάλλει [h]τὰ‖ ἀγαθά· καὶ ὁ πονηρὸς ἄνθρω-
of the heart puts forth the good things; and the wicked man
πος ἐκ τοῦ πονηροῦ θησαυροῦ ἐκβάλλει πονηρά. 36 λέγω.δὲ
out of the wicked treasure puts forth wicked things. But I say
ὑμῖν, ὅτι πᾶν ῥῆμα ἀργὸν ὃ.[i]ἐὰν‖ [k]λαλήσωσιν‖ οἱ ἄνθρωποι,
to you, that every [2]word [1]idle whatsoever [2]may [3]speak [1]men,
ἀποδώσουσιν περὶ αὐτοῦ λόγον ἐν ἡμέρᾳ κρίσεως. 37 ἐκ
they shall render of it an account in day of judgment. [2]By
γὰρ τῶν.λόγων.σου δικαιωθήσῃ, καὶ ἐκ τῶν.λόγων.σου
[1]for thy words thou shalt be justified, and by thy words
καταδικασθήσῃ.
thou shalt be condemned.

38 Then certain of
the scribes and of the
Pharisees answered,
saying, Master, we
would see a sign from
thee. 39 But he an-
swered and said unto
them, An evil and a-
dulterous generation
seeketh after a sign;
and there shall no sign
be given to it, but the
sign of the prophet
Jonas: 40 for as Jonas
was three days and
three nights in the
whale's belly; so shall
the Son of man be
three days and three
nights in the heart of
the earth. 41 The men
of Nineveh shall rise
in judgment with this
generation, and shall
condemn it: because
they repented at the
preaching of Jonas;
and, behold, a greater
than Jonas *is* here.
42 The queen of the
south shall rise up in
the judgment with
this generation, and
shall condemn it: for
she came from the ut-
termost parts of the
earth to hear the
wisdom of Solomon;
and, behold, a greater
than Solomon *is* here.
43 When the unclean
spirit is gone out of
a man, he walketh
through dry places,
seeking rest, and find-
eth none. 44 Then he
saith, I will return

38 Τότε ἀπεκρίθησάν[l] τινες τῶν γραμματέων [m]καὶ Φαρι-
Then answered, some of the scribes and Phari-
σαίων,‖ λέγοντες, Διδάσκαλε, θέλομεν ἀπὸ σοῦ σημεῖον ἰδεῖν.
sees, saying, Teacher, we wish from thee a sign to see.
39 Ὁ.δὲ ἀποκριθεὶς εἶπεν αὐτοῖς, Γενεὰ πονηρὰ καὶ μοι-
But he answering said to them, A generation wicked and adul-
χαλὶς σημεῖον ἐπιζητεῖ· καὶ σημεῖον οὐ.δοθήσεται αὐτῇ,
terous a sign seeks for, and a sign shall not be given to it,
εἰ.μὴ τὸ σημεῖον Ἰωνᾶ τοῦ προφήτου. 40 ὥσπερ.γὰρ ἦν Ἰωνᾶς
except the sign of Jonas the prophet. For even as was Jonas
ἐν τῇ κοιλίᾳ τοῦ κήτους τρεῖς ἡμέρας καὶ τρεῖς νύκτας, οὕτως
in the belly of the great fish three days and three nights, thus
ἔσται ὁ υἱὸς τοῦ ἀνθρώπου ἐν τῇ καρδίᾳ τῆς γῆς τρεῖς
shall be the Son of man in the heart of the earth three
ἡμέρας καὶ τρεῖς νύκτας. 41 Ἄνδρες [n]Νινευῖται‖ ἀναστήσονται
days and three nights. Men Ninevites shall stand up
ἐν τῇ κρίσει μετὰ τῆς.γενεᾶς.ταύτης, καὶ κατακρινοῦσιν αὐτήν·
in the judgment with this generation, and shall condemn it;
ὅτι μετενόησαν εἰς τὸ κήρυγμα Ἰωνᾶ· καὶ ἰδού, πλεῖον
for they repented at the proclamation of Jonas; and behold, more
Ἰωνᾶ ὧδε. 42 βασίλισσα νότου ἐγερθήσεται ἐν τῇ κρίσει
than Jonas here. A queen of [the] south shall rise up in the judgment
μετὰ τῆς.γενεᾶς.ταύτης, καὶ κατακρινεῖ αὐτήν· ὅτι ἦλθεν
with this generation, and shall condemn it; for she came
ἐκ τῶν περάτων τῆς γῆς ἀκοῦσαι τὴν σοφίαν [o]Σολομῶντος·‖
from the ends of the earth to hear the wisdom of Solomon;
καὶ ἰδού, πλεῖον [o]Σολομῶντος‖ ὧδε. 43 Ὅταν.δὲ τὸ ἀκάθαρτον
and behold, more than Solomon here. But when the unclean
πνεῦμα ἐξέλθῃ ἀπὸ τοῦ ἀνθρώπου, διέρχεται δι' ἀνύδρων
spirit is gone out from the man, he goes through waterless
τόπων, ζητοῦν ἀνάπαυσιν, καὶ οὐχ.εὑρίσκει. 44 τότε λέγει,
places, seeking rest, and finds not [it]. Then he says,

[g] — τῆς καρδίας GLTTrAW. [h] — τὰ LTrW. [i] — ἐὰν (*read* which) LTTrA. [k] λαλήσουσιν shall speak TTrA. [l] + αὐτῷ him LTTrA. [m] — καὶ Φαρισαίων L. [n] Νινευεῖται TTrA. [o] Σολομῶνος GLTTrAW.

[q]Ἐπιστρέψω εἰς τὸν.οἶκόν.μου,|| ὅθεν ἐξῆλθον· καὶ ἐλθὸν
I will return to my house, whence I came out. And having come
εὑρίσκει σχολάζοντα, [r]σεσαρωμένον καὶ κεκοσμημένον. 45 τότε
he finds [it] unoccupied, swept and adorned. Then
πορεύεται καὶ παραλαμβάνει μεθ' ἑαυτοῦ ἑπτὰ ἕτερα πνεύματα
he goes and takes with himself seven other spirits
πονηρότερα ἑαυτοῦ, καὶ εἰσελθόντα κατοικεῖ ἐκεῖ· καὶ γίνεται
more wicked than himself and entering in they dwell there; and [6]becomes
τὰ ἔσχατα τοῦ.ἀνθρώπου.ἐκείνου χείρονα τῶν πρώτων. οὕτως
[1]the [2]last [3]of [4]that [5]man worse than the first. Thus
ἔσται καὶ τῇ.γενεᾷ.ταύτῃ τῇ πονηρᾷ.
it shall be also to this generation the wicked.

46 [s]Ἔτι.[s]δὲ|| αὐτοῦ λαλοῦντος τοῖς ὄχλοις, ἰδού, ἡ μήτηρ
But while yet he was speaking to the crowds, behold, [his] mother
καὶ οἱ.ἀδελφοὶ.[t]αὐτοῦ|| εἱστήκεισαν ἔξω, ζητοῦντες αὐτῷ λα-
and his brethren were standing without, seeking [3]to [4]him [1]to
λῆσαι. [v]47 εἶπεν.δέ τις αὐτῷ, Ἰδού, ἡ.μήτηρ.σου καὶ οἱ ἀδελφοί
[2]speak. Then said one to him, Behold, thy mother and [2]brethren
σου ἔξω ἑστήκασιν, ζητοῦντές σοι λαλῆσαι.|| 48 Ὁ.δὲ ἀπο-
[1]thy without are standing, seeking [3]to [4]thee [1]to [2]speak. But he an-
κριθεὶς εἶπεν τῷ [w]εἰπόντι|| αὐτῷ, Τίς ἐστιν ἡ.μήτηρ.μου;
swering said to him who spoke to him, Who is my mother?
καὶ τίνες εἰσὶν οἱ.ἀδελφοί.μου; 49 Καὶ ἐκτείνας τὴν χεῖρα
and who are my brethren? And stretching out [2]hand
[x]αὐτοῦ|| ἐπὶ τοὺς.μαθητὰς.αὐτοῦ εἶπεν, Ἰδού, ἡ.μήτηρ.μου καὶ
[1]his to his disciples he said, Behold, my mother and
οἱ.ἀδελφοί.μου. 50 ὅστις.γὰρ ἂν [y]ποιήσῃ|| τὸ θέλημα τοῦ
my brethren. For whosoever shall do the will
πατρός.μου τοῦ ἐν οὐρανοῖς, αὐτός μου ἀδελφὸς καὶ
of my Father who [is] in [the] heavens, he my brother and
ἀδελφὴ καὶ μήτηρ ἐστίν.
sister and mother is.

13 Ἐν.[z]δὲ|| τῇ.ἡμέρᾳ.ἐκείνῃ ἐξελθὼν ὁ Ἰησοῦς [a]ἀπὸ||
And in that day [2]having [3]gone [4]forth [1]Jesus from
τῆς οἰκίας ἐκάθητο παρὰ τὴν θάλασσαν· 2 καὶ συνήχθησαν
the house sat down by the sea. And were gathered together
πρὸς αὐτὸν ὄχλοι πολλοί, ὥστε αὐτὸν εἰς [b]τὸ|| πλοῖον ἐμ-
to [4]him [2]crowds [1]great, so that he into the ship having
βάντα καθῆσθαι, καὶ πᾶς ὁ ὄχλος ἐπὶ τὸν αἰγιαλὸν εἱστήκει.
entered sat down, and all the crowd on the shore stood.
3 καὶ ἐλάλησεν αὐτοῖς πολλὰ ἐν παραβολαῖς, λέγων, Ἰδού,
And he spoke to them many things in parables, saying, Behold,
ἐξῆλθεν ὁ σπείρων τοῦ σπείρειν. 4 καὶ ἐν.τῷ.σπείρειν.αὐτὸν
[3]went [4]out [1]the [2]sower to sow. And as he sowed
ἃ.μὲν ἔπεσεν παρὰ τὴν ὁδόν, καὶ [c]ἦλθεν|| τὰ πετεινὰ [d]καὶ||
some fell by the way, and [3]came [1]the [2]birds and
κατέφαγεν αὐτά. 5 ἄλλα.δὲ ἔπεσεν ἐπὶ τὰ πετρώδη, ὅπου
devoured them. And some fell upon the rocky places, where
οὐκ.εἶχεν γῆν πολλήν, καὶ εὐθέως ἐξανέτειλεν διὰ τὸ μὴ
they had not [2]earth [1]much, and immediately sprang up because of not
ἔχειν βάθος [e] γῆς· 6 ἡλίου.δὲ ἀνατείλαντος ἐκαυματίσθη,
having depth of earth; and [the] sun having risen they were scorched,

into my house from whence I came out; and when he is come, he findeth *it* empty, swept, and garnished. 45 Then goeth he, and taketh with himself seven other spirits more wicked than himself, and they enter in and dwell there: and the last *state* of that man is worse than the first. Even so shall it be also unto this wicked generation.

46 While he yet talked to the people, behold, *his* mother and his brethren stood without, desiring to speak with him. 47 Then one said unto him, Behold, thy mother and thy brethren stand without, desiring to speak with thee. 48 But he answered and said unto him that told him, Who is my mother? and who are my brethren? 49 And he stretched forth his hand toward his disciples, and said, Behold my mother and my brethren! 50 For whosoever shall do the will of my Father which is in heaven, the same is my brother, and sister, and mother.

XIII. The same day went Jesus out of the house, and sat by the sea side. 2 And great multitudes were gathered together unto him, so that he went into a ship, and sat; and the whole multitude stood on the shore. 3 And he spake many things unto them in parables, saying, Behold, a sower went forth to sow; 4 and when he sowed, some *seeds* fell by the way side, and the fowls came and devoured them up: 5 some fell upon stony places, where they had not much earth: and forthwith they sprung up, because they had no deepness of earth: 6 and when the sun was up, they were scorched; and because

---

[q] εἰς τὸν οἶκόν μου ἐπιστρέψω LTTrA. [r] + καὶ and [L]T. [s] — δὲ but LTTrA. [t] [αὐτοῦ] L. [v] Verse 47 in [ ] T. [w] λέγοντι LTTrA. [x] — αὐτοῦ (*read* [his] hand) T. [y] ποιῇ A. [z] — δὲ and LTTrA. [a] ἐκ out of LT; — ἀπὸ (*read* ἐξελ. having gone out of) Tr. [b] — τὸ (*read* a ship) LTTrA. [c] ἦλθον LTr; ἐλθόντα having come A. [d] — καὶ A. [e] + τῆς L.

they had no root, they
withered away. 7 And
some fell among
thorns ; and the thorns
sprung up, and choked
them : 8 but other fell
into good ground, and
brought forth fruit,
some an hundredfold,
some sixtyfold, some
thirtyfold. 9 Who hath
ears to hear, let him
hear.

10 And the disciples
came, and said unto
him, Why speakest
thou unto them in pa-
rables ? 11 He answered
and said unto them, Be-
cause it is given unto
you to know the myste-
ries of the kingdom of
heaven, but to them
it is not given. 12 For
whosoever hath, to him
shall be given, and he
shall have more abun-
dance : but whosoever
hath not, from him
shall be taken away
even that he hath.
13 Therefore speak I
to them in parables :
because they seeing
see not ; and hearing
they hear not, neither
do they understand.
14 And in them is ful-
filled the prophecy of
Esaias, which saith, By
hearing ye shall hear,
and shall not under-
stand ; and seeing ye
shall see, and shall not
perceive : 15 for this
people's heart is waxed
gross, and *their* ears
are dull of hearing,
and their eyes they
have closed; lest at any
time they should see
with *their* eyes, and
hear with *their* ears,
and should understand
with *their* heart, and
should be converted,
and I should heal them.
16 But blessed *are* your
eyes, for they see : and
your ears, for they
hear. 17 For verily I
say unto you, That
many prophets and
righteous *men* have de-
sired to see *those things*
which ye see, and have
not seen *them;* and to
hear *those things* which
ye hear, and have not
heard *them.*

18 Hear ye therefore
the parable of the
sower. 19 When any
one heareth the word
of the kingdom, and

καὶ διὰ τὸ.μὴ.ἔχειν ῥίζαν ἐξηράνθη. 7 ἄλλα.δὲ ἔπεσεν ἐπὶ
and because of not having root were dried up. And some fell upon
τὰς ἀκάνθας, καὶ ἀνέβησαν αἱ ἄκανθαι καὶ [f]ἀπέπνιξαν‖ αὐτά.
the thorns, and [3]grew [4]up [1]the [2]thorns and choked them.
8 ἄλλα.δὲ ἔπεσεν ἐπὶ τὴν γῆν τὴν καλήν, καὶ ἐδίδου καρπόν,
And some fell upon the ground the good, and yielded fruit,
ὃ.μὲν ἑκατόν, ὃ.δὲ ἑξήκοντα, ὃ.δὲ τριάκοντα. 9 ὁ ἔχων
one a hundred, another sixty, another thirty. He that has
ὦτα [g]ἀκούειν‖ ἀκουέτω.
ears to hear let him hear.

10 Καὶ προσελθόντες οἱ μαθηταὶ[h] [i]εἶπον‖ αὐτῷ, [k]Διατί‖
And [3]having [4]come [5]to[6him] [1]the [2]disciples said to him, Why
ἐν παραβολαῖς λαλεῖς αὐτοῖς; 11 Ὁ.δὲ ἀποκριθεὶς εἶπεν
in parables speakest thou to them? And he answering said
[l]αὐτοῖς,‖ Ὅτι ὑμῖν δέδοται γνῶναι τὰ μυστήρια τῆς
to them, Because to you it has been given to know the mysteries of the
βασιλείας τῶν.οὐρανῶν, ἐκείνοις.δὲ οὐ.δέδοται. 12 ὅστις
kingdom of the heavens, but to them it has not been given. [2]Whosoever
γὰρ ἔχει, δοθήσεται αὐτῷ, καὶ περισσευθήσεται· ὅστις.δὲ
[1]for has, [3]shall [4]be [5]given [1]to [2]him, and he shall be in abundance; but whosoever
οὐκ.ἔχει, καὶ ὃ ἔχει ἀρθήσεται ἀπ' αὐτοῦ. 13 διὰ τοῦτο
has not, even what he has shall be taken away from him. Because of this
ἐν παραβολαῖς αὐτοῖς λαλῶ, ὅτι βλέποντες οὐ.βλέπουσιν,
in parables to them I speak, because seeing they see not,
καὶ ἀκούοντες οὐκ.ἀκούουσιν, οὐδὲ συνιοῦσιν. 14 καὶ ἀνα-
and hearing they hear not, nor do they understand. And [3]is
πληροῦται [m]ἐπ'‖ αὐτοῖς ἡ προφητεία Ἠσαΐου, ἡ λέγουσα,
[4]filled [5]up [1]in [2]them the prophecy of Esaias, which says,
Ἀκοῇ ἀκούσετε, καὶ οὐ.μὴ.συνῆτε· καὶ βλέποντες βλέ-
In hearing ye shall hear, and in no wise understand; and seeing ye shall
ψετε, καὶ οὐ.μὴ.ἴδητε. 15 ἐπαχύνθη.γὰρ ἡ καρδία τοῦ
see, and in no wise perceive: for [6]has [7]grown [8]fat the [2]heart
λαοῦ.τούτου, καὶ τοῖς ὠσὶν[n] βαρέως ἤκουσαν, καὶ τοὺς
[3]of [4]this [5]people, and with the ears heavily they have heard, and
ὀφθαλμοὺς.αὐτῶν ἐκάμμυσαν· μήποτε ἴδωσιν τοῖς ὀφ-
their eyes they have closed; lest they should see with the
θαλμοῖς, καὶ τοῖς ὠσὶν ἀκούσωσιν, καὶ τῇ καρδίᾳ συν-
eyes, and with the ears they should hear, and with the heart they should
ῶσιν, καὶ ἐπιστρέψωσιν καὶ [o]ἰάσωμαι‖ αὐτούς. 16 Ὑμῶν.δὲ
understand, and should be converted and I should heal them. But of you
μακάριοι οἱ ὀφθαλμοί, ὅτι βλέπουσιν· καὶ τὰ ὦτα [p]ὑμῶν,‖
blessed [are] the eyes, because they see; and the ears of you,
ὅτι [q]ἀκούει.‖ 17 ἀμὴν.[r]γὰρ‖ λέγω ὑμῖν, ὅτι πολλοὶ προφῆται
because they hear. For verily I say to you, that many prophets
καὶ δίκαιοι ἐπεθύμησαν ἰδεῖν ἃ βλέπετε, καὶ οὐκ [s]εἶδον·‖
and righteous [men] desired to see what ye see, and [2]not [1]saw;
καὶ ἀκοῦσαι ἃ ἀκούετε, καὶ οὐκ.ἤκουσαν.
and to hear what ye hear, and heard not.

18 Ὑμεῖς οὖν ἀκούσατε τὴν παραβολὴν τοῦ [t]σπείροντος.‖
[2]Ye [3]therefore [1]hear the parable of the sower.
19 Παντὸς.ἀκούοντος τὸν λόγον τῆς βασιλείας καὶ μὴ
When any one hears the word of the kingdom and not [it]

---

[f] ἔπνιξαν T. [g] — ἀκούειν T[Tr]A. [h] + αὐτοῦ (*read* his disciples) L. [i] εἶπαν TTrA. [k] διὰ τί LTrA. [l] — αὐτοῖς T. [m] — ἐπ' (*read* αὐτοῖς in them) GLTTrAW. [n] + [αὐτῶν] (*read* their ears) L. [o] ἰάσομαι I shall heal LTTrA. [p] — ὑμῶν L[TrA]. [q] ἀκούουσιν LTTrA. [r] — γὰρ for T. [s] εἶδαν LTr; ἴδαν T. [t] σπείραντος LTTrA.

συνιέντος, ἔρχεται ὁ πονηρὸς καὶ ἁρπάζει τὸ ἐσπαρμένον
understands, [4]comes [1]the [2]wicked [3]one and catches away that which was sown
ἐν τῇ.καρδίᾳ.αὐτοῦ· οὗτός ἐστιν ὁ παρὰ τὴν ὁδὸν σπαρείς.
in his heart. This is he who by the way was sown.
20 Ὁ.δὲ ἐπὶ τὰ πετρώδη σπαρείς, οὗτός ἐστιν ὁ τὸν λόγον
And he who upon the rocky places was sown, this is he who the word
ἀκούων καὶ εὐθὺς μετὰ χαρᾶς λαμβάνων αὐτόν· 21 οὐκ
hears and immediately with joy receives it; [3]no
ἔχει δὲ ῥίζαν ἐν ἑαυτῷ, ἀλλὰ πρόσκαιρός ἐστιν· γενομένης.δὲ
[2]has [1]but root in himself, but temporary is; but [4]having [5]risen
θλίψεως ἢ διωγμοῦ διὰ τὸν λόγον, εὐθὺς σκαν-
[1]tribulation [2]or [3]persecution on account of the word, immediately he is
δαλίζεται. 22 Ὁ.δὲ εἰς τὰς ἀκάνθας σπαρείς, οὗτός ἐστιν
offended. And he who among the thorns was sown, this is
ὁ τὸν λόγον ἀκούων, καὶ ἡ μέριμνα τοῦ.αἰῶνος.[v]τούτου‖
he who the word hears, and the care of this life
καὶ ἡ ἀπάτη τοῦ πλούτου [w]συμπνίγει‖ τὸν λόγον, καὶ ἄκαρπος
and the deceit of riches choke the word, and unfruitful
γίνεται. 23 Ὁ.δὲ ἐπὶ τὴν [x]γῆν τὴν καλὴν‖ σπαρείς, οὗτός
it becomes. But he who on the ground the good was sown, this
ἐστιν ὁ τὸν λόγον ἀκούων καὶ [y]συνιών·‖ ὃς δὴ καρ-
is he who the word hears and understands; who indeed brings
ποφορεῖ, καὶ ποιεῖ [z]ὃ‖.μὲν ἑκατόν, [z]ὃ‖.δὲ ἑξήκοντα, [z]ὃ‖.δὲ
forth fruit, and produces one a hundred, another sixty, another
τριάκοντα.
thirty.

understandeth *it* not, then cometh the wicked *one*, and catcheth away that which was sown in his heart. This is he which received seed by the way side. 20 But he that received the seed into stony places, the same is he that heareth the word, and anon with joy receiveth it; 21 yet hath he not root in himself, but dureth for a while: for when tribulation or persecution ariseth because of the word, by and by he is offended. 22 He also that received seed among the thorns is he that heareth the word; and the care of this world, and the deceitfulness of riches, choke the word, and he becometh unfruitful. 23 But he that received seed into the good ground is he that heareth the word, and understandeth *it*; which also beareth fruit, and bringeth forth, some an hundredfold, some sixty, some thirty.

24 Ἄλλην παραβολὴν παρέθηκεν αὐτοῖς, λέγων, Ὡμοιώ-
Another parable put he before them, saying, [6]has [7]become
θη ἡ βασιλεία τῶν οὐρανῶν ἀνθρώπῳ [a]σπείροντι‖ καλὸν
[8]like [1]the [2]kingdom [3]of [4]the [5]heavens to a man sowing good
σπέρμα ἐν τῷ.ἀγρῷ.αὐτοῦ· 25 ἐν.δὲ.τῷ.καθεύδειν τοὺς ἀνθρώ-
seed in his field; but while [3]slept [1]the [2]men
πους ἦλθεν αὐτοῦ ὁ ἐχθρὸς καὶ [b]ἔσπειρεν‖ ζιζάνια ἀνὰ μέσον
came his enemy and sowed darnel in [the] midst
τοῦ σίτου, καὶ ἀπῆλθεν. 26 ὅτε.δὲ ἐβλάστησεν ὁ χόρτος,
of the wheat, and went away. And when [3]sprouted [1]the [2]blade,
καὶ καρπὸν ἐποίησεν, τότε ἐφάνη καὶ τὰ ζιζάνια. 27 προσελ-
and fruit produced, then appeared also the darnel. [2]Having [3]come
θόντες δὲ οἱ δοῦλοι τοῦ οἰκοδεσπότου εἶπον αὐτῷ, Κύριε,
[4]to [5][him] [1]and the bondmen of the master of the house said to him, Sir,
οὐχὶ καλὸν σπέρμα [c]ἔσπειρας‖ ἐν τῷ σῷ ἀγρῷ; πόθεν οὖν
[3]not [5]good [6]seed [1]didst [2]thou [4]sow in thy field? whence then
ἔχει [d]τὰ‖ ζιζάνια; 28 Ὁ.δὲ ἔφη αὐτοῖς, Ἐχθρὸς ἄνθρωπος
has it the darnel? And he said to them, [3]an [4]enemy [1]a [2]man
τοῦτο ἐποίησεν. οἱ.δὲ [e]δοῦλοι‖ [f]εἶπον αὐτῷ,‖ Θέλεις οὖν
[6]this [5]did. And the bondmen said to him, Wilt thou then
ἀπελθόντες συλλέξωμεν αὐτά; 29 Ὁ.δὲ [g]ἔφη,‖ Οὔ·
[that] having gone forth we should gather them? But he said, No;
μήποτε συλλέγοντες τὰ ζιζάνια, ἐκριζώσητε ἅμα αὐτοῖς τὸν
lest gathering the darnel, ye should uproot with them the
σῖτον. 30 ἄφετε συναυξάνεσθαι ἀμφότερα [h]μέχρὶ‖ τοῦ θερισμοῦ·
wheat. Suffer to grow together both until the harvest;

24 Another parable put he forth unto them, saying, The kingdom of heaven is likened unto a man which sowed good seed in his field: 25 but while men slept, his enemy came and sowed tares among the wheat, and went his way. 26 But when the blade was sprung up, and brought forth fruit, then appeared the tares also. 27 So the servants of the householder came and said unto him, Sir, didst not thou sow good seed in thy field? from whence then hath it tares? 28 He said unto them, An enemy hath done this. The servants said unto him, Wilt thou then that we go and gather them up? 29 But he said, Nay; lest while ye gather up the tares, ye root up also the wheat with them. 30 Let both grow together until the harvest: and in

---

[v] — τουτου (*read* of life) LTTrA. [w] συνπνίγει TA. [x] καλὴν γῆν LTTrA. [y] συνιείς LTTr. [z] ὃ LT. [a] σπείραντι [who] sowed LTTrA. [b] ἐπέσπειρεν sowed over LTTrA. [c] ἔσπειρες Tr. [d] — τα GLTTrAW. [e] — δοῦλοι (*read* οἱ δὲ and they) A. [f] αὐτῷ λέγουσιν say to him LTrA; λέγουσιν αὐτῷ T. [g] φησιν says LTTrA. [h] ἕως until LTrA.

the time of harvest I will say to the reapers, Gather ye together first the tares, and bind them in bundles to burn them: but gather the wheat into my barn.

31 Another parable put he forth unto them, saying, The kingdom of heaven is like to a grain of mustard seed, which a man took, and sowed in his field: 32 which indeed is the least of all seeds: but when it is grown, it is the greatest among herbs, and becometh a tree, so that the birds of the air come and lodge in the branches thereof.

33 Another parable spake he unto them; The kingdom of heaven is like unto leaven, which a woman took, and hid in three measures of meal, till the whole was leavened.

34 All these things spake Jesus unto the multitude in parables; and without a parable spake he not unto them: 35 that it might be fulfilled which was spoken by the prophet, saying, I will open my mouth in parables; I will utter things which have been kept secret from the foundation of the world.

36 Then Jesus sent the multitude away, and went into the house: and his disciples came unto him, saying, Declare unto us the parable of the tares of the field. 37 He answered and said unto them, He that soweth the good seed is the Son of man; 38 the field is the world; the good seed are the children of the kingdom; but the tares are the children of the wicked *one;* 39 the enemy that sowed them is the devil; the harvest is the end of

καὶ ἐν [i]τῷ‖ καιρῷ τοῦ θερισμοῦ ἐρῶ τοῖς θερισταῖς, Συλ-
and in the time of the harvest I will say to the harvest men, Ga-
λέξατε πρῶτον τὰ ζιζάνια, καὶ δήσατε αὐτὰ [j]εἰς‖ δέσμας
ther first the darnel, and bind them into bundles
πρὸς.τὸ.κατακαῦσαι αὐτά· τὸν.δὲ σῖτον [k]συναγάγετε‖ εἰς τὴν
to burn them; but the wheat bring together into
ἀποθήκην.μου.
my granary.

31 Ἄλλην παραβολὴν παρέθηκεν αὐτοῖς, λέγων, Ὁμοία
Another parable put he before them, saying, Like
ἐστὶν ἡ βασιλεία τῶν οὐρανῶν κόκκῳ σινάπεως, ὃν λα-
is the kingdom of the heavens to a grain of mustard, which having
βὼν ἄνθρωπος ἔσπειρεν ἐν τῷ.ἀγρῷ.αὐτοῦ· 32 ὃ μικρότερον
taken, a man sowed in his field; which less
μέν ἐστιν πάντων τῶν σπερμάτων, ὅταν.δὲ αὐξηθῇ
indeed is than all the seeds, but when it be grown,
μεῖζον τῶν λαχάνων ἐστίν, καὶ γίνεται δένδρον, ὥστε
greater than the herbs is, and becomes a tree, so that
ἐλθεῖν τὰ πετεινὰ τοῦ οὐρανοῦ καὶ [l]κατασκηνοῦν‖ ἐν τοῖς
come the birds of the heaven and roost in the
κλάδοις αὐτοῦ.
branches of it.

33 Ἄλλην παραβολὴν ἐλάλησεν αὐτοῖς, Ὁμοία ἐστὶν ἡ
Another parable spoke he to them, Like is the
βασιλεία τῶν οὐρανῶν ζύμῃ, ἣν λαβοῦσα γυνὴ ἐνέκρυψεν
kingdom of the heavens to leaven, which having taken, a woman hid
εἰς ἀλεύρου σάτα τρία, ἕως.οὗ ἐζυμώθη ὅλον.
in [3]of [4]meal [2]seahs [1]three, until [2]was [3]leavened [1]all.

34 Ταῦτα πάντα ἐλάλησεν ὁ Ἰησοῦς ἐν παραβολαῖς τοῖς
[2]These [3]things [1]all spoke Jesus in parables to the
ὄχλοις, καὶ χωρὶς παραβολῆς [m]οὐκ‖ ἐλάλει αὐτοῖς· 35 ὅπως
crowds, and without a parable [3]not [1]he [2]spoke to them; so that
πληρωθῇ τὸ ῥηθὲν διὰ τοῦ προφήτου[n], λέγοντος,
might be fulfilled that which was spoken by the prophet, saying,
Ἀνοίξω ἐν παραβολαῖς τὸ.στόμα.μου· ἐρεύξομαι κεκρυμμένα
I will open in parables my mouth: I will utter things hidden
ἀπὸ καταβολῆς [o]κόσμου.‖
from [the] foundation of [the] world.

36 Τότε ἀφεὶς τοὺς ὄχλους, ἦλθεν εἰς τὴν οἰκίαν
Then having dismissed the crowds, [2]went [3]into [4]the [5]house
[p]ὁ Ἰησοῦς·‖ καὶ [q]προσῆλθον‖ αὐτῷ οἱ.μαθηταὶ.αὐτοῦ, λέγοντες,
[1]Jesus; and came to him his disciples, saying,
[r]Φράσον‖ ἡμῖν τὴν παραβολὴν τῶν ζιζανίων τοῦ ἀγροῦ.
Expound to us the parable of the darnel of the field.
37 Ὁ.δὲ ἀποκριθεὶς εἶπεν [s]αὐτοῖς,‖ Ὁ σπείρων τὸ καλὸν
And he answering said to them, He who sows the good
σπέρμα ἐστὶν ὁ υἱὸς τοῦ ἀνθρώπου· 38 ὁ.δὲ ἀγρός ἐστιν ὁ
seed is the Son of man; and the field is the
κόσμος· τὸ.δὲ καλὸν σπέρμα, οὗτοί εἰσιν οἱ υἱοὶ τῆς βασιλείας·
world; and the good seed, these are the sons of the kingdom;
τὰ.δὲ ζιζάνιά εἰσιν οἱ υἱοὶ τοῦ πονηροῦ· 39 ὁ.δὲ ἐχθρὸς
but the darnel are the sons of the evil [one]; and the enemy
[t]ὁ σπείρας αὐτά ἐστιν‖ ὁ διάβολος· ὁ.δὲ θερισμὸς συν-
who sowed them is the devil; and the harvest [the] com-

---

[i] — τῷ GLTTrAW. [j] — εἰς (*read* [in]) [Tr]A. [k] συνάγετε LTr. [l] κατασκηνοῖν LTTrA. [m] οὐδὲν nothing LTTrA. [n] + Ἠσαΐου Isaiah T. [o] — κόσμου LTTrA. [p] — ὁ Ἰησοῦς (*read* he went) LTTrA. [q] προσῆλθαν LTr. [r] διασάφησον explain LTr. [s] — αὐτοῖς LTTrA. [t] ἐστιν ὁ σπείρας αὐτὰ L.

τέλεια [v]τοῦ‖ αἰῶνός ἐστιν· οἱ.δὲ θερισταὶ ἄγγελοί εἰσιν.
pletion of the age is, and the harvest men angels are.
40 ὥσπερ οὖν συλλέγεται τὰ ζιζάνια, καὶ πυρὶ [w]κατα-
As therefore is gathered the darnel, and in fire is con-
καίεται,‖ οὕτως ἔσται ἐν τῇ συντελείᾳ τοῦ.αἰῶνος.[x]τούτου.‖
sumed, thus it shall be in the completion of this age.
41 ἀποστελεῖ ὁ υἱὸς τοῦ ἀνθρώπου τοὺς ἀγγέλους.αὐτοῦ,
[5]shall [6]send [7]forth [1]the [2]Son [3]of [4]man his angels,
καὶ συλλέξουσιν ἐκ τῆς.βασιλείας.αὐτοῦ πάντα τὰ σκάνδαλα
and they shall gather out of his kingdom all the offences
καὶ τοὺς ποιοῦντας τὴν ἀνομίαν, 42 καὶ βαλοῦσιν αὐτοὺς
and those who practise lawlessness, and they shall cast them
εἰς τὴν κάμινον τοῦ πυρός· ἐκεῖ ἔσται ὁ κλαυθμὸς καὶ ὁ
into the furnace of the fire: there shall be the weeping and the
βρυγμὸς τῶν ὀδόντων. 43 τότε οἱ δίκαιοι ἐκλάμψουσιν ὡς
gnashing of the teeth. Then the righteous shall shine forth as
ὁ ἥλιος ἐν τῇ βασιλείᾳ τοῦ.πατρὸς.αὐτῶν. Ὁ ἔχων ὦτα
the sun in the kingdom of their Father. He that has ears
[y]ἀκούειν‖ ἀκουέτω.
to hear let him hear.

44 [z]Πάλιν‖ ὁμοία ἐστὶν ἡ βασιλεία τῶν οὐρανῶν θησαυρῷ
Again like is the kingdom of the heavens to treasure
κεκρυμμένῳ ἐν τῷ ἀγρῷ, ὃν εὑρὼν ἄνθρωπος ἔκρυψεν,
hid in the field, which [3]having [4]found [1]a [2]man hid,
καὶ ἀπὸ τῆς χαρᾶς αὐτοῦ ὑπάγει καὶ [a]πάντα ὅσα ἔχει
and for the joy of it goes and all things as many as he has
πωλεῖ,‖ καὶ ἀγοράζει τὸν.ἀγρὸν.ἐκεῖνον.
he sells, and buys that field.

45 Πάλιν ὁμοία ἐστὶν ἡ βασιλεία τῶν οὐρανῶν ἀνθρώπῳ
Again like is the kingdom of the heavens to a man
ἐμπόρῳ, ζητοῦντι καλοὺς μαργαρίτας· 46 [b]ὃς εὑρὼν‖ ἕνα
a merchant, seeking beautiful pearls; who having found one
πολύτιμον μαργαρίτην, ἀπελθὼν πέπρακεν πάντα ὅσα
very precious pearl, having gone away has sold all things as many as
εἶχεν, καὶ ἠγόρασεν αὐτόν.
he had, and bought it.

47 Πάλιν ὁμοία ἐστὶν ἡ βασιλεία τῶν οὐρανῶν σαγήνῃ
Again like is the kingdom of the heavens to a drag net
βληθείσῃ εἰς τὴν θάλασσαν, καὶ ἐκ παντὸς γένους συναγα-
cast into the sea, and of every kind gathering
γούσῃ· 48 ἣν ὅτε ἐπληρώθη ἀναβιβάσαντες[c] [d]ἐπὶ τὸν
together; which when it was filled having drawn up on the
αἰγιαλόν, καὶ‖ καθίσαντες συνέλεξαν τὰ καλὰ εἰς [e]ἀγγεῖα,‖
shore, and having sat down they collected the good into vessels,
τὰ.δὲ σαπρὰ ἔξω ἔβαλον. 49 οὕτως ἔσται ἐν τῇ συντελείᾳ
and the corrupt [3]out [1]they [2]cast. Thus shall it be in the completion
τοῦ αἰῶνος· ἐξελεύσονται οἱ ἄγγελοι, καὶ ἀφοριοῦσιν τοὺς
of the age: [3]shall [4]go [5]out [1]the [2]angels, and shall separate the
πονηροὺς ἐκ μέσου τῶν δικαίων, 50 καὶ βαλοῦσιν αὐτοὺς
wicked from [the] midst of the righteous, and shall cast them
εἰς τὴν κάμινον τοῦ πυρός· ἐκεῖ ἔσται ὁ κλαυθμὸς καὶ ὁ
into the furnace of the fire: there shall be the wailing and the
βρυγμὸς τῶν ὀδόντων.
gnashing of the teeth.

the world; and the reapers are the angels.
40 As therefore the tares are gathered and burned in the fire; so shall it be in the end of this world.
41 The Son of man shall send forth his angels, and they shall gather out of his kingdom all things that offend, and them which do iniquity;
42 and shall cast them into a furnace of fire: there shall be wailing and gnashing of teeth.
43 Then shall the righteous shine forth as the sun in the kingdom of their Father. Who hath ears to hear, let him hear.

44 Again, the kingdom of heaven is like unto treasure hid in a field; the which when a man hath found, he hideth, and for joy thereof goeth and selleth all that he hath, and buyeth that field.

45 Again, the kingdom of heaven is like unto a merchant man, seeking goodly pearls:
46 who, when he had found one pearl of great price, went and sold all that he had, and bought it.

47 Again, the kingdom of heaven is like unto a net, that was cast into the sea, and gathered of every kind:
48 which, when it was full, they drew to shore, and sat down, and gathered the good into vessels, but cast the bad away.
49 So shall it be at the end of the world: the angels shall come forth, and sever the wicked from among the just,
50 and shall cast them into the furnace of fire: there shall be wailing and gnashing of teeth.

---

[v] — τοῦ (*read* of [the]) LTTrA. [w] καίεται is burned GTrA. [x] — τούτου (*read* the age) LTTr[A]. [y] — ἀκούειν [L]T[Tr]A. [z] — πάλιν [L]TTrA. [a] πωλεῖ πάντα ὅσα ἔχει LTTrA. [b] εὑρὼν δὲ GLTTrA. [c] + αὐτὴν it L[A]. [d] καὶ ἐπὶ τὸν αἰγιαλὸν L; ἐπὶ τὸν αἰγιαλὸν [καὶ] A. [e] ἄγγη TTrA.

51 Jesus saith unto
them, Have ye under-
stood all these things?
They say unto him,
Yea, Lord. 52 Then
said he unto them,
Therefore every scribe
which is instructed un-
to the kingdom of
heaven is like unto a
man *that is* an house-
holder, which bringeth
forth out of his trea-
sure *things* new and
old.

53 And it came to
pass, *that* when Jesus
had finished these
parables, he departed
thence. 54 And when
he was come into his
own country, he taught
them in their syna-
gogue, insomuch that
they were astonished,
and said, Whence hath
this *man* this wisdom,
and *these* mighty
works? 55 Is not this
the carpenter's son?
is not his mother
called Mary? and his
brethren, James, and
Joses, and Simon, and
Judas? 56 and his sis-
ters, are they not all
with us? Whence then
hath this *man* all these
things? 57 And they
were offended in him.
But Jesus said unto
them, A prophet is not
without honour, save
in his own country,
and in his own house.
58 And he did not many
mighty works there
because of their un-
belief.

XIV. At that time
Herod the tetrarch
heard of the fame of
Jesus, 2 and said unto
his servants, This is
John the Baptist; he
is risen from the dead;
and therefore mighty
works do shew forth
themselves in him.
3 For Herod had laid
hold on John, and
bound him, and put
him in prison for
Herodias' sake, his
brother Philip's wife.
4 For John said unto
him, It is not lawful
for thee to have her.
5 And when he would
have put him to death,

51 [g]Λέγει αὐτοῖς ὁ Ἰησοῦς,‖ Συνήκατε ταῦτα πάντα;
[2]Says [3]to [4]them [1]Jesus, Have ye understood [2]these [3]things [1]all?
Λέγουσιν αὐτῷ, Ναί, [h]κύριε.‖ 52 Ὁ.δὲ [i]εἶπεν‖ αὐτοῖς, Διὰ
They say to him, Yea, Lord. And he said to them, Because of
τοῦτο πᾶς γραμματεὺς μαθητευθεὶς [k]εἰς τὴν βασιλείαν‖ τῶν
this every scribe discipled into the kingdom of the
οὐρανῶν ὅμοιός ἐστιν ἀνθρώπῳ οἰκοδεσπότῃ, ὅστις ἐκβάλλει
heavens [2]like [1]is to a man a master of a house, who puts forth
ἐκ τοῦ.θησαυροῦ.αὐτοῦ καινὰ καὶ παλαιά.
out of his treasure [things] new and old.

53 Καὶ ἐγένετο ὅτε ἐτέλεσεν ὁ Ἰησοῦς τὰς παραβολὰς
And it came to pass when [2]had [3]finished [1]Jesus [2]parables
ταύτας, μετῆρεν ἐκεῖθεν· 54 καὶ ἐλθὼν εἰς τὴν πατρίδα
[1]these, he withdrew thence; and having come into [3]country
αὐτοῦ, ἐδίδασκεν αὐτοὺς ἐν τῇ.συναγωγῇ.αὐτῶν, ὥστε [l]ἐκπλήτ-
[1]his [[2]own], he taught them in their synagogue, so that [2]were
τεσθαι‖ αὐτοὺς καὶ λέγειν, Πόθεν τούτῳ ἡ.σοφία.αὕτη καὶ
[3]astonished [1]they and said, Whence to this [man] this wisdom and
αἱ δυνάμεις; 55 οὐχ οὗτός ἐστιν ὁ τοῦ τέκτονος υἱός;
the works of power? [2]not [3]this [1]is [4]the [6]of [7]the [8]carpenter [5]son? [Is]
[m]οὐχὶ‖ ἡ.μήτηρ.αὐτοῦ λέγεται Μαριάμ, καὶ οἱ.ἀδελφοὶ.αὐτοῦ
not his mother called Mary, and his brethren
Ἰάκωβος καὶ [n]Ἰωσῆς‖ καὶ Σίμων καὶ Ἰούδας; 56 καὶ αἱ
James and Joses and Simon and Judas? and
ἀδελφαὶ.αὐτοῦ οὐχὶ πᾶσαι πρὸς ἡμᾶς εἰσιν; πόθεν οὖν τούτῳ
[3]his [4]sisters [2]not [5]all [6]with [7]us [1]are? whence then to this
ταῦτα πάντα; 57 Καὶ ἐσκανδαλίζοντο ἐν αὐτῷ. Ὁ δὲ
[man] [2]these [3]things [1]all? And they were offended in him. But
Ἰησοῦς εἶπεν αὐτοῖς, Οὐκ ἔστιν προφήτης ἄτιμος εἰ.μὴ
Jesus said to them, [4]not [3]is [1]a [2]prophet without honour except
ἐν τῇ[o].πατρίδι.[p]αὐτοῦ‖ καὶ ἐν τῇ.οἰκίᾳ.αὐτοῦ. 58 Καὶ οὐκ
in his [own] country and in his [own] house. And [3]not
ἐποίησεν ἐκεῖ δυνάμεις πολλὰς διὰ τὴν.ἀπιστίαν.αὐτῶν.
[1]he [2]did there [2]works [3]of [4]power [1]many because of their unbelief.

14 Ἐν ἐκείνῳ τῷ καιρῷ ἤκουσεν Ἡρώδης ὁ [q]τετράρχης‖
At that time heard Herod the tetrarch
τὴν ἀκοὴν Ἰησοῦ, 2 καὶ εἶπεν τοῖς.παισὶν.αὐτοῦ, Οὗτός ἐστιν
the fame of Jesus, and said to his servants, This is
Ἰωάννης ὁ βαπτιστής· αὐτὸς ἠγέρθη ἀπὸ τῶν νεκρῶν, καὶ
John the Baptist: he is risen from the dead, and
διὰ τοῦτο αἱ δυνάμεις ἐνεργοῦσιν ἐν αὐτῷ. 3 Ὁ γὰρ
because of this the works of power operate in him. For
Ἡρώδης κρατήσας τὸν Ἰωάννην ἔδησεν [r]αὐτὸν‖ καὶ [s]ἔθετο
Herod having seized John bound him and put
ἐν φυλακῇ,‖ διὰ Ἡρωδιάδα τὴν γυναῖκα [t]Φιλίππου‖
[him] in prison, on account of Herodias the wife [4]Philip
τοῦ.ἀδελφοῦ.αὐτοῦ. 4 ἔλεγεν.γὰρ [v]αὐτῷ ὁ Ἰωάννης,‖ Οὐκ
[1]of [2]his [3]brother. For [2]said [3]to [4]him [1]John, [7]Not
ἔξεστίν σοι ἔχειν αὐτήν. 5 Καὶ θέλων αὐτὸν ἀποκτεῖναι,
[5]it [6]is lawful for thee to have her. And wishing [3]him [1]to [2]kill,

[g] — Λέγει αὐτοῖς ὁ Ἰησοῦς LTTrA. [h] — κύριε LTTrA. [i] λέγει says L. [k] ἐν τῇ βασιλείᾳ in the kingdom L; τῇ βασιλείᾳ to the kingdom GTTrA. [l] ἐκπλήσσεσθαι LTTrAW. [m] οὐχ LTTrA. [n] Ἰωσὴφ Joseph LTTrA. [o] + ἰδίᾳ own T. [p] — αὐτοῦ (*read* [his]) LTTrA. [q] τετραάρχης T. [r] — αὐτὸν T. [s] ἐν τῇ (— τῇ T) φυλακῇ ἀπέθετο in the prison put [him] aside LTTrA. [t] — Φιλίππου [T]A. [v] ὁ (— ὁ T) Ἰωάννης αὐτῷ LT.

ἐφοβήθη τὸν ὄχλον, ὅτι ὡς προφήτην αὐτὸν εἶχον.
he feared the multitude, because as a prophet him they held.
6 [w]γενεσίων.δὲ ἀγομένων[‖] τοῦ.Ἡρώδου, ὠρχήσατο ἡ θυγάτηρ
But a birthday being celebrated of Herod, [5]danced [1]the [2]daughter
τῆς Ἡρωδιάδος ἐν τῷ μέσῳ, καὶ ἤρεσεν τῷ Ἡρώδῃ· 7 ὅθεν
[3]of [4]Herodias in the midst, and pleased Herod; Whereupon
μεθ' ὅρκου ὡμολόγησεν αὐτῇ δοῦναι ὃ.[x]ἐὰν[‖] αἰτήσηται. 8 Ἡ.δὲ
with oath he promised to her to give whatever she should ask. But she
προβιβασθεῖσα ὑπὸ τῆς.μητρὸς.αὐτῆς, Δός μοι, φησίν, ὧδε
being urged on by her mother, Give me, she says, here
ἐπὶ πίνακι τὴν κεφαλὴν Ἰωάννου τοῦ βαπτιστοῦ. 9 Καὶ
upon a dish the head of John the Baptist. And
[y]ἐλυπήθη[‖] ὁ βασιλεύς· διὰ.[z]δὲ[‖] τοὺς ὅρκους καὶ τοὺς
[3]was [4]grieved [1]the [2]king; but on account of the oaths and those who
συνανακειμένους ἐκέλευσεν δοθῆναι· 10 καὶ πέμψας
reclined with [him at table] he commanded [it] to be given. And having sent
ἀπεκεφάλισεν [a]τὸν[‖] Ἰωάννην ἐν τῇ φυλακῇ. 11 καὶ ἠνέχθη
he beheaded John in the prison. And [3]was [4]brought
ἡ.κεφαλὴ.αὐτοῦ ἐπὶ πίνακι, καὶ ἐδόθη τῷ κορασίῳ· καὶ ἤν-
[1]his [2]head on a dish, and was given to the damsel, and she
εγκεν τῇ.μητρὶ.αὐτῆς. 12 καὶ προσελθόντες οἱ.μαθηταὶ.αὐτοῦ
brought [it] to her mother. And having come his disciples
ἦραν τὸ [b]σῶμα,[‖] καὶ ἔθαψαν [c]αὐτό·[‖] καὶ ἐλθόντες ἀπήγγειλαν
took the body, and buried it; and having come told
τῷ Ἰησοῦ. 13 [d]καὶ ἀκούσας[‖] ὁ Ἰησοῦς ἀνεχώρησεν ἐκεῖθεν
[it] to Jesus. And [2]having [3]heard [1]Jesus withdrew thence
ἐν πλοίῳ εἰς ἔρημον τόπον κατ'.ἰδίαν.
by ship to a desert place apart.

he feared the multitude, because they counted him as a prophet. 6 But when Herod's birthday was kept, the daughter of Herodias danced before them, and pleased Herod. 7 Whereupon he promised with an oath to give her whatsoever she would ask. 8 And she, being before instructed of her mother, said, Give me here John Baptist's head in a charger. 9 And the king was sorry: nevertheless for the oath's sake, and them which sat with him at meat, he commanded *it* to be given *her*. 10 And he sent, and beheaded John in the prison. 11 And his head was brought in a charger, and given to the damsel: and she brought *it* to her mother. 12 And his disciples came, and took up the body, and buried it, and went and told Jesus. 13 When Jesus heard *of it*, he departed thence by ship into a desert place apart.

Καὶ ἀκούσαντες οἱ ὄχλοι ἠκολούθησαν αὐτῷ [e]πεζῇ[‖]
And having heard [of it] the crowds followed him on foot
ἀπὸ τῶν πόλεων. 14 Καὶ ἐξελθὼν [f]ὁ Ἰησοῦς[‖] εἶδεν πολὺν
from the cities. And having gone out Jesus saw [2]great
ὄχλον, καὶ ἐσπλαγχνίσθη ἐπ' [g]αὐτούς,[‖] καὶ ἐθεράπευσεν
[1]a crowd, and was moved with compassion towards them, and healed
τοὺς.ἀῤῥώστους.αὐτῶν. 15 Ὀψίας.δὲ γενομένης [h]προσῆλθον[‖]
their infirm. And evening having come came
αὐτῷ οἱ.μαθηταὶ.[i]αὐτοῦ,[‖] λέγοντες, Ἔρημός ἐστιν ὁ τόπος,
to him his disciples, saying, Desert is the place,
καὶ ἡ ὥρα [k]ἤδη παρῆλθεν·[‖] ἀπόλυσον [l]τοὺς ὄχλους, ἵνα
and the time already is gone by: dismiss the crowds, that
ἀπελθόντες εἰς τὰς κώμας ἀγοράσωσιν ἑαυτοῖς βρώματα.
having gone into the villages they may buy for themselves meat.
16 Ὁ.δὲ.[m]Ἰησοῦς[‖] εἶπεν αὐτοῖς, Οὐ χρείαν ἔχουσιν ἀπελθεῖν·
But Jesus said to them, [3]No [4]need [1]they [2]have to go away:
δότε αὐτοῖς ὑμεῖς φαγεῖν. 17 Οἱ.δὲ λέγουσιν αὐτῷ, Οὐκ.ἔχομεν
give [2]to [3]them [1]ye to eat. But they say to him, We have not
ὧδε εἰ.μὴ πέντε ἄρτους καὶ δύο ἰχθύας. 18 Ὁ.δὲ εἶπεν, Φέρετέ
here except five loaves and two fishes. And he said, Bring
μοι [n]αὐτοὺς ὧδε.[‖] 19 Καὶ κελεύσας τοὺς ὄχλους ἀνα-
[2]to [3]me [1]them here. And having commanded the crowds to re-
κλιθῆναι ἐπὶ [o]τοὺς χόρτους,[‖] [p]καὶ[‖] λαβὼν τοὺς πέντε ἄρτους
cline on the grass, and having taken the five loaves

And when the people had heard *thereof*, they followed him on foot out of the cities. 14 And Jesus went forth, and saw a great multitude, and was moved with compassion toward them, and he healed their sick. 15 And when it was evening, his disciples came to him, saying, This is a desert place, and the time is now past; send the multitude away, that they may go into the villages, and buy themselves victuals. 16 But Jesus said unto them, They need not depart; give ye them to eat. 17 And they say unto him, We have here but five loaves, and two fishes. 18 He said, Bring them hither to me. 19 And he commanded the multitude to sit down on the grass, and took the five loaves, and the

---

[w] γενεσίοις δὲ γενομένοις LTTrA. [x] ἂν LTrA. [y] λυπηθεὶς being grieved LTTrA. [z] — δὲ but LTTrA. [a] — τὸν LTTrA. [b] πτῶμα corpse LTTr. [c] αὐτόν him TTrA. [d] ἀκούσας δὲ LTTrA. [e] πεζοὶ T. [f] — ὁ Ἰησοῦς (*read* he saw) LTTrA. [g] αὐτοῖς GLTTrAW. [h] προσῆλθαν LTr. [i] — αὐτοῦ (*read* the disciples) LTTrA. [k] παρῆλθεν ἤδη T. [l] + οὖν therefore T [A]. [m] — Ἰησοῦς (*read* he said) T. [n] ὧδε αὐτούς LTTrA. [o] τοῦ χόρτου LTTr. [p] — καὶ GLTTrAW.

two fishes, and looking
up to heaven, he bles-
ed, and brake, and gave
the loaves to *his* dis-
ciples, and the disci-
ples to the multitude.
20 And they did all
eat, and were filled:
and they took up of
the fragments that re-
mained twelve baskets
full. 21 And they that
had eaten were about
five thousand men,
beside women and
children

22 And straightway
Jesus constrained his
disciples to get into a
ship, and to go before
him unto the other
side, while he sent
the multitudes away.
23 And when he had
sent the multitudes
away, he went up into
a mountain apart to
pray: and when the
evening was come, he
was there alone. 24 But
the ship was now in
the midst of the sea,
tossed with waves:
for the wind was con-
trary. 25 And in the
fourth watch of the
night Jesus went unto
them, walking on the
sea. 26 And when the
disciples saw him
walking on the sea,
they were troubled,
saying, It is a spirit;
and they cried out for
fear. 27 But straight-
way Jesus spake unto
them, saying, Be of
good cheer; it is I;
be not afraid. 28 And
Peter answered him
and said, Lord, if it be
thou, bid me come un-
to thee on the water.
29 And he said, Come.
And when Peter was
come down out of the
ship, he walked on the
water, to go to Jesus.
30 But when he saw
the wind boisterous,
he was afraid; and
beginning to sink, he
cried, saying, Lord,
save me. 31 And
immediately Jesus
stretched forth *his*
hand, and caught him,
and said unto him, O

καὶ τοὺς δύο ἰχθύας, ἀναβλέψας εἰς τὸν οὐρανὸν [q]εὐλόγησεν·‖
and the two fishes, having looked up to the heaven he blessed;
καὶ κλάσας ἔδωκεν τοῖς μαθηταῖς τοὺς ἄρτους, οἱ.δὲ μα-
and having broken he gave to the disciples the loaves, and the dis-
θηταὶ τοῖς ὄχλοις. 20 καὶ ἔφαγον πάντες καὶ ἐχορτάσθησαν·
ciples to the crowds. And [2]ate [1]all and were satisfied;
καὶ ἦραν τὸ περισσεῦον τῶν κλασμάτων, δώδεκα
and they took up that which was over and above of the fragments, twelve
κοφίνους πλήρεις. 21 οἱ.δὲ ἐσθίοντες ἦσαν ἄνδρες ὡσεὶ
hand-baskets full. And those who ate were men about
πεντακισχίλιοι, χωρὶς [r]γυναικῶν καὶ παιδίων.‖
five thousand, besides women and children.

22 Καὶ [s]εὐθέως‖ ἠνάγκασεν [t]ὁ Ἰησοῦς‖ τοὺς.μαθητὰς.[v]αὐτοῦ‖
And immediately [2]compelled [1]Jesus — his disciples
ἐμβῆναι εἰς [w]τὸ‖ πλοῖον καὶ προάγειν αὐτὸν εἰς τὸ πέραν,
to enter into the ship and to go before him to the other side,
ἕως.οὗ ἀπολύσῃ τοὺς ὄχλους. 23 καὶ ἀπολύσας τοὺς
until he should have dismissed the crowds. And having dismissed the
ὄχλους ἀνέβη εἰς τὸ ὄρος κατ᾽.ἰδίαν προσεύξασθαι. Ὀψί-
crowds he went up into the mountain apart to pray. [2]Even-
ας δὲ γενομένης μόνος ἦν ἐκεῖ. 24 τὸ.δὲ πλοῖον ἤδη [x]μέσον
ing [1]and being come alone he was there. But the ship now in [the] midst
τῆς θαλάσσης ἦν,‖ βασανιζόμενον ὑπὸ τῶν κυμάτων· ἦν γὰρ
of the sea was, tossed by the waves, [4]was [5]for
ἐναντίος ὁ ἄνεμος. 25 Τετάρτῃ.δὲ φυλακῇ τῆς νυκτὸς
[6]contrary [2]the [3]wind. But in [the] fourth watch of the night
[y]ἀπῆλθεν‖ πρὸς αὐτοὺς [z]ὁ Ἰησοῦς,‖ περιπατῶν ἐπὶ [a]τῆς θαλάσ-
[2]went [3]to [4]them [1]Jesus, walking on the sea.
σης.‖ 26 [b]καὶ ἰδόντες αὐτὸν οἱ μαθηταὶ‖ ἐπὶ [c]τὴν θάλασσαν‖
And [3]seeing [4]him [1]the [2]disciples on the sea
περιπατοῦντα ἐταράχθησαν, λέγοντες, Ὅτι φάντασμά ἐστιν·
walking were troubled, saying, An apparition it is:
καὶ ἀπὸ τοῦ φόβου ἔκραξαν. 27 [d]εὐθέως‖.δὲ ἐλάλησεν [e]αὐ-
and through fear they cried out. But immediately [2]spoke [3]to
τοῖς ὁ Ἰησοῦς,‖ λέγων, Θαρσεῖτε, ἐγώ.εἰμι, μὴ.φοβεῖσθε.
[4]them [1]Jesus, saying, Be of good courage, I am [he], fear not.
28 Ἀποκριθεὶς δὲ [f]αὐτῷ ὁ Πέτρος εἶπεν,‖ Κύριε, εἰ σὺ.εἶ,
And answering him Peter said, Lord, if it be thou,
κέλευσόν με [g]πρός σε ἐλθεῖν‖ ἐπὶ τὰ ὕδατα. 29 Ὁ.δὲ εἶπεν,
bid me [3]to [4]thee [1]to [2]come upon the waters. And he said,
Ἐλθέ. Καὶ καταβὰς ἀπὸ τοῦ πλοίου [h]ὁ‖ Πέτρος περιεπά-
Come. And having descended from the ship Peter walk-
τησεν ἐπὶ τὰ ὕδατα, [i]ἐλθεῖν‖ πρὸς τὸν Ἰησοῦν. 30 βλέπων.δὲ
ed upon the waters, to go to Jesus. But seeing
τὸν ἄνεμον [k]ἰσχυρὸν‖ ἐφοβήθη, καὶ ἀρξάμενος καταπον-
the wind strong he was affrighted, and beginning to
τίζεσθαι ἔκραξεν, λέγων, Κύριε, σῶσόν με. 31 Εὐθέως.δὲ
sink he cried out, saying, Lord, save me. And immediately
ὁ Ἰησοῦς ἐκτείνας τὴν χεῖρα ἐπελάβετο αὐτοῦ, καὶ λέγει
Jesus having stretched out the hand took hold of him, and says

q ηὐλόγησεν LTrA. r παιδίων καὶ γυναικῶν L. s — εὐθέως T. t — ὁ Ἰησοῦς (*read* he compelled) GLTTrAW. v — αὐτοῦ (*read* the disciples) GTTrAW. w — τὸ (*read* a ship) Tr. x σταδίους πολλοὺς ἀπὸ τῆς γῆς ἀπεῖχεν many stadia from the land was distant Tr. y ἦλθεν LTTr. z — ὁ Ἰησοῦς (*read* he went) GLTTrAW. a τὴν θάλασσαν LTTrA. b οἱ δὲ μαθηταὶ ἰδόντες αὐτὸν L; ἰδόντες δὲ αὐτὸν T. c τῆς θαλάσσης LTTrA. d εὐθὺς LTTr. e ὁ Ἰησοῦς αὐτοῖς L, — ὁ Ἰησοῦς T; αὐτοῖς [ὁ Ἰησοῦς] A. f ὁ Πέτρος εἶπεν αὐτῷ L. g ἐλθεῖν πρός σε LTTrA. h — ὁ LTTrA. i καὶ ἦλθεν and he went T. k — ἰσχυρὸν T.

αὐτῷ, Ὀλιγόπιστε, εἰς.τί ἐδίστασας; 32 Καὶ [l]ἐμβάντων[ll]
to him, O [thou] of little faith, why didst thou doubt? And [4]having [3]entered
αὐτῶν εἰς τὸ πλοῖον ἐκόπασεν ὁ ἄνεμος· 33 οἱ.δὲ ἐν τῷ
[1]they into the ship [3]ceased [1]the [2]wind. And those in the
πλοίῳ [m]ἐλθόντες[ll] προσεκύνησαν αὐτῷ, λέγοντες, Ἀληθῶς
ship having come worshipped him, saying, Truly
θεοῦ υἱὸς εἶ.
[2]of [3]God [1]Son thou art!

34 Καὶ διαπεράσαντες ἦλθον [n]εἰς[ll] τὴν γῆν[o] [p]Γεννησαρέτ.[ll]
And having passed over they came to the land of Gennesaret.
35 καὶ ἐπιγνόντες αὐτὸν οἱ ἄνδρες τοῦ.τόπου.ἐκείνου ἀπέ-
And having recognized him the men of that place sent
στειλαν εἰς ὅλην τὴν.περίχωρον.ἐκείνην, καὶ προσήνεγκαν αὐτῷ
to all that country round, and brought to him
πάντας τοὺς κακῶς.ἔχοντας· 36 καὶ παρεκάλουν αὐτὸν ἵνα
all those who were ill; and besought him that
μόνον ἅψωνται τοῦ κρασπέδου τοῦ.ἱματίου.αὐτοῦ· καὶ
only they might touch the border of his garment; and
ὅσοι ἥψαντο διεσώθησαν.
as many as touched were cured.

15 Τότε προσέρχονται τῷ Ἰησοῦ [q]οἱ[ll] ἀπὸ Ἱεροσολύμων
Then come to Jesus the [4]from [5]Jerusalem
[r]γραμματεῖς καὶ Φαρισαῖοι,[ll] λέγοντες, 2 [s]Διατί[ll] οἱ μαθηταί
[1]scribes [2]and [3]Pharisees, saying, Why [3]disciples
σου παραβαίνουσιν τὴν παράδοσιν τῶν πρεσβυτέρων; οὐ
[2]thy [1]transgress the tradition of the elders? [4]not
γὰρ νίπτονται τὰς.χεῖρας.[t]αὐτῶν[ll] ὅταν ἄρτον ἐσθίωσιν. 3 Ὁ.δὲ
[1]for [2]they [3]wash their hands when bread they eat. But he
ἀποκριθεὶς εἶπεν αὐτοῖς, [s]Διατί[ll] καὶ ὑμεῖς παραβαίνετε τὴν
answering said to them, Why [3]also [2]ye [1]transgress the
ἐντολὴν τοῦ θεοῦ διὰ τὴν.παράδοσιν.ὑμῶν; 4 Ὁ γὰρ
commandment of God on account of your tradition? For
θεὸς [v]ἐνετείλατο, λέγων,[ll] Τίμα τὸν.πατέρα.[w]σου[ll] καὶ τὴν
God commanded, saying, Honour thy father and
μητέρα· καὶ Ὁ κακολογῶν πατέρα ἢ μητέρα, θανάτῳ τε-
mother; and, He who speaks evil of father or mother, by death let
λευτάτω. 5 ὑμεῖς.δὲ λέγετε, Ὃς.ἂν εἴπῃ τῷ πατρὶ ἢ τῇ
him die. But ye say, Whoever shall say to father or
μητρί, Δῶρον, ὃ.ἐὰν ἐξ ἐμοῦ ὠφεληθῇς, [x]καὶ[ll]
mother, [It is] a gift whatever by me thou mightest be profited—: and
οὐ.μὴ [y]τιμήσῃ[ll] τὸν.πατέρα.αὐτοῦ [z]ἢ τὴν.μητέρα.αὐτοῦ·[ll]
in no wise honour his father or his mother:
6 καὶ ἠκυρώσατε [a]τὴν ἐντολὴν[ll] τοῦ θεοῦ διὰ τὴν παρά-
and ye made void the commandment of God on account of [2]tra-
δοσιν ὑμῶν. 7 Ὑποκριταί, καλῶς [b]προεφήτευσεν[ll] περὶ ὑμῶν
dition [1]your. Hypocrites! well prophesied concerning you
Ἡσαΐας, λέγων, 8 [c]Ἐγγίζει μοι[ll] ὁ.λαὸς.οὗτος [d]τῷ στόματι
Esaias, saying, Draws near to me this people with [2]mouth
αὐτῶν, καὶ[ll] τοῖς.χείλεσίν με τιμᾷ· ἡ.δὲ.καρδία.αὐτῶν πόῤῥω
[1]their, and with the lips [3]me [1]it [2]honours; but their heart far

thou of little faith, wherefore didst thou doubt? 32 And when they were come into the ship, the wind ceased. 33 Then they that were in the ship came and worshipped him, saying, Of a truth thou art the Son of God.

34 And when they were gone over, they came into the land of Gennesaret. 35 And when the men of that place had knowledge of him, they sent out into all that country round about, and brought unto him all that were diseased; 36 and besought him that they might only touch the hem of his garment: and as many as touched were made perfectly whole.

XV. Then came to Jesus scribes and Pharisees, which were of Jerusalem, saying, 2 Why do thy disciples transgress the tradition of the elders? for they wash not their hands when they eat bread. 3 But he answered and said unto them, Why do ye also transgress the commandment of God by your tradition? 4 For God commanded, saying, Honour thy father and mother: and, He that curseth father or mother, let him die the death. 5 But ye say, Whosoever shall say to *his* father or *his* mother, *It is* a gift, by whatsoever thou mightest be profited by me; 6 and honour not his father or his mother, *he shall be free*. Thus have ye made the commandment of God of none effect by your tradition. 7 *Ye* hypocrites, well did Esaias prophesy of you, saying, 8 This people draweth nigh unto me with their mouth, and honoureth me with *their* lips; but their heart is far from me.

---

[l] ἀναβάντων having gone up LTTrA. [m] — ἐλθόντες T[A]. [n] ἐπὶ TTr. [o] + εἰς (*read* at Gennesaret) TTr. [p] Γεννησαρέθ LW. [q] — οἱ LTTr. [r] Φαρισαῖοι καὶ γραμματεῖς TTr. [s] διὰ τί LTrA. [t] — αὐτῶν (*read* the hands) T[Tr]. [v] εἶπεν said LTr. [w] — σου (*read* [thy]) GLTTrAW. [x] — καὶ LTTr[A]. [y] τιμήσει will he honour LTTrA. [z] — ἢ τὴν μητέρα αὐτοῦ L[A]. [a] τὸν λόγον the word LTr; τὸν νόμον the law TA. [b] ἐπροφήτευσεν LTTrA. [c] — Ἐγγίζει μοι GLTTrA. [d] — τῷ στόματι αὐτῶν καὶ GLTTrA.

9 But in vain they do
worship me, teaching
for doctrines the com-
mandments of men.
10 And he called the
multitude, and said
unto them, Hear, and
understand: 11 not
that which goeth into
the mouth defileth a
man; but that which
cometh out of the
mouth, this defileth a
man.

12 Then came his dis-
ciples, and said unto
him, Knowest thou
that the Pharisees were
offended, after they
heard this saying?
13 But he answered
and said, Every plant,
which my heavenly
Father hath not plant-
ed, shall be rooted up.
14 Let them alone:
they be blind leaders
of the blind. And if
the blind lead the
blind, both shall fall
into the ditch. 15 Then
answered Peter and
said unto him, Declare
unto us this parable.
16 And Jesus said, Are
ye also yet without
understanding? 17 Do
not ye yet understand,
that whatsoever enter-
eth in at the mouth
goeth into the belly,
and is cast out into
the draught? 18 But
those things which
proceed out of the
mouth come forth
from the heart; and
they defile the man.
19 For out of the heart
proceed evil thoughts,
murders, adulteries,
fornications, thefts,
false witness, blasphe-
mies: 20 these are *the*
things which defile a
man: but to eat with
unwashen hands de-
fileth not a man.

21 Then Jesus went
thence, and departed
into the coasts of Tyre
and Sidon. 22 And,
behold, a woman of
Canaan came out of
the same coasts, and
cried unto him, say-
ing, Have mercy on
me, O Lord, *thou* son
of David; my daugh-
ter is grievously vexed
with a devil. 23 But
he answered her not a
word. And his disci-

ἀπέχει ἀπ' ἐμοῦ. 9 μάτην.δὲ σέβονταί με, διδάσκοντες
is away from me: But in vain they worship me, teaching [as]
διδασκαλίας ἐντάλματα ἀνθρώπων. 10 Καὶ προσκαλεσάμενος
teachings injunctions of men. And having called to [him]
τὸν ὄχλον εἶπεν αὐτοῖς, Ἀκούετε καὶ συνίετε. 11 οὐ
the crowd he said to them, Hear and understand! not
τὸ εἰσερχόμενον εἰς τὸ στόμα κοινοῖ τὸν ἄνθρωπον·
that which enters into the mouth defiles the man;
ἀλλὰ τὸ ἐκπορευόμενον ἐκ τοῦ στόματος, τοῦτο κοινοῖ
but that which goes forth out of the mouth, this defiles
τὸν ἄνθρωπον.
the man.

12 Τότε προσελθόντες οἱ.μαθηταὶ.[e]αὐτοῦ‖ [f]εἶπον‖ αὐτῷ,
Then having come to [him] his disciples said to him,
Οἶδας ὅτι οἱ Φαρισαῖοι ἀκούσαντες τὸν λόγον ἐσκανδαλί-
Knowest thou that the Pharisees having heard the saying were of-
σθησαν; 13 ὁ.δὲ ἀποκριθεὶς εἶπεν, Πᾶσα φυτεία ἣν οὐκ
fended? But he answering said, Every plant which [6]not
ἐφύτευσεν ὁ.πατήρ.μου ὁ.οὐράνιος, ἐκριζωθήσεται. 14 ἄφετε
[5]has [7]planted [1]my [2]Father [3]the [4]heavenly, shall be rooted up. Leave
αὐτούς· [g]ὁδηγοί εἰσιν τυφλοὶ‖ τυφλῶν· τυφλὸς.δὲ τυφλὸν
them; [4]leaders [1]they [2]are [3]blind of blind; [3]blind [1]and [5]blind
ἐὰν ὁδηγῇ, ἀμφότεροι εἰς βόθυνον πεσοῦνται. 15 Ἀποκριθεὶς.δὲ
[2]if [4]lead, both into a pit will fall. And answering
ὁ Πέτρος εἶπεν αὐτῷ, Φράσον ἡμῖν τὴν.παραβολὴν.[h]ταύτην.‖
Peter said to him, Expound to us this parable.
16 Ὁ.δὲ.[i]Ἰησοῦς‖ εἶπεν, Ἀκμὴν καὶ ὑμεῖς ἀσύνετοί ἐστε;
But Jesus said, [4]Still [3]also [2]ye [5]without [6]understanding [1]are?
17 [k]οὔπω‖ νοεῖτε ὅτι πᾶν τὸ εἰσπορευόμενον εἰς τὸ
[3]not [4]yet [1]perceive [2]ye that everything which enters into the
στόμα εἰς τὴν κοιλίαν χωρεῖ, καὶ εἰς ἀφεδρῶνα ἐκβάλλεται;
mouth into the belly goes, and into [the] draught is cast forth?
18 τὰ.δὲ ἐκπορευόμενα ἐκ τοῦ στόματος ἐκ τῆς
But the things which go forth out of the mouth out of the
καρδίας ἐξέρχεται, κἀκεῖνα κοινοῖ τὸν ἄνθρωπον. 19 ἐκ.γὰρ
heart come forth, and these defile the man. For out of
τῆς καρδίας ἐξέρχονται διαλογισμοὶ πονηροί, φόνοι, μοιχεῖαι,
the heart come forth [2]reasonings [1]evil, murders, adulteries,
πορνεῖαι, κλοπαί, ψευδομαρτυρίαι, βλασφημίαι. 20 ταῦτά
fornications, thefts, false-witnessings, blasphemies. These things
ἐστιν τὰ κοινοῦντα τὸν ἄνθρωπον· τὸ.δὲ ἀνίπτοις
are they which defile the man; but the [2]with [3]unwashed
χερσὶν φαγεῖν οὐ.κοινοῖ τὸν ἄνθρωπον.
[4]hands [1]eating defiles not the man.

21 Καὶ ἐξελθὼν ἐκεῖθεν ὁ Ἰησοῦς ἀνεχώρησεν εἰς τὰ μέρη
And going forth thence Jesus withdrew to the parts
Τύρου καὶ Σιδῶνος. 22 καὶ ἰδού, γυνὴ Χαναναία ἀπὸ
of Tyre and Sidon; and behold, a [2]woman [1]Canaanæan from
τῶν.ὁρίων.ἐκείνων ἐξελθοῦσα [l]ἐκραύγασεν‖ [m]αὐτῷ,‖ λέγουσα,
those borders having come out cried to him, saying,
Ἐλέησόν με, κύριε, [n]υἱὲ Δαβίδ·‖ ἡ.θυγάτηρ.μου κακῶς δαι-
Have pity on me, Lord, Son of David; my daughter miserably is pos-
μονίζεται. 23 Ὁ.δὲ οὐκ.ἀπεκρίθη αὐτῇ λόγον. καὶ προσ-
sessed by a demon. But he answered [2]not [1]her a word. And having

[e] — αὐτοῦ (*read* the disciples) LTA. [f] λέγουσιν say LTTrA. [g] τυφλοί εἰσιν ὁδηγοὶ LTr.
[h] — ταύτην (*read* the parable) LTTr[A]. [i] — Ἰησοῦς (*read* he said) LTTrA. [k] οὐ not LTTr.
[l] ἔκραζεν LTr; ἔκραξεν T. [m] — αὐτῷ LTTrA. [n] υἱὲ Δαυὶδ GW; υἱὸς Δαυείδ LTTrA.

ἐλθόντες οἱ.μαθηταὶ.αὐτοῦ °ἠρώτων‖ αὐτόν, λέγοντες,
come to [him] his disciples asked him, saying,
Ἀπόλυσον αὐτήν, ὅτι κράζει ὄπισθεν ἡμῶν. 24 Ὁ.δὲ ἀποκρι-
Dismiss her, for she cries after us. But he answer-
θεὶς εἶπεν, Οὐκ.ἀπεστάλην εἰ.μὴ εἰς τὰ πρόβατα τὰ ἀπολωλότα
ing said, I was not sent except to the sheep the lost
οἴκου Ἰσραήλ. 25 Ἡ.δὲ ἐλθοῦσα προσεκύνει αὐτῷ,
of [the] house of Israel. But she having come did homage to him,
λέγουσα, Κύριε, βοήθει μοι. 26 Ὁ.δὲ ἀποκριθεὶς εἶπεν, Οὐκ
saying, Lord, help me! But he answering said, [3]Not
ᵖἔστιν καλὸν‖ λαβεῖν τὸν ἄρτον τῶν τέκνων, καὶ βαλεῖν
[1]it [2]is good to take the bread of the children, and to cast [it]
τοῖς κυναρίοις. 27 Ἡ.δὲ εἶπεν, Ναί, κύριε· καὶ.γὰρ τὰ κυνάρια
to the little dogs. But she said, Yea, Lord: for even the little dogs
ἐσθίει ἀπὸ τῶν ψιχίων τῶν πιπτόντων ἀπὸ τῆς τραπέζης
eat of the crumbs which fall from the table
τῶν.κυρίων.αὐτῶν. 28 Τότε ἀποκριθεὶς ὁ Ἰησοῦς εἶπεν αὐτῇ,
of their masters. Then answering Jesus said to her,
Ὦ γύναι, μεγάλη σου ἡ πίστις· γενηθήτω σοι ὡς θέλεις.
O woman, great [is] thy faith: be it to thee as thou desirest.
Καὶ ἰάθη ἡ.θυγάτηρ.αὐτῆς ἀπὸ τῆς.ὥρας.ἐκείνης.
And was healed her daughter from that hour.

29 Καὶ μεταβὰς ἐκεῖθεν ὁ Ἰησοῦς ἦλθεν παρὰ τὴν θάλασ-
And having departed thence Jesus came towards the sea
σαν τῆς Γαλιλαίας· καὶ ἀναβὰς εἰς τὸ ὄρος ἐκάθητο
of Galilee; and having gone up into the mountain he was sitting
ἐκεῖ. 30 καὶ προσῆλθον αὐτῷ ὄχλοι πολλοί, ἔχοντες μεθ'
there. And came to him [2]crowds [1]great, having with
ἑαυτῶν χωλούς, τυφλούς, κωφούς, κυλλούς, καὶ ἑτέρους πολ-
them lame, blind, dumb, maimed, and [2]others [1]many,
λούς, καὶ ᵠἔῤῥιψαν‖ αὐτοὺς παρὰ τοὺς πόδας ʳτοῦ Ἰησοῦ·‖
and they cast down them at the feet of Jesus,
καὶ ἐθεράπευσεν αὐτούς· 31 ὥστε ˢτοὺς ὄχλους‖ θαυμάσαι,
and he healed them; so that the crowds wondered,
βλέποντας κωφοὺς λαλοῦντας, κυλλοὺς ὑγιεῖς, ᵗ χωλοὺς περι-
seeing dumb speaking, maimed sound, lame walk-
πατοῦντας, καὶ τυφλοὺς βλέποντας· καὶ ᵛἐδόξασαν‖ τὸν θεὸν
ing, and blind seeing; and they glorified the God
Ἰσραήλ. 32 Ὁ.δὲ.Ἰησοῦς προσκαλεσάμενος τοὺς μαθητὰς
of Israel. But Jesus having called to [him] [2]disciples
αὐτοῦ εἶπεν, Σπλαγχνίζομαι ἐπὶ τὸν ὄχλον, ὅτι ἤδη
[1]his said, I am moved with compassion towards the crowd, because already
ʷἡμέρας‖ τρεῖς προσμένουσίν μοι, καὶ οὐκ.ἔχουσιν τί φάγω-
[2]days [1]three they continue with me, and have not what they may
σιν· καὶ ἀπολῦσαι αὐτοὺς νήστεις οὐ.θέλω, μήποτε ἐκλυθῶσιν
eat; and to send away them fasting I am not willing, lest they faint
ἐν τῇ ὁδῷ. 33 Καὶ λέγουσιν αὐτῷ οἱ.μαθηταὶ.ˣαὐτοῦ,‖ Πόθεν
in the way. And [3]say [4]to [5]him [1]his [2]disciples, Whence
ἡμῖν ἐν ἐρημίᾳ ἄρτοι τοσοῦτοι ὥστε χορτάσαι ὄχλον τοσοῦτον;
to us in a desert loaves so many as to satisfy a crowd so great?
34 Καὶ λέγει αὐτοῖς ὁ Ἰησοῦς, Πόσους ἄρτους ἔχετε; Οἱ.δὲ
And [2]says [3]to [4]them [1]Jesus, How many loaves have ye? And they
εἶπον, Ἑπτά, καὶ ὀλίγα ἰχθύδια. 35 Καὶ ʸἐκέλευσεν τοῖς
said, Seven, and a few small fishes. And he commanded the

ples came and besought him, saying, Send her away; for she crieth after us. 24 But he answered and said, I am not sent but unto the lost sheep of the house of Israel. 25 Then came she and worshipped him, saying, Lord, help me. 26 But he answered and said, It is not meet to take the children's bread, and to cast *it* to dogs. 27 And she said, Truth, Lord: yet the dogs eat of the crumbs which fall from their masters' table. 28 Then Jesus answered and said unto her, O woman, great *is* thy faith: be it unto thee even as thou wilt. And her daughter was made whole from that very hour.

29 And Jesus departed from thence, and came nigh unto the sea of Galilee; and went up into a mountain, and sat down there. 30 And great multitudes came unto him, having with them *those that were* lame, blind, dumb, maimed, and many others, and cast them down at Jesus' feet; and he healed them: 31 insomuch that the multitude wondered, when they saw the dumb to speak, the maimed to be whole, the lame to walk, and the blind to see: and they glorified the God of Israel. 32 Then Jesus called his disciples *unto him*, and said, I have compassion on the multitude, because they continue with me now three days, and have nothing to eat: and I will not send them away fasting, lest they faint in the way. 33 And his disciples say unto him, Whence should we have so much bread in the wilderness, as to fill so great a multitude? 34 And Jesus saith unto them, How many loaves have ye? And they said, Seven, and a few little fishes. 35 And he commanded the multitude to sit

° ἠρώτουν LTTrA. ᵖ ἔξεστιν it is allowed LTA. ᵠ ἔριψαν T. ʳ αὐτοῦ of him LTTrA. ˢ τὸν ὄχλον the crowd TA. ᵗ + καὶ and LTTrA. ᵛ ἐδόξαζον T. ʷ ἡμέραι GLTTrAW. ˣ — αὐτοῦ (*read* the disciples) [L]T[Tr]A. ʸ παραγγείλας τῷ ὄχλῳ having commanded the crowd LTTr.

down on the ground.
36 And he took the
seven loaves and the
fishes, and gave thanks,
and brake *them*, and
gave to his disciples,
and the disciples to the
multitude. 37 And
they did all eat, and
were filled: and they
took up of the broken
meat that was left
seven baskets full.
38 And they that did
eat were four thousand
men, beside women
and children. 39 And
he sent away the mul-
titude, and took ship,
and came into the
coasts of Magdala.

XVI. The Pharisees
also with the Saddu-
cees came, and tempt-
ing desired him that
he would shew them a
sign from heaven.
2 He answered and
said unto them, When
it is evening, ye say,
It will be fair weather:
for the sky is red.
3 And in the morning,
It will be foul weather
to day: for the sky is
red and lowring. O *ye*
hypocrites, ye can dis-
cern the face of the
sky; but can ye not
discern the signs of the
times? 4 A wicked and
adulterous generation
seeketh after a sign;
and there shall no sign
be given unto it, but
the sign of the prophet
Jonas. And he left
them, and departed.

5 And when his dis-
ciples were come to the
other side, they had
forgotten to take
bread. 6 Then Jesus
said unto them, Take
heed and beware of
the leaven of the Pha-
risees and of the Sad-
ducees. 7 And they
reasoned among them-
selves, saying, *It is* because we have taken
no bread. 8 *Which*
when Jesus perceived,
he said unto them, O
ye of little faith, why
reason ye among your-
selves, because ye have
brought no bread?
9 Do ye not yet under-
stand, neither remem-
ber the five loaves of

ὄχλοις‖ *ἀναπεσεῖν ἐπὶ τὴν γῆν·* 36 [z]*καὶ λαβὼν*‖ *τοὺς ἑπτὰ*
crowds to recline on the ground; and having taken the seven
ἄρτους καὶ τοὺς ἰχθύας,[a] *εὐχαριστήσας ἔκλασεν καὶ* [b]*ἔδωκεν*‖
loaves and the fishes, having given thanks he broke and gave
τοῖς-μαθηταῖς-[c]*αὐτοῦ,*‖ *οἱ.δὲ μαθηταὶ* [d]*τῷ ὄχλῳ.*‖ 37 *Καὶ*
to his disciples, and the disciples to the crowd. And
ἔφαγον πάντες, καὶ ἐχορτάσθησαν καὶ [e]*ἦραν τὸ περισ-*
[2]ate [1]all, and were satisfied; and they took up that which was over
σεῦον τῶν κλασμάτων‖ *ἑπτὰ σπυρίδας πλήρεις.* 38 *οἱ.δὲ*
and above of the fragments seven baskets full; and they who
ἐσθίοντες ἦσαν τετρακισχίλιοι ἄνδρες, χωρὶς [f]*γυναικῶν καὶ*
ate were four thousand men, besides women and
παιδίων.‖ 39 *Καὶ ἀπολύσας τοὺς ὄχλους* [g]*ἐνέβη*‖ *εἰς τὸ*
children. And having dismissed the crowds he entered into the
πλοῖον, καὶ ἦλθεν εἰς τὰ ὅρια [h]*Μαγδαλά.*‖
ship, and came to the borders of Magdala.

16 *Καὶ προσελθόντες οἱ Φαρισαῖοι καὶ Σαδδουκαῖοι*
And having come to [him] the Pharisees and Sadducees
πειράζοντες [i]*ἐπηρώτησαν*‖ *αὐτὸν σημεῖον ἐκ τοῦ οὐρανοῦ*
tempting [him] asked him a sign out of the heaven
ἐπιδεῖξαι αὐτοῖς 2 *ὁ.δὲ ἀποκριθεὶς εἶπεν αὐτοῖς,* [k]*Ὀψίας*
to shew them. But he answering said to them, Evening
γενομένης λέγετε, Εὐδία· πυῤῥάζει.γὰρ ὁ οὐρανός. 3 *καὶ*
having come ye say, Fine weather; for [3]is [4]red [1]the [2]heaven. And
πρωΐ, Σήμερον χειμών· πυῤῥάζει.γὰρ στυγνάζων ὁ οὐρανός.
at morning, To-day a storm; for [3]is [4]red [5]lowering [1]the [2]heaven.
[l]*ὑποκριταί,*[l] *τὸ μὲν πρόσωπον τοῦ οὐρανοῦ γινώσκετε*
Hypocrites! the [5]indeed [1]face [2]of [3]the [4]heaven ye know [how]
διακρίνειν, τὰ.δὲ σημεῖα τῶν καιρῶν οὐ.δύνασθε;‖ 4 *γενεὰ*
to discern, but the signs of the times ye cannot! A generation
πονηρὰ καὶ μοιχαλὶς σημεῖον ἐπιζητεῖ· καὶ σημεῖον οὐ.δοθή-
wicked and adulterous a sign seeks, and a sign shall not be
σεται αὐτῇ, εἰ.μὴ τὸ σημεῖον Ἰωνᾶ [m]*τοῦ προφήτου.*‖ *Καὶ*
given to it, except the sign of Jonas the prophet. And
καταλιπὼν αὐτοὺς ἀπῆλθεν.
leaving them he went away.

5 *Καὶ ἐλθόντες οἱ.μαθηταὶ* [n]*αὐτοῦ*‖ *εἰς τὸ πέραν ἐπελάθοντο*
And [3]having [4]come [1]his [2]disciples to the other side they forgot
ἄρτους λαβεῖν. 6 *ὁ.δὲ.Ἰησοῦς εἶπεν αὐτοῖς, Ὁρᾶτε καὶ προσ-*
[2]loaves [1]to [2]take. And Jesus said to them, See and be-
έχετε ἀπὸ τῆς ζύμης τῶν Φαρισαίων καὶ Σαδδουκαίων. 7 *Οἱ.δὲ*
ware of the leaven of the Pharisees and Sadducees. And they
διελογίζοντο ἐν ἑαυτοῖς, λέγοντες, Ὅτι ἄρτους οὐκ ἐλά-
reasoned among themselves, saying, Because loaves [3]not [1]we
βομεν. 8 *Γνοὺς.δὲ ὁ Ἰησοῦς εἶπεν* [o]*αὐτοῖς,*‖ *Τί δια-*
[2]took. And having known [this] Jesus said to them, Why rea-
λογίζεσθε ἐν ἑαυτοῖς, ὀλιγόπιστοι, ὅτι ἄρτους οὐκ
son ye among yourselves, O [ye] of little faith, because loaves [3]not
[p]*ἐλάβετε;*‖ 9 *οὔπω.νοεῖτε, οὐδὲ μνημονεύετε τοὺς πέντε*
[1]ye [2]took? Do ye not yet perceive, nor remember the five

---

[z] *ἔλαβεν* he took LTTr. [a] + *καὶ* and LT. [b] *ἐδίδου* TTr. [c] — *αὐτοῦ* (*read* the disciples) [L]T[Tr]A. [d] *τοῖς ὄχλοις* to the crowds TTrA. [e] *τὸ περισσεῦον τῶν κλασμάτων ἦραν* LTTrA. [f] *παιδίων καὶ γυναικῶν* T. [g] *ἀνέβη* he went up GTrAW. [h] *Μαγαδάν* Magadan LTTrA. [i] *ἐπηρώτων* T. [k] *Ὀψίας* . . . *to end of verse* 3 [TA]. [l] — *ὑποκριταί* LTTrA; + *καὶ* and L. [m] — *τοῦ προφήτου* LTTrA. [n] — *αὐτοῦ* (*read* the disciples) LTTrA. [o] — *αὐτοῖς* GLTTrA. [p] *ἔχετε* ye have L.

ἄρτους τῶν πεντακισχιλίων, καὶ πόσους κοφίνους ἐλάβετε,
loaves of the five thousand, and how many hand-baskets ye took [up]?
10 οὐδὲ τοὺς ἑπτὰ ἄρτους τῶν τετρακισχιλίων, καὶ πόσας
nor the seven loaves of the four thousand, and how many
[q]σπυρίδας‖ ἐλάβετε; 11 πῶς οὐ.νοεῖτε ὅτι οὐ περὶ
baskets ye took [up]? How perceive ye not that not concerning
[r]ἄρτου‖ εἶπον ὑμῖν [s]προσέχειν‖ ἀπὸ τῆς ζύμης τῶν Φαρισαίων
bread I spoke to you to beware of the leaven of the Pharisees
καὶ Σαδδουκαίων; 12 Τότε συνῆκαν ὅτι οὐκ.εἶπεν προσέχειν
and Sadducees? Then they understood that he said not to beware
ἀπὸ τῆς ζύμης [t]τοῦ ἄρτου,‖ [v]ἀλλ'‖ ἀπὸ τῆς διδαχῆς τῶν
of the leaven of bread, but of the teaching of the
Φαρισαίων καὶ Σαδδουκαίων.
Pharisees and Sadducees.

13 Ἐλθὼν.δὲ ὁ Ἰησοῦς εἰς τὰ μέρη Καισαρείας τῆς
And [2]having [3]come [1]Jesus into the parts of Cæsarea
Φιλίππου ἠρώτα τοὺς.μαθητὰς.αὐτοῦ, λέγων, Τίνα [w]με‖
Philippi he questioned his disciples, saying, Whom [4]me
λέγουσιν οἱ.ἄνθρωποι εἶναι τὸν υἱὸν τοῦ ἀνθρώπου; 14 Οἱ.δὲ
[1]do [3]pronounce [2]men [9]to [10]be [5]the [6]Son [7]of [8]man? And they
[x]εἶπον,‖ Οἱ.μὲν Ἰωάννην τὸν βαπτιστήν· [y]ἄλλοι‖.δὲ [z]Ἠλίαν‖
said, Some John the Baptist; and others Elias;
ἕτεροι.δὲ Ἱερεμίαν, ἢ ἕνα τῶν προφητῶν. 15 Λέγει αὐτοῖς,[a]
and others Jeremias, or one of the prophets. He says to them,
Ὑμεῖς.δὲ τίνα με λέγετε εἶναι; 16 [b]Ἀποκριθεὶς.δὲ‖ Σί-
But ye whom [4]me [1]do [2]ye [3]pronounce to be? And answering Si-
μων Πέτρος εἶπεν, Σὺ εἶ ὁ χριστός, ὁ υἱὸς τοῦ θεοῦ τοῦ
mon Peter said, Thou art the Christ, the Son of God the
ζῶντος. 17 [c]Καὶ ἀποκριθεὶς‖ ὁ Ἰησοῦς εἶπεν αὐτῷ, Μακάριος
living. And answering Jesus said to him, Blessed
εἶ, Σίμων [d]Βὰρ Ἰωνᾶ,‖ ὅτι σὰρξ καὶ αἷμα οὐκ.ἀπεκάλυψέν
art thou, Simon Bar-Jonas, for flesh and blood revealed [it] not
σοι, ἀλλ' ὁ.πατήρ.μου ὁ ἐν [e]τοῖς‖ οὐρανοῖς. 18 Κἀγὼ.δέ
to thee, but my Father who [is] in the heavens. And I also
σοι λέγω, ὅτι σὺ εἶ Πέτρος, καὶ ἐπὶ ταύτῃ τῇ πέτρᾳ οἰκοδο-
to thee say, That thou art Peter, and on this rock I will
μήσω μου τὴν ἐκκλησίαν, καὶ πύλαι ᾅδου οὐ.κατισχύσουσιν
build my assembly, and gates of hades shall not prevail against
αὐτῆς. 19 [f]καὶ‖ δώσω σοὶ τὰς [g]κλεῖς‖ τῆς βασιλείας τῶν
it. And I will give to thee the keys of the kingdom of the
οὐρανῶν· καὶ ὃ.[h]ἐὰν‖ δήσῃς ἐπὶ τῆς γῆς, ἔσται δεδεμένον
heavens: and whatever thou mayest bind on the earth, shall be bound
ἐν τοῖς οὐρανοῖς· καὶ ὃ.[i]ἐὰν‖ λύσῃς ἐπὶ τῆς γῆς, ἔσται
in the heavens; and whatever thou mayest loose on the earth, shall be
λελυμένον ἐν τοῖς οὐρανοῖς. 20 Τότε [k]διεστείλατο‖ τοῖς μαθη-
loosed in the heavens. Then charged he [2]dis-
ταῖς [l]αὐτοῦ‖ ἵνα μηδενὶ εἴπωσιν ὅτι αὐτός ἐστιν [m]Ἰησοῦς‖
ciples [1]his that to no one they should say that he is Jesus
ὁ χριστός.
the Christ.

the five thousand, and how many baskets ye took up? 10 Neither the seven loaves of the four thousand, and how many baskets ye took up? 11 How is it that ye do not understand that I spake *it* not to you concerning bread, that ye should beware of the leaven of the Pharisees and of the Sadducees? 12 Then understood they how that he bade *them* not beware of the leaven of bread, but of the doctrine of the Pharisees and of the Sadducees.

13 When Jesus came into the coasts of Cæsarea Philippi, he asked his disciples, saying, Whom do men say that I the Son of man am? 14 And they said, Some *say that thou art* John the Baptist: some, Elias; and others, Jeremias, or one of the prophets. 15 He saith unto them, But whom say ye that I am? 16 And Simon Peter answered and said, Thou art the Christ, the Son of the living God. 17 And Jesus answered and said unto him, Blessed art thou, Simon Bar-jona: for flesh and blood hath not revealed *it* unto thee, but my Father which is in heaven. 18 And I say also unto thee, That thou art Peter, and upon this rock I will build my church; and the gates of hell shall not prevail against it. 19 And I will give unto thee the keys of the kingdom of heaven: and whatsoever thou shalt bind on earth shall be bound in heaven: and whatsoever thou shalt loose on earth shall be loosed in heaven. 20 Then charged he his disciples that they should tell no man that he was Jesus the Christ.

---

[q] σφυρίδας L. [r] ἄρτων loaves LTTrAW. [s] ; (*the question ends at* you) προσέχετε δὲ but beware LTTrA. [t] τῶν ἄρτων of the loaves LTrA; τῶν Φαρισαίων καὶ Σαδδουκαίων of the Pharisees and Sadducees T. [v] ἀλλὰ TTrAW. [w] — με [L]TTrA. [x] εἶπαν LTTr. [y] οἱ L. [z] Ἡλείαν T. [a] + [ὁ Ἰησοῦς] Jesus (says) L. [b] καὶ ἀποκριθεὶς W. [c] ἀποκριθεὶς δὲ LTTrA. [d] Βαριωνᾶ LTA. [e] — τοῖς (*read* [the]) L[Tr]. [f] — καὶ T[A]. [g] κλεῖδας LTTrA. [h] ἂν LTrA. [i] ἂν Tr. [k] ἐπετίμησεν he earnestly charged L. [l] — αὐτοῦ (*read* the disciples) LTTrA. [m] — Ἰησοῦς GLTTrAW.

21 From that time forth began Jesus to shew unto his disciples, how that he must go unto Jerusalem, and suffer many things of the elders and chief priests and scribes, and be killed, and be raised again the third day. 22 Then Peter took him, and began to rebuke him, saying, Be it far from thee, Lord: this shall not be unto thee. 23 But he turned, and said unto Peter, Get thee behind me, Satan: thou art an offence unto me: for thou savourest not the things that be of God, but those that be of men. 24 Then said Jesus unto his disciples, If any *man* will come after me, let him deny himself, and take up his cross, and follow me. 25 For whosoever will save his life shall lose it: and whosoever will lose his life for my sake shall find it. 26 For what is a man profited, if he shall gain the whole world, and lose his own soul? or what shall a man give in exchange for his soul? 27 For the Son of man shall come in the glory of his Father with his angels; and then he shall reward every man according to his works. 28 Verily I say unto you, There be some standing here, which shall not taste of death, till they see the Son of man coming in his kingdom.

21 Ἀπὸ τότε ἤρξατο [n]ὁ[‖] Ἰησοῦς δεικνύειν τοῖς μαθηταῖς
From that time began Jesus to shew to [2]disciples
αὐτοῦ, ὅτι δεῖ αὐτὸν [o]ἀπελθεῖν εἰς Ἱεροσόλυμα,[‖] καὶ
[1]his that it is necessary for him to go away to Jerusalem, and
πολλὰ παθεῖν ἀπὸ τῶν πρεσβυτέρων καὶ ἀρχιερέων καὶ
many things to suffer from the elders and chief priests and
γραμματέων, καὶ ἀποκτανθῆναι, καὶ τῇ τρίτῃ ἡμέρᾳ ἐγερθῆναι.
scribes, and to be killed, and the third day to be raised.
22 καὶ προσλαβόμενος αὐτὸν ὁ Πέτρος [p]ἤρξατο[‖] [q]ἐπιτιμᾷν
And [2]having [3]taken [5]to [[6]him] [4]him [1]Peter began to rebuke
αὐτῷ, λέγων,[‖] Ἵλεώς σοι, κύριε· οὐ.μὴ ἔσται σοι
him, saying, [God be] favourable to thee, Lord: in no wise shall be to thee
τοῦτο. 23 Ὁ.δὲ στραφεὶς εἶπεν τῷ Πέτρῳ, Ὕπαγε ὀπίσω μου,
this. But he having turned said to Peter, Get behind me,
σατανᾶ, σκάνδαλόν [r]μου εἶ·[‖] ὅτι οὐ.φρονεῖς τὰ
Satan: an offence to me thou art, for thy thoughts are not of the things
τοῦ θεοῦ, ἀλλὰ τὰ τῶν ἀνθρώπων. 24 Τότε ὁ Ἰησοῦς εἶπεν
of God, but the things of men. Then Jesus said
τοῖς.μαθηταῖς.αὐτοῦ, Εἴ τις θέλει ὀπίσω μου ἐλθεῖν, ἀπαρ-
to his disciples, If any one desires after me to come, let
νησάσθω ἑαυτόν, καὶ ἀράτω τὸν.σταυρὸν.αὐτοῦ, καὶ ἀκο-
him deny himself, and let him take up his cross, and let
λουθείτω μοι. 25 ὃς.γὰρ.[s]ἂν[‖] θέλῃ τὴν.ψυχὴν.αὐτοῦ σῶσαι,
him follow me. For whoever may desire his life to save,
ἀπολέσει αὐτήν· ὃς.δ᾽.ἂν ἀπολέσῃ τὴν.ψυχὴν.αὐτοῦ ἕνεκεν
shall lose it; but whoever may lose his life on account of
ἐμοῦ, εὑρήσει αὐτήν· 26 τί.γὰρ [t]ὠφελεῖται[‖] ἄνθρωπος, ἐὰν
me, shall find it. For what is [3]profited [1]a [2]man, if
τὸν κόσμον ὅλον κερδήσῃ, τὴν.δὲ.ψυχὴν.αὐτοῦ ζημιωθῇ; ἢ
the [2]world [1]whole he gain, and his soul lose? or
τί δώσει ἄνθρωπος ἀντάλλαγμα τῆς.ψυχῆς.αὐτοῦ; 27 μέλ-
what will [3]give [1]a [2]man [as] an exchange for his soul? For [5]is
λει.γὰρ ὁ υἱὸς τοῦ.ἀνθρώπου ἔρχεσθαι ἐν τῇ δόξῃ τοῦ πατρὸς
[6]about [1]the [2]Son [3]of [4]man to come in the glory [3]Father
αὐτοῦ μετὰ τῶν.ἀγγέλων.αὐτοῦ· καὶ τότε ἀποδώσει ἑκάστῳ
[1]of [2]his with his angels; and then he will render to each
κατὰ τὴν.πρᾶξιν.αὐτοῦ. 28 Ἀμὴν λέγω ὑμῖν, [v] εἰσίν
according to his doing. Verily I say to you, There are
τινες [w]τῶν ὧδε ἑστηκότων,[‖] οἵτινες οὐ.μὴ γεύσωνται θανάτου
some of those here standing who in no wise shall taste of death
ἕως ἂν ἴδωσιν τὸν υἱὸν τοῦ ἀνθρώπου ἐρχόμενον ἐν τῇ
until they have seen the Son of man coming in
βασιλείᾳ.αὐτοῦ.
his kingdom.

XVII. And after six days Jesus taketh Peter, James, and John his brother, and bringeth them up into an high mountain apart, 2 and was transfigured before them: and his face did shine as the sun, and his raiment

17 Καὶ μεθ᾽ ἡμέρας ἓξ παραλαμβάνει ὁ Ἰησοῦς τὸν Πέτρον
And after [2]days [1]six [4]takes [5]with [[6]him] [3]Jesus Peter
καὶ Ἰάκωβον καὶ Ἰωάννην τὸν.ἀδελφὸν.αὐτοῦ, καὶ ἀναφέρει
and James and John his brother, and brings up
αὐτοὺς εἰς ὄρος ὑψηλὸν κατ᾽.ἰδίαν. 2 καὶ μετεμορφώθη
them into a [2]mountain [1]high apart. And he was transfigured
ἔμπροσθεν αὐτῶν, καὶ ἔλαμψεν τὸ.πρόσωπον.αὐτοῦ ὡς ὁ ἥλιος,
before them, and [3]shone [1]his [2]face as the sun,

---

[n] — ὁ L[Tr]A. [o] εἰς Ἱεροσόλυμα ἀπελθεῖν LTTrA. [p] — ἤρξατο A. [q] αὐτῷ ἐπιτιμᾶν λέγων L; λέγει αὐτῷ ἐπιτιμῶν says to him rebuking [him] A. [r] εἶ ἐμοῦ LTTrA. [s] ἐὰν LTTrA. [t] ὠφεληθήσεται shall be profited LTTrA. [v] + ὅτι that LT. [w] τῶν ὧδε ἑστώτων GLTTrA; ὧδε ἑστῶτες W.

τὰ.δὲ.ἱμάτια.αὐτοῦ ἐγένετο λευκὰ ὡς τὸ φῶς. 3 καὶ ἰδού, [x]ὤφ-
and his garments became white as the light; and behold, [4]ap-
θησαν‖ αὐτοῖς [y]Μωσῆς‖ καὶ [z]Ἠλίας,‖ [a]μετ' αὐτοῦ συλλαλοῦντες.‖
peared [5]to [6]them [1]Moses [2]and [3]Elias [8]with [9]him [7]talking.
4 ἀποκριθεὶς.δὲ ὁ Πέτρος εἶπεν τῷ Ἰησοῦ, Κύριε, καλόν ἐστιν
And answering Peter said to Jesus, Lord, good it is
ἡμᾶς ὧδε εἶναι· εἰ θέλεις, [b]ποιήσωμεν‖ ὧδε τρεῖς σκηνάς,
for us here to be. If thou wilt, let us make here three tabernacles:
σοὶ μίαν, καὶ [c]Μωσῇ‖ μίαν, καὶ [d]μίαν Ἡλίᾳ.‖ 5 Ἔτι αὐτοῦ
for thee one, and for Moses one, and one for Elias. While yet he
λαλοῦντος, ἰδού, νεφέλη [e]φωτεινὴ‖ ἐπεσκίασεν αὐτούς· καὶ
was speaking, behold, a [2]cloud [1]bright overshadowed them: and
ἰδού, φωνὴ ἐκ τῆς νεφέλης, λέγουσα, Οὗτός ἐστιν ὁ.υἱός.μου
lo, a voice out of the cloud, saying, This is my Son
ὁ ἀγαπητός, ἐν ᾧ [f]εὐδόκησα·‖ [g]αὐτοῦ ἀκούετε.‖ 6 Καὶ
the beloved, in whom I have found delight: [3]him [1]hear [2]ye. And
ἀκούσαντες οἱ μαθηταὶ [h]ἔπεσον‖ ἐπὶ πρόσωπον.αὐτῶν, καὶ
hearing [it] the disciples fell upon their face, and
ἐφοβήθησαν σφόδρα. 7 καὶ [i]προσελθὼν‖ ὁ Ἰησοῦς [k]ἥψατο‖
were terrified greatly. And having come to [them] Jesus touched
αὐτῶν, [l]καὶ‖ εἶπεν, Ἐγέρθητε, καὶ μὴ.φοβεῖσθε. 8 Ἐπάραντες
them, and said, Rise up, and be not terrified. [2]Having [3]lifted [4]up
δὲ τοὺς.ὀφθαλμοὺς.αὐτῶν οὐδένα εἶδον εἰ.μὴ τὸν Ἰησοῦν
[1]and their eyes [3]no [4]one [1]they [2]saw except Jesus
μόνον.
alone.

was white as the light.
3 And, behold, there
appeared unto them
Moses and Elias talk-
ing with him. 4 Then
answered Peter, and
said unto Jesus, Lord,
it is good for us to be
here: if thou wilt, let
us make here three
tabernacles; one for
thee, and one for Mo-
ses, and one for Elias.
5 While he yet spake,
behold, a bright cloud
overshadowed them:
and behold a voice out
of the cloud, which
said, This is my be-
loved Son, in whom I
am well pleased; hear
ye him. 6 And when
the disciples heard *it*,
they fell on their face,
and were sore afraid.
7 And Jesus came and
touched them, and
said, Arise, and be not
afraid. 8 And when
they had lifted up
their eyes, they saw no
man, save Jesus only.

9 Καὶ καταβαινόντων αὐτῶν [m]ἀπὸ‖ τοῦ ὄρους ἐνετείλατο
And as [2]were [3]descending [1]they from the mountain [2]charged
αὐτοῖς ὁ Ἰησοῦς, λέγων, Μηδενὶ εἴπητε τὸ ὅραμα, ἕως.οὗ ὁ
[3]them [1]Jesus, saying, To no one tell the vision, until the
υἱὸς τοῦ ἀνθρώπου ἐκ νεκρῶν [n]ἀναστῇ.‖ 10 Καὶ ἐπη-
Son of man from among [the] dead be risen. And [3]ask-
ρώτησαν αὐτὸν οἱ.μαθηταὶ.[o]αὐτοῦ,‖ λέγοντες, Τί οὖν οἱ γραμ-
ed [4]him [1]his [2]disciples, saying, Why then [2]the [3]scribes
ματεῖς λέγουσιν ὅτι [p]Ἡλίαν‖ δεῖ ἐλθεῖν πρῶτον; 11 Ὁ δὲ
[1]say that Elias must come first? And
[q]Ἰησοῦς‖ ἀποκριθεὶς εἶπεν [r]αὐτοῖς,‖ [s]Ἡλίας‖ μὲν ἔρχεται
Jesus answering said to them, Elias indeed comes
[t]πρῶτον‖ καὶ ἀποκαταστήσει πάντα· 12 λέγω δὲ ὑμῖν ὅτι
first and shall restore all things. But I say to you that
[s]Ἡλίας‖ ἤδη ἦλθεν, καὶ οὐκ.ἐπέγνωσαν αὐτόν, [v]ἀλλ'‖ ἐποίη-
Elias already is come, and they knew not him, but did
σαν ἐν αὐτῷ ὅσα ἠθέλησαν· οὕτως καὶ ὁ υἱὸς τοῦ ἀνθρώπου
to him whatever they desired. Thus also the Son of man
μέλλει πάσχειν ὑπ' αὐτῶν. 13 Τότε συνῆκαν οἱ μαθηταὶ ὅτι
is about to suffer from them. Then understood the disciples that
περὶ Ἰωάννου τοῦ βαπτιστοῦ εἶπεν αὐτοῖς.
concerning John the Baptist he spoke to them.

9 And as they came
down from the moun-
tain, Jesus charged
them, saying, Tell the
vision to no man, until
the Son of man be
risen again from the
dead. 10 And his dis-
ciples asked him, say-
ing, Why then say the
scribes that Elias must
first come? 11 And Je-
sus answered and said
unto them, Elias truly
shall first come, and
restore all things.
12 But I say unto you,
That Elias is come al-
ready, and they knew
him not, but have done
unto him whatsoever
they listed. Likewise
shall also the Son of
man suffer of them.
13 Then the disciples
understood that he
spake unto them of
John the Baptist.

14 Καὶ ἐλθόντων [w]αὐτῶν‖ πρὸς τὸν ὄχλον προσῆλθεν
And [2]having [3]come [1]they to the crowd [3]came

14 And when they
were come to the mul-
titude, there came to

[x] ὤφθη LTTrA. [y] Μωϋσῆς LTTrAW. [z] Ἠλείας T. [a] συλλαλοῦντες (συνλαλ. T) μετ' αὐτοῦ LTTr. [b] ποιήσω I will make LTA. [c] Μωυσεῖ LTTrA; Μωϋσῇ W. [d] Ἡλίᾳ (Ἠλείᾳ T) μίαν LTTrA. [e] φωτὸς of light G. [f] ηὐδόκησα LTr. [g] ἀκούετε αὐτοῦ LTTrA. [h] ἔπεσαν LTTrA. [i] προσῆλθεν came to LTTr. [k] καὶ ἁψάμενος and touching LT; καὶ ἥψατο Tr. [l] — καὶ LT. [m] ἐκ GLTTrAW. [n] ἐγερθῇ be raised LTTrA. [o] — αὐτοῦ (*read* the disciples) LTTr. [p] Ἠλείαν T. [q] — Ἰησοῦς (*read* he said) LTTrA. [r] — αὐτοῖς LTTr[A]. [s] Ἠλείας T. [t] — πρῶτον LTTrA. [v] ἀλλὰ TrA. [w] — αὐτῶν LTTrA.

him a *certain* man,
kneeling down to him,
and saying, 15 Lord,
have mercy on my son:
for he is lunatick, and
sore vexed: for oft-
times he falleth into
the fire, and oft into
the water. 16 And I
brought him to thy
disciples, and they
could not cure him.
17 Then Jesus answer-
ed and said, O faith-
less and perverse
generation, how long
shall I be with you?
how long shall I suffer
you? bring him hither
to me. 18 And Jesus
rebuked the devil; and
he departed out of
him: and the child
was cured from that
very hour. 19 Then
came the disciples to
Jesus apart, and said,
Why could not we cast
him out? 20 And Jesus
said unto them, Be-
cause of your unbelief:
for verily I say unto
you, If ye have faith
as a grain of mustard
seed, ye shall say unto
this mountain, Re-
move hence to yonder
place; and it shall
remove; and nothing
shall be impossible
unto you. 21 Howbeit
this kind goeth not
out but by prayer and
fasting.

22 And while they
abode in Galilee, Jesus
said unto them, The
Son of man shall be
betrayed into the
hands of men: 23 and
they shall kill him,
and the third day he
shall be raised again.
And they were exceed-
ing sorry.

24 And when they
were come to Caper-
naum, they that re-
ceived tribute *money*
came to Peter, and
said, Doth not your
master pay tribute?
25 He saith, Yes. And
when he was come into
the house, Jesus pre-
vented him, saying,
What thinkest thou,
Simon? of whom do
the kings of the earth
take custom or tribute?
of their own children,
or of strangers? 26 Pe-

αὐτῷ ἄνθρωπος γονυπετῶν [x]αὐτῷ,ǁ 15 καὶ λέγων, Κύριε,
[4]to [5]him [1]a [2]man kneeling down to him, and saying, Lord,
ἐλέησόν μου τὸν υἱόν, ὅτι σεληνιάζεται καὶ [y]κακῶς πάσχει·ǁ
have pity on my son, for he is lunatic and miserably suffers:
πολλάκις-γὰρ πίπτει εἰς τὸ πῦρ, καὶ πολλάκις εἰς τὸ ὕδωρ.
for often he falls into the fire, and often into the water.
16 καὶ προσήνεγκα αὐτὸν τοῖς-μαθηταῖς-σου, καὶ οὐκ-ἠδυνή-
And I brought him to thy disciples, and they were not
θησαν αὐτὸν θεραπεῦσαι. 17 Ἀποκριθεὶς-δὲ ὁ Ἰησοῦς εἶπεν,
able him to heal. And answering Jesus said,
Ὦ γενεὰ ἄπιστος καὶ διεστραμμένη, ἕως πότε [z]ἔσομαι
O generation unbelieving and perverted, until when shall I be
μεθ' ὑμῶν;ǁ ἕως πότε ἀνέξομαι ὑμῶν; φέρετέ μοι αὐτὸν ὧδε.
with you? until when shall I bear with you? Bring to me him here.
18 Καὶ ἐπετίμησεν αὐτῷ ὁ Ἰησοῦς, καὶ ἐξῆλθεν ἀπ' αὐτοῦ τὸ
And [2]rebuked [3]him [1]Jesus, and went out from him the
δαιμόνιον, καὶ ἐθεραπεύθη ὁ παῖς ἀπὸ τῆς-ὥρας-ἐκείνης.
demon, and was healed the boy from that hour.
19 Τότε προσελθόντες οἱ μαθηταὶ τῷ Ἰησοῦ κατ'-ἰδίαν εἶπον,
Then [3]having [4]come [1]the [2]disciples to Jesus apart said,
[a]Διατίǁ ἡμεῖς οὐκ-ἠδυνήθημεν ἐκβαλεῖν αὐτό; 20 Ὁ-δὲ-[b]Ἰησοῦςǁ
Why [3]we [1]were [2]not able to cast out him? And Jesus
[c]εἶπενǁ αὐτοῖς, Διὰ τὴν [d]ἀπιστίανǁ ὑμῶν. ἀμὴν-γὰρ λέγω
said to them, Because of [2]unbelief [1]your. For verily I say
ὑμῖν, ἐὰν ἔχητε πίστιν ὡς κόκκον σινάπεως, ἐρεῖτε τῷ ὄρει
to you, If ye have faith as a grain of mustard, ye shall say [3]mountain
τούτῳ, [e]Μετάβηθι ἐντεῦθενǁ ἐκεῖ, καὶ μεταβήσεται· καὶ οὐδὲν
[1]to [2]this, Remove hence thither, and it shall remove; and nothing
ἀδυνατήσει ὑμῖν. 21 [f]τοῦτο-δὲ-τὸ-γένος οὐκ-ἐκπορεύεται
shall be impossible to you. But this kind goes not out
εἰ-μὴ ἐν προσευχῇ καὶ νηστείᾳ.ǁ
except by prayer and fasting.

22 [g]Ἀναστρεφομένωνǁ-δὲ αὐτῶν ἐν τῇ Γαλιλαίᾳ, εἶπεν αὐτοῖς
And while [2]were [3]abiding [1]they in Galilee, [2]said [3]to [4]them
ὁ Ἰησοῦς, Μέλλει ὁ υἱὸς τοῦ ἀνθρώπου παραδίδοσθαι εἰς
[1]Jesus, [9]is [10]about [5]the [6]Son [7]of [8]man to be delivered up into
χεῖρας ἀνθρώπων, 23 καὶ ἀποκτενοῦσιν αὐτόν, καὶ τῇ τρίτῃ
[the] hands of men, and they will kill him; and the third
ἡμέρᾳ [h]ἐγερθήσεται.ǁ Καὶ ἐλυπήθησαν σφόδρα.
day he shall be raised up. And they were grieved greatly.

24 Ἐλθόντων-δὲ αὐτῶν εἰς [i]Καπερναοὺμǁ προσῆλθον οἱ
And [2]having [3]come [1]they to Capernaum [6]came [1]those [2]who
τὰ δίδραχμα λαμβάνοντες τῷ Πέτρῳ καὶ [k]εἶπον,ǁ Ὁ διδάσ-
[4]the [5]didrachmas [3]received to Peter and said, [2]Teach-
καλος ὑμῶν οὐ-τελεῖ [l]τὰǁ δίδραχμα; 25 Λέγει, Ναί. Καὶ
er [1]your does he not pay the didrachmas? He says, Yes. And
[m]ὅτε εἰσῆλθενǁ εἰς τὴν οἰκίαν προέφθασεν αὐτὸν ὁ Ἰησοῦς,
when he entered into the house [2]anticipated [3]him [1]Jesus,
λέγων, Τί σοι-δοκεῖ, Σίμων; οἱ βασιλεῖς τῆς γῆς ἀπὸ τίνων
saying, What thinkest thou, Simon? The kings of the earth from whom
λαμβάνουσιν τέλη ἢ κῆνσον; ἀπὸ τῶν-υἱῶν-αὐτῶν, ἢ ἀπὸ
do they receive custom or tribute? from their sons, or from

---

[x] αὐτόν GLTTrAW. [y] κακῶς ἔχει is ill LTr. [z] μεθ' ὑμῶν ἔσομαι LTTrA. [a] διὰ τί LTTrAW.
[b] — Ἰησοῦς LTTrA. [c] λέγει he says LTTrA. [d] ὀλιγοπιστίαν little faith LTTrA. [e] Μετάβα
ἔνθεν LTTrA. [f] — *verse* 21 T[TrA]. [g] Συστρεφομένων were abiding together LTTr.
[h] ἀναστήσεται he shall rise again L. [i] Καφαρναοὺμ LTTrAW. [k] εἶπαν LTTrA. [l] — τὰ T.
[m] εἰσελθόντα entering LT; ἐλθόντα having come TrA.

τῶν ἀλλοτρίων; 26 [n]Λέγει αὐτῷ‖ [o]ὁ Πέτρος,‖ Ἀπὸ τῶν ἀλ-
the strangers? [2]says [3]to [4]him [1]Peter, From the stran-
λοτρίων. Ἔφη αὐτῷ ὁ Ἰησοῦς, [p]Ἄραγε‖ ἐλεύθεροί εἰσιν οἱ
gers. [2]said [3]to [4]him [1]Jesus, Then indeed free are the
υἱοί. 27 ἵνα.δὲ μὴ.[q]σκανδαλίσωμεν‖ αὐτούς, πορευθεὶς εἰς
sons. But that we may not offend them, having gone to
[r]τὴν‖ θάλασσαν βάλε ἄγκιστρον, καὶ τὸν ἀναβάντα πρῶτον
the sea cast a hook, and the [3]coming [4]up [2]first
ἰχθὺν ἆρον· καὶ ἀνοίξας τὸ.στόμα.αὐτοῦ εὑρήσεις στα-
[1]fish take, and having opened its mouth thou shalt find a sta-
τῆρα· ἐκεῖνον λαβὼν δὸς αὐτοῖς ἀντὶ ἐμοῦ καὶ σοῦ.
ter; that having taken give to them for me and thee.

18 Ἐν ἐκείνῃ τῇ [s]ὥρᾳ‖ προσῆλθον οἱ μαθηταὶ τῷ Ἰησοῦ,
In that hour came the disciples to Jesus,
λέγοντες, Τίς.ἄρα μείζων ἐστὶν ἐν τῇ βασιλείᾳ τῶν οὐ-
saying, Who then [[2]the] [3]greater [1]is in the kingdom of the hea-
ρανῶν; 2 Καὶ προσκαλεσάμενος [t]ὁ Ἰησοῦς‖ παιδίον, ἔστησεν
vens? And [2]having [3]called [4]to [[5]him] [1]Jesus a little child, he set
αὐτὸ ἐν μέσῳ.αὐτῶν, 3 καὶ εἶπεν, Ἀμὴν λέγω ὑμῖν, ἐὰν.μὴ
it in their midst, and said, Verily I say to you, Unless
στραφῆτε καὶ γένησθε ὡς τὰ παιδία, οὐ.μὴ εἰσέλθητε εἰς
ye are converted and become as the little children, in no wise shall ye enter into
τὴν βασιλείαν τῶν οὐρανῶν. 4 ὅστις οὖν [v]ταπεινώσῃ‖
the kingdom of the heavens. Whosoever therefore will humble
ἑαυτὸν ὡς τὸ.παιδίον.τοῦτο, οὗτός ἐστιν ὁ μείζων ἐν τῇ βασι-
himself as this little child, he is the greater in the king-
λείᾳ τῶν οὐρανῶν. 5 καὶ ὃς.[w]ἐὰν‖ δέξηται [x]παιδίον τοιοῦτον
dom of the heavens; and whoever will receive [3]little [4]child [2]such
ἓν‖ ἐπὶ τῷ.ὀνόματί.μου, ἐμὲ δέχεται· 6 ὃς.δ'.ἂν σκανδαλίσῃ
[1]one in my name, [2]me [1]receives. But whoever shall cause [6]to [7]offend
ἕνα τῶν.μικρῶν.τούτων τῶν πιστευόντων εἰς ἐμέ, συμφέρει
[1]one [2]of [3]these [4]little [5]ones who believe in me, it is profitable
αὐτῷ ἵνα κρεμασθῇ μύλος ὀνικὸς [y]ἐπὶ‖ τὸν
for him that should be hung [4]a [5]millstone [6]turned [7]by [8]an [9]ass [1]upon
τράχηλον.αὐτοῦ, καὶ καταποντισθῇ ἐν τῷ πελάγει τῆς θαλάσ-
[2]his [3]neck, and he be sunk in the depth of the sea.
σης. 7 Οὐαὶ τῷ κόσμῳ ἀπὸ τῶν σκανδάλων· ἀνάγκη.γάρ
Woe to the world because of the offences! For necessary
[z]ἐστιν‖ ἐλθεῖν τὰ σκάνδαλα, πλὴν οὐαὶ τῷ.ἀνθρώπῳ.[a]ἐκείνῳ‖
it is [3]to [4]come [1]the [2]offences, yet woe to that man
δι' οὗ τὸ σκάνδαλον ἔρχεται. 8 Εἰ.δὲ ἡ.χείρ.σου ἢ ὁ.πούς.σου
by whom the offence comes! And if thy hand or thy foot
σκανδαλίζει σε, ἔκκοψον [b]αὐτὰ‖ καὶ βάλε ἀπὸ σοῦ· καλόν
cause [2]to [3]offend [1]thee, cut off them and cast [them] from thee; good
σοι ἐστὶν εἰσελθεῖν εἰς τὴν ζωὴν [c]χωλὸν ἢ κυλλόν,‖ ἢ
for thee it is to enter into life lame or maimed, [rather] than
δύο χεῖρας ἢ δύο πόδας ἔχοντα βληθῆναι εἰς τὸ πῦρ τὸ αἰώνιον.
two hands or two feet having to be cast into the fire the eternal.
9 καὶ εἰ ὁ.ὀφθαλμός.σου σκανδαλίζει σε, ἔξελε αὐτὸν καὶ βάλε
And if thine eye cause [2]to [3]offend [1]thee, pluck out it and cast
ἀπὸ σοῦ· καλόν σοι ἐστὶν μονόφθαλμον εἰς τὴν ζωὴν
[it] from thee; good for thee it is one eyed into life

ter saith unto him, Of strangers. Jesus saith unto him, Then are the children free. 27 Notwithstanding, lest we should offend them, go thou to the sea, and cast an hook, and take up the fish that first cometh up; and when thou hast opened his mouth, thou shalt find a piece of money: that take, and give unto them for me and thee.

XVIII. At the same time came the disciples unto Jesus, saying, Who is the greatest in the kingdom of heaven? 2 And Jesus called a little child unto him, and set him in the midst of them, 3 and said, Verily I say unto you, Except ye be converted, and become as little children, ye shall not enter into the kingdom of heaven. 4 Whosoever therefore shall humble himself as this little child, the same is greatest in the kingdom of heaven. 5 And whoso shall receive one such little child in my name receiveth me. 6 But whoso shall offend one of these little ones which believe in me, it were better for him that a millstone were hanged about his neck, and *that* he were drowned in the depth of the sea. 7 Woe unto the world because of offences! for it must needs be that offences come; but woe to that man by whom the offence cometh! 8 Wherefore if thy hand or thy foot offend thee, cut them off, and cast *them* from thee: it is better for thee to enter into life halt or maimed, rather than having two hands or two feet to be cast into everlasting fire. 9 And if thine eye offend thee, pluck it out, and cast *it* from thee: it is better for thee to enter into life with one eye, rather

---

[n] εἰπόντος δὲ and having said LTTr. [o] — ὁ Πέτρος LTTrA. [p] Ἄρα γε TrA. [q] σκανδαλίζωμεν T. [r] — τὴν (*read* [the]) LTTrAW. [s] ἡμέρᾳ day L. [t] — ὁ Ἰησοῦς TTrA. [v] ταπεινώσει LTTrAW. [w] ἂν LTr. [x] ἓν παιδίον τοιοῦτον (— ν T) LTTrA. [y] περὶ about LTTr; εἰς to A. [z] — ἐστιν (*read* [it is]) LTrA. [a] — ἐκείνῳ (*read* to the man) LTTr. [b] αὐτὸν it (and cast [it]) LTTrA. [c] κυλλὸν ἢ χωλόν LT.

than having two eyes to be cast into hell fire. 10 Take heed that ye despise not one of these little ones; for I say unto you, That in heaven their angels do always behold the face of my Father which is in heaven. 11 For the Son of man is come to save that which was lost. 12 How think ye? if a man have an hundred sheep, and one of them be gone astray, doth he not leave the ninety and nine, and goeth into the mountains, and seeketh that which is gone astray? 13 And if so be that he find it, verily I say unto you, he rejoiceth more of that *sheep*, than of the ninety and nine which went not astray. 14 Even so it is not the will of your Father which is in heaven, that one of these little ones should perish.

15 Moreover if thy brother shall trespass against thee, go and tell him his fault between thee and him alone: if he shall hear thee, thou hast gained thy brother. 16 But if he will not hear *thee*, *then* take with thee one or two more, that in the mouth of two or three witnesses every word may be established. 17 And if he shall neglect to hear them, tell *it* unto the church: but if he neglect to hear the church, let him be unto thee as an heathen man and a publican. 18 Verily I say unto you, Whatsoever ye shall bind on earth shall be bound in heaven: and whatsoever ye shall loose on earth shall be loosed in heaven. 19 Again I say unto you, That if two of you shall agree on earth as touching any thing that they shall ask, it shall be done for them of my Father which is in

εἰσελθεῖν, ἢ δύο ὀφθαλμοὺς ἔχοντα βληθῆναι εἰς τὴν
to enter, [rather] than two eyes having to be cast into the
γέενναν τοῦ πυρός. 10 Ὁρᾶτε μὴ.καταφρονήσητε ἑνὸς τῶν
Gehenna of the fire. See , ye despise not one
μικρῶν.τούτων· λέγω.γὰρ ὑμῖν, ὅτι οἱ.ἄγγελοι.αὐτῶν [d]ἐν
of these little ones, for I say to you, that their angels in [the]
οὐρανοῖς‖ διὰ.παντὸς βλέπουσιν τὸ πρόσωπον τοῦ.πατρός.μου
heavens continually behold the face of my Father
τοῦ ἐν οὐρανοῖς. 11 [e]ἦλθεν.γὰρ ὁ υἱὸς τοῦ ἀνθρώπου
who [is] in [the] heavens. For is come the Son of man
σῶσαι τὸ ἀπολωλός.‖ 12 Τί ὑμῖν.δοκεῖ; ἐὰν γένηταί
to save that which has been lost. What think ye? If there should be
τινι ἀνθρώπῳ ἑκατὸν πρόβατα, καὶ πλανηθῇ ἓν ἐξ αὐτῶν,
to any man a hundred sheep, and be gone astray one of them,
οὐχὶ [f]ἀφεὶς‖ τὰ [g]ἐννενηκονταεννέα‖ ἐπὶ τὰ ὄρη
[does he] not, having left the ninety-nine on the mountains,
[h]πορευθεὶς ζητεῖ τὸ πλανώμενον; 13 καὶ ἐὰν γένηται
having gone seek that which is gone astray? and if it should be
εὑρεῖν αὐτό, ἀμὴν λέγω ὑμῖν, ὅτι χαίρει ἐπ' αὐτῷ μᾶλλον
that he find it, verily I say to you, that he rejoices over it more
ἢ ἐπὶ τοῖς [g]ἐννενηκονταεννέα‖ τοῖς μὴ.πεπλανημένοις. 14 οὕ-
than over the ninety-nine which have not gone astray. So
τως οὐκ.ἔστιν θέλημα ἔμπροσθεν τοῦ πατρὸς [i]ὑμῶν‖ τοῦ
it is not [the] will before [2]Father [1]your who [is]
ἐν οὐρανοῖς, ἵνα ἀπόληται [k]εἷς‖ τῶν.μικρῶν.τούτων.
in [the] heavens, that should perish one of these little ones.

15 Ἐὰν.δὲ ἁμαρτήσῃ [l]εἰς σὲ‖ ὁ.ἀδελφός.σου, ὕπαγε [m]καὶ‖
But if [3]sin [4]against [5]thee [1]thy [2]brother, go and
ἔλεγξον αὐτὸν μεταξὺ σοῦ καὶ αὐτοῦ μόνου. ἐάν σου ἀκούσῃ,
reprove him between thee and him alone. If thee he will hear,
ἐκέρδησας τὸν.ἀδελφόν.σου· 16 ἐὰν.δὲ μὴ.ἀκούσῃ, παράλαβε
thou hast gained thy brother. But if he will not hear, take
[n]μετὰ σοῦ‖ ἔτι ἕνα ἢ δύο[o], ἵνα ἐπὶ στόματος δύο μαρτύρων
with thee besides one or two, that upon [the] mouth of two witnesses
ἢ τριῶν σταθῇ πᾶν ῥῆμα. 17 ἐὰν.δὲ παρακούσῃ αὐτῶν,
or of three may stand every word. But if he fail to listen to them,
[p]εἰπὲ‖ τῇ ἐκκλησίᾳ· ἐὰν.δὲ καὶ τῆς ἐκκλησίας παρακούσῃ,
tell [it] to the assembly. And if also the assembly he fail to listen to,
ἔστω σοι ὥσπερ ὁ ἐθνικὸς καὶ ὁ τελώνης. 18 Ἀμὴν λέγω
let him be to thee as the heathen and the taxgatherer. Verily I say
ὑμῖν, ὅσα.[q]ἐὰν‖ δήσητε ἐπὶ τῆς γῆς, ἔσται δεδεμένα ἐν [r]τῷ‖
to you, Whatsoever ye shall bind on the earth, shall be bound in the
οὐρανῷ· καὶ ὅσα.ἐὰν λύσητε ἐπὶ τῆς γῆς, ἔσται λελυμένα
heaven; and whatsoever ye shall loose on the earth, shall be loosed
ἐν [r]τῷ‖ οὐρανῷ. 19 [s]Πάλιν‖ λέγω ὑμῖν, ὅτι ἐὰν δύο [t]ὑμῶν
in the heaven. Again I say to you, that if two of you
συμφωνήσωσιν‖ ἐπὶ τῆς γῆς περὶ παντὸς πράγματος οὗ.ἐὰν
may agree on the earth concerning any matter whatever
αἰτήσωνται, γενήσεται αὐτοῖς παρὰ τοῦ.πατρός.μου τοῦ
they shall ask, it shall be done to them from my Father who [is]

---

[d] ἐν τῷ οὐρανῷ in the heaven [L]A. [e] — *verse* 11 LTTr[A]. [f] ἀφήσει (*read* will not leave) LTr. [g] ἐνενήκοντα ἐννέα LTTr; ἐνενηκονταεννέα W. [h] + καὶ and LTr. [i] μου my LTr. [k] ἓν LTTr. [l] — εἰς σὲ LT[A]. [m] — καὶ GLTTrA. [n] — μετὰ σοῦ L; μετὰ σεαυτοῦ with thyself T. [o] + μετὰ σοῦ L. [p] εἰπὸν T. [q] ἂν LTrA. [r] — τῷ LT[Tr]A. [s] ἀμὴν verily L; πάλιν ἀμὴν TrA. [t] συμφωνήσωσιν ἐξ ὑμῶν L; συμφωνήσουσιν ἐξ ὑμῶν of you shall agree TTrA.

ἐν οὐρανοῖς. 20 οὗ.γάρ εἰσιν δύο ἢ τρεῖς συνηγμένοι εἰς
in [the] heavens. For where are two or three gathered together unto
τὸ ἐμὸν ὄνομα, ἐκεῖ εἰμὶ ἐν μέσῳ αὐτῶν.
my name, there am I in [the] midst of them.
21 Τότε προσελθὼν [u]αὐτῷ ὁ Πέτρος εἶπεν,‖ Κύριε, ποσάκις
Then having come to him Peter said, Lord, how often
ἁμαρτήσει εἰς ἐμὲ ὁ.ἀδελφός.μου καὶ ἀφήσω αὐτῷ; ἕως
shall [3]sin [4]against [5]me [1]my [2]brother and I forgive him? until
ἑπτάκις; 22 Λέγει αὐτῷ ὁ Ἰησοῦς, Οὐ.λέγω σοι ἕως ἑπτάκις,
seven times? [2]Says [3]to [4]him [1]Jesus, I say not to thee until seven times,
[v]ἀλλ'‖ ἕως ἑβδομηκοντάκις ἑπτά. 23 Διὰ.τοῦτο ὡμοιώθη
but until seventy times seven. Because of this [6]has [7]become [8]like
ἡ βασιλεία τῶν οὐρανῶν ἀνθρώπῳ βασιλεῖ, ὃς ἠθέλησεν
[1]the [2]kingdom [3]of [4]the [5]heavens to a man a king, who would
συνᾶραι.λόγον μετὰ τῶν.δούλων.αὐτοῦ. 24 ἀρξαμένου.δὲ αὐτοῦ
take account with his bondmen. And [2]having [3]begun [1]he
συναίρειν, [w]προσηνέχθη‖ [x]αὐτῷ εἷς‖ ὀφειλέτης μυρίων
to reckon, there was brought to him one debtor of ten thousand
ταλάντων. 25 μὴ.ἔχοντος.δὲ αὐτοῦ ἀποδοῦναι, ἐ-
talents. But [2]not [3]having [1]he [wherewith] to pay, [3]com-
κέλευσεν αὐτὸν ὁ.κύριος.[y]αὐτοῦ‖ πραθῆναι, καὶ τὴν γυναῖκα
manded [4]him [1]his [2]lord to be sold, and [2]wife
[z]αὐτοῦ‖ καὶ τὰ τέκνα, καὶ πάντα ὅσα [a]εἶχεν,‖ καὶ ἀποδο-
[1]his and the children, and all as much as he had, and payment to
θῆναι. 26 πεσὼν οὖν ὁ δοῦλος[b] προσεκύνει αὐτῷ,
be made. Having fallen down therefore the bondman did homage to him,
λέγων, [c]Κύριε,‖ μακροθύμησον ἐπ' [d]ἐμοί,‖ καὶ πάντα [e]σοι
saying, Lord, have patience with me, and [3]all [4]to [5]thee
ἀποδώσω.‖ 27 σπλαγχνισθεὶς.δὲ ὁ κύριος τοῦ δούλου
[1]I [2]will [3]pay. And having been moved with compassion the lord [3]bondman
[f]ἐκείνου‖ ἀπέλυσεν αὐτόν, καὶ τὸ δάνειον ἀφῆκεν αὐτῷ.
[1]of [2]that released him, and [3]the [4]loan [1]forgave [2]him.
28 Ἐξελθὼν.δὲ ὁ.δοῦλος.[g]ἐκεῖνος‖ εὗρεν ἕνα τῶν συνδούλων
But having gone out that bondman found one [3]fellow [4]bondmen
αὐτοῦ, ὃς ὤφειλεν αὐτῷ ἑκατὸν δηνάρια, καὶ κρατήσας αὐτὸν
[1]of [2]his, who owed him a hundred denarii, and having seized him
ἔπνιγεν, λέγων, Ἀπόδος [h]μοι‖ [i]ὅ τι‖ ὀφείλεις. 29 πε-
he throttled [him], saying, Pay me what thou owest. [5]Having [6]fallen
σὼν οὖν ὁ.σύνδουλος.αὐτοῦ [k]εἰς τοὺς.πόδας.αὐτοῦ‖ παρε-
[7]down [4]therefore [1]his [2]fellow [3]bondman at his feet be-
κάλει αὐτόν, λέγων, Μακροθύμησον ἐπ' [l]ἐμοί,‖ καὶ [m]πάντα‖
sought him, saying, Have patience with me, and all
ἀποδώσω σοι. 30 Ὁ.δὲ οὐκ.ἤθελεν, [n]ἀλλὰ‖ ἀπελθὼν ἔβαλεν
I will pay thee. But he would not, but having gone he cast
αὐτὸν εἰς φυλακήν, ἕως.[o]οὗ‖ ἀποδῷ τὸ ὀφειλόμενον.
him into prison, until he should pay that which was owing.
31 ἰδόντες [p]δὲ οἱ.σύνδουλοι.αὐτοῦ‖ τὰ [q]γενόμενα‖
[5]Having [6]seen [1]but [2]his [3]fellow [4]bondmen what things had taken place,
ἐλυπήθησαν σφόδρα· καὶ ἐλθόντες διεσάφησαν τῷ.κυρίῳ.[r]αὐτῶν‖
were grieved greatly, and having gone narrated to their lord

heaven. 20 For where
two or three are gath-
ered together in my
name, there am I in
the midst of them.

21 Then came Peter
to him, and said, Lord,
how oft shall my bro-
ther sin against me,
and I forgive him? till
seven times? 22 Jesus
saith unto him, I say
not unto thee, Until
seven times: but,
Until seventy times
seven. 23 Therefore is
the kingdom of hea-
ven likened unto a
certain king, which
would take account of
his servants. 24 And
when he had begun
to reckon, one was
brought unto him,
which owed him ten
thousand talents. 25
But forasmuch as he
had not to pay, his
lord commanded him
to be sold, and his
wife, and children, and
all that he had, and
payment to be made.
26 The servant there-
fore fell down, and wor-
shipped him, saying,
Lord, have patience
with me, and I will
pay thee all. 27 Then
the lord of that ser-
vant was moved with
compassion, and loosed
him, and forgave him
the debt. 28 But the
same servant went
out, and found one of
his fellowservants,
which owed him an
hundred pence: and
he laid hands on him,
and took *him* by the
throat, saying, Pay
me that thou owest.
29 And his fellowser-
vant fell down at his
feet, and besought
him, saying, Have
patience with me, and
I will pay thee all.
30 And he would not:
but went and cast him
into prison, till he
should pay the debt.
31 So when his fellow-
servants saw what was
done, they were very
sorry, and came and
told unto their lord all

---

[u] ὁ Πέτρος εἶπεν αὐτῷ LTTrA. [v] ἀλλὰ LTrA. [w] προσήχθη was conducted LTrA. [x] εἷς αὐτῷ T. [y] — αὐτοῦ (*read* [his] lord) TTrA. [z] — αὐτοῦ (*read* [his] wife) T[A]. [a] ἔχει he has LTrA. [b] + ἐκεῖνος (*read* that bondman) T. [c] — Κύριε LTTrA. [d] ἐμέ Tr. [e] ἀποδώσω σοι ([σοὶ] A) LTTrA. [f] — ἐκείνου (*read* of the bondman) L. [g] — ἐκεῖνος (*read* the bondman) L. [h] — μοι LTTrAW. [i] εἴ τι if anything GLTTrAW. [k] — εἰς τοὺς πόδας αὐτοῦ GLTTr[A]. [l] ἐμέ LTrA. [m] — πάντα [L]TTrAW. [n] ἀλλ' EG. [o] — οὗ LTTrA. [p] οὖν (therefore) αὐτοῦ οἱ σύνδουλοι L; οὖν οἱ σύνδουλοι αὐτοῦ TTrA. [q] γινόμενα were taking place T. [r] ἑαυτῶν LTTrA.

that was done. 32 Then his lord, after that he had called him, said unto him, O thou wicked servant, I forgave thee all that debt, because thou desiredst me: 33 shouldest not thou also have had compassion on thy fellowservant, even as I had pity on thee? 34 And his lord was wroth, and delivered him to the tormentors, till he should pay all that was due unto him. 35 So likewise shall my heavenly Father do also unto you, if ye from your hearts forgive not every one his brother their trespasses.

XIX. And it came to pass, *that* when Jesus had finished these sayings, he departed from Galilee, and came into the coasts of Judæa beyond Jordan; 2 and great multitudes followed him; and he healed them there.

3 The Pharisees also came unto him, tempting him, and saying unto him, Is it lawful for a man to put away his wife for every cause? 4 And he answered and said unto them, Have ye not read, that he which made *them* at the beginning made them male and female, 5 and said, For this cause shall a man leave father and mother, and shall cleave to his wife: and they twain shall be one flesh? 6 Wherefore they are no more twain, but one flesh. What therefore God hath joined together, let not man put asunder. 7 They say unto him, Why did Moses then command to give a writing of divorcement, and to put her away? 8 He saith unto them, Moses because of the hardness of your hearts suffered you to put away your wives: but from the beginning it was not so.

πάντα τὰ γενόμενα. 32 Τότε προσκαλεσάμενος αὐτὸν ὁ
all that had taken place. Then [3]having [4]called [6]to [[7]him] [5]him
κύριος.αὐτοῦ λέγει αὐτῷ, Δοῦλε πονηρέ, πᾶσαν τὴν ὀφειλὴν
[1]his [2]lord says to him, [2]Bondman [1]wicked, all [2]debt
ἐκείνην ἀφῆκά σοι, ἐπεὶ παρεκάλεσάς με· 33 οὐκ.ἔδει καὶ
[1]that I forgave thee, since thou besoughtest me; did it not behove [2]also
σὲ ἐλεῆσαι τὸν.σύνδουλόν.σου, ὡς [s]καὶ ἐγώ‖ σε ἠλέησα;
[1]thee to have pitied thy fellow bondman, as also I thee had pitied?
34 καὶ ὀργισθεὶς ὁ.κύριος.αὐτοῦ παρέδωκεν αὐτὸν τοῖς βασανι-
And being angry his lord delivered up him to the tormen-
σταῖς, ἕως.[t]οὗ‖ ἀποδῷ πᾶν τὸ ὀφειλόμενον [v]αὐτῷ.‖ 35 Οὕτως
tors, until he should pay all that was owing to him. Thus
καὶ ὁ.πατήρ.μου ὁ [w]ἐπουράνιος‖ ποιήσει ὑμῖν ἐὰν.μὴ ἀφῆτε
also my Father the heavenly will do to you unless ye forgive
ἕκαστος τῷ.ἀδελφῷ.αὐτοῦ ἀπὸ τῶν.καρδιῶν.ὑμῶν [x]τὰ παρα-
each his brother from your hearts [2]of-
πτώματα αὐτῶν.‖
fences [1]their.

19 Καὶ ἐγένετο ὅτε ἐτέλεσεν ὁ Ἰησοῦς τοὺς λόγους
And it came to pass when [2]had [3]finished [1]Jesus [5]words
τούτους, μετῆρεν ἀπὸ [y]τῆς‖ Γαλιλαίας, καὶ ἦλθεν εἰς τὰ ὅρια
[4]these, he withdrew from Galilee, and came to the borders
τῆς Ἰουδαίας πέραν τοῦ Ἰορδάνου. 2 καὶ ἠκολούθησαν αὐτῷ
of Judæa beyond the Jordan: and [3]followed [4]him
ὄχλοι πολλοί, καὶ ἐθεράπευσεν αὐτοὺς ἐκεῖ.
[2]crowds [1]great, and he healed them there.

3 Καὶ προσῆλθον αὐτῷ [z]οἱ‖ Φαρισαῖοι πειράζοντες αὐτόν,
And [3]came [4]to [5]him [1]the [2]Pharisees tempting him,
καὶ λέγοντες [a]αὐτῷ,‖ Εἰ.ἔξεστιν [b]ἀνθρώπῳ‖ ἀπολῦσαι τὴν
and saying to him, Is it lawful for a man to put away
γυναῖκα.αὐτοῦ κατὰ πᾶσαν αἰτίαν; 4 Ὁ.δὲ ἀποκριθεὶς εἶπεν
his wife for every cause? But he answering said
[c]αὐτοῖς,‖ Οὐκ.ἀνέγνωτε ὅτι ὁ [d]ποιήσας‖ ἀπ' ἀρ-
to them, Have ye not read that he who made [them] from [the] begin-
χῆς ἄρσεν καὶ θῆλυ ἐποίησεν αὐτούς, 5 καὶ εἶπεν, [e]Ἕνεκεν‖
ning male and female made them, and said, On account of
τούτου καταλείψει ἄνθρωπος τὸν πατέρα καὶ τὴν μητέρα, καὶ
this [3]shall [4]leave [1]a [2]man father and mother, and
[f]προσκολληθήσεται‖ τῇ.γυναικὶ.αὐτοῦ, καὶ ἔσονται οἱ δύο εἰς
shall be joined to his wife, and [3]shall [4]be [1]the [2]two [5]for
σάρκα μίαν; 6 ὥστε οὐκέτι εἰσὶν δύο, ἀλλὰ σὰρξ μία· ὃ
[7]flesh [6]one? So that no longer are they two, but [2]flesh [1]one. What
οὖν ὁ θεὸς συνέζευξεν, ἄνθρωπος μὴ.χωριζέτω. 7 Λέγουσιν
therefore God united together, [3]man [1]let [2]not separate. They say
αὐτῷ, Τί οὖν [g]Μωσῆς‖ ἐνετείλατο δοῦναι βιβλίον ἀπο-
to him, Why then [2]Moses [1]did command to give a bill of di-
στασίου, καὶ ἀπολῦσαι [h]αὐτήν;‖ 8 Λέγει αὐτοῖς, Ὅτι [g]Μωσῆς‖
vorce, and to put away her? He says to them, Moses
πρὸς τὴν.σκληροκαρδίαν.ὑμῶν ἐπέτρεψεν ὑμῖν ἀπολῦσαι
in view of your hard-heartedness allowed you to put away
τὰς.γυναῖκας.ὑμῶν· ἀπ' ἀρχῆς δὲ οὐ.γέγονεν οὕτως.
your wives; from [the] beginning however it was not thus.

[s] κἀγώ LTTrA. [t] — οὗ L. [v] — αὐτῷ LTrA. [w] οὐράνιος LTTr; [ἐπ]ουράνιος A. [x] — τὰ παραπτώματα αὐτῶν GLTTrA. [y] — τῆς E. [z] — οἱ LTrA. [a] — αὐτῷ LTTrA. [b] — ἀνθρώπῳ (*read* one's wife) LTA. [c] — αὐτοῖς LTTrA. [d] κτίσας created Tr. [e] Ἕνεκα LTTrA. [f] κολληθήσεται LTTrAW. [g] Μωϋσῆς LTTrAW. [h] — αὐτήν LTTr.

9 λέγω.δὲ ὑμῖν, ⁱὅτι‖ ὃς.ἂν ἀπολύσῃ τὴν.γυναῖκα.αὐτοῦ
And I say to you, that whoever shall put away his wife
ᵏεἰ‖ ˡμὴ ἐπὶ πορνείᾳ,‖ καὶ γαμήσῃ ἄλλην, μοιχᾶται· ᵐκαὶ
if not for fornication, and shall marry another, commits adultery; and
ὁ ἀπολελυμένην γαμήσας μοιχᾶται.‖ 10 Λέγουσιν
he who ²her [³that ⁴is] ⁵put ⁶away ¹marries commits adultery. ³Say
αὐτῷ οἱ.μαθηταὶ.ⁿαὐτοῦ,‖ Εἰ οὕτως ἐστὶν ἡ αἰτία τοῦ ἀνθρώ-
⁴to ⁵him ¹his ²disciples, If thus is the case of the man
που μετὰ τῆς γυναικός, οὐ.συμφέρει γαμῆσαι. 11 Ὁ.δὲ εἶπεν
with the wife, it is not profitable to marry. But he said
αὐτοῖς, Οὐ πάντες χωροῦσιν τὸν.λόγον.ᵒτοῦτον,‖ ἀλλ'
to them, Not all receive this word, but [those]
οἷς δέδοται. 12 εἰσὶν.γὰρ εὐνοῦχοι οἵτινες ἐκ κοιλίας
to whom it has been given; for there are eunuchs who from [the] womb
μητρὸς ἐγεννήθησαν οὕτως, καί εἰσιν εὐνοῦχοι οἵτινες
of [their] mother were born thus, and there are eunuchs who
εὐνουχίσθησαν ὑπὸ τῶν ἀνθρώπων, καί εἰσιν εὐνοῦχοι οἵτινες
were made eunuchs by men, and there are eunuchs who
εὐνούχισαν ἑαυτοὺς διὰ τὴν βασιλείαν τῶν οὐρανῶν.
made eunuchs of themselves for the sake of the kingdom of the heavens.
ὁ δυνάμενος χωρεῖν χωρείτω.
He who is able to receive [it] let him receive [it].

13 Τότε ᵖπροσηνέχθη‖ αὐτῷ παιδία, ἵνα τὰς χεῖρας
Then were brought to him little children, that [his] hands
ἐπιθῇ αὐτοῖς, καὶ προσεύξηται· οἱ.δὲ μαθηταὶ ἐπετίμησαν
he might lay on them, and might pray; but the disciples rebuked
αὐτοῖς· 14 ὁ.δὲ.Ἰησοῦς εἶπενᑫ, Ἄφετε τὰ παιδία, καὶ μὴ
them. But Jesus said, Suffer the little children, and ²not
κωλύετε αὐτὰ ἐλθεῖν πρός ʳμε·‖ τῶν.γὰρ.τοιούτων ἐστὶν ἡ
¹do forbid them to come to me; for of such is the
βασιλεία τῶν οὐρανῶν. 15 Καὶ ἐπιθεὶς ˢαὐτοῖς τὰς χεῖρας‖
kingdom of the heavens. And having laid upon them [his] hands
ἐπορεύθη ἐκεῖθεν.
he departed thence.

16 Καὶ ἰδού, εἷς προσελθὼν ᵗεἶπεν αὐτῷ,‖ Διδάσκαλε
And behold, one having come to [him] said to him, ²Teacher
ᵛἀγαθέ,‖ τί ἀγαθὸν ποιήσω ἵνα ʷἔχω‖ ζωὴν αἰώνιον;
¹good, what good [thing] shall I do that I may have life eternal?
17 Ὁ.δὲ εἶπεν.αὐτῷ, ˣΤί με λέγεις ἀγαθόν; οὐδεὶς ἀγαθὸς
And he said to him, Why me callest thou good? no one [is] good
εἰ.μὴ εἷς, ὁ θεός.‖ εἰ.δὲ θέλεις ʸεἰσελθεῖν εἰς τὴν ζωήν,‖
except one, God. But if thou desirest to enter into life,
ᶻτήρησον‖ τὰς ἐντολάς. 18 ᵃΛέγει αὐτῷ,‖ Ποίας; ᵇὉ.δὲ.Ἰη-
keep the commandments. He says to him, Which? And Je-
σοῦς εἶπεν, Τό, οὐ.φονεύσεις· οὐ.μοιχεύσεις·
sus said, Thou shalt not commit murder; Thou shalt not commit adultery;
οὐ.κλέψεις· οὐ.ψευδομαρτυρήσεις· 19 τίμα τὸν πατέρα
Thou shalt not steal; Thou shalt not bear false witness; Honour ²father
ᶜσου‖ καὶ τὴν μητέρα· καὶ ἀγαπήσεις τὸν.πλησίον.σου ὡς
¹thy and mother; and Thou shalt love thy neighbour as

9 And I say unto you, Whosoever shall put away his wife, except *it be* for fornication, and shall marry another, committeth adultery: and whoso marrieth her which is put away doth commit adultery. 10 His disciples say unto him, If the case of the man be so with *his* wife, it is not good to marry. 11 But he said unto them, All *men* cannot receive this saying, save *they* to whom it is given. 12 For there are some eunuchs, which were so born from *their* mother's womb: and there are some eunuchs, which were made eunuchs of men: and there be eunuchs, which have made themselves eunuchs for the kingdom of heaven's sake. He that is able to receive *it*, let him receive *it*.

13 Then were there brought unto him little children, that he should put *his* hands on them, and pray: and the disciples rebuked them. 14 But Jesus said, Suffer little children, and forbid them not, to come unto me: for of such is the kingdom of heaven. 15 And he laid *his* hands on them, and departed thence.

16 And, behold, one came and said unto him, Good Master, what good thing shall I do, that I may have eternal life? 17 And he said unto him, Why callest thou me good? *there is* none good but one, *that is*, God: but if thou wilt enter into life, keep the commandments. 18 He saith unto him, Which? Jesus said, Thou shalt do no murder, Thou shalt not commit adultery, Thou shalt not steal, Thou shalt not bear false witness, 19 Honour thy father and *thy* mother: and, Thou shalt love thy neighbour as thyself.

ⁱ — ὅτι LTrA. ᵏ — εἰ GLTTrAW. ˡ παρεκτὸς λόγου πορνείας except for cause of fornication L. ᵐ — καὶ ὁ ἀπολελυμένην γαμήσας μοιχᾶται T[Tr]. ⁿ — αὐτοῦ (*read* the disciples) T[A]. ᵒ [τοῦτον] L. ᵖ προσηνέχθησαν LTTrA. ᑫ + αὐτοῖς to them T. ʳ ἐμέ T. ˢ τὰς χεῖρας αὐτοῖς LTTrA. ᵗ αὐτῷ εἶπεν LTTrA. ᵛ — ἀγαθέ LTTrA. ʷ σχῶ LTTrA. ˣ Τί με ἐρωτᾷς περὶ τοῦ ἀγαθοῦ; εἷς ἐστιν ὁ ἀγαθός Why askest thou me concerning the good? One is good (+ ὁ θεός God W) GLTTrAW. ʸ εἰς τὴν ζωὴν εἰσελθεῖν LTTrAW. ᶻ τήρει LTrA. ᵃ ἔφη αὐτῷ he said to him L; — λέγει αὐτῷ T. ᵇ + φησίν he says T. ᶜ — σου GLTTrAW.

20 The young man saith unto him, All these things have I kept from my youth up: what lack I yet? 21 Jesus said unto him, If thou wilt be perfect, go *and* sell that thou hast, and give to the poor, and thou shalt have treasure in heaven: and come *and* follow me. 22 But when the young man heard that saying, he went away sorrowful: for he had great possessions.

σεαυτόν. 20 Λέγει αὐτῷ ὁ νεανίσκος, [d]Πάντα ταῦτα‖
thyself. [4]Says [5]to [6]him [1]the [2]young [3]man, All these
[e]ἐφυλαξάμην‖ [f]ἐκ νεότητός-μου·‖ τί ἔτι ὑστερῶ; 21 [g]Ἔφη‖ αὐτῷ
have I kept from my youth, what yet lack I? [2]Said [3]to [4]him
ὁ Ἰησοῦς, Εἰ θέλεις τέλειος εἶναι, ὕπαγε πώλησόν σου τὰ
[1]Jesus, If thou desirest perfect to be, go sell thy
ὑπάρχοντα καὶ δὸς [h]πτωχοῖς, καὶ ἕξεις θησαυρὸν ἐν
property and give to [the] poor, and thou shalt have treasure in
[i]οὐρανῷ·‖ καὶ δεῦρο ἀκολούθει μοι. 22 Ἀκούσας-δὲ ὁ νεανίσκος
heaven; and come follow me. But [4]having [5]heard [1]the [2]young [3]man
[k]τὸν λόγον‖ [l] ἀπῆλθεν λυπούμενος, ἦν-γὰρ-ἔχων κτήματα
the word went away grieved, for he had [2]possessions
πολλά.
[1]many.

23 Then said Jesus unto his disciples, Verily I say unto you, That a rich man shall hardly enter into the kingdom of heaven. 24 And again I say unto you, It is easier for a camel to go through the eye of a needle, than for a rich man to enter into the kingdom of God. 25 When his disciples heard *it*, they were exceedingly amazed, saying, Who then can be saved? 26 But Jesus beheld *them*, and said unto them, With men this is impossible; but with God all things are possible.

23 Ὁ-δὲ Ἰησοῦς εἶπεν τοῖς-μαθηταῖς-αὐτοῦ, Ἀμὴν λέγω
And Jesus said to his disciples, Verily I say
ὑμῖν, ὅτι [m]δυσκόλως πλούσιος‖ εἰσελεύσεται εἰς τὴν βασι-
to you, that with difficulty a rich man shall enter into the king-
λείαν τῶν οὐρανῶν. 24 πάλιν-δὲ λέγω ὑμῖν, [n] εὐκοπώτερόν ἐστιν
dom of the heavens. And again I say to you, easier is it
κάμηλον διὰ τρυπήματος ῥαφίδος [o]διελθεῖν,‖ ἢ πλού-
a camel through [the] eye of a needle to pass, than a rich
σιον [p] εἰς τὴν βασιλείαν [q]τοῦ θεοῦ‖ [r]εἰσελθεῖν.‖ 25 Ἀκούσαντες
man into the kingdom of God to enter. [2]Having [3]heard
δὲ οἱ-μαθηταὶ-[s]αὐτοῦ‖ ἐξεπλήσσοντο σφόδρα, λέγοντες,
[1]and [this] his disciples were astonished exceedingly, saying,
Τίς ἄρα δύναται σωθῆναι; 26 Ἐμβλέψας-δὲ ὁ Ἰησοῦς
Who then is able to be saved? But looking on [them] Jesus
εἶπεν αὐτοῖς, Παρὰ ἀνθρώποις τοῦτο ἀδύνατόν ἐστιν, παρὰ-δὲ
said to them, With men this impossible is, but with
θεῷ [t]πάντα δυνατά‖ [v]ἐστιν.‖
God all things possible are.

27 Then answered Peter and said unto him, Behold, we have forsaken all, and followed thee; what shall we have therefore? 28 And Jesus said unto them, Verily I say unto you, That ye which have followed me, in the regeneration when the Son of man shall sit in the throne of his glory, ye also shall sit upon twelve thrones, judging the twelve tribes of Israel. 29 And every one that hath forsaken houses, or brethren, or sisters, or father, or mother, or wife, or children, or lands, for my name's sake, shall receive an hundredfold, and shall

27 Τότε ἀποκριθεὶς ὁ Πέτρος εἶπεν αὐτῷ, Ἰδού, ἡμεῖς ἀφή-
Then answering Peter said to him, Lo, we left
καμεν πάντα καὶ ἠκολουθήσαμέν σοι· τί ἄρα ἔσται ἡμῖν;
all things and followed thee; what then shall be to us?
28 Ὁ-δὲ-Ἰησοῦς εἶπεν αὐτοῖς, Ἀμὴν λέγω ὑμῖν, ὅτι ὑμεῖς οἱ
And Jesus said to them, Verily I say to you, that ye who
ἀκολουθήσαντές μοι, ἐν τῇ [w]παλιγγενεσίᾳ,‖ ὅταν καθίσῃ
have followed me, in the regeneration, when shall sit down
ὁ υἱὸς τοῦ ἀνθρώπου ἐπὶ θρόνου δόξης-αὐτοῦ, καθίσεσθε
the Son of man upon [the] throne of his glory, [3]shall [4]sit
καὶ [x]ὑμεῖς‖ ἐπὶ δώδεκα θρόνους, κρίνοντες τὰς δώδεκα φυλὰς
[2]also [1]ye on twelve thrones, judging the twelve tribes
τοῦ Ἰσραήλ. 29 καὶ πᾶς [y]ὃς‖ ἀφῆκεν [z]οἰκίας, ἢ‖ ἀδελφούς,
of Israel. And every one who has left houses, or brothers,
ἢ ἀδελφάς, ἢ πατέρα, ἢ μητέρα, [a]ἢ γυναῖκα,‖ ἢ τέκνα, ἢ
or sisters, or father, or mother, or wife, or children, or
ἀγρούς,[b] [c]ἕνεκεν‖ τοῦ-[da]ὀνόματός-μου,‖ [ea]ἑκατονταπλασίονα
lands, for the sake of my name, a hundredfold

[d] ταῦτα πάντα LTr. [e] ἐφύλαξα LTTrA. [f] — ἐκ νεότητός μου LTTrA. [g] λέγει says L. [h] + τοῖς to the LTrA. [i] οὐρανοῖς [the] heavens TrA. [k] — τὸν λόγον T. [l] + [τοῦτον] (*read* this word) LA. [m] πλούσιος δυσκόλως LTTrA. [n] + ὅτι that T. [o] εἰσελθεῖν to enter GTTrA. [p] + εἰσελθεῖν to enter L[Tr]. [q] τῶν οὐρανῶν of the heavens LTTrA. [r] — εἰσελθεῖν LTTrA. [s] — αὐτοῦ (*read* the disciples) GLTTrAW. [t] δυνατὰ πάντα T. [v] — ἐστιν (*read* [are]) GLTTrAW. [w] παλινγενεσίᾳ T. [x] αὐτοὶ yourselves TTr. [y] ὅστις LTTrAW. [z] — οἰκίας ἢ TTrA. [a] — ἢ γυναῖκα LTTrA. [b] + ἢ οἰκίας or houses TTrA. [c] ἕνεκα T. [da] ἐμοῦ ὀνόματός T. [ea] πολλαπλασίονα λήμψεται many times more shall receive LTTrA.

λήψεται," καὶ ζωὴν αἰώνιον κληρονομήσει. 30 πολλοὶ.δὲ
shall receive, and life eternal shall inherit; but many
ἔσονται πρῶτοι ἔσχατοι, καὶ ἔσχατοι πρῶτοι. 20 Ὁμοία.γάρ
[2]shall [3]be [1]first last, and last first. For [7]like
ἐστιν ἡ βασιλεία τῶν οὐρανῶν ἀνθρώπῳ οἰκοδεσπότῃ, ὅστις
[6]is [1]the [2]kingdom [3]of [4]the [5]heavens to a man a master of a house, who
ἐξῆλθεν ἅμα πρωῒ μισθώσασθαι ἐργάτας εἰς τὸν ἀμπελῶνα
went out with [the] morning to hire workmen for [2]vineyard
αὐτοῦ. 2 συμφωνήσας.δὲ μετὰ τῶν ἐργατῶν ἐκ δηναρίου τὴν
[1]his. And having agreed with the workmen for a denarius the
ἡμέραν, ἀπέστειλεν αὐτοὺς εἰς τὸν.ἀμπελῶνα.αὐτοῦ. 3 Καὶ
day, he sent them into his vineyard. And
ἐξελθὼν περὶ [f]τὴν" τρίτην ὥραν, εἶδεν ἄλλους ἑστῶτας
having gone out about the third hour, he saw others standing
ἐν τῇ ἀγορᾷ ἀργούς· 4 [g]κἀκείνοις" εἶπεν, Ὑπάγετε καὶ
in the marketplace idle; and to them he said, Go also
ὑμεῖς εἰς τὸν ἀμπελῶνα, καὶ ὃ.ἐὰν ᾖ δίκαιον δώσω ὑμῖν.
ye into the vineyard, and whatever may be just I will give you.
5 οἱ.δὲ ἀπῆλθον. Πάλιν[h] ἐξελθὼν περὶ ἕκτην καὶ
And they went. Again having gone out about [the] sixth and
[i]ἐννάτην' ὥραν, ἐποίησεν ὡσαύτως. 6 Περὶ.δὲ τὴν ἑνδεκάτην
ninth hour, he did likewise. And about the eleventh
[k]ὥραν" ἐξελθὼν εὗρεν ἄλλους ἑστῶτας [l]ἀργούς," καὶ λέγει
hour having gone out he found others standing idle, and says
αὐτοῖς, Τί ὧδε ἑστήκατε ὅλην τὴν ἡμέραν ἀργοί; 7 λέγουσιν
to them, Why here stand ye all the day idle? They say
αὐτῷ, Ὅτι οὐδεὶς ἡμᾶς ἐμισθώσατο. λέγει αὐτοῖς, Ὑπάγετε
to him, Because no one [3]us [1]has [2]hired. He says to them, Go
καὶ ὑμεῖς εἰς τὸν ἀμπελῶνα,[m] [n]καὶ ὃ.ἐὰν ᾖ δίκαιον λή-
also ye into the vineyard, and whatever may be just ye shall
ψεσθε." 8 Ὀψίας.δὲ γενομένης λέγει ὁ κύριος τοῦ ἀμπελῶνος
receive. But evening being come [6]says [1]the [2]lord [3]of [4]the [5]vineyard
τῷ.ἐπιτρόπῳ.αὐτοῦ, Κάλεσον τοὺς ἐργάτας, καὶ ἀπόδος [o]αὐ-
to his steward, Call the workmen, and pay them
τοῖς" τὸν μισθόν, ἀρξάμενος ἀπὸ τῶν ἐσχάτων ἕως τῶν
[their] hire, beginning from the last unto the
πρώτων. 9 [p]καὶ ἐλθόντες" οἱ περὶ τὴν ἑνδεκάτην
first. And [7]having [8]come [1]those [[2]hired] [3]about [4]the [5]eleventh
ὥραν ἔλαβον ἀνὰ δηνάριον. 10 [q]ἐλθόντες.δὲ" οἱ πρῶτοι
[6]hour they received each a denarius. And [3]having [4]come [1]the [2]first
ἐνόμισαν ὅτι [r]πλείονα λήψονται·" καὶ ἔλαβον [s]καὶ αὐτοὶ
they thought that more they would receive, and they received also themselves
ἀνὰ δηνάριον." 11 λαβόντες.δὲ ἐγόγγυζον κατὰ τοῦ
each a denarius. And having received [it] they murmured against the
οἰκοδεσπότου, 12 λέγοντες, [t]Ὅτι" οὗτοι οἱ ἔσχατοι μίαν
master of the house, saying, These last one
ὥραν ἐποίησαν, καὶ ἴσους [v]ἡμῖν αὐτοὺς" ἐποίησας, τοῖς
hour have worked, and [5]equal [6]to [7]us [4]them [1]thou [2]hast [3]made, who
βαστάσασιν τὸ βάρος τῆς ἡμέρας καὶ τὸν καύσωνα.[w] 13 ὁ.δὲ
have borne the burden of the day and the heat. But he
ἀποκριθεὶς [x]εἶπεν ἑνὶ αὐτῶν," Ἑταῖρε, οὐκ.ἀδικῶ σε· οὐχὶ
answering said to one of them, Friend, I do not wrong thee. [3]Not

inherit everlasting life. 30 But many *that are* first shall be last; and the last *shall be* first. XX. For the kingdom of heaven is like unto a man *that is* an householder, which went out early in the morning to hire labourers into his vineyard. 2 And when he had agreed with the labourers for a penny a day, he sent them into his vineyard. 3 And he went out about the third hour, and saw others standing idle in the marketplace, 4 and said unto them; Go ye also into the vineyard, and whatsoever is right I will give you. And they went their way. 5 Again he went out about the sixth and ninth hour, and did likewise. 6 And about the eleventh hour he went out, and found others standing idle, and saith unto them, Why stand ye here all the day idle? 7 They say unto him, Because no man hath hired us. He saith unto them, Go ye also into the vineyard; and whatsoever is right, *that* shall ye receive. 8 So when even was come, the lord of the vineyard saith unto his steward, Call the labourers, and give them *their* hire, beginning from the last unto the first. 9 And when they came that *were hired* about the eleventh hour, they received every man a penny. 10 But when the first came, they supposed that they should have received more; and they likewise received every man a penny. 11 And when they had received *it*, they murmured against the goodman of the house, 12 saying, These last have wrought *but* one hour, and thou hast made them equal unto us, which have borne the burden and heat of the day. 13 But he answered one of them, and said, Friend, I do thee no wrong: didst

[f] — τὴν (*read* [the]) GLTTrAW. [g] καὶ ἐκείνοις TA. [h] + δὲ and (again) TTrA. [i] ἐνάτην LTTrAW. [k] — ὥραν LTTrA. [l] — ἀργούς GLTTrA. [m] + [μου] my (vineyard) L. [n] — καὶ ὃ ἐὰν ᾖ δίκαιον λήψεσθε LTTrA. [o] — αὐτοῖς T[TrA]. [p] ἐλθόντες δὲ L. [q] καὶ ἐλθόντες TrA. [r] πλεῖον λήμψονται LTrA; πλείονα λήμψονται T. [s] τὸ ([τὸ] A) ἀνὰ δηνάριον καὶ αὐτοί TTrA. [t] — ὅτι LTTr[A]. [v] αὐτοὺς ἡμῖν LT. [w] ; (*read* hast thou made, &c.?) L. [x] ἑνὶ αὐτῶν εἶπεν T.

not thou agree with me for a penny? 14 Take *that* thine *is*, and go thy way: I will give unto this last, even as unto thee. 15 Is it not lawful for me to do what I will with mine own? Is thine eye evil, because I am good? 16 So the last shall be first, and the first last: for many be called, but few chosen.

δηναρίου συνεφώνησάς μοι; 14 ἆρον τὸ.σὸν καὶ
[7]for [8]a [9]denarius [1]didst [2]thou [4]agree [5]with [6]me? Take thine own and
ὕπαγε. θέλω.[y]δὲ‖ τούτῳ τῷ ἐσχάτῳ δοῦναι ὡς καὶ σοί· 15 [z]ἢ‖
go. But I will to this last give as also to thee: or
οὐκ.ἔξεστίν μοι [a]ποιῆσαι ὃ θέλω‖ ἐν τοῖς ἐμοῖς; [b]εἰ‖
is it not lawful for me to do what I will in that which [is] mine?
ὁ.ὀφθαλμός.σου πονηρός ἐστιν ὅτι ἐγὼ ἀγαθός εἰμι; 16 οὕτως
[2]thine [3]eye [4]evil [1]is because I good am? Thus
ἔσονται οἱ ἔσχατοι πρῶτοι, καὶ οἱ πρῶτοι ἔσχατοι· [c]πολλοὶ.γάρ
shall be the last first, and the first last: for many
εἰσιν κλητοί, ὀλίγοι.δὲ ἐκλεκτοί.‖
are called, but few chosen.

17 And Jesus going up to Jerusalem took the twelve disciples apart in the way, and said unto them, 18 Behold, we go up to Jerusalem; and the Son of man shall be betrayed unto the chief priests and unto the scribes, and they shall condemn him to death, 19 and shall deliver him to the Gentiles to mock, and to scourge, and to crucify *him*: and the third day he shall rise again.

17 Καὶ ἀναβαίνων ὁ Ἰησοῦς εἰς Ἱεροσόλυμα παρέλαβεν
And [2]going [3]up [1]Jesus to Jerusalem took
τοὺς δώδεκα [d]μαθητὰς‖ κατ᾽.ἰδίαν [e]ἐν τῇ ὁδῷ, καὶ‖ εἶπεν αὐτοῖς,
the twelve disciples apart in the way, and said to them,
18 Ἰδού, ἀναβαίνομεν εἰς Ἱεροσόλυμα, καὶ ὁ υἱὸς τοῦ ἀνθρώ-
Behold, we go up to Jerusalem, and the Son of man
που παραδοθήσεται τοῖς ἀρχιερεῦσιν καὶ γραμματεῦσιν, καὶ
will be delivered up to the chief priests and scribes, and
κατακρινοῦσιν αὐτὸν [f]θανάτῳ,‖ 19 καὶ παραδώσουσιν αὐτὸν
they will condemn him to death, and they will deliver up him
τοῖς ἔθνεσιν εἰς τὸ ἐμπαῖξαι καὶ μαστιγῶσαι καὶ σταυρῶσαι·
to the Gentiles to mock and to scourge and to crucify;
καὶ τῇ τρίτῃ ἡμέρᾳ [g]ἀναστήσεται.‖
and the third day he will rise again.

20 Then came to him the mother of Zebedee's children with her sons, worshipping *him*, and desiring a certain thing of him. 21 And he said unto her, What wilt thou? She saith unto him, Grant that these my two sons may sit, the one on thy right hand, and the other on the left, in thy kingdom. 22 But Jesus answered and said, Ye know not what ye ask. Are ye able to drink of the cup that I shall drink of, and to be baptized with the baptism that I am baptized with? They say unto him, We are able. 23 And he saith unto them, Ye shall drink indeed of my cup, and be baptized with the baptism that I am baptized with: but to sit on my right hand, and on my left, is not mine to give, but *it shall be given to them* for whom it is prepared of my

20 Τότε προσῆλθεν αὐτῷ ἡ μήτηρ τῶν υἱῶν Ζεβεδαίου μετὰ
Then came to him the mother of the sons of Zebedee with
τῶν.υἱῶν.αὐτῆς, προσκυνοῦσα καὶ αἰτοῦσά τι [h]παρ᾽‖ αὐτοῦ.
her sons, doing homage and asking something from him.
21 ὁ.δὲ εἶπεν αὐτῇ, Τί θέλεις; Λέγει αὐτῷ, Εἰπὲ ἵνα
And he said to her, What dost thou desire? She says to him, Say that
καθίσωσιν [i]οὗτοι‖ οἱ δύο υἱοί μου εἷς ἐκ δεξιῶν.[k]σου‖ καὶ εἷς
[5]may [6]sit [1]these [3]two [4]sons [2]my one on thy right hand and one
ἐξ εὐωνύμων[l] ἐν τῇ.βασιλείᾳ.σου. 22 Ἀποκριθεὶς.δὲ ὁ
on [thy] left in thy kingdom. But answering
Ἰησοῦς εἶπεν, Οὐκ.οἴδατε τί αἰτεῖσθε. δύνασθε πιεῖν τὸ
Jesus said, Ye know not what ye ask for. Are ye able to drink the
ποτήριον ὃ ἐγὼ μέλλω πίνειν, [m]καὶ τὸ βάπτισμα ὃ ἐγὼ
cup which I am about to drink, and [5]the [6]baptism [7]which [8]I
βαπτίζομαι βαπτισθῆναι;‖ Λέγουσιν αὐτῷ, Δυνά-
[9]am [10]baptized [[11]with] [1]to [2]be [3]baptized [[4]with]? They say to him, We are
μεθα. 23 [n]Καὶ‖ λέγει αὐτοῖς, Τὸ μὲν ποτήριόν μου πίεσθε,
able. And he says to them, [3]Indeed [2]cup [1]my ye shall drink,
[o]καὶ τὸ βάπτισμα ὃ ἐγὼ βαπτίζομαι βαπτισθήσεσθε·‖
and the baptism which I am baptized [with] ye shall be baptized
τὸ.δὲ.καθίσαι ἐκ δεξιῶν.μου καὶ ἐξ εὐωνύμων.[p]μου‖ οὐκ
[with]; but to sit on my right hand and on my left [2]not
ἔστιν ἐμὸν[q] δοῦναι, ἀλλ᾽ οἷς ἡτοίμασται ὑπὸ τοῦ
[1]is mine to give, but [to those] for whom it has been prepared by

[y] — δὲ but W. [z] — ἢ LTr[A]. [a] ὃ θέλω ποιῆσαι LTTrA. [b] ἢ or EGLTTrAW. [c] — πολλοὶ γάρ εἰσιν κλητοί, ὀλίγοι δὲ ἐκλεκτοί T[TrA]. [d] — μαθητὰς TTr. [e] καὶ ἐν τῇ ὁδῷ LTTrA. [f] εἰς θάνατον T. [g] ἐγερθήσεται he shall be raised TTrA. [h] ἀπ᾽ LTrA. [i] [οὗτοι] L. [k] — σου (*read* [thy] right hand) LT. [l] + σου thy (left) GLTTrAW. [m] — καὶ τὸ βάπτισμα, ὃ ἐγὼ βαπτίζομαι, βαπτισθῆναι GLTTrA. [n] — καὶ LTTrA. [o] — καὶ τὸ βάπτισμα ὃ ἐγὼ βαπτίζομαι βαπτισθήσεσθε GLTTrA. [p] — μου (*read* [my] left) LTTrA. [q] + τοῦτο this (is not mine) TA.

πατρός.μου. 24 [r]Καὶ ἀκούσαντες[‖] οἱ δέκα ἠγανάκτησαν
my Father. And having heard [this] the ten were indignant
περὶ τῶν δύο ἀδελφῶν. 25 ὁ.δὲ.Ἰησοῦς προσκαλεσάμενος
about the two brothers. But Jesus having called [2]to [[3]him]
αὐτοὺς εἶπεν, Οἴδατε ὅτι οἱ ἄρχοντες τῶν ἐθνῶν κατακυριεύου-
[1]them said, Ye know that the rulers of the nations exercise lordship
σιν αὐτῶν, καὶ οἱ μεγάλοι κατεξουσιάζουσιν αὐτῶν. 26 οὐχ
over them, and the great ones exercise authority over them. Not
οὕτως [s]δὲ[‖] [t]ἔσται[‖] ἐν ὑμῖν· ἀλλ' ὃς.[v]ἐὰν[‖] θέλῃ [w]ἐν
thus however shall it be among you; but whoever would among
ὑμῖν[‖] μέγας γενέσθαι, [x]ἔστω[‖] ὑμῶν διάκονος· 27 καὶ ὃς.[y]ἐὰν[‖]
you great become, let him be your servant; and whoever
θέλῃ ἐν ὑμῖν εἶναι πρῶτος, [z]ἔστω[‖] ὑμῶν δοῦλος· 28 ὥσπερ
would among you be first, let him be your bondman; even as
ὁ υἱὸς τοῦ ἀνθρώπου οὐκ.ἦλθεν διακονηθῆναι, ἀλλὰ διακονῆ-
the Son of man came not to be served, but to serve,
σαι καὶ δοῦναι τὴν.ψυχὴν.αὐτοῦ λύτρον ἀντὶ πολλῶν.
and to give his life a ransom for many.

29 Καὶ ἐκπορευομένων αὐτῶν ἀπὸ [a]Ἱεριχὼ[‖] ἠκολούθησεν
And as [2]were [3]going [4]out [1]they from Jericho [4]followed
αὐτῷ ὄχλος πολύς. 30 καὶ ἰδού, δύο τυφλοὶ καθήμενοι
[5]him [1]a [3]crowd [2]great. And behold, two blind [men] sitting
παρὰ τὴν ὁδόν, ἀκούσαντες ὅτι Ἰησοῦς παράγει ἔκραξαν,
beside the way, having heard that Jesus is passing by cried out,
λέγοντες, [b]Ἐλέησον ἡμᾶς, κύριε,[‖] [c]υἱὸς[‖] [d]Δαβίδ.[‖] 31 Ὁ.δὲ.ὄχλος
saying, Have pity on us, Lord, Son of David. But the crowd
ἐπετίμησεν αὐτοῖς ἵνα σιωπήσωσιν. οἱ.δὲ μεῖζον [e]ἔκρα-
rebuked them that they should be silent. But they the more cried
ζον,[‖] λέγοντες, [f]Ἐλέησον ἡμᾶς, κύριε,[‖] [c]υἱὸς[‖] [d]Δαβίδ[‖]. 32 Καὶ
out, saying, Have pity on us, Lord, Son of David. And
στὰς ὁ Ἰησοῦς ἐφώνησεν αὐτούς, καὶ εἶπεν, Τί θέλετε
having stopped, Jesus called them, and said, What do ye desire
[g]ποιήσω ὑμῖν; 33 Λέγουσιν αὐτῷ, Κύριε, ἵνα [h]ἀνοιχθῶσιν[‖]
I should do to you? They say to him, Lord, that [3]may [4]be [5]opened
[i]ἡμῶν οἱ ὀφθαλμοί.[‖] 34 Σπλαγχνισθεὶς.δὲ ὁ Ἰησοῦς ἥψατο
[1]our [2]eyes. And moved with compassion Jesus touched
τῶν [k]ὀφθαλμῶν[‖].αὐτῶν· καὶ εὐθέως ἀνέβλεψαν [l]αὐτῶν οἱ
their eyes; and immediately [3]received [4]sight [1]their
ὀφθαλμοί,[‖] καὶ ἠκολούθησαν αὐτῷ.
[2]eyes, and they followed him.

21 Καὶ ὅτε ἤγγισαν εἰς Ἱεροσόλυμα καὶ ἦλθον εἰς Βηθ-
And when they drew near to Jerusalem and came to Beth-
φαγῆ [m]πρὸς[‖] τὸ ὄρος τῶν ἐλαιῶν, τότε [n]ὁ[‖] Ἰησοῦς ἀπέστειλεν
phage towards the mount of Olives, then Jesus sent
δύο μαθητάς, 2 λέγων αὐτοῖς, [o]Πορεύθητε[‖] εἰς τὴν κώμην τὴν
two disciples, saying to them, Go into the village, that
[p]ἀπέναντι[‖] ὑμῶν, καὶ [q]εὐθέως[‖] εὑρήσετε ὄνον δεδεμένην, καὶ
opposite you, and immediately ye will find an ass tied, and
πῶλον μετ' αὐτῆς· λύσαντες [ra]ἀγάγετέ[‖] μοι. 3 καὶ ἐάν
a colt with her; having loosed [them] bring [them] to me. And if

Father. 24 And when the ten heard *it*, they were moved with indignation against the two brethren. 25 But Jesus called them *unto him*, and said, Ye know that the princes of the Gentiles exercise dominion over them, and they that are great exercise authority upon them. 26 But it shall not be so among you: but whosoever will be great among you, let him be your minister; 27 and whosoever will be chief among you, let him be your servant: 28 even as the Son of man came not to be ministered unto, but to minister, and to give his life a ransom for many.

29 And as they departed from Jericho, a great multitude followed him. 30 And, behold, two blind men sitting by the way side, when they heard that Jesus passed by, cried out, saying, Have mercy on us, O Lord, *thou* son of David. 31 And the multitude rebuked them, because they should hold their peace: but they cried the more, saying, Have mercy on us, O Lord, *thou* son of David. 32 And Jesus stood still, and called them, and said, What will ye that I shall do unto you? 33 They say unto him, Lord, that our eyes may be opened. 34 So Jesus had compassion *on them*, and touched their eyes: and immediately their eyes received sight, and they followed him.

XXI. And when they drew nigh unto Jerusalem, and were come to Bethphage, unto the mount of Olives, then sent Jesus two disciples, 2 saying unto them, Go into the village over against you, and straightway ye shall find an ass tied, and a colt with her: loose *them*, and bring *them* unto me. 3 And

---

[r] ἀκούσαντες δὲ TA. [s] — δὲ GLTTrA. [t] ἐστὶν is it LTr. [v] ἂν LTr. [w] ὑμῶν of you A. [x] ἔσται he shall be LTTrA. [y] ἂν LTTrA. [z] ἔσται he shall be LTTr. [a] Ἱερειχὼ T. [b] Κύριε, ἐλέησον ἡμᾶς LTrA; — κύριε T. [c] υἱὲ LT. [d] Δαυίδ GW; Δαυείδ LTTrA. [e] ἔκραξαν LTTrA. [f] Κύριε, ἐλέησον ἡμᾶς LTTrA. [g] + [ἵνα] that LA. [h] ἀνοιγῶσιν LTTrA. [i] οἱ ὀφθαλμοὶ ἡμῶν LTTrA. [k] ὀμμάτων LTTrA. [l] — αὐτῶν οἱ ὀφθαλμοί LTTrA. [m] εἰς to LTTrA. [n] — ὁ T. [o] Πορεύεσθε LTTrA. [p] κατέναντι LTTr. [q] εὐθὺς T. [ra] ἄγετέ LTrA.

if any *man* say ought
unto you, ye shall say,
The Lord hath need of
them; and straight-
way he will send them.
4 All this was done,
that it might be ful-
filled which was spo-
ken by the prophet,
saying, 5 Tell ye the
daughter of Sion,
Behold, thy King com-
eth unto thee, meek,
and sitting upon an
ass, and a colt the foal
of an ass. 6 And the
disciples went, and did
as Jesus commanded
them, 7 and brought
the ass, and the colt,
and put on them their
clothes, and they set
him thereon. 8 And a
very great multitude
spread their garments
in the way; others cut
down branches from
the trees, and strawed
them in the way. 9 And
the multitudes that
went before, and that
followed, cried, say-
ing, Hosanna to the
son of David: Blessed
is he that cometh in
the name of the Lord;
Hosanna in the high-
est. 10 And when he
was come into Jerusa-
lem, all the city was
moved, saying, Who is
this? 11 And the mul-
titude said, This is
Jesus the prophet of
Nazareth of Galilee.

12 And Jesus went
into the temple of God,
and cast out all them
that sold and bought
in the temple, and
overthrew the tables
of the money changers,
and the seats of them
that sold doves, 13 and
said unto them, It is
written, My house
shall be called the
house of prayer; but
ye have made it a den
of thieves. 14 And the
blind and the lame
came to him in the
temple; and he healed
them. 15 And when
the chief priests and
scribes saw the won-

τις ὑμῖν εἴπῃ τι, ἐρεῖτε, Ὅτι ὁ κύριος αὐτῶν χρείαν
any one to you say anything, ye shall say, The Lord [3]of [4]them [2]need
ἔχει· [s]εὐθέως‖.δὲ [t]ἀποστελεῖ‖ αὐτούς. 4 Τοῦτο.δὲ [u]ὅλον‖ γέ-
[1]has. And immediately he will send them. But this all came
γονεν ἵνα πληρωθῇ τὸ ῥηθὲν διὰ τοῦ προφήτου,
to pass that might be fulfilled that which was spoken by the prophet,
λέγοντος, 5 Εἴπατε τῇ θυγατρὶ Σιών, Ἰδού, ὁ.βασιλεύς.σου
saying, Say to the daughter of Sion, Behold, thy king
ἔρχεταί σοι, πραῢς [v]καὶ‖ ἐπιβεβηκὼς ἐπὶ ὄνον καὶ [w] πῶλον
comes to thee, meek and mounted on an ass and a colt [the]
υἱὸν ὑποζυγίου. 6 Πορευθέντες.δὲ οἱ μαθηταί, καὶ ποιήσαν-
foal of a beast of burden. And [3]having [4]gone [1]the [2]disciples, and having
τες καθὼς [x]προσέταξεν‖ αὐτοῖς ὁ Ἰησοῦς, 7 ἤγαγον τὴν
done as [2]ordered [3]them [1]Jesus, they brought the
ὄνον καὶ τὸν πῶλον, καὶ ἐπέθηκαν [y]ἐπάνω‖ αὐτῶν τὰ.ἱμάτια
ass and the colt, and put upon them [2]garments
[z]αὐτῶν,‖ καὶ [a]ἐπεκάθισεν‖ ἐπάνω αὐτῶν. 8 ὁ.δὲ πλεῖστος
[1]their, and he sat on them. And the greater part [of the]
ὄχλος ἔστρωσαν ἑαυτῶν τὰ ἱμάτια ἐν τῇ ὁδῷ, ἄλλοι.δὲ ἔκοπ-
crowd strewed their garments on the way, and others were cutting
τον κλάδους ἀπὸ τῶν δένδρων καὶ [b]ἐστρώννυον‖ ἐν τῇ
down branches from the trees and were strewing [them] on the
ὁδῷ. 9 οἱ.δὲ ὄχλοι οἱ προάγοντες[c] καὶ οἱ ἀκολουθοῦντες
way. And the crowds those going before and those following
ἔκραζον, λέγοντες, Ὡσαννὰ τῷ υἱῷ [d]Δαβίδ·‖ εὐλογημένος
were crying out, saying, Hosanna to the Son of David; blessed
ὁ ἐρχόμενος ἐν ὀνόματι κυρίου· Ὡσαννὰ ἐν τοῖς
[be] he who comes in [the] name of [the] Lord. Hosanna in the
ὑψίστοις. 10 Καὶ εἰσελθόντος.αὐτοῦ εἰς Ἱεροσόλυμα ἐσείσθη
highest. And as he entered into Jerusalem [4]was [5]moved
πᾶσα ἡ πόλις, λέγουσα, Τίς ἐστιν οὗτος; 11 Οἱ.δὲ ὄχλοι
[1]all [2]the [3]city, saying, Who is this? And the crowds
ἔλεγον, Οὗτός ἐστιν [e]Ἰησοῦς ὁ προφήτης,‖ ὁ ἀπὸ [f]Να-
said, This is Jesus the prophet, he who [is] from Na-
ζαρὲτ‖ τῆς Γαλιλαίας.
zareth of Galilee.

12 Καὶ εἰσῆλθεν [g]ὁ‖ Ἰησοῦς εἰς τὸ ἱερὸν [h]τοῦ θεοῦ,‖ καὶ
And [2]entered [1]Jesus into the temple of God, and
ἐξέβαλεν πάντας τοὺς πωλοῦντας καὶ ἀγοράζοντας ἐν τῷ
cast out all those selling and buying in the
ἱερῷ, καὶ τὰς τραπέζας τῶν κολλυβιστῶν κατέστρεψεν, καὶ
temple, and the tables of the money changers he overthrew, and
τὰς καθέδρας τῶν πωλούντων τὰς περιστεράς. 13 καὶ λέγει
the seats of those selling the doves. And he says
αὐτοῖς, Γέγραπται, Ὁ.οἶκός.μου οἶκος προσευχῆς κληθή-
to them, It has been written, My house a house of prayer shall be
σεται· ὑμεῖς.δὲ αὐτὸν [i]ἐποιήσατε‖ σπήλαιον λῃστῶν. 14 Καὶ
called; but ye it have made a den of robbers. And
προσῆλθον αὐτῷ τυφλοὶ καὶ χωλοὶ ἐν τῷ ἱερῷ, καὶ ἐθεράπευ-
[4]came [5]to [6]him [1]blind [2]and [3]lame in the temple, and he healed
σεν αὐτούς. 15 Ἰδόντες.δὲ οἱ ἀρχιερεῖς καὶ οἱ γραμματεῖς
them. But [7]seeing [1]the [2]chief [3]priests [4]and [5]the [6]scribes

---

[s] εὐθὺς TTr. [t] ἀποστέλλει he sends G. [u] — ὅλον LTTrA. [v] — καὶ A. [w] + ἐπὶ on LTTrA. [x] συνέταξεν did direct LTrA. [y] ἐπ' LTTrA. [z] — αἰ τῶν [L]TTrA. [a] ἐπεκάθισαν they set [him] E. [b] ἔστρωσαν strewed T. [c] + αὐτὸν him LTTrA. [d] Δαυίδ GW; Δαυείδ LTTrA. [e] ὁ προφήτης Ἰησοῦς LTTrA. [f] Ναζαρὲθ ELTTrAW. [g] — ὁ LTTrA. [h] — τοῦ θεοῦ LTr. [i] ποιεῖτε make LTTrA.

τὰ θαυμάσια ἃ ἐποίησεν, καὶ τοὺς παῖδας ᵏκράζοντας ἐν τῷ
the wonders which he wrought, and the children crying in the
ἱερῷ. καὶ λέγοντας, Ὡσαννὰ τῷ υἱῷ ˡΔαβίδ,ˡ ἠγανάκτησαν,
temple, and saying, Hosanna to the Son of David, they were indignant,
16 καὶ ᵐεἶπονˡ αὐτῷ, Ἀκούεις τί οὗτοι λέγουσιν; Ὁ.δὲ.Ἰη-
and said to him, Hearest thou what these say? And Je-
σοῦς λέγει αὐτοῖς, Ναί· οὐδέποτε ἀνέγνωτε, Ὅτι ἐκ στόμα-
sus says to them, Yea; [3]never [1]did [2]ye read, Out of [the] mouth
τος νηπίων καὶ θηλαζόντων κατηρτίσω αἶνον; 17 Καὶ
of babes and sucklings thou hast perfected praise? And
καταλιπὼν αὐτοὺς ἐξῆλθεν ἔξω τῆς πόλεως εἰς Βηθανίαν, καὶ
having left them, he went out of the city to Bethany, and
ηὐλίσθη ἐκεῖ.
passed the night there.

18 ⁿΠρωΐαςˡ.δὲ ᵒἐπανάγωνˡ εἰς τὴν πόλιν ἐπείνασεν,
Now early in the morning coming back into the city he hungered,
19 καὶ ἰδὼν συκῆν μίαν ἐπὶ τῆς ὁδοῦ, ἦλθεν ἐπ' αὐτήν, καὶ
and seeing [2]fig-tree [1]one by the way, he came to it, and
οὐδὲν εὗρεν ἐν αὐτῇ εἰ.μὴ φύλλα μόνον· καὶ λέγει αὐτῇ,
nothing found on it except leaves only. And he says to it,
ᵖ Μηκέτι ἐκ σοῦ καρπὸς γένηται εἰς τὸν.αἰῶνα. Καὶ ἐξηράνθη
Never more of thee fruit let there be for ever. And [4]dried [5]up
παραχρῆμα ἡ συκῆ. 20 Καὶ ἰδόντες οἱ μαθηταὶ ἐθαύμασαν,
[1]immediately [2]the [3]fig-tree. And seeing [it] the disciples wondered,
λέγοντες, Πῶς παραχρῆμα ἐξηράνθη ἡ συκῆ; 21 Ἀποκριθεὶς
saying, How immediately is dried up the fig-tree! [2]Answering
δὲ ὁ Ἰησοῦς εἶπεν αὐτοῖς, Ἀμὴν λέγω ὑμῖν, ἐὰν ἔχητε πίστιν,
[1]and Jesus said to them, Verily, I say to you, If ye have faith,
καὶ μὴ.διακριθῆτε, οὐ μόνον τὸ τῆς συκῆς ποιήσετε,
and do not doubt, not only the [miracle] of the fig-tree shall ye do,
ἀλλὰ κἂν τῷ.ὄρει.τούτῳ εἴπητε, Ἄρθητι καὶ βλήθητι
but even if to this mountain ye should say, Be thou taken away and be thou cast
εἰς τὴν θάλασσαν, γενήσεται· 22 καὶ πάντα ὅσα.ᵠἂνˡ
into the sea, it shall come to pass. And all things whatsoever
αἰτήσητε ἐν τῇ προσευχῇ, πιστεύοντες, ʳλήψεσθε.ˡ
ye may ask in prayer, believing, ye shall receive.

23 Καὶ ˢἐλθόντι.αὐτῷˡ εἰς τὸ ἱερὸν προσῆλθον αὐτῷ
And on his coming into the temple there came up to him, [when]
διδάσκοντι οἱ ἀρχιερεῖς καὶ οἱ πρεσβύτεροι τοῦ λαοῦ, λέγον-
teaching, the chief priests and the elders of the people, say-
τες, Ἐν ποίᾳ ἐξουσίᾳ ταῦτα ποιεῖς; καὶ τίς σοι ἔδωκεν τὴν
ing, By what authority these things doest thou? and who to thee gave
ἐξουσίαν.ταύτην; 24 Ἀποκριθεὶς.ᵗδὲˡ ὁ Ἰησοῦς εἶπεν αὐτοῖς,
this authority? And answering Jesus said to them,
Ἐρωτήσω ὑμᾶς κἀγὼ λόγον ἕνα, ὃν ἐὰν εἴπητέ μοι, κἀγὼ
[3]Will [4]ask [5]you [1]I [2]also [7]thing [6]one, which if ye tell me, I also
ὑμῖν ἐρῶ ἐν ποίᾳ ἐξουσίᾳ ταῦτα ποιῶ. 25 τὸ βάπτισμα
to you will say by what authority these things I do. The baptism
ᵛ Ἰωάννου πόθεν ἦν; ἐξ οὐρανοῦ, ἢ ἐξ ἀνθρώπων;
of John, whence was it? from heaven, or from men?
Οἱ.δὲ διελογίζοντο ʷπαρ'ˡ ἑαυτοῖς, λέγοντες, Ἐὰν εἴπω-
And they reasoned with themselves, saying, If we should
μεν, Ἐξ οὐρανοῦ, ἐρεῖ ἡμῖν, ˣΔιατίˡ οὖν οὐκ.ἐπιστεύσατε
say, From heaven, he will say to us, Why then did ye not believe

derful things that he did, and the children crying in the temple, and saying, Hosanna to the Son of David; they were sore displeased, 16 and said unto him, Hearest thou what these say? And Jesus saith unto them, Yea; have ye never read, Out of the mouth of babes and sucklings thou hast perfected praise? 17 And he left them, and went out of the city into Bethany; and he lodged there.

18 Now in the morning as he returned into the city, he hungered. 19 And when he saw a fig tree in the way, he came to it, and found nothing thereon, but leaves only, and said unto it, Let no fruit grow on thee henceforward for ever. And presently the fig tree withered away. 20 And when the disciples saw *it*, they marvelled, saying, How soon is the fig tree withered away! 21 Jesus answered and said unto them, Verily I say unto you, If ye have faith, and doubt not, ye shall not only do this *which is done* to the fig tree, but also if ye shall say unto this mountain, Be thou removed, and be thou cast into the sea; it shall be done. 22 And all things, whatsoever ye shall ask in prayer, believing, ye shall receive.

23 And when he was come into the temple, the chief priests and the elders of the people came unto him as he was teaching, and said, By what authority doest thou these things? and who gave thee this authority? 24 And Jesus answered and said unto them, I also will ask you one thing, which if ye tell me, I in like wise will tell you by what authority I do these things. 25 The baptism of John, whence was it? from heaven, or of men? And they reasoned with themselves, saying, If we shall say, From heaven; he will say unto us, Why did ye not then be-

---

ᵏ + τοὺς (*read* who were) LTTrA. ˡ Δαυίδ GW; Δαυείδ LTTrA. ᵐ εἶπαν LTTrA. ⁿ Πρωῒ Tr. ᵒ ἐπαναγαγὼν LTA. ᵖ + Οὐ LT[A]. ᵠ ἐὰν Tr. ʳ λήμψεσθε LTTrA. ˢ ἐλθόντος αὐτοῦ LTTr. ᵗ — δὲ and L. ᵛ + τὸ that LTTrA. ʷ ἐν among LTr. ˣ διὰ τί LTTrA.

lieve him? 26 But if
we shall say, Of men;
we fear the people; for
all hold John as a pro-
phet. 27 And they an-
swered Jesus, and said,
We cannot tell. And
he said unto them,
Neither tell I you by
what authority I do
these things. 28 But
what think ye? A *cer-*
tain man had two
sons; and he came to
the first, and said,
Son, go work to day in
my vineyard. 29 He
answered and said, I
will not: but after-
ward he repented, and
went. 30 And he came
to the second, and
said likewise. And he
answered and said, I
go, sir: and went not.
31 Whether of them
twain did the will of
his father? They say
unto him, The first.
Jesus saith unto them,
Verily I say unto you,
That the publicans
and the harlots go into
the kingdom of God
before you. 32 For
John came unto you
in the way of right-
eousness, and ye be-
lieved him not: but
the publicans and the
harlots believed him:
and ye, when ye had
seen *it*, repented not
afterward, that ye
might believe him.

33 Hear another pa-
rable: There was a
certain householder,
which planted a vine-
yard, and hedged it
round about, and dig-
ged a winepress in it,
and built a tower, and
let it out to husband-
men, and went into a
far country: 34 and
when the time of the
fruit drew near, he
sent his servants to
the husbandmen, that
they might receive the
fruits of it. 35 And
the husbandmen took
his servants, and beat
one, and killed an-
other, and stoned an-
other. 36 Again, he
sent other servants
more than the first:
and they did unto

αὐτῷ; 26 ἐὰν-δὲ εἴπωμεν, Ἐξ ἀνθρώπων, φοβούμεθα τὸν
him? but if we should say, From men, we fear the
ὄχλον· πάντες-γὰρ [y]ἔχουσιν τὸν Ἰωάννην ὡς προφήτην.‖
multitude; for all hold John as a prophet.
27 Καὶ ἀποκριθέντες τῷ Ἰησοῦ [z]εἶπον,‖ Οὐκ-οἴδαμεν. Ἔφη
And answering Jesus they said, We know not. [3]Said
αὐτοῖς καὶ αὐτός, Οὐδὲ ἐγὼ λέγω ὑμῖν ἐν ποίᾳ ἐξουσίᾳ
[4]to [5]them [2]also [1]he, Neither [2]I [1]tell you by what authority
ταῦτα ποιῶ. 28 Τί-δὲ ὑμῖν-δοκεῖ; ἄνθρωπος[a] εἶχεν [b]τέκνα
these things I do. But what think ye? a man had [2]children
δύο,‖ [c]καὶ‖ προσελθὼν τῷ πρώτῳ εἶπεν, Τέκνον, ὕπαγε
[1]two, and having come to the first he said, Child, go
σήμερον ἐργάζου ἐν τῷ-ἀμπελῶνί-[d]μου.‖ 29 Ὁ-δὲ ἀποκριθεὶς
to-day work in my vineyard. And he answering
εἶπεν, Οὐ-θέλω· ὕστερον-[e]δὲ‖ μεταμεληθεὶς ἀπῆλθεν. 30 [f]Καὶ
said, I will not; but afterwards having repented he went. And
προσελθὼν‖ τῷ [g]δευτέρῳ‖ εἶπεν ὡσαύτως. ὁ-δὲ ἀποκριθεὶς
having come to the second he said likewise. And he answering
εἶπεν, Ἐγώ, κύριε· καὶ οὐκ-ἀπῆλθεν. 31 Τίς ἐκ τῶν δύο ἐποίη-
said, I [go], sir, and went not. Which of the two did
σεν τὸ θέλημα τοῦ πατρός; Λέγουσιν [h]αὐτῷ,‖ [i]Ὁ πρῶτος.‖
the will of the father? They say to him, The first.
Λέγει αὐτοῖς ὁ Ἰησοῦς, Ἀμὴν λέγω ὑμῖν, ὅτι οἱ τελῶναι καὶ
[2]Says [3]to [4]them [1]Jesus, Verily I say to you, that the tax-gatherers and
αἱ πόρναι προάγουσιν ὑμᾶς εἰς τὴν βασιλείαν τοῦ θεοῦ.
the harlots go before you into the kingdom of God.
32 ἦλθεν-γὰρ [k]πρὸς ὑμᾶς Ἰωάννης‖ ἐν ὁδῷ δικαιοσύνης,
For [2]came [3]to [4]you [1]John in [the] way of righteousness,
καὶ οὐκ-ἐπιστεύσατε αὐτῷ, οἱ-δὲ τελῶναι καὶ αἱ πόρναι
and ye did not believe him, but the tax-gatherers and the harlots
ἐπίστευσαν αὐτῷ· ὑμεῖς-δὲ ἰδόντες [l]οὐ‖-μετεμελήθητε ὕστερον
believed him; but ye having seen did not repent afterwards
τοῦ πιστεῦσαι αὐτῷ.
to believe him.

33 Ἄλλην παραβολὴν ἀκούσατε. Ἄνθρωπός [m]τις‖ ἦν
Another parable hear. A [2]man [1]certain there was
οἰκοδεσπότης, ὅστις ἐφύτευσεν ἀμπελῶνα, καὶ φραγμὸν αὐτῷ
a master of a house, who planted a vineyard, and [4]a [5]fence [3]it
περιέθηκεν, καὶ ὤρυξεν ἐν αὐτῷ ληνόν, καὶ ᾠκοδόμησεν
[1]placed [2]about, and dug in it a winepress, and built
πύργον, καὶ [n]ἐξέδοτο‖ αὐτὸν γεωργοῖς, καὶ ἀπεδήμησεν.
a tower, and let out it to husbandmen, and left the country.
34 ὅτε-δὲ ἤγγισεν ὁ καιρὸς τῶν καρπῶν, ἀπέστειλεν τοὺς
And when drew near the season of the fruits, he sent
δούλους-αὐτοῦ πρὸς τοὺς γεωργοὺς λαβεῖν τοὺς-καρποὺς-αὐτοῦ.
his bondmen to the husbandmen to receive his fruits.
35 καὶ λαβόντες οἱ γεωργοὶ τοὺς-δούλους-αὐτοῦ, ὃν-μὲν
And [3]having [4]taken [1]the [2]husbandmen his bondmen, one
ἔδειραν, ὃν-δὲ ἀπέκτειναν, ὃν-δὲ ἐλιθοβόλησαν. 36 πάλιν
they beat, and another they killed, and another they stoned. Again
ἀπέστειλεν ἄλλους δούλους πλείονας τῶν πρώτων, καὶ ἐποίη-
he sent other bondmen more than the first, and they

[y] ὡς προφήτην ἔχουσιν τὸν Ἰωάννην LTTrA. [z] εἶπαν T. [a] + τις (*read* a certain man) L. [b] δύο τέκνα L. [c] — καὶ T. [d] — μου (*read* the vineyard) TTrA. [e] — δὲ but [L]T. [f] προσελθὼν δὲ LTTrA. [g] ἑτέρῳ other GTAW. [h] — αὐτῷ LTTrA. [i] ὁ ὕστερος he who afterwards [obeyed] LTr. [k] Ἰωάννης πρὸς ὑμᾶς LTTrA. [l] οὐδὲ (*read* did neither repent) LTr; οὐ[δὲ] A. [m] — τις GLTTrAW. [n] ἐξέδετο TA.

σαν αὐτοῖς ὡσαύτως. 37 ὕστερον.δὲ ἀπέστειλεν πρὸς αὐτοὺς
did to them in like manner. And at last he sent to them
τὸν.υἱὸν.αὐτοῦ, λέγων, Ἐντραπήσονται τὸν.υἱόν.μου.
his son, saying, They will have respect for my son.
38 Οἱ.δὲ γεωργοὶ ἰδόντες τὸν υἱὸν εἶπον ἐν ἑαυτοῖς, Οὗτός
But the husbandmen seeing the son said among themselves, This
ἐστιν ὁ κληρονόμος· δεῦτε, ἀποκτείνωμεν αὐτόν, καὶ [o]κατά-
is the heir; come, let us kill him, and gain pos-
σχωμεν‖ τὴν.κληρονομίαν.αὐτοῦ. 39 καὶ λαβόντες αὐτὸν
session of his inheritance. And having taken him
ἐξέβαλον ἔξω τοῦ ἀμπελῶνος καὶ ἀπέκτειναν. 40 ὅταν οὖν
they cast [him] out of the vineyard and killed [him]. When therefore
ἔλθῃ ὁ κύριος τοῦ ἀμπελῶνος, τί ποιήσει τοῖς γεωργοῖς
shall come the lord of the vineyard, what will he do [3]husbandmen
ἐκείνοις; 41 Λέγουσιν αὐτῷ, Κακοὺς κακῶς ἀπολέσει
[1]to [2]those? They say to him, Evil [men]! miserably he will destroy
αὐτούς, καὶ τὸν ἀμπελῶνα [p]ἐκδόσεται‖ ἄλλοις γεωργοῖς,
them, and the vineyard he will let out to other husbandmen,
οἵτινες ἀποδώσουσιν αὐτῷ τοὺς καρποὺς ἐν τοῖς.καιροῖς.αὐτῶν.
who will render to him the fruits in their seasons.
42 Λέγει αὐτοῖς ὁ Ἰησοῦς, Οὐδέποτε.ἀνέγνωτε ἐν ταῖς γρα-
[2]Says [3]to [4]them [1]Jesus, Did ye never read in the scrip-
φαῖς, Λίθον ὃν ἀπεδοκίμασαν οἱ οἰκοδομοῦντες, οὗτος
tures, [The] stone which [4]rejected [1]those [2]who [3]build, this
ἐγενήθη εἰς κεφαλὴν γωνίας· παρὰ κυρίου ἐγένετο αὕτη,
is become head of [the] corner: from [the] Lord was this,
καὶ ἔστιν θαυμαστὴ ἐν ὀφθαλμοῖς.ἡμῶν; 43 Διὰ τοῦτο λέγω
and it is wonderful in our eyes? Because of this I say
ὑμῖν, ὅτι ἀρθήσεται ἀφ' ὑμῶν ἡ βασιλεία τοῦ θεοῦ, καὶ
to you, that [3]shall [4]be [5]taken [1]from [2]you the kingdom of God, and
δοθήσεται ἔθνει ποιοῦντι τοὺς καρποὺς αὐτῆς. 44 [q]καὶ
it shall be given to a nation producing the fruits of it. And
ὁ πεσὼν ἐπὶ τὸν.λίθον.τοῦτον συνθλασθήσεται· ἐφ'.ὃν.δ'.ἂν
he who falls on this stone shall be broken; but on whomsoever
πέσῃ, λικμήσει αὐτόν.‖ 45 [r]Καὶ ἀκούσαντες‖ οἱ
it shall fall it will grind to powder him. And [7]hearing [1]the
ἀρχιερεῖς καὶ οἱ Φαρισαῖοι τὰς.παραβολὰς.αὐτοῦ ἔγνωσαν
[2]chief [3]priests [4]and [5]the [6]Pharisees his parables knew
ὅτι περὶ αὐτῶν λέγει. 46 καὶ ζητοῦντες αὐτὸν κρατῆσαι,
that about them he speaks. And seeking him to lay hold of,
ἐφοβήθησαν τοὺς ὄχλους, [s]ἐπειδὴ‖ [t]ὡς‖ προφήτην αὐτὸν εἶχον.
they feared the crowds, because as a prophet him they held.

22 Καὶ ἀποκριθεὶς ὁ Ἰησοῦς πάλιν εἶπεν [v]αὐτοῖς ἐν παρα-
And answering Jesus again spoke to them in para-
βολαῖς,‖ λέγων, 2 Ὡμοιώθη ἡ βασιλεία τῶν οὐρανῶν
bles, saying, [6]Has [7]become [8]like [1]the [2]kingdom [3]of [4]the [5]heavens
ἀνθρώπῳ βασιλεῖ, ὅστις ἐποίησεν γάμους τῷ.υἱῷ.αὐτοῦ·
to a man a king, who made a wedding feast for his son:
3 καὶ ἀπέστειλεν τοὺς.δούλους.αὐτοῦ καλέσαι τοὺς κεκλη-
and sent his bondmen to call those who had been
μένους εἰς τοὺς γάμους, καὶ οὐκ.ἤθελον ἐλθεῖν. 4 Πάλιν
invited to the wedding feast, and they would not come. Again
ἀπέστειλεν ἄλλους δούλους, λέγων, Εἴπατε τοῖς κεκλη-
he sent other bondmen, saying, Say to those who had been

them likewise. 37 But
last of all he sent unto
them his son, saying,
They will reverence
my son. 38 But when
the husbandmen saw
the son, they said a-
mong themselves, This
is the heir; come, let
us kill him, and let us
seize on his inherit-
ance. 39 And they
caught him, and cast
him out of the vine-
yard, and slew *him.*
40 When the lord
therefore of the vine-
yard cometh, what will
he do unto those hus-
bandmen? 41 They say
unto him, He will mi-
serably destroy those
wicked men, and will
let out *his* vineyard
unto other husband-
men, which shall ren-
der him the fruits in
their seasons. 42 Jesus
saith unto them, Did
ye never read in the
scriptures, The stone
which the builders
rejected, the same is
become the head of
the corner: this is the
Lord's doing, and it is
marvellous in our eyes?
43 Therefore say I unto
you, The kingdom of
God shall be taken
from you, and given
to a nation bringing
forth the fruits there-
of. 44 And whosoever
shall fall on this stone
shall be broken: but
on whomsoever it shall
fall, it will grind him
to powder. 45 And
when the chief priests
and Pharisees had
heard his parables,
they perceived that he
spake of them. 46 But
when they sought to
lay hands on him, they
feared the multitude,
because they took him
for a prophet.

XXII. And Jesus
answered and spake
unto them again by pa-
rables, and said, 2 The
kingdom of heaven is
like unto a certain
king, which made a
marriage for his son,
3 and sent forth his
servants to call them
that were bidden to
the wedding: and they
would not come. 4 A-
gain, he sent forth
other servants, say-
ing, Tell them which
are bidden, Behold, I

---

[o] σχῶμεν let us possess LTTrA. [p] ἐκδώσεται GLTTrAW. [q] — *verse* 44 [L] T. [r] ἀκούσαντες δὲ T. [s] ἐπεὶ TTrA. [t] εἰς for LTTrA. [v] ἐν παραβολαῖς αὐτοῖς LTTrA.

have prepared my dinner: my oxen and my
fatlings *are* killed, and
all things *are* ready:
come unto the mar-
riage. 5 But they
made light of *it*, and
went their ways, one
to his farm, another
to his merchandise:
6 and the remnant
took his servants, and
entreated *them* spite-
fully, and slew *them*.
7 But when the king
heard *thereof*, he was
wroth: and he sent
forth his armies, and
destroyed those mur-
derers, and burned up
their city. 8 Then saith
he to his servants, The
wedding is ready, but
they which were bid-
den were not worthy.
9 Go ye therefore into
the highways, and as
many as ye shall find,
bid to the marriage.
10 So those servants
went out into the
highways, and gather-
ed together all as many
as they found, both
bad and good: and the
wedding was furnish-
ed with guests. 11 And
when the king came in
to see the guests, he
saw there a man which
had not on a wedding
garment: 12 and he
saith unto him, Friend,
how camest thou in
hither not having
a wedding garment?
And he was speechless.
13 Then said the king
to the servants, Bind
him hand and foot, and
take him away, and
cast *him* into outer
darkness; there shall
be weeping and gnash-
ing of teeth. 14 For
many are called, but
few *are* chosen.

15 Then went the
Pharisees, and took
counsel how they
might entangle him in
his talk. 16 And they
sent out unto him their
disciples with the He-
rodians, saying, Mas-
ter, we know that thou
art true, and teachest
the way of God in
truth, neither carest

μένοις, Ἰδού, τὸ.ἄριστόν.μου [w]ἡτοίμασα,‖ οἱ.ταῦροί.μου καὶ
invited, Behold, my dinner I prepared, my oxen and
τὰ σιτιστὰ τεθυμένα, καὶ πάντα ἕτοιμα· δεῦτε εἰς τοὺς
the fatted beasts are killed, and all things [are] ready; come to the
γάμους. 5 Οἱ.δὲ ἀμελήσαντες ἀπῆλθον, [x]ὁ‖.μὲν εἰς τὸν
wedding feast. But they being negligent of [it] went away, one to
ἴδιον ἀγρόν, [y]ὁ‖.δὲ [z]εἰς‖ τὴν.ἐμπορίαν.αὐτοῦ. 6 οἱ.δὲ λοιποὶ
his own field, and another to his commerce. And the rest,
κρατήσαντες τοὺς.δούλους.αὐτοῦ ὕβρισαν καὶ ἀπέκτειναν.
having laid hold of his bondmen, insulted and killed [them].
7 [a]Ἀκούσας.δὲ ὁ βασιλεὺς ὠργίσθη, καὶ πέμψας τὰ
And having heard [it] the king was wroth, and having sent
στρατεύματα.αὐτοῦ ἀπώλεσεν τοὺς.φονεῖς.ἐκείνους, καὶ τὴν
his forces he destroyed those murderers, and
πόλιν.αὐτῶν ἐνέπρησεν. 8 Τότε λέγει τοῖς.δούλοις.αὐτοῦ, Ὁ
their city he burnt. Then he says to his bondmen, The
μὲν γάμος ἕτοιμός ἐστιν, οἱ.δὲ κεκλημένοι οὐκ.ἦσαν
[3]indeed [1]wedding [2]feast [5]ready [4]is, but those who had been invited were not
ἄξιοι· 9 πορεύεσθε οὖν ἐπὶ τὰς διεξόδους τῶν ὁδῶν, καὶ
worthy; Go therefore into the thoroughfares of the highways, and
ὅσους [b]ἂν‖.εὕρητε, καλέσατε εἰς τοὺς γάμους. 10 Καὶ
as many as ye shall find, invite to the wedding feast. And
ἐξελθόντες οἱ.δοῦλοι.ἐκεῖνοι εἰς τὰς ὁδοὺς συνήγαγον πάντας
[3]having [4]gone [5]out [1]those [2]bondmen into the highways brought together all
ὅσους εὗρον, πονηρούς τε καὶ ἀγαθούς· καὶ ἐπλήσθη ὁ
as many as they found, [2]evil [1]both and good; and [4]became [5]full [1]the
[c]γάμος‖ ἀνακειμένων. 11 εἰσελθὼν.δὲ ὁ βασιλεὺς θεάσα-
[2]wedding [3]feast of guests. And [3]coming [4]in [1]the [2]king to see
σθαι τοὺς ἀνακειμένους εἶδεν ἐκεῖ ἄνθρωπον οὐκ ἐνδεδυμένον
the guests beheld there a man not clothed
ἔνδυμα γάμου· 12 καὶ λέγει αὐτῷ, Ἑταῖρε, πῶς
with a garment of [the] wedding feast; and he says to him, Friend, how
εἰσῆλθες ὧδε μὴ ἔχων ἔνδυμα γάμου; Ὁ.δὲ
didst thou enter here not having a garment of [the] wedding feast? But he
ἐφιμώθη. 13 τότε [d]εἶπεν ὁ βασιλεὺς‖ τοῖς διακόνοις, Δήσαν-
was speechless. Then said the king to the servants, Having
τες αὐτοῦ πόδας καὶ χεῖρας [e]ἄρατε αὐτὸν καὶ‖ ἐκβάλετε [f]
bound his feet and hands take away him and cast out [him]
εἰς τὸ σκότος τὸ ἐξώτερον· ἐκεῖ ἔσται ὁ κλαυθμὸς καὶ ὁ
into the darkness the outer: there shall be the weeping and the
βρυγμὸς τῶν ὀδόντων. 14 πολλοὶ.γάρ εἰσιν κλητοί, ὀλίγοι.δὲ
gnashing of the teeth. For many are called, but few
ἐκλεκτοί.
chosen.

15 Τότε πορευθέντες οἱ Φαρισαῖοι συμβούλιον ἔλαβον ὅπως
Then having gone the Pharisees [2]counsel [1]took how
αὐτὸν παγιδεύσωσιν ἐν λόγῳ. 16 καὶ ἀποστέλλουσιν αὐτῷ
him they might ensnare in discourse. And they send to him
τοὺς.μαθητὰς.αὐτῶν μετὰ τῶν Ἡρωδιανῶν, [g]λέγοντες,‖ Διδά-
their disciples with the Herodians, saying, Teacher,
σκαλε, οἴδαμεν ὅτι ἀληθὴς εἶ, καὶ τὴν ὁδὸν τοῦ θεοῦ ἐν ἀληθείᾳ
we know that true thou art, and the way of God in truth

---

[w] ἡτοίμακα I have prepared LTTrA. [x] ὅς LTTrA. [y] ὅς LTTrA. [z] ἐπὶ LTTrA.
[a] ὁ δὲ βασιλεὺς ἀκούσας L; ὁ δὲ βασιλεὺς TTrA; καὶ ἀκούσας ὁ βασ. W. [b] ἐὰν LTTrAW.
[c] νυμφὼν bridechamber T. [d] ὁ.βασιλεὺς εἶπεν LTTrA. [e] — ἄρατε αὐτὸν καὶ LTTrA.
[f] + αὐτὸν him LTTrA. [g] λέγοντας LTTr.

διδάσκεις, καὶ οὐ μέλει σοι περὶ οὐδενός, οὐ.γὰρ βλέπεις
teachest, and there is care to thee about no one, for [3]not [1]thou [2]lookest
εἰς πρόσωπον ἀνθρώπων· 17 [h]εἰπὲ[‖] οὖν ἡμῖν, τί [*]σοι
on [the] appearance of men; tell therefore us, what [2]thou
δοκεῖ; ἔξεστιν δοῦναι κῆνσον Καίσαρι ἢ οὔ; 18 Γνοὺς.δὲ
[1]thinkest? Is it lawful to give tribute to Cæsar or not? But [2]knowing
ὁ Ἰησοῦς τὴν.πονηρίαν.αὐτῶν εἶπεν, Τί με πειράζετε, ὑπο-
[1]Jesus their wickedness said, Why me do ye tempt, hypo-
κριταί; 19 ἐπιδείξατέ μοι τὸ νόμισμα τοῦ κήνσου. Οἱ.δὲ
crites? Shew me the coin of the tribute. And they
προσήνεγκαν αὐτῷ δηνάριον. 20 καὶ λέγει αὐτοῖς[i], Τίνος
presented to him a denarius. And he says to them, Whose [is]
ἡ.εἰκὼν.αὕτη καὶ ἡ ἐπιγραφή; 21 Λέγουσιν [k]αὐτῷ,[‖] Καίσαρος.
this image and the inscription? They say to him, Cæsar's.
Τότε λέγει αὐτοῖς, Ἀπόδοτε οὖν τὰ Καίσαρος Καίσαρι,
Then he says to them, Render then the things of Cæsar to Cæsar,
καὶ τὰ τοῦ θεοῦ τῷ θεῷ. 22 Καὶ ἀκούσαντες ἐθαύμασαν·
and the things of God to God. And having heard they wondered;
καὶ ἀφέντες αὐτὸν [l]ἀπῆλθον.[‖]
and leaving him went away.

23 Ἐν ἐκείνῃ τῇ ἡμέρᾳ προσῆλθον αὐτῷ Σαδδουκαῖοι, [m]οἱ[‖]
On that day came to him Sadducees, who
λέγοντες μὴ.εἶναι ἀνάστασιν, καὶ ἐπηρώτησαν αὐτόν, 24 λέ-
say there is not a resurrection, and they questioned him, say-
γοντες, Διδάσκαλε, [n]Μωσῆς[‖] εἶπεν, Ἐάν τις ἀποθάνῃ μὴ
ing, Teacher, Moses said, If any one should die not
ἔχων τέκνα, [o]ἐπιγαμβρεύσει ὁ.ἀδελφὸς.αὐτοῦ τὴν γυναῖκα
having children, [3]shall [4]marry [1]his [2]brother [6]wife
αὐτοῦ, καὶ ἀναστήσει σπέρμα τῷ.ἀδελφῷ.αὐτοῦ. 25 Ἦσαν.δὲ
[5]his, and shall raise up seed to his brother. Now there were
παρ' ἡμῖν ἑπτὰ ἀδελφοί· καὶ ὁ πρῶτος [p]γαμήσας[‖] ἐτελεύτη-
with us seven brothers; and the first having married died,
σεν, καὶ μὴ ἔχων σπέρμα ἀφῆκεν τὴν.γυναῖκα.αὐτοῦ τῷ
and not having seed left his wife
ἀδελφῷ.αὐτοῦ. 26 ὁμοίως καὶ ὁ δεύτερος, καὶ ὁ τρίτος,
to his brother. In like manner also the second, and the third,
ἕως τῶν ἑπτά. 27 ὕστερον.δὲ πάντων ἀπέθανεν [q]καὶ[‖] ἡ γυνή.
unto the seven. And last of all died also the woman.
28 ἐν τῇ [r]οὖν ἀναστάσει[‖] τίνος τῶν ἑπτὰ ἔσται γυνή;
[2]In [3]the [1]therefore resurrection of which of the seven shall she be wife?
πάντες.γὰρ ἔσχον αὐτήν. 29 Ἀποκριθεὶς.δὲ ὁ Ἰησοῦς εἶπεν
for all had her. And answering Jesus said
αὐτοῖς, Πλανᾶσθε, μὴ εἰδότες τὰς γραφάς, μηδὲ τὴν δύναμιν
to them, Ye err, not knowing the scriptures, nor the power
τοῦ θεοῦ. 30 ἐν.γὰρ τῇ ἀναστάσει οὔτε γαμοῦσιν οὔτε
of God. For in the resurrection neither do they marry nor
[s]ἐκγαμίζονται,[‖] ἀλλ' ὡς ἄγγελοι [t]τοῦ[‖] [v]θεοῦ[‖] ἐν [w] οὐρανῷ
are given in marriage, but as angels of God in heaven
εἰσιν. 31 περὶ.δὲ τῆς ἀναστάσεως τῶν νεκρῶν, οὐκ.ἀνέγνωτε
they are. But concerning the resurrection of the dead, have ye not read
τὸ ῥηθὲν ὑμῖν ὑπὸ τοῦ θεοῦ, λέγοντος, 32 Ἐγώ εἰμι
that which was spoken to you by God, saying, I am

thou for any *man*: for
thou regardest not the
person of men. 17 Tell
us therefore, What
thinkest thou? Is it
lawful to give tribute
unto Cæsar, or not?
18 But Jesus perceived
their wickedness, and
said, Why tempt ye
me, *ye* hypocrites?
19 Shew me the tribute
money. And they
brought unto him a
penny. 20 And he
saith unto them, Whose
is this image and su-
perscription? 21 They
say unto him, Cæsar's.
Then saith he unto
them, Render therefore
unto Cæsar the things
which are Cæsar's;
and unto God the
things that are God's.
22 When they had
heard *these words*,
they marvelled, and
left him, and went
their way.

23 The same day
came to him the Sad-
ducees, which say that
there is no resurrec-
tion, and asked him,
24 saying, Master, Mo-
ses said, If a man die,
having no children,
his brother shall marry
his wife, and raise up
seed unto his brother.
25 Now there were with
us seven brethren: and
the first, when he had
married a wife, de-
ceased, and, having no
issue, left his wife unto
his brother: 26 like-
wise the second also,
and the third, unto the
seventh. 27 And last
of all the woman died
also. 28 Therefore in
the resurrection whose
wife shall she be of the
seven? for they all
had her. 29 Jesus an-
swered and said unto
them, Ye do err, not
knowing the scrip-
tures, nor the power of
God. 30 For in the
resurrection they nei-
ther marry, nor are
given in marriage, but
are as the angels of
God in heaven. 31 But
as touching the resur-
rection of the dead,
have ye not read that
which was spoken unto
you by God, saying,
32 I am the God of

[h] εἰπὸν T. [i] + ὁ Ἰησοῦς Jesus (says) LT. [k] — αὐτῷ T[A]. [l] ἀπῆλθαν LTTrA.
[m] — οἱ (*read* saying) LTTrA. [n] Μωϋσῆς LTTrAW. [o] + ἵνα that L. [p] γήμας LTTrA.
[q] — καὶ T[Tr]A. [r] ἀναστάσει οὖν LTTrA. [s] γαμίζονται LTTrA. [t] — τοῦ LTTrA.
[v] — θεοῦ LTr[A]. [w] + τῷ the LTTrA.

Abraham, and the God
of Isaac, and the God
of Jacob? God is not
the God of the dead,
but of the living.
33 And when the mul-
titude heard *this*, they
were astonished at his
doctrine.

34 But when the
Pharisees had heard
that he had put the
Sadducees to silence,
they were gathered
together. 35 Then one
of them, *which was* a
lawyer, asked *him a
question*, tempting
him, and saying,
36 Master, which *is*
the great command-
ment in the law?
37 Jesus said unto him,
Thou shalt love the
Lord thy God with all
thy heart, and with all
thy soul, and with all
thy mind. 38 This is
the first and great com-
mandment. 39 And the
second *is* like unto it,
Thou shalt love thy
neighbour as thyself.
40 On these two com-
mandments hang all
the law and the pro-
phets.

41 While the Pha-
risees were gathered
together, Jesus asked
them, 42 saying, What
think ye of Christ?
whose son is he? They
say unto him, *The Son*
of David. 43 He saith
unto them, How then
doth David in spirit
call him Lord, saying,
44 The LORD said unto
my Lord, Sit thou on
my right hand, till I
make thine enemies
thy footstool? 45 If
David then call him
Lord, how is he his
son? 46 And no man
was able to answer
him a word, neither
durst any *man* from
that day forth ask
him any more *ques-
tions*.

XXIII. Then spake
Jesus to the multitude,
and to his disciples,
2 saying, The scribes
and the Pharisees sit
in Moses' seat: 3 all
therefore whatsoever
they bid you observe,

ὁ θεὸς Ἀβραὰμ καὶ ὁ θεὸς Ἰσαὰκ καὶ ὁ θεὸς Ἰακώβ; οὐκ
the God of Abraham and the God of Isaac and the God of Jacob? [3]Not
ἔστιν [x]ὁ θεὸς‖ [y]θεὸς‖ νεκρῶν, ἀλλὰ ζώντων. 33 Καὶ ἀκού-
[2]is [1]God God of [the] dead, but of [the] living. And having
σαντες οἱ ὄχλοι ἐξεπλήσσοντο ἐπὶ τῇ.διδαχῇ.αὐτοῦ.
heard, the crowds were astonished at his teaching.

34 Οἱ.δὲ Φαρισαῖοι ἀκούσαντες ὅτι ἐφίμωσεν τοὺς Σαδ-
But the Pharisees, having heard that he had silenced the Sad-
δουκαίους, συνήχθησαν ἐπὶ.τὸ.αὐτό, 35 καὶ ἐπηρώτησεν
ducees, were gathered together, and [9]questioned [[10]him]
εἷς ἐξ αὐτῶν νομικός, πειράζων αὐτόν, [z]καὶ λέγων,‖
[1]one [2]of [3]them [4]a [5]doctor [6]of [7]the [8]law, tempting him, and saying,
36 Διδάσκαλε, ποία ἐντολὴ μεγάλη ἐν τῷ νόμῳ;
Teacher, which [4]commandment [[1]is [2]the] [3]great in the law?
37 [a]Ὁ.δὲ.Ἰησοῦς εἶπεν αὐτῷ,‖ Ἀγαπήσεις κύριον τὸν θεόν
And Jesus said to him, Thou shalt love [the] Lord [2]God
σου ἐν ὅλῃ [b]τῇ‖.καρδίᾳ σου, καὶ ἐν ὅλῃ τῇ.ψυχῇ.σου, καὶ ἐν
[1]thy with all thy heart, and with all thy soul, and with
ὅλῃ τῇ.διανοίᾳ.σου. 38 αὕτη ἐστὶν [c]πρώτη καὶ μεγάλη‖
all thy mind. This is [the] first and great
ἐντολή. 39 δευτέρα.[d]δὲ‖ ὁμοία αὐτῇ, Ἀγαπήσεις τὸν
commandment. And [the] second [is] like it, Thou shalt love
πλησίον.σου ὡς σεαυτόν. 40 ἐν ταύταις ταῖς δυσὶν ἐντολαῖς
thy neighbour as thyself. On these two commandments
ὅλος ὁ νόμος [e]καὶ οἱ προφῆται κρέμανται.‖
all the law and the prophets hang.

41 Συνηγμένων.δὲ τῶν Φαρισαίων ἐπηρώτησεν
But [3]having [4]been [5]assembled [6]together [1]the [2]Pharisees [8]questioned
αὐτοὺς ὁ Ἰησοῦς, 42 λέγων, Τί ὑμῖν δοκεῖ περὶ τοῦ χριστοῦ;
[9]them [7]Jesus, saying, What [2]ye [1]think concerning the Christ?
τίνος υἱός ἐστιν; Λέγουσιν αὐτῷ, Τοῦ.[f]Δαβίδ.‖ 43 Λέγει
of whom [3]son [1]is [2]he? They say to him, Of David. He says
αὐτοῖς, Πῶς οὖν [f]Δαβὶδ‖ ἐν πνεύματι [g]κύριον αὐτὸν καλεῖ;‖
to them, How then [2]David [3]in [4]spirit [7]Lord [6]him [1]does [5]call?
λέγων, 44 Εἶπεν [h]ὁ‖ κύριος τῷ.κυρίῳ.μου, Κάθου ἐκ δεξιῶν.μου
saying, [3]Said [1]the [2]Lord to my Lord, Sit on my right hand
ἕως.ἂν θῶ τοὺς.ἐχθρούς.σου [i]ὑποπόδιον‖ τῶν.ποδῶν.σου.
until I place thine enemies [as] a footstool for thy feet.
45 Εἰ οὖν [f]Δαβὶδ‖ καλεῖ αὐτὸν κύριον, πῶς υἱὸς.αὐτοῦ
If therefore David calls him Lord, how his son
ἐστιν; 46 Καὶ οὐδεὶς ἐδύνατο [k]αὐτῷ ἀποκριθῆναι‖ λόγον,
is he? And no one was able him to answer a word,
οὐδὲ ἐτόλμησέν τις ἀπ' ἐκείνης τῆς ἡμέρας ἐπερωτῆσαι αὐτὸν
nor dared anyone from that day to question him
οὐκέτι.
any more (*lit.* no more).

23 Τότε ὁ Ἰησοῦς ἐλάλησεν τοῖς ὄχλοις καὶ τοῖς.μαθηταῖς
Then Jesus spoke to the crowds and to [2]disciples
αὐτοῦ, 2 λέγων, Ἐπὶ τῆς [l]Μωσέως‖ καθέδρας ἐκάθισαν οἱ
[1]his, saying, On the [2]of [3]Moses [1]seat have sat down the
γραμματεῖς καὶ οἱ Φαρισαῖοι· 3 πάντα οὖν ὅσα.[m]ἂν‖ εἴπω-
scribes and the Pharisees; all things therefore whatever they may

[x] — ὁ θεὸς (*read* he is not) T. [y] — θεὸς LTr[A]. [z] — καὶ λέγων LTTr. [a] ὁ δὲ Ἰησοῦς ἔφη αὐτῷ G; ὁ δὲ ἔφη αὐτῷ LTTrA; ἔφη αὐτῷ Ἰησοῦς W. [b] [τῇ] A. [c] ἡ μεγάλη καὶ πρώτη LTTrAW. [d] — δὲ and T. [e] κρέμαται καὶ οἱ προφῆται LTTrAW. [f] Δαυΐδ GW; Δαυείδ LTTrA. [g] καλεῖ αὐτὸν κύριον LTrA; καλεῖ κύριον αὐτὸν T. [h] — ὁ (*read* [the]) LTTrA. [i] ὑποκάτω under (thy feet) LTTrA. [k] ἀποκριθῆναι αὐτῷ LTTrA. [l] Μωϋσέως LTTrAW. [m] ἐὰν TW.

σιν ὑμῖν [n]τηρεῖν,‖ [o]τηρεῖτε καὶ ποιεῖτε·‖ κατὰ.δὲ τὰ.ἔργα.αὐτῶν
tell you to keep, keep and do. But after their works
μὴ.ποιεῖτε λέγουσιν.γὰρ καὶ οὐ.ποιοῦσιν. 4 δεσμεύουσιν [p]γὰρ‖
do not; for they say and do not. [2]They [3]bind [1]for
φορτία βαρέα [q]καὶ δυσβάστακτα,‖ καὶ ἐπιτιθέασιν ἐπὶ τοὺς
burdens heavy and hard to bear, and lay [them] on the
ὤμους τῶν ἀνθρώπων· [r]τῷ δὲ.δακτύλῳ.αὐτῶν‖ οὐ.θέλουσιν
shoulders of men, but with their own finger they will not
κινῆσαι αὐτά. 5 πάντα.δὲ τὰ.ἔργα.αὐτῶν ποιοῦσιν πρὸς τὸ
move them. And all their works they do to
θεαθῆναι τοῖς ἀνθρώποις. πλατύνουσιν [s]δὲ‖ τὰ φυλακτήρια
be seen by men. [2]They [3]make [4]broad [1]and [6]phylacteries
αὐτῶν, καὶ μεγαλύνουσιν τὰ κράσπεδα [t]τῶν.ἱματίων.αὐτῶν·‖
[5]their, and enlarge the borders of their garments,
6 φιλοῦσίν [v]τε‖ τὴν πρωτοκλισίαν ἐν τοῖς δείπνοις, καὶ τὰς
[2]love [1]and the first place in the suppers, and the
πρωτοκαθεδρίας ἐν ταῖς συναγωγαῖς, 7 καὶ τοὺς ἀσπασμοὺς ἐν
first seats in the synagogues, and the salutations in
ταῖς ἀγοραῖς, καὶ καλεῖσθαι ὑπὸ τῶν ἀνθρώπων [w]ῥαββί, ῥαββί·‖
the market-places, and to be called by men Rabbi, Rabbi.
8 ὑμεῖς.δὲ μὴ.κληθῆτε [x]ῥαββί·‖ εἷς.γάρ ἐστιν ὑμῶν ὁ [y]καθηγητής,‖
But [3]ye [1]be [2]not called Rabbi; for one is your leader,
[z]ὁ χριστός·‖ πάντες.δὲ ὑμεῖς ἀδελφοί ἐστε. 9 καὶ πατέρα μὴ
the Christ, and all ye brethren are. And [6]father [2]not
καλέσητε ὑμῶν ἐπὶ τῆς γῆς· εἷς.γάρ ἐστιν [a]ὁ.πατὴρ.ὑμῶν,‖
[1]call [5]your [[3]any [4]one] on the earth; for one is your father,
[b]ὁ ἐν τοῖς οὐρανοῖς.‖ 10 μηδὲ κληθῆτε καθηγηταί· [c]εἷς.γὰρ
who [is] in the heavens. Neither be called leaders; for one
ὑμῶν ἐστιν ὁ καθηγητής,‖ ὁ χριστός. 11 ὁ.δὲ μείζων ὑμῶν
[2]your [1]is leader, the Christ. But the greater of you
ἔσται ὑμῶν διάκονος. 12 ὅστις.δὲ ὑψώσει ἑαυτὸν ταπεινωθή-
shall be your servant. And whosoever will exalt himself shall be
σεται· καὶ ὅστις ταπεινώσει ἑαυτὸν ὑψωθήσεται.
humbled; and whosoever will humble himself shall be exalted.

13 (14) [d]Οὐαὶ.[e]δὲ‖ ὑμῖν, γραμματεῖς καὶ Φαρισαῖοι, ὑποκριταί,
But woe to you, scribes and Pharisees, hypocrites,
ὅτι κατεσθίετε τὰς οἰκίας τῶν χηρῶν, καὶ προφάσει μακρὰ
for ye devour the houses of widows, and as a pretext [2]at [3]great [4]length
προσευχόμενοι· διὰ τοῦτο λήψεσθε περισσότερον κρίμα.‖
[1]praying. Because of this ye shall receive more abundant judgment.
14 (13) Οὐαὶ[f] ὑμῖν, γραμματεῖς καὶ Φαρισαῖοι, ὑποκριταί, ὅτι
Woe to you, scribes and Pharisees, hypocrites, for
κλείετε τὴν βασιλείαν τῶν οὐρανῶν ἔμπροσθεν τῶν ἀνθρώπων·
ye shut up the kingdom of the heavens before men;
ὑμεῖς.γὰρ οὐκ.εἰσέρχεσθε, οὐδὲ τοὺς εἰσερχομένους ἀφίετε
for ye do not enter, nor even those who are entering do ye suffer
εἰσελθεῖν. 15 Οὐαὶ ὑμῖν, γραμματεῖς καὶ Φαρισαῖοι, ὑποκριταί,
to enter. Woe to you, scribes and Pharisees, hypocrites,
ὅτι περιάγετε τὴν θάλασσαν καὶ τὴν ξηρὰν ποιῆσαι ἕνα
for ye go about the sea and the dry [land] to make one

that observe and do; but do not ye after their works: for they say, and do not. 4 For they bind heavy burdens and grievous to be borne, and lay *them* on men's shoulders; but they *themselves* will not move them with one of their fingers. 5 But all their works they do for to be seen of men: they make broad their phylacteries, and enlarge the borders of their garments, 6 and love the uppermost rooms at feasts, and the chief seats in the synagogues, 7 and greetings in the markets, and to be called of men, Rabbi, Rabbi. 8 But be not ye called Rabbi: for one is your Master, *even* Christ; and all ye are brethren. 9 And call no *man* your father upon the earth: for one is your Father, which is in heaven. 10 Neither be ye called masters: for one is your Master, *even* Christ. 11 But he that is greatest among you shall be your servant. 12 And whosoever shall exalt himself shall be abased; and he that shall humble himself shall be exalted.

13 But woe unto you, scribes and Pharisees, hypocrites! for ye shut up the kingdom of heaven against men: for ye neither go in *yourselves*, neither suffer ye them that are entering to go in. 14 Woe unto you, scribes and Pharisees, hypocrites! for ye devour widows' houses, and for a pretence make long prayer: therefore ye shall receive the greater damnation. 15 Woe unto you, scribes and Pharisees, hypocrites! for ye compass sea and land to make one pros-

[n] — τηρεῖν LTTrA. [o] ποιήσατε καὶ τηρεῖτε LTTrA. [p] δὲ but LTTrA. [q] — καὶ δυσβάστακτα T[Tr]A. [r] αὐτοὶ δὲ τῷ δακτύλῳ αὐτῶν but they themselves with their finger LTTrA. [s] γὰρ for LTTrA. [t] — τῶν ἱματίων αὐτῶν LTTrA. [v] δὲ LTTrA. [w] ῥαββί LTr; ῥαββεί T; ῥαββὶ [ῥαββί] A. [x] ῥαββεί T. [y] διδάσκαλος teacher LTTrAW. [z] — ὁ χριστός GLTTrAW. [a] ὑμῶν ὁ πατὴρ LTTr. [b] ὁ οὐράνιος the heavenly LTTrA. [c] ὅτι καθηγητὴς ὑμῶν ἐστιν εἷς LTTrA. [d] *Verse* 13 *placed after* 14 E; — *verse* 13 LTTrA. [e] — δὲ but E. [f] + δὲ but (woe) ELTTrA.

elyte, and when he is
made, ye make him
twofold more the child
of hell than your-
selves. 16 Woe unto
you, *ye* blind guides,
which say, Whosoever
shall swear by the tem-
ple, it is nothing; but
whosoever shall swear
by the gold of the tem-
ple, he is a debtor!
17 *Ye* fools and blind:
for whether is greater,
the gold, or the temple
that sanctifieth the
gold? 18 And, Who-
soever shall swear by
the altar, it is nothing;
but whosoever sweareth
by the gift that is
upon it, he is guilty.
19 *Ye* fools and blind:
for whether *is* greater,
the gift, or the altar
that sanctifieth the
gift? 20 Whoso there-
fore shall swear by the
altar, sweareth by it,
and by all things there-
on. 21 And whoso shall
swear by the temple,
sweareth by it, and
by him that dwelleth
therein. 22 And he that
shall swear by heaven,
sweareth by the throne
of God, and by him
that sitteth thereon.
23 Woe unto you,
scribes and Pharisees,
hypocrites! for ye pay
tithe of mint and anise
and cummin, and have
omitted the weightier
matters of the law,
judgment, mercy, and
faith: these ought ye
to have done, and not
to leave the other un-
done. 24 *Ye* blind
guides, which strain at
a gnat, and swallow a
camel. 25 Woe unto
you, scribes and Pha-
risees, hypocrites! for
ye make clean the out-
side of the cup and of
the platter, but within
they are full of ex-
tortion and excess.
26 *Thou* blind Pha-
risee, cleanse first that
which is within the cup
and platter, that the
outside of them may
be clean also. 27 Woe
unto you, scribes and
Pharisees, hypocrites!
for ye are like unto
whited sepulchres,
which indeed appear
beautiful outward, but
are within full of dead
men's bones, and of all

προσήλυτον, καὶ ὅταν γένηται, ποιεῖτε αὐτὸν υἱὸν γε-
proselyte, and when he has become [so], ye make him a son of Ge-
έννης διπλότερον ὑμῶν. 16 Οὐαὶ ὑμῖν, ὁδηγοὶ τυφλοί, οἱ
henna twofold more than yourselves. Woe to you, [2]guides [1]blind, who
λέγοντες, Ὃς.ἂν ὀμόσῃ ἐν τῷ ναῷ, οὐδέν ἐστιν· ὃς.δ᾽.ἂν
say, Whoever shall swear by the temple, nothing it is; but whoever
ὀμόσῃ ἐν τῷ χρυσῷ τοῦ ναοῦ, ὀφείλει. 17 μωροὶ καὶ τυφλοί·
shall swear by the gold of the temple, is a debtor. Fools and blind,
[g]τίς‖.γὰρ [h]μείζων‖ ἐστίν, ὁ χρυσός, ἢ ὁ ναὸς ὁ [i]ἁγιάζων‖
for which [2]greater [1]is, the gold, or the temple which sanctifies
τὸν χρυσόν; 18 καί, Ὃς.[k]ἐὰν‖ ὀμόσῃ ἐν τῷ θυσιαστηρίῳ,
the gold? And, Whoever shall swear by the altar,
οὐδέν ἐστιν· ὃς.δ᾽.ἂν ὀμόσῃ ἐν τῷ δώρῳ τῷ ἐπάνω αὐτοῦ,
nothing it is; but whoever shall swear by the gift that [is] upon it,
ὀφείλει. 19 [l]μωροὶ καὶ‖ τυφλοί, τί γὰρ μεῖζον, τὸ δῶρον,
is a debtor. Fools and blind, for which [is] greater, the gift,
ἢ τὸ θυσιαστήριον τὸ ἁγιάζον τὸ δῶρον; 20 ὁ οὖν ὀμόσας
or the altar which sanctifies the gift? He [2]that [1]therefore swears
ἐν τῷ θυσιαστηρίῳ ὀμνύει ἐν αὐτῷ καὶ ἐν πᾶσιν τοῖς ἐπάνω
by the altar swears by it and by all things that [are] upon
αὐτοῦ· 21 καὶ ὁ ὀμόσας ἐν τῷ ναῷ ὀμνύει ἐν αὐτῷ καὶ ἐν
it. And he that swears by the temple swears by it and by
τῷ [m]κατοικοῦντι‖ αὐτόν· 22 καὶ ὁ ὀμόσας ἐν τῷ οὐρανῷ
him who dwells in it. And he that swears by the heaven
ὀμνύει ἐν τῷ θρόνῳ τοῦ θεοῦ καὶ ἐν τῷ καθημένῳ ἐπάνω
swears by the throne of God and by him who sits upon
αὐτοῦ. 23 Οὐαὶ ὑμῖν, γραμματεῖς καὶ Φαρισαῖοι, ὑποκριταί, ὅτι
it. Woe to you, scribes and Pharisees, hypocrites, for
ἀποδεκατοῦτε τὸ ἡδύοσμον καὶ τὸ ἄνηθον καὶ τὸ κύμινον, καὶ
ye pay tithes of the mint and the anise and the cummin, and
ἀφήκατε τὰ βαρύτερα τοῦ νόμου, τὴν κρίσιν καὶ [n]τὸν
ye have left aside the weightier [matters] of the law, judgment, and
ἔλεον‖ καὶ τὴν πίστιν· ταῦτα[o] ἔδει ποιῆσαι, κἀκεῖνα μὴ
mercy and faith: these it behoved [you] to do, and those not
[p]ἀφιέναι.‖ 24 ὁδηγοὶ τυφλοί, [q]οἱ‖ διϋλίζοντες τὸν κώνωπα,
to be leaving aside. [2]Guides [1]blind, who filter out the gnat,
τὴν.δὲ κάμηλον καταπίνοντες. 25 Οὐαὶ ὑμῖν, γραμματεῖς καὶ
but the camel swallow. Woe to you, scribes and
Φαρισαῖοι, ὑποκριταί, ὅτι καθαρίζετε τὸ ἔξωθεν τοῦ ποτηρίου
Pharisees, hypocrites, for ye cleanse the outside of the cup
καὶ τῆς παροψίδος, ἔσωθεν.δὲ γέμουσιν [r]ἐξ‖ ἁρπαγῆς καὶ
and of the dish, but within they are full of plunder and
[s]ἀκρασίας.‖ 26 Φαρισαῖε τυφλέ, καθάρισον πρῶτον τὸ ἐντὸς
incontinence. [2]Pharisee [1]blind, cleanse first the inside
τοῦ ποτηρίου [t]καὶ τῆς παροψίδος,‖ ἵνα γένηται καὶ τὸ ἐκτὸς
of the cup and of the dish, that [6]may [7]become [5]also [1]the [2]outside
[v]αὐτῶν‖ καθαρόν. 27 Οὐαὶ ὑμῖν, γραμματεῖς καὶ Φαρισαῖοι,
[3]of [4]them clean. Woe to you, scribes and Pharisees,
ὑποκριταί, ὅτι [w]παρομοιάζετε‖ τάφοις κεκονιαμένοις, οἵτινες
hypocrites, for ye are like [2]sepulchres [1]whited, which
ἔξωθεν μὲν φαίνονται ὡραῖοι, ἔσωθεν.δὲ γέμουσιν ὀστέων
outwardly indeed appear beautiful, but within are full of bones

---

[g] τί L. [h] μεῖζόν L. [i] ἁγιάσας sanctified LTTrA. [k] ἂν LTTrA. [l] — μωροὶ καὶ [L]TTrA. [m] κατοικήσαντι dwelt in GTrAW. [n] τὸ ἔλεος LTTrA. [o] + δὲ but GLTrAW. [p] ἀφεῖναι to leave aside LTTrA. [q] — οἱ (*read* filtering out.... swallowing) LTrA. [r] — ἐξ L [Tr]. [s] ἀδικίας unrighteousness GW. [t] — καὶ τῆς παροψίδος TA. [v] αὐτοῦ of it LTTrA. [w] ὁμοιάζετε LTr.

νεκρῶν καὶ πάσης ἀκαθαρσίας. 28 οὕτως καὶ ὑμεῖς ἔξωθεν
of [the] dead and of all uncleanness. Thus also ye outwardly
μὲν φαίνεσθε τοῖς ἀνθρώποις δίκαιοι, ἔσωθεν.δὲ [x]μεστοί ἐστε[‖]
indeed appear to men righteous, but within [2]full [1]are
ὑποκρίσεως καὶ ἀνομίας. 29 Οὐαὶ ὑμῖν, γραμματεῖς καὶ Φα-
of hypocrisy and lawlessness. Woe to you, scribes and Pha-
ρισαῖοι, ὑποκριταί, ὅτι οἰκοδομεῖτε τοὺς τάφους τῶν προφητῶν,
risees, hypocrites, for ye build the sepulchres of the prophets,
καὶ κοσμεῖτε τὰ μνημεῖα τῶν δικαίων, 30 καὶ λέγετε, Εἰ [y]ἦμεν[‖]
and adorn the tombs of the righteous, and ye say, If we had been
ἐν ταῖς ἡμέραις τῶν.πατέρων.ἡμῶν, οὐκ.ἂν.[y]ἦμεν[‖] [z]κοινωνοὶ
in the days of our fathers we would not have been partakers
αὐτῶν[‖] ἐν τῷ αἵματι τῶν προφητῶν. 31 ὥστε μαρτυρεῖτε
with them in the blood of the prophets. So that ye bear witness
ἑαυτοῖς, ὅτι υἱοί ἐστε τῶν φονευσάντων τοὺς προφήτας·
to yourselves, that sons ye are of those who murdered the prophets;
32 καὶ ὑμεῖς πληρώσατε τὸ μέτρον τῶν.πατέρων.ὑμῶν. 33 ὄφεις,
and ye, fill ye up the measure of your fathers. Serpents,
γεννήματα ἐχιδνῶν, πῶς φύγητε ἀπὸ τῆς κρίσεως τῆς γε-
offspring of vipers, how shall ye escape from the judgment of Ge-
έννης; 34 Διὰ τοῦτο, ἰδού, ἐγὼ ἀποστέλλω πρὸς ὑμᾶς προ-
henna? Because of this, behold, I send to you pro-
φήτας καὶ σοφοὺς καὶ γραμματεῖς· [a]καὶ[‖] ἐξ αὐτῶν ἀπο-
phets and wise [men] and scribes; and [some] of them ye will
κτενεῖτε καὶ σταυρώσετε, καὶ ἐξ αὐτῶν μαστιγώσετε ἐν ταῖς
kill and crucify, and [some] of them ye will scourge in
συναγωγαῖς.ὑμῶν, καὶ διώξετε ἀπὸ πόλεως εἰς πόλιν·
your synagogues, and will persecute from city to city;
35 ὅπως ἔλθῃ ἐφ' ὑμᾶς πᾶν αἷμα δίκαιον [b]ἐκχυνόμενον[‖]
so that should come upon you all [the] [2]blood [1]righteous poured out
ἐπὶ τῆς γῆς, ἀπὸ [c]τοῦ[‖] αἵματος Ἄβελ τοῦ δικαίου, ἕως τοῦ
upon the earth from the blood of Abel the righteous, to the
αἵματος Ζαχαρίου υἱοῦ Βαραχίου, ὃν ἐφονεύσατε μεταξὺ τοῦ
blood of Zacharias son of Barachias, whom ye murdered between the
ναοῦ καὶ τοῦ θυσιαστηρίου. 36 ἀμὴν λέγω ὑμῖν, [d]ἥξει
temple and the altar. Verily I say to you, [4]shall [5]come
[e]ταῦτα πάντα[‖] ἐπὶ τὴν.γενεὰν.ταύτην. 37 Ἱερουσαλήμ,
[2]these [3]things [1]all upon this generation. Jerusalem,
Ἱερουσαλήμ, ἡ ἀποκτείνουσα τοὺς προφήτας καὶ λιθοβολοῦσα
Jerusalem, who killest the prophets and stonest
τοὺς ἀπεσταλμένους πρὸς αὐτήν, ποσάκις ἠθέλησα ἐπισυν-
those who have been sent to her, how often would I have gath-
αγαγεῖν τὰ.τέκνα.σου, ὃν.τρόπον [f]ἐπισυνάγει ὄρνις[‖] τὰ
ered together thy children, in the way [3]gathers [4]together [1]a [2]hen
νοσσία.[g]ἑαυτῆς[‖] ὑπὸ τὰς πτέρυγας[h], καὶ οὐκ.ἠθελήσατε;
her brood under [her] wings, and ye would not!
38 ἰδού, ἀφίεται ὑμῖν ὁ.οἶκος.ὑμῶν [i]ἔρημος.[‖] 39 λέγω.γὰρ
Behold, is left to you your house desolate; for I say
ὑμῖν, Οὐ.μή με ἴδητε ἀπ'.ἄρτι ἕως.ἂν εἴπητε, Εὐλογη-
to you, In no wise me shall ye see henceforth until ye say, Bless-
μένος ὁ ἐρχόμενος ἐν ὀνόματι κυρίου.
ed [is] he who comes in [the] name of [the] Lord.

uncleanness. 28 Even so ye also outwardly appear righteous unto men, but within ye are full of hypocrisy and iniquity. 29 Woe unto you, scribes and Pharisees, hypocrites! because ye build the tombs of the prophets, and garnish the sepulchres of the righteous, 30 and say, If we had been in the days of our fathers, we would not have been partakers with them in the blood of the prophets. 31 Wherefore ye be witnesses unto yourselves, that ye are the children of them which killed the prophets. 32 Fill ye up then the measure of your fathers. 33 *Ye* serpents, *ye* generation of vipers, how can ye escape the damnation of hell? 34 Wherefore, behold, I send unto you prophets, and wise men, and scribes: and *some* of them ye shall kill and crucify; and *some* of them shall ye scourge in your synagogues, and persecute *them* from city to city: 35 that upon you may come all the righteous blood shed upon the earth, from the blood of righteous Abel unto the blood of Zacharias son of Barachias, whom ye slew between the temple and the altar. 36 Verily I say unto you, All these things shall come upon this generation. 37 O Jerusalem, Jerusalem, *thou* that killest the prophets, and stonest them which are sent unto thee, how often would I have gathered thy children together, even as a hen gathereth her chickens under *her* wings, and ye would not! 38 Behold, your house is left unto you desolate. 39 For I say unto you, Ye shall not see me henceforth, till ye shall say, Blessed *is* he that cometh in the name of the Lord.

---

[x] ἐστε μεστοὶ LTTrA. [y] ἤμεθα GLTTrAW. [z] αὐτῶν κοινωνοὶ LTrA. [a] — καὶ LTTrA. [b] ἐκχυννόμενον LTTrA. [c] — τοῦ W. [d] + ὅτι that G[A]W. [e] πάντα ταῦτα LTrA. [f] ὄρνις ἐπισυνάγει LTTrA. [g] αὐτῆς T[Tr]AW; — ἑαυτῆς (*read* [her]) L. [h] + [αὐτῆς] her (wings) L. [i] — ἔρημος L.

XXIV. And Jesus
went out, and departed
from the temple: and
his disciples came to
him for to shew him
the buildings of the
temple. 2 And Jesus
said unto them, See ye
not all these things?
verily I say unto you,
There shall not be left
here one stone upon
another, that shall not
be thrown down. 3 And
as he sat upon the
mount of Olives, the
disciples came unto
him privately, saying,
Tell us, when shall
these things be? and
what *shall be* the sign
of thy coming, and of
the end of the world?
4 And Jesus answered
and said unto them,
Take heed that no man
deceive you. 5 For
many shall come in my
name, saying, I am
Christ; and shall deceive
many. 6 And ye
shall hear of wars and
rumours of wars: see
that ye be not troubled:
for all *these
things* must come to
pass, but the end is not
yet. 7 For nation shall
rise against nation,
and kingdom against
kingdom: and there
shall be famines, and
pestilences, and earthquakes,
in divers
places. 8 All these *are*
the beginning of sorrows.
9 Then shall
they deliver you up to
be afflicted, and shall
kill you: and ye shall
be hated of all nations
for my name's sake.
10 And then shall
many be offended, and
shall betray one another,
and shall hate
one another. 11 And
many false prophets
shall rise, and shall
deceive many. 12 And
because iniquity shall
abound, the love of
many shall wax cold.
13 But he that shall
endure unto the end,
the same shall be
saved. 14 And this
gospel of the kingdom
shall be preached in
all the world for a
witness unto all nations;
and then shall
the end come. 15 When
ye therefore shall see
the abomination of
desolation, spoken of
by Daniel the prophet,
stand in the holy place,

24 Καὶ ἐξελθὼν ὁ Ἰησοῦς [k]ἐπορεύετο ἀπὸ τοῦ ἱεροῦ,‖ καὶ
And going forth Jesus went away from the temple, and
προσῆλθον οἱ.μαθηταὶ.αὐτοῦ ἐπιδεῖξαι αὐτῷ τὰς οἰκοδομὰς
[3]came [4]to [[5]him] [1]his [2]disciples to point out to him the buildings
τοῦ ἱεροῦ. 2 ὁ.δὲ.[l]Ἰησοῦς‖ εἶπεν αὐτοῖς, Οὐ.βλέπετε [m]πάντα
of the temple. But Jesus said to them, See ye not all
ταῦτα;‖ ἀμὴν λέγω ὑμῖν, οὐ.μὴ ἀφεθῇ ὧδε λίθος ἐπὶ λίθον
these things? Verily I say to you, not at all shall be left here stone upon stone
ὃς οὐ.[n]μὴ‖.καταλυθήσεται. 3 Καθημένου.δὲ αὐτοῦ ἐπὶ τοῦ
which shall not be thrown down. And as [2]was [3]sitting [1]he upon the
ὄρους τῶν ἐλαιῶν προσῆλθον αὐτῷ οἱ μαθηταὶ[o] κατ᾽.ἰδίαν, λέ-
mount of Olives [3]came [4]to [5]him [1]the [2]disciples apart, say-
γοντες, Εἰπὲ ἡμῖν, πότε ταῦτα ἔσται; καὶ τί τὸ σημεῖον
ing, Tell us, when [2]these [3]things [1]shall be? and what [is] the sign
τῆς.σῆς παρουσίας καὶ [p]τῆς‖ συντελείας τοῦ αἰῶνος; 4 Καὶ
of thy coming, and of the completion of the age? And
ἀποκριθεὶς ὁ Ἰησοῦς εἶπεν αὐτοῖς, Βλέπετε, μή τις ὑμᾶς
answering Jesus said to them, Take heed, lest any one [2]you
πλανήσῃ. 5 πολλοὶ.γὰρ ἐλεύσονται ἐπὶ τῷ.ὀνόματί.μου, λέ-
[1]mislead. For many will come in my name,
γοντες, Ἐγώ εἰμι ὁ χριστός· καὶ πολλοὺς πλανήσουσιν.
saying, I am the Christ; and many they will mislead.
6 Μελλήσετε.δὲ ἀκούειν πολέμους καὶ ἀκοὰς πολέμων. ὁρᾶτε,
But ye shall be about to hear of wars and rumours of wars. See,
μὴ.θροεῖσθε· δεῖ.γὰρ [q]πάντα‖ γενέσθαι· ἀλλ᾽ οὔπω
be not disturbed; for it is necessary all [these] things to take place, but not yet
ἐστὶν τὸ τέλος. 7 Ἐγερθήσεται.γὰρ ἔθνος [r]ἐπὶ‖ ἔθνος, καὶ
is the end. For [2]shall [3]rise [4]up [1]nation against nation, and
βασιλεία ἐπὶ βασιλείαν· καὶ ἔσονται λιμοὶ [s]καὶ λοιμοὶ‖
kingdom against kingdom; and there shall be famines and pestilences
καὶ σεισμοὶ κατὰ τόπους. 8 πάντα.δὲ ταῦτα ἀρχὴ ὠδί-
and earthquakes in [different] places. But all these [are] a beginning of
νων. 9 Τότε παραδώσουσιν ὑμᾶς εἰς θλίψιν, καὶ ἀποκτενοῦσιν
throes. Then will they deliver up you to tribulation, and will kill
ὑμᾶς· καὶ ἔσεσθε μισούμενοι ὑπὸ πάντων [t]τῶν‖ ἐθνῶν διὰ
you; and ye will be hated by all the nations on account of
τὸ.ὄνομά.μου. 10 καὶ τότε σκανδαλισθήσονται πολλοί, καὶ
my name. And then will be offended many, and
ἀλλήλους παραδώσουσιν καὶ μισήσουσιν ἀλλήλους· 11 καὶ
one another they will deliver up and will hate one another; and
πολλοὶ ψευδοπροφῆται ἐγερθήσονται, καὶ πλανήσουσιν πολ-
many false prophets will arise, and will mislead
λούς· 12 καὶ διὰ τὸ.πληθυνθῆναι τὴν ἀνομίαν, ψυγήσεται
many; and because shall have been multiplied lawlessness, [6]will [7]grow [8]cold
ἡ ἀγάπη τῶν πολλῶν· 13 ὁ.δὲ ὑπομείνας εἰς τέλος,
[1]the [2]love [3]of [4]the [5]many; but he who endures to [the] end
οὗτος σωθήσεται. 14 καὶ κηρυχθήσεται τοῦτο.τὸ.εὐαγγέλιον
he shall be saved. And there shall be proclaimed these glad tidings
τῆς βασιλείας ἐν ὅλῃ τῇ οἰκουμένῃ, εἰς μαρτύριον πᾶσιν τοῖς
of the kingdom in all the habitable earth, for a testimony to all the
ἔθνεσιν· καὶ τότε ἥξει τὸ τέλος. 15 Ὅταν οὖν ἴδητε τὸ
nations; and then shall come the end. When therefore ye shall see the
βδέλυγμα τῆς ἐρημώσεως, τὸ ῥηθὲν διὰ Δανιὴλ τοῦ προ-
abomination of desolation, which was spoken of by Daniel the pro-

[k] ἀπὸ (ἐκ out of L) τοῦ ἱεροῦ ἐπορεύετο LTTrA. [l] ἀποκριθεὶς answering (he said) LTTrA.
[m] ταῦτα πάντα LTTrA. [n] — μὴ GLTTrAW. [o] + [αὐτοῦ] of him L. [p] — τῆς LTTrA.
[q] — πάντα LTTr[A]. [r] ἐπ᾽ T. [s] — καὶ λοιμοί LTTrA. [t] — τῶν E.

φήτου, [v]ἑστὸς‖ ἐν τόπῳ ἁγίῳ· ὁ ἀναγινώσκων [w]νοεί-
phet, standing in [the] [2]place [1]holy (he who reads let him un-
τω·‖ 16 τότε οἱ ἐν τῇ Ἰουδαίᾳ φευγέτωσαν [x]ἐπὶ‖ τὰ
derstand), then those in Judea let them flee to the
ὄρη· 17 ὁ ἐπὶ τοῦ δώματος μὴ.[y]καταβαινέτω‖ ἆραί [z]τι‖
mountains; he on the housetop let him not come down to take anything
ἐκ τῆς.οἰκίας.αὐτοῦ· 18 καὶ ὁ ἐν τῷ ἀγρῷ μὴ.ἐπιστρεψάτω
out of his house; and he in the field let him not return
ὀπίσω ἆραι [a]τὰ ἱμάτια‖ αὐτοῦ. 19 οὐαὶ.δὲ ταῖς ἐν.γαστρὶ.ἐ-
back to take [2]garments [1]his. But woe to those that are with
χούσαις καὶ ταῖς θηλαζούσαις ἐν ἐκείναις ταῖς ἡμέραις.
child and to those that give suck in those days.
20 προσεύχεσθε.δὲ ἵνα μὴ.γένηται ἡ.φυγὴ.ὑμῶν χειμῶνος, μηδὲ
And pray that [3]may [4]not [5]be [1]your [2]flight in winter, nor
[b]ἐν‖ σαββάτῳ. 21 Ἔσται.γὰρ τότε θλῖψις μεγάλη, οἵα [c]οὐ
on sabbath: for there shall be then [2]tribulation [1]great such as [2]not
γέγονεν‖ ἀπ' ἀρχῆς κόσμου ἕως τοῦ νῦν, οὐδ'.οὐ.μὴ
[1]has been from [the] beginning of [the] world until now, no, nor ever
γένηται. 22 καὶ εἰ.μὴ ἐκολοβώθησαν αἱ.ἡμέραι.ἐκεῖναι, οὐκ
shall be; and unless [3]had [4]been [5]shortened [1]those [2]days, [8]not
ἂν.ἐσώθη πᾶσα σάρξ· διὰ.δὲ τοὺς ἐκλεκτοὺς
[6]there [7]would have been saved any flesh, but on account of the elect
κολοβωθήσονται αἱ.ἡμέραι.ἐκεῖναι. 23 Τότε ἐάν τις ὑμῖν
[3]shall [4]be [5]shortened [1]those [2]days. Then if anyone to you
εἴπῃ, Ἰδού, ὧδε ὁ χριστός, ἢ ὧδε, μὴ.[d]πιστεύσητε.‖ 24 Ἐγερ-
say, Behold, here [is] the Christ, or here, believe [it] not. [2]There [3]will
θήσονται γὰρ ψευδόχριστοι καὶ ψευδοπροφῆται, καὶ δώσουσιν
[4]arise [1]for false Christs and false prophets, and will give
σημεῖα μεγάλα καὶ τέρατα, ὥστε [e]πλανῆσαι‖, εἰ δυνατόν, καὶ
[2]signs [1]great and wonders, so as to mislead, if possible, even
τοὺς ἐκλεκτούς. 25 Ἰδού, προείρηκα ὑμῖν. 26 ἐὰν οὖν εἴπωσιν
the elect. Lo, I have foretold [it] to you. If therefore they say
ὑμῖν, Ἰδού, ἐν τῇ ἐρήμῳ ἐστίν, μὴ.ἐξέλθητε· Ἰδού, ἐν
to you, Behold, in the wilderness he is, go not forth: Behold, [he is] in
τοῖς ταμείοις, μὴ.πιστεύσητε. 27 ὥσπερ.γὰρ ἡ ἀστραπὴ ἐξέρ-
the chambers, believe [it] not. For as the lightning comes
χεται ἀπὸ ἀνατολῶν καὶ φαίνεται ἕως δυσμῶν, οὕτως
forth from [the] east and appears as far as [the] west, so
ἔσται [f]καὶ‖ ἡ παρουσία τοῦ υἱοῦ τοῦ ἀνθρώπου. 28 ὅπου.[g]γὰρ‖
shall be also the coming of the Son of man. For wherever
ἐὰν ᾖ τὸ πτῶμα, ἐκεῖ συναχθήσονται οἱ ἀετοί. 29 Εὐ-
may be the carcase, there will be gathered together the eagles. [2]Immedi-
θέως δὲ μετὰ τὴν θλῖψιν τῶν.ἡμερῶν.ἐκείνων ὁ ἥλιος σκοτι-
ately, [1]but after the tribulation of those days the sun shall be
σθήσεται, καὶ ἡ σελήνη οὐ.δώσει τὸ.φέγγος.αὐτῆς, καὶ οἱ
darkened, and the moon shall not give her light, and the
ἀστέρες πεσοῦνται [h]ἀπὸ‖ τοῦ οὐρανοῦ, καὶ αἱ δυνάμεις τῶν
stars shall fall from the heaven, and the powers of the
οὐρανῶν σαλευθήσονται. 30 καὶ τότε φανήσεται τὸ σημεῖον
heavens shall be shaken. And then shall appear the sign
τοῦ υἱοῦ τοῦ ἀνθρώπου ἐν [i]τῷ‖ οὐρανῷ· καὶ [k]τότε‖ κό-
of the Son of man in the heaven; and then shall

(whoso readeth, let him
understand:) 16 then
let them which be in
Judæa flee into the
mountains: 17 let him
which is on the house-
top not come down to
take any thing out of
his house: 18 neither
let him which is in
the field return back
to take his clothes.
19 And woe unto them
that are with child,
and to them that give
suck in those days!
20 But pray ye that
your flight be not in
the winter, neither on
the sabbath day: 21 for
then shall be great
tribulation, such as
was not since the be-
ginning of the world
to this time, no, nor
ever shall be. 22 And
except those days
should be shortened,
there should no flesh
be saved: but for the
elect's sake those days
shall be shortened.
23 Then if any man
shall say unto you, Lo,
here *is* Christ, or there;
believe *it* not. 24 For
there shall arise false
Christs, and false pro-
phets, and shall shew
great signs and won-
ders; insomuch that,
if *it were* possible, they
shall deceive the very
elect. 25 Behold, I
have told you before.
26 Wherefore if they
shall say unto you,
Behold, he is in the
desert; go not forth:
behold, *he is* in the
secret chambers; be-
lieve *it* not. 27 For as
the lightning cometh
out of the east, and
shineth even unto the
west; so shall also the
coming of the Son of
man be. 28 For where-
soever the carcase is,
there will the eagles
be gathered together.
29 Immediately after
the tribulation of
those days shall the
sun be darkened, and
the moon shall not
give her light, and the
stars shall fall from
heaven, and the powers
of the heavens shall be
shaken: 30 and then
shall appear the sign
of the Son of man in
heaven: and then shall

---

[v] ἑστὼς EG. [w] νοείτω; does he understand? Tr. [x] εἰς LTr. [y] καταβάτω LTTr. [z] τὰ the things GLTTrAW. [a] τὸ ἱμάτιον garment LTTr. [b] — ἐν GLTTrAW. [c] οὐκ ἐγένετο T. [d] πιστεύετε L. [e] πλανηθῆναι T; πλανᾶσθαι (*read* so that will be misled) Tr. [f] — καὶ LTTrAW. [g] — γὰρ for LTTrA. [h] ἐκ out of T. [i] — τῷ LTTrA. [k] — τότε T.

all the tribes of the
earth mourn, and they
shall see the Son of
man coming in the
clouds of heaven with
power and great glory.
31 And he shall send
his angels with a great
sound of a trumpet,
and they shall gather
together his elect from
the four winds, from
one end of heaven to
the other. 32 Now learn
a parable of the fig
tree; When his branch
is yet tender, and put-
teth forth leaves, ye
know that summer *is*
nigh: 33 so likewise
ye, when ye shall see
all these things, know
that it is near, *even* at
the doors. 34 Verily I
say unto you, This
generation shall not
pass, till all these
things be fulfilled.
35 Heaven and earth
shall pass away, but
my words shall not
pass away. 36 But of
that day and hour
knoweth no *man*, no,
not the angels of hea-
ven, but my Father
only. 37 But as the
days of Noe *were*, so
shall also the coming
of the Son of man be.
38 For as in the days
that were before the
flood they were eating
and drinking, marry-
ing and giving in mar-
riage, until the day
that Noe entered into
the ark, 39 and knew
not until the flood
came, and took them
all away; so shall also
the coming of the Son
of man be. 40 Then
shall two be in the field;
the one shall be taken,
and the other left.
41 Two *women shall be*
grinding at the mill;
the one shall be taken,
and the other left.
42 Watch therefore:
for ye know not what
hour your Lord doth
come. 43 But know
this, that if the good-
man of the house had

ψονται πᾶσαι αἱ φυλαὶ τῆς γῆς. καὶ ὄψονται τὸν υἱὸν τοῦ
wail all the tribes of the land, and they shall see the Son
ἀνθρώπου, ἐρχόμενον ἐπὶ τῶν νεφελῶν τοῦ οὐρανοῦ μετὰ δυ-
of man, coming on the clouds of heaven with
νάμεως καὶ δόξης πολλῆς. 31 καὶ ἀποστελεῖ τοὺς ἀγγέλους
power and [2]glory [1]great. And he shall send [2]angels
αὐτοῦ μετὰ σάλπιγγος [l]φωνῆς‖ μεγάλης, καὶ ἐπισυνάξουσιν
[1]his with [3]of [4]a [5]trumpet [2]sound [1]great, and they shall gather together
τοὺς.ἐκλεκτοὺς.αὐτοῦ ἐκ τῶν τεσσάρων ἀνέμων, ἀπ' ἄκρων
his elect from the four winds, from [the] extremities
οὐρανῶν ἕως [m] ἄκρων αὐτῶν. 32 Ἀπὸ.δὲ τῆς συκῆς
of [the] heavens to [the] extremities of them. But from the fig-tree
μάθετε τὴν παραβολήν· ὅταν ἤδη ὁ.κλάδος.αὐτῆς γένηται
learn the parable: When already its branch is become
ἁπαλός, καὶ τὰ φύλλα [n]ἐκφύῃ,‖ γινώσκετε ὅτι ἐγγὺς τὸ
tender, and the leaves it puts forth, ye know that near [is] the
θέρος· 33 οὕτως καὶ ὑμεῖς, ὅταν ἴδητε [o]πάντα ταῦτα,‖
summer. Thus also ye, when ye see all these things,
γινώσκετε ὅτι ἐγγύς ἐστιν ἐπὶ θύραις. 34 ἀμὴν λέγω ὑμῖν,[p]
know that near it is, at [the] doors. Verily I say to you,
οὐ.μὴ παρέλθῃ ἡ.γενεὰ.αὕτη ἕως.ἂν πάντα ταῦτα
In no wise will have passed away this generation until all these things
γένηται. 35 Ὁ οὐρανὸς καὶ ἡ γῆ [q]παρελεύσονται,‖
shall have taken place. The heaven and the earth shall pass away,
οἱ.δὲ.λόγοι.μου οὐ.μὴ παρέλθωσιν. 36 Περὶ.δὲ τῆς ἡμέρας
but my words in no wise shall pass away. But concerning [2]day
ἐκείνης καὶ [r]τῆς‖ ὥρας οὐδεὶς οἶδεν, οὐδὲ οἱ ἄγγελοι τῶν
[1]that and the hour no one knows, not even the angels of the
οὐρανῶν, [s] εἰ.μὴ ὁ.πατήρ.[t]μου‖ μόνος. 37 Ὥσπερ.[v]δὲ‖ αἱ ἡμέραι
heavens, but my Father only. But as the days
τοῦ.Νῶε, οὕτως ἔσται [w]καὶ‖ ἡ παρουσία τοῦ υἱοῦ τοῦ ἀνθρώ-
of Noe, so shall be also the coming of the Son of
που. 38 [x]ὥσπερ‖ γὰρ ἦσαν ἐν ταῖς ἡμέραις[y] [z]ταῖς πρὸ‖
man. [2]As [1]for they were in the days which [were] before
τοῦ κατακλυσμοῦ, τρώγοντες καὶ πίνοντες, γαμοῦντες καὶ
the flood, eating and drinking, marrying and
[a]ἐκγαμίζοντες,‖ ἄχρι ἧς.ἡμέρας εἰσῆλθεν Νῶε εἰς τὴν κιβωτόν,
giving in marriage, until the day when [2]entered [1]Noe into the ark,
39 καὶ οὐκ.ἔγνωσαν, ἕως ἦλθεν ὁ κατακλυσμὸς καὶ ἦρεν
and they knew not till [3]came [1]the [2]flood and took away
ἅπαντας, οὕτως ἔσται [b]καὶ‖ ἡ παρουσία τοῦ υἱοῦ τοῦ ἀνθρώπου.
all; thus shall be also the coming of the Son of man.
40 Τότε [c]δύο ἔσονται‖ ἐν τῷ ἀγρῷ· [d]ὁ‖ εἷς παραλαμβάνεται,
Then two will be in the field, the one is taken,
καὶ [d]ὁ‖ εἷς ἀφίεται. 41 δύο ἀλήθουσαι ἐν τῷ [e]μύλωνι·‖ μία
and the one is left; two [women] grinding at the mill, one
παραλαμβάνεται, καὶ μία ἀφίεται. 42 Γρηγορεῖτε οὖν, ὅτι
is taken, and one is left. Watch therefore, for
οὐκ.οἴδατε ποίᾳ [f]ὥρᾳ‖ ὁ.κύριος.ὑμῶν ἔρχεται. 43 ἐκεῖνο.δὲ
ye know not in what hour your Lord comes. But this

---

[l] — φωνῆς (*read* a great trumpet) T. [m] + τῶν the Tr. [n] ἐκφυῇ are put forth LTrA.
[o] ταῦτα πάντα TTr. [p] + ὅτι that LTr. [q] παρελεύσεται GLTTrA. [r] — τῆς GLTTrA.
[s] + οὐδὲ ὁ υἱὸς nor the son LT. [t] — μου (*read* the Father) GLTTr[A]. [v] γὰρ for (as) LTr.
[w] — καὶ LTTrA. [x] ὡς as LTA; ὣς so Tr. [y] + ἐκείναις (*read* those days) L[Tr]
[z] — ταῖς πρὸ (*read* of the flood) A. [a] γαμίσκοντες L; γαμίζοντες T. [b] — καὶ LTrA.
[c] ἔσονται δύο LT. [d] — ὁ LTTrA. [e] μύλῳ LTTrA. [f] ἡμέρᾳ day LTTrA.

γινώσκετε, ὅτι εἰ ᾔδει ὁ οἰκοδεσπότης ποίᾳ φυλακῇ
know, that if [6]had [7]known [1]the [2]master [3]of [4]the [5]house in what watch

ὁ κλέπτης ἔρχεται, ἐγρηγόρησεν.ἂν, καὶ οὐκ ἂν.εἴασεν [g]διο-
the thief comes, he would have watched, and not have suffered [3]to [4]be

ρυγῆναι‖ τὴν.οἰκίαν.αὐτοῦ. 44 διὰ.τοῦτο καὶ ὑμεῖς γίνεσθε
[5]dug [6]through [1]his [2]house. Wherefore also [2]ye [1]be

ἕτοιμοι· ὅτι ᾗ.[h]ὥρᾳ οὐ.δοκεῖτε‖ ὁ υἱὸς τοῦ ἀνθρώπου ἔρχεται.
ready, for in what hour ye think not the Son of man comes.

45 Τίς ἄρα ἐστὶν ὁ πιστὸς δοῦλος καὶ φρόνιμος, ὃν κατέ-
Who then is the faithful bondman and prudent, whom [3]has

στησεν ὁ.κύριος.[i]αὐτοῦ‖ ἐπὶ τῆς.[k]θεραπείας‖.αὐτοῦ, τοῦ [l]διδόναι‖
[4]set [1]his [2]lord over his household, to give

αὐτοῖς τὴν τροφὴν ἐν καιρῷ; 46 μακάριος ὁ.δοῦλος.ἐκεῖνος, ὃν
to them the food in season? Blessed that bondman, whom

ἐλθὼν ὁ.κύριος.αὐτοῦ εὑρήσει [m]ποιοῦντα οὕτως.‖ 47 Ἀμὴν
[3]having [4]come [1]his [2]lord will find doing thus. Verily

λέγω ὑμῖν, ὅτι ἐπὶ πᾶσιν τοῖς.ὑπάρχουσιν.αὐτοῦ καταστήσει
I say to you, that over all his property he will set

αὐτόν. 48 Ἐὰν.δὲ εἴπῃ ὁ κακὸς δοῦλος [n]ἐκεῖνος‖ ἐν τῇ
him. But if [4]should [5]say [2]evil [3]bondman [1]that in

καρδίᾳ.αὐτοῦ, Χρονίζει [o]ὁ.κύριός.μου‖ [p]ἐλθεῖν,‖ 49 καὶ ἄρξηται
his heart, [3]Delays [1]my [2]lord to come, and should begin

τύπτειν τοὺς συνδούλους[q], [r]ἐσθίειν‖.δὲ καὶ [s]πίνειν‖ μετὰ τῶν
to beat [his] fellow-bondmen, and to eat and to drink with the

μεθυόντων, 50 ἥξει ὁ κύριος τοῦ.δούλου ἐκείνου ἐν ἡμέρᾳ
drunken, [6]will [7]come [1]the [2]lord [3]of [4]that [5]bondman in a day

ᾗ οὐ.προσδοκᾷ, καὶ ἐν ὥρᾳ ᾗ οὐ.γινώσκει, 51 καὶ
in which he does not expect, and in an hour which he knows not, and

διχοτομήσει αὐτόν, καὶ τὸ.μέρος.αὐτοῦ μετὰ τῶν ὑποκριτῶν
will cut [2]in [3]two [1]him, and his portion with the hypocrites

θήσει· ἐκεῖ ἔσται ὁ κλαυθμὸς καὶ ὁ βρυγμὸς τῶν ὀδόντων.
will appoint: there will be the weeping and the gnashing of the teeth.

25 Τότε ὁμοιωθήσεται ἡ βασιλεία τῶν οὐρανῶν δέκα
Then [6]will [7]be [8]made [9]like [1]the [2]kingdom [3]of [4]the [5]heavens [to] ten

παρθένοις, αἵτινες λαβοῦσαι τὰς.λαμπάδας.[t]αὐτῶν‖ ἐξῆλθον
virgins, who having taken their lamps went forth

εἰς.[v]ἀπάντησιν‖ τοῦ νυμφίου. 2 πέντε.δὲ [w]ἦσαν ἐξ αὐτῶν‖
to meet the bridegroom. And five [3]were [1]of [2]them

[x]φρόνιμοι,‖ καὶ [y]αἱ‖ πέντε [z]μωραί.‖ 3 [a]αἵτινες‖ μωραί, λα-
prudent, and five foolish. They who [were] foolish, hav-

βοῦσαι τὰς.λαμπάδας.[b]ἑαυτῶν,‖ οὐκ.ἔλαβον μεθ' ἑαυτῶν
ing taken their lamps, did not take with themselves

ἔλαιον· 4 αἱ.δὲ φρόνιμοι ἔλαβον ἔλαιον ἐν τοῖς ἀγγείοις
oil; but the prudent took oil in [2]vessels

[c]αὐτῶν‖ μετὰ τῶν.λαμπάδων.[d]αὐτῶν.‖ 5 χρονίζοντος.δὲ τοῦ
[1]their with their lamps. But [3]tarrying [1]the

νυμφίου, ἐνύσταξαν πᾶσαι καὶ ἐκάθευδον. 6 μέσης.δὲ
[2]bridegroom, they [2]became [3]drowsy [1]all and slept. But in [the] middle

νυκτὸς κραυγὴ γέγονεν, Ἰδού, ὁ νυμφίος [e]ἔρχεται,‖ ἐξέρ-
of [the] night [3]a [4]cry [1]there [2]was, Behold, the bridegroom comes, go

known in what watch the thief would come, he would have watched, and would not have suffered his house to be broken up. 44 Therefore be ye also ready: for in such an hour as ye think not the Son of man cometh. 45 Who then is a faithful and wise servant, whom his lord hath made ruler over his household, to give them meat in due season? 46 Blessed *is* that servant, whom his lord when he cometh shall find so doing. 47 Verily I say unto you, That he shall make him ruler over all his goods. 48 But and if that evil servant shall say in his heart, My lord delayeth his coming; 49 and shall begin to smite *his* fellowservants, and to eat and drink with the drunken; 50 the lord of that servant shall come in a day when he looketh not for *him*, and in an hour that he is not aware of, 51 and shall cut him asunder, and appoint *him* his portion with the hypocrites: there shall be weeping and gnashing of teeth.

XXV. Then shall the kingdom of heaven be likened unto ten virgins, which took their lamps, and went forth to meet the bridegroom. 2 And five of them were wise, and five *were* foolish. 3 They that *were* foolish took their lamps, and took no oil with them: 4 but the wise took oil in their vessels with their lamps. 5 While the bridegroom tarried, they all slumbered and slept. 6 And at midnight there was a cry made, Behold, the bridegroom cometh;

---

[g] διορυχθῆναι TTr. [h] οὐ δοκεῖτε ὥρᾳ LTTrA. [i] — αὐτοῦ (*read* [his]) LTTrA. [k] οἰκετείας LTTrA. [l] δοῦναι GLTTrA. [m] οὕτως ποιοῦντα LTTrA. [n] — ἐκεῖνος (*read* the evil bondman) T. [o] μου ὁ κύριος LTTrA. [p] — ἐλθεῖν LTTr. [q] + αὐτοῦ his (fellow bondmen) LTTrAW. [r] ἐσθίῃ should eat GLTTrAW. [s] πίνῃ should drink GLTTrAW. [t] ἑαυτῶν LTrA; αὐτῶν TW. [v] ὑπάντησιν LTTrA. [w] ἐξ αὐτῶν ἦσαν LTTrA. [x] μωραὶ foolish LTTrA. [y] — αἱ EGLTTrAW. [z] φρόνιμοι prudent LTTrA. [a] αἱ δὲ but the L; αἳ γὰρ for those who Tr; αἱ γὰρ for the TA. [b] αὐτῶν GW; αὐτῶν LTrA; — ἑαυτῶν T. [c] — αὐτῶν (*read* the vessels) LTTrA. [d] ἑαυτῶν LT; αὐτῶν TrA. [e] — ἔρχεται LTTrA.

go ye out to meet him.
7 Then all those vir-
gins arose, and trim-
med their lamps. 8 And
the foolish said unto
the wise, Give us of
your oil; for our lamps
are gone out. 9 But
the wise answered, say-
ing, *Not so;* lest there
be not enough for us
and you: but go ye
rather to them that
sell, and buy for your-
selves. 10 And while
they went to buy, the
bridegroom came; and
they that were ready
went in with him to
the marriage: and the
door was shut. 11 Af-
terward came also the
other virgins, saying,
Lord, Lord, open to
us. 12 But he answer-
ed and said, Verily I
say unto you, I know
you not. 13 Watch
therefore, for ye know
neither the day nor the
hour wherein the Son
of man cometh.

14 For *the kingdom
of heaven is* as a man
travelling into a far
country, *who* called
his own servants, and
delivered unto them
his goods. 15 And unto
one he gave five ta-
lents, to another two,
and to another one;
to every man accord-
ing to his several abi-
lity; and straightway
took his journey.
16 Then he that had
received the five ta-
lents went and traded
with the same, and
made *them* other five
talents. 17 And like-
wise he that *had re-
ceived* two, he also
gained other two.
18 But he that had re-
ceived one went and
digged in the earth,
and hid his lord's
money. 19 After a long
time the lord of those
servants cometh, and
reckoneth with them.
20 And so he that had
received five talents
came and brought
other five talents, say-
ing, Lord, thou deliv-
eredst unto me five

χεσθε εἰς.ἀπάντησιν [f]αὐτοῦ.‖ 7 Τότε ἠγέρθησαν πᾶσαι αἱ
forth to meet him. Then arose all

παρθένοι.ἐκεῖναι, καὶ ἐκόσμησαν τὰς.λαμπάδας.[g]αὐτῶν.‖ 8 αἱ.δὲ
those virgins, and trimmed their lamps. And the

μωραὶ ταῖς φρονίμοις [h]εἶπον,‖ Δότε ἡμῖν ἐκ τοῦ.ἐλαίου.ὑμῶν,
foolish to the prudent said, Give us of your oil,

ὅτι αἱ.λαμπάδες.ἡμῶν σβέννυνται. 9 Ἀπεκρίθησαν.δὲ αἱ
for our lamps are going out. But [3]answered [1]the

φρόνιμοι, λέγουσαι, Μήποτε [i]οὐκ‖ ἀρκέσῃ ἡμῖν καὶ ὑμῖν·
[2]prudent, saying, [No,] lest [3]not [1]it [2]may suffice for us and you:

πορεύεσθε.[k]δὲ‖ μᾶλλον πρὸς τοὺς πωλοῦντας, καὶ ἀγοράσατε
but go rather to those who sell, and buy

ἑαυταῖς. 10 ἀπερχομένων.δὲ αὐτῶν ἀγοράσαι, ἦλθεν ὁ
for yourselves. But as [2]went [3]away [1]they to buy, [3]came [1]the

νυμφίος· καὶ αἱ ἕτοιμοι εἰσῆλθον μετ' αὐτοῦ εἰς τοὺς γά-
[2]bridegroom, and those ready went in with him to the wedding

μους, καὶ ἐκλείσθη ἡ θύρα. 11 ὕστερον.δὲ ἔρχονται [l]καὶ‖ αἱ
feast, and [3]was [4]shut [1]the [2]door. And afterwards come also the

λοιπαὶ παρθένοι, λέγουσαι, Κύριε, κύριε, ἄνοιξον ἡμῖν. 12 Ὁ.δὲ
other virgins, saying, Lord, Lord, open to us. But he

ἀποκριθεὶς εἶπεν, Ἀμὴν λέγω ὑμῖν, οὐκ.οἶδα ὑμᾶς. 13 Γρη-
answering said, Verily I say to you, I do not know you. Watch

γορεῖτε οὖν, ὅτι οὐκ.οἴδατε τὴν ἡμέραν οὐδὲ τὴν ὥραν [m]ἐν
therefore, for ye do not know the day nor the hour in

ᾗ ὁ υἱὸς τοῦ ἀνθρώπου ἔρχεται.‖
which the Son of man comes.

14 Ὥσπερ.γὰρ ἄνθρωπος ἀποδημῶν ἐκάλεσεν τοὺς.ἰδίους
For [it is] as [if] a man leaving the country called his own

δούλους, καὶ παρέδωκεν αὐτοῖς τὰ.ὑπάρχοντα.αὐτοῦ. 15 καὶ
bondmen, and delivered to them his property. And

ᾧ.μὲν ἔδωκεν πέντε τάλαντα, ᾧ.δὲ δύο, ᾧ.δὲ ἕν,
to one he gave five talents, and to another two, and to another one,

ἑκάστῳ κατὰ τὴν.ἰδίαν δύναμιν καὶ [n]ἀπεδήμησεν εὐθέως.
to each according to his respective ability; and left the country immediately.

16 πορευθεὶς‖ [o]δὲ‖ ὁ τὰ πέντε τάλαντα λαβὼν [p]εἰργάσατο‖
And [2]having [3]gone [1]he who the five talents received trafficked

ἐν αὐτοῖς, καὶ [q]ἐποίησεν‖ ἄλλα πέντε [r]τάλαντα.‖ 17 ὡσαύτως
with them, and made other five talents. In like manner

[s]καὶ‖ ὁ τὰ δύο ἐκέρδησεν [t]καὶ αὐτὸς‖ ἄλλα δύο.
also he who [received] the two [3]gained [2]also [1]he other two.

18 ὁ.δὲ τὸ ἓν[v] λαβὼν ἀπελθὼν ὤρυξεν [w]ἐν τῇ γῇ,‖ καὶ
But he who the one received having gone away dug in the earth, and

[x]ἀπέκρυψεν‖ τὸ ἀργύριον τοῦ.κυρίου.αὐτοῦ. 19 Μετὰ.δὲ [y]χρόνον
hid the money of his lord. And after a [2]time

πολὺν‖ ἔρχεται ὁ κύριος τῶν.δούλων.ἐκείνων, καὶ συναίρει
[1]long comes the lord of those bondmen, and takes

[z]μετ' αὐτῶν λόγον.‖ 20 καὶ προσελθὼν ὁ τὰ πέντε τά-
[2]with [3]them [1]account. And [2]having [3]come [1]he who the five ta-

λαντα λαβὼν, προσήνεγκεν ἄλλα πέντε τάλαντα, λέγων,
lents received, brought to [him] other five talents, saying,

---

f — αὐτοῦ (*read* [him]) TA. g ἑαυτῶν LTTrA. h εἶπαν TTrA. i οὐ μὴ not at all LTrAW. k — δὲ but GLTTrAW. l — καὶ L[Tr]. m — ἐν ᾗ ὁ υἱὸς τοῦ ἀνθρώπου ἔρχεται GLTTrA. n ἀπεδήμησεν. εὐθέως πορευθεὶς left the country. Immediately having gone T. o — δὲ and [L]T[Tr]. p ἠργάσατο TA. q ἐκέρδησεν gained LTr. r — τάλαντα LTr[A]. s — καὶ [L]T. t — καὶ αὐτὸς LTTr[A]. v + τάλαντον talent L. w γῆν [the] earth TTrA. x ἔκρυψεν LTTrA. y πολὺν χρόνον LTTrA. z λόγον μετ' αὐτῶν LTTrA.

Κύριε, πέντε τάλαντά μοι παρέδωκας· ἴδε, ἄλλα πέντε
Lord, five talents to me thou didst deliver: behold, other five
ᵃτάλαντα‖ ἐκέρδησα ᵇἐπ' αὐτοῖς.‖ 21 Ἔφη-ᶜδὲ‖ αὐτῷ ὁ κύριος
talents have I gained besides them. And [3]said [4]to [5]him [2]lord
αὐτοῦ, Εὖ, δοῦλε ἀγαθὲ καὶ πιστέ, ἐπὶ ὀλίγα ἦς
[1]his, Well! bondman good and faithful, over a few things thou wast
πιστός, ἐπὶ πολλῶν σε καταστήσω· εἴσελθε εἰς τὴν χαρὰν
faithful, over many things thee will I set: enter into the joy
τοῦ.κυρίου.σου. 22 Προσελθὼν-ᵈδὲ‖ καὶ ὁ τὰ δύο τά-
of thy lord. And having come to [him] [2]also [1]he who the two ta-
λαντα ᵉλαβὼν‖ εἶπεν, Κύριε, δύο τάλαντά μοι παρέδωκας·
lents received said, Lord, two talents to me thou didst deliver;
ἴδε, ἄλλα δύο τάλαντα ἐκέρδησα ᵇἐπ' αὐτοῖς.‖ 23 Ἔφη
behold, other two talents have I gained besides them. [3]Said
αὐτῷ ὁ.κύριος.αὐτοῦ, Εὖ, δοῦλε ἀγαθὲ καὶ πιστέ, ἐπὶ
[4]to [5]him [1]his [2]Lord, Well! bondman good and faithful, over
ὀλίγα ἦς πιστός, ἐπὶ πολλῶν σε καταστήσω· εἴσελθε
a few things thou wast faithful, over many things thee will I set: enter
εἰς τὴν χαρὰν τοῦ.κυρίου.σου. 24 Προσελθὼν.δὲ καὶ ὁ
into the joy of thy Lord. And having come to [him] [2]also [1]he who
τὸ ἓν τάλαντον εἰληφὼς εἶπεν, Κύριε, ἔγνων σε ὅτι σκληρὸς
the one talent had received said, Lord, I knew thee that [4]hard
εἶ ἄνθρωπος, θερίζων ὅπου οὐκ.ἔσπειρας, καὶ συνάγων
[1]thou [2]art [3]a [5]man, reaping where thou didst not sow, and gathering
ὅθεν οὐ.διεσκόρπισας· 25 καὶ φοβηθείς, ἀπελθὼν ἔκρυψα
whence thou didst not scatter, and being afraid, having gone away I hid
τὸ.τάλαντόν.σου ἐν τῇ γῇ· ἴδε, ἔχεις τὸ.σόν. 26 Ἀπο-
thy talent in the earth; behold, thou hast thine own. [4]An-
κριθεὶς δὲ ὁ.κύριος.αὐτοῦ εἶπεν αὐτῷ, ᶠΠονηρὲ δοῦλε‖ καὶ
swering [1]and [2]his [3]Lord said to him, Wicked [3]bondman [1]and
ὀκνηρέ, ᾔδεις ὅτι θερίζω ὅπου οὐκ.ἔσπειρα, καὶ συνάγω ὅθεν
[2]slothful, thou knewest that I reap where I sowed not, and gather whence
οὐ.διεσκόρπισα; 27 ἔδει ᵍοὖν σε‖ βαλεῖν ʰτὸ.ἀργύριόν‖.μου
I scattered not; it behoved [2]therefore [1]thee to put my money
τοῖς ⁱτραπεζίταις·‖ καὶ ἐλθὼν ἐγὼ ἐκομισάμην.ἂν τὸ.ἐμὸν σὺν
to the money changers, and coming I should have received mine own with
τόκῳ. 28 ἄρατε οὖν ἀπ' αὐτοῦ τὸ τάλαντον, καὶ δότε τῷ
interest. Take therefore from him the talent, and give [it] to him who
ἔχοντι τὰ δέκα τάλαντα. 29 Τῷ.γὰρ ἔχοντι παντὶ δοθή-
has the ten talents. For [4]who [5]has [1]to [2]every [3]one shall
σεται, καὶ περισσευθήσεται· ᵏἀπὸ δὲ τοῦ‖ μὴ.ἔχοντος, καὶ
be given, and [he] shall be in abundance; [2]from [1]but him who has not, even
ὃ ἔχει ἀρθήσεται ἀπ' αὐτοῦ. 30 Καὶ τὸν ἀχρεῖον δοῦλον
that which he has shall be taken from him. And the useless bondman
ˡἐκβάλλετε‖ εἰς τὸ σκότος τὸ ἐξώτερον· ἐκεῖ ἔσται ὁ κλαυθμὸς
cast ye out into the darkness the outer: there shall be the weeping
καὶ ὁ βρυγμὸς τῶν ὀδόντων.
and the gnashing of the teeth.

31 Ὅταν.δὲ ἔλθῃ ὁ υἱὸς τοῦ ἀνθρώπου ἐν τῇ.δόξῃ.αὐτοῦ,
But when [5]comes [1]the [2]Son [3]of [4]man in his glory,
καὶ πάντες οἱ ᵐἅγιοι‖ ἄγγελοι μετ' αὐτοῦ, τότε καθίσει ἐπὶ
and all the holy angels with him, then will he sit upon [the]

talents: behold, I have gained beside them five talents more. 21 His lord said unto him, Well done, *thou* good and faithful servant: thou hast been faithful over a few things, I will make thee ruler over many things: enter thou into the joy of thy lord. 22 He also that had received two talents came and said, Lord, thou deliveredst unto me two talents: behold, I have gained two other talents beside them. 23 His lord said unto him, Well done, good and faithful servant; thou hast been faithful over a few things, I will make thee ruler over many things: enter thou into the joy of thy lord. 24 Then he which had received the one talent came and said, Lord, I knew thee that thou art an hard man, reaping where thou hast not sown, and gathering where thou hast not strawed: 25 and I was afraid, and went and hid thy talent in the earth: lo, *there* thou hast *that* is thine. 26 His lord answered and said unto him, *Thou* wicked and slothful servant, thou knewest that I reap where I sowed not, and gather where I have not strawed: 27 thou oughtest therefore to have put my money to the exchangers, and *then* at my coming I should have received mine own with usury. 28 Take therefore the talent from him, and give *it* unto him which hath ten talents. 29 For unto every one that hath shall be given, and he shall have abundance: but from him that hath not shall be taken away even that which he hath. 30 And cast ye the unprofitable servant into outer darkness: there shall be weeping and gnashing of teeth.

31 When the Son of man shall come in his glory, and all the holy angels with him, then shall he sit upon the

---

ᵃ [τάλαντα] Tr. ᵇ — ἐπ' αὐτοῖς LTTr. ᶜ — δὲ and GLTTrAW. ᵈ — δὲ and T. ᵉ — λαβὼν (*read* [received]) LTTrA. ᶠ Δοῦλε πονηρὲ L. ᵍ σε οὖν TTrA. ʰ τὰ ἀργύριά T. ⁱ τραπεζείταις T. ᵏ τοῦ δὲ but of him who LTTrA. ˡ ἐκβάλετε GLTTrAW. ᵐ — ἅγιοι GLTTrA.

throne of his glory:
32 and before him shall
be gathered all nations:
and he shall
separate them one
from another, as a
shepherd divideth *his*
sheep from the goats:
33 and he shall set the
sheep on his right
hand, but the goats on
the left. 34 Then shall
the King say unto
them on his right
hand, Come, ye blessed
of my Father, inherit
the kingdom prepared
for you from the foundation
of the world:
35 for I was an hungred,
and ye gave me
meat: I was thirsty,
and ye gave me drink:
I was a stranger, and
ye took me in: 36 naked,
and ye clothed
me: I was sick, and ye
visited me: I was in
prison, and ye came
unto me. 37 Then shall
the righteous answer
him, saying, Lord,
when saw we thee an
hungred, and fed
thee? or thirsty, and
gave *thee* drink?
38 When saw we thee
a stranger, and took
thee in? or naked, and
clothed *thee?* 39 Or
when saw we thee sick,
or in prison, and came
unto thee? 40 And
the King shall answer
and say unto them,
Verily I say unto you,
Inasmuch as ye have
done *it* unto one of
the least of these my
brethren, ye have done
it unto me. 41 Then
shall he say also unto
them on the left hand,
Depart from me, ye
cursed, into everlasting
fire, prepared for
the devil and his angels:
42 for I was an
hungred, and ye gave
me no meat: I was
thirsty, and ye gave
me no drink: 43 I was
a stranger, and ye took
me not in: naked, and
ye clothed me not:
sick, and in prison, and
ye visited me not.
44 Then shall they
also answer him, saying,
Lord, when saw
we thee an hungred,
or athirst, or a stranger,
or naked, or sick,
or in prison, and did
not minister unto
thee? 45 Then shall he
answer them, saying,
Verily I say unto you,

θρόνου δόξης.αὐτοῦ, 32 καὶ [n]συναχθήσεται‖ ἔμπροσθεν αὐτοῦ
throne of his glory, and shall be gathered before him
πάντα τὰ ἔθνη, καὶ [o]ἀφοριεῖ‖ αὐτοὺς ἀπ᾽ ἀλλήλων, ὥσπερ ὁ
all the nations, and he will separate them from one another, as the
ποιμὴν ἀφορίζει τὰ πρόβατα ἀπὸ τῶν ἐρίφων, 33 καὶ στήσει
shepherd separates the sheep from the goats; and he will set
τὰ μὲν πρόβατα ἐκ δεξιῶν αὐτοῦ, τὰ.δὲ ἐρίφια ἐξ εὐωνύμων.
the sheep on [2]right [3]hand [1]his, but the goats on [his] left.
34 Τότε ἐρεῖ ὁ βασιλεὺς τοῖς ἐκ δεξιῶν αὐτοῦ, Δεῦτε, οἱ
Then [3]will [4]say [1]the [2]king to those on [2]right [3]hand [1]his, Come, the
εὐλογημένοι τοῦ.πατρός.μου, κληρονομήσατε τὴν ἡτοιμασμένην
blessed of my Father, inherit the [2]prepared
ὑμῖν βασιλείαν ἀπὸ καταβολῆς κόσμου. 35 ἐπείνασα.γάρ,
[3]for [4]you [1]kingdom from [the] foundation of [the] world. For I hungered,
καὶ ἐδώκατέ μοι φαγεῖν· ἐδίψησα, καὶ ἐποτίσατέ με· ξένος
and ye gave me to eat; I thirsted, and ye gave [2]to [3]drink [1]me; a stranger
ἤμην, καὶ συνηγάγετέ με· 36 γυμνός, καὶ περιεβάλετέ με· ἠσθέ-
I was, and ye took [2]in [1]me; naked, and ye clothed me; I was
νησα, καὶ ἐπεσκέψασθέ με· ἐν φυλακῇ ἤμην, καὶ [p]ἤλθετε‖ πρός
sick, and ye visited me; in prison I was, and ye came to
με. 37 Τότε ἀποκριθήσονται αὐτῷ οἱ δίκαιοι, λέγοντες, Κύριε,
me. Then will answer him the righteous, saying, Lord,
πότε σὲ [q]εἴδομεν‖ πεινῶντα, καὶ ἐθρέψαμεν; ἢ διψῶντα, καὶ
when [3]thee [1]saw [2]we hungering, and fed [thee]? or thirsting, and
ἐποτίσαμεν; 38 πότε.δέ σε εἴδομεν ξένον, καὶ συνηγάγομεν;
gave [thee] to drink? and when [3]thee [1]saw [2]we a stranger, and took [thee] in?
ἢ γυμνόν, καὶ περιεβάλομεν; 39 πότε.δέ σε εἴδομεν [r]ἀσθενῆ,‖
or naked, and clothed [thee]? And when [3]thee [1]saw [2]we sick,
ἢ ἐν φυλακῇ, καὶ ἤλθομεν πρός σε; 40 Καὶ ἀποκριθεὶς ὁ
or in prison, and came to thee? And answering the
βασιλεὺς ἐρεῖ αὐτοῖς, Ἀμὴν λέγω ὑμῖν, ἐφ᾽.ὅσον ἐποιήσατε
king will say to them, Verily I say to you, Inasmuch as ye did [it]
ἑνὶ τούτων [s]τῶν.ἀδελφῶν.μου‖ τῶν ἐλαχίστων, ἐμοὶ ἐποιή-
to one of these my brethren the least, to me ye
σατε. 41 Τότε ἐρεῖ καὶ τοῖς ἐξ εὐωνύμων, Πορεύεσθε ἀπ᾽
did [it]. Then will he say also to those on [the] left, Go from
ἐμοῦ, [t]οἱ‖ κατηραμένοι, εἰς τὸ πῦρ τὸ αἰώνιον, τὸ ἡτοιμα-
me, the cursed, into the fire the eternal, which has been
σμένον τῷ διαβόλῳ καὶ τοῖς.ἀγγέλοις.αὐτοῦ. 42 ἐπείνασα.γάρ,
prepared for the devil and his angels. For I hungered,
καὶ οὐκ.ἐδώκατέ μοι φαγεῖν· ἐδίψησα, καὶ οὐκ.ἐποτίσατέ με·
and ye gave not to me to eat; I thirsted, and ye gave [2]not [3]to [4]drink [1]me;
43 ξένος ἤμην, καὶ οὐ.συνηγάγετέ με· γυμνός, καὶ οὐ.περιεβά-
a stranger I was, and ye took [2]not [3]in [1]me; naked, and ye did not
λετέ με· ἀσθενής, καὶ ἐν φυλακῇ, καὶ οὐκ.ἐπεσκέψασθέ με.
clothe me; sick, and in prison, and ye did not visit me.
44 Τότε ἀποκριθήσονται [v]αὐτῷ‖ καὶ αὐτοί, λέγοντες, Κύριε,
Then [3]will [4]answer [5]him [2]also [1]they, saying, Lord,
πότε σὲ εἴδομεν πεινῶντα, ἢ διψῶντα, ἢ ξένον, ἢ γυμνόν, ἢ
when [3]thee [1]saw [2]we hungering, or thirsting, or a stranger, or naked, or
ἀσθενῆ, ἢ ἐν φυλακῇ, καὶ οὐ.διηκονήσαμέν σοι; 45 Τότε ἀπο-
sick, or in prison, and did not minister to thee? Then will
κριθήσεται αὐτοῖς, λέγων, Ἀμὴν λέγω ὑμῖν, ἐφ᾽.ὅσον οὐκ.ἐποι-
he answer them, saying, Verily I say to you, Inasmuch as ye did not

---

[n] συναχθήσονται LTTrA. [o] ἀφορίσει T. [p] ἤλθατε LTTrA. [q] εἴδαμεν Tr. [r] ἀσθενοῦντα LTTrA. [s] [τῶν ἀδελφῶν μου] L. [t] — οἱ T. [v] — αὐτῷ GLTTrAW.

ησατε ἑνὶ τούτων τῶν ἐλαχίστων, οὐδὲ ἐμοὶ ἐποιήσατε. 46 Καὶ
[it] to one of these the least, neither to me did ye [it]. And
ἀπελεύσονται οὗτοι εἰς κόλασιν αἰώνιον· οἱ.δὲ δίκαιοι εἰς ζωὴν
[2]shall [3]go [4]away [1]these into punishment eternal, but the righteous into life
αἰώνιον.
eternal.

26 Καὶ ἐγένετο ὅτε ἐτέλεσεν ὁ Ἰησοῦς πάντας τοὺς
And it came to pass when [2]had [3]finished [1]Jesus all
λόγους.τούτους, εἶπεν τοῖς.μαθηταῖς.αὐτοῦ. 2 Οἴδατε ὅτι μετὰ
these sayings he said to his disciples, Ye know that after
δύο ἡμέρας τὸ πάσχα γίνεται, καὶ ὁ υἱὸς τοῦ ἀνθρώπου
two days the passover takes place, and the Son of man
παραδίδοται εἰς.τὸ.σταυρωθῆναι. 3 Τότε συνήχθησαν οἱ
is delivered up to be crucified. Then were gathered together the
ἀρχιερεῖς [w]καὶ οἱ γραμματεῖς‖ καὶ οἱ πρεσβύτεροι τοῦ λαοῦ
chief priests and the scribes and the elders of the people
εἰς τὴν αὐλὴν τοῦ ἀρχιερέως τοῦ λεγομένου Καϊάφα, 4 καὶ
to the court of the high priest who was called Caiaphas, and
συνεβουλεύσαντο ἵνα τὸν Ἰησοῦν [x]κρατήσωσιν δόλῳ,‖
took counsel together in order that Jesus they might seize by guile,
καὶ ἀποκτείνωσιν. 5 ἔλεγον.δέ, Μὴ ἐν τῇ ἑορτῇ, ἵνα μὴ
and kill [him]; but they said, Not during the feast, that [3]not
θόρυβος γένηται ἐν τῷ λαῷ.
[4]a [5]tumult [1]there [2]be among the people.

6 Τοῦ.δὲ.Ἰησοῦ γενομένου ἐν Βηθανίᾳ ἐν οἰκίᾳ Σίμωνος
Now Jesus being in Bethany in [the] house of Simon
τοῦ λεπροῦ, 7 προσῆλθεν αὐτῷ γυνὴ [y]ἀλάβαστρον μύρου
the leper, [3]came [4]to [5]him [1]a [2]woman, an alabaster flask of ointment
ἔχουσα‖ [z]βαρυτίμου,‖ καὶ κατέχεεν ἐπὶ [a]τὴν.κεφαλὴν.‖αὐτοῦ
having, very precious, and poured [it] on his head
ἀνακειμένου. 8 ἰδόντες.δὲ οἱ.μαθηταὶ.[b]αὐτοῦ‖ ἠγανάκ-
as he reclined [at table]. But seeing [it] his disciples became
τησαν, λέγοντες, Εἰς τί ἡ.ἀπώλεια.αὕτη; 9 [c]ἠδύνατο‖.γὰρ τοῦτο
indignant, saying, For what this waste? for [3]could [1]this
[d]τὸ.μύρον‖ πραθῆναι πολλοῦ, καὶ δοθῆναι [e] πτωχοῖς.
[2]ointment have been sold for much, and have been given to [the] poor.
10 Γνοὺς.δὲ ὁ Ἰησοῦς εἶπεν αὐτοῖς, Τί κόπους παρέχετε
But knowing [this] Jesus said to them, Why trouble do ye cause
τῇ γυναικί; ἔργον.γὰρ καλὸν [f]εἰργάσατο‖ εἰς ἐμέ. 11 πάν-
to the woman? for a [2]work [1]good she wrought towards me. [2]Al-
τοτε γὰρ τοὺς πτωχοὺς ἔχετε μεθ' ἑαυτῶν, ἐμὲ.δὲ οὐ πάντοτε
ways [1]for the poor ye have with you, but me not always
ἔχετε. 12 βαλοῦσα.γὰρ αὕτη τὸ.μύρον.τοῦτο ἐπὶ τοῦ
ye have. For [3]in [4]pouring [1]this [[2]woman] this ointment on
σώματός.μου πρὸς τὸ.ἐνταφιάσαι.με ἐποίησεν. 13 ἀμὴν λέγω
my body for my burying she did [it]. Verily I say
ὑμῖν, ὅπου.ἐὰν κηρυχθῇ τὸ.εὐαγγέλιον.τοῦτο ἐν ὅλῳ
to you, Wheresoever shall be proclaimed these glad tidings in all
τῷ κόσμῳ, λαληθήσεται καὶ ὃ ἐποίησεν αὕτη, εἰς
the world, shall be spoken of also that which [3]did [1]this [[2]woman], for
μνημόσυνον αὐτῆς.
a memorial of her.

Inasmuch as ye did *it* not to one of the least of these, ye did *it* not to me. 46 And these shall go away into everlasting punishment: but the righteous into life eternal.

XXVI. And it came to pass, when Jesus had finished all these sayings, he said unto his disciples, 2 Ye know that after two days is *the feast of* the passover, and the Son of man is betrayed to be crucified. 3 Then assembled together the chief priests, and the scribes, and the elders of the people, unto the palace of the high priest, who was called Caiaphas, 4 and consulted that they might take Jesus by subtilty, and kill *him*. 5 But they said, Not on the feast *day*, lest there be an uproar among the people.

6 Now when Jesus was in Bethany, in the house of Simon the leper, 7 there came unto him a woman having an alabaster box of very precious ointment, and poured it on his head, as he sat *at meat*. 8 But when his disciples saw *it*, they had indignation, saying, To what purpose *is* this waste? 9 for this ointment might have been sold for much, and given to the poor. 10 When Jesus understood *it*, he said unto them, Why trouble ye the woman? for she hath wrought a good work upon me. 11 For ye have the poor always with you; but me ye have not always. 12 For in that she hath poured this ointment on my body, she did *it* for my burial. 13 Verily I say unto you, Wheresoever this gospel shall be preached in the whole world, *there* shall also this, that this woman hath done, be told for a memorial of her.

---

[w] — καὶ οἱ γραμματεῖς LTTrA. [x] δόλῳ κρατήσωσιν GLTTrAW. [y] ἔχουσα ἀλάβαστρον μύρου LTTr. [z] πολυτίμου LT. [a] τῆς κεφαλῆς LTTr. [b] — αὐτοῦ (*read* the disciples) LTTrA. [c] ἐδύνατο TA. [d] — τὸ μύρον GLTTrAW. [e] + τοῖς (*read* to the poor) LW. [f] ἠργάσατο T.

14 Then one of the twelve, called Judas Iscariot, went unto the chief priests, 15 and said *unto them*, What will ye give me, and I will deliver him unto you? And they covenanted with him for thirty pieces of silver. 16 And from that time he sought opportunity to betray him.

14 Τότε πορευθεὶς εἷς τῶν δώδεκα, ὁ λεγόμενος Ἰούδας
Then [10]having [11]gone [1]one [2]of [3]the [4]twelve, [5]who [6]was [7]called [8]Judas
Ἰσκαριώτης, πρὸς τοὺς ἀρχιερεῖς, 15 εἶπεν, Τί θέλετέ μοι
[9]Iscariote, to the chief priests, said, What are ye willing [3]me
δοῦναι, [g]κἀγὼ ὑμῖν παραδώσω αὐτόν; Οἱ.δὲ ἔστησαν αὐτῷ
[1]to [2]give, and I to you will deliver up him? And they appointed to him
τριάκοντα ἀργύρια. 16 καὶ ἀπὸ τότε ἐζήτει εὐκαιρίαν
thirty pieces of silver. And from that time he sought an opportunity
ἵνα αὐτὸν παραδῷ.
that him he might deliver up.

17 Now the first *day* of the *feast of* unleavened bread the disciples came to Jesus, saying unto him, Where wilt thou that we prepare for thee to eat the passover? 18 And he said, Go into the city to such a man, and say unto him, The Master saith, My time is at hand; I will keep the passover at thy house with my disciples. 19 And the disciples did as Jesus had appointed them; and they made ready the passover.

17 Τῇ.δὲ πρώτῃ τῶν.ἀζύμων προσῆλθον οἱ μαθη-
Now on the first [day] of unleavened [bread] came the disci-
ταὶ τῷ Ἰησοῦ, λέγοντες [h]αὐτῷ,‖ Ποῦ θέλεις ἑτοιμάσωμέν
ples to Jesus, saying to him, Where wilt thou [that] we should prepare
σοι φαγεῖν τὸ πάσχα; 18 Ὁ.δὲ εἶπεν, Ὑπάγετε εἰς τὴν
for thee to eat the passover? And he said, Go into the
πόλιν πρὸς τὸν.δεῖνα, καὶ εἴπατε αὐτῷ, Ὁ διδάσκαλος λέγει,
city unto such a one, and say to him, The teacher says,
Ὁ.καιρός.μου ἐγγύς ἐστιν· πρὸς σὲ ποιῶ τὸ πάσχα μετὰ
My time [2]near [1]is; with thee I will keep the passover with
τῶν.μαθητῶν.μου. 19 Καὶ ἐποίησαν οἱ μαθηταὶ ὡς συνέταξεν
my disciples. And [3]did [1]the [2]disciples [4]as [6]directed
αὐτοῖς ὁ Ἰησοῦς, καὶ ἡτοίμασαν τὸ πάσχα.
[7]them [5]Jesus, and prepared the passover.

20 Now when the even was come, he sat down with the twelve. 21 And as they did eat, he said, Verily I say unto you, that one of you shall betray me. 22 And they were exceeding sorrowful, and began every one of them to say unto him, Lord, is it I? 23 And he answered and said, He that dippeth *his* hand with me in the dish, the same shall betray me. 24 The Son of man goeth as it is written of him: but woe unto that man by whom the Son of man is betrayed! it had been good for that man if he had not been born. 25 Then Judas, which betrayed him, answered and said, Master, is it I? He said unto him, Thou hast said.

20 Ὀψίας.δὲ γενομένης ἀνέκειτο μετὰ τῶν δώδεκα[i].
And evening being come he reclined [at table] with the twelve.
21 καὶ ἐσθιόντων.αὐτῶν εἶπεν, Ἀμὴν λέγω ὑμῖν, ὅτι εἷς ἐξ
And as they were eating he said, Verily I say to you, that one of
ὑμῶν παραδώσει με. 22 Καὶ λυπούμενοι σφόδρα ἤρξαντο
you will deliver up me. And being grieved exceedingly they began
λέγειν αὐτῷ [k]ἕκαστος αὐτῶν,‖ Μήτι ἐγώ εἰμι, κύριε; 23 Ὁ.δὲ
to say to him, each of them, [2]I [1]am [he], Lord? But he
ἀποκριθεὶς εἶπεν, Ὁ ἐμβάψας μετ᾽ ἐμοῦ [l]ἐν τῷ τρυβλίῳ
answering said, He who dipped with me in the dish
τὴν χεῖρα,‖ οὗτός με παραδώσει. 24 ὁ μὲν υἱὸς τοῦ ἀνθρώ-
[his] hand, he me will deliver up. The [4]indeed [1]Son [2]of [3]man
που ὑπάγει, καθὼς γέγραπται περὶ αὐτοῦ, οὐαὶ.δὲ τῷ
goes, as it has been written concerning him, but woe
ἀνθρώπῳ.ἐκείνῳ δι᾽ οὗ ὁ υἱὸς τοῦ ἀνθρώπου παραδίδοται·
to that man by whom the Son of man is delivered up;
καλὸν ἦν αὐτῷ εἰ οὐκ.ἐγεννήθη ὁ.ἄνθρωπος.ἐκεῖνος.
good were it for him if [3]had [4]not [5]been [6]born that [2]man.
25 Ἀποκριθεὶς.δὲ Ἰούδας ὁ παραδιδοὺς αὐτὸν εἶπεν, Μήτι
And answering Judas, who was delivering up him, said,
ἐγώ εἰμι, [m]ῥαββί;‖ Λέγει αὐτῷ, Σὺ εἶπας.
[2]I [1]am [he], Rabbi? He says to him, Thou hast said.

26 And as they were eating, Jesus took bread, and blessed *it*, and brake *it*, and gave *it* to the disciples, and said, Take, eat; this is my body. 27 And he took the cup, and gave thanks, and gave *it* to them, saying, Drink

26 Ἐσθιόντων.δὲ.αὐτῶν, λαβὼν ὁ Ἰησοῦς [n]τὸν‖ ἄρτον,
And as they were eating, [2]having [3]taken [1]Jesus the bread,
καὶ εὐλογήσας, ἔκλασεν καὶ [o]ἐδίδου‖ τοῖς μαθηταῖς, [p]καὶ‖
and having blessed, broke and gave to the disciples, and
εἶπεν, Λάβετε, φάγετε· τοῦτό ἐστιν τὸ.σῶμά.μου. 27 Καὶ
said, Take, eat; this is my body. And
λαβὼν [q]τὸ‖ ποτήριον, [r]καὶ‖ εὐχαριστήσας, ἔδωκεν αὐτοῖς,
having taken the cup, and having given thanks, he gave [it] to them,

[g] καὶ ἐγὼ T. [h] — αὐτῷ LTTrAW. [i] + μαθητῶν disciples LT. [k] εἷς ἕκαστος each one LTTrA. [l] τὴν χεῖρα ἐν τῷ τρυβλίῳ LTTrA. [m] ῥαββεί T. [n] — τὸν LTTr[A]. [o] δοὺς having given LTTr. [p] — καὶ LTTr. [q] — τὸ (*read* a cup) TTrA. [r] — καὶ L[Tr].

λέγων, Πίετε ἐξ αὐτοῦ πάντες· 28 τοῦτο.γάρ ἐστιν τὸ.αἷμά.μου,
saying, [2]Drink [3]of [4]it [1]all. For this is my blood,
[t]τὸ" τῆς [v]καινῆς" διαθήκης, τὸ περὶ πολλῶν [w]ἐκχυνόμενον" εἰς
that of the new covenant, which for many is poured out for
ἄφεσιν ἁμαρτιῶν. 29 λέγω.δὲ ὑμῖν, [x]ὅτι" οὐ.μὴ πίω ἀπ'
remission of sins. But I say to you, that not at all will I drink hence-
ἄρτι ἐκ τούτου τοῦ [y]γεννήματος" τῆς ἀμπέλου, ἕως τῆς ἡμέρας
forth of this fruit of the vine, until [2]day
ἐκείνης ὅταν αὐτὸ πίνω μεθ' ὑμῶν καινὸν ἐν τῇ βασιλείᾳ τοῦ
[1]that when it I drink with you new in the kingdom
πατρός.μου. 30 Καὶ ὑμνήσαντες ἐξῆλθον εἰς τὸ ὄρος τῶν
of my father. And having sung a hymn they went out to the mount
ἐλαιῶν. 31 τότε λέγει αὐτοῖς ὁ Ἰησοῦς, Πάντες ὑμεῖς σκανδα-
of Olives. Then [2]says [3]to [4]them [1]Jesus, All ye will be
λισθήσεσθε ἐν ἐμοὶ ἐν τῇ.νυκτὶ.ταύτῃ. γέγραπται.γάρ,
offended in me during this night. For it has been written,
Πατάξω τὸν ποιμένα, καὶ [z]διασκορπισθήσεται" τὰ πρόβατα
I will smite the shepherd, and will be scattered abroad the sheep
τῆς ποίμνης. 32 μετὰ.δὲ τὸ.ἐγερθῆναί.με προάξω ὑμᾶς
of the flock; but after my being raised I will go before you
εἰς τὴν Γαλιλαίαν. 33 Ἀποκριθεὶς.δὲ ὁ Πέτρος εἶπεν αὐτῷ,
into Galilee. And answering Peter said to him,
Εἰ [a]καὶ" πάντες σκανδαλισθήσονται ἐν σοί, ἐγὼ οὐδέποτε
If even all will be offended in thee, I never
σκανδαλισθήσομαι. 34 Ἔφη αὐτῷ ὁ Ἰησοῦς, Ἀμὴν λέγω σοι,
will be offended. [2]Said [3]to [4]him [1]Jesus, Verily I say to thee,
ὅτι ἐν ταύτῃ τῇ νυκτί, πρὶν ἀλέκτορα φωνῆσαι, τρὶς
that during this night, before [the] cock crows, thrice
ἀπαρνήσῃ με. 35 Λέγει αὐτῷ ὁ Πέτρος, Κἂν δέῃ με
thou wilt deny me. [2]Says [3]to [4]him [1]Peter, Even if it were needful for me
σὺν σοὶ ἀποθανεῖν, οὐ.μή σε ἀπαρνήσομαι. Ὁμοίως [b] καὶ
with thee to die, in nowise thee will I deny. Likewise also
πάντες οἱ μαθηταὶ εἶπον.
all the disciples said.

ye all of it: 28 for this
is my blood of the
new testament, which
is shed for many for
the remission of sins.
29 But I say unto you,
I will not drink hence-
forth of this fruit of
the vine, until that
day when I drink
it new with you in
my Father's kingdom.
30 And when they
had sung an hymn,
they went out into
the mount of Olives.
31 Then saith Jesus
unto them, All ye shall
be offended because of
me this night: for it
is written, I will smite
the shepherd, and the
sheep of the flock shall
be scattered abroad.
32 But after I am risen
again, I will go before
you into Galilee. 33 Pe-
ter answered and said
unto him, Though all
men shall be offended
because of thee, *yet*
will I never be offend-
ed. 34 Jesus said unto
him, Verily I say unto
thee, That this night,
before the cock crow,
thou shalt deny me
thrice. 35 Peter said
unto him, Though I
should die with thee,
yet will I not deny
thee. Likewise also
said all the disciples.

36 Τότε ἔρχεται μετ' αὐτῶν ὁ Ἰησοῦς εἰς χωρίον λεγόμενον
Then comes with them Jesus to a place called
[c]Γεθσημανῆ," καὶ λέγει τοῖς μαθηταῖς[d], Καθίσατε αὐτοῦ, ἕως.οὗ[e]
Gethsemane, and he says to the disciples, Sit here, until
ἀπελθὼν [f]προσεύξωμαι ἐκεῖ." 37 Καὶ παραλαβὼν τὸν
having gone away I shall pray yonder. And having taken with [him]
Πέτρον καὶ τοὺς δύο υἱοὺς Ζεβεδαίου, ἤρξατο λυπεῖσθαι καὶ
Peter and the two sons of Zebedee, he began to be sorrowful and
ἀδημονεῖν. 38 τότε λέγει αὐτοῖς[g], Περίλυπός ἐστιν ἡ.ψυχή.μου
deeply depressed. Then he says to them, Very sorrowful is my soul
ἕως θανάτου· μείνατε ὧδε καὶ γρηγορεῖτε μετ' ἐμοῦ. 39 Καὶ
even to death; remain here and watch with me. And
[h]προελθὼν" μικρὸν ἔπεσεν ἐπὶ πρόσωπον.αὐτοῦ προσευχό-
having gone forward a little he fell upon his face pray-
μενος, καὶ λέγων, Πάτερ.[i]μου," εἰ δυνατόν ἐστιν [k]παρελθέτω"
ing, and saying, my Father, if possible it is let pass
ἀπ' ἐμοῦ τὸ.ποτήριον.τοῦτο· πλὴν οὐχ ὡς ἐγὼ θέλω, ἀλλ' ὡς
from me this cup; nevertheless not as I will, but as

36 Then cometh Je-
sus with them unto
a place called Geth-
semane, and saith unto
the disciples, Sit ye
here, while I go and
pray yonder. 37 And
he took with him Pe-
ter and the two sons
of Zebedee, and began
to be sorrowful and
very heavy. 38 Then
saith he unto them,
My soul is exceeding
sorrowful, even unto
death: tarry ye here,
and watch with me.
39 And he went a little
farther, and fell on
his face, and prayed,
saying, O my Father,
if it be possible, let
this cup pass from me:
nevertheless not as I
will, but as thou *wilt*.

---

[t] — τὸ LTTrA. [v] — καινῆς T[A]. [w] ἐκχυννόμενον LTTrA. [x] — ὅτι LTTrA. [y] γενήματος LTTrAW. [z] διασκορπισθήσονται LTTrA. [a] — καὶ GLTTrAW. [b] + δὲ and (likewise) W. [c] Γεθσημανεῖ LTrAW; Γεθσημανεί T. [d] + αὐτοῦ of him L. [e] + ἂν L. [f] ἐκεῖ προσεύξωμαι LTTrA. [g] + ὁ Ἰησοῦς Jesus (says) W. [h] προσελθὼν having come towards [them] TTr. [i] — μου my T[Tr]. [k] παρελθάτω LTTrA.

40 And he cometh unto the disciples, and findeth them asleep, and saith unto Peter, What, could ye not watch with me one hour? 41 Watch and pray, that ye enter not into temptation: the spirit indeed *is* willing, but the flesh *is* weak. 42 He went away again the second time, and prayed, saying, O my Father, if this cup may not pass away from me, except I drink it, thy will be done. 43 And he came and found them asleep again: for their eyes were heavy. 44 And he left them, and went away again, and prayed the third time, saying the same words. 45 Then cometh he to his disciples, and saith unto them, Sleep on now and take *your* rest: behold, the hour is at hand, and the Son of man is betrayed into the hands of sinners. 46 Rise, let us be going: behold, he is at hand that doth betray me.

σύ. 40 Καὶ ἔρχεται πρὸς τοὺς μαθητὰς καὶ εὑρίσκει αὐτοὺς
thou. And he comes to the disciples and finds them
καθεύδοντας, καὶ λέγει τῷ Πέτρῳ, Οὕτως οὐκ.ἰσχύσατε μίαν
sleeping, and says to Peter, Thus were ye not able one
ὥραν γρηγορῆσαι μετ' ἐμοῦ; 41 γρηγορεῖτε καὶ προσεύχεσθε,
hour to watch with me? Watch and pray,
ἵνα μὴ.εἰσέλθητε εἰς πειρασμόν. τὸ μὲν πνεῦμα πρόθυμον,
that ye enter not into temptation: the [2]indeed [1]spirit [is] ready,
ἡ.δὲ.σὰρξ ἀσθενής. 42 Πάλιν ἐκ.δευτέρου ἀπελθὼν προσ-
but the flesh weak. Again a second time having gone away he
ηύξατο, λέγων, Πάτερ.μου, εἰ οὐ.δύναται τοῦτο [l]τὸ ποτήριον"
prayed, saying, My Father, if [3]cannot [1]this [2]cup
παρελθεῖν [m]ἀπ' ἐμοῦ ἐὰν.μὴ αὐτὸ πίω, γενηθήτω τὸ θέλημά
pass from me unless [3]it [1]I [2]drink, [6]be [7]done [5]will
σου. 43 Καὶ ἐλθὼν [n]εὑρίσκει αὐτοὺς πάλιν" καθεύδοντας,
[4]thy. And having come he finds them again sleeping,
ἦσαν.γὰρ αὐτῶν.οἱ.ὀφθαλμοὶ βεβαρημένοι. 44 Καὶ ἀφεὶς
for [3]were [1]their [2]eyes heavy. And leaving
αὐτούς, [o]ἀπελθὼν πάλιν" προσηύξατο [p]ἐκ.τρίτου," τὸν αὐτὸν
them, having gone away again he prayed a third time, [2]the [3]same
λόγον εἰπών[q]. 45 τότε ἔρχεται πρὸς τοὺς.μαθητὰς.[r]αὐτοῦ,"
[4]thing [1]saying. Then he comes to his disciples
καὶ λέγει αὐτοῖς, Καθεύδετε [s]τὸ".λοιπὸν καὶ ἀναπαύεσθε·
and says to them, Sleep on now and take your rest;
ἰδού, ἤγγικεν ἡ ὥρα, καὶ ὁ υἱὸς τοῦ ἀνθρώπου παραδιδο-
lo, [3]has [4]drawn [5]near [1]the [2]hour, and the Son of man is delivered
ται εἰς χεῖρας ἁμαρτωλῶν. 46 ἐγείρεσθε, ἄγωμεν· ἰδού,
up into [the] hands of sinners. Rise up, let us go; behold,
ἤγγικεν ὁ παραδιδούς με.
[2]has [3]drawn [4]near [1]he who is delivering up me.

47 And while he yet spake, lo, Judas, one of the twelve, came, and with him a great multitude with swords and staves, from the chief priests and elders of the people. 48 Now he that betrayed him gave them a sign, saying, Whomsoever I shall kiss, that same is he: hold him fast. 49 And forthwith he came to Jesus, and said, Hail, master; and kissed him. 50 And Jesus said unto him, Friend, wherefore art thou come? Then came they, and laid hands on Jesus, and took him. 51 And, behold, one of them which were with Jesus stretched out *his* hand, and drew his sword, and struck a servant of the high priest's, and smote off his ear.

47 Καὶ ἔτι αὐτοῦ.λαλοῦντος, ἰδού, Ἰούδας εἷς τῶν δώδεκα
And [4]yet [1]as [2]he [3]is speaking behold, Judas, one of the twelve,
ἦλθεν, καὶ μετ' αὐτοῦ ὄχλος πολὺς μετὰ μαχαιρῶν καὶ ξύλων,
came, and with him a [2]crowd [1]great with swords and staves,
ἀπὸ τῶν ἀρχιερέων καὶ πρεσβυτέρων τοῦ λαοῦ. 48 ὁ.δὲ
from the chief priests and elders of the people. And he who
παραδιδοὺς αὐτὸν ἔδωκεν αὐτοῖς σημεῖον, λέγων, "Ον.[t]ἂν"
was delivering up him gave them a sign, saying, Whomsoever
φιλήσω, αὐτός ἐστιν· κρατήσατε αὐτόν. 49 Καὶ εὐθέως
I shall kiss, he it is: seize him. And immediately
προσελθὼν τῷ Ἰησοῦ εἶπεν, Χαῖρε, [v]ῥαββί," καὶ κατεφίλησεν
having come up to Jesus he said, Hail, Rabbi, and ardently kissed
αὐτόν. 50 ὁ.δὲ.Ἰησοῦς εἶπεν αὐτῷ, Ἑταῖρε, ἐφ' [w]ᾧ"
him. But Jesus said to him, Friend, for what [purpose]
πάρει; Τότε προσελθόντες ἐπέβαλον τὰς χεῖρας ἐπὶ
art thou come? Then having come to [him] they laid hands on
τὸν Ἰησοῦν, καὶ ἐκράτησαν αὐτόν. 51 Καὶ ἰδού, εἷς τῶν
Jesus, and seized him. And behold, one of those
μετὰ Ἰησοῦ, ἐκτείνας τὴν χεῖρα ἀπέσπασεν τὴν μάχαι-
with Jesus, having stretched out [his] hand drew [2]sword
ραν αὐτοῦ, καὶ πατάξας τὸν δοῦλον τοῦ ἀρχιερέως ἀφεῖλεν
[1]his, and smiting the bondman of the high priest took off

---

l — τὸ ποτήριον LTTrA. m — ἀπ' ἐμοῦ [L]TTrA. n πάλιν εὗρεν αὐτοὺς again he found them LTTrA. o πάλιν ἀπελθὼν LTTrA. p — ἐκ τρίτου [L]A. q + πάλιν again T. r — αὐτοῦ (read the disciples) LTTrA. s — τὸ [Tr]A. t ἐὰν TA. v ῥαββεί T. w ὃ GLTTrAW.

αὐτοῦ τὸ ὠτίον. 52 τότε λέγει αὐτῷ ὁ Ἰησοῦς, Ἀπόστρεψόν
his ear. Then [2]says [3]to [4]him [1]Jesus, Return
[x]σου τὴν μάχαιραν‖ εἰς τὸν.τόπον.αὐτῆς· πάντες.γὰρ οἱ λα-
thy sword to its place; for all who
βόντες μάχαιραν ἐν [y]μαχαίρᾳ‖ ἀπολοῦνται. 53 ἢ δο-
take [the] sword by [the] sword shall perish. Or think-
κεῖς ὅτι οὐ.δύναμαι [z]ἄρτι‖ παρακαλέσαι τὸν.πατέρα.μου,
est thou that I am not able now to call upon my Father,
καὶ παραστήσει μοι [a] [b]πλείους‖ [c]ἢ‖ δώδεκα [d]λεγεῶνας‖ ἀγ-
and he will furnish to me more than twelve legions of
γέλων; 54 πῶς οὖν πληρωθῶσιν αἱ γραφαὶ ὅτι οὕτως
angels? How then should be fulfilled the scriptures that thus
δεῖ γενέσθαι;
it must be?

52 Then said Jesus unto him, Put up again thy sword into his place: for all they that take the sword shall perish with the sword.
53 Thinkest thou that I cannot now pray to my Father, and he shall presently give me more than twelve legions of angels?
54 But how then shall the scriptures be fulfilled, that thus it must be?

55 Ἐν ἐκείνῃ τῇ ὥρᾳ εἶπεν ὁ Ἰησοῦς τοῖς ὄχλοις, Ὡς ἐπὶ
In that hour said Jesus to the crowds, As against
ληστὴν [e]ἐξήλθετε‖ μετὰ μαχαιρῶν καὶ ξύλων συλλαβεῖν με;
a robber are ye come out with swords and staves to take me?
καθ᾽.ἡμέραν [f]πρὸς ὑμᾶς‖ [g]ἐκαθεζόμην διδάσκων ἐν τῷ ἱερῷ,‖
Daily with you I sat teaching in the temple,
καὶ οὐκ.ἐκρατήσατέ με. 56 τοῦτο.δὲ ὅλον γέγονεν ἵνα πλη-
and ye did not seize me. But this all is come to pass that may
ρωθῶσιν αἱ γραφαὶ τῶν προφητῶν. Τότε οἱ μαθηταὶ[h] πάντες
be fulfilled the scriptures of the prophets. Then the disciples all
ἀφέντες αὐτὸν ἔφυγον.
forsaking him fled.

55 In that same hour said Jesus to the multitudes, Are ye come out as against a thief with swords and staves for to take me? I sat daily with you teaching in the temple, and ye laid no hold on me.
56 But all this was done, that the scriptures of the prophets might be fulfilled. Then all the disciples forsook him, and fled.

57 Οἱ.δὲ κρατήσαντες τὸν Ἰησοῦν ἀπήγαγον πρὸς Καϊ-
But they who had seized Jesus led [him] away to Cai-
άφαν τὸν ἀρχιερέα, ὅπου οἱ γραμματεῖς καὶ οἱ πρεσβύτεροι
aphas the high priest, where the scribes and the elders
συνήχθησαν. 58 Ὁ.δὲ.Πέτρος ἠκολούθει αὐτῷ [i]ἀπὸ‖ μακρό-
were gathered together. And Peter followed him from afar
θεν, ἕως τῆς αὐλῆς τοῦ ἀρχιερέως· καὶ εἰσελθὼν ἔσω ἐκάθητο
even to the court of the high priest; and having entered within he sat
μετὰ τῶν ὑπηρετῶν ἰδεῖν τὸ τέλος. 59 Οἱ.δὲ ἀρχιερεῖς [k]καὶ οἱ
with the officers to see the end. And the chief priests and the
πρεσβύτεροι‖ καὶ τὸ συνέδριον ὅλον ἐζήτουν ψευδομαρτυρίαν
elders and the [2]sanhedrim [1]whole sought false evidence
κατὰ τοῦ Ἰησοῦ, ὅπως [l]αὐτὸν θανατώσωσιν,‖ 60 καὶ οὐχ
against Jesus, so that him they might put to death, and [2]not
εὗρον· [m]καὶ‖ πολλῶν [n]ψευδομαρτύρων προσελθόντων‖ [o]οὐχ
[1]found [[3]any]: even many false witnesses having come forward [3]not
εὗρον.‖ 61 ὕστερον.δὲ προσελθόντες δύο [p]ψευδομάρτυρες‖
[1]they [2]found [any]. But at last having come forward two false witnesses
εἶπον, Οὗτος ἔφη, Δύναμαι καταλῦσαι τὸν ναὸν τοῦ θεοῦ,
said, This [man] said, I am able to destroy the temple of God,
καὶ διὰ τριῶν ἡμερῶν [q]οἰκοδομῆσαι αὐτόν.‖ 62 Καὶ ἀναστὰς
and in three days to build it. And having stood up
ὁ ἀρχιερεὺς εἶπεν αὐτῷ, Οὐδὲν ἀποκρίνῃ; τί οὗτοί σου
the high priest said to him, Nothing answerest thou? What [2]these [5]thee

57 And they that had laid hold on Jesus led *him* away to Caiaphas the high priest, where the scribes and the elders were assembled.
58 But Peter followed him afar off unto the high priest's palace, and went in, and sat with the servants, to see the end.
59 Now the chief priests, and elders, and all the council, sought false witness against Jesus, to put him to death;
60 but found none: yea, though many false witnesses came, *yet* found they none. At the last came two false witnesses,
61 and said, This *fellow* said, I am able to destroy the temple of God, and to build it in three days.
62 And the high priest arose, and said unto him, Answerest thou nothing? what *is it which* these witness against thee?
63 But

---

[x] τὴν μάχαιράν σου LTTrA. [y] μαχαίρῃ LTTrA. [z] — ἄρτι TTr. [a] + ἄρτι now TTr. [b] πλείω LTTrA. [c] — ἢ (read [than]) [L]TTrA. [d] λεγιώνων T. [e] ἐξήλθατε LTTrA. [f] — πρὸς ὑμᾶς T[Tr]A [g] ἐκαθεζόμην ἐν τῷ ἱερῷ διδάσκων L; ἐν τῷ ἱερῷ ἐκαθεζόμην διδάσκων TTrA. [h] + αὐτοῦ of him [L]. [i] — ἀπὸ T. [k] — καὶ οἱ πρεσβύτεροι LTTrA. [l] αὐτὸν θανατώσουσιν LTTrA; θανατώσωσιν αὐτὸν W. [m] — καὶ GLTTr. [n] προσελθόντων ψευδομαρτύρων LTTrA. [o] — οὐχ εὗρον G[L]TTrA. [p] — ψευδομάρτυρες TTrA. [q] αὐτὸν οἰκοδομῆσαι T; — αὐτὸν TrA.

Jesus held his peace. And the high priest answered and said unto him, I adjure thee by the living God, that thou tell us whether thou be the Christ, the Son of God. 64 Jesus saith unto him, Thou hast said: nevertheless I say unto you, Hereafter shall ye see the Son of man sitting on the right hand of power, and coming in the clouds of heaven. 65 Then the high priest rent his clothes, saying, He hath spoken blasphemy; what further need have we of witnesses? behold, now ye have heard his blasphemy. 66 What think ye? They answered and said, He is guilty of death. 67 Then did they spit in his face, and buffeted him; and others smote *him* with the palms of their hands, 68 saying, Prophesy unto us, thou Christ, Who is he that smote thee?

καταμαρτυροῦσιν; 63 Ὁ.δὲ.Ἰησοῦς ἐσιώπα. καὶ [s]ἀποκριθεὶς‖ ὁ
[1]do [3]witness [2]against? But Jesus was silent. And answering the
ἀρχιερεὺς εἶπεν αὐτῷ, Ἐξορκίζω σὲ κατὰ τοῦ θεοῦ τοῦ ζῶντος,
high priest said to him, I adjure thee by [3]God [1]the [2]living,
ἵνα ἡμῖν εἴπῃς, εἰ σὺ εἶ ὁ χριστός, ὁ υἱὸς τοῦ θεοῦ. 64 Λέγει
that us thou tell if thou art the Christ, the Son of God. [2]Says
αὐτῷ ὁ Ἰησοῦς, Σὺ εἶπας. πλὴν λέγω ὑμῖν, ἀπ'.ἄρτι ὄψεσθε
[3]to [4]him [1]Jesus, Thou hast said. Moreover I say to you, Henceforth ye shall see
τὸν υἱὸν τοῦ ἀνθρώπου καθήμενον ἐκ δεξιῶν τῆς δυνάμεως καὶ
the Son of man sitting at [the] right hand of power, and
ἐρχόμενον ἐπὶ τῶν νεφελῶν τοῦ οὐρανοῦ. 65 Τότε ὁ ἀρχιερεὺς
coming on the clouds of heaven. Then the high priest
διέῤῥηξεν τὰ.ἱμάτια.αὐτοῦ, λέγων, [t]"Οτι‖ ἐβλασφήμησεν· τί
rent his garments, saying, He has blasphemed; why
ἔτι χρείαν ἔχομεν μαρτύρων; ἴδε, νῦν ἠκούσατε τὴν βλασ-
any more [3]need [1]have [2]we of witnesses? lo, now ye have heard the blas-
φημίαν [v]αὐτοῦ.‖ 66 τί ὑμῖν.δοκεῖ; Οἱ.δὲ ἀποκριθέντες εἶπον,
phemy of him. What do ye think? And they answering said,
"Ενοχος θανάτου ἐστίν. 67 Τότε ἐνέπτυσαν εἰς τὸ πρόσωπον
Deserving of death he is. Then they spat in [2]face
αὐτοῦ, καὶ ἐκολάφισαν αὐτόν, οἱ.δὲ [w]ἐῤῥάπισαν,‖
[1]his, and buffeted him, and some struck [him] with the palm of the
68 λέγοντες, Προφήτευσον ἡμῖν, χριστέ, τίς ἐστιν ὁ
hand, saying, Prophesy to us, Christ, Who is he that
παίσας σε;
struck thee?

69 Now Peter sat without in the palace: and a damsel came unto him, saying, Thou also wast with Jesus of Galilee. 70 But he denied before *them* all, saying, I know not what thou sayest. 71 And when he was gone out into the porch, another *maid* saw him, and said unto them that were there, This *fellow* was also with Jesus of Nazareth. 72 And again he denied with an oath, I do not know the man. 73 And after a while came unto *him* they that stood by, and said to Peter, Surely thou also art *one* of them; for thy speech bewrayeth thee. 74 Then began he to curse and to swear, *saying*, I know not the man. And immediately the cock crew. 75 And Peter remembered the word of Jesus, which said unto him, Before the cock crow, thou shalt deny me thrice. And he went out, and wept bitterly.

69 Ὁ.δὲ.Πέτρος [x]ἔξω ἐκάθητο‖ ἐν τῇ αὐλῇ, καὶ προσῆλθεν
But Peter [3]without [1]was [2]sitting in the court, and [3]came
αὐτῷ μία.παιδίσκη, λέγουσα, Καὶ σὺ ἦσθα μετὰ Ἰησοῦ τοῦ
[4]to [5]him [1]a [2]maid, saying, And thou wast with Jesus the
Γαλιλαίου. 70 Ὁ.δὲ ἠρνήσατο ἔμπροσθεν [y]πάντων, λέγων, Οὐκ
Galilæan. But he denied before all, saying, [3]Not
οἶδα τί λέγεις. 71 Ἐξελθόντα.δὲ [z]αὐτὸν‖ εἰς τὸν πυλῶνα
[1]I [2]know what thou sayest. And [2]having [3]gone [4]out [1]he into the porch
εἶδεν αὐτὸν ἄλλη, καὶ λέγει [a]τοῖς‖ ἐκεῖ, [b]Καὶ‖ οὗτος
[3]saw [4]him [1]another [[2]maid], and says to those there, And this [man]
ἦν μετὰ Ἰησοῦ τοῦ Ναζωραίου. 72 Καὶ πάλιν ἠρνήσατο
was with Jesus the Nazaræan. And again he denied
[c]μεθ'‖ ὅρκου, "Οτι οὐκ.οἶδα τὸν ἄνθρωπον. 73 Μετὰ μικρὸν.δὲ
with an oath, I know not the man. After a little also
προσελθόντες οἱ ἑστῶτες εἶπον τῷ Πέτρῳ, Ἀληθῶς
[5]having [6]come [7]to [[8]him] [1]those [2]who [3]stood [4]by said to Peter, Truly
καὶ σὺ ἐξ αὐτῶν εἶ· καὶ.γὰρ ἡ.λαλιά.σου δῆλόν σε ποιεῖ.
also thou of them art, for even thy speech [3]manifest [2]thee [1]makes.
74 Τότε ἤρξατο [d]καταναθεματίζειν‖ καὶ ὀμνύειν, "Οτι οὐκ.οἶδα
Then he began to curse and to swear, I know not
τὸν ἄνθρωπον. Καὶ [e]εὐθέως‖ ἀλέκτωρ ἐφώνησεν. 75 καὶ
the man. And immediately a cock crew. And
ἐμνήσθη ὁ Πέτρος τοῦ ῥήματος [f]τοῦ‖ Ἰησοῦ εἰρηκότος [g]αὐτῷ‖,
[2]remembered [1]Peter the word of Jesus, who had said to him,
"Οτι πρὶν ἀλέκτορα φωνῆσαι, τρὶς ἀπαρνήσῃ με· καὶ
Before [the] cock crow, thrice thou wilt deny me. And
ἐξελθὼν ἔξω ἔκλαυσεν πικρῶς.
having gone out he wept bitterly.

[s] — ἀποκριθεὶς Tr. [t] — ὅτι LTTrA. [v] — αὐτοῦ [L]TTrA. [w] ἐράπισαν LTTrA. [x] ἐκάθητο ἔξω LTTrA. [y] + αὐτῶν them G. [z] — αὐτὸν [L] Tr. [a] αὐτοῖς to them AW. [b] — καὶ T. [c] μετὰ LTTrA. [d] καταθεματίζειν GLTTrAW. [e] εὐθὺς Tr. [f] — τοῦ LTTrA. [g] — αὐτῷ [L]TTrA.

27 Πρωΐας.δὲ γενομένης, συμβούλιον ἔλαβον πάντες οἱ
And morning being come, [12]counsel [11]took [1]all [2]the
ἀρχιερεῖς καὶ οἱ πρεσβύτεροι τοῦ λαοῦ κατὰ τοῦ Ἰησοῦ,
[3]chief [4]priests [5]and [6]the [7]elders [8]of [9]the [10]people against Jesus,
ὥστε θανατῶσαι αὐτόν· 2 καὶ δήσαντες αὐτὸν ἀπήγα-
so that they might put to death him; and having bound him they led
γον καὶ παρέδωκαν [i]αὐτὸν‖ [k]Ποντίῳ‖ [l]Πιλάτῳ‖ τῷ
away [him] and delivered up him to Pontius Pilate the
ἡγεμόνι.
governor.

3 Τότε ἰδὼν Ἰούδας ὁ [m]παραδιδοὺς‖ αὐτὸν ὅτι κατ-
Then [6]having [7]seen [1]Judas [2]who [3]delivered [5]up [4]him that he was
εκρίθη, μεταμεληθεὶς [n]ἀπέστρεψεν‖ τὰ τριάκοντα ἀργύ-
condemned, having regretted [it] returned the thirty pieces of
ρια τοῖς ἀρχιερεῦσιν καὶ [o]τοῖς‖ πρεσβυτέροις, 4 λέγων,
silver to the chief priests and the elders, saying,
Ἥμαρτον παραδοὺς αἷμα [p]ἀθῷον‖. Οἱ.δὲ εἶπον, Τί
I sinned delivering up [2]blood [1]guiltless. But they said, What [is that]
πρὸς ἡμᾶς; σὺ [q]ὄψει.‖ 5 Καὶ ῥίψας τὰ ἀργύρια
to us? thou wilt see [to it]. And having cast down the pieces of silver
[r]ἐν τῷ ναῷ‖ ἀνεχώρησεν, καὶ ἀπελθὼν ἀπήγξατο. 6 Οἱ.δὲ
in the temple he withdrew, and having gone away hanged himself. And the
ἀρχιερεῖς λαβόντες τὰ ἀργύρια [s]εἶπον,‖ Οὐκ.ἔξεστιν βαλεῖν
chief priests having taken the pieces of silver said, It is not lawful to put
αὐτὰ εἰς τὸν κορβανᾶν, ἐπεὶ τιμὴ αἵματός ἐστιν. 7 Συμ-
them into the treasury, since [the] price of blood it is. [4]Coun-
βούλιον δὲ λαβόντες, ἠγόρασαν ἐξ αὐτῶν τὸν ἀγρὸν τοῦ
sel [1]and [2]having [3]taken, they bought with them the field of the
κεραμέως, εἰς ταφὴν τοῖς ξένοις. 8 διὸ ἐκλήθη ὁ
potter, for a burying ground for strangers. Wherefore [3]was [4]called
ἀγρὸς.ἐκεῖνος ἀγρὸς αἵματος ἕως τῆς.σήμερον. 9 τότε
[1]that [2]field Field of blood to this day. Then
ἐπληρώθη τὸ ῥηθὲν διὰ Ἱερεμίου τοῦ προφήτου, λέγον-
was fulfilled that which was spoken by Jeremias the prophet, say-
τος, Καὶ ἔλαβον τὰ τριάκοντα ἀργύρια, τὴν τιμὴν τοῦ
ing, And I took the thirty pieces of silver, the price of him who
τετιμημένου, ὃν ἐτιμήσαντο ἀπὸ υἱῶν Ἰσραήλ, 10 καὶ
was set a price on, whom they [6]set [7]a [8]price [9]on [1]of [[2]the] [3]sons [4]of [5]Israel, and
ἔδωκαν αὐτὰ εἰς τὸν ἀγρὸν τοῦ κεραμέως, καθὰ συνέταξέν
gave them for the field of the potter, according as [3]directed
μοι κύριος.
[4]me [[1]the] [2]Lord.

XXVII. When the morning was come, all the chief priests and elders of the people took counsel against Jesus to put him to death: 2 and when they had bound him, they led *him* away, and delivered him to Pontius Pilate the governor.

3 Then Judas, which had betrayed him, when he saw that he was condemned, repented himself, and brought again the thirty pieces of silver to the chief priests and elders, 4 saying, I have sinned in that I have betrayed the innocent blood. And they said, What *is that* to us? see thou *to that*. 5 And he cast down the pieces of silver in the temple, and departed, and went and hanged himself. 6 And the chief priests took the silver pieces, and said, It is not lawful for to put them into the treasury, because it is the price of blood. 7 And they took counsel, and bought with them the potter's field, to bury strangers in. 8 Wherefore that field was called, The field of blood, unto this day. 9 Then was fulfilled that which was spoken by Jeremy the prophet, saying, And they took the thirty pieces of silver, the price of him that was valued, whom they of the children of Israel did value; 10 and gave them for the potter's field, as the Lord appointed me.

11 Ὁ.δὲ.Ἰησοῦς [t]ἔστη‖ ἔμπροσθεν τοῦ ἡγεμόνος· καὶ ἐπηρώ-
But Jesus stood before the governor; and [3]ques-
τησεν αὐτὸν ὁ ἡγεμών, λέγων, Σὺ εἶ ὁ βασιλεὺς τῶν
tioned [4]him [1]the [2]governor, saying, [2]Thou [1]art the king of the
Ἰουδαίων; Ὁ.δὲ.Ἰησοῦς ἔφη [v]αὐτῷ,‖ Σὺ λέγεις. 12 Καὶ
Jews? And Jesus said to him, Thou sayest. And
ἐν.τῷ.κατηγορεῖσθαι αὐτὸν ὑπὸ τῶν ἀρχιερέων καὶ [w]τῶν‖ πρεσ-
when [2]was [3]accused [1]he by the chief priests and the el-
βυτέρων, οὐδὲν ἀπεκρίνατο. 13 τότε λέγει αὐτῷ ὁ [x]Πιλάτος,‖
ders, nothing he answered. Then [2]says [3]to [4]him [1]Pilate,

11 And Jesus stood before the governor: and the governor asked him, saying, Art thou the king of the Jews? And Jesus said unto him, Thou sayest. 12 And when he was accused of the chief priests and elders, he answered nothing. 13 Then said Pilate unto him, Hearest

---

[i] — αὐτὸν LTTrA. [k] — Ποντίῳ TTr. [l] Πειλάτῳ T. [m] παραδοὺς had delivered up LTr. [n] ἔστρεψεν TTrA. [o] — τοῖς LTTrA. [p] ἀθῷον LTA. [q] ὄψῃ LTTrA. [r] εἰς τὸν ναὸν into the temple TTr. [s] εἶπαν LTTr. [t] ἐστάθη LTTrA. [v] — αὐτῷ T. [w] — τῶν T[A]. [x] Πιλᾶτος LTr; Πειλᾶτος T.

Οὐκ.ἀκούεις πόσα σοῦ καταμαρτυροῦσιν; 14 Καὶ
Hearest thou not how many things [4]thee [1]they [2]witness [3]against? And

οὐκ.ἀπεκρίθη αὐτῷ πρὸς οὐδὲ ἓν ῥῆμα, ὥστε θαυμάζειν τὸν
he did not answer him to even one word, so that [3]wondered [1]the

ἡγεμόνα λίαν.
[2]governor exceedingly.

15 Κατὰ.δὲ ἑορτὴν εἰώθει ὁ ἡγεμὼν ἀπολύειν ἕνα
Now at [the] feast [3]was [4]accustomed [1]the [2]governor to release one

τῷ ὄχλῳ δέσμιον, ὃν ἤθελον. 16 εἶχον.δὲ τότε δέσ-
[2]to [3]the [4]multitude [1]prisoner, whom they wished. And they had then a [2]pri-

μιον ἐπίσημον, λεγόμενον Βαραββᾶν. 17 συνηγμένων
soner [1]notable, called Barabbas. [3]Being [4]gathered [5]together

οὖν αὐτῶν εἶπεν αὐτοῖς ὁ [y]Πιλάτος,|| Τίνα θέλετε ἀπο-
[2]therefore [1]they [7]said [8]to [9]them [6]Pilate, Whom will ye [that] I

λύσω ὑμῖν; Βαραββᾶν, ἢ Ἰησοῦν τὸν λεγόμενον χριστόν;
release to you? Barabbas, or Jesus who is called Christ?

18 ᾔδει.γὰρ ὅτι διὰ φθόνον παρέδωκαν αὐτόν. 19 Καθη-
For he knew that through envy they delivered up him. [2]As [4]was

μένου δὲ αὐτοῦ ἐπὶ τοῦ βήματος ἀπέστειλεν πρὸς αὐτὸν ἡ
[5]sitting [1]but [3]he on the judgment seat [3]sent [4]to [5]him

γυνὴ.αὐτοῦ, λέγουσα, Μηδὲν σοὶ καὶ τῷ δικαίῳ
[1]his [2]wife, saying, [Let there be] nothing between thee and [2]righteous

ἐκείνῳ· πολλὰ.γὰρ ἔπαθον σήμερον κατ' ὄναρ δι'
[1]that [man]; for many things I suffered to-day in a dream because of

αὐτόν. 20 Οἱ.δὲ ἀρχιερεῖς καὶ οἱ πρεσβύτεροι ἔπεισαν τοὺς
him. But the chief priests and the elders persuaded the

ὄχλους ἵνα αἰτήσωνται τὸν Βαραββᾶν, τὸν.δὲ.Ἰησοῦν ἀπολ-
crowds that they should beg for Barabbas, and [3]Jesus [1]should

έσωσιν. 21 ἀποκριθεὶς.δὲ ὁ ἡγεμὼν εἶπεν αὐτοῖς, Τίνα θέλετε
[2]destroy. And [3]answering [1]the [2]governor said to them, Which will ye

ἀπὸ τῶν δύο ἀπολύσω ὑμῖν; Οἱ.δὲ [z]εἶπον,|| [a]Βαραββᾶν.
of the two [that] I release to you? And they said, Barabbas.

22 Λέγει αὐτοῖς ὁ [y]Πιλάτος,|| Τί οὖν ποιήσω Ἰησοῦν, τὸν
[2]Says [3]to [4]them [1]Pilate, What then shall I do with Jesus, who

λεγόμενον χριστόν; Λέγουσιν [b]αὐτῷ|| πάντες, Σταυρωθήτω.
is called Christ? They [2]say [3]to [4]him [1]all, Let [him] be crucified.

23 Ὁ.δὲ [c]ἡγεμὼν|| ἔφη, Τί γὰρ κακὸν ἐποίησεν; Οἱ.δὲ
And the governor said, What [2]then [1]evil did he commit? But they

περισσῶς ἔκραζον, λέγοντες, Σταυρωθήτω. 24 Ἰδὼν.δὲ ὁ
the more cried out, saying, Let [him] be crucified. And [2]seeing

[y]Πιλάτος|| ὅτι οὐδὲν ὠφελεῖ, ἀλλὰ μᾶλλον θόρυβος γίνεται,
[1]Pilate that nothing it availed, but rather a tumult is arising,

λαβὼν ὕδωρ ἀπενίψατο τὰς χεῖρας [d]ἀπέναντι|| τοῦ ὄχλου,
having taken water he washed [his] hands before the crowd,

λέγων, [e]Ἀθῷός|| εἰμι ἀπὸ τοῦ αἵματος [f]τοῦ.δικαίου.τούτου·||
saying, Guiltless I am of the blood of this righteous [man];

ὑμεῖς ὄψεσθε. 25 Καὶ ἀποκριθεὶς πᾶς ὁ λαὸς εἶπεν, Τὸ
ye will see [to it]. And [4]answering [1]all [2]the [3]people said,

αἷμα.αὐτοῦ ἐφ' ἡμᾶς καὶ ἐπὶ τὰ.τέκνα.ἡμῶν. 26 Τότε ἀπέλυ-
His blood [be] on us and on our children. Then he re-

σεν αὐτοῖς τὸν Βαραββᾶν· τὸν.δὲ.Ἰησοῦν φραγελλώσας
leased to them Barabbas; but [3]Jesus [1]having [2]scourged

παρέδωκεν ἵνα σταυρωθῇ.
he delivered up [him] that he might be crucified.

thou not how many things they witness against thee? 14 And
he answered him to never a word; insomuch that the governor marvelled greatly.

15 Now at *that* feast the governor was wont to release unto the people a prisoner, whom they would.
16 And they had then a notable prisoner, called Barabbas.
17 Therefore when they were gathered together, Pilate said unto them, Whom will ye that I release unto you? Barabbas, or Jesus which is called Christ?
18 For he knew that for envy they had delivered him.
19 When he was set down on the judgment seat, his wife sent unto him, saying, Have thou nothing to do with that just man: for I have suffered many things this day in a dream because of him.
20 But the chief priests and elders persuaded the multitude that they should ask Barabbas, and destroy Jesus.
21 The governor answered and said unto them, Whether of the twain will ye that I release unto you? They said, Barabbas.
22 Pilate saith unto them, What shall I do then with Jesus which is called Christ? *They* all say unto him, Let him be crucified.
23 And the governor said, Why, what evil hath he done? But they cried out the more, saying, Let him be crucified.
24 When Pilate saw that he could prevail nothing, but *that* rather a tumult was made, he took water, and washed *his* hands before the multitude, saying, I am innocent of the blood of this just person: see ye *to it*.
25 Then answered all the people, and said, His blood *be* on us, and on our children.
26 Then released he Barabbas unto them: and when he had scourged Jesus, he delivered *him* to be crucified.

y Πιλᾶτος LTr; Πειλᾶτος T. z εἶπαν TTr. a + τὸν TTr. b — αὐτῷ LTTrA. c — ἡγεμὼν (*read* and he said) TTrA. d κατέναντι LTr. e ἀθῷός LTA. f τούτου [τοῦ δικαίου] L; — τοῦ δικαίου (*read* of this [man]) T[Tr]A.

27 Τότε οἱ στρατιῶται τοῦ ἡγεμόνος, παραλαβόντες
Then the soldiers of the governor, having taken with [them]
τὸν Ἰησοῦν εἰς τὸ πραιτώριον, συνήγαγον ἐπ' αὐτὸν ὅλην
Jesus to the prætorium, gathered against him all
τὴν σπεῖραν· 28 καὶ [g]ἐκδύσαντες‖ αὐτὸν [h]περιέθηκαν αὐτῷ
the band; and having stripped him they put round him
χλαμύδα κοκκίνην‖ 29 καὶ πλέξαντες στέφανον ἐξ ἀκανθῶν
a [2]cloak [1]scarlet; And having platted a crown of thorns
ἐπέθηκαν ἐπὶ [i]τὴν.κεφαλὴν‖.αὐτοῦ, καὶ κάλαμον [k]ἐπὶ τὴν
they put [it] on his head, and a reed in
δεξιὰν‖ αὐτοῦ· καὶ γονυπετήσαντες ἔμπροσθεν αὐτοῦ [l]ἐνέ-
[2]right [3]hand [1]his; and bowing the knees before him they
παιζον‖ αὐτῷ, λέγοντες, Χαῖρε, [m]ὁ βασιλεὺς‖ τῶν Ἰουδαίων·
mocked him, saying, Hail, king of the Jews!
30 καὶ ἐμπτύσαντες εἰς αὐτὸν ἔλαβον τὸν κάλαμον καὶ ἔτυπ-
And having spit upon him they took the reed and struck
τον εἰς τὴν.κεφαλὴν.αὐτοῦ. 31 Καὶ ὅτε ἐνέπαιξαν αὐτῷ
[him] on his head. And when they had mocked him
[n]ἐξέδυσαν‖ αὐτὸν τὴν χλαμύδα, [o]καὶ‖ ἐνέδυσαν αὐτὸν τὰ
they took off him the cloak, and they put on him
ἱμάτια.αὐτοῦ· καὶ ἀπήγαγον αὐτὸν εἰς τὸ.σταυρῶσαι.
his own garments; and led [2]away [1]him to crucify.

32 Ἐξερχόμενοι.δὲ εὗρον ἄνθρωπον Κυρηναῖον, ὀνόματι
And going forth they found a man a Cyrenæan, by name
Σίμωνα· τοῦτον ἠγγάρευσαν ἵνα ἄρῃ τὸν.σταυρὸν.αὐτοῦ.
Simon; him they compelled that he might carry his cross.
33 Καὶ ἐλθόντες εἰς τόπον λεγόμενον [p]Γολγοθᾶ,‖ [q]ὅς‖ ἐστιν
And having come to a place called Golgotha, which is
[r]λεγόμενος κρανίου τόπος,‖ 34 ἔδωκαν αὐτῷ [s]πιεῖν‖ [t]ὄξος‖
called [2]of [3]a [4]skull [1]place, they gave him to drink vinegar
μετὰ χολῆς μεμιγμένον· καὶ γευσάμενος οὐκ.[v]ἤθελεν‖ [s]πιεῖν.‖
with gall mingled; and having tasted he would not drink.
35 Σταυρώσαντες.δὲ αὐτὸν διεμερίσαντο τὰ.ἱμάτια.αὐτοῦ,
And having crucified him they divided his garments,
[w]βάλλοντες‖ κλῆρον· [x]ἵνα πληρωθῇ τὸ ῥηθὲν ὑπὸ
casting a lot; that might be fulfilled that which was spoken by
τοῦ προφήτου, Διεμερίσαντο τὰ.ἱμάτιά.μου ἑαυτοῖς, καὶ
the prophet, They divided my garments among themselves, and
ἐπὶ τὸν.ἱματισμόν.μου ἔβαλον κλῆρον.‖ 36 Καὶ καθήμενοι
for my vesture they cast a lot. And sitting down
ἐτήρουν αὐτὸν ἐκεῖ. 37 Καὶ ἐπέθηκαν ἐπάνω τῆς
they kept guard over him there. And they put up over
κεφαλῆς.αὐτοῦ τὴν.αἰτίαν.αὐτοῦ γεγραμμένην, Οὗτός ἐστιν
his head his accusation written: This is
Ἰησοῦς ὁ βασιλεὺς τῶν Ἰουδαίων. 38 Τότε σταυροῦνται σὺν
Jesus the king of the Jews. Then are crucified with
αὐτῷ δύο λῃσταί, εἷς ἐκ δεξιῶν καὶ εἷς ἐξ εὐωνύμων.
him two robbers, one at [the] right hand and one at [the] left.

39 Οἱ.δὲ παραπορευόμενοι ἐβλασφήμουν αὐτόν, κινοῦντες
But those passing by railed at him, shaking
τὰς.κεφαλὰς.αὐτῶν, 40 καὶ λέγοντες, Ὁ καταλύων τὸν ναὸν
their heads, and saying, Thou who destroyest the temple

27 Then the soldiers
of the governor took
Jesus into the common
hall, and gathered unto him the whole band
of soldiers. 28 And
they stripped him, and
put on him a scarlet
robe. 29 And when
they had platted a
crown of thorns, they
put *it* upon his head,
and a reed in his right
hand: and they bowed
the knee before him,
and mocked him, saying, Hail, King of the
Jews! 30 And they
spit upon him, and
took the reed, and
smote him on the head.
31 And after that they
had mocked him, they
took the robe off from
him, and put his own
raiment on him, and
led him away to crucify *him*.

32 And as they came
out, they found a
man of Cyrene, Simon
by name: him they
compelled to bear his
cross. 33 And when
they were come unto
a place called Golgotha, that is to say,
a place of a skull,
34 They gave him vinegar to drink mingled
with gall: and when
he had tasted *thereof*,
he would not drink.
35 And they crucified
him, and parted his
garments, casting lots:
that it might be fulfilled which was spoken by the prophet,
They parted my garments among them,
and upon my vesture
did they cast lots.
36 And sitting down
they watched him
there; 37 and set up
over his head his accusation written, THIS
IS JESUS THE
KING OF THE
JEWS. 38 Then were
there two thieves crucified with him, one
on the right hand, and
another on the left.

39 And they that
passed by reviled him,
wagging their heads,
40 and saying, Thou
that destroyest the
temple, and buildest

[g] ἐνδύσαντες having clothed L. [h] χλαμύδα κοκκίνην περιέθηκαν αὐτῷ LTTrA. [i] τῆς κεφαλῆς TTrA. [k] ἐν τῇ δεξιᾷ LTTrA. [l] ἐνέπαιξαν T. [m] βασιλεῦ O king LTr. [n] ἐκδύσαντες having taken off T. [o] — καὶ T. [p] Γολγοθά Tr. [q] ὅ GLTTrAW. [r] κρανίου τόπος λεγόμενος LTTrA. [s] πεῖν T. [t] οἶνον wine LTTr. [v] ἠθέλησεν LTTr; ἐθέλησεν A. [w] βαλόντες having cast LTA. [x] — ἵνα πληρωθῇ *to end of verse* GLTTrA.

it in three days, save thyself. If thou be the Son of God, come down from the cross. 41 Likewise also the chief priests mocking *him*, with the scribes and elders, said, 42 He saved others; himself he cannot save. If he be the King of Israel, let him now come down from the cross, and we will believe him. 43 He trusted in God; let him deliver him now, if he will have him: for he said, I am the Son of God. 44 The thieves also, which were crucified with him, cast the same in his teeth.

45 Now from the sixth hour there was darkness over all the land unto the ninth hour. 46 And about the ninth hour Jesus cried with a loud voice, saying, ELI, ELI, LAMA SABACHTHANI? that is to say, My God, my God, why hast thou forsaken me? 47 Some of them that stood there, when they heard *that*, said, This *man* calleth for Elias. 48 And straightway one of them ran, and took a spunge, and filled *it* with vinegar, and put *it* on a reed, and gave him to drink. 49 The rest said, Let be, let us see whether Elias will come to save him.

50 Jesus, when he had cried again with a loud voice, yielded up the ghost. 51 And, behold, the veil of the temple was rent in twain from the top to the bottom; and the earth did quake, and the rocks rent; 52 and the graves were opened; and many bodies of the saints which slept arose, 53 and

καὶ ἐν τρισὶν ἡμέραις οἰκοδομῶν, σῶσον σεαυτόν· [y]εἰ υἱὸς
and in three days buildest [it], save thyself. If son

[y]εἶ τοῦ θεοῦ," [z]κατάβηθι ἀπὸ τοῦ σταυροῦ. 41 Ὁμοίως
thou art of God, descend from the cross. [2]In [3]like [4]manner

[a]δὲ καὶ" οἱ ἀρχιερεῖς ἐμπαίζοντες μετὰ τῶν γραμματέων καὶ
[1]and also the chief priests, mocking, with the scribes and

πρεσβυτέρων ἔλεγον, 42 Ἄλλους ἔσωσεν, ἑαυτὸν οὐ.δύναται
elders, said, Others he saved, himself he is not able

σῶσαι. [b]εἰ" βασιλεὺς Ἰσραήλ ἐστιν, καταβάτω νῦν ἀπὸ τοῦ
to save. If king of Israel he is, let him descend now from the

σταυροῦ, καὶ [c]πιστεύσομεν" [d]αὐτῷ." 43 πέποιθεν ἐπὶ [e]τὸν θεόν·"
cross, and we will believe him. He trusted on God:

ῥυσάσθω νῦν [f]αὐτόν," εἰ θέλει αὐτόν. εἶπεν.γάρ, Ὅτι θεοῦ
let him deliver [2]now [1]him, if he will [have] him. For he said, [4]Of [5]God

εἰμι υἱός. 44 Τὸ.δ'.αὐτὸ καὶ οἱ λῃσταὶ οἱ [g]συσταυρωθέν-
[1]I [2]am [3]Son. And [with] the same thing also the robbers who were crucified to-

τες" [h]αὐτῷ ὠνείδιζον [i]αὐτῷ."
gether with him reproached him.

45 Ἀπὸ.δὲ ἕκτης ὥρας σκότος ἐγένετο ἐπὶ πᾶσαν τὴν
Now from [2]sixth [[1]the] hour darkness was over all the

γῆν ἕως ὥρας [k]ἐννάτης" 46 περὶ.δὲ τὴν [l]ἐννάτην" ὥραν
land until [the] [2]hour [1]ninth; and about the ninth hour

[m]ἀνεβόησεν" ὁ Ἰησοῦς φωνῇ μεγάλῃ, λέγων, [n]Ἠλί, Ἠλί,"
[2]cried [3]out [1]Jesus [4]with [5]a [7]voice [6]loud, saying, Eli, Eli,

[o]λαμὰ" [p]σαβαχθανί;" τοῦτ' ἔστιν, Θεέ.μου, θεέ.μου, [q]ἱνατί" με
lama sabachthani? that is, My God, my God, why me

ἐγκατέλιπες; 47 Τινὲς.δὲ τῶν ἐκεῖ [r]ἑστώτων" ἀκού-
hast thou forsaken? And some of those who there were standing having

σαντες, ἔλεγον, Ὅτι [s]Ἠλίαν" φωνεῖ οὗτος. 48 Καὶ εὐθέως
heard, said, [4]Elias [3]calls [1]this [[2]man]. And immediately

δραμὼν εἷς ἐξ αὐτῶν καὶ λαβὼν σπόγγον, πλήσας.τε
[4]having [5]run [1]one [2]of [3]them and taken a sponge, and filled [it]

ὄξους καὶ περιθεὶς καλάμῳ, ἐπότιζεν αὐτόν· 49 οἱ.δὲ
with vinegar and put [it] on a reed, gave [2]to [3]drink [1]him. But the

λοιποὶ [t]ἔλεγον," Ἄφες, ἴδωμεν εἰ ἔρχεται [v]Ἠλίας" σώσων
rest said, Let be; let us see [2]comes [1]Elias to save

αὐτόν.
him.

50 Ὁ.δὲ.Ἰησοῦς πάλιν κράξας φωνῇ μεγάλῃ ἀφῆκεν
And Jesus again having cried with a [2]voice [1]loud yielded up

τὸ πνεῦμα. 51 Καὶ ἰδού, τὸ καταπέτασμα τοῦ ναοῦ ἐσχίσθη
[his] spirit. And behold, the veil of the temple was rent

[w]εἰς δύο" [x]ἀπὸ" ἄνωθεν ἕως κάτω[w]· καὶ ἡ γῆ ἐσείσθη, καὶ
into two from top to bottom; and the earth was shaken, and

αἱ πέτραι ἐσχίσθησαν, 52 καὶ τὰ μνημεῖα ἀνεῴχθησαν, καὶ
the rocks were rent, and the tombs were opened, and

πολλὰ σώματα τῶν κεκοιμημένων ἁγίων [ya]ἠγέρθη," 53 καὶ
many bodies of the [2]fallen [3]asleep [1]saints arose, and

---

[y] θεοῦ εἶ L. [z] + καὶ and LT. [a] [δὲ] καὶ TrA; — δὲ καὶ [L]T. [b] — εἰ TTrA. [c] πιστεύομεν we believe L; πιστεύσωμεν let us believe T. [d] ἐπ' αὐτόν on him TTr; ἐπ' αὐτῷ W. [e] τῷ θεῷ L. [f] — αὐτόν T[Tr]. [g] συνσταυρωθέντες LTTrA. [h] + σὺν with (him) LTTrA. [i] αὐτόν GLTTrAW. [k] ἐνάτης LTTrA. [l] ἐνάτην LTTrA. [m] ἐβόησεν cried Tr. [n] Ἠλὶ ἠλὶ LA; Ἠλεὶ ἠλεὶ T. [o] λημὰ L; λεμὰ TTrA. [p] σαβακθανί L; σαβαχθανεί TTr. [q] ἵνα τί A. [r] ἑστηκότων TTr. [s] Ἠλείαν T. [t] εἶπαν LTr. [v] Ἠλείας T. [w] εἰς δύο placed after κάτω TTrA. [x] ἀπ' Tr; — ἀπὸ T. [ya] ἠγέρθησαν LTTrA.

ἐξελθόντες ἐκ τῶν μνημείων μετὰ τὴν.ἔγερσιν.αὐτοῦ, εἰσῆλ-
having gone forth out of the tombs after his arising, entered
θον εἰς τὴν ἁγίαν πόλιν καὶ ἐνεφανίσθησαν πολλοῖς.
into the holy city and appeared to many.
54 Ὁ.δὲ [z]ἑκατόνταρχος‖ καὶ οἱ μετ' αὐτοῦ τηροῦντες
But the centurion and they who with him kept guard over
τὸν Ἰησοῦν, ἰδόντες τὸν σεισμὸν καὶ τὰ [a]γενόμενα,‖
Jesus, having seen the earthquake and the things that took place,
ἐφοβήθησαν σφόδρα, λέγοντες, Ἀληθῶς [b]θεοῦ υἱὸς‖ ἦν οὗτος.
feared greatly, saying, Truly [3]God's [4]Son [2]was [1]this.
55 Ἦσαν.δὲ ἐκεῖ γυναῖκες πολλαὶ ἀπὸ μακρόθεν θεωροῦ-
And there were there [2]women [1]many from afar off looking
σαι, αἵτινες ἠκολούθησαν τῷ Ἰησοῦ ἀπὸ τῆς Γαλιλαίας δια-
on, who followed Jesus from Galilee min-
κονοῦσαι αὐτῷ, 56 ἐν αἷς ἦν Μαρία ἡ Μαγδαληνή, καὶ
istering to him, among whom was Mary the Magdalene, and
Μαρία ἡ τοῦ Ἰακώβου καὶ [c]Ἰωσῆ‖ μήτηρ, καὶ ἡ μήτηρ τῶν
Mary the [2]of [3]James [4]and [5]Joses [1]mother; and the mother of the
υἱῶν Ζεβεδαίου.
sons of Zebedee.

57 Ὀψίας.δὲ γενομένης ἦλθεν ἄνθρωπος πλούσιος ἀπὸ
And evening being come [4]came [1]a [3]man [2]rich from
[d]Ἀριμαθαίας,‖ τοὔνομα Ἰωσήφ, ὃς καὶ αὐτὸς [e]ἐμαθήτευσεν‖
Arimathea, by name Joseph, who also himself was discipled
τῷ Ἰησοῦ· 58 οὗτος προσελθὼν τῷ [f]Πιλάτῳ‖ ᾐτήσατο τὸ σῶμα
to Jesus. He having gone to Pilate begged the body
τοῦ Ἰησοῦ. τότε ὁ [g]Πιλάτος‖ ἐκέλευσεν ἀποδοθῆναι [h]τὸ σῶμα.‖
of Jesus. Then Pilate commanded to be given up the body.
59 καὶ λαβὼν τὸ σῶμα ὁ Ἰωσὴφ ἐνετύλιξεν αὐτὸ [i] σινδόνι
And having taken the body Joseph wrapped it in a [2]linen [3]cloth
καθαρᾷ, 60 καὶ ἔθηκεν αὐτὸ ἐν τῷ.καινῷ.αὐτοῦ μνημείῳ ὃ
[1]clean, and placed it in his new tomb which
ἐλατόμησεν ἐν τῇ πέτρᾳ καὶ προσκυλίσας λίθον μέγαν
he had hewn in the rock; and having rolled a [2]stone [1]great
[k]τῇ θύρᾳ τοῦ μνημείου ἀπῆλθεν. 61 ἦν.δὲ ἐκεῖ [l]Μαρία‖
to the door of the tomb went away. And there was there Mary
ἡ Μαγδαληνὴ καὶ ἡ ἄλλη Μαρία, καθήμεναι ἀπέναντι τοῦ
the Magdalene and the other Mary, sitting opposite the
τάφου.
sepulchre.

62 Τῇ.δὲ ἐπαύριον, ἥτις ἐστὶν μετὰ τὴν παρασκευήν,
Now on the morrow, which is after the preparation,
συνήχθησαν οἱ ἀρχιερεῖς καὶ οἱ Φαρισαῖοι πρὸς [m]Πι-
were gathered together the chief priests and the Pharisees to Pi-
λάτον,‖ 63 λέγοντες, Κύριε, ἐμνήσθημεν ὅτι ἐκεῖνος
late, saying, Sir, we have called to mind that that
ὁ πλάνος εἶπεν ἔτι ζῶν, Μετὰ τρεῖς ἡμέρας ἐγείρομαι. 64 κέ-
deceiver said whilst living, After three days I arise. Com-
λευσον οὖν ἀσφαλισθῆναι τὸν τάφον ἕως τῆς τρίτης ἡμέρας·
mand therefore to be secured the sepulchre until the third day,
μήποτε ἐλθόντες οἱ.μαθηταὶ.[n]αὐτοῦ‖ [o]νυκτὸς‖ κλέψωσιν αὐτόν,
lest [3]coming [1]his [2]disciples by night steal [2]away [1]him,

came out of the graves after his resurrection, and went into the holy city, and appeared unto many.

54 Now when the centurion, and they that were with him, watching Jesus, saw the earthquake, and those things that were done, they feared greatly, saying, Truly this was the Son of God.

55 And many women were there beholding afar off, which followed Jesus from Galilee, ministering unto him: 56 among which was Mary Magdalene, and Mary the mother of James and Joses, and the mother of Zebedee's children.

57 When the even was come, there came a rich man of Arimathæa, named Joseph, who also himself was Jesus' disciple: 58 he went to Pilate, and begged the body of Jesus. Then Pilate commanded the body to be delivered. 59 And when Joseph had taken the body, he wrapped it in a clean linen cloth, 60 and laid it in his own new tomb, which he had hewn out in the rock: and he rolled a great stone to the door of the sepulchre, and departed. 61 And there was Mary Magdalene, and the other Mary, sitting over against the sepulchre.

62 Now the next day, that followed the day of the preparation, the chief priests and Pharisees came together unto Pilate, 63 saying, Sir, we remember that that deceiver said, while he was yet alive, After three days I will rise again. 64 Command therefore that the sepulchre be made sure until the third day, lest his disciples come by night, and steal him away, and

[z] ἑκατοντάρχης T. [a] γινόμενα were taking place LTTrA. [b] υἱὸς θεοῦ LTrA. [c] Ἰωσὴφ Joseph T. [d] Ἀριμαθείας W. [e] ἐμαθητεύθη LTTr. [f] Πειλάτῳ T. [g] Πιλᾶτος LTr; Πειλᾶτος T. [h] — τὸ σῶμα (read [it]) T[Tr]. [i] + ἐν in (a linen cloth) TrA. [k] + ἐπὶ over (the door) L. [l] Μαριὰμ T. [m] Πιλᾶτον LTr; Πειλᾶτον T. [n] — αὐτοῦ (read the disciples) T. [o] — νυκτὸς GLTTrA.

say unto the people, He is risen from the dead: so the last error shall be worse than the first. 65 Pilate said unto them, Ye have a watch: go your way, make *it* as sure as ye can. 66 So they went, and made the sepulchre sure, sealing the stone, and setting a watch.

XXVIII. In the end of the sabbath, as it began to dawn toward the first *day* of the week, came Mary Magdalene and the other Mary to see the sepulchre.

2 And, behold, there was a great earthquake: for the angel of the Lord descended from heaven, and came and rolled back the stone from the door, and sat upon it. 3 His countenance was like lightning, and his raiment white as snow: 4 and for fear of him the keepers did shake, and became as dead *men*. 5 And the angel answered and said unto the women, Fear not ye: for I know that ye seek Jesus, which was crucified. 6 He is not here: for he is risen, as he said. Come, see the place where the Lord lay. 7 And go quickly, and tell his disciples that he is risen from the dead; and, behold, he goeth before you into Galilee; there shall ye see him: lo, I have told you. 8 And they departed quickly from the sepulchre with fear and great joy; and did run to bring his disciples word. 9 And as they went to tell his disciples, behold, Jesus met them, saying, All hail. And they came and held him by the feet, and worshipped him. 10 Then said Jesus unto them, Be not afraid: go tell my brethren

καὶ εἴπωσιν τῷ λαῷ, Ἠγέρθη ἀπὸ τῶν νεκρῶν· καὶ ἔσται
and say to the people, He is risen from the dead; and [4]shall [5]be
ἡ ἐσχάτη πλάνη χείρων τῆς πρώτης. 65 Ἔφη.[p]δὲ‖ αὐτοῖς
[1]the [2]last [3]deception worse than the first. And [2]said [3]to [4]them
ὁ [q]Πιλάτος,‖ Ἔχετε κουστωδίαν· ὑπάγετε ἀσφαλίσασθε ὡς
[1]Pilate, Ye have a guard: Go make [it as] secure as
οἴδατε. 66 Οἱ.δὲ πορευθέντες ἠσφαλίσαντο τὸν τάφον
ye know [how]. And they having gone made [3]secure [1]the [2]sepulchre
σφραγίσαντες τὸν λίθον, μετὰ τῆς κουστωδίας.
[7]sealing [8]the [9]stone, [4]with [5]the [6]guard.

28 Ὀψὲ.δὲ σαββάτων, τῇ.ἐπιφωσκούσῃ εἰς μίαν
Now late on Sabbath, as it was getting dusk toward [the] first [day]
σαββάτων, ἦλθεν [r]Μαρία‖ ἡ Μαγδαληνὴ καὶ ἡ ἄλλη Μαρία
of [the] week, came Mary the Magdalene and the other Mary
θεωρῆσαι τὸν τάφον.
to see the sepulchre.

2 Καὶ ἰδού, σεισμὸς ἐγένετο μέγας· ἄγγελος.γὰρ κυρίου
And behold, [3]a [5]earthquake [1]there [2]was [4]great; for an angel of [the] Lord
καταβὰς ἐξ οὐρανοῦ, [s] προσελθὼν ἀπεκύλισεν τὸν λίθον
having descended out of heaven, having come rolled away the stone
[t]ἀπὸ τῆς θύρας,‖ καὶ ἐκάθητο ἐπάνω αὐτοῦ. 3 ἦν.δὲ ἡ [v]ἰδέα‖
from the door, and was sitting upon it. And [3]was [2]look
αὐτοῦ ὡς ἀστραπή, καὶ τὸ.ἔνδυμα.αὐτοῦ λευκὸν [w]ὡσεὶ‖ χιών.
[1]his as lightning, and his raiment white as snow.
4 ἀπὸ.δὲ τοῦ φόβου αὐτοῦ ἐσείσθησαν οἱ τηροῦντες, καὶ [x]ἐγέ-
And from the fear of him [4]trembled [1]those [2]keeping [3]guard, and be-
νοντο ὡσεὶ‖ νεκροί. 5 Ἀποκριθεὶς.δὲ ὁ ἄγγελος εἶπεν ταῖς
came as dead [men]. But [3]answering [1]the [2]angel said to the
γυναιξίν, Μὴ.φοβεῖσθε ὑμεῖς· οἶδα.γὰρ ὅτι Ἰησοῦν τὸν ἐσταυ-
women, Fear not ye; for I know that Jesus who has been
ρωμένον ζητεῖτε. 6 οὐκ.ἔστιν ὧδε· ἠγέρθη.γάρ, καθὼς εἶπεν.
crucified ye seek. He is not here, for he is risen, as he said.
δεῦτε ἴδετε τὸν τόπον ὅπου ἔκειτο [y]ὁ κύριος.‖ 7 καὶ ταχὺ
Come see the place where [3]was [4]lying [1]the [2]Lord. And [2]quickly
πορευθεῖσαι εἴπατε τοῖς.μαθηταῖς.αὐτοῦ, ὅτι ἠγέρθη ἀπὸ τῶν
[1]going say to his disciples, that he is risen from the
νεκρῶν· καὶ ἰδού, προάγει ὑμᾶς εἰς τὴν Γαλιλαίαν· ἐκεῖ
dead; and behold, he goes before you into Galilee; there
αὐτὸν ὄψεσθε. ἰδού, εἶπον ὑμῖν. 8 Καὶ [z]ἐξελθοῦσαι‖ ταχὺ
him ye shall see. Lo, I have told you. And having gone out quickly
ἀπὸ τοῦ μνημείου μετὰ φόβου καὶ χαρᾶς μεγάλης, ἔδραμον
from the tomb with fear and [2]joy [1]great, they ran
ἀπαγγεῖλαι τοῖς.μαθηταῖς.αὐτοῦ. 9 [a]ὡς.δὲ ἐπορεύοντο
to tell [it] to his disciples. But as they were going
ἀπαγγεῖλαι τοῖς.μαθηταῖς.αὐτοῦ,‖ καὶ ἰδού, [b]ὁ‖ Ἰησοῦς [c]ἀπήν-
to tell [it] to his disciples, [2]also [1]behold, Jesus met
τησεν‖ αὐταῖς, λέγων, Χαίρετε. Αἱ.δὲ προσελθοῦσαι ἐκρά-
them, saying, Hail! And they having come to [him] seized
τησαν αὐτοῦ τοὺς πόδας, καὶ προσεκύνησαν αὐτῷ. 10 τότε
hold of his feet, and worshipped him. Then
λέγει αὐταῖς ὁ Ἰησοῦς, Μὴ.φοβεῖσθε· ὑπάγετε, ἀπαγγείλατε
[2]says [3]to [4]them [1]Jesus, Fear not: Go, tell

---

p — δὲ and GLTTrAW. q Πιλᾶτος LTr; Πειλᾶτος T. r Μαριὰμ T. s + καὶ and TTr. t — ἀπὸ τῆς θύρας LTTrA. v εἰδέα TTr. w ὡς LTTrA. x ἐγενήθησαν ὡς LTTrA. y — ὁ κύριος (*read* he was lying) T[TrA]. z ἀπελθοῦσαι having departed TTrA. a — ὡς δὲ ἐπορεύοντο ἀπαγγεῖλαι τοῖς μαθηταῖς αὐτοῦ LTTrA. b — ὁ TA. c ὑπήντησεν TTr.

τοῖς.ἀδελφοῖς.μου ἵνα ἀπέλθωσιν εἰς τὴν Γαλιλαίαν, [d]κἀκεῖ‖ με
my brethren that they go into Galilee, and there me
ὄψονται.
shall they see.

11 Πορευομένων.δὲ αὐτῶν, ἰδού, τινὲς τῆς κουστωδίας ἐλ-
And as [2]were [3]going [1]they, lo, some of the guard hav-
θόντες εἰς τὴν πόλιν [e]ἀπήγγειλαν‖ τοῖς ἀρχιερεῦσιν ἅπαντα
ing gone into the city reported to the chief priests all things
τὰ γενόμενα. 12 καὶ συναχθέντες μετὰ τῶν πρεσ-
that were done. And having been gathered together with the el-
βυτέρων, συμβούλιόν.τε λαβόντες, ἀργύρια ἱκανὰ ἔδωκαν
ders, and counsel having taken, [2]money [1]much they gave
τοῖς στρατιώταις, 13 λέγοντες, Εἴπατε ὅτι οἱ.μαθηταὶ.αὐτοῦ
to the soldiers, saying, Say that his disciples
νυκτὸς ἐλθόντες ἔκλεψαν αὐτὸν ἡμῶν κοιμωμένων· 14 καὶ
by night having come stole him, we being asleep. And
ἐὰν ἀκουσθῇ τοῦτο [f]ἐπὶ‖ τοῦ ἡγεμόνος, ἡμεῖς πείσομεν [g]αὐτὸν‖
if [2]be [3]heard [1]this by the governor, we will persuade him
καὶ ὑμᾶς ἀμερίμνους ποιήσομεν. 15 Οἱ.δὲ λαβόντες τὰ
and [3]you [4]free [5]from [6]care [1]will [2]make. And they having taken the
ἀργύρια ἐποίησαν ὡς ἐδιδάχθησαν. καὶ [h]διεφημίσθη‖ ὁ λόγος
money did as they were taught. And [3]is [4]spread [5]abroad [2]report
οὗτος παρὰ Ἰουδαίοις μέχρι τῆς σήμερον[i].
[1]this among [the] Jews until the present.

16 Οἱ.δὲ ἕνδεκα μαθηταὶ ἐπορεύθησαν εἰς τὴν Γαλιλαίαν,
But the eleven disciples went into Galilee,
εἰς τὸ ὄρος οὗ ἐτάξατο αὐτοῖς ὁ Ἰησοῦς. 17 καὶ ἰδόντες
to the mountain whither [2]appointed [3]them [1]Jesus. And seeing
αὐτὸν προσεκύνησαν [k]αὐτῷ·‖ οἱ.δὲ ἐδίστασαν. 18 καὶ προσ-
him they worshipped him: but some doubted. And having
ελθὼν ὁ Ἰησοῦς ἐλάλησεν αὐτοῖς, λέγων, Ἐδόθη μοι
come to [them] Jesus spoke to them, saying, [3]Has [4]been [5]given [6]to [7]me
πᾶσα ἐξουσία ἐν οὐρανῷ καὶ ἐπὶ [l]γῆς. 19 πορευθέντες [m]οὖν‖
[1]all [2]authority in heaven and on earth. Going therefore
μαθητεύσατε πάντα τὰ ἔθνη, [n]βαπτίζοντες‖ αὐτοὺς εἰς τὸ
disciple all the nations, baptizing them to the
ὄνομα τοῦ πατρὸς καὶ τοῦ υἱοῦ καὶ τοῦ ἁγίου πνεύματος,
name of the Father and of the Son and of the Holy Spirit;
20 διδάσκοντες αὐτοὺς τηρεῖν πάντα ὅσα ἐνετειλάμην
teaching them to observe all things whatsoever I commanded
ὑμῖν· καὶ ἰδού, ἐγὼ μεθ' ὑμῶν εἰμι πάσας τὰς ἡμέρας ἕως τῆς
you. And lo, I with you am all the days until the
συντελείας τοῦ αἰῶνος. [o]Ἀμήν.‖ [p]
completion of the age. Amen.

that they go into Galilee, and there shall they see me.

11 Now when they were going, behold, some of the watch came into the city, and shewed unto the chief priests all the things that were done. 12 And when they were assembled with the elders, and had taken counsel, they gave large money unto the soldiers, 13 saying, Say ye, His disciples came by night, and stole him *away* while we slept. 14 And if this come to the governor's ears, we will persuade him, and secure you. 15 So they took the money, and did as they were taught: and this saying is commonly reported among the Jews until this day.

16 Then the eleven disciples went away into Galilee, into a mountain where Jesus had appointed them. 17 And when they saw him, they worshipped him: but some doubted. 18 And Jesus came and spake unto them, saying, All power is given unto me in heaven and in earth. 19 Go ye therefore, and teach all nations, baptizing them in the name of the Father, and of the Son, and of the Holy Ghost: 20 teaching them to observe all things whatsoever I have commanded you: and, lo, I am with you alway, *even* unto the end of the world. Amen.

---

[d] καὶ ἐκεῖ T. [e] ἀνήγγειλαν announced T. [f] ὑπὸ LTr. [g] — αὐτὸν (*read* [him]) T[Tr]. [h] ἐφημίσθη is spoken of T. [i] + ἡμέρας day LTrA. [k] — αὐτῷ LTTrA. [l] + τῆς the LTrA. [m] — οὖν G[L]T[Tr]A. [n] βαπτίσαντες having baptized Tr. [o] — Ἀμήν GLTTrA. [p] + κατὰ Μαθθαῖον according to Matthew TrA.

[a]ΤΟ ΚΑΤΑ ΜΑΡΚΟΝ ΑΓΙΟΝ ΕΥΑΓΓΕΛΙΟΝ.[a]
THE [4]ACCORDING [5]TO [6]MARK [1]HOLY [2]GLAD [3]TIDINGS.

THE beginning of
the gospel of Jesus
Christ, the Son of God;
2 as it is written in
the prophets, Behold,
I send my messenger
before thy face, which
shall prepare thy way
before thee. 3 The
voice of one crying in
the wilderness, Prepare ye the way of the
Lord, make his paths
straight.

ΑΡΧΗ τοῦ εὐαγγελίου Ἰησοῦ χριστοῦ, [b]υἱοῦ τοῦ θεοῦ·[b]
BEGINNING of the glad tidings of Jesus Christ, Son of God;
2 [c]ὡς[c] γέγραπται ἐν [d]τοῖς.προφήταις,[d] Ἰδού, [e]ἐγὼ[e] ἀποστέλλω
as it has been written in the prophets, Behold, I send
τὸν.ἄγγελόν.μου πρὸ προσώπου.σου, ὃς κατασκευάσει τὴν
my messenger before thy face, who shall prepare
ὁδόν.σου [f]ἔμπροσθέν σου.[f] 3 Φωνὴ βοῶντος ἐν τῇ ἐρήμῳ,
thy way before thee. [The] voice of one crying in the wilderness,
Ἑτοιμάσατε τὴν ὁδὸν κυρίου, εὐθείας ποιεῖτε τὰς τρίβους
Prepare the way of [the] Lord, straight make [2]paths
αὐτοῦ.
[1]his.

4 John did baptize
in the wilderness, and
preach the baptism of
repentance for the remission of sins. 5 And
there went out unto
him all the land of
Judæa, and they of
Jerusalem, and were
all baptized of him in
the river of Jordan,
confessing their sins.
6 And John was clothed with camel's hair,
and with a girdle of a
skin about his loins;
and he did eat locusts
and wild honey; 7 and
preached, saying, There
cometh one mightier
than I after me, the
latchet of whose shoes
I am not worthy to
stoop down and unloose. 8 I indeed have
baptized you with
water: but he shall
baptize you with the
Holy Ghost.

4 Ἐγένετο Ἰωάννης [g] βαπτίζων ἐν τῇ ἐρήμῳ, [h]καὶ[h] κηρύσ-
[2]Came [1]John baptizing in the wilderness, and proclaim-
σων βάπτισμα μετανοίας εἰς ἄφεσιν ἁμαρτιῶν. 5 καὶ
ing [the] baptism of repentance for remission of sins. And
ἐξεπορεύετο πρὸς αὐτὸν πᾶσα ἡ Ἰουδαία χώρα, καὶ οἱ [i]Ἱερο-
went out to him all the [2]of [3]Judæa [1]country, and they of Je-
σολυμῖται,[i] [k]καὶ ἐβαπτίζοντο πάντες[k] [l]ἐν τῷ Ἰορδάνῃ ποταμῷ
rusalem, and were [2]baptized [1]all in the [2]Jordan [1]river
ὑπ' αὐτοῦ,[l] ἐξομολογούμενοι τὰς.ἁμαρτίας.αὐτῶν. 6 [m]ἦν.δὲ[m]
by him, confessing their sins. And [2]was
[n]Ἰωάννης ἐνδεδυμένος τρίχας καμήλου, καὶ ζώνην δερματίνην
[1]John clothed in hair of a camel, and a girdle of leather
περὶ τὴν.ὀσφὺν.αὐτοῦ, καὶ [o]ἐσθίων[o] ἀκρίδας καὶ μέλι ἄγριον.
about his loins, and eating locusts and [2]honey [1]wild.
7 Καὶ ἐκήρυσσεν, λέγων, Ἔρχεται ὁ ἰσχυρότερός μου ὀπίσω
And he proclaimed, saying, He comes who [is] mightier than I after
μου, οὗ οὐκ.εἰμὶ ἱκανὸς κύψας λῦσαι τὸν ἱμάντα
me, of whom I am not fit having stooped down to loose the thong
τῶν.ὑποδημάτων.αὐτοῦ. 8 ἐγὼ [p]μὲν[p] ἐβάπτισα ὑμᾶς [q]ἐν[q] ὕδατι,
of his sandals. I indeed baptized you with water,
αὐτὸς.δὲ βαπτίσει ὑμᾶς [r]ἐν[r] πνεύματι ἁγίῳ.
but he will baptize you with [the] [2]Spirit [1]Holy.

9 And it came to pass
in those days, that Jesus came from Nazareth of Galilee, and
was baptized of John
in Jordan. 10 And
straightway coming
up out of the water,
he saw the heavens
opened, and the Spirit
like a dove descending
upon him: 11 and there
came a voice from

9 [s]Καὶ[s] ἐγένετο ἐν ἐκείναις ταῖς ἡμέραις ἦλθεν Ἰησοῦς
And it came to pass in those days [that] [2]came [1]Jesus
ἀπὸ [t]Ναζαρὲτ[t] τῆς Γαλιλαίας, καὶ ἐβαπτίσθη [v]ὑπὸ Ἰωάν-
from Nazareth of Galilee, and was baptized by John
νου εἰς τὸν Ἰορδάνην.[v] 10 καὶ [w]εὐθέως[w] ἀναβαίνων [x]ἀπὸ[x] τοῦ
in the Jordan. And immediately going up from the
ὕδατος, εἶδεν σχιζομένους τοὺς οὐρανούς, καὶ τὸ πνεῦμα
water, he saw parting asunder the heavens, and the Spirit
[y]ὡσεὶ[y] περιστερὰν καταβαῖνον [z]ἐπ'[z] αὐτόν· 11 καὶ φωνὴ [aa]ἐγένε-
as a dove descending upon him. And a voice came

---

[a] Εὐαγγέλιον κατὰ Μάρκον GLTrAW; κατὰ Μάρκον T. [b] — υἱοῦ τοῦ θεοῦ T; — τοῦ LTrA. [c] καθὼς according as TTr. [d] τῷ (— τῷ [Tr]GW) Ἠσαΐᾳ τῷ προφήτῃ Isaiah the prophet GLTTrAW. [e] — ἐγὼ (read ἀποσ. I send) LTrA. [f] — ἔμπροσθέν σου GLTTrAW. [g] + ὁ TTrA. [h] — καὶ [Tr]A. [i] Ἱεροσολυμεῖται T. [k] πάντες, καὶ ἐβαπτίζοντο GLTTrA. [l] ὑπ' αὐτοῦ ἐν τῷ Ἰορδάνῃ ποταμῷ TTrA. [m] καὶ ἦν LTTrA. [n] + ὁ TTrA. [o] ἔσθων TTrA. [p] — μὲν [L]TTrA. [q] — ἐν (read ὕδατι with water) T[Tr]A. [r] — ἐν (read πνεύματι with [the] Spirit) [L]Tr]A. [s] [καὶ] L. [t] Ναζαρὲθ ETrW. [v] εἰς τὸν Ἰορδάνην ὑπὸ Ἰωάννου LTTrA. [w] εὐθὺς TTrA. [x] ἐκ out of LTTrA. [y] ὡς GLTTrAW. [z] εἰς on LTTrA. [aa] — ἐγένετο (read [came]) T.

το" ἐκ τῶν οὐρανῶν, Σὺ εἶ ὁ.υἱός.μου ὁ ἀγαπητός, ἐν [b]ᾧ"
out of the heavens, Thou art my Son the beloved, in whom
εὐδόκησα.
I have found delight.

12 Καὶ [c]εὐθὺς" τὸ πνεῦμα αὐτὸν ἐκβάλλει εἰς τὴν ἔρη-
And immediately the Spirit [2]him [1]drives out into the wilder-
μον. 13 καὶ ἦν [d]ἐκεῖ" ἐν τῇ ἐρήμῳ [e]ἡμέρας τεσσαράκοντα,"
ness. And he was there in the wilderness [2]days [1]forty,
πειραζόμενος ὑπὸ τοῦ σατανᾶ, καὶ ἦν μετὰ τῶν θηρίων· καὶ
tempted by Satan, and was with the beasts; and
οἱ ἄγγελοι διηκόνουν αὐτῷ.
the angels ministered to him.

14 [f]Μετὰ.δὲ" τὸ.παραδοθῆναι τὸν Ἰωάννην ἦλθεν ὁ Ἰησοῦς
And after [2]was [3]delivered [4]up [1]John came Jesus
εἰς τὴν Γαλιλαίαν, κηρύσσων τὸ εὐαγγέλιον [g]τῆς βασιλείας"
into Galilee, proclaiming the glad tidings of the kingdom
τοῦ θεοῦ, 15 [h]καὶ λέγων," Ὅτι πεπλήρωται ὁ καιρός, καὶ ἤγ-
of God, and saying, [3]Has [4]been [5]fulfilled [1]the [2]time, and has
γικεν ἡ βασιλεία τοῦ θεοῦ· μετανοεῖτε, καὶ πιστεύετε ἐν τῷ
drawn near the kingdom of God; repent, and believe in the
εὐαγγελίῳ. 16 [i]Περιπατῶν.δὲ" παρὰ τὴν θάλασσαν τῆς Γαλι-
glad tidings. And walking by the sea of Ga-
λαίας εἶδεν Σίμωνα καὶ Ἀνδρέαν τὸν ἀδελφὸν [k]αὐτοῦ" [l]βάλ-
lilee he saw Simon and Andrew the brother of him cast-
λοντας" [m]ἀμφίβληστρον" ἐν τῇ θαλάσσῃ· ἦσαν.γὰρ [n]ἁλιεῖς·"
ing a large net in the sea; for they were fishers.
17 καὶ εἶπεν αὐτοῖς ὁ Ἰησοῦς, Δεῦτε ὀπίσω μου, καὶ ποιήσω
And [2]said [3]to [4]them [1]Jesus, Come after me, and I will make
ὑμᾶς γενέσθαι [n]ἁλιεῖς" ἀνθρώπων. 18 Καὶ [o]εὐθέως" ἀφέντες
you to become fishers of men. And immediately having left
τὰ.δίκτυα.[p]αὐτῶν" ἠκολούθησαν αὐτῷ. 19 Καὶ προβὰς
their nets they followed him. And having gone on
[q]ἐκεῖθεν" ὀλίγον εἶδεν Ἰάκωβον τὸν τοῦ Ζεβεδαίου, καὶ
thence a little he saw James the [son] of Zebedee, and
Ἰωάννην τὸν.ἀδελφὸν.αὐτοῦ, καὶ αὐτοὺς ἐν τῷ πλοίῳ
John his brother, and these [were] in the ship
καταρτίζοντας τὰ δίκτυα. 20 καὶ [r]εὐθέως" ἐκάλεσεν αὐτούς·
mending the nets. And immediately he called them;
καὶ ἀφέντες τὸν πατέρα.αὐτῶν Ζεβεδαῖον ἐν τῷ πλοίῳ μετὰ
and having left their father Zebedee in the ship with
τῶν μισθωτῶν, ἀπῆλθον ὀπίσω αὐτοῦ.
the hired servants, they went away after him.

21 Καὶ εἰσπορεύονται εἰς [s]Καπερναούμ·" καὶ [t]εὐθέως" τοῖς
And they go into Capernaum; and immediately on the
σάββασιν [v]εἰσελθὼν" [w]εἰς τὴν συναγωγὴν ἐδίδασκεν." 22 καὶ
sabbaths having entered into the synagogue he taught. And
ἐξεπλήσσοντο ἐπὶ τῇ.διδαχῇ.αὐτοῦ· ἦν.γὰρ διδάσκων αὐτοὺς
they were astonished at his teaching: for he was teaching them
ὡς ἐξουσίαν ἔχων, καὶ οὐχ ὡς οἱ γραμματεῖς[x]. 23 Καὶ [y] ἦν
as [2]authority [1]having, and not as the scribes. And there was

heaven, *saying*, Thou art my beloved Son, in whom I am well pleased.

12 And immediately the spirit driveth him into the wilderness.
13 And he was there in the wilderness forty days, tempted of Satan; and was with the wild beasts; and the angels ministered unto him.

14 Now after that John was put in prison, Jesus came into Galilee, preaching the gospel of the kingdom of God, 15 and saying, The time is fulfilled, and the kingdom of God is at hand: repent ye, and believe the gospel. 16 Now as he walked by the sea of Galilee, he saw Simon and Andrew his brother casting a net into the sea: for they were fishers. 17 And Jesus said unto them, Come ye after me, and I will make you to become fishers of men. 18 And straightway they forsook their nets, and followed him. 19 And when he had gone a little farther thence, he saw James the *son* of Zebedee, and John his brother, who also were in the ship mending their nets. 20 And straightway he called them: and they left their father Zebedee in the ship with the hired servants, and went after him.

21 And they went into Capernaum; and straightway on the sabbath day he entered into the synagogue, and taught. 22 And they were astonished at his doctrine: for he taught them as one that had authority, and not as the scribes.
23 And there was in

[b] σοὶ thee LTTrA. [c] εὐθέως LW. [d] — ἐκεῖ GLTTrAW. [e] τεσσεράκοντα ἡμέρας TTr; ἡμέρας τεσσε. A. [f] καὶ μετὰ LTrA. [g] — τῆς βασιλείας [L]TTrA. [h] — καὶ λέγων T; — καὶ A. [i] καὶ παράγων and passing on LTTrA. [k] τοῦ Σίμωνος of Simon L; Σίμωνος TTrAW. [l] ἀμφιβάλλοντας casting around GLTTrAW. [m] — ἀμφίβληστρον (*read* [a net]) TTrA. [n] ἁλεεῖς TA. [o] εὐθὺς T. [p] — αὐτῶν (*read* the nets) LTTr[A]. [q] — ἐκεῖθεν [L]TTrA. [r] εὐθὺς TTrA. [s] Καφαρναούμ LTTrAW. [t] εὐθὺς T. [v] — εἰσελθὼν T[Tr]A. [w] ἐδίδασκεν εἰς τὴν συναγωγήν TA; — τὴν E. [x] + [αὐτῶν] (*read* their scribes) L. [y] + εὐθὺς immediately TA.

their synagogue a man
with an unclean spirit;
and he cried out,
24 saying, Let *us*
alone; what have we
to do with thee, thou
Jesus of Nazareth?
art thou come to de-
stroy us? I know thee
who thou art, the Holy
One of God. 25 And
Jesus rebuked him,
saying, Hold thy peace,
and come out of him.
26 And when the un-
clean spirit had torn
him, and cried with
a loud voice, he came
out of him. 27 And
they were all amazed,
insomuch that they
questioned among
themselves, saying,
What thing is this?
what new doctrine *is*
this? for with au-
thority commandeth
he even the unclean
spirits, and they do
obey him. 28 And im-
mediately his fame
spread abroad through-
out all the region
round about Galilee.

29 And forthwith,
when they were come
out of the synagogue,
they entered into the
house of Simon and
Andrew, with James
and John. 30 But Si-
mon's wife's mother
lay sick of a fever, and
anon they tell him of
her. 31 And he came
and took her by the
hand, and lifted her
up; and immediately
the fever left her, and
she ministered unto
them. 32 And at even,
when the sun did set,
they brought unto
him all that were dis-
eased, and them that
were possessed with
devils. 33 And all the
city was gathered to-
gether at the door.
34 And he healed many
that were sick of di-
vers diseases, and cast
out many devils; and
suffered not the devils
to speak, because they
knew him.

35 And in the morn-
ing, rising up a great
while before day, he
went out, and departed

ἐν τῇ.συναγωγῇ.αὐτῶν ἄνθρωπος ἐν πνεύματι.ἀκαθάρτῳ, καὶ
in their synagogue a man with an unclean spirit, and
ἀνέκραξεν, 24 λέγων, [z]Ἔα,‖ τί ἡμῖν καὶ σοί, Ἰησοῦ Ναζαρηνέ;
he cried out, saying, Ah! what to us and to thee, Jesus, Nazarene?
ἦλθες ἀπολέσαι ἡμᾶς; [a]οἶδά‖ σε τίς εἶ, ὁ ἅγιος
art thou come to destroy us? I know thee who thou art, the Holy [One]
τοῦ θεοῦ. 25 Καὶ ἐπετίμησεν αὐτῷ ὁ Ἰησοῦς, [b]λέγων,‖ Φιμώ-
of God. And [2]rebuked [3]him [1]Jesus, saying, Be
θητι, καὶ ἔξελθε ἐξ αὐτοῦ. 26 Καὶ σπαράξαν
silent, and come forth out of him. And [5]having [6]thrown [8]into [9]convulsions
αὐτὸν τὸ πνεῦμα τὸ ἀκάθαρτον, καὶ [c]κράξαν‖ φωνῇ μεγάλῃ,
[7]him [1]the [2]spirit [3]the [4]unclean, and having cried with a [2]voice [1]loud,
ἐξῆλθεν [d]ἐξ‖ αὐτοῦ. 27 καὶ ἐθαμβήθησαν [e]πάντες,‖ ὥστε
came forth out of him. And [2]were [3]astonished [1]all, so that
[f]συζητεῖν‖ [g]πρὸς‖ [h]αὐτούς,‖ λέγοντας, Τί ἐστιν τοῦτο;
they questioned together among themselves, saying, What is this?
[i]τίς ἡ διδαχὴ ἡ καινὴ αὕτη, ὅτι‖ κατ' ἐξουσίαν καὶ τοῖς πνεύ-
what [3]teaching [2]new [1]this, that with authority even the spirits
μασιν τοῖς ἀκαθάρτοις ἐπιτάσσει, καὶ ὑπακούουσιν αὐτῷ;
the unclean he commands, and they obey him!
28 [k]Ἐξῆλθεν.δὲ‖ ἡ ἀκοὴ αὐτοῦ [l]εὐθὺς‖ [m]εἰς ὅλην τὴν περί-
And went out the fame of him immediately in all the [2]around
χωρον τῆς Γαλιλαίας.
[1]country Galilee.

29 Καὶ [n]εὐθέως‖ ἐκ τῆς συναγωγῆς [o]ἐξελθόντες ἦλθον‖
And immediately out of the synagogue having gone forth they came
εἰς τὴν οἰκίαν Σίμωνος καὶ Ἀνδρέου, μετὰ Ἰακώβου καὶ Ἰωάν-
into the house of Simon and Andrew, with James and John.
νου. 30 ἡ.δὲ πενθερὰ Σίμωνος κατέκειτο πυρέσσουσα· καὶ
And the mother-in-law of Simon was lying in a fever. And
[p]εὐθέως‖ λέγουσιν αὐτῷ περὶ αὐτῆς. 31 καὶ προσελθὼν
immediately they speak to him about her. And having come to [her]
ἤγειρεν αὐτήν, κρατήσας τῆς.χειρὸς.[q]αὐτῆς·‖ καὶ ἀφῆκεν
he raised up her, having taken her hand. And [3]left
αὐτὴν ὁ πυρετὸς [r]εὐθέως,‖ καὶ διηκόνει αὐτοῖς. 32 Ὀψίας
[4]her [1]the [2]fever immediately, and she ministered to them. [2]Evening
δὲ γενομένης, ὅτε [s]ἔδυ‖ ὁ ἥλιος, ἔφερον πρὸς αὐτὸν
[1]and being come, when went down the sun, they brought to him
πάντας τοὺς κακῶς ἔχοντας καὶ τοὺς δαιμονιζομένους· 33 καὶ
all who [2]ill [1]were and those possessed by demons; and
[t]ἡ πόλις ὅλη ἐπισυνηγμένη ἦν‖ πρὸς τὴν θύραν. 34 καὶ
the [2]city [1]whole [4]gathered [5]together [3]was at the door. And
ἐθεράπευσεν πολλοὺς κακῶς.ἔχοντας ποικίλαις νόσοις, καὶ
he healed many that were ill of various diseases, and
δαιμόνια πολλὰ ἐξέβαλεν, καὶ οὐκ.ἤφιεν λαλεῖν τὰ δαιμόνια,
[2]demons [1]many he cast out, and suffered not [3]to [4]speak [1]the [2]demons,
ὅτι ᾔδεισαν αὐτόν.
because they knew him.

35 Καὶ πρωῒ [v]ἔννυχον‖.λίαν ἀναστὰς ἐξῆλθεν καὶ
And very early while yet night having risen up he went out and

---

[z] — Ἔα LTTrA. [a] οἴδαμέν we know T. [b] — λέγων T. [c] φωνῆσαν TTrA. [d] ἀπ' from L. [e] ἅπαντες TTrA. [f] συνζητεῖν LTTrA. [g] — πρὸς T. [h] αὐτούς E: ἑαυτοὺς LTrAW. [i] διδαχὴ καινή a new teaching LTTrA. [k] καὶ ἐξῆλθεν LTTrA. [l] [εὐθὺς] Tr. [m] + πανταχοῦ everywhere T[Tr]A. [n] εὐθὺς LTTrA. [o] ἐξελθὼν ἦλθεν having gone forth he came LTr. [p] εὐθὺς LTTrA. [q] — αὐτῆς (*read* [her] hand) LT[Tr]A. [r] — εὐθέως TTr. [s] ἔδυσεν LTrA. [t] ἦν ὅλη ἡ πόλις ἐπισυνηγμένη LTTrA. [v] ἔννυχα LTTrA.

ἀπῆλθεν εἰς ἔρημον τόπον, [w]κἀκεῖ‖ προσηύχετο. 36 καὶ
departed into [2]desert [1]a place, and there was praying. And
[x]κατεδίωξαν‖ αὐτὸν [y]ὁ‖ Σίμων καὶ οἱ μετ' αὐτοῦ· 37 καὶ
[6]went [7]after [8]him [1]Simon [2]and [3]those [4]with [5]him; and
[z]εὑρόντες αὐτὸν‖ λέγουσιν αὐτῷ, Ὅτι πάντες [a]ζητοῦσίν σε.‖
having found him they say to him, All seek thee.
38 Καὶ λέγει αὐτοῖς, Ἄγωμεν[b] εἰς τὰς ἐχομένας κωμοπόλεις,
And he says to them, Let us go into the neighbouring country towns,
ἵνα [c]κἀκεῖ‖ κηρύξω· εἰς τοῦτο γὰρ [d]ἐξελήλυθα.‖ 39 Καὶ
that there also I may preach; [2]for [3]this [1]because have I come forth. And
[e]ἦν‖ κηρύσσων [f]ἐν ταῖς συναγωγαῖς‖ αὐτῶν εἰς ὅλην τὴν Γαλι-
he was preaching in their synagogues in all Ga-
λαίαν, καὶ τὰ δαιμόνια ἐκβάλλων.
lilee, and the demons casting out.

40 Καὶ ἔρχεται πρὸς αὐτὸν λεπρός, παρακαλῶν αὐτὸν [g]καὶ
And [3]comes [4]to [5]him [1]a [2]leper, beseeching him and
γονυπετῶν αὐτόν,‖ [h]καὶ‖ λέγων αὐτῷ, Ὅτι ἐὰν θέλῃς δύνασαί
kneeling down to him, and saying to him, If thou wilt thou art able
με καθαρίσαι. 41 [i]Ὁ δὲ Ἰησοῦς‖ σπλαγχνισθείς, ἐκ-
me to cleanse. And Jesus being moved with compassion, having
τείνας τὴν χεῖρα [k]ἥψατο αὐτοῦ,‖ καὶ λέγει [l]αὐτῷ,‖
stretched out [his] hand he touched him, and says to him,
Θέλω, καθαρίσθητι. 42 Καὶ [m]εἰπόντος αὐτοῦ,‖ [n]εὐθέως‖ ἀπῆλ-
I will, be thou cleansed. And he having spoken, immediately depart-
θεν ἀπ' αὐτοῦ ἡ λέπρα, καὶ [o]ἐκαθαρίσθη.‖ 43 Καὶ ἐμβριμησά-
ed from him the leprosy, and he was cleansed. And having strictly
μενος αὐτῷ, [p]εὐθέως‖ ἐξέβαλεν αὐτόν, 44 καὶ λέγει αὐτῷ,
charged him, immediately he sent away him, And says to him,
Ὅρα μηδενὶ [q]μηδὲν‖ εἴπῃς· [r]ἀλλ'‖ ὕπαγε, σεαυτὸν δεῖξον
See to no one anything thou speak; but go, thyself shew
(*lit.* nothing)
τῷ ἱερεῖ, καὶ προσένεγκε περὶ τοῦ καθαρισμοῦ σου ἃ προσ-
to the priest, and offer for thy cleansing what [2]or-
έταξεν [s]Μωσῆς,‖ εἰς μαρτύριον αὐτοῖς. 45 Ὁ δὲ ἐξελθὼν
dered [1]Moses, for a testimony to them. But he having gone out
ἤρξατο κηρύσσειν πολλὰ καὶ διαφημίζειν τὸν λόγον, ὥστε
began to proclaim [it] much and to spread abroad the matter, so that
μηκέτι αὐτὸν δύνασθαι [t]φανερῶς εἰς πόλιν‖ εἰσελθεῖν·
no longer he was able openly into [the] city to enter;
[v]ἀλλ'‖ ἔξω [wa]ἐν‖ ἐρήμοις τόποις [xa]ἦν,‖ καὶ ἤρχοντο πρὸς αὐτὸν
but without in desert places was, and they came to him
[ya]πανταχόθεν.‖
from every quarter.

2 Καὶ [za]πάλιν εἰσῆλθεν‖ εἰς [aa]Καπερναοὺμ‖ δι' ἡμερῶν,
And again he entered into Capernaum after [some] days,
[ba]καὶ‖ ἠκούσθη ὅτι [ca]εἰς οἶκόν‖ ἐστιν· 2 καὶ [da]εὐθέως‖ συνη-
and it was heard that in [the] house he is; and immediately were
χθησαν πολλοί, ὥστε μηκέτι χωρεῖν μηδὲ τὰ
gathered together many, so that there was no longer any room not even

into a solitary place, and there prayed.
36 And Simon and they that were with him followed after him.
37 And when they had found him, they said unto him, All *men* seek for thee.
38 And he said unto them, Let us go into the next towns, that I may preach there also: for therefore came I forth.
39 And he preached in their synagogues throughout all Galilee, and cast out devils.
40 And there came a leper to him, beseeching him, and kneeling down to him, and saying unto him, If thou wilt, thou canst make me clean.
41 And Jesus, moved with compassion, put forth *his* hand, and touched him, and saith unto him, I will; be thou clean.
42 And as soon as he had spoken, immediately the leprosy departed from him, and he was cleansed.
43 And he straitly charged him, and forthwith sent him away;
44 and saith unto him, See thou say nothing to any man: but go thy way, shew thyself to the priest, and offer for thy cleansing those things which Moses commanded, for a testimony unto them.
45 But he went out, and began to publish *it* much, and to blaze abroad the matter, insomuch that Jesus could no more openly enter into the city, but was without in desert places: and they came to him from every quarter.

II. And again he entered into Capernaum, after *some* days; and it was noised that he was in the house.
2 And straightway many were gathered together, insomuch that there was no room to receive *them*, no, not so much as about

[w] καὶ ἐκεῖ L. [x] κατεδίωξεν T. [y] — ὁ T[Tr]A. [z] εὗρον αὐτον καὶ found him and TTrA. [a] σε ζητοῦσιν LW. [b] + ἀλλαχοῦ elsewhere TTrA. [c] καὶ ἐκεῖ GW. [d] ἐξῆλθον I came forth TTrA. [e] ἦλθεν he went TTr. [f] εἰς τὰς συναγωγὰς GLTTrAW. [g] — καὶ γονυπετῶν αὐτόν L[TrA]; — αὐτόν T. [h] — καὶ T[A]. [i] καὶ and LTTr. [k] αὐτοῦ ἥψατο LTTrA. [l] — αὐτῷ T. [m] — εἰπόντος αὐτοῦ LTTr. [n] εὐθὺς TTrA. [o] ἐκαθερίσθη TA. [p] εὐθὺς LTTrA. [q] — μηδὲν L[Tr]. [r] ἀλλὰ LTTrAW. [s] Μωϋσῆς LTTrAW. [t] εἰς πόλιν φανερῶς T. [v] ἀλλὰ LTrA. [wa] ἐπ' TTrA. [xa] [ἦν] L. [ya] πάντοθεν LTTrAW. [za] εἰσῆλθεν πάλιν LW; εἰσελθὼν πάλιν he having entered again TTrA. [aa] Καφαρναοὺμ LTTrAW. [ba] — καὶ [L]TTrA [ca] ἐν οἴκῳ LTTr. [da] — εὐθέως [LTr]T.

the door: and he
preached the word
unto them. 3 And they
come unto him, bring-
ing one sick of the
palsy, which was borne
of four. 4 And when
they could not come
nigh unto him for the
press, they uncovered
the roof where he was:
and when they had
broken *it* up, they let
down the bed wherein
the sick of the palsy
lay. 5 When Jesus saw
their faith, he said
unto the sick of the
palsy, Son, thy sins be
forgiven thee. 6 But
there were certain of
the scribes sitting
there, and reasoning in
their hearts, 7 Why
doth this *man* thus
speak blasphemies?
who can forgive sins
but God only? 8 And
immediately when Je-
sus perceived in his
spirit that they so
reasoned within them-
selves, he said unto
them, Why reason ye
these things in your
hearts? 9 Whether is
it easier to say to the
sick of the palsy, *Thy*
sins be forgiven thee;
or to say, Arise, and
take up thy bed, and
walk? 10 But that ye
may know that the
Son of man hath power
on earth to forgive
sins, (he saith to the
sick of the palsy,)
11 I say unto thee,
Arise, and take up thy
bed, and go thy way
into thine house.
12 And immediately
he arose, took up the
bed, and went forth
before them all; inso-
much that they were
all amazed, and glori-
fied God, saying, We
never saw it on this
fashion.

πρὸς τὴν θύραν· καὶ ἐλάλει αὐτοῖς τὸν λόγον. 3 Καὶ ἔρχονται
at the door; and he spoke to them the word. And they come
[e]πρὸς αὐτόν, παραλυτικὸν φέροντες,‖ αἰρόμενον ὑπὸ τεσσάρων.
to him, [2]a [3]paralytic [1]bringing, borne by four.
4 καὶ μὴ δυνάμενοι [f]προσεγγίσαι‖ αὐτῷ διὰ τὸν ὄχλον,
And not being able to come near to him on account of the crowd,
ἀπεστέγασαν τὴν.στέγην ὅπου ἦν, καὶ ἐξορύξαντες χα-
they uncovered the roof where he was, and having broken up [it] they
λῶσιν τὸν [g]κράββατον‖ [h]ἐφ' ᾧ‖ ὁ παραλυτικὸς κατέκειτο.
let down the couch on which the paralytic was lying.
5 [i]ἰδὼν.δὲ‖ ὁ Ἰησοῦς τὴν.πίστιν.αὐτῶν λέγει τῷ παραλυτικῷ,
And [2]seeing [1]Jesus their faith says to the paralytic,
Τέκνον, [k]ἀφέωνταί‖ [l]σοι αἱ.ἁμαρτίαι.σου.‖ 6 Ἦσαν.δέ τινες
Child, [3]have [4]been [5]forgiven [6]thee [1]thy [2]sins. But there were some
τῶν γραμματέων ἐκεῖ καθήμενοι, καὶ διαλογιζόμενοι ἐν ταῖς
of the scribes [2]there [1]sitting, and reasoning in
καρδίαις.αὐτῶν, 7 Τί οὗτος οὕτως λαλεῖ [m]βλασφημίας‖;
their hearts, Why [2]this [[3]man] [4]thus [1]does [5]speak blasphemies?
τίς δύναται ἀφιέναι ἁμαρτίας, εἰ.μὴ εἷς, ὁ θεός; 8 Καὶ
who is able to forgive sins, except one, [that is] God? And
[n]εὐθέως‖ ἐπιγνοὺς ὁ Ἰησοῦς τῷ.πνεύματι.αὐτοῦ ὅτι [o]οὕτως‖ [p]
immediately [2]knowing [1]Jesus in his spirit that thus
διαλογίζονται ἐν ἑαυτοῖς, [q]εἶπεν‖ αὐτοῖς, Τί ταῦτα δια-
they are reasoning within themselves, said to them, Why these things rea-
λογίζεσθε ἐν ταῖς.καρδίαις.ὑμῶν; 9 τί ἐστιν εὐκοπώτερον,
son ye in your hearts? which is easier,
εἰπεῖν τῷ παραλυτικῷ, [r]Ἀφέωνταί‖ [s]σοι‖ αἱ ἁμαρτίαι,
to say to the paralytic, [3]Have [4]been [5]forgiven [6]thee [[1]thy] [2]sins,
ἢ εἰπεῖν, [t]Ἔγειραι,‖ [v]καὶ‖ ἆρόν [w]σου τὸν κράββατον‖ καὶ
or to say, Arise, and take up thy couch and
[x]περιπάτει‖; 10 ἵνα.δὲ εἰδῆτε ὅτι ἐξουσίαν ἔχει ὁ υἱὸς τοῦ
walk? but that ye may know that [6]authority [5]has [1]the [2]Son
ἀνθρώπου [y]ἀφιέναι ἐπὶ τῆς γῆς‖ ἁμαρτίας, λέγει τῷ παρα-
[3]of [4]man to forgive on the earth sins,— he says to the para-
λυτικῷ, 11 Σοὶ λέγω, [z]ἔγειραι,‖ [a]καὶ‖ ἆρον τὸν [g]κράββατόν‖
lytic, To thee I say, arise, and take up [2]couch
σου καὶ ὕπαγε εἰς τὸν.οἶκόν.σου. 12 Καὶ ἠγέρθη [b]εὐθέως, καὶ‖
[1]thy and go to thy house. And he arose immediately, and
ἄρας τὸν [g]κράββατον‖ ἐξῆλθεν [c]ἐναντίον‖ πάντων,
having taken up the couch went forth before all,
ὥστε ἐξίστασθαι πάντας, καὶ δοξάζειν τὸν θεόν, [d]λέγοντας,‖
so that [2]were [3]amazed [1]all, and glorified God, saying,
Ὅτι [ea]οὐδέποτε οὕτως‖ [fa]εἴδομεν.‖
Never thus did we see [it].

13 And he went forth
again by the sea side;
and all the multitude
resorted unto him,
and he taught them.
14 And as he passed

13 Καὶ ἐξῆλθεν πάλιν [ga]παρὰ‖ τὴν θάλασσαν, καὶ πᾶς ὁ
And he went forth again by the sea, and all the
ὄχλος ἤρχετο πρὸς αὐτόν, καὶ ἐδίδασκεν αὐτούς. 14 Καὶ
crowd came to him, and he taught them. And

---

[e] πρὸς αὐτὸν φέροντες παραλυτικὸν LTr; φέροντες πρὸς αὐτὸν παραλυτικὸν TA. [f] προσενέγκαι to bring near T. [g] κράβαττον LTTrAW. [h] ὅπου where LTTrA. [i] καὶ ἰδὼν T. [k] ἀφίενταί are forgiven LTTr. [l] σου αἱ ἁμαρτίαι GTTrA; σοι αἱ ἁμαρτίαι [σου] L. [m]; βλασφημεῖ· (*read* Why does this [man] thus speak? he blasphemes.) LTTrA. [n] εὐθὺς LTTrA. [o] — οὕτως L. [p] + αὐτοὶ they (are reasoning) G[A]W. [q] λέγει says TTrA. [r] Ἀφίενταί are forgiven LTTr. [s] σου thy (sins) GTTrAW. [t] Ἔγειρε GLTW; Ἐγείρου TrA. [v] — καὶ G[Tr]AW. [w] τὸν κράβαττόν σου LTTrAW. [x] ὕπαγε go T. [y] ἐπὶ τῆς γῆς ἀφιέναι GLTTrW. [z] ἔγειρε GLTTrAW. [a] — καὶ G[L]TTrAW. [b] καὶ εὐθὺς TTrA. [c] ἔμπροσθεν T. [d] — λέγοντας [L]A. [ea] οὕτως οὐδέποτε TTrA. [fa] εἴδαμεν LTTrA. [ga] εἰς to T.

παράγων εἶδεν [h]Λευῒν‖ τὸν τοῦ Ἀλφαίου καθήμενον ἐπὶ τὸ
passing on he saw Levi the [son] of Alphæus sitting at the
τελώνιον, καὶ λέγει αὐτῷ, Ἀκολούθει μοι. Καὶ ἀναστὰς
tax office, and says to him, Follow me. And having arisen
ἠκολούθησεν αὐτῷ. 15 Καὶ [i]ἐγένετο‖ [k]ἐν.τῷ‖.κατακεῖσθαι.αὐ-
he followed him. And it came to pass as he reclined
τὸν ἐν τῇ.οἰκίᾳ.αὐτοῦ, καὶ πολλοὶ τελῶναι καὶ ἁμαρτω-
[at table] in his house, that many tax-gatherers and sin-
λοὶ συνανέκειντο τῷ Ἰησοῦ καὶ τοῖς.μαθηταῖς.αὐτοῦ·
ners were reclining [at table] with Jesus and his disciples;
ἦσαν.γὰρ πολλοί, καὶ [l]ἠκολούθησαν‖ αὐτῷ. 16 καὶ [m]οἱ‖ γραμ-
for they were many, and they followed him. And the scribes
ματεῖς [n]καὶ οἱ Φαρισαῖοι,‖ [o]ἰδόντες [p]αὐτὸν ἐσθίοντα‖ μετὰ
and the Pharisees, having seen him eating with
τῶν [q]τελωνῶν καὶ ἁμαρτωλῶν,‖ ἔλεγον τοῖς.μαθηταῖς.αὐτοῦ,
the tax-gatherers and sinners, said to his disciples,
[r]Τί‖ ὅτι μετὰ τῶν [s]τελωνῶν καὶ ἁμαρτωλῶν‖ ἐσθίει [t]καὶ
Why [is it] that with the tax-gatherers and sinners he eats and
πίνει;‖ 17 Καὶ ἀκούσας ὁ Ἰησοῦς λέγει αὐτοῖς, Οὐ χρείαν
drinks? And [2]having [3]heard [1]Jesus says to them, [6]Not [7]need
ἔχουσιν οἱ ἰσχύοντες ἰατροῦ, ἀλλ' οἱ κακῶς ἔχον-
[5]have [1]they [2]who [3]are [4]strong of a physician, but they who ill are.
τες. οὐκ.ἦλθον καλέσαι δικαίους, ἀλλὰ ἁμαρτωλοὺς [v]εἰς
I came not to call righteous [ones], but sinners to
μετάνοιαν.‖
repentance.

by, he saw Levi the *son* of Alphæus sitting at the receipt of custom, and said unto him, Follow me. And he arose and followed him. 15 And it came to pass, that, as Jesus sat at meat in his house, many publicans and sinners sat also together with Jesus and his disciples: for there were many, and they followed him. 16 And when the scribes and Pharisees saw him eat with publicans and sinners, they said unto his disciples, How is it that he eateth and drinketh with publicans and sinners? 17 When Jesus heard *it*, he saith unto them, They that are whole have no need of the physician, but they that are sick: I came not to call the righteous, but sinners to repentance.

18 Καὶ ἦσαν οἱ μαθηταὶ Ἰωάννου καὶ [w]οἱ τῶν Φαρισαίων‖
And [10]were [1]the [2]disciples [3]of [4]John [5]and [6]those [7]of [8]the [9]Pharisees
νηστεύοντες· καὶ ἔρχονται καὶ λέγουσιν αὐτῷ, [x]Διατί‖ οἱ μαθη-
fasting; and they come and say to him, Why [2]the [3]disci-
ταὶ Ἰωάννου καὶ οἱ [y] τῶν Φαρισαίων νηστεύουσιν, οἱ δὲ σοὶ
ples [4]of [5]John [6]and [7]those [8]of [9]the [10]Pharisees [1]fast, but thy
μαθηταὶ οὐ.νηστεύουσιν; 19 Καὶ εἶπεν αὐτοῖς ὁ Ἰησοῦς, Μὴ
disciples fast not? And [2]said [3]to [4]them [1]Jesus,
δύνανται οἱ υἱοὶ τοῦ νυμφῶνος, ἐν.ᾧ ὁ νυμφίος μετ' αὐτῶν
Can the sons of the bridechamber, while the bridegroom with them
ἐστιν, νηστεύειν; ὅσον.χρόνον [z]μεθ' ἑαυτῶν ἔχουσιν τὸν νυμ-
is, fast? as long as with them they have the bride-
φίον,‖ οὐ.δύνανται νηστεύειν· 20 ἐλεύσονται.δὲ ἡμέραι ὅταν
groom, they are not able to fast. But will come days when
ἀπαρθῇ ἀπ' αὐτῶν ὁ νυμφίος, καὶ τότε νη-
will have been taken away from them the bridegroom, and then they
στεύσουσιν ἐν [a]ἐκείναις ταῖς ἡμέραις.‖ 21 [b]καὶ‖ οὐδεὶς ἐπίβλημα
will fast in those days. And no one a piece
[c]ῥάκους‖ ἀγνάφου [d]ἐπιῤῥάπτει‖ ἐπὶ [e]ἱματίῳ.παλαιῷ‖· εἰ.δὲ.μή,
of [2]cloth [1]unfulled sews on an old garment; otherwise,
αἴρει [f] τὸ πλήρωμα[g] [ha]αὐτοῦ‖ τὸ καινὸν τοῦ παλαιοῦ, καὶ
[7]takes [8]away [1]the [3]filling [4]up [5]of [6]it [2]new from the old, and

18 And the disciples of John and of the Pharisees used to fast: and they come and say unto him, Why do the disciples of John and of the Pharisees fast, but thy disciples fast not? 19 And Jesus said unto them, Can the children of the bridechamber fast, while the bridegroom is with them? as long as they have the bridegroom with them, they cannot fast. 20 But the days will come, when the bridegroom shall be taken away from them, and then shall they fast in those days. 21 No man also seweth a piece of new cloth on an old garment: else the new piece that filled it up taketh away from the old, and the rent is

---

[h] Λευεὶν TA. [i] γίνεται it comes to pass TTrA. [k] — ἐν τῷ T[Tr]. [l] ἠκολούθουν they were following TTrA. [m] — οἱ T. [n] τῶν Φαρισαίων of the Pharisees TTr. [o] + καὶ also [L]TTr. [p] ὅτι ἐσθίει L; ὅτι ἤσθιεν that he was eating TTr. [q] ἁμαρτωλῶν καὶ τελωνῶν LTrA. [r] — Τί TTrA. [s] ἁμαρτωλῶν καὶ τῶν τελωνῶν LTr. [t] [καὶ πίνει] L. [v] — εἰς μετάνοιαν GLTTrAW. [w] οἱ Φαρισαῖοι the Pharisees GLTTrAW. [x] Διὰ τί LTrA. [y] + μαθηταὶ (οἱ the) disciples TTrA. [z] ἔχουσιν τὸν νυμφίον μετ' αὐτῶν (μεθ' ἑαυτῶν L) LTTrA. [a] ἐκείνῃ τῇ ἡμέρᾳ that day GLTTrAW. [b] — καὶ GLTTrAW. [c] ῥάκκους L. [d] ἐπιράπτει TTrA. [e] ἱμάτιον παλαιόν LTTrA. [f] + ἀπ' αὐτοῦ from it A. [g] + ἀπ' from LT. [ha] — αὐτοῦ [Tr]A.

made worse. 22 And no man putteth new wine into old bottles: else the new wine doth burst the bottles, and the wine is spilled, and the bottles will be marred: but new wine must be put into new bottles.

23 And it came to pass, that he went through the corn fields on the sabbath day; and his disciples began, as they went, to pluck the ears of corn. 24 And the Pharisees said unto him, Behold, why do they on the sabbath day that which is not lawful? 25 And he said unto them, Have ye never read what David did, when he had need, and was an hungred, he, and they that were with him? 26 How he went into the house of God in the days of Abiathar the high priest, and did eat the shewbread, which is not lawful to eat but for the priests, and gave also to them which were with him? 27 And he said unto them, The sabbath was made for man, and not man for the sabbath: 28 therefore the Son of man is Lord also of the sabbath.

III. And he entered again into the synagogue; and there was a man there which had a withered hand. 2 And they watched him, whether he would heal him on the sabbath day; that they might accuse him. 3 And he saith unto the man which had the withered hand, Stand forth. 4 And he saith unto them, Is it lawful to do good on the sabbath days, or to do evil? to save life, or to kill? But they held their peace. 5 And when he had looked round about on them with anger, being grieved

χεῖρον σχίσμα γίνεται. 22 καὶ οὐδεὶς βάλλει οἶνον νέον εἰς
[2]worse [1]a rent takes place. And no one puts [2]wine [1]new into
ἀσκοὺς παλαιούς· εἰ.δὲ.μή, [i]ῥήσσει‖ ὁ οἶνος [k]ὁ νέος‖ τοὺς ἀσ-
[2]skins [1]old; otherwise, [4]bursts [1]the [3]wine [2]new the skins,
κούς, καὶ ὁ οἶνος [l]ἐκχεῖται καὶ οἱ ἀσκοὶ ἀπολοῦνται·‖ [m]ἀλλὰ
and the wine is poured out, and the skins will be destroyed; but
οἶνον νέον εἰς ἀσκοὺς καινοὺς βλητέον.‖
[2]wine [1]new [3]into [5]skins [4]new is to be put.

23 Καὶ ἐγένετο [n]παραπορεύεσθαι.αὐτὸν ἐν τοῖς σάββασιν‖
And it came to pass that he went on the sabbath
διὰ τῶν σπορίμων, καὶ [o]ἤρξαντο οἱ.μαθηταὶ.αὐτοῦ‖ [p]ὁδὸν
through the corn-fields, and [3]began [1]his [2]disciples [their] way
ποιεῖν‖ τίλλοντες τοὺς στάχυας. 24 καὶ οἱ Φαρισαῖοι ἔλεγον
to make, plucking the ears. And the Pharisees said
αὐτῷ, Ἴδε, τί ποιοῦσιν [q]ἐν‖ τοῖς σάββασιν ὃ οὐκ.ἔξεστιν;
to him, Behold, why do they on the sabbath that which is not lawful?
25 Καὶ [r]αὐτὸς‖ [s]ἔλεγεν‖ αὐτοῖς, Οὐδέποτε ἀνέγνωτε τί ἐποίη-
And he said to them, [3]Never [1]did [2]ye read what [2]did
σεν [t]Δαβίδ,‖ ὅτε χρείαν ἔσχεν καὶ ἐπείνασεν, αὐτὸς καὶ οἱ
[1]David, when need he had and hungered, he and those
μετ' αὐτοῦ; 26 [v]πῶς‖ εἰσῆλθεν εἰς τὸν οἶκον τοῦ θεοῦ ἐπὶ
with him? how he entered into the house of God in
[w]Ἀβιάθαρ [w]τοῦ‖ ἀρχιερέως, καὶ τοὺς ἄρτους τῆς
[the days of] Abiathar the high priest, and the loaves of the
προθέσεως ἔφαγεν, οὓς οὐκ.ἔξεστιν φαγεῖν εἰ.μὴ [x]τοῖς ἱερεῦ-
presentation ate, which it is not lawful to eat except for the priests,
σιν,‖ καὶ ἔδωκεν καὶ τοῖς σὺν αὐτῷ οὖσιν; 27 Καὶ ἔλεγεν
and gave even to those who with him were? And he said
αὐτοῖς, Τὸ σάββατον διὰ τὸν ἄνθρωπον ἐγένετο, [y]οὐχ ὁ
to them, The sabbath on account of man was made, not
ἄνθρωπος διὰ τὸ σάββατον. 28 ὥστε κύριός ἐστιν ὁ
man on account of the sabbath: so then Lord is the
υἱὸς τοῦ ἀνθρώπου καὶ τοῦ σαββάτου.
Son of man also of the sabbath.

3 Καὶ εἰσῆλθεν πάλιν εἰς [z]τὴν‖ συναγωγήν, καὶ [a]ἦν‖ ἐκεῖ
And he entered again into the synagogue, and there was there
ἄνθρωπος ἐξηραμμένην ἔχων τὴν χεῖρα, 2 καὶ [b]παρ-
a man [4]withered [1]having [[2]his] [3]hand, and they
ετήρουν‖ αὐτὸν εἰ [c] τοῖς σάββασιν [d]θεραπεύσει‖ αὐτόν,
were watching him whether on the sabbath he will heal him,
ἵνα [e]κατηγορήσωσιν‖ αὐτοῦ. 3 καὶ λέγει τῷ ἀνθρώπῳ
in order that they might accuse him. And he says to the man
τῷ [f]ἐξηραμμένην ἔχοντι τὴν χεῖρα,‖ [g]Ἔγειραι‖ εἰς τὸ
who [3]withered [1]had [2]the hand, Arise [and come] into the
μέσον. 4 Καὶ λέγει αὐτοῖς, Ἔξεστιν τοῖς σάββασιν [h]ἀγαθο-
midst. And he says to them, Is it lawful on the sabbaths to do
ποιῆσαι,‖ ἢ κακοποιῆσαι; ψυχὴν σῶσαι, ἢ ἀποκτεῖναι; Οἱ.δὲ
good, or to do evil? [3]life [1]to [2]save, or to kill? But they
ἐσιώπων. 5 καὶ περιβλεψάμενος αὐτοὺς μετ' ὀργῆς, [ia]συλ-
were silent. And having looked around on them with anger, being

[i] ῥήξει will burst LTTrA. [k] — ὁ νέος LTTrA. [l] ἀπόλλυται καὶ οἱ ἀσκοὶ is destroyed and the skins TTrA. [m] — ἀλλὰ....βλητέον T[Tr]A. [n] αὐτὸν ἐν τοῖς σάββασιν παραπορεύεσθαι (διαπορεύεσθαι LTr) LTTrA. [o] οἱ μαθηταὶ αὐτοῦ ἤρξαντο LTTrA. [p] ὁδοποιεῖν L. [q] — ἐν LTTrA. [r] — αὐτὸς [L]TTr. [s] λέγει he says LTTr. [t] Δαυεὶδ LTTrA; Δαυὶδ GW. [v] [πῶς] TrA. [w] — τοῦ LTTrAW. [x] τοὺς ἱερεῖς T. [y] + καὶ and TTrA. [z] — τὴν (read [the]) T[Tr]A. [a] — ἦν (read [was]) L[Tr]. [b] παρετηροῦντο L. [c] + ἐν on (the) T. [d] θεραπεύει he heals T. [e] κατηγορήσουσιν they shall accuse LTr. [f] τὴν χεῖρα ἔχοντι ξηράν LTrA; τὴν ξηρὰν χεῖρα ἔχοντι T. [g] Ἔγειρε GLTTrA. [h] ἀγαθὸν ποιῆσαι T. [ia] συνλυπούμενος TA.

λυπούμενος‖ ἐπὶ τῇ πωρώσει τῆς-καρδίας-αὐτῶν, λέγει τῷ
grieved at the hardness of their heart, he says to the
ἀνθρώπῳ, 'Ἔκτεινον τὴν-χεῖρά-[k]σου.‖ Καὶ ἐξέτεινεν, καὶ
man, Stretch out thy hand. And he stretched out [it], and
[l]ἀποκατεστάθη‖ ἡ-χεὶρ-αὐτοῦ [m]ὑγιὴς ὡς ἡ ἄλλη.‖ 6 καὶ ἐξελ-
[3]was [4]restored [1]his [2]hand sound as the other. And having
θόντες οἱ Φαρισαῖοι [n]εὐθέως‖ μετὰ τῶν Ἡρωδιανῶν συμβούλιον
gone out the Pharisees immediately with the Herodians [2]counsel
[o]ἐποίουν‖ κατ' αὐτοῦ, ὅπως αὐτὸν ἀπολέσωσιν.
[1]took against him, how him they might destroy.

7 Καὶ ὁ Ἰησοῦς [p]ἀνεχώρησεν μετὰ τῶν-μαθητῶν-αὐτοῦ‖ [q]πρὸς‖
And Jesus withdrew with his disciples to
τὴν θάλασσαν· καὶ πολὺ πλῆθος ἀπὸ τῆς Γαλιλαίας
the sea; and [2]great [1]a multitude from Galilee
[r]ἠκολούθησαν‖ [s]αὐτῷ,‖ καὶ ἀπὸ τῆς Ἰουδαίας, 8 καὶ ἀπὸ Ἱε-
followed him, and from Judea, and from Je-
ροσολύμων, καὶ ἀπὸ τῆς Ἰδουμαίας, καὶ πέραν τοῦ Ἰορδάνου·
rusalem, and from Idumea, and beyond the Jordan;
καὶ [t]οἱ‖ περὶ Τύρον καὶ Σιδῶνα, πλῆθος πολύ, [v]ἀκούσαντες‖
and they around Tyre and Sidon, a [2]multitude [1]great, having heard
ὅσα [w]ἐποίει‖ ἦλθον πρὸς αὐτόν. 9 καὶ εἶπεν τοῖς-μαθη-
how much he was doing came to him. And he spoke to his dis-
ταῖς-αὐτοῦ, ἵνα πλοιάριον προσκαρτερῇ αὐτῷ διὰ τὸν
ciples, that a small ship might wait upon him, on account of the
ὄχλον, ἵνα μὴ-θλίβωσιν αὐτόν. 10 πολλοὺς-γὰρ ἐθερά-
crowd, that they might not press upon him. For many he
πευσεν, ὥστε ἐπιπίπτειν αὐτῷ, ἵνα αὐτοῦ ἅψωνται, ὅσοι
healed, so that they beset him, that him they might touch, as many as
εἶχον μάστιγας· 11 καὶ τὰ πνεύματα τὰ ἀκάθαρτα, ὅταν αὐτὸν
had scourges; and the spirits the unclean, when him
[x]ἐθεώρει, προσέπιπτεν‖ αὐτῷ, καὶ [y]ἔκραζεν‖, [z]λέγοντα,‖ Ὅτι σὺ
they beheld, fell down before him, and cried, saying, Thou
εἶ ὁ υἱὸς τοῦ θεοῦ. 12 Καὶ πολλὰ ἐπετίμα αὐτοῖς, ἵνα μὴ
art the Son of God. And much he rebuked them, so that [3]not
[a]αὐτὸν φανερὸν‖ [b]ποιήσωσιν‖ [c].
[5]him [6]manifest [1]they [2]should [4]make.

13 Καὶ ἀναβαίνει εἰς τὸ ὄρος, καὶ προσκαλεῖται οὓς
And he goes up into the mountain, and calls to [him] whom
ἤθελεν αὐτός· καὶ ἀπῆλθον πρὸς αὐτόν. 14 καὶ ἐποίησεν
[2]would [1]he; and they went to him. And he appointed
δώδεκα ἵνα ὦσιν μετ' αὐτοῦ, καὶ ἵνα ἀποστέλλῃ αὐτοὺς
twelve that they might be with him, and that he might send them
κηρύσσειν, 15 καὶ ἔχειν ἐξουσίαν [d]θεραπεύειν τὰς νόσους καὶ‖
to preach, and to have authority to heal diseases and
ἐκβάλλειν τὰ δαιμόνια. 16 [e]καὶ ἐπέθηκεν [f]τῷ Σίμωνι ὄνομα‖
to cast out demons. And he added to Simon [the] name
Πέτρον· 17 καὶ Ἰάκωβον τὸν τοῦ Ζεβεδαίου, καὶ Ἰωάννην
Peter; and James the [son] of Zebedee, and John
τὸν ἀδελφὸν τοῦ Ἰακώβου· καὶ ἐπέθηκεν αὐτοῖς ὀνόματα
the brother of James; and he added to them [the] names

for the hardness of their hearts, he saith unto the man, Stretch forth thine hand. And he stretched *it* out: and his hand was restored whole as the other. 6 And the Pharisees went forth, and straightway took counsel with the Herodians against him, how they might destroy him.

7 But Jesus withdrew himself with his disciples to the sea: and a great multitude from Galilee followed him, and from Judæa, 8 and from Jerusalem, and from Idumæa, and *from* beyond Jordan; and they about Tyre and Sidon, a great multitude, when they had heard what great things he did, came unto him. 9 And he spake to his disciples, that a small ship should wait on him because of the multitude, lest they should throng him. 10 For he had healed many; insomuch that they pressed upon him for to touch him, as many as had plagues. 11 And unclean spirits, when they saw him, fell down before him, and cried, saying, Thou art the Son of God. 12 And he straitly charged them that they should not make him known.

13 And he goeth up into a mountain, and calleth *unto him* whom he would: and they came unto him. 14 And he ordained twelve, that they should be with him, and that he might send them forth to preach, 15 and to have power to heal sicknesses, and to cast out devils: 16 and Simon he surnamed Peter; 17 and James the *son* of Zebedee, and John the brother of James; and he surnamed them Boan-

[k] — σου (*read* [thy]) hand T[Tr]A. [l] ἀπεκατεστάθη GLTTrAW. [m] — ὑγιὴς ὡς ἡ ἄλλη GLTTrAW. [n] εὐθὺς TTrA. [o] ἐποίησαν T; ἐδίδουν gave TrA. [p] μετὰ τῶν μαθητῶν αὐτοῦ ἀνεχώρησεν GLTTrA. [q] εἰς GLT. [r] ἠκολούθησεν LTrA; ἠκολούθησαν *placed after* Ἰουδαίας T. [s] — αὐτῷ [L]TTrA. [t] — οἱ [L]TTr[A]. [v] ἀκούοντες hearing LTTrA. [w] ποιεῖ he is doing TrA. [x] ἐθεώρουν, προσέπιπτον LTTrAW. [y] ἔκραζον LTTrAW. [z] λέγοντες T. [a] φανερὸν αὐτὸν GW. [b] ποιῶσιν TTrA. [c] + [ὅτι ᾔδεισαν τὸν χριστὸν αὐτὸν εἶναι] because they had known him to be the Christ L. [d] — θεραπεύειν τὰς νόσους καὶ TTrA. [e] + καὶ ἐποίησεν τοὺς δώδεκα, and he appointed the twelve T. [f] ὄνομα τῷ Σίμωνι TTrA.

erges, which is, The sons of thunder: 18 and Andrew, and Philip, and Bartholomew, and Matthew, and Thomas, and James the *son* of Alphæus, and Thaddæus, and Simon the Canaanite, 19 and Judas Iscariot, which also betrayed him:

And they went into an house. 20 And the multitude cometh together again, so that they could not so much as eat bread. 21 And when his friends heard *of it*, they went out to lay hold on him: for they said, He is beside himself. 22 And the scribes which came down from Jerusalem said, He hath Beelzebub, and by the prince of the devils casteth he out devils. 23 And he called them *unto him*, and said unto them in parables, How can Satan cast out Satan? 24 And if a kingdom be divided against itself, that kingdom cannot stand. 25 And if a house be divided against itself, that house cannot stand. 26 And if Satan rise up against himself, and be divided, he cannot stand, but hath an end. 27 No man can enter into a strong man's house, and spoil his goods, except he will first bind the strong man; and then he will spoil his house. 28 Verily I say unto you, All sins shall be forgiven unto the sons of men, and blasphemies wherewith soever they shall blaspheme: 29 but he that shall blaspheme against the Holy Ghost hath never forgiveness, but is in danger of eternal damnation: 30 because they said, He hath an unclean spirit.

[g]Βοανεργές,‖ ὅ ἐστιν υἱοὶ βροντῆς· 18 καὶ Ἀνδρέαν, καὶ
Boanerges, which is Sons of thunder; and Andrew, and
Φίλιππον, καὶ Βαρθολομαῖον, καὶ [h]Ματθαῖον,‖ καὶ Θωμᾶν,
Philip, and Bartholomew, and Matthew, and Thomas,
καὶ Ἰάκωβον τὸν τοῦ Ἀλφαίου, καὶ Θαδδαῖον, καὶ Σίμωνα
and James the [son] of Alphæus, and Thaddæus, and Simon
τὸν [i]Κανανίτην,‖ 19 καὶ Ἰούδαν [k]Ἰσκαριώτην,‖ ὃς καὶ παρέ-
the Cananite, and Judas Iscariote, who also deliver-
δωκεν αὐτόν.
ed up him.

Καὶ [l]ἔρχονται‖ εἰς οἶκον· 20 καὶ συνέρχεται πάλιν [m]ὄχλος,
And they come to a house: and [3]comes [4]together [5]again [1]a [2]crowd,
ὥστε μὴ-δύνασθαι-αὐτοὺς-[n]μήτε‖ ἄρτον φαγεῖν. 21 καὶ ἀκού-
so that they are not able so much as [3]bread [1]to [2]eat. And having
σαντες οἱ παρ' αὐτοῦ ἐξῆλθον κρατῆσαι αὐτόν·
heard [of it], those belonging to him went out to lay hold of him;
ἔλεγον-γάρ, Ὅτι ἐξέστη. 22 Καὶ οἱ γραμματεῖς οἱ ἀπὸ
for they said, He is beside himself. And the scribes who from
Ἱεροσολύμων καταβάντες ἔλεγον, Ὅτι Βεελζεβοὺλ ἔχει· καὶ
Jerusalem came down said, Beelzebul he has; and
Ὅτι ἐν τῷ ἄρχοντι τῶν δαιμονίων ἐκβάλλει τὰ δαιμόνια.
By the prince of the demons he casts out the demons.
23 Καὶ προσκαλεσάμενος αὐτοὺς ἐν παραβολαῖς ἔλεγεν
And having called to [him] them in parables he said
αὐτοῖς, Πῶς δύναται σατανᾶς σατανᾶν ἐκβάλλειν; 24 καὶ
to them, How can Satan [3]Satan [1]cast [2]out? and
ἐὰν βασιλεία ἐφ' ἑαυτὴν μερισθῇ, οὐ-δύναται σταθῆναι ἡ
if a kingdom against itself be divided, [3]is [4]not [5]able [6]to [7]stand
βασιλεία-ἐκείνη· 25 καὶ ἐὰν οἰκία ἐφ' ἑαυτὴν μερισθῇ, [o]οὐ
[1]that [2]kingdom: and if a house against itself be divided, [4]not
δύναται‖ [p]σταθῆναι ἡ-οἰκία-ἐκείνη·‖ 26 καὶ εἰ ὁ σατανᾶς ἀνέστη
[3]is [5]able [6]to [7]stand [1]that [2]house: and if Satan has risen up
ἐφ' ἑαυτὸν [q]καὶ μεμέρισται,‖ οὐ-δύναται [r]σταθῆναι,‖ ἀλλὰ
against himself and has been divided, he is not able to stand, but
τέλος ἔχει. 27 [s] [t]οὐ-δύναται-οὐδεὶς‖ [v]τὰ σκεύη τοῦ ἰσχυροῦ,
an end has. No one in any wise is able the goods of the strong man,
εἰσελθὼν εἰς τὴν-οἰκίαν‖-αὐτοῦ, διαρπάσαι, ἐὰν-μὴ πρῶτον
having entered into his house, to plunder, unless first
τὸν ἰσχυρὸν δήσῃ, καὶ τότε τὴν-οἰκίαν-αὐτοῦ διαρπάσει. 28 ἀ-
the strong man he bind, and then his house he will plunder. Ve-
μὴν λέγω ὑμῖν, ὅτι πάντα ἀφεθήσεται [w]τὰ ἁμαρτήματα τοῖς
rily I say to you, that all [3]shall [4]be [5]forgiven [1]the [2]sins to the
υἱοῖς τῶν ἀνθρώπων,‖ καὶ [x] βλασφημίαι [y]ὅσας‖-[z]ἂν‖ βλασ-
sons of men, and blasphemies whatsoever they shall
φημήσωσιν· 29 ὃς-δ'-ἂν βλασφημήσῃ εἰς τὸ πνεῦμα τὸ
have blasphemed; but whosoever shall blaspheme against the Spirit the
ἅγιον, οὐκ-ἔχει ἄφεσιν εἰς τὸν αἰῶνα, [a]ἀλλ'‖ ἔνοχός [b]ἐστιν‖
Holy, has not forgiveness to eternity, but [2]liable [3]to [1]is
αἰωνίου [c]κρίσεως.‖ 30 ὅτι ἔλεγον, Πνεῦμα-ἀκάθαρτον ἔχει.
eternal judgment; because they said, An unclean spirit he has.

---

[g] βοανηργές LTTrA. [h] Μαθθαῖον LTTrA. [i] Καναναῖον Cananæan LTTrAW. [k] Ἰσκαριώθ LTTrAW. [l] ἔρχεται he comes T. [m] + ὁ the (crowd) LTrA. [n] μηδὲ LTrAW. [o] οὐ δυνήσεται will not be able TTrA. [p] ἡ οἰκία ἐκείνη σταθῆναι (στῆναι TrA) LTTrA. [q] ἐμερίσθη, καὶ he is divided, and T. [r] στῆναι TTrA. [s] + ἀλλ' but TTrA. [t] οὐδεὶς δύναται GLTrW. [v] εἰς τὴν οἰκίαν τοῦ ἰσχυροῦ εἰσελθὼν τὰ σκεύη TTr. [w] τοῖς υἱοῖς τῶν ἀνθρώπων τὰ ἁμαρτήματα GLTTrAW. [x] + αἱ the GLTTrAW. [y] ὅσα LTTrA. [z] ἐὰν TrA. [a] ἀλλὰ LTTrA. [b] ἔσται shall be T. [c] ἁμαρτήματος sin (*read* guilty of eternal sin) LTTrA.

31 [d]″Ερχονται.οὖν‖ [e]οἱ ἀδελφοὶ καὶ ἡ.μητηρ.αὐτοῦ,‖ καὶ
Then come [his] brethren and his mother, and
ἔξω [f]ἑστῶτες‖ ἀπέστειλαν πρὸς αὐτόν, [g]φωνοῦντες‖ αὐτόν.
²without ¹standing sent to him, calling him.
32 καὶ ἐκάθητο [h]ὄχλος περὶ αὐτόν·‖ [i]εἶπον.δὲ‖ αὐτῷ, Ἰδού,
And ³sat ¹a ²crowd around him: and they said to him, Behold,
ἡ.μήτηρ.σου καὶ οἱ.ἀδελφοί.σου [k] ἔξω ζητοῦσίν σε. 33 Καὶ
thy mother and thy brethren without seek thee. And
[l]ἀπεκρίθη αὐτοῖς, λέγων,‖ Τίς ἐστιν ἡ.μήτηρ.μου [m]ἢ‖ οἱ ἀδελ-
he answered them, saying, Who is my mother or ²breth-
φοί [n]μου‖; 34 Καὶ περιβλεψάμενος [o]κύκλῳ τοὺς περὶ
ren ¹my? And having looked around on ³in ⁴a ⁵circuit ¹those ²who around
αὐτὸν‖ καθημένους, λέγει, [p]″Ιδε,‖ ἡ.μήτηρ.μου καὶ οἱ ἀδελφοί
him were sitting, he says, Behold, my mother and ²brethren
μου· 35 ὃς.[q]γὰρ‖.ἂν ποιήσῃ [r]τὸ θέλημα‖ τοῦ θεοῦ, οὗτος ἀδελ-
¹my: for whoever shall do the will of God, he ²bro-
φός μου καὶ ἀδελφή.[s]μου‖ καὶ μήτηρ ἐστίν.
ther ¹my and my sister and mother is.

31 There came then his brethren and his mother, and, standing without, sent unto him, calling him. 32 And the multitude sat about him, and they said unto him, Behold, thy mother and thy brethren without seek for thee. 33 And he answered them, saying, Who is my mother, or my brethren? 34 And he looked round about on them which sat about him, and said, Behold my mother and my brethren! 35 For whosoever shall do the will of God, the same is my brother, and my sister, and mother.

4 Καὶ πάλιν ἤρξατο διδάσκειν παρὰ τὴν θάλασσαν· καὶ
And again he began to teach by the sea. And
[t]συνήχθη‖ πρὸς αὐτὸν ὄχλος [v]πολύς,‖ ὥστε αὐτὸν [w]ἐμ-
was gathered together to him a ²crowd ¹great, so that he having
βάντα εἰς τὸ πλοῖον‖ καθῆσθαι ἐν τῇ θαλάσσῃ, καὶ πᾶς ὁ
entered into the ship sat in the sea, and all the
ὄχλος πρὸς τὴν θάλασσαν ἐπὶ τῆς γῆς [x]ἦν.‖ 2 καὶ ἐδίδασκεν
crowd close to the sea on the land was. And he taught
αὐτοὺς ἐν παραβολαῖς πολλά, καὶ ἔλεγεν αὐτοῖς ἐν τῇ δι-
them in parables many things, and said to them in ²teach-
δαχῇ.αὐτοῦ, 3 Ἀκούετε· ἰδού, ἐξῆλθεν ὁ σπείρων [y]τοῦ‖ σπεῖραι
ing ¹his, Hearken: behold, went out the sower to sow.
4 καὶ ἐγένετο ἐν.τῷ.σπείρειν, ὃ.μὲν ἔπεσεν παρὰ τὴν ὁδόν,
And it came to pass as he sowed, one fell by the way,
καὶ ἦλθεν τὰ πετεινὰ [z]τοῦ.οὐρανοῦ‖ καὶ κατέφαγεν αὐτό.
and came the birds of the heaven and devoured it.
5 [a]ἄλλο.δὲ‖ ἔπεσεν ἐπὶ τὸ πετρῶδες, [b] ὅπου οὐκ.εἶχεν γῆν
And another fell upon the rocky place, where it had not ²earth
πολλήν· καὶ [c]εὐθέως‖ ἐξανέτειλεν, διὰ τὸ.μὴ.ἔχειν βάθος[da]
¹much, and immediately it sprang up, because of not having depth
γῆς· 6 [ea]ἡλίου.δὲ ἀνατείλαντος‖ [fa]ἐκαυματίσθη,‖ καὶ διὰ
of earth; and [the] sun having arisen it was scorched, and because of
τὸ.μὴ.ἔχειν ῥίζαν ἐξηράνθη. 7 καὶ ἄλλο ἔπεσεν εἰς [ga]τὰς‖
not having root it withered away. And another fell among the
ἀκάνθας· καὶ ἀνέβησαν αἱ ἄκανθαι, καὶ συνέπνιξαν αὐτό, καὶ
thorns, and ³grew ⁴up ¹the ²thorns, and choked it, and
καρπὸν οὐκ.ἔδωκεν. 8 καὶ [ha]ἄλλο‖ ἔπεσεν εἰς τὴν γῆν τὴν
fruit it yielded not. And another fell into the ground the

IV. And he began again to teach by the sea side: and there was gathered unto him a great multitude, so that he entered into a ship, and sat in the sea; and the whole multitude was by the sea on the land. 2 And he taught them many things by parables, and said unto them in his doctrine, 3 Hearken; Behold, there went out a sower to sow: 4 and it came to pass, as he sowed, some fell by the way side, and the fowls of the air came and devoured it up. 5 And some fell on stony ground, where it had not much earth; and immediately it sprang up, because it had no depth of earth: 6 but when the sun was up, it was scorched; and because it had no root, it withered away. 7 And some fell among thorns, and the thorns grew up, and choked it, and it yielded no fruit. 8 And other fell on good ground, and did yield

---

[d] καὶ ἔρχονται LTrAW; καὶ ἔρχεται T. [e] ἡ μήτηρ αὐτοῦ καὶ οἱ ἀδελφοὶ αὐτοῦ GLTTrW; οἱ ἀδελφοὶ αὐτοῦ καὶ ἡ μήτηρ αὐτοῦ A. [f] στήκοντες TTrA. [g] καλοῦντες LTTrA. [h] περὶ αὐτὸν ὄχλος LTTrAW. [i] καὶ λέγουσιν and they say LTTrAW. [k] + καὶ αἱ (— αἱ W) ἀδελφαί σου and thy sisters LT[A]W. [l] ἀποκριθεὶς αὐτοῖς λέγει answering them he says TTrA. [m] καὶ and LTTr. [n] — μου [Tr]A. [o] τοὺς περὶ αὐτὸν κύκλῳ LTTr. [p] Ἰδοὺ L. [q] — γὰρ for LT[Tr]A. [r] τὰ θελήματα (read the things God wills) A. [s] — μου my LTTrA. [t] συνάγεται is gathered together LTTrAW. [v] πλεῖστος very great TTrAW. [w] εἰς τὸ (— τὸ TTrW) πλοῖον ἐμβάντα LTTrW. [x] ἦσαν were TTrA. [y] — τοῦ LT[Tr]A. [z] — τοῦ οὐρανοῦ GLTTrAW. [a] καὶ ἄλλο LTTrA. [b] + καὶ and [LTr]A. [c] εὐθὺς LTTrA. [da] + τῆς L. [ea] καὶ ὅτε ἀνέτειλεν ὁ ἥλιος and when the sun was risen LTTrA. [fa] ἐκαυματίσθησαν they were scorched Tr. [ga] — τὰς G. [ha] ἄλλα others TA.

fruit that sprang up
and increased; and
brought forth, some
thirty, and some sixty,
and some an hundred.
9 And he said unto
them, He that hath
ears to hear, let him
hear. 10 And when he
was alone, they that
were about him with
the twelve asked of
him the parable.
11 And he said unto
them, Unto you it is
given to know the mys-
tery of the kingdom of
God: but unto them
that are without, all
these things are done
in parables: 12 that
seeing they may see,
and not perceive; and
hearing they may hear,
and not understand;
lest at any time they
should be converted,
and *their* sins should
be forgiven them.
13 And he said unto
them, Know ye not
this parable? and how
then will ye know all
parables? 14 The sower
soweth the word.
15 And these are they
by the way side, where
the word is sown; but
when they have heard,
Satan cometh immedi-
ately, and taketh away
the word that was
sown in their hearts.
16 And these are they
likewise which are
sown on stony ground;
who, when they have
heard the word, imme-
diately receive it with
gladness; 17 and have
no root in themselves,
and so endure but for
a time: afterward,
when affliction or per-
secution ariseth for
the word's sake, im-
mediately they are of-
fended. 18 And these
are they which are
sown among thorns;
such as hear the word,
19 and the cares of this
world, and the deceit-
fulness of riches, and
the lusts of other
things entering in,
choke the word, and it
becometh unfruitful.
20 And these are they
which are sown on
good ground; such as

καλήν· καὶ ἐδίδου καρπὸν ἀναβαίνοντα καὶ [i]αὐξάνοντα,‖ καὶ
good, and yielded fruit, growing up and increasing, and
ἔφερεν [k]ἓν‖ τριάκοντα, καὶ [k]ἓν‖ ἑξήκοντα, καὶ [k]ἓν‖ ἑκατόν.
bore one thirty, and one sixty, and one a hundred.
9 Καὶ ἔλεγεν [l]αὐτοῖς,‖ [m]Ὁ ἔχων‖ ὦτα ἀκούειν ἀκουέτω.
And he said to them, He that has ears to hear let him hear.
10 [n]Ὅτε.δὲ‖ ἐγένετο [o]καταμόνας,‖ [p]ἠρώτησαν‖ αὐτὸν οἱ περὶ
And when he was alone, [7]asked [8]him [1]those [2]about
αὐτὸν σὺν τοῖς δώδεκα [q]τὴν παραβολήν.‖ 11 καὶ ἔλεγεν
[3]him [4]with [5]the [6]twelve [as to] the parable. And he said
αὐτοῖς, Ὑμῖν [r]δέδοται γνῶναι τὸ μυστήριον‖ τῆς βασιλείας
to them, To you has been given to know the mystery of the kingdom
τοῦ θεοῦ· ἐκείνοις.δὲ τοῖς ἔξω, ἐν παραβολαῖς [s]τὰ‖.πάντα
of God: but to those who are without, in parables all things
γίνεται· 12 ἵνα βλέποντες βλέπωσιν, καὶ μὴ ἴδωσιν· καὶ
are done, that seeing they may see, and not perceive; and
ἀκούοντες ἀκούωσιν, καὶ μὴ συνιῶσιν· μήποτε ἐπιστρέψω-
hearing they may hear, and not understand, lest they should be con-
σιν, καὶ ἀφεθῇ αὐτοῖς [t]τὰ ἁμαρτήματα.‖ 13 Καὶ
verted, and [3]should [4]be [5]forgiven [6]them [[1]their] [2]sins. And
λέγει αὐτοῖς, Οὐκ.οἴδατε τὴν.παραβολὴν.ταύτην; καὶ πῶς
he says to them, Perceive ye not this parable? and how
πάσας τὰς παραβολὰς γνώσεσθε; 14 ὁ σπείρων τὸν λόγον
all the parables will ye know? The sower the word
σπείρει. 15 οὗτοι.δέ εἰσιν οἱ παρὰ τὴν ὁδόν, ὅπου σπείρεται
sows. And these are they by the way, where is sown
ὁ λόγος, καὶ ὅταν ἀκούσωσιν, [v]εὐθέως‖ ἔρχεται ὁ σατανᾶς
the word, and when they hear, immediately comes Satan
καὶ αἴρει τὸν λόγον τὸν ἐσπαρμένον [w]ἐν ταῖς.καρδίαις.αὐ-
and takes away the word that has been sown in their hearts.
τῶν.‖ 16 καὶ οὗτοί [x]εἰσιν ὁμοίως‖ οἱ ἐπὶ τὰ πετρώδη
And these are in like manner they who upon the rocky places
σπειρόμενοι, οἵ, ὅταν ἀκούσωσιν τὸν λόγον, [y]εὐθέως‖ μετὰ
are sown, who, when they hear the word, immediately with
χαρᾶς λαμβάνουσιν αὐτόν, 17 καὶ οὐκ.ἔχουσιν ῥίζαν ἐν ἑαυ-
joy receive it, and have not root in them-
τοῖς, ἀλλὰ πρόσκαιροί εἰσιν· εἶτα γενομένης θλίψεως ἢ
selves, but temporary are; then having arisen tribulation or
διωγμοῦ διὰ τὸν λόγον, [v]εὐθέως‖ σκανδαλίζονται. 18 καὶ
persecution on account of the word, immediately they are offended. And
[z]οὗτοί‖ εἰσιν οἱ [a]εἰς‖ τὰς ἀκάνθας σπειρόμενοι, οὗτοί
these are they who among the thorns are sown, these
εἰσιν οἱ τὸν λόγον [b]ἀκούοντες,‖ 19 καὶ αἱ μέριμναι τοῦ
are they who the word hear, and the cares
αἰῶνος.[c]τούτου‖ καὶ ἡ ἀπάτη τοῦ πλούτου καὶ αἱ περὶ
of this life and the deceit of riches and the [2]of
τὰ.λοιπὰ ἐπιθυμίαι εἰσπορευόμεναι [d]συμπνίγουσιν‖ τὸν λόγον,
[3]other [4]things [1]desires entering in choke the word,
καὶ ἄκαρπος γίνεται. 20 καὶ [e]οὗτοί‖ εἰσιν οἱ ἐπὶ τὴν γῆν
and unfruitful it becomes. And these are they who upon the ground

[i] αὐξανόμενον LTTrAW. [k] εἰς A; εἰς unto TTr. [l] — αὐτοῖς GLTTrAW. [m] ὃς ἔχει LTTrAW. [n] καὶ ὅτε LTTrA. [o] κατὰ μόνας LTTr. [p] ἠρώτων LTrA; ἠρώτουν T. [q] τὰς παραβολάς the parables TTrA. [r] — γνῶναι LTTrA; τὸ μυστήριον δέδοται TTrA. [s] — τὰ T. [t] — τὰ ἁμαρτήματα (*read* [their sins]) [L]TTrA. [v] εὐθὺς TTrA. [w] ἐν αὐτοῖς in them T; εἰς αὐτούς in them TrA. [x] ὁμοίως εἰσὶν T. [y] εὐθὺς LTTrA. [z] ἄλλοι others GLTTrAW. [a] ἐπὶ about T. [b] ἀκούσαντες heard TTrA. [c] — τούτου this GLTTrA. [d] συνπνίγουσιν TA [e] ἐκεῖνοί those TTrA.

τὴν καλὴν σπαρέντες, οἵτινες ἀκούουσιν τὸν λόγον καὶ
the good have been sown, such as hear the word and
παραδέχονται, καὶ καρποφοροῦσιν, [f]ἓν‖ τριάκοντα, καὶ [f]ἓν‖
receive [it], and bring forth fruit, one thirty, and one
ἑξήκοντα, καὶ [f]ἓν‖ ἑκατόν. 21 Καὶ ἔλεγεν αὐτοῖς, [g]Μήτι [h]ὁ
sixty, and one a hundred. And he said to them, [2]The
λύχνος ἔρχεται‖ ἵνα ὑπὸ τὸν μόδιον τεθῇ ἢ ὑπὸ τὴν
[3]lamp [1]comes that under the corn measure it may be put or under the
κλίνην; οὐχ ἵνα ἐπὶ τὴν λυχνίαν [i]ἐπιτεθῇ‖; 22 οὐ-γάρ
couch? [Is it] not that upon the lampstand it may be put? for not
ἐστίν [k]τι‖ κρυπτόν, [l]ὃ‖ ἐὰν-μὴ [m] φανερωθῇ· οὐδὲ
[2]is [1]anything hidden, unless it should be made manifest, nor
ἐγένετο ἀπόκρυφον, ἀλλ᾽ ἵνα [n]εἰς φανερὸν ἔλθῃ.‖
has [4]taken [5]place [1]a [2]secret [3]thing, but that to light it should come.
23 εἴ τις ἔχει ὦτα ἀκούειν, ἀκουέτω. 24 Καὶ ἔλεγεν αὐτοῖς,
If anyone has ears to hear, let him hear. And he said to them,
Βλέπετε τί ἀκούετε. ἐν ᾧ μέτρῳ μετρεῖτε μετρηθήσεται
Take heed what ye hear: with what measure ye mete it shall be measured
ὑμῖν, [o]καὶ προστεθήσεται ὑμῖν‖ [p]τοῖς ἀκούουσιν.‖ 25 ὃς-γὰρ [q]ἂν
to you, and [5]shall [6]be [7]added [1]to [2]you [3]who [4]hear; for whoever
ἔχῃ,‖ δοθήσεται αὐτῷ· καὶ ὃς οὐκ-ἔχει, καὶ ὃ ἔχει
may have, [3]shall [4]be [5]given [1]to [2]him; and he who has not, even that which he has
ἀρθήσεται ἀπ᾽ αὐτοῦ.
shall be taken from him.

26 Καὶ ἔλεγεν, Οὕτως ἐστὶν ἡ βασιλεία τοῦ θεοῦ, ὡς [r]ἐὰν‖
And he said, Thus is the kingdom of God, as if
ἄνθρωπος βάλῃ τὸν σπόρον ἐπὶ τῆς γῆς, 27 καὶ καθεύδῃ
a man should cast the seed upon the earth, and should sleep
καὶ ἐγείρηται νύκτα καὶ ἡμέραν, καὶ ὁ σπόρος [s]βλαστάνῃ‖
and rise night and day, and the seed should sprout
καὶ μηκύνηται ὡς οὐκ-οἶδεν αὐτός· 28 αὐτομάτη [t]γὰρ‖ ἡ γῆ
and be lengthened how [2]knows [3]not [1]he; [2]of [3]itself [1]for the earth
καρποφορεῖ, πρῶτον χόρτον, [v]εἶτα‖ στάχυν, [v]εἶτα‖ [w]πλήρη
brings forth fruit, first a blade, then an ear, then full
σῖτον‖ ἐν τῷ στάχυϊ. 29 ὅταν-δὲ [x]παραδῷ‖ ὁ καρπός,
corn in the ear. And when [3]offers [4]itself [1]the [2]fruit,
[y]εὐθέως‖ ἀποστέλλει τὸ δρέπανον, ὅτι παρέστηκεν ὁ θερισμός.
immediately he sends the sickle, for has come the harvest.

30 Καὶ ἔλεγεν, [z]Τίνι‖ ὁμοιώσωμεν τὴν βασιλείαν τοῦ θεοῦ;
And he said, To what shall we liken the kingdom of God?
ἢ ἐν [a]ποίᾳ παραβολῇ παραβάλωμεν αὐτήν;‖ 31 ὡς [b]κόκκῳ‖
or with what parable shall we compare it? As to a grain
σινάπεως, ὅς, ὅταν σπαρῇ ἐπὶ τῆς γῆς, [c]μικρότερος‖
of mustard, which, when it has been sown upon the earth, less
πάντων τῶν σπερμάτων [d]ἐστὶν‖ [e]τῶν ἐπὶ τῆς γῆς·‖ 32 καὶ
than all the seeds is which [are] upon the earth, and
ὅταν σπαρῇ, ἀναβαίνει, καὶ γίνεται [f]πάντων τῶν λαχάνων
when it has been sown, it grows up, and becomes [2]than [3]all [4]the [5]herbs
μείζων‖ καὶ ποιεῖ κλάδους μεγάλους, ὥστε δύνασθαι ὑπὸ
[1]greater, and produces [2]branches [1]great, so that [6]are [7]able [1]under

hear the word, and
receive *it*, and bring
forth fruit, some
thirtyfold, some sixty,
and some an hundred.
21 And he said unto
them, Is a candle
brought to be put un-
der a bushel, or under
a bed? and not to be
set on a candlestick?
22 For there is nothing
hid, which shall not be
manifested; neither
was any thing kept
secret, but that it
should come abroad.
23 If any man have
ears to hear, let him
hear. 24 And he said
unto them, Take heed
what ye hear: with
what measure ye mete,
it shall be measured
to you: and unto you
that hear shall more
be given. 25 For he
that hath, to him shall
be given: and he that
hath not, from him
shall be taken even
that which he hath.

26 And he said, So is
the kingdom of God,
as if a man should cast
seed into the ground;
27 and should sleep,
and rise night and day,
and the seed should
spring and grow up,
he knoweth not how.
28 For the earth bring-
eth forth fruit of her-
self; first the blade,
then the ear, after that
the full corn in the
ear. 29 But when the
fruit is brought forth,
immediately he put-
teth in the sickle, be-
cause the harvest is
come.

30 And he said,
Whereunto shall we
liken the kingdom of
God? or with what
comparison shall we
compare it? 31 *It is*
like a grain of mus-
tard seed, which, when
it is sown in the earth,
is less than all the
seeds that be in the
earth: 32 but when it
is sown, it groweth up,
and becometh greater
than all herbs, and
shooteth out great
branches; so that the

---

[f] ἐν in TTr. [g] + ὅτι that TA. [h] ἔρχεται ὁ λύχνος LTTrA. [i] τεθῇ LTTrAW. [k] — τι (*read* it is not) [L]Tr[A]. [l] — ὃ LTTrA. [m] + ἵνα that LT[A]. [n] ἔλθῃ εἰς φανερόν TTrA. [o] — καὶ προσ. ὑμῖν G. [p] — τοῖς ἀκούουσιν GLTTrA. [q] ἔχει has LTTrA. [r] — ἐὰν TTrA. [s] βλαστᾷ LTTrA. [t] — γὰρ LTTrA. [v] εἶτεν T. [w] πλήρης σῖτος LTTrA. [x] παραδοῖ LTTrA. [y] εὐθὺς TTrA. [z] Πῶς how TTrA. [a] τίνι αὐτὴν παραβολῇ θῶμεν what parable shall we represent it? LTTrA. [b] κόκκον a grain GLTrAW. [c] μικρότερον ὂν being less LTTrA. [d] — ἐστὶν LTTrA. [e] [τῶν ἐπὶ τῆς γῆς] L. [f] μείζων (μεῖζον T) πάντων τῶν λαχάνων LTTrA.

fowls of the air may lodge under the shadow of it. 33 And with many such parables spake he the word unto them, as they were able to hear *it*. 34 But without a parable spake he not unto them: and when they were alone, he expounded all things to his disciples.

τὴν σκιὰν αὐτοῦ τὰ πετεινὰ τοῦ οὐρανοῦ κατασκηνοῦν.
[2]the [3]shadow [4]of [5]it the birds of the heaven to roost.
33 Καὶ τοιαύταις παραβολαῖς πολλαῖς ἐλάλει αὐτοῖς τὸν
And with [2]such [3]parables [1]many he spoke to them the
λόγον, καθὼς [g]ἠδύναντο‖ ἀκούειν, 34 χωρὶς.δὲ παραβολῆς
word, as they were able to hear, but without a parable
οὐκ.ἐλάλει αὐτοῖς· κατ'.ἰδίαν.δὲ [h]τοῖς.μαθηταῖς.αὐτοῦ‖ ἐπέλυεν
spoke he not to them; and apart to his disciples he explained
πάντα.
all things.

35 And the same day, when the even was come, he saith unto them, Let us pass over unto the other side. 36 And when they had sent away the multitude, they took him even as he was in the ship. And there were also with him other little ships. 37 And there arose a great storm of wind, and the waves beat into the ship, so that it was now full. 38 And he was in the hinder part of the ship, asleep on a pillow: and they awake him, and say unto him, Master, carest thou not that we perish? 39 And he arose, and rebuked the wind, and said unto the sea, Peace, be still. And the wind ceased, and there was a great calm. 40 And he said unto them, Why are ye so fearful? how is it that ye have no faith? 41 And they feared exceedingly, and said one to another, What manner of man is this, that even the wind and the sea obey him?

35 Καὶ λέγει αὐτοῖς ἐν ἐκείνῃ τῇ ἡμέρᾳ, ὀψίας γενομένης,
And he says to them on that day, evening being come,
Διέλθωμεν εἰς τὸ πέραν. 36 Καὶ ἀφέντες τὸν ὄχλον,
Let us pass over to the other side. And having dismissed the crowd,
παραλαμβάνουσιν αὐτὸν ὡς ἦν ἐν τῷ πλοίῳ· καὶ ἄλλα
they take with [them] him as he was in the ship; [2]also [3]other
[i]δὲ‖ [k]πλοιάρια‖ [l]ἦν‖ μετ' αὐτοῦ. 37 καὶ γίνεται λαῖλαψ
[1]but small ships were with him. And comes a [2]storm
[m]ἀνέμου μεγάλη,‖ [n]τὰ.δὲ‖ κύματα ἐπέβαλλεν εἰς τὸ πλοῖον,
[3]of [4]wind [1]violent, and the waves beat into the ship,
ὥστε [o]αὐτὸ ἤδη γεμίζεσθαι.‖ 38 καὶ ἦν αὐτὸς [p]ἐπὶ‖ τῇ πρύ-
so that it already was filled. And [2]was [1]he on the stern
μνῃ ἐπὶ τὸ προσκεφάλαιον καθεύδων· καὶ [q]διεγείρουσιν‖
on the cushion sleeping. And they arouse
αὐτόν, καὶ λέγουσιν αὐτῷ, Διδάσκαλε, οὐ.μέλει σοι ὅτι
him, and say to him, Teacher, is it no concern to thee that
ἀπολλύμεθα; 39 Καὶ διεγερθεὶς ἐπετίμησεν τῷ ἀνέμῳ,
we perish? And having been aroused he rebuked the wind,
καὶ εἶπεν τῇ θαλάσσῃ, Σιώπα, πεφίμωσο. Καὶ ἐκόπασεν ὁ
and said to the sea, Silence, be quiet. And [3]fell [1]the
ἄνεμος, καὶ ἐγένετο γαλήνη μεγάλη. 40 καὶ εἶπεν αὐτοῖς,
[2]wind, and there was a [2]calm [1]great. And he said to them,
Τί δειλοί ἐστε [r]οὕτως; πῶς οὐκ‖ ἔχετε πίστιν; 41 Καὶ ἐφο-
Why fearful are ye thus? How [3]not [1]have [2]ye faith? And they
βήθησαν φόβον μέγαν, καὶ ἔλεγον πρὸς.ἀλλήλους, Τίς
feared [with] [2]fear [1]great, and said one to another, Who
ἄρα οὗτός ἐστιν, ὅτι καὶ ὁ ἄνεμος καὶ ἡ θάλασσα [s]ὑπακούου-
then [2]this [1]is, that even the wind and the sea obey
σιν αὐτῷ‖;
him?

V. And they came over unto the other side of the sea, into the country of the Gadarenes. 2 And when he was come out of the ship, immediately there met him out of the tombs a man with an unclean spirit, 3 who had *his* dwelling among the tombs; and no man could bind him, no, not with chains:

5 Καὶ ἦλθον εἰς τὸ πέραν τῆς θαλάσσης, εἰς τὴν χώραν
And they came to the other side of the sea, to the country
τῶν [t]Γαδαρηνῶν.‖ 2 καὶ [u]ἐξελθόντι.αὐτῷ‖ ἐκ τοῦ πλοίου,
of the Gadarenes. And on his having gone forth out of the ship,
[v]εὐθέως‖ [w]ἀπήντησεν‖ αὐτῷ ἐκ τῶν μνημείων ἄνθρωπος
immediately met him out of the tombs a man
ἐν πνεύματι.ἀκαθάρτῳ, 3 ὃς τὴν κατοίκησιν εἶχεν ἐν τοῖς
with an unclean spirit, who [his] dwelling had in the
[x]μνημείοις·‖ καὶ [y]οὔτε‖ [z]ἁλύσεσιν‖ [a] οὐδεὶς [b]ἠδύνατο‖ αὐτὸν
tombs; and not even with chains anyone was able him
(*lit.* no one)

---

[g] ἐδύναντο LTr [h] τοῖς ἰδίοις μαθηταῖς to his own disciples TA. [i] — δὲ LTr[A]. [k] πλοῖα ships GLTTrA. [l] ἦσαν T. [m] μεγάλη ἀνέμου LTTrA. [n] καὶ τὰ LTTrA. [o] ἤδη γεμίζεσθαι τὸ πλοῖον already was filled the ship LTTrA. [p] ἐν in GLTTrAW. [q] ἐγείρουσιν they awake TTrA. [r] ; οὔπω [3]not [4]yet LTr. [s] αὐτῷ ὑπακούει T ; ὑπακούει αὐτῷ TrA. [t] Γερασηνῶν Gerasenes LTTr ; Γεργεσηνῶν Gergesenes A. [u] ἐξελθόντος αὐτοῦ LTTr. [v] — εὐθέως L ; εὐθὺς T[Tr]A. [w] ὑπήντησεν LTTr. [x] μνήμασιν (— ν GW) GLTTrAW. [y] οὐδὲ LTTrAW. [z] ἁλύσει with a chain LTTrA. [a] + οὐκέτι any longer (*lit.* no longer) LTTrAW. [b] ἐδύνατο LTTrA.

δῆσαι, 4 διὰ τὸ αὐτὸν πολλάκις πέδαις καὶ ἁλύσεσιν δε-
to bind, because that he often with fetters and chains had
δέσθαι, καὶ διεσπᾶσθαι ὑπ' αὐτοῦ τὰς ἁλύσεις, καὶ
been bound, and [3]had [4]been [5]torn [6]asunder [7]by [8]him [1]the [2]chains, and
τὰς πέδας συντετρίφθαι, καὶ οὐδεὶς [c]αὐτὸν ἴσχυεν‖ δαμάσαι·
the fetters had been shattered, and no one him was able to subdue.
5 καὶ [d]διαπαντὸς‖ νυκτὸς καὶ ἡμέρας ἐν τοῖς [e]ὄρεσιν καὶ ἐν
And continually night and day in the mountains and in
τοῖς μνήμασιν‖ ἦν κράζων καὶ κατακόπτων ἑαυτὸν λίθοις.
the tombs he was crying and cutting himself with stones.
6 [f]Ἰδὼν.δὲ‖ τὸν Ἰησοῦν ἀπὸ μακρόθεν, ἔδραμεν καὶ προσ-
And having seen Jesus from afar, he ran and did
εκύνησεν [g]αὐτῷ,‖ 7 καὶ κράξας φωνῇ μεγάλῃ [h]εἶπεν,‖ Τί ἐμοὶ
homage to him, and crying with a [2]voice [1]loud he said, What to me
καὶ σοί, Ἰησοῦ, υἱὲ τοῦ θεοῦ τοῦ ὑψίστου; ὁρκίζω σε τὸν
and to thee, Jesus, Son of God the Most High? I adjure thee
θεόν, μή με βασανίσῃς. 8 ἔλεγεν.γὰρ αὐτῷ, Ἔξελθε, τὸ
by God, [3]not [2]me [1]torment. For he was saying to him, Come forth, the
πνεῦμα τὸ ἀκάθαρτον, ἐκ τοῦ ἀνθρώπου. 9 Καὶ ἐπηρώτα
spirit the unclean, out of the man. And he asked
αὐτόν, Τί [i]σοι.ὄνομα‖; Καὶ [k]ἀπεκρίθη, λέγων,‖ [l]Λεγεὼν‖
him, What [is] thy name? And he answered, saying, Legion
ὄνομά.μοι,[m] ὅτι πολλοί ἐσμεν. 10 Καὶ παρεκάλει αὐτὸν
my name [is], because many we are. And he besought him
πολλά, ἵνα μὴ [n]αὐτοὺς‖ ἀποστείλῃ ἔξω τῆς χώρας. 11 ἦν.δὲ
much, that not them he would send out of the country. Now there was
ἐκεῖ πρὸς [o]τὰ ὄρη‖ ἀγέλη χοίρων μεγάλη βοσκομένη· 12 καὶ
there just at the mountains a [2]herd [3]of [4]swine [1]great feeding; and
παρεκάλεσαν αὐτὸν [p]πάντες οἱ δαίμονες,‖ λέγοντες, Πέμψον
[4]besought [5]him [1]all [2]the [3]demons, saying, Send
ἡμᾶς εἰς τοὺς χοίρους, ἵνα εἰς αὐτοὺς εἰσέλθωμεν. 13 Καὶ
us into the swine, that into them we may enter. And
ἐπέτρεψεν αὐτοῖς [q]εὐθέως ὁ Ἰησοῦς.‖ καὶ ἐξελθόντα τὰ
[2]allowed [3]them [4]immediately [1]Jesus. And having gone out the
πνεύματα τὰ ἀκάθαρτα εἰσῆλθον εἰς τοὺς χοίρους· καὶ ὥρμησεν
spirits the unclean entered into the swine, and [3]rushed
ἡ ἀγέλη κατὰ τοῦ κρημνοῦ εἰς τὴν θάλασσαν· [r]ἦσαν δὲ‖
[1]the [2]herd down the steep into the sea, (now they were
ὡς δισχίλιοι· καὶ ἐπνίγοντο ἐν τῇ θαλάσσῃ. 14 [s]Οἱ.δὲ‖
about two thousand), and they were choked in the sea. And those who
βόσκοντες [t]τοὺς χοίρους‖ ἔφυγον, καὶ [v]ἀνήγγειλαν‖ εἰς τὴν
fed the swine fled, and announced [it] to the
πόλιν καὶ εἰς τοὺς ἀγρούς. καὶ [w]ἐξῆλθον‖ ἰδεῖν τί ἐστιν τὸ
city and to the country. And they went out to see what it is that
γεγονός· 15 καὶ ἔρχονται πρὸς τὸν Ἰησοῦν, καὶ θεωροῦσιν
has been done. And they come to Jesus, and see
τὸν δαιμονιζόμενον καθήμενον [x]καὶ‖ ἱματισμένον καὶ σωφρο-
the possessed by demons sitting and clothed and of sound
νοῦντα, τὸν.ἐσχηκότα τὸν [y]λεγεῶνα·‖ καὶ ἐφοβήθησαν. 16 καὶ
mind, him who had the legion: and they were afraid. And

4 because that he had
been often bound with
fetters and chains, and
the chains had been
plucked asunder by
him, and the fetters
broken in pieces: nei-
ther could any *man*
tame him. 5 And al-
ways, night and day,
he was in the moun-
tains, and in the
tombs, crying, and
cutting himself with
stones. 6 But when he
saw Jesus afar off, he
ran and worshipped
him, 7 and cried with
a loud voice, and said,
What have I to do
with thee, Jesus, *thou*
Son of the most high
God? I adjure thee
by God, that thou tor-
ment me not. 8 For he
said unto him, Come
out of the man, *thou*
unclean spirit. 9 And
he asked him, What
is thy name? And he
answered, saying, My
name *is* Legion: for
we are many. 10 And
he besought him much
that he would not send
them away out of the
country. 11 Now there
was there nigh unto
the mountains a great
herd of swine feeding.
12 And all the devils
besought him, saying,
Send us into the swine,
that we may enter into
them. 13 And forth-
with Jesus gave them
leave. And the unclean
spirits went out, and
entered into the swine:
and the herd ran vio-
lently down a steep
place into the sea,
(they were about two
thousand;) and were
choked in the sea.
14 And they that fed
the swine fled, and
told *it* in the city, and
in the country. And
they went out to see
what it was that was
done. 15 And they
come to Jesus, and see
him that was possessed
with the devil, and
had the legion, sitting,
and clothed, and in
his right mind: and
they were afraid.
16 And they that saw

[c] ἴσχυεν αὐτὸν LTTrAW. [d] διὰ παντὸς AL. [e] μνήμασιν (— ν GW) καὶ ἐν τοῖς ὄρεσιν GLTTrAW. [f] καὶ ἰδὼν TTrA. [g] αὐτόν A. [h] λέγει he says LTTrAW. [i] ὄνομά σοι LTTrA. [k] λέγει αὐτῷ he says to him GLTTrAW. [l] Λεγιὼν LTTrA. [m] + ἐστιν is L. [n] αὐτὰ TTr. [o] τῷ ὄρει the mountain GLTTrAW. [p] — πάντες GW[L]; — πάντες οἱ δαίμονες (*read* they besought) TTrA. [q] — εὐθέως ὁ Ἰησοῦς (*read* he allowed) [L]TTr[A]. [r] — ἦσαν δὲ [L]TTrA. [s] καὶ οἱ LTTrA. [t] αὐτοὺς them GLTTrAW. [v] ἀπήγγειλαν told GLTTrAW. [w] ἦλθον they went LTTrAW. [x] — καὶ LTTrA. [y] λεγιῶνα LTTrA.

it told them how it
befell to him that was
possessed with the de-
vil, and *also* concern-
ing the swine. 17 And
they began to pray
him to depart out of
their coasts. 18 And
when he was come into
the ship, he that had
been possessed with
the devil prayed him
that he might be with
him. 19 Howbeit Jesus
suffered him not, but
saith unto him, Go
home to thy friends,
and tell them how
great things the Lord
hath done for thee,
and hath had com-
passion on thee. 20 And
he departed, and began
to publish in Decapolis
how great things Jesus
had done for him: and
all *men* did marvel.

21 And when Jesus
was passed over again
by ship unto the other
side, much people ga-
thered unto him: and
he was nigh unto the
sea. 22 And, behold,
there cometh one of
the rulers of the syna-
gogue, Jairus by name;
and when he saw him,
he fell at his feet,
23 and besought him
greatly, saying, My
little daughter lieth
at the point of death:
I pray thee, come and
lay thy hands on her,
that she may be heal-
ed; and she shall live.
24 And *Jesus* went
with him; and much
people followed him,
and thronged him.
25 And a certain wo-
man, which had an
issue of blood twelve
years, 26 and had suf-
fered many things of
many physicians, and
had spent all that she
had, and was nothing
bettered, but rather
grew worse, 27 when
she had heard of Jesus,
came in the press be-
hind, and touched his
garment. 28 For she
said, If I may touch
but his clothes, I shall
be whole. 29 And

διηγήσαντο αὐτοῖς οἱ ἰδόντες, πῶς ἐγένετο τῷ δαι-
[6]related [7]to [8]them [1]those [2]who [3]had [4]seen [[5]it] how it happened to him pos-
μονιζομένῳ, καὶ περὶ τῶν χοίρων. 17 καὶ ἤρξαντο παρα-
sessed by demons, and concerning the swine. And they began to be-
καλεῖν αὐτὸν ἀπελθεῖν ἀπὸ τῶν.ὁρίων.αὐτῶν. 18 Καὶ
seech him to depart from their borders. And
[z]ἐμβάντος‖ αὐτοῦ εἰς τὸ πλοῖον, παρεκάλει αὐτὸν ὁ
[2]having [3]entered [1]he into the ship, [8]besought [9]him [1]he [2]who
δαιμονισθείς, ἵνα [a]ᾖ μετ᾽ αὐτοῦ.‖ 19 [b]ὁ δὲ‖
[3]had [4]been [5]possessed [6]by [7]demons that he might be with him. But
[c]Ἰησοῦς‖ οὐκ.ἀφῆκεν αὐτόν, ἀλλὰ λέγει αὐτῷ, Ὕπαγε εἰς τὸν
Jesus did not suffer him, but says to him, Go to
οἶκόν.σου πρὸς τοὺς.σούς, καὶ [d]ἀνάγγειλον‖ αὐτοῖς ὅσα [e]σοι
thy house to thine own, and announce to them how much for thee
ὁ κύριος‖ [f]ἐποίησεν,‖ καὶ ἠλέησέν σε. 20 Καὶ ἀπῆλθεν καὶ
the Lord did, and pitied thee. And he departed and
ἤρξατο κηρύσσειν ἐν τῇ Δεκαπόλει, ὅσα ἐποίησεν αὐτῷ ὁ
began to proclaim in Decapolis, how much [2]had [3]done [4]for [5]him
Ἰησοῦς· καὶ πάντες ἐθαύμαζον.
[1]Jesus; and all wondered.

21 Καὶ διαπεράσαντος τοῦ Ἰησοῦ ἐν τῷ πλοίῳ [g]πάλιν εἰς
And [2]having [3]passed [4]over [1]Jesus in the ship again to
τὸ πέραν,‖ συνήχθη ὄχλος πολὺς ἐπ᾽ αὐτόν, καὶ ἦν
the other side, [4]was [5]gathered [1]a [3]crowd [2]great to him, and he was
παρὰ τὴν θάλασσαν. 22 Καὶ [h]ἰδού,‖ ἔρχεται εἷς τῶν ἀρχι-
by the sea. And behold, comes one of the rulers of
συναγώγων, ὀνόματι Ἰάειρος, καὶ ἰδὼν αὐτόν, πίπτει πρὸς
the synagogue, by name Jairus, and seeing him, falls at
τοὺς.πόδας.αὐτοῦ· 23 καὶ [i]παρεκάλει‖ αὐτὸν πολλά, λέγων,
his feet; and he besought him much, saying
Ὅτι τὸ.θυγάτριόν.μου ἐσχάτως.ἔχει· ἵνα ἐλθὼν
My little daughter is at the last extremity, [I pray] that having come
ἐπιθῇς [k]αὐτῇ τὰς χεῖρας,‖ [l]ὅπως‖ σωθῇ καὶ
thou wouldest lay on her [thy] hands, so that she may be cured, and
[m]ζήσεται.‖ 24 Καὶ ἀπῆλθεν μετ᾽ αὐτοῦ, καὶ ἠκολούθει αὐτῷ
she shall live. And he departed with him, and [4]followed [5]him
ὄχλος πολύς, καὶ συνέθλιβον αὐτόν. 25 Καὶ γυνή [n]τις‖
[1]a [3]crowd [2]great, and pressed on him. And a [2]woman [1]certain
οὖσα ἐν ῥύσει αἵματος [o]ἔτη δώδεκα,‖ 26 καὶ πολλὰ παθοῦσα
being with a flux of blood [2]years [1]twelve, and much having suffered
ὑπὸ πολλῶν ἰατρῶν, καὶ δαπανήσασα τὰ.παρ᾽.[p]ἑαυτῆς‖
under many physicians, and having spent [2]her [3]means
πάντα, καὶ μηδὲν ὠφεληθεῖσα ἀλλὰ μᾶλλον εἰς τὸ.χεῖρον
[1]all, and in no way having benefited but rather [3]to [4]worse
ἐλθοῦσα, 27 ἀκούσασα [q] περὶ τοῦ Ἰησοῦ, ἐλθοῦσα ἐν
[1]having [2]come, having heard concerning Jesus, having come in
τῷ ὄχλῳ.ὄπισθεν, ἥψατο τοῦ.ἱματίου.αὐτοῦ· 28 ἔλεγεν.γάρ,
the crowd behind, touched his garment; for she said,
Ὅτι [r]κἂν τῶν.ἱματίων.αὐτοῦ ἅψωμαι.‖ σωθήσομαι. 29 Καὶ
If but his garments I shall touch, I shall be cured. And

---

[z] ἐμβαίνοντος [was] entering LTTrAW. [a] μετ᾽ αὐτοῦ ᾖ LTTrAW. [b] καὶ and GLTTrAW. [c] — Ἰησοῦς (read he did not suffer) G[L]TTrAW. [d] ἀπάγγειλον tell LTTrAW. [e] ὁ κύριός σοι TTrA. [f] πεποίηκεν has done GLTTrAW. [g] εἰς τὸ πέραν πάλιν T. [h] — ἰδού [L]TTrA. [i] παρακαλεῖ he beseeches TTrA. [k] τὰς χεῖρας αὐτῇ LTTrA. [l] ἵνα in order that LTTrA. [m] ζήσῃ may live LTTrA. [n] — τις LTTr[A]. [o] δώδεκα ἔτη T. [p] αὐτῆς GLTrAW. [q] + τὰ the things T[A]. [r] ἐὰν ἅψωμαι κἂν τῶν ἱματίων αὐτοῦ TA.

[s]εὐθέως‖ ἐξηράνθη ἡ πηγὴ τοῦ.αἵματος.αὐτῆς, καὶ ἔγνω
immediately was dried up the fountain of her blood, and she knew
τῷ σώματι ὅτι ἴαται ἀπὸ τῆς μάστιγος. 30 καὶ [s]εὐθέως‖
in [her] body that she was healed from the scourge. And immediately
ὁ Ἰησοῦς, ἐπιγνοὺς ἐν ἑαυτῷ τὴν ἐξ αὐτοῦ δύναμιν
Jesus, knowing in himself [that] the [2]out [3]of [4]him [1]power
ἐξελθοῦσαν, ἐπιστραφεὶς ἐν τῷ ὄχλῳ, ἔλεγεν, Τίς μου ἥψατο
had gone forth, having turned in the crowd, said, Who of me touched
τῶν ἱματίων; 31 Καὶ ἔλεγον αὐτῷ οἱ.μαθηταὶ.αὐτοῦ, Βλέπεις
the garments? And [3]said [4]to [5]him [1]his [2]disciples, Thou seest
τὸν ὄχλον συνθλίβοντά σε, καὶ λέγεις, Τίς μου ἥψατο;
the crowd pressing on thee, and sayest thou, Who me touched?
32 Καὶ περιεβλέπετο ἰδεῖν τὴν τοῦτο ποιήσασαν. 33 ἡ.δὲ
And he looked round to see her who this had done. But the
γυνὴ φοβηθεῖσα καὶ τρέμουσα, εἰδυῖα ὃ γέγονεν [t]ἐπ'‖
woman being frightened and trembling, knowing what had been done upon
αὐτῇ, ἦλθεν καὶ προσέπεσεν αὐτῷ, καὶ εἶπεν αὐτῷ πᾶσαν
her, came and fell down before him, and told him all
τὴν ἀλήθειαν. 34 ὁ.δὲ [v] εἶπεν αὐτῇ, [w]Θύγατερ,‖ ἡ.πίστις.σου
the truth. And he said to her, Daughter, thy faith
σέσωκέν σε· ὕπαγε εἰς εἰρήνην, καὶ ἴσθι ὑγιὴς ἀπὸ τῆς μάστι-
has cured thee; go in peace, and be sound from [2]scourge
γός σου. 35 Ἔτι αὐτοῦ.λαλοῦντος, ἔρχονται ἀπὸ τοῦ ἀρχι-
[1]thy. [While] yet he is speaking, they come from the ruler of
συναγώγου, λέγοντες, Ὅτι ἡ.θυγάτηρ.σου ἀπέθανεν· τί ἔτι
the synagogue's [house], saying, Thy daughter is dead; why still
σκύλλεις τὸν διδάσκαλον; 36 Ὁ.δὲ.Ἰησοῦς [x]εὐθέως‖ [y]ἀκού-
troublest thou the teacher? But Jesus immediately, having
σας‖ τὸν λόγον λαλούμενον λέγει τῷ ἀρχισυναγώγῳ, Μὴ
heard the word spoken, says to the ruler of the synagogue, [2]Not
φοβοῦ· μόνον πίστευε. 37 Καὶ οὐκ.ἀφῆκεν οὐδένα [z]αὐτῷ‖
[1]fear; only believe. And he suffered no one him
[a]συνακολουθῆσαι,‖ εἰ.μὴ [b] Πέτρον καὶ Ἰάκωβον καὶ Ἰωάννην
to accompany, except Peter and James and John
τὸν ἀδελφὸν Ἰακώβου. 38 καὶ [c]ἔρχεται‖ εἰς τὸν οἶκον τοῦ
the brother of James. And he comes to the house of the
ἀρχισυναγώγου, καὶ θεωρεῖ θόρυβον, [d] κλαίοντας καὶ
ruler of the synagogue, and he beholds a tumult, [people] weeping and
ἀλαλάζοντας πολλά. 39 καὶ εἰσελθὼν λέγει αὐτοῖς, Τί
wailing greatly. And having entered he says to them, Why
θορυβεῖσθε καὶ κλαίετε; τὸ παιδίον οὐκ.ἀπέθανεν, ἀλλὰ
make ye a tumult and weep? the child is not dead, but
καθεύδει. 40 Καὶ κατεγέλων αὐτοῦ. [e]ὁ‖.δὲ ἐκβαλὼν [f]ἅπαν-
sleeps. And they laughed at him. But he having put out all,
τας,‖ παραλαμβάνει τὸν πατέρα τοῦ παιδίου καὶ τὴν
takes with [him] the father of the child and the
μητέρα καὶ τοὺς μετ' αὐτοῦ, καὶ εἰσπορεύεται ὅπου ἦν τὸ
mother and those with him, and enters in where [3]was [1]the
παιδίον [g]ἀνακείμενον.‖ 41 καὶ κρατήσας τῆς χειρὸς τοῦ
[2]child lying. And having taken the hand of the
παιδίου, λέγει αὐτῇ, Ταλιθά, [h]κοῦμι·‖ ὅ ἐστιν μεθερμηνευό-
child, he says to her, Talitha, koumi; which is, being inter-

straightway the fountain of her blood was dried up; and she felt in *her* body that she was healed of that plague.
30 And Jesus, immediately knowing in himself that virtue had gone out of him, turned him about in the press, and said, Who touched my clothes?
31 And his disciples said unto him, Thou seest the multitude thronging thee, and sayest thou, Who touched me?
32 And he looked round about to see her that had done this thing.
33 But the woman fearing and trembling, knowing what was done in her, came and fell down before him, and told him all the truth.
34 And he said unto her, Daughter, thy faith hath made thee whole; go in peace, and be whole of thy plague.
35 While he yet spake, there came from the ruler of the synagogue's *house certain* which said, Thy daughter is dead: why troublest thou the Master any further?
36 As soon as Jesus heard the word that was spoken, he saith unto the ruler of the synagogue, Be not afraid, only believe.
37 And he suffered no man to follow him, save Peter, and James, and John the brother of James.
38 And he cometh to the house of the ruler of the synagogue, and seeth the tumult, and them that wept and wailed greatly.
39 And when he was come in, he saith unto them, Why make ye this ado, and weep? the damsel is not dead, but sleepeth.
40 And they laughed him to scorn. But when he had put them all out, he taketh the father and the mother of the damsel, and them that were with him, and entereth in where the damsel was lying.
41 And he took the damsel by the hand, and said unto her, Talitha cumi; which is, being interpret-

[s] εὐθὺς TTrA. [t] — ἐπ' (*read* to her) [L]TTrA. [v] + Ἰησοῦς Jesus L. [w] Θυγάτηρ LTrA. [x] — εὐθέως [L]TTr[A]. [y] παρακούσας having disregarded TTrA. [z] μετ' αὐτοῦ with him TTrA. [a] ἀκολουθῆσαι to follow L. [b] + τὸν TTrA. [c] ἔρχονται they come LTTrAW. [d] + καὶ and GLTTrAW. [e] αὐτὸς LTTr. [f] πάντας GLTTrAW [g] — ἀνακείμενον G[L]TTrA. [h] κούμ T; κοῦμ TrA.

ed, Damsel, I say unto thee, arise.
42 And straightway the damsel arose, and walked; for she was *of the age* of twelve years. And they were astonished with a great astonishment.
43 And he charged them straitly that no man should know it; and commanded that something should be given her to eat.

VI. And he went out from thence, and came into his own country; and his disciples follow him.
2 And when the sabbath day was come, he began to teach in the synagogue: and many hearing *him* were astonished, saying, From whence hath this *man* these things? and what wisdom *is* this which is given unto him, that even such mighty works are wrought by his hands?
3 Is not this the carpenter, the son of Mary, the brother of James, and Joses, and of Juda, and Simon? and are not his sisters here with us? And they were offended at him.
4 But Jesus said unto them, A prophet is not without honour, but in his own country, and among his own kin, and in his own house.
5 And he could there do no mighty work, save that he laid his hands upon a few sick folk, and healed *them*.
6 And he marvelled because of their unbelief. And he went round about the villages, teaching.

7 And he called *unto him* the twelve, and began to send them forth by two and two; and gave them power over unclean spirits;
8 and commanded them that they should take nothing for *their* journey, save a staff only; no scrip, no bread, no money in *their* purse:
9 but *be* shod with sandals; and

μενον, Τὸ κοράσιον, σοὶ λέγω, [i]ἔγειραι.‖ 42 Καὶ [k]εὐθέως‖
preted, Damsel, to thee I say, arise. And immediately
ἀνέστη τὸ κοράσιον καὶ περιεπάτει, ἦν-γὰρ ἐτῶν δώδεκα.
arose the damsel and walked, for she was [2]years [1]twelve [old].
καὶ ἐξέστησαν [l] ἐκστάσει μεγάλῃ. 43 καὶ διεστείλατο
And they were amazed with [2]amazement [1]great. And he charged
αὐτοῖς πολλὰ ἵνα μηδεὶς [m]γνῷ‖ τοῦτο· καὶ εἶπεν
them much that no one should know this; and he said [that some-
δοθῆναι αὐτῇ φαγεῖν.
thing] should be given to her to eat.

6 Καὶ ἐξῆλθεν ἐκεῖθεν, καὶ [n]ἦλθεν‖ εἰς τὴν-πατρίδα-αὐτοῦ·
And he went out thence, and came into his [own] country;
καὶ ἀκολουθοῦσιν αὐτῷ οἱ-μαθηταὶ-αὐτοῦ· 2 καὶ γενομένου
and [3]follow [4]him [1]his [2]disciples. And [2]being [3]come
σαββάτου ἤρξατο [o]ἐν τῇ συναγωγῇ διδάσκειν·‖ καὶ [p] πολλοὶ
[1]sabbath he began in the synagogue to teach; and many
ἀκούοντες ἐξεπλήσσοντο, λέγοντες, Πόθεν τούτῳ ταῦτα;
hearing were astonished, saying, Whence to this [man] these things?
καὶ τίς ἡ σοφία ἡ δοθεῖσα [q]αὐτῷ,‖ [r]ὅτι‖ καὶ δυνάμεις
and what the wisdom that has been given to him, that even [2]works [3]of [4]power
τοιαῦται διὰ τῶν-χειρῶν-αὐτοῦ [s]γίνονται;‖ 3 οὐχ οὗτός ἐστιν
[1]such by his hands are done? [2]not [3]this [1]is
ὁ τέκτων, ὁ υἱὸς [t]Μαρίας, [v]ἀδελφὸς-δὲ‖ Ἰακώβου καὶ [w]Ἰωσῆ‖
the carpenter, the son of Mary, and brother of James and Joses
καὶ Ἰούδα καὶ Σίμωνος; καὶ οὐκ-εἰσὶν αἱ-ἀδελφαὶ-αὐτοῦ ὧδε
and Judas and Simon? and are not his sisters here
πρὸς ἡμᾶς; Καὶ ἐσκανδαλίζοντο ἐν αὐτῷ. 4 [x]ἔλεγεν-δὲ‖ αὐτοῖς
with us? And they were offended in him. But [2]said [3]to [4]them
ὁ Ἰησοῦς, Ὅτι οὐκ ἔστιν προφήτης ἄτιμος, εἰ-μὴ ἐν τῇ
[1]Jesus, [8]Not [7]is [5]a [6]prophet without honour, except in
πατρίδι-[y]αὐτοῦ‖ καὶ ἐν τοῖς [z]συγγενέσιν‖ [a] καὶ ἐν τῇ
his [own] country and among [his] kinsmen and in
οἰκίᾳ-[b]αὐτοῦ‖. 5 Καὶ οὐκ [c]ἠδύνατο‖ ἐκεῖ [d]οὐδεμίαν δύναμιν
his [own] house. And he was [2]able [3]there [1]not any work of power
ποιῆσαι,‖ εἰ-μὴ ὀλίγοις ἀῤῥώστοις ἐπιθεὶς τὰς χεῖρας
to do, except on a few infirm having laid [his] hands
ἐθεράπευσεν. 6 καὶ [e]ἐθαύμαζεν‖ διὰ τὴν-ἀπιστίαν-αὐ-
he healed [them]. And he wondered because of their unbelief.
τῶν· καὶ περιῆγεν τὰς κώμας κύκλῳ διδάσκων.
And he went about the villages in a circuit teaching.

7 Καὶ προσκαλεῖται τοὺς δώδεκα, καὶ ἤρξατο αὐτοὺς
And he calls to [him] the twelve, and began them
ἀποστέλλειν δύο-δύο, καὶ ἐδίδου αὐτοῖς ἐξουσίαν τῶν πνευμά-
to send forth two and two, and gave to them authority over the spirits
των τῶν ἀκαθάρτων· 8 καὶ παρήγγειλεν αὐτοῖς ἵνα μηδὲν
the unclean; and he charged them that nothing
αἴρωσιν εἰς ὁδόν, εἰ-μὴ ῥάβδον μόνον· μὴ [f]πήραν,
they should take for [the] way, except a staff only; no provision bag,
μὴ ἄρτον,‖ μὴ εἰς τὴν ζώνην χαλκόν· 9 [g]ἀλλ'‖ ὑποδεδεμένους
nor bread, nor in the belt money; but be shod

---

[i] ἔγειρε GLTTrAW. [k] εὐθὺς TTrA. [l] + εὐθὺς immediately T[Tr]A. [m] γνοῖ LTTrA. [n] ἔρχεται comes TTrAW. [o] διδάσκειν ἐν τῇ συναγωγῇ TTr. [p] + οἱ the T[A]. [q] τούτῳ to this [man] TTrA. [r] — ὅτι GLTTrAW. [s] γινόμεναι Tr. [t] + τῆς TTrA. [v] καὶ ἀδελφὸς LTTrAW. [w] Ἰωσῆτος LTTrA. [x] καὶ ἔλεγεν and [2]said LTTrA. [y] αὐτοῦ LTrAW; ἑαυτοῦ T. [z] συγγενεῦσιν TTr. [a] + αὐτοῦ his (kinsmen) [L]TTrA [b] αὐτοῦ LTTrAW. [c] ἐδύνατο TTrA. [d] ποιῆσαι οὐδεμίαν δύναμιν LTTrA. [e] ἐθαύμασεν T. [f] ἄρτον, μὴ πήραν TTrA. [g] ἀλλὰ LTTrAW.

σανδάλια· καὶ μὴ.[h]ἐνδύσησθε‖ δύο χιτῶνας. 10 Καὶ ἔλεγεν
with sandals; and put not on two tunics. And he said
αὐτοῖς, "Οπου.[i]ἐὰν‖ εἰσέλθητε εἰς οἰκίαν, ἐκεῖ μένετε ἕως ἂν
to them, Wherever ye enter into a house, there remain until
ἐξέλθητε ἐκεῖθεν. 11 καὶ [k]ὅσοι.ἂν μὴ.δέξωνται‖ ὑμᾶς, μηδὲ
ye go out thence. And as many as will not receive you, nor
ἀκούσωσιν ὑμῶν, ἐκπορευόμενοι ἐκεῖθεν, ἐκτινάξατε τὸν χοῦν
hear you, departing thence, shake off the dust
τὸν ὑποκάτω τῶν.ποδῶν.ὑμῶν, εἰς μαρτύριον αὐτοῖς. [l]ἀμὴν
which [is] under your feet, for a testimony to them. Verily
λέγω ὑμῖν, ἀνεκτότερον ἔσται Σοδόμοις ἢ Γομόῤῥοις ἐν ἡμέρᾳ
I say to you, more tolerable it shall be for Sodom or Gomorrha in day
κρίσεως, ἢ τῇ.πόλει.ἐκείνῃ.‖ 12 Καὶ ἐξελθόντες [m]ἐκήρυσ-
of judgment than for that city. And having gone out they pro-
σον‖ ἵνα [n]μετανοήσωσιν.‖ 13 καὶ δαιμόνια πολλὰ ἐξέβαλλον,
claimed that [men] should repent. And [2]demons [1]many they cast out,
καὶ ἤλειφον ἐλαίῳ πολλοὺς ἀῤῥώστους καὶ ἐθεράπευον.
and anointed with oil many infirm and healed [them].

14 Καὶ ἤκουσεν ὁ βασιλεὺς Ἡρώδης, φανερὸν.γὰρ
And [4]heard [2]the [3]king [1]Herod [of him], for public
ἐγένετο τὸ.ὄνομα.αὐτοῦ, καὶ [o]ἔλεγεν,‖ "Οτι Ἰωάννης ὁ βαπ-
became his name, and he said, John the Bap-
τίζων [p]ἐκ νεκρῶν ἠγέρθη,‖ καὶ διὰ τοῦτο ἐνεργοῦ-
tist from among [the] dead is risen, and because of this [5]ope-
σιν αἱ δυνάμεις ἐν αὐτῷ. 15 "Αλλοι[q] ἔλεγον, "Οτι [r]Ἠλίας‖
rate [1]the [2]works [3]of [4]power in him. Others said, Elias
ἐστίν· ἄλλοι.δὲ ἔλεγον, "Οτι προφήτης [s]ἐστίν,‖ [t]ἢ‖ ὡς εἷς τῶν
it is; and others said, A prophet it is, or as one of the
προφητῶν. 16 Ἀκούσας.δὲ ὁ Ἡρώδης [v]εἶπεν,‖ [w]"Οτι‖ ὃν
prophets. But having heard Herod said, [2]Whom
ἐγὼ ἀπεκεφάλισα Ἰωάννην, οὗτός [x]ἐστιν· αὐτὸς‖ ἠγέρθη
[3]I [4]beheaded [1]John, he it is. He is risen
[y]ἐκ νεκρῶν.‖ 17 Αὐτὸς.γὰρ ὁ Ἡρώδης ἀποστείλας
from among [the] dead. For [2]himself [1]Herod having sent
ἐκράτησεν τὸν Ἰωάννην, καὶ ἔδησεν αὐτὸν ἐν [z]τῇ‖ φυλακῇ,
seized John, and bound him in the prison,
διὰ Ἡρωδιάδα τὴν γυναῖκα Φιλίππου τοῦ.ἀδελφοῦ.αὐτοῦ,
on account of Herodias the wife of Philip his brother,
ὅτι αὐτὴν ἐγάμησεν. 18 ἔλεγεν.γὰρ ὁ Ἰωάννης τῷ Ἡρώδῃ,
because her he had married. For [2]said [1]John to Herod,
"Οτι οὐκ.ἔξεστίν σοι ἔχειν τὴν γυναῖκα τοῦ.ἀδελφοῦ.σου.
It is not lawful for thee to have the wife of thy brother.
19 Ἡ.δὲ.Ἡρωδιὰς ἐνεῖχεν αὐτῷ, καὶ [a]ἤθελεν‖ αὐτὸν ἀπο-
But Herodias held it against him, and wished [3]him [1]to
κτεῖναι· καὶ οὐκ.ἠδύνατο. 20 ὁ.γὰρ.Ἡρώδης ἐφοβεῖτο τὸν
[2]kill, and was not able: for Herod feared
Ἰωάννην, εἰδὼς αὐτὸν ἄνδρα δίκαιον καὶ ἅγιον, καὶ
John, knowing him [to be] a man just and holy, and
συνετήρει αὐτόν· καὶ ἀκούσας αὐτοῦ, πολλὰ [b]ἐποίει,‖ καὶ
kept [2]safe [1]him; and having heard him, many things did, and

not put on two coats. 10 And he said unto them, In what place soever ye enter into an house, there abide till ye depart from that place. 11 And whosoever shall not receive you, nor hear you, when ye depart thence, shake off the dust under your feet for a testimony against them. Verily I say unto you, It shall be more tolerable for Sodom and Gomorrha in the day of judgment, than for that city. 12 And they went out, and preached that men should repent. 13 And they cast out many devils, and anointed with oil many that were sick, and healed *them.*

14 And king Herod heard *of him;* (for his name was spread abroad:) and he said, That John the Baptist was risen from the dead, and therefore mighty works do shew forth themselves in him. 15 Others said, That it is Elias. And others said, That it is a prophet, or as one of the prophets. 16 But when Herod heard *thereof,* he said, It is John, whom I beheaded: he is risen from the dead. 17 For Herod himself had sent forth and laid hold upon John, and bound him in prison for Herodias' sake, his brother Philip's wife: for he had married her. 18 For John had said unto Herod, It is not lawful for thee to have thy brother's wife. 19 Therefore Herodias had a quarrel against him, and would have killed him; but she could not: 20 for Herod feared John, knowing that he was a just man and an holy, and observed him; and when he heard him, he did many things, and

---

[h] ἐνδύσασθαι E. [i] ἂν LTr. [k] ἐὰν *for* ἂν L; ὃς ἂν τόπος μὴ δέξηται whatsoever place will not receive TTrA. [l] — ἀμὴν λέγω .... τῇ πόλει ἐκείνῃ G[L]TTrA. [m] ἐκήρυξαν TTrA. [n] μετανοῶσιν LTTrA. [o] ἔλεγον they said L. [p] ἐγήγερται (has risen) ἐκ νεκρῶν LTTr; ἐκ νεκρῶν ἀνέστη A. [q] + δὲ also LTTrAW. [r] Ἠλείας T. [s] — ἐστίν [L]TTrA. [t] — ἢ GLTTrAW. [v] ἔλεγεν TTrA. [w] — "Οτι LTTrA. [x] — ἐστιν· αὐτὸς G[L]TTrA. [y] — ἐκ νεκρῶν T[Tr]A. [z] — τῇ GLTTrAW. [a] ἐζήτει sought L. [b] ἠπόρει was at a loss [about] T.

heard him gladly.
21 And when a con-
venient day was come,
that Herod on his
birthday made a sup-
per to his lords, high
captains, and chief
estates of Galilee;
22 and when the daugh
ter of the said Herodias,
came in, and danced,
and pleased Herod and
them that sat with
him, the king said unto
the damsel, Ask of me
whatsoever thou wilt,
and I will give *it* thee.
23 And he sware unto
her, Whatsoever thou
shalt ask of me, I will
give *it* thee, unto the
half of my kingdom.
24 And she went forth,
and said unto her mo-
ther, What shall I ask?
And she said, The head
of John the Baptist.
25 And she came in
straightway with
haste unto the king,
and asked, saying, I
will that thou give me
by and by in a charger
the head of John the
Baptist. 26 And the
king was exceeding
sorry; *yet* for his oath's
sake, and for their
sakes which sat with
him, he would not re-
ject her. 27 And im-
mediately the king
sent an executioner,
and commanded his
head to be brought:
and he went and be-
headed him in the
prison, 28 and brought
his head in a charger,
and gave it to the dam-
sel: and the damsel
gave it to her mother.
29 And when his disci-
ples heard *of it*, they
came and took up his
corpse, and laid it in
a tomb.

30 And the apostles
gathered themselves
together unto Jesus,
and told him all things,
both what they had
done, and what they
had taught. 31 And he
said unto them, Come
ye yourselves apart

ἡδέως αὐτοῦ ἤκουεν. 21 καὶ γενομένης ἡμέρας-εὐκαίρου, [c]ὅτε‖
gladly him heard. And [4]being [5]come [1]an [2]opportune [3]day, when
Ἡρώδης τοῖς-γενεσίοις-αὐτοῦ δεῖπνον [d]ἐποίει‖ τοῖς μεγιστᾶσιν
Herod on his birthday a supper made to [2]great [3]men
αὐτοῦ καὶ τοῖς χιλιάρχοις καὶ τοῖς πρώτοις τῆς Γαλιλαίας,
[1]his and to the chief captains and to the first [men] of Galilee;
22 καὶ εἰσελθούσης τῆς θυγατρὸς αὐτῆς τῆς Ἡρωδιάδος, καὶ
and [6]having [7]come [8]in [1]the [2]daughter [3]of [5]herself [4]Herodias, and
ὀρχησαμένης, [e]καὶ ἀρεσάσης‖ τῷ Ἡρώδῃ καὶ τοῖς συνανα-
having danced, and pleased Herod and those reclining
κειμένοις, [f]εἶπεν ὁ βασιλεὺς‖ τῷ κορασίῳ, Αἴτησόν με
[at table] with [him], [3]said [1]the [2]king to the damsel, Ask me
ὃ-ἐὰν θέλῃς, καὶ δώσω σοί· 23 καὶ ὤμοσεν αὐτῇ, Ὅτι
whatever thou wilt, and I will give to thee. And he swore to her,
ὃ-ἐὰν με αἰτήσῃς, δώσω σοί, ἕως ἡμίσους τῆς βασιλείας
Whatever me thou mayest ask, I will give thee, to half of [2]kingdom
μου. 24 [g]Ἡ-δὲ‖ ἐξελθοῦσα εἶπεν τῇ-μητρὶ-αὐτῆς, Τί [h]αἰτή-
[1]my. And she having gone out said to her mother, What shall I
σομαι;‖ Ἡ-δὲ εἶπεν, Τὴν κεφαλὴν Ἰωάννου τοῦ [i]βαπτιστοῦ.‖
ask? And she said, The head of John the Baptist.
25 Καὶ εἰσελθοῦσα [k]εὐθέως‖ μετὰ σπουδῆς πρὸς τὸν βασιλέα,
And having entered immediately with haste to the king,
ᾐτήσατο, λέγουσα, Θέλω ἵνα [l]μοι δῷς ἐξ-αὐτῆς‖ ἐπὶ πίνακι
she asked, saying, I desire that to me thou give at once upon a dish
τὴν κεφαλὴν Ἰωάννου τοῦ βαπτιστοῦ. 26 Καὶ περίλυπος
the head of John the Baptist. And [5]very [6]sorrowful
γενόμενος ὁ βασιλεύς, διὰ τοὺς ὅρκους καὶ τοὺς
[[3]while] [4]made [1]the [2]king, on account of the oaths and those who
[m]συνανακειμένους‖ οὐκ-ἠθέλησεν [n]αὐτὴν ἀθετῆσαι.‖ 27 καὶ
reclined [at table] with [him], would not [2]her [1]reject. And
[o]εὐθέως‖ ἀποστείλας ὁ βασιλεὺς [p]σπεκουλάτωρα‖ ἐπέταξεν
immediately [3]having [4]sent [1]the [2]king a guardsman ordered
[q]ἐνεχθῆναι‖ τὴν-κεφαλὴν-αὐτοῦ[r]. 28 [s]ὁ-δὲ‖ ἀπελθὼν ἀπεκε-
to be brought his head. And he having gone be-
φάλισεν αὐτὸν ἐν τῇ φυλακῇ, καὶ ἤνεγκεν τὴν-κεφαλὴν-αὐτοῦ
headed him in the prison, and brought his head
ἐπὶ πίνακι, καὶ ἔδωκεν αὐτὴν τῷ κορασίῳ· καὶ τὸ κοράσιον
upon a dish, and gave it to the damsel, and the damsel
ἔδωκεν αὐτὴν τῇ-μητρὶ-αὐτῆς. 29 Καὶ ἀκούσαντες οἱ μαθηταὶ
gave it to her mother. And having heard [it] [2]disciples
αὐτοῦ [t]ἦλθον,‖ καὶ ἦραν τὸ-πτῶμα-αὐτοῦ, καὶ ἔθηκαν [u]αὐτὸ‖
[1]his came, and took up his corpse, and laid it
ἐν [v]τῷ‖ μνημείῳ.
in the tomb.

30 Καὶ συνάγονται οἱ ἀπόστολοι πρὸς τὸν Ἰησοῦν, καὶ
And [3]are [4]gathered [5]together [1]the [2]apostles to Jesus, and
ἀπήγγειλαν αὐτῷ πάντα, [w]καὶ‖ ὅσα ἐποίησαν καὶ [x]ὅσα‖
they related to him all things, both what they had done and what
ἐδίδαξαν. 31 καὶ [y]εἶπεν‖ αὐτοῖς, Δεῦτε ὑμεῖς αὐτοὶ
they had taught. And he said to them, Come ye yourselves

---

[c] ὅ τε L. [d] ἐποίησεν LTTrA. [e] ἤρεσεν she pleased LTTrA. [f] εἶπεν δὲ ὁ βασιλεὺς L; ὁ δὲ βασιλεὺς εἶπεν and the king said TTrA. [g] καὶ and TTrA. [h] αἰτήσωμαι should I ask LTTrAW. [i] βαπτίζοντος TTrA. [k] εὐθὺς LTTrA. [l] ἐξαυτῆς δῷς μοι LTTrA. [m] ἀνακειμένους reclined [at table] TTrA. [n] ἀθετῆσαι αὐτήν TTrA. [o] εὐθὺς TTrA. [p] σπεκουλάτορα LTTrAW. [q] ἐνέγκαι [him] to bring TTrA. [r] + [ἐπὶ πίνακι] on a dish L. [s] καὶ (*read* and having gone he beheaded) LTTrA. [t] ἦλθαν TTrA. [u] αὐτὸν him T. [v] — τῷ (*read* a tomb) EGLTTrAW. [w] — καὶ LTTrAW. [x] — ὅσα T. [y] λέγει he says TTrAW.

κατ᾽.ἰδίαν εἰς ἔρημον τόπον, καὶ [z]ἀναπαύεσθε‖ ὀλίγον. Ἦσαν
apart into [2]desert [1]a place, and rest a little. [7]Were
γὰρ οἱ.ἐρχόμενοι καὶ οἱ ὑπάγοντες πολλοί, καὶ οὐδὲ φαγεῖν
[1]for [2]those [3]coming [4]and [5]those [6]going many, and not even to eat
[a]ηὐκαίρουν.‖ 32 καὶ ἀπῆλθον [b]εἰς ἔρημον τόπον τῷ
had they opportunity. And they went away into [2]desert [1]a place by the
πλοίῳ‖ κατ᾽.ἰδίαν. 33 Καὶ εἶδον αὐτοὺς ὑπάγοντας [c]οἱ ὄχλοι,‖
ship apart. And [3]saw [4]them [5]going [1]the [2]crowds,
καὶ [d]ἐπέγνωσαν‖ [e]αὐτὸν‖ πολλοί, καὶ πεζῇ ἀπὸ πασῶν τῶν
[6]and [8]recognized [9]him [7]many, and on foot from all the
πόλεων συνέδραμον ἐκεῖ, [f]καὶ προῆλθον αὐτούς,‖ [g]καὶ συνῆλ-
cities ran together there, and went before them, and came to-
θον πρὸς αὐτόν.‖ 34 καὶ ἐξελθὼν [h]εἶδεν ὁ Ἰησοῦς‖ πολὺν
gether to him. And having gone out [2]saw [1]Jesus [4]great
ὄχλον, καὶ ἐσπλαγχνίσθη ἐπ᾽ [i]αὐτοῖς,‖ ὅτι ἦσαν
[3]a crowd, and was moved with compassion towards them, because they were
ὡς πρόβατα μὴ ἔχοντα ποιμένα· καὶ ἤρξατο διδάσκειν αὐτοὺς
as sheep not having a shepherd. And he began to teach them
πολλά. 35 Καὶ ἤδη ὥρας.πολλῆς [k]γενομένης,‖ προσελ-
many things. And already a late hour [it] being, com-
θόντες [l]αὐτῷ‖ οἱ.μαθηταὶ.[m]αὐτοῦ‖ [n]λέγουσιν,‖ Ὅτι ἔρημός ἐστιν
ing to him his disciples say, Desert is
ὁ τόπος, καὶ ἤδη ὥρα.πολλή· 36 ἀπόλυσον αὐτούς, ἵνα
the place, and already [it is] a late hour; dismiss them, that
ἀπελθόντες εἰς τοὺς κύκλῳ ἀγροὺς καὶ κώμας, ἀγοράσωσιν
having gone [4]to [5]the [1]in [2]a [3]circuit country and villages, they may buy
ἑαυτοῖς [o]ἄρτους·‖ τί [p]γὰρ‖ φάγωσιν [q]οὐκ.ἔχουσιν.‖
for themselves bread; [2]something [1]for to eat they have not.
37 Ὁ.δὲ ἀποκριθεὶς εἶπεν αὐτοῖς, Δότε αὐτοῖς ὑμεῖς φαγεῖν.
But he answering said to them, Give [2]to [3]them [1]ye to eat.
Καὶ λέγουσιν αὐτῷ, Ἀπελθόντες ἀγοράσωμεν [r]διακοσίων
And they say to him, Having gone shall we buy two hundred
δηναρίων‖ ἄρτους, καὶ [s]δῶμεν‖ αὐτοῖς φαγεῖν; 38 Ὁ.δὲ λέγει
denarii of bread, and give them to eat? And he says
αὐτοῖς, Πόσους ἄρτους ἔχετε; ὑπάγετε [t]καὶ‖ ἴδετε. Καὶ γνόν-
to them, How many loaves have ye? go and see. And having
τες λέγουσιν[v], Πέντε, καὶ δύο ἰχθύας. 39 Καὶ ἐπέταξεν αὐτοῖς
known they say, Five, and two fishes. And he ordered them
[w]ἀνακλῖναι‖ πάντας συμπόσια.συμπόσια ἐπὶ τῷ χλωρῷ χόρτῳ.
to make [2]recline [1]all by companies on the green grass.
40 καὶ [x]ἀνέπεσον‖ πρασιαὶ.πρασιαί, [y]ἀνὰ‖ ἑκατὸν καὶ [y]ἀνὰ‖
And they sat down in ranks, by hundreds and by
πεντήκοντα. 41 καὶ λαβὼν τοὺς πέντε ἄρτους καὶ τοὺς δύο
fifties. And having taken the five loaves and the two
ἰχθύας, ἀναβλέψας εἰς τὸν οὐρανὸν εὐλόγησεν καὶ κατέκλα-
fishes, having looked up to the heaven he blessed and broke
σεν τοὺς ἄρτους, καὶ ἐδίδου τοῖς.μαθηταῖς.[za]αὐτοῦ‖ ἵνα [aa]παρα-
the loaves, and gave to his disciples that they might

into a desert place, and rest a while: for there were many coming and going, and they had no leisure so much as to eat. 32 And they departed into a desert place by ship privately. 33 And the people saw them departing, and many knew him, and ran afoot thither out of all cities, and outwent them, and came together unto him. 34 And Jesus, when he came out, saw much people, and was moved with compassion toward them, because they were as sheep not having a shepherd: and he began to teach them many things. 35 And when the day was now far spent, his disciples came unto him, and said, This is a desert place, and now the time *is* far passed: 36 send them away, that they may go into the country round about, and into the villages, and buy themselves bread: for they have nothing to eat. 37 He answered and said unto them, Give ye them to eat. And they say unto him, Shall we go and buy two hundred pennyworth of bread, and give them to eat? 38 He saith unto them, How many loaves have ye? go and see. And when they knew, they say, Five, and two fishes. 39 And he commanded them to make all sit down by companies upon the green grass. 40 And they sat down in ranks, by hundreds and by fifties. 41 And when he had taken the five loaves and the two fishes, he looked up to heaven, and blessed, and brake the loaves, and gave *them* to his disciples to set before

---

[z] ἀναπαύσασθε TTrA. [a] εὐκαίρουν LTTrA. [b] ἐν τῷ πλοίῳ εἰς ἔρημον τόπον L. [c] — οἱ ὄχλοι (*read* they saw) GLTTrAW. [d] ἔγνωσαν knew LTrA. [e] αὐτοὺς them T; — αὐτὸν GLTrA. [f] — καὶ προῆλθον αὐτούς G. [g] — καὶ συνῆλθον πρὸς αὐτόν GLTTrAW. [h] — ὁ Ἰησοῦς (*read* he saw) GTTrAW; [ὁ Ἰησοῦς] εἶδεν L. [i] αὐτούς LTTrA. [k] γινομένης T. [l] — αὐτῷ T. [m] [αὐτοῦ] L. [n] ἔλεγον said TTrA. [o] — ἄρτους [L]TTrA. [p] — γὰρ [L]TTrA. [q] — οὐκ ἔχουσιν (*read* buy for themselves something to eat) [L]TTrA. [r] δηναρίων διακοσίων GLTTrAW. [s] δώσομεν shall we give LTrA; δώσωμεν T. [t] — καὶ [L]TTrA. [v] + [αὐτῷ] to him L. [w] ἀνακλιθῆναι L. [x] ἀνέπεσαν TTrA. [y] κατὰ LTTrA. [za] — αὐτοῦ (*read* the disciples) TTrA. [aa] παρατιθῶσιν TA.

them; and the two
fishes divided he a-
mong them all. 42 And
they did all eat, and
were filled. 43 And
they took up twelve
baskets full of the
fragments, and of the
fishes. 44 And they
that did eat of the
loaves were about five
thousand men. 45 And
straightway he con-
strained his disciples
to get into the ship,
and to go to the other
side before unto Beth-
saida, while he sent a-
way the people. 46 And
when he had sent them
away, he departed into
a mountain to pray.
47 And when even was
come, the ship was in
the midst of the sea,
and he alone on the
land. 48 And he saw
them toiling in row-
ing; for the wind was
contrary unto them:
and about the fourth
watch of the night he
cometh unto them,
walking upon the sea,
and would have passed
by them. 49 But when
they saw him walking
upon the sea they sup-
posed it had been a
spirit, and cried out:
50 for they all saw
him, and were trou-
bled. And immedi-
ately he talked with
them, and saith unto
them, Be of good cheer:
it is I; be not afraid.
51 And he went up
unto them into the
ship; and the wind
ceased: and they were
sore amazed in them-
selves beyond measure,
and wondered. 52 For
they considered not
the miracle of the
loaves: for their heart
was hardened.

53 And when they
had passed over, they
came into the land of
Gennesaret, and drew
to the shore. 54 And
when they were come
out of the ship,
straightway they knew
him, 55 and ran
through that whole
region round about,
and began to carry
about in beds those

θῶσιν‖ αὐτοῖς· καὶ τοὺς δύο ἰχθύας ἐμέρισεν πᾶσιν. 42 καὶ
set before them. And the two fishes he divided among all. And
ἔφαγον πάντες, καὶ ἐχορτάσθησαν. 43 καὶ ἦραν [b]κλασμά-
[2]ate [1]all, and were satisfied. And they took up of frag-
των‖ δώδεκα [c]κοφίνους‖ [d]πλήρεις,‖ καὶ ἀπὸ τῶν ἰχθύων. 44 καὶ
ments twelve hand-baskets full, and of the fishes. And
ἦσαν οἱ φαγόντες τοὺς ἄρτους [e]ὡσεὶ‖ πεντακισχίλιοι
[7]were [1]those [2]that [3]ate [4]of [5]the [6]loaves about five thousand
ἄνδρες. 45 Καὶ [f]εὐθέως‖ ἠνάγκασεν τοὺς-μαθητὰς-αὐτοῦ
men. And immediately he compelled his disciples
ἐμβῆναι εἰς τὸ πλοῖον, καὶ προάγειν εἰς τὸ πέραν πρὸς Βηθ-
to enter into the ship, and to go before to the other side to Beth-
σαϊδάν, ἕως αὐτὸς [g]ἀπολύσῃ‖ τὸν ὄχλον. 46 καὶ ἀποταξάμενος
saida, until he should dismiss the crowd. And having taken leave of
αὐτοῖς, ἀπῆλθεν εἰς τὸ ὄρος προσεύξασθαι. 47 Καὶ ὀψίας
them, he departed into the mountain to pray. And evening
γενομένης, ἦν τὸ πλοῖον ἐν μέσῳ τῆς θαλάσσης, καὶ αὐτὸς
being come, [3]was [1]the [2]ship in the midst of the sea, and he
μόνος ἐπὶ τῆς γῆς. 48 Καὶ [h]εἶδεν‖ αὐτοὺς βασανιζομένους
alone upon the land. And he saw them labouring
ἐν τῷ ἐλαύνειν, ἦν-γὰρ ὁ ἄνεμος ἐναντίος αὐτοῖς· [i]καὶ‖ περὶ
in the rowing, for [3]was [1]the [2]wind contrary to them; and about
τετάρτην φυλακὴν τῆς νυκτὸς ἔρχεται πρὸς αὐτούς, περιπα-
[the] fourth watch of the night he comes to them, walk-
τῶν ἐπὶ τῆς θαλάσσης, καὶ ἤθελεν παρελθεῖν αὐτούς. 49 οἱ-δὲ
ing on the sea, and would have passed by them. But they,
ἰδόντες αὐτὸν [k]περιπατοῦντα ἐπὶ τῆς θαλάσσης,‖ ἔδοξαν [l]
seeing him walking on the sea, thought [it]
φάντασμα [m]εἶναι,‖ καὶ ἀνέκραξαν. 50 πάντες-γὰρ αὐτὸν
[3]an [4]apparition [1]to [2]be, and cried out: for all [2]him
[n]εἶδον,‖ καὶ ἐταράχθησαν. [o]καὶ εὐθέως‖ ἐλάλησεν μετ' αὐτῶν,
[1]saw, and were troubled. And immediately he spoke with them,
καὶ λέγει αὐτοῖς, Θαρσεῖτε· ἐγώ εἰμι, μὴ-φοβεῖσθε.
and says to them, Be of good courage: I am [he]; fear not.
51 Καὶ ἀνέβη πρὸς αὐτοὺς εἰς τὸ πλοῖον, καὶ ἐκόπασεν ὁ
And he went up to them into the ship, and [3]fell [1]the
ἄνεμος· καὶ λίαν [p]ἐκ-περισσοῦ‖ ἐν ἑαυτοῖς ἐξίσταντο,
[2]wind. And exceedingly beyond measure in themselves they were amazed,
[q]καὶ ἐθαύμαζον·‖ 52 οὐ-γὰρ-συνῆκαν ἐπὶ τοῖς ἄρτοις· [r]ἦν-γὰρ‖
and wondered; for they understood not by the loaves, for [3]was
[s]ἡ-καρδία-αὐτῶν‖ πεπωρωμένη.
[1]their [2]heart hardened.

53 Καὶ διαπεράσαντες [t]ἦλθον ἐπὶ τὴν γῆν‖ [v]Γεννησαρέτ,‖
And having passed over they came to the land of Gennesaret.
καὶ προσωρμίσθησαν. 54 καὶ ἐξελθόντων-αὐτῶν ἐκ τοῦ
and drew to shore. And on their coming out of the
πλοίου, [f]εὐθέως‖ ἐπιγνόντες αὐτόν[w], 55 [x]περιδραμόντες‖
ship, immediately having recognized him, running through
ὅλην τὴν-[y]περίχωρον‖-ἐκείνην [z] ἤρξαντο ἐπὶ τοῖς [a]κραββάτοις‖
all that country around they began on couches

---

[b] κλάσματα A. [c] κοφίνων TA. [d] πληρώματα TTrA. [e] — ὡσεὶ GLTTrAW. [f] εὐθὺς TTrA. [g] ἀπολύει dismisses LTTrA. [h] ἰδὼν seeing LTTrA. [i] — καὶ LTTrA. [k] ἐπὶ τῆς θαλάσσης περιπατοῦντα T. [l] + ὅτι that T. [m] ἐστιν it is T. [n] εἶδαν TTr. [o] καὶ εὐθὺς LTrA; ὁ δὲ εὐθὺς T. [p] [ἐκ περισσοῦ] Tr. [q] — καὶ ἐθαύμαζον [L] TTrA. [r] ἀλλ' ἦν but was TTr. [s] αὐτῶν ἡ καρδία LTTrAW. [t] ἐπὶ τὴν γῆν ἦλθον εἰς T. [v] Γεννησαρὲτ LTTrAW. [w] + [οἱ ἄνδρες τοῦ τόπου ἐκείνου] the men of that place L. [x] περιέδραμον they ran through TTr. [y] χώραν (omit around) TTrA. [z] + καὶ and TTr. [a] κραβάττοις LTTrAW.

τοὺς κακῶς-ἔχοντας περιφέρειν, ὅπου ἤκουον ὅτι
those that were ill to carry about, where they were hearing that
[c]ἐκεῖ‖ ἐστιν. 56 καὶ ὅπου [d]ἂν‖ εἰσεπορεύετο εἰς κώμας ἢ [e]
there he was. (lit. he is.) And wherever he entered into villages or
πόλεις ἢ [e] ἀγρούς, ἐν ταῖς ἀγοραῖς [f]ἐτίθουν‖ τοὺς ἀσθενοῦν-
cities or fields, in the marketplaces they laid those who were sick,
τας, καὶ παρεκάλουν αὐτὸν ἵνα κἂν τοῦ κρασπέδου τοῦ
and besought him that if only the border
ἱματίου-αὐτοῦ ἅψωνται· καὶ ὅσοι ἂν [g]ἥπτοντο‖ αὐτοῦ
of his garment they might touch; and as many as touched him
ἐσώζοντο.
were healed.

7 Καὶ συνάγονται πρὸς αὐτὸν οἱ Φαρισαῖοι καί τινες
And are gathered together to him the Pharisees and some
τῶν γραμματέων, ἐλθόντες ἀπὸ Ἱεροσολύμων· 2 καὶ ἰδόντες
of the scribes, having come from Jerusalem; and having seen
τινὰς τῶν-μαθητῶν-αὐτοῦ [h] κοιναῖς χερσίν, [i]τοῦτ' ἔστιν‖
some of his disciples with defiled hands, that is
ἀνίπτοις, [k]ἐσθίοντας‖ [l]ἄρτους, [m]ἐμέμψαντο·‖ 3 οἱ-γὰρ Φαρι-
unwashed, eating bread, they found fault; for the Phari-
σαῖοι καὶ πάντες οἱ Ἰουδαῖοι, ἐὰν-μὴ [n]πυγμῇ‖ νίψωνται τὰς
sees and all the Jews, unless with the fist they wash the
χεῖρας, οὐκ-ἐσθίουσιν, κρατοῦντες τὴν παράδοσιν τῶν πρεσ-
hands, eat not, holding the tradition of the el-
βυτέρων· 4 καὶ [o]ἀπὸ‖ ἀγορᾶς, ἐὰν-μὴ βαπτίσωνται
ders; and [on coming] from the market, unless they wash themselves
οὐκ-ἐσθίουσιν· καὶ ἄλλα πολλά ἐστιν ἃ παρέλαβον
they eat not; and ²other ³things ¹many there are which they received
κρατεῖν, βαπτισμοὺς ποτηρίων καὶ ξεστῶν καὶ χαλκίων [p]καὶ
to hold, washings of cups and vessels and brazen utensils and
κλινῶν·‖ 5 [q]ἔπειτα‖ ἐπερωτῶσιν αὐτὸν οἱ Φαρισαῖοι καὶ οἱ
couches: then question him the Pharisees and the
γραμματεῖς, [r]Διατί‖ [s]οἱ-μαθηταί-σου οὐ-περιπατοῦσιν‖ κατὰ
scribes, Why ³thy ⁴disciples ¹walk ²not according to
τὴν παράδοσιν τῶν πρεσβυτέρων, ἀλλὰ [t]ἀνίπτοις‖ χερσὶν
the tradition of the elders, but with unwashed hands
ἐσθίουσιν τὸν ἄρτον; 6 Ὁ-δὲ [v]ἀποκριθεὶς‖ εἶπεν αὐτοῖς, [w]Ὅτι‖
eat bread? But he answering said to them,
καλῶς [x]προεφήτευσεν‖ Ἡσαΐας περὶ ὑμῶν τῶν ὑποκριτῶν,
Well prophesied Esaias concerning you, hypocrites,
ὡς γέγραπται, [y] [z]Οὗτος ὁ λαὸς‖ τοῖς χείλεσίν με τιμᾷ,
as it has been written, This people with the lips me honour,
ἡ-δὲ-καρδία-αὐτῶν πόῤῥω ἀπέχει ἀπ' ἐμοῦ. 7 μάτην-δὲ σέβον-
but their heart far is away from me. But in vain they wor-
ταί με, διδάσκοντες διδασκαλίας ἐντάλματα ἀνθρώπων.
ship me, teaching [as] teachings injunctions of men.
8 Ἀφέντες-[a]γὰρ‖ τὴν ἐντολὴν τοῦ θεοῦ, κρατεῖτε τὴν παρά-
For, leaving the commandment of God, ye hold the tra-
δοσιν τῶν ἀνθρώπων, [b]βαπτισμοὺς ξεστῶν καὶ ποτηρίων, καὶ
dition of men, washings of vessels and cups, and

that were sick, where they heard he was. 56 And whithersoever he entered, into villages, or cities, or country, they laid the sick in the streets, and besought him that they might touch if it were but the border of his garment: and as many as touched him were made whole.

VII. Then came together unto him the Pharisees, and certain of the scribes, which came from Jerusalem. 2 And when they saw some of his disciples eat bread with defiled, that is to say, with unwashen, hands, they found fault. 3 For the Pharisees, and all the Jews, except they wash *their* hands oft, eat not, holding the tradition of the elders. 4 And *when they come* from the market, except they wash, they eat not. And many other things there be, which they have received to hold, *as* the washing of cups, and pots, brasen vessels, and of tables. 5 Then the Pharisees and scribes asked him, Why walk not thy disciples according to the tradition of the elders, but eat bread with unwashen hands? 6 He answered and said unto them, Well hath Esaias prophesied of you hypocrites, as it is written, This people honoureth me with *their* lips, but their heart is far from me. 7 Howbeit in vain do they worship me, teaching *for* doctrines the commandments of men. 8 For laying aside the commandment of God, ye hold the tradition of men, *as* the washing of pots and cups: and many

[c] — ἐκεῖ LT[Tr]. [d] ἐὰν T. [e] + εἰς into [L]TTrA. [f] ἐτίθεσαν TTrA. [g] ἥψαντο LTTr. [h] + ὅτι that TTr. [i] τουτέστιν LA. [k] ἐσθίουσιν they eat TTr. [l] + τοὺς LTTrA. [m] — ἐμέμψαντο (*read verses 3 and 4 in parenthesis*) GLTTrAW. [n] πυκνὰ often T. [o] ἀπ' LTrA. [p] — καὶ κλινῶν T. [q] καὶ and LTTrA. [r] διὰ τί LTrA. [s] οὐ περιπατοῦσιν οἱ μαθηταί σου TTrA. [t] κοιναῖς with defiled GLTTrAW. [v] — ἀποκριθεὶς TTrA. [w] — Ὅτι [L]T[TrA]. [x] ἐπροφήτευσεν LTTrA. [y] + ὅτι T. [z] Ὁ λαὸς οὗτος L. [a] — γὰρ for LTTrA. [b] — βαπτισμοὺς .... ποιεῖτε T[TrA].

other such like things
ye do. 9 And he said
unto them, Full well
ye reject the com-
mandment of God,
that ye may keep your
own tradition. 10 For
Moses said, Honour
thy father and thy
mother; and, Whoso
curseth father or mo-
ther, let him die the
death: 11 but ye say,
If a man shall say to
his father or mother,
It is Corban, that is to
say, a gift, by whatso-
ever thou mightest be
profited by me; *he
shall be free.* 12 And
ye suffer him no more
to do ought for his fa-
ther or his mother;
13 making the word of
God of none effect
through your tradi-
tion, which ye have
delivered: and many
such like things do ye.
14 And when he had
called all the people
unto him, he said unto
them, Hearken unto
me every one *of
you,* and understand:
15 there is nothing
from without a man,
that entering into him
can defile him: but
the things which come
out of him, those are
they that defile the
man. 16 If any man
have ears to hear, let
him hear. 17 And when
he was entered into
the house from the
people, his disciples
asked him concerning
the parable. 18 And
he saith unto them,
Are ye so without un-
derstanding also? Do
ye not perceive, that
whatsoever thing from
without entereth into
the man, *it* cannot
defile him; 19 because
it entereth not into
his heart, but into the
belly, and goeth out
into the draught,
purging all meats?
20 And he said, That
which cometh out of
the man, that defileth
the man. 21 For from
within, out of the
heart of men, proceed
evil thoughts, adul-
teries, fornications,
murders, 22 thefts,
covetousness, wicked-

ἄλλα παρόμοια τοιαῦτα πολλὰ ποιεῖτε.‖ 9 Καὶ ἔλεγεν
[2]other [4]like [[5]things] [3]such [1]many ye do. And he said
αὐτοῖς, Καλῶς ἀθετεῖτε τὴν ἐντολὴν τοῦ θεοῦ, ἵνα τὴν
to them, Well do ye set aside the commandment of God, that
παράδοσιν.ὑμῶν τηρήσητε. 10 [c]Μωσῆς‖.γὰρ εἶπεν, Τίμα
your tradition ye may observe. For Moses said, Honour
τὸν.πατέρα.σου καὶ τὴν.μητέρα.σου· καί, Ὁ κακολογῶν πατέρα
thy father and thy mother; and, He who speaks evil of father
ἢ μητέρα θανάτῳ τελευτάτω. 11 Ὑμεῖς.δὲ λέγετε, Ἐὰν εἴπῃ
or mother by death let him die. But ye say, If [3]say
ἄνθρωπος τῷ πατρὶ ἢ τῇ μητρί, Κορβᾶν ὅ ἐστιν, δῶρον,
[1]a [2]man to father or mother, [It is] a corban, (that is, a gift,)
ὃ.ἐὰν ἐξ ἐμοῦ ὠφεληθῇς· 12 [d]καὶ‖ οὐκέτι ἀφίετε
whatever from me thou mightest be profited by :— and no longer ye suffer
αὐτὸν οὐδὲν ποιῆσαι τῷ.πατρὶ.[e]αὐτοῦ‖ ἢ τῇ.μητρὶ.[e]αὐτοῦ,‖
him anything (*lit.* nothing) to do for his father or his mother,
13 ἀκυροῦντες τὸν λόγον τοῦ θεοῦ τῇ.παραδόσει.ὑμῶν ᾗ
making void the word of God by your tradition which
παρεδώκατε· καὶ παρόμοια τοιαῦτα πολλὰ ποιεῖτε.
ye have delivered; and [3]like [[4]things] [2]such [1]many ye do.
14 Καὶ προσκαλεσάμενος [f]πάντα‖ τὸν ὄχλον, ἔλεγεν αὐτοῖς,
And having called to [him] all the crowd, he said to them,
[g]Ἀκούετέ‖ μου πάντες, καὶ [h]συνίετε.‖ 15 οὐδέν ἐστιν ἔξω-
Hear ye me, all, and understand: Nothing there is from with-
θεν τοῦ ἀνθρώπου εἰσπορευόμενον εἰς αὐτόν, ὃ δύναται
out the man entering into him, which is able
[i]αὐτὸν κοινῶσαι·‖ ἀλλὰ τὰ [k]ἐκπορευόμενα ἀπ' αὐτοῦ,‖
him to defile; but the things which go out from him,
[l]ἐκεῖνά‖ ἐστιν τὰ κοινοῦντα τὸν ἄνθρωπον. 16 [m]εἴ τις
those are the things which defile the man. If anyone
ἔχει ὦτα ἀκούειν, ἀκουέτω.‖ 17 Καὶ ὅτε εἰσῆλθεν εἰς [n] οἶκον
have ears to hear, let him hear. And when he went into a house
ἀπὸ τοῦ ὄχλου, ἐπηρώτων αὐτὸν οἱ.μαθηταὶ.αὐτοῦ [o]περὶ τῆς
from the crowd, [3]asked [4]him [1]his [2]disciples concerning the
παραβολῆς.‖ 18 καὶ λέγει αὐτοῖς, Οὕτως καὶ ὑμεῖς ἀσύνε-
parable. And he says to them, [4]Thus [3]also [2]ye [5]without [6]un-
τοί ἐστε; οὐ.νοεῖτε ὅτι πᾶν τὸ ἔξωθεν εἰσπο-
derstanding [1]are? Perceive ye not that everything which from without en-
ρευόμενον εἰς τὸν ἄνθρωπον οὐ.δύναται αὐτὸν κοινῶσαι;
ters into the man is not able him to defile?
19 ὅτι οὐκ.εἰσπορεύεται αὐτοῦ εἰς τὴν καρδίαν, ἀλλ' εἰς τὴν
because it enters not [4]of [5]him [1]into [2]the [3]heart, but into the
κοιλίαν· καὶ εἰς τὸν ἀφεδρῶνα ἐκπορεύεται, [p]καθαρίζον‖ πάντα
belly, and into the draught goes out, purifying all
τὰ βρώματα. 20 Ἔλεγεν.δέ, Ὅτι τὸ ἐκ τοῦ ἀνθρώπου
the food. And he said, That which out of the man
ἐκπορευόμενον, ἐκεῖνο κοινοῖ τὸν ἄνθρωπον. 21 ἔσωθεν.γὰρ
goes forth, that defiles the man. For from within
ἐκ τῆς καρδίας τῶν ἀνθρώπων οἱ διαλογισμοὶ οἱ κακοὶ ἐκ-
out of the heart of men [2]reasonings [1]evil go
πορεύονται, [q]μοιχεῖαι, πορνεῖαι, φόνοι, 22 κλοπαί,‖ πλεον-
forth, adulteries, fornications, murders, thefts, covetous

[c] Μωϋσῆς LTTrAW. [d] — καὶ LTTr[A]. [e] — αὐτοῦ (*read* [his]) LTTrA. [f] πάλιν again LTTrA. [g] ἀκούσατέ LTTrA. [h] σύνετε LTTrA. [i] κοινῶσαι αὐτόν T. [k] ἐκ τοῦ ἀνθρώπου ἐκπορευόμενα from the man go out LTTrA. [l] — ἐκεῖνά T[Tr]. [m] — *verse* 16 T[TrA]. [n] + τὸν the (house) T. [o] τὴν παραβολὴν the parable LTTrA. [p] καθαρίζων LTTrA. [q] πορνεῖαι, κλοπαί, φόνοι, μοιχεῖαι TTrA.

ἐξίαι, πονηρίαι, δόλος, ἀσέλγεια, ὀφθαλμὸς πονηρός,
desires, wickednesses, guile, licentiousness, an eye wicked,
βλασφημία, ὑπερηφανία, ἀφροσύνη· 23 πάντα ταῦτα τὰ
blasphemy, haughtiness, folly: all these
πονηρὰ ἔσωθεν ἐκπορεύεται, καὶ κοινοῖ τὸν ἄνθρωπον.
evils from within go forth, and defile the man.

24 [r]Καὶ ἐκεῖθεν‖ ἀναστὰς ἀπῆλθεν εἰς τὰ [s]μεθόρια‖
And thence having risen up he went away into the borders
Τύρου [t]καὶ Σιδῶνος‖. καὶ εἰσελθὼν εἰς [v]τὴν‖ οἰκίαν, οὐδένα
of Tyre and Sidon; and having entered into the house, no one
[w]ἤθελεν‖ γνῶναι, καὶ οὐκ.[x]ἠδυνήθη‖ λαθεῖν. 25 [y]ἀκούσασα
he wished to know [it], and he could not be hid. ⁴Having ⁵heard
γὰρ‖ γυνὴ περὶ αὐτοῦ, ἧς εἶχεν τὸ.θυγάτριον.αὐτῆς πνεῦμα
¹for ²a ³woman about him, of whom ⁴had ¹her ²little ³daughter a spirit
ἀκάθαρτον, [z]ἐλθοῦσα‖ προσέπεσεν πρὸς τοὺς.πόδας.αὐτοῦ·
unclean, having come fell at his feet,
26 [a]ἦν.δὲ ἡ γυνὴ‖ Ἑλληνίς, [b]Συροφοίνισσα‖ τῷ γένει· καὶ
(now ³was ¹the ²woman a Greek, Syrophenician by race), and
ἠρώτα αὐτὸν ἵνα τὸ δαιμόνιον [c]ἐκβάλλῃ‖ ἐκ τῆς θυγατρὸς
asked him that the demon he should cast forth out of ²daughter
αὐτῆς. 27 [d]ὁ.δὲ.Ἰησοῦς εἶπεν‖ αὐτῇ, Ἄφες πρῶτον χορτασ-
¹her. But Jesus said to her, Suffer first to be satis-
θῆναι τὰ τέκνα· οὐ.γάρ [e]καλόν ἐστιν‖ λαβεῖν τὸν ἄρτον τῶν
fied the children; for not good is it to take the bread of the
τέκνων, καὶ [f]βαλεῖν τοῖς κυναρίοις.‖ 28 Ἡ.δὲ ἀπεκρίθη καὶ
children, and cast [it] to the dogs. But she answered and
λέγει αὐτῷ, Ναί, κύριε· καὶ.[g]γὰρ‖ τὰ κυνάρια ὑποκάτω τῆς
says to him, Yea, Lord; for even the little dogs under the
τραπέζης [h]ἐσθίει‖ ἀπὸ τῶν ψιχίων τῶν παιδίων. 29 Καὶ εἶπεν
table eat of the crumbs of the children. And he said
αὐτῇ, Διὰ τοῦτον τὸν λόγον ὕπαγε· ἐξελήλυθεν [i]τὸ δαι-
to her, Because of this word go; has gone forth the de-
μόνιον ἐκ τῆς.θυγατρός.σου.‖ 30 Καὶ ἀπελθοῦσα εἰς τὸν
mon out of thy daughter. And having gone away to
οἶκον.αὐτῆς, εὗρεν [k]τὸ δαιμόνιον ἐξεληλυθός, καὶ τὴν θυγα-
her house, she found the demon had gone forth, and the daugh-
τέρα βεβλημένην ἐπὶ τῆς κλίνης.‖
ter laid on the bed.

31 Καὶ πάλιν ἐξελθὼν ἐκ τῶν ὁρίων Τύρου [l]καὶ Σιδῶνος,
And again having departed from the borders of Tyre and Sidon,
ἦλθεν‖ [m]πρὸς‖ τὴν θάλασσαν τῆς Γαλιλαίας, ἀνὰ μέσον
he came to the sea of Galilee, through [the] midst
τῶν ὁρίων Δεκαπόλεως. 32 καὶ φέρουσιν αὐτῷ κωφὸν [n]
of the borders of Decapolis. And they bring to him a deaf man
[o]μογιλάλον,‖ καὶ παρακαλοῦσιν αὐτὸν ἵνα ἐπιθῇ
who spoke with difficulty, and they beseech him that he might lay
αὐτῷ τὴν χεῖρα. 33 καὶ ἀπολαβόμενος αὐτὸν ἀπὸ τοῦ
on him [his] hand. And having taken away him from the

ness, deceit, lasciviousness, an evil eye, blasphemy, pride, foolishness: 23 all these evil things come from within, and defile the man.

24 And from thence he arose, and went into the borders of Tyre and Sidon, and entered into an house, and would have no man know *it*: but he could not be hid.
25 For a *certain* woman, whose young daughter had an unclean spirit, heard of him, and came and fell at his feet: 26 the woman was a Greek, a Syrophenician by nation; and she besought him that he would cast forth the devil out of her daughter.
27 But Jesus said unto her, Let the children first be filled: for it is not meet to take the children's bread, and to cast *it* unto the dogs. 28 And she answered and said unto him, Yes, Lord: yet the dogs under the table eat of the children's crumbs. 29 And he said unto her, For this saying go thy way; the devil is gone out of thy daughter.
30 And when she was come to her house, she found the devil gone out, and her daughter laid upon the bed.

31 And again, departing from the coasts of Tyre and Sidon, he came unto the sea of Galilee, through the midst of the coasts of Decapolis. 32 And they bring unto him one that was deaf, and had an impediment in his speech; and they beseech him to put his hand upon him. 33 And he took him aside from the multitude, and

---

[r] Ἐκεῖθεν δὲ TA. [s] ὅρια LTTr. [t] — καὶ Σιδῶνος TA. [v] — τὴν (*read* a house) LTTrAW. [w] ἠθέλησεν T. [x] ἠδυνάσθη T. [y] ἀλλ' εὐθὺς ἀκούσασα but immediately having heard TTrA. [z] εἰσελθοῦσα having come in T. [a] ἡ δὲ γυνὴ ἦν LTA; ἡ γυνὴ δὲ ἦν Tr. [b] Συραφοινίκισσα G; Συροφοινίκισσα LTW; Σύρα Φοινίκισσα TrA. [c] ἐκβάλῃ GLTTrAW. [d] καὶ ἔλεγεν and he said LTTrA. [e] ἐστιν καλὸν LTTrA. [f] τοῖς κυναρίοις βαλεῖν TTrA. [g] — γὰρ for [L]TTr. [h] ἐσθίουσιν LTTrAW. [i] ἐκ τῆς θυγατρός σου τὸ δαιμόνιον TA. [k] τὸ παιδίον (the child) βεβλημένον ἐπὶ τὴν κλίνην καὶ τὸ δαιμόνιον ἐξεληλυθός LTTrA. [l] ἦλθεν διὰ Σιδῶνος he came through Sidon LTTrA. [m] εἰς unto GLTTrA. [n] + καὶ and LTTr. [o] μογγιλάλον Tr.

put his fingers into his ears, and he spit, and touched his tongue; 34 and looking up to heaven, he sighed, and saith unto him, Ephphatha, that is, Be opened. 35 And straightway his ears were opened, and the string of his tongue was loosed, and he spake plain. 36 And he charged them that they should tell no man: but the more he charged them, so much the more a great deal they published *it*; 37 and were beyond measure astonished, saying, He hath done all things well: he maketh both the deaf to hear, and the dumb to speak.

VIII. In those days the multitude being very great, and having nothing to eat, Jesus called his disciples *unto him*, and saith unto them, 2 I have compassion on the multitude, because they have now been with me three days, and have nothing to eat: 3 and if I send them away fasting to their own houses, they will faint by the way: for divers of them came from far. 4 And his disciples answered him, From whence can a man satisfy these *men* with bread here in the wilderness? 5 And he asked them, How many loaves have ye? And they said, Seven. 6 And he commanded the people to sit down on the ground: and he took the seven loaves, and gave thanks, and brake, and gave to his disciples to set before *them*; and they did set *them* before the people. 7 And they had a few small fishes: and he blessed, and commanded to set

ὄχλον κατ'.ἰδίαν, ἔβαλεν τοὺς.δακτύλους.[p]αὐτοῦ" εἰς τὰ ὦτα
crowd apart, he put his fingers to [2]ears
αὐτοῦ, καὶ πτύσας ἥψατο τῆς.γλώσσης.αὐτοῦ, 34 καὶ ἀνα-
[1]his, and having spit he touched his tongue, and having
βλέψας εἰς τὸν οὐρανὸν ἐστέναξεν, καὶ λέγει αὐτῷ, Ἐφφαθά,
looked up to the heaven he groaned, and says to him, Ephphatha,
ὅ.ἐστιν, Διανοίχθητι. 35 Καὶ [q]εὐθέως" [r]διηνοίχθησαν" αὐτοῦ
that is, Be opened. And immediately were opened his
αἱ ἀκοαί, καὶ [s] ἐλύθη ὁ δεσμὸς τῆς.γλώσσης.αὐτοῦ, καὶ ἐλάλει
ears, and was loosed the band of his tongue, and he spoke
ὀρθῶς. 36 καὶ διεστείλατο αὐτοῖς ἵνα μηδενὶ [t]εἴπωσιν·"
rightly. And he charged them that no one they should tell.
ὅσον.δὲ [v]αὐτὸς" αὐτοῖς διεστέλλετο, [w]μᾶλλον περισσότερον
But as much as he them charged, exceeding more abundantly
ἐκήρυσσον. 37 καὶ ὑπερπερισσῶς ἐξεπλήσσοντο, λέγοντες,
they proclaimed [it]: and above measure they were astonished, saying,
Καλῶς πάντα πεποίηκεν· καὶ τοὺς κωφοὺς ποιεῖ ἀκούειν,
[6]Well [4]all [5]things [1]he [2]has [3]done: both the deaf he makes to hear,
καὶ [x]τοὺς" ἀλάλους λαλεῖν.
and the dumb to speak.

8 Ἐν ἐκείναις.ταῖς.ἡμέραις [y]παμπόλλου" ὄχλου ὄντος,
In those days very great [the] crowd being,
καὶ μὴ ἐχόντων τί φάγωσιν, προσκαλεσάμενος [z]ὁ Ἰη-
and not having what they may eat, [2]having [3]called [4]to [[5]him] [1]Je-
σοῦς" τοὺς.μαθητὰς.[a]αὐτοῦ" λέγει αὐτοῖς, 2 Σπλαγχνίζομαι
sus his disciples he says to them, I am moved with compassion
ἐπὶ τὸν ὄχλον· ὅτι ἤδη [b]ἡμέρας" τρεῖς προσμένουσίν [c]μοι,"
on the crowd, because already [2]days [1]three they continue with me
καὶ οὐκ.ἔχουσιν τί φάγωσιν· 3 καὶ ἐὰν ἀπολύσω αὐτοὺς
and have not what they may eat; and if I shall send away them
[d]νήστεις" εἰς οἶκον.αὐτῶν, ἐκλυθήσονται ἐν τῇ ὁδῷ· [e]τινὲς.γὰρ"
fasting to their home, they will faint in the way; for some
αὐτῶν [f] μακρόθεν [g]ἥκασιν." 4 Καὶ ἀπεκρίθησαν αὐτῷ οἱ μαθη-
of them from afar are come. And [3]answered [4]him [2]disci-
ταὶ αὐτοῦ, [h]Πόθεν τούτους δυνήσεταί τις ὧδε χορτάσαι
ples [1]his, Whence [6]these [1]shall [3]be [4]able [2]anyone [5]here to satisfy
ἄρτων ἐπ'.ἐρημίας; 5 Καὶ [i]ἐπηρώτα" αὐτούς, Πόσους ἔχετε
with bread in a desert? And he asked them, How many [2]have [3]ye
ἄρτους; Οἱ.δὲ [k]εἶπον," Ἑπτά. 6 Καὶ [l]παρήγγειλεν" τῷ ὄχλῳ
[1]loaves? And they said, Seven. And he ordered the crowd
ἀναπεσεῖν ἐπὶ τῆς γῆς· καὶ λαβὼν τοὺς ἑπτὰ ἄρτους,
to recline on the ground. And having taken the seven loaves,
[m]εὐχαριστήσας ἔκλασεν καὶ ἐδίδου τοῖς.μαθηταῖς.αὐτοῦ, ἵνα
having given thanks he broke and gave to his disciples, that
[n]παραθῶσιν·" καὶ παρέθηκαν τῷ ὄχλῳ. 7 καὶ
they might set before [them]. And they set [it] before the crowd. And
[o]εἶχον" ἰχθύδια ὀλίγα· καὶ [pa] εὐλογήσας [qa]εἶπεν παρα-
they had small fishes a few; and having blessed he desired [3]to [4]be [5]set

---

[p] — αὐτοῦ (*read* [his] fingers) T. [q] — εὐθέως [L]TTrA. [r] ἠνοίγησαν LTTrA. [s] + εὐθὺς immediately T. [t] λέγωσιν TTrA. [v] — αὐτὸς (*read* he charged) LTTrAW. [w] + αὐτοὶ they LTTrA. [x] — τοὺς TTrA. [y] πάλιν πολλοῦ again great LTTrA. [z] — ὁ Ἰησοῦς GLTTrAW. [a] — αὐτοῦ (*read* the disciples) TTr. [b] ἡμέραι GLTTrAW. [c] — μοι L[Tr]A. [d] νῆστις T. [e] καί τινες and some LTTrA. [f] + ἀπὸ from (afar) TTrA. [g] ἥκουσι EW; εἰσίν are A. [h] + ὅτι TTrA. [i] ἠρώτα TTrA. [k] εἶπαν TTrA. [l] παραγγέλλει he orders LTTrA. [m] + [καὶ] and L. [n] παρατιθῶσιν TTrA. [o] εἶχαν LTTrA. [pa] + ταῦτα these L [qa] εἶπεν παρατεθῆναι καὶ αὐτὰ L; αὐτὰ εἶπεν καὶ ταῦτα παρατιθέναι Tr; αὐτὰ παρέθηκεν he set these before [them] TA.

θεῖναι καὶ αὐτά.ǁ 8 ʳἔφαγον.δὲǁ καὶ ἐχορτάσθησαν. καὶ
ᵉbefore [⁷them] ²also ¹these. And they ate and were satisfied. And

ἦραν περισσεύματα κλασμάτων ἑπτὰ ˢσπυρίδας.ǁ 9 ἦσαν.δὲ
they took up ³over ⁴and ⁵above ¹of ²fragments seven baskets. And ⁵were

ᵗοἱ φαγόντεςǁ ὡς τετρακισχίλιοι· καὶ ἀπέλυσεν αὐτούς.
¹those ²who ³had ⁴eaten about four thousand; and he sent ²away ¹them.

10 Καὶ ᵛεὐθέωςǁ ἐμβὰςʷ εἰς τὸ πλοῖον μετὰ τῶν μαθητῶν
And immediately having entered into the ship with ²disciples

αὐτοῦ, ἦλθεν εἰς τὰ μέρη Δαλμανουθά. 11 καὶ ἐξῆλθον οἱ
¹his, he came into the parts of Dalmanutha. And ³went ⁴out ¹the

Φαρισαῖοι καὶ ἤρξαντο ˣσυζητεῖνǁ αὐτῷ, ζητοῦντες παρ᾽
²Pharisees and began to dispute with him, seeking from

αὐτοῦ σημεῖον ἀπὸ τοῦ οὐρανοῦ, πειράζοντες αὐτόν. 12 καὶ
him a sign from the heaven, tempting him. And

ἀναστενάξας τῷ.πνεύματι.αὐτοῦ λέγει, Τί ἡ.γενεὰ.αὕτη
having groaned in his spirit he says, Why ²this ³generation

ʸσημεῖον ἐπιζητεῖ;ǁ ἀμὴν λέγω ᶻὑμῖν,ǁ εἰ.δοθήσεται τῇ
⁴a ⁵sign ¹seeks? Verily I say to you, If there shall be given

γενεᾷ.ταύτῃ σημεῖον. 13 Καὶ ἀφεὶς αὐτούς, ᵃἐμβὰς
to this generation a sign. And having left them, having entered

πάλινǁ ᵇεἰς τὸ πλοῖονǁ ἀπῆλθεν εἰς τὸ πέραν.
again into the ship he went away to the other side.

14 Καὶ ἐπελάθοντο λαβεῖν ἄρτους, καὶ εἰ.μὴ ἕνα ἄρτον
And they forgot to take loaves, and except one loaf

οὐκ.εἶχον μεθ᾽ ἑαυτῶν ἐν τῷ πλοίῳ. 15 καὶ διεστέλλετο
they had not [any] with them in the ship. And he charged

αὐτοῖς, λέγων, Ὁρᾶτε, ᶜβλέπετε ἀπὸ τῆς ζύμης τῶν Φαρισαίων
them, saying, See, take heed of the leaven of the Pharisees

καὶ τῆς ζύμης Ἡρώδου. 16 Καὶ διελογίζοντο πρὸς ἀλλήλους,
and of the leaven of Herod. And they reasoned with one another,

ᵈλέγοντες,ǁ Ὅτι ἄρτους οὐκ ᵉἔχομεν.ǁ 17 Καὶ γνοὺς
saying, Because loaves ³not ¹we ²have. And knowing [it]

ᶠὁ Ἰησοῦςǁ λέγει αὐτοῖς, Τί διαλογίζεσθε ὅτι ἄρτους οὐκ
Jesus says to them, Why reason ye because loaves ³not

ἔχετε; οὔπω.νοεῖτε οὐδὲ.συνίετε; ᵍἔτιǁ πεπωρωμένην
¹ye ²have? Do ye not yet perceive nor understand? Yet hardened

ἔχετε τὴν.καρδίαν.ὑμῶν; 18 ὀφθαλμοὺς ἔχοντες οὐ.βλέπετε;
have ye your heart? Eyes having, do ye not see?

καὶ ὦτα ἔχοντες οὐκ.ἀκούετε; καὶ οὐ.μνημονεύετε; 19 ὅτε
and ears having, do ye not hear? and do ye not remember? When

τοὺς πέντε ἄρτους ἔκλασα εἰς τοὺς πεντακισχιλίους, ʰ πόσους
the five loaves I broke to the five thousand, how many

κοφίνους ⁱπλήρεις κλασμάτωνǁ ἤρατε; Λέγουσιν αὐτῷ,
hand-baskets full of fragments took ye up? They say to him,

Δώδεκα. 20 Ὅτε.ᵏδὲǁ τοὺς ἑπτὰ ˡ εἰς τοὺς τετρακισχιλίους,
Twelve. And when the seven to the four thousand,

πόσων σπυρίδων πληρώματα κλασμάτων ἤρατε; ᵐΟἱ.δὲ
of how many baskets [the] fillings of fragments took ye up? And they

εἶπον,ǁ Ἑπτά. 21 Καὶ ἔλεγεν αὐτοῖς, ⁿΠῶςǁ ᵒοὐǁ συνίετε;
said, Seven. And he said to them, How ³not ¹do ²ye understand?

them also before *them*.
8 So they did eat, and were filled: and they took up of the broken *meat* that was left seven baskets. 9 And they that had eaten were about four thousand: and he sent them away.

10 And straightway he entered into a ship with his disciples, and came into the parts of Dalmanutha. 11 And the Pharisees came forth, and began to question with him, seeking of him a sign from heaven, tempting him. 12 And he sighed deeply in his spirit, and saith, Why doth this generation seek after a sign? verily I say unto you, There shall no sign be given unto this generation. 13 And he left them, and entering into the ship again departed to the other side.

14 Now *the disciples* had forgotten to take bread, neither had they in the ship with them more than one loaf. 15 And he charged them, saying, Take heed, beware of the leaven of the Pharisees, and *of* the leaven of Herod. 16 And they reasoned among themselves, saying, *It is* because we have no bread. 17 And when Jesus knew *it*, he saith unto them, Why reason ye, because ye have no bread? perceive ye not yet, neither understand? have ye your heart yet hardened? 18 Having eyes, see ye not? and having ears, hear ye not? and do ye not remember? 19 When I brake the five loaves among five thousand, how many baskets full of fragments took ye up? They say unto him, Twelve. 20 And when the seven among four thousand, how many baskets full of fragments took ye up? And they said, Seven. 21 And he said unto them, How is it that ye do not understand?

ʳ καὶ ἔφαγον LTTr. ˢ σφυρίδας L. ᵗ — οἱ φαγόντες (*read* and they were) T[Tr]A. ᵛ εὐθὺς LTTrA. ʷ + [αὐτὸς] he L. ˣ συνζητεῖν LTTrA. ʸ ζητεῖ σημεῖον LTTrA. ᶻ [ὑμῖν] A. ᵃ πάλιν ἐμβὰς LTTrA. ᵇ — τὸ LTrW; [εἰς πλοῖον] Tr; — εἰς τὸ πλοῖον (*read* ἐμβὰς having embarked) TA. ᶜ + [καὶ] and L. ᵈ — λέγοντες LTTrA. ᵉ ἔχουσιν they have LTrA. ᶠ — ὁ Ἰησοῦς (*read* he says) T[Tr]A. ᵍ — ἔτι LTTrA. ʰ + καὶ T. ⁱ κλασμάτων πλήρεις LTTrAW. ᵏ [δὲ] TrA; καὶ T. ˡ + [ἄρτους] loaves L. ᵐ καὶ λέγουσιν T; καὶ λέγουσιν αὐτῷ and they say to him A. ⁿ — Πῶς TA. ᵒ οὔπω not yet LTTrA.

22 Καὶ [p]ἔρχεται" εἰς Βηθσαϊδάν· καὶ φέρουσιν αὐτῷ τυφλόν,
And he comes to Bethsaida; and they bring to him a blind

καὶ παρακαλοῦσιν αὐτὸν ἵνα αὐτοῦ ἅψηται. 23 καὶ
[man], and beseech him that him he might touch. And

ἐπιλαβόμενος τῆς χειρὸς τοῦ τυφλοῦ [q]ἐξήγαγεν" αὐτὸν
taking hold of the hand of the blind [man] he led forth him

ἔξω τῆς κώμης, καὶ πτύσας εἰς τὰ.ὄμματα.αὐτοῦ, ἐπιθεὶς
out of the village, and having spit upon his eyes, having laid

τὰς χεῖρας αὐτῷ ἐπηρώτα αὐτὸν εἴ τι [r]βλέπει." 24 καὶ
[his] hands upon him he asked him if anything he beholds. And

ἀναβλέψας ἔλεγεν, Βλέπω τοὺς ἀνθρώπους, [s]ὅτι ὡς δένδρα
having looked up he said, I behold the men, for as trees

ὁρῶ" περιπατοῦντας. 25 Εἶτα πάλιν [t]ἐπέθηκεν" τὰς
I see [them] walking. Then again he laid [his]

χεῖρας ἐπὶ τοὺς.ὀφθαλμοὺς.αὐτοῦ, καὶ [v]ἐποίησεν αὐτὸν ἀνα-
hands upon his eyes, and made him look

βλέψαι." καὶ [w]ἀποκατεστάθη," καὶ [x]ἐνέβλεψεν" [y]τηλαυγῶς"
up. And he was restored, and [2]looked [3]on [1]clearly

[z]ἅπαντας." 26 καὶ ἀπέστειλεν αὐτὸν εἰς [a]τὸν." οἶκον.αὐτοῦ,
all [men]. And he sent him to his house,

λέγων, [b]Μηδὲ" εἰς τὴν κώμην εἰσέλθῃς, [c]μηδὲ εἴπῃς
saying, Neither into the village mayest thou enter, nor mayest tell [it]

τινὶ ἐν τῇ κώμῃ."
to any one in the village.

27 Καὶ ἐξῆλθεν ὁ Ἰησοῦς καὶ οἱ.μαθηταὶ.αὐτοῦ εἰς τὰς κώ-
And [2]went [3]forth [1]Jesus and his disciples into the vil-

μας Καισαρείας τῆς Φιλίππου· καὶ ἐν τῇ ὁδῷ ἐπηρώτα
lages of Cæsarea Philippi. And by the way he was questioning

τοὺς.μαθητὰς.αὐτοῦ, λέγων [d]αὐτοῖς," Τίνα με λέγουσιν οἱ
his disciples, saying to them, Whom [4]me [1]do [3]pronounce

ἄνθρωποι εἶναι; 28 Οἱ.δὲ [e]ἀπεκρίθησαν" [f], [g]Ἰωάννην τὸν βαπ-
[2]men to be? And they answered, John the Bap-

τιστήν· καὶ ἄλλοι [h]Ἠλίαν·" ἄλλοι.δὲ [i]ἕνα" τῶν.προφητῶν.
tist; and others, Elias; but others, one of the prophets.

29 Καὶ αὐτὸς [k]λέγει αὐτοῖς," Ὑμεῖς.δὲ τίνα με λέγετε
And he says to them, But ye, whom [4]me [1]do [2]ye [3]pronounce

εἶναι; [l]Ἀποκριθεὶς [m]δὲ" ὁ Πέτρος λέγει αὐτῷ, Σὺ.εἶ ὁ χριστός.
to be? [2]Answering [1]and Peter says to him, Thou art the Christ.

30 Καὶ ἐπετίμησεν αὐτοῖς ἵνα μηδενὶ [n]λέγωσιν" περὶ
And he strictly charged them that no one they should tell concerning

αὐτοῦ. 31 Καὶ ἤρξατο διδάσκειν αὐτοὺς ὅτι δεῖ τὸν
him. And he began to teach them that it is necessary for the

υἱὸν τοῦ ἀνθρώπου πολλὰ παθεῖν, καὶ ἀποδοκιμασθῆναι
Son of man many things to suffer, and to be rejected

[o]ἀπὸ" τῶν πρεσβυτέρων καὶ [pa]ἀρχιερέων καὶ [pa]γραμματέων, καὶ
of the elders and chief priests and scribes, and

ἀποκτανθῆναι, καὶ μετὰ τρεῖς ἡμέρας ἀναστῆναι· 32 καὶ
to be killed, and after three days to rise [again]. And

παῤῥησίᾳ τὸν λόγον ἐλάλει. Καὶ προσλαβόμενος [qa]αὐτὸν
openly the word he spoke. And [2]having [3]taken [5]to [[6]him] [4]him

22 And he cometh to Bethsaida; and they bring a blind man unto him, and besought him to touch him. 23 And he took the blind man by the hand, and led him out of the town; and when he had spit on his eyes, and put his hands upon him, he asked him if he saw ought. 24 And he looked up, and said, I see men as trees, walking. 25 After that he put *his* hands again upon his eyes, and made him look up: and he was restored, and saw every man clearly. 26 And he sent him away to his house, saying, Neither go into the town, nor tell *it* to any in the town.

27 And Jesus went out, and his disciples, into the towns of Cæsarea Philippi: and by the way he asked his disciples, saying unto them, Whom do men say that I am? 28 And they answered, John the Baptist: but some *say*, Elias; and others, One of the prophets. 29 And he saith unto them, But whom say ye that I am? And Peter answereth and saith unto him, Thou art the Christ. 30 And he charged them that they should tell no man of him. 31 And he began to teach them, that the Son of man must suffer many things, and be rejected of the elders, and *of* the chief priests, and scribes, and be killed, and after three days rise again. 32 And he spake that saying openly. And Peter took him, and began

---

[p] ἔρχονται they come LTTrA. [q] ἐξήνεγκεν he brought forth TTrA. [r] βλέπεις thou beholdest A. [s] ὡς δένδρα G. [t] ἔθηκεν TrA. [v] διέβλεψεν he saw distinctly TTrA. [w] ἀπεκατεστάθη L; ἀπεκατέστη TTrA. [x] ἐνέβλεπεν LTTrA. [y] δηλαυγῶς T. [z] ἅπαντα all things LTTrAW. [a] — τὸν GLTTrAW. [b] μὴ not T. [c] — μηδὲ .... κώμῃ T. [d] [αὐτοῖς] Tr. [e] εἶπαν spake TA. [f] + αὐτῷ λέγοντες to him saying LTTrA. [g] + ὅτι TA. [h] Ἠλείαν T. [i] ὅτι εἷς LTTrA. [k] ἐπηρώτα αὐτούς asked them LTTrA. [l] + καὶ and L. [m] — δὲ LTTrA. [n] εἴπωσιν L. [o] ὑπὸ by LTTrAW. [pa] + τῶν of the GLTTrAW. [qa] ὁ Πέτρος αὐτὸν LTTrA.

ὁ Πέτρος" ἤρξατο ἐπιτιμᾷν αὐτῷ. 33 ὁ.δὲ ἐπιστραφεὶς καὶ
[2]Peter began to rebuke him. But he, turning and
ἰδὼν τοὺς.μαθητὰς.αὐτοῦ, ἐπετίμησεν [r]τῷ" Πέτρῳ, [s]λεγων,"
seeing his disciples, rebuked Peter, saying,
Ὕπαγε ὀπίσω μου, σατανᾶ· ὅτι οὐ.φρονεῖς τὰ
Get behind me, Satan, for thy thoughts are not of the things
τοῦ θεοῦ, ἀλλὰ τὰ τῶν ἀνθρώπων.
of God, but the things of men.

34 Καὶ προσκαλεσάμενος τὸν ὄχλον σὺν τοῖς μαθηταῖς
And having called to [him] the crowd with [2]disciples
αὐτοῦ εἶπεν αὐτοῖς, [t]Ὅστις" θέλει ὀπίσω μου [v]ἐλθεῖν," ἀπαρ-
[1]his he said to them, Whosoever desires after me to come, let
νησάσθω ἑαυτόν, καὶ ἀράτω τὸν.σταυρὸν.αὐτοῦ, καὶ
him deny himself, and let him take up his cross, and
ἀκολουθείτω μοι. 35 ὃς.γὰρ.[w]ἂν" θέλῃ τὴν.ψυχὴν.αὐτοῦ
let him follow me. For whoever may desire his life
σῶσαι, ἀπολέσει αὐτήν· ὃς.δ'.ἂν [x]ἀπολέσῃ" τὴν.[y]ψυχὴν.αὐτοῦ"
to save, shall lose it, but whoever may lose his life
ἕνεκεν ἐμοῦ καὶ τοῦ εὐαγγελίου, [z]οὗτος" σώσει αὐτήν.
on account of me and of the glad tidings, he shall save it.
36 τί.γὰρ [a]ὠφελήσει" [b]ἄνθρωπον [c]ἐὰν κερδήσῃ" τὸν κόσμον
For what shall it profit a man if he gain the [2]world
ὅλον καὶ [d]ζημιωθῇ" τὴν.ψυχὴν.αὐτοῦ; 37 [e]ἢ τί δώσει
[1]whole and lose his soul? or what shall [3]give
ἄνθρωπος" ἀντάλλαγμα τῆς.ψυχῆς.αὐτοῦ; 38 ὃς.γὰρ.[f]ἂν"
[1]a [2]man [as] an exchange for his soul? For whoever
ἐπαισχυνθῇ με καὶ τοὺς ἐμοὺς λόγους ἐν τῇ.γενεᾷ.ταύτῃ
may have been ashamed of me and my words in this generation
τῇ μοιχαλίδι καὶ ἁμαρτωλῷ, καὶ ὁ υἱὸς τοῦ ἀνθρώπου ἐπαισ-
the adulterous and sinful, also the Son of man will be
χυνθήσεται αὐτόν, ὅταν ἔλθῃ ἐν τῇ δόξῃ τοῦ.πατρὸς.αὐτοῦ
ashamed of him when he shall come in the glory of his Father
μετὰ τῶν ἀγγέλων τῶν ἁγίων. 9 Καὶ ἔλεγεν αὐτοῖς, Ἀμὴν
with the angels the holy. And he said to them, Verily
λέγω ὑμῖν, ὅτι εἰσίν τινες [g]τῶν ὧδε" ἑστηκότων, οἵτινες
I say to you, That there are some of those here standing, who
οὐ.μὴ γεύσωνται θανάτου ἕως.ἂν ἴδωσιν τὴν βασιλείαν τοῦ
in no wise shall taste of death until they see the kingdom
θεοῦ ἐληλυθυῖαν ἐν δυνάμει.
of God having come in power.

2 Καὶ [h]μεθ'" ἡμέρας ἓξ παραλαμβάνει ὁ Ἰησοῦς τὸν
And after [2]days [1]six [4]takes [5]with [[6]him] [3]Jesus
Πέτρον καὶ [i]τὸν" Ἰάκωβον καὶ [k]τὸν" Ἰωάννην, καὶ ἀναφέρει
Peter and James and John, and brings up
αὐτοὺς εἰς ὄρος ὑψηλὸν κατ'.ἰδίαν μόνους· καὶ μετεμορ-
them into a [2]mountain [1]high apart alone. And he was trans-
φώθη ἔμπροσθεν αὐτῶν, 3 καὶ τὰ.ἱμάτια.αὐτοῦ [l]ἐγένετο"
figured before them; and his garments became
στίλβοντα, λευκὰ λίαν [m]ὡς χιών," οἷα γναφεὺς ἐπὶ τῆς
shining, white exceedingly as snow, such as a fuller on the

to rebuke him. 33 But when he had turned about and looked on his disciples, he rebuked Peter, saying, Get thee behind me, Satan: for thou savourest not the things that be of God, but the things that be of men.

34 And when he had called the people *unto him* with his disciples also, he said unto them, Whosoever will come after me, let him deny himself, and take up his cross, and follow me. 35 For whosoever will save his life shall lose it; but whosoever shall lose his life for my sake and the gospel's, the same shall save it. 36 For what shall it profit a man, if he shall gain the whole world, and lose his own soul? 37 Or what shall a man give in exchange for his soul? 38 Whosoever therefore shall be ashamed of me and of my words in this adulterous and sinful generation; of him also shall the Son of man be ashamed, when he cometh in the glory of his Father with the holy angels. IX. And he said unto them, Verily I say unto you, That there be some of them that stand here, which shall not taste of death, till they have seen the kingdom of God come with power.

2 And after six days Jesus taketh *with him* Peter, and James, and John, and leadeth them up into an high mountain apart by themselves: and he was transfigured before them. 3 And his raiment became shining, exceeding white as snow; so as no fuller on earth can white

---

[r] — τῷ LTTrA. [s] καὶ λέγει and says TTrA. [t] Εἴ τις If any one LTr. [v] ἀκολουθεῖν to follow GTTrAW. [w] ἐὰν TTrA. [x] ἀπολέσει shall lose TTrA. [y] ἑαυτοῦ ψυχὴν GTrW. [z] — οὗτος GLTTrAW. [a] ὠφελεῖ does it profit TA. [b] + τὸν the (man) LTr[A]W. [c] κερδῆσαι to gain TA. [d] ζημιωθῆναι to lose TA. [e] τί γὰρ δοῖ ἄνθρωπος (read for what, &c) TTr; τί γὰρ [δώσει ἄνθρωπος] A. [f] ἐὰν LTTrA. [g] ὧδε τῶν TTrA. [h] μετὰ LTTrA. [i] — τὸν W. [k] — τὸν GLTrA. [l] ἐγένοντο LTrAW. [m] — ὡς χιών TTrA.

them. 4 And there
appeared unto them
Elias with Moses: and
they were talking with
Jesus. 5 And Peter
answered and said to
Jesus, Master, it is
good for us to be here:
and let us make three
tabernacles; one for
thee, and one for Mo-
ses, and one for Elias.
6 For he wist not what
to say; for they were
sore afraid. 7 And
there was a cloud that
overshadowed them:
and a voice came out
of the cloud, saying,
This is my beloved
Son: hear him. 8 And
suddenly, when they
had looked round a-
bout, they saw no man
any more, save Jesus
only with themselves.
9 And as they came
down from the moun-
tain, he charged them
that they should tell
no man what things
they had seen, till the
Son of man were risen
from the dead. 10 And
they kept that saying
with themselves, ques-
tioning one with an-
other what the rising
from the dead should
mean. 11 And they
asked him, saying,
Why say the scribes
that Elias must first
come? 12 And he an-
swered and told them,
Elias verily cometh
first, and restoreth all
things; and how it is
written of the Son of
man, that he must
suffer many things,
and be set at nought.
13 But I say unto you,
That Elias is indeed
come, and they have
done unto him what-
soever they listed, as
it is written of him.

14 And when he
came to *his* disciples,
he saw a great multi-
tude about them, and
the scribes questioning
with them. 15 And
straightway all the
people, when they be-
held him, were greatly
amazed, and running

γῆς οὐ.δύναται [n]λευκᾶναι. 4 καὶ ὤφθη αὐτοῖς [o]Ἠλίας‖ σὺν
earth is not able to whiten. And [4]appeared [5]to [6]them [1]Elias [2]with
[p]Μωσεῖ,‖ καὶ ἦσαν [q]συλλαλοῦντες‖ τῷ Ἰησοῦ. 5 καὶ ἀποκριθεὶς
[3]Moses, and they were talking with Jesus. And [2]answering
ὁ.Πέτρος λέγει τῷ Ἰησοῦ, [r]Ῥαββί,‖ καλόν ἐστιν ἡμᾶς ὧδε
[1]Peter says to Jesus, Rabbi, good it is for us here
εἶναι· καὶ ποιήσωμεν [s]σκηνὰς τρεῖς,‖ σοὶ μίαν, καὶ [p]Μω-
to be; and let us make [2]tabernacles [1]three, for thee one, and for Mo-
σεῖ‖ μίαν, καὶ [t]Ἠλίᾳ‖ μίαν. 6 οὐ.γὰρ.ᾔδει τί [v]λαλήσῃ·‖
ses one, and for Elias one. For he knew not what he should say,
[w]ἦσαν.γὰρ ἔκφοβοι.‖ 7 καὶ ἐγένετο νεφέλη ἐπισκιάζουσα
for they were greatly afraid. And there came a cloud overshadowing
αὐτοῖς· καὶ [x]ἦλθεν‖ φωνὴ ἐκ τῆς νεφέλης, [y]λέγουσα,‖ Οὗτός
them; and there came a voice out of the cloud, saying, This
ἐστιν ὁ.υἱός.μου ὁ ἀγαπητός· [z]αὐτοῦ ἀκούετε.‖ 8 Καὶ ἐξάπινα
is my Son the beloved: [3]him [1]hear [2]ye. And suddenly
περιβλεψάμενοι οὐκέτι.οὐδένα εἶδον, [a]ἀλλὰ‖ τὸν Ἰησοῦν
having looked around no longer any one they saw, but Jesus
μόνον μεθ' ἑαυτῶν. 9 [b]Καταβαινόντων.δὲ‖ αὐτῶν [c]ἀπὸ‖ τοῦ
alone with themselves. And as [2]were [3]descending [1]they from the
ὄρους διεστείλατο αὐτοῖς ἵνα μηδενὶ [d]διηγήσωνται ἃ εἶ-
mountain he charged them that to no one they should relate what they
δον,‖ εἰ.μὴ ὅταν ὁ υἱὸς τοῦ ἀνθρώπου ἐκ νεκρῶν
had seen except when the Son of man from among [the] dead
ἀναστῇ. 10 καὶ τὸν λόγον ἐκράτησαν πρὸς ἑαυτούς, [e]συζη-
be risen. And that saying they kept among themselves, ques-
τοῦντες‖ τί ἐστιν τὸ ἐκ νεκρῶν ἀναστῆναι.
tioning what is the [2]from [3]among [[4]the] [5]dead [1]rising.
11 Καὶ ἐπηρώτων αὐτόν, λέγοντες, [f]Ὅτι‖ λέγουσιν [g]οἱ γραμ-
And they asked him, saying, That [3]say [1]the [2]scribes
ματεῖς ὅτι [h]Ἠλίαν‖ δεῖ ἐλθεῖν πρῶτον; 12 Ὁ.δὲ [i]ἀποκριθεὶς
that Elias must come first? And he answering
εἶπεν‖ αὐτοῖς, [k]Ἠλίας‖ [l]μὲν‖ ἐλθὼν πρῶτον, [m]ἀποκαθιστᾷ‖
said to them, Elias indeed having come first, restores
πάντα· καὶ πῶς γέγραπται ἐπὶ τὸν υἱὸν τοῦ ἀνθρώπου[na]
all things; and how it has been written of the Son of man
ἵνα πολλὰ πάθῃ καὶ [oa]ἐξουδενωθῇ.‖ 13 ἀλλὰ λέγω
that many things he should suffer and be set at nought: but I say
ὑμῖν, ὅτι καὶ [k]Ἠλίας‖ ἐλήλυθεν, καὶ ἐποίησαν αὐτῷ ὅσα
to you, that also Elias has come, and they did to him whatever
[pa]ἠθέλησαν,‖ καθὼς γέγραπται ἐπ' αὐτόν.
they desired, as it has been written of him.

14 Καὶ [qa]ἐλθὼν‖ πρὸς τοὺς μαθητὰς [ra]εἶδεν‖ ὄχλον πολὺν
And having come to the disciples he saw a [2]crowd [1]great
περὶ αὐτούς, καὶ γραμματεῖς [sa]συζητοῦντας‖ [ta]αὐτοῖς.‖ 15 καὶ
around them, and scribes discussing with them. And
[va]εὐθέως‖ πᾶς ὁ ὄχλος [wa]ἰδὼν‖ αὐτὸν [xa]ἐξεθαμβήθη,‖ καὶ
immediately all the crowd seeing him were greatly amazed, and

[n] + οὕτως thus TTrA. [o] Ἠλείας T. [p] Μωϋσεῖ LTW; Μωυσῇ TrA. [q] συνλαλοῦντες T. [r] Ῥαββεί TA. [s] τρεῖς σκηνάς LTTrA. [t] Ἠλείᾳ T. [v] ἀποκριθῇ he should answer TTrA. [w] ἔκφοβοι γὰρ ἐγένοντο for they became greatly afraid LTTrA. [x] ἐγένετο T. [y] — λέγουσα GTTrAW. [z] ἀκούετε αὐτοῦ LTTrA. [a] εἰ μὴ L. [b] καὶ καταβαινόντων LTTr. [c] ἐκ L. [d] ἃ εἶδον διηγήσωνται LTTrA. [e] συνζητοῦντες LTTrA. [f] Ὅ τι wherefore LW. [g] + οἱ Φαρισαῖοι καὶ the Pharisees and [L]T. [h] Ἠλείαν T. [i] ἔφη said TTrA. [k] Ἠλείας T. [l] — μὲν T[Tr]. [m] ἀποκαθιστάνει LTTrA. [na] ; (*read* and how has it been written, &c.) LT. [oa] ἐξουδενηθῇ (; A) LTrA; ἐξουθενωθῇ T. [pa] ἤθελον TTrA. [qa] ἐλθόντες TTr. [ra] εἶδον they saw TTr. [sa] συνζητοῦντας LTrA. [ta] πρὸς αὐτούς with them TTr. [va] εὐθὺς TTrA. [wa] ἰδόντες LTTrA. [xa] ἐξεθαμβήθησαν LTTrA.

προστρέχοντες , ἠσπάζοντο αὐτόν. 16 καὶ ἐπηρώτησεν [y]τοὺς
running to [him] saluted him. And he asked the
γραμματεῖς,‖ Τί [z]συζητεῖτε‖ πρὸς [a]αὐτούς;‖ 17 Καὶ [b]ἀπο-
scribes, What discuss ye with them? And an-
κριθεὶς‖ εἷς ἐκ τοῦ ὄχλου [c]εἶπεν,‖ Διδάσκαλε, ἤνεγκα τὸν υἱόν
swering one out of the crowd said, Teacher, I brought [2]son
μου πρός σε, ἔχοντα πνεῦμα ἄλαλον. 18 καὶ ὅπου.[d]ἂν‖ αὐτὸν
[1]my to thee, having a [2]spirit [1]dumb; and wheresoever him
καταλάβῃ ῥήσσει [e]αὐτόν·‖ καὶ ἀφρίζει, καὶ τρίζει τοὺς
it seizes it dashes [2]down [1]him; and he foams, and gnashes
ὀδόντας.[f]αὐτοῦ,‖ καὶ ξηραίνεται· καὶ [g]εἶπον‖ τοῖς μαθηταῖς
his teeth, and is withering away. And I spoke to [2]disciples
σου ἵνα αὐτὸ ἐκβάλωσιν, καὶ οὐκ.ἴσχυσαν. 19 Ὁ.δὲ ἀπο-
[1]thy that it they might cast out, and they had not power. But he an-
κριθεὶς [h]αὐτῷ‖ λέγει, Ὦ γενεὰ ἄπιστος, ἕως πότε πρὸς ὑμᾶς
swering him says, O [2]generation [1]unbelieving! until when with you
ἔσομαι; ἕως πότε ἀνέξομαι ὑμῶν; φέρετε αὐτὸν πρός με.
shall I be? until when shall I bear with you? Bring him to me.
20 Καὶ ἤνεγκαν αὐτὸν πρὸς αὐτόν· καὶ ἰδὼν αὐτὸν [i]εὐθέως
And they brought him to him. And seeing him immediately
τὸ πνεῦμα‖ [k]ἐσπάραξεν‖ αὐτόν, καὶ πεσὼν ἐπὶ τῆς
the spirit threw [2]into [3]convulsions [1]him, and having fallen upon the
γῆς ἐκυλίετο ἀφρίζων. 21 Καὶ ἐπηρώτησεν τὸν.πατέρα.αὐτοῦ,
earth he rolled foaming. And he asked his father,
Πόσος χρόνος ἐστὶν ὡς τοῦτο γέγονεν αὐτῷ; Ὁ.δὲ εἶπεν,
How long a time is it that this has been with him? And he said,
[l]Παιδιόθεν. 22 καὶ πολλάκις [m]αὐτὸν καὶ εἰς πῦρ‖ ἔβαλεν καὶ
From childhood. And often him both into fire it cast and
εἰς ὕδατα, ἵνα ἀπολέσῃ αὐτόν· [n]ἀλλ'‖ εἴ τι [o]δύνασαι,‖
into waters, that it might destroy him: but if anything thou art able
βοήθησον ἡμῖν, σπλαγχνισθεὶς ἐφ' ἡμᾶς. 23 Ὁ.δὲ.Ἰη-
[to do], help us, being moved with pity on us. And Je-
σοῦς εἶπεν αὐτῷ, Τὸ εἰ [o]δύνασαι‖ [p]πιστεῦσαι,‖ πάντα δυνατὰ
sus said to him, If thou art able to believe, all things are possible
τῷ πιστεύοντι. 24 [q]Καὶ‖ [r]εὐθέως‖ κράξας ὁ πατὴρ τοῦ
to him that believes. And immediately crying out the father of the
παιδίου [s]μετὰ δακρύων‖ ἔλεγεν, Πιστεύω, [t]Κύριε,‖ βοήθει
little child with tears said, I believe, Lord, help
μου.τῇ.ἀπιστίᾳ. 25 Ἰδὼν.δὲ ὁ Ἰησοῦς ὅτι ἐπισυντρέχει [v]
mine unbelief. But [2]seeing [1]Jesus that [3]was [4]running [5]together
ὄχλος, ἐπετίμησεν τῷ πνεύματι τῷ ἀκαθάρτῳ, λέγων αὐτῷ,
[1]a [2]crowd, rebuked the spirit the unclean, saying to it,
Τὸ [w]πνεῦμα τὸ ἄλαλον καὶ κωφόν,‖ ἐγὼ [x]σοι ἐπιτάσσω,‖ ἔξελθε
Spirit dumb and deaf, I thee command, come
[ya]ἐξ‖ αὐτοῦ, καὶ μηκέτι εἰσέλθῃς εἰς αὐτόν. 26 Καὶ [za]κρά-
out of him, and no more mayest thou enter into him. And having
ξαν,‖ καὶ πολλὰ [aa]σπαράξαν‖ [ba]αὐτόν,‖ ἐξῆλθεν· καὶ
cried out, and [3]much [1]thrown [4]into [5]convulsions , [2]him, it came out; and
ἐγένετο ὡσεὶ νεκρός, ὥστε [ca]πολλοὺς λέγειν ὅτι ἀπέθανεν.
he became as if dead, so that many said that he was dead.

to *him* saluted him.
16 And he asked the
scribes, What question
ye with them? 17 And
one of the multitude
answered and said,
Master, I have brought
unto thee my son,
which hath a dumb
spirit; 18 and where-
soever he taketh him,
he teareth him: and
he foameth, and gnash-
eth with his teeth, and
pineth away: and I
spake to thy disciples
that they should cast
him out; and they
could not. 19 He an-
swereth him, and saith,
O faithless generation,
how long shall I be
with you? how long
shall I suffer you?
bring him unto me.
20 And they brought
him unto him: and
when he saw him,
straightway the spirit
tare him; and he fell
on the ground, and
wallowed foaming.
21 And he asked his
father, How long is it
ago since this came
unto him? And he
said, Of a child. 22 And
ofttimes it hath cast
him into the fire, and
into the waters, to
destroy him: but if
thou canst do any
thing, have compas-
sion on us, and help
us. 23 Jesus said unto
him, If thou canst be-
lieve, all things *are*
possible to him that
believeth. 24 And
straightway the father
of the child cried out,
and said with tears,
Lord, I believe; help
thou mine unbelief.
25 When Jesus saw
that the people came
running together, he
rebuked the foul
spirit, saying unto
him, *Thou* dumb and
deaf spirit, I charge
thee, come out of him,
and enter no more
into him. 26 And *the*
spirit cried, and rent
him sore, and came
out of him: and he
was as one dead; in-
somuch that many
said, He is dead.

[y] αὐτούς them GLTTrA. [z] συνζητεῖτε LTTrA. [a] αὐτούς E. [b] ἀπεκρίθη αὐτῷ answered him LTTrA. [c] — εἶπεν LTTrA. [d] ἐὰν LTTrA. [e] — αὐτόν (*read* [him]) T. [f] — αὐτοῦ (*read* [his] teeth) [L]TTrA. [g] εἶπα TTrA. [h] αὐτοῖς them GLTTrAW. [i] τὸ πνεῦμα εὐθὺς LTTrA. [k] συνεσπάραξεν LT. [l] + ἐκ since LTTrAW. [m] καὶ εἰς πῦρ αὐτὸν TA. [n] ἀλλὰ T. [o] δύνῃ LTTrA. [p] — πιστεῦσαι TTr[A]. [q] — καὶ [L]T[Tr]A. [r] εὐθὺς TTrA. [s] — μετὰ δακρύων LTTrA. [t] — Κύριε GLTTrAW. [v] + ὁ the (crowd) T. [w] ἄλαλον καὶ κωφὸν πνεῦμα LTTrA. [x] ἐπιτάσσω σοι TTrA. [ya] ἀπ' from L. [za] κράξας GLTTrAW. [aa] σπαράξας GLTTrAW. [ba] — αὐτόν G[L]TTrA. [ca] + τοὺς the LTTrA.

27 But Jesus took him by the hand, and lifted him up; and he arose.

28 And when he was come into the house, his disciples asked him privately, Why could not we cast him out? 29 And he said unto them, This kind can come forth by nothing, but by prayer and fasting.

30 And they departed thence, and passed through Galilee; and he would not that any man should know *it*. 31 For he taught his disciples, and said unto them, The Son of man is delivered into the hands of men, and they shall kill him; and after that he is killed, he shall rise the third day. 32 But they understood not that saying, and were afraid to ask him.

33 And he came to Capernaum: and being in the house he asked them, What was it that ye disputed among yourselves by the way? 34 But they held their peace: for by the way they had disputed among themselves, who *should be* the greatest. 35 And he sat down, and called the twelve, and saith unto them, If any man desire to be first, *the same* shall be last of all, and servant of all. 36 And he took a child, and set him in the midst of them: and when he had taken him in his arms, he said unto them, 37 Whosoever shall receive one of such children in my name, receiveth me: and whosoever shall receive me, receiveth not me, but him that sent me. 38 And John answered him, saying, Master, we saw one casting out devils in thy name, and he followeth not us: and

27 ὁ.δὲ.Ἰησοῦς κρατήσας [d]αὐτὸν τῆς χειρός" ἤγειρεν αὐτόν,
But Jesus, having taken him by the hand, raised [2]up [1]him,
καὶ ἀνέστη.
and he arose.

28 Καὶ [e]εἰσελθόντα.αὐτὸν" εἰς οἶκον οἱ.μαθηταὶ.αὐτοῦ
And when he was entered into a house his disciples
[f]ἐπηρώτων αὐτὸν κατ'.ἰδίαν," [g]"Ὅτι" ἡμεῖς οὐκ.ἠδυνή-
asked him apart, Because [of what] [2]we [1]were not
θημεν ἐκβαλεῖν αὐτό; 29 Καὶ εἶπεν αὐτοῖς, Τοῦτο τὸ γένος
able to cast out it? And he said to them, This kind
ἐν οὐδενὶ δύναται ἐξελθεῖν εἰ.μὴ ἐν προσευχῇ [h]καὶ νηστείᾳ."
by nothing can go out except by prayer and fasting.

30 [i]Καὶ ἐκεῖθεν" ἐξελθόντες [k]παρεπορεύοντο" διὰ τῆς
And from thence having gone forth they went through
Γαλιλαίας· καὶ οὐκ.ἤθελεν ἵνα τις [l]γνῷ·" 31 ἐδίδασ-
Galilee; and he would not that anyone should know [it]; [2]he [3]was [4]teach-
κεν γὰρ τοὺς.μαθητὰς.αὐτοῦ, καὶ ἔλεγεν αὐτοῖς, "Ὅτι ὁ υἱὸς
ing [1]for his disciples, and said to them, The Son
τοῦ ἀνθρώπου παραδίδοται εἰς χεῖρας ἀνθρώπων, καὶ
of man is delivered into [the] hands of men, and
ἀποκτενοῦσιν αὐτόν· καὶ ἀποκτανθείς, [m]τῇ τρίτῃ ἡμέρᾳ"
they will kill him; and having been killed, on the third day
ἀναστήσεται. 32 Οἱ.δὲ ἠγνόουν τὸ ῥῆμα, καὶ ἐφοβοῦντο
he will arise. But they understood not the saying, and were afraid
αὐτὸν ἐπερωτῆσαι.
[3]him [1]to [2]ask.

33 Καὶ [n]ἦλθεν" εἰς [o]Καπερναούμ·" καὶ ἐν τῇ οἰκίᾳ γενόμενος
And he came to Capernaum; and [2]in [3]the [4]house [1]being
ἐπηρώτα αὐτούς, Τί ἐν τῇ ὁδῷ [p]πρὸς ἑαυτοὺς" διελογίζεσθε;
he asked them, What in the way among yourselves were ye discussing?
34 Οἱ.δὲ ἐσιώπων· πρὸς ἀλλήλους γὰρ διελέχθησαν [q]ἐν
But they were silent; [2]with [3]one [4]another [1]for they had been discussing by
τῇ ὁδῷ," τίς μείζων. 35 καὶ καθίσας ἐφώνησεν τοὺς
the way, who [was] greater. And sitting down he called the
δώδεκα, καὶ λέγει αὐτοῖς, Εἴ τις θέλει πρῶτος εἶναι, ἔσται
twelve, and he says to them, If anyone desires [3]first [1]to [2]be, he shall be
πάντων ἔσχατος καὶ πάντων διάκονος. 36 Καὶ λαβὼν
[2]of [3]all [1]last and [2]of [3]all [1]servant. And having taken
παιδίον ἔστησεν αὐτὸ ἐν μέσῳ.αὐτῶν· καὶ ἐναγκαλισάμενος
a little child he set it in their midst; and having taken [2]in [3his] [4]arms
αὐτὸ εἶπεν αὐτοῖς, 37 "Ὃς ἐὰν" ἓν τῶν [s]τοιούτων παιδίων"
[1]it he said to them, Whoever one of such little children
δέξηται ἐπὶ τῷ.ὀνόματί.μου, ἐμὲ δέχεται· καὶ ὃς [r]ἐὰν" ἐμὲ
shall receive in my name, me receives; and whoever me
[t]δέξηται," οὐκ ἐμὲ δέχεται, ἀλλὰ τὸν ἀποστείλαντά με.
shall receive, not me receives, but him who sent me.
38 [u]Ἀπεκρίθη.δὲ" αὐτῷ [v]ὁ" Ἰωάννης [w]λέγων," Διδάσκαλε, εἴδομέν
And [2]answered [3]him [1]John saying, Teacher, we saw
τινα [x]τῷ.ὀνόματί.σου ἐκβάλλοντα δαιμόνια, [y]ὃς οὐκ.ἀκολουθεῖ
some one in thy name casting out demons, who follows not

---

[d] τῆς χειρὸς αὐτοῦ his hand LTTr. [e] εἰσελθόντος αὐτοῦ LTTr. [f] κατ' ἰδίαν ἐπηρώτων αὐτόν LTTrA. [g] Ὅ τι wherefore LW. [h] — καὶ νηστείᾳ T[A]. [i] Κἀκεῖθεν LTTrA. [k] ἐπορεύοντο LTr. [l] γνοῖ LTTrA. [m] μετὰ τρεῖς ἡμέρας after three days LTTrA. [n] ἦλθον they came LTTrA. [o] Καφαρναούμ LTTrAW. [p] — πρὸς ἑαυτοὺς LTTrA. [q] [ἐν τῇ ὁδῷ] L. [r] ἂν LTTrA. [s] παιδίων τούτων of these little children T. [t] δέχηται should receive TTrA. [u] ἀπεκρίθη [δὲ] L; ἔφη spoke (to him) TTrA. [v] — ὁ GLW. [w] — λέγων T. [x] + ἐν ELTTrAW. [y] — ὃς οὐκ ἀκολουθεῖ ἡμῖν G.

ἡμῖν·‖ καὶ [z]ἐκωλύσαμεν‖ αὐτόν, [a]ὅτι οὐκ.ἀκολουθεῖ ἡμῖν.‖
us, and we forbade him, because he follows not us.
39 Ὁ.δὲ.Ἰησοῦς εἶπεν, Μὴ.κωλύετε αὐτόν· οὐδεὶς.γάρ ἐστιν
But Jesus said, Forbid not him; for no one there is
ὃς ποιήσει δύναμιν ἐπὶ τῷ.ὀνόματί.μου, καὶ δυνήσεται
who shall do a work of power in my name, and be able
ταχὺ κακολογῆσαί με. 40 ὃς.γὰρ οὐκ.ἔστιν καθ' [b]ὑμῶν,‖ ὑπὲρ
readily to speak evil of me; for he who is not against you, for
[b]ὑμῶν‖ ἐστιν. 41 ὃς.γὰρ.ἂν ποτίσῃ ὑμᾶς ποτήριον
you is. For whoever may give [2]to [3]drink [1]you a cup
ὕδατος ἐν [c]τῷ‖.ὀνόματί.[d]μου,‖ ὅτι χριστοῦ ἐστε, ἀμὴν λέγω
of water in my name, because Christ's [1]ye [2]are, verily I say
ὑμῖν, [e]οὐ.μὴ [f]ἀπολέσῃ‖ τὸν.μισθὸν.αὐτοῦ. 42 Καὶ ὃς.ἂν
to you, in no wise should he lose his reward. And whoever
σκανδαλίσῃ ἕνα τῶν μικρῶν [g]τῶν [h]πιστευόντων εἰς
may cause [6]to [7]offend [1]one [2]of [3]the [4]little [5]ones who believe in
ἐμέ,‖ καλόν ἐστιν αὐτῷ μᾶλλον εἰ περίκειται [i]λίθος.μυλικὸς‖
me, good it is for him rather if is put a millstone
περὶ τὸν.τράχηλον.αὐτοῦ, καὶ βέβληται εἰς τὴν θάλασσαν.
about his neck, and he has been cast into the sea.
43 Καὶ ἐὰν [k]σκανδαλίζῃ‖ σε ἡ.χείρ.σου, ἀπόκοψον αὐτήν·
And if [3]should [4]cause [6]to [7]offend [5]thee [1]thy [2]hand, cut off it:
καλόν [l]σοι ἐστὶν‖ κυλλὸν· [m]εἰς τὴν ζωὴν εἰσελθεῖν,‖
good for thee it is maimed into life to enter, [rather]
ἢ τὰς δύο χεῖρας ἔχοντα ἀπελθεῖν εἰς τὴν γέενναν, εἰς τὸ
than the two hands having to go away into the Gehenna, into the
πῦρ τὸ ἄσβεστον, 44 [n]ὅπου ὁ.σκώληξ.αὐτῶν οὐ.τελευτᾷ, καὶ
fire the unquenchable, where their worm dies not, and
τὸ πῦρ οὐ.σβέννυται.‖ 45 καὶ ἐὰν ὁ.πούς.σου σκανδαλίζῃ
the fire is not quenched. And if thy foot should cause [2]to [3]offend
σε, ἀπόκοψον αὐτόν· καλόν [o][p]ἐστίν σοι‖ εἰσελθεῖν εἰς τὴν
[1]thee, cut off it: good it is for thee to enter into
ζωὴν χωλόν, ἢ τοὺς δύο πόδας ἔχοντα βληθῆναι εἰς
life lame, [rather] than the two feet having to be cast into
τὴν γέενναν, [q]εἰς τὸ πῦρ τὸ ἄσβεστον,‖ 46 [r]ὅπου ὁ σκώληξ
the Gehenna, into the fire the unquenchable, where [2]worm
αὐτῶν οὐ.τελευτᾷ, καὶ τὸ πῦρ οὐ.σβέννυται.‖ 47 καὶ ἐὰν ὁ
[1]their dies not, and the fire is not quenched. And if
ὀφθαλμός.σου σκανδαλίζῃ σε, ἔκβαλε αὐτόν· καλόν
thine eye should cause [2]to [3]offend [1]thee, cast out it: good
[s]σοι ἐστὶν‖ μονόφθαλμον εἰσελθεῖν εἰς τὴν βασιλείαν τοῦ
for thee it is with one eye to enter into the kingdom
θεοῦ, ἢ δύο ὀφθαλμοὺς ἔχοντα βληθῆναι εἰς τὴν γέεν-
of God, [rather] than two eyes having to be cast into the Gehen-
ναν [t]τοῦ πυρός,‖ 48 ὅπου ὁ.σκώληξ.αὐτῶν οὐ.τελευτᾷ, καὶ τὸ
na of fire, where their worm dies not, and the
πῦρ οὐ.σβέννυται. 49 Πᾶς.γὰρ πυρὶ ἁλισθήσεται, [u]καὶ
fire is not quenched. For everyone with fire shall be salted, and
πᾶσα θυσία ἁλὶ ἁλισθήσεται.‖ 50 καλὸν τὸ [v]ἅλας,‖
every sacrifice with salt shall be salted. Good [is] the salt,

we forbad him, because he followeth not us. 39 But Jesus said, Forbid him not: for there is no man which shall do a miracle in my name, that can lightly speak evil of me. 40 For he that is not against us is on our part. 41 For whosoever shall give you a cup of water to drink in my name, because ye belong to Christ, verily I say unto you, he shall not lose his reward. 42 And whosoever shall offend one of *these* little ones that believe in me, it is better for him that a millstone were hanged about his neck, and he were cast into the sea. 43 And if thy hand offend thee, cut it off: it is better for thee to enter into life maimed, than having two hands to go into hell, into the fire that never shall be quenched: 44 where their worm dieth not, and the fire is not quenched. 45 And if thy foot offend thee, cut it off: it is better for thee to enter halt into life, than having two feet to be cast into hell, into the fire that never shall be quenched: 46 where their worm dieth not, and the fire is not quenched. 47 And if thine eye offend thee, pluck it out: it is better for thee to enter into the kingdom of God with one eye, than having two eyes to be cast into hell fire: 48 where their worm dieth not, and the fire is not quenched. 49 For every one shall be salted with fire, and every sacrifice shall be salted with salt. 50 Salt *is* good:

---

[z] ἐκωλύομεν TTrA. [a] [ὅτι οὐκ ἀκολουθεῖ ἡμῖν] Tr; ὅτι οὐκ ἠκολούθει ἡμῖν because he was not following us T. [b] ἡμῶν us ELTTrAW. [c] — τῷ GLTTrAW. [d] — μου (*read* [my]) GLTrA. [e] + ὅτι that [L]TTrA. [f] ἀπολέσει shall he lose LTr. [g] + τούτων (*read* of these little ones) LTTr[A]. [h] πίστιν ἐχόντων have faith A; — εἰς ἐμέ T. [i] μύλος ὀνικὸς, millstone turned by an ass LTTrA. [k] σκανδαλίσῃ T. [l] ἐστίν σε LTTrA. [m] εἰσελθεῖν εἰς τὴν ζωὴν LTTrAW. [n] — *verse* 44 T[Tr]. [o] + [γὰρ] for L. [p] ἐστίν σε LTTrAW. [q] — εἰς τὸ πῦρ τὸ ἄσβεστον [L]TTr[A]. [r] — *verse* 46 T[Tr]. [s] σέ ἐστιν TTrA. [t] — τοῦ πυρός LTTrA. [u] — καὶ πᾶσα θυσία ἁλὶ ἁλισθήσεται T[Tr]. [v] ἅλα T.

but if the salt have
lost his saltness, where-
with will ye season it?
Have salt in your-
selves, and have peace
one with another.

X. And he arose
from thence, and com-
eth into the coasts of
Judæa by the farther
side of Jordan: and
the people resort unto
him again; and, as he
was wont, he taught
them again. 2 And the
Pharisees came to him,
and asked him, Is it
lawful for a man to
put away *his* wife?
tempting him. 3 And
he answered and said
unto them, What did
Moses command you?
4 And they said, Moses
suffered to write a bill
of divorcement, and to
put *her* away. 5 And
Jesus answered and
said unto them, For the
hardness of your heart
he wrote you this pre-
cept. 6 But from the
beginning of the cre-
ation God made them
male and female. 7 For
this cause shall a man
leave his father and
mother, and cleave to
his wife; 8 and they
twain shall be one
flesh: so then they are
no more twain, but
one flesh. 9 What
therefore God hath
joined together, let
not man put asunder.
10 And in the house
his disciples asked him
again of the same
matter. 11 And he
saith unto them, Who-
soever shall put away
his wife, and marry
another, committeth
adultery against her.
12 And if a woman
shall put away her
husband, and be mar-
ried to another, she
committeth adultery.

13 And they brought
young children to him,
that he should touch
them: and *his* disci-
ples rebuked those that
brought *them*. 14 But
when Jesus saw *it*, he
was much displeased,
and said unto them,
Suffer the little child-
ren to come unto me,

ἐὰν.δὲ τὸ [w]ἅλας‖ ἄναλον γένηται, ἐν τίνι αὐτὸ ἀρτύσετε;
but if the salt saltless is become, with what it will ye season?
ἔχετε ἐν ἑαυτοῖς [x]ἅλας,‖ καὶ εἰρηνεύετε ἐν ἀλλήλοις.
Have in yourselves salt, and be at peace with one another.

10 [y]Κἀκεῖθεν‖ ἀναστὰς ἔρχεται εἰς τὰ ὅρια τῆς Ἰουδαίας,
And thence rising up he comes into the borders of Judæa,
[z]διὰ τοῦ‖ πέραν τοῦ Ἰορδάνου· καὶ [a]συμπορεύονται‖ πάλιν
by the other side of the Jordan. And come together again
ὄχλοι πρὸς αὐτόν, καὶ ὡς εἰώθει πάλιν ἐδίδασκεν
crowds to him, and as he had been accustomed again he taught
αὐτούς. 2 Καὶ προσελθόντες [b]οἱ‖ Φαρισαῖοι [c]ἐπηρώτησαν‖
them. And coming to [him] the Pharisees asked
αὐτὸν εἰ ἔξεστιν ἀνδρὶ γυναῖκα ἀπολῦσαι, πειράζοντες
him if it is lawful for a husband a wife to put away, tempting
αὐτόν. 3 ὁ.δὲ ἀποκριθεὶς εἶπεν αὐτοῖς, Τί ὑμῖν ἐνετείλατο
him. But he answering said to them, What [4]you [1]did [3]command
[d]Μωσῆς;‖ 4 Οἱ.δὲ [e]εἶπον,‖ [f]Μωσῆς ἐπέτρεψεν‖ βιβλίον ἀπο-
[2]Moses? And they said, Moses allowed a bill of di-
στασίου γράψαι, καὶ ἀπολῦσαι. 5 [g]Καὶ ἀποκριθεὶς ὁ‖ Ἰησοῦς
vorce to write, and to put away. And answering Jesus
εἶπεν αὐτοῖς, Πρὸς τὴν.σκληροκαρδίαν.ὑμῶν ἔγραψεν ὑμῖν
said to them, In view of your hardheartedness he wrote for you
τὴν.ἐντολὴν.ταύτην· 6 ἀπὸ.δὲ ἀρχῆς κτίσεως ἄρσεν καὶ
this commandment; but from [the] beginning of creation male and
θῆλυ ἐποίησεν αὐτοὺς [h]ὁ θεός.‖ 7 ἕνεκεν τούτου καταλείψει
female, [2]made [3]them [1]God. On account of this shall [3]leave
ἄνθρωπος τὸν.πατέρα.αὐτοῦ καὶ τὴν μητέρα, [i]καὶ προσκολ-
[1]a [2]man his father and mother, and shall be
ληθήσεται‖ [k]πρὸς τὴν.γυναῖκα‖.αὐτοῦ, 8 καὶ ἔσονται οἱ δύο
joined to his wife, and [3]shall [4]be [1]the [2]two
εἰς σάρκα μίαν· ὥστε οὐκέτι εἰσὶν δύο, ἀλλὰ μία σάρξ. 9 ὃ
[5]for [7]flesh [6]one; so that no longer are they two, but one flesh. What
οὖν ὁ θεὸς συνέζευξεν, ἄνθρωπος μὴ.χωριζέτω. 10 Καὶ [l]ἐν
therefore God united together, [3]man [1]let [2]not separate. And in
τῇ οἰκίᾳ‖ πάλιν οἱ.μαθηταὶ.[m]αὐτοῦ‖ περὶ [n]τοῦ.αὐτοῦ‖ [o]ἐπη-
the house again his disciples concerning the same thing
ρώτησαν‖ αὐτόν. 11 καὶ λέγει αὐτοῖς, Ὃς.[p]ἐὰν‖ ἀπολύσῃ
asked him. And he says to them, Whoever should put away
τὴν.γυναῖκα.αὐτοῦ καὶ γαμήσῃ ἄλλην, μοιχᾶται ἐπ᾽
his wife and should marry another, commits adultery against
αὐτήν. 12 καὶ ἐὰν [q]γυνὴ ἀπολύσῃ‖ τὸν.ἄνδρα.αὐτῆς [r]καὶ‖
her. And if a woman should put away her husband and
[s]γαμηθῇ ἄλλῳ,‖ μοιχᾶται.
be married to another, she commits adultery.

13 Καὶ προσέφερον αὐτῷ παιδία, ἵνα ἅψηται αὐτῶν·
And they brought to him little children, that he might touch them.
οἱ.δὲ μαθηταὶ ἐπετίμων τοῖς προσφέρουσιν. 14 ἰδὼν.δὲ
But the disciples rebuked those who brought them. But having seen [it]
ὁ Ἰησοῦς ἠγανάκτησεν, καὶ εἶπεν αὐτοῖς, Ἄφετε τὰ παιδία
Jesus was indignant, and said to them, Suffer the little children

---

[w] ἅλα T. [x] ἅλα LTTrA. [y] καὶ ἐκεῖθεν LTTrAW. [z] καὶ and LTTrA. [a] συνπορεύονται TA.
[b] — οἱ GLTrAW. [c] ἐπηρώτων were asking LTTrA. [d] Μωϋσῆς LTTrAW. [e] εἶπαν LTTrA.
[f] ἐπέτρεψεν Μωϋσῆς LTTrA; Μωϋσῆς ἐπέτ. W. [g] ὁ δὲ but TTrA. [h] — ὁ θεός (*read* he
made them) [L]TTr[A]. [i] — καὶ προσκολληθήσεται T. [k] τῇ γυναικὶ L; — πρὸς τὴν
γυναῖκα T. [l] εἰς τὴν οἰκίαν LTTrA. [m] — αὐτοῦ (*read* the disciples) [L]TTr[A]. [n] τούτου
this LTTrA. [o] ἐπηρώτων were asking TA. [p] ἂν LTTrA. [q] αὐτὴ ἀπολύσασα she putting
away TTrA. [r] — καὶ TTrA. [s] γαμήσῃ ἄλλον should marry another LTTrA.

ἔρχεσθαι πρός με, [t]καὶ[‖] μὴ.κωλύετε αὐτά· τῶν.γὰρ.τοιούτων
to come to me, and do not hinder them; for of such
ἐστιν ἡ βασιλεία τοῦ θεοῦ· 15 ἀμὴν λέγω ὑμῖν, ὃς.[v]ἐὰν[‖]
is the kingdom of God. Verily I say to you, Whoever
μὴ.δέξηται τὴν βασιλείαν τοῦ θεοῦ ὡς παιδίον, οὐ.μὴ
shall not receive the kingdom of God as a little child, in no wise
εἰσέλθῃ εἰς αὐτήν. 16 Καὶ ἐναγκαλισάμενος αὐτά, [w]
shall enter into it. And having taken [2]in [[3]his] [4]arms [1]them,
τιθεὶς τὰς χεῖρας ἐπ' αὐτὰ [x]ηὐλόγει αὐτά.[‖]
having laid [his] hands on them he blessed them.

17 Καὶ ἐκπορευομένου.αὐτοῦ εἰς ὁδόν, προσδραμὼν εἷς καὶ
And as he went forth into [the] way, [2]running [3]up [1]one and
γονυπετήσας αὐτὸν ἐπηρώτα αὐτόν, Διδάσκαλε ἀγαθέ, τί
kneeling down to him asked him, [2]Teacher [1]good, what
ποιήσω ἵνα ζωὴν αἰώνιον κληρονομήσω; 18 Ὁ.δὲ.Ἰησοῦς
shall I do that life eternal I may inherit? But Jesus
εἶπεν αὐτῷ, Τί με λέγεις ἀγαθόν; οὐδεὶς ἀγαθὸς εἰ.μὴ
said to him, Why me callest thou good? No one [is] good except
εἷς, ὁ θεός. 19 τὰς ἐντολὰς οἶδας, [y]Μὴ.μοιχεύσῃς·
one, God. The commandments thou knowest: Thou shouldest not commit
μὴ.φονεύσῃς·[‖] μὴ.κλέψῃς·
adultery; thou shouldest not commit murder; thou shouldest not steal; thou
μὴ.ψευδομαρτυρήσῃς· μὴ.ἀποστερήσῃς· τίμα τὸν
shouldest not bear false witness; thou shouldest not defraud; honour
πατέρα.σου καὶ τὴν μητέρα[z]. 20 Ὁ.δὲ [a]ἀποκριθεὶς[‖] [b]εἶπεν[‖]
thy father and mother. And he answering said
αὐτῷ, Διδάσκαλε, [c]ταῦτα πάντα[‖] [d]ἐφυλαξάμην[‖] ἐκ νεότητός
to him, Teacher, [2]these [1]all have I kept from [2]youth
μου. 21 Ὁ.δὲ.Ἰησοῦς ἐμβλέψας αὐτῷ ἠγάπησεν αὐτόν, καὶ
[1]my. And Jesus looking upon him loved him, and
εἶπεν αὐτῷ, Ἕν [e]σοι[‖] ὑστερεῖ· ὕπαγε, ὅσα ἔχεις πώλη-
said to him, One thing to thee is lacking: go, as much as thou hast sell
σον καὶ δὸς [f]τοῖς[‖] πτωχοῖς, καὶ ἕξεις θησαυρὸν ἐν
and give to the poor, and thou shalt have treasure in
οὐρανῷ· καὶ δεῦρο, ἀκολούθει μοι, [g]ἄρας τὸν σταυρόν.[‖] 22 Ὁ.δὲ
heaven; and come, follow me, taking up the cross. But he,
στυγνάσας ἐπὶ τῷ λόγῳ ἀπῆλθεν λυπούμενος· ἦν.γὰρ.ἔχων
being sad at the word, went away grieved, for he had
κτήματα πολλά. 23 Καὶ περιβλεψάμενος ὁ Ἰησοῦς λέγει τοῖς
[2]possessions [1]many. And looking around Jesus says
μαθηταῖς.αὐτοῦ, Πῶς δυσκόλως οἱ τὰ χρήματα ἔχοντες εἰς
to his disciples, How difficultly those [2]riches [1]having into
τὴν βασιλείαν τοῦ θεοῦ εἰσελεύσονται. 24 Οἱ.δὲ μαθηταὶ ἐθαμ-
the kingdom of God shall enter! And the disciples were as-
βοῦντο ἐπὶ τοῖς.λόγοις.αὐτοῦ. Ὁ.δὲ.Ἰησοῦς πάλιν ἀποκριθεὶς
tonished at his words. And Jesus again answering
λέγει αὐτοῖς, [h]Τέκνα,[‖] πῶς δύσκολόν ἐστιν [i]τοὺς πεποιθότας
says to them, Children, how difficult it is [for] those who trust
ἐπὶ [k]τοῖς[‖] χρήμασιν[‖] εἰς τὴν βασιλείαν τοῦ θεοῦ εἰσελθεῖν.
in riches into the kingdom of God to enter!
25 εὐκοπώτερόν ἐστιν κάμηλον διὰ [l]τῆς[‖] τρυμαλιᾶς [l]τῆς[‖]
Easier it is [for] a camel through the eye of the

and forbid them not: for of such is the kingdom of God. 15 Verily I say unto you, Whosoever shall not receive the kingdom of God as a little child, he shall not enter therein. 16 And he took them up in his arms, put *his* hands upon them, and blessed them.

17 And when he was gone forth into the way, there came one running, and kneeled to him, and asked him, Good Master, what shall I do that I may inherit eternal life? 18 And Jesus said unto him, Why callest thou me good? *there is* none good but one, *that is*, God. 19 Thou knowest the commandments, Do not commit adultery, Do not kill, Do not steal, Do not bear false witness, Defraud not, Honour thy father and mother. 20 And he answered and said unto him, Master, all these have I observed from my youth. 21 Then Jesus beholding him loved him, and said unto him, One thing thou lackest: go thy way, sell whatsoever thou hast, and give to the poor, and thou shalt have treasure in heaven: and come, take up the cross, and follow me. 22 And he was sad at that saying, and went away grieved: for he had great possessions. 23 And Jesus looked round about, and saith unto his disciples, How hardly shall they that have riches enter into the kingdom of God! 24 And the disciples were astonished at his words. But Jesus answereth again, and saith unto them, Children, how hard is it for them that trust in riches to enter into the kingdom of God! 25 It is easier for a camel to go through the eye of a needle,

[t] — καὶ GTTrAW [v] ἂν LTTrA. [w] + κατευλόγει he blesses [them] TTrA. [x] εὐλόγει αὐτά he blesses them LW; — ηὐλόγει αὐτά TTrA. [y] Μὴ φονεύσῃς, μὴ μοιχεύσῃς L. [z] — σου thy (mother) LT. [a] — ἀποκριθεὶς T. [b] ἔφη TTrA. [c] πάντα ταυτα L. [d] ἐφύλαξα L. [e] σε thee TA. [f] — τοῖς LTrAW. [g] — ἄρας τὸν σταυρόν [L]TTr. [h] τεκνία L. [i] — τοὺς πεποιθότας ἐπὶ τοῖς χρήμασιν T. [k] — τοῖς LTrAW. [l] — τῆς (read an eye of a needle) LTrW.

than for a rich man
to enter into the king-
dom of God. 26 And
they were astonished
out of measure, saying
among themselves,
Who then can be saved?
27 And Jesus looking
upon them saith, With
men *it is* impossible,
but not with God: for
with God all things
are possible. 28 Then
Peter began to say
unto him, Lo, we have
left all, and have fol-
lowed thee. 29 And
Jesus answered and
said, Verily I say unto
you, There is no man
that hath left house,
or brethren, or sisters,
or father, or mother,
or wife, or children,
or lands, for my sake,
and the gospel's, 30 but
he shall receive an
hundredfold now in
this time, houses, and
brethren, and sisters,
and mothers, and
children, and lands,
with persecutions; and
in the world to come
eternal life. 31 But
many *that are* first
shall be last; and the
last first.

ῥαφίδος [m]εἰσελθεῖν," ἢ πλούσιον εἰς τὴν βασιλείαν τοῦ θεοῦ
needle to pass, than [for] a rich man into the kingdom of God
εἰσελθεῖν. 26 Οἱ.δὲ περισσῶς ἐξεπλήσσοντο, λέγοντες πρὸς
to enter. And they exceedingly were astonished, saying among
ἑαυτούς, Καὶ τίς δύναται σωθῆναι; 27 Ἐμβλέψας.[n]δὲ" αὐτοῖς
themselves, And who is able to be saved? But looking on them
ὁ Ἰησοῦς λέγει, Παρὰ ἀνθρώποις [o] ἀδύνατον, ἀλλ' οὐ παρὰ
Jesus says, With men [it is] impossible, but not with
[p]τῷ" θεῷ· πάντα.γὰρ δυνατά [q]ἐστιν" παρὰ τῷ θεῷ. 28 [r]Καὶ"
God; for all things [2]possible [1]are with God. And
ἤρξατο [s]ὁ Πέτρος λέγειν" αὐτῷ, Ἰδού, ἡμεῖς ἀφήκαμεν πάντα,
[2]began [1]Peter to say to him, Lo, we left all,
καὶ [t]ἠκολουθήσαμέν" σοι. 29 [v]Ἀποκριθεὶς.δὲ ὁ Ἰησοῦς εἶπεν,"
and followed thee. But answering Jesus said,
Ἀμὴν λέγω ὑμῖν, οὐδείς ἐστιν ὃς ἀφῆκεν οἰκίαν, ἢ ἀδελφούς,
Verily I say to you, No one there is who has left house, or brothers,
ἢ ἀδελφάς, [w]ἢ πατέρα, ἢ μητέρα," [x]ἢ γυναῖκα," ἢ τέκνα, ἢ
or sisters, or father, or mother, or wife, or children, or
ἀγρούς, ἕνεκεν ἐμοῦ καὶ [y] τοῦ εὐαγγελίου, 30 ἐὰν.μὴ.λάβῃ
lands, for the sake of me and of the glad tidings, that shall not receive
ἑκατονταπλασίονα νῦν ἐν τῷ.καιρῷ.τούτῳ, οἰκίας καὶ ἀδελ-
a hundredfold now in this time: houses and bro-
φοὺς καὶ ἀδελφὰς καὶ [z]μητέρας" καὶ τέκνα καὶ ἀγρούς, μετὰ
thers and sisters and mothers and children and lands, with
διωγμῶν, καὶ ἐν τῷ αἰῶνι τῷ.ἐρχομένῳ ζωὴν αἰώνιον. 31 πολ-
persecutions, and in the age that is coming life eternal. [2]Many
λοὶ δὲ ἔσονται πρῶτοι ἔσχατοι, καὶ [a]οἱ" ἔσχατοι πρῶτοι.
[1]but [4]shall [5]be [3]first last, and the last first.

32 And they were in
the way going up to
Jerusalem; and Jesus
went before them: and
they were amazed; and
as they followed, they
were afraid. And he
took again the twelve,
and began to tell them
what things should
happen unto him,
33 *saying*, Behold, we
go up to Jerusalem;
and the Son of man
shall be delivered unto
the chief priests, and
unto the scribes; and
they shall condemn
him to death, and shall
deliver him to the
Gentiles: 34 and they
shall mock him, and
shall scourge him, and
shall spit upon him,
and shall kill him:
and the third day he
shall rise again.

32 Ἦσαν.δὲ ἐν τῇ ὁδῷ ἀναβαίνοντες εἰς Ἱεροσόλυμα· καὶ
And they were in the way going up to Jerusalem, and
ἦν προάγων αὐτοὺς ὁ Ἰησοῦς, καὶ ἐθαμβοῦντο, [b]καὶ"
[2]was [3]going [4]on [5]before [6]them [1]Jesus, and they were astonished, and
ἀκολουθοῦντες ἐφοβοῦντο. καὶ παραλαβὼν πάλιν τοὺς
following were afraid. And having taken to [him] again the
δώδεκα, ἤρξατο αὐτοῖς λέγειν τὰ μέλλοντα αὐτῷ
twelve, he began them to tell the things which were about [3]to [4]him
συμβαίνειν· 33 Ὅτι, ἰδού, ἀναβαίνομεν εἰς Ἱεροσόλυμα, καὶ
[1]to [2]happen: Behold, we go up to Jerusalem, and
ὁ υἱὸς τοῦ ἀνθρώπου παραδοθήσεται τοῖς ἀρχιερεῦσιν καὶ
the Son of man will be delivered up to the chief priests and
[c]τοῖς" γραμματεῦσιν, καὶ κατακρινοῦσιν αὐτὸν θανάτῳ, καὶ
to the scribes, and they will condemn him to death, and
παραδώσουσιν αὐτὸν τοῖς ἔθνεσιν, 34 καὶ ἐμπαίξουσιν αὐτῷ,
will deliver up him to the Gentiles. And they will mock him,
[d]καὶ μαστιγώσουσιν αὐτόν, καὶ ἐμπτύσουσιν αὐτῷ," καὶ ἀπο-
and will scourge him, and will spit upon him, and will
κτενοῦσιν [e]αὐτόν·" καὶ [f]τῇ τρίτῃ ἡμέρᾳ" ἀναστήσεται.
kill him; and on the third day he will rise again.

35 And James and
John, the sons of Ze-
bedee, come unto him,

35 Καὶ προσπορεύονται αὐτῷ Ἰάκωβος καὶ Ἰωάννης [g]οἱ"
And come up to him James and John, the

---

[m] διελθεῖν EGLTTrAW. [n] — δὲ but TTrA. [o] + [τοῦτο] this [is] L. [p] — τῷ TTrAW.
[q] — ἐστιν (*read* [are]) TTr. [r] — καὶ GLTTrAW. [s] λέγειν ὁ Πέτρος TA. [t] ἠκολουθήκαμέν
have followed LTTrAW. [v] ἀποκριθεὶς (*omit* but) ὁ Ἰησοῦς εἶπεν GLTrW; ἔφη ὁ Ἰησοῦς
Jesus said (— ἀποκ. δὲ) TA. [w] ἢ μητέρα, ἢ πατέρα LTTrA. [x] — ἢ γυναῖκα LTTrA.
[y] + ἕνεκεν for the sake G[L]TTrAW. [z] μητέρα mother LTr. [a] — οἱ GLW. [b] οἱ δὲ
and those TTr. [c] — τοῖς L. [d] καὶ ἐμπτύσουσιν αὐτῷ, καὶ μαστιγώσουσιν αὐτὸν LTTrA.
[e] — αὐτόν (*read* [him]) [L]T[Tr]. [f] μετὰ τρεῖς ἡμέρας after three days LTTrA. [g] — οἱ A.

υἱοὶ Ζεβεδαίου, λέγοντες[h], Διδάσκαλε, θέλομεν ἵνα ὃ.ἐὰν
sons of Zebedee, saying, Teacher, we desire that whatever
αἰτήσωμεν [i] ποιήσῃς ἡμῖν. 36 Ὁ.δὲ εἶπεν αὐτοῖς, Τί θέλετε
we may ask thou wouldest do for us. And he said to them, What do ye desire
[k]ποιῆσαί με‖ ὑμῖν; 37 Οἱ.δὲ [l]εἶπον‖ αὐτῷ, Δὸς ἡμῖν, ἵνα εἷς
[2]to [3]do [1]me for you? And they said to him, Give to us, that one
[m]ἐκ δεξιῶν.σου‖ καὶ εἷς [n] ἐξ [o]εὐωνύμων‖.[p]σου‖ καθίσωμεν. ἐν
at thy right hand and one at thy left hand we may sit in
τῇ.δόξῃ.σου. 38 Ὁ.δὲ.Ἰησοῦς εἶπεν αὐτοῖς, Οὐκ.οἴδατε τί
thy glory. But Jesus said to them, Ye know not what
αἰτεῖσθε. δύνασθε πιεῖν τὸ ποτήριον ὃ ἐγὼ πίνω, [q]καὶ‖ τὸ
ye ask. Are ye able to drink the cup which I drink, and [5]the
βάπτισμα ὃ ἐγὼ βαπτίζομαι, βαπτισθῆναι;
[6]baptism [7]which [8]I [9]am [10]baptized [[11]with], [1]to [2]be [3]baptized [[4]with]?
39 Οἱ.δὲ [r]εἶπον‖ αὐτῷ, Δυνάμεθα. Ὁ.δὲ.Ἰησοῦς εἶπεν αὐτοῖς,
And they said to him, We are able. But Jesus said to them,
Τὸ [s]μὲν‖ ποτήριον ὃ ἐγὼ πίνω, πίεσθε· καὶ τὸ βάπτισμα
The [2]indeed [1]cup which I drink, ye shall drink; and the baptism
ὃ ἐγὼ βαπτίζομαι, βαπτισθήσεσθε· 40 τὸ.δὲ.καθί-
which I am baptized [with], ye shall be baptized [with]; but to sit
σαι ἐκ δεξιῶν.μου· [q]καὶ‖ ἐξ εὐωνύμων.[t]μου‖ οὐκ.ἔστιν ἐμὸν
at my right hand and at my left hand is not mine
δοῦναι, ἀλλ' οἷς ἡτοίμασται. 41 Καὶ ἀκούσαν-
to give, but [to those] for whom it has been prepared. And having
τες οἱ δέκα ἤρξαντο ἀγανακτεῖν περὶ Ἰακώβου καὶ
heard [this] the ten began to be indignant about James and
Ἰωάννου 42 [v]ὁ.δὲ.Ἰησοῦς προσκαλεσάμενος αὐτοὺς‖ λέγει
John. But Jesus having called [2]to [[3]him] [1]them says
αὐτοῖς, Οἴδατε ὅτι οἱ δοκοῦντες ἄρχειν τῶν ἐθνῶν
to them, Ye know that those who are accounted to rule over the nations
κατακυριεύουσιν αὐτῶν· καὶ οἱ.μεγάλοι.αὐτῶν κατεξουσιάζου-
exercise lordship over them; and their great ones exercise authority
σιν αὐτῶν. 43 οὐχ οὕτως δὲ [w]ἔσται‖ ἐν ὑμῖν· ἀλλ'
over them; not thus however shall it be among you; but
ὃς.[x]ἐὰν‖ θέλῃ [y]γενέσθαι μέγας‖ ἐν ὑμῖν, ἔσται [z]διάκονος
whoever desires to become great among you, shall be [2]servant
ὑμῶν.‖ 44 καὶ ὃς.[a]ἂν‖ θέλῃ [b]ὑμῶν‖ [c]γενέσθαι‖ πρῶτος, ἔσται
[1]your; and whoever desires of you to become first, shall be
πάντων δοῦλος· 45 καὶ.γὰρ ὁ υἱὸς τοῦ ἀνθρώπου οὐκ.ἦλθεν
[2]of [3]all [1]bondman. For even the Son of man came not
διακονηθῆναι, ἀλλὰ διακονῆσαι, καὶ δοῦναι τὴν.ψυχὴν.αὐτοῦ
to be served, but to serve, and to give his life
λύτρον ἀντὶ πολλῶν.
a ransom for many.

46 Καὶ [d]ἔρχονται‖ εἰς [e]Ἱεριχώ·‖ καὶ ἐκπορευομένου.αὐτοῦ
And they come to Jericho; and as he was going out
ἀπὸ [e]Ἱεριχώ,‖ καὶ τῶν.μαθητῶν.αὐτοῦ, καὶ ὄχλου ἱκανοῦ,
from Jericho, and his disciples, and a [2]crowd [1]large,
[f]υἱὸς Τιμαίου Βαρτίμαιος [g]ὁ‖ τυφλὸς [ha] ἐκάθητο παρὰ τὴν
a son of Timæus, Bartimæus the blind [man], was sitting beside the

saying, Master, we would that thou shouldest do for us whatsoever we shall desire. 36 And he said unto them, What would ye that I should do for you? 37 They said unto him, Grant unto us that we may sit, one on thy right hand, and the other on thy left hand, in thy glory. 38 But Jesus said unto them, Ye know not what ye ask: can ye drink of the cup that I drink of? and be baptized with the baptism that I am baptized with? 39 And they said unto him, We can. And Jesus said unto them, Ye shall indeed drink of the cup that I drink of; and with the baptism that I am baptized withal shall ye be baptized: 40 but to sit on my right hand and on my left hand is not mine to give; but *it shall be given to them* for whom it is prepared. 41 And when the ten heard *it*, they began to be much displeased with James and John. 42 But Jesus called them *to him*, and saith unto them, Ye know that they which are accounted to rule over the Gentiles exercise lordship over them; and their great ones exercise authority upon them. 43 But so shall it not be among you: but whosoever will be great among you, shall be your minister: 44 and whosoever of you will be the chiefest, shall be servant of all. 45 For even the Son of man came not to be ministered unto, but to minister, and to give his life a ransom for many.

46 And they came to Jericho: and as he went out of Jericho with his disciples and a great number of people, blind Bartimæus, the son of Timæus, sat by the highway side begging. 47 And when

---

[h] + αὐτῷ to him [L]TTrA. [i] + σε thee LTTrAW. [k] ποιήσω I should do LTr; με ποιήσω T. [l] εἶπαν LTTrA. [m] σου ἐκ δεξιῶν TTrA. [n] + σου thy T. [o] ἀριστερῶν TTrA. [p] — σου (*read* [thy] left hand) [L]TTrA. [q] ἢ or LTTrA. [r] εἶπαν LTTrA. [s] — μὲν TTrA. [t] — μου (*read* [my] left hand) GLTTrAW. [v] καὶ προσκαλεσάμενος αὐτοὺς ὁ Ἰησοῦς LTTrA. [w] ἐστιν it is LTTrA. [x] ἂν LTTr. [y] μέγας γενέσθαι TTr. [z] ὑμῶν διάκονος GLTTrAW. [a] ἐὰν GTrA. [b] ἐν ὑμῖν among you L. [c] εἶναι to be LTr. [d] ἔρχεται he comes L. [e] Ἰερειχώ T. [f] + ὁ the (son) LTTrAW. [g] — ὁ (*read* a blind [man]) LTTrA. [ha] + προσαίτης a beggar TTrA.

he heard that it was
Jesus of Nazareth, he
began to cry out, and
say, Jesus, *thou* Son
of David, have mercy
on me. 48 And many
charged him that he
should hold his peace:
but he cried the more
a great deal, *Thou* Son
of David, have mercy
on me. 49 And Jesus
stood still, and commanded
him to be
called. And they call
the blind man, saying
unto him, Be of good
comfort, rise; he
calleth thee. 50 And
he, casting away his
garment, rose, and
came to Jesus. 51 And
Jesus answered and
said unto him, What
wilt thou that I should
do unto thee? The
blind man said unto
him, Lord, that I
might receive my
sight. 52 And Jesus
said unto him, Go thy
way; thy faith hath
made thee whole. And
immediately he received
his sight, and followed
Jesus in the way.

XI. And when they
came nigh to Jerusalem,
unto Bethphage
and Bethany, at the
mount of Olives, he
sendeth forth two of
his disciples, 2 and
saith unto them, Go
your way into the village
over against you:
and as soon as ye be
entered into it, ye
shall find a colt tied,
whereon never man
sat; loose him, and
bring *him*. 3 And if
any man say unto you,
Why do ye this? say
ye that the Lord hath
need of him; and
straightway he will
send him hither. 4 And
they went their way,
and found the colt tied
by the door without in
a place where two ways
met; and they loose
him. 5 And certain of
them that stood there
said unto them, What
do ye, loosing the colt?
6 And they said unto
them even as Jesus had
commanded: and they

ὁδὸν [i]προσαιτῶν.‖ 47 καὶ ἀκούσας ὅτι Ἰησοῦς ὁ [k]Ναζωραιός‖
way, begging. And having heard that Jesus the Nazaræan
ἐστιν, ἤρξατο κράζειν καὶ λέγειν, [l]Ὁ υἱὸς‖ [m]Δαβίδ,‖ Ἰησοῦ,
it was, (*lit.* it is) he began to cry out and to say, Son of David, Jesus,
ἐλέησόν με. 48 Καὶ ἐπετίμων αὐτῷ πολλοὶ ἵνα σιωπήσῃ·
have pity on me. And ²rebuked ³him ¹many that he should be silent;
ὁ.δὲ πολλῷ μᾶλλον ἔκραζεν, Υἱὲ [m]Δαβίδ,‖ ἐλέησόν με.
but he much more cried out, Son of David, have pity on me.
49 Καὶ στὰς ὁ Ἰησοῦς [n]εἶπεν αὐτὸν φωνηθῆναι·‖ καὶ
And ²having ³stopped ¹Jesus asked for him to be called. And
φωνοῦσιν τὸν τυφλόν, λέγοντες αὐτῷ, Θάρσει·
they call the blind [man], saying to him, Be of good courage;
[o]ἔγειραι,‖ φωνεῖ σε. 50 Ὁ.δὲ ἀποβαλὼν τὸ.ἱμάτιον.αὐτοῦ,
rise up, he calls thee. And he casting away his garment,
[p]ἀναστὰς‖ ἦλθεν πρὸς τὸν Ἰησοῦν. 51 καὶ ἀποκριθεὶς [q]λέγει
having risen up he came to Jesus. And answering ²says
αὐτῷ ὁ Ἰησοῦς,‖ Τί [r]θέλεις ποιήσω σοί;‖ Ὁ.δὲ τυφλὸς
³to ⁴him ¹Jesus, What dost thou desire I should do to thee? And the blind
εἶπεν αὐτῷ, [s]Ῥαββονί,‖ ἵνα ἀναβλέψω. 52 Ὁ.δὲ.Ἰη-
[man] said to him, Rabboni, that I may receive sight. And Je-
σοῦς εἶπεν αὐτῷ, Ὕπαγε· ἡ.πίστις.σου σέσωκέν σε. Καὶ
sus said to him, Go, thy faith has healed thee. And
[t]εὐθέως‖ ἀνέβλεψεν, καὶ ἠκολούθει [v]τῷ Ἰησοῦ‖ ἐν τῇ ὁδῷ.
immediately he received sight, and followed Jesus in the way.

11 Καὶ ὅτε ἐγγίζουσιν εἰς [w]Ἱερουσαλήμ,‖ [x]εἰς Βηθφαγὴ
And when they drew near to Jerusalem, to Bethphage
καὶ Βηθανίαν,‖ πρὸς τὸ ὄρος τῶν Ἐλαιῶν, [y]ἀποστέλλει‖ δύο
and Bethany, towards the mount of Olives, he sends two
τῶν.μαθητῶν.αὐτοῦ, 2 καὶ λέγει αὐτοῖς, Ὑπάγετε εἰς τὴν
of his disciples, and says to them, Go into the
κώμην τὴν.κατέναντι ὑμῶν· καὶ [z]εὐθέως‖ εἰσπορευόμενοι εἰς
village, that opposite you, and immediately entering into
αὐτὴν εὑρήσετε πῶλον δεδεμένον, ἐφ' ὃν οὐδεὶς[a] ἀνθρώπων[b]
it ye will find a colt tied, upon which no one of men
κεκάθικεν· [c]λύσαντες αὐτὸν‖ [d]ἀγάγετε.‖ 3 καὶ ἐάν τις ὑμῖν
has sat: having loosed it lead [it]. And if anyone to you
εἴπῃ, Τί ποιεῖτε τοῦτο; εἴπατε, [e]Ὅτι‖ ὁ κύριος αὐτοῦ χρείαν
say, Why do ye this? say, The Lord ³of ⁴it ²need
ἔχει· καὶ [f]εὐθέως‖ αὐτὸν [g]ἀποστελεῖ‖ [h] ὧδε. 4 [ia]Ἀπῆλθον.δέ,‖
¹has, and immediately it he will send hither. And they departed,
καὶ εὗρον [ka]τὸν‖ πῶλον δεδεμένον πρὸς [la]τὴν‖ θύραν ἔξω ἐπὶ
and found the colt tied at the door without, by
τοῦ ἀμφόδου, καὶ λύουσιν αὐτόν. 5 καί τινες τῶν ἐκεῖ ἑστη-
the cross way, and they loose it. And some of those there stand-
κότων ἔλεγον αὐτοῖς, Τί ποιεῖτε λύοντες τὸν πῶλον; 6 Οἱ.δὲ
ing said to them, What are ye doing loosing the colt? And they
[ma]εἶπον‖ αὐτοῖς καθὼς [na]ἐνετείλατο‖ ὁ Ἰησοῦς· καὶ ἀφῆκαν
said to them as ²commanded ¹Jesus. And they allowed

[i] — προσαιτῶν TTrA. [k] Ναζαρηνός LTTrA. [l] Υἱὲ LTTr. [m] Δαυείδ LTTrA; Δαυίδ GW. [n] εἶπεν, φωνήσατε αὐτόν said, call ye him TTrA. [o] ἔγειρε GLTTrAW. [p] ἀναπηδήσας having leaped up LTTrAW. [q] αὐτῷ ὁ Ἰησοῦς εἶπεν Jesus said to him TTrA. [r] σοι θέλεις ποιήσω; T. [s] Ῥαββουνί GLTTrAW. [t] εὐθὺς TTrA. [v] αὐτῷ him GLTTrAW. [w] Ἱεροσόλυμα LTTrAW. [x] καὶ εἰς Βηθανίαν LT. [y] ἀπέστειλεν he sent L. [z] εὐθὺς TTrA. [a] + οὔπω not yet (*read* no one yet) LTr. [b] + οὔπω T. [c] λύσατε αὐτὸν καὶ loose it and LTTrA. [d] φέρετε bring TTrA. [e] — Ὅτι LTTrA. [f] εὐθὺς LTTrA. [g] ἀποστέλλει he sends GLTTrAW. [h] + πάλιν back TTr. [ia] καὶ ἀπῆλθον LTTrA. [ka] — τὸν (*read* a colt) GLTrAW. [la] — τὴν (*read* a door) TrA. [ma] εἶπαν T. [na] εἶπεν said LTTrA.

αὐτούς. 7 καὶ [o]ἤγαγον" τὸν πῶλον πρὸς τὸν Ἰησοῦν· καὶ
them. And they led the colt to Jesus. And
[p]ἐπέβαλον" αὐτῷ τὰ.ἱμάτια.αὐτῶν, καὶ ἐκάθισεν ἐπ' [q]αὐτῷ·"
they cast upon it their garments, and he sat on it;
8 [r]πολλοὶ.δὲ" τὰ.ἱμάτια.αὐτῶν ἔστρωσαν εἰς τὴν ὁδόν· ἄλλοι.δὲ
and many their garments strewed on the way, and others
[s]στοιβάδας" [t]ἔκοπτον" ἐκ τῶν [v]δένδρων," [w]καὶ ἐστρώννυον
branches were cutting down from the trees, and were strewing
εἰς τὴν ὁδόν." 9 καὶ οἱ προάγοντες καὶ οἱ ἀκολουθοῦν-
[them] on the way. And those going before and those follow-
τες ἔκραζον, [x]λέγοντες," Ὡσαννά· εὐλογημένος ὁ
ing were crying out, saying, Hosanna! blessed [be] he who
ἐρχόμενος ἐν ὀνόματι κυρίου. 10 εὐλογημένη ἡ ἐρχο-
comes in [the] name of [the] Lord. Blessed [be] the com-
μένη βασιλεία [y]ἐν ὀνόματι κυρίου" τοῦ.πατρὸς.ἡμῶν
ing kingdom [5]in [6the] [7]name [8]of [9the] [10]Lord [1]of [2]our [3]father
[z]Δαβίδ·" Ὡσαννὰ ἐν τοῖς ὑψίστοις. 11 Καὶ εἰσῆλθεν εἰς
[4]David. Hosanna in the highest! And [2]entered [3]into
Ἱεροσόλυμα [a]ὁ Ἰησοῦς καὶ" εἰς τὸ ἱερόν· καὶ περιβλεψάμενος
[4]Jerusalem [1]Jesus and into the temple; and having looked round on
πάντα, [b]ὀψίας" ἤδη οὔσης τῆς ὥρας, ἐξῆλθεν εἰς Βηθανίαν
all things, late already being the hour, he went out to Bethany
μετὰ τῶν δώδεκα.
with the twelve.

12 Καὶ τῇ ἐπαύριον ἐξελθόντων αὐτῶν ἀπὸ Βηθανίας,
And on the morrow [2]having [3]gone [4]out [1]they from Bethany,
ἐπείνασεν· 13 καὶ ἰδὼν συκῆν [c] μακρόθεν ἔχουσαν φύλλα,
he hungered. And seeing a fig-tree afar off having leaves,
ἦλθεν εἰ ἄρα [d]εὑρήσει τι" ἐν αὐτῇ· καὶ ἐλθὼν ἐπ'
he went if perhaps he will find anything on it. And having come to
αὐτήν, οὐδὲν εὗρεν εἰ.μὴ φύλλα·[e] [f]οὐ.γὰρ.ἦν καιρὸς" σύκων.
it, nothing he found except leaves, for it was not [the] season of figs.
14 καὶ ἀποκριθεὶς [g]ὁ Ἰησοῦς" εἶπεν αὐτῇ, Μηκέτι [h]ἐκ σοῦ εἰς
And [2]answering [1]Jesus said to it, No more of thee for
τὸν αἰῶνα" [i]μηδεὶς" καρπὸν φάγοι. Καὶ ἤκουον οἱ μαθηταὶ
ever [2]any [3]one [5]fruit [1]let [4]eat. And [3]heard [2]disciples
(lit. no one)
αὐτοῦ. 15 Καὶ ἔρχονται εἰς Ἱεροσόλυμα· καὶ εἰσελθὼν
[1]his. And they come to Jerusalem; and [2]having [3]entered
[k]ὁ Ἰησοῦς" εἰς τὸ ἱερὸν ἤρξατο ἐκβάλλειν τοὺς πωλοῦντας
[1]Jesus into the temple he began to cast out those selling
καὶ [l] ἀγοράζοντας ἐν τῷ ἱερῷ· καὶ τὰς τραπέζας τῶν κολλυ-
and buying in the temple, and the tables of the money
βιστῶν καὶ τὰς καθέδρας τῶν πωλούντων τὰς περιστερὰς
changers and the seats of those selling the doves
κατέστρεψεν· 16 καὶ οὐκ.ἤφιεν ἵνα τις διενέγκῃ σκεῦος
he overthrew, and suffered not that anyone should carry a vessel
διὰ τοῦ ἱεροῦ. 17 καὶ ἐδίδασκεν, [m]λέγων" [n]αὐτοῖς," Οὐ
through the temple. And he taught, saying to them, [3]Not

let them go. 7 And
they brought the colt
to Jesus, and cast their
garments on him;
and he sat upon him.
8 And many spread
their garments in the
way: and others cut
down branches off the
trees, and strawed
them in the way. 9 And
they that went before,
and they that fol-
lowed, cried, saying,
Hosanna; Blessed *is*
he that cometh in the
name of the Lord:
10 blessed *be* the king-
dom of our father
David, that cometh in
the name of the Lord:
Hosanna in the high-
est. 11 And Jesus en-
tered into Jerusalem,
and into the temple:
and when he had look-
ed round about upon
all things, and now
the eventide was come,
he went out unto Beth-
any with the twelve.

12 And on the mor-
row, when they were
come from Bethany,
he was hungry: 13 and
seeing a fig tree afar
off having leaves, he
came, if haply he
might find any thing
thereon: and when he
came to it, he found
nothing but leaves;
for the time of figs
was not *yet*. 14 And
Jesus answered and
said unto it, No man
eat fruit of thee here-
after for ever. And
his disciples heard *it*.
15 And they come to
Jerusalem: and Jesus
went into the temple,
and began to cast out
them that sold and
bought in the temple,
and overthrew the
tables of the money-
changers, and the seats
of them that sold
doves; 16 and would
not suffer that any
man should carry *any*
vessel through the
temple. 17 And he
taught, saying unto

---

[o] φέρουσιν they bring TTrA. [p] ἐπιβάλλουσιν they cast upon GLTTrAW. [q] αὐτόν LTTrA. [r] καὶ πολλοὶ TTrA. [s] στιβάδας LTTrA. [t] κόψαντες having cut [them] down TTrA. [v] ἀγρῶν fields TTrA. [w] — καὶ ἐστρώννυον εἰς τὴν ὁδόν TTrA. [x] — λέγοντες [L]TTrA. [y] — ἐν ὀνόματι κυρίου GLTTrAW. [z] Δαυείδ LTTrA; Δαυῒδ GW. [a] — ὁ Ἰησοῦς καὶ (*read* he entered) LTTrA. [b] ὀψὲ T. [c] + ἀπὸ from LTTrAW. [d] τι εὑρήσει LTTrAW. [e] + [μόνα] only L. [f] οὐ γὰρ ἦν ὁ καιρὸς L; ὁ γὰρ καιρὸς οὐκ ἦν TTrA. [g] — ὁ Ἰησοῦς (*read* he said) GLTTrAW. [h] εἰς τὸν αἰῶνα ἐκ σοῦ LTTrA. [i] οὐδεὶς E. [k] — ὁ Ἰησοῦς GLTTrAW. [l] + τοὺς these LTTrAW. [m] καὶ ἔλεγεν and said TTrA. [n] — αὐτοῖς [L]A.

them, Is it not written, My house shall be called of all nations the house of prayer? but ye have made it a den of thieves. 18 And the scribes and chief priests heard *it*, and sought how they might destroy him: for they feared him, because all the people was astonished at his doctrine. 19 And when even was come, he went out of the city.

20 And in the morning, as they passed by, they saw the fig tree dried up from the roots. 21 And Peter calling to remembrance saith unto him, Master, behold, the fig tree which thou cursedst is withered away. 22 And Jesus answering saith unto them, Have faith in God. 23 For verily I say unto you, That whosoever shall say unto this mountain, Be thou removed, and be thou cast into the sea; and shall not doubt in his heart, but shall believe that those things which he saith shall come to pass; he shall have whatsoever he saith. 24 Therefore I say unto you, What things soever ye desire, when ye pray, believe that ye receive *them*, and ye shall have *them*. 25 And when ye stand praying, forgive, if ye have ought against any: that your Father also which is in heaven may forgive you your trespasses. 26 But if ye do not forgive, neither will your Father which is in heaven forgive your trespasses.

27 And they come again to Jerusalem: and as he was walking in the temple, there come to him the chief priests, and the scribes, and the elders, 28 and say unto him, By what authority doest thou these things? and who gave thee this authority to do these things? 29 And Jesus

γέγραπται, [o]"Ὅτι" ὁ.οἶκός.μου οἶκος προσευχῆς κληθήσεται
[1]has [2]it been written, My house a house of prayer shall be called
πᾶσιν τοῖς ἔθνεσιν; ὑμεῖς.δὲ [p]ἐποιήσατε" αὐτὸν σπήλαιον
for all the nations? but ye made it a den
λῃστῶν. 18 Καὶ ἤκουσαν οἱ [q]γραμματεῖς καὶ οἱ ἀρχιερεῖς,"
of robbers. And [7]heard [[8]it] [1]the [2]scribes [3]and [4]the [5]chief [6]priests,
καὶ ἐζήτουν πῶς αὐτὸν [r]ἀπολέσουσιν·" ἐφοβοῦντο.γὰρ [s]αὐτόν,"
and they sought how him they shall destroy; for they feared him,
[t]ὅτι πᾶς" ὁ ὄχλος [v]ἐξεπλήσσετο" ἐπὶ τῇ.διδαχῇ.αὐτοῦ.
because all the crowd were astonished at his teaching.
19 Καὶ [w]ὅτε" ὀψὲ ἐγένετο [x]ἐξεπορεύετο" ἔξω τῆς πόλεως.
And when evening came he went forth out of the city.
20 Καὶ [y]πρωῒ παραπορευόμενοι" εἶδον τὴν συκῆν
And in the morning passing by they saw the fig-tree
ἐξηραμμένην ἐκ ῥιζῶν. 21 καὶ ἀναμνησθεὶς ὁ Πέτρος
dried up from [the] roots. And [2]having [3]remembered [1]Peter
λέγει αὐτῷ, [z]Ῥαββί," ἴδε, ἡ συκῆ ἣν κατηράσω ἐξήρανται.
says to him Rabbi, see, the fig-tree which thou cursedst is dried up.
22 Καὶ ἀποκριθεὶς [a]Ἰησοῦς λέγει αὐτοῖς, Ἔχετε πίστιν θεοῦ.
And [2]answering [1]Jesus says to them, Have faith in God.
23 ἀμὴν.[b]γὰρ" λέγω ὑμῖν, ὅτι ὃς.ἂν εἴπῃ τῷ.ὄρει.τούτῳ,
For verily I say to you, that whoever shall say to this mountain,
Ἄρθητι καὶ βλήθητι εἰς τὴν θάλασσαν, καὶ μὴ.διακριθῇ ἐν τῇ.καρδίᾳ.αὐτοῦ, ἀλλὰ [c]πιστεύσῃ" ὅτι [d]ἃ" [e]λέγει"
Be thou taken away and be thou cast into the sea, and shall not doubt in his heart, but shall believe that what he says
γίνεται· ἔσται αὐτῷ [f]ὃ.ἐὰν εἴπῃ." 24 διὰ.τοῦτο λέγω
takes place, there shall be to him whatever he shall say. For this reason I say
ὑμῖν, Πάντα ὅσα.[g]ἂν" [h]προσευχόμενοι", αἰτεῖσθε, πιστεύετε
to you, All things whatsoever praying ye ask, believe
ὅτι [i]λαμβάνετε," καὶ ἔσται ὑμῖν. 25 Καὶ ὅταν [k]στήκητε"
that ye receive, and [they] shall be to you. And when ye may stand
προσευχόμενοι, ἀφίετε εἴ τι ἔχετε κατά τινος· ἵνα καὶ
praying, forgive if anything ye have against anyone, that also
ὁ.πατὴρ.ὑμῶν ὁ ἐν τοῖς οὐρανοῖς ἀφῇ ὑμῖν τὰ παραπτώματα ὑμῶν. 26 [l]εἰ.δὲ ὑμεῖς οὐκ.ἀφίετε, οὐδὲ ὁ.πατὴρ.ὑμῶν
your Father who [is] in the heavens may forgive you [2]offences [1]your. But if ye forgive not, neither your Father
ὁ ἐν [m]τοῖς| οὐρανοῖς ἀφήσει τὰ.παραπτώματα.ὑμῶν."
who [is] in the heavens will forgive your offences.
27 Καὶ ἔρχονται πάλιν εἰς Ἱεροσόλυμα· καὶ ἐν τῷ ἱερῷ
And they come again to Jerusalem. And in the temple
περιπατοῦντος.αὐτοῦ ἔρχονται πρὸς αὐτὸν οἱ ἀρχιερεῖς καὶ
as he is walking come to him the chief priests and
οἱ γραμματεῖς καὶ οἱ πρεσβύτεροι, 28 καὶ [n]λέγουσιν" αὐτῷ,
the scribes and the elders, and they say to him,
Ἐν ποίᾳ ἐξουσίᾳ ταῦτα ποιεῖς; [oa]καὶ" τίς σοι [pa]τὴν ἐξουσίαν
By what authority these things doest thou? and who thee [2]authority
ταύτην ἔδωκεν," ἵνα ταῦτα ποιῇς; 29 Ὁ.δὲ.Ἰησοῦς
[1]this gave, that these things thou shouldst do? And Jesus

o — Ὅτι L. p πεποιήκατε have made TTrA. q ἀρχιερεῖς καὶ οἱ γραμματεῖς LTTrAW. r ἀπολέσωσιν they might destroy LTTrAW. s [αὐτόν] L. t πᾶς γὰρ for all TTrA. v ἐξεπλήσσοντο T. w ὅταν TTr. x ἐξεπορεύοντο they went forth LTr. y παραπορευόμενοι πρωῒ LTTrA. z Ῥαββεί TA. a + ὁ GLTTrAW. b — γὰρ for LT[Tr]A. c πιστεύῃ TA. d ὃ what TTrA. e λαλεῖ LTTrA. f — ὃ ἐὰν εἴπῃ TTr[A]. g — ἂν LTTrAW. h προσεύχεσθε καὶ ye pray and LTTrA. i ἐλάβετε ye received LTTrA. k στήκετε ye stand LTTrA. l — verse 26 TTrA. m — τοῖς LA. n ἔλεγον they said TTrA. oa ἢ or TA. pa ἔδωκεν τὴν ἐξουσίαν ταύτην LTr.

[r]ἀποκριθεὶς" εἶπεν αὐτοῖς, Ἐπερωτήσω [s]ὑμᾶς κἀγὼ' ἕνα λόγον,
answering said to them ²Will ³ask ⁴you ¹I also one thing,
καὶ ἀποκρίθητέ μοι, καὶ ἐρῶ ὑμῖν ἐν ποίᾳ ἐξουσίᾳ ταῦτα
and answer me, and I will tell you by what authority these things
ποιῶ. 30 Τὸ βάπτισμα [t]Ἰωάννου ἐξ οὐρανοῦ ἦν ἢ ἐξ
I do: The baptism of John from heaven was it or from
ἀνθρώπων; ἀποκρίθητέ μοι. 31 Καὶ [v]ἐλογίζοντο" πρὸς ἑαυ-
men? answer me. And they reasoned with them-
τούς, λέγοντες, Ἐὰν εἴπωμεν, Ἐξ οὐρανοῦ, ἐρεῖ, [w]Διατί"
selves, saying, If we should say, From heaven, he will say, Why
[x]οὖν" οὐκ.ἐπιστεύσατε αὐτῷ; 32 [y]ἀλλ' ἐὰν" εἴπωμεν, Ἐξ
then did ye not believe him? but if we should say, From
ἀνθρώπων, ἐφοβοῦντο τὸν λαόν· [z]ἅπαντες".γὰρ εἶχον τὸν
men,— they feared the people; for all held
Ἰωάννην [a]ὅτι ὄντως" προφήτης ἦν. 33 καὶ ἀποκριθέντες [b]λέ-
John that indeed a prophet he was. And answering they
γουσιν τῷ Ἰησοῦ," Οὐκ.οἴδαμεν. Καὶ [c]ὁ Ἰησοῦς ἀποκριθεὶς" λέγει
say to Jesus, We know not. And Jesus answering says
αὐτοῖς, Οὐδὲ ἐγὼ λέγω ὑμῖν ἐν ποίᾳ ἐξουσίᾳ ταῦτα ποιῶ.
to them, Neither ²I ¹tell you by what authority these things I do.

12 Καὶ ἤρξατο αὐτοῖς ἐν παραβολαῖς [d]λέγειν," Ἀμπελῶνα
And he began to them in parables to say, ⁴A ⁵vineyard
[e]ἐφύτευσεν ἄνθρωπος," καὶ περιέθηκεν φραγμόν, καὶ ὤρυξεν
³planted ¹a ²man, and placed about [it] a fence, and dug
ὑπολήνιον, καὶ ᾠκοδόμησεν πύργον, καὶ [f]ἐξέδοτο" αὐτὸν
a wine-vat, and built a tower, and let out it
γεωργοῖς, καὶ ἀπεδήμησεν. 2 καὶ ἀπέστειλεν πρὸς τοὺς
to husbandmen, and left the country. And he sent to the
γεωργοὺς τῷ καιρῷ δοῦλον, ἵνα παρὰ τῶν γεωργῶν
husbandmen at the season a bondman, that from the husbandmen
λάβῃ ἀπὸ [g]τοῦ καρποῦ" τοῦ ἀμπελῶνος 3 [h]οἱ.δὲ" λα-
he might receive from the fruit of the vineyard. But they having
βόντες αὐτὸν ἔδειραν, καὶ ἀπέστειλαν κενόν. 4 καὶ πάλιν
taken ²him ¹beat, and sent [him] away empty. And again
ἀπέστειλεν πρὸς αὐτοὺς ἄλλον δοῦλον· κἀκεῖνον [i]λιθοβολή-
he sent to them another bondman, and him having
σαντες" [j]ἐκεφαλαίωσαν," καὶ [k]ἀπέστειλαν ἠτιμωμένον."
stoned they struck on the head, and sent [him] away having insulted [him].
5 καὶ [l]πάλιν" ἄλλον ἀπέστειλεν· κἀκεῖνον ἀπέκτειναν· καὶ
And again another he sent, and him they killed; also
πολλοὺς ἄλλους, [m]τοὺς" μὲν δέροντες, [m]τοὺς".δὲ [n]ἀποκτείνον-
many others, ²some ¹beating, and ²others ¹killing.
τες." 6 ἔτι [o]οὖν" ἕνα [p]υἱὸν ἔχων" ἀγαπητὸν [q]αὐτοῦ,"
Yet therefore ²one ³son ¹having ⁶beloved ⁴his ⁵own,
ἀπέστειλεν [ra]καὶ" αὐτὸν [sa]πρὸς αὐτοὺς ἔσχατον," λέγων, Ὅτι
he sent also him to them last, saying,
ἐντραπήσονται τὸν.υἱόν.μου. 7 ἐκεῖνοι.δὲ οἱ γεωργοὶ [ta]εἶπον
They will have respect for my son. But those husbandmen said

answered and said unto them, I will also ask of you one question, and answer me, and I will tell you by what authority I do these things. 30 The baptism of John, was it from heaven, or of men? answer me. 31 And they reasoned with themselves, saying, If we shall say, From heaven; he will say, Why then did ye not believe him? 32 But if we shall say, Of men; they feared the people: for all *men* counted John, that he was a prophet indeed. 33 And they answered and said unto Jesus, We cannot tell. And Jesus answering saith unto them, Neither do I tell you by what authority I do these things.

XII. And he began to speak unto them by parables. A *certain* man planted a vineyard, and set an hedge about *it*, and digged *a place for* the winefat, and built a tower, and let it out to husbandmen, and went into a far country. 2 And at the season he sent to the husbandmen a servant, that he might receive from the husbandmen of the fruit of the vineyard. 3 And they caught *him*, and beat him, and sent *him* away empty. 4 And again he sent unto them another servant; and at him they cast stones, and wounded *him* in the head, and sent *him* away shamefully handled. 5 And again he sent another; and him they killed, and many others; beating some, and killing some. 6 Having yet therefore one son, his wellbeloved, he sent him also last unto them, saying, They will reverence my son. 7 But those husbandmen said among them-

---

[r] — ἀποκριθεὶς TTrA. [s] κἀγὼ ὑμᾶς L; — κἀγὼ (*read* ἐπερ. I will ask) TTrA. [t] + τὸ LTTrAW. [v] διελογίζοντο LTTrAW. [w] Διὰ τί LTrA. [x] — οὖν LTrAW. [y] ἀλλὰ (*read* but should we say) LTTrAW. [z] πάντες L. [a] ὄντως ὅτι TTrA. [b] τῷ Ἰησοῦ λέγουσιν TTrA. [c] [ἀποκριθεὶς] ὁ Ἰησοῦς L; — ἀποκριθεὶς TTrA. [d] λαλεῖν LTTrA. [e] ἄνθρωπος ἐφύτευσεν T. [f] ἐξέδετο TA. [g] τῶν καρπῶν the fruits TTrA. [h] καὶ and LTTrA. [i] — λιθοβολήσαντες LTTrA. [j] ἐκεφαλίωσαν T. [k] ἠτίμησαν insulted LTr; ἠτίμασαν TA. [l] — πάλιν GLTTrA. [m] οὓς LTTrA. [n] ἀποκτέννοντες GLTTrA. [o] — οὖν [L]TTrA. [p] ἔχων υἱὸν L; εἶχεν υἱὸν TTrA. [q] — αὐτοῦ LTTrA; αὐτοῦ W. [ra] — καὶ [L]TTrA. [sa] ἔσχατον πρὸς αὐτούς LTTrA. [ta] πρὸς ἑαυτοὺς εἶπαν TTrA; εἶπαν πρὸς ἑαυτοὺς L.

selves, This is the heir; come, let us kill him, and the inheritance shall be ours. 8 And they took him, and killed *him*, and cast *him* out of the vineyard. 9 What shall therefore the lord of the vineyard do? he will come and destroy the husbandmen, and will give the vineyard unto others. 10 And have ye not read this scripture; The stone which the builders rejected is become the head of the corner: 11 this was the Lord's doing, and it is marvellous in our eyes? 12 And they sought to lay hold on him, but feared the people: for they knew that he had spoken the parable against them: and they left him, and went their way.

13 And they send unto him certain of the Pharisees and of the Herodians, to catch him in *his* words. 14 And when they were come, they say unto him, Master, we know that thou art true, and carest for no man: for thou regardest not the person of men, but teachest the way of God in truth: Is it lawful to give tribute to Cæsar, or not? 15 Shall we give, or shall we not give? But he, knowing their hypocrisy, said unto them, Why tempt ye me? bring me a penny, that I may see *it*. 16 And they brought *it*. And he saith unto them, Whose *is* this image and superscription? And they said unto him, Cæsar's. 17 And Jesus answering said unto them, Render to Cæsar the things that are Cæsar's, and to God the things that are God's. And they marvelled at him.

18 Then come unto him the Sadducees, which say there is no resurrection; and they asked him, saying,

πρὸς ἑαυτούς,‖ Ὅτι οὗτός ἐστιν ὁ κληρονόμος· δεῦτε, ἀπο-
among themselves, This is the heir: come, let us
κτείνωμεν αὐτόν, καὶ ἡμῶν ἔσται ἡ κληρονομία. 8 καὶ λαβόντες
kill him, and ours will be the inheritance. And having taken
[v]αὐτὸν ἀπέκτειναν,‖ καὶ ἐξέβαλον [w] ἔξω τοῦ ἀμπελῶνος.
him they killed [him], and cast forth [him] outside the vineyard.
9 τί [x]οὖν‖ ποιήσει ὁ κύριος τοῦ ἀμπελῶνος; ἐλεύσεται καὶ
What therefore will do the lord of the vineyard? He will come and
ἀπολέσει τοὺς γεωργούς, καὶ δώσει τὸν ἀμπελῶνα ἄλλοις.
will destroy the husbandmen, and will give the vineyard to others.
10 Οὐδὲ τὴν-γραφὴν-ταύτην ἀνέγνωτε; Λίθον ὃν
[3]Not [4]even [6]this [7]scripture [1]did [2]ye [5]read? [The] stone which
ἀπεδοκίμασαν οἱ οἰκοδομοῦντες, οὗτος ἐγενήθη εἰς κεφαλὴν
[4]rejected [1]those [2]who [3]build, this is become head
γωνίας. 11 παρὰ κυρίου ἐγένετο αὕτη, καὶ ἔστιν θαυ-
of [the] corner: from [the] Lord was this, and it is won-
μαστὴ ἐν ὀφθαλμοῖς-ἡμῶν. 12 Καὶ ἐζήτουν αὐτὸν κρατῆσαι,
derful in our eyes. And they sought him to lay hold of,
καὶ ἐφοβήθησαν τὸν ὄχλον· ἔγνωσαν-γὰρ ὅτι πρὸς αὐτοὺς
and they feared the crowd; for they knew that against them
τὴν παραβολὴν εἶπεν· καὶ ἀφέντες αὐτὸν ἀπῆλθον.
the parable he speaks. And leaving him they went away.

13 Καὶ ἀποστέλλουσιν πρὸς αὐτόν τινας τῶν Φαρισαίων
And they send to him some of the Pharisees
καὶ τῶν Ἡρωδιανῶν, ἵνα αὐτὸν ἀγρεύσωσιν λόγῳ. 14 [y]οἱ-δὲ‖
and of the Herodians, that him they might catch in discourse. And they
ἐλθόντες λέγουσιν αὐτῷ, Διδάσκαλε, οἴδαμεν ὅτι ἀληθὴς εἶ,
having come say to him, Teacher, we know that true thou art,
καὶ οὐ μέλει σοι περὶ οὐδενός· οὐ-γὰρ βλέπεις εἰς
and there is care to thee about no one; for [3]not [1]thou [2]lookest on [the]
πρόσωπον ἀνθρώπων, ἀλλ' ἐπ' ἀληθείας τὴν ὁδὸν τοῦ θεοῦ
appearance of men, but with truth the way of God
διδάσκεις. [z]ἔξεστιν [a]κῆνσον Καίσαρι δοῦναι‖ ἢ οὔ; 15 δῶμεν
teachest: Is it lawful tribute to Cæsar to give or not? Should we give
ἢ μὴ-δῶμεν; Ὁ-δὲ [b]εἰδὼς‖ αὐτῶν-τὴν-ὑπόκρισιν εἶπεν
or should we not give? But he knowing their hypocrisy said
αὐτοῖς, Τί με πειράζετε; φέρετέ μοι δηνάριον ἵνα ἴδω.
to them, Why me do ye tempt? Bring me a denarius that I may see [it].
16 Οἱ-δὲ ἤνεγκαν. Καὶ λέγει αὐτοῖς, Τίνος ἡ-εἰκὼν-αὕτη καὶ
And they brought [it]. And he says to them, Whose [is] this image and
ἡ ἐπιγραφή; [c]Οἱ-δὲ‖ [d]εἶπον‖ αὐτῷ, Καίσαρος. 17 [e]Καὶ
the inscription? And they said to him, Cæsar's. And
ἀποκριθεὶς ὁ‖ Ἰησοῦς εἶπεν [f]αὐτοῖς,‖ [g]Ἀπόδοτε τὰ Καί-
[2]answering [1]Jesus said to them, Render the things of Cæ-
σαρος‖ Καίσαρι, καὶ τὰ τοῦ θεοῦ τῷ θεῷ. Καὶ [h]ἐθαύμασαν‖
sar to Cæsar, and the things of God to God. And they wondered
ἐπ' αὐτῷ,
at him.

18 Καὶ ἔρχονται Σαδδουκαῖοι πρὸς αὐτόν, οἵτινες λέγουσιν
And [2]come [1]Sadducees to him, who say
ἀνάστασιν μὴ-εἶναι· καὶ [i]ἐπηρώτησαν‖ αὐτόν, λέγοντες,
a resurrection there is not. And they questioned him, saying,

---

[v] ἀπέκτειναν αὐτόν TTrA. [w] + αὐτὸν him LTTrAW. [x] — οὖν TA. [y] καὶ and (*read* they say) LTTrA. [z] + εἰπὲ οὖν ἡμῖν tell us therefore L. [a] δοῦναι κῆνσον Καίσαρι LTr. [b] ἰδὼν having known T. [c] [οἱ δὲ] L. [d] εἶπαν LTTrA. [e] ὁ δὲ and (Jesus) LTTrA. [f] — αὐτοῖς A. [g] Τὰ Καίσαρος ἀπόδοτε TTrA. [h] ἐθαύμαζον LTrA; ἐξεθαύμαζον greatly wondered T. [i] ἐπηρώτων LTTrA.

19 Διδάσκαλε, [k]Μωσῆς‖ ἔγραψεν ἡμῖν, ὅτι ἐάν τινος ἀδελ-
Teacher, Moses wrote for us, that if of anyone a bro-
φὸς ἀποθάνῃ καὶ καταλίπῃ γυναῖκα καὶ [l]τέκνα μὴ.ἀφῇ,‖
ther should die and leave behind a wife and children leave not,
ἵνα λάβῃ ὁ.ἀδελφὸς.αὐτοῦ τὴν γυναῖκα· [m]αὐτοῦ‖ καὶ
that [3]should [4]take [1]his [2]brother the wife of him and
ἐξαναστήσῃ σπέρμα τῷ.ἀδελφῷ.αὐτοῦ. 20 ἑπτὰ [n] ἀδελφοὶ
raise up seed to his brother. Seven brethren
ἦσαν· καὶ ὁ πρῶτος ἔλαβεν γυναῖκα, καὶ ἀποθνήσκων
there were; and the first took a wife, and dying
οὐκ.ἀφῆκεν σπέρμα· 21 καὶ ὁ δεύτερος ἔλαβεν αὐτήν, καὶ
left no seed; and the second took her, and
ἀπέθανεν, [o]καὶ οὐδὲ αὐτὸς ἀφῆκεν‖ σπέρμα· καὶ ὁ τρίτος
died, and neither he left seed; and the third
ὡσαύτως· 22 καὶ [p]ἔλαβον αὐτὴν‖ οἱ ἑπτά, [q]καὶ‖ οὐκ.ἀφῆκαν
likewise. And [3]took [4]her [1]the [2]seven, and left no
σπέρμα. [r]ἐσχάτη‖ πάντων [s]ἀπέθανεν καὶ ἡ γυνή.‖ 23 ἐν.τῇ
seed. Last of all died also the woman. In the
[t]οὖν‖ ἀναστάσει, [v]ὅταν ἀναστῶσιν,‖ τίνος αὐτῶν ἔσται
[2]therefore [1]resurrection, when they shall arise, of which of them shall she be
γυνή; οἱ.γὰρ ἑπτὰ ἔσχον αὐτὴν γυναῖκα. 24 [w]Καὶ ἀποκριθεὶς
wife? for the seven had her as wife. And [2]answering
ὁ Ἰησοῦς εἶπεν αὐτοῖς,‖ Οὐ διὰ.τοῦτο πλανᾶσθε, μὴ εἰδότες
[1]Jesus said to them, [3]Not [4]therefore [1]do [2]ye err, not knowing
τὰς γραφὰς μηδὲ τὴν δύναμιν τοῦ θεοῦ; 25 ὅταν.γὰρ ἐκ
the scriptures nor the power of God? For when from among
νεκρῶν ἀναστῶσιν, οὔτε γαμοῦσιν οὔτε [x]γαμίσκονται,‖
[the] dead they rise, neither do they marry nor are given in marriage,
ἀλλ' εἰσὶν ὡς ἄγγελοι [y]οἱ‖ ἐν τοῖς οὐρανοῖς. 26 περὶ.δὲ
but are as angels who [are] in the heavens. But concerning
τῶν νεκρῶν, ὅτι ἐγείρονται, οὐκ.ἀνέγνωτε ἐν τῇ βίβλῳ
the dead, that they rise, have ye not read in the book
[z]Μωσέως,‖ ἐπὶ [a]τῆς‖ βάτου, [b]ὡς‖ εἶπεν αὐτῷ ὁ θεός,
of Moses, [in the part] on the bush, how [2]spoke [3]to [4]him [1]God,
λέγων, Ἐγὼ ὁ θεὸς Ἀβραὰμ καὶ [c]ὁ‖ θεὸς Ἰσαὰκ καὶ [c]ὁ‖
saying, I [am] the God of Abraham and the God of Isaac and the
θεὸς Ἰακώβ; 27 Οὐκ.ἔστιν [c]ὁ‖ θεὸς νεκρῶν, ἀλλὰ [d]θεὸς‖
God of Jacob? He is not the God of [the] dead, but God
ζώντων· [e]ὑμεῖς οὖν‖ πολὺ πλανᾶσθε. 28 Καὶ προσελθὼν
of [the] living. Ye therefore greatly err. And [5]having [6]come [7]up
εἷς τῶν γραμματέων, ἀκούσας αὐτῶν [f]συνζητούντων,‖ [g]εἰδὼς‖
[1]one [2]of [3]the [4]scribes, having heard them reasoning together, perceiving
ὅτι καλῶς [h]αὐτοῖς ἀπεκρίθη,‖ ἐπηρώτησεν αὐτόν, Ποία ἐστὶν
that well them he answered, questioned him, Which is
[i]πρώτη πασῶν ἐντολή‖; 29 [ka]Ὁ.δὲ.Ἰησοῦς ἀπεκρίθη‖
[the] first [2]of [3]all [1]commandment? And Jesus answered
[la]αὐτῷ,‖ Ὅτι πρώτη [ma]πασῶν τῶν ἐντολῶν,‖ Ἄκουε,
him, [The] first of all the commandments [is], Hear,

19 Master, Moses wrote
unto us, If a man's
brother die, and leave
his wife *behind him*,
and leave no children,
that his brother should
take his wife, and raise
up seed unto his bro-
ther. 20 Now there
were seven brethren:
and the first took a
wife, and dying left
no seed. 21 And the
second took her, and
died, neither left he
any seed: and the third
likewise. 22 And the
seven had her, and left
no seed: last of all the
woman died also. 23 In
the resurrection there-
fore, when they shall
rise, whose wife shall
she be of them? for
the seven had her to
wife. 24 And Jesus
answering said unto
them, Do ye not there-
fore err, because ye
know not the scrip-
tures, neither the
power of God? 25 For
when they shall rise
from the dead, they
neither marry, nor are
given in marriage; but
are as the angels which
are in heaven. 26 And
as touching the dead,
that they rise: have
ye not read in the book
of Moses, how in the
bush God spake unto
him, saying, I *am* the
God of Abraham, and
the God of Isaac, and
the God of Jacob?
27 He is not the God
of the dead, but the
God of the living: ye
therefore do greatly
err. 28 And one of the
scribes came, and hav-
ing heard them rea-
soning together, and
perceiving that he had
answered them well,
asked him, Which is
the first command-
ment of all? 29 And
Jesus answered him,
The first of all the
commandments *is*,
Hear, O Israel; The

[k] Μωϋσῆς LTTrAW. [l] μὴ ἀφῇ τέκνον leave no child TA. [m] — αὐτοῦ TTrA. [n] + οὖν therefore EW. [o] μὴ καταλιπὼν having left behind no TTrA. [p] — ἔλαβον αὐτὴν [L]TTrA. [q] — καὶ TTrA. [r] ἔσχατον LTTrA. [s] καὶ ἡ γυνὴ ἀπέθανεν LTTrA. [t] — οὖν TTrA. [v] — ὅταν ἀναστῶσιν [L]Tr. [w] ἔφη αὐτοῖς ὁ Ἰησοῦς Jesus said to them TTrA. [x] γαμίζονται LTTrAW. [y] — οἱ GLT[Tr]W. [z] Μωϋσέως LTTrAW. [a] τοῦ GLTTrAW. [b] πῶς TTrA. [c] — ὁ LTrAW. [d] — θεὸς GLTTrAW. [e] — ὑμεῖς οὖν (*read* πλαν. ye err) T[Tr]A. [f] συνζητούντων LTTrA. [g] ἰδὼν having seen LTTr. [h] ἀπεκρίθη αὐτοῖς TTrA. [i] πρώτη πάντων ἐντολή GLW; ἐντολὴ πρώτη πάντων TTrA. [ka] ἀπεκρίθη ὁ Ἰησοῦς TTrA. [la] — αὐτῷ T[Tr]A. [ma] πάντων ἐντολή GW; πάντων [ἐντολή ἐστιν] commandment of all is L; ἐστίν (*read* [The] first is) TTrA.

Lord our God is one
Lord: 30 and thou
shalt love the Lord thy
God with all thy heart,
and with all thy soul,
and with all thy mind,
and with all thy
strength: this *is* the
first commandment.
31 And the second *is*
like, *namely* this, Thou
shalt love thy neigh-
bour as thyself. There
is none other com-
mandment greater
than these. 32 And
the scribe said unto
him, Well, Master,
thou hast said the
truth: for there is one
God; and there is none
other but he: 33 and
to love him with all
the heart, and with
all the understanding,
and with all the soul,
and with all the
strength, and to love
his neighbour as him-
self, is more than all
whole burnt offerings
and sacrifices. 34 And
when Jesus saw that
he answered discreet-
ly, he said unto him,
Thou art not far from
the kingdom of God.
And no man after that
durst ask him *any*
question.

35 And Jesus an-
swered and said, while
he taught in the tem-
ple, How say the
scribes that Christ is
the Son of David?
36 For David himself
said by the Holy Ghost,
The LORD said to my
Lord, Sit thou on my
right hand, till I make
thine enemies thy
footstool. 37 David
therefore himself call-
eth him Lord; and
whence is he *then* his
son? And the com-
mon people heard him
gladly.

38 And he said unto
them in his doctrine,
Beware of the scribes;
which love to go in
long clothing, and *love*

Ἰσραήλ· κύριος ὁ.θεὸς.ἡμῶν κύριος εἷς ἐστίν. 30 καὶ
Israel: [the] Lord our God [3]Lord [2]one [1]is. And
ἀγαπήσεις κύριον τὸν.θεόν.σου ἐξ ὅλης τῆς.καρδίας.σου
thou shalt love [the] Lord thy God with all thy heart
καὶ ἐξ ὅλης τῆς.ψυχῆς.σου καὶ ἐξ ὅλης τῆς.διανοίας.σου
and with all thy soul and with all thy mind
καὶ ἐξ ὅλης τῆς.ἰσχύος.σου. [n]αὕτη πρώτη ἐντολή."
and with all thy strength. This [is the] first commandment.
31 [o]καὶ" δευτέρα [p]ὁμοία" [q]αὕτη," Ἀγαπήσεις τὸν πλη-
And [the] second like [it is] this: Thou shalt love [2]neigh-
σίον σου ὡς σεαυτόν. Μείζων τούτων ἄλλη ἐντολὴ
bour [1]thy as thyself. Greater than these another commandment
οὐκ.ἔστιν. 32 Καὶ εἶπεν αὐτῷ ὁ γραμματεύς, Καλῶς, διδάσ-
there is not. And [3]said [4]to [5]him [1]the [2]scribe, Right, teach-
καλε, ἐπ' ἀληθείας [r]εἶπας" ὅτι εἷς ἐστιν [s]θεός," καὶ
er, according to truth thou hast said that [3]one [2]is [1]God, and
οὐκ.ἔστιν ἄλλος πλὴν αὐτοῦ. 33 καὶ τὸ ἀγαπᾷν αὐτὸν ἐξ
there is not another besides him: and to love him with
ὅλης τῆς καρδίας καὶ ἐξ ὅλης τῆς συνέσεως [t]καὶ ἐξ ὅλης
all the heart and with all the understanding and with all
τῆς ψυχῆς" καὶ ἐξ ὅλης τῆς ἰσχύος, καὶ τὸ ἀγαπᾷν
the soul and with all the strength, and to love [one's]
τὸν πλησίον ὡς ἑαυτόν, [v]πλεῖόν" ἐστιν πάντων τῶν ὁλοκαυ-
neighbour as oneself, [2]more [1]is than all the burnt
τωμάτων καὶ [w]τῶν" θυσιῶν. 34 Καὶ ὁ Ἰησοῦς ἰδὼν [x]αὐτὸν"
offerings and the sacrifices. And Jesus seeing him
ὅτι νουνεχῶς ἀπεκρίθη, εἶπεν αὐτῷ, Οὐ μακρὰν εἶ
that intelligently he answered, said to him, Not far art thou
ἀπὸ τῆς βασιλείας τοῦ θεοῦ. Καὶ οὐδεὶς.οὐκέτι ἐτόλμα αὐτὸν
from the kingdom of God. And no one any more dared [3]him
ἐπερωτῆσαι.
[1]to [2]question.

35 Καὶ ἀποκριθεὶς ὁ Ἰησοῦς ἔλεγεν, διδάσκων ἐν τῷ ἱερῷ,
And [2]answering [1]Jesus said, teaching in the temple,
Πῶς λέγουσιν οἱ γραμματεῖς ὅτι ὁ χριστὸς υἱός [y]ἐστιν Δαβίδ";
How say the scribes that the Christ [2]son [1]is of David?
36 αὐτὸς [z]γὰρ" [a]Δαβὶδ" [b]εἶπεν" ἐν [c]τῷ" πνεύματι [c]τῷ" ἁγίῳ,
[3]himself [1]for [2]David said by the Spirit the Holy,
[d]Εἶπεν" [e]ὁ" κύριος τῷ.κυρίῳ.μου, [f]Κάθου" ἐκ δεξιῶν.μου ἕως.ἂν
[3]Said [1]the [2]Lord to my Lord, Sit at my right hand until
θῶ τοὺς.ἐχθρούς.σου [g]ὑποπόδιον" τῶν.ποδῶν.σου. 37 Αὐτὸς
I place thine enemies [as] a footstool for thy feet. [2]Himself
[h]οὖν" [a]Δαβὶδ" λέγει αὐτὸν κύριον· καὶ πόθεν [i]υἱὸς.αὐτοῦ
[3]therefore [1]David calls him Lord, and whence his son
ἐστιν;" Καὶ ὁ πολὺς ὄχλος ἤκουεν αὐτοῦ ἡδέως.
is he? And the great crowd heard him gladly.

38 Καὶ [k]ἔλεγεν αὐτοῖς ἐν τῇ.διδαχῇ.αὐτοῦ," Βλέπετε ἀπὸ
And he said to them in his teaching, Take heed of
τῶν γραμματέων, τῶν θελόντων ἐν στολαῖς περιπατεῖν, καὶ
the scribes, who like in robes to walk about, and

---

[n] — αὕτη πρώτη ἐντολή TA. [o] — καὶ [L]TTrA. [p] — ὁμοία TA. [q] αὐτῇ (*read* [is] like it) LTr. [r] εἶπες T. [s] — θεός (*read* he is one) GLTTrAW. [t] — καὶ ἐξ ὅλης τῆς ψυχῆς [L]T. [v] περισσότερόν abundantly more TTr. [w] — τῶν GLTrAW. [x] [αὐτὸν] Tr. [y] Δαυείδ ἐστιν TTrA; ἐστιν Δαυείδ L; ἐστιν Δαυΐδ GW. [z] — γὰρ [L]T[Tr]A. [a] Δαυεὶδ LTTrA; Δαυΐδ GW. [b] λέγει says W. [c] — τῷ GW. [d] λέγει says GTr. [e] — ὁ (*read* [the]) LTrA. [f] κάθισον TrA. [g] ὑποκάτω (*read* beneath thy feet) A. [h] — οὖν [L]TTrA. [i] αὐτοῦ ἐστιν υἱός TTrA. [k] ἐν τῇ διδαχῇ αὐτοῦ ἔλεγεν TTrA.

ἀσπασμοὺς ἐν ταῖς ἀγοραῖς 39 καὶ πρωτοκαθεδρίας ἐν ταῖς
salutations in the market-places and first seats in the
συναγωγαῖς καὶ πρωτοκλισίας ἐν τοῖς δείπνοις· 40 οἱ [l]κατεσ-
synagogues and first places at the suppers; who de-
θίοντες‖ τὰς οἰκίας τῶν χηρῶν, καὶ προφάσει μακρὰ
vour the houses of widows, and as a pretext [2]at [3]great [4]length
προσευχόμενοι· οὗτοι [m]λήψονται‖ περισσότερον κρίμα.
[1]pray. These shall receive more abundant judgment.

41 Καὶ καθίσας [n]ὁ Ἰησοῦς‖ [o]κατέναντι‖ τοῦ γαζοφυλα-
And [2]having [3]sat [4]down [1]Jesus opposite the treasury,
κίου ἐθεώρει πῶς ὁ ὄχλος βάλλει χαλκὸν εἰς τὸ γαζοφυλά-
he saw how the crowd cast money into the treasury;
κιον· καὶ πολλοὶ πλούσιοι ἔβαλλον πολλά. 42 καὶ ἐλθοῦσα
and many rich were casting [in] much. And [4]having [5]come
μία χήρα πτωχὴ ἔβαλεν λεπτὰ δύο, ὅ ἐστιν κοδράντης.
[1]one [3]widow [2]poor cast [in] [2]lepta [1]two, which is a kodrantes.
43 καὶ προσκαλεσάμενος τοὺς.μαθητὰς.αὐτοῦ [p]λέγει‖ αὐτοῖς,
And having called to [him] his disciples he says to them,
Ἀμὴν λέγω ὑμῖν, ὅτι ἡ.χήρα.αὕτη ἡ πτωχὴ πλεῖον πάντων
Verily I say to you, that this [2]widow [1]poor more than all
[q]βέβληκεν‖ τῶν [r]βαλόντων‖ εἰς τὸ γαζοφυλάκιον. 44 πάν-
has cast [in] of those casting into the treasury. [2]All
τες γὰρ ἐκ τοῦ περισσεύοντος αὐτοῖς ἔβαλον· αὕτη.δὲ
[1]for out of that which was abounding to them cast [in], but she
ἐκ τῆς.ὑστερήσεως.αὐτῆς πάντα ὅσα εἶχεν ἔβαλεν,
out of her destitution [3]all [4]as [5]much [6]as [7]she [8]had [1]cast [[2]in],
ὅλον τὸν.βίον.αὐτῆς.
[10]whole [9]her [11]livelihood.

13 Καὶ ἐκπορευομένου.αὐτοῦ ἐκ τοῦ ἱεροῦ λέγει αὐτῷ
And as he was going forth out of the temple [5]says [6]to [7]him
εἷς [s] τῶν.μαθητῶν.αὐτοῦ, Διδάσκαλε, ἴδε, ποταποὶ λίθοι καὶ
[1]one [2]of [3]his [4]disciples, Teacher, see, what stones and
ποταπαὶ οἰκοδομαί. 2 Καὶ [t]ὁ Ἰησοῦς ἀποκριθεὶς‖ εἶπεν αὐτῷ,
what buildings! And Jesus answering said to him,
Βλέπεις ταύτας τὰς μεγάλας οἰκοδομάς; οὐ.μὴ ἀφεθῇ [u]
Seest thou these great buildings? not at all shall be left
λίθος ἐπὶ [v]λίθῳ‖ ὃς οὐ.μὴ.καταλυθῇ. 3 Καὶ καθημένου
stone upon stone which shall not be thrown down. And as [2]was [3]sitting
αὐτοῦ εἰς τὸ ὄρος τῶν Ἐλαιῶν κατέναντι τοῦ ἱεροῦ, [w]ἐπηρώ-
[1]he upon the mount of Olives opposite the temple, [8]ask-
των‖ αὐτὸν κατ᾽.ἰδίαν [x]Πέτρος καὶ Ἰάκωβος καὶ Ἰωάννης καὶ
ed [9]him [10]apart [1]Peter [2]and [3]James [4]and [5]John [6]and
Ἀνδρέας, 4 [y]Εἰπὲ‖ ἡμῖν πότε ταῦτα ἔσται; καὶ τί τὸ
[7]Andrew, Tell us when [2]these [3]things [1]shall be? and what the
σημεῖον ὅταν μέλλῃ [z]πάντα ταῦτα συντελεῖσθαι‖;
sign when [4]should [5]be [6]about [1]all [2]these [3]things to be accomplished?
5 Ὁ.δὲ.Ἰησοῦς [a]ἀποκριθεὶς‖ [b]αὐτοῖς ἤρξατο λέγειν,‖ Βλέπετε
And Jesus answering to them began to say, Take heed
μή τις ὑμᾶς πλανήσῃ. 6 πολλοὶ.[c]γὰρ‖ ἐλεύσονται ἐπὶ τῷ
lest anyone [2]you [1]mislead. For many will come in
ὀνόματί.μου, λέγοντες, Ὅτι ἐγώ εἰμι· καὶ πολλοὺς πλανή-
my name, saying, I am [he], and many they will

salutations in the market-places, 39 and the chief seats in the synagogues, and the uppermost rooms at feasts: 40 which devour widows' houses, and for a pretence make long prayers: these shall receive greater damnation.
41 And Jesus sat over against the treasury, and beheld how the people cast money into the treasury: and many that were rich cast in much.
42 And there came a certain poor widow, and she threw in two mites, which make a farthing. 43 And he called *unto him* his disciples, and saith unto them, Verily I say unto you, That this poor widow hath cast more in, than all they which have cast into the treasury: 44 for all *they* did cast in of their abundance; but she of her want did cast in all that she had, *even* all her living.

XIII. And as he went out of the temple, one of his disciples saith unto him, Master, see what manner of stones and what buildings *are here!* 2 And Jesus answering said unto him, Seest thou these great buildings? there shall not be left one stone upon another, that shall not be thrown down. 3 And as he sat upon the mount of Olives over against the temple, Peter and James and John and Andrew asked him privately, 4 Tell us, when shall these things be? and what *shall be* the sign when all these things shall be fulfilled? 5 And Jesus answering them began to say, Take heed lest any *man* deceive you: 6 for many shall come in my name, saying, I am *Christ;* and shall deceive many. 7 And when ye shall hear of wars

---

[l] κατέσθοντες TrA. [m] λήμψονται LTTrA. [n] — ὁ Ἰησοῦς [L]TTrA. [o] ἀπέναντι Tr. [p] εἶπεν he said GLTTr. [q] ἔβαλεν did cast [in] LTr. [r] βαλλόντων LTTrAW. [s] + ἐκ of Tr[A]. [t] ἀποκριθεὶς ὁ Ἰησοῦς L; — ἀποκριθεὶς TTrA. [u] + ὧδε here LTr. [v] λίθον TTr. [w] ἐπηρώτα TTrA. [x] + ὁ T. [y] εἰπὸν LTTrA. [z] ταῦτα πάντα συντελεῖσθαι L; ταῦτα συντελεῖσθαι πάντα TTrA. [a] — ἀποκριθεὶς TTrA. [b] ἤρξατο λέγειν αὐτοῖς LTTrA. [c] — γὰρ for TA.

and rumours of wars,
be ye not troubled:
for *such things* must
needs be; but the end
shall not *be* yet. 8 For
nation shall rise a-
gainst nation, and
kingdom against king-
dom: and there shall
be earthquakes in di-
vers places, and there
shall be famines and
troubles: these *are*
the beginnings of sor-
rows. 9 But take heed
to yourselves: for they
shall deliver you up
to councils; and in the
synagogues ye shall be
beaten: and ye shall
be brought before ru-
lers and kings for my
sake, for a testimony
against them. 10 And
the gospel must first
be published among all
nations. 11 But when
they shall lead *you*,
and deliver you up,
take no thought be-
forehand what ye
shall speak, neither do
ye premeditate: but
whatsoever shall be
given you in that hour,
that speak ye: for it
is not ye that speak,
but the Holy Ghost.
12 Now the brother
shall betray the bro-
ther to death, and the
father the son; and
children shall rise up
against *their* parents,
and shall cause them
to be put to death.
13 And ye shall be
hated of all *men* for
my name's sake: but
he that shall endure
unto the end, the
same shall be saved.
14 But when ye shall
see the abomination of
desolation, spoken of
by Daniel the prophet,
standing where it
ought not, (let him
that readeth under-
stand,) then let them
that be in Judæa flee
to the mountains:
15 and let him that is
on the housetop not
go down into the house,
neither enter *therein*,
to take any thing out
of his house: 16 and
let him that is in the
field not turn back
again for to take up
his garment. 17 But
woe to them that are

σουσιν. 7 ὅταν.δὲ [d]ἀκούσητε‖ πολέμους καὶ ἀκοὰς πολέμων,
mislead. But when ye shall hear of wars and rumours of wars,
μὴ.θροεῖσθε· δεῖ [e]γὰρ‖ γενέσθαι· ἀλλ' οὔπω τὸ
be not disturbed; [2]it [3]must [4]needs [1]for come to pass, but [4]not [5]yet [[3]is] [1]the
τέλος. 8 Ἐγερθήσεται.γὰρ ἔθνος [f]ἐπὶ‖ ἔθνος καὶ βασιλεία
[2]end. For [2]shall [3]rise [4]up [1]nation against nation and kingdom
ἐπὶ βασιλείαν· [g]καὶ‖ ἔσονται σεισμοὶ κατὰ.τόπους, [h]καὶ‖
against kingdom; and there shall be earthquakes in different places, and
ἔσονται λιμοὶ [i]καὶ ταραχαί.‖ [k]ἀρχαὶ‖ ὠδίνων ταῦτα.
there shall be famines and troubles. Beginnings of throes [are] these.
9 Βλέπετε.δὲ ὑμεῖς ἑαυτούς. παραδώσουσιν.[l]γὰρ‖ ὑμᾶς εἰς
But take heed ye to yourselves; for they will deliver up you to
συνέδρια καὶ εἰς συναγωγὰς· δαρήσεσθε, καὶ ἐπὶ ἡγεμόνων
sanhedrims and to synagogues: ye will be beaten, and before governors
καὶ βασιλέων σταθήσεσθε ἕνεκεν.ἐμοῦ, εἰς μαρτύριον αὐτοῖς·
and kings ye will be brought for my sake, for a testimony to them;
10 καὶ εἰς πάντα τὰ ἔθνη [m]δεῖ πρῶτον‖ κηρυχθῆναι τὸ
and to all the nations must first be proclaimed the
εὐαγγέλιον. 11 [n]ὅταν.δὲ‖ [o]ἀγάγωσιν‖ ὑμᾶς παραδιδόντες,
glad tidings. But whenever they may lead away you delivering [you] up,
μὴ.προμεριμνᾶτε τί λαλήσητε, [p]μηδὲ μελετᾶτε·‖
be not careful beforehand what ye should say, nor meditate [your reply];
ἀλλ' ὃ.[q]ἐὰν‖ δοθῇ ὑμῖν ἐν ἐκείνῃ.τῇ.ὥρᾳ, τοῦτο λαλεῖτε·
but whatever may be given to you in that hour, that speak;
οὐ.γάρ ἐστε ὑμεῖς οἱ λαλοῦντες, ἀλλὰ τὸ πνεῦμα τὸ ἅγιον.
for [3]not [2]are [1]ye they who speak, but the Spirit the Holy.
12 [r]παραδώσει.δὲ‖ ἀδελφὸς ἀδελφὸν εἰς θάνατον, καὶ πατὴρ
And [2]will [3]deliver [4]up [1]brother brother to death, and father
τέκνον· καὶ ἐπαναστήσονται τέκνα ἐπὶ γονεῖς, καὶ θανατώ-
child; and [2]will [3]rise [4]up [1]children against parents, and will put to
σουσιν αὐτούς· 13 καὶ ἔσεσθε μισούμενοι ὑπὸ πάντων διὰ
death them. And ye will be hated by all on account of
τὸ.ὄνομά.μου· ὁ.δὲ ὑπομείνας εἰς τέλος, οὗτος σωθήσε-
my name; but he who endures to [the] end, he shall be
ται. 14 Ὅταν.δὲ ἴδητε τὸ βδέλυγμα τῆς ἐρημώσεως [s]τὸ
saved. But when ye see the abomination of the desolation which
ῥηθὲν ὑπὸ Δανιὴλ τοῦ προφήτου,‖ [t]ἑστὸς‖ ὅπου οὐ.δεῖ·
was spoken of by Daniel the prophet, standing where it should not
ὁ ἀναγινώσκων νοείτω· τότε οἱ ἐν τῇ Ἰουδαίᾳ φευ-
(he who reads let him understand), then those in Judæa let
γέτωσαν εἰς.τὰ ὄρη· 15 ὁ [v]δὲ‖ ἐπὶ τοῦ δώματος μὴ κατα-
them flee to the mountains, [2]he [1]and upon the housetop [3]not [4]let [2]him
βάτω [w]εἰς τὴν οἰκίαν,‖ μηδὲ [x]εἰσελθέτω‖ [y]ἆραί τι‖ ἐκ
come down into the house, nor go in to take any thing out of
τῆς.οἰκίας.αὐτοῦ· 16 καὶ ὁ εἰς τὸν ἀγρὸν [z]ὢν‖ μὴ.ἐπιστρεψάτω
his house; and he that in the field is let him not return
εἰς τὰ ὀπίσω ἆραι τὸ.ἱμάτιον.αὐτοῦ. 17 οὐαὶ.δὲ ταῖς
to the things behind to take his garment. But woe to those that
ἐν.γαστρὶ.ἐχούσαις καὶ ταῖς θηλαζούσαις ἐν ἐκείναις ταῖς
are with child and to those that give suck in those

---

[d] ἀκούετε ye hear of Tr [e] — γὰρ T[Tr]A. [f] ἐπ' TA. [g] — καὶ TTrA. [h] — καὶ T[Tr]A.
[i] — καὶ ταραχαί LTTr[A]. [k] ἀρχὴ a beginning LTTr. [l] — γὰρ for T[Tr]A. [m] πρῶτον δεῖ
LTTrA. [n] καὶ ὅταν and when LTTrA. [o] ἄγωσιν GLTTrAW. [p] — μηδὲ μελετᾶτε [L]TTr[A].
[q] ἂν L. [r] καὶ παραδώσει LTTrA. [s] — τὸ ῥηθὲν ὑπὸ Δανιὴλ τοῦ προφήτου G[L]TTrA.
[t] ἑστὼς EG; ἑστηκὸς L; ἑστηκότα TTrA. [v] — δὲ L[Tr]. [w] — εἰς τὴν οἰκίαν [L]T.
[x] εἰσελθάτω LTTr. [y] τι ἆραι TrA. [z] — ὢν (*read* [is]) LTTr.

ἡμέραις. 18 προσεύχεσθε.δὲ ἵνα μὴ.γένηται [a]ἡ.φυγὴ.ὑμῶν‖
days! And pray that ³may ⁴not ⁵be ¹your ²flight
χειμῶνος. 19 ἔσονται.γὰρ αἱ.ἡμέραι.ἐκεῖναι θλίψις, οἵα
in winter; for ⁴shall ⁵be [¹in] ²those ³days tribulation, such as
οὐ.γέγονεν τοιαύτη ἀπ' ἀρχῆς κτίσεως [b]ἧς‖ ἔκτισεν ὁ
has not been the like from [the] beginning of creation which ²created
θεὸς ἕως τοῦ νῦν, καὶ οὐ.μὴ γένηται. 20 καὶ εἰ.μὴ [c]κύριος
¹God until now, and not at all shall be; and unless [the] Lord
ἐκολόβωσεν‖ τὰς ἡμέρας, οὐκ.ἂν.ἐσώθη πᾶσα σάρξ·
had shortened the days, there would not have been saved any flesh;
ἀλλὰ διὰ τοὺς ἐκλεκτοὺς οὓς ἐξελέξατο, ἐκολόβωσεν τὰς
but on account of the elect whom he chose, he has shortened the
ἡμέρας. 21 Καὶ τότε ἐάν τις ὑμῖν εἴπῃ, [d]Ἰδού,‖ ὧδε ὁ
days. And then if anyone to you say, Behold, here [is] the
χριστός, [e]ἤ‖ [f]ἰδού,‖ ἐκεῖ, [g]μὴ.πιστεύσητε.‖ 22 ἐγερθήσονται
Christ, or Behold, there, ye shall not believe [it] ²There ³will ⁴arise
[h]γὰρ‖ [i]ψευδόχριστοι καὶ‖ ψευδοπροφῆται, καὶ [j]δώσουσιν‖ σημεῖα
¹for false Christs and false prophets, and will give signs
καὶ τέρατα, πρὸς τὸ ἀποπλανᾶν εἰ δυνατὸν [k]καὶ‖ τοὺς ἐκλεκ-
and wonders, to deceive if possible even the elect.
τούς. 23 ὑμεῖς.δὲ βλέπετε· [l]ἰδού,‖ προείρηκα ὑμῖν πάντα.
But ²ye ¹take heed: lo, I have foretold to you all things.
24 [m]Ἀλλ'‖ ἐν ἐκείναις ταῖς ἡμέραις, μετὰ τὴν.θλίψιν.ἐκείνην,
But in those days, after that tribulation,
ὁ ἥλιος σκοτισθήσεται, καὶ ἡ σελήνη οὐ.δώσει τὸ φέγγος
the sun shall be darkened, and the moon shall not give ²light
αὐτῆς, 25 καὶ οἱ ἀστέρες [n]τοῦ οὐρανοῦ ἔσονται ἐκπίπτοντες,‖
¹her; and the stars of the heaven shall be falling out,
καὶ αἱ δυνάμεις αἱ ἐν τοῖς οὐρανοῖς σαλευθήσονται.
and the powers which [are] in the heavens shall be shaken;
26 καὶ τότε ὄψονται τὸν υἱὸν τοῦ ἀνθρώπου ἐρχόμενον ἐν
and then shall they see the Son of man coming in
νεφέλαις μετὰ δυνάμεως [o]πολλῆς καὶ δόξης.‖ 27 καὶ τότε
clouds with ²power ¹great and glory; and then
ἀποστελεῖ τοὺς.ἀγγέλους.[p]αὐτοῦ,‖ καὶ ἐπισυνάξει τοὺς
he will send his angels, and will gather together
ἐκλεκτοὺς.[q]αὐτοῦ‖ ἐκ τῶν τεσσάρων ἀνέμων, ἀπ' ἄκρου
his elect from the four winds, from [the] extremity
γῆς ἕως ἄκρου οὐρανοῦ. 28 Ἀπὸ.δὲ τῆς συκῆς μάθετε
of earth to [the] extremity of heaven. But from the fig-tree learn
τὴν παραβολήν· ὅταν [r]αὐτῆς ἤδη ὁ κλάδος‖ ἁπαλὸς γένη-
the parable: when of it already the branch tender is be-
ται, καὶ [s]ἐκφυῇ‖ τὰ φύλλα, [t]γινώσκετε‖ ὅτι ἐγγὺς τὸ θέρος
come, and it puts forth the leaves, ye know that near the summer
ἐστίν· 29 οὕτως καὶ ὑμεῖς, ὅταν [u]ταῦτα ἴδητε‖ γινόμενα,
is. So also ye, when these things ye see coming to pass,
γινώσκετε ὅτι ἐγγύς ἐστιν ἐπὶ θύραις. 30 Ἀμὴν λέγω ὑμῖν,
know that near it is, at [the] doors. Verily I say to you,
ὅτι οὐ.μὴ παρέλθῃ ἡ.γενεὰ.αὕτη, μέχρις οὗ [v]πάντα
that in no wise will have passed away this generation, until all

with child, and to
them that give suck in
those days! 18 And
pray ye that your
flight be not in the
winter. 19 For *in* those
days shall be affliction,
such as was not from
the beginning of the
creation which God
created unto this
time, neither shall be.
20 And except that the
Lord had shortened
those days, no flesh
should be saved: but
for the elect's sake,
whom he hath chosen,
he hath shortened the
days. 21 And then if
any man shall say to
you, Lo, here *is* Christ;
or, lo, *he is* there; believe *him* not: 22 for
false Christs and false
prophets shall rise,
and shall shew signs
and wonders, to se-
duce, if *it were* pos-
sible, even the elect.
23 But take ye heed:
behold, I have foretold
you all things. 24 But
in those days, after
that tribulation, the
sun shall be darkened,
and the moon shall
not give her light,
25 and the stars of
heaven shall fall, and
the powers that are
in heaven shall be
shaken. 26 And then
shall they see the Son
of man coming in
the clouds with great
power and glory.
27 And then shall he
send his angels, and
shall gather together
his elect from the four
winds, from the utter-
most part of the earth
to the uttermost part
of heaven. 28 Now
learn a parable of the
fig tree; When her
branch is yet tender,
and putteth forth
leaves, ye know that
summer is near: 29 so
ye in like manner,
when ye shall see these
things come to pass,
know that it is nigh,
even at the doors.
30 Verily I say unto
you, that this gene-
ration shall not pass,
till all these things be

[a] — ἡ φυγὴ ὑμῶν (*read* it may not be) LTTrA. [b] ἣν LTTr. [c] ἐκολόβωσεν κύριος T. [d] ἴδε TTrA. [e] — ἢ TA. [f] ἴδε LTTrA. [g] μὴ πιστεύετε believe [it] not GLTTrAW. [h] δὲ and T. [i] — ψευδόχριστοι καὶ A. [j] ποιήσουσιν will work TA. [k] — καὶ T[Tr]A. [l] — ἰδού [L]TTrA. [m] Ἀλλὰ LTTrA. [n] ἔσονται ἐκ τοῦ οὐρανοῦ πίπτοντες LTTrA. [o] καὶ δόξης πολλῆς L. [p] — αὐτοῦ (*read* the angels) [L]TTrA. [q] — αὐτοῦ (*read* the elect) TTrA. [r] ἤδη ὁ κλάδος αὐτῆς LTr. [s] ἐκφύῃ EGT. [t] γινώσκεται it is known A. [u] ἴδητε ταῦτα LTTr. [v] ταῦτα πάντα TTrA.

done. 31 Heaven and earth shall pass away: but my words shall not pass away. 32 But of that day and *that* hour knoweth no man, no, not the angels which are in heaven, neither the Son, but the Father. 33 Take ye heed, watch and pray: for ye know not when the time is. 34 *For the Son of man is* as a man taking a far journey, who left his house, and gave authority to his servants, and to every man his work, and commanded the porter to watch. 35 Watch ye therefore: for ye know not when the master of the house cometh, at even, or at midnight, or at the cockcrowing, or in the morning: 36 lest coming suddenly he find you sleeping. 37 And what I say unto you I say unto all, Watch.

XIV. After two days was *the feast of* the passover, and of unleavened bread: and the chief priests and the scribes sought how they might take him by craft, and put *him* to death. 2 But they said, Not on the feast *day*, lest there be an uproar of the people.

3 And being in Bethany in the house of Simon the leper, as he sat at meat, there came a woman having an alabaster box of ointment of spikenard very precious; and she brake the box, and poured *it* on his head. 4 And there were some that had indignation within themselves, and said, Why was this waste of the ointment made? 5 for it might have been sold for more than three hundred pence, and have been given to the poor. And they murmured against her. 6 And Jesus said, Let her alone; why trouble ye her? she hath

ταῦτα‖ γένηται. 31 ὁ οὐρανὸς καὶ ἡ γῆ [w]παρε-
these things shall have taken place. The heaven and the earth shall
λεύσονται·‖ οἱ.δὲ.λόγοι.μου οὐ.[x]μὴ‖ [y]παρέλθωσιν.‖ 32 Περὶ.δὲ
pass away, but my words in no wise shall pass away. But concerning
τῆς.ἡμέρας.ἐκείνης [z]καὶ‖ τῆς ὥρας, οὐδεὶς οἶδεν, οὐδὲ [a]οἱ ἄγ-
that day and the hour, no one knows, not even the an-
γελοι‖ [b]οἱ‖ ἐν οὐρανῷ, οὐδὲ ὁ υἱός, εἰ.μὴ ὁ πατήρ. 33 Βλέπετε,
gels those in heaven, nor the Son, but the Father. Take heed,
ἀγρυπνεῖτε [c]καὶ προσεύχεσθε·‖ οὐκ.οἴδατε.γὰρ πότε ὁ καιρός
watch and pray; for ye know not when the time
ἐστιν 34 ὡς ἄνθρωπος ἀπόδημος ἀφεὶς τὴν οἰκίαν
is; as a man going out of the country, leaving [2]house
αὐτοῦ, καὶ δοὺς τοῖς.δούλοις.αὐτοῦ τὴν ἐξουσίαν, [d]καὶ‖ ἑκάστῳ
[1]his, and giving to his bondmen the authority, and to each one
τὸ.ἔργον.αὐτοῦ, καὶ τῷ θυρωρῷ ἐνετείλατο ἵνα γρηγορῇ.
his work, and [2]the [3]door-keeper [1]commanded that he should watch.
35 γρηγορεῖτε οὖν· οὐκ.οἴδατε.γὰρ πότε ὁ.κύριος τῆς οἰκίας
Watch therefore, for ye know not when the master of the house
ἔρχεται. [e]ὀψέ, ἢ [f]μεσονυκτίου,‖ ἢ ἀλεκτοροφωνίας, ἢ πρωΐ·
comes: at evening, or at midnight, or at cock-crowing, or morning;
36 μὴ ἐλθὼν ἐξαίφνης εὕρῃ ὑμᾶς καθεύδοντας. 37 [g]ἃ‖.δὲ
lest coming suddenly he should find you sleeping. And what
ὑμῖν λέγω, πᾶσιν λέγω, Γρηγορεῖτε.
to you I say, to all I say, Watch.

14 Ἦν.δὲ τὸ πάσχα καὶ τὰ ἄζυμα μετὰ δύο
Now it was the passover and the [feast of] unleavened bread after two
ἡμέρας· καὶ ἐζήτουν οἱ ἀρχιερεῖς καὶ οἱ γραμματεῖς πῶς
days. And [7]were [8]seeking [1]the [2]chief [3]priests [4]and [5]the [6]scribes how
αὐτὸν ἐν δόλῳ κρατήσαντες ἀποκτείνωσιν· 2 ἔλεγον [h]δέ,‖
him by guile getting hold of they might kill [him]. [2]They [3]said [1]but,
Μὴ ἐν τῇ ἑορτῇ, μήποτε [i]θόρυβος ἔσται‖ τοῦ λαοῦ.
Not in the feast, lest a tumult there shall be of the people.

3 Καὶ ὄντος αὐτοῦ ἐν Βηθανίᾳ, ἐν τῇ οἰκίᾳ Σίμωνος τοῦ
And [2]being [1]he in Bethany, in the house of Simon the
λεπροῦ, κατακειμένου.αὐτοῦ, ἦλθεν γυνὴ ἔχουσα ἀλά-
leper, as he reclined [at table], [3]came [1]a [2]woman having an ala-
βαστρον μύρου νάρδου πιστικῆς πολυτελοῦς· [k]καὶ‖ συν-
baster flask of ointment of [2]nard [1]pure of great price; and having
τρίψασα [l]τὸ‖ ἀλάβαστρον, κατέχεεν αὐτοῦ [m]κατὰ‖ τῆς
broken the alabaster flask, she poured [it] [2]his [1]on
κεφαλῆς. 4 ἦσαν.δέ τινες ἀγανακτοῦντες πρὸς.ἑαυτούς, [n]καὶ
head. And [2]were [1]some indignant within themselves, and
λέγοντες,‖ Εἰς τί ἡ.ἀπώλεια.αὕτη τοῦ μύρου γέγονεν;
saying, For what [2]this [3]waste [4]of [5]the [6]ointment [1]has been made?
5 ἠδύνατο.γὰρ τοῦτο [o] πραθῆναι ἐπάνω [p]τριακοσίων
for it was possible [for] this to have been sold for above three hundred
δηναρίων,‖ καὶ δοθῆναι τοῖς πτωχοῖς· καὶ [q]ἐνεβριμῶντο‖
denarii, and to have been given to the poor. And they murmured
αὐτῇ. 6 Ὁ.δὲ.Ἰησοῦς εἶπεν, Ἄφετε αὐτήν· τί αὐτῇ κόπους
at her. But Jesus said, Let [2]alone [1]her; why to her trouble

---

[w] παρελεύσεται GW. [x] — μὴ TrA. [y] παρελεύσονται TTrA. [z] ἢ or GLTTrAW. [a] ἄγγελος an angel A. [b] — οἱ TTrA. [c] — καὶ προσεύχεσθε LT[Tr]A. [d] — καὶ LTTrA. [e] + ἢ either TTrA. [f] μεσονύκτιον TTrA. [g] ὃ LTTrA. [h] γάρ for LTTrA. [i] ἔσται θόρυβος TTrA. [k] — καὶ TA. [l] τὸν LTW; τὴν TrA. [m] — κατὰ (*read* αὐτοῦ on his) LTTrA. [n] — καὶ λέγοντες T[Tr]A. [o] + τὸ μύρον ointment GLTTrAW. [p] δηναρίων τριακοσίων LTTrAW. [q] ἐνεβριμοῦντο T.

παρέχετε; καλὸν ἔργον [r]εἰργάσατο‖ [s]εἰς ἐμέ.‖ 7 πάντοτε.γὰρ
do ye cause? a good work she wrought towards me. For always
τοὺς πτωχοὺς ἔχετε μεθ' ἑαυτῶν, καὶ ὅταν θέλητε δύνασθε
the poor ye have with you, and whenever ye desire ye are able
[t]αὐτοὺς‖ εὖ.ποιῆσαι· ἐμὲ.δὲ οὐ πάντοτε ἔχετε. 8 ὃ [v]εἶχεν‖
[3]them [1]to [2]do good; but me not always ye have. What [2]could
[w]αὕτη,‖ ἐποίησεν· προέλαβεν μυρίσαι [x]μου.τὸ.σῶμα‖ εἰς
[1]she, she did. She came beforehand to anoint my body for
τὸν ἐνταφιασμόν. 9 ἀμὴν[y] λέγω ὑμῖν, ὅπου.[z]ἂν‖ κηρυχθῇ
the burial. Verily I say to you, Wheresoever shall be proclaimed
τὸ.εὐαγγέλιον.[a]τοῦτο‖ εἰς ὅλον τὸν κόσμον, καὶ ὃ ἐποίησεν
this glad tidings in [2]whole [1]the world, also what [3]has [4]done
αὕτη λαληθήσεται εἰς μνημόσυνον αὐτῆς.
[1]this [[2]woman] shall be spoken of for a memorial of her.

10 Καὶ [b]ὁ‖ Ἰούδας [b]ὁ‖ [c]Ἰσκαριώτης,‖ [d] εἷς τῶν δώδεκα,
And Judas the Iscariote, one of the twelve,
ἀπῆλθεν πρὸς τοὺς ἀρχιερεῖς, ἵνα [e]παραδῷ αὐτὸν‖
went away to the chief priests, that he might deliver up him
αὐτοῖς. 11 Οἱ.δὲ ἀκούσαντες ἐχάρησαν, καὶ ἐπηγγείλαντο
to them. And they having heard rejoiced, and promised
αὐτῷ ἀργύριον δοῦναι· καὶ ἐζήτει πῶς [f]εὐκαίρως αὐτὸν
[3]him [4]money [1]to [2]give. And he sought how [3]conveniently [5]him
παραδῷ.‖
[1]he [2]might [4]deliver [6]up.

12 Καὶ τῇ πρώτῃ ἡμέρᾳ τῶν ἀζύμων, ὅτε τὸ πάσχα
And on the first day of unleavened [bread], when the passover
ἔθυον, λέγουσιν αὐτῷ οἱ.μαθηταὶ.αὐτοῦ, Ποῦ θέλεις
they killed, [3]say [4]to [5]him [1]his [2]disciples, Where desirest thou [that]
ἀπελθόντες ἑτοιμάσωμεν ἵνα φάγῃς τὸ πάσχα; 13 Καὶ
going we should prepare that thou mayest eat the passover? And
ἀποστέλλει δύο τῶν.μαθητῶν.αὐτοῦ, καὶ λέγει αὐτοῖς, Ὑπάγετε
he sends forth two of his disciples, and says to them, Go
εἰς τὴν πόλιν· καὶ ἀπαντήσει ὑμῖν ἄνθρωπος κεράμιον ὕδατος
into the city, and [3]will [4]meet [5]you [1]a [2]man a pitcher of water
βαστάζων· ἀκολουθήσατε αὐτῷ, 14 καὶ ὅπου.[g]ἐὰν‖ εἰσέλθῃ,
carrying; follow him; and wherever he may enter,
εἴπατε τῷ οἰκοδεσπότῃ, Ὅτι ὁ διδάσκαλος λέγει, Ποῦ
say to the master of the house, The teacher says, Where
ἐστιν τὸ κατάλυμα [h] ὅπου τὸ πάσχα μετὰ τῶν.μαθητῶν.μου
is the guest-chamber where the passover with my disciples
φάγω; 15 καὶ αὐτὸς ὑμῖν δείξει [i]ἀνώγεον‖ μέγα ἐστρω-
I may eat? and he [2]you [1]will [3]shew an upper room large, fur-
μένον [k]ἕτοιμον.‖ [l]ἐκεῖ‖ ἑτοιμάσατε ἡμῖν. 16 Καὶ ἐξῆλθον οἱ
nished ready. There prepare for us. And went away
μαθηταὶ.[m]αὐτοῦ,‖ καὶ ἦλθον εἰς τὴν πόλιν, καὶ εὗρον καθὼς
his disciples, and came into the city, and found as
εἶπεν αὐτοῖς, καὶ ἡτοίμασαν τὸ πάσχα. 17 Καὶ ὀψίας
he had said to them, and they prepared the passover. And evening
γενομένης ἔρχεται μετὰ τῶν δώδεκα· 18 καὶ ἀνακειμένων
being come he comes with the twelve. And as [2]were [3]reclining

wrought a good work
on me. 7 For ye have
the poor with you
always, and whensoever
ye will ye may do
them good: but me
ye have not always.
8 She hath done what
she could: she is come
aforehand to anoint
my body to the burying.
9 Verily I say
unto you, Wheresoever
this gospel shall be
preached throughout
the whole world, *this*
also that she hath done
shall be spoken of for
a memorial of her.

10 And Judas Iscariot,
one of the twelve,
went unto the chief
priests, to betray him
unto them. 11 And
when they heard *it*,
they were glad, and
promised to give him
money. And he sought
how he might conveniently
betray him.

12 And the first day
of unleavened bread,
when they killed the
passover, his disciples
said unto him, Where
wilt thou that we go
and prepare that thou
mayest eat the passover?
13 And he sendeth
forth two of his
disciples, and saith
unto them, Go ye into
the city, and there
shall meet you a man
bearing a pitcher of
water: follow him.
14 And wheresoever
he shall go in, say ye
to the goodman of the
house, The Master
saith, Where is the
guestchamber, where
I shall eat the passover
with my disciples?
15 And he will shew
you a large upper room
furnished *and* prepared:
there make
ready for us. 16 And
his disciples went
forth, and came into
the city, and found as
he had said unto them:
and they made ready
the passover. 17 And
in the evening he cometh
with the twelve.
18 And as they sat and
did eat, Jesus said,

---

[r] ἠργάσατο T. [s] ἐν ἐμοί to me GLTTrAW. [t] αὐτοῖς LTrA; — αὐτοὺς T. [v] ἔσχεν GLTTrAW. [w] — αὕτη (*read* εἶχεν she could) [L]T[Tr]A. [x] τὸ σῶμά μου LTr. [y] + δὲ and (verily) [L]TTrA. [z] ἐὰν TA. [a] — τοῦτο (*read* the glad tidings) [L]TTrA. [b] — ὁ LTTrAW. [c] Ἰσκαριὼθ TA. [d] + ὁ the TTrA. [e] παραδοῖ αὐτὸν L; αὐτὸν παραδοῖ TTrA. [f] αὐτὸν εὐκαίρως παραδοῖ LTTrA; αὐτὸν εὐκ. παραδῷ W. [g] ἂν LTrA. [h] + μου (*read* my guest-chamber) [L]TTrA. [i] ἀνάγαιον GLTTrAW. [k] [ἕτοιμον] L. [l] καὶ ἐκεῖ and there TrA; κἀκεῖ T. [m] — αὐτοῦ (*read* the disciples) T[Tr].

Verily I say unto you,
One of you which eat-
eth with me shall be-
tray me. 19 And they
began to be sorrowful,
and to say unto him
one by one, *Is* it I?
and another *said*, *Is*
it I? 20 And he an-
swered and said unto
them, *It is* one of the
twelve, that dippeth
with me in the dish.
21 The Son of man in-
deed goeth, as it is
written of him: but
woe to that man by
whom the Son of man
is betrayed! good were
it for that man if he
had never been born.

22 And as they did
eat, Jesus took bread,
and blessed, and brake
it, and gave to them,
and said, Take, eat:
this is my body. 23 And
he took the cup, and
when he had given
thanks, he gave *it* to
them: and they all
drank of it. 24 And
he said unto them,
This is my blood of
the new testament,
which is shed for
many. 25 Verily I say
unto you, I will drink
no more of the fruit of
the vine, until that
day that I drink it
new in the kingdom
of God.

26 And when they
had sung an hymn,
they went out into
the mount of Olives.
27 And Jesus saith
unto them, All ye
shall be offended be-
cause of me this night:
for it is written, I will
smite the shepherd,
and the sheep shall be
scattered. 28 But after
that I am risen, I will
go before you into
Galilee. 29 But Peter
said unto him, Al-
though all shall be
offended, yet *will* not
I. 30 And Jesus saith
unto him, Verily I say
unto thee, That this

αὐτῶν καὶ ἐσθιόντων [n]εἶπεν ὁ Ἰησοῦς,‖ Ἀμὴν λέγω
[[4]at [5]table] [1]they and were eating [2]said [1]Jesus, Verily I say
ὑμῖν, ὅτι εἷς ἐξ ὑμῶν παραδώσει με, ὁ ἐσθίων μετ' ἐμοῦ.
to you, that one of you will deliver up me, who is eating with me.
19 [o]Οἱ.δὲ‖ ἤρξαντο λυπεῖσθαι, καὶ λέγειν αὐτῷ, εἷς [p]καθ'‖ εἷς,
And they began to be grieved, and to say to him, one by one,
Μή τι ἐγώ; [q]Καὶ ἄλλος, Μή τι ἐγώ;‖ 20 Ὁ.δὲ [r]ἀπο-
[Is it] I? And another, [Is it] I? But he an-
κριθεὶς‖ εἶπεν αὐτοῖς, Εἷς [s]ἐκ‖ τῶν δώδεκα, ὁ ἐμβαπτό-
swering said to them, [It is] one of the twelve, who is dip-
μενος μετ' ἐμοῦ [t]εἰς τὸ τρυβλίον. 21 [v]ὁ μὲν υἱὸς τοῦ ἀνθρώπου
ping with me in the dish. The [5]indeed [1]Son [2]of [3]man
ὑπάγει, καθὼς γέγραπται περὶ αὐτοῦ· οὐαὶ.δὲ τῷ
[4]goes, as it has been written concerning him; but woe
ἀνθρώπῳ.ἐκείνῳ δι' οὗ ὁ υἱὸς τοῦ ἀνθρώπου παραδίδοται·
to that man by whom the Son of man is delivered up;
καλὸν [w]ἦν‖ αὐτῷ εἰ οὐκ.ἐγεννήθη ὁ.ἄνθρωπος.ἐκεῖνος.
good were it for him if [3]had [4]not [5]been [6]born [1]that [2]man.

22 Καὶ ἐσθιόντων.αὐτῶν, λαβὼν [x]ὁ Ἰησοῦς‖ ἄρτον,
And as they were eating, [2]having [3]taken [1]Jesus a loaf,
εὐλογήσας ἔκλασεν, καὶ ἔδωκεν αὐτοῖς, καὶ εἶπεν, Λάβετε,
having blessed he brake, and gave to them, and said, Take,
[y]φάγετε·‖ τοῦτό ἐστιν τὸ.σῶμά.μου. 23 Καὶ λαβὼν [z]τὸ‖
eat; this is my body. And having taken the
ποτήριον, εὐχαριστήσας ἔδωκεν αὐτοῖς· καὶ ἔπιον ἐξ αὐτοῦ
cup, having given thanks he gave to them, and they [2]drank [3]of [4]it
πάντες· 24 καὶ εἶπεν αὐτοῖς, Τοῦτό ἐστιν τὸ.αἷμά.μου [a]τὸ‖
[1]all And he said to them, This is my blood that
τῆς [b]καινῆς‖ διαθήκης, τὸ [c]περὶ πολλῶν ἐκχυνόμενον.‖
of the new covenant, which for many is poured out.
25 ἀμὴν λέγω ὑμῖν, ὅτι οὐκέτι.οὐ.μὴ πίω ἐκ τοῦ
Verily I say to you, that not any more in any wise will I drink of the
[d]γεννήματος‖ τῆς ἀμπέλου, ἕως τῆς.ἡμέρας.ἐκείνης ὅταν αὐτὸ
fruit of the vine, until that day when it
πίνω καινὸν ἐν τῇ βασιλείᾳ τοῦ θεοῦ.
I drink new in the kingdom of God.

26 Καὶ ὑμνήσαντες ἐξῆλθον εἰς τὸ ὄρος τῶν Ἐλαιῶν.
And having sung a hymn they went out to the mount of Olives.
27 καὶ λέγει αὐτοῖς ὁ Ἰησοῦς, Ὅτι πάντες σκανδαλισθήσεσθε
And [2]says [3]to [4]them [1]Jesus, All ye will be offended
[e]ἐν ἐμοὶ‖ [f]ἐν τῇ.νυκτὶ.ταύτῃ·‖ ὅτι γέγραπται, Πατάξω τὸν
in me in this night; for it has been written, I will smite the
ποιμένα, καὶ [g]διασκορπισθήσεται τὰ πρόβατα.‖ 28 Ἀλλὰ
shepherd, and will be scattered abroad the sheep. But
μετὰ τὸ.ἐγερθῆναί.με, προάξω ὑμᾶς εἰς τὴν Γαλιλαίαν.
after my arising, I will go before you into Galilee.
29 Ὁ.δὲ.Πέτρος ἔφη αὐτῷ, [h]Καὶ εἰ‖ πάντες σκανδαλισθήσονται,
But Peter said to him, Even if all shall be offended,
ἀλλ' οὐκ ἐγώ. 30 Καὶ λέγει αὐτῷ ὁ Ἰησοῦς, Ἀμὴν λέγω σοι,
yet not I. And [2]says [3]to [4]him [1]Jesus, Verily I say to thee,

---

[n] ὁ Ἰησοῦς εἶπεν TA. [o] — Οἱ δὲ (*read* ἤρξαντο they began) TA. [p] κατὰ TA. [q] — καὶ ἄλλος, Μή τι ἐγώ; TTr. [r] — ἀποκριθεὶς LTTrA. [s] — ἐκ (*read* τῶν of the) T[Tr]. [t] + τὴν χεῖρα the hand L. [v] + ὅτι for T[Tr]A. [w] — ἦν [L]T[Tr]A. [x] — ὁ Ἰησοῦς [L]T[Tr]A. [y] — φάγετε GLTTrAW. [z] — τὸ (*read* a cup) LTTrA. [a] — τὸ [L]TA. [b] — καινῆς TTrA. [c] ὑπὲρ πολλῶν ἐκχυννόμενον L; ἐκχυννόμενον ὑπὲρ πολλῶν TTrA. [d] γενήματος TTrAW. [e] — ἐν ἐμοὶ TTrA. [f] — ἐν τῇ νυκτὶ ταύτῃ [L]TTrAW. [g] διασκορπισθήσονται τὰ πρόβατα L; τὰ πρόβατα διασκορπισθήσονται TTrA. [h] Εἰ καὶ TTrA.

ὅτι [i] σήμερον [j]ἐν τῇ.νυκτὶ.ταύτῃ,‖ πρὶν ἢ δὶς ἀλέκτορα
that to-day in this night, before that twice [the] cock
φωνῆσαι, τρίς [k]ἀπαρνήσῃ με.‖ 31 Ὁ.δὲ [l]ἐκ.περισσοῦ ἔλεγεν
crow, thrice thou wilt deny me. But he [3]vehemently [4]said
μᾶλλον,‖ Ἐάν [m]με.δέῃ‖ συναποθανεῖν σοι, οὐ.μή σε
[1]the [2]more, If it were needful for me to die with thee, in no wise thee
[n]ἀπαρνήσομαι.‖ Ὡσαύτως.δὲ καὶ πάντες ἔλεγον.
will I deny. And in like manner also [3]all [2]they [1]spake.
32 Καὶ ἔρχονται εἰς χωρίον [o]οὗ τὸ‖ ὄνομα [p]Γεθσημανῆ·‖
And they come to a place of which the name [is] Gethsemane;
καὶ λέγει τοῖς.μαθηταῖς.αὐτοῦ, Καθίσατε ὧδε, ἕως προσεύξω-
and he says to his disciples, Sit here, while I shall
μαι. 33 Καὶ παραλαμβάνει τὸν Πέτρον καὶ [q]τὸν‖ Ἰάκωβον
pray. And he takes Peter and James
καὶ Ἰωάννην [r]μεθ' ἑαυτοῦ.‖ Καὶ ἤρξατο ἐκθαμβεῖσθαι καὶ
and John with him; and he began to be greatly amazed and
ἀδημονεῖν. 34 καὶ λέγει αὐτοῖς, Περίλυπός ἐστιν ἡ.ψυχή.μου
deeply depressed. And he says to them, Very sorrowful is my soul
ἕως θανάτου· μείνατε ὧδε καὶ γρηγορεῖτε. 35 Καὶ [s]προελ-
even to death; remain here and watch. And having gone
θὼν‖ μικρὸν [t]ἔπεσεν‖ ἐπὶ τῆς γῆς, καὶ προσηύχετο ἵνα, εἰ
forward a little he fell upon the earth, and prayed that, if
δυνατόν ἐστιν, παρέλθῃ ἀπ' αὐτοῦ ἡ ὥρα. 36 καὶ ἔλεγεν,
possible it is, might pass from him the hour. And he said,
Ἀββᾶ, ὁ πατήρ, πάντα δυνατά σοι· παρένεγκε τὸ ποτή-
Abba, Father, all things [are] possible to thee; take away [2]cup
ριον [v]ἀπ' ἐμοῦ τοῦτο·‖ ἀλλ' οὐ τί ἐγὼ θέλω, ἀλλὰ τί σύ.
[3]from [4]me [1]this; but not what I will, but what thou.
37 Καὶ ἔρχεται καὶ εὑρίσκει αὐτοὺς καθεύδοντας· καὶ λέγει τῷ
And he comes and finds them sleeping. And he says
Πέτρῳ, Σίμων, καθεύδεις; οὐκ.ἴσχυσας μίαν ὥραν γρη-
to Peter, Simon, sleepest thou? wast thou not able one hour to
γορῆσαι; 38 γρηγορεῖτε καὶ προσεύχεσθε, ἵνα μὴ.[w]εἰσέλθητε‖
watch? Watch and pray, that ye enter not
εἰς πειρασμόν. τὸ μὲν πνεῦμα πρόθυμον, ἡ.δὲ σάρξ
into temptation. The [2]indeed [1]spirit [is] ready, but the flesh
ἀσθενής. 39 Καὶ πάλιν ἀπελθὼν προσηύξατο, τὸν αὐτὸν
weak. And again having gone away he prayed, [2]the [3]same
λόγον εἰπών. 40 καὶ [x]ὑποστρέψας‖ εὗρεν αὐτοὺς [y]πάλιν‖
[4]thing [1]saying. And having returned he found them again
καθεύδοντας· ἦσαν.γὰρ [z]οἱ.ὀφθαλμοὶ.αὐτῶν‖ [a]βεβαρημένοι.‖
sleeping, for [3]were [1]their [2]eyes heavy;
καὶ οὐκ.ᾔδεισαν τί [b]αὐτῷ ἀποκριθῶσιν.‖ 41 Καὶ ἔρχεται
and they knew not what [4]him [1]they [2]should [3]answer. And he comes
τὸ τρίτον, καὶ λέγει αὐτοῖς, Καθεύδετε [c]τὸ‖ λοιπὸν καὶ
the third time, and says to them, Sleep on now and
ἀναπαύεσθε. ἀπέχει· ἦλθεν ἡ ὥρα· ἰδού, παραδίδοται
take your rest. It is enough; has come the hour; lo, [5]is [6]delivered [7]up
ὁ υἱὸς τοῦ ἀνθρώπου εἰς τὰς χεῖρας τῶν ἁμαρτωλῶν. 42 ἐγεί-
[1]the [2]Son [3]of [4]man into the hands of sinners. Rise,
ρεσθε, ἄγωμεν· ἰδού, ὁ παραδιδούς με [d]ἤγγικεν.‖
let us go; behold, he who is delivering up me has drawn near.

day, *even* in this night,
before the cock crow
twice, thou shalt deny
me thrice. 31 But he
spake the more vehe-
mently, If I should die
with thee, I will not
deny thee in any wise.
Likewise also said
they all.
32 And they came to
a place which was
named Gethsemane:
and he saith to his
disciples, Sit ye here,
while I shall pray.
33 And he taketh with
him Peter and James
and John, and began
to be sore amazed,
and to be very heavy;
34 and saith unto
them, My soul is ex-
ceeding sorrowful un-
to death: tarry ye here,
and watch. 35 And he
went forward a little,
and fell on the ground,
and prayed that, if it
were possible, the hour
might pass from him.
36 And he said, Abba,
Father, all things *are*
possible unto thee;
take away this cup
from me: nevertheless
not what I will, but
what thou wilt. 37 And
he cometh, and find-
eth them sleeping,
and saith unto Peter,
Simon, sleepest thou?
couldest not thou
watch one hour?
38 Watch ye and pray,
lest ye enter into temp-
tation. The spirit
truly *is* ready, but the
flesh *is* weak. 39 And
again he went away,
and prayed, and spake
the same words. 40 And
when he returned, he
found them asleep a-
gain, (for their eyes
were heavy,) neither
wist they what to an-
swer him. 41 And he
cometh the third time,
and saith unto them,
Sleep on now, and
take *your* rest: it is
enough, the hour is
come; behold, the Son
of man is betrayed into
the hands of sinners.
42 Rise up, let us go;
lo, he that betrayeth
me is at hand.

---

[i] + σὺ thou GLTTrAW. [j] ταύτῃ τῇ νυκτὶ LTTrA. [k] με ἀπαρνήσῃ LTTrAW. [l] ἐκπερισσῶς ἐλάλει LTTrA. [m] δέῃ με LTr. [n] ἀπαρνήσωμαι T. [o] ᾧ L. [p] Γεθσημανεί LTTrAW. [q] — τὸν GLTTrAW. [r] μετ' αὐτοῦ LTTrA. [s] προσελθὼν Tr. [t] ἔπιπτεν TA. [v] τοῦτο ἀπ' ἐμοῦ LTTrAW. [w] ἔλθητε TA. [x] πάλιν ἐλθὼν again coming LA; ἐλθὼν Tr. [y] — πάλιν LTrA. [z] αὐτῶν οἱ ὀφθαλμοὶ T. [a] καταβαρυνόμενοι LTTrAW. [b] ἀποκριθῶσιν αὐτῷ LTTrAW. [c] — τὸ LTrAW. [d] ἤγγισεν T.

43 And immediately,
while he yet spake,
cometh Judas, one of
the twelve, and with
him a great multi-
tude with swords and
staves, from the chief
priests and the scribes
and the elders. 44 And
he that betrayed him
had given them a
token, saying, Whom-
soever I shall kiss, that
same is he; take him,
and lead *him* away
safely. 45 And as soon
as he was come, he
goeth straightway to
him, and saith, Master,
master; and kissed
him. 46 And they laid
their hands on him,
and took him. 47 And
one of them that stood
by drew a sword, and
smote a servant of the
high priest, and cut off
his ear. 48 And Jesus
answered and said
unto them, Are ye
come out, as against
a thief, with swords
and *with* staves to take
me? 49 I was daily
with you in the tem-
ple teaching, and ye
took me not: but the
scriptures must be ful-
filled. 50 And they all
forsook him, and fled.
51 And there followed
him a certain young
man, having a linen
cloth cast about *his*
naked *body*; and the
young men laid hold
on him: 52 and he left
the linen cloth, and
fled from them naked.

53 And they led Je-
sus away to the high
priest: and with him
were assembled all the
chief priests and the
elders and the scribes.
54 And Peter followed
him afar off, even into
the palace of the high
priest: and he sat with
the servants, and
warmed himself at the
fire. 55 And the chief
priests and all the
council sought for wit-

43 Καὶ [e]εὐθέως‖ ἔτι αὐτοῦ.λαλοῦντος παραγίνεται [f]Ἰού-
And immediately [4]yet [1]as [2]he [3]is speaking, comes up Ju-
δας[g], εἷς [h]ὢν‖ τῶν δώδεκα, καὶ μετ' αὐτοῦ ὄχλος [i]πολὺς‖
das, [2]one [1]being of the twelve, and with him a [2]crowd [1]great,
μετὰ μαχαιρῶν καὶ ξύλων, παρὰ τῶν ἀρχιερέων καὶ τῶν
with swords and staves, from the chief priests and the
γραμματέων καὶ [k]τῶν‖ πρεσβυτέρων. 44 δεδώκει.δὲ ὁ
scribes and the elders. Now [7]had [8]given [1]he [2]who
παραδιδοὺς αὐτὸν [l]σύσσημον‖ αὐτοῖς, λέγων, Ὃν.ἂν
[3]was [4]delivering [6]up [5]him a sign to them, saying, Whomsoever
φιλήσω αὐτός ἐστιν· κρατήσατε αὐτόν, καὶ [m]ἀπαγάγετε‖
I shall kiss [2]he [1]is; seize him, and lead [him] away
ἀσφαλῶς. 45 Καὶ ἐλθών, [e]εὐθέως‖ προσελθὼν αὐτῷ λέγει,
safely. And being come, immediately coming up to him he says,
[n]Ῥαββί, ῥαββί‖ καὶ κατεφίλησεν αὐτόν. 46 Οἱ.δὲ [o]ἐπέβαλον‖
Rabbi, Rabbi; and ardently kissed him. And they laid
[p]ἐπ' αὐτὸν τὰς χεῖρας αὐτῶν,‖ καὶ ἐκράτησαν αὐτόν. 47 Εἷς.δέ
upon him [2]hands [1]their, and seized him. But [3]one
[q]τις‖ τῶν παρεστηκότων σπασάμενος τὴν μάχαιραν
[1]a [2]certain of those standing by, having drawn the sword
ἔπαισεν τὸν δοῦλον τοῦ ἀρχιερέως καὶ ἀφεῖλεν αὐτοῦ τὸ
struck the bondman of the high priest and took off his
[r]ὠτίον.‖ 48 Καὶ ἀποκριθεὶς ὁ Ἰησοῦς εἶπεν αὐτοῖς, Ὡς ἐπὶ
ear. And [2]answering [1]Jesus said to them, As against
λῃστὴν [s]ἐξήλθετε‖ μετὰ μαχαιρῶν καὶ ξύλων συλλαβεῖν με;
a robber are ye come out with swords and staves to take me?
49 καθ'.ἡμέραν ἤμην πρὸς ὑμᾶς ἐν τῷ ἱερῷ διδάσκων, καὶ
Daily I was with you in the temple teaching, and
οὐκ ἐκρατήσατέ με· ἀλλ' ἵνα πληρωθῶσιν αἱ γραφαί.
ye did not seize me: but [it is] that [2]may [4]be [5]fulfilled [1]the [3]scriptures.
50 Καὶ ἀφέντες αὐτὸν [t]πάντες ἔφυγον.‖ 51 Καὶ [u]εἷς τις
And leaving him all fled. And one a certain
νεανίσκος‖ [v]ἠκολούθει‖ αὐτῷ, περιβεβλημένος σινδόνα ἐπὶ
young man was following him, having cast a linen cloth about
γυμνοῦ· καὶ κρατοῦσιν αὐτὸν [w]οἱ νεανίσκοι·‖ 52 ὁ δὲ
[his] naked [body]; and [4]seize [5]him [1]the [2]young [3]men, but he,
καταλιπὼν τὴν σινδόνα γυμνὸς ἔφυγεν [x]ἀπ' αὐτῶν.‖
leaving behind the linen cloth, [2]naked [1]fled from them.

53 Καὶ ἀπήγαγον τὸν Ἰησοῦν πρὸς τὸν ἀρχιερέα· καὶ
And they led away Jesus to the high priest. And
συνέρχονται [y]αὐτῷ πάντες οἱ ἀρχιερεῖς καὶ οἱ [z]πρεσβύτεροι
there come together to him all the chief priests and the elders
καὶ οἱ γραμματεῖς.‖ 54 Καὶ ὁ Πέτρος ἀπὸ μακρόθεν ἠκολού-
and the scribes. And Peter from afar off fol-
θησεν αὐτῷ ἕως ἔσω εἰς τὴν αὐλὴν τοῦ ἀρχιερέως· καὶ ἦν
lowed him as far as within to the court of the high priest; and he was
[a]συγκαθήμενος‖ μετὰ τῶν ὑπηρετῶν, καὶ θερμαινόμενος πρὸς
sitting with the officers, and warming himself at
[b]τὸ‖ φῶς. 55 Οἱ.δὲ ἀρχιερεῖς καὶ ὅλον τὸ συνέδριον ἐζήτουν
the fire (*lit.* light). And the chief priests and [2]whole [1]the sanhedrim sought

[e] εὐθὺς LTTrA. [f] + ὁ LTrAW. [g] + ὁ Ἰσκαριώτης Iscariote LT[Tr]A. [h] — ὢν LTTr[A]. [i] — πολὺς [L]TTrA. [k] — τῶν T. [l] σύνσημον T. [m] ἀπάγετε LTTrA. [n] Ῥαββί LTr; ῥαββεί T; ῥαββεί [ῥαββεί] A. [o] ἐπέβαλαν T. [p] τὰς χεῖρας ἐπ' αὐτὸν L; τὰς χεῖρας αὐτῷ TTrA. [q] — τις LTrAW. [r] ὠτάριον LTTrA. [s] ἐξήλθατε LTTrAW. [t] ἔφυγον πάντες TTrA. [u] νεανίσκος τις LTr. [v] συνηκολούθει was following with LTTrA; ἠκολούθησεν followed W. [w] — οἱ νεανίσκοι (*read* they seize) LTTrA. [x] — ἀπ' αὐτῶν [L]TTr. [y] — αὐτῷ T. [z] γραμματεῖς καὶ οἱ πρεσβύτεροι L. [a] συνκαθήμενος T. [b] — τὸ E.

κατὰ τοῦ Ἰησοῦ μαρτυρίαν, εἰς τὸ θανατῶσαι αὐτόν· καὶ οὐχ
against Jesus testimony, to put to death him, and [2]not
[d]εὕρισκον.‖ 56 πολλοὶ.γὰρ ἐψευδομαρτύρουν κατ αὐτοῦ,
[1]did find [any]. For many bore false testimony against him,
καὶ ἴσαι αἱ μαρτυρίαι οὐκ.ἦσαν. 57 καί τινες ἀναστάντες
and alike their testimonies were not. And some having risen up
ἐψευδομαρτύρουν κατ' αὐτοῦ, λέγοντες, 58 Ὅτι ἡμεῖς ἠκούσα-
bore false testimony against him, saying, We heard
μεν αὐτοῦ λέγοντος, Ὅτι ἐγὼ καταλύσω τὸν.ναὸν.τοῦτον τὸν
him saying, I will destroy this temple the
χειροποίητον, καὶ διὰ τριῶν ἡμερῶν ἄλλον ἀχειροποίητον
[one] made with hands, and in three days another not made with hands
οἰκοδομήσω. 59 Καὶ οὐδὲ οὕτως ἴση ἦν ἡ.μαρτυρία.αὐτῶν.
I will build. And neither thus alike was their testimony.
60 Καὶ ἀναστὰς ὁ ἀρχιερεὺς εἰς [e]τὸ‖ μέσον ἐπηρώτησεν
And [4]having [5]stood [6]up [1]the [2]high [3]priest in the midst questioned
τὸν Ἰησοῦν, λέγων, Οὐκ ἀποκρίνῃ οὐδέν; τί οὗτοί σου
Jesus, saying, Answerest thou nothing? What [2]these [4]thee
καταμαρτυροῦσιν; 61 Ὁ.δὲ ἐσιώπα, καὶ [f]οὐδὲν ἀπεκρίνατο.‖
[1]testify [3]against? But he was silent, and nothing answered.
Πάλιν ὁ ἀρχιερεὺς ἐπηρώτα αὐτόν, καὶ λέγει αὐτῷ, Σὺ
Again the high priest was questioning him, and says to him, [2]Thou
εἶ ὁ χριστός, ὁ υἱὸς τοῦ εὐλογητοῦ; 62 Ὁ.δὲ.Ἰησοῦς εἶπεν,
[1]art the Christ, the Son of the blessed? And Jesus said,
Ἐγώ εἰμι. καὶ ὄψεσθε τὸν υἱὸν τοῦ ἀνθρώπου [g]καθήμενον
I am. And ye shall see the Son of man sitting
ἐκ δεξιῶν‖ τῆς δυνάμεως, καὶ ἐρχόμενον μετὰ τῶν νεφελῶν
at [the] right hand of power, and coming with the clouds
τοῦ οὐρανοῦ. 63 Ὁ.δὲ ἀρχιερεὺς διαῤῥήξας τοὺς.χιτῶνας.αὐτοῦ
of the heaven. And the high priest having rent his garments
λέγει, Τί ἔτι χρείαν ἔχομεν μαρτύρων; 64 ἠκούσατε [h]τῆς
says, What any more need have we of witnesses? Ye heard the
βλασφημίας·‖ τί ὑμῖν φαίνεται; Οἱ.δὲ πάντες κατέκριναν
blasphemy: what [2]to [3]you [1]appears? And they all condemned
αὐτὸν [i]εἶναι ἔνοχον‖ θανάτου. 65 Καὶ ἤρξαντό τινες ἐμπτύειν
him to be deserving of death. And [2]began [1]some to spit upon
αὐτῷ, καὶ περικαλύπτειν [k]τὸ.πρόσωπον.αὐτοῦ,‖ καὶ κολα-
him, and to cover up his face, and to buf-
φίζειν αὐτόν, καὶ λέγειν αὐτῷ, Προφήτευσον· καὶ οἱ ὑπηρέται
fet him, and to say to him, Prophesy; and the officers
ῥαπίσμασιν αὐτὸν [m]ἔβαλλον.‖
with the palm of the hand [2]him [1]struck.

66 Καὶ ὄντος τοῦ Πέτρου [n]ἐν τῇ αὐλῇ κάτω,‖ ἔρχεται μία
And [2]being [1]Peter in the court below, comes one
τῶν παιδισκῶν τοῦ ἀρχιερέως, 67 καὶ ἰδοῦσα τὸν Πέτρον
of the maids of the high priest, and seeing Peter
θερμαινόμενον, ἐμβλέψασα αὐτῷ λέγει, Καὶ σὺ μετὰ τοῦ
warming himself, having looked at him says, And thou [2]with [3]the
Ναζαρηνοῦ [o]Ἰησοῦ ἦσθα.‖ 68 Ὁ.δὲ ἠρνήσατο, λέγων, [p]Οὐκ‖
[4]Nazarene [5]Jesus [1]wast. But he denied, saying, [3]Not
οἶδα [q]οὐδὲ‖ ἐπίσταμαι [r]τί σὺ‖ λέγεις. Καὶ ἐξῆλθεν ἔξω
[1]I [2]know nor even understand what thou sayest. And he went forth out

ness against Jesus to
put him to death; and
found none. 56 For
many bare false wit-
ness against him, but
their witness agreed
not together. 57 And
there arose certain,
and bare false witness
against him, saying,
58 We heard him say,
I will destroy this
temple that is made
with hands, and with-
in three days I will
build another made
without hands. 59 But
neither so did their
witness agree together.
60 And the high priest
stood up in the midst,
and asked Jesus, say-
ing, Answerest thou
nothing? what *is it*
which these witness
against thee? 61 But
he held his peace, and
answered nothing. A-
gain the high priest
asked him, and said
unto him, Art thou
the Christ, the Son of
the Blessed? 62 And
Jesus said, I am: and
ye shall see the Son of
man sitting on the
right hand of power,
and coming in the
clouds of heaven.
63 Then the high priest
rent his clothes, and
saith, What need we
any further witnesses?
64 Ye have heard
the blasphemy: what
think ye? And they
all condemned him to
be guilty of death.
65 And some began to
spit on him, and to
cover his face, and to
buffet him, and to say
unto him, Prophesy:
and the servants did
strike him with the
palms of their hands.

66 And as Peter was
beneath in the palace,
there cometh one of
the maids of the high
priest: 67 and when
she saw Peter warming
himself, she looked up-
on him, and said, And
thou also wast with
Jesus of Nazareth.
68 But he denied, say-
ing, I know not, nei-
ther understand I
what thou sayest. And
he went out into the

---

[d] ηὕρισκον LTrA. [e] — τὸ (*read* [the]) GLTTrAW. [f] οὐκ ἀπεκρίνατο ουδέν TTr. [g] ἐκ δεξιῶν καθήμενον GLTTrAW. [h] τὴν βλασφημίαν L. [i] ενοχον εἶναι TTrA. [k] αὐτοῦ τὸ πρόσωπον TTrA. [m] ἔβαλον W; ἔλαβον (*read* received him with buffets) LTTrA. [n] κάτω ἐν τῇ αὐλῇ TTrA. [o] ἦσθα τοῦ Ἰησοῦ LTTrA. [p] οὔτε neither (know I) LTTrA. [q] οὔτε nor LTTrAW. [r] σὺ τί LTTrA.

porch; and the cock crew. 69 And a maid saw him again, and began to say to them that stood by, This is *one* of them. 70 And he denied it again. And a little after, they that stood by said again to Peter, Surely thou art *one* of them: for thou art a Galilæan, and thy speech agreeth *thereto*. 71 But he began to curse and to swear, *saying*, I know not this man of whom ye speak. 72 And the second time the cock crew. And Peter called to mind the word that Jesus said unto him, Before the cock crow twice, thou shalt deny me thrice. And when he thought thereon, he wept.

XV. And straightway in the morning the chief priests held a consultation with the elders and scribes and the whole council, and bound Jesus, and carried *him* away, and delivered *him* to Pilate. 2 And Pilate asked him, Art thou the King of the Jews? And he answering said unto him, Thou sayest *it*. 3 And the chief priests accused him of many things: but he answered nothing. 4 And Pilate asked him again, saying, Answerest thou nothing? behold how many things they witness against thee. 5 But Jesus yet answered nothing; so that Pilate marvelled. 6 Now at *that* feast he released unto them one prisoner, whomsoever they desired. 7 And there was *one* named Barabbas, *which lay* bound with them that had made insurrection with him, who had committed murder in the insurrection. 8 And the multitude crying aloud began to desire *him to do* as he had ever done unto them.

εἰς το προαύλιον· [s]καὶ ἀλέκτωρ ἐφώνησεν.‖ 69 Καὶ ἡ παιδίσκη
into the porch, and a cock crew. And the maid
ἰδοῦσα αὐτὸν [t]πάλιν ἤρξατο‖ λέγειν τοῖς [v]παρεστηκόσιν,‖ "Οτι
seeing him again began to say to those standing by,
οὗτος ἐξ αὐτῶν ἐστιν. 70 Ὁ.δὲ πάλιν ἠρνεῖτο. Καὶ μετὰ
This [[2]one] [3]of [4]them [1]is. And he again denied. And after
μικρὸν πάλιν οἱ παρεστῶτες ἔλεγον τῷ Πέτρῳ, Ἀληθῶς
a little again those standing by said to Peter, Truly
ἐξ αὐτῶν εἶ· καὶ.γὰρ Γαλιλαῖος εἶ, [w]καὶ ἡ λαλιά
from among them thou art, for both a Galilean thou art, and [2]speech
σου ὁμοιάζει.‖ 71 Ὁ.δὲ ἤρξατο ἀναθεματίζειν καὶ [x]ὀμνύειν,‖
[1]thy agrees. But he began to curse and to swear,
"Οτι οὐκ.οἶδα τὸν.ἄνθρωπον.τοῦτον ὃν λέγετε. 72 Καὶ [y]
I know not this man whom ye speak of. And
ἐκ.δευτέρου ἀλέκτωρ ἐφώνησεν. Καὶ ἀνεμνήσθη ὁ Πέτρος [z]τοῦ
the second time a cock crew. And [2]remembered [1]Peter the
ῥήματος οὗ‖ εἶπεν αὐτῷ ὁ Ἰησοῦς, "Οτι πρὶν ἀλέκτορα
word that [2]said [3]to [4]him [1]Jesus, Before [the] cock
[a]φωνῆσαι δίς‖ [b]ἀπαρνήσῃ με τρίς·‖ καὶ ἐπιβαλὼν
crow twice thou wilt deny me thrice; and having thought thereon
ἔκλαιεν.
he wept.

15 Καὶ [c]εὐθέως‖ [d]ἐπὶ τὸ‖ πρωῒ συμβούλιον [e]ποιήσαντες‖
And immediately in the morning [6]a [7]counsel [4]having [5]formed
οἱ ἀρχιερεῖς μετὰ τῶν πρεσβυτέρων καὶ [f]γραμματέων καὶ
[1]the [2]chief [3]priests with the elders and scribes and
ὅλον τὸ συνέδριον, δήσαντες τὸν Ἰησοῦν ἀπήνεγκαν καὶ
[2]whole [1]the sanhedrim, having bound Jesus carried [him] away and
παρέδωκαν [g]τῷ‖ [h]Πιλάτῳ.‖ 2 καὶ ἐπηρώτησεν αὐτὸν ὁ
delivered up [him] to Pilate. And [2]questioned [3]him
[i]Πιλάτος,‖ Σὺ εἶ ὁ βασιλεὺς τῶν Ἰουδαίων; Ὁ.δὲ ἀπο-
[1]Pilate, [5]Thou [4]art the King of the Jews? And he an-
κριθεὶς [j]εἶπεν αὐτῷ,‖ Σὺ λέγεις. 3 Καὶ κατηγόρουν αὐτοῦ οἱ
swering said to him, Thou sayest. And [4]were [5]accusing [6]him [1]the
ἀρχιερεῖς πολλά· 4 ὁ.δὲ.[i]Πιλάτος‖ πάλιν [k]ἐπηρώτησεν‖ αὐτόν,
[2]chief [3]priests urgently. And Pilate again questioned him,
[l]λέγων,‖ Οὐκ ἀποκρίνῃ οὐδέν; ἴδε, πόσα σου
saying, Answerest thou nothing? See, of how many things [4]thee
[m]καταμαρτυροῦσιν.‖ 5 Ὁ.δὲ.Ἰησοῦς οὐκέτι.οὐδὲν ἀπεκρίθη,
[1]they [2]witness [3]against. But Jesus not any more any thing answered,
ὥστε θαυμάζειν τὸν [n]Πιλάτον.‖ 6 Κατὰ.δὲ ἑορτὴν ἀπέλυεν
so that [2]wondered [1]Pilate. Now at [the] feast he released
αὐτοῖς ἕνα δέσμιον, [o]ὅνπερ ᾐτοῦντο.‖ 7 ἦν.δὲ ὁ λεγό-
to them one prisoner, whomsoever they asked. And there was the [one] call-
μενος Βαραββᾶς μετὰ τῶν [p]συστασιαστῶν‖ δεδεμένος,
ed Barabbas with the associates in insurrection bound,
οἵτινες ἐν τῇ στάσει φόνον πεποιήκεισαν. 8 καὶ [q]ἀναβοήσας‖
who in the insurrection murder had committed. And crying out
ὁ ὄχλος ἤρξατο αἰτεῖσθαι καθὼς [r]ἀεὶ‖ ἐποίει αὐτοῖς
the crowd began to beg [him to do] as always he did to them.

---

[s] [καὶ ἀλέκτωρ ἐφώνησεν] L. [t] ἤρξατο πάλιν T; — πάλιν A. [v] παρεστῶσιν TTrA. [w] — καὶ ἡ λαλιά σου ὁμοιάζει LTTrA. [x] ὀμνύναι GLTTrAW. [y] + εὐθὺς immediately LTTr. [z] τὸ ῥῆμα ὡς LTTrA; τὸ ῥῆμα ὃ W. [a] δὶς φωνῆσαι LTrA. [b] τρίς με ἀπαρνήσῃ LTTrA. [c] εὐθὺς TTrA. [d] — ἐπὶ τὸ (*read* πρωῒ early) LTTr[A]. [e] ἑτοιμάσαντες T. [f] + τῶν the T. [g] — τῷ LTTrA. [h] Πειλάτῳ T. [i] Πειλᾶτος T. [j] αὐτῷ λέγει to him says TTrA. [k] ἐπηρώτα TTrA. [l] — λέγων T. [m] κατηγοροῦσιν they accuse LTTrA. [n] Πειλᾶτον T. [o] ὃν παρῃτοῦντο T. [p] στασιαστῶν LTTrA. [q] ἀναβὰς coming up LTTrA. [r] — ἀεὶ T.

9 ὁ.δὲ.[s]Πιλάτος‖ ἀπεκρίθη αὐτοῖς, λέγων, Θέλετε ἀπολύσω
But Pilate answered them, saying, Will ye I should release
ὑμῖν τὸν βασιλέα τῶν Ἰουδαίων; 10 Ἐγίνωσκεν.γὰρ ὅτι διὰ
to you the King of the Jews? for he knew that through
φθόνον παραδεδώκεισαν αὐτὸν οἱ ἀρχιερεῖς. 11 οἱ.δὲ ἀρχ-
envy [4]had [5]delivered [7]up [6]him [1]the [2]chief [3]priests. But the chief
ιερεῖς ἀνέσεισαν τὸν ὄχλον ἵνα μᾶλλον τὸν Βαραββᾶν
priests stirred up the crowd that rather Barabbas
ἀπολύσῃ αὐτοῖς· 12 ὁ.δὲ.[s]Πιλάτος‖ [t]ἀποκριθεὶς πάλιν‖
he might release to them. And Pilate answering again
[v]εἶπεν‖ αὐτοῖς, Τί οὖν [w]θέλετε‖ ποιήσω [x]ὃν λέγετε‖
said to them, What then will ye I should do [to him] whom ye call
[y] βασιλέα τῶν Ἰουδαίων; 13 Οἱ.δὲ πάλιν ἔκραξαν,[z] Σταύρω-
King of the Jews? But they again cried out Cruci-
σον αὐτόν. 14 Ὁ.δὲ.[s]Πιλάτος‖ ἔλεγεν αὐτοῖς, Τί γὰρ [a]κακὸν
fy him. And Pilate said to them, What [2]then [1]evil
ἐποίησεν‖; Οἱ.δὲ [b]περισσοτέρως‖ [c]ἔκραξαν,‖ Σταύρωσον αὐ-
did he commit? But they much more cried out, Crucify him.
τόν. 15 Ὁ.δὲ.[s]Πιλάτος‖ βουλόμενος [d]τῷ ὄχλῳ τὸ
And Pilate, desiring [7]to [8]the [9]crowd [3]that [4]which [[5]was]
ἱκανὸν ποιῆσαι,‖ ἀπέλυσεν αὐτοῖς τὸν Βαραββᾶν· καὶ παρέ-
[6]satisfactory [1]to [2]do, released to them Barabbas, and de-
δωκεν τὸν Ἰησοῦν, φραγελλώσας, ἵνα σταυρωθῇ.
livered up Jesus, having scourged [him], that he might be crucified.

16 Οἱ.δὲ στρατιῶται ἀπήγαγον αὐτὸν ἔσω τῆς αὐλῆς, ὅ
And the soldiers led away him within the court, which
ἐστιν πραιτώριον, καὶ [e]συγκαλοῦσιν‖ ὅλην τὴν σπεῖραν·
is [the] prætorium, and they call together [2]whole [1]the band.
17 καὶ [f]ἐνδύουσιν‖ αὐτὸν πορφύραν, καὶ περιτιθέασιν αὐτῷ
And they put on him purple, and placed on him
πλέξαντες ἀκάνθινον στέφανον, 18 καὶ ἤρξαντο ἀσπάζε-
having platted [it] [2]thorny [1]a crown, and they began to sa-
σθαι αὐτόν, Χαῖρε, [g]βασιλεῦ‖ τῶν Ἰουδαίων· 19 καὶ ἔτυπτον
lute him, Hail, King of the Jews! And they struck
αὐτοῦ τὴν κεφαλὴν καλάμῳ, καὶ ἐνέπτυον αὐτῷ, καὶ τιθέντες
his head with a reed, and spat on him, and bending
τὰ γόνατα προσεκύνουν αὐτῷ. 20 Καὶ ὅτε ἐνέπαιξαν αὐτῷ,
the knees did homage to him. And when they had mocked him,
ἐξέδυσαν αὐτὸν τὴν πορφύραν, καὶ ἐνέδυσαν αὐτὸν τὰ
they took off him the purple, and put on him
[h]ἱμάτια.τὰ.ἴδια·‖ καὶ [i]ἐξάγουσιν‖ αὐτὸν ἵνα [k]σταυρώσωσιν‖
his own garments; and they lead [2]out [1]him that they may crucify
[l]αὐτόν.‖ 21 καὶ ἀγγαρεύουσιν παράγοντά τινα Σίμωνα Κυ-
him. And they compel [2]passing [3]by [1]one, Simon a Cy-
ρηναῖον, ἐρχόμενον [m]ἀπ'‖ ἀγροῦ, τὸν πατέρα Ἀλεξάνδρου καὶ
renian, coming from a field, the father of Alexander and
Ῥούφου, ἵνα ἄρῃ τὸν.σταυρὸν.αὐτοῦ.
Rufus, that he might carry his cross.

22 Καὶ φέρουσιν αὐτὸν ἐπὶ [n]Γολγοθᾶ‖ τόπον, ὅ ἐστιν
And they bring him to [3]Golgotha [1]a [2]place, which is
μεθερμηνευόμενον, κρανίου τόπος. 23 Καὶ ἐδίδουν αὐτῷ
being interpreted, [2]of [3]a [4]skull [1]place. And they gave him

9 But Pilate answered them, saying, Will ye that I release unto you the King of the Jews? 10 For he knew that the chief priests had delivered him for envy. 11 But the chief priests moved the people, that he should rather release Barabbas unto them. 12 And Pilate answered and said again unto them, What will ye then that I shall do *unto him* whom ye call the King of the Jews? 13 And they cried out again, Crucify him. 14 Then Pilate said unto them, Why, what evil hath he done? And they cried out the more exceedingly, Crucify him. 15 And *so* Pilate, willing to content the people, released Barabbas unto them, and delivered Jesus, when he had scourged *him*, to be crucified.

16 And the soldiers led him away into the hall, called Prætorium; and they call together the whole band. 17 And they clothed him with purple, and platted a crown of thorns, and put it about his *head*, 18 and began to salute him, Hail, King of the Jews! 19 And they smote him on the head with a reed, and did spit upon him, and bowing *their* knees worshipped him. 20 And when they had mocked him, they took off the purple from him, and put his own clothes on him, and led him out to crucify him. 21 And they compel one Simon a Cyrenian, who passed by, coming out of the country, the father of Alexander and Rufus, to bear his cross.

22 And they bring him unto the place Golgotha, which is, being interpreted, The place of a skull. 23 And they gave him to drink wine

[s] Πειλᾶτος T. [t] πάλιν ἀποκριθεὶς LTTrA. [v] ἔλεγεν TTrA. [w] [θέλετε] Tr. [x] — ὃν λέγετε LTr. [y] + τὸν the LTTrAW. [z] + λέγοντες saying L. [a] ἐποίησεν κακόν TTrA. [b] περισσῶς GLTTrAW. [c] ἔκραζον L. [d] ποιῆσαι τὸ ἱκανὸν τῷ ὄχλῳ T. [e] συνκαλοῦσιν T. [f] ἐνδιδύσκουσιν LTTrA. [g] ὁ βασιλεὺς GAW. [h] ἱμάτια αὐτοῦ L; ἴδια ἱμάτια αὐτοῦ T. [i] ἄγουσιν they lead L. [k] σταυρώσουσιν they shall crucify LTTrA. [l] — αὐτόν T. [m] ἀπὸ LTr. [n] τὸν Γολγοθᾶν T; Γολγοθᾶν A; [τὸν] Γολγοθὰ Tr.

mingled with myrrh: but he received *it* not. 24 And when they had crucified him, they parted his garments, casting lots upon them, what every man should take. 25 And it was the third hour, and they crucified him. 26 And the superscription of his accusation was written over, THE KING OF THE JEWS. 27 And with him they crucify two thieves; the one on his right hand, and the other on his left. 28 And the scripture was fulfilled, which saith, And he was numbered with the transgressors. 29 And they that passed by railed on him, wagging their heads, and saying, Ah, thou that destroyest the temple, and buildest *it* in three days, 30 save thyself, and come down from the cross. 31 Likewise also the chief priests mocking said among themselves with the scribes, He saved others; himself he cannot save. 32 Let Christ the King of Israel descend now from the cross, that we may see and believe. And they that were crucified with him reviled him. 33 And when the sixth hour was come, there was darkness over the whole land until the ninth hour. 34 And at the ninth hour Jesus cried with a loud voice, saying, ELOI, ELOI, LAMA SABACHTHANI? which is, being interpreted, My God, my God, why hast thou forsaken me? 35 And some of them that stood by, when they heard *it*, said, Behold, he calleth Elias. 36 And one ran and filled a spunge full of vinegar, and put *it* on a reed, and gave him to drink, saying, Let alone; let us see whether Elias will come to take him down.

[o]πιεῖν‖ ἐσμυρνισμένον οἶνον· [p]ὁ.δὲ‖ οὐκ.ἔλαβεν. 24 Καὶ
to drink [2]medicated [3]with [4]myrrh [1]wine; but he did not take [it]. And
[q]σταυρώσαντες αὐτὸν‖ [r]διεμέριζον‖ τὰ.ἱμάτια.αὐτοῦ, βάλλον-
having crucified him they divided his garments, cast-
τες κλῆρον ἐπ' αὐτά, τίς τί ἄρῃ. 25 ἦν.δὲ
ing a lot on them, who [and] what [each] should take. And it was [the]
ὥρα τρίτη, καὶ ἐσταύρωσαν αὐτόν. 26 Καὶ ἦν ἡ ἐπιγραφὴ
[2]hour [1]third, and they crucified him. And [6]was [1]the [2]inscription
τῆς.αἰτίας.αὐτοῦ ἐπιγεγραμμένη, Ὁ βασιλεὺς τῶν Ἰουδαίων.
[3]of [4]his [5]accusation written up, The King of the Jews.
27 Καὶ σὺν αὐτῷ σταυροῦσιν δύο λῃστάς, ἕνα ἐκ δεξιῶν
And with him they crucify two robbers, one at [the] right hand
καὶ ἕνα ἐξ εὐωνύμων αὐτοῦ. 28 [s]καὶ ἐπληρώθη ἡ γραφὴ
and one at [the] left of him. And was fulfilled the scripture
ἡ λέγουσα, Καὶ μετὰ ἀνόμων ἐλογίσθη.‖ 29 Καὶ οἱ
which says, And with [the] lawless he was reckoned. And those
παραπορευόμενοι ἐβλασφήμουν αὐτόν, κινοῦντες τὰς κεφαλὰς
passing by railed at him, shaking [2]heads
αὐτῶν, καὶ λέγοντες, [t]Οὐά,‖ ὁ.καταλύων τὸν ναὸν καὶ [v]ἐν
[1]their, and saying, Aha, thou who destroyest the temple and in
τρισὶν ἡμέραις οἰκοδομῶν,‖ 30 σῶσον σεαυτόν, [w]καὶ κατάβα‖
three days buildest [it], save thyself, and descend
ἀπὸ τοῦ σταυροῦ. 31 Ὁμοίως.[x]δὲ‖ καὶ οἱ ἀρχιερεῖς, ἐμπαί-
from the cross. And in like manner also the chief priests, mock-
ζοντες πρὸς ἀλλήλους μετὰ τῶν γραμματέων, ἔλεγον, Ἄλλους
ing among one another with the scribes, said, Others
ἔσωσεν, ἑαυτὸν οὐ.δύναται σῶσαι. 32 ὁ χριστὸς ὁ βασιλεὺς
he saved, himself he is not able to save. The Christ the King
[y]τοῦ‖ Ἰσραὴλ καταβάτω νῦν ἀπὸ τοῦ σταυροῦ, ἵνα ἴδωμεν
of Israel! let him descend now from the cross, that we may see
καὶ πιστεύσωμεν[z]. Καὶ οἱ συνεσταυρωμένοι[a] αὐτῷ ὠνείδιζον
and believe. And they who were crucified with him reproached
αὐτόν. 33 [b]Γενομένης.δὲ‖ ὥρας ἕκτης, σκότος ἐγένετο ἐφ'
him. And [4]being [5]come [[1]the] [3]hour [2]sixth, darkness came over
ὅλην τὴν γῆν, ἕως ὥρας [c]ἐννάτης·‖ 34 καὶ τῇ [d]ὥρᾳ τῇ
all the land, until [the] [2]hour [1]ninth; and at the hour the
ἐννάτῃ‖ ἐβόησεν ὁ Ἰησοῦς φωνῇ μεγάλῃ, [e]λέγων,‖ [f]Ἐλωΐ,
ninth [2]cried [1]Jesus with a [2]voice [1]loud, saying, Eloi,
Ἐλωΐ,‖ [g]λαμμᾶ‖ [h]σαβαχθανί;‖ ὅ ἐστιν μεθερμηνευόμενον,
Eloi, lama sabachthani? which is being interpreted,
Ὁ.θεός.μου, ὁ.θεός.μου, εἰς.τί [i]με ἐγκατέλιπες‖; 35 Καὶ τινὲς
My God, My God, why me hast thou forsaken? And some
τῶν [k]παρεστηκότων‖ ἀκούσαντες ἔλεγον, [l]Ἰδού,‖ [m]Ἠλίαν‖
of those standing by having heard said, Lo, Elias
φωνεῖ. 36 Δραμὼν.δὲ [n]εἷς‖ [oa]καὶ‖ γεμίσας σπόγγον ὄξους,
he calls. And [2]having [3]run [1]one and filled a sponge with vinegar,
περιθείς [pa]τε‖ καλάμῳ ἐπότιζεν αὐτόν, λέγων, Ἄφετε,
[2]having [3]put [[4]it] [5]on [1]and a reed gave [2]to [3]drink [1]him, saying, Let be,
ἴδωμεν εἰ ἔρχεται [qa]Ἠλίας‖ καθελεῖν αὐτόν.
let us see if [2]comes [1]Elias to take down him.

[o] — πιεῖν TTrA. [p] ὃς δὲ who however TTr. [q] σταυροῦσιν αὐτόν, καὶ they crucify him and TTrA. [r] διαμερίζονται they divide GLTTrAW. [s] — *verse* 28 T[Tr]A. [t] Οὐᾶ T. [v] οἰκοδομῶν τρισὶν ἡμέραις LTTrA. [w] καταβὰς descending LTTrA. [x] — δὲ and GLTTrAW. [y] — τοῦ LTTr. [z] + αὐτῷ him L. [a] + σὺν with (*read* crucified along with) LT. [b] καὶ γενομένης LTTrA. [c] ἐνάτης LTTrA. [d] ἐνάτῃ ὥρᾳ LTTrA. [e] — λέγων TTrA. [f] Ἐλωΐ ἐλωΐ LTA. [g] λεμὰ LT; λαμὰ TrAW. [h] σαβαχθανεί TTr. [i] ἐγκατέλιπές με LTTrA. [k] παρεστώτων T. [l] Ἴδε TTrA. [m] Ἠλείαν T. [n] τις TTrA. [oa] — καὶ L[Tr]A. [pa] — τε LTTrA. [qa] Ἠλείας T.

37 Ὁ.δὲ.Ἰησοῦς ἀφεὶς φωνὴν μεγάλην ἐξέπνευσεν.
And Jesus having uttered a [2]cry [1]loud expired.
38 καὶ τὸ καταπέτασμα τοῦ ναοῦ ἐσχίσθη εἰς δύο, [r]ἀπὸ‖ ἄνω-
And the veil of the temple was rent into two, from top
θεν ἕως κάτω. 39 Ἰδὼν.δὲ ὁ κεντυρίων ὁ παρεστηκὼς
to bottom. And [8]having [9]seen [1]the [2]centurion [3]who [4]stood [5]by
ἐξ.ἐναντίας αὐτοῦ ὅτι οὕτως [s]κράξας‖ ἐξέπνευσεν, εἶπεν,
[6]opposite [7]him that thus having cried out he expired, said,
Ἀληθῶς [t]ὁ.ἄνθρωπος.οὗτος‖ υἱὸς ἦν θεοῦ. 40 [v]Ἦσαν.δὲ καὶ
Truly this man [2]Son [1]was of God. And there were also
γυναῖκες ἀπὸ μακρόθεν θεωροῦσαι, ἐν αἷς [v]ἦν‖ καὶ Μαρία
women from afar off looking on, among whom was also Mary
ἡ Μαγδαληνή, καὶ Μαρία [w]ἡ‖ [x]τοῦ‖ Ἰακώβου τοῦ μικροῦ καὶ
the Magdalene, and Mary the [2]of [3]James [4]the [5]less [6]and
[y]Ἰωσῆ‖ μήτηρ, καὶ Σαλώμη, 41 αἳ [z]καὶ‖ ὅτε ἦν ἐν τῇ Γαλι-
[7]of [8]Joses [1]mother, and Salome; who also when he was in Gali-
λαίᾳ ἠκολούθουν αὐτῷ καὶ διηκόνουν αὐτῷ, καὶ ἄλλαι πολλαὶ
lee followed him and ministered to him, and [2]others [1]many
αἱ συναναβᾶσαι αὐτῷ εἰς Ἱεροσόλυμα.
who came up with him to Jerusalem.

42 Καὶ ἤδη ὀψίας γενομένης, ἐπεὶ ἦν παρασκευή,
And already evening being come, since it was [the] preparation,
ὅ ἐστιν [a]προσάββατον, 43 [b]ἦλθεν‖ Ἰωσὴφ ὁ ἀπὸ
that is [the day] before sabbath, came Joseph who [was] from
Ἀριμαθαίας, εὐσχήμων βουλευτής, ὃς καὶ αὐτὸς ἦν προσ-
Arimathæa, [an] honourable counsellor, who also himself was wait-
δεχόμενος τὴν βασιλείαν τοῦ θεοῦ· τολμήσας εἰσῆλθεν πρὸς[c]
ing for the kingdom of God, having boldness he went in to
[d]Πιλάτον‖ καὶ ᾐτήσατο τὸ σῶμα τοῦ Ἰησοῦ. 44 ὁ.δὲ.[e]Πιλάτος
Pilate and begged the body of Jesus. And Pilate
ἐθαύμασεν‖ εἰ ἤδη τέθνηκεν· καὶ προσκαλεσάμενος τὸν
wondered if already he were dead; and having called to [him] the
κεντυρίωνα ἐπηρώτησεν αὐτὸν εἰ [f]πάλαι‖ ἀπέθανεν· 45 καὶ
centurion he questioned him if long he had died. And
γνοὺς ἀπὸ τοῦ κεντυρίωνος ἐδωρήσατο τὸ [g]σῶμα‖ τῷ
having known [it] from the centurion he granted the body
Ἰωσήφ. 46 καὶ ἀγοράσας σινδόνα, [h]καὶ‖ καθελὼν
to Joseph. And having bought a linen cloth, and having taken [2]down
αὐτὸν ἐνείλησεν τῇ σινδόνι, καὶ [i]κατέθηκεν‖ αὐτὸν ἐν
[1]him he wrapped [him] in the linen cloth, and laid him in
[k]μνημείῳ,‖ ὃ ἦν λελατομημένον ἐκ πέτρας· καὶ προσ-
a tomb, which was cut out of a rock, and roll-
εκύλισεν λίθον ἐπὶ τὴν θύραν τοῦ μνημείου. 47 ἡ.δὲ.Μαρία ἡ
ed a stone to the door of the tomb. And Mary the
Μαγδαληνὴ καὶ Μαρία [l]Ἰωσῆ‖ ἐθεώρουν ποῦ [m]τίθεται.‖
Magdalene and Mary [mother] of Joses saw where he is laid.

16 Καὶ διαγενομένου τοῦ σαββάτου, Μαρία ἡ Μαγδαληνὴ
And [3]being [4]past [1]the [2]sabbath, Mary the Magdalene
καὶ Μαρία ἡ [n]τοῦ‖ Ἰακώβου καὶ Σαλώμη ἠγόρασαν
and Mary the [mother] of James and Salome bought
ἀρώματα, ἵνα ἐλθοῦσαι ἀλείψωσιν αὐτόν. 2 καὶ λίαν πρωῒ
aromatics, that having come they might anoint him. And very early

37 And Jesus cried with a loud voice, and gave up the ghost. 38 And the veil of the temple was rent in twain from the top to the bottom. 39 And when the centurion, which stood over against him, saw that he so cried out, and gave up the ghost, he said, Truly this man was the Son of God. 40 There were also women looking on afar off: among whom was Mary Magdalene, and Mary the mother of James the less and of Joses, and Salome; 41 (who also, when he was in Galilee, followed him, and ministered unto him;) and many other women which came up with him unto Jerusalem.

42 And now when the even was come, because it was the preparation, that is, the day before the sabbath, 43 Joseph of Arimathæa, an honourable counsellor, which also waited for the kingdom of God, came, and went in boldly unto Pilate, and craved the body of Jesus. 44 And Pilate marvelled if he were already dead: and calling *unto him* the centurion, he asked him whether he had been any while dead. 45 And when he knew *it* of the centurion, he gave the body to Joseph. 46 And he bought fine linen, and took him down, and wrapped him in the linen, and laid him in a sepulchre which was hewn out of a rock, and rolled a stone unto the door of the sepulchre. 47 And Mary Magdalene and Mary *the mother* of Joses beheld where he was laid.

XVI. And when the sabbath was past, Mary Magdalene, and Mary the *mother* of James, and Salome, had bought sweet spices, that they might come and anoint him. 2 And very early in the morning the first *day* of the week, they

---

[r] ἀπ' LTrA. [s] — κράξας T[Tr]A. [t] οὗτος ὁ ἄνθρωπος LTTrA. [v] — ἦν (*read* [was]) T[TrA]. [w] [ἡ] Tr. [x] — τοῦ LTTrA. [y] Ἰωσῆτος LTTrA. [z] — καὶ LT[Tr] [a] πρὸς σάββατον LTr. [b] ἐλθὼν having come LTTrAW. [c] + τὸν TTr. [d] Πειλᾶτον T. [e] Πειλᾶτος ἐθαύμαζεν T. [f] ἤδη already LTr. [g] πτῶμα corpse LTTrA. [h] — καὶ LTTrAW. [i] ἔθηκεν LTr. [k] μνήματι T. [l] ἡ Ἰωσῆτος LTTrA. [m] τέθειται he has been laid LTTrA. [n] — τοῦ T[Tr].

came unto the sepul-
chre at the rising of
the sun. 3 And they
said among them-
selves, Who shall roll
us away the stone
from the door of the
sepulchre? 4 And
when they looked,
they saw that the
stone was rolled a-
way: for it was very
great. 5 And entering
into the sepulchre,
they saw a young man
sitting on the right
side, clothed in a long
white garment; and
they were affrighted.
6 And he saith unto
them, Be not affright-
ed: Ye seek Jesus of
Nazareth, which was
crucified: he is risen;
he is not here: behold
the place where they
laid him. 7 But go
your way, tell his dis-
ciples and Peter that
he goeth before you
into Galilee: there
shall ye see him, as he
said unto you. 8 And
they went out quick-
ly, and fled from the
sepulchre; for they
trembled and were a-
mazed: neither said
they any thing to any
man; for they were
afraid.

9 Now when *Jesus*
was risen early the
first *day* of the week,
he appeared first to
Mary Magdalene, out
of whom he had cast
seven devils. 10 *And*
she went and told
them that had been
with him, as they
mourned and wept.
11 And they, when
they had heard that
he was alive, and had
been seen of her, be-
lieved not. 12 After
that he appeared in
another form unto
two of them, as they
walked, and went into
the country. 13 And
they went and told *it*
unto the residue: nei-
ther believed they
them. 14 Afterward
he appeared unto the
eleven as they sat at
meat, and upbraided
them with their unbe-
lief and hardness of
heart, because they be-
lieved not them which
had seen him after he
was risen. 15 And he

[o]τῆς μιᾶς‖ σαββάτων ἔρχονται ἐπὶ τὸ [p]μνημεῖον,‖ ἀνατεί-
on the first [day] of the week they come to the tomb, [3]having
λαντος τοῦ ἡλίου. 3 καὶ ἔλεγον πρὸς ἑαυτάς, Τίς ἀποκυλίσει
[4]risen [1]the [2]sun. And they said among themselves, Who will roll away
ἡμῖν τὸν λίθον [q]ἐκ‖ τῆς θύρας τοῦ μνημείου; 4 Καὶ ἀνα-
for us the stone out of the door of the tomb? And having
βλέψασαι θεωροῦσιν ὅτι [r]ἀποκεκύλισται‖ ὁ λίθος· ἦν.γὰρ
looked up they see that has been rolled away the stone: for it was
μέγας σφόδρα. 5 καὶ [s]εἰσελθοῦσαι‖ εἰς τὸ μνημεῖον, εἶδον
[2]great [1]very. And having entered into the tomb, they saw
νεανίσκον καθήμενον ἐν τοῖς δεξιοῖς, περιβεβλημένον στολὴν
a young man sitting on the right, clothed with a [2]robe
λευκήν· καὶ ἐξεθαμβήθησαν. 6 ὁ.δὲ λέγει αὐταῖς, Μὴ
[1]white, and they were greatly amazed. But he says to them, [2]Not
ἐκθαμβεῖσθε. Ἰησοῦν ζητεῖτε τὸν Ναζαρηνὸν τὸν ἐσταυ-
[1]be amazed. [3]Jesus [1]ye [2]seek the Nazarene, who has been
ρωμένον· ἠγέρθη, οὐκ.ἔστιν ὧδε· ἴδε ὁ τόπος ὅπου ἔθηκαν
crucified. He is risen, he is not here; behold the place where they laid
αὐτόν· 7 [t]ἀλλ'‖ ὑπάγετε, εἴπατε τοῖς.μαθηταῖς.αὐτοῦ καὶ τῷ
him. But go, say to his disciples and
Πέτρῳ, ὅτι προάγει ὑμᾶς εἰς τὴν Γαλιλαίαν· ἐκεῖ αὐτὸν
to Peter, that he goes before you into Galilee; there him
ὄψεσθε, καθὼς εἶπεν ὑμῖν. 8 Καὶ ἐξελθοῦσαι [v]ταχὺ‖
shall ye see, as he said to you. And having gone out quickly
ἔφυγον ἀπὸ τοῦ μνημείου· εἶχεν.[w]δὲ‖ αὐτὰς τρόμος καὶ
they fled from the tomb. And [4]possessed [5]them [1]trembling [2]and
ἔκστασις· καὶ οὐδενὶ [x]οὐδὲν‖ εἶπον, ἐφοβοῦντο.γάρ.[y]
[3]amazement, and to no one anything they spoke, for they were afraid.
(*lit.* nothing)

9 [z]Ἀναστὰς.δὲ πρωῒ πρώτῃ σαββάτου ἐφάνη πρῶ-
Now having risen early [the] first [day] of the week he appeared first
τον Μαρίᾳ τῇ Μαγδαληνῇ, [a]ἀφ'‖ ἧς ἐκβεβλήκει ἑπτὰ δαιμό-
to Mary the Magdalene, from whom he had cast out seven demons.
νια. 10 ἐκείνη[b] πορευθεῖσα ἀπήγγειλεν τοῖς μετ' αὐτοῦ γε-
She having gone told [it] to those who with him had
νομένοις, πενθοῦσιν καὶ κλαίουσιν. 11 κἀκεῖνοι ἀκούσαντες
been, [who were] grieving and weeping. And they having heard
ὅτι ζῇ καὶ ἐθεάθη ὑπ' αὐτῆς ἠπίστησαν. 12 Μετὰ.δὲ
that he is alive and has been seen by her disbelieved [it]. And after
ταῦτα δυσὶν ἐξ αὐτῶν περιπατοῦσιν ἐφανερώθη ἐν ἑτέρᾳ
these things to two of them as they walked he was manifested in another
μορφῇ, πορευομένοις εἰς ἀγρόν. 13 κἀκεῖνοι ἀπελθόντες ἀπ-
form, going into [the] country; and they having gone
ήγγειλαν τοῖς λοιποῖς· οὐδὲ ἐκείνοις ἐπίστευσαν. 14 Ὕστερον[c]
told [it] to the rest; neither them did they believe. Afterwards
ἀνακειμένοις αὐτοῖς τοῖς ἕνδεκα ἐφανερώθη, καὶ ὠνεί-
as [2]reclined [[3]at [4]table] [1]they to the eleven he was manifested, and re-
δισεν τὴν.ἀπιστίαν.αὐτῶν καὶ σκληροκαρδίαν, ὅτι τοῖς
proached their unbelief and hardness of heart, because [4]those [5]who
θεασαμένοις αὐτὸν ἐγηγερμένον [d] οὐκ.ἐπίστευσαν. 15 Καὶ εἶπεν
[6]had [7]seen [8]him [9]arisen [1]they [2]believed [3]not. And he said
αὐτοῖς, Πορευθέντες εἰς τὸν κόσμον ἅπαντα κηρύξατε τὸ εὐαγ-
to them, Having gone into [2]the [3]world [1]all proclaim the glad

[o] μιᾷ τῶν LTr; τῇ μιᾷ τῶν T. [p] μνῆμα T. [q] ἀπὸ from LTr. [r] ἀνακεκύλισται TTrA. [s] ἐλθοῦσαι having gone A. [t] ἀλλὰ LTTrA. [v] — ταχὺ GLTTrAW. [w] γὰρ for LTTr. [x] — οὐδὲν L. [y] + κατὰ Μάρκον according to Mark Tr; [εὐαγγέλιον] κατὰ Μάρκον glad tidings according to Mark A. [z] — verses 9 to 20 T[A]. [a] παρ' LTr. [b] + δὲ and (she) L. [c] + δὲ and (afterwards) LTr. [d] + ἐκ νεκρῶν from among [the] dead L.

γέλιον πάσῃ τῇ κτίσει. 16 ὁ πιστεύσας καὶ βαπτισθεὶς σωθήσε-
tidings to all the creation. He that believes and is baptized shall be
ται· ὁ.δὲ ἀπιστήσας κατακριθήσεται. 17 σημεῖα.δὲ τοῖς
saved, and he that disbelieves shall be condemned. And [2]signs [5]those [6]that
πιστεύσασιν [e]ταῦτα παρακολουθήσει‖. ἐν τῷ.ὀνόματί.μου δαι-
[7]believe [1]these [3]shall [4]follow: in my name de-
μόνια ἐκβαλοῦσιν· γλώσσαις λαλήσουσιν [f]καιναῖς·‖
mons they shall cast out; with [2]tongues [3]they [4]shall [5]speak [1]new;
18 [g]ὄφεις ἀροῦσιν· κἂν θανάσιμόν τι πίωσιν οὐ.μὴ
serpents they shall take up; and if [2]deadly [1]anything they drink in no wise
αὐτοὺς [h]βλάψει·‖ ἐπὶ ἀῤῥώστους χεῖρας ἐπιθήσουσιν, καὶ
them shall it injure; upon [the] infirm [4]hands [1]they [2]shall [3]lay, and
καλῶς ἕξουσιν.
[4]well [1]they [2]shall [3]be.

19 Ὁ μὲν οὖν κύριος[i] μετὰ τὸ λαλῆσαι αὐτοῖς [k]ἀνελή-
The [2]indeed [3]therefore [1]Lord after speaking to them was taken
φθη‖ εἰς τὸν οὐρανόν, καὶ ἐκάθισεν ἐκ δεξιῶν τοῦ θεοῦ·
up into the heaven, and sat at [the] right hand of God.
20 ἐκεῖνοι.δὲ ἐξελθόντες ἐκήρυξαν πανταχοῦ, τοῦ κυρίου συνερ-
And they having gone forth preached everywhere, the Lord working
γοῦντος, καὶ τὸν λόγον βεβαιοῦντος διὰ τῶν ἐπακολουθούν-
with [them], and the word confirming by the [2]following [3]upon
των σημείων. [l]Ἀμήν.‖
[4it] [1]signs. Amen.

[m]Τὸ κατὰ Μάρκον εὐαγγέλιον.‖
The [3]according [4]to [5]Mark [1]glad [2]tidings.

said unto them, Go ye into all the world, and preach the gospel to every creature. 16 He that believeth and is baptized shall be saved; but he that believeth not shall be damned. 17 And these signs shall follow them that believe; In my name shall they cast out devils; they shall speak with new tongues; 18 they shall take up serpents; and if they drink any deadly thing, it shall not hurt them; they shall lay hands on the sick, and they shall recover.

19 So then after the Lord had spoken unto them, he was received up into heaven, and sat on the right hand of God. 20 And they went forth, and preached every where, the Lord working with *them*, and confirming the word with signs following. Amen.

---

[a]ΤΟ ΚΑΤΑ ΛΟΥΚΑΝ ΑΓΙΟΝ ΕΥΑΓΓΕΛΙΟΝ.‖

THE [4]ACCORDING [5]TO [6]LUKE [1]HOLY [2]GLAD [3]TIDINGS.

ἘΠΕΙΔΗΠΕΡ πολλοὶ ἐπεχείρησαν ἀνατάξασθαι διήγησιν
FORASMUCH AS many took in hand to draw up a narration
περὶ τῶν πεπληροφορημένων ἐν ἡμῖν πραγμά-
concerning the [2]which [3]have [4]been [5]fully [6]believed [7]among [8]us [1]mat-
των, 2 καθὼς παρέδοσαν ἡμῖν οἱ ἀπ' ἀρχῆς
ters, as they delivered [them] to us, they [3]from [4the] [5]beginning
αὐτόπται καὶ ὑπηρέται γενόμενοι τοῦ λόγου, 3 ἔδοξεν
[6]eye-witnesses [7]and [8]attendants [1]having [2]been of the Word, it seemed good
κἀμοί, παρηκολουθηκότι ἄνωθεν πᾶσιν ἀκριβῶς, κα-
also to me, having been acquainted from the first with all things accurately, with
θεξῆς σοι γράψαι, κράτιστε Θεόφιλε, 4 ἵνα ἐπιγνῷς
method to thee to write, most excellent Theophilus, that thou mightest know
περὶ ὧν κατηχήθης λόγων τὴν ἀσφάλειαν.
[6]concerning [7]which [8]thou [9]wast [10]instructed [3]of [4the] [5]things [1]the [2]certainty.
5 Ἐγένετο ἐν ταῖς ἡμέραις Ἡρώδου [b]τοῦ‖ βασιλέως τῆς
There was in the days of Herod the king
Ἰουδαίας ἱερεύς τις ὀνόματι Ζαχαρίας, ἐξ ἐφημερίας
of Judæa a [2]priest [1]certain, by name Zacharias, of [the] course
Ἀβιά· καὶ [c]ἡ.γυνὴ.αὐτοῦ‖ ἐκ τῶν θυγατέρων Ἀαρών, καὶ τὸ
of Abia, and his wife of the daughters of Aaron, and

FORASMUCH as many have taken in hand to set forth in order a declaration of those things which are most surely believed among us, 2 even as they delivered them unto us, which from the beginning were eyewitnesses, and ministers of the word; 3 it seemed good to me also, having had perfect understanding of all things from the very first, to write unto thee in order, most excellent Theophilus, 4 that thou mightest know the certainty of those things, wherein thou hast been instructed.

5 THERE was in the days of Herod, the king of Judæa, a certain priest named

---

[e] παρακολουθήσει ταῦτα L; ἀκολουθήσει ταῦτα Tr. [f] — καιναῖς Tr. [g] + καὶ ἐν ταῖς χερσὶν and in the hands Tr. [h] βλάψῃ should it injure GLTrAW. [i] + Ἰησοῦς Jesus LTr. [k] ἀνελήμφθη LTrA. [l] — Ἀμήν EGLTrAW. [m] — Τὸ κατὰ Μάρκον εὐαγγέλιον EGLTW; Κατὰ Μᾶρκον Tr; Εὐαγγέλιον κατὰ Μάρκον [A].

[a] Εὐαγγέλιον ([Εὐαγ.] A) κατὰ Λουκᾶν GLTrAW; κατὰ Λουκᾶν T. [b] — τοῦ TTr[A]. [c] γυνὴ αὐτῷ LTTrA.

Zacharias, of the course
of Abia: and his wife
was of the daughters
of Aaron, and her
name *was* Elisabeth.
6 And they were both
righteous before God,
walking in all the
commandments and
ordinances of the Lord
blameless. 7 And they
had no child, because
that Elisabeth was
barren, and they both
were *now* well stricken
in years. 8 And it
came to pass, that
while he executed the
priest's office before
God in the order of his
course, 9 according to
the custom of the
priest's office, his lot
was to burn incense
when he went into the
temple of the Lord.
10 And the whole mul-
titude of the people
were praying without
at the time of incense.
11 And there appeared
unto him an angel of
the Lord standing on
the right side of the
altar of incense. 12 And
when Zacharias saw
him, he was troubled,
and fear fell upon him.
13 But the angel said
unto him, Fear not,
Zacharias: for thy
prayer is heard; and
thy wife Elisabeth
shall bear thee a son,
and thou shalt call his
name John. 14 And
thou shalt have joy
and gladness; and
many shall rejoice at
his birth. 15 For he
shall be great in the
sight of the Lord, and
shall drink neither
wine nor strong drink;
and he shall be filled
with the Holy Ghost,
even from his mother's
womb. 16 And many
of the children of Is-
rael shall he turn to
the Lord their God.
17 And he shall go be-
fore him in the spirit
and power of Elias, to
turn the hearts of the
fathers to the children,
and the disobedient to
the wisdom of the just;
to make ready a people
prepared for the Lord.
18 And Zacharias said
unto the angel, Where-
by shall I know this?
for I am an old man,
and my wife well
stricken in years.
19 And the angel an-
swering said unto him,

ὄνομα.αὐτῆς Ἐλισάβετ. 6 ἦσαν.δὲ δίκαιοι ἀμφότεροι [d]ἐνώ-
her name Elizabeth. And they were [2]just [1]both be-
πιον‖ τοῦ θεοῦ. πορευόμενοι ἐν πάσαις ταῖς ἐντολαῖς καὶ
fore God, walking in all the commandments and
δικαιώμασιν τοῦ κυρίου ἄμεμπτοι. 7 καὶ οὐκ.ἦν αὐτοῖς
ordinances of the Lord blameless. And there was not to them
τέκνον, καθότι [e]ἡ Ἐλισάβετ ἦν‖ στεῖρα, καὶ ἀμφότεροι προ-
a child, inasmuch as Elizabeth was barren, and both ad-
βεβηκότες ἐν ταῖς.ἡμέραις.αὐτῶν ἦσαν. 8 Ἐγένετο.δὲ ἐν
vanced in their days were. And it came to pass in
τῷ.ἱερατεύειν.αὐτὸν ἐν τῇ τάξει τῆς.ἐφημερίας.αὐτοῦ ἔναντι
fulfilling his priestly service in the order of his course before
τοῦ θεοῦ, 9 κατὰ τὸ ἔθος τῆς ἱερατείας, ἔλαχεν
God, according to the custom of the priestly service, it fell to him by lot
τοῦ θυμιᾶσαι εἰσελθὼν εἰς τὸν ναὸν τοῦ κυρίου· 10 καὶ
to burn incense, having entered into the temple of the Lord. And
πᾶν τὸ πλῆθος [f]τοῦ λαοῦ ἦν‖ προσευχόμενον ἔξω τῇ ὥρᾳ
all the multitude of the people were praying without at the hour
τοῦ θυμιάματος. 11 ὤφθη.δὲ αὐτῷ ἄγγελος κυρίου, ἑ-
of incense. And [6]appeared [7]to [8]him [1]an [2]angel [3]of [[4]the] [5]Lord, stand-
στὼς ἐκ δεξιῶν τοῦ θυσιαστηρίου τοῦ θυμιάματος· 12 καὶ
ing at [the] right of the altar of incense. and
ἐταράχθη Ζαχαρίας ἰδών, καὶ φόβος ἐπέπεσεν ἐπ' αὐτόν.
[4]was [3]troubled [1]Zacharias [2]seeing [[3]him], and fear fell upon him.
13 Εἶπεν.δὲ πρὸς αὐτὸν ὁ ἄγγελος, Μὴ.φοβοῦ, Ζαχαρία·
But [3]said [4]to [5]him [1]the [2]angel, Fear not, Zacharias,
διότι εἰσηκούσθη ἡ.δέησίς.σου, καὶ ἡ.γυνή.σου Ἐλισάβετ γεν-
because has been heard thy supplication, and thy wife Elizabeth shall
νήσει υἱόν σοι, καὶ καλέσεις τὸ.ὄνομα.αὐτοῦ [g]Ἰωάννην.‖
bear a son to thee, and thou shalt call his name John.
14 καὶ ἔσται χαρά σοι καὶ ἀγαλλίασις, καὶ πολλοὶ ἐπὶ τῇ
And he shall be joy to thee and exultation, and many at
[h]γεννήσει‖.αὐτοῦ χαρήσονται. 15 ἔσται.γὰρ μέγας ἐνώπιον
his birth shall rejoice. For he shall be great before
[i]τοῦ‖ κυρίου· καὶ οἶνον καὶ σίκερα οὐ.μὴ πίῃ, καὶ
the Lord; and wine and strong drink in no wise shall he drink, and
πνεύματος ἁγίου πλησθήσεται ἔτι ἐκ κοιλίας μητρὸς
with [the] [2]Spirit [1]Holy he shall be filled even from [the] womb [3]mother
αὐτοῦ. 16 καὶ πολλοὺς τῶν υἱῶν Ἰσραὴλ ἐπιστρέψει ἐπὶ
[1]of [2]his. And many of the sons of Israel shall he turn to [the]
κύριον τὸν.θεὸν.αὐτῶν. 17 καὶ αὐτὸς προελεύσεται ἐνώπιον
Lord their God. And he shall go forth before
αὐτοῦ ἐν πνεύματι καὶ δυνάμει [k]Ἡλίου,‖ ἐπιστρέψαι καρδίας
him in [the] spirit and power of Elias, to turn hearts
πατέρων ἐπὶ τέκνα, καὶ ἀπειθεῖς ἐν φρονήσει δι-
of fathers to children, and [the] disobedient to [the] wisdom of [the]
καίων, ἑτοιμάσαι κυρίῳ λαὸν κατεσκευασμένον. 18 Καὶ
righteous, to make ready for [the] Lord a people prepared. And
εἶπεν Ζαχαρίας πρὸς τὸν ἄγγελον, Κατὰ τί γνώσομαι τοῦτο;
[2]said [1]Zacharias to the angel, By what shall I know this?
ἐγὼ.γάρ εἰμι πρεσβύτης, καὶ ἡ.γυνή.μου προβεβηκυῖα ἐν ταῖς
for I am an old man, and my wife advanced in
ἡμέραις.αὐτῆς. 19 Καὶ ἀποκριθεὶς ὁ ἄγγελος εἶπεν αὐτῷ,
her days. And [3]answering [1]the [2]angel said to him,

---

[d] ἐναντίον TTrA. [e] ἦν ἡ (— ἡ L[Tr]) Ἐλισάβετ LTTrA. [f] ἦν τοῦ λαοῦ GLTTrAW.
[g] Ἰωάνην Tr. [h] γενέσει GLTTrAW. [i] — τοῦ (read [the]) GT[Tr]W. [k] Ἠλείᾳ T.

Ἐγώ εἰμι Γαβριὴλ ὁ παρεστηκὼς ἐνώπιον τοῦ θεοῦ· καὶ
I am Gabriel, who stand before God, and
ἀπεστάλην λαλῆσαι πρός σε, καὶ εὐαγγελίσασθαί σοι
I was sent to speak to thee, and to announce [2]glad [3]tidings [4]to [5]thee
ταῦτα. 20 καὶ ἰδού, ἔσῃ σιωπῶν καὶ μὴ δυνάμενος λαλῆσαι
[1]these; and lo, thou shalt be silent and not able to speak
ἄχρι ἧς.ἡμέρας γένηται ταῦτα· ἀνθ'.ὧν οὐκ.ἐπίστευσας
till the day in which shall take place these things, because thou didst not believe
τοῖς.λόγοις.μου, οἵτινες πληρωθήσονται εἰς τὸν.καιρὸν.αὐτῶν.
my words, which shall be fulfilled in their season.
21 Καὶ ἦν ὁ λαὸς προσδοκῶν τὸν Ζαχαρίαν· καὶ ἐθαύμαζον ἐν
And [3]were [1]the [2]people expecting Zacharias, and they wondered at
τῷ.χρονίζειν.αὐτὸν ἐν τῷ ναῷ. 22 ἐξελθὼν.δὲ οὐκ.[l]ἠδύνατο‖
his delaying in the temple. But having come out he was not able
λαλῆσαι αὐτοῖς· καὶ ἐπέγνωσαν ὅτι ὀπτασίαν ἑώρακεν ἐν
to speak to them, and they recognized that a vision he has seen in
τῷ ναῷ· καὶ αὐτὸς ἦν διανεύων αὐτοῖς, καὶ διέμενεν κωφός.
the temple. And he was making signs to them, and continued dumb.
23 καὶ ἐγένετο ὡς ἐπλήσθησαν αἱ ἡμέραι τῆς λειτουργίας
And it came to pass, when were fulfilled the days [3]service
αὐτοῦ ἀπῆλθεν εἰς τὸν.οἶκον.αὐτοῦ.
[1]of [2]his he departed to his house.

24 Μετὰ.δὲ ταύτας τὰς ἡμέρας συνέλαβεν Ἐλισάβετ ἡ
Now after these days [4]conceived [1]Elizabeth
γυνὴ.αὐτοῦ, καὶ περιέκρυβεν ἑαυτὴν μῆνας πέντε, λέγουσα,
[2]his [3]wife, and hid herself [2]months [1]five, saying,
25 "Ὅτι.οὕτως μοι πεποίηκεν [m]ὁ‖ κύριος ἐν ἡμέραις αἷς
Thus to me has done the Lord in [the] days in which
ἐπεῖδεν ἀφελεῖν [n]τὸ‖.ὄνειδός.μου ἐν ἀνθρώποις.
he looked upon [me] to take away my reproach among men.

26 Ἐν.δὲ τῷ μηνὶ τῷ ἕκτῳ ἀπεστάλη ὁ ἄγγελος Γαβριὴλ
And in the month the sixth was sent the angel Gabriel
[o]ὑπὸ‖ τοῦ θεοῦ εἰς πόλιν τῆς Γαλιλαίας, ᾗ ὄνομα [p]Να-
by God to a city of Galilee, whose name [was] Na-
ζαρέτ,‖ 27 πρὸς παρθένον [q]μεμνηστευμένην‖ ἀνδρὶ ᾧ ὄνομα
zareth, to a virgin betrothed to a man whose name
Ἰωσήφ, ἐξ οἴκου [r]Δαβίδ·‖ καὶ τὸ ὄνομα τῆς παρθένου
[was] Joseph, of [the] house of David, and the name of the virgin
Μαριάμ. 28 καὶ εἰσελθὼν [s]ὁ ἄγγελος‖ πρὸς αὐτὴν [t] εἶπεν,
[was] Mary. And [3]coming [1]the [2]angel to her said,
Χαῖρε, κεχαριτωμένη· ὁ κύριος μετὰ σοῦ, [v]εὐλογημένη
Hail, [thou] favoured one! the Lord [is] with thee, blessed [art]
σὺ ἐν γυναιξίν.‖ 29 Ἡ.δὲ [w]ἰδοῦσα‖ [x]διεταράχθη ἐπὶ
thou amongst women. But she seeing [him] was troubled at
τῷ.λόγῳ.αὐτοῦ,‖ καὶ διελογίζετο ποταπὸς εἴη ὁ ἀσπασμὸς
his word, and was reasoning of what kind might be [2]salutation
οὗτος. 30 Καὶ εἶπεν ὁ ἄγγελος αὐτῇ, Μὴ.φοβοῦ, Μαριάμ·
[1]this. And [3]said [1]the [2]angel to her, Fear not, Mary,
εὗρες.γὰρ χάριν παρὰ τῷ θεῷ· 31 καὶ ἰδού, [y]συλλήψῃ‖
for thou hast found favour with God; and lo, thou shalt conceive
ἐν γαστρὶ καὶ τέξῃ υἱόν, καὶ καλέσεις τὸ.ὄνομα.αὐτοῦ
in [thy] womb and bring forth a son, and thou shalt call his name

I am Gabriel, that stand in the presence of God; and am sent to speak unto thee, and to shew thee these glad tidings. 20 And, behold, thou shalt be dumb, and not able to speak, until the day that these things shall be performed, because thou believest not my words, which shall be fulfilled in their season. 21 And the people waited for Zacharias, and marvelled that he tarried so long in the temple. 22 And when he came out, he could not speak unto them: and they perceived that he had seen a vision in the temple: for he beckoned unto them, and remained speechless. 23 And it came to pass, that, as soon as the days of his ministration were accomplished, he departed to his own house.

24 And after those days his wife Elisabeth conceived, and hid herself five months, saying, 25 Thus hath the Lord dealt with me in the days wherein he looked on *me*, to take away my reproach among men.

26 And in the sixth month the angel Gabriel was sent from God unto a city of Galilee, named Nazareth, 27 to a virgin espoused to a man whose name was Joseph, of the house of David; and the virgin's name *was* Mary. 28 And the angel came in unto her, and said, Hail, *thou that art* highly favoured, the Lord *is* with thee: blessed *art* thou among women. 29 And when she saw *him*, she was troubled at his saying, and cast in her mind what manner of salutation this should be. 30 And the angel said unto her, Fear not, Mary: for thou hast found favour with God. 31 And, behold, thou shalt conceive in thy womb, and bring forth a son, and shalt call his name

---

[l] ἐδύνατο LTTrA. [m] — ὁ (*read* [the]) LTTr[A]. [n] — τὸ TTr[A]. [o] ἀπὸ from TTrA. [p] Ναζαρέθ LTW. [q] ἐμνηστευμένην LTTr. [r] Δαυείδ LTTrA; Δαυΐδ GW. [s] — ὁ ἄγγελος T[Tr]A. [t] + ὁ ἄγγελος the angel T. [v] — εὐλογημένη σὺ ἐν γυναιξίν T[Tr]A. [w] — ἰδοῦσα GTTrA [x] ἐπὶ.τῷ.λόγῳ διεταράχθη GTTrA. [y] συλλήμψῃ LTTrA.

JESUS. 32 He shall
be great, and shall be
called the Son of the
Highest: and the Lord
God shall give unto
him the throne of his
father David: 33 and
he shall reign over the
house of Jacob for
ever; and of his king-
dom there shall be no
end. 34 Then said
Mary unto the angel,
How shall this be, see-
ing I know not a man?
35 And the angel an-
swered and said unto
her, The Holy Ghost
shall come upon thee,
and the power of the
Highest shall over-
shadow thee: therefore
also that holy thing
which shall be born of
thee shall be called the
Son of God. 36 And,
behold, thy cousin
Elisabeth, she hath
also conceived a son
in her old age: and
this is the sixth month
with her, who was
called barren. 37 For
with God nothing shall
be impossible. 38 And
Mary said, Behold the
handmaid of the Lord;
be it unto me accord-
ing to thy word. And
the angel departed
from her.

39 And Mary arose
in those days, and went
into the hill country
with haste, into a city
of Juda; 40 and enter-
ed into the house of
Zacharias, and saluted
Elisabeth. 41 And it
came to pass, that,
when Elisabeth heard
the salutation of Mary,
the babe leaped in her
womb; and Elisabeth
was filled with the
Holy Ghost: 42 and
she spake out with a
loud voice, and said,
Blessed *art* thou a-
mong women, and
blessed *is* the fruit of
thy womb. 43 And
whence *is* this to me,
that the mother of my
Lord should come to
me? 44 For, lo, as soon
as the voice of thy
salutation sounded in
mine ears, the babe
leaped in my womb for
joy. 45 And blessed *is*
she that believed: for
there shall be a perfor-
mance of those things
which were told her
from the Lord.

Ἰησοῦν. 32 οὗτος ἔσται μέγας, καὶ υἱὸς ὑψίστου κληθήσε-
Jesus. He shall be great, and Son of [the] Highest shall be

ται· καὶ δώσει αὐτῷ κύριος ὁ θεὸς τὸν θρόνον [z]Δαβὶδ‖
called; and [4]shall [5]give [6]him [[1]the] [2]Lord [3]God the throne of David

τοῦ.πατρὸς.αὐτοῦ, 33 καὶ βασιλεύσει ἐπὶ τὸν οἶκον Ἰακὼβ εἰς
his father; and he shall reign over the house of Jacob to

τοὺς αἰῶνας, καὶ τῆς.βασιλείας.αὐτοῦ οὐκ.ἔσται τέλος.
the ages, and of his kingdom there shall not be an end.

34 Εἶπεν.δὲ Μαριὰμ πρὸς τὸν ἄγγελον, Πῶς ἔσται τοῦτο ἐπεὶ
But [2]said [1]Mary to the angel, How shall [2]be [1]this since

ἄνδρα οὐ.γινώσκω; 35 Καὶ ἀποκριθεὶς ὁ ἄγγελος εἶπεν αὐτῇ,
a man I know not? And answering the angel said to her,

Πνεῦμα ἅγιον ἐπελεύσεται ἐπὶ σέ, καὶ δύναμις ὑψίστου
[The] [2]Spirit [1]Holy shall come upon thee, and power of [the] Highest

ἐπισκιάσει σοι· διὸ καὶ τὸ γεννώμενον[a] ἅγιον κληθή-
shall overshadow thee; wherefore also the [3]born [1]holy [2]thing shall be

σεται υἱὸς θεοῦ. 36 καὶ ἰδού, Ἐλισάβετ ἡ.[b]συγγενής‖.σου καὶ
called Son of God. And lo, Elizabeth thy kinswoman [2]also

αὐτὴ [c]συνειληφυῖα‖ υἱὸν ἐν [d]γήρᾳ‖.αὐτῆς· καὶ οὗτος μὴν
[1]she has conceived a son in her old age, and this [the] [2]month

ἕκτος ἐστὶν αὐτῇ τῇ καλουμένῃ στείρᾳ· 37 ὅτι οὐκ ἀδυνα-
[1]sixth is to her who [was] called barren; for not [3]shall [4]be

τήσει παρὰ [e]τῷ θεῷ‖ πᾶν ῥῆμα. 38 Εἶπεν.δὲ Μαριάμ,
[5]impossible [6]with [7]God [1]any [2]thing. And [2]said [1]Mary,
(*lit.* every)

Ἰδού, ἡ δούλη κυρίου· γένοιτό μοι κατὰ τὸ.ῥῆμά.σου.
Behold, the bondmaid of [the] Lord; be it to me according to thy word.

Καὶ ἀπῆλθεν ἀπ' αὐτῆς ὁ ἄγγελος.
And departed from her the angel.

39 Ἀναστᾶσα.δὲ Μαριὰμ ἐν ταῖς.ἡμέραις.ταύταις ἐπορεύθη
And [2]rising [3]up [1]Mary in those days went

εἰς τὴν ὀρεινὴν μετὰ σπουδῆς, εἰς πόλιν Ἰούδα, 40 καὶ
into the hill-country with haste, to a city of Judah, and

εἰσῆλθεν εἰς τὸν οἶκον Ζαχαρίου καὶ ἠσπάσατο τὴν Ἐλισάβετ.
entered into the house of Zacharias and saluted Elizabeth.

41 καὶ ἐγένετο ὡς ἤκουσεν [f]ἡ Ἐλισάβετ τὸν ἀσπασμὸν τῆς
And it came to pass as [2]heard [1]Elizabeth the salutation

Μαρίας,‖ ἐσκίρτησεν τὸ βρέφος ἐν τῇ.κοιλίᾳ.αὐτῆς· καὶ ἐπλήσθη
of Mary, [3]leaped [1]the [2]babe in her womb; and [2]was [3]filled

πνεύματος ἁγίου ἡ Ἐλισάβετ, 42 καὶ ἀνεφώνησεν [g]φωνῇ‖
[4]with [[5]the] [7]Spirit [6]Holy [1]Elizabeth, and cried out with a [2]voice

μεγάλῃ καὶ εἶπεν, Εὐλογημένη σὺ ἐν γυναιξίν, καὶ εὐλο-
[1]loud and said, Blessed [art] thou among women, and bless-

γημένος ὁ καρπὸς τῆς.κοιλίας.σου. 43 καὶ πόθεν μοι τοῦτο,
ed the fruit of thy womb. And whence to me this,

ἵνα ἔλθῃ ἡ μήτηρ τοῦ.κυρίου.μου πρός [h]με‖; 44 ἰδοὺ.γάρ,
that should come the mother of my Lord to me? For lo,

ὡς ἐγένετο ἡ φωνὴ τοῦ.ἀσπασμοῦ.σου εἰς τὰ.ὦτά.μου ἐσκίρ-
as came the voice of thy salutation into mine ears, leap-

τησεν [i]ἐν ἀγαλλιάσει τὸ βρέφος‖ ἐν τῇ.κοιλίᾳ.μου. 45 καὶ
ed in exultation the babe in my womb; and

μακαρία ἡ πιστεύσασα, ὅτι ἔσται τελείωσις τοῖς
blessed [is] she who believed, for there shall be a fulfilment to the things

λελαλημένοις αὐτῇ παρὰ κυρίου
spoken to her from [the] Lord.

---

[z] Δαυείδ LTTrA; Δαυΐδ GW. [a] + [ἐκ σοῦ] of thee L. [b] συγγενίς LTW. [c] συνειληφεν Tr. [d] γήρει GLTTrAW. [e] τοῦ θεοῦ TTrA. [f] τὸν ἀσπασμὸν τῆς Μαρίας ἡ Ἐλισάβετ LTTrA. [g] κραυγῇ with a [2]cry TTrA. [h] ἐμέ T. [i] τὸ βρέφος ἐν ἀγαλλιάσει GW.

46 Καὶ εἶπεν Μαριάμ, Μεγαλύνει ἡ.ψυχή.μου τὸν κύριον,
And said Mary, [3]Magnifies [1]my [2]soul the Lord,
47 καὶ ἠγαλλίασεν τὸ.πνεῦμά.μου ἐπὶ τῷ θεῷ τῷ.σωτῆρί.μου·
and [3]exulted [1]my [2]spirit in God my Saviour.
48 ὅτι ἐπέβλεψεν ἐπὶ τὴν ταπείνωσιν τῆς.δούλης.αὐτοῦ· ἰδοὺ
For he looked upon the humiliation of his bondmaid; [2]lo
γάρ, ἀπὸ τοῦ.νῦν μακαριοῦσίν.με πᾶσαι αἱ γενεαί. 49 ὅτι
[1]for, from henceforth [3]will [4]count [5]me [6]blessed [1]all [2]generations. For
ἐποίησέν μοι [k]μεγαλεῖα‖ ὁ δυνατός, καὶ ἅγιον τὸ ὄνομα
[4]has [5]done [6]to [7]me [8]great [9]things [1]the [2]mighty [3]one, and holy [is] [2]name
αὐτοῦ· 50 καὶ τὸ.ἔλεος.αὐτοῦ εἰς γενεὰς [l]γενεῶν‖ τοῖς
[1]his; and his mercy [is] to generations of generations to those
φοβουμένοις αὐτόν. 51 ἐποίησεν κράτος ἐν βραχίονι.αὐτοῦ·
fearing him. He wrought strength with his arm,
διεσκόρπισεν ὑπερηφάνους διανοίᾳ καρδίας.αὐτῶν.
he scattered [the] haughty in [the] thought of their heart.
52 καθεῖλεν δυνάστας ἀπὸ θρόνων, καὶ ὕψωσεν ταπεινούς.
He put down rulers from thrones, and exalted [the] lowly:
53 πεινῶντας ἐνέπλησεν ἀγαθῶν, καὶ πλουτοῦντας
[the] hungry he filled with good things, and [the] rich
ἐξαπέστειλεν κενούς. 54 ἀντελάβετο Ἰσραὴλ παιδὸς αὐτοῦ,
he sent away empty. He helped Israel [2]servant [1]his,
μνησθῆναι ἐλέους, 55 καθὼς ἐλάλησεν πρὸς τοὺς
[in order] to remember mercy, according as he spoke to
πατέρας.ἡμῶν, τῷ Ἀβραὰμ καὶ τῷ.σπέρματι.αὐτοῦ [m]εἰς τὸν
our fathers, to Abraham and to his seed for
αἰῶνα.‖ 56 Ἔμεινεν.δὲ Μαριὰμ σὺν αὐτῇ [n]ὡσεὶ‖ μῆνας τρεῖς,
ever. And [2]abode [1]Mary with her about [2]months [1]three,
καὶ ὑπέστρεψεν εἰς τὸν.οἶκον.αὐτῆς.
and returned to her house.

57 Τῇ.δὲ.Ἐλισάβετ ἐπλήσθη ὁ χρόνος τοῦ.τεκεῖν.αὐτήν,
Now to Elizabeth was fulfilled the time that she should bring forth,
καὶ ἐγέννησεν υἱόν· 58 καὶ ἤκουσαν οἱ περίοικοι καὶ οἱ συγ-
and she bore a son. And [3]heard [1]the [2]neighbours and [2]kins-
γενεῖς αὐτῆς ὅτι ἐμεγάλυνεν κύριος τὸ.ἔλεος.αὐτοῦ μετ'
folk [1]her that [3]was [4]magnifying [[1]the] [2]Lord his mercy with
αὐτῆς, καὶ συνέχαιρον αὐτῇ. 59 Καὶ ἐγένετο ἐν τῇ [o]ὀγδόῃ
her, and they rejoiced with her. And it came to pass on the eighth
ἡμέρᾳ‖ ἦλθον περιτεμεῖν τὸ παιδίον· καὶ ἐκάλουν αὐτὸ
day they came to circumcise the little child, and were calling it
ἐπὶ τῷ ὀνόματι τοῦ.πατρὸς.αὐτοῦ Ζαχαρίαν. 60 καὶ ἀπο-
after the name of his father Zacharias. And [3]an-
κριθεῖσα ἡ.μήτηρ.αὐτοῦ εἶπεν, Οὐχί, ἀλλὰ κληθήσεται [p]Ἰωάν-
swering [1]his [2]mother said, No; but he shall be called John.
νης.‖ 61 Καὶ [q]εἶπον‖ πρὸς αὐτήν, Ὅτι οὐδείς ἐστιν [r]ἐν τῇ
And they said to her, No one is among the
συγγενείᾳ‖ σου ὃς καλεῖται τῷ.ὀνόματι.τούτῳ. 62 Ἐνένευον
kinsfolk of thee who is called by this name. [2]They [3]made [4]signs
δὲ τῷ.πατρὶ.αὐτοῦ τὸ.τί ἂν.θέλοι καλεῖσθαι [s]αὐτόν.‖
[1]and to his father [as to] what he might wish [2]to [3]be [4]called [1]him.
63 καὶ αἰτήσας πινακίδιον ἔγραψεν, λέγων, [p]Ἰωάννης‖
And having asked for a writing tablet he wrote, saying, John
ἐστὶν [t]τὸ‖.ὄνομα.αὐτοῦ· καὶ ἐθαύμασαν πάντες. 64 Ἀνεῴχθη.δὲ
is his name. And they [2]wondered [1]all. And was opened

46 And Mary said,
My soul doth magnify
the Lord, 47 and my
spirit hath rejoiced in
God my Saviour. 48 For
he hath regarded the
low estate of his hand-
maiden: for, behold,
from henceforth all
generations shall call
me blessed. 49 For he
that is mighty hath
done to me great
things; and holy *is* his
name. 50 And his
mercy *is* on them that
fear him from genera-
tion to generation.
51 He hath shewed
strength with his arm;
he hath scattered the
proud in the imagina-
tion of their hearts.
52 He hath put down
the mighty from *their*
seats, and exalted them
of low degree. 53 He
hath filled the hungry
with good things; and
the rich he hath sent
empty away. 54 He
hath holpen his ser-
vant Israel, in remem-
brance of *his* mercy;
55 as he spake to our
fathers, to Abraham,
and to his seed for
ever. 56 And Mary a-
bode with her about
three months, and re-
turned to her own
house.

57 Now Elisabeth's
full time came that she
should be delivered;
and she brought forth
a son. 58 And her
neighbours and her
cousins heard how the
Lord had shewed great
mercy upon her; and
they rejoiced with her.
59 And it came to pass,
that on the eighth day
they came to circum-
cise the child; and they
called him Zacharias,
after the name of his
father. 60 And his
mother answered and
said, Not *so*; but he
shall be called John.
61 And they said unto
her, There is none of
thy kindred that is
called by this name.
62 And they made signs
to his father, how he
would have him called.
63 And he asked for a
writing table, and
wrote, saying, His
name is John. And
they marvelled all.
64 And his mouth was
opened immediately,

---

[k] μεγάλα LTTr. [l] καὶ γενεὰς and generations TTrA. [m] ἕως αἰῶνος G. [n] ὡς LTTr. [o] ἡμέρᾳ τῇ ὀγδόῃ LTTrA. [p] Ἰωάνης Tr. [q] εἶπαν TTr. [r] ἐκ τῆς συγγενείας from among the kinsfolk LTTrA. [s] αὐτό it LTTrA. [t] — τὸ Tr[A].

and his tongue *loosed*, and he spake, and praised God. 65 And fear came on all that dwelt round about them: and all these sayings were noised abroad throughout all the hill country of Judæa. 66 And all they that heard *them* laid *them* up in their hearts, saying, What manner of child shall this be! And the hand of the Lord was with him.

67 And his father Zacharias was filled with the Holy Ghost, and prophesied, saying, 68 Blessed *be* the Lord God of Israel; for he hath visited and redeemed his people, 69 and hath raised up an horn of salvation for us in the house of his servant David; 70 as he spake by the mouth of his holy prophets, which have been since the world began: 71 that we should be saved from our enemies, and from the hand of all that hate us; 72 to perform the mercy *promised* to our fathers, and to remember his holy covenant; 73 the oath which he sware to our father Abraham, 74 that he would grant unto us, that we being delivered out of the hand of our enemies might serve him without fear, 75 in holiness and righteousness before him, all the days of our life. 76 And thou, child, shalt be called the prophet of the Highest: for thou shalt go before the face of the Lord to prepare his ways; 77 to give knowledge of salvation unto his people by the remission of their sins, 78 through the tender mercy of our God; whereby the dayspring from on high hath visited us, 79 to give light to them that sit in darkness and *in* the shadow of death, to guide our feet

τὸ.στόμα.αὐτοῦ παραχρῆμα καὶ ἡ.γλῶσσα.αὐτοῦ, καὶ
his mouth immediately and his tongue [loosed], and

ἐλάλει εὐλογῶν τὸν θεόν. 65 Καὶ ἐγένετο ἐπὶ πάντας φόβος
he spoke, blessing God. And [2]came [3]upon [4]all [1]fear

τοὺς περιοικοῦντας αὐτούς· καὶ ἐν ὅλῃ τῇ ὀρεινῇ τῆς
those who dwelt around them; and in [2]whole [1]the hill-country

Ἰουδαίας διελαλεῖτο πάντα τὰ.ῥήματα.ταῦτα· 66 καὶ
of Judæa [4]were [5]being [6]talked [7]of [1]all [2]these [3]things. And

ἔθεντο πάντες οἱ ἀκούσαντες ἐν τῇ.καρδίᾳ.αὐτῶν, λέ-
[4]laid [[5]them] [6]up [1]all [2]who [3]heard in their heart, say-

γοντες, Τί ἄρα τὸ.παιδίον.τοῦτο ἔσται; Καὶ [w] χεὶρ
ing, What then [3]this [4]little [5]child [1]will [2]be? And [the] hand

κυρίου ἦν μετ' αὐτοῦ.
of [the] Lord was with him.

67 Καὶ Ζαχαρίας ὁ.πατὴρ.αὐτοῦ ἐπλήσθη πνεύματος
And Zacharias his father was filled with [the] [2]Spirit

ἁγίου, καὶ [x]προεφήτευσεν,‖ λέγων, 68 Εὐλογητὸς κύριος ὁ
[1]Holy, and prophesied, saying, Blessed be [the] Lord the

θεὸς τοῦ Ἰσραήλ, ὅτι ἐπεσκέψατο καὶ ἐποίησεν λύτρωσιν
God of Israel, because he looked upon and wrought redemption

τῷ.λαῷ.αὐτοῦ· 69 καὶ ἤγειρεν κέρας σωτηρίας ἡμῖν ἐν [y]τῷ‖
for his people, and raised up a horn of salvation for us in the

οἴκῳ [z]Δαβὶδ‖ [a]τοῦ‖.παιδὸς.αὐτοῦ· 70 καθὼς ἐλάλησεν διὰ
house of David his servant; according as he spoke by [the]

στόματος τῶν ἁγίων [b]τῶν‖.ἀπ'.αἰῶνος προφητῶν αὐτοῦ·
mouth [3]holy [5]since [6]time [7]began [4]prophets [1]of [2]his;

71 σωτηρίαν ἐξ ἐχθρῶν.ἡμῶν καὶ ἐκ χειρὸς πάντων
salvation from our enemies and from [the] hand of all

τῶν μισούντων ἡμᾶς· 72 ποιῆσαι ἔλεος μετὰ τῶν πατέρων
those who hate us; to fulfil mercy with [2]fathers

ἡμῶν, καὶ μνησθῆναι διαθήκης ἁγίας αὐτοῦ, 73 ὅρκον ὃν
[1]our, and to remember [3]covenant [2]holy [1]his, [the] oath which

ὤμοσεν πρὸς Ἀβραὰμ τὸν.πατέρα.ἡμῶν, τοῦ δοῦναι ἡμῖν
he swore to Abraham our father, to give us [that]

74 ἀφόβως ἐκ χειρὸς [c]τῶν‖.ἐχθρῶν.[d]ἡμῶν‖ ῥυσθέντας,
without fear out of [the] hand of our enemies being saved,

λατρεύειν αὐτῷ 75 ἐν ὁσιότητι καὶ δικαιοσύνῃ ἐνώπιον αὐτοῦ
we should serve him in holiness and righteousness before him,

πάσας τὰς ἡμέρας [e]τῆς.ζωῆς‖.ἡμῶν. 76 Καὶ σύ[f], παιδίον,
all the days of our life. And thou, little child,

προφήτης ὑψίστου κληθήσῃ· προπορεύσῃ.γὰρ πρὸ
prophet of [the] Highest shalt be called; for thou shalt go before [the]

προσώπου κυρίου ἑτοιμάσαι ὁδοὺς.αὐτοῦ· 77 τοῦ δοῦναι
face of [the] Lord to prepare his ways; to give

γνῶσιν σωτηρίας τῷ.λαῷ.αὐτοῦ ἐν ἀφέσει ἁμαρτιῶν.αὐτῶν,
knowledge of salvation to his people in remission of their sins,

78 διὰ σπλάγχνα ἐλέους θεοῦ.ἡμῶν, ἐν οἷς ἐπεσκέψατο
through [the] bowels of compassion of our God, in which has visited

ἡμᾶς ἀνατολὴ ἐξ ὕψους, 79 ἐπιφᾶναι τοῖς ἐν σκότει
us [the] day-spring from on high, to shine upon those [2]in [3]darkness

καὶ σκιᾷ θανάτου καθημένοις· τοῦ κατευθῦναι τοὺς
[4]and [5]in [[6]the] [7]shadow [8]of [9]death [1]sitting; to direct

---

[w] + γὰρ (*read* For also) LTTrA. [x] ἐπροφήτευσεν LTTrA. [y] — τῷ (*read* [the]) LTTrA.
[z] Δαυείδ LTTrA; Δαυΐδ GW. [a] — τοῦ LTTrA. [b] — τῶν TTrA. [c] — τῶν LTTrA.
[d] — ἡμῶν (*read* of [our] enemies) [L]TTrA. [e] — τῆς ζωῆς (*read* all our days) GLTTrAW.
[f] + δὲ also TTrA.

πόδας.ἡμῶν εἰς ὁδὸν εἰρήνης. 80 Τὸ.δὲ παιδίον ηὔξανεν
our feet into [the] way of peace. And the little child grew
καὶ ἐκραταιοῦτο πνεύματι· καὶ ἦν ἐν ταῖς ἐρήμοις ἕως
and was strengthened in spirit; and he was in the deserts until [the]
ἡμέρας ἀναδείξεως.αὐτοῦ πρὸς τὸν Ἰσραήλ.
day of his shewing to Israel.

2 Ἐγένετο.δὲ ἐν ταῖς.ἡμέραις.ἐκείναις ἐξῆλθεν δόγμα
And it came to pass in those days [3]went [4]out [1]a [2]decree
παρὰ Καίσαρος Αὐγούστου, ἀπογράφεσθαι πᾶσαν τὴν
from Cæsar Augustus, that should be registered all the
οἰκουμένην· 2 αὕτη.[g]ἡ.ἀπογραφὴ [h]πρώτη ἐγένετο[‖] ἡγε-
habitable world; this registration first took place when
μονεύοντος τῆς Συρίας [i]Κυρηνίου.[‖] 3 καὶ ἐπορεύοντο πάντες
[2]was [3]governor [4]of [5]Syria [1]Cyrenius. And [2]went [1]all
ἀπογράφεσθαι, ἕκαστος εἰς τὴν.[k]ἰδίαν[‖].πόλιν. 4 Ἀνέβη.δὲ καὶ
to be registered, each to his own city: and [3]went [4]up [2]also
Ἰωσὴφ ἀπὸ τῆς Γαλιλαίας ἐκ πόλεως [l]Ναζαρέτ[‖] εἰς τὴν
[1]Joseph from Galilee out of [the] city Nazareth to
Ἰουδαίαν, εἰς πόλιν [m]Δαβίδ[‖] ἥτις καλεῖται Βηθλεέμ, διὰ
Judæa, to a city of David which is called Bethlehem, because
τὸ.εἶναι.αὐτὸν ἐξ οἴκου καὶ πατριᾶς [m]Δαβίδ,[‖] 5 [n]ἀπο-
of his being of [the] house and family of David, to re-
γράψασθαι[‖] σὺν Μαριὰμ τῇ [o]μεμνηστευμένῃ[‖] αὐτῷ [p]γυναικί,[‖]
gister himself with Mary who was betrothed to him as wife,
οὔσῃ ἐγκύῳ. 6 Ἐγένετο.δὲ ἐν τῷ εἶναι.αὐτοὺς
she being great with child. And it came to pass in the [time] they were
ἐκεῖ ἐπλήσθησαν αἱ ἡμέραι τοῦ.τεκεῖν.αὐτήν· 7 καὶ ἔτε-
there [3]were [4]fulfilled [1]the [2]days for her bringing forth, and she brought
κεν τὸν.υἱὸν.αὐτῆς τὸν πρωτότοκον, καὶ ἐσπαργάνωσεν
forth her son the first-born, and wrapped [2]in [3]swaddling [4]clothes
αὐτόν, καὶ ἀνέκλινεν αὐτὸν ἐν [q]τῇ[‖] φάτνῃ, διότι οὐκ.ἦν
[1]him, and laid him in the manger, because there was not
αὐτοῖς τόπος ἐν τῷ καταλύματι.
for them a place in the inn.

8 Καὶ ποιμένες ἦσαν ἐν τῇ χώρᾳ τῇ αὐτῇ, ἀγραυλοῦντες
And shepherds were in the [2]country [1]same, lodging in the fields
καὶ φυλάσσοντες φυλακὰς τῆς νυκτὸς ἐπὶ τὴν.ποίμνην.αὐτῶν.
and keeping watch by night over their flock;
9 καὶ [r]ἰδού,[‖] ἄγγελος κυρίου ἐπέστη αὐτοῖς, καὶ δόξα
and behold, an angel of [the] Lord stood by them, and [the] glory
κυρίου περιέλαμψεν αὐτούς· καὶ ἐφοβήθησαν φόβον
of [the] Lord shone around them, and they feared [with] [2]fear
μέγαν. 10 καὶ εἶπεν αὐτοῖς ὁ ἄγγελος, Μὴ.φοβεῖσθε· ἰδοὺ
[1]great. And [3]said [4]to [5]them [1]the [2]angel, Fear not; [2]behold
γάρ, εὐαγγελίζομαι ὑμῖν χαρὰν μεγάλην, ἥτις ἔσται
[1]for, I announce glad tidings to you [of] [2]joy [1]great, which shall be
παντὶ τῷ λαῷ· 11 ὅτι ἐτέχθη ὑμῖν σήμερον σωτήρ, ὅς ἐστιν
to all the people; for was born to you to-day a Saviour, who is
χριστὸς κύριος, ἐν πόλει [s]Δαβίδ.[‖] 12 καὶ τοῦτο ὑμῖν
Christ [the] Lord, in [the] city of David. And this [is] to you
τὸ σημεῖον· εὑρήσετε βρέφος ἐσπαργανωμένον, [t] [v]κεί-
the sign: ye shall find a babe wrapped in swaddling clothes, ly-

into the way of peace. 80 And the child grew, and waxed strong in spirit, and was in the deserts till the day of his shewing unto Israel.

II. And it came to pass in those days, that there went out a decree from Cæsar Augustus, that all the world should be taxed. 2 (*And* this taxing was first made when Cyrenius was governor of Syria.) 3 And all went to be taxed, every one into his own city. 4 And Joseph also went up from Galilee, out of the city of Nazareth, into Judæa, unto the city of David, which is called Bethlehem; (because he was of the house and lineage of David:) 5 to be taxed with Mary his espoused wife, being great with child. 6 And so it was, that, while they were there, the days were accomplished that she should be delivered. 7 And she brought forth her firstborn son, and wrapped him in swaddling clothes, and laid him in a manger; because there was no room for them in the inn.

8 And there were in the same country shepherds abiding in the field, keeping watch over their flock by night. 9 And, lo, the angel of the Lord came upon them, and the glory of the Lord shone round about them: and they were sore afraid. 10 And the angel said unto them, Fear not: for, behold, I bring you good tidings of great joy, which shall be to all people. 11 For unto you is born this day in the city of David a Saviour, which is Christ the Lord. 12 And this *shall be* a sign unto you; Ye shall find the babe wrapped in swaddling clothes, lying in a manger.

---

[g] — ἡ LTTrA. [h] ἐγένετο πρώτη T. [i] Κυρίνου Cyrenus L. [k] ἑαυτοῦ (*read* his city) LTTr. [l] Ναζαρὰθ L; Ναζαρὲθ TW. [m] Δαυείδ LTTrA; Δαυΐδ GW. [n] ἀπογράφεσθαι L. [o] ἐμνηστευμένῃ LTTrA. [p] — γυναικί LTTrA. [q] — τῇ (*read* a manger) LTTrA. [r] — ἰδοὺ T[Tr]A. [s] Δαυείδ LTTrA; Δαυΐδ GW. [t] + καὶ and [L]TrA. [v] — κείμενον T.

13 And suddenly there was with the angel a multitude of the heavenly host praising God, and saying, 14 Glory to God in the highest, and on earth peace, good will toward men. 15 And it came to pass, as the angels were gone away from them into heaven, the shepherds said one to another, Let us now go even unto Bethlehem, and see this thing which is come to pass, which the Lord hath made known unto us. 16 And they came with haste, and found Mary, and Joseph, and the babe lying in a manger. 17 And when they had seen *it*, they made known abroad the saying which was told them concerning this child. 18 And all they that heard *it* wondered at those things which were told them by the shepherds. 19 But Mary kept all these things, and pondered *them* in her heart. 20 And the shepherds returned, glorifying and praising God for all the things that they had heard and seen, as it was told unto them.

21 And when eight days were accomplished for the circumcising of the child, his name was called JESUS, which was so named of the angel before he was conceived in the womb.

22 And when the days of her purification according to the law of Moses were accomplished, they brought him to Jerusalem, to present *him* to the Lord; 23 (as it is written in the law of the Lord, Every male that openeth the womb shall be called holy to the Lord;) 24 and to offer a sacrifice according to that

μενον" ἐν [w]τῇ" φάτνῃ. 13 Καὶ ἐξαίφνης ἐγένετο σὺν τῷ
ing in the manger. And suddenly there was with the

ἀγγέλῳ πλῆθος στρατιᾶς [x]οὐρανίου," αἰνούντων τὸν θεόν,
angel a multitude of [the] [2]host [1]heavenly, praising God,

καὶ λεγόντων, 14 Δόξα ἐν ὑψίστοις θεῷ, καὶ ἐπὶ γῆς
and saying, Glory in [the] highest to God, and on earth

εἰρήνη, ἐν ἀνθρώποις [y]εὐδοκία." 15 Καὶ ἐγένετο, ὡς ἀπῆλ-
peace, in men good pleasure. And it came to pass, as [3]depart-

θον ἀπ' αὐτῶν εἰς τὸν οὐρανὸν οἱ ἄγγελοι, [z]καὶ οἱ ἄνθρωποι"
ed [4]from [5]them [6]into [7]the [8]heaven [1]the [2]angels, that the men

οἱ ποιμένες [a]εἶπον" πρὸς ἀλλήλους, Διέλθωμεν δὴ ἕως
the shepherds said to one another, Let us go through indeed as far as

Βηθλεέμ, καὶ ἴδωμεν τὸ.ῥῆμα.τοῦτο τὸ γεγονὸς ὃ ὁ
Bethlehem, and let us see this thing that has come to pass which the

κύριος ἐγνώρισεν ἡμῖν. 16 Καὶ [b]ἦλθον" σπεύσαντες καὶ
Lord made known to us. And they came having hasted and

[c]ἀνεῦρον" τήν.τε.Μαριὰμ καὶ τὸν Ἰωσήφ, καὶ τὸ βρέφος κεί-
found both Mary and Joseph, and the babe ly-

μενον ἐν τῇ φάτνῃ. 17 ἰδόντες.δὲ [d]διεγνώρισαν"
ing in the manger. And having seen, they made known abroad

περὶ τοῦ ῥήματος τοῦ λαληθέντος αὐτοῖς περὶ τοῦ
concerning the saying which had been told them concerning

παιδίου.τούτου. 18 καὶ πάντες οἱ ἀκούσαντες ἐθαύμασαν
this little child. And all who heard wondered

περὶ τῶν λαληθέντων ὑπὸ τῶν ποιμένων πρὸς
concerning the things which had been spoken by the shepherds to

αὐτούς. 19 ἡ.δὲ.[e]Μαριὰμ" πάντα συνετήρει τὰ.ῥήματα.ταῦτα,
them. But Mary [2]all [1]kept these sayings,

[f]συμβάλλουσα" ἐν τῇ.καρδίᾳ.αὐτῆς. 20 καὶ [g]ἐπέστρεψαν"
pondering [them] in her heart. And [3]returned

οἱ ποιμένες, δοξάζοντες καὶ αἰνοῦντες τὸν θεὸν ἐπὶ πᾶσιν
[1]the [2]shepherds, glorifying and praising God for all things

οἷς ἤκουσαν καὶ [h]εἶδον," καθὼς ἐλαλήθη πρὸς αὐτούς.
which they had heard and seen, as it was said to them.

21 Καὶ ὅτε ἐπλήσθησαν ἡμέραι ὀκτὼ τοῦ περιτεμεῖν [i]τὸ
And when were fulfilled [2]days [1]eight for the circumcising the

παιδίον," καὶ ἐκλήθη τὸ.ὄνομα.αὐτοῦ Ἰησοῦς, τὸ κλη-
little child, [3]was [4]called [1]his [2]name Jesus, which [he] was

θὲν ὑπὸ τοῦ ἀγγέλου πρὸ τοῦ [k]συλληφθῆναι" αὐτὸν ἐν τῇ
called by the angel before [2]was [3]conceived [1]he in the

κοιλίᾳ.
womb.

22 Καὶ ὅτε ἐπλήσθησαν αἱ ἡμέραι τοῦ.καθαρισμοῦ.[l]αὐτῶν"
And when were fulfilled the days for their purification

κατὰ τὸν νόμον [m]Μωσέως," ἀνήγαγον αὐτὸν εἰς Ἱεροσό-
according to the law of Moses, they brought him to Jerusa-

λυμα παραστῆσαι τῷ κυρίῳ, 23 καθὼς γέγραπται ἐν [n]"
lem to present to the Lord, as it has been written in [the]

νόμῳ κυρίου, Ὅτι πᾶν ἄρσεν διανοῖγον μήτραν ἅγιον
law of [the] Lord, That every male opening a womb [4]holy

τῷ κυρίῳ κληθήσεται· 24 καὶ τοῦ δοῦναι θυσίαν κατὰ
[5]to [6]the [7]Lord [1]shall [2]be [3]called; and to offer a sacrifice according to

---

w — τῇ (*read* a manger) GLTTrAW. x οὐρανοῦ of heaven Tr. y εὐδοκίας of good pleasure ETTrA. z — καὶ οἱ ἄνθρωποι [L]T[TrA]. a ἐλάλουν T. b ἦλθαν TTrA. c ἀνεῦραν TTr. d ἐγνώρισαν they made known LTTrA. e Μαρία LTTrA. f συνβάλλουσα T. g ὑπέστρεψαν GLTTrAW. h ἴδον T. i αὐτόν him GLTTrAW. k συλλημφθῆναι LTTrA. l αὐτῆς (*read* her purification) E. m Μωϋσέως LTTrAW. n + τῷ the L.

τὸ εἰρημένον ἐν [o] νόμῳ κυρίου, Ζεῦγος τρυγόνων
that which has been said in [the] law of [the] Lord, A pair of turtle doves
ἢ δύο [p]νεοσσοὺς‖ περιστερῶν.
or two young of pigeons.

25 Καὶ ἰδού, [q]ἦν ἄνθρωπος‖ ἐν Ἱερουσαλὴμ ᾧ ὄνομα
And behold, there was a man in Jerusalem whose name
Συμεών, καὶ ὁ.ἄνθρωπος.οὗτος δίκαιος καὶ εὐλαβής,
[was] Simeon; and this man [was] just and pious,
προσδεχόμενος παράκλησιν τοῦ Ἰσραήλ, καὶ πνεῦμα
waiting for [the] consolation of Israel, and [the] [2]Spirit
[r]ἅγιον ἦν‖ ἐπ' αὐτόν· 26 καὶ ἦν αὐτῷ κεχρηματισμένον ὑπὸ
[1]Holy was upon him. And it was to him divinely communicated by
τοῦ πνεύματος τοῦ ἁγίου μὴ.ἰδεῖν θάνατον πρὶν [s]ἢ‖
the Spirit the Holy that he should not see death before
ἴδῃ τὸν χριστὸν κυρίου. 27 καὶ ἦλθεν ἐν τῷ πνεύματι
he should see the Christ of [the] Lord. And he came in the Spirit
εἰς τὸ ἱερόν· καὶ ἐν.τῷ.εἰσαγαγεῖν τοὺς γονεῖς τὸ παιδίον Ἰη-
into the temple; and when [3]brought [4]in [1]the [2]parents the little child Je-
σοῦν, τοῦ.ποιῆσαι.αὐτοὺς κατὰ τὸ.εἰθισμένον
sus, that they might do [3]according [4]to [5]what [6]had [7]become [8]customary
τοῦ νόμου περὶ αὐτοῦ, 28 καὶ.αὐτὸς ἐδέξατο αὐτὸ εἰς τὰς ἀγκά-
[9]by [10]the [11]law [1]for [2]him, he also received him into [2]arms,
λας [t]αὐτοῦ,‖ καὶ εὐλόγησεν τὸν θεόν, καὶ εἶπεν, 29 Νῦν ἀπολύεις
[1]his, and blessed God, and said, Now thou lettest go
τὸν.δοῦλόν.σου, δέσποτα, κατὰ τὸ.ῥῆμά.σου, ἐν εἰρήνῃ·
thy bondman, O Master, according to thy word, in peace;
30 ὅτι εἶδον οἱ.ὀφθαλμοί.μου τὸ.σωτήριόν.σου, 31 ὃ
for [3]have [4]seen [1]mine [2]eyes thy salvation, which
ἡτοίμασας κατὰ πρόσωπον πάντων τῶν λαῶν· 32 φῶς
thou hast prepared before [the] face of all the peoples; a light
εἰς ἀποκάλυψιν ἐθνῶν καὶ δόξαν λαοῦ.σου Ἰσραήλ.
for revelation of [the] Gentiles and glory of thy people Israel.
33 Καὶ ἦν [u] [v]Ἰωσὴφ‖ καὶ ἡ.μήτηρ.[w]αὐτοῦ‖ θαυμάζοντες ἐπὶ
And [5]were [1]Joseph [2]and [3]his [4]mother wondering at
τοῖς λαλουμένοις περὶ αὐτοῦ. 34 καὶ εὐλόγησεν
the things which were spoken concerning him. And [2]blessed
αὐτοὺς Συμεών, καὶ εἶπεν πρὸς Μαριὰμ τὴν.μητέρα αὐτοῦ,
[3]them [1]Simeon, and said to Mary his mother,
Ἰδού, οὗτος κεῖται εἰς πτῶσιν καὶ ἀνάστασιν πολλῶν
Lo, this [child] is set for [the] fall and rising up of many
ἐν τῷ Ἰσραήλ, καὶ εἰς σημεῖον ἀντιλεγόμενον· 35 καὶ σοῦ [x]δὲ‖
in Israel, and for a sign spoken against; (and of thee also
αὐτῆς τὴν ψυχὴν διελεύσεται ῥομφαία· ὅπως ἂν.ἀποκαλυ-
[6]thy [7]soul [3]shall [4]go [5]through [1]a [2]sword;) so that may be re-
φθῶσιν ἐκ πολλῶν καρδιῶν διαλογισμοί.
vealed of many hearts [the] reasonings.

36 Καὶ ἦν Ἄννα προφῆτις, θυγάτηρ Φανουήλ, ἐκ
And there was Anna a prophetess, daughter of Phanuel, of [the]
φυλῆς Ἀσήρ· αὕτη προβεβηκυῖα ἐν ἡμέραις πολλαῖς, ζήσασα
tribe of Asher, she was advanced in [2]days [1]many, having lived
[y]ἔτη μετὰ ἀνδρὸς‖ ἑπτὰ ἀπὸ τῆς.[z]παρθενίας‖.αὐτῆς, 37 καὶ
[2]years [3]with [4]a [5]husband [1]seven from her virginity, and

which is said in the law of the Lord, A pair of turtledoves, or two young pigeons.

25 And, behold, there was a man in Jerusalem, whose name *was* Simeon; and the same man *was* just and devout, waiting for the consolation of Israel: and the Holy Ghost was upon him. 26 And it was revealed unto him by the Holy Ghost, that he should not see death, before he had seen the Lord's Christ. 27 And he came by the Spirit into the temple: and when the parents brought in the child Jesus, to do for him after the custom of the law, 28 then took he him up in his arms, and blessed God, and said, 29 Lord, now lettest thou thy servant depart in peace, according to thy word: 30 for mine eyes have seen thy salvation, 31 which thou hast prepared before the face of all people; 32 a light to lighten the Gentiles, and the glory of thy people Israel. 33 And Joseph and his mother marvelled at those things which were spoken of him. 34 And Simeon blessed them, and said unto Mary his mother, Behold, this *child* is set for the fall and rising again of many in Israel; and for a sign which shall be spoken against; 35 (yea, a sword shall pierce through thy own soul also,) that the thoughts of many hearts may be revealed.

36 And there was one Anna, a prophetess, the daughter of Phanuel, of the tribe of Aser: she was of a great age, and had lived with an husband seven years from her virginity; 37 and she

---

[o] + τῷ the LTTr. [p] νοσσοὺς TA. [q] ἄνθρωπος ἦν T. [r] ἦν ἅγιον GLTTrAW. [s] ἢ ἂν T; ἂν Tr. [t] — αὐτοῦ (*read* [his] arms) [L]T[TrA]. [u] + ὁ L. [v] ὁ πατὴρ αὐτοῦ his father GTTrA. [w] — αὐτοῦ (*read* [his] mother) GTrA. [x] [δὲ] LTr. [y] μετὰ ἀνδρὸς ἔτη LTTr. [z] παρθενείας A.

was a widow of about fourscore and four years, which departed not from the temple, but served *God* with fastings and prayers night and day. 38 And she coming in that instant gave thanks likewise unto the Lord, and spake of him to all them that looked for redemption in Jerusalem.

39 And when they had performed all things according to the law of the Lord, they returned into Galilee, to their own city Nazareth. 40 And the child grew, and waxed strong in spirit, filled with wisdom: and the grace of God was upon him.

41 Now his parents went to Jerusalem every year at the feast of the passover. 42 And when he was twelve years old, they went up to Jerusalem after the custom of the feast. 43 And when they had fulfilled the days, as they returned, the child Jesus tarried behind in Jerusalem; and Joseph and his mother knew not *of it*. 44 But they, supposing him to have been in the company, went a day's journey; and they sought him among *their* kinsfolk and acquaintance. 45 And when they found him not, they turned back again to Jerusalem, seeking him. 46 And it came to pass, that after three days they found him in the temple, sitting in the midst of the doctors, both hearing them, and asking them questions. 47 And all that heard him were astonished at his understanding and answers. 48 And when they saw him, they were amazed: and his mother said unto him, Son, why hast thou thus dealt with us?

[b]αὕτη‖ χήρα [c]ὡς‖ ἐτῶν ὀγδοηκοντατεσσάρων, ἣ οὐκ
she [was] a widow ²about ⁴years ¹of ³eighty-four, ⁵who ⁷not

ἀφίστατο [d]ἀπὸ‖ τοῦ ἱεροῦ, νηστείαις καὶ δεήσεσιν λατρεύουσα
⁶departed from the temple, with fastings and supplications serving

νύκτα καὶ ἡμέραν. 38 καὶ [e]αὕτη‖ αὐτῇ.τῇ ὥρᾳ ἐπιστᾶσα
night and day: and she at the same hour coming up

ἀνθωμολογεῖτο τῷ [f]κυρίῳ,‖ καὶ ἐλάλει περὶ αὐτοῦ πᾶσιν
gave praise to the Lord, and spoke concerning him to all

τοῖς προσδεχομένοις λύτρωσιν [g]ἐν‖ Ἱερουσαλήμ.
those waiting for redemption in Jerusalem.

39 Καὶ ὡς ἐτέλεσαν [h]ἅπαντα‖ [i]τὰ‖ κατὰ τὸν νόμον
And when they had completed all things according to the law

κυρίου, [k]ὑπέστρεψαν‖ εἰς τὴν Γαλιλαίαν, εἰς [l]τὴν‖ πόλιν
of [the] Lord they returned to Galilee, to ³city

[m]αὐτῶν‖ [n]Ναζαρέτ.‖ 40 Τὸ.δὲ παιδίον ηὔξανεν καὶ ἐκρα-
¹their [²own], Nazareth. And the little child grew, and became

ταιοῦτο [o]πνεύματι,‖ πληρούμενον [p]σοφίας,‖ καὶ χάρις
strong in spirit, being filled with wisdom, and [the] grace

θεοῦ ἦν ἐπ' αὐτό.
of God was upon him.

41 Καὶ ἐπορεύοντο οἱ.γονεῖς.αὐτοῦ κατ'.ἔτος εἰς Ἱερουσαλὴμ
And ³went ¹his ²parents yearly to Jerusalem

τῇ ἑορτῇ τοῦ πάσχα. 42 καὶ ὅτε ἐγένετο ἐτῶν δώδεκα,
at the feast of the passover. And when he was ²years [³old] ¹twelve,

[q]ἀναβάντων‖ αὐτῶν [r]εἰς Ἱεροσόλυμα‖ κατὰ τὸ ἔθος τῆς
⁵having ⁶gone ⁷up ⁴they to Jerusalem according to the custom of the

ἑορτῆς, 43 καὶ τελειωσάντων τὰς ἡμέρας, ἐν.τῷ.ὑποστρέφειν
feast, and having completed the days, as ²returned

αὐτοὺς ὑπέμεινεν [s]Ἰησοῦς‖ ὁ παῖς ἐν Ἱερουσαλήμ, καὶ
¹they ⁶remained ⁷behind ⁵Jesus ³the ⁴child in Jerusalem, and

[t]οὐκ.ἔγνω Ἰωσὴφ καὶ ἡ.μήτηρ.αὐτοῦ·‖ 44 νομίσαντες.δὲ αὐτὸν
⁵knew [⁶it] ⁷not ¹Joseph ²and ³his ⁴mother; but supposing him

[v]ἐν τῇ συνοδίᾳ εἶναι‖ ἦλθον ἡμέρας ὁδόν, καὶ ἀνεζήτουν
in the company to be they went a day's journey, and sought

αὐτὸν ἐν τοῖς συγγενέσιν καὶ [w]ἐν‖ τοῖς γνωστοῖς· 45 καὶ
him among the relations and among the acquaintances: and

μὴ εὑρόντες [x]αὐτὸν ὑπέστρεψαν εἰς Ἱερουσαλήμ, [y]ζητοῦντες‖
not having found him they returned to Jerusalem, seeking

αὐτόν. 46 Καὶ ἐγένετο [z]μεθ'‖ ἡμέρας τρεῖς εὗρον αὐτὸν ἐν
him. And it came to pass after ²days ¹three they found him in

τῷ ἱερῷ, καθεζόμενον ἐν μέσῳ τῶν διδασκάλων, καὶ ἀκού-
the temple, sitting in [the] midst of the teachers, both hear-

οντα αὐτῶν καὶ ἐπερωτῶντα αὐτούς. 47 ἐξίσταντο.δὲ πάντες
ing them and questioning them. And ⁵were ⁶amazed ¹all

οἱ ἀκούοντες αὐτοῦ ἐπὶ τῇ συνέσει καὶ ταῖς ἀποκρίσεσιν
²those ³hearing ⁴him at [his] understanding and ²answers

αὐτοῦ. 48 Καὶ ἰδόντες αὐτὸν ἐξεπλάγησαν· καὶ [a]πρὸς αὐτὸν
¹his. And seeing him they were astonished: and to him

ἡ.μήτηρ.αὐτοῦ εἶπεν,‖ Τέκνον, τί ἐποίησας ἡμῖν οὕτως;
his mother said, Child, why hast thou done to us thus?

---

[b] αὐτὴ herself TTrA. [c] ἕως up to LTTrA. [d] — ἀπὸ (*read* left not) TTrA. [e] αὐτὴ W; — αὕτη (*read* ἀνθωμολ. she gave praise) LTTrA. [f] θεῷ (*read* to God) LTTrA. [g] — ἐν (*read* [in]) LTTr[A]. [h] πάντα TTr. [i] — τὰ T. [k] ἐπέστρεψαν T. [l] — τὴν LTTrA. [m] ἑαυτῶν LTTrAW. [n] Ναζαρέθ TTrAW. [o] — πνεύματι LTTrA. [p] σοφίᾳ TrA. [q] ἀναβαινόντων going up LTTrA. [r] — εἰς Ἱεροσόλυμα T[Tr]A. [s] [Ἰησοῦς] A. [t] οὐκ ἔγνωσαν οἱ γονεῖς αὐτοῦ his parents knew it not LTTrA. [v] εἶναι ἐν τῇ συνοδίᾳ LTTrA. [w] — ἐν GLTTrAW. [x] — αὐτόν (*read* [him]) G[L]TTrA. [y] ἀναζητοῦντες LTTrA. [z] μετὰ TTrA. [a] εἶπεν πρὸς αὐτὸν ἡ μήτηρ αὐτοῦ LTTrA.

ἰδού, ὁ.πατήρ.σου κἀγὼ ὀδυνώμενοι ἐζητοῦμέν σε. 49 Καὶ
behold, thy father and I distressed were seeking thee. And
εἶπεν πρὸς αὐτούς, Τί ὅτι ἐζητεῖτέ με; οὐκ.ᾔδειτε ὅτι
he said to them, Why [is it] that ye were seeking me? knew ye not that
ἐν τοῖς τοῦ.πατρός.μου δεῖ εἶναί με; 50 Καὶ αὐτοὶ
in the [affairs] of my Father it behoves [2]to [3]be [1]me? And they
οὐ.συνῆκαν τὸ ῥῆμα ὃ ἐλάλησεν αὐτοῖς. 51 Καὶ κατέβη
understood not the word which he spoke to them. And he went down
μετ' αὐτῶν καὶ ἦλθεν εἰς [b]Ναζαρέτ·‖ καὶ ἦν ὑποτασσόμενος
with them and came to Nazareth, and he was subject
αὐτοῖς. καὶ ἡ.μήτηρ.αὐτοῦ διετήρει [c]πάντα τὰ.ῥήματα‖ [d]ταῦτα‖
to them. And his mother kept all these things
ἐν τῇ.καρδίᾳ.αὐτῆς. 52 καὶ Ἰησοῦς προέκοπτεν [e] [f]σοφίᾳ καὶ
in her heart. And Jesus advanced in wisdom and
ἡλικίᾳ,‖ καὶ χάριτι παρὰ θεῷ καὶ ἀνθρώποις.
stature, and in favour with God and men.

3 Ἐν ἔτει δὲ πεντεκαιδεκάτῳ τῆς ἡγεμονίας Τιβερίου
[2]In [5]year [1]now [[3]the] [4]fifteenth of the government of Tiberius
Καίσαρος, ἡγεμονεύοντος Ποντίου [g]Πιλάτου‖ τῆς Ἰουδαίας,
Cæsar, [3]being [4]governor [1]Pontius [2]Pilate of Judæa,
καὶ [h]τετραρχοῦντος‖ τῆς Γαλιλαίας Ἡρώδου, Φιλίππου.δὲ τοῦ
and [2]being [3]tetrarch [4]of [5]Galilee [1]Herod, and Philip
ἀδελφοῦ.αὐτοῦ [h]τετραρχοῦντος‖ τῆς Ἰτουραίας καὶ Τραχωνί-
his brother being tetrarch of Ituræa and [3]of [4]Tracho-
τιδος χώρας, καὶ Λυσανίου τῆς Ἀβιληνῆς [h]τετραρχοῦντος,‖
nitis [[1]the] [2]region, and Lysanias [3]of [4]Abilene [1]being [2]tetrarch,
2 [i]ἐπ' ἀρχιερέων‖ Ἄννα καὶ [k]Καϊάφα,‖ ἐγένετο ῥῆμα
in [the] high-priesthood of Annas and Caiaphas, came [the] word
θεοῦ ἐπὶ [l]Ἰωάννην‖ τὸν [m]τοῦ‖ Ζαχαρίου υἱὸν ἐν τῇ ἐρήμῳ·
of God upon John the [2]of [3]Zacharias [1]son in the wilderness.
3 καὶ ἦλθεν εἰς πᾶσαν [n]τὴν‖ περίχωρον τοῦ Ἰορδάνου,
And he went into all the country around the Jordan,
κηρύσσων βάπτισμα μετανοίας εἰς ἄφεσιν ἁμαρτιῶν·
proclaiming [the] baptism of repentance for remission of sins;
4 ὡς γέγραπται ἐν βίβλῳ λόγων Ἡσαΐου τοῦ
as it has been written in [the] book of [the] words of Esaias the
προφήτου, [o]λέγοντος,‖ Φωνὴ βοῶντος ἐν τῇ ἐρήμῳ,
prophet, saying, [The] voice of one crying in the wilderness,
Ἑτοιμάσατε τὴν ὁδὸν κυρίου· εὐθείας ποιεῖτε τὰς τρίβους
Prepare the way of [the] Lord; [2]straight [1]make [4]paths
αὐτοῦ. 5 πᾶσα φάραγξ πληρωθήσεται, καὶ πᾶν ὄρος καὶ
[3]his. Every ravine shall be filled up, and every mountain and
βουνὸς ταπεινωθήσεται· καὶ ἔσται τὰ σκολιὰ εἰς
hill shall be made low; and [4]shall [5]become [1]the [2]crooked [[3]places] into
[p]εὐθεῖαν,‖ καὶ αἱ τραχεῖαι εἰς ὁδοὺς λείας· 6 καὶ ὄψεται
a straight [path], and the rough into [2]ways [1]smooth; and [3]shall [4]see
πᾶσα σὰρξ τὸ σωτήριον τοῦ θεοῦ. 7 Ἔλεγεν οὖν τοῖς
[1]all [2]flesh the salvation of God. He said therefore to the
ἐκπορευομένοις ὄχλοις βαπτισθῆναι ὑπ' αὐτοῦ, Γεννήματα
[2]coming [3]out [1]crowds to be baptized by him, Offspring
ἐχιδνῶν, τίς ὑπέδειξεν ὑμῖν φυγεῖν ἀπὸ τῆς μελλούσης ὀργῆς;
of vipers, who forewarned you to flee from the coming wrath?

behold, thy father and I have sought thee sorrowing. 49 And he said unto them, How is it that ye sought me? wist ye not that I must be about my Father's business? 50 And they understood not the saying which he spake unto them. 51 And he went down with them, and came to Nazareth, and was subject unto them: but his mother kept all these sayings in her heart. 52 And Jesus increased in wisdom and stature, and in favour with God and man.

III. Now in the fifteenth year of the reign of Tiberius Cæsar, Pontius Pilate being governor of Judæa, and Herod being tetrarch of Galilee, and his brother Philip tetrarch of Ituræa and of the region of Trachonitis, and Lysanias the tetrarch of Abilene, 2 Annas and Caiaphas being the high priests, the word of God came unto John the son of Zacharias in the wilderness. 3 And he came into all the country about Jordan, preaching the baptism of repentance for the remission of sins; 4 as it is written in the book of the words of Esaias the prophet, saying, The voice of one crying in the wilderness, Prepare ye the way of the Lord, make his paths straight. 5 Every valley shall be filled, and every mountain and hill shall be brought low; and the crooked shall be made straight, and the rough ways *shall be* made smooth; 6 and all flesh shall see the salvation of God. 7 Then said he to the multitude that came forth to be baptized of him, O generation of vipers, who hath warned you to flee from the wrath to come? 8 Bring forth therefore fruits worthy of repentance, and begin not to say within yourselves, We have Abraham to *our* fa-

---

[b] Ναζαρέθ TTrAW. [c] τὰ ῥήματα πάντα L. [d] — ταῦτα these [L]T[A]. [e] + ἐν τῇ in (wisdom) T. [f] ἡλικίᾳ καὶ σοφίᾳ Tr. [g] Πειλάτου T. [h] τετρααρχοῦντος T. [i] ἐπὶ ἀρχιερέως GLTTrAW. [k] Καϊφα L. [l] Ἰωάνην Tr. [m] — τοῦ GLTTrAW. [n] — τὴν (*read* every country around) LTTrA. [o] — λέγοντος LTTrA. [p] εὐθείας straight [paths] LTTrA.

ther: for I say unto
you, That God is able
of these stones to raise
up children unto Abra-
ham. 9 And now also
the axe is laid unto
the root of the trees:
every tree therefore
which bringeth not
forth good fruit is
hewn down, and cast
into the fire. 10 And
the people asked him,
saying, What shall we
do then? 11 He an-
swereth and saith unto
them, He that hath
two coats, let him im-
part to him that hath
none; and he that hath
meat, let him do like-
wise. 12 Then came
also publicans to be
baptized, and said unto
him, Master, what
shall we do? 13 And
he said unto them,
Exact no more than
that which is appoint-
ed you. 14 And the
soldiers likewise de-
manded of him, say-
ing, And what shall
we do? And he said
unto them, Do violence
to no man, neither ac-
cuse *any* falsely; and
be content with your
wages.

15 And as the people
were in expectation,
and all men mused in
their hearts of John,
whether he were the
Christ, or not; 16 John
answered, saying unto
them all, I indeed bap-
tize you with water;
but one mightier than
I cometh, the latchet
of whose shoes I am
not worthy to unloose:
he shall baptize you
with the Holy Ghost
and with fire: 17 whose
fan *is* in his hand, and
he will throughly
purge his floor, and
will gather the wheat
into his garner; but
the chaff he will burn
with fire unquench-
able. 18 And many
other things in his ex-
hortation preached he
unto the people. 19 But
Herod the tetrarch,
being reproved by him
for Herodias his bro-
ther Philip's wife, and
for all the evils
which Herod had done,
20 added yet this above
all, that he shut up
John in prison.

8 ποιήσατε οὖν καρποὺς ἀξίους τῆς μετανοίας· καὶ μὴ
Produce therefore fruits worthy of repentance; and [2]not
ἄρξησθε λέγειν ἐν ἑαυτοῖς, Πατέρα ἔχομεν τὸν Ἀβραάμ·
[1]begin to say in yourselves, [[4]For] [5]father [1]we [2]have [3]Abraham,
λέγω.γὰρ ὑμῖν, ὅτι δύναται ὁ θεὸς ἐκ τῶν.λίθων.τούτων
for I say to you, that [2]is [3]able [1]God from these stones
ἐγεῖραι τέκνα τῷ Ἀβραάμ. 9 ἤδη.δὲ καὶ ἡ ἀξίνη πρὸς τὴν
to raise up children to Abraham. But already also the axe to the
ῥίζαν τῶν δένδρων κεῖται· πᾶν οὖν δένδρον μὴ ποιοῦν
root of the trees is applied: [2]every [1]therefore tree not producing
καρπὸν [r]καλὸν[||] ἐκκόπτεται καὶ εἰς πῦρ βάλλεται. 10 Καὶ
[2]fruit [1]good is cut down and into [the] fire is cast. And
ἐπηρώτων αὐτὸν οἱ ὄχλοι, λέγοντες, Τί οὖν [s]ποιήσομεν[||];
[3]asked [4]him [1]the [2]crowds, saying, What then shall we do?
11 Ἀποκριθεὶς.δὲ [t]λέγει[||] αὐτοῖς, Ὁ ἔχων δύο χιτῶνας μετα-
And answering he says to them, He that has two tunics let him
δότω τῷ μὴ.ἔχοντι· καὶ ὁ ἔχων βρώματα ὁμοίως
impart to him that has not; and he that has victuals [4]likewise
ποιείτω. 12 Ἦλθον.δὲ καὶ τελῶναι βαπτισθῆναι, καὶ
[1]let [2]him [3]do. And [3]came [2]also [1]tax-gatherers to be baptized, and
[v]εἶπον[||] πρὸς αὐτόν, Διδάσκαλε, τί [s]ποιήσομεν[||]; 13 Ὁ.δὲ εἶπεν
they said to him, Teacher, what shall we do? And he said
πρὸς αὐτούς, Μηδὲν πλέον παρὰ τὸ διατεταγμένον
to them, [2]Nothing [3]more [4]beyond [5]that [6]which [7]is [8]appointed
ὑμῖν πράσσετε. 14 Ἐπηρώτων.δὲ αὐτὸν καὶ στρατευόμενοι,
[9]to [10]you [1]exact. And asked him also those who were soldiers,
λέγοντες, [w]Καὶ ἡμεῖς τί ποιήσομεν[||]; Καὶ εἶπεν [x]πρὸς αὐτούς,[||]
saying, And we what shall we do? And he said to them,
Μηδένα διασείσητε [y]μηδὲ[||] συκοφαντήσητε, καὶ ἀρκεῖσθε τοῖς
[2]No [3]one [1]oppress nor accuse falsely, and be satisfied
ὀψωνίοις.ὑμῶν.
with your wages.

15 Προσδοκῶντος.δὲ τοῦ λαοῦ, καὶ διαλογιζομένων πάν-
But as [3]were [4]in [5]expectation [1]the [2]people, and [2]were [3]reasoning [1]all
των ἐν ταῖς.καρδίαις.αὐτῶν περὶ τοῦ [z]Ἰωάννου,[||] μήποτε
in their hearts concerning John, whether or not
αὐτὸς εἴη ὁ χριστός, 16 ἀπεκρίνατο [a]ὁ Ἰωάννης ἅπασιν,
he might be the Christ, [2]answered [1]John all,
λέγων,[||] Ἐγὼ μὲν ὕδατι βαπτίζω ὑμᾶς[b]· ἔρχεται.δὲ ὁ
saying, I indeed with water baptize you, but he comes who [is]
ἰσχυρότερός μου, οὗ οὐκ.εἰμὶ ἱκανὸς λῦσαι τὸν ἱμάντα τῶν
mightier than I, of whom I am not fit to loose the thong
ὑποδημάτων.αὐτοῦ· αὐτὸς ὑμᾶς βαπτίσει ἐν πνεύματι
of his sandals; he [3]you [1]will [2]baptize with [the] [2]Spirit
ἁγίῳ καὶ πυρί· 17 οὗ τὸ πτύον ἐν τῇ.χειρὶ.αὐτοῦ,
[1]Holy and with fire; of whom the winnowing fan [is] in his hand,
[c]καὶ διακαθαριεῖ[||] τὴν.ἅλωνα.αὐτοῦ, καὶ [d]συνάξει[||] τὸν
and he will thoroughly purge his floor, and will gather the
σῖτον εἰς τὴν.ἀποθήκην.αὐτοῦ, τὸ.δὲ ἄχυρον κατακαύσει
wheat into his granary, but the chaff he will burn
πυρὶ ἀσβέστῳ. 18 Πολλὰ μὲν.οὖν καὶ ἕτερα παρακαλῶν
with fire unquenchable. [3]Many [2]therefore [1]and other things exhorting

---

[r] [καλὸν] L. [s] ποιήσωμεν should we do LTTrAW. [t] ἔλεγεν he said LTTrA. [v] εἶπαν LTTr. [w] τί ποιήσομεν (ποιήσωμεν should we do TAW) καὶ ἡμεῖς LTTrA. [x] αὐτοῖς to them LTrA. [y] μηδένα no one T. [z] Ἰωάνου Tr. [a] ὁ Ἰωάνης ἅπασιν λέγων Tr; λέγων πᾶσιν ὁ Ἰωάνης T. [b] + εἰς μετάνοιαν to repentance L. [c] διακαθᾶραι to thoroughly purge T. [d] συναγαγεῖν to gather T.

εὐηγγελίζετο τὸν λαόν. 19 Ὁ.δὲ.Ἡρώδης ὁ [e]τε-
he announced the glad tidings to the people. But Herod the te-
τράρχης‖ ἐλεγχόμενος ὑπ' αὐτοῦ περὶ Ἡρωδιάδος τῆς
trarch being reproved by him concerning Herodias the
γυναικὸς [f]Φιλίππου‖ τοῦ.ἀδελφοῦ.αὐτοῦ, καὶ περὶ πάντων
wife of Philip his brother, and concerning all
ὧν ἐποίησεν πονηρῶν ὁ Ἡρώδης, 20 προσέθηκεν [g]καὶ‖
[3]which [5]had [6]done [[1]the] [2]evils [4]Herod, added also
τοῦτο ἐπὶ πᾶσιν [h]καὶ‖ κατέκλεισεν τὸν [i]Ἰωάννην‖ ἐν [k]τῇ‖
this to all that he shut up John in the
φυλακῇ.
prison.

21 Ἐγένετο.δὲ ἐν.τῷ.βαπτισθῆναι ἅπαντα τὸν λαόν, καὶ
Now it came to pass [4]having [5]been [6]baptized [1]all [2]the [3]people, and
Ἰησοῦ βαπτισθέντος καὶ προσευχομένου, ἀνεῳχθῆναι τὸν
Jesus having been baptized and praying, [3]was [4]opened [1]the
οὐρανόν, 22 καὶ καταβῆναι τὸ πνεῦμα τὸ ἅγιον σωματικῷ
[2]heaven, and descended the Spirit the Holy in a bodily
εἴδει [l]ὡσεὶ‖ περιστερὰν ἐπ' αὐτόν, καὶ φωνὴν ἐξ οὐρανοῦ
form as a dove upon him, and a voice out of heaven
γενέσθαι, [m]λέγουσαν,‖ Σὺ εἶ ὁ.υἱός.μου ὁ ἀγαπητός, ἐν σοὶ
came, saying, Thou art my Son the beloved, in thee
[n]ηὐδόκησα.‖
I have found delight.

23 Καὶ αὐτὸς ἦν [o]ὁ‖ Ἰησοῦς [p]ὡσεὶ ἐτῶν τριάκοντα
And [2]himself [3]was [1]Jesus [7]about [9]years [[10]old] [8]thirty
ἀρχόμενος,‖ [q]ὤν, ὡς ἐνομίζετο, υἱὸς‖ Ἰωσήφ, τοῦ [r]Ἡλί,‖
[4]beginning [[5]to [6]be], being, as was supposed, son of Joseph, of Eli,
24 τοῦ [s]Ματθάτ,‖ τοῦ [t]Λευΐ,‖ τοῦ [v]Μελχί,‖ τοῦ [w]Ἰαννά,‖ τοῦ
of Matthat, of Levi, of Melchi, of Janna,
Ἰωσήφ, 25 τοῦ [x]Ματταθίου,‖ τοῦ Ἀμώς, τοῦ Ναούμ, τοῦ [y]Ἐσλί,‖
of Joseph, of Mattathias, of Amos, of Naoum, of Esli,
τοῦ Ναγγαί, 26 τοῦ Μαάθ, τοῦ Ματταθίου, τοῦ [z]Σεμεΐ,‖ τοῦ
of Naggai, of Maath, of Mattathias, of Semei,
[a]Ἰωσήφ,‖ τοῦ [b]Ἰούδα,‖ 27 τοῦ [c]Ἰωαννᾶ,‖ τοῦ Ῥησά, τοῦ Ζορο-
of Joseph, of Juda, of Joannes, of Rhesa, of Zoro-
βάβελ, τοῦ Σαλαθιήλ, τοῦ [d]Νηρί,‖ 28 τοῦ [v]Μελχί,‖ τοῦ [ea]Ἀδδί,‖
babel of Salathiel, of Neri, of Melchi, of Addi,
τοῦ Κωσάμ, τοῦ [fa]Ἐλμωδάμ,‖ τοῦ Ἤρ, 29 τοῦ [ga]Ἰωσή,‖ τοῦ Ἐλι-
of Cosam, of Elmodam, of Er, of Joses, of Eli-
έζερ, τοῦ Ἰωρείμ, τοῦ [ha]Ματθάτ,‖ τοῦ [ia]Λευΐ,‖ 30 τοῦ Συμεών,
ezer, of Joreim, of Matthat, of Levi, of Simeon,
τοῦ Ἰούδα, τοῦ Ἰωσήφ, τοῦ [ka]Ἰωνάν,‖ τοῦ Ἐλιακείμ, 31 τοῦ [la]Με-
of Juda, of Joseph, of Jonan, of Eliakim, of Me-
λεᾶ,‖ [ma]τοῦ Μαϊνάν,‖ τοῦ Ματταθά, τοῦ [na]Ναθάν,‖ τοῦ [oa]Δα-
leas, of Menna, of Mattatha, of Nathan, of Da-
βίδ,‖ 32 τοῦ Ἰεσσαί, τοῦ [pa]Ὠβήδ,‖ τοῦ [qa]Βοόζ,‖ τοῦ [ra]Σαλμών,‖
vid, of Jesse, of Obed, of Booz, of Salmon,

21 Now when all the
people were baptized,
it came to pass, that
Jesus also being bap-
tized, and praying, the
heaven was opened,
22 and the Holy Ghost
descended in a bodily
shape like a dove upon
him, and a voice came
from heaven, which
said, Thou art my be-
loved Son; in thee I
am well pleased.
23 And Jesus him-
self began to be about
thirty years of age, be-
ing (as was supposed)
the son of Joseph,
which was *the son* of
Heli, 24 which was *the*
son of Matthat, which
was *the son* of Levi,
which was *the son* of
Melchi, which was *the*
son of Janna, which
was *the son* of Joseph,
25 which was *the son*
of Mattathias, which
was *the son* of Amos,
which was *the son* of
Naum, which was *the*
son of Esli, which was
the son of Nagge,
26 which was *the son*
of Maath, which was
the son of Mattathias,
which was *the son* of
Semei, which was *the*
son of Joseph, which
was *the son* of Juda,
27 which was *the son*
of Joanna, which was
the son of Rhesa, which
was *the son* of Zoro-
babel, which was *the*
son of Salathiel, which
was *the son* of Neri,
28 which was *the son* of
Melchi, which was *the*
son of Addi, which was
the son of Cosam, which
was *the son* of Elmo-
dam, which was *the*
son of Er, 29 which
was *the son* of Jose,
which was *the son* of
Eliezer, which was *the*
son of Jorim, which
was *the son* of Matthat,
which was *the son* of
Levi, 30 which was
the son of Simeon,
which was *the son* of
Juda, which was *the*
son of Joseph, which
was *the son* of Jonan,
which was *the son* of
Eliakim, 31 which was
the son of Melea, which

---

[e] τετραάρχης T. [f] — Φιλίππου (*read* of his) GLTTrAW. [g] [καὶ] L. [h] — καὶ T[A]. [i] Ἰωάνην Tr. [k] — τῇ LTTrA. [l] ὡς LTTrA. [m] — λέγουσαν LTTrA. [n] εὐδόκησα LTTrA. [o] — ὁ TTrA. [p] ἀρχόμενος ὡσεὶ ἐτῶν τριάκοντα TTr. [q] ὢν υἱὸς ὡς ἐνομίζετο LTTrA. [r] Ἡλεί TTrA. [s] Μαθθάθ T. [t] Λευεί TTrA. [v] Μελχεί TTrA. [w] Ἰανναί LTTrA. [x] Μαθθαθίου Tr. [y] Ἐσλεί TTrA. [z] Σεμεείν TTrA. [a] Ἰωσήχ Josech TTrA [b] Ἰωδά TTrA. [c] Ἰωανάν LTTrA. [d] Νηρεί TTrA. [ea] Ἀδδεί TTrA. [fa] Ἐλμαδάμ LTTrA. [ga] Ἰησοῦ Jesus LTTrA. [ha] Μαθθάθ T; Μαθθάτ TrA. [ia] Λευεί TTrA. [ka] Ἰωνάμ TTrA. [la] Μελεά TTr. [ma] τοῦ Μεννά [L]TTrA. [na] Ναθάμ T. [oa] Δαυείδ LTTrA; Δαυΐδ GW. [pa] Ἰωβήδ Jobed LTTrA. [qa] Βοός LTTrA. [ra] Σαλά T.

was *the son* of Menan, which was *the son* of Mattatha, which was *the son* of Nathan, which was *the son* of David, 32 which was *the son* of Jesse, which was *the son* of Obed, which was *the son* of Booz, which was *the son* of Salmon, which was *the son* of Naasson, 33 which was *the son* of Aminadab, which was *the son* of Aram, which was *the son* of Esrom, which was *the son* of Phares, which was *the son* of Juda, 34 which was *the son* of Jacob, which was *the son* of Isaac, which was *the son* of Abraham, which was *the son* of Thara, which was *the son* of Nachor, 35 which was *the son* of Saruch, which was *the son* of Ragau, which was *the son* of Phalec, which was *the son* of Heber, which was *the son* of Sala, 36 which was *the son* of Cainan, which was *the son* of Arphaxad, which was *the son* of Sem, which was *the son* of Noe, which was *the son* of Lamech, 37 which was *the son* of Mathusala, which was *the son* of Enoch, which was *the son* of Jared, which was *the son* of Maleleel, which was *the son* of Cainan, 38 which was *the son* of Enos, which was *the son* of Seth, which was *the son* of Adam, which was *the son* of God.

IV. And Jesus being full of the Holy Ghost returned from Jordan, and was led by the Spirit into the wilderness, 2 being forty days tempted of the devil. And in those days he did eat nothing: and when they were ended, he afterward hungered. 3 And the devil said unto him, If thou be the Son of God, command this stone that it be made bread. 4 And Jesus answered him, saying, It is written, That man shall not live by bread alone, but by every word of

τοῦ Ναασσών, 33 τοῦ [s]'Αμιναδάβ,‖ τοῦ [t]'Αράμ,‖ τοῦ [v]'Εσρώμ,‖
of Naasson, of Aminadab, of Aram, of Esrom,

τοῦ Φαρές, τοῦ 'Ιούδα, 34 τοῦ 'Ιακώβ, τοῦ 'Ισαάκ, τοῦ 'Αβραάμ,
of Phares, of Juda, of Jacob, of Isaac, of Abraham,

τοῦ Θάρα, τοῦ Ναχώρ, 35 τοῦ [w]Σαρούχ,‖ τοῦ 'Ραγαῦ, τοῦ Φαλέκ,
of Terah, of Nachor, of Saruch, of Ragau, of Phalek,

τοῦ [x]"Εβερ,‖ τοῦ Σαλά, 36 τοῦ [y]Καϊνάν,‖ τοῦ 'Αρφαξάδ, τοῦ
of Eber, of Sala, of Cainan, of Arphaxad,

Σήμ, τοῦ Νῶε, τοῦ Λάμεχ, 37 τοῦ Μαθουσάλα, τοῦ 'Ενώχ,
of Sem, of Noe, of Lamech, of Mathusala, of Enoch,

τοῦ [z]'Ιαρέδ,‖ τοῦ [a]Μαλελεήλ,‖ τοῦ [b]Καϊνάν,‖ 38 τοῦ 'Ενώς,
of Jared, of Maleleel, of Cainan, of Enos,

τοῦ Σήθ, τοῦ 'Αδάμ, τοῦ θεοῦ.
of Seth, of Adam, of God.

4 'Ιησοῦς.δὲ [c]πνεύματος ἁγίου πλήρης‖ ὑπέστρεψεν ἀπὸ
And Jesus, [2]of [[3]the] [5]Spirit [4]Holy [1]full, returned from

τοῦ 'Ιορδάνου· καὶ ἤγετο ἐν τῷ πνεύματι [d]εἰς τὴν ἔρημον‖
the Jordan, and was led by the Spirit into the wilderness

2 ἡμέρας [e]τεσσαράκοντα,‖ πειραζόμενος ὑπὸ τοῦ διαβόλου·
[2]days [1]forty, being tempted by the devil;

καὶ οὐκ ἔφαγεν οὐδὲν ἐν ταῖς.ἡμέραις.ἐκείναις, καὶ συντελεσ-
and he ate nothing in those days, and [2]being

θεισῶν αὐτῶν [f]ὕστερον‖ ἐπείνασεν. 3 [g]καὶ εἶπεν‖ αὐτῷ ὁ
[3]ended [1]they afterwards he hungered. And [3]said [4]to [5]him [1]the

διάβολος, Εἰ υἱὸς εἶ τοῦ θεοῦ, εἰπὲ τῷ.λίθῳ.τούτῳ ἵνα
[2]devil, If Son thou art of God, speak to this stone that

γένηται ἄρτος. 4 Καὶ ἀπεκρίθη [h]'Ιησοῦς πρὸς αὐτόν,‖ [i]λέγων,‖
it become bread. And [2]answered [1]Jesus to him, saying,

Γέγραπται, "Οτι οὐκ ἐπ' ἄρτῳ μόνῳ ζήσεται ὁ ἄνθρωπος,
It has been written, That not on bread alone shall [2]live [1]man,

[k]ἀλλ' ἐπὶ παντὶ ῥήματι θεοῦ.‖ 5 Καὶ ἀναγαγὼν αὐτὸν [l]ὁ
but on every word of God. And [3]leading [5]up [4]him [1]the

διάβολος‖ [m]εἰς ὄρος ὑψηλὸν‖ ἔδειξεν αὐτῷ πάσας τὰς βασι-
[2]devil into a [2]mountain [1]high shewed him all the king-

λείας τῆς οἰκουμένης ἐν στιγμῇ χρόνου· 6 καὶ εἶπεν αὐτῷ
doms of the habitable world in a moment of time. And [3]said [4]to [5]him

ὁ διάβολος, Σοὶ δώσω τὴν.ἐξουσίαν.ταύτην ἅπασαν καὶ
[1]the [2]devil, To thee will I give [2]this [3]authority [1]all and

τὴν.δόξαν.αὐτῶν· ὅτι ἐμοὶ παραδέδοται, καὶ ᾧ.[n]ἐὰν‖ θέλω
their glory; for to me it has been delivered, and to whomsoever I wish

δίδωμι αὐτήν· 7 σὺ οὖν ἐὰν προσκυνήσῃς ἐνώπιόν [o]μου,‖
I give it. Thou therefore if thou wilt worship before me,

ἔσται σου [p]πάντα.‖ 8 Καὶ ἀποκριθεὶς [q]αὐτῷ εἶπεν ὁ 'Ιησοῦς,‖
[3]shall [4]be [5]thine [1]all [2]things. And answering him [2]said [1]Jesus,

[r]"Υπαγε ὀπίσω μου, σατανᾶ·‖ γέγραπται.[sa]γάρ,‖ [ta]Προσκυνή-
Get thee behind me, Satan; for it has been written, Thou shalt wor-

σεις κύριον τὸν.θεόν.σου,‖ καὶ αὐτῷ μόνῳ λατρεύσεις.
ship [the] Lord thy God, and him only shalt thou serve.

9 [va]Καὶ ἤγαγεν‖ αὐτὸν εἰς 'Ιερουσαλήμ, καὶ ἔστησεν [wa]αὐτὸν‖
And he led him to Jerusalem, and set him

[s] 'Αμειναδάβ A. [t] 'Αδμείν, τοῦ 'Αρνεί of Admin, of Arni, TA. [v] 'Εσρών EL. [w] Σερούχ GLTTrAW. [x] "Εβερ TrA. [y] Καϊνάμ TA. [z] 'Ιάρεθ L; 'Ιάρετ T. [a] Μελελεήλ T. [b] Καϊνάμ T. [c] πλήρης πνεύμ. ἁγίου LTTrA. [d] ἐν τῇ ἐρήμῳ LTTrA. [e] τεσσεράκοντα TTrA. [f] — ὕστερον LTTrA. [g] εἶπεν δὲ LTTrA. [h] πρὸς αὐτὸν ὁ 'Ιησοῦς LTTrA. [i] — λέγων TTrA. [k] — ἀλλ' ἐπὶ παντὶ ῥήματι θεοῦ T[Tr]A. [l] — ὁ διάβολος (*read* he shewed) TTrA. [m] — εἰς ὄρος ὑψηλὸν [L]TTrA. [n] ἂν LTrA. [o] ἐμοῦ LTTrAW. [p] πᾶσα all GLTTrAW. [q] [ὁ] A; εἶπεν αὐτῷ ὁ 'Ιησοῦς L; ὁ 'Ιησοῦς εἶπεν αὐτῷ T. [r] — ὕπαγε ὀπίσω μου, σατανᾶ G[L]TTrA. [sa] — γάρ for GLTTrAW. [ta] κύριον τὸν θεόν σου προσκυνήσεις LTr. [va] ἤγαγεν δὲ TTrA. [wa] — αὐτὸν (*read* [him]) T[Tr]A.

ἐπὶ τὸ πτερύγιον τοῦ ἱεροῦ, καὶ εἶπεν αὐτῷ, Εἰ [x]ὁ‖ υἱὸς εἶ
upon the edge of the temple, and said to him, If the Son thou art
τοῦ θεοῦ, βάλε σεαυτὸν ἐντεῦθεν κάτω. 10 γέγραπται.γάρ,
of God, cast thyself ²hence ¹down; for it has been written,
Ὅτι τοῖς.ἀγγέλοις.αὐτοῦ ἐντελεῖται περὶ σοῦ, τοῦ δια-
That to his angels he will give charge concerning thee, to
φυλάξαι σε· 11 καὶ ὅτι ἐπὶ χειρῶν ἀροῦσίν σε, μήποτε
keep thee; and that in [their] hands shall they bear thee, lest
προσκόψῃς πρὸς λίθον τὸν.πόδα.σου. 12 Καὶ ἀποκριθεὶς εἶπεν
thou strike against a stone thy foot. And answering ²said
αὐτῷ ὁ Ἰησοῦς, Ὅτι εἴρηται, Οὐκ.ἐκπειράσεις κύριον
³to ⁴him ¹Jesus, It has been said, Thou shalt not tempt [the] Lord
τὸν.θεόν.σου. 13 Καὶ συντελέσας πάντα πειρασμὸν ὁ διά-
thy God. And having finished every temptation the de-
βολος ἀπέστη ἀπ' αὐτοῦ ἄχρι.καιροῦ.
vil departed from him for a time.
14 Καὶ ὑπέστρεψεν ὁ Ἰησοῦς ἐν τῇ δυνάμει τοῦ πνεύματος
And ²returned ¹Jesus in the power of the Spirit
εἰς τὴν Γαλιλαίαν· καὶ φήμη ἐξῆλθεν καθ' ὅλης τῆς περι-
to Galilee; and a rumour went out into ²whole ¹the country
χώρου περὶ αὐτοῦ. 15 καὶ αὐτὸς ἐδίδασκεν ἐν ταῖς συν-
around concerning him. and he taught in ²syn-
αγωγαῖς αὐτῶν, δοξαζόμενος ὑπὸ πάντων. 16 καὶ ἦλθεν εἰς
agogues ¹their, being glorified by all. And he came to
[y]τὴν‖ [z]Ναζαρέτ,‖ οὗ ἦν [a]τεθραμμένος·‖ καὶ εἰσῆλθεν κατὰ
Nazareth, where he was brought up; and he entered according to
τὸ.εἰωθὸς.αὐτῷ ἐν τῇ ἡμέρᾳ τῶν σαββάτων εἰς τὴν συναγωγήν,
his custom on the day of the sabbaths into the synagogue,
καὶ ἀνέστη ἀναγνῶναι. 17 καὶ ἐπεδόθη αὐτῷ βιβλίον
and stood up to read. And there was given to him [the] book
[b]Ἡσαΐου τοῦ προφήτου,‖ καὶ [c]ἀναπτύξας‖ τὸ βιβλίον εὗρεν
of Esaias the prophet, and having unrolled the book he found
[d]τὸν‖ τόπον οὗ ἦν γεγραμμένον, 18 Πνεῦμα κυρίου
the place where it was written, [The] Spirit of [the] Lord [is]
ἐπ' ἐμέ, οὗ.[e]ἕνεκεν‖ ἔχρισέν με [f]εὐαγγελίζεσθαι‖
upon me, on account of which he anointed me to announce the glad tidings
πτωχοῖς, ἀπέσταλκέν με [g]ἰάσασθαι τοὺς συντετριμμένους
to [the] poor, he has sent me to heal the broken
τὴν καρδίαν,‖ κηρύξαι αἰχμαλώτοις ἄφεσιν καὶ τυφλοῖς
in heart, to proclaim to captives deliverance and to [the] blind
ἀνάβλεψιν, ἀποστεῖλαι τεθραυσμένους ἐν ἀφέσει· 19 κηρύ-
recovery of sight, to send forth [the] crushed in deliverance, to pro-
ξαι ἐνιαυτὸν κυρίου δεκτόν. 20 Καὶ πτύξας τὸ
claim [the] ²year ³of [⁴the] ⁵Lord ¹acceptable. And having rolled up the
βιβλίον, ἀποδοὺς τῷ ὑπηρέτῃ ἐκάθισεν, καὶ πάντων
book, having delivered [it] to the attendant he sat down, and ³of ⁴all
[h]ἐν τῇ συναγωγῇ οἱ ὀφθαλμοὶ ἦσαν‖ ἀτενίζοντες αὐτῷ.
⁵in ⁶the ⁷synagogue ¹the ²eyes were fixed upon him.
21 Ἤρξατο.δὲ λέγειν πρὸς αὐτούς, Ὅτι σήμερον πεπλήρωται
And he began to say to them, To-day is fulfilled
ἡ.γραφὴ.αὕτη ἐν τοῖς.ὠσὶν.ὑμῶν. 22 Καὶ πάντες ἐμαρτύρουν
this scripture in your ears. And all bore witness

God. 5 And the devil,
taking him up into an
high mountain, shewed
unto him all the king-
doms of the world in
a moment of time.
6 And the devil said
unto him, All this
power will I give thee,
and the glory of them:
for that is delivered
unto me; and to whom-
soever I will I give it.
7 If thou therefore wilt
worship me, all shall
be thine. 8 And Jesus
answered and said un-
to him, Get thee be-
hind me, Satan: for it
is written, Thou shalt
worship the Lord thy
God, and him only
shalt thou serve. 9 And
he brought him to Je-
rusalem, and set him
on a pinnacle of the
temple, and said unto
him, If thou be the Son
of God, cast thyself
down from hence:
10 for it is written, He
shall give his angels
charge over thee, to
keep thee: 11 and in
their hands they shall
bear thee up, lest at
any time thou dash thy
foot against a stone.
12 And Jesus answer-
ing said unto him, It
is said, Thou shalt not
tempt the Lord thy
God. 13 And when the
devil had ended all the
temptation, he depart-
ed from him for a
season.

14 And Jesus return-
ed in the power of the
Spirit into Galilee:
and there went out a
fame of him through
all the region round
about. 15 And he
taught in their syna-
gogues, being glorified
of all. 16 And he came
to Nazareth, where he
had been brought up:
and, as his custom
was, he went into the
synagogue on the sab-
bath day, and stood up
for to read. 17 And
there was delivered
unto him the book of
the prophet Esaias.
And when he had
opened the book, he
found the place where
it was written, 18 The
Spirit of the Lord *is*
upon me, because he
hath anointed me to
preach the gospel to

[x] — ὁ GLTTrAW. [y] — τὴν LTTrA. [z] Ναζαρέθ W; Ναζαρά Nazara T. [a] ἀνατεθραμμένος T. [b] τοῦ προφήτου Ἡσαΐου LTTrA. [c] ἀνοίξας having opened LTr. [d] — τὸν T. [e] εἵνεκεν GLTTrAW. [f] εὐαγγελίσασθαι GLTTrAW. [g] — ἰάσασθαι τοὺς συντετριμμένους τὴν καρδίαν G[L]TTrA. [h] ἐν τῇ συναγωγῇ ἦσαν οἱ ὀφθαλμοὶ L; οἱ ὀφθαλμοὶ ἐν τῇ συναγωγῇ ἦσαν TTrA.

the poor; he hath sent me to heal the brokenhearted, to preach deliverance to the captives, and recovering of sight to the blind, to set at liberty them that are bruised, 19 to preach the acceptable year of the Lord. 20 And he closed the book, and he gave *it* again to the minister, and sat down. And the eyes of all them that were in the synagogue were fastened on him. 21 And he began to say unto them, This day is this scripture fulfilled in your ears. 22 And all bare him witness, and wondered at the gracious words which proceeded out of his mouth. And they said, Is not this Joseph's son? 23 And he said unto them, Ye will surely say unto me this proverb, Physician, heal thyself: whatsoever we have heard done in Capernaum, do also here in thy country. 24 And he said, Verily I say unto you, No prophet is accepted in his own country. 25 But I tell you of a truth, many widows were in Israel in the days of Elias, when the heaven was shut up three years and six months, when great famine was throughout all the land; 26 but unto none of them was Elias sent, save unto Sarepta, *a city* of Sidon, unto a woman *that was* a widow. 27 And many lepers were in Israel in the time of Eliseus the prophet; and none of them was cleansed, saving Naaman the Syrian. 28 And all they in the synagogue, when they heard these things, were filled with wrath, 29 and rose up, and thrust him out of the city, and led him unto the brow of the hill whereon their city was built, that they might cast him down headlong. 30 But he passing through the midst of them went his way,

31 And came down

αὐτῷ, καὶ ἐθαύμαζον ἐπὶ τοῖς λόγοις τῆς χάριτος τοῖς ἐκπορευο-
to him, and wondered at the words of grace which pro-
μένοις ἐκ τοῦ.στόματος.αὐτοῦ, καὶ ἔλεγον, [i]Οὐχ‖ [k]οὗτός ἐστιν
ceeded out of his mouth; and they said, [2]Not [3]this [1]is
[l]ὁ‖ υἱὸς Ἰωσήφ‖; 23 Καὶ εἶπεν πρὸς αὐτούς, Πάντως ἐρεῖτέ
the son of Joseph? And he said to them, Surely ye will say
μοι τὴν.παραβολὴν.ταύτην, Ἰατρέ, θεράπευσον σεαυτόν·
to me this parable, Physician, heal thyself;
ὅσα ἠκούσαμεν γενόμενα [m]ἐν τῇ‖ [n]Καπερναούμ,‖ ποίησον
whatsoever we have heard being done in Capernaum, do
καὶ ὧδε ἐν τῇ.πατρίδι.σου. 24 Εἶπεν.δέ, Ἀμὴν λέγω ὑμῖν, ὅτι
also here in thine [own] country. But he said, Verily I say to you, that
οὐδεὶς προφήτης δεκτός ἐστιν ἐν τῇ.πατρίδι.[o]αὐτοῦ.‖ 25 ἐπ'
no prophet acceptable is in his [own] country. [2]In
ἀληθείας.δὲ λέγω ὑμῖν, [p] πολλαὶ χῆραι ἦσαν ἐν ταῖς ἡμέραις
[1]but truth I say to you, many widows were in the days
[q]Ἡλίου‖ ἐν τῷ Ἰσραήλ, ὅτε ἐκλείσθη ὁ οὐρανὸς [r]ἐπὶ‖ ἔτη
of Elias in Israel, when [3]was [4]shut [5]up [1]the [2]heaven for [2]years
τρία καὶ μῆνας ἕξ, ὡς ἐγένετο λιμὸς μέγας ἐπὶ πᾶσαν τὴν
[1]three and [2]months [1]six, when there was a [2]famine [1]great upon all the
γῆν, 26 καὶ πρὸς οὐδεμίαν αὐτῶν ἐπέμφθη [s]Ἡλίας‖ εἰ.μὴ εἰς
land, and to none of them was sent Elias except to
[t]Σάρεπτα‖ τῆς [v]Σιδῶνος,‖ πρὸς γυναῖκα χήραν. 27 καὶ πολλοὶ
Sarepta of Sidonia, to a [2]woman [1]widow. And many
λεπροὶ ἦσαν [w]ἐπὶ Ἐλισσαίου τοῦ προφήτου ἐν τῷ Ἰσραήλ,‖
lepers were in the time of Elisha the prophet in Israel,
καὶ οὐδεὶς αὐτῶν ἐκαθαρίσθη εἰ.μὴ [x]Νεεμὰν‖ ὁ Σύρος. 28 Καὶ
and none of them was cleansed except Naaman the Syrian. And
ἐπλήσθησαν πάντες θυμοῦ ἐν τῇ συναγωγῇ, ἀκούοντες
[5]were [6]filled [1]all [7]with [8]indignation [2]in [3]the [4]synagogue, hearing
ταῦτα. 29 καὶ ἀναστάντες ἐξέβαλον αὐτὸν ἔξω τῆς
these things; and having risen up they cast him out of [the]
πόλεως, καὶ ἤγαγον αὐτὸν ἕως [y]τῆς‖ ὀφρύος τοῦ ὄρους ἐφ'
city, and led him unto the brow of the mountain upon
οὗ ἡ.πόλις.[z]αὐτῶν ᾠκοδόμητο,‖ [a]εἰς τὸ‖ κατακρημνίσαι
which their city had been built, for to throw [2]down [3]headlong
αὐτόν· 30 αὐτὸς.δὲ διελθὼν διὰ μέσου αὐτῶν ἐπορεύετο
[1]him; but he passing through [the] midst of them went away.
31 Καὶ κατῆλθεν εἰς [b]Καπερναοὺμ‖ πόλιν τῆς Γαλιλαίας·
And he went down to Capernaum a city of Galilee,
καὶ ἦν διδάσκων αὐτοὺς ἐν τοῖς σάββασιν. 32 καὶ ἐξεπλήσ-
and was teaching them on the sabbaths. And they were as-
σοντο ἐπὶ τῇ.διδαχῇ.αὐτοῦ, ὅτι ἐν ἐξουσίᾳ ἦν ὁ.λόγος.αὐτοῦ.
tonished at his teaching, for with authority was his word.
33 Καὶ ἐν τῇ συναγωγῇ ἦν ἄνθρωπος ἔχων πνεῦμα δαιμονίου
And in the synagogue was a man having a spirit of a demon
ἀκαθάρτου, καὶ ἀνέκραξεν φωνῇ μεγάλῃ, 34 [c]λέγων,‖ Ἔα,
unclean; and he cried out with a [2]voice [1]loud, saying, Ah!
τί ἡμῖν καὶ σοί, Ἰησοῦ Ναζαρηνέ; ἦλθες ἀπολέσαι ἡμᾶς;
what to us and to thee, Jesus, Nazarene? Art thou come to destroy us?
οἶδά σε τίς εἶ, ὁ ἅγιος τοῦ θεοῦ. 35 Καὶ ἐπετίμησεν
I know thee who thou art, the Holy [One] of God. And [2]rebuked

[i] οὐχὶ LTTrA. [k] υἱός ἐστιν Ἰωσὴφ οὗτος TA. [l] [ὁ] Tr. [m] εἰς GLTr; εἰς τὴν TA. [n] Καφαρναούμ LTTrAW. [o] ἑαυτοῦ T. [p] + ὅτι that T. [q] Ἠλείου T. [r] — ἐπὶ LTr[A] [s] Ἠλείας T. [t] Σάρεφθα W. [v] Σιδωνίας LTTrA. [w] ἐν τῷ Ἰσραὴλ ἐπὶ Ἐλισαίου (Ἐλισαίου LT) τοῦ προφήτου LTTrA. [x] Ναιμὰν LTTrA. [y] — τῆς (read a brow) GTTrAW. [z] ᾠκοδόμητο αὐτῶν TTrA. [a] ὥστε so as GLTTrA. [b] Καφαρναούμ LTTrAW. [c] — λέγων T[Tr]A.

αὐτῷ ὁ Ἰησοῦς, λέγων, Φιμώθητι, καὶ ἔξελθε [d]ἐξ‖ αὐτοῦ.
[3]him [1]Jesus, saying, Hold thy peace, and come forth out of him.
Καὶ ῥίψαν αὐτὸν τὸ δαιμόνιον εἰς [e]τὸ‖ μέσον ἐξῆλθεν
And [3]having [4]thrown [5]him [1]the [2]demon into the midst came out
ἀπ' αὐτοῦ, μηδὲν βλάψαν αὐτόν. 36 καὶ ἐγένετο θάμβος
from him, in nothing having hurt him. And [2]came [1]astonishment
ἐπὶ πάντας, καὶ συνελάλουν πρὸς ἀλλήλους, λέγοντες, Τίς
upon all, and they spoke to one another, saying, What
ὁ λόγος οὗτος, ὅτι ἐν ἐξουσίᾳ καὶ δυνάμει ἐπιτάσσει τοῖς
word [is] this, that with authority and power he commands the
ἀκαθάρτοις πνεύμασιν, καὶ ἐξέρχονται; 37 Καὶ ἐξεπορεύετο
unclean spirits, and they come out? And [3]went [4]out
ἦχος περὶ αὐτοῦ εἰς πάντα τόπον τῆς περιχώρου.
[1]a [2]rumour concerning him into every place of the country around.

38 Ἀναστὰς-δὲ [f]ἐκ‖ τῆς συναγωγῆς εἰσῆλθεν εἰς τὴν οἰκίαν
And rising up out of the synagogue he entered into the house
Σίμωνος· [g]ἡ‖ πενθερὰ δὲ τοῦ Σίμωνος ἦν συνεχομένη
of Simon. [2]The [3]mother-in-law [1]and of Simon was oppressed with
πυρετῷ μεγάλῳ· καὶ ἠρώτησαν αὐτὸν περὶ αὐτῆς. 39 καὶ
a [2]fever [1]great; and they asked him for her. And
ἐπιστὰς ἐπάνω αὐτῆς ἐπετίμησεν τῷ πυρετῷ, καὶ ἀφῆκεν αὐτήν·
standing over her he rebuked the fever, and it left her;
παραχρῆμα-δὲ ἀναστᾶσα διηκόνει αὐτοῖς.
and immediately arising she served them.

40 Δύνοντος-δὲ τοῦ ἡλίου πάντες ὅσοι εἶχον
And at the going down of the sun all as many as had [persons]
ἀσθενοῦντας νόσοις ποικίλαις ἤγαγον αὐτοὺς πρὸς αὐτόν·
sick with [2]diseases [1]various brought them to him,
ὁ-δὲ ἑνὶ ἑκάστῳ αὐτῶν τὰς χεῖρας [h]ἐπιθεὶς‖ [i]ἐθεράπευ-
and he [4]on [6]one [5]each [7]of [8]them [3]hands [1]having [2]laid healed
σεν‖ αὐτούς· 41 [k]ἐξήρχετο‖-δὲ καὶ δαιμόνια ἀπὸ πολλῶν,
them; and [2]went [3]out [4]also [1]demons from many,
[l]κράζοντα‖ καὶ λέγοντα, Ὅτι σὺ εἶ [m]ὁ χριστὸς‖ ὁ υἱὸς τοῦ
crying out and saying, Thou art the Christ the Son
θεοῦ. Καὶ ἐπιτιμῶν οὐκ-εἴα αὐτὰ λαλεῖν ὅτι ᾔδεισαν
of God. And rebuking he suffered not them to speak because they knew
τὸν χριστὸν αὐτὸν εἶναι.
[4]the [5]Christ [1]him [2]to [3]be.

42 Γενομένης-δὲ ἡμέρας ἐξελθὼν ἐπορεύθη εἰς ἔρημον
And [2]being [3]come [1]day having gone out he went into a desert
τόπον, καὶ οἱ ὄχλοι [n]ἐζήτουν‖ αὐτόν, καὶ ἦλθον ἕως αὐτοῦ
place, and the crowds sought him, and came up to him
καὶ κατεῖχον αὐτὸν τοῦ-μὴ-πορεύεσθαι ἀπ' αὐτῶν. 43 ὁ-δὲ
and were detaining him that he might not go from them. But he
εἶπεν πρὸς αὐτούς, Ὅτι καὶ ταῖς ἑτέραις πόλεσιν εὐαγ-
said to them, Also to the other cities [4]to [5]announce
γελίσασθαί [o]με-δεῖ‖ τὴν βασιλείαν τοῦ θεοῦ· ὅτι
[6]the [7]glad [8]tidings [1]it [2]behoves [3]me, the kingdom of God; because
[p]εἰς‖ τοῦτο [q]ἀπέσταλμαι.‖ 44 Καὶ ἦν κηρύσσων [r]ἐν ταῖς
for this have I been sent forth. And he was preaching in the
συναγωγαῖς‖ τῆς [s]Γαλιλαίας.‖
synagogues of Galilee.

to Capernaum, a city
of Galilee, and taught
them on the sabbath
days. 32 And they
were astonished at his
doctrine: for his word
was with power.
33 And in the syna-
gogue there was a man,
which had a spirit of
an unclean devil, and
cried out with a loud
voice, 34 saying, Let
us alone; what have
we to do with thee,
thou Jesus of Naza-
reth? art thou come to
destroy us? I know
thee who thou art;
the Holy One of God.
35 And Jesus rebuked
him, saying, Hold thy
peace, and come out of
him. And when the
devil had thrown him
in the midst, he came
out of him, and hurt
him not. 36 And they
were all amazed, and
spake among them-
selves, saying, What a
word *is* this! for with
authority and power
he commandeth the
unclean spirits, and
they come out. 37 And
the fame of him went
out into every place of
the country round
about.

38 And he arose out
of the synagogue, and
entered into Simon's
house. And Simon's
wife's mother was ta-
ken with a great fever;
and they besought him
for her. 39 And he
stood over her, and re-
buked the fever; and
it left her: and imme-
diately she arose and
ministered unto them.
40 Now when the sun
was setting, all they
that had any sick with
divers diseases brought
them unto him; and
he laid his hands on
every one of them, and
healed them. 41 And
devils also came out of
many, crying out, and
saying, Thou art Christ
the Son of God. And
he rebuking *them* suf-
fered them not to
speak: for they knew
that he was Christ.

42 And when it was
day, he departed and
went into a desert
place: and the people
sought him, and came
unto him, and stayed

---

[d] ἀπ' from LTTrA. [e] — τὸ G. [f] ἀπὸ from TTrA. [g] — ἡ (*read* [the]) GLTTrAW. [h] ἐπιτιθεὶς laying LTTrA. [i] ἐθεράπευεν TTrA. [k] ἐξήρχοντο T. [l] κραυγάζοντα LT. [m] — ὁ χριστὸς GLTTrA. [n] ἐπεζήτουν sought after GLTTrAW. [o] δεῖ με L. [p] ἐπὶ LTTrA. [q] ἀπεστάλην I was sent forth LTTrA. [r] εἰς τὰς συναγωγὰς TTrA. [s] Ἰουδαίας of Judea A.

him, that he should
not depart from them.
43 And he said unto
them, I must preach
the kingdom of God
to other cities also:
for therefore am I
sent. 44 And he preach-
ed in the synagogues
of Galilee.

V. And it came to
pass, that, as the peo-
ple pressed upon him
to hear the word of
God, he stood by the
lake of Gennesaret,
2 and saw two ships
standing by the lake:
but the fishermen were
gone out of them, and
were washing *their*
nets. 3 And he enter-
ed into one of the ships,
which was Simon's,
and prayed him that
he would thrust out a
little from the land.
And he sat down, and
taught the people out
of the ship. 4 Now
when he had left
speaking, he said unto
Simon, Launch out in-
to the deep, and let
down your nets for a
draught. 5 And Simon
answering said unto
him, Master, we have
toiled all the night,
and have taken no-
thing: nevertheless at
thy word I will let
down the net. 6 And
when they had this
done, they inclosed a
great multitude of
fishes: and their net
brake. 7 And they
beckoned unto *their*
partners, which were
in the other ship, that
they should come and
help them. And they
came, and filled both
the ships, so that they
began to sink. 8 When
Simon Peter saw *it*,
he fell down at Jesus'
knees, saying, Depart
from me; for I am a
sinful man, O Lord.
9 For he was asto-
nished, and all that
were with him, at the
draught of the fishes
which they had taken:
10 and so *was* also
James, and John, the
sons of Zebedee, which
were partners with Si-
mon. And Jesus said
unto Simon, Fear not;

5 Ἐγένετο.δὲ ἐν τῷ τὸν ὄχλον ἐπικεῖσθαι αὐτῷ
And it came to pass during the [time] the crowd pressed on him
[t]τοῦ‖ ἀκούειν τὸν λόγον τοῦ θεοῦ, καὶ αὐτὸς ἦν ἑστὼς παρὰ
to hear the word of God, that he was standing by
τὴν λίμνην Γεννησαρέτ· 2 καὶ [v]εἶδεν‖ δύο [w]πλοῖα‖ ἑστῶτα
the lake of Gennesaret: and he saw two ships standing
παρὰ τὴν λίμνην· οἱ.δὲ [x]ἁλιεῖς‖ [y]ἀποβάντες ἀπ' αὐτῶν‖
by the lake, but the fishermen having gone out from them
[z]ἀπέπλυναν‖ τὰ δίκτυα. 3 ἐμβὰς.δὲ εἰς ἓν τῶν πλοίων
washed the nets. And having entered into one of the ships
ὃ ἦν [a]τοῦ‖ Σίμωνος, ἠρώτησεν αὐτὸν ἀπὸ τῆς γῆς ἐπαναγα-
which was Simon's, he asked him from the land to put
γεῖν ὀλίγον· [b]καὶ καθίσας‖ [c]ἐδίδασκεν ἐκ τοῦ πλοίου‖ τοὺς
off a little; and having sat down he taught from the ship the
ὄχλους. 4 Ὡς.δὲ ἐπαύσατο λαλῶν εἶπεν πρὸς τὸν Σίμωνα,
crowds. And when he ceased speaking he said to Simon,
Ἐπανάγαγε εἰς τὸ βάθος καὶ χαλάσατε τὰ.δίκτυα.ὑμῶν εἰς
Put off into the deep and let down your nets for
ἄγραν. 5 Καὶ ἀποκριθεὶς [d]ὁ‖ Σίμων εἶπεν [e]αὐτῷ,‖ Ἐπιστάτα,
a haul. And answering Simon said to him, Master,
δι' ὅλης [f]τῆς‖ νυκτὸς κοπιάσαντες οὐδὲν ἐλάβομεν·
through [2]whole [1]the night having laboured, nothing have we taken,
ἐπὶ.δὲ τῷ.ῥήματί.σου χαλάσω [g]τὸ δίκτυον.‖ 6 Καὶ τοῦτο
but at thy word I will let down the net. And this
ποιήσαντες συνέκλεισαν [h]ἰχθύων πλῆθος‖ πολύ· [i]διεῤῥήγνυτο‖
having done they enclosed of fishes a [2]shoal [1]great; [6]was [7]breaking
δὲ [j]τὸ δίκτυον‖ αὐτῶν. 7 καὶ κατένευσαν τοῖς μετόχοις
[3]and [5]net [4]their. And they beckoned to the partners
[k]τοῖς‖ ἐν τῷ ἑτέρῳ πλοίῳ, τοῦ.ἐλθόντας συλλαβέσθαι αὐτοῖς·
those in the other ship, that coming they should help them;
καὶ [l]ἦλθον,‖ καὶ ἔπλησαν ἀμφότερα τὰ πλοῖα, ὥστε βυθίζε-
and they came, and filled both the ships, so that [2]were [3]sink-
σθαι αὐτά. 8 ἰδὼν.δὲ Σίμων Πέτρος προσέπεσεν τοῖς γόνασιν
ing [1]they. And [3]having [4]seen [1]Simon [2]Peter fell at the knees
[m]τοῦ‖ Ἰησοῦ, λέγων, Ἔξελθε ἀπ' ἐμοῦ, ὅτι ἀνὴρ ἁμαρτωλός
of Jesus, saying, Depart from me, for a man a sinner
εἰμι, κύριε. 9 Θάμβος.γὰρ περιέσχεν αὐτὸν καὶ πάντας τοὺς
am I, Lord. For astonishment laid hold on him and all those
σὺν αὐτῷ, ἐπὶ τῇ ἄγρᾳ τῶν ἰχθύων [n]ᾗ‖ συνέλαβον·
with him, at the haul of the fishes which they had taken;
10 ὁμοίως.δὲ καὶ Ἰάκωβον καὶ [o]Ἰωάννην,‖ υἱοὺς Ζεβεδαίου,
and in like manner also James and John, sons of Zebedee,
οἳ ἦσαν κοινωνοὶ τῷ Σίμωνι. Καὶ εἶπεν πρὸς τὸν Σίμωνα
who were partners with Simon. And [2]said [3]to [4]Simon
[p]ὁ‖ Ἰησοῦς, Μὴ.φοβοῦ· ἀπὸ τοῦ.νῦν ἀνθρώπους ἔσῃ
[1]Jesus, Fear not; from henceforth men thou shalt be
ζωγρῶν. 11 Καὶ καταγαγόντες τὰ πλοῖα ἐπὶ τὴν γῆν, ἀφέντες
capturing. And having brought the ships to land, leaving
[q]ἅπαντα‖ ἠκολούθησαν αὐτῷ.
all they followed him.

---

[t] καὶ also TTrA. [v] ἴδεν T. [w] πλοιάρια small ships TA. [x] ἁλεεῖς T. [y] ἀπ' αὐτῶν ἀποβάντες TTrA. [z] ἔπλυνον were washing LTrA; ἔπλυναν T. [a] — τοῦ LTTrA. [b] καθίσας δὲ TA. [c] ἐν (in) τῷ πλοίῳ ἐδίδασκεν T; ἐκ τοῦ πλοίου ἐδίδασκεν A. [d] — ὁ TTrA. [e] — αὐτῷ T. [f] — τῆς (*read* a whole night) LTTrA. [g] τὰ δίκτυα the nets TTr. [h] πλῆθος ἰχθύων GTTrAW. [i] διερήγνυτο L; διερήσσετο TTrA. [j] τὰ δίκτυα nets (*read* διερ. were breaking) TTrA. [k] — τοῖς [L]TTrA. [l] ἦλθαν T. [m] — τοῦ LTTrAW. [n] ὧν Tr. [o] Ἰωάνην Tr. [p] — ὁ [Tr]A. [q] πάντα LTTr.

12 Καὶ ἐγένετο ἐν.τῷ.εἶναι αὐτὸν ἐν μιᾷ τῶν πόλεων,
And it came to pass as ²was ¹he in one of the cities,
καὶ ἰδού, ἀνὴρ πλήρης λέπρας· ʳκαὶ ἰδὼν‖ τὸν Ἰησοῦν, πεσὼν
that behold, a man full of leprosy, and seeing Jesus, falling
ἐπὶ πρόσωπον ἐδεήθη αὐτοῦ, λέγων, Κύριε, ἐὰν θέλῃς·
upon [his] face he besought him, saying, Lord, if thou wilt
δύνασαί με καθαρίσαι. 13 Καὶ ἐκτείνας τὴν χεῖρα
thou art able me to cleanse. And having stretched out [his] hand
ἥψατο αὐτοῦ, ˢεἰπών,‖ Θέλω, καθαρίσθητι. Καὶ εὐθέως ἡ
he touched him, saying, I will; be thou cleansed. And immediately the
λέπρα ἀπῆλθεν ἀπ' αὐτοῦ. 14 καὶ αὐτὸς παρήγγειλεν αὐτῷ
leprosy departed from him. And he charged him
μηδενὶ εἰπεῖν· ἀλλὰ ἀπελθὼν δεῖξον σεαυτὸν τῷ ἱερεῖ, καὶ
no one to tell; but having gone shew thyself to the priest, and
προσένεγκε περὶ τοῦ.καθαρισμοῦ.σου, καθὼς προσέταξεν ᵗΜω-
offer for thy cleansing, as ²ordered ¹Mo-
σῆς,‖ εἰς μαρτύριον αὐτοῖς. 15 Διήρχετο.δὲ μᾶλλον ὁ
ses, for a testimony to them. But was spread abroad still more the
λόγος περὶ αὐτοῦ· καὶ συνήρχοντο ὄχλοι πολλοὶ ἀκούειν,
report concerning him; and ³were ⁴coming ²crowds ¹great to hear,
καὶ θεραπεύεσθαι ᵛὑπ' αὐτοῦ‖ ἀπὸ τῶν.ἀσθενειῶν.αὐτῶν·
and to be healed by him from their infirmities.
16 αὐτὸς.δὲ ἦν ὑποχωρῶν ἐν ταῖς ἐρήμοις καὶ προσευχό-
But he was retiring in the deserts and pray-
μενος.
ing.

17 Καὶ ἐγένετο ἐν μιᾷ τῶν ἡμερῶν καὶ αὐτὸς.ἦν διδάσ-
And it came to pass on one of the days that he was teach-
κων, καὶ ἦσαν καθήμενοι ʷΦαρισαῖοι καὶ νομοδιδάσκαλοι,
ing, and there were sitting by Pharisees and teachers of the law,
οἳ ἦσαν ˣἐληλυθότες‖ ἐκ πάσης κώμης τῆς Γαλιλαίας καὶ
who were come out of every village of Galilee and
Ἰουδαίας καὶ Ἱερουσαλήμ· καὶ δύναμις κυρίου ἦν εἰς
of Judæa and of Jerusalem: and power of [the] Lord was [there] for
τὸ ἰᾶσθαι ʸαὐτούς.‖ 18 καὶ ἰδού, ἄνδρες φέροντες ἐπὶ κλίνης
to heal them. And behold, men carrying upon a couch
ἄνθρωπον ὃς ἦν παραλελυμένος, καὶ ἐζήτουν αὐτὸν εἰσενεγ-
a man who was paralysed, and they sought ³him ¹to ²bring
κεῖν καὶ θεῖναι ᶻ ἐνώπιον αὐτοῦ· 19 καὶ μὴ εὑρόντες ᵃδιὰ‖
in and to place [him] before him. And not having found by
ποίας εἰσενέγκωσιν αὐτὸν διὰ τὸν ὄχλον, ἀναβάντες
what way they should bring in him on account of the crowd, going up
ἐπὶ τὸ δῶμα, διὰ τῶν κεράμων καθῆκαν αὐτὸν σὺν τῷ
on the housetop, through the tiles they let down him with the
κλινιδίῳ εἰς τὸ μέσον ἔμπροσθεν τοῦ Ἰησοῦ. 20 καὶ ἰδὼν τὴν
little couch into the midst before Jesus. And seeing
πίστιν.αὐτῶν εἶπεν ᵇαὐτῷ,‖ Ἄνθρωπε, ἀφέωνταί σοι
their faith he said to him, Man, ³have ⁴been ⁵forgiven ⁶thee
αἱ.ἁμαρτίαι.σου. 21 Καὶ ἤρξαντο διαλογίζεσθαι οἱ γραμματεῖς
¹thy ²sins. And began to reason the scribes
καὶ οἱ Φαρισαῖοι, λέγοντες, Τίς ἐστιν οὗτος ὃς λαλεῖ βλασ-
and the Pharisees, saying, Who is this who speaks blas-
φημίας; τίς δύναται ᶜἀφιέναι ἁμαρτίας,‖ εἰ.μὴ μόνος ὁ θεός;
phemies? who is able to forgive sins, except ²alone ¹God?

from henceforth thou shalt catch men. 11 And when they had brought their ships to land, they forsook all, and followed him.

12 And it came to pass, when he was in a certain city, behold a man full of leprosy: who seeing Jesus fell on *his* face, and besought him, saying, Lord, if thou wilt, thou canst make me clean. 13 And he put forth *his* hand, and touched him, saying, I will: be thou clean. And immediately the leprosy departed from him. 14 And he charged him to tell no man: but go, and shew thyself to the priest, and offer for thy cleansing, according as Moses commanded, for a testimony unto them. 15 But so much the more went there a fame abroad of him: and great multitudes came together to hear, and to be healed by him of their infirmities. 16 And he withdrew himself into the wilderness, and prayed.

17 And it came to pass on a certain day, as he was teaching, that there were Pharisees and doctors of the law sitting by, which were come out of every town of Galilee, and Judæa, and Jerusalem: and the power of the Lord was *present* to heal them. 18 And, behold, men brought in a bed a man which was taken with a palsy: and they sought *means* to bring him in, and to lay *him* before him. 19 And when they could not find by what *way* they might bring him in because of the multitude, they went upon the housetop, and let him down through the tiling with *his* couch into the midst before Jesus. 20 And when he saw their faith, he said unto him, Man, thy sins are forgiven thee. 21 And the scribes and the Pharisees began to reason, saying, Who is this which speaketh blasphemies? Who can forgive sins, but God alone? 22 But when

ʳ ἰδὼν δὲ T. ˢ λέγων LTr. ᵗ Μωϋσῆς LTTrAW. ᵛ — ὑπ' αὐτοῦ LTTrA. ʷ + οἱ the L. ˣ συνεληλυθότες come together L. ʸ αὐτόν him (*read* was for his healing) TA. ᶻ + αὐτὸν him A. ᵃ — διὰ GLTTrAW. ᵇ — αὐτῷ GLTTrA. ᶜ ἁμαρτίας ἀφεῖναι LTTrA.

Jesus perceived their
thoughts, he answer-
ing said unto them,
What reason ye in
your hearts? 23 Whe-
ther is easier, to say,
Thy sins be forgiven
thee; or to say, Rise
up and walk? 24 But
that ye may know that
the Son of man hath
power upon earth to
forgive sins, (he said
unto the sick of the
palsy,) I say unto thee,
Arise, and take up thy
couch, and go into
thine house. 25 And
immediately he rose up
before them, and took
up that whereon he
lay, and departed to
his own house, glorify-
ing God. 26 And they
were all amazed, and
they glorified God, and
were filled with fear,
saying, We have seen
strange things to day.

22 Ἐπιγνοὺς.δὲ ὁ Ἰησοῦς τοὺς.διαλογισμοὺς.αὐτῶν [d]ἀπο-
But [2]knowing [1]Jesus their reasonings an-
κριθεὶς" εἶπεν πρὸς αὐτούς, Τί διαλογίζεσθε ἐν ταῖς καρδίαις
swering said to them, Why reason ye in [2]hearts
ὑμῶν; 23 τί ἐστιν εὐκοπώτερον, εἰπεῖν, Ἀφέωνταί σοι
[1]your? which is easier, to say, Have been forgiven thee
αἱ.ἁμαρτίαι.σου, ἢ εἰπεῖν, [e]Ἔγειραι" καὶ περιπάτει; 24 ἵνα.δὲ
thy sins, or to say, Arise and walk? But that
εἰδῆτε ὅτι [f]ἐξουσίαν ἔχει ὁ υἱὸς τοῦ ἀνθρώπου" ἐπὶ τῆς
ye may know that authority has the Son of man on the
γῆς ἀφιέναι ἁμαρτίας, εἶπεν τῷ [g]παραλελυμένῳ," Σοὶ λέγω,
earth to forgive sins, he said to the paralysed, To thee I say,
[h]ἔγειραι," καὶ ἄρας τὸ.κλινίδιόν.σου πορεύου εἰς τὸν οἶκόν
Arise, and having taken up thy little couch go to [2]house
σου. 25 Καὶ παραχρῆμα ἀναστὰς ἐνώπιον αὐτῶν, ἄρας
[1]thy. And immediately having stood up before them, having taken up
ἐφ' [i]ᾧ" κατέκειτο, ἀπῆλθεν εἰς τὸν.οἶκον.αὐτοῦ, δοξάζων
[that] on which he was lying, he departed to his house, glorifying
τὸν θεόν. 26 καὶ ἔκστασις ἔλαβεν ἅπαντας, καὶ ἐδόξαζον
God. And amazement seized all, and they glorified
τὸν θεόν, καὶ ἐπλήσθησαν φόβου, λέγοντες, Ὅτι εἴδομεν
God, and were filled with fear, saying, We have seen
παράδοξα σήμερον.
strange things to-day.

27 And after these
things he went forth,
and saw a publican,
named Levi, sitting at
the receipt of custom:
and he said unto him,
Follow me. 28 And he
left all, rose up, and
followed him. 29 And
Levi made him a great
feast in his own house:
and there was a great
company of publicans
and of others that
sat down with them.
30 But their scribes
and Pharisees mur-
mured against his dis-
ciples, saying, Why do
ye eat and drink with
publicans and sinners?
31 And Jesus answer-
ing said unto them,
They that are whole
need not a physician;
but they that are sick.
32 I came not to call
the righteous, but sin-
ners to repentance.
33 And they said unto
him, Why do the dis-
ciples of John fast

27 Καὶ μετὰ ταῦτα ἐξῆλθεν, καὶ ἐθεάσατο τελώνην,
And after these things he went forth, and saw a tax-gatherer,
ὀνόματι [j]Λευΐν," καθήμενον ἐπὶ τὸ τελώνιον, καὶ εἶπεν αὐτῷ,
by name Levi, sitting at the tax office, and said to him,
Ἀκολούθει μοι. 28 Καὶ καταλιπὼν [k]ἅπαντα," ἀναστὰς [l]ἠκο-
Follow me. And having left all, having arisen he fol-
λούθησεν" αὐτῷ. 29 Καὶ ἐποίησεν δοχὴν μεγάλην [m]ὁ"
lowed him. And [2]made [5]entertainment [3]a [4]great
[n]Λευΐς" αὐτῷ ἐν τῇ.οἰκίᾳ.αὐτοῦ, καὶ ἦν ὄχλος [o]τελω-
[1]Levi for him in his house, and there was a [2]multitude [3]of [4]tax-
νῶν πολύς" καὶ ἄλλων οἳ ἦσαν μετ' αὐτῶν κατακείμενοι.
gatherers [1]great and others who were with them reclining
30 καὶ ἐγόγγυζον οἱ.[p]γραμματεῖς.αὐτῶν καὶ οἱ Φαρι-
[at table]. And murmured their scribes and the Phari-
σαῖοι" πρὸς τοὺς.μαθητὰς.αὐτοῦ, λέγοντες, [q]Διατί" μετὰ
sees at his disciples, saying, Why with
[r]τελωνῶν [s]καὶ ἁμαρτωλῶν" ἐσθίετε καὶ πίνετε; 31 καὶ ἀπο-
tax-gatherers and sinners do ye eat and drink? And an-
κριθεὶς ὁ Ἰησοῦς εἶπεν πρὸς αὐτούς, Οὐ χρείαν ἔχουσιν οἱ
swering Jesus said to them, No need have they who
ὑγιαίνοντες ἰατροῦ, [t]ἀλλ'" οἱ κακῶς ἔχοντες. 32 οὐκ
are in health of a physician, but they who ill are. [3]Not
ἐλήλυθα καλέσαι δικαίους, ἀλλὰ ἁμαρτωλοὺς εἰς μετά-
[1]I [2]have come to call righteous [ones], but sinners to repent-
νοιαν. 33 Οἱ.δὲ [v]εἶπον" πρὸς αὐτόν, [w]Διατί" οἱ μαθηταὶ
ance. And they said to him, Why [2]the [3]disciples

---

[d] — ἀποκριθεὶς L[Tr]. [e] Ἔγειρε GLTTrAW. [f] ὁ υἱὸς τοῦ ἀνθρώπου ἐξουσίαν ἔχει TTrA. [g] παραλυτικῷ paralytic L. [h] ἔγειρε GLTTrAW. [i] ὃ TTrA. [j] Λευεὶν A; Λευείν TTr. [k] πάντα LTTrA. [l] ἠκολούθει LTTrA. [m] — ὁ GLTTrAW. [n] Λευεὶς A; Λευεὶς TTr. [o] πολὺς τελωνῶν LTTrA. [p] Φαρισαῖοι καὶ οἱ γραμματεῖς αὐτῶν ([αὐτῶν] Tr) LTTrAW. [q] Διὰ τί LTrA. [r] + τῶν the GLTTrAW. [s] — καὶ ἁμαρτωλῶν A. [t] ἀλλὰ LTTrA. [v] εἶπαν LTTrA. [w] Διὰ τί L[Tr]; — Διατί TA.

[x]Ἰωάννου‖ νηστεύουσιν πυκνὰ καὶ δεήσεις ποιοῦνται, ὁ-
[4]of [5]John [1]fast often and supplications make, in like
μοίως καὶ οἱ τῶν Φαρισαίων, οἱ.δὲ σοὶ ἐσθίουσιν καὶ
manner also those of the Pharisees, but those of thee eat and
πίνουσιν; 34 Ὁ.δὲ [y] εἶπεν πρὸς αὐτούς, Μὴ δύνασθε τοὺς
drink? And he said to them, Are ye able [3]the
υἱοὺς τοῦ νυμφῶνος, ἐν.ᾧ ὁ νυμφίος μετ' αὐτῶν ἐστιν
[4]sons [5]of [6]the [7]bridechamber [10]while [11]the [12]bridegroom [14]with [15]them [13]is
ποιῆσαι [z]νηστεύειν‖; 35 ἐλεύσονται.δὲ ἡμέραι [a]καὶ‖ ὅταν
[1]to [2]make [8]to [9]fast? But will come days [2]also [1]when
ἀπαρθῇ ἀπ' αὐτῶν ὁ νυμφίος, τότε νηστεύσουσιν ἐν
shall be taken away from them the bridegroom, then they will fast in
ἐκείναις ταῖς ἡμέραις. 36 Ἔλεγεν.δὲ καὶ παραβολὴν πρὸς
those days. And he spoke also a parable to
αὐτούς, Ὅτι οὐδεὶς ἐπίβλημα [b] ἱματίου καινοῦ [c] ἐπιβάλλει ἐπὶ
them, No one a piece of a [2]garment [1]new puts on
ἱμάτιον παλαιόν· εἰ.δὲ.μήγε καὶ τὸ καινὸν [d]σχίζει,‖ καὶ
[3]garment [1]an [2]old, otherwise both the new he rends, and
τῷ παλαιῷ [e]οὐ.συμφωνεῖ‖. [f] ἐπίβλημα τὸ ἀπὸ τοῦ
with the old does not agree [the] piece which [is] from the
καινοῦ. 37 καὶ οὐδεὶς βάλλει οἶνον νέον εἰς ἀσκοὺς παλαιούς·
new. And no one puts [2]wine [1]new into [2]skins [1]old,
εἰ.δὲ.μήγε ῥήξει [g]ὁ νέος οἶνος‖ τοὺς ἀσκούς, καὶ αὐτὸς
otherwise [4]will [5]burst [1]the [2]new [3]wine the skins, and it
ἐκχυθήσεται, καὶ οἱ ἀσκοὶ ἀπολοῦνται· 38 ἀλλὰ οἶνον νέον
will be poured out, and the skins will be destroyed; but [2]wine [1]new
εἰς ἀσκοὺς καινοὺς βλητέον, [h]καὶ ἀμφότεροι συντηροῦνται.‖
into [2]skins [1]new is to be put, and both are preserved together.
39 καὶ οὐδεὶς πιὼν παλαιὸν [i]εὐθέως‖ θέλει νέον·
And no one having drunk old [wine] immediately desires new;
λέγει.γάρ, Ὁ παλαιὸς [k]χρηστότερός‖ ἐστιν.
for he says, The old [2]better [1]is.

6 Ἐγένετο.δὲ ἐν σαββάτῳ [l]δευτεροπρώτῳ‖ διαπο-
And it came to pass on [4]sabbath [[1]the] [2]second [3]first [6]passed
ρεύεσθαι αὐτὸν διὰ [m]τῶν‖ σπορίμων· καὶ ἔτιλλον οἱ
[7]along [5]he through the corn fields; and [3]were [4]plucking
μαθηταὶ.αὐτοῦ [n]τοὺς στάχυας, καὶ ἤσθιον,‖ ψώχοντες
[1]his [2]disciples the ears, and were eating, rubbing [them]
ταῖς χερσίν[o]. 2 τινὲς.δὲ τῶν Φαρισαίων εἶπον [p]αὐτοῖς,‖ Τί
in the hands. But some of the Pharisees said to them, Why
ποιεῖτε ὃ οὐκ.ἔξεστιν [q]ποιεῖν ἐν‖ τοῖς σάββασιν; 3 Καὶ
do ye that which it is not lawful to do on the sabbaths? And
ἀποκριθεὶς [r]πρὸς αὐτοὺς εἶπεν ὁ Ἰησοῦς,‖ Οὐδὲ τοῦτο ἀνέγνωτε,
answering to them [2]said [1]Jesus, Not even this did ye read,
ὃ ἐποίησεν [s]Δαβίδ,‖ [t]ὁπότε‖ ἐπείνασεν αὐτὸς καὶ οἱ
that which [2]did [1]David, when he hungered, himself and those who
μετ' αὐτοῦ [v]ὄντες‖; 4 [w]ὡς‖ εἰσῆλθεν εἰς τὸν οἶκον τοῦ θεοῦ,
with him were? how he entered into the house of God,
καὶ τοὺς ἄρτους τῆς προθέσεως [xa]ἔλαβεν, καὶ‖ ἔφαγεν, καὶ
and the loaves of the presentation took, and ate, and

often, and make prayers, and likewise *the* *disciples* of the Pharisees; but thine eat and drink? 34 And he said unto them, Can ye make the children of the bridechamber fast, while the bridegroom is with them? 35 But the days will come, when the bridegroom shall be taken away from them, and then shall they fast in those days. 36 And he spake also a parable unto them; No man putteth a piece of a new garment upon an old; if otherwise, then both the new maketh a rent, and the piece that was *taken* out of the new agreeth not with the old. 37 And no man putteth new wine into old bottles; else the new wine will burst the bottles, and be spilled, and the bottles shall perish. 38 But new wine must be put into new bottles; and both are preserved. 39 No man also having drunk old *wine* straightway desireth new: for he saith, The old is better.

VI. And it came to pass on the second sabbath after the first, that he went through the corn fields; and his disciples plucked the ears of corn, and did eat, rubbing *them* in *their* hands. 2 And certain of the Pharisees said unto them, Why do ye that which is not lawful to do on the sabbath days? 3 And Jesus answering them said, Have ye not read so much as this, what David did, when himself was an hungered, and they which were with him; 4 how he went into the house of God, and did take and eat the shewbread, and gave

[x] Ἰωάνου Tr. [y] + Ἰησοῦς (And) Jesus TTrA. [z] νηστεῦσαι TTrA. [a] [καὶ] L. [b] + ἀπὸ from (a garment) [L]TTrA. [c] + σχίσας having rent (*read* puts [it]) TTrA. [d] σχίσει he will rend LTTrA. [e] οὐ συμφωνήσει will not agree LTTrA. [f] + τὸ the TTrA. [g] ὁ οἶνος ὁ νέος LTTrAW. [h] — καὶ ἀμφότεροι συντηροῦνται T[Tr]A. [i] — εὐθέως TTrA. [k] χρηστός good TTrA. [l] — δευτεροπρώτῳ [L]Tr[A]. [m] — τῶν LTTrA. [n] καὶ ἤσθιον τοὺς στάχυας TrA. [o] + [αὐτῶν] of them L. [p] — αὐτοῖς [L]TTrA. [q] — ἐν T; — ποιεῖν ἐν (*read* τοῖς on the) LTrA. [r] ὁ Ἰησοῦς εἶπεν πρὸς αὐτούς L; ὁ Ἰησοῦς πρὸς αὐτοὺς εἶπεν T. [s] Δαυΐδ GW; Δαυείδ LTTrA. [t] ὅτε LTr. [v] — ὄντες LTr. [w] πῶς L; [ὡς] Tr. [xa] λαβὼν having taken LTrA.

also to them that
were with him; which
it is not lawful to eat
but for the priests
alone? 5 And he said
unto them, That the
Son of man is Lord
also of the sabbath.

6 And it came to
pass also on another
sabbath, that he en-
tered into the syna-
gogue and taught: and
there was a man whose
right hand was with-
ered. 7 And the scribes
and Pharisees watched
him, whether he would
heal on the sabbath
day; that they might
find an accusation a-
gainst him. 8 But he
knew their thoughts,
and said to the man
which had the with-
ered hand, Rise up,
and stand forth in
the midst. And he
arose and stood forth.
9 Then said Jesus unto
them, I will ask you
one thing; Is it law-
ful on the sabbath
days to do good, or to
do evil? to save life,
or to destroy *it*? 10 And
looking round about
upon them all, he said
unto the man, Stretch
forth thy hand. And
he did so: and his hand
was restored whole as
the other. 11 And they
were filled with mad-
ness; and communed
one with another what
they might do to Jesus.

12 And it came to
pass in those days, that
he went out into a
mountain to pray, and
continued all night in
prayer to God. 13 And
when it was day, he
called *unto him* his disciples: and of them he
chose twelve, whom
also he named apo-
stles; 14 Simon, (whom
he also named Peter,)
and Andrew his bro-
ther, James and John,
Philip and Bartholo-
mew, 15 Matthew and
Thomas, James the *son*

ἔδωκεν [y]καὶ‖ τοῖς μετ' αὐτοῦ, οὓς οὐκ-ἔξεστιν φαγεῖν εἰ-μὴ
gave also to those with him, which it is not lawful to eat except
μόνους τοὺς ἱερεῖς; 5 Καὶ ἔλεγεν αὐτοῖς, [z]"Οτι‖ κύριός ἐστιν
[3]only [1]the [2]priests? And he said to them, [6]Lord [5]is
ὁ υἱὸς τοῦ ἀνθρώπου καὶ τοῦ σαββάτου.
[1]the [2]Son [3]of [4]man also of the sabbath.
6 Ἐγένετο-δὲ [a]καὶ‖ ἐν ἑτέρῳ σαββάτῳ εἰσελθεῖν αὐτὸν
And it came to pass also on another sabbath [2]entered [1]he
εἰς τὴν συναγωγὴν καὶ διδάσκειν· καὶ ἦν [b]ἐκεῖ ἄνθρωπος,‖
into the synagogue and taught; and there was there a man,
καὶ ἡ-χεὶρ-αὐτοῦ ἡ δεξιὰ ἦν ξηρά. 7 [c]παρετήρουν‖-δὲ [d]αὐτὸν‖
and his hand the right was withered. And [6]were [7]watching [8]him
οἱ γραμματεῖς καὶ οἱ Φαρισαῖοι, εἰ ἐν τῷ σαββάτῳ [e]θερα-
[1]the [2]scribes [3]and [4]the [5]Pharisees, whether on the sabbath he will
πεύσει,‖ ἵνα εὕρωσιν [f]κατηγορίαν‖ αὐτοῦ. 8 αὐτὸς-δὲ
heal, that they might find an accusation against him. But he
ᾔδει τοὺς-διαλογισμοὺς-αὐτῶν, [g]καὶ εἶπεν‖ τῷ [h]ἀνθρώπῳ‖ τῷ
knew their reasonings, and said to the man who
ξηρὰν ἔχοντι τὴν χεῖρα, [i]Ἔγειραι,‖ καὶ στῆθι εἰς τὸ μέσον.
[3]withered [1]had [2]the hand, Arise, and stand in the midst.
[k]Ὁ-δὲ‖ ἀναστὰς ἔστη. 9 Εἶπεν [l]οὖν‖ ὁ Ἰησοῦς πρὸς αὐτούς,
And he having risen up stood. [3]Said [1]then [2]Jesus to them,
[m]Ἐπερωτήσω‖ ὑμᾶς, [n]τί‖ ἔξεστιν [o]τοῖς σάββασιν‖ ἀγαθο-
I will ask you, whether it is lawful on the sabbaths to do
ποιῆσαι ἢ κακοποιῆσαι; ψυχὴν σῶσαι ἢ [p]ἀπολέσαι‖; 10 Καὶ
good or to do evil? [3]life [1]to [2]save or to destroy? And
περιβλεψάμενος πάντας αὐτοὺς εἶπεν [q]τῷ ἀνθρώπῳ,‖
having looked around on all them he said to the man,
Ἔκτεινον τὴν-χεῖρά-σου. Ὁ-δὲ ἐποίησεν [r]οὕτως·‖ καὶ [s]ἀπο-
Stretch out thy hand. And he did so, and [3]was
κατεστάθη‖ ἡ-χεὶρ-αὐτοῦ [t]ὑγιὴς‖ [v]ὡς ἡ ἄλλη.‖ 11 αὐτοὶ-δὲ
[4]restored [1]his [2]hand sound as the other. But they
ἐπλήσθησαν ἀνοίας, καὶ διελάλουν πρὸς ἀλλήλους τί
were filled with madness, and consulted with one another [as to] what
ἂν [w]ποιήσειαν‖ τῷ Ἰησοῦ.
they should do to Jesus.

12 Ἐγένετο-δὲ ἐν ταῖς-ἡμέραις-ταύταις [x]ἐξῆλθεν‖ εἰς τὸ
And it came to pass in those days he went out into the
ὄρος προσεύξασθαι· καὶ ἦν διανυκτερεύων ἐν τῇ προσευχῇ
mountain to pray, and he was spending the night in prayer
τοῦ θεοῦ. 13 καὶ ὅτε ἐγένετο ἡμέρα προσεφώνησεν τοὺς
of God. And when it became day he called to [him]
μαθητὰς-αὐτοῦ· καὶ ἐκλεξάμενος ἀπ' αὐτῶν δώδεκα, οὓς καὶ
his disciples, and chose out from them twelve, whom also
ἀποστόλους ὠνόμασεν, 14 Σίμωνα ὃν καὶ ὠνόμασεν Πέτρον
[3]apostles [1]he [2]named: Simon whom also he named Peter
καὶ Ἀνδρέαν τὸν-ἀδελφὸν-αὐτοῦ, [ya]Ἰάκωβον καὶ [za]Ἰωάννην,‖
and Andrew his brother, James and John,
[ya]Φίλιππον καὶ Βαρθολομαῖον, 15 [ya] [aa]Ματθαῖον‖ καὶ Θωμᾶν,
Philip and Bartholomew, Matthew and Thomas,

---

[y] — καὶ LTrA. [z] [ὅτι] Tr. [a] — καὶ LTTr[A]. [b] ἄνθρωπος ἐκεῖ TTrA. [c] παρετηροῦντο LTTrAW. [d] — αὐτὸν LTTrAW. [e] θεραπεύει he heals LTTrA. [f] κατηγορεῖν to accuse TTrA. [g] εἶπεν δὲ TTrA. [h] ἀνδρὶ man TTrA. [i] Ἔγειρε GLTTrAW. [k] καὶ LTTrA. [l] δὲ and LTTr. [m] Ἐπερωτῶ I ask TTrA. [n] εἰ if LTTrA. [o] τῷ σαββάτῳ on the sabbath LTTrA. [p] ἀποκτεῖναι to kill GW. [q] αὐτῷ to him GLTTrAW. [r] — οὕτως GTTrAW. [s] ἀπεκατεστάθη GLTTrA. [t] — ὑγιὴς GLTTrAW. [v] — ὡς ἡ ἄλλη [L]T[Tr]A. [w] ποιήσαιεν LTTrA. [x] ἐξελθεῖν αὐτὸν he went out TTrA. [ya] + καὶ and LTTrA. [za] Ἰωάνην Tr. [aa] Μαθθαῖον LTTrA.

a 'Ἰάκωβον bτὸν τοῦ‖ Ἀλφαίου καὶ Σίμωνα τὸν καλού-
James the [son] of Alphæus and Simon who [was] call-
μενον Ζηλωτήν, 16 c Ἰούδαν Ἰακώβου, καὶ Ἰούδαν
ed Zealot, Judas [brother] of James, and Judas
d Ἰσκαριώτην,‖ ὃς eκαὶ‖ ἐγένετο προδότης· 17 καὶ καταβὰς
Iscariote, who also became [the] betrayer. And descending
μετ' αὐτῶν ἔστη ἐπὶ τόπου πεδινοῦ, καὶ ὄχλος f μαθητῶν
with them he stood on a ²place ¹level, and a crowd of ²disciples
αὐτοῦ καὶ πλῆθος πολὺ τοῦ λαοῦ ἀπὸ πάσης τῆς Ἰουδαίας
¹his and a ²multitude ¹great of the people from all Judæa
καὶ Ἱερουσαλὴμ καὶ τῆς παραλίου Τύρου καὶ Σιδῶνος, οἳ
and Jerusalem and the sea coast of Tyre and Sidon, who
ἦλθον ἀκοῦσαι αὐτοῦ, καὶ ἰαθῆναι ἀπὸ τῶν.νόσων.αὐτῶν,
came to hear him, and to be healed of their diseases,
18 καὶ οἱ gὀχλούμενοι‖ hὑπὸ‖ πνευμάτων ἀκαθάρτων, iκαὶ‖
and those beset by ²spirits ¹unclean, and
ἐθεραπεύοντο. 19 καὶ πᾶς ὁ ὄχλος kἐζήτει‖ ἅπτεσθαι αὐτοῦ·
they were healed. And all the crowd sought to touch him;
ὅτι δύναμις παρ' αὐτοῦ ἐξήρχετο καὶ ἰᾶτο πάντας.
for power from him went out and healed all.

of Alphæus, and Simon called Zelotes, 16 and Judas *the brother* of James, and Judas Iscariot, which also was the traitor. 17 And he came down with them, and stood in the plain, and the company of his disciples, and a great multitude of people out of all Judæa and Jerusalem, and from the sea coast of Tyre and Sidon, which came to hear him, and to be healed of their diseases; 18 and they that were vexed with unclean spirits: and they were healed. 19 And the whole multitude sought to touch him: for there went virtue out of him, and healed *them* all.

20 Καὶ αὐτὸς ἐπάρας τοὺς.ὀφθαλμοὺς.αὐτοῦ εἰς τοὺς μαθη-
And he lifting up his eyes upon ²disci-
τὰς αὐτοῦ ἔλεγεν, Μακάριοι οἱ πτωχοί, ὅτι ὑμετέρα ἐστὶν
ples ¹his said, Blessed [are] the poor, for yours is
ἡ βασιλεία τοῦ θεοῦ. 21 μακάριοι οἱ πεινῶντες νῦν, ὅτι
the kingdom of God. Blessed [ye] who hunger now, for
χορτασθήσεσθε. μακάριοι οἱ κλαίοντες νῦν, ὅτι γελάσετε.
ye shall be filled. Blessed [ye] who weep now, for ye shall laugh.
22 μακάριοί ἐστε ὅταν μισήσωσιν ὑμᾶς οἱ ἄνθρωποι, καὶ ὅταν
Blessed are ye when ²shall ³hate ⁴you ¹men, and when
ἀφορίσωσιν ὑμᾶς, καὶ ὀνειδίσωσιν, καὶ ἐκβάλωσιν τὸ
they shall cut ²off ¹you, and shall reproach [you], and cast out
ὄνομα.ὑμῶν ὡς πονηρόν, lἕνεκα‖ τοῦ υἱοῦ τοῦ ἀνθρώπου·
your name as wicked, on account of the Son of man:
23 mχαίρετε‖ ἐν ἐκείνῃ τῇ ἡμέρᾳ καὶ σκιρτήσατε· ἰδοὺ.γάρ, ὁ
rejoice in that day and leap for joy; for lo,
μισθὸς.ὑμῶν πολὺς ἐν τῷ οὐρανῷ· κατὰ nταῦτα‖ γὰρ
your reward [is] great in the heaven, ²according ³to ⁴these ⁵things ¹for
ἐποίουν τοῖς προφήταις οἱ.πατέρες.αὐτῶν. 24 Πλὴν οὐαὶ
did ³to ⁴the ⁵prophets ¹their ²fathers. But woe
ὑμῖν τοῖς πλουσίοις, ὅτι ἀπέχετε τὴν.παράκλησιν.ὑμῶν.
to you the rich, for ye are receiving your consolation.
25 οὐαὶ ὑμῖν οἱ ἐμπεπλησμένοιo, ὅτι πεινάσετε. οὐαὶ pὑμῖν‖
Woe to you who have been filled, for ye shall hunger. Woe to you
οἱ γελῶντες νῦν, ὅτι πενθήσετε καὶ κλαύσετε. 26 οὐαὶ qὑμῖν‖
who laugh now, for ye shall mourn and weep. Woe to you
ὅταν καλῶς rὑμᾶς εἴπωσιν‖ sπάντες‖ οἱ ἄνθρωποι· κατὰ
when well of you speak all men, ²according ³to
nταῦτα‖ γὰρ ἐποίουν τοῖς ψευδοπροφήταις οἱ.πατέρες.αὐτῶν.
⁴these ⁵things ¹for did ³to ⁴the ⁵false ⁶prophets ¹their ²fathers.
27 t'Ἀλλ'‖ ὑμῖν λέγω τοῖς ἀκούουσιν, Ἀγαπᾶτε τοὺς ἐχθροὺς
But to you I say who hear, Love ²enemies

20 And he lifted up his eyes on his disciples, and said, Blessed *be ye* poor: for yours is the kingdom of God. 21 Blessed *are ye* that hunger now: for ye shall be filled. Blessed *are ye* that weep now: for ye shall laugh. 22 Blessed are ye, when men shall hate you, and when they shall separate you *from their company*, and shall reproach *you*, and cast out your name as evil, for the Son of man's sake. 23 Rejoice ye in that day, and leap for joy: for, behold, your reward *is* great in heaven: for in the like manner did their fathers unto the prophets. 24 But woe unto you that are rich! for ye have received your consolation. 25 Woe unto you that are full! for ye shall hunger. Woe unto you that laugh now! for ye shall mourn and weep. 26 Woe unto you, when all men shall speak well of you! for so did their fathers to the false prophets. 27 But I say unto you which hear, Love your enemies, do good to them which hate you, 28 bless them that

a + καὶ and T. b — τὸν τοῦ TTrA. c + καὶ and LTTrA. d Ἰσκαριώθ LTTrA. e — καὶ LT[Tr]A. f + πολὺς great T. g ἐνοχλούμενοι TTrA. h ἀπὸ GLTTrAW. i — καὶ (omit and they) LTTrA. k ἐζήτουν TTrA. l ἕνεκεν L. m χάρητε GLTTrAW. n τὰ αὐτὰ the same things LTTrA. o + νῦν now T[Tr]A. p — ὑμῖν TTrA. q — ὑμῖν GLTTrAW. r εἴπωσιν ὑμᾶς T. s — πάντες G. t Ἀλλὰ LTTrAW.

curse you, and pray
for them which de-
spitefully use you.
29 And unto him that
smiteth thee on the
one cheek offer also the
other; and him that
taketh away thy cloke
forbid not *to take thy*
coat also. 30 Give to
every man that asketh
of thee; and of him
that taketh away thy
goods ask *them* not
again. 31 And as ye
would that men should
do to you, do ye also to
them likewise. 32 For
if ye love them which
love you, what thank
have ye? for sinners
also love those that
love them. 33 And if
ye do good to them
which do good to you,
what thank have ye?
for sinners also do even
the same. 34 And if
ye lend *to them* of
whom ye hope to re-
ceive, what thank have
ye? for sinners also
lend to sinners, to re-
ceive as much again.
35 But love ye your
enemies, and do good,
and lend, hoping for
nothing again; and
your reward shall be
great, and ye shall be
the children of the
Highest: for he is kind
unto the unthankful
and *to* the evil. 36 Be
ye therefore merciful,
as your Father also is
merciful. 37 Judge not,
and ye shall not be
judged: condemn not,
and ye shall not be
condemned: forgive,
and ye shall be for-
given: 38 give, and
it shall be given
unto you; good mea-
sure, pressed down,
and shaken together,
and running over,
shall men give into
your bosom. For with
the same measure that
ye mete withal it shall
be measured to you

ὑμῶν, καλῶς ποιεῖτε τοῖς μισοῦσιν ὑμᾶς, 28 εὐλογεῖτε
[1]your, [4]well [3]do to those who hate you, bless
τοὺς καταρωμένους [v]ὑμῖν,‖ [w]καὶ‖ προσεύχεσθε [x]ὑπὲρ‖ τῶν
those who curse you, and pray for those who
ἐπηρεαζόντων ὑμᾶς. 29 τῷ τύπτοντί σε [y]ἐπὶ‖ τὴν σιαγόνα,
despitefully use you. To him who strikes thee on the cheek,
πάρεχε καὶ τὴν ἄλλην· καὶ ἀπὸ τοῦ αἴροντός σου τὸ
offer also the other; and from him who takes away thy
ἱμάτιον, καὶ τὸν χιτῶνα μὴ.κωλύσῃς. 30 παντὶ [z]δὲ τῷ‖
cloak, also the tunic do not forbid. [2]To [3]every [4]one [1]and who
αἰτοῦντί σε, δίδου· καὶ ἀπὸ τοῦ αἴροντος τὰ.σά,
asks thee, give; and from him who takes away what [is] thine,
μὴ.ἀπαίτει. 31 καὶ καθὼς θέλετε ἵνα ποιῶσιν ὑμῖν οἱ
ask [it] not back; and according as ye desire that [2]should [3]do [4]to [5]you
ἄνθρωποι, [a]καὶ ὑμεῖς‖ ποιεῖτε αὐτοῖς ὁμοίως. 32 καὶ εἰ
[1]men, also [2]ye [1]do to them in like manner. And if
ἀγαπᾶτε τοὺς ἀγαπῶντας ὑμᾶς, ποία ὑμῖν χάρις ἐστίν;
ye love those who love you, what [4]to [5]you [1]thank [2]is [3]it?
καὶ.γὰρ οἱ ἁμαρτωλοὶ τοὺς ἀγαπῶντας αὐτοὺς ἀγαπῶσιν.
for even sinners [2]those [3]who [4]love [5]them [1]love.
33 καὶ [b] ἐὰν ἀγαθοποιῆτε τοὺς ἀγαθοποιοῦντας ὑμᾶς,
And if ye do good to those who do good to you,
ποία ὑμῖν [c]χάρις ἐστίν‖; καὶ [d]γὰρ‖ οἱ ἁμαρτωλοὶ τὸ αὐτὸ
what [2]to [3]you [1]thank is it? [2]even [1]for sinners [2]the [3]same
ποιοῦσιν. 34 καὶ ἐὰν [e]δανείζητε‖ παρ᾽ ὧν ἐλπίζετε
[1]do. And if ye lend [to those] from whom ye hope
[f]ἀπολαβεῖν,‖ ποία ὑμῖν χάρις ἐστίν; καὶ [g]γὰρ‖ [h]οἱ‖ ἁμαρτωλοὶ
to receive, what [2]to [3]you [1]thank is it? [2]even [1]for sinners
ἁμαρτωλοῖς [i]δανείζουσιν,‖ ἵνα ἀπολάβωσιν τὰ [k]ἴσα.‖ 35 πλὴν
[2]to [3]sinners [1]lend, that they may receive the like. But
ἀγαπᾶτε τοὺς.ἐχθροὺς.ὑμῶν, καὶ ἀγαθοποιεῖτε, καὶ [l]δανείζετε‖
love your enemies, and do good, and lend,
[m]μηδὲν‖ [n]ἀπελπίζοντες·‖ καὶ ἔσται ὁ.μισθὸς.ὑμῶν πολύς[o],
[3]nothing [1]hoping [2]for again; and [3]shall [4]be your [2]reward great,
καὶ ἔσεσθε υἱοὶ [p]τοῦ‖ ὑψίστου· ὅτι αὐτὸς χρηστός ἐστιν ἐπὶ
and ye shall be sons of the Highest; for he [2]good [1]is to
τοὺς ἀχαρίστους καὶ πονηρούς. 36 γίνεσθε [q]οὖν‖ οἰκτίρμονες,
the unthankful and wicked. Be ye therefore compassionate,
καθὼς [r]καὶ‖ ὁ.πατὴρ.ὑμῶν οἰκτίρμων ἐστίν. 37 καὶ μὴ.κρίνετε,
as also your father [2]compassionate [1]is. And judge not,
[s]καὶ οὐ‖.μὴ κριθῆτε· [t] μὴ.καταδικάζετε, καὶ οὐ.μὴ κατα-
that in no wise ye be judged; condemn not, that in no wise ye be
δικασθῆτε. ἀπολύετε, καὶ ἀπολυθήσεσθε· 38 δίδοτε, καὶ
condemned. Release, and ye shall be released. Give, and
δοθήσεται ὑμῖν. μέτρον καλόν πεπιεσμένον [va]καὶ‖ σεσαλευ-
it shall be given to you, [2]measure [1]good, pressed down and shaken to-
μένον [va]καὶ‖ [wa]ὑπερεκχυνόμενον‖ δώσουσιν εἰς τὸν κόλπον
gether and running over shall they give into [2]bosom
ὑμῶν· [xa]τῷ γὰρ αὐτῷ μέτρῳ ᾧ‖ μετρεῖτε, ἀντιμε-
[1]your: [4]with [5]the [3]for same measure with which ye mete, it shall be

---

[v] ὑμᾶς GLTTrA. [w] — καὶ GLTTrAW. [x] περὶ TA. [y] εἰς T. [z] [δὲ τῷ] L; — δὲ τῷ T; [δὲ] τῷ Tr. [a] [καὶ ὑμεῖς] L. [b] + γὰρ (*read* for if ye also) T. [c] ἐστὶν χάρις L. [d] — γὰρ T. [e] δανείσητε L; δανίσητε T; δανείζετε TrA. [f] λαβεῖν TTrA. [g] — γὰρ T[Tr]A. [h] — οἱ LTTrA. [i] δανίζουσιν T. [k] ἴσα LTAW. [l] δανίζετε T. [m] μηδένα T. [n] ἀφελπίζοντες L. [o] + [ἐν τοῖς οὐρανοῖς] in the heavens L. [p] — τοῦ (*read* of [the]) GLTTrAW. [q] — οὖν LTTrA. [r] — καὶ [L]T[Tr]. [s] ἵνα (*read* that ye be not judged) L. [t] + καὶ and TA. [va] — καὶ LTTrA. [wa] ὑπερεκχυννόμενον LTTrA. [xa] ᾧ γὰρ μέτρῳ LTTr.

τρηθήσεται ὑμῖν. 39 Εἶπεν.δὲ [y] παραβολὴν αὐτοῖς, Μήτι
measured again to you. And he spoke a parable to them,
δύναται τυφλὸς τυφλὸν ὁδηγεῖν; οὐχὶ ἀμφότεροι εἰς
Is [4]able [1]a [2]blind [[3]man] a blind [man] to lead? [2]not [3]both [4]into
βόθυνον [z]πεσοῦνται‖; 40 οὐκ ἔστιν μαθητὴς ὑπὲρ τὸν διδάσκα-
[5]a [6]pit [1]will fall? [4]not [3]is [1]a [2]disciple above the teacher
λον [a]αὐτοῦ·‖ κατηρτισμένος.δὲ πᾶς ἔσται ὡς ὁ διδάσκαλος
of him; but [3]perfected [1]every [2]one shall be as [2]teacher
αὐτοῦ. 41 τί.δὲ βλέπεις τὸ κάρφος τὸ ἐν τῷ ὀφθαλμῷ
[1]his. But why lookest thou on the mote that [is] in the eye
τοῦ.ἀδελφοῦ.σου, τὴν.δὲ δοκὸν τὴν ἐν τῷ.ἰδίῳ ὀφθαλμῷ
of thy brother, but the beam that [is] in thine own eye
οὐ.κατανοεῖς; 42 [b]ἢ‖ πῶς δύνασαι λέγειν τῷ.ἀδελφῷ.σου,
perceivest not? or how art thou able to say to thy brother,
Ἀδελφέ, ἄφες ἐκβάλω τὸ κάρφος τὸ ἐν τῷ ὀφθαλμῷ
Brother, suffer [that] I may cast out the mote that [is] in [2]eye
σου, αὐτὸς τὴν ἐν τῷ.ὀφθαλμῷ.σου δοκὸν οὐ βλέπων; ὑπο-
[1]thine, thyself the [2]in [3]thine [[4]own] [5]eye [1]beam not seeing? Hypo-
κριτά, ἔκβαλε πρῶτον τὴν δοκὸν ἐκ τοῦ.ὀφθαλμοῦ.σου, καὶ
crite, cast out first the beam out of thine [own] eye, and
τότε διαβλέψεις [c]ἐκβαλεῖν‖ τὸ κάρφος τὸ ἐν τῷ ὀφθαλμῷ
then thou wilt see clearly to cast out the mote that [is] in the eye
τοῦ.ἀδελφοῦ.σου[d]. 43 οὐ.γάρ ἐστιν δένδρον καλὸν ποιοῦν
of thy brother. For [3]not [1]there [2]is [4]a [6]tree [5]good producing
καρπὸν σαπρόν· οὐδὲ[e] δένδρον σαπρὸν ποιοῦν καρπὸν καλόν·
[2]fruit [1]corrupt; nor a [2]tree [1]corrupt producing [2]fruit [1]good;
44 ἕκαστον.γὰρ δένδρον ἐκ τοῦ.ἰδίου καρποῦ γινώσκεται· οὐ.γὰρ
for each tree by its own fruit is known, for not
ἐξ ἀκανθῶν συλλέγουσιν σῦκα, οὐδὲ ἐκ βάτου [f]τρυγῶσιν
from thorns do they gather figs, nor from a bramble gather they
σταφυλήν.‖ 45 ὁ ἀγαθὸς ἄνθρωπος ἐκ τοῦ ἀγαθοῦ θησαυροῦ
a bunch of grapes. The good man out of the good treasure
τῆς.καρδίας.[g]αὐτοῦ‖ προφέρει τὸ ἀγαθόν· καὶ ὁ πονη-
of his heart brings forth that which [is] good; and the wick-
ρὸς [h]ἄνθρωπος‖ ἐκ τοῦ πονηροῦ [i]θησαυροῦ τῆς καρδίας
ed man out of the wicked treasure of [2]heart
αὐτοῦ‖ προφέρει τὸ πονηρόν· ἐκ.γὰρ [k]τοῦ‖ περισσεύ-
[1]his brings forth that which [is] wicked; for out of the abun-
ματος [l]τῆς‖ καρδίας [m]λαλεῖ τὸ.στόμα.αὐτοῦ.‖ 46 Τί.δέ με
dance of the heart [3]speaks [1]his [2]mouth. And why me
καλεῖτε Κύριε, κύριε, καὶ οὐ.ποιεῖτε ἃ λέγω; 47 πᾶς ὁ ἐρ-
do ye call Lord, Lord, and do not what I say? Every one who
χόμενος πρός με καὶ ἀκούων μου.τῶν.λόγων καὶ ποιῶν αὐτούς,
is coming to me and hearing my words and doing them,
ὑποδείξω ὑμῖν τίνι ἐστὶν ὅμοιος. 48 ὅμοιός ἐστιν ἀνθρώπῳ
I will shew you to whom he is like. Like he is to a man
οἰκοδομοῦντι οἰκίαν, ὃς ἔσκαψεν καὶ ἐβάθυνεν, καὶ ἔθηκεν
building a house, who dug and deepened, and laid
θεμέλιον ἐπὶ τὴν πέτραν· [n]πλημμύρας‖.δὲ γενομένης [o]προσέρ-
a foundation on the rock; and a flood having come [3]burst
ῥηξεν‖ ὁ ποταμὸς τῇ.οἰκίᾳ.ἐκείνῃ, καὶ οὐκ.ἴσχυσεν σαλεῦσαι
[4]upon [1]the [2]stream that house, and could not shake

again. 39 And he spake a parable unto them, Can the blind lead the blind? shall they not both fall into the ditch? 40 The disciple is not above his master: but every one that is perfect shall be as his master. 41 And why beholdest thou the mote that is in thy brother's eye, but perceivest not the beam that is in thine own eye? 42 Either how canst thou say to thy brother, Brother, let me pull out the mote that is in thine eye, when thou thyself beholdest not the beam that is in thine own eye? Thou hypocrite, cast out first the beam out of thine own eye, and then shalt thou see clearly to pull out the mote that is in thy brother's eye. 43 For a good tree bringeth not forth corrupt fruit; neither doth a corrupt tree bring forth good fruit. 44 For every tree is known by his own fruit. For of thorns men do not gather figs, nor of a bramble bush gather they grapes. 45 A good man out of the good treasure of his heart bringeth forth that which is good; and an evil man out of the evil treasure of his heart bringeth forth that which is evil: for of the abundance of the heart his mouth speaketh. 46 And why call ye me, Lord, Lord, and do not the things which I say? 47 Whosoever cometh to me, and heareth my sayings, and doeth them, I will shew you to whom he is like: 48 he is like a man which built an house, and digged deep, and laid the foundation on a rock: and when the flood arose, the stream beat vehemently upon that house, and could not shake it: for it

---

[y] + καὶ also LTTrA. [z] ἐμπεσοῦνται LTTrA. [a] — αὐτοῦ LTTrA. [b] — ἢ T[Tr]A. [c] — ἐκβαλεῖν TA. [d] + ἐκβαλεῖν to cast out TA. [e] + πάλιν again [L]T[Tr]A. [f] σταφυλὴν τρυγῶσιν TTrA. [g] — αὐτοῦ (read [his] heart) T. [h] — ἄνθρωπος [L]TTrA. [i] — θησαυροῦ τῆς καρδίας αὐτοῦ [L]TTrA. [k] — τοῦ LTTrA. [l] — τῆς (read of [the]) LTTrA. [m] τὸ στόμα αὐτοῦ λαλεῖ L. [n] πλημμύρης TTrA. [o] προσέρηξεν TTr.

was founded upon a rock. 49 But he that heareth, and doeth not, is like a man that without a foundation built an house upon the earth; against which the stream did beat vehemently, and immediately it fell; and the ruin of that house was great.

VII. Now when he had ended all his sayings in the audience of the people, he entered into Capernaum. 2 And a certain centurion's servant, who was dear unto him, was sick, and ready to die. 3 And when he heard of Jesus, he sent unto him the elders of the Jews, beseeching him that he would come and heal his servant. 4 And when they came to Jesus, they besought him instantly, saying, That he was worthy for whom he should do this: 5 for he loveth our nation, and he hath built us a synagogue. 6 Then Jesus went with them. And when he was now not far from the house, the centurion sent friends to him, saying unto him, Lord, trouble not thyself: for I am not worthy that thou shouldest enter under my roof: 7 wherefore neither thought I myself worthy to come unto thee: but say in a word, and my servant shall be healed. 8 For I also am a man set under authority, having under me soldiers, and I say unto one, Go, and he goeth; and to another, Come, and he cometh; and to my servant, Do this, and he doeth *it*. 9 When Jesus heard these things, he marvelled at him, and turned him about, and said unto the people that followed him, I say

αὐτήν· [p]τεθεμελίωτο.γὰρ ἐπὶ τὴν πέτραν.‖ 49 ὁ.δὲ ἀκούσας
it, for it had been founded upon the rock. But he who heard
καὶ μὴ.ποιήσας ὅμοιός ἐστιν ἀνθρώπῳ [q]οἰκοδομήσαντι‖ οἰκίαν
and did not [2]like [1]is to a man having built a house
ἐπὶ τὴν γῆν χωρὶς θεμελίου· ᾗ [r]προσέῤῥηξεν‖ ὁ ποτα-
on the earth without a foundation; on which [3]burst [1]the [2]stream,
μός, καὶ [s]εὐθέως ἔπεσεν,‖ καὶ ἐγένετο τὸ ῥῆγμα τῆς οἰκίας
and immediately it fell, and [6]was [1]the [2]ruin [3]of [5]house
ἐκείνης μέγα.
[4]that great.

7 [t]Ἐπεὶ.δὲ‖ ἐπλήρωσεν πάντα τὰ.ῥήματα.αὐτοῦ εἰς τὰς
And when he had completed all his words in the
ἀκοὰς τοῦ λαοῦ εἰσῆλθεν εἰς [u]Καπερναούμ.‖ 2 Ἑκατοντάρχου
ears of the people he entered into Capernaum. [4]Of [5]a [7]centurion
δέ τινος δοῦλος κακῶς ἔχων ἤμελλεν τελευτᾷν, ὃς ἦν
[1]and [6]certain [2]a [3]bondman [9]ill [8]being was about to die, who was
αὐτῷ ἔντιμος. 3 ἀκούσας.δὲ περὶ τοῦ Ἰησοῦ ἀπέστειλεν πρὸς
by him honoured. And having heard about Jesus he sent to
αὐτὸν πρεσβυτέρους τῶν Ἰουδαίων, ἐρωτῶν αὐτὸν ὅπως
him elders of the Jews, begging him that
ἐλθὼν διασώσῃ τὸν.δοῦλον.αὐτοῦ. 4 οἱ.δὲ παραγενόμενοι
having come he might cure his bondman. And they having come
πρὸς τὸν Ἰησοῦν [v]παρεκάλουν‖ αὐτὸν σπουδαίως, λέγοντες,
to Jesus besought him diligently, saying,
Ὅτι ἄξιός ἐστιν ᾧ [w]παρέξει‖ τοῦτο· 5 ἀγαπᾷ.γὰρ τὸ
that [3]worthy [1]he [2]is to whom he shall grant this, for he loves
ἔθνος.ἡμῶν καὶ τὴν συναγωγὴν αὐτὸς ᾠκοδόμησεν ἡμῖν.
our nation and the synagogue he built for us.
6 Ὁ.δὲ.Ἰησοῦς ἐπορεύετο σὺν αὐτοῖς· ἤδη.δὲ αὐτοῦ οὐ μακρὰν
And Jesus went with them; but already he [2]not [3]far
ἀπέχοντος [x]ἀπὸ‖ τῆς οἰκίας, ἔπεμψεν [y]πρὸς αὐτὸν‖ [z]ὁ ἑκατόν-
[1]being distant from the house, [3]sent [4]to [5]him [1]the [2]cen-
ταρχος φίλους,‖ λέγων [a]αὐτῷ,‖ Κύριε, μὴ.σκύλλου· οὐ
turion friends, saying to him, Lord, trouble not [thyself], [4]not
γάρ [b]εἰμι ἱκανὸς‖ ἵνα [c]ὑπὸ τὴν.στέγην.μου‖ εἰσέλθῃς·
[1]for [2]I [3]am worthy that under my roof thou shouldest come;
7 διὸ οὐδὲ ἐμαυτὸν ἠξίωσα πρός σε ἐλθεῖν· ἀλλὰ
wherefore neither myself counted I worthy [3]to [4]thee [1]to [2]come; but
εἰπὲ λόγῳ, καὶ [d]ἰαθήσεται‖ ὁ.παῖς.μου. 8 καὶ.γὰρ ἐγὼ ἄν-
say by a word, and shall be healed my servant. For also I a
θρωπός εἰμι ὑπὸ ἐξουσίαν τασσόμενος, ἔχων ὑπ' ἐμαυτὸν
man am under authority appointed, having under myself
στρατιώτας, καὶ λέγω τούτῳ Πορεύθητι, καὶ πορεύεται·
soldiers, and I say to this [one] Go, and he goes;
καὶ ἄλλῳ, Ἔρχου. καὶ ἔρχεται· καὶ τῷ.δούλῳ.μου, Ποίησον
and to another, Come, and he comes; and to my bondman, Do
τοῦτο, καὶ ποιεῖ. 9 Ἀκούσας δὲ ταῦτα ὁ Ἰησοῦς ἐθαύ-
this, and he does [it]. And having heard these things Jesus won-
μασεν αὐτόν· καὶ στραφεὶς τῷ ἀκολουθοῦντι αὐτῷ ὄχλῳ
dered at him; and turning to the [2]following [3]him [1]crowd

---

[p] διὰ τὸ καλῶς οἰκοδομεῖσθαι (οἰκοδομῆσθαι T) αὐτήν because it was well built TTrA. [q] οἰκοδομοῦντι building L. [r] προσέρηξεν TTr. [s] εὐθὺς συνέπεσεν immediately it fell together TTrA. [t] Ἐπειδὴ after that LTTrA. [u] Καφαρναούμ LTTrAW. [v] ἠρώτων asked T. [w] παρέξῃ he should grant LTTrA. [x] — ἀπὸ (*read* τῆς from the) T. [y] — πρὸς αὐτὸν T. [z] φίλους ὁ ἑκατόνταρχος (ἑκατοντάρχης T) TTrA. [a] — αὐτῷ T. [b] ἱκανός εἰμι TTrA. [c] μου ὑπὸ τὴν στέγην W. [d] ἰαθήτω let be healed TTrA.

εἶπεν, Λέγω ὑμῖν, οὐδὲ ἐν τῷ Ἰσραὴλ τοσαύτην πίστιν εὗρον.
said, I say to you, not even in Israel so great faith did I find.
10 Καὶ ὑποστρέψαντες [e]οἱ πεμφθέντες εἰς τὸν οἶκον‖ εὗρον
And [3]having [4]returned [1]those [2]sent to the house found
τὸν [f]ἀσθενοῦντα‖ δοῦλον ὑγιαίνοντα.
the sick bondman in good health.
11 Καὶ ἐγένετο ἐν [g]τῇ‖ ἑξῆς [h]ἐπορεύετο‖ εἰς πόλιν
And it came to pass on the next [day] he went into a city
καλουμένην Ναΐν, καὶ συνεπορεύοντο αὐτῷ οἱ.μαθηταὶ.αὐτοῦ
called Nain, and went with him his [2]disciples
[i]ἱκανοὶ‖ καὶ ὄχλος πολύς. 12 ὡς.δὲ ἤγγισεν τῇ πύλῃ τῆς
[1]many and a [2]crowd [1]great. And as he drew near to the gate of the
πόλεως καὶ ἰδού, ἐξεκομίζετο [k]τεθνηκώς,‖ [l]υἱὸς μονο-
city [2]also [1]behold, was being carried out [one] who had died, an [2]son [1]only
γενὴς‖ τῇ.μητρὶ.αὐτοῦ, καὶ [m]αὕτη ἦν‖ χήρα· καὶ ὄχλος τῆς
to his mother, and she was a widow, and a [2]crowd [3]of [4]the
πόλεως ἱκανὸς [n] σὺν αὐτῇ. 13 καὶ ἰδὼν αὐτὴν ὁ κύριος
[5]city [1]considerable [was] with her. And seeing her the Lord
ἐσπλαγχνίσθη ἐπ' [o]αὐτῇ‖ καὶ εἶπεν αὐτῇ, Μὴ.κλαῖε.
was moved with compassion on her and said to her, Weep not.
14 Καὶ προσελθὼν ἥψατο τῆς σοροῦ· οἱ.δὲ βαστάζοντες
And coming up he touched the bier, and those bearing [it]
ἔστησαν· καὶ εἶπεν, Νεανίσκε, σοὶ λέγω, ἐγέρθητι. 15 Καὶ
stopped. And he said, Young man, to thee I say, Arise. And
ἀνεκάθισεν ὁ νεκρὸς καὶ ἤρξατο λαλεῖν· καὶ ἔδωκεν αὐτὸν τῇ
[3]sat [4]up [1]the [2]dead and began to speak, and he gave him
μητρὶ.αὐτοῦ. 16 ἔλαβεν.δὲ φόβος [p]ἅπαντας,‖ καὶ ἐδόξαζον
to his mother. And [2]seized [1]fear all, and they glorified
τὸν θεόν, λέγοντες, Ὅτι προφήτης μέγας [q]ἐγήγερται‖ ἐν
God, saying, A [2]prophet [1]great has risen up amongst
ἡμῖν, καὶ Ὅτι ἐπεσκέψατο ὁ θεὸς τὸν.λαὸν.αὐτοῦ. 17 Καὶ
us; and [2]Has [3]visited [1]God his people. And
ἐξῆλθεν ὁ.λόγος.οὗτος ἐν ὅλῃ τῇ Ἰουδαίᾳ περὶ αὐτοῦ, καὶ
went out this report in all Judæa concerning him, and
[r]ἐν‖ πάσῃ τῇ περιχώρῳ.
in all the country around.

18 Καὶ ἀπήγγειλαν [s]Ἰωάννῃ‖ οἱ.μαθηταὶ.αὐτοῦ περὶ
And [5]brought [6]word [1]to [2]John [3]his [4]disciples concerning
πάντων τούτων. 19 καὶ προσκαλεσάμενος δύο τινὰς τῶν
all these things. And having called to [him] [2]two [1]certain
μαθητῶν.αὐτοῦ ὁ [t]Ἰωάννης‖ ἔπεμψεν πρὸς [v]τὸν Ἰησοῦν,‖
of his disciples John sent [them] to Jesus,
λέγων, Σὺ.εἶ ὁ ἐρχόμενος ἢ [w]ἄλλον‖ προσδοκῶμεν;
saying, Art thou the coming [one] or another are we to look for?
20 Παραγενόμενοι.δὲ πρὸς αὐτὸν οἱ ἄνδρες [x]εἶπον,‖ [y]Ἰωάν-
And having come to him the men said, John
νης‖ ὁ βαπτιστὴς ἀπέσταλκεν ἡμᾶς πρός σε, λέγων, Σὺ.εἶ
the Baptist has sent us to thee, saying, Art thou
ὁ ἐρχόμενος ἢ ἄλλον προσδοκῶμεν; 21 Ἐν [z]αὐτῇ‖ [a]δὲ‖
the coming [one] or another are we to look for? [2]In [3]the [4]same [1]and
τῇ ὥρᾳ ἐθεράπευσεν πολλοὺς ἀπὸ νόσων καὶ μαστίγων καὶ
hour he healed many of diseases and scourges and

unto you, I have not found so great faith, no, not in Israel. 10 And they that were sent, returning to the house, found the servant whole that had been sick.

11 And it came to pass the day after, that he went into a city called Nain; and many of his disciples went with him, and much people. 12 Now when he came nigh to the gate of the city, behold, there was a dead man carried out, the only son of his mother, and she was a widow: and much people of the city was with her. 13 And when the Lord saw her, he had compassion on her, and said unto her, Weep not. 14 And he came and touched the bier: and they that bare *him* stood still. And he said, Young man, I say unto thee, Arise. 15 And he that was dead sat up, and began to speak. And he delivered him to his mother. 16 And there came a fear on all: and they glorified God, saying, That a great prophet is risen up among us; and, That God hath visited his people. 17 And this rumour of him went forth throughout all Judæa, and throughout all the region round about.

18 And the disciples of John shewed him of all these things. 19 And John calling *unto him* two of his disciples sent *them* to Jesus, saying, Art thou he that should come? or look we for another? 20 When the men were come unto him, they said, John Baptist hath sent us unto thee, saying, Art thou he that should come? or look we for another? 21 And in that same hour he cured many of *their* infirmities and plagues, and of evil

---

[e] εἰς τὸν οἶκον οἱ πεμφθέντες LTTr. [f] — ἀσθενοῦντα LTTr[A]. [g] τῷ Tr. [h] ἐπορεύθη T. [i] — ἱκανοὶ [L]Tr[A]. [k] [τεθνηκὼς] L. [l] μονογενὴς υἱὸς TTrA. [m] αὐτὴ W; — ἦν EGW. [n] + ἦν was EGT[TrA]. [o] αὐτὴν T. [p] πάντας GTrA. [q] ἠγέρθη is risen LTTrA. [r] — ἐν [L]T[Tr]A. [s] Ἰωάννει T; Ἰωάνει Tr. [t] Ἰωάνης Tr. [v] τὸν κύριον the Lord TTrA. [w] ἕτερον Tr. [x] εἶπαν LTTrA. [y] Ἰωάνης Tr. [z] ἐκείνῃ that TTrA. [a] — δὲ LTTrA.

spirits; and unto many
that were blind he gave
sight. 22 Then Jesus
answering said unto
them, Go your way,
and tell John what
things ye have seen
and heard; how that
the blind see, the lame
walk, the lepers are
cleansed, the deaf hear,
the dead are raised, to
the poor the gospel
is preached. 23 And
blessed is *he*, whoso-
ever shall not be of-
fended in me.

24 And when the
messengers of John
were departed, he
began to speak unto
the people concerning
John, What went ye
out into the wilderness
for to see? A reed
shaken with the wind?
25 But what went ye
out for to see? A man
clothed in soft rai-
ment? Behold, they
which are gorgeously
apparelled, and live
delicately, are in kings'
courts. 26 But what
went ye out for to see?
A prophet? Yea, I
say unto you, and
much more than a
prophet. 27 This is *he*,
of whom it is written,
Behold, I send my
messenger before thy
face, which shall pre-
pare thy way before
thee. 28 For I say
unto you, Among those
that are born of women
there is not a greater
prophet than John the
Baptist: but he that is
least in the kingdom
of God is greater than
he. 29 And all the
people that heard *him*,
and the publicans, jus-
tified God, being bap-
tized with the baptism
of John. 30 But the
Pharisees and lawyers
rejected the counsel of
God against them-
selves, being not bap-
tized of him. 31 And
the Lord said, Where-
unto then shall I liken
the men of this gene-
ration? and to what
are they like? 32 They
are like unto children
sitting in the market-
place, and calling one
to another, and say-

πνευμάτων πονηρῶν, καὶ τυφλοῖς πολλοῖς ἐχαρίσατο [b]τὸ‖
[2]spirits [1]evil, and to [2]blind [1]many he granted
βλέπειν. 22 καὶ ἀποκριθεὶς [c]ὁ Ἰησοῦς‖.εἶπεν αὐτοῖς, Πορευθέν-
to see. And [2]answering [1]Jesus said to them, Having
τες ἀπαγγείλατε [d]Ἰωάννῃ‖ ἃ εἴδετε καὶ ἠκούσατε· [e]ὅτι‖
gone relate to John what ye have seen and heard; that
τυφλοὶ ἀναβλέπουσιν, χωλοὶ περιπατοῦσιν, λεπροὶ καθαρίζον-
blind receive sight, lame walk, lepers are cleansed,
ται, κωφοὶ ἀκούουσιν, νεκροὶ ἐγείρονται, πτωχοὶ εὐαγγελίζονται·
deaf hear, dead are raised, poor are evangelized;
23 καὶ μακάριός ἐστιν ὃς.ἐὰν μὴ.σκανδαλισθῇ ἐν ἐμοί.
and blessed is whoever shall not be offended in me.

24 Ἀπελθόντων.δὲ τῶν ἀγγέλων [f]Ἰωάννου‖ ἤρξατο λέγειν
And [5]having [6]departed [1]the [2]messengers [3]of [4]John he began to speak
πρὸς τοὺς ὄχλους περὶ [f]Ἰωάννου,‖ Τί [g]ἐξεληλύθατε‖ εἰς
to the crowds concerning John: What have ye gone out into
τὴν ἔρημον θεάσασθαι; κάλαμον ὑπὸ ἀνέμου σαλευό-
the wilderness to look at? a reed by [the] wind shaken?
μενον; 25 ἀλλὰ τί [g]ἐξεληλύθατε‖ ἰδεῖν; ἄνθρωπον ἐν μαλα-
But what have ye gone out to see? a man in soft
κοῖς ἱματίοις ἠμφιεσμένον; ἰδού, οἱ ἐν ἱματισμῷ ἐνδόξῳ
clothing arrayed? Behold, they who in [2]clothing [1]splendid
καὶ τρυφῇ ὑπάρχοντες ἐν τοῖς βασιλείοις εἰσίν. 26 ἀλλὰ τί
and in luxury are living [2]in [3]the [4]palaces [1]are. But what
[g]ἐξεληλύθατε‖ ἰδεῖν; προφήτην; ναί, λέγω ὑμῖν, καὶ
have ye gone out to see? a prophet? Yea, I say to you, and [one]
περισσότερον προφήτου. 27 οὗτός ἐστιν περὶ οὗ γέ-
more excellent than a prophet. This is he concerning whom it has
γραπται, Ἰδού, [h]ἐγὼ‖ ἀποστέλλω τὸν.ἄγγελόν.μου πρὸ
been written, Behold, I send my messenger before
προσώπου.σου, ὃς κατασκευάσει τὴν.ὁδόν.σου ἔμπροσθέν σου.
thy face, who shall prepare thy way before thee.
28 Λέγω [i]γὰρ‖ ὑμῖν, μείζων ἐν γεννητοῖς γυναικῶν
[2]I [3]say [1]for to you, [6]a [7]greater [1]among [[2]those] [3]born [4]of [5]women
[k]προφήτης‖ [f]Ἰωάννου‖ [l]τοῦ βαπτιστοῦ‖ οὐδείς ἐστιν· ὁ.δὲ
prophet than John the Baptist no one is; but he that [is]
μικρότερος ἐν τῇ βασιλείᾳ τοῦ θεοῦ μείζων αὐτοῦ ἐστιν. 29 Καὶ
less in the kingdom of God greater than he is. And
πᾶς ὁ λαὸς ἀκούσας καὶ οἱ τελῶναι ἐδικαίωσαν τὸν θεόν,
all the people having heard and the tax-gatherers justified God,
βαπτισθέντες τὸ βάπτισμα [f]Ἰωάννου·‖ 30 οἱ.δὲ Φα-
having been baptized [with] the baptism of John; but the Pha-
ρισαῖοι καὶ οἱ νομικοὶ τὴν βουλὴν τοῦ θεοῦ ἠθέτησαν
risees and the doctors of the law the counsel of God set aside
εἰς ἑαυτούς, μὴ βαπτισθέντες ὑπ' αὐτοῦ. 31 [m]εἶπεν.δὲ ὁ
as to themselves, not having been baptized by him. And [3]said [1]the
κύριος,‖ Τίνι οὖν ὁμοιώσω τοὺς ἀνθρώπους τῆς γενεᾶς
[2]Lord, To what therefore shall I liken the men of [2]generation
ταύτης; καὶ τίνι εἰσὶν ὅμοιοι; 32 ὅμοιοί εἰσιν παιδίοις
[1]this? and to what are they like? Like are they to little children
τοῖς ἐν ἀγορᾷ καθημένοις, καὶ προσφωνοῦσιν ἀλλήλοις
in a market-place sitting, and calling one to another

---

[b] — τὸ LTTrAW. [c] — ὁ Ἰησοῦς (*read* he said) [L]TTrA. [d] Ἰωάννει T; Ἰωάνει Tr. [e] — ὅτι L[Tr]. [f] Ἰωάνου Tr. [g] ἐξήλθατε went ye out LTr. [h] — ἐγὼ (*read* ἀποστ. I send) LTTrA. [i] — γὰρ TTrA. [k] — προφήτης L[TrA]. [l] — τοῦ βαπτιστοῦ TTrA. [m] — εἶπεν δὲ ὁ κύριος GLTTrAW.

[n]καὶ λέγουσιν,‖ Ηὐλήσαμεν ὑμῖν, καὶ οὐκ.ὠρχήσασθε· ἐθρη-
and saying, We piped to you, and ye did not dance; we
νήσαμεν [o]ὑμῖν,‖ καὶ οὐκ.ἐκλαύσατε. 33 ἐλήλυθεν.γὰρ [p]Ἰωάννης‖
mourned to you, and ye did not weep. For [4]has [5]come [1]John
ὁ βαπτιστὴς [q]μήτε‖ [r]ἄρτον ἐσθίων‖ [s]μήτε‖ [t]οἶνον πίνων,‖
[2]the [3]Baptist neither [2]bread [1]eating nor [2]wine [1]drinking,
καὶ λέγετε, Δαιμόνιον ἔχει. 34 ἐλήλυθεν ὁ υἱὸς τοῦ ἀνθρώπου
and ye say, A demon he has. [5]Has [6]come [1]the [2]Son [3]of [4]man
ἐσθίων καὶ πίνων, καὶ λέγετε, Ἰδού, ἄνθρωπος φάγος καὶ
eating and drinking, and ye say, Behold, a man a glutton and
οἰνοπότης, [v]τελωνῶν φίλος‖ καὶ ἁμαρτωλῶν. 35 καὶ ἐδι-
a wine-bibber, of tax-gatherers a friend and of sinners; and [2]was
καιώθη ἡ σοφία ἀπὸ [w]τῶν.τέκνων.αὐτῆς πάντων.‖
[3]justified [1]wisdom by [2]her [3]children [1]all.

36 Ἠρώτα.δέ τις αὐτὸν τῶν Φαρισαίων ἵνα φάγῃ μετ'
And [5]asked [1]one. [6]him [2]of [3]the [4]Pharisees that he should eat with
αὐτοῦ· καὶ εἰσελθὼν εἰς [x]τὴν οἰκίαν‖ τοῦ Φαρισαίου [y]ἀνε-
him And having entered into the house of the Pharisee he re-
κλίθη.‖ 37 Καὶ ἰδού, γυνὴ [z]ἐν τῇ πόλει ἥτις ἦν‖
clined [at table]; and behold, a woman in the city who was
ἁμαρτωλός, [a]ἐπιγνοῦσα ὅτι [b]ἀνάκειται‖ ἐν τῇ οἰκίᾳ
a sinner, having known that he had reclined [at table] in the house
τοῦ Φαρισαίου, κομίσασα ἀλάβαστρον μύρου, 38 καὶ στᾶσα
of the Pharisee, having taken an alabaster flask of ointment, and standing
[c]παρὰ τοὺς.πόδας.αὐτοῦ ὀπίσω‖ κλαίουσα, [d]ἤρξατο βρέχειν
at his feet behind weeping, began to bedew
τοὺς.πόδας.αὐτοῦ τοῖς.δάκρυσιν,‖ καὶ ταῖς θριξὶν τῆς κεφαλῆς
his feet with tears, and with the hairs of [2]head
αὐτῆς [e]ἐξέμασσεν,‖ καὶ κατεφίλει τοὺς.πόδας.αὐτοῦ,
[1]her she was wiping [them], and was ardently kissing his feet,
καὶ ἤλειφεν τῷ μύρῳ. 39 ἰδὼν.δὲ ὁ Φαρισαῖος
and was anointing [them] with the ointment. But having seen, the Pharisee
ὁ καλέσας αὐτὸν εἶπεν ἐν ἑαυτῷ, λέγων, Οὗτος εἰ
who invited him spoke within himself, saying, This [person] if
ἦν προφήτης, ἐγίνωσκεν.ἂν τίς καὶ ποταπὴ ἡ γυνὴ
he were a prophet, would have known who and what the woman [is]
ἥτις ἅπτεται αὐτοῦ, ὅτι ἁμαρτωλός ἐστιν. 40 Καὶ ἀποκριθεὶς
who touches him, for a sinner she is. And [2]answering
ὁ Ἰησοῦς εἶπεν πρὸς αὐτόν, Σίμων, ἔχω σοί τι εἰπεῖν.
[1]Jesus said to him, Simon, I have to thee something to say.
Ὁ.δέ [f]φησιν, Διδάσκαλε, εἰπέ.‖ 41 Δύο [g]χρεωφειλέται‖ ἦσαν
And he says, Teacher, say [it]. Two debtors there were
[h]δανειστῇ‖ τινι· ὁ εἷς ὤφειλεν δηνάρια πεντακόσια, ὁ.δὲ
to a [2]creditor [1]certain; the one owed [3]denarii [1]five [2]hundred, and the
ἕτερος πεντήκοντα. 42 μὴ.ἐχόντων.[i]δὲ‖ αὐτῶν ἀπο-
other fifty. But [2]not [3]having [1]they [wherewith] to
δοῦναι ἀμφοτέροις ἐχαρίσατο· τίς οὖν αὐτῶν, [k]εἰπέ,‖ πλεῖον
pay, both he forgave: which therefore of them, say, [4]most
[l]αὐτὸν ἀγαπήσει‖; 43 Ἀποκριθεὶς.[i]δὲ‖ [m]ὁ‖ Σίμων εἶπεν, Ὑπο-
[3]him [1]will [2]love? And [2]answering [1]Simon said, I

ing, We have piped unto you, and ye have not danced; we have mourned to you, and ye have not wept. 33 For John the Baptist came neither eating bread nor drinking wine; and ye say, He hath a devil. 34 The Son of man is come eating and drinking; and ye say, Behold a gluttonous man, and a winebibber, a friend of publicans and sinners! 35 But wisdom is justified of all her children.

36 And one of the Pharisees desired him that he would eat with him. And he went into the Pharisee's house, and sat down to meat. 37 And, behold, a woman in the city, which was a sinner, when she knew that *Jesus* sat at meat in the Pharisee's house, brought an alabaster box of ointment, 38 and stood at his feet behind *him* weeping, and began to wash his feet with tears, and did wipe *them* with the hairs of her head, and kissed his feet, and anointed *them* with the ointment. 39 Now when the Pharisee which had bidden him saw *it*, he spake within himself, saying, This man, if he were a prophet, would have known who and what manner of woman *this is* that toucheth him: for she is a sinner. 40 And Jesus answering said unto him, Simon, I have somewhat to say unto thee. And he saith, Master, say on. 41 There was a certain creditor which had two debtors: the one owed five hundred pence, and the other fifty. 42 And when they had nothing to pay, he frankly forgave them both. Tell me therefore, which of them will love him most? 43 Simon answered and said, I sup-

---

[n] λέγοντες TTrA. [o] — ὑμῖν TTr. [p] Ἰωάνης Tr. [q] μὴ not TA. [r] ἔσθων ἄρτον LTrA; ἐσθίων ἄρτον T. [s] μηδὲ T. [t] πίνων οἶνον LTTrA. [v] φίλος τελωνῶν GLTTrAW. [w] πάντων τῶν τέκνων αὐτῆς LTrA. [x] τὸν οἶκον LTTrA. [y] κατεκλίθη LTTrA. [z] ἥτις ἦν ἐν τῇ πόλει LTTrA. [a] + καὶ and LTTrAW. [b] κατάκειται LTTrA. [c] ὀπίσω παρὰ τοὺς πόδας αὐτοῦ GLTTrA. [d] τοῖς δάκρυσιν ἤρξατο βρέχειν τοὺς πόδας αὐτοῦ LTTrA. [e] ἐξέμαξεν T. [f] Διδάσκαλε, ειπέ, φησίν TTrA. [g] χρεοφειλέται LTTrA. [h] δανιστῇ T. [i] — δὲ [L]TTrA. [k] — εἰπέ LTTr[A]. [l] ἀγαπήσει αὐτόν LTTrA. [m] — ὁ T[Tr].

pose that *he*, to whom he forgave most. And he said unto him, Thou hast rightly judged.
44 And he turned to the woman, and said unto Simon, Seest thou this woman? I entered into thine house, thou gavest me no water for my feet: but she hath washed my feet with tears, and wiped *them* with the hairs of her head.
45 Thou gavest me no kiss: but this woman since the time I came in hath not ceased to kiss my feet.
46 My head with oil thou didst not anoint: but this woman hath anointed my feet with ointment.
47 Wherefore I say unto thee, Her sins, which are many, are forgiven; for she loved much: but to whom little is forgiven, *the same* loveth little.
48 And he said unto her, Thy sins are forgiven.
49 And they that sat at meat with him began to say within themselves, Who is this that forgiveth sins also?
50 And he said to the woman, Thy faith hath saved thee; go in peace.

VIII. And it came to pass afterward, that he went throughout every city and village, preaching and shewing the glad tidings of the kingdom of God: and the twelve *were* with him,
2 and certain women, which had been healed of evil spirits and infirmities, Mary called Magdalene, out of whom went seven devils,
3 and Joanna the wife of Chuza Herod's steward, and Susanna, and many others, which ministered unto him of their substance.
4 And when much people were gathered together, and were come to him out of every city, he spake by a parable:
5 A sower went out to sow his seed: and as he sowed, some fell by the way side; and it was trodden down, and the

λαμβάνω ὅτι ᾧ τὸ πλεῖον ἐχαρίσατο. Ὁ.δὲ εἶπεν αὐτῷ,
take it that [he] to whom the more he forgave. And he said to him,
Ὀρθῶς ἔκρινας. 44 Καὶ στραφεὶς πρὸς τὴν γυναῖκα, τῷ
Rightly thou hast judged. And having turned to the woman,
Σίμωνι ἔφη, Βλέπεις ταύτην τὴν γυναῖκα; εἰσῆλθόν σου εἰς
to Simon he said, Seest thou this woman? I entered [2]thy [1]into
τὴν οἰκίαν, ὕδωρ [n]ἐπὶ τοὺς.πόδας.μου[||] οὐκ.ἔδωκας· αὕτη.δὲ
house, water for my feet thou gavest not, but she
τοῖς δάκρυσιν ἔβρεξέν μου τοὺς πόδας, καὶ ταῖς θριξὶν [o]τῆς
with tears bedewed my feet, and with the hairs
κεφαλῆς[||] αὐτῆς ἐξέμαξεν. 45 φίλημά μοι οὐκ.ἔδωκας·
[3]head [1]of [2]her wiped [them]. A kiss to me thou gavest not,
αὕτη.δὲ ἀφ' ἧς εἰσῆλθον οὐ.[p]διέλιπεν[||] καταφιλοῦσά
but she from which [time] I came in ceased not ardently kissing
[q]μου τοὺς πόδας.[||] 46 ἐλαίῳ τὴν.κεφαλήν.μου οὐκ.ἤλειψας·
my feet. With oil my head thou didst not anoint,
αὕτη.δὲ μύρῳ ἤλειψέν [r]μου τοὺς πόδας.[||] 47 οὗ.χάριν
but she with ointment anointed my feet. For which cause
λέγω σοι, ἀφέωνται [s]αἱ.ἁμαρτίαι.αὐτῆς[||] αἱ πολλαί, ὅτι
I say to thee, forgiven have been her [2]sins [1]many; for
ἠγάπησεν πολύ· ᾧ.δὲ ὀλίγον ἀφίεται ὀλίγον ἀγαπᾷ.
she loved much; but to whom little is forgiven little he loves.
48 Εἶπεν.δὲ αὐτῇ, Ἀφέωνταί σου αἱ ἁμαρτίαι. 49 Καὶ
And he said to her, Forgiven have been thy sins. And
ἤρξαντο οἱ συνανακείμενοι λέγειν ἐν ἑαυτοῖς, Τίς [t]οὗτός
began those reclining with [him] to say within themselves, Who [2]this
ἐστιν[||] ὃς καὶ ἁμαρτίας ἀφίησιν; 50 Εἶπεν.δὲ πρὸς τὴν γυ-
[1]is who even [2]sins [1]forgives? But he said to the wo-
ναῖκα, Ἡ.πίστις.σου σέσωκέν σε· πορεύου εἰς εἰρήνην.
man, Thy faith has saved thee; go in peace.

8 Καὶ ἐγένετο ἐν.τῷ.καθεξῆς καὶ αὐτὸς διώδευεν
And it came to pass afterwards that he journeyed through
κατὰ.πόλιν καὶ κώμην, κηρύσσων καὶ εὐαγγελιζό-
city by city and village by village, preaching and announcing the glad
μενος τὴν βασιλείαν τοῦ θεοῦ· καὶ οἱ δώδεκα σὺν αὐτῷ,
tidings, the kingdom of God, and the twelve [were] with him,
2 καὶ γυναῖκές τινες αἳ ἦσαν.τεθεραπευμέναι ἀπὸ πνευμάτων
and [2]women [1]certain who had been cured from [2]spirits
πονηρῶν καὶ ἀσθενειῶν, Μαρία ἡ καλουμένη Μαγδαληνή,
[1]wicked and infirmities, Mary who is called Magdalene,
ἀφ' ἧς δαιμόνια ἑπτὰ ἐξεληλύθει, 3 καὶ [v]Ἰωάννα[||] γυνὴ
from whom [2]demons [1]seven had gone out; and Joanna wife
Χουζᾶ ἐπιτρόπου Ἡρώδου, καὶ Σουσάννα, καὶ ἕτεραι πολλαί,
of Chuza a steward of Herod; and Susanna, and [2]others [1]many,
αἵτινες διηκόνουν [w]αὐτῷ[||] [x]ἀπὸ[||] τῶν.ὑπαρχόντων.αὐταῖς.
who were ministering to him of their property.
4 Συνιόντος.δὲ ὄχλου πολλοῦ, καὶ τῶν κατὰ.πόλιν ἐπι-
And [4]assembling [1]a [3]crowd [2]great, and those who from each city were
πορευομένων πρὸς αὐτόν, εἶπεν διὰ παραβολῆς. 5 Ἐξῆλθεν
coming to him, he spoke by a parable. [3]Went [4]out
ὁ σπείρων τοῦ σπεῖραι τὸν.σπόρον.αὐτοῦ· καὶ ἐν.τῷ.σπείρειν
[1]the [2]sower to sow his seed; and as [2]sowed
αὐτὸν ὃ.μὲν ἔπεσεν παρὰ τὴν ὁδόν, καὶ κατεπατήθη, καὶ τὰ
[1]he some fell by the way, and it was trampled upon, and the

[n] μου ἐπὶ τοὺς πόδας T; μοι ἐπὶ πόδας TrA. [o] — τῆς κεφαλῆς (*read* with her hairs) GLTTrAW. [p] διέλειπεν T. [q] τοὺς πόδας μου L. [r] τοὺς πόδας μου GLTrA. [s] αὐτῇ (αὐτῆς T) αἱ ἁμαρτίαι LT. [t] ἐστιν οὗτος L. [v] Ἰώανα Tr. [w] αὐτοῖς to them TTrA. [x] ἐκ out of LTTrA.

πετεινὰ τοῦ οὐρανοῦ κατέφαγεν αὐτό. 6 καὶ ἕτερον [y]ἔπεσεν‖
birds of the heaven devoured it. And other fell
ἐπὶ τὴν πέτραν, καὶ φυὲν ἐξηράνθη, διὰ τὸ μὴ-ἔχειν.
upon the rock, and having sprung up it withered, because it had not
ἰκμάδα. 7 καὶ ἕτερον ἔπεσεν ἐν μέσῳ τῶν ἀκανθῶν, καὶ
moisture; and other fell in [the] midst of the thorns, and
[z]συμφυεῖσαι‖ αἱ ἄκανθαι ἀπέπνιξαν αὐτό. 8 καὶ ἕτερον
having sprung up together the thorns choked it; and other
ἔπεσεν [a]ἐπὶ‖ τὴν γῆν τὴν ἀγαθήν, καὶ φυὲν ἐποίησεν
fell upon the ground the good, and having sprung up produced
καρπὸν ἑκατονταπλασίονα. Ταῦτα λέγων ἐφώνει, Ὁ ἔχων
fruit a hundredfold. These things saying he cried, He that has
ὦτα ἀκούειν ἀκουέτω. 9 Ἐπηρώτων-δὲ αὐτὸν οἱ-μαθηταὶ-αὐτοῦ,
ears to hear let him hear. And [3]asked [4]him [1]his [2]disciples,
[b]λέγοντες,‖ Τίς [c]εἴη ἡ-παραβολὴ-αὕτη‖; 10 Ὁ-δὲ εἶπεν,
saying, What may be this parable? And he said,
Ὑμῖν δέδοται γνῶναι τὰ μυστήρια τῆς βασιλείας τοῦ
To you it has been given to know the mysteries of the kingdom
θεοῦ· τοῖς-δὲ λοιποῖς ἐν παραβολαῖς, ἵνα βλέποντες μὴ
of God, but to the rest in parables, that seeing [3]not
βλέπωσιν, καὶ ἀκούοντες μὴ-συνιῶσιν. 11 Ἔστιν-δὲ
[1]they [2]may see, and hearing they may not understand. Now [3]is
αὕτη ἡ παραβολή· ὁ σπόρος ἐστὶν ὁ λόγος τοῦ θεοῦ· 12 οἱ-δὲ
[4]this [1]the [2]parable: The seed is the word of God: and those
παρὰ τὴν ὁδὸν εἰσὶν οἱ [d]ἀκούοντες,‖ εἶτα ἔρχεται ὁ διά-
by the way are those who hear; then comes the de-
βολος καὶ αἴρει τὸν λόγον ἀπὸ τῆς-καρδίας-αὐτῶν, ἵνα-μὴ
vil and takes away the word from their heart, lest
πιστεύσαντες σωθῶσιν. 13 οἱ-δὲ ἐπὶ [e]τῆς πέτρας,‖ οἳ
having believed they should be saved. And those upon the rock, those who
ὅταν ἀκούσωσιν, μετὰ χαρᾶς δέχονται τὸν λόγον, καὶ οὗτοι
when they hear, with joy receive the word, and these
ῥίζαν οὐκ-ἔχουσιν, οἳ πρὸς καιρὸν πιστεύουσιν, καὶ ἐν καιρῷ
a root have not, who for a time believe, and in time
πειρασμοῦ ἀφίστανται. 14 τὸ-δὲ εἰς τὰς ἀκάνθας πεσόν,
of trial fall away. And that which into the thorns fell,
οὗτοί εἰσιν οἱ ἀκούσαντες, καὶ ὑπὸ μεριμνῶν καὶ πλούτου
these are they who having heard, and under cares and riches
καὶ ἡδονῶν τοῦ βίου πορευόμενοι [f]συμπνίγονται,‖ καὶ οὐ
and pleasures of life moving along are choked, and [2]not
τελεσφοροῦσιν. 15 τὸ-δὲ ἐν τῇ καλῇ γῇ, οὗτοί εἰσιν
[1]do bring to perfection. And that in the good ground, these are
οἵτινες ἐν καρδίᾳ καλῇ καὶ ἀγαθῇ ἀκούσαντες τὸν λόγον
they who in a heart right and good having heard the word
κατέχουσιν, καὶ καρποφοροῦσιν ἐν ὑπομονῇ. 16 Οὐδεὶς-δὲ
keep [it], and bring forth fruit with endurance. And no one
λύχνον ἅψας καλύπτει αὐτὸν σκεύει, ἢ ὑποκάτω κλίνης
a lamp having lighted covers it with a vessel, or under a couch
τίθησιν· [g]ἀλλ'‖ ἐπὶ λυχνίας [h]ἐπιτίθησιν,‖ ἵνα οἱ
puts [it], but on a lamp-stand puts [it], that they who
εἰσπορευόμενοι βλέπωσιν τὸ φῶς. 17 οὐ-γάρ ἐστιν
enter in may see the light. For not [anything] is
κρυπτὸν ὃ οὐ φανερὸν γενήσεται· οὐδὲ ἀπόκρυφον ὃ
hidden which [2]not [4]manifest [1]shall [3]become; nor secret which

fowls of the air devoured it. 6 And some fell upon a rock; and as soon as it was sprung up, it withered away, because it lacked moisture. 7 And some fell among thorns; and the thorns sprang up with it, and choked it. 8 And other fell on good ground, and sprang up, and bare fruit an hundredfold. And when he had said these things, he cried, He that hath ears to hear, let him hear. 9 And his disciples asked him, saying, What might this parable be? 10 And he said, Unto you it is given to know the mysteries of the kingdom of God: but to others in parables; that seeing they might not see, and hearing they might not understand. 11 Now the parable is this: The seed is the word of God. 12 Those by the way side are they that hear; then cometh the devil, and taketh away the word out of their hearts, lest they should believe and be saved. 13 They on the rock *are they*, which, when they hear, receive the word with joy; and these have no root, which for a while believe, and in time of temptation fall away. 14 And that which fell among thorns are they, which, when they have heard, go forth, and are choked with cares and riches and pleasures of *this* life, and bring no fruit to perfection. 15 But that on the good ground are they, which in an honest and good heart, having heard the word, keep *it*, and bring forth fruit with patience. 16 No man, when he hath lighted a candle, covereth it with a vessel, or putteth *it* under a bed; but setteth *it* on a candlestick, that they which enter in may see the light. 17 For nothing is secret, that shall not be made

---

[y] κατέπεσεν fell down TTrA. [z] συνφυεῖσαι T. [a] εἰς into GLTTrAW. [b] — λέγοντες LTTr[A]. [c] αὕτη εἴη ἡ παραβολή T. [d] ἀκούσαντες heard TTr. [e] τὴν πέτραν T. [f] συνπνίγονται TA. [g] ἀλλὰ Tr. [h] τίθησιν LTTrA.

manifest; neither *any thing* hid, that shall not be known and come abroad. 18 Take heed therefore how ye hear: for whosoever hath, to him shall be given; and whosoever hath not, from him shall be taken even that which he seemeth to have.

[i]οὐ.γνωσθήσεται‖ καὶ εἰς φανερὸν ἔλθῃ. 18 βλέπετε οὖν
shall not be known and to light come. Take heed therefore
πῶς ἀκούετε· ὃς.[k]γὰρ.ἂν‖ ἔχῃ, δοθήσεται αὐτῷ· καὶ
how ye hear; for whoever may have, [3]shall [4]be [5]given [1]to [2]him; and
ὃς.[l]ἂν‖ μὴ.ἔχῃ, καὶ ὃ δοκεῖ ἔχειν ἀρθήσεται ἀπ' αὐτοῦ.
whoever may not have, even what he seems to have shall be taken from him.

19 Then came to him *his* mother and his brethren, and could not come at him for the press. 20 And it was told him *by certain* which said, Thy mother and thy brethren stand without, desiring to see thee. 21 And he answered and said unto them, My mother and my brethren are these which hear the word of God, and do it.

19 [m]Παρεγένοντο‖.δὲ πρὸς αὐτὸν ἡ μήτηρ[n] καὶ οἱ ἀδελ-
And came to him [his] mother and [2]breth-
φοὶ αὐτοῦ, καὶ οὐκ.ἠδύναντο συντυχεῖν αὐτῷ διὰ τὸν
ren [1]his, and were not able to get to him because of the
ὄχλον. 20 [o]καὶ ἀπηγγέλη‖ αὐτῷ, [p]λεγόντων,‖ [q]Ἡ.μήτηρ.σου
crowd. And it was told him, saying, Thy mother
καὶ οἱ.ἀδελφοί.σου ἑστήκασιν ἔξω, ἰδεῖν [r]σε θέλοντες.‖
and thy brethren are standing without, [2]to [3]see [4]thee [1]wishing.
21 Ὁ.δὲ ἀποκριθεὶς εἶπεν [s]πρὸς αὐτούς,‖ Μήτηρ.μου καὶ
And he answering said to them, My mother and
ἀδελφοί.μου οὗτοί εἰσιν οἱ τὸν λόγον τοῦ θεοῦ ἀκούοντες καὶ
my brethren [2]those [1]are who the word of God are hearing and
ποιοῦντες [t]αὐτόν.‖
doing it.

22 Now it came to pass on a certain day, that he went into a ship with his disciples: and he said unto them, Let us go over unto the other side of the lake. And they launched forth. 23 But as they sailed he fell asleep: and there came down a storm of wind on the lake; and they were filled *with water*, and were in jeopardy. 24 And they came to him, and awoke him, saying, Master, master, we perish. Then he arose, and rebuked the wind and the raging of the water: and they ceased, and there was a calm. 25 And he said unto them, Where is your faith? And they being afraid wondered, saying one to another, What manner of man is this! for he commandeth even the winds and water, and they obey him.

22 [v]Καὶ ἐγένετο‖ ἐν μιᾷ τῶν ἡμερῶν καὶ αὐτὸς ἐνέβη
And it came to pass on one of the days that he entered
εἰς πλοῖον καὶ οἱ.μαθηταὶ.αὐτοῦ, καὶ εἶπεν πρὸς αὐτούς,
into a ship, and his disciples, and he said to them,
Διέλθωμεν εἰς τὸ πέραν τῆς λίμνης· καὶ ἀνήχθησαν.
Let us pass over to the other side of the lake; and they put off.
23 πλεόντων.δὲ.αὐτῶν ἀφύπνωσεν· καὶ κατέβη λαῖλαψ
And as they sailed he fell asleep; and came down a storm
ἀνέμου εἰς τὴν λίμνην, καὶ συνεπληροῦντο, καὶ ἐκινδύνευον.
of wind on the lake, and they were being filled, and were in danger.
24 προσελθόντες.δὲ διήγειραν αὐτόν, λέγοντες, Ἐπιστάτα,
And having come to [him] they aroused him, saying, Master,
ἐπιστάτα, ἀπολλύμεθα. Ὁ.δὲ [w]ἐγερθεὶς‖ ἐπετίμησεν τῷ
Master, we are perishing. And he having arisen rebuked the
ἀνέμῳ καὶ τῷ κλύδωνι τοῦ ὕδατος· καὶ ἐπαύσαντο, καὶ ἐγένετο
wind and the raging of the water; and they ceased, and there was
γαλήνη. 25 εἶπεν.δὲ αὐτοῖς, Ποῦ [x]ἐστιν‖ ἡ.πίστις.ὑμῶν;
a calm. And he said to them, Where is your faith?
Φοβηθέντες.δὲ ἐθαύμασαν, λέγοντες πρὸς ἀλλήλους, Τίς ἄρα
And being afraid they wondered, saying to one another, Who then
οὗτός ἐστιν, ὅτι καὶ τοῖς ἀνέμοις ἐπιτάσσει καὶ τῷ ὕδατι,
[2]this [1]is, that even the winds he commands and the water,
καὶ ὑπακούουσιν αὐτῷ;
and they obey him?

26 And they arrived at the country of the Gadarenes, which is over against Galilee. 27 And when he went forth to land, there met him out of the city a certain man, which had

26 Καὶ κατέπλευσαν εἰς τὴν χώραν τῶν [y]Γαδαρηνῶν,‖
And they sailed down to the country of the Gadarenes,
ἥτις ἐστὶν [z]ἀντιπέραν‖ τῆς Γαλιλαίας. 27 ἐξελθόντι.δὲ.αὐτῷ
which is over against Galilee. And on his having gone forth
ἐπὶ τὴν γῆν ὑπήντησεν [a]αὐτῷ‖ ἀνήρ τις ἐκ τῆς πόλεως,
upon the land [4]met [5]him [1]a [3]man [2]certain out of the city,

---

[i] οὐ μὴ γνωσθῇ in any wise should not be known LTTrA. [k] ἂν γὰρ TTrA. [l] ἐὰν L. [m] Παρεγένετο TTr. [n] + αὐτοῦ his T. [o] ἀπηγγέλη δὲ LTTrA. [p] — λεγόντων LTTr[A]. [q] + ὅτι T. [r] θέλοντές σε Tr. [s] αὐτοῖς L. [t] — αὐτόν GLTTrA. [v] ἐγένετο δὲ LTTrA. [w] διεγερθεὶς having been aroused TTr. [x] — ἐστιν (*read* [is]) LTTrAW. [y] Γερασηνῶν Gerasenes LTrA; Γεργεσηνῶν Gergesenes T. [z] ἀντιπέρα LTrAW; ἀντίπερα T. [a] — αὐτῷ (*read* [him]) T[TrA].

[b]ὃς εἶχεν" δαιμόνια [c]ἐκ χρόνων.ἱκανῶν, καὶ ἱμάτιον οὐκ
who had demons for a long time, and a garment [2]not
ἐνεδιδύσκετο," καὶ ἐν οἰκίᾳ οὐκ.ἔμενεν, ἀλλ' ἐν τοῖς μνήμασιν.
[1]was wearing, and in a house did not abide, but in the tombs.
28 ἰδὼν.δὲ τὸν Ἰησοῦν [d]καὶ" ἀνακράξας προσέπεσεν αὐτῷ,
But having seen Jesus and having cried out he fell down before him,
καὶ φωνῇ μεγάλῃ εἶπεν, Τί ἐμοὶ καὶ σοί, Ἰησοῦ, υἱὲ τοῦ
and with a [2]voice [1]loud said, What to me and to thee, Jesus, Son
θεοῦ τοῦ ὑψίστου; δέομαί σου μή με βασανίσῃς.
of God the Most High? I beseech of thee [3]not [5]me [1]thou [2]mayest [4]torment.
29 [e]Παρήγγελλεν".γὰρ τῷ πνεύματι τῷ ἀκαθάρτῳ ἐξελθεῖν
For he was charging the spirit the unclean to come out
ἀπὸ τοῦ ἀνθρώπου· πολλοῖς.γὰρ χρόνοις συνηρπάκει αὐτόν,
from the man. For many times it had seized him;
καὶ [f]ἐδεσμεῖτο," ἁλύσεσιν καὶ πέδαις φυλασσόμενος, καὶ [g]διαρ-
and he was bound, with chains and fetters being kept, and break-
ρήσσων" τὰ δεσμὰ ἠλαύνετο ὑπὸ τοῦ [h]δαίμονος" εἰς τὰς
ing the bonds he was driven by the demon into the
ἐρήμους. 30 ἐπηρώτησεν.δὲ αὐτὸν ὁ Ἰησοῦς, [i]λέγων," Τί σοι
deserts. And [2]asked [3]him [1]Jesus, saying, What [2]thy
[k]ἐστὶν ὄνομα"; Ὁ.δὲ εἶπεν, [l]Λεγεών·" ὅτι [m]δαιμόνια πολλὰ
[1]is name? And he said, Legion, because demons many
εἰσῆλθεν" εἰς αὐτόν. 31 καὶ [n]παρεκάλει" αὐτὸν ἵνα μὴ ἐπι-
had entered into him. And he besought him that [3]not [1]he [2]would
τάξῃ αὐτοῖς εἰς τὴν ἄβυσσον ἀπελθεῖν. 32 ἦν.δὲ ἐκεῖ
command them into the abyss to go away. Now there was there
ἀγέλη χοίρων ἱκανῶν [o]βοσκομένων" ἐν τῷ ὄρει· καὶ [p]παρε-
a herd of [2]swine [1]many feeding in the mountain, and they be-
κάλουν" αὐτὸν ἵνα ἐπιτρέψῃ αὐτοῖς εἰς ἐκείνους εἰσελθεῖν.
sought him that he would allow them into those to enter;
καὶ ἐπέτρεψεν αὐτοῖς. 33 ἐξελθόντα.δὲ τὰ δαιμόνια ἀπὸ τοῦ
and he allowed them. And having gone out the demons from the
ἀνθρώπου [q]εἰσῆλθεν" εἰς τοὺς χοίρους· καὶ ὥρμησεν ἡ ἀγέλη
man they entered into the swine, and [3]rushed [1]the [2]herd
κατὰ τοῦ κρημνοῦ εἰς τὴν λίμνην, καὶ ἀπεπνίγη 34 ἰδόντες.δὲ
down the steep into the lake, and were choked. And [5]having [6]seen
οἱ βόσκοντες τὸ [r]γεγενημένον" ἔφυγον, καὶ [s]ἀπελ-
[1]those [2]who [3]fed [[4]them] what had taken place fled, and having
θόντες" ἀπήγγειλαν εἰς τὴν πόλιν καὶ εἰς τοὺς ἀγρούς.
gone away related [it] to the city and to the country.
35 ἐξῆλθον.δὲ ἰδεῖν τὸ γεγονός· καὶ [t]ἦλθον" πρὸς τὸν
And they went out to see what had taken place, and came to
Ἰησοῦν, καὶ [v]εὗρον" καθήμενον τὸν ἄνθρωπον ἀφ' οὗ τὰ
Jesus, and found seated the man from whom the
δαιμόνια [w]ἐξεληλύθει," ἱματισμένον καὶ σωφρονοῦντα, παρὰ
demons had gone out, clothed and of sound mind, at
τοὺς πόδας τοῦ Ἰησοῦ. καὶ ἐφοβήθησαν. 36 ἀπήγγειλαν.δὲ
the feet of Jesus. And they were afraid. And [7]related
αὐτοῖς [x]καὶ" οἱ ἰδόντες πῶς ἐσώθη ὁ δαι-
[8]to [9]them [2]also [1]those [3]who [4]had [5]seen [[6]it] how was healed he who had been pos-

devils long time, and
ware no clothes, nei-
ther abode in *any*
house, but in the
tombs. 28 When he
saw Jesus, he cried out,
and fell down before
him, and with a loud
voice said, What have
I to do with thee, Jesus,
thou Son of God most
high? I beseech thee,
torment me not. 29 (For
he had commanded
the unclean spirit to
come out of the man.
For oftentimes it had
caught him: and he
was kept bound with
chains and in fetters;
and he brake the bands,
and was driven of the
devil into the wilder-
ness.) 30 And Jesus
asked him, saying,
What is thy name?
And he said, Legion:
because many devils
were entered into him.
31 And they besought
him that he would not
command them to go
out into the deep.
32 And there was there
an herd of many swine
feeding on the moun-
tain: and they be-
sought him that he
would suffer them to
enter into them. And
he suffered them.
33 Then went the de-
vils out of the man,
and entered into the
swine: and the herd
ran violently down a
steep place into the
lake, and were choked.
34 When they that fed
them saw what was
done, they fled, and
went and told *it* in the
city and in the coun-
try. 35 Then they went
out to see what was
done; and came to Je-
sus, and found the
man, out of whom the
devils were departed,
sitting at the feet of
Jesus, clothed, and in
his right mind: and
they were afraid.
36 They also which saw
it told them by what
means he that was
possessed of the devils

---

[b] ἔχων having T. [c] καὶ χρόνῳ ἱκανῷ οὐκ ἐνεδύσατο ἱμάτιον and for a long time did not put on a garment TTr. [d] — καὶ LTTrA. [e] Παρήγγειλε he charged EG. [f] ἐδεσμεύετο TTr. [g] διαρήσσων LTTrA. [h] δαιμονίου LTTrA. [i] — λέγων L. [k] ὄνομα ἐστίν LTTr. [l] Λεγιών TTr. [m] εἰσῆλθεν δαιμόνια πολλὰ LT. [n] παρεκάλουν they besought LTTrA. [o] βοσκομένη L. [p] παρεκάλεσαν LTTrA. [q] εἰσῆλθον LTTrAW. [r] γεγονὸς GLTTrAW. [s] — ἀπελθόντες GLTTrAW. [t] ἦλθαν Tr. [v] εὗραν Tr. [w] ἐξῆλθεν went out T. [x] — καὶ LTTr[A].

was healed. 37 Then the whole multitude of the country of the Gadarenes round about besought him to depart from them; for they were taken with great fear: and he went up into the ship, and returned back again. 38 Now the man out of whom the devils were departed besought him that he might be with him: but Jesus sent him away, saying, 39 Return to thine own house, and shew how great things God hath done unto thee. And he went his way, and published throughout the whole city how great things Jesus had done unto him.

40 And it came to pass, that, when Jesus was returned, the people *gladly* received him: for they were all waiting for him. 41 And, behold, there came a man named Jairus, and he was a ruler of the synagogue: and he fell down at Jesus' feet, and besought him that he would come into his house: 42 for he had one only daughter, about twelve years of age, and she lay a dying. But as he went the people thronged him. 43 And a woman having an issue of blood twelve years, which had spent all her living upon physicians, neither could be healed of any, 44 came behind *him*, and touched the border of his garment: and immediately her issue of blood stanched. 45 And Jesus said, Who touched me? When all denied, Peter and they that were with him said, Master, the multitude throng thee and press *thee*, and sayest thou, Who touched me? 46 And Jesus said, Somebody hath touched me: for I perceive that virtue is gone out of me. 47 And

μονισθείς. 37 καὶ [y]ἠρώτησαν‖ αὐτὸν ἅπαν τὸ πλῆθος τῆς
sessed by demons. And asked him all the multitude of the
περιχώρου τῶν [z]Γαδαρηνῶν‖ ἀπελθεῖν ἀπ' αὐτῶν, ὅτι φόβῳ
country around of the Gadarenes to depart from them, for with [2]fear
μεγάλῳ συνείχοντο· αὐτὸς.δὲ ἐμβὰς εἰς [a]τὸ‖ πλοῖον
[1]great they were possessed. And he having entered into the ship
ὑπέστρεψεν. 38 [b]ἐδέετο‖.δὲ αὐτοῦ ὁ ἀνὴρ ἀφ' οὗ ἐξελη-
returned. And [9]was [10]begging [11]him [1]the [2]man [3]from [4]whom [5]had
λύθει τὰ δαιμόνια εἶναι σὺν αὐτῷ. ἀπέλυσεν.δὲ αὐτὸν
[6]gone [7]the [8]demons to be [taken] with him. But [2]sent [4]away [3]him
[c]ὁ Ἰησοῦς,‖ λέγων, 39 Ὑπόστρεφε εἰς τὸν.οἶκόν.σου καὶ διηγοῦ
[1]Jesus, saying, Return to thy house and relate
ὅσα [d]ἐποίησέν σοι‖ ὁ θεός. Καὶ ἀπῆλθεν, καθ' ὅλην τὴν
all that [2]has [3]done [4]for [5]thee [1]God. And he departed, through [2]whole [1]the
πόλιν κηρύσσων ὅσα ἐποίησεν αὐτῷ ὁ Ἰησοῦς.
city proclaiming all that [2]had [3]done [4]for [5]him [1]Jesus.

40 [e]Ἐγένετο δὲ ἐν‖ τῷ [f]ὑποστρέψαι‖ τὸν Ἰησοῦν ἀπ-
[2]It [3]came [4]to [5]pass [1]and [6]on [8]returning [7]Jesus, gladly
εδέξατο αὐτὸν ὁ ὄχλος· ἦσαν.γὰρ πάντες προσδοκῶντες
received him the crowd, for they were all looking for
αὐτόν. 41 Καὶ ἰδού, ἦλθεν ἀνὴρ ᾧ ὄνομα Ἰάειρος, καὶ
him. And behold, [3]came [1]a [2]man whose name [was] Jairus, and
[g]αὐτὸς‖ ἄρχων τῆς συναγωγῆς ὑπῆρχεν, καὶ πεσὼν παρὰ
he a ruler of the synagogue was, and having fallen at
τοὺς πόδας [h]τοῦ‖ Ἰησοῦ παρεκάλει αὐτὸν εἰσελθεῖν εἰς τὸν
the feet of Jesus he besought him to come to
οἶκον.αὐτοῦ· 42 ὅτι θυγάτηρ μονογενὴς ἦν αὐτῷ ὡς ἐτῶν
his house, because [3]daughter [1]an [2]only was to him, about [2]years
δώδεκα, καὶ αὕτη ἀπέθνησκεν. [i]Ἐν.δὲ.τῷ.ὑπάγειν αὐτὸν‖
[[3]old] [1]twelve, and she was dying. And as [2]went [1]he
οἱ ὄχλοι συνέπνιγον αὐτόν. 43 Καὶ γυνὴ οὖσα ἐν ῥύσει
the crowds thronged him. And a woman being with a flux
αἵματος ἀπὸ ἐτῶν δώδεκα, ἥτις [k]εἰς ἰατροὺς‖ προσαναλώσασα
of blood since [2]years [1]twelve, who on physicians having spent
ὅλον τὸν βίον [l] οὐκ ἴσχυσεν [m]ὑπ'‖ οὐδενὸς θεραπευθῆναι,
[2]whole [3]living [[1]her] could by no one be cured,
44 προσελθοῦσα ὄπισθεν ἥψατο τοῦ κρασπέδου τοῦ ἱματίου
having come behind touched the border of [2]garment
αὐτοῦ, καὶ παραχρῆμα ἔστη ἡ ῥύσις τοῦ.αἵματος.αὐτῆς.
[1]his, and immediately stopped the flux of her blood.
45 καὶ εἶπεν ὁ Ἰησοῦς, Τίς ὁ ἁψάμενός μου; Ἀρνου-
And [2]said [1]Jesus, Who [is it] that was touching me? [3]Deny-
μένων δὲ πάντων, εἶπεν ὁ Πέτρος καὶ οἱ [n]μετ' αὐτοῦ,‖ Ἐπι-
ing [1]and [2]all, [9]said [4]Peter [5]and [6]those [7]with [8]him, Mas-
στάτα, οἱ ὄχλοι συνέχουσίν σε καὶ ἀποθλίβουσιν, [o]καὶ λέγεις,
ter, the crowds throng thee and press, and sayest thou,
Τίς ὁ ἁψάμενός μου;‖ 46 Ὁ.δὲ.Ἰησοῦς εἶπεν, Ἥψατό
Who [is it] that was touching me? And Jesus said, [3]Touched
μου τίς· ἐγὼ.γὰρ ἔγνων δύναμιν [p]ἐξελθοῦσαν‖ ἀπ'
[4]me [1]some [2]one, for I knew [that] power went out from

---

[y] ἠρώτησεν LTrA. [z] Γερασηνῶν Gerasenes LTrA; Γεργεσηνῶν Gergesenes T. [a] — τὸ (*read* a ship) LTTrA. [b] ἐδεεῖτο L; ἐδεῖτο TrA. [c] — ὁ Ἰησοῦς (*read* he sent) [L]TTrA. [d] σοι ἐποίησεν LTTrA. [e] Ἐν δὲ Tr. [f] ὑποστρέφειν T. [g] οὗτος this LTr. [h] — τοῦ T[Tr]. [i] καὶ ἐγένετο ἐν τῷ πορεύεσθαι αὐτὸν and it came to pass as he proceeded L. [k] ἰατροῖς GLTTrAW. [l] + αὐτῆς her L. [m] ἀπ' LTTrA. [n] σὺν αὐτῷ GLTTrA. [o] — καὶ λέγεις, Τίς ὁ ἁψάμενός μου; T[TrA]. [p] ἐξεληλυθυῖαν had gone out TTrA.

-μου. 47 Ἰδοῦσα.δὲ η γυνὴ ὅτι οὐκ.ἔλαθεν, τρέμουσα ἦλ-
me. And [3]seeing [1]the [2]woman that she was not hid, trembling she
θεν, καὶ προσπεσοῦσα αὐτῷ, δι' ἣν αἰτίαν ἥψατο
came, and having fallen down before him, for what cause she touched
αὐτοῦ ἀπήγγειλεν [q]αὐτῷ‖ ἐνώπιον παντὸς τοῦ λαοῦ, καὶ ὡς
him she declared to him before all the people, and how
ἰάθη παραχρῆμα. 48 ὁ.δὲ εἶπεν αὐτῇ, [r]Θάρσει,‖
she was healed immediately. And he said to her, Be of good courage,
[s]θύγατερ,‖ ἡ.πίστις.σου σέσωκέν σε· πορεύου εἰς εἰρήνην.
daughter, thy faith has cured thee: go in peace.
49 Ἔτι.αὐτοῦ.λαλοῦντος ἔρχεταί τις [t]παρὰ‖ τοῦ ἀρχισυναγώ-
As yet he was speaking comes one from the ruler of the syna-
γου, λέγων [v]αὐτῷ,‖ Ὅτι τέθνηκεν ἡ.θυγάτηρ.σου· [w]μὴ‖ σκύλλε
gogue, saying to him, [3]Has [4]died [1]thy [2]daughter; [6]not [5]trouble
τὸν διδάσκαλον. 50 Ὁ.δὲ.Ἰησοῦς ἀκούσας ἀπεκρίθη αὐτῷ,
the teacher. But Jesus having heard answered him,
[x]λέγων,‖ Μὴ.φοβοῦ· μόνον [y]πίστευε.‖ καὶ σωθήσεται.
saying, Fear not; only believe, and she shall be restored.
51 [z]Εἰσελθὼν‖.δὲ εἰς τὴν οἰκίαν οὐκ.ἀφῆκεν εἰσελθεῖν [a]οὐδένα‖
And having entered into the house he did not suffer [3]to [4]go [5]in [1]any [2]one (lit. no one)
εἰ.μὴ Πέτρον καὶ [b]Ἰάκωβον καὶ Ἰωάννην,‖ καὶ τὸν πατέρα
except Peter and James and John, and the father
τῆς παιδὸς καὶ τὴν μητέρα. 52 ἔκλαιον.δὲ πάντες καὶ
of the child and the mother. And they were [2]weeping [1]all and
ἐκόπτοντο αὐτήν. ὁ.δὲ εἶπεν, Μὴ.κλαίετε· [c]οὐκ‖.ἀπέθανεν,
bewailing her. But he said, Weep not; she is not dead,
ἀλλὰ καθεύδει. 53 Καὶ κατεγέλων αὐτοῦ, εἰδότες ὅτι ἀπέ-
but sleeps. And they laughed at him, knowing that she was
θανεν. 54 αὐτὸς.δὲ [d]ἐκβαλὼν ἔξω πάντας, καὶ‖ κρατήσας
dead. But he having put out all, and having taken hold
τῆς.χειρὸς.αὐτῆς, ἐφώνησεν, λέγων, Ἡ παῖς, [e]ἐγείρου.‖ 55 Καὶ
of her hand, cried, saying, Child, arise. And
ἐπέστρεψεν τὸ.πνεῦμα.αὐτῆς, καὶ ἀνέστη παραχρῆμα· καὶ
[3]returned [1]her [2]spirit, and she arose immediately; and
διέταξεν αὐτῇ δοθῆναι φαγεῖν. 56 καὶ
he directed [that] [5]to [6]her [[1]something] [2]should [3]be [4]given to eat. And
ἐξέστησαν οἱ.γονεῖς.αὐτῆς· ὁ.δὲ παρήγγειλεν αὐτοῖς μηδενὶ
[3]were [4]amazed [1]her [2]parents; and he charged them to no one
εἰπεῖν τὸ γεγονός.
to tell what had happened.

9 [f]Συγκαλεσάμενος‖.δὲ τοὺς δώδεκα [g]μαθητὰς αὐτοῦ‖ ἔδωκεν
And having called together the twelve disciples of him he gave
αὐτοῖς δύναμιν καὶ ἐξουσίαν ἐπὶ πάντα τὰ δαιμόνια, καὶ
to them power and authority over all the demons, and
νόσους θεραπεύειν· 2 καὶ ἀπέστειλεν αὐτοὺς κηρύσσειν τὴν
diseases to heal, and sent them to proclaim the
βασιλείαν τοῦ θεοῦ, καὶ ἰᾶσθαι [h]τοὺς ἀσθενοῦντας.‖ 3 καὶ
kingdom of God, and to heal those being sick. And
εἶπεν πρὸς αὐτούς, Μηδὲν αἴρετε εἰς τὴν ὁδόν· μήτε [i]ῥάβδους,‖
he said to them, Nothing take for the way; neither staves,

when the woman saw that she was not hid, she came trembling, and falling down before him, she declared unto him before all the people for what cause she had touched him, and how she was healed immediately. 48 And he said unto her, Daughter, be of good comfort: thy faith hath made thee whole; go in peace. 49 While he yet spake, there cometh one from the ruler of the synagogue's *house*, saying to him, Thy daughter is dead; trouble not the Master. 50 But when Jesus heard *it*, he answered him, saying, Fear not: believe only, and she shall be made whole. 51 And when he came into the house, he suffered no man to go in, save Peter, and James, and John, and the father and the mother of the maiden. 52 And all wept, and bewailed her: but he said, Weep not; she is not dead, but sleepeth. 53 And they laughed him to scorn, knowing that she was dead. 54 And he put them all out, and took her by the hand, and called, saying, Maid, arise. 55 And her spirit came again, and she arose straightway: and he commanded to give her meat. 56 And her parents were astonished: but he charged them that they should tell no man what was done.

IX. Then he called his twelve disciples together, and gave them power and authority over all devils, and to cure diseases. 2 And he sent them to preach the kingdom of God, and to heal the sick. 3 And he said unto them, Take nothing for *your* journey, neither staves, nor

[q] — αὐτῷ LTTrA. [r] — Θάρσει LTTrA. [s] θυγάτηρ Tr. [t] ἀπὸ L. [v] — αὐτῷ T[Tr]. [w] μηκέτι no longer LTTr. [x] — λέγων LTTr[A]. [y] πίστευσον TTrA. [z] ἐλθὼν having gone GLTTrW. [a] τινὰ σὺν αὐτῷ any one with him LTTrA. [b] Ἰωάννην (Ἰωάνην Tr) καὶ Ἰάκωβον GLTTrAW. [c] οὐ γὰρ (read for she is not dead) LTrA. [d] — ἐκβαλὼν ἔξω πάντας καὶ LTTrA. [e] ἔγειρε LTrA. [f] Συνκαλεσάμενος T. [g] — μαθητὰς αὐτοῦ GTTrAW. [h] τοὺς ἀσθενεῖς the sick L[Tr]; — τοὺς ἀσθενοῦντας TA. [i] ῥάβδον staff GLTTrA.

scrip, neither bread,
neither money; neither
have two coats apiece.
4 And whatsoever
house ye enter into,
there abide, and thence
depart. 5 And whoso-
ever will not receive
you, when ye go out
of that city, shake off
the very dust from
your feet for a testi-
mony against them.
6 And they departed,
and went through the
towns, preaching the
gospel, and healing
every where.

7 Now Herod the
tetrarch heard of all
that was done by him:
and he was perplexed,
because that it was
said of some, that John
was risen from the
dead; 8 and of some,
that Elias had appear-
ed; and of others, that
one of the old pro-
phets was risen again.
9 And Herod said, John
have I beheaded: but
who is this, of whom
I hear such things?
And he desired to see
him.

10 And the apostles,
when they were re-
turned, told him all
that they had done.
And he took them, and
went aside privately
into a desert place
belonging to the
city called Bethsaida.
11 And the people,
when they knew *it*,
followed him: and he
received them, and
spake unto them of
the kingdom of God,
and healed them that
had need of healing.
12 And when the day
began to wear away,
then came the twelve,
and said unto him,
Send the multitude a-
way, that they may
go into the towns
and country round a-
bout, and lodge, and
get victuals: for we
are here in a desert
place. 13 But he said
unto them, Give ye
them to eat. And they
said, We have no more
but five loaves and

μήτε πήραν, μήτε ἄρτον, μήτε ἀργύριον, μήτε [k]ἀνὰ‖ δύο
nor provision bag, nor bread, nor money, nor each two
χιτῶνας ἔχειν. 4 καὶ εἰς ἣν.ἂν οἰκίαν εἰσέλθητε, ἐκεῖ μένετε,
tunics to have. And into whatever house ye may enter, there remain,
καὶ ἐκεῖθεν ἐξέρχεσθε. 5 καὶ ὅσοι ἂν μὴ.[l]δέξωνται‖ ὑμᾶς,
and thence go forth. And as many as may not receive you,
ἐξερχόμενοι ἀπὸ τῆς.πόλεως.ἐκείνης [m]καὶ‖ τὸν κονιορτὸν ἀπὸ
going forth from that city even the dust from
τῶν.ποδῶν.ὑμῶν [n]ἀποτινάξατε,‖ εἰς μαρτύριον ἐπ' αὐτούς.
your feet shake off, for a testimony against them.
6 Ἐξερχόμενοι.δὲ διήρχοντο κατὰ τὰς κώμας, εὐαγγελιζό-
And going forth they passed through the villages, announcing the
μενοι καὶ θεραπεύοντες πανταχοῦ.
glad tidings and healing everywhere.

7 Ἤκουσεν.δὲ Ἡρώδης ὁ [o]τετράρχης‖ τὰ γινόμενα
And [4]heard [5]of [1]Herod [2]the [3]tetrarch [7]the [8]things [9]being [10]done
[p]ὑπ' αὐτοῦ‖ πάντα· καὶ διηπόρει, διὰ τὸ λέγεσθαι ὑπό
[11]by [12]him [6]all, and was perplexed, because it was said by
τινων, Ὅτι [q]Ἰωάννης‖ [r]ἐγήγερται‖ ἐκ νεκρῶν·
some, John has been raised from among [the] dead;
8 ὑπό τινων δέ, Ὅτι [s]Ἠλίας‖ ἐφάνη· ἄλλων δέ, Ὅτι
by some also, that Elias had appeared; by others also, that
προφήτης [t]εἷς‖ τῶν ἀρχαίων ἀνέστη. 9 [v]Καὶ εἶπεν‖ [w]ὁ‖
a prophet one of the ancients had arisen. And [2]said
Ἡρώδης, [x]Ἰωάννην‖ ἐγὼ ἀπεκεφάλισα· τίς.δέ ἐστιν οὗτος
[1]Herod, John I beheaded, but who is this
περὶ οὗ [y]ἐγὼ‖ ἀκούω τοιαῦτα; Καὶ ἐζήτει ἰδεῖν αὐτόν.
concerning whom I hear such things? And he sought to see him.

10 Καὶ ὑποστρέψαντες οἱ ἀπόστολοι διηγήσαντο αὐτῷ
And [3]having [4]returned [1]the [2]apostles related to him
ὅσα ἐποίησαν· καὶ παραλαβὼν αὐτοὺς ὑπεχώρησεν
whatsoever they had done. And having taken them he retired
κατ'.ἰδίαν εἰς [z]τόπον ἔρημον πόλεως καλουμένης‖ Βηθσαϊδά.
apart into a [2]place [1]desert of a city called Bethsaida.
11 οἱ.δὲ ὄχλοι γνόντες ἠκολούθησαν αὐτῷ· καὶ [a]δεξά-
But the crowds having known [it] followed him; and having
μενος‖ αὐτοὺς ἐλάλει αὐτοῖς περὶ τῆς βασιλείας τοῦ θεοῦ,
received them he spoke to them concerning the kingdom of God,
καὶ τοὺς χρείαν ἔχοντας θεραπείας ἰᾶτο. 12 Ἡ.δὲ ἡμέρα
and those [2]need [1]having of healing he cured. But the day
ἤρξατο κλίνειν· προσελθόντες.δὲ οἱ δώδεκα εἶπον αὐτῷ, Ἀπό-
began to decline, and having come the twelve said to him, Dis-
λυσον τὸν ὄχλον, ἵνα [b]ἀπελθόντες‖ εἰς τὰς κύκλῳ κώμας καὶ
miss the crowd, that having gone into the [2]around [1]villages and
[c]τοὺς‖ ἀγροὺς καταλύσωσιν, καὶ εὕρωσιν ἐπισιτισμόν· ὅτι ὧδε
the country they may lodge, and may find provisions; for here
ἐν ἐρήμῳ τόπῳ ἐσμέν. 13 Εἶπεν.δὲ πρὸς αὐτούς, Δότε αὐτοῖς
in [2]desert [1]a place we are. But he said to them, Give [2]to [3]them
[d]ὑμεῖς φαγεῖν.‖ Οἱ.δὲ [e]εἶπον,‖ Οὐκ.εἰσὶν ἡμῖν πλεῖον ἢ
[1]ye to eat. But they said, There are not to us more than

---

[k] [ἀνὰ] TrL. [l] δέχωνται LTTrA. [m] — καὶ [L]TrA. [n] ἀποτινάσσετε TA. [o] τετραάρχης T. [p] — ὑπ' αὐτοῦ [L]TTrA. [q] Ἰωάνης Tr. [r] ἠγέρθη was raised LTTr. [s] Ἡλείας T. [t] τις some one TA; τὶς Tr. [v] εἶπεν δὲ LTTrA. [w] — ὁ GLTTrAW. [x] Ἰωάνην Tr. [y] — ἐγὼ (*read* ἀκούω I hear) T[Tr]. [z] πόλιν καλουμένην a city called TTrA. [a] ἀποδεξάμενος having gladly received LTTrA. [b] πορευθέντες GLTTrA. [c] — τοὺς T[Tr]A. [d] φάγετε ὑμεῖς LTA. [e] εἶπαν LTTrA.

[f]πέντε ἄρτοι‖ καὶ [g]δύο ἰχθύες,‖ εἰ.[h]μήτι‖ πορευθέντες ἡμεῖς
five loaves and two fishes, unless indeed having gone we
ἀγοράσωμεν εἰς πάντα τὸν.λαὸν.τοῦτον βρώματα. 14 [i]Ἦσαν
should buy for all this people victuals; ²they ³were
γὰρ‖ ὡσεὶ ἄνδρες πεντακισχίλιοι. Εἶπεν.δὲ πρὸς τοὺς μαθητὰς
¹for about ³men ¹five ²thousand. But he said to ²disciples
αὐτοῦ, Κατακλίνατε αὐτοὺς κλισίας [k] ἀνὰ πεντήκοντα. 15 Καὶ
¹his, Make ²recline ¹them in companies by fifties. And
ἐποίησαν οὕτως, καὶ [l]ἀνέκλιναν‖ ἅπαντας. 16 Λαβὼν.δὲ
they did so, and made ²recline ¹all. And having taken
τοὺς πέντε ἄρτους καὶ τοὺς δύο ἰχθύας, ἀναβλέψας εἰς τὸν
the five loaves and the two fishes, having looked up to the
οὐρανὸν εὐλόγησεν αὐτοὺς καὶ κατέκλασεν, καὶ ἐδίδου τοῖς
heaven he blessed them and broke, and gave to the
μαθηταῖς [m]παρατιθέναι‖ τῷ ὄχλῳ. 17 καὶ ἔφαγον καὶ ἐχορ-
disciples to set before the crowd. And they ate and were
τάσθησαν πάντες· καὶ ἤρθη τὸ περισσεῦσαν αὐτοῖς
²satisfied ¹all; and was taken up that which was over and above to them
κλασμάτων κόφινοι δώδεκα.
of fragments ²hand ³baskets ¹twelve.

18 Καὶ ἐγένετο ἐν.τῷ.εἶναι αὐτὸν προσευχόμενον [n]κατα-
And it came to pass as ²was ¹he praying a-
μόνας,‖ συνῆσαν αὐτῷ οἱ μαθηταί· καὶ ἐπηρώτησεν αὐτούς,
lone, ³were ⁴with ⁵him ¹the ²disciples, and he questioned them,
λέγων, Τίνα με [o]λέγουσιν οἱ ὄχλοι‖ εἶναι; 19 Οἱ.δὲ ἀπο-
saying, Whom ⁵me ¹do ⁴pronounce ²the ³crowds to be? And they an-
κριθέντες [p]εἶπον,‖ [q]Ἰωάννην‖ τὸν βαπτιστήν· ἄλλοι.δὲ
swering said, John the Baptist; and others,
[r]Ἠλίαν·‖ ἄλλοι.δέ, ὅτι προφήτης τις τῶν ἀρχαίων ἀνέστη.
Elias; and others, that ²prophet ¹some of the ancients has arisen.
20 Εἶπεν.δὲ αὐτοῖς, Ὑμεῖς.δὲ τίνα με λέγετε εἶναι;
And he said to them, But ye whom ⁴me ¹do ²ye ³pronounce to be?
[s]Ἀποκριθεὶς.δὲ ὁ Πέτρος‖ εἶπεν, Τὸν χριστὸν τοῦ θεοῦ. 21 Ὁ.δὲ
And answering Peter said, The Christ of God. And he
ἐπιτιμήσας αὐτοῖς παρήγγειλεν μηδενὶ [t]εἰπεῖν‖ τοῦτο,
strictly enjoining them charged [them] to no one to tell this,
22 εἰπών, Ὅτι δεῖ τὸν υἱὸν τοῦ ἀνθρώπου πολλὰ
saying, It is necessary for the Son of man many things
παθεῖν, καὶ ἀποδοκιμασθῆναι ἀπὸ τῶν πρεσβυτέρων καὶ ἀρχ-
to suffer, and to be rejected by the elders and chief
ιερέων καὶ γραμματέων, καὶ ἀποκτανθῆναι, καὶ τῇ τρίτῃ
priests and scribes, and to be killed, and the third
ἡμέρᾳ [v]ἐγερθῆναι.‖ 23 [i]Ἔλεγεν.δὲ πρὸς πάντας, Εἴ τις θέλει
day to be raised. And he said to all, If any one desires
ὀπίσω μου [w]ἐλθεῖν, ἀπαρνησάσθω‖ ἑαυτόν, καὶ ἀράτω
after me to come, let him deny himself, and let him take up
τὸν.σταυρὸν.αὐτοῦ [x]καθ᾽.ἡμέραν,‖ καὶ ἀκολουθείτω μοι.
his cross daily, and let him follow me;
24 ὃς.γὰρ.[y]ἂν‖ θέλῃ τὴν.ψυχὴν.αὐτοῦ σῶσαι, ἀπολέσει αὐ-
for whoever may desire his life to save, shall lose it;
τήν· ὃς.δ᾽.ἂν ἀπολέσῃ τὴν.ψυχὴν.αὐτοῦ ἕνεκεν ἐμοῦ, οὗτος
but whoever may lose his life on account of me, he

two fishes; except we should go and buy meat for all this people. 14 For they were about five thousand men. And he said to his disciples, Make them sit down by fifties in a company. 15 And they did so, and made them all sit down. 16 Then he took the five loaves and the two fishes, and looking up to heaven, he blessed them, and brake, and gave to the disciples to set before the multitude. 17 And they did eat, and were all filled: and there was taken up of fragments that remained to them twelve baskets.

18 And it came to pass, as he was alone praying, his disciples were with him: and he asked them, saying, Whom say the people that I am? 19 They answering said, John the Baptist; but some *say*, Elias; and others *say*, that one of the old prophets is risen again. 20 He said unto them, But whom say ye that I am? Peter answering said, The Christ of God. 21 And he straitly charged them, and commanded *them* to tell no man that thing; 22 Saying, The Son of man must suffer many things, and be rejected of the elders and chief priests and scribes, and be slain, and be raised the third day. 23 And he said to *them* all, If any *man* will come after me, let him deny himself, and take up his cross daily, and follow me. 24 For whosoever will save his life shall lose it: but whosoever will lose his life for my sake, the same shall save it.

---

[f] ἄρτοι πέντε T. [g] ἰχθύες δύο GLTTrAW. [h] μή τι LTrA. [i] δὲ and T. [k] + ὡσεὶ (*read* about fifty each) [LTr]A. [l] κατέκλιναν TTr. [m] παραθεῖναι TTrA. [n] κατὰ μόνας LTTr. [o] οἱ ὄχλοι λέγουσιν TTrA. [p] εἶπαν LTTrA. [q] Ἰωάνην Tr. [r] Ἡλείαν T. [s] Πέτρος δὲ ἀποκριθεὶς TTrA. [t] λέγειν GLTTrA. [v] ἀναστῆναι to arise LA. [w] ἔρχεσθαι, ἀρνησάσθω GLTTrA. [x] — καθ᾽ ἡμέραν L. [y] ἐὰν T.

σώσει αὐτήν. 25 τί.γὰρ ὠφελεῖται ἄνθρωπος, κερδήσας
shall save it. For what is [3]profited [1]a [2]man, having gained

τὸν κόσμον ὅλον, ἑαυτὸν.δὲ ἀπολέσας ἢ ζημιωθείς;
the [2]world [1]whole, but himself having destroyed or suffered the loss of?

26 ὃς.γὰρ.ἂν ἐπαισχυνθῇ με καὶ τοὺς ἐμοὺς λόγους,
For whoever may have been ashamed of me and my words,

τοῦτον ὁ υἱὸς τοῦ ἀνθρώπου ἐπαισχυνθήσεται ὅταν ἔλθῃ
him the Son of man will be ashamed of when he shall come

ἐν τῇ δόξῃ αὐτοῦ καὶ τοῦ πατρὸς καὶ τῶν ἁγίων ἀγγέλων.
in the glory of himself and of the Father and of the holy angels.

27 Λέγω.δὲ ὑμῖν ἀληθῶς, εἰσίν τινες τῶν [z]ὧδε[‖] [a]ἑστηκό-
But I say to you of a truth, there are some of those here stand-

των,[‖] οἳ οὐ.μὴ [b]γεύσονται[‖] θανάτου ἕως.ἂν ἴδωσιν
ing who in no wise shall taste of death until they shall have seen

τὴν βασιλείαν τοῦ θεοῦ.
the kingdom of God.

28 Ἐγένετο.δὲ μετὰ τοὺς.λόγους.τούτους ὡσεὶ ἡμέραι ὀκτὼ
And it came to pass after these words about [2]days [1]eight

[c]καὶ[‖] παραλαβὼν [d]τὸν[‖] Πέτρον καὶ [e]Ἰωάννην[‖] καὶ Ἰάκωβον
that having taken Peter and John and James

ἀνέβη εἰς τὸ ὄρος προσεύξασθαι. 29 καὶ ἐγένετο
he went up into the mountain to pray. And it came to pass

ἐν.τῷ.προσεύχεσθαι αὐτὸν τὸ εἶδος τοῦ.προσώπου.αὐτοῦ
as [2]prayed [1]he the appearance of his face

ἕτερον, καὶ ὁ.ἱματισμὸς.αὐτοῦ λευκὸς ἐξαστράπτων.
[became] altered, and his clothing white effulgent.

30 Καὶ ἰδού, ἄνδρες δύο συνελάλουν αὐτῷ, οἵτινες ἦσαν
And behold, [2]men [1]two talked with him, who were

[f]Μωσῆς[‖] καὶ [g]Ἠλίας[‖] 31 οἳ ὀφθέντες ἐν δόξῃ ἔλεγον[h] τὴν
Moses and Elias, who appearing in glory spoke of

ἔξοδον.αὐτοῦ ἣν [i]ἔμελλεν[‖] πληροῦν ἐν Ἱερουσαλήμ.
his departure which he was about to accomplish in Jerusalem.

32 ὁ.δὲ.Πέτρος καὶ οἱ σὺν αὐτῷ ἦσαν βεβαρημένοι ὕπνῳ.
But Peter and those with him were oppressed with sleep.

διαγρηγορήσαντες.δὲ [k]εἶδον[‖] τὴν.δόξαν.αὐτοῦ, καὶ τοὺς δύο
and having awoke fully they saw his glory, and the two

ἄνδρας τοὺς συνεστῶτας αὐτῷ. 33 καὶ ἐγένετο ἐν.τῷ.δια-
men who stood with him. And it came to pass as [2]de-

χωρίζεσθαι αὐτοὺς ἀπ' αὐτοῦ, εἶπεν ὁ Πέτρος πρὸς τὸν
parted [1]these from him, [2]said [1]Peter to

Ἰησοῦν, Ἐπιστάτα, καλόν ἐστιν ἡμᾶς ὧδε εἶναι· καὶ ποιήσωμεν
Jesus, Master, good it is for us here to be; and let us make

σκηνὰς τρεῖς, μίαν σοί, καὶ [l]Μωσεῖ μίαν,[‖] καὶ μίαν
[2]tabernacles [1]three, one for thee, and for Moses one, and one

[m]Ἠλίᾳ,[‖] μὴ εἰδὼς ὃ λέγει. 34 ταῦτα δὲ αὐτοῦ.λέγοντος
for Elias, not knowing what he is saying. But these things as he was saying

ἐγένετο νεφέλη καὶ [n]ἐπεσκίασεν[‖] αὐτούς· ἐφοβήθησαν.δὲ ἐν.τῷ
[3]came [1]a [2]cloud and overshadowed them, and they feared as

[o]ἐκείνους εἰσελθεῖν[‖] εἰς τὴν νεφέλην. 35 καὶ φωνὴ ἐγένετο ἐκ
those entered into the cloud: and a voice came out of

τῆς νεφέλης, λέγουσα, Οὗτός ἐστιν ὁ.υἱός.μου ὁ [p]ἀγαπητός·[‖]
the cloud, saying, This is my Son the beloved;

25 For what is a man advantaged, if he gain the whole world, and lose himself, or be cast away? 26 For whosoever shall be ashamed of me and of my words, of him shall the Son of man be ashamed, when he shall come in his own glory, and *in his* Father's, and of the holy angels. 27 But I tell you of a truth, there be some standing here, which shall not taste of death, till they see the kingdom of God.

28 And it came to pass about an eight days after these sayings, he took Peter and John and James, and went up into a mountain to pray. 29 And as he prayed, the fashion of his countenance was altered, and his raiment *was* white *and* glistering. 30 And, behold, there talked with him two men, which were Moses and Elias: 31 who appeared in glory, and spake of his decease which he should accomplish at Jerusalem. 32 But Peter and they that were with him were heavy with sleep: and when they were awake, they saw his glory, and the two men that stood with him. 33 And it came to pass, as they departed from him, Peter said unto Jesus, Master, it is good for us to be here: and let us make three tabernacles; one for thee, and one for Moses, and one for Elias: not knowing what he said. 34 While he thus spake, there came a cloud, and overshadowed them: and they feared as they entered into the cloud. 35 And there came a voice out of the cloud, saying, This is my beloved Son: hear him. 36 And

---

[z] αὐτοῦ TTrA [a] ἑστώτων GLTTrAW. [b] γεύσωνται should taste GLTTrAW. [c] [καὶ] L.
[d] — τὸν GLTTrAW. [e] Ἰωάνην Tr. [f] Μωϋσῆς LTTrAW. [g] Ἠλείας T. [h] + [δὲ] and L.
[i] ἤμελλεν T. [k] εἶδαν T. [l] μίαν Μωσεῖ G; μίαν Μωϋσεῖ LTTrAW. [m] Ἠλείᾳ T.
[n] ἐπεσκίαζεν TTrA. [o] εἰσελθεῖν αὐτοὺς they entered TTrA. [p] ἐκλελεγμένος chosen TTrA.

αὐτοῦ ἀκούετε. 36 Καὶ ἐν.τῷ γενέσθαι τὴν φωνὴν εὑρέθη
[3]him [1]hear [2]ye. And as occurred the voice [2]was [3]found
[q]ὁ‖ Ἰησοῦς μόνος. Καὶ αὐτοὶ ἐσίγησαν, καὶ οὐδενὶ ἀπήγγειλαν
[1]Jesus alone: and they were silent, and to no one they told
ἐν ἐκείναις ταῖς ἡμέραις οὐδὲν ὧν [r]ἑωράκασιν.‖
in those days anything of what they had seen.

37 Ἐγένετο.δὲ [s]ἐν‖ τῇ ἑξῆς ἡμέρᾳ, κατελθόντων.αὐτῶν
And it came to pass on the next day, on their having come down
ἀπὸ τοῦ ὄρους, συνήντησεν αὐτῷ ὄχλος πολύς. 38 Καὶ
from the mountain, [4]met [5]him [1]a [3]crowd [2]great. And
ἰδού, ἀνὴρ ἀπὸ τοῦ ὄχλου [t]ἀνεβόησεν,‖ λέγων, Διδάσκαλε,
behold, a man from the crowd cried out, saying, Teacher,
δέομαί σου [v]ἐπίβλεψον‖ ἐπὶ τὸν.υἱόν.μου, ὅτι μονογενής
I beseech thee look upon my son, for an only child
[w]ἐστίν μοι·‖ 39 καὶ ἰδού, πνεῦμα λαμβάνει αὐτὸν καὶ ἐξ-
he is to me: and behold, a spirit takes him and sud-
αίφνης κράζει, καὶ σπαράσσει αὐτὸν μετὰ ἀφροῦ,
denly he cries out, and it throws [2]into [3]convulsions [1]him with foaming,
καὶ μόγις ἀποχωρεῖ ἀπ' αὐτοῦ, συντρίβον αὐτόν. 40 καὶ
and with difficulty departs from him, bruising him. And
ἐδεήθην τῶν.μαθητῶν.σου ἵνα [x]ἐκβάλλωσιν‖ αὐτό, καὶ οὐκ
I besought thy disciples that they might cast out it, and [3]not
ἠδυνήθησαν. 41 Ἀποκριθεὶς.δὲ ὁ Ἰησοῦς εἶπεν, Ὦ γενεὰ
[1]they [2]were able. And [2]answering [1]Jesus said, O generation
ἄπιστος καὶ διεστραμμένη, ἕως πότε ἔσομαι πρὸς ὑμᾶς καὶ
unbelieving and perverted, until when shall I be with you and
ἀνέξομαι ὑμῶν; προσάγαγε [y]ὧδε τὸν.υἱόν.σου.‖ 42 Ἔτι.δὲ
bear with you? Bring hither thy son. But [4]yet
προσερχομένου.αὐτοῦ ἔρρηξεν αὐτὸν τὸ δαιμόνιον καὶ συν-
[1]as [2]he [3]was coming near [3]dashed [5]down [4]him [1]the [2]demon and threw
εσπάραξεν· ἐπετίμησεν.δὲ ὁ Ἰησοῦς τῷ πνεύματι τῷ
[him] into convulsions. And [2]rebuked [1]Jesus the spirit the
ἀκαθάρτῳ, καὶ ἰάσατο τὸν παῖδα, καὶ ἀπέδωκεν αὐτὸν τῷ
unclean, and healed the child, and gave back him to
πατρὶ.αὐτοῦ. 43 ἐξεπλήσσοντο.δὲ πάντες ἐπὶ τῇ μεγαλειότητι
his father. And [2]were [3]astonished [1]all at the majesty
τοῦ θεοῦ.
of God.

Πάντων.δὲ θαυμαζόντων ἐπὶ πᾶσιν οἷς [z]ἐποίησεν‖ [a]ὁ Ἰη-
And [as] all were wondering at all which [2]did [1]Je-
σοῦς,‖ εἶπεν πρὸς τοὺς.μαθητὰς.αὐτοῦ, 44 Θέσθε ὑμεῖς εἰς τὰ
sus, he said to his disciples, Lay [2]by [1]ye into
ὦτα.ὑμῶν τοὺς.λόγους.τούτους· ὁ.γὰρ.υἱὸς τοῦ ἀνθρώπου μέλ-
your ears these words: For the Son of man is a-
λει παραδίδοσθαι εἰς χεῖρας ἀνθρώπων. 45 Οἱ.δὲ ἠγνόουν
bout to be delivered up into [the] hands of men. But they understood not
τὸ.ῥῆμα.τοῦτο, καὶ ἦν παρακεκαλυμμένον ἀπ' αὐτῶν ἵνα
this saying, and it was veiled from them that
μὴ.αἴσθωνται αὐτό· καὶ ἐφοβοῦντο [b]ἐρωτῆσαι‖ αὐτὸν
they should not perceive it. And they feared to ask him
περὶ τοῦ ῥήματος τούτου. 46 Εἰσῆλθεν.δὲ διαλογισμὸς ἐν
concerning [2]saying [1]this. But [3]came [4]up [1]a [2]reasoning among
αὐτοῖς, τό, τίς ἂν εἴη μείζων αὐτῶν. 47 ὁ.δὲ.Ἰησοῦς [c]ἰδὼν‖
them, this, who might be greatest of them. And Jesus having seen

when the voice was past, Jesus was found alone. And they kept *it* close, and told no man in those days any of those things which they had seen.

37 And it came to pass, that on the next day, when they were come down from the hill, much people met him. 38 And, behold, a man of the company cried out, saying, Master, I beseech thee, look upon my son: for he is mine only child. 39 And, lo, a spirit taketh him, and he suddenly crieth out; and it teareth him that he foameth again, and bruising him hardly departeth from him. 40 And I besought thy disciples to cast him out; and they could not. 41 And Jesus answering said, O faithless and perverse generation, how long shall I be with you, and suffer you? Bring thy son hither. 42 And as he was yet a coming, the devil threw him down, and tare *him*. And Jesus rebuked the unclean spirit, and healed the child, and delivered him again to his father. 43 And they were all amazed at the mighty power of God.

But while they wondered every one at all things which Jesus did, he said unto his disciples, 44 Let these sayings sink down into your ears: for the Son of man shall be delivered into the hands of men. 45 But they understood not this saying, and it was hid from them, that they perceived it not: and they feared to ask him of that saying. 46 Then there arose a reasoning among them, which of them should be greatest. 47 And Jesus, perceiving the thought of

[q] — ὁ LTTrAW. [r] ἑώρακαν TTrA. [s] — ἐν T[Tr]A. [t] ἐβόησεν LTTrA. [v] ἐπιβλέψαι GTTrAW. [w] μοι ἐστιν LTTrAW. [x] ἐκβάλωσιν GLTTrAW. [y] τὸν υἱόν σου ὧδε GW. [z] ἐποίει GLTTrA. [a] — ὁ Ἰησοῦς (read ἐποίει he was doing) TTrA. [b] ἐπερωτῆσαι L. [c] εἰδὼς T.

their heart, took a
child, and set him by
him, 48 and said unto
them, Whosoever shall
receive this child in
my name receiveth
me: and whosoever
shall receive me re-
ceiveth him that sent
me: for he that is least
among you all, the
same shall be great.
49 And John answered
and said, Master, we
saw one casting out
devils in thy name;
and we forbad him,
because he followeth
not with us. 50 And
Jesus said unto him,
Forbid *him* not: for
he that is not against
us is for us.

51 And it came to
pass, when the time
was come that he
should be received up,
he stedfastly set his
face to go to Jerusa-
lem, 52 and sent mes-
sengers before his face:
and they went, and
entered into a village
of the Samaritans, to
make ready for him.
53 And they did not
receive him, because
his face was as though
he would go to Jeru-
salem. 54 And when
his disciples James
and John saw *this*,
they said, Lord, wilt
thou that we command
fire to come down
from heaven, and con-
sume them, even as
Elias did? 55 But he
turned, and rebuked
them, and said, Ye
know not what man-
ner of spirit ye are of.
56 For the Son of man
is not come to destroy
men's lives, but to save
them. And they went
to another village.

57 And it came to
pass, that, as they went
in the way, a certain
man said unto him,
Lord, I will follow
thee whithersoever
thou goest. 58 And Je-

τὸν διαλογισμὸν τῆς.καρδίας.αὐτῶν, ἐπιλαβόμενος [d]παιδίου‖
the reasoning of their heart, having taken hold of a little child
ἔστησεν αὐτὸ παρ' ἑαυτῷ, 48 καὶ εἶπεν αὐτοῖς, ῝Ος.[e]ἐὰν‖
he set it by him, and said to them, Whoever
δέξηται τοῦτο τὸ παιδίον ἐπὶ τῷ.ὀνόματί.μου, ἐμὲ δέχεται·
shall receive this little child in my name, me receives;
καὶ ὃς.[f]ἐὰν‖ ἐμὲ δέξηται, δέχεται τὸν ἀποστείλαντά με.
and whoever me shall receive, receives him who sent me.
ὁ.γὰρ μικρότερος ἐν πᾶσιν ὑμῖν ὑπάρχων οὗτος [g]ἔσται‖
For he who [2]less [3]among [5]all [4]you [1]is he shall be
μέγας. 49 Ἀποκριθεὶς.δὲ [h]ὁ‖ [i]Ἰωάννης‖ εἶπεν, Ἐπιστάτα,
great. And answering John said, Master,
εἴδομέν τινα ἐπὶ τῷ.ὀνόματί.σου ἐκβάλλοντα [k]τὰ‖ δαιμόνια·
we saw some one in thy name casting out the demons,
καὶ ἐκωλύσαμεν αὐτόν, ὅτι οὐκ.ἀκολουθεῖ μεθ' ἡμῶν. 50 [l]Καὶ
and we forbade him, because he follows not with us. And
εἶπεν‖ πρὸς αὐτὸν [m]ὁ‖ Ἰησοῦς, Μὴ.κωλύετε· ὃς.γὰρ οὐκ
[2]said [3]to [4]him [1]Jesus, Forbid not; for whosoever [2]not
ἔστιν καθ' [n]ἡμῶν,‖ ὑπὲρ [n]ἡμῶν‖ ἐστιν.
[1]is against us, for us is.

51 Ἐγένετο.δὲ ἐν.τῷ.συμπληροῦσθαι τὰς ἡμέρας τῆς
And it came to pass when were being fulfilled the days of the
[o]ἀναλήψεως‖.αὐτοῦ, καὶ αὐτὸς τὸ.πρόσωπον.[p]αὐτοῦ‖ [q]ἐστή-
receiving him up, that he his face sted-
ριξεν‖ τοῦ πορεύεσθαι εἰς Ἱερουσαλήμ. 52 καὶ ἀπέστειλεν
fastly set to go to Jerusalem. And he sent
ἀγγέλους πρὸ προσώπου αὐτοῦ. καὶ πορευθέντες εἰσῆλθον
messengers before [2]face [1]his. And having gone they entered
εἰς [r]κώμην Σαμαρειτῶν,‖ ὥστε ἑτοιμάσαι αὐτῷ. 53 καὶ οὐκ
into a village of Samaritans, so as to make ready for him. And [3]not
ἐδέξαντο αὐτόν, ὅτι τὸ.πρόσωπον.αὐτοῦ ἦν πορευό-
[1]they [2]did receive him, because his face was [as] go-
μενον εἰς Ἱερουσαλήμ. 54 ἰδόντες.δὲ οἱ.μαθηταὶ.[s]αὐτοῦ‖
ing to Jerusalem. And seeing [it] his disciples
Ἰάκωβος καὶ [t]Ἰωάννης‖ [w]εἶπον,‖ Κύριε, θέλεις εἴπω-
James and John said, Lord, wilt thou [that] we should
μεν πῦρ καταβῆναι [x]ἀπὸ‖ τοῦ οὐρανοῦ, καὶ ἀναλῶσαι αὐτούς,
call fire to come down from the heaven, and consume them,
[y]ὡς καὶ Ἠλίας ἐποίησεν‖; 55 Στραφεὶς.δὲ ἐπετίμησεν αὐτοῖς,
as also Elias did? But turning he rebuked them,
[z]καὶ εἶπεν, Οὐκ.οἴδατε οἵου πνεύματός ἐστε ὑμεῖς· 56 [z]ὁ.γὰρ
and said, Ye know not of what spirit [2]are [1]ye. For the
υἱὸς τοῦ ἀνθρώπου οὐκ.ἦλθεν ψυχὰς ἀνθρώπων ἀπολέσαι,
Son of man did not come [the] lives of men to destroy,
ἀλλὰ σῶσαι.‖ Καὶ ἐπορεύθησαν εἰς ἑτέραν κώμην.
but to save. And they went to another village.

57 [a]Ἐγένετο.δὲ‖ πορευομένων.αὐτῶν ἐν τῇ ὁδῷ εἶπέν τις
And it came to pass as they were going in the way [3]said [1]some [2]one
πρὸς αὐτόν, Ἀκολουθήσω σοι ὅπου [b]ἂν‖ ἀπέρχῃ, [c]κύριε.‖
to him, I will follow thee wherever thou mayest go, Lord.

[d] παιδίον TrA. [e] ἂν L. [f] ἂν T. [g] ἐστιν is LTTrA. [h] — ὁ LTrA. [i] Ἰωάνης Tr.
[k] — τὰ LTTrAW. [l] εἶπεν δὲ LTTrA. [m] — ὁ T[A]. [n] ὑμῶν you GLTTrA. [o] ἀναλήμψεως
LTTrA. [p] [αὐτοῦ] LTrA. [q] ἐστήρισεν TTrA. [r] πόλιν Σαμαριτῶν a city of Samaritans T.
[s] — αὐτοῦ (*read* the disciples) T[TrA] [t] Ἰωάνης Tr. [w] εἶπαν TTrA. [x] ἐκ out of L.
[y] — ὡς καὶ Ἠλίας ἐποίησεν TTr[A]. [z] — καὶ εἶπεν (*verse* 55) .... σῶσαι (*verse* 56) LTTrA;
— ὁ γὰρ .... σῶσαι G. [a] Καὶ and TTrA. [b] ἐὰν LTrA. [c] — κύριε LTTr[A].

58 Καὶ εἶπεν αὐτῷ ὁ Ἰησοῦς, Αἱ ἀλώπεκες φωλεοὺς ἔχουσιν,
And [2]said [3]to [4]him [1]Jesus, The foxes holes have,
καὶ τὰ πετεινὰ τοῦ οὐρανοῦ κατασκηνώσεις· ὁ.δὲ υἱὸς τοῦ
and the birds of the heaven nests; but the Son
ἀνθρώπου οὐκ.ἔχει ποῦ τὴν κεφαλὴν κλίνῃ. 59 Εἶπεν.δὲ
of man has not where the head he may lay. And he said
πρὸς ἕτερον, Ἀκολούθει μοι. Ὁ.δὲ εἶπεν, [d]Κύριε,‖ ἐπίτρεψόν
to another, Follow me. But he said, Lord, allow
μοι [e]ἀπελθόντι πρῶτον‖ θάψαι τὸν.πατέρα.μου. 60 Εἶπεν.δὲ
me going away first to bury my father. But [2]said
αὐτῷ [f]ὁ Ἰησοῦς,‖ Ἄφες τοὺς νεκροὺς θάψαι τοὺς ἑαυτῶν
[3]to [4]him [1]Jesus, Leave the dead to bury their own
νεκρούς· σὺ.δὲ ἀπελθὼν διάγγελλε τὴν βασιλείαν τοῦ θεοῦ.
dead; but thou going forth declare the kingdom of God.
61 Εἶπεν.δὲ καὶ ἕτερος, Ἀκολουθήσω σοι, κύριε· πρῶτον.δὲ
And [2]said [3]also [1]another, I will follow thee, Lord, but first
ἐπίτρεψόν μοι ἀποτάξασθαι τοῖς εἰς τὸν.οἶκόν.μου. 62 Εἶπεν.δὲ
allow me to take leave of those at my house. But [2]said
[g]πρὸς αὐτὸν ὁ Ἰησοῦς,‖ Οὐδεὶς [h]ἐπιβαλὼν‖ τὴν.χεῖρα.[i]αὐτοῦ‖
[3]to [4]him [1]Jesus, No one having laid his hand
ἐπ' ἄροτρον, καὶ βλέπων εἰς τὰ ὀπίσω, εὔθετός ἐστιν
upon [the] plough, and looking on the things behind, [2]fit [1]is
[k]εἰς τὴν βασιλείαν‖ τοῦ θεοῦ.
for the kingdom of God.

sus said unto him, Foxes have holes, and birds of the air *have* nests; but the Son of man hath not where to lay *his* head. 59 And he said unto another, Follow me. But he said, Lord, suffer me first to go and bury my father. 60 Jesus said unto him, Let the dead bury their dead: but go thou and preach the kingdom of God. 61 And another also said, Lord, I will follow thee; but let me first go bid them farewell, which are at home at my house. 62 And Jesus said unto him, No man, having put his hand to the plough, and looking back, is fit for the kingdom of God.

10 Μετὰ.δὲ ταῦτα ἀνέδειξεν ὁ κύριος [l]καὶ‖ ἑτέρους ἑβδο-
Now after these things [3]appointed [1]the [2]Lord [6]also [5]others [4]seven-
μήκοντα[m], καὶ ἀπέστειλεν αὐτοὺς ἀνὰ.δύο πρὸ προσώπου
ty, and sent them two and two before [2]face
αὐτοῦ, εἰς πᾶσαν πόλιν καὶ τόπον οὗ [n]ἔμελλεν‖ αὐτὸς
[1]his, into every city and place where he was about himself
ἔρχεσθαι. 2 Ἔλεγεν [o]οὖν‖ πρὸς αὐτούς, Ὁ μὲν θερισμὸς
to come. He said therefore to them, The [2]indeed [1]harvest [is]
πολύς, οἱ.δὲ ἐργάται ὀλίγοι· δεήθητε οὖν τοῦ κυρίου
great, but the workmen [are] few. Supplicate therefore the Lord
τοῦ θερισμοῦ, ὅπως [p]ἐκβάλλῃ ἐργάτας‖ εἰς τὸν θερισμὸν
of the harvest, that he may send out workmen into [2]harvest
αὐτοῦ. 3 Ὑπάγετε· ἰδού, [q]ἐγὼ‖ ἀποστέλλω ὑμᾶς ὡς ἄρνας ἐν
[1]his. Go; lo, I send forth you as lambs in
μέσῳ λύκων. 4 μὴ βαστάζετε [r]βαλάντιον‖ μὴ πήραν
[the] midst of wolves. Neither carry purse nor provision bag
[s]μηδὲ‖ ὑποδήματα· [t]καὶ‖ μηδένα κατὰ τὴν ὁδὸν ἀσπάσησθε.
nor sandals, and no one on the way salute.
5 Εἰς.ἣν.δ'.ἂν [v]οἰκίαν εἰσέρχησθε,‖ πρῶτον λέγετε, Εἰρήνη τῷ
And into whatever house ye may enter, first say, Peace
οἴκῳ.τούτῳ. 6 καὶ ἐὰν [w]μὲν‖ ᾖ ἐκεῖ [x]υἱὸς εἰρήνης, [y]ἐπανα-
to this house. And if indeed be there a son of peace, [3]shall
παύσεται‖ ἐπ' αὐτὸν ἡ.εἰρήνη.ὑμῶν· εἰ.δὲ μήγε, ἐφ' ὑμᾶς
[4]rest [5]upon [6]it [1]your [2]peace; but if not so, to you
ἀνακάμψει. 7 ἐν αὐτῇ δὲ τῇ οἰκίᾳ μένετε, [z]ἐσθίοντες‖ καὶ
it shall return. [2]In [3]the [4]same [1]and house abide, eating and

X. After these things the Lord appointed other seventy also, and sent them two and two before his face into every city and place, whither he himself would come. 2 Therefore said he unto them, The harvest truly *is* great, but the labourers *are* few: pray ye therefore the Lord of the harvest, that he would send forth labourers into his harvest. 3 Go your ways: behold, I send you forth as lambs among wolves. 4 Carry neither purse, nor scrip, nor shoes: and salute no man by the way. 5 And into whatsoever house ye enter, first say, Peace *be* to this house. 6 And if the son of peace be there, your peace shall rest upon it: if not, it shall turn to you again. 7 And in the same house remain, eating and drinking such things as they give: for the labourer is worthy

[d] — Κύριε T. [e] πρῶτον ἀπελθεῖν first to go away L; πρῶτον ἀπελθόντι TTr. [f] — ὁ Ἰησοῦς (*read* he said) [L]TTrA. [g] ὁ Ἰησοῦς πρὸς αὐτόν LTTr; — πρὸς αὐτὸν A. [h] ἐπιβάλλων L. [i] [αὐτοῦ] Tr. [k] τῇ βασιλείᾳ LTTrA. [l] [καὶ] TrA. [m] + [δύο] two L. [n] ἤμελλεν LTTrAW. [o] δὲ and (he said) LTTrA. [p] ἐκβάλῃ ἐργάτας GLW; ἐργάτας ἐκβάλῃ TTrA. [q] — ἐγὼ (*read* ἀποσ. I send forth) LTTrA. [r] βαλλάντιον LTTrAW. [s] μὴ TTrA. [t] — καὶ T. [v] εἰσέλθητε οἰκίαν TTrA; οἰκίαν εἰσέλθητε L. [w] — μὲν GLTTrAW. [x] + ὁ the (son) E. [y] ἐπαναπαήσεται T. [z] ἔσθοντες LTTrA.

of his hire. Go not from house to house.
8 And into whatsoever city ye enter, and they receive you, eat such things as are set before you:
9 and heal the sick that are therein, and say unto them, The kingdom of God is come nigh unto you.
10 But into whatsoever city ye enter, and they receive you not, go your ways out into the streets of the same, and say,
11 Even the very dust of your city, which cleaveth on us, we do wipe off against you: notwithstanding be ye sure of this, that the kingdom of God is come nigh unto you.
12 But I say unto you, that it shall be more tolerable in that day for Sodom, than for that city.
13 Woe unto thee, Chorazin! woe unto thee, Bethsaida! for if the mighty works had been done in Tyre and Sidon, which have been done in you, they had a great while ago repented, sitting in sackcloth and ashes.
14 But it shall be more tolerable for Tyre and Sidon at the judgment, than for you.
15 And thou, Capernaum, which art exalted to heaven, shalt be thrust down to hell.
16 He that heareth you heareth me; and he that despiseth you despiseth me; and he that despiseth me despiseth him that sent me.

17 And the seventy returned again with joy, saying, Lord, even the devils are subject unto us through thy name.
18 And he said unto them, I beheld Satan as lightning fall from heaven.
19 Behold, I give unto you power to tread on serpents and scorpions, and over all the power of the enemy: and nothing shall by any means hurt you.

πίνοντες τὰ παρ' αὐτῶν· ἄξιος-γὰρ ὁ ἐργάτης
drinking the things [supplied] by them; for worthy ²the ³workman
τοῦ-μισθοῦ-αὐτοῦ ᵃἐστιν.ǁ μὴ-μεταβαίνετε ἐξ οἰκίας εἰς οἰκίαν.
⁴of ⁵his ⁶hire ¹is. Remove not from house to house.
8 καὶ εἰς ἣν-ᵇδ'ǁ-ἂν πόλιν εἰσέρχησθε, καὶ δέχωνται ὑμᾶς,
And into whatever ²also ¹city ye may enter, and they receive you,
ἐσθίετε τὰ παρατιθέμενα ὑμῖν, 9 καὶ θεραπεύετε τοὺς ἐν
eat the things set before you, and heal the ²in
αὐτῇ ἀσθενεῖς, καὶ λέγετε αὐτοῖς, Ἤγγικεν ἐφ' ὑμᾶς ἡ βασι-
³it ¹sick, and say to them, Has drawn near to you the king-
λεία τοῦ θεοῦ. 10 εἰς-ἣν-δ'-ἂν πόλιν ᶜεἰσέρχησθε,ǁ καὶ μὴ
dom of God. But into whatever city ye may enter, and ³not
δέχωνται ὑμᾶς, ἐξελθόντες εἰς τὰς-πλατείας-αὐτῆς, εἴπατε,
¹they ²do receive you, having gone out into its streets, say,
11 Καὶ τὸν κονιορτὸν τὸν κολληθέντα ἡμῖν ἐκ τῆς πόλεως
Even the dust which clung to us out of ²city
ὑμῶν ᵈ ἀπομασσόμεθα ὑμῖν· πλὴν τοῦτο γινώσκετε, ὅτι
¹your we wipe off against you; yet this know, that
ἤγγικεν ᵉἐφ' ὑμᾶςǁ ἡ βασιλεία τοῦ θεοῦ. 12 λέγω-ᶠδὲǁ ὑμῖν,
has drawn near to you the kingdom of God. And I say to you,
ὅτι Σοδόμοις ἐν τῇ-ἡμέρᾳ-ἐκείνῃ ἀνεκτότερον ἔσται ἢ τῇ
that for Sodom in that day more tolerable it shall be than
πόλει-ἐκείνῃ. 13 Οὐαί σοι, ᵍΧωραζίν,ǁ οὐαί σοι, Βηθσαϊδά·
for that city. Woe to thee, Chorazin! woe to thee, Bethsaida!
ὅτι εἰ ἐν Τύρῳ καὶ Σιδῶνι ʰἐγένοντοǁ αἱ δυνάμεις αἱ
for if in Tyre and Sidon had taken place the works of power which
γενόμεναι ἐν ὑμῖν, πάλαι ἂν ἐν σάκκῳ καὶ σποδῷ
have been taking place in you, long ago in sackcloth and ashes
ⁱκαθήμεναιǁ μετενόησαν. 14 πλὴν Τύρῳ καὶ Σιδῶνι ἀνεκ-
sitting they had repented. But for Tyre and Sidon more
τότερον ἔσται ἐν τῇ κρίσει ἢ ὑμῖν. 15 καὶ σύ, ᵏΚαπερ-
tolerable will it be in the judgment than for you. And thou, Caper-
ναούμ,ǁ ˡἡǁ ἕως ᵐτοῦǁ οὐρανοῦ ⁿὑψωθεῖσα,ǁ ἕως ᵒ ᾅδου
naum, who to the heaven hast been lifted up, to hades
καταβιβασθήσῃ. 16 Ὁ ἀκούων ὑμῶν ἐμοῦ ἀκούει· καὶ
thou shalt be brought down. He that hears you ²me ¹hears, and
ὁ ἀθετῶν ὑμᾶς ἐμὲ ἀθετεῖ· ὁ-δὲ ἐμὲ ἀθετῶν ἀθετεῖ τὸν
he that rejects you ²me ¹rejects, and he that ²me ¹rejects rejects him
ἀποστείλαντά με.
who sent me.

17 Ὑπέστρεψαν-δὲ οἱ ἑβδομήκονταᵖ μετὰ χαρᾶς, λέγοντες,
And ³returned ¹the ²seventy with joy, saying,
Κύριε, καὶ τὰ δαιμόνια ὑποτάσσεται ἡμῖν ἐν τῷ ὀνόματί
Lord, even the demons are subject to us through ²name
σου. 18 Εἶπεν-δὲ αὐτοῖς, Ἐθεώρουν τὸν σατανᾶν ὡς ἀστραπὴν
¹thy. And he said to them, I beheld Satan as lightning
ἐκ τοῦ οὐρανοῦ πεσόντα. 19 ἰδού, ᵍδίδωμιǁ ὑμῖν τὴν ἐξουσίαν
out of the heaven falling. Lo, I give you the authority
τοῦ πατεῖν ἐπάνω ὄφεων καὶ σκορπίων, καὶ ἐπὶ πᾶσαν τὴν
to tread upon serpents and scorpions, and upon all the
δύναμιν τοῦ ἐχθροῦ· καὶ οὐδὲν ὑμᾶς οὐ-μὴ ʳἀδικήσῃ.ǁ
power of the enemy, and nothing you in anywise shall injure.
(lit. in no wise)

ᵃ — ἐστιν (read [is]) LTTrA. ᵇ — δ' also LTTrA. ᶜ εἰσέλθητε LTTrA. ᵈ + εἰς τοὺς πόδας to the feet (+[ἡμῶν] of us A) LTTrA. ᵉ — ἐφ' ὑμᾶς GLTTrA. ᶠ — δὲ and G[L]TrAW. ᵍ Χοραζίν EGLW; Χοραζείν TTrA. ʰ ἐγενήθησαν LTTrA. ⁱ καθήμενοι LTTrA. ᵏ Καφαρναούμ LTTrAW. ˡ μὴ LTTrA. ᵐ — τοῦ LTTr. ⁿ ὑψωθήσῃ; wilt thou be lifted up? LTTrA. ᵒ + τοῦ the TrA. ᵖ + [δύο] two L. ᵍ δέδωκα I have given TTrA. ʳ ἀδικήσει ELTTrA.

20 πλὴν ἐν τούτῳ μὴ.χαίρετε, ὅτι τὰ πνεύματα ὑμῖν ὑποτάσ-
Yet in this rejoice not, that the spirits to you are sub-
σεται· χαίρετε.δὲ [s]μᾶλλον‖ ὅτι τὰ.ὀνόματα.ὑμῶν [t]ἐγράφη‖
jected, but rejoice rather that your names are written
ἐν τοῖς οὐρανοῖς. 21 Ἐν αὐτῇ.τῇ ὥρᾳ ἠγαλλιάσατο [v] τῷ
in the heavens. In the same hour [2]rejoiced [3]in [4]the
πνεύματι[w] [x]ὁ Ἰησοῦς,‖ καὶ εἶπεν, Ἐξομολογοῦμαί σοι, πάτερ,
[5]Spirit [1]Jesus, and said, I praise thee, O Father,
κύριε τοῦ οὐρανοῦ καὶ τῆς γῆς, ὅτι ἀπέκρυψας ταῦτα ἀπὸ
Lord of the heaven and of the earth, that thou didst hide these things from
σοφῶν καὶ συνετῶν, καὶ ἀπεκάλυψας αὐτὰ νηπίοις· ναί, ὁ πα-
wise and prudent, and didst reveal them to babes: yea, Fa-
τήρ, ὅτι οὕτως [y]ἐγένετο εὐδοκία‖ ἔμπροσθέν σου. 22 [z]Καὶ
ther, for thus was it well pleasing before thee. And
στραφεὶς πρὸς τοὺς μαθητὰς εἶπεν,‖ Πάντα [a]παρεδόθη μοι‖
having turned to the disciples he said, All things were delivered to me
ὑπὸ τοῦ.πατρός.μου· καὶ οὐδεὶς γινώσκει τίς ἐστιν ὁ υἱὸς εἰ.μὴ
by my Father, and no one knows who is the Son except
ὁ πατήρ, καὶ τίς ἐστιν ὁ πατήρ, εἰ.μὴ ὁ υἱός, καὶ ᾧ.[b]ἐὰν‖
the Father, and who is the Father, except the Son, and he to whomsoever
βούληται ὁ υἱὸς ἀποκαλύψαι. 23 Καὶ στραφεὶς πρὸς
[3]may [4]will [1]the [2]Son to reveal [him]. And having turned to
τοὺς μαθητὰς κατ'.ἰδίαν εἶπεν, Μακάριοι οἱ ὀφθαλμοὶ
the disciples apart he said, Blessed [are] the eyes
οἱ βλέποντες ἃ βλέπετε. 24 λέγω.γὰρ ὑμῖν, ὅτι πολλοὶ
which see what ye see. For I say to you, that many
προφῆται καὶ βασιλεῖς ἠθέλησαν ἰδεῖν ἃ ὑμεῖς βλέπετε,
prophets and kings desired to see what ye see,
καὶ οὐκ [c]εἶδον·‖ καὶ ἀκοῦσαι ἃ ἀκούετε, καὶ οὐκ.ἤκουσαν.
and saw not; and to hear what ye hear, and heard not.

25 Καὶ ἰδού, νομικός τις ἀνέστη, ἐκπειράζων
And behold, a [2]doctor [3]of [4]the [5]law [1]certain stood up, tempting
αὐτόν, [d]καὶ‖ λέγων, Διδάσκαλε, τί ποιήσας ζωὴν αἰώνιον
him, and saying, Teacher, [3]what [1]having [2]done life eternal
κληρονομήσω; 26 Ὁ.δὲ εἶπεν πρὸς αὐτόν, Ἐν τῷ νόμῳ τί
shall I inherit? And he said to him, In the law what
γέγραπται; πῶς ἀναγινώσκεις; 27 Ὁ.δὲ ἀποκριθεὶς εἶπεν,
has been written? how readest thou? And he answering said,
Ἀγαπήσεις κύριον τὸν.θεόν.σου ἐξ ὅλης [e]τῆς‖ καρδίας
Thou shalt love [the] Lord thy God with all [2]heart
σου καὶ [f]ἐξ ὅλης τῆς.ψυχῆς.σου καὶ ἐξ ὅλης τῆς.ἰσχύος‖.σου
[1]thy and with all thy soul and with all thy strength
καὶ [g]ἐξ ὅλης τῆς.διανοίας‖.σου· καὶ τὸν.πλησίον.σου ὡς σεαυ-
and with all thy mind; and thy neighbour as thy-
τόν. 28 Εἶπεν.δὲ αὐτῷ, Ὀρθῶς ἀπεκρίθης· τοῦτο ποίει,
self. And he said to him, Rightly thou hast answered: this do,
καὶ ζήσῃ. 29 Ὁ.δὲ θέλων [h]δικαιοῦν‖ ἑαυτὸν εἶπεν πρὸς
and thou shalt live. But he desiring to justify himself said to
τὸν Ἰησοῦν, Καὶ τίς ἐστίν μου πλησίον; 30 Ὑπολαβὼν.[i]δὲ‖
Jesus, And who is my neighbour? And taking [it] up
ὁ Ἰησοῦς εἶπεν, Ἄνθρωπός τις κατέβαινεν ἀπὸ Ἱερουσαλὴμ
Jesus said, A [2]man [1]certain was going down from Jerusalem

20 Notwithstanding in
this rejoice not, that
the spirits are subject
unto you; but rather
rejoice, because your
names are written in
heaven. 21 In that
hour Jesus rejoiced in
spirit, and said, I thank
thee, O Father, Lord
of heaven and earth,
that thou hast hid
these things from the
wise and prudent, and
hast revealed them un-
to babes: even so, Fa-
ther; for so it seemed
good in thy sight.
22 All things are de-
livered to me of my
Father: and no man
knoweth who the Son
is, but the Father; and
who the Father is, but
the Son, and he to
whom the Son will re-
veal *him*. 23 And he
turned him unto *his*
disciples, and said pri-
vately, Blessed *are* the
eyes which see the
things that ye see:
24 for I tell you, that
many prophets and
kings have desired to
see those things which
ye see, and have not
seen *them*; and to
hear those things
which ye hear, and
have not heard *them*.

25 And, behold, a
certain lawyer stood
up, and tempted him,
saying, Master, what
shall I do to inherit
eternal life? 26 He
said unto him, What
is written in the law?
how readest thou?
27 And he answering
said, Thou shalt love
the Lord thy God with
all thy heart, and with
all thy soul, and with
all thy strength, and
with all thy mind; and
thy neighbour as thy-
self. 28 And he said
unto him, Thou hast
answered right: this
do, and thou shalt live.
29 But he, willing to
justify himself, said
unto Jesus, And who
is my neighbour?
30 And Jesus answer-
ing said, A certain *man*
went down from Jeru-
salem to Jericho, and

---

[s] — μᾶλλον GLTTrAW. [t] ἐνγέγραπται have been inscribed T; ἐγγέ. TrA. [v] + ἐν in (the) T. [w] + τῷ ἁγίῳ the Holy LTTrA. [x] — ὁ Ἰησοῦς (*read* ἠγαλ. he rejoiced) LTTrA. [y] εὐδοκία ἐγένετο LTrA. [z] — καὶ στραφεὶς πρὸς τοὺς μαθητὰς εἶπεν EGTr[A]. [a] μοι παρεδόθη GLTTrAW. [b] ἂν LTrA. [c] ἴδαν T; εἶδαν TrA. [d] — καὶ T[Tr]A. [e] [τῆς] Tr. [f] ἐν ὅλῃ τῇ ψυχῇ σου καὶ ἐν ὅλῃ τῇ ἰσχύϊ LTTr. [g] ἐν ὅλῃ τῇ διανοίᾳ LTTr. [h] δικαιῶσαι LTTrA. [i] — δὲ and T.

fell among thieves,
which stripped him
of his raiment, and
wounded *him*, and de-
parted, leaving *him*
half dead. 31 And by
chance there came
down a certain priest
that way: and when he
saw him, he passed by
on the other side.
32 And likewise a Le-
vite, when he was at
the place, came and
looked *on him*, and
passed by on the other
side. 33 But a cer-
tain Samaritan, as he
journeyed, came where
he was: and when he
saw him, he had com-
passion *on him*, 34 and
went to *him*, and bound
up his wounds, pour-
ing in oil and wine,
and set him on his
own beast, and brought
him to an inn, and
took care of him.
35 And on the mor-
row when he departed,
he took out two pence,
and gave *them* to the
host, and said unto
him, Take care of him;
and whatsoever thou
spendest more, when I
come again, I will re-
pay thee. 36 Which
now of these three,
thinkest thou, was
neighbour unto him
that fell among the
thieves? 37 And he
said, He that shewed
mercy on him. Then
said Jesus unto him,
Go, and do thou like-
wise.

38 Now it came to
pass, as they went, that
he entered into a cer-
tain village: and a
certain woman named
Martha received him
into her house. 39 And
she had a sister called
Mary, which also sat
at Jesus' feet, and
heard his word. 40 But
Martha was cumbered
about much serving,
and came to him, and
said, Lord, dost thou
not care that my sis-
ter hath left me to
serve alone? bid her

εἰς [k]Ἱεριχώ,‖ καὶ λῃσταῖς περιέπεσεν, οἳ καὶ ἐκδύσαντες
to Jericho, and [3]robbers [1]fell [2]among, who both having stripped
αὐτὸν καὶ πληγὰς ἐπιθέντες ἀπῆλθον, ἀφέντες ἡμιθανῆ
him and wounds having inflicted went away, leaving [him], half dead
[l]τυγχάνοντα.‖ 31 κατὰ συγκυρίαν δὲ ἱερεύς τις κατ-
being. [2]By [3]a [4]coincidence [1]now [5]a [7]priest [6]certain went
έβαινεν ἐν τῇ.ὁδῷ.ἐκείνῃ, καὶ ἰδὼν αὐτὸν ἀντιπαρῆλ-
down in that road, and having seen him he passed by on the op-
θεν· 32 ὁμοίως.δὲ καὶ [m]Λευΐτης,‖ [n]γενόμενος‖ κατὰ τὸν
posite side; and in like manner also a Levite, being at the
τόπον, ἐλθὼν καὶ ἰδὼν [o] ἀντιπαρῆλθεν. 33 [p]Σα-
spot, having come and having seen passed by on the opposite side. [2]A [4]Sa-
μαρείτης‖ δέ τις ὁδεύων ἦλθεν κατ' αὐτόν, καὶ ἰδὼν
maritan [1]but [3]certain journeying, came to him, and having seen
[q]αὐτὸν‖ ἐσπλαγχνίσθη· 34 καὶ προσελθὼν κατέδησεν τὰ
him was moved with compassion, and having approached bound up
τραύματα.αὐτοῦ, ἐπιχέων ἔλαιον καὶ οἶνον· [r]ἐπιβιβάσας.δὲ‖
his wounds, pouring on oil and wine; and having put
αὐτὸν ἐπὶ τὸ.ἴδιον κτῆνος ἤγαγεν αὐτὸν εἰς [s]πανδοχεῖον,‖ καὶ
him on his own beast brought him to an inn, and
ἐπεμελήθη αὐτοῦ. 35 καὶ ἐπὶ τὴν αὔριον [t]ἐξελθών,‖ ἐκβαλὼν
took care of him. And on the morrow going forth, taking out
δύο δηνάρια ἔδωκεν τῷ [v]πανδοχεῖ,‖ καὶ εἶπεν [w]αὐτῷ,‖
two denarii he gave [them] to the innkeeper, and said to him,
Ἐπιμελήθητι αὐτοῦ· καὶ ὅ.τι.ἂν προσδαπανήσῃς, ἐγὼ ἐν
Take care of him, and whatsoever thou mayest expend more, I on
τῷ.ἐπανέρχεσθαί.με ἀποδώσω σοι. 36 Τίς [x]οὖν‖ τούτων
my coming back will repay thee. Which therefore of these
τῶν τριῶν [y]δοκεῖ σοι πλησίον‖ γεγονέναι τοῦ ἐμπεσόντος
three seems to thee [4]neighbour [1]to [2]have [3]been of him who fell
εἰς τοὺς λῃστάς; 37 Ὁ.δὲ εἶπεν, Ὁ ποιήσας τὸ ἔλεος
among the robbers? And he said, He who shewed compassion
μετ' αὐτοῦ. Εἶπεν [z]οὖν‖ αὐτῷ ὁ Ἰησοῦς, Πορεύου, καὶ
towards him. [3]Said [2]therefore [4]to [5]him [1]Jesus, Go [2]and
σὺ ποίει ὁμοίως.
[1]thou do likewise.

38 [a]Ἐγένετο.δὲ.ἐν‖ τῷ.πορεύεσθαι αὐτοὺς [b]καὶ‖ αὐτὸς εἰσῆλ-
And it came to pass as [2]proceeded [1]they that he enter-
θεν εἰς κώμην τινά· γυνὴ.δέ τις ὀνόματι Μάρθα ὑπ-
ed into a [2]village [1]certain; and a [2]woman [1]certain by name Martha re-
εδέξατο αὐτὸν εἰς [c]τὸν.οἶκον‖.[d]αὐτῆς.‖ 39 καὶ τῇδε.ἦν ἀδελφὴ
ceived him into her house. And she had a sister
καλουμένη [e]Μαρία,‖ ἣ καὶ [f]παρακαθίσασα‖ [g]παρὰ‖ τοὺς πόδας
called Mary, who also having sat down at the feet
[h]τοῦ Ἰησοῦ‖ ἤκουεν τὸν.λόγον.αὐτοῦ. 40 ἡ.δὲ.Μάρθα
of Jesus was listening to his word. But Martha
περιεσπᾶτο περὶ πολλὴν διακονίαν· ἐπιστᾶσα.δὲ εἶπεν, Κύριε,
was distracted about much service; and coming up she said, Lord,
οὐ.μέλει σοι ὅτι ἡ.ἀδελφή.μου μόνην με [i]κατέλιπεν‖ δια-
is it no concern to thee that my sister [3]alone [2]me [1]left to

---

[k] Ἱερειχώ T. [l] — τυγχάνοντα LTTr[A]. [m] Λευείτης TTrA. [n] — γενόμενος Tr. [o] + αὐτὸν him L. [p] Σαμαρίτης T. [q] — αὐτὸν [L]T[Tr]A. [r] καὶ ἐπιβιβάσας L. [s] πανδοκίον T. [t] — ἐξελθών LTTr[A]. [v] πανδοκεῖ T. [w] — αὐτῷ [L]TTr[A]. [x] — οὖν [L]T[Tr]A. [y] πλησίον δοκεῖ σοι GTTrAW. [z] δὲ [1]and ([2]Jesus) GLTTrA. [a] Ἐν δὲ And as Tr. [b] [καὶ] LTr. [c] τὴν οἰκίαν T. [d] — αὐτῆς (read the house) T[Tr]. [e] Μαριάμ T. [f] παρακαθεσθεῖσα TTrA. [g] πρὸς against TTrA. [h] τοῦ κυρίου of the Lord LTTrAW. [i] κατέλειπεν TrA.

κονεῖν; [k]εἰπὲǁ οὖν αὐτῇ ἵνα μοι συναντιλάβηται. 41 Ἀπο-
serve? Speak therefore to her that me she may help. [3]An-
κριθεὶς δὲ εἶπεν αὐτῇ [l]ὁ Ἰησοῦς,ǁ Μάρθα, Μάρθα, μεριμνᾷς
swering [1]but [4]said [5]to [6]her [2]Jesus, Martha, Martha, thou art careful
καὶ [m]τυρβάζῃǁ περὶ πολλά· 42 ἑνὸς.δέ ἐστιν χρεία· Μαρία
and troubled about many things; but of one there is need; [2]Mary
[n]δὲǁ τὴν ἀγαθὴν μερίδα ἐξελέξατο, ἥτις οὐκ.ἀφαιρεθήσεται
[1]and the good part chose, which shall not be taken
[o]ἀπ'ǁ αὐτῆς.
from her.

11 Καὶ ἐγένετο ἐν.τῷ.εἶναι αὐτὸν ἐν τόπῳ τινὶ προσ-
And it came to pass as [2]was [1]he in a [2]place [1]certain pray-
ευχόμενον, ὡς ἐπαύσατο, εἶπέν τις τῶν.μαθητῶν.αὐτοῦ πρὸς
ing, when he ceased, said one of his disciples to
αὐτόν, Κύριε, δίδαξον ἡμᾶς προσεύχεσθαι, καθὼς καὶ [p]Ἰωάν-
him, Lord, teach us to pray, as also John
νηςǁ ἐδίδαξεν τοὺς.μαθητὰς.αὐτοῦ. 2 Εἶπεν.δὲ αὐτοῖς, Ὅταν
taught his disciples. And he said to them, When
προσεύχησθε λέγετε, Πάτερ [q]ἡμῶν ὁ ἐν τοῖς οὐρανοῖς,ǁ
ye pray say, [2]Father [1]our, who [art] in the heavens,
ἁγιασθήτω τὸ.ὄνομά.σου· [r]ἐλθέτωǁ [s]ἡ.βασιλεία.σου·ǁ [t]γενηθήτω
sanctified be thy name; let come thy kingdom; let be done
τὸ.θέλημά.σου,ǁ [v]ὡς ἐν οὐρανῷ, καὶ ἐπὶ τῆς γῆς.ǁ 3 τὸν
thy will, as in heaven, [so] also upon the earth.
ἄρτον.ἡμῶν τὸν ἐπιούσιον δίδου ἡμῖν τὸ.καθ'.ἡμέραν· 4 καὶ
Our bread the needed give us daily; and
ἄφες ἡμῖν τὰς.ἁμαρτίας.ἡμῶν, καὶ.γὰρ αὐτοὶ [w]ἀφίεμενǁ
forgive us our sins, for [3]also [2]ourselves [1]we forgive
παντὶ ὀφείλοντι ἡμῖν· καὶ μὴ.εἰσενέγκῃς ἡμᾶς εἰς πειρασμόν,
every one indebted to us; and lead not us into temptation,
[x]ἀλλὰ ῥῦσαι ἡμᾶς ἀπὸ τοῦ πονηροῦ.ǁ 5 Καὶ εἶπεν πρὸς
but deliver us from evil. And he said to
αὐτούς, Τίς ἐξ ὑμῶν ἕξει φίλον, καὶ πορεύσεται πρὸς
them, Who among you shall have a friend, and shall go to
αὐτὸν μεσονυκτίου, καὶ [y]εἴπῃǁ αὐτῷ, Φίλε, χρῆσόν μοι τρεῖς
him at midnight, and say to him, Friend, lend me three
ἄρτους, 6 ἐπειδὴ φίλος μου παρεγένετο ἐξ ὁδοῦ πρός με,
loaves, since a friend of mine is come off a journey to me,
καὶ οὐκ.ἔχω ὃ παραθήσω αὐτῷ· 7 κἀκεῖνος ἔσωθεν
and I have not what I shall set before him; and he from within
ἀποκριθεὶς εἴπῃ, Μή μοι κόπους πάρεχε· ἤδη ἡ θύρα
answering should say, [3]Not [2]me [4]trouble [1]cause; already the door
κέκλεισται, καὶ τὰ.παιδία.μου μετ' ἐμοῦ εἰς τὴν κοίτην εἰσίν·
has been shut, and my children with me in bed are;
οὐ.δύναμαι ἀναστὰς δοῦναί σοι. 8 Λέγω ὑμῖν, εἰ καὶ οὐ
I cannot rise up to give to thee. I say to you, if even [3]not
δώσει αὐτῷ ἀναστάς, διὰ τὸ.εἶναι [z]αὐτοῦ φίλον,ǁ
[1]he [2]will give to him, having risen up, because of [his] being his friend,
διά.γε τὴν.[a]ἀναίδειανǁ.αὐτοῦ ἐγερθεὶς δώσει αὐτῷ
yet because of his importunity having risen he will give him
ὅσων χρῄζει. 9 Κἀγὼ ὑμῖν λέγω, Αἰτεῖτε, καὶ δοθήσεται
as many as he needs. And I to you say, Ask, and it shall be given

therefore that she help me. 41 And Jesus answered and said unto her, Martha, Martha, thou art careful and troubled about many things: 42 but one thing is needful: and Mary hath chosen that good part, which shall not be taken away from her.

XI. And it came to pass, that, as he was praying in a certain place, when he ceased, one of his disciples said unto him, Lord, teach us to pray, as John also taught his disciples. 2 And he said unto them, When ye pray, say, Our Father which art in heaven, Hallowed be thy name. Thy kingdom come. Thy will be done, as in heaven, so in earth. 3 Give us day by day our daily bread. 4 And forgive us our sins; for we also forgive every one that is indebted to us. And lead us not into temptation; but deliver us from evil. 5 And he said unto them, Which of you shall have a friend, and shall go unto him at midnight, and say unto him, Friend, lend me three loaves; 6 for a friend of mine in his journey is come to me, and I have nothing to set before him? 7 And he from within shall answer and say, Trouble me not: the door is now shut, and my children are with me in bed; I cannot rise and give thee. 8 I say unto you, Though he will not rise and give him, because he is his friend, yet because of his importunity he will rise and give him as many as he needeth. 9 And I say unto you, Ask, and it shall be given you.

[k] εἰπὸν T. [l] ὁ κύριος the Lord T. [m] θορυβάζῃ agitated LTTrA. [n] γὰρ for T; [δὲ] A.
[o] — ἀπ' [L]T[TrA]. [p] Ἰωάνης Tr. [q] — ἡμῶν ὁ ἐν τοῖς οὐρανοῖς GTTrA. [r] ἐλθάτω TTr.
[s] σου ἡ βασιλεία G. [t] — γενηθήτω τὸ θέλημά σου GTTrA. [v] — ὡς ἐν οὐρανῷ καὶ ἐπὶ τῆς γῆς G[L]TTrA. [w] ἀφίομεν LTTrA. [x] — ἀλλὰ ῥῦσαι ἡμᾶς ἀπὸ τοῦ πονηροῦ GTTrA.
[y] ἐρεῖ L. [z] φίλον αὐτοῦ TTrA. [a] ἀναιδίαν T.

seek, and ye shall find;
knock, and it shall
be opened unto you.
10 For every one that
asketh receiveth; and
he that seeketh find-
eth; and to him that
knocketh it shall be
opened. 11 If a son
shall ask bread of any
of you that is a father,
will he give him a
stone? or if *he ask* a
fish, will he for a fish
give him a serpent?
12 Or if he shall ask an
egg, will he offer him a
scorpion? 13 If ye then,
being evil, know how
to give good gifts unto
your children: how
much more shall *your*
heavenly Father give
the Holy Spirit to them
that ask him?

14 And he was cast-
ing out a devil, and it
was dumb. And it
came to pass, when the
devil was gone out,
the dumb spake; and
the people wondered.
15 But some of them
said, He casteth out
devils through Beelze-
bub the chief of the
devils. 16 And others,
tempting *him*, sought
of him a sign from hea-
ven. 17 But he, know-
ing their thoughts, said
unto them, Every king-
dom divided against
itself is brought to
desolation; and a house
divided against a house
falleth. 18 If Satan
also be divided against
himself, how shall his
kingdom stand? be-
cause ye say that I cast
out devils through
Beelzebub. 19 And if I
by Beelzebub cast out
devils, by whom do
your sons cast *them*
out? therefore shall
they be your judges.
20 But if I with the
finger of God cast out
devils, no doubt the
kingdom of God is
come upon you.
21 When a strong man
armed keepeth his
palace, his goods are in
peace: 22 but when a
stronger than he shall

ὑμῖν· ζητεῖτε, καὶ εὑρήσετε· κρούετε, καὶ [b]ἀνοιγήσεται" ὑμῖν.
to you; seek, and ye shall find; knock, and it shall be opened to you.
10 πᾶς-γὰρ ὁ αἰτῶν λαμβάνει· καὶ ὁ ζητῶν εὑρίσκει· και
For every one that asks receives; and he that seeks finds; and
τῷ κρούοντι [c]ἀνοιγήσεται." 11 τίνα.δὲ [d] ὑμῶν τὸν
to him that knocks it will be opened. And which of you who [is]
πατέρα αἰτήσει ὁ υἱὸς ἄρτον, μὴ λίθον ἐπιδώσει αὐτῷ;
a father shall ³ask ⁴for ¹the ²son bread, a stone will he give to him?
[e]εἰ" καὶ ἰχθύν, μὴ ἀντὶ ἰχθύος ὄφιν [f]ἐπιδώσει αὐτῷ"; 12 ἢ
if also a fish, instead of a fish a serpent will he give to him? or
καὶ [g]ἐὰν" [h]αἰτήσῃ" ᾠόν, μὴ ἐπιδώσει αὐτῷ σκορπίον; 13 εἰ
also if he should ask an egg, will he give to him a scorpion? If
οὖν ὑμεῖς πονηροὶ ὑπάρχοντες οἴδατε [i]ἀγαθὰ δόματα"
therefore ye, ²evil ¹being, know [how] good gifts
διδόναι τοῖς.τέκνοις.ὑμῶν, πόσῳ μᾶλλον ὁ πατὴρ[k] ὁ ἐξ
to give to your children, how much more the Father who [is] of
οὐρανοῦ δώσει πνεῦμα ἅγιον τοῖς αἰτοῦσιν αὐτόν;
heaven will give [the] ²Spirit ¹Holy to those that ask him?

14 Καὶ ἦν ἐκβάλλων δαιμόνιον, [l]καὶ αὐτὸ ἦν" κωφόν·
And he was casting out a demon, and it was dumb;
ἐγένετο.δὲ τοῦ.δαιμονίου [m]ἐξελθόντος," ἐλάλησεν ὁ κωφός·
and it came to pass on the demon having gone out, ³spoke ¹the ²dumb.
καὶ ἐθαύμασαν οἱ ὄχλοι. 15 τινὲς.δὲ ἐξ αὐτῶν [n]εἶπον," Ἐν
And ³wondered ¹the ²crowds. But some of them said, By
Βεελζεβοὺλ [o] ἄρχοντι τῶν δαιμονίων ἐκβάλλει τὰ δαιμόνια.
Beelzebul prince of the demons he casts out the demons.
16 Ἕτεροι.δὲ πειράζοντες σημεῖον [p]παρ' αὐτοῦ ἐζήτουν ἐξ
And others, tempting, a sign from him were seeking from
οὐρανοῦ." 17 Αὐτὸς.δὲ εἰδὼς [q]αὐτῶν τὰ διανοήματα" εἶπεν
heaven. But he knowing their thoughts said
αὐτοῖς, Πᾶσα βασιλεία [r]ἐφ' ἑαυτὴν διαμερισθεῖσα" ἐρη-
to them, Every kingdom ²against ³itself ¹divided is brought to
μοῦται· καὶ οἶκος ἐπὶ οἶκον πίπτει. 18 εἰ.δὲ καὶ ὁ σατανᾶς
desolation; and a house against a house falls. And if also Satan
ἐφ' ἑαυτὸν διεμερίσθη, πῶς σταθήσεται ἡ.βασιλεία.αὐτοῦ;
against himself be divided, how shall stand his kingdom?
ὅτι λέγετε, ἐν Βεελζεβοὺλ ἐκβάλλειν.με τὰ δαιμόνια. 19 εἰ.δὲ
because ye say, by Beelzebul I cast out the demons. And if
ἐγὼ ἐν Βεελζεβοὺλ ἐκβάλλω τὰ δαιμόνια, [s]οἱ".υἱοὶ.ὑμῶν ἐν
I by Beelzebul cast out the demons, your sons by
τίνι ἐκβάλλουσιν; διὰ τοῦτο [t]κριταὶ ὑμῶν αὐτοὶ ἔσον-
whom do they cast out? on account of this judges of you they shall
ται." 20 εἰ.δὲ ἐν δακτύλῳ θεοῦ [v]ἐκβάλλω τὰ δαιμόνια,
be. But if by [the] finger of God I cast out the demons,
ἄρα ἔφθασεν ἐφ' ὑμᾶς ἡ βασιλεία τοῦ θεοῦ. 21 ὅταν ὁ
then is come upon you the kingdom of God. When the
ἰσχυρὸς καθωπλισμένος φυλάσσῃ τὴν.ἑαυτοῦ.αὐλήν, ἐν
strong [man] being armed may keep his own dwelling, in
εἰρήνῃ ἐστὶν τὰ.ὑπάρχοντα.αὐτοῦ· 22 ἐπὰν.δὲ [w]ὁ" ἰσχυρό-
peace are his goods; but as soon as the stronger

---

[b] ἀνοιχθήσεται TA. [c] ἀνοιχθήσεται LTAW. [d] + ἐξ LTTrAW. [e] ἢ or GLTTrAW. [f] αὐτῷ ἐπιδώσει TTrA. [g] — ἐὰν TTr[A]. [h] αἰτήσει he shall ask ETTrA. [i] δόματα ἀγαθὰ GLTTrAW. [k] + ὑμῶν (*read* your father) L. [l] [καὶ αὐτὸ ἦν] TrA. [m] ἐκβληθέντος having been cast out L. [n] εἶπαν TrA. [o] + τῷ the LTTrAW. [p] ἐξ οὐρανοῦ ἐζήτουν παρ' αὐτοῦ LTTrAW. [q] τὰ διανοήματα αὐτῶν L. [r] διαμερισθεῖσα ἐφ' ἑαυτὴν T. [s] — οἱ L. [t] αὐτοὶ ὑμῶν κριταὶ ἔσονται LA; αὐτοὶ κριταὶ ἔσονται ὑμῶν T; αὐτοὶ κριταὶ ὑμῶν ἔσονται Tr. [v] + [ἐγὼ] Tr. [w] — ὁ (*read* a stronger) LTTrA.

τερος αὐτοῦ ἐπελθὼν νικήσῃ αὐτόν, τὴν πανοπλίαν
than he coming upon [him] shall overcome him, ²panoply
αὐτοῦ αἴρει ἐφ' ᾗ ἐπεποίθει, καὶ τὰ.σκῦλα.αὐτοῦ δια-
¹his he takes away in which he had trusted, and his spoils he
δίδωσιν. 23 ὁ μὴ.ὢν μετ' ἐμοῦ κατ' ἐμοῦ ἐστιν· καὶ ὁ
divides. He that is not with me against me is, and he that
μὴ.συνάγων μετ' ἐμοῦ σκορπίζει. 24 Ὅταν τὸ ἀκάθαρτον
gathers not with me scatters. When the unclean
πνεῦμα ἐξέλθῃ ἀπὸ τοῦ ἀνθρώπου, διέρχεται δι' ἀνύδρων
spirit is gone out from the man, he goes through waterless
τόπων, ζητοῦν ἀνάπαυσιν· καὶ μὴ εὑρίσκον ˣλέγει, Ὑπο-
places, seeking rest; and not finding [any] he says, I will
στρέψω εἰς τὸν.οἶκόν.μου ὅθεν ἐξῆλθον· 25 καὶ ἐλθὸν
return to my house whence I came out. And having come
εὑρίσκει σεσαρωμένον καὶ κεκοσμημένον. 26 τότε πορεύεται
he finds [it] swept and adorned. Then he goes
καὶ παραλαμβάνει ʸἑπτὰ ἕτερα πνεύματα πονηρότερα ἑαυτοῦ,‖
and takes seven other spirits more wicked than himself,
καὶ εἰσελθόντα κατοικεῖ ἐκεῖ· καὶ γίνεται τὰ ἔσχατα τοῦ
and having entered they dwell there; and becomes the last
ἀνθρώπου ἐκείνου χείρονα τῶν πρώτων. 27 Ἐγένετο.δὲ
³man ¹of ²that worse than the first. And it came to pass
ἐν.τῷ.λέγειν αὐτὸν ταῦτα, ἐπάρασά τις ᶻγυνὴ φωνὴν‖
as ²spoke ¹he these things, ⁴lifting ⁵up ²certain ¹a ³woman [her] voice
ἐκ τοῦ ὄχλου εἶπεν αὐτῷ, Μακαρία ἡ κοιλία ἡ βαστάσασά
from the crowd said to him, Blessed the womb that bore
σε, καὶ μαστοὶ οὓς ἐθήλασας. 28 Αὐτὸς.δὲ εἶπεν, ᵃΜεν-
thee, and [the] breasts which thou didst suck. But he said, Yea
οῦνγε‖ μακάριοι οἱ ἀκούοντες τὸν λόγον τοῦ θεοῦ καὶ
rather blessed they who hear the word of God and
φυλάσσοντες ᵇαὐτόν.‖
keep it.

29 Τῶν.δὲ ὄχλων ἐπαθροιζομένων ἤρξατο λέγειν, Ἡ γενεὰ
But the crowds being thronged together he began to say, ²generation
αὕτη ᶜ πονηρά ἐστιν· σημεῖον ᵈἐπιζητεῖ,‖ καὶ σημεῖον οὐ
¹this ⁴wicked ³is; a sign it seeks after, and a sign ²not
δοθήσεται αὐτῇ, εἰ.μὴ τὸ σημεῖον Ἰωνᾶ ᵉτοῦ προφήτου.‖
¹shall be given to it except the sign of Jonas the prophet.
30 καθὼς.γὰρ ἐγένετο Ἰωνᾶς ᶠσημεῖον τοῖς Νινευΐταις,‖ οὕτως
For as was Jonas a sign to the Ninevites, thus
ἔσται καὶ ὁ υἱὸς τοῦ ἀνθρώπου τῇ.γενεᾷ.ταύτῃ. 31 Βασίλισσα
shall be also the Son of man to this generation. A queen
νότου ἐγερθήσεται ἐν τῇ κρίσει μετὰ τῶν ἀνδρῶν τῆς
of [the] south shall rise up in the judgment with the men
γενεᾶς.ταύτης, καὶ κατακρινεῖ αὐτούς· ὅτι ἦλθεν ἐκ τῶν
of this generation, and shall condemn them; for she came from the
περάτων τῆς γῆς ἀκοῦσαι τὴν σοφίαν ᵍΣολομῶντος,‖ καὶ ἰδού,
ends of the earth to hear the wisdom of Solomon, and behold,
πλεῖον ᵍΣολομῶντος‖ ὧδε. 32 ἄνδρες ʰΝινευῒ‖ ἀναστήσονται
more than Solomon here. Men of Nineveh shall stand up
ἐν τῇ κρίσει μετὰ τῆς.γενεᾶς.ταύτης, καὶ κατακρινοῦσιν αὐτήν·
in the judgment with this generation, and shall condemn it,

come upon him, and overcome him, he taketh from him all his armour wherein he trusted, and divideth his spoils.
23 He that is not with me is against me: and he that gathereth not with me scattereth.
24 When the unclean spirit is gone out of a man, he walketh through dry places, seeking rest; and finding none, he saith, I will return unto my house whence I came out.
25 And when he cometh, he findeth *it* swept and garnished.
26 Then goeth he, and taketh *to him* seven other spirits more wicked than himself; and they enter in, and dwell there: and the last *state* of that man is worse than the first.
27 And it came to pass, as he spake these things, a certain woman of the company lifted up her voice, and said unto him, Blessed *is* the womb that bare thee, and the paps which thou hast sucked.
28 But he said, Yea rather, blessed *are* they that hear the word of God, and keep it.

29 And when the people were gathered thick together, he began to say, This is an evil generation: they seek a sign; and there shall no sign be given it, but the sign of Jonas the prophet.
30 For as Jonas was a sign unto the Ninevites, so shall also the Son of man be to this generation.
31 The queen of the south shall rise up in the judgment with the men of this generation, and condemn them: for she came from the utmost parts of the earth to hear the wisdom of Solomon; and, behold, a greater than Solomon *is* here.
32 The men of Nineve shall rise up in the judgment with this generation, and shall condemn it: for they repented at

ˣ + [. τότε] then L. ʸ ἕτερα πνεύματα πονηρότερα ἑαυτοῦ ἑπτά TTrA. ᶻ φωνὴν γυνὴ LTA. ᵃ μενοῦν TTr; μὲν οὖν A. ᵇ — αὐτόν (*read* [it]) GLTTrA. ᶜ + γενεὰ a generation LTTrA. ᵈ ζητεῖ it seeks TTrA. ᵉ — τοῦ προφήτου GLTTrA. ᶠ τοῖς Νινευείταις (Νινευΐταις TrA) σημεῖον TTrA. ᵍ Σολομῶνος GLTTrAW. ʰ Νινευὴ A; Νινευῖται Ninevites LTrW; Νινευεῖται T.

the preaching of Jo-
nas; and, behold, a
greater than Jonas *is*
here. 33 No man, when
he hath lighted a can-
dle, putteth *it* in a
secret place, neither
under a bushel, but on
a candlestick, that
they which come in
may see the light.
34 The light of the
body is the eye: there-
fore when thine eye is
single, thy whole body
also is full of light;
but when *thine eye* is
evil, thy body also *is*
full of darkness.
35 Take heed there-
fore that the light
which is in thee be not
darkness. 36 If thy
whole body therefore
be full of light, having
no part dark, the whole
shall be full of light,
as when the bright
shining of a candle
doth give thee light.

37 And as he spake,
a certain Pharisee be-
sought him to dine
with him: and he went
in, and sat down to
meat. 38 And when
the Pharisee saw *it*, he
marvelled that he had
not first washed before
dinner. 39 And the
Lord said unto him,
Now do ye Pharisees
make clean the outside
of the cup and the
platter; but your in-
ward part is full of ra-
vening and wicked-
ness. 40 *Ye* fools, did
not he that made that
which is without make
that which is within
also? 41 But rather
give alms of such
things as ye have; and,
behold, all things are
clean unto you. 42 But
woe unto you, Phari-
sees! for ye tithe mint
and rue and all man-
ner of herbs, and pass
over judgment and the
love of God: these
ought ye to have done,
and not to leave the
other undone. 43 Woe
unto you, Pharisees!
for ye love the upper-
most seats in the syna-
gogues, and greetings
in the markets. 44 Woe
unto you, scribes and
Pharisees, hypocrites!

ὅτι μετενόησαν εἰς τὸ κήρυγμα Ἰωνᾶ. καὶ ἰδού, πλεῖον
because they repented at the proclamation of Jonas: and behold, more
Ἰωνᾶ ὧδε. 33 Οὐδεὶς.[i]δὲ" λύχνον ἅψας εἰς [k]κρυπτὸν"
than Jonas here. But no one a lamp having lit [3]in [4]secret
τίθησιν, οὐδὲ ὑπὸ τὸν μόδιον, [l]ἀλλ'" ἐπὶ τὴν λυχνίαν,
[1]sets [2]it, nor under the corn-measure, but upon the lampstand,
ἵνα οἱ εἰσπορευόμενοι τὸ [m]φέγγος" βλέπωσιν. 34 ὁ λύχνος
that they who enter in the light may see. The lamp
τοῦ σώματός ἐστιν ὁ ὀφθαλμός[n]· ὅταν [o]οὖν" ὁ.ὀφθαλμός.σου
of the body is the eye: when therefore thine eye
ἁπλοῦς ᾖ, [p]καὶ" ὅλον τὸ.σῶμά.σου φωτεινόν ἐστιν· ἐπὰν.δὲ
[2]single [1]be, also [2]whole [1]thy body light is; but when
πονηρὸς ᾖ, καὶ τὸ.σῶμά.σου σκοτεινόν. 35 σκόπει οὖν
evil it be, also thy body [is] dark. See therefore
μὴ τὸ φῶς τὸ ἐν σοὶ σκότος ἐστίν. 36 εἰ οὖν τὸ σῶμά
lest the light that [is] in thee [2]darkness [1]is. If therefore [3]body
σου ὅλον φωτεινόν, μὴ ἔχον [q]τὶ μέρος" σκοτεινόν, ἔσται
[1]thy [2]whole [is] light, not having any part dark, it shall be
φωτεινὸν ὅλον, ὡς ὅταν ὁ λύχνος τῇ.ἀστραπῇ φωτίζῃ σε.
[2]light [1]all, as when the lamp with [its] brightness may light thee.
37 Ἐν.δὲ.τῷ.λαλῆσαι [r] [s]ἠρώτα" αὐτὸν Φαρισαῖός [t]τις"
Now as [2]was [3]speaking [[1]he] asked him [1]a [3]Pharisee [2]certain
ὅπως ἀριστήσῃ παρ' αὐτῷ· εἰσελθὼν.δὲ ἀνέπεσεν.
that he would dine with him: and having entered he reclined himself.
38 ὁ.δὲ Φαρισαῖος ἰδὼν ἐθαύμασεν ὅτι οὐ πρῶτον ἐβαπτίσθη
But the Pharisee seeing [it] wondered that not first he washed
πρὸ τοῦ ἀρίστου. 39 εἶπεν.δὲ ὁ κύριος πρὸς αὐτόν, Νῦν ὑμεῖς
before the dinner. But said the Lord to him, Now ye
οἱ Φαρισαῖοι τὸ ἔξωθεν τοῦ ποτηρίου καὶ τοῦ πίνακος καθαρίζετε,
Pharisees the outside of the cup and of the dish ye cleanse,
τὸ.δὲ ἔσωθεν ὑμῶν γέμει ἁρπαγῆς καὶ πονηρίας. 40 ἄφρονες,
but the inside of you is full of plunder and wickedness. Fools,
οὐχ ὁ ποιήσας τὸ ἔξωθεν καὶ τὸ ἔσωθεν ἐποίησεν;
[did] not he who made the outside also the inside make?
41 πλὴν τὰ.ἐνόντα δότε ἐλεημοσύνην, καὶ ἰδού,
But [of] the things which are within give alms, and lo,
πάντα καθαρὰ ὑμῖν ἐστιν. 42 [v]ἀλλ'" οὐαὶ ὑμῖν τοῖς Φαρισαίοις,
all things clean to you are. But woe to you Pharisees,
ὅτι ἀποδεκατοῦτε τὸ ἡδύοσμον καὶ τὸ πήγανον καὶ πᾶν
for ye pay tithes of the mint and the rue and every
λάχανον, καὶ παρέρχεσθε τὴν κρίσιν καὶ τὴν ἀγάπην τοῦ θεοῦ·
herb, and pass by the judgment and the love of God:
ταῦτα [w] ἔδει ποιῆσαι, κἀκεῖνα μὴ [x]ἀφιέναι."
These things it behoved [you] to do, and those not to be leaving aside.
43 οὐαὶ ὑμῖν τοῖς Φαρισαίοις, ὅτι ἀγαπᾶτε τὴν πρωτοκαθεδρίαν
Woe to you Pharisees, for ye love the first seat
ἐν ταῖς συναγωγαῖς καὶ τοὺς ἀσπασμοὺς ἐν ταῖς ἀγοραῖς[y].
in the synagogues and the salutations in the market-places.
44 οὐαὶ ὑμῖν, [z]γραμματεῖς καὶ Φαρισαῖοι, ὑποκριταί," ὅτι ἐστὲ
Woe to you, scribes and Pharisees, hypocrites, for ye are

---

[i] — δὲ but TTrA. [k] κρυπτὴν secret place EGLTTrAW. [l] ἀλλὰ EW. [m] φῶς LTrA. [n] + σου (*read* thine eye) LTTrA. [o] — οὖν LTTrA. [p] — καὶ L. [q] μέρος τι ([τι] A) LTrA. [r] + αὐτὸν he L. [s] ἐρωτᾷ asks LTA; ἐρώτα Tr. [t] — τις TTrA. [v] ἀλλὰ T. [w] + δὲ now [L]Tr. [x] παρεῖναι to pass by LTTrA. [y] + [καὶ τὰς πρωτοκλισίας ἐν τοῖς δείπνοις] and the first places at the suppers L. [z] — γραμματεῖς καὶ Φαρισαῖοι ὑποκριταί G[L]TTrA.

ὡς τὰ μνημεῖα τὰ ἄδηλα, καὶ οἱ ἄνθρωποι [a]οἱ‖ περιπατοῦντες
as the ²tombs ¹unseen, and the men who walk

ἐπάνω οὐκ.οἴδασιν. 45 Ἀποκριθεὶς.δέ τις τῶν νομι-
over [them] do not know [it]. And answering one of the doctors of the

κῶν λέγει αὐτῷ, Διδάσκαλε, ταῦτα λέγων καὶ ἡμᾶς ὑβρίζεις.
law says to him, Teacher, these things saying ²also ¹us thou insultest.

46 Ὁ.δὲ εἶπεν, Καὶ ὑμῖν τοῖς νομικοῖς οὐαί, ὅτι φορτίζετε
And he said, Also to you the doctors of the law woe, for ye burden

τοὺς ἀνθρώπους φορτία δυσβάστακτα, καὶ αὐτοὶ ἑνὶ
men [with] burdens heavy to bear, and yourselves with one

τῶν.δακτύλων.ὑμῶν οὐ.προσψαύετε τοῖς φορτίοις. 47 οὐαὶ
of your fingers do not touch the burdens. Woe

ὑμῖν, ὅτι οἰκοδομεῖτε τὰ μνημεῖα τῶν προφητῶν, [b]οἱ δὲ‖ πα-
to you, for ye build the tombs of the prophets, and ²fa-

τέρες ὑμῶν ἀπέκτειναν αὐτούς. 48 ἄρα [c]μαρτυρεῖτε‖ καὶ
thers ¹your killed them. Hence ye bear witness and

συνευδοκεῖτε τοῖς ἔργοις τῶν.πατέρων.ὑμῶν· ὅτι αὐτοὶ μὲν
consent to the works of your fathers; for they indeed

ἀπέκτειναν αὐτούς, ὑμεῖς.δὲ οἰκοδομεῖτε [d]αὐτῶν τὰ μνημεῖα.‖
killed them, and ye build their tombs.

49 διὰ τοῦτο καὶ ἡ σοφία τοῦ θεοῦ εἶπεν, Ἀποστελῶ εἰς
Because of this also the wisdom of God said, I will send to

αὐτοὺς προφήτας καὶ ἀποστόλους, καὶ ἐξ αὐτῶν ἀποκτε-
them prophets and apostles, and [some] of them they will

νοῦσιν καὶ [e]ἐκδιώξουσιν·‖ 50 ἵνα ἐκζητηθῇ τὸ αἷμα πάντων
kill and drive out, that may be required the blood of all

τῶν προφητῶν [f]τὸ ἐκχυνόμενον‖ ἀπὸ καταβολῆς κόσμου
the prophets poured out from [the] foundation of [the] world,

ἀπὸ τῆς.γενεᾶς.ταύτης, 51 ἀπὸ [g]τοῦ‖ αἵματος Ἄβελ ἕως [g]τοῦ‖
of this generation, from the blood of Abel to the

αἵματος Ζαχαρίου τοῦ ἀπολομένου μεταξὺ τοῦ θυσιαστηρίου
blood of Zacharias, who perished between the altar

καὶ τοῦ οἴκου· ναί, λέγω ὑμῖν, ἐκζητηθήσεται ἀπὸ τῆς γενεᾶς
and the house; yea, I say to you, it shall be required of ²generation

ταύτης. 52 Οὐαὶ ὑμῖν τοῖς νομικοῖς, ὅτι ἤρατε τὴν
¹this. Woe to you the doctors of the law, for ye took away the

κλεῖδα τῆς γνώσεως· αὐτοὶ οὐκ.[h]εἰσήλθετε,‖ καὶ τοὺς εἰσερ-
key of knowledge; yourselves did not enter, and those who were

χομένους ἐκωλύσατε. 53 [i]Λέγοντος.δὲ αὐτοῦ ταῦτα πρὸς
entering ye hindered. And as ²was ³saying ¹he these things to

αὐτοὺς‖ ἤρξαντο οἱ γραμματεῖς καὶ οἱ Φαρισαῖοι δεινῶς ἐν-
them began the scribes and the Pharisees urgently to press

έχειν, καὶ ἀποστοματίζειν αὐτὸν περὶ πλειόνων, 54 ἐνε-
upon [him], and to make ²speak ¹him about many things; watch-

δρεύοντες [k]αὐτὸν‖ [l]καὶ‖ [m]ζητοῦντες‖ θηρεῦσαί τι ἐκ τοῦ
ing him and seeking to catch something out of

στόματος.αὐτοῦ [n]ἵνα κατηγορήσωσιν αὐτοῦ.‖
his mouth that they might accuse him.

12 Ἐν οἷς ἐπισυναχθεισῶν τῶν μυριάδων τοῦ
During which [things] being gathered together the myriads of the

ὄχλου, ὥστε καταπατεῖν ἀλλήλους, ἤρξατο λέγειν πρὸς τοὺς
crowd, so as to trample upon one another, he began to say to

for ye are as graves
which appear not, and
the men that walk over
them are not aware *of*
them. 45 Then answer-
ed one of the lawyers,
and said unto him,
Master, thus saying
thou reproachest us
also. 46 And he said,
Woe unto you also, *ye*
lawyers! for ye lade
men with burdens grie-
vous to be borne, and
ye yourselves touch not
the burdens with one
of your fingers. 47 Woe
unto you! for ye build
the sepulchres of the
prophets, and your
fathers killed them.
48 Truly ye bear wit-
ness that ye allow
the deeds of your fa-
thers: for they indeed
killed them, and ye
build their sepulchres.
49 Therefore also said
the wisdom of God, I
will send them pro-
phets and apostles, and
some of them they shall
slay and persecute:
50 That the blood of
all the prophets, which
was shed from the
foundation of the
world, may be required
of this generation;
51 from the blood of
Abel unto the blood
of Zacharias, which
perished between the
altar and the temple:
verily I say unto you,
It shall be required of
this generation. 52 Woe
unto you, lawyers! for
ye have taken away the
key of knowledge: ye
entered not in your-
selves, and them that
were entering in ye
hindered. 53 And as he
said these things unto
them, the scribes and
the Pharisees began to
urge *him* vehemently,
and to provoke him to
speak of many things:
54 laying wait for
him, and seeking to
catch something out of
his mouth, that they
might accuse him.

XII. In the mean
time, when there were
gathered together an
innumerable multi-
tude of people, inso-
much that they trode
one upon another, he
began to say unto his

[a] — οἱ (*read* περιπ. walking) L[A]W. [b] καὶ οἱ T. [c] μάρτυρές ἐστε witnesses ye are TTrA. [d] — αὐτῶν τὰ μνημεῖα [L]TTrA. [e] [ἐκ]διώξουσιν TrA. [f] τὸ ἐκχυννόμενον LTA; τὸ ἐκκεχυμένον which has been poured out Tr. [g] — τοῦ (*read* [the]) LTTrA. [h] εἰσήλθατε GLTTrA. [i] Κἀκεῖθεν ἐξελθόντος αὐτοῦ and as he went out thence TTrA. [k] — αὐτόν T. [l] — καὶ GLTTrAW. [m] — ζητοῦντες T[Tr]A. [n] — ἵνα κατηγορήσωσιν αὐτοῦ T[Tr]A.

disciples first of all, Beware ye of the leaven of the Pharisees, which is hypocrisy. 2 For there is nothing covered, that shall not be revealed; neither hid, that shall not be known. 3 Therefore whatsoever ye have spoken in darkness shall be heard in the light; and that which ye have spoken in the ear in closets shall be proclaimed upon the housetops. 4 And I say unto you my friends, Be not afraid of them that kill the body, and after that have no more that they can do. 5 But I will forewarn you whom ye shall fear: Fear him, which after he hath killed hath power to cast into hell; yea, I say unto you, Fear him. 6 Are not five sparrows sold for two farthings, and not one of them is forgotten before God? 7 But even the very hairs of your head are all numbered. Fear not therefore: ye are of more value than many sparrows. 8 Also I say unto you, Whosoever shall confess me before men, him shall the Son of man also confess before the angels of God: 9 but he that denieth me before men shall be denied before the angels of God. 10 And whosoever shall speak a word against the Son of man, it shall be forgiven him: but unto him that blasphemeth against the Holy Ghost it shall not be forgiven. 11 And when they bring you unto the synagogues, and *unto* magistrates, and powers, take ye no thought how or what thing ye shall answer, or what ye shall say: 12 for the Holy Ghost shall teach you in the same hour what ye ought to say.

13 And one of the company said unto him, Master, speak to

μαθητὰς.αὐτοῦ πρῶτον, Προσέχετε ἑαυτοῖς ἀπὸ τῆς ζύμης
his disciples first, Take heed to yourselves of the leaven
τῶν Φαρισαίων, ἥτις ἐστὶν ὑπόκρισις. 2 οὐδὲν.δὲ συγκεκαλυμ-
of the Pharisees, which is hypocrisy; but nothing [2]covered
μένον ἐστὶν ὃ οὐκ.ἀποκαλυφθήσεται, καὶ κρυπτὸν ὃ οὐ
[3]up [1]is which shall not be uncovered, nor hidden which [2]not
γνωσθήσεται. 3 ἀνθ'.ὧν ὅσα ἐν τῇ σκοτίᾳ εἴπατε, ἐν τῷ
[1]shall be known; wherefore whatever in the darkness ye said, in the
φωτὶ ἀκουσθήσεται· καὶ ὃ πρὸς τὸ οὖς ἐλαλήσατε ἐν τοῖς
light shall be heard; and what in the ear ye spoke in
ταμείοις, κηρυχθήσεται ἐπὶ τῶν δωμάτων. 4 Λέγω.δὲ ὑμῖν
chambers, shall be proclaimed upon the housetops. But I say to you,
τοῖς.φίλοις.μου, Μὴ.φοβηθῆτε ἀπὸ τῶν [p]ἀποκτεινόντων‖
my friends, Ye should not fear because of those who kill
τὸ σῶμα, καὶ μετὰ ταῦτα μὴ.ἐχόντων [q]περισσότερόν‖.τι
the body, and after these things are not able anything more
ποιῆσαι. 5 ὑποδείξω.δὲ ὑμῖν τίνα φοβηθῆτε· φοβήθητε
to do. But I will shew you whom ye should fear: Fear
τὸν μετὰ τὸ ἀποκτεῖναι [r]ἐξουσίαν ἔχοντα‖ ἐμβαλεῖν εἰς τὴν
him who after having killed, authority has to cast into the
γέενναν· ναί, λέγω ὑμῖν, τοῦτον φοβήθητε. 6 Οὐχὶ πέντε
gehenna; yea, I say to you, [2]him [1]fear. [2]Not [3]five
στρουθία [s]πωλεῖται‖ ἀσσαρίων δύο; καὶ ἓν ἐξ αὐτῶν οὐκ
[4]sparrows [1]are sold for [2]assaria [1]two? and one of them [2]not
ἔστιν ἐπιλελησμένον ἐνώπιον τοῦ θεοῦ· 7 ἀλλὰ.καὶ αἱ τρίχες
[1]is forgotten before God. But even the hairs
τῆς.κεφαλῆς.ὑμῶν πᾶσαι ἠρίθμηνται. μὴ [t]οὖν‖ φοβεῖσθε·
of your head [2]all [1]have been numbered. [2]Not [3]therefore [1]fear,
πολλῶν στρουθίων διαφέρετε. 8 Λέγω.δὲ ὑμῖν, Πᾶς ὃς.ἂν
than many sparrows ye are better. But I say to you, Every one whoever
ὁμολογήσῃ ἐν ἐμοὶ ἔμπροσθεν τῶν ἀνθρώπων, καὶ ὁ υἱὸς τοῦ
may confess me before men, also the Son
ἀνθρώπου ὁμολογήσει ἐν αὐτῷ ἔμπροσθεν τῶν ἀγγέλων τοῦ
of man will confess him before the angels
θεοῦ· 9 ὁ.δὲ ἀρνησάμενός με [v]ἐνώπιον‖ τῶν ἀνθρώπων
of God; but he that has denied me before men
ἀπαρνηθήσεται ἐνώπιον τῶν ἀγγέλων τοῦ θεοῦ. 10 καὶ πᾶς
will be denied before the angels of God; and every one
ὃς ἐρεῖ λόγον εἰς τὸν υἱὸν τοῦ ἀνθρώπου, ἀφεθήσεται
who shall say a word against the Son of man, it will be forgiven
αὐτῷ· τῷ.δὲ εἰς τὸ ἅγιον πνεῦμα βλασφημήσαντι
him; but to him who against the Holy Spirit has blasphemed
οὐκ.ἀφεθήσεται. 11 ὅταν.δὲ [w]προσφέρωσιν‖ ὑμᾶς ἐπὶ τὰς
it will not be forgiven. But when they bring you before the
συναγωγὰς καὶ τὰς ἀρχὰς καὶ τὰς ἐξουσίας, [x]μὴ.μεριμνᾶτε‖
synagogues and the rulers and the authorities, be not careful
πῶς [y]ἢ τί‖ ἀπολογήσησθε, ἢ τί εἴπητε· 12 τὸ.γὰρ
how or what ye shall reply in defence, or what ye should say; for the
ἅγιον πνεῦμα διδάξει ὑμᾶς ἐν αὐτῇ.τῇ ὥρᾳ ἃ δεῖ
Holy Spirit will teach you in that same hour what it behoves [you]
εἰπεῖν.
to say.

13 Εἶπεν.δέ τις [z]αὐτῷ ἐκ τοῦ ὄχλου,‖ Διδάσκαλε, εἰπὲ τῷ
And [2]said [1]one to him from the crowd, Teacher, speak

[p] ἀποκτενόντων G; ἀποκτεννόντων LTTrA. [q] περισσόν L. [r] ἔχοντα ἐξουσίαν LTTrA. [s] πωλοῦνται TTrA. [t] — οὖν [L]TTrA. [v] ἔμπροσθεν L. [w] εἰσφέρωσιν TTrA. [x] μὴ μεριμνήσητε ye should not be careful TTr. [y] [ἢ τί] TrA. [z] ἐκ τοῦ ὄχλου αὐτῷ T.

ἀδελφῷ-μου μερίσασθαι μετ' ἐμοῦ τὴν κληρονομίαν. 14 Ὁ.δὲ
to my brother to divide with me the inheritance. But he
εἶπεν αὐτῷ, Ἄνθρωπε, τίς με κατέστησεν [a]δικαστὴν‖ ἢ μεριστὴν
said to him, Man, who [2]me [1]appointed a judge or a di-
τὴν ἐφ' ὑμᾶς; 15 Εἶπεν.δὲ πρὸς αὐτούς, Ὁρᾶτε καὶ φυλάσ-
vider over you? And he said to them, See and keep your-
σεσθε ἀπὸ [b]τῆς‖ πλεονεξίας· ὅτι οὐκ ἐν τῷ περισσεύειν
selves from covetousness; for not in the abundance
τινὶ ἡ.ζωὴ.αὐτοῦ ἐστιν ἐκ τῶν ὑπαρχόντων.[c]αὐτοῦ.‖
[7]to [8]anyone [9]his [10]life [6]is [1]of [2]that [3]which [4]he [5]possesses.
16 Εἶπεν.δὲ παραβολὴν πρὸς αὐτούς, λέγων, Ἀνθρώπου
And he spoke a parable to them, saying, [3]Of [4]a [7]man
τινὸς πλουσίου [d]εὐφόρησεν‖ ἡ χώρα· 17 καὶ
[5]certain [6]rich [8]brought [9]forth [10]abundantly [1]the [2]ground. And
διελογίζετο ἐν ἑαυτῷ, λέγων, Τί ποιήσω, ὅτι οὐκ.ἔχω
he was reasoning within himself, saying, What shall I do, for I have not
ποῦ συνάξω τοὺς.καρπούς.μου; 18 καὶ εἶπεν, Τοῦτο ποιήσω·
where I shall lay up my fruit? and he said, This will I do:
καθελῶ μου τὰς ἀποθήκας, καὶ μείζονας οἰκοδομήσω, καὶ
I will take away my granaries, and greater will build, and
συνάξω ἐκεῖ πάντα [e]τὰ.γενήματά‖.[f]μου‖ καὶ τὰ.ἀγαθά.μου,
will lay up there all my produce and my good things,
19 καὶ ἐρῶ τῇ.ψυχῇ.μου, Ψυχή, ἔχεις πολλὰ ἀγαθὰ
and I will say to my soul, Soul, thou hast many good things
κείμενα εἰς ἔτη πολλά· ἀναπαύου, φάγε, πίε, εὐφραίνου.
laid by for [2]years [1]many; take thy rest, eat, drink, be merry.
20 εἶπεν.δὲ αὐτῷ ὁ θεός, [g]Ἄφρων,‖ ταύτῃ τῇ νυκτὶ τὴν ψυχήν
But [2]said [3]to [4]him [1]God, Fool, this night [2]soul
σου [h]ἀπαιτοῦσιν‖ ἀπὸ σοῦ· ἃ.δὲ ἡτοίμασας τίνι
[1]thy they require of thee; and [5]what [6]thou [7]didst [8]prepare [1]to [2]whom
ἔσται; 21 οὕτως ὁ θησαυρίζων [i]ἑαυτῷ,‖ καὶ μὴ εἰς
[3]shall [4]be? Thus [is] he who treasures up for himself, and not toward
θεὸν πλουτῶν. 22 Εἶπεν.δὲ πρὸς τοὺς.μαθητὰς.[k]αὐτοῦ,‖ Διὰ
God is rich. And he said to his disciples, Because of
τοῦτο [l]ὑμῖν λέγω,‖ μὴ.μεριμνᾶτε τῇ.ψυχῇ.[m]ὑμῶν‖ τί φάγητε,
this to you I say, Be not careful as to your life what ye should eat,
μηδὲ τῷ σώματι[n] τί ἐνδύσησθε. 23 ἡ[o] ψυχὴ πλεῖόν ἐστιν
nor as to the body what ye should put on. The life more is
τῆς τροφῆς, καὶ τὸ σῶμα τοῦ ἐνδύματος. 24 Κατανοήσατε
than the food, and the body than the raiment. Consider
τοὺς κόρακας, ὅτι [p]οὐ‖ σπείρουσιν [q]οὐδὲ‖ θερίζουσιν, οἷς
the ravens, for [3]not [1]they [2]sow nor reap, to which
οὐκ.ἔστιν ταμεῖον οὐδὲ ἀποθήκη, καὶ ὁ θεὸς τρέφει αὐτούς·
there is not storehouse nor granary, and God feeds them.
πόσῳ μᾶλλον ὑμεῖς διαφέρετε τῶν πετεινῶν; 25 τίς.δὲ ἐξ
How much more [2]ye [1]are better than the birds? And who of
ὑμῶν [r]μεριμνῶν‖ δύναται [s]προσθεῖναι ἐπὶ τὴν.ἡλικίαν.αὐτοῦ‖
you [by] being careful is able to add to his stature
πῆχυν [t]ἕνα‖; 26 εἰ οὖν [v]οὔτε‖ ἐλάχιστον δύνασθε,
[2]cubit [1]one? If therefore not even [the] least ye are able [to do],
τί περὶ τῶν λοιπῶν μεριμνᾶτε; 27 Κατανοήσατε τὰ κρίνα,
why about the rest are ye careful? Consider the lilies,

my brother, that he
divide the inheritance
with me. 14 And he
said unto him, Man,
who made me a judge
or a divider over you?
15 And he said unto
them, Take heed, and
beware of covetous-
ness: for a man's life
consisteth not in the
abundance of the
things which he pos-
sesseth. 16 And he
spake a parable unto
them, saying, The
ground of a certain
rich man brought forth
plentifully: 17 and he
thought within him-
self, saying, What shall
I do, because I have no
room where to bestow
my fruits? 18 And he
said, This will I do: I
will pull down my
barns, and build great-
er; and there will I be-
stow all my fruits and
my goods. 19 And I
will say to my soul,
Soul, thou hast much
goods laid up for many
years; take thine ease,
eat, drink, *and* be mer-
ry. 20 But God said
unto him, *Thou* fool,
this night thy soul
shall be required of
thee: then whose shall
those things be, which
thou hast provided?
21 So *is* he that layeth
up treasure for him-
self, and is not rich
toward God. 22 And he
said unto his disciples,
Therefore I say unto
you, Take no thought
for your life, what ye
shall eat; neither for
the body, what ye shall
put on. 23 The life is
more than meat, and
the body *is more* than
raiment. 24 Consider
the ravens: for they
neither sow nor reap;
which neither have
storehouse nor barn;
and God feedeth them:
how much more are
ye better than the
fowls? 25 And which
of you with taking
thought can add to
his stature one cubit?
26 If ye then be not
able to do that thing
which is least, why
take ye thought for the
rest? 27 Consider the
lilies how they grow:

[a] κριτὴν LTTrA. [b] πάσης all LTTrAW. [c] αὐτῷ LTTrA. [d] ηὐφόρησεν L. [e] τὰ γεννήματα E; τὸν σῖτον the wheat Tr. [f] — μου Tr[A]. [g] ἄφρον GW. [h] αἰτοῦσιν TrA. [i] αὐτῷ T. [k] [αὐτοῦ] L. [l] λέγω ὑμῖν TrA. [m] — ὑμῶν (*read* as to the life) LTTrA. [n] + [ὑμῶν] (*read* your body) L. [o] + [γὰρ] (*read* for the) LTrA. [p] οὔτε neither TA. [q] οὔτε TA. [r] [μεριμνῶν] A. [s] ἐπὶ τὴν ἡλικίαν αὐτοῦ προσθεῖναι A. [t] — ἕνα (*read* a cubit) T[Tr]A. [v] οὐδὲ LTTrA.

they toil not, they spin
not; and yet I say unto
you, that Solomon in
all his glory was not
arrayed like one of
these. 28 If then God
so clothe the grass,
which is to day in the
field, and to morrow is
cast into the oven; how
much more *will he*
clothe you, O ye of little faith? 29 And seek
not ye what ye shall
eat, or what ye shall
drink, neither be ye of
doubtful mind. 30 For
all these things do the
nations of the world
seek after: and your
Father knoweth that
ye have need of these
things. 31 But rather
seek ye the kingdom of
God; and all these
things shall be added
unto you. 32 Fear not,
little flock; for it is
your Father's good
pleasure to give you
the kingdom. 33 Sell
that ye have, and give
alms; provide your-
selves bags which wax
not old, a treasure in
the heavens that fail-
eth not, where no
thief approacheth, nei-
ther moth corrupteth.
34 For where your trea-
sure is, there will your
heart be also. 35 Let
your loins be girded
about, and *your* lights
burning; 36 and ye
yourselves like unto
men that wait for their
lord, when he will re-
turn from the wed-
ding; that when he
cometh and knock-
eth, they may open
unto him immediately.
37 Blessed *are* those
servants, whom the
lord when he cometh
shall find watching:
verily I say unto you,
that he shall gird him-
self, and make them to
sit down to meat, and
will come forth and
serve them. 38 And if
he shall come in the se-
cond watch, or come in
the third watch, and
find *them* so, blessed
are those servants.
39 And this know, that
if the goodman of the
house had known what
hour the thief would

πῶς [w]αὐξάνει· οὐ.κοπιᾷ, οὐδὲ νήθει·‖ λέγω.δὲ ὑμῖν,[x]
how they grow; they labour not, nor do they spin; but I say to you,
οὐδὲ Σολομὼν ἐν πάσῃ τῇ.δόξῃ.αὐτοῦ περιεβάλετο ὡς ἓν
Not even Solomon in all his glory was clothed as one
τούτων. 28 εἰ.δὲ [y]τὸν χόρτον ἐν τῷ ἀγρῷ σήμερον ὄντα,‖ καὶ
of these. But if the grass [3]in [4]the [5]field [6]to-day [1]which [2]is, and
αὔριον εἰς κλίβανον βαλλόμενον, ὁ θεὸς οὕτως [z]ἀμφιέννυσιν,‖
to-morrow into an oven is cast, God thus arrays,
πόσῳ μᾶλλον ὑμᾶς, ὀλιγόπιστοι; 29 καὶ ὑμεῖς μὴ.ζητεῖτε
how much rather you, O [ye] of little faith? And ye seek ye not
τί φάγητε [a]ἢ‖ τί πίητε, καὶ μὴ.μετεωρίζεσθε. 30 ταῦτα
what ye may eat or what ye may drink, and be not in anxiety; [2]these [3]things
γὰρ πάντα τὰ ἔθνη τοῦ κόσμου [b]ἐπιζητεῖ·‖ ὑμῶν.δὲ ὁ πατὴρ
[1]for all the nations of the world seek after; and your Father
οἶδεν ὅτι χρῄζετε τούτων. 31 πλὴν ζητεῖτε τὴν βασιλείαν
knows that ye have need of these things. But seek ye the kingdom
[c]τοῦ θεοῦ,‖ καὶ ταῦτα [d]πάντα‖ προστεθήσεται ὑμῖν. 32 μὴ
of God, and [2]these [3]things [1]all shall be added to you. [2]Not
φοβοῦ, τὸ μικρὸν ποίμνιον· ὅτι εὐδόκησεν ὁ.πατὴρ.ὑμῶν
[1]fear, little flock, for [3]took [4]delight [1]your [2]Father
δοῦναι ὑμῖν τὴν βασιλείαν. 33 πωλήσατε τὰ.ὑπάρχοντα.ὑμῶν,
in giving you the kingdom. Sell your possessions,
καὶ δότε ἐλεημοσύνην· ποιήσατε ἑαυτοῖς [e]βαλάντια‖ μὴ
and give alms; make to yourselves purses not
παλαιούμενα, θησαυρὸν ἀνέκλειπτον ἐν τοῖς οὐρανοῖς, ὅπου
growing old, a treasure unfailing in the heavens, where
κλέπτης οὐκ.ἐγγίζει, οὐδὲ σὴς διαφθείρει· 34 ὅπου.γάρ ἐστιν
thief does not draw near, nor moth destroy. For where is
ὁ.θησαυρὸς.ὑμῶν, ἐκεῖ καὶ ἡ.καρδία.ὑμῶν ἔσται. 35 Ἔστωσαν
your treasure, there also your heart will be. Let be
[f]ὑμῶν αἱ ὀσφύες‖ περιεζωσμέναι καὶ οἱ λύχνοι καιόμενοι· 36 καὶ
your loins girded about and lamps burning; and
ὑμεῖς ὅμοιοι ἀνθρώποις προσδεχομένοις τὸν.κύριον.ἑαυτῶν,
ye like to men waiting for their lord,
πότε [g]ἀναλύσει‖ ἐκ τῶν γάμων, ἵνα ἐλθόντος καὶ κρού-
whenever he shall return from the wedding feasts, that having come and having
σαντος, εὐθέως ἀνοίξωσιν αὐτῷ. 37 μακάριοι οἱ δοῦλοι
knocked, immediately they may open to him. Blessed [2]bondmen
ἐκεῖνοι οὓς ἐλθὼν ὁ κύριος εὑρήσει γρηγοροῦντας. ἀμὴν
[1]those whom coming the Lord shall find watching. Verily
λέγω ὑμῖν, ὅτι περιζώσεται καὶ ἀνακλινεῖ αὐτούς, καὶ
I say to you, that he will gird himself and will make [2]recline [1]them, and
παρελθὼν διακονήσει αὐτοῖς. 38 [h]καὶ ἐὰν ἔλθῃ ἐν τῇ δευτέρᾳ
coming up will serve them. And if he come in the second
φυλακῇ, καὶ‖ ἐν τῇ τρίτῃ φυλακῇ ἔλθῃ, καὶ εὕρῃ οὕτως,
watch, and in the third watch he come, and find [them] thus,
μακάριοί εἰσιν [i]οἱ δοῦλοι ἐκεῖνοι.‖ 39 τοῦτο.δὲ γινώσκετε, ὅτι
blessed are [2]bondmen [1]those. But this know, that
εἰ ᾔδει ὁ οἰκοδεσπότης ποίᾳ ὥρᾳ ὁ κλέπτης ἔρχεται,
if [6]had [7]known [1]the [2]master [3]of [4]the [5]house in what hour the thief is coming,

---

[w] οὔτε νήθει οὔτε ὑφαίνει they neither spin nor weave TA. [x] + [ὅτι] that L. [y] ἐν ἀγρῷ τὸν χόρτον ὄντα σήμερον TA; τὸν χόρτον σήμερον ἐν ἀγρῷ ὄντα LTr. [z] ἀμφιάζει L; ἀμφιέζει TTrA. [a] καὶ and TTr. [b] ἐπιζητοῦσιν TTrA. [c] αὐτοῦ (*read* his kingdom) LTTrA. [d] — πάντα [L]TTrA. [e] βαλλάντια LTTrAW. [f] αἱ ὀσφύες ὑμῶν L. [g] ἀναλύσῃ he may return LTTrA. [h] κἂν ἐν τῇ δευτέρᾳ, κἂν and if in the second and if TTrA. [i] [οἱ δοῦλοι] ἐκεῖνοι TrA; — οἱ δοῦλοι ἐκεῖνοι (*read* are they) T.

[k]ἐγρηγόρησεν ἄν, καὶ" οὐκ.[l]ἂν".ἀφῆκεν [m]διορυγῆναι"
he would have watched, and would not have suffered to be dug through
τὸν.οἶκον.αὐτοῦ. 40 καὶ ὑμεῖς [n]οὖν" γίνεσθε ἕτοιμοι· ὅτι
his house. And ye therefore be ye ready; for
ᾗ ὥρᾳ οὐ.δοκεῖτε, ὁ υἱὸς τοῦ ἀνθρώπου ἔρχεται. 41 Εἶπεν.δὲ
in the hour ye think not, the Son of man comes. And [2]said
[o]αὐτῷ" ὁ Πέτρος, Κύριε, πρὸς ἡμᾶς τὴν.παραβολὴν.ταύτην
[3]to [4]him [1]Peter, Lord, to us this parable
λέγεις, ἢ καὶ πρὸς πάντας; 42 [p]Εἶπεν.δὲ" ὁ κύριος, Τίς
speakest thou, or also to all? And said the Lord, Who
ἄρα ἐστὶν ὁ πιστὸς οἰκονόμος [q]καὶ" φρόνιμος, ὃν καταστήσει
then is the faithful steward and prudent, whom [3]will [4]set
ὁ κύριος ἐπὶ τῆς.θεραπείας.αὐτοῦ, [r]τοῦ" διδόναι ἐν καιρῷ [s]τὸ"
[1]the [2]Lord over his household, to give in season the
σιτομέτριον; 43 μακάριος ὁ.δοῦλος.ἐκεῖνος ὃν ἐλθὼν
measure of corn? Blessed that bondman whom [3]having [4]come
ὁ.κύριος.αὐτοῦ εὑρήσει ποιοῦντα οὕτως. 44 ἀληθῶς λέγω ὑμῖν,
[1]his [2]Lord will find doing thus. Of a truth I say to you,
ὅτι ἐπὶ πᾶσιν τοῖς.ὑπάρχουσιν.αὐτοῦ καταστήσει αὐτόν.
that over all his possessions he will set him.
45 Ἐὰν.δὲ εἴπῃ ὁ.δοῦλος.ἐκεῖνος ἐν τῇ.καρδίᾳ.αὐτοῦ, Χρο-
But if [3]should [4]say [1]that [2]bondman in his heart, [3]De-
νίζει ὁ.κύριός.μου ἔρχεσθαι· καὶ ἄρξηται τύπτειν τοὺς
lays [1]my [2]Lord to come, and should begin to beat the
παῖδας καὶ τὰς παιδίσκας, ἐσθίειν.τε καὶ πίνειν καὶ με-
men-servants and the maid-servants, and to eat and to drink and to be
θύσκεσθαι· 46 ἥξει ὁ κύριος τοῦ.δούλου.ἐκείνου ἐν ἡμέρᾳ
drunken, [6]will [7]come [1]the [2]Lord [3]of [4]that [5]bondman in a day
ᾗ οὐ.προσδοκᾷ, καὶ ἐν ὥρᾳ ᾗ οὐ.γινώσκει, καὶ
in which he does not expect, and in an hour which he knows not, and
διχοτομήσει αὐτόν, καὶ τὸ.μέρος.αὐτοῦ μετὰ τῶν ἀπίστων
will cut [2]in [3]two [1]him, and his portion with the unbelievers
θήσει. 47 ἐκεῖνος.δὲ ὁ δοῦλος ὁ γνοὺς τὸ θέλημα τοῦ
will appoint. But that bondman who knew the will
κυρίου.[t]ἑαυτοῦ," καὶ μὴ.ἑτοιμάσας [v]μηδὲ" ποιήσας πρὸς
of his Lord, and prepared not nor did according to
τὸ.θέλημα.αὐτοῦ, δαρήσεται πολλάς· 48 ὁ.δὲ μὴ
his will, shall be beaten with many [stripes]; but he who [2]not
γνούς, ποιήσας.δὲ ἄξια πληγῶν, δαρήσεται ὀλίγας.
[1]knew, and did [things] worthy of stripes, shall be beaten with few.
παντὶ.δὲ ᾧ ἐδόθη πολύ, πολὺ ζητηθήσεται παρ' αὐτοῦ·
And everyone to whom was given much, much will be required from him;
καὶ ᾧ παρέθεντο πολύ, περισσότερον αἰτήσουσιν αὐτόν.
and to whom was committed much, the more will they ask of him.
49 Πῦρ ἦλθον βαλεῖν [w]εἰς" τὴν γῆν, καὶ τί θέλω εἰ ἤδη
Fire I came to cast into the earth, and what will I if already
ἀνήφθη; 50 βάπτισμα.δὲ ἔχω βαπτισθῆναι, καὶ πῶς συν-
it be kindled? But a baptism I have to be baptized [with], and how am I
έχομαι ἕως.[x]οὗ" τελεσθῇ. 51 δοκεῖτε ὅτι εἰρήνην παρε-
straitened until it be accomplished! Think ye that peace I
γενόμην δοῦναι ἐν τῇ γῇ; οὐχί, λέγω ὑμῖν, ἀλλ' ἢ
came to give in the earth? No, I say to you, but rather

come, he would have
watched, and not have
suffered his house to be
broken through. 40 Be
ye therefore ready al-
so: for the Son of man
cometh at an hour
when ye think not.
41 Then Peter said un-
to him, Lord, speakest
thou this parable unto
us, or even to all?
42 And the Lord said,
Who then is that faith-
ful and wise steward,
whom *his* lord shall
make ruler over his
household, to give *them*
their portion of meat
in due season? 43 Bless-
ed *is* that servant,
whom his lord when he
cometh shall find so
doing. 44 Of a truth I
say unto you, that he
will make him ruler
over all that he hath.
45 But and if that ser-
vant say in his heart,
My lord delayeth his
coming; and shall be-
gin to beat the menser-
vants and maidens, and
to eat and drink, and
to be drunken; 46 the
lord of that servant
will come in a day
when he looketh not
for *him*, and at an hour
when he is not aware,
and will cut him in sun-
der, and will appoint
him his portion with
the unbelievers. 47 And
that servant, which
knew his lord's will,
and prepared not *him-*
self, neither did according to his will, shall be
beaten with many
stripes. 48 But he that
knew not, and did com-
mit things worthy of
stripes, shall be beat-
en with few *stripes*.
For unto whomsoever
much is given, of him
shall be much requir-
ed: and to whom men
have committed much,
of him they will ask
the more. 49 I am come
to send fire on the
earth; and what will
I, if it be already kin-
dled? 50 But I have a
baptism to be baptized
with; and how am I
straitened till it be
accomplished! 51 Sup-
pose ye that I am come
to give peace on earth?
I tell you, Nay; but ra-
ther division: 52 for

---

[k] — ἐγρηγόρησεν ἄν, καὶ (*read* he would not have suffered) T. [l] — ἂν TrA. [m] διορυχθῆναι TA. [n] — οὖν LTTrA. [o] — αὐτῷ LTr[A]. [p] καὶ εἶπεν TTrA. [q] ὁ the LTTrA; καὶ ὁ and the W. [r] — τοῦ L[TrA]. [s] — τὸ (*read* a measure of corn) TrA. [t] αὐτοῦ LTTrA. [v] ἢ or T. [w] ἐπὶ upon LTTrAW. [x] ὅτου LTTrAW.

from henceforth there shall be five in one house divided, three against two, and two against three. 53 The father shall be divided against the son, and the son against the father; the mother against the daughter, and the daughter against the mother; the mother in law against her daughter in law, and the daughter in law against her mother in law.

διαμερισμόν. 52 ἔσονται.γὰρ ἀπὸ τοῦ.νῦν πέντε ἐν [y]οἴκῳ
division; for there will be from henceforth five in [2]house
ἑνὶ[||] διαμεμερισμένοι, τρεῖς ἐπὶ δυσὶν καὶ δύο ἐπὶ [z]τρισίν.
[1]one divided, three against two and two against three.
53 διαμερισθήσεται[||] πατὴρ [a]ἐφ'[||] υἱῷ, καὶ υἱὸς ἐπὶ πατρί·
[2]Will [3]be [4]divided [1]father against son, and son against father
μήτηρ ἐπὶ [b]θυγατρί,[||] καὶ θυγάτηρ ἐπὶ [c]μητρί·[||] πενθερὰ
mother against daughter, and daughter against mother; mother-in-law
ἐπὶ τὴν νύμφην [d]αὐτῆς,[||] καὶ νύμφη ἐπὶ τὴν
against [2]daughter-in-law [1]her, and daughter-in-law against
πενθερὰν [e]αὐτῆς.[||]
[2]mother-in-law [1]her.

54 And he said also to the people, When ye see a cloud rise out of the west, straightway ye say, There cometh a shower; and so it is. 55 And when *ye see* the south wind blow, ye say, There will be heat; and it cometh to pass. 56 *Ye* hypocrites, ye can discern the face of the sky and of the earth; but how is it that ye do not discern this time? 57 Yea, and why even of yourselves judge ye not what is right? 58 When thou goest with thine adversary to the magistrate, *as thou art* in the way, give diligence that thou mayest be delivered from him; lest he hale thee to the judge, and the judge deliver thee to the officer, and the officer cast thee into prison. 59 I tell thee, thou shalt not depart thence, till thou hast paid the very last mite.

54 Ἔλεγεν.δὲ καὶ τοῖς ὄχλοις, Ὅταν ἴδητε [f]τὴν[||] νεφέλην
And he said also to the crowds, When ye see the cloud
ἀνατέλλουσαν [g]ἀπὸ[||] δυσμῶν, εὐθέως λέγετε, [h]Ὄμβρος
rising up from [the] west, immediately ye say, A shower
ἔρχεται· καὶ γίνεται οὕτως. 55 καὶ ὅταν νότον πνέοντα,
is coming; and it happens so. And when a south wind [is] blowing,
λέγετε, Ὅτι καύσων ἔσται· καὶ γίνεται. 56 ὑποκριταί, τὸ
ye say, Heat there will be; and it happens. Hypocrites, the
πρόσωπον τῆς γῆς καὶ τοῦ οὐρανοῦ οἴδατε δοκιμάζειν·
appearance of the earth and of the heaven ye know [how] to discern,
τὸν.δὲ.καιρὸν.τοῦτον πῶς [i]οὐ.δοκιμάζετε[||]; 57 τί.δὲ καὶ ἀφ'
but this time how do ye not discern? And why even of
ἑαυτῶν οὐ.κρίνετε τὸ δίκαιον; 58 ὡς.γὰρ ὑπάγεις μετὰ
yourselves judge ye not what [is] right? For as thou goest with
τοῦ.ἀντιδίκου.σου ἐπ' ἄρχοντα, ἐν τῇ ὁδῷ δὸς ἐργασίαν
thine adverse party before a magistrate, in the way give diligence
ἀπηλλάχθαι ἀπ' αὐτοῦ· μήποτε κατασύρῃ σε πρὸς
to be set free from him, lest he should drag away thee to
τὸν κριτήν, καὶ ὁ κριτής σε [k]παραδῷ[||] τῷ πράκτορι, καὶ
the judge, and the judge thee should deliver to the officer, and
ὁ πράκτωρ σε [l]βάλλῃ[||] εἰς φυλακήν. 59 λέγω σοι, οὐ.μὴ
the officer thee should cast into prison. I say to thee, In no wise
ἐξέλθῃς ἐκεῖθεν ἕως.[m]οὗ[||] καὶ τὸ ἔσχατον λεπτὸν
shalt thou come out thence until even the last lepton
ἀποδῷς.
thou shalt have paid.

XIII. There were present at that season some that told him of the Galilæans, whose blood Pilate had mingled with their sacrifices. 2 And Jesus answering said unto them, Suppose ye that these Galilæans were sinners above all the Galilæans, because they suffered such things? 3 I tell you, Nay: but, except ye repent, ye shall all likewise perish. 4 Or

13 Παρῆσαν.δέ τινες ἐν αὐτῷ.τῷ καιρῷ ἀπαγγέλλοντες
And [2]were [3]present [1]some at the same time telling
αὐτῷ περὶ τῶν Γαλιλαίων, ὧν τὸ αἷμα [n]Πιλάτος[||] ἔμιξεν
him about the Galileans, of whom the blood Pilate mingled
μετὰ τῶν.θυσιῶν.αὐτῶν. 2 καὶ ἀποκριθεὶς [o]ὁ Ἰησοῦς[||] εἶπεν
with their sacrifices. And answering Jesus said
αὐτοῖς, Δοκεῖτε ὅτι οἱ.Γαλιλαῖοι.οὗτοι ἁμαρτωλοὶ παρὰ πάν-
to them, Think ye that these Galileans sinners beyond all
τας τοὺς Γαλιλαίους ἐγένοντο, ὅτι [p]τοιαῦτα[||] πεπόνθασιν;
the Galileans were, because such things they have suffered?
3 οὐχί, λέγω ὑμῖν· ἀλλ' ἐὰν μὴ.[q]μετανοῆτε,[||] πάντες [r]ὡσαύ-
No, I say to you; but if ye repent not, all [2]in [3]like

---

[y] ἑνὶ οἴκῳ LTTrA. [z] τρισὶν διαμερισθήσονται· (*read* three will be divided:) LTTrA. [a] ἐπὶ TTrA. [b] θυγατέρα LTTrA. [c] μητέρα T; τὴν μητέρα LTrA. [d] — αὐτῆς T. [e] — αὐτῆς TTrA. [f] — τὴν (*read* a cloud) LTTr[A]. [g] ἐπὶ at T. [h] + ὅτι that [L]TTrA. [i] οὐκ οἴδατε δοκιμάζειν know ye not to discern? Tr. [k] παραδώσει shall deliver LTTrA. [l] βάλῃ GW; βαλεῖ shall cast LTTrA. [m] — οὗ TTr. [n] Πειλᾶτος T. [o] — ὁ Ἰησοῦς (*read* he said) [L]TTrA. [p] ταῦτα these things TTr. [q] μετανοήσητε L. [r] ὁμοίως LTTrA.

τως" ἀπολεῖσθε. 4 ἢ ἐκεῖνοι οἱ [s]δέκα.καὶ.ὀκτὼ" ἐφ' οὓς
[4]manner [1]ye shall perish. Or those eighteen on whom
ἔπεσεν ὁ πύργος ἐν τῷ Σιλωὰμ καὶ ἀπέκτεινεν αὐτούς, δοκεῖτε
fell the tower in Siloam and killed them, think ye
ὅτι [t]οὗτοι" ὀφειλέται ἐγένοντο παρὰ πάντας [v] ἀνθρώπους
that these debtors were beyond all men
τοὺς κατοικοῦντας [w]ἐν" Ἱερουσαλήμ; 5 οὐχί, λέγω ὑμῖν· ἀλλ'
who dwelt in Jerusalem? No, I say to you; but
ἐὰν μὴ.[x]μετανοῆτε," πάντες [y]ὁμοίως" ἀπολεῖσθε.
if ye repent not, all [2]in [3]like [4]manner [1]ye shall perish.

6 Ἔλεγεν.δὲ ταύτην τὴν παραβολήν· Συκῆν εἶχέν τις
And he spoke this parable: [5]A [6]fig-tree [4]had [1]a [2]certain
[z]ἐν τῷ.ἀμπελῶνι.αὐτοῦ πεφυτευμένην·" καὶ ἦλθεν [a]καρπὸν
[[3]man] in his vineyard planted; and he came fruit
ζητῶν" ἐν αὐτῇ καὶ οὐχ.εὗρεν. 7 εἶπεν.δὲ πρὸς τὸν ἀμ-
seeking on it and did not find [any]. And he said to the vine-
πελουργόν, Ἰδού, τρία ἔτη[b] ἔρχομαι ζητῶν καρπὸν ἐν τῇ
dresser, Behold, three years I come seeking fruit on
συκῇ.ταύτῃ καὶ οὐχ.εὑρίσκω· ἔκκοψον [c] αὐτήν· [d]ἱνατί" καὶ
this fig-tree and do not find [any]: cut [2]down [1]it, why even
τὴν γῆν καταργεῖ; 8 ὁ.δὲ ἀποκριθεὶς λέγει αὐτῷ,
the ground does it render useless? But he answering says to him,
Κύριε, ἄφες αὐτὴν καὶ τοῦτο τὸ ἔτος, ἕως.ὅτου σκάψω περὶ
Sir, let [2]alone [1]it also this year, until I shall dig about
αὐτὴν καὶ βάλω [e]κοπρίαν·" 9 κἂν μὲν ποιήσῃ [f]καρπόν·
it and put manure, and if indeed it should bear fruit—;
εἰ.δὲ μήγε, εἰς.τὸ μέλλον". ἐκκόψεις αὐτήν.
but if not, hereafter thou shalt cut [2]down [1]it.

10 Ἦν.δὲ διδάσκων ἐν μιᾷ τῶν συναγωγῶν ἐν τοῖς σάβ-
And he was teaching in one of the synagogues on the sab-
βασιν· 11 καὶ ἰδού, γυνὴ [g]ἦν" πνεῦμα ἔχουσα ἀσθενείας
baths. And behold, a woman there was [2]a [3]spirit [1]having of infirmity
ἔτη [s]δέκα.καὶ.ὀκτώ," καὶ ἦν [h]συγκύπτουσα" καὶ μὴ.δυναμένη
[2]years [1]eighteen, and she was bent together and [2]unable
ἀνακύψαι εἰς.τὸ.παντελές. 12 ἰδὼν.δὲ αὐτὴν ὁ Ἰησοῦς
[3]to [4]lift [5]up [6]herself [1]wholly. And seeing her Jesus
προσεφώνησεν καὶ εἶπεν αὐτῇ, Γύναι, ἀπολέλυσαι [i]
called to [her] and said to her, Woman, thou hast been loosed from
τῆς.ἀσθενείας.σοῦ. 13 Καὶ ἐπέθηκεν αὐτῇ τὰς χεῖρας·
thine infirmity. And he laid upon her [his] hands,
καὶ παραχρῆμα [k]ἀνωρθώθη," καὶ ἐδόξαζεν τὸν θεόν.
and immediately she was made straight, and glorified God.
14 Ἀποκριθεὶς.δὲ ὁ ἀρχισυνάγωγος, ἀγανακτῶν ὅτι
But [6]answering [1]the [2]ruler [3]of [4]the [5]synagogue, indignant because
τῷ σαββάτῳ ἐθεράπευσεν ὁ Ἰησοῦς, ἔλεγεν τῷ ὄχλῳ,[l]
on the sabbath [2]healed [1]Jesus, said to the crowd,
Ἓξ ἡμέραι εἰσίν, ἐν αἷς δεῖ ἐργάζεσθαι· ἐν [m]ταύ-
Six days there are, in which it behoves [men] to work; in these
ταις" οὖν ἐρχόμενοι θεραπεύεσθε, καὶ μὴ τῇ ἡμέρᾳ τοῦ
therefore coming be healed, and not on the [2]day

those eighteen, upon whom the tower in Siloam fell, and slew them, think ye that they were sinners above all men that dwelt in Jerusalem?
5 I tell you, Nay: but, except ye repent, ye shall all likewise perish.

6 He spake also this parable; A certain *man* had a fig tree planted in his vineyard; and he came and sought fruit thereon, and found none.
7 Then said he unto the dresser of his vineyard, Behold, these three years I come seeking fruit on this fig tree, and find none: cut it down; why cumbereth it the ground?
8 And he answering said unto him, Lord, let it alone this year also, till I shall dig about it, and dung *it:*
9 and if it bear fruit, *well:* and if not, *then* after that thou shalt cut it down.

10 And he was teaching in one of the synagogues on the sabbath.
11 And, behold, there was a woman which had a spirit of infirmity eighteen years, and was bowed together, and could in no wise lift up *herself.*
12 And when Jesus saw her, he called *her to him,* and said unto her, Woman, thou art loosed from thine infirmity.
13 And he laid *his* hands on her: and immediately she was made straight, and glorified God.
14 And the ruler of the synagogue answered with indignation, because that Jesus had healed on the Sabbath day, and said unto the people, There are six days in which men ought to work: in them therefore come and be healed, and not on the sabbath day.
15 The

---

[s] δέκα [καὶ] ὀκτὼ LTrA; δεκαοκτὼ T. [t] αὐτοὶ they LTTrA. [v] + τοὺς the LTTrA. [w] — ἐν (*read* [in]) TrA. [x] μετανοήσητε LTTrA. [y] ὡσαύτως TTrA. [z] πεφυτευμένην ἐν τῷ ἀμπελῶνι αὐτοῦ LTTrA. [a] ζητῶν καρπὸν GLTTrAW. [b] + ἀφ' οὗ since (three years) TTrA. [c] + οὖν therefore (cut) L. [d] ἵνα τί LTrA. [e] κόπρια EGLTTrAW. [f] καρπὸν εἰς τὸ μέλλον· εἰ δὲ μήγε (*read* bear fruit hereafter; but if not) TTrA. [g] — ἦν LTTrA. [h] συνκύπτουσα T. [i] + ἀπὸ from LT. [k] ἀνορθώθη LTTrA. [l] + ὅτι that TA. [m] αὐταῖς them LTTrA.

Lord then answered him, and said, *Thou* hypocrite, doth not each one of you on the sabbath loose his ox or *his* ass from the stall, and lead *him* away to watering? 16 And ought not this woman, being a daughter of Abraham, whom Satan hath bound, lo, these eighteen years, be loosed from this bond on the sabbath day? 17 And when he had said these things, all his adversaries were ashamed: and all the people rejoiced for all the glorious things that were done by him.

18 Then said he, Unto what is the kingdom of God like? and whereunto shall I resemble it? 19 It is like a grain of mustard seed, which a man took, and cast into his garden; and it grew, and waxed a great tree; and the fowls of the air lodged in the branches of it. 20 And again he said, Whereunto shall I liken the kingdom of God? 21 It is like leaven, which a woman took and hid in three measures of meal, till the whole was leavened.

22 And he went through the cities and villages, teaching, and journeying toward Jerusalem. 23 Then said one unto him, Lord, are there few that be saved? And he said unto them, 24 Strive to enter in at the strait gate: for many, I say unto you, will seek to enter in, and shall not be able. 25 When once the master of the house is risen up, and hath shut to the door, and ye begin to stand without, and to knock at the door, saying, Lord, Lord, open unto us; and he shall answer and say unto you, I know you not whence ye are: 26 then shall ye begin to say, We have eaten and drunk in thy presence, and thou hast taught in

σαββάτου. 15 Ἀπεκρίθη °οὖν‖ αὐτῷ ὁ κύριος, και εἶπεν,
1sabbath. 4Answered 1therefore 5him 2the 3Lord, and said,
p'Ὑποκριτά,‖ ἕκαστος ὑμῶν τῷ σαββάτῳ οὐ.λύει τὸν
Hypocrite, each one of you on the sabbath does he not loose
βοῦν.αὐτοῦ ἢ τὸν ὄνον ἀπὸ τῆς φάτνης, καὶ ἀπαγαγὼν
his ox or ass from the manger, and having led [it] away
ποτίζει; 16 ταύτην.δὲ θυγατέρα Ἀβραὰμ οὖσαν,
give [it] drink? And this [woman], 2a 3daughter 4of 5Abraham 1being,
ἣν ἔδησεν ὁ σατανᾶς, ἰδού, δέκα.καὶ.ὀκτὼ ἔτη, οὐκ.ἔδει
whom 2has 3bound 1Satan, lo, eighteen years, ought [she] not
λυθῆναι ἀπὸ τοῦ.δεσμοῦ.τούτου τῇ ἡμέρᾳ τοῦ σαββάτου;
to be loosed from this bond on the 2day 1sabbath?
17 Καὶ ταῦτα λέγοντος.αὐτοῦ κατῃσχύνοντο πάντες οἱ
And 4these 5things 1on 2his 3saying 7were 8ashamed 6all who
ἀντικείμενοι αὐτῷ· καὶ πᾶς ὁ ὄχλος ἔχαιρεν ἐπὶ πᾶσιν
were opposed to him; and all the crowd were rejoicing at all
τοῖς ἐνδόξοις τοῖς γινομένοις ὑπ' αὐτοῦ.
the glorious things which were being done by him.

18 "Ἔλεγεν qδέ,‖ Τίνι ὁμοία ἐστὶν ἡ βασιλεία τοῦ θεοῦ;
2He 3said 1and, To what 2like 1is the kingdom of God?
καὶ τίνι ὁμοιώσω αὐτήν; 19 ὁμοία ἐστὶν κόκκῳ σινάπεως,
and to what shall I liken it? Like it is to a grain of mustard,
rὃν‖ λαβὼν ἄνθρωπος ἔβαλεν εἰς κῆπον ἑαυτοῦ· καὶ
which 3having 4taken 1a 2man cast into 2garden 1his; and
ηὔξησεν.καὶ ἐγένετο εἰς δένδρον sμέγα,‖ καὶ.τὰ πετεινὰ τοῦ
it grew and came into a 2tree 1great, and the birds of the
οὐρανοῦ κατεσκήνωσεν ἐν τοῖς.κλάδοις.αὐτοῦ. 20 tΚαὶ‖ πάλιν
heaven roosted in its branches. And again
εἶπεν, Τίνι ὁμοιώσω τὴν βασιλείαν τοῦ θεοῦ; 21 ὁμοία
he said, To what shall I liken the kingdom of God? Like
ἐστὶν ζύμῃ, ἣν λαβοῦσα γυνὴ vἐνέκρυψεν‖ εἰς ἀλεύρου
it is to leaven, which 3having 4taken 1a 2woman hid in 3of 4meal
σάτα τρία, ἕως.οὗ ἐζυμώθη ὅλον.
2seahs 1three, until 2was 3leavened 1all.

22 Καὶ διεπορεύετο κατὰ πόλεις καὶ κώμας διδάσκων, καὶ
And he went through by cities and villages teaching, and
πορείαν ποιούμενος εἰς wἹερουσαλήμ.‖ 23 εἶπεν.δέ τις αὐτῷ,
2progress 1making towards Jerusalem. And said one to him,
Κύριε, εἰ ὀλίγοι οἱ σωζόμενοι; Ὁ.δὲ εἶπεν πρὸς αὐτούς,
Lord, [are] 4few 1those 2being 3saved? But he said to them,
24 Ἀγωνίζεσθε εἰσελθεῖν διὰ τῆς στενῆς xπύλης·‖ ὅτι
Strive with earnestness to enter in through the narrow gate; for
πολλοί, λέγω ὑμῖν, ζητήσουσιν εἰσελθεῖν, καὶ οὐκ.ἰσχύσουσιν.
many, I say to you, will seek to enter in, and will not be able.
25 ἀφ'.οὗ.ἂν ἐγερθῇ ὁ οἰκοδεσπότης, καὶ ἀπο-
From the time 6shall 7have 8risen 9up 1the 2master 3of 4the 5house, and shall
κλείσῃ τὴν θύραν, καὶ ἄρξησθε ἔξω ἑστάναι καὶ κρούειν τὴν
have shut the door, and ye begin without to stand and to knock at the
θύραν, λέγοντες, Κύριε, yκύριε,‖ ἄνοιξον ἡμῖν· καὶ ἀποκριθεὶς
door, saying, Lord, Lord, open to us; and he answering
ἐρεῖ ὑμῖν, Οὐκ οἶδα ὑμᾶς πόθεν ἐστέ. 26 τότε ἄρξεσθε
will say to you, I do not know you whence ye are. Then will ye begin
λέγειν, Ἐφάγομεν ἐνώπιόν.σου καὶ ἐπίομεν, καὶ ἐν ταῖς
to say, We ate in thy presence and drank, and in

° δὲ but LTTrA. p Ὑποκριταί hypocrites LTTrAW. q οὖν therefore TTrA. r ὃ E. s — μέγα [L]T[TrA]. t — καὶ W. v ἔκρυψεν TTrA. w Ἱεροσόλυμα T. x θύρας door LTTrA. y — κύριε [L]TTrA.

πλατείαις.ἡμῶν ἐδίδαξας. 27 καὶ ἐρεῖ, Λέγω ὑμῖν, οὐκ
our streets thou didst teach. And he will say, I tell you, [3]Not
οἶδα [z]ὑμᾶς‖ πόθεν ἐστέ· ἀπόστητε ἀπ' ἐμοῦ πάντες
[1]I [2]do know you whence ye are; depart from me, all [ye]
[a]οἱ‖ ἐργάται [b]τῆς‖ ἀδικίας. 28 ἐκεῖ ἔσται ὁ κλαυθμὸς καὶ
the workers of unrighteousness. There shall be the weeping and
ὁ βρυγμὸς τῶν ὀδόντων, ὅταν [c]ὄψησθε‖ Ἀβραὰμ καὶ Ἰσαὰκ
the gnashing of the teeth, when ye see Abraham and Isaac
καὶ Ἰακὼβ καὶ πάντας τοὺς προφήτας ἐν τῇ βασιλείᾳ τοῦ
and Jacob and all the prophets in the kingdom
θεοῦ, ὑμᾶς.δὲ ἐκβαλλομένους ἔξω. 29 καὶ ἥξουσιν ἀπὸ
of God, but yourselves being cast out. And they shall come from
ἀνατολῶν καὶ δυσμῶν, καὶ [d]ἀπὸ‖ βοῤῥᾶ καὶ νότου, καὶ ἀνα-
east and west, and from north and south, and shall
κλιθήσονται ἐν τῇ βασιλείᾳ τοῦ θεοῦ. 30 καὶ ἰδού, εἰσὶν
recline in the kingdom of God. And lo, there are
ἔσχατοι οἳ ἔσονται πρῶτοι, καί εἰσιν πρῶτοι οἳ ἔσονται
last who shall be first, and there are first who shall be
ἔσχατοι.
last.

our streets. 27 But he shall say, I tell you, I know you not whence ye are; depart from me, all *ye* workers of iniquity. 28 There shall be weeping and gnashing of teeth, when ye shall see Abraham, and Isaac, and Jacob, and all the prophets, in the kingdom of God, and you *yourselves* thrust out. 29 And they shall come from the east, and *from* the west, and from the north, and *from* the south, and shall sit down in the kingdom of God. 30 And, behold, there are last which shall be first, and there are first which shall be last.

31 Ἐν.αὐτῇ τῇ [e]ἡμέρᾳ‖ [f]προσῆλθόν‖ τινες Φαρισαῖοι,
On the same day came to [him] certain Pharisees,
λέγοντες αὐτῷ, Ἔξελθε καὶ πορεύου ἐντεῦθεν, ὅτι Ἡρώδης
saying to him, Go out and proceed hence, for Herod
θέλει σε ἀποκτεῖναι. 32 Καὶ εἶπεν αὐτοῖς, Πορευθέντες
desires [3]thee [1]to [2]kill. And he said to them, Having gone
εἴπατε τῇ.ἀλώπεκι.ταύτῃ, Ἰδού, ἐκβάλλω δαιμόνια καὶ ἰάσεις
say to that fox, Lo, I cast out demons and cures
[g]ἐπιτελῶ‖ σήμερον καὶ αὔριον, καὶ τῇ τρίτῃ[h] τελειοῦμαι.
I complete to-day and to-morrow, and the third [day] I am perfected;
33 πλὴν δεῖ με σήμερον καὶ αὔριον καὶ τῇ ἐχομένῃ
but it behoves me to-day and to-morrow and the [day] following
πορεύεσθαι· ὅτι οὐκ.ἐνδέχεται προφήτην ἀπολέσθαι ἔξω
to proceed; for it is not possible [for] a prophet to perish out of
Ἱερουσαλήμ. 34 Ἱερουσαλήμ, Ἱερουσαλήμ, ἡ ἀποκτείνουσα
Jerusalem. Jerusalem, Jerusalem, who killest
τοὺς προφήτας, καὶ λιθοβολοῦσα τοὺς ἀπεσταλμένους πρὸς
the prophets, and stonest those who have been sent to
αὐτήν, ποσάκις ἠθέλησα ἐπισυνάξαι τὰ.τέκνα.σου, ὃν.τρόπον
her, how often would I have gathered thy children, in the way
[i]ὄρνις‖ [k]τὴν‖ ἑαυτῆς [l]νοσσιὰν‖ ὑπὸ τὰς πτέρυγας,
a hen [gathers] her brood under [her] wings,
καὶ οὐκ.ἠθελήσατε. 35 ἰδού, ἀφίεται ὑμῖν ὁ.οἶκος.ὑμῶν [m]ἔρη-
and ye would not. Behold, is left to you your house de-
μος·‖ [n]ἀμὴν δὲ λέγω‖ ὑμῖν, [o]ὅτι‖ οὐ.μή [p]με ἴδητε‖ ἕως.[q]ἂν‖
solate; [2]verily [1]and I say to you, that not at all me shall ye see until
[r]ἥξῃ,‖ [s]ὅτε‖ εἴπητε, Εὐλογημένος ὁ ἐρχόμενος ἐν ὀνό-
it come when ye say, Blessed [is] he who comes in [the] name
ματι κυρίου.
of [the] Lord.

31 The same day there came certain of the Pharisees, saying unto him, Get thee out, and depart hence: for Herod will kill thee. 32 And he said unto them, Go ye, and tell that fox, Behold, I cast out devils, and I do cures to day and to morrow, and the third *day* I shall be perfected. 33 Nevertheless I must walk to day, and to morrow, and the *day* following: for it cannot be that a prophet perish out of Jerusalem. 34 O Jerusalem, Jerusalem, which killest the prophets, and stonest them that are sent unto thee; how often would I have gathered thy children together, as a hen *doth gather* her brood under *her* wings, and ye would not! 35 Behold, your house is left unto you desolate: and verily I say unto you, Ye shall not see me, until *the time* come when ye shall say, Blessed *is* he that cometh in the name of the Lord.

14 Καὶ ἐγένετο ἐν τῷ.ἐλθεῖν.αὐτὸν εἰς οἶκόν τινος τῶν
And it came to pass on his having gone into a house of one of the

XIV. And it came to pass, as he went into the house of one of the

---

[z] — ὑμᾶς [L]TrA. [a] — οἱ TTrA. [b] — τῆς LTTrA. [c] ὄψεσθε ye shall see TTr. [d] — ἀπὸ [L]T[TrA]. [e] ὥρᾳ hour TA. [f] προσῆλθάν TTrA. [g] ἀποτελῶ LTTrA. [h] + [ἡμέρᾳ] day L. [i] ὄρνιξ T. [k] τὰ L. [l] νοσσία L. [m] — ἔρημος GLTTrAW. [n] λέγω δὲ GLTrAW; λέγω T. [o] — ὅτι [L]T[A]. [p] ἴδητέ με LTTrA. [q] — ἂν TTrA. [r] ἥξει it shall come LT[TrA]. [s] [ὅτε] TrA.

chief Pharisees to eat
bread on the sabbath
day, that they watched
him. 2 And, behold,
there was a certain
man before him which
had the dropsy. 3 And
Jesus answering spake
unto the lawyers and
Pharisees, saying, Is
it lawful to heal on the
sabbath day? 4 And
they held their peace.
And he took *him*, and
healed him, and let
him go; 5 and an-
swered them, saying,
Which of you shall
have an ass or an ox
fallen into a pit, and
will not straightway
pull him out on the
sabbath day? 6 And
they could not answer
him again to these
things.

ἀρχόντων [t]τῶν‖ Φαρισαίων σαββάτῳ φαγεῖν ἄρτον, καὶ αὐτοὶ
rulers of the Pharisees on a sabbath to eat bread, that they
ἦσαν παρατηρούμενοι αὐτόν. 2 καὶ ἰδού, ἄνθρωπός τις
were watching him. And behold, a [2]man [1]certain
ἦν ὑδρωπικὸς ἔμπροσθεν αὐτοῦ. 3 καὶ ἀποκριθεὶς ὁ Ἰησοῦς
there was dropsical before him. And answering Jesus
εἶπεν πρὸς τοὺς νομικοὺς καὶ Φαρισαίους, [v]λέγων,‖ [w]Εἰ‖
spoke to the doctors of the law and to [the] Pharisees, saying,
ἔξεστιν τῷ σαββάτῳ [x]θεραπεύειν‖ [y]; 4 Οἱ.δὲ ἡσύχασαν.
Is it lawful on the sabbath to heal? But they were silent.
καὶ ἐπιλαβόμενος ἰάσατο αὐτόν, καὶ ἀπέλυσεν. 5 καὶ
And taking hold [of him] he healed him, and let [him] go. And
[z]ἀποκριθεὶς‖ [a]πρὸς αὐτοὺς εἶπεν,‖ Τίνος ὑμῶν [b]ὄνος‖ ἢ βοῦς
answering to them he said, Of which of you [2]an [3]ass [4]or [5]an [6]ox
εἰς φρέαρ [c]ἐμπεσεῖται,‖ καὶ οὐκ εὐθέως ἀνασπάσει αὐτὸν
[8]into [9]a [10]pit [1]shall [7]fall, and [3]not [4]immediately [1]he [2]will pull up him
[d]ἐν‖ [e]τῇ‖ ἡμέρᾳ τοῦ σαββάτου; 6 Καὶ οὐκ.ἴσχυσαν ἀνταπο-
on the [2]day [1]sabbath? And they were not able to re-
κριθῆναι [f]αὐτῷ‖ πρὸς ταῦτα.
ply to him as to these things.

7 And he put forth a
parable to those which
were bidden, when he
marked how they chose
out the chief rooms;
saying unto them,
8 When thou art bid-
den of any *man* to a
wedding, sit not down
in the highest room;
lest a more honourable
man than thou be bid-
den of him; 9 and he
that bade thee and him
come and say to thee,
Give this man place;
and thou begin with
shame to take the low-
est room. 10 But when
thou art bidden, go and
sit down in the lowest
room; that when he
that bade thee cometh,
he may say unto thee,
Friend, go up higher:
then shalt thou have
worship in the presence
of them that sit at meat
with thee. 11 For who-
soever exalteth him-
self shall be abased;
and he that humbleth
himself shall be ex-
alted.

7 Ἔλεγεν.δὲ πρὸς τοὺς κεκλημένους παραβολήν, ἐπέχων
And he spoke to those who were invited a parable, remarking
πῶς τὰς πρωτοκλισίας ἐξελέγοντο, λέγων πρὸς αὐτούς,
how the first places they were choosing out, saying to them,
8 Ὅταν κληθῇς ὑπό τινος εἰς γάμους, μὴ.κατακλιθῇς
When thou art invited by anyone to wedding feasts, do not recline
εἰς τὴν πρωτοκλισίαν, μήποτε ἐντιμότερός σου ᾖ.κεκλη-
in the first place, lest a more honourable than thou may have
μένος ὑπ᾽ αὐτοῦ, 9 καὶ ἐλθὼν ὁ σὲ καὶ αὐτὸν καλέσας
been invited by him, and having come he who thee and him invited
ἐρεῖ σοι, Δὸς τούτῳ τόπον· καὶ τότε ἄρξῃ [g]μετ᾽‖
shall say to thee, Give [2]to [3]this [4]one [1]place, and then thou begin with
αἰσχύνης τὸν ἔσχατον τόπον κατέχειν. 10 ἀλλ᾽ ὅταν κλη-
shame the last place to take. But when thou art
θῇς, πορευθεὶς [h]ἀνάπεσον‖ εἰς τὸν ἔσχατον τόπον· ἵνα
invited, having gone recline in the last place, that
ὅταν ἔλθῃ ὁ κεκληκώς σε, [i]εἴπῃ‖ σοι, Φίλε, προσ-
when he may come who has invited thee, he may say to thee, Friend, come
ανάβηθι ἀνώτερον· τότε ἔσται σοι δόξα ἐνώπιον [k] τῶν
up higher. Then shall be to thee glory before those who
συνανακειμένων σοί. 11 ὅτι πᾶς ὁ ὑψῶν ἑαυτὸν ταπεινω-
recline [at table] with thee; for everyone that exalts himself shall be
θήσεται· καὶ ὁ ταπεινῶν ἑαυτὸν ὑψωθήσεται.
humbled, and he that humbles himself shall be exalted.

12 Then said he also
to him that bade him,
When thou makest a
dinner or a supper,
call not thy friends,
nor thy brethren, nei-
ther thy kinsmen, nor
thy rich neighbours;
lest they also bid thee
again, and a recom-
pence be made thee.

12 Ἔλεγεν.δὲ καὶ τῷ κεκληκότι.αὐτόν, Ὅταν ποιῇς
And he said also to him who had invited him, When thou makest
ἄριστον ἢ δεῖπνον, μὴ.φώνει τοὺς.φίλους.σου μηδὲ τοὺς ἀδελ-
a dinner or a supper, call not thy friends nor [2]breth-
φούς σου μηδὲ τοὺς.συγγενεῖς.σου μηδὲ γείτονας πλουσίους·
ren [1]thy nor thy kinsfolk nor [2]neighbours [1]rich,
μήποτε καὶ αὐτοί [l]σε ἀντικαλέσωσιν,‖ καὶ γένηταί [m]σοι
lest also they thee should invite in return, and [3]be [4]made [5]thee

---

[t] [τῶν] A. [v] [λέγων] L. [w] — Εἰ TTrA. [x] θεραπεῦσαι LTTrA. [y] + ἢ οὔ or not [L]TTrA. [z] — ἀποκριθεὶς LTr[A]. [a] εἶπεν πρὸς αὐτούς L. [b] υἱὸς a son LTTrAW. [c] πεσεῖται LTTrA. [d] — ἐν (read τῇ on the) [L]Tr. [e] — τῇ T. [f] — αὐτῷ TTrA. [g] μετὰ LTTrAW. [h] ἀνάπεσαι G; ἀνάπεσε LTTrAW. [i] ἐρεῖ he will say TTr. [k] + πάντων all LTTrA. [l] ἀντικαλέσωσίν σε LTTrA. [m] ἀνταπόδομά σοι TTrA.

ἀνταπόδομα.ǁ 13 ἀλλ' ὅταν ποιῇς δοχήν, κάλει πτωχούς,
[1]a [2]recompense; but when thou makest a feast, call poor,
[n]ἀναπήρους,ǁ χωλούς, τυφλούς· 14 καὶ μακάριος ἔσῃ·
crippled, lame, blind; and blessed thou shalt be;
ὅτι οὐκ.ἔχουσιν ἀνταποδοῦναί σοι· ἀνταποδοθήσεται
for they have not [wherewith] to recompense thee; [2]it [3]shall [4]be [5]recompensed
[o]γάρǁ σοι ἐν τῇ ἀναστάσει τῶν δικαίων.
[1]for thee in the resurrection of the just.

15 Ἀκούσας.δέ τις τῶν συνανακειμένων ταῦ-
And [9]having [10]heard [1]one [2]of [3]those [4]reclining [[5]at [6]table] [7]with [[8]him] these
τα εἶπεν αὐτῷ, Μακάριος [p]ὃςǁ φάγεται ἄρτον ἐν τῇ
things said to him, Blessed [he] who shall eat bread in the
βασιλείᾳ τοῦ θεοῦ. 16 Ὁ.δὲ εἶπεν αὐτῷ, Ἄνθρωπός τις
kingdom of God. But he said to him, A [2]man [1]certain
[q]ἐποίησενǁ δεῖπνον [r]μέγα,ǁ καὶ.ἐκάλεσεν πολλούς· 17 καὶ ἀπέ-
made a [2]supper [1]great, and invited many. And he
στειλεν τὸν.δοῦλον.αὐτοῦ τῇ ὥρᾳ τοῦ δείπνου εἰπεῖν τοῖς
sent his bondman at the hour of the supper to say to those who
κεκλημένοις, Ἔρχεσθε, ὅτι ἤδη ἕτοιμά [s]ἐστινǁ [t]πάντα.ǁ 18 Καὶ
had been invited, Come, for now [3]ready [2]is [1]all. And
ἤρξαντο ἀπὸ μιᾶς [v]παραιτεῖσθαι πάντες.ǁ [w] ὁ πρῶ-
[2]began [3]with [4]one [[5]consent] [6]to [7]excuse [8]themselves [1]all. The first
τος εἶπεν αὐτῷ, Ἀγρὸν ἠγόρασα, καὶ [x]ἔχω ἀνάγκηνǁ
said to him, [4]A [5]field [1]I [2]have [3]bought, and I have need
[y]ἐξελθεῖν καὶǁ ἰδεῖν αὐτόν· ἐρωτῶ σε ἔχε με παρῃτημένον.
to go out and to see it; I pray thee hold me excused.
19 καὶ ἕτερος εἶπεν, Ζεύγη βοῶν ἠγόρασα πέντε, καὶ
And another said, [5]Pairs [6]of [7]oxen [1]I [2]have [3]bought [4]five, and
πορεύομαι δοκιμάσαι αὐτά· ἐρωτῶ σε ἔχε με.παρῃτημένον.
I go to prove them; I pray thee hold me excused.
20 καὶ ἕτερος εἶπεν, Γυναῖκα ἔγημα, καὶ διὰ τοῦτο
And another said, A wife I have married, and because of this
οὐ.δύναμαι ἐλθεῖν. 21 καὶ παραγενόμενος ὁ.δοῦλος.[z]ἐκεῖνοςǁ
I am unable to come. And having come that bondman
ἀπήγγειλεν τῷ.κυρίῳ.αὐτοῦ ταῦτα. Τότε ὀργισθεὶς ὁ οἰκο-
reported to his lord these things. Then being angry the master
δεσπότης εἶπεν τῷ.δούλῳ.αὐτοῦ, Ἔξελθε ταχέως εἰς τὰς
of the house said to his bondman, Go out quickly into the
πλατείας καὶ ῥύμας τῆς πόλεως, καὶ τοὺς πτωχοὺς καὶ [a]ἀνα-
streets and lanes of the city, and the poor and crip-
πήρουςǁ καὶ [b]χωλοὺς καὶ τυφλοὺςǁ εἰσάγαγε ὧδε. 22 Καὶ εἶπεν
pled and lame and blind bring in here. And said
ὁ δοῦλος, Κύριε, γέγονεν [c]ὡςǁ ἐπέταξας, καὶ ἔτι
the bondman, Sir, it has been done as thou didst command, and still
τόπος ἐστίν. 23 Καὶ εἶπεν ὁ κύριος πρὸς τὸν δοῦλον,
room there is. And said the lord to the bondman,
Ἔξελθε εἰς τὰς ὁδοὺς καὶ φραγμούς, καὶ ἀνάγκασον εἰσελθεῖν,
Go out into the ways and hedges, and compel to come in,
ἵνα γεμισθῇ [d]ὁ.οἶκός.μου.ǁ 24 λέγω.γὰρ ὑμῖν, ὅτι οὐδεὶς τῶν
that may be filled my house; for I say to you, that not one
ἀνδρῶν.ἐκείνων τῶν κεκλημένων γεύσεταί μου τοῦ δείπνου.
of those men who have been invited shall taste of my supper.

13 But when thou makest a feast, call the poor, the maimed, the lame, the blind: 14 and thou shalt be blessed; for they cannot recompense thee: for thou shalt be recompensed at the resurrection of the just.

15 And when one of them that sat at meat with him heard these things, he said unto him, Blessed *is* he that shall eat bread in the kingdom of God.
16 Then said he unto him, A certain man made a great supper, and bade many: 17 and sent his servant at supper time to say to them that were bidden, Come; for all things are now ready. 18 And they all with one *consent* began to make excuse. The first said unto him, I have bought a piece of ground, and I must needs go and see it: I pray thee have me excused. 19 And another said, I have bought five yoke of oxen, and I go to prove them: I pray thee have me excused. 20 And another said, I have married a wife, and therefore I cannot come. 21 So that servant came, and shewed his lord these things. Then the master of the house being angry said to his servant, Go out quickly into the streets and lanes of the city, and bring in hither the poor, and the maimed, and the halt, and the blind. 22 And the servant said, Lord, it is done as thou hast commanded, and yet there is room. 23 And the lord said unto the servant, Go out into the highways and hedges, and compel *them* to come in, that my house may be filled. 24 For I say unto you, That none of those men which were bidden shall taste of my supper.

---

[n] ἀναπείρους LTTrA. [o] δέ but T. [p] ὅστις whosoever TTrA. [q] ἐποίει TTrA. [r] μέγαν L. [s] εἰσιν are T. [t] — πάντα (read [all]) [L]T[TrA]. [v] πάντες παραιτεῖσθαι LTTrA. [w] + [καὶ] and L. [x] ἀνάγκην ἔχω L. [y] ἐξελθὼν having gone out TTrA. [z] — ἐκεῖνος (read the bondman) LTTrA. [a] ἀναπείρους LTrA. [b] τυφλοὺς καὶ χωλοὺς LTTrA. [c] ὃ which TTrA. [d] μου ὁ οἶκος TTrA.

25 And there went
great multitudes with
him: and he turned,
and said unto them,
26 If any *man* come
to me, and hate not his
father, and mother,
and wife, and children,
and brethren, and sis-
ters, yea, and his own
life also, he cannot be
my disciple. 27 And
whosoever doth not
bear his cross, and
come after me, cannot
be my disciple. 28 For
which of you, intend-
ing to build a tower,
sitteth not down first,
and counteth the cost,
whether he have *suffi-
cient* to finish *it*?
29 Lest haply, after he
hath laid the founda-
tion, and is not able to
finish *it*, all that be-
hold *it* begin to mock
him, 30 saying, This
man began to build,
and was not able to
finish. 31 Or what king,
going to make war a-
gainst another king,
sitteth not down first,
and consulteth whe-
ther he be able with
ten thousand to meet
him that cometh a-
gainst him with twen-
ty thousand? 32 Or
else, while the other
is yet a great way off,
he sendeth an ambas-
sage, and desireth con-
ditions of peace. 33 So
likewise, whosoever he
be of you that forsak-
eth not all that he hath,
he cannot be my disci-
ple. 34 Salt *is* good:
but if the salt have
lost his savour, where-
with shall it be sea-
soned? 35 It is neither
fit for the land, nor
yet for the dunghill;
but men cast it out.
He that hath ears to
hear, let him hear.

25 Συνεπορεύοντο.δὲ αὐτῷ ὄχλοι πολλοί· καὶ στραφεὶς
And [3]were [4]going [5]with [6]him [2]crowds [1]great; and having turned
εἶπεν πρὸς αὐτούς, 26 Εἴ τις ἔρχεται πρός με, καὶ οὐ.μισεῖ
he said to them, If any one comes to me, and hates not
τὸν.πατέρα.[f]ἑαυτοῦ‖ καὶ τὴν μητέρα καὶ τὴν γυναῖκα καὶ τὰ
his father and mother and wife and
τέκνα καὶ τοὺς ἀδελφοὺς καὶ τὰς ἀδελφάς, ἔτι.[g]δὲ‖ καὶ τὴν
children and brothers and sisters, and besides also
ἑαυτοῦ.ψυχήν, οὐ.δύναταί [h]μου.μαθητὴς εἶναι·‖ 27 [i]καὶ‖ ὅστις
his own life, he cannot my disciple be; and whosoever
οὐ.βαστάζει τὸν.σταυρὸν.[k]αὐτοῦ,‖ καὶ ἔρχεται ὀπίσω μου,
carries not his cross, and comes after me,
οὐ.δύναταί [l]μου εἶναι‖ μαθητής. 28 τίς.γὰρ ἐξ ὑμῶν θέλων
cannot [2]my [1]be disciple. For which of you desiring
πύργον οἰκοδομῆσαι, οὐχὶ πρῶτον καθίσας ψηφίζει τὴν
a tower to build, [5]not [6]first [1]having [2]sat [3]down [4]counts the
δαπάνην, εἰ ἔχει [m]τὰ‖ [n]πρὸς‖ ἀπαρτισμόν; 29 ἵνα μήποτε
cost, if he has the [means] for [its] completion? that lest
θέντος αὐτοῦ θεμέλιον καὶ μὴ ἰσχύοντος ἐκτελέσαι, πάντες
having laid of it a foundation and not being able to finish, all
οἱ θεωροῦντες ἄρξωνται [o]ἐμπαίζειν αὐτῷ,‖ 30 λέγοντες, Ὅτι
who see [it] should begin to mock at him, saying,
οὗτος ὁ ἄνθρωπος ἤρξατο οἰκοδομεῖν, καὶ οὐκ.ἴσχυσεν ἐκτελέσαι.
This man began to build, and was not able to finish.
31 Ἢ τίς βασιλεὺς πορευόμενος [p]συμβαλεῖν ἑτέρῳ βασι-
Or what king proceeding to engage with another king
λεῖ‖ εἰς πόλεμον οὐχὶ καθίσας πρῶτον [q]βουλεύεται‖
in war [6]not [1]having [2]sat [3]down [4]first [5]takes [7]counsel
εἰ δυνατός ἐστιν ἐν δέκα χιλιάσιν [r]ἀπαντῆσαι‖ τῷ μετὰ
whether able he is with ten thousand to meet him with
εἴκοσι χιλιάδων ἐρχομένῳ ἐπ' αὐτόν; 32 εἰ.δὲ μήγε, ἔτι
twenty thousand who comes against him? But if not, [2]still
[s]αὐτοῦ πόῤῥω‖ ὄντος, πρεσβείαν ἀποστείλας ἐρωτᾷ τὰ
[1]he [4]far [5]off [3]being, an embassy having sent he asks the [terms]
πρὸς εἰρήνην. 33 οὕτως οὖν πᾶς ἐξ ὑμῶν ὃς οὐκ ἀπο-
for peace. Thus therefore everyone of you who [2]not [1]does take
τάσσεται πᾶσιν τοῖς ἑαυτοῦ ὑπάρχουσιν, οὐ.δύναταί [t]μου
leave of all that he himself possesses, cannot [2]my
εἶναι‖ μαθητής. 34 καλὸν [v] τὸ [w]ἅλας·‖ ἐὰν.δὲ [x] τὸ [w]ἅλας‖
[1]be disciple. Good [is] the salt, but if the salt
μωρανθῇ ἐν τίνι ἀρτυθήσεται; 35 οὔτε εἰς γῆν οὔτε
become tasteless with what shall it be seasoned? Neither for land nor
εἰς κοπρίαν εὔθετόν ἐστιν· ἔξω βάλλουσιν αὐτό. Ὁ ἔχων
for manure fit is it: [4]out [1]they [2]cast [3]it. He that has
ὦτα [y]ἀκούειν‖ ἀκουέτω.
ears to hear let him hear.

XV. Then drew near
unto him all the pub-
licans and sinners for
to hear him. 2 And the
Pharisees and scribes
murmured, saying,

15 Ἦσαν.δὲ [z]ἐγγίζοντες αὐτῷ‖ πάντες οἱ τελῶναι καὶ
And were drawing near to him all the tax-gatherers and
οἱ ἁμαρτωλοὶ ἀκούειν αὐτοῦ· 2 καὶ διεγόγγυζον οἱ [a]Φαρισαῖοι
the sinners to hear him; and murmured the Pharisees

---

[f] αὐτοῦ LTTrA. [g] τε LTrA. [h] εἶναί μου μαθητής TTrA. [i] — καὶ T. [k] ἑαυτοῦ LTA. [l] εἶναί μου TTrA. [m] — τὰ (*read* [the means]) GTTrA. [n] εἰς to GLTTrAW. [o] αὐτῷ ἐμπαίζειν LTTrA. [p] ἑτέρῳ βασιλεῖ συμβαλεῖν LTTrA. [q] βουλεύσεται will take counsel T. [r] ὑπαντῆσαι LTTrAW. [s] πόῤῥω αὐτοῦ W. [t] εἶναί μου LTTr. [v] + οὖν therefore T[Tr]A. [w] ἅλα T. [x] + καὶ also LTTrA. [y] — ἀκούειν T. [z] αὐτῷ ἐγγίζοντες LTTrAW. [a] + τε both (the) LTTrA.

καὶ οἱ γραμματεῖς, λέγοντες, Ὅτι οὗτος ἁμαρτωλοὺς
and the scribes, saying, This [man] sinners
προσδέχεται καὶ συνεσθίει αὐτοῖς. 3 Εἶπεν.δὲ πρὸς αὐτοὺς
receives and eats with them. And he spoke to them
τὴν.παραβολὴν.ταύτην, λέγων, 4 Τίς ἄνθρωπος ἐξ ὑμῶν
this parable, saying, What man of you
ἔχων ἑκατὸν πρόβατα, καὶ [b]ἀπολέσας‖ [c]ἓν ἐξ αὐτῶν,‖ οὐ
having a hundred sheep, and having lost one of them, [2]not
καταλείπει τὰ [d]ἐννενηκονταεννέα‖ ἐν τῇ ἐρήμῳ καὶ πορεύεται
[1]leaves the ninety nine in the wilderness and goes
ἐπὶ τὸ ἀπολωλός, ἕως εὕρῃ αὐτό; 5 καὶ εὑρὼν
after that which has been lost, until he find it? And having found [it]
ἐπιτίθησιν ἐπὶ τοὺς.ὤμους.[e]ἑαυτοῦ‖ χαίρων, 6 καὶ ἐλθὼν
he lays [it] on his shoulders rejoicing, and having come
εἰς τὸν οἶκον [f]συγκαλεῖ‖ τοὺς φίλους καὶ τοὺς γείτονας, λέ-
to the house he calls together friends and neighbours, say-
γων αὐτοῖς, [g]Συγχάρητέ‖ μοι, ὅτι εὗρον τὸ.πρόβατόν.μου
ing to them, Rejoice with me, for I have found my sheep
τὸ ἀπολωλός. 7 λέγω ὑμῖν, ὅτι οὕτως χαρὰ [h]ἔσται ἐν τῷ
that was lost. I say to you, that thus joy shall be in the
οὐρανῷ‖ ἐπὶ ἑνὶ ἁμαρτωλῷ μετανοοῦντι, ἢ ἐπὶ [d]ἐννενη-
heaven over one sinner repenting, [more] than over ninety
κονταεννέα‖ δικαίοις, οἵτινες οὐ χρείαν ἔχουσιν μετανοίας.
nine righteous ones, who [2]no [3]need [1]have of repentance.
8 Ἢ τίς γυνὴ δραχμὰς ἔχουσα δέκα, ἐὰν ἀπολέσῃ δραχμὴν
Or what woman [3]drachmas [1]having [2]ten, if she should lose [2]drachma
μίαν, οὐχὶ.ἅπτει λύχνον καὶ σαροῖ τὴν οἰκίαν καὶ ζητεῖ ἐπι-
[1]one, lights not a lamp and sweeps the house and seeks care-
μελῶς ἕως.[i]ὅτου‖ εὕρῃ; 9 καὶ εὑροῦσα [f]συγκαλεῖται‖
fully until she find [it]? and having found [it] she calls together
τὰς φίλας καὶ [k]τὰς‖ γείτονας, λέγουσα, [g]Συγχάρητέ‖ μοι, ὅτι
friends and neighbours, saying, Rejoice with me, for
εὗρον τὴν δραχμὴν ἣν ἀπώλεσα. 10 οὕτως, λέγω ὑμῖν,
I have found the drachma which I lost. Thus, I say to you,
[l]χαρὰ γίνεται‖ ἐνώπιον τῶν ἀγγέλων τοῦ θεοῦ ἐπὶ ἑνὶ ἁμαρ-
joy there is before the angels of God over one sin-
τωλῷ μετανοοῦντι.
ner repenting.

11 Εἶπεν.δέ, Ἄνθρωπός τις εἶχεν δύο υἱούς· 12 καὶ εἶπεν
And he said, A [2]man [1]certain had two sons; and said
ὁ νεώτερος αὐτῶν τῷ.πατρί, Πάτερ, δός μοι τὸ ἐπιβάλ-
the younger of them to [his] father, Father, give to me that [2]fall-
λον μέρος τῆς οὐσίας. [m]καὶ‖ διεῖλεν αὐτοῖς τὸν βίον.
ing [[3]to [4]me] [1]portion of the property. And he divided to them the living.
13 καὶ μετ' οὐ πολλὰς ἡμέρας συναγαγὼν [n]ἅπαντα‖
And after not many days having gathered together all
ὁ νεώτερος υἱὸς ἀπεδήμησεν εἰς χώραν μακράν, καὶ ἐκεῖ
the younger son went away into a [2]country [1]distant, and there
διεσκόρπισεν τὴν.οὐσίαν.αὐτοῦ, ζῶν ἀσώτως. 14 δαπανή-
wasted his property, living dissolutely. [3]Having
σαντος δὲ αὐτοῦ πάντα ἐγένετο λιμὸς [o]ἰσχυρὸς‖ κατὰ
[4]spent [1]but [2]he all there arose a [2]famine [1]violent throughout
τὴν.χώραν.ἐκείνην, καὶ αὐτὸς ἤρξατο ὑστερεῖσθαι. 15 καὶ
that country, and he began to be in want. And

This man receiveth sinners, and eateth with them. 3 And he spake this parable unto them, saying, 4 What man of you, having an hundred sheep, if he lose one of them, doth not leave the ninety and nine in the wilderness, and go after that which is lost, until he find it? 5 And when he hath found *it*, he layeth *it* on his shoulders, rejoicing. 6 And when he cometh home, he calleth together *his* friends and neighbours, saying unto them, Rejoice with me; for I have found my sheep which was lost. 7 I say unto you, that likewise joy shall be in heaven over one sinner that repenteth, more than over ninety and nine just persons, which need no repentance. 8 Either what woman having ten pieces of silver, if she lose one piece, doth not light a candle, and sweep the house, and seek diligently till she find *it*? 9 And when she hath found *it*, she calleth *her* friends and *her* neighbours together, saying, Rejoice with me; for I have found the piece which I had lost. 10 Likewise, I say unto you, there is joy in the presence of the angels of God, over one sinner that repenteth.

11 And he said, A certain man had two sons: 12 and the younger of them said to *his* father, Father, give me the portion of goods that falleth *to me*. And he divided unto them *his* living. 13 And not many days after the younger son gathered all together, and took his journey into a far country, and there wasted his substance with riotous living. 14 And when he had spent all, there arose a mighty famine in that land; and he began to be in want. 15 And he went and

---

[b] ἀπολέσῃ should he lose Tr. [c] ἐξ αὐτῶν ἕν TTrA. [d] ἐνενήκοντα ἐννέα LTTr. [e] αὐτοῦ TTrA. [f] συνκαλεῖ T. [g] συνχάρητέ T. [h] ἐν τῷ οὐρανῷ ἔσται TA. [i] οὗ Tr. [k] — τὰς LTTrA. [l] γίνεται χαρὰ TTrA. [m] ὁ δὲ LTrA. [n] πάντα LTrA. [o] ἰσχυρὰ LTTrAW.

joined himself to a
citizen of that country;
and he sent him into
his fields to feed swine.
16 And he would fain
have filled his belly
with the husks that the
swine did eat: and no
man gave unto him.
17 And when he came
to himself, he said,
How many hired ser-
vants of my father's
have bread enough and
to spare, and I perish
with hunger! 18 I will
arise and go to my
father, and will say
unto him, Father, I
have sinned against
heaven, and before
thee, 19 and am no
more worthy to be
called thy son: make
me as one of thy hired
servants. 20 And he
arose, and came to his
father. But when he
was yet a great way
off, his father saw him,
and had compassion,
and ran, and fell on his
neck, and kissed him.
21 And the son said un-
to him, Father, I have
sinned against heaven,
and in thy sight, and
am no more worthy to
be called thy son.
22 But the father said
to his servants, Bring
forth the best robe, and
put *it* on him; and put
a ring on his hand,
and shoes on *his* feet:
23 and bring hither
the fatted calf, and
kill *it*; and let us eat,
and be merry: 24 for
this my son was dead,
and is alive again; he
was lost, and is found.
And they began to be
merry. 25 Now his
elder son was in the
field: and as he came
and drew nigh to the
house, he heard musick
and dancing. 26 And
he called one of the
servants, and asked
what these things
meant. 27 And he said
unto him, Thy brother
is come; and thy father
hath killed the fatted
calf, because he hath

πορευθεὶς ἐκολλήθη ἑνὶ τῶν πολιτῶν τῆς-χώρας-ἐκείνης·
having gone he joined himself to one of the citizens of that country,
καὶ ἔπεμψεν αὐτὸν εἰς τοὺς-ἀγροὺς-αὐτοῦ βόσκειν χοίρους.
and he sent him into his fields to feed swine.
16 καὶ ἐπεθύμει γεμίσαι τὴν-κοιλίαν-αὐτοῦ ἀπὸ τῶν κερατίων
And he was longing to fill his belly from the husks
ὧν ἤσθιον οἱ χοῖροι· καὶ οὐδεὶς ἐδίδου αὐτῷ. 17 Εἰς
which [3]were [4]eating [1]the [2]swine; and no one gave to him. [4]To
ἑαυτὸν δὲ ἐλθὼν [p]εἶπεν,‖ Πόσοι μίσθιοι τοῦ πατρός
[5]himself [1]but [2]having [3]come he said, How many hired servants [3]father
μου [q]περισσεύουσιν‖ ἄρτων, ἐγὼ-δὲ [r] λιμῷ [s] ἀπόλλυμαι;
[1]of my have abundance of bread, and I with famine am perishing?
18 ἀναστὰς πορεύσομαι πρὸς τὸν-πατέρα-μου, καὶ ἐρῶ
Having risen up I will go to my father, and I will say
αὐτῷ, Πάτερ, ἥμαρτον εἰς τὸν οὐρανὸν καὶ ἐνώπιόν σου·
to him, Father, I have sinned against heaven and before thee;
19 [t]καὶ‖ οὐκέτι εἰμὶ ἄξιος κληθῆναι υἱός-σου· ποίησόν με ὡς
and no longer am I worthy to be called thy son: make me as
ἕνα τῶν-μισθίων-σου. 20 καὶ ἀναστὰς ἦλθεν πρὸς τὸν πα-
one of thy hired servants. And having risen up he went to [2]fa-
τέρα [v]ἑαυτοῦ.‖ Ἔτι-δὲ αὐτοῦ μακρὰν ἀπέχοντος εἶδεν αὐτὸν
ther [1]his. But [2]yet [1]he [4]far [3]being distant [3]saw [4]him
ὁ-πατὴρ-αὐτοῦ καὶ ἐσπλαγχνίσθη, καὶ δραμὼν ἐπέπεσεν
[1]his [2]father and was moved with compassion, and running fell
ἐπὶ τὸν-τράχηλον-αὐτοῦ καὶ κατεφίλησεν αὐτόν. 21 εἶπεν-δὲ
upon his neck and ardently kissed him. And [3]said
[w]αὐτῷ ὁ υἱός,‖ Πάτερ, ἥμαρτον εἰς τὸν οὐρανὸν καὶ ἐνώ-
[4]to [5]him [1]the [2]son, Father, I have sinned against heaven and be-
πιόν σου, [x]καὶ‖ οὐκέτι εἰμὶ ἄξιος κληθῆναι υἱός-σου. 22 Εἶπεν
fore thee, and no longer am I worthy to be called thy son. [2]Said
δὲ ὁ πατὴρ πρὸς τοὺς-δούλους-αὐτοῦ, [y] Ἐξενέγκατε [z]τὴν‖
[1]but the father to his bondmen, Bring out the
στολὴν τὴν πρώτην καὶ ἐνδύσατε αὐτόν, καὶ δότε δακτύλιον
robe the best and clothe him, and give a ring
εἰς τὴν-χεῖρα-αὐτοῦ καὶ ὑποδήματα εἰς τοὺς πόδας· 23 καὶ
for his hand and sandals for the feet; and
[a]ἐνέγκαντες‖ τὸν μόσχον τὸν σιτευτὸν θύσατε, καὶ φαγόντες
having brought the [2]calf [1]fattened kill [it], and eating
εὐφρανθῶμεν· 24 ὅτι οὗτος ὁ-υἱός-μου νεκρὸς ἦν, καὶ ἀνέζη-
let us be merry: for this my son [2]dead [1]was, and is alive
σεν· [b]καὶ ἀπολωλὼς ἦν,‖ καὶ εὑρέθη. Καὶ ἤρξαντο εὐ-
again; and [2]lost [1]was, and is found. And they began to
φραίνεσθαι. 25 Ἦν-δὲ ὁ-υἱὸς-αὐτοῦ ὁ πρεσβύτερος ἐν ἀγρῷ·
be merry. And [5]was [1]his [2]son [3]the [4]elder in a field;
καὶ ὡς ἐρχόμενος ἤγγισεν τῇ οἰκίᾳ ἤκουσεν συμφωνίας
and as coming [up] he drew near to the house he heard music
καὶ χορῶν· 26 καὶ προσκαλεσάμενος ἕνα τῶν-παίδων-[c]αὐτοῦ,‖
and dancing. And having called near one of his servants,
ἐπυνθάνετο τί [d] εἴη ταῦτα. 27 ὁ-δὲ εἶπεν αὐτῷ, Ὅτι
he inquired what might be these things. And he said to him,
ὁ-ἀδελφός-σου ἥκει· καὶ ἔθυσεν ὁ-πατήρ-σου τὸν μόσχον τὸν
Thy brother is come, and [3]killed [1]thy [2]father the [2]calf

---

p ἔφη T. q περισσεύονται TrA. r + ὧδε here GTrA. s + ὧδε here LT. t — καὶ GLTTrAW. v αὐτοῦ LTTr. w ὁ υἱὸς αὐτῷ A. x — καὶ LTTrA. y + Ταχὺ Quickly L[Tr]A. z — τὴν (read a robe) LTTrA. a φέρετε bring TTrA. b ἦν ἀπολωλὼς LTTrA; ἀπολ. ἦν W. c — αὐτοῦ (read the servants) EGLTTrAW. d + ἂν [L]Tr[A].

σιτευτόν, ὅτι ὑγιαίνοντα αὐτὸν ἀπέλαβεν. 28 Ὠργίσθη
[1]fattened, because safe and well [3]him [1]he [2]received. [2]He [3]was [4]angry
δὲ καὶ οὐκ.ἤθελεν εἰσελθεῖν. ὁ [e]οὖν‖ πατὴρ αὐτοῦ
[1]but and was not willing to go in. [2]The [1]therefore father of him
ἐξελθὼν παρεκάλει αὐτόν. 29 ὁ.δὲ ἀποκριθεὶς εἶπεν τῷ.πα-
having gone besought him. But he answering said to [2]fa-
τρί[f], Ἰδού, τοσαῦτα ἔτη δουλεύω σοι καὶ οὐδέποτε ἐντολήν
ther [[1]his], Lo, so many years I serve thee and never [4]commandment
σου παρῆλθον, καὶ ἐμοὶ οὐδέποτε ἔδωκας ἔριφον ἵνα μετὰ
[3]thy [1]transgressed [2]I, and to me never didst thou give a kid that with
τῶν.φίλων.μου εὐφρανθῶ· 30 ὅτε.δὲ ὁ.υἱός.σου οὗτος
my friends I might make merry; but when [2]thy [3]son [1]this
ὁ καταφαγών σου τὸν βίον μετὰ [g] πορνῶν ἦλθεν, ἔθυσας
who devoured thy living with harlots came, thou didst kill
αὐτῷ τὸν [h]μόσχον τὸν σιτευτόν.‖ 31 ὁ.δὲ εἶπεν αὐτῷ, Τέκνον,
for him the [2]calf [1]fattened. But he said to him, Child,
σὺ πάντοτε μετ' ἐμοῦ εἶ, καὶ πάντα τὰ ἐμὰ σά ἐστιν.
thou always with me art, and all that [is] mine [2]thine [1]is.
32 εὐφρανθῆναι.δὲ καὶ χαρῆναι ἔδει, ὅτι ὁ.ἀδελφός.σου
But to make merry and rejoice was becoming, because [2]thy [3]brother
οὗτος νεκρὸς ἦν, καὶ [i]ἀνέζησεν·‖ [k]καὶ‖ ἀπολωλὼς [l]ἦν,‖ καὶ
[1]this [5]dead [4]was, and is alive again; and [2]lost [1]was, and
εὑρέθη.
is found.

16 Ἔλεγεν.δὲ καὶ πρὸς τοὺς.μαθητὰς.[m]αὐτοῦ,‖ Ἄνθρωπός
And he said also to his disciples, A [3]man
τις ἦν πλούσιος, ὃς εἶχεν οἰκονόμον· καὶ οὗτος διε-
[1]certain [4]there [5]was [2]rich, who had a steward, and he was
βλήθη αὐτῷ ὡς διασκορπίζων τὰ.ὑπάρχοντα.αὐτοῦ. 2 καὶ
accused to him as wasting his goods. And
φωνήσας αὐτὸν εἶπεν αὐτῷ, Τί τοῦτο ἀκούω περὶ
having called him he said to him, What [is] this I hear concerning
σοῦ; ἀπόδος τὸν λόγον τῆς.οἰκονομίας.σου· οὐ.γὰρ.[n]δυνήσῃ‖
thee? render the account of thy stewardship; for thou canst not
ἔτι οἰκονομεῖν. 3 Εἶπεν.δὲ ἐν ἑαυτῷ ὁ οἰκονόμος,
any longer be steward. And [3]said [4]within [5]himself [1]the [2]steward,
Τί ποιήσω, ὅτι ὁ.κύριός.μου ἀφαιρεῖται τὴν οἰκονομίαν ἀπ'
What shall I do, for my lord is taking away the stewardship from
ἐμοῦ; σκάπτειν οὐκ.ἰσχύω, ἐπαιτεῖν αἰσχύνομαι. 4 ἔγνων
me? To dig I am unable; to beg I am ashamed. I know
τί ποιήσω, ἵνα, ὅταν μετασταθῶ [o] τῆς οἰκονο-
what I will do, that, when I shall have been removed [from] the steward-
μίας, δέξωνταί με εἰς τοὺς.οἴκους.[p]αὐτῶν.‖ 5 Καὶ προσ-
ship, they may receive me into their houses. And call-
καλεσάμενος ἕνα ἕκαστον τῶν [q]χρεωφειλετῶν‖ τοῦ κυρίου
ing to [him] [2]one [1]each of the debtors [3]lord
ἑαυτοῦ ἔλεγεν τῷ πρώτῳ, Πόσον ὀφείλεις τῷ.κυρίῳ.μου;
[1]of [2]his he said to the first, How much owest thou to my lord?
6 Ὁ.δὲ εἶπεν, Ἑκατὸν βάτους ἐλαίου. [r]Καὶ‖ εἶπεν αὐτῷ,
And he said, A hundred baths of oil. And he said to him,
Δέξαι σου [s]τὸ γράμμα‖ καὶ καθίσας ταχέως γράψον πεντή-
Take thy bill and sitting down quickly write fifty.

received him safe and
sound. 28 And he was
angry, and would not
go in: therefore came
his father out, and in-
treated him. 29 And
he answering said to
his father, Lo, these
many years do I serve
thee, neither trans-
gressed I at any time
thy commandment:
and yet thou never
gavest me a kid, that I
might make merry
with my friends:
30 but as soon as this
thy son was come,
which hath devoured
thy living with har-
lots, thou hast killed
for him the fatted calf.
31 And he said unto
him, Son, thou art ever
with me, and all that
I have is thine. 32 It
was meet that we
should make merry,
and be glad: for this
thy brother was dead,
and is alive again; and
was lost, and is found.

XVI. And he said
also unto his disciples,
There was a certain
rich man, which had a
steward; and the same
was accused unto him
that he had wasted his
goods. 2 And he called
him, and said unto
him, How is it that I
hear this of thee? give
an account of thy
stewardship; for thou
mayest be no longer
steward. 3 Then the
steward said within
himself, What shall I
do? for my lord taketh
away from me the
stewardship: I cannot
dig; to beg I am
ashamed. 4 I am re-
solved what to do, that,
when I am put out of
the stewardship, they
may receive me into
their houses. 5 So he
called every one of his
lord's debtors *unto him*,
and said unto the first,
How much owest thou
unto my lord? 6 And
he said, An hundred
measures of oil. And
he said unto him, Take
thy bill, and sit down
quickly, and write
fifty. 7 Then said he

---

[e] δὲ but LTTrA. [f] + αὐτοῦ his LTTrA. [g] + τῶν the LTTrA. [h] σιτευτὸν μόσχον TTrA. [i] ἔζησεν is alive TTrA. [k] — καὶ T. [l] — ἦν (*read* ἀπολωλὼς had been lost) LTTrA. [m] — αὐτοῦ (*read* the disciples) TTrA. [n] δύνῃ TTrA. [o] + ἐκ from [L]TTrA. [p] ἑαυτῶν TTrA. [q] χρεοφειλετῶν LTTrA. [r] ὁ δὲ LTTrA. [s] τὰ γράμματα bills LTTrA.

to another, And how
much owest thou? And
he said, An hundred
measures of wheat.
And he said unto him,
Take thy bill, and
write fourscore. 8 And
the lord commended
the unjust steward,
because he had done
wisely: for the child-
ren of this world are in
their generation wiser
than the children of
light. 9 And I say un-
to you, Make to your-
selves friends of the
mammon of unright-
eousness; that, when
ye fail, they may re-
ceive you into ever-
lasting habitations.
10 He that is faithful
in that which is least
is faithful also in
much: and he that is
unjust in the least is
unjust also in much.
11 If therefore ye have
not been faithful in
the unrighteous mam-
mon, who will commit
to your trust the true
riches? 12 And if ye
have not been faithful
in that which is ano-
ther man's, who shall
give you that which is
your own? 13 No ser-
vant can serve two
masters: for either he
will hate the one, and
love the other; or else
he will hold to the one,
and despise the other.
Ye cannot serve God
and mammon.

14 And the Pharisees
also, who were cove-
tous, heard all these
things: and they de-
rided him. 15 And he
said unto them, Ye are
they which justify
yourselves before men;
but God knoweth your
hearts: for that which
is highly esteemed a-
mong men is abomina-
tion in the sight of
God. 16 The law and
the prophets *were* until
John: since that time
the kingdom of God is
preached, and every
man presseth into it.
17 And it is easier for
heaven and earth to
pass, than one tittle of
the law to fail. 18 Who-
soever putteth away
his wife, and marrieth
another, committeth

κοντα. 7 [s]Ἔπειτα ἑτέρῳ εἶπεν, Σὺ.δὲ πόσον ὀφείλεις;
Then to another he said, And thou how much owest thou?
Ὁ.δὲ εἶπεν, Ἑκατὸν κόρους σίτου. [t]Καὶ‖ λέγει αὐτῷ, Δέξαι
And he said, A hundred cors of wheat. And he says to him, Take
σου [u]τὸ γράμμα‖ καὶ γράψον ὀγδοήκοντα. 8 Καὶ ἐπῄνεσεν
thy bill and write eighty. And [3]praised
ὁ κύριος τὸν οἰκονόμον τῆς ἀδικίας ὅτι φρονίμως ἐποίη-
[1]the [2]lord the [2]steward [1]unrighteous because prudently he had
σεν· ὅτι οἱ υἱοὶ τοῦ.αἰῶνος.τούτου φρονιμώτεροι ὑπὲρ τοὺς
done. For the sons of this age [6]more [7]prudent [8]than [9]the
υἱοὺς τοῦ φωτὸς εἰς τὴν γενεὰν τὴν.ἑαυτῶν εἰσιν. 9 [v]Κἀγὼ‖
[10]sons [11]of [12]the [13]light [2]in [5]generation [3]their [4]own [1]are. And I
ὑμῖν λέγω, [w]Ποιήσατε ἑαυτοῖς‖ φίλους ἐκ τοῦ μαμωνᾶ τῆς
to you say, Make to yourselves friends by the mammon
ἀδικίας, ἵνα ὅταν [x]ἐκλίπητε‖ δέξωνται ὑμᾶς εἰς τὰς
of unrighteousness, that when ye fail they may receive you into the
αἰωνίους σκηνάς[y]. 10 Ὁ πιστὸς ἐν ἐλαχίστῳ καὶ
eternal dwellings. He that [is] faithful in [the] least also
ἐν πολλῷ πιστός ἐστιν· καὶ ὁ ἐν ἐλαχίστῳ ἄδικος
in much faithful is; and he that in [the] least [is] unrighteous
καὶ ἐν πολλῷ ἄδικός ἐστιν. 11 εἰ οὖν ἐν τῷ ἀδίκῳ
also in much unrighteous is. If therefore in the unrighteous
μαμωνᾷ πιστοὶ οὐκ.ἐγένεσθε, τὸ ἀληθινὸν τίς ὑμῖν πιστεύσει;
mammon faithful ye have not been, the true who to you will entrust?
12 καὶ εἰ ἐν τῷ ἀλλοτρίῳ πιστοὶ οὐκ.ἐγένεσθε, τὸ
And if in that which [is] another's faithful ye have not been,
ὑμέτερον τίς [z]ὑμῖν δώσει;‖ 13 Οὐδεὶς οἰκέτης δύναται δυσὶ
your own who to you will give? No servant is able two
κυρίοις δουλεύειν· ἢ.γὰρ τὸν ἕνα μισήσει, καὶ τὸν ἕτερον
lords to serve, for either the one he will hate, and the other
ἀγαπήσει· ἢ ἑνὸς ἀνθέξεται, καὶ τοῦ ἑτέρου καταφρονήσει.
he will love; or one he will hold to, and the other he will despise.
οὐ.δύνασθε θεῷ δουλεύειν καὶ μαμωνᾷ.
Ye are unable [3]God [1]to [2]serve and mammon.

14 Ἤκουον.δὲ ταῦτα πάντα [a]καὶ‖ οἱ Φαρισαῖοι, φιλάρ-
And [4]heard [2]these [3]things [1]all also the Pharisees, [2]covet-
γυροι ὑπάρχοντες, καὶ ἐξεμυκτήριζον αὐτόν. 15 καὶ εἶπεν
ous [1]being, and they derided him. And he said
αὐτοῖς, Ὑμεῖς ἐστε οἱ δικαιοῦντες ἑαυτοὺς ἐνώπιον τῶν
to them, Ye are they who justify themselves before
ἀνθρώπων, ὁ.δὲ.θεὸς γινώσκει τὰς.καρδίας.ὑμῶν· ὅτι τὸ ἐν
men, but God knows your hearts; for that [4]among
ἀνθρώποις ὑψηλὸν βδέλυγμα ἐνώπιον τοῦ θεοῦ [b]ἐστιν.‖
[5]men [1]highly [2]thought [3]of an abomination before God is.
16 Ὁ νόμος καὶ οἱ προφῆται [c]ἕως‖ [d]Ἰωάννου·‖ ἀπὸ
The law and the prophets [were] until John: from
τότε ἡ βασιλεία τοῦ θεοῦ εὐαγγελίζεται, καὶ πᾶς εἰς
that time the kingdom of God is announced, and everyone [2]into
αὐτὴν βιάζεται. 17 Εὐκοπώτερον.δέ ἐστιν τὸν οὐρανὸν καὶ
[3]it [1]forces. But easier it is [for] the heaven and
τὴν γῆν παρελθεῖν, ἢ τοῦ νόμου μίαν κεραίαν πεσεῖν.
the earth to pass away, than of the law one tittle to fail.
18 Πᾶς ὁ ἀπολύων τὴν.γυναῖκα.αὐτοῦ καὶ γαμῶν ἑτέραν
Everyone who puts away his wife and marries another

---

t — καὶ LTTrA. u τὰ γράμματα bills LTTrA. v καὶ ἐγὼ TTrA. w ἑαυτοῖς ποιήσατε TA. x ἐκλίπῃ it shall fail LTTrA. y + [αὐτῶν] (*read* their eternal dwellings) L. z δώσει ὑμῖν TTr. a — καὶ TTr[A]. b — ἐστιν (*read* [is]) GLTTrAW. c μέχρι TTrA. d Ἰωάνου Tr.

μοιχεύει· καὶ [e]πᾶς‖ ὁ ἀπολελυμένην ἀπὸ ἀνδρὸς
commits adultery; and everyone who [2]her [3]put [4]away [5]from [6]a [7]husband
γαμῶν μοιχεύει.
[1]marries commits adultery.
19 Ἄνθρωπος-δέ τις ἦν πλούσιος, καὶ ἐνεδιδύσκετο
Now [3]a [6]man [4]certain [1]there [2]was [5]rich, and he was clothed in
πορφύραν καὶ βύσσον, εὐφραινόμενος καθ'.ἡμέραν λαμπρῶς.
purple and fine linen, making good cheer daily in splendour.
20 πτωχὸς-δέ τις [f]ἦν‖ ὀνόματι Λάζαρος, [g]ὃς‖ ἐβέβλητο
And a [2]poor [3]man [1]certain there was, by name Lazarus, who was laid
πρὸς τὸν-πυλῶνα-αὐτοῦ [h]ἡλκωμένος,‖ 21 καὶ ἐπιθυμῶν χορ-
at his porch being full of sores, and desiring to be
τασθῆναι ἀπὸ [i]τῶν ψιχίων τῶν‖ πιπτόντων ἀπὸ τῆς τραπέζης
satisfied from the crumbs which fell from the table
τοῦ πλουσίου· ἀλλὰ καὶ οἱ κύνες ἐρχόμενοι [k]ἀπέλειχον‖ τὰ
of the rich man; but even the dogs coming licked
ἕλκη-αὐτοῦ. 22 ἐγένετο-δὲ ἀποθανεῖν τὸν πτωχόν, καὶ
his sores. And it came to pass [4]died [1]the [2]poor [3]man, and
ἀπενεχθῆναι αὐτὸν ὑπὸ τῶν ἀγγέλων εἰς τὸν κόλπον [l]τοῦ‖
[2]was [3]carried [4]away [1]he by the angels into the bosom
Ἀβραάμ· ἀπέθανεν-δὲ καὶ ὁ πλούσιος, καὶ ἐτάφη. 23 καὶ ἐν
of Abraham. And died also the rich man, and was buried. And in
τῷ ᾅδῃ ἐπάρας τοὺς ὀφθαλμοὺς-αὐτοῦ, ὑπάρχων ἐν βα-
the hades having lifted up his eyes, being in tor-
σάνοις, ὁρᾷ [m]τὸν‖ Ἀβραὰμ ἀπὸ-μακρόθεν, καὶ Λάζαρον ἐν
ments, he sees Abraham afar off, and Lazarus in
τοῖς-κόλποις-αὐτοῦ· 24 καὶ αὐτὸς φωνήσας εἶπεν, Πάτερ
his bosom. And he crying out said, Father
Ἀβραάμ, ἐλέησόν με, καὶ πέμψον Λάζαρον, ἵνα βάψῃ
Abraham, have compassion on me, and send Lazarus, that he may dip
τὸ ἄκρον τοῦ-δακτύλου-αὐτοῦ ὕδατος, καὶ καταψύξῃ τὴν γλῶσ-
the tip of his finger in water, and cool [2]tongue
σάν μου· ὅτι ὀδυνῶμαι ἐν τῇ-φλογὶ-ταύτῃ. 25 Εἶπεν-δὲ
[1]my; for I am suffering in this flame. But [2]said
Ἀβραάμ, Τέκνον, μνήσθητι ὅτι ἀπέλαβες [n]σὺ‖ τὰ
[1]Abraham, Child, recollect that [2]didst [3]fully [4]receive [1]thou
ἀγαθά-σου ἐν τῇ-ζωῇ-σου, καὶ Λάζαρος ὁμοίως τὰ-κακά·
thy good things in thy lifetime, and Lazarus likewise evil things.
νῦν-δὲ [o]ὅδε‖ παρακαλεῖται, σὺ-δὲ ὀδυνᾶσαι. 26 καὶ [p]ἐπὶ‖
But now he is comforted, and thou art suffering. And besides
πᾶσιν τούτοις, μεταξὺ ἡμῶν καὶ ὑμῶν χάσμα μέγα ἐστήρικ-
all these things, between us and you a [2]chasm [1]great has been
ται, ὅπως οἱ θέλοντες διαβῆναι [q]ἐντεῦθεν‖ πρὸς ὑμᾶς
fixed, so that they who desire to pass hence to you
μὴ-δύνωνται, μηδὲ [r]οἱ‖ ἐκεῖθεν πρὸς ἡμᾶς διαπερῶσιν.
are unable, nor [2]they [4]thence [5]to [6]us [1]can [3]pass
27 Εἶπεν-δέ, Ἐρωτῶ [s]οὖν σε,‖ πάτερ, ἵνα πέμψῃς
And he said, I beseech [2]then [1]thee, father, that thou wouldest send
αὐτὸν εἰς τὸν οἶκον τοῦ-πατρός-μου, 28 ἔχω-γὰρ πέντε ἀδελ-
him to the house of my father, for I have five bro-
φούς· ὅπως διαμαρτύρηται αὐτοῖς, ἵνα μὴ καὶ αὐτοὶ
thers, so that he may earnestly testify to them, that [4]not [2]also [1]they

adultery: and whosoever marrieth her that is put away from *her* husband committeth adultery.

19 There was a certain rich man, which was clothed in purple and fine linen, and fared sumptuously every day: 20 and there was a certain beggar named Lazarus, which was laid at his gate, full of sores, 21 and desiring to be fed with the crumbs which fell from the rich man's table: moreover the dogs came and licked his sores. 22 And it came to pass, that the beggar died, and was carried by the angels into Abraham's bosom: the rich man also died, and was buried; 23 and in hell he lift up his eyes, being in torments, and seeth Abraham afar off, and Lazarus in his bosom. 24 And he cried and said, Father Abraham, have mercy on me, and send Lazarus, that he may dip the tip of his finger in water, and cool my tongue; for I am tormented in this flame. 25 But Abraham said, Son, remember that thou in thy lifetime receivedst thy good things, and likewise Lazarus evil things: but now he is comforted, and thou art tormented. 26 And beside all this, between us and you there is a great gulf fixed: so that they which would pass from hence to you cannot; neither can they pass to us, that *would come* from thence. 27 Then he said, I pray thee therefore, father, that thou wouldest send him to my father's house: 28 for I have five brethren; that he may testify unto them, lest they also come in-

---

e — πᾶς LTTrA. f — ἦν [L]TTrA. g — ὃς [L]TTrA. h εἱλκωμένος LTTrAW.
i — ψιχίων τῶν (*read* τῶν that which) [L]TA; [τῶν ψιχίων] τῶν Tr. k ἐπέλειχον LTTrA.
l — τοῦ GLTTrAW. m — τὸν LTTrA. n — σὺ (*read* ἀπέλαβες thou didst fully receive) GTTrA.
o ὧδε here (*read* παρακ. he is comforted) LTTrAW. p ἐν before T. q ἔνθεν GLTTrAW.
r — οἱ (*read* διαπ. can they pass) L[A]. s σε οὖν LTrAW.

to this place of tor-
ment. 29 Abraham
saith unto him, They
have Moses and the
prophets; let them
hear them. 30 And he
said, Nay, father Abra-
ham: but if one went
unto them from the
dead, they will repent.
31 And he said unto
him, If they hear not
Moses and the pro-
phets, neither will they
be persuaded, though
one rose from the dead.

XVII. Then said he
unto the disciples, It is
impossible but that of-
fences will come: but
woe *unto him*, through
whom they come! 2 It
were better for him
that a millstone were
hanged about his neck,
and he cast into the
sea, than that he should
offend one of these lit-
tle ones. 3 Take heed
to yourselves: If thy
brother trespass a-
gainst thee, rebuke
him; and if he repent,
forgive him. 4 And if
he trespass against thee
seven times in a day,
and seven times in a
day turn again to thee,
saying, I repent; thou
shalt forgive him.

5 And the apostles
said unto the Lord, In-
crease our faith. 6 And
the Lord said, If ye had
faith as a grain of mus-
tard seed, ye might say
unto this sycamine
tree, Be thou plucked
up by the root, and be
thou planted in the sea;
and it should obey you.
7 But which of you,
having a servant plow-
ing or feeding cattle,
will say unto him by
and by, when he is
come from the field, Go
and sit down to meat?
8 And will not rather
say unto him, Make
ready wherewith I may
sup, and gird thyself,
and serve me, till I
have eaten and drunk-

ἔλθωσιν εἰς τὸν.τόπον.τοῦτον τῆς βασάνου· 29 λέγει[t] [v]αὐτῷ‖
may come to this place of torment. [2]Says [3]to [4]him
Ἀβραάμ, Ἔχουσιν [w]Μωσέα‖ καὶ τοὺς προφήτας· ἀκουσάτωσαν
[1]Abraham, They have Moses and the prophets: let them hear
αὐτῶν. 30 Ὁ.δὲ εἶπεν, Οὐχί, πάτερ Ἀβραάμ· ἀλλ' ἐάν τις
them. But he said, No, father Abraham, but if one
ἀπὸ νεκρῶν πορευθῇ πρὸς αὐτούς, μετανοήσουσιν.
from [the] dead should go to them, they will repent.
31 Εἶπεν.δὲ αὐτῷ, Εἰ [x]Μωσέως‖ καὶ τῶν προφητῶν οὐκ
And he said to him, If Moses and the prophets [3]not
ἀκούουσιν, [y]οὐδὲ‖ ἐάν τις ἐκ νεκρῶν ἀναστῇ πεισθή-
[1]they [2]hear, not even if one from [the] dead should rise will they
σονται.
be persuaded.

17 Εἶπεν.δὲ πρὸς τοὺς μαθητάς,[z] Ἀνένδεκτόν ἐστιν [a]τοῦ‖
And he said to the disciples, Impossible it is that
[b]μὴ.ἐλθεῖν τὰ σκάνδαλα·‖ [c]οὐαὶ.δὲ‖ δι' οὗ ἔρχεται.
[2]should [3]not [4]come [1]offences, but woe [to him] by whom they come.
2 λυσιτελεῖ αὐτῷ εἰ [d]μύλος ὀνικὸς‖ περίκειται περὶ
It is profitable for him if a millstone turned by an ass is put about
τὸν.τράχηλον.αὐτοῦ, καὶ ἔρριπται εἰς τὴν θάλασσαν, ἢ ἵνα
his neck, and he is cast into the sea, than that
σκανδαλίσῃ [e]ἕνα τῶν.μικρῶν.τούτων.‖ 3 προσέχετε
he should cause [6]to [7]offend [1]one [2]of [3]these [4]little [5]ones. Take heed
ἑαυτοῖς. ἐὰν.[f]δὲ‖ ἁμάρτῃ [g]εἰς σὲ‖ ὁ.ἀδελφός.σου, ἐπι-
to yourselves: and if [3]should [4]sin [5]against [6]thee [1]thy [2]brother, re-
τίμησον αὐτῷ· καὶ ἐὰν μετανοήσῃ, ἄφες αὐτῷ. 4 καὶ ἐὰν
buke him; and if he should repent, forgive him. And if
ἑπτάκις τῆς ἡμέρας [h]ἁμάρτῃ‖ εἰς σέ, καὶ [i]ἑπτάκις [k]τῆς
seven times in the day he should sin against thee, and seven times in the
ἡμέρας‖ ἐπιστρέψῃ [l]ἐπὶ σέ,‖ λέγων, Μετανοῶ, ἀφήσεις
day should return to thee, saying, I repent, thou shalt forgive
αὐτῷ.
him.

5 Καὶ [m]εἶπον‖ οἱ ἀπόστολοι τῷ κυρίῳ, Πρόσθες ἡμῖν
And said the apostles to the Lord, Give more [2]to [3]us
πίστιν. 6 Εἶπεν.δὲ ὁ κύριος, Εἰ [n]εἴχετε‖ πίστιν, ὡς κόκκον
[1]faith. But [3]said [1]the [2]Lord, If ye had faith, as a grain
σινάπεως, ἐλέγετε.ἂν τῇ.συκαμίνῳ.ταύτῃ, Ἐκριζώθητι, καὶ
of mustard, ye might say to this sycamine tree, Be thou rooted up, and
φυτεύθητι ἐν τῇ θαλάσσῃ· καὶ ὑπήκουσεν.ἂν ὑμῖν. 7 Τίς.δὲ
be thou planted in the sea, and it would obey you. But which
[o]ἐξ‖ ὑμῶν δοῦλον ἔχων ἀροτριῶντα ἢ ποιμαίνοντα, ὃς
of you [2]a [3]bondman [1]having ploughing or shepherding, who
εἰσελθόντι ἐκ τοῦ ἀγροῦ ἐρεῖ [p] [q]εὐθέως, Παρελθὼν‖
[to him] come in out of the field will say immediately, Having come
[r]ἀνάπεσαι‖; 8 ἀλλ' οὐχὶ.ἐρεῖ αὐτῷ, Ἑτοίμασον τί
recline [at table]? but will he not say to him, Prepare what
δειπνήσω, καὶ περιζωσάμενος διακόνει μοι, ἕως φάγω καὶ
I may sup on, and girding thyself about serve me, while I eat and

[t] + δὲ (*read* but Abraham) LTTrAW. [v] — αὐτῷ T[TrA]. [w] Μωϋσέα LTTrAW. [x] Μωϋσέως LTTrAW. [y] οὐδ' LTrA. [z] + αὐτοῦ (*read* his disciples) LTTrAW. [a] — τοῦ E. [b] τὰ σκάνδαλα μὴ ἐλθεῖν TTrA. [c] πλὴν οὐαὶ yet woe LTr. [d] λίθος μυλικὸς a millstone LTTrA. [e] τῶν μικρῶν τούτων ἕνα TTrA. [f] — δὲ and LTTrA. [g] — εἰς σὲ LTTrA. [h] ἁμαρτήσῃ LTTrAW. [i] + [ἐὰν] if L. [k] — τῆς ἡμέρας LTTrA. [l] — ἐπὶ σέ G; πρός σε LTTrAW. [m] εἶπαν LTTrA. [n] ἔχετε ye have TTrA. [o] [ἐξ] Tr. [p] + αὐτῷ to him [L]TTrA. [q] Εὐθέως παρελθὼν (*read* Having come immediately recline) LTTrA. [r] ἀνάπεσε LTTrAW.

πίω· καὶ μετὰ ταῦτα φάγεσαι καὶ πίεσαι σύ; 9 Μὴ
drink; and after these things [2]shalt [3]eat [4]and [5]drink [1]thou?
[s]χάριν.ἔχει‖ τῷ.δούλῳ.[t]ἐκείνῳ‖ ὅτι ἐποίησεν τὰ διατα-
Is he thankful to that bondman because he did the things com-
χθέντα [v]αὐτῷ‖; [w]οὐ.δοκῶ.‖ 10 οὕτως καὶ ὑμεῖς, ὅταν
manded him? I judge not. Thus also ye, when
ποιήσητε πάντα.τὰ διαταχθέντα ὑμῖν, λέγετε, [x]"Ὅτι‖ δοῦ-
ye may have done all things commanded you, say, [2]Bond-
λοι ἀχρεῖοί ἐσμεν· [y]ὅτι‖ ὃ ὠφείλομεν ποιῆσαι πεποιή-
men [1]unprofitable are we, for that which we were bound to do we have
καμεν.
done.

11 Καὶ ἐγένετο ἐν τῷ.πορεύεσθαι.[z]αὐτὸν‖ εἰς Ἱερουσαλὴμ
And it came to pass in his going up to Jerusalem
καὶ αὐτὸς διήρχετο διὰ [a]μέσου‖ [b]Σαμαρείας‖ καὶ Γαλι-
that he passed through [the] midst of Samaria and Gali-
λαίας. 12 καὶ εἰσερχομένου.αὐτοῦ εἴς τινα κώμην [c]ἀπήντησαν‖
lee. And on his entering into a certain village [4]met
[d]αὐτῷ‖ δέκα λεπροὶ ἄνδρες, οἳ ἔστησαν πόῤῥωθεν· 13 καὶ
[5]him [1]ten [2]leprous [3]men, who stood afar off. And
αὐτοὶ ἦραν φωνὴν λέγοντες, Ἰησοῦ, ἐπιστάτα, ἐλέη-
they lifted up [their] voice saying, Jesus, Master, have compas-
σον ἡμᾶς. 14 Καὶ ἰδὼν εἶπεν αὐτοῖς, Πορευθέντες
sion on us. And seeing [them] he said to them, Having gone
ἐπιδείξατε ἑαυτοὺς τοῖς ἱερεῦσιν. Καὶ ἐγένετο ἐν τῷ ὑπά-
shew yourselves to the priests. And it came to pass in [2]go-
γειν αὐτοὺς ἐκαθαρίσθησαν. 15 εἷς.δὲ ἐξ αὐτῶν, ἰδὼν ὅτι
ing [1]their they were cleansed. And one of them, seeing that
ἰάθη, ὑπέστρεψεν, μετὰ φωνῆς μεγάλης δοξάζων τὸν
he was healed, turned back, with a [2]voice [1]loud glorifying
θεόν· 16 καὶ ἔπεσεν ἐπὶ πρόσωπον παρὰ τοὺς.πόδας.αὐτοῦ,
God, and fell on [his] face at his feet,
εὐχαριστῶν αὐτῷ· καὶ αὐτὸς ἦν [e]Σαμαρείτης.‖ 17 ἀποκριθεὶς
giving thanks to him: and he was a Samaritan. [2]Answering
δὲ ὁ Ἰησοῦς εἶπεν, [f]Οὐχὶ‖ οἱ δέκα ἐκαθαρίσθησαν; οἱ.[g]δὲ‖
[1]and Jesus said, [2]Not [3]the [4]ten [1]were cleansed? but [3]the
ἐννέα ποῦ; 18 οὐχ.εὑρέθησαν ὑποστρέψαντες δοῦναι
[4]nine [1]where [[2]are]? Were there not found [any] returning to give
δόξαν τῷ θεῷ εἰ.μὴ ὁ.ἀλλογενὴς.οὗτος; 19 Καὶ εἶπεν αὐτῷ,
glory to God except this stranger? And he said to him,
Ἀναστὰς πορεύου· ἡ.πίστις.σου σέσωκέν σε.
Having risen up go forth; thy faith has cured thee.

20 Ἐπερωτηθεὶς.δὲ ὑπὸ τῶν Φαρισαίων, πότε ἔρχεται ἡ
And having been asked by the Pharisees, when is coming the
βασιλεία τοῦ θεοῦ, ἀπεκρίθη αὐτοῖς καὶ εἶπεν, Οὐκ.ἔρχεται ἡ
kingdom of God, he answered them and said, [5]Comes [6]not [1]the
βασιλεία τοῦ θεοῦ μετὰ παρατηρήσεως· 21 οὐδὲ ἐροῦσιν,
[2]kingdom [3]of [4]God with observation; nor shall they say,
Ἰδοὺ ὧδε, ἢ [h]ἰδοὺ‖ ἐκεῖ· ἰδοὺ.γάρ, ἡ βασιλεία τοῦ θεοῦ ἐντὸς
Lo here, or Lo there; for lo, the kingdom of God in the midst
ὑμῶν ἐστιν. 22 Εἶπεν.δὲ πρὸς τοὺς μαθητάς,[i] Ἐλεύσονται
of you is. And he said to the disciples, [2]Will [3]come

en; and afterward thou shalt eat and drink?
9 Doth he thank that servant because he did the things that were commanded him? I trow not.
10 So likewise ye, when ye shall have done all those things which are commanded you, say, We are unprofitable servants: we have done that which was our duty to do.

11 And it came to pass, as he went to Jerusalem, that he passed through the midst of Samaria and Galilee.
12 And as he entered into a certain village, there met him ten men that were lepers, which stood afar off:
13 and they lifted up *their* voices, and said, Jesus, Master, have mercy on us.
14 And when he saw *them*, he said unto them, Go shew yourselves unto the priests. And it came to pass, that, as they went, they were cleansed.
15 And one of them, when he saw that he was healed, turned back, and with a loud voice glorified God,
16 and fell down on *his* face at his feet, giving him thanks: and he was a Samaritan.
17 And Jesus answering said, Were there not ten cleansed? but where *are* the nine?
18 There are not found that returned to give glory to God, save this stranger.
19 And he said unto him, Arise, go thy way: thy faith hath made thee whole.

20 And when he was demanded of the Pharisees, when the kingdom of God should come, he answered them and said, The kingdom of God cometh not with observation:
21 neither shall they say, Lo here! or, lo there! for, behold, the kingdom of God is within you.
22 And he said unto the disciples, The days will come,

---

[s] ἔχει χάριν LTTrA. [t] — ἐκείνῳ (*read* the bondman) LTTrA. [v] — αὐτῷ GLTTrAW. [w] — οὐ δοκῶ [L]TTrA. [x] — ὅτι L. [y] — ὅτι LTTrAW. [z] — αὐτὸν (*read* in the going up) T[TrA]. [a] μέσον LTTrA. [b] Σαμαρίας T. [c] ὑπήντησαν T. [d] — αὐτῷ (*read* [him]) L[TrA]. [e] Σαμαρίτης T. [f] οὐχ LTr. [g] — δὲ but LT[Tr]. [h] — ἰδοὺ TA. [i] + αὐτοῦ (*read* his disciples) L.

when ye shall desire to
see one of the days of
the Son of man, and ye
shall not see *it*. 23 And
they shall say to you,
See here; or, see there:
go not after *them*, nor
follow *them*. 24 For as
the lightning, that
lighteneth out of the
one *part* under hea-
ven, shineth unto the
other *part* under hea-
ven; so shall also the
Son of man be in his
day. 25 But first must
he suffer many things,
and be rejected of this
generation. 26 And as
it was in the days of
Noe, so shall it be also
in the days of the Son
of man. 27 They did
eat, they drank, they
married wives, they
were given in marriage,
until the day that Noe
entered into the ark,
and the flood came, and
destroyed them all.
28 Likewise also as it
was in the days of Lot:
they did eat, they
drank, they bought,
they sold, they plant-
ed, they builded; 29 but
the same day that Lot
went out of Sodom it
rained fire and brim-
stone from heaven, and
destroyed *them* all.
30 Even thus shall it
be in the day when the
Son of man is revealed.
31 In that day, he
which shall be upon the
housetop, and his stuff
in the house, let him
not come down to take
it away: and he that is
in the field, let him
likewise not return
back. 32 Remember
Lot's wife. 33 Whoso-
ever shall seek to save
his life shall lose it;
and whosoever shall
lose his life shall pre-
serve it. 34 I tell you, in
that night there shall
be two *men* in one bed;
the one shall be taken,
and the other shall be
left. 35 Two *women*
shall be grinding to-
gether; the one shall
be taken, and the other

ἡμέραι, ὅτε ἐπιθυμήσετε μίαν τῶν ἡμερῶν τοῦ υἱοῦ τοῦ ἀν-
[1]days, when ye will desire one of the days of the Son of
θρώπου ἰδεῖν, καὶ οὐκ.ὄψεσθε. 23 καὶ ἐροῦσιν ὑμῖν, Ἰδοὺ
man to see, and shall not see [it]. And they will say to you, Lo
[k]ὧδε, ἢ ἰδοὺ ἐκεῖ·‖ μὴ.ἀπέλθητε μηδὲ διώξητε. 24 ὥσπερ.γὰρ
here, or Lo there; go not forth nor follow. For as
ἡ ἀστραπὴ [l]ἡ‖ ἀστράπτουσα ἐκ τῆς [m]ὑπ'‖ οὐρανὸν
the lightning which lightens from the [one end] under heaven
εἰς τὴν ὑπ' οὐρανὸν λάμπει, οὕτως ἔσται [n]καὶ‖ ὁ
to the [other end] under heaven shines, thus will be also the
υἱὸς τοῦ ἀνθρώπου [o]ἐν τῇ.ἡμέρᾳ.αὐτοῦ.‖ 25 πρῶτον.δὲ δεῖ
Son of man in his day. But first it behoves
αὐτὸν πολλὰ παθεῖν, καὶ ἀποδοκιμασθῆναι ἀπὸ τῆς γενεᾶς
him many things to suffer, and to be rejected of [2]generation
ταύτης. 26 καὶ καθὼς ἐγένετο ἐν ταῖς ἡμέραις [p]τοῦ‖ Νῶε,
[1]this. And as it came to pass in the days of Noe,
οὕτως ἔσται καὶ ἐν ταῖς ἡμέραις [q]τοῦ‖ υἱοῦ τοῦ ἀνθρώπου.
thus shall it be also in the days of the Son of man.
27 ἤσθιον, ἔπινον, ἐγάμουν, [r]ἐξεγα-
They were eating, they were drinking, they were marrying, they were being
μίζοντο,‖ ἄχρι ἧς.ἡμέρας εἰσῆλθεν Νῶε εἰς τὴν κιβωτόν,
given in marriage, until the day [2]entered [1]Noe into the ark,
καὶ ἦλθεν ὁ κατακλυσμὸς καὶ ἀπώλεσεν [s]ἅπαντας.‖ 28 ὁμοίως
and came the flood and destroyed all. [2]In [3]like [4]manner
[t]καὶ ὡς‖ ἐγένετο ἐν ταῖς ἡμέραις Λώτ· ἤσθιον, ἔπι-
[1]and as it came to pass in the days of Lot; they were eating, they were
νον, ἠγόραζον, ἐπώλουν, ἐφύτευον, ᾠκοδό-
drinking, they were buying, they were selling, they were planting, they were
μουν· 29 ᾗ.δὲ ἡμέρᾳ ἐξῆλθεν Λὼτ ἀπὸ Σοδόμων ἔβρεξεν
building; but on the day [2]went [3]out [1]Lot from Sodom it rained
πῦρ καὶ θεῖον ἀπ' οὐρανοῦ καὶ ἀπώλεσεν [s]ἅπαντας·‖ 30 κα-
fire and sulphur from heaven and destroyed all. In
τὰ.[v]ταῦτα‖ ἔσται ᾗ.ἡμέρᾳ ὁ υἱὸς τοῦ ἀνθρώπου ἀποκαλύπ-
this way shall it be in the day the Son of man is revealed.
τεται. 31 ἐν ἐκείνῃ τῇ ἡμέρᾳ ὃς ἔσται ἐπὶ τοῦ δώματος, καὶ
In that day [he] who shall be on the housetop, and
τὰ.σκεύη.αὐτοῦ ἐν τῇ οἰκίᾳ, μὴ.καταβάτω ἆραι αὐτά·
his goods in the house, let him not come down to take away them;
καὶ ὁ ἐν [w]τῷ‖ ἀγρῷ ὁμοίως μὴ.ἐπιστρεψάτω εἰς τὰ ὀπίσω.
and he in the field likewise let him not return to the things behind.
32 μνημονεύετε τῆς γυναικὸς Λώτ. 33 ὃς.ἐὰν ζητήσῃ τὴν
Remember the wife of Lot. Whoever may seek
ψυχὴν.αὐτοῦ [x]σῶσαι,‖ ἀπολέσει αὐτήν· καὶ ὃς.[y]ἐὰν‖ [z]ἀπολέσῃ‖
his life to save, shall lose it; and whoever may lose
[a]αὐτήν,‖ ζωογονήσει αὐτήν. 34 λέγω ὑμῖν, ταύτῃ τῇ νυκτὶ
it, shall preserve it. I say to you, In that night
ἔσονται δύο ἐπὶ κλίνης [b]μιᾶς·‖ [c]ὁ‖ εἷς [d]παραληφθήσε-
there shall be two [men] upon [2]bed [1]one; the one shall be ta-
ται,‖ καὶ ὁ ἕτερος ἀφεθήσεται. 35 [e]δύο ἔσονται‖ ἀλή-
ken, and the other shall be left. Two [women] shall be grind-

---

[k] ἐκεῖ, ἢ (— ἢ TTr) ἰδοὺ ὧδε TTrA. [l] — ἡ T[TrA]. [m] ὑπὸ τὸν under the LTTrA. [n] — καὶ G[L]TTrAW. [o] — ἐν τῇ ἡμέρᾳ αὐτοῦ L. [p] — τοῦ GLTTrAW. [q] — τοῦ E. [r] ἐγαμίζοντο LTTrA. [s] πάντας LTTrA. [t] καθὼς according as TTrA. [v] ταὐτὰ in the same way GLW; τὰ αὐτὰ in the same way TTrA. [w] — τῷ (*read* a field) TTrA. [x] περιποιήσασθαι to gain TTrA. [y] ἂν TrA. [z] ἀπολέσει shall lose T. [a] — αὐτήν (*read* [it]) [L]TTrA. [b] [μιᾶς] L. [c] — ὁ GLTTrAW. [d] παραλημφθήσεται LTTrA. [e] ἔσονται δύο LTTrA.

θουσαι ἐπὶ τὸ.αὐτό· [f] μία [g]παραληφθήσεται,‖ [h]καὶ ἡ‖ ἑτέρα
ing together; one shall be taken, and the other
ἀφεθήσεται. [i] 37 Καὶ ἀποκριθέντες λέγουσιν αὐτῷ, Ποῦ,
shall be left. And answering they say to him, Where,
κύριε; Ὁ.δὲ εἶπεν αὐτοῖς, Ὅπου τὸ σῶμα ἐκεῖ [j]συναχθή-
Lord? And he said to them, Where the body [is] there will be gathered
σονται οἱ ἀετοί.‖
together the eagles.

18 Ἔλεγεν.δὲ [k]καὶ‖ παραβολὴν αὐτοῖς πρὸς.τὸ δεῖν
And he spoke also a parable to them to the purport that it behoves
πάντοτε προσεύχεσθαι, [l] καὶ μὴ [m]ἐκκακεῖν,‖ 2 λέγων,
[2]always [3]to [4]pray [[1]them] and not to faint, saying,
Κριτής τις ἦν ἔν τινι πόλει, τὸν θεὸν μὴ φοβούμενος
A [2]judge [1]certain there was in [2]certain [1]a city, God not fearing
καὶ ἄνθρωπον μὴ ἐντρεπόμενος. 3 χήρα.δὲ [n] ἦν ἐν τῇ
and man not respecting. And a widow there was in
πόλει.ἐκείνῃ, καὶ ἤρχετο πρὸς αὐτόν, λέγουσα, Ἐκδίκησόν
that city, and she was coming to him, saying, Avenge
με ἀπὸ τοῦ.ἀντιδίκου.μου. 4 Καὶ οὐκ.[o]ἠθέλησεν‖ ἐπὶ χρόνον·
me of mine adverse party. And he would not for a time;
μετὰ.[p]δὲ.ταῦτα‖ εἶπεν ἐν ἑαυτῷ, Εἰ καὶ τὸν θεὸν οὐ.φοβοῦμαι
but afterwards he said within himself, If even God I fear not
[q]καὶ‖ ἄνθρωπον οὐκ‖ ἐντρέπομαι· 5 διά.γε τὸ παρέχειν μοι
and man [2]not [1]respect, yet because [3]causes [4]me
κόπον τὴν.χήραν.ταύτην ἐκδικήσω αὐτήν, ἵνα.μὴ εἰς.τέλος
[5]trouble [1]this [2]widow I will avenge her, lest perpetually
ἐρχομένη ὑπωπιάζῃ με. 6 Εἶπεν.δὲ ὁ κύριος, Ἀκούσατε τί
coming she harass me. And said the Lord, Hear what
ὁ κριτὴς τῆς ἀδικίας λέγει· 7 ὁ.δὲ.θεὸς οὐ.μὴ [r]ποιήσει‖ τὴν
the [2]judge [1]unrighteous says. And [3]God [2]not [1]shall execute the
ἐκδίκησιν τῶν.ἐκλεκτῶν.αὐτοῦ τῶν βοώντων [s]πρὸς αὐτὸν‖
avenging of his elect who cry to him
ἡμέρας καὶ νυκτός, καὶ [t]μακροθυμῶν‖ ἐπ' αὐτοῖς; 8 λέγω
day and night, and [is] being patient over them? I say
ὑμῖν, ὅτι ποιήσει τὴν ἐκδίκησιν αὐτῶν ἐν.τάχει. πλὴν
to you, that he will execute the avenging of them speedily. Nevertheless
ὁ υἱὸς τοῦ ἀνθρώπου ἐλθὼν ἄρα εὑρήσει τὴν πίστιν
the Son of man having come [3]indeed [1]will [2]he find faith
ἐπὶ τῆς γῆς;
on the earth?

9 Εἶπεν.δὲ [v]καὶ‖ πρός τινας τοὺς πεποιθότας ἐφ' ἑαυτοῖς
And he spoke also to some who trusted in themselves
ὅτι εἰσὶν δίκαιοι καὶ ἐξουθενοῦντας τοὺς λοιποὺς τὴν παρα-
that they are righteous and despised the rest [2]para-
βολὴν ταύτην. 10 Ἄνθρωποι δύο ἀνέβησαν εἰς τὸ ἱερὸν
ble [1]this: [2]Men [1]two went up into the temple
προσεύξασθαι· [w]ὁ‖ εἷς Φαρισαῖος καὶ ὁ ἕτερος τελώνης 11 ὁ
to pray; the one a Pharisee and the other a tax-gatherer. The
Φαρισαῖος σταθεὶς [x]πρὸς ἑαυτὸν ταῦτα‖ προσηύχετο, Ὁ θεός,
Pharisee standing, with himself thus was praying, God,

left. 36 Two *men* shall be in the field; the one shall be taken, and the other left. 37 And they answered and said unto him, Where, Lord? And he said unto them, Wheresoever the body *is*, thither will the eagles be gathered together.

XVIII. And he spake a parable unto them *to this end*, that men ought always to pray, and not to faint; 2 saying, There was in a city a judge, which feared not God, neither regarded man: 3 and there was a widow in that city; and she came unto him, saying, Avenge me of mine adversary. 4 And he would not for a while: but afterward he said within himself, Though I fear not God, nor regard man; 5 yet because this widow troubleth me, I will avenge her, lest by her continual coming she weary me. 6 And the Lord said, Hear what the unjust judge saith. 7 And shall not God avenge his own elect, which cry day and night unto him, though he bear long with them? 8 I tell you that he will avenge them speedily. Nevertheless when the Son of man cometh, shall he find faith on the earth?

9 And he spake this parable unto certain which trusted in themselves that they were righteous, and despised others: 10 Two men went up into the temple to pray; the one a Pharisee, and the other a publican. 11 The Pharisee stood and prayed thus with himself, God, I thank thee, that

[f] + ἡ the EGLT[Tr]A. [g] παραλημφθήσεται LTTrA. [h] ἡ δὲ TTrA. [i] + *verse* 36, Δύο ἔσονται ἐν τῷ ἀγρῷ· ὁ εἷς παραληφθήσεται, καὶ ὁ ἕτερος ἀφεθήσεται, Two [men] shall be in the field: the one shall be taken, and the other left E. [j] συναχθήσονται [καὶ also] οἱ ἀετοί L; καὶ οἱ ἀετοὶ ἐπισυναχθήσονται TTrA. [k] — καὶ LT[TrA]. [l] + αὐτοὺς them LTTrAW. [m] ἐγκακεῖν LTrAW; ἐνκακεῖν T. [n] + τις certain E. [o] ἤθελεν LTTrAW. [p] ταῦτα δὲ TrA. [q] οὐδὲ ἄνθρωπον nor man LTTr. [r] ποιήσῃ LTTrA. [s] αὐτῷ TTrA. [t] μακροθυμεῖ is patient LTTrA. [v] [καὶ] L. [w] — ὁ LTTrA. [x] ταῦτα πρὸς ἑαυτὸν Tr; — πρὸς ἑαυτὸν T.

I am not as other men
are, extortioners, un-
just, adulterers, or
even as this publican.
12 I fast twice in the
week, I give tithes of
all that I possess.
13 And the publican,
standing afar off,
would not lift up so
much as *his* eyes unto
heaven, but smote up-
on his breast, saying,
God be merciful to me
a sinner. 14 I tell you,
this man went down to
his house justified *ra-
ther* than the other:
for every one that
exalteth himself shall
be abased; and he
that humbleth him-
self shall be exalted.

εὐχαριστῶ σοι ὅτι οὐκ.εἰμὶ [y]ὥσπερ‖ οἱ λοιποὶ τῶν ἀνθρώπων,
I thank thee that I am not as, the rest of men,
ἅρπαγες, ἄδικοι, μοιχοί, ἢ καὶ ὡς οὗτος ὁ τελώνης. 12 νη-
rapacious, unrighteous, adulterers, or even as this tax-gatherer. I
στεύω δὶς τοῦ σαββάτου, [z]ἀποδεκατῶ‖ πάντα ὅσα κτῶμαι.
fast twice in the week, I tithe all things as many as I gain.
13 [a]Καὶ ὁ‖ τελώνης μακρόθεν ἑστὼς οὐκ ἤθελεν οὐδὲ τοὺς
And the tax-gatherer afar off standing would not even the
ὀφθαλμοὺς [b]εἰς τὸν οὐρανὸν ἐπᾶραι‖· ἀλλ' ἔτυπτεν [c]εἰς‖ τὸ
eyes to the heaven lift up, but was striking upon
στῆθος.[d]αὐτοῦ,‖ λέγων, Ὁ θεός, ἱλάσθητί μοι τῷ ἁμαρτωλῷ.
his breast, saying, God, be propitious to me the sinner.
14 Λέγω ὑμῖν, [e] κατέβη οὗτος δεδικαιωμένος εἰς τὸν οἶκον
I say to you, Went down this one justified to [2]house
αὐτοῦ [f]ἢ ἐκεῖνος.‖ ὅτι πᾶς ὁ ὑψῶν ἑαυτὸν ταπεινω-
[1]his rather than that. For everyone that exalts himself shall be
θήσεται [g]ὁ.δὲ‖ ταπεινῶν ἑαυτὸν ὑψωθήσεται.
humbled; and he that humbles himself shall be exalted.

15 And they brought
unto him also infants,
that he would touch
them: but when *his*
disciples saw *it*, they
rebuked them. 16 But
Jesus called them *unto
him*, and said, Suffer
little children to come
unto me, and forbid
them not: for of such
is the kingdom of God.
17 Verily I say unto
you, Whosoever shall
not receive the king-
dom of God as a little
child shall in no wise
enter therein.

15 Προσέφερον.δὲ αὐτῷ καὶ τὰ βρέφη, ἵνα αὐτῶν ἅπτη-
And they brought to him also the babes, that them he might
ται· ἰδόντες.δὲ οἱ μαθηταὶ [h]ἐπετίμησαν‖ αὐτοῖς. 16 ὁ δὲ
touch; but having seen [it] the disciples rebuked them. But
Ἰησοῦς [i]προσκαλεσάμενος αὐτὰ εἶπεν,‖ Ἄφετε τὰ παιδία
Jesus having called [2]to [[3]him] [1]them said, Suffer the little children
ἔρχεσθαι πρός με, καὶ μὴ.κωλύετε αὐτά· τῶν.γὰρ.τοιούτων
to come to me, and do not forbid them; for of such
ἐστὶν ἡ βασιλεία τοῦ θεοῦ. 17 ἀμὴν λέγω ὑμῖν, ὃς.[k]ἐὰν‖ μὴ
is the kingdom of God. Verily I say to you, Whoever [2]not
δέξηται τὴν βασιλείαν τοῦ θεοῦ ὡς παιδίον οὐ.μὴ εἰσέλθη
[1]shall receive the kingdom of God as a little child in no wise shall enter
εἰς αὐτήν.
into it.

18 And a certain ruler
asked him, saying,
Good Master, what
shall I do to inherit
eternal life? 19 And
Jesus said unto him,
Why callest thou me
good? none *is* good,
save one, *that is*, God.
20 Thou knowest the
commandments, Do
not commit adultery,
Do not kill, Do not
steal, Do not bear false
witness, Honour thy
father and thy mother.
21 And he said, All
these have I kept from
my youth up. 22 Now
when Jesus heard these
things, he said unto
him, Yet lackest thou
one thing: sell all that
thou hast, and distri-
bute unto the poor,
and thou shalt have
treasure in heaven:

18 Καὶ ἐπηρώτησέν τις αὐτὸν ἄρχων, λέγων, Διδάσκαλε
And [4]asked [1]a [2]certain [5]him [3]ruler, saying, [2]Teacher
ἀγαθέ, τί ποιήσας ζωὴν αἰώνιον κληρονομήσω; 19 Εἶπεν
[1]good, [5]what [3]having [4]done life eternal shall I inherit? [3]Said
δὲ αὐτῷ ὁ Ἰησοῦς, Τί με λέγεις ἀγαθόν; οὐδεὶς ἀγαθὸς
[1]but [4]to [5]him [2]Jesus, Why me callest thou good? No one [is] good
εἰ.μὴ εἷς, [l]ὁ‖ θεός. 20 τὰς ἐντολὰς οἶδας· Μὴ.μοι-
except one, God. The commandments thou knowest: Thou shouldest not
χεύσῃς· μὴ.φονεύσῃς· μὴ.κλέψῃς·
commit adultery; thou shouldest not commit murder; thou shouldest not steal;
μὴ.ψευδομαρτυρήσῃς· τίμα τὸν.πατέρα.σου καὶ τὴν
thou shouldest not bear false witness; honour thy father and
μητέρα.[m]σου.‖ 21 Ὁ.δὲ εἶπεν, Ταῦτα πάντα [n]ἐφυλαξάμην‖ ἐκ
thy mother. And he said, [2]These [1]all have I kept from
νεότητός [o]μου.‖ 22 Ἀκούσας.δὲ [p]ταῦτα‖ ὁ Ἰησοῦς εἶπεν
[2]youth [1]my. And having heard these things Jesus said
αὐτῷ, Ἔτι ἕν σοι λείπει· πάντα ὅσα ἔχεις πώλη-
to him, Yet one thing to thee is lacking; all as much as thou hast sell,
σον, καὶ [q]διάδος‖ πτωχοῖς, καὶ ἕξεις θησαυρὸν ἐν [r]οὐ-
and distribute to [the] poor, and thou shalt have treasure in hea-

---

[y] ὡς LTr. [z] ἀποδεκατεύω T. [a] ὁ δὲ T. [b] ἐπᾶραι εἰς τὸν οὐρανόν TTrA. [c] — εἰς LTTr[A]. [d] ἑαυτοῦ TrA. [e] + [ὅτι] that L. [f] παρ' ἐκεῖνον LTrA; ἢ γὰρ ἐκεῖνος GTW. [g] καὶ ὁ L. [h] ἐπετίμων LTTrA. [i] προσεκαλέσατο αὐτὰ λέγων called them to [him] saying TTrA. [k] ἂν LTTrA. [l] — ὁ TA. [m] — σου thy LTrAW. [n] ἐφύλαξα LTTrA. [o] — μου T[Tr]A. [p] — ταῦτα LTTrA. [q] δὸς give L. [r] οὐρανοῖς T; τοῖς οὐρανοῖς the heavens LTrA.

ρανῷ·" καὶ δεῦρο ἀκολούθει μοι. 23 Ὁ.δὲ ἀκούσας ταῦτα
ven, and come follow me. But he having heard these things
περίλυπος [s]ἐγένετο·" ἦν.γὰρ πλούσιος σφόδρα. 24 Ἰδὼν.δὲ
very sorrowful became, for he was [2]rich [1]very. But [2]seeing
αὐτὸν ὁ Ἰησοῦς [t]περίλυπον γενόμενον" εἶπεν, Πῶς δυσκό-
[3]him [1]Jesus [6]very [7]sorrowful [4]having [5]become said, How diffi-
λως οἱ τὰ χρήματα ἔχοντες [v]εἰσελεύσονται εἰς τὴν βασιλείαν
cultly those [2]riches [1]having shall enter into the kingdom
τοῦ θεοῦ." 25 Εὐκοπώτερον.γάρ ἐστιν κάμηλον διὰ [w]τρυμαλιᾶς
of God. For easier it is a camel through an eye
ῥαφίδος" [x]εἰσελθεῖν" ἢ πλούσιον εἰς τὴν βασιλείαν τοῦ θεοῦ
of a needle to enter than a rich man into the kingdom of God
εἰσελθεῖν. 26 [y]Εἶπον".δὲ οἱ ἀκούσαντες, Καὶ τίς δύναται
to enter. And said those who heard, [2]Then [1]who is able
σωθῆναι; 27 Ὁ.δὲ εἶπεν, Τὰ ἀδύνατα παρὰ ἀνθρώποις
to be saved? But he said, The things impossible with men
δυνατά [z]ἐστιν παρὰ τῷ θεῷ." 28 Εἶπεν.δὲ [a]ὁ" Πέτρος, Ἰδού,
[2]possible [1]are with God. And [2]said [1]Peter, Lo,
ἡμεῖς [b]ἀφήκαμεν πάντα καὶ" ἠκολουθήσαμέν σοι. 29 Ὁ.δὲ
we left all and followed thee. And he
εἶπεν αὐτοῖς, Ἀμὴν λέγω ὑμῖν, [c]ὅτι" οὐδείς ἐστιν ὃς ἀφῆκεν
said to them, Verily I say to you, That no one there is who has left
οἰκίαν [d]ἢ γονεῖς ἢ ἀδελφοὺς ἢ γυναῖκα" ἢ τέκνα [e]ἕνεκεν"
house or parents or brethren or wife or children for the sake of
τῆς βασιλείας τοῦ θεοῦ, 30 ὃς [f]οὐ" μὴ.[g]ἀπολάβῃ" πολ-
the kingdom of God, who shall not receive mani-
λαπλασίονα ἐν τῷ.καιρῷ.τούτῳ, καὶ ἐν τῷ αἰῶνι τῷ.ἐρχομένῳ
fold more in this time, and in the age that is coming
ζωὴν αἰώνιον.
life eternal.

and come, follow me.
23 And when he heard
this, he was very sor-
rowful: for he was very
rich. 24 And when Je-
sus saw that he was
very sorrowful, he said,
How hardly shall they
that have riches enter
into the kingdom of
God! 25 For it is easier
for a camel to go
through a needle's eye,
than for a rich man to
enter into the kingdom
of God. 26 And they
that heard *it* said,
Who then can be
saved? 27 And he said,
The things which are
impossible with men
are possible with God.
28 Then Peter said, Lo,
we have left all, and
followed thee. 29 And
he said unto them,
Verily I say unto you,
There is no man that
hath left house, or pa-
rents, or brethren, or
wife, or children, for
the kingdom of God's
sake, 30 who shall not
receive manifold more
in this present time,
and in the world to
come life everlasting.

31 Παραλαβὼν.δὲ τοὺς δώδεκα εἶπεν πρὸς αὐτούς,
And having taken to [him] the twelve he said to them,
Ἰδού, ἀναβαίνομεν εἰς [h]Ἱεροσόλυμα," καὶ τελεσθήσεται
Behold, we go up to Jerusalem, and [3]shall [4]be [5]accomplished
πάντα τὰ γεγραμμένα διὰ τῶν προφητῶν τῷ υἱῷ τοῦ
[1]all [2]things which have been written by the prophets about the Son
ἀνθρώπου. 32 παραδοθήσεται.γὰρ τοῖς ἔθνεσιν, καὶ ἐμπαι-
of man; for he will be delivered up to the Gentiles, and will be
χθήσεται καὶ ὑβρισθήσεται καὶ ἐμπτυσθήσεται. 33 καὶ μα-
mocked and will be insulted and will be spit upon. And having
στιγώσαντες ἀποκτενοῦσιν αὐτόν· καὶ τῇ ἡμέρᾳ τῇ τρίτῃ
scourged they will kill him; and on the [2]day [1]third
ἀναστήσεται. 34 Καὶ αὐτοὶ οὐδὲν τούτων συνῆκαν, καὶ
he will rise again. And they nothing of these things understood, and
ἦν τὸ.ῥῆμα.τοῦτο κεκρυμμένον ἀπ' αὐτῶν, καὶ οὐκ.ἐγίνωσκον
[3]was [1]this [2]saying hid from them, and they knew not
τὰ λεγόμενα.
that which was said.

31 Then he took *unto*
him the twelve, and
said unto them, Be-
hold, we go up to Jeru-
salem, and all things
that are written by
the prophets concern-
ing the Son of man
shall be accomplished.
32 For he shall be de-
livered unto the Gen-
tiles, and shall be
mocked, and spitefully
entreated, and spitted
on: 33 and they shall
scourge *him*, and put
him to death: and the
third day he shall rise
again. 34 And they un-
derstood none of these
things: and this saying
was hid from them,
neither knew they the
things which were spo-
ken.

35 Ἐγένετο.δὲ ἐν.τῷ.ἐγγίζειν.αὐτὸν εἰς [i]Ἱεριχώ," τυφλός
And it came to pass as he drew near to Jericho, a [2]blind
τις ἐκάθητο παρὰ τὴν ὁδὸν [k]προσαιτῶν" 36 ἀκούσας
[3man] [1]certain sat beside the way begging. [2]Having [3]heard

35 And it came to
pass, that as he was
come nigh unto Je-
richo, a certain blind
man sat by the way
side begging: 36 and

---

[s] ἐγενήθη TTrA. [t] — περίλυπον γενόμενον T[Tr]A. [v] εἰς τὴν βασιλείαν τοῦ θεοῦ εἰσπορεύονται TTrA. [w] τρήματος βελόνης LTTrA. [x] διελθεῖν to pass L. [y] εἶπαν T. [z] παρὰ τῷ (— τῷ L[Tr]) θεῷ ἐστίν LTTrA. [a] — ὁ T[A]W. [b] ἀφέντες τὰ ἴδια having left our own LTTrA. [c] — ὅτι T. [d] ἢ γυναῖκα ἢ ἀδελφοὺς ἢ γονεῖς TA. [e] εἵνεκεν T. [f] οὐχὶ TA. [g] λάβῃ L. [h] Ἰερουσαλήμ TTrA. [i] Ἰερειχώ T. [k] ἐπαιτῶν LTTrA.

15

hearing the multitude pass by, he asked what it meant. 37 And they told him, that Jesus of Nazareth passeth by. 38 And he cried, saying, Jesus, *thou* Son of David, have mercy on me. 39 And they which went before rebuked him, that he should hold his peace: but he cried so much the more, *Thou* Son of David, have mercy on me. 40 And Jesus stood, and commanded him to be brought unto him: and when he was come near, he asked him, 41 saying, What wilt thou that I shall do unto thee? And he said, Lord, that I may receive my sight. 42 And Jesus said unto him, Receive thy sight: thy faith hath saved thee. 43 And immediately he received his sight, and followed him, glorifying God: and all the people, when they saw *it*, gave praise unto God.

XIX. And *Jesus* entered and passed through Jericho. 2 And, behold, *there was* a man named Zacchæus, which was the chief among the publicans, and he was rich. 3 And he sought to see Jesus who he was; and could not for the press, because he was little of stature. 4 And he ran before, and climbed up into a sycomore tree to see him: for he was to pass that *way*. 5 And when Jesus came to the place, he looked up, and saw him, and said unto him, Zacchæus, make haste, and come down; for to day I must abide at thy house. 6 And he made haste, and came down, and received him joyfully. 7 And when they saw *it*, they all murmured, saying, That he was gone to be guest with a man that is a sinner. 8 And Zacchæus stood, and said unto the Lord; Behold, Lord, the half of my goods I give to the poor; and if I have

δὲ ὄχλου διαπορευομένου ἐπυνθάνετο τί [1] εἴη τοῦτο.
and a crowd passing along he asked what [2]might [3]be [1]this.

37 ἀπήγγειλαν.δὲ αὐτῷ, "Οτι Ἰησοῦς ὁ Ναζωραῖος παρέρχεται.
And they told him, Jesus the Nazaræan is passing by.

38 Καὶ ἐβόησεν λέγων, Ἰησοῦ, υἱὲ [m]Δαβίδ,‖ ἐλέησόν με.
And he called out saying, Jesus, Son of David, have pity on me.

39 Καὶ οἱ προάγοντες ἐπετίμων αὐτῷ ἵνα [n]σιωπήσῃ·‖
And those going before rebuked him that he should be silent,

αὐτὸς.δὲ πολλῷ μᾶλλον ἔκραζεν, Υἱὲ [m]Δαβίδ,‖ ἐλέησόν με.
but he much more cried out, Son of David, have pity on me.

40 Σταθεὶς.δὲ [o]ὁ‖ Ἰησοῦς ἐκέλευσεν αὐτὸν ἀχθῆναι πρὸς
And [2]having [3]stopped [1]Jesus commanded him to be brought to

αὐτόν· ἐγγίσαντος.δὲ αὐτοῦ ἐπηρώτησεν αὐτόν, 41 [p]λέ-
him. And having drawn near he asked him, say-

γων,‖ Τί σοι θέλεις ποιήσω; Ὁ.δὲ εἶπεν, Κύριε, ἵνα
ing, What [6]to [7]thee [1]desirest [2]thou [3]I [4]shall [5]do? And he said, Lord, that

ἀναβλέψω. 42 Καὶ ὁ Ἰησοῦς εἶπεν αὐτῷ, Ἀνάβλεψον·
I may receive sight. And Jesus said to him, Receive sight:

ἡ.πίστις.σου σέσωκέν σε. 43 Καὶ παραχρῆμα ἀνέβλεψεν,
thy faith hath healed thee. And immediately he received sight,

καὶ ἠκολούθει αὐτῷ, δοξάζων τὸν θεόν· καὶ πᾶς ὁ λαὸς
and followed him, glorifying God. And all the people

ἰδὼν ἔδωκεν αἶνον τῷ θεῷ.
having seen [it] gave praise to God.

19 Καὶ εἰσελθὼν διήρχετο τὴν [q]Ἱεριχώ.‖ 2 καὶ ἰδού,
And having entered he passed through Jericho. And behold,

ἀνὴρ ὀνόματι καλούμενος Ζακχαῖος, καὶ αὐτὸς ἦν ἀρχι-
a man by name called Zacchæus, and he was a chief

τελώνης, καὶ [r]οὗτος ἦν‖ πλούσιος· 3 καὶ ἐζήτει ἰδεῖν τὸν
tax-gatherer, and he was rich. And he was seeking to see

Ἰησοῦν τίς ἐστιν, καὶ οὐκ.ἠδύνατο ἀπὸ τοῦ ὄχλου, ὅτι τῇ
Jesus— who he is: and he was not able for the crowd, because

ἡλικίᾳ μικρὸς ἦν. 4 καὶ προδραμὼν [s]ἔμπροσθεν ἀνέβη
in stature small he was. And having run forward before, he went up

ἐπὶ [t]συκομωραίαν,‖ ἵνα ἴδῃ αὐτόν· ὅτι [v]δι'‖ ἐκείνης
into a sycomore, that he might see him, for by that [way]

ἤμελλεν διέρχεσθαι. 5 καὶ ὡς ἦλθεν ἐπὶ τὸν τόπον, ἀνα-
he was about to pass. And as he came to the place, look-

βλέψας ὁ Ἰησοῦς [w]εἶδεν αὐτόν, καὶ‖ εἶπεν πρὸς αὐτόν,
ing up Jesus saw him, and said to him,

Ζακχαῖε, σπεύσας κατάβηθι· σήμερον.γὰρ ἐν τῷ.οἴκῳ.σου
Zacchæus, making haste come down, for to-day in thy house

δεῖ με μεῖναι. 6 Καὶ σπεύσας κατέβη καὶ ὑπεδέξατο
it behoveth me to remain. And making haste he came down and received

αὐτὸν χαίρων. 7 καὶ ἰδόντες [x]ἅπαντες‖ διεγόγγυζον,
him rejoicing. And having seen [it] all murmured,

λέγοντες, "Οτι παρὰ ἁμαρτωλῷ ἀνδρὶ εἰσῆλθεν καταλῦσαι.
saying, With a sinful man he has entered to lodge.

8 Σταθεὶς.δὲ Ζακχαῖος εἶπεν πρὸς τὸν κύριον, Ἰδού, τὰ
But standing Zacchæus said to the Lord, Lo, the

[y]ἡμίση‖ [z]τῶν.ὑπαρχόντων.μου,‖ κύριε, [a]δίδωμι τοῖς πτωχοῖς·‖
half of my possessions, Lord, I give to the poor,

---

[1] + [ἂν] LTr. [m] Δαυὶδ GW; Δαυείδ LTTrA. [n] σιγήσῃ LTTrA. [o] [ὁ] Tr. [p] — λέγων T[Tr]A. [q] Ἱερειχώ T. [r] αὐτὸς (— ἦν [L]TrA) LTrA; — οὗτος T. [s] + εἰς τὸ to the (*read* ἔμπρ. front,) T[A]. [t] συκομορέαν EGTTrAW; συκομωρέαν L. [v] — δι' GLTTrAW. [w] — εἶδεν αὐτόν, καὶ TTr[A]. [x] πάντες LTTrAW. [y] ἡμίσεα L; ἡμισειά TTrA. [z] μου τῶν ὑπαρχόντων TTrA. [a] τοῖς πτωχοῖς δίδωμι TTrA.

καὶ εἴ τινός τι ἐσυκοφάντησα, ἀποδίδωμι τετρα-
and if of anyone anything I took by false accusation, I return four-
πλοῦν. 9 Εἶπεν.δὲ πρὸς αὐτὸν ὁ Ἰησοῦς, Ὅτι σήμερον σωτηρία
fold. And [2]said [3]to [4]him [1]Jesus, To-day salvation
τῷ.οἴκῳ.τούτῳ ἐγένετο, καθότι καὶ αὐτὸς υἱὸς Ἀβραάμ
to this house is come, inasmuch as also he a son of Abraham
[b]ἐστιν·‖ 10 ἦλθεν.γὰρ ὁ υἱὸς τοῦ ἀνθρώπου ζητῆσαι καὶ σῶσαι
is: for [5]came [1]the [2]Son [3]of [4]man to seek and to save
τὸ ἀπολωλός.
that which has been lost.

11 Ἀκουόντων.δὲ αὐτῶν ταῦτα, προσθεὶς εἶπεν παρα-
But as [2]were [3]hearing [1]they these things, adding he spoke a para-
βολήν, διὰ τὸ ἐγγὺς [c]αὐτὸν εἶναι Ἱερουσαλήμ,‖ καὶ δοκεῖν
ble, because [3]near [1]he [2]was Jerusalem, and [2]thought
αὐτοὺς ὅτι παραχρῆμα μέλλει ἡ βασιλεία τοῦ θεοῦ ἀνα-
[1]they that immediately was about the kingdom of God to be
φαίνεσθαι· 12 εἶπεν οὖν, Ἄνθρωπός τις εὐγενὴς ἐπορεύθη
manifested. He said therefore, A [2]man [1]certain high born proceeded
εἰς χώραν μακράν, λαβεῖν ἑαυτῷ βασιλείαν καὶ ὑποστρέψαι.
to a [2]country [1]distant, to receive for himself a kingdom and to return.
13 καλέσας.δὲ δέκα δούλους.ἑαυτοῦ ἔδωκεν αὐτοῖς δέκα μνᾶς,
And having called ten of his bondmen he gave to them ten minas,
καὶ εἶπεν πρὸς αὐτούς, Πραγματεύσασθε [d]ἕως‖ ἔρχομαι.
and said to them, Trade until I come.
14 Οἱ.δὲ.πολῖται.αὐτοῦ ἐμίσουν αὐτόν, καὶ ἀπέστειλαν πρεσ-
But his citizens hated him and sent an em-
βείαν ὀπίσω αὐτοῦ, λέγοντες, Οὐ.θέλομεν τοῦτον
bassy after him, saying, We are unwilling [for] this [man]
βασιλεῦσαι ἐφ' ἡμᾶς. 15 Καὶ ἐγένετο ἐν τῷ ἐπανελθεῖν
to reign over us. And it came to pass on [2]coming [3]back [4]again
αὐτὸν λαβόντα τὴν βασιλείαν, καὶ εἶπεν φωνηθῆναι αὐτῷ
[1]his having received the kingdom, that he directed to be called to him
τοὺς.δούλους.τούτους οἷς [e]ἔδωκεν‖ τὸ ἀργύριον, ἵνα
these bondmen to whom he gave the money, in order that
[f]γνῷ‖ [g]τίς.τί διεπραγματεύσατο.‖ 16 παρεγένετο.δὲ ὁ
he might know what each had gained by trading. And came up the
πρῶτος, λέγων, Κύριε, ἡ.μνᾶ.σου [h]προσειργάσατο δέκα‖ μνᾶς.
first, saying, Lord, thy mina has produced ten minas.
17 Καὶ εἶπεν αὐτῷ, [i]Εὖ,‖ ἀγαθὲ δοῦλε· ὅτι ἐν ἐλαχίστῳ
And he said to him, Well! good bondman; because in a very little
πιστὸς ἐγένου, ἴσθι ἐξουσίαν ἔχων ἐπάνω δέκα πόλεων.
faithful thou wast, be thou [2]authority [1]having over ten cities.
18 Καὶ ἦλθεν ὁ δεύτερος, λέγων, [k]Κύριε, ἡ.μνᾶ.σου‖ ἐποίησεν
And came the second, saying, Lord, thy mina has made
πέντε μνᾶς. 19 Εἶπεν.δὲ καὶ τούτῳ, Καὶ σὺ [l]γίνου ἐπάνω‖
five minas. And he said also to this one, And [2]thou [1]be over
πέντε πόλεων. 20 Καὶ [m]ἕτερος ἦλθεν, λέγων, Κύριε, ἰδοὺ ἡ
five cities. And another came, saying, Lord, behold
μνᾶ.σου, ἣν εἶχον ἀποκειμένην ἐν σουδαρίῳ· 21 ἐφοβούμην
thy mina, which I kept laid up in a handkerchief. [2]I [3]feared
γάρ σε, ὅτι ἄνθρωπος αὐστηρὸς εἶ· αἴρεις ὃ
[1]for thee, because a man harsh thou art; thou takest up what

taken any thing from any man by false accusation, I restore *him* fourfold. 9 And Jesus said unto him, This day is salvation come to this house, forsomuch as he also is a son of Abraham. 10 For the Son of man is come to seek and to save that which was lost.

11 And as they heard these things, he added and spake a parable, because he was nigh to Jerusalem, and because they thought that the kingdom of God should immediately appear. 12 He said therefore, A certain nobleman went into a far country to receive for himself a kingdom, and to return. 13 And he called his ten servants, and delivered them ten pounds, and said unto them, Occupy till I come. 14 But his citizens hated him, and sent a message after him, saying, We will not have this *man* to reign over us. 15 And it came to pass, that when he was returned, having received the kingdom, then he commanded these servants to be called unto him, to whom he had given the money, that he might know how much every man had gained by trading. 16 Then came the first, saying, Lord, thy pound hath gained ten pounds. 17 And he said unto him, Well, thou good servant: because thou hast been faithful in a very little, have thou authority over ten cities. 18 And the second came, saying, Lord, thy pound hath gained five pounds. 19 And he said likewise to him, Be thou also over five cities. 20 And another came, saying, Lord, behold, *here is* thy pound, which I have kept laid up in a napkin: 21 for I feared thee, because thou art an austere man: thou takest up that

---

[b] — ἐστιν (*read* [is]) T. [c] εἶναι αὐτὸν Ἱερουσαλὴμ L; εἶναι Ἱερουσαλὴμ αὐτὸν TTrA. [d] ἐν ᾧ LTTrA. [e] δεδώκει he had given LTTrA. [f] γνοῖ LTTrA. [g] τί διεπραγματεύσαντο what they had gained by trading TrA. [h] δέκα προσηργάσατο (προσειρ. Tr) LTTrA. [i] εὖγε well done LTTrA. [k] ἡ μνᾶ σου, κύριε, TTrA. [l] ἐπάνω γίνου TA. [m] + ὁ the (ἕτερος other) LTTrA.

thou layedst not down, and reapest that thou didst not sow. 22 And he saith unto him, Out of thine own mouth will I judge thee, *thou* wicked servant. Thou knewest that I was an austere man, taking up that I laid not down, and reaping that I did not sow: 23 wherefore then gavest not thou my money into the bank, that at my coming I might have required mine own with usury? 24 And he said unto them that stood by, Take from him the pound, and give *it* to him that hath ten pounds. 25 (And they said unto him, Lord, he hath ten pounds.) 26 For I say unto you, That unto every one which hath shall be given; and from him that hath not, even that he hath shall be taken away from him. 27 But those mine enemies, which would not that I should reign over them, bring hither, and slay *them* before me.

28 And when he had thus spoken, he went before, ascending up to Jerusalem. 29 And it came to pass, when he was come nigh to Bethphage and Bethany, at the mount called *the mount* of Olives, he sent two of his disciples, 30 saying, Go ye into the village over against *you;* in the which at your entering ye shall find a colt tied, whereon yet never man sat: loose him, and bring *him hither.* 31 And if any man ask you, Why do ye loose *him?* thus shall ye say unto him, Because the Lord hath need of him. 32 And they that were sent went their way, and found even as he had said unto them. 33 And as they were loosing the colt, the owners thereof said unto them, Why loose ye the colt? 34 And they said, The Lord hath need of him. 35 And they brought him to Jesus: and they

οὐκ.ἔθηκας καὶ θερίζεις ὃ οὐκ.ἔσπειρας. 22 Λέγει
thou didst not lay down and thou reapest what thou didst not sow. [2]He [3]says
[n]δὲ‖ αὐτῷ, Ἐκ τοῦ.στόματός.σου κρινῶ σε, πονηρὲ δοῦ-
[1]but to him, Out of thy mouth I will judge thee, wicked bond-
λε. ᾔδεις ὅτι ἐγὼ ἄνθρωπος αὐστηρός εἰμι, αἴρων ὃ
man: thou knewest that I [2]a [4]man [3]harsh [1]am, taking up what
οὐκ.ἔθηκα καὶ θερίζων ὃ οὐκ.ἔσπειρα. 23 καὶ [o]διατί‖
I did not lay down and reaping what I did not sow! and why
οὐκ.ἔδωκας [p]τὸ.ἀργύριόν.μου‖ ἐπὶ [q]τὴν‖ τράπεζαν, [r]καὶ ἐγὼ‖
didst thou not give my money to the bank, that I
ἐλθὼν σὺν τόκῳ ἂν.[s]ἔπραξα αὐτό‖; 24 Καὶ τοῖς παρε-
coming with interest might have required it? And to those stand-
στῶσιν εἶπεν, Ἄρατε ἀπ' αὐτοῦ τὴν μνᾶν, καὶ δότε τῷ
ing by he said, Take from him the mina, and give [it] to him who
τὰς δέκα μνᾶς ἔχοντι. 25 Καὶ [t]εἶπον‖ αὐτῷ, Κύριε, ἔχει
the ten minas has. (And they said to him, Lord, he has
δέκα μνᾶς. 26 Λέγω.[v]γὰρ‖ ὑμῖν, ὅτι παντὶ τῷ ἔχοντι δο-
ten minas.) For I say to you, that to everyone who has shall be
θήσεται· ἀπὸ.δὲ τοῦ μὴ.ἔχοντος, καὶ ὃ ἔχει ἀρθήσεται
given; but from him who has not, even that which he has shall be taken
[w]ἀπ' αὐτοῦ.‖ 27 Πλὴν τοὺς.ἐχθρούς.μου [x]ἐκείνους‖ τοὺς
from him. Moreover [2]mine [3]enemies [1]those who
μὴ.θελήσαντάς με βασιλεῦσαι ἐπ' αὐτούς, ἀγάγετε ὧδε
were unwilling [for] me to reign over them, bring here
καὶ κατασφάξατε [y] ἔμπροσθέν μου.
and slay [them] before me.

28 Καὶ εἰπὼν ταῦτα ἐπορεύετο ἔμπροσθεν, ἀναβαίνων
And having said these things he went on before, going up
εἰς Ἱεροσόλυμα. 29 Καὶ ἐγένετο ὡς ἤγγισεν εἰς Βηθ-
to Jerusalem. And it came to pass as he drew near to Beth-
φαγὴ καὶ [z]Βηθανίαν,‖ πρὸς τὸ ὄρος τὸ καλούμενον ἐλαιῶν,
phage and Bethany, towards the mount called of Olives,
ἀπέστειλεν δύο τῶν.μαθητῶν.[a]αὐτοῦ,‖ 30 [b]εἰπών,‖ Ὑπάγετε εἰς
he sent two of his disciples, saying, Go into
τὴν κατέναντι κώμην· ἐν ᾗ εἰσπορευόμενοι εὑρήσετε
the [2]opposite [[3]you] [1]village, in which entering ye will find
πῶλον δεδεμένον, ἐφ' ὃν οὐδεὶς πώποτε ἀνθρώπων ἐκάθισεν·
a colt tied, on which no one [3]ever [4]yet [1]of [2]men sat:
[c]λύσαντες αὐτὸν ἀγάγετε. 31 καὶ ἐάν τις ὑμᾶς ἐρωτᾷ,
having loosed it bring [it]. And if anyone [2]you [1]ask,
[d]Διατί‖ λύετε; οὕτως ἐρεῖτε [e]αὐτῷ,‖ Ὅτι ὁ κύριος
Why do ye loose [it]? thus shall ye say to him, Because the Lord
αὐτοῦ χρείαν ἔχει. 32 Ἀπελθόντες.δὲ οἱ ἀπεσταλμένοι
[3]of [4]it [2]need [1]has. And having departed those who had been sent
εὗρον καθὼς εἶπεν αὐτοῖς. 33 λυόντων.δὲ.αὐτῶν τὸν πῶλον
found as he had said to them. And on their loosing the colt
[f]εἶπον‖ οἱ κύριοι αὐτοῦ πρὸς αὐτούς, Τί λύετε τὸν πῶλον;
[5]said [1]the [2]masters [3]of [4]it to them, Why loose ye the colt?
34 Οἱ.δὲ [f]εἶπον,‖ [g]Ὁ κύριος αὐτοῦ χρείαν ἔχει. 35 Καὶ ἤγαγον
And they said, The Lord [3]of [4]it [2]need [1]has. And they led
αὐτὸν πρὸς τὸν Ἰησοῦν· καὶ [h]ἐπιρρίψαντες‖ [i]ἑαυτῶν‖ τὰ ἱμά-
it to Jesus; and having cast their gar-

[n] — δὲ but TTrA. [o] διὰ τί LTrA. [p] μου τὸ ἀργύριον LTTrA. [q] — τὴν (*read* a bank) LTTrAW. [r] κἀγὼ LTTrA. [s] αὐτὸ ἔπραξα LTTrA. [t] εἶπαν LTTrA. [v] — γὰρ for [L]T[Tr]A. [w] — ἀπ' αὐτοῦ [L]TA. [x] τούτους these TTrA. [y] + αὐτοὺς them TTrA. [z] Βηθανιά A. [a] — αὐτοῦ (*read* the disciples) T[Tr]A. [b] λέγων LTr. [c] + καὶ and TTrA. [d] διὰ τί LTrA. [e] — αὐτῷ [L]TTr[A]. [f] εἶπαν LTTrA. [g] + ὅτι because LTTrA. [h] ἐπιρίψαντες LTTrA. [i] αὐτῶν LTTrA.

τια· ἐπὶ τὸν πῶλον, ἐπεβίβασαν τὸν Ἰησοῦν. 36 πορευο-
ments on the colt, they put [2]on [3it] [1]Jesus.
μένου.δὲ.αὐτοῦ ὑπεστρώννυον τὰ.ἱμάτια.[k]αὐτῶν ἐν τῇ ὁδῷ.
And as he went they were strewing their garments in the way.
37 Ἐγγίζοντος.δὲ.αὐτοῦ ἤδη πρὸς τῇ καταβάσει τοῦ ὄρους
And as he drew near already at the descent of the mount
τῶν ἐλαιῶν ἤρξαντο ἅπαν τὸ πλῆθος τῶν μαθητῶν χαίρον-
of Olives began all the multitude of the disciples, rejoic-
τες αἰνεῖν τὸν θεὸν φωνῇ μεγάλῃ περὶ [l]πασῶν ὧν
ing, to praise God with a [2]voice [1]loud for all [5]which
εἶδον δυνάμεων, 38 λέγοντες, Εὐλογημένος ὁ
[6]they [7]had [8]seen [[1]the] [2]works [3]of [4]power, saying, Blessed the
[m]ἐρχόμενος βασιλεὺς ἐν ὀνόματι κυρίου· [n]εἰρήνη ἐν
[2]coming [1]king in [the] name of [the] Lord. Peace in
οὐρανῷ καὶ δόξα ἐν ὑψίστοις. 39 Καί τινες τῶν Φαρισαίων
heaven and glory in [the] highest. And some of the Pharisees
ἀπὸ τοῦ ὄχλου [o]εἶπον πρὸς αὐτόν, Διδάσκαλε, ἐπιτίμησον
from the crowd said to him, Teacher, rebuke
τοῖς.μαθηταῖς.σου. 40 Καὶ ἀποκριθεὶς εἶπεν [p]αὐτοῖς, Λέγω
thy disciples. And answering he said to them, I say
ὑμῖν, [q]ὅτι ἐὰν οὗτοι [r]σιωπήσωσιν οἱ λίθοι [s]κεκράξονται.
to you, that if these should be silent the stones will cry out.
41 Καὶ ὡς ἤγγισεν, ἰδὼν τὴν πόλιν ἔκλαυσεν ἐπ' [t]αὐτῇ,
And as he drew near, seeing the city he wept over it,
42 λέγων, Ὅτι εἰ ἔγνως καὶ σύ, [v]καί.γε ἐν τῇ ἡμέρᾳ
saying, If thou hadst known, even thou, even at least in [3]day
[w]σου ταύτῃ, τὰ πρὸς εἰρήνην [x]σου· νῦν.δὲ ἐκρύβη ἀπὸ
[2]thy [1]this, the things for [2]peace [1]thy: but now they are hid from
ὀφθαλμῶν.σου· 43 ὅτι ἥξουσιν ἡμέραι ἐπὶ σὲ καὶ [y]περιβα-
thine eyes; for [2]shall [3]come [1]days upon thee that [3]shall [4]cast
λοῦσιν οἱ.ἐχθροί.σου χάρακά σοι, καὶ περικυκλώσουσίν σε
[5]about [1]thine [2]enemies [7]a [8]rampart [6]thee, and shall close around thee
καὶ συνέξουσίν σε πάντοθεν, 44 καὶ ἐδαφιοῦσίν
and keep in thee on every side, and shall level [2]with [3]the [4]ground
σε καὶ τὰ.τέκνα.σου ἐν σοί, καὶ οὐκ.ἀφήσουσιν [z]ἐν σοὶ λίθον
[1]thee and thy children in thee, and shall not leave in thee a stone
ἐπὶ λίθῳ· ἀνθ'.ὧν οὐκ.ἔγνως τὸν καιρὸν τῆς ἐπισκοπῆς
upon a stone, because thou knewest not the season of [2]visitation
σου.
[1]thy.

45 Καὶ εἰσελθὼν εἰς τὸ ἱερὸν ἤρξατο ἐκβάλλειν τοὺς
And having entered into the temple he began to cast out those
πωλοῦντας [a]ἐν αὐτῷ καὶ ἀγοράζοντας, 46 λέγων αὐτοῖς,
selling in it and buying, saying to them,
Γέγραπται, [b]Ὁ.οἶκός.μου οἶκος προσευχῆς [c]ἐστίν· ὑμεῖς.δὲ
It has been written, My house a house of prayer is; but ye
αὐτὸν ἐποιήσατε σπήλαιον λῃστῶν. 47 Καὶ ἦν διδάσκων
it have made a den of robbers. And he was teaching
τὸ.καθ'.ἡμέραν ἐν τῷ ἱερῷ· οἱ.δὲ ἀρχιερεῖς καὶ οἱ γραμματεῖς
day by day in the temple; and the chief priests and the scribes

cast their garments upon the colt, and they set Jesus thereon.
36 And as he went, they spread their clothes in the way.
37 And when he was come nigh, even now at the descent of the mount of Olives, the whole multitude of the disciples began to rejoice and praise God with a loud voice for all the mighty works that they had seen;
38 saying, Blessed *be* the King that cometh in the name of the Lord: peace in heaven, and glory in the highest.
39 And some of the Pharisees from among the multitude said unto him, Master, rebuke thy disciples.
40 And he answered and said unto them, I tell you that, if these should hold their peace, the stones would immediately cry out.
41 And when he was come near, he beheld the city, and wept over it,
42 saying, If thou hadst known, even thou, at least in this thy day, the things *which belong* unto thy peace! but now they are hid from thine eyes.
43 For the days shall come upon thee, that thine enemies shall cast a trench about thee, and compass thee round, and keep thee in on every side,
44 and shall lay thee even with the ground, and thy children within thee; and they shall not leave in thee one stone upon another; because thou knewest not the time of thy visitation.

45 And he went into the temple, and began to cast out them that sold therein, and them that bought;
46 saying unto them, It is written, My house is the house of prayer: but ye have made it a den of thieves.
47 And he taught daily in the temple. But the chief priests and the scribes

---

[k] ἑαυτῶν Tr. [l] πάντων LTr. [m] — ἐρχόμενος T. [n] ἐν οὐρανῷ εἰρήνη TTrA. [o] εἶπαν LTTrA. [p] — αὐτοῖς T[Tr]A. [q] [ὅτι] Tr. [r] σιωπήσουσιν shall be silent LTTrA. [s] κράξουσιν TTrA. [t] αὐτήν LTTrAW. [v] καίγε GT; — καί γε [L]Tr[A]. [w] — σου LTr[A]. [x] [σου] LTrA. [y] παρεμβαλοῦσιν shall place near T. [z] λίθον ἐπὶ λίθον (λίθῳ L) ἐν σοί LTTrA. [a] — ἐν αὐτῷ καὶ ἀγοράζοντας TTrA. [b] + ὅτι L; + καὶ ἔσται and shall be TTrA. [c] — ἐστίν TTrA.

and the chief of the people sought to destroy him, 48 and could not find what they might do: for all the people were very attentive to hear him.

XX. And it came to pass, *that* on one of those days, as he taught the people in the temple, and preached the gospel, the chief priests and the scribes came upon *him* with the elders, 2 and spake unto him, saying, Tell us, by what authority doest thou these things? or who is he that gave thee this authority? 3 And he answered and said unto them, I will also ask you one thing; and answer me: 4 The baptism of John, was it from heaven, or of men? 5 And they reasoned with themselves, saying, If we shall say, From heaven; he will say, Why then believed ye him not? 6 But and if we say, Of men; all the people will stone us: for they be persuaded that John was a prophet. 7 And they answered, that they could not tell whence *it was*. 8 And Jesus said unto them, Neither tell I you by what authority I do these things.

9 Then began he to speak to the people this parable; A certain man planted a vineyard, and let it forth to husbandmen, and went into a far country for a long time. 10 And at the season he sent a servant to the husbandmen, that they should give him of the fruit of the vineyard: but the husbandmen beat him, and sent *him* away empty. 11 And again he sent another servant: and they beat him also, and entreated *him* shamefully, and sent *him* away empty. 12 And again he sent a third: and

ἐζήτουν αὐτὸν ἀπολέσαι, καὶ οἱ πρῶτοι τοῦ λαοῦ· 48 καὶ
[7]were [8]seeking [11]him [9]to [10]destroy, [1]and [2]the [3]first [4]of [5]the [6]people, and
οὐχ.[d]εὕρισκον‖ τὸ τί ποιήσωσιν, ὁ.λαὸς.γὰρ ἅπας [e]ἐξεκρέματο‖
found not what they might do, for [2]the [3]people [1]all [5]were [6]hanging [7]on
αὐτοῦ ἀκούων.
[8]him [4]listening.

20 Καὶ ἐγένετο ἐν μιᾷ τῶν.ἡμερῶν.[f]ἐκείνων,‖ διδάσκον-
And it came to pass on one of those days, as [2]was [3]teach-
τος αὐτοῦ τὸν λαὸν ἐν τῷ ἱερῷ καὶ εὐαγγελιζομένου,
ing [1]he the people in the temple and announcing the glad tidings,
ἐπέστησαν οἱ [g]ἀρχιερεῖς‖ καὶ οἱ γραμματεῖς σὺν τοῖς πρεσβυ-
came up the chief priests and the scribes with the elders
τέροις, 2 καὶ [h]εἶπον‖ [i]πρὸς αὐτόν, λέγοντες,‖ [k]Εἰπὲ‖ ἡμῖν ἐν
and spoke to him, saying, Tell us by
ποίᾳ ἐξουσίᾳ ταῦτα ποιεῖς, ἢ τίς ἐστιν ὁ δούς σοι τὴν
what authority these things thou doest, or who it is who gave to thee
ἐξουσίαν.ταύτην; 3 Ἀποκριθεὶς.δὲ εἶπεν πρὸς αὐτούς, Ἐρω-
this authority? And answering he said to them, [3]Will
τήσω ὑμᾶς κἀγὼ [l]ἕνα‖ λόγον, καὶ εἴπατέ μοι· 4 Τὸ βάπτισμα
[4]ask [5]you [1]I [2]also one thing, and tell me, The baptism
[m] [n]Ἰωάννου‖ ἐξ οὐρανοῦ ἦν ἢ ἐξ ἀνθρώπων; 5 Οἱ.δὲ
of John from heaven was it or from men? And they
[o]συνελογίσαντο‖ πρὸς ἑαυτούς, λέγοντες, Ὅτι ἐὰν εἴπωμεν
reasoned among themselves, saying, If we should say
Ἐξ οὐρανοῦ, ἐρεῖ [p] [q]Διατί‖ [r]οὖν‖ οὐκ.ἐπιστεύσατε αὐτῷ;
From heaven, he will say Why then did ye not believe him?
6 ἐὰν.δὲ εἴπωμεν Ἐξ ἀνθρώπων, [s]πᾶς ὁ λαὸς‖ καταλιθάσει
But if we should say From men, all the people will stone
ἡμᾶς· πεπεισμένος.γάρ.ἐστιν [t]Ἰωάννην‖ προφήτην εἶναι.
us; for they are persuaded [that] John [2]a [3]prophet [1]was.
7 Καὶ ἀπεκρίθησαν μὴ.εἰδέναι πόθεν. 8 καὶ ὁ Ἰησοῦς εἶπεν
And they answered they knew not whence. And Jesus said
αὐτοῖς, Οὐδὲ ἐγὼ λέγω ὑμῖν ἐν ποίᾳ ἐξουσίᾳ ταῦτα ποιῶ.
to them, Neither [2]I [1]tell you by what authority these things I do.
9 Ἤρξατο δὲ [v]πρὸς τὸν λαὸν λέγειν‖ τὴν.παραβολὴν.ταύτην·
And he began to the people to speak this parable:
[w]Ἄνθρωπός [x]τις‖ ἐφύτευσεν ἀμπελῶνα,‖ καὶ [y]ἐξέδοτο‖ αὐτὸν
A [2]man [1]certain planted a vineyard, and let out it
γεωργοῖς, καὶ ἀπεδήμησεν χρόνους.ἱκανούς. 10 καὶ [z]ἐν‖
to husbandmen, and left the country for a long time. And in [the]
καιρῷ ἀπέστειλεν πρὸς τοὺς γεωργοὺς δοῦλον, ἵνα ἀπὸ τοῦ
season he sent to the husbandmen a bondman, that from the
καρποῦ τοῦ ἀμπελῶνος [a]δῶσιν‖ αὐτῷ· οἱ.δὲ γεωργοὶ
fruit of the vineyard they might give to him; but the husbandmen
[b]δείραντες αὐτὸν ἐξαπέστειλαν‖ κενόν. 11 καὶ προσέθετο
having beat him sent [him] away empty. And he added
[c]πέμψαι ἕτερον‖ δοῦλον· οἱ.δὲ κἀκεῖνον δείραντες καὶ ἀτι-
to send another bondman; but they [4]also [3]him [1]having [2]beat and dis-
μάσαντες ἐξαπέστειλαν κενόν. 12 καὶ προσέθετο [d]πέμψαι
honoured [him] sent [him] away empty. And he added to send

---

[d] ηὕρισκον LTr. [e] ἐξεκρέμετο T. [f] — ἐκείνων (*read* one of the days) LTTrA. [g] ἱερεῖς priests TA. [h] εἶπαν TTrA. [i] λέγοντες πρὸς αὐτὸν LT; — λέγοντες TrA. [k] Εἰπὸν TTrA. [l] — ἕνα (*read* [one]) LTTrA. [m] + τὸ T. [n] Ἰωάνου Tr. [o] συνελογίζοντο L. [p] + ἡμῖν to us L. [q] Διὰ τί ELTrA. [r] — οὖν [L]TTrA. [s] ὁ λαὸς ἅπας TTrA. [t] Ἰωάνην Tr. [v] λέγειν πρὸς τὸν λαὸν L. [w] Ἀμπελῶνα ἐφύτευσεν ἄνθρωπος L [x] — τις GLTTrAW. [y] ἐξέδετο TA. [z] — ἐν (*read* καιρῷ at [the] season LTTrA. [a] δώσουσιν they shall give LTTrA. [b] ἐξαπέστειλαν αὐτὸν δείραντες TA. [c] ἕτερον πέμψαι LTTrA. [d] τρίτον πέμψαι LTTrA.

τρίτον·‖ οἱ.δὲ [e]καὶ τοῦτον‖ τραυματίσαντες ἐξέβαλον.
a third; and they [4]also [3]him [1]having [2]wounded cast [him] out.
13 εἶπεν.δὲ ὁ κύριος τοῦ ἀμπελῶνος, Τί ποιήσω; πέμψω
And said the lord of the vineyard, What shall I do? I will send
τὸν.υἱόν.μου τὸν ἀγαπητόν· ἴσως τοῦτον [f]ἰδόντες‖ ἐντρα-
my son the beloved; perhaps him having seen they will
πήσονται. 14 Ἰδόντες.δὲ αὐτὸν οἱ γεωργοὶ [g]διελογίζοντο‖
respect. But having seen him the husbandmen reasoned
πρὸς [h]ἑαυτούς,‖ λέγοντες, Οὗτός ἐστιν ὁ κληρονόμος· [i]δεῦτε‖
among themselves, saying, This is the heir; come
ἀποκτείνωμεν αὐτόν, ἵνα ἡμῶν γένηται ἡ κληρονομία.
let us kill him, that [5]ours [3]may [4]become [1]the [2]inheritance.
15 Καὶ ἐκβαλόντες αὐτὸν ἔξω τοῦ ἀμπελῶνος ἀπέκτειναν.
And having cast forth him outside the vineyard they killed
Τί οὖν ποιήσει αὐτοῖς ὁ κύριος τοῦ ἀμπελῶνος;
[him]. What therefore will do to them the lord of the vineyard?
16 ἐλεύσεται καὶ ἀπολέσει τοὺς.γεωργοὺς.τούτους, καὶ δώσει
He will come and will destroy these husbandmen, and will give
τὸν ἀμπελῶνα ἄλλοις. [k]Ἀκούσαντες.δὲ‖ [l]εἶπον,‖ Μὴ
the vineyard to others. And having heard [it] they said, [3]Not
γένοιτο. 17 Ὁ.δὲ ἐμβλέψας αὐτοῖς εἶπεν, Τί οὖν ἐστιν τὸ
[1]may [2]it be! But he looking at them said, What then is [2]that
γεγραμμένον τοῦτο, Λίθον ὃν ἀπεδοκίμασαν οἱ
[3]has [4]been [5]written [1]this, [The] stone which [4]rejected [1]they [2]that
οἰκοδομοῦντες, οὗτος ἐγενήθη εἰς κεφαλὴν γωνίας; 18 Πᾶς
[3]build, this is become head of [the] corner? Everyone
ὁ πεσὼν ἐπ' ἐκεῖνον τὸν λίθον συνθλασθήσεται· ἐφ'.ὃν.δ'.ἂν
that falls on that stone will be broken, but on whomsoever
πέσῃ λικμήσει αὐτόν. 19 Καὶ [m]ἐζήτησαν‖ οἱ
it may fall it will grind [2]to [3]powder [1]him. And [7]sought [1]the
[n]ἀρχιερεῖς καὶ οἱ γραμματεῖς‖ ἐπιβαλεῖν ἐπ' αὐτὸν τὰς χεῖρας
[2]chief [3]priests [4]and [5]the [6]scribes to lay [2]on [3]him [1]hands
ἐν αὐτῇ.τῇ.ὥρᾳ, καὶ ἐφοβήθησαν τὸν λαόν· ἔγνωσαν.γὰρ ὅτι
in that hour, and they feared the people; for they knew that
πρὸς αὐτοὺς [o]τὴν.παραβολὴν.ταύτην εἶπεν.‖
against them this parable he speaks.

20 Καὶ παρατηρήσαντες ἀπέστειλαν [p]ἐγκαθέτους,‖ ὑπο-
And having watched [him] they sent secret agents, feign-
κρινομένους ἑαυτοὺς δικαίους εἶναι, ἵνα ἐπιλάβωνται
ing themselves [3]righteous [1]to [2]be, that they might take hold
αὐτοῦ [q]λόγου,‖ [r]εἰς τὸ‖ παραδοῦναι αὐτὸν τῇ ἀρχῇ καὶ
of him in discourse, to the [end] to deliver up him to the power and
τῇ ἐξουσίᾳ τοῦ ἡγεμόνος. 21 καὶ ἐπηρώτησαν αὐτόν, λέγον-
to the authority of the governor. And they questioned him, say-
τες, Διδάσκαλε, οἴδαμεν ὅτι ὀρθῶς λέγεις καὶ διδάσκεις, καὶ
ing, Teacher, we know that rightly thou sayest and teachest, and
οὐ.λαμβάνεις πρόσωπον, ἀλλ' ἐπ' ἀληθείας τὴν ὁδὸν
acceptest not [any man's] person, but with truth the way
τοῦ θεοῦ διδάσκεις. 22 ἔξεστιν [s]ἡμῖν‖ Καίσαρι φόρον δοῦναι
of God teachest: is it lawful for us [4]to [5]Cæsar [3]tribute [1]to [2]give
ἢ οὔ; 23 Κατανοήσας.δὲ αὐτῶν τὴν.πανουργίαν εἶπεν πρὸς
or not? But perceiving their craftiness he said to

they wounded him also, and cast *him* out. 13 Then said the lord of the vineyard, What shall I do? I will send my beloved son: it may be they will reverence *him* when they see him. 14 But when the husbandmen saw him, they reasoned among themselves, saying, This is the heir: come, let us kill him, that the inheritance may be ours. 15 So they cast him out of the vineyard, and killed *him*. What therefore shall the lord of the vineyard do unto them? 16 He shall come and destroy these husbandmen, and shall give the vineyard to others. And when they heard *it*, they said, God forbid. 17 And he beheld them, and said, What is this then that is written, The stone which the builders rejected, the same is become the head of the corner? 18 Whosoever shall fall upon that stone shall be broken; but on whomsoever it shall fall, it will grind him to powder. 19 And the chief priests and the scribes the same hour sought to lay hands on him; and they feared the people: for they perceived that he had spoken this parable against them.

20 And they watched *him*, and sent forth spies, which should feign themselves just men, that they might take hold of his words, that so they might deliver him unto the power and authority of the governor. 21 And they asked him, saying, Master, we know that thou sayest and teachest rightly, neither acceptest thou the person *of any*, but teachest the way of God truly: 22 is it lawful for us to give tribute unto Cæsar, or no? 23 But he perceived their craftiness, and said unto them, Why

---

[e] κἀκεῖνον L. [f] — ἰδόντες LTTr[A]. [g] διελογίσαντο L. [h] ἀλλήλους one another TTrA. [i] — δεῦτε LTTrA. [k] οἱ δὲ ἀκούσαντες L. [l] εἶπαν LTTrA. [m] ἐζήτουν L. [n] γραμματεῖς καὶ οἱ ἀρχιερεῖς LTTrA. [o] εἶπεν τὴν παραβολὴν ταύτην LTTrA. [p] ἐνκαθέτους T. [q] λόγον (read of his discourse) Tr. [r] ὥστε so as LTTrA. [s] ἡμᾶς TTrA.

tempt ye me? 24 Shew me a penny. Whose image and superscription hath it? They answered and said, Cæsar's. 25 And he said unto them, Render therefore unto Cæsar the things which be Cæsar's, and unto God the things which be God's. 26 And they could not take hold of his words before the people: and they marvelled at his answer, and held their peace.

27 Then came to *him* certain of the Sadducees, which deny that there is any resurrection; and they asked him, 28 saying, Master, Moses wrote unto us, If any man's brother die, having a wife, and he die without children, that his brother should take his wife, and raise up seed unto his brother. 29 There were therefore seven brethren: and the first took a wife, and died without children. 30 And the second took her to wife, and he died childless. 31 And the third took her; and in like manner the seven also: and they left no children, and died. 32 Last of all the woman died also. 33 Therefore in the resurrection whose wife of them is she? for seven had her to wife. 34 And Jesus answering said unto them, The children of this world marry, and are given in marriage: 35 but they which shall be accounted worthy to obtain that world, and the resurrection from the dead, neither marry, nor are given in marriage: 36 neither can they die any more: for they are equal unto the angels; and are the children of God, being the children of the resurrection. 37 Now that the dead are raised, even Moses shewed at the bush, when he

αὐτούς, [t]Τί με πειράζετε‖; 24 [v]ἐπιδείξατέ‖ μοι δηνάριον·[w]
them, Why me do ye tempt? Shew me a denarius:
τίνος ἔχει εἰκόνα καὶ ἐπιγραφήν; [x]Ἀποκριθέντες‖.δὲ [y]εἶπον,‖
whose [4]has [5]it [1]image [2]and [3]inscription? And answering they said,
Καίσαρος. 25 Ὁ.δὲ εἶπεν [z]αὐτοῖς,‖ [a]Ἀπόδοτε τοίνυν‖ τὰ
Cæsar's. And he said to them, Render therefore the things
Καίσαρος [b] Καίσαρι, καὶ τὰ τοῦ θεοῦ τῷ θεῷ. 26 Καὶ
of Cæsar to Cæsar, and the things of God to God. And
οὐκ.ἴσχυσαν ἐπιλαβέσθαι [c]αὐτοῦ‖.ῥήματος ἐναντίον τοῦ
they were not able to take hold of his speech before the
λαοῦ· καὶ θαυμάσαντες ἐπὶ τῇ.ἀποκρίσει.αὐτοῦ ἐσίγησαν.
people; and wondering at his answer they were silent.

27 Προσελθόντες.δέ τινες τῶν Σαδδουκαίων, οἱ [d]ἀντι-
And having come to [him] some of the Sadducees, who deny
λεγοντες‖ ἀνάστασιν μὴ εἶναι, ἐπηρώτησαν αὐτόν, 28 λέγον-
[3]a [4]resurrection [1]there [2]is, they questioned him, say-
τες, Διδάσκαλε, [e]Μωσῆς‖ ἔγραψεν ἡμῖν, ἐάν τινος ἀδελφὸς
ing, Teacher, Moses wrote to us, If anyone's brother
ἀποθάνῃ ἔχων γυναῖκα, καὶ οὗτος ἄτεκνος [f]ἀποθάνῃ,‖ ἵνα
should die having a wife, and he childless should die, that
λάβῃ ὁ.ἀδελφὸς.αὐτοῦ τὴν γυναῖκα καὶ ἐξαναστήσῃ σπέρμα
[3]should [4]take [1]his [2]brother the wife and should raise up seed
τῷ.ἀδελφῷ.αὐτοῦ. 29 ἑπτὰ οὖν ἀδελφοὶ ἦσαν· καὶ ὁ πρῶτος
to his brother. [4]Seven [3]then [5]brethren [1]there [2]were; and the first
λαβὼν γυναῖκα ἀπέθανεν ἄτεκνος· 30 καὶ [g]ἔλαβεν‖ ὁ
having taken a wife died childless; and [3]took [1]the
δεύτερος [h]τὴν γυναῖκα, καὶ οὗτος ἀπέθανεν ἄτεκνος·‖ 31 καὶ
[2]second the woman, and he died childless; and
ὁ τρίτος ἔλαβεν αὐτήν[i]· ὡσαύτως.δὲ καὶ οἱ ἑπτὰ [k] οὐ.κατ-
the third took her; and likewise also the seven did not
έλιπον τέκνα, καὶ ἀπέθανον· 32 ὕστερον [l]δὲ πάντων‖ [m]ἀπέ-
leave children, and died; [2]last [1]and of all died
θανεν καὶ ἡ γυνή.‖ 33 [n]ἐν.τῇ.οὖν‖ ἀναστάσει τίνος αὐτῶν
also the woman. Therefore in the resurrection of which of them
γίνεται γυνή; οἱ.γὰρ ἑπτὰ ἔσχον αὐτὴν γυναῖκα. 34 Καὶ
does she become wife? for the seven had her as wife. And
[o]ἀποκριθεὶς‖ εἶπεν αὐτοῖς ὁ Ἰησοῦς, Οἱ υἱοὶ τοῦ.αἰῶνος.τούτου
answering [2]said [3]to [4]them [1]Jesus, The sons of this age
γαμοῦσιν καὶ [p]ἐκγαμίσκονται·‖ 35 οἱ.δὲ καταξιωθέντες τοῦ
marry and are given in marriage; but those accounted worthy
αἰῶνος.ἐκείνου τυχεῖν καὶ τῆς ἀναστάσεως τῆς ἐκ
[3]that [4]age [1]to [2]obtain and the resurrection which [is] from among
νεκρῶν οὔτε γαμοῦσιν οὔτε [q]ἐκγαμίσκονται·‖ 36 [r]οὔτε‖
[the] dead neither marry nor are given in marriage; [2]neither
γὰρ ἀποθανεῖν ἔτι δύνανται· ἰσάγγελοι.γάρ εἰσιν, καὶ
[1]for [5]die [6]any [7]more [4]they [3]can; for equal to angels they are, and
υἱοί εἰσιν [s]τοῦ‖ θεοῦ, τῆς ἀναστάσεως υἱοὶ ὄντες. 37 Ὅτι.δὲ
sons are of God, [3]of [4]the [5]resurrection [2]sons [1]being. But that
ἐγείρονται οἱ νεκροί, καὶ [e]Μωσῆς‖ ἐμήνυσεν ἐπὶ τῆς
are raised the dead, even Moses shewed [in the part] on the

[t] — Τί με πειράζετε TTrA. [v] δείξατέ GLTTrAW. [w] + [οἱ δὲ ἔδειξαν. καὶ εἶπεν] and they shewed [it]. And he said L. [x] οἱ (*read* and they said) T. [y] εἶπαν TTrA. [z] πρὸς αὐτούς TTrA. [a] Τοίνυν ἀπόδοτε TTrA. [b] + τῷ Tr. [c] τοῦ (*read* [his]) A. [d] λέγοντες (*read* who say there is not (μὴ) a resurrection) Tr. [e] Μωϋσῆς LTTrAW. [f] ᾖ should be LTTrA. [g] — ἔλαβεν TTrA. [h] — τὴν γυναῖκα, καὶ οὗτος ἀπέθανεν ἄτεκνος TTrA. [i] + [ὡσαύτως] likewise L. [k] + καὶ even E. [l] — δὲ πάντων LTTrA. [m] καὶ ἡ γυνὴ ἀπέθανεν TTrA. [n] ἡ γυνὴ οὖν ἐν τῇ the woman therefore in the TA. [o] — ἀποκριθεὶς LTTrA. [p] γαμίσκονται LTTrA. [q] γαμίζονται LTTr; γαμίσκονται A. [r] οὐδὲ LTrA. [s] — τοῦ TTrA.

βάτου, ὡς λέγει κύριον τὸν θεὸν Ἀβραὰμ καὶ [t]τὸν‖ θεὸν
bush, when he called [the] Lord the God of Abraham and the God
Ἰσαὰκ καὶ [t]τὸν‖ θεὸν Ἰακώβ· 38 θεὸς.δὲ οὐκ.ἔστιν νεκρῶν,
of Isaac and the God of Jacob; but God he is not of [the] dead,
ἀλλὰ ζώντων. πάντες.γὰρ αὐτῷ ζῶσιν. 39 Ἀποκριθέν-
but of [the] living; for all for him live. [2]Answering
τες δέ τινες τῶν γραμματέων [v]εἶπον,‖ Διδάσκαλε, καλῶς
[1]and some of the scribes said, Teacher, well
εἶπας. 40 Οὐκέτι [x]δὲ‖ ἐτόλμων ἐπερωτᾷν αὐτὸν
thou hast spoken. [2]Not [3]any [4]more [1]and did they dare to ask him
οὐδέν.
anything.
(lit. nothing.)

calleth the Lord the God of Abraham, and the God of Isaac, and the God of Jacob. 38 For he is not a God of the dead, but of the living: for all live unto him. 39 Then certain of the scribes answering said, Master, thou hast well said. 40 And after that they durst not ask him any *question at all.*

41 Εἶπεν.δὲ πρὸς αὐτούς, Πῶς λέγουσιν τὸν χριστὸν [y]υἱὸν
And he said to them, How do they say the Christ [2]Son
[z]Δαβὶδ‖ εἶναι‖; 42 [a]καὶ αὐτὸς‖ [z]Δαβὶδ‖ λέγει ἐν βίβλῳ
[3]of [4]David [1]is? and [2]himself [1]David says in [the] book
[b]ψαλμῶν, Εἶπεν [c]ὁ‖ κύριος τῷ.κυρίῳ.μου, Κάθου ἐκ δεξιῶν.μου,
of Psalms, [3]Said [1]the [2]Lord to my Lord, Sit on my right hand,
43 ἕως.ἂν θῶ τοὺς.ἐχθρούς.σου ὑποπόδιον τῶν.ποδῶν.σου.
until I place thine enemies [as] a footstool for thy feet.
44 [z]Δαβὶδ‖ οὖν [d]κύριον αὐτὸν‖ καλεῖ, καὶ πῶς [e]υἱὸς.αὐτοῦ‖
David therefore [3]Lord [2]him [1]calls, and how his son
ἐστιν;
is he?

41 And he said unto them, How say they that Christ is David's son? 42 And David himself saith in the book of Psalms, The LORD said unto my Lord, Sit thou on my right hand, 43 till I make thine enemies thy footstool. 44 David therefore calleth him Lord, how is he then his son?

45 Ἀκούοντος.δὲ παντὸς τοῦ λαοῦ εἶπεν [f]τοῖς μαθηταῖς
And as were listening all the people he said to [2]disciples
αὐτοῦ,‖ 46 Προσέχετε ἀπὸ τῶν γραμματέων τῶν θελόντων
[1]his, Beware of the scribes who like
περιπατεῖν ἐν στολαῖς, καὶ φιλούντων ἀσπασμοὺς ἐν ταῖς
to walk in robes, and love salutations in the
ἀγοραῖς καὶ πρωτοκαθεδρίας ἐν ταῖς συναγωγαῖς καὶ πρω-
market-places and first seats in the synagogues and first
τοκλισίας ἐν τοῖς δείπνοις· 47 [g]οἳ κατεσθίουσιν‖ τὰς οἰκίας
places in the suppers; who devour the houses
τῶν χηρῶν, καὶ προφάσει μακρὰ [h]προσεύχονται.‖ οὗτοι
of widows, and as a pretext [2]at [3]great [4]length [1]pray. These
[i]λήψονται‖ περισσότερον κρίμα.
shall receive more abundant judgment.

45 Then in the audience of all the people he said unto his disciples, 46 Beware of the scribes, which desire to walk in long robes, and love greetings in the markets, and the highest seats in the synagogues, and the chief rooms at feasts; 47 which devour widows' houses, and for a shew make long prayers: the same shall receive greater damnation.

21 Ἀναβλέψας.δὲ εἶδεν τοὺς βάλλοντας [k]τὰ.δῶρα.αὐτῶν
And having looked up he saw the [2]casting [3]their [4]gifts
εἰς τὸ γαζοφυλάκιον‖ πλουσίους· 2 εἶδεν.δὲ [l]καί τινα‖
[5]into [6]the [7]treasury [1]rich, and he saw also a certain
χήραν πενιχρὰν βάλλουσαν ἐκεῖ [m]δύο λεπτά·‖ 3 καὶ εἶπεν,
[2]widow [1]poor casting therein two lepta. And he said,
Ἀληθῶς λέγω ὑμῖν, ὅτι ἡ χήρα [n]ἡ πτωχὴ αὕτη‖ [o]πλεῖον‖
Of a truth I say to you, that [3]widow [2]poor [1]this more
πάντων ἔβαλεν· 4 [p]ἅπαντες‖.γὰρ οὗτοι ἐκ τοῦ περισ-
than all cast in; for all these out of that which was
σεύοντος αὐτοῖς ἔβαλον εἰς τὰ δῶρα [q]τοῦ θεοῦ,‖ αὕτη.δὲ
abounding to them cast into the gifts of God; but she

XXI. And he looked up, and saw the rich men casting their gifts into the treasury. 2 And he saw also a certain poor widow casting in thither two mites. 3 And he said, Of a truth I say unto you, that this poor widow hath cast in more than they all: 4 for all these have of their abundance cast in unto the offerings of God: but she

[t] — τὸν LTTrA. [v] εἶπαν LTTrA. [x] γὰρ for TTrA. [y] εἶναι Δαυεὶδ υἱόν TA. [z] Δαυῒδ GW; Δαυεὶδ LTTrA. [a] αὐτὸς γὰρ for [2]himself T. [b] + τῶν the L. [c] — ὁ (read [the]) LTrA. [d] αὐτὸν κύριον TrA. [e] αὐτοῦ υἱός TTrA. [f] — αὐτοῦ (read the disciples) TTr; πρὸς αὐτούς to them A. [g] οἱ κατεσθίοντες those devouring L. [h] προσευχόμενοι praying L. [i] λήμψονται LTTrA. [k] εἰς τὸ γαζοφυλάκιον τὰ δῶρα αὐτῶν TTrA. [l] [καί] τινα L; τινα [καὶ] A; — καὶ TTr. [m] λεπτὰ δύο Tr. [n] αὕτη ἡ πτωχὴ LTr. [o] πλείω LTA. [p] πάντες L. [q] — τοῦ θεοῦ T[Tr]A.

of her penury hath
cast in all the living
that she had.

5 And as some spake
of the temple, how it
was adorned with
goodly stones and
gifts, he said, 6 *As
for* these things which
ye behold, the days
will come, in the which
there shall not be left
one stone upon an-
other, that shall not
be thrown down.
7 And they asked him,
saying, Master, but
when shall these things
be? and what sign
will there be when
these things shall come
to pass? 8 And he said,
Take heed that ye
be not deceived: for
many shall come in
my name, saying, I am
Christ; and the time
draweth near: go ye
not therefore after
them. 9 But when ye
shall hear of wars and
commotions, be not
terrified: for these
things must first come
to pass; but the end *is*
not by and by. 10 Then
said he unto them,
Nation shall rise a-
gainst nation, and
kingdom against king-
dom: 11 and great
earthquakes shall be
in divers places, and
famines, and pesti-
lences; and fearful
sights and great signs
shall there be from
heaven. 12 But before
all these, they shall
lay their hands on you,
and persecute *you,* de-
livering *you* up to the
synagogues, and into
prisons, being brought
before kings and rulers
for my name's sake.
13 And it shall turn to
you for a testimony.
14 Settle *it* therefore
in your hearts, not to
meditate before what
ye shall answer: 15 for
I will give you a mouth
and wisdom, which all
your adversaries shall
not be able to gainsay
nor resist. 16 And ye
shall be betrayed both
by parents, and breth-

ἐκ τοῦ.ὑστερήματος.αὐτῆς [r]ἅπαντα‖ τὸν βίον ὃν εἶχεν
out of her poverty all the livelihood which she had

ἔβαλεν.
did cast.

5 Καί τινων λεγόντων περὶ τοῦ ἱεροῦ, ὅτι λίθοις καλοῖς
And as some were speaking about the temple, that with [2]stones [1]goodly

καὶ [s]ἀναθήμασιν‖ κεκόσμηται, εἶπεν, 6 Ταῦτα ἃ θεω-
and consecrated gifts it was adorned, he said, [As to] these things which ye are

ρεῖτε, ἐλεύσονται ἡμέραι ἐν αἷς οὐκ.ἀφεθήσεται λίθος ἐπὶ
beholding, [2]will [3]come [1]days in which shall not be left stone upon

λίθῳ [t] ὃς οὐ.καταλυθήσεται. 7 Ἐπηρώτησαν.δὲ αὐτόν, λέ-
stone which shall not be thrown down. And they asked him, say-

γοντες, Διδάσκαλε, πότε οὖν ταῦτα ἔσται; καὶ τί τὸ
ing, Teacher, when then [2]these [3]things [1]will be? and what the

σημεῖον ὅταν μέλλῃ ταῦτα γίνεσθαι; 8 Ὁ.δὲ εἶπεν,
sign when [3]are [4]about [1]these [2]things to take place? And he said,

Βλέπετε μὴ.πλανηθῆτε· πολλοὶ.γὰρ ἐλεύσονται ἐπὶ τῷ
Take heed ye be not led astray; for many will come in

ὀνόματί.μου, λέγοντες, [v]Ὅτι‖ ἐγώ εἰμι· καί, Ὁ καιρὸς ἤγ-
my name, saying, I am [he]; and, The time is

γικεν. μὴ [w]οὖν‖ πορευθῆτε ὀπίσω αὐτῶν. 9 ὅταν.δὲ
drawn near. [3]Not [4]therefore [1]go [2]ye after them. And when

ἀκούσητε πολέμους καὶ ἀκαταστασίας, μὴ.πτοηθῆτε· δεῖ
ye shall hear of wars and commotions, be not terrified; [4]must

γὰρ [x]ταῦτα γενέσθαι‖ πρῶτον, ἀλλ' οὐκ εὐθέως τὸ
[1]for [2]these [3]things take place first, but not immediately [is] the

τέλος. 10 Τότε ἔλεγεν αὐτοῖς, Ἐγερθήσεται ἔθνος [y]ἐπὶ‖
end. Then he was saying to them, [2]Shall [3]rise [4]up [1]nation against

ἔθνος, καὶ βασιλεία ἐπὶ βασιλείαν· 11 σεισμοί.τε μεγάλοι
nation, and kingdom against kingdom; also [2]earthquakes [1]great

[z]κατὰ τόπους καὶ‖ [a]λιμοὶ καὶ λοιμοὶ‖ ἔσονται, [b]φόβη-
in different places and famines and pestilences shall there be, [2]fearful

τρά‖ τε καὶ [c]σημεῖα ἀπ' οὐρανοῦ‖ μεγάλα ἔσται. 12 Πρὸ
[3]sights [1]and and [2]signs [3]from [4]heaven [1]great shall there be. [2]Before

δὲ τούτων [d]ἁπάντων‖ ἐπιβαλοῦσιν ἐφ' ὑμᾶς τὰς χεῖρας
[1]but [4]these [5]things [3]all they will lay upon you [2]hands

αὐτῶν, καὶ διώξουσιν, παραδιδόντες εἰς [e] συναγωγὰς καὶ
[1]their, and will persecute [you], delivering up to synagogues and

φυλακάς, [f]ἀγομένους‖ ἐπὶ βασιλεῖς καὶ ἡγεμόνας, ἕνεκεν
prisons, bringing [you] before kings and governors, on account of

τοῦ.ὀνόματός.μου. 13 ἀποβήσεται.[g]δὲ‖ ὑμῖν εἰς μαρτύριον·
my name; but it shall turn out to you for a testimony.

14 [h]θέσθε‖ οὖν [i]εἰς τὰς καρδίας‖.ὑμῶν μὴ προμελετᾷν ἀπο-
Settle therefore in your hearts not to premeditate to make

λογηθῆναι· 15 ἐγὼ.γὰρ δώσω ὑμῖν στόμα καὶ σοφίαν, ᾗ
a defence; for I will give you a mouth and wisdom, which

οὐ.δυνήσονται [k]ἀντειπεῖν [l]οὐδὲ[l] ἀντιστῆναι‖ [m]πάντες‖ οἱ
[5]shall [6]not [7]be [8]able [9]to [10]reply [11]to [12]nor [13]to [14]resist [1]all [2]those

ἀντικείμενοι ὑμῖν. 16 παραδοθήσεσθε.δὲ καὶ ὑπὸ γονέων καὶ
[3]opposing [4]you. But ye will be delivered up even by parents and

---

[r] πάντα LTr. [s] ἀναθέμασιν LT. [t] + ὧδε here L. [v] — ὅτι [L]T[TrA]. [w] — οὖν LTTrA.
[x] γενέσθαι ταῦτα A. [y] ἐπ' LTTrA. [z] καὶ κατὰ τόπους TTrA. [a] λοιμοὶ καὶ λιμοὶ LTrA.
[b] φόβηθρά LTrA. [c] ἀπ' οὐρανοῦ σημεῖα L. [d] πάντων GLTTrAW. [e] + τὰς the TTr[A].
[f] ἀπαγομένους leading [you] away TTrA. [g] — δὲ but T[TrA]. [h] θέτε LTTrA. [i] ἐν ταῖς
καρδίαις LTTrA. [k] ἀντιστῆναι οὐδὲ ἀντειπεῖν L; ἀντιστῆναι ἢ ἀντειπεῖν ([ἢ ἀντειπ.] Tr) TTrA.
[l] ἢ or G. [m] ἅπαντες TTrA.

ἀδελφῶν καὶ συγγενῶν καὶ φίλων, καὶ θανατώσουσιν
brethren and relations and friends, and they will put to death [some]
ἐξ ὑμῶν· 17 καὶ ἔσεσθε μισούμενοι ὑπὸ πάντων διὰ
from among you, and ye will be hated by all because of
τὸ.ὄνομά.μου. 18 καὶ θρὶξ ἐκ τῆς.κεφαλῆς.ὑμῶν οὐ.μὴ ἀπό-
my name. And a hair of your head in no wise may
ληται. 19 ἐν τῇ.ὑπομονῇ.ὑμῶν [n]κτήσασθε‖ τὰς.ψυχὰς.ὑμῶν.
perish. By your patient endurance gain your souls.
20 Ὅταν.δὲ ἴδητε κυκλουμένην ὑπὸ στρατοπέδων [o]τὴν‖ Ἱερου-
But when ye see [2]being [3]encircled [4]with [5]armies [1]Jeru-
σαλήμ, τότε γνῶτε ὅτι ἤγγικεν ἡ.ἐρήμωσις.αὐτῆς. 21 τότε
salem then know that has drawn near her desolation. Then
οἱ ἐν τῇ Ἰουδαίᾳ φευγέτωσαν εἰς τὰ ὄρη· καὶ οἱ ἐν
those in Judæa let them flee to the mountains; and those in
μέσῳ.αὐτῆς ἐκχωρείτωσαν· καὶ οἱ ἐν ταῖς χώραις μὴ εἰσερχέ-
her midst let them depart out, and those in the countries [3]not [1]let [2]them
σθωσαν εἰς αὐτήν. 22 ὅτι ἡμέραι ἐκδικήσεως αὗταί εἰσιν, τοῦ
enter into her; for days of avenging these are,
[p]πληρωθῆναι‖ πάντα τὰ γεγραμμένα. 23 οὐαὶ.[q]δὲ‖ ταῖς
that may be accomplished all things that have been written. But woe to those
ἐν.γαστρὶ.ἐχούσαις καὶ ταῖς θηλαζούσαις ἐν ἐκείναις ταῖς ἡμέ-
with child and to those giving suck in those days,
ραις· ἔσται.γὰρ ἀνάγκη μεγάλη ἐπὶ τῆς γῆς καὶ ὀργὴ [r]ἐν‖
for there shall be [2]distress [1]great upon the land and wrath among
τῷ.λαῷ.τούτῳ. 24 καὶ πεσοῦνται στόματι [s]μαχαίρας,‖ καὶ
this people. And they shall fall by [the] mouth of [the] sword, and
αἰχμαλωτισθήσονται εἰς [t]πάντα τὰ ἔθνη·‖ καὶ Ἱερουσαλὴμ
shall be led captive into all the nations; and Jerusalem
ἔσται πατουμένη ὑπὸ ἐθνῶν [v]ἄχρι‖ [w] πληρωθῶσιν
shall be trodden down by [the] nations until be fulfilled [the]
καιροὶ ἐθνῶν. 25 Καὶ [x]ἔσται‖ σημεῖα ἐν ἡλίῳ καὶ σελήνῃ
times of [the] nations. And there shall be signs in sun and moon
καὶ ἄστροις, καὶ ἐπὶ τῆς γῆς συνοχὴ ἐθνῶν ἐν ἀπορίᾳ,
and stars, and upon the earth distress of nations with perplexity,
[y]ἠχούσης‖ θαλάσσης καὶ σάλου, 26 ἀποψυχόντων ἀνθρώ-
roaring of [the] sea and rolling surge, [2]fainting [3]at [4]heart [1]men
πων ἀπὸ φόβου καὶ προσδοκίας τῶν ἐπερχομένων τῇ
from fear and expectation of that which is coming on the
οἰκουμένῃ· αἱ.γὰρ δυνάμεις τῶν οὐρανῶν σαλευθήσονται.
habitable earth; for the powers of the heavens shall be shaken.
27 καὶ τότε ὄψονται τὸν υἱὸν τοῦ ἀνθρώπου ἐρχόμενον ἐν
And then shall they see the Son of man coming in
νεφέλῃ μετὰ δυνάμεως καὶ δόξης πολλῆς. 28 Ἀρχομένων.δὲ
a cloud with power and [2]glory [1]great. But [3]beginning
τούτων γίνεσθαι ἀνακύψατε καὶ ἐπάρατε τὰς κεφαλὰς
[1]these [2]things to come to pass look up and lift up [2]heads
ὑμῶν· διότι ἐγγίζει ἡ.ἀπολύτρωσις.ὑμῶν. 29 Καὶ εἶπεν
[1]your, because draws near your redemption. And he spoke
παραβολὴν αὐτοῖς, Ἴδετε τὴν συκῆν καὶ πάντα τὰ δένδρα.
a parable to them: Behold the fig-tree and all the trees:
30 ὅταν προβάλωσιν ἤδη, βλέποντες ἀφ' ἑαυτῶν
when [2]they [3]sprout [1]already, looking [on them] of yourselves

ren, and kinsfolks, and
friends; and *some* of
you shall they cause
to be put to death.
17 And ye shall be
hated of all *men* for
my name's sake. 18 But
there shall not an hair
of your head perish.
19 In your patience
possess ye your souls.
20 And when ye shall
see Jerusalem com-
passed with armies,
then know that the de-
solation thereof is
nigh. 21 Then let them
which are in Judæa
flee to the mountains;
and let them which are
in the midst of it de-
part out; and let not
them that are in the
countries enter there-
into. 22 For these be
the days of vengeance,
that all things which
are written may be
fulfilled. 23 But woe
unto them that are
with child, and to
them that give suck,
in those days! for there
shall be great distress
in the land, and wrath
upon this people.
24 And they shall fall
by the edge of the
sword, and shall be
led away captive into
all nations: and Jeru-
salem shall be trodden
down of the Gentiles,
until the times of the
Gentiles be fulfilled.
25 And there shall be
signs in the sun, and
in the moon, and in
the stars; and upon
the earth distress of
nations, with per-
plexity; the sea and
the waves roaring;
26 men's hearts failing
them for fear, and for
looking after those
things which are com-
ing on the earth: for
the powers of heaven
shall be shaken. 27 And
then shall they see the
Son of man coming in
a cloud with power and
great glory. 28 And
when these things be-
gin to come to pass,
then look up, and
lift up your heads;
for your redemption
draweth nigh. 29 And
he spake to them a pa-
rable; Behold the fig
tree, and all the trees;
30 when they now
shoot forth, ye see and

---

[n] κτήσεσθε ye shall gain LTrA. [o] — τὴν LTTrA. [p] πλησθῆναι GLTTrAW. [q] — δὲ but LTTrA. [r] — ἐν (*read* to this people) GLTTrAW. [s] μαχαίρης TTr. [t] τὰ ἔθνη πάντα LTTrA. [v] ἄχρις L. [w] + οὗ LTTrA. [x] ἔσονται LTTrA. [y] ἤχους at [the] sound GLTTrAW.

know of your own
selves that summer is
now nigh at hand.
31 So likewise ye, when
ye see these things
come to pass, know ye
that the kingdom of
God is nigh at hand.
32 Verily I say unto
you, This generation
shall not pass away,
till all be fulfilled.
33 Heaven and earth
shall pass away: but
my words shall not
pass away. 34 And
take heed to your-
selves, lest at any time
your hearts be over-
charged with surfeit-
ing, and drunkenness,
and cares of this life,
and *so* that day come
upon you unawares.
35 For as a snare shall
it come on all them
that dwell on the face
of the whole earth.
36 Watch ye therefore,
and pray always, that
ye may be accounted
worthy to escape all
these things that shall
come to pass, and to
stand before the Son
of man.

37 And in the day
time he was teaching
in the temple; and at
night he went out, and
abode in the mount
that is called *the mount*
of Olives. 38 And all
the people came early
in the morning to him
in the temple, for to
hear him.

XXII. Now the feast
of unleavened bread
drew nigh, which is
called the Passover.
2 And the chief priests
and scribes sought
how they might kill
him; for they feared
the people. 3 Then
entered Satan into Ju-
das surnamed Iscariot,
being of the number
of the twelve. 4 And
he went his way, and
communed with the
chief priests and cap-
tains, how he might
betray him unto them.
5 And they were glad,
and covenanted to
give him money.
6 And he promised,

γινώσκετε ὅτι ἤδη ἐγγὺς τὸ θέρος ἐστίν. 31 οὕτως καὶ ὑμεῖς,
ye know that already near the summer is. So also ye,
ὅταν ἴδητε ταῦτα γινόμενα γινώσκετε ὅτι ἐγγύς ἐστιν ἡ
when ye see these things coming to pass know that near is the
βασιλεία τοῦ θεοῦ. 32 ἀμὴν λέγω ὑμῖν, ὅτι οὐ.μὴ παρ-
kingdom of God. Verily I say to you, that in no wise will have
έλθῃ ἡ.γενεὰ.αὕτη ἕως.ἂν πάντα γένηται. 33 ὁ
passed away this generation until all shall have taken place. The
οὐρανὸς καὶ ἡ γῆ παρελεύσονται, οἱ.δὲ.λόγοι.μου οὐ.μὴ
heaven and the earth shall pass away, but my words in no wise
[z]παρέλθωσιν.‖ 34 Προσέχετε.δὲ ἑαυτοῖς, μήποτε [a]βαρυνθῶ-
may pass away. But take heed to yourselves, lest be laden
σιν‖ [b]ὑμῶν αἱ καρδίαι‖ ἐν κραιπάλῃ καὶ μέθῃ καὶ μερίμναις
your hearts with surfeiting and drinking and cares
βιωτικαῖς, καὶ [c]αἰφνίδιος ἐφ' ὑμᾶς ἐπιστῇ‖ ἡ.ἡμέρα.ἐκείνη·
of life, and suddenly upon you should come that day;
35 ὡς.[d]παγὶς.γὰρ ἐπελεύσεται‖ ἐπὶ πάντας τοὺς καθημένους
for as a snare shall it come upon all those sitting
ἐπὶ πρόσωπον πάσης τῆς γῆς. 36 ἀγρυπνεῖτε [e]οὖν‖ ἐν
upon the face of all the earth. Watch therefore at
παντὶ καιρῷ δεόμενοι, ἵνα [f]καταξιωθῆτε‖ ἐκφυγεῖν ταῦ-
every season praying, that ye may be accounted worthy to escape [2]these
τα πάντα τὰ μέλλοντα γίνεσθαι, καὶ σταθῆναι ἔμπρο-
[3]things [1]all which are about to come to pass, and to stand before
σθεν τοῦ υἱοῦ τοῦ ἀνθρώπου.
the Son of man.

37 Ἦν.δὲ τὰς.ἡμέρας [g]ἐν τῷ ἱερῷ διδάσκων·‖ τὰς.δὲ.νύκτας
And he was by day in the temple teaching, and by night
ἐξερχόμενος ηὐλίζετο εἰς τὸ ὄρος τὸ καλούμενον ἐλαιῶν·
going out he lodged on the mount called of Olives;
38 καὶ πᾶς ὁ λαὸς ὤρθριζεν πρὸς αὐτὸν ἐν τῷ
and all the people came early in the morning to him in the
ἱερῷ ἀκούειν αὐτοῦ.
temple to hear him.

22 Ἤγγιζεν.δὲ ἡ ἑορτὴ τῶν.ἀζύμων ἡ λεγομένη
And drew near the feast of unleavened [bread] which [is] called
πάσχα· 2 καὶ ἐζήτουν οἱ ἀρχιερεῖς καὶ οἱ γραμματεῖς
passover; and [7]were [8]seeking [1]the [2]chief [3]priests [4]and [5]the [6]scribes
τὸ.πῶς ἀνέλωσιν αὐτόν· ἐφοβοῦντο.γὰρ τὸν λαόν.
as to how they might put [2]to [3]death [1]him, for they feared the people.
3 Εἰσῆλθεν.δὲ [h]ὁ‖ σατανᾶς εἰς Ἰούδαν τὸν [i]ἐπικαλούμενον‖
And [2]entered [1]Satan into Judas who is surnamed
Ἰσκαριώτην, ὄντα ἐκ τοῦ ἀριθμοῦ τῶν δώδεκα· 4 καὶ ἀπελ-
Iscariote, being of the number of the twelve. And having gone
θὼν συνελάλησεν τοῖς ἀρχιερεῦσιν [k] καὶ [l]τοῖς‖ στρατηγοῖς
away he spoke with the chief priests and the captains
τὸ.πῶς [m]αὐτὸν παραδῷ αὐτοῖς.‖ 5 καὶ ἐχάρησαν, καὶ
as to how him he might deliver up to them. And they rejoiced, and
συνέθεντο αὐτῷ ἀργύριον δοῦναι· 6 [n]καὶ ἐξωμολόγησεν,‖ καὶ
agreed [3]him [4]money [1]to [2]give. And he promised, and

---

[z] παρελεύσονται shall pass away LTTrA. [a] βαρηθῶσιν GLTTrAW. [b] αἱ καρδίαι ὑμῶν LTr. [c] αἰφνίδιος ἐπιστῇ ἐφ' ὑμᾶς L; ἐπιστῇ ἐφ' ὑμᾶς αἰφνίδιος TTrA. [d] παγίς· ἐπεισελεύσεται γὰρ (*read* that day as a snare: for it shall come in) LTTrA. [e] δὲ but (watch) LTTrA. [f] κατισχύσητε ye may prevail TTrA. [g] διδάσκων εν τῷ ἱερῷ Tr. [h] — ὁ GLTTrAW. [i] καλούμενον is called TTrA. [k] + καὶ τοῖς γραμματεῦσιν and the scribes L. [l] — τοῖς TTrA. [m] αὐτοῖς παραδῷ αὐτόν LTTrA. [n] — καὶ ἐξωμολόγησεν (*read* he sought) L.

ἐζήτει εὐκαιρίαν τοῦ παραδοῦναι αὐτὸν [o]αὐτοῖς ἄτερ
sought opportunity to deliver up him to them away from [the]
ὄχλου.‖
crowd.
7 [r]Ἦλθεν.δὲ ἡ ἡμέρα τῶν.ἀζύμων [p]ἐν‖ ᾗ ἔδει
And came the day of unleavened [bread] in which was needful
θύεσθαι τὸ πάσχα. 8 καὶ ἀπέστειλεν Πέτρον καὶ [q]Ἰωάννην,‖
to be killed the passover. And he sent Peter and John,
εἰπών, Πορευθέντες ἑτοιμάσατε ἡμῖν τὸ πάσχα, ἵνα φάγω-
saying, Having gone prepare for us the passover, that we may
μεν. 9 Οἱ.δὲ [r]εἶπον‖ αὐτῷ, Ποῦ θέλεις ἑτοιμάσωμεν[s];
eat [it]. But they said to him, Where willest thou we should prepare?
10 Ὁ.δὲ εἶπεν αὐτοῖς, Ἰδού, εἰσελθόντων.ὑμῶν εἰς τὴν πόλιν
And he said to them, Lo, on your having entered into the city
συναντήσει ὑμῖν ἄνθρωπος κεράμιον ὕδατος βαστάζων· ἀκο-
[3]will [4]meet [5]you [1]a [2]man, a pitcher of water carrying; fol-
λουθήσατε αὐτῷ εἰς τὴν οἰκίαν [t]οὗ‖ εἰσπορεύεται· 11 καὶ
low him into the house where he enters; and
ἐρεῖτε τῷ οἰκοδεσπότῃ τῆς οἰκίας, Λέγει σοι ὁ διδάσ-
ye shall say to the master of the house, [3]Says [4]to [5]thee [1]the [2]teach-
καλος, Ποῦ ἐστιν τὸ κατάλυμα ὅπου τὸ πάσχα μετὰ τῶν
er, Where is the guest-chamber where the passover with
μαθητῶν.μου φάγω; 12 Κἀκεῖνος ὑμῖν δείξει [v]ἀνώγεον‖
my disciples I may eat? And he [3]you [1]will [2]shew [6]upper [7]room
μέγα ἐστρωμένον· ἐκεῖ ἑτοιμάσατε. 13 Ἀπελθόντες.δὲ εὗρον
[4]a [5]large furnished: there prepare. And having gone they found
καθὼς [w]εἰρήκεν‖ αὐτοῖς· καὶ ἡτοίμασαν τὸ πάσχα.
as he had said to them; and they prepared the passover.
14 Καὶ ὅτε ἐγένετο ἡ ὥρα ἀνέπεσεν, καὶ οἱ [x]δώδεκα‖
And when was come the hour he reclined [at table], and the twelve
ἀπόστολοι σὺν αὐτῷ. 15 καὶ εἶπεν πρὸς αὐτούς, Ἐπιθυμίᾳ
apostles with him. And he said to them, With desire
ἐπεθύμησα τοῦτο τὸ πάσχα φαγεῖν μεθ' ὑμῶν πρὸ τοῦ.με.πα-
I desired this passover to eat with you before I suf-
θεῖν· 16 λέγω.γὰρ ὑμῖν, ὅτι [y]οὐκέτι‖ οὐ.μὴ φάγω [z]ἐξ
fer. For I say to you, that [4]any [5]more [1]not [2]at [3]all will I eat of
(lit. no more)
αὐτοῦ‖ ἕως.ὅτου πληρωθῇ ἐν τῇ βασιλείᾳ τοῦ θεοῦ. 17 Καὶ
it until it be fulfilled in the kingdom of God. And
δεξάμενος [a]ποτήριον, εὐχαριστήσας εἶπεν, Λάβετε τοῦτο,
having received a cup having given thanks he said, Take this,
καὶ διαμερίσατε [b]ἑαυτοῖς·‖ 18 λέγω.γὰρ ὑμῖν, [c]ὅτι‖ οὐ.μὴ
and divide [it] among yourselves. For I say to you, that not at all
πίω [d]ἀπὸ τοῦ [e]γεννήματος‖ τῆς ἀμπέλου ἕως.[f]ὅτου‖ ἡ
will I drink of the fruit of the vine until the
βασιλεία τοῦ θεοῦ ἔλθῃ. 19 Καὶ λαβὼν ἄρτον, εὐχαριστή-
kingdom of God be come. And having taken a loaf, having given
σας ἔκλασεν, καὶ ἔδωκεν αὐτοῖς, λέγων, Τοῦτό ἐστιν τὸ σῶμά
thanks he broke, and gave to them, saying, This is [2]body
μου, τὸ ὑπὲρ ὑμῶν διδόμενον· τοῦτο ποιεῖτε [g]εἰς‖ τὴν ἐμὴν
[1]my, which for you is given: this do in the [2]of [3]me
ἀνάμνησιν. 20 [h]Ὡσαύτως καὶ τὸ ποτήριον‖ μετὰ τὸ.δειπνῆ-
[1]remembrance. In like manner also the cup after having supped,

and sought opportu-
nity to betray him
unto them in the ab-
sence of the multitude.

7 Then came the day
of unleavened bread,
when the passover
must be killed. 8 And
he sent Peter and John,
saying, Go and pre-
pare us the passover,
that we may eat. 9 And
they said unto him,
Where wilt thou that
we prepare? 10 And
he said unto them, Be-
hold, when ye are en-
tered into the city,
there shall a man meet
you, bearing a pitcher
of water; follow him
into the house where
he entereth in. 11 And
ye shall say unto the
good man of the house,
The Master saith unto
thee, Where is the
guestchamber, where
I shall eat the pass-
over with my disci-
ples? 12 And he shall
shew you a large up-
per room furnished:
there make ready.
13 And they went, and
found as he had said
unto them: and they
made ready the pass-
over.

14 And when the
hour was come, he sat
down, and the twelve
apostles with him.
15 And he said unto
them, With desire I
have desired to eat
this passover with you
before I suffer: 16 for
I say unto you, I will
not any more eat
thereof, until it be
fulfilled in the king-
dom of God. 17 And
he took the cup, and
gave thanks, and said,
Take this, and divide
it among yourselves:
18 for I say unto you,
I will not drink of the
fruit of the vine, until
the kingdom of God
shall come. 19 And he
took bread, and gave
thanks, and brake *it*,
and gave unto them,
saying, This is my
body which is given
for you: this do in re-
membrance of me.
20 Likewise also the
cup after supper, say-

[o] ἄτερ ὄχλου αὐτοῖς LTTrA. [p] — ἐν (read ᾗ in which) TrA. [q] Ἰωάνην Tr. [r] εἶπαν LTTrA. [s] + [σοι] for thee L. [t] εἰς ἣν in which LTTrA. [v] ἀνάγαιον GLTTrAW. [w] εἰρήκει LTTrA. [x] — δώδεκα LTTrA. [y] — οὐκέτι [LTr]A. [z] αὐτὸ it LTTrA. [a] + τὸ the (cup) L. [b] εἰς ἑαυτούς LTTrA. [c] — ὅτι TrA. [d] + ἀπὸ τοῦ νῦν henceforth T[TrA]. [e] γενήματος LTTrAW. [f] οὗ TrA. [g] [εἰς] A. [h] καὶ τὸ ποτήριον ὡσαύτως TTrA.

ing, This cup *is* the
new testament in my
blood, which is shed
for you. 21 But, be-
hold, the hand of him
that betrayeth me *is*
with me on the table.
22 And truly the Son
of man goeth, as it
was determined: but
woe unto that man by
whom he is betrayed!
23 And they began to
inquire among them-
selves, which of them
it was that should do
this thing.

24 And there was
also a strife among
them, which of them
should be accounted
the greatest. 25 And
he said unto them,
The kings of the Gen-
tiles exercise lordship
over them; and they
that exercise authority
upon them are called
benefactors. 26 But ye
shall not *be* so: but he
that is greatest among
you, let him be as the
younger; and he that
is chief, as he that
doth serve. 27 For
whether *is* greater, he
that sitteth at meat,
or he that serveth?
is not he that sitteth
at meat? but I am
among you as he that
serveth. 28 Ye are
they which have con-
tinued with me in my
temptations. 29 And
I appoint unto you a
kingdom, as my Fa-
ther hath appointed
unto me; 30 that ye
may eat and drink at
my table in my king-
dom, and sit on thrones
judging the twelve
tribes of Israel.

31 And the Lord said,
Simon, Simon, behold,
Satan hath desired *to
have* you, that he may
sift *you* as wheat:
32 but I have prayed
for thee, that thy faith
fail not: and when
thou art converted,
strengthen thy breth-
ren. 33 And he said
unto him, Lord, I am
ready to go with thee,
both into prison, and
to death. 34 And he
said, I tell thee, Peter,

σαι, λέγων, Τοῦτο τὸ ποτήριον ἡ καινὴ διαθήκη ἐν τῷ
saying, This cup [is] the new covenant in
αἵματί.μου, τὸ ὑπὲρ ὑμῶν [i]ἐκχυνόμενον.‖ 21 Πλὴν ἰδού,
my blood, which for you is poured out. Moreover, behold,
ἡ χεὶρ τοῦ παραδιδόντος με μετ' ἐμοῦ ἐπὶ τῆς τραπέζης.
the hand of him delivering up me [is] with me on the table;
22 [k]καὶ ὁ.μὲν.υἱὸς‖ τοῦ ἀνθρώπου [l]πορεύεται κατὰ τὸ
and indeed the Son of man goes according as
ὡρισμένον·‖ πλὴν οὐαὶ τῷ.ἀνθρώπῳ.ἐκείνῳ δι' οὗ παρα-
it has been determined, but woe to that man by whom he is de-
δίδοται. 23 Καὶ αὐτοὶ ἤρξαντο [m]συζητεῖν‖ πρὸς ἑαυτούς,
livered up. And they began to question together among themselves,
τό, τίς ἄρα εἴη ἐξ αὐτῶν ὁ τοῦτο μέλλων πράσσειν.
this, who then it might be of them who this was about to do.

24 Ἐγένετο.δὲ καὶ φιλονεικία ἐν αὐτοῖς, τό, τίς αὐτῶν
And there was also a strife among them, this, which of them
δοκεῖ εἶναι μείζων. 25 ὁ.δὲ εἶπεν αὐτοῖς, Οἱ βασιλεῖς
is thought to be [the] greater. And he said to them, The kings
τῶν ἐθνῶν κυριεύουσιν αὐτῶν, καὶ οἱ ἐξουσιάζοντες
of the nations rule over them, and those exercising authority over
αὐτῶν εὐεργέται καλοῦνται. 26 ὑμεῖς.δὲ οὐχ οὕτως· ἀλλ'
them well-doers are called. But ye not thus [shall be]; but
ὁ μείζων ἐν ὑμῖν [n]γενέσθω‖ ὡς ὁ νεώτερος· καὶ ὁ
the greater among you let him be as the younger, and he that
ἡγούμενος ὡς ὁ διακονῶν. 27 τίς.γὰρ μείζων, ὁ
leads as he that serves. For which [is] greater, he that
ἀνακείμενος ἢ ὁ διακονῶν; οὐχὶ ὁ ἀνακείμε-
reclines [at table] or he that serves? [Is] not he that reclines
νος; ἐγὼ.δέ [o]εἰμι ἐν μέσῳ ὑμῶν‖ ὡς ὁ διακονῶν.
[at table]? But I am in [the] midst of you as he that serves.
28 Ὑμεῖς.δέ ἐστε οἱ διαμεμενηκότες μετ' ἐμοῦ ἐν τοῖς
But ye are they who have continued with me in
πειρασμοῖς.μου· 29 κἀγὼ διατίθεμαι ὑμῖν, καθὼς διέθετό
my temptations. And I appoint to you, as [3]appointed
μοι ὁ.πατήρ.μου, βασιλείαν, 30 ἵνα [p]ἐσθίητε‖ καὶ πίνητε
[4]to [5]me [1]my [2]father, a kingdom, that ye may eat and may drink
ἐπὶ τῆς.τραπέζης.μου ἐν τῇ.βασιλείᾳ.μου, καὶ [q]καθίσησθε‖ ἐπὶ
at my table in my kingdom, and may sit on
θρόνων, κρίνοντες τὰς δώδεκα φυλὰς τοῦ Ἰσραήλ.
thrones, judging the twelve tribes of Israel.

31 [r]Εἶπεν.δὲ ὁ κύριος,‖ Σίμων, Σίμων, ἰδού, ὁ σατανᾶς
And [3]said [1]the [2]Lord, Simon, Simon, lo, Satan
ἐξῃτήσατο ὑμᾶς, τοῦ σινιάσαι ὡς τὸν σῖτον· 32 ἐγὼ
demanded to have you, for the sifting [you] as wheat; [2]I
δὲ ἐδεήθην περὶ σοῦ, ἵνα μὴ.[s]ἐκλείπῃ‖ ἡ.πίστις.σου· καὶ σύ
[1]but besought for thee, that may not fail thy faith; and [2]thou
ποτε ἐπιστρέψας [t]στήριξον‖ τοὺς.ἀδελφούς.σου. 33 Ὁ.δὲ
[1]when hast turned back confirm thy brethren. And he
εἶπεν αὐτῷ, Κύριε, μετὰ σοῦ ἕτοιμός εἰμι καὶ εἰς φυλακὴν καὶ
said to him, Lord, with thee ready I am both to prison and
εἰς θάνατον πορεύεσθαι. 34 Ὁ.δὲ εἶπεν, Λέγω σοι, Πέτρε,
to death to go. And he said, I tell thee, Peter.

[i] ἐκχυννόμενον LTTrA. [k] ὅτι (for) ὁ υἱὸς μὲν TTrA. [l] κατὰ τὸ ὡρισμένον πορεύεται LTTrA. [m] συνζητεῖν LTTrA. [n] γινέσθω TTrA. [o] ἐν μέσῳ ὑμῶν εἰμι TTrA. [p] ἔσθητε LTTrA. [q] καθίσεσθε ye shall sit GLW; καθήσεσθε ye shall sit TTr; κάθησθε A. [r] — Εἶπεν δὲ ὁ κύριος T[Tr]A. [s] ἐκλίπῃ LTTrA. [t] στήρισον LTTrA.

οὐ.[v]μὴ" φωνήσει σήμερον ἀλέκτωρ [w]πρὶν.ἢ" τρὶς [x]ἀπαρ-
in no wise shall crow to-day [the] a cock before that thrice thou wilt
νήσῃ [y]μὴ' εἰδέναι με."
deny knowing me.

35 Καὶ εἶπεν αὐτοῖς, Ὅτε ἀπέστειλα ὑμᾶς ἄτερ [z]βαλαν-
And he said to them, When I sent you without purse
τίου" καὶ πήρας καὶ ὑποδημάτων, μή τινος ὑστερήσατε;
and provision bag and sandals, anything did ye lack?
Οἱ.δὲ [a]εἶπον," [b]Οὐδενός." 36 [c]Εἶπεν οὖν" αὐτοῖς, Ἀλλὰ
And they said, Nothing. He said therefore to them, [2]However
νῦν ὁ ἔχων [d]βαλάντιον" ἀράτω, ὁμοίως καὶ πήραν·
[1]now he who has a purse let him take [it], in like manner also provision bag;
καὶ ὁ μὴ.ἔχων πωλησάτω τὸ.ἱμάτιον.αὐτοῦ καὶ ἀγορασάτω
and he who has not [one] let him sell his garment and buy
μάχαιραν· 37 λέγω.γὰρ ὑμῖν, ὅτι [e]ἔτι" τοῦτο τὸ γεγραμμένον
a sword; for I say to you, that yet this that has been written
δεῖ τελεσθῆναι ἐν ἐμοί, [f]τὸ" Καὶ μετὰ ἀνόμων ἐλογίσθη·
must be accomplished in me, And with [the] lawless he was reckoned:
καὶ.[g]γὰρ" [h]τὰ" περὶ ἐμοῦ τέλος ἔχει. 38 Οἱ.δὲ [a]εἶπον,"
for also the things concerning me an end have. And they said,
Κύριε, ἰδού, μάχαιραι ὧδε δύο. Ὁ.δὲ εἶπεν αὐτοῖς,
Lord, behold, [4]swords [1]here [2are] [3]two. And he said to them,
Ἱκανόν ἐστιν.
[3]Enough [1]it [2]is.

39 Καὶ ἐξελθὼν ἐπορεύθη κατὰ τὸ ἔθος εἰς τὸ ὄρος
And going forth he went according to custom to the mount
τῶν ἐλαιῶν· ἠκολούθησαν.δὲ αὐτῷ καὶ οἱ.μαθηταὶ.[i]αὐτοῦ."
of Olives, and followed him also his disciples.
40 γενόμενος.δὲ ἐπὶ τοῦ τόπου εἶπεν αὐτοῖς, Προσεύχεσθε
And having arrived at the place he said to them, Pray
μὴ.εἰσελθεῖν εἰς πειρασμόν. 41 Καὶ αὐτὸς ἀπεσπάσθη ἀπ'
not to enter into temptation. And he was withdrawn from
αὐτῶν ὡσεὶ λίθου βολήν, καὶ θεὶς.τὰ.γόνατα προσηύχετο,
them about a stone's throw, and falling on [his] knees he prayed,
42 λέγων, Πάτερ, εἰ βούλει [k]παρενεγκεῖν" [l]τὸ ποτήριον
saying, Father, if thou art willing to take away [2]cup
τοῦτο" ἀπ' ἐμοῦ· πλὴν μὴ τὸ.θέλημά.μου, ἀλλὰ τὸ.σὸν [m]γε-
[1]this from me—; but not my will, but thine be
νέσθω." 43 [n]Ὤφθη.δὲ αὐτῷ ἄγγελος [o]ἀπ' οὐρανοῦ ἐνισχύων
done. And appeared to him an angel from heaven strengthening
αὐτόν. 44 καὶ γενόμενος ἐν ἀγωνίᾳ ἐκτενέστερον προσηύχετο.
him. And being in conflict more intently he prayed.
[p]ἐγένετο.δὲ ὁ' ἱδρὼς.αὐτοῦ ὡσεὶ θρόμβοι αἵματος [q]κατα-
And became his sweat as great drops of blood falling
βαίνοντες' ἐπὶ τὴν γῆν." 45 Καὶ ἀναστὰς ἀπὸ τῆς
down to the earth. And having risen up from
προσευχῆς, ἐλθὼν πρὸς τοὺς μαθητὰς[r] εὗρεν [s]αὐτοὺς κοιμω-
prayer, coming to the disciples he found them sleep-

the cock shall not crow this day, before that thou shalt thrice deny that thou knowest me.

35 And he said unto them, When I sent you without purse, and scrip, and shoes, lacked ye any thing? And they said, Nothing.
36 Then said he unto them, But now, he that hath a purse, let him take *it*, and likewise *his* scrip: and he that hath no sword, let him sell his garment, and buy one.
37 For I say unto you, that this that is written must yet be accomplished in me, And he was reckoned among the transgressors: for the things concerning me have an end. 38 And they said, Lord, behold, here *are* two swords. And he said unto them, It is enough.

39 And he came out, and went, as he was wont, to the mount of Olives; and his disciples also followed him.
40 And when he was at the place, he said unto them, Pray that ye enter not into temptation. 41 And he was withdrawn from them about a stone's cast, and kneeled down, and prayed, 42 saying, Father, if thou be willing, remove this cup from me: nevertheless not my will, but thine, be done.
43 And there appeared an angel unto him from heaven, strengthening him. 44 And being in an agony he prayed more earnestly: and his sweat was as it were great drops of blood falling down to the ground. 45 And when he rose up from prayer, and was come to his disciples, he found them sleeping

[v] — μὴ (*read* shall not crow) TTrA. [w] ἕως until LTTrA. [x] με ἀπαρνήσῃ εἰδέναι LTr. [y] [μὴ] A. [z] βαλλαντίου LTTrAW. [a] εἶπαν LTTrA. [b] Οὐθενός TTrA. [c] ὁ δὲ εἶπεν but he said T; εἶπεν δὲ Tr. [d] βαλλάντιον LTTrAW. [e] — ἔτι LTTrA. [f] ὅτι L. [g] [γὰρ] LTr. [h] τὸ that (concerning me has an end) TTrA. [i] — αὐτοῦ (*read* the disciples) TTrA. [k] παρενέγκαι T; παρένεγκε take away LTr. [l] τοῦτο τὸ ποτήριον TTrA. [m] γινέσθω TTrAW. [n] *verses* 43, 44 *in* [ ] L. [o] ἀπὸ τοῦ from the LTr. [p] καὶ ἐγένετο ὁ ([ὁ] A) TA. [q] καταβαίνοντος TA. [r] + αὐτοῦ (*read* his disciples) E. [s] κοιμωμένους αὐτοὺς TTrA.

for sorrow, 46 and said
unto them, Why sleep
ye? rise and pray, lest
ye enter into temptation.

47 And while he yet
spake, behold a multitude,
and he that was
called Judas, one of
the twelve, went before
them, and drew
near unto Jesus to
kiss him. 48 But Jesus
said unto him, Judas,
betrayest thou the Son
of man with a kiss?
49 When they which
were about him saw
what would follow,
they said unto him,
Lord, shall we smite
with the sword? 50 And
one of them smote the
servant of the high
priest, and cut off his
right ear. 51 And Jesus
answered and said,
Suffer ye thus far.
And he touched his
ear, and healed him.
52 Then Jesus said
unto the chief priests,
and captains of the
temple, and the elders,
which were come to
him, Be ye come out,
as against a thief, with
swords and staves?
53 When I was daily
with you in the temple,
ye stretched forth
no hands against me:
but this is your hour,
and the power of darkness.

54 Then took they
him, and led *him*, and
brought him into the
high priest's house.
And Peter followed
afar off. 55 And when
they had kindled a fire
in the midst of the
hall, and were set
down together, Peter
sat down among them.
56 But a certain maid
beheld him as he sat
by the fire, and earnestly
looked upon him,
and said, This man was
also with him. 57 And
he denied him, saying,
Woman, I know him
not. 58 And after a
little while another
saw him, and said,

μένους‖ ἀπὸ τῆς λύπης, 46 καὶ εἶπεν αὐτοῖς, Τί καθεύδετε;
ing from grief, and he said to them, Why sleep ye?
ἀναστάντες προσεύχεσθε, ἵνα μὴ.εἰσέλθητε εἰς πειρασμόν.
Having risen up pray, that ye may not enter into temptation.

47 [v]Ἔτι.[v]δὲ‖ αὐτοῦ.λαλοῦντος, ἰδοὺ ὄχλος, καὶ ὁ λεγό-
And [4]yet [1]as [2]he [3]was speaking, behold a crowd, and he who was
μενος Ἰούδας, εἷς τῶν δώδεκα, προήρχετο [w]αὐτῶν,‖ καὶ
called Judas, one of the twelve, was going before them, and
ἤγγισεν τῷ Ἰησοῦ φιλῆσαι αὐτόν. 48 [x]ὁ.δὲ.Ἰησοῦς‖ εἶπεν
drew near to Jesus to kiss him. But Jesus said
αὐτῷ, Ἰούδα, φιλήματι τὸν υἱὸν τοῦ ἀνθρώπου παραδίδως;
to him, Judas, with a kiss the Son of man deliverest thou up?
49 Ἰδόντες.δὲ οἱ περὶ αὐτὸν τὸ ἐσόμενον [y]εἶπον‖
And [4]seeing [1]those [2]around [3]him what was about to happen said
[z]αὐτῷ,‖ Κύριε, εἰ πατάξομεν ἐν [a]μαχαίρᾳ‖; 50 Καὶ ἐπά-
to him, Lord, shall we smite with [the] sword? And [6]smote
ταξεν εἷς τις ἐξ αὐτῶν [b]τὸν δοῦλον τοῦ ἀρχιερέως,‖ καὶ
[3]one [1]a [2]certain [4]of [5]them the bondman of the high priest, and
ἀφεῖλεν [c]αὐτοῦ τὸ οὖς‖ τὸ δεξιόν. 51 ἀποκριθεὶς.δὲ ὁ Ἰησοῦς
took off his [2]ear [1]right. And answering Jesus
εἶπεν, Ἐᾶτε ἕως.τούτου. Καὶ ἁψάμενος τοῦ ὠτίου [d]αὐτοῦ‖
said, Suffer thus far. And having touched the ear of him
ἰάσατο αὐτόν. 52 Εἶπεν.δὲ [e]ὁ‖ Ἰησοῦς πρὸς τοὺς παρα-
he healed him. And [2]said [1]Jesus to those who were
γενομένους [f]ἐπ'‖ αὐτὸν ἀρχιερεῖς καὶ στρατηγοὺς τοῦ ἱεροῦ
come against him, chief priests and captains of the temple
καὶ πρεσβυτέρους, Ὡς ἐπὶ λῃστὴν [g]ἐξεληλύθατε‖ μετὰ
and elders, As against a robber have ye come out with
μαχαιρῶν καὶ ξύλων; 53 καθ'.ἡμέραν ὄντος.μου μεθ' ὑμῶν
swords and staves? Daily when I was with you
ἐν τῷ ἱερῷ οὐκ.ἐξετείνατε τὰς χεῖρας ἐπ' ἐμέ. [h]ἀλλ'‖
in the temple ye stretched not out [your] hands against me; but
αὕτη [i]ὑμῶν ἐστιν‖ ἡ ὥρα, καὶ ἡ ἐξουσία τοῦ σκότους.
this [2]your [1]is hour, and the power of darkness.

54 Συλλαβόντες.δὲ αὐτὸν ἤγαγον, καὶ εἰσήγαγον
And having seized him they led [him away], and led
[k]αὐτὸν‖ εἰς [l]τὸν οἶκον‖ τοῦ ἀρχιερέως· ὁ.δὲ.Πέτρος ἠκολούθει
him into the house of the high priest. And Peter was following
μακρόθεν. 55 [m]ἁψάντων‖.δὲ πῦρ ἐν μέσῳ τῆς αὐλῆς,
afar off. And having kindled a fire in [the] midst of the court,
καὶ [n]συγκαθισάντων‖ [o]αὐτῶν‖ ἐκάθητο ὁ Πέτρος [p]ἐν.μέσῳ‖
and [2]having [3]sat [4]down [5]together [1]they [7]sat [6]Peter among
αὐτῶν. 56 ἰδοῦσα.δὲ αὐτὸν παιδίσκη τις καθήμενον πρὸς
them. And [4]having [5]seen [6]him [1]a [3]maid [2]certain sitting by
τὸ φῶς, καὶ ἀτενίσασα αὐτῷ, εἶπεν, Καὶ οὗτος σὺν
the light, and having looked intently on him, said, And this one with
αὐτῷ ἦν. 57 Ὁ.δὲ ἠρνήσατο [q]αὐτόν,‖ λέγων, [r]Γύναι, οὐκ
him was. But he denied him, saying, Woman, [3]not
οἶδα αὐτόν.‖ 58 Καὶ μετὰ βραχὺ ἕτερος ἰδὼν αὐτὸν ἔφη,
[1]I [2]do know him. And after a little another seeing him said,

---

[v] — δὲ and LTTrAW. [w] αὐτούς GLTTrAW. [x] Ἰησοῦς δὲ TTrA. [y] εἶπαν LTTrA. [z] — αὐτῷ TTrA. [a] μαχαίρῃ TTrA. [b] τοῦ ἀρχιερέως τὸν δοῦλον TTrA. [c] τὸ οὖς αὐτοῦ LTTrA. [d] — αὐτοῦ TTrA. [e] — ὁ LTTrA. [f] πρὸς T. [g] ἐξήλθατε came ye out LTr. [h] ἀλλὰ TrA. [i] ἐστὶν ὑμῶν LTTrA. [k] — αὐτὸν (*read* [him]) LTTrA. [l] τὴν οἰκίαν TTrA. [m] περιαψάντων TTrA. [n] περικαθισάντων, having sat around L; συνκαθισάντων T. [o] — αὐτῶν LTTrA. [p] μέσος TTrA. [q] — αὐτὸν LTr[A]. [r] οὐκ οἶδα αὐτόν, γύναι TTrA.

Καὶ σὺ ἐξ αὐτῶν εἶ. Ὁ.δὲ.Πέτρος [s]εἶπεν," Ἄνθρωπε, οὐκ.εἰμί.
And thou of them art. But Peter said, Man, I am not.
59 Καὶ διαστάσης ὡσεὶ ὥρας μιᾶς, ἄλλος τις διϊσχυρίζετο,
And having elapsed about [2]hour [1]one, [5]other [3]a [4]certain strongly affirmed,
λέγων, Ἐπ' ἀληθείας καὶ οὗτος μετ' αὐτοῦ ἦν· καὶ.γὰρ Γαλι-
saying, In truth also this one with him was; for also a Gali-
λαῖός ἐστιν. 60 Εἶπεν.δὲ ὁ Πέτρος, Ἄνθρωπε, οὐκ.οἶδα ὃ
lean he is. And [2]said [1]Peter, Man, I know not what
λέγεις. Καὶ παραχρῆμα, ἔτι λαλοῦντος.αὐτοῦ, ἐφώνησεν
thou sayest. And immediately, [2]yet [1]as he was speaking, [3]crew
[t]ὁ" ἀλέκτωρ· 61 καὶ στραφεὶς ὁ κύριος ἐνέβλεψεν τῷ Πέτρῳ·
[1]the [2]cock. And having turned, the Lord looked at Peter;
καὶ ὑπεμνήσθη ὁ Πέτρος τοῦ λόγου τοῦ κυρίου, ὡς εἶπεν αὐτῷ,
and [2]remembered [1]Peter the word of the Lord, how he said to him,
Ὅτι πρὶν ἀλέκτορα φωνῆσαι [v] ἀπαρνήσῃ με τρίς. 62 Καὶ
Before [the] cock crow thou wilt deny me thrice. And
ἐξελθὼν ἔξω [w]ὁ Πέτρος" ἔκλαυσεν πικρῶς.
having gone forth outside Peter wept bitterly.

Thou art also of them. And Peter said, Man, I am not. 59 And about the space of one hour after another confidently affirmed, saying, Of a truth this *fellow* also was with him: for he is a Galilæan. 60 And Peter said, Man, I know not what thou sayest. And immediately, while he yet spake, the cock crew. 61 And the Lord turned, and looked upon Peter. And Peter remembered the word of the Lord, how he had said unto him, Before the cock crow, thou shalt deny me thrice. 62 And Peter went out, and wept bitterly.

63 Καὶ οἱ ἄνδρες οἱ συνέχοντες [x]τὸν Ἰησοῦν" ἐνέπαιζον
And the men who were holding Jesus mocked
αὐτῷ, δέροντες· 64 καὶ περικαλύψαντες αὐτὸν [y]ἔτυπτον
him, beating [him]; and having covered up him they were striking
αὐτοῦ τὸ πρόσωπον, καὶ" ἐπηρώτων [z]αὐτόν," λέγοντες, Προ-
his face, and were asking him, saying, Pro-
φήτευσον, τίς ἐστιν ὁ παίσας σε; 65 Καὶ ἕτερα πολλὰ
phesy, who is it that struck thee? And [2]other [3]things [1]many
βλασφημοῦντες ἔλεγον εἰς αὐτόν.
blasphemously they said to him.

63 And the men that held Jesus mocked him, and smote *him*. 64 And when they had blindfolded him, they struck him on the face, and asked him, saying, Prophesy, who is it that smote thee? 65 And many other things blasphemously spake they against him.

66 Καὶ ὡς [a]ἐγένετο ἡμέρα συνήχθη τὸ πρεσβυτέριον
And when it became day were gathered together the elderhood
τοῦ λαοῦ, ἀρχιερεῖς.τε καὶ γραμματεῖς, καὶ [a]ἀνήγαγον" αὐτὸν
of the people, both chief priests and scribes, and they led him
εἰς τὸ συνέδριον [b]ἑαυτῶν," λέγοντες, 67 Εἰ σὺ εἶ ὁ χριστός,
into [2]sanhedrim [1]their, saying, If thou art the Christ,
[c]εἰπὲ" ἡμῖν. Εἶπεν.δὲ αὐτοῖς, Ἐὰν ὑμῖν εἴπω, οὐ.μὴ
tell us. And he said to them, If you I should tell, not at all
πιστεύσητε· 68 ἐὰν.δὲ [d]καὶ" ἐρωτήσω, οὐ.μὴ ἀποκρι-
would ye believe; and if also I should ask [you], not at all would ye
θῆτέ [e]μοι, ἢ ἀπολύσητε." 69 ἀπὸ.τοῦ.νῦν [f] ἔσται ὁ υἱὸς τοῦ
answer me, nor let [me] go. Henceforth shall be the Son
ἀνθρώπου καθήμενος ἐκ δεξιῶν τῆς δυνάμεως τοῦ θεοῦ.
of man sitting at [the] right hand of the power of God.
70 [g]Εἶπον".δὲ πάντες, Σὺ οὖν εἶ ὁ υἱὸς τοῦ θεοῦ; Ὁ.δὲ
And they [2]said [1]all, Thou then art the Son of God? And he
πρὸς αὐτοὺς ἔφη, Ὑμεῖς λέγετε, ὅτι ἐγώ εἰμι. 71 Οἱ.δὲ [h]εἶπον,"
to them said, Ye say, that I am. And they said,
Τί ἔτι [i]χρείαν ἔχομεν μαρτυρίας"; αὐτοὶ.γὰρ ἠκούσαμεν
What any more need have we of witness? for ourselves have heard
ἀπὸ τοῦ.στόματος.αὐτοῦ.
from his [own] mouth.

66 And as soon as it was day, the elders of the people and the chief priests and the scribes came together, and led him into their council, saying, 67 Art thou the Christ? tell us. And he said unto them, If I tell you ye will not believe: 68 and if I also ask *you*, ye will not answer me, nor let *me* go. 69 Hereafter shall the Son of man sit on the right hand of the power of God. 70 Then said they all, Art thou then the Son of God? And he said unto them, Ye say that I am. 71 And they said, What need we any further witness? for we ourselves have heard of his own mouth.

23 Καὶ ἀναστὰν ἅπαν τὸ πλῆθος αὐτῶν [k]ἤγαγεν"
And having risen up all the multitude of them led

XXIII. And the whole multitude of them arose, and led

---

[s] ἔφη TTrA. [t] — ὁ (read [the]) GLTTrAW. [v] + σήμερον to-day TTrA. [w] — ὁ Πέτρος (read he wept) GTTr[A]. [x] αὐτὸν him LTTrA. [y] — ἔτυπτον αὐτοῦ τὸ πρόσωπον, καὶ [L]TTrA. [z] — αὐτὸν TTrA. [a] ἀπήγαγον they led away TTrA. [b] αὐτῶν TTrAW. [c] εἰπὸν TTrA. [d] — καὶ LTTrA. [e] — μοι ἢ ἀπολύσητε T[TrA]. [f] + δὲ however LTTrA. [g] εἶπαν TTrA. [h] εἶπαν LTTrA. [i] ἔχομεν μαρτυρίας χρείαν TTrA. [k] ἤγαγον GLTTrAW.

him unto Pilate. 2 And
they began to accuse
him, saying, We found
this *fellow* perverting
the nation, and for-
bidding to give tribute
to Cæsar, saying that
he himself is Christ a
King. 3 And Pilate
asked him, saying, Art
thou the King of the
Jews? And he answer-
ed him and said, Thou
sayest *it*. 4 Then said
Pilate to the chief
priests and *to* the peo-
ple, I find no fault in
this man. 5 And they
were the more fierce,
saying, He stirreth up
the people, teaching
throughout all Jewry,
beginning from Ga-
lilee to this place.
6 When Pilate heard
of Galilee, he asked
whether the man were
a Galilæan. 7 And as
soon as he knew that
he belonged unto He-
rod's jurisdiction, he
sent him to Herod,
who himself also was
at Jerusalem at that
time. 8 And when
Herod saw Jesus, he
was exceeding glad:
for he was desirous to
see him of a long
season, because he had
heard many things of
him; and he hoped to
have seen some mi-
racle done by him.
9 Then he questioned
with him in many
words; but he answer-
ed him nothing. 10 And
the chief priests and
scribes stood and ve-
hemently accused him.
11 And Herod with his
men of war set him at
nought, and mocked
him, and arrayed him
in a gorgeous robe,
and sent him again to
Pilate. 12 And the
same day Pilate and
Herod were made
friends together: for
before th‿y were at en-
mity between them-
selves.

13 And Pilate, when
he had called together
the chief priests and
the rulers and the peo-
ple, 14 said unto them,
Ye have brought this

αὐτὸν ἐπὶ τὸν [l]Πιλατον.‖ 2 ἤρξαντο.δὲ κατηγορεῖν αὐτοῦ,
him to Pilate. And they began to accuse him,
λέγοντες, Τοῦτον [m]εὕρομεν‖ διαστρέφοντα τὸ ἔθνος[n], καὶ
saying, This [man] we found perverting the nation, and
κωλύοντα [o]Καίσαρι φόρους‖ διδόναι, [p]λέγοντα ἑαυτὸν χριστὸν
forbidding [4]to [5]Cæsar [3]tribute [1]to [2]give, saying himself [2]Christ
βασιλέα εἶναι. 3 Ὁ.δὲ.[q]Πιλάτος‖ [r]ἐπηρώτησεν‖ αὐτόν, λέγων,
[3]a [4]king [1]is. And Pilate questioned him, saying,
Σὺ εἶ ὁ βασιλεὺς τῶν Ἰουδαίων; Ὁ.δὲ ἀποκριθεὶς αὐτῷ
[2]Thou [1]art the king of the Jews? And he answering him
ἔφη, Σὺ λέγεις. 4 Ὁ.δὲ.[q]Πιλάτος‖ εἶπεν πρὸς τοὺς ἀρχιερεῖς
said, Thou sayest. And Pilate said to the chief priests
καὶ τοὺς ὄχλους, Οὐδὲν εὑρίσκω αἴτιον ἐν τῷ.ἀνθρώπῳ.τούτῳ.
and the crowds, Nothi‿ find I blamable in this man.
5 Οἱ.δὲ ἐπίσχυον, λέγοντες, Ὅτι ἀνασείει τὸν λαόν, διδάσ-
But they were insisting, saying, He stirs up the people, teach-
κων καθ' ὅλης τῆς Ἰουδαίας, [s]ἀρξάμενος ἀπὸ τῆς Γαλι-
ing throughout [2]whole [1]the of Judæa, beginning from Gali-
λαίας ἕως ὧδε. 6 [q]Πιλάτος‖.δὲ ἀκούσας [t]Γαλιλαίαν‖
lee even to here. But Pilate having heard Galilee [named]
ἐπηρώτησεν εἰ ὁ ἄνθρωπος Γαλιλαῖός ἐστιν· 7 καὶ ἐπι-
asked whether the man [2]a [3]Galilean [1]is; and having
γνοὺς ὅτι ἐκ τῆς ἐξουσίας Ἡρώδου ἐστίν, ἀνέπεμψεν αὐτὸν
known that from the jurisdiction of Herod he is, he sent [2]up [1]him
πρὸς [v] Ἡρώδην, ὄντα καὶ αὐτὸν ἐν Ἱεροσολύμοις ἐν ταύταις
to Herod, [3]being [2]also [1]he at Jerusalem in those
ταῖς ἡμέραις. 8 ὁ.δὲ.Ἡρώδης ἰδὼν τὸν Ἰησοῦν ἐχάρη λίαν
days. And Herod seeing Jesus rejoiced greatly,
ἦν.γὰρ [w]θέλων ἐξ.ἱκανοῦ‖ ἰδεῖν αὐτόν, διὰ τὸ ἀκούειν
for he was wishing for long to see him, because of hearing
[x]πολλὰ‖ περὶ αὐτοῦ· καὶ ἤλπιζέν τι σημεῖον ἰδεῖν ὑπ'
many things concerning him; and he was hoping some sign to see [2]by
αὐτοῦ γινόμενον. 9 ἐπηρώτα.δὲ αὐτὸν ἐν λόγοις ἱκανοῖς·
[3]him [1]done. And he questioned him in [2]words [1]many,
αὐτὸς.δὲ οὐδὲν ἀπεκρίνατο αὐτῷ. 10 εἱστήκεισαν.δὲ οἱ ἀρχ-
but he nothing answered him. And [7]had [8]stood [1]the [2]chief
ιερεῖς καὶ οἱ γραμματεῖς, εὐτόνως κατηγοροῦντες αὐτοῦ.
[3]priests [4]and [5]the [6]scribes, violently accusing him.
11 ἐξουθενήσας.δὲ αὐτὸν [y] ὁ Ἡρώδης σὺν τοῖς στρατεύμασιν
And [2]having [3]set [5]at [6]nought [4]him [1]Herod with [2]troops
αὐτοῦ, καὶ ἐμπαίξας, περιβαλὼν [z]αὐτὸν‖ ἐσθῆτα λαμ-
[1]his, and having mocked [him], having put on him [2]apparel [1]splen-
πρὰν ἀνέπεμψεν αὐτὸν τῷ [a]Πιλάτῳ.‖ 12 ἐγένοντο.δὲ φίλοι
did he sent [2]back [1]him to Pilate. And became friends
ὅ.τε.[b]Πιλάτος καὶ ὁ Ἡρώδης‖ ἐν αὐτῇ.τῇ ἡμέρᾳ μετ' ἀλλήλων·
both Pilate and Herod on that same day with one another;
προϋπῆρχον.γὰρ ἐν ἔχθρᾳ ὄντες πρὸς [c]ἑαυτούς.‖
for before they were at enmity between themselves.

13 [q]Πιλάτος‖.δὲ [d]συγκαλεσάμενος‖ τοὺς ἀρχιερεῖς καὶ τοὺς
And Pilate having called together the chief priests and the
ἄρχοντας καὶ τὸν λαόν, 14 εἶπεν πρὸς αὐτούς, Προσηνέγκατέ
rulers and the people, said to them, Ye brought

---

[l] Πειλᾶτον T. [m] εὕραμεν TTrA. [n] + ἡμῶν (*read* our nation) LTTr[A]W. [o] φόρους Καίσαρι LTTrA. [p] + καὶ and [L]TTr[A]. [q] Πειλᾶτος T. [r] ἠρώτησεν TTrA. [s] + καὶ even TTr[A]. [t] — Γαλιλαίαν T[A]. [v] + τὸν L. [w] ἐξ ἱκανῶν χρόνων θέλων many times wishing LTTrA. [x] — πολλὰ TTrA. [y] + καὶ also T. [z] — αὐτὸν (*read* [him]) [L]T[Tr]A. [a] Πειλάτῳ T. [b] Ἡρώδης καὶ ὁ Πιλάτος (Πειλ. T) TTrA. [c] αὐτούς TTrA. [d] συνκαλεσάμενος T.

μοι τὸν.ἄνθρωπον.τοῦτον, ὡς ἀποστρέφοντα τὸν λαόν· καὶ
to me this man, as turning away the people; and

ἰδού, ἐγὼ ἐνώπιον ὑμῶν ἀνακρίνας [e]οὐδὲν‖ εὗρον ἐν τῷ
behold, I before you having examined [him] [2]nothing [1]found in

ἀνθρώπῳ.τούτῳ αἴτιον ὧν κατηγορεῖτε
this man blamable [as to the things] of which ye bring accusation

κατ' αὐτοῦ· 15 ἀλλ'.οὐδὲ Ἡρώδης· [f]ἀνέπεμψα.γὰρ ὑμᾶς πρὸς
against him; nor even Herod, for I sent [2]up [1]you to

αὐτόν,‖ καὶ ἰδού, οὐδὲν ἄξιον θανάτου ἐστὶν πεπραγμένον
him, and lo, nothing worthy of death is done

αὐτῷ. 16 παιδεύσας οὖν αὐτὸν ἀπολύσω. 17 [g]Ἀνάγκην
by him. Having [2]chastised [1]therefore him I will release [him]. [4]Necessity

δὲ εἶχεν ἀπολύειν αὐτοῖς κατὰ ἑορτὴν ἕνα.‖ 18 [h]ἀνέ-
[1]now [2]he [3]had to release to them at [the] feast one. [2]they

κραξαν‖ δὲ [k]παμπληθεί,‖ λέγοντες, Αἶρε τοῦτον, ἀπόλυ-
[3]cried [4]out [1]but in a mass, saying, Away with this [man], [2]re-

σον δὲ ἡμῖν τὸν Βαραββᾶν· 19 ὅστις ἦν διὰ στάσιν
lease [1]and to us Barabbas; who was on account of [3]insurrection

τινὰ γενομένην ἐν τῇ πόλει καὶ φόνον [l]βεβλημένος εἰς
[1]a [2]certain made in the city and murder cast into

φυλακήν.‖ 20 Πάλιν [m]οὖν‖ ὁ [n]Πιλάτος‖ προσεφώνησεν[o],
prison. Again therefore Pilate called to [them],

θέλων ἀπολῦσαι τὸν Ἰησοῦν. 21 οἱ.δὲ ἐπεφώνουν, λέγοντες,
wishing to release Jesus. But they were crying out, saying,

[p]Σταύρωσον, σταύρωσον‖ αὐτόν. 22 Ὁ.δὲ τρίτον εἶπεν
Crucify, crucify him. And he a third [time] said

πρὸς αὐτούς, Τί γὰρ κακὸν ἐποίησεν οὗτος; οὐδὲν
to them, What [2]then [1]evil did [3]commit [1]this [[2]man]? No

αἴτιον θανάτου εὗρον ἐν αὐτῷ· παιδεύσας οὖν αὐτὸν
cause of death found I in him. Having [2]chastised [1]therefore him

ἀπολύσω. 23 Οἱ.δὲ ἐπέκειντο φωναῖς μεγάλαις, αἰτού-
I will release [him]. But they were urgent with [2]voices [1]loud, asking

μενοι αὐτὸν σταυρωθῆναι· καὶ κατίσχυον αἱ φωναὶ αὐτῶν
for him to be crucified. And prevailed the voices of them

[q]καὶ τῶν ἀρχιερέων.‖ 24 [r]Ὁ.δὲ‖.[n]Πιλάτος‖ ἐπέκρινεν γενέσθαι
and of the chief priests. And Pilate adjudged [3]to [4]be [5]done

τὸ.αἴτημα.αὐτῶν. 25 ἀπέλυσεν.δὲ [s]αὐτοῖς‖ τὸν διὰ
[1]their [2]request. And he released to them him who on account of

στάσιν καὶ φόνον βεβλημένον εἰς [t]τὴν‖ φυλακήν, ὃν
insurrection and murder had been cast into the prison, whom

ᾐτοῦντο· τὸν.δὲ.Ἰησοῦν παρέδωκεν τῷ.θελήματι.αὐτῶν.
they asked for; but Jesus he delivered up to their will.

26 Καὶ ὡς ἀπήγαγον αὐτόν, ἐπιλαβόμενοι [v]Σίμωνός
And as they led [2]away [1]him, having laid hold on [3]Simon

τινος Κυρηναίου [w]τοῦ‖ ἐρχομένου‖ [x]ἀπ'‖ ἀγροῦ, ἐπέθηκαν
[1]a [2]certain a Cyrenian coming from a field, they put upon

αὐτῷ τὸν σταυρὸν φέρειν ὄπισθεν τοῦ Ἰησοῦ. 27 Ἠκολούθει
him the cross to bear [it] behind Jesus. [2]Were [3]following

δὲ αὐτῷ πολὺ πλῆθος τοῦ λαοῦ καὶ γυναικῶν, αἳ [y]καὶ‖
[1]and him a great multitude of the people and of women, who also

man unto me, as one that perverteth the people: and, behold, I, having examined *him* before you, have found no fault in this man touching those things whereof ye accuse him:
15 no, nor yet Herod: for I sent you to him; and, lo, nothing worthy of death is done unto him.
16 I will therefore chastise him, and release *him*.
17 (For of necessity he must release one unto them at the feast.)
18 And they cried out all at once, saying, Away with this *man*, and release unto us Barabbas:
19 (who for a certain sedition made in the city, and for murder, was cast into prison.)
20 Pilate therefore, willing to release Jesus, spake again to them.
21 But they cried, saying, Crucify *him*, crucify him.
22 And he said unto them the third time, Why, what evil hath he done? I have found no cause of death in him: I will therefore chastise him, and let *him* go.
23 And they were instant with loud voices, requiring that he might be crucified. And the voices of them and of the chief priests prevailed.
24 And Pilate gave sentence that it should be as they required.
25 And he released unto them him that for sedition and murder was cast into prison, whom they had desired; but he delivered Jesus to their will.

26 And as they led him away, they laid hold upon one Simon, a Cyrenian, coming out of the country, and on him they laid the cross, that he might bear *it* after Jesus.
27 And there followed him a great company of people, and of women, which also be-

---

[e] οὐθὲν TTr. [f] ἀνέπεμψεν γὰρ αὐτὸν πρὸς ἡμᾶς for he sent him back to us T. [g] — verse 17 [L]TTr[A]. [h] ἀνέκραγον TTrA. [k] πανπληθεί T. [l] βληθεὶς ([βληθεὶς] A) ἐν τῇ φυλακῇ TTrA. [m] δὲ however LTTrA. [n] Πειλᾶτος T. [o] + αὐτοῖς them L. [p] Σταύρου σταύρου LTTrA. [q] — καὶ τῶν ἀρχιερέων [L]T[TrA]. [r] καὶ LTTrA. [s] — αὐτοῖς G[L]TTrAW. [t] — τὴν LTTrA. [v] Σίμωνά τινα Κυρηναῖον ἐρχόμενον LTTrA. [w] — τοῦ GW. [x] ἀπὸ L. [y] — καὶ LTTrA.

wailed and lamented
him. 28 But Jesus turn-
ing unto them said,
Daughters of Jerusa-
lem, weep not for me,
but weep for your-
selves, and for your
children. 29 For, be-
hold, the days are
coming, in the which
they shall say, Blessed
are the barren, and
the wombs that never
bare, and the paps
which never gave suck.
30 Then shall they be-
gin to say to the moun-
tains, Fall on us; and
to the hills, Cover us.
31 For if they do these
things in a green tree,
what shall be done in
the dry? 32 And there
were also two other,
malefactors, led with
him to be put to death.
33 And when they were
come to the place,
which is called Cal-
vary, there they cru-
cified him, and the
malefactors, one on
the right hand, and
the other on the left.
34 Then said Jesus,
Father, forgive them;
for they know not
what they do. And
they parted his rai-
ment, and cast lots.
35 And the people stood
beholding. And the
rulers also with them
derided *him*, saying,
He saved others; let
him save himself, if
he be Christ, the cho-
sen of God. 36 And
the soldiers also mock-
ed him, coming to
him, and offering him
vinegar, 37 and saying,
If thou be the king of
the Jews, save thyself.
38 And a superscrip-
tion also was written
over him in letters of
Greek, and Latin, and
Hebrew, THIS IS
THE KING OF THE
JEWS

39 And one of the
malefactors which
were hanged railed on
him, saying, If thou
be Christ, save thyself
and us. 40 But the
other answering re-
buked him, saying,

ἐκόπτοντο καὶ ἐθρήνουν αὐτόν. 28 στραφεὶς.δὲ πρὸς αὐτὰς
were bewailing and lamenting him. And turning to them
[z]ὁ'' Ἰησοῦς εἶπεν, Θυγατέρες Ἱερουσαλήμ, μὴ.κλαίετε ἐπ' ἐμέ,
Jesus said, Daughters of Jerusalem, weep not for me,
πλὴν ἐφ' ἑαυτὰς κλαίετε καὶ ἐπὶ τὰ.τέκνα.ὑμῶν· 29 ὅτι ἰδού,
but [2]for [3]yourselves [1]weep and for your children: for lo,
ἔρχονται ἡμέραι ἐν αἷς ἐροῦσιν, Μακάριαι αἱ στεῖραι
are coming days in which they will say, Blessed [are] the barren
καὶ [a]κοιλίαι αἳ οὐκ.ἐγέννησαν καὶ μαστοὶ οἳ [b]οὐκ.ἐθήλασαν.''
and wombs which did not bear and breasts which gave not suck.
30 τότε ἄρξονται λέγειν τοῖς ὄρεσιν, [c]Πέσετε'' ἐφ' ἡμᾶς
Then shall they begin to say to the mountains, Fall upon us;
καὶ τοῖς βουνοῖς, Καλύψατε ἡμᾶς. 31 ὅτι εἰ ἐν [d]τῷ'' ὑγρῷ
and to the hills, Cover us: for if in the green
ξύλῳ ταῦτα ποιοῦσιν, ἐν τῷ ξηρῷ τί γένηται; 32 Ἤγοντο
tree these things they do, in the dry what may take place? [2]Were [3]led
δὲ καὶ ἕτεροι δύο κακοῦργοι σὺν αὐτῷ ἀναιρεθῆναι. 33 Καὶ
[4]and also [2]other [1]two malefactors with him to be put to death. And
ὅτε [e]ἀπῆλθον'' ἐπὶ τὸν τόπον τὸν καλούμενον κρανίον ἐκεῖ
when they came to the place called a Skull there
ἐσταύρωσαν αὐτόν, καὶ τοὺς κακούργους, ὃν.μὲν ἐκ δεξιῶν
they crucified him, and the malefactors, the one on [the] right
ὃν.δὲ ἐξ ἀριστερῶν. 34 [f]ὁ.δὲ.Ἰησοῦς ἔλεγεν, Πάτερ, ἄφες
and one on [the] left. And Jesus said, Father, forgive
αὐτοῖς· οὐ.γὰρ.οἴδασιν τί ποιοῦσιν.'' Διαμεριζόμενοι.δὲ τὰ
them, for they know not what they do. And dividing
ἱμάτια.αὐτοῦ ἔβαλον [g]κλῆρον.'' 35 καὶ εἱστήκει ὁ λαὸς θεω-
his garments they cast a lot. And [3]stood [1]the [2]people behold-
ρῶν· ἐξεμυκτήριζον.δὲ [h]καὶ'' οἱ ἄρχοντες [i]σὺν αὐτοῖς,'' λέγον-
ing, and [4]were [5]deriding [3]also [1]the [2]rulers with them, say-
τες, Ἄλλους ἔσωσεν, σωσάτω ἑαυτόν εἰ οὗτός ἐστιν ὁ χριστὸς
ing, Others he saved, let him save himself if this is the Christ
[k]ὁ τοῦ θεοῦ'' ἐκλεκτός. 36 [l]Ἐνέπαιζον''.δὲ αὐτῷ καὶ οἱ στρα-
the [2]of [3]God [1]chosen. And mocked him also the sol-
τιῶται, προσερχόμενοι [m]καὶ'' ὄξος προσφέροντες αὐτῷ, 37 καὶ
diers, coming near and [3]vinegar [1]offering [2]him, and
λέγοντες, [n]Εἰ'' σὺ εἶ ὁ βασιλεὺς τῶν Ἰουδαίων, σῶσον σεαυ-
saying, If thou art the king of the Jews, save thy-
τόν. 38 Ἦν.δὲ καὶ ἐπιγραφὴ [o]γεγραμμένη'' ἐπ' αὐτῷ
self. And there was also an inscription written over him
[p]γράμμασιν Ἑλληνικοῖς καὶ Ῥωμαϊκοῖς καὶ Ἑβραϊκοῖς,''
in letters Greek and Latin and Hebrew:
[q]Οὗτός ἐστιν ὁ βασιλεὺς τῶν Ἰουδαίων.''
This is the king of the Jews.

39 Εἷς.δὲ τῶν κρεμασθέντων κακούργων ἐβλασφήμει
Now one of the [2]who [3]had [4]been [5]hanged [1]malefactors railed at
αὐτόν, [r]λέγων,'' [s]Εἰ σὺ εἶ ὁ χριστός,'' σῶσον σεαυτὸν καὶ
him, saying, If thou art the Christ, save thyself and
ἡμᾶς. 40 Ἀποκριθεὶς.δὲ ὁ ἕτερος [t]ἐπετίμα αὐτῷ, λέγων,''
us. But answering the other rebuked him, saying,

---

[z] — ὁ TTrA. [a] + αἱ the TTrA. [b] οὐκ ἔθρεψαν nourished not LTTrA. [c] Πέσατε TTrA.
[d] [τῷ] Tr. [e] ἦλθον LTrA. [f] [ὁ δὲ .... ποιοῦσιν] L. [g] κλήρους lots TA. [h] — καὶ LT.
[i] — σὺν αὐτοῖς [L]TTrA. [k] τοῦ θεοῦ ὁ TA. [l] ἐνέπαιξαν TA. [m] — καὶ [L]TTrA.
[n] [Εἰ] L. [o] ἐπιγεγραμμένη L[Tr]; — γεγραμμένη TA. [p] — γράμμασιν .... Ἑβραϊκοῖς [L]TTr[A]. [q] ὁ βασιλεὺς τῶν Ἰουδαίων οὗτος ([οὗτος] L) LTTrA. [r] — λέγων T[Tr]A.
[s] Οὐχὶ σὺ εἶ ὁ χριστός; Art not thou the Christ? TTrA. [t] ἐπιτιμῶν αὐτῷ ἔφη rebuking him said TTrA.

Οὐδὲ φοβῇ σὺ τὸν θεόν, ὅτι ἐν τῷ αὐτῷ κρίματι εἶ;
[2]Not [3]even [1]dost [5]fear [4]thou God, [thou] that under the same judgment art?

41 καὶ ἡμεῖς μὲν δικαίως· ἄξια.γὰρ ὧν ἐπράξαμεν
And we indeed justly; for [3]a [4]due [5]recompense [6]of [7]what [8]we [9]did

ἀπολαμβάνομεν· οὗτος.δὲ οὐδὲν ἄτοπον ἔπραξεν. 42 Καὶ
[1]we [2]receive; but this [man] [2]nothing [3]amiss [1]did. And

ἔλεγεν [v]τῷ[‖] Ἰησοῦ, Μνήσθητί μου, [w]κύριε,[‖] ὅταν ἔλθῃς ἐν
he said to Jesus, Remember me, Lord, when thou comest in

τῇ.βασιλείᾳ.σου. 43 Καὶ εἶπεν αὐτῷ [x]ὁ Ἰησοῦς,[‖] Ἀμὴν [y]λέγω
thy kingdom. And [2]said [3]to [4]him [1]Jesus, Verily I say

σοι,[‖] σήμερον μετ' ἐμοῦ ἔσῃ ἐν τῷ παραδείσῳ.
to thee, To-day with me thou shalt be in Paradise.

44 [z]Ἦν.δὲ[‖] ὡσεὶ ὥρα ἕκτη, καὶ σκότος ἐγένετο ἐφ' ὅλην
And it was about [the] [2]hour [1]sixth, and darkness came over [2]whole

τὴν γῆν ἕως ὥρας [a]ἐννάτης·[‖] 45 [b]καὶ ἐσκοτίσθη ὁ ἥλιος,[‖]
[1]the land until [the] [2]hour [1]ninth; and [3]was [4]darkened [1]the [2]sun;

[c]καὶ ἐσχίσθη[‖] τὸ καταπέτασμα τοῦ ναοῦ μέσον· 46 καὶ
and [6]was [7]rent [1]the [2]veil [3]of [4]the [5]temple in [the] midst. And

φωνήσας φωνῇ μεγάλῃ ὁ Ἰησοῦς εἶπεν, Πάτερ, εἰς χεῖράς
having cried with a [2]voice [1]loud Jesus said, Father, into [2]hands

σου [d]παραθήσομαι[‖] τὸ.πνεῦμά μου. [e]Καὶ ταῦτα[‖] εἰπὼν
[1]thy I will commit my spirit. And these things having said

ἐξέπνευσεν. 47 Ἰδὼν.δὲ ὁ [f]ἑκατόνταρχος[‖] τὸ γενόμενον
he expired. Now [3]having [4]seen [1]the [2]centurion that which took place

[g]ἐδόξασεν[‖] τὸν θεόν, λέγων, Ὄντως ὁ.ἄνθρωπος.οὗτος δίκαιος
glorified God, saying, Indeed this man [2]just

ἦν. 48 Καὶ πάντες οἱ [h]συμπαραγενόμενοι[‖] ὄχλοι ἐπὶ τὴν
[1]was. And all the [2]who [3]were [4]come [5]together [1]crowds to

θεωρίαν.ταύτην, [i]θεωροῦντες[‖] τὰ γενόμενα, τύπτοντες
this sight, seeing the things which took place, beating

[k]ἑαυτῶν[‖] τὰ στήθη ὑπέστρεφον. 49 εἱστήκεισαν.δὲ πάντες
their breasts returned. And [6]stood [1]all

οἱ γνωστοὶ [l]αὐτοῦ[‖] [m]μακρόθεν, καὶ γυναῖκες αἱ [n]συν-
[2]those [3]who [4]knew [5]him afar off, also women who fol-

ακολουθήσασαι[‖] αὐτῷ ἀπὸ τῆς Γαλιλαίας, ὁρῶσαι ταῦτα.
lowed with him from Galilee, beholding these things.

50 Καὶ ἰδού, ἀνὴρ ὀνόματι Ἰωσήφ, βουλευτὴς ὑπάρχων,
And behold, a man by name Joseph, a counsellor being,

[o]ἀνὴρ ἀγαθὸς καὶ δίκαιος, 51 οὗτος οὐκ.ἦν.[p]συγκατατεθειμένος[‖]
a man good and just, (he had not assented

τῇ βουλῇ καὶ τῇ πράξει αὐτῶν, ἀπὸ Ἀριμαθαίας πόλεως
to the counsel and the deed of them,) from Arimathæa a city

τῶν Ἰουδαίων, ὃς.[q]καὶ[‖] προσεδέχετο [r]καὶ αὐτὸς[‖] τὴν βασι-
of the Jews, and who [3]was [4]waiting [5]for [1]also [2]himself the king-

λείαν τοῦ θεοῦ, 52 οὗτος προσελθὼν τῷ [s]Πιλάτῳ[‖] ᾐτήσατο τὸ
dom of God, he having gone to Pilate begged the

σῶμα τοῦ Ἰησοῦ. 53 καὶ καθελὼν [t]αὐτὸ[‖] ἐνετύλιξεν αὐτὸ
body of Jesus. And having taken [2]down [1]it he wrapped it

Dost not thou fear
God, seeing thou art
in the same condem-
nation? 41 and we in-
deed justly; for we
receive the due reward
of our deeds: but this
man hath done nothing
amiss. 42 And he said
unto Jesus, Lord, re-
member me when thou
comest into thy king-
dom. 43 And Jesus
said unto him, Verily
I say unto thee, To
day shalt thou be with
me in paradise.

44 And it was about
the sixth hour, and
there was a darkness
over all the earth until
the ninth hour. 45 And
the sun was darkened,
and the veil of the
temple was rent in the
midst. 46 And when
Jesus had cried with
a loud voice, he said,
Father, into thy hands
I commend my spirit:
and having said thus,
he gave up the ghost.
47 Now when the cen-
turion saw what was
done, he glorified God,
saying, Certainly this
was a righteous man.
48 And all the people
that came together to
that sight, beholding
the things which were
done, smote their
breasts, and returned.
49 And all his ac-
quaintance, and the
women that followed
him from Galilee,
stood afar off, behold-
ing these things.

50 And, behold, *there*
was a man named
Joseph, a counseller;
and he was a good man,
and a just: 51 (the
same had not consent-
ed to the counsel and
deed of them;) *he was*
of Arimathæa, a city
of the Jews: who also
himself waited for
the kingdom of God.
52 This *man* went unto
Pilate, and begged the
body of Jesus. 53 And
he took it down, and
wrapped it in linen,

---

[v] — τῷ (*read* he said, Jesus, remember) TTrA. [w] — κύριε [L]TTrA. [x] — ὁ Ἰησοῦς (*read* he said) T[Tr]A. [y] σοι λέγω TTrA. [z] καὶ ἦν ἤδη ([ἤδη] TrA) and it was now LTTrA. [a] ἐνάτης LTTrA. [b] τοῦ ἡλίου ἐκλιπόντος (darkness came) from the sun failing T. [c] ἐσχίσθη δὲ T. [d] παρατίθεμαι I commit LTTrAW. [e] καὶ τοῦτο and this L; τοῦτο δὲ TTrA. [f] ἑκατοντάρχης TTr. [g] ἐδόξαζεν LTTrA. [h] συνπαραγενόμενοι TA. [i] θεωρήσαντες having seen LTTrA. [k] — ἑαυτῶν (*read* the breasts) TTrA. [l] αὐτῷ LTTrA. [m] + ἀπὸ from LT. [n] συνακολουθοῦσαι TTrA. [o] + καὶ and T. [p] συνκατατιθέμενος T; συνκατατεθειμένος A. [q] — καὶ and LTTrA. [r] — καὶ αὐτὸς LTTrA. [s] Πειλάτῳ T. [t] — αὐτὸ (*read* [it]) LTTrA.

and laid it in a sepulchre that was hewn in stone, wherein never man before was laid. 54 And that day was the preparation, and the sabbath drew on.

55 And the women also, which came with him from Galilee, followed after, and beheld the sepulchre, and how his body was laid. 56 And they returned, and prepared spices and ointments; and rested the sabbath day according to the commandment. XXIV. Now upon the first *day* of the week, very early in the morning, they came unto the sepulchre, bringing the spices which they had prepared, and certain *others* with them. 2 And they found the stone rolled away from the sepulchre. 3 And they entered in, and found not the body of the Lord Jesus. 4 And it came to pass, as they were much perplexed thereabout, behold, two men stood by them in shining garments: 5 and as they were afraid, and bowed down *their* faces to the earth, they said unto them, Why seek ye the living among the dead? 6 He is not here, but is risen: remember how he spake unto you when he was yet in Galilee, 7 saying, The Son of man must be delivered into the hands of sinful men, and be crucified, and the third day rise again. 8 And they remembered his words, 9 and returned from the sepulchre, and told all these things unto the eleven, and to all the rest. 10 It was Mary Magdalene, and Joanna, and Mary *the mother* of James, and other *women that were* with them, which told these things unto the apostles. 11 And their

σινδόνι καὶ ἔθηκεν [v]αὐτὸ‖ ἐν μνήματι λαξευτῷ, οὗ
in a linen cloth and placed it in a tomb hewn in a rock, in which
οὐκ ἦν [w]οὐδέπω.οὐδεὶς‖ κείμενος. 54 καὶ ἡμέρα ἦν [x]παρα-
³was ¹no ²one ever yet laid. And ⁴day ¹it ²was ³pre-
σκευή,‖ καὶ σάββατον ἐπέφωσκεν.
paration, and Sabbath was coming on.

55 Κατακολουθήσασαι.δὲ [y]καὶ‖ [z] γυναῖκες, αἵτινες ἦσαν
And ³having ⁴followed ²also ¹women, who were
συνεληλυθυῖαι [a]αὐτῷ‖ ἐκ τῆς Γαλιλαίας[b], ἐθεάσαντο τὸ
come with him out of Galilee, saw the
μνημεῖον, καὶ ὡς ἐτέθη τὸ.σῶμα.αὐτοῦ. 56 ὑποστρέψασαι.δὲ
tomb, and how was laid his body. And having returned
ἡτοίμασαν ἀρώματα καὶ μύρα. καὶ τὸ.μὲν.σάββατον ἡσύχα-
they prepared aromatics and ointments, and on the sabbath remained
σαν κατὰ τὴν ἐντολήν. 24 τῇ.δὲ μιᾷ τῶν σαβ-
quiet, according to the commandment. But on the first [day] of the week
βάτων ὄρθρου.[c]βαθέος‖ [d]ἦλθον ἐπὶ τὸ μνῆμα,‖ φέρουσαι ἃ
at early dawn they came to the tomb, bringing ²which
ἡτοίμασαν ἀρώματα, [e]καί τινες σὺν αὐταῖς.‖ 2 Εὗ-
³they ⁴had ⁵prepared ¹aromatics, and some [others] with them. ²They
ρον δὲ τὸν λίθον ἀποκεκυλισμένον ἀπὸ τοῦ μνημείου, 3 [f]καὶ
³found ¹and the stone rolled away from the tomb; and
εἰσελθοῦσαι‖ οὐχ.εὗρον τὸ σῶμα τοῦ κυρίου Ἰησοῦ. 4 καὶ
having entered they found not the body of the Lord Jesus. And
ἐγένετο ἐν.τῷ.[g]διαπορεῖσθαι‖ αὐτὰς περὶ τούτου, καὶ ἰδού,
it came to pass as ²were ³perplexed ¹they about this, that behold,
[h]δύο ἄνδρες‖ ἐπέστησαν αὐταῖς ἐν [i]ἐσθήσεσιν ἀστραπτούσαις.‖
two men stood by them in ²garments ¹shining.
5 ἐμφόβων δὲ γενομένων αὐτῶν καὶ κλινουσῶν [k]τὸ πρόσω-
And ³filled ⁴with ⁵fear ²becoming ¹they and bowing the face
πον‖ εἰς τὴν γῆν, [l]εἶπον‖ πρὸς αὐτάς, Τί ζητεῖτε τὸν ζῶντα
to the earth, they said to them, Why seek ye the living
μετὰ τῶν νεκρῶν; 6 οὐκ.ἔστιν ὧδε, [m]ἀλλ'‖ ἠγέρθη· μνήσθητε
with the dead? He is not here, but is risen: remember
ὡς ἐλάλησεν ὑμῖν, ἔτι ὢν ἐν τῇ Γαλιλαίᾳ, 7 λέγων, [n]Ὅτι
how he spoke to you, yet being in Galilee, saying,
δεῖ τὸν υἱὸν τοῦ ἀνθρώπου‖ παραδοθῆναι εἰς χεῖρας
It behoveth the Son of man to be delivered up into hands
ἀνθρώπων ἁμαρτωλῶν, καὶ σταυρωθῆναι, καὶ τῇ τρίτῃ ἡμέρᾳ
of ²men ¹sinful, and to be crucified, and the third day
ἀναστῆναι. 8 Καὶ ἐμνήσθησαν τῶν.ῥημάτων.αὐτοῦ· 9 καὶ
to arise. And they remembered his words; and
ὑποστρέψασαι ἀπὸ τοῦ μνημείου ἀπήγγειλαν [o]ταῦτα πάντα‖
having returned from the tomb they related ²these ³things ¹all
τοῖς ἕνδεκα καὶ πᾶσιν τοῖς λοιποῖς. 10 [p]ἦσαν.δὲ‖ ἡ Μαγδαληνὴ
to the eleven and to all the rest. Now it was ²Magdalene
Μαρία καὶ [q]Ἰωάννα‖ καὶ Μαρία [r] Ἰακώβου, καὶ αἱ λοιπαὶ σὺν
¹Mary and Joanna and Mary of James, and the rest with
αὐταῖς, [s]αἳ‖ ἔλεγον, πρὸς τοὺς ἀποστόλους ταῦτα. 11 Καὶ
them, who told to the apostles these things. And

[v] αὐτὸν him LTTrA. [w] οὐδεὶς οὐδέπω T; οὐδεὶς οὔπω LTrA. [x] παρασκευῆς LTTrA. [y] — καὶ LTTrAW. [z] + αἱ the LTr. [a] — αὐτῷ T[Tr]A. [b] + αὐτῷ him TA. [c] βαθέως LTTrAW. [d] ἐπὶ τὸ μνῆμα ἦλθον T. [e] — καί τινες σὺν αὐταῖς LTTrA. [f] εἰσελθοῦσαι δὲ LTTrA. [g] ἀπορεῖσθαι LTTrA. [h] ἄνδρες δύο GLTTrAW. [i] ἐσθῆτι ἀστραπτούσῃ shining raiment LTTrA. [k] τὰ πρόσωπα the faces TTr. [l] εἶπαν LTTrA. [m] ἀλλὰ TTrA. [n] τὸν υἱὸν τοῦ ἀνθρώπου ὅτι δεῖ TTrA. [o] πάντα ταῦτα T. [p] [ἦσαν δὲ] TrA. [q] Ἰωάνα Tr. [r] + ἡ the [...] LTTr[A]W. [s] — αἳ LTTr[A].

ἐφάνησαν ἐνώπιον αὐτῶν ὡσεὶ λῆρος τὰ.ῥήματα [t]αὐτῶν,‖
[3]appeared [4]before [5]them [6]like [7]idle [8]talk [2]words [1]their,
καὶ ἠπίστουν αὐταῖς. 12 [v]ὁ.δὲ.Πέτρος ἀναστὰς ἔδραμεν
and they disbelieved them. But Peter having risen up ran
ἐπὶ τὸ μνημεῖον, καὶ παρακύψας βλέπει τὰ ὀθόνια
to the tomb, and having stooped down he sees the linen clothes
[w]κείμενα μόνα·‖ καὶ ἀπῆλθεν πρὸς.[x]ἑαυτὸν‖ θαυμάζων τὸ
lying alone, and went away home wondering at that which
γεγονός.‖
had come to pass.

13 Καὶ ἰδού, δύο ἐξ αὐτῶν [y]ἦσαν πορευόμενοι ἐν αὐτῇ τῇ
And lo, two of them were going on [2]same [1]the
ἡμέρᾳ‖ εἰς κώμην ἀπέχουσαν σταδίους ἑξήκοντα ἀπὸ Ἱερου-
day to a village being distant [2]furlongs [1]sixty from Jeru-
σαλήμ, ᾗ ὄνομα Ἐμμαούς· 14 καὶ αὐτοὶ ὡμίλουν πρὸς
salem, whose name [is] Emmaus; and they were conversing with
ἀλλήλους περὶ πάντων τῶν συμβεβηκότων τούτων. 15 καὶ
one another about all [3]which [4]had [5]taken [6]place [1]these [2]things. And
ἐγένετο ἐν.τῷ.ὁμιλεῖν.αὐτοὺς καὶ [z]συζητεῖν,‖ καὶ αὐτὸς [a]ὁ‖
it came to pass as they conversed and reasoned, that [2]himself
Ἰησοῦς ἐγγίσας συνεπορεύετο αὐτοῖς· 16 οἱ.δὲ ὀφθαλμοὶ
[1]Jesus having drawn near went with them; but the eyes
αὐτῶν ἐκρατοῦντο τοῦ μὴ ἐπιγνῶναι αὐτόν. 17 Εἶπεν.δὲ
of them were holden [so as] not to know him. And he said
πρὸς αὐτούς, Τίνες οἱ λόγοι οὗτοι οὓς ἀντιβάλλετε πρὸς
to them, What words [are] these which ye exchange with
ἀλλήλους περιπατοῦντες, [b]καί ἐστε σκυθρωποί;‖
one another as ye walk, and are downcast in countenance?
18 Ἀποκριθεὶς.δὲ [c]ὁ‖ εἷς[d], [e]ᾧ ὄνομα‖ Κλεόπας, εἶπεν πρὸς
And answering the one, whose name [was] Cleopas, said to
αὐτόν, Σὺ μόνος παροικεῖς [f]ἐν‖ Ἱερουσαλήμ, καὶ οὐκ.ἔγνως
him, [2]Thou [3]alone [1]sojournest in Jerusalem, and hast not known
τὰ γενόμενα ἐν αὐτῇ ἐν ταῖς.ἡμέραις.ταύταις;
the things which are come to pass in it in these days?
19 Καὶ εἶπεν αὐτοῖς, Ποῖα; Οἱ.δὲ [g]εἶπον‖ αὐτῷ, Τὰ
And he said to them, What things? And they said to him, The things
περὶ Ἰησοῦ τοῦ [h]Ναζωραίου,‖ ὃς ἐγένετο ἀνὴρ προφήτης,
concerning Jesus the Nazaræan, who was a man a prophet,
δυνατὸς ἐν ἔργῳ καὶ [i] λόγῳ ἐναντίον τοῦ θεοῦ καὶ παντὸς τοῦ
mighty in deed and word before God and all the
λαοῦ· 20 ὅπως.τε [k]παρέδωκαν αὐτὸν‖ οἱ ἀρχιερεῖς καὶ οἱ
people; and how [7]delivered [8]up [9]him [1]the [2]chief [3]priests [4]and
ἄρχοντες.ἡμῶν εἰς κρίμα θανάτου, καὶ ἐσταύρωσαν αὐτόν·
[5]our [6]rulers to judgment of death, and crucified him.
21 ἡμεῖς.δὲ ἠλπίζομεν ὅτι αὐτός ἐστιν ὁ μέλλων λυτροῦσθαι
But we were hoping he it is who is about to redeem
τὸν Ἰσραήλ. ἀλλά.γε [l] σὺν πᾶσιν τούτοις τρίτην ταύτην
Israel. But then with all these things [4]third [3]this
ἡμέραν ἄγει [m]σήμερον‖ ἀφ'.οὗ ταῦτα ἐγένετο. 22 ἀλλὰ.καὶ
[5]day [2]brings [1]to-day since these things came to pass. And withal
γυναῖκές τινες ἐξ ἡμῶν ἐξέστησαν ἡμᾶς, γενόμεναι
[2]women [1]certain from amongst us astonished us, having been

words seemed to them as idle tales, and they believed them not. 12 Then arose Peter, and ran unto the sepulchre; and stooping down, he beheld the linen clothes laid by themselves, and departed, wondering in himself at that which was come to pass.

13 And, behold, two of them went that same day to a village called Emmaus, which was from Jerusalem *about* threescore furlongs. 14 And they talked together of all these things which had happened. 15 And it came to pass, that, while they communed *together* and reasoned, Jesus himself drew near, and went with them. 16 But their eyes were holden that they should not know him. 17 And he said unto them, What manner of communications *are* these that ye have one to another, as ye walk, and are sad? 18 And the one of them, whose name was Cleopas, answering said unto him, Art thou only a stranger in Jerusalem, and hast not known the things which are come to pass there in these days? 19 And he said unto them, What things? And they said unto him, Concerning Jesus of Nazareth, which was a prophet mighty in deed and word before God and all the people: 20 and how the chief priests and our rulers delivered him to be condemned to death, and have crucified him. 21 But we trusted that it had been he which should have redeemed Israel: and beside all this, to day is the third day since these things were done. 22 Yea, and certain women also of our company made us astonished, which were early at

[t] ταῦτα these LTTrA. [v] — *verse* 12 [L]T[Tr]. [w] [κείμενα μόνα] A; — κείμενα Tr. [x] αὐτὸν Tr. [y] ἐν αὐτῇ τῇ ἡμέρᾳ ἦσαν πορευόμενοι T. [z] συνζητεῖν LTTrA. [a] — ὁ TTrA. [b] ; καὶ ἐστάθησαν ([; καὶ ἐστά.] A) σκυθρωποί. (*question ends at* walk) And they stood downcast in countenance. TTrA. [c] — ὁ LTTrA. [d] + [ἐξ αὐτῶν] of them L. [e] ὀνόματι by name TrA. [f] — ἐν (*read* [in]) GTTrAW. [g] εἶπαν TTr. [h] Ναζαρηνοῦ TTrA. [i] + [ἐν] in L. [k] αὐτὸν παρέδωκαν L. [l] + καὶ also LTTrA. [m] — σήμερον (*read* it brings) T[TrA].

the sepulchre; 23 and
when they found not
his body, they came,
saying, that they had
also seen a vision of
angels, which said that
he was alive. 24 And
certain of them which
were with us went
to the sepulchre, and
found *it* even so as the
women had said: but
him they saw not.
25 Then he said unto
them, O fools, and slow
of heart to believe all
that the prophets have
spoken: 26 ought not
Christ to have suffered
these things, and to
enter into his glory?
27 And beginning at
Moses and all the prophets, he expounded
unto them in all the
scriptures the things
concerning himself.
28 And they drew nigh
unto the village, whither they went: and he
made as though he
would have gone further. 29 But they constrained him, saying,
Abide with us: for it
is toward evening, and
the day is far spent.
And he went in to
tarry with them.
30 And it came to pass,
as he sat at meat with
them, he took bread,
and blessed *it*, and
brake, and gave to
them. 31 And their
eyes were opened, and
they knew him; and
he vanished out of
their sight. 32 And
they said one to another, Did not our
heart burn within us,
while he talked with
us by the way, and
while he opened to us
the scriptures? 33 And
they rose up the same
hour, and returned to
Jerusalem, and found
the eleven gathered
together, and them
that were with them,
34 saying, The Lord is
risen indeed, and hath
appeared to Simon.
35 And they told what
things *were done* in
the way, and how he
was known of them in
breaking of bread.

[n]ὄρθριαι‖ ἐπὶ τὸ μνημεῖον· 23 καὶ μὴ εὑροῦσαι τὸ.σῶμα.αὐτοῦ
early to the tomb, and not having found his body
ἦλθον, λέγουσαι καὶ ὀπτασίαν ἀγγέλων ἑωρακέναι, οἳ λέγουσιν
came, declaring also a vision of angels to have seen, who say
αὐτὸν ζῆν. 24 καὶ ἀπῆλθόν τινες τῶν σὺν ἡμῖν ἐπὶ τὸ
he is living. And [6]went [1]some [2]of [3]those [4]with [5]us to the
μνημεῖον καὶ εὗρον οὕτως καθὼς [o]καὶ‖ αἱ γυναῖκες εἶπον,
tomb and found [it] so as also the women said,
αὐτὸν.δὲ οὐκ.εἶδον. 25 Καὶ αὐτὸς εἶπεν πρὸς αὐτούς, Ὦ
but him they saw not. And he said to them, O
ἀνόητοι καὶ βραδεῖς τῇ καρδίᾳ τοῦ πιστεύειν ἐπὶ πᾶσιν οἷς
senseless and slow of heart to believe in all which
ἐλάλησαν οἱ προφῆται· 26 οὐχὶ ταῦτα ἔδει
spoke the prophets. [3]Not [10]these [11]things [1]was [2]it [4]needful [5]for
παθεῖν τὸν χριστόν, καὶ εἰσελθεῖν εἰς τὴν.δόξαν.αὐτοῦ;
[8]to [9]suffer [6]the [7]Christ, and to enter into his glory?
27 Καὶ ἀρξάμενος ἀπὸ [p]Μωσέως‖ καὶ ἀπὸ πάντων τῶν προ-
And beginning from Moses and from all the pro-
φητῶν [q]διηρμήνευεν‖ αὐτοῖς ἐν πάσαις ταῖς γραφαῖς τὰ
phets he interpreted to them in all the scriptures the things
περὶ [r]ἑαυτοῦ.‖ 28 Καὶ ἤγγισαν εἰς τὴν κώμην οὗ
concerning himself. And they drew near to the village where
ἐπορεύοντο, καὶ αὐτὸς [s]προσεποιεῖτο‖ [t]πορρωτέρω‖ πορεύεσθαι.
they were going, and he appeared [4]farther [1]to [2]be [3]going.
29 καὶ παρεβιάσαντο αὐτόν, λέγοντες, Μεῖνον μεθ' ἡμῶν, ὅτι
And they constrained him, saying, Abide with us, for
πρὸς ἑσπέραν ἐστίν, καὶ κέκλικεν [v] ἡ ἡμέρα. Καὶ εἰσῆλθεν
towards evening it is, and has declined the day. And he entered in
τοῦ μεῖναι σὺν αὐτοῖς. 30 καὶ ἐγένετο ἐν.τῷ.κατακλιθῆναι
to abide with them. And it came to pass as [2]reclined
αὐτὸν μετ' αὐτῶν, λαβὼν τὸν ἄρτον [w]εὐλόγησεν,‖
[[3]at [4]table] [1]he with them, having taken the bread he blessed,
καὶ κλάσας ἐπεδίδου αὐτοῖς. 31 αὐτῶν.δὲ διηνοίχθησαν οἱ
and having broken he gave [it] to them. And their [2]were [3]opened
ὀφθαλμοί καὶ ἐπέγνωσαν αὐτόν· καὶ αὐτὸς ἄφαντος.ἐγένετο
[1]eyes and they knew him. And he disappeared
ἀπ' αὐτῶν. 32 Καὶ [x]εἶπον‖ πρὸς ἀλλήλους, Οὐχὶ ἡ καρδία
from them. And they said to one another, [2]Not [4]heart
ἡμῶν καιομένη ἦν [y]ἐν ἡμῖν‖ ὡς ἐλάλει ἡμῖν ἐν τῇ ὁδῷ,
[3]our [5]burning [1]was in us as he was speaking to us in the way,
[z]καὶ‖ ὡς διήνοιγεν ἡμῖν τὰς γραφάς; 33 Καὶ ἀναστάντες
and as he was opening to us the scriptures? And rising up
αὐτῇ.τῇ ὥρᾳ ὑπέστρεψαν εἰς Ἱερουσαλήμ, καὶ εὗρον [a]συνη-
the same hour they returned to Jerusalem, and they found gathered
θροισμένους‖ τοὺς ἕνδεκα καὶ τοὺς σὺν αὐτοῖς, 34 λέγοντας,
together the eleven and those with them, saying,
Ὅτι [b]ἠγέρθη ὁ κύριος ὄντως,‖ καὶ ὤφθη Σίμωνι. 35 Καὶ
[3]Is [4]risen [1]the [2]Lord indeed, and appeared to Simon. And
αὐτοὶ ἐξηγοῦντο τὰ ἐν τῇ ὁδῷ, καὶ ὡς ἐγνώσθη αὐτοῖς
they related the things in the way, and how he was known to them
ἐν τῇ κλάσει τοῦ ἄρτου.
in the breaking of the bread.

---

[n] ὀρθριναὶ LTTrAW. [o] — καὶ LTrA. [p] Μωϋσέως LTTrAW. [q] διερμήνευεν L; διερμήνευσεν TTrA. [r] αὐτοῦ EG; αὑτοῦ LTr. [s] προσεποιήσατο LTTrA. [t] πορρώτερον LTrA. [v] + ἤδη already [L]TTrA. [w] ηὐλόγησεν L. [x] εἶπαν TTrA. [y] [ἐν ἡμῖν] TrA. [z] — καὶ LTTrA. [a] ἠθροισμένους gathered LTTrA. [b] ὄντως ἠγέρθη ὁ κύριος LTTrA.

36 Ταῦτα.δὲ αὐτῶν.λαλούντων, αὐτὸς [c]ὁ Ἰησοῦς‖ ἔστη ἐν
And these things as they were telling, [2]himself [1]Jesus stood in
μέσῳ αὐτῶν [d]καὶ λέγει αὐτοῖς, Εἰρήνη ὑμῖν.‖ [e] 37 Πτοηθέντες
[2]midst [1]their and says to them, Peace to you. [3]Terrified
δὲ καὶ ἔμφοβοι γενόμενοι ἐδόκουν πνεῦμα θεωρεῖν.
[1]but [4]and [5]filled [6]with [7]fear [2]being they thought a spirit they beheld.
38 καὶ εἶπεν αὐτοῖς, Τί τεταραγμένοι ἐστέ; καὶ [f]διατί‖ δια-
And he said to them, Why troubled are ye? and wherefore [2]rea-
λογισμοὶ ἀναβαίνουσιν ἐν [g]ταῖς καρδίαις‖ ὑμῶν; 39 ἴδετε
sonings [1]do come up in [2]hearts [1]your? see
τὰς.χεῖράς.μου καὶ τοὺς.πόδας.μου, ὅτι [h]αὐτὸς ἐγώ εἰμι.‖
my hands and my feet, that [3]he [1]I [2]am.
ψηλαφήσατέ με καὶ ἴδετε· ὅτι πνεῦμα [i]σάρκα‖ καὶ ὀστέα οὐκ
Handle me and see, for a spirit flesh and bones [2]not
ἔχει, καθὼς ἐμὲ θεωρεῖτε ἔχοντα. 40 [k]Καὶ τοῦτο εἰπὼν
[1]has, as [3]me [1]ye [2]see having. And this having said
[l]ἐπέδειξεν[l] αὐτοῖς τὰς χεῖρας καὶ τοὺς πόδας.‖ 41 ἔτι.δὲ
he shewed to them [his] hands and feet. But yet
ἀπιστούντων.αὐτῶν [m]ἀπὸ τῆς χαρᾶς καὶ θαυμαζόντων,‖ εἶπεν
while they were disbelieving for joy and were wondering, he said
αὐτοῖς, Ἔχετέ τι βρώσιμον ἐνθάδε; 42 Οἱ.δὲ ἐπέδωκαν
to them, Have ye anything eatable here? And they gave
αὐτῷ ἰχθύος ὀπτοῦ μέρος [n]καὶ ἀπὸ μελισσίου.κηρίου.‖ 43 καὶ
to him [2]of [3]a [5]fish [4]broiled [1]part and of a honeycomb. And
λαβὼν ἐνώπιον αὐτῶν ἔφαγεν. 44 Εἶπεν.δὲ [o]αὐτοῖς,‖
having taken [it] [3]before [4]them [1]he [2]ate. And he said to them,
Οὗτοι οἱ λόγοι[p] οὓς ἐλάλησα πρὸς ὑμᾶς ἔτι ὢν σὺν ὑμῖν,
These [are] the words which I spoke to you yet being with you,
ὅτι δεῖ πληρωθῆναι πάντα τὰ γεγραμμένα ἐν τῷ.νόμῳ
that must be fulfilled all things that have been written in the law
[q]Μωσέως‖ καὶ [r] προφήταις καὶ ψαλμοῖς περὶ ἐμοῦ. 45 Τότε
of Moses and prophets and psalms concerning me. Then
διήνοιξεν αὐτῶν τὸν νοῦν τοῦ συνιέναι τὰς γραφάς·
he opened their understanding to understand the scriptures,
46 καὶ εἶπεν αὐτοῖς, Ὅτι οὕτως γέγραπται, [s]καὶ οὕτως
and said to them, Thus it has been written, and thus
ἔδει‖ παθεῖν τὸν χριστὸν καὶ ἀναστῆναι ἐκ νεκρῶν
it behoved [3]to [4]suffer [1]the [2]Christ and to rise from among [the] dead
τῇ τρίτῃ ἡμέρᾳ, 47 καὶ κηρυχθῆναι ἐπὶ τῷ.ὀνόματι.αὐτοῦ
the third day; and should be proclaimed in his name
μετάνοιαν [t]καὶ‖ ἄφεσιν ἁμαρτιῶν εἰς πάντα τὰ ἔθνη, [u]ἀρξά-
repentance and remission of sins to all nations, begin-
μενον‖ ἀπὸ Ἱερουσαλήμ. 48 ὑμεῖς [v]δέ ἐστε‖ μάρτυρες τούτων.
ning at Jerusalem. [2]Ye [1]and are witnesses of these things.
49 [w]καὶ ἰδού, ἐγὼ‖ [x]ἀποστέλλω‖ τὴν ἐπαγγελίαν τοῦ πατρός
And lo, I send the promise of [2]Father
μου.ἐφ᾽ ὑμᾶς· ὑμεῖς.δὲ καθίσατε ἐν τῇ πόλει [y]Ἱερουσαλὴμ‖
[1]my upon you; but [2]ye [1]remain in the city of Jerusalem
ἕως.οὗ ἐνδύσησθε [z]δύναμιν ἐξ ὕψους.‖
till ye be clothed with power from on high.

36 And as they thus
spake, Jesus himself
stood in the midst of
them, and saith unto
them, Peace *be* unto
you. 37 But they were
terrified and affright-
ed, and supposed that
they had seen a spirit.
38 And he said unto
them, Why are ye
troubled? and why do
thoughts arise in your
hearts? 39 Behold my
hands and my feet,
that it is I myself:
handle me, and see;
for a spirit hath not
flesh and bones, as ye
see me have. 40 And
when he had thus spo-
ken, he shewed them
his hands and *his* feet.
41 And while they yet
believed not for joy,
and wondered, he said
unto them, Have ye
here any meat? 42 And
they gave him a piece
of a broiled fish, and
of an honeycomb.
43 And he took *it*, and
did eat before them.
44 And he said unto
them, These *are* the
words which I spake
unto you, while I was
yet with you, that all
things must be ful-
filled, which were
written in the law of
Moses, and *in* the pro-
phets, and *in* the
psalms, concerning
me. 45 Then opened he
their understanding,
that they might under-
stand the scriptures,
46 and said unto them,
Thus it is written, and
thus it behoved Christ
to suffer, and to rise
from the dead the
third day: 47 and that
repentance and remis-
sion of sins should be
preached in his name
among all nations, be-
ginning at Jerusalem.
48 And ye are wit-
nesses of these things.
49 And, behold, I send
the promise of my Fa-
ther upon you: but
tarry ye in the city of
Jerusalem, until ye be
endued with power
from on high.

---

[c] — ὁ Ἰησοῦς GLTTrA. [d] — καὶ λέγει αὐτοῖς, Εἰρήνη ὑμῖν T. [e] + [ἐγώ εἰμι, μὴ φοβεῖσθε] I am [he], fear not L. [f] διὰ τί LTrA. [g] τῇ καρδίᾳ heart LTTrA. [h] ἐγώ εἰμι αὐτός LTTrA. [i] σάρκας T. [k] — *verse* 40 T[Tr]. [l] ἔδειξεν LTr; [ἐπ]έδειξεν A. [m] καὶ θαυμαζόντων ἀπὸ τῆς χαρᾶς L. [n] — καὶ ἀπὸ μελισσίου κηρίου LT[TrA]. [o] πρὸς αὐτούς TTrA. [p] + μου (*read* my words) [L]TTrA. [q] Μωϋσέως LTTrAW. [r] + [τοῖς] the Tr. [s] — καὶ οὕτως ἔδει [L]TTrA. [t] εἰς to T. [u] ἀρξάμενοι TTrA. [v] — δέ ἐστε ([ἐστε] Tr) (*read* [are]) TTrA. [w] κἀγὼ and I T. [x] ἐξαποστέλλω send out TTrA. [y] — Ἱερουσαλήμ GLTTrA. [z] ἐξ ὕψους δύναμιν TTrA.

50 And he led them out as far as to Bethany, and he lifted up his hands, and blessed them. 51 And it came to pass, while he blessed them, he was parted from them, and carried up into heaven. 52 And they worshipped him, and returned to Jerusalem with great joy: 53 and were continually in the temple, praising and blessing God. Amen.

50 Ἐξήγαγεν.δὲ αὐτοὺς [a]ἔξω‖ ἕως [b]εἰς‖ Βηθανίαν, καὶ
And he led them out as far as to Bethany, and
ἐπάρας τὰς.χεῖρας.αὐτοῦ εὐλόγησεν αὐτούς. 51 καὶ
having lifted up his hands he blessed them. And
ἐγένετο ἐν.τῷ.εὐλογεῖν αὐτὸν αὐτοὺς διέστη ἀπ' αὐτῶν
it came to pass as [2]was [3]blessing [1]he them he was separated from them
[c]καὶ ἀνεφέρετο εἰς τὸν οὐρανόν.‖ 52 καὶ αὐτοὶ [d]προσκυνή-
and was carried up into the heaven. And they having wor-
σαντες αὐτὸν‖ ὑπέστρεψαν εἰς Ἱερουσαλὴμ μετὰ χαρᾶς μεγά-
shipped him returned to Jerusalem with [2]joy [1]great,
λης· 53 καὶ ἦσαν [e]διαπαντὸς‖ ἐν τῷ ἱερῷ, [f]αἰνοῦντες καὶ
and were continually in the temple, praising and
εὐλογοῦντες‖ τὸν θεόν. [g]Ἀμήν.‖
blessing God. Amen.

[h]Τὸ κατὰ Λουκᾶν εὐαγγέλιον.‖
The [3]according [4]to [5]Luke [1]glad [2]tidings..

---

[i]ΤΟ ΚΑΤΑ ΙΩΑΝΝΗΝ ΑΓΙΟΝ ΕΥΑΓΓΕΛΙΟΝ.‖
THE [4]ACCORDING [5]TO [6]JOHN [1]HOLY [2]GLAD [3]TIDINGS.

IN the beginning was the Word, and the Word was with God, and the Word was God. 2 The same was in the beginning with God. 3 All things were made by him; and without him was not any thing made that was made. 4 In him was life; and the life was the light of men. 5 And the light shineth in darkness; and the darkness comprehended it not.

ἘΝ ἀρχῇ ἦν ὁ λόγος, καὶ ὁ λόγος ἦν πρὸς τὸν θεόν,
In [the] beginning was the Word, and the Word was with God,
καὶ θεὸς ἦν ὁ λόγος. 2 οὗτος ἦν ἐν ἀρχῇ πρὸς τὸν
and [4]God [3]was [1]the [2]Word. He was in [the] beginning with
θεόν. 3 Πάντα δι' αὐτοῦ ἐγένετο, καὶ χωρὶς αὐτοῦ
God. All things through him came into being, and without him
ἐγένετο οὐδὲ [k]ἓν ὃ γέγονεν. 4 ἐν‖ αὐτῷ ζωὴ
came into being not even one [thing] which has come into being. In him [2]life
[l]ἦν,‖ καὶ ἡ ζωὴ ἦν τὸ φῶς τῶν ἀνθρώπων· 5 καὶ τὸ φῶς ἐν
[1]was, and the life was the light of men. And the light in
τῇ σκοτίᾳ φαίνει, καὶ ἡ σκοτία αὐτὸ οὐ.κατέλαβεν.
the darkness appears, and the darkness [2]it [1]apprehended not.

6 There was a man sent from God, whose name was John. 7 The same came for a witness, to bear witness of the Light, that all *men* through him might believe. 8 He was not that Light, but *was sent* to bear witness of that Light. 9 *That* was the true Light, which lighteth every man that cometh into the world. 10 He was in the world, and the world was made by him, and the world knew him not. 11 He came unto his own, and his own received him not. 12 But as many as received him, to them gave he power

6 Ἐγένετο ἄνθρωπος ἀπεσταλμένος παρὰ θεοῦ, ὄνομα
There was a man sent from God, [2]name
αὐτῷ [m]Ἰωάννης.‖ 7 οὗτος ἦλθεν εἰς μαρτυρίαν, ἵνα μαρτυ-
[1]his John. He came for a witness, that he might
ρήσῃ περὶ τοῦ φωτός, ἵνα πάντες πιστεύσωσιν δι' αὐτοῦ.
witness concerning the light, that all might believe through him.
8 οὐκ.ἦν ἐκεῖνος τὸ φῶς, ἀλλ' ἵνα μαρτυρήσῃ περὶ τοῦ
[3]Was [2]not [1]he the light, but that he might witness concerning the
φωτός. 9 ἦν τὸ φῶς τὸ ἀληθινόν ὃ φωτίζει πάντα
light. [4]Was [1]the [3]light [2]true that which lightens every
ἄνθρωπον ἐρχόμενον εἰς τὸν κόσμον. 10 ἐν τῷ κόσμῳ ἦν,
man coming into the world. In the world he was,
καὶ ὁ κόσμος δι' αὐτοῦ ἐγένετο, καὶ ὁ κόσμος αὐτὸν
and the world through him came into being, and the world him
οὐκ.ἔγνω. 11 εἰς τὰ.ἴδια ἦλθεν, καὶ οἱ.ἴδιοι αὐτὸν οὐ.παρέλα-
knew not. To his own he came, and his own him received not;
βον· 12 ὅσοι.δὲ [n]ἔλαβον‖ αὐτὸν ἔδωκεν αὐτοῖς ἐξουσίαν
but as many as received him he gave to them authority

---

[a] — ἔξω [L]TTr[A]. [b] πρὸς LTTrA. [c] — καὶ ἀνεφέρετο εἰς τὸν οὐρανόν T. [d] — προσκυνήσαντες αὐτόν T. [e] διὰ παντὸς LA. [f] [αἰνοῦντες καὶ] εὐλογοῦντες TrA; — καὶ εὐλογοῦντες T. [g] — Ἀμήν G[L]TTrA. [h] Κατὰ Λουκᾶν TrA; — Τὸ κατὰ Λουκᾶν εὐαγγέλιον EGLTW.

[i] — ἅγιον E; Εὐαγγέλιον κατὰ Ἰωάννην (Ἰωάνην Tr) GLTrAW; κατὰ Ἰωάννην T. [k] ἕν. ὃ γέγονεν ἐν (*read* one [thing]. That which was in him was life) LTr. [l] ἐστιν is LT. [m] Ἰωάνης Tr. [n] ἔλαβαν Tr.

τέκνα θεοῦ γενέσθαι, τοῖς πιστεύουσιν εἰς τὸ ὄνομα
children of God to be, to those that believe on [2]name
αὐτοῦ· 13 οἳ οὐκ ἐξ αἱμάτων οὐδὲ ἐκ θελήματος σαρκὸς οὐδὲ
[1]his; who not of bloods nor of will of flesh nor
ἐκ θελήματος ἀνδρὸς ἀλλ' ἐκ θεοῦ ἐγεννήθησαν.
of will of man but of God were born.

14 Καὶ ὁ λόγος σὰρξ ἐγένετο, καὶ ἐσκήνωσεν ἐν ἡμῖν,
And the Word flesh became, and tabernacled among us,
καὶ ἐθεασάμεθα τὴν.δόξαν.αὐτοῦ, δόξαν ὡς μονογενοῦς παρὰ
(and we discerned his glory, a glory as of an only-begotten with
πατρός, πλήρης χάριτος καὶ ἀληθείας. 15 [o]Ἰωάννης[ǁ] μαρτυρεῖ
a father, full of grace and truth. John witnesses
περὶ αὐτοῦ, καὶ κέκραγεν, λέγων, Οὗτος ἦν ὃν εἶπον,
concerning him, and cried, saying, This was he of whom I said,
Ὁ ὀπίσω μου ἐρχόμενος, ἔμπροσθέν μου γέγονεν· ὅτι
He who after me comes, [2]precedence [3]of [4]me [1]has, for
πρῶτός μου ἦν. 16 [p]Καὶ[ǁ] ἐκ τοῦ.πληρώματος.αὐτοῦ ἡμεῖς
before me he was. And of his fulness we
πάντες ἐλάβομεν, καὶ χάριν ἀντὶ χάριτος· 17 ὅτι ὁ νόμος
all received, and grace upon grace. For the law
διὰ [q]Μωσέως[ǁ] ἐδόθη, ἡ χάρις καὶ ἡ ἀλήθεια διὰ Ἰησοῦ
through Moses was given; the grace and the truth through Jesus
χριστοῦ ἐγένετο. 18 θεὸν οὐδεὶς ἑώρακεν πώποτε· [r]ὁ[ǁ] μονο-
Christ came. [5]God [1]no [2]one [3]has [4]seen at any time; the only-
γενὴς [s]υἱός,[ǁ] ὁ ὢν εἰς τὸν κόλπον τοῦ πατρός, ἐκεῖνος ἐξη-
begotten Son, who is in the bosom of the Father, he de-
γήσατο. 19 Καὶ αὕτη ἐστὶν ἡ μαρτυρία τοῦ [t]Ἰωάννου,[ǁ]
clared [him]. And this is the witness of John,
ὅτε ἀπέστειλαν[v] οἱ Ἰουδαῖοι ἐξ Ἱεροσολύμων ἱερεῖς καὶ
when [3]sent [1]the [2]Jews from Jerusalem priests and
[w]Λευΐτας,[ǁ] ἵνα ἐρωτήσωσιν αὐτόν, Σὺ τίς εἶ; 20 Καὶ
Levites, that they might ask him, Thou who art thou? And
ὡμολόγησεν καὶ οὐκ.ἠρνήσατο, καὶ ὡμολόγησεν, Ὅτι [x]οὐκ εἰμὶ
he confessed and denied not, and confessed, [3]Not [2]am
ἐγὼ[ǁ] ὁ χριστός. 21 Καὶ ἠρώτησαν αὐτόν, [y]Τί οὖν; Ἠλίας
[1]I the Christ. And they asked him, What then? Elias
εἶ σύ; [z]Καὶ[ǁ] λέγει, Οὐκ.εἰμί. Ὁ προφήτης εἶ σύ; Καὶ
art thou? And he says, I am not. The prophet art thou? And
ἀπεκρίθη, Οὔ. 22 [a]Εἶπον[ǁ] [b]οὖν[ǁ] αὐτῷ, Τίς εἶ; ἵνα ἀπό-
he answered, No. They said therefore to him, Who art thou? that an
κρισιν δῶμεν τοῖς πέμψασιν ἡμᾶς· τί λέγεις περὶ
answer we may give to those who sent us: what sayest thou about
σεαυτοῦ; 23 Ἔφη, Ἐγὼ φωνὴ βοῶντος ἐν τῇ ἐρήμῳ,
thyself? He said, I [am] a voice crying in the wilderness,
Εὐθύνατε τὴν ὁδὸν κυρίου· καθὼς εἶπεν Ἠσαΐας ὁ προ-
Make straight the way of [the] Lord, as said Esaias the pro-
φήτης. 24 Καὶ [c]οἱ[ǁ] ἀπεσταλμένοι ἦσαν ἐκ τῶν Φαρι-
phet. And those who had been sent were from among the Phari-
σαίων. 25 καὶ ἠρώτησαν αὐτὸν καὶ [d]εἶπον[ǁ] αὐτῷ, Τί οὖν
sees. And they asked him and said to him, Why then
βαπτίζεις, εἰ σὺ οὐκ.εἶ ὁ χριστός, [e]οὔτε[ǁ] [f]Ἠλίας,[ǁ] [e]οὔτε[ǁ]
baptizest thou, if thou art not the Christ, nor Elias, nor

to become the sons of God, *even* to them that believe on his name:
13 which were born, not of blood, nor of the will of the flesh, nor of the will of man, but of God.

14 And the Word was made flesh, and dwelt among us, (and we beheld his glory, the glory as of the only begotten of the Father,) full of grace and truth.
15 John bare witness of him, and cried, saying, This was he of whom I spake, He that cometh after me is preferred before me: for he was before me.
16 And of his fulness have all we received, and grace for grace.
17 For the law was given by Moses, *but* grace and truth came by Jesus Christ.
18 No man hath seen God at any time; the only begotten Son, which is in the bosom of the Father, he hath declared *him*.
19 And this is the record of John, when the Jews sent priests and Levites from Jerusalem to ask him, Who art thou?
20 And he confessed, and denied not; but confessed, I am not the Christ.
21 And they asked him, What then? Art thou Elias? And he saith, I am not. Art thou that prophet? And he answered, No.
22 Then said they unto him, Who art thou? that we may give an answer to them that sent us. What sayest thou of thyself?
23 He said, I *am* the voice of one crying in the wilderness, Make straight the way of the Lord, as said the prophet Esaias.
24 And they which were sent were of the Pharisees.
25 And they asked him, and said unto him, Why baptizest thou then, if thou be not that Christ, nor Elias, neither that prophet?

[o] Ἰωάνης Tr. [p] ὅτι for GLTTrA. [q] Μωϋσέως LTTrAW. [r] — ὁ (*read* [the]) Tr. [s] θεὸς God Tr. [t] Ἰωάνου Tr. [v] + πρὸς αὐτὸν to him LTrA. [w] Λευείτας TTrA. [x] ἐγὼ οὐκ εἰμὶ LTTrA. [y] τί οὖν; Ἠλείας εἶ; T: τί οὖν; σὺ Ἠλίας εἶ; Tr: σὺ οὖν τί; Ἠλίας εἶ; A. [z] — καὶ T. [a] εἶπαν LTTrA. [b] — οὖν L. [c] — οἱ (*read* [those who]) TTrA. [d] εἶπαν LTTrA. [e] οὐδὲ LTTrA. [f] Ἠλείας T.

26 John answered
them, saying, I bap-
tize with water: but
there standeth one a-
mong you, whom ye
know not; 27 he it is,
who coming after me
is preferred before me,
whose shoe's latchet I
am not worthy to un-
loose. 28 These things
were done in Beth-
abara beyond Jordan,
where John was bap-
tizing.

ὁ προφήτης; 26 Ἀπεκρίθη αὐτοῖς ὁ [g]Ἰωάννης‖ λέγων, Ἐγὼ
the prophet? [2]Answered [3]them [1]John saying, I
βαπτίζω ἐν ὕδατι· μέσος.[h]δὲ‖ ὑμῶν [i]ἕστηκεν‖ ὃν ὑμεῖς
baptize with water; but in [the] midst of you stands [one] whom ye
οὐκ.οἴδατε· 27 [k]αὐτός ἐστιν‖ [l]ὁ‖ ὀπίσω μου ἐρχόμενος, [m]ὃς
know not; [1]he [2]it is who after me comes, who
ἔμπροσθέν μου γέγονεν·‖ οὗ [n]ἐγὼ‖ οὐκ εἰμὶ [o] ἄξιος ἵνα
[2]precedence [3]of [4]me [1]has, of whom I [2]not [1]am worthy that
λύσω αὐτοῦ τὸν ἱμάντα τοῦ ὑποδήματος. 28 Ταῦτα ἐν
I should loose of him the thong of the sandal. These things in
[p]Βηθαβαρᾶ‖ ἐγένετο πέραν τοῦ Ἰορδάνου, ὅπου ἦν [q] [r]Ἰωάν-
Bethabara took place across the Jordan, where [2]was [1]John
νης‖ βαπτίζων.
baptizing.

29 The next day
John seeth Jesus com-
ing unto him, and
saith, Behold the Lamb
of God, which taketh
away the sin of the
world. 30 This is he
of whom I said, After
me cometh a man
which is preferred be-
fore me: for he was
before me. 31 And I
knew him not: but
that he should be made
manifest to Israel,
therefore am I come
baptizing with water.
32 And John bare re-
cord, saying, I saw the
Spirit descending from
heaven like a dove, and
it abode upon him.
33 And I knew him
not: but he that sent
me to baptize with
water, the same said
unto me, Upon whom
thou shalt see the Spi-
rit descending, and re-
maining on him, the
same is he which bap-
tizeth with the Holy
Ghost. 34 And I saw,
and bare record that
this is the Son of God.

29 Τῇ ἐπαύριον βλέπει [s]ὁ Ἰωάννης‖ τὸν Ἰησοῦν ἐρχόμενον
On the morrow [2]sees [1]John Jesus coming
πρὸς αὐτόν, καὶ λέγει, Ἴδε ὁ ἀμνὸς τοῦ θεοῦ, ὁ αἴρων
to him, and says, Behold the Lamb of God, who takes away
τὴν ἁμαρτίαν τοῦ κόσμου. 30 οὗτός ἐστιν [t]περὶ‖ οὗ ἐγὼ
the sin of the world. He it is concerning whom I
εἶπον, Ὀπίσω μου ἔρχεται ἀνήρ, ὃς ἔμπροσθέν μου γέγονεν,
said, After me comes a man, who [2]precedence [3]of [4]me [1]has,
ὅτι πρῶτός μου ἦν. 31 κἀγὼ οὐκ.ᾔδειν αὐτόν· ἀλλ' ἵνα
because before me he was. And I knew not him; but that
φανερωθῇ τῷ Ἰσραήλ, διὰ.τοῦτο ἦλθον ἐγὼ ἐν [v]τῷ‖
he might be manifested to Israel, therefore came I with
ὕδατι βαπτίζων. 32 Καὶ ἐμαρτύρησεν [r]Ἰωάννης‖ λέγων, Ὅτι
water baptizing. And [2]bore [3]witness [1]John saying,
τεθέαμαι τὸ πνεῦμα καταβαῖνον [w]ὡσεὶ‖ περιστερὰν ἐξ οὐ-
I have beheld the Spirit descending as a dove out of hea-
ρανοῦ, καὶ ἔμεινεν ἐπ' αὐτόν. 33 κἀγὼ οὐκ.ᾔδειν αὐτόν· ἀλλ'
ven, and it abode upon him. And I knew not him; but
ὁ πέμψας με βαπτίζειν ἐν ὕδατι, ἐκεῖνός μοι εἶπεν, Ἐφ'
he who sent me to baptize with water, he to me said, Upon
ὃν ἂν ἴδῃς τὸ πνεῦμα καταβαῖνον καὶ μένον ἐπ'
whom thou shalt see the Spirit descending and abiding on
αὐτόν, οὗτός ἐστιν ὁ βαπτίζων ἐν πνεύματι ἁγίῳ.
him, he it is who baptizes with [the] [2]Spirit [1]Holy.
34 κἀγὼ ἑώρακα, καὶ μεμαρτύρηκα ὅτι οὗτός ἐστιν ὁ υἱὸς
And I have seen, and have borne witness that this is the Son
τοῦ θεοῦ.
of God.

35 Again the next
day after John stood,
and two of his disci-
ples; 36 and looking
upon Jesus as he walk-
ed, he saith, Behold
the Lamb of God!
37 And the two disci-
ples heard him speak,
and they followed Je-

35 Τῇ ἐπαύριον πάλιν εἱστήκει [x]ὁ‖ [r]Ἰωάννης,‖ καὶ ἐκ
On the morrow again [2]was [3]standing [1]John, and [2]of
τῶν.μαθητῶν.αὐτοῦ δύο. 36 καὶ ἐμβλέψας τῷ Ἰησοῦ περιπα-
[3]his [4]disciples [1]two. And looking at Jesus walk-
τοῦντι, λέγει, Ἴδε ὁ ἀμνὸς τοῦ θεοῦ[y]. 37 [z]Καὶ‖ ἤκουσαν
ing, he says, Behold the Lamb of God! And [4]heard
[a]αὐτοῦ οἱ δύο μαθηταὶ‖ λαλοῦντος, καὶ ἠκολούθησαν τῷ
[5]him [1]the [2]two [3]disciples speaking, and followed

---

[g] Ἰωάνης Tr. [h] — δὲ but TTrA. [i] στήκει TTrA. [k] — αὐτός ἐστιν G[L]TTrA. [l] [ὁ] TrA. [m] — ὃς ἔμπροσθέν μου γέγονεν G[L]TTrA. [n] — ἐγὼ [L]TTrA. [o] + ἐγὼ I T[Tr]A. [p] Βηθαβαρᾶ E; Βηθανίᾳ Bethany GLTTrAW. [q] + ὁ LTTr[A]. [r] Ἰωάνης Tr. [s] — ὁ Ἰωάννης (read he sees) GLTTrAW. [t] ὑπὲρ LTTrA. [v] — τῷ LTT[A]. [w] ὡς GLTTrAW [x] — ὁ LTrA. [y] + [ὁ αἴρων τὴν ἁμαρτίαν τοῦ κόσμου] who takes away the sin of the world L. [z] — καὶ T. [a] οἱ δύο μαθηταὶ αὐτοῦ T.

Ἰησοῦ. 38 στραφεὶς [c]δὲ‖ ὁ Ἰησοῦς, καὶ θεασάμενος αὐτοὺς
Jesus. [3]Having [4]turned [1]but [2]Jesus, and beheld them
ἀκολουθοῦντας, λέγει αὐτοῖς, 39 Τί ζητεῖτε; Οἱ.δὲ [d]εἶπον‖
following, says to them, What seek ye? And they said
αὐτῷ, [e]Ῥαββί,‖ ὃ λέγεται [f]ἑρμηνευόμενον‖ διδάσκαλε, ποῦ
to him, Rabbi, which is to say being interpreted Teacher, where
μένεις; 40 Λέγει αὐτοῖς, Ἔρχεσθε καὶ [g]ἴδετε.‖ [h]Ἦλθον‖
abidest thou? He says to them, Come and see. They went
[i]καὶ [k]εἶδον‖ ποῦ μένει· καὶ παρ' αὐτῷ ἔμειναν τὴν ἡμέραν
and saw where he abides; and with him they abode [2]day
ἐκείνην· ὥρα [l]δὲ‖ ἦν ὡς δεκάτη. 41 Ἦν [m]Ἀνδρέας
[1]that. [[2]The] [3]hour [1]now was about [the] tenth. [7]Was [1]Andrew
ὁ ἀδελφὸς Σίμωνος Πέτρου εἷς ἐκ τῶν δύο τῶν ἀκουσάντων
[2]the [3]brother [4]of [5]Simon [6]Peter one of the two who heard
παρὰ [n]Ἰωάννου,‖ καὶ ἀκολουθησάντων αὐτῷ. 42 εὑρίσκει
[this] from John, and followed him. [3]Finds
οὗτος [o]πρῶτος‖ τὸν.ἀδελφὸν τὸν.ἴδιον Σίμωνα, καὶ λέγει
[1]he [2]first [6]brother [4]his [5]own Simon, and says
αὐτῷ, Εὑρήκαμεν τὸν μεσσίαν, ὅ ἐστιν μεθερμηνευόμενον
to him, We have found the Messias, which is being interpreted
[p]ὁ‖ χριστός· 43 [q]καὶ‖ ἤγαγεν αὐτὸν πρὸς τὸν Ἰησοῦν.
the Christ. And he led him to Jesus.
ἐμβλέψας.[r]δὲ‖ αὐτῷ ὁ Ἰησοῦς εἶπεν, Σὺ εἶ Σίμων ὁ υἱὸς
And looking at him Jesus said, Thou art Simon the son
[s]Ἰωνᾶ·‖ σὺ κληθήσῃ Κηφᾶς, ὃ ἑρμηνεύεται Πέτρος.
of Jonas; thou shalt be called Cephas, which is interpreted Stone.
44 Τῇ ἐπαύριον ἠθέλησεν [t]ὁ Ἰησοῦς‖ ἐξελθεῖν εἰς τὴν
On the morrow [2]desired [1]Jesus to go forth into
Γαλιλαίαν· καὶ εὑρίσκει Φίλιππον καὶ λέγει αὐτῷ[v], Ἀκολούθει
Galilee, and he finds Philip and says to him, Follow
μοι. 45 Ἦν.δὲ ὁ Φίλιππος ἀπὸ Βηθσαϊδά, ἐκ τῆς πόλεως
me. Now [2]was [1]Philip from Bethsaida, of the city
Ἀνδρέου καὶ Πέτρου. 46 Εὑρίσκει Φίλιππος τὸν Ναθαναὴλ
of Andrew and Peter. [2]Finds [1]Philip Nathanael
καὶ λέγει αὐτῷ, Ὃν ἔγραψεν [w]Μωσῆς‖ ἐν τῷ νόμῳ καὶ
and says to him, [Him] whom [2]wrote [3]of [1]Moses in the law and
οἱ προφῆται, εὑρήκαμεν, Ἰησοῦν [x]τὸν‖ υἱὸν τοῦ Ἰωσὴφ τὸν
the prophets, we have found, Jesus the son of Joseph who
ἀπὸ [y]Ναζαρέτ.‖ 47 [z]Καὶ‖ εἶπεν αὐτῷ Ναθαναήλ, Ἐκ
[is] from Nazareth. And [2]said [3]to [4]him [1]Nathanael, Out of
[y]Ναζαρὲτ‖ δύναταί τι ἀγαθὸν εἶναι; Λέγει αὐτῷ [a]Φίλιππος,
Nazareth can any good thing be? [2]Says [3]to [4]him [1]Philip,
Ἔρχου καὶ ἴδε. 48 Εἶδεν [b]ὁ‖ Ἰησοῦς τὸν Ναθαναὴλ ἐρχόμενον
Come and see. [2]Saw [1]Jesus Nathanael coming
πρὸς αὐτόν, καὶ λέγει περὶ αὐτοῦ, Ἴδε ἀληθῶς [ca]Ἰσραηλ-
to him, and says concerning him, Behold truly an Israel-
ίτης,‖ ἐν ᾧ δόλος οὐκ.ἔστιν. 49 Λέγει αὐτῷ Ναθαναήλ,
ite, in whom guile is not. [2]Says [3]to [4]him [1]Nathanael,
Πόθεν με γινώσκεις; Ἀπεκρίθη [da]ὁ‖ Ἰησοῦς καὶ εἶπεν αὐτῷ,
Whence me knowest thou? [2]Answered [1]Jesus and said to him,

sus. 38 Then Jesus turned, and saw them following, and saith unto them, What seek ye? They said unto him, Rabbi, (which is to say, being interpreted, Master,) where dwellest thou? 39 He saith unto them, Come and see. They came and saw where he dwelt, and abode with him that day: for it was about the tenth hour. 40 One of the two which heard John *speak*, and followed him, was Andrew, Simon Peter's brother. 41 He first findeth his own brother Simon, and saith unto him, We have found the Messias, which is, being interpreted, the Christ. 42 And he brought him to Jesus. And when Jesus beheld him, he said, Thou art Simon the son of Jona: thou shalt be called Cephas, which is by interpretation, A stone. 43 The day following Jesus would go forth into Galilee, and findeth Philip, and saith unto him, Follow me.

44 Now Philip was of Bethsaida, the city of Andrew and Peter. 45 Philip findeth Nathanael, and saith unto him, We have found him, of whom Moses in the law, and the prophets, did write, Jesus of Nazareth, the son of Joseph. 46 And Nathanael said unto him, Can there any good thing come out of Nazareth? Philip saith unto him, Come and see. 47 Jesus saw Nathanael coming to him, and saith of him, Behold an Israelite indeed, in whom is no guile! 48 Nathanael saith unto him, Whence knowest thou me? Jesus answered and said unto him, Before that

---

[c] — δὲ T. [d] εἶπαν LTTrA. [e] Ῥαββεί T. [f] μεθερμηνευόμενον LTrA. [g] ὄψεσθε ye shall see TTrA. [h] ἦλθαν TTrA. [i] + οὖν therefore [L]TTrA. [k] εἶδαν LTTrA. [l] — δὲ GLTTrAW. [m] + [δὲ] and L. [n] Ἰωάνου Tr. [o] πρῶτον LTrA. [p] — ὁ GLTTrAW. [q] — καὶ [L]TTrA. [r] — δὲ and GTTrAW. [s] Ἰωάνου of John LTr; Ἰωάννου TA. [t] — ὁ Ἰησοῦς (read he desired) GLTTrAW. [v] + ὁ Ἰησοῦς Jesus (finds) LTTrAW. [w] Μωϋσῆς LTTrAW. [x] — τὸν LT[Tr]. [y] Ναζαρέθ EGW. [z] — καὶ T. [a] + ὁ LTrA. [b] — ὁ LTTrAW. [ca] Ἰσραηλείτης TTr. [da] — ὁ GLTTrAW.

Philip called thee, when thou wast under the fig tree, I saw thee. 49 Nathanael answered and saith unto him, Rabbi, thou art the Son of God; thou art the King of Israel. 50 Jesus answered and said unto him, Because I said unto thee, I saw thee under the fig tree, believest thou? thou shalt see greater things than these. 51 And he saith unto him, Verily, verily, I say unto you, Hereafter ye shall see heaven open, and the angels of God ascending and descending upon the Son of man.

II. And the third day there was a marriage in Cana of Galilee; and the mother of Jesus was there: 2 and both Jesus was called, and his disciples, to the marriage. 3 And when they wanted wine, the mother of Jesus saith unto him, They have no wine. 4 Jesus saith unto her, Woman, what have I to do with thee? mine hour is not yet come. 5 His mother saith unto the servants, Whatsoever he saith unto you, do *it*. 6 And there were set there six waterpots of stone, after the manner of the purifying of the Jews, containing two or three firkins apiece. 7 Jesus saith unto them, Fill the waterpots with water. And they filled them up to the brim. 8 And he saith unto them, Draw out now, and bear unto the governor of the feast. And they bare *it*. 9 When the ruler of the feast had tasted the water that was made wine, and knew not whence it was: (but the servants which drew the water knew;) the governor of the feast called the bridegroom, 10 and saith unto him, Every man at the beginning doth set forth good wine; and when men

Πρὸ τοῦ σε Φίλιππον φωνῆσαι, ὄντα ὑπὸ τὴν συκῆν,
Before that ³thee ¹Philip ²called, [thou] being under the fig-tree,
εἶδόν σε. 50 Ἀπεκρίθη[e] Ναθαναὴλ [f]καὶ λέγει[ǁ] [g]αὐτῷ,[ǁ] [h]Ῥαββί,[ǁ]
I saw thee. ²Answered ¹Nathanael and says to him, Rabbi,
σὺ εἶ ὁ υἱὸς τοῦ θεοῦ, σὺ [i]εἶ ὁ βασιλεὺς[ǁ] τοῦ Ἰσραήλ.
thou art the Son of God, thou art the King of Israel.
51 Ἀπεκρίθη Ἰησοῦς καὶ εἶπεν αὐτῷ, Ὅτι εἶπόν σοι, [k]Εἶδόν
²Answered ¹Jesus and said to him, Because I said to thee, I saw
σε ὑποκάτω τῆς συκῆς, πιστεύεις; μείζω τούτων
thee under the fig-tree, believest thou? Greater things than these
[l]ὄψει.[ǁ] 52 Καὶ λέγει αὐτῷ, Ἀμὴν ἀμὴν λέγω ὑμῖν,
thou shalt see. And he says to him, Verily verily I say to you,
[m]ἀπ᾽.ἄρτι[ǁ] ὄψεσθε τὸν οὐρανὸν ἀνεῳγότα, καὶ τοὺς ἀγ-
Henceforth ye shall see the heaven opened, and the an-
γέλους τοῦ θεοῦ ἀναβαίνοντας καὶ καταβαίνοντας ἐπὶ τὸν
gels of God ascending and descending on the
υἱὸν τοῦ ἀνθρώπου.
Son of man.

2 Καὶ [n]τῇ ἡμέρᾳ τῇ τρίτῃ[ǁ] γάμος ἐγένετο ἐν [o]Κανᾷ[ǁ]
And on the ²day ¹third a marriage took place in Cana
τῆς Γαλιλαίας· καὶ ἦν ἡ μήτηρ τοῦ Ἰησοῦ ἐκεῖ. 2 ἐκλήθη.δὲ
of Galilee, and ³was ¹the ²mother ³of ⁴Jesus there. And ³was ⁴invited
καὶ ὁ Ἰησοῦς καὶ οἱ μαθηταὶ.αὐτοῦ εἰς τὸν γάμον. 3 καὶ
²also ¹Jesus and his disciples to the marriage. And
[p]ὑστερήσαντος οἴνου[ǁ] λέγει ἡ μήτηρ τοῦ Ἰησοῦ πρὸς αὐτόν,
being deficient of wine ⁵says ¹the ²mother ³of ⁴Jesus to him,
[q]Οἶνον οὐκ.ἔχουσιν.[ǁ] 4 [r]Λέγει αὐτῇ ὁ Ἰησοῦς, Τί ἐμοὶ καὶ
Wine they have not. ²Says ³to ⁴her ¹Jesus, What to me and
σοί, γύναι; οὔπω ἥκει ἡ.ὥρα.μου. 5 Λέγει ἡ.μήτηρ.αὐτοῦ
to thee, woman? not yet is come mine hour. ³Says ¹his ²mother
τοῖς διακόνοις, Ὅ.τι ἂν λέγῃ ὑμῖν, ποιήσατε. 6 Ἦσαν
to the servants, Whatever he may say to you, do. ²There ³were
δὲ ἐκεῖ [s]ὑδρίαι λίθιναι[ǁ] ἓξ [t]κείμεναι[ǁ] κατὰ τὸν καθα-
¹and there ²water-vessels ³of ⁴stone ¹six standing according to the puri-
ρισμὸν τῶν Ἰουδαίων[t], χωροῦσαι ἀνὰ μετρητὰς δύο ἢ τρεῖς.
fication of the Jews, ²holding ¹each metretæ two or three.
7 λέγει αὐτοῖς ὁ Ἰησοῦς, Γεμίσατε τὰς ὑδρίας ὕδατος.
²Says ³to ⁴them ¹Jesus, Fill the water-vessels with water.
Καὶ ἐγέμισαν αὐτὰς ἕως ἄνω. 8 Καὶ λέγει αὐτοῖς, Ἀν-
And they filled them unto [the] brim. And he says to them, Draw
τλήσατε νῦν καὶ φέρετε τῷ ἀρχιτρικλίνῳ. [v]Καὶ[ǁ] ἤνεγκαν.
out now and carry to the master of the feast. And they carried [it].
9 ὡς.δὲ ἐγεύσατο ὁ ἀρχιτρίκλινος τὸ ὕδωρ οἶνον γεγενη-
But when ⁶had ⁷tasted ¹the ²master ³of ⁴the ⁵feast the water ⁴wine ¹that ²had
μένον, καὶ οὐκ.ᾔδει πόθεν ἐστίν· οἱ.δὲ διάκονοι ᾔδεισαν οἱ
³become, and knew not whence it is, (but the servants knew who
ἠντληκότες τὸ ὕδωρ· φωνεῖ τὸν νυμφίον ὁ ἀρχιτρίκλινος
had drawn the water,) ⁶calls ⁷the ⁸bridegroom ¹the ²master ³of ⁴the ⁵feast
10 καὶ λέγει αὐτῷ, Πᾶς ἄνθρωπος πρῶτον τὸν καλὸν οἶνον
and says to him, Every man first the good wine

---

[e] + αὐτῷ ³him [L]TTrA. [f] — καὶ λέγει [L]TTrA. [g] — αὐτῷ LTTrA. [h] Ῥαββεί T. [i] ὁ βασιλεὺς εἶ L; βασιλεὺς εἶ TTrA. [k] + ὅτι that LTTrA. [l] ὄψῃ GLTTrAW. [m] — ἀπ᾽ ἄρτι LTTrA. [n] τῇ τρίτῃ ἡμέρᾳ TrA. [o] Κανὰ ELTTr. [p] οἶνον οὐκ εἶχον, ὅτι συνετελέσθη ὁ οἶνος τοῦ γάμου. εἶτα wine they had not, for the wine of the marriage feast was finished. Then T. [q] οἶνος οὐκ ἔστιν wine there is not T. [r] + καὶ and (Jesus) [L]TrA. [s] λιθιναι ὑδρίαι LTTrA. [t] κείμεναι placed after Ἰουδαίων TTrA. [v] οἱ δὲ and they (carried) TTrA.

τίθησιν, και ὅταν μεθυσθῶσιν [x]τότε[ǁ] τὸν ἐλάσσω·
sets on, and when they may have drunk freely then the inferior;
σὺ τετήρηκας τὸν καλὸν οἶνον ἕως ἄρτι. 11 Ταύτην ἐποίησεν
thou hast kept the good wine until now. This [5]did
[y]τὴν[ǁ] ἀρχὴν τῶν σημείων ὁ Ἰησοῦς ἐν [z]Κανᾷ[ǁ] τῆς Γαλιλαίας,
[1]beginning [2]of [3]the [4]signs Jesus in Cana of Galilee,
καὶ ἐφανέρωσεν τὴν.δόξαν.αὐτοῦ· καὶ ἐπίστευσαν εἰς αὐτὸν
and manifested his glory; and [3]believed [4]on [5]him
οἱ.μαθηταὶ.αὐτοῦ.
[1]his [2]disciples.

12 Μετὰ τοῦτο κατέβη εἰς [a]Καπερναούμ,[ǁ] αὐτὸς καὶ ἡ
After this he went down to Capernaum, he and
μήτηρ.αὐτοῦ καὶ οἱ ἀδελφοὶ [b]αὐτοῦ[ǁ] καὶ οἱ.μαθηταὶ.αὐτοῦ, καὶ
his mother and [2]brethren [1]his and his disciples, and
ἐκεῖ ἔμειναν οὐ πολλὰς ἡμέρας. 13 Καὶ ἐγγὺς ἦν τὸ πάσχα
there they abode not many days. And near was the passover
τῶν Ἰουδαίων, καὶ ἀνέβη εἰς Ἱεροσόλυμα ὁ Ἰησοῦς. 14 καὶ
of the Jews, and [2]went [3]up [4]to [5]Jerusalem [1]Jesus. And
εὗρεν ἐν τῷ ἱερῷ τοὺς πωλοῦντας βόας καὶ πρόβατα καὶ
he found in the temple those who sold oxen and sheep and
περιστεράς, καὶ τοὺς κερματιστὰς καθημένους· 15 καὶ ποιή-
doves, and the money-changers sitting; and having
σας φραγέλλιον ἐκ σχοινίων πάντας ἐξέβαλεν ἐκ τοῦ
made a scourge of cords [4]all [1]he [2]drove [3]out from the
ἱεροῦ, τά.τε πρόβατα καὶ τοὺς βόας. καὶ τῶν κολλυβιστῶν
temple, both the sheep and the oxen; and of the money-changers
ἐξέχεεν [c]τὸ κέρμα[ǁ] καὶ τὰς τραπέζας ἀνέστρεψεν. 16 καὶ
he poured out the coin and the tables overthrew. And
τοῖς τὰς περιστερὰς πωλοῦσιν εἶπεν, Ἄρατε ταῦτα
to those who [2]the [3]doves [1]sold he said, Take these things
ἐντεῦθεν· [d]μὴ.ποιεῖτε τὸν οἶκον τοῦ.πατρός.μου οἶκον ἐμ-
hence; make not the house of my father a house of mer-
πορίου. 17 Ἐμνήσθησαν.[e]δὲ[ǁ] οἱ.μαθηταὶ.αὐτοῦ ὅτι γε-
chandise. And [3]remembered [1]his [2]disciples that writ-
γραμμένον ἐστίν, Ὁ ζῆλος τοῦ.οἴκου.σου [f]κατέφαγέν[ǁ] με.
ten it is, The zeal of thine house has eaten [2]up [1]me.
18 Ἀπεκρίθησαν οὖν οἱ Ἰουδαῖοι καὶ [g]εἶπον[ǁ] αὐτῷ, Τί
[4]Answered [3]therefore [1]the [2]Jews and said to him, What
σημεῖον δεικνύεις ἡμῖν ὅτι ταῦτα ποιεῖς; 19 Ἀπεκρίθη
sign shewest thou to us that these things thou doest? [2]Answered
[h]ὁ[ǁ] Ἰησοῦς καὶ εἶπεν αὐτοῖς, Λύσατε τὸν.ναὸν.τοῦτον, καὶ [i]ἐν[ǁ]
[1]Jesus and said to them, Destroy this temple, and in
τρισὶν ἡμέραις ἐγερῶ αὐτόν. 20 [g]Εἶπον[ǁ] οὖν οἱ Ἰουδαῖοι,
three days I will raise up it. [4]Said [3]therefore [1]the [2]Jews,
[k]Τεσσαράκοντα[ǁ] καὶ ἓξ ἔτεσιν [l]ᾠκοδομήθη[ǁ] ὁ.ναὸς.οὗτος, καὶ
Forty and six years was building this temple, and
σὺ ἐν τρισὶν ἡμέραις ἐγερεῖς αὐτόν; 21 Ἐκεῖνος.δὲ ἔλεγεν
thou in three days wilt raise up it? But he spoke
περὶ τοῦ ναοῦ τοῦ.σώματος.αὐτοῦ. 22 ὅτε οὖν ἠγέρ-
concerning the temple of his body. When therefore he was
θη ἐκ νεκρῶν ἐμνήσθησαν οἱ.μαθηταὶ.αὐτοῦ ὅτι
raised up from among [the] dead [3]remembered [1]his [2]disciples that

have well drunk, then that which is worse: *but* thou hast kept the good wine until now. 11 This beginning of miracles did Jesus in Cana of Galilee, and manifested forth his glory; and his disciples believed on him.

12 After this he went down to Capernaum, he, and his mother, and his brethren, and his disciples: and they continued there not many days. 13 And the Jews' passover was at hand, and Jesus went up to Jerusalem, 14 and found in the temple those that sold oxen and sheep and doves, and the changers of money sitting: 15 and when he had made a scourge of small cords, he drove them all out of the temple, and the sheep, and the oxen; and poured out the changers' money, and overthrew the tables; 16 and said unto them that sold doves, Take these things hence; make not my Father's house an house of merchandise. 17 And his disciples remembered that it was written, The zeal of thine house hath eaten me up. 18 Then answered the Jews and said unto him, What sign shewest thou unto us, seeing that thou doest these things? 19 Jesus answered and said unto them, Destroy this temple, and in three days I will raise it up. 20 Then said the Jews, Forty and six years was this temple in building, and wilt thou rear it up in three days? 21 But he spake of the temple of his body. 22 When therefore he was risen from the dead, his disciples remembered that he

---

[x] — τότε [L]T[TrA]. [y] — τὴν LTTrA. [z] Κανᾶ ELTTr. [a] Καφαρναούμ LTTrAW. [b] — αὐτοῦ [L]Tr[A]. [c] τα κέρματα the coins TrA. [d] + [καὶ] and L. [e] — δὲ and [L]TTrA. [f] καταφάγεταί will eat up GLTTrAW. [g] εἶπαν LTTrA. [h] — ὁ LTTrAW. [i] [ἐν] Tr. [k] Τεσσεράκοντα TTrA. [l] οἰκοδομήθη T.

τοῦτο ἔλεγεν [m]αὐτοῖς,‖ καὶ ἐπίστευσαν τῇ γραφῇ καὶ τῷ
this he had said to them, and believed the scripture and the
λόγῳ [n]ᾧ‖ εἶπεν ὁ Ἰησοῦς.
word which [2]had [3]spoken [1]Jesus.
23 Ὡς.δὲ ἦν ἐν [o]Ἱεροσολύμοις ἐν τῷ πάσχα, [p]ἐν‖ τῇ
But when he was in Jerusalem at the passover, at the
ἑορτῇ, πολλοὶ ἐπίστευσαν εἰς τὸ.ὄνομα.αὐτοῦ, θεωροῦντες αὐτοῦ
feast, many believed on his name, beholding his
τὰ σημεῖα ἃ ἐποίει. 24 αὐτὸς.δὲ [q]ὁ‖ Ἰησοῦς οὐκ.ἐπίστευεν
signs which he was doing. But [2]himself [1]Jesus did not trust
[r]ἑαυτὸν‖ αὐτοῖς, διὰ τὸ.αὐτὸν.γινώσκειν πάντας, 25 καὶ
himself to them, because of his knowing all [men], and
ὅτι οὐ χρείαν εἶχεν ἵνα τις μαρτυρήσῃ περὶ [s]τοῦ‖ ἀνθρώ-
that [3]no [4]need [1]he [2]had that any should testify concerning man,
που· αὐτὸς.γὰρ ἐγίνωσκεν τί ἦν ἐν τῷ ἀνθρώπῳ.
for he knew what was in man.
3 Ἦν.δὲ ἄνθρωπος ἐκ τῶν Φαρισαίων, Νικόδημος ὄνομα
But there was a man of the Pharisees, Nicodemus [2]name
αὐτῷ, ἄρχων τῶν Ἰουδαίων· 2 οὗτος ἦλθεν πρὸς [t]τὸν Ἰησοῦν‖
[1]his, a ruler of the Jews; he came to Jesus
νυκτός, καὶ εἶπεν αὐτῷ, [v]Ῥαββί,‖ οἴδαμεν ὅτι ἀπὸ θεοῦ ἐλή-
by night, and said to him, Rabbi, we know that from God thou
λυθας διδάσκαλος· οὐδεὶς γὰρ [w]ταῦτα τὰ σημεῖα δύναται‖
hast come a teacher, for no one these signs is able
ποιεῖν ἃ σὺ ποιεῖς ἐὰν.μὴ ᾖ ὁ θεὸς μετ' αὐτοῦ. 3 Ἀπεκρίθη
to do which thou doest unless [2]be [1]God with him. [2]Answered
[x]ὁ‖ Ἰησοῦς καὶ εἶπεν αὐτῷ, Ἀμὴν ἀμὴν λέγω σοι, ἐὰν.μή
[1]Jesus and said to him, Verily verily I say to thee, Unless
τις γεννηθῇ ἄνωθεν, οὐ.δύναται ἰδεῖν τὴν βασιλείαν τοῦ
anyone be born anew, he cannot see the kingdom
θεοῦ. 4 Λέγει πρὸς αὐτὸν [y]ὁ‖ Νικόδημος, Πῶς δύναται ἄν-
of God. [2]Says [3]to [4]him [1]Nicodemus, How can a
θρωπος γεννηθῆναι γέρων ὤν; μὴ δύναται εἰς τὴν κοιλίαν
man be born [2]old [1]being? can he into the womb
τῆς.μητρὸς.αὐτοῦ δεύτερον εἰσελθεῖν καὶ γεννηθῆναι; 5 Ἀπε-
of his mother a second time enter and be born? [2]An-
κρίθη [z]ὁ‖ Ἰησοῦς, Ἀμὴν ἀμὴν λέγω σοι, ἐὰν.μή τις γεννηθῇ
swered [1]Jesus, Verily verily I say to thee, Unless anyone be born
ἐξ ὕδατος καὶ πνεύματος οὐ.δύναται εἰσελθεῖν εἰς τὴν βασιλείαν
of water and of Spirit he cannot enter into the kingdom
[a]τοῦ θεοῦ.‖ 6 τὸ [b]γεγεννημένον‖ ἐκ τῆς σαρκὸς σάρξ ἐστιν·
of God. That which has been born of the flesh flesh is;
καὶ τὸ [b]γεγεννημένον‖ ἐκ τοῦ πνεύματος πνεῦμά ἐστιν.
and that which has been born of the Spirit spirit is.
7 μὴ.θαυμάσῃς ὅτι εἶπόν σοι, Δεῖ ὑμᾶς γεννηθῆναι
Do not wonder that I said to thee, It is needful for you to be born
ἄνωθεν. 8 τὸ πνεῦμα ὅπου θέλει πνεῖ, καὶ τὴν.φωνὴν.αὐτοῦ
anew. The wind [2]where [3]it [4]wills [1]blows, and its sound
ἀκούεις, [c]ἀλλ'‖ οὐκ.οἶδας πόθεν ἔρχεται [d]καὶ‖ ποῦ ὑπάγει
thou hearest, but knowest not whence it comes and where it goes:
οὕτως ἐστὶν πᾶς ὁ γεγεννημένος ἐκ τοῦ πνεύματος. 9 Ἀπε-
thus is everyone that has been born of the Spirit. [2]An-

had said this unto
them; and they be-
lieved the scripture,
and the word which
Jesus had said.

23 Now when he was
in Jerusalem at the
passover, in the feast
day, many believed in
his name, when they
saw the miracles which
he did. 24 But Jesus
did not commit him-
self unto them, be-
cause he knew all *men*,
25 and needed not that
any should testify of
man: for he knew
what was in man.

III. There was a
man of the Pharisees,
named Nicodemus, a
ruler of the Jews:
2 the same came to
Jesus by night, and
said unto him, Rabbi,
we know that thou art
a teacher come from
God: for no man can
do these miracles that
thou doest, except God
be with him. 3 Jesus
answered and said un-
to him, Verily, verily,
I say unto thee, Except
a man be born again,
he cannot see the king-
dom of God. 4 Nico-
demus saith unto him,
How can a man be
born when he is old?
can he enter the second
time into his mother's
womb, and be born?
5 Jesus answered, Ve-
rily, verily, I say unto
thee, Except a man
be born of water and
of the Spirit, he cannot
enter into the kingdom
of God. 6 That which
is born of the flesh is
flesh; and that which
is born of the Spirit is
spirit. 7 Marvel not
that I said unto thee,
Ye must be born again.
8 The wind bloweth
where it listeth, and
thou hearest the sound
thereof, but canst not
tell whence it cometh,
and whither it goeth:
so is every one that is
born of the Spirit.
9 Nicodemus answered

---

[m] — αὐτοῖς GLTTrAW. [n] ὃν LTTrA. [o] + τοῖς GLTTrA. [p] [ἐν] LTr. [q] — ὁ LTTrA. [r] αὐτὸν LTTrA. [s] — τοῦ L. [t] αὐτὸν him GLTTrAW. [v] Ῥαββεί T. [w] δύναται ταῦτα τὰ σημεῖα LTTrA. [x] — ὁ LTTrAW. [y] — ὁ Tr. [z] — ὁ GLT[TrA]W. [a] τῶν οὐρανῶν of the heavens. T. [b] γεγενημένον E. [c] ἀλλὰ Tr. [d] ἢ or L.

κρίθη Νικόδημος καὶ εἶπεν αὐτῷ, Πῶς δύναται ταῦτα γενέ-
swered [1]Nicodemus and said to him, How can these things be?
σθαι; 10 Ἀπεκρίθη [e]ὁ‖ Ἰησοῦς καὶ εἶπεν αὐτῷ, Σὺ εἶ ὁ
[2]Answered [1]Jesus and said to him, Thou art the
διδάσκαλος τοῦ Ἰσραήλ, καὶ ταῦτα οὐ.γινώσκεις; 11 ἀμὴν
teacher of Israel, and these things knowest not? Verily
ἀμὴν λέγω σοι, ὅτι ὃ οἴδαμεν λαλοῦμεν, καὶ ὃ ἑωρά-
verily I say to thee, That which we know we speak, and that which we
καμεν μαρτυροῦμεν· καὶ τὴν.μαρτυρίαν.ἡμῶν οὐ.λαμβάνετε.
have seen we bear witness of; and our witness ye receive not.
12 εἰ τὰ.ἐπίγεια εἶπον ὑμῖν, καὶ οὐ.πιστεύετε, πῶς ἐὰν εἴπω
If earthly things I said to you, and ye believe not, how if I say
ὑμῖν τὰ.ἐπουράνια πιστεύσετε; 13 καὶ οὐδεὶς ἀναβέβηκεν
to you heavenly things will ye believe? And no one has gone up
εἰς τὸν οὐρανὸν εἰ.μὴ ὁ ἐκ τοῦ οὐρανοῦ καταβάς, ὁ υἱὸς
into the heaven except he who out of the heaven came down, the Son
τοῦ ἀνθρώπου ὁ ὢν ἐν τῷ οὐρανῷ· 14 καὶ καθὼς [f]Μωσῆς‖
of man who is in the heaven. And even as Moses
ὕψωσεν τὸν ὄφιν ἐν τῇ ἐρήμῳ, οὕτως ὑψωθῆναι δεῖ
lifted up the serpent in the wilderness, thus to be lifted up it behoves
τὸν υἱὸν τοῦ ἀνθρώπου· 15 ἵνα πᾶς ὁ πιστεύων [g]εἰς αὐτὸν‖
the Son of man, that everyone that believes on him
[h]μὴ.ἀπόληται, ἀλλ'‖ ἔχῃ ζωὴν αἰώνιον. 16 οὕτως.γὰρ
may not perish, but may have life eternal. For [2]so
ἠγάπησεν ὁ θεὸς τὸν κόσμον ὥστε τὸν.υἱὸν.[i]αὐτοῦ‖ τὸν μονο-
[3]loved [1]God the world that his Son the only be-
γενῆ ἔδωκεν, ἵνα πᾶς ὁ πιστεύων εἰς αὐτὸν μὴ.ἀπόληται,
gotten he gave, that everyone who believes on him may not perish,
[k]ἀλλ'‖ ἔχῃ ζωὴν αἰώνιον. 17 οὐ.γὰρ.ἀπέστειλεν ὁ θεὸς τὸν
but may have life eternal. For [2]sent [3]not [1]God
υἱὸν.[l]αὐτοῦ‖ εἰς τὸν κόσμον ἵνα κρίνῃ τὸν κόσμον, ἀλλ'
his Son into the world that he might judge the world, but
ἵνα σωθῇ ὁ κόσμος δι' αὐτοῦ. 18 ὁ πιστεύων εἰς
that [3]might [4]be [5]saved [1]the [2]world through him. He that believes on
αὐτὸν οὐ.κρίνεται· ὁ.[m]δὲ‖ μὴ.πιστεύων ἤδη κέκριται,
him is not judged; but he that believes not already has been judged,
ὅτι μὴ.πεπίστευκεν εἰς τὸ ὄνομα τοῦ μονογενοῦς υἱοῦ τοῦ
because he has not believed on the name of the only begotten Son
θεοῦ. 19 αὕτη.δέ ἐστιν ἡ κρίσις, ὅτι τὸ φῶς ἐλήλυθεν εἰς
of God. And this is the judgment, that the light has come into
τὸν κόσμον, καὶ ἠγάπησαν οἱ ἄνθρωποι μᾶλλον τὸ σκότος
the world, and [2]loved [1]men [5]rather [3]the [4]darkness
ἢ τὸ φῶς· ἦν.γὰρ [n]πονηρὰ αὐτῶν‖ τὰ ἔργα. 20 πᾶς.γὰρ
than the light; for [2]were [1]evil their works. For everyone
ὁ φαῦλα πράσσων μισεῖ τὸ φῶς, καὶ οὐκ.ἔρχεται πρὸς τὸ
that evil does hates the light, and comes not to the
φῶς, ἵνα μὴ.ἐλεγχθῇ τὰ.ἔργα.αὐτοῦ· 21 ὁ.δὲ ποιῶν τὴν
light, that may not be exposed his works; but he that practises the
ἀλήθειαν ἔρχεται πρὸς τὸ φῶς, ἵνα φανερωθῇ αὐτοῦ τὰ
truth comes to the light, that may be manifested his
ἔργα ὅτι ἐν θεῷ ἐστιν.εἰργασμένα.
works that in God they have been wrought.

22 Μετὰ ταῦτα ἦλθεν ὁ Ἰησοῦς καὶ οἱ.μαθηταὶ.αὐτοῦ εἰς
After these things came Jesus and his disciples into

and said unto him,
How can these things
be? 10 Jesus answered
and said unto him, Art
thou a master of Is-
rael, and knowest not
these things? 11 Veri-
ly, verily, I say unto
thee, We speak that we
do know, and testify
that we have seen;
and ye receive not
our witness. 12 If I
have told you earthly
things, and ye believe
not, how shall ye be-
lieve, if I tell you
of heavenly things?
13 And no man hath
ascended up to heaven,
but he that came down
from heaven, *even* the
Son of man which is
in heaven. 14 And as
Moses lifted up the
serpent in the wilder-
ness, even so must the
Son of man be lifted
up: 15 that whoso-
ever believeth in him
should not perish,
but have eternal life.
16 For God so loved
the world, that he gave
his only begotten Son,
that whosoever believ-
eth in him should not
perish, but have ever-
lasting life. 17 For God
sent not his Son into
the world to condemn
the world; but that
the world through him
might be saved. 18 He
that believeth on him
is not condemned: but
he that believeth not
is condemned already,
because he hath not
believed in the name
of the only begotten
Son of God. 19 And
this is the condemna-
tion, that light is come
into the world, and
men loved darkness
rather than light, be-
cause their deeds were
evil. 20 For every one
that doeth evil hateth
the light, neither com-
eth to the light, lest
his deeds should be
reproved. 21 But he
that doeth truth com-
eth to the light, that
his deeds may be
made manifest, that
they are wrought in
God.

22 After these things
came Jesus and his
disciples into the land

---

[e] — ὁ GLTTrAW. [f] Μωϋσῆς LTTrAW. [g] ἐπ' αὐτὸν L; ἐν αὐτῷ in him TTrA. [h] — μὴ ἀπόληται ἀλλ' [L]TTrA. [i] — αὐτοῦ (*read* the Son) T. [k] ἀλλὰ Tr. [l] — αὐτοῦ (*read* the Son) T[TrA]. [m] — δὲ but [L]T[Tr]A. [n] αὐτῶν πονηρὰ LTTrA.

of Judæa; and there
he tarried with them,
and baptized. 23 And
John also was bap-
tizing in Ænon near
to Salim, because there
was much water there:
and they came, and
were baptized. 24 For
John was not yet cast
into prison. 25 Then
there arose a question
between *some* of John's
disciples and the
Jews about purifying.
26 And they came un-
to John, and said unto
him, Rabbi, he that
was with thee beyond
Jordan, to whom thou
barest witness, behold,
the same baptizeth,
and all *men* come to
him. 27 John answered
and said, A man can
receive nothing, except
it be given him from
heaven. 28 Ye your-
selves bear me witness,
that I said, I am not
the Christ, but that I
am sent before him.
29 He that hath the
bride is the bride-
groom: but the friend
of the bridegroom,
which standeth and
heareth him, rejoiceth
greatly because of the
bridegroom's voice:
this my joy therefore
is fulfilled. 30 He
must increase, but I
must decrease. 31 He
that cometh from a-
bove is above all: he
that is of the earth is
earthly, and speaketh
of the earth: he that
cometh from heaven is
above all. 32 And
what he hath seen
and heard, that he tes-
tifieth; and no man
receiveth his testi-
mony. 33 He that hath
received his testimony
hath set to his seal
that God is true.
34 For he whom God
hath sent speaketh the
words of God: for God
giveth not the Spirit
by measure *unto him*.
35 The Father loveth
the Son, and hath giv-
en all things into his
hand. 36 He that be-
lieveth on the Son
hath everlasting life:
and he that believeth
not the Son shall not

τὴν Ἰουδαίαν.γῆν. καὶ ἐκεῖ διέτριβεν μετ' αὐτῶν καὶ ἐβάπ-
the land of Judæa; and there he stayed with them and was bap-
τιζεν. 23 ἦν.δὲ καὶ [o]Ἰωάννης‖ βαπτίζων ἐν Αἰνὼν ἐγγὺς
tizing. And [3]was [2]also [1]John baptizing in Ænon, near
τοῦ Σαλείμ, ὅτι ὕδατα.πολλὰ ἦν ἐκεῖ· καὶ παρεγίνοντο καὶ
Salim, because [2]waters [1]many were there; and they were coming and
ἐβαπτίζοντο. 24 οὔπω.γὰρ ἦν βεβλημένος εἰς τὴν φυλακὴν
being baptized. For not yet was [2]cast [3]into [4]the [5]prison
[p]ὁ‖ [o]Ἰωάννης.‖ 25 Ἐγένετο οὖν ζήτησις ἐκ τῶν μαθητῶν
[1]John. Arose then a question [on the part] of the disciples
[q]Ἰωάννου‖ μετὰ [r]Ἰουδαίων‖ περὶ καθαρισμοῦ· 26 καὶ [s]ἦλθον‖
of John with [some] Jews about purification. And they came
πρὸς τὸν [t]Ἰωάννην‖ καὶ [v]εἶπον‖ αὐτῷ, [w]Ῥαββί,‖ ὃς ἦν μετὰ
to John and said to him, Rabbi, he who was with
σοῦ πέραν τοῦ Ἰορδάνου, ᾧ σὺ μεμαρτύρηκας, ἴδε οὗτος
thee beyond the Jordan, to whom thou hast borne witness, behold he
βαπτίζει, καὶ πάντες ἔρχονται πρὸς αὐτόν. 27 Ἀπεκρίθη
baptizes, and all come to him. [2]Answered
[o]Ἰωάννης‖ καὶ εἶπεν. Οὐ δύναται ἄνθρωπος λαμβάνειν οὐδὲν
[1]John and said, [3]Is [4]able [1]a [2]man to receive nothing
ἐὰν.μὴ ᾖ δεδομένον αὐτῷ ἐκ τοῦ οὐρανοῦ. 28 αὐτοὶ.ὑμεῖς
unless it be given to him from the heaven. Ye yourselves
μοι μαρτυρεῖτε ὅτι εἶπον, [x]Οὐκ.εἰμὶ ἐγὼ‖ ὁ χριστός, ἀλλ' ὅτι
to me bear witness that I said, [2]Am [3]not [1]I the Christ, but that
ἀπεσταλμένος εἰμὶ ἔμπροσθεν ἐκείνου. 29 ὁ ἔχων τὴν νύμ-
[3]sent [1]I [2]am before him. He that has the bride
φην, νυμφίος ἐστίν· ὁ.δὲ φίλος τοῦ νυμφίου, ὁ ἑστηκὼς καὶ
[2]bridegroom [1]is; but the friend of the bridegroom, who stands and
ἀκούων αὐτοῦ, χαρᾷ χαίρει διὰ τὴν φωνὴν τοῦ νυμφίου·
hears him, with joy rejoices because of the voice of the bridegroom,
αὕτη οὖν ἡ χαρὰ ἡ ἐμὴ πεπλήρωται. 30 ἐκεῖνον δεῖ
this then [2]joy [1]my is fulfilled. [3]Him [1]it [2]behoves
αὐξάνειν, ἐμὲ.δὲ ἐλαττοῦσθαι. 31 ὁ ἄνωθεν ἐρχόμενος ἐπάνω
to increase, but me to decrease. He who from above comes, above
πάντων ἐστίν. ὁ ὢν ἐκ τῆς γῆς ἐκ τῆς γῆς ἐστιν, καὶ
all is. He who is from the earth from the earth is, and
ἐκ τῆς γῆς λαλεῖ· ὁ ἐκ τοῦ οὐρανοῦ ἐρχόμενος [y]ἐπάνω
from the earth speaks. He who from the heaven comes above
πάντων ἐστίν,‖ 32 [z]καὶ‖ ὃ ἑώρακεν καὶ ἤκουσεν [a]τοῦτο‖
all is, and what he has seen and heard this
μαρτυρεῖ· καὶ τὴν.μαρτυρίαν.αὐτοῦ οὐδεὶς λαμβάνει. 33 ὁ
he testifies; and his testimony no one receives. He that
λαβὼν αὐτοῦ τὴν μαρτυρίαν ἐσφράγισεν ὅτι ὁ θεὸς ἀληθής
has received his testimony has set to his seal that God [2]true
ἐστιν. 34 ὃν.γὰρ ἀπέστειλεν ὁ θεὸς τὰ ῥήματα τοῦ θεοῦ
[1]is; for he whom [2]sent [1]God the words of God
λαλεῖ· οὐ.γὰρ ἐκ μέτρου δίδωσιν [b]ὁ θεὸς‖ τὸ πνεῦμα. 35 ὁ
speaks; for not by measure [2]gives [1]God the Spirit. The
πατὴρ ἀγαπᾷ τὸν υἱόν, καὶ πάντα δέδωκεν ἐν τῇ.χειρὶ.αὐ-
Father loves the Son, and all things has given into his hand.
τοῦ. 36 ὁ πιστεύων εἰς τὸν υἱὸν ἔχει ζωὴν αἰώνιον· ὁ.[c]δὲ‖
He that believes on the Son has life eternal; and he that

---

o Ἰωάνης Tr. p — ὁ T[TrA]. q Ἰωάνου Tr. r Ἰουδαίου a Jew GLTTrAW. s ἦλθαν TrA. t Ἰωάνην Tr. v εἶπαν TrA. w Ῥαββεί T. x Ἐγὼ οὐκ εἰμὶ L. y — ἐπάνω πάντων ἐστίν T. z — καὶ [L]TTrA. a — τοῦτο T. b — ὁ θεὸς (*read* he gives) [L]T[Tr]A. c — δὲ and T.

ἀπειθῶν τῷ υἱῷ·οὐκ.ὄψεται ζωήν, ἀλλ' ἡ ὀργὴ τοῦ θεοῦ
is not subject to the Son shall not see life, but the wrath of God
μένει ἐπ' αὐτόν.
abides on him.

4 Ὡς οὖν ἔγνω ὁ [d]κύριος‖ ὅτι ἤκουσαν οἱ Φαρισαῖοι,
When therefore [3]knew [1]the [2]Lord that [3]heard [1]the [2]Pharisees,
ὅτι Ἰησοῦς πλείονας μαθητὰς ποιεῖ καὶ βαπτίζει ἢ [e]Ἰωάν-
that Jesus more disciples makes and baptizes than John
νης·‖ 2 καίτοιγε Ἰησοῦς αὐτὸς οὐκ.ἐβάπτιζεν, ἀλλ' οἱ
(although indeed Jesus himself was not baptizing but
μαθηταὶ.αὐτοῦ· 3 ἀφῆκεν τὴν Ἰουδαίαν, καὶ ἀπῆλθεν πάλιν
his disciples), he left Judæa, and went away again
εἰς τὴν Γαλιλαίαν. 4 ἔδει.δὲ αὐτὸν διέρχεσθαι διὰ τῆς
into Galilee. And it was necessary for him to pass through
[f]Σαμαρείας.‖ 5 ἔρχεται οὖν εἰς πόλιν τῆς [f]Σαμαρείας‖ λεγο-
Samaria. He comes therefore to a city of Samaria call-
μένην [g]Συχάρ,‖ πλησίον τοῦ χωρίου [h]ὃ‖ ἔδωκεν Ἰακὼβ
ed Sychar, near the land which [2]gave [1]Jacob
Ἰωσὴφ τῷ.υἱῷ.αὐτοῦ. 6 ἦν.δὲ ἐκεῖ πηγὴ τοῦ Ἰακώβ.
to Joseph his son. Now [3]was [4]there [2]fountain [1]Jacob's;
ὁ.οὖν.Ἰησοῦς κεκοπιακὼς ἐκ τῆς ὁδοιπορίας ἐκαθέζετο οὕτως
Jesus therefore, being wearied from the journey, sat thus
ἐπὶ τῇ πηγῇ. ὥρα ἦν [i]ὡσεὶ‖ ἕκτη. 7 Ἔρχεται γυνὴ
at the fountain. [The] hour was about [the] sixth. Comes a woman
ἐκ τῆς [f]Σαμαρείας‖ ἀντλῆσαι ὕδωρ. λέγει αὐτῇ ὁ Ἰησοῦς,
out of Samaria to draw water. [2]Says [3]to [4]her [1]Jesus,
Δός μοι [k]πιεῖν·‖ 8 οἱ.γὰρ.μαθηταὶ.αὐτοῦ ἀπεληλύθεισαν εἰς
Give me to drink; for his disciples had gone away into
τὴν πόλιν, ἵνα τροφὰς ἀγοράσωσιν. 9 Λέγει [l]οὖν‖ αὐτῷ
the city, that provisions they might buy. [5]Says [4]therefore [6]to [7]him
ἡ γυνὴ ἡ [m]Σαμαρεῖτις,‖ Πῶς σὺ Ἰουδαῖος ὢν παρ' ἐμοῦ
[1]the [3]woman [2]Samaritan, How [2]thou [4]a [5]Jew [3]being [9]from [10]me
[n]πιεῖν‖ αἰτεῖς; [o]οὔσης γυναικὸς Σαμαρείτιδος‖; [p]οὐ.γὰρ
[7]to [8]drink [1]dost [6]ask, being a [2]woman [1]Samaritan? For [3]no
συγχρῶνται Ἰουδαῖοι Σαμαρείταις.‖ 10 Ἀπεκρίθη Ἰησοῦς
[2]have [4]intercourse [1]Jews with Samaritans. [2]Answered [1]Jesus
καὶ εἶπεν αὐτῇ, Εἰ ᾔδεις τὴν δωρεὰν τοῦ θεοῦ, καὶ τίς
and said to her, If thou hadst known the gift of God, and who
ἐστιν ὁ λέγων σοι, Δός μοι [k]πιεῖν,‖ σὺ ἂν.ᾔτησας
it is that says to thee, Give me to drink, thou wouldest have asked
αὐτόν, καὶ ἔδωκεν.ἂν σοι ὕδωρ ζῶν. 11 Λέγει αὐτῷ [q]ἡ
him, and he would have given to thee [2]water [1]living. [3]Says [4]to [5]him [1]the
γυνή,‖ Κύριε, οὔτε ἄντλημα ἔχεις, καὶ τὸ φρέαρ ἐστὶν
[2]woman, Sir, nothing to draw with thou hast, and the well is
βαθύ· πόθεν [l]οὖν‖ ἔχεις τὸ ὕδωρ τὸ ζῶν; 12 μὴ σὺ.μείζων.εἶ
deep; whence then hast thou the [2]water [1]living? Art thou greater
τοῦ.πατρὸς.ἡμῶν Ἰακώβ, ὃς ἔδωκεν ἡμῖν τὸ φρέαρ, καὶ αὐτὸς
than our father Jacob, who gave us the well, and himself
ἐξ αὐτοῦ ἔπιεν, καὶ οἱ.υἱοὶ.αὐτοῦ καὶ τὰ.θρέμματα.αὐτοῦ;
of it drank, and his sons and his cattle?
13 Ἀπεκρίθη [r]ὁ‖ Ἰησοῦς καὶ εἶπεν αὐτῇ, Πᾶς ὁ πίνων ἐκ
[2]Answered [1]Jesus and said to her, Everyone that drinks of

see life; but the wrath of God abideth on him.

IV. When therefore the Lord knew how the Pharisees had heard that Jesus made and baptized more disciples than John, 2 (though Jesus himself baptized not, but his disciples,) 3 he left Judæa, and departed again into Galilee. 4 And he must needs go through Samaria. 5 Then cometh he to a city of Samaria, which is called Sychar, near to the parcel of ground that Jacob gave to his son Joseph. 6 Now Jacob's well was there. Jesus therefore, being wearied with *his* journey, sat thus on the well: *and* it was about the sixth hour. 7 There cometh a woman of Samaria to draw water: Jesus saith unto her, Give me to drink. 8 (For his disciples were gone away unto the city to buy meat.) 9 Then saith the woman of Samaria unto him, How is it that thou, being a Jew, askest drink of me, which am a woman of Samaria? for the Jews have no dealings with the Samaritans. 10 Jesus answered and said unto her, If thou knewest the gift of God, and who it is that saith to thee, Give me to drink; thou wouldest have asked of him, and he would have given thee living water. 11 The woman saith unto him, Sir, thou hast nothing to draw with, and the well is deep: from whence then hast thou that living water? 12 Art thou greater than our father Jacob, which gave us the well, and drank thereof himself, and his children, and his cattle? 13 Jesus answered and said unto her, Whosoever drinketh of this water

---

[d] Ἰησοῦς Jesus T. [e] Ἰωάνης Tr. [f] Σαμαρίας T. [g] Σιχάρ E. [h] οὗ GL. [i] ὡς LTTrAW. [k] πεῖν TTrA. [l] — οὖν T. [m] Σαμαρῖτις T. [n] πῖν L; πεῖν TTrA. [o] γυναικὸς Σαμαρείτιδος (Σαμαρίτιδος T) οὔσης LTTrA. [p] — οὐ γὰρ συγχρῶνται Ἰουδαῖοι Σαμαρείταις T. [q] [ἡ γυνή] A. [r] — ὁ GLTTrAW.

shall thirst again:
14 but whosoever
drinketh of the water
that I shall give him
shall never thirst; but
the water that I shall
give him shall be in
him a well of water
springing up into ever-
lasting life. 15 The
woman saith unto him,
Sir, give me this water,
that I thirst not, nei-
ther come hither to
draw. 16 Jesus saith
unto her, Go, call thy
husband, and come
hither. 17 The woman
answered and said, I
have no husband. Je-
sus said unto her, Thou
hast well said, I have
no husband: 18 for
thou hast had five hus-
bands; and he whom
thou now hast is not
thy husband: in that
saidst thou truly.
19 The woman saith
unto him, Sir, I per-
ceive that thou art a
prophet. 20 Our fa-
thers worshipped in
this mountain; and ye
say, that in Jerusalem
is the place where men
ought to worship.
21 Jesus saith unto her,
Woman, believe me,
the hour cometh, when
ye shall neither in this
mountain, nor yet at
Jerusalem, worship the
Father. 22 Ye worship
ye know not what: we
know what we wor-
ship: for salvation is
of the Jews. 23 But
the hour cometh, and
now is, when the true
worshippers shall wor-
ship the Father in
spirit and in truth: for
the Father seeketh
such to worship him.
24 God *is* a Spirit: and
they that worship him
must worship *him* in
spirit and in truth.
25 The woman saith
unto him, I know that
Messias cometh, which
is called Christ: when
he is come, he will tell
us all things. 26 Jesus
saith unto her, I that
speak unto thee am *he*.
27 And upon this came

τοῦ.ὕδατος.τούτου διψήσει πάλιν· 14 ὃς.δ᾽.ἂν πίῃ ἐκ τοῦ
this water will thirst again; but whoever may drink of the
ὕδατος οὗ ἐγὼ δώσω αὐτῷ [v]οὐ.μὴ [w]διψήσῃ‖ εἰς τὸν.αἰῶνα·
water which I will give him in no wise shall thirst for ever,
ἀλλὰ τὸ ὕδωρ ὃ [x] δώσω αὐτῷ‖ γενήσεται ἐν αὐτῷ πηγὴ
but the water which I will give to him shall become in him a fountain
ὕδατος ἁλλομένου εἰς ζωὴν αἰώνιον. 15 Λέγει πρὸς αὐτὸν
of water springing up into life eternal. [3]Says [4]to [5]him
ἡ γυνή, Κύριε, δός μοι τοῦτο τὸ ὕδωρ, ἵνα μὴ.διψῶ
[1]the [2]woman, Sir, give me this water, that I may not thirst
μηδὲ [y]ἔρχωμαι‖ ἐνθάδε ἀντλεῖν. 16 Λέγει αὐτῇ [z]ὁ‖ [a]Ἰησοῦς,‖
nor come here to draw. [2]Says [3]to [4]her [1]Jesus,
Ὕπαγε, φώνησον [b]τὸν.ἄνδρα.σοῦ‖ καὶ ἐλθὲ ἐνθάδε. 17 Ἀπε-
Go, call thy husband and come here. [3]An-
κρίθη ἡ γυνὴ καὶ εἶπεν[c], [d]Οὐκ.ἔχω ἄνδρα.‖ Λέγει αὐτῇ ὁ
swered [1]the [2]woman and said, I have not a husband. [2]Says [3]to [4]her
Ἰησοῦς, Καλῶς [e]εἶπας,‖ Ὅτι ἄνδρα οὐκ.ἔχω· 18 πέντε
[1]Jesus, Well didst thou say, A husband I have not; [2]five
γὰρ ἄνδρας ἔσχες. καὶ νῦν ὃν ἔχεις οὐκ.ἔστιν σου
[1]for husbands thou hast had, and now he whom thou hast is not thy
ἀνήρ· τοῦτο ἀληθὲς εἴρηκας. 19 Λέγει αὐτῷ ἡ γυνή,
husband: this truly thou hast spoken. [3]Says [4]to [5]him [1]the [2]woman,
Κύριε, θεωρῶ ὅτι προφήτης εἶ σύ. 20 οἱ.πατέρες.ἡμῶν ἐν
Sir, I perceive that a prophet [2]art [1]thou. Our fathers in
[f]τούτῳ τῷ ὄρει‖ προσεκύνησαν· καὶ ὑμεῖς λέγετε ὅτι ἐν Ἱε-
this mountain worshipped, and ye say that in Je-
ροσολύμοις ἐστὶν ὁ τόπος ὅπου [g]δεῖ προσκυνεῖν.‖ 21 Λέγει
rusalem is the place where it is necessary to worship. [2]Says
αὐτῇ ὁ Ἰησοῦς, [h]Γύναι, πίστευσόν μοι,‖ ὅτι ἔρχεται ὥρα ὅτε
[3]to [4]her [1]Jesus, Woman, believe me, that is coming an hour when
οὔτε ἐν τῷ.ὄρει.τούτῳ οὔτε ἐν Ἱεροσολύμοις προσκυνήσετε
neither in this mountain nor in Jerusalem shall ye worship
τῷ πατρί. 22 ὑμεῖς προσκυνεῖτε ὃ οὐκ.οἴδατε· ἡμεῖς προσ-
the Father. Ye worship what ye know not: we wor-
κυνοῦμεν ὃ οἴδαμεν· ὅτι ἡ σωτηρία ἐκ τῶν Ἰουδαίων ἐστίν.
ship what we know; for salvation of the Jews is.
23 [i]ἀλλ᾽‖ ἔρχεται ὥρα καὶ νῦν ἐστιν, ὅτε οἱ ἀληθινοὶ προσ-
But is coming an hour and now is, when the true wor-
κυνηταὶ προσκυνήσουσιν τῷ πατρὶ ἐν πνεύματι καὶ ἀληθείᾳ·
shippers will worship the Father in spirit and truth;
καὶ.γὰρ ὁ πατὴρ τοιούτους ζητεῖ τοὺς προσκυνοῦντας αὐτόν.
for also the Father [2]such [1]seeks who worship him.
24 Πνεῦμα ὁ θεός· καὶ τοὺς προσκυνοῦντας [k]αὐτὸν‖ ἐν
A spirit God [is], and they that worship him, in
πνεύματι καὶ ἀληθείᾳ [l]δεῖ προσκυνεῖν.‖ 25 Λέγει αὐτῷ ἡ
spirit and truth must worship. [3]Says [4]to [5]him [1]the
γυνή, Οἶδα ὅτι μεσσίας ἔρχεται, ὁ λεγόμενος χριστός· ὅταν
[2]woman, I know that Messias is coming, who is called Christ; when
ἔλθῃ ἐκεῖνος ἀναγγελεῖ ἡμῖν [m]πάντα.‖ 26 Λέγει αὐτῇ ὁ Ἰη-
[2]comes [1]he he will tell us all things. [2]Says [3]to [4]her [1]Je-
σοῦς, Ἐγώ εἰμι, ὁ λαλῶν σοι. 27 Καὶ ἐπὶ τούτῳ
sus, I [6]am [[7]he], [1]who [2]am [3]speaking [4]to [5]thee. And upon this

---

[v] [οὐ μὴ διψήσει .... ὃ δώσω αὐτῷ] L [w] διψήσει LTTrA. [x] + ἐγὼ I T. [y] ἔρχομαι Tr; διέρχωμαι TA. [z] — ὁ LT[Tr]A. [a] — Ἰησοῦς (*read* he says) [L]T[Tr]A. [b] σου τὸν ἄνδρα A. [c] + αὐτῷ to him [L]A. [d] ἄνδρα οὐκ ἔχω T. [e] εἶπες T. [f] τῷ ὄρει τούτῳ GLTTrAW. [g] προσκυνεῖν δεῖ LTTrAW. [h] Γύναι, πίστευέ μοι L; Πίστευέ μοι, γύναι TTrA. [i] ἀλλὰ LTTrAW. [k] — αὐτὸν T. [l] προσκυνεῖν δεῖ T. [m] ἅπαντα TTrA.

[n]ἦλθον‖ οἱ.μαθηταὶ.αὐτοῦ, καὶ [o]ἐθαύμασαν‖ ὅτι μετὰ γυναικὸς
came his disciples, and wondered that with a woman
ἐλάλει· οὐδεὶς μέντοι εἶπεν, Τί ζητεῖς; ἤ Τί λα-
he was speaking; no one however said, What seekest thou? or Why speakest
λεῖς μετ' αὐτῆς;
thou with her?

28 Ἀφῆκεν οὖν τὴν.ὑδρίαν.αὐτῆς ἡ γυνὴ καὶ ἀπῆλθεν εἰς
[4]Left [3]then [5]her [6]waterpot [1]the [2]woman and went away into
τὴν πόλιν, καὶ λέγει τοῖς ἀνθρώποις, 29 Δεῦτε, ἴδετε ἄνθρω-
the city, and says to the men, Come, see a man
πον ὃς εἶπέν μοι πάντα [p]ὅσα‖ ἐποίησα· μήτι οὗτός ἐστιν
who told me all things whatsoever I did: [3]perchance [2]this [1]is
ὁ χριστός; 30 [q]Ἐξῆλθον [r]οὖν‖ ἐκ τῆς πόλεως, καὶ ἤρ-
the Christ! They went forth therefore out of the city, and came
χοντο πρὸς αὐτόν.
unto him.

31 Ἐν.[s]δὲ‖ τῷ μεταξὺ ἠρώτων αὐτὸν οἱ μαθηταί, λέ-
But in the meantime [3]were [4]asking [5]him [1]the [2]disciples, say-
γοντες, [t]Ῥαββί,‖ φάγε. 32 Ὁ.δὲ εἶπεν αὐτοῖς, Ἐγὼ βρῶσιν
ing, Rabbi, eat. But he said to them, I meat
ἔχω φαγεῖν ἣν ὑμεῖς οὐκ.οἴδατε. 33 Ἔλεγον [v]οὖν‖ οἱ μαθη-
have to eat which ye know not. [4]Said [3]therefore [1]the [2]disci-
ταὶ πρὸς ἀλλήλους, Μή τις ἤνεγκεν αὐτῷ φαγεῖν;
ples to one another, [2]Anyone [1]did bring him [anything] to eat?
34 Λέγει αὐτοῖς ὁ Ἰησοῦς, Ἐμὸν βρῶμά ἐστιν ἵνα [x]ποιῶ‖ τὸ
[2]Says [3]to [4]them [1]Jesus, My meat is that I should do the
θέλημα τοῦ πέμψαντός με, καὶ τελειώσω αὐτοῦ τὸ ἔργον.
will of him who sent me, and should finish his work.
35 οὐχ ὑμεῖς λέγετε, ὅτι ἔτι [y]τετράμηνόν‖ ἐστιν καὶ ὁ θερισμὸς
[2]Not [3]ye [1]say, that yet four months it is and the harvest
ἔρχεται; ἰδού, λέγω ὑμῖν, Ἐπάρατε τοὺς.ὀφθαλμοὺς.ὑμῶν καὶ
comes? Behold, I say to you, Lift up your eyes and
θεάσασθε τὰς χώρας, ὅτι λευκαί εἰσιν πρὸς θερισμὸν [z]ἤδη.‖
see the fields, for white they are to harvest already.
36 [a]καὶ‖ ὁ θερίζων μισθὸν λαμβάνει, καὶ συνάγει καρπὸν
And he that reaps a reward receives, and gathers fruit
εἰς ζωὴν αἰώνιον· ἵνα [b]καὶ‖ ὁ σπείρων ὁμοῦ χαίρῃ
unto life eternal, that both he that sows [7]together [5]may [6]rejoice
καὶ ὁ θερίζων. 37 ἐν.γὰρ τούτῳ ὁ λόγος ἐστὶν [c]ὁ‖ ἀλη-
[1]and [2]he [3]that [4]reaps. For in this the saying is true,
θινός, ὅτι ἄλλος ἐστὶν ὁ σπείρων, καὶ ἄλλος ὁ θερίζων.
That [3]one [1]it [2]is who sows, and another who reaps.
38 ἐγὼ [d]ἀπέστειλα‖ ὑμᾶς θερίζειν ὃ οὐχ ὑμεῖς κεκοπιάκατε·
I sent you to reap on which [3]not [1]ye [2]have laboured;
ἄλλοι κεκοπιάκασιν, καὶ ὑμεῖς εἰς τὸν.κόπον.αὐτῶν εἰσεληλύ-
others have laboured, and ye into their labour have en-
θατε.
tered.

39 Ἐκ.δὲ τῆς.πόλεως.ἐκείνης πολλοὶ ἐπίστευσαν εἰς αὐτὸν
But out of that city many believed on him
τῶν [e]Σαμαρειτῶν,‖ διὰ τὸν λόγον τῆς γυναικὸς μαρ-
of the Samaritans, because of the word of the woman tes-

his disciples, and marvelled that he talked with the woman: yet no man said, What seekest thou? or, Why talkest thou with her?

28 The woman then left her waterpot, and went her way into the city, and saith to the men, 29 Come, see a man, which told me all things that ever I did: is not this the Christ? 30 Then they went out of the city, and came unto him.

31 In the mean while his disciples prayed him, saying, Master, eat. 32 But he said unto them, I have meat to eat that ye know not of. 33 Therefore said the disciples one to another, Hath any man brought him *ought* to eat? 34 Jesus saith unto them, My meat is to do the will of him that sent me, and to finish his work. 35 Say not ye, There are yet four months, and *then* cometh harvest? behold, I say unto you, Lift up your eyes, and look on the fields; for they are white already to harvest. 36 And he that reapeth receiveth wages, and gathereth fruit unto life eternal: that both he that soweth and he that reapeth may rejoice together. 37 And herein is that saying true, One soweth, and another reapeth. 38 I sent you to reap that whereon ye bestowed no labour: other men laboured, and ye are entered into their labours.

39 And many of the Samaritans of that city believed on him for the saying of the woman, which testi-

---

[n] ἦλθαν TTr. [o] ἐθαύμαζον were wondering GLTTrAW. [p] ἃ which T. [q] + [καὶ] and L. [r] — οὖν GLTTrAW. [s] — δὲ but [L]TTrA. [t] Ῥαββεί T. [v] — οὖν W. [x] ποιήσω LTrA. [y] τετράμηνός GLTTrAW. [z] . ἤδη (read already he that reaps) T. [a] — καὶ G[L]TTrA. [b] — καὶ Tr[A]. [c] — ὁ TTr[A]. [d] ἀπέσταλκα have sent T. [e] Σαμαριτῶν T.

fied, He told me all
that ever I did. 40 So
when the Samaritans
were come unto him,
they besought him
that he would tarry
with them: and he
abode there two days.
41 And many more be-
lieved because of his
own word; 42 and said
unto the woman, Now
we believe, not be-
cause of thy saying:
for we have heard *him*
ourselves, and know
that this is indeed the
Christ, the Saviour of
the world.

43 Now after two
days he departed
thence, and went into
Galilee. 44 For Jesus
himself testified, that
a prophet hath no
honour in his own
country. 45 Then when
he was come into Ga-
lilee, the Galilæans
received him, having
seen all the things that
he did at Jerusalem at
the feast: for they
also went unto the
feast.

46 So Jesus came
again into Cana of
Galilee, where he made
the water wine. And
there was a certain no-
bleman, whose son was
sick at Capernaum.
47 When he heard that
Jesus was come out of
Judæa into Galilee, he
went unto him, and
besought him that he
would come down,
and heal his son: for
he was at the point of
death. 48 Then said
Jesus unto him, Ex-
cept ye see signs and
wonders, ye will not
believe. 49 The no-
bleman saith unto him,
Sir, come down ere my
child die. 50 Jesus
saith unto him, Go
thy way; thy son liv-
eth. And the man be-
lieved the word that
Jesus had spoken unto
him, and he went his
way. 51 And as he was
now going down, his
servants met him, and

τυρούσης, "Ὅτι εἶπέν μοι πάντα [f]ὅσα" ἐποίησα. 40 Ὡς
tifying, He told me all things whatsoever I did. When
οὖν ἦλθον πρὸς αὐτὸν οἱ [g]Σαμαρεῖται," ἠρώτων αὐτὸν
therefore came to him the Samaritans, they asked him
μεῖναι παρ' αὐτοῖς· καὶ ἔμεινεν ἐκεῖ δύο ἡμέρας. 41 καὶ
to abide with them, and he abode there two days. And
πολλῷ.πλείους ἐπίστευσαν διὰ τὸν.λόγον.αὐτοῦ· 42 τῇ.τε
many more believed because of his word; and to the
γυναικὶ ἔλεγον, [h]"Ὅτι" οὐκέτι διὰ τὴν σὴν λαλιὰν πισ-
woman they said, No longer because of thy saying we
τεύομεν· αὐτοὶ.γὰρ ἀκηκόαμεν, καὶ οἴδαμεν ὅτι οὗτός ἐστιν
believe, for ourselves have heard, and we know that this is
ἀληθῶς ὁ σωτὴρ τοῦ κόσμου, [i]ὁ χριστός."
truly the Saviour of the world, the Christ.

43 Μετὰ.δὲ τὰς δύο ἡμέρας ἐξῆλθεν ἐκεῖθεν, [k]καὶ ἀπῆλ-
But after the two days he went forth thence, and went
θεν" εἰς τὴν Γαλιλαίαν. 44 αὐτὸς.γὰρ [l]ὁ" Ἰησοῦς ἐμαρτύρη-
away into Galilee; for [2]himself [1]Jesus testified,
σεν, ὅτι προφήτης ἐν τῇ.ἰδίᾳ πατρίδι τιμὴν οὐκ.ἔχει.
that a prophet in his own country honour has not.
45 [m]"Ὅτε" οὖν ἦλθεν εἰς τὴν Γαλιλαίαν ἐδέξαντο αὐτὸν
When therefore he came into Galilee [3]received [4]him
οἱ Γαλιλαῖοι, πάντα ἑωρακότες [n]ἃ" ἐποίησεν ἐν Ἰε-
[1]the [2]Galileans, all things having seen which he did in Je-
ροσολύμοις ἐν τῇ ἑορτῇ· καὶ.αὐτοὶ.γὰρ ἦλθον εἰς τὴν
rusalem during the feast, for they also went to the
ἑορτήν.
feast.

46 Ἦλθεν οὖν [o]ὁ Ἰησοῦς" πάλιν [p] εἰς τὴν Κανᾶ τῆς
[2]Came [3]therefore [1]Jesus again to Cana
Γαλιλαίας, ὅπου ἐποίησεν τὸ ὕδωρ οἶνον. [q]καὶ ἦν" τις
of Galilee, where he made the water wine. And there was a certain
βασιλικός, οὗ ὁ υἱὸς ἠσθένει ἐν [r]Καπερναούμ." 47 οὗτος
courtier, whose son was sick in Capernaum. He
ἀκούσας ὅτι Ἰησοῦς ἥκει ἐκ τῆς Ἰουδαίας εἰς τὴν Γαλι-
having heard that Jesus had come out of Judæa into Gali-
λαίαν, ἀπῆλθεν πρὸς αὐτόν, καὶ ἠρώτα [s]αὐτὸν" ἵνα κατα-
lee, went to him, and asked him that he would
βῇ καὶ ἰάσηται αὐτοῦ τὸν υἱόν· ἤμελλεν.γὰρ ἀποθνήσκειν.
come down and heal his son; for he was about to die.
48 εἶπεν οὖν ὁ Ἰησοῦς πρὸς αὐτόν, Ἐὰν.μὴ σημεῖα καὶ
[3]Said [2]therefore [1]Jesus to him, Unless signs and
τέρατα ἴδητε οὐ.μὴ πιστεύσητε. 49 Λέγει πρὸς αὐτὸν ὁ
wonders ye see in no wise will ye believe. [3]Says [4]to [5]him [1]the
βασιλικός, Κύριε, κατάβηθι πρὶν ἀποθανεῖν τὸ.παιδίον.μου.
[2]courtier, Sir, come down before [4]dies [1]my [2]little [3]child.
50 Λέγει αὐτῷ ὁ Ἰησοῦς, Πορεύου· ὁ.υἱός.σου ζῇ. [t]Καὶ"
[2]Says [3]to [4]him [1]Jesus, Go, thy son lives. And
ἐπίστευσεν ὁ ἄνθρωπος τῷ λόγῳ [v]ᾧ" εἶπεν αὐτῷ [w] Ἰησοῦς,
[3]believed [1]the [2]man the word which [2]said [3]to [4]him [1]Jesus,
καὶ ἐπορεύετο. 51 ἤδη.δὲ αὐτοῦ.καταβαίνοντος οἱ.δοῦλοι.[x]αὐ-
and went away. But already as he was going down his bondmen

---

[f] ἃ which TTrA. [g] Σαμαρῖται T. [h] [ὅτι] L. [i] — ὁ χριστός LTTrA. [k] — καὶ ἀπῆλθεν [L]TTrA. [l] — ὁ GLTTrAW. [m] ὡς T. [n] ὅσα whatsoever LTrA. [o] — ὁ Ἰησοῦς (*read* he came GLTTrAW. [p] + ὁ Ἰησοῦς Jesus W. [q] Ἦν δέ T. [r] Καφαρναούμ LTTrAW. [s] — αὐτὸν [L]TTrA. [t] — καὶ [L]T[Tr]A. [v] ὃν LTTrA. [w] + ὁ LTTrAW. [x] — αὐτοῦ (*read* the bondmen) T.

τοῦ‖ [y]ἀπήντησαν‖ αὐτῷ, [z]καὶ ἀπήγγειλαν‖ [a]λέγοντες,‖ ″Ὅτι
met him, and reported, saying,
ὁ.παῖς.[b]σου‖ ζῇ. 52 Ἐπύθετο οὖν [c]παρ' αὐτῶν τὴν ὥραν‖
Thy child lives. He inquired therefore from them the hour
ἐν ᾗ κομψότερον ἔσχεν. [d]καὶ εἶπον‖ αὐτῷ, ″Ὅτι [e]χθὲς‖
in which [3]better [1]he [2]got. And they said to him, Yesterday
ὥραν ἑβδόμην ἀφῆκεν αὐτὸν ὁ πυρετός. 53 ″Ἔγνω
[at the] [2]hour [1]seventh left him the fever. [3]Knew
οὖν ὁ πατὴρ ὅτι [f]ἐν‖ ἐκείνῃ τῇ ὥρᾳ ἐν ᾗ εἶπεν
[4]therefore [1]the [2]father that [it was] at that hour in which [2]said
αὐτῷ ὁ Ἰησοῦς, [g]″Ὅτι‖ ὁ.υἱός.σου ζῇ. Καὶ ἐπίστευσεν αὐτὸς
[3]to [4]him [1]Jesus, Thy son lives. And he [2]believed [1]himself
καὶ ἡ.οἰκία.αὐτοῦ ὅλη. 54 τοῦτο [h] πάλιν δεύτερον σημεῖον
and his [2]house [1]whole. This again a second sign
ἐποίησεν ὁ Ἰησοῦς, ἐλθὼν ἐκ τῆς Ἰουδαίας εἰς τὴν Γα-
did Jesus, having come out of Judæa into Ga-
λιλαίαν.
lilee.

told *him*, saying, Thy
son liveth. 52 Then in-
quired he of them the
hour when he began
to amend. And they
said unto him, Yester-
day at the seventh
hour the fever left
him. 53 So the father
knew that *it was* at
the same hour, in the
which Jesus said unto
him, Thy son liveth:
and himself believed,
and his whole house.
54 This *is* again the
second miracle *that*
Jesus did, when he
was come out of Ju-
dæa into Galilee.

5 Μετὰ ταῦτα ἦν [i] ἑορτὴ τῶν Ἰουδαίων, καὶ ἀνέβη [k]ὁ‖
After these things was a feast of the Jews, and [2]went [3]up
Ἰησοῦς εἰς Ἱεροσόλυμα. 2 ἔστιν.δὲ ἐν τοῖς Ἱεροσολύμοις
[1]Jesus to Jerusalem. And there is in Jerusalem
ἐπὶ τῇ προβατικῇ κολυμβήθρα, [l]ἡ ἐπιλεγομένη‖ Ἑβραϊστὶ
at the sheepgate a pool, which [is] called in Hebrew
[m]Βηθεσδά,‖ πέντε στοὰς ἔχουσα. 3 ἐν ταύταις κατέκειτο
Bethesda, five porches having. In these were lying
πλῆθος [n]πολὺ‖ τῶν ἀσθενούντων, τυφλῶν, χωλῶν,
a [2]multitude [1]great of those who were sick, blind, lame,
ξηρῶν, [o]ἐκδεχομένων τὴν τοῦ ὕδατος κίνησιν. 4 ἄγγελος
withered, awaiting the [2]of [3]the [4]water [1]moving. [2]An [3]angel
γὰρ [p] κατὰ.καιρὸν κατέβαινεν ἐν τῇ κολυμβήθρᾳ, καὶ ἐτά-
[1]for from time to time descended in the pool, and agi-
ρασσεν τὸ ὕδωρ· ὁ οὖν πρῶτος ἐμβὰς μετὰ τὴν ταραχὴν
tated the water. He who therefore first entered after the agitation
τοῦ ὕδατος, ὑγιὴς ἐγίνετο, [q]ᾧ.δήποτε‖ κατείχετο νοσήματι.‖
of the water, [2]well [1]became, whatever [2]he [3]was [4]held [5]by [1]disease.
5 ″Ἦν.δέ τις ἄνθρωπος ἐκεῖ [r]τριακονταοκτὼ‖ ἔτη ἔχων ἐν
But [4]was [1]a [2]certain [3]man there [2]thirty [3]eight [4]years [1]being in
τῇ ἀσθενείᾳ[s]. 6 τοῦτον ἰδὼν ὁ Ἰησοῦς κατακείμενον, καὶ
infirmity. [3]Him [2]seeing [1]Jesus lying, and
γνοὺς ὅτι πολὺν ἤδη χρόνον ἔχει, λέγει αὐτῷ, Θέλεις
knowing that a long [2]already [1]time he has been, says to him, Desirest thou
ὑγιὴς γενέσθαι; 7 ἀπεκρίθη αὐτῷ ὁ ἀσθενῶν, Κύριε, ἄν-
well to become? [4]Answered [5]him [1]the [2]infirm [[3]man], Sir, a
θρωπον οὐκ.ἔχω, ἵνα ὅταν ταραχθῇ τὸ ὕδωρ [t]βάλλῃ‖
man I have not, that when [3]has [4]been [5]agitated [1]the [2]water he may put
με εἰς τὴν κολυμβήθραν· ἐν.ᾧ.δὲ ἔρχομαι ἐγὼ ἄλλος πρὸ
me into the pool; but while [2]am [3]coming [1]I another before
ἐμοῦ καταβαίνει. 8 Λέγει αὐτῷ ὁ Ἰησοῦς, [v]″Ἔγειραι,‖ [w] ἆρον
me descends. [2]Says [3]to [4]him [1]Jesus, Arise, take up

V. After this there
was a feast of the
Jews; and Jesus went
up to Jerusalem. 2 Now
there is at Jerusalem
by the sheep *market* a
pool, which is called in
the Hebrew tongue
Bethesda, having five
porches. 3 In these lay
a great multitude of
impotent folk, of blind,
halt, withered, wait-
ing for the moving of
the water. 4 For an
angel went down at
a certain season into
the pool, and troubled
the water: whosoever
then first after the
troubling of the
water stepped in
was made whole of
whatsoever disease he
had. 5 And a cer-
tain man was there,
which had an infirmity
thirty and eight years.
6 When Jesus saw him
lie, and knew that he
had been now a long
time *in that case*, he
saith unto him, Wilt
thou be made whole?
7 The impotent man
answered him, Sir, I
have no man, when the
water is troubled, to
put me into the pool:
but while I am com-
ing, another steppeth
down before me. 8 Je-
sus saith unto him,
Rise, take up thy bed,

---

[y] ὑπήντησαν LTTrA. [z] καὶ ἤγγειλαν T; [καὶ ἀπήγγειλαν] TrA. [a] — λέγοντες T. [b] αὐτοῦ (*read* that his child lives) LTTrA. [c] τὴν ὥραν παρ' αὐτῶν LTTrA. [d] εἶπον οὖν therefore they said TTrA. [e] ἐχθὲς LTTrAW. [f] — ἐν T[Tr]. [g] — ″Ὅτι LTTrA. [h] + δὲ now (this) Tr[A]. [i] + ἡ the (feast) T. [k] — ὁ LTTrAW. [l] τὸ λεγόμενον T. [m] Βηθζαθά Bethzatha T. [n] — πολὺ [L]TTrA. [o] — ἐκδεχομένων *to end of verse* 4 [G]TTrA. [p] + [κυρίου] of [the] Lord L [q] οἱῳδηποτοῦν L. [r] τριάκοντα καὶ (— καὶ [L]Tr) ὀκτὼ GLTTrAW. [s] + αὐτοῦ his (infirmity) [L]TTrA. [t] βάλῃ GLTTrAW. [v] ″Ἔγειρε LTTrAW. [w] + [καὶ] and L.

and walk. 9 And im-
mediately the man
was made whole, and
took up his bed, and
walked: and on the
same day was the sab-
bath. 10 The Jews
therefore said unto
him that was cured,
It is the sabbath day:
it is not lawful for
thee to carry *thy* bed.
11 He answered them,
He that made me
whole, the same said
unto me, Take up thy
bed, and walk. 12 Then
asked they him, What
man is that which said
unto thee, Take up
thy bed, and walk?
13 And he that was
healed wist not who
it was: for Jesus had
conveyed himself a-
way, a multitude be-
ing in *that* place.
14 Afterward Jesus
findeth him in the
temple, and said unto
him, Behold, thou art
made whole: sin no
more, lest a worse
thing come unto thee.
15 The man departed,
and told the Jews that
it was Jesus, which
had made him whole.
16 And therefore did
the Jews persecute Je-
sus, and sought to
slay him, because he
had done these things
on the sabbath day.
17 But Jesus answer-
ed them, My Father
worketh hitherto, and
I work. 18 Therefore
the Jews sought the
more to kill him, be-
cause he not only had
broken the sabbath,
but said also that God
was his Father, mak-
ing himself equal with
God. 19 Then answer-
ed Jesus and said unto
them, Verily, verily, I
say unto you, The Son
can do nothing of him-
self, but what he seeth
the Father do: for
what things soever he
doeth, these also do-
eth the Son likewise.
20 For the Father
loveth the Son, and

τὸν.[x]κράββατόν‖.σου, καὶ περιπάτει. 9 Καὶ [y]εὐθέως‖ ἐγένετο
thy bed, and walk. And immediately [3]became
ὑγιὴς ὁ ἄνθρωπος, καὶ ἦρεν τὸν.[x]κράββατον‖.αὐτοῦ, καὶ
[4]well [1]the [2]man, and took up his bed, and
περιεπάτει· ἦν.δὲ σάββατον ἐν ἐκείνῃ τῇ ἡμέρᾳ. 10 [z]Ἔλεγον
walked; and it was sabbath on that day. [3]Said
οὖν οἱ Ἰουδαῖοι τῷ τεθεραπευμένῳ, Σάββατόν ἐστιν·
[4]therefore [1]the [2]Jews to him who had been healed, Sabbath it is,
[z]οὐκ.ἔξεστίν σοι ἆραι τὸν [x]κράββατον‖[a]. 11 [b]Ἀπεκρίθη
it is not lawful for thee to take up the bed. He answered
αὐτοῖς, Ὁ ποιήσας με ὑγιῆ, ἐκεῖνός μοι εἶπεν, [r]Ἆρον τὸν
them, He who made me well, he to me said, Take up
[x]κράββατόν‖.σου καὶ περιπάτει. 12 Ἠρώτησαν [c]οὖν‖ αὐτόν,
thy bed and walk. They asked [2]therefore [1]him,
Τίς ἐστιν ὁ ἄνθρωπος ὁ εἰπών σοι, [r]Ἆρον [d]τὸν [e]κράββατόν
Who is the man who said to thee, Take up [2]bed
σου‖ καὶ περιπάτει; 13 Ὁ.δὲ [f]ἰαθεὶς‖ οὐκ.ᾔδει τίς ἐστιν·
[1]thy and walk? But he who had been healed knew not who it is,
ὁ.γὰρ.Ἰησοῦς ἐξένευσεν, ὄχλου ὄντος ἐν τῷ τόπῳ. 14 Μετὰ
for Jesus had moved away, a crowd being in the place. After
ταῦτα εὑρίσκει αὐτὸν ὁ Ἰησοῦς ἐν τῷ ἱερῷ, καὶ εἶπεν αὐτῷ,
these things [2]finds [3]him [1]Jesus in the temple, and said to him,
Ἴδε ὑγιὴς γέγονας· μηκέτι ἁμάρτανε, ἵνα μὴ χεῖρόν
Behold, well thou hast become: [2]no [3]more [1]sin, that [4]not [2]worse
[g]τί σοι‖ γένηται. 15 [h]Ἀπῆλθεν ὁ ἄνθρωπος καὶ [i]ἀνήγ-
[1]something [5]to [6]thee [3]happens. Went away the man and told
γειλεν‖ τοῖς Ἰουδαίοις ὅτι Ἰησοῦς ἐστιν ὁ ποιήσας αὐτὸν
the Jews that Jesus it is who made him
ὑγιῆ. 16 Καὶ διὰ τοῦτο ἐδίωκον [k]τὸν Ἰησοῦν οἱ Ἰουδαῖοι,‖
well. And because of this [3]persecuted [4]Jesus [1]the [2]Jews,
[l]καὶ ἐζήτουν αὐτὸν ἀποκτεῖναι,‖ ὅτι ταῦτα ἐποίει ἐν σαβ-
and sought him to kill, because these things he did on a sab-
βάτῳ. 17 ὁ.δὲ.[m]Ἰησοῦς‖ ἀπεκρίνατο αὐτοῖς, Ὁ.πατήρ.μου
bath. But Jesus answered them, My Father
ἕως.ἄρτι ἐργάζεται, κἀγὼ ἐργάζομαι. 18 Διὰ τοῦτο [n]οὖν‖
until now works, and I work. Because of this therefore
μᾶλλον ἐζήτουν αὐτὸν οἱ Ἰουδαῖοι ἀποκτεῖναι, ὅτι οὐ μόνον
the more sought [5]him [1]the [2]Jews [3]to [4]kill, because not only
ἔλυεν τὸ σάββατον, ἀλλὰ καὶ πατέρα ἴδιον ἔλεγεν τὸν
did he break the sabbath, but also [5]Father [3]his [4]own [1]called
θεόν, ἴσον ἑαυτὸν ποιῶν τῷ θεῷ. 19 Ἀπεκρίνατο οὖν ὁ
[2]God, equal [2]himself [1]making to God. [3]Answered [2]therefore
Ἰησοῦς καὶ [o]εἶπεν‖ αὐτοῖς, Ἀμὴν ἀμὴν λέγω ὑμῖν, οὐ δύναται
[1]Jesus and said to them, Verily verily I say to you, [3]is [4]able
ὁ υἱὸς ποιεῖν ἀφ' ἑαυτοῦ οὐδέν, [p]ἐὰν‖.μή τι βλέπῃ
[1]the [2]Son to do from himself nothing, unless anything he may see
τὸν πατέρα ποιοῦντα· ἃ.γὰρ.[q]ἂν‖ ἐκεῖνος ποιῇ, ταῦτα καὶ
the Father doing: for whatever he does, these things also
ὁ υἱὸς [r]ὁμοίως ποιεῖ.‖ 20 ὁ.γὰρ πατὴρ φιλεῖ τὸν υἱόν, καὶ
the Son in like manner does. For the Father loves the Son, and

---

[x] κράβαττον LTTrAW. [y] — εὐθέως T. [z] + καὶ and [L]T[Tr]A. [a] + σου (*read* thy bed) L. [b] + ὃς δὲ who however LTr. [c] — οὖν [L]T[Tr]A. [d] — τὸν κράββατόν σου T[Tr]A. [e] κράβαττόν L[Tr]W. [f] ἀσθενῶν was impotent T. [g] σοί τι GLTTrAW. [h] + [καὶ] and L. [i] εἶπεν T. [k] οἱ Ἰουδαῖοι τὸν Ἰησοῦν LTTrA. [l] — καὶ ἐζήτουν αὐτὸν ἀποκτεῖναι G[L]TTrA. [m] — Ἰησοῦς (*read* he answered) T. [n] — οὖν T. [o] ἔλεγεν T. [p] ἂν T. [q] [ἂν] Tr. [r] ποιεῖ ὁμοίως T.

πάντα δείκνυσιν αὐτῷ ἃ αὐτὸς ποιεῖ· καὶ μείζονα τού-
all things shews to him which [2]himself [1]he does; and greater [2]than
των δείξει αὐτῷ ἔργα, ἵνα ὑμεῖς [s]θαυμάζητε.‖ 21 ὥσπερ
[3]these [4]he [5]will [6]shew [7]him [1]works, that ye may wonder. [2]Even [3]as
γὰρ ὁ πατὴρ ἐγείρει τοὺς νεκροὺς καὶ ζωοποιεῖ, οὕτως καὶ ὁ
[1]for the Father raises up the dead and quickens, thus also the
υἱὸς οὓς θέλει ζωοποιεῖ. 22 οὐδὲ γὰρ ὁ πατὴρ κρίνει οὐδένα,
Son whom he will quickens; for the Father judges no one,
ἀλλὰ τὴν κρίσιν πᾶσαν δέδωκεν τῷ υἱῷ, 23 ἵνα πάντες
but [2]judgment [1]all has given to the Son, that all
τιμῶσιν τὸν υἱὸν καθὼς τιμῶσιν τὸν πατέρα. ὁ μὴ-τιμῶν
may honour the Son even as they honour the Father. He that honours not
τὸν υἱὸν οὐ-τιμᾷ τὸν πατέρα τὸν πέμψαντα αὐτόν. 24 Ἀμὴν
the Son honours not the Father who sent him. Verily
ἀμὴν λέγω ὑμῖν, ὅτι ὁ τὸν-λόγον-μου ἀκούων, καὶ πιστεύων
verily I say to you, that he that my word hears, and believes
τῷ πέμψαντί με, ἔχει ζωὴν αἰώνιον, καὶ εἰς κρίσιν οὐκ
him who sent me, has life eternal, and into judgment [2]not
ἔρχεται, ἀλλὰ μεταβέβηκεν ἐκ τοῦ θανάτου εἰς τὴν ζωήν.
[1]comes, but has passed out of death into life.
25 Ἀμὴν ἀμὴν λέγω ὑμῖν, ὅτι ἔρχεται ὥρα καὶ νῦν ἐστιν,
Verily verily I say to you, that is coming an hour and now is,
ὅτε οἱ νεκροὶ [t]ἀκούσονται‖ τῆς φωνῆς τοῦ υἱοῦ τοῦ θεοῦ, καὶ
when the dead shall hear the voice of the Son of God, and
οἱ ἀκούσαντες [v]ζήσονται.‖ 26 ὥσπερ-γὰρ ὁ πατὴρ ἔχει
those having heard shall live. For even as the Father has
ζωὴν ἐν ἑαυτῷ, οὕτως [w]ἔδωκεν καὶ τῷ υἱῷ‖ ζωὴν ἔχειν
life in himself, so he gave also to the Son life to have
ἐν ἑαυτῷ. 27 καὶ ἐξουσίαν ἔδωκεν αὐτῷ [x]καὶ‖ κρίσιν
in himself, and authority gave to him also judgment
ποιεῖν, ὅτι υἱὸς ἀνθρώπου ἐστίν. 28 μὴ-θαυμάζετε τοῦτο·
to execute, because Son of man he is. Wonder not at this,
ὅτι ἔρχεται ὥρα ἐν ᾗ πάντες οἱ ἐν τοῖς μνημείοις [t]ἀκού-
for [3]is [4]coming [1]an [2]hour in which all those in the tombs shall
σονται‖ τῆς-φωνῆς-αὐτοῦ, 29 καὶ ἐκπορεύσονται, οἱ τὰ
hear his voice, and shall come forth, those that
ἀγαθὰ ποιήσαντες εἰς ἀνάστασιν ζωῆς, οἱ [y]δὲ‖ τὰ φαῦλα
good practised to a resurrection of life, and those that evil
πράξαντες εἰς ἀνάστασιν κρίσεως. 30 οὐ δύναμαι-ἐγὼ ποιεῖν
did to a resurrection of judgment. [2]Am [3]able [1]I to do
ἀπ' ἐμαυτοῦ οὐδέν· καθὼς ἀκούω κρίνω, καὶ ἡ κρίσις ἡ
from myself nothing; even as I hear I judge, and [2]judgment
ἐμὴ δικαία ἐστίν· ὅτι οὐ-ζητῶ τὸ θέλημα τὸ ἐμόν, ἀλλὰ τὸ
[1]my [4]just [3]is, because I seek not [2]will [1]my, but the
θέλημα τοῦ πέμψαντός με [z]πατρός.‖ 31 Ἐὰν ἐγὼ μαρτυρῶ
will of the [2]who [3]sent [4]me [1]Father. If I bear witness
περὶ ἐμαυτοῦ, ἡ-μαρτυρία-μου οὐκ-ἔστιν ἀληθής. 32 ἄλλος
concerning myself, my witness is not true. Another
ἐστὶν ὁ μαρτυρῶν περὶ ἐμοῦ, καὶ [a]οἶδα‖ ὅτι ἀληθής ἐστιν
it is who bears witness concerning me, and I know that true is
ἡ μαρτυρία ἣν μαρτυρεῖ περὶ ἐμοῦ. 33 Ὑμεῖς ἀπεστάλ-
the witness which he witnesses concerning me. Ye have
κατε πρὸς [b]Ἰωάννην‖ καὶ μεμαρτύρηκεν τῇ ἀληθείᾳ· 34 ἐγὼ
sent unto John and he has borne witness to the truth. [2]I

sheweth him all things
that himself doeth
and he will shew him
greater works than
these, that ye may
marvel. 21 For as the
Father raiseth up the
dead, and quickeneth
them; even so the Son
quickeneth whom he
will. 22 For the Fa-
ther judgeth no man,
but hath committed
all judgment unto the
Son: 23 that all *men*
should honour the Son,
even as they honour
the Father. He that
honoureth not the Son
honoureth not the Fa-
ther which hath sent
him. 24 Verily, verily,
I say unto you, He
that heareth my word,
and believeth on him
that sent me, hath
everlasting life, and
shall not come into
condemnation; but is
passed from death un-
to life. 25 Verily, ve-
rily, I say unto you,
The hour is coming,
and now is, when the
dead shall hear the
voice of the Son of
God: and they that
hear shall live. 26 For
as the Father hath life
in himself; so hath he
given to the Son to
have life in himself;
27 and hath given him
authority to execute
judgment also, be-
cause he is the Son of
man. 28 Marvel not
at this: for the hour
is coming, in the which
all that are in the
graves shall hear his
voice, 29 and shall
come forth; they that
have done good, unto
the resurrection of
life; and they that
have done evil, unto
the resurrection of
damnation. 30 I can
of mine own self do
nothing: as I hear, I
judge: and my judg-
ment is just; because
I seek not mine own
will, but the will of
the Father which hath
sent me. 31 If I bear
witness of myself, my
witness is not true.
32 There is another
that beareth witness
of me; and I know
that the witness which
he witnesseth of me is
true. 33 Ye sent unto
John, and he bare wit-
ness unto the truth.

[s] θαυμάζετε wonder T. [t] ἀκούσουσιν TTr. [v] ζήσουσιν LTTrA. [w] καὶ τῷ υἱῷ ἔδωκεν TTrA. [x] — καὶ LTTrA. [y] — δὲ and [L]T[Tr]A. [z] — πατρός (*read* of him who sent me) GLTTrAW. [a] οἴδατε ye know T. [b] Ἰωάνην Tr.

34 But I receive not
testimony from man:
but these things I say,
that ye might be saved.
35 He was a burning
and a shining light:
and ye were willing
for a season to rejoice
in his light. 36 But I
have greater witness
than *that* of John: for
the works which the
Father hath given me
to finish, the same
works that I do, bear
witness of me, that
the Father hath sent
me. 37 And the Father
himself, which hath
sent me, hath borne
witness of me. Ye
have neither heard his
voice at any time, nor
seen his shape. 38 And
ye have not his word
abiding in you: for
whom he hath sent,
him ye believe not.
39 Search the scrip-
tures; for in them ye
think ye have eternal
life: and they are they
which testify of me.
40 And ye will not
come to me, that ye
might have life. 41 I
receive not honour
from men. 42 But I
know you, that ye have
not the love of God in
you. 43 I am come in
my Father's name, and
ye receive me not: if
another shall come in
his own name, him ye
will receive. 44 How
can ye believe, which
receive honour one of
another, and seek not
the honour that *com-
eth* from God only?
45 Do not think that
I will accuse you to
the Father: there is
one that accuseth you,
even Moses, in whom
ye trust. 46 For had
ye believed Moses, ye
would have believed
me: for he wrote of
me. 47 But if ye be-
lieve not his writings,
how shall ye believe
my words?

δὲ οὐ παρὰ ἀνθρώπου τὴν μαρτυρίαν λαμβάνω, ἀλλὰ ταῦ-
[1]but [4]not [6]from [7]man [5]witness [3]receive, but these

τα λέγω ἵνα ὑμεῖς σωθῆτε. 35 ἐκεῖνος ἦν ὁ λύχνος ὁ
things I say that ye may be saved. He was the [4]lamp

καιόμενος καὶ φαίνων, ὑμεῖς.δὲ ἠθελήσατε [c]ἀγαλλιασθῆναι‖
[1]burning [2]and [3]shining, and ye were willing to rejoice

πρὸς ὥραν ἐν τῷ.φωτὶ.αὐτοῦ. 36 ἐγὼ.δὲ ἔχω τὴν μαρτυρίαν
for an hour in his light. But I have the witness

[d]μείζω‖ τοῦ [e]Ἰωάννου·‖ τὰ.γὰρ ἔργα ἃ [f]ἔδωκέν‖ μοι ὁ
greater than John's for the works which [3]gave [4]me [1]the

πατὴρ ἵνα τελειώσω αὐτά, αὐτὰ.τὰ.ἔργα ἃ [g]ἐγὼ‖
[2]Father that I should complete them, the works themselves which I

ποιῶ, μαρτυρεῖ περὶ ἐμοῦ ὅτι ὁ πατήρ με ἀπέσταλκεν.
do, bear witness concerning me that the Father me has sent.

37 καὶ ὁ πέμψας με πατήρ, [h]αὐτὸς‖ μεμαρτύρηκεν περὶ
And the [2]who [3]sent [4]me [1]Father, himself has borne witness concerning

ἐμοῦ. οὔτε φωνὴν.αὐτοῦ [i]ἀκηκόατε πώποτε,‖ οὔτε εἶδος
me. Neither his voice have ye heard at any time, nor [2]form

αὐτοῦ ἑωράκατε. 38 καὶ τὸν.λόγον.αὐτοῦ οὐκ.ἔχετε [k]μένοντα
[1]his have ye seen. And his word ye have not abiding

ἐν ὑμῖν,‖ ὅτι ὃν ἀπέστειλεν ἐκεῖνος, τούτῳ ὑμεῖς οὐ.πιστεύετε.
in you, for whom [2]sent [1]he, him ye believe not.

39 [l]Ἐρευνᾶτε‖ τὰς γραφάς, ὅτι ὑμεῖς δοκεῖτε ἐν αὐταῖς ζωὴν
Ye search the scriptures, for ye think in them life

αἰώνιον ἔχειν, καὶ ἐκεῖναί εἰσιν αἱ μαρτυροῦσαι περὶ
eternal to have, and they are they which bear witness concerning

ἐμοῦ· 40 καὶ οὐ.θέλετε ἐλθεῖν πρός με, ἵνα ζωὴν ἔχητε.
me; and ye are unwilling to come to me, that life ye may have.

41 Δόξαν παρὰ ἀνθρώπων οὐ.λαμβάνω· 42 [m]ἀλλ'‖ ἔγνωκα
Glory from men I receive not; but I have known

ὑμᾶς ὅτι [n]τὴν ἀγάπην τοῦ θεοῦ οὐκ.ἔχετε‖ ἐν ἑαυτοῖς. 43 ἐγὼ
you that the love of God ye have not in yourselves. I

ἐλήλυθα ἐν τῷ ὀνόματι τοῦ.πατρός.μου, καὶ οὐ.λαμβάνετέ με·
have come in the name of my Father, and ye receive not me;

ἐὰν ἄλλος ἔλθῃ ἐν τῷ ὀνόματι τῷ.ἰδίῳ, ἐκεῖνον [o]λήψεσθε.‖
if another should come in [3]name [1]his [2]own, him ye will receive.

44 πῶς δύνασθε.ὑμεῖς πιστεῦσαι, δόξαν [p]παρὰ‖ ἀλλήλων
How are ye able to believe, [3]glory [4]from [5]one [6]another

λαμβάνοντες, καὶ τὴν δόξαν τὴν παρὰ τοῦ μόνου [q]θεοῦ‖
[1]who [2]receive, and the glory which [is] from the only God

οὐ.ζητεῖτε; 45 μὴ.δοκεῖτε ὅτι ἐγὼ κατηγορήσω ὑμῶν πρὸς τὸν
ye seek not? Think not that I will accuse you to the

πατέρα· ἔστιν ὁ κατηγορῶν ὑμῶν, [r]Μωσῆς,‖ εἰς ὃν
Father: there is [one] who accuses you, Moses, in whom

ὑμεῖς ἠλπίκατε. 46 εἰ.γὰρ ἐπιστεύετε [s]Μωσῇ,‖ ἐπιστεύετε.ἂν
ye have hoped. For if ye believed Moses, ye would have believed

ἐμοί· περὶ.γὰρ ἐμοῦ ἐκεῖνος ἔγραψεν. 47 εἰ.δὲ τοῖς ἐκείνου
me, for concerning me he wrote. But if his

γράμμασιν οὐ.πιστεύετε, πῶς τοῖς.ἐμοῖς.ῥήμασιν πιστεύ-
writings ye believe not, how my words shall ye

σετε;
believe?

---

[c] ἀγαλλιαθῆναι GLTTrAW. [d] μείζων LTrA. [e] Ἰωάνου Tr. [f] δέδωκέν has given TTrA. [g] — ἐγὼ (*read* ποιῶ I do) LTTrA [h] ἐκεῖνος TTrA. [i] πώποτε ἀκηκόατε LTTrAW. [k] ἐν ὑμῖν μένοντα TTrA. [l] ἐραυνᾶτε TTrA. [m] ἀλλὰ LTTrAW. [n] οὐκ ἔχετε τὴν ἀγάπην τοῦ θεοῦ T. [o] λήμψεσθε LTTrA. [p] παρ' A. [q] [θεοῦ] L. [r] Μωϋσῆς LTTrAW. [s] Μωϋσεῖ LTTrA; Μωϋσῇ W.

6 Μετὰ ταῦτα ἀπῆλθεν ὁ Ἰησοῦς πέραν τῆς θαλάσσης
After these things [2]went [3]away [1]Jesus over the sea
τῆς Γαλιλαίας τῆς Τιβεριάδος· 2 [t]καὶ ἠκολούθει‖ αὐτῷ ὄχλος
of Galilee (of Tiberias), and [4]followed [5]him [1]a [3]crowd
πολύς, ὅτι [v]ἑώρων‖ [w]αὐτοῦ‖ τὰ σημεῖα ἃ ἐποίει ἐπὶ
[2]great, because they saw of him the signs which he wrought upon
τῶν ἀσθενούντων. 3 ἀνῆλθεν.δὲ εἰς τὸ ὄρος [x]ὁ‖ Ἰησοῦς,
those who were sick. And [2]went [3]up [4]into [5]the [6]mountain [1]Jesus,
καὶ ἐκεῖ [y]ἐκάθητο‖ μετὰ τῶν.μαθητῶν.αὐτοῦ. 4 ἦν δὲ ἐγγὺς
and there sat with his disciples; and [3]was [4]near
τὸ πάσχα ἡ ἑορτὴ τῶν Ἰουδαίων. 5 ἐπάρας οὖν [z]ὁ Ἰη-
[1]the [2]passover, the feast of the Jews. [3]Having [4]lifted [5]up [2]then [1]Je-
σοῦς τοὺς ὀφθαλμούς,‖ καὶ θεασάμενος ὅτι πολὺς ὄχλος
sus [his] eyes, and having seen that a great crowd
ἔρχεται πρὸς αὐτόν, λέγει πρὸς [a]τὸν‖ Φίλιππον, Πόθεν
is coming to him, he says to Philip, Whence
[b]ἀγοράσομεν‖ ἄρτους ἵνα φάγωσιν οὗτοι; 6 Τοῦτο.δὲ ἔλεγεν
shall we buy loaves that [2]may [3]eat [1]these? But this he said
πειράζων αὐτόν· αὐτὸς.γὰρ ᾔδει τί ἔμελλεν ποιεῖν. 7 [c]ἀπε-
trying him, for he knew what he was about to do. An-
κρίθη‖ αὐτῷ [d] Φίλιππος, Διακοσίων δηναρίων ἄρτοι οὐκ
swered him Philip, [2]For [3]two [4]hundred [5]denarii [1]loaves [7]not
ἀρκοῦσιν αὐτοῖς ἵνα ἕκαστος [e]αὐτῶν‖ βραχύ.[f]τι‖ λάβῃ.
[6]are sufficient for them that each of them some little may receive.
8 Λέγει αὐτῷ εἷς ἐκ τῶν.μαθητῶν.αὐτοῦ, Ἀνδρέας ὁ ἀδελφὸς
Says to him one of his disciples, Andrew the brother
Σίμωνος Πέτρου, 9 Ἔστιν παιδάριον [g]ἓν‖ ὧδε, [h]ὃ‖ ἔχει πέντε
of Simon Peter, [4]Is [2]little [3]boy [1]a here, who has five
ἄρτους κριθίνους καὶ δύο ὀψάρια· ἀλλὰ ταῦτα τί ἐστιν εἰς
[2]loaves [1]barley and two small fishes; but [3]these [1]what [2]are for
τοσούτους; 10 Εἶπεν.[i]δὲ‖ ὁ Ἰησοῦς, Ποιήσατε τοὺς ἀνθρώπους
so many? And [2]said [1]Jesus, Make the men
ἀναπεσεῖν. ἦν.δὲ χόρτος πολὺς ἐν τῷ τόπῳ. [k]ἀνέπεσον‖
to recline. Now [3]was [2]grass [1]much in the place: reclined
οὖν οἱ ἄνδρες τὸν ἀριθμὸν [l]ὡσεὶ‖ πεντακισχίλιοι. 11 ἔλαβεν
therefore the men, the number about five thousand. [3]Took
[m]δὲ‖ τοὺς ἄρτους ὁ Ἰησοῦς, καὶ [n]εὐχαριστήσας διέδωκεν‖ [o]τοῖς
[1]and [4]the [5]loaves [2]Jesus, and having given thanks distributed to the
μαθηταῖς, οἱ.δὲ μαθηταὶ‖ τοῖς ἀνακειμένοις· ὁμοίως.καὶ
disciples, and the disciples to those reclining; and in like manner
ἐκ τῶν ὀψαρίων ὅσον ἤθελον. 12 ὡς.δὲ ἐνεπλήσθησαν
of the small fishes as much as they wished. And when they were filled
λέγει τοῖς.μαθηταῖς.αὐτοῦ, Συναγάγετε τὰ περισσεύσαντα
he says to his disciples, Gather together the [2]over [3]and [4]above
κλάσματα, ἵνα μή.τι ἀπόληται. 13 Συνήγαγον οὖν
[1]fragments, that nothing may be lost. They gathered together therefore
καὶ ἐγέμισαν δώδεκα κοφίνους κλασμάτων ἐκ τῶν πέντε
and filled twelve hand-baskets of fragments from the five
ἄρτων τῶν κριθίνων ἃ [p]ἐπερίσσευσεν‖ τοῖς βεβρω-
[2]loaves [1]barley which were over and above to those who had

VI. After these
things Jesus went
over the sea of Gali-
lee, which is *the sea* of
Tiberias. 2 And a
great multitude fol-
lowed him, because
they saw his miracles
which he did on them
that were diseased.
3 And Jesus went up
into a mountain, and
there he sat with his
disciples. 4 And the
passover, a feast of
the Jews, was nigh.
5 When Jesus then
lifted up *his* eyes, and
saw a great company
come unto him, he
saith unto Philip,
Whence shall we buy
bread, that these may
eat? 6 And this he
said to prove him: for
he himself knew what
he would do. 7 Philip
answered him, Two
hundred pennyworth
of bread is not suffici-
ent for them, that
every one of them may
take a little. 8 One of
his disciples, Andrew,
Simon Peter's brother,
saith unto him, 9 There
is a lad here, which
hath five barley loaves,
and two small fishes:
but what are they a-
mong so many? 10 And
Jesus said, Make the
men sit down. Now
there was much grass
in the place. So the
men sat down, in num-
ber about five thou-
sand. 11 And Jesus
took the loaves; and
when he had given
thanks, he distributed
to the disciples, and
the disciples to them
that were set down;
and likewise of the
fishes as much as they
would. 12 When they
were filled, he said
unto his disciples, Ga-
ther up the fragments
that remain, that no-
thing be lost. 13 There-
fore they gathered
them together, and filled twelve baskets with
the fragments of the
five barley loaves,
which remained over
and above unto them
that had eaten. 14 Then

---

[t] ἠκολούθει δὲ LTTrA. [v] ἐθεώρουν LTrA. [w] — αὐτοῦ GLTTrAW. [x] — ὁ LTTrA. [y] ἐκαθέζετο T. [z] τοὺς ὀφθαλμοὺς ὁ Ἰησοῦς LTTrAW. [a] — τὸν LTTrA. [b] ἀγοράσωμεν should we buy LTTrAW. [c] ἀποκρίνεται answers T. [d] + ὁ T. [e] — αὐτῶν LTTrA. [f] — τι (*read* a little) [L]Tr[A]. [g] — ἓν (*read* παιδ. a little boy) [L]TTr[A]. [h] ὃς LTTrAW [i] — δὲ and [L]TTrA. [k] ἀνέπεσαν LTTrA. [l] ὡς TTrA. [m] οὖν therefore (took) LTTrA. [n] εὐχαρίστησεν καὶ ἔδωκεν gave thanks and distributed T. [o] — τοῖς μαθηταῖς, οἱ δὲ μαθηταὶ LTTrA. [p] ἐπερίσσευσαν LTTrA.

those men, when they
had seen the miracle
that Jesus did, said,
This is of a truth that
prophet that should
come into the world.
15 When Jesus there-
fore perceived that
they would come and
take him by force, to
make him a king, he
departed again into a
mountain himself a-
lone.

16 And when even
was *now* come, his dis-
ciples went down unto
the sea, 17 and entered
into a ship, and went
over the sea toward
Capernaum. And it
was now dark, and Je-
sus was not come to
them. 18 And the sea
arose by reason of a
great wind that blew.
19 So when they had
rowed about five and
twenty or thirty fur-
longs, they see Jesus
walking on the sea,
and drawing nigh unto
the ship: and they were
afraid. 20 But he saith
unto them, It is I; be
not afraid. 21 Then
they willingly received
him into the ship: and
immediately the ship
was at the land whi-
ther they went.

22 The day following,
when the people which
stood on the other side
of the sea saw that
there was none other
boat there, save that
one whereinto his dis-
ciples were entered, and
that Jesus went not
with his disciples into
the boat, but *that* his
disciples were gone a-
way alone; 23 (howbeit
there came other boats
from Tiberias nigh un-
to the place where they
did eat bread, after
that the Lord had
given thanks:) 24 when
the people therefore
saw that Jesus was
not there, neither his
disciples, they also took
shipping, and came to
Capernaum, seeking

κόσιν. 14 οἱ.οὖν.ἄνθρωποι ἰδόντες ὃ ἐποίησεν σημεῖον
eaten. The men therefore having seen what [3]had [4]done [1]sign
[q]ὁ Ἰησοῦς,‖ ἔλεγον, Ὅτι οὗτός ἐστιν ἀληθῶς ὁ προφήτης ὁ
[2]Jesus, said, This is truly the prophet who
[r]ἐρχόμενος εἰς τὸν κόσμον.‖ 15 Ἰησοῦς οὖν γνοὺς ὅτι μέλ-
is coming into the world. Jesus therefore knowing that they
λουσιν ἔρχεσθαι καὶ ἁρπάζειν αὐτόν, ἵνα ποιήσωσιν [s]αὐτὸν‖
are about to come and seize him, that they may make him
βασιλέα, [t]ἀνεχώρησεν‖ πάλιν εἰς τὸ ὄρος αὐτὸς μόνος.
king, withdrew again to the mountain himself alone.

16 Ὡς.δὲ ὀψία ἐγένετο κατέβησαν οἱ.μαθηταὶ.αὐτοῦ ἐπὶ
And when evening it became [3]went [4]down [1]his [2]disciples to
τὴν θάλασσαν, 17 καὶ ἐμβάντες εἰς [v]τὸ‖ πλοῖον ἤρχοντο
the sea, and having entered into the ship they were going
πέραν τῆς θαλάσσης εἰς [w]Καπερναούμ.‖ [x]καὶ σκοτία ἤδη
over the sea to Capernaum. And dark already
ἐγεγόνει,‖ καὶ [y]οὐκ‖ ἐληλύθει [z]πρὸς αὐτοὺς ὁ Ἰησοῦς,‖ 18 ἥ.τε
it had become, and [3]not [2]had [4]come [5]to [6]them [1]Jesus, and the
θάλασσα ἀνέμου μεγάλου πνέοντος [a]διηγείρετο.‖ 19 ἐληλα-
sea by a [2]wind [1]strong blowing was agitated. Having
κότες οὖν [b]ὡς‖ [c]σταδίους‖ [d]εἰκοσιπέντε‖ ἢ τριάκοντα θεωροῦσιν
rowed then about [4]furlongs [1]twenty-five [2]or [3]thirty they see
τὸν Ἰησοῦν περιπατοῦντα ἐπὶ τῆς θαλάσσης, καὶ ἐγγὺς τοῦ
Jesus walking on the sea, and near the
πλοίου γινόμενον· καὶ ἐφοβήθησαν. 20 ὁ.δὲ λέγει αὐτοῖς,
ship coming, and they were frightened. But he says to them,
Ἐγώ εἰμι· μὴ.φοβεῖσθε. 21 Ἤθελον οὖν λαβεῖν αὐτὸν
I am [he]; fear not. They were willing then to receive him
εἰς τὸ πλοῖον, καὶ εὐθέως [e]τὸ πλοῖον ἐγένετο‖ ἐπὶ [f]τῆς γῆς‖
into the ship, and immediately the ship was at the land
εἰς ἣν ὑπῆγον.
to which they were going.

22 Τῇ ἐπαύριον ὁ ὄχλος ὁ ἑστηκὼς πέραν τῆς θα-
On the morrow the crowd which stood the other side of the
λάσσης, [g]ἰδὼν‖ ὅτι πλοιάριον ἄλλο οὐκ ἦν ἐκεῖ εἰ.μὴ ἓν
sea, having seen that [3]small [4]ship [2]other [1]no was there except one
[h]ἐκεῖνο εἰς ὃ ἐνέβησαν οἱ.μαθηταὶ.αὐτοῦ,‖ καὶ ὅτι οὐ
that into which entered his disciples, and that [3]not
συνεισῆλθεν τοῖς.μαθηταῖς.αὐτοῦ ὁ Ἰησοῦς εἰς τὸ [i]πλοιάριον,‖
[2]went [4]with [5]his [6]disciples [1]Jesus into the small ship,
ἀλλὰ μόνοι οἱ.μαθηταὶ.αὐτοῦ ἀπῆλθον, 23 ἄλλα.[k]δὲ‖ [l]ἦλθεν‖
but alone his disciples went away, (but other [3]came
[m]πλοιάρια‖ ἐκ Τιβεριάδος ἐγγὺς τοῦ τόπου ὅπου ἔφαγον τὸν
[1]small [2]ships from Tiberias near the place where they ate the
ἄρτον, εὐχαριστήσαντος τοῦ κυρίου· 24 ὅτε οὖν εἶδεν ὁ
bread, [3]having [4]given [5]thanks [1]the [2]Lord;) when therefore [3]saw [1]the
ὄχλος ὅτι Ἰησοῦς οὐκ ἔστιν ἐκεῖ οὐδὲ οἱ.μαθηταὶ.αὐτοῦ, ἐνέ-
[2]crowd that Jesus [2]not [1]is there nor his disciples, they
βησαν [n]καὶ‖ αὐτοὶ εἰς τὰ [o]πλοῖα‖ καὶ ἦλθον εἰς [p]Καπερ-
[3]entered [1]also [2]themselves into the ships and came to Caper-

---

[q] — ὁ Ἰησοῦς (*read* he had done) TTrA. [r] εἰς τὸν κόσμον ἐρχόμενος T. [s] — αὐτὸν (*read* [him]) LTTrA. [t] φεύγει escapes T. [v] — τὸ (*read* a ship) TTrA. [w] Καφαρναούμ LTTrAW. [x] κατέλαβεν δὲ αὐτοὺς ἡ σκοτία and darkness overtook them T. [y] οὔπω not yet LTTrA. [z] Ἰησοῦς πρὸς αὐτούς T. [a] διεγείρετο TrA. [b] ὡσεὶ L. [c] στάδια T. [d] εἴκοσι πέντε LTTr. [e] ἐγένετο τὸ πλοῖον LTTrA. [f] τὴν γῆν T. [g] εἶδον saw LTTrA. [h] — ἐκεῖνο εἰς ὃ ἐνέβησαν οἱ μαθηταὶ αὐτοῦ GLTTrA. [i] πλοῖον ship GLTTrA. [k] — δὲ but TTr[A]. [l] ἦλθον T. [m] πλοῖα ships L. [n] — καὶ GLTTrAW. [o] πλοιάρια small ships LTTrA. [p] Καφαρναούμ LTTrAW.

ναούμ,ˡ ζητοῦντες τὸν Ἰησοῦν. 25 καὶ εὑρόντες αὐτὸν
naum, seeking Jesus. And having found him
πέραν τῆς θαλάσσης, εἶπον αὐτῷ, [q]Ῥαββί,ˡ πότε ὧδε
the other side of the sea, they said to him, Rabbi, when here
γέγονας; 26 Ἀπεκρίθη αὐτοῖς ὁ Ἰησοῦς καὶ εἶπεν, Ἀμὴν
hast thou come? [2]Answered [3]them [1]Jesus and said, Verily
ἀμὴν λέγω ὑμῖν, ζητεῖτέ με, οὐχ ὅτι εἴδετε σημεῖα, ἀλλ'
verily I say to you, Ye seek me, not because ye saw signs, but
ὅτι ἐφάγετε ἐκ τῶν ἄρτων καὶ ἐχορτάσθητε. 27 ἐργάζεσθε
because ye ate of the loaves and were satisfied. Work
μὴ τὴν βρῶσιν τὴν ἀπολλυμένην, ἀλλὰ τὴν βρῶσιν
not [for] the food which perishes, but [for] the food
τὴν μένουσαν εἰς ζωὴν αἰώνιον, ἣν ὁ υἱὸς τοῦ ἀνθρώπου
which abides unto life eternal, which the Son of man
[r]ὑμῖν δώσει·ˡ τοῦτον.γὰρ ὁ πατὴρ ἐσφράγισεν ὁ θεός.
to you will give; for him the Father sealed, [even] God.
28 Εἶπον οὖν πρὸς αὐτόν, Τί [s]ποιοῦμεν,ˡ ἵνα ἐργαζώμεθα
They said therefore to him, What do we, that we may work
τὰ ἔργα τοῦ θεοῦ; 29 Ἀπεκρίθη [t]ὁˡ Ἰησοῦς καὶ εἶπεν αὐτοῖς,
the works of God? [2]Answered [1]Jesus and said to them,
Τοῦτό ἐστιν τὸ ἔργον τοῦ θεοῦ, ἵνα [v]πιστεύσητεˡ εἰς ὃν
This is the work of God, that ye should believe on him whom
ἀπέστειλεν ἐκεῖνος. 30 Εἶπον οὖν αὐτῷ, Τί οὖν ποιεῖς
[2]sent [1]he. They said therefore to him, What [2]then [3]doest
σὺ σημεῖον, ἵνα ἴδωμεν καὶ πιστεύσωμέν σοι; τί ἐργάζῃ;
[4]thou [1]sign, that we may see and may believe thee? what dost thou work?
31 οἱ.πατέρες.ἡμῶν τὸ μάννα ἔφαγον ἐν τῇ ἐρήμῳ, καθώς
Our fathers the manna ate in the wilderness, as
ἐστιν γεγραμμένον, Ἄρτον ἐκ τοῦ οὐρανοῦ ἔδωκεν αὐτοῖς
it is written, Bread out of the heaven he gave them
φαγεῖν. 32 Εἶπεν οὖν αὐτοῖς ὁ Ἰησοῦς, Ἀμὴν ἀμὴν λέγω
to eat. [2]Said [3]therefore [4]to [5]them [1]Jesus, Verily verily I say
ὑμῖν, Οὐ [w]Μωσῆςˡ [x]δέδωκενˡ ὑμῖν τὸν ἄρτον ἐκ τοῦ οὐρα-
to you, [3]Not [1]Moses [2]has [4]given you the bread out of the hea-
νοῦ· ἀλλ' ὁ.πατήρ.μου δίδωσιν ὑμῖν τὸν ἄρτον ἐκ τοῦ οὐ-
ven; but my Father gives you the [2]bread [3]out [4]of [5]the [6]hea-
ρανοῦ τὸν ἀληθινόν. 33 ὁ.γὰρ ἄρτος [y] τοῦ θεοῦ ἐστιν ὁ
ven [1]true. For the bread of God is he who
καταβαίνων ἐκ τοῦ οὐρανοῦ, καὶ ζωὴν διδοὺς τῷ κόσμῳ.
comes down out of the heaven, and life gives to the world.
34 Εἶπον οὖν πρὸς αὐτόν, Κύριε, πάντοτε δὸς ἡμῖν τὸν
They said therefore to him, Lord, always give to us
ἄρτον.τοῦτον. 35 Εἶπεν [z]δὲˡ αὐτοῖς ὁ Ἰησοῦς, Ἐγώ εἰμι ὁ
this bread. [3]Said [1]and [4]to [5]them [2]Jesus, I am the
ἄρτος τῆς ζωῆς· ὁ ἐρχόμενος πρός [a]μεˡ οὐ.μὴ [b]πεινάσῃ·ˡ
bread of life: he that comes to me in no wise may hunger,
καὶ ὁ πιστεύων εἰς ἐμὲ οὐ.μὴ [c]διψήσῃˡ πώποτε. 36 ἀλλ'
and he that believes on me in no wise may thirst at any time. But
εἶπον ὑμῖν ὅτι καὶ ἑωράκατέ [d]μεˡ καὶ οὐ.πιστεύετε. 37 πᾶν
I said to you that also ye have seen me and believe not. All
ὃ δίδωσίν μοι ὁ πατὴρ πρὸς ἐμὲ ἥξει· καὶ τὸν ἐρχό-
that [3]gives [4]me [1]the [2]Father to me shall come, and him that comes

for Jesus. 25 And when they had found him on the other side of the sea, they said unto him, Rabbi, when camest thou hither? 26 Jesus answered them and said, Verily, verily, I say unto you, Ye seek me, not because ye saw the miracles, but because ye did eat of the loaves, and were filled. 27 Labour not for the meat which perisheth, but for that meat which endureth unto everlasting life, which the Son of man shall give unto you: for him hath God the Father sealed. 28 Then said they unto him, What shall we do, that we might work the works of God? 29 Jesus answered and said unto them, This is the work of God, that ye believe on him whom he hath sent. 30 They said therefore unto him, What sign shewest thou then, that we may see, and believe thee? what dost thou work? 31 Our fathers did eat manna in the desert; as it is written, He gave them bread from heaven to eat. 32 Then Jesus said unto them, Verily, verily, I say unto you, Moses gave you not that bread from heaven; but my Father giveth you the true bread from heaven. 33 For the bread of God is he which cometh down from heaven, and giveth life unto the world. 34 Then said they unto him, Lord, evermore give us this bread. 35 And Jesus said unto them, I am the bread of life: he that cometh to me shall never hunger; and he that believeth on me shall never thirst. 36 But I said unto you, That ye also have seen me, and believe not. 37 All that the Father giveth me shall come to me; and him that cometh

---

q Ῥαββεί T. r δίδωσιν ὑμῖν gives to you T. s ποιῶμεν should we do EGLTTrAW. t — ὁ T. v πιστεύητε TTrA. w Μωϋσῆς LTTrAW. x ἔδωκεν gave LTrA. y + ὁ T. z οὖν therefore T; — δὲ [L]TrA. a ἐμὲ TTrA. b πεινάσει shall hunger L. c διψήσει shall thirst LTTrA. d — με [L]T.

to me I will in no wise
cast out. 38 For I
came down from hea-
ven, not to do mine
own will, but the will
of him that sent me.
39 And this is the Fa-
ther's will which hath
sent me, that of all
which he hath given
me I should lose no-
thing, but should raise
it up again at the last
day. 40 And this is
the will of him that
sent me, that every
one which seeth the
Son, and believeth on
him, may have ever-
lasting life: and I
will raise him up at
the last day. 41 The
Jews then murmured
at him, because he
said, I am the bread
which came down from
heaven. 42 And they
said, Is not this Jesus,
the son of Joseph,
whose father and mo-
ther we know? how is
it then that he saith,
I came down from
heaven? 43 Jesus there-
fore answered and said
unto them, Murmur
not among yourselves.
44 No man can come
to me, except the Fa-
ther which hath sent
me draw him: and I
will raise him up at
the last day. 45 It is
written in the pro-
phets, And they shall
be all taught of God.
Every man therefore
that hath heard, and
hath learned of the
Father, cometh unto
me. 46 Not that any
man hath seen the Fa-
ther, save he which is
of God, he hath seen
the Father. 47 Verily,
verily, I say unto you,
He that believeth on
me hath everlasting
life. 48 I am that
bread of life. 49 Your
Fathers did eat manna
in the wilderness, and
are dead. 50 This is
the bread which com-
eth down from hea-
ven, that a man may

μενον πρός [e]με‖ οὐ.μὴ ἐκβάλω ἔξω· 38 ὅτι καταβέβηκα
to me not at all will I cast out. For I have come down

[f]ἐκ‖ τοῦ οὐρανοῦ, οὐχ ἵνα [g]ποιῶ‖ τὸ θέλημα τὸ ἐμόν, ἀλλὰ
out of the heaven, not that I should do ²will ¹my, but

τὸ θέλημα τοῦ πέμψαντός με. 39 τοῦτο.δέ ἐστιν τὸ
the will of him who sent me. And this is the

θέλημα τοῦ πέμψαντός με [h]πατρός,‖ ἵνα πᾶν ὃ δέδωκέν
will of the ²who ³sent ⁴me ¹Father, that [of] all that he has given

μοι, μὴ.ἀπολέσω ἐξ.αὐτοῦ, ἀλλὰ ἀναστήσω αὐτὸ [i]ἐν‖
me, I should not lose [any] of it, but should raise up it in

τῇ ἐσχάτῃ ἡμέρᾳ. 40 τοῦτο.[k]δέ‖ ἐστιν τὸ θέλημα [l]τοῦ
the last day. And this is the will of him who

πέμψαντός με,‖ ἵνα πᾶς ὁ θεωρῶν τὸν υἱὸν καὶ πιστεύων
sent me, that everyone who sees the Son and believes

εἰς αὐτόν, ἔχῃ ζωὴν αἰώνιον, καὶ ἀναστήσω αὐτὸν [m]ἐγὼ‖
on him, should have life eternal; and ²will ³raise ⁴up ⁵him ¹I

[n]τῇ ἐσχάτῃ ἡμέρᾳ. 41 Ἐγόγγυζον οὖν οἱ Ἰουδαῖοι περὶ
at the last day. Were murmuring therefore the Jews about

αὐτοῦ, ὅτι εἶπεν, Ἐγώ εἰμι ὁ ἄρτος ὁ καταβὰς ἐκ τοῦ
him, because he said, I am the bread which came down out of the

οὐρανοῦ. 42 καὶ ἔλεγον, [o]Οὐχ‖.οὗτός.ἐστιν Ἰησοῦς ὁ υἱὸς
heaven. And were saying, Is not this Jesus the Son

Ἰωσήφ, οὗ ἡμεῖς οἴδαμεν τὸν πατέρα καὶ τὴν μητέρα;
of Joseph, of whom we know the father and the mother?

πῶς [p]οὖν‖ λέγει [q]οὗτος,‖ Ὅτι ἐκ τοῦ οὐρανοῦ καταβέβηκα;
how therefore says he, Out of the heaven I have come down?

43 Ἀπεκρίθη [r]οὖν‖ [s]ὁ‖ Ἰησοῦς καὶ εἶπεν αὐτοῖς, Μὴ.γογγύζετε
³Answered ²therefore ¹Jesus and said to them, Murmur not

[t]μετ'‖ ἀλλήλων. 44 οὐδεὶς δύναται ἐλθεῖν πρός [v]με‖ ἐὰν.μὴ
with one another. No one is able to come to me unless

ὁ πατὴρ ὁ πέμψας με ἑλκύσῃ αὐτόν, [w]καὶ ἐγὼ‖ ἀναστήσω
the Father who sent me draw him, and I will raise up

αὐτὸν [x] τῇ ἐσχάτῃ ἡμέρᾳ. 45 ἔστιν γεγραμμένον ἐν τοῖς προ-
him at the last day. It is written in the pro-

φήταις, Καὶ ἔσονται πάντες διδακτοὶ [y]τοῦ‖ θεοῦ. Πᾶς
phets, And they shall be all taught of God. Everyone

[z]οὖν‖ ὁ ἀκούσας παρὰ τοῦ πατρὸς καὶ μαθών, ἔρχεται
therefore that has heard from the Father and has learnt, comes

πρός [a]με·‖ 46 οὐχ ὅτι τὸν πατέρα [b]τις ἑώρακεν,‖ εἰ.μὴ ὁ
to me: not that ⁴the ⁵Father ¹anyone ²has ³seen, except he who

ὢν παρὰ τοῦ θεοῦ, οὗτος ἑώρακεν τὸν [c]πατέρα.‖ 47 ἀμὴν
is from God, he has seen the Father. Verily

ἀμὴν λέγω ὑμῖν, ὁ πιστεύων [d]εἰς ἐμὲ‖ ἔχει ζωὴν αἰώνιον.
verily I say to you, He that believes on me has life eternal.

48 ἐγώ εἰμι ὁ ἄρτος τῆς ζωῆς. 49 οἱ.πατέρες.ὑμῶν ἔφαγον
I am the bread of life. Your Fathers ate

[e]τὸ μάννα ἐν τῇ ἐρήμῳ,‖ καὶ ἀπέθανον· 50 οὗτός ἐστιν ὁ
the manna in the desert, and died. This is the

ἄρτος ὁ ἐκ τοῦ οὐρανοῦ καταβαίνων, ἵνα τις ἐξ αὐτοῦ
bread which out of heaven comes down, that anyone of it

---

[e] ἐμὲ T. [f] ἀπὸ from LTTrA. [g] ποιήσω T. [h] — πατρός (*read* of him who sent) GLTTrAW. [i] — ἐν (*read* at the) TrA. [k] γάρ for (this) GLTTrAW. [l] τοῦ πατρός μου of my father LTTrA. [m] [ἐγὼ] L. [n] + ἐν in (the) LT. [o] Οὐχὶ Tr. [p] νῦν now TTrA. [q] — οὗτος (*read* λέγει says he) [L]TrA. [r] — οὖν G[L]TTrAW. [s] — ὁ TTr. [t] μετὰ Tr. [v] ἐμὲ TrA. [w] κἀγὼ LTTrA. [x] + ἐν in (the) GLTTrAW. [y] — τοῦ GLTTrAW. [z] — οὖν GLTTrA. [a] ἐμέ TTrW. [b] ἑώρακέν τις LTTrAW. [c] θεόν God T. [d] — εἰς ἐμέ T[TrA]. [e] ἐν τῇ ἐρήμῳ τὸ μάννα LTTrA.

φάγῃ καὶ μὴ ἀποθάνῃ. 51 ἐγώ εἰμι ὁ ἄρτος ὁ ζῶν, ὁ
may eat and not die. I am the [2]bread [1]living, which
ἐκ τοῦ οὐρανοῦ καταβάς· ἐάν τις φάγῃ [f]ἐκ τούτου
out of the heaven came down: if anyone shall have eaten of this
τοῦ ἄρτου ζήσεται‖ εἰς.τὸν.αἰῶνα. καὶ ὁ ἄρτος δὲ ὃν ἐγὼ
bread he shall live for ever; and the bread also which I
δώσω, [g]ἡ.σάρξ.μου ἐστίν, [h]ἣν ἐγὼ δώσω‖ ὑπὲρ τῆς τοῦ
will give, my flesh is, which I will give for the [2]of [3]the
κόσμου ζωῆς.‖ 52 Ἐμάχοντο οὖν [i]πρὸς ἀλλήλους οἱ Ἰου-
[4]world [1]life. Were contending therefore with one another the Jews
δαῖοι,‖ λέγοντες, Πῶς δύναται [k]οὗτος ἡμῖν‖ δοῦναι τὴν
saying, How is [2]able [1]he [5]us. [3]to [4]give
σάρκα[l] φαγεῖν; 53 Εἶπεν οὖν αὐτοῖς ὁ Ἰησοῦς, Ἀμὴν
[7]flesh [[6]his] to eat? [3]Said [2]therefore [4]to [5]them [1]Jesus, Verily
ἀμὴν λέγω ὑμῖν, ἐὰν.μὴ φάγητε τὴν σάρκα τοῦ υἱοῦ
verily I say to you, Unless ye shall have eaten the flesh of the Son
τοῦ ἀνθρώπου καὶ πίητε αὐτοῦ τὸ αἷμα, οὐκ.ἔχετε ζωὴν
of man and shall have drunk his blood, ye have not life
ἐν ἑαυτοῖς. 54 ὁ τρώγων μου τὴν σάρκα, καὶ πίνων μου
in yourselves. He that eats my flesh, and drinks my
τὸ αἷμα, ἔχει ζωὴν αἰώνιον, [m]καὶ ἐγὼ‖ ἀναστήσω αὐτὸν [n] τῇ
blood, has life eternal, and I will raise up him in the
ἐσχάτῃ ἡμέρᾳ· 55 ἡ.γὰρ.σάρξ.μου [o]ἀληθῶς‖ ἐστιν βρῶσις, καὶ
last day; for my flesh truly is food, and
τὸ.αἷμά.μου [o]ἀληθῶς‖ ἐστιν πόσις. 56 ὁ τρώγων μου τὴν
my blood truly is drink. He that eats my
σάρκα καὶ πίνων μου τὸ αἷμά, ἐν ἐμοὶ μένει, κἀγὼ ἐν αὐτῷ.
flesh and drinks my blood, in me abides, and I in him.
57 καθὼς ἀπέστειλέν με ὁ ζῶν πατήρ, κἀγὼ ζῶ διὰ
As [4]sent [5]me [1]the [2]living [3]Father, and I live because of
τὸν πατέρα· καὶ ὁ τρώγων με, κἀκεῖνος [p]ζήσεται‖ δι'
the Father, also he that eats me, he also shall live because of
ἐμέ. 58 οὗτός ἐστιν ὁ ἄρτος ὁ [q]ἐκ τοῦ‖ οὐρανοῦ καταβάς·
me. This is the bread which out of the heaven came down.
οὐ καθὼς ἔφαγον οἱ πατέρες [r]ὑμῶν‖ [s]τὸ μάννα,‖ καὶ ἀπέθα-
Not as [5]ate [1]the [2]fathers [3]of [4]you the manna, and died:
νον· ὁ τρώγων τοῦτον τὸν ἄρτον [t]ζήσεται‖ εἰς.τὸν.αἰῶνα.
he that eats this bread shall live for ever.
59 Ταῦτα εἶπεν ἐν συναγωγῇ διδάσκων ἐν [v]Καπερναούμ.‖
These things he said in [the] synagogue teaching in Capernaum.
60 Πολλοὶ οὖν ἀκούσαντες ἐκ τῶν.μαθητῶν.αὐτοῦ εἶπον,
Many therefore [4]having [5]heard [1]of [2]his [3]disciples said,
Σκληρός ἐστιν [w]οὗτος ὁ λόγος·‖ τίς δύναται αὐτοῦ ἀκούειν;
Hard is this word; who is able it to hear?
61 Εἰδὼς δὲ ὁ Ἰησοῦς ἐν ἑαυτῷ ὅτι γογγύζουσιν περὶ
[3]Knowing [1]but [2]Jesus in himself that [3]murmur [4]concerning
τούτου οἱ.μαθηταὶ.αὐτοῦ εἶπεν αὐτοῖς, Τοῦτο ὑμᾶς σκανδα-
[5]this [1]his [2]disciples said to them, [2]This [4]you [1]does [3]of-
λίζει; 62 ἐὰν οὖν θεωρῆτε τὸν υἱὸν τοῦ ἀνθρώπου ἀνα-
fend? If then ye should see the Son of man ascend-
βαίνοντα ὅπου ἦν τὸ πρότερον; 63 τὸ πνεῦμά ἐστιν τὸ
ing up where he was before? The Spirit it is which

eat thereof, and not
die. 51 I am the liv-
ing bread which came
down from heaven:
if any man eat of
this bread, he shall
live for ever: and the
bread that I will give
is my flesh, which I
will give for the life
of the world. 52 The
Jews therefore strove
among themselves,
saying, How can this
man give us *his* flesh
to eat? 53 Then Jesus
said unto them, Verily,
verily, I say unto you,
Except ye eat the flesh
of the Son of man,
and drink his blood,
ye have no life in you.
54 Whoso eateth my
flesh, and drinketh my
blood, hath eternal
life; and I will raise
him up at the last day.
55 For my flesh is meat
indeed, and my blood
is drink indeed. 56 He
that eateth my flesh,
and drinketh my blood,
dwelleth in me, and I
in him. 57 As the liv-
ing Father hath sent
me, and I live by the
Father: so he that eat-
eth me, even he shall
live by me. 58 This
is that bread which
came down from hea-
ven: not as your fa-
thers did eat manna,
and are dead: he that
eateth of this bread
shall live for ever.
59 These things said
he in the synagogue,
as he taught in Caper-
naum. 60 Many there-
fore of his disciples,
when they had heard
this, said, This is an
hard saying; who can
hear it? 61 When Jesus
knew in himself that
his disciples murmur-
ed at it, he said unto
them, Doth this offend
you? 62 *What* and if
ye shall see the Son
of man ascend up
where he was before?
63 It is the spirit that

---

[f] ἐκ τοῦ ἐμοῦ ἄρτου, ζήσει of my bread, he shall live T. [g] ὑπὲρ τῆς τοῦ κόσμου ζωῆς, ἡ σάρξ μου ἐστίν T. [h] — ἣν ἐγὼ δώσω LTTrA. [i] οἱ Ἰουδαῖοι πρὸς ἀλλήλους L. [k] ἡμῖν οὗτος T. [l] + αὐτοῦ his L. [m] κἀγὼ LTTrA. [n] + [ἐν] L. [o] ἀληθής (is) true LTTrA. [p] ζήσει LTTrA. [q] ἐξ out of LTTrA. [r] — ὑμῶν LTTrA. [s] — τὸ μάννα GTTrA. [t] ζήσει TTrA. [v] Καφαρναούμ LTTrAW. [w] ὁ λόγος οὗτος LTTrA.

quickeneth; the flesh
profiteth nothing: the
words that I speak
unto you, *they* are
spirit, and *they* are life.
64 But there are some
of you that believe
not. For Jesus knew
from the beginning
who they were that
believed not, and who
should betray him.
65 And he said, There-
fore said I unto you,
that no man can come
unto me, except it were
given unto him of my
Father. 66 From that
time many of his dis-
ciples went back, and
walked no more with
him. 67 Then said Je-
sus unto the twelve,
Will ye also go away?
68 Then Simon Peter
answered him, Lord,
to whom shall we go?
thou hast the words of
eternal life. 69 And
we believe and are sure
that thou art that
Christ, the Son of the
living God. 70 Jesus
answered them, Have
not I chosen you
twelve, and one of you
is a devil? 71 He
spake of Judas Isca-
riot *the son* of Simon:
for he it was that
should betray him,
being one of the twelve.

ζωοποιοῦν, ἡ σὰρξ οὐκ ὠφελεῖ οὐδέν· τὰ ῥήματα ἃ ἐγὼ
quickens, the flesh profits nothing; the words which I
[x]λαλῶ‖ ὑμῖν. πνεῦμά ἐστιν καὶ ζωή ἐστιν. 64 [y]ἀλλ'‖ εἰσὶν
speak to you, spirit are and life are; but there are
ἐξ ὑμῶν τινες οἳ οὐ.πιστεύουσιν. ᾔδει.γὰρ ἐξ ἀρχῆς
of you some who believe not. For [2]knew [3]from [[4]the] [5]beginning
ὁ Ἰησοῦς τίνες εἰσὶν οἱ μὴ.πιστεύοντες, καὶ τίς ἐστιν ὁ
[1]Jesus who they are who believe not, and who is he who
παραδώσων αὐτόν. 65 καὶ ἔλεγεν, Διὰ.τοῦτο εἴρηκα ὑμῖν,
shall deliver up him. And he said, Therefore have I said to you,
ὅτι οὐδεὶς δύναται ἐλθεῖν πρός [z]με‖ ἐὰν.μὴ ᾖ δεδομένον
that no one is able to come to me unless it be given
αὐτῷ ἐκ τοῦ.πατρός.[a]μου.‖ 66 Ἐκ τούτου [b] πολλοὶ [c]
to him from my Father. From that [time] many
[d]ἀπῆλθον τῶν.μαθητῶν.αὐτοῦ‖ εἰς.τὰ.ὀπίσω, καὶ οὐκέτι μετ'
[4]went [5]away [1]of [2]his [3]disciples back, and no more with
αὐτοῦ περιεπάτουν. 67 εἶπεν οὖν ὁ Ἰησοῦς τοῖς δώδεκα,
him walked. [2]Said [3]therefore [1]Jesus to the twelve,
Μὴ καὶ ὑμεῖς θέλετε ὑπάγειν; 68 Ἀπεκρίθη [e]οὖν‖ αὐτῷ
[3]Also [2]ye [1]are [4]wishing to go away? [4]Answered [3]therefore [5]him
Σίμων Πέτρος, Κύριε, πρὸς τίνα ἀπελευσόμεθα; ῥήματα ζωῆς
[1]Simon [2]Peter, Lord, to whom shall we go? words of life
αἰωνίου ἔχεις· 69 καὶ ἡμεῖς πεπιστεύκαμεν καὶ ἐγνώκαμεν
eternal thou hast; and we have believed and have known
ὅτι σὺ εἶ [f]ὁ χριστὸς ὁ υἱὸς‖ τοῦ θεοῦ [g]τοῦ ζῶντος.‖ 70 Ἀπε-
that thou art the Christ the Son of [3]God [1]the [2]living. An-
κρίθη αὐτοῖς ὁ Ἰησοῦς, Οὐκ ἐγὼ ὑμᾶς τοὺς δώδεκα ἐξελεξάμην,
swered them Jesus, [3]Not [2]I [5]you [6]the [7]twelve [1]did [4]choose,
καὶ ἐξ ὑμῶν εἷς διάβολός ἐστιν; 71 Ἔλεγεν.δὲ τὸν Ἰούδαν
and of you one a devil is? But he spoke of Judas
Σίμωνος [h]Ἰσκαριώτην·‖ οὗτος.γὰρ [i]ἤμελλεν‖ [k]αὐτὸν παρα-
Simon's [son], Iscariote, for he was about him to de-
διδόναι,‖ εἷς [l]ὢν‖ ἐκ τῶν δώδεκα.
liver up, [2]one [1]being of the twelve.

VII. After these
things Jesus walked in
Galilee: for he would
not walk in Jewry,
because the Jews
sought to kill him.
2 Now the Jews' feast
of tabernacles was at
hand. 3 His brethren
therefore said unto
him, Depart hence,
and go into Judæa,
that thy disciples also
may see the works
that thou doest. 4 For
there is no man *that*
doeth any thing in se-
cret, and he himself
seeketh to be known
openly. If thou do
these things, shew thy-

7 [m]Καὶ‖ [n]περιεπάτει ὁ Ἰησοῦς μετὰ ταῦτα‖ ἐν τῇ Γαλι-
And [2]was [3]walking [1]Jesus after these things in Gali-
λαίᾳ· οὐ γὰρ ἤθελεν ἐν τῇ Ἰουδαίᾳ περιπατεῖν, ὅτι
lee, [4]not [1]for [2]he [3]did desire in Judæa to walk, because
ἐζήτουν αὐτὸν οἱ Ἰουδαῖοι ἀποκτεῖναι. 2 Ἦν.δὲ ἐγγὺς ἡ
[3]were [4]seeking [5]him [1]the [2]Jews to kill. Now was near the
ἑορτὴ τῶν Ἰουδαίων ἡ σκηνοπηγία. 3 εἶπον οὖν πρὸς αὐτὸν
feast of the Jews, the tabernacles. [3]Said [4]therefore [5]to [6]him
οἱ.ἀδελφοὶ.αὐτοῦ, Μετάβηθι ἐντεῦθεν, καὶ ὕπαγε εἰς τὴν Ἰου-
[1]his [2]brethren, Remove hence, and go into Ju-
δαίαν, ἵνα καὶ οἱ.μαθηταί.σου [o]θεωρήσωσιν‖ [p]τὰ.ἔργα.σου‖ ἃ
dæa, that also thy disciples may see thy works which
ποιεῖς· 4 οὐδεὶς.γὰρ [q]ἐν κρυπτῷ τι‖ ποιεῖ, καὶ ζητεῖ
thou doest; for no one in secret anything does, and seeks
[r]αὐτὸς‖ ἐν παῤῥησίᾳ εἶναι. εἰ ταῦτα ποιεῖς, φανέρωσον
himself [3]in [4]public [1]to [2]be. If these things thou doest, manifest

[x] λελάληκα have spoken LTTrAW. [y] ἀλλὰ TrW. [z] ἐμὲ T. [a] — μου (*read* the Father) LTTrA. [b] + οὖν therefore T. [c] + ἐκ [L]Tr[A]. [d] τῶν μαθητῶν αὐτοῦ ἀπῆλθον LTTrA. [e] — οὖν GLTTrA. [f] ὁ ἅγιος the holy [one] GLTTrA. [g] — τοῦ ζῶντος GLTTrA. [h] Ἰσκαριώτου (*read* son of Simon Iscariote) LTTrA. [i] ἔμελλεν LTTrA. [k] παραδιδόναι αὐτόν LTrA. [l] — ὢν LTrA. [m] — καὶ T. [n] μετὰ ταῦτα περιεπάτει ὁ ([ὁ] Tr) Ἰησοῦς LTTrAW. [o] θεωρήσουσιν shall see TTrA. [p] σου τὰ ἔργα L. [q] τι ἐν κρυπτῷ LTTrA. [r] αὐτὸ it L.

σεαυτὸν τῷ κόσμῳ. 5 Οὐδὲ.γὰρ οἱ.ἀδελφοὶ.αὐτοῦ ἐπίστευον
thyself to the world. For neither [2]his [3]brethren [1]believed
εἰς αὐτόν. 6 Λέγει [a]οὖν‖ αὐτοῖς ὁ Ἰησοῦς, Ὁ.καιρὸς ὁ.ἐμὸς
on him. [3]Says [2]therefore [4]to [5]them [1]Jesus, [7]Time [6]my
οὔπω πάρεστιν· ὁ.δὲ.καιρὸς ὁ ὑμέτερος πάντοτέ ἐστιν ἕτοιμος.
not yet is come, but [2]time [1]your always is ready.
7 οὐ.δύναται ὁ κόσμος μισεῖν ὑμᾶς· ἐμὲ.δὲ μισεῖ, ὅτι ἐγὼ
[3]Is [4]unable [1]the [2]world to hate you, but me it hates, because I
μαρτυρῶ περὶ αὐτοῦ, ὅτι τὰ ἔργα αὐτοῦ πονηρά ἐστιν.
bear witness concerning it, that the works of it evil are.
8 ὑμεῖς ἀνάβητε εἰς τὴν.ἑορτὴν.[t]ταύτην‖ ἐγὼ [v]οὔπω‖ ἀνα-
Ye, go ye up to this feast. I not yet am
βαίνω εἰς τὴν.ἑορτὴν.ταύτην, ὅτι ὁ [w]καιρὸς ὁ ἐμὸς‖ οὔπω
going up to this feast, for [2]time [1]my not yet
πεπλήρωται. 9 Ταῦτα.[x]δὲ‖ εἰπὼν [y]αὐτοῖς‖ ἔμεινεν ἐν τῇ
has been fulfilled. And these things having said to them he abode in
Γαλιλαίᾳ. 10 Ὡς.δὲ ἀνέβησαν οἱ.ἀδελφοὶ.αὐτοῦ [z]τότε καὶ
Galilee. But when were gone up his brethren then also
αὐτὸς ἀνέβη εἰς τὴν ἑορτήν,‖ οὐ φανερῶς, [a]ἀλλ'‖ [b]ὡς‖ ἐν
he went up to the feast, not openly, but as in
κρυπτῷ. 11 Οἱ οὖν Ἰουδαῖοι ἐζήτουν αὐτὸν ἐν τῇ ἑορτῇ,
secret. The [2]therefore [1]Jews were seeking him at the feast,
καὶ ἔλεγον, Ποῦ ἐστιν ἐκεῖνος; 12 Καὶ γογγυσμὸς [c]πολὺς
and said, Where is he? And [2]murmuring [1]much
περὶ αὐτοῦ ἦν‖ ἐν [d]τοῖς ὄχλοις‖ οἱ.μὲν ἔλεγον,
concerning him there was among the crowds. Some said,
Ὅτι ἀγαθός ἐστιν· ἄλλοι.[e]δὲ‖ ἔλεγον, Οὔ· ἀλλὰ πλανᾷ τὸν
[3]Good [1]he [2]is; but others said, No; but he deceives the
ὄχλον. 13 Οὐδεὶς μέντοι παῤῥησίᾳ ἐλάλει περὶ αὐτοῦ,
crowd. No one however publicly spoke concerning him,
διὰ τὸν φόβον τῶν Ἰουδαίων.
because of the fear of the Jews.

14 Ἤδη.δὲ τῆς ἑορτῆς μεσούσης ἀνέβη [f]ὁ‖ Ἰησοῦς
But now [5]of [6]the [7]feast [[1]it] [2]being [3]the [4]middle went up Jesus
εἰς τὸ ἱερόν, καὶ ἐδίδασκεν. 15 [g]καὶ ἐθαύμαζον‖ οἱ Ἰουδαῖοι
into the temple, and was teaching: and [3]were [4]wondering [1]the [2]Jews
λέγοντες, Πῶς οὗτος γράμματα οἶδεν, μὴ μεμαθηκώς;
saying, How [2]this [3]one [4]letters [1]knows, not having learned?
16 Ἀπεκρίθη [h]αὐτοῖς [i]ὁ‖ Ἰησοῦς καὶ εἶπεν, Ἡ.ἐμὴ.διδαχὴ οὐκ
[2]Answered [3]them [1]Jesus and said, My teaching [2]not
ἔστιν ἐμή, ἀλλὰ τοῦ πέμψαντός με· 17 ἐάν τις θέλῃ τὸ
[1]is mine, but his who sent me. If anyone desire
θέλημα.αὐτοῦ ποιεῖν, γνώσεται περὶ τῆς διδαχῆς πότερον
his will to practise, he shall know concerning the teaching whether
ἐκ [k]τοῦ‖ θεοῦ ἐστιν, ἢ ἐγὼ ἀπ' ἐμαυτοῦ λαλῶ. 18 ὁ ἀφ'
from God it is, or I from myself speak. He that from
ἑαυτοῦ λαλῶν, τὴν.δόξαν.τὴν.ἰδίαν ζητεῖ· ὁ.δὲ ζητῶν τὴν
himself speaks, his own glory seeks; but he that seeks the
δόξαν τοῦ πέμψαντος αὐτόν, οὗτος ἀληθής ἐστιν, καὶ
glory of him that sent him, he true is, and
ἀδικία ἐν αὐτῷ οὐκ.ἔστιν. 19 οὐ [l]Μωσῆς‖ [m]δέδωκεν‖
unrighteousness in him is not. [2]Not [3]Moses [1]has given

self to the world.
5 For neither did his brethren believe in him.
6 Then Jesus said unto them, My time is not yet come: but your time is alway ready.
7 The world cannot hate you; but me it hateth, because I testify of it, that the works thereof are evil.
8 Go ye up unto this feast: I go not up yet unto this feast; for my time is not yet full come.
9 When he had said these words unto them he abode *still* in Galilee.
10 But when his brethren were gone up, then went he also up unto the feast, not openly, but as it were in secret.
11 Then the Jews sought him at the feast, and said, Where is he?
12 And there was much murmuring among the people concerning him: for some said, He is a good man: others said, Nay; but he deceiveth the people.
13 Howbeit no man spake openly of him for fear of the Jews.

14 Now about the midst of the feast Jesus went up into the temple, and taught.
15 And the Jews marvelled, saying, How knoweth this man letters, having never learned?
16 Jesus answered them, and said, My doctrine is not mine, but his that sent me.
17 If any man will do his will, he shall know of the doctrine, whether it be of God, or *whether* I speak of myself.
18 He that speaketh of himself seeketh his own glory: but he that seeketh his glory that sent him, the same is true, and no unrighteousness is in him.
19 Did not Moses give you the

[s] — οὖν T. [t] — ταύτην (*read* the feast) LTTrAW. [v] οὐκ not GTTrA. [w] ἐμὸς καιρὸς LTTrA. [x] — δὲ and GTTr. [y] αὐτὸς he (abode) T. [z] εἰς τὴν ἑορτήν, τότε καὶ αὐτὸς ἀνέβη LTTrA. [a] ἀλλὰ LTrA. [b] — ὡς T. [c] περὶ αὐτοῦ ἦν πολὺς LTrA; ἦν περὶ αὐτοῦ πολὺς T. [d] τῷ ὄχλῳ the crowd T. [e] — δὲ and GTW. [f] — ὁ LTTrA. [g] ἐθαύμαζον οὖν were wondering therefore LTTrAW. [h] + οὖν therefore LTTrAW. [i] — ὁ TTr. [k] — τοῦ T. [l] Μωϋσῆς LTTrAW. [m] ἔδωκεν gave LTrA.

law, and *yet* none of
you keepeth the law?
Why go ye about to
kill me? 20 The peo-
ple answered and said,
Thou hast a devil:
who goeth about to kill
thee? 21 Jesus an-
swered and said unto
them, I have done one
work, and ye all mar-
vel. 22 Moses there-
fore gave unto you
circumcision; (not be-
cause it is of Moses,
but of the fathers;)
and ye on the sabbath
day circumcise a man.
23 If a man on the
sabbath day receive
circumcision, that the
law of Moses should
not be broken; are ye
angry at me, because I
have made a man every
whit whole on the
sabbath day? 24 Judge
not according to the
appearance, but judge
righteous judgment.
25 Then said some of
them of Jerusalem, Is
not this he, whom they
seek to kill? 26 But,
lo, he speaketh boldly,
and they say nothing
unto him. Do the
rulers know indeed
that this is the very
Christ? 27 Howbeit
we know this man
whence he is: but when
Christ cometh, no man
knoweth whence he is.
28 Then cried Jesus in
the temple as he
taught, saying, Ye
both know me, and ye
know whence I am:
and I am not come of
myself, but he that
sent me is true, whom
ye know not. 29 But
I know him: for I am
from him, and he hath
sent me. 30 Then they
sought to take him:
but no man laid hands
on him, because his
hour was not yet come.
31 And many of the
people believed on him,
and said, When Christ
cometh, will he do
more miracles than
these which this *man*

ὑμῖν τὸν νόμον, καὶ οὐδεὶς ἐξ ὑμῶν ποιεῖ τὸν νόμον; τί
you the law, and no one of you practises the law? Why
με ζητεῖτε ἀποκτεῖναι; 20 Ἀπεκρίθη ὁ ὄχλος [n]καὶ εἶπεν,‖
me do ye seek to kill? [3]Answered [1]the [2]crowd and said,
Δαιμόνιον ἔχεις· τίς σε ζητεῖ ἀποκτεῖναι; 21 Ἀπεκρίθη
A demon thou hast; who thee seeks to kill? [2]Answered
[o]ὁ‖ Ἰησοῦς καὶ εἶπεν αὐτοῖς, Ἓν ἔργον ἐποίησα, καὶ πάντες
[1]Jesus and said to them, One work I did, and [2]all
[p]θαυμάζετε. 22 διὰ.τοῦτο‖ [q]Μωσῆς‖ δέδωκεν ὑμῖν τὴν περι-
[1]ye wonder. Therefore Moses has given you circum-
τομήν, οὐχ ὅτι ἐκ τοῦ [r]Μωσέως‖ ἐστίν, ἀλλ᾽ ἐκ τῶν πατέρων·
cision, not that of Moses it is, but of the fathers,
καὶ [s]ἐν‖ σαββάτῳ περιτέμνετε ἄνθρωπον. 23 εἰ περιτομὴν
and on sabbath ye circumcise a man. If [4]circumcision
λαμβάνει ἄνθρωπος ἐν σαββάτῳ ἵνα μὴ.λυθῇ ὁ νόμος [t]
[3]receives [1]a [2]man on sabbath, that may not be broken the law
[r]Μωσέως,‖ ἐμοὶ χολᾶτε ὅτι ὅλον ἄνθρωπον ὑγιῆ ἐποίησα
of Moses, with me are ye angry because entirely [2]a [3]man [1]sound I made
ἐν σαββάτῳ; 24 μὴ.κρίνετε κατ᾽ ὄψιν, ἀλλὰ τὴν δικαίαν
on sabbath? Judge not according to sight, but righteous
κρίσιν [v]κρίνατε.‖ 25 Ἔλεγον οὖν τινες ἐκ τῶν [w]Ἱεροσο-
judgment judge. [7]Said [6]therefore [1]some [2]of [3]those [4]of [5]Jeru-
λυμιτῶν,‖ Οὐχ.οὗτός.ἐστιν ὃν ζητοῦσιν ἀποκτεῖναι; 26 καὶ
salem, Is not this he whom they seek to kill? and
ἴδε, παῤῥησίᾳ λαλεῖ, καὶ οὐδὲν αὐτῷ λέγουσιν. μήποτε
lo, publicly he speaks, and nothing to him they say.
ἀληθῶς ἔγνωσαν οἱ ἄρχοντες, ὅτι οὗτός ἐστιν
[5]Truly [1]have [6]recognized [2]those [3]who [4]rule, that this is
[x]ἀληθῶς‖ ὁ χριστός; 27 ἀλλὰ τοῦτον οἴδαμεν πόθεν ἐστίν·
truly the Christ? But this one we know whence he is.
ὁ.δὲ.χριστὸς ὅταν [y]ἔρχηται,‖ οὐδεὶς γινώσκει πόθεν ἐστίν.
But the Christ, whenever he may come, no one knows whence he is.
28 Ἔκραξεν οὖν ἐν τῷ ἱερῷ διδάσκων ὁ Ἰησοῦς καὶ λέγων,
[3]Cried [2]therefore [4]in [5]the [6]temple [7]teaching [1]Jesus and saying,
Κἀμὲ οἴδατε, καὶ οἴδατε πόθεν εἰμί· καὶ ἀπ᾽ ἐμαυτοῦ οὐκ
Both me ye know, and ye know whence I am; and of myself [3]not
ἐλήλυθα, ἀλλ᾽ ἔστιν ἀληθινὸς ὁ πέμψας με, ὃν ὑμεῖς
[1]I [2]have come, but [5]is [6]true [1]he [2]who [3]sent [4]me, whom ye
οὐκ.οἴδατε· 29 ἐγὼ.[z]δὲ‖ οἶδα αὐτόν, ὅτι παρ᾽ αὐτοῦ εἰμι,
know not. But I know him, because from him I am,
κἀκεῖνός με [a]ἀπέστειλεν.‖ 30 Ἐζήτουν οὖν αὐτὸν πιά-
and he me sent. They were seeking therefore him to
σαι· καὶ οὐδεὶς ἐπέβαλεν ἐπ᾽ αὐτὸν τὴν χεῖρα, ὅτι οὔπω
take, but no one laid upon him [his] hand, because not yet
ἐληλύθει ἡ.ὥρα.αὐτοῦ. 31 [b]Πολλοὶ.δὲ ἐκ τοῦ ὄχλου ἐπίστευ-
had come his hour. But many of the crowd believed
σαν‖ εἰς αὐτόν, καὶ ἔλεγον, [c]Ὅτι‖ ὁ χριστὸς ὅταν ἔλθῃ
on him, and said, The Christ, when he comes,
[d]μήτι‖ πλείονα σημεῖα [e]τούτων‖ ποιήσει ὧν οὗτος
[4]more [5]signs [6]than [7]these [1]will [2]he [3]do which this [man]

---

[n] — καὶ εἶπεν LTTrA. [o] — ὁ TTrA. [p] θαυμάζετε διὰ τοῦτο. (*read* ye wonder therefore.) GLTrW; — διὰ τοῦτο, + ὁ T. [q] Μωϋσῆς LTTrAW. [r] Μωϋσέως LTTrAW. [s] [ἐν] L. [t] + ὁ T. [v] κρίνετε LTrA. [w] Ἱεροσολυμειτῶν T. [x] — ἀληθῶς GLTTrAW. [y] ἔρχεται he comes E. [z] — δὲ but GLTTrAW. [a] ἀπέσταλκεν has sent T. [b] Ἐκ τοῦ ὄχλου δὲ πολλοὶ ἐπίστευσαν LTrA; πολλοὶ δὲ ἐπίστευσαν ἐκ τοῦ ὄχλου T. [c] — Ὅτι LTTrA. [d] μὴ LTTrA. [e] — τούτων (*read* ὧν than [these] which) LTTrAW.

[f]ἐποίησεν‖; 32 Ἤκουσαν οἱ Φαρισαῖοι τοῦ ὄχλου γογγύζοντος
did? 3Heard 1the 2Pharisees of the crowd murmuring
περὶ αὐτοῦ ταῦτα· καὶ ἀπέστειλαν [g]οἱ Φαρισαῖοι καὶ
5concerning 6him 1these 2things, and 7sent 1the 2Pharisees 3and
οἱ ἀρχιερεῖς ὑπηρέτας,‖ ἵνα πιάσωσιν αὐτόν. 33 εἶπεν
4the 5chief 6priests officers, that they might take him. 2Said
οὖν [h]αὐτοῖς‖ ὁ Ἰησοῦς, Ἔτι [i]μικρὸν χρόνον‖ μεθ' ὑμῶν
3therefore 4to 5them 1Jesus, Yet a little time with you
εἰμι, καὶ ὑπάγω πρὸς τὸν πέμψαντά με. 34 ζητήσετέ με καὶ
I am, and I go to him who sent me. Ye will seek me and
οὐχ.εὑρήσετε[k]· καὶ ὅπου εἰμὶ ἐγὼ ὑμεῖς οὐ.δύνασθε ἐλθεῖν.
shall not find [me], and where 2am 1I ye are unable to come.
35 Εἶπον οὖν οἱ Ἰουδαῖοι πρὸς ἑαυτούς, Ποῦ [l]οὗτος
4Said 3therefore 1the 2Jews among themselves, Where 2he
μέλλει‖ πορεύεσθαι ὅτι [m]ἡμεῖς‖ οὐχ.εὑρήσομεν αὐτόν; μὴ εἰς
1is about to go that we shall not find him? to
τὴν διασπορὰν τῶν Ἑλλήνων μέλλει πορεύεσθαι, καὶ
the dispersion among the Greeks is he about to go, and
διδάσκειν τοὺς Ἕλληνας; 36 τίς ἐστιν [n]οὗτος ὁ λόγος‖ ὃν
teach the Greeks? What is this word which
εἶπεν, Ζητήσετέ με, καὶ οὐχ.εὑρήσετε[k]· καὶ Ὅπου εἰμὶ ἐγὼ
he said, Ye will seek me, and shall not find [me]; and Where 2am 1I
ὑμεῖς οὐ.δύνασθε ἐλθεῖν;
ye are unable to come?

37 Ἐν.δὲ τῇ ἐσχάτῃ ἡμέρᾳ τῇ μεγάλῃ τῆς ἑορτῆς εἱστήκει
And in the last 3day 1the 2great of the feast stood
ὁ Ἰησοῦς, καὶ [o]ἔκραξεν‖ λέγων, Ἐάν τις διψᾷ, ἐρχέσθω
Jesus, and cried, saying, If anyone thirst, let him come
[p]πρός με‖ καὶ πινέτω· 38 ὁ πιστεύων εἰς ἐμέ, καθὼς εἶπεν
to me and drink. He that believes on me, as said
ἡ γραφή, ποταμοὶ ἐκ τῆς.κοιλίας.αὐτοῦ ῥεύσουσιν ὕδατος
the scripture, rivers out of his belly shall flow of 2water
ζῶντος. 39 Τοῦτο.δὲ εἶπεν περὶ τοῦ πνεύματος οὗ [q]ἔμελ-
1living. But this he said concerning the Spirit which 5were
λον‖ λαμβάνειν οἱ [r]πιστεύοντες‖ εἰς αὐτόν· οὔπω.γὰρ ἦν
6about 7to 8receive 1those 2believing 3on 4him; for not yet was
πνεῦμα [s]ἅγιον‖[t]; ὅτι [v]ὁ‖ Ἰησοῦς [w]οὐδέπω‖ ἐδοξάσθη.
[the] 2Spirit 1Holy, because Jesus not yet was glorified.
40 [x]πολλοὶ οὖν ἐκ τοῦ ὄχλου‖ ἀκούσαντες [y]τὸν λόγον‖
Many therefore out of the crowd having heard the word
ἔλεγον, [z] Οὗτός ἐστιν ἀληθῶς ὁ προφήτης. 41 Ἄλλοι[a] ἔλεγον,
said, This is truly the prophet. Others said,
Οὗτός ἐστιν ὁ χριστός. [b]Ἄλλοι‖ [c]δὲ‖ ἔλεγον, Μὴ γὰρ ἐκ
This is the Christ. 2Others 1and said, 4Then 5out 6of
τῆς Γαλιλαίας ὁ χριστὸς ἔρχεται; 42 [d]οὐχὶ‖ ἡ γραφὴ εἶπεν,
7Galilee 2the 3Christ 1comes? 9Not 10the 11scripture 8said,
ὅτι ἐκ τοῦ σπέρματος [e]Δαβίδ,‖ καὶ ἀπὸ Βηθλεὲμ τῆς κώμης
that out of the seed of David, and from Bethlehem the village
ὅπου ἦν [e]Δαβίδ,‖ [fa]ὁ χριστὸς ἔρχεται;‖ 43 Σχίσμα οὖν [ga]ἐν
where 2was 1David, the Christ comes? A division therefore in

hath done? 32 The Pharisees heard that the people murmured such things concerning him; and the Pharisees and the chief priests sent officers to take him. 33 Then said Jesus unto them, Yet a little while am I with you, and *then* I go unto him that sent me. 34 Ye shall seek me, and shall not find *me*: and where I am, *thither* ye cannot come. 35 Then said the Jews among themselves, Whither will he go, that we shall not find him? will he go unto the dispersed among the Gentiles, and teach the Gentiles? 36 What *manner of* saying is this that he said, Ye shall seek me, and shall not find *me*: and where I am, *thither* ye cannot come?

37 In the last day, that great *day* of the feast, Jesus stood and cried, saying, If any man thirst, let him come unto me, and drink. 38 He that believeth on me, as the scripture hath said, out of his belly shall flow rivers of living water. 39 (But this spake he of the Spirit, which they that believe on him should receive: for the Holy Ghost was not yet *given*; because that Jesus was not yet glorified.) 40 Many of the people therefore, when they heard this saying, said, Of a truth this is the prophet. 41 Others said, This is the Christ. But some said, Shall Christ come out of Galilee? 42 Hath not the scripture said, That Christ cometh of the seed of David, and out of the town of Bethlehem, where David was? 43 So there was a division among

[f] ποιεῖ does T. [g] οἱ ἀρχιερεῖς καὶ οἱ Φαρισαῖοι ὑπηρέτας LTrAW; ὑπηρέτας οἱ ἀρχιερεῖς καὶ οἱ Φαρισαῖοι T. [h] — αὐτοῖς GLTTrAW. [i] χρόνον μικρὸν LTTrA. [k] + με me LA. [l] μέλλει οὗτος T. [m] — ἡμεῖς (*read* εὑρή. we shall find) T. [n] ὁ λόγος οὗτος LTTrA. [o] ἔκραζεν T. [p] — πρός με T. [q] ἤμελλον T. [r] πιστεύσαντες having believed LTrA. [s] — ἅγιον LT[TrA]. [t] + δεδομένον given L. [v] — ὁ LTTrAW. [w] οὔπω LTrA. [x] ἐκ τοῦ ὄχλου οὖν [some] out of the crowd therefore LTTrA. [y] τῶν λόγων τούτων these words (— τούτων W) LTTrAW. [z] + [ὅτι] A. [a] + [δὲ] and L. [b] οἱ they LTrA. [c] — δὲ T. [d] οὐχ LTrA. [e] Δαυῒδ GW; Δαυεὶδ LTTrA. [fa] ἔρχεται ὁ χριστός LTrA. [ga] ἐγένετο ἐν τῷ ὄχλῳ LTTrA.

the people because of him. 44 And some of them would have taken him; but no man laid hands on him. 45 Then came the officers to the chief priests and Pharisees; and they said unto them, Why have ye not brought him? 46 The officers answered, Never man spake like this man. 47 Then answered them the Pharisees, Are ye also deceived? 48 Have any of the rulers or of the Pharisees believed on him? 49 But this people who knoweth not the law are cursed. 50 Nicodemus saith unto them, (he that came to Jesus by night, being one of them,) 51 Doth our law judge *any* man, before it hear him, and know what he doeth? 52 They answered and said unto him, Art thou also of Galilee? Search, and look: for out of Galilee ariseth no prophet. 53 And every man went unto his own house.

τῷ ὄχλῳ ἐγένετο‖ δι' αὐτόν. 44 τινὲς.δὲ ἤθελον ἐξ αὐτῶν
the crowd occurred because of him. But some [3]desired [1]of [2]them
πιάσαι αὐτόν, ἀλλ' οὐδεὶς [h]ἐπέβαλεν‖ ἐπ' αὐτὸν τὰς χεῖρας.
to take him, but no one laid [2]on [3]him [1]hands.
45 ἦλθον οὖν οἱ ὑπηρέται πρὸς τοὺς ἀρχιερεῖς καὶ Φαρι-
Came therefore the officers to the chief priests and Phari-
σαίους· καὶ εἶπον αὐτοῖς ἐκεῖνοι, [i]Διατί‖ οὐκ.ἠγάγετε αὐτόν;
sees, and [2]said [3]to [4]them [1]they, Why did ye not bring him?
46 Ἀπεκρίθησαν οἱ ὑπηρέται, Οὐδέποτε [k]οὕτως ἐλάλησεν‖
[3]Answered [1]the [2]officers, Never thus spoke
ἄνθρωπος [l]ὡς οὗτος [m]ὁ ἄνθρωπος.‖ 47 Ἀπεκρίθησαν [n]οὖν‖
man as this man. [4]Answered [3]therefore
[o]αὐτοῖς‖ οἱ Φαρισαῖοι, Μὴ καὶ ὑμεῖς πεπλάνησθε; 48 μή
[5]them [1]the [2]Pharisees, [8]also [7]ye [6]have been deceived?
τις ἐκ τῶν ἀρχόντων ἐπίστευσεν εἰς αὐτόν, ἢ ἐκ τῶν
[2]Any [3]one [4]of [5]the [6]rulers [1]has believed on him, or of the
Φαρισαίων; 49 [p]ἀλλ'‖ ὁ.ὄχλος.οὗτος ὁ μὴ.γινώσκων τὸν
Pharisees? But this crowd, which knows not the
νόμον [q]ἐπικατάρατοί‖ εἰσιν. 50 Λέγει Νικόδημος πρὸς αὐτούς,
law, accursed are. [2]Says [1]Nicodemus to them,
[r]ὁ ἐλθὼν [s]νυκτὸς‖ πρὸς αὐτόν,‖ [t]εἷς ὢν ἐξ αὐτῶν, 51 Μὴ
(he who came by night to him, [2]one [1]being of themselves,)
ὁ.νόμος.ἡμῶν κρίνει τὸν ἄνθρωπον, ἐὰν.μὴ ἀκούσῃ [v]παρ'
[2]Our [3]law [1]does judge the man, unless it have heard from
αὐτοῦ πρότερον,‖ καὶ γνῷ τί ποιεῖ; 52 Ἀπεκρίθησαν καὶ
himself first, and known what he does? They answered and
[w]εἶπον‖ αὐτῷ, Μὴ καὶ σὺ ἐκ τῆς Γαλιλαίας εἶ; [x]ἐρεύνησον‖
said to him, [3]Also [2]thou [4]of [5]Galilee [1]art? Search
καὶ ἴδε, ὅτι [y]προφήτης ἐκ τῆς Γαλιλαίας‖ [z]οὐκ.ἐγήγερται.‖
and look, that a prophet out of Galilee has not arisen.
53 [a]Καὶ ἐπορεύθη ἕκαστος εἰς τὸν.οἶκον.αὐτοῦ.
And [2]went [1]each to his house.

VIII. Jesus went unto the mount of Olives. 2 And early in the morning he came again into the temple, and all the people came unto him; and he sat down, and taught them. 3 And the scribes and Pharisees brought unto him a woman taken in adultery; and when they had set her in the midst, 4 they say unto him, Master, this woman was taken in adultery, in the very act. 5 Now Moses in the law commanded us, that such should be stoned: but what sayest thou? 6 This they said, tempting him, that they might have to accuse him.

8 Ἰησοῦς.δὲ ἐπορεύθη εἰς τὸ ὄρος τῶν ἐλαιῶν· 2 ὄρθρου.δὲ
But Jesus went to the mount of Olives. And at dawn
πάλιν παρεγένετο εἰς τὸ ἱερόν, καὶ πᾶς ὁ λαὸς ἤρχετο πρὸς
again he came into the temple, and all the people came to
αὐτόν· καὶ καθίσας ἐδίδασκεν αὐτούς. 3 ἄγουσιν δὲ οἱ
him; and having sat down he was teaching them. [7]Bring [1]and [2]the
γραμματεῖς καὶ οἱ Φαρισαῖοι πρὸς αὐτὸν γυναῖκα ἐν μοιχείᾳ
[3]scribes [4]and [5]the [6]Pharisees to him a woman in adultery
κατειλημμένην, καὶ στήσαντες αὐτὴν ἐν μέσῳ, 4 λέγουσιν
having been taken, and having set her in [the] midst, they say
αὐτῷ, Διδάσκαλε, αὕτη ἡ γυνὴ κατειλήφθη [b]ἐπαυτοφώρῳ‖
to him, Teacher, this woman was taken in the very act
μοιχευομένη. 5 ἐν.δὲ τῷ νόμῳ [c]Μωσῆς‖ ἡμῖν ἐνετείλατο
committing adultery. Now in the law Moses us commanded
τὰς τοιαύτας [d]λιθοβολεῖσθαι·‖ σὺ οὖν τί λέγεις[e];
such to be stoned: thou therefore what sayest thou?
6 Τοῦτο.δὲ ἔλεγον πειράζοντες αὐτὸν ἵνα ἔχωσιν κατη-
But this they said tempting him that they might have to ac-

---

[h] ἔβαλεν LTTrA. [i] Διὰ τί LTrAW. [k] ἐλάλησεν οὕτως LTTrA. [l] — ὡς οὗτος ὁ ἄνθρωπος L[TrA]. [m] + λαλεῖ speaks T. [n] — οὖν TA. [o] [αὐτοῖς] Tr. [p] ἀλλὰ LTTrAW. [q] ἐπάρατοί LTTrA. [r] — ὁ ἐλθὼν νυκτὸς πρὸς αὐτόν T. [s] ← νυκτὸς LTrA. [t] + πρότερον formerly LTrA. [v] πρῶτον παρ' αὐτοῦ LTTrA. [w] εἶπαν LTTrA. [x] ἐραύνησον TTrA. [y] ἐκ τῆς Γαλιλαίας προφήτης LTrA. [z] οὐκ ἐγείρεται does not arise LTTrA. [a] — καὶ ἐπορεύθη .... ἁμάρτανε (viii. 11) [G]LTTrA. [b] ἐπ' αὐτοφώρῳ W. [c] Μωϋσῆς W. [d] λιθάζειν to stone W. [e] + περὶ αὐτῆς concerning her W.

γορεῖν αὐτοῦ. ὁ δὲ.Ἰησοῦς κάτω.κύψας, τῷ δακτύλῳ
cuse him. But Jesus having stooped down, with [his] finger
ἔγραφεν εἰς τὴν γῆν. 7 ὡς.δὲ ἐπέμενον ἐρωτῶντες αὐτόν,
wrote on the ground. But as they continued asking him,
ἀνακύψας εἶπεν πρὸς αὐτούς, Ὁ ἀναμάρτητος ὑ-
having lifted up himself he said to them, The sinless one among
μῶν πρῶτος τὸν λίθον ἐπ' αὐτῇ βαλέτω. 8 καὶ πάλιν
you [5]first [4]the [6]stone [7]at [8]her [1]let [2]him [3]cast. And again
κάτω.κύψας ἔγραφεν εἰς τὴν γῆν. 9 οἱ.δὲ ἀκούσαντες,
having stooped down he wrote on the ground. But they having heard,
καὶ ὑπὸ τῆς συνειδήσεως ἐλεγχόμενοι, ἐξήρχοντο εἷς καθ' εἷς,
and by the conscience being convicted, went out one by one,
ἀρξάμενοι ἀπὸ τῶν πρεσβυτέρων ἕως τῶν ἐσχάτων· καὶ
beginning from the elder ones until the last; and
κατελείφθη μόνος ὁ Ἰησοῦς, καὶ ἡ γυνὴ ἐν μέσῳ [f]ἑστῶσα.‖
was left alone Jesus, and the woman in [the] midst standing.
10 ἀνακύψας.δὲ ὁ Ἰησοῦς, καὶ μηδένα θεασάμενος
And [2]having [3]lifted [4]up [5]himself [1]Jesus, and [2]no [3]one [1]seeing
πλὴν τῆς γυναικός, εἶπεν αὐτῇ, [g]Ἡ γυνή,‖ ποῦ εἰσιν ἐκεῖνοι
but the woman, said to her, Woman, where are those
οἱ.κατήγοροί.σου, οὐδείς σε κατέκρινεν; 11 Ἡ.δὲ εἶπεν,
thine accusers, [2]no [3]one [5]thee [1]did [4]condemn? And she said,
Οὐδείς, κύριε. Εἶπεν.δὲ αὐτῇ ὁ Ἰησοῦς, Οὐδὲ ἐγώ σε κατα-
No one, Sir. And [2]said [3]to [4]her [1]Jesus, Neither [2]I [4]thee [1]do
κρίνω· πορεύου καὶ μηκέτι ἁμάρτανε.‖
[3]condemn: go, and no more sin.

12 Πάλιν οὖν [h]ὁ Ἰησοῦς αὐτοῖς ἐλάλησεν,‖ λέγων, Ἐγώ
Again therefore Jesus to them spoke, saying, I
εἰμι τὸ φῶς τοῦ κόσμου· ὁ ἀκολουθῶν [i]ἐμοὶ‖ οὐ.μὴ
am the light of the world; he that follows me in no wise
[k]περιπατήσει‖ ἐν τῇ σκοτίᾳ, ἀλλ' ἕξει τὸ φῶς τῆς ζωῆς.
shall walk in the darkness, but shall have the light of the life.
13 Εἶπον οὖν αὐτῷ οἱ Φαρισαῖοι, Σὺ περὶ σεαυτοῦ
[3]Said [4]therefore [5]to [6]him [1]the [2]Pharisees, Thou concerning thyself
μαρτυρεῖς· ἡ.μαρτυρία.σου οὐκ.ἔστιν ἀληθής. 14 Ἀπεκρίθη
bearest witness; thy witness is not true. [2]Answered
Ἰησοῦς καὶ εἶπεν αὐτοῖς, Κἂν ἐγὼ μαρτυρῶ περὶ ἐμαυτοῦ,
[1]Jesus and said to them, Even if I bear witness concerning myself,
ἀληθής ἐστιν ἡ.μαρτυρία.μου, ὅτι οἶδα πόθεν ἦλθον καὶ
true is my witness, because I know whence I came and
ποῦ ὑπάγω· ὑμεῖς.[l]δὲ‖ οὐκ.οἴδατε πόθεν ἔρχομαι [m]καὶ‖ ποῦ
whither I go: but ye know not whence I come and whither
ὑπάγω. 15 ὑμεῖς κατὰ τὴν σάρκα κρίνετε· ἐγὼ οὐ κρίνω
I go. Ye according to the flesh judge, I judge
οὐδένα. 16 καὶ ἐὰν κρίνω δὲ ἐγώ, ἡ κρίσις ἡ ἐμὴ [n]ἀληθής‖
no one. And if [3]judge [2]also [1]I, [5]judgment [4]my true
ἐστιν· ὅτι μόνος οὐκ.εἰμί, ἀλλ' ἐγὼ καὶ ὁ πέμψας με [o]πα-
is, because alone I am not, but I and the [2]who [3]sent [4]me [1]Fa-
τήρ.‖ 17 καὶ ἐν τῷ νόμῳ δὲ τῷ ὑμετέρῳ [p]γέγραπται,‖ ὅτι
ther. And in [2]law [3]also [1]your it has been written, that
δύο ἀνθρώπων ἡ μαρτυρία ἀληθής ἐστιν. 18 ἐγώ εἰμι ὁ
of two men the witness true is. I am [one] who

But Jesus stooped
down, and with his
finger wrote on the
ground, *as though he
heard them not.* 7 So
when they continued
asking him, he lifted
up himself, and said
unto them, He that is
without sin among
you, let him first cast
a stone at her. 8 And
again he stooped down,
and wrote on the
ground. 9 And they
which heard *it,* being
convicted by *their own*
conscience, went out
one by one, beginning
at the eldest, *even* unto
the last: and Jesus
was left alone, and the
woman standing in the
midst. 10 When Jesus
had lifted up himself,
and saw none but the
woman, he said unto
her, Woman, where are
those thine accusers?
hath no man condemned
thee? 11 She said,
No man, Lord. And
Jesus said unto her,
Neither do I condemn
thee: go, and sin no
more.

12 Then spake Jesus
again unto them, saying,
I am the light of
the world: he that followeth
me shall not
walk in darkness, but
shall have the light of
life. 13 The Pharisees
therefore said unto
him, Thou bearest record
of thyself; thy
record is not true.
14 Jesus answered and
said unto them,
Though I bear record
of myself, *yet* my record
is true: for I
know whence I came,
and whither I go; but
ye cannot tell whence
I come, and whither I
go. 15 Ye judge after
the flesh; I judge no
man. 16 And yet if I
judge, my judgment
is true: for I am not
alone, but I and the
Father that sent me.
17 It is also written in
your law, that the
testimony of two men
is true. 18 I am one
that bear witness of

---

f οὖσα being W. g — Ἡ γυνή W. h αὐτοῖς ἐλάλησεν ὁ ([ὁ] Tr) Ἰησοῦς LTTrA.
i μοι LTr. k περιπατήσῃ should walk LTTrAW. l — δὲ but T. m ἢ or GTTrAW.
n ἀληθινή LTTrA. o — πατήρ (read he who sent me) T. p γεγραμμένον ἐστὶν it is
written T.

μαρτυρῶν περὶ ἐμαυτοῦ, καὶ μαρτυρεῖ περὶ ἐμοῦ ὁ
bears witness concerning myself, and [6]bears [7]witness [8]concerning [9]me [1]the
πέμψας με πατήρ. 19 Ἔλεγον οὖν αὐτῷ, Ποῦ ἐστιν ὁ
[3]who [4]sent [5]me [2]Father. They said therefore to him, Where is
πατήρ.σου; Ἀπεκρίθη [q]ὁ‖ Ἰησοῦς, Οὔτε ἐμὲ οἴδατε οὔτε τὸν
thy Father? [2]Answered [1]Jesus, Neither me ye know nor
πατέρα.μου· εἰ ἐμὲ ᾔδειτε, καὶ τὸν.πατέρα.μου [r]ᾔδειτε.ἄν.‖
my Father. If me ye had known, also my Father ye would have known.
20 Ταῦτα τὰ ῥήματα ἐλάλησεν [s]ὁ Ἰησοῦς‖ ἐν τῷ γαζοφυλακίῳ,
These words spoke Jesus in the treasury,
διδάσκων ἐν τῷ ἱερῷ· καὶ οὐδεὶς ἐπίασεν αὐτόν, ὅτι οὔπω
teaching in the temple; and no one took him, for not yet
ἐληλύθει ἡ.ὥρα.αὐτοῦ.
had come his hour.

21 Εἶπεν οὖν πάλιν αὐτοῖς [t]ὁ Ἰησοῦς,‖ Ἐγω ὑπάγω,
[2]Said [3]therefore [4]again [5]to [6]them [1]Jesus, I go away,
καὶ ζητήσετέ με, καὶ ἐν τῇ.ἁμαρτίᾳ.ὑμῶν ἀποθανεῖσθε· ὅπου
and ye will seek me, and in your sin ye will die; where
ἐγὼ ὑπάγω ὑμεῖς οὐ.δύνασθε ἐλθεῖν. 22 Ἔλεγον οὖν οἱ
I go ye are unable to come. [4]Said [3]therefore [1]the
Ἰουδαῖοι, Μήτι ἀποκτενεῖ ἑαυτόν, ὅτι λέγει, Ὅπου.ἐγὼ ὑπάγω
[2]Jews, Will he kill himself, that he says, Where I go
ὑμεῖς οὐ.δύνασθε ἐλθεῖν; 23 Καὶ [v]εἶπεν‖ αὐτοῖς, Ὑμεῖς ἐκ
ye are unable to come? And he said to them, Ye from
τῶν.κάτω ἐστέ, ἐγὼ ἐκ τῶν.ἄνω εἰμί· ὑμεῖς ἐκ [w]τοῦ κόσμου
beneath are, I from above am; Ye of [2]world
τούτου‖ ἐστέ, ἐγὼ οὐκ.εἰμὶ ἐκ τοῦ.κόσμου.τούτου. 24 εἶπον
[1]this are, I am not of this world. I said
οὖν ὑμῖν ὅτι ἀποθανεῖσθε ἐν ταῖς.ἁμαρτίαις.ὑμῶν· ἐὰν.γὰρ
therefore to you that ye will die in your sins; for if
μὴ.πιστεύσητε ὅτι ἐγώ εἰμι, ἀποθανεῖσθε ἐν ταῖς ἁμαρτίαις
ye believe not that I am [he], ye will die in [2]sins
ὑμῶν. 25 Ἔλεγον οὖν αὐτῷ, Σὺ τίς εἶ; [x]Καὶ‖ εἶπεν
[1]your. They said therefore to him, [3]Thou [1]who [2]art? And [2]said
αὐτοῖς [y]ὁ‖ Ἰησοῦς, Τὴν.ἀρχὴν ὅ.τι καὶ λαλῶ ὑμῖν.
[3]to [4]them [1]Jesus, Altogether that which also I say to you.
26 πολλὰ ἔχω περὶ ὑμῶν λαλεῖν καὶ κρίνειν· ἀλλ' ὁ
Many things I have concerning you to say and to judge; but he who
πέμψας με ἀληθής ἐστιν, κἀγὼ ἃ ἤκουσα παρ' αὐτοῦ, ταῦτα
sent me true is, and I what I heard from him, these things
[z]λέγω‖ εἰς τὸν κόσμον. 27 Οὐκ.ἔγνωσαν ὅτι τὸν πατέρα αὐτοῖς
I say to the world. They knew not that the Father to them
ἔλεγεν. 28 Εἶπεν οὖν [a]αὐτοῖς‖ ὁ Ἰησοῦς, Ὅταν ὑψώ-
he spoke of. [2]Said [3]therefore [4]to [5]them [1]Jesus, When ye shall have
σητε τὸν υἱὸν τοῦ ἀνθρώπου, τότε γνώσεσθε ὅτι ἐγώ εἰμι·
lifted up the Son of man, then ye shall know that I am [he],
καὶ ἀπ' ἐμαυτοῦ ποιῶ οὐδέν, ἀλλὰ καθὼς ἐδίδαξέν με ὁ
and from myself I do nothing, but as [3]taught [4]me
πατήρ.[b]μου,‖ ταῦτα λαλῶ. 29 καὶ ὁ πέμψας με, μετ'
[1]my [2]Father, these things I speak. And he who sent me, with
ἐμοῦ ἐστιν· οὐκ.ἀφῆκέν με μόνον [c]ὁ πατήρ,‖ ὅτι ἐγὼ τὰ
me is; [3]left [5]not [4]me [6]alone [1]the [2]Father, because I the things

myself, and the Father
that sent me beareth
witness of me. 19 Then
said they unto him,
Where is thy Father?
Jesus answered, Ye
neither know me, nor
my Father: if ye had
known me, ye should
have known my Father also. 20 These
words spake Jesus in
the treasury, as he
taught in the temple:
and no man laid hands
on him; for his hour
was not yet come.

21 Then said Jesus
again unto them, I go
my way, and ye shall
seek me, and shall die
in your sins: whither
I go, ye cannot come.
22 Then said the Jews,
Will he kill himself?
because he saith, Whither I go, ye cannot
come. 23 And he said
unto them, Ye are from
beneath; I am from
above: ye are of this
world; I am not of this
world. 24 I said therefore unto you, that ye
shall die in your sins:
for if ye believe not
that I am *he*, ye shall
die in your sins.
25 Then said they unto
him, Who art thou?
And Jesus saith unto
them, Even *the same*
that I said unto you
from the beginning.
26 I have many things
to say and to judge of
you: but he that sent
me is true; and I speak
to the world those
things which I have
heard of him. 27 They
understood not that he
spake to them of the
Father. 28 Then said
Jesus unto them, When
ye have lifted up the
Son of man, then shall
ye know that I am *he*,
and *that* I do nothing
of myself; but as my
Father hath taught
me, I speak these
things. 29 And he that
sent me is with me:
the Father hath not
left me alone; for I do

---

[q] — ὁ GLTTrAW. [r] ἂν ᾔδειτε LTTrA. [s] — ὁ Ἰησοῦς (*read* he spoke) GLTTrAW. [t] — ὁ Ἰησοῦς (*read* he said) LTTrAW. [v] ἔλεγεν LTTrA. [w] τούτου τοῦ κόσμου LTrA. [x] — καὶ LTTrAW. [y] [ὁ] Tr. [z] λαλῶ LTTrA. [a] — αὐτοῖς LTTrA. [b] — μου (*read* the Father) LTTrA. [c] — ὁ πατήρ (*read* he left not) LTTrA.

ἀρεστὰ αὐτῷ ποιῶ πάντοτε. 30 Ταῦτα αὐτοῦ.λαλοῦντος
pleasing to him do always. [4]These [5]things [1]as [2]he [3]spoke
πολλοὶ ἐπίστευσαν εἰς αὐτόν.
many believed on him.
31 Ἔλεγεν οὖν ὁ Ἰησοῦς πρὸς τοὺς πεπιστευκότας αὐτῷ
[3]Said [2]therefore [1]Jesus to the [2]who [3]had [4]believed [5]on [6]him
Ἰουδαίους, Ἐὰν ὑμεῖς μείνητε ἐν τῷ λόγῳ τῷ ἐμῷ, ἀληθῶς
[1]Jews, If ye abide in [2]word [1]my, truly
μαθηταί μου ἐστέ· 32 καὶ γνώσεσθε τὴν ἀλήθειαν, καὶ ἡ
[2]disciples [1]my ye are. And ye shall know the truth, and the
ἀλήθεια ἐλευθερώσει ὑμᾶς. 33 Ἀπεκρίθησαν [d]αὐτῷ,[‖] Σπέρμα
truth shall set free you. They answered him, [2]Seed
Ἀβραάμ ἐσμεν, καὶ οὐδενὶ δεδουλεύκαμεν πώποτε· πῶς
[1]Abraham's we are, and to anyone have been under bondage never; how
(*lit.* to no one)
σὺ λέγεις, Ὅτι ἐλεύθεροι γενήσεσθε; 34 Ἀπεκρίθη αὐτοῖς
[2]thou [1]sayest, Free ye shall become? [2]Answered [3]them
[e]ὁ[‖] Ἰησοῦς, Ἀμὴν ἀμὴν λέγω ὑμῖν, ὅτι πᾶς ὁ ποιῶν
[1]Jesus, Verily verily I say to you, that everyone that practises
τὴν ἁμαρτίαν δοῦλός ἐστιν τῆς ἁμαρτίας. 35 ὁ.δὲ δοῦλος
sin a bondman is of sin. Now the bondman
οὐ.μένει ἐν τῇ οἰκίᾳ εἰς.τὸν.αἰῶνα· ὁ υἱὸς μένει εἰς.τὸν.αἰῶνα.
abides not in the house for ever; the Son abides for ever.
36 ἐὰν οὖν ὁ υἱὸς ὑμᾶς ἐλευθερώσῃ, ὄντως ἐλεύθεροι ἔσ-
If therefore the Son [3]you [1]shall [2]set free, really free ye
εσθε. 37 οἶδα ὅτι σπέρμα Ἀβραάμ ἐστε· ἀλλὰ ζητεῖτέ με
shall be. I know that [2]seed [1]Abraham's ye are; but ye seek me
ἀποκτεῖναι, ὅτι ὁ λόγος ὁ ἐμὸς οὐ.χωρεῖ ἐν ὑμῖν. 38 [f]ἐγὼ
to kill, because [2]word [1]my has no entrance in you. I
ὃ[‖] ἑώρακα παρὰ τῷ.πατρί.[g]μου[‖] λαλῶ· καὶ ὑμεῖς οὖν [h]ὃ
what I have seen with my Father speak; and ye therefore what
ἑωράκατε[‖] παρὰ [i]τῷ.πατρὶ.ὑμῶν[‖] ποιεῖτε. 39 Ἀπεκρίθησαν
ye have seen with your father do. They answered
καὶ [k]εἶπον[‖] αὐτῷ, Ὁ.πατὴρ.ἡμῶν Ἀβραάμ ἐστιν. Λέγει αὐτοῖς
and said to him, [3]Our [4]Father [1]Abraham [2]is. [6]Says [7]to [8]them
[l]ὁ[‖] Ἰησοῦς, Εἰ τέκνα τοῦ Ἀβραὰμ [m]ἦτε,[‖] τὰ ἔργα τοῦ.Ἀβραὰμ
[5]Jesus, If children of Abraham ye were, the works of Abraham
ἐποιεῖτε.[n]ἄν·[‖] 40 νῦν.δὲ ζητεῖτέ με ἀποκτεῖναι, ἄνθρωπον ὃς
ye would do; but now ye seek me to kill, a man who
τὴν ἀλήθειαν ὑμῖν λελάληκα, ἣν ἤκουσα παρὰ τοῦ θεοῦ·
the truth to you has spoken, which I heard from God:
τοῦτο Ἀβραὰμ οὐκ.ἐποίησεν. 41 ὑμεῖς ποιεῖτε τὰ ἔργα τοῦ
this Abraham did not. Ye do the works
πατρὸς.ὑμῶν. [o]Εἶπον[‖] [p]οὖν[‖] αὐτῷ, Ἡμεῖς ἐκ πορνείας [q]οὐ
of your father. They said therefore to him, We of fornication [2]not
γεγεννήμεθα.[‖] ἕνα πατέρα ἔχομεν, τὸν θεόν. 42 Εἶπεν [r]οὖν[‖]
[1]have been born; one Father we have, God. [3]Said [2]therefore
αὐτοῖς [s]ὁ[‖] Ἰησοῦς, Εἰ ὁ θεὸς [t] πατὴρ ὑμῶν ἦν, ἠγαπᾶτε.ἂν
[4]to [5]them [1]Jesus, If God Father of you were, ye would have loved
ἐμέ· ἐγὼ.γὰρ ἐκ τοῦ θεοῦ ἐξῆλθον καὶ ἥκω· οὐδὲ.γὰρ ἀπ'
me, for I from God came forth and am come; for neither of
ἐμαυτοῦ ἐλήλυθα, ἀλλ' ἐκεῖνός με ἀπέστειλεν. 43 [v]διατί[‖] τὴν
myself have I come, but he [2]me [1]sent. Why

always those things that please him. 30 As he spake these words, many believed on him.

31 Then said Jesus to those Jews which believed on him, If ye continue in my word, *then* are ye my disciples indeed; 32 and ye shall know the truth, and the truth shall make you free. 33 They answered him, We be Abraham's seed, and were never in bondage to any man: how sayest thou, Ye shall be made free? 34 Jesus answered them, Verily, verily, I say unto you, Whosoever committeth sin is the servant of sin. 35 And the servant abideth not in the house for ever: *but* the Son abideth ever. 36 If the Son therefore shall make you free, ye shall be free indeed. 37 I know that ye are Abraham's seed; but ye seek to kill me, because my word hath no place in you. 38 I speak that which I have seen with my Father: and ye do that which ye have seen with your father. 39 They answered and said unto him, Abraham is our father. Jesus saith unto them, If ye were Abraham's children, ye would do the works of Abraham. 40 But now ye seek to kill me, a man that hath told you the truth, which I have heard of God: this did not Abraham. 41 Ye do the deeds of your father. Then said they to him, We be not born of fornication; we have one Father, *even* God. 42 Jesus said unto them, If God were your Father, ye would love me: for I proceeded forth and came from God; neither came I of myself, but he sent me. 43 Why

---

[d] πρὸς αὐτόν to him LTTrA. [e] — ὁ L[Tr]. [f] ἃ ἐγὼ LTTr; ἐγὼ ἃ A. [g] — μου (*read* the Father) LTTrA. [h] ἃ ἠκούσατε what ye have heard LTTrA. [i] τοῦ πατρὸς the father LTTrA. [k] εἴπαν LTTrA. [l] [ὁ] Tr. [m] ἐστε ye are GLTTrA. [n] — ἄν GTTrA. [o] εἶπαν T. [p] — οὖν LTTrA. [q] οὐκ ἐγεννήθημεν were not born LTrA. [r] — οὖν GLTTrA. [s] — ὁ L[Tr] [t] + ὁ the L. [v] διὰ τί LTrA.

do ye not understand
my speech? *even* be-
cause ye cannot hear
my word. 44 Ye are of
your father the devil,
and the lusts of your
father ye will do. He
was a murderer from
the beginning, and a-
bode not in the truth,
because there is no
truth in him. When
he speaketh a lie, he
speaketh of his own:
for he is a liar, and the
father of it. 45 And
because I tell *you* the
truth, ye believe me
not. 46 Which of you
convinceth me of sin?
And if I say the truth,
why do ye not believe
me? 47 He that is of
God heareth God's
words: ye therefore
hear *them* not, because
ye are not of God.
48 Then answered the
Jews, and said unto
him, Say we not well
that thou art a Sama-
ritan, and hast a devil?
49 Jesus answered, I
have not a devil; but
I honour my Father,
and ye do dishonour
me. 50 And I seek not
mine own glory: there
is one that seeketh and
judgeth. 51 Verily,
verily, I say unto you,
If a man keep my say-
ing, he shall never see
death. 52 Then said
the Jews unto him,
Now we know that
thou hast a devil. A-
braham is dead, and
the prophets; and thou
sayest, If a man keep
my saying, he shall
never taste of death.
53 Art thou greater
than our father Abra-
ham, which is dead?
and the prophets are
dead: whom makest
thou thyself? 54 Jesus
answered, If I honour
myself, my honour is
nothing: it is my Fa-
ther that honoureth
me; of whom ye say,
that he is your God:
55 yet ye have not
known him; but I
know him: and if I

λαλιὰν τὴν ἐμὴν οὐ.γινώσκετε; ὅτι οὐ.δύνασθε ἀκούειν τὸν
[2]speech [1]my do ye not know? Because ye are unable to hear

λόγον τὸν ἐμόν. 44 ὑμεῖς ἐκ [w] πατρὸς τοῦ διαβόλου ἐστέ,
[2]word [1]my. Ye of [the] father the devil are,

καὶ τὰς ἐπιθυμίας τοῦ.πατρὸς.ὑμῶν θέλετε ποιεῖν. ἐκεῖνος
and the lusts of your father ye desire to do. He

ἀνθρωποκτόνος ἦν ἀπ' ἀρχῆς, καὶ ἐν τῇ ἀληθείᾳ [x]οὐχ"
a murderer was from [the] beginning, and in the truth [2]not

ἕστηκεν· ὅτι οὐκ.ἔστιν ἀλήθεια ἐν αὐτῷ. ὅταν λαλῇ
[1]has stood, because there is not truth in him. Whenever he may speak

τὸ ψεῦδος, ἐκ τῶν.ἰδίων λαλεῖ· ὅτι ψεύστης ἐστὶν καὶ ὁ
falsehood, from his own he speaks; for a liar he is and the

πατὴρ αὐτοῦ. 45 ἐγὼ δὲ ὅτι τὴν ἀλήθειαν λέγω[y], οὐ
father of it. [3]I [1]and [2]because the truth speak, [3]not

πιστεύετέ μοι. 46 τίς ἐξ ὑμῶν ἐλέγχει με περὶ ἁμαρτίας;
[1]ye [2]do believe me. Which of you convinces me concerning sin?

εἰ.[z]δὲ" ἀλήθειαν λέγω, [a]διατί" ὑμεῖς οὐ.πιστεύετέ μοι; 47 ὁ
But if truth I speak, why [2]ye [1]do [3]not believe me? He that

ὢν ἐκ τοῦ θεοῦ τὰ ῥήματα τοῦ θεοῦ ἀκούει· διὰ.τοῦτο ὑμεῖς
is of God the words of God hears: therefore ye

οὐκ.ἀκούετε, ὅτι ἐκ τοῦ θεοῦ οὐκ.ἐστέ. 48 Ἀπεκρίθησαν
hear not, because of God ye are not. Answered

[b]οὖν" οἱ Ἰουδαῖοι καὶ [c]εἶπον" αὐτῷ, Οὐ καλῶς λέγομεν ἡμεῖς
therefore the Jews and said to him, [3]Not [4]well [1]say [2]we

ὅτι [d]Σαμαρείτης" εἶ σύ, καὶ δαιμόνιον ἔχεις; 49 Ἀπεκρίθη
that a Samaritan [2]art [1]thou, and a demon hast? [2]Answered

Ἰησοῦς, Ἐγὼ δαιμόνιον οὐκ.ἔχω, ἀλλὰ τιμῶ τὸν.πατέρα.μου,
[1]Jesus, I a demon have not; but I honour my Father,

καὶ ὑμεῖς ἀτιμάζετέ με. 50 ἐγὼ.δὲ οὐ.ζητῶ τὴν.δόξαν.μου·
and ye dishonour me. But I seek not my glory:

ἔστιν ὁ ζητῶν καὶ κρίνων. 51 ἀμὴν ἀμὴν λέγω ὑμῖν, ἐάν
there is he who seeks and judges. Verily verily I say to you, If

τις τὸν [e]λόγον τὸν ἐμὸν" τηρήσῃ, θάνατον οὐ.μὴ θεωρήσῃ
anyone [3]word [2]my [1]keep, death in no wise shall he see

εἰς.τὸν.αἰῶνα. 52 [f]Εἶπον" [g]οὖν" αὐτῷ οἱ Ἰουδαῖοι, Νῦν
for ever. [4]Said [3]therefore [5]to [6]him [1]the [2]Jews, Now

ἐγνώκαμεν ὅτι δαιμόνιον ἔχεις. Ἀβραὰμ ἀπέθανεν καὶ οἱ
we know that a demon thou hast. Abraham died and the

προφῆται, καὶ σὺ λέγεις, Ἐάν τις τὸν.λόγον.μου τηρήσῃ,
prophets, and thou sayest, If anyone [2]my [3]word [1]keep,

οὐ.μὴ [h]γεύσεται" θανάτου εἰς.τὸν.αἰῶνα. 53 μὴ σὺ μείζων
in no wise shall he taste of death for ever. [2]Thou [3]greater

εἶ τοῦ.πατρὸς.ἡμῶν Ἀβραάμ, ὅστις ἀπέθανεν; καὶ οἱ προ-
[1]art than our father Abraham, who died? and the pro-

φῆται ἀπέθανον· τίνα σεαυτὸν [i]σὺ" ποιεῖς; 54 Ἀπεκρίθη
phets died! whom [3]thyself [2]thou [1]makest? [5]Answered

Ἰησοῦς, Ἐὰν ἐγὼ [k]δοξάζω" ἐμαυτόν, ἡ.δόξα.μου οὐδέν ἐστιν·
[4]Jesus, If I glorify myself, my glory nothing is;

ἔστιν ὁ.πατήρ.μου ὁ δοξάζων με, ὃν ὑμεῖς λέγετε, ὅτι
it is my Father who glorifies me, [of] whom ye say, that

θεὸς [l]ὑμῶν" ἐστιν, 55 καὶ οὐκ.ἐγνώκατε αὐτόν, ἐγὼ.δὲ οἶδα
[2]God [1]your he is. And ye have not known him, but I know

---

[w] + τοῦ the GLTTrA. [x] οὐκ T. [y] + [ὑμῖν] to thee L. [z] — δὲ but GLTTrA. [a] διὰ τί LTrA. [b] — οὖν GLTTrA. [c] εἶπαν LTTrA. [d] Σαμαρίτης T. [e] ἐμὸν λόγον LTTrA. [f] εἶπαν T. [g] — οὖν LTTrA. [h] γεύσηται should he taste GLTTrAW. [i] — σὺ (*read* ποιεῖς makest thou) GLTTrA. [k] δοξάσω shall glorify LTTrA. [l] ἡμῶν our TTrAW.

αὐτόν· [m]καὶ ἐὰν|| εἴπω ὅτι οὐκ.οἶδα αὐτόν, ἔσομαι ὅμοιος
him; and if I say that I know not him, I shall be like
[n]ὑμῶν,|| ψεύστης· [o]ἀλλ'|| οἶδα αὐτόν, καὶ τὸν.λόγον.αὐτοῦ
you, a liar. But I know him, and his word
τηρῶ. 56 Ἀβραὰμ ὁ.πατὴρ.ὑμῶν ἠγαλλιάσατο ἵνα [p]ἴδῃ||
I keep. Abraham your Father exulted in that he should see
τὴν ἡμέραν τὴν ἐμήν· καὶ εἶδεν καὶ ἐχάρη. 57 [q]Εἶπον|| οὖν
[2]day [1]my, and he saw and rejoiced. Said therefore
οἱ Ἰουδαῖοι πρὸς αὐτόν, Πεντήκοντα ἔτη οὔπω ἔχεις,
the Jews to him, Fifty years [old] not yet art thou,
καὶ Ἀβραὰμ ἑώρακας; 58 Εἶπεν αὐτοῖς [r]ὁ|| Ἰησοῦς, Ἀμὴν
and Abraham hast thou seen? [2]Said [3]to [4]them [1]Jesus, Verily
ἀμὴν λέγω ὑμῖν, πρὶν Ἀβραὰμ γενέσθαι ἐγώ εἰμι. 59 Ἦραν
verily I say to you, Before Abraham was I am. They took up
οὖν λίθους ἵνα βάλωσιν ἐπ' αὐτόν· Ἰησοῦς.δὲ ἐκρύβη,
therefore stones that they might cast at him; but Jesus hid himself,
καὶ ἐξῆλθεν ἐκ τοῦ ἱεροῦ, [s]διελθὼν διὰ μέσου αὐτῶν·
and went forth out of the temple, going through the midst of them,
καὶ παρῆγεν οὕτως.||
and [2]passed [3]on [1]thus.

9 Καὶ παράγων εἶδεν ἄνθρωπον τυφλὸν ἐκ γενετῆς. 2 καὶ
And passing on he saw a man blind from birth. And
ἠρώτησαν αὐτὸν οἱ.μαθηταὶ.αὐτοῦ λέγοντες, [t]Ῥαββί,|| τίς
[3]asked [4]him [1]his [2]disciples saying, Rabbi, who
ἥμαρτεν, οὗτος ἢ οἱ.γονεῖς.αὐτοῦ, ἵνα τυφλὸς γεννηθῇ;
sinned, this [man] or his parents, that blind he should be born?
3 Ἀπεκρίθη [u]ὁ|| Ἰησοῦς, Οὔτε οὗτος ἥμαρτεν οὔτε οἱ.γονεῖς
[2]Answered [1]Jesus, Neither this [man] sinned nor [2]parents
αὐτοῦ ἀλλ' ἵνα φανερωθῇ τὰ ἔργα τοῦ θεοῦ ἐν αὐτῷ.
[1]his; but that should be manifested the works of God in him.
4 [v]ἐμὲ|| δεῖ ἐργάζεσθαι τὰ ἔργα τοῦ πέμψαντός [w]με||
[3]Me [1]it [2]behoves to work the works of him who sent me
ἕως ἡμέρα ἐστίν· ἔρχεται νύξ, ὅτε οὐδεὶς δύναται ἐργάζεσθαι.
while day it is; [2]comes [1]night, when no one is able to work.
5 ὅταν ἐν τῷ κόσμῳ ὦ, φῶς εἰμι τοῦ κόσμου. 6 Ταῦ-
While in the world I may be, [the] light I am of the world. These
τα εἰπών, ἔπτυσεν χαμαί, καὶ ἐποίησεν πηλὸν ἐκ
things having said, he spat on [the] ground, and made clay of
τοῦ πτύσματος, καὶ ἐπέχρισεν [x] τὸν πηλὸν ἐπὶ τοὺς ὀφθαλμοὺς
the spittle, and applied the clay to the eyes
[y]τοῦ τυφλοῦ·|| 7 καὶ εἶπεν αὐτῷ, Ὕπαγε, [z]νίψαι|| εἰς τὴν
of the blind [man]. And he said to him, Go, wash in the
κολυμβήθραν τοῦ Σιλωάμ, ὃ ἑρμηνεύεται, ἀπεσταλμένος.
pool of Siloam, which is interpreted, Sent.
ἀπῆλθεν οὖν καὶ ἐνίψατο, καὶ ἦλθεν βλέπων. 8 Οἱ οὖν
He went therefore and washed, and came seeing. The [2]therefore
γείτονες καὶ οἱ θεωροῦντες αὐτὸν τὸ πρότερον ὅτι [a]τυφλὸς||
[1]neighbours and those who saw him before that blind
ἦν, ἔλεγον, Οὐχ οὗτός ἐστιν ὁ καθήμενος καὶ προσαιτῶν;
he was, said, [2]Not [3]this [1]is he who was sitting and begging?
9 Ἄλλοι ἔλεγον, Ὅτι οὗτός ἐστιν· ἄλλοι.[b]δέ,|| [c]Ὅτι|| ὅμοιος
Some said, [3]He [1]it [2]is, but others, [3]Like

should say, I know
him not, I shall be a
liar like unto you: but
I know him, and keep
his saying. 56 Your
father Abraham re-
joiced to see my day:
and he saw *it*, and was
glad. 57 Then said the
Jews unto him, Thou
art not yet fifty years
old, and hast thou seen
Abraham? 58 Jesus
said unto them, Verily,
verily, I say unto you,
Before Abraham was,
I am. 59 Then took
they up stones to cast
at him: but Jesus hid
himself, and went out
of the temple, going
through the midst of
them, and so passed
by.

IX. And as *Jesus*
passed by, he saw a
man which was blind
from *his* birth. 2 And
his disciples asked
him, saying, Master,
who did sin, this man,
or his parents, that he
was born blind? 3 Je-
sus answered, Neither
hath this man sinned,
nor his parents: but
that the works of God
should be made mani-
fest in him. 4 I must
work the works of
him that sent me,
while it is day: the
night cometh, when no
man can work. 5 As
long as I am in the
world, I am the light
of the world. 6 When
he had thus spoken, he
spat on the ground,
and made clay of the
spittle, and he anoint-
ed the eyes of the blind
man with the clay,
7 and said unto him,
Go, wash in the pool
of Siloam, (which is by
interpretation, Sent.)
He went his way there-
fore, and washed, and
came seeing. 8 The
neighbours therefore,
and they which before
had seen him that he
was blind, said, Is not
this he that sat and
begged? 9 Some said,
This is he: others *said*,
He is like him: *but* he

---

[m] κἂν LTTr. [n] ὑμῖν LTr. [o] ἀλλὰ LTTrAW. [p] εἴδῃ T. [q] Εἶπαν T. [r] — ὁ TTr. [s] — διελθὼν .... οὕτως GLTTrA. [t] Ῥαββεί T. [u] — ὁ GLTTrAW. [v] ἡμᾶς us TTr. [w] ἡμᾶς us T. [x] + αὐτοῦ on him LTTrA. [y] — τοῦ τυφλοῦ [L]TTrA. [z] [νίψαι] L. [a] προσαίτης a beggar GLTTrAW. [b] — δέ but [L]TTrA. [c] ἔλεγον, Οὐχί, ἀλλ' (ἀλλὰ T) said, No, but TTrA; ἔλεγον [Οὐχί, ἀλλ'] L.

said, I am *he*. 10 Therefore said they unto
him, How were thine
eyes opened? 11 He
answered and said, A
man that is called Je-
sus made clay, and an-
ointed mine eyes, and
said unto me, Go to
the pool of Siloam,
and wash: and I went
and washed, and I re-
ceived sight. 12 Then
said they unto him,
Where is he? He said,
I know not.

13 They brought to
the Pharisees him that
aforetime was blind.
14 And it was the
sabbath day when
Jesus made the clay,
and opened his eyes.
15 Then again the Pha-
risees also asked him
how he had received
his sight. He said un-
to them, He put clay
upon mine eyes, and I
washed, and do see.
16 Therefore said some
of the Pharisees, This
man is not of God, be-
cause he keepeth not
the sabbath day.
Others said, How can
a man that is a sinner
do such miracles? And
there was a division
among them. 17 They
say unto the blind man
again, What sayest
thou of him, that he
hath opened thine
eyes? He said, He is
a prophet. 18 But the
Jews did not believe
concerning him, that
he had been blind, and
received his sight, un-
til they called the pa-
rents of him that had
received his sight.
19 And they asked
them, saying, Is this
your son, who ye say
was born blind? how
then doth he now see?
20 His parents answer-
ed them and said, We
know that this is our
son, and that he was
born blind: 21 but by
what means he now

αὐτῷ ἐστιν. Ἐκεῖνος[d] ἔλεγεν, ″Οτι ἐγώ εἰμι. 10 ″Ἔλεγον
[4]him [1]he [2]is. He said, I am [he]. They said
οὖν αὐτῷ, Πῶς[e] [f]ἀνεῴχθησάν‖ [g]σου‖ οἱ ὀφθαλμοί; 11 Ἀπ-
therefore to him, How were opened thine eyes? [2]An-
εκρίθη ἐκεῖνος [h]καὶ εἶπεν,‖ [i] ″Ἄνθρωπος [i] λεγόμενος Ἰησοῦς
swered [1]he and said, A man called Jesus
πηλὸν ἐποίησεν καὶ ἐπέχρισέν μου τοὺς ὀφθαλμούς, καὶ εἶπέν
clay made and applied to mine eyes, and said
μοι,[k] ″Ὕπαγε εἰς [l]τὴν κολυμβήθραν τοῦ‖ Σιλωὰμ καὶ νίψαι.
to me, Go to the pool of Siloam and wash:
ἀπελθὼν [m]δὲ‖ καὶ νιψάμενος ἀνέβλεψα. 12 [n] [o]Εἶπον‖ [p]οὖν‖
[2]having [3]gone [1]and and washed I received sight. They said therefore
αὐτῷ, Ποῦ ἐστιν ἐκεῖνος; Λέγει, Οὐκ.οἶδα.
to him, Where is he? He says, I know not.

13 ″Ἄγουσιν αὐτὸν πρὸς τοὺς Φαρισαίους, τόν ποτε
They bring [4]him [1]to [2]the [3]Pharisees, who once [was]
τυφλόν. 14 ἦν.δὲ σάββατον [q]ὅτε‖ τὸν πηλὸν ἐποίησεν ὁ
blind. Now it was sabbath when [3]the [4]clay [2]made
Ἰησοῦς καὶ ἀνέῳξεν αὐτοῦ τοὺς ὀφθαλμούς. 15 πάλιν οὖν
[1]Jesus and opened his eyes. Again therefore
ἠρώτων αὐτὸν καὶ οἱ Φαρισαῖοι πῶς ἀνέβλεψεν. ὁ.δὲ εἶπεν
asked him also the Pharisees how he received sight. And he said
αὐτοῖς, Πηλὸν ἐπέθηκεν [r]ἐπὶ τοὺς.ὀφθαλμούς.μου,‖ καὶ ἐνι-
to them, Clay he put on mine eyes, and I
ψάμην, καὶ βλέπω. 16 ″Ἔλεγον οὖν ἐκ τῶν Φαρισαίων τινές,
washed, and I see. Said therefore [2]of [3]the [4]Pharisees [1]some,
[s]Οὗτος ὁ ἄνθρωπος οὐκ.ἔστιν παρὰ τοῦ θεοῦ,‖ ὅτι τὸ σάββατον
This man is not from God, for the sabbath
οὐ.τηρεῖ. ″Ἄλλοι ἔλεγον, Πῶς δύναται ἄνθρωπος ἁμαρτωλὸς
he does not keep. Others said, How can a man a sinner
τοιαῦτα σημεῖα ποιεῖν; Καὶ σχίσμα ἦν ἐν αὐτοῖς. 17 Λέ-
such signs do? And a division was among them. They
γουσιν[t] τῷ τυφλῷ πάλιν, [v]Σὺ τί‖ λέγεις περὶ αὐτοῦ,
say to the blind [man] again, [3]Thou [1]what [2]sayest concerning him,
ὅτι [w]ἤνοιξέν‖ σου τοὺς ὀφθαλμούς; Ὁ.δὲ εἶπεν, ″Οτι προ-
for he opened thine eyes? And he said, A pro-
φήτης ἐστίν. 18 Οὐκ.ἐπίστευσαν οὖν οἱ Ἰουδαῖοι περὶ
phet he is. [4]Did [5]not [6]believe [3]therefore [1]the [2]Jews concerning
αὐτοῦ, ὅτι [x]τυφλὸς ἦν‖ καὶ ἀνέβλεψεν, ἕως.ὅτου ἐφώνησαν
him, that [3]blind [1]he [2]was and received sight, until they called
τοὺς γονεῖς αὐτοῦ τοῦ ἀναβλέψαντος· 19 καὶ ἠρώτησαν
the parents of him who had received sight. And they asked
αὐτοὺς λέγοντες, Οὗτός ἐστιν ὁ.υἱὸς.ὑμῶν ὃν ὑμεῖς λέγετε
them saying, [2]This [1]is your son, of whom ye say
ὅτι τυφλὸς ἐγεννήθη; πῶς οὖν [y]ἄρτι βλέπει‖; 20 Ἀπεκρίθη-
that blind he was born? how then now does he see? [3]Answered
σαν[z] [a]αὐτοῖς‖ οἱ.γονεῖς.αὐτοῦ καὶ [b]εἶπον,‖ Οἴδαμεν ὅτι οὗτός
[4]them [1]his [2]parents and said, We know that this
ἐστιν ὁ.υἱὸς.ἡμῶν, καὶ ὅτι τυφλὸς ἐγεννήθη· 21 πῶς.δὲ νῦν
is our son, and that blind he was born; but how now

---

[d] + δὲ however L. [e] + οὖν then [L]T[A]. [f] ἠνεῴχθησάν LTTrA. [g] σοι E. [h] — καὶ εἶπεν [L]TTrA. [i] + ὁ (*read* the man that is called) TTr[A]. [k] + ὅτι TTr. [l] τὸν (*read* Go to Siloam) GLTTrA. [m] οὖν therefore LTTrA. [n] + [καὶ] and Tr. [o] εἶπαν LTTrA. [p] — οὖν LTTrA. [q] ἐν ᾗ ἡμέρᾳ in which day LTTrA. [r] μου ἐπὶ τοὺς ὀφθαλμούς GLTTrAW [s] Οὐκ ἔστιν οὗτος παρὰ θεοῦ ὁ ἄνθρωπος LTTrA. [t] + οὖν therefore LTTrAW. [v] Τί σὺ TrA. [w] ἠνέῳξέν TrA. [x] ἦν τυφλὸς TTrA. [y] βλέπει ἄρτι LTTrA. [z] + οὖν therefore LT. [a] — αὐτοῖς [L]TTrA. [b] εἶπαν TTrA.

βλέπει οὐκ.οἴδαμεν, ἢ τίς ἤνοιξεν αὐτοῦ τοὺς ὀφθαλμοὺς
he sees we know not, or who opened his eyes
ἡμεῖς οὐκ.οἴδαμεν· [d]αὐτὸς ἡλικίαν.ἔχει, αὐτὸν ἐρωτήσατε,‖
we know not; he is of age, [2]him [1]ask,
αὐτὸς περὶ [e]αὐτοῦ‖ λαλήσει. 22 Ταῦτα εἶπον οἱ γονεῖς
he concerning himself shall speak. These things said [2]parents
αὐτοῦ, ὅτι ἐφοβοῦντο τοὺς Ἰουδαίους· ἤδη.γὰρ συνε-
[1]his, because they feared the Jews; for already had agreed
τέθειντο οἱ Ἰουδαῖοι, ἵνα ἐάν τις αὐτὸν ὁμολογήσῃ
together the Jews, that if anyone him should confess [to be the]
χριστόν, ἀποσυνάγωγος γένηται. 23 διὰ τοῦτο οἱ γονεῖς
Christ, put out of the synagogue he should be. Because of this [2]parents
αὐτοῦ [f]εἶπον,‖ Ὅτι ἡλικίαν.ἔχει, αὐτὸν [g]ἐρωτήσατε.‖ 24 Ἐφώ-
[1]his said, He is of age, [2]him [1]ask. They
νησαν οὖν [h]ἐκ.δευτέρου τὸν ἄνθρωπον‖ ὃς ἦν τυφλός, καὶ
called therefore a second time the man who was blind, and
[f]εἶπον‖ αὐτῷ, Δὸς δόξαν τῷ θεῷ· ἡμεῖς οἴδαμεν ὅτι [i]ὁ ἄνθρω-
said to him, Give glory to God; we know that [2]man
πος οὗτος‖ ἁμαρτωλός ἐστιν. 25 Ἀπεκρίθη οὖν ἐκεῖνος
[1]this a sinner is. [3]Answered [2]therefore [1]he
[k]καὶ εἶπεν,‖ Εἰ ἁμαρτωλός ἐστιν οὐκ.οἶδα· ἓν οἶδα, ὅτι
and said, If a sinner he is I know not. One [thing] I know, that
τυφλὸς ὢν ἄρτι βλέπω. 26 Εἶπον.[l]δὲ‖ αὐτῷ [m]πάλιν,‖ Τί
[2]blind [1]being now I see. And they said to him again, What
ἐποίησέν σοι; πῶς ἤνοιξέν σου τοὺς ὀφθαλμούς; 27 Ἀπε-
did he to thee? how opened he thine eyes? He an-
κρίθη αὐτοῖς, Εἶπον ὑμῖν ἤδη, καὶ οὐκ.ἠκούσατε· τί πάλιν
swered them, I told you already, and ye did not hear: why again
θέλετε ἀκούειν; μὴ καὶ ὑμεῖς.θέλετε αὐτοῦ μαθηταὶ γενέσθαι;
do ye wish to hear? [3]also [1]do [2]ye wish his disciples to become?
28 [n]Ἐλοιδόρησαν [o]οὖν‖ αὐτόν, καὶ [p]εἶπον,‖ Σὺ [q]εἶ μαθητὴς‖
They [2]railed [3]at [1]therefore him, and said, Thou art [2]disciple
ἐκείνου· ἡμεῖς.δὲ τοῦ [r]Μωσέως‖ ἐσμὲν μαθηταί. 29 ἡμεῖς οἴδα-
[1]his, but we of Moses are disciples. We know
μεν ὅτι [s]Μωσῇ‖ λελάληκεν ὁ θεός· τοῦτον.δὲ οὐκ.οἴδαμεν
that to Moses [2]has [3]spoken [1]God; but this [man] we know not
πόθεν ἐστίν. 30 Ἀπεκρίθη ὁ ἄνθρωπος καὶ εἶπεν αὐτοῖς, Ἐν
whence he is. [3]Answered [1]the [2]man and said to them, [2]In
[t]γὰρ τούτῳ‖ [v]θαυμαστόν ἐστιν, ὅτι ὑμεῖς οὐκ.οἴδατε πόθεν
[1]indeed this a wonderful thing is, that ye know not whence
ἐστίν, καὶ [w]ἀνέῳξέν‖ μου τοὺς ὀφθαλμούς. 31 οἴδαμεν.[x]δὲ‖ ὅτι
he is, and he opened mine eyes. But we know that
[y]ἁμαρτωλῶν ὁ θεὸς‖ οὐκ.ἀκούει· ἀλλ' ἐάν τις θεοσεβὴς ᾖ,
sinners God does not hear; but if anyone God-fearing be,
καὶ τὸ θέλημα αὐτοῦ ποιῇ, τούτου ἀκούει. 32 ἐκ.τοῦ.αἰῶνος
and the will of him do, him he hears. [4]Ever
οὐκ.ἠκούσθη, ὅτι [z]ἤνοιξέν‖ τις ὀφθαλμοὺς τυφλοῦ
[1]it [2]was [3]not heard that [2]opened [1]anyone [the] eyes of [one] [4]blind
γεγεννημένου. 33 εἰ μὴ ἦν οὗτος παρὰ θεοῦ οὐκ ἠ-
[1]having [2]been [3]born. If [4]not [3]were [1]this [[2]man] from God he
δύνατο ποιεῖν οὐδέν. 34 Ἀπεκρίθησαν καὶ [a]εἶπον‖ αὐτῷ, Ἐν
could do nothing. They answered and said to him, In

seeth, we know not;
or who hath opened
his eyes, we know not:
he is of age; ask him:
he shall speak for him-
self. 22 These *words*
spake his parents, be-
cause they feared the
Jews: for the Jews had
agreed already, that if
any man did confess
that he was Christ, he
should be put out
of the synagogue.
23 Therefore said his
parents, He is of age;
ask him. 24 Then a-
gain called they the
man that was blind,
and said unto him,
Give God the praise:
we know that this
man is a sinner. 25 He
answered and said,
Whether he be a sin-
ner *or no*, I know not:
one thing I know,
that, whereas I was
blind, now I see.
26 Then said they to
him again, What did
he to thee? how open-
ed he thine eyes? 27 He
answered them, I have
told you already, and
ye did not hear: where-
fore would ye hear *it*
again? will ye also be
his disciples? 28 Then
they reviled him, and
said, Thou art his dis-
ciple; but we are
Moses' disciples. 29 We
know that God spake
unto Moses: *as for* this
fellow, we know not
from whence he is.
30 The man answered
and said unto them,
Why herein is a mar-
vellous thing, that ye
know not from whence
he is, and *yet* he hath
opened mine eyes.
31 Now we know that
God heareth not sin-
ners: but if any man
be a worshipper of
God, and doeth his
will, him he heareth.
32 Since the world be-
gan was it not heard
that any man opened
the eyes of one that
was born blind. 33 If
this man were not of
God, he could do no-
thing. 34 They an-
swered and said unto
him, Thou wast alto-

---

[d] αὐτὸν ἐρωτήσατε, αὐτὸς (— αὐτὸς TTrA) ἡλικίαν ἔχει LTTrA. [e] ἑαυτοῦ TTr. [f] εἶπαν LTTrA. [g] ἐπερωτήσατε T. [h] τὸν ἄνθρωπον ἐκ δευτέρου LTTrA. [i] οὗτος ὁ ἄνθρωπος L. [k] — καὶ εἶπεν LTTrAW. [l] οὖν therefore (they said) LTTrA. [m] — πάλιν LTTrA. [n] + οἱ δὲ (*read* But they railed) Tr. [o] — οὖν GLTTrAW. [p] εἶπαν T. [q] μαθητὴς εἶ LTTrA. [r] Μωϋσέως LTTrAW. [s] Μωϋσεῖ LTTrA; Μώϋσῇ W [t] τούτῳ γὰρ TTrA. [v] + τὸ the (wonderful thing) TTr. [w] ἤνοιξέν LTTr. [x] — δὲ but LTTrA. [y] ὁ θεὸς ἁμαρτωλῶν LTrA. [z] ἠνέῳξέν Tr. [a] εἶπαν LTTrA.

ἁμαρτίαις σὺ ἐγεννήθης ὅλος, καὶ σὺ διδάσκεις ἡμᾶς; Καὶ
sins thou wast born wholly, and ²thou ¹teachest us? And
ἐξέβαλον αὐτὸν ἔξω. 35 "Ηκουσεν [b]ὁ" Ἰησοῦς ὅτι ἐξέβαλον
they cast him out. ²Heard ¹Jesus that they cast
αὐτὸν ἔξω· καὶ εὑρὼν αὐτὸν εἶπεν [c]αὐτῷ," Σὺ πιστεύεις
him out, and having found him said to him, ²Thou ¹believest
εἰς τὸν υἱὸν τοῦ [d]θεοῦ;" 36 Ἀπεκρίθη ἐκεῖνος [e]καὶ εἶπεν," [f]Τίς
on the Son of God? ²Answered ¹he and said, Who
ἐστιν, κύριε, ἵνα πιστεύσω εἰς αὐτόν; 37 Εἶπεν.[g]δὲ" αὐτῷ
is he, Lord, that I may believe on him? And ²said ³to ⁴him
ὁ Ἰησοῦς, Καὶ ἑώρακας αὐτόν, καὶ ὁ λαλῶν μετὰ σοῦ
¹Jesus, ⁷Both ⁵thou ⁶hast seen him, and he who speaks with thee
ἐκεῖνός ἐστιν. 38 Ὁ.δὲ ἔφη, Πιστεύω, κύριε· καὶ προσεκύνη-
²he ¹is. And he said, I believe, Lord: and he worshipped
σεν αὐτῷ. 39 καὶ εἶπεν ὁ Ἰησοῦς, Εἰς κρίμα ἐγὼ εἰς τὸν
him. And ²said ¹Jesus, For judgment I into
κόσμον.τοῦτον ἦλθον, ἵνα οἱ μὴ.βλέποντες βλέπωσιν, καὶ
this world came, that they that see not might see, and
οἱ βλέποντες τυφλοὶ γένωνται. 40 [h]Καὶ" ἤκουσαν ἐκ τῶν
they that see blind might become. And ⁹heard ²of ³the
Φαρισαίων [i]ταῦτα" οἱ [k]ὄντες μετ' αὐτοῦ," καὶ [l]εἶ-
⁴Pharisees ¹⁰these ¹¹things ¹those ⁵who ⁶were ⁷with ⁸him, and they
πον" αὐτῷ, Μὴ καὶ ἡμεῖς τυφλοί ἐσμεν; 41 Εἶπεν αὐτοῖς ὁ
said to him, ³Also ²we ⁴blind ¹are? Said to them
Ἰησοῦς, Εἰ τυφλοὶ ἦτε, οὐκ.ἂν.εἴχετε ἁμαρτίαν· νῦν.δὲ λέ-
Jesus, If blind ye were, ye would not have sin; but now ye
γετε, Ὅτι βλέπομεν· ἡ [m]οὖν" ἁμαρτία ὑμῶν μένει.
say We see, the ²therefore ¹sin of you remains.

10 Ἀμὴν ἀμὴν λέγω ὑμῖν, ὁ μὴ.εἰσερχόμενος διὰ τῆς
Verily verily I say to you, He that enters not in by the
θύρας εἰς τὴν αὐλὴν τῶν προβάτων, ἀλλὰ ἀναβαίνων ἀλ-
door to the fold of the sheep, but mounts up else-
λαχόθεν, ἐκεῖνος κλέπτης ἐστὶν καὶ λῃστής· 2 ὁ.δὲ εἰσερ-
where, he a thief is and a robber; but he that en-
χόμενος διὰ τῆς θύρας ποιμήν ἐστιν τῶν προβάτων. 3 τούτῳ
ters in by the door shepherd is of the sheep. To him
ὁ θυρωρὸς ἀνοίγει, καὶ τὰ πρόβατα τῆς.φωνῆς.αὐτοῦ ἀκούει,
the door-keeper opens, and the sheep his voice hear,
καὶ τὰ.ἴδια πρόβατα [n]καλεῖ" κατ' ὄνομα, καὶ ἐξάγει αὐτά.
and his own sheep he calls by name, and leads ²out ¹them.
4 [o]καὶ" ὅταν τὰ.ἴδια [p]πρόβατα" ἐκβάλῃ ἔμπροσθεν αὐτῶν
And when his own sheep he puts forth before them
πορεύεται· καὶ τὰ πρόβατα αὐτῷ ἀκολουθεῖ, ὅτι οἴδασιν
he goes; and the sheep him follow, because they know
τὴν.φωνὴν.αὐτοῦ. 5 ἀλλοτρίῳ.δὲ οὐ.μὴ [q]ἀκολουθήσωσιν,"
his voice. But a stranger in no wise they should follow,
ἀλλὰ φεύξονται ἀπ' αὐτοῦ· ὅτι οὐκ.οἴδασιν τῶν ἀλλοτρίων
but will flee from him, because they know not of strangers
τὴν φωνήν. 6 Ταύτην τὴν παροιμίαν εἶπεν αὐτοῖς ὁ Ἰησοῦς,
the voice. This allegory ²spoke ³to ⁴them ¹Jesus,
ἐκεῖνοι.δὲ οὐκ.ἔγνωσαν τίνα [r]ἦν" ἃ ἐλάλει αὐτοῖς.
but they knew not what it was which he spoke to them.

gether born in sins, and dost thou teach us? And they cast him out. 35 Jesus heard that they had cast him out; and when he had found him, he said unto him, Dost thou believe on the Son of God? 36 He answered and said, Who is he, Lord, that I might believe on him? 37 And Jesus said unto him, Thou hast both seen him, and it is he that talketh with thee. 38 And he said, Lord, I believe. And he worshipped him. 39 And Jesus said, For judgment I am come into this world, that they which see not might see; and that they which see might be made blind. 40 And *some* of the Pharisees which were with him heard these words, and said unto him, Are we blind also? 41 Jesus said unto them, If ye were blind, ye should have no sin: but now ye say, We see; therefore your sin remaineth.

X. Verily, verily, I say unto you, He that entereth not by the door into the sheepfold, but climbeth up some other way, the same is a thief and a robber. 2 But he that entereth in by the door is the shepherd of the sheep. 3 To him the porter openeth; and the sheep hear his voice: and he calleth his own sheep by name, and leadeth them out. 4 And when he putteth forth his own sheep, he goeth before them, and the sheep follow him: for they know his voice. 5 And a stranger will they not follow, but will flee from him: for they know not the voice of strangers. 6 This parable spake Jesus unto them: but they understood not what things they were which he spake unto them.

---

b — ὁ T[Tr]. c — αὐτῷ T[TrA]. d ἀνθρώπου of man T. e — καὶ εἶπεν L[A]. f + καὶ and GTTrAW. g — δὲ and LTTrA. h — καὶ TTrA. i — ταῦτα T. k μετ' αὐτοῦ ὄντες LTTrA. l εἶπαν T. m — οὖν [L]TTrA. n φωνεῖ he calls LTTrA. o — καὶ TTrA. p πάντα all (his own) LTTrA. q ἀκολουθήσουσιν will they follow LTTrAW. r ᾖ it might be Tr.

7 Εἶπεν οὖν [s]πάλιν αὐτοῖς‖ ὁ Ἰησοῦς, Ἀμὴν ἀμὴν λέγω
[2]Said [3]therefore [4]again [5]to [6]them [1]Jesus, Verily verily I say
ὑμῖν, [t]ὅτι‖ ἐγώ εἰμι ἡ θύρα τῶν προβάτων. 8 πάντες ὅσοι
to you, that I am the door of the sheep. All whoever
[v]πρὸ ἐμοῦ ἦλθον‖ κλέπται εἰσὶν καὶ λῃσταί· ἀλλ' οὐκ.ἤκουσαν
before me came thieves are and robbers; but [3]did [4]not [5]hear
αὐτῶν τὰ πρόβατα. 9 ἐγώ εἰμι ἡ θύρα· δι' ἐμοῦ ἐάν τις
[6]them [1]the [2]sheep. I am the door: by me if anyone
εἰσέλθῃ σωθήσεται, καὶ εἰσελεύσεται καὶ ἐξελεύσεται, καὶ
enter in he shall be saved, and shall go in and shall go out, and
νομὴν εὑρήσει. 10 ὁ κλέπτης οὐκ.ἔρχεται εἰ.μὴ ἵνα κλέψῃ
pasture shall find. The thief comes not except that he may steal
καὶ θύσῃ καὶ ἀπολέσῃ· ἐγὼ ἦλθον ἵνα ζωὴν ἔχωσιν,
and may kill and may destroy: I came that life they might have,
καὶ περισσὸν ἔχωσιν. 11 Ἐγώ εἰμι ὁ ποιμὴν ὁ καλός· ὁ
and abundantly might have [it]. I am the [2]shepherd [1]good. The
ποιμὴν ὁ καλὸς τὴν.ψυχὴν.αὐτοῦ τίθησιν ὑπὲρ τῶν προβά-
[2]shepherd [1]good his life lays down for the sheep:
των. 12 ὁ.μισθωτὸς.[w]δέ,‖ καὶ οὐκ.ὢν ποιμήν, οὗ οὐκ
but the hired servant, and who is not [the] shepherd, whose [5]not
[x]εἰσὶν‖ τὰ πρόβατα ἴδια, θεωρεῖ τὸν λύκον ἐρχόμενον, καὶ
[4]are [2]the [3]sheep [1]own, sees the wolf coming, and
ἀφίησιν τὰ πρόβατα καὶ φεύγει· καὶ ὁ λύκος ἁρπάζει αὐτὰ
leaves the sheep, and flees; and the wolf seizes them
καὶ σκορπίζει [y]τὰ πρόβατα. 13 ὁ.δὲ μισθωτὸς φεύγει‖ ὅτι
and scatters the sheep. Now the hired servant flees because
μισθωτός ἐστιν, καὶ οὐ.μέλει.αὐτῷ περὶ τῶν προβάτων.
a hired servant he is, and is not himself concerned about the sheep.
14 ἐγώ εἰμι ὁ ποιμὴν ὁ καλός· καὶ γινώσκω τὰ ἐμά,
I am the [2]shepherd [1]good; and I know those that [are] mine,
καὶ [z]γινώσκομαι ὑπὸ τῶν ἐμῶν.‖ 15 καθὼς γινώσκει
and am known of those that [are] mine. As [3]knows
με ὁ πατήρ, κἀγὼ γινώσκω τὸν πατέρα· καὶ τὴν.ψυχήν.μου
[4]me [1]the [2]Father, I also know the Father; and my life
τίθημι ὑπὲρ τῶν προβάτων. 16 καὶ ἄλλα πρόβατα ἔχω,
I lay down for the sheep. And other sheep I have,
ἃ οὐκ.ἔστιν ἐκ τῆς.αὐλῆς.ταύτης· κἀκεῖνά [a]με δεῖ‖
which are not of this fold; those also [3]me [1]it [2]behoves
ἀγαγεῖν, καὶ τῆς.φωνῆς.μου ἀκούσουσιν· καὶ [b]γενήσεται‖ μία
to bring, and my voice they will hear; and there shall be one
ποίμνη, εἷς ποιμήν. 17 διὰ.τοῦτο [c]ὁ πατήρ με‖ ἀγαπᾷ,
flock, one shepherd. On this account the Father me loves,
ὅτι ἐγὼ τίθημι τὴν.ψυχήν.μου, ἵνα πάλιν λάβω αὐτήν.
because I lay down my life, that again I may take it.
18 οὐδεὶς αἴρει αὐτὴν ἀπ' ἐμοῦ, ἀλλ' ἐγὼ τίθημι αὐτὴν ἀπ'
No one takes it from me, but I lay down it of
ἐμαυτοῦ. ἐξουσίαν ἔχω θεῖναι αὐτήν, καὶ ἐξουσίαν ἔχω
myself. Authority I have to lay down it, and authority I have
πάλιν λαβεῖν αὐτήν· ταύτην τὴν ἐντολὴν ἔλαβον παρὰ
again to take it. This commandment I received from
τοῦ.πατρός.μου. 19 Σχίσμα [d]οὖν‖ πάλιν ἐγένετο ἐν τοῖς
my Father. A division therefore again there was among the

7 Then said Jesus
unto them again, Ve-
rily, verily, I say unto
you, I am the door of
the sheep. 8 All that
ever came before me
are thieves and rob-
bers: but the sheep
did not hear them.
9 I am the door: by
me if any man enter
in, he shall be saved,
and shall go in and
out, and find pasture.
10 The thief cometh
not, but for to steal, and
to kill, and to destroy:
I am come that they
might have life, and
that they might have
it more abundantly.
11 I am the good shep-
herd: the good shep-
herd giveth his life for
the sheep. 12 But he
that is an hireling,
and not the shepherd,
whose own the sheep
are not, seeth the wolf
coming, and leaveth
the sheep, and fleeth:
and the wolf catcheth
them, and scattereth
the sheep. 13 The hire-
ling fleeth, because he
is an hireling, and car-
eth not for the sheep.
14 I am the good shep-
herd, and know my
sheep, and am known
of mine. 15 As the
Father knoweth me,
even so know I the Fa-
ther: and I lay down
my life for the sheep.
16 And other sheep I
have, which are not of
this fold: them also I
must bring, and they
shall hear my voice;
and there shall be one
fold, *and* one shep-
herd. 17 Therefore
doth my Father love
me, because I lay down
my life, that I might
take it again. 18 No
man taketh it from
me, but I lay it down
of myself. I have
power to lay it down,
and I have power to
take it again. This
commandment have I
received of my Father.
19 There was a division
therefore again among
the Jews for these

[s] αὐτοῖς πάλιν L; — πάλιν αὐτοῖς T; — αὐτοῖς A. [t] — ὅτι [L]Tr[A]. [v] ἦλθον πρὸ ἐμοῦ GLTrA; — πρὸ ἐμοῦ T. [w] — δέ but T[Tr]. [x] ἔστιν LTTrA. [y] — τὰ πρόβατα. ([τὰ πρόβατα] A) ὁ δὲ μισθωτὸς φεύγει [L]TTrA. [z] γινώσκουσίν με τὰ ἐμά those that [are] mine know me LTTrA. [a] δεῖ με LTTrA. [b] γενήσονται TrA. [c] με ὁ πατὴρ LTTrA. [d] — οὖν LTTrA.

sayings. 20 And many
of them said, He hath
a devil, and is mad;
why hear ye him?
21 Others said, These
are not the words of
him that hath a devil.
Can a devil open the
eyes of the blind?

22 And it was at
Jerusalem the feast of
the dedication, and it
was winter. 23 And
Jesus walked in the
temple in Solomon's
porch. 24 Then came
the Jews round about
him, and said unto
him, How long dost
thou make us to
doubt? If thou be the
Christ, tell us plain-
ly. 25 Jesus answered
them, I told you, and
ye believed not: the
works that I do in my
Father's name, they
bear witness of me.
26 But ye believe not,
because ye are not of
my sheep, as I said
unto you. 27 My sheep
hear my voice, and I
know them, and they
follow me: 28 and I
give unto them eter-
nal life; and they
shall never perish, nei-
ther shall any *man*
pluck them out of my
hand. 29 My Father,
which gave *them* me,
is greater than all;
and no *man* is able to
pluck *them* out of my
Father's hand. 30 I
and *my* Father are one.
31 Then the Jews took
up stones again to
stone him. 32 Jesus
answered them, Many
good works have I
shewed you from my
Father; for which of
those works do ye
stone me? 33 The Jews
answered him, saying,
For a good work we

Ἰουδαίοις διὰ τοὺς.λόγους.τούτους. 20 ἔλεγον [e]δὲ‖
Jews on account of these words; [2]said [1]but

πολλοὶ ἐξ αὐτῶν, Δαιμόνιον ἔχει καὶ μαίνεται· τί αὐτοῦ
many of them, A demon he has and is mad; why him

ἀκούετε; 21 Ἄλλοι ἔλεγον, Ταῦτα τὰ ῥήματα οὐκ.ἔστιν
do ye hear? Others said, These sayings are not [those]

δαιμονιζομένου· μὴ δαιμόνιον δύναται τυφλῶν
of one possessed by a demon. [2]A [3]demon [1]is able of [the] blind [the]

ὀφθαλμοὺς [f]ἀνοίγειν‖;
eyes to open?

22 Ἐγένετο.δὲ τὰ [g]ἐγκαίνια‖ ἐν [h]τοῖς‖ Ἱεροσολύμοις,
And took place the feast of dedication at Jerusalem,

[i]καὶ‖ χειμὼν ἦν· 23 καὶ περιεπάτει [k]ὁ‖ Ἰησοῦς ἐν τῷ ἱερῷ
and winter it was. And [2]was [3]walking [1]Jesus in the temple

ἐν τῇ στοᾷ [l]τοῦ Σολομῶντος.‖ 24 ἐκύκλωσαν οὖν αὐτὸν
in the porch of Solomon. [4]Encircled [3]therefore [5]him

οἱ Ἰουδαῖοι, καὶ ἔλεγον αὐτῷ, Ἕως πότε τὴν.ψυχὴν.ἡμῶν
[1]the [2]Jews, and said to him, Until when our soul

αἴρεις; εἰ σὺ εἶ ὁ χριστός, [m]εἰπὲ‖ ἡμῖν παρ-
holdest thou in suspense? If thou art the Christ, tell us plain-

ῥησίᾳ. 25 Ἀπεκρίθη [n]αὐτοῖς‖ [k]ὁ‖ Ἰησοῦς, Εἶπον ὑμῖν, καὶ
ly. [2]Answered [3]them [1]Jesus, I told you, and

οὐ.πιστεύετε. τὰ ἔργα ἃ ἐγὼ ποιῶ ἐν τῷ ὀνόματι τοῦ πατρός
ye believe not. The works which I do in the name of [2]Father

μου, ταῦτα μαρτυρεῖ περὶ ἐμοῦ· 26 [o]ἀλλ'‖ ὑμεῖς οὐ
[1]my, these bear witness concerning me: but ye [2]not

πιστεύετε· [p]οὐ.γάρ‖.ἐστε ἐκ τῶν προβάτων τῶν ἐμῶν, [q]καθὼς
[1]believe, for ye are not of [2]sheep [1]my, as

εἶπον ὑμῖν.‖ 27 τὰ πρόβατα τὰ ἐμὰ τῆς.φωνῆς.μου [r]ἀκούει,‖
I said to you. [2]Sheep [1]my my voice hear,

κἀγὼ γινώσκω αὐτά· καὶ ἀκολουθοῦσίν μοι, 28 κἀγὼ [s]ζωὴν
and I know them, and they follow me; and I life

αἰώνιον δίδωμι αὐτοῖς·‖ καὶ οὐ.μὴ ἀπόλωνται εἰς τὸν
eternal give them; and in no wise shall they perish for

αἰῶνα, καὶ οὐχ.ἁρπάσει τις αὐτὰ ἐκ τῆς.χειρός.μου. 29 ὁ
ever, and [3]shall [1]not [4]seize [2]anyone them out of my hand.

πατήρ.[t]μου‖ [v]ὃς‖ δέδωκέν μοι [w]μείζων πάντων‖ ἐστίν· καὶ
My Father who has given [them] to me greater than all is, and

οὐδεὶς δύναται ἁρπάζειν ἐκ τῆς χειρὸς τοῦ.πατρός.[x]μου.‖
no one is able to seize out of the hand of my Father.

30 ἐγὼ καὶ ὁ πατὴρ ἕν ἐσμεν. 31 Ἐβάστασαν [y]οὖν‖ πάλιν
I and the Father one are. [5]Took [6]up [3]therefore [4]again

λίθους οἱ Ἰουδαῖοι ἵνα λιθάσωσιν αὐτόν. 32 ἀπεκρίθη
[7]stones [1]the [2]Jews that they might stone him. [2]Answered

αὐτοῖς ὁ Ἰησοῦς, Πολλὰ [z]καλὰ ἔργα‖ ἔδειξα ὑμῖν ἐκ τοῦ
[3]them [1]Jesus, Many good works I shewed you from

πατρός.[a]μου·‖ διὰ ποῖον αὐτῶν ἔργον [b]λιθάζετέ με‖;
my Father; because of which [2]of [3]them [1]work do ye stone me?

33 Ἀπεκρίθησαν αὐτῷ οἱ Ἰουδαῖοι [c]λέγοντες,‖ Περὶ καλοῦ
[3]Answered [4]him [1]the [2]Jews, saying, For a good

---

[e] οὖν then T. [f] ἀνοῖξαι to have opened TTrA. [g] ἐνκαίνια T. [h] — τοῖς T. [i] — καὶ TTrA. [k] [ὁ] Tr. [l] Σολομῶνος GLTAW; τοῦ Σολομῶνος Tr. [m] εἰπὸν T. [n] — αὐτοῖς T. [o] ἀλλὰ LTTrAW. [p] ὅτι οὐκ TTr. [q] — καθὼς εἶπον ὑμῖν [L]TTr[A]. [r] ἀκούουσιν [are] hearing TTrA. [s] δίδωμι αὐτοῖς ζωὴν αἰώνιον TTrA. [t] — μου (*read* The Father) T. [v] ὃ what (he has given) TTrA. [w] πάντων μεῖζόν TTrA. [x] — μου (*read* the Father) T[Tr]A. [y] — οὖν T[Tr]. [z] ἔργα καλὰ LT. [a] — μου (*read* the Father) [L]T[Tr]A. [b] ἐμὲ λιθάζετε TTrA. [c] — λέγοντες LTTrAW.

ἔργου οὐ.λιθάζομέν σε, ἀλλὰ περὶ βλασφημίας, καὶ ὅτι
work we do not stone thee, but for blasphemy, and because
σὺ ἄνθρωπος ὢν ποιεῖς σεαυτὸν θεόν. 34 Ἀπεκρίθη αὐτοῖς
thou ²a ³man ¹being makest thyself God. ²Answered ³them
[d]ὁ Ἰησοῦς, Οὐκ.ἔστιν γεγραμμένον ἐν τῷ.νόμῳ.ὑμῶν, [e]Ἐγὼ
¹Jesus, Is it not written in your law, I
[f]εἶπα, θεοί ἐστε; 35 Εἰ ἐκείνους εἶπεν θεούς, πρὸς οὓς ὁ
said, ³gods ¹ye ²are? If them he called gods, to whom the
λόγος [g]τοῦ θεοῦ ἐγένετο, καὶ οὐ.δύναται λυθῆναι ἡ γραφή·
word of God came, (and ³cannot ⁴be ⁵broken ¹the ²scripture,)
36 ὃν ὁ πατὴρ ἡγίασεν καὶ ἀπέστειλεν εἰς τὸν κόσμον,
[of him] whom the Father sanctified and sent into the world,
ὑμεῖς.λέγετε, Ὅτι βλασφημεῖς, ὅτι εἶπον, Υἱὸς [h]τοῦ θεοῦ
do ye say, Thou blasphemest, because I said, Son of God
εἰμι; 37 εἰ οὐ.ποιῶ τὰ ἔργα τοῦ.πατρός.μου, μὴ.πιστεύετέ
I am? If I do not the works of my Father, believe not
μοι· 38 εἰ.δὲ ποιῶ, κἂν ἐμοὶ μὴ.[i]πιστεύητε, τοῖς ἔργοις
me; but if I do, even if me ye believe not, the works
[k]πιστεύσατε, ἵνα γνῶτε καὶ [l]πιστεύσητε ὅτι ἐν ἐμοὶ
believe, that ye may perceive and may believe that in me [is]
ὁ πατήρ, κἀγὼ ἐν [m]αὐτῷ. 39 Ἐζήτουν [n]οὖν [o]πάλιν
the Father, and I in him. They sought therefore again
αὐτὸν πιάσαι· καὶ ἐξῆλθεν ἐκ τῆς.χειρὸς.αὐτῶν. 40 Καὶ
him to take, and he went forth out of their hand; and
ἀπῆλθεν πάλιν πέραν τοῦ Ἰορδάνου, εἰς τὸν τόπον ὅπου ἦν
departed again beyond the Jordan, to the place where was
[p]Ἰωάννης τὸ πρῶτον βαπτίζων· καὶ [q]ἔμεινεν ἐκεῖ. 41 καὶ
John first baptizing; and he abode there. And
πολλοὶ ἦλθον πρὸς αὐτόν, καὶ ἔλεγον, Ὅτι [p]Ἰωάννης μὲν
many came to him, and said, John indeed
σημεῖον ἐποίησεν οὐδέν· πάντα.δὲ ὅσα εἶπεν [p]Ἰωάννης
³sign ¹did ²no; but all whatsoever ²said ¹John
περὶ τούτου, ἀληθῆ ἦν. 42 Καὶ [r]ἐπίστευσαν πολλοὶ
concerning this [man], true were. And ²believed ¹many
ἐκεῖ εἰς αὐτόν.
there on him.

11 Ἦν.δέ τις ἀσθενῶν Λάζαρος ἀπὸ Βηθανίας,
Now there was a certain [man] sick, Lazarus of Bethany,
ἐκ τῆς κώμης [s]Μαρίας καὶ Μάρθας τῆς.ἀδελφῆς.αὐτῆς. 2 ἦν
of the village of Mary and Martha her sister. ²It ³was
δὲ [t]Μαρία ἡ ἀλείψασα τὸν κύριον μύρῳ καὶ ἐκμάξασα
¹and Mary who anointed the Lord with ointment and wiped
τοὺς.πόδας.αὐτοῦ ταῖς.θριξὶν.αὐτῆς, ἧς ὁ ἀδελφὸς Λάζαρος
his feet with her hair, whose brother Lazarus
ἠσθένει. 3 ἀπέστειλαν οὖν αἱ ἀδελφαὶ πρὸς αὐτὸν λέγου-
was sick. ⁴Sent ³therefore ¹the ²sisters to him, say-
σαι, Κύριε, ἴδε ὃν φιλεῖς ἀσθενεῖ. 4 Ἀκούσας.δὲ ὁ Ἰησοῦς
ing, Lord, lo, he whom thou lovest is sick. But ²having ³heard ¹Jesus
εἶπεν, Αὕτη ἡ ἀσθένεια οὐκ.ἔστιν πρὸς θάνατον, ἀλλ' ὑπὲρ
said, This sickness is not unto death, but for
τῆς δόξης τοῦ θεοῦ, ἵνα δοξασθῇ ὁ υἱὸς τοῦ θεοῦ δι'
the glory of God, that may be glorified the Son of God by

stone thee not; but for blasphemy; and because that thou, being a man, makest thyself God. 34 Jesus answered them, Is it not written in your law, I said, Ye are gods? 35 If he called them gods, unto whom the word of God came, and the scripture cannot be broken; 36 say ye of him, whom the Father hath sanctified, and sent into the world, Thou blasphemest; because I said, I am the Son of God? 37 If I do not the works of my Father, believe me not. 38 But if I do, though ye believe not me, believe the works: that ye may know, and believe, that the Father *is* in me, and I in him. 39 Therefore they sought again to take him: but he escaped out of their hand, 40 and went away again beyond Jordan into the place where John at first baptized; and there he abode. 41 And many resorted unto him, and said, John did no miracle: but all things that John spake of this man were true. 42 And many believed on him there.

XI. Now a certain *man* was sick, *named* Lazarus, of Bethany, the town of Mary and her sister Martha. 2 (It was *that* Mary which anointed the Lord with ointment, and wiped his feet with her hair, whose brother Lazarus was sick.) 3 Therefore his sisters sent unto him, saying, Lord, behold, he whom thou lovest is sick. 4 When Jesus heard *that*, he said, This sickness is not unto death, but for the glory of God, that the Son of God might be glorified

---

d [ὁ] Tr. e + ὅτι that LTTrA. f εἶπον L. g ἐγένετο τοῦ θεοῦ T. h — τοῦ T. i πιστεύετε T. k πιστεύετε LTTr. l γινώσκητε may know LTTrA. m τῷ πατρί the Father LTTrA. n [οὖν] TrA. o — πάλιν T. p Ἰωάνης Tr. q ἔμενεν L. r πολλοὶ ἐπίστευσαν εἰς αὐτὸν ἐκεῖ LTTrA. s + τῆς T. t Μαριὰμ Tr.

thereby. 5 Now Jesus loved Martha, and her sister, and Lazarus. 6 When he had heard therefore that he was sick, he abode two days still in the same place where he was. 7 Then after that saith he to *his* disciples, Let us go into Judæa again. 8 *His* disciples say unto him, Master, the Jews of late sought to stone thee; and goest thou thither again? 9 Jesus answered, Are there not twelve hours in the day? If any man walk in the day, he stumbleth not, because he seeth the light of this world. 10 But if a man walk in the night, he stumbleth, because there is no light in him. 11 These things said he: and after that he saith unto them, Our friend Lazarus sleepeth; but I go, that I may awake him out of sleep. 12 Then said his disciples, Lord, if he sleep, he shall do well. 13 Howbeit Jesus spake of his death: but they thought that he had spoken of taking of rest in sleep. 14 Then said Jesus unto them plainly, Lazarus is dead. 15 And I am glad for your sakes that I was not there, to the intent ye may believe; nevertheless let us go unto him. 16 Then said Thomas, which is called Didymus, unto his fellowdisciples, Let us also go, that we may die with him.

17 Then when Jesus came, he found that he had *lain* in the grave four days already. 18 Now Bethany was nigh unto Jerusalem, about fifteen furlongs off: 19 and many of the Jews came to Martha and Mary, to comfort them concerning their

αὐτῆς. 5 Ἠγάπα δὲ ὁ Ἰησοῦς τὴν Μάρθαν καὶ τὴν ἀδελφὴν
it. [3]Loved [1]now [2]Jesus Martha and [2]sister

αὐτῆς καὶ τὸν Λάζαρον. 6 ὡς οὖν ἤκουσεν ὅτι ἀσθενεῖ,
[1]her and Lazarus. When therefore he heard that he is sick,

τότε μὲν ἔμεινεν ἐν ᾧ ἦν τόπῳ δύο ἡμέρας. 7 Ἔπειτα
then indeed he remained in which [2]he [3]was [1]place two days. Then

μετὰ τοῦτο λέγει τοῖς μαθηταῖς,[w] Ἄγωμεν εἰς τὴν Ἰουδαίαν
after this he says to the disciples, Let us go into Judæa

πάλιν. 8 Λέγουσιν αὐτῷ οἱ μαθηταί, [x]Ῥαββί,‖ νῦν ἐζή-
again. [3]Say [4]to [5]him [1]the [2]disciples, Rabbi, just now [3]were

τουν σε λιθάσαι οἱ Ἰουδαῖοι, καὶ πάλιν ὑπάγεις ἐκεῖ;
[4]seeking [7]thee [5]to [6]stone [1]the [2]Jews, and again goest thou thither?

9 Ἀπεκρίθη [y]ὁ‖ Ἰησοῦς, Οὐχὶ δώδεκά [z]εἰσιν ὧραι‖ τῆς
[2]Answered [1]Jesus, [5]Not [6]twelve [3]are [4]there hours in the

ἡμέρας; ἐάν τις περιπατῇ ἐν τῇ ἡμέρᾳ, οὐ.προσκόπτει,
day? If anyone walk in the day, he stumbles not,

ὅτι τὸ φῶς τοῦ.κόσμου.τούτου βλέπει· 10 ἐὰν.δέ τις
because the light of this world he sees; but if anyone

περιπατῇ ἐν τῇ νυκτί, προσκόπτει, ὅτι τὸ φῶς οὐκ.ἔστιν ἐν
walk in the night, he stumbles, because the light is not in

αὐτῷ. 11 Ταῦτα εἶπεν, καὶ μετὰ τοῦτο λέγει αὐτοῖς, Λά-
him. These things he said; and after this he says to them, La-

ζαρος ὁ.φίλος.ἡμῶν κεκοίμηται· ἀλλὰ πορεύομαι ἵνα ἐξ-
zarus our friend has fallen asleep; but I go that I may

υπνίσω αὐτόν. 12 Εἶπον οὖν[a] [b]οἱ.μαθηταὶ‖.[c]αὐτοῦ,‖ Κύριε,
awake him. [2]Said [1]therefore his disciples, Lord,

εἰ κεκοίμηται σωθήσεται. 13 Εἰρήκει.δὲ ὁ Ἰησοῦς περὶ
if he has fallen asleep he will get well. But [2]had [3]spoken [1]Jesus of

τοῦ.θανάτου.αὐτοῦ· ἐκεῖνοι.δὲ ἔδοξαν ὅτι περὶ τῆς κοιμήσεως
his death, but they thought that of the rest

τοῦ ὕπνου λέγει. 14 τότε [d]οὖν‖ εἶπεν αὐτοῖς ὁ Ἰησοῦς
of sleep he speaks. Then therefore [2]said [3]to [4]them [1]Jesus

παῤῥησίᾳ, Λάζαρος ἀπέθανεν· 15 καὶ χαίρω δι᾽.ὑμᾶς,
plainly, Lazarus died. And I rejoice on your account,

ἵνα πιστεύσητε, ὅτι οὐκ.ἤμην ἐκεῖ· [e]ἀλλ᾽‖ ἄγωμεν πρὸς
in order that ye may believe, that I was not there. But let us go to

αὐτόν. 16 Εἶπεν οὖν Θωμᾶς, ὁ λεγόμενος Δίδυμος, τοῖς
him. [2]Said [1]therefore Thomas, called Didymus, to the

[f]συμμαθηταῖς,‖ Ἄγωμεν καὶ ἡμεῖς, ἵνα ἀποθάνωμεν μετ᾽
fellow-disciples, Let [3]go [2]also [1]us, that we may die with

αὐτοῦ.
him.

17 [g]Ἐλθὼν‖ οὖν ὁ Ἰησοῦς [h] εὗρεν αὐτὸν τέσσαρας
[3]Having [4]come [2]therefore [1]Jesus found him four

[i]ἡμέρας ἤδη‖ ἔχοντα ἐν τῷ μνημείῳ. 18 ἦν.δὲ [k]ἡ‖ Βηθανία
days already having been in the tomb. Now [2]was [1]Bethany

ἐγγὺς τῶν Ἱεροσολύμων, ὡς ἀπὸ σταδίων δεκαπέντε 19 [l]καὶ
near to Jerusalem, about [3]off [2]furlongs [1]fifteen, and

πολλοὶ‖ ἐκ τῶν Ἰουδαίων ἐληλύθεισαν πρὸς [m]τὰς περὶ‖
many of the Jews had come unto those around

Μάρθαν καὶ [n]Μαρίαν,‖ ἵνα παραμυθήσωνται αὐτὰς περὶ
Martha and Mary, that they might console them concerning

---

[w] + [αὐτοῦ] (*read* his disciples) L. [x] Ῥαββεί T. [y] — ὁ GLTTrAW. [z] ὧραί εἰσιν LTTrAW. [a] + αὐτῷ to him LT. [b] [οἱ μαθηταὶ] A. [c] — αὐτοῦ (*read* the disciples) LT; αὐτῷ to him TrA. [d] [οὖν] L. [e] ἀλλὰ LTTrA. [f] συνμαθηταῖς T. [g] Ἦλθεν came L. [h] + καὶ and L. [i] ἤδη ἡμέρας TrA; — ἤδη T. [k] — ἡ T. [l] πολλοὶ δὲ LTTrA. [m] τὴν (*read* had come to Martha) LTrA. [n] Μαριάμ LTTrA.

τοῦ.ἀδελφοῦ.[o]αὐτῶν.[‖] 20 ἡ.οὖν.Μάρθα ὡς ἤκουσεν ὅτι [p]ὁ[‖]
their brother. Martha therefore when she heard that
Ἰησοῦς ἔρχεται, ὑπήντησεν αὐτῷ· Μαρία.δὲ ἐν τῷ οἴκῳ ἐκα-
Jesus is coming, met him; but Mary in the house was
θέζετο. 21 εἶπεν.οὖν [q]ἡ[‖] Μάρθα πρὸς [r]τὸν[‖] Ἰησοῦν, Κύριε, εἰ
sitting. Then said Martha to Jesus, Lord, if
ἦς ὧδε, [s]ὁ.ἀδελφός.μου οὐκ.ἂν.ἐτεθνήκει.[‖] 22 [t]ἀλλὰ[‖]
thou hadst been here, my brother had not died; but
καὶ νῦν οἶδα ὅτι ὅσα ἂν.αἰτήσῃ τὸν θεόν, δώσει
even now I know that whatsoever thou mayest ask of God, ²will ³give
σοι ὁ θεός. 23 Λέγει αὐτῇ ὁ Ἰησοῦς, Ἀναστήσεται ὁ ἀδελφός
⁴thee ¹God. Says to her Jesus, ³Will ⁴rise ⁵again ²brother
σου. 24 Λέγει αὐτῷ [v] Μάρθα, Οἶδα ὅτι ἀναστήσεται ἐν τῇ
¹thy. Says to him Martha, I know that he will rise again in the
ἀναστάσει ἐν τῇ ἐσχάτῃ ἡμέρᾳ. 25 Εἶπεν αὐτῇ ὁ Ἰησοῦς,
resurrection in the last day. ²Said ³to ⁴her ¹Jesus,
Ἐγώ εἰμι ἡ ἀνάστασις καὶ ἡ ζωή. ὁ πιστεύων εἰς ἐμέ,
I am the resurrection and the life: he that believes on me,
κἂν ἀποθάνῃ ζήσεται· 26 καὶ πᾶς ὁ ζῶν καὶ πιστεύων
though he die he shall live; and everyone who lives and believes
εἰς ἐμέ, οὐ.μὴ ἀποθάνῃ εἰς.τὸν.αἰῶνα. πιστεύεις τοῦτο;
on me, in no wise shall die for ever. Believest thou this?
27 Λέγει αὐτῷ, Ναί, κύριε· ἐγὼ πεπίστευκα ὅτι σὺ εἶ ὁ
She says to him, Yea, Lord; I have believed that thou art the
χριστός, ὁ υἱὸς τοῦ θεοῦ, ὁ εἰς τὸν κόσμον ἐρχόμενος.
Christ, the Son of God, who into the world comes.
28 Καὶ [w]ταῦτα[‖] εἰποῦσα ἀπῆλθεν, καὶ ἐφώνησεν [x]Μαρίαν[‖]
And these things having said she went away, and called Mary
τὴν.ἀδελφὴν.αὐτῆς [y]λάθρα,[‖] [z]εἰποῦσα,[‖] Ὁ διδάσκαλος πάρ-
her sister secretly, saying, The teacher is
εστιν καὶ φωνεῖ σε. 29 Ἐκείνη [a] ὡς ἤκουσεν [b]ἐγείρεται[‖] ταχὺ
come and calls thee. She when she heard rises up quickly
καὶ [c]ἔρχεται[‖] πρὸς αὐτόν. 30 οὔπω.δὲ ἐληλύθει ὁ Ἰησοῦς
and comes to him. Now not yet had ²come ¹Jesus
εἰς τὴν κώμην, ἀλλ' ἦν [d] ἐν τῷ τόπῳ ὅπου ὑπήντησεν αὐτῷ
into the village, but was in the place where ²met ³him
ἡ Μάρθα. 31 οἱ.οὖν.Ἰουδαῖοι οἱ ὄντες μετ' αὐτῆς ἐν τῇ οἰκίᾳ
¹Martha. The Jews therefore who were with her in the house
καὶ παραμυθούμενοι αὐτήν, ἰδόντες τὴν [e]Μαρίαν[‖] ὅτι ταχέως
and consoling her, having seen Mary that quickly
ἀνέστη καὶ ἐξῆλθεν, ἠκολούθησαν αὐτῇ, [f]λέγοντες,[‖] Ὅτι
she rose up and went out, followed her, saying,
ὑπάγει εἰς τὸ μνημεῖον ἵνα κλαύσῃ ἐκεῖ. 32 Ἡ.οὖν.[g]Μαρία[‖]
She is going to the tomb that she may weep there. Mary therefore
ὡς ἦλθεν ὅπου ἦν [h]ὁ[‖] Ἰησοῦς, ἰδοῦσα αὐτὸν ἔπεσεν [i]εἰς
when she came where ²was ¹Jesus, seeing him, fell at
τοὺς.πόδας.αὐτοῦ,[‖] λέγουσα αὐτῷ, Κύριε, εἰ ἦς ὧδε
his feet, saying to him, Lord, if thou hadst been here
οὐκ.ἂν.[k]ἀπέθανέν μου[‖] ὁ ἀδελφός. 33 Ἰησοῦς οὖν ὡς εἶδεν
³had ⁴not ⁵died ¹my ²brother. Jesus therefore when he saw

brother. 20 Then Martha, as soon as she heard that Jesus was coming, went and met him: but Mary sat *still* in the house. 21 Then said Martha unto Jesus, Lord, if thou hadst been here, my brother had not died. 22 But I know, that even now, whatsoever thou wilt ask of God, God will give *it* thee. 23 Jesus saith unto her, Thy brother shall rise again. 24 Martha saith unto him, I know that he shall rise again in the resurrection at the last day. 25 Jesus said unto her, I am the resurrection, and the life: he that believeth in me, though he were dead, yet shall he live: 26 and whosoever liveth and believeth in me shall never die. Believest thou this? 27 She saith unto him, Yea, Lord: I believe that thou art the Christ, the Son of God, which should come into the world. 28 And when she had so said, she went her way, and called Mary her sister secretly, saying, The Master is come, and calleth for thee. 29 As soon as she heard *that*, she arose quickly, and came unto him. 30 Now Jesus was not yet come into the town, but was in that place where Martha met him. 31 The Jews then which were with her in the house, and comforted her, when they saw Mary, that she rose up hastily and went out, followed her, saying, She goeth unto the grave to weep there. 32 Then when Mary was come where Jesus was, and saw him, she fell down at his feet, saying unto him, Lord, if thou hadst been here, my brother had not died. 33 When Jesus therefore saw her weeping,

---

[o] — αὐτῶν (*read* [their] brother) TTrA. [p] — ὁ GLTTrAW. [q] — ἡ GL. [r] — τὸν T[Tr]. [s] οὐκ ἂν ἀπέθανεν (ἐτεθνήκει A) ὁ ἀδελφός μου LTTrA. [t] — ἀλλὰ [L]TTrA. [v] + ἡ LTTrA. [w] τοῦτο this TTrA. [x] Μαριὰμ LTTrA. [y] λάθρᾳ L. [z] εἴπασα Tr. [a] + δὲ and (she) Tr[A]. [b] ἠγέρθη rose up LTrA. [c] ἤρχετο came TrA. [d] + ἔτι yet LTr[A]. [e] Μαριὰμ LTTrA. [f] δόξαντες thinking TTrA. [g] Μαριὰμ TTrA. [h] — ὁ LTTrA. [i] αὐτοῦ εἰς (πρὸς TTrA) τοὺς πόδας GTTrAW. [k] μου ἀπέθανεν TTrA.

and the Jews also weeping which came with her, he groaned in the spirit, and was troubled, 34 and said, Where have ye laid him? They said unto him, Lord, come and see. 35 Jesus wept. 36 Then said the Jews, Behold how he loved him! 37 And some of them said, Could not this man, which opened the eyes of the blind, have caused that even this man should not have died? 38 Jesus therefore again groaning in himself cometh to the grave. It was a cave, and a stone lay upon it. 39 Jesus said, Take ye away the stone. Martha, the sister of him that was dead, saith unto him, Lord, by this time he stinketh: for he hath been *dead* four days. 40 Jesus saith unto her, Said I not unto thee, that, if thou wouldest believe, thou shouldest see the glory of God? 41 Then they took away the stone *from the place* where the dead was laid. And Jesus lifted up *his* eyes, and said, Father, I thank thee that thou hast heard me. 42 And I knew that thou hearest me always: but because of the people which stand by I said *it*, that they may believe that thou hast sent me. 43 And when he thus had spoken, he cried with a loud voice, Lazarus, come forth. 44 And he that was dead came forth, bound hand and foot with graveclothes: and his face was bound about with a napkin. Jesus saith unto them, Loose him, and let him go.

αὐτὴν κλαίουσαν, καὶ τοὺς συνελθόντας αὐτῇ Ἰουδαίους
her weeping, and the [2]who [3]came [4]with [5]her [1]Jews
κλαίοντας, ἐνεβριμήσατο τῷ πνεύματι, καὶ ἐτάραξεν ἑαυτόν,
weeping, he groaned in spirit, and troubled himself,
34 καὶ εἶπεν, Ποῦ τεθείκατε αὐτόν; Λέγουσιν αὐτῷ, Κύριε,
and said, Where have ye laid him; They say to him, Lord,
ἔρχου καὶ ἴδε. 35 Ἐδάκρυσεν ὁ Ἰησοῦς. 36 ἔλεγον οὖν οἱ
come and see. [2]Wept [1]Jesus. [3]Said [4]therefore [1]the
Ἰουδαῖοι, Ἴδε πῶς ἐφίλει αὐτόν. 37 Τινὲς.δὲ ἐξ αὐτῶν
[2]Jews, Behold how he loved him! But some of them
εἶπον, Οὐκ.[l]ἠδύνατο[ǁ] οὗτος ὁ ἀνοίξας τοὺς ὀφθαλμοὺς
said, Was not [3]able [1]this [[2]man] who opened the eyes
τοῦ τυφλοῦ, ποιῆσαι ἵνα καὶ οὗτος μὴ.ἀποθάνῃ;
of the blind [man], to have caused that also this one should not have died?
38 Ἰησοῦς οὖν πάλιν [m]ἐμβριμώμενος[ǁ] ἐν ἑαυτῷ ἔρχεται
Jesus therefore again groaning in himself comes
εἰς τὸ μνημεῖον. ἦν.δὲ σπήλαιον, καὶ λίθος ἐπέκειτο ἐπ'
to the tomb. Now it was a cave, and a stone was lying upon
αὐτῷ. 39 λέγει [n]ὁ[ǁ] Ἰησοῦς, Ἄρατε τὸν λίθον. Λέγει αὐτῷ
it. [2]Says [1]Jesus, Take away the stone. [3]Says [1]to [2]him
ἡ ἀδελφὴ τοῦ [o]τεθνηκότος[ǁ] Μάρθα, Κύριε, ἤδη ὄζει·
[5]the [6]sister [7]of [8]him [9]who [10]has [11]died, [4]Martha, Lord, already he stinks,
τεταρταῖος γάρ ἐστιν. 40 Λέγει αὐτῇ ὁ Ἰησοῦς, Οὐκ.εἶπόν
[4]four [5]days [1]for [2]it [3]is. [2]Says [3]to [4]her [1]Jesus, Said I not
σοι, ὅτι ἐὰν πιστεύσῃς, [p]ὄψει[ǁ] τὴν δόξαν τοῦ θεοῦ;
to thee, that if thou shouldest believe, thou shalt see the glory of God?
41 [q]Ἦραν οὖν τὸν λίθον [q]οὗ ἦν ὁ τεθνηκὼς κείμενος.[q]
They took away therefore the stone where [3]was [1]the [2]dead [4]laid.
Ὁ.δὲ.Ἰησοῦς ἦρεν τοὺς ὀφθαλμοὺς ἄνω, καὶ εἶπεν, Πά-
And Jesus lifted [his] eyes upwards, and said, Fa-
τερ, εὐχαριστῶ σοι ὅτι ἤκουσάς μου. 42 ἐγὼ.δὲ ᾔδειν ὅτι
ther, I thank thee that thou heardest me; and I knew that
πάντοτέ μου ἀκούεις· ἀλλὰ διὰ τὸν ὄχλον τὸν περι-
always me thou hearest; but on account of the crowd who stand
εστῶτα εἶπον ἵνα πιστεύσωσιν ὅτι σύ με ἀπέστειλας.
around I said [it], that they might believe that thou me didst send.
43 Καὶ ταῦτα εἰπών, φωνῇ μεγάλῃ ἐκραύγασεν, Λά-
And these things having said, with a [2]voice [1]loud he cried, La-
ζαρε, δεῦρο ἔξω. 44 [r]Καὶ[ǁ] ἐξῆλθεν ὁ τεθνηκώς, δεδεμένος
zarus, come forth. And came forth he who had been dead, bound
τοὺς πόδας καὶ τὰς χεῖρας κειρίαις, καὶ ἡ.ὄψις.αὐτοῦ
feet and hands with grave clothes, and his face
σουδαρίῳ περιεδέδετο. λέγει αὐτοῖς ὁ Ἰησοῦς, Λύσατε
with a handkerchief bound about. [2]Says [3]to [4]them [1]Jesus, Loose
αὐτὸν καὶ ἄφετε [s] ὑπάγειν.
him and let [him] go.

45 Then many of the Jews which came to Mary, and had seen the things which Jesus did, believed on him. 46 But some of them went their ways to the Pharisees, and told

45 Πολλοὶ οὖν ἐκ τῶν Ἰουδαίων οἱ ἐλθόντες πρὸς τὴν
Many therefore of the Jews who came to
[t]Μαρίαν[ǁ] καὶ θεασάμενοι [v]ἃ[ǁ] ἐποίησεν [w]ὁ Ἰησοῦς,[ǁ] ἐπίστευσαν
Mary and saw what [2]did [1]Jesus, believed
εἰς αὐτόν. 46 τινὲς.δὲ ἐξ αὐτῶν ἀπῆλθον πρὸς τοὺς Φαρι-
on him; but some of them went to the Phari-

---

[l] ἐδύνατο LTTrA. [m] ἐμβριμούμενος T. [n] — ὁ L[Tr]. [o] τετελευτηκότος LTTrAW. [p] ὄψῃ thou shouldest see LTTrAW. [q] — οὗ ἦν ὁ τεθνηκὼς κείμενος GLTTrA. [r] — καὶ GTTrA. [s] + αὐτὸν him T[Tr]A. [t] Μαριὰμ LTTrA. [v] ὃ TrA. [w] — ὁ Ἰησοῦς (read he did) GLTTrAW.

σαίους καὶ [x]εἶπον‖ αὐτοῖς [y]ἃ‖ ἐποίησεν [z]ὁ‖ Ἰησοῦς. 47 συνήγα-
sees and told them what [2]did [1]Jesus. Gathered

γον οὖν οἱ ἀρχιερεῖς καὶ οἱ Φαρισαῖοι συνέδριον, καὶ ἔλεγον,
therefore the chief priests and the Pharisees a council, and said,

Τί ποιοῦμεν; ὅτι οὗτος ὁ ἄνθρωπος πολλὰ [a]σημεῖα ποιεῖ.‖
What do we? for this man many signs does.

48 ἐὰν ἀφῶμεν αὐτὸν οὕτως, πάντες πιστεύσουσιν εἰς αὐτόν·
If we let alone him thus, all will believe on him,

καὶ ἐλεύσονται οἱ Ῥωμαῖοι καὶ ἀροῦσιν ἡμῶν καὶ τὸν τόπον
and will come the Romans and will take away from us both the place

καὶ τὸ ἔθνος. 49 Εἷς.δέ.τις ἐξ αὐτῶν, Καϊάφας, ἀρχιερεὺς
and the nation. But a certain one of them, Caiaphas, high priest

ὢν τοῦ.ἐνιαυτοῦ.ἐκείνου, εἶπεν αὐτοῖς, Ὑμεῖς οὐκ οἴδατε
being of that year, said to them, Ye know

οὐδέν, 50 οὐδὲ [b]διαλογίζεσθε‖ ὅτι συμφέρει [c]ἡμῖν‖ ἵνα εἷς
nothing, nor consider that it is profitable for us that one

ἄνθρωπος ἀποθάνῃ ὑπὲρ τοῦ λαοῦ, καὶ μὴ ὅλον τὸ ἔθνος
man should die for the people, and not [2]whole [1]the nation

ἀπόληται. 51 Τοῦτο.δὲ ἀφ' ἑαυτοῦ οὐκ.εἶπεν, ἀλλὰ ἀρχ-
should perish. But this from himself he said not, but high

ιερεὺς ὢν τοῦ.ἐνιαυτοῦ.ἐκείνου, [d]προεφήτευσεν‖ ὅτι [e]ἔμελλεν‖
priest being of that year, prophesied that [2]was [3]about

[f]ὁ‖ Ἰησοῦς ἀποθνήσκειν ὑπὲρ τοῦ ἔθνους, 52 καὶ οὐχ ὑπὲρ
[1]Jesus to die for the nation; and not for

τοῦ ἔθνους μόνον, ἀλλ' ἵνα καὶ τὰ τέκνα τοῦ θεοῦ τὰ διεσκορ-
the nation only, but that also the children of God who have been

πισμένα συναγάγῃ εἰς ἕν. 53 ἀπ' ἐκείνης οὖν
scattered abroad he might gather together into one. From that [2]therefore

τῆς ἡμέρας [g]συνεβουλεύσαντο‖ ἵνα ἀποκτείνωσιν αὐτόν.
[1]day they took counsel together that they might kill him.

54 [h]Ἰησοῦς οὖν‖ [i]οὐκ. ἔτι‖ παῤῥησίᾳ περιεπάτει ἐν τοῖς
Jesus therefore no longer publicly walked among the

Ἰουδαίοις, ἀλλὰ ἀπῆλθεν ἐκεῖθεν εἰς τὴν χώραν ἐγγὺς τῆς
Jews, but went away thence into the country near the

ἐρήμου, εἰς Ἐφραῒμ λεγομένην πόλιν, κἀκεῖ [k]διέτριβεν‖
desert, to [4]Ephraim [3]called [1]a [2]city, and there he stayed

μετὰ τῶν.μαθητῶν.[l]αὐτοῦ.‖
with his disciples.

55 Ἦν.δὲ ἐγγὺς τὸ πάσχα τῶν Ἰουδαίων, καὶ ἀνέβησαν
Now [6]was [7]near [1]the [2]passover [3]of [4]the [5]Jews, and went up

πολλοὶ εἰς Ἱεροσόλυμα ἐκ τῆς χώρας πρὸ τοῦ πάσχα, ἵνα
many to Jerusalem out of the country before the passover, that

ἁγνίσωσιν ἑαυτούς. 56 ἐζήτουν οὖν τὸν Ἰησοῦν, καὶ
they might purify themselves. They were seeking therefore Jesus, and

[m]ἔλεγον‖ μετ' ἀλλήλων ἐν τῷ ἱερῷ ἑστηκότες, Τί δοκεῖ
were saying among one another in the temple standing, What does it seem

ὑμῖν, ὅτι οὐ.μὴ ἔλθῃ εἰς τὴν ἑορτήν; 57 Δεδώκεισαν.δὲ
to you, that in no wise he will come to the feast? Now had given

[n]καὶ‖ οἱ ἀρχιερεῖς καὶ οἱ Φαρισαῖοι [o]ἐντολήν,‖ ἵνα ἐάν τις
both the chief priests and the Pharisees a command, that if anyone

γνῷ ποῦ ἐστιν μηνύσῃ, ὅπως πιάσωσιν αὐτόν.
should know where he is he should shew [it], that they might take him.

them what things Jesus had done. 47 Then gathered the chief priests and the Pharisees a council, and said, What do we? for this man doeth many miracles. 48 If we let him thus alone, all *men* will believe on him: and the Romans shall come and take away both our place and nation. 49 And one of them, *named* Caiaphas, being the high priest that same year, said unto them, Ye know nothing at all, 50 nor consider that it is expedient for us, that one man should die for the people, and that the whole nation perish not. 51 And this spake he not of himself: but being high priest that year, he prophesied that Jesus should die for that nation; 52 and not for that nation only, but that also he should gather together in one the children of God that were scattered abroad. 53 Then from that day forth they took counsel together for to put him to death. 54 Jesus therefore walked no more openly among the Jews; but went thence unto a country near to the wilderness, into a city called Ephraim, and there continued with his disciples.

55 And the Jews' passover was nigh at hand: and many went out of the country up to Jerusalem before the passover, to purify themselves. 56 Then sought they for Jesus, and spake among themselves, as they stood in the temple, What think ye, that he will not come to the feast? 57 Now both the chief priests and the Pharisees had given a commandment, that, if any man knew where he were, he should shew *it*, that they might take him.

---

[x] εἶπαν T. [y] ὃ L. [z] — ὁ LTTrA. [a] ποιεῖ σημεῖα LTTrAW. [b] λογίζεσθε LTTrAW. [c] ὑμῖν for you TTrA. [d] ἐπροφήτευσεν LTTrAW. [e] ἤμελλεν LTTrAW. [f] — ὁ GLTTrAW. [g] ἐβουλεύσαντο they took counsel LTTr. [h] ὁ οὖν Ἰησοῦς TrA. [i] οὐκέτι GLTTr. [k] ἔμεινεν TrA. [l] — αὐτοῦ (*read* the disciples) TTrA. [m] ἔλεγαν T. [n] — καὶ LTTrAW. [o] ἐντολὰς commands TTrA.

XII. Then Jesus six days before the passover came to Bethany, where Lazarus was which had been dead, whom he raised from the dead. 2 There they made him a supper; and Martha served: but Lazarus was one of them that sat at the table with him. 3 Then took Mary a pound of ointment of spikenard, very costly, and anointed the feet of Jesus, and wiped his feet with her hair: and the house was filled with the odour of the ointment. 4 Then saith one of his disciples, Judas Iscariot, Simon's *son*, which should betray him, 5 Why was not this ointment sold for three hundred pence, and given to the poor? 6 This he said, not that he cared for the poor; but because he was a thief, and had the bag, and bare what was put therein. 7 Then said Jesus, Let her alone: against the day of my burying hath she kept this. 8 For the poor always ye have with you; but me ye have not always.

12 Ὁ.οὖν.Ἰησοῦς πρὸ ἓξ ἡμερῶν τοῦ πάσχα ἦλθεν εἰς
Jesus therefore [3]before [1]six [2]days the passover came to
Βηθανίαν, ὅπου ἦν Λάζαρος [p]ὁ τεθνηκώς,ǁ ὃν ἤγειρεν
Bethany, where was Lazarus who had died, whom he raised
ἐκ νεκρῶν[q]. 2 ἐποίησαν οὖν αὐτῷ δεῖπνον ἐκεῖ,
from among [the] dead. They made therefore him a supper there,
καὶ ἡ Μάρθα διηκόνει· ὁ.δὲ.Λάζαρος εἷς ἦν [r] τῶν [s]συνανα-
and Martha served, but Lazarus one was of those re-
κειμένωνǁ αὐτῷ. 3 Ἡ.οὖν.[t]Μαρίαǁ λαβοῦσα λίτραν μύρου
clining with him. Mary therefore having taken a pound of ointment
νάρδου πιστικῆς πολυτίμου, ἤλειψεν τοὺς πόδας [v]τοῦǁ Ἰησοῦ,
of [2]nard [1]pure of great price, anointed the feet of Jesus,
καὶ ἐξέμαξεν ταῖς.θριξὶν.αὐτῆς τοὺς.πόδας.αὐτοῦ· ἡ.δὲ οἰκία
and wiped with her hair his feet; and the house
ἐπληρώθη ἐκ τῆς ὀσμῆς τοῦ μύρου. 4 λέγει [w]οὖνǁ [x]εἷς ἐκ
was filled with the odour of the ointment. Says therefore one of
τῶν.μαθητῶν.αὐτοῦ, Ἰούδας, Σίμωνος Ἰσκαριώτης,ǁ ὁ
his disciples, Judas, Simon's [son] Iscariote, who
μέλλων αὐτὸν παραδιδόναι, 5 [y]Διατίǁ τοῦτο τὸ μύρον οὐκ
was about him to deliver up, Why [3]this [4]ointment [2]not
ἐπράθη τριακοσίων δηναρίων, καὶ ἐδόθη πτωχοῖς; 6 Εἶπεν
[1]was sold for three hundred denarii, and given to [the] poor? [2]he [3]said
δὲ τοῦτο, οὐχ ὅτι περὶ τῶν πτωχῶν ἔμελεν.αὐτῷ, ἀλλ' ὅτι
[1]but this, not that for the poor he was caring, but because
κλέπτης ἦν, καὶ τὸ γλωσσόκομον [z]εἶχεν, καὶǁ τὰ βαλλόμενα
a thief he was, and the bag had, and what was put into
ἐβάσταζεν. 7 εἶπεν οὖν ὁ Ἰησοῦς, Ἄφες αὐτήν· [a] εἰς
[it] carried. [3]Said [2]therefore [1]Jesus, Let [2]alone [1]her: for
τὴν ἡμέραν τοῦ.ἐνταφιασμοῦ.μου [b]τετήρηκενǁ αὐτό. 8 τοὺς
the day of my burial has she kept it: [2]the
πτωχοὺς γὰρ πάντοτε ἔχετε μεθ' ἑαυτῶν, ἐμὲ.δὲ οὐ πάντοτε
[3]poor [1]for always ye have with you, but me not always
ἔχετε.
ye have.

9 Much people of the Jews therefore knew that he was there: and they came not for Jesus' sake only, but that they might see Lazarus also, whom he had raised from the dead. 10 But the chief priests consulted that they might put Lazarus also to death; 11 because that by reason of him many of the Jews went away, and believed on Jesus.

9 Ἔγνω οὖν [c] ὄχλος πολὺς ἐκ τῶν Ἰουδαίων ὅτι ἐκεῖ
[7]Knew [8]therefore [1]a [3]crowd [2]great [4]of [5]the [6]Jews that there
ἐστιν, καὶ ἦλθον, οὐ διὰ τὸν Ἰησοῦν μόνον, ἀλλ' ἵνα
he is; and they came, not because of Jesus only, but that
καὶ τὸν Λάζαρον ἴδωσιν ὃν ἤγειρεν ἐκ νεκρῶν.
also Lazarus they might see whom he raised from among [the] dead.
10 ἐβουλεύσαντο.δὲ οἱ ἀρχιερεῖς ἵνα καὶ τὸν Λάζαρον ἀπο-
But [4]took [5]counsel [1]the [2]chief [3]priests that also Lazarus they
κτείνωσιν, 11 ὅτι πολλοὶ δι' αὐτὸν ὑπῆγον
might kill, because many [4]by [5]reason [6]of [7]him [8]were [9]going [10]away
τῶν Ἰουδαίων καὶ ἐπίστευον εἰς τὸν Ἰησοῦν.
[1]of [2]the [3]Jews and were believing on Jesus.

12 On the next day much people that were come to the feast, when they heard that Jesus was coming to Jerusalem, 13 took branches of palm trees, and went forth to meet him, and

12 Τῇ.ἐπαύριον ὄχλος πολὺς ὁ ἐλθὼν εἰς τὴν ἑορτήν,
On the morrow a [2]crowd [1]great who came to the feast,
ἀκούσαντες ὅτι ἔρχεται [d]ὁǁ Ἰησοῦς εἰς Ἱεροσόλυμα, 13 ἔλα-
having heard that [2]is [3]coming [1]Jesus into Jerusalem, took
βον τὰ βαΐα τῶν φοινίκων καὶ ἐξῆλθον εἰς ὑπάντησιν [e]αὐτῷ,ǁ
branches of the palms and went out to meet him,

[p] — ὁ τεθνηκὼς [L]T[TrA]. [q] + ὁ (— ὁ T) Ἰησοῦς Jesus (raised) LTTrAW. [r] + ἐκ of (those) TA. [s] ἀνακειμένων σὺν GLTTrAW. [t] Μαριὰμ Tr. [v] [τοῦ] Tr. [w] δὲ but (says) T. [x] Ἰούδας ὁ Ἰσκαριώτης εἷς ἐκ (— ἐκ Tr) τῶν μαθητῶν αὐτοῦ TTrA. [y] Διὰ τί LTrA. [z] ἔχων having TTrA. [a] + ἵνα that LTTrAW. [b] τηρήσῃ she may keep LTTrAW. [c] + ὁ the (crowd) T. [d] — ὁ GLTTrAW. [e] αὐτῶν them W

καὶ [f]ἔκραζον,‖ [g]Ὡσαννά, εὐλογημένος ὁ ἐρχόμενος ἐν
and were crying, Hosanna, blessed [is] he who comes in [the]
ὀνόματι κυρίου, [h] ὁ βασιλεὺς τοῦ Ἰσραήλ. 14 Εὑρὼν δὲ
name of [the] Lord, the king of Israel. [3]Having [4]found [1]and
ὁ Ἰησοῦς ὀνάριον ἐκάθισεν ἐπ' αὐτό, καθώς ἐστιν γεγραμ-
[2]Jesus a young ass sat upon it, as it is writ-
μένον, 15 Μὴ.φοβοῦ, [i]θύγατερ‖ Σιών· ἰδού, ὁ.βασιλεύς.σου
ten, Fear not, daughter of Sion: behold, thy king
ἔρχεται, καθήμενος ἐπὶ πῶλον ὄνου 16 ταῦτα [k]δὲ‖ οὐκ
comes, sitting on a colt of an ass. [2]These [3]things [1]now [7]not
ἔγνωσαν [l]οἱ.μαθηταὶ.αὐτοῦ‖ τὸ.πρῶτον, ἀλλ' ὅτε ἐδοξάσθη
[8]knew [4]his [5]disciples at the first, but when was glorified
[m]ὁ‖ Ἰησοῦς τότε ἐμνήσθησαν ὅτι ταῦτα ἦν ἐπ' αὐτῷ
Jesus then they remembered that these things were of him
γεγραμμένα, καὶ ταῦτα ἐποίησαν αὐτῷ. 17 ἐμαρτύρει οὖν
written, and these things they did to him. Bore witness therefore
ὁ ὄχλος ὁ ὢν μετ' αὐτοῦ, [n]ὅτε‖ τὸν Λάζαρον ἐφώνησεν ἐκ
the crowd that was with him, when Lazarus he called out of
τοῦ μνημείου, καὶ ἤγειρεν αὐτὸν ἐκ νεκρῶν. 18 διὰ
the tomb, and raised him from among [the] dead. On account of
τοῦτο [o]καὶ‖ ὑπήντησεν αὐτῷ ὁ ὄχλος, ὅτι [p]ἤκουσεν‖ τοῦτο
this also met him the crowd, because it heard [5]this
αὐτὸν.πεποιηκέναι τὸ σημεῖον. 19 οἱ οὖν Φαρισαῖοι [q]εἶπον‖
[1]of [2]his [3]having [4]done sign. The [2]therefore [1]Pharisees said
πρὸς ἑαυτούς, Θεωρεῖτε ὅτι οὐκ ὠφελεῖτε οὐδέν; ἴδε, ὁ κόσμος
among themselves, Do ye see that ye gain nothing? lo, the world
ὀπίσω αὐτοῦ ἀπῆλθεν.
after him is gone.

20 Ἦσαν.δέ [r]τινες Ἕλληνες‖ ἐκ τῶν ἀναβαινόντων ἵνα
And there were certain Greeks among those coming up that
[s]προσκυνήσωσιν‖ ἐν τῇ ἑορτῇ· 21 οὗτοι οὖν προσῆλθον
they might worship in the feast; these therefore came
Φιλίππῳ, τῷ ἀπὸ Βηθσαϊδὰ τῆς Γαλιλαίας, καὶ ἠρώτων
to Philip, who was from Bethsaida of Galilee, and they asked
αὐτὸν λέγοντες, Κύριε, θέλομεν τὸν Ἰησοῦν ἰδεῖν. 22 [v]Ἔρχε-
him saying, Sir, we desire [3]Jesus [1]to [2]see. [5]Comes
ται [t] Φίλιππος καὶ λέγει τῷ Ἀνδρέᾳ· [v]καὶ πάλιν‖ Ἀνδρέας
[4]Philip and tells Andrew, and again Andrew
καὶ Φίλιππος [w] λέγουσιν τῷ Ἰησοῦ. 23 ὁ.δὲ.Ἰησοῦς [x]ἀπε-
and Philip tell Jesus. But Jesus an-
κρίνατο‖ αὐτοῖς λέγων, Ἐλήλυθεν ἡ ὥρα ἵνα δοξασθῇ
swered them saying, [3]Has [4]come [1]the [2]hour that should be glorified
ὁ υἱὸς τοῦ ἀνθρώπου. 24 ἀμὴν ἀμὴν λέγω ὑμῖν, ἐὰν.μὴ ὁ
the Son of man. Verily verily I say to you, Unless the
κόκκος τοῦ σίτου πεσὼν εἰς τὴν γῆν ἀποθάνῃ, αὐτὸς μόνος
grain of wheat falling into the ground should die, it alone
μένει· ἐὰν.δὲ ἀποθάνῃ, πολὺν καρπὸν φέρει. 25 ὁ φιλῶν
abides; but if it should die, much fruit it bears. He that loves
τὴν.ψυχὴν.αὐτοῦ [y]ἀπολέσει‖ αὐτήν, καὶ ὁ μισῶν τὴν
his life shall lose it, and he that hates
ψυχὴν αὐτοῦ ἐν τῷ.κόσμῳ.τούτῳ εἰς ζωὴν αἰώνιον φυλάξει
[2]life [1]his in this world to life eternal shall keep

cried, Hosanna: Blessed is the King of Israel that cometh in the name of the Lord.
14 And Jesus, when he had found a young ass, sat thereon; as it is written, 15 Fear not, daughter of Sion: behold, thy King cometh, sitting on an ass's colt.
16 These things understood not his disciples at the first: but when Jesus was glorified, then remembered they that these things were written of him, and *that* they had done these things unto him.
17 The people therefore that was with him when he called Lazarus out of his grave, and raised him from the dead, bare record.
18 For this cause the people also met him, for that they heard that he had done this miracle. 19 The Pharisees therefore said among themselves, Perceive ye how ye prevail nothing? behold, the world is gone after him.

20 And there were certain Greeks among them that came up to worship at the feast:
21 the same came therefore to Philip, which was of Bethsaida of Galilee, and desired him, saying, Sir, we would see Jesus.
22 Philip cometh and telleth Andrew: and again Andrew and Philip tell Jesus. 23 And Jesus answered them, saying, The hour is come, that the Son of man should be glorified. 24 Verily, verily, I say unto you, Except a corn of wheat fall into the ground and die, it abideth alone: but if it die, it bringeth forth much fruit. 25 He that loveth his life shall lose it; and he that hateth his life in this world shall keep it unto life eternal. 26 If

---

[f] ἐκραύγαζον LTTrA. [g] + [λέγοντες] saying L. [h] + καὶ and TTrA. [i] θυγάτηρ LTTrAW.
[k] — δὲ [L]TTrA. [l] αὐτοῦ οἱ μαθηταὶ T. [m] — ὁ TTrAW. [n] ὅτι because EGLTW.
[o] — καὶ Tr. [p] ἤκουσαν they heard GLTTrAW. [q] εἶπαν TTr. [r] Ἕλληνές τινες LTTrA.
[s] προσκυνήσουσιν they shall worship LTrA. [t] + ὁ TrA. [v] ἔρχεται (Andrew) comes LTTrA.
[w] + καὶ and LTTrA. [x] ἀποκρίνεται answers TTr. [y] ἀπολλύει loses TTr.

any man serve me, let him follow me; and where I am, there shall also my servant be: if any man serve me, him will *my* Father honour.

27 Now is my soul troubled; and what shall I say? Father, save me from this hour: but for this cause came I unto this hour.
28 Father, glorify thy name. Then came there a voice from heaven, *saying*, I have both glorified *it*, and will glorify *it* again.
29 The people therefore, that stood by, and heard *it*, said that it thundered: others said, An angel spake to him.
30 Jesus answered and said, This voice came not because of me, but for your sakes.
31 Now is the judgment of this world: now shall the prince of this world be cast out.
32 And I, if I be lifted up from the earth, will draw all *men* unto me.
33 This he said, signifying what death he should die.
34 The people answered him, We have heard out of the law that Christ abideth for ever: and how sayest thou, The Son of man must be lifted up? who is this Son of man?
35 Then Jesus said unto them, Yet a little while is the light with you. Walk while ye have the light, lest darkness come upon you: for he that walketh in darkness knoweth not whither he goeth.
36 While ye have light, believe in the light, that ye may be the children of light. These things spake Jesus, and departed, and did hide himself from them.
37 But though he had done so many miracles before them, yet they believed not on him:
38 that the saying of Esaias the prophet might be ful-

αὐτήν. 26 ἐὰν ἐμοὶ [z]διακονῇ τις,‖ ἐμοὶ ἀκολουθείτω· καὶ
it. If ³me ²serve ¹anyone, me let him follow; and
ὅπου εἰμὶ ἐγὼ ἐκεῖ καὶ ὁ διάκονος ὁ ἐμὸς ἔσται· [a]καὶ‖ ἐάν
where ²am ¹I there also ²servant ¹my shall be. And if
τις ἐμοὶ διακονῇ, τιμήσει αὐτὸν ὁ πατήρ.
anyone me serve, ²will ⁵honour ¹him ³the ⁴Father.
27 Νῦν ἡ.ψυχή.μου τετάρακται, καὶ τί εἴπω; Πάτερ,
Now my soul has been troubled, and what shall I say? Father,
σῶσόν με ἐκ τῆς.ὥρας.ταύτης.[b] ἀλλὰ διὰ τοῦτο ἦλθον
save me from this hour. But on account of this I came
εἰς τὴν.ὥραν.ταύτην. 28 Πάτερ, δόξασόν σου τὸ ὄνομα.
to this hour. Father, glorify thy name.
Ἦλθεν.οὖν φωνὴ ἐκ τοῦ οὐρανοῦ, Καὶ ἐδόξασα καὶ πάλιν
Therefore came a voice out of heaven, ²Both ¹I glorified and again
δοξάσω. 29 Ὁ.[c]οὖν‖.ὄχλος ὁ [d]ἑστὼς‖ [e]καὶ‖ ἀκούσας
will glorify [it]. Therefore the crowd which stood [there] and heard
ἔλεγεν βροντὴν.γεγονέναι. ἄλλοι ἔλεγον, Ἄγγελος αὐτῷ
said, Thunder there has been: others said, An angel to him
λελάληκεν. 30 Ἀπεκρίθη [f]ὁ‖ Ἰησοῦς καὶ εἶπεν, Οὐ δι' ἐμὲ
has spoken. ²Answered ¹Jesus and said, Not because of me
[g]αὕτη ἡ φωνὴ‖ γέγονεν, ἀλλὰ δι' ὑμᾶς. 31 νῦν κρίσις
this voice has come, but because of you. Now judgment
ἐστὶν τοῦ.κόσμου.τούτου· νῦν ὁ ἄρχων τοῦ.κόσμου.τούτου
is of this world; now the prince of this world
ἐκβληθήσεται ἔξω· 32 κἀγὼ ἐὰν ὑψωθῶ ἐκ τῆς γῆς, πάν-
shall be cast out: and I if I be lifted up from the earth, ³all
τας ἑλκύσω πρὸς ἐμαυτόν. 33 Τοῦτο.δὲ ἔλεγεν, σημαίνων
¹will ²draw to myself. But this he said, signifying
ποίῳ θανάτῳ ἤμελλεν ἀποθνήσκειν. 34 ἀπεκρίθη [h] αὐτῷ
by what death he was about to die. ³Answered ⁴him
ὁ ὄχλος, Ἡμεῖς ἠκούσαμεν ἐκ τοῦ νόμου ὅτι ὁ χριστὸς
¹the ²crowd, We heard out of the law that the Christ
μένει εἰς.τὸν.αἰῶνα, καὶ πῶς [i]σὺ λέγεις,‖ Ὅτι δεῖ ὑψωθῆναι
abides for ever, and how ²thou ¹sayest, that must be lifted up
τὸν υἱὸν τοῦ ἀνθρώπου; τίς ἐστιν οὗτος ὁ υἱὸς τοῦ ἀνθρώπου;
the Son of man? Who is this Son of man?
35 Εἶπεν οὖν αὐτοῖς ὁ Ἰησοῦς, Ἔτι μικρὸν χρόνον τὸ
³Said ²therefore ⁴to ⁵them ¹Jesus, Yet a little while the
φῶς [k]μεθ' ὑμῶν‖ ἐστιν. περιπατεῖτε [l]ἕως‖ τὸ φῶς ἔχετε, ἵνα
light with you is. Walk while the light ye have, that
μὴ σκοτία ὑμᾶς καταλάβῃ· καὶ ὁ περιπατῶν ἐν τῇ
⁵not ¹darkness ³you ²may ⁴overtake. And he who walks in the
σκοτίᾳ οὐκ.οἶδεν ποῦ ὑπάγει. 36 [l]ἕως‖ τὸ φῶς ἔχετε, πισ-
darkness knows not where he goes. While the light ye have, be-
τεύετε εἰς τὸ φῶς, ἵνα υἱοὶ φωτὸς γένησθε. Ταῦτα
lieve in the light, that sons of light ye may become. These things
ἐλάλησεν [m]ὁ‖ Ἰησοῦς, καὶ ἀπελθὼν ἐκρύβη ἀπ' αὐτῶν.
spoke Jesus, and going away was hid from them.
37 Τοσαῦτα.δὲ αὐτοῦ σημεῖα πεποιηκότος ἔμπροσθεν αὐτῶν
But [though] so many ²he ¹signs had done before them
οὐκ.ἐπίστευον εἰς αὐτόν, 38 ἵνα ὁ λόγος Ἡσαΐου τοῦ προ-
they believed not on him, that the word of Esaias the pro-

---

[z] τις διακονῇ LTTrAW. [a] — καὶ GLTTrA. [b] ταυτης; (*continue the question to the word* hour) GLTr. [c] [οὖν] LTr. [d] ἑστηκὼς L. [e] — καὶ T. [f] — ὁ TTrA. [g] ἡ φωνὴ αὕτη LTTrAW. [h] + οὖν therefore TA. [i] λέγεις σύ TTrA. [k] ἐν ὑμῖν among you GLTTrA. [l] ὡς LTTrA. [m] — ὁ LTTrA.

φήτου πληρωθῇ, ὃν εἶπεν, Κύριε, τίς ἐπίστευσεν τῇ
phet might be fulfilled, which he said, Lord, who believed
ἀκοῇ.ἡμῶν; καὶ ὁ βραχίων κυρίου τίνι ἀπεκαλύφθη;
our report? and the arm of [the] Lord to whom was it revealed?
39 Διὰ.τοῦτο οὐκ.ἠδύναντο πιστεύειν, ὅτι πάλιν εἶπεν
On this account they could not believe, because again said
Ἡσαΐας, 40 Τετύφλωκεν αὐτῶν τοὺς ὀφθαλμοὺς καὶ [n]πε-
Esaias, He has blinded their eyes and has
πώρωκεν‖ αὐτῶν τὴν καρδίαν· ἵνα μὴ.ἴδωσιν τοῖς ὀφ-
hardened their heart, that they should not see with the
θαλμοῖς καὶ νοήσωσιν τῇ καρδίᾳ καὶ [o]ἐπιστραφῶσιν,‖ καὶ
eyes and understand with the heart and be converted, and
[p]ἰάσωμαι‖ αὐτούς. 41 Ταῦτα εἶπεν Ἡσαΐας, [q]ὅτε‖ εἶδεν
I should heal them. These things said Esaias, when he saw
τὴν.δόξαν.αὐτοῦ, καὶ ἐλάλησεν περὶ αὐτοῦ. 42 ὅμως μέντοι
his glory, and spoke concerning him. Although indeed
καὶ ἐκ τῶν ἀρχόντων πολλοὶ ἐπίστευσαν εἰς αὐτόν·
even from among the rulers many believed on him,
ἀλλὰ διὰ τοὺς Φαρισαίους οὐχ.ὡμολόγουν, ἵνα μὴ
but on account of the Pharisees they confessed not, that not
ἀποσυνάγωγοι γένωνται. 43 ἠγάπησαν.γὰρ τὴν δόξαν
put out of the synagogue they might be; for they loved the glory
τῶν ἀνθρώπων μᾶλλον ἤπερ τὴν δόξαν τοῦ θεοῦ. 44 Ἰησοῦς
of men more than the glory of God. [2]Jesus
δὲ ἔκραξεν καὶ εἶπεν, Ὁ πιστεύων εἰς ἐμέ, οὐ.πιστεύει εἰς
[1]but cried and said, He that believes on me, believes not on
ἐμέ, [r]ἀλλ'‖ εἰς τὸν πέμψαντά με· 45 καὶ ὁ θεωρῶν ἐμέ,
me, but on him who sent me; and he that beholds me,
θεωρεῖ τὸν πέμψαντά με. 46 ἐγὼ φῶς εἰς τὸν κόσμον
beholds him who sent me. I a light into the world
ἐλήλυθα, ἵνα πᾶς ὁ πιστεύων εἰς ἐμὲ ἐν τῇ σκοτίᾳ μὴ
have come, that everyone that believes on me in the darkness [2]not
μείνῃ. 47 καὶ ἐάν τις μου ἀκούσῃ τῶν ῥημάτων καὶ μὴ
[1]may abide. And if anyone [4]of [5]me [1]hear [2]the [3]words and [2]not
[s]πιστεύσῃ,‖ ἐγὼ οὐ.κρίνω αὐτόν· οὐ.γὰρ.ἦλθον ἵνα κρίνω
[1]believe, I do not judge him, for I came not that I might judge
τὸν κόσμον, ἀλλ' ἵνα σώσω τὸν κόσμον. 48 ὁ ἀθετῶν
the world, but that I might save the world. He that rejects
ἐμὲ καὶ μὴ.λαμβάνων τὰ.ῥήματά.μου, ἔχει τὸν κρίνοντα
me and does not receive my words, has him who judges
αὐτόν· ὁ λόγος ὃν ἐλάλησα, ἐκεῖνος κρινεῖ αὐτὸν ἐν τῇ
him: the word which I spoke, that shall judge him in the
ἐσχάτῃ ἡμέρᾳ. 49 ὅτι ἐγὼ ἐξ ἐμαυτοῦ οὐκ.ἐλάλησα· ἀλλ'
last day; for I from myself spoke not, but
ὁ πέμψας με πατήρ, αὐτός μοι ἐντολὴν [t]ἔδωκεν‖ τί
the [2]who [3]sent [4]me [1]Father, himself me commandment gave what
εἴπω καὶ τί λαλήσω· 50 καὶ οἶδα ὅτι ἡ.ἐντολὴ.αὐτοῦ
I should say and what I should speak; and I know that his commandment
ζωὴ αἰώνιός ἐστιν· ἃ οὖν [v]λαλῶ ἐγώ,‖ καθὼς εἴρηκέν μοι
life eternal is. What therefore [2]speak [1]I, as has said to me
ὁ πατήρ, οὕτως λαλῶ.
the Father, so I speak.

13 Πρὸ.δὲ τῆς ἑορτῆς τοῦ πάσχα, εἰδὼς ὁ Ἰησοῦς ὅτι
Now before the feast of the passover, [2]knowing [1]Jesus that

filled, which he spake, Lord, who hath believed our report? and to whom hath the arm of the Lord been revealed? 39 Therefore they could not believe, because that Esaias said again, 40 He hath blinded their eyes, and hardened their heart; that they should not see with *their* eyes, nor understand with *their* heart, and be converted, and I should heal them. 41 These things said Esaias, when he saw his glory, and spake of him. 42 Nevertheless among the chief rulers also many believed on him; but because of the Pharisees they did not confess *him*, lest they should be put out of the synagogue: 43 for they loved the praise of men more than the praise of God. 44 Jesus cried and said, He that believeth on me, believeth not on me, but on him that sent me. 45 And he that seeth me seeth him that sent me. 46 I am come a light into the world, that whosoever believeth on me should not abide in darkness. 47 And if any man hear my words, and believe not, I judge him not: for I came not to judge the world, but to save the world. 48 He that rejecteth me, and receiveth not my words, hath one that judgeth him: the word that I have spoken, the same shall judge him in the last day. 49 For I have not spoken of myself; but the Father which sent me, he gave me a commandment, what I should say, and what I should speak. 50 And I know that his commandment is life everlasting: whatsoever I speak therefore, even as the Father said unto me, so I speak.

XIII. Now before the feast of the passover, when Jesus knew that

[n] ἐπώρωσεν hardened TTrA. [o] στραφῶσιν LTTrA. [p] ἰάσομαι I shall heal LTTrA. [q] ὅτι because GLTTrA. [r] ἀλλὰ LTTrA. [s] φυλάξῃ keep [them] LTTrAW. [t] δέδωκεν has given LTTrAW. [v] ἐγὼ λαλῶ LTTrA.

his hour was come that
he should depart out
of this world unto the
Father, having loved
his own which were in
the world, he loved
them unto the end.
2 And supper being
ended, the devil having
now put into the heart
of Judas Iscariot, Si-
mon's *son*, to betray
him; 3 Jesus knowing
that the Father had
given all things into
his hands, and that he
was come from God,
and went to God; 4 he
riseth from supper, and
laid aside his gar-
ments; and took a
towel, and girded him-
self. 5 After that he
poureth water into a
bason, and began to
wash the disciples' feet,
and to wipe *them* with
the towel wherewith
he was girded. 6 Then
cometh he to Simon
Peter: and Peter saith
unto him, Lord, dost
thou wash my feet?
7 Jesus answered and
said unto him, What I
do thou knowest not
now; but thou shalt
know hereafter. 8 Pe-
ter saith unto him,
Thou shalt never wash
my feet. Jesus answer-
ed him, If I wash thee
not, thou hast no part
with me. 9 Simon Peter
saith unto him, Lord,
not my feet only, but
also *my* hands and *my*
head. 10 Jesus saith to
him, He that is washed
needeth not save to
wash *his* feet, but is
clean every whit: and
ye are clean, but not
all. 11 For he knew
who should betray
him; therefore said he,
Ye are not all clean.
12 So after he had
washed their feet, and
had taken his gar-
ments, and was set
down again, he said
unto them, Know ye
what I have done to
you? 13 Ye call me

[w]ἐλήλυθεν‖ αὐτοῦ ἡ ὥρα ἵνα μεταβῇ ἐκ τοῦ.κόσμου.τού-
has come his hour that he should depart out of this world
του πρὸς τὸν πατέρα, ἀγαπήσας τοὺς.ἰδίους τοὺς ἐν τῷ
to the Father, having loved his own which [were] in the
κόσμῳ εἰς τέλος ἠγάπησεν αὐτούς. 2 καὶ δείπνου [x]γενο-
world to [the] end he loved them. And supper taking
μένου,‖ τοῦ διαβόλου ἤδη βεβληκότος εἰς τὴν καρδίαν
place, the devil already having put into the heart
[y]Ἰούδα Σίμωνος Ἰσκαριώτου, ἵνα αὐτὸν παραδῷ,‖
of Judas, Simon's [son] Iscariote, that him he should deliver up,
3 εἰδὼς [z]ὁ Ἰησοῦς‖ ὅτι πάντα [a]δέδωκεν‖ αὐτῷ ὁ πατὴρ
[2]knowing [1]Jesus [3]that [9]all [10]things [6]has [7]given [8]him [4]the [5]Father
εἰς τὰς χεῖρας, καὶ ὅτι ἀπὸ θεοῦ ἐξῆλθεν καὶ πρὸς τὸν
into [his] hands, and that from God he came out and to
θεὸν ὑπάγει, 4 ἐγείρεται ἐκ τοῦ δείπνου καὶ τίθησιν τὰ
God goes, he rises from the supper and lays aside [his]
ἱμάτια, καὶ λαβὼν λέντιον διέζωσεν ἑαυτόν· 5 εἶτα βάλ-
garments and having taken a towel he girded himself: afterwards he
λει ὕδωρ εἰς τὸν νιπτῆρα, καὶ ἤρξατο νίπτειν τοὺς πόδας
pours water into the washing-basin, and began to wash the feet
τῶν μαθητῶν, καὶ ἐκμάσσειν τῷ λεντίῳ ᾧ ἦν
of the disciples, and to wipe [them] with the towel with which he was
διεζωσμένος. 6 ἔρχεται οὖν πρὸς Σίμωνα Πέτρον· [b]καὶ‖
girded, He comes therefore to Simon Peter, and
λέγει αὐτῷ [c]ἐκεῖνος,‖ Κύριε, σύ μου νίπτεις τοὺς πόδας;
[2]says [3]to [4]him [1]he, Lord, [2]thou [3]of [4]me [1]dost wash the feet?
7 Ἀπεκρίθη Ἰησοῦς καὶ εἶπεν αὐτῷ, Ὃ ἐγὼ ποιῶ σὺ οὐκ
[2]Answered [1]Jesus and said to him, What I do thou [2]not
οἶδας ἄρτι, γνώσῃ.δὲ μετὰ.ταῦτα. 8 Λέγει αὐτῷ Πέ-
[1]knowest now, but thou shalt know hereafter. [2]Says [3]to [4]him [1]Pe-
τρος, Οὐ.μὴ νίψῃς [d]τοὺς.πόδας.μου‖ εἰς.τὸν.αἰῶνα.
ter, In no wise mayest thou wash my feet for ever.
Ἀπεκρίθη [e]αὐτῷ ὁ Ἰησοῦς,‖ Ἐὰν.μὴ νίψω σε, οὐκ.ἔχεις
[2]Answered [3]him [1]Jesus, Unless I wash thee, thou hast not
μέρος μετ' ἐμοῦ. 9 Λέγει αὐτῷ Σίμων Πέτρος, Κύριε, μὴ
part with me. [3]Says [4]to [5]him [1]Simon [2]Peter, Lord, not
τοὺς.πόδας.μου μόνον, ἀλλὰ καὶ τὰς χεῖρας καὶ τὴν κεφαλήν.
my feet only, but also the hands and the head.
10 Λέγει αὐτῷ [f]ὁ‖ Ἰησοῦς, Ὁ λελουμένος [g]οὐ χρείαν
[2]Says [3]to [4]him [1]Jesus, He that has been laved [2]not [3]need
ἔχει‖ [h]ἢ‖ [i]τοὺς πόδας‖ νίψασθαι, ἀλλ' ἔστιν καθαρὸς
[1]has [other] than the feet to wash, but is clean
ὅλος· καὶ ὑμεῖς καθαροί ἐστε, ἀλλ' οὐχὶ πάντες. 11 ᾔδει.γὰρ
wholly; and ye clean are, but not all. For he knew
τὸν παραδιδόντα αὐτόν· διὰ τοῦτο εἶπεν, [k]Οὐχὶ πάν-
him who was delivering up him: on account of this he said, [3]Not [4]all
τες καθαροί ἐστε. 12 Ὅτε οὖν ἔνιψεν τοὺς.πόδας.αὐτῶν,
[5]clean [1]ye [2]are. When therefore he had washed their feet,
[l]καὶ‖ ἔλαβεν τὰ.ἱμάτια.αὐτοῦ, [m] [n]ἀναπεσὼν‖ πάλιν, εἶπεν
and taken his garments, having reclined again, he said
αὐτοῖς, Γινώσκετε τί πεποίηκα ὑμῖν; 13 ὑμεῖς φωνεῖτέ με
to them, Do ye know what I have done to you? Ye call me

[w] ἦλθεν was come LTTrA. [x] γινομένου TTr. [y] ἵνα παραδοῖ αὐτὸν Ἰούδας Σίμωνος Ἰσκαριώτης TTrA; Ἰούδα Σίμ. Ἰσκ. ἵνα παραδοῖ αὐτόν L. [z] — ὁ Ἰησοῦς (*read* [Jesus] [L]TTrA. [a] ἔδωκεν gave TTr. [b] — καὶ TTrA. [c] — ἐκεῖνος (*read* λέγει he says) LT[Tr]A. [d] μου τοὺς πόδας LTTrA. [e] Ἰησοῦς αὐτῷ LTTrA. [f] — ὁ T[Tr]. [g] οὐκ ἔχει χρείαν LTTrAW. [h] εἰ μὴ except LTrA; — ἢ T. [i] — τοὺς πόδας T. [k] + ὅτι LTTrA. [l] — καὶ L. [m] + καὶ LTTrA. [n] ἀνέπεσεν reclined TTrA.

ὁ διδάσκαλος καὶ ὁ κύριος, καὶ καλῶς λέγετε, εἰμὶ γάρ.
the Teacher and the Lord, and well ye say, [2]I [3]am [[4]so] [1]for.
14 εἰ οὖν ἐγὼ ἔνιψα ὑμῶν τοὺς πόδας, ὁ κύριος καὶ ὁ
If therefore I washed your feet, the Lord and the
διδάσκαλος, καὶ ὑμεῖς ὀφείλετε ἀλλήλων νίπτειν τοὺς πόδας.
Teacher, also ye ought of one another to wash the feet;
15 ὑπόδειγμα.γὰρ [o]ἔδωκα‖ ὑμῖν, ἵνα καθὼς ἐγὼ ἐποίησα ὑμῖν,
for an example I gave you, that as I did to you,
καὶ ὑμεῖς ποιῆτε. 16 ἀμὴν ἀμὴν λέγω ὑμῖν, οὐκ.ἔστιν δοῦλος
also ye should do. Verily verily I say to you, [3]Is [4]not [1]a [2]bondman
μείζων τοῦ.κυρίου.αὐτοῦ, οὐδὲ ἀπόστολος μείζων τοῦ.πέμψαν-
greater than his lord, nor a messenger greater than he who sent
τος αὐτόν. 17 εἰ ταῦτα οἴδατε, μακάριοί ἐστε ἐὰν ποιῆτε
him. If these things ye know, blessed are ye if ye do
αὐτά. 18 οὐ περὶ πάντων ὑμῶν λέγω· ἐγὼ[p] οἶδα [q]οὓς‖
them. Not of [2]all [1]you I speak. I know whom
ἐξελεξάμην· ἀλλ' ἵνα ἡ γραφὴ πληρωθῇ, Ὁ τρώγων
I chose, but that the scripture might be fulfilled, He that eats
[r]μετ' ἐμοῦ‖ τὸν ἄρτον [s]ἐπῆρεν‖ ἐπ' ἐμὲ τὴν.πτέρναν.αὐτοῦ.
[2]with [3]me [1]bread lifted up against me his heel.
19 [t]ἀπ'.ἄρτι‖ λέγω ὑμῖν πρὸ τοῦ.γενέσθαι, ἵνα [v]ὅταν γένη-
From this time I tell you, before it comes to pass, that when it come
ται, πιστεύσητε‖ ὅτι ἐγώ εἰμι. 20 ἀμὴν ἀμὴν λέγω ὑμῖν,
to pass, ye may believe that I am [he]. Verily verily I say to you,
Ὁ λαμβάνων [w]ἐάν‖.τινα πέμψω, ἐμὲ λαμβάνει· ὁ.δὲ
He that receives whomsoever I shall send, me receives; and he that
ἐμὲ λαμβάνων, λαμβάνει τὸν πέμψαντά με. 21 Ταῦτα
me receives, receives him who sent me. These things
εἰπὼν [x]ὁ‖ Ἰησοῦς ἐταράχθη τῷ πνεύματι, καὶ ἐμαρτύρησεν
saying Jesus was troubled in spirit, and testified
καὶ εἶπεν, Ἀμὴν ἀμὴν λέγω ὑμῖν, ὅτι εἷς ἐξ ὑμῶν παραδώσει
and said, Verily verily I say to you, that one of you will deliver up
με. 22 Ἔβλεπον [y]οὖν‖ εἰς ἀλλήλους οἱ μαθηταί, ἀπορού-
me. [4]Looked [3]therefore [5]upon [6]one [7]another [1]the [2]disciples, doubt-
μενοι περὶ τίνος λέγει. 23 ἦν.[z]δὲ‖ ἀνακείμενος εἷς [a] τῶν
ing of whom he speaks. But there was reclining one
μαθητῶν.αὐτοῦ ἐν τῷ κόλπῳ τοῦ.Ἰησοῦ, ὃν ἠγάπα ὁ Ἰησοῦς·
of his disciples in the bosom of Jesus, whom [2]loved [1]Jesus.
24 νεύει οὖν τούτῳ Σίμων Πέτρος [b]πυθέσθαι τίς
[6]Makes [7]a [8]sign [5]therefore [9]to [10]him [3]Simon [4]Peter to ask who
ἂν.εἴη‖ περὶ οὗ λέγει. 25 [c]ἐπιπεσὼν‖ [d]δὲ‖ ἐκεῖνος[e] ἐπὶ τὸ
it might be of whom he speaks. [3]Having [4]leaned [1]and [2]he on the
στῆθος τοῦ Ἰησοῦ, λέγει αὐτῷ, Κύριε, τίς ἐστιν; 26 Ἀπο-
breast of Jesus, says to him, Lord, who is it? [2]An-
κρίνεται[f] [g]ὁ‖ Ἰησοῦς, Ἐκεῖνός ἐστιν ᾧ ἐγὼ [h]βάψας‖ τὸ
swers [1]Jesus, He it is to whom I, having dipped the
ψωμίον [i]ἐπιδώσω.‖ [k]Καὶ ἐμβάψας‖ τὸ ψωμίον [l] δίδωσιν
morsel, shall give [it]. And having dipped the morsel he gives [it]
Ἰούδᾳ Σίμωνος [m]Ἰσκαριώτῃ.‖ 27 καὶ μετὰ τὸ ψωμίον,
to Judas, Simon's [son] Iscariote. And after the morsel,

Master and Lord: and ye say well; for *so* I am. 14 If I then, *your* Lord and Master, have washed your feet; ye also ought to wash one another's feet. 15 For I have given you an example, that ye should do as I have done to you. 16 Verily, verily, I say unto you, The servant is not greater than his lord; neither he that is sent greater than he that sent him. 17 If ye know these things, happy are ye if ye do them. 18 I speak not of you all: I know whom I have chosen: but that the scripture may be fulfilled, He that eateth bread with me hath lifted up his heel against me. 19 Now I tell you before it come, that, when it is come to pass, ye may believe that I am *he*. 20 Verily, verily, I say unto you, He that receiveth whomsoever I send receiveth me; and he that receiveth me receiveth him that sent me. 21 When Jesus had thus said, he was troubled in spirit, and testified, and said, Verily, verily, I say unto you, that one of you shall betray me. 22 Then the disciples looked one on another, doubting of whom he spake. 23 Now there was leaning on Jesus' bosom one of his disciples, whom Jesus loved. 24 Simon Peter therefore beckoned to him, that he should ask who it should be of whom he spake. 25 He then lying on Jesus' breast saith unto him, Lord, who is it? 26 Jesus answered, He it is, to whom I shall give a sop, when I have dipped *it*. And when he had dipped the sop, he gave *it* to Judas Iscariot, *the son* of Simon. 27 And after the sop

[o] δέδωκα I have given T. [p] + [γὰρ] for (I) L. [q] τίνας TTrA. [r] μου my TrA. [s] ἐπῆρκεν has lifted up T. [t] ἀπάρτι T. [v] πιστεύσητε (πιστεύητε Tr) ὅταν γένηται TTrA. [w] ἄν LTTrA. [x] — ὁ TTrA. [y] — οὖν T[Tr]A. [z] — δὲ but TTrA. [a] + ἐκ of (his) GLTTrAW. [b] καὶ λέγει αὐτῷ Εἰπὲ τίς ἐστιν and says to him, Say who it is LTTrA. [c] ἀναπεσὼν having leaned back LTrA. [d] — δὲ TrA; οὖν therefore T. [e] + οὕτως thus T[Tr]AW. [f] + οὖν therefore [L]A. [g] [ὁ] Tr. [h] ἐμβάψας L; βάψω shall dip TTrA. [i] καὶ δώσω αὐτῷ and shall give to him TTrA. [k] βάψας οὖν having dipped therefore TTrA. [l] + λαμβάνει καὶ he takes and TTrA. [m] Ἰσκαριώτου (*read* son of Simon Iscariote.) TTrA.

Satan entered into him. Then said Jesus unto him, That thou doest, do quickly. 28 Now no man at the table knew for what intent he spake this unto him. 29 For some *of them* thought, because Judas had the bag, that Jesus had said unto him, Buy *those things* that we have need of against the feast; or, that he should give something to the poor. 30 He then having received the sop went immediately out: and it was night.

31 Therefore, when he was gone out, Jesus said, Now is the Son of man glorified, and God is glorified in him. 32 If God be glorified in him, God shall also glorify him in himself, and shall straightway glorify him. 33 Little children, yet a little while I am with you. Ye shall seek me: and as I said unto the Jews, Whither I go, ye cannot come; so now I say to you. 34 A new commandment I give unto you, That ye love one another; as I have loved you, that ye also love one another. 35 By this shall all *men* know that ye are my disciples, if ye have love one to another. 36 Simon Peter said unto him, Lord, whither goest thou? Jesus answered him, Whither I go, thou canst not follow me now; but thou shalt follow me afterwards. 37 Peter said unto him, Lord, why cannot I follow thee now? I will lay down my life for thy sake. 38 Jesus answered him, Wilt thou lay down thy life for my sake? Verily, verily, I say unto thee, The cock shall not crow, till thou hast denied me thrice.

τότε εἰσῆλθεν εἰς ἐκεῖνον ὁ σατανᾶς. λέγει οὖν αὐτῷ [n]ὁ"
then entered into him Satan. [3]Says [2]therefore [4]to [5]him
Ἰησοῦς, Ὃ ποιεῖς, ποίησον τάχιον. 28 Τοῦτο.δὲ οὐδεὶς
[1]Jesus, What thou doest, do quickly. But this no one
ἔγνω τῶν ἀνακειμένων πρὸς.τί εἶπεν αὐτῷ. 29 τινὲς.γὰρ
knew of those reclining wherefore he spoke to him; for some
ἐδόκουν, ἐπεὶ τὸ γλωσσόκομον εἶχεν [o]ὁ" Ἰούδας, ὅτι λέγει
thought, since [3]the [4]bag [2]had [1]Judas, that [2]is [3]saying
αὐτῷ [p]ὁ" Ἰησοῦς, Ἀγόρασον ὧν χρείαν ἔχομεν εἰς
[4]to [5]him [1]Jesus, Buy what things need [of] we have for
τὴν ἑορτήν· ἢ τοῖς πτωχοῖς ἵνα τι δῷ. 30 λα-
the feast; or to the poor that something he should give. Having
βὼν οὖν τὸ ψωμίον ἐκεῖνος [q]εὐθέως ἐξῆλθεν·" ἦν.δὲ
received therefore the morsel he immediately went out; and it was
νύξ.
night.

31 Ὅτε [r] ἐξῆλθεν λέγει [s]ὁ" Ἰησοῦς, Νῦν ἐδοξάσθη
When he was gone out [2]says [1]Jesus, Now has been glorified
ὁ υἱὸς τοῦ ἀνθρώπου, καὶ ὁ θεὸς ἐδοξάσθη ἐν αὐτῷ. 32 [t]εἰ
the Son of man, and God has been glorified in him. If
ὁ θεὸς ἐδοξάσθη ἐν αὐτῷ," καὶ ὁ θεὸς δοξάσει αὐτὸν ἐν
God has been glorified in him, also God shall glorify him in
[v]ἑαυτῷ," καὶ εὐθὺς δοξάσει αὐτόν. 33 Τεκνία, ἔτι
himself, and immediately shall glorify him. Little children, yet
μικρὸν μεθ' ὑμῶν εἰμι. ζητήσετέ με, καὶ καθὼς εἶπον τοῖς
a little while with you I am. Ye will seek me; and, as I said to the
Ἰουδαίοις, Ὅτι ὅπου [w]ὑπάγω ἐγώ," ὑμεῖς οὐ.δύνασθε ἐλθεῖν,
Jews, That where [2]go [1]I, ye are not able to come,
καὶ ὑμῖν λέγω ἄρτι. 34 ἐντολὴν καινὴν δίδωμι ὑμῖν, ἵνα
also to you I say now. A [2]commandment [1]new I give to you, that
ἀγαπᾶτε ἀλλήλους· καθὼς ἠγάπησα ὑμᾶς, ἵνα καὶ ὑμεῖς
ye should love one another; according as I loved you, that [2]also [1]ye
ἀγαπᾶτε ἀλλήλους. 35 ἐν τούτῳ γνώσονται πάντες ὅτι ἐμοὶ
should love one another. By this shall [2]know [1]all that to me
μαθηταί ἐστε, ἐὰν ἀγάπην ἔχητε ἐν ἀλλήλοις. 36 Λέγει
disciples ye are, if love ye have among one another. [3]Says
αὐτῷ Σίμων Πέτρος, Κύριε, ποῦ ὑπάγεις; ἀπεκρίθη [x]αὐτῷ
[4]to [5]him [1]Simon [2]Peter, Lord, where goest thou? [2]Answered [3]him
ὁ" Ἰησοῦς, Ὅπου[y] ὑπάγω οὐ.δύνασαί μοι νῦν ἀκολουθῆσαι·
[1]Jesus, Where I go thou art not able me now to follow,
[z]ὕστερον.δὲ ἀκολουθήσεις μοι." 37 Λέγει αὐτῷ [a]ὁ" Πέτρος,
but afterwards thou shalt follow me. [2]Says [3]to [4]him [1]Peter,
Κύριε, [b]διατί" οὐ.δύναμαί σοι [c]ἀκολουθῆσαι" ἄρτι; τὴν ψυχήν
Lord, why am I not able thee to follow now? [2]life
μου ὑπὲρ σοῦ θήσω. 38 [d]Ἀπεκρίθη αὐτῷ ὁ" Ἰησοῦς,
[1]my for thee I will lay down. [2]Answered [3]him [1]Jesus,
Τὴν.ψυχήν.σου ὑπὲρ ἐμοῦ θήσεις; ἀμὴν ἀμὴν λέγω
Thy life for me thou wilt lay down! Verily verily I say
σοι, οὐ.μὴ ἀλέκτωρ [e]φωνήσει" ἕως.οὗ [f]ἀπαρνήσῃ" με
to thee, in no wise [the] cock will crow until thou wilt deny me
τρίς.
thrice.

---

[n] — ὁ TTrA. [o] — ὁ LTTrA. [p] — ὁ T[Tr]A. [q] ἐξῆλθεν εὐθύς LTTrA. [r] + οὖν therefore ELTTrA. [s] — ὁ TTrA. [t] [εἰ ὁ θεὸς ἐδοξάσθη ἐν αὐτῷ] LTrA. [v] αὐτῷ TTr. [w] ἐγὼ ὑπάγω GLTTrAW. [x] — αὐτῷ ὁ LTTrA. [y] + ἐγὼ I (go) T. [z] ἀκολουθήσεις δὲ ὕστερον LTTrA. [a] — ὁ GLTTrAW. [b] διὰ τί LTrA. [c] ἀκολουθεῖν Tr. [d] ἀποκρίνεται answers LTTrAW. [e] φωνήσῃ LTTrA. [f] ἀρνήσῃ LTTrA.

14 Μὴ.ταρασσέσθω ὑμῶν ἡ καρδία· πιστεύετε εἰς τὸν θεόν,
Let not be troubled your heart; ye believe on God,
καὶ εἰς ἐμὲ πιστεύετε. 2 ἐν τῇ οἰκίᾳ τοῦ.πατρός.μου μοναὶ
also on me believe. In the house of my Father [2]abodes
πολλαί εἰσιν· εἰ.δὲ.μή, εἶπον.ἂν ὑμῖν· [g]πορεύομαι ἑτοι-
[1]many there are; otherwise I would have told you; I go to pre-
μάσαι τόπον ὑμῖν. 3 καὶ ἐὰν.πορευθῶ [h]καὶ‖ ἑτοιμάσω [i]ὑμῖν
pare a place for you; and if I go and prepare for you
τόπον,‖ πάλιν ἔρχομαι καὶ [k]παραλήψομαι‖ ὑμᾶς πρὸς ἐμαυ-
a place, again I am coming and will receive you to my-
τόν· ἵνα ὅπου εἰμὶ ἐγώ, καὶ ὑμεῖς ἦτε. 4 καὶ ὅπου [l]ἐγὼ‖
self, that where [2]am [1]I [4]also [3]ye may be. And where I
ὑπάγω οἴδατε [m]καὶ‖ τὴν ὁδὸν [n]οἴδατε.‖ 5 Λέγει αὐτῷ Θωμᾶς,
go ye know and the way ye know. [2]Says [3]to [4]him [1]Thomas,
Κύριε, οὐκ.οἴδαμεν ποῦ ὑπάγεις, [o]καὶ‖ πῶς [p]δυνάμεθα τὴν
Lord, we know not where thou goest, and how can we the
ὁδὸν εἰδέναι;‖ 6 Λέγει αὐτῷ [q]ὁ‖ Ἰησοῦς, Ἐγώ εἰμι ἡ ὁδὸς
way know? [2]Says [3]to [4]him [1]Jesus, I am the way
καὶ ἡ ἀλήθεια καὶ ἡ ζωή· οὐδεὶς ἔρχεται πρὸς τὸν πατέρα
and the truth and the life. No one comes to the Father
εἰ.μὴ δι' ἐμοῦ. 7 εἰ [r]ἐγνώκειτέ με,‖ καὶ τὸν.πατέρα.μου
but by me. If ye had known me, also my Father
[s]ἐγνώκειτε.ἄν·‖ [t]καὶ‖ [v]ἀπ'.ἄρτι‖ γινώσκετε αὐτόν, καὶ ἑωρά-
ye would have known; and henceforth ye know him, and have
κατε [w]αὐτόν.‖ 8 Λέγει αὐτῷ Φίλιππος, Κύριε, δεῖξον ἡμῖν
seen him. [2]Says [3]to [4]him [1]Philip, Lord, shew us
τὸν πατέρα, καὶ ἀρκεῖ ἡμῖν. 9 Λέγει αὐτῷ ὁ Ἰησοῦς,
the Father, and it suffices us. [2]Says [3]to [4]him [1]Jesus,
[x]Τοσοῦτον χρόνον‖ μεθ' ὑμῶν εἰμι, καὶ οὐκ.ἔγνωκάς με,
So long a time with you am I, and thou hast not known me,
Φίλιππε; ὁ ἑωρακὼς ἐμέ, ἑώρακεν τὸν πατέρα· [y]καὶ‖ πῶς
Philip? He that has seen me, has seen the Father; and how
σὺ λέγεις, Δεῖξον ἡμῖν τὸν πατέρα; 10 οὐ.πιστεύεις ὅτι
[2]thou [1]sayest, Shew us the Father? Believest thou not that
ἐγὼ ἐν τῷ πατρί, καὶ ὁ πατὴρ ἐν ἐμοί ἐστιν; τὰ ῥήματα
I [am] in the Father, and the Father [2]in [3]me [1]is? The words
ἃ ἐγὼ [z]λαλῶ‖ ὑμῖν, ἀπ' ἐμαυτοῦ οὐ.λαλῶ· ὁ.δὲ πατὴρ
which I speak to you, from myself I speak not; but the Father
[a]ὁ‖ ἐν ἐμοὶ μένων [b]αὐτὸς ποιεῖ τὰ ἔργα‖ [c]. 11 πιστεύετέ μοι
who in me abides he does the works. Believe me
ὅτι ἐγὼ ἐν τῷ πατρί, καὶ ὁ πατὴρ ἐν ἐμοί[d]· εἰ.δὲ μή,
that I [am] in the Father, and the Father in me; but if not,
διὰ τὰ ἔργα αὐτὰ πιστεύετέ [e]μοι.‖ 12 Ἀμὴν ἀμὴν λέγω
because of the works themselves believe me. Verily verily I say
ὑμῖν, ὁ πιστεύων εἰς ἐμέ, τὰ ἔργα ἃ ἐγὼ ποιῶ, κἀκεῖνος
to you, He that believes on me, the works which I do, also he
ποιήσει, καὶ μείζονα τούτων ποιήσει, ὅτι ἐγὼ πρὸς τὸν
shall do, and greater than these he shall do, because I to
πατέρα.[f]μου‖ πορεύομαι. 13 καὶ ὅ.τι.ἂν αἰτήσητε ἐν τῷ
my Father go. And whatsoever ye may ask in

XIV. Let not your
heart be troubled: ye
believe in God, believe
also in me. 2 In my
Father's house are
many mansions: if *it*
were not *so*, I would
have told you. I go to
prepare a place for you.
3 And if I go and pre-
pare a place for you,
I will come again, and
receive you unto my-
self; that where I am,
there ye may be also.
4 And whither I go
ye know, and the way
ye know. 5 Thomas
saith unto him, Lord,
we know not whither
thou goest; and how
can we know the way?
6 Jesus saith unto him,
I am the way, the
truth, and the life: no
man cometh unto the
Father, but by me. 7 If
ye had known me, ye
should have known my
Father also: and from
henceforth ye know
him, and have seen
him. 8 Philip saith
unto him, Lord, shew
us the Father, and it
sufficeth us. 9 Jesus
saith unto him, Have I
been so long time with
you, and yet hast thou
not known me, Philip?
he that hath seen me
hath seen the Father;
and how sayest thou
then, Shew us the Fa-
ther? 10 Believest thou
not that I am in the
Father, and the Father
in me? the words that
I speak unto you I
speak not of myself:
but the Father that
dwelleth in me, he do-
eth the works. 11 Be-
lieve me that I *am* in
the Father, and the Fa-
ther in me: or else be-
lieve me for the very
works' sake. 12 Verily,
verily, I say unto you,
He that believeth on
me, the works that I
do shall he do also; and
greater *works* than
these shall he do; be-
cause I go unto my
Father. 13 And what-
soever ye shall ask in

---

[g] + ὅτι for LTTrAW. [h] — καὶ L. [i] τόπον ὑμῖν TTrA. [k] παραλήμψομαι LTTrA. [l] [ἐγὼ] L. [m] — καὶ [L]TTrA. [n] — οἴδατε [L]TTrA. [o] — καὶ LTr. [p] οἴδαμεν τὴν ὁδόν know we the way LTTrA. [q] — ὁ T. [r] ἐγνώκατε ἐμέ ye have known me T. [s] ἂν ᾔδειτε TrA; γνώσεσθε ye will know T. [t] — καὶ [L]TrA. [v] ἀπάρτι T. [w] [αὐτόν] LTrA. [x] τοσούτῳ χρόνῳ LT. [y] — καὶ LT[Tr]. [z] λέγω TTrA. [a] [ὁ] LTrA. [b] ποιεῖ τὰ ἔργα αὐτοῦ does his works TTrA. [c] + [αὐτοῦ] (*read* his works) L. [d] + ἐστίν is E. [e] — μοι T[Tr]. [f] — μου (*read* the father) LTTrA.

my name, that will I
do, that the Father
may be glorified in the
Son. 14 If ye shall
ask any thing in my
name, I will do it.
15 If ye love me, keep
my commandments.
16 And I will pray the
Father, and he shall
give you another Com-
forter, that he may
abide with you for
ever; 17 *even* the Spirit
of truth; whom the
world cannot receive,
because it seeth him
not, neither knoweth
him: but ye know him;
for he dwelleth with
you, and shall be in
you. 18 I will not
leave you comfortless:
I will come to you.
19 Yet a little while,
and the world seeth
me no more; but ye see
me: because I live, ye
shall live also. 20 At
that day ye shall know
that I *am* in my Fa-
ther, and ye in me, and
I in you. 21 He that
hath my command-
ments, and keepeth
them, he it is that lov-
eth me: and he that
loveth me shall be lov-
ed of my Father, and I
will love him, and will
manifest myself to
him. 22 Judas saith
unto him, not Iscariot,
Lord, how is it that
thou wilt manifest
thyself unto us, and
not unto the world?
23 Jesus answered and
said unto him, If a man
love me, he will keep
my words: and my Fa-
ther will love him, and
we will come unto
him, and make our a-
bode with him. 24 He
that loveth me not
keepeth not my say-
ings: and the word
which ye hear is not
mine, but the Fa-
ther's which sent me.
25 These things have I
spoken unto you, being
yet present with you.
26 But the Comforter,
which is the Holy
Ghost, whom the Fa-
ther will send in my
name, he shall teach
you all things, and
bring all things to
your remembrance,

ὀνόματί.μου, τοῦτο ποιήσω, ἵνα δοξασθῇ ὁ πατὴρ ἐν τῷ
my name, this will I do, that may be glorified the Father in the
υἱῷ. 14 ἐάν τι αἰτήσητε [g] ἐν τῷ.ὀνόματί.μου, ἐγὼ ποιήσω.
Son. If anything ye ask in my name, I will do [it].
15 ἐὰν ἀγαπᾶτέ με, τὰς ἐντολὰς τὰς ἐμὰς [h]τηρήσατε.‖
If ye love me, [2]commandments [1]my keep.
16 [i]καὶ ἐγὼ‖ ἐρωτήσω τὸν πατέρα, καὶ ἄλλον παράκλητον
And I will ask the Father, and another Paraclete
δώσει ὑμῖν, ἵνα [k]μένῃ μεθ' ὑμῶν εἰς.τὸν.αἰῶνα,‖ 17 τὸ
he will give you, that he may remain with you for ever, the
πνεῦμα τῆς ἀληθείας, ὃ ὁ κόσμος οὐ.δύναται λαβεῖν, ὅτι
Spirit of truth, whom the world cannot receive, because
οὐ.θεωρεῖ αὐτό, οὐδὲ γινώσκει [l]αὐτό·‖ ὑμεῖς.[m]δὲ‖ γινώσκετε
it does not see him, nor know him; but ye know
αὐτό, ὅτι παρ' ὑμῖν μένει, καὶ ἐν ὑμῖν [n]ἔσται.‖ 18 οὐκ.ἀφήσω
him, for with you he abides, and in you shall be. I will not leave
ὑμᾶς ὀρφανούς· ἔρχομαι πρὸς ὑμᾶς. 19 ἔτι μικρὸν καὶ ὁ
you orphans, I am coming to you. Yet a little while and the
κόσμος με [o]οὐκ ἔτι‖ θεωρεῖ, ὑμεῖς.δὲ θεωρεῖτέ με· ὅτι ἐγὼ
world me no longer sees, but ye see me: because I
ζῶ, καὶ ὑμεῖς [p]ζήσεσθε.‖ 20 ἐν ἐκείνῃ τῇ ἡμέρᾳ [q]γνώσεσθε
live, [2]also [1]ye shall live. In that day shall [2]know
ὑμεῖς‖ ὅτι ἐγὼ ἐν τῷ.πατρί.μου, καὶ ὑμεῖς ἐν ἐμοί, κἀγὼ
[1]ye that I [am] in my Father, and ye in me, and I
ἐν ὑμῖν· 21 ὁ ἔχων τὰς.ἐντολάς.μου καὶ τηρῶν αὐτάς,
in you. He that has my commandments and keeps them,
ἐκεῖνός ἐστιν ὁ ἀγαπῶν με· ὁ.δὲ ἀγαπῶν με, ἀγαπηθήσε-
he it is that loves me; but he that loves me, shall be loved
ται ὑπὸ τοῦ.πατρός.μου· [r]καὶ ἐγὼ‖ ἀγαπήσω αὐτόν, καὶ
by my Father; and I will love him, and
ἐμφανίσω αὐτῷ ἐμαυτόν. 22 Λέγει αὐτῷ Ἰούδας οὐχ
will manifest to him myself. [2]Says [3]to [4]him [1]Judas, (not
ὁ Ἰσκαριώτης, Κύριε, [s] τί γέγονεν ὅτι ἡμῖν μέλλεις
the Iscariote,) Lord, what has occurred that to us thou art about
ἐμφανίζειν σεαυτόν, καὶ οὐχὶ τῷ κόσμῳ; 23 Ἀπεκρίθη [t]ὁ‖
to manifest thyself, and not to the world? [2]Answered
Ἰησοῦς καὶ εἶπεν αὐτῷ, Ἐάν τις ἀγαπᾷ με, τὸν.λόγον.μου
[1]Jesus and said to him, If anyone love me, my word
τηρήσει, καὶ ὁ.πατήρ.μου ἀγαπήσει αὐτόν, καὶ πρὸς αὐτὸν
he will keep, and my Father will love him, and to him
ἐλευσόμεθα, καὶ μονὴν παρ' αὐτῷ [v]ποιήσομεν.‖ 24 ὁ μὴ
we will come, and an abode with him will make. He that [2]not
ἀγαπῶν με, τοὺς.λόγους.μου οὐ.τηρεῖ· καὶ ὁ λόγος ὃν
[1]loves me, my words does not keep; and the word which
ἀκούετε οὐκ.ἔστιν ἐμός, ἀλλὰ τοῦ πέμψαντός με πατρός.
ye hear is not mine, but of the [2]who [3]sent [4]me [1]Father.
25 Ταῦτα λελάληκα ὑμῖν παρ' ὑμῖν μένων· 26 ὁ.δὲ παρά-
These things I have said to you, with you abiding; but the Para-
κλητος, τὸ πνεῦμα τὸ ἅγιον, ὃ πέμψει ὁ πατὴρ ἐν τῷ
clete, the Spirit the Holy, whom [3]will [4]send [1]the [2]Father in
ὀνόματί.μου, ἐκεῖνος ὑμᾶς διδάξει πάντα, καὶ ὑπο-
my name, he [3]you [1]will [2]teach all things, and will bring to [2]re-

[g] + με me [L]T. [h] τηρήσετε ye will keep TTr. [i] κἀγὼ LTTrA. [k] μεθ' ὑμῶν εἰς τὸν αἰῶνα ᾖ he may be with you for ever L; μεθ' ὑμῶν ᾖ εἰς τὸν αἰῶνα T; ᾖ μεθ' ὑμῶν εἰς τὸν αἰῶνα TrA. [l] [αὐτό] L. [m] — δὲ but [L]T[Tr]A. [n] ἐστίν is LTrA. [o] οὐκέτι GLT. [p] ζήσετε TTrA. [q] ὑμεῖς ([ὑμεῖς] L) γνώσεσθε LTrA. [r] κἀγὼ LTTrAW. [s] + καὶ then GT[A]W. [t] — ὁ GLTTrAW. [v] ποιησόμεθα LTTrA.

μνήσει ὑμᾶς πάντα ἃ εἶπον ὑμῖν. 27 εἰρήνην ἀφίημι
membrance [1]your all things which I said to you. Peace I leave
ὑμῖν, εἰρήνην τὴν ἐμὴν δίδωμι ὑμῖν· οὐ καθὼς ὁ κόσμος
with you; [2]peace [1]my I give to you; not as the world
δίδωσιν, ἐγὼ δίδωμι ὑμῖν· μὴ.ταρασσέσθω ὑμῶν ἡ καρδία, μηδὲ
gives, [2]I [1]give to you. Let not be troubled your heart, nor
δειλιάτω. 28 ἠκούσατε ὅτι ἐγὼ εἶπον ὑμῖν, Ὑπάγω καὶ
let it fear. Ye heard that I said to you, I am going away and
ἔρχομαι πρὸς ὑμᾶς. εἰ ἠγαπᾶτέ με, ἐχάρητε.ἂν ὅτι
I am coming to you. If ye loved me, ye would have rejoiced that
[w]εἶπον,‖ Πορεύομαι πρὸς τὸν πατέρα· ὅτι ὁ.πατήρ.[x]μου‖
I said, I am going to the Father, for my Father
μείζων μου ἐστίν. 29 καὶ νῦν εἴρηκα ὑμῖν πρὶν γενέ-
[2]greater [3]than [4]I [1]is. And now I have told you before it comes to
σθαι, ἵνα ὅταν γένηται πιστεύσητε. 30 [y]οὐκ ἔτι‖
pass, that when it shall have come to pass ye may believe. No longer
πολλὰ λαλήσω μεθ' [z]ὑμῶν·‖ ἔρχεται.γὰρ ὁ τοῦ κόσμου
much I will speak with you, for comes the [2]of [4]world
[a]τούτου‖ ἄρχων, καὶ ἐν ἐμοὶ οὐκ ἔχει οὐδέν· 31 ἀλλ' ἵνα
[3]this [1]ruler, and in me he has nothing; but that
γνῷ ὁ κόσμος ὅτι ἀγαπῶ τὸν πατέρα, [b]καὶ‖ καθὼς
[3]may [4]know [1]the [2]world that I love the Father, and as
[c]ἐνετείλατό‖ μοι ὁ πατήρ, οὕτως ποιῶ· ἐγείρεσθε, ἄγωμεν
[3]commanded [4]me [1]the [2]Father, thus I do. Rise up, let us go
ἐντεῦθεν.
hence.

15 Ἐγώ εἰμι ἡ ἄμπελος ἡ ἀληθινή, καὶ ὁ.πατήρ.μου ὁ
I am the [2]vine [1]true, and my Father the
γεωργός ἐστιν. 2 πᾶν κλῆμα ἐν ἐμοὶ μὴ φέρον καρπόν,
husbandman is. Every branch in me not bearing fruit,
αἴρει αὐτό· καὶ πᾶν τὸ καρπὸν φέρον, καθαίρει αὐτὸ
he takes away it; and everyone that fruit bears, he cleanses it
ἵνα [d]πλείονα καρπὸν‖ φέρῃ. 3 ἤδη ὑμεῖς καθαροί ἐστε
that more fruit it may bear. Already ye clean are
διὰ τὸν λόγον ὃν λελάληκα ὑμῖν. 4 μείνατε ἐν ἐμοί,
by reason of the word which I have spoken to you. Abide in me,
κἀγὼ ἐν ὑμῖν. καθὼς τὸ κλῆμα οὐ.δύναται καρπὸν φέρειν ἀφ'
and I in you. As the branch is not able fruit to bear of
ἑαυτοῦ ἐὰν.μὴ [e]μείνῃ‖ ἐν τῇ ἀμπέλῳ, οὕτως οὐδὲ ὑμεῖς
itself unless it abide in the vine, so neither [can] ye
ἐὰν.μὴ ἐν ἐμοὶ [f]μείνητε.‖ 5 ἐγώ εἰμι ἡ ἄμπελος, ὑμεῖς τὰ
unless in me ye abide. I am the vine, ye [are] the
κλήματα. ὁ μένων ἐν ἐμοί, κἀγὼ ἐν αὐτῷ, οὗτος φέρει
branches. He that abides in me, and I in him, he bears
καρπὸν πολύν· ὅτι χωρὶς ἐμοῦ οὐ δύνασθε ποιεῖν οὐδέν.
[2]fruit [1]much; for apart from me ye are able to do nothing.
6 ἐὰν.μή τις [g]μείνῃ‖ ἐν ἐμοί, ἐβλήθη ἔξω ὡς τὸ κλῆμα, καὶ
Unless anyone abide in me, he is cast out as the branch, and
ἐξηράνθη, καὶ συνάγουσιν [h]αὐτὰ‖ καὶ εἰς [i]πῦρ βάλλουσιν, καὶ
is dried up, and they gather them and into a fire cast, and
καίεται. 7 ἐὰν μείνητε ἐν ἐμοί, καὶ τὰ.ῥήματά.μου ἐν ὑμῖν
it is burned. If ye abide in me, and my words in you

whatsoever I have said unto you. 27 Peace I leave with you, my peace I give unto you: not as the world giveth, give I unto you. Let not your heart be troubled, neither let it be afraid. 28 Ye have heard how I said unto you, I go away, and come *again* unto you. If ye loved me, ye would rejoice, because I said, I go unto the Father: for my Father is greater than I. 29 And now I have told you before it come to pass, that, when it is come to pass, ye might believe. 30 Hereafter I will not talk much with you: for the prince of this world cometh, and hath nothing in me. 31 But that the world may know that I love the Father; and as the Father gave me commandment, even so I do. Arise, let us go hence.

XV. I am the true vine, and my Father is the husbandman. 2 Every branch in me that beareth not fruit he taketh away: and every *branch* that beareth fruit, he purgeth it, that it may bring forth more fruit. 3 Now ye are clean through the word which I have spoken unto you. 4 Abide in me, and I in you. As the branch cannot bear fruit of itself, except it abide in the vine; no more can ye, except ye abide in me. 5 I am the vine, ye *are* the branches: He that abideth in me, and I in him, the same bringeth forth much fruit: for without me ye can do nothing. 6 If a man abide not in me, he is cast forth as a branch, and is withered; and men gather them, and cast *them* into the fire, and they are burned. 7 If ye abide in me, and my words abide in you,

---

[w] — εἶπον GLTTrAW. [x] — μου (*read* the Father) [L]TTrA. [y] οὐκέτι GLT. [z] ὑμῖν W. [a] — τούτου (*read* of the world) GLTTrAW. [b] [καὶ] L. [c] ἐντολὴν ἔδωκέν gave (me) commandment LTr. [d] καρπὸν πλείονα LTTrA. [e] μένῃ T. [f] μένητε LTTrA. [g] μενῃ LTr. [h] αὐτὸ it L. [i] + τὸ the (fire) TTrAW.

ye shall ask what ye
will, and it shall be
done unto you. 8 Here-
in is my Father glori-
fied, that ye bear much
fruit; so shall ye be my
disciples. 9 As the Fa-
ther hath loved me, so
have I loved you: con-
tinue ye in my love.
10 If ye keep my com-
mandments, ye shall
abide in my love; even
as I have kept my Fa-
ther's commandments,
and abide in his love.
11 These things have I
spoken unto you, that
my joy might remain
in you, and *that* your
joy might be full.
12 This is my com-
mandment, That ye
love one another, as
I have loved you.
13 Greater love hath
no man than this, that
a man lay down his
life for his friends.
14 Ye are my friends,
if ye do whatsoever
I command you.
15 Henceforth I call
you not servants; for
the servant knoweth
not what his lord do-
eth: but I have called
you friends; for all
things that I have
heard of my Father I
have made known unto
you. 16 Ye have not
chosen me, but I have
chosen you, and or-
dained you, that ye
should go and bring
forth fruit, and *that*
your fruit should re-
main: that whatsoever
ye shall ask of the Fa-
ther in my name, he
may give it you.
17 These things I com-
mand you, that ye love
one another. 18 If the
world hate you, ye
know that it hated me
before *it hated* you.
19 If ye were of the
world, the world would
love his own: but be-
cause ye are not of the
world, but I have cho-
sen you out of the
world, therefore the
world hateth you.
20 Remember the word
that I said unto you,
The servant is not
greater than his lord.
If they have persecut-
ed me, they will also
persecute you; if they

μείνῃ, ὃ.[k]ἐὰν" θέλητε [l]αἰτήσεσθε," καὶ γενήσεται ὑμῖν.
abide, whatever ye will ye shall ask, and it shall come to pass to you.
8 ἐν τούτῳ ἐδοξάσθη ὁ.πατήρ.μου, ἵνα καρπὸν πολὺν φέρητε,
In this is glorified my Father, that [2]fruit [1]much ye should bear,
καὶ [m]γενήσεσθε" ἐμοὶ μαθηταί. 9 καθὼς ἠγάπησέν με ὁ
and ye shall become [2]to [3]me [1]disciples. As loved me the
πατήρ, κἀγὼ [n]ἠγάπησα ὑμᾶς·" μείνατε ἐν τῇ ἀγάπῃ τῇ ἐμῇ.
Father, I also loved you: abide in [2]love [1]my.
10 ἐὰν τὰς.ἐντολάς.μου τηρήσητε, μενεῖτε ἐν τῇ.ἀγάπῃ.μου·
If my commandments ye keep, ye shall abide in my love,
καθὼς [o]ἐγὼ" [p]τὰς ἐντολὰς τοῦ.πατρός".[q]μου" τετήρηκα, καὶ
as I the commandments of my Father have kept, and
μένω αὐτοῦ ἐν τῇ ἀγάπῃ. 11 ταῦτα λελάληκα ὑμῖν, ἵνα
abide [2]his [1]in love. These things I have spoken to you, that
ἡ χαρὰ ἡ ἐμὴ ἐν ὑμῖν [r]μείνῃ," καὶ ἡ.χαρὰ.ὑμῶν πληρωθῇ.
[2]joy [1]my in you may abide, and your joy may be full.
12 αὕτη ἐστὶν ἡ ἐντολὴ ἡ ἐμή, ἵνα ἀγαπᾶτε ἀλλήλους,
This is [2]commandment [1]my, that ye love one another,
καθὼς ἠγάπησα ὑμᾶς. 13 μείζονα ταύτης ἀγάπην οὐδεὶς
as I loved you. Greater than this love no one
ἔχει, ἵνα [s]τις" τὴν.ψυχὴν.αὐτοῦ θῇ ὑπὲρ τῶν φίλων
has, that one his life should lay down for [2]friends
αὐτοῦ. 14 ὑμεῖς φίλοι μου ἐστὲ ἐὰν ποιῆτε [t]ὅσα" ἐγὼ
[1]his. Ye [2]friends [1]my are if ye practise whatsoever I
ἐντέλλομαι ὑμῖν. 15 οὐκέτι [v]ὑμᾶς λέγω" δούλους, ὅτι ὁ δοῦ-
command you. No longer you I call bondmen, for the bond-
λος οὐκ.οἶδεν τί ποιεῖ αὐτοῦ ὁ κύριος· ὑμᾶς.δὲ εἴρηκα
man knows not what [3]is [4]doing [1]his [2]master. But you I have called
φίλους, ὅτι πάντα ἃ ἤκουσα παρὰ τοῦ.πατρός.μου ἐγνώ-
friends, for all things which I heard of my Father I made
ρισα ὑμῖν. 16 οὐχ ὑμεῖς με ἐξελέξασθε, ἀλλ' ἐγὼ ἐξελεξάμην
known to you. [3]Not [1]ye [4]me [2]chose, but I chose
ὑμᾶς, καὶ ἔθηκα ὑμᾶς ἵνα ὑμεῖς ὑπάγητε καὶ καρπὸν φέ-
you, and appointed you that ye should go and fruit ye should
ρητε, καὶ ὁ.καρπὸς.ὑμῶν μένῃ· ἵνα ὅ.τι.ἂν αἰτήσητε τὸν
bear, and your fruit should abide; that whatsoever ye may ask the
πατέρα ἐν τῷ.ὀνόματί.μου δῷ ὑμῖν. 17 ταῦτα ἐντέλ-
Father in my name he may give you. These things I com-
λομαι ὑμῖν, ἵνα ἀγαπᾶτε ἀλλήλους. 18 Εἰ ὁ κόσμος ὑμᾶς
mand you, that ye love one another. If the world you
μισεῖ, γινώσκετε ὅτι ἐμὲ πρῶτον [w]ὑμῶν" μεμίσηκεν. 19 εἰ ἐκ
hates, ye know that me before you it has hated. If of
τοῦ κόσμου ἦτε, ὁ κόσμος ἂν.τὸ.ἴδιον.ἐφίλει· ὅτι.δὲ ἐκ τοῦ
the world ye were, the world would love its own; but because of the
κόσμου οὐκ.ἐστέ, ἀλλ' ἐγὼ ἐξελεξάμην ὑμᾶς ἐκ τοῦ κόσμου,
world ye are not, but I chose you out of the world,
διὰ τοῦτο μισεῖ ὑμᾶς ὁ κόσμος. 20 μνημονεύετε τοῦ
on account of this [3]hates [4]you [1]the [2]world. Remember the
λόγου οὗ ἐγὼ εἶπον ὑμῖν, Οὐκ.ἔστιν δοῦλος μείζων τοῦ
word which I said to you, [3]Is [4]not [1]a [2]bondman greater
κυρίου.αὐτοῦ. εἰ ἐμὲ ἐδίωξαν, καὶ ὑμᾶς διώξουσιν· εἰ
than his master. If me they persecuted, also you they will persecute; if

---

[k] ἂν L. [l] αἰτήσασθε ask ye LTTrAW. [m] γένησθε ye should become LTrA. [n] ὑμᾶς ἠγάπησα LTrA. [o] κἀγὼ I also T. [p] τοῦ πατρὸς (+ μου T) τὰς ἐντολὰς TA. [q] — μου (*read* the Father) LTA. [r] ᾖ may be LTTrA. [s] — τις T. [t] ἃ what LTTrA. [v] λεγω ὑμᾶς LTTrA. [w] — ὑμῶν T.

τον.λόγον.μου ἐτήρησαν, καὶ τὸν ὑμέτερον τηρήσουσιν. 21 ἀλλὰ
my word they kept, also yours they will keep. But
ταῦτα πάντα ποιήσουσιν [x]ὑμῖν‖ διὰ τὸ.ὄνομά.μου,
[2]these [3]things [1]all they will do to you on account of my name,
ὅτι οὐκ.οἴδασιν τὸν πέμψαντά με. 22 εἰ μὴ.ἦλθον καὶ
because they know not him who sent me. If I had not come and
ἐλάλησα αὐτοῖς, ἁμαρτίαν οὐκ.[y]εἶχον·‖ νῦν.δὲ πρόφασιν
spoken to them, sin they had not had; but now a pretext
οὐκ.ἔχουσιν περὶ τῆς.ἁμαρτίας.αὐτῶν. 23 ὁ ἐμὲ μισῶν, καὶ
they have not for their sin. He that [2]me [1]hates, [3]also
τον.πατέρα.μου μισεῖ. 24 εἰ τὰ ἔργα μὴ.ἐποίησα ἐν
[5]my [6]Father [4]hates. If [7]the [8]works [1]I [2]had [3]not [4]done [5]among
αὐτοῖς ἃ οὐδεὶς.ἄλλος [z]πεποίηκεν,‖ ἁμαρτίαν οὐκ.[a]εἶχον·‖
[6]them which no other one has done, sin they had not had;
νῦν.δὲ καὶ ἑωράκασιν καὶ μεμισήκασιν καὶ ἐμὲ καὶ τὸν πατέρα
but now both they have seen and have hated both me and [2]Father
μου· 25 ἀλλ' ἵνα πληρωθῇ ὁ λόγος ὁ [b]γεγραμμένος ἐν
[1]my. But that might be fulfilled the word that has been written in
τῷ.νόμῳ.αὐτῶν,‖ Ὅτι ἐμίσησάν με δωρεάν. 26 Ὅταν.[c]δὲ‖
their law, They hated me without cause. But when
ἔλθῃ ὁ παράκλητος, ὃν ἐγὼ πέμψω ὑμῖν παρὰ τοῦ πατρός,
is come the Paraclete, whom I will send to you from the Father,
τὸ πνεῦμα τῆς ἀληθείας, ὃ παρὰ τοῦ πατρὸς ἐκπορεύεται,
the Spirit of truth, who from the Father goes forth,
ἐκεῖνος μαρτυρήσει περὶ ἐμοῦ· 27 καὶ ὑμεῖς δὲ μαρ-
he will bear witness concerning me; [3]also [2]ye [1]and bear
τυρεῖτε, ὅτι ἀπ' ἀρχῆς μετ' ἐμοῦ ἐστε.
witness, because from [the] beginning with me ye are.

16 Ταῦτα λελάληκα ὑμῖν ἵνα μὴ.σκανδαλισθῆτε. 2 ἀπο-
These things I have spoken to you that ye may not be offended. Out of
συναγώγους ποιήσουσιν ὑμᾶς· ἀλλ' ἔρχεται ὥρα ἵνα πᾶς
the synagogues they will put you; but is coming an hour that everyone
ὁ ἀποκτείνας ὑμᾶς δόξῃ λατρείαν προσφέρειν τῷ θεῷ.
who kills you will think service to render to God;
3 καὶ ταῦτα ποιήσουσιν [d]ὑμῖν‖ ὅτι οὐκ.ἔγνωσαν τὸν πα-
and these things they will do to you because they know not the Fa-
τέρα οὐδὲ ἐμέ. 4 ἀλλὰ ταῦτα λελάληκα ὑμῖν, ἵνα ὅταν
ther nor me. But these things I have said to you, that when
ἔλθῃ ἡ ὥρα [e] μνημονεύητε [f]αὐτῶν‖ ὅτι ἐγὼ εἶπον
may have come the hour ye may remember them that I said [them]
ὑμῖν· ταῦτα.δὲ ὑμῖν ἐξ ἀρχῆς οὐκ.εἶπον ὅτι
to you. But these things to you from [the] beginning I did not say, because
μεθ' ὑμῶν ἤμην. 5 νῦν.δὲ ὑπάγω πρὸς τὸν πέμψαντά με,
with you I was. But now I go to him who sent me,
καὶ οὐδεὶς ἐξ ὑμῶν ἐρωτᾷ με, Ποῦ ὑπάγεις; 6 ἀλλ' ὅτι
and none of you asks me, Where goest thou? But because
ταῦτα λελάληκα ὑμῖν ἡ λύπη πεπλήρωκεν ὑμῶν τὴν
these things I have said to you grief has filled your
καρδίαν. 7 ἀλλ' ἐγὼ τὴν ἀλήθειαν λέγω ὑμῖν, συμφέρει
heart. But I the truth say to you, It is profitable
ὑμῖν ἵνα [g]ἐγὼ ἀπέλθω· ἐὰν.γὰρ μὴ.ἀπέλθω ὁ παράκλη-
for you that I should go away; for if I go not away the Paraclete
τος [h]οὐκ.ἐλεύσεται‖ πρὸς ὑμᾶς· ἐὰν.δὲ πορευθῶ, πέμψω
will not come to you; but if I go, I will send

have kept my saying,
they will keep yours
also. 21 But all these
things will they do un-
to you for my name's
sake, because they
know not him that
sent me. 22 If I had
not come and spoken
unto them, they had
not had sin: but now
they have no cloke for
their sin. 23 He that
hateth me hateth my
Father also. 24 If I had
not done among them
the works which none
other man did, they
had not had sin: but
now have they both
seen and hated both
me and my Father.
25 But *this cometh to
pass*, that the word
might be fulfilled that
is written in their law,
They hated me with-
out a cause. 26 But
when the Comforter is
come, whom I will
send unto you from the
Father, *even* the Spirit
of truth, which pro-
ceedeth from the Fa-
ther, he shall testify of
me: 27 and ye also
shall bear witness, be-
cause ye have been
with me from the be-
ginning.

XVI. These things
have I spoken unto
you, that ye should not
be offended. 2 They
shall put you out of
the synagogues: yea,
the time cometh, that
whosoever killeth you
will think that he do-
eth God service. 3 And
these things will they
do unto you, because
they have not known
the Father, nor me.
4 But these things have
I told you, that when
the time shall come, ye
may remember that I
told you of them. And
these things I said not
unto you at the begin-
ning, because I was
with you. 5 But now I
go my way to him that
sent me; and none of
you asketh me, Whi-
ther goest thou? 6 But
because I have said
these things unto you,
sorrow hath filled your
heart. 7 Nevertheless
I tell you the truth;
It is expedient for you
that I go away: for
if I go not away, the
Comforter will not
come unto you; but if
I depart, I will send

[x] εἰς ὑμᾶς to you LTTrA. [y] εἴχοσαν LTTrA. [z] ἐποίησεν did LTTrA. [a] εἴχοσαν LTTrA. [b] ἐν τῷ νόμῳ αὐτῶν γεγραμμένος LTTrA. [c] — δὲ T[TrA]. [d] — ὑμῖν GLTTrAW. [e] + αὐτῶν (read their hour) LTrA. [f] [αὐτῶν] Tr. [g] + ἐγὼ L[A]W. [h] οὐ μὴ ἔλθῃ in no wise should come Tr.

him unto you. 8 And when he is come, he will reprove the world of sin, and of righteousness, and of judgment: 9 of sin, because they believe not on me; 10 of righteousness, because I go to my Father, and ye see me no more; 11 of judgment, because the prince of this world is judged. 12 I have yet many things to say unto you, but ye cannot bear them now. 13 Howbeit when he, the Spirit of truth, is come, he will guide you into all truth: for he shall not speak of himself; but whatsoever he shall hear, *that* shall he speak: and he will shew you things to come. 14 He shall glorify me: for he shall receive of mine, and shall shew *it* unto you. 15 All things that the Father hath are mine: therefore said I, that he shall take of mine, and shall shew *it* unto you. 16 A little while, and ye shall not see me: and again, a little while, and ye shall see me, because I go to the Father. 17 Then said *some* of his disciples among themselves, What is this that he saith unto us, A little while, and ye shall not see me: and again, a little while, and ye shall see me: and, Because I go to the Father? 18 They said therefore, What is this that he saith, A little while? we cannot tell what he saith. 19 Now Jesus knew that they were desirous to ask him, and said unto them, Do ye inquire among yourselves of that I said, A little while, and ye shall not see me: and again, a little while, and ye shall see me? 20 Verily, verily, I say unto you, That ye shall weep and lament, but the world shall rejoice: and ye

αὐτὸν πρὸς ὑμᾶς· 8 καὶ ἐλθὼν ἐκεῖνος ἐλέγξει τὸν κόσμον
him to you. And having come he will convict the world

περὶ ἁμαρτίας καὶ περὶ δικαιοσύνης καὶ περὶ κρίσεως.
concerning sin and concerning righteousness and concerning judgment.

9 περὶ ἁμαρτίας μέν, ὅτι οὐ.πιστεύουσιν εἰς ἐμέ· 10 περὶ
Concerning sin, because they believe not on me; concerning

δικαιοσύνης δέ, ὅτι πρὸς τὸν.πατέρα.[i]μου" ὑπάγω, καὶ [k]οὐκ
righteousness because to my Father I go away, and no

ἔτι" θεωρεῖτέ με· 11 περὶ.δὲ κρίσεως, ὅτι ὁ ἄρχων τοῦ
longer ye behold me; and concerning judgment, because the ruler

κόσμου.τούτου κέκριται. 12 [l]Ἔτι πολλὰ ἔχω [l]λέγειν
of this world has been judged. Yet many things I have to say

ὑμῖν," ἀλλ' οὐ.δύνασθε βαστάζειν ἄρτι· 13 ὅταν.δὲ ἔλθῃ
to you, but ye are not able to bear them now. But when [2]may [3]have [4]come

ἐκεῖνος, τὸ πνεῦμα τῆς ἀληθείας, ὁδηγήσει ὑμᾶς [m]εἰς πᾶσαν
[1]he, the Spirit of truth, he will guide you into all

τὴν ἀλήθειαν·" οὐ γὰρ λαλήσει ἀφ' ἑαυτοῦ, ἀλλ' ὅσα.[n]ἂν"
the truth; [4]not [1]for [2]he [3]will speak from himself, but whatsoever

[o]ἀκούσῃ" λαλήσει, καὶ τὰ ἐρχόμενα ἀναγγελεῖ ὑμῖν.
he may hear he will speak; and the things coming he will announce to you.

14 ἐκεῖνος ἐμὲ δοξάσει, ὅτι ἐκ τοῦ ἐμοῦ [p]λήψεται," καὶ ἀναγ-
He me will glorify, for of mine he will receive, and will an-

γελεῖ ὑμῖν. 15 πάντα ὅσα ἔχει ὁ πατὴρ ἐμά ἐστιν·
nounce to you. All things whatsoever [3]has [1]the [2]Father [5]mine [4]are;

διὰ τοῦτο εἶπον, ὅτι ἐκ τοῦ ἐμοῦ [q]λήψεται," καὶ ἀναγ-
because of this I said, that of mine he will receive, and will an-

γελεῖ ὑμῖν. 16 Μικρὸν καὶ [r]οὐ".θεωρεῖτέ με, καὶ πάλιν
nounce to you. A little [while] and ye do not behold me; and again

μικρὸν, καὶ ὄψεσθέ με, [s]ὅτι ἐγὼ ὑπάγω πρὸς τὸν πα-
a little [while] and ye shall see me, because I go away to the Fa-

τέρα." 17 Εἶπον οὖν ἐκ τῶν.μαθητῶν.αὐτοῦ πρὸς
ther. Said therefore [some] of his disciples to

ἀλλήλους, Τί ἐστιν τοῦτο ὃ λέγει ἡμῖν, Μικρὸν καὶ
one another, What is this which he says to us, A little [while] and

οὐ.θεωρεῖτέ με, καὶ πάλιν μικρὸν καὶ ὄψεσθέ με; καὶ
ye do not behold me; and again a little [while] and ye shall see me? and

Ὅτι [t]ἐγὼ" ὑπάγω πρὸς τὸν πατέρα; 18 Ἔλεγον οὖν,
Because I go away to the Father? They said therefore,

[v]Τοῦτο τί ἐστιν" ὃ λέγει, [w]τὸ" μικρόν; οὐκ.οἴδαμεν
[3]This [1]what [2]is which he says, the little [while]? We do not know

τί λαλεῖ. 19 Ἔγνω [x]οὖν" [y]ὁ" Ἰησοῦς ὅτι ἤθελον αὐτὸν
what he speaks. [2]Knew [3]therefore [1]Jesus that they desired [3]him

ἐρωτᾷν, καὶ εἶπεν αὐτοῖς, Περὶ τούτου ζητεῖτε μετ'
[1]to [2]ask, and said to them, Concerning this do ye inquire among

ἀλλήλων, ὅτι εἶπον, Μικρὸν καὶ οὐ.θεωρεῖτέ με, καὶ
one another, that I said, A little [while] and ye do not behold me; and

πάλιν μικρὸν καὶ ὄψεσθέ με; 20 ἀμὴν ἀμὴν λέγω ὑμῖν,
again a little [while] and ye shall see me? Verily verily I say to you,

ὅτι κλαύσετε καὶ θρηνήσετε ὑμεῖς, ὁ.δὲ κόσμος χαρήσεται·
that [2]will [3]weep [4]and [5]will [6]lament [1]ye, but the world will rejoice;

---

[i] — μου (*read* the Father) TTr[A]. [k] οὐκέτι GLT. [l] ὑμῖν λέγειν TTrA. [m] εἰς τὴν ἀλήθειαν πᾶσαν LTrA; ἐν τῇ ἀληθείᾳ πάσῃ T. [n] — ἂν LTTrA. [o] ἀκούσει he shall hear TrA; ἀκούει he hears T. [p] λήμψεται LTTrA. [q] λαμβάνει receives GLTTrAW. [r] οὐκέτι no longer (do ye behold) LTA; οὐκ ἔτι Tr. [s] — ὅτι ἐγὼ ὑπάγω πρὸς τὸν πατέρα TTrA; ὅτι ὑπάγω πρὸς τὸν πατέρα G[L]W. [t] — ἐγὼ (*read* ὑπάγω I go away) LTTrAW. [v] Τί ἐστιν τοῦτο LTr. [w] — τὸ (*read* a little [while]) TrA. [x] — οὖν GTTrAW. [y] — ὁ TTrA.

ὑμεῖς [z]δὲ‖ λυπηθήσεσθε, [a]ἀλλ'‖ ἡ.λύπη.ὑμῶν εἰς χαρὰν γενή-
but ye will be grieved, but your grief to joy shall be-
σεται. 21 ἡ γυνὴ ὅταν τίκτῃ, λύπην ἔχει, ὅτι ἦλθεν
come. The woman when she gives birth, grief has, because is come
ἡ.ὥρα.αὐτῆς· ὅταν.δὲ γεννήσῃ τὸ παιδίον, [b]οὐκ ἔτι‖
her hour; but when she brings forth the child, no longer
μνημονεύει τῆς θλίψεως, διὰ τὴν χαρὰν ὅτι ἐγεννήθη
she remembers the tribulation, on account of the joy that has been born
ἄνθρωπος εἰς τὸν κόσμον. 22 καὶ ὑμεῖς οὖν [c]λύπην μὲν
a man into the world. And ye therefore grief indeed
νῦν [d]ἔχετε·‖ πάλιν.δὲ ὄψομαι ὑμᾶς, καὶ χαρήσεται ὑμῶν
now have; but again I will see you, and [3]shall [4]rejoice [1]your
ἡ καρδία, καὶ τὴν.χαρὰν.ὑμῶν οὐδεὶς [e]αἴρει‖ ἀφ' ὑμῶν. 23 καὶ
[2]heart, and your joy no one takes from you. And
ἐν ἐκείνῃ τῇ ἡμέρᾳ ἐμὲ οὐκ ἐρωτήσετε οὐδέν. Ἀμὴν ἀμὴν
in that day of me ye shall ask nothing. Verily verily
λέγω ὑμῖν, [f]ὅτι‖ [g]ὅσα.ἂν‖ αἰτήσητε τὸν πατέρα [h]ἐν τῷ
I say to you, That whatsoever ye may ask the Father in
ὀνόματί.μου δώσει ὑμῖν.‖ 24 ἕως.ἄρτι οὐκ ᾐτήσατε οὐδὲν
my name he will give you. Hitherto ye asked nothing
ἐν τῷ.ὀνόματί.μου· αἰτεῖτε, καὶ [i]λήψεσθε,‖ ἵνα ἡ.χαρὰ.ὑμῶν
in my name: ask, and ye shall receive, that your joy
ᾖ πεπληρωμένη. 25 ταῦτα ἐν παροιμίαις λελάληκα ὑμῖν·
may be full. These things in allegories I have spoken to you;
[k]ἀλλ'‖ ἔρχεται ὥρα ὅτε [l]οὐκ ἔτι‖ ἐν παροιμίαις λαλήσω
but is coming an hour when no longer in allegories I will speak
ὑμῖν, ἀλλὰ παῤῥησίᾳ περὶ τοῦ πατρὸς [m]ἀναγγελῶ‖ ὑμῖν.
to you, but plainly concerning the Father I will announce to you.
26 ἐν ἐκείνῃ τῇ ἡμέρᾳ ἐν τῷ.ὀνόματί.μου αἰτήσεσθε· καὶ οὐ
In that day in my name ye shall ask; and [3]not
λέγω ὑμῖν ὅτι ἐγὼ ἐρωτήσω τὸν πατέρα περὶ ὑμῶν· 27 αὐ-
[1]I [2]say to you that I will beseech the Father for you, [4]him-
τὸς γὰρ ὁ πατὴρ φιλεῖ ὑμᾶς, ὅτι ὑμεῖς ἐμὲ πεφιλήκατε, καὶ
self [1]for [2]the [3]Father loves you, because ye me have loved, and
πεπιστεύκατε ὅτι ἐγὼ παρὰ [n]τοῦ θεοῦ‖ ἐξῆλθον. 28 ἐξῆλθον
have believed that I from God came out. I came out
[o]παρὰ‖ τοῦ πατρὸς καὶ ἐλήλυθα εἰς τὸν κόσμον· πάλιν ἀφίημι
from the Father and have come into the world; again I leave
τὸν κόσμον καὶ πορεύομαι πρὸς τὸν πατέρα. 29 Λέγουσιν
the world and go to the Father. [3]Say
[p]αὐτῷ‖ οἱ.μαθηταὶ.αὐτοῦ, Ἴδε, νῦν [q]παῤῥησίᾳ λαλεῖς, καὶ
[4]to [5]him [1]his [2]disciples, Lo, now plainly thou speakest, and
παροιμίαν οὐδεμίαν λέγεις. 30 νῦν οἴδαμεν ὅτι οἶδας
[2]allegory [1]no speakest. Now we know that thou knowest
πάντα, καὶ οὐ χρείαν ἔχεις ἵνα τίς σε ἐρωτᾷ. ἐν τούτῳ
all things, and [2]not [3]need [1]hast that anyone thee should ask. By this
πιστεύομεν ὅτι ἀπὸ θεοῦ ἐξῆλθες. 31 Ἀπεκρίθη αὐτοῖς
we believe that from God thou camest forth. [2]Answered [3]them
[r]ὁ‖ Ἰησοῦς, Ἄρτι πιστεύετε; 32 ἰδού, ἔρχεται ὥρα καὶ [s]νῦν
[1]Jesus, [6]Now [4]do [5]ye [7]believe? Lo, is coming an hour and now
ἐλήλυθεν· ἵνα σκορπισθῆτε ἕκαστος εἰς τὰ.ἴδια, [t]καὶ ἐμὲ‖
has come, that ye will be scattered each to his own, and me

shall be sorrowful, but your sorrow shall be turned into joy. 21 A woman when she is in travail hath sorrow, because her hour is come: but as soon as she is delivered of the child, she remembereth no more the anguish, for joy that a man is born into the world. 22 And ye now therefore have sorrow: but I will see you again, and your heart shall rejoice, and your joy no man taketh from you. 23 And in that day ye shall ask me nothing. Verily, verily, I say unto you, Whatsoever ye shall ask the Father in my name, he will give *it* you. 24 Hitherto have ye asked nothing in my name: ask, and ye shall receive, that your joy may be full. 25 These things have I spoken unto you in proverbs: but the time cometh, when I shall no more speak unto you in proverbs, but I shall shew you plainly of the Father. 26 At that day ye shall ask in my name: and I say not unto you, that I will pray the Father for you: 27 for the Father himself loveth you, because ye have loved me, and have believed that I came out from God. 28 I came forth from the Father, and am come into the world: again, I leave the world, and go to the Father. 29 His disciples said unto him, Lo, now speakest thou plainly, and speakest no proverb. 30 Now are we sure that thou knowest all things, and needest not that any man should ask thee: by this we believe that thou camest forth from God. 31 Jesus answered them, Do ye now believe? 32 Behold, the hour cometh, yea, is now come, that ye shall be scattered, every man to his own, and shall leave me a-

[z] — δὲ but LTTrA. [a] ἀλλὰ TrA. [b] οὐκέτι GLT. [c] νῦν μὲν λυπην LTTrA. [d] ἕξετε shall have L. [e] ἀρεῖ shall take LTrA. [f] — ὅτι [L]TTrA. [g] ἄν τι if anything LTTrA. [h] δώσει ὑμῖν ἐν τῷ ὀνόματί μου TTrA. [i] λήμψεσθε LTTrA. [k] — ἀλλ G[L]TTrAW. [l] οὐκέτι GLT. [m] ἀπαγγελῶ LTTrAW. [n] — τοῦ L; τοῦ πατρὸς the Father TrA. [o] ἐκ LTTrA. [p] — αὐτῷ [L]TTrA. [q] + ἐν LTTrA. [r] — ὁ TTrA. [s] — νῦν LTTrA. [t] κἀμὲ TTrA.

lone: and yet I am not
alone, because the Fa-
ther is with me.
33 These things I have
spoken unto you, that
in me ye might have
peace. In the world ye
shall have tribulation:
but be of good cheer;
I have overcome the
world.

XVII. These words
spake Jesus, and lifted
up his eyes to heaven,
and said, Father, the
hour is come; glorify
thy Son, that thy Son
also may glorify thee:
2 as thou hast given
him power over all
flesh, that he should
give eternal life to as
many as thou hast
given him. 3 And this
is life eternal, that
they might know thee
the only true God, and
Jesus Christ, whom
thou hast sent. 4 I have
glorified thee on the
earth: I have finished
the work which thou
gavest me to do. 5 And
now, O Father, glorify
thou me with thine
own self with the glory
which I had with thee
before the world was.
6 I have manifested
thy name unto the
men which thou gavest
me out of the world:
thine they were, and
thou gavest them me;
and they have kept
thy word. 7 Now they
have known that all
things whatsoever
thou hast given me
are of thee. 8 For I
have given unto them
the words which thou
gavest me; and they
have received *them*,
and have known sure-
ly that I came out
from thee, and they
have believed that
thou didst send me.
9 I pray for them: I
pray not for the world,
but for them which
thou hast given me; for
they are thine. 10 And
all mine are thine, and
thine are mine; and
I am glorified in them.
11 And now I am no
more in the world, but
these are in the world,

μονον ἀφῆτε· καὶ οὐκ.εἰμὶ μόνος, ὅτι ὁ πατὴρ μετ'
alone ye.will leave; and [yet] I am not alone, for the Father with
ἐμοῦ ἐστιν. 33 ταῦτα λελάληκα ὑμῖν ἵνα ἐν ἐμοὶ εἰρήνην
me is. These things I have spoken to you that in me peace
ἔχητε. ἐν τῷ κόσμῳ θλίψιν [v]ἔχετε·‖ ἀλλὰ θαρσεῖτε,
ye may have. In the world tribulation ye have; but be of good courage,
ἐγὼ νενίκηκα τὸν κόσμον.
I have overcome the world.

17 Ταῦτα ἐλάλησεν [w]ὁ‖ Ἰησοῦς, καὶ [x]ἐπῆρεν‖ τοὺς ὀφθαλ-
These things spoke Jesus, and lifted up [2]eyes
μοὺς αὐτοῦ εἰς τὸν οὐρανὸν [y]καὶ‖ εἶπεν, Πάτερ, ἐλήλυθεν ἡ
[1]his to the heaven and said, Father, [3]has [4]come [1]the
ὥρα· δόξασόν σου τὸν υἱόν, ἵνα [z]καὶ‖ ὁ.υἱός.[a]σου‖ δοξάσῃ
[2]hour; glorify thy Son, that also thy Son may glorify
σε· 2 καθὼς ἔδωκας αὐτῷ ἐξουσίαν πάσης σαρκός, ἵνα
thee; as thou gavest him authority over all flesh, that [of]
πᾶν ὃ δέδωκας αὐτῷ, [b]δώσῃ‖ αὐτοῖς ζωὴν αἰώνιον.
all which thou hast given him, he should give to them life eternal.
3 αὕτη.δέ ἐστιν ἡ αἰώνιος ζωή, ἵνα [c]γινώσκωσίν‖ σε τὸν
And this is the eternal life, that they should know thee the
μόνον ἀληθινὸν θεόν, καὶ ὃν ἀπέστειλας Ἰησοῦν χριστόν.
only true God, and [3]whom [4]thou [5]didst [6]send [1]Jesus [2]Christ.
4 ἐγώ σε ἐδόξασα ἐπὶ τῆς γῆς· τὸ ἔργον [d]ἐτελείωσα‖ ὃ
I thee glorified on the earth; the work I completed which
δέδωκάς μοι ἵνα ποιήσω· 5 καὶ νῦν δόξασόν με σύ, πά-
thou hast given me that I should do; and now glorify me thou, Fa-
τερ, παρὰ σεαυτῷ, τῇ δόξῃ ᾗ εἶχον πρὸ τοῦ τὸν κόσμον
ther, with thyself, with the glory which I had before the world
εἶναι παρὰ σοί. 6 Ἐφανέρωσά σου τὸ ὄνομα τοῖς ἀνθρώποις
was with thee. I manifested thy name to the men
οὓς [e]δέδωκάς‖ μοι ἐκ τοῦ κόσμου· σοὶ ἦσαν, [f]καὶ ἐμοὶ‖
whom thou hast given me out of the world. Thine they were, and to me
αὐτοὺς [e]δέδωκας·‖ καὶ τὸν.λόγον.σου [g]τετηρήκασιν.‖ 7 νῦν
them thou hast given, and thy word they have kept. Now
ἔγνωκαν ὅτι πάντα ὅσα [h]δέδωκάς‖ μοι, παρὰ σοῦ
they have known that all things whatsoever thou hast given me, of thee
[i]ἐστιν·‖ 8 ὅτι τὰ ῥήματα ἃ [k]δέδωκάς‖ μοι δέδωκα αὐτοῖς·
are; for the words which thou hast given me I have given them,
καὶ αὐτοὶ ἔλαβον, [l]καὶ ἔγνωσαν‖ ἀληθῶς ὅτι παρὰ σοῦ
and they received [them], and knew truly that from thee
ἐξῆλθον, καὶ ἐπίστευσαν ὅτι σύ με ἀπέστειλας. 9 ἐγὼ περὶ
I came out, and they believed that thou me didst send. I concerning
αὐτῶν ἐρωτῶ· οὐ περὶ τοῦ κόσμου ἐρωτῶ, ἀλλὰ
them make request; not concerning the world make I request, but
περὶ ὧν δέδωκάς μοι, ὅτι σοί εἰσιν. 10 καὶ τὰ
concerning whom thou hast given me, for thine they are: (and [3]things
ἐμὰ πάντα σά ἐστιν, καὶ τὰ.σὰ ἐμά· καὶ δεδόξασμαι
[2]my [1]all [5]thine [4]are, and thine [are] mine:) and I have been glorified
ἐν αὐτοῖς. 11 καὶ [m]οὐκ ἔτι‖ εἰμὶ ἐν τῷ κόσμῳ, καὶ [n]οὗτοι‖ ἐν
in them. And no longer I am in the world, and these in

---

[v] ἕξετε ye will have EL. [w] — ὁ T. [x] ἐπάρας having lifted up LTTrA. [y] — καὶ LTTrA. [z] — καὶ LTTrAW. [a] — σου (*read* the Son) TTr[A]. [b] δώσει he shall give A. [c] γινώσκουσιν they know TTr. [d] τελειώσας having completed LTTrA. [e] ἔδωκάς thou gavest LTTr. [f] κἀμοὶ Tr. [g] τετήρηκαν LTTrA. [h] ἔδωκάς thou gavest L. [i] εἰσίν TTrA. [k] ἔδωκάς thou gavest LTTrA. [l] [καὶ ἔγνωσαν] L. [m] οὐκέτι LTW. [n] αὐτοὶ they T.

τῷ κόσμῳ εἰσίν, [o]καὶ ἐγὼ‖ πρός σε ἔρχομαι. πάτερ ἅγιε, τήρη-
the world are, and I to thee come. [2]Father [1]Holy, keep

σον αὐτοὺς ἐν τῷ.ὀνόματί.σου [p]οὓς‖ δέδωκάς μοι, ἵνα
them in thy name whom thou hast given me, that

ὦσιν ἕν, καθὼς [q] ἡμεῖς. 12 ὅτε ἤμην μετ' αὐτῶν [r]ἐν τῷ
they may be one, as we. When I was with them in the

κόσμῳ ἐγὼ ἐτήρουν αὐτοὺς ἐν τῷ.ὀνόματί.σου [s]οὓς‖ δέ-
world I was keeping them in thy name: whom thou

δωκάς μοι [t] ἐφύλαξα, καὶ οὐδεὶς ἐξ αὐτῶν ἀπώλετο, εἰ.μὴ ὁ
hast given me I guarded, and no one of them perished, except the

υἱὸς τῆς ἀπωλείας, ἵνα ἡ γραφὴ πληρωθῇ. 13 νῦν.δὲ
son of perdition, that the scripture might be fulfilled. And now

πρός σε ἔρχομαι, καὶ ταῦτα λαλῶ ἐν τῷ κόσμῳ ἵνα ἔχω-
to thee I come; and these things I speak in the world that they may

σιν τὴν χαρὰν τὴν ἐμὴν πεπληρωμένην ἐν [u]αὐτοῖς.‖ 14 ἐγὼ
have [2]joy [1]my fulfilled in them. I

δέδωκα αὐτοῖς τὸν.λόγον.σου, καὶ ὁ κόσμος ἐμίσησεν αὐτούς,
have given them thy word, and the world hated them,

ὅτι οὐκ.εἰσὶν ἐκ τοῦ κόσμου, καθὼς ἐγὼ οὐκ.εἰμὶ ἐκ τοῦ
because they are not of the world, as I am not of the

κόσμου. 15 οὐκ.ἐρωτῶ ἵνα ἄρῃς αὐτοὺς ἐκ τοῦ
world. I do not make request that thou shouldest take them out of the

κόσμου, ἀλλ' ἵνα τηρήσῃς αὐτοὺς ἐκ τοῦ πονηροῦ.
world, but that thou shouldest keep them out of the evil.

16 ἐκ τοῦ κόσμου οὐκ.εἰσίν, καθὼς ἐγὼ [v]ἐκ τοῦ κόσμου οὐκ
Of the world they are not, as I of the world [2]not

εἰμί.‖ 17 ἁγίασον αὐτοὺς ἐν τῇ.ἀληθείᾳ.[w]σου.‖ ὁ λόγος ὁ σὸς
[1]am. Sanctify them by thy truth; [2]word [1]thy

ἀλήθειά ἐστιν. 18 καθὼς ἐμὲ ἀπέστειλας εἰς τὸν κόσμον,
truth is. As me thou didst send into the world,

κἀγὼ ἀπέστειλα αὐτοὺς εἰς τὸν κόσμον· 19 καὶ ὑπὲρ αὐτῶν
I also sent them into the world; and for them

[x]ἐγὼ‖ ἁγιάζω ἐμαυτόν, ἵνα [y]καὶ αὐτοὶ ὦσιν‖ ἡγιασμένοι ἐν
I sanctify myself, that also they may be sanctified in

ἀληθείᾳ. 20 Οὐ περὶ τούτων δὲ ἐρωτῶ μόνον, ἀλλὰ
truth. [2]Not [3]for [4]these [1]and [7]make [6]I [8]request [5]only, but

καὶ περὶ τῶν [z]πιστευσόντων‖ διὰ τοῦ.λόγου.αὐτῶν εἰς
also for those who shall believe through their word on

ἐμέ· 21 ἵνα πάντες ἓν ὦσιν, καθὼς σύ, [a]πάτερ,‖ ἐν ἐμοί,
me; that all one may be, as thou, Father, [art] in me,

κἀγὼ ἐν σοί, ἵνα καὶ αὐτοὶ ἐν ἡμῖν [b]ἓν‖ ὦσιν· ἵνα ὁ κόσμος
and I in thee, that also they in us one may be, that the world

[c]πιστεύσῃ‖ ὅτι σύ με ἀπέστειλας. 22 [d]καὶ ἐγὼ‖ τὴν δόξαν
may believe that thou me didst send. And I the glory

ἣν [e]δέδωκάς‖ μοι δέδωκα αὐτοῖς, ἵνα ὦσιν ἕν, καθὼς
which thou hast given me have given them, that they may be one, as

ἡμεῖς ἕν [f]ἐσμεν·‖ 23 ἐγὼ ἐν αὐτοῖς, καὶ σὺ ἐν ἐμοί, ἵνα
we one are: I in them, and thou in me, that

ὦσιν τετελειωμένοι εἰς ἕν, [g]καὶ‖ ἵνα γινώσκῃ ὁ κόσμος
they may be perfected into one, and that [3]may [4]know [1]the [2]world

and I come to thee.
Holy Father, keep
through thine own
name those whom
thou hast given me,
that they may be
one, as we *are*.
12 While I was with
them in the world, I
kept them in thy name:
those that thou gavest
me I have kept, and
none of them is lost,
but the son of perdi-
tion; that the scrip-
ture might be fulfilled.
13 And now come I to
thee; and these things
I speak in the world,
that they might have
my joy fulfilled in
themselves. 14 I have
given them thy word;
and the world hath
hated them, because
they are not of the
world, even as I am
not of the world. 15 I
pray not that thou
shouldest take them
out of the world, but
that thou shouldest
keep them from the
evil. 16 They are not
of the world, even as
I am not of the world.
17 Sanctify them
through thy truth:
thy word is truth.
18 As thou hast sent
me into the world, even
so have I also sent
them into the world.
19 And for their sakes
I sanctify myself, that
they also might be
sanctified through the
truth. 20 Neither pray
I for these alone, but
for them also which
shall believe on me
through their word;
21 that they all may be
one; as thou, Father,
art in me, and I in
thee, that they also
may be one in us: that
the world may believe
that thou hast sent
me. 22 And the glory
which thou gavest me
I have given them;
that they may be one,
even as we are one:
23 I in them, and thou
in me, that they may
be made perfect in one;
and that the world
may know that thou

---

[o] κἀγὼ LTTrA. [p] ᾧ which GLTTrAW. [q] + καὶ also Tr. [r] — ἐν τῷ κόσμῳ LTTrA. [s] ᾧ which TTrA. [t] + καὶ and (*read* I was keeping them in thy name which thou hast given me, and I guarded [them]) [L]TTrA. [u] ἑαυτοῖς TTrA. [v] οὐκ εἰμὶ ἐκ τοῦ κόσμου LTTrAW. [w] — σου (*read* the truth) LTTrA. [x] — ἐγὼ (*read* ἁγ. I sanctify) [L]T. [y] ὦσιν καὶ αὐτοὶ LTTrAW. [z] πιστευόντων believe GLTTrAW. [a] πατὴρ TTrA. [b] — ἓν [L]TTrA. [c] πιστεύῃ TTr. [d] κἀγὼ LTTrA. [e] ἔδωκας thou gavest L. [f] — ἐσμεν (*read* [are]) TTrA. [g] — καὶ LTTrA.

hast sent me, and hast loved them, as thou hast loved me. 24 Father, I will that they also, whom thou hast given me, be with me where I am; that they may behold my glory, which thou hast given me: for thou lovedst me before the foundation of the world. 25 O righteous Father, the world hath not known thee: but I have known thee, and these have known that thou hast sent me. 26 And I have declared unto them thy name, and will declare *it*: that the love wherewith thou hast loved me may be in them, and I in them.

ὅτι σύ με ἀπέστειλας, καὶ ἠγάπησας αὐτοὺς καθὼς ἐμὲ ἠγά-
that thou me didst send, and lovedst them as me thou
πησας. 24 [h]Πάτερ,‖ [i]οὓς‖ [j]δέδωκάς‖ μοι θέλω ἵνα ὅπου εἰμὶ
lovedst. Father, whom thou hast given me I desire that where [2]am
ἐγὼ κἀκεῖνοι ὦσιν μετ' ἐμοῦ, ἵνα θεωρῶσιν τὴν δόξαν τὴν
[1]I they also may be with me, that they may behold [2]glory
ἐμὴν ἣν [k]ἔδωκάς‖ μοι, ὅτι ἠγάπησάς με πρὸ καταβολῆς
[1]my which thou gavest me, for thou lovedst me before [the] foundation
κόσμου 25 [l]Πάτερ‖ δίκαιε, καὶ ὁ κόσμος σε οὐκ.ἔγνω,
of [the] world. [2]Father [1]righteous, and the world thee knew not,
ἐγὼ.δέ σε ἔγνων, καὶ οὗτοι ἔγνωσαν ὅτι σύ με ἀπέστειλας·
but I thee knew, and these knew that thou me didst send.
26 καὶ ἐγνώρισα αὐτοῖς τὸ.ὄνομά.σου, καὶ γνωρίσω·
And I made known to them thy name, and will make [it] known;
ἵνα ἡ ἀγάπη ἣν ἠγάπησάς με ἐν αὐτοῖς ᾖ, κἀγὼ
that the love with which thou lovedst me in them may be; and I
ἐν αὐτοῖς.
in them.

XVIII. When Jesus had spoken these words, he went forth with his disciples over the brook Cedron, where was a garden, into the which he entered, and his disciples. 2 And Judas also, which betrayed him, knew the place: for Jesus ofttimes resorted thither with his disciples. 3 Judas then, having received a band *of men* and officers from the chief priests and Pharisees, cometh thither with lanterns and torches and weapons. 4 Jesus therefore, knowing all things that should come upon him, went forth, and said unto them, Whom seek ye? 5 They answered him, Jesus of Nazareth. Jesus saith unto them, I am *he*. And Judas also, which betrayed him, stood with them. 6 As soon then as he had said unto them, I am *he*, they went backward, and fell to the ground. 7 Then asked he them again, Whom seek ye? And they said, Jesus of Nazareth. 8 Jesus answered, I have told you that I am *he*: if therefore ye seek me, let these go their way:

18 Ταῦτα εἰπὼν [m]ὁ‖ Ἰησοῦς ἐξῆλθεν σὺν τοῖς μαθηταῖς
[4]These [5]things [2]having [3]said [1]Jesus went out with [2]disciples
αὐτοῦ πέραν τοῦ χειμάῤῥου [n]τῶν Κέδρων,‖ ὅπου ἦν κῆπος,
[1]his beyond the winter stream of Kedron, where was a garden,
εἰς ὃν εἰσῆλθεν αὐτὸς καὶ οἱ.μαθηταὶ.αὐτοῦ. 2 ᾔδει.δὲ καὶ
into which [2]entered [1]he and his disciples. And [8]knew [2]also
Ἰούδας ὁ παραδιδοὺς αὐτὸν τὸν τόπον· ὅτι πολλάκις
[1]Judas [3]who [4]was [5]delivering [7]up [6]him the place, because [3]often
συνήχθη [o]ὁ‖ Ἰησοῦς ἐκεῖ μετὰ τῶν.μαθητῶν.αὐτοῦ. 3 ὁ οὖν
[2]was [4]gathered [1]Jesus there with his disciples. [2]Therefore
Ἰούδας λαβὼν τὴν σπεῖραν, καὶ ἐκ τῶν ἀρχιερέων καὶ [p]
[1]Judas having received the band, and [2]from [3]the [4]chief [5]priests [6]and
Φαρισαίων ὑπηρέτας, ἔρχεται ἐκεῖ μετὰ φανῶν καὶ λαμπάδων
[7]Pharisees [1]officers, comes there with torches and lamps
καὶ ὅπλων. 4 Ἰησοῦς [q]οὖν‖ εἰδὼς πάντα τὰ ἐρχόμενα
and weapons. Jesus therefore knowing all things that were coming
ἐπ' αὐτόν, [r]ἐξελθὼν εἶπεν‖ αὐτοῖς, Τίνα ζητεῖτε; 5 Ἀπε-
upon him, having gone forth said to them, Whom seek ye? They
κρίθησαν αὐτῷ, Ἰησοῦν τὸν Ναζωραῖον. Λέγει αὐτοῖς [s]ὁ
answered him, Jesus the Nazaræan. [2]Says [3]to [4]them
Ἰησοῦς,‖ Ἐγώ εἰμι. Εἱστήκει.δὲ καὶ Ἰούδας ὁ παρα-
[1]Jesus, I am [he]. And [8]was [9]standing [2]also [1]Judas [3]who [4]was [5]de-
διδοὺς αὐτὸν μετ' αὐτῶν. 6 Ὡς οὖν εἶπεν αὐτοῖς, [t]Ὅτι‖
livering [7]up [6]him with them. When therefore he said to them,
ἐγώ εἰμι, [v]ἀπῆλθον‖ εἰς.τὰ.ὀπίσω καὶ [w]ἔπεσον‖ χαμαί.
I am [he], they went backward and fell to [the] ground.
7 πάλιν οὖν [x]αὐτοὺς ἐπηρώτησεν,‖ Τίνα ζητεῖτε; Οἱ.δὲ
Again therefore [3]them [1]he [2]questioned, Whom seek ye? And they
εἶπον, Ἰησοῦν τὸν Ναζωραῖον. 8 Ἀπεκρίθη [y]ὁ‖ Ἰησοῦς, Εἶπον
said, Jesus the Nazaræan. [2]Answered [1]Jesus, I told
ὑμῖν ὅτι ἐγώ εἰμι. εἰ οὖν ἐμὲ ζητεῖτε, ἄφετε τούτους ὑπά-
you that I am [he]. If therefore me ye seek, suffer these to go

---

[h] πατήρ LTTrA. [i] ὃ what TTrA. [j] ἔδωκάς thou gavest L. [k] δέδωκάς thou hast given LTTrAW. [l] πατὴρ LTTrA. [m] — ὁ TTrA. [n] τοῦ Κεδρών GL; τοῦ κέδρου T. [o] — ὁ TTrA. [p] + τῶν LTr[A]; + ἐκ τῶν from the T. [q] δὲ and (Jesus) Tr. [r] ἐξῆλθεν καὶ λέγει went forth and says LTTrA. [s] — ὁ T; — ὁ Ἰησοῦς (*read* he says) TrA. [t] — ὅτι LTTr. [v] ἀπῆλθαν LTTrA. [w] ἔπεσαν LTTrA. [x] ἐπηρώτησεν αὐτούς LTrA; αὐτὸς ἐπηρώτησεν W. [y] — ὁ GLTTrAW.

γειν· 9 ἵνα πληρωθῇ ὁ λόγος ὃν εἶπεν. ʺΟτι οὓς δέ-
away; that might be fulfilled the word which he said, Whom thou
δωκάς μοι οὐκ ἀπώλεσα ἐξ αὐτῶν οὐδένα. 10 Σίμων οὖν
hast given me I lost of them not one. Simon [2]therefore
Πέτρος ἔχων μάχαιραν, εἵλκυσεν αὐτήν, καὶ ἔπαισεν τὸν
[1]Peter having a sword, drew it, and smote the
τοῦ ἀρχιερέως δοῦλον, καὶ ἀπέκοψεν αὐτοῦ τὸ [z]ὠτίονǁ τὸ
[3]of [4]the [6]high [5]priest [1]bondman, and cut off his [2]ear
δεξιόν. ἦν.δὲ ὄνομα τῷ δούλῳ Μάλχος. 11 εἶπεν οὖν
[1]right. And [4]was [3]name [1]the [2]bondman's Malchus. [3]Said [2]therefore
ὁ Ἰησοῦς τῷ Πέτρῳ, Βάλε τὴν.μάχαιράν.[a]σουǁ εἰς τὴν θήκην.
[1]Jesus to Peter, Put thy sword into the sheath;
τὸ ποτήριον ὃ δέδωκέν μοι ὁ πατὴρ οὐ.μὴ.πίω αὐτό;
the cup which [3]has [4]given [5]me [1]the [2]Father should I not drink it?

12 Ἡ οὖν σπεῖρα καὶ ὁ χιλίαρχος καὶ οἱ ὑπηρέται τῶν
The [2]therefore [1]band and the chief captain and the officers of the
Ἰουδαίων συνέλαβον τὸν Ἰησοῦν, καὶ ἔδησαν αὐτόν, 13 καὶ
Jews took hold of Jesus, and bound him; and
[b]ἀπήγαγον αὐτὸνǁ πρὸς ʺΑνναν πρῶτον· ἦν.γὰρ πενθερὸς
they led away him to Annas first; for he was father-in-law
τοῦ Καϊάφα, ὃς ἦν ἀρχιερεὺς τοῦ.ἐνιαυτοῦ.ἐκείνου. 14 ἦν.δὲ
of Caiaphas, who was high priest that year. And it was
Καϊάφας ὁ συμβουλεύσας τοῖς Ἰουδαίοις, ὅτι συμφέρει
Caiaphas who gave counsel to the Jews, that it is profitable
ἕνα ἄνθρωπον [c]ἀπολέσθαιǁ ὑπὲρ τοῦ λαοῦ. 15 Ἠκολούθει.δὲ
for one man to perish for the people. Now there followed
τῷ Ἰησοῦ Σίμων Πέτρος καὶ [d]ὁǁ ἄλλος μαθητής. ὁ δὲ μαθητὴς
Jesus Simon Peter and the other disciple. And [2]disciple
ἐκεῖνος ἦν γνωστὸς τῷ ἀρχιερεῖ, καὶ συνεισῆλθεν τῷ Ἰησοῦ
[1]that was known to the high priest, and entered with Jesus
εἰς τὴν αὐλὴν τοῦ ἀρχιερέως· 16 ὁ.δὲ.Πέτρος εἱστήκει πρὸς
into the court of the high priest, but Peter stood at
τῇ θύρᾳ ἔξω. ἐξῆλθεν οὖν ὁ μαθητὴς ὁ ἄλλος [e]ὃς ἦνǁ
the door without. Went out therefore the [2]disciple [1]other who was
γνωστὸς [f]τῷ ἀρχιερεῖ,ǁ καὶ εἶπεν τῇ θυρωρῷ καὶ εἰσήγα-
known to the high priest, and spoke to the door-keeper and brought
γεν τὸν Πέτρον. 17 λέγει οὖν [g]ἡ παιδίσκη ἡ θυρωρὸς τῷ
in Peter. [6]Says [5]therefore [1]the [2]maid [3]the [4]door-keeper
Πέτρῳ, Μὴ καὶ σὺ ἐκ τῶν μαθητῶν εἶ τοῦ ἀνθρώπου
to Peter, [2]not [4]also [3]thou [5]of [6]the [7]disciples [1]art of [2]man
τούτου; Λέγει ἐκεῖνος, Οὐκ.εἰμί. 18 Εἱστήκεισαν.δὲ οἱ δοῦλοι
[1]this? [4]Says [3]he, I am not. But [6]were [7]standing [1]the [2]bondmen
καὶ οἱ ὑπηρέται ἀνθρακιὰν πεποιηκότες, ὅτι ψῦχος ἦν,
[3]and [4]the [5]officers, a fire of coals having made, for cold it was,
καὶ ἐθερμαίνοντο· ἦν.δὲ [h]μετ' αὐτῶν ὁ Πέτροςǁ ἑστὼς
and were warming themselves; and [2]was [3]with [4]them [1]Peter standing
καὶ θερμαινόμενος. 19 Ὁ.οὖν.ἀρχιερεὺς ἠρώτησεν τὸν Ἰη-
and warming himself. The high priest therefore questioned Je-
σοῦν περὶ τῶν.μαθητῶν.αὐτοῦ, καὶ περὶ τῆς διδαχῆς
sus concerning his disciples, and concerning [2]teaching
αὐτοῦ. 20 ἀπεκρίθη [i]αὐτῷǁ [k]ὁǁ Ἰησοῦς, Ἐγὼ παρρησίᾳ
[1]his. [2]Answered [3]him [1]Jesus, I openly

9 that the saying might
be fulfilled, which he
spake, Of them which
thou gavest me have I
lost none. 10 Then
Simon Peter having a
sword drew it, and
smote the high priest's
servant, and cut off
his right ear. The
servant's name was
Malchus. 11 Then said
Jesus unto Peter, Put
up thy sword into the
sheath: the cup which
my Father hath given
me, shall I not drink
it?

12 Then the band and
the captain and offi-
cers of the Jews took
Jesus, and bound him,
13 and led him away
to Annas first; for he
was father in law to
Caiaphas, which was
the high priest that
same year. 14 Now
Caiaphas was he, which
gave counsel to the
Jews, that it was ex-
pedient that one man
should die for the peo-
ple. 15 And Simon
Peter followed Jesus,
and *so did* another dis-
ciple: that disciple was
known unto the high
priest, and went in
with Jesus into the pa-
lace of the high priest.
16 But Peter stood at
the door without.
Then went out that
other disciple, which
was known unto the
high priest, and spake
unto her that kept the
door, and brought in
Peter. 17 Then saith
the damsel that kept
the door unto Peter,
Art not thou also *one*
of this man's disci-
ples? He saith, I am
not. 18 And the ser-
vants and officers stood
there, who had made
a fire of coals; for it
was cold: and they
warmed themselves:
and Peter stood with
them, and warmed
himself. 19 The high
priest then asked Je-
sus of his disciples, and
of his doctrine. 20 Je-
sus answered him, I
spake openly to the

---

[z] ὠτάριον TTrA. [a] — σου (*read* the sword) GLTTrAW. [b] ἤγαγον [αὐτὸν] they led him L; ἤγαγον TTr; [ἀπ]ήγαγον αὐτὸν A. [c] ἀποθανεῖν to die LTTrA. [d] — ὁ (*read* another LT[Tr]A]. [e] ὁ TTrA. [f] τοῦ ἀρχιερέως of the high priest TTrA [g] τῷ Πέτρῳ ἡ παιδίσκη ἡ θυρωρός LTTrA. [h] καὶ (also) ὁ Πέτρος μετ' αὐτῶν LTTrA. [i] [αὐτῷ] L. [k] — ὁ TTr.

world; I ever taught in the synagogue, and in the temple, whither the Jews always resort; and in secret have I said nothing. 21 Why askest thou me? ask them which heard me, what I have said unto them: behold, they know what I said. 22 And when he had thus spoken, one of the officers which stood by struck Jesus with the palm of his hand, saying, Answerest thou the high priest so? 23 Jesus answered him, If I have spoken evil, bear witness of the evil: but if well, why smitest thou me? 24 Now Annas had sent him bound unto Caiaphas the high priest.

25 And Simon Peter stood and warmed himself. They said therefore unto him, Art not thou also *one* of his disciples? He denied *it*, and said, I am not. 26 One of the servants of the high priest, being *his* kinsman whose ear Peter cut off, saith, Did not I see thee in the garden with him? 27 Peter then denied again: and immediately the cock crew.

28 Then led they Jesus from Caiaphas unto the hall of judgment: and it was early; and they themselves went not into the judgment hall, lest they should be defiled; but that they might eat the passover. 29 Pilate then went out unto them, and said, What accusation bring ye against this man? 30 They answered and said unto him, If he were not a malefactor, we would not have delivered him up unto thee. 31 Then said Pilate unto them, Take ye him, and judge him according to your law. The Jews therefore said unto him, It is not

[l]ἐλάλησα‖ τῷ κόσμῳ· ἐγὼ πάντοτε ἐδίδαξα ἐν [m]τῇ‖ συνα-
spoke to the world; I always taught in the syna-
γωγῇ καὶ ἐν τῷ ἱερῷ, ὅπου [n]πάντοτε‖ οἱ Ἰουδαῖοι συνέρχον-
gogue and in the temple, where always the Jews come to-
ται, καὶ ἐν κρυπτῷ ἐλάλησα οὐδέν. 21 τί με [o]ἐπερωτᾷς;
gether, and in secret I spoke nothing. Why me dost thou question?
ἐπερώτησον‖ τοὺς ἀκηκοότας τί ἐλάλησα αὐτοῖς· ἴδε οὗτοι
question those who have heard what I spoke to them; lo, they
οἴδασιν ἃ εἶπον ἐγώ. 22 Ταῦτα.δὲ αὐτοῦ.εἰπόντος εἷς [p]τῶν
know what [2]said [1]I. But [4]these [5]things [1]on [2]his [3]saying one of the
ὑπηρετῶν παρεστηκὼς‖ ἔδωκεν ῥάπισμα τῷ
officers standing by gave a blow with the palm of the hand
Ἰησοῦ, εἰπών, Οὕτως ἀποκρίνῃ τῷ ἀρχιερεῖ; 23 Ἀπεκρίθη
to Jesus, saying, Thus answerest thou the high priest? [2]Answered
αὐτῷ [q]ὁ‖ Ἰησοῦς, Εἰ κακῶς ἐλάλησα, μαρτύρησον περὶ τοῦ
[3]him [1]Jesus, If evil I spoke, bear witness concerning the
κακοῦ· εἰ.δὲ καλῶς, τί με δέρεις; 24 Ἀπέστειλεν [r] αὐτὸν
evil; but if well, why me strikest thou? [2]Sent [3]him
ὁ Ἄννας δεδεμένον πρὸς Καϊάφαν τὸν ἀρχιερέα.
[1]Annas bound to Caiaphas the high priest.

25 Ἦν.δὲ Σίμων Πέτρος ἑστὼς καὶ θερμαινόμενος·
Now [3]was [1]Simon [2]Peter standing and warming himself.
εἶπον οὖν αὐτῷ, Μὴ καὶ σὺ ἐκ τῶν.μαθητῶν.αὐτοῦ
They said therefore to him, [2]Not [4]also [3]thou [5]of [6]his [7]disciples
εἶ; Ἠρνήσατο.ἐκεῖνος, καὶ εἶπεν, Οὐκ.εἰμί. 26 Λέγει εἷς
[1]art? He denied, and said, I am not. Says one
ἐκ τῶν δούλων τοῦ ἀρχιερέως, συγγενὴς ὢν οὗ
of the bondmen of the high priest, kinsman being [of him] of whom
ἀπέκοψεν Πέτρος τὸ ὠτίον, Οὐκ.ἐγώ σε εἶδον ἐν τῷ κήπῳ
[2]cut [3]off [1]Peter the ear, [2]I [3]not [4]thee [1]saw in the garden
μετ' αὐτοῦ; 27 Πάλιν οὖν ἠρνήσατο [s]ὁ‖ Πέτρος, καὶ εὐθέως
with him? Again therefore [2]denied [1]Peter, and immediately
ἀλέκτωρ ἐφώνησεν.
a cock crew.

28 Ἄγουσιν οὖν τὸν Ἰησοῦν ἀπὸ τοῦ Καϊάφα εἰς τὸ
They lead therefore Jesus from Caiaphas into the
πραιτώριον· ἦν.δὲ [t]πρωΐα·‖ καὶ αὐτοὶ οὐκ.εἰσῆλθον εἰς τὸ
prætorium, and it was early. And they entered not into the
πραιτώριον, ἵνα μὴ.μιανθῶσιν, [v]ἀλλ' ἵνα‖ φάγωσιν τὸ
prætorium, that they might not be defiled, but that they might eat the
πάσχα. 29 ἐξῆλθεν οὖν ὁ [w]Πιλάτος‖ [x] πρὸς αὐτούς, καὶ
passover. [3]Went [4]forth [2]therefore [1]Pilate to them, and
[y]εἶπεν,‖ Τίνα κατηγορίαν φέρετε [z]κατὰ‖ τοῦ.ἀνθρώπου.τούτου;
said, What accusation bring ye against this man?
30 Ἀπεκρίθησαν καὶ [a]εἶπον‖ αὐτῷ, Εἰ μὴ.ἦν οὗτος [b]κακο-
They answered and said to him, If [2]were [3]not [1]he an evil
ποιός,‖ οὐκ ἄν σοι παρεδώκαμεν αὐτόν. 31 Εἶπεν
doer, [3]not [4]to [5]thee [1]we [2]would have delivered up him. [3]Said
[c]οὖν‖ αὐτοῖς [d]ὁ‖ [w]Πιλάτος,‖ Λάβετε αὐτὸν ὑμεῖς, καὶ
[2]therefore [4]to [5]them [1]Pilate, Take him ye, and
κατὰ τὸν.νόμον.ὑμῶν κρίνατε [e]αὐτόν.‖ Εἶπον [f]οὖν‖
according to your law judge him. [4]Said [3]therefore

[l] λελάληκα have spoken LTTrAW. [m] — τῇ (read a) GLTTrAW. [n] πάντοθεν E; πάντες all GLTTrAW. [o] ἐρωτᾷς; ἐρώτησον (ἐπερ. W) LTTrAW. [p] παρεστηκὼς τῶν ὑπηρετῶν LTTrA. [q] — ὁ LTTrA. [r] + οὖν therefore ELT[Tr]A. [s] — ὁ LTTrAW. [t] πρωΐ GLTTrAW. [v] ἀλλὰ LTTrA. [w] Πειλᾶτος T. [x] + ἔξω out LTTrA. [y] φησίν says TTrA. [z] — κατὰ T. [a] εἶπαν LTTrA. [b] κακὸν ποιῶν TTrA. [c] [οὖν] L. [d] — ὁ TrA. [e] — αὐτόν T. [f] — οὖν LTrA.

αὐτῷ οἱ Ἰουδαῖοι, Ἡμῖν οὐκ ἔξεστιν ἀποκτεῖναι οὐδένα·
[5]to [6]him [1]the [2]Jews, To us it is permitted to put [3]to [4]death [1]no [2]one;
32 ἵνα ὁ λόγος τοῦ Ἰησοῦ πληρωθῇ ὃν εἶπεν σημαίνων
that the word of Jesus might be fulfilled which he spoke signifying
ποίῳ θανάτῳ ἤμελλεν ἀποθνήσκειν. 33 Εἰσῆλθεν οὖν
by what death he was about to die. [2]Entered [3]therefore
[g]εἰς τὸ πραιτώριον πάλιν‖ ὁ [h]Πιλάτος,‖ καὶ ἐφώνησεν τὸν
[4]into [5]the [6]prætorium [7]again [1]Pilate, and called
Ἰησοῦν, καὶ εἶπεν αὐτῷ, Σὺ εἶ ὁ βασιλεὺς τῶν Ἰουδαίων;
Jesus, and said to him, [2]Thou [1]art the king of the Jews?
34 Ἀπεκρίθη [i]αὐτῷ ὁ‖ Ἰησοῦς, [k]Ἀφ' ἑαυτοῦ‖ σὺ τοῦτο
[2]Answered [3]him [1]Jesus, From thyself [2]thou [3]this
λέγεις, ἢ ἄλλοι [l]σοι εἶπον‖ περὶ ἐμοῦ; 35 Ἀπεκρίθη
[1]sayest, [4]or [6]others [7]to [8]thee [5]did say [it] concerning me? [2]Answered
ὁ [h]Πιλάτος,‖ Μήτι ἐγὼ Ἰουδαῖός εἰμι; τὸ ἔθνος τὸ σὸν καὶ
[1]Pilate, [4]I [5]a [6]Jew [3]am? [8]Nation [7]thy and
οἱ ἀρχιερεῖς παρέδωκάν σε ἐμοί· τί ἐποίησας; 36 Ἀπεκρίθη
the chief priests delivered up thee to me: what didst thou? [2]Answered
[m]ὁ‖ Ἰησοῦς, Ἡ βασιλεία ἡ ἐμὴ οὐκ ἔστιν ἐκ τοῦ κόσμου τούτου·
[1]Jesus, [4]kingdom [3]my is not of this world;
εἰ ἐκ τοῦ κόσμου τούτου ἦν ἡ βασιλεία ἡ ἐμή, οἱ ὑπηρέται [n]ἂν
if of this world were [2]kingdom [1]my, [4]attendants
οἱ ἐμοὶ ἠγωνίζοντο‖ ἵνα μὴ παραδοθῶ τοῖς Ἰουδαίοις·
[3]my would fight that I might not be delivered up to the Jews;
νῦν δὲ ἡ βασιλεία ἡ ἐμὴ οὐκ ἔστιν ἐντεῦθεν. 37 Εἶπεν οὖν
but now [2]kingdom [1]my is not from hence. [3]Said [2]therefore
αὐτῷ ὁ [h]Πιλάτος,‖ Οὐκοῦν βασιλεὺς εἶ σύ; Ἀπεκρίθη [o]ὁ‖
[4]to [5]him [1]Pilate, Then a king art thou? [2]Answered
Ἰησοῦς, Σὺ λέγεις, ὅτι βασιλεύς εἰμι [p]ἐγώ.‖ [q]ἐγὼ‖ εἰς τοῦτο
[1]Jesus, Thou sayest [it], for a king [2]am [1]I. I for this
γεγέννημαι, καὶ εἰς τοῦτο ἐλήλυθα εἰς τὸν κόσμον, ἵνα
have been born, and for this I have come into the world, that
μαρτυρήσω τῇ ἀληθείᾳ. πᾶς ὁ ὢν ἐκ τῆς ἀληθείας
I may bear witness to the truth. Everyone that is of the truth
ἀκούει μου τῆς φωνῆς. 38 Λέγει αὐτῷ ὁ [h]Πιλάτος,‖ Τί ἐστιν
hears my voice. [2]Says [3]to [4]him [1]Pilate, What is
ἀλήθεια; Καὶ τοῦτο εἰπών, πάλιν ἐξῆλθεν πρὸς τοὺς
truth? And this having said, again he went out to the
Ἰουδαίους, καὶ λέγει αὐτοῖς, Ἐγὼ οὐδεμίαν [r]αἰτίαν εὑρίσκω ἐν
Jews, and says to them, I not any fault find in
αὐτῷ.‖ 39 ἔστιν δὲ συνήθεια ὑμῖν ἵνα ἕνα [s]ὑμῖν ἀπολύσω‖
him. But it is a custom with you that one to you I should release
ἐν τῷ πάσχα· βούλεσθε οὖν [t]ὑμῖν ἀπολύσω‖ τὸν βασιλέα
at the passover; will ye therefore to you I should release the king
τῶν Ἰουδαίων; 40 Ἐκραύγασαν οὖν πάλιν [u]πάντες,‖ λέ-
of the Jews? They [3]cried [4]out [2]therefore [5]again [1]all, say-
γοντες, Μὴ τοῦτον, ἀλλὰ τὸν Βαραββᾶν· ἦν δὲ ὁ Βαραβ-
ing, Not this one, but Barabbas. Now [2]was [1]Barab-
βᾶς λῃστής. 19 Τότε οὖν ἔλαβεν ὁ [h]Πιλάτος‖ τὸν Ἰησοῦν
bas a robber. Then therefore [2]took [1]Pilate Jesus
καὶ ἐμαστίγωσεν. 2 καὶ οἱ στρατιῶται πλέξαντες στέφανον
and scourged [him]. And the soldiers having platted a crown

lawful for us to put any man to death: 32 that the saying of Jesus might be fulfilled, which he spake, signifying what death he should die. 33 Then Pilate entered into the judgment hall again, and called Jesus, and said unto him, Art thou the King of the Jews? 34 Jesus answered him, Sayest thou this thing of thyself, or did others tell it thee of me? 35 Pilate answered, Am I a Jew? Thine own nation and the chief priests have delivered thee unto me: what hast thou done? 36 Jesus answered, My kingdom is not of this world: if my kingdom were of this world, then would my servants fight, that I should not be delivered to the Jews: but now is my kingdom not from hence. 37 Pilate therefore said unto him, Art thou a king then? Jesus answered, Thou sayest that I am a king. To this end was I born, and for this cause came I into the world, that I should bear witness unto the truth. Every one that is of the truth heareth my voice. 38 Pilate saith unto him, What is truth? And when he had said this, he went out again unto the Jews, and saith unto them, I find in him no fault *at all*. 39 But ye have a custom, that I should release unto you one at the passover: will ye therefore that I release unto you the King of the Jews? 40 Then cried they all again, saying, Not this man, but Barabbas. Now Barabbas was a robber. XIX. Then Pilate therefore took Jesus, and scourged *him*. 2 And the soldiers platted a crown

---

[g] πάλιν εἰς τὸ πραιτώριον LTTrAW. [h] Πειλᾶτος T. [i] — αὐτῷ ὁ LTTrA; — αὐτῷ W. [k] ἀπὸ σεαυτοῦ LTrA. [l] εἶπόν σοι TrA. [m] — ὁ GLTTrAW. [n] οἱ ἐμοὶ ἠγωνίζοντο ἂν Tr. [o] — ὁ [A]W. [p] — ἐγώ (*read* εἰμι I am) TTr[A]. [q] [ἐγὼ] L. [r] εὑρίσκω ἐν αὐτῷ αἰτίαν LTTrA. [s] ἀπολύσω ὑμῖν LTTr. [t] ἀπολύσω ὑμῖν LTTrW. [u] — πάντες T.

of thorns, and put *it*
on his head, and they
put on him a purple
robe, 3 and said, Hail,
King of the Jews! and
they smote him with
their hands. 4 Pilate
therefore went forth
again, and saith unto
them, Behold, I bring
him forth to you, that
ye may know that I
find no fault in him.
5 Then came Jesus
forth, wearing the
crown of thorns, and
the purple robe. And
Pilate saith unto
them, Behold the
man! 6 When the chief
priests therefore and
officers saw him, they
cried out, saying, Cru-
cify *him*, crucify *him*.
Pilate saith unto
them, Take ye him,
and crucify *him*: for I
find no fault in him.
7 The Jews answered
him, We have a law,
and by our law he
ought to die, because
he made himself the
Son of God. 8 When
Pilate therefore heard
that saying, he was
the more afraid; 9 and
went again into the
judgment hall, and
saith unto Jesus,
Whence art thou? But
Jesus gave him no an-
swer. 10 Then saith
Pilate unto him,
Speakest thou not un-
to me? knowest thou
not that I have power
to crucify thee, and
have power to release
thee? 11 Jesus an-
swered, Thou couldest
have no power *at all*
against me, except it
were given thee from
above: therefore he
that delivered me un-
to thee hath the great-
er sin. 12 And from
thenceforth Pilate
sought to release him:
but the Jews cried out,
saying, If thou let
this man go, thou art

ἐξ ἀκανθῶν ἐπέθηκαν αὐτοῦ τῇ κεφαλῇ, καὶ ἱμάτιον πορ-
of thorns put [it] on his head, and a [2]cloak [1]pur-
φυροῦν περιέβαλον αὐτόν, 3 [v]καὶ ἔλεγον, Χαῖρε, ὁ βασιλεὺς
ple cast around him, and said, Hail, king
τῶν Ἰουδαίων· καὶ [w]ἐδίδουν‖ αὐτῷ ῥαπίσματα.
of the Jews! and they gave him blows with the palm of the hand.
4 [x]Ἐξῆλθεν [y]οὖν‖ πάλιν [z]ἔξω ὁ Πιλάτος,‖ καὶ λέγει αὐτοῖς,
[4]Went [2]therefore [3]again [5]out [1]Pilate, and says to them,
Ἴδε, ἄγω ὑμῖν αὐτὸν ἔξω, ἵνα γνῶτε ὅτι [a]ἐν αὐτῷ
Behold, I bring [3]to [4]you [1]him [2]out, that ye may know that in him
οὐδεμίαν αἰτίαν εὑρίσκω.‖ 5 Ἐξῆλθεν οὖν [b]ὁ‖ Ἰησοῦς ἔξω,
not any fault I find. Went therefore Jesus out,
φορῶν τὸν ἀκάνθινον στέφανον καὶ τὸ πορφυροῦν ἱμάτιον.
wearing the thorny crown and the purple cloak;
καὶ λέγει αὐτοῖς, [c]Ἴδε‖ ὁ ἄνθρωπος. 6 Ὅτε οὖν [d]εἶδον‖
and he says to them, Behold the man! When therefore saw
αὐτὸν οἱ ἀρχιερεῖς καὶ οἱ ὑπηρέται ἐκραύγασαν [e]λέγοντες,‖
him the chief priests and the officers they cried out saying,
Σταύρωσον, σταύρωσον[f]. Λέγει αὐτοῖς ὁ [g]Πιλάτος,‖ Λάβετε
Crucify, crucify [him]. [2]Says [3]to [4]them [1]Pilate, Take
αὐτὸν ὑμεῖς καὶ σταυρώσατε· ἐγὼ.γὰρ οὐχ.εὑρίσκω ἐν αὐτῷ
him ye and crucify [him], for I find not in him
αἰτίαν. 7 Ἀπεκρίθησαν [h]αὐτῷ‖ οἱ Ἰουδαῖοι, Ἡμεῖς νόμον
a fault. [3]Answered [4]him [1]the [2]Jews, We a law
ἔχομεν, καὶ κατὰ τὸν.νόμον.[i]ἡμῶν‖ ὀφείλει ἀποθανεῖν,
have, and according to our law he ought to die,
ὅτι [k]ἑαυτὸν υἱὸν θεοῦ‖ ἐποίησεν. 8 Ὅτε οὖν ἤκουσεν
because himself Son of God he made. When therefore [2]heard
ὁ [g]Πιλάτος‖ τοῦτον τὸν λόγον μᾶλλον ἐφοβήθη, 9 καὶ
[1]Pilate this word [the] more he was afraid, and
εἰσῆλθεν εἰς τὸ πραιτώριον πάλιν, καὶ λέγει τῷ Ἰησοῦ, Πόθεν
went into the prætorium again, and says to Jesus, Whence
εἶ σύ; Ὁ.δὲ.Ἰησοῦς ἀπόκρισιν οὐκ.ἔδωκεν αὐτῷ. 10 λέγει
art thou? But Jesus an answer did not give him. [3]Says
[l]οὖν‖ αὐτῷ ὁ [g]Πιλάτος,‖ Ἐμοὶ οὐ.λαλεῖς; οὐκ.οἶδας
[2]therefore [4]to [5]him [1]Pilate, To me speakest thou not? Knowest not thou
ὅτι ἐξουσίαν ἔχω [m]σταυρῶσαί σε, καὶ ἐξουσίαν ἔχω ἀπο-
that authority I have to crucify thee, and authority I have to re-
λῦσαί σε‖; 11 Ἀπεκρίθη[n] [o]ὁ‖ Ἰησοῦς, Οὐκ [p]εἶχες‖ ἐξουσίαν
lease thee? [2]Answered [1]Jesus, Thou hadst [3]authority
[q]οὐδεμίαν κατ' ἐμοῦ‖ εἰ μὴ.ἦν [r]σοι δεδομένον‖ ἄνωθεν·
[1]not [2]any against me if it were not to thee given from above.
διὰ.τοῦτο ὁ [s]παραδιδούς‖ μέ σοι μείζονα ἁμαρτίαν
On this account he who delivers up me to thee greater sin
ἔχει. 12 Ἐκ τούτου [t]ἐζήτει ὁ Πιλάτος‖ ἀπολῦσαι αὐτόν.
has. From this sought Pilate to release him;
οἱ.δὲ Ἰουδαῖοι [va]ἔκραζον,‖ λέγοντες, Ἐὰν τοῦτον ἀπο-
but the Jews cried out, saying, If this [man] thou re-

---

[v] + καὶ ἤρχοντο πρὸς αὐτὸν and came to him LTTrA. [w] ἐδίδοσαν LTTrA. [x] + καὶ and LTrA. [y] — οὖν GLTTrA. [z] ὁ Πειλᾶτος ἔξω T. [a] οὐδεμίαν αἰτίαν εὑρίσκω ἐν αὐτῷ LTr; αἰτίαν ἐν αὐτῷ οὐδεμίαν εὑρίσκω A; αἰτίαν οὐχ εὑρίσκω T. [b] [ὁ] Tr. [c] Ἰδοὺ TTrA. [d] ἴδον T. [e] — λέγοντες T. [f] + αὐτόν him GLW. [g] Πειλᾶτος T. [h] — αὐτῷ T. [i] — ἡμῶν (*read* the law) LTTrA. [k] ἑαυτὸν υἱὸν τοῦ θεοῦ E; υἱὸν θεοῦ ἑαυτὸν LTTrA. [l] — οὖν T[A]. [m] ἀπολῦσαί σε, καὶ ἐξουσίαν ἔχω σταυρῶσαί σε LTTrA. [n] + αὐτῷ him [L]Tr[A]. [o] — ὁ GLTTrAW. [p] ἔχεις thou hast T. [q] κατ' ἐμοῦ οὐδεμίαν LTTrAW. [r] δεδομένον σοι LTTrA. [s] παραδούς delivered up LT. [t] ὁ Πιλάτος (Πειλᾶτος T) ἐζήτει LTTrA. [va] ἐκραύγαζον LT; ἐκραύγασαν Tr.

λύσῃς οὐκ.εἶ φίλος τοῦ Καίσαρος. πᾶς ὁ βασιλέα
lease thou art not a friend of Cæsar. Everyone [3]the [4]king
[w]αὑτὸν‖ ποιῶν ἀντιλέγει τῷ Καίσαρι. 13 Ὁ οὖν.[x]Πιλάτος‖
[2]himself [1]making speaks against Cæsar. Pilate therefore
ἀκούσας [y]τοῦτον τὸν λόγον,‖ ἤγαγεν ἔξω τὸν Ἰησοῦν, καὶ
having heard this word, led out Jesus, and
ἐκάθισεν ἐπὶ [z]τοῦ‖ βήματος, εἰς τόπον λεγόμενον Λιθό-
sat down upon the judgment-seat, at a place called Pave-
στρωτον, Ἑβραϊστὶ.δὲ Γαββαθᾶ· 14 ἦν.δὲ παρασκευὴ
ment, but in Hebrew Gabbatha: (and it was [the] preparation
τοῦ πάσχα, ὥρα [a]δὲ ὡσεὶ‖ ἕκτη· καὶ λέγει τοῖς Ἰου-
of the passover, [[2]the] [3]hour [1]and about the sixth;) and he says to the Jews,
δαίοις, Ἴδε ὁ.βασιλεὺς.ὑμῶν. 15 [b]Οἱ.δὲ ἐκραύγασαν,‖ Ἆρον
Behold your king! But they cried out, Away,
ἆρον, σταύρωσον αὐτόν. Λέγει αὐτοῖς ὁ [x]Πιλάτος,‖ Τὸν
away, crucify him. [2]Says [3]to [4]them [1]Pilate,
βασιλέα.ὑμῶν σταυρώσω; Ἀπεκρίθησαν οἱ ἀρχιερεῖς, Οὐκ
Your king shall I crucify? [4]Answered [1]the [2]chief [3]priests, [7]Not
ἔχομεν βασιλέα εἰ.μὴ Καίσαρα. 16 Τότε οὖν παρέδωκεν
[5]we [6]have a king except Cæsar. Then therefore he delivered up
αὐτὸν αὐτοῖς ἵνα σταυρωθῇ. Παρέλαβον [c]δὲ‖ τὸν Ἰη-
him to them that he might be crucified. [2]They [3]took [1]and Je-
σοῦν [d]καὶ ἀπήγαγον·‖ 17 καὶ βαστάζων [e]τὸν.σταυρὸν.αὐτοῦ‖
sus and led [him] away. And bearing his cross
ἐξῆλθεν εἰς τὸν λεγόμενον κρανίου τόπον, [f]ὃς‖ λέγεται
he went out to the [2]called [3]of [4]a [5]skull [1]place, which is called
Ἑβραϊστὶ Γολγοθᾶ. 18 ὅπου αὐτὸν ἐσταύρωσαν, καὶ μετ᾽
in Hebrew Golgotha: where him they crucified, and with
αὐτοῦ ἄλλους δύο ἐντεῦθεν καὶ ἐντεῦθεν, μέσον.δὲ
him [2]others [1]two on this side and on that side [one], and in the middle
τὸν Ἰησοῦν. 19 Ἔγραψεν.δὲ καὶ τίτλον ὁ [x]Πιλάτος‖ καὶ
Jesus. And [3]wrote [2]also [4]a [5]title [1]Pilate and
ἔθηκεν ἐπὶ τοῦ σταυροῦ· ἦν.δὲ γεγραμμένον. Ἰησοῦς ὁ
put on the cross. And it was written, Jesus the
Ναζωραῖος, ὁ βασιλεὺς τῶν Ἰουδαίων. 20 Τοῦτον οὖν
Nazaræan, the king of the Jews. This [2]therefore
τὸν τίτλον πολλοὶ ἀνέγνωσαν τῶν Ἰουδαίων, ὅτι ἐγγὺς ἦν
[1]title [4]many [5]read of the Jews, for near [3]was
[g]τῆς πόλεως ὁ τόπος,‖ ὅπου ἐσταυρώθη ὁ Ἰησοῦς· καὶ ἦν
[1]the [2]city the place, where was crucified Jesus; and it was
γεγραμμένον Ἑβραϊστί, [h]Ἑλληνιστί, Ῥωμαϊστί.‖ 21 ἔλεγον
written in Hebrew, in Greek, in Latin. [7]Said
οὖν τῷ [i]Πιλάτῳ‖ οἱ ἀρχιερεῖς τῶν Ἰουδαίων, Μὴ.γράφε,
[8]therefore [9]to [10]Pilate [1]the [2]chief [3]priests [4]of [5]the [6]Jews, Write not,
Ὁ βασιλεὺς τῶν Ἰουδαίων· ἀλλ᾽ ὅτι ἐκεῖνος εἶπεν, Βασιλεύς
The king of the Jews, but that he said, King
[k]εἰμι τῶν Ἰουδαίων.‖ 22 Ἀπεκρίθη ὁ [x]Πιλάτος,‖ Ὃ γέ-
I am of the Jews. [2]Answered [1]Pilate, What I have
γραφα γέγραφα. 23 Οἱ οὖν στρατιῶται, ὅτε ἐσταύρωσαν
written I have written. The [2]therefore [1]soldiers, when they crucified
τὸν Ἰησοῦν ἔλαβον τὰ.ἱμάτια.αὐτοῦ, καὶ ἐποίησαν [l]τέσσαρα‖
Jesus took his garments, and made four

not Cæsar's friend: whosoever maketh himself a king speaketh against Cæsar.
13 When Pilate therefore heard that saying, he brought Jesus forth, and sat down in the judgment seat in a place that is called the Pavement, but in the Hebrew, Gabbatha.
14 And it was the preparation of the passover, and about the sixth hour: and he saith unto the Jews, Behold your King!
15 But they cried out, Away with *him*, away with *him*, crucify him. Pilate saith unto them, Shall I crucify your King? The chief priests answered, We have no king but Cæsar.
16 Then delivered he him therefore unto them to be crucified. And they took Jesus, and led *him* away.
17 And he bearing his cross went forth into a place called *the place* of a skull, which is called in the Hebrew Golgotha:
18 where they crucified him, and two other with him, on either side one, and Jesus in the midst.
19 And Pilate wrote a title, and put *it* on the cross. And the writing was, JESUS OF NAZARETH, THE KING OF THE JEWS.
20 This title then read many of the Jews: for the place where Jesus was crucified was nigh to the city: and it was written in Hebrew, *and* Greek, *and* Latin.
21 Then said the chief priests of the Jews to Pilate, Write not, The King of the Jews; but that he said, I am King of the Jews.
22 Pilate answered, What I have written I have written.
23 Then the soldiers, when they had crucified Jesus, took his garments, and made four parts, to

[w] ἑαυτὸν GLTTrAW. [x] Πειλᾶτος T. [y] τῶν λόγων τούτων these words LTTrAW. [z] — τοῦ (*read* a judgment seat) LTTrAW. [a] ἦν ὡς was about LTTrAW. [b] ἐκραύγασαν οὖν ἐκεῖνοι they therefore cried out TTrA. [c] οὖν therefore LTTrA. [d] καὶ ἤγαγον G; — καὶ ἀπήγαγον LTTrA. [e] αὐτῷ (ἑαυτῷ T) τὸν σταυρὸν LTTrA. [f] ὃ LTTrA. [g] ὁ τόπος τῆς πόλεως GLTTrAW. [h] Ῥωμαιστί, Ἑλληνιστί TTrA. [i] Πειλάτῳ T. [k] τῶν Ἰουδαίων εἰμί TrA. [l] τέσσερα TTrA.

μέρη, ἑκάστῳ στρατιώτῃ μέρος, καὶ τὸν χιτῶνα. ἦν.δὲ ὁ
parts, to each soldier a part, and the tunic; but [3]was [1]the
χιτὼν [m]ἄρραφος,‖ ἐκ τῶν ἄνωθεν ὑφαντὸς δι'.ὅλου. 24 [n]εἶ-
[2]tunic seamless, from the top woven throughout. They
πον‖ οὖν πρὸς ἀλλήλους, Μὴ.σχίσωμεν αὐτόν, ἀλλὰ
said therefore to one another, Let us not rend it, but
λάχωμεν περὶ αὐτοῦ τίνος ἔσται· ἵνα ἡ γραφὴ πλη-
let us cast lots for it whose it shall be; that the scripture [1]might be
ρωθῇ [o]ἡ λέγουσα,‖ Διεμερίσαντο τὰ.ἱμάτιά.μου ἑαυτοῖς.
fulfilled which says, They divided my garments among them,
καὶ ἐπὶ τὸν.ἱματισμόν.μου ἔβαλον κλῆρον. Οἱ μὲν οὖν
and for my vesture they cast a lot. The [2]therefore
στρατιῶται ταῦτα ἐποίησαν.
[1]soldiers these things did.

25 Εἱστήκεισαν.δὲ παρὰ τῷ σταυρῷ τοῦ Ἰησοῦ ἡ.μήτηρ.αὐ-
And stood by the cross of Jesus his mother,
τοῦ, καὶ ἡ ἀδελφὴ τῆς.μητρὸς.αὐτοῦ, [p]Μαρία‖ ἡ τοῦ
and the sister of his mother, Mary the [wife]
Κλωπᾶ, καὶ [p]Μαρία‖ ἡ Μαγδαληνή. 26 Ἰησοῦς οὖν ἰδὼν
of Clopas, and Mary the Magdalene. Jesus therefore seeing
τὴν μητέρα, καὶ τὸν μαθητὴν παρεστῶτα ὃν ἠγάπα, λέγει
[his] mother, and the disciple standing by whom he loved, says
τῇ.μητρὶ.[q]αὐτοῦ,‖ Γύναι, [r]ἰδοὺ‖ ὁ.υἱός.σου. 27 Εἶτα λέγει τῷ
to his mother, Woman, behold thy son. Then he says to the
μαθητῇ, [r]Ἰδοὺ‖ ἡ.μήτηρ.σου. Καὶ ἀπ' ἐκείνης τῆς ὥρας
disciple, Behold thy mother. And from that hour
ἔλαβεν [s]αὐτὴν ὁ μαθητὴς‖ εἰς τὰ.ἴδια. 28 Μετὰ τοῦτο
[3]took [4]her [1]the [2]disciple to his own [home]. After this,
εἰδὼς ὁ Ἰησοῦς ὅτι [t]πάντα ἤδη‖ τετέλεσται, ἵνα τελειωθῇ
[2]knowing [1]Jesus that all things now have been finished, that might be fulfilled
ἡ γραφὴ λέγει, Διψῶ. 29 Σκεῦος [v]οὖν‖ ἔκειτο ὄξους
the scripture he says, I thirst. A vessel therefore was set [2]of [3]vinegar
μεστόν· [w]οἱ.δὲ πλήσαντες σπόγγον ὄξους, καὶ ὑσσώπῳ‖
[1]full, and they having filled a sponge with vinegar, and [5]hyssop
περιθέντες προσήνεγκαν αὐτοῦ τῷ.στόματι. 30 ὅτε
[1]having [2]put [[3]it] [4]on they brought it to [his] mouth. When
οὖν ἔλαβεν τὸ ὄξος [x]ὁ Ἰησοῦς‖ εἶπεν, Τετέλεσται· καὶ
therefore [2]took [3]the [4]vinegar [1]Jesus he said, It has been finished; and
κλίνας τὴν κεφαλὴν παρέδωκεν τὸ πνεῦμα. 31 Οἱ
having bowed the head he yielded up [his] spirit. The
οὖν Ἰουδαῖοι, [y]ἵνα μὴ.μείνῃ ἐπὶ τοῦ σταυροῦ τὰ
[2]therefore [1]Jews, that might not remain on the cross the
σώματα ἐν τῷ σαββάτῳ, [y]ἐπεὶ παρασκευὴ ἦν,‖ ἦν.γὰρ
bodies on the sabbath, because [the] preparation it was, (for [4]was
μεγάλη ἡ ἡμέρα [z]ἐκείνου‖ τοῦ σαββάτου, ἠρώτησαν τὸν [a]Πι-
[5]great [3]day [1]that [2]sabbath,) requested Pi-
λάτον‖ ἵνα κατεαγῶσιν αὐτῶν τὰ σκέλη, καὶ ἀρθῶσιν.
late that [3]might [4]be [5]broken [1]their [2]legs, and taken away.
32 ἦλθον οὖν οἱ στρατιῶται, καὶ τοῦ μὲν πρώτου κατέαξαν
Came therefore the soldiers, and of the first broke
τὰ σκέλη καὶ τοῦ ἄλλου τοῦ [b]συσταυρωθέντος‖ αὐτῷ· 33 ἐπὶ.δὲ
the legs and of the other who was crucified with him; but to

every soldier a part; and also *his* coat: now the coat was without seam, woven from the top throughout.
24 They said therefore among themselves, Let us not rend it, but cast lots for it, whose it shall be: that the scripture might be fulfilled, which saith, They parted my raiment among them, and for my vesture they did cast lots. These things therefore the soldiers did.

25 Now there stood by the cross of Jesus his mother, and his mother's sister, Mary the *wife* of Cleophas, and Mary Magdalene.
26 When Jesus therefore saw his mother, and the disciple standing by, whom he loved, he saith unto his mother, Woman, behold thy son!
27 Then saith he to the disciple, Behold thy mother! And from that hour that disciple took her unto his own *home*.
28 After this, Jesus knowing that all things were now accomplished, that the scripture might be fulfilled, saith, I thirst.
29 Now there was set a vessel full of vinegar: and they filled a spunge with vinegar, and put *it* upon hyssop, and put *it* to his mouth.
30 When Jesus therefore had received the vinegar, he said, It is finished: and he bowed his head, and gave up the ghost.
31 The Jews therefore, because it was the preparation, that the bodies should not remain upon the cross on the sabbath day, (for that sabbath day was an high day,) besought Pilate that their legs might be broken, and *that* they might be taken away.
32 Then came the soldiers, and brake the legs of the first, and of the other which was crucified with him.
33 But when they came to Je-

[m] ἄραφος TTrA. [n] εἶπαν T. [o] — ἡ λέγουσα LT. [p] Μαριὰμ T. [q] — αὐτοῦ (*read* [his]) [L]TTr[A]. [r] ἴδε GLTTrA. [s] ὁ μαθητὴς αὐτὴν GTrAW. [t] ἤδη πάντα LTTrAW. [v] — οὖν LTTrAW. [w] σπόγγον οὖν μεστὸν τοῦ (— τοῦ T) ὄξους ὑσσώπῳ (ὑσώπῳ L) a sponge therefore full of the vinegar, [5]hyssop LTTrA. [x] [ὁ] Tr; — ὁ Ἰησοῦς T. [y] ἐπεὶ παρασκευὴ ἦν *placed after* Ἰουδαῖοι TTrA. [z] ἐκείνη E. [a] Πειλᾶτον T. [b] συνσταυρωθέντος LTTrA.

τὸν Ἰησοῦν ἐλθόντες, ὡς εἶδον [c]αὐτὸν ἤδη‖ τεθνηκότα,
Jesus having come, when they saw he already was dead,
οὐ.κατέαξαν αὐτοῦ τὰ σκέλη· 34 ἀλλ' εἷς τῶν στρατιωτῶν
they did not break his legs, but one of the soldiers
λόγχῃ αὐτοῦ τὴν πλευρὰν ἔνυξεν, καὶ [d]εὐθὺς ἐξῆλθεν‖
with a spear his side pierced, and immediately came out
αἷμα καὶ ὕδωρ. 35 καὶ ὁ ἑωρακὼς μεμαρτύρηκεν, καὶ
blood and water. And he who has seen has borne witness, and
ἀληθινὴ αὐτοῦ ἐστιν ἡ μαρτυρία, [e]κἀκεῖνος‖ οἶδεν ὅτι ἀληθῆ
true [2]his [1]is witness, and he knows that true
λέγει, ἵνα [f] ὑμεῖς [g]πιστεύσητε.‖ 36 ἐγένετο.γὰρ ταῦτα ἵνα
he says, that ye may believe. For [3]took [4]place [1]these [2]things that
ἡ γραφὴ πληρωθῇ, Ὀστοῦν.οὐ συντριβήσεται αὐτοῦ.
the scripture might be fulfilled, Not a bone shall be broken of him.
37 καὶ πάλιν ἑτέρα γραφὴ λέγει, Ὄψονται εἰς ὃν
And again another scripture says, They shall look on him whom
ἐξεκέντησαν.
they pierced.

38 Μετὰ.δὲ ταῦτα ἠρώτησεν τὸν [h]Πιλάτον‖ [i]ὁ‖ Ἰωσὴφ
And after these things asked Pilate Joseph
[k]ὁ‖ ἀπὸ Ἀριμαθαίας, ὢν μαθητὴς τοῦ Ἰησοῦ, κεκρυμμένος.δὲ
(from Arimathæa, being a disciple of Jesus, but concealed
διὰ τὸν φόβον τῶν Ἰουδαίων, ἵνα ἄρῃ τὸ σῶμα
through fear of the Jews,) that he might take away the body
τοῦ Ἰησοῦ· καὶ ἐπέτρεψεν ὁ [l]Πιλάτος.‖ [m]ἦλθεν‖ οὖν καὶ
of Jesus: and [2]gave [3]leave [1]Pilate. He came therefore and
[n]ἦρεν‖ [o]τὸ σῶμα‖ [p]τοῦ Ἰησοῦ.‖ 39 ἦλθεν.δὲ καὶ Νικόδημος,
took away the body of Jesus. And came also Nicodemus,
ὁ ἐλθὼν πρὸς [q]τὸν Ἰησοῦν‖ νυκτὸς τὸ.πρῶτον, φέρων μίγμα
who came to Jesus by night at first, bearing a mixture
σμύρνης καὶ ἀλόης [r]ὡσεὶ‖ λίτρας ἑκατόν. 40 ἔλαβον οὖν
of myrrh and aloes about [3]pounds [1]a [2]hundred. They took therefore
τὸ σῶμα τοῦ Ἰησοῦ, καὶ ἔδησαν αὐτὸ [s] ὀθονίοις μετὰ τῶν
the body of Jesus, and bound it in linen cloths with the
ἀρωμάτων, καθὼς ἔθος ἐστὶν τοῖς Ἰουδαίοις ἐντα-
aromatics, as a custom is among the Jews to prepare for
φιάζειν. 41 ἦν.δὲ ἐν τῷ τόπῳ ὅπου ἐσταυρώθη κῆπος,
burial. Now there was in the place where he was crucified a garden,
καὶ ἐν τῷ κήπῳ μνημεῖον καινόν, ἐν ᾧ οὐδέπω.οὐδεὶς ἐτέθη.
and in the garden a [2]tomb [1]new, in which no one ever was laid.
42 ἐκεῖ οὖν διὰ τὴν παρασκευὴν τῶν Ἰουδαίων, ὅτι
There therefore on account of the preparation of the Jews, because
ἐγγὺς ἦν τὸ μνημεῖον, ἔθηκαν τὸν Ἰησοῦν.
near was the tomb, they laid Jesus.

20 Τῇ.δὲ μιᾷ τῶν σαββάτων [t]Μαρία‖ ἡ Μαγδαληνὴ
But on the first [day] of the week Mary the Magdalene
ἔρχεται πρωΐ σκοτίας ἔτι οὔσης εἰς τὸ μνημεῖον, καὶ βλέπει
comes early [4]dark [3]still [1]it [2]being to the tomb, and sees
τὸν λίθον ἠρμένον ἐκ τοῦ μνημείου. 2 τρέχει οὖν καὶ
the stone taken away from the tomb. She runs therefore and
ἔρχεται πρὸς Σίμωνα Πέτρον καὶ πρὸς τὸν ἄλλον μαθητὴν
comes to Simon Peter and to the other disciple

sus, and saw that he was dead already, they brake not his legs: 34 but one of the soldiers with a spear pierced his side, and forthwith came there out blood and water. 35 And he that saw *it* bare record, and his record is true: and he knoweth that he saith true, that ye might believe. 36 For these things were done, that the scripture should be fulfilled, A bone of him shall not be broken. 37 And again another scripture saith, They shall look on him whom they pierced.

38 And after this Joseph of Arimathæa, being a disciple of Jesus, but secretly for fear of the Jews, besought Pilate that he might take away the body of Jesus: and Pilate gave *him* leave. He came therefore, and took the body of Jesus. 39 And there came also Nicodemus, which at the first came to Jesus by night, and brought a mixture of myrrh and aloes, about an hundred pound *weight*. 40 Then took they the body of Jesus, and wound it in linen clothes with the spices, as the manner of the Jews is to bury. 41 Now in the place where he was crucified there was a garden; and in the garden a new sepulchre, wherein was never man yet laid. 42 There laid they Jesus therefore because of the Jews' preparation *day*; for the sepulchre was nigh at hand.

XX. The first *day* of the week cometh Mary Magdalene early, when it was yet dark, unto the sepulchre, and seeth the stone taken away from the sepulchre. 2 Then she runneth, and cometh to Simon Peter, and to the other disciple,

[c] ἤδη αὐτὸν TTrA. [d] ἐξῆλθεν εὐθὺς TTrA. [e] καὶ ἐκεῖνος LTr. [f] + καὶ also GLTTrAW. [g] πιστεύητε T. [h] Πειλᾶτον T. [i] — ὁ LTTrAW. [k] — ὁ LTrA. [l] Πειλᾶτος T. [m] ἦλθον they came T. [n] ἦραν T. [o] — τὸ σῶμα T. [p] αὐτοῦ of him LTrA; αὐτόν him T. [q] αὐτὸν him LTTrAW. [r] ὡς GLTTrAW. [s] + ἐν W. [t] Μαριὰμ T.

whom Jesus loved, and
saith unto them, They
have taken away the
Lord out of the sepul-
chre, and we know not
where they have laid
him. 3 Peter there-
fore went forth, and
that other disciple,and
came to the sepulchre.
4 So they ran both to-
gether : and the other
disciple did outrun Pe-
ter, and came first to
the sepulchre. 5 And
he stooping down, *and*
looking in, saw the li-
nen clothes lying ; yet
went he not in. 6 Then
cometh Simon Peter
following him, and
went into the sepul-
chre, and seeth the li-
nen clothes lie, 7 and
the napkin, that was
about his head, not ly-
ing with the linen
clothes, but wrapped
together in a place by
itself. 8 Then went in
also that other disci-
ple, which came first to
the sepulchre, and he
saw, and believed.
9 For as yet they knew
not the scripture, that
he must rise again
from the dead. 10 Then
the disciples went a-
way again unto their
own home. 11 But
Mary stood without at
the sepulchre weeping:
and as she wept, she
stooped down, *and*
looked into the sepul-
chre, 12 and seeth two
angels in white sitting,
the one at the head,
and the other at the
feet, where the body
of Jesus had lain.
13 And they say unto
her, Woman, why
weepest thou? She
saith unto them, Be-
cause they have taken
away my Lord, and I
know not where they
have laid him. 14 And
when she had thus
said, she turned her-
self back, and saw Je-
sus standing,and knew
not that it was Jesus.
15 Jesus saith unto
her, Woman, why
weepest thou? whom
seekest thou? She,
supposing him to be
the gardener, saith un-
to him, Sir, if thou
have borne him hence,
tell me where thou
hast laid him, and I
will take him away.
16 Jesus saith unto her,
Mary. She turned her-

ὃν ἐφίλει ὁ Ἰησοῦς, καὶ λέγει αὐτοῖς, Ἦραν τὸν κύριον
whom [2]loved [1]Jesus, and says to them, They took away the Lord
ἐκ τοῦ μνημείου, καὶ οὐκ.οἴδαμεν ποῦ ἔθηκαν αὐτόν.
out of the tomb, and we know not where they laid him.
3 Ἐξῆλθεν οὖν ὁ Πέτρος καὶ ὁ ἄλλος μαθητής, καὶ ἤρχοντο
[3]Went [4]forth [2]therefore [1]Peter and the other disciple, and came
εἰς τὸ μνημεῖον. 4 ἔτρεχον.δὲ οἱ δύο ὁμοῦ· [v]καὶ ὁ‖ ἄλλος
to the tomb. And [3]ran [1]the [2]two together, and the other
μαθητὴς προέδραμεν τάχιον τοῦ Πέτρου, καὶ ἦλθεν πρῶτος
disciple ran forward faster than Peter, and came first
εἰς τὸ μνημεῖον, 5 καὶ παρακύψας βλέπει [w]κείμενα τὰ ὀθόνια,‖
to the tomb, and stooping down he sees lying the linen cloths;
οὐ μέντοι εἰσῆλθεν. 6 ἔρχεται οὖν [x] Σίμων Πέτρος ἀκολου-
[3]not [4]however [1]he [2]entered. Comes then Simon Peter follow-
θῶν αὐτῷ, καὶ εἰσῆλθεν εἰς τὸ μνημεῖον, καὶ θεωρεῖ τὰ
ing him, and entered into the tomb, and sees the
ὀθόνια κείμενα, 7 καὶ τὸ σουδάριον ὃ ἦν ἐπὶ τῆς κεφαλῆς
linen cloths lying, and the handkerchief which was upon [2]head
αὐτοῦ, οὐ μετὰ τῶν ὀθονίων κείμενον, ἀλλὰ χωρὶς ἐν-
[1]his, not with the linen cloths lying, but [6]by [7]itself
τετυλιγμένον εἰς ἕνα τόπον. 8 τότε οὖν εἰσῆλθεν καὶ ὁ
[1]folded [2]up [3]in [4]a [5]place. Then therefore entered also the
ἄλλος μαθητὴς ὁ ἐλθὼν πρῶτος εἰς τὸ μνημεῖον, καὶ εἶδεν
other disciple who came first to the tomb, and saw
καὶ ἐπίστευσεν· 9 οὐδέπω.γὰρ ᾔδεισαν τὴν γραφήν, ὅτι
and believed; for not yet knew they the scripture, that
δεῖ αὐτὸν ἐκ νεκρῶν ἀναστῆναι. 10 ἀπῆλθον
it behoves him from among [the] dead to rise. Went away
οὖν πάλιν πρὸς [y]ἑαυτοὺς‖ οἱ μαθηταί. 11 [z]Μαρία‖.δὲ
therefore again to their [home] the disciples. But Mary
εἱστήκει πρὸς [a]τὸ μνημεῖον‖ [b]κλαίουσα ἔξω.‖ ὡς οὖν
stood at the tomb [2]weeping [1]outside. As therefore
ἔκλαιεν, παρέκυψεν εἰς τὸ μνημεῖον, 12 καὶ θεωρεῖ δύο ἀγ-
she wept, she stooped down into the tomb, and beholds two an-
γέλους ἐν λευκοῖς καθεζομένους, ἕνα πρὸς τῇ κεφαλῇ καὶ ἕνα
gels in white sitting, one at the head and one
πρὸς τοῖς ποσίν, ὅπου ἔκειτο τὸ σῶμα τοῦ Ἰησοῦ. 13 [c]καὶ‖
at the feet, where was laid the body of Jesus. And
λέγουσιν αὐτῇ ἐκεῖνοι, Γύναι, τί κλαίεις; Λέγει αὐτοῖς,
[2]say [3]to [4]her [1]they, Woman, why weepest thou? She says to them,
Ὅτι ἦραν τὸν.κύριόν.μου, καὶ οὐκ.οἶδα ποῦ ἔθηκαν
Because they took away my Lord, and I know not where they laid
αὐτόν. 14 [d]Καὶ‖ ταῦτα εἰποῦσα ἐστράφη εἰς.τὰ.ὀπίσω, καὶ
him. And these things having said she turned backward, and
θεωρεῖ τὸν Ἰησοῦν ἑστῶτα· καὶ οὐκ.ᾔδει ὅτι [e]ὁ‖ Ἰησοῦς ἐστιν.
beholds Jesus standing, and knew not that Jesus it is.
15 λέγει αὐτῇ *ὁ‖ Ἰησοῦς, Γύναι, τί κλαίεις; τίνα ζητεῖς;
[2]Says [3]to [4]her [1]Jesus, Woman, why weepest thou? Whom seekest thou?
Ἐκείνη δοκοῦσα ὅτι ὁ κηπουρός ἐστιν, λέγει αὐτῷ, Κύριε, εἰ
She thinking that the gardener it is, says to him, Sir, if
σὺ ἐβάστασας αὐτόν, εἰπέ μοι ποῦ [f]αὐτὸν ἔθηκας·‖ κἀγὼ
thou didst carry off him, tell me where him thou didst lay, and I
αὐτὸν ἀρῶ. 16 Λέγει αὐτῇ [g]ὁ‖ Ἰησοῦς, [h]Μαρία.‖ Στρα-
him will take away. [2]Says [3]to [4]her [1]Jesus, Mary. Turn-

[v] ὁ δὲ L. [w] τὰ ὀθόνια κείμενα L. [x] + καὶ also TrA. [y] αὐτοὺς TTr. [z] Μαριάμ T.
[a] τῷ μνημείῳ GLTTrAW [b] ἔξω κλαίουσα TTrA; — ἔξω L. [c] — καὶ T. [d] — καὶ GLTTrAW.
[e] — ὁ GLTTrAW. * — ὁ LTTrAW. [f] ἔθηκας αὐτόν GLTTrAW. [g] — ὁ LTTrA. [h] Μαριάμ TTrA.

φεῖσα ἐκείνη λέγει αὐτῷ[i], Ῥαββουνί· ὃ.λέγεται, διδάσκαλε.
ing round she says to him, Rabboni, that is to say, Teacher.
17 λέγει αὐτῇ [k]ὁ" Ἰησοῦς, Μή μου ἅπτου, οὔπω.γὰρ ἀναβέ-
[2]Says [3]to [4]her [1]Jesus, [7]Not [6]me [5]touch, for not yet have I
βηκα πρὸς τὸν.πατέρα.[l]μου·" πορεύου.δὲ πρὸς τοὺς ἀδελφούς
ascended to my Father; but go to [2]brethren
μου, καὶ εἰπὲ αὐτοῖς, Ἀναβαίνω πρὸς τὸν.πατέρα.μου καὶ
[1]my, and say to them, I ascend to my Father and
πατέρα.ὑμῶν, καὶ θεόν.μου καὶ θεὸν.ὑμῶν. 18 Ἔρχεται
your Father, and my God and your God. [4]Comes
[m]Μαρία" ἡ Μαγδαληνὴ [n]ἀπαγγέλλουσα" τοῖς μαθηταῖς ὅτι
[1]Mary [2]the [3]Magdalene bringing word to the disciples
[o]ἑώρακεν" τὸν κύριον, καὶ ταῦτα εἶπεν αὐτῇ. 19 Οὔσης.οὖν
she has seen the Lord, and these things he said to her. It being therefore
ὀψίας τῇ.ἡμέρᾳ.ἐκείνῃ, τῇ μιᾷ [p]τῶν".σαββάτων, καὶ τῶν
evening on that day, the first [day] of the week, and the
θυρῶν κεκλεισμένων ὅπου ἦσαν οἱ μαθηταὶ [q]συνηγμένοι," διὰ
doors having been shut where [3]were [1]the [2]disciples assembled, through
τὸν φόβον τῶν Ἰουδαίων, ἦλθεν ὁ Ἰησοῦς καὶ ἔστη εἰς τὸ
fear of the Jews, [2]came [1]Jesus and stood in the
μέσον, καὶ λέγει αὐτοῖς, Εἰρήνη ὑμῖν. 20 Καὶ τοῦτο εἰπὼν
midst, and says to them, Peace to you. And this having said
ἔδειξεν [r]αὐτοῖς τὰς χεῖρας καὶ τὴν πλευρὰν αὐτοῦ." ἐχάρη-
he shewed to them the hands and the side of himself. [3]Rejoiced
σαν οὖν οἱ μαθηταὶ ἰδόντες τὸν κύριον. 21 εἶπεν οὖν
[4]therefore [1]the [2]disciples having seen the Lord. [3]Said [2]therefore
αὐτοῖς [s]ὁ Ἰησοῦς" πάλιν, Εἰρήνη ὑμῖν· καθὼς ἀπέσταλκέν
[4]to [5]them [1]Jesus again, Peace to you: as [3]has [4]sent [5]forth
με ὁ πατήρ, κἀγὼ πέμπω ὑμᾶς. 22 Καὶ τοῦτο εἰπὼν
[6]me [1]the [2]Father, I also send you. And this having said
ἐνεφύσησεν, καὶ λέγει αὐτοῖς, Λάβετε πνεῦμα ἅγιον.
he breathed into [them], and says to them, Receive [the] [2]Spirit [1]Holy:
23 [t]ἄν".τινων ἀφῆτε τὰς ἁμαρτίας, [v]ἀφίενται" αὐτοῖς·
of whomsoever ye may remit the sins, they are remitted to them;
[t]ἄν".τινων κρατῆτε, κεκράτηνται. 24 Θωμᾶς.δέ, εἷς ἐκ
of whomsoever ye may retain, they have been retained. But Thomas, one of
τῶν δώδεκα ὁ λεγόμενος Δίδυμος, οὐκ.ἦν μετ' αὐτῶν ὅτε
the twelve called Didymus, was not with them when
ἦλθεν [w]ὁ" Ἰησοῦς. 25 ἔλεγον οὖν αὐτῷ οἱ ἄλλοι μαθηταί,
[2]came [1]Jesus. [4]Said [5]therefore [6]to [7]him [1]the [2]other [3]disciples,
Ἑωράκαμεν τὸν κύριον. Ὁ.δὲ εἶπεν αὐτοῖς, Ἐὰν.μὴ ἴδω ἐν
We have seen the Lord. But he said to them, Unless I see in
ταῖς.χερσὶν.αὐτοῦ τὸν τύπον τῶν ἥλων, καὶ βάλω [x]τὸν δάκτυ-
his hands the mark of the nails, and put [2]finger
λόν μου" εἰς τὸν [y]τύπον" τῶν ἥλων, καὶ βάλω [z]τὴν.χεῖρά.μου"
[1]my into the mark of the nails, and put my hand
εἰς τὴν.πλευρὰν.αὐτοῦ, οὐ.μὴ πιστεύσω. 26 Καὶ μεθ' ἡμέρας
into his side, not at all will I believe. And after [2]days
ὀκτὼ πάλιν ἦσαν ἔσω οἱ.μαθηταὶ.αὐτοῦ, καὶ Θωμᾶς μετ'
[1]eight again were [3]within [1]his [2]disciples, and Thomas with
αὐτῶν. ἔρχεται ὁ Ἰησοῦς, τῶν θυρῶν κεκλεισμένων, καὶ ἔστη
them. Comes Jesus, the doors having been shut, and stood

self, and saith unto him, Rabboni; which is to say, Master. 17 Jesus saith unto her, Touch me not; for I am not yet ascended to my Father: but go to my brethren, and say unto them, I ascend unto my Father, and your Father; and *to* my God, and your God. 18 Mary Magdalene came and told the disciples that she had seen the Lord, and *that* he had spoken these things unto her. 19 Then the same day at evening, being the first *day* of the week, when the doors were shut where the disciples were assembled for fear of the Jews, came Jesus and stood in the midst, and saith unto them, Peace *be* unto you. 20 And when he had so said, he shewed unto them *his* hands and his side. Then were the disciples glad, when they saw the Lord. 21 Then said Jesus to them again, Peace *be* unto you: as *my* Father hath sent me, even so send I you. 22 And when he had said this, he breathed on *them*, and saith unto them, Receive ye the Holy Ghost: 23 whose soever sins ye remit, they are remitted unto them; *and* whose soever *sins* ye retain, they are retained. 24 But Thomas, one of the twelve, called Didymus, was not with them when Jesus came. 25 The other disciples therefore said unto him, We have seen the Lord. But he said unto them, Except I shall see in his hands the print of the nails, and put my finger into the print of the nails, and thrust my hand into his side, I will not believe. 26 And after eight days again his disciples were within, and Thomas with them: *then* came Jesus, the doors being shut, and stood in the

---

[i] + Ἑβραϊστί in Hebrew [L]TTrA. [k] — ὁ LTTrA. [l] — μου (*read* the Father) [L]TTrA. [m] Μαριὰμ TTrA. [n] ἀγγέλλουσα LTTrA. [o] ἑώρακα I have seen TTrA. [p] — τῶν LTTrAW. [q] — συνηγμένοι LTTrA. [r] καὶ (— καὶ T) τὰς χεῖρας καὶ τὴν πλευρὰν αὐτοῖς LTTrA. [s] — ὁ Ἰησοῦς (*read* he said) TTr[A]. [t] ἐὰν L. [v] ἀφέωνται they have been remitted LTTrA. [w] — ὁ LTTrA. [x] μου τὸν δάκτυλον T. [y] τόπον place LT. [z] μου τὴν χεῖρα TTrA.

midst, and said, Peace be unto you. 27 Then saith he to Thomas, Reach hither thy finger, and behold my hands; and reach hither thy hand, and thrust *it* into my side: and be not faithless, but believing. 28 And Thomas answered and said unto him, My Lord and my God. 29 Jesus saith unto him, Thomas, because thou hast seen me, thou hast believed: blessed *are* they that have not seen, and *yet* have believed.

30 And many other signs truly did Jesus in the presence of his disciples, which are not written in this book: 31 but these are written, that ye might believe that Jesus is the Christ, the Son of God; and that believing ye might have life through his name.

εἰς τὸ μέσον καὶ εἶπεν, Εἰρήνη ὑμῖν. 27 Εἶτα λέγει τῷ Θωμᾷ,
in **the midst** and said, Peace to you. Then he says to Thomas,
Φέρε τὸν.δάκτυλόν.σου ὧδε, καὶ ἴδε τὰς.χεῖράς.μου· καὶ
Bring thy finger here, and see my hands; and
φέρε τὴν.χεῖρά.σου, καὶ βάλε εἰς τὴν.πλευράν.μου· καὶ
bring thy hand, and put [it] into my side; and
μὴ.γίνου ἄπιστος, ἀλλὰ πιστός. 28 [a]Καὶ[a] ἀπεκρίθη [b]ὁ[b]
be not unbelieving, but believing. And [2]answered
Θωμᾶς καὶ εἶπεν αὐτῷ, Ὁ.κύριός.μου καὶ ὁ.θεός.μου. 29 Λέγει
[1]Thomas and said to him, My Lord and my God. [2]Says
αὐτῷ [c]ὁ[c] Ἰησοῦς, Ὅτι ἑώρακάς με, [d]Θωμᾶ,[d] πεπίστευκας·
[3]to [4]him [1]Jesus, Because thou hast seen me, Thomas, thou hast believed:
μακάριοι οἱ μὴ.ἰδόντες καὶ πιστεύσαντες.
blessed they who have not seen and have believed.

30 Πολλὰ μὲν οὖν καὶ ἄλλα σημεῖα ἐποίησεν ὁ Ἰη-
Many [3]therefore [4]also [1]other [2]signs did Je-
σοῦς ἐνώπιον τῶν.μαθητῶν.[e]αὐτοῦ,[e] ἃ οὐκ.ἔστιν γεγραμ-
sus in presence of his disciples, which are not written
μένα ἐν τῷ.βιβλίῳ.τούτῳ. 31 ταῦτα.δὲ γέγραπται ἵνα
in this book; but these have been written that
[f]πιστεύσητε[f] ὅτι [g]ὁ[g] Ἰησοῦς ἐστιν ὁ χριστὸς ὁ υἱὸς τοῦ
ye may believe that Jesus is the Christ the Son
θεοῦ, καὶ ἵνα πιστεύοντες ζωὴν [h] ἔχητε ἐν τῷ ὀνόματι
of God, and that believing, life ye may have in [2]name
αὐτοῦ.
[1]his.

XXI. After these things Jesus shewed himself again to the disciples at the sea of Tiberias; and on this wise shewed he *himself*. 2 There were together Simon Peter, and Thomas called Didymus, and Nathanael of Cana in Galilee, and the *sons* of Zebedee, and two other of his disciples. 3 Simon Peter saith unto them, I go a fishing. They say unto him, We also go with thee. They went forth, and entered into a ship immediately; and that night they caught nothing. 4 But when the morning was now come, Jesus stood on the shore: but the disciples knew not that it was Jesus. 5 Then Jesus saith unto them, Children, have ye any meat? They answered him, No. 6 And he said unto them, Cast the net on the right side of the ship, and

21 Μετὰ ταῦτα ἐφανέρωσεν ἑαυτὸν πάλιν [i]ὁ Ἰησοῦς[i]
After these things [3]manifested [4]himself [2]again [1]Jesus
τοῖς μαθηταῖς ἐπὶ τῆς θαλάσσης τῆς Τιβεριάδος· ἐφανέρωσεν.δὲ
to the disciples at the sea of Tiberias. And he manifested
οὕτως· 2 ἦσαν ὁμοῦ Σίμων Πέτρος, καὶ Θωμᾶς ὁ
[himself] thus: There were together Simon Peter, and Thomas
λεγόμενος Δίδυμος, καὶ Ναθαναὴλ ὁ ἀπὸ Κανᾶ τῆς Γαλι-
called Didymus, and Nathanael from Cana of Gali-
λαίας, καὶ οἱ τοῦ Ζεβεδαίου, καὶ ἄλλοι ἐκ τῶν μαθητῶν
lee, and the [sons] of Zebedee, and [2]others [3]of [5]disciples
αὐτοῦ δύο. 3 λέγει αὐτοῖς Σίμων Πέτρος, Ὑπάγω ἁλιεύειν.
[4]his [1]two. [8]Says [9]to [10]them [6]Simon [7]Peter, I go to fish.
Λέγουσιν αὐτῷ, Ἐρχόμεθα καὶ ἡμεῖς σὺν σοί. [k]Ἐξῆλθον
They say to him, [3]Come [2]also [1]we with thee. They went forth
καὶ [l]ἀνέβησαν[l] εἰς τὸ πλοῖον [m]εὐθύς,[m] καὶ ἐν ἐκείνῃ τῇ
and went up into the ship immediately, and during that
νυκτὶ ἐπίασαν οὐδέν. 4 πρωΐας.δὲ ἤδη [n]γενομένης[n] ἔστη [o]ὁ[o]
night they took nothing. And morning already being come [2]stood
Ἰησοῦς [p]εἰς[p] τὸν αἰγιαλόν· οὐ μέντοι ᾔδεισαν οἱ μαθηταὶ ὅτι
[1]Jesus on the shore; [5]not [3]however [4]knew [1]the [2]disciples that
Ἰησοῦς ἐστιν. 5 λέγει οὖν αὐτοῖς [q]ὁ Ἰησοῦς,[q] Παιδία,
Jesus it is. [3]Says [2]therefore [4]to [5]them [1]Jesus, Little children,
μή τι προσφάγιον ἔχετε; Ἀπεκρίθησαν αὐτῷ, Οὔ. 6 [r]Ὁ.δὲ
any food have ye? They answered him, No. And he
εἶπεν[r] αὐτοῖς, Βάλετε εἰς τὰ δεξιὰ μέρη τοῦ πλοίου τὸ δίκτυον,
said to them, Cast to the right side of the ship the net,

---

[a] — καὶ GLTTrAW. [b] — ὁ GLTTrAW. [c] [ὁ] Tr. [d] — Θωμᾶ GLTTrAW. [e] — αὐτοῦ (*read* the disciples) LTTrA. [f] πιστεύητε T. [g] — ὁ GLTTrAW. [h] + [αἰώνιον] eternal L. [i] — ὁ Ἰησοῦς (*read* he manifested) A; — ὁ TTr. [k] + [καὶ] and L. [l] ἐνέβησαν entered GLTTrAW. [m] — εὐθύς LTTrA. [n] γινομένης breaking TTrW. [o] — ὁ LTTrA. [p] ἐπὶ LT. [q] [ὁ Ἰησοῦς] L; [ὁ] Ἰησοῦς Tr; — ὁ TA. [r] λέγει he says T.

καὶ εὑρήσετε. Ἔβαλον οὖν, καὶ [s]οὐκ ἔτι‖ αὐτὸ ἑλκῦσαι
and ye shall find. They cast therefore, and no longer it to draw
[t]ἴσχυσαν‖ ἀπὸ τοῦ πλήθους τῶν ἰχθύων. 7 λέγει οὖν
were they able from the multitude of the fishes. Says therefore
ὁ.μαθητὴς.ἐκεῖνος ὃν ἠγάπα ὁ Ἰησοῦς τῷ Πέτρῳ, Ὁ κύριός
that disciple whom [2]loved [1]Jesus to Peter, The Lord
ἐστιν. Σίμων οὖν Πέτρος, ἀκούσας ὅτι ὁ κύριός ἐστιν,
it is. Simon [2]therefore [1]Peter, having heard that the Lord it is,
τὸν ἐπενδύτην διεζώσατο· ἦν.γὰρ γυμνός· καὶ ἔβαλεν
[his] upper garment he girded on, for he was naked, and cast
ἑαυτὸν εἰς τὴν θάλασσαν. 8 οἱ.δὲ ἄλλοι μαθηταὶ τῷ
himself into the sea. And the other disciples in the
πλοιαρίῳ ἦλθον· οὐ.γὰρ ἦσαν μακρὰν ἀπὸ τῆς γῆς, [v]ἀλλ'‖
small ship came, for not were they far from the land, but
ὡς.ἀπὸ πηχῶν διακοσίων, σύροντες τὸ δίκτυον τῶν
somewhere about [3]cubits [1]two [2]hundred, dragging the net
ἰχθύων. 9 Ὡς οὖν ἀπέβησαν εἰς τὴν γῆν βλέπουσιν
of fishes. When therefore they went up on the land they see
ἀνθρακιὰν κειμένην καὶ ὀψάριον ἐπικείμενον, καὶ ἄρτον.
a fire of coals lying and fish lying on [it], and bread.
10 λέγει αὐτοῖς [w]ὁ‖ Ἰησοῦς, Ἐνέγκατε ἀπὸ τῶν ὀψαρίων ὧν
[2]Says [3]to [4]them [1]Jesus, Bring of the fishes which
ἐπιάσατε νῦν. 11 Ἀνέβη [x] Σίμων Πέτρος, καὶ εἵλκυσεν τὸ
ye took just now. Went up Simon Peter, and drew the
δίκτυον [y]ἐπὶ τῆς γῆς,‖ μεστὸν [z]ἰχθύων μεγάλων‖ ἑκατὸν
net to the land, full of [2]fishes [1]large a hundred [and]
[a]πεντηκοντατριῶν·‖ καὶ τοσούτων ὄντων οὐκ.ἐσχίσθη τὸ
fifty three; and [though] so many there were was not rent the
δίκτυον. 12 Λέγει αὐτοῖς [b]ὁ‖ Ἰησοῦς, Δεῦτε ἀριστήσατε.
net. [2]Says [3]to [4]them [1]Jesus, Come ye, dine.
οὐδεὶς.[c]δὲ‖ ἐτόλμα τῶν μαθητῶν ἐξετάσαι αὐτόν, Σὺ τίς
But none [4]ventured [1]of [2]the [3]disciples to ask him, [3]Thou [1]who
εἶ; εἰδότες ὅτι ὁ κύριός ἐστιν· 13 ἔρχεται [d]οὖν ὁ‖ Ἰησοῦς
[2]art? knowing that the Lord it is. [3]Comes [2]therefore [1]Jesus
καὶ λαμβάνει τὸν ἄρτον καὶ δίδωσιν αὐτοῖς, καὶ τὸ ὀψάριον
and takes the bread and gives to them, and the fish
ὁμοίως. 14 τοῦτο ἤδη τρίτον ἐφανερώθη [e]ὁ‖ Ἰησοῦς
in like manner. This [is] now the third time [2]was [3]manifested [1]Jesus
τοῖς.μαθηταῖς.[f]αὐτοῦ‖ ἐγερθεὶς ἐκ νεκρῶν.
to his disciples having been raised from among [the] dead.
15 Ὅτε οὖν ἠρίστησαν, λέγει τῷ Σίμωνι Πέτρῳ ὁ Ἰησοῦς,
When therefore they had dined, [2]says [3]to [4]Simon [5]Peter [1]Jesus,
Σίμων [g]Ἰωνᾶ,‖ ἀγαπᾷς με [h]πλεῖον‖ τούτων; Λέγει αὐτῷ,
Simon [son] of Jonas, lovest thou me more than these? He says to him,
Ναί, κύριε· σὺ οἶδας ὅτι φιλῶ σε. Λέγει αὐτῷ,
Yea, Lord; thou knowest that I have affection for thee. He says to him,
Βόσκε τὰ.ἀρνία.μου. 16 Λέγει αὐτῷ πάλιν δεύτερον, Σίμων
Feed my lambs. He says to him again a second time, Simon
[g]Ἰωνᾶ,‖ ἀγαπᾷς με; Λέγει αὐτῷ, Ναί κύριε· σὺ οἶδας
[son] of Jonas, lovest thou me? He says to him, Yea, Lord; thou knowest
ὅτι φιλῶ σε. Λέγει αὐτῷ, Ποίμαινε τὰ [i]πρόβατά‖
that I have affection for thee. He says to him, Shepherd [2]sheep

ye shall find. They
cast therefore, and now
they were not able to
draw it for the multi-
tude of fishes. 7 There-
fore that disciple
whom Jesus loved
saith unto Peter, It is
the Lord. Now when
Simon Peter heard
that it was the Lord,
he girt *his* fisher's
coat *unto him*, (for he
was naked,) and did
cast himself into the
sea. 8 And the other
disciples came in a lit-
tle ship; (for they
were not far from
land, but as it were
two hundred cubits,)
dragging the net with
fishes. 9 As soon then
as they were come to
land, they saw a fire
of coals there, and fish
laid thereon, and
bread. 10 Jesus saith
unto them, Bring of
the fish which ye have
now caught. 11 Simon
Peter went up, and
drew the net to land
full of great fishes, an
hundred and fifty and
three: and for all there
were so many, yet was
not the net broken.
12 Jesus saith unto
them, Come *and* dine.
And none of the disci-
ples durst ask him,
Who art thou? know-
ing that it was the
Lord. 13 Jesus then
cometh, and taketh
bread, and giveth
them, and fish like-
wise. 14 This is now
the third time that
Jesus shewed himself
to his disciples, after
that he was risen from
the dead. 15 So when
they had dined, Jesus
saith to Simon Peter,
Simon, *son* of Jonas,
lovest thou me more
than these? He saith
unto him, Yea, Lord;
thou knowest that I
love thee. He saith
unto him, Feed my
lambs. 16 He saith to
him again the second
time, Simon, *son* of
Jonas, lovest thou me?
He saith unto him, Yea,
Lord; thou knowest
that I love thee. He
saith unto him, Feed
my sheep. 17 He saith

---

[s] οὐκέτι GLTW. [t] ἴσχυον LTTrA. [v] ἀλλὰ TTrA. [w] [ὁ] Tr. [x] + οὖν therefore TrA. [y] εἰς τὴν γῆν LTTrA. [z] μεγάλων ἰχθύων L. [a] πεντήκοντα τριῶν LTTr. [b] [ὁ] Tr. [c] — δὲ but [Tr]A. [d] — οὖν G; — οὖν ὁ LTTrA. [e] — ὁ LTTrA. [f] — αὐτοῦ (*read* the disciples) LTTrAW. [g] Ἰωάνου John LTr; Ἰωάννου TA. [h] πλέον LTTrA. [i] προβάτια little sheep T.

μου. 17 Λέγει αὐτῷ τὸ τρίτον, Σίμων [k]Ἰωνᾶ,‖ φι-
my. He says to him the third time, Simon [son] of Jonas, hast thou
λεῖς με; Ἐλυπήθη ὁ Πέτρος ὅτι εἶπεν αὐτῷ τὸ
affection for me? [2]Was [3]grieved [1]Peter because he said to him the
τρίτον, Φιλεῖς με; [l]καὶ‖ [m]εἶπεν‖ αὐτῷ, Κύριε, [n]σὺ
third time, Hast thou affection for me? and said to him, Lord, thou
πάντα‖ οἶδας· σὺ γινώσκεις ὅτι φιλῶ σε. Λέγει
all things knowest; thou knowest that I have affection for thee. [2]Says
αὐτῷ [o]ὁ Ἰησοῦς,‖ Βόσκε τὰ.[p]πρόβατά‖.μου. 18 ἀμὴν ἀμὴν
[3]to [4]him [1]Jesus, Feed my sheep. Verily verily
λέγω σοι, ὅτε ἦς νεώτερος ἐζώννυες σεαυτόν, καὶ
I say to thee, When thou wast younger thou girdedst thyself, and
περιεπάτεις ὅπου ἤθελες· ὅταν.δὲ γηράσῃς ἐκ-
walkedst where thou didst desire; but when thou shalt be old thou shalt
τενεῖς τὰς.χεῖράς.σου, καὶ ἄλλος [q]σε ζώσει,‖ καὶ οἴσει [r]
stretch forth thy hands, and another thee shall gird, and bring [thee]
ὅπου οὐ.θέλεις. 19 Τοῦτο.δὲ εἶπεν σημαίνων ποίῳ
where thou dost not desire. But this he said signifying by what
θανάτῳ δοξάσει τὸν θεόν. καὶ τοῦτο εἰπὼν λέγει αὐτῷ,
death he should glorify God. And this having said he says to him,
Ἀκολούθει μοι. 20 Ἐπιστραφεὶς.[s]δὲ‖ ὁ Πέτρος βλέπει τὸν
Follow me. But having turned Peter sees the
μαθητὴν ὃν ἠγάπα ὁ Ἰησοῦς ἀκολουθοῦντα, ὃς καὶ ἀνέπεσεν
disciple whom [2]loved [1]Jesus following, who also reclined
ἐν τῷ δείπνῳ ἐπὶ τὸ.στῆθος.αὐτοῦ καὶ εἶπεν, Κύριε, τίς ἐστιν
at the supper on his breast and said, Lord, who is it
ὁ παραδιδούς σε; 21 Τοῦτον [t] ἰδὼν ὁ Πέτρος λέγει τῷ Ἰη-
who is delivering up thee? [3]Him [2]seeing [1]Peter says to Je-
σοῦ, Κύριε, οὗτος.δὲ τί; 22 Λέγει αὐτῷ ὁ Ἰησοῦς, Ἐὰν
sus, Lord, but of this one what? [2]Says [3]to [4]him [1]Jesus, If
αὐτὸν θέλω μένειν ἕως ἔρχομαι, τί πρός σε; σύ
[3]him [1]I [2]desire to abide till I come, what [is it] to thee? [2]Thou
[v]ἀκολούθει μοι.‖ 23 Ἐξῆλθεν οὖν [w]ὁ.λόγος.οὗτος‖ εἰς
[1]follow me. Went out therefore this word among
τοὺς ἀδελφούς, Ὅτι ὁ.μαθητὴς.ἐκεῖνος οὐκ.ἀποθνήσκει· [x]καὶ
the brethren, That that disciple does not die. However
οὐκ εἶπεν‖ αὐτῷ ὁ Ἰησοῦς, ὅτι οὐκ ἀποθνήσκει· ἀλλ', Ἐὰν
[3]not [2]said [4]to [5]him [1]Jesus, That he does not die; but, If
αὐτὸν θέλω μένειν ἕως ἔρχομαι, [y]τί πρός σε;‖
[3]him [1]I [2]desire to abide till I come, what [is it] to thee?
24 Οὗτός ἐστιν ὁ μαθητὴς ὁ μαρτυρῶν περὶ τούτων,
This is the disciple who bears witness concerning these things,
καὶ [z] γράψας ταῦτα· καὶ οἴδαμεν ὅτι ἀληθής [a]ἐστιν ἡ
and [who] wrote these things: and we know that true is
μαρτυρία.αὐτοῦ.‖ 25 [b]ἔστιν.δὲ καὶ ἄλλα πολλὰ [c]ὅσα‖
his witness. And there are also [2]other [3]things [1]many whatsoever
ἐποίησεν ὁ Ἰησοῦς, ἅτινα ἐὰν γράφηται καθ'.ἕν, [d]οὐδὲ‖
[2]did [1]Jesus, which if they should be written one by one, [3]not [4]even
αὐτὸν οἶμαι τὸν κόσμον [e]χωρῆσαι‖ τὰ γραφόμενα βιβλία.
[7]itself [1]I [2]suppose [5]the [6]world would contain the [2]written [1]books.
[f]Ἀμήν.‖ ‖ [g]
Amen.

unto him the third
time, Simon, *son* of
Jonas, lovest thou me?
Peter was grieved be-
cause he said unto him
the third time, Lovest
thou me? And he said
unto him, Lord, thou
knowest all things;
thou knowest that I
love thee. Jesus saith
unto him, Feed my
sheep. 18 Verily, ve-
rily, I say unto thee,
When thou wast
young, thou girdedst
thyself, and walkedst
whither thou would-
est: but when thou
shalt be old, thou
shalt stretch forth thy
hands, and another
shall gird thee, and
carry *thee* whither
thou wouldest not.
19 This spake he, sig-
nifying by what death
he should glorify God.
And when he had spo-
ken this, he saith un-
to him, Follow me.
20 Then Peter, turning
about, seeth the disci-
ple whom Jesus loved
following; which also
leaned on his breast at
supper, and said, Lord,
which is he that be-
trayeth thee? 21 Pe-
ter seeing him saith
to Jesus, Lord, and
what *shall* this man
do? 22 Jesus saith
unto him, If I will
that he tarry till I
come, what *is that* to
thee? follow thou me.
23 Then went this say-
ing abroad among the
brethren, that that
disciple should not
die: yet Jesus said not
unto him, He shall not
die; but, If I will that
he tarry till I come,
what *is that* to thee?

24 This is the disci-
ple which testifieth
of these things, and
wrote these things:
and we know that his
testimony is true.
25 And there are also
many other things
which Jesus did, the
which, if they should
be written every one,
I suppose that even
the world itself could
not contain the books
that should be writ-
ten. Amen.

k Ἰωάνου John LTr; Ἰωάννου TA. l [καὶ] L. m λέγει says T. n πάντα σὺ LTTrA. o — ὁ LTTrA; — Ἰησοῦς (*read* he says) T[Tr]. p προβάτιά little sheep TTrA. q ζώσει σε TrA. r + [σε] thee L. s — δὲ but LTTrAW. t + οὖν therefore LTTrA. v μοι ἀκολούθει LTTrAW. w οὗτος ὁ λόγος LTTrA. x οὐκ εἶπεν δὲ Tr. y — τί πρός σε T. z + ὁ who LTr[A]. a αὐτοῦ ἡ μαρτυρία ἐστίν TTrA. b — *verse* 25 T. c ἃ which LTrA. d οὐδ' LTrA. e χωρήσειν Tr. f — Ἀμήν GLTrA. g + κατὰ Ἰωάνην (Ἰωάννην A) according to John TrA.

ΠΡΑΞΕΙΣ [h]ΤΩΝ ΑΓΙΩΝ‖ [i]ΑΠΟΣΤΟΛΩΝ.‖
ACTS OF THE HOLY APOSTLES.

ΤΟΝ μὲν πρῶτον λόγον ἐποιησάμην περὶ πάντων, ὦ
The [3]indeed [1]first [2]account I made concerning all things, O
Θεόφιλε, ὧν ἤρξατο [j]ὁ‖ Ἰησοῦς ποιεῖν-τε καὶ διδάσκειν,
Theophilus, which [2]began [1]Jesus both to do and to teach,
2 ἄχρι ἧς-ἡμέρας ἐντειλάμενος τοῖς ἀποστόλοις διὰ
until the day in which, having given command [5]to [6]the [7]apostles [1]by
πνεύματος ἁγίου οὓς ἐξελέξατο, [k]ἀνελήφθη.‖ 3 οἷς
[[2]the] [4]Spirit [3]Holy whom he chose, he was taken up: to whom
καὶ παρέστησεν ἑαυτὸν ζῶντα μετὰ τὸ-παθεῖν-αὐτόν, ἐν
also he presented himself living after he had suffered, with
πολλοῖς τεκμηρίοις, δι' ἡμερῶν [l]τεσσαράκοντα‖ ὀπτανόμενος
many proofs, during [2]days [1]forty being seen
αὐτοῖς, καὶ λέγων τὰ περὶ τῆς βασιλείας τοῦ θεοῦ.
by them, and speaking the things concerning the kingdom of God:
4 καὶ συναλιζόμενος [m]παρήγγειλεν αὐτοῖς‖ ἀπὸ Ἱερο-
and being assembled with [him] he charged them from Jeru-
σολύμων μὴ χωρίζεσθαι, ἀλλὰ περιμένειν τὴν ἐπαγγελίαν
salem not to depart, but to await the promise
τοῦ πατρός, ἣν ἠκούσατέ μου· 5 ὅτι [n]Ἰωάννης‖ μὲν
of the Father, which [said he] ye heard of me. For John indeed
ἐβάπτισεν ὕδατι, ὑμεῖς-δὲ [o]βαπτισθήσεσθε ἐν πνεύμα-
baptized with water, but ye shall be baptized with [the] [2]Spirit
τι‖ ἁγίῳ οὐ μετὰ πολλὰς ταύτας ἡμέρας. 6 Οἱ μὲν οὖν
[1]Holy [4]not [3]after many days. They indeed therefore
συνελθόντες [p]ἐπηρώτων‖ αὐτὸν λέγοντες, Κύριε, εἰ ἐν
having come together asked him, saying, Lord, [3]at
τῷ-χρόνῳ-τούτῳ ἀποκαθιστάνεις τὴν βασιλείαν τῷ Ἰσραήλ;
[4]this [5]time [1]restorest [2]thou the kingdom to Israel?
7 Εἶπεν-[q]δὲ‖ πρὸς αὐτούς, Οὐχ ὑμῶν ἐστιν γνῶναι χρόνους
And he said to them, [3]Not [4]yours [1]it [2]is to know times
ἢ καιροὺς οὓς ὁ πατὴρ ἔθετο ἐν τῇ-ἰδίᾳ ἐξουσίᾳ· 8 ἀλλὰ
or seasons which the Father placed in his own authority; but
[r]λήψεσθε‖ δύναμιν, ἐπελθόντος τοῦ ἁγίου πνεύματος ἐφ'
ye will receive power, [4]having [5]come [1]the [2]Holy [3]Spirit upon
ὑμᾶς, καὶ ἔσεσθέ [s]μοι‖ μάρτυρες ἔν-τε Ἱερουσαλὴμ καὶ [t]ἐν‖
you, and ye shall be to me witnesses both in Jerusalem and in
πάσῃ [v]τῇ‖ Ἰουδαίᾳ καὶ [w]Σαμαρείᾳ‖ καὶ ἕως ἐσχάτου
all Judæa and Samaria and to [the] uttermost part
τῆς γῆς. 9 Καὶ ταῦτα εἰπών, βλεπόντων αὐτῶν
of the earth. And these things having said, [2]beholding [[3]him] [1]they
ἐπήρθη, καὶ νεφέλη ὑπέλαβεν αὐτὸν ἀπὸ τῶν ὀφθαλμῶν
he was taken up, and a cloud withdrew him from [2]eyes
αὐτῶν.
[1]their.

10 Καὶ ὡς ἀτενίζοντες ἦσαν εἰς τὸν οὐρανὸν πορευομένου
And as [3]looking [4]intently [1]they [2]were into the heaven as [2]was [3]going

THE former treatise
have I made, O Theo-
philus, of all that
Jesus began both to
do and teach, 2 until
the day in which he
was taken up, after
that he through the
Holy Ghost had given
commandments unto
the apostles whom he
had chosen: 3 to whom
also he shewed himself
alive after his pas-
sion by many infalli-
ble proofs, being seen
of them forty days,
and speaking of the
things pertaining to
the kingdom of God:
4 and, being assem-
bled together with
them, commanded
them that they should
not depart from Jeru-
salem, but wait for
the promise of the Fa-
ther, which, *saith he*,
ye have heard of me.
5 For John truly bap-
tized with water; but
ye shall be baptized
with the Holy Ghost
not many days hence.
6 When they therefore
were come together,
they asked of him,
saying, Lord, wilt
thou at this time re-
store again the king-
dom to Israel? 7 And
he said unto them, It
is not for you to know
the times or the sea-
sons, which the Father
hath put in his own
power. 8 But ye shall
receive power, after
that the Holy Ghost is
come upon you: and
ye shall be witnesses
unto me both in Jeru-
salem, and in all Ju-
dæa, and in Samaria,
and unto the utter-
most part of the
earth. 9 And when he
had spoken these
things, while they be-
held, he was taken up;
and a cloud received
him out of their sight.

10 And while they
looked stedfastly to-
ward heaven as he

---

h — ἁγίων G; — τῶν ἁγίων (read of [the]) LTTrAW. i — ἀποστόλων T. j — ὁ LTrAW. k ἀνελήμφθη LTTrA. l τεσσεράκοντα LTTrA. m αὐτοῖς παρήγγειλεν AW. n Ἰωάνης Tr. o ἐν πνεύματι βαπτισθήσεσθε LTTrA. p ἠρώτων LTTrA. q — δὲ and TTr. r λήμψεσθε LTTrA. s μου of me LTTrAW. t — ἐν L[TrA]. v — τῇ A. w Σαμαρίᾳ T.

went up, behold, two
men stood by them in
white apparel; 11 which
also said, Ye men of
Galilee, why stand ye
gazing up into heaven?
this same Jesus, which
is taken up from you
into heaven, shall so
come in like manner
as ye have seen him go
into heaven. 12 Then
returned they unto Je-
rusalem from the
mount called Olivet,
which is from Jerusa-
lem a sabbath day's
journey. 13 And when
they were come in,
they went up into an
upper room, where
abode both Peter, and
James, and John, and
Andrew, Philip, and
Thomas, Bartholo-
mew, and Matthew,
James *the son* of Al-
phæus, and Simon Ze-
lotes, and Judas *the
brother* of James.
14 These all continued
with one accord in
prayer and supplica-
tion, with the women,
and Mary the mother
of Jesus, and with his
brethren.

15 And in those days
Peter stood up in the
midst of the disciples,
and said, (the number
of names together
were about an hun-
dred and twenty,)
16 Men *and* brethren,
this scripture must
needs have been ful-
filled, which the Holy
Ghost by the mouth
of David spake before
concerning Judas,
which was guide to
them that took Jesus.
17 For he was number-
ed with us, and had
obtained part of this
ministry. 18 Now this
man purchased a field
with the reward of
iniquity; and falling
headlong, he burst a-
sunder in the midst,
and all his bowels
gushed out. 19 And it

αὐτου, καὶ ἰδοὺ ἄνδρες δύο παρειστήκεισαν αὐτοῖς ἐν [x]ἐσθῆτι
[1]he, [5]also [4]behold [7]men [6]two stood by them in [2]apparel
λευκῇ,‖ 11 οἳ καὶ [y]εἶπον,‖ Ἄνδρες Γαλιλαῖοι, τί ἑστήκατε [z]ἐμ-
[1]white, who also said, Men Galileans, why do ye stand look-
βλέποντες‖ εἰς τὸν οὐρανόν; οὗτος ὁ Ἰησοῦς ὁ [a]ἀναληφθεὶς‖
ing into the heaven? This Jesus who was taken up
ἀφ' ὑμῶν εἰς τὸν οὐρανὸν οὕτως ἐλεύσεται ὃν.τρόπον
from you into the heaven thus will come in the manner
ἐθεάσασθε αὐτὸν πορευόμενον εἰς τὸν οὐρανόν. 12 Τότε
ye beheld him going into the heaven. Then
ὑπέστρεψαν εἰς Ἱερουσαλὴμ ἀπὸ ὄρους τοῦ καλουμένου
they returned to Jerusalem from [the] mount called
ἐλαιῶνος, ὅ ἐστιν ἐγγὺς Ἱερουσαλήμ, σαββάτου ἔχον
of Olives, which is near Jerusalem, [3]a [4]sabbath's [1]being [2]distant
ὁδόν. 13 Καὶ ὅτε εἰσῆλθον [b]ἀνέβησαν εἰς τὸ ὑπερῷον,‖
journey. And when they had entered they went up to the upper chamber,
οὗ ἦσαν καταμένοντες ὅ.τε.Πέτρος καὶ [c]Ἰάκωβος καὶ Ἰωάν-
where were staying both Peter and James and John
νης‖ καὶ Ἀνδρέας, Φίλιππος καὶ Θωμᾶς, Βαρθολομαῖος καὶ
and Andrew, Philip and Thomas, Bartholomew and
[d]Ματθαῖος,‖ Ἰάκωβος Ἀλφαίου καὶ Σίμων ὁ Ζηλωτής,
Matthew, James [son] of Alphæus and Simon the Zealot,
καὶ Ἰούδας Ἰακώβου. 14 οὗτοι πάντες ἦσαν προσκαρ-
and Jude [brother] of James. These all were [4]steadfastly
τεροῦντες ὁμοθυμαδὸν τῇ προσευχῇ [e]καὶ τῇ δεήσει,‖ σὺν
[5]continuing [1]with [2]one [3]accord in prayer and supplication, with [the]
γυναιξὶν καὶ [f]Μαρίᾳ‖ τῇ μητρὶ τοῦ Ἰησοῦ, καὶ [g]σὺν‖ τοῖς
women and Mary the mother of Jesus, and with
ἀδελφοῖς.αὐτοῦ.
his brethren.

15 Καὶ ἐν ταῖς.ἡμέραις.ταύταις ἀναστὰς Πέτρος ἐν
And in those days [2]having [3]stood [4]up [1]Peter in
μέσῳ τῶν [h]μαθητῶν‖ εἶπεν· ἦν τε ὄχλος ὀνομάτων
[the] midst of the disciples said, ([7]was [1]and [[2]the] [3]number [4]of [5]names
ἐπὶ.τὸ.αὐτὸ [i]ὡς‖ ἑκατὸν.[k]εἴκοσιν·‖ 16 Ἄνδρες ἀδελφοί, ἔδει
[6]together about a hundred and twenty,) Men brethren, it was neces-
πληρωθῆναι τὴν.γραφὴν.[l]ταύτην,‖ ἣν προεῖπεν τὸ
sary [3]to [4]have [5]been [6]fulfilled [1]this [2]scripture, which [5]spoke [6]before [1]the
πνεῦμα τὸ ἅγιον διὰ στόματος [m]Δαβὶδ‖ περὶ Ἰούδα τοῦ
[2]Spirit [3]the [4]Holy by [the] mouth of David concerning Judas who
γενομένου ὁδηγοῦ τοῖς συλλαβοῦσιν [n]τὸν‖ Ἰησοῦν· 17 ὅτι
became guide to those who took Jesus; for
κατηριθμημένος ἦν [o]σὺν‖ ἡμῖν, καὶ ἔλαχεν τὸν κλῆρον τῆς
numbered he was with us, and obtained a part
διακονίας.ταύτης. 18 Οὗτος μὲν οὖν ἐκτήσατο χωρίον
in this service. This [man] indeed then got a field
ἐκ [p]τοῦ‖ μισθοῦ τῆς ἀδικίας, καὶ πρηνὴς γενόμενος
out of the reward of unrighteousness, and [3]headlong [1]having [2]fallen
ἐλάκησεν μέσος, καὶ ἐξεχύθη πάντα τὰ.σπλάγχνα.αὐτοῦ.
burst in [the] midst, and [4]gushed [5]out [1]all [2]his [3]bowels.

---

[x] ἐσθήσεσι(ν A) λευκαῖς LTTrA. [y] εἶπαν LTTrA. [z] βλέποντες TTr. [a] ἀναλημφθεὶς LTTrA. [b] εἰς τὸ ὑπερῷον ἀνέβησαν LTTrA. [c] Ἰωάννης (Ἰωάνης Tr) καὶ Ἰάκωβος LTTrAW. [d] Μαθθαῖος LTTrA. [e] — καὶ τῇ δεήσει GLTTrAW. [f] Μαριὰμ TTr. [g] — σὺν LT[Tr]AW. [h] ἀδελφῶν brethren LTTrAW. [i] ὡσεὶ T. [k] εἴκοσι LTA. [l] — ταύτην (*read* the scripture) LTTr[A]W. [m] Δαυεὶδ LTTrA; Δαυὶδ GW. [n] — τὸν LTTrA [o] ἐν among GLTTrAW. [p] — τοῦ (*read* a reward) GLTTrAW

19 [q]καὶ γνωστὸν ἐγένετο πᾶσιν τοῖς κατοικοῦσιν Ἱερουσαλήμ,
And known it became to all those dwelling in Jerusalem,
ὥστε κληθῆναι τὸ.χωρίον.ἐκεῖνο τῇ.[r]ἰδίᾳ‖.διαλέκτῳ.αὐτῶν
so that was called that field in their own language
[s]Ἀκελδαμά,‖ [t]τουτέστιν‖ χωρίον αἵματος. 20 γέγραπται.γὰρ
Aceldama; that is, field of blood. For it has been written
ἐν βίβλῳ ψαλμῶν, Γενηθήτω ἡ.ἔπαυλις.αὐτοῦ ἔρημος,
in [the] book of Psalms, Let [3]become [1]his [2]homestead desolate,
καὶ μὴ.ἔστω ὁ κατοικῶν ἐν αὐτῇ. καί, Τὴν ἐπισκοπὴν
and let there not be [one] dwelling in it; and, [5]Overseership
αὐτοῦ [v]λάβοι‖ ἕτερος. 21 Δεῖ οὖν τῶν συνελθόντων
[4]his [1]let [3]take [2]another. It behoves therefore of those [2]consorting
ἡμῖν ἀνδρῶν ἐν παντὶ χρόνῳ [w]ἐν‖ ᾧ εἰσῆλθεν καὶ
[3]with [4]us [1]men during all [the] time in which came in and
ἐξῆλθεν ἐφ' ἡμᾶς ὁ κύριος Ἰησοῦς, 22 ἀρξάμενος ἀπὸ τοῦ
went out among us the Lord Jesus, beginning from the
βαπτίσματος [x]Ἰωάννου‖ [y]ἕως‖ τῆς ἡμέρας ἧς [z]ἀνελήφθη‖
baptism of John until the day in which he was taken up
ἀφ' ἡμῶν, μάρτυρα τῆς.ἀναστάσεως.αὐτοῦ· [a]γενέσθαι σὺν
from us, [8]a [9]witness [10]of [11]his [12]resurrection. [4]to [5]become [6]with
ἡμῖν‖ ἕνα τούτων. 23 Καὶ ἔστησαν δύο, Ἰωσὴφ τὸν καλού-
[7]us [1]one [2]of [3]these. And they set forth two, Joseph call-
μενον [b]Βαρσαβᾶν,‖ ὃς ἐπεκλήθη Ἰοῦστος, καὶ [c]Ματθίαν.‖
ed Barsabas, who was surnamed Justus, and Matthias.
24 καὶ προσευξάμενοι [d]εἶπον,‖ Σὺ κύριε, καρδιογνῶστα
And praying they said, Thou Lord, knower of the hearts
πάντων, ἀνάδειξον [e]ἐκ τούτων τῶν δύο ἕνα ὃν ἐξελέξω‖
of all, shew of these two [2]one [1]which thou didst choose
25 λαβεῖν τὸν [f]κλῆρον‖ τῆς.διακονίας.ταύτης καὶ ἀποστολῆς,
to receive the part of this service and apostleship,
[g]ἐξ‖ ἧς παρέβη Ἰούδας, πορευθῆναι εἰς τὸν τόπον
from which [2]transgressing [3]fell [1]Judas, to go to his [2]place
τὸν ἴδιον. 26 Καὶ ἔδωκαν κλήρους [h]αὐτῶν,‖ καὶ ἔπεσεν ὁ
[1]own. And they gave [2]lots [1]their, and [3]fell [1]the
κλῆρος ἐπὶ [c]Ματθίαν,‖ καὶ [i]συγκατεψηφίσθη‖ μετὰ τῶν ἕνδεκα
[2]lot on Matthias, and he was numbered with the eleven
ἀποστόλων.
apostles.

2 Καὶ ἐν τῷ [k]συμπληροῦσθαι‖ τὴν ἡμέραν τῆς πεντη-
And during the accomplishing of the day of Pente-
κοστῆς ἦσαν [l]ἅπαντες ὁμοθυμαδὸν‖ ἐπὶ.τὸ.αὐτό. 2 καὶ
cost they were all with one accord in the same place. And
ἐγένετο ἄφνω ἐκ τοῦ οὐρανοῦ ἦχος ὥσπερ φερομένης
[2]came [1]suddenly out of the heaven a sound as [5]rushing
πνοῆς βιαίας, καὶ ἐπλήρωσεν ὅλον τὸν οἶκον οὗ ἦσαν
[1]of [2]a [4]breath [3]violent, and filled [2]whole [1]the house where they were
[m]καθήμενοι·‖ 3 καὶ ὤφθησαν αὐτοῖς διαμεριζόμεναι γλῶσσαι
sitting. And there appeared to them divided tongues
ὡσεὶ πυρός, [n]ἐκάθισέν.τε‖ ἐφ' ἕνα ἕκαστον αὐτῶν· 4 καὶ
as of fire, and sat upon [2]one [1]each of them. And

was known unto all the dwellers at Jerusalem; insomuch as that field is called in their proper tongue, Aceldama, that is to say, The field of blood. 20 For it is written in the book of Psalms, Let his habitation be desolate, and let no man dwell therein: and his bishoprick let another take. 21 Wherefore of these men which have companied with us all the time that the Lord Jesus went in and out among us, 22 beginning from the baptism of John, unto that same day that he was taken up from us, must one be ordained to be a witness with us of his resurrection. 23 And they appointed two, Joseph called Barsabas, who was surnamed Justus, and Matthias. 24 And they prayed, and said, Thou, Lord, which knowest the hearts of all *men*, shew whether of these two thou hast chosen, 25 that he may take part of this ministry and apostleship, from which Judas by transgression fell, that he might go to his own place. 26 And they gave forth their lots; and the lot fell upon Matthias; and he was numbered with the eleven apostles.

II. And when the day of Pentecost was fully come, they were all with one accord in one place. 2 And suddenly there came a sound from heaven as of a rushing mighty wind, and it filled all the house where they were sitting. 3 And there appeared unto them cloven tongues like as of fire, and it sat upon each of them. 4 And they were all

---

[q] + ὁ T. [r] [ἰδίᾳ] TrA. [s] Ἀκελδαμάχ Aceldamach LA; Ἀχελδαμάχ Acheldamach TTr. [t] τοῦτ' ἔστιν GTTr. [v] λαβέτω LTTrAW. [w] — ἐν (read ᾧ in which) LTTrA. [x] Ἰωάνου Tr. [y] ἄχρι T. [z] ἀνελήμφθη LTTrA. [a] σὺν ἡμῖν γενέσθαι LTTrAW. [b] Βαρσαββᾶν LTTrA. [c] Μαθθίαν TTrA. [d] εἶπαν LTTrAW. [e] ὃν ἐξελέξω ἐκ τούτων τῶν δύο ἕνα GLTTrAW. [f] τόπον place LTTrA. [g] ἀφ' LTTrAW. [h] αὐτοῖς on them LTTrA. [i] συν- T. [k] συν- TA. [l] πάντες ὁμοῦ all together LTTrA. [m] καθεζόμενοι L. [n] καὶ ἐκάθισεν LTTr.

filled with the Holy
Ghost, and began to
speak with other
tongues, as the Spirit
gave them utterance.
5 And there were
dwelling at Jerusalem
Jews, devout men, out
of every nation under
heaven. 6 Now when
this was noised abroad,
the multitude came
together, and were
confounded, because
that every man heard
them speak in his own
language. 7 And they
were all amazed and
marvelled, saying one
to another, Behold, are
not all these which
speak Galilæans?
8 And how hear we
every man in our own
tongue, wherein we
were born? 9 Par-
thians, and Medes, and
Elamites, and the
dwellers in Mesopo-
tamia, and in Judæa,
and Cappadocia, in
Pontus, and Asia,
10 Phrygia, and Pam-
phylia, in Egypt, and
in the parts of Libya
about Cyrene, and
strangers of Rome,
Jews and proselytes,
11 Cretes and Arabi-
ans, we do hear them
speak in our tongues
the wonderful works
of God. 12 And they
were all amazed, and
were in doubt, saying
one to another, What
meaneth this? 13 O-
thers mocking said,
These men are full of
new wine. 14 But Pe-
ter, standing up with
the eleven, lifted up
his voice, and said
unto them, Ye men of
Judæa, and all *ye* that
dwell at Jerusalem, be
this known unto you,
and hearken to my
words: 15 for these
are not drunken, as ye
suppose, seeing it is
but the third hour of
the day. 16 But this
is that which was spo-
ken by the prophet
Joel; 17 And it shall
come to pass in the
last days, saith God, I

ἐπλήσθησαν [o]ἅπαντες‖ πνεύματος ἁγίου, καὶ ἤρξαντο λαλεῖν
they were [2]filled [1]all with [the] [2]Spirit [1]Holy, and began to speak
ἑτέραις γλώσσαις, καθὼς τὸ πνεῦμα ἐδίδου [p]αὐτοῖς ἀποφθέγ-
with other tongues, as the Spirit gave to them to utter
γεσθαι.‖ 5 Ἦσαν.δὲ [q]ἐν‖ Ἱερουσαλὴμ κατοικοῦντες Ἰουδαῖοι,
forth. Now [3]were [1]in [2]Jerusalem dwelling Jews,
ἄνδρες εὐλαβεῖς ἀπὸ παντὸς ἔθνους τῶν ὑπὸ τὸν οὐρανόν.
[2]men [1]pious from every nation of those under the heaven.
6 γενομένης.δὲ τῆς φωνῆς ταύτης, συνῆλθεν τὸ πλῆθος
But [5]having [6]arisen [1]the [2]rumour [3]of [4]this, [9]came [10]together [7]the [8]multitude
καὶ συνεχύθη· ὅτι ἤκουον εἷς ἕκαστος τῇ.ἰδίᾳ διαλέκτῳ
and were confounded, because [3]heard [2]one [1]each in his own language
λαλούντων αὐτῶν. 7 ἐξίσταντο.δὲ [r]πάντες‖ καὶ ἐθαύμαζον,
[2]speaking [1]them. And [2]were [3]amazed [1]all and wondered,
λέγοντες [s]πρὸς ἀλλήλους,‖ [t]Οὐκ‖ ἰδοὺ [v]πάντες‖ οὗτοί εἰσιν οἱ
saying to one another, [3]Not [1]lo [4]all [5]these [2]are who
λαλοῦντες Γαλιλαῖοι; 8 καὶ πῶς ἡμεῖς ἀκούομεν ἕκαστος
are speaking Galileans? and how [2]we [1]hear each
τῇ.ἰδίᾳ.διαλέκτῳ.ἡμῶν ἐν ᾗ ἐγεννήθημεν, 9 Πάρθοι καὶ
in our own language in which we were born, Parthians and
Μῆδοι καὶ [w]Ἐλαμῖται,‖ καὶ οἱ κατοικοῦντες τὴν Μεσοπο-
Medes and Elamites, and those who inhabit Mesopo-
ταμίαν, Ἰουδαίαν.τε καὶ Καππαδοκίαν, Πόντον καὶ τὴν Ἀσίαν,
tamia, and Judæa and Cappadocia, Pontus and Asia,
10 Φρυγίαν.τε καὶ Παμφυλίαν, Αἴγυπτον καὶ τὰ μέρη τῆς
both Phrygia and Pamphylia, Egypt and the parts
Λιβύης τῆς κατὰ Κυρήνην, καὶ οἱ ἐπιδημοῦντες
of Libya which [is] about Cyrene, and the [2]sojourning [[3]here]
Ῥωμαῖοι, Ἰουδαῖοί.τε καὶ προσήλυτοι, 11 Κρῆτες καὶ Ἄραβες,
[1]Romans, both Jews and proselytes, Cretans and Arabians,
ἀκούομεν λαλούντων αὐτῶν ταῖς.ἡμετέραις γλώσσαις τὰ
we hear [2]speaking [1]them in our own tongues the
μεγαλεῖα τοῦ θεοῦ; 12 Ἐξίσταντο.δὲ πάντες καὶ [x]διηπόρουν,‖
great things of God? And [2]were [3]amazed [1]all and were in perplexity,
ἄλλος.πρὸς.ἄλλον λέγοντες, Τί [y]ἂν.θέλοι‖ τοῦτο εἶναι;
one to another saying, What would this be?
13 Ἕτεροι.δὲ [z]χλευάζοντες‖ ἔλεγον, Ὅτι γλεύκους μεμεστω-
But others mocking said, Of new wine [3]full
μένοι εἰσίν. 14 Σταθεὶς.δὲ [a]Πέτρος σὺν τοῖς ἕνδεκα ἐπῆρεν
[1]they [2]are. But [2]standing [3]up [1]Peter with the eleven lifted up
τὴν.φωνὴν.αὐτοῦ καὶ ἀπεφθέγξατο αὐτοῖς, Ἄνδρες Ἰουδαῖοι,
his voice and spoke forth to them, Men Jews,
καὶ οἱ κατοικοῦντες Ἱερουσαλὴμ [o]ἅπαντες,‖ τοῦτο ὑμῖν
and [2]ye [3]who [4]inhabit [5]Jerusalem [1]all, [7]this [10]to [11]you
γνωστὸν ἔστω, καὶ ἐνωτίσασθε τὰ.ῥήματά.μου. 15 οὐ.γὰρ ὡς
[9]known [8]let [6]be, and give heed to my words: for not as
ὑμεῖς ὑπολαμβάνετε, οὗτοι μεθύουσιν· ἔστιν.γὰρ ὥρα
ye take it, [2]these [1]are drunken, for it is [the] [2]hour
τρίτη τῆς ἡμέρας· 16 ἀλλὰ τοῦτό ἐστιν τὸ εἰρημένον
[1]third of the day; but this is that which has been spoken
διὰ τοῦ προφήτου [b]Ἰωήλ,‖ 17 [c]Καὶ‖ ἔσται ἐν ταῖς ἐσχάταις
by the prophet Joel, And it shall be in the last

---

[o] πάντες LTTr. [p] ἀποφθέγγεσθαι αὐτοῖς LTTrAW. [q] εἰς T. [r] — πάντες (*read* they were amazed) L[Tr]A. [s] — πρὸς ἀλλήλους LTTrA. [t] Οὐχ LT; Οὐχὶ TrA. [v] ἅπαντες LTA. [w] Ἐλαμεῖται T. [x] διηπορουῦντο TTrA. [y] θέλει LTTr. [z] διαχλευάζοντες GLTTrAW. [a] + ὁ LTTrA. [b] — Ἰωήλ A. [c] — καὶ A.

ἡμέραις, λέγει ὁ θεός, ἐκχεῶ ἀπὸ τοῦ.πνεύματός.μου ἐπὶ
days, says God, I will pour out of my Spirit upon
πᾶσαν σάρκα, καὶ προφητεύσουσιν οἱ.υἱοὶ.ὑμῶν καὶ αἱ θυγα-
all flesh; and shall prophesy your sons and [2]daugh-
τέρες ὑμῶν· καὶ οἱ.νεανίσκοι.ὑμῶν ὁράσεις ὄψονται, καὶ οἱ
ters [1]your; and your young men visions shall see, and
πρεσβύτεροι.ὑμῶν [e]ἐνύπνια‖ ἐνυπνιασθήσονται· 18 [f]καί γε‖
your elders dreams shall dream; and even
ἐπὶ τοὺς.δούλους.μου καὶ ἐπὶ τὰς.δούλας.μου ἐν ταῖς ἡμέραις
upon my bondmen and upon my bondwomen in [2]days
ἐκείναις ἐκχεῶ ἀπὸ τοῦ.πνεύματός.μου, καὶ προφητεύ-
[1]those will I pour out of my Spirit, and they shall pro-
σουσιν. 19 καὶ δώσω τέρατα ἐν τῷ οὐρανῷ ἄνω καὶ σημεῖα
phesy; and I will give wonders in the heaven above and signs
ἐπὶ τῆς γῆς κάτω, αἷμα καὶ πῦρ καὶ ἀτμίδα καπνοῦ. 20 ὁ
on the earth below, blood and fire and vapour of smoke. The
ἥλιος μεταστραφήσεται εἰς σκότος καὶ ἡ σελήνη εἰς αἷμα,
sun shall be turned into darkness and the moon into blood,
πρὶν [g]ἢ‖ ἐλθεῖν [h]τὴν‖ ἡμέραν κυρίου τὴν μεγάλην [i]καὶ
before come [5]day [6]of [[7]the] [8]Lord [1]the [2]great [3]and
ἐπιφανῆ.‖ 21 καὶ ἔσται, πᾶς ὃς.[k]ἂν‖ ἐπικαλέσηται τὸ
[4]manifest. And it shall be, everyone whoever shall call upon the
ὄνομα κυρίου σωθήσεται. 22 Ἄνδρες [l]Ἰσραηλῖται,‖ ἀκούσατε
name of [the] Lord shall be saved. Men Israelites, hear
τοὺς.λόγους.τούτους· Ἰησοῦν τὸν Ναζωραῖον, ἄνδρα [m]ἀπὸ
these words: Jesus the Nazaræan, a man by
τοῦ θεοῦ ἀποδεδειγμένον‖ εἰς ὑμᾶς δυνάμεσιν καὶ τέρασιν
God set forth to you by works of power and wonders
καὶ σημείοις, οἷς ἐποίησεν δι' αὐτοῦ ὁ θεὸς ἐν μέσῳ ὑμῶν,
and signs, which [2]wrought [3]by [4]him [1]God in [2]midst [1]your,
καθὼς [n]καὶ‖ αὐτοὶ οἴδατε, 23 τοῦτον τῇ ὡρισμένῃ βουλῇ
as also yourselves know: him, [3]by [4]the [5]determinate [6]counsel
καὶ προγνώσει τοῦ θεοῦ ἔκδοτον [o]λαβόντες‖ διὰ [p]χειρῶν‖
[7]and [8]foreknowledge [9]of [10]God [1]given [2]up, having taken by [2]hands
ἀνόμων προσπήξαντες [q]ἀνείλετε·‖ 24 ὃν ὁ θεὸς ἀνέστησεν,
[1]lawless, having crucified ye put to death. Whom God raised up,
λύσας τὰς ὠδῖνας τοῦ θανάτου, καθότι οὐκ.ἦν δυνατὸν
having loosed the throes of death, inasmuch as it was not possible
κρατεῖσθαι αὐτὸν ὑπ' αὐτοῦ. 25 [r]Δαβὶδ‖.γὰρ λέγει εἰς
[for] [2]to [3]be [4]held [1]him by it; for David says as to
αὐτόν, [s]Προωρώμην‖ τὸν κύριον [t]ἐνώπιόν μου [v]διὰ.παντός,‖
him, I foresaw the Lord before me continually,
ὅτι ἐκ δεξιῶν.μου ἐστίν, ἵνα μὴ.σαλευθῶ. 26 διὰ.τοῦτο
because at my right hand he is, that I may not be shaken. Therefore
[w]εὐφράνθη‖ [x]ἡ.καρδία.μου‖ καὶ ἠγαλλιάσατο ἡ.γλῶσσά.μου·
[3]rejoiced [1]my [2]heart and [3]exulted [1]my [2]tongue;
ἔτι.δὲ καὶ ἡ.σάρξ.μου κατασκηνώσει [y]ἐπ'‖ ἐλπίδι· 27 ὅτι οὐκ
yea more, also my flesh shall rest in hope, for [3]not
[z]ἐγκαταλείψεις‖ τὴν.ψυχήν.μου εἰς [a]ᾅδου,‖ οὐδὲ δώσεις τὸν
[1]thou [2]wilt leave my soul in hades, nor wilt thou give

will pour out of my
Spirit upon all flesh:
and your sons and your
daughters shall pro-
phesy, and your young
men shall see visions,
and your old men shall
dream dreams: 18 and
on my servants and on
my handmaidens I
will pour out in those
days of my Spirit;
and they shall prophe-
sy: 19 and I will shew
wonders in heaven
above, and signs in
the earth beneath;
blood, and fire, and va-
pour of smoke: 20 the
sun shall be turned
into darkness, and the
moon into blood, be-
fore that great and
notable day of the
Lord come: 21 and it
shall come to pass,
that whosoever shall
call on the name of
the Lord shall be
saved. 22 Ye men of
Israel, hear these
words; Jesus of Na-
zareth, a man approv-
ed of God among you
by miracles and won-
ders and signs, which
God did by him in the
midst of you, as ye
yourselves also know:
23 him, being delivered
by the determinate
counsel and fore-
knowledge of God, ye
have taken, and by
wicked hands have
crucified and slain:
24 whom God hath
raised up, having
loosed the pains of
death: because it was
not possible that he
should be holden of it.
25 For David speak-
eth concerning him, I
foresaw the Lord al-
ways before my face,
for he is on my right
hand, that I should not
be moved: 26 therefore
did my heart rejoice,
and my tongue was
glad; moreover also
my flesh shall rest in
hope: 27 because thou
wilt not leave my soul
in hell, neither wilt

---

[e] ενυπνίοις with dreams GLTTrAW. [f] καίγε GT. [g] — ἢ LTTr. [h] — τὴν LTTrA. [i] — καὶ ἐπιφανῆ T. [k] ἐὰν TrA. [l] Ἰσραηλεῖται T. [m] ἀποδεδειγμένον ἀπὸ τοῦ θεοῦ TTr. [n] — καὶ LTTrA. [o] — λαβόντες LTTrA. [p] χειρὸς hand (*read* by [the] hand of lawless [ones]) LTTrA. [q] ἀνείλατε GLTTrAW. [r] Δαυεὶδ LTTrA; Δαυῒδ GW. [s] Προορώμην LTTrA. [t] + μου (*read* my Lord) T. [v] διαπαντός GT. [w] ηὐφράνθη LTTrAW. [x] μου ἡ καρδία TTrA. [y] ἐφ' LT. [z] ἐνκαταλείψεις T. [a] ᾅδην LTTrAW.

ou suffer thine Holy
One to see corruption.
28 Thou hast made
known to me the ways
of life; thou shalt
make me full of joy
with thy countenance.
29 Men *and* brethren,
let me freely speak
unto you of the patri-
arch David, that he is
both dead and buried,
and his sepulchre is
with us unto this day.
30 Therefore being a
prophet, and knowing
that God had sworn
with an oath to him,
that of the fruit of his
loins, according to the
flesh, he would raise
up Christ to sit on his
throne: 31 he seeing
this before spake of
the resurrection of
Christ, that his soul
was not left in hell,
neither his flesh did
see corruption. 32 This
Jesus hath God raised
up, whereof we all are
witnesses. 33 There-
fore being by the right
hand of God exalted,
and having received
of the Father the pro-
mise of the Holy
Ghost, he hath shed
forth this, which ye
now see and hear.
34 For David is not
ascended into the hea-
vens: but he saith him-
self, The LORD said
unto my Lord, Sit
thou on my right
hand, 35 until I make
thy foes thy footstool.
36 Therefore let all the
house of Israel know
assuredly, that God
hath made that same
Jesus, whom ye have
crucified, both Lord
and Christ.

37 Now when they
heard *this*, they were
pricked in their heart,
and said unto Peter
and to the rest of the
apostles, Men *and*
brethren, what shall
we do? 38 Then Peter
said unto them, Re-
pent, and be baptized
every one of you in the
name of Jesus Christ

ὅσιόν σου ἰδεῖν διαφθοράν. 28 ἐγνώρισάς μοι ὁδοὺς
[2]holy [3]one [1]thy to see corruption. Thou didst make known to me paths
ζωῆς· πληρώσεις με εὐφροσύνης μετὰ τοῦ-προσώπου-σου.
of life, thou wilt fill me with joy with thy countenance.
29 Ἄνδρες ἀδελφοί, ἐξὸν εἰπεῖν μετὰ παῤῥησίας
Men brethren, it is permitted [me] to speak with freedom
πρὸς ὑμᾶς περὶ τοῦ πατριάρχου [b]Δαβίδ," ὅτι καὶ ἐτελεύτη-
to you concerning the patriarch David, that both he died
σεν καὶ ἐτάφη, καὶ τὸ-μνῆμα-αὐτοῦ ἐστιν ἐν ἡμῖν ἄχρι
and was buried, and his tomb is amongst us unto
τῆς-ἡμέρας-ταύτης. 30 προφήτης οὖν ὑπάρχων, καὶ εἰδὼς
this day. A prophet therefore being, and knowing
ὅτι ὅρκῳ ὤμοσεν αὐτῷ ὁ θεός, ἐκ καρποῦ τῆς ὀσφύος
that with an oath [2]swore [3]to [4]him [1]God, of [the] fruit of [4]loins
αὐτοῦ [c]τὸ-κατὰ σάρκα ἀναστήσειν τὸν χριστόν," καθίσαι ἐπὶ
[1]his as concerning flesh to raise up the Christ, to sit upon
[d]τοῦ-θρόνου"-αὐτοῦ, 31 προϊδὼν ἐλάλησεν περὶ τῆς ἀνα-
his throne, foreseeing he spoke concerning the resur-
στάσεως τοῦ χριστοῦ, ὅτι [e]οὐ" [f]κατελείφθη" [g]ἡ-ψυχὴ-αὐτοῦ" εἰς
rection of the Christ, that was not left his soul in
[h]ᾅδου," [i]οὐδὲ" ἡ-σὰρξ-αὐτοῦ εἶδεν διαφθοράν. 32 τοῦτον τὸν
hades, nor his flesh saw corruption. This
Ἰησοῦν ἀνέστησεν ὁ θεὸς οὗ πάντες ἡμεῖς ἐσμεν μάρτυρες.
Jesus [2]raised [3]up [1]God whereof all we are witnesses.
33 τῇ δεξιᾷ οὖν τοῦ θεοῦ ὑψωθείς, τήν-τε ἐπαγ-
By the right hand therefore of God having been exalted, and the pro-
γελίαν τοῦ [k]ἁγίου πνεύματος" λαβὼν παρὰ τοῦ πατρός,
mise of the Holy Spirit having received from the Father,
ἐξέχεεν τοῦτο ὃ [l]νῦν" ὑμεῖς [m]βλέπετε καὶ ἀκούετε. 34 οὐ
he poured out this which now ye behold and hear. [4]Not
γὰρ [b]Δαβὶδ" ἀνέβη εἰς τοὺς οὐρανούς, λέγει-δὲ αὐτός,
[1]for [2]David [3]ascended into the heavens, but he says himself,
Εἶπεν [n]ὁ" κύριος τῷ-κυρίῳ-μου, Κάθου ἐκ δεξιῶν-μου· 35 ἕως
Said the Lord to my Lord, Sit at my right hand, until
ἂν θῶ τοὺς-ἐχθρούς-σου ὑποπόδιον τῶν-ποδῶν-σου. 36 Ἀ-
I place thine enemies a footstool of thy feet. As-
σφαλῶς οὖν γινωσκέτω πᾶς [o]οἶκος Ἰσραήλ, ὅτι [p]καὶ"
suredly therefore let know all [the] house of Israel, that both
κύριον [q]καὶ χριστὸν αὐτὸν" [r]ὁ θεὸς ἐποίησεν," τοῦτον τὸν
Lord and Christ him God made, this
Ἰησοῦν ὃν ὑμεῖς ἐσταυρώσατε.
Jesus whom ye crucified.

37 Ἀκούσαντες-δὲ κατενύγησαν [s]τῇ-καρδίᾳ," εἶπόν-τε πρὸς
And having heard they were pricked in heart, and said to
τὸν Πέτρον καὶ τοὺς λοιποὺς ἀποστόλους, Τί [t]ποιήσομεν,"
Peter and the other apostles, What shall we do,
ἄνδρες ἀδελφοί; 38 Πέτρος-δὲ [v]ἔφη" πρὸς αὐτούς, Μετανοή-
men brethren? And Peter said to them, Repent,
σατε[w], καὶ βαπτισθήτω ἕκαστος ὑμῶν [x]ἐπὶ" τῷ ὀνόματι Ἰησοῦ
and be baptized each of you in the name of Jesus

---

[b] Δαυεὶδ LTTrA; Δαυῒδ GW. [c] — τὸ κατὰ σάρκα ἀναστήσειν τὸν χριστόν GLTTrA. [d] τὸν θρόνον LTTrA. [e] οὔτε LTTrAW. [f] ἐγκατελείφθη LTrA; ἐνκ- T. [g] — ἡ ψυχὴ αὐτοῦ GLTTrA. [h] ᾅδην T. [i] οὔτε LTTrAW. [k] πνεύματος τοῦ ἁγίου LTTrA. [l] — νῦν GLTTrA. [m] + καὶ also T[A]. [n] — ὁ (read [the]) TTrA. [o] + ὁ the L. [p] — καὶ E. [q] αὐτὸν καὶ χριστὸν GLTTrAW. [r] ἐποίησεν ὁ θεός T. [s] τὴν καρδίαν LTTrA. [t] ποιήσωμεν should we do TTrA. [v] — ἔφη LTTrA. [w] + φησίν says T. [x] ἐν LTr.

χριστοῦ, εἰς ἄφεσιν [y]ἁμαρτιῶν,‖ καὶ [z]λήψεσθε‖ τὴν δωρεὰν
Christ, for remission of sins, and ye will receive the gift
τοῦ ἁγίου πνεύματος. 39 ὑμῖν.γάρ ἐστιν ἡ ἐπαγγελία καὶ
of the Holy Spirit. For to you is the promise and
τοῖς.τέκνοις.ὑμῶν, καὶ πᾶσιν τοῖς εἰς μακράν, [a]ὅσους‖ ἂν
to your children, and to all those at a distance, as many as
προσκαλέσηται κύριος ὁ.θεὸς.ἡμῶν. 40 Ἑτέροις.τε λόγοις
[5]may [6]call [[1]the] [2]Lord [3]our [4]God. And with [2]other [3]words
πλείοσιν [b]διεμαρτύρετο‖ καὶ παρεκάλει [c] λέγων, Σώθητε ἀπὸ
[1]many he earnestly testified and exhorted, saying, Be saved from
τῆς γενεᾶς τῆς.σκολιᾶς.ταύτης. 41 Οἱ.μὲν.οὖν [d]ἀσμένως‖
[3]generation [1]this [2]crooked. Those therefore who gladly
ἀποδεξάμενοι τὸν.λόγον.αὐτοῦ ἐβαπτίσθησαν· καὶ προσετέθη-
had welcomed his word were baptized; and were added
σαν [e] τῇ.ἡμέρᾳ.ἐκείνῃ ψυχαὶ ὡσεὶ τρισχίλιαι. 42 Ἦσαν.δὲ
that day [4]souls [1]about [2]three [3]thousand. And they were
προσκαρτεροῦντες [f] τῇ διδαχῇ τῶν ἀποστόλων καὶ τῇ κοινωνίᾳ
steadfastly continuing in the teaching of the apostles and in fellowship,
[g]καὶ‖ τῇ κλάσει τοῦ ἄρτου καὶ ταῖς προσευχαῖς. 43 [h]ἐγένετο‖
and the breaking of bread and prayers. [2]There [3]came
δὲ πάσῃ ψυχῇ φόβος, πολλά.[i]τε‖ τέρατα καὶ σημεῖα διὰ
[1]and upon every soul fear, and many wonders and signs through
τῶν ἀποστόλων ἐγίνετο.[j] 44 [k] πάντες.δὲ οἱ [l]πιστεύοντες‖ ἦσαν
the apostles took place. And all who believed were
ἐπὶ.τὸ.αὐτὸ καὶ εἶχον ἅπαντα κοινά, 45 καὶ τὰ κτήματα
together and had all things common, and [their] possessions
καὶ τὰς ὑπάρξεις ἐπίπρασκον, καὶ διεμέριζον αὐτὰ πᾶσιν,
and goods they sold, and divided them to all,
καθότι ἄν τις χρείαν εἶχεν. 46 καθ'.ἡμέραν.τε προσκαρ-
according as anyone [2]need [1]had. And every day steadfastly
τεροῦντες ὁμοθυμαδὸν ἐν τῷ ἱερῷ, κλῶντές.τε κατ'.οἶκον
continuing with one accord in the temple, and breaking [2]in [[3]their] [4]houses
ἄρτον, μετελάμβανον τροφῆς ἐν ἀγαλλιάσει καὶ ἀφελότητι
[1]bread, they partook of food with gladness and simplicity
καρδίας, 47 αἰνοῦντες τὸν θεὸν, καὶ ἔχοντες χάριν πρὸς ὅλον
of heart, praising God, and having favour with [2]whole
τὸν λαόν. ὁ.δὲ κύριος προσετίθει τοὺς σωζομένους
[1]the people; and the Lord added [2]those [3]who [4]were [5]being [6]saved
καθ'.ἡμέραν [m]τῇ ἐκκλησίᾳ.‖
[1]daily to the assembly.

3 [n]Ἐπὶ.τὸ.αὐτὸ‖ [o]δὲ Πέτρος‖ καὶ [p]Ἰωάννης‖ ἀνέβαινον
[5]Together [1]and [2]Peter [3]and [4]John went up
εἰς τὸ ἱερὸν ἐπὶ τὴν ὥραν τῆς προσευχῆς τὴν [q]ἐννάτην.‖
into the temple at the hour of prayer, the ninth;
2 καί τις ἀνὴρ χωλὸς ἐκ κοιλίας μητρὸς αὐτοῦ ὑπάρχων
and a certain man [2]lame [3]from [6]womb [5]mother's [4]his [1]being
ἐβαστάζετο· ὃν ἐτίθουν καθ'.ἡμέραν πρὸς τὴν θύραν τοῦ
was being carried, whom they placed daily at the door of the
ἱεροῦ τὴν λεγομένην Ὡραίαν, τοῦ αἰτεῖν ἐλεημοσύνην παρὰ
temple called Beautiful, to ask alms from

for the remission of sins, and ye shall receive the gift of the Holy Ghost. 39 For the promise is unto you, and to your children, and to all that are afar off, *even* as many as the Lord our God shall call. 40 And with many other words did he testify and exhort, saying, Save yourselves from this untoward generation. 41 Then they that gladly received his word were baptized: and the same day there were added *unto them* about three thousand souls. 42 And they continued stedfastly in the apostles' doctrine and fellowship, and in breaking of bread, and in prayers. 43 And fear came upon every soul: and many wonders and signs were done by the apostles. 44 And all that believed were together, and had all things common; 45 and sold their possessions and goods, and parted them to all *men*, as every man had need. 46 And they, continuing daily with one accord in the temple, and breaking bread from house to house, did eat their meat with gladness and singleness of heart, 47 praising God, and having favour with all the people. And the Lord added to the church daily such as should be saved.

III. Now Peter and John went up together into the temple at the hour of prayer, *being* the ninth *hour*. 2 And a certain man lame from his mother's womb was carried, whom they laid daily at the gate of the temple which is called Beautiful, to ask alms of them that entered

[y] τῶν ἁμαρτιῶν ὑμῶν of your sins LTTr. [z] λήμψεσθε LTTrA. [a] οὓς whom L. [b] διεμαρτύρατο LTTrAW. [c] + αὐτοὺς them LTTrAW. [d] — ἀσμένως LTTrA. [e] + ἐν in LTTr[A]. [f] + [ἐν] L. [g] — καὶ LTTrA. [h] ἐγίνετο LTTrA. [i] δὲ T. [j] + ἐν Ἱερουσαλήμ, φόβος τε ἦν μέγας ἐπὶ πάντας. in Jerusalem, and great fear was upon all. T. [k] + καὶ (*read* And all also) T. [l] πιστεύσαντες T. [m] — τῇ ἐκκλησίᾳ LTTrA. [n] ἐπὶ τὸ αὐτό *joined to chapter* ii. LTTrA. [o] Πέτρος δὲ LTTrA. [p] Ἰωάνης Tr. [q] ἐνάτην LTTrAW.

into the temple: 3 who
seeing Peter and John
about to go into the
temple asked an alms.
4 And Peter, fastening
his eyes upon him
with John, said, Look
on us. 5 And he gave
heed unto them, ex-
pecting to receive
something of them.
6 Then Peter said, Sil-
ver and gold have I
none; but such as I
have give I thee: In
the name of Jesus
Christ of Nazareth
rise up and walk.
7 And he took him by
the right hand, and
lifted *him* up: and im-
mediately his feet and
ancle bones received
strength. 8 And he
leaping up stood, and
walked, and entered
with them into the
temple, walking, and
leaping, and praising
God. 9 And all the
people saw him walk-
ing and praising God:
10 and they knew that
it was he which sat
for alms at the Beau-
tiful gate of the tem-
ple: and they were
filled with wonder and
amazement at that
which had happened
unto him. 11 And as
the lame man which
was healed held Peter
and John, all the peo-
ple ran together unto
them in the porch that
is called Solomon's,
greatly wondering.
12 And when Peter
saw *it*, he answered
unto the people, Ye
men of Israel, why
marvel ye at this? or
why look ye so earn-
estly on us, as though
by our own power or
holiness we had made
this man to walk?
13 The God of Abra-
ham, and of Isaac,
and of Jacob, the God
of our fathers, hath
glorified his Son Je-
sus; whom ye de-
livered up, and denied
him in the presence of
Pilate, when he was
determined to let *him*

των εἰσπορευομένων εἰς τὸ ἱερόν. 3 ὃς ἰδὼν Πέτρον καὶ
those who were going into the temple; who seeing Peter and
[r]Ἰωάννην‖ μέλλοντας εἰσιέναι εἰς τὸ ἱερόν, ἠρώτα ἐλεημοσύ-
John being about to enter into the temple, asked [3]alms
νην λαβεῖν. 4 ἀτενίσας.δὲ Πέτρος εἰς αὐτὸν σὺν τῷ [s]Ἰωάν-
[1]to [2]receive. And [2]looking [3]intently [1]Peter upon him with John
νῃ‖ εἶπεν, Βλέψον εἰς ἡμᾶς. 5 Ὁ.δὲ ἐπεῖχεν αὐτοῖς, προσδοκῶν
said, Look on us. And he gave heed to them, expecting
τι παρ' αὐτῶν λαβεῖν. 6 εἶπεν.δὲ Πέτρος, Ἀργύριον καὶ
something from them to receive. But said Peter, Silver and
χρυσίον οὐχ.ὑπάρχει μοι· ὃ.δὲ ἔχω, τοῦτό σοι δίδωμι.
gold there is not to me, but what I have, this to thee I give:
ἐν τῷ ὀνόματι Ἰησοῦ χριστοῦ τοῦ Ναζωραίου [t]ἔγειραι καὶ‖
In the name of Jesus Christ the Nazaræan rise up and
περιπάτει. 7 Καὶ πιάσας αὐτὸν τῆς δεξιᾶς χειρὸς ἤγειρεν[v]·
walk. And having taken him by the right hand he raised up
παραχρῆμα.δὲ ἐστερεώθησαν [w]αὐτοῦ αἱ βάσεις‖ καὶ τὰ
[him], and immediately were strengthened his feet and
[x]σφυρά·‖ 8 καὶ ἐξαλλόμενος ἔστη καὶ περιεπάτει, καὶ εἰσῆλ-
ankle bones. And leaping up he stood and walked, and entered
θεν σὺν αὐτοῖς εἰς τὸ ἱερόν, περιπατῶν καὶ ἁλλόμενος [y]καὶ‖
with them into the temple, walking and leaping and
αἰνῶν τὸν θεόν. 9 καὶ εἶδεν [z]αὐτὸν πᾶς ὁ λαὸς‖ περιπα-
praising God. And [4]saw [5]him [1]all [2]the [3]people walk-
τοῦντα καὶ αἰνοῦντα τὸν θεόν· 10 ἐπεγίνωσκόν.[a]τε‖ αὐτὸν
ing and praising God. And they recognized him
ὅτι [b]οὗτος‖ ἦν ὁ πρὸς τὴν ἐλεημοσύνην καθήμενος ἐπὶ
that he it was who for alms [was] sitting at
τῇ Ὡραίᾳ πύλῃ τοῦ ἱεροῦ· καὶ ἐπλήσθησαν θάμβους καὶ
the Beautiful gate of the temple, and they were filled with wonder and
ἐκστάσεως ἐπὶ τῷ συμβεβηκότι αὐτῷ. 11 Κρατοῦντος.δὲ
amazement at that which had happened to him. And as [8]held
[c]τοῦ ἰαθέντος χωλοῦ‖ τὸν Πέτρον καὶ [d] [e]Ἰωάννην,‖
[1]the [4]who [5]had [6]been [7]healed [2]lame [[3]man] Peter and John,
συνέδραμεν [f]πρὸς αὐτοὺς πᾶς ὁ λαὸς‖ ἐπὶ τῇ στοᾷ τῇ
ran together to them all the people in the porch
καλουμένῃ [g]Σολομῶντος,‖ ἔκθαμβοι. 12 ἰδὼν.δὲ [h] Πέτρος
called Solomon's, greatly amazed. And seeing [it] Peter
ἀπεκρίνατο πρὸς τὸν λαόν, Ἄνδρες [i]Ἰσραηλῖται,‖ τί θαυ-
answered to the people, Men Israelites, why won-
μάζετε ἐπὶ τούτῳ, ἢ ἡμῖν τί ἀτενίζετε ὡς ἰδίᾳ δυνάμει
der ye at this? or on us why look intently as if by [our] own power
ἢ εὐσεβείᾳ πεποιηκόσιν τοῦ περιπατεῖν αὐτόν; 13 ὁ θεὸς
or piety [we] had made [2]to [3]walk [1]him? The God
Ἀβραὰμ καὶ [k] Ἰσαὰκ καὶ [k] Ἰακώβ, ὁ θεὸς τῶν.πατέρων.ἡμῶν,
of Abraham and Isaac and Jacob, the God of our fathers,
ἐδόξασεν τὸν.παῖδα.αὐτοῦ Ἰησοῦν· ὃν ὑμεῖς [l] παρεδώκατε,
glorified his servant Jesus, whom ye delivered up,
καὶ ἠρνήσασθε [m]αὐτὸν‖ κατὰ.πρόσωπον [n]Πιλάτου,‖ κρίναντος
and denied him in the presence of Pilate, [2]having [3]adjudged

---

[r] Ἰωάνην Tr. [s] Ἰωάνῃ Tr. [t] ἔγειρε καὶ L[Tr]; — ἔγειραι καὶ T[A]. [v] + αὐτόν him LTTrA. [w] αἱ βάσεις αὐτοῦ LTTrA. [x] σφυδρά T. [y] [καὶ] L. [z] πᾶς ὁ λαὸς αὐτὸν LTTrAW. [a] δὲ LTTrA. [b] αὐτὸς LT. [c] αὐτοῦ he (held) GLTTrAW. [d] + τὸν LTTr. [e] Ἰωάνην Tr. [f] πᾶς ὁ λαὸς πρὸς αὐτοὺς LTTrA. [g] Σολομῶνος GTrW. [h] + ὁ LTTrA. [i] Ἰσραηλεῖται T. [k] + θεὸς God L; + ὁ θεὸς T. [l] + μὲν indeed GLTTrAW. [m] — αὐτὸν LT[TrA]. [n] Πειλάτου T.

ἐκείνου ἀπολύειν. 14 ὑμεῖς.δὲ τὸν ἅγιον καὶ δίκαιον
[1]he to release [him]. But ye the holy and righteous one
ἠρνήσασθε, καὶ ᾐτήσασθε ἄνδρα φονέα χαρισθῆναι ὑμῖν,
denied, and requested a man a murderer to be granted to you,
15 τὸν.δὲ ἀρχηγὸν τῆς ζωῆς ἀπεκτείνατε· ὃν ὁ θεὸς ἤγειρεν
but the Author of life ye killed, whom God raised up
ἐκ νεκρῶν, οὗ ἡμεῖς μάρτυρές ἐσμεν. 16 καὶ ἐπὶ
from among [the] dead, whereof we witnesses are: and by
τῇ πίστει τοῦ.ὀνόματος.αὐτοῦ τοῦτον ὃν θεωρεῖτε καὶ
faith in his name this [man] whom ye behold and
οἴδατε ἐστερέωσεν τὸ.ὄνομα.αὐτοῦ· καὶ ἡ πίστις ἡ δι'
know [3]made [4]strong [1]his [2]name; and the faith which [is] by
αὐτοῦ ἔδωκεν αὐτῷ τὴν.ὁλοκληρίαν.ταύτην ἀπέναντι πάντων
him gave to him this complete soundness before all
ὑμῶν. 17 καὶ νῦν, ἀδελφοί, οἶδα ὅτι κατὰ ἄγνοιαν ἐπράξατε,
of you. And now, brethren, I know that in ignorance ye acted,
ὥσπερ καὶ οἱ.ἄρχοντες.ὑμῶν· 18 ὁ.δὲ.θεὸς ἃ προκατήγγειλεν
as also your rulers; but [2]God [1]what before announced
διὰ στόματος πάντων τῶν.προφητῶν.[o]αὐτοῦ‖ παθεῖν
by [the] mouth of all his prophets [that] [3]should [4]suffer
τὸν χριστόν[p], ἐπλήρωσεν οὕτως. 19 μετανοήσατε οὖν καὶ
[1]the [2]Christ, he fulfilled thus. Repent therefore and
ἐπιστρέψατε, [q]εἰς‖ τὸ ἐξαλειφθῆναι ὑμῶν τὰς ἁμαρτίας, ὅπως
be converted, for the blotting out of your sins, so that
ἂν.ἔλθωσιν καιροὶ ἀναψύξεως ἀπὸ προσώπου τοῦ κυρίου,
may come times of refreshing from [the] presence of the Lord,
20 καὶ ἀποστείλῃ τὸν [r]προκεκηρυγμένον‖ ὑμῖν, [s]Ἰησοῦν
and [that] he may send him who was before proclaimed to you, Jesus
χριστόν,‖ 21 ὃν δεῖ οὐρανὸν μὲν δέξασθαι ἄχρι χρόνων
Christ, whom [2]must [1]heaven indeed receive till times
ἀποκαταστάσεως πάντων, ὧν ἐλάλησεν ὁ θεὸς διὰ
of restoration of all things, of which [2]spoke [1]God by [the]
στόματος [t]πάντων‖ ἁγίων [v]αὐτοῦ προφητῶν ἀπ' αἰῶνος.‖
mouth of all [3]holy [1]his prophets from of old.
22 [w]Μωσῆς‖ μὲν [x]γὰρ‖ [y]πρὸς τοὺς πατέρας‖ εἶπεν, Ὅτι
[2]Moses [3]indeed [1]for to the fathers said,
προφήτην ὑμῖν ἀναστήσει κύριος ὁ θεὸς [z]ὑμῶν‖ ἐκ
A prophet to you will [5]raise [6]up [[1]the] [2]Lord [4]God [3]your from among
τῶν.ἀδελφῶν.ὑμῶν, ὡς ἐμέ· αὐτοῦ ἀκούσεσθε κατὰ πάντα
your brethren, like me: him shall ye hear in all things
ὅσα.ἂν λαλήσῃ πρὸς ὑμᾶς. 23 ἔσται.δὲ πᾶσα ψυχὴ
whatsoever he may say to you. And it shall be [that] every soul
ἥτις [a]ἂν‖.μὴ.ἀκούσῃ τοῦ.προφήτου.ἐκείνου [b]ἐξολοθρευθήσεται‖
which may not hear that prophet shall be destroyed
ἐκ τοῦ λαοῦ. 24 Καὶ πάντες.δὲ οἱ προφῆται ἀπὸ
from among the people. And indeed all the prophets from
Σαμουὴλ καὶ τῶν καθεξῆς, ὅσοι ἐλάλησαν καὶ [c]προκατήγ-
Samuel and those subsequent, as many as spoke also before an-
γειλαν‖ τὰς.ἡμέρας.ταύτας. 25 ὑμεῖς ἐστε [d]υἱοὶ τῶν προφητῶν
nounced these days. Ye are sons of the prophets
καὶ τῆς διαθήκης ἧς [e]διέθετο ὁ θεὸς‖ πρὸς τοὺς πατέρας
and of the covenant which [2]appointed [1]God to [2]fathers

go. 14 But ye denied
the Holy One and the
Just, and desired a
murderer to be grant-
ed unto you; 15 and
killed the Prince of
life, whom God hath
raised from the dead;
whereof we are wit-
nesses. 16 And his
name through faith in
his name hath made
this man strong, whom
ye see and know: yea,
the faith which is by
him hath given him
this perfect soundness
in the presence of
you all. 17 And now,
brethren, I wot that
through ignorance ye
did *it*, as *did* also your
rulers. 18 But those
things, which God
before had shewed by
the mouth of all his
prophets, that Christ
should suffer, he hath
so fulfilled. 19 Repent
ye therefore, and be
converted, that your
sins may be blotted
out, when the times
of refreshing shall
come from the pre-
sence of the Lord;
20 and he shall send
Jesus Christ, which
before was preached
unto you: 21 whom
the heaven must re-
ceive until the times
of restitution of all
things, which God
hath spoken by the
mouth of all his holy
prophets since the
world began. 22 For
Moses truly said unto
the fathers, A prophet
shall the Lord your
God raise up unto you
of your brethren, like
unto me; him shall
ye hear in all things
whatsoever he shall
say unto you. 23 And
it shall come to pass,
that every soul, which
will not hear that pro-
phet, shall be de-
stroyed from among
the people. 24 Yea,
and all the prophets
from Samuel and
those that follow af-
ter, as many as have
spoken, have likewise
foretold of these days.
25 Ye are the children
of the prophets, and
of the covenant which
God made with our
fathers, saying unto

---

[o] — αὐτοῦ (*read* the prophets) LTTrA. [p] + αὐτοῦ (*read* his Christ) LTTrAW. [q] πρὸς T. [r] προκεχειρισμένον was foreordained GLTTrAW. [s] χριστὸν Ἰησοῦν LTTrA. [t] τῶν (*omit* all) GLTTrAW. [v] ἀπ' αἰῶνος αὐτοῦ προφητῶν LTTrA. [w] Μωϋσῆς GLTTrAW. [x] — γὰρ GLTTrAW. [y] — πρὸς τοὺς πατέρας LTTrA. [z] ἡμῶν our T. [a] ἐὰν TA. [b] ἐξολεθρευθήσεται LTTrA. [c] κατήγγειλαν announced GLTTrAW. [d] + οἱ the GLTTrAW. [e] ὁ θεὸς διέθετο L.

Abraham, And in thy
seed shall all the kin-
dreds of the earth be
blessed. 26 Unto you
first God, having
raised up his Son Je-
sus, sent him to bless
you, in turning away
every one of you from
his iniquities.

IV. And as they
spake unto the people,
the priests, and the
captain of the temple,
and the Sadducees,
came upon them,
2 being grieved that
they taught the peo-
ple, and preached
through Jesus the re-
surrection from the
dead. 3 And they laid
hands on them, and
put *them* in hold un-
to the next day: for
it was now eventide.
4 Howbeit many of
them which heard the
word believed; and
the number of the men
was about five thou-
sand.

5 And it came to
pass on the morrow,
that their rulers, and
elders, and scribes,
6 and Annas the high
priest, and Caiaphas,
and John, and Alex-
ander, and as many as
were of the kindred
of the high priest,
were gathered toge-
ther at Jerusalem.
7 And when they had
set them in the midst,
they asked, By what
power, or by what
name, have ye done
this? 8 Then Peter,
filled with the Holy
Ghost, said unto them,
Ye rulers of the peo-
ple, and elders of Is-
rael, 9 if we this day
be examined of the
good deed done to
the impotent man, by
what means he is
made whole; 10 be it
known unto you all,
and to all the people
of Israel, that by the
name of Jesus Christ
of Nazareth, whom ye
crucified, whom God
raised from the dead,
even by him doth this

[f]ἡμῶν,‖ λέγων πρὸς Ἀβραάμ, Καὶ [g]τῷ.σπέρματί.σου ἐνευλο-
[1]our, saying to Abraham, And in thy seed shall be
γηθήσονται πᾶσαι αἱ πατριαὶ τῆς γῆς. 26 ὑμῖν πρῶτον
blessed all the families of the earth. To you first
[h]ὁ θεὸς ἀναστήσας‖ τὸν.παῖδα.αὐτοῦ [i]Ἰησοῦν,‖ ἀπέστειλεν
God, having raised up his servant Jesus, sent
αὐτὸν εὐλογοῦντα ὑμᾶς ἐν τῷ ἀποστρέφειν ἕκαστον ἀπὸ
him, blessing you in turning each from
τῶν πονηριῶν [k]ὑμῶν.‖
[2]wickedness [1]your.

4 Λαλούντων.δὲ αὐτῶν πρὸς τὸν λαόν, ἐπέστησαν αὐτοῖς
And as [2]were [3]speaking [1]they to the people, came upon them
οἱ ἱερεῖς καὶ ὁ στρατηγὸς τοῦ ἱεροῦ καὶ οἱ Σαδδουκαῖοι,
the priests and captain of the temple and the Sadducees,
2 διαπονούμενοι διὰ τὸ διδάσκειν αὐτοὺς τὸν λαόν, καὶ
being distressed because [2]teach [1]they the people, and
καταγγέλλειν ἐν τῷ Ἰησοῦ τὴν ἀνάστασιν τὴν ἐκ
announce in Jesus the resurrection which [is] from among
νεκρῶν· 3 καὶ ἐπέβαλον αὐτοῖς τὰς χεῖρας καὶ ἔθεντο [l]
[the] dead; and they laid [2]on [3]them [1]hands and put
εἰς τήρησιν εἰς τὴν αὔριον· ἦν.γὰρ ἑσπέρα ἤδη.
[them] in hold till the morrow; for it was evening already.
4 πολλοὶ.δὲ τῶν ἀκουσάντων τὸν λόγον ἐπίστευσαν,
But many of those who had heard the word believed,
καὶ ἐγενήθη [m]ὁ‖ ἀριθμὸς τῶν ἀνδρῶν [n]ὡσεὶ‖ χιλιάδες πέντε.
and [6]became [1]the [2]number [3]of [4]the [5]men about [2]thousand [1]five.

5 Ἐγένετο.δὲ ἐπὶ τὴν αὔριον συναχθῆναι αὐτῶν
And it came to pass on the morrow were gathered together their
τοὺς ἄρχοντας καὶ [o]πρεσβυτέρους καὶ [o]γραμματεῖς [p]εἰς‖ Ἱε-
rulers and elders and scribes at Je-
ρουσαλήμ, 6 καὶ [q]Ἄνναν τὸν ἀρχιερέα καὶ Καϊάφαν καὶ
rusalem, and Annas the high priest and Caiaphas and
Ἰωάννην καὶ Ἀλέξανδρον,‖ καὶ ὅσοι ἦσαν ἐκ γένους
John and Alexander, and as many as were of [2]family
ἀρχιερατικοῦ. 7 καὶ στήσαντες αὐτοὺς ἐν [r]τῷ‖ μέσῳ ἐπυν-
[1]high-priestly. And having placed them in the midst they
θάνοντο, Ἐν ποίᾳ δυνάμει ἢ ἐν ποίῳ ὀνόματι [s]ἐποιήσατε
inquired, In what power or in what name did
τοῦτο‖ ὑμεῖς; 8 Τότε Πέτρος πλησθεὶς πνεύματος ἁγίου
[2]this [1]ye? Then Peter, filled with [the] [2]Spirit [1]Holy,
εἶπεν πρὸς αὐτούς, Ἄρχοντες τοῦ λαοῦ καὶ πρεσβύτεροι
said to them, Rulers of the people and elders
[t]τοῦ Ἰσραήλ,‖ 9 εἰ ἡμεῖς σήμερον ἀνακρινόμεθα ἐπὶ εὐεργεσίᾳ
of Israel, If we this day are examined as to a good work
ἀνθρώπου.ἀσθενοῦς, ἐν τίνι οὗτος [v]σέσωσται,‖ 10 γνωστὸν
[to the] infirm man, by what he has been cured, [3]known
ἔστω πᾶσιν ὑμῖν καὶ παντὶ τῷ λαῷ Ἰσραήλ, ὅτι ἐν τῷ
[1]be [2]it to all you and to all the people of Israel, that in the
ὀνόματι Ἰησοῦ χριστοῦ τοῦ Ναζωραίου, ὃν ὑμεῖς ἐσταυ-
name of Jesus Christ the Nazaræan, whom ye cruci-
ρώσατε, ὃν ὁ θεὸς ἤγειρεν ἐκ νεκρῶν, ἐν τούτῳ
fied, whom God raised from among [the] dead, by him

---

[f] ὑμῶν your TrA. [g] + ἐν GLTTrAW. [h] ἀναστήσας ὁ θεὸς TA. [i] — Ἰησοῦν GLTTrA.
[k] αὐτῶν their L. [l] + αὐτοὺς them W. [m] — ὁ LT[Tr]A. [n] [ὡς] LTrA; — ὡσεὶ T.
[o] + τοὺς the LTTrA. [p] ἐν LTrAW. [q] Ἄννας ὁ ἀρχιερεὺς καὶ Καϊάφας καὶ Ἰωάννης καὶ
Ἀλέξανδρος LTTrA. [r] — τῷ G[A]. [s] τοῦτο ἐποιήσατε T. [t] — τοῦ Ἰσραήλ LTTr[A].
[v] σέσωται T.

οὗτος παρέστηκεν ἐνώπιον ὑμῶν ὑγιής. 11 οὗτός ἐστιν ὁ
this [man] stands before you sound. This is the
λίθος ὁ ἐξουθενηθεὶς ὑφ' ὑμῶν τῶν [w]οἰκοδομούντων,‖
stone which has been set at nought by you the builders,
ὁ γενόμενος εἰς κεφαλὴν γωνίας. 12 καὶ οὐκ ἔστιν
which is become head of [the] corner. And there is
ἐν ἄλλῳ οὐδενὶ ἡ σωτηρία· [x]οὔτε‖-γὰρ ὄνομά ἐστιν ἕτερον
in [2]other [1]no one salvation, for neither [4]name [1]is [2]there [3]another
ὑπὸ τὸν οὐρανὸν τὸ δεδομένον ἐν ἀνθρώποις, ἐν ᾧ
under the heaven which has been given among men, by which
δεῖ σωθῆναι ἡμᾶς.
[2]must [3]be [4]saved [1]we.

13 Θεωροῦντες-δὲ τὴν τοῦ Πέτρου παῤῥησίαν καὶ [y]Ἰωάν-
But seeing the [2]of [3]Peter [1]boldness and of John,
νου,‖ καὶ καταλαβόμενοι ὅτι ἄνθρωποι ἀγράμματοί εἰσιν
and having perceived that [3]men [4]unlettered [1]they [2]are
καὶ ἰδιῶται, ἐθαύμαζον, ἐπεγίνωσκόν-τε αὐτοὺς ὅτι σὺν τῷ
and uninstructed, they wondered, and they recognized them that with
Ἰησοῦ ἦσαν. 14 τὸν-[z]δὲ‖ ἄνθρωπον βλέποντες σὺν αὐτοῖς
Jesus they were. But [2]the [3]man [1]beholding [5]with [6]them
ἑστῶτα τὸν τεθεραπευμένον, οὐδὲν εἶχον ἀντειπεῖν. 15 κελεύ-
[4]standing who had been healed, nothing they had to gainsay. [2]Having
σαντες δὲ αὐτοὺς ἔξω τοῦ συνεδρίου ἀπελθεῖν [a]συνέβαλον‖
[3]commanded [1]but them outside the sanhedrim to go they conferred
πρὸς ἀλλήλους, 16 λέγοντες, Τί [b]ποιήσομεν‖ τοῖς ἀνθρώ-
with one another, saying, What shall we do to [2]men
ποις τούτοις; ὅτι-μὲν-γὰρ γνωστὸν σημεῖον γέγονεν
[1]these? for that indeed a known sign has come to pass
δι' αὐτῶν, πᾶσιν τοῖς κατοικοῦσιν Ἱερουσαλὴμ φανερόν,
through them, [3]to [4]all [5]those [6]inhabiting [7]Jerusalem [[1]is] [2]manifest,
καὶ οὐ-δυνάμεθα [c]ἀρνήσασθαι·‖ 17 ἀλλ' ἵνα μὴ ἐπὶ-πλεῖον
and we are unable to deny [it]. But that not further
διανεμηθῇ εἰς τὸν λαόν, [d]ἀπειλῇ‖ ἀπειλησώμεθα αὐτοῖς
it may spread among the people, with a threat let us threaten them
μηκέτι λαλεῖν ἐπὶ τῷ-ὀνόματι-τούτῳ μηδενὶ ἀνθρώπων.
no longer to speak in this name to any man.
(*lit.* to no)
18 Καὶ καλέσαντες αὐτοὺς παρήγγειλαν [e]αὐτοῖς‖ [f]τὸ‖ καθόλου
And having called them they charged them [2]at [3]all
μὴ φθέγγεσθαι μηδὲ διδάσκειν ἐπὶ τῷ ὀνόματι τοῦ Ἰησοῦ.
[1]not to speak nor to teach in the name of Jesus.
19 ὁ-δὲ-Πέτρος καὶ [g]Ἰωάννης‖ ἀποκριθέντες [h]πρὸς αὐτοὺς
But Peter and John answering to them
εἶπον,‖ Εἰ δίκαιόν ἐστιν ἐνώπιον τοῦ θεοῦ ὑμῶν ἀκούειν
said, Whether right it is before God [3]to [4]you [1]to [2]listen
μᾶλλον ἢ τοῦ θεοῦ κρίνατε. 20 οὐ-δυνάμεθα γὰρ ἡμεῖς ἃ
rather than God, judge ye; [3]cannot [1]for [2]we [6]what
[i]εἴδομεν‖ καὶ ἠκούσαμεν μὴ-λαλεῖν. 21 Οἱ-δὲ προσαπειλη-
[7]we [8]saw [9]and [10]heard [4]but [5]speak. But they having further
σάμενοι ἀπέλυσαν αὐτούς, μηδὲν εὑρίσκοντες τὸ-πῶς κολά-
threatened let [2]go [1]them, nothing finding as to how they might
σωνται αὐτοὺς διὰ τὸν λαόν, ὅτι πάντες ἐδόξαζον
punish them on account of the people, because all were glorifying

man stand here before you whole. 11 This is the stone which was set at nought of you builders, which is become the head of the corner. 12 Neither is there salvation in any other: for there is none other name under heaven given among men, whereby we must be saved.

13 Now when they saw the boldness of Peter and John, and perceived that they were unlearned and ignorant men, they marvelled; and they took knowledge of them, that they had been with Jesus. 14 And beholding the man which was healed standing with them, they could say nothing against it. 15 But when they had commanded them to go aside out of the council, they conferred among themselves, 16 saying, What shall we do to these men? for that indeed a notable miracle hath been done by them *is* manifest to all them that dwell in Jerusalem; and we cannot deny *it*. 17 But that it spread no further among the people, let us straitly threaten them, that they speak henceforth to no man in this name. 18 And they called them, and commanded them not to speak at all nor teach in the name of Jesus. 19 But Peter and John answered and said unto them, Whether it be right in the sight of God to hearken unto you more than unto God, judge ye. 20 For we cannot but speak the things which we have seen and heard. 21 So when they had further threatened them, they let them go, finding nothing how they might punish them, because of the people: for all *men* glorified God for that

---

[w] οἰκοδόμων LTTrA. [x] οὐδὲ LTTrW. [y] Ἰωάνου Tr. [z] τε and LTTr A. [a] συνέβαλλον LTTrA. [b] ποιήσωμεν should we do TTrA. [c] ἀρνεῖσθαι LTTrA. [d] — ἀπειλῇ LTT [A]. [e] — αὐτοῖς (*read* [them]) LTTrA. [f] — τὸ LT. [g] Ἰωάνης Tr. [h] εἶπον (εἶπαν Tr) πρὸς αὐτούς LTTrAW. [i] εἴδαμεν LTTrA.

τὸν θεὸν ἐπὶ τῷ γεγονότι. 22 ἐτῶν.γὰρ ἦν
God for that which has taken place; for [6]years [7old] [3]was
πλειόνων [k]τεσσαράκοντα‖ ὁ ἄνθρωπος ἐφ' ὃν [l]ἐγεγόνει‖
[4]above [5]forty [1]the [2]man on whom had taken place
τὸ.σημεῖον.τοῦτο τῆς ἰάσεως.
this sign of healing.
23 Ἀπολυθέντες.δὲ ἦλθον πρὸς τοὺς.ἰδίους, καὶ
And having been let go they came to their own [company], and
ἀπήγγειλαν ὅσα πρὸς αὐτοὺς οἱ ἀρχιερεῖς καὶ οἱ πρεσ-
reported whatever to them the chief priests and the el-
βύτεροι [m]εἶπον.‖ 24 οἱ.δὲ ἀκούσαντες, ὁμοθυμαδὸν ἦραν
ders said. And they having heard, with one accord lifted up
φωνὴν πρὸς τὸν θεόν, καὶ [m]εἶπον,‖ Δέσποτα, σὺ [n]ὁ
[their] voice to God, and said, O master, thou [art] the
θεὸς‖ ὁ ποιήσας τὸν οὐρανὸν καὶ τὴν γῆν καὶ τὴν θάλασσαν
God who made the heaven and the earth and the sea
καὶ πάντα τὰ ἐν αὐτοῖς, 25 [o]ὁ διὰ στόματος‖ [p]Δαβὶδ‖
and all that [are] in them, who by [the] mouth of David
[q]τοῦ‖.παιδός.σου εἰπών, [r]Ἱνατί‖ ἐφρύαξαν ἔθνη, καὶ
thy servant didst say, Why did [2]rage [3]haughtily [1]nations, and
λαοὶ ἐμελέτησαν κενά; 26 παρέστησαν οἱ βασιλεῖς τῆς
[2]peoples [1]did meditate vain things? Stood up the kings of the
γῆς, καὶ οἱ ἄρχοντες συνήχθησαν ἐπὶ.τὸ.αὐτὸ κατὰ τοῦ
earth, and the rulers were gathered together against the
κυρίου καὶ κατὰ τοῦ.χριστοῦ.αὐτοῦ. 27 Συνήχθησαν.γὰρ
Lord and against his Christ. For were gathered together
ἐπ'.ἀληθείας [s] ἐπὶ τὸν ἅγιον παῖδά σου Ἰησοῦν, ὃν
of a truth against [2]holy [3]servant [1]thy Jesus, whom
ἔχρισας, Ἡρώδης.τε καὶ Πόντιος [t]Πιλάτος,‖ σὺν ἔθνεσιν
thou didst anoint, both Herod and Pontius Pilate, with nations
καὶ λαοῖς Ἰσραήλ, 28 ποιῆσαι ὅσα ἡ.χείρ.σου καὶ ἡ βουλή
and peoples of Israel, to do whatever thy hand and [2]counsel
[u]σου‖ προώρισεν γενέσθαι. 29 καὶ τὰ νῦν, κύριε, [v]ἔπιδε‖
[1]thy predetermined to come to pass. And now, Lord, look
ἐπὶ τὰς.ἀπειλὰς.αὐτῶν, καὶ δὸς τοῖς.δούλοις.σου μετὰ παρ-
upon their threatenings, and give to thy bondmen with [2]bold-
ῥησίας πάσης λαλεῖν τὸν.λόγον.σου, 30 ἐν τῷ τὴν.χεῖρά.[w]σου‖
ness [1]all to speak thy word, in that thy hand
ἐκτείνειν [x]σε‖ εἰς ἴασιν, καὶ.σημεῖα καὶ τέρατα γίνεσθαι
[2]stretchest [3]out [1]thou for healing, and signs and wonders take place
διὰ τοῦ ὀνόματος τοῦ ἁγίου παιδός σου Ἰησοῦ. 31 Καὶ
through the name [3]holy [4]servant [1]of [2]thy Jesus. And
δεηθέντων αὐτῶν ἐσαλεύθη ὁ τόπος ἐν ᾧ ἦσαν συνηγ-
[2]having [3]prayed [1]they [6]was [7]shaken [4]the [5]place in which they were assem-
μένοι, καὶ ἐπλήσθησαν ἅπαντες [y]πνεύματος ἁγίου,‖ καὶ
bled, and they were [2]filled [1]all with [the] [2]Spirit [1]Holy, and
ἐλάλουν τὸν λόγον τοῦ θεοῦ μετὰ παῤῥησίας.
spoke the word of God with boldness.
32 Τοῦ.δὲ πλήθους τῶν πιστευσάντων ἦν [z]ἡ‖ καρδία
And of the multitude of those that believed [6]were [1]the [2]heart

which was done. 22 For
the man was above
forty years old, on
whom this miracle of
healing was shewed.

23 And being let go,
they went to their own
company, and reported
all that the chief
priests and elders had
said unto them. 24 And
when they heard that,
they lifted up their
voice to God with one
accord, and said, Lord,
thou *art* God, which
hast made heaven,
and earth, and the
sea, and all that in
them is: 25 who by the
mouth of thy servant
David hast said, Why
did the heathen rage,
and the people ima-
gine vain things?
26 The kings of the
earth stood up, and
the rulers were ga-
thered together a-
gainst the Lord, and
against his Christ.
27 For of a truth a-
gainst thy holy child
Jesus, whom thou hast
anointed, both Herod,
and Pontius Pilate,
with the Gentiles, and
the people of Israel,
were gathered toge-
ther, 28 for to do what-
soever thy hand and
thy counsel determin-
ed before to be done.
29 And now, Lord,
behold their threat-
enings: and grant
unto thy servants,
that with all boldness
they may speak thy
word, 30 by stretch-
ing forth thine hand
to heal; and that
signs and wonders
may be done by the
name of thy holy
child Jesus. 31 And
when they had prayed,
the place was shaken
where they were as-
sembled together; and
they were all filled
with the Holy Ghost,
and they spake the
word of God with
boldness.

32 And the multi-
tude of them that be-
lieved were of one

---

[k] τεσσεράκοντα TTrA. [l] γεγόνει LTTrA. [m] εἶπαν LTTrA. [n] — ὁ θεὸς (*read* he who) LTTr[A]. [o] ὁ τοῦ πατρὸς ἡμῶν διὰ πνεύματος ἁγίου στόματος who by [the] Holy Spirit by [the] mouth of our father LTTrA. [p] Δαυεὶδ LTTrA; Δαυὶδ GW. [q] — τοῦ GLTTrAW. [r] Ἵνα τί LTrAW. [s] + ἐν τῇ πόλει ταύτῃ in this city GLTTrAW. [t] Πειλᾶτος T. [u] — σου L[Tr]. [v] ἔφιδε L. [w] — σου (*read* [thy]) LTr. [x] [σε] A. [y] τοῦ ἁγίου πνεύματος LTTrAW. [z] — ἡ LTTrA.

καὶ [a]ἡ‖ ψυχὴ μία· καὶ [b]οὐδὲ‖ εἷς τι τῶν ὑπαρ-
[3]and [4]the [5]soul one, and not one [2]anything [3]of [4]that [5]which [7]pos-
χόντων αὐτῷ ἔλεγεν ἴδιον εἶναι, ἀλλ' ἦν αὐτοῖς [c]ἅπαντα‖
sessed [6]he [1]said [9]his [10]own [8]was, [11]but [14]were [15]to [16]them [12]all [13]things
κοινά. 33 καὶ [d]μεγάλῃ δυνάμει‖ ἀπεδίδουν τὸ μαρτύριον
common. And with great power [3]gave [4]testimony
οἱ ἀπόστολοι [e]τῆς ἀναστάσεως τοῦ κυρίου Ἰησοῦ,‖ χάρις.τε
[1]the [2]apostles of the resurrection of the Lord Jesus, and [2]grace
μεγάλη ἦν ἐπὶ πάντας αὐτούς. 34 οὐδὲ.γὰρ ἐνδεής τις
[1]great was upon all them. For neither in want [2]anyone
[f]ὑπῆρχεν‖ ἐν αὐτοῖς· ὅσοι.γὰρ κτήτορες χωρίων ἢ οἰκιῶν
[1]was among them; for as many as owners of estates or houses
ὑπῆρχον, πωλοῦντες ἔφερον τὰς τιμὰς τῶν πιπρα-
were, selling [them] brought the values of those sold,
σκομένων, 35 καὶ ἐτίθουν παρὰ τοὺς πόδας τῶν ἀπο-
and laid [them] at the feet of the apos-
στόλων· [g]διεδίδοτο‖.δὲ ἑκάστῳ καθότι.ἂν τις χρείαν
tles; and distribution was made to each according as anyone [2]need
εἶχεν.
[1]had.

36 [h]Ἰωσῆς‖.δὲ ὁ ἐπικληθεὶς Βαρνάβας [i]ὑπὸ‖ τῶν ἀπο-
And Joses who was surnamed Barnabas by the apos-
στόλων, ὅ ἐστιν μεθερμηνευόμενον, υἱὸς παρακλήσεως,
tles (which is, being interpreted, Son of consolation),
[k]Λευΐτης,‖ Κύπριος τῷ.γένει, 37 ὑπάρχοντος αὐτῷ ἀγροῦ,
a Levite, a Cypriot by birth, having land,
πωλήσας ἤνεγκεν τὸ χρῆμα καὶ ἔθηκεν [l]παρὰ‖ τοὺς πόδας
having sold [it] brought the money and laid [it] at the feet
τῶν ἀποστόλων. 5 Ἀνὴρ.δέ τις [m]Ἀνανίας ὀνόματι,‖
of the apostles. But [3]man [1]a [2]certain, Ananias by name,
σὺν [n]Σαπφείρῃ‖ τῇ.γυναικὶ.αὐτοῦ, ἐπώλησεν κτῆμα, 2 καὶ
with Sapphira his wife, sold a possession, and
ἐνοσφίσατο ἀπὸ τῆς τιμῆς, [o]συνειδυίας‖ καὶ τῆς γυναικὸς
kept back from the value, being aware of [it] also [2]wife
[p]αὐτοῦ,‖ καὶ ἐνέγκας μέρος.τι παρὰ τοὺς πόδας τῶν
[1]his, and having brought a certain part [3]at [4]the [5]feet [6]of [7]the
ἀποστόλων ἔθηκεν. 3 εἶπεν.δὲ [q] Πέτρος, Ἀνανία, [r]διατί‖
[8]apostles [1]laid [[2]it]. But said Peter, Ananias, why
ἐπλήρωσεν ὁ σατανᾶς τὴν.καρδίαν.σου, ψεύσασθαί σε τὸ
did [2]fill [1]Satan thy heart, [3]to [4]lie [5]to [[1]for] [2]thee the
πνεῦμα τὸ ἅγιον, καὶ νοσφίσασθαι [s] ἀπὸ τῆς τιμῆς τοῦ
Spirit the Holy, and to keep back from the value of the
χωρίου; 4 οὐχὶ μένον σοὶ ἔμενεν; καὶ πραθὲν
estate? [6]Not [1]remaining [2]to [3]thee [4]did [5]it remain? and having been sold,
ἐν τῇ.σῇ ἐξουσίᾳ ὑπῆρχεν; τί ὅτι ἔθου ἐν τῇ
in thine own authority was it [not]? why didst thou purpose in
καρδίᾳ.σου τὸ.πρᾶγμα.τοῦτο; οὐκ.ἐψεύσω ἀνθρώποις, ἀλλὰ
thy heart this thing? Thou didst not lie to men, but
τῷ θεῷ. 5 Ἀκούων.δὲ [t] Ἀνανίας τοὺς.λόγους.τούτους, πεσὼν
to God. And [2]hearing [1]Ananias these words, falling down

heart and of one soul:
neither said any *of*
them that ought of the
things which he pos-
sessed was his own;
but they had all things
common. 33 And with
great power gave the
apostles witness of the
resurrection of the
Lord Jesus: and great
grace was upon them
all. 34 Neither was
there any among them
that lacked: for as
many as were possess-
ors of lands or houses
sold them, and brought
the prices of the things
that were sold, 35 and
laid *them* down at the
apostles' feet: and dis-
tribution was made
unto every man ac-
cording as he had
need.

36 And Joses, who
by the apostles was
surnamed Barnabas,
(which is, being in-
terpreted, The son of
consolation,) a Levite,
and of the country of
Cyprus, 37 having
land, sold *it*, and
brought the money,
and laid *it* at the
apostles' feet. V. But
a certain man named
Ananias, with Sapphi-
ra his wife, sold a
possession, 2 and kept
back *part* of the price,
his wife also being
privy *to it*, and brought
a certain part, and
laid *it* at the apostles'
feet. 3 But Peter said,
Ananias, why hath Sa-
tan filled thine heart
to lie to the Holy
Ghost, and to keep
back *part* of the price
of the land? 4 Whiles
it remained, was it not
thine own? and after
it was sold, was it not
in thine own power?
why hast thou con-
ceived this thing in
thine heart? thou
hast not lied unto
men, but unto God.
5 And Ananias hear-
ing these words fell
down, and gave up the

---

[a] — ἡ LTTrA. [b] οὐδ' E. [c] πάντα L. [d] δυνάμει μεγάλῃ LTTrA. [e] τοῦ κυρίου Ἰησοῦ [χριστοῦ Christ] τῆς ἀναστάσεως L; τῆς ἀναστάσεως Ἰησοῦ χριστοῦ τοῦ κυρίου T. [f] ἦν LTTr. [g] διεδίδετο LTTrA. [h] Ἰωσὴφ Joseph LTTrAW. [i] ἀπὸ LTTrAW. [k] Λευείτης T\. [l] πρὸς T. [m] ὀνόματι Ἀνανίας L. [n] Σαπφείρᾳ LTr. [o] συνειδυίης LTTrA. [p] — αὐτοῦ (read {his]) LTTrA. [q] + ὁ LTTrA. [r] διὰ τί LTrA. [s] + [σε] thee (to keep back) A. [t] + ὁ GLTTrAW.

ghost: and great fear
came on all them that
heard these things.
6 And the young men
arose, wound him up,
and carried *him* out,
and buried *him*. 7 And
it was about the space
of three hours after,
when his wife, not
knowing what was
done, came in. 8 And
Peter answered unto
her, Tell me whether
ye sold the land for so
much? And she said,
Yea, for so much.
9 Then Peter said unto
to her, How is it that
ye have agreed together
ther to tempt the Spirit
rit of the Lord? behold,
hold, the feet of them
which have buried thy
husband *are* at the
door, and shall carry
thee out. 10 Then fell
she down straightway
at his feet, and yielded
up the ghost: and the
young men came in,
and found her dead,
and, carrying *her*
forth, buried *her* by
her husband. 11 And
great fear came upon
all the church, and
upon as many as heard
these things. 12 And
by the hands of the
apostles were many
signs and wonders
wrought among the
people; (and they
were all with one accord
cord in Solomon's
porch. 13 And of the
rest durst no man join
himself to them: but
the people magnified
them. 14 And believers
ers were the more added
ed to the Lord, multitudes
titudes both of men
and women.) 15 Insomuch
somuch that they
brought forth the sick
into the streets, and
laid *them* on beds and
couches, that at the
least the shadow of Peter
ter passing by might
overshadow some of
them. 16 There came
also a multitude *out*
of the cities round
about unto Jerusalem,
bringing sick folks,
and them which were
vexed with unclean
spirits: and they were
healed every one.

ἐξέψυξεν· καὶ ἐγένετο φόβος μέγας ἐπὶ πάντας τοὺς
expired. And [3]came [2]fear [1]great upon all who
ἀκούοντας [v]ταῦτα.‖ 6 ἀναστάντες.δὲ οἱ νεώτεροι συνέ-
heard these things. And having risen the younger [men] swathed
στειλαν αὐτόν, καὶ ἐξενέγκαντες ἔθαψαν. 7 Ἐγένετο.δὲ
him, and having carried out buried [him]. And it came to pass
ὡς ὡρῶν τριῶν διάστημα καὶ ἡ.γυνὴ.αὐτοῦ μὴ εἰδυῖα τὸ
about [2]hours [1]three afterwards also his wife, not knowing what
γεγονὸς εἰσῆλθεν. 8 ἀπεκρίθη.δὲ [w]αὐτῇ‖ [x]ὁ‖ Πέτρος,
had come to pass, came in. And answered her Peter,
Εἰπέ μοι εἰ τοσούτου τὸ χωρίον ἀπέδοσθε; Ἡ.δὲ εἶπεν,
Tell me if for so much the estate ye sold? And she said,
Ναί, τοσούτου. 9 Ὁ.δὲ.Πέτρος [y]εἶπεν‖ πρὸς αὐτήν, Τί
Yes, for so much. And Peter said to her, Why [is it]
ὅτι συνεφωνήθη.ὑμῖν πειράσαι τὸ πνεῦμα κυρίου; ἰδού, οἱ
that ye agreed together to tempt the Spirit of [the] Lord? Lo, the
πόδες τῶν θαψάντων τὸν.ἄνδρα.σου ἐπὶ τῇ θύρᾳ, καὶ
feet of those who buried thy husband [are] at the door, and
ἐξοίσουσίν σε. 10 [z]Ἔπεσεν.δὲ παραχρῆμα [z]παρὰ‖ τοὺς
they shall carry out thee. And she fell down immediately at
πόδας.αὐτοῦ καὶ ἐξέψυξεν· εἰσελθόντες.δὲ οἱ νεανίσκοι
his feet and expired. And having come in the young [men]
[a]εὗρον‖ αὐτὴν νεκράν, καὶ ἐξενέγκαντες ἔθαψαν πρὸς
found her dead; and having carried out they buried [her] by
τὸν.ἄνδρα.αὐτῆς. 11 καὶ ἐγένετο φόβος μέγας ἐφ' ὅλην τὴν
her husband. And [3]came [2]fear [1]great upon [2]whole [1]the
ἐκκλησίαν, καὶ ἐπὶ πάντας τοὺς ἀκούοντας ταῦτα. 12 Διὰ.δὲ
assembly, and upon all who heard these things. And by
τῶν χειρῶν τῶν ἀποστόλων [b]ἐγένετο‖ σημεῖα καὶ τέρατα
the hands of the apostles came to pass [2]signs [3]and [4]wonders
[c]ἐν τῷ λαῷ πολλά·‖ καὶ ἦσαν ὁμοθυμαδὸν [d]ἅπαντες‖
[5]among [6]the [7]people [1]many; (and they were [2]with [3]one [4]accord [1]all
ἐν τῇ στοᾷ [e]Σολομῶντος·‖ 13 τῶν.δὲ λοιπῶν οὐδεὶς ἐτόλμα
in the porch of Solomon, but of the rest no one durst
κολλᾶσθαι αὐτοῖς, ἀλλ' ἐμεγάλυνεν αὐτοὺς ὁ λαός· 14 μᾶλλον
join them, but [3]magnified [4]them [1]the [2]people; [8]the [9]more
δὲ προσετίθεντο πιστεύοντες τῷ κυρίῳ, πλήθη ἀνδρῶν.τε
[5]and [7]were [10]added [6]believers to the Lord, multitudes both of men
καὶ γυναικῶν· 15 ὥστε [f]κατὰ‖ τὰς πλατείας ἐκφέρειν τοὺς
and women;) so as in the streets to bring out the
ἀσθενεῖς καὶ τιθέναι ἐπὶ [g]κλινῶν‖ καὶ [h]κραββάτων,‖ ἵνα
sick, and put [them] on beds and couches, that
ἐρχομένου Πέτρου κἂν ἡ σκιὰ [i]ἐπισκιάσῃ‖ τινὶ
[7]coming [5]of [6]Peter [1]at [2]least [3]the [4]shadow might overshadow some one
αὐτῶν. 16 συνήρχετο.δὲ καὶ τὸ πλῆθος τῶν πέριξ
of them. And came together also the multitude of the [2]round [3]about
πόλεων [k]εἰς‖ Ἱερουσαλήμ, φέροντες ἀσθενεῖς καὶ ὀχλου-
[1]cities to Jerusalem, bringing sick ones and those
μένους ὑπὸ πνευμάτων ἀκαθάρτων, οἵτινες ἐθεραπεύοντο
beset by [2]spirits [1]unclean. who were [2]healed
ἅπαντες.
[1]all.

---

[v] — ταῦτα LTTrA. [w] πρὸς αὐτὴν to her LTTrA. [x] — ὁ LTTrA. [y] — εἶπεν (read [said] LTTrA. [z] πρὸς LTTrA. [a] εὗραν Tr. [b] ἐγίνετο EGLTTrAW. [c] πολλὰ ἐν τῷ λαῷ LTTrAW. [d] πάντες LTr. [e] Σολομῶνος GTrAW. [f] καὶ εἰς even into LTTr. [g] κλιναρίων LTTrA. [h] κραβάττων LTTrAW. [i] ἐπισκιάσει shall overshadow Tr. [k] — εἰς LTTrA.

17 Ἀναστὰς.δὲ ὁ ἀρχιερεὺς καὶ πάντες οἱ σὺν αὐτῷ,
And having risen up the high priest and all those with him,
ἡ οὖσα αἵρεσις τῶν Σαδδουκαίων, ἐπλήσθησαν ζήλου,
which is [the] sect of the Sadducees, were filled with anger,
18 καὶ ἐπέβαλον τὰς χεῖρας [l]αὐτῶν‖ ἐπὶ τοὺς ἀποστόλους καὶ
and laid [2]hands [1]their on the apostles and
ἔθεντο αὐτοὺς ἐν τηρήσει δημοσίᾳ. 19 ἄγγελος.δὲ κυρίου
put them in [the] [2]hold [1]public. But an angel of [the] Lord
διὰ [m]τῆς‖ νυκτὸς [n]ἤνοιξεν‖ τὰς θύρας τῆς φυλακῆς,
during the night opened the doors of the prison,
ἐξαγαγών.τε αὐτοὺς εἶπεν, 20 Πορεύεσθε, καὶ σταθέντες
and having brought [2]out [1]them said, Go ye, and standing
λαλεῖτε ἐν τῷ ἱερῷ τῷ λαῷ πάντα τὰ ῥήματα τῆς ζωῆς
speak in the temple to the people all the words of [2]life
ταύτης. 21 Ἀκούσαντες.δὲ εἰσῆλθον ὑπὸ τὸν ὄρθρον εἰς τὸ
[1]this. And having heard they entered at the dawn into the
ἱερόν, καὶ ἐδίδασκον. παραγενόμενος.δὲ ὁ ἀρχιερεὺς καὶ οἱ
temple, and were teaching. But having come the high priest and those
σὺν αὐτῷ, συνεκάλεσαν τὸ συνέδριον καὶ πᾶσαν τὴν γερου-
with him, they called together the sanhedrim and all the elder-
σίαν τῶν υἱῶν Ἰσραήλ, καὶ ἀπέστειλαν εἰς τὸ δεσμωτήριον
hood of the sons of Israel, and sent to the prison
ἀχθῆναι.αὐτούς. 22 οἱ.δὲ [o]ὑπηρέται παραγενόμενοι‖ οὐχ
to have them brought. But the officers having come [2]not
εὗρον αὐτοὺς ἐν τῇ φυλακῇ· ἀναστρέψαντες.δὲ ἀπήγγειλαν,
[1]did find them in the prison; and having returned they reported,
23 λέγοντες, Ὅτι τὸ [p]μὲν‖ δεσμωτήριον εὕρομεν κεκλεισ-
saying, The [2]indeed [1]prison we found shut
μένον ἐν πάσῃ ἀσφαλείᾳ, καὶ τοὺς φύλακας [q]ἔξω‖ ἑστῶτας
with all security, and the keepers without standing
[r]πρὸ‖ τῶν θυρῶν· ἀνοίξαντες.δέ, ἔσω οὐδένα εὕρομεν.
before the doors; but having opened, within no one we found.
24 Ὡς.δὲ ἤκουσαν τοὺς.λόγους.τούτους ὅ.τε [s]ἱερεὺς καὶ
And when they heard these words both the priest and
ὁ‖ στρατηγὸς τοῦ ἱεροῦ καὶ οἱ ἀρχιερεῖς διηπόρουν περὶ
the captain of the temple and the chief priests were perplexed concerning
αὐτῶν, τί ἂν.γένοιτο τοῦτο. 25 παραγενόμενος.δέ τις
them, what [2]might [3]be [1]this. But having come a certain one
ἀπήγγειλεν αὐτοῖς [t]λέγων,‖ Ὅτι ἰδοὺ οἱ ἄνδρες οὓς ἔθεσθε
reported to them, saying, Lo, the men whom ye put
ἐν τῇ φυλακῇ εἰσὶν ἐν τῷ ἱερῷ ἑστῶτες καὶ διδάσκοντες τὸν
in the prison are in the temple standing and teaching the
λαόν. 26 Τότε ἀπελθὼν ὁ στρατηγὸς σὺν τοῖς ὑπηρέταις
people. Then [3]having [4]gone [1]the [2]captain with the officers
[v]ἤγαγεν‖ αὐτούς, οὐ μετὰ βίας, ἐφοβοῦντο.γὰρ τὸν λαόν,
brought them, not with violence, for they feared the people,
[w]ἵνα‖ μὴ.λιθασθῶσιν. 27 ἀγαγόντες.δὲ αὐτοὺς ἔστησαν
that they might not be stoned. And having brought them they set
ἐν τῷ συνεδρίῳ· καὶ ἐπηρώτησεν αὐτοὺς ὁ ἀρχιερεύς,
[them] in the sanhedrim. And [4]asked [5]them [1]the [2]high [3]priest,
28 λέγων, [x]Οὐ‖ παραγγελίᾳ παρηγγείλαμεν ὑμῖν μὴ διδάσ-
saying, [3]Not [4]by [5]a [6]charge [1]did [2]we charge you not to teach

17 Then the high priest rose up, and all they that were with him, (which is the sect of the Sadducees,) and were filled with indignation, 18 and laid their hands on the apostles, and put them in the common prison. 19 But the angel of the Lord by night opened the prison doors, and brought them forth, and said, 20 Go, stand and speak in the temple to the people all the words of this life. 21 And when they heard *that*, they entered into the temple early in the morning, and taught. But the high priest came, and they that were with him, and called the council together, and all the senate of the children of Israel, and sent to the prison to have them brought. 22 But when the officers came, and found them not in the prison, they returned, and told, 23 saying, The prison truly found we shut with all safety, and the keepers standing without before the doors: but when we had opened, we found no man within. 24 Now when the high priest and the captain of the temple and the chief priests heard these things, they doubted of them whereunto this would grow. 25 Then came one and told them, saying, Behold, the men whom ye put in prison are standing in the temple, and teaching the people. 26 Then went the captain with the officers, and brought them without violence: for they feared the people, lest they should have been stoned. 27 And when they had brought them, they set *them* before the council: and the high priest asked them, 28 saying, Did not we straitly command you that ye should not teach in

[l] — αὐτῶν LTTrAW. [m] — τῆς LTTrA. [n] ἀνοίξας having opened T. [o] παραγενόμενοι ὑπηρέται LTTrA. [p] — μὲν LTTrAW. [q] — ἔξω GLTTrAW. [r] ἐπὶ LTTrA. [s] — ἱερεὺς καὶ ὁ LTTrA. [t] — λέγων GLTTrAW. [v] ἦγεν T. [w] — ἵνα (*read* lest they should be stoned) LTTr[A]. [x] — Οὐ (*read* We did charge you by a charge, &c.) LTTrA.

this name? and, be
hold, ye have filled
Jerusalem with your
doctrine, and intend to
bring this man's blood
upon us. 29 Then Pe-
ter and the *other* apos-
tles answered and said,
We ought to obey
God rather than men.
30 The God of our fa-
thers raised up Jesus,
whom ye slew and
hanged on a tree.
31 Him hath God
exalted with his right
hand *to be* a Prince
and a Saviour, for to
give repentance to Is-
rael, and forgiveness
of sins. 32 And we are
his witnesses of these
things; and *so is* also
the Holy Ghost, whom
God hath given to
them that obey him.
33 When they heard
that, they were cut *to*
the heart, and took
counsel to slay them.
34 Then stood there up
one in the council, a
Pharisee, named Ga-
maliel, a doctor of the
law, had in reputation
among all the people,
and commanded to put
the apostles forth a
little space; 35 and
said unto them, Ye
men of Israel, take
heed to yourselves
what ye intend to do
as touching these men.
36 For before these
days rose up Theudas,
boasting himself to be
somebody; to whom a
number of men, about
four hundred, joined
themselves: who was
slain; and all, as many
as obeyed him, were
scattered, and brought
to nought. 37 After
this man rose up Ju-
das of Galilee in the
days of the taxing,
and drew away much
people after him: he
also perished; and all,
even as many as obeyed
him, were dispersed.
38 And now I say unto
you, Refrain from
these men, and let
them alone: for if
this counsel or this

κειν ἐπι τῷ.ὀνόματι.τούτῳ [x];‖ καὶ ἰδοὺ πεπληρώκατε τὴν Ἰε-
in this name? and lo, ye have filled Je-
ρουσαλὴμ τῆς.διδαχῆς.ὑμῶν, καὶ βούλεσθε ἐπαγαγεῖν ἐφ
rusalem with your teaching, and purpose to bring upon
ἡμᾶς τὸ αἷμα τοῦ.ἀνθρώπου.τούτου. 29 Ἀποκριθεὶς.δὲ [y]ὁ‖
us the blood of this man. But [5]answering
Πέτρος καὶ οἱ ἀπόστολοι [z]εἶπον,‖ Πειθαρχεῖν δεῖ
[1]Peter [2]and [3]the [4]apostles said, [4]To [5]obey [1]it [2]is [3]necessary
θεῷ μᾶλλον ἢ ἀνθρώποις. 30 ὁ θεὸς τῶν.πατέρων.ἡμῶν
God rather than men. The God of our fathers
ἤγειρεν Ἰησοῦν, ὃν ὑμεῖς διεχειρίσασθε κρεμάσαντες ἐπὶ
raised up Jesus, whom ye killed, having hanged on
ξύλου· 31 τοῦτον ὁ θεὸς ἀρχηγὸν καὶ σωτῆρα ὕψωσεν τῇ
a tree. Him God a chief and Saviour exalted by the
δεξιᾷ αὐτοῦ, [a]δοῦναι μετάνοιαν τῷ Ἰσραὴλ καὶ ἄφεσιν
right hand of him, to give repentance to Israel and remission
ἁμαρτιῶν. 32 καὶ ἡμεῖς [b]ἐσμεν αὐτοῦ μάρτυρες‖ τῶν ῥημάτων
of sins. And we are of him witnesses of [2]things
τούτων, καὶ τὸ πνεῦμα [c]δὲ‖ τὸ ἅγιον, ὃ ἔδωκεν ὁ θεὸς
[1]these, and [2]the [3]Spirit [1]also the Holy, which [2]gave [1]God
τοῖς πειθαρχοῦσιν αὐτῷ. 33 Οἱ.δὲ ἀκούσαντες διεπρίοντο,
to those that obey him. But they having heard were cut
καὶ [d]ἐβουλεύοντο‖ ἀνελεῖν αὐτούς. 34 ἀναστὰς
[to the heart], and took counsel to put to death them. [5]Having [6]risen [7]up
δέ τις ἐν τῷ συνεδρίῳ Φαρισαῖος, ὀνόματι Γα-
[1]but [2]a [3]certain [[4]man] in the sanhedrim a Pharisee, by name Ga-
μαλιήλ, νομοδιδάσκαλος, τίμιος παντὶ τῷ λαῷ, ἐκέλευσεν
maliel, a teacher of the law, honoured by all the people, commanded
ἔξω βραχύ.[e]τι‖ [f]τοὺς ἀποστόλους‖ ποιῆσαι, 35 εἶπέν.τε
[3]out [4]for [5]a [6]short [7]while [8]the [9]apostles [1]to [2]put, and said
πρὸς αὐτούς, Ἄνδρες [g]Ἰσραηλῖται,‖ προσέχετε ἑαυτοῖς
to them, Men Israelites, take heed to yourselves
ἐπὶ τοῖς.ἀνθρώποις.τούτοις τί μέλλετε πράσσειν. 36 πρὸ
as regards these men what ye are about to do; [2]before
γὰρ τούτων τῶν ἡμερῶν ἀνέστη Θευδᾶς, λέγων εἶναί τινα
[1]for these days rose up Theudas, affirming [2]to [3]be [4]somebody
ἑαυτόν, ᾧ [h]προσεκολλήθη ἀριθμὸς ἀνδρῶν, ὡσεὶ‖ τετρα-
[1]himself, to whom were joined a number of men, about four
κοσίων· ὃς ἀνῃρέθη, καὶ πάντες ὅσοι ἐπείθοντο αὐτῷ
hundred; who was put to death, and all as many as were persuaded by him
διελύθησαν καὶ ἐγένοντο εἰς οὐδέν. 37 μετὰ τοῦτον ἀνέστη
were dispersed and came to nothing. After this one rose up
Ἰούδας ὁ Γαλιλαῖος ἐν ταῖς ἡμέραις τῆς ἀπογραφῆς, καὶ
Judas the Galilean in the days of the registration, and
ἀπέστησεν λαὸν [i]ἱκανὸν‖ ὀπίσω αὐτοῦ· κἀκεῖνος ἀπώλετο,
drew away [2]people [1]much after him; and he perished,
καὶ πάντες ὅσοι ἐπείθοντο αὐτῷ διεσκορπίσθησαν. 38 καὶ
and all as many as were persuaded by him were scattered abroad. And
τὰ νῦν λέγω ὑμῖν, ἀπόστητε ἀπὸ τῶν.ἀνθρώπων.τούτων, καὶ
now I say to you, Withdraw from these men, and
[k]ἐάσατε‖ αὐτούς· ὅτι ἐὰν ᾖ ἐξ ἀνθρώπων ἡ.βουλὴ.αὕτη ἢ
let [2]alone [1]them, for if [6]be [7]from [8]men [1]this [2]counsel [3]or

---

[x] — ; LTTrA. [y] — ὁ LTTrA. [z] εἶπαν LTTrA. [a] + τοῦ T. [b] ἐν αὐτῷ μάρτυρές ἐσμεν L; — αὐτοῦ TTr. [c] — δὲ LTTr[A]. [d] ἐβούλοντο resolved LTr. [e] — τι LTTrAW. [f] τοὺς ἀνθρώπους the men LTTrA. [g] Ἰσραηλεῖται T. [h] προσεκλίθη ἀνδρῶν ἀριθμὸς ὡς LTTrAW [i] — ἱκανὸν LTTrA. [k] ἄφετε LTTrA.

τὸ.ἔργον.τοῦτο, καταλυθήσεται· 39 εἰ.δὲ ἐκ θεοῦ ἐστιν,
[4]this [5]work, it will be overthrown; but if from God it be,
[l]οὐ.δύνασθε[ǁ] καταλῦσαι [m]αὐτό,[ǁ] μήποτε καὶ θεομάχοι
ye are not able to overthrow it, lest also fighters against God
εὑρεθῆτε. 40 Ἐπείσθησαν.δὲ αὐτῷ· καὶ προσκαλεσάμενοι
ye be found. And they were persuaded by him; and having called to
τοὺς ἀποστόλους, δείραντες παρήγγειλαν μὴ λαλεῖν
[them] the apostles, having beaten they enjoined [them] not to speak
ἐπὶ τῷ ὀνόματι τοῦ Ἰησοῦ, καὶ ἀπέλυσαν [n]αὐτούς.[ǁ] 41 Οἱ
in the name of Jesus, and released them. They
μὲν οὖν ἐπορεύοντο χαίροντες ἀπὸ προσώπου τοῦ
therefore departed rejoicing from [the] presence of the
συνεδρίου ὅτι [o]ὑπὲρ τοῦ ὀνόματος αὐτοῦ κατηξιώθησαν[ǁ]
sanhedrim that for the name of him they were accounted worthy
ἀτιμασθῆναι· 42 πᾶσάν.τε ἡμέραν ἐν τῷ ἱερῷ καὶ κατ'.οἶκον
to be dishonoured. And every day in the temple and in the houses
οὐκ.ἐπαύοντο διδάσκοντες καὶ εὐαγγελιζόμενοι [p]Ἰησοῦν
they ceased not teaching and announcing the glad tidings— Jesus
τὸν χριστόν.[ǁ]
the Christ.

work be of men, it will come to nought: 39 but if it be of God, ye cannot overthrow it; lest haply ye be found even to fight against God. 40 And to him they agreed: and when they had called the apostles, and beaten *them*, they commanded that they should not speak in the name of Jesus, and let them go. 41 And they departed from the presence of the council, rejoicing that they were counted worthy to suffer shame for his name. 42 And daily in the temple, and in every house, they ceased not to teach and preach Jesus Christ.

6 Ἐν.δὲ ταῖς.ἡμέραις.ταύταις πληθυνόντων τῶν μαθητῶν
But in those days [3]multiplying [1]the [2]disciples
ἐγένετο γογγυσμὸς τῶν Ἑλληνιστῶν πρὸς τοὺς Ἑβραίους,
there arose a murmuring of the Hellenists against the Hebrews,
ὅτι παρεθεωροῦντο ἐν τῇ διακονίᾳ τῇ καθημερινῇ αἱ
because were overlooked in the [2]ministration [1]daily
χῆραι.αὐτῶν. 2 προσκαλεσάμενοι.δὲ οἱ δώδεκα τὸ πλῆθος
their widows. And [3]having [4]called [5]to [[6]them] [1]the [2]twelve the multitude
τῶν μαθητῶν, [q]εἶπον,[ǁ] Οὐκ ἀρεστόν ἐστιν ἡμᾶς, καταλείψαν-
of the disciples, said, Not seemly it is [for] us, leaving
τας τὸν λόγον τοῦ θεοῦ, διακονεῖν τραπέζαις. 3 ἐπισκέψασθε
the word of God, to attend tables. Look out
[r]οὖν,[ǁ] [s]ἀδελφοί,[ǁ] ἄνδρας ἐξ ὑμῶν μαρτυρουμένους
therefore, brethren, [2]men [3]from [4]among [5]yourselves, [6]borne [7]witness [8]to
ἑπτά, πλήρεις πνεύματος [t]ἁγίου[ǁ] καὶ σοφίας, οὓς [v]κατα-
[1]seven, full of [the] [2]Spirit [1]Holy and wisdom, whom we will
στήσομεν[ǁ] ἐπὶ τῆς.χρείας.ταύτης· 4 ἡμεῖς.δὲ τῇ προσευχῇ
appoint over this business; but we to prayer
καὶ τῇ διακονίᾳ τοῦ λόγου προσκαρτερήσομεν. 5 Καὶ
and the ministry of the word will steadfastly continue. And
ἤρεσεν ὁ λόγος ἐνώπιον παντὸς τοῦ πλήθους· καὶ
[3]was [4]pleasing [1]the [2]saying before all the multitude; and
ἐξελέξαντο Στέφανον, ἄνδρα [w]πλήρη[ǁ] πίστεως καὶ πνεύ-
they chose Stephen, a man full of faith and [the] [2]Spi-
ματος ἁγίου, καὶ Φίλιππον, καὶ Πρόχορον, καὶ Νικάνορα, καὶ
rit [1]Holy, and Philip, and Prochorus, and Nicanor, and
Τίμωνα, καὶ Παρμενᾶν, καὶ Νικόλαον προσήλυτον Ἀντιοχέα,
Timon, and Parmenas, and Nicolas a proselyte of Antioch,
6 οὓς ἔστησαν ἐνώπιον τῶν ἀποστόλων· καὶ προσευξάμενοι
whom they set before the apostles; and having prayed
ἐπέθηκαν αὐτοῖς τὰς χεῖρας. 7 καὶ ὁ λόγος τοῦ θεοῦ
they laid [2]on [3]them [1]hands. And the word of God

VI. And in those days, when the number of the disciples was multiplied, there arose a murmuring of the Grecians against the Hebrews, because their widows were neglected in the daily ministration. 2 Then the twelve called the multitude of the disciples *unto them*, and said, It is not reason that we should leave the word of God, and serve tables. 3 Wherefore, brethren, look ye out among you seven men of honest report, full of the Holy Ghost and wisdom, whom we may appoint over this business. 4 But we will give ourselves continually to prayer, and to the ministry of the word. 5 And the saying pleased the whole multitude: and they chose Stephen, a man full of faith and of the Holy Ghost, and Philip, and Prochorus, and Nicanor, and Timon, and Parmenas, and Nicolas a proselyte of Antioch: 6 whom they set before the apostles: and when they had prayed, they laid *their* hands on them. 7 And the word of God increased;

---

[l] οὐ δυνήσεσθε ye will not be able LTTr. [m] αὐτούς them GLTTrA. [n] — αὐτούς (*read* [them]) TTrA. [o] — αὐτοῦ GLTTrAW; κατηξιώθησαν ὑπὲρ τοῦ ὀνόματος LTTrA. [p] τὸν χριστὸν Ἰησοῦν LTTrA. [q] εἶπαν LTTrA. [r] δή indeed L; δέ but T. [s] — ἀδελφοί L. [t] — ἁγίου GLTTrA. [v] καταστήσωμεν we may appoint EW. [w] πλήρης L.

and the number of the disciples multiplied in Jerusalem greatly; and a great company of the priests were obedient to the faith.

8 And Stephen, full of faith and power, did great wonders and miracles among the people. 9 Then there arose certain of the synagogue, which is called *the synagogue* of the Libertines, and Cyrenians, and Alexandrians, and of them of Cilicia and of Asia, disputing with Stephen. 10 And they were not able to resist the wisdom and the spirit by which he spake. 11 Then they suborned men, which said, We have heard him speak blasphemous words against Moses, and *against* God. 12 And they stirred up the people, and the elders, and the scribes, and came upon *him*, and caught him, and brought *him* to the council, 13 and set up false witnesses, which said, This man ceaseth not to speak blasphemous words against this holy place, and the law: 14 for we have heard him say, that this Jesus of Nazareth shall destroy this place, and shall change the customs which Moses delivered us. 15 And all that sat in the council, looking stedfastly on him, saw his face as it had been the face of an angel.

VII. Then said the high priest, Are these things so? 2 And he said, Men, brethren, and fathers, hearken; The God of glory appeared unto our father Abraham, when he was in Mesopotamia, before he dwelt in Charran, 3 and said unto him, Get thee out of thy country, and from thy kindred, and

ηὔξανεν, καὶ ἐπληθύνετο ὁ ἀριθμὸς τῶν μαθητῶν ἐν Ἱε-
increased, and [6]was [7]multiplied [1]the [2]number [3]of [4]the [5]disciples in Je-
ρουσαλὴμ σφόδρα, πολύς.τε ὄχλος τῶν ἱερέων ὑπήκουον
rusalem exceedingly, and a great multitude of the priests were obedient
τῇ πίστει.
to the faith.

8 Στέφανος.δὲ πλήρης [x]πίστεως‖ καὶ δυνάμεως ἐποίει
And Stephen, full of faith and power, wrought
τέρατα καὶ σημεῖα μεγάλα ἐν τῷ λαῷ. 9 ἀνέστησαν.δέ
wonders and [2]signs [1]great among the people. And arose
τινες τῶν ἐκ τῆς συναγωγῆς [y]τῆς λεγομένης‖ Λιβερτίνων,
certain of those of the synagogue called Libertines,
καὶ Κυρηναίων, καὶ Ἀλεξανδρέων, καὶ τῶν ἀπὸ Κιλικίας
and of Cyrenians, and of Alexandrians, and of those from Cilicia
[z]καὶ Ἀσίας,‖ [a]συζητοῦντες‖ τῷ Στεφάνῳ· 10 καὶ οὐκ.ἴσχυον
and Asia, disputing with Stephen. And they were not able
ἀντιστῆναι τῇ σοφίᾳ καὶ τῷ πνεύματι ᾧ ἐλάλει. 11 τότε
to resist the wisdom and the spirit by which he spoke. Then
ὑπέβαλον ἄνδρας, λέγοντας, Ὅτι ἀκηκόαμεν αὐτοῦ λαλοῦν-
they suborned men, saying, We have heard him speaking
τος ῥήματα βλάσφημα εἰς [b]Μωσῆν‖ καὶ τὸν θεόν. 12 Συν-
[2]words [1]blasphemous against Moses and God. [2]They
εκίνησάν τε τὸν λαὸν καὶ τοὺς πρεσβυτέρους καὶ τοὺς
[3]stirred [4]up [1]and the people and the elders and the
γραμματεῖς, καὶ ἐπιστάντες συνήρπασαν αὐτόν, καὶ ἤγαγον
scribes, and coming upon they seized him, and brought
εἰς τὸ συνέδριον, 13 ἔστησάν.τε μάρτυρας ψευδεῖς,
[him] to the sanhedrim, And they set [2]witnesses [1]false,
λέγοντας, Ὁ.ἄνθρωπος.οὗτος οὐ.παύεται [c]ῥήματα βλάσφημα
saying, This man does not cease [3]words [2]blasphemous
λαλῶν‖ κατὰ τοῦ τόπου τοῦ ἁγίου [d]τούτου‖ καὶ τοῦ νόμου.
[1]speaking against [3]place [2]holy [1]this and the law;
14 ἀκηκόαμεν.γὰρ αὐτοῦ λέγοντος, Ὅτι Ἰησοῦς ὁ Ναζω-
for we have heard him saying, That [2]Jesus [3]the [4]Naza-
ραῖος οὗτος καταλύσει τὸν.τόπον.τοῦτον, καὶ ἀλλάξει τὰ
ræan [1]this will destroy this place, and will change the
ἔθη ἃ παρέδωκεν ἡμῖν Μωϋσῆς. 15 Καὶ ἀτενίσαντες εἰς
customs which [2]delivered [3]to [4]us [1]Moses. And looking intently on
αὐτὸν [e]ἅπαντες‖ οἱ καθεζόμενοι ἐν τῷ συνεδρίῳ [f]εἶδον‖ τὸ
him all who sat in the sanhedrim saw
πρόσωπον.αὐτοῦ ὡσεὶ πρόσωπον ἀγγέλου.
his face as [the] face of an angel.

7 Εἶπεν.δὲ ὁ ἀρχιερεύς, Εἰ [g]ἄρα‖ ταῦτα οὕτως [h]ἔχει‖;
And [4]said [1]the [2]high [3]priest, [6]Then [7]these [8]things [9]so [5]are?
2 Ὁ.δὲ ἔφη, Ἄνδρες ἀδελφοὶ καὶ πατέρες, ἀκούσατε. ὁ θεὸς
And he said, Men brethren and fathers, hearken. The God
τῆς δόξης ὤφθη τῷ.πατρὶ.ἡμῶν Ἀβραὰμ ὄντι ἐν τῇ Μεσο-
of glory appeared to our father Abraham being in Meso-
ποταμίᾳ, πρὶν ἢ κατοικῆσαι αὐτὸν ἐν Χαῤῥάν, 3 καὶ εἶπεν
potamia, before [2]dwelt [1]he in Charran, and said
πρὸς αὐτόν, Ἔξελθε ἐκ τῆς.γῆς.σου καὶ [i]ἐκ‖ τῆς συγγενείας
to him, Go out from thy land and from [2]kindred

---

[x] χάριτος of grace GLTTrAW. [y] τῶν λεγομένων T. [z] — καὶ Ἀσίας L. [a] συνζητοῦντες LTTrA. [b] Μωϋσῆν GLTTrAW. [c] βλάσφημα GLTTrAW; λαλῶν ῥήματα TTr. [d] — τούτου (*read* the holy place) GLTTrAW. [e] πάντες LTTr. [f] εἶδαν Tr. [g] — ἄρα LTTr[A]. [h] — ἔχει (*read* [are]) W. [i] — ἐκ [L]Tr[A].

σου, καὶ δεῦρο εἰς [k] γῆν ἣν ἄν σοι δείξω. 4 Τότε ἐξελθὼν
[1]thy and come into land which to thee I will shew. Then going out
ἐκ γῆς Χαλδαίων, κατῴκησεν ἐν Χαῤῥάν, κἀκεῖθεν
from [the] land of Chaldeans, he dwelt in Charran, and thence
μετὰ τὸ ἀποθανεῖν τὸν.πατέρα.αὐτοῦ, μετῴκισεν αὐτὸν εἰς
after [3]died [1]his [2]father, he removed him into
τὴν.γῆν.ταύτην εἰς ἣν ὑμεῖς νῦν κατοικεῖτε· 5 καὶ οὐκ
this land in which ye now dwell. And [3]not
ἔδωκεν αὐτῷ κληρονομίαν ἐν αὐτῇ, οὐδὲ βῆμα.ποδός·
[1]he [2]did give to him an inheritance in it, not even a foot's tread;
καὶ ἐπηγγείλατο [l]αὐτῷ δοῦναι‖ εἰς κατάσχεσιν [m]αὐτήν,‖ καὶ
and promised to him to give [2]for [3]a [4]possession [1]it, and
τῷ.σπέρματι.αὐτοῦ μετ' αὐτόν, οὐκ.ὄντος αὐτῷ τέκνου.
to his seed after him, there not being to him a child.
6 ἐλάλησεν.δὲ οὕτως ὁ θεός, Ὅτι ἔσται τὸ.σπέρμα.αὐτοῦ
And [2]spoke [3]thus [1]God: That [3]shall [4]be [1]his [2]seed
πάροικον ἐν γῇ ἀλλοτρίᾳ, καὶ δουλώσουσιν αὐτὸ καὶ
a sojourner in a [2]land [1]strange, and they will enslave it and
κακώσουσιν ἔτη τετρακόσια. 7 καὶ τὸ ἔθνος ᾧ [n]ἐὰν‖
ill-treat [it] [3]years [1]four [2]hundred; and the nation to which
[o]δουλεύσωσιν,‖ κρινῶ ἐγώ, [p]εἶπεν ὁ θεός·‖ καὶ μετὰ
they may be in bondage will [2]judge [1]I, said God; and after
ταῦτα ἐξελεύσονται καὶ λατρεύσουσίν μοι ἐν τῷ τόπῳ
these things they shall come forth and serve me in [2]place
τούτῳ. 8 Καὶ ἔδωκεν αὐτῷ διαθήκην περιτομῆς· καὶ οὕτως
[1]this. And he gave to him a covenant of circumcision; and thus
ἐγέννησεν τὸν Ἰσαάκ, καὶ περιέτεμεν αὐτὸν τῇ ἡμέρᾳ τῇ
he begat Isaac, and circumcised him the [2]day
ὀγδόῃ· καὶ [q]ὁ‖ Ἰσαὰκ τὸν Ἰακώβ, καὶ [q]ὁ‖ Ἰακὼβ τοὺς
[1]eighth; and Isaac [begat] Jacob, and Jacob the
δώδεκα πατριάρχας. 9 καὶ οἱ πατριάρχαι ζηλώσαντες τὸν
twelve patriarchs. And the patriarchs, envying
Ἰωσὴφ ἀπέδοντο εἰς Αἴγυπτον· καὶ ἦν ὁ θεὸς μετ'
Joseph, sold [him] into Egypt. And [2]was [1]God with
αὐτοῦ, 10 καὶ [r]ἐξείλετο‖ αὐτὸν ἐκ πασῶν τῶν.θλίψεων.αὐτοῦ,
him, and delivered him out of all his tribulations,
καὶ ἔδωκεν αὐτῷ χάριν καὶ σοφίαν [s]ἐναντίον‖ Φαραὼ βασι-
and gave him favour and wisdom before Pharaoh king
λέως Αἰγύπτου, καὶ κατέστησεν αὐτὸν ἡγούμενον ἐπ' Αἴγυπ-
of Egypt, and he appointed him ruler over Egypt
τον καὶ [t] ὅλον τὸν.οἶκον.αὐτοῦ. 11 ἦλθεν.δὲ λιμὸς ἐφ' ὅλην
and [2]whole [1]his house. But [3]came [1]a [2]famine upon [2]whole
τὴν [v]γῆν Αἰγύπτου‖ καὶ Χαναάν, καὶ θλίψις μεγάλη· καὶ
[1]the land of Egypt and Canaan, and [2]tribulation [1]great, and
οὐχ.[w]εὕρισκον‖ χορτάσματα οἱ.πατέρες.ἡμῶν. 12 ἀκούσας.δὲ
[3]did [4]not [5]find [6]sustenance [1]our [2]fathers. But [2]having [3]heard
Ἰακὼβ ὄντα [x]σῖτα ἐν Αἰγύπτῳ,‖ ἐξαπέστειλεν τοὺς πατέρας
[1]Jacob [5]was [4]corn in Egypt, sent forth [2]fathers
ἡμῶν πρῶτον· 13 καὶ ἐν τῷ δευτέρῳ [y]ἀνεγνωρίσθη‖ Ἰωσὴφ
[1]our first; and at the second time was made known Joseph
τοῖς.ἀδελφοῖς.αὐτοῦ, καὶ φανερὸν ἐγένετο τῷ Φαραὼ τὸ γένος
to his brethren, and [2]known [1]became to Pharaoh the family

come into the land
which I shall shew
thee. 4 Then came he
out of the land of the
Chaldæans, and dwelt
in Charran: and from
thence, when his father
was dead, he removed
him into this land,
wherein ye now dwell.
5 And he gave him
none inheritance in
it, no, not *so much as*
to set his foot on: yet
he promised that he
would give it to him
for a possession, and
to his seed after him,
when *as yet* he had no
child. 6 And God spake
on this wise, That his
seed should sojourn in
a strange land; and
that they should bring
them into bondage, and
entreat *them* evil four
hundred years. 7 And
the nation to whom
they shall be in bon-
dage will I judge, said
God: and after that
shall they come forth,
and serve me in this
place. 8 And he gave
him the covenant of
circumcision: and so
Abraham begat Isaac,
and circumcised him
the eighth day; and
Isaac *begat* Jacob; and
Jacob *begat* the twelve
patriarchs. 9 And the
patriarchs, moved with
envy, sold Joseph into
Egypt: but God was
with him, 10 and de-
livered him out of all
his afflictions, and
gave him favour and
wisdom in the sight
of Pharaoh king of
Egypt; and he made
him governor over
Egypt and all his
house. 11 Now there
came a dearth over all
the land of Egypt and
Chanaan, and great af-
fliction: and our fa-
thers found no suste-
nance. 12 But when
Jacob heard that there
was corn in Egypt, he
sent out our fathers
first. 13 And at the
second *time* Joseph
was made known to
his brethren; and Jo-
seph's kindred was
made known unto Pha-

---

[k] + τὴν the LTTrAW. [l] δοῦναι αὐτῷ LTTrA; δοῦναι αὐτὴν to give it w. [m] αὐτῷ to him w. [n] ἂν LTr. [o] δουλεύσουσιν they will be in bondage TTrA. [p] ὁ θεὸς εἶπεν LTTrAW. [q] — ὁ LTTrA. [r] ἐξείλατο GLTTrAW. [s] ἔναντι T. [t] + ἐφ' over T. [v] Αἴγυπτον (*read* over all Egypt) LTTrA. [w] ηὕρισκον TrA. [x] σιτία εἰς Αἴγυπτον LTTrAW. [y] ἐγνωρίσθη Tr.

raoh. 14 Then sent Jo-
seph, and called his fa-
ther Jacob to *him*, and
all his kindred, three-
score and fifteen souls.
15 So Jacob went down
into Egypt, and died,
he, and our fathers,
16 and were carried
over into Sychem, and
laid in the sepulchre
that Abraham bought
for a sum of money of
the sons of Emmor *the
father* of Sychem.
17 But when the time
of the promise drew
nigh, which God had
sworn to Abraham, the
people grew and mul-
tiplied in Egypt, 18 till
another king arose,
which knew not Jo-
seph. 19 The same
dealt subtilly with
our kindred, and
evil entreated our
fathers, so that they
cast out their young
children, to the end
they might not live.
20 In which time Mo-
ses was born, and was
exceeding fair, and
nourished up in his
father's house three
months: 21 and when
he was cast out, Pha-
raoh's daughter took
him up, and nourished
him for her own son.
22 And Moses was
learned in all the wis-
dom of the Egyptians,
and was mighty in
words and in deeds.
23 And when he was
full forty years old, it
came into his heart to
visit his brethren the
children of Israel.
24 And seeing one *of
them* suffer wrong, he
defended *him*, and a-
venged him that was
oppressed, and smote
the Egyptian: 25 for
he supposed his breth-
ren would have under-
stood how that God by
his hand would deliver
them: but they under-
stood not. 26 And the

[z]τοῦ‖ [a]Ἰωσήφ.‖ 14 ἀποστείλας.δὲ Ἰωσὴφ μετεκαλέσατο [b]τὸν
of Joseph. And having sent Joseph he called for
πατέρα.αὐτοῦ Ἰακώβ,‖ καὶ πᾶσαν τὴν.συγγένειαν.[c]αὐτοῦ,‖ ἐν
his father Jacob, and all his kindred, in
ψυχαῖς ἑβδομήκοντα πέντε. 15 [d]κατέβη.δὲ‖ Ἰακὼβ εἰς Αἴγυπ-
[3]souls [1]seventy [2]five. And went down Jacob into Egypt
τον, καὶ ἐτελεύτησεν αὐτὸς καὶ οἱ.πατέρες.ἡμῶν· 16 καὶ
and died, he and our fathers, and
μετετέθησαν εἰς Συχέμ, καὶ ἐτέθησαν ἐν τῷ μνήματι [e]ὃ‖
were carried over to Sychem, and were placed in the tomb which
ὠνήσατο Ἀβραὰμ τιμῆς ἀργυρίου παρὰ τῶν υἱῶν [f]Ἐμμὸρ‖
[2]bought [1]Abraham for a sum of money from the sons of Emmor
[g]τοῦ‖ [h]Συχέμ. 17 Καθὼς.δὲ ἤγγιζεν ὁ χρόνος τῆς ἐπαγ-
of Sychem. But as drew near the time of the pro-
γελίας ἧς [i]ὤμοσεν‖ ὁ θεὸς τῷ Ἀβραάμ, ηὔξησεν ὁ λαὸς καὶ
mise which [2]swore [1]God to Abraham, [3]increased [1]the [2]people and
ἐπληθύνθη ἐν Αἰγύπτῳ, 18 [k]ἄχρις‖ οὗ ἀνέστη βασιλεὺς
multiplied in Egypt, until arose [2]king
ἕτερος,[l] ὃς οὐκ.ᾔδει τὸν Ἰωσήφ. 19 οὗτος κατασοφισάμενος
[1]another, who knew not Joseph. He having dealt subtilly with
τὸ.γένος.ἡμῶν, ἐκάκωσεν τοὺς.πατέρας.[m]ἡμῶν,‖ τοῦ ποιεῖν
our race, ill-treated our fathers, making
[n]ἔκθετα τὰ.βρέφη‖.αὐτῶν εἰς.τὸ μὴ.ζωογονεῖσθαι. 20 Ἐν ᾧ
[3]exposed [1]their [2]babes that they might not live. In which
καιρῷ ἐγεννήθη [o]Μωσῆς,‖ καὶ ἦν ἀστεῖος τῷ θεῷ· ὃς ἀνε-
time was born Moses, and was beautiful to God; who was
τράφη μῆνας τρεῖς ἐν τῷ οἴκῳ τοῦ.πατρὸς.[p]αὐτοῦ.‖
brought up [2]months [1]three in the house of his father.
21 [q]ἐκτεθέντα.δὲ αὐτόν,‖ [r]ἀνείλετο‖ αὐτὸν ἡ θυγάτηρ Φαραώ,
And [2]being [3]exposed [1]he, took up him the daughter of Pharaoh,
καὶ ἀνεθρέψατο αὐτὸν ἑαυτῇ εἰς υἱόν. 22 καὶ ἐπαιδεύθη
and brought up him for herself for a son. And [2]was [3]instructed
[o]Μωσῆς‖ [s]πάσῃ σοφίᾳ Αἰγυπτίων· ἦν.δὲ δυνατὸς ἐν
[1]Moses in all [the] wisdom of [the] Egyptians, and he was mighty in
λόγοις καὶ [t]ἐν‖ ἔργοις[v]. 23 Ὡς.δὲ ἐπληροῦτο αὐτῷ [w]τεσ-
words and in deeds. And when was fulfilled to him [3]of
σαρακονταετὴς‖ χρόνος, ἀνέβη ἐπὶ τὴν.καρδίαν.αὐτοῦ ἐπι-
[4]forty [5]years [1]a [2]period, it came into his heart to
σκέψασθαι τοὺς.ἀδελφοὺς.αὐτοῦ τοὺς υἱοὺς Ἰσραήλ. 24 καὶ
look upon his brethren the sons of Israel; and
ἰδών τινα ἀδικούμενον, ἠμύνατο καὶ ἐποίησεν.ἐκδίκησιν
seeing a certain one being wronged, he defended [him] and avenged
τῷ καταπονουμένῳ, πατάξας τὸν Αἰγύπτιον. 25 ἐνόμιζεν.δὲ
him being oppressed, having smitten the Egyptian. For he thought
συνιέναι τοὺς.ἀδελφοὺς.[x]αὐτοῦ‖ ὅτι ὁ θεὸς διὰ χειρὸς
[3]would [4]understand [1]his [2]brethren that God by [2]hand
αὐτοῦ δίδωσιν [y]αὐτοῖς σωτηρίαν.‖ οἱ.δὲ οὐ.συνῆκαν.
[1]his is giving them salvation. But they understood not.

---

[z] — τοῦ LTTrA. [a] αὐτοῦ (*read* his family) T. [b] Ἰακὼβ τὸν πατέρα αὐτοῦ LTTrAW.
[c] — αὐτοῦ (*read* [his]) GLTTrA. [d] καὶ κατέβη LTTrAW. [e] ᾧ GLTTrAW [f] Ἐμμὼρ LTTrAW.
[g] — τοῦ TTr. [h] + ἐν in LTTr. [i] ὡμολόγησεν promised LTTrAW. [k] ἄχρι LTTrA.
[l] + ἐπ' Αἴγυπτον over Egypt LTTr. [m] — ἡμῶν (*read* the fathers) LTTrA. [n] τὰ βρέφη
ἔκθετα LTTrA. [o] Μωϋσῆς GLTTrAW. [p] — αὐτοῦ (*read* [his]) GLTTrAW. [q] ἐκτεθέντος δὲ
αὐτοῦ LTTrA. [r] ἀνείλατο GLTTrAW. [s] + ἐν in (*read* πάσῃ all) TTrAW. [t] — ἐν LTTrA.
[v] + αὐτοῦ (*read* his deeds) GLTTrAW. [w] τεσσερακονταετὴς TTrA. [x] — αὐτοῦ (*read*
[his]) TTr[A]. [y] σωτηρίαν αὐτοῖς LTTrAW.

26 τῇ.[z]τε‖ ἐπιούσῃ ἡμέρᾳ ὤφθη αὐτοῖς μαχομένοις, καὶ
And on the following day he appeared to those who were contending, and
[a]συνήλασεν‖ αὐτοὺς εἰς εἰρήνην, εἰπών, Ἄνδρες ἀδελφοί ἐστε
urged them to peace, saying, Men [3]brethren [2]are
[b]ὑμεῖς·‖ [c]ἱνατί‖ ἀδικεῖτε ἀλλήλους; 27 Ὁ.δὲ ἀδικῶν
[1]ye, why wrong ye one another? But he who was wronging [his]
τὸν πλησίον ἀπώσατο αὐτόν, εἰπών, Τίς σε κατέστησεν
neighbour thrust away him, saying, Who [2]thee [1]appointed
ἄρχοντα καὶ δικαστὴν ἐφ' [d]ἡμᾶς‖; 28 μὴ ἀνελεῖν με
ruler and judge over us? To put to death me
σὺ θέλεις, ὃν.τρόπον ἀνεῖλες [e]χθὲς‖ τὸν Αἰγύπτιον;
[2]thou [1]wishest, in the way thou puttest to death yesterday the Egyptian?
29 Ἔφυγεν.δὲ [f]Μωσῆς‖ ἐν τῷ.λόγῳ.τούτῳ, καὶ ἐγένετο
And [2]fled [1]Moses at this saying, and became
πάροικος ἐν γῇ Μαδιάμ, οὗ ἐγέννησεν υἱοὺς δύο.
a sojourner in [the] land of Madiam, where he begat [2]sons [1]two.
30 Καὶ πληρωθέντων ἐτῶν [g]τεσσαράκοντα‖ ὤφθη αὐτῷ ἐν
And [3]being [4]fulfilled [2]years [1]forty appeared to him in
τῇ ἐρήμῳ τοῦ ὄρους Σινᾶ ἄγγελος [h]κυρίου‖ ἐν φλογὶ
the desert of the Mount Sina an angel of [the] Lord in a flame
πυρὸς βάτου. 31 ὁ.δὲ.[f]Μωσῆς‖ ἰδὼν [i]ἐθαύμασεν‖ τὸ
of fire of a bush. And Moses seeing [it] wondered at the
ὅραμα· προσερχομένου.δὲ αὐτοῦ κατανοῆσαι, ἐγένετο φωνὴ
vision; and [2]coming [3]near [1]he to consider [it], there was a voice
κυρίου [k]πρὸς αὐτόν,‖ 32 Ἐγὼ ὁ θεὸς τῶν.πατέρων.σου,
of [the] Lord to him, I [am] the God of thy fathers,
ὁ θεὸς Ἀβραὰμ καὶ [l]ὁ θεὸς‖ Ἰσαὰκ καὶ [l]ὁ θεὸς‖ Ἰακώβ.
the God of Abraham and the God of Isaac and the God of Jacob.
Ἔντρομος.δὲ γενόμενος [f]Μωσῆς‖ οὐκ.ἐτόλμα κατανοῆσαι.
And [4]trembling [2]having [3]become [1]Moses he durst not consider [it].
33 εἶπεν.δὲ αὐτῷ ὁ κύριος, Λῦσον τὸ ὑπόδημα τῶν ποδῶν
And [3]said [4]to [5]him [1]the [2]Lord, Loose the sandal of [2]feet
σου· ὁ.γὰρ τόπος [m]ἐν‖ ᾧ ἕστηκας, γῆ ἁγία ἐστίν. 34 ἰδὼν
[1]thy, for the place on which thou standest, [3]ground [2]holy [1]is. Seeing,
εἶδον τὴν κάκωσιν τοῦ.λαοῦ.μου τοῦ ἐν Αἰγύπτῳ, καὶ τοῦ
I saw the ill-treatment of my people in Egypt, and
στεναγμοῦ.[n]αὐτῶν‖ ἤκουσα· καὶ κατέβην ἐξελέσθαι αὐτούς·
their groaning heard, and came down to take [2]out [1]them;
καὶ νῦν δεῦρο, [o]ἀποστελῶ‖ σε εἰς Αἴγυπτον. 35 Τοῦτον τὸν
and now come, I will send thee to Egypt. This
Μωϋσῆν ὃν ἠρνήσαντο εἰπόντες, Τίς σε κατέστησεν ἄρ-
Moses, whom they refused, saying, Who [2]thee [1]appointed ru-
χοντα καὶ δικαστήν; τοῦτον ὁ θεὸς [p] ἄρχοντα καὶ λυτρωτὴν
ler and judge? him God [[2]as] [3]ruler [4]and [5]deliverer
[q]ἀπέστειλεν ἐν‖ χειρὶ ἀγγέλου τοῦ ὀφθέντος αὐτῷ ἐν τῇ
[1]sent by [the] hand of [the] angel who appeared to him in the
βάτῳ. 36 οὗτος ἐξήγαγεν αὐτούς, ποιήσας τέρατα καὶ
bush. This one led out them, having wrought wonders and
σημεῖα ἐν [r]γῇ‖ [s]Αἰγύπτου‖ καὶ ἐν ἐρυθρᾷ θαλάσσῃ,
signs in [the] land of Egypt and in [the] Red Sea,

next day he shewed himself unto them as they strove, and would have set them at one again, saying, Sirs, ye are brethren; why do ye wrong one to another? 27 But he that did his neighbour wrong thrust him away, saying, Who made thee a ruler and a judge over us? 28 Wilt thou kill me, as thou diddest the Egyptian yesterday? 29 Then fled Moses at this saying, and was a stranger in the land of Madian, where he begat two sons. 30 And when forty years were expired, there appeared to him in the wilderness of mount Sina an angel of the Lord in a flame of fire in a bush. 31 When Moses saw *it*, he wondered at the sight: and as he drew near to behold *it*, the voice of the Lord came unto him, 32 *saying*, I *am* the God of thy fathers, the God of Abraham, and the God of Isaac, and the God of Jacob. Then Moses trembled, and durst not behold. 33 Then said the Lord to him, Put off thy shoes from thy feet: for the place where thou standest is holy ground. 34 I have seen, I have seen the affliction of my people which is in Egypt, and I have heard their groaning, and am come down to deliver them. And now come, I will send thee into Egypt. 35 This Moses whom they refused, saying, Who made thee a ruler and a judge? the same did God send *to be* a ruler and a deliverer by the hand of the angel which appeared to him in the bush. 36 He brought them out, after that he had shewed wonders and signs in the land of Egypt, and in the Red sea, and in the wil-

---

z δὲ EGW. a συνήλλασσεν LTTrW. b — ὑμεῖς (*read* ἐστε ye are) LTTr[A]W. c ἵνα τί LTrA. d ἡμῶν LTTrW. e ἐχθὲς LTTrA. f Μωϋσῆς GLTTrAW. g τεσσεράκοντα TTrA. h — κυρίου LTTrA. i ἐθαύμαζεν GTAW. k — πρὸς αὐτόν LTTrA. l — ὁ θεὸς LTTrA. m ἐφ' LTTrA. n αὐτοῦ (*read* [their]) LTr. o ἀποστείλω LTTrAW. p + καὶ both LT[Tr]A. q ἀπέσταλκεν σὺν has sent with LTTrAW. r τῇ (*read* in Egypt) LTr. s Αἰγύπτῳ GLTTrA.

derness forty years.
37 This is that Moses,
which said unto the
children of Israel,
A prophet shall the
Lord your God raise
up unto you of your
brethren, like unto me;
him shall ye hear.
38 This is he, that was
in the church in the
wilderness with the
angel which spake to
him in the mount
Sina, and *with* our fa-
thers: who received
the lively oracles to
give unto us: 39 to
whom our fathers
would not obey, but
thrust *him* from
them, and in their
hearts turned back
again into Egypt,
40 saying unto Aaron,
Make us gods to go
before us: for *as for*
this Moses, which
brought us out of the
land of Egypt, we wot
not what is become of
him. 41 And they made
a calf in those days,
and offered sacrifice
unto the idol, and re-
joiced in the works
of their own hands.
42 Then God turned,
and gave them up to
worship the host of
heaven; as it is writ-
ten in the book of the
prophets, O ye house
of Israel, have ye of-
fered to me slain beasts
and sacrifices *by the
space of* forty years in
the wilderness? 43 Yea,
ye took up the ta-
bernacle of Moloch,
and the star of your
god Remphan, figures
which ye made to wor-
ship them: and I will
carry you away beyond
Babylon. 44 Our fa-
thers had the taber-
nacle of witness in the
wilderness, as he had
appointed, speaking
unto Moses, that he
should make it accor-
ding to the fashion
that he had seen.
45 Which also our fa-
thers that came after
brought in with Jesus
into the possession of
the Gentiles, whom
God drave out before
the face of our fathers,

καὶ ἐν τῇ ἐρήμῳ ἔτη [v]τεσσαράκοντα.‖ 37 Οὗτός ἐστιν ὁ
and in the wilderness [2]years [1]forty. This is the
Μωϋσῆς ὁ [w]εἰπὼν‖ τοῖς υἱοῖς Ἰσραήλ, Προφήτην ὑμῖν
Moses who said to the sons of Israel, A prophet to you
ἀναστήσει [x]κύριος‖ ὁ θεὸς [y]ὑμῶν‖ ἐκ τῶν ἀδελφῶν
[5]will [6]raise [7]up [[1]the] [2]Lord [4]God [3]your from among [2]brethren
ὑμῶν ὡς ἐμέ· [z]αὐτοῦ ἀκούσεσθε.‖ 38 Οὗτός ἐστιν ὁ γενό-
[1]your like me, him ye shall hear. This is he who was
μενος ἐν τῇ ἐκκλησίᾳ ἐν τῇ ἐρήμῳ μετὰ τοῦ ἀγγέλου τοῦ
in the assembly in the wilderness with the angel who
λαλοῦντος αὐτῷ ἐν τῷ ὄρει Σινᾶ, καὶ τῶν.πατέρων.ἡμῶν,
spoke to him in the mount Sina, and with our fathers;
ὃς ἐδέξατο λόγια ζῶντα δοῦναι ἡμῖν· 39 ᾧ οὐκ.ἠθέλησαν
who received [2]oracles [1]living to give to us: to whom [5]would [4]not
ὑπήκοοι γενέσθαι οἱ.πατέρες.ἡμῶν, [a]ἀλλ'‖ ἀπώσαντο, καὶ
[6]subject [3]be [1]our [2]fathers, but thrust [him] away, and
ἐστράφησαν [b]ταῖς.καρδίαις.αὐτῶν εἰς Αἴγυπτον, 40 εἰπόντες
turned back their hearts to Egypt, saying
τῷ Ἀαρών, Ποίησον ἡμῖν θεοὺς οἳ προπορεύσονται ἡμῶν·
to Aaron, Make us gods who shall go before us;
ὁ γὰρ [c]Μωσῆς‖ οὗτος ὃς ἐξήγαγεν ἡμᾶς ἐκ γῆς Αἰγύπ-
for [3]Moses [1]that who brought [2]out us from [the] land of Egypt,
του, οὐκ.οἴδαμεν τί [d]γέγονεν‖ αὐτῷ. 41 Καὶ ἐμοσχοποίησαν
we know not what has happened to him. And they made a calf
ἐν ταῖς.ἡμέραις.ἐκείναις, καὶ ἀνήγαγον θυσίαν τῷ εἰδώλῳ,
in those days, and offered sacrifice to the idol,
καὶ εὐφραίνοντο ἐν τοῖς ἔργοις τῶν.χειρῶν.αὐτῶν. 42 Ἔστρεψεν
and rejoiced in the works of their hands. [3]Turned
δὲ ὁ θεὸς καὶ παρέδωκεν αὐτοὺς λατρεύειν τῇ στρατιᾷ τοῦ
[1]but [2]God and delivered up them to serve the host of the
οὐρανοῦ· καθὼς γέγραπται ἐν βίβλῳ τῶν προφητῶν,
heaven; as it has been written in [the] book of the prophets,
Μὴ σφάγια καὶ θυσίας προσηνέγκατέ μοι ἔτη [v]τεσσαρά-
[4]Slain [5]beasts [6]and [7]sacrifices [1]did [2]ye [3]offer to me [2]years [1]forty
κοντα‖ ἐν τῇ ἐρήμῳ, οἶκος Ἰσραήλ; 43 καὶ ἀνελάβετε τὴν
in the wilderness, O house of Israel? And ye took up the
σκηνὴν τοῦ Μολόχ, καὶ τὸ ἄστρον τοῦ.θεοῦ.[e]ὑμῶν‖ [f]Ῥεμφάν,‖
tabernacle of Moloch, and the star of your god Remphan,
τοὺς τύπους οὓς ἐποιήσατε προσκυνεῖν αὐτοῖς· καὶ μετοικιῶ
the models which ye made to worship them; and I will remove
ὑμᾶς ἐπέκεινα Βαβυλῶνος. 44 Ἡ σκηνὴ τοῦ μαρτυρίου ἦν
you beyond Babylon. The tabernacle of the testimony was
[g]ἐν‖ τοῖς.πατράσιν.ἡμῶν ἐν τῇ ἐρήμῳ, καθὼς διετάξατο
among our fathers in the wilderness, as commanded
ὁ λαλῶν τῷ.[h]Μωσῇ,‖ ποιῆσαι αὐτὴν κατὰ τὸν τύπον
he who spoke to Moses, to make it according to the model
ὃν ἑωράκει· 45 ἣν καὶ εἰσήγαγον διαδεξάμενοι
which he had seen; which also [7]brought [8]in [3]having [4]received [5]by [6]succession
οἱ.πατέρες.ἡμῶν μετὰ Ἰησοῦ ἐν τῇ κατασχέσει τῶν ἐθνῶν,
[1]our [2]fathers with Joshua in the taking possession of the nations,
ὧν [i]ἐξῶσεν‖ ὁ θεὸς ἀπὸ προσώπου τῶν.πατέρων.ἡμῶν,
whom [2]drove [3]out [1]God from [the] face of our fathers,

---

[v] τεσσεράκοντα TTrA. [w] εἴπας LTTrA. [x] — κύριος LTTrA. [y] — ὑμῶν GLTTrA.
[z] — αὐτοῦ ἀκούσεσθε LTTrA. [a] ἀλλὰ LTTrA. [b] + ἐν LTTrA. [c] Μωϋσῆς GLTTrAW.
[d] ἐγένετο happened LTTrA. [e] — ὑμῶν (*read* the God) LTTrA. [f] Ῥεφάν Rephan LTrAW;
Ῥομφάν Romphan T. [g] — ἐν (*read* to our) LTTrA. [h] Μωϋσῇ GLTTrAW. [i] ἐξέωσεν T.

ἕως τῶν ἡμερῶν [l]Δαβίδ·‖ 46 ὃς εὗρεν χάριν ἐνώπιον τοῦ
until the days of David; who found favour before
θεοῦ, καὶ ᾐτήσατο εὑρεῖν σκήνωμα τῷ [m]θεῷ‖ Ἰακώβ.
God, and asked to find a tabernacle for the God of Jacob;
47 [n]Σολομῶν‖.δὲ [o]ᾠκοδόμησεν‖ αὐτῷ οἶκον. 48 Ἀλλ' οὐχ ὁ
but Solomon built him a house. But [4]not [1]the
ὕψιστος ἐν χειροποιήτοις [p]ναοῖς‖ κατοικεῖ, καθὼς ὁ προ-
[2]Most [3]High in hand-made temples dwells; as the pro-
φήτης λέγει, 49 Ὁ οὐρανός μοι θρόνος ἡ.δὲ γῆ ὑπο-
phet says, The heaven [is] to me a throne and the earth a foot-
πόδιον τῶν.ποδῶν.μου· ποῖον οἶκον οἰκοδομήσετέ μοι; λέγει
stool of my feet: what house will ye build me? says
κύριος· ἢ τίς τόπος τῆς.καταπαύσεώς.μου; 50 οὐχὶ
[the] Lord, or what [the] place of my rest? [2]not
ἡ.χείρ.μου ἐποίησεν ταῦτα πάντα; 51 σκληροτράχηλοι καὶ
[3]my [4]hand [1]made [6]these [7]things [5]all? O stiffnecked and
ἀπερίτμητοι [q]τῇ καρδίᾳ‖ καὶ τοῖς ὠσίν, ὑμεῖς ἀεὶ τῷ πνεύματι
uncircumcised in heart and ears, ye always the Spirit
τῷ ἁγίῳ ἀντιπίπτετε, [r]ὡς‖ οἱ.πατέρες.ὑμῶν, καὶ ὑμεῖς. 52 τίνα
the Holy resist; as your fathers, also ye. Which
τῶν προφητῶν οὐκ.ἐδίωξαν οἱ.πατέρες.ὑμῶν; καὶ ἀπέ-
of the prophets did not [3]persecute [1]your [2]fathers? and they
κτειναν τοὺς προκαταγγείλαντας περὶ τῆς ἐλεύσεως τοῦ
killed those who before announced concerning the coming of the
δικαίου, οὗ νῦν ὑμεῖς προδόται καὶ φονεῖς [s]γεγένησθε·‖
Just One, of whom now ye betrayers and murderers have become!
53 οἵτινες ἐλάβετε τὸν νόμον εἰς διαταγὰς ἀγγέλων, καὶ
who received the law by [the] disposition of angels, and
οὐκ.ἐφυλάξατε.
kept [it] not.

54 Ἀκούοντες.δὲ ταῦτα διεπρίοντο ταῖς.καρδίαις.αὐτῶν,
And hearing these things they were cut to their hearts,
καὶ ἔβρυχον τοὺς ὀδόντας ἐπ' αὐτόν. 55 Ὑπάρχων.δὲ πλήρης
and gnashed the teeth at him. But being full
πνεύματος ἁγίου, ἀτενίσας εἰς τὸν οὐρανόν, εἶδεν
of [the] [2]Spirit [1]Holy, having looked intently into heaven, he saw
δόξαν θεοῦ, καὶ Ἰησοῦν ἑστῶτα ἐκ δεξιῶν τοῦ θεοῦ,
[the] glory of God, and Jesus standing at the right hand of God,
56 καὶ εἶπεν, Ἰδού, θεωρῶ τοὺς οὐρανοὺς [t]ἀνεῳγμένους,‖ καὶ
and said, Lo, I behold the heavens opened, and
τὸν υἱὸν τοῦ ἀνθρώπου ἐκ δεξιῶν ἑστῶτα τοῦ θεοῦ.
the Son of man [2]at [3]the [4]right [[5]hand] [1]standing of God.
57 Κράξαντες.δὲ φωνῇ μεγάλῃ συνέσχον τὰ.ὦτα.αὐτῶν
And crying out with a [2]voice [1]loud they held their ears
καὶ ὥρμησαν ὁμοθυμαδὸν ἐπ' αὐτόν, 58 καὶ ἐκβαλόντες
and rushed with one accord upon him, and having cast [him]
ἔξω τῆς πόλεως ἐλιθοβόλουν. καὶ οἱ μάρτυρες ἀπέθεντο
out of the city they stoned [him]. And the witnesses laid aside
τὰ.ἱμάτια.αὐτῶν παρὰ τοὺς πόδας νεανίου καλουμένου
their garments at the feet of a young man called
Σαύλου. 59 καὶ ἐλιθοβόλουν τὸν Στέφανον, ἐπικαλούμενον
Saul. And they stoned Stephen, invoking
καὶ λέγοντα, Κύριε Ἰησοῦ, δέξαι τὸ.πνεῦμά.μου. 60 θεὶς.δὲ
and saying, Lord Jesus, receive my spirit. And having bowed

unto the days of David; 46 who found favour before God, and desired to find a tabernacle for the God of Jacob. 47 But Solomon built him an house. 48 Howbeit the most High dwelleth not in temples made with hands; as saith the prophet, 49 Heaven *is* my throne, and earth *is* my footstool: what house will ye build me? saith the Lord: or what *is* the place of my rest? 50 Hath not my hand made all these things? 51 Ye stiffnecked and uncircumcised in heart and ears, ye do always resist the Holy Ghost: as your fathers *did*, so *do* ye. 52 Which of the prophets have not your fathers persecuted? and they have slain them which shewed before of the coming of the Just One; of whom ye have been now the betrayers and murderers: 53 who have received the law by the disposition of angels, and have not kept *it*.

54 When they heard these things, they were cut to the heart, and they gnashed on him with *their* teeth. 55 But he, being full of the Holy Ghost, looked up stedfastly into heaven, and saw the glory of God, and Jesus standing on the right hand of God, 56 and said, Behold, I see the heavens opened, and the Son of man standing on the right hand of God. 57 Then they cried out with a loud voice, and stopped their ears, and ran upon him with one accord, 58 and cast *him* out of the city, and stoned *him*: and the witnesses laid down their clothes at a young man's feet, whose name was Saul. 59 And they stoned Stephen, calling upon *God*, and saying, Lord Jesus, receive my spirit. 60 And he kneeled

[l] Δαυείδ LTTrA; Δαυΐδ GW. [m] οἴκῳ house LT. [n] Σαλωμὼν T. [o] οἰκοδόμησεν Tr. [p] — ναοῖς (*read* [places]) GLTTrAW. [q] καρδίαις hearts LTTr; ταῖς καρδίαις W. [r] καθὼς L. [s] ἐγένεσθε became LTTrAW. [t] διηνοιγμένους LTTrAW.

down, and cried with a loud voice, Lord, lay not this sin to their charge. And when he had said this, he fell asleep. VIII. And Saul was consenting unto his death.

And at that time there was a great persecution against the church which was at Jerusalem; and they were all scattered abroad throughout the regions of Judæa and Samaria, except the apostles. 2 And devout men carried Stephen *to his burial*, and made great lamentation over him. 3 As for Saul, he made havock of the church, entering into every house, and haling men and women committed *them* to prison.

4 Therefore they that were scattered abroad went every where preaching the word. 5 Then Philip went down to the city of Samaria, and preached Christ unto them. 6 And the people with one accord gave heed unto those things which Philip spake, hearing and seeing the miracles which he did. 7 For unclean spirits, crying with loud voice, came out of many that were possessed *with them*: and many taken with palsies, and that were lame, were healed. 8 And there was great joy in that city.

9 But there was a certain man, called Simon, which beforetime in the same city used sorcery, and bewitched the people of Samaria, giving out that himself was some great one: 10 to whom they all gave heed, from the least to the greatest, saying, This man is the great power of God. 11 And to him they had regard, because that of long time he had bewitched them with sorceries. 12 But when they believed Philip preaching the things concerning the

τὰ γόνατα ἔκραξεν φωνῇ μεγάλῃ, Κύριε, μὴ.στήσῃς αὐτοῖς
the knees he cried with a [2]voice [1]loud, Lord, lay not to them
[v]τὴν.ἁμαρτίαν.ταύτην.‖ Καὶ τοῦτο εἰπὼν ἐκοιμήθη.
this sin. And this having said he fell asleep.
8 Σαῦλος.δὲ ἦν συνευδοκῶν τῇ ἀναιρέσει αὐτοῦ.
And Saul was consenting to the killing of him.
Ἐγένετο.δὲ ἐν ἐκείνῃ τῇ ἡμέρᾳ διωγμὸς μέγας ἐπὶ τὴν
And took place on that day a [2]persecution [1]great against the
ἐκκλησίαν τὴν ἐν Ἱεροσολύμοις· πάντες.[w]τε‖ διεσπάρησαν
assembly which [was] in Jerusalem, and all were scattered
κατὰ τὰς χώρας τῆς Ἰουδαίας καὶ [x]Σαμαρείας‖.πλὴν τῶν
throughout the countries of Judæa and Samaria except the
ἀποστόλων. 2 συνεκόμισαν.δὲ τὸν Στέφανον ἄνδρες εὐλαβεῖς,
apostles. And [3]buried [4]Stephen [2]men [1]pious,
καὶ [y]ἐποιήσαντο‖ κοπετὸν μέγαν ἐπ' αὐτῷ. 3 Σαῦλος.δὲ
and made [2]lamentation [1]great over him. But Saul
ἐλυμαίνετο τὴν ἐκκλησίαν, κατὰ.τοὺς.οἴκους εἰσπορευόμενος,
was ravaging the assembly, [2]house [3]by [4]house [1]entering,
σύρων.τε ἄνδρας καὶ γυναῖκας παρεδίδου εἰς φυλακήν.
and dragging men and women delivered [them] up to prison.
4 Οἱ μὲν οὖν διασπαρέντες διῆλθον, εὐαγγελιζό-
They who therefore had been scattered passed through, announcing the
μενοι τὸν λόγον. 5 Φίλιππος.δὲ κατελθὼν εἰς [z] πόλιν
glad tidings— the word. And Philip, going down to a city
τῆς [x]Σαμαρείας‖ ἐκήρυσσεν αὐτοῖς τὸν χριστόν. 6 προσεῖχόν
of Samaria, proclaimed to them the Christ; [4]gave [5]heed
[a]τε‖ οἱ ὄχλοι τοῖς λεγομένοις ὑπὸ τοῦ Φιλίππου ὁμο-
[1]and [2]the [3]crowds to the things spoken by Philip with
θυμαδόν, ἐν.τῷ.ἀκούειν.αὐτοὺς καὶ βλέπειν τὰ σημεῖα ἃ
one accord, when they heard and saw the signs which
ἐποίει. 7 [b]πολλῶν‖.γὰρ τῶν ἐχόντων πνεύματα ἀκά-
he did. For of many of those who had spirits un-
θαρτα, βοῶντα [c]μεγάλῃ φωνῇ ἐξήρχετο·‖ πολλοὶ.δὲ
clean, [4]crying [5]with [6]a [7]loud [8]voice [1]they [2]went [3]out; and many
παραλελυμένοι καὶ χωλοὶ ἐθεραπεύθησαν. 8 [d]καὶ ἐγένετο
having been paralysed and lame were healed. And [3]was
χαρὰ μεγάλη‖ ἐν τῇ.πόλει.ἐκείνῃ.
[2]joy [1]great in that city.
9 Ἀνὴρ.δέ.τις ὀνόματι Σίμων προϋπῆρχεν ἐν τῇ πόλει
But a certain man, by name Simon, was formerly in the city
μαγεύων καὶ [e]ἐξιστῶν‖ τὸ ἔθνος τῆς [x]Σαμαρείας,‖ λέγων
using magic arts and amazing the nation of Samaria, saying
εἶναί τινα ἑαυτὸν μέγαν· 10 ᾧ προσεῖχον πάντες
[2]to [3]be [4]some [1]himself great one. To whom [2]were [3]giving [4]heed [1]all
ἀπὸ μικροῦ ἕως μεγάλου, λέγοντες, Οὗτός ἐστιν ἡ δύναμις
from small to great, saying, This one is the power
τοῦ θεοῦ ἡ [f] μεγάλη. 11 Προσεῖχον.δὲ αὐτῷ, διὰ
of God which [is] great. And they were giving heed to him, because
τὸ.ἱκανῷ χρόνῳ ταῖς [g]μαγείαις‖ ἐξεστακέναι αὐτούς.
that for a long time with the magic arts [he] had amazed them.
12 Ὅτε.δὲ ἐπίστευσαν τῷ Φιλίππῳ εὐαγγελιζομένῳ
But when they believed Philip announcing the glad tidings—

---

[v] ταύτην τὴν ἁμαρτίαν LTrA W. [w] δὲ LTrA; — τε T. [x] Σαμαρίας T. [y] ἐποίησαν LTTrAW. [z] + τὴν the (city) LT. [a] δὲ LTTrAW. [b] πολλοὶ LTTrA. [c] φωνῇ μεγάλῃ ἐξήρχοντο (ἐξήρχετο G) GLTTrAW. [d] ἐγένετο δὲ πολλὴ χαρὰ LTTrA. [e] ἐξιστάνων LTTrA. [f] + καλουμένη called GLTTrAW. [g] μαγίαις T.

[h]τὰ[‖] περὶ τῆς βασιλείας τοῦ θεοῦ καὶ τοῦ ὀνόματος
the things concerning the kingdom of God and the name
[i]τοῦ[‖] Ἰησοῦ χριστοῦ, ἐβαπτίζοντο ἄνδρες-τε καὶ γυναῖκες.
of Jesus Christ, they were baptized both men and women.
13 ὁ.δὲ.Σίμων καὶ αὐτὸς ἐπίστευσεν, καὶ βαπτισθεὶς ἦν
And Simon also himself believed, and having been baptized was
προσκαρτερῶν τῷ Φιλίππῳ· θεωρῶν τε [k]σημεῖα καὶ δυνά-
steadfastly continuing with Philip; [2]beholding [4]and signs and [5]works [3]of
μεις μεγάλας γινομένας,[‖] ἐξίστατο. 14 Ἀκούσαντες.δὲ οἱ
[6]power [1]great being done, was amazed. And [5]having [6]heard [1]the
ἐν Ἱεροσολύμοις ἀπόστολοι ὅτι δέδεκται ἡ [l]Σαμάρεια[‖] τὸν
[3]in [4]Jerusalem [2]apostles that [2]had [3]received [1]Samaria the
λόγον τοῦ θεοῦ, ἀπέστειλαν πρὸς αὐτοὺς [m]τὸν[‖] Πέτρον καὶ
word of God, they sent to them Peter and
[n]Ἰωάννην·[‖] 15 οἵτινες καταβάντες προσηύξαντο περὶ
John; who having come down prayed for
αὐτῶν, ὅπως λάβωσιν πνεῦμα ἅγιον. 16 [o]οὔπω[‖].γὰρ
them, that they might receive [the] [2]Spirit [1]Holy; for not yet
ἦν ἐπ' οὐδενὶ αὐτῶν ἐπιπεπτωκός, μόνον.δὲ βεβαπ-
was he upon any (*lit.* no one) of them fallen, but only [3]bap-
τισμένοι ὑπῆρχον εἰς τὸ ὄνομα τοῦ κυρίου Ἰησοῦ. 17 τότε
tized [1]they [2]were to the name of the Lord Jesus. Then
[p]ἐπετίθουν[‖] τὰς χεῖρας ἐπ' αὐτούς, καὶ ἐλάμβανον πνεῦμα
they laid hands upon them, and they received [the] [2]Spirit
ἅγιον. 18 [q]Θεασάμενος[‖].δὲ ὁ Σίμων ὅτι διὰ τῆς ἐπιθέσεως
[1]Holy. But [2]having [3]seen [1]Simon that by the laying on
τῶν χειρῶν τῶν ἀποστόλων δίδοται τὸ πνεῦμα [r]τὸ ἅγιον,[‖]
of the hands of the apostles was given the Spirit the Holy,
προσήνεγκεν αὐτοῖς χρήματα, 19 λέγων, Δότε κἀμοὶ τὴν
he offered to them riches, saying, Give also to me
ἐξουσίαν.ταύτην, ἵνα ᾧ.[s]ἂν[‖] ἐπιθῶ τὰς χεῖρας, λαμ-
this authority, that on whomsoever I may lay hands, he may re-
βάνῃ πνεῦμα ἅγιον. 20 Πέτρος.δὲ εἶπεν πρὸς αὐτόν,
ceive [the] [2]Spirit [1]Holy. But Peter said to him,
Τὸ.ἀργύριόν.σου σὺν σοὶ εἴη εἰς ἀπώλειαν· ὅτι τὴν
Thy money with thee may it be to destruction, because the
δωρεὰν τοῦ θεοῦ ἐνόμισας διὰ χρημάτων κτᾶσθαι. 21 οὐκ
gift of God thou didst think by riches to be obtained. [3]Not
ἔστιν σοι μερὶς οὐδὲ κλῆρος ἐν τῷ.λόγῳ.τούτῳ· ἡ.γὰρ
[4]there [2]is to thee part nor lot in this matter; for the
καρδία σου οὐκ.ἔστιν εὐθεῖα [t]ἐνώπιον[‖] τοῦ θεοῦ. 22 μετανόη-
heart of thee is not right before God. Repent
σον οὖν ἀπὸ τῆς.κακίας.σου ταύτης, καὶ δεήθητι [v]τοῦ θεοῦ,[‖]
therefore of [2]thy [3]wickedness [1]this, and supplicate God,
εἰ ἄρα ἀφεθήσεταί σοι ἡ ἐπίνοια τῆς.καρδίας.σου. 23 εἰς
if indeed may be forgiven to thee the thought of thy heart; [2]in
γὰρ χολὴν πικρίας καὶ σύνδεσμον ἀδικίας ὁρῶ σε
[1]for a gall of bitterness and a bond of unrighteousness I see thee
ὄντα. 24 Ἀποκριθεὶς.δὲ ὁ Σίμων εἶπεν, Δεήθητε ὑμεῖς ὑπὲρ
to be. And [2]answering [1]Simon said, Supplicate ye on behalf
ἐμοῦ πρὸς τὸν κύριον, ὅπως μηδὲν ἐπέλθῃ ἐπ' ἐμὲ ὧν
of me to the Lord, so that nothing may come upon me of which

kingdom of God, and the name of Jesus Christ, they were baptized, both men and women. 13 Then Simon himself believed also: and when he was baptized, he continued with Philip, and wondered, beholding the miracles and signs which were done. 14 Now when the apostles which were at Jerusalem heard that Samaria had received the word of God, they sent unto them Peter and John: 15 who, when they were come down, prayed for them, that they might receive the Holy Ghost: 16 (for as yet he was fallen upon none of them: only they were baptized in the name of the Lord Jesus.) 17 Then laid they *their* hands on them, and they received the Holy Ghost. 18 And when Simon saw that through laying on of the apostles' hands the Holy Ghost was given, he offered them money, 19 saying, Give me also this power, that on whomsoever I lay hands, he may receive the Holy Ghost. 20 But Peter said unto him, Thy money perish with thee, because thou hast thought that the gift of God may be purchased with money. 21 Thou hast neither part nor lot in this matter: for thy heart is not right in the sight of God. 22 Repent therefore of this thy wickedness, and pray God, if perhaps the thought of thine heart may be forgiven thee. 23 For I perceive that thou art in the gall of bitterness, and *in* the bond of iniquity. 24 Then answered Simon, and said, Pray ye to the Lord for me, that none of these things which ye have spoken come upon me.

---

[h] — τὰ LTTrAW. [i] — τοῦ GLTTrAW. [k] δυνάμεις καὶ σημεῖα μεγάλα γινόμενα GW. [l] Σαμαρία T. [m] — τὸν LTTrAW. [n] Ἰωάνην Tr. [o] οὐδέπω LTTrAW. [p] ἐπετίθεσαν LTTrA [q] ἰδὼν GLTTrAW. [r] — τὸ ἅγιον T[Tr]A. [s] ἐὰν EGLTTrAW. [t] ἔναντι GLTTrAW. [v] τοῦ κυρίου the Lord LTTrAW.

25 And they, when
they had testified and
preached the word of
the Lord, returned
to Jerusalem, and
preached the gospel
in many villages of the
Samaritans.

26 And the angel
of the Lord spake
unto Philip, saying,
Arise, and go toward
the south unto the
way that goeth down
from Jerusalem unto
Gaza, which is desert.
27 And he arose and
went: and, behold, a
man of Ethiopia, an
eunuch of great autho-
rity under Candace
queen of the Ethio-
pians, who had the
charge of all her trea-
sure, and had come to
Jerusalem for to wor-
ship, 28 was returning,
and sitting in his cha-
riot read Esaias the
prophet. 29 Then the
Spirit said unto Philip,
Go near, and join thy-
self to this chariot.
30 And Philip ran
thither to *him*, and
heard him read the
prophet Esaias, and
said, Understandest
thou what thou read-
est? 31 And he said,
How can I, except
some man should guide
me? And he desired
Philip that he would
come up and sit with
him. 32 The place of
the scripture which he
read was this, He was
led as a sheep to the
slaughter; and like a
lamb dumb before his
shearer, so opened he
not his mouth: 33 in his
humiliation his judg-
ment was taken away:
and who shall declare
his generation? for his
life is taken from the
earth. 34 And the eu-
nuch answered Philip,
and said, I pray thee,
of whom speaketh the
prophet this? of him-
self, or of some other
man? 35 Then Philip
opened his mouth, and
began at the same

εἰρήκατε. 25 Οἱ μὲν οὖν διαμαρτυράμενοι καὶ λαλή-
ye have spoken. They therefore having earnestly testified and having
σαντες τὸν λόγον τοῦ κυρίου, [w]ὑπέστρεψαν" εἰς [x]Ἱερουσαλήμ,"
spoken the word of the Lord, returned to Jerusalem,
πολλάς.τε κώμας τῶν [y]Σαμαρειτῶν" [z]εὐηγγελίσαντο."
and [to] many villages of the Samaritans announced the glad tidings.

26 Ἄγγελος.δὲ κυρίου ἐλάλησεν πρὸς Φίλιππον, λέγων,
But an angel of [the] Lord spoke to Philip, saying,
Ἀνάστηθι καὶ [a]πορεύου" κατὰ μεσημβρίαν, ἐπὶ τὴν ὁδὸν
Rise up and go towards [the] south, on the way
τὴν καταβαίνουσαν ἀπὸ Ἱερουσαλὴμ εἰς Γάζαν· αὕτη
which goes down from Jerusalem to Gaza: the same
ἐστὶν ἔρημος. 27 καὶ ἀναστὰς ἐπορεύθη· καὶ ἰδού, ἀνὴρ
is desert. And having risen up he went. And lo, a man
Αἰθίοψ εὐνοῦχος δυνάστης Κανδάκης [b]τῆς" βασιλίσσης
an Ethiopian, a eunuch, one in power under Candace the queen
Αἰθιόπων, ὃς ἦν ἐπὶ πάσης τῆς.γάζης.αὐτῆς, [c]ὃς"
of [the] Ethiopians, who was over all her treasure, who
ἐληλύθει προσκυνήσων εἰς Ἱερουσαλήμ, 28 ἦν.τε ὑποστρέφων
had come ³to ⁴worship ¹to ²Jerusalem, and was returning
καὶ καθήμενος ἐπὶ τοῦ.ἅρματος.αὐτοῦ, [d]καὶ" ἀνεγίνωσκεν [e]
and sitting in his chariot, and he was reading
τὸν προφήτην Ἡσαΐαν. 29 εἶπεν.δὲ τὸ πνεῦμα τῷ Φιλίππῳ,
the prophet Esaias. And said the Spirit to Philip,
Πρόσελθε καὶ κολλήθητι τῷ.ἅρματι.τούτῳ. 30 Προσδραμὼν.δὲ
Go near and join thyself to this chariot. And running up
ὁ Φίλιππος ἤκουσεν αὐτοῦ ἀναγινώσκοντος [f]τὸν προφήτην
Philip heard him reading the prophet
Ἡσαΐαν," καὶ εἶπεν, [g]Ἆρά.γε" γινώσκεις ἃ ἀναγινώσκεις;
Esaias, and said, ³Then ¹dost ²thou know what thou readest?
31 Ὁ.δὲ εἶπεν, Πῶς.γὰρ ἂν.δυναίμην ἐὰν.μή τις [h]ὁδη-
But he said, [No,] for how should I be able unless some one should
γήσῃ" με; Παρεκάλεσέν.τε τὸν Φίλιππον ἀναβάντα καθίσαι
guide me? And he besought Philip having come up to sit
σὺν αὐτῷ. 32 ἡ.δὲ περιοχὴ τῆς γραφῆς ἣν ἀνεγίνωσκεν
with him. And the passage of the scripture which he was reading
ἦν αὕτη, Ὡς πρόβατον ἐπὶ σφαγὴν ἤχθη, καὶ ὡς ἀμνὸς
was this, As a sheep to slaughter he was led, and as a lamb
ἐναντίον τοῦ [i]κείροντος" αὐτὸν ἄφωνος, οὕτως οὐκ.ἀνοίγει
before him who shears him [is] dumb, thus he opens not
τὸ.στόμα.αὐτοῦ. 33 ἐν τῇ.ταπεινώσει.[k]αὐτοῦ" ἡ.κρίσις.αὐτοῦ
his mouth. In his humiliation his judgment
ἤρθη, τὴν.[l]δὲ" γενεὰν αὐτοῦ τίς διηγήσεται; ὅτι
was taken away, and the generation of him who shall declare? for
αἴρεται ἀπὸ τῆς γῆς ἡ.ζωὴ.αὐτοῦ. 34 Ἀποκριθεὶς.δὲ ὁ εὐνοῦχος
is taken from the earth his life. And answering the eunuch
τῷ Φιλίππῳ εἶπεν, Δέομαί σου, περὶ τίνος ὁ προφήτης
²to ³Philip ¹said, I pray thee, concerning whom ²the ³prophet
λέγει τοῦτο; περὶ ἑαυτοῦ, ἢ περὶ ἑτέρου.τινός;
¹says this? concerning himself, or concerning some other?
35 Ἀνοίξας.δὲ ὁ Φίλιππος τὸ.στόμα.αὐτοῦ, καὶ ἀρξάμενος
And ²having ³opened ¹Philip his mouth, and having begun

---

[w] ὑπέστρεφον were returning LTTrAW. [x] Ἱεροσόλυμα LTTrA. [y] Σαμαριτῶν T. [z] εὐηγγελίζοντο were announcing the glad tidings LTTrAW. [a] πορεύθητι L. [b] — τῆς LTTrAW. [c] — ὃς LT[Tr]. [d] — καὶ LT[Tr]W. [e] + τε, and L. [f] Ἡσαΐαν τὸν προφήτην LTTrA. [g] ἆράγε GT. [h] ὁδηγήσει shall guide TTr. [i] κείραντος TA. [k] — αὐτοῦ (*read* the humiliation) LTTr. [l] — δὲ and LTTr[A].

ἀπὸ τῆς.γραφῆς.ταύτης, εὐηγγελίσατο.αὐτῷ τὸν Ἰη-
from this scripture, announced to him the glad tidings— Je-
σοῦν. 36 ὡς.δὲ ἐπορεύοντο κατὰ τὴν ὁδόν, ἦλθον ἐπί
sus. And as they were going along the way, they came upon
τι ὕδωρ· καί φησιν ὁ εὐνοῦχος, Ἰδοὺ ὕδωρ· τί κωλύει
a certain water, and [3]says [1]the [2]eunuch, Behold water; what hinders
με βαπτισθῆναι; 37 [n]Εἶπεν δὲ ὁ Φίλιππος, Εἰ πιστεύεις ἐξ
me to be baptized? And [2]said [1]Philip, If thou believest from
ὅλης τῆς καρδίας, ἔξεστιν. Ἀποκριθεὶς.δὲ εἶπεν, Πιστεύω
[2]whole [1]the heart, it is lawful. And answering he said, I believe
τὸν υἱὸν τοῦ θεοῦ εἶναι τὸν Ἰησοῦν χριστόν.‖ 38 Καὶ ἐκέλευ-
[5]the [6]Son [7]of [8]God [3]to [4]be [1]Jesus [2]Christ. And he com-
σεν στῆναι τὸ ἅρμα· καὶ κατέβησαν ἀμφότεροι εἰς
manded [3]to [4]stand [5]still [1]the [2]chariot. And they went down both to
τὸ ὕδωρ, ὅ.τε.Φίλιππος καὶ ὁ εὐνοῦχος· καὶ ἐβάπτισεν αὐτόν.
the water, both Philip and the eunuch, and he baptized him.
39 ὅτε.δὲ ἀνέβησαν ἐκ τοῦ ὕδατος πνεῦμα κυρίου
But when they came up out of the water [the] Spirit of [the] Lord
ἥρπασεν τὸν Φίλιππον· καὶ οὐκ εἶδεν αὐτὸν οὐκέτι ὁ
caught away Philip, and [3]saw [4]him [5]no [6]longer [1]the
εὐνοῦχος, ἐπορεύετο.γὰρ τὴν.ὁδὸν.αὐτοῦ χαίρων. 40 Φίλιππος
[2]eunuch, for he went his way rejoicing. [2]Philip
δὲ εὑρέθη εἰς Ἄζωτον· καὶ διερχόμενος εὐηγ-
[1]but was found at Azotus, and passing through he announced the
γελίζετο τὰς πόλεις πάσας, ἕως τοῦ.ἐλθεῖν.αὐτὸν εἰς
glad tidings [to] [2]the [3]cities [1]all, till he came to
[o]Καισάρειαν.‖
Cæsarea.

9 Ὁ.δὲ.Σαῦλος ἔτι [p]ἐμπνέων‖ ἀπειλῆς καὶ φόνου εἰς
But Saul, still breathing out threatenings and slaughter towards
τοὺς μαθητὰς τοῦ κυρίου, προσελθὼν τῷ ἀρχιερεῖ 2 ᾐτήσατο
the disciples of the Lord, having come to the high priest asked
παρ' αὐτοῦ ἐπιστολὰς εἰς Δαμασκὸν πρὸς τὰς συναγωγάς,
from him letters to Damascus, to the synagogues,
ὅπως [q]ἐάν‖ τινας εὕρῃ [r]τῆς ὁδοῦ ὄντας‖ ἄνδρας.τε καὶ
so that if any he found [2]of [3]the [4]way [1]being both men and
γυναῖκας, δεδεμένους ἀγάγῃ εἰς Ἱερουσαλήμ. 3 ἐν.δὲ
women, having bound he might bring [them] to Jerusalem. But in
τῷ πορεύεσθαι ἐγένετο αὐτὸν ἐγγίζειν τῇ Δαμασκῷ, [s]καὶ
proceeding it came to pass he drew near to Damascus, and
ἐξαίφνης‖ [t]περιήστραψεν αὐτὸν‖ φῶς [v]ἀπὸ‖ τοῦ οὐρανοῦ·
suddenly shone round about him a light from the heaven,
4 καὶ πεσὼν ἐπὶ τὴν γῆν ἤκουσεν φωνὴν λέγουσαν αὐτῷ,
and having fallen on the earth he heard a voice saying to him,
Σαοὺλ, Σαοὺλ, τί με διώκεις; 5 Εἶπεν.δέ, Τίς εἶ[w],
Saul, Saul, why me dost thou persecute? And he said, Who art thou,
κύριε; Ὁ.δὲ [x]κύριος εἶπεν,‖ Ἐγώ εἰμι Ἰησοῦς [y] ὃν σὺ
Lord? And the Lord said, I am Jesus whom thou
διώκεις· [z]σκληρόν σοι πρὸς κέντρα λακτίζειν.
persecutest. [It is] hard for thee against [the] goads to kick.
6 Τρέμων.τε καὶ θαμβῶν εἶπεν, Κύριε, τί με θέλεις
And trembling and astonished he said, Lord, What me desirest thou

scripture, and preached
unto him Jesus. 36 And
as they went on *their*
way, they came unto
a certain water: and
the eunuch said, See,
here is water; what
doth hinder me to be
baptized? 37 And Phi-
lip said, If thou believ-
est with all thine heart,
thou mayest. And he
answered and said, I
believe that Jesus
Christ is the Son of
God. 38 And he com-
manded the chariot to
stand still: and they
went down both into
the water, both Philip
and the eunuch; and he
baptized him. 39 And
when they were come
up out of the water,
the Spirit of the Lord
caught away Philip,
that the eunuch saw
him no more: and he
went on his way re-
joicing. 40 But Philip
was found at Azotus:
and passing through
he preached in all the
cities, till he came to
Cæsarea.

IX. And Saul, yet
breathing out threat-
enings and slaughter
against the disciples of
the Lord, went unto
the high priest, 2 and
desired of him letters
to Damascus to the
synagogues, that if he
found any of this way,
whether they were men
or women, he might
bring them bound un-
to Jerusalem. 3 And
as he journeyed, he
came near Damascus:
and suddenly there
shined round about
him a light from hea-
ven: 4 and he fell to
the earth, and heard a
voice saying unto him,
Saul, Saul, why perse-
cutest thou me? 5 And
he said, Who art thou,
Lord? And the Lord
said, I am Jesus whom
thou persecutest: *it is*
hard for thee to kick a-
gainst the pricks. 6 And
he trembling and asto-
nished said, Lord, what
wilt thou have me to

---

[n] — *verse* 37 GLTTrA. [o] Καισαρίαν T. [p] ἐνπνέων T. [q] ἄν T. [r] ὄντας τῆς ὁδοῦ, T.
[s] ἐξαίφνης τε LTTrAW. [t] περιέστραψεν αὐτὸν E; αὐτὸν περιέ- L; αὐτὸν περιή- TTrAW.
[v] ἐκ out of LTTrW. [w] + [σύ] A. [x] — κύριος εἶπεν (*read* he [said]) LTTrAW. [y] + ὁ
Ναζωραῖος the Nazarene [L]W. [z] — σκληρόν .... πρὸς αὐτόν (*verse* 6) GLTTrAW.

do? And the Lord
said unto him, Arise,
and go into the city,
and it shall be told
thee what thou must
do. 7 And the men
which journeyed with
him stood speechless,
hearing a voice, but
seeing no man. 8 And
Saul arose from the
earth; and when his
eyes were opened, he
saw no man: but they
led him by the hand,
and brought *him* into
Damascus. 9 And he
was three days with-
out sight, and neither
did eat nor drink.
10 And there was a
certain disciple at Da-
mascus, named Ana-
nias; and to him said
the Lord in a vision,
Ananias. And he said,
Behold, I *am here*,
Lord. 11 And the
Lord *said* unto him,
Arise, and go into the
street which is called
Straight, and inquire
in the house of Judas
for *one* called Saul, of
Tarsus: for, behold, he
prayeth, 12 and hath
seen in a vision a man
named Ananias com-
ing in, and putting
his hand on him, that
he might receive his
sight. 13 Then Ananias
answered, Lord, I have
heard by many of this
man, how much evil he
hath done to thy saints
at Jerusalem: 14 and
here he hath authority
from the chief priests
to bind all that call on
thy name. 15 But the
Lord said unto him,
Go thy way: for he is
a chosen vessel unto
me, to bear my name
before the Gentiles,
and kings, and the
children of Israel:
16 for I will shew him
how great things he
must suffer for my
name's sake. 17 And
Ananias went his way,
and entered into the
house; and putting his
hands on him said,
Brother Saul, the Lord,

ποιῆσαι; Καὶ ὁ κύριος πρὸς αὐτόν,‖ [a]Ἀνάστηθι καὶ
to do? And the Lord [said] to him, Rise up and
εἴσελθε εἰς τὴν πόλιν, καὶ λαληθήσεταί σοι [b]τί‖ σε δεῖ
enter into the city, and it shall be told thee what thee it behoves
ποιεῖν. 7 Οἱ.δὲ ἄνδρες οἱ συνοδεύοντες αὐτῷ εἱστήκεισαν
to do. But the men who were travelling with him stood
[c]ἐννεοί,‖ ἀκούοντες .μὲν τῆς φωνῆς μηδένα.δὲ θεωροῦντες.
speechless, hearing indeed the voice but no one seeing.
8 ἠγέρθη.δὲ [d]ὁ‖ Σαῦλος ἀπὸ τῆς γῆς· [e]ἀνεῳγμένων‖.δὲ τῶν
And rose up Saul from the earth, and having been opened
ὀφθαλμῶν.αὐτοῦ [f]οὐδένα‖ ἔβλεπεν. χειραγωγοῦντες.δὲ αὐτὸν
his eyes no one he saw. But leading [2]by [3]the [4]hand [1]him
εἰσήγαγον εἰς Δαμασκόν. 9 καὶ ἦν ἡμέρας τρεῖς μὴ βλέ-
they brought [him] to Damascus. And he was [2]days [1]three not see-
πων, καὶ οὐκ.ἔφαγεν οὐδὲ ἔπιεν. 10 Ἦν.δέ τις μαθητὴς
ing, and did not eat nor drink. And there was a certain disciple
ἐν Δαμασκῷ ὀνόματι Ἀνανίας· καὶ εἶπεν πρὸς αὐτὸν [g]ὁ κύριος
in Damascus by name Ananias. And [3]said [4]to [5]him [1]the [2]Lord
ἐν ὁράματι,‖ Ἀνανία. Ὁ.δὲ εἶπεν, Ἰδοὺ ἐγώ, κύριε.
in a vision, Ananias. And he said, Behold [here am] I, Lord.
11 Ὁ.δὲ κύριος πρὸς αὐτόν, [h]Ἀναστὰς‖ πορεύθητι ἐπὶ
And the Lord to him [said], Having risen up go into
τὴν ῥύμην τὴν καλουμένην Εὐθεῖαν, καὶ ζήτησον ἐν οἰκίᾳ
the street which is called Straight, and seek in [the] house
Ἰούδα Σαῦλον ὀνόματι, Ταρσέα. ἰδοὺ.γὰρ προσεύχεται,
of Judas [one] Saul by name, of Tarsus: for lo he prays,
12 καὶ εἶδεν [i]ἐν ὁράματι ἄνδρα‖ [k]ὀνόματι Ἀνανίαν‖ εἰσελθόντα
and he saw in a vision a man by name Ananias coming
καὶ ἐπιθέντα αὐτῷ [l]χεῖρα,‖ ὅπως ἀναβλέψῃ. 13 Ἀπε-
and putting on him a hand, so that he should receive sight. [2]An-
κρίθη δὲ [m]ὁ‖ Ἀνανίας, Κύριε, [n]ἀκήκοα‖ ἀπὸ πολλῶν περὶ
swered [1]and Ananias, Lord, I have heard from many concerning
τοῦ.ἀνδρὸς.τούτου, ὅσα κακὰ [o]ἐποίησεν τοῖς.ἁγίοις.σου‖ ἐν
this man, how many evils he did to thy saints in
Ἰερουσαλήμ· 14 καὶ ὧδε ἔχει ἐξουσίαν παρὰ τῶν ἀρχιερέων
Jerusalem; and here he has authority from the chief priests
δῆσαι πάντας τοὺς ἐπικαλουμένους τὸ.ὄνομά.σου. 15 Εἶπεν.δὲ
to bind all who call on thy name. And [3]said
πρὸς αὐτὸν ὁ κύριος, Πορεύου, ὅτι σκεῦος ἐκλογῆς [p]μοί
[4]to [5]him [1]the [2]Lord, Go, for a vessel of election to me
ἐστιν‖ οὗτος, τοῦ βαστάσαι τὸ.ὄνομά.μου ἐνώπιον [q]ἐθνῶν [r]
is this [man], to bear my name before Gentiles
καὶ βασιλέων, υἱῶν.τε Ἰσραήλ. 16 ἐγὼ.γὰρ ὑποδείξω
and kings, and [the] sons of Israel: for I will shew
αὐτῷ ὅσα δεῖ αὐτὸν ὑπὲρ τοῦ.ὀνόματός.μου παθεῖν.
to him how much it behoves him for my name to suffer.
17 Ἀπῆλθεν.δὲ Ἀνανίας καὶ εἰσῆλθεν εἰς τὴν οἰκίαν, καὶ
And [2]went [3]away [1]Ananias and entered into the house; and
ἐπιθεὶς ἐπ' αὐτὸν τὰς χεῖρας εἶπεν, Σαοὺλ ἀδελφέ, ὁ
having laid upon him [his] hands he said, [2]Saul [1]brother, the

---

[a] + ἀλλὰ but GLTTrAW. [b] ὅ τι LTTrA. [c] ἐνεοί LTTrAW. [d] — ὁ LTTrAW. [e] ἠνεῳγμένων LA; ἠνοιγμένων T. [f] οὐδὲν nothing LTTrW. [g] ἐν ὁράματι ὁ κύριος LTTrAW. [h] Ἀνάστα Rise up L. [i] — ἐν ὁράματι LTA; ἄνδρα [ἐν ὁράματι] Tr. [k] Ἀνανίαν ὀνόματι LTTrA. [l] τὰς (— τὰς TTr) χεῖρας the hands LTTr. [m] — ὁ GLTTrAW. [n] ἤκουσα I heard LTTrA. [o] τοῖς ἁγίοις σου ἐποίησεν LTTrA. [p] ἐστίν μοι LTTrAW. [q] + τῶν the L. [r] + τε both (Gentiles) LTTrAW.

κύριος ἀπέσταλκέν με, Ἰησοῦς ὁ ὀφθείς σοι ἐν τῇ ὁδῷ
Lord has sent me, Jesus who appeared to thee in the way
ᾗ ἤρχου, ὅπως ἀναβλέψῃς καὶ πλησθῇς πνεύ-
in which thou camest, that thou mightest receive sight and be filled with [the]
ματος ἁγίου. 18 Καὶ εὐθέως [s]ἀπέπεσον ἀπὸ τῶν ὀφθαλμῶν
[3]Spirit [1]Holy. And immediately fell from [2]eyes
αὐτοῦ‖ [t]ὡσεὶ‖ λεπίδες, ἀνέβλεψέν.τε [v]παραχρῆμα,‖ καὶ
[1]his as it were scales, and he received sight instantly, and
ἀναστὰς ἐβαπτίσθη, 19 καὶ λαβὼν τροφὴν ἐνίσχυσεν·
having risen up was baptized; and having taken food he was strengthened.
Ἐγένετο.δὲ [w]ὁ Σαῦλος‖ μετὰ τῶν ἐν Δαμασκῷ μαθητῶν ἡμέρας
And [2]was [1]Saul with the [2]in [3]Damascus [1]disciples [5]days
τινάς· 20 καὶ εὐθέως ἐν ταῖς συναγωγαῖς ἐκήρυσσεν
[4]certain. And immediately in the synagogues he was proclaiming
τὸν [x]χριστόν,‖ ὅτι οὗτός ἐστιν ὁ υἱὸς τοῦ θεοῦ. 21 ἐξίσταντο.δὲ
Christ, that he is the Son of God. And [2]were [3]amazed
πάντες οἱ ἀκούοντες, καὶ ἔλεγον, Οὐχ οὗτός ἐστιν ὁ πορθήσας
[1]all who heard, and said, [2]Not [3]this [1]is he who destroyed
[y]ἐν‖ Ἱερουσαλὴμ τοὺς ἐπικαλουμένους τὸ.ὄνομα.τοῦτο, καὶ
in Jerusalem those who called on this name, and
ὧδε εἰς τοῦτο ἐληλύθει ἵνα δεδεμένους αὐτοὺς ἀγάγῃ
here for this had come that [5]bound [4]them [1]he [2]might [3]bring
ἐπὶ τοὺς ἀρχιερεῖς; 22 Σαῦλος.δὲ μᾶλλον ἐνεδυναμοῦτο, καὶ
to the chief priests? But Saul more increased in power, and
[z]συνέχυνεν‖ [a]τοὺς‖ Ἰουδαίους τοὺς κατοικοῦντας ἐν Δαμασκῷ,
confounded the Jews who dwelt in Damascus,
συμβιβάζων ὅτι οὗτός ἐστιν ὁ χριστός. 23 ὡς.δὲ ἐπληροῦντο
proving that this is the Christ. Now when were fulfilled
ἡμέραι ἱκαναί, συνεβουλεύσαντο οἱ Ἰουδαῖοι ἀνελεῖν αὐ-
[2]days [1]many, [5]consulted [6]together [3]the [4]Jews to put to death him.
τόν· 24 ἐγνώσθη.δὲ τῷ Σαύλῳ ἡ.ἐπιβουλὴ.αὐτῶν. [b]παρε-
But became known to Saul their plot. [2]They [3]were
τήρουν‖ [c]τε‖ τὰς πύλας ἡμέρας.τε καὶ νυκτός, ὅπως αὐτὸν
[4]watching [1]and the gates both day and night, that him
ἀνέλωσιν· 25 λαβόντες.δὲ [d]αὐτὸν οἱ μαθηταὶ‖ νυκτὸς
they might put to death; but taking him the disciples by night
[e]καθῆκαν διὰ τοῦ τείχους‖ [f], χαλάσαντες ἐν σπυρίδι.
let down [2]through [3]the [4]wall [[1]him], lowering [him] in a basket.

even Jesus, that appeared unto thee in the way as thou camest, hath sent me, that thou mightest receive thy sight, and be filled with the Holy Ghost. 18 And immediately there fell from his eyes as it had been scales: and he received sight forthwith, and arose, and was baptized. 19 And when he had received meat, he was strengthened. Then was Saul certain days with the disciples which were at Damascus. 20 And straightway he preached Christ in the synagogues, that he is the Son of God. 21 But all that heard *him* were amazed, and said; Is not this he that destroyed them which called on this name in Jerusalem, and came hither for that intent, that he might bring them bound unto the chief priests? 22 But Saul increased the more in strength, and confounded the Jews which dwelt at Damascus, proving that this is very Christ. 23 And after that many days were fulfilled, the Jews took counsel to kill him: 24 but their laying await was known of Saul. And they watched the gates day and night to kill him. 25 Then the disciples took him by night, and let *him* down by the wall in a basket.

26 Παραγενόμενος.δὲ [g]ὁ Σαῦλος‖ [h]εἰς‖ Ἱερουσαλήμ, [i]ἐπει-
And [2]having [3]arrived [1]Saul at Jerusalem, he at-
ρᾶτο‖ κολλᾶσθαι τοῖς μαθηταῖς· καὶ πάντες ἐφοβοῦντο
tempted to join himself to the disciples, and all were afraid of
αὐτόν, μὴ πιστεύοντες ὅτι ἐστὶν μαθητής. 27 Βαρνάβας.δὲ
him, not believing that he is a disciple. But Barnabas
ἐπιλαβόμενος αὐτόν, ἤγαγεν πρὸς τοὺς ἀποστόλους, καὶ
having taken him, brought [him] to the apostles, and
διηγήσατο αὐτοῖς πῶς ἐν τῇ ὁδῷ εἶδεν τὸν κύριον, καὶ ὅτι
related to them how in the way he saw the Lord, and that
ἐλάλησεν αὐτῷ, καὶ πῶς ἐν Δαμασκῷ ἐπαῤῥησιάσατο ἐν τῷ
he spoke to him, and how in Damascus he spoke boldly in the
ὀνόματι [k]τοῦ‖ Ἰησοῦ. 28 καὶ ἦν μετ' αὐτῶν εἰσπορευόμενος
name of Jesus. And he was with them coming in

26 And when Saul was come to Jerusalem, he assayed to join himself to the disciples: but they were all afraid of him, and believed not that he was a disciple. 27 But Barnabas took him, and brought *him* to the apostles, and declared unto them how he had seen the Lord in the way, and that he had spoken to him, and how he had preached boldly at Damascus in the name of Jesus. 28 And he was with them coming in and going out

---

[s] ἀπέπεσαν αὐτοῦ ἀπὸ τῶν ὀφθαλμῶν LTTrA. [t] ὡς LTTr. [v] — παραχρῆμα GLTTrA. [w] — ὁ Σαῦλος (*read* he was) GLTTrAW. [x] Ἰησοῦν Jesus GLTTrAW. [y] εἰς at T. [z] συνέχυννεν TA. [a] — τοὺς T. [b] παρετηροῦντο LTTrAW. [c] δὲ καὶ and also LTTrA. [d] οἱ μαθηταὶ αὐτοῦ his disciples LTTrA. [e] διὰ τοῦ τείχους καθῆκαν LTTrA. [f] + αὐτὸν him LTTrA. [g] — ὁ Σαῦλος GLTTrAW. [h] ἐν in L. [i] ἐπείραζεν LTTr. [k] — τοῦ LTTrA.

at Jerusalem. 29 And
he spake boldly in the
name of the Lord Je-
sus, and disputed a-
gainst the Grecians:
but they went about to
slay him. 30 *Which*
when the brethren
knew, they brought
him down to Cæsarea,
and sent him forth to
Tarsus. 31 Then had
the churches rest
throughout all Judæa
and Galilee and Sama-
ria, and were edified;
and walking in the
fear of the Lord, and
in the comfort of the
Holy Ghost, were mul-
tiplied.

32 And it came to
pass, as Peter passed
throughout all *quar-
ters*, he came down
also to the saints which
dwelt at Lydda. 33 And
there he found a cer-
tain man named Æne-
as, which had kept
his bed eight years,
and was sick of the
palsy. 34 And Peter
said unto him, Æneas,
Jesus Christ maketh
thee whole: arise, and
make thy bed. And
he arose immediately.
35 And all that dwelt
at Lydda and Saron
saw him, and turned
to the Lord.

36 Now there was at
Joppa a certain disci-
ple named Tabitha,
which by interpreta-
tion is called Dorcas:
this woman was full
of good works and
almsdeeds which she
did. 37 And it came
to pass in those days,
that she was sick, and
died: whom when they
had washed, they laid
her in an upper cham-
ber. 38 And forasmuch
as Lydda was nigh to
Joppa, and the disci-
ples had heard that
Peter was there, they
sent unto him two men,
desiring *him* that he

καὶ ἐκπορευόμενος [l]ἐν‖ Ἱερουσαλήμ. [m]καὶ‖ παῤῥησιαζόμενος
and going out in Jerusalem, and speaking boldly
ἐν τῷ ὀνόματι τοῦ κυρίου [n]Ἰησοῦ·‖ 29 ἐλάλει.τε καὶ συνεζήτει
in the name of the Lord Jesus. And he spoke and discussed
πρὸς τοὺς Ἑλληνιστάς· οἱ.δὲ ἐπεχείρουν [o]αὐτὸν ἀνε-
with the Hellenists; but they took in hand [3]him [1]to [2]put to
λεῖν.‖ 30 ἐπιγνόντες.δὲ οἱ ἀδελφοὶ κατήγαγον αὐτὸν εἰς
death. But having known [it] the brethren brought down him to
[p]Καισάρειαν,‖ καὶ ἐξαπέστειλαν [q]αὐτὸν‖ εἰς Ταρσόν. 31 [r]Αἱ‖
Cæsarea, and sent away him to Tarsus. The
μὲν οὖν [s]ἐκκλησίαι‖ καθ' ὅλης τῆς Ἰουδαίας καὶ Γαλι-
[2]indeed [3]then [1]assemblies throughout [2]whole [1]the of Judæa and Gali-
λαίας καὶ [t]Σαμαρείας‖ [v]εἶχον‖ εἰρήνην, [w]οἰκοδομούμεναι καὶ
lee and Samaria had peace, being built up and
πορευόμεναι‖ τῷ φόβῳ τοῦ κυρίου, καὶ τῇ παρακλήσει τοῦ
going on in the fear of the Lord, and in the comfort of the
ἁγίου πνεύματος [x]ἐπληθύνοντο.‖
Holy Spirit were increased.

32 Ἐγένετο.δὲ Πέτρον διερχόμενον διὰ πάντων,
Now it came to pass [that] Peter, passing through all
κατελθεῖν καὶ πρὸς τοὺς ἁγίους τοὺς κατοικοῦντας
[quarters], went down also to the saints that inhabited
[y]Λύδδαν.‖ 33 εὗρεν.δὲ ἐκεῖ ἄνθρωπόν.τινα [z]Αἰνέαν ὀνόματι,‖
Lydda, And he found there a certain man, Æneas by name,
ἐξ ἐτῶν ὀκτὼ κατακείμενον ἐπὶ [a]κραββάτῳ,‖ ὃς ἦν παρα-
for [2]years [1]eight lying on a couch, who was para-
λελυμένος. 34 καὶ εἶπεν αὐτῷ ὁ Πέτρος, Αἰνέα, ἰᾶταί σε
lysed. And [2]said [3]to [4]him [1]Peter, Æneas, [4]heals [5]thee
Ἰησοῦς [b]ὁ‖ χριστός· ἀνάστηθι καὶ στρῶσον σεαυτῷ.
[1]Jesus [2]the [3]Christ; rise up, and spread [a couch] for thyself.
Καὶ εὐθέως ἀνέστη· 35 καὶ [c]εἶδον‖ αὐτὸν πάντες οἱ
And immediately he rose up. And saw him all those
κατοικοῦντες [y]Λύδδαν‖ καὶ τὸν [d]Σαρωνᾶν,‖ οἵτινες ἐπέστρεψαν
inhabiting Lydda and the Saron, who turned
ἐπὶ τὸν κύριον.
to the Lord.

36 Ἐν.Ἰόππῃ.δὲ τις ἦν μαθήτρια ὀνόματι Ταβιθά,
And in Joppa [2]a [3]certain [1]was disciple, by name Tabitha,
ἣ διερμηνευομένη λέγεται Δορκάς· αὕτη ἦν πλήρης [e]ἀγαθῶν
which being interpreted is called Dorcas, She was full of good
ἔργων‖ καὶ ἐλεημοσυνῶν ὧν ἐποίει· 37 ἐγένετο.δὲ ἐν ταῖς
works and of alms which she did. And it came to pass in
ἡμέραις.ἐκείναις ἀσθενήσασαν αὐτὴν ἀποθανεῖν· λούσαν-
those days [that] having sickened she died; [2]having
τες δὲ [f]αὐτὴν ἔθηκαν‖ ἐν [g] ὑπερῴῳ. 38 ἐγγὺς.δὲ
[3]washed [1]and her they put [her] in an upper room. And [3]near
οὔσης [h]Λύδδης‖ τῇ Ἰόππῃ, οἱ μαθηταὶ ἀκούσαντες ὅτι Πέτρος
[2]being [1]Lydda to Joppa, the disciples having heard that Peter
ἐστὶν ἐν αὐτῇ ἀπέστειλαν δύο ἄνδρας πρὸς αὐτόν, παρα-
is in it sent two men to him, beseech-

---

[l] εἰς at LTTrAW. [m] — καὶ LTTrA. [n] — Ἰησοῦ LTTrAW. [o] ἀνελεῖν αὐτόν LTTrAW. [p] Καισαρίαν T. [q] — αὐτὸν L. [r] Ἡ LTTrAW. [s] ἐκκλησία assembly LTTrAW. [t] Σαμαρίας T. [v] εἶχεν LTTrAW. [w] οἰκοδομουμένη καὶ πορευομένη LTTrAW. [x] ἐπληθύνετο was increased LTTrAW. [y] Λύδδα LTTrA. [z] ὀνόματι Αἰνέαν LTTrAW. [a] κραβάττου LTTrAW. [b] — ὁ LTTrW. [c] εἶδαν LTTrA. [d] Σάρωνα EGLTTrAW. [e] ἔργων ἀγαθῶν LTrW. [f] ἔθηκαν αὐτὴν TTr. [g] + τῷ the L. [h] Λύδδας TTrA.

καλοῦντες [i]μὴ ὀκνῆσαι‖ διελθεῖν ἕως [k]αὐτῶν.‖ 39 ἀναστὰς
ing [him] not to delay to come to them. [2]Having [3]risen [4]up

δὲ Πέτρος συνῆλθεν αὐτοῖς· ὃν παραγενόμενον ἀνήγαγον
[1]and Peter went with them, whom, having arrived they brought

εἰς τὸ ὑπερῷον, καὶ παρέστησαν αὐτῷ πᾶσαι αἱ χῆραι
into the upper room, and stood by him all the widows

κλαίουσαι καὶ ἐπιδεικνύμεναι χιτῶνας καὶ ἱμάτια ὅσα ἐ-
weeping and shewing tunics and garments which [2]was

ποίει μετ' αὐτῶν οὖσα ἡ Δορκάς. 40 ἐκβαλὼν.δὲ ἔξω πάντας
[3]making [5]with [6]them [4]being [1]Dorcas. But [2]having [3]put [5]out [4]all

ὁ Πέτρος, [l]θεὶς τὰ γόνατα προσηύξατο· καὶ ἐπιστρέψας
[1]Peter, having bowed the knees he prayed. And having turned

πρὸς τὸ σῶμα εἶπεν, Ταβιθά, ἀνάστηθι. Ἡ.δὲ ἤνοιξεν
to the body he said, Tabitha, Arise. And she opened

τοὺς.ὀφθαλμοὺς.αὐτῆς· καὶ ἰδοῦσα τὸν Πέτρον ἀνεκάθισεν.
her eyes, and seeing Peter she sat up.

41 δοὺς.δὲ αὐτῇ χεῖρα ἀνέστησεν αὐτήν, φωνήσας.δὲ
And having given her [his] hand he raised up her, and having called

τοὺς ἁγίους καὶ τὰς χήρας παρέστησεν αὐτὴν ζῶσαν. 42 γνω-
the saints and the widows he presented her living. [4]Known

στὸν δὲ ἐγένετο καθ' ὅλης [m]τῆς‖ Ἰόππης, καὶ [n]πολλοὶ
[1]and [2]it [3]became throughout [2]whole [1]the of Joppa, and many

ἐπίστευσαν‖ ἐπὶ τὸν κύριον· 43 ἐγένετο.δὲ [o]ἡμέρας
believed on the Lord. And it came to pass [that] [4]days

ἱκανὰς μεῖναι αὐτὸν‖ ἐν Ἰόππῃ παρά τινι Σίμωνι βυρσεῖ.
[3]many [2]abode [1]he in Joppa with a certain Simon a tanner.

10 Ἀνὴρ.δέ.τις [p]ἦν‖ ἐν [q]Καισαρείᾳ‖ ὀνόματι Κορνήλιος,
But a certain man was in Cæsarea by name Cornelius,

ἑκατοντάρχης ἐκ σπείρης τῆς καλουμένης Ἰταλικῆς, 2 εὐ-
a centurion of a band which is called Italic, pious

σεβὴς καὶ φοβούμενος τὸν θεὸν σὺν παντὶ τῷ.οἴκῳ.αὐτοῦ,
and fearing God with all his house,

ποιῶν.[r]τε‖ ἐλεημοσύνας πολλὰς τῷ λαῷ, καὶ δεόμενος
both doing [2]alms [1]much to the people, and supplicating

τοῦ θεοῦ [s]διαπαντός.‖ 3 εἶδεν ἐν ὁράματι φανερῶς, ὡσεὶ [t]
God continually, He saw in a vision plainly, about

ὥραν [v]ἐννάτην‖ τῆς ἡμέρας, ἄγγελον τοῦ θεοῦ εἰσελθόντα
[3]hour [1]the [2]ninth of the day, an angel of God coming

πρὸς αὐτόν, καὶ εἰπόντα αὐτῷ, Κορνήλιε. 4 Ὁ.δὲ ἀτε-
to him, and saying to him, Cornelius. But he having looked

νίσας αὐτῷ καὶ ἔμφοβος γενόμενος εἶπεν, Τί ἐστιν, κύριε;
intently on him and [2]afraid [1]becoming said, What is it, Lord?

εἶπεν.δὲ αὐτῷ, Αἱ.προσευχαί.σου καὶ αἱ.ἐλεημοσύναι.σου
And he said to him, Thy prayers and thine alms

ἀνέβησαν εἰς μνημόσυνον [w]ἐνώπιον‖ τοῦ θεοῦ. 5 καὶ νῦν
are gone up for a memorial before God. And now

πέμψον [x]εἰς Ἰόππην ἄνδρας,‖ καὶ μετάπεμψαι Σίμωνα [y] ὃς
send [2]to [3]Joppa [1]men, and send for Simon who

ἐπικαλεῖται Πέτρος· 6 οὗτος ξενίζεται παρά τινι Σίμωνι
is surnamed Peter. He lodges with a certain Simon

βυρσεῖ, ᾧ ἐστιν οἰκία παρὰ θάλασσαν· [z]οὗτος λαλήσει σοι
a tanner, whose [2]is [1]house by [the] sea; he shall tell thee

would not delay to come to them. 39 Then Peter arose and went with them. When he was come, they brought him into the upper chamber: and all the widows stood by him weeping, and shewing the coats and garments which Dorcas made, while she was with them. 40 But Peter put them all forth, and kneeled down, and prayed; and turning *him* to the body said, Tabitha, arise. And she opened her eyes: and when she saw Peter, she sat up. 41 And he gave her *his* hand, and lifted her up, and when he had called the saints and widows, presented her alive. 42 And it was known throughout all Joppa; and many believed in the Lord. 43 And it came to pass, that he tarried many days in Joppa with one Simon a tanner.

X. There was a certain man in Cæsarea called Cornelius, a centurion of the band called the Italian *band*, 2 *a* devout *man*, and one that feared God with all his house, which gave much alms to the people, and prayed to God alway. 3 He saw in a vision evidently about the ninth hour of the day an angel of God coming in to him, and saying unto him, Cornelius. 4 And when he looked on him, he was afraid, and said, What is it, Lord? And he said unto him, Thy prayers and thine alms are come up for a memorial before God. 5 And now send men to Joppa, and call for *one* Simon, whose surname is Peter: 6 he lodgeth with one Simon a tanner, whose house is by the sea side: he shall tell thee what

[i] μὴ ὀκνήσῃς delay not LTTrAW. [k] ἡμῶν us LTTrAW. [l] + καὶ and LTTrAW. [m] [τῆς] Tr. [n] ἐπίστευσαν πολλοὶ LTTrAW. [o] αὐτὸν ἡμέρας ἱκανὰς μεῖναι LTr; — αὐτὸν T. [p] — ἦν GLTTrAW. [q] Καισαρίᾳ T. [r] — τε LTTrAW. [s] διὰ παντός LTrA. [t] + περὶ LTTrAW. [v] ἐνάτην LTTrAW. [w] ἔμπροσθεν LTTrA. [x] ἄνδρας εἰς Ἰόππην LTTrAW. [y] + τινα a certain (Simon) LTTrA. [z] — οὗτος λαλήσει σοι τί σε δεῖ ποιεῖν GLTTrAW.

thou oughtest to do.
7 And when the angel
which spake unto Cor-
nelius was departed, he
called two of his house-
hold servants, and a
devout soldier of them
that waited on him
continually; 8 and
when he had declared
all *these* things unto
them, he sent them to
Joppa. 9 On the mor-
row, as they went on
their journey, and
drew nigh unto the
city, Peter went up
upon the housetop to
pray about the sixth
hour: 10 and he be-
came very hungry, and
would have eaten: but
while they made ready,
he fell into a trance,
11 and saw heaven
opened, and a certain
vessel descending unto
him, as it had been a
great sheet knit at the
four corners, and let
down to the earth:
12 wherein were all
manner of fourfooted
beasts of the earth,
and wild beasts, and
creeping things, and
fowls of the air. 13 And
there came a voice to
him, Rise, Peter; kill,
and eat. 14 But Peter
said, Not so, Lord; for
I have never eaten any
thing that is common
or unclean. 15 And the
voice *spake* unto him
again the second time,
What God hath cleans-
ed, *that* call not thou
common. 16 This was
done thrice: and the
vessel was received up
again into heaven.
17 Now while Peter
doubted in himself
what this vision which
he had seen should
mean, behold, the men
which were sent from
Cornelius had made
inquiry for Simon's
house, and stood be-
fore the gate, 18 and
called, and asked
whether Simon, which
was surnamed Peter,
were lodged there.
19 While Peter thought
on the vision, the Spi-
rit said unto him, Be-

τί σε δεῖ ποιεῖν.‖ 7 Ὡς.δὲ ἀπῆλθεν ὁ ἄγγελος ὁ
what [3]thee [1]it [2]behoves to do. And when [3]departed [1]the [2]angel who

λαλῶν [a]τῷ Κορνηλίῳ,‖ φωνήσας δύο τῶν.οἰκετῶν.[b]αὐτοῦ,‖
spoke to Cornelius, having called two of his servants,

καὶ στρατιώτην εὐσεβῆ τῶν προσκαρτερούντων αὐτῷ, 8 καὶ
and a [2]soldier [1]pious of those continually waiting on him, and

ἐξηγησάμενος [c]αὐτοῖς ἅπαντα‖ ἀπέστειλεν αὐτοὺς εἰς τὴν
having related to them all things he sent them to

Ἰόππην. 9 Τῇ.δὲ ἐπαύριον ὁδοιπορούντων [d]ἐκείνων‖ καὶ
Joppa. And on the morrow, as [2]are [3]journeying [1]these and

τῇ πόλει ἐγγιζόντων, ἀνέβη Πέτρος ἐπὶ τὸ δῶμα προσ-
to the city drawing near, [2]went [3]up [1]Peter on the housetop to

εύξασθαι, περὶ ὥραν ἕκτην. 10 ἐγένετο.δὲ πρόσπεινος,
pray, about [3]hour [1]the [2]sixth. And he became very hungry,

καὶ ἤθελεν γεύσασθαι· παρασκευαζόντων.δὲ [e]ἐκείνων‖ [f]ἐπέ-
and wished to eat. But as [2]were [3]making [4]ready [1]they [7]fell

πεσεν‖ ἐπ' αὐτὸν ἔκστασις, 11 καὶ θεωρεῖ τὸν οὐρανὸν ἀνεῳγ-
[8]upon [9]him [5]a [6]trance, and he beholds the heaven opened,

μένον, καὶ καταβαῖνον [g]ἐπ' αὐτὸν‖ σκεῦός τι ὡς ὀθόνην
and descending upon him a [2]vessel [1]certain, as a [2]sheet

μεγάλην, τέσσαρσιν ἀρχαῖς [h]δεδεμένον, καὶ‖ καθιέμενον ἐπὶ
[1]great, by four corners bound, and let down upon

τῆς γῆς· 12 ἐν ᾧ ὑπῆρχεν πάντα τὰ τετράποδα [i]τῆς γῆς
the earth; in which were all the quadrupeds of the earth

καὶ τὰ θηρία καὶ τὰ ἑρπετὰ‖ καὶ [k]τὰ‖ πετεινὰ τοῦ οὐ-
and the wild beasts and the creeping things and the birds of the hea-

ρανοῦ. 13 καὶ ἐγένετο φωνὴ πρὸς αὐτόν, Ἀναστάς, Πέτρε,
ven. And came a voice to him, Having risen up, Peter,

θῦσον καὶ φάγε. 14 Ὁ.δὲ.Πέτρος εἶπεν, Μηδαμῶς, κύριε· ὅτι
kill and eat. But Peter said, In no wise, Lord; for

οὐδέποτε ἔφαγον πᾶν κοινὸν [l]ἢ‖ ἀκάθαρτον. 15 Καὶ φωνὴ
never did I eat anything common or unclean. And a voice

πάλιν ἐκ.δευτέρου πρὸς αὐτόν, Ἃ ὁ θεὸς [m]ἐκαθάρισεν,‖
[came] again the second time to him, What God cleansed,

σὺ μὴ κοίνου. 16 Τοῦτο.δὲ ἐγένετο ἐπὶ.τρίς· καὶ [n]πάλιν‖
[3]thou [2]not [1]make common. And this took place thrice, and again

[o]ἀνελήφθη‖ τὸ σκεῦος εἰς τὸν οὐρανόν. 17 Ὡς.δὲ ἐν ἑαυτῷ
was taken up the vessel into the heaven. And as [4]in [5]himself

διηπόρει ὁ Πέτρος τί ἂν.εἴη τὸ ὅραμα ὃ εἶδεν, [p]καὶ‖
[2]was [3]perplexed [1]Peter what might be the vision which he saw, [2]also

ἰδού, οἱ ἄνδρες οἱ ἀπεσταλμένοι [q]ἀπὸ‖ τοῦ Κορνηλίου, διε-
[1]behold, the men who were sent from Cornelius, having

ρωτήσαντες τὴν οἰκίαν [r]Σίμωνος, ἐπέστησαν ἐπὶ τὸν πυλῶνα·
inquired for the house of Simon, stood at the porch;

18 καὶ φωνήσαντες ἐπυνθάνοντο εἰ Σίμων ὁ ἐπικαλού-
and having called out they asked if Simon who [is] surnamed

μενος Πέτρος ἐνθάδε ξενίζεται. 19 Τοῦ.δὲ.Πέτρου [s]ἐνθυμου-
Peter [2]here [1]lodges. But as Peter was think-

μένου‖ περὶ τοῦ ὁράματος, εἶπεν [t]αὐτῷ τὸ πνεῦμα,‖ Ἰδού,
ing over the vision, [3]said [4]to [5]him [1]the [2]Spirit, Behold,

---

[a] αὐτῷ to him GLTTrAW. [b] — αὐτοῦ (*read* of the servants) LTTrAW. [c] ἅπαντα αὐτοῖς LTTrA. [d] αὐτῶν they T. [e] αὐτῶν LTTrAW. [f] ἐγένετο came LTTrAW. [g] — ἐπ' αὐτὸν GLTTrAW. [h] — δεδεμένον καὶ LTTr[A]. [i] καὶ τὰ (— τὰ LTTrA) ἑρπετὰ της γῆς LTTrAW. [k] — τὰ LTTrA. [l] καὶ and LTTrA. [m] ἐκαθέρισεν Tr. [n] εὐθὺς immediately LTTrAW. [o] ἀνελήμφθη LTTrA. [p] — καὶ LTTr[A]. [q] ὑπὸ T. [r] + τοῦ LTTrAW. [s] διενθυμουμένου was pondering GLTTrAW. [t] τὸ πνεῦμα αὐτῷ LTTrA.

ἄνδρες [v]τρεῖς‖ [w]ζητοῦσίν‖ σε· 20 ἀλλὰ ἀναστὰς κατάβηθι,
[2]men [1]three seek thee; but having risen go down,
καὶ πορεύου σὺν αὐτοῖς, μηδὲν διακρινόμενος· [x]διότι‖ ἐγὼ
and proceed with them, nothing doubting, because I
ἀπέσταλκα αὐτούς. 21 Καταβὰς.δὲ Πέτρος πρὸς τοὺς
have sent them. And [2]having [3]gone [4]down [1]Peter to the
ἄνδρας [y]τοὺς ἀπεσταλμένους ἀπὸ τοῦ Κορνηλίου πρὸς αὐτόν,‖
men who were sent from Cornelius to him,
εἶπεν, Ἰδού, ἐγώ εἰμι ὃν ζητεῖτε· τίς ἡ αἰτία δι' ἣν
said, Behold, I am whom ye seek; what [is] the cause for which
πάρεστε; 22 οἱ.δὲ [z]εἶπον,‖ Κορνήλιος ἑκατοντάρχης, ἀνὴρ
ye are come? And they said, Cornelius a centurion, a [2]man
δίκαιος καὶ φοβούμενος τὸν θεόν, μαρτυρούμενός.τε ὑπὸ ὅλου
[1]righteous and fearing God, and borne witness to by [2]whole
τοῦ ἔθνους τῶν Ἰουδαίων, ἐχρηματίσθη ὑπὸ ἀγγέλου
[1]the nation of the Jews, was divinely instructed by [3]angel
ἁγίου, μεταπέμψασθαί σε εἰς τὸν.οἶκον.αὐτοῦ, καὶ ἀκοῦσαι
[1]a [2]holy, to send for thee to his house, and to hear
ῥήματα παρὰ σοῦ. 23 Εἰσκαλεσάμενος οὖν αὐτοὺς ἐξένισεν.
words from thee. Having called [2]in [3]therefore [1]them he lodged
Τῇ.δὲ ἐπαύριον [a]ὁ Πέτρος‖ ἐξῆλθεν σὺν αὐτοῖς, καί
[them]. And on the morrow Peter went forth with them, and
τινες τῶν ἀδελφῶν τῶν ἀπὸ [b]τῆς‖ Ἰόππης συνῆλθον αὐτῷ.
certain of the brethren those from Joppa went with him.
24 [c]καὶ τῇ‖ ἐπαύριον [d]εἰσῆλθον‖ εἰς τὴν [e]Καισάρειαν·‖
And on the morrow they entered into Cæsarea.
ὁ.δὲ.Κορνήλιος ἦν προσδοκῶν αὐτούς, [f]συγκαλεσάμενος‖ τοὺς
And Cornelius was expecting them, having called together
συγγενεῖς.αὐτοῦ καὶ τοὺς ἀναγκαίους φίλους. 25 Ὡς.δὲ
his kinsmen and intimate friends. And as
ἐγένετο [g] εἰσελθεῖν τὸν Πέτρον, συναντήσας αὐτῷ ὁ Κορνήλιος,
[2]was [3]coming [4]in [1]Peter, [6]having [7]met [8]him [5]Cornelius,
πεσὼν ἐπὶ τοὺς πόδας προσεκύνησεν. 26 ὁ.δὲ.Πέτρος
having fallen at [his] feet did homage. But Peter
[h]αὐτὸν ἤγειρεν,‖ λέγων, Ἀνάστηθι· [i]κἀγὼ‖ αὐτὸς ἄνθρωπός
[2]him [1]raised, saying, Rise up: I also myself a man
εἰμι. 27 Καὶ συνομιλῶν αὐτῷ εἰσῆλθεν, καὶ εὑρίσκει συνελη-
am. And talking with him he went in, and finds gathered to-
λυθότας πολλούς. 28 ἔφη.τε πρὸς αὐτούς, Ὑμεῖς ἐπίστασθε
gether many. And he said to them, Ye know
ὡς ἀθέμιτόν ἐστιν ἀνδρὶ Ἰουδαίῳ κολλᾶσθαι ἢ προσέρ-
how unlawful it is for a man a Jew to unite himself or come
χεσθαι ἀλλοφύλῳ· [k]καὶ ἐμοὶ‖ [l]ὁ θεὸς ἔδειξεν‖ μηδένα
near to one of another race. And to me God shewed [3]no
κοινὸν ἢ ἀκάθαρτον λέγειν ἄνθρωπον· 29 διὸ καὶ ἀναν-
[5]common [6]or [7]unclean [1]to [2]call [4]man. Wherefore also without
τιρρήτως ἦλθον μεταπεμφθείς. πυνθάνομαι οὖν, τίνι
gainsaying I came, having been sent for. I inquire therefore, for what
λόγῳ [m]μετεπέμψασθέ‖ με; 30 Καὶ ὁ Κορνήλιος ἔφη, Ἀπὸ
reason did ye send for me? And Cornelius said, [3]Ago
τετάρτης ἡμέρας μέχρι ταύτης τῆς ὥρας ἤμην [n]νηστεύων, καὶ‖
[1]four [2]days until this hour I was fasting, and

hold, three men seek thee. 20 Arise therefore, and get thee down, and go with them, doubting nothing: for I have sent them. 21 Then Peter went down to the men which were sent unto him from Cornelius; and said, Behold, I am he whom ye seek: what *is* the cause wherefore ye are come? 22 And they said, Cornelius the centurion, a just man, and one that feareth God, and of good report among all the nation of the Jews, was warned from God by an holy angel to send for thee into his house, and to hear words of thee. 23 Then called he them in, and lodged *them*. And on the morrow Peter went away with them, and certain brethren from Joppa accompanied him. 24 And the morrow after they entered into Cæsarea. And Cornelius waited for them, and had called together his kinsmen and near friends. 25 And as Peter was coming in, Cornelius met him, and fell down at his feet, and worshipped *him*. 26 But Peter took him up, saying, Stand up; I myself also am a man. 27 And as he talked with him, he went in, and found many that were come together. 28 And he said unto them, Ye know how that it is an unlawful thing for a man that is a Jew to keep company, or come unto one of another nation; but God hath shewed me that I should not call any man common or unclean. 29 Therefore came I *unto you* without gainsaying, as soon as I was sent for: I ask therefore for what intent ye have sent for me? 30 And Cornelius said, Four days ago I was fasting until this hour; and at the ninth hour I prayed in my

[v] — τρεῖς TA. [w] ζητοῦντές TA. [x] ὅτι GLTTrAW. [y] — τοὺς ἀπεσταλμένους ἀπὸ τοῦ Κορνηλίου πρὸς αὐτόν GLTTrAW. [z] εἶπαν LTTrA. [a] ἀναστὰς having arisen (he went forth) GLTTrAW. [b] — τῆς GLTTrAW. [c] τῇ δὲ LTTrAW. [d] εἰσῆλθεν he entered LTr; εἰσηλθαν T. [e] Καισαρίαν T. [f] συν- T [g] + τοῦ GLTTrAW. [h] ἤγειρεν αὐτὸν LTTrAW. [i] καὶ ἐγὼ TTrA. [k] κἀμοί LTTrA. [l] ἔδειξεν ὁ θεὸς T. [m] μεταπέμψασθέ A. [n] — νηστεύων καὶ LTTr[A].

house, and, behold, a
man stood before me
in bright clothing,
31 and said, Cornelius,
thy prayer is heard,
and thine alms are had
in remembrance in the
sight of God. 32 Send
therefore to Joppa, and
call hither Simon,
whose surname is Peter;
he is lodged in the
house of *one* Simon a
tanner by the sea side:
who, when he cometh,
shall speak unto thee.
33 Immediately therefore
I sent to thee;
and thou hast well
done that thou art
come. Now therefore
are we all here present
before God, to hear all
things that are commanded
thee of God.
34 Then Peter opened
his mouth, and said,
Of a truth I perceive
that God is no respecter
of persons: 35 but
in every nation he that
feareth him, and worketh
righteousness, is
accepted with him.
36 The word which
God sent unto the
children of Israel,
preaching peace by
Jesus Christ: (he is
Lord of all:) 37 that
word, *I say*, ye know,
which was published
throughout all Judæa,
and began from Galilee,
after the baptism
which John preached;
38 how God anointed
Jesus of Nazareth with
the Holy Ghost and
with power: who went
about doing good, and
healing all that were
oppressed of the devil;
for God was with him.
39 And we are witnesses
of all things
which he did both in
the land of the Jews,
and in Jerusalem;
whom they slew and
hanged on a tree:
40 him God raised up
the third day, and
shewed him openly;
41 not to all the people,
but unto witnesses

τὴν [o]ἐννάτην‖ [p]ὥραν‖ προσευχόμενος ἐν τῷ.οἴκῳ.μου· καὶ ἰδού,
the ninth hour praying in my house; and behold,
ἀνὴρ ἔστη ἐνώπιόν μου ἐν ἐσθῆτι λαμπρᾷ, 31 καί φησιν,
a man stood before me in [2]apparel [1]bright, and said,
Κορνήλιε, εἰσηκούσθη σου ἡ προσευχὴ καὶ αἱ.ἐλεημοσύναι.σου
Cornelius, [3]was [4]heard [1]thy [2]prayer and thine alms
ἐμνήσθησαν ἐνώπιον τοῦ θεοῦ. 32 πέμψον οὖν εἰς Ἰόππην,
were remembered before God. Send therefore to Joppa,
καὶ μετακάλεσαι Σίμωνα ὃς ἐπικαλεῖται Πέτρος· οὗτος ξενίζεται
and call for Simon who is surnamed Peter; he lodges
ἐν οἰκίᾳ Σίμωνος βυρσέως παρὰ θάλασσαν· [q]ὃς
in [the] house of Simon a tanner by [the] sea; who,
παραγενόμενος λαλήσει σοι.‖ 33 [r]Ἐξαυτῆς‖ οὖν ἔπεμψα
having come will speak to thee. At once therefore I sent
πρός σε· σύ.τε καλῶς ἐποίησας παραγενόμενος. νῦν οὖν
to thee; and thou [2]well [1]didst having come. Now therefore
πάντες ἡμεῖς ἐνώπιον τοῦ θεοῦ πάρεσμεν ἀκοῦσαι πάντα τὰ
all we before God are present to hear all things that
προστεταγμένα σοι [s]ὑπὸ‖ [t]τοῦ θεοῦ.‖ 34 Ἀνοίξας.δὲ Πέτρος
have been ordered thee by God. And [2]opening [1]Peter
τὸ στόμα εἶπεν, Ἐπ᾽.ἀληθείας καταλαμβάνομαι ὅτι οὐκ
[his] mouth said, Of a truth I perceive that [3]not
ἔστιν [v]προσωπολήπτης‖ ὁ θεός, 35 ἀλλ᾽ ἐν παντὶ ἔθνει ὁ
[2]is [4]a [5]respecter [6]of [7]persons [1]God, but in every nation he that
φοβούμενος αὐτὸν καὶ ἐργαζόμενος δικαιοσύνην, δεκτὸς αὐτῷ
fears him and works righteousness, acceptable to him
ἐστιν. 36 τὸν λόγον [w]ὃν‖ ἀπέστειλεν τοῖς υἱοῖς Ἰσραήλ,
is. The word which he sent to the sons of Israel,
εὐαγγελιζόμενος εἰρήνην διὰ Ἰησοῦ χριστοῦ, οὗτός ἐστιν
announcing the glad tidings— peace by Jesus Christ, (he is
πάντων κύριος, 37 ὑμεῖς οἴδατε· τὸ γενόμενον ῥῆμα
[2]of [3]all [1]Lord), ye know; the [2]which [3]came [1]declaration
καθ᾽ ὅλης τῆς Ἰουδαίας, [x]ἀρξάμενον‖ [y] ἀπὸ τῆς Γαλιλαίας,
through [2]whole [1]the of Judæa, beginning from Galilee,
μετὰ τὸ βάπτισμα ὃ ἐκήρυξεν [z]Ἰωάννης·‖ 38 Ἰησοῦν τὸν
after the baptism which [2]proclaimed [1]John: Jesus who
ἀπὸ [a]Ναζαρέτ,‖ ὡς ἔχρισεν αὐτὸν ὁ θεὸς πνεύματι
[was] from Nazareth, how [2]anointed [3]him [1]God with [the] [2]Spirit
ἁγίῳ καὶ δυνάμει, ὃς διῆλθεν εὐεργετῶν καὶ ἰώμενος
[1]Holy and with power, who went through, doing good and healing
πάντας τοὺς καταδυναστευομένους ὑπὸ τοῦ διαβόλου, ὅτι
all that were being oppressed by the devil, because
ὁ θεὸς ἦν μετ᾽ αὐτοῦ· 39 καὶ ἡμεῖς [b]ἐσμεν‖ μάρτυρες πάντων
God was with him. And we are witnesses of all things
ὧν ἐποίησεν ἔν.τε τῇ χώρᾳ τῶν Ἰουδαίων καὶ [c]ἐν‖ Ἰερουσαλήμ·
which he did both in the country of the Jews and in Jerusalem;
ὃν [d] [e]ἀνεῖλον‖ κρεμάσαντες ἐπὶ ξύλου.
whom they put to death having hanged [him] on a tree.
40 τοῦτον ὁ θεὸς ἤγειρεν [f] τῇ τρίτῃ ἡμέρᾳ, καὶ ἔδωκεν αὐτὸν
This one God raised up on the third day, and gave him
ἐμφανῆ γενέσθαι, 41 οὐ παντὶ τῷ λαῷ, ἀλλὰ μάρτυσιν τοῖς
[3]manifest [1]to [2]become, not to all the people, but to witnesses who

---

[o] ἐνάτην LTTrA. [p] — ὥραν LTTrA. [q] — ὃς παραγενόμενος λαλήσει σοι LTTr[A]. [r] ἐξ αὐτῆς A. [s] ἀπὸ from LA. [t] τοῦ κυρίου the Lord LTTr. [v] προσωπολήμπτης LTTrA. [w] — ὃν L[Tr]. [x] ἀρξάμενος TTrA. [y] + [γὰρ] L. [z] Ἰωάνης Tr. [a] Ναζαρέθ ELTTrA. [b] — ἐσμεν (read [are]) GLTTrAW. [c] — ἐν [L]Tr. [d] + καὶ also GLTTrAW. [e] ἀνεῖλαν LTTrA. [f] + ἐν T.

προκεχειροτονημένοις ὑπὸ τοῦ θεοῦ, ἡμῖν, οἵτινες συνεφάγομεν
had been chosen before by God, to us, who did eat with
καὶ συνεπίομεν αὐτῷ μετὰ τὸ.ἀναστῆναι.αὐτὸν ἐκ
and did drink with him after he had risen from among [the]
νεκρῶν· 42 καὶ παρήγγειλεν ἡμῖν κηρύξαι τῷ λαῷ, καὶ
dead. And he charged us to proclaim to the people, and
διαμαρτύρασθαι ὅτι [g]αὐτός[||] ἐστιν ὁ ὡρισμένος ὑπὸ τοῦ
to testify fully that he it is who has been appointed by
θεοῦ κριτὴς ζώντων καὶ νεκρῶν. 43 τούτῳ πάντες οἱ προφῆται
God judge of living and dead. To him all the prophets
μαρτυροῦσιν, ἄφεσιν ἁμαρτιῶν λαβεῖν διὰ τοῦ ὀνόματος
bear witness, [that] [8]remission [9]of [10]sins [7]receives [11]through [13]name
αὐτοῦ πάντα τὸν πιστεύοντα εἰς αὐτόν.
[12]his [1]every [2]one [3]that [4]believes [5]on [6]him.
44 Ἔτι λαλοῦντος τοῦ Πέτρου τὰ.ῥήματα.ταῦτα, [h]ἐπέπεσεν[||]
[4]Yet [1]as [3]is [5]speaking [2]Peter these words, [5]fell
τὸ πνεῦμα τὸ ἅγιον ἐπὶ πάντας τοὺς ἀκούοντας τὸν λόγον.
[1]the [2]Spirit [3]the [4]Holy upon all those hearing the word.
45 καὶ ἐξέστησαν οἱ ἐκ περιτομῆς πιστοὶ [i]ὅσοι[||] [k]συνῆλ-
And were amazed the [2]of [3]the [4]circumcision [1]believers as many as came
θον[||] τῷ Πέτρῳ, ὅτι καὶ ἐπὶ τὰ ἔθνη ἡ δωρεὰ τοῦ [l]ἁγίου
with Peter, that also upon the Gentiles the gift of the Holy
πνεύματος[||] ἐκκέχυται· 46 ἤκουον.γὰρ αὐτῶν λαλούν-
Spirit had been poured out; for they heard them speak-
των γλώσσαις καὶ μεγαλυνόντων τὸν θεόν. τότε ἀπεκρίθη
ing with tongues and magnifying God. Then answered
[m]ὁ[||] Πέτρος, 47 Μήτι τὸ ὕδωρ [n]κωλῦσαι δύναταί[||] τις
Peter, [5]The [6]water [4]forbid [1]can [2]any [3]one
τοῦ μὴ.βαπτισθῆναι τούτους, οἵτινες τὸ πνεῦμα τὸ ἅγιον
that should not be baptized these, who the Spirit the Holy
ἔλαβον [o]καθὼς[||] καὶ ἡμεῖς; 48 προσέταξέν.[p]τε[||] [q]αὐτοὺς[||] [r]βαπ-
received as also we? And he ordered them to be
τισθῆναι ἐν τῷ ὀνόματι τοῦ κυρίου.[||] τότε ἠρώτησαν αὐτὸν
baptized in the name of the Lord. Then they begged him
ἐπιμεῖναι ἡμέρας τινάς.
to remain [2]days [1]some.

11 Ἤκουσαν.δὲ οἱ.ἀπόστολοι καὶ οἱ ἀδελφοὶ οἱ ὄντες κατὰ
And [3]heard [1]the [2]apostles and the brethren who were in
τὴν Ἰουδαίαν, ὅτι καὶ τὰ ἔθνη ἐδέξαντο τὸν λόγον τοῦ θεοῦ.
Judæa, that also the Gentiles received the word of God;
2 [s]καὶ ὅτε[||] ἀνέβη Πέτρος εἰς [t]Ἱεροσόλυμα,[||] διεκρίνοντο πρὸς
and when [2]went [3]up [1]Peter to Jerusalem, [5]contended [6]with
αὐτὸν οἱ ἐκ περιτομῆς, 3 λέγοντες, Ὅτι [v] πρὸς ἄνδρας
[7]him [1]those [2]of [[3]the] [4]circumcision, saying, To men
ἀκροβυστίαν.ἔχοντας [v]εἰσῆλθες,[||] καὶ [w]συνέφαγες[||] αὐτοῖς.
uncircumcised thou wentest in, and didst eat with them.
4 Ἀρξάμενος.δὲ [x]ὁ[||] Πέτρος ἐξετίθετο αὐτοῖς καθεξῆς λέ-
But [2]having [3]begun [1]Peter he set [it] forth to them in order say-
γων, 5 Ἐγὼ ἤμην ἐν πόλει Ἰόππῃ προσευχόμενος, καὶ
ing, I was in [the] city of Joppa praying, and
εἶδον ἐν ἐκστάσει ὅραμα, καταβαῖνον σκεῦός τι ὡς ὀθόνην
I saw in a trance a vision, [4]descending [1]a [3]vessel [2]certain like a [2]sheet

chosen before of God,
even to us, who did eat
and drink with him
after he rose from the
dead. 42 And he com-
manded us to preach
unto the people, and
to testify that it is he
which was ordained of
God *to be* the Judge of
quick and dead. 43 To
him give all the pro-
phets witness, that
through his name who-
soever believeth in
him shall receive re-
mission of sins.

44 While Peter yet
spake these words, the
Holy Ghost fell on all
them which heard the
word. 45 And they
of the circumcision
which believed were
astonished, as many
as came with Peter,
because that on the
Gentiles also was
poured out the gift of
the Holy Ghost. 46 For
they heard them speak
with tongues, and
magnify God. Then
answered Peter, 47 Can
any man forbid water,
that these should not
be baptized, which
have received the Holy
Ghost as well as we?
48 And he commanded
them to be baptized in
the name of the Lord.
Then prayed they him
to tarry certain days.

XI. And the apo-
stles and brethren that
were in Judæa heard
that the Gentiles had
also received the word
of God. 2 And when
Peter was come up to
Jerusalem, they that
were of the circumci-
sion contended with
him, 3 saying, Thou
wentest in to men
uncircumcised, and
didst eat with them.
4 But Peter rehearsed
the matter from the
beginning, and ex-
pounded *it* by order
unto them, saying, 5 I
was in the city of Jop-
pa praying: and in a
trance I saw a vision,
A certain vessel de-
scend, as it had been a
great sheet, let down

---

[g] οὗτός LTr. [h] ἔπεσε L. [i] οἳ who L. [k] συνῆλθαν TTr. [l] πνεύματος τοῦ ἁγίου L. [m] — ὁ LTTrA. [n] δύναται κωλῦσαί LTTrA. [o] ὡς LTTrA. [p] δὲ TTr. [q] αὐτοῖς T. [r] ἐν τῷ ὀνόματι Ἰησοῦ χριστοῦ (Jesus Christ) βαπτισθῆναι LTTr; ἐν τῷ ὀνόματι τοῦ κυρίου βαπ. A. [s] ὅτε δὲ LTTrA. [t] Ἱερουσαλήμ LTTrA. [v] εἰσῆλθες (εἰσῆλθεν he went in Tr) *placed before* πρὸς LTTrAW. [w] συνέφαγεν did eat with Tr. [x] — ὁ LTTrAW.

from heaven by four corners; and it came even to me: 6 upon the which when I had fastened mine eyes, I considered, and saw fourfooted beasts of the earth, and wild beasts, and creeping things, and fowls of the air. 7 And I heard a voice saying unto me, Arise, Peter; slay and eat. 8 But I said, Not so, Lord: for nothing common or unclean hath at any time entered into my mouth. 9 But the voice answered me again from heaven, What God hath cleansed, *that* call not thou common. 10 And this was done three times: and all were drawn up again into heaven. 11 And, behold, immediately there were three men already come unto the house where I was, sent from Cæsarea unto me. 12 And the spirit bade me go with them, nothing doubting. Moreover these six brethren accompanied me, and we entered into the man's house: 13 and he shewed us how he had seen an angel in his house, which stood and said unto him, Send men to Joppa, and call for Simon, whose surname is Peter; 14 who shall tell thee words, whereby thou and all thy house shall be saved. 15 And as I began to speak, the Holy Ghost fell on them, as on us at the beginning. 16 Then remembered I the word of the Lord, how that he said, John indeed baptized with water; but ye shall be baptized with the Holy Ghost. 17 Forasmuch then as God gave them the like gift as *he did* unto us, who believed on the Lord Jesus Christ; what was I, that I could withstand God? 18 When they heard these things, they held their peace, and

μεγάλην, τέσσαρσιν ἀρχαῖς καθιεμένην ἐκ τοῦ οὐρανοῦ. καὶ
[1]great, by four corners let down out of the heaven, and
ἦλθεν [y]ἄχρις ἐμοῦ. 6 εἰς ἣν ἀτενίσας κατενόουν,
it came as far as me: on which having looked intently I considered,
καὶ εἶδον τὰ τετράποδα τῆς γῆς καὶ τὰ θηρία καὶ τὰ ἑρ-
and saw the quadrupeds of the earth and the wild beasts and the creeping
πετὰ καὶ τὰ πετεινὰ τοῦ οὐρανοῦ. 7 ἤκουσα.δὲ [z] φωνῆς λε-
things and the birds of the heaven. And I heard a voice say-
γούσης μοι, Ἀναστάς, Πέτρε, θῦσον καὶ φάγε. 8 εἶπον.δέ,
ing to me, Having risen up, Peter, kill and eat. But I said,
Μηδαμῶς, κύριε· ὅτι [a]πᾶν κοινὸν ἢ ἀκάθαρτον οὐδέποτε
In no wise, Lord, for anything common or unclean never
εἰσῆλθεν εἰς τὸ.στόμα.μου. 9 ἀπεκρίθη.δέ [b]μοι φωνὴ ἐκ.δευ-
entered into my mouth. But [3]answered [4]me [1]a [2]voice the second
τέρου ἐκ τοῦ οὐρανοῦ, Ἃ ὁ θεὸς [c]ἐκαθάρισεν, σὺ μὴ
time out of the heaven, What God cleansed, [3]thou [2]not
κοίνου. 10 τοῦτο.δὲ ἐγένετο ἐπὶ.τρίς, καὶ [d]πάλιν ἀνε-
[1]make common. And this took place thrice, and again was
σπάσθη ἅπαντα εἰς τὸν οὐρανόν. 11 καὶ ἰδού, [e]ἐξαυτῆς τρεῖς
drawn up all into the heaven. And lo, at once three
ἄνδρες ἐπέστησαν ἐπὶ τὴν οἰκίαν ἐν ᾗ [f]ἤμην, ἀπεσταλμένοι
men stood at the house in which I was, sent
ἀπὸ [g]Καισαρείας πρός με. 12 εἶπεν.δέ [h]μοι τὸ πνεῦμα,
from Cæsarea to me. And [3]said [4]to [5]me [1]the [2]Spirit,
συνελθεῖν αὐτοῖς, [i]μηδὲν διακρινόμενον· ἦλθον.δὲ σὺν ἐμοὶ
to go with them, nothing doubting. And went with me
καὶ οἱ ἓξ ἀδελφοὶ οὗτοι, καὶ εἰσήλθομεν εἰς τὸν οἶκον τοῦ
also [2]six [3]brethren [1]these, and we entered into the house of the
ἀνδρός, 13 ἀπήγγειλέν.[k]τε ἡμῖν πῶς εἶδεν τὸν ἄγγελον ἐν
man, and he related to us how he saw the angel in
τῷ.οἴκῳ.αὐτοῦ σταθέντα καὶ εἰπόντα [l]αὐτῷ, Ἀπόστειλον εἰς
his house standing and saying to him, Send [2]to
Ἰόππην [m]ἄνδρας, καὶ μετάπεμψαι Σίμωνα τὸν ἐπικαλούμενον
[3]Joppa [1]men, and send for Simon who is surnamed
Πέτρον, 14 ὃς λαλήσει ῥήματα πρός σε ἐν.οἷς σωθήσῃ
Peter, who shall speak words to thee whereby shalt be saved
σὺ καὶ πᾶς ὁ.οἶκός.σου. 15 ἐν.δὲ τῷ.ἄρξασθαί.με λαλεῖν
thou and all thy house. And in my beginning to speak
ἐπέπεσεν τὸ πνεῦμα τὸ ἅγιον ἐπ' αὐτούς, ὥσπερ καὶ ἐφ'
[5]fell [1]the [2]Spirit [3]the [4]Holy upon them, even as also upon
ἡμᾶς ἐν ἀρχῇ. 16 ἐμνήσθην.δὲ τοῦ ῥήματος [n] κυρίου,
us in [the] beginning. And I remembered the word of [the] Lord,
ὡς ἔλεγεν, [o]Ἰωάννης μὲν ἐβάπτισεν ὕδατι, ὑμεῖς.δὲ
how he said, John indeed baptized with water, but ye
βαπτισθήσεσθε ἐν πνεύματι ἁγίῳ. 17 Εἰ οὖν τὴν ἴσην
shall be baptized with [the] [2]Spirit [1]Holy. If then the like
δωρεὰν ἔδωκεν αὐτοῖς ὁ θεὸς ὡς καὶ ἡμῖν, πιστεύσασιν ἐπὶ
gift [2]gave [3]to [4]them [1]God as also to us, having believed on
τὸν κύριον Ἰησοῦν χριστόν, ἐγὼ.[p]δὲ τίς ἤμην δυνατὸς
the Lord Jesus Christ, and I, who was I, [to be] able
κωλῦσαι τὸν θεόν; 18 Ἀκούσαντες.δὲ ταῦτα ἡσύχασαν,
to forbid God? And having heard these things they were silent,

---

[y] ἄχρι TTrA. [z] + καὶ also LTTrA. [a] — πᾶν GLTTrAW. [b] — μοι LTTrA. [c] ἐκαθέρισεν Tr. [d] ἀνεσπάσθη πάλιν LTTrA. [e] ἐξ αὐτῆς A. [f] ἦμεν we were LTTr. [g] Καισαρίας T. [h] τὸ πνεῦμά μοι LTTrA. [i] μηδὲν διακρίναντα LTTr; — μηδὲν διακρινόμενον A. [k] δὲ LTTr. [l] — αὐτῷ LTTr. [m] — ἄνδρας GLTTrAW. [n] + τοῦ of the GLTTrAW. [o] Ἰωάνης Tr. [p] — δὲ and LTTr[A].

καὶ ᵠἐδόξαζον‖ τὸν θεόν, λέγοντες, ʳἌραγε‖ καὶ τοῖς ἔθνεσιν
and glorified God, saying, Then indeed also to the Gentiles
ὁ θεὸς τὴν μετάνοιαν ˢἔδωκεν εἰς ζωήν.‖
God [2]repentance [1]gave unto life.

19 Οἱ μὲν οὖν διασπαρέντες ἀπὸ τῆς θλίψεως τῆς
They indeed therefore who were scattered by the tribulation that
γενομένης ἐπὶ ᵗΣτεφάνῳ,‖ διῆλθον ἕως Φοινίκης καὶ Κύπρου
took place upon Stephen, passed through to Phœnicia and Cyprus
καὶ Ἀντιοχείας, μηδενὶ λαλοῦντες τὸν λόγον εἰ.μὴ μόνον
and Antioch, to no one speaking the word except [3]only
Ἰουδαίοις. 20 ἦσαν.δέ τινες ἐξ αὐτῶν ἄνδρες Κύπριοι καὶ
[1]to [2]Jews. But were certain [2]of [3]them [1]men Cypriots and
Κυρηναῖοι, οἵτινες ᵛεἰσελθόντες‖ εἰς Ἀντιόχειαν, ἐλάλουν ʷ
Cyrenians, who having come into Antioch, spoke
πρὸς τοὺς ˣἙλληνιστὰς‖ εὐαγγελιζόμενοι τὸν κύριον
to the Hellenists, announcing the glad tidings— the Lord
Ἰησοῦν. 21 καὶ ἦν χεὶρ κυρίου μετ᾽ αὐτῶν· πολύς.τε
Jesus. And [6]was [[1]the] [2]hand [3]of [[4]the] [5]Lord with them, and a great
ἀριθμὸς ʸ πιστεύσας ἐπέστρεψεν ἐπὶ τὸν κύριον. 22 Ἠκούσθη
number having believed turned to the Lord. [4]Was [5]heard
δὲ ὁ λόγος εἰς τὰ ὦτα τῆς ἐκκλησίας τῆς ᶻ ἐν ᵃἹερο-
[1]and [2]the [3]report in the ears of the assembly which [was] in Jeru-
σολύμοις‖ περὶ αὐτῶν· καὶ ἐξαπέστειλαν Βαρνάβαν ᵇδιελ-
salem concerning them; and they sent forth Barnabas to go
θεῖν‖ ἕως Ἀντιοχείας. 23 ὃς παραγενόμενος καὶ ἰδὼν
through as far as Antioch: who having come and having seen
τὴν χάριν ᶜ τοῦ θεοῦ ἐχάρη, καὶ παρεκάλει πάντας τῇ.προθέσει
the grace of God rejoiced, and exhorted all with purpose
τῆς καρδίας προσμένειν τῷ κυρίῳ· 24 ὅτι ἦν ἀνὴρ ἀγαθὸς
of heart to abide with the Lord; for he was a [2]man [1]good
καὶ πλήρης πνεύματος ἁγίου καὶ πίστεως. καὶ προσετέθη
and full of [the] [2]Spirit [1]Holy and of faith. And was added
ὄχλος ἱκανὸς τῷ κυρίῳ. 25 Ἐξῆλθεν.δὲ εἰς Ταρσὸν ᵈὁ Βαρ-
a [2]crowd [1]large to the Lord. And [2]went [3]forth [4]to [5]Tarsus [1]Bar-
νάβας‖ ἀναζητῆσαι Σαῦλον, 26 καὶ εὑρὼν ᵉαὐτὸν‖ ἤγαγεν
nabas to seek Saul; and having found him he brought
ᵉαὐτὸν‖ εἰς Ἀντιόχειαν. ἐγένετο.δὲ ᶠαὐτοὺς‖ ἐνιαυτὸν
him to Antioch. And it came to pass they a [2]year
ὅλον συναχθῆναι ἐν τῇ ἐκκλησίᾳ, καὶ διδάξαι ὄχλον
[1]whole were gathered together in the assembly, and taught a [2]crowd
ἱκανόν, χρηματίσαι.τε ᵍπρῶτον‖ ἐν Ἀντιοχείᾳ τοὺς μαθητὰς
[1]large: and [3]were [5]called [4]first [7]in [8]Antioch [1]the [2]disciples
Χριστιανούς.
[6]Christians.

27 Ἐν.ταύταις.δὲ ταῖς ἡμέραις κατῆλθον ἀπὸ Ἱεροσολύμων
And in these days came down from Jerusalem
προφῆται εἰς Ἀντιόχειαν. 28 ἀναστὰς.δὲ εἷς ἐξ
prophets to Antioch; and [5]having [6]risen [7]up [1]one [2]from [3]among
αὐτῶν ὀνόματι Ἄγαβος, ʰἐσήμανεν‖ διὰ τοῦ πνεύματος,
[4]them, by name Agabus, he signified by the Spirit,
Λιμὸν ⁱμέγαν‖ μέλλειν ἔσεσθαι ἐφ᾽ ὅλην τὴν οἰκουμένην·
A [2]famine [1]great is about to be over [2]whole [1]the habitable world;

glorified God, saying, Then hath God also to the Gentiles granted repentance unto life.

19 Now they which were scattered abroad upon the persecution that arose about Stephen travelled as far as Phenice, and Cyprus, and Antioch, preaching the word to none but unto the Jews only. 20 And some of them were men of Cyprus and Cyrene, which, when they were come to Antioch, spake unto the Grecians, preaching the Lord Jesus. 21 And the hand of the Lord was with them: and a great number believed, and turned unto the Lord. 22 Then tidings of these things came unto the ears of the church which was in Jerusalem: and they sent forth Barnabas, that he should go as far as Antioch. 23 Who, when he came, and had seen the grace of God, was glad, and exhorted them all, that with purpose of heart they would cleave unto the Lord. 24 For he was a good man, and full of the Holy Ghost and of faith: and much people was added unto the Lord. 25 Then departed Barnabas to Tarsus, for to seek Saul: 26 and when he had found him, he brought him unto Antioch. And it came to pass, that a whole year they assembled themselves with the church, and taught much people. And the disciples were called Christians first in Antioch.

27 And in these days came prophets from Jerusalem unto Antioch. 28 And there stood up one of them named Agabus, and signified by the spirit that there should be great dearth throughout all the world:

ᵠ ἐδόξασαν LTTr. ʳ Ἄρα then LTTr; Ἄρα [γε] A. ˢ εἰς ζωὴν ἔδωκεν LTTrAW. ᵗ Στεφάνου L. ᵛ ἐλθόντες GLTTrAW. ʷ + καὶ also LTTrA. ˣ Ἕλληνας Greeks GLTTrA. ʸ + ὁ LTTrA. ᶻ + οὔσης was TTr. ᵃ Ἰερουσαλὴμ LTTrAW. ᵇ — διελθεῖν LTTr. ᶜ + τὴν which [was] LTTrA. ᵈ — ὁ Βαρνάβας (read he went forth) LTTrA. ᵉ — αὐτὸν (read [him]) LTTrA. ᶠ αὐτοῖς καὶ to them even LTTrA. ᵍ πρώτως TTrA. ʰ ἐσήμαινεν L. ⁱ μεγάλην LTTrAW.

which came to pass in the days of Claudius Cæsar. 29 Then the disciples, every man according to his ability, determined to send relief unto the brethren which dwelt in Judæa: 30 which also they did, and sent it to the elders by the hands of Barnabas and Saul.

XII. Now about that time Herod the king stretched forth *his* hands to vex certain of the church. 2 And he killed James the brother of John with the sword. 3 And because he saw it pleased the Jews, he proceeded further to take Peter also. (Then were the days of unleavened bread.) 4 And when he had apprehended him, he put *him* in prison, and delivered *him* to four quaternions of soldiers to keep him; intending after Easter to bring him forth to the people. 5 Peter therefore was kept in prison: but prayer was made without ceasing of the church unto God for him. 6 And when Herod would have brought him forth, the same night Peter was sleeping between two soldiers, bound with two chains: and the keepers before the door kept the prison. 7 And, behold, the angel of the Lord came upon *him*, and a light shined in the prison: and he smote Peter on the side, and raised him up, saying, Arise up quickly. And his chains fell off from *his* hands. 8 And the angel said unto him, Gird thyself, and bind on thy sandals. And so he did. And he saith unto him, Cast thy garment about thee, and follow me. 9 And he went out, and followed him; and wist not that it was true which was done by the angel; but thought he saw a vision.

[k]ὅστις[‖] [l]καὶ[‖] ἐγένετο ἐπὶ Κλαυδίου [m]Καίσαρος.[‖] 29 τῶν.δὲ
which also came to pass under Claudius Cæsar. And the
μαθητῶν καθὼς [n]ηὐπορεῖτό[‖] τις, ὥρισαν ἕκαστος αὐ-
disciples according as [3]was [4]prospered [1]any [2]one, determined, each of
τῶν εἰς διακονίαν πέμψαι τοῖς κατοικοῦσιν ἐν τῇ Ἰουδαίᾳ
them, for ministration to send to the [2]dwelling [3]in [4]Judæa
ἀδελφοῖς· 30 ὃ καὶ ἐποίησαν, ἀποστείλαντες πρὸς τοὺς
[1]brethren; which also they did, sending [it] to the
πρεσβυτέρους διὰ χειρὸς Βαρνάβα καὶ Σαύλου.
elders by [the] hand of Barnabas and Saul.

12 Κατ᾽.ἐκεῖνον.δὲ τὸν.καιρὸν ἐπέβαλεν [o]Ἡρώδης ὁ βασι-
And at that time [4]put [5]forth [1]Herod [2]the [3]king
λεὺς[‖] τὰς χεῖρας κακῶσαί τινας τῶν ἀπὸ τῆς ἐκκλησίας.
[his] hands to ill-treat some of those of the assembly;
2 ἀνεῖλεν.δὲ Ἰάκωβον τὸν ἀδελφὸν [p]Ἰωάννου[‖] [q]μαχαίρᾳ.[‖]
and he put to death James the brother of John with a sword.
3 [r]καὶ ἰδὼν[‖] ὅτι ἀρεστόν ἐστιν τοῖς Ἰουδαίοις προσέθετο
And having seen that pleasing it is to the Jews he added
συλλαβεῖν καὶ Πέτρον· ἦσαν.δὲ [s]ἡμέραι τῶν.ἀζύμων·)
to take also Peter: (and they were days of unleavened bread:)
4 ὃν καὶ πιάσας ἔθετο εἰς φυλακήν, παραδοὺς τέσσαρ-
whom also having seized he put in prison, having delivered to four
σιν τετραδίοις στρατιωτῶν φυλάσσειν αὐτόν, βουλόμενος μετὰ
sets of four soldiers to guard him, purposing after
τὸ πάσχα ἀναγαγεῖν αὐτὸν τῷ λαῷ. 5 ὁ.μὲν.οὖν.Πέτρος
the passover to bring out him to the people. Peter therefore indeed
ἐτηρεῖτο ἐν τῇ φυλακῇ· προσευχὴ.δὲ ἦν [t]ἐκτενὴς[‖] γινομένη
was kept in the prison; but [2]prayer [3]was [1]fervent made
ὑπὸ τῆς ἐκκλησίας πρὸς τὸν θεὸν [v]ὑπὲρ[‖] αὐτοῦ. 6 Ὅτε.δὲ
by the assembly to God concerning him. But when
[w]ἔμελλεν[‖] [x]αὐτὸν προάγειν[‖] ὁ Ἡρώδης, τῇ.νυκτὶ.ἐκείνῃ ἦν
[2]was [3]about [6]him [4]to [5]bring [7]forth [1]Herod, in that night was
ὁ Πέτρος κοιμώμενος μεταξὺ δύο στρατιωτῶν, δεδεμένος ἁλύ-
Peter sleeping between two soldiers, bound with
σεσιν δυσίν, φύλακές τε πρὸ τῆς θύρας ἐτήρουν τὴν φυλακήν.
[2]chains [1]two, guards also before the door kept the prison.
7 καὶ ἰδού, ἄγγελος κυρίου ἐπέστη, καὶ φῶς ἔλαμψεν ἐν
And behold, an angel of [the] Lord stood by, and a light shone in
τῷ οἰκήματι. πατάξας.δὲ τὴν πλευρὰν τοῦ Πέτρου ἤγειρεν
the building. And having smitten the side of Peter he roused up
αὐτὸν λέγων, Ἀνάστα ἐν τάχει. Καὶ [y]ἐξέπεσον[‖] αὐτοῦ αἱ
him, saying, Rise up in haste. And fell off of him the
ἁλύσεις ἐκ τῶν χειρῶν. 8 εἶπέν.[z]τε[‖] ὁ ἄγγελος πρὸς
chains from [his] hands. And [3]said [1]the [2]angel to
αὐτόν, [a]Περίζωσαι,[‖] καὶ ὑπόδησαι τὰ.σανδάλιά.σου. Ἐποίη-
him, Gird thyself about, and bind on thy sandals. [2]He [3]did
σεν δὲ οὕτως. καὶ λέγει αὐτῷ, Περιβαλοῦ τὸ.ἱμάτιόν.σου,
[1]and so. And he says to him, Cast about [thee] thy garment,
καὶ ἀκολούθει μοι. 9 Καὶ ἐξελθὼν ἠκολούθει [b]αὐτῷ·[‖] καὶ
and follow me. And going forth he followed him, and
οὐκ.ᾔδει ὅτι ἀληθές ἐστιν τὸ γινόμενον διὰ τοῦ ἀγ-
did not know that real it is which is happening by means of the an-

---

[k] ἥτις LTTrAW. [l] — καὶ LTTr[A]. [m] — Καίσαρος GLTTrAW. [n] εὐπορεῖτό LTTrA. [o] ὁ βασιλεὺς Ἡρώδης T. [p] Ἰωάνου Tr. [q] μαχαίρῃ TTrA. [r] ἰδὼν δὲ LTTrA. [s] + αἱ the GL[A]W. [t] ἐκτενῶς fervently LTTrA. [v] περὶ LTTr. [w] ἤμελλεν TTrA. [x] προαγαγεῖν αὐτὸν LTA; προάγειν αὐτὸν Tr. [y] ἐξέπεσαν LTTrA. [z] δὲ LTr. [a] Ζῶσαι gird thyself LTTrA. [b] — αὐτῷ LTTrA.

γέλον, ἐδόκει.δὲ ὅραμα βλέπειν. 10 διελθόντες.δὲ πρώτην
gel, but thought a vision he saw. And having passed through a first
φυλακὴν καὶ δευτέραν, [c]ἦλθον" ἐπὶ τὴν πύλην τὴν σιδηρᾶν
guard and a second, they came to the [2]gate [1]iron
τὴν φέρουσαν εἰς τὴν πόλιν, ἥτις αὐτομάτη [d]ἠνοίχθη" αὐτοῖς·
that leads into the city, which of itself opened to them;
καὶ ἐξελθόντες προῆλθον ῥύμην μίαν, καὶ εὐθέως
and having gone out they went on through [2]street [1]one, and immediately
ἀπέστη ὁ ἄγγελος ἀπ' αὐτοῦ. 11 καὶ ὁ Πέτρος [e]γενόμενος
departed the angel from him. And Peter having come
ἐν.ἑαυτῷ" εἶπεν, Νῦν οἶδα ἀληθῶς ὅτι ἐξαπέστειλεν
to himself said, Now I know of a truth that [3]sent [4]forth [[1]the]
κύριος τὸν.ἄγγελον.αὐτοῦ, καὶ [f]ἐξείλετό" με ἐκ χειρὸς
[2]Lord his angel, and delivered me out of [the] hand
Ἡρώδου καὶ πάσης τῆς προσδοκίας τοῦ λαοῦ τῶν Ἰουδαίων.
of Herod and all the expectation of the people of the Jews.
12 συνιδών.τε ἦλθεν ἐπὶ τὴν οἰκίαν [g] Μαρίας τῆς μητρὸς
And considering [it] he came to the house of Mary the mother
[h]Ἰωάννου" τοῦ ἐπικαλουμένου Μάρκου, οὗ ἦσαν ἱκανοὶ
of John who is surnamed Mark, where were many
συνηθροισμένοι καὶ προσευχόμενοι. 13 Κρούσαντος.δὲ [i]τοῦ
gathered together and praying. And [2]having [3]knocked
Πέτρου" τὴν θύραν τοῦ πυλῶνος, προσῆλθεν παιδίσκη ὑπα-
[1]Peter [at] the door of the porch, [3]came [1]a [2]damsel to
κοῦσαι, ὀνόματι Ῥόδη· 14 καὶ ἐπιγνοῦσα τὴν φωνὴν τοῦ
listen, by name Rhoda; and having recognized the voice
Πέτρου, ἀπὸ τῆς χαρᾶς οὐκ.ἤνοιξεν τὸν πυλῶνα, εἰσδρα-
of Peter, from joy she opened not the porch, [2]having
μοῦσα δὲ ἀπήγγειλεν ἑστάναι τὸν Πέτρον πρὸ τοῦ
[3]run [4]in [1]but she reported [2]to [3]be [4]standing [1]Peter before the
πυλῶνος. 15 οἱ.δὲ πρὸς αὐτὴν [k]εἶπον," Μαίνῃ. Ἡ.δὲ
porch. But they to her said, Thou art mad. But she
διϊσχυρίζετο οὕτως ἔχειν. οἱ.[l]δ' ἔλεγον," Ὁ ἄγγελος [m]αὐ-
strongly affirmed thus it was. And they said, The angel of
τοῦ ἐστιν." 16 Ὁ.δὲ.Πέτρος ἐπέμενεν κρούων· ἀνοίξαντες.δὲ
him it is. But Peter continued knocking: and having opened
[n]εἶδον" αὐτόν, καὶ ἐξέστησαν. 17 κατασείσας.δὲ αὐτοῖς
they saw him, and were amazed. And having made a sign to them
τῇ χειρὶ σιγᾶν διηγήσατο [o]αὐτοῖς" πῶς ὁ κύριος αὐτὸν
with the hand to be silent he related to them how the Lord him
ἐξήγαγεν ἐκ τῆς φυλακῆς. εἶπεν.[p]δέ," Ἀπαγγείλατε Ἰακώβῳ
brought out of the prison. And he said, Report to James
καὶ τοῖς ἀδελφοῖς ταῦτα. Καὶ ἐξελθὼν ἐπορεύθη εἰς ἕτερον
and to the brethren these things. And having gone out he went to another
τόπον. 18 γενομένης.δὲ ἡμέρας ἦν τάραχος οὐκ ὀλίγος
place. And [2]having [3]come [1]day there was [3]disturbance [1]no [2]small
ἐν τοῖς στρατιώταις, τί ἄρα ὁ Πέτρος ἐγένετο. 19 Ἡρώδης
among the soldiers, what then [[3]of] [4]Peter [1]was [2]become. [6]Herod
δὲ ἐπιζητήσας αὐτὸν καὶ μὴ εὑρών, ἀνακρίνας τοὺς
[5]and having sought after [6]him [1]and [2]not [3]having [4]found, having examined the
φύλακας ἐκέλευσεν ἀπαχθῆναι· καὶ κατελθὼν
guards he commanded [them] to be led away [to death]. And having gone down

10 When they were
past the first and the
second ward, they
came unto the iron
gate that leadeth unto
the city; which opened
to them of his own
accord: and they went
out, and passed on
through one street;
and forthwith the an-
gel departed from him.
11 And when Peter
was come to himself,
he said, Now I know
of a surety, that the
Lord hath sent his an-
gel, and hath delivered
me out of the hand of
Herod, and *from* all
the expectation of the
people of the Jews.
12 And when he had
considered *the thing,*
he came to the house
of Mary the mother
of John, whose sur-
name was Mark;
where many were ga-
thered together pray-
ing. 13 And as Peter
knocked at the door of
the gate, a damsel
came to hearken,
named Rhoda. 14 And
when she knew Peter's
voice, she opened not
the gate for gladness,
but ran in, and told
how Peter stood before
the gate. 15 And they
said unto her, Thou
art mad. But she
constantly affirmed
that it was even so.
Then said they, It is
his angel. 16 But Pe-
ter continued knock-
ing: and when they
had opened *the door,*
and saw him, they
were astonished. 17 But
he, beckoning unto
them with the hand to
hold their peace, de-
clared unto them how
the Lord had brought
him out of the prison.
And he said, Go shew
these things unto
James, and to the
brethren. And he de-
parted, and went into
another place. 18 Now
as soon as it was day,
there was no small
stir among the sol-
diers, what was be-
come of Peter. 19 And
when Herod had
sought for him, and
found him not, he ex-
amined the keepers,
and commanded that
they should be put to

---

[c] ἦλθαν LTTrA. [d] ἠνοίγη LTTrA. [e] ἐν ἑαυτῷ γενόμενος LTTrAW. [f] ἐξείλατό GLTTrAW. [g] + τῆς LTTrAW. [h] Ἰωάνου Tr. [i] αὐτοῦ he GLTTrAW. [k] εἶπαν LTTrA. [l] δὲ εἶπαν L; δὲ ἔλεγον GTTrAW. [m] ἐστιν αὐτοῦ LTTrA. [n] εἶδαν LTTrA. [o] — αὐτοῖς T[Tr]. [p] τε LTTrA.

death. And he went
down from Judæa to
Cæsarea, and *there* a-
bode. 20 And Herod
was highly displeased
with them of Tyre and
Sidon: but they came
with one accord to
him, and, having made
Blastus the king's
chamberlain their
friend, desired peace;
because their coun-
try was nourished by
the king's *country*.
21 And upon a set
day Herod, arrayed in
royal apparel, sat up-
on his throne, and
made an oration un-
to them. 22 And
the people gave a
shout, *saying*, *It is* the
voice of a god, and not
of a man. 23 And im-
mediately the angel of
the Lord smote him,
because he gave not
God the glory: and he
was eaten of worms,
and gave up the ghost.
24 But the word of God
grew and multiplied.
25 And Barnabas and
Saul returned from
Jerusalem, when they
had fulfilled *their* ministry, and took with
them John, whose sur-
name was Mark.

XIII. Now there
were in the church
that was at Antioch
certain prophets and
teachers; as Barna-
bas, and Simeon that
was called Niger, and
Lucius of Cyrene, and
Manaen, which had
been brought up with
Herod the tetrarch,
and Saul. 2 As they
ministered to the Lord,
and fasted, the Holy
Ghost said, Separate
me Barnabas and Saul
for the work where-
unto I have called
them. 3 And when
they had fasted and
prayed, and laid *their*
hands on them, they
sent *them* away. 4 So
they, being sent forth
by the Holy Ghost, de-
parted unto Seleucia;
and from thence they
sailed to Cyprus. 5 And
when they were at Sa-
lamis, they preached
the word of God in
the synagogues of the

ἀπὸ τῆς Ἰουδαίας εἰς [q]τὴν" [r]Καισάρειαν" διέτριβεν. 20 [r]Ἦν
from Judæa to Cæsarea he stayed [there]. [3]Was

δὲ [s]ὁ Ἡρώδης" θυμομαχῶν Τυρίοις καὶ Σιδωνίοις·
[1]and [2]Herod in bitter hostility with [the] Tyrians and Sidonians;

ὁμοθυμαδὸν.δὲ παρῆσαν πρὸς αὐτόν, καὶ πείσαντες Βλάστον
but with one accord they came to him, and having gained Blastus

τὸν ἐπὶ τοῦ κοιτῶνος τοῦ βασιλέως, ᾐτοῦντο εἰρήνην,
who [was] over the bedchamber of the king, sought peace,

διὰ τὸ τρέφεσθαι αὐτῶν τὴν χώραν ἀπὸ τῆς βασιλικῆς.
because was nourished their country by the king's.

21 Τακτῇ.δὲ ἡμέρᾳ ὁ Ἡρώδης ἐνδυσάμενος ἐσθῆτα βασιλικήν,
And on a set day Herod having put on [2]apparel [1]royal,

[t]καὶ" καθίσας ἐπὶ τοῦ βήματος, ἐδημηγόρει πρὸς αὐ-
and having sat on the tribunal, was making an oration to them.

τούς. 22 ὁ.δὲ δῆμος ἐπεφώνει, Θεοῦ φωνὴ καὶ οὐκ
And the people were crying out, [3]Of [4]a [5]god [[1]the] [2]voice and not

ἀνθρώπου. 23 παραχρῆμα.δὲ ἐπάταξεν αὐτὸν ἄγγελος κυ-
of a man! And immediately [6]smote [7]him [1]an [2]angel [3]of [[4]the]

ρίου, ἀνθ'.ὧν οὐκ ἔδωκεν [v]τὴν" δόξαν τῷ θεῷ· καὶ γενόμενος
[5]Lord, because he gave not the glory to God, and having been

σκωληκόβρωτος ἐξέψυξεν. 24 ὁ.δὲ λόγος τοῦ θεοῦ ηὔξανεν
eaten of worms he expired. But the word of God grew

καὶ ἐπληθύνετο. 25 Βαρνάβας.δὲ καὶ Σαῦλος ὑπέστρεψαν ἐξ
and multiplied. And Barnabas and Saul returned from

Ἱερουσαλήμ, πληρώσαντες τὴν διακονίαν, [w]συμπαραλαβόν-
Jerusalem, having fulfilled the ministration, having taken with

τες" [x]καὶ" [y]Ἰωάννην" τὸν ἐπικληθέντα Μάρκον.
[them] also John who was surnamed Mark.

13 [r]Ἦσαν.δὲ [z]τινες" ἐν Ἀντιοχείᾳ κατὰ τὴν οὖσαν
Now there were certain in Antioch in the [2]which [3]was [[4]there]

ἐκκλησίαν προφῆται καὶ διδάσκαλοι, ὅ.τε.Βαρνάβας καὶ Συμεὼν
[1]assembly prophets and teachers, both Barnabas and Simeon

ὁ καλούμενος Νίγερ, καὶ Λούκιος ὁ Κυρηναῖος, Μαναήν.τε
who was called Niger, and Lucius the Cyrenian, and Manaen,

Ἡρώδου τοῦ [a]τετράρχου" σύντροφος, καὶ Σαῦλος. 2 λειτουρ-
of Herod the tetrarch a foster-brother, and Saul. [2]As [4]were [5]min-

γούντων δὲ αὐτῶν τῷ κυρίῳ καὶ νηστευόντων, εἶπεν τὸ
istering [1]and [3]they to the Lord and fasting, [5]said [1]the

πνεῦμα τὸ ἅγιον, Ἀφορίσατε δή μοι τόν.[b]τε".Βαρνάβαν καὶ
[2]Spirit [3]the [4]Holy, Separate indeed to me both Barnabas and

[c]τὸν" Σαῦλον εἰς τὸ ἔργον ὃ προσκέκλημαι αὐτούς. 3 Τότε
Saul for the work to which I have called them. Then

νηστεύσαντες καὶ προσευξάμενοι, καὶ ἐπιθέντες τὰς χεῖρας
having fasted and prayed, and having laid hands

αὐτοῖς, ἀπέλυσαν. 4 [d]Οὗτοι" μὲν οὖν ἐκπεμφθέντες
on them, they let [them] go. They indeed therefore having been sent forth

ὑπὸ τοῦ [e]πνεύματος τοῦ ἁγίου," κατῆλθον εἰς [f]τὴν" [g]Σελεύ-
by the Spirit the Holy, went down to Seleu-

κειαν," ἐκεῖθέν.τε ἀπέπλευσαν εἰς [f]τὴν" Κύπρον. 5 καὶ γενό-
cia, and thence sailed away to Cyprus. And having

μενοι ἐν Σαλαμῖνι κατήγγελλον τὸν λόγον τοῦ θεοῦ ἐν ταῖς
come into Salamis they announced the word of God in the

---

[q] — τὴν LTTrAW. [r] Καισαρίαν T. [s] — ὁ Ἡρώδης (read he was) GLTTrAW. [t] — καὶ [L]T[Tr]. [v] — τὴν GL. [w] συν- T. [x] — καὶ LTTr[A]. [y] Ἰωάνην Tr. [z] — τινες LTTrA. [a] τετραάρχου T. [b] — τε GLTTrAW. [c] — τὸν LTTrAW. [d] αὐτοὶ LTTrA. [e] ἁγίου πνεύματος LTTrA. [f] — τὴν LTTrA. [g] Σελευκίαν T.

συναγωγαῖς τῶν Ἰουδαίων· εἶχον.δὲ καὶ [h]Ἰωάννην‖
synagogues of the Jews. And they had also John [as]

ὑπηρέτην. 6 διελθόντες.δὲ [i] τὴν νῆσον ἄχρι Πάφου
an attendant. And having passed through the island as far as Paphos

εὗρόν [j] τινα μάγον ψευδοπροφήτην Ἰουδαῖον, ᾧ ὄνομα
they found a certain magician, a false prophet a Jew, whose name

[k]Βαριησοῦς,‖ 7 ὃς ἦν σὺν τῷ ἀνθυπάτῳ Σεργίῳ Παύλῳ,
[was] Barjesus, who was with the proconsul Sergius Paulus,

ἀνδρὶ συνετῷ. οὗτος προσκαλεσάμενος Βαρνάβαν καὶ
[3]man [1]an [2]intelligent. He having called to [him] Barnabas and

Σαῦλον ἐπεζήτησεν ἀκοῦσαι τὸν λόγον τοῦ θεοῦ· 8 ἀνθίστατο.δὲ
Saul desired to hear the word of God. But there withstood

αὐτοῖς Ἐλύμας ὁ μάγος· οὕτως.γὰρ μεθερμηνεύεται τὸ ὄνομα
them Elymas the magician, (for so is interpreted [2]name

αὐτοῦ· ζητῶν διαστρέψαι τὸν ἀνθύπατον ἀπὸ τῆς πίστεως.
[1]his), seeking to pervert the proconsul from the faith.

9 Σαῦλος.δέ, ὁ καὶ Παῦλος, πλησθεὶς πνεύματος ἁγίου,
But Saul, who also [is] Paul, being filled with [the] [2]Spirit [1]Holy,

[l]καὶ‖ ἀτενίσας εἰς αὐτὸν 10 εἶπεν, Ὦ πλήρης παν-
and having looked steadfastly upon him said, O full of

τὸς δόλου καὶ πάσης ῥᾳδιουργίας, υἱὲ διαβόλου, ἐχθρὲ πάσης
all guile and all craft, son of [the] devil, enemy of all

δικαιοσύνης, οὐ.παύσῃ διαστρέφων τὰς ὁδοὺς κυρίου
righteousness, wilt thou not cease perverting the [2]ways [3]of [4the] [5]Lord

τὰς εὐθείας; 11 καὶ νῦν ἰδού, χεὶρ [m]τοῦ‖ κυρίου ἐπὶ σέ,
[1]straight? And now lo, [the] hand of the Lord [is] upon thee,

καὶ ἔσῃ τυφλός, μὴ βλέπων τὸν ἥλιον ἄχρι καιροῦ.
and thou shalt be blind, not seeing the sun for a season.

Παραχρῆμα.[n]δὲ‖ [o]ἐπέπεσεν‖ ἐπ' αὐτὸν ἀχλὺς καὶ σκότος, καὶ
And immediately fell upon him a mist and darkness, and

περιάγων ἐζήτει χειραγωγούς. 12 τότε ἰδὼν
going about he sought some to lead [him] by the hand. Then [3]having [4]seen

ὁ ἀνθύπατος τὸ γεγονὸς ἐπίστευσεν, [p]ἐκπλησσόμενος‖ ἐπὶ
[1]the [2]proconsul what had happened believed, being astonished at

τῇ διδαχῇ τοῦ κυρίου.
the teaching of the Lord.

13 Ἀναχθέντες.δὲ ἀπὸ τῆς Πάφου οἱ περὶ [q]τὸν‖
And having sailed from Paphos [2with] [3]those [4]about [5him]

Παῦλον ἦλθον εἰς Πέργην τῆς Παμφυλίας. [r]Ἰωάννης‖.δὲ
[1]Paul came to Perga of Pamphylia; and John

ἀποχωρήσας ἀπ' αὐτῶν ὑπέστρεψεν εἰς Ἱεροσόλυμα. 14 αὐ-
having departed from them returned to Jerusalem. [2]They

τοὶ δὲ διελθόντες ἀπὸ τῆς Πέργης παρεγένοντο εἰς Ἀν-
[1]but, having passed through from Perga, came to An-

τιόχειαν [s]τῆς Πισιδίας,‖ καὶ [t]εἰσελθόντες‖ εἰς τὴν συναγωγὴν
tioch of Pisidia, and having gone into the synagogue

τῇ ἡμέρᾳ τῶν σαββάτων ἐκάθισαν. 15 Μετὰ.δὲ τὴν ἀνά-
on the [2]day [1]sabbath they sat down. And after the read-

γνωσιν τοῦ νόμου καὶ τῶν προφητῶν ἀπέστειλαν οἱ ἀρχισυνά-
ing of the law and of the prophets [6]sent [1]the [2]rulers [3]of

γωγοι πρὸς αὐτούς, λέγοντες, Ἄνδρες ἀδελφοί, εἰ [v] ἔστιν
[4]the [5]synagogue to them, saying, Men brethren, if there is

Jews: and they had also John to *their* minister. 6 And when they had gone through the isle unto Paphos, they found a certain sorcerer, a false prophet, a Jew, whose name *was* Bar-jesus: 7 which was with the deputy of the country, Sergius Paulus, a prudent man; who called for Barnabas and Saul, and desired to hear the word of God. 8 But Elymas the sorcerer (for so is his name by interpretation) withstood them, seeking to turn away the deputy from the faith. 9 Then Saul, (who also *is called* Paul,) filled with the Holy Ghost, set his eyes on him, 10 and said, O full of all subtilty and all mischief, *thou* child of the devil, *thou* enemy of all righteousness, wilt thou not cease to pervert the right ways of the Lord? 11 And now, behold, the hand of the Lord *is* upon thee, and thou shalt be blind, not seeing the sun for a season. And immediately there fell on him a mist and a darkness; and he went about seeking some to lead him by the hand. 12 Then the deputy, when he saw what was done, believed, being astonished at the doctrine of the Lord.

13 Now when Paul and his company loosed from Paphos, they came to Perga in Pamphylia: and John departing from them returned to Jerusalem. 14 But when they departed from Perga, they came to Antioch in Pisidia, and went into the synagogue on the sabbath day, and sat down. 15 And after the reading of the law and the prophets the rulers of the synagogue sent unto them, saying, *Ye* men *and* brethren, if ye have

---

[h] Ἰωάνην Tr. [i] + ὅλην (the) whole GLTTrAW. [j] + ἄνδρα a man LTTrAW. [k] Βαριησοῦ T. [l] — καὶ LTTrA. [m] — τοῦ (*read* of [the]) GLTTrAW. [n] τε T. [o] ἔπεσεν LTTr. [p] ἐκπληττόμενος Tr. [q] — τὸν LTTrAW. [r] Ἰωάνης Tr. [s] τὴν Πισιδίαν LTTrA. [t] ἐλθόντες TTr. [v] + τις any (word) LTTrAW.

any word of exhorta-
tion for the people,
say on. 16 Then Paul
stood up, and beck-
oning with *his* hand
said, Men of Israel,
and ye that fear God,
give audience. 17 The
God of this people of
Israel chose our fa-
thers, and exalted the
people when they
dwelt as strangers in
the land of Egypt, and
with an high arm
brought he them out
of it. 18 And about
the time of forty years
suffered he their man-
ners in the wilderness.
19 And when he had
destroyed seven na-
tions in the land of
Chanaan, he divided
their land to them by
lot. 20 And after that
he gave *unto them*
judges about the space
of four hundred and
fifty years, until Samu-
el the prophet. 21 And
afterward they desired
a king: and God gave
unto them Saul the
son of Cis, a man of
the tribe of Benjamin,
by the space of forty
years. 22 And when he
had removed him, he
raised up unto them
David to be their king;
to whom also he gave
testimony, and said,
I have found David
the *son* of Jesse, a man
after mine own heart,
which shall fulfil all
my will. 23 Of this
man's seed hath God
according to *his* pro-
mise raised unto Is-
rael a Saviour, Jesus:
24 when John had first
preached before his
coming the baptism
of repentance to all
the people of Israel.
25 And as John ful-
filled his course, he
said, Whom think ye
that I am? I am not
he. But, behold, there
cometh one after me,
whose shoes of *his* feet
I am not worthy to
loose. 26 Men *and*
brethren, children of
the stock of Abraham,
and whosoever among
you feareth God, to

[w]λόγος ἐν ὑμῖν‖ παρακλήσεως πρὸς τὸν λαόν, λέγετε.
a word among you of exhortation to the people, speak.
16 Ἀναστὰς.δὲ Παῦλος, καὶ κατασείσας τῇ χειρί, εἶπεν,
And [2]having [3]risen [4]up [1]Paul, and making a sign with the hand, said,
Ἄνδρες [x]Ἰσραηλῖται,‖ καὶ οἱ φοβούμενοι τὸν θεόν, ἀκούσατε.
Men Israelites, and those fearing God, hearken.
17 ὁ θεὸς τοῦ.λαοῦ.τούτου [y]Ἰσραὴλ‖ ἐξελέξατο τοὺς πατέρας
The God of this people Israel chose [2]fathers
ἡμῶν· καὶ τὸν λαὸν ὕψωσεν ἐν τῇ παροικίᾳ ἐν γῇ
[1]our, and [2]the [3]people [1]exalted in the sojourning in [the] land
[z]Αἰγύπτῳ,‖ καὶ μετὰ βραχίονος ὑψηλοῦ ἐξήγαγεν αὐτοὺς ἐξ
of Egypt, and with [3]arm [1]a [2]high brought them out of
αὐτῆς· 18 καὶ ὡς [a]τεσσαρακονταετῆ‖ χρόνον [b]ἐτροπο-
it, and about [3]forty [4]years [[1]the] [2]time he bore
φόρησεν αὐτοὺς‖ ἐν τῇ ἐρήμῳ. 19 καὶ καθελὼν ἔθνη ἑπτὰ
[2]manners [1]their in the desert. And having destroyed [2]nations [1]seven
ἐν γῇ Χαναάν, [c]κατεκληροδότησεν‖ [d]αὐτοῖς‖ τὴν.γῆν.αὐ-
in [the] land of Canaan, he gave by lot to them their land.
τῶν. 20 [e]καὶ μετὰ ταῦτα, ὡς ἔτεσιν τετρακοσίοις καὶ
And after these things about [5]years [1]four [2]hundred [3]and
πεντήκοντα‖ ἔδωκεν κριτὰς ἕως Σαμουὴλ [f]τοῦ‖ προφήτου·
[4]fifty he gave judges until Samuel the prophet.
21 κἀκεῖθεν ᾐτήσαντο βασιλέα, καὶ ἔδωκεν αὐτοῖς ὁ θεὸς
And then they asked for a king, and [2]gave [3]to [4]them [1]God
τὸν Σαοὺλ υἱὸν [g]Κίς,‖ ἄνδρα ἐκ φυλῆς [h]Βενιαμίν,‖ ἔτη
Saul son of Cis, a man of [the] tribe of Benjamin, [2]years
[i]τεσσαράκοντα.‖ 22 καὶ μεταστήσας αὐτὸν ἤγειρεν [k]αὐτοῖς
[1]forty. And having removed him he raised up to them
τὸν Δαβὶδ‖ εἰς βασιλέα, ᾧ καὶ εἶπεν μαρτυρήσας,
David for king, to whom also [4]he [5]said [1]having [2]borne [3]witness,
Εὗρον [l]Δαβὶδ‖ τὸν τοῦ Ἰεσσαί, ἄνδρα κατὰ τὴν καρδίαν
I found David the [son] of Jesse, a man according to [2]heart
μου, ὃς ποιήσει πάντα τὰ.θελήματά.μου. 23 Τούτου
[1]my, who will do all my will. [4]Of [5]this [[6]man,]
ὁ θεὸς ἀπὸ τοῦ σπέρματος κατ' ἐπαγγελίαν [m]ἤγειρεν‖ τῷ
[7]God [1]of [2]the [3]seed according to promise raised up
Ἰσραὴλ σωτῆρα Ἰησοῦν, 24 προκηρύξαντος [n]Ἰωάννου‖
to Israel a Saviour Jesus, [2]having [3]before [4]proclaimed [1]John
πρὸ προσώπου τῆς.εἰσόδου.αὐτοῦ βάπτισμα μετανοίας
before [the] face of his entrance a baptism of repentance
παντὶ τῷ λαῷ Ἰσραήλ. 25 ὡς.δὲ ἐπλήρου [o]ὁ‖ [p]Ἰωάννης‖
to all the people of Israel. And as [2]was [3]fulfilling [1]John
τὸν δρόμον, ἔλεγεν, [q]Τίνα με‖ ὑπονοεῖτε εἶναι; οὐκ εἰμὶ
[his] course, he said, Whom me do ye suppose to be? [3]Not [2]am
ἐγώ, ἀλλ' ἰδού, ἔρχεται μετ' ἐμέ, οὗ οὐκ.εἰμὶ ἄξιος τὸ ὑπό-
[1]I [he], but lo, he comes after me, of whom I am not worthy the san-
δημα τῶν ποδῶν λῦσαι. 26 Ἄνδρες ἀδελφοί, υἱοὶ γένους
dal of the feet to loose. Men brethren, sons of [the] race
Ἀβραάμ, καὶ οἱ ἐν ὑμῖν φοβούμενοι τὸν θεόν, [r]ὑμῖν‖ ὁ
of Abraham, and those among you fearing God, to you the

---

[w] ἐν ὑμῖν λόγος LTTrW. [x] Ἰσραηλεῖται T. [y] — Ἰσραὴλ G. [z] Αἰγύπτου LTr. [a] τεσσερακονταέτη TTrA. [b] ἐτροφοφόρησεν αὐτοὺς he nourished them GLTAW. [c] κατεκληρονόμησεν GLTTrAW. [d] — αὐτοῖς TTr[A]. [e] ὡς ἔτεσιν τετρακοσίοις καὶ πεντήκοντα· καὶ μετὰ ταῦτα (*read* their land about four hundred and fifty years. And after these things he gave, &c.) LTTrW. [f] — τοῦ TTr[A]. [g] Κείς Keis LTTrA. [h] Βενιαμείν LTTrA. [i] τεσσεράκοντα TTrA. [k] τὸν Δαυεὶδ αὐτοῖς LTTrA; Δαυῒδ GW. [l] Δαυεὶδ LTTrA; Δαυῒδ GW. [m] ἤγαγεν brought GLTTrAW. [n] Ἰωάνου Tr. [o] — ὁ LTTrA. [p] Ἰωάνης Tr [q] Τί ἐμὲ LTTrA. [r] ἡμῖν to us TA.

λύγος τῆς.σωτηρίας.ταύτης [s]ἀπεστάλη·‖ 27 οἱ.γὰρ κατοικοῦν-
word of this salvation was sent: for those dwelling
τες ἐν Ἱερουσαλὴμ καὶ οἱ.ἄρχοντες.αὐτῶν, τοῦτον ἀγνοήσαντες
in Jerusalem and their rulers, him not having known
καὶ τὰς φωνὰς τῶν προφητῶν τὰς κατὰ πᾶν σάββατον ἀνα-
and the voices of the prophets who on every sabbath are
γινωσκομένας, κρίναντες ἐπλήρωσαν· 28 καὶ μηδεμίαν
read, [3]having [4]judged [[5]him] [1]they [2]fulfilled. And no one
αἰτίαν θανάτου εὑρόντες ᾐτήσαντο [t]Πιλάτον‖ ἀναιρεθῆναι
cause of death having found they begged Pilate to put [2]to [3]death
αὐτόν. 29 ὡς.δὲ ἐτέλεσαν [v]ἅπαντα‖ τὰ περὶ αὐτοῦ γε-
[1]him. And when they finished all things that concerning him had
γραμμένα, καθελόντες ἀπὸ τοῦ ξύλου, ἔθηκαν εἰς
been written, having taken [him] down from the tree, they put [him] in
μνημεῖον· 30 ὁ.δὲ.θεὸς ἤγειρεν αὐτὸν ἐκ νεκρῶν,
a tomb; but God raised him from among [the] dead,
31 ὃς ὤφθη ἐπὶ ἡμέρας πλείους τοῖς συναναβᾶσιν αὐτῷ
who appeared for [2]days [1]many to those who came up with him
ἀπὸ τῆς Γαλιλαίας εἰς Ἱερουσαλήμ, οἵτινές [w] εἰσιν μάρτυρες
from Galilee to Jerusalem, who are [2]witnesses
αὐτοῦ πρὸς τὸν λαόν. 32 καὶ ἡμεῖς [x] ὑμᾶς εὐαγγελιζόμεθα
[1]his to the people. And we to you announce the glad tidings—
τὴν πρὸς τοὺς πατέρας ἐπαγγελίαν γενομένην, ὅτι ταύτην
the, [3]to [4]the [5]fathers [1]promise [2]made, that this
ὁ θεὸς ἐκπεπλήρωκεν τοῖς τέκνοις [y]αὐτῶν ἡμῖν,‖ ἀναστήσας
God has fulfilled [4]children [3]their [1]to [2]us, having raised up
Ἰησοῦν· 33 ὡς καὶ ἐν [z]τῷ ψαλμῷ τῷ δευτέρῳ γέγραπται,‖
Jesus; as also in the [2]psalm [1]second it has been written,
Υἱός μου εἶ σύ, ἐγὼ σήμερον γεγέννηκά σε. 34 Ὅτι.δὲ
[4]Son [3]my [1]thou [2]art, I to-day have begotten thee. And that
ἀνέστησεν αὐτὸν ἐκ νεκρῶν, μηκέτι μέλλοντα ὑπο-
he raised him from among [the] dead, no more to be about to
στρέφειν εἰς διαφθοράν, οὕτως εἴρηκεν, Ὅτι δώσω ὑμῖν τὰ
return to corruption, thus he spoke: I will give to you the
ὅσια [a]Δαβὶδ‖ τὰ πιστά. 35 [b]διὸ‖ καὶ ἐν ἑτέρῳ λέγει,
[2]mercies [3]of [4]David [1]faithful. Wherefore also in another he says,
Οὐ.δώσεις τὸν.ὅσιόν.σου ἰδεῖν διαφθοράν. 36 [a]Δαβὶδ‖
Thou wilt not suffer thy Holy One to see corruption. [2]David
μὲν γὰρ ἰδίᾳ γενεᾷ ὑπηρετήσας τῇ τοῦ θεοῦ βουλῇ
[3]indeed [1]for to his own generation having ministered by the [2]of [3]God [1]counsel
ἐκοιμήθη, καὶ προσετέθη πρὸς τοὺς.πατέρας.αὐτοῦ, καὶ εἶδεν
fell asleep, and was added to his fathers, and saw
διαφθοράν. 37 ὃν.δὲ ὁ θεὸς ἤγειρεν οὐκ.εἶδεν διαφθοράν.
corruption. But he whom God raised up did not see corruption.
38 Γνωστὸν οὖν ἔστω ὑμῖν, ἄνδρες ἀδελφοί, ὅτι διὰ τού-
[4]Known [3]therefore [1]be [2]it to you, men brethren, that through this
του ὑμῖν ἄφεσις ἁμαρτιῶν καταγγέλλεται· 39 [c]καὶ‖ ἀπὸ
one to you remission of sins is announced, and from
πάντων ὧν οὐκ.ἠδυνήθητε ἐν [d]τῷ‖ νόμῳ [e]Μωσέως‖ δι-
all things from which ye could not in the law of Moses be
καιωθῆναι, ἐν τούτῳ πᾶς ὁ πιστεύων δικαιοῦται. 40 βλέ-
justified, in him everyone that believes is justified. Take

you is the word of this salvation sent. 27 For they that dwell at Jerusalem, and their rulers, because they knew him not, nor yet the voices of the prophets which are read every sabbath day, they have fulfilled *them* in condemning *him*. 28 And though they found no cause of death *in him*, yet desired they Pilate that he should be slain. 29 And when they had fulfilled all that was written of him, they took *him* down from the tree, and laid *him* in a sepulchre. 30 But God raised him from the dead: 31 and he was seen many days of them which came up with him from Galilee to Jerusalem, who are his witnesses unto the people. 32 And we declare unto you glad tidings, how that the promise which was made unto the fathers, 33 God hath fulfilled the same unto us their children, in that he hath raised up Jesus again; as it is also written in the second psalm, Thou art my Son, this day have I begotten thee. 34 And as concerning that he raised him up from the dead, *now* no more to return to corruption, he said on this wise, I will give you the sure mercies of David. 35 Wherefore he saith also in another *psalm*, Thou shalt not suffer thine Holy One to see corruption. 36 For David, after he had served his own generation by the will of God, fell on sleep, and was laid unto his fathers, and saw corruption: 37 but he, whom God raised again, saw no corruption. 38 Be it known unto you therefore, men *and* brethren, that through this man is preached unto you the forgiveness of sins: 39 and by him all that believe are justified from all things, from which ye could not be justified by the law of Moses.

[s] ἐξαπεστάλη was sent forth LTTrAW. [t] Πειλᾶτον T. [v] πάντα GLTTrAW. [w] + νῦν now LTTrAW. [x] + νῦν now W. [y] ἡμῶν to our LTTr; αὐτῶν ἡμῶν W. [z] τῷ πρώτῳ (first) ψαλμῷ γέγραπται GTTr; τῷ ψαλμῷ γέγ. τῷ πρώτῳ (δευτέρῳ AW) LAW. [a] Δαυεὶδ LTTrA; Δαυῖδ GW. [b] διότι LTTrA. [c] — καὶ LT[TrA]. [d] — τῷ LTTrA. [e] Μωϋσέως GLTTrAW.

40 Beware therefore, lest that come upon you, which is spoken of in the prophets; 41 Behold, ye despisers, and wonder, and perish: for I work a work in your days, a work which ye shall in no wise believe, though a man declare it unto you. 42 And when the Jews were gone out of the synagogue, the Gentiles besought that these words might be preached to them the next sabbath. 43 Now when the congregation was broken up, many of the Jews and religious proselytes followed Paul and Barnabas: who, speaking to them, persuaded them to continue in the grace of God.

44 And the next sabbath day came almost the whole city together to hear the word of God. 45 But when the Jews saw the multitudes, they were filled with envy, and spake against those things which were spoken by Paul, contradicting and blaspheming. 46 Then Paul and Barnabas waxed bold, and said, It was necessary that the word of God should first have been spoken to you: but seeing ye put it from you, and judge yourselves unworthy of everlasting life, lo, we turn to the Gentiles. 47 For so hath the Lord commanded us, *saying*, I have set thee to be a light of the Gentiles, that thou shouldest be for salvation unto the ends of the earth. 48 And when the Gentiles heard this, they were glad, and glorified the word of the Lord: and as many as were ordained to eternal life believed. 49 And the word of the Lord was published throughout all the region. 50 But the Jews stirred up the devout and honourable women, and the chief

πετε οὖν μὴ.ἐπέλθῃ [f]ἐφ' ὑμᾶς‖ τὸ εἰρημένον ἐν
heed therefore that it may not come upon you that which has been said in

τοῖς προφήταις, 41 Ἴδετε, οἱ.καταφρονηταί, καὶ θαυμάσατε
the prophets, Behold, ye despisers, and wonder

καὶ ἀφανίσθητε· ὅτι ἔργον [g]ἐγὼ ἐργάζομαι‖ ἐν ταῖς ἡμέραις
and perish; for a work I work in [2]days

ὑμῶν, ἔργον [h]ᾧ‖ οὐ.μὴ πιστεύσητε ἐάν τις ἐκδιηγῆται
[1]your, a work which in no wise ye would believe if one should declare it

ὑμῖν. 42 Ἐξιόντων.δὲ [i]ἐκ τῆς συναγωγῆς τῶν Ἰουδαίων,‖
to you. But [3]having [4]departed [5]from [6]the [7]synagogue [1]the [2]Jews,

παρεκάλουν [k]τὰ ἔθνη‖ εἰς τὸ μεταξὺ σάββατον λαληθῆναι
[10]besought [8]the [9]Gentiles on the next sabbath [3]to [4]be [5]spoken

αὐτοῖς τὰ.ῥήματα.ταῦτα. 43 λυθείσης.δὲ τῆς συναγωγῆς,
[6]to [7]them [1]these [2]words. And [3]having [4]broken [5]up [1]the [2]synagogue,

ἠκολούθησαν πολλοὶ τῶν Ἰουδαίων καὶ τῶν σεβομένων
[15]followed [6]many [7]of [8]the [9]Jews [10]and [11]of [12]the [13]worshipping

προσηλύτων τῷ Παύλῳ καὶ τῷ Βαρνάβᾳ· οἵτινες προσλα-
[14]proselytes Paul and Barnabas, who speak-

λοῦντες αὐτοῖς, ἔπειθον αὐτοὺς [l]ἐπιμένειν‖ τῇ χάριτι τοῦ
ing to them persuaded them to continue in the grace

θεοῦ.
of God.

44 Τῷ.[m]δὲ‖ [n]ἐρχομένῳ‖ σαββάτῳ σχεδὸν πᾶσα ἡ πόλις
And on the coming sabbath almost all the city

συνήχθη ἀκοῦσαι τὸν λόγον [o]τοῦ θεοῦ.‖ 45 ἰδόντες.δὲ
was gathered together to hear the word of God. But [3]having [4]seen

οἱ Ἰουδαῖοι τοὺς ὄχλους, ἐπλήσθησαν ζήλου, καὶ ἀντέλεγον
[1]the [2]Jews the crowds, were filled with envy, and contradicted

τοῖς ὑπὸ [p]τοῦ‖ Παύλου [q]λεγομένοις,‖ [r]ἀντιλέγοντες καὶ‖
the things [2]by [3]Paul [1]spoken, contradicting and

βλασφημοῦντες. 46 παῤῥησιασάμενοι.[s]δὲ‖ ὁ Παῦλος καὶ ὁ Βαρ-
blaspheming. But [4]speaking [5]boldly [1]Paul [2]and [3]Bar-

νάβας [t]εἶπον,‖ Ὑμῖν ἦν ἀναγκαῖον πρῶτον λαληθῆναι τὸν
nabas said, To you was necessary first to be spoken the

λόγον τοῦ θεοῦ· ἐπειδὴ.[v]δὲ‖ ἀπωθεῖσθε αὐτόν, καὶ οὐκ ἀξίους
word of God; but since ye thrust away it, and not worthy

κρίνετε ἑαυτοὺς τῆς αἰωνίου ζωῆς, ἰδοὺ στρεφόμεθα εἰς τὰ
ye judge yourselves of eternal life, lo, we turn to the

ἔθνη· 47 οὕτως.γὰρ ἐντέταλται ἡμῖν ὁ κύριος, Τέθεικά σε
Gentiles; for thus has enjoined us the Lord, I have set thee

εἰς φῶς ἐθνῶν, τοῦ.εἶναί.σε εἰς σωτηρίαν ἕως ἐσχά-
for a light of [the] Gentiles, that thou be for salvation to [the] uttermost

του τῆς γῆς. 48 Ἀκούοντα.δὲ τὰ ἔθνη ἔχαιρον, καὶ ἐδόξα-
part of the earth. And hearing [it] the Gentiles rejoiced, and glori-

ζον τὸν λόγον τοῦ κυρίου, καὶ ἐπίστευσαν ὅσοι ἦσαν
fied the word of the Lord, and believed as many as were

τεταγμένοι εἰς ζωὴν αἰώνιον. 49 διεφέρετο.δὲ ὁ λόγος τοῦ
appointed to life eternal. And was carried the word of the

κυρίου [w]δι'‖ ὅλης τῆς χώρας. 50 οἱ.δὲ Ἰουδαῖοι παρώτρυναν
Lord through [2]whole [1]the country. But the Jews excited

τὰς σεβομένας γυναῖκας [x]καὶ‖ τὰς εὐσχήμονας καὶ τοὺς πρώ-
the worshipping [3]women [1]and [2]honourable and the principal

---

[f] — ἐφ' ὑμᾶς LTTr[A]. [g] ἐργάζομαι ἐγὼ LTTrAW. [h] ὃ LTTrAW. [i] αὐτῶν they (having departed) GLTTrAW. [k] — τὰ ἔθνη (*read* they besought) GLTTrAW. [l] προσμένειν GLTTrAW. [m] τε GA. [n] ἐχομένῳ following GLAW. [o] τοῦ κυρίου of the Lord LTTr. [p] — τοῦ LTTr[A]. [q] λαλουμένοις LTTr. [r] — ἀντιλέγοντες καὶ LTr[A]. [s] τε LTTrA. [t] εἶπαν LTTrA. [v] — δὲ but LTTr. [w] καθ' T. [x] — καὶ GLTTrAW.

τους τῆς πόλεως, καὶ ἐπήγειραν διωγμὸν ἐπὶ τὸν Παῦλον
men of the city, and stirred up a persecution against Paul
καὶ [y]τὸν‖ Βαρνάβαν, καὶ ἐξέβαλον αὐτοὺς ἀπὸ τῶν.ὁρίων.αὐ-
and Barnabas, and cast out them from their borders.
τῶν. 51 οἱ.δὲ ἐκτιναξάμενοι τὸν κονιορτὸν τῶν.ποδῶν.[z]αὐτῶν‖
But they having shaken off the dust of their feet
ἐπ' αὐτούς, ἦλθον εἰς Ἰκόνιον. 52 οἱ.[a]δὲ‖ μαθηταὶ ἐπλη-
against them, came to Iconium. And the disciples were
ροῦντο χαρᾶς καὶ πνεύματος ἁγίου.
filled with joy and [the] [2]Spirit [1]Holy.

14 Ἐγένετο.δὲ ἐν Ἰκονίῳ κατὰ.τὸ.αὐτὸ εἰσελθεῖν αὐτοὺς
And it came to pass in Iconium [2]together [3]entered [1]they
εἰς τὴν συναγωγὴν τῶν Ἰουδαίων, καὶ λαλῆσαι οὕτως ὥστε
into the synagogue of the Jews, and spoke so that
πιστεῦσαι Ἰουδαίων.τε καὶ Ἑλλήνων πολὺ πλῆθος. 2 οἱ.δὲ
[9]believed [1]both [2]of [3]Jews [4]and [5]Hellenists [6]a [7]great [8]number. But the
[b]ἀπειθοῦντες‖ Ἰουδαῖοι ἐπήγειραν καὶ ἐκάκωσαν τὰς ψυχὰς
disobeying Jews stirred up and made evil-affected the souls
τῶν ἐθνῶν κατὰ τῶν ἀδελφῶν. 3 ἱκανὸν μὲν οὖν χρόνον
of the Gentiles against the brethren. A long [2]therefore [1]time
διέτριψαν παῤῥησιαζόμενοι ἐπὶ τῷ κυρίῳ, τῷ μαρτυ-
they stayed, speaking boldly, [confiding] in the Lord, who bore wit-
ροῦντι [c]τῷ λόγῳ τῆς.χάριτος.αὐτοῦ, [d]καὶ‖ [e]διδόντι‖ σημεῖα καὶ
ness to the word of his grace, and giving signs and
τέρατα γίνεσθαι διὰ τῶν.χειρῶν.αὐτῶν. 4 ἐσχίσθη.δὲ τὸ
wonders to be done through their hands. And was divided the
πλῆθος τῆς πόλεως· καὶ οἱ.μὲν ἦσαν σὺν τοῖς Ἰουδαίοις
multitude of the city, and some were with the Jews
οἱ.δὲ σὺν τοῖς ἀποστόλοις. 5 Ὡς.δὲ ἐγένετο ὁρμὴ τῶν
and some with the apostles. And when there was a rush [2]of [3]the
ἐθνῶν τε καὶ Ἰουδαίων σὺν τοῖς.ἄρχουσιν.αὐτῶν, ὑβρίσαι
[4]Gentiles [1]both and Jews with their rulers, to insult
καὶ λιθοβολῆσαι αὐτούς, 6 συνιδόντες κατέφυγον εἰς τὰς
and to stone them, being aware they fled to the
πόλεις τῆς Λυκαονίας, [f]Λύστραν, καὶ Δέρβην, καὶ τὴν περί-
cities of Lycaonia, Lystra, and Derbe, and the country
χωρον, 7 κἀκεῖ [g]ἦσαν εὐαγγελιζόμενοι.‖
around, and there they were announcing the glad tidings.

8 Καί τις ἀνὴρ [h]ἐν Λύστροις ἀδύνατος‖ τοῖς ποσὶν ἐκά-
And a certain man in Lystra, impotent in the feet, sat,
θητο, χωλὸς ἐκ κοιλίας μητρὸς.αὐτοῦ [i]ὑπάρχων,‖ ὃς
lame from [the] womb of his mother being, who
οὐδέποτε [k]περιπεπατήκει.‖ 9 οὗτος [l]ἤκουεν‖ τοῦ Παύλου
never had walked. This [man] heard Paul
λαλοῦντος· ὃς ἀτενίσας αὐτῷ, καὶ ἰδὼν ὅτι [m]πίστιν
speaking, who, having looked intently on him, and seeing that faith
ἔχει‖ τοῦ σωθῆναι, 10 εἶπεν μεγάλῃ [n]τῇ‖ φωνῇ, [o]Ἀνάστηθι
he has to be healed, said with a loud voice, Stand up
ἐπὶ τοὺς.πόδας.σου ὀρθός. Καὶ [p]ἥλλετο‖ καὶ περιεπάτει.
on thy feet upright. And he sprang up and walked.

men of the city, and raised persecution against Paul and Barnabas, and expelled them out of their coasts. 51 But they shook off the dust of their feet against them, and came unto Iconium. 52 And the disciples were filled with joy, and with the Holy Ghost.

XIV. And it came to pass in Iconium, that they went both together into the synagogue of the Jews, and so spake, that a great multitude both of the Jews and also of the Greeks believed. 2 But the unbelieving Jews stirred up the Gentiles, and made their minds evil affected against the brethren. 3 Long time therefore abode they speaking boldly in the Lord, which gave testimony unto the word of his grace, and granted signs and wonders to be done by their hands. 4 But the multitude of the city was divided: and part held with the Jews, and part with the apostles. 5 And when there was an assault made both of the Gentiles, and also of the Jews with their rulers, to use *them* despitefully, and to stone them, 6 they were ware of *it*, and fled unto Lystra and Derbe, cities of Lycaonia, and unto the region that lieth round about: 7 and there they preached the gospel.

8 And there sat a certain man at Lystra, impotent in his feet, being a cripple from his mother's womb, who never had walked: 9 the same heard Paul speak: who stedfastly beholding him, and perceiving that he had faith to be healed, 10 said with a loud voice, Stand upright on thy feet. And he leaped and walked.

---

[y] — τὸν LTTrA. [z] — αὐτῶν (*read* of the feet) LTTrA. [a] τε LTrA. [b] ἀπειθήσαντες LTTrA. [c] + ἐπὶ to (the) T. [d] — καὶ GLTTrAW. [e] διδόντος T. [f] + εἰς to L. [g] εὐαγγελιζόμενοι ἦσαν LTTrA. [h] ἀδύνατος ἐν Λύστροις T. [i] — ὑπάρχων GLTTrAW. [k] περιεπεπατήκει E; περιεπάτησεν walked LTTrA. [l] ἤκουσεν LTTr. [m] ἔχει πίστιν LTTrA. [n] — τῇ LTTr. [o] + Σοὶ λέγω ἐν τῷ ὀνόματι τοῦ κυρίου Ἰησοῦ χριστοῦ To thee I say in the name of the Lord Jesus Christ L. [p] ἥλατο GLTTrAW.

11 And when the peo-
ple saw what Paul had
done, they lifted up
their voices, saying in
the speech of Lycaonia,
The gods are come
down to us in the like-
ness of men. 12 And
they called Barnabas,
Jupiter; and Paul,
Mercurius, because he
was the chief speaker.
13 Then the priest of
Jupiter, which was be-
fore their city, brought
oxen and garlands
unto the gates, and
would have done sacri-
fice with the people.
14 *Which* when the
apostles, Barnabas and
Paul, heard *of*, they
rent their clothes, and
ran in among the peo-
ple, crying out, 15 and
saying, Sirs, why do ye
these things? We also
are men of like pas-
sions with you, and
preach unto you that
ye should turn from
these vanities unto
the living God, which
made heaven, and
earth, and the sea, and
all things that are
therein: 16 who in
times past suffered all
nations to walk in
their own ways. 17 Ne-
vertheless he left not
himself without wit-
ness, in that he did
good, and gave us rain
from heaven, and
fruitful seasons, fill-
ing our hearts with
food and gladness.
18 And with these say-
ings scarce restrained
they the people, that
they had not done
sacrifice unto them.
19 And there came
thither *certain* Jews
from Antioch and Ico-
nium, who persuaded
the people, and, having
stoned Paul, drew *him*
out of the city, sup-
posing he had been
dead. 20 Howbeit, as
the disciples stood
round about him, he
rose up, and came in-
to the city: and the
next day he departed
with Barnabas to Der-
be. 21 And when they
had preached the gos-
pel to that city, and had
taught many, they re-
turned again to Lys-

11 Οἱ.[r]δὲ‖ ὄχλοι ἰδόντες ὃ ἐποίησεν [s]ὁ‖ Παῦλος, ἐπῆραν
And the crowds having seen what [2]did [1]Paul, lifted up
τὴν.φωνὴν.αὐτῶν Λυκαονιστὶ λέγοντες, Οἱ θεοὶ ὁμοιωθέντες
their voice in Lycaonian saying, The gods, having become like
ἀνθρώποις κατέβησαν πρὸς ἡμᾶς· 12 ἐκάλουν.τε τὸν [t]μὲν‖
men, are come down to us. And they called
Βαρνάβαν Δία· τὸν.δὲ.Παῦλον Ἑρμῆν, ἐπειδὴ αὐτὸς ἦν ὁ
Barnabas Zeus; and Paul Hermes, because he was the
ἡγούμενος τοῦ λόγου. 13 [v]ὁ.δὲ‖ ἱερεὺς τοῦ Διὸς τοῦ ὄντος
leader in speaking. And the priest of Zeus who was
πρὸ τῆς.πόλεως.[w]αὐτῶν,‖ ταύρους καὶ στέμματα ἐπὶ τοὺς
before their city, oxen and garlands to the
πυλῶνας ἐνέγκας, σὺν τοῖς ὄχλοις ἤθελεν θύειν. 14 Ἀκού-
gates having brought, with the crowds wished to sacrifice. [7]Having
σαντες δὲ οἱ ἀπόστολοι Βαρνάβας καὶ Παῦλος, διαῤῥήξαντες
[8]heard [1]but [2]the [3]apostles [4]Barnabas [5]and [6]Paul, having rent
τὰ.ἱμάτια.αὐτῶν [x]εἰσεπήδησαν‖ εἰς τὸν ὄχλον, κράζοντες
their garments, rushed in to the crowd, crying
15 καὶ λέγοντες, Ἄνδρες, τί ταῦτα ποιεῖτε; καὶ ἡμεῖς
and saying, Men, why these things do ye? also we
ὁμοιοπαθεῖς ἐσμεν ὑμῖν ἄνθρωποι, εὐαγγελιζόμενοι
[3]of [4]like [5]feelings [1]are [6]with [7]you [2]men, announcing the glad tidings to
ὑμᾶς ἀπὸ τούτων τῶν ματαίων ἐπιστρέφειν ἐπὶ [y]τὸν‖ θεὸν
you from these vanities to turn to God
[y]τὸν‖ ζῶντα, ὃς ἐποίησεν τὸν οὐρανὸν καὶ τὴν γῆν καὶ τὴν
the living, who made the heaven and the earth and the
θάλασσαν καὶ πάντα τὰ ἐν αὐτοῖς· 16 ὃς ἐν ταῖς παρ-
sea and all the things in them; who in the
ῳχημέναις γενεαῖς εἴασεν πάντα τὰ ἔθνη πορεύεσθαι ταῖς
past generations suffered all the nations to go
ὁδοῖς.αὐτῶν· 17 [z]καί.τοι.γε‖ οὐκ ἀμάρτυρον [a]ἑαυτὸν‖ ἀφῆ-
in their [own] ways, though indeed not without witness himself he
κεν [b]ἀγαθοποιῶν,‖ οὐρανόθεν [c]ἡμῖν‖ ὑετοὺς διδοὺς καὶ καιροὺς
left, doing good, from heaven to us [2]rains [1]giving and [2]seasons
καρποφόρους, ἐμπιπλῶν τροφῆς καὶ εὐφροσύνης τὰς καρδίας
[1]fruitful, filling with food and gladness the hearts
[d]ἡμῶν.‖ 18 Καὶ ταῦτα λέγοντες μόλις κατέπαυσαν τοὺς
of us. And these things saying hardly they stopped the
ὄχλους τοῦ.μὴ.θύειν αὐτοῖς. 19 [e]Ἐπῆλθον‖.δὲ ἀπὸ Ἀντιοχείας
crowds from sacrificing to them. But thither came from Antioch
καὶ Ἰκονίου Ἰουδαῖοι, καὶ πείσαντες τοὺς ὄχλους, καὶ λιθά-
and Iconium Jews, and having persuaded the crowds, and having
σαντες τὸν Παῦλον, ἔσυρον ἔξω τῆς πόλεως, [f]νομίσαντες‖
stoned Paul, drew [him] outside the city, supposing
αὐτὸν [g]τεθνάναι.‖ 20 κυκλωσάντων.δὲ [h]αὐτὸν τῶν μαθητῶν,‖
him to have died. But [3]having [4]surrounded [5]him [1]the [2]disciples,
ἀναστὰς εἰσῆλθεν εἰς τὴν πόλιν· καὶ τῇ ἐπαύριον ἐξῆλ-
having risen up he entered into the city. And on the morrow he went
θεν σὺν τῷ Βαρνάβᾳ εἰς Δέρβην. 21 [i]εὐαγγελισάμενοί‖.τε
away with Barnabas to Derbe. And having announced the glad tidings to
τὴν.πόλιν.ἐκείνην, καὶ μαθητεύσαντες ἱκανοὺς ὑπέστρεψαν εἰς
that city, and having discipled many they returned to

---

[r] τε LTA. [s] — ὁ LTTrAW. [t] — μὲν LTTrA. [v] ὅ τε LTTrA. [w] — αὐτῶν (*read* the city) GLTTrAW. [x] ἐξεπήδησαν rushed out GLTTrAW. [y] — τὸν LTTrAW. [z] καίτοι LT; καιτοιγε GAW; — γε LTTr. [a] αὐτὸν LTTr. [b] ἀγαθουργῶν LTTrAW. [c] ὑμῖν to you GLT[Tr]A. [d] ὑμῶν of you GLTTrA. [e] ἐπῆλθαν LTTrA. [f] νομίζοντες LTTrA. [g] τεθνηκέναι LTTrA. [h] τῶν μαθητῶν αὐτὸν LTTrA. [i] εὐαγγελιζόμενοί announcing &c. LT.

τὴν Λύστραν καὶ [k]Ἰκόνιον καὶ [k]Ἀντιόχειαν· 22 ἐπιστηρίζοντες
Lystra and Iconium and Antioch, establishing
τὰς ψυχὰς τῶν μαθητῶν, παρακαλοῦντες ἐμμένειν τῇ
the souls of the disciples, exhorting [them] to continue in the
πίστει, καὶ ὅτι διὰ πολλῶν θλίψεων δεῖ ἡμᾶς εἰσελθεῖν εἰς
faith, and that through many tribulations must we enter into
τὴν βασιλείαν τοῦ θεοῦ. 23 χειροτονήσαντες.δὲ αὐτοῖς [l]πρεσ-
the kingdom of God. And having chosen for them el-
βυτέρους κατ'.ἐκκλησίαν,‖ προσευξάμενοι μετὰ νηστειῶν πα-
ders in every assembly, having prayed with fastings they
ρέθεντο αὐτοὺς τῷ κυρίῳ εἰς ὃν πεπιστεύκεισαν. 24 καὶ
committed them to the Lord, on whom they had believed. And
διελθόντες τὴν Πισιδίαν ἦλθον εἰς [m]Παμφυλίαν· 25 καὶ
having passed through Pisidia they came to Pamphylia, and
λαλήσαντες [n]ἐν Πέργῃ‖ τὸν λόγον κατέβησαν εἰς [o]Ἀττάλειαν·‖
having spoken in Perga the word they came down to Attalia;
26 κἀκεῖθεν ἀπέπλευσαν εἰς Ἀντιόχειαν, ὅθεν ἦσαν παρα-
and thence they sailed to Antioch, whence they had been
δεδομένοι τῇ χάριτι τοῦ θεοῦ εἰς τὸ ἔργον ὃ ἐπλήρωσαν.
committed to the grace of God for the work which they fulfilled.
27 παραγενόμενοι.δὲ καὶ συναγαγόντες τὴν ἐκκλησίαν
And having arrived and having gathered together the assembly
[p]ἀνήγγειλαν‖ ὅσα ἐποίησεν ὁ θεὸς μετ' αὐτῶν, καὶ ὅτι ἤνοιξεν
they declared all that [2]did [1]God with them, and that he opened
τοῖς ἔθνεσιν θύραν πίστεως. 28 διέτριβον.δὲ [q]ἐκεῖ‖ χρόνον
to the nations a door of faith. And they stayed there [4]time
οὐκ ὀλίγον σὺν τοῖς μαθηταῖς.
[1]not [2]a [3]little with the disciples.

15 Καί τινες κατελθόντες ἀπὸ τῆς Ἰουδαίας ἐδίδασκον
And certain having come down from Judæa were teaching
τοὺς ἀδελφούς, Ὅτι ἐὰν.μὴ [r]περιτέμνησθε‖ τῷ ἔθει [s]Μωϋ-
the brethren, Unless ye be circumcised after the custom of Mo-
σέως οὐ.δύνασθε σωθῆναι. 2 Γενομένης [t]οὖν‖ στάσεως
ses ye cannot be saved. Having taken place therefore a commotion
καὶ [v]συζητήσεως‖ οὐκ ὀλίγης τῷ Παύλῳ καὶ τῷ Βαρνάβᾳ πρὸς
and discussion not a little by Paul and Barnabas with
αὐτούς, ἔταξαν ἀναβαίνειν Παῦλον καὶ Βαρνάβαν καί
them, they appointed [4]to [5]go [6]up [1]Paul [2]and [3]Barnabas and
τινας ἄλλους ἐξ αὐτῶν πρὸς τοὺς ἀποστόλους καὶ
certain others from amongst them to the apostles and
πρεσβυτέρους εἰς Ἱερουσαλήμ, περὶ τοῦ.ζητήματος.τούτου.
elders to Jerusalem, about this question.
3 οἱ μὲν οὖν προπεμφθέντες ὑπὸ τῆς ἐκκλησίας διήρ-
They indeed therefore having been sent forward by the assembly passed
χοντο τὴν [w]Φοινίκην καὶ [x]Σαμάρειαν,‖ ἐκδιηγούμενοι τὴν
through Phœnicia and Samaria, relating the
ἐπιστροφὴν τῶν ἐθνῶν· καὶ ἐποίουν χαρὰν μεγάλην πᾶσιν
conversion of the nations. And they caused [2]joy [1]great to all
τοῖς ἀδελφοῖς. 4 παραγενόμενοι.δὲ εἰς [y]Ἱερουσαλὴμ‖ [z]ἀπε-
the brethren. And having come to Jerusalem they were
δέχθησαν‖ [a]ὑπὸ‖ τῆς ἐκκλησίας καὶ τῶν ἀποστόλων καὶ τῶν
welcomed by the assembly and the apostles and the

tra, and *to* Iconium, and Antioch, 22 confirming the souls of the disciples, *and* exhorting them to continue in the faith, and that we must through much tribulation enter into the kingdom of God. 23 And when they had ordained them elders in every church, and had prayed with fasting, they commended them to the Lord, on whom they believed. 24 And after they had passed throughout Pisidia, they came to Pamphylia. 25 And when they had preached the word in Perga, they went down into Attalia: 26 and thence sailed to Antioch, from whence they had been recommended to the grace of God for the work which they fulfilled. 27 And when they were come, and had gathered the church together, they rehearsed all that God had done with them, and how he had opened the door of faith unto the Gentiles. 28 And there they abode long time with the disciples.

XV. And certain men which came down from Judæa taught the brethren, *and said*, Except ye be circumcised after the manner of Moses, ye cannot be saved. 2 When therefore Paul and Barnabas had no small dissension and disputation with them, they determined that Paul and Barnabas, and certain other of them, should go up to Jerusalem unto the apostles and elders about this question. 3 And being brought on their way by the church, they passed through Phenice and Samaria, declaring the conversion of the Gentiles: and they caused great joy unto all the brethren. 4 And when they were come to Jerusalem, they were received of the church, and *of*

---

[k] + εἰς to LTTrA. [l] κατ' ἐκκλησίαν πρεσβυτέρους LTTrAW. [m] + τὴν TTr. [n] εἰς τὴν Πέργην T. [o] Ἀτταλίαν TA. [p] ἀνήγγελλον LTTrA. [q] — ἐκεῖ GLTTrAW. [r] περιτμηθῆτε ye have been circumcised LTTrA. [s] + τῷ LTTrA. [t] δὲ but (having taken place) TTr. [v] ζητήσεως GLTTrAW. [w] + τε both LTTrA. [x] Σαμαρίαν T. [y] Ἱεροσόλυμα Tr. [z] παρεδέχθησαν they were received LTTrAW. [a] ἀπὸ Tr.

the apostles and elders,
and they declared all
things that God had
done with them. 5 But
there rose up certain
of the sect of the Pha-
risees which believed,
saying, That it was
needful to circumcise
them, and to command
them to keep the law
of Moses. 6 And the
apostles and elders
came together for to
consider of this matter.
7 And when there had
been much disputing,
Peter rose up, and
said unto them, Men
and brethren, ye know
how that a good while
ago God made choice
among us, that the
Gentiles by my mouth
should hear the word
of the gospel, and be-
lieve. 8 And God,
which knoweth the
hearts, bare them wit-
ness, giving them the
Holy Ghost, even as
he did unto us; 9 and
put no difference be-
tween us and them,
purifying their hearts
by faith. 10 Now
therefore why tempt
ye God, to put a yoke
upon the neck of the
disciples, which nei-
ther our fathers nor
we were able to bear?
11 But we believe that
through the grace of
the Lord Jesus Christ
we shall be saved, even
as they. 12 Then all
the multitude kept si-
lence, and gave audi-
ence to Barnabas and
Paul, declaring what
miracles and wonders
God had wrought a-
mong the Gentiles by
them. 13 And after
they had held their
peace, James answer-
ed, saying, Men *and*
brethren, hearken unto
me: 14 Simeon hath
declared how God at
the first did visit the
Gentiles, to take out
of them a people for
his name. 15 And to
this agree the words
of the prophets; as it
is written, 16 After
this I will return, and
will build again the
tabernacle of David,
which is fallen down;
and I will build again
the ruins thereof, and

πρεσβυτέρων, ἀνήγγειλάν-τε ὅσα ὁ θεὸς ἐποίησεν μετ' αὐτῶν.
elders, and they declared all that God did with them.
5 ἐξανέστησαν-δέ τινες τῶν ἀπὸ τῆς αἱρέσεως τῶν Φαρισαίων
And rose up certain of those of the sect of the Pharisees
πεπιστευκότες, λέγοντες, Ὅτι δεῖ περιτέμνειν αὐτούς,
who believed, saying, It is necessary to circumcise them,
παραγγέλλειν-τε τηρεῖν τὸν νόμον Μωϋσέως. 6 Συνήχ-
and charge [them] to keep the law of Moses. [2]Were [3]gathered
θησαν [b]δὲ" οἱ ἀπόστολοι καὶ οἱ πρεσβύτεροι ἰδεῖν περὶ τοῦ
[4]together [1]and the apostles and the elders to see about
λόγου-τούτου. 7 πολλῆς-δὲ [c]συζητήσεως" γενομένης, ἀνα-
this matter. And much discussion having taken place, [2]having
στὰς Πέτρος εἶπεν πρὸς αὐτούς, Ἄνδρες ἀδελφοί, ὑμεῖς
[3]risen [4]up [1]Peter said to them, Men brethren, ye
ἐπίστασθε ὅτι ἀφ' ἡμερῶν ἀρχαίων [d]ὁ θεὸς ἐν ἡμῖν ἐξελέξατο"
know that from [2]days [1]early God among us chose
διὰ τοῦ-στόματός-μου ἀκοῦσαι τὰ ἔθνη τὸν λόγον τοῦ
by my mouth [for] [3]to [4]hear [1]the [2]nations the word of the
εὐαγγελίου, καὶ πιστεῦσαι. 8 καὶ ὁ καρδιογνώστης θεὸς ἐμαρ-
glad tidings, and to believe. And the heart-knowing God bore
τύρησεν αὐτοῖς, δοὺς [e]αὐτοῖς" τὸ πνεῦμα τὸ ἅγιον, καθὼς καὶ
witness to them, giving to them the Spirit the Holy, as also
ἡμῖν· 9 καὶ [f]οὐδὲν"-διέκρινεν μεταξὺ ἡμῶν [g]τε" καὶ αὐτῶν,
to us, and put no difference between [2]us [1]both and them,
τῇ πίστει καθαρίσας τὰς-καρδίας-αὐτῶν. 10 νῦν οὖν τί
by the faith having purified their hearts. Now therefore why
πειράζετε τὸν θεόν, ἐπιθεῖναι ζυγὸν ἐπὶ τὸν τράχηλον τῶν
tempt ye God to put a yoke upon the neck of the
μαθητῶν, ὃν οὔτε οἱ-πατέρες-ἡμῶν οὔτε ἡμεῖς ἰσχύσαμεν
disciples, which neither our fathers nor we were able
βαστάσαι; 11 ἀλλὰ διὰ τῆς χάριτος [h] κυρίου Ἰησοῦ [i]χριστοῦ"
to bear? But by the grace of [the] Lord Jesus Christ
πιστεύομεν σωθῆναι, καθ' ὃν-τρόπον κἀκεῖνοι. 12 Ἐσίγησεν
we believe to be saved, in the same manner as they also. [2]Kept [3]silence
δὲ πᾶν τὸ πλῆθος, καὶ ἤκουον Βαρνάβα καὶ Παύλου ἐξη-
[1]and all the multitude, and heard Barnabas and Paul — re-
γουμένων ὅσα ἐποίησεν ὁ θεὸς σημεῖα καὶ τέρατα ἐν τοῖς
lating what [5]did [4]God [1]signs [2]and [3]wonders among the
ἔθνεσιν δι' αὐτῶν. 13 Μετὰ-δὲ τὸ-σιγῆσαι αὐτοὺς ἀπεκρίθη
nations by them. And after [2]were [3]silent [1]they [5]answered
Ἰάκωβος λέγων, Ἄνδρες ἀδελφοί, ἀκούσατέ μου. 14 Συμεὼν
[4]James, saying, Men brethren, hear me. Simeon
ἐξηγήσατο καθὼς πρῶτον ὁ θεὸς ἐπεσκέψατο λαβεῖν ἐξ
related how first God visited to take out of
ἐθνῶν λαὸν [k]ἐπὶ" τῷ-ὀνόματι-αὐτοῦ. 15 καὶ τούτῳ συμφω-
nations a people for his name. And with this agree
νοῦσιν οἱ λόγοι τῶν προφητῶν, καθὼς γέγραπται, 16 Μετὰ
the words of the prophets: as it has been written, After
ταῦτα ἀναστρέψω καὶ ἀνοικοδομήσω τὴν σκηνὴν [l]Δαβὶδ"
these things I will return and will build again the tabernacle of David
τὴν πεπτωκυῖαν· καὶ τὰ [m]κατεσκαμμένα" αὐτῆς ἀνοικοδομήσω,
which is fallen; and the ruins of it I will build again,

---

[b] τε TrA. [c] συνζητήσεως LA; ζητήσεως TTr. [d] ἐν ὑμῖν you (ἡμῖν W) ἐξελέξατο ὁ θεὸς LTTrAW. [e] — αὐτοῖς TTrA. [f] οὐθὲν TTrA. [g] — τε W. [h] + τοῦ of the GLTTrAW. [i] — χριστοῦ GTTrAW. [k] — ἐπὶ (read τῷ ὀν. αὐτοῦ for his name) LTTrAW. [l] Δαυεὶδ LTTrA; Δαυὶδ GW. [m] κατεστραμμένα T; κατεστρευμένα Tr.

καὶ ἀνορθώσω αὐτήν, 17 ὅπως ἂν.ἐκζητήσωσιν οἱ κατάλοιποι
and will set up it, so that [5]may [6]seek [7]out [1]the [2]residue
τῶν ἀνθρώπων τὸν κύριον, καὶ πάντα τὰ ἔθνη ἐφ' οὓς ἐπι-
[3]of [4]men the Lord, and all the nations upon whom has
κέκληται τὸ.ὄνομά.μου ἐπ' αὐτούς· λέγει κύριος [u]ὁ[ǁ] ποιῶν
been called my name upon them, says [the] Lord who does
ταῦτα [o]πάντα.[ǁ] 18 [p]Γνωστὰ[ǁ] ἀπ' αἰῶνός [q]ἐστιν τῷ θεῷ
[2]these [3]things [1]all: known from eternity are to God
πάντα τὰ.ἔργα.αὐτοῦ.[ǁ] 19 διὸ ἐγὼ κρίνω μὴ παρενοχλεῖν
all his works. Wherefore I judge not to trouble
τοῖς ἀπὸ τῶν ἐθνῶν ἐπιστρέφουσιν ἐπὶ τὸν θεόν· 20 ἀλλὰ
those who from the nations turn to God; but
ἐπιστεῖλαι αὐτοῖς τοῦ ἀπέχεσθαι [r]ἀπὸ[ǁ] τῶν ἀλισγημάτων τῶν
to write to them to abstain from the pollutions of the
εἰδώλων καὶ τῆς πορνείας καὶ [s]τοῦ[ǁ] πνικτοῦ καὶ τοῦ αἵματος.
idols and fornication and what is strangled and blood.
21 [t]Μωσῆς[ǁ].γὰρ ἐκ γενεῶν ἀρχαίων κατὰ.πόλιν τοὺς κη-
For Moses from generations of old in every city [2]those [3]pro-
ρύσσοντας αὐτὸν ἔχει ἐν ταῖς συναγωγαῖς κατὰ.πᾶν σάββατον
claiming [4]him [1]has in the synagogues, every sabbath
ἀναγινωσκόμενος.
being read.

22 Τότε ἔδοξεν τοῖς ἀποστόλοις καὶ τοῖς πρεσβυτέροις
Then it seemed good to the apostles and to the elders
σὺν ὅλῃ τῇ ἐκκλησίᾳ, ἐκλεξαμένους ἄνδρας ἐξ αὐτῶν
with [2]whole [1]the assembly, chosen men from among them
πέμψαι εἰς Ἀντιόχειαν σὺν τῷ Παύλῳ καὶ Βαρνάβᾳ, Ἰούδαν
to send to Antioch with Paul and Barnabas, Judas
τὸν [v]ἐπικαλούμενον[ǁ] [w]Βαρσαβᾶν,[ǁ] καὶ Σίλαν, ἄνδρας ἡγου-
surnamed Barsabas, and Silas, [2]men [1]lead-
μένους ἐν τοῖς ἀδελφοῖς, 23 γράψαντες διὰ χειρὸς.αὐτῶν
ing among the brethren, having written by their hand
[x]τάδε,[ǁ] Οἱ ἀπόστολοι καὶ οἱ πρεσβύτεροι [y]καὶ οἱ[ǁ] ἀδελφοί,
thus: The apostles and the elders and the brethren,
τοῖς κατὰ τὴν Ἀντιόχειαν καὶ Συρίαν καὶ Κιλικίαν ἀδελφοῖς
to those in Antioch and Syria and Cilicia, brethren
τοῖς ἐξ ἐθνῶν, χαίρειν. 24 Ἐπειδὴ ἠκούσαμεν ὅτι
from among [the] nations, greeting. Inasmuch as we have heard that
τινὲς ἐξ ἡμῶν ἐξελθόντες ἐτάραξαν ὑμᾶς λόγοις,
certain from amongst us having gone out troubled you by words,
ἀνασκευάζοντες τὰς.ψυχὰς.ὑμῶν, [z]λέγοντες περιτέμνεσθαι
upsetting your souls, saying [ye must] be circumcised
καὶ τηρεῖν τὸν νόμον,[ǁ] οἷς οὐ.διεστειλάμεθα· 25 ἔδοξεν
and keep the law; to whom we gave no [such] command; it seemed good
ἡμῖν γενομένοις ὁμοθυμαδόν, [a]ἐκλεξαμένους[ǁ] ἄνδρας πέμψαι
to us having come with one accord, chosen men to send
πρὸς ὑμᾶς, σὺν τοῖς.ἀγαπητοῖς.ἡμῶν Βαρνάβᾳ καὶ Παύλῳ,
to you, with our beloved Barnabas and Paul,
26 ἀνθρώποις παραδεδωκόσιν τὰς.ψυχὰς.αὐτῶν ὑπὲρ τοῦ
men who have given up their lives for the
ὀνόματος τοῦ.κυρίου.ἡμῶν Ἰησοῦ χριστοῦ. 27 ἀπεστάλκαμεν
name of our Lord Jesus Christ. We have sent

I will set it up: 17 that the residue of men might seek after the Lord, and all the Gentiles, upon whom my name is called, saith the Lord, who doeth all these things.
18 Known unto God are all his works from the beginning of the world. 19 Wherefore my sentence is, that we trouble not them, which from among the Gentiles are turned to God: 20 but that we write unto them, that they abstain from pollutions of idols, and *from* fornication, and *from* things strangled, and *from* blood. 21 For Moses of old time hath in every city them that preach him, being read in the synagogues every sabbath day.

22 Then pleased it the apostles and elders, with the whole church, to send chosen men of their own company to Antioch with Paul and Barnabas; *namely*, Judas surnamed Barsabas, and Silas, chief men among the brethren: 23 and they wrote *letters* by them after this manner; The apostles and elders and brethren *send* greeting unto the brethren which are of the Gentiles in Antioch and Syria and Cilicia: 24 forasmuch as we have heard, that certain which went out from us have troubled you with words, subverting your souls, saying, *Ye must* be circumcised, and keep the law: to whom we gave no *such* commandment: 25 it seemed good unto us, being assembled with one accord, to send chosen men unto you with our beloved Barnabas and Paul, 26 men that have hazarded their lives for the name of our Lord Jesus Christ. 27 We have sent there-

---

[u] — ὁ LTTr. [o] — πάντα GLTTrAW. [p] γνωστὸν LW. [q] τῷ κυρίῳ τὸ ἔργον αὐτοῦ to the Lord his work L; ἐστιν τῷ θεῷ τὸ ἔργον αὐτοῦ W; — ἐστιν τῷ θεῷ παντα τὰ ἔργα αὐτοῦ GTTrA. [r] — ἀπὸ (*read* τῶν from the) LTTr[A]. [s] — τοῦ LTr. [t] Μωϋσῆς GLTTrAW. [v] καλουμενον called LTTrAW. [w] Βαρσαββᾶν LTTrA. [x] — τάδε LTTrA. [y] — καὶ οἱ (*read* elder brethren) LTTrA. [z] — λέγοντες περιτέμνεσθαι καὶ τηρεῖν τὸν νόμον LTTrA. [a] ἐκλεξαμένοις having chosen LTrW.

fore Judas and Silas, who shall also tell *you* the same things by mouth. 28 For it seemed good to the Holy Ghost, and to us, to lay upon you no greater burden than these necessary things; 29 that ye abstain from meats offered to idols, and from blood, and from things strangled, and from fornication: from which if ye keep yourselves, ye shall do well. Fare ye well. 30 So when they were dismissed, they came to Antioch: and when they had gathered the multitude together, they delivered the epistle: 31 *which* when they had read, they rejoiced for the consolation. 32 And Judas and Silas, being prophets also themselves, exhorted the brethren with many words, and confirmed *them*. 33 And after they had tarried *there* a space, they were let go in peace from the brethren unto the apostles. 34 Notwithstanding it pleased Silas to abide there still. 35 Paul also and Barnabas continued in Antioch, teaching and preaching the word of the Lord, with many others also.

36 And some days after Paul said unto Barnabas, Let us go again and visit our brethren in every city where we have preached the word of the Lord, *and see* how they do. 37 And Barnabas determined to take with them John, whose surname was Mark. 38 But Paul thought not good to take him with them, who departed from them from Pamphylia, and went not with them to the work. 39 And the contention was so sharp between them, that they departed asunder one from the other: and so Barnabas took Mark, and

οὖν Ἰούδαν καὶ Σίλαν, καὶ αὐτοὺς διὰ λόγου ἀπαγγέλ-
therefore Judas and Silas, [2]also [1]themselves by word telling
λοντας τὰ αὐτά. 28 ἔδοξεν.γὰρ [b]τῷ ἁγίῳ πνεύματι‖
[you] the same things. For it seemed good to the Holy Spirit
καὶ ἡμῖν, μηδὲν πλέον ἐπιτίθεσθαι ὑμῖν βάρος πλὴν [c]τῶν
and to us, no further [2]to [3]lay [4]upon [5]you [1]burden than
ἐπάναγκες.τούτων,‖ 29 ἀπέχεσθαι εἰδωλοθύτων καὶ
these necessary things: to abstain from things sacrificed to idols, and
αἵματος καὶ [d]πνικτοῦ‖ καὶ πορνείας· ἐξ ὧν
from blood and from what is strangled, and from fornication; from which
διατηροῦντες ἑαυτούς, εὖ πράξετε. ἔρρωσθε. 30 Οἱ μὲν
keeping yourselves, well ye will do. Farewell. They
οὖν ἀπολυθέντες [e]ἦλθον‖ εἰς Ἀντιόχειαν· καὶ συναγαγόντες
therefore, being let go went to Antioch, and having gathered
τὸ πλῆθος ἐπέδωκαν τὴν ἐπιστολήν. 31 ἀναγνόντες.δὲ ἐχά-
the multitude delivered the epistle. And having read they
ρησαν ἐπὶ τῇ παρακλήσει. 32 Ἰούδας.[f]τε‖ καὶ Σιλας, καὶ αὐ-
rejoiced at the consolation. And Judas and Silas, [2]also [1]them-
τοὶ προφῆται ὄντες, διὰ λόγου πολλοῦ παρεκάλεσαν τοὺς
selves [4]prophets [3]being, by [2]discourse [1]much exhorted the
ἀδελφούς, καὶ ἐπεστήριξαν. 33 Ποιήσαντες.δὲ χρόνον ἀπε-
brethren, and established [them]. And having continued a time they
λύθησαν μετ' εἰρήνης ἀπὸ τῶν ἀδελφῶν πρὸς [g]τοὺς ἀποστό-
were let go in peace from the brethren to the apostles;
λους.‖ 34 [h]ἔδοξεν.δὲ τῷ Σίλᾳ ἐπιμεῖναι αὐτοῦ.‖ 35 Παῦλος.δὲ
but it seemed good to Silas to remain there. And Paul
καὶ Βαρνάβας διέτριβον ἐν Ἀντιοχείᾳ, διδάσκοντες καὶ εὐαγ-
and Barnabas stayed in Antioch, teaching and [5]an-
γελιζόμενοι μετὰ καὶ ἑτέρων πολλῶν, τὸν λόγον τοῦ
nouncing [6]the [7]glad [8]tidings [1]with [4]also [3]others [2]many— the word of the
κυρίου.
Lord.

36 Μετὰ.δέ τινας ἡμέρας εἶπεν [i]Παῦλος πρὸς Βαρνάβαν,‖
But after certain days said Paul to Barnabas,
Ἐπιστρέψαντες δὴ ἐπισκεψώμεθα τοὺς.ἀδελφοὺς.[k]ἡμῶν‖ κατὰ
Having turned back [3]indeed [1]let [2]us look after our brethren in
[l]πᾶσαν πόλιν‖ ἐν αἷς κατηγγείλαμεν τὸν λόγον τοῦ κυρίου,
every city in which we have announced the word of the Lord,
πῶς ἔχουσιν. 37 Βαρνάβας.δὲ [m]ἐβουλεύσατο‖ [n]συμπαρα-
how they are. And Barnabas purposed to take
λαβεῖν‖ [o] [p]τὸν‖ [q]Ἰωάννην‖ τὸν καλούμενον Μάρκον· 38 Παῦ-
with [them] John called Mark; [2]Paul
λος δὲ ἠξίου τὸν ἀποστάντα ἀπ' αὐτῶν ἀπὸ Παμ-
[1]but thought it well him who withdrew from them from Pam-
φυλίας, καὶ μὴ.συνελθόντα αὐτοῖς εἰς τὸ ἔργον, μὴ [r]συμπαρα-
phylia, and went not with them to the work, not to take
λαβεῖν‖ τοῦτον. 39 ἐγένετο [s]οὖν‖ παροξυσμός, ὥστε
[2]with [[3]them] [1]him. Arose therefore a sharp contention so that
ἀποχωρισθῆναι αὐτοὺς ἀπ' ἀλλήλων, τόν.τε.Βαρνάβαν παρα-
[2]departed [1]they from one another, and Barnabas having

---

[b] τῷ πνεύματι τῷ ἁγίῳ TTrW. [c] τούτων τῶν ἐπάναγκες LTTr; — τούτων A. [d] πνικτῶν LTTrA. [e] κατῆλθον LTTrA. [f] δὲ E. [g] τοὺς ἀποστείλαντας αὐτούς, those who sent them GLTTrAW. [h] — *verse* 34 LTTrAW. [i] πρὸς Βαρνάβαν Παῦλος, LTTrA. [k] — ἡμῶν (*read* the brethren) GLTTrAW. [l] πόλιν πᾶσαν LTTrA. [m] ἐβούλετο LTTrAW. [n] συν- TA. [o] + καὶ also GLTTrA. [p] — τὸν GLA. [q] Ἰωάνην Tr. [r] συμ-(συν- TA)παραλαμβάνειν LTTrA. [s] δὲ and (arose) LTTrA.

λαβόντα τὸν Μάρκον ἐκπλεῦσαι εἰς Κύπρον· 40 Παῦλος.δὲ
taken Mark sailed to Cyprus; but Paul
ἐπιλεξάμενος Σίλαν ἐξῆλθεν, παραδοθεὶς τῇ χάριτι
having chosen Silas went forth, having been committed to the grace
ᵛτοῦ θεοῦ‖ ὑπὸ τῶν ἀδελφῶν. 41 διήρχετο.δὲ τὴν Συρίαν
of God by the brethren. And he passed through Syria
καὶ ʷ Κιλικίαν, ἐπιστηρίζων τὰς ἐκκλησίας. 16 Κατήντησεν.δὲ ˣ
and Cilicia, establishing the assemblies. And he arrived
εἰς Δέρβην καὶ ʸ Λύστραν· καὶ ἰδού, μαθητής τις ἦν ἐκεῖ,
at Derbe and Lystra: and behold, a ²disciple ¹certain was there,
ὀνόματι Τιμόθεος, υἱὸς γυναικός ᶻτινος‖ Ἰουδαίας πιστῆς
by name Timotheus, son of a ⁴woman ¹certain ²Jewish ³believing
πατρὸς.δὲ "Ἕλληνος· 2 ὃς ἐμαρτυρεῖτο ὑπὸ τῶν ἐν Λύσ-
but [the] father a Greek, who was borne witness to by the ²in ³Lys-
τροις καὶ Ἰκονίῳ ἀδελφῶν. 3 τοῦτον ἠθέλησεν ὁ Παῦλος σὺν
tra ⁴and ⁵Iconium ¹brethren. This one ²wished ¹Paul with
αὐτῷ ἐξελθεῖν, καὶ λαβὼν περιέτεμεν αὐτὸν διὰ τοὺς
him to go forth, and having taken he circumcised him on account of the
Ἰουδαίους τοὺς ὄντας ἐν τοῖς.τόποις.ἐκείνοις· ᾔδεισαν.γὰρ
Jews who were in those places, for they ²knew
ᵃἅπαντες τὸν.πατέρα.αὐτοῦ ὅτι "Ἕλλην‖ ὑπῆρχεν. 4 ὡς.δὲ
¹all his father that a Greek he was. And as
διεπορεύοντο τὰς πόλεις ᵇπαρεδίδουν‖ αὐτοῖς φυλάσσειν
they passed through the cities they delivered to them to keep
τὰ δόγματα τὰ κεκριμένα ὑπὸ τῶν ἀποστόλων καὶ ᶜτῶν‖
the decrees decided on by the apostles and the
πρεσβυτέρων τῶν ἐν ᵈἹερουσαλήμ.‖ 5 αἱ μὲν οὖν ἐκ-
elders in Jerusalem. The ²therefore ¹as-
κλησίαι ἐστερεοῦντο τῇ πίστει, καὶ ἐπερίσσευον τῷ ἀριθμῷ
semblies were strengthened in the faith, and abounded in number
καθ'.ἡμέραν.
every day.

6 ᵉΔιελθόντες‖ δὲ τὴν Φρυγίαν καὶ ᶠτὴν‖ Γαλατικὴν
²Having ³passed ⁴through ¹and Phrygia and the Galatian
χώραν, κωλυθέντες ὑπὸ τοῦ ἁγίου πνεύματος λαλῆσαι
country, having been forbidden by the Holy Spirit to speak
τὸν λόγον ἐν τῇ Ἀσίᾳ, 7 ἐλθόντες ᵍ κατὰ τὴν Μυσίαν ἐπείρα-
the word in Asia, having come down to Mysia they at-
ζον ʰκατὰ‖ ⁱτὴν‖ Βιθυνίαν ᵏπορεύεσθαι·‖ καὶ οὐκ.εἴασεν
tempted to Bithynia to go; and ³did ⁴not ⁵suffer
αὐτοὺς τὸ πνεῦμα ˡ. 8 παρελθόντες.δὲ τὴν Μυσίαν κατέβη-
⁶them ¹the ²Spirit; and having passed by Mysia they came
σαν εἰς Τρωάδα. 9 καὶ ὅραμα διὰ ᵐτῆς‖ νυκτὸς ⁿὤφθη τῷ
down to Troas. And a vision during the night appeared
Παύλῳ·‖ Ἀνήρ ᵒτις ἦν Μακεδὼν‖ ἑστώς, ᵖ παρακαλῶν
to Paul: A ²man ¹certain ⁵was ³of ⁴Macedonia standing, beseeching
αὐτὸν καὶ λέγων, Διαβὰς εἰς Μακεδονίαν βοήθησον
him and saying, Having passed over into Macedonia help
ἡμῖν. 10 Ὡς.δὲ τὸ ὅραμα εἶδεν, εὐθέως ἐζητήσαμεν ἐξελθεῖν
us. And when the vision he saw, immediately we sought to go forth

sailed unto Cyprus;
40 and Paul chose Si-
las, and departed, be-
ing recommended by
the brethren unto the
grace of God. 41 And
he went through Sy-
ria and Cilicia, con-
firming the churches.
XVI. Then came he
to Derbe and Lystra:
and, behold, a certain
disciple was there,
named Timotheus, the
son of a certain wo-
man, which was a
Jewess, and believed;
but his father was a
Greek: 2 which was
well reported of by the
brethren that were at
Lystra and Iconium.
3 Him would Paul
have to go forth with
him; and took and
circumcised him be-
cause of the Jews
which were in those
quarters: for they
knew all that his fa-
ther was a Greek.
4 And as they went
through the cities,
they delivered them
the decrees for to keep,
that were ordained of
the apostles and elders
which were at Jerusa-
lem. 5 And so were the
churches established
in the faith, and in-
creased in number
daily.

6 Now when they
had gone throughout
Phrygia and the re-
gion of Galatia, and
were forbidden of the
Holy Ghost to preach
the word in Asia, 7 af-
ter they were come to
Mysia, they assayed to
go into Bithynia: but
the Spirit suffered
them not. 8 And they
passing by Mysia came
down to Troas. 9 And
a vision appeared to
Paul in the night;
There stood a man of
Macedonia, and pray-
ed him, saying, Come
over into Macedonia,
and help us. 10 And
after he had seen the
vision, immediately
we endeavoured to go

ᵛ τοῦ κυρίου of the Lord LTTrAW. ʷ + τὴν L. ˣ + καὶ also L[Tr]. ʸ + εἰς at LTTr. ᶻ — τινος GLTTrAW. ᵃ πάντες (ἅπαντες Tr) ὅτι Ἕλλην ὁ πατὴρ αὐτοῦ LTr. ᵇ παρεδίδοσαν LTTrAW. ᶜ — τῶν LTTrAW. ᵈ Ἱεροσολύμοις LTTrAW. ᵉ διῆλθον they passed through LTTrAW. ᶠ — τὴν LTTrA. ᵍ + δὲ and (having come) LTTrAW. ʰ εἰς GLTTrAW. ⁱ — τὴν W. ᵏ πορευθῆναι LTTrA. ˡ + Ἰησοῦ of Jesus GLTTrAW. ᵐ — τῆς LTTr[A]W ⁿ τῷ Παυλῳ ὤφθη TTrA. ᵒ Μακεδών τις ἦν (— ἦν A) LTTrAW. ᵖ + καὶ and LTTr.

into Macedonia, as-
suredly gathering that
the Lord had called
us for to preach the
gospel unto them.
11 Therefore loosing
from Troas, we came
with a straight course
to Samothracia, and
the next *day* to Nea-
polis; 12 and from
thence to Philippi,
which is the chief city
of that part of Mace-
donia, *and* a colony:
and we were in that
city abiding certain
days. 13 And on the
sabbath we went out
of the city by a river
side, where prayer was
wont to be made; and
we sat down, and spake
unto the women which
resorted *thither*. 14 And
a certain woman nam-
ed Lydia, a seller of
purple, of the city of
Thyatira, which wor-
shipped God, heard *us*:
whose heart the Lord
opened, that she at-
tended unto the things
which were spoken of
Paul. 15 And when
she was baptized, and
her household, she be-
sought *us*, saying, If
ye have judged me to
be faithful to the Lord,
come into my house,
and abide *there*. And
she constrained us.
16 And it came to pass,
as we went to prayer,
a certain damsel pos-
sessed with a spirit of
divination met us,
which brought her
masters much gain by
soothsaying: 17 the
same followed Paul
and us, and cried, say-
ing, These men are the
servants of the most
high God, which shew
unto us the way of
salvation. 18 And this
did she many days.
But Paul, being griev-
ed, turned and said to
the spirit, I command
thee in the name of
Jesus Christ to come
out of her. And he
came out the same
hour. 19 And when
her masters saw that
the hope of their gains
was gone, they caught

εἰς [q]τὴν‖ Μακεδονίαν, συμβιβάζοντες ὅτι προσκέκληται ἡμᾶς
to Macedonia, concluding that [3]had [4]called [5]us
[r]ὁ κύριος‖ εὐαγγελίσασθαι αὐτούς. 11 Ἀναχθέντες
[1]the [2]Lord to announce the glad tidings to them. Having sailed
[s]οὖν‖ ἀπὸ [t]τῆς‖ Τρῳάδος εὐθυδρομήσαμεν εἰς Σαμο-
therefore from Troas we came with a straight course to Samo-
θρᾴκην, τῇ.[v]τε‖ ἐπιούσῃ εἰς [w]Νεάπολιν,‖ 12 [x]ἐκεῖθέν.τε‖
thracia, and on the following day to Neapolis, and thence
εἰς Φιλίππους, ἥτις ἐστὶν πρώτη τῆς μερίδος [y]τῆς‖
to Philippi, which is [the] first [2]of [[3]that] [4]part
Μακεδονίας πόλις, κολώνια. Ἦμεν.δὲ ἐν ταύτῃ τῇ πόλει δια-
[5]of [6]Macedonia [1]city, a colony. And we were in this city stay-
τρίβοντες ἡμέρας τινάς, 13 τῇ.τε ἡμέρᾳ τῶν σαββάτων
ing [2]days [1]certain. And on the day of the sabbath
ἐξήλθομεν [z]ἔξω‖ τῆς [a]πόλεως‖ παρὰ ποταμόν, οὗ [b]ἐνομίζετο
we went forth outside the city by a river, where was customary
προσευχὴ‖ εἶναι, καὶ καθίσαντες ἐλαλοῦμεν ταῖς συνελ-
prayer to be, and having sat down we spoke to the [2]who [3]came
θούσαις γυναιξίν. 14 Καί τις γυνὴ ὀνόματι Λυδία, πορ-
[4]together [1]women. And a certain woman, by name Lydia, a seller
φυρόπωλις πόλεως Θυατείρων, σεβομένη τὸν θεόν, ἤκουεν·
of purple of [the] city of Thyatira, who worshipped God, was hearing;
ἧς ὁ κύριος διήνοιξεν τὴν καρδίαν προσέχειν τοῖς
of whom the Lord opened the heart to attend to the things
λαλουμένοις ὑπὸ [c]τοῦ‖ Παύλου. 15 ὡς.δὲ ἐβαπτίσθη καὶ
spoken by Paul. And when she was baptized and
ὁ.οἶκος.αὐτῆς παρεκάλεσεν λέγουσα, Εἰ κεκρίκατέ με πιστὴν
her house she besought saying, If ye have judged me faithful
τῷ κυρίῳ εἶναι, εἰσελθόντες εἰς τὸν.οἶκόν.μου, [d]μείνατε·‖
to the Lord to be, having entered into my house, abide.
καὶ παρεβιάσατο ἡμᾶς. 16 Ἐγένετο.δὲ πορευομένων.ἡμῶν
And she constrained us. And it came to pass as we were going
εἰς [e] προσευχήν, παιδίσκην τινὰ ἔχουσαν πνεῦμα [f]Πύθωνος‖
to prayer, a [2]damsel [1]certain, having a spirit of Python,
[g]ἀπαντῆσαι‖ ἡμῖν, ἥτις ἐργασίαν πολλὴν παρεῖχεν τοῖς
met us, who [2]gain [1]much brought
κυρίοις.αὐτῆς μαντευομένη. 17 αὕτη [h]κατακολουθήσασα‖ τῷ
to her masters by divining. She having followed
Παύλῳ καὶ ἡμῖν ἔκραζεν λέγουσα, Οὗτοι οἱ ἄνθρωποι δοῦλοι
Paul and us cried saying, These men bondmen
τοῦ θεοῦ τοῦ ὑψίστου εἰσίν, οἵτινες καταγγέλλουσιν [i]ἡμῖν‖
of the [3]God [1]Most [2]High are, who announce to us [the]
ὁδὸν σωτηρίας. 18 Τοῦτο.δὲ ἐποίει ἐπὶ πολλὰς ἡμέρας· δια-
way of salvation. And this she did for many days. [3]Being
πονηθεὶς δὲ [k]ὁ‖ Παῦλος, καὶ ἐπιστρέψας τῷ πνεύματι εἶπεν,
[4]distressed [1]but [2]Paul, and having turned to the spirit said,
Παραγγέλλω σοι ἐν [l]τῷ‖ ὀνόματι Ἰησοῦ χριστοῦ ἐξελθεῖν
I charge thee in the name of Jesus Christ to come out
ἀπ' αὐτῆς. Καὶ ἐξῆλθεν αὐτῇ.τῇ ὥρᾳ. 19 Ἰδόντες.δὲ οἱ κύριοι
from her. And it came out the same hour. And [3]seeing [2]masters
αὐτῆς ὅτι ἐξῆλθεν ἡ ἐλπὶς τῆς.ἐργασίας.αὐτῶν, ἐπιλαβόμενοι
[1]her that was gone the hope of their gain, having taken hold of

---

[q] — τὴν LTTr. [r] ὁ θεὸς God LTTrA. [s] δὲ and (having sailed) TA. [t] — τῆς LTTrA. [v] δὲ LTTrA. [w] Νέαν πόλιν TTr. [x] κἀκεῖθεν LTTrAW. [y] — τῆς LTTr. [z] — ἔξω W. [a] πύλης gate LTTrAW. [b] ἐνομίζομεν προσευχὴν we supposed prayer LTTr. [c] — τοῦ Tr. [d] μένετε LTTrW. [e] + τὴν the [place for] LTTrAW. [f] Πύθωνα LTTrA. [g] ὑπαντῆσαι TTrA. [h] κατακολουθοῦσα following TTr. [i] ὑμῖν to you ETTr. [k] — ὁ TTr. [l] — τῷ LTTrA.

τὸν Παῦλον καὶ [m]τὸν‖ Σίλαν εἵλκυσαν εἰς τὴν ἀγορὰν
Paul and Silas they dragged [them] into the market
ἐπὶ τοὺς ἄρχοντας· 20 καὶ προσαγαγόντες αὐτοὺς τοῖς
before the magistrates; and having brought up them to the
στρατηγοῖς [n]εἶπον,‖ Οὗτοι οἱ ἄνθρωποι ἐκταράσσουσιν ἡμῶν
captains said, These men [3]exceedingly [4]trouble [5]our
τὴν πόλιν, Ἰουδαῖοι ὑπάρχοντες· 21 καὶ καταγγέλλουσιν ἔθη
[6]city, [2]Jews [1]being, and announce customs
ἃ οὐκ.ἔξεστιν ἡμῖν παραδέχεσθαι οὐδὲ ποιεῖν, Ῥωμαίοις
which it is not lawful for us to receive nor to do, [2]Romans
οὖσιν. 22 Καὶ συνεπέστη ὁ ὄχλος κατ' αὐτῶν, καὶ οἱ στρα-
[1]being. And rose up together the crowd against them, and the cap-
τηγοὶ [o]περιῤῥήξαντες‖ αὐτῶν τὰ ἱμάτια ἐκέλευον ῥαβδί-
tains having torn off of them the garments commanded to beat [them]
ζειν· 23 πολλάς.τε ἐπιθέντες αὐτοῖς πληγὰς ἔβαλον
with rods. And [3]many [1]having [2]laid [5]on [6]them [4]stripes they cast [them]
εἰς φυλακήν, παραγγείλαντες τῷ δεσμοφύλακι ἀσφαλῶς τηρεῖν
into prison, charging the jailor safely to keep
αὐτούς· 24 ὃς παραγγελίαν τοιαύτην [p]εἰληφὼς‖ ἔβαλεν αὐτοὺς
them; who [2]a [3]charge [1]such having received thrust them
εἰς τὴν ἐσωτέραν φυλακήν, καὶ τοὺς.πόδας.[q]αὐτῶν ἠσφαλί-
into the inner prison, and their feet secured
σατο‖ εἰς τὸ ξύλον. 25 Κατὰ.δὲ τὸ μεσονύκτιον Παῦλος καὶ
to the stocks. And towards midnight Paul and
Σίλας προσευχόμενοι ὕμνουν τὸν θεόν· ἐπηκροῶντο
Silas praying were singing praises to God, [4]listened [5]to
δὲ αὐτῶν οἱ δέσμιοι. 26 ἄφνω.δὲ σεισμὸς ἐγένετο μέγας,
[1]and [6]them [2]the [3]prisoners. And suddenly [5]earthquake [1]there [2]was [3]a [4]great,
ὥστε σαλευθῆναι τὰ θεμέλια τοῦ δεσμωτηρίου· [r]ἀνεῴχθησάν‖
so that were shaken the foundations of the prison, [2]were [3]opened
[s]τε‖ παραχρῆμα αἱ θύραι πᾶσαι, καὶ πάντων τὰ δεσμὰ ἀνέθη.
[1]and immediately [2]the [3]doors [1]all, and [3]of [4]all [1]the [2]bonds were loosed.
27 ἔξυπνος.δὲ γενόμενος ὁ δεσμοφύλαξ, καὶ ἰδὼν ἀνεῳγ-
And [4]awoke [5]out [6]of [7]sleep [3]being [1]the [2]jailor, and seeing opened
μένας τὰς θύρας τῆς φυλακῆς, σπασάμενος [t] μάχαιραν [v]ἔμελ-
the doors of the prison, having drawn a sword was
λεν‖ ἑαυτὸν ἀναιρεῖν, νομίζων ἐκπεφευγέναι τοὺς δεσμίους.
about himself to put to death, supposing had escaped the prisoners.
28 ἐφώνησεν.δὲ [w]φωνῇ μεγάλῃ ὁ Παῦλος‖ λέγων, Μηδὲν
But [2]called [3]out [4]with [5]a [7]voice [6]loud [1]Paul saying, [4]No
πράξῃς σεαυτῷ κακόν· ἅπαντες.γάρ ἐσμεν ἐνθάδε. 29 Αἰ-
[1]do [2]to [3]thyself injury; for [2]all [1]we [3]are here. [2]Having
τήσας δὲ φῶτα εἰσεπήδησεν, καὶ ἔντρομος.γενόμενος προσ-
[3]asked [4]for [1]and lights he rushed in, and trembling fell
έπεσεν τῷ Παύλῳ καὶ [x]τῷ‖ Σίλᾳ· 30 καὶ προαγαγὼν αὐτοὺς
down before Paul and Silas. And having brought them
ἔξω ἔφη, Κύριοι, τί με.δεῖ ποιεῖν ἵνα σωθῶ;
out he said, Sirs, what is necessary for me to do that I may be saved?
31 Οἱ.δὲ [y]εἶπον,‖ Πίστευσον ἐπὶ τὸν κύριον Ἰησοῦν [z]χριστόν,‖
And they said, Believe on the Lord Jesus Christ,
καὶ σωθήσῃ, σὺ καὶ ὁ.οἶκός.σου. 32 Καὶ ἐλάλησαν αὐτῷ
and thou shalt be saved, thou and thy house. And they spoke to him

Paul and Silas, and
drew *them* into the
marketplace unto the
rulers, 20 and brought
them to the magis-
trates, saying, These
men, being Jews, do ex-
ceedingly trouble our
city, 21 and teach cus-
toms, which are not
lawful for us to re-
ceive, neither to ob-
serve, being Romans.
22 And the multitude
rose up together a-
gainst them: and the
magistrates rent off
their clothes, and com-
manded to beat *them*.
23 And when they had
laid many stripes up-
on them, they cast
them into prison,
charging the jailor to
keep them safely:
24 who, having receiv-
ed such a charge, thrust
them into the inner
prison, and made their
feet fast in the stocks.
25 And at midnight
Paul and Silas prayed,
and sang praises unto
God: and the prisoners
heard them. 26 And
suddenly there was a
great earthquake, so
that the foundations
of the prison were
shaken: and imme-
diately all the doors
were opened, and every
one's bands were loos-
ed. 27 And the keeper
of the prison awaking
out of his sleep, and
seeing the prison doors
open, he drew out his
sword, and would have
killed himself, suppos-
ing that the prisoners
had been fled. 28 But
Paul cried with a loud
voice, saying, Do thy-
self no harm: for we
are all here. 29 Then
he called for a light,
and sprang in, and
came trembling, and
fell down before
Paul and Silas, 30 and
brought them out, and
said, Sirs, what must
I do to be saved?
31 And they said, Be-
lieve on the Lord Jesus
Christ, and thou shalt
be saved, and thy
house. 32 And they
spake unto him the

m — τὸν A. n εἶπαν LTTrA. o περιρήξαντες LTTrA. p λαβὼν LTTrAW. q ἠσφαλίσατο αὐτῶν LTTrA. r ἠνεῴχθησαν LTrA; ἠνοίχθησαν T. s δὲ LTTrA. t + τὴν the (sword) LTrA. v ἤμελλεν LTTrA. w — ὁ LTTr; Παῦλος φωνῇ μεγάλῃ L. x — τῷ LTrA. y εἶπαν LTTrA. z — χριστόν LTTrA.

word of the Lord, and
to all that were in
his house. 33 And
he took them the same
hour of the night,
and washed *their*
stripes; and was bap-
tized, he and all his,
straightway. 34 And
when he had brought
them into his house,
he set meat before
them, and rejoiced, be-
lieving in God with all
his house. 35 And
when it was day, the
magistrates sent the
serjeants, saying, Let
those men go. 36 And
the keeper of the pri-
son told this saying to
Paul, The magistrates
have sent to let you
go: now therefore de-
part, and go in peace.
37 But Paul said unto
them, They have beat-
en us openly uncon-
demned, being Ro-
mans, and have cast *us*
into prison; and now
do they thrust us out
privily? nay verily;
but let them come
themselves and fetch
us out. 38 And the
serjeants told these
words unto the magis-
trates: and they feared,
when they heard that
they were Romans.
39 And they came and
besought them, and
brought *them* out, and
desired *them* to depart
out of the city. 40 And
they went out of the
prison, and entered in-
to *the house of* Lydia:
and when they had
seen the brethren, they
comforted them, and
departed.

XVII. Now when they
had passed through
Amphipolis and Apol-
lonia, they came to
Thessalonica, where
was a synagogue of
the Jews: 2 and Paul,
as his manner was,
went in unto them, and
three sabbath days
reasoned with them
out of the scriptures,
3 opening and alleg-
ing, that Christ must
needs have suffered,

τὸν λόγον τοῦ κυρίου, [a]καὶ πᾶσιν‖ τοῖς ἐν τῇ.οἰκίᾳ.αὐτοῦ.
the word of the Lord, and to all those in his house.
33 καὶ παραλαβὼν αὐτοὺς ἐν ἐκείνῃ τῇ ὥρᾳ τῆς νυκτὸς ἔλου-
And having taken them in that hour of the night he wash-
σεν ἀπὸ τῶν πληγῶν, καὶ ἐβαπτίσθη αὐτὸς καὶ οἱ αὐτοῦ
ed [them] from the stripes; and [2]was [3]baptized [1]he and [2]his
[b]πάντες‖ παραχρῆμα. 34 ἀναγαγών.τε αὐτοὺς εἰς τὸν οἶκον
[1]all immediately. And having brought them into [2]house
[c]αὐτοῦ‖ παρέθηκεν τράπεζαν, καὶ [d]ἠγαλλιάσατο‖ [e]παν-
[1]his he laid a table [for them], and exulted with all
οικὶ‖ πεπιστευκὼς τῷ θεῷ. 35 Ἡμέρας.δὲ γενομένης ἀπέ-
[his] house, having believed in God. And day having come
στειλαν οἱ στρατηγοὶ τοὺς ῥαβδούχους λέγοντες, Ἀπόλυσον
[3]sent [1]the [2]captains the serjeants, saying, Let [3]go
τοὺς.ἀνθρώπους.ἐκείνους. 36 [i]Ἀπήγγειλεν.δὲ ὁ δεσμοφύλαξ
[1]those [2]men. And [3]reported [1]the [2]jailor
τοὺς.λόγους.[f]τούτους‖ πρὸς τὸν Παῦλον, Ὅτι [g]ἀπεστάλκασιν‖
these words to Paul, [3]Have [4]sent
οἱ στρατηγοὶ ἵνα ἀπολυθῆτε· νῦν οὖν ἐξελθόντες πο-
[1]the [2]captains that ye may be let go. Now therefore having gone out de-
ρεύεσθε ἐν εἰρήνῃ. 37 Ὁ.δὲ.Παῦλος ἔφη πρὸς αὐτούς, Δείραντες
part in peace. But Paul said to them, Having beaten
ἡμᾶς δημοσίᾳ ἀκατακρίτους, ἀνθρώπους Ῥωμαίους ὑπάρχον-
us publicly uncondemned, men Romans being,
τας, [h]ἔβαλον‖ εἰς φυλακήν, καὶ νῦν λάθρα ἡμᾶς ἐκβάλλου-
they cast [us] into prison, and now secretly us do they thrust
σιν; οὐ γάρ· ἀλλὰ ἐλθόντες αὐτοὶ ἡμᾶς ἐξαγαγέτωσαν.
out? no indeed, but having come themselves us let them bring out.
38 [i]Ἀνήγγειλαν‖.[k]δὲ‖ τοῖς στρατηγοῖς οἱ ῥαβδοῦχοι τὰ ῥήματα
And [3]reported [4]to [5]the [6]captains [1]the [2]serjeants [8]words
ταῦτα· [l]καὶ ἐφοβήθησαν‖ ἀκούσαντες ὅτι Ῥωμαῖοί εἰσιν.
[7]these. And they were afraid having heard that Romans they are.
39 καὶ ἐλθόντες παρεκάλεσαν αὐτούς, καὶ ἐξαγαγόντες
And having come they besought them, and having brought out
ἠρώτων [m]ἐξελθεῖν‖ τῆς πόλεως. 40 ἐξελθόντες.δὲ [n]ἐκ‖
they asked [them] to go out of the city. And having gone forth out of
τῆς φυλακῆς εἰσῆλθον [o]εἰς‖ τὴν Λυδίαν· καὶ ἰδόντες [p]τοὺς
the prison they came to Lydia; and having seen the
ἀδελφοὺς παρεκάλεσαν αὐτούς,‖ καὶ [q]ἐξῆλθον.‖
brethren they exhorted them, and went away.

17 Διοδεύσαντες.δὲ τὴν Ἀμφίπολιν καὶ [r]Ἀπολλωνίαν
And having journeyed through Amphipolis and Apollonia
ἦλθον εἰς Θεσσαλονίκην, ὅπου ἦν [s]ἡ‖ συναγωγὴ τῶν Ἰου-
they came to Thessalonica, where was the synagogue of the Jews.
δαίων. 2 κατὰ.δὲ τὸ εἰωθὸς τῷ Παύλῳ εἰσῆλθεν πρὸς αὐτούς,
And according to the custom with Paul he went in to them,
καὶ ἐπὶ σάββατα τρία [t]διελέγετο‖ αὐτοῖς ἀπὸ τῶν γραφῶν,
and for [2]sabbaths [1]three reasoned with them from the scriptures,
3 διανοίγων καὶ παρατιθέμενος ὅτι τὸν χριστὸν ἔδει πα-
opening and setting forth that [3]the [4]Christ [1]it [2]behoved to have

---

[a] σὺν πᾶσιν with all GLTTrAW. [b] ἅπαντες T. [c] — αὐτοῦ (*read* the house) LT[Tr]A. [d] ἠγαλλιᾶτο A. [e] πανοικεὶ TA. [f] — τούτους (*read* the words) LTr. [g] ἀπέσταλκαν LTTrA. [h] ἔβαλαν LTTrA. [i] ἀπήγγειλαν LTTrAW. [k] τε T. [l] ἐφοβήθησαν δὲ LTTrA. [m] ἀπελθεῖν ἀπὸ to depart from (the) LTTrA. [n] ἀπὸ from T. [o] πρὸς GLTTrAW. [p] παρεκάλεσαν τοὺς ἀδελφούς LTTrA. [q] ἐξῆλθαν TTr. [r] + τὴν LTTr. [s] — ἡ (*read* a synagogue) LTTr[A]. [t] διελέξατο LTTr.

θεῖν καὶ ἀναστῆναι ἐκ νεκρῶν, καὶ ὅτι οὗτός ἐστιν
suffered and to have risen from among [the] dead, and that this is
[w]ὁ|| χριστὸς [x] Ἰησοῦς, ὃν ἐγὼ καταγγέλλω ὑμῖν. 4 Καί τινες
the Christ Jesus, whom I announce to you. And some
ἐξ αὐτῶν ἐπείσθησαν, καὶ προσεκληρώθησαν τῷ Παύλῳ καὶ
of them were obedient, and joined themselves to Paul and
τῷ Σίλᾳ, τῶν.τε σεβομένων [y] Ἑλλήνων [z]πολὺ πλῆθος,||
to Silas, and of the worshipping Greeks a great multitude,
γυναικῶν.τε τῶν πρώτων οὐκ ὀλίγαι. 5 [a]ζηλώσαντες.δὲ
and of 3women 1the 2chief not a few. But 4having 5become 6envious
οἱ ἀπειθοῦντες Ἰουδαῖοι, καὶ προσλαβόμενοι|| τῶν
1the 2disobeying 3Jews, and having taken to [them] 2of 3the
ἀγοραίων [b]τινὰς ἄνδρας|| πονηρούς, καὶ ὀχλοποιήσαντες
4market-loungers 1certain 6men 5evil, and having collected a crowd
ἐθορύβουν τὴν πόλιν· [c]ἐπιστάντες.τε|| τῇ οἰκίᾳ Ἰάσονος
roused 3in 4tumult 1the 2city; and having assaulted the house of Jason
ἐζήτουν αὐτοὺς [d]ἀγαγεῖν|| εἰς τὸν δῆμον· 6 μὴ.εὑρόντες.δὲ
they sought 3them 1to 2bring out to the people; but not having found
αὐτοὺς ἔσυρον [e]τὸν|| Ἰάσονα καί τινας ἀδελφοὺς ἐπὶ τοὺς
them they dragged Jason and certain brethren before the
πολιτάρχας, βοῶντες, "Ὅτι οἱ τὴν οἰκουμένην ἀνα-
city magistrates, crying out, Those who 5the 6habitable 7world 1have 2set
στατώσαντες οὗτοι καὶ ἐνθάδε πάρεισιν, 7 οὓς ὑποδέδεκται
3in 4confusion these 4also 3here 1are 2come, whom 2has 3received
Ἰάσων· καὶ οὗτοι πάντες ἀπέναντι τῶν δογμάτων Καίσαρος
1Jason; and these all contrary to the decrees of Cæsar
[f]πράττουσιν,|| βασιλέα [g]λέγοντες ἕτερον|| εἶναι, Ἰησοῦν.
do, 3king 1saying 2another there is— Jesus.
8 Ἐτάραξαν.δὲ τὸν ὄχλον καὶ τοὺς πολιτάρχας ἀκούοντας
And they troubled the crowd and the city magistrates hearing
ταῦτα. 9 καὶ λαβόντες τὸ ἱκανὸν παρὰ τοῦ Ἰάσονος καὶ
these things. And having taken security from Jason and
τῶν λοιπῶν ἀπέλυσαν αὐτούς. 10 Οἱ.δὲ ἀδελφοὶ εὐθέως διὰ
the rest they let 2go 1them. But the brethren immediately by
[h]τῆς|| νυκτὸς ἐξέπεμψαν τόν.τε.Παῦλον καὶ τὸν Σίλαν εἰς Βέ-
night sent away both Paul and Silas to Be-
ροιαν· οἵτινες παραγενόμενοι, εἰς τὴν συναγωγὴν [i]τῶν Ἰου-
rœa; who, being arrived, into the synagogue of the Jews
δαίων ἀπῄεσαν.|| 11 οὗτοι.δὲ ἦσαν εὐγενέστεροι τῶν ἐν
went. And these were more noble than those in
Θεσσαλονίκῃ, οἵτινες ἐδέξαντο τὸν λόγον μετὰ πάσης προθυ-
Thessalonica, who received the word with all readi-
μίας, [k]τὸ|| καθ'.ἡμέραν ἀνακρίνοντες τὰς γραφὰς εἰ ἔχοι
ness, daily examining the scriptures if were
ταῦτα οὕτως. 12 πολλοὶ μὲν οὖν ἐξ αὐτῶν ἐπί-
these things so. Many indeed therefore from among them be-
στευσαν, καὶ τῶν Ἑλληνίδων γυναικῶν τῶν εὐσχημόνων καὶ
lieved, and of the 2Grecian 3women 1honourable and
ἀνδρῶν οὐκ ὀλίγοι. 13 ὡς.δὲ ἔγνωσαν οἱ ἀπὸ τῆς Θεσσαλο-
men not a few. But when 5knew 1the 3from 4Thessalo-
νίκης Ἰουδαῖοι ὅτι καὶ ἐν τῇ Βεροίᾳ κατηγγέλη ὑπὸ τοῦ
nica 2Jews that also in Berœa was announced by

and risen again from
the dead; and that this
Jesus, whom I preach
unto you, is Christ.
4 And some of them
believed, and consorted
with Paul and Silas;
and of the devout
Greeks a great multi-
tude, and of the chief
women not a few. 5 But
the Jews which be-
lieved not, moved with
envy, took unto them
certain lewd fellows of
the baser sort, and ga-
thered a company, and
set all the city on an
uproar, and assaulted
the house of Jason, and
sought to bring them
out to the people.
6 And when they found
them not, they drew
Jason and certain bre-
thren unto the rulers
of the city, crying,
These that have turned
the world upside down
are come hither also;
7 whom Jason hath re-
ceived: and these all
do contrary to the de-
crees of Cæsar, saying
that there is another
king, *one* Jesus. 8 And
they troubled the peo-
ple and the rulers of
the city, when they
heard these things.
9 And when they had
taken security of Ja-
son, and of the other,
they let them go.
10 And the brethren
immediately sent a-
way Paul and Silas by
night unto Berea: who
coming *thither* went
into the synagogue of
the Jews. 11 These
were more noble than
those in Thessalonica,
in that they received
the word with all rea-
diness of mind, and
searched the scrip-
tures daily, whether
those things were so.
12 Therefore many of
them believed; also
of honourable women
which were Greeks,
and of men, not a few.
13 But when the Jews
of Thessalonica had
knowledge that the
word of God was
preached of Paul at
Berea, they came thi-

---

[w] — ὁ LTTr. [x] + ὁ A. [y] + καὶ L. [z] πλῆθος πολύ LTTrAW. [a] προσλαβόμενοι δὲ οἱ Ἰουδαῖοι G; — ἀπειθοῦντες LTTrAW. [b] ἄνδρας τινὰς LTrAW. [c] καὶ ἐπιστάντες LTTrA. [d] προαγαγεῖν LTTrA. [e] — τὸν LTTr[A]. [f] πράσσουσιν LTTrAW. [g] ἕτερον λέγοντες LTTr. [h] — τῆς LTTrA. [i] ἀπῄεσαν τῶν Ἰουδαίων A. [k] — τὸ LTTr.

ther also, and stirred up the people. 14 And then immediately the brethren sent away Paul to go as it were to the sea: but Silas and Timotheus abode there still. 15 And they that conducted Paul brought him unto Athens: and receiving a commandment unto Silas and Timotheus for to come to him with all speed, they departed.

Παῦλον ὁ λόγος τοῦ θεοῦ, ἦλθον κἀκεῖ σαλεύοντες [l] τοὺς
Paul the word of God, they came also there stirring up the
ὄχλους. 14 εὐθέως.δὲ τότε τὸν Παῦλον ἐξαπέστειλαν οἱ
crowds. And immediately then [5]Paul [3]sent [4]away [1]the
ἀδελφοὶ πορεύεσθαι [m]ὡς ἐπὶ τὴν θάλασσαν· [n]ὑπέμενον.δὲ
[2]brethren to go as to the sea; but remained
ὅ.τε.Σίλας καὶ ὁ Τιμόθεος ἐκεῖ. 15 Οἱ.δὲ [o]καθιστῶντες τὸν
both Silas and Timotheus there. But those conducting
Παῦλον ἤγαγον [p]αὐτὸν ἕως Ἀθηνῶν· καὶ λαβόντες ἐντολὴν
Paul brought him unto Athens; and having received a command
πρὸς τὸν Σίλαν καὶ [q] Τιμόθεον, ἵνα ὡς τάχιστα ἔλθω-
to Silas and Timotheus, that as quickly as possible they should
σιν πρὸς αὐτόν, ἐξῄεσαν.
come to him, they departed.

16 Now while Paul waited for them at Athens, his spirit was stirred in him, when he saw the city wholly given to idolatry. 17 Therefore disputed he in the synagogue with the Jews, and with the devout persons, and in the market daily with them that met with him. 18 Then certain philosophers of the Epicureans, and of the Stoicks, encountered him. And some said, What will this babbler say? Other some, He seemeth to be a setter forth of strange gods: because he preached unto them Jesus, and the resurrection. 19 And they took him, and brought him unto Areopagus, saying, May we know what this new doctrine, whereof thou speakest, *is?* 20 For thou bringest certain strange things to our ears: we would know therefore what these things mean. 21 (For all the Athenians and strangers which were there spent their time in nothing else, but either to tell, or to hear some new thing.) 22 Then Paul stood in the midst of Mars' hill, and said, *Ye* men of Athens, I perceive that in all things ye

16 Ἐν.δὲ ταῖς Ἀθήναις ἐκδεχομένου αὐτοὺς τοῦ Παύλου,
But in Athens [2]waiting [3]for [4]them [1]Paul,
παρωξύνετο τὸ.πνεῦμα.αὐτοῦ ἐν αὐτῷ [r]θεωροῦντι κατ-
[7]was [8]painfully [9]excited [5]his [6]spirit in him seeing [4]full
είδωλον οὖσαν τὴν πόλιν. 17 διελέγετο μὲν οὖν ἐν τῇ
[5]of [6]idols [3]being [1]the [2]city. He reasoned indeed therefore in the
συναγωγῇ τοῖς Ἰουδαίοις καὶ τοῖς σεβομένοις, καὶ ἐν τῇ
synagogue with the Jews and those who worshipped, and in the
ἀγορᾷ κατὰ.πᾶσαν.ἡμέραν πρὸς τοὺς παρατυγχάνον-
market-place every day with those who met with
τας. 18 τινὲς.δὲ [s] τῶν [t]Ἐπικουρείων καὶ [v]τῶν [w]Στωϊκῶν
[him]. But some of the Epicureans and the Stoics,
φιλοσόφων συνέβαλλον αὐτῷ· καί τινες ἔλεγον, Τί ἂν θέλοι
philosophers, encountered him. And some said, What may [3]desire
ὁ.σπερμολόγος.οὗτος λέγειν; Οἱ.δέ, Ξένων δαιμονίων δοκεῖ
[1]this [2]chatterer to say? And some, Of foreign gods he seems
(*lit.* demons)
καταγγελεὺς εἶναι· ὅτι τὸν Ἰησοῦν καὶ τὴν ἀνάστασιν
a proclaimer to be, because [of] Jesus and the resurrection
[x]αὐτοῖς εὐηγγελίζετο. 19 ἐπιλαβόμενοί.[y]τε αὐτοῦ,
to them he announced the glad tidings. And having taken hold of him,
ἐπὶ τὸν [z]Ἄρειον πάγον ἤγαγον λέγοντες, Δυνάμεθα
to the Mars' hill they brought [him], saying, Are we able
γνῶναι τίς ἡ.καινὴ.αὕτη [a]ἡ ὑπὸ σοῦ λαλουμένη διδαχή;
to know what [is] this new [2]which [3]by [4]thee [5]is [6]spoken [1]teaching?
20 ξενίζοντα.γάρ τινα εἰσφέρεις εἰς τὰς.ἀκοὰς.ἡμῶν. βου-
For [2]strange [3]things [1]certain thou bringest to our ears. We
λόμεθα οὖν γνῶναι [b]τί ἂν.θέλοι ταῦτα εἶναι. 21 Ἀθη-
wish therefore to know what [3]may [4]mean [1]these [2]things. [7]Athe-
ναῖοι δὲ πάντες καὶ οἱ ἐπιδημοῦντες ξένοι εἰς οὐδὲν ἕτερον
nians [5]now [6]all and the sojourning strangers in nothing else
[c]εὐκαίρουν ἢ λέγειν τι [d]καὶ ἀκούειν [e] καινότερον.
spent their leisure than to tell [4]something [1]and [2]to [3]hear newer.
22 Σταθεὶς.δὲ [f]ὁ Παῦλος ἐν μέσῳ τοῦ [g]Ἀρείου πάγου
And [2]having [3]stood [1]Paul in [the] midst of Mars' hill
ἔφη, Ἄνδρες Ἀθηναῖοι, κατὰ πάντα ὡς δεισιδαιμονεστέρους
said, Men Athenians, in all things very religious
(*lit.* very reverent to demons)

---

[l] + καὶ ταράσσοντες and troubling LTTrA. [m] ἕως as far as LTTr. [n] ὑπέμεινέν (-νάν TTr) τε LTTrA. [o] καθιστάνοντες LTTrA. [p] — αὐτὸν (*read* [him]) LTTrA. [q] + τὸν TTr. [r] θεωροῦντος LTTrAW. [s] + καὶ also LTTrAW. [t] Ἐπικουρίων T. [v] — τῶν LTTrA. [w] Στοϊκῶν LTA. [x] εὐηγγελίζετο αὐτοῖς ([αὐτοῖς] A) LA; — αὐτοῖς TTr. [y] δὲ Tr. [z] Ἄριον T. [a] — ἡ L[Tr]. [b] τίνα θέλει what mean LTTrA. [c] ηὐκαίρουν LTTrA. [d] ἢ or LTTrA. [e] + τι something LT[Tr]. [f] — ὁ LTTr. [g] Ἀρίου T.

ὑμᾶς θεωρῶ. 23 διερχόμενος.γὰρ καὶ ἀναθεωρῶν τὰ σεβάσ-
you I behold; for, passing through and beholding [2]objects [3]of
ματα ὑμῶν, εὗρον καὶ βωμὸν ἐν ᾧ ἐπεγέγραπτο,
[4]veneration [1]your, I found also an altar on which had been inscribed,
Ἀγνώστῳ θεῷ. [h]ὃν" οὖν ἀγνοοῦντες εὐσεβεῖτε, [i]τοῦτον"
To an unknown God. Whom therefore not knowing ye reverence, him
ἐγὼ καταγγέλλω ὑμῖν. 24 ὁ θεὸς ὁ ποιήσας τὸν κόσμον καὶ
I announce to you. The God who made the world and
πάντα τὰ ἐν αὐτῷ, οὗτος οὐρανοῦ καὶ γῆς [k]κύριος
all things that [are] in it, he of heaven and earth Lord
ὑπάρχων," οὐκ ἐν χειροποιήτοις ναοῖς κατοικεῖ, 25 οὐδὲ ὑπὸ
being, not in hand-made temples dwells, nor by
χειρῶν [l]ἀνθρώπων" θεραπεύεται προσδεόμενός τινος, αὐτὸς
hands of men is served as needing anything, himself
διδοὺς πᾶσιν ζωὴν καὶ πνοὴν [m]κατὰ.πάντα·" 26 ἐποίησέν.τε
giving to all life and breath in every [respect]; and he made
ἐξ ἑνὸς [n]αἵματος" πᾶν ἔθνος ἀνθρώπων, κατοικεῖν ἐπὶ [o]πᾶν
of one blood every nation of men, to dwell upon all
τὸ πρόσωπον" τῆς γῆς, ὁρίσας [p]προτεταγμένους" και-
the face of the earth, having determined fore-arranged times
ροὺς καὶ τὰς ὁροθεσίας τῆς.κατοικίας.αὐτῶν· 27 ζητεῖν [q]τὸν
and the boundaries of their dwelling— to seek the
κύριον," εἰ ἄρα.γε ψηλαφήσειαν αὐτὸν [r]καὶ" εὕροιεν,
Lord; if perhaps they might feel after him and might find him,
[s]καίτοιγε" οὐ μακρὰν ἀπὸ ἑνὸς ἑκάστου ἡμῶν ὑπάρχοντα.
though indeed [2]not [3]far [4]from [6]one [5]each [7]of [8]us [1]being;
28 ἐν.αὐτῷ.γὰρ ζῶμεν καὶ κινούμεθα καί ἐσμεν· ὡς καί τινες
for in him we live and move and are; as also some
τῶν καθ' ὑμᾶς ποιητῶν εἰρήκασιν, Τοῦ.γὰρ καὶ γένος
of the [2]among [3]you [1]poets have said, For of him [2]also [1]offspring
ἐσμέν. 29 Γένος οὖν ὑπάρχοντες τοῦ θεοῦ, οὐκ.ὀφείλομεν
we are. Offspring therefore being of God, we ought not
νομίζειν χρυσῷ ἢ ἀργύρῳ ἢ λίθῳ, χαράγματι τέχνης καὶ
to think to gold or to silver or to stone, a graven thing of art and
ἐνθυμήσεως ἀνθρώπου, τὸ θεῖον εἶναι ὅμοιον. 30 Τοὺς
imagination of man, that which [is] divine to be like. The
μὲν οὖν χρόνους τῆς ἀγνοίας ὑπεριδὼν ὁ θεός, [t]τὰ
[2]indeed [3]therefore [1]times of ignorance [2]having [3]overlooked [1]God,
νῦν" [v]παραγγέλλει" τοῖς ἀνθρώποις [w]πᾶσιν" πανταχοῦ μετα-
now charges men all everywhere to re-
νοεῖν· 31 [x]διότι" ἔστησεν ἡμέραν ἐν ᾗ μέλλει κρίνειν τὴν
pent, because he set a day in which he is about to judge the
οἰκουμένην ἐν δικαιοσύνῃ, ἐν ἀνδρὶ ᾧ ὥρισεν, πίστιν
habitable world in righteousness, by a man whom he appointed; [3]proof
παρασχὼν πᾶσιν ἀναστήσας αὐτὸν ἐκ νεκρῶν.
[1]having [2]given to all [in] having raised him from among [the] dead.
32 Ἀκούσαντες.δὲ ἀνάστασιν νεκρῶν, οἱ μὲν ἐχλεύαζον·
And having heard a resurrection of [the] dead, some mocked,
οἱ.δὲ [y]εἶπον," Ἀκουσόμεθά σου [z]πάλιν περὶ τούτου."
and some said, We will hear thee again concerning this.

are too superstitious.
23 For as I passed by, and beheld your devotions, I found an altar with this inscription, TO THE UNKNOWN GOD. Whom therefore ye ignorantly worship, him declare I unto you.
24 God that made the world and all things therein, seeing that he is Lord of heaven and earth, dwelleth not in temples made with hands;
25 neither is worshipped with men's hands, as though he needed any thing, seeing he giveth to all life, and breath, and all things;
26 and hath made of one blood all nations of men for to dwell on all the face of the earth, and hath determined the times before appointed, and the bounds of their habitation;
27 that they should seek the Lord, if haply they might feel after him, and find him, though he be not far from every one of us:
28 for in him we live, and move, and have our being; as certain also of your own poets have said, For we are also his offspring.
29 Forasmuch then as we are the offspring of God, we ought not to think that the Godhead is like unto gold, or silver, or stone, graven by art and man's device.
30 And the times of this ignorance God winked at; but now commandeth all men every where to repent:
31 because he hath appointed a day, in the which he will judge the world in righteousness by *that* man whom he hath ordained; *whereof* he hath given assurance unto all *men*, in that he hath raised him from the dead.
32 And when they heard of the resurrection of the dead, some mocked: and others said, We will hear thee again of this

---

[h] ὃ what LTTrAW. [i] τοῦτο this LTTrAW. [k] ὑπάρχων κύριος LTTrA. [l] ἀνθρωπίνων (*read* human hands) LTTrA. [m] καὶ τὰ πάντα and all things EGLTTrAW. [n] — αἵματος (*read* made from one) LTTr[A]. [o] παντὸς προσώπου LTTrA. [p] προστεταγμένους arranged GTTrAW; πρὸς τεταγμένους L. [q] τὸν θεόν God GLTTrA. [r] ἢ or L. [s] καὶ γε LTrA; καιγε T. [t] ταννῦν EGW. [v] ἀπαγγέλλει sends word (to all) T. [w] πάντας LTTrA. [x] καθότι inasmuch as LTTrAW. [y] εἶπαν TTrA. [z] περὶ τούτου καὶ (also) πάλιν LTTrA.

matter. 33 So Paul departed from among them. 34 Howbeit certain men clave unto him, and believed: among the which *was* Dionysius the Areopagite, and a woman named Damaris, and others with them.

XVIII. After these things Paul departed from Athens, and came to Corinth; 2 and found a certain Jew named Aquila, born in Pontus, lately come from Italy, with his wife Priscilla; (because that Claudius had commanded all Jews to depart from Rome:) and came unto them. 3 And because he was of the same craft, he abode with them, and wrought: for by their occupation they were tentmakers. 4 And he reasoned in the synagogue every sabbath, and persuaded the Jews and the Greeks. 5 And when Silas and Timotheus were come from Macedonia, Paul was pressed in the spirit and testified to the Jews *that* Jesus *was* Christ. 6 And when they opposed themselves, and blasphemed, he shook *his* raiment, and said unto them, Your blood *be* upon your own heads; I *am* clean: from henceforth I will go unto the Gentiles. 7 And he departed thence, and entered into a certain man's house, named Justus, *one* that worshipped God, whose house joined hard to the synagogue. 8 And Crispus, the chief ruler of the synagogue, believed on the Lord with all his house; and many of the Corinthians hearing believed, and were baptized. 9 Then spake the Lord to Paul in the night by a vision, Be not afraid, but speak, and hold not thy peace: 10 for I am with thee,

33 [a]Καὶ‖ οὕτως ὁ Παῦλος ἐξῆλθεν ἐκ μέσου αὐτῶν.
And thus Paul went out from [the] midst of them.
34 τινὲς.δὲ ἄνδρες κολληθέντες αὐτῷ ἐπίστευσαν· ἐν οἷς
But some men joining themselves to him believed; among whom
καὶ Διονύσιος [b]ὁ‖ [c]Ἀρεοπαγίτης,‖ καὶ γυνὴ ὀνόματι Δά-
also [was] Dionysius the Areopagite, and a woman by name Da-
μαρις, καὶ ἕτεροι σὺν αὐτοῖς.
maris, and others with them.

18 Μετὰ.[d]δὲ‖ ταῦτα χωρισθεὶς [e]ὁ Παῦλος‖ ἐκ τῶν
And after these things [2]having [3]departed [1]Paul from
Ἀθηνῶν ἦλθεν εἰς.Κόρινθον· 2 καὶ εὑρών τινα Ἰουδαῖον
Athens, came to Corinth; and having found a certain Jew
ὀνόματι Ἀκύλαν, Ποντικὸν τῷ.γένει, προσφάτως ἐληλυθότα
by name Aquila, of Pontus by race, lately come
ἀπὸ τῆς Ἰταλίας, καὶ Πρίσκιλλαν γυναῖκα.αὐτοῦ, διὰ τὸ
from Italy, and Priscilla his wife, because
[f]διατεταχέναι‖ Κλαύδιον χωρίζεσθαι πάντας τοὺς Ἰουδαίους
[2]had [3]ordered [1]Claudius to depart all the Jews
[g]ἐκ‖ τῆς Ῥώμης, προσῆλθεν αὐτοῖς· 3 καὶ διὰ τὸ ὁμό-
out of Rome, he came to them, and because of [2]the [3]same
τεχνον εἶναι, ἔμενεν παρ' αὐτοῖς καὶ [h]εἰργάζετο·‖ ἦσαν.γὰρ
[4]trade [1]being, he abode with them and worked; for they were
σκηνοποιοὶ [i]τὴν.τέχνην.‖ 4 διελέγετο.δὲ ἐν τῇ συναγωγῇ
tent makers by trade. And he reasoned in the synagogue
κατὰ.πᾶν.σάββατον, ἔπειθέν.τε Ἰουδαίους καὶ Ἕλληνας.
every sabbath, and persuaded Jews and Greeks.
5 Ὡς.δὲ κατῆλθον ἀπὸ τῆς Μακεδονίας ὅ.τε.Σίλας καὶ ὁ Τι-
And when came down from Macedonia both Silas and Ti-
μόθεος [k]συνείχετο τῷ πνεύματι‖ ὁ Παῦλος διαμαρτυρόμενος
motheus [2]was [3]pressed [4]in [5]spirit [1]Paul earnestly testifying
τοῖς Ἰουδαίοις [l] τὸν χριστὸν Ἰησοῦν. 6 ἀντιτασ-
to the Jews [[2]to [3]be] [4]the [5]Christ [1]Jesus. [7]As [9]set [10]themselves [11]in
σομένων δὲ αὐτῶν καὶ βλασφημούντων, ἐκτιναξάμενος
[12]opposition [6]but [8]they and were blaspheming, having shaken [his]
τὰ ἱμάτια, εἶπεν πρὸς αὐτούς, Τὸ.αἷμα.ὑμῶν ἐπὶ τὴν
garments, he said to them, Your blood [be] upon
κεφαλὴν.ὑμῶν· καθαρὸς ἐγὼ ἀπὸ τοῦ.νῦν εἰς τὰ ἔθνη
your head: [2]pure [[3]from [4]it] [1]I from henceforth to the nations
πορεύσομαι. 7 Καὶ μεταβὰς ἐκεῖθεν [m]ἦλθεν‖ εἰς οἰκίαν
will go. And having departed thence he came to [the] house
τινὸς ὀνόματι [n]Ἰούστου, σεβομένου τὸν θεόν, οὗ
of a certain one by name Justus, who worshipped God, of whom
ἡ οἰκία ἦν συνομοροῦσα τῇ συναγωγῇ. 8 Κρίσπος.δὲ ὁ
the house was adjoining the synagogue. But Crispus the
ἀρχισυνάγωγος ἐπίστευσεν τῷ κυρίῳ σὺν ὅλῳ τῷ.οἴκῳ.αὐ-
ruler of the synagogue believed in the Lord with [2]whole [1]his house;
τοῦ· καὶ πολλοὶ τῶν Κορινθίων ἀκούοντες ἐπίστευον καὶ
and many of the Corinthians hearing believed and
ἐβαπτίζοντο. 9 Εἶπεν.δὲ ὁ κύριος [o]δι' ὁράματος ἐν νυκτὶ‖
were baptized. And said the Lord by a vision in [the] night
τῷ Παύλῳ, Μὴ.φοβοῦ, ἀλλὰ λάλει καὶ μὴ.σιωπήσῃς· 10 διότι
to Paul, Fear not, but speak and be not silent; because

[a] — καὶ LTTrA. [b] — ὁ L[Tr]. [c] Ἀρεοπαγείτης T; Ἀρειοπαγίτης W. [d] — δὲ and LTTr[A]. [e] — ὁ Παῦλος (*read* he having departed) LTTrA. [f] τεταχέναι T. [g] ἀπὸ from LTTrAW. [h] ἠργάζετο LTrA: ἠργάζοντο they worked T. [i] τῇ τέχνῃ LTTrAW. [k] συνείχετο τῷ λόγῳ [2]was [3]engrossed [4]with [5]the [6]word GLTTrAW. [l] + εἶναι to be LTTr. [m] εἰσῆλθεν LT. [n] + Τιτίου Titius T[Tr]. [o] ἐν νυκτὶ δι' ὁράματος LTTrA.

ἐγώ εἰμι μετὰ σοῦ, καὶ οὐδεὶς ἐπιθήσεταί σοι τοῦ κακῶσαί σε·
I am with thee, and no one shall set on thee to ill-treat thee;
διότι λαός ἐστίν μοι πολὺς ἐν τῇ.πόλει.ταύτῃ. 11 Ἐκάθισέν
because people there is to me much in this city. [2]He [3]remained
[p]τε[||] ἐνιαυτὸν καὶ μῆνας ἓξ διδάσκων ἐν αὐτοῖς τὸν λόγον
[1]and a year and [2]months [1]six, teaching among them the word
τοῦ θεοῦ.
of God.

12 Γαλλίωνος.δὲ [q]ἀνθυπατεύοντος[||] τῆς Ἀχαΐας, κατεπ-
But Gallio being proconsul of Achaia, [6]rose
έστησαν ὁμοθυμαδὸν οἱ Ἰουδαῖοι τῷ Παύλῳ, καὶ ἤγαγον
[7]against [3]with [4]one [5]accord [1]the [2]Jews Paul, and led
αὐτὸν ἐπὶ τὸ βῆμα, 13 λέγοντες, Ὅτι παρὰ τὸν νόμον
him to the judgment seat, saying, That contrary to the law
[r]οὗτος ἀναπείθει[||] τοὺς ἀνθρώπους σέβεσθαι τὸν θεόν.
this [man] persuades men to worship God.
14 Μέλλοντος.δὲ τοῦ Παύλου ἀνοίγειν τὸ στόμα, εἶπεν ὁ
But [2]being [3]about [1]Paul to open [his] mouth, [2]said
Γαλλίων πρὸς τοὺς Ἰουδαίους, Εἰ μὲν [s]οὖν[||] ἦν ἀδί-
[1]Gallio to the Jews, If indeed therefore it was [2]unrighteous-
κημά τι ἢ ῥᾳδιούργημα πονηρόν, ὦ Ἰουδαῖοι, κατὰ λόγον
ness [1]some or [2]criminality [1]wicked, O Jews, according to reason
ἂν [t]ἠνεσχόμην[||] ὑμῶν, 15 εἰ.δὲ [v]ζήτημά[||] ἐστιν περὶ
I should have borne with you, but if a question it be about
λόγου καὶ ὀνομάτων καὶ νόμου τοῦ καθ' ὑμᾶς, ὄψεσθε
a word and names and a law which [is] among you, ye will see
αὐτοί· κριτὴς.[w]γὰρ[||] ἐγὼ τούτων οὐ.βούλομαι εἶναι.
[to it] yourselves; for a judge I of these things do not wish to be.
16 Καὶ ἀπήλασεν αὐτοὺς ἀπὸ τοῦ βήματος· 17 ἐπιλαβό-
And he drove them from the judgment seat. [5]Having [6]laid
μενοι δὲ πάντες [x]οἱ Ἕλληνες[||] Σωσθένην τὸν ἀρχισυνάγωγον
[7]hold [8]on [1]and [2]all [3]the [4]Greeks Sosthenes the ruler of the synagogue,
ἔτυπτον ἔμπροσθεν τοῦ βήματος· καὶ οὐδὲν τού-
they beat [him] before the judgment seat. And [5]nothing [6]about [7]these
των τῷ Γαλλίωνι ἔμελεν.
[8]things [4]to [3]Gallio [1]it [2]mattered.

18 Ὁ.δὲ.Παῦλος ἔτι προσμείνας ἡμέρας ἱκανάς, τοῖς ἀδελ-
But Paul yet having remained [2]days [1]many, [7]the [8]breth-
φοῖς ἀποταξάμενος, ἐξέπλει εἰς τὴν Συρίαν, καὶ σὺν αὐτῷ
ren [3]having [4]taken [5]leave [6]of sailed away to Syria, and with him
Πρίσκιλλα καὶ Ἀκύλας, κειράμενος [y]τὴν κεφαλὴν ἐν Κεγ-
Priscilla and Aquila, having shorn [his] head in Cen-
χρεαῖς·[||] εἶχεν.γὰρ εὐχήν. 19 [z]κατήντησεν[||].δὲ εἰς Ἔφεσον, κά-
chrea, for he had a vow: and he came to Ephesus, and
κείνους κατέλιπεν [a]αὐτοῦ·[||] αὐτὸς.δὲ εἰσελθὼν εἰς τὴν
[2]them [1]left there. But he himself having entered into the
συναγωγὴν [b]διελέχθη[||] τοῖς Ἰουδαίοις. 20 ἐρωτώντων.δὲ
synagogue reasoned with the Jews. And [2]asking [[3]him]
αὐτῶν ἐπὶ πλείονα χρόνον μεῖναι [c]παρ' αὐτοῖς[||] οὐκ.ἐπένευσεν·
[1]they for a longer time to remain with them he did not accede,
21 [d]ἀλλ' ἀπετάξατο αὐτοῖς,[||] εἰπών, [e]Δεῖ με πάντως τὴν
but took leave of them, saying, It behoves me by all means the

and no man shall set on thee to hurt thee: for I have much people in this city. 11 And he continued *there* a year and six months, teaching the word of God among them.

12 And when Gallio was the deputy of Achaia, the Jews made insurrection with one accord against Paul, and brought him to the judgment seat, 13 saying, This *fellow* persuadeth men to worship God contrary to the law. 14 And when Paul was now about to open *his* mouth, Gallio said unto the Jews, If it were a matter of wrong or wicked lewdness, O *ye* Jews, reason would that I should bear with you: 15 but if it be a question of words and names, and *of* your law, look ye *to it*; for I will be no judge of such *matters*. 16 And he drave them from the judgment seat. 17 Then all the Greeks took Sosthenes, the chief ruler of the synagogue, and beat *him* before the judgment seat. And Gallio cared for none of those things.

18 And Paul *after this* tarried *there* yet a good while, and then took his leave of the brethren, and sailed thence into Syria, and with him Priscilla and Aquila; having shorn *his* head in Cenchrea: for he had a vow. 19 And he came to Ephesus, and left them there: but he himself entered into the synagogue, and reasoned with the Jews. 20 When they desired *him* to tarry longer time with them, he consented not; 21 but bade them farewell, saying, I must by all means keep this

---

p δὲ LTTrA. q ἀνθυπάτου ὄντος LTTrA. r ἀναπείθει οὗτος LTTrAW. s — οὖν LTTr[A]W. t ἀνεσχόμην LTTr. v ζητήματά questions LTTrA. w — γὰρ LTTrAW. x — οἱ Ἕλληνες LTTrAW. y ἐν Κεγχρεαῖς (Κενχρεαῖς T) τὴν κεφαλήν LTTrA. z κατήντησαν they came LTTrA. a ἐκεῖ L. b διελέξατο LTTr. c — παρ' αὐτοῖς LTTrA. d ἀλλὰ ἀποταξάμενος καὶ but taking leave and LTTrA. e — Δεῖ με .... Ἱεροσόλυμα LTTrA.

feast that cometh in
Jerusalem : but I will
return again unto you,
if God will. And he
sailed from Ephesus.
22 And when he had
landed at Cæsarea, and
gone up, and saluted
the church, he went
down to Antioch.
23 And after he had
spent some time *there*,
he departed, and went
over *all* the country of
Galatia and Phrygia
in order, strengthen-
ing all the disciples.

24 And a certain
Jew named Apollos,
born at Alexandria,
an eloquent man,
and mighty in the
scriptures, came to
Ephesus. 25 This man
was instructed in the
way of the Lord ; and
being fervent in the
spirit, he spake and
taught diligently the
things of the Lord,
knowing only the bap-
tism of John. 26 And
he began to speak
boldly in the syna-
gogue : whom when
Aquila and Priscilla
had heard, they took
him unto *them*, and
expounded unto him
the way of God more
perfectly. 27 And when
he was disposed to pass
into Achaia, the breth-
ren wrote, exhorting
the disciples to receive
him : who, when he
was come, helped them
much which had be-
lieved through grace :
28 for he mightily con-
vinced the Jews, *and
that* publickly, shew-
ing by the scriptures
that Jesus was Christ.

XIX. And it came to
pass, that, while A-
pollos was at Corinth,
Paul having passed
through the upper
coasts came to Ephe-
sus : and finding cer-
tain disciples, 2 he said
unto them, Have ye
received the Holy
Ghost since ye believ-
ed ? And they said un-
to him, We have not so
much as heard whe-
ther there be any Holy
Ghost. 3 And he said

ἑορτὴν τὴν ἐρχομένην ποιῆσαι εἰς Ἱεροσόλυμα· πάλιν [f]δὲ
[2]feast [1]coming to keep at Jerusalem, but again
ἀνακάμψω πρὸς ὑμᾶς, τοῦ θεοῦ θέλοντος. [g]Καὶ ἀνήχθη ἀπὸ
I will return to you, God willing. And he sailed from
τῆς Ἐφέσου· 22 καὶ κατελθὼν εἰς [h]Καισάρειαν, ἀναβὰς
Ephesus. And having landed at Cæsarea, having gone up
καὶ ἀσπασάμενος τὴν ἐκκλησίαν κατέβη εἰς Ἀντιόχειαν.
and having saluted the assembly he went down to Antioch.
23 καὶ ποιήσας χρόνον τινὰ ἐξῆλθεν, διερχόμενος καθεξῆς
And having stayed [2]time [1]some he went forth, passing through [6]in [7]order
τὴν Γαλατικὴν χώραν καὶ Φρυγίαν, [i]ἐπιστηρίζων πάντας
[1]the [2]Galatian [5]country [3]and [4]Phrygian, establishing all
τοὺς μαθητάς.
the disciples.

24 Ἰουδαῖος.δέ τις Ἀπολλὼς ὀνόματι, Ἀλεξανδρεὺς τῷ
But a [2]Jew [1]certain, Apollos by name, an Alexandrian
γένει, ἀνὴρ λόγιος, κατήντησεν εἰς Ἔφεσον, δυνατὸς ὢν
by birth, [3]man [1]an [2]eloquent, came to Ephesus, [2]mighty [1]being
ἐν ταῖς γραφαῖς. 25 οὗτος ἦν κατηχημένος τὴν ὁδὸν τοῦ
in the scriptures. He was instructed in the way of the
κυρίου, καὶ ζέων τῷ πνεύματι, ἐλάλει καὶ ἐδίδασκεν
Lord, and being fervent in spirit, he spoke and taught
ἀκριβῶς τὰ περὶ [k]τοῦ κυρίου, ἐπιστάμενος μόνον τὸ
accurately the things concerning the Lord, knowing only the
βάπτισμα [l]Ἰωάννου· 26 οὗτός.τε ἤρξατο παῤῥησιάζεσθαι ἐν
baptism of John. And he began to speak boldly in
τῇ συναγωγῇ. ἀκούσαντες.δὲ αὐτοῦ [m]Ἀκύλας καὶ Πρίσκιλλα
the synagogue. And [4]having [5]heard [6]him [1]Aquila [2]and [3]Priscilla
προσελάβοντο αὐτόν, καὶ ἀκριβέστερον αὐτῷ ἐξέθεντο τὴν
they took [2]to [[3]them] [1]him, and more accurately to him expounded the
[n]τοῦ θεοῦ ὁδόν. 27 βουλομένου.δὲ αὐτοῦ διελθεῖν εἰς τὴν
[2]of [3]God [1]way. And [2]being [3]minded [1]he to pass through into
Ἀχαΐαν, προτρεψάμενοι οἱ ἀδελφοὶ ἔγραψαν τοῖς μαθηταῖς
Achaia, [7]exhorting [[8]them] [1]the [2]brethren [3]wrote [4]to [5]the [6]disciples
ἀποδέξασθαι αὐτόν· ὃς παραγενόμενος συνεβάλετο πολὺ τοῖς
to welcome him, who having arrived helped much those who
πεπιστευκόσιν διὰ τῆς χάριτος· 28 εὐτόνως.γὰρ τοῖς Ἰου-
believed through grace. For powerfully the Jews
δαίοις διακατηλέγχετο δημοσίᾳ, ἐπιδεικνὺς διὰ τῶν γραφῶν,
he confuted publicly, shewing by the scriptures
εἶναι τὸν χριστὸν Ἰησοῦν.
[2]to [3]be [4]the [5]Christ [1]Jesus.

19 Ἐγένετο.δὲ ἐν.τῷ τὸν Ἀπολλὼ εἶναι ἐν Κορίνθῳ, Παῦ-
And it came to pass, while Apollos was in Corinth, Paul,
λον διελθόντα τὰ ἀνωτερικὰ μέρη, [o]ἐλθεῖν εἰς Ἔφεσον·
having passed through the upper parts, came to Ephesus,
καὶ [p]εὑρών τινας μαθητὰς 2 εἶπεν [q] πρὸς αὐτούς, Εἰ
and having found certain disciples he said to them, [The]
πνεῦμα ἅγιον ἐλάβετε πιστεύσαντες; Οἱ.δὲ [r]εἶπον πρὸς
[2]Spirit [1]Holy did ye receive, having believed? And they said to
αὐτόν, Ἀλλ' [s]οὐδὲ εἰ πνεῦμα ἅγιόν ἐστιν, ἠκούσαμεν.
him, Not even if [the] [2]Spirit [1]Holy is, did we hear.

[f] — δὲ but LTTrA. [g] — καὶ LTTrA. [h] Καισαρίαν T. [i] στηρίζων LTTrA. [k] τοῦ Ἰησοῦ Jesus LTTrAW. [l] Ἰωάνου Tr. [m] Πρίσκιλλα καὶ Ἀκύλας LTTrA. [n] ὁδὸν τοῦ θεοῦ LTTr ; — τοῦ θεοῦ A. [o] κατελθεῖν T. [p] εὑρεῖν found LTTrA. [q] + τε and (he said) LTTrA. [r] — εἶπον (*read* [said]) LTTrAW. [s] οὐδ' LTA

3 [t]Εἶπέν.τε[‖] [v]πρὸς αὐτούς,[‖] Εἰς τί οὖν ἐβαπτίσθητε; Οἱ.δὲ
And he said to them, To what then were ye baptized? And they
[w]εἶπον,[‖] Εἰς τὸ [x]Ἰωάννου[‖] βάπτισμα. 4 Εἶπεν.δὲ Παῦλος,
said, To the [2]of [3]John [1]baptism. And [2]said [1]Paul,
[y]Ἰωάννης[‖] [z]μὲν[‖] ἐβάπτισεν βάπτισμα μετανοίας, τῷ
John indeed baptized [with] a baptism of repentance, to the
λαῷ λέγων, εἰς τὸν ἐρχόμενον μετ' αὐτὸν ἵνα πιστεύσωσιν,
people saying, [2]On [3]him [4]coming [5]after [6]him [1]that they should believe,
[a]τουτέστιν[‖] εἰς τὸν [b]χριστὸν[‖] Ἰησοῦν. 5 Ἀκούσαντες.δὲ ἐβαπ-
that is, on [2]the [3]Christ [1]Jesus. And having heard they
τίσθησαν εἰς τὸ ὄνομα τοῦ κυρίου Ἰησοῦ. 6 καὶ ἐπιθέντος
were baptized to the name of the Lord Jesus. And [2]having [3]laid
αὐτοῖς τοῦ Παύλου [c]τὰς[‖] χεῖρας ἦλθεν τὸ πνεῦμα τὸ ἅγιον
[5]on [6]them [1]Paul [4]hands came the Spirit the Holy
ἐπ' αὐτούς, ἐλάλουν.τε γλώσσαις καὶ [d]προεφήτευον.[‖]
upon them, and they were speaking with tongues and prophesying.
7 ἦσαν.δὲ οἱ πάντες ἄνδρες ὡσεὶ [e]δεκαδύο.[‖] 8 Εἰσελθὼν.δὲ
And [4]were [2]the [1]all [3]men about twelve. And having entered
εἰς τὴν συναγωγὴν ἐπαῤῥησιάζετο, ἐπὶ μῆνας τρεῖς διαλεγό-
into the synagogue he spoke boldly, for [2]months [1]three reason-
μενος καὶ πείθων [f]τὰ[‖] περὶ τῆς βασιλείας τοῦ θεοῦ.
ing and persuading the things concerning the kingdom of God.
9 Ὡς.δέ τινες ἐσκληρύνοντο καὶ ἠπείθουν, κακολογοῦντες τὴν
But when some were hardened and disobeyed, speaking evil of the
ὁδὸν ἐνώπιον τοῦ πλήθους, ἀποστὰς ἀπ' αὐτῶν ἀφώρισεν
way before the multitude, having departed from them he separated
τοὺς μαθητάς, καθ'.ἡμέραν διαλεγόμενος ἐν τῇ σχολῇ Τυράν-
the disciples, daily reasoning in the school of [3]Tyran-
νου [g]τινός.[‖] 10 Τοῦτο.δὲ ἐγένετο ἐπὶ ἔτη δύο, ὥστε πάντας
nus [1]a [2]certain. And this was for [2]years [1]two, so that all
τοὺς κατοικοῦντας τὴν Ἀσίαν ἀκοῦσαι τὸν λόγον τοῦ κυρίου
those who inhabited Asia heard the word of the Lord
[h]Ἰησοῦ,[‖] Ἰουδαίους.τε καὶ Ἕλληνας· 11 Δυνάμεις.τε οὐ τὰς
Jesus, both Jews and Greeks. And works of power not
τυχούσας [i]ἐποίει ὁ θεὸς[‖] διὰ τῶν χειρῶν Παύλου, 12 ὥστε καὶ
common [2]wrought [1]God by the hands of Paul, so that even
ἐπὶ τοὺς ἀσθενοῦντας [k]ἐπιφέρεσθαι[‖] ἀπὸ τοῦ.χρωτὸς.αὐτοῦ
to those being sick were brought from his skin
σουδάρια ἢ σιμικίνθια, καὶ ἀπαλλάσσεσθαι ἀπ' αὐτῶν τὰς
handkerchiefs or aprons, and departed from them the
νόσους, τά.τε πνεύματα τὰ πονηρὰ [l]ἐξέρχεσθαι ἀπ' αὐτῶν.[‖]
diseases, and the [2]spirits [1]wicked went out from them.
13 Ἐπεχείρησαν.δέ τινες [m]ἀπὸ τῶν[‖] περιερχομένων Ἰουδαίων
But [7]took [8]in [9]hand [1]certain [2]from [3]the [4]wandering [5]Jews,
ἐξορκιστῶν ὀνομάζειν ἐπὶ τοὺς ἔχοντας τὰ πνεύματα τὰ
[6]exorcists, to name over those who had the [2]spirits
πονηρὰ τὸ ὄνομα τοῦ κυρίου Ἰησοῦ, λέγοντες, [n]Ὁρκίζομεν[‖]
[1]wicked the name of the Lord Jesus, saying, We adjure
ὑμᾶς τὸν Ἰησοῦν ὃν [o]ὁ[‖] Παῦλος κηρύσσει. 14 Ἦσαν.δέ
you [by] Jesus. whom Paul proclaims. And there were

unto them, Unto what then were ye baptized? And they said, Unto John's baptism. 4 Then said Paul, John verily baptized with the baptism of repentance, saying unto the people, that they should believe on him which should come after him, that is, on Christ Jesus. 5 When they heard *this*, they were baptized in the name of the Lord Jesus. 6 And when Paul had laid *his* hands upon them, the Holy Ghost came on them; and they spake with tongues, and prophesied. 7 And all the men were about twelve. 8 And he went into the synagogue, and spake boldly for the space of three months, disputing and persuading the things concerning the kingdom of God. 9 But when divers were hardened, and believed not, but spake evil of that way before the multitude, he departed from them, and separated the disciples, disputing daily in the school of one Tyrannus. 10 And this continued by the space of two years; so that all they which dwelt in Asia heard the word of the Lord Jesus, both Jews and Greeks. 11 And God wrought special miracles by the hands of Paul: 12 so that from his body were brought unto the sick handkerchiefs or aprons, and the diseases departed from them, and the evil spirits went out of them. 13 Then certain of the vagabond Jews, exorcists, took upon them to call over them which had evil spirits the name of the Lord Jesus, saying, We adjure you by Jesus whom Paul preacheth. 14 And there were seven sons

---

[t] ὁ δὲ εἶπεν T. [v] — πρὸς αὐτούς LTTrAW. [w] εἶπαν LTTrA. [x] Ἰωάνου Tr. [y] Ἰωάνης Tr. [z] — μὲν GLTTrA. [a] τοῦτ' ἔστιν GT. [b] — χριστὸν GLTTrA. [c] — τὰς LTTrA. [d] ἐπροφήτευον LTTrA. [e] δώδεκα LTTrAW. [f] — τὰ LTr. [g] — τινός LTTrA. [h] — Ἰησοῦ GLTTrAW. [i] ὁ θεὸς ἐποίει LTTrAW. [k] ἀποφέρεσθαι LTTrA. [l] ἐκπορεύεσθαι (— ἀπ' αὐτῶν) GLTTrAW. [m] καὶ τῶν also of the LTTrA. [n] Ὁρκίζω I adjure GLTTrAW. [o] — ὁ LTTrA.

of *one* Sceva, a Jew,
and chief of the priests,
which did so. 15 And
the evil spirit answer-
ed and said, Jesus I
know, and Paul I
know; but who are ye?
16 And the man in
whom the evil spirit
was leaped on them,
and overcame them,
and prevailed against
them, so that they fled
out of that house na-
ked and wounded.
17 And this was known
to all the Jews and
Greeks also dwelling
at Ephesus; and fear
fell on them all,
and the name of the
Lord Jesus was magni-
fied. 18 And many that
believed came, and
confessed, and shewed
their deeds. 19 Many
of them also which
used curious arts
brought their books
together, and burned
them before all *men:*
and they counted the
price of them, and
found *it* fifty thousand
pieces of silver. 20 So
mightily grew the
word of God and pre-
vailed.

21 After these things
were ended, Paul pur-
posed in the spirit,
when he had passed
through Macedonia
and Achaia, to go to
Jerusalem, saying, Af-
ter I have been there,
I must also see Rome.
22 So he sent into Ma-
cedonia two of them
that ministered unto
him, Timotheus and
Erastus; but he him-
self stayed in Asia for
a season. 23 And the
same time there arose
no small stir about
that way. 24 For a
certain *man* named
Demetrius, a silver-
smith, which made sil-
ver shrines for Diana,
brought no small gain
unto the craftsmen;
25 whom he called to-
gether with the work-

[p]τινες‖ [q]υἱοὶ‖ Σκευᾶ Ἰουδαίου ἀρχιερέως ἑπτὰ [q] [r]οἱ‖ τοῦτο
certain [men] [2]sons [3]of [4]Sceva [5]a [6]Jew, [7]a [8]high [9]priest [1]seven who this
ποιοῦντες. 15 ἀποκριθὲν.δὲ τὸ πνεῦμα τὸ πονηρὸν εἶπεν[s],
were doing. But answering the [2]spirit [1]wicked said,
Τὸν Ἰησοῦν γινώσκω, καὶ τὸν Παῦλον ἐπίσταμαι· ὑμεῖς
Jesus I know, and Paul I am acquainted with; [2]ye
δὲ τίνες ἐστέ; 16 Καὶ [t]ἐφαλλόμενος‖ [v]ἐπ' αὐτοὺς ὁ ἄνθρω-
[1]but, who are ye? And leaping on them the man
πος‖ ἐν ᾧ ἦν τὸ πνεῦμα τὸ πονηρόν, [w]καὶ‖ κατακυριεύσας
in whom was the [2]spirit [1]wicked, and having mastered
[x]αὐτῶν‖ ἴσχυσεν κατ' αὐτῶν, ὥστε γυμνοὺς καὶ τετραυματισ-
them prevailed against them, so that naked and wounded
μένους ἐκφυγεῖν ἐκ τοῦ.οἴκου.ἐκείνου. 17 τοῦτο.δὲ ἐγένετο
they escaped out of that house. And this became
γνωστὸν πᾶσιν Ἰουδαίοις.τε καὶ Ἕλλησιν τοῖς κατοικοῦσιν τὴν
known to all both Jews and Greeks, those inhabiting
Ἔφεσον, καὶ [y]ἐπέπεσεν‖ φόβος ἐπὶ πάντας αὐτούς, καὶ ἐμεγα-
Ephesus, and [2]fell [1]fear upon [2]all [1]them, and was mag-
λύνετο τὸ ὄνομα τοῦ κυρίου Ἰησοῦ. 18 Πολλοί.τε τῶν
nified the name of the Lord Jesus. And many of those who
πεπιστευκότων ἤρχοντο ἐξομολογούμενοι καὶ ἀναγγέλλοντες
believed came confessing and declaring
τὰς.πράξεις.αὐτῶν. 19 ἱκανοὶ.δὲ τῶν τὰ περίεργα πρα-
their deeds. And many of those who the curious arts prac-
ξάντων συνενέγκαντες τὰς βίβλους κατέκαιον ἐνώπιον
tised having brought the books burnt [them] before
πάντων· καὶ συνεψήφισαν τὰς τιμὰς αὐτῶν, καὶ εὗρον
all. And they reckoned up the prices of them, and found [it]
ἀργυρίου μυριάδας πέντε. 20 οὕτως κατὰ κράτος [z]ὁ λόγος τοῦ
[3]of [4]silver [2]myriads [1]five. Thus with might the word of the
κυρίου‖ ηὔξανεν καὶ ἴσχυεν.
Lord increased and prevailed.

21 Ὡς.δὲ ἐπληρώθη ταῦτα ἔθετο ὁ Παῦλος ἐν τῷ πνεύ-
And when were fulfilled these things [2]purposed [1]Paul in the spirit,
ματι, [a]διελθὼν‖ τὴν Μακεδονίαν καὶ [b]Ἀχαΐαν πορεύε-
having passed through Macedonia and Achaia, to
σθαι εἰς [c]Ἱερουσαλήμ,‖ εἰπών, Ὅτι μετὰ τὸ γενέσθαι με ἐκεῖ
go to Jerusalem, saying, After [2]having [3]been [1]my there
δεῖ με καὶ Ῥώμην ἰδεῖν. 22 Ἀποστείλας.δὲ εἰς [d]τὴν‖
it behoves me also Rome to see. And having sent into
Μακεδονίαν δύο τῶν διακονούντων αὐτῷ, Τιμόθεον καὶ
Macedonia two of those who ministered to him, Timotheus and
Ἔραστον, αὐτὸς ἐπέσχεν χρόνον εἰς τὴν Ἀσίαν· 23 Ἐγένετο
Erastus, he remained a time in Asia. [2]Came [3]to [4]pass
δὲ κατὰ τὸν.καιρὸν.ἐκεῖνον τάραχος οὐκ ὀλίγος περὶ τῆς
[1]and at that time [3]disturbance [1]no [2]small about the
ὁδοῦ. 24 Δημήτριος.γάρ τις ὀνόματι, ἀργυροκόπος,
way. For [4]Demetrius [1]a [2]certain [[3]man] by name, a silversmith,
ποιῶν ναοὺς ἀργυροῦς Ἀρτέμιδος, [e]παρείχετο‖ τοῖς τεχνίταις
making [2]temples [1]silver of Artemis, brought to the artificers
[f]ἐργασίαν οὐκ ὀλίγην·‖ 25 οὓς συναθροίσας, καὶ τοὺς
[3]gain [1]no [2]little; whom having brought together, and the

[p] τινος (*read* seven sons of a certain one) LTr. [q] υἱοὶ *placed after* ἑπτὰ LTTrA. [r] — οἱ LTTr[A]. [s] + αὐτοῖς to them LTTrAW. [t] ἐφαλόμενος LTTrA. [v] ὁ ἄνθρωπος ἐπ' αὐτούς LTTrA. [w] — καὶ LTTrAW. [x] ἀμφοτέρων both LTTrA. [y] ἔπεσεν LTr. [z] τοῦ κυρίου ὁ λόγος LTTrA. [a] διελθεῖν to have passed through L. [b] + τὴν L. [c] Ἱεροσόλυμα LTTrAW. [d] — τὴν T. [e] παρεῖχε L. [f] οὐκ ὀλίγην ἐργασίαν LTTrA.

περὶ τὰ.τοιαῦτα ἐργάτας, εἶπεν, Ἄνδρες, ἐπίστασθε ὅτι ἐκ
[2]in [3]such [4]things [1]workmen, he said, Men, ye know that from
ταύτης τῆς ἐργασίας. ἡ εὐπορία [g]ἡμῶν‖ ἐστιν· 26 καὶ θεωρεῖτε
this gain the wealth of us is; and ye see
καὶ ἀκούετε ὅτι οὐ μόνον Ἐφέσου ἀλλὰ [h]σχεδὸν πάσης τῆς
and hear that not only of Ephesus but almost of all
Ἀσίας ὁ.Παῦλος.οὗτος πείσας μετέστησεν ἱκανὸν.ὄχλον,
Asia this Paul having persuaded turned away a great multitude,
λέγων ὅτι οὐκ.εἰσὶν θεοὶ οἱ διὰ χειρῶν γινόμενοι. 27 οὐ
saying that they are not gods which by hands are made. [2]Not
μόνον δὲ τοῦτο κινδυνεύει ἡμῖν τὸ μέρος εἰς ἀπελεγμὸν
[3]only [1]now [5]this [4]is dangerous to us [lest] the business [2]into [3]disrepute
ἐλθεῖν, ἀλλὰ καὶ τὸ τῆς μεγάλης θεᾶς [i]Ἀρτέμιδος ἱερὸν‖ εἰς
[1]come, but also the [2]of [3]the [4]great [5]goddess [6]Artemis [1]temple for
[k]οὐδὲν‖ [l]λογισθῆναι, μέλλειν‖ [m]δὲ‖ καὶ καθαιρεῖσθαι [n]τὴν μεγα-
nothing be reckoned, and be about also to be destroyed the ma-
λειότητα‖ αὐτῆς, ἣν ὅλη [o]ἡ‖ Ἀσία καὶ ἡ οἰκουμένη σέβεται.
jesty of her, whom all Asia and the habitable world worships.
28 Ἀκούσαντες.δὲ καὶ γενόμενοι πλήρεις θυμοῦ, ἔκρα-
And having heard, and having become full of indignation, they cried
ζον λέγοντες, Μεγάλη ἡ Ἄρτεμις Ἐφεσίων. 29 Καὶ
out saying, Great the Artemis of [the] Ephesians. And
ἐπλήσθη ἡ πόλις [p]ὅλη‖ [q]συγχύσεως· ὥρμησάν.τε ὁμοθυ-
was [5]filled [1]the [3]city [2]whole with confusion, and they rushed with one
μαδὸν εἰς τὸ θέατρον, συναρπάσαντες Γάϊον καὶ Ἀρί-
accord to the theatre, having seized with [them] Gaius and Ari-
σταρχον Μακεδόνας, συνεκδήμους [r]τοῦ‖ Παύλου. 30 [r]τοῦ‖ [s]δὲ
starchus, Macedonians, fellow-travellers of Paul. But
Παύλου‖ βουλομένου εἰσελθεῖν εἰς τὸν δῆμον, οὐκ.εἴων αὐτὸν
Paul intending to go in to the people, [3]did [4]not [5]suffer [6]him
οἱ μαθηταί· 31 τινὲς.δὲ καὶ τῶν Ἀσιαρχῶν ὄντες αὐτῷ
[1]the [2]disciples, and some also of the chiefs of Asia being [2]to [3]him
φίλοι, πέμψαντες πρὸς αὐτόν, παρεκάλουν μὴ δοῦναι ἑαυτὸν
[1]friends, having sent to him, urged [him] not to venture himself
εἰς τὸ θέατρον. 32 ἄλλοι.μὲν.οὖν.ἄλλο.τι ἔκραζον.
into the theatre. Some therefore one thing and some another were crying out;
ἦν.γὰρ ἡ.ἐκκλησία [t]συγκεχυμένη,‖ καὶ οἱ πλείους οὐκ.ᾔδεισαν
for [3]was [1]the [2]assembly confused, and the most did not know
τίνος [v]ἕνεκεν‖ συνεληλύθεισαν. 33 ἐκ.δὲ τοῦ ὄχλου
for what cause they had come together. But from among the crowd
[w]προεβίβασαν‖ Ἀλέξανδρον, [x]προβαλόντων‖ αὐτὸν τῶν
they put forward Alexander, [3]thrusting [5]forward [4]him [1]the
Ἰουδαίων· ὁ.δὲ.Ἀλέξανδρος κατασείσας τὴν χεῖρα,
[2]Jews. And Alexander, having made a sign with the hand,
ἤθελεν ἀπολογεῖσθαι τῷ δήμῳ. 34 [y]ἐπιγνόντων‖.δὲ ὅτι
wished to make a defence to the people. But having recognized that
Ἰουδαῖός ἐστιν, φωνὴ ἐγένετο μία ἐκ πάντων, ὡς.ἐπὶ ὥρας
a Jew he is, [4]cry [1]there [2]was [3]one from all, for about [2]hours
δύο [z]κραζόντων,‖ Μεγάλη ἡ Ἄρτεμις Ἐφεσίων. 35 Κατα-
[1]two crying out, Great the Artemis of [the] Ephesians. [4]Having
στείλας δὲ ὁ γραμματεὺς τὸν ὄχλον φησίν, Ἄνδρες Ἐφέσιοι,
[5]calmed [1]and [2]the [3]recorder the crowd says, Men Ephesians,

men of like occupa-
tion, and said, Sirs, ye
know that by this craft
we have our wealth.
26 Moreover ye see and
hear, that not alone at
Ephesus, but almost
throughout all Asia,
this Paul hath per-
suaded and turned a-
way much people, say-
ing that they be no
gods, which are made
with hands: 27 so that
not only this our craft
is in danger to be set
at nought; but also
that the temple of the
great goddess Diana
should be despised,
and her magnificence
should be destroyed,
whom all Asia and
the world worshippeth.
28 And when they
heard *these sayings*,
they were full of wrath,
and cried out, saying,
Great *is* Diana of the
Ephesians. 29 And the
whole city was filled
with confusion: and
having caught Gaius
and Aristarchus, men
of Macedonia, Paul's
companions in travel,
they rushed with one
accord into the thea-
tre. 30 And when Paul
would have entered in
unto the people, the
disciples suffered him
not. 31 And certain of
the chief of Asia, which
were his friends, sent
unto him, desiring *him*
that he would not ad-
venture himself into
the theatre. 32 Some
therefore cried one
thing, and some an-
other: for the as-
sembly was confused;
and the more part
knew not wherefore
they were come to-
gether. 33 And they
drew Alexander out
of the multitude, the
Jews putting him for-
ward. And Alexander
beckoned with the
hand, and would have
made his defence unto
the people. 34 But
when they knew that
he was a Jew, all with
one voice about the
space of two hours
cried out, Great *is*
Diana of the Ephe-
sians. 35 And when the
townclerk had ap-
peased the people, he
said, *Ye* men of Ephe-

---

[g] ἡμῖν to us LTTrA. [h] + καὶ also L. [i] ἱερὸν Ἀρτέμιδος TA. [k] οὐθὲν LTTrA.
[l] λογισθήσεται (shall be counted), μέλλει L. [m] τε EGLTTrA. [n] τῆς μεγαλειότητος LTTrA.
[o] [ἡ] Tr. [p] — ὅλη LTTrA. [q] + τῆς GTTrAW. [r] — τοῦ GLTTrAW. [s] Παύλου δὲ LTTrAW.
[t] συν- T. [v] ἕνεκα LTTrA. [w] συνεβίβασαν they instructed LTTr. [x] προβαλλόντων EGL.
[y] ἐπιγνόντες GLTTrAW. [z] κράζοντες T.

sus, what man is there that knoweth not how that the city of the Ephesians is a worshipper of the great goddess Diana, and of the *image* which fell down from Jupiter? 36 Seeing then that these things cannot be spoken against, ye ought to be quiet, and to do nothing rashly. 37 For ye have brought hither these men, which are neither robbers of churches, nor yet blasphemers of your goddess. 38 Wherefore if Demetrius, and the craftsmen which are with him, have a matter against any man, the law is open, and there are deputies: let them implead one another. 39 But if ye inquire any thing concerning other matters, it shall be determined in a lawful assembly. 40 For we are in danger to be called in question for this day's uproar, there being no cause whereby we may give an account of this concourse. 41 And when he had thus spoken, he dismissed the assembly.

XX. And after the uproar was ceased, Paul called unto *him* the disciples, and embraced *them*, and departed for to go into Macedonia. 2 And when he had gone over those parts, and had given them much exhortation, he came into Greece. 3 And *there* abode three months. And when the Jews laid wait for him, as he was about to sail into Syria, he purposed to return through Macedonia. 4 And there accompanied him into Asia Sopater of Berea; and of the Thessalonians, Aristarchus and Secundus; and Gaius of Derbe, and Timotheus; and of Asia, Tychicus and Trophimus. 5 These going before tarried for us at

τίς γάρ ἐστιν [a]ἄνθρωπος‖ ὃς οὐ.γινώσκει τὴν Ἐφεσίων
[2]what [1]for [4]is [5]there [3]man who knows not the [2]of [[3]the] [4]Ephesians

πόλιν νεωκόρον οὖσαν τῆς μεγάλης [b]θεᾶς‖ Ἀρτέμιδος καὶ
[1]city [7]temple-keepers [5]as [6]being of the great goddess Artemis, and

τοῦ Διοπετοῦς; 36 ἀναντιῤῥήτων οὖν ὄντων τούτων,
of that fallen from Zeus? Undeniable therefore being these things

δέον ἐστὶν ὑμᾶς κατεσταλμένους ὑπάρχειν, καὶ μηδὲν προ-
necessary it is for you calm to be, and [3]nothing [4]head-

πετὲς [c]πράττειν.‖ 37 ἠγάγετε.γὰρ τοὺς.ἄνδρας.τούτους,
long [1]to [2]do. For ye brought these men, [who are]

οὔτε ἱεροσύλους οὔτε βλασφημοῦντας τὴν [d]θεὰν‖ [e]ὑμῶν.‖
neither temple plunderers nor are defaming [2]goddess [1]your.

38 εἰ μὲν οὖν Δημήτριος καὶ οἱ σὺν αὐτῷ τεχνῖται [f]πρός
If indeed therefore Demetrius and the [2]with [3]him [1]artificers against

τινα λόγον ἔχουσιν,‖ ἀγοραῖοι ἄγονται, καὶ ἀνθύπατοί εἰσιν·
anyone a matter have, courts are held, and proconsuls there are:

ἐγκαλείτωσαν ἀλλήλοις. 39 εἰ.δέ τι [g]περὶ ἑτέρων‖
let them accuse one another. But if anything concerning other matters

ἐπιζητεῖτε, ἐν τῇ ἐννόμῳ ἐκκλησίᾳ ἐπιλυθήσεται. 40 καὶ.γὰρ
ye inquire, in the lawful assembly it shall be solved. For also

κινδυνεύομεν ἐγκαλεῖσθαι στάσεως περὶ τῆς.σήμερον,
we are in danger to be accused of insurrection in regard to this day,

μηδενὸς αἰτίου ὑπάρχοντος περὶ οὗ [h] δυνησόμεθα ἀπο-
not one cause existing concerning which we shall be able to

δοῦναι λόγον [i] της.συστροφῆς.ταύτης. 41 Καὶ ταῦτα εἰπών,
give a reason for this concourse. And these things having said,

ἀπέλυσεν τὴν ἐκκλησίαν.
he dismissed the assembly.

20 Μετὰ.δὲ τὸ παύσασθαι τὸν θόρυβον, [k]προσκαλεσάμενος‖
But after [3]ceased [1]the [2]tumult, [5]having [6]called [7]to

ὁ Παῦλος τοὺς μαθητάς, καὶ [l] ἀσπασάμενος, ἐξῆλθεν
[[8]him] [4]Paul the disciples, and saluted [them], went away

[m]πορευθῆναι‖ εἰς [n]τὴν‖ Μακεδονίαν. 2 διελθὼν.δὲ τὰ
to go to Macedonia. And having passed through

μέρη.ἐκεῖνα, καὶ παρακαλέσας αὐτοὺς λόγῳ πολλῷ, ἦλ-
those parts, and having exhorted them with [2]discourse [1]much, he

θεν εἰς τὴν Ἑλλάδα· 3 ποιήσας.τε μῆνας τρεῖς, γενο-
came to Greece. And having continued [2]months [1]three, having been

μένης [o]αὐτῷ ἐπιβουλῆς‖ ὑπὸ τῶν Ἰουδαίων μέλλοντι
made against them a plot by the Jews being about

ἀνάγεσθαι εἰς τὴν Συρίαν, ἐγένετο [p]γνώμη‖ τοῦ ὑποστρέφειν
to sail into Syria, [3]arose [1]a [2]purpose to return

διὰ Μακεδονίας. 4 συνείπετο.δὲ αὐτῷ [q]ἄχρι τῆς Ἀσίας‖
through Macedonia. And accompanied him as far as Asia

Σώπατρος [r] Βεροιαῖος· Θεσσαλονικέων.δὲ Ἀρίσταρχος καὶ
Sopater a Berœan, and of Thessalonians Aristarchus and

Σεκοῦνδος, καὶ Γάϊος Δερβαῖος καὶ Τιμόθεος· Ἀσιανοὶ.δὲ
Secundus, and Gaius of Derbe and Timotheus, and of Asia

Τυχικὸς καὶ Τρόφιμος. 5 οὗτοι [s] [t]προελθόντες‖ ἔμενον ἡμᾶς
Tychicus and Trophimus. These having gone before waited for us

---

[a] ἀνθρώπων (read τις who) of men LTTrA. [b] — θεᾶς GLTTrAW. [c] πράσσειν LTTrA. [d] θεὸν GLTTrAW. [e] ἡμῶν our LTTrA. [f] ἔχουσιν πρός τινα λόγον GLTTrAW. [g] περαιτέρω further LTr. [h] + οὐ TTr[A]. [i] + περὶ concerning (this concourse) LTTr. [k] μεταπεμψάμενος having sent for TTr. [l] + παρακαλέσας having exhorted [and] LTTrA. [m] πορεύεσθαι LTTr. [n] — τὴν LTTr[A]. [o] ἐπιβουλῆς αὐτῷ LTTr. [p] γνώμης TTrA. [q] — ἄχρι τῆς Ἀσίας T[Tr]. [r] + Πύῤῥου of Pyrrhus GLTTrAW. [s] + δὲ and (these) LTTr[A]. [t] προσελθόντες having gone Tr.

ἐν [v]Τρωάδι·‖ 6 ἡμεῖς.δὲ ἐξεπλεύσαμεν μετὰ τὰς ἡμέρας τῶν
in Troas; but we sailed away after the days of the
ἀζύμων ἀπὸ Φιλίππων, καὶ ἤλθομεν πρὸς αὐτοὺς εἰς
unleavened bread from Philippi, and came to them at
τὴν [w]Τρωάδα‖ [x]ἄχρις‖ ἡμερῶν πέντε, [y]οὗ‖ διετρίψαμεν ἡμέρας
Troas in [2]days [1]five, where we stayed [2]days
ἑπτά. 7 Ἐν.δὲ τῇ μιᾷ τῶν σαββάτων, συνηγμένων
[1]seven. And on the first [day] of the week, [3]having [4]been [5]assembled
[z]τῶν μαθητῶν τοῦ‖ κλάσαι ἄρτον, ὁ Παῦλος διελέγετο αὐτοῖς,
[1]the [2]disciples to break bread, Paul discoursed to them,
μέλλων ἐξιέναι τῇ ἐπαύριον, παρέτεινέν.τε τὸν λόγον μέχρι
about to depart on the morrow; and he continued the discourse till
μεσονυκτίου· 8 ἦσαν.δὲ λαμπάδες ἱκαναὶ ἐν τῷ ὑπερῴῳ οὗ
midnight. And [3]were [2]lamps [1]many in the upper room where
[a]ἦσαν‖ συνηγμένοι. 9 [b]καθήμενος‖.δέ τις νεανίας ὀνόματι
they were assembled. And was sitting a certain youth, by name
Εὔτυχος ἐπὶ τῆς θυρίδος, καταφερόμενος ὕπνῳ βαθεῖ, δια-
Eutychus, by the window, overpowered by [2]sleep [1]deep, as
λεγομένου τοῦ Παύλου ἐπὶ.πλεῖον, κατενεχθεὶς ἀπὸ
[2]discoursed [1]Paul for a longer time, having been overpowered by
τοῦ ὕπνου ἔπεσεν ἀπὸ τοῦ τριστέγου κάτω, καὶ ἤρθη
the sleep he fell [2]from [3]the [4]third [5]story [1]down, and was taken up
νεκρός. 10 καταβὰς.δὲ ὁ Παῦλος ἐπέπεσεν αὐτῷ, καὶ [c]συμ-
dead. But [2]having [3]descended [1]Paul fell upon him, and having
περιλαβὼν‖ εἶπεν, Μὴ.θορυβεῖσθε· ἡ.γὰρ ψυχὴ αὐτοῦ ἐν
embraced [him] said, Do not make a tumult, for the life of him in
αὐτῷ ἐστιν. 11 Ἀναβὰς.δὲ καὶ κλάσας [d] ἄρτον καὶ γευσά-
him is. And having gone up and having broken bread and having
μενος, ἐφ᾽.ἱκανόν.τε ὁμιλήσας [e]ἄχρις‖ αὐγῆς, οὕτως ἐξῆλ-
eaten, and for long having conversed until day-break, so he de-
θεν. 12 ἤγαγον.δὲ τὸν παῖδα ζῶντα, καὶ παρεκλήθησαν οὐ
parted. And they brought the boy alive, and were comforted not
μετρίως. 13 Ἡμεῖς.δὲ [f]προελθόντες‖ ἐπὶ τὸ πλοῖον ἀνήχθημεν
a little. But we having gone before to the ship sailed
[g]εἰς‖ τὴν Ἄσσον, ἐκεῖθεν μέλλοντες ἀναλαμβάνειν τὸν Παῦ-
to Assos, [3]there [1]being [2]about to take in Paul;
λον· οὕτως.γὰρ [h]ἦν.διατεταγμένος,‖ μέλλων αὐτὸς πεζεύειν.
for so he had appointed, [2]being [3]about [1]himself to go on foot.
14 ὡς.δὲ [i]συνέβαλεν‖ ἡμῖν εἰς τὴν Ἄσσον, ἀναλαβόντες αὐτὸν
And when he met with us at Assos, having taken [2]in [1]him
ἤλθομεν εἰς Μιτυλήνην· 15 κἀκεῖθεν ἀποπλεύσαντες τῇ
we came to Mitylene; and thence having sailed away, on the
ἐπιούσῃ κατηντήσαμεν [k]ἀντικρὺ‖ Χίου· τῇ.δὲ ἑτέρᾳ
following [day] arrived opposite Chios, and the next [day]
παρεβάλομεν εἰς Σάμον· [l]καὶ μείναντες ἐν Τρωγυλλίῳ,‖ τῇ [m]
we arrived at Samos; and having remained at Trogyllium, the
ἐχομένῃ ἤλθομεν εἰς Μίλητον. 16 [n]ἔκρινεν‖.γὰρ ὁ Παῦλος
next [day] we came to Miletus: for [2]had [3]decided [1]Paul
παραπλεῦσαι τὴν Ἔφεσον, ὅπως μὴ.γένηται αὐτῷ χρονο-
to sail by Ephesus, so that it might not happen to him to spend
τριβῆσαι ἐν τῇ Ἀσίᾳ· ἔσπευδεν.γὰρ εἰ δυνατὸν [o]ἦν‖ αὐτῷ
time in Asia; for he hastened if possible it was for him

Troas. 6 And we sailed away from Philippi after the days of unleavened bread, and came unto them to Troas in five days; where we abode seven days. 7 And upon the first *day* of the week, when the disciples came together to break bread, Paul preached unto them, ready to depart on the morrow; and continued his speech until midnight. 8 And there were many lights in the upper chamber, where they were gathered together. 9 And there sat in a window a certain young man named Eutychus, being fallen into a deep sleep: and as Paul was long preaching, he sunk down with sleep, and fell down from the third loft, and was taken up dead. 10 And Paul went down, and fell on him, and embracing *him* said, Trouble not yourselves; for his life is in him. 11 When he therefore was come up again, and had broken bread, and eaten, and talked a long while, even till break of day, so he departed. 12 And they brought the young man alive, and were not a little comforted. 13 And we went before to ship, and sailed unto Assos, there intending to take in Paul: for so had he appointed, minding himself to go afoot. 14 And when he met with us at Assos, we took him in, and came to Mitylene. 15 And we sailed thence, and came the next *day* over against Chios; and the next *day* we arrived at Samos, and tarried at Trogyllium; and the next *day* we came to Miletus. 16 For Paul had determined to sail by Ephesus, because he would not spend the time in Asia: for he hasted, if it were possible for him, to be at

[v] Τρῳάδι LT. [w] Τρῳάδα LT. [x] ἄχρι LTTrA. [y] ὅπου T. [z] ἡμῶν we (having been assembled) GLTTrAW. [a] ἦμεν we were GLTTrAW. [b] καθεζόμενος LTTrAW. [c] συν- T. [d] + τὸν the LTTrAW. [e] ἄχρι TTrA. [f] προσελθόντες having gone Tr. [g] ἐπὶ LTTrA. [h] διατεταγμένος ἦν LTTrA. [i] συνέβαλλεν LTTrA. [k] ἄντικρυς LTTrA. [l] Τρωγυλίῳ A; — καὶ μείναντες ἐν Τρω. LTTr. [m] + δὲ and (the) LTTr. [n] κεκρίκει GLTTrAW. [o] εἴη it might be LTTrA.

Jerusalem the day of
Pentecost. 17 And from
Miletus he sent to
Ephesus, and called the
elders of the church.
18 And when they were
come to him, he said
unto them, Ye know,
from the first day that
I came into Asia, after
what manner I have
been with you at all
seasons, 19 serving the
Lord with all humi-
lity of mind, and with
many tears, and temp-
tations, which befell
me by the lying in wait
of the Jews: 20 *and*
how I kept back no-
thing that was profit-
able *unto you*, but have
shewed you, and have
taught you publickly,
and from house to
house, 21 testifying
both to the Jews, and
also to the Greeks,
repentance toward
God, and faith toward
our Lord Jesus Christ.
22 And now, behold,
I go bound in the spi-
rit unto Jerusalem,
not knowing the things
that shall befall me
there: 23 save that
the Holy Ghost wit-
nesseth in every city,
saying that bonds and
afflictions abide me.
24 But none of these
things move me, nei-
ther count I my life
dear unto myself, so
that I might finish my
course with joy, and
the ministry, which I
have received of the
Lord Jesus, to testify
the gospel of the grace
of God. 25 And now,
behold, I know that
ye all, among whom I
have gone preaching
the kingdom of God,
shall see my face no
more. 26 Wherefore I
take you to record
this day, that I *am*
pure from the blood of
all *men*. 27 For I have
not shunned to declare
unto you all the coun-

τὴν ἡμέραν τῆς πεντηκοστῆς γενέσθαι εἰς [p]Ἱεροσόλυμα.‖
the day of Pentecost to be in Jerusalem.
17 Ἀπὸ.δὲ τῆς Μιλήτου πέμψας εἰς Ἔφεσον μετεκαλέσατο
And from Miletus having sent to Ephesus he called for
τοὺς.πρεσβυτέρους τῆς ἐκκλησίας. 18 ὡς.δὲ παρεγένοντο πρὸς
the elders of the assembly. And when they were come to
αὐτὸν [q] εἶπεν αὐτοῖς, Ὑμεῖς ἐπίστασθε, ἀπὸ πρώτης ἡμέρας
him he said to them, Ye know, from the first day
ἀφ' ἧς ἐπέβην εἰς τὴν Ἀσίαν, πῶς μεθ' ὑμῶν τὸν.πάντα
on which I arrived in Asia, how with you all the
χρόνον ἐγενόμην, 19 δουλεύων τῷ κυρίῳ μετὰ πάσης ταπεινο-
time I was, serving the Lord with all humi-
φροσύνης καὶ [r]πολλῶν‖ δακρύων καὶ πειρασμῶν, τῶν-συμ-
lity and many tears and temptations, which hap-
βάντων μοι ἐν ταῖς ἐπιβουλαῖς τῶν Ἰουδαίων· 20 ὡς
pened to me through the plots of the Jews; how
οὐδὲν ὑπεστειλάμην τῶν συμφερόντων τοῦ.μὴ ἀναγγεῖλαι
nothing I kept back of what is profitable so as not to announce [it]
ὑμῖν, καὶ διδάξαι ὑμᾶς δημοσίᾳ καὶ κατ'.οἴκους, 21 διαμαρ-
to you, and to teach you publicly and from house to house, earnestly
τυρόμενος Ἰουδαίοις.τε καὶ Ἕλλησιν τὴν εἰς [s]τὸν‖ θεὸν
testifying both to Jews and Greeks [2]toward [3]God
μετάνοιαν καὶ πίστιν [t]τὴν‖ εἰς τὸν.κύριον.ἡμῶν Ἰησοῦν
[1]repentance and faith toward our Lord Jesus
[v]χριστόν.‖ 22 καὶ νῦν ἰδοὺ [w]ἐγὼ δεδεμένος‖ τῷ πνεύματι
Christ. And now, lo, I, bound in the spirit,
πορεύομαι εἰς Ἱερουσαλήμ, τὰ ἐν αὐτῇ συναντήσοντά
go to Jerusalem, the things which in it shall happen
[x]μοι‖ μὴ εἰδώς, 23 πλὴν ὅτι τὸ πνεῦμα τὸ ἅγιον κατὰ.πόλιν
to me not knowing; except that the Spirit the Holy in every city
διαμαρτύρεται[y] [z]λέγον‖ ὅτι δεσμά [a]με καὶ θλίψεις‖ μένουσιν.
fully testifies, saying that bonds [4]me [1]and [2]tribulations [3]await.
24 ἀλλ' οὐδενὸς [b]λόγον‖ [c]ποιοῦμαι, οὐδὲ ἔχω‖ τὴν ψυχήν
But [4]of [5]nothing [3]account [1]I [2]make, nor hold I [2]life
[d]μου‖ τιμίαν ἐμαυτῷ, ὡς τελειῶσαι τὸν.δρόμον.μου [e]μετὰ
[1]my dear to myself, so as to finish my course with
χαρᾶς,‖ καὶ τὴν διακονίαν ἣν ἔλαβον παρὰ τοῦ κυρίου Ἰη-
joy, and the ministry which I received from the Lord Je-
σοῦ, διαμαρτύρασθαι τὸ εὐαγγέλιον τῆς χάριτος τοῦ θεοῦ.
sus, to testify fully the glad tidings of the grace of God.
25 καὶ νῦν ἰδοὺ ἐγὼ οἶδα ὅτι οὐκέτι ὄψεσθε τὸ.πρόσωπόν.μου
And now, lo, I know that no more [3]will [4]see [5]my [6]face
ὑμεῖς πάντες, ἐν οἷς διῆλθον κηρύσσων τὴν βασιλείαν
[1]ye [2]all, among whom I have gone about proclaiming the kingdom
[f]τοῦ θεοῦ.‖ 26 [g]διὸ‖ μαρτύρομαι ὑμῖν ἐν τῇ.σήμερον.ἡμέρᾳ,
of God. Wherefore I testify to you in this day
ὅτι καθαρὸς [h]ἐγὼ‖ ἀπὸ τοῦ αἵματος πάντων· 27 οὐ.γὰρ
that pure I [am] from the blood of all, for [3]not
ὑπεστειλάμην τοῦ μὴ ἀναγγεῖλαι [i]ὑμῖν‖ πᾶσαν τὴν βουλὴν
[1]I [2]kept back from announcing to you all the counsel

---

[p] Ἱερουσαλήμ T. [q] + ὁμοῦ ὄντων αὐτῶν they being together L. [r] — πολλῶν GLTTrAW. [s] — τὸν TTrA. [t] — τὴν LTTrA. [v] — χριστόν L[Tr]A. [w] δεδεμένος ἐγὼ GLTTrAW. [x] ἐμοὶ T. [y] + μοι to me GLTTrAW. [z] λέγων A. [a] καὶ θλίψεις με LTTrA. [b] λόγου TTrA. [c] ἔχω, οὐδὲ ποιοῦμαι L; — οὐδὲ ἔχω TTrA. [d] — μου LTTrA. [e] — μετὰ χαρᾶς LTTrA. [f] — τοῦ θεοῦ LTTrAW. [g] διότι TA. [h] εἰμι am LTTrA. [i] — ὑμῖν LTTrA.

τοῦ.θεοῦ [j]. 28 προσέχετε [k]οὖν‖ ἑαυτοῖς καὶ παντὶ τῷ
of God. Take heed therefore to yourselves and to all the

ποιμνίῳ. ἐν.ᾧ ὑμᾶς τὸ πνεῦμα τὸ ἅγιον ἔθετο ἐπισκόπους,
flock, wherein [7]you [1]the [2]Spirit [3]the [4]Holy [5]did [6]set overseers,

ποιμαίνειν τὴν ἐκκλησίαν [l]τοῦ θεοῦ,‖ ἣν περιεποιήσατο διὰ
to shepherd the assembly of God, which he purchased with

τοῦ [m]ἰδίου αἵματος.‖ 29 ἐγὼ.[n]γὰρ‖ οἶδα [o]τοῦτο,‖ ὅτι εἰσελεύ-
the [2]of [3]his [4]own [1]blood. For I know this, that will

σονται μετὰ τὴν.ἄφιξίν.μου λύκοι βαρεῖς εἰς ὑμᾶς, μὴ
come in after my departure [2]wolves [1]grievous amongst you, not

φειδόμενοι τοῦ ποιμνίου· 30 καὶ ἐξ ὑμῶν.αὐτῶν ἀνα-
sparing the flock; and from amongst your own selves will

στήσονται ἄνδρες λαλοῦντες διεστραμμένα, τοῦ ἀποσπᾷν τοὺς
rise up men speaking perverted things, to draw away the

μαθητὰς ὀπίσω [p]αὐτῶν.‖ 31 διὸ γρηγορεῖτε, μνημονεύοντες
disciples after themselves. Wherefore watch, remembering

ὅτι τριετίαν νύκτα καὶ ἡμέραν οὐκ.ἐπαυσάμην μετὰ δακρύων
that three years night and day I ceased not with tears

νουθετῶν ἕνα ἕκαστον. 32 καὶ [q]τανῦν‖ παρατίθεμαι ὑμᾶς,
admonishing [2]one [1]each. And now I commit you,

[r]ἀδελφοί,‖ τῷ θεῷ καὶ τῷ λόγῳ τῆς.χάριτος.αὐτοῦ, τῷ δυνα-
brethren, to God and to the word of his grace, which is

μένῳ [s]ἐποικοδομῆσαι‖ καὶ δοῦναι [t]ὑμῖν‖ [v] κληρονομίαν ἐν
able to build up and to give you an inheritance among

τοῖς ἡγιασμένοις πᾶσιν. 33 ἀργυρίου ἢ χρυσίου ἢ ἱματισμοῦ
[2]the [3]sanctified [1]all. Silver or gold or clothing

[w]οὐδενὸς‖ ἐπεθύμησα· 34 αὐτοὶ.[x]δὲ‖ γινώσκετε ὅτι ταῖς
of no one I desired. But yourselves know that

χρείαις.μου καὶ τοῖς οὖσιν μετ' ἐμοῦ ὑπηρέτησαν αἱ
to my needs and to those who were with me did [3]minister

χεῖρες.αὗται. 35 πάντα ὑπέδειξα ὑμῖν ὅτι οὕτως κοπιῶντας
[1]these [2]hands. All things I shewed you that thus labouring

δεῖ ἀντιλαμβάνεσθαι τῶν ἀσθενούντων, μνημονεύειν.τε
it behoves [us] to aid those being weak, and to remember

τῶν λόγων τοῦ κυρίου Ἰησοῦ ὅτι αὐτὸς εἶπεν, Μακάριόν ἐστιν
the words of the Lord Jesus that himself said, [2]Blessed [3]it [4]is

[y]διδόναι μᾶλλον‖ ἢ λαμβάνειν. 36 Καὶ ταῦτα εἰπών,
[5]to [6]give [1]more than to receive. And these things having said

θεὶς τὰ.γόνατα.αὐτοῦ σὺν πᾶσιν αὐτοῖς προσηύξατο.
having bowed his knees with [2]all [1]them he prayed.

37 Ἱκανὸς.δὲ [z]ἐγένετο κλαυθμὸς‖ πάντων· καὶ ἐπιπεσόντες
And [3]much [1]there [2]was weeping of all: and falling

ἐπὶ τὸν τράχηλον τοῦ Παύλου κατεφίλουν αὐτόν· 38 ὀδυνώ-
upon the neck of Paul they ardently kissed him, dis-

μενοι μάλιστα ἐπὶ τῷ λόγῳ ᾧ εἰρήκει, ὅτι οὐκέτι μέλ-
tressed most of all for the word which he had said, that no more they

λουσιν τὸ.πρόσωπον.αὐτοῦ θεωρεῖν. προέπεμπον.δὲ αὐτὸν
are about his face to see. And they accompanied him

εἰς τὸ πλοῖον.
to the ship.

sel of God. 28 Take heed therefore unto yourselves, and to all the flock, over the which the Holy Ghost hath made you overseers, to feed the church of God, which he hath purchased with his own blood. 29 For I know this, that after my departing shall grievous wolves enter in among you, not sparing the flock. 30 Also of your own selves shall men arise, speaking perverse things, to draw away disciples after them. 31 Therefore watch, and remember, that by the space of three years I ceased not to warn every one night and day with tears. 32 And now, brethren, I commend you to God, and to the word of his grace, which is able to build you up, and to give you an inheritance among all them which are sanctified. 33 I have coveted no man's silver, or gold, or apparel. 34 Yea, ye yourselves know, that these hands have ministered unto my necessities, and to them that were with me. 35 I have shewed you all things, how that so labouring ye ought to support the weak, and to remember the words of the Lord Jesus, how he said, It is more blessed to give than to receive. 36 And when he had thus spoken, he kneeled down, and prayed with them all. 37 And they all wept sore, and fell on Paul's neck, and kissed him, 38 sorrowing most of all for the words which he spake, that they should see his face no more. And they accompanied him unto the ship.

21 Ὡς.δὲ ἐγένετο ἀναχθῆναι ἡμᾶς ἀποσπασθέντας ἀπ'
And when it was [2]sailed [1]we, having drawn away from

XXI. And it came to pass, that after we were gotten from

---

[j] + ὑμῖν to you LTTrA. [k] — οὖν [L]TTr. [l] τοῦ κυρίου of the Lord GLTTr. [m] αἵματος τοῦ ἰδίου GLTTrAW. [n] — γὰρ for LTTrAW. [o] — τοῦτο LTTrAW. [p] ἑαυτῶν TTrA. [q] τὰ νῦν LTTrA. [r] — ἀδελφοί LTTrA. [s] οἰκοδομῆσαι to build LTTrAW. [t] — ὑμῖν LTTrA. [v] + τὴν (*read* the inheritance) TTrA. [w] οὐθενὸς T. [x] — δὲ but GLTTrAW. [y] μᾶλλον διδόναι GLTTrAW. [z] κλαυθμὸς ἐγένετο LTTrAW.

them, and had launch-
ed, we came with a
straight course unto
Coos, and the *day* fol-
lowing unto Rhodes,
and from thence unto
Patara : 2 and find-
ing a ship sailing over
unto Phenicia, we
went aboard, and set
forth. 3 Now when we
had discovered Cyprus,
we left it on the left
hand, and sailed into
Syria, and landed at
Tyre : for there the
ship was to unlade
her burden. 4 And
finding disciples, we
tarried there seven
days : who said to
Paul through the Spi-
rit, that he should not
go up to Jerusalem.
5 And when we had
accomplished those
days, we departed and
went our way ; and
they all brought us on
our way, with wives
and children, till *we*
were out of the city :
and we kneeled down
on the shore, and pray-
ed. 6 And when we
had taken our leave
one of another, we
took ship ; and they
returned home again.
7 And when we had
finished *our* course
from Tyre, we came
to Ptolemais, and sa-
luted the brethren, and
abode with them one
day. 8 And the next
day we that were of
Paul's company de-
parted, and came unto
Cæsarea : and we en-
tered into the house
of Philip the evangel-
ist, which was *one* of
the seven ; and abode
with him. 9 And the
same man had four
daughters, virgins,
which did prophesy.
10 And as we tarried
there many days, there
came down from Ju-
dæa a certain pro-
phet, named Agabus.
11 And when he was
come unto us, he
took Paul's girdle,
and bound his own
hands and feet, and
said, Thus saith the
Holy Ghost, So shall
the Jews at Jerusalem
bind the man that

αὐτῶν, εὐθυδρομήσαντες ἤλθομεν εἰς τὴν [a]Κῶν," τῇ.δὲ ἑξῆς
them, having run direct we came to Cos, and on the next
εἰς τὴν Ῥόδον, κἀκεῖθεν εἰς Πάταρα. 2 καὶ εὑρόντες
[day] to Rhodes, and thence to Patara. And having found
πλοῖον διαπερῶν εἰς Φοινίκην, ἐπιβάντες ἀνήχθημεν.
a ship passing over into Phœnicia, having gone on board we sailed ;
3 [b]ἀναφάναντες".δὲ τὴν Κύπρον, καὶ καταλιπόντες αὐτὴν
and having sighted Cyprus, and having left it
εὐώνυμον ἐπλέομεν εἰς Συρίαν, καὶ [c]κατήχθημεν" εἰς Τύρον·
on the left we sailed to Syria, and brought to at Tyre,
ἐκεῖσε.γὰρ [d]ἦν τὸ πλοῖον" ἀποφορτιζόμενον τὸν γόμον. 4 [e]καὶ
for there was the ship discharging the lading. And
ἀνευρόντες" τοὺς μαθητάς, ἐπεμείναμεν [f]αὐτοῦ" ἡμέρας ἑπτά·
having found out the ^ disciples, we remained there [2]days [1]seven ;
οἵτινες τῷ Παύλῳ ἔλεγον διὰ τοῦ πνεύματος, μὴ [g]ἀναβαίνειν"
who to Paul said by the Spirit, not to go up
εἰς [h]Ἱερουσαλήμ." 5 ὅτε.δὲ ἐγένετο [i]ἡμᾶς ἐξαρτίσαι" τὰς ἡμέ-
to Jerusalem. But when it was we completed the days,
ρας, ἐξελθόντες ἐπορευόμεθα, προπεμπόντων ἡμᾶς πάντων
having set out we journeyed, [2]accompanying [3]us [1]all
σὺν γυναιξὶν καὶ τέκνοις ἕως ἔξω τῆς πόλεως· καὶ θέντες
with wives and children as far as outside the city. And having bowed
τὰ γόνατα ἐπὶ τὸν αἰγιαλὸν [k]προσηυξάμεθα. 6 καὶ ἀσπασά-
the knees on the shore we prayed. And having
μενοι" ἀλλήλους [l] [m]ἐπέβημεν" εἰς τὸ πλοῖον, ἐκεῖνοι.δὲ ὑπέ-
saluted one another we went up into the ship, and they re-
στρεψαν εἰς τὰ.ἴδια. 7 Ἡμεῖς.δὲ τὸν πλοῦν διανύσαντες
turned to their own [homes]. And we, the voyage having completed
ἀπὸ Τύρου κατηντήσαμεν εἰς Πτολεμαΐδα, καὶ ἀσπασάμενοι
from Tyre, arrived at Ptolemais, and having saluted
τοὺς ἀδελφοὺς ἐμείναμεν ἡμέραν μίαν παρ' αὐτοῖς. 8 τῇ.δὲ
the brethren we abode [2]day [1]one with them. And on the
ἐπαύριον ἐξελθόντες [n]οἱ.περὶ.τὸν.Παῦλον" [o]ἦλθον" εἰς
morrow [6]having [7]gone [8]forth [1]Paul [2]and [3]those [4]with [5]him they came to
[p]Καισάρειαν·" καὶ εἰσελθόντες εἰς τὸν οἶκον Φιλίππου τοῦ
Cæsarea ; and having entered into the house of Philip the
εὐαγγελιστοῦ, [q]τοῦ" ὄντος ἐκ τῶν ἑπτά, ἐμείναμεν παρ' αὐτῷ.
evangelist, being of the seven, we abode with him.
9 τούτῳ.δὲ ἦσαν θυγατέρες [r]παρθένοι τέσσαρες" προφη-
Now to this [man] there were [2]daughters [3]virgins [1]four who pro-
τεύουσαι. 10 ἐπιμενόντων.δὲ [s]ἡμῶν" ἡμέρας πλείους κατῆλθέν
phesied. And [2]remaining [1]we [4]days [3]many [8]came [9]down
τις ἀπὸ τῆς Ἰουδαίας προφήτης ὀνόματι Ἄγαβος·
[5]a [6]certain [7]one from Judæa, a prophet, by name Agabus ;
11 καὶ ἐλθὼν πρὸς ἡμᾶς, καὶ ἄρας τὴν ζώνην τοῦ
and having come to us, and having taken the girdle
Παύλου, δήσας.[t]τε" [v]αὐτοῦ τὰς χεῖρας καὶ τοὺς πόδας"
of Paul, and having bound of himself the hands and the feet
εἶπεν, Τάδε λέγει τὸ πνεῦμα τὸ ἅγιον, Τὸν ἄνδρα οὗ ἐστιν
said, Thus says the Spirit the Holy, The man of whom is

---

[a] Κῶ GLTTrAW. [b] ἀναφανέντες EGLTrAW. [c] κατήλθομεν landed LTTrA. [d] τὸ πλοῖον ἦν LTTrAW. [e] ἀνευρόντες δὲ LTTrAW. [f] αὐτοῖς with them L. [g] ἐπιβαίνειν LTTrA. [h] Ἱεροσόλυμα GLTTrAW. [i] ἐξαρτίσαι ἡμᾶς LTrAW. [k] προσευξάμενοι ἀπησπασάμεθα having prayed we took our leave LTTrAW. [l] + καὶ and LTTrAW. [m] ἐνέβημεν LTr ; ἀνέβημεν TAW. [n] — οἱ περὶ τὸν Παῦλον GLTTrAW. [o] ἤλθομεν we came EGLTAW ; ἤλθαμεν Tr. [p] Καισαρίαν T. [q] — τοῦ GLTTrAW. [r] τέσσαρες παρθένοι LTTrA. [s] — ἡμῶν LTTrAW. [t] — τε and LTTrAW. [v] ἑαυτοῦ τοὺς πόδας καὶ τὰς χεῖρας LTTrAW.

ἡ.ζώνη.αὕτη οὕτως δήσουσιν ἐν Ἱερουσαλὴμ οἱ Ἰουδαῖοι, καὶ
this girdle thus shall [3]bind [4]in [5]Jerusalem [1]the [2]Jews, and
παραδώσουσιν εἰς χεῖρας ἐθνῶν. 12 Ὡς.δὲ ἠκούσαμεν
deliver up into [the] hands of [the] nations. And when we heard
ταῦτα, παρεκαλοῦμεν ἡμεῖς.τε καὶ οἱ ἐντόπιοι τοῦ
these things, [8]besought [1]both [2]we [3]and [4]those [5]of [[6]the] [7]place
μὴ ἀναβαίνειν αὐτὸν εἰς Ἱερουσαλήμ. 13 [w]ἀπεκρίθη.[x]δὲ‖ ὁ
[10]not [11]to [12]go [13]up [9]him to Jerusalem. But [2]answered
Παῦλος, [y]Τί ποιεῖτε κλαίοντες καὶ συνθρύπτοντές μου τὴν
[1]Paul, What do ye weeping and breaking my
καρδίαν; ἐγὼ.γὰρ οὐ μόνον δεθῆναι ἀλλὰ καὶ ἀποθανεῖν εἰς
heart? for I not only to be bound but also to die at
Ἱερουσαλὴμ ἑτοίμως.ἔχω ὑπὲρ τοῦ ὀνόματος τοῦ κυρίου Ἰησοῦ.
Jerusalem am ready for the name of the Lord Jesus.
14 Μὴ.πειθομένου.δὲ αὐτοῦ ἡσυχάσαμεν εἰπόντες, [z]Τὸ θέλημα
And [2]not [3]being [4]persuaded [1]he we were silent, saying, The will
τοῦ κυρίου γενέσθω.‖
of the Lord be done.

15 Μετὰ.δὲ τὰς.ἡμέρας ταύτας [a]ἀποσκευασάμενοι‖ ἀνε-
And after these days, having packed the baggage we
βαίνομεν εἰς [b]Ἱερουσαλήμ.‖ 16 συνῆλθον.δὲ καὶ τῶν
went up to Jerusalem. And went also [some] of the
μαθητῶν ἀπὸ [c]Καισαρείας‖ σὺν ἡμῖν, ἄγοντες παρ' ᾧ
disciples from Cæsarea with us, bringing [one] with whom
ξενισθῶμεν, Μνάσωνί.τινι Κυπρίῳ, ἀρχαίῳ μαθητῇ. 17 Γενο-
we might lodge, a certain Mnason, a Cypriot, an old disciple. [3]Having
μένων δὲ ἡμῶν εἰς Ἱεροσόλυμα ἀσμένως [d]ἐδέξαντο‖ ἡμᾶς οἱ
[4]arrived [1]and [2]we at Jerusalem [3]gladly [4]received [5]us [1]the
ἀδελφοί. 18 τῇ.[e]δὲ‖ ἐπιούσῃ εἰσῄει ὁ Παῦλος σὺν ἡμῖν
[2]brethren. And on the following [day] [2]went [3]in [1]Paul with us
πρὸς Ἰάκωβον, πάντες.τε παρεγένοντο οἱ πρεσβύτεροι. 19 καὶ
to James, and all [3]assembled [1]the [2]elders. And
ἀσπασάμενος αὐτοὺς ἐξηγεῖτο καθ'.ἓν.ἕκαστον ὧν ἐποίησεν
having saluted them he related one by one what things [2]wrought
ὁ θεὸς ἐν τοῖς ἔθνεσιν διὰ τῆς.διακονίας.αὐτοῦ. 20 οἱ.δὲ
[1]God among the nations by his ministry. And they
ἀκούσαντες ἐδόξαζον [f]τὸν κύριον·‖ [g]εἶπόν.τε‖ αὐτῷ, Θεωρεῖς,
having heard glorified the Lord. And they said to him, Thou seest,
ἀδελφέ, πόσαι μυριάδες εἰσὶν [h]Ἰουδαίων‖ τῶν πεπι-
brother, how many myriads there are of Jews who have be-
στευκότων, καὶ πάντες ζηλωταὶ τοῦ νόμου ὑπάρχουσιν.
lieved, and all zealous ones of the law are.
21 κατηχήθησαν.δὲ περὶ σοῦ, ὅτι ἀποστασίαν διδάσκεις
And they were informed concerning thee, that [9]apostasy [1]thou [2]teachest
ἀπὸ [i]Μωσέως‖ τοὺς κατὰ τὰ ἔθνη [k]πάντας‖ Ἰουδαίους,
[10]from [11]Moses [4]the [6]among [7]the [8]nations [3]all [5]Jews,
λέγων μὴ περιτέμνειν αὐτοὺς τὰ τέκνα, μηδὲ τοῖς ἔθεσιν
telling [2]not [3]to [4]circumcise [1]them the children, nor in the customs
περιπατεῖν. 22 τί οὖν ἐστιν; πάντως [l]δεῖ πλῆθος
to walk. What then is it? certainly [3]must [1]a [2]multitude

owneth this girdle, and shall deliver *him* into the hands of the Gentiles. 12 And when we heard these things, both we, and they of that place, besought him not to go up to Jerusalem. 13 Then Paul answered, What mean ye to weep and to break mine heart? for I am ready not to be bound only, but also to die at Jerusalem for the name of the Lord Jesus. 14 And when he would not be persuaded, we ceased, saying, The will of the Lord be done.

15 And after those days we took up our carriages, and went up to Jerusalem. 16 There went with us also *certain* of the disciples of Cæsarea, and brought with them one Mnason of Cyprus, an old disciple, with whom we should lodge. 17 And when we were come to Jerusalem, the brethren received us gladly. 18 And the *day* following Paul went in with us unto James; and all the elders were present. 19 And when he had saluted them, he declared particularly what things God had wrought among the Gentiles by his ministry. 20 And when they heard *it*, they glorified the Lord, and said unto him, Thou seest, brother, how many thousands of Jews there are which believe; and they are all zealous of the law: 21 and they are informed of thee, that thou teachest all the Jews which are among the Gentiles to forsake Moses, saying that they ought not to circumcise *their* children, neither to walk after the customs. 22 What is it therefore? the multitude must

---

[w] + τότε then LTTrAW. [x] — δὲ but LTTrAW. [y] + καὶ εἶπεν and said T. [z] Τοῦ κυρίου τὸ θέλημα γινέσθω LTTrAW. [a] ἐπισκευασάμενοι LTTrAW. [b] Ἱεροσόλυμα LTTrAW. [c] Καισαρίας T. [d] ἀπεδέξαντο welcomed LTTrAW. [e] τε T. [f] τὸν θεόν God GLTTrAW. [g] εἰπόντες saying L; εἶπάν τε TTr. [h] ἐν τοῖς Ἰουδαιοῖς among the Jews LTrAW; — Ἰουδαίων T. [i] Μωϋσέως GLTTrAW. [k] — πάντας L[Tr]. [l] δεῖ συνελθεῖν πλῆθος LTA; — δεῖ πλῆθος συνελθεῖν Tr.

needs come together:
for they will hear that
thou art come. 23 Do
therefore this that we
say to thee: We have
four men which have a
vow on them; 24 them
take, and purify thy-
self with them, and be
at charges with them,
that they may shave
their heads: and all
may know that those
things, whereof they
were informed con-
cerning thee, are no-
thing; but *that* thou
thyself also walkest
orderly, and keepest
the law. 25 As touch-
ing the Gentiles which
believe, we have writ-
ten *and* concluded that
they observe no such
thing, save only that
they keep themselves
from *things* offered to
idols, and from blood,
and from strangled,
and from fornication.
26 Then Paul took the
men, and the next day
purifying himself with
them entered into the
temple, to signify the
accomplishment of the
days of purification,
until that an offering
should be offered for
every one of them.
27 And when the seven
days were almost end-
ed, the Jews which
were of Asia, when
they saw him in the
temple, stirred up all
the people, and laid
hands on him, 28 cry-
ing out, Men of Israel,
help: This is the man,
that teacheth all *men*
every where against
the people, and the
law, and this place:
and further brought
Greeks also into the
temple, and hath pol-
luted this holy place.
29 (For they had seen
before with him in
the city Trophimus an
Ephesian, whom they
supposed that Paul
had brought into the
temple.) 30 And all
the city was moved,
and the people ran to-
gether: and they took
Paul, and drew him
out of the temple: and
forthwith the doors
were shut. 31 And as
they went about to kill
him, tidings came un-

συνελθεῖν·‖ ἀκούσονται.[m]γὰρ‖ ὅτι ἐλήλυθας. 23 τοῦτο οὖν
come together; for they will hear that thou hast come. This therefore
ποίησον ὅ σοι λέγομεν· εἰσὶν ἡμῖν ἄνδρες τέσσαρες εὐχὴν
do thou what [3]to [4]thee [1]we [2]say: There are with us [2]men [1]four a vow
ἔχοντες ἐφ' ἑαυτῶν· 24 τούτους παραλαβὼν ἁγνίσθητι σὺν
having on themselves; these having taken be purified with
αὐτοῖς, καὶ δαπάνησον ἐπ' αὐτοῖς, ἵνα [n]ξυρήσωνται‖ τὴν
them, and be at expense for them, that they may shave the
κεφαλήν, καὶ [o]γνῶσιν‖ πάντες ὅτι ὧν κατήχηνται
head; and [2]may [3]know [1]all that of which they have been informed
περὶ σοῦ οὐδέν ἐστιν, ἀλλὰ στοιχεῖς καὶ αὐτὸς
about thee [2]nothing [1]is, but thou [3]walkest [4]orderly [2]also [1]thyself
[p]τὸν νόμον φυλάσσων.‖ 25 περὶ.δὲ τῶν πεπιστευκότων
[6]the [7]law [5]keeping. But concerning those who have believed
ἐθνῶν ἡμεῖς [q]ἐπεστείλαμεν,‖ κρίναντες [r]μηδὲν.τοιοῦτον
of the nations we wrote, judging [4]no [5]such [6]thing
τηρεῖν αὐτούς, εἰ.μὴ‖ φυλάσσεσθαι αὐτοὺς τό τε εἰδωλό-
[2]to [3]observe [1]them, except to keep [2]from [1]themselves things offered
θυτον καὶ [s]τὸ‖ αἷμα καὶ πνικτὸν καὶ πορνείαν. 26 Τότε
to idols, and blood, and what is strangled, and fornication. Then
ὁ Παῦλος παραλαβὼν τοὺς ἄνδρας, τῇ ἐχομένῃ ἡμέρᾳ σὺν
Paul having taken the men, on the next day with
αὐτοῖς ἁγνισθεὶς εἰσῄει εἰς τὸ ἱερόν, διαγγέλλων τὴν
them having been purified entered into the temple, declaring the
ἐκπλήρωσιν τῶν ἡμερῶν τοῦ ἁγνισμοῦ, ἕως οὗ προσηνέχθη
fulfilment of the days of the purification, until was offered
ὑπὲρ ἑνὸς ἑκάστου αὐτῶν ἡ προσφορά. 27 ὡς.δὲ ἔμελλον
for [2]one [1]each of them the offering. But when [4]were [5]about
αἱ ἑπτὰ ἡμέραι συντελεῖσθαι οἱ ἀπὸ τῆς Ἀσίας Ἰουδαῖοι
[1]the [2]seven [3]days to be completed the [2]from [3]Asia [1]Jews
θεασάμενοι αὐτὸν ἐν τῷ ἱερῷ, [t]συνέχεον‖ πάντα τὸν ὄχλον,
having seen him in the temple, stirred up all the crowd,
καὶ [v]ἐπέβαλον‖ [w]τὰς χεῖρας ἐπ' αὐτόν,‖ 28 κράζοντες, Ἄνδρες
and laid hands upon him, crying, Men
[x]Ἰσραηλῖται,‖ βοηθεῖτε. οὗτός ἐστιν ὁ ἄνθρωπος ὁ κατὰ
Israelites, help! this is the man who against
τοῦ λαοῦ καὶ τοῦ νόμου καὶ τοῦ.τόπου.τούτου πάντας [y]παν-
the people and the law and this place all every-
ταχοῦ‖ διδάσκων· ἔτι.τε καὶ Ἕλληνας εἰσήγαγεν εἰς τὸ ἱερόν,
where teaches, and further also Greeks he brought into the temple,
καὶ κεκοίνωκεν τὸν ἅγιον τόπον τοῦτον. 29 Ἦσαν.γὰρ.προ-
and defiled [2]holy [3]place [1]this. For they had before
εωρακότες Τρόφιμον τὸν Ἐφέσιον ἐν τῇ πόλει σὺν αὐτῷ, ὃν
seen Trophimus the Ephesian in the city with him, whom
ἐνόμιζον ὅτι εἰς τὸ ἱερὸν εἰσήγαγεν ὁ Παῦλος. 30 ἐκινήθη
they supposed that into the temple [2]brought [1]Paul. [4]Was [5]moved
τε ἡ πόλις ὅλη, καὶ ἐγένετο συνδρομὴ τοῦ λαοῦ· καὶ ἐπι-
[3]and [6]the [8]city [7]whole, and there was a concourse of the people; and having
λαβόμενοι τοῦ Παύλου, εἷλκον αὐτὸν ἔξω τοῦ ἱεροῦ· καὶ
laid hold of Paul, they drew him outside the temple, and
εὐθέως ἐκλείσθησαν αἱ θύραι. 31 ζητούντων.[z]δὲ‖ αὐτὸν
immediately were shut the doors. But as they were seeking him

---

[m] — γὰρ for Tr. [n] ξυρήσονται they shall shave TTrA. [o] γνώσονται will know GLTTrAW. [p] φυλάσσων τὸν νόμον LTTrAW. [q] ἀπεστείλαμεν LTr. [r] — μηδὲν τοιοῦτον τηρεῖν αὐτούς, εἰ μὴ LTTr. [s] — τὸ LTTr[A]W. [t] συνέχεαν L. [v] ἐπέβαλαν TTr. [w] ἐπ' αὐτὸν τὰς χεῖρας GLTTrAW. [x] Ἰσραηλεῖται T. [y] πανταχῇ LTr; πανταχῆ TAW. [z] τε And LTTrA.

ἀποκτεῖναι ἀνέβη φάσις τῷ χιλιάρχῳ τῆς σπείρης,
to kill there came a representation to the chief captain of the band,
ὅτι ὅλη [a]συγκέχυται‖ Ἱερουσαλήμ. 32 ὃς [b]ἐξαυτῆς‖ [c]παρα-
that all [2]was [3]in [4]a [5]tumult [1]Jerusalem; who at once having
λαβὼν‖ στρατιώτας καὶ [d]ἑκατοντάρχους‖ κατέδραμεν ἐπ'
taken with [him] soldiers and centurions ran down upon
αὐτούς. οἱ.δὲ ἰδόντες [e]τὸν‖ χιλίαρχον καὶ τοὺς στρατιώτας
them. And they having seen the chief captain and the soldiers
ἐπαύσαντο τύπτοντες τὸν Παῦλον. 33 τότε ἐγγίσας
ceased beating Paul. Then [4]having [5]drawn [6]near
ὁ χιλίαρχος ἐπελάβετο αὐτοῦ, καὶ ἐκέλευσεν δεθῆναι
[1]the [2]chief [3]captain laid hold of him, and commanded [him] to be bound
ἁλύσεσιν δυσίν· καὶ ἐπυνθάνετο τίς [f]ἂν‖.εἴη, καὶ τί
with [2]chains [1]two, and inquired who he might be, and what
ἐστιν.πεποιηκώς. 34 ἄλλοι.δὲ.ἄλλο.τι [g]ἐβόων‖
he had been doing. But some [3]one [4]thing [5]and [6]some [7]another [1]were [2]crying
ἐν τῷ ὄχλῳ· [h]μὴ.δυνάμενος.δὲ‖ γνῶναι τὸ ἀσφαλὲς διὰ
in the crowd. And not being able to know the certainty on account of
τὸν θόρυβον, ἐκέλευσεν ἄγεσθαι αὐτὸν εἰς τὴν παρεμ-
the tumult, he commanded [2]to [3]be [4]brought [1]him into the for-
βολήν. 35 ὅτε.δὲ ἐγένετο ἐπὶ τοὺς ἀναβαθμοὺς συνέβη
tress. But when he came on the stairs it happened
βαστάζεσθαι αὐτὸν ὑπὸ τῶν στρατιωτῶν διὰ τὴν βίαν
[2]was [3]borne [1]he by the soldiers because of the violence
τοῦ ὄχλου. 36 ἠκολούθει.γὰρ τὸ πλῆθος τοῦ λαοῦ [i]κράζον,‖
of the crowd. For followed the multitude of the people, crying,
Αἶρε αὐτόν. 37 Μέλλων.τε εἰσάγεσθαι εἰς τὴν παρεμβολὴν
Away with him. But being about to be brought into the fortress
ὁ Παῦλος λέγει τῷ χιλιάρχῳ, Εἰ ἔξεστίν μοι εἰπεῖν τι
Paul says to the chief captain, Is it permitted to me to say something
πρός σε; Ὁ.δὲ ἔφη, Ἑλληνιστὶ γινώσκεις; 38 οὐκ ἄρα
to thee? And he said, Greek dost thou know? [3]Not [4]then
σὺ εἶ ὁ Αἰγύπτιος ὁ πρὸ τούτων τῶν ἡμερῶν ἀναστα-
[2]thou [1]art the Egyptian who before these days caused a
τώσας καὶ ἐξαγαγὼν εἰς τὴν ἔρημον τοὺς τετρακισχιλίους
confusion and led out into the desert the four thousand
ἄνδρας τῶν σικαρίων; 39 Εἶπεν.δὲ ὁ Παῦλος, Ἐγὼ ἄνθρωπος
men of the assassins? But [2]said [1]Paul, I a man
μέν εἰμι Ἰουδαῖος Ταρσεύς, τῆς Κιλικίας οὐκ ἀσήμου πόλεως
indeed am a Jew of Tarsus, [7]of [8]Cilicia [4]no [3]of [5]insignificant [6]city
πολίτης· δέομαι.δέ σου, ἐπίτρεψόν μοι λαλῆσαι πρὸς τὸν
[1]a [2]citizen, and I beseech thee, allow me to speak to the
λαόν. 40 Ἐπιτρέψαντος.δὲ αὐτοῦ, ὁ Παῦλος ἑστὼς ἐπὶ
people. And [2]having [3]allowed [[4]him] [1]he, Paul standing on
τῶν ἀναβαθμῶν κατέσεισεν τῇ χειρὶ τῷ λαῷ· πολλῆς.δὲ
the stairs made a sign with the hand to the people; and great
σιγῆς γενομένης προσεφώνησεν τῇ Ἑβραΐδι διαλέκτῳ
silence having taken place he spoke to [them] in the Hebrew language
λέγων, 22 Ἄνδρες ἀδελφοὶ καὶ πατέρες, ἀκούσατέ μου τῆς
saying, Men, brethren and fathers, hear my
πρὸς ὑμᾶς [k]νῦν‖ ἀπολογίας. 2 Ἀκούσαντες.δὲ ὅτι τῇ Ἑβραΐδι
[2]to [3]you [4]now [1]defence. And having heard that in the Hebrew

to the chief captain of the band, that all Jerusalem was in an uproar. 32 Who immediately took soldiers and centurions, and ran down unto them: and when they saw the chief captain and the soldiers, they left beating of Paul. 33 Then the chief captain came near, and took him, and commanded *him* to be bound with two chains; and demanded who he was, and what he had done. 34 And some cried one thing, some another, among the multitude: and when he could not know the certainty for the tumult, he commanded him to be carried into the castle. 35 And when he came upon the stairs, so it was, that he was borne of the soldiers for the violence of the people. 36 For the multitude of the people followed after, crying, Away with him. 37 And as Paul was to be led into the castle, he said unto the chief captain, May I speak unto thee? who said, Canst thou speak Greek? 38 Art not thou that Egyptian, which before these days madest an uproar, and leddest out into the wilderness four thousand men that were murderers? 39 But Paul said, I am a man *which am* a Jew of Tarsus, *a city* in Cilicia, a citizen of no mean city: and, I beseech thee, suffer me to speak unto the people. 40 And when he had given him licence, Paul stood on the stairs, and beckoned with the hand unto the people. And when there was made a great silence, he spake unto *them* in the Hebrew tongue, saying,
XXII. Men, brethren, and fathers, hear ye my defence *which I make* now unto you. 2 (And when they heard that he spake in the Hebrew tongue to

---

[a] συγ(συν- T)χύννεται LTTrA; συγχύνεται W. [b] ἐξ αὐτῆς A. [c] λαβὼν having taken L. [d] ἑκατοντάρχας LTTrAW. [e] — τὸν W. [f] — ἂν LTTr[A]W. [g] ἐπεφώνουν LTTrAW. [h] μὴ δυναμένου δὲ αὐτοῦ he not being able LTTrAW. [i] κράζοντες LTTrAW. [k] νυνὶ GLTTrW.

them, they kept the
more silence: and he
saith,) 3 I am verily a
man *which am* a Jew,
born in Tarsus, *a city*
in Cilicia, yet brought
up in this city at the
feet of Gamaliel, *and*
taught according to
the perfect manner of
the law of the fathers,
and was zealous to-
ward God, as ye all
are this day. 4 And I
persecuted this way
unto the death, bind-
ing and delivering into
prisons both men and
women. 5 As also the
high priest doth bear
me witness, and all
the estate of the elders:
from whom also I re-
ceived letters unto the
brethren, and went to
Damascus, to bring
them which were there
bound unto Jerusalem,
for to be punished.
6 And it came to pass,
that, as I made my
journey, and was come
nigh unto Damascus
about noon, suddenly
there shone from hea-
ven a great light round
about me. 7 And I
fell unto the ground,
and heard a voice say-
ing unto me, Saul,
Saul, why persecutest
thou me? 8 And I an-
swered, Who art thou,
Lord? And he said un-
to me, I am Jesus of
Nazareth, whom thou
persecutest. 9 And they
that were with me saw
indeed the light, and
were afraid; but they
heard not the voice of
him that spake to me.
10 And I said, What
shall I do, Lord? And
the Lord said unto me,
Arise, and go into Da-
mascus; and there it
shall be told thee of
all things which are
appointed for thee to
do. 11 And when I
could not see for the
glory of that light,
being led by the hand
of them that were
with me, I came into
Damascus. 12 And one
Ananias, a devout man
according to the law,
having a good report
of all the Jews which
dwelt *there*, 13 came
unto me, and stood,
and said unto me,
Brother Saul, receive
thy sight. And the

διαλέκτῳ προσεφώνει αὐτοῖς, μᾶλλον παρέσχον ἡσυχίαν. καί
language he spoke to them, [3]the [4]more [1]they [2]kept quiet; and
φησιν, 3 Ἐγὼ [l]μέν‖ εἰμι ἀνὴρ Ἰουδαῖος, γεγεννημένος ἐν
he says, I indeed am a man a Jew, born in
Ταρσῷ τῆς Κιλικίας, ἀνατεθραμμένος.δὲ ἐν τῇ.πόλει.ταύτῃ
Tarsus of Cilicia, but brought up in this city
παρὰ τοὺς πόδας Γαμαλιήλ, πεπαιδευμένος κατὰ
at the feet of Gamaliel, having been instructed according to [the]
ἀκρίβειαν τοῦ πατρῴου νόμου, ζηλωτὴς ὑπάρχων τοῦ θεοῦ,
exactness of the ancestral law, [2]a [3]zealous [4]one [1]being for God,
καθὼς πάντες ὑμεῖς ἐστε σήμερον· 4 ὃς ταύτην τὴν ὁδὸν
even as all ye are this day; who this way
ἐδίωξα ἄχρι θανάτου, δεσμεύων καὶ παραδιδοὺς εἰς φυλακὰς
persecuted unto death, binding and delivering up to prisons
ἄνδρας.τε καὶ γυναῖκας, 5 ὡς καὶ ὁ ἀρχιερεὺς μαρτυρεῖ μοι,
both men and women; as also the high priest bears witness to me,
καὶ πᾶν τὸ πρεσβυτέριον· παρ' ὧν καὶ ἐπιστολὰς δεξάμενος
and all the elderhood; from whom also letters having received
πρὸς τοὺς ἀδελφούς, εἰς Δαμασκὸν ἐπορευόμην, ἄξων καὶ τοὺς
to the brethren, to Damascus I went, to bring also those
ἐκεῖσε ὄντας, δεδεμένους εἰς Ἱερουσαλήμ, ἵνα τιμωρη-
there who were, bound to Jerusalem, in order that they might
θῶσιν. 6 ἐγένετο.δέ μοι πορευομένῳ καὶ ἐγγίζοντι τῇ
be punished. And it came to pass to me journeying and drawing near
Δαμασκῷ περὶ μεσημβρίαν ἐξαίφνης ἐκ τοῦ οὐρανοῦ περι-
to Damascus, about mid-day suddenly out of the heaven
αστράψαι φῶς ἱκανὸν περὶ ἐμέ· 7 [m]ἔπεσόν‖.τε εἰς τὸ ἔδαφος,
shone a [2]light [1]great about me. And I fell to the ground,
καὶ ἤκουσα φωνῆς λεγούσης μοι, Σαούλ, Σαούλ, τί με διώ-
and heard a voice saying to me, Saul, Saul, why me perse-
κεις; 8 Ἐγὼ.δὲ ἀπεκρίθην, Τίς εἶ, κύριε; Εἶπέν.τε
cutest thou? And I answered, Who art thou, Lord? And he said
πρός [n]με,‖ Ἐγώ εἰμι Ἰησοῦς ὁ Ναζωραῖος ὃν σὺ διώκεις.
to me, I am Jesus the Nazaræan, whom thou persecutest.
9 Οἱ.δὲ σὺν ἐμοὶ ὄντες τὸ μὲν φῶς ἐθεάσαντο, [o]καὶ ἔμ-
But those [2]with [3]me [1]being the [2]indeed [1]light beheld, and a-
φοβοι ἐγένοντο·‖ τὴν.δὲ φωνὴν οὐκ.ἤκουσαν τοῦ λαλοῦντός
larmed were, but the voice did not hear of him speaking
μοι. 10 εἶπον.δέ, Τί ποιήσω κύριε; Ὁ.δὲ κύριος εἶπεν
to me. And I said, What shall I do, Lord? And the Lord said
πρός με, Ἀναστὰς πορεύου εἰς Δαμασκόν, κἀκεῖ σοι λα-
to me, Having risen up go to Damascus, and there thee it
ληθήσεται περὶ πάντων ὧν τέτακταί σοι ποιῆσαι.
shall be told concerning all things which it has been appointed thee to do.
11 Ὡς.δὲ οὐκ.ἐνέβλεπον ἀπὸ τῆς δόξης τοῦ.φωτὸς.ἐκείνου,
And as I did not see from the glory of that light,
χειραγωγούμενος ὑπὸ τῶν συνόντων μοι, ἦλθον εἰς Δαμασ-
being led by the hand by those being with me, I came to Damas-
κόν. 12 Ἀνανίας.δέ.τις, ἀνὴρ [p]εὐσεβὴς‖ κατὰ τὸν νόμον,
cus. And a certain Ananias, a [2]man [1]pious according to the law,
μαρτυρούμενος ὑπὸ πάντων τῶν κατοικούντων Ἰουδαίων,
borne witness to by all the [2]dwelling [[3]there] [1]Jews,
13 ἐλθὼν πρός [q]με‖ καὶ ἐπιστὰς εἶπέν μοι, Σαοὺλ ἀδελφέ,
coming to me and standing by said to me, [2]Saul [1]brother,

---

[l] — μέν LTTrAW. [m] ἔπεσα LTTrA. [n] ἐμέ LTTr. [o] — καὶ ἔμφοβοι ἐγένοντο LTTr[A].
[p] εὐλαβὴς LTTrA. [q] ἐμὲ LTTr.

ἀνάβλεψον. Κἀγὼ αὐτῇ.τῇ.ὥρᾳ ἀνέβλεψα εἰς αὐτόν. 14 ὁ.δὲ
look up. And I in the same hour looked up on him. And he

εἶπεν, Ὁ θεὸς τῶν.πατέρων.ἡμῶν προεχειρίσατό σε γνῶναι
said, The God of our fathers appointed thee to know

τὸ.θέλημα.αὐτοῦ, καὶ ἰδεῖν τὸν δίκαιον καὶ ἀκοῦσαι φωνὴν
his will, and to see the Just One, and to hear a voice

ἐκ τοῦ.στόματος.αὐτοῦ· 15 ὅτι ἔσῃ μάρτυς αὐτῷ
out of his mouth; for thou shalt be a witness for him

πρὸς πάντας ἀνθρώπους ὧν ἑώρακας καὶ ἤκουσας. 16 καὶ
to all men of what thou hast seen and heard. And

νῦν τί μέλλεις; ἀναστὰς βάπτισαι καὶ ἀπόλουσαι τὰς
now why delayest thou? Having arisen be baptized and wash away

ἁμαρτίας.σου, ἐπικαλεσάμενος τὸ ὄνομα [r]τοῦ κυρίου.‖ 17 Ἐ-
thy sins, calling on the name of the Lord. [2]It [3]came

γένετο δέ μοι ὑποστρέψαντι εἰς Ἱερουσαλήμ, καὶ προσευ-
to [4]pass [1]and to me having returned to Jerusalem, and on [2]pray-

χομένου μου ἐν τῷ ἱερῷ, γενέσθαι.με ἐν ἐκστάσει, 18 καὶ [s]ἰδεῖν‖
ing [1]my in the temple, I became in a trance, and saw

αὐτὸν λέγοντά μοι, Σπεῦσον καὶ ἔξελθε ἐν τάχει ἐξ Ἱε-
him saying to me, Make haste and go away with speed out of Je-

ρουσαλήμ, διότι οὐ.παραδέξονταί σοῦ [t]τὴν‖ μαρτυρίαν
rusalem, because they will not receive thy testimony

περὶ ἐμοῦ. 19 Κἀγὼ εἶπον, Κύριε, αὐτοὶ ἐπίστανται,
concerning me. And I said, Lord, themselves know

ὅτι ἐγὼ ἤμην φυλακίζων καὶ δέρων κατὰ.τὰς.συναγωγὰς τοὺς
that I was imprisoning and beating in every synagogue those

πιστεύοντας ἐπὶ σέ· 20 καὶ ὅτε [v]ἐξεχεῖτο‖ τὸ αἷμα Στεφάνου
believing on thee; and when was poured out the blood of Stephen

τοῦ.μάρτυρός.σου, καὶ αὐτὸς ἤμην ἐφεστὼς καὶ συνευδοκῶν
thy witness, also myself was standing by and consenting

[w]τῇ ἀναιρέσει αὐτοῦ,‖ καὶ φυλάσσων τὰ ἱμάτια τῶν
to the putting to death of him, and keeping the garments of those who

ἀναιρούντων αὐτόν. 21 Καὶ εἶπεν πρός με, Πορεύου, ὅτι ἐγὼ
killed him. And he said to me, Go, for I

εἰς ἔθνη μακρὰν ἐξαποστελῶ σε. 22 Ἤκουον.δὲ αὐτοῦ ἄχρι
to nations afar off will send forth thee. And they heard him until

τούτου τοῦ λόγου, καὶ ἐπῆραν τὴν.φωνὴν.αὐτῶν λέγοντες,
this word, and lifted up their voice, saying,

Αἶρε ἀπὸ τῆς γῆς τὸν.τοιοῦτον· οὐ.γὰρ [x]καθῆκον‖ αὐτὸν
Away with [4]from [5]the [6]earth [1]such [2]a [3]one, for [3]not [1]it [2]is fit he

ζῆν. 23 Κραυγαζόντων.[y]δὲ‖ αὐτῶν, καὶ ῥιπτούντων
should live. And as [2]were [3]crying [4]out [1]they, and casting off [their]

τὰ ἱμάτια, καὶ κονιορτὸν βαλλόντων εἰς τὸν ἀέρα, 24 ἐκέλευσεν
garments, and [2]dust [1]throwing into the air, [4]commanded

[z]αὐτὸν ὁ χιλίαρχος ἄγεσθαι‖ εἰς τὴν παρεμβολήν, [a]εἰπὼν‖
[5]him [1]the [2]chief [3]captain to be brought into the fortress, bidding

μάστιξιν ἀνετάζεσθαι αὐτόν, ἵνα ἐπιγνῷ δι' ἣν αἰτίαν
[5]by [6]scourges [2]to [3]be [4]examined [1]him, that he might know for what cause

οὕτως ἐπεφώνουν αὐτῷ. 25 ὡς.δὲ [b]προέτεινεν‖ αὐτὸν
thus they cried out against him. But as he stretched forward him

τοῖς ἱμᾶσιν εἶπεν πρὸς τὸν ἑστῶτα ἑκατόνταρχον [c]ὁ
with the thongs [2]said [3]to [4]the [6]who [7]stood [8]by [5]centurion

same hour I looked up upon him. 14 And he said, The God of our fathers hath chosen thee, that thou shouldest know his will, and see that Just One, and shouldest hear the voice of his mouth. 15 For thou shalt be his witness unto all men of what thou hast seen and heard. 16 And now why tarriest thou? arise, and be baptized, and wash away thy sins, calling on the name of the Lord. 17 And it came to pass, that, when I was come again to Jerusalem, even while I prayed in the temple, I was in a trance; 18 and saw him saying unto me, Make haste, and get thee quickly out of Jerusalem: for they will not receive thy testimony concerning me. 19 And I said, Lord, they know that I imprisoned and beat in every synagogue them that believed on thee: 20 and when the blood of thy martyr Stephen was shed, I also was standing by, and consenting unto his death, and kept the raiment of them that slew him. 21 And he said unto me, Depart: for I will send thee far hence unto the Gentiles. 22 And they gave him audience unto this word, and *then* lifted up their voices, and said, Away with such a *fellow* from the earth: for it is not fit that he should live. 23 And as they cried out, and cast off *their* clothes, and threw dust into the air, 24 the chief captain commanded him to be brought into the castle, and bade that he should be examined by scourging; that he might know wherefore they cried so against him. 25 And as they bound him with thongs, Paul said unto the centurion that

---

[r] αὐτοῦ (*read* his name) GLTTrAW. [s] ἴδον T. [t] — τὴν LTTr[A]. [v] ἐξεχύννετο LTTrA. [w] — τῇ ἀναιρέσει αὐτοῦ GLTTrAW. [x] καθῆκεν GLTTrAW. [y] τε LTrAW. [z] ὁ χιλίαρχος εἰσάγεσθαι αὐτὸν GLTTrAW. [a] εἴπας LTTrAW. [b] προέτειναν they stretched forward GLTTrAW. [c] [ὁ Παῦλος] A.

stood by, Is it lawful
for you to scourge a
man that is a Roman,
and uncondemned?
26 When the centurion
heard *that*, he went
and told the chief cap-
tain, saying, Take
heed what thou doest:
for this man is a Ro-
man. 27 Then the chief
captain came, and said
unto him, Tell me, art
thou a Roman? He
said, Yea. 28 And the
chief captain answer-
ed, With a great sum
obtained I this free-
dom. And Paul said,
But I was *free* born.
29 Then straightway
they departed from
him which should
have examined him:
and the chief captain
also was afraid, after
he knew that he was
a Roman, and because
he had bound him.
30 On the morrow, be-
cause he would have
known the certainty
wherefore he was ac-
cused of the Jews, he
loosed him from *his*
bands, and command-
ed the chief priests
and all their council
to appear, and brought
Paul down, and set
him before them.

XXIII. And Paul,
earnestly beholding
the council, said, Men
and brethren, I have
lived in all good con-
science before God un-
til this day. 2 And the
high priest Ananias
commanded them that
stood by him to smite
him on the mouth.
3 Then said Paul unto
him, God shall smite
thee, *thou* whited wall:
for sittest thou to
judge me after the law,
and commandest me
to be smitten contrary
to the law? 4 And
they that stood by
said, Revilest thou
God's high priest?
5 Then said Paul, I
wist not, brethren, that
he was the high priest:
for it is written, Thou
shalt not speak evil of
the ruler of thy peo-
ple. 6 But when Paul
perceived that the one
part were Sadducees,

Παῦλος,‖ Εἰ ἄνθρωπον Ῥωμαῖον καὶ ἀκατάκριτον ἔξεστιν
[1]Paul, A man a Roman and uncondemned is it lawful
ὑμῖν μαστίζειν; 26 Ἀκούσας.δὲ ὁ [d]ἑκατόνταρχος,‖ προσ-
for you to scourge? And [3]having [4]heard [[5]it] [1]the [2]centurion, having
ελθὼν [e]ἀπήγγειλεν τῷ χιλιάρχῳ‖ λέγων, [f]Ὅρα‖ τί μέλ-
gone he reported [it] to the chief captain saying, See what art
λεις ποιεῖν; ὁ.γὰρ.ἄνθρωπος.οὗτος Ῥωμαῖός ἐστιν.
thou about to do? For this man a Roman is.
27 Προσελθὼν.δὲ ὁ χιλίαρχος εἶπεν αὐτῷ, Λέγε μοι, [g]εἶ‖ σὺ
And having come up the chief captain said to him, Tell me, [2]thou
Ῥωμαῖος εἶ; Ὁ.δὲ ἔφη, Ναί. 28 Ἀπεκρίθη.[h]τε‖ ὁ χιλίαρχος,
[3]a [4]Roman [1]art? And he said, Yes. And [4]answered [1]the [2]chief [3]captain,
Ἐγὼ πολλοῦ κεφαλαίου τὴν.πολιτείαν.ταύτην ἐκτησάμην.
I with a great sum this citizenship bought.
Ὁ.δὲ.Παῦλος ἔφη, Ἐγὼ.δὲ καὶ γεγέννημαι. 29 Εὐθέως οὖν
And Paul said, But I also was [free] born. Immediately therefore
ἀπέστησαν ἀπ' αὐτοῦ οἱ μέλλοντες αὐτὸν ἀνετάζειν· καὶ
departed from him those being about [3]him [1]to [2]examine, and
ὁ χιλίαρχος δὲ ἐφοβήθη, ἐπιγνοὺς ὅτι Ῥωμαῖός ἐστιν,
the chief captain also was afraid, having ascertained that a Roman he is,
καὶ ὅτι [i]ἦν.αὐτὸν‖.δεδεκώς. 30 Τῇ.δὲ ἐπαύριον βουλόμενος
and because he had bound him. And on the morrow, desiring
γνῶναι τὸ ἀσφαλὲς τὸ.τί κατηγορεῖται [k]παρὰ‖ τῶν Ἰουδαίων,
to know the certainty wherefore he is accused by the Jews,
ἔλυσεν αὐτὸν [l]ἀπὸ τῶν δεσμῶν,‖ καὶ ἐκέλευσεν [m]ἐλθεῖν‖ τοὺς
he loosed him from the bonds, and commanded to come the
ἀρχιερεῖς καὶ [n]ὅλον‖ τὸ.συνέδριον.[o]αὐτῶν·‖ καὶ καταγαγὼν
chief priests and [2]whole [1]their sanhedrim, and having brought down
τὸν Παῦλον ἔστησεν εἰς αὐτούς.
Paul he set [him] among them.

23 Ἀτενίσας.δὲ [p]ὁ Παῦλος τῷ συνεδρίῳ‖ εἶπεν,
And [2]having [3]looked [4]intently [1]Paul on the sanhedrim said,
Ἄνδρες ἀδελφοί, ἐγὼ πάσῃ συνειδήσει ἀγαθῇ πεπολίτευμαι
Men brethren, I in all [2]conscience [1]good have conducted myself
τῷ θεῷ ἄχρι ταύτης τῆς ἡμέρας. 2 Ὁ.δὲ ἀρχιερεὺς Ἀνα-
towards God unto this day. But the high priest Ana-
νίας ἐπέταξεν τοῖς παρεστῶσιν αὐτῷ τύπτειν αὐτοῦ τὸ στόμα
nias ordered those standing by him to smite his mouth.
3 τότε ὁ Παῦλος πρὸς αὐτὸν εἶπεν, Τύπτειν σε μέλλει ὁ
Then Paul to him said, [4]To [5]smite [6]thee [2]is [3]about
θεός, τοῖχε κεκονιαμένε· καὶ σὺ κάθῃ κρίνων με κατὰ
[1]God, [8]wall [7]whited. And thou dost thou sit judging me according to
τὸν νόμον, καὶ παρανομῶν κελεύεις με τύπτεσθαι; 4 Οἱ.δὲ
the law, and contrary to law commandest me to be smitten? And those who
παρεστῶτες [q]εἶπον,‖ Τὸν ἀρχιερέα τοῦ θεοῦ λοιδορεῖς;
stood by said, [4]The [5]high [6]priest [7]of [8]God [1]railest [2]thou [3]at?
5 Ἔφη.τε ὁ Παῦλος, Οὐκ.ᾔδειν, ἀδελφοί, ὅτι ἐστὶν ἀρχ-
And [2]said [1]Paul, I was not conscious, brethren, that he is a high
ιερεύς· γέγραπται.γάρ, [r]Ἄρχοντα τοῦ.λαοῦ.σου οὐκ ἐ-
priest; for it has been written, A ruler of thy people [3]not [1]thou [2]shalt
ρεῖς κακῶς. 6 Γνοὺς.δὲ ὁ Παῦλος ὅτι τὸ ἓν μέρος ἐστὶν
speak [2]of [1]evil. But [2]having [3]known [1]Paul that the one part consists

---

d ἑκατοντάρχης LT. e τῷ χιλιάρχῳ ἀπήγγειλεν GLTTrA. f — Ὅρα GLTTrAW. g — εἶ GLTTrAW. h δὲ LTTr; — τε A. i αὐτὸν ἦν LTTrAW. k ὑπὸ LTTrAW. l — ἀπὸ τῶν δεσμῶν GLTTrAW. m συνελθεῖν to come together GLTTrAW. n πᾶν all GLTTrAW. o — αὐτῶν (*read* the sanhedrim) GLTTrAW. p τῷ συνεδρίῳ ὁ Παῦλος LTTr. q εἶπαν TTr. r + ὅτι TTr[A].

Σαδδουκαίων τὸ.δὲ ἕτερον Φαρισαίων [s]ἔκραξεν‖ ἐν τῷ συν-
of Sadducees and the other of Pharisees cried out in the sanhe-
εδρίῳ, Ἄνδρες ἀδελφοί, ἐγὼ Φαρισαῖός εἰμι, υἱὸς [t]Φαρισαίου·‖
drim, Men brethren, I a Pharisee am, son of a Pharisee:
περὶ ἐλπίδος καὶ ἀναστάσεως νεκρῶν ἐγὼ κρίνομαι.
concerning a hope and resurrection of [the] dead I am judged.
7 Τοῦτο.δὲ αὐτοῦ [v]λαλήσαντος‖ ἐγένετο στάσις τῶν Φαρι-
And this he having spoken there was a dissension of the Phari-
σαίων καὶ [w]τῶν‖ Σαδδουκαίων, καὶ ἐσχίσθη [x] τὸ πλῆθος·
sees and the Sadducees, and was divided the multitude.
8 Σαδδουκαῖοι [y]μὲν‖ γὰρ λέγουσιν μὴ.εἶναι ἀνάστασιν [z]μηδὲ‖
[2]Sadducees [3]indeed [1]for say there is no resurrection nor
ἄγγελον μήτε πνεῦμα· Φαρισαῖοι.δὲ ὁμολογοῦσιν τὰ ἀμφότερα.
angel nor spirit; but Pharisees confess both.
9 ἐγένετο.δὲ κραυγὴ μεγάλη· καὶ ἀναστάντες [a]οἱ‖ [b]γραμ-
And there was a [2]clamour [1]great, and having risen up the scribes
ματεῖς τοῦ μέρους‖ τῶν Φαρισαίων διεμάχοντο λέγοντες,
of the part of the Pharisees they were contending, saying,
Οὐδὲν κακὸν εὑρίσκομεν ἐν τῷ.ἀνθρώπῳ.τούτῳ· εἰ.δὲ πνεῦμα
Nothing evil we find in this man; and if a spirit
ἐλάλησεν αὐτῷ ἢ ἄγγελος[c], μὴ.θεομαχῶμεν.‖ 10 Πολλῆς.δὲ
spoke to him or an angel, let us not fight against God. And a great
[d]γενομένης στάσεως, εὐλαβηθεὶς‖ ὁ χιλίαρχος μὴ δια-
[2]arising [1]dissension, [6]fearing [3]the [4]chief [5]captain lest [2]should [3]be
σπασθῇ ὁ Παῦλος ὑπ' αὐτῶν, ἐκέλευσεν τὸ στράτευμα
[4]torn [5]in [6]pieces [1]Paul by them, commanded the troop
καταβὰν ἁρπάσαι αὐτὸν ἐκ μέσου αὐτῶν, ἄγειν.τε
having gone down to take by force him from [2]midst [1]their, and to bring
εἰς τὴν παρεμβολήν. 11 Τῇ.δὲ ἐπιούσῃ νυκτὶ ἐπιστὰς
[him] into the fortress. But the following night [3]standing [4]by
αὐτῷ ὁ κύριος εἶπεν, Θάρσει [e]Παῦλε·‖ ὡς.γὰρ διε-
[5]him [1]the [2]Lord said, Be of good courage, Paul; for as thou didst
μαρτύρω τὰ περὶ ἐμοῦ εἰς Ἱερουσαλήμ, οὕτως σε.δεῖ
fully testify the things concerning me at Jerusalem, so thou must
καὶ εἰς Ῥώμην μαρτυρῆσαι. 12 Γενομένης.δὲ ἡμέρας, ποιή-
also at Rome bear witness. And it being day, [5]having
σαντές [f]τινες τῶν Ἰουδαίων συστροφὴν‖ ἀνεθεμάτισαν
[6]made [1]some [2]of [3]the [4]Jews a combination put [2]under [3]a [4]curse
ἑαυτούς, λέγοντες μήτε φαγεῖν μήτε πιεῖν ἕως.οὗ ἀποκτεί-
[1]themselves, declaring neither to eat nor to drink till they should
νωσιν τὸν Παῦλον· 13 ἦσαν.δὲ πλείους [g]τεσσαράκοντα‖ οἱ
kill Paul. And they were more than forty who
ταύτην τὴν συνωμοσίαν [h]πεποιηκότες·‖ 14 οἵτινες προσελ-
this conspiracy had made; who having
θόντες τοῖς ἀρχιερεῦσιν καὶ τοῖς πρεσβυτέροις [i]εἶπον,‖ Ἀνα-
come to the chief priests and the elders said, With a
θέματι ἀνεθεματίσαμεν ἑαυτούς, [k]μηδενὸς‖ γεύσασθαι ἕως.οὗ
curse we have cursed ourselves, nothing to taste until
ἀποκτείνωμεν τὸν Παῦλον. 15 νῦν οὖν ὑμεῖς ἐμφανίσατε
we should kill Paul. Now therefore ye make a representation

and the other Pharisees, he cried out in the council, Men *and* brethren, I am a Pharisee, the son of a Pharisee: of the hope and resurrection of the dead I am called in question.
7 And when he had so said, there arose a dissension between the Pharisees and the Sadducees: and the multitude was divided.
8 For the Sadducees say that there is no resurrection, neither angel, nor spirit: but the Pharisees confess both.
9 And there arose a great cry: and the scribes *that were* of the Pharisees' part arose, and strove, saying, We find no evil in this man: but if a spirit or an angel hath spoken to him, let us not fight against God.
10 And when there arose a great dissension, the chief captain, fearing lest Paul should have been pulled in pieces of them, commanded the soldiers to go down, and to take him by force from among them, and to bring *him* into the castle.
11 And the night following the Lord stood by him, and said, Be of good cheer, Paul: for as thou hast testified of me in Jerusalem, so must thou bear witness also at Rome.
12 And when it was day, certain of the Jews banded together, and bound themselves under a curse, saying that they would neither eat nor drink till they had killed Paul.
13 And they were more than forty which had made this conspiracy.
14 And they came to the chief priests and elders, and said, We have bound ourselves under a great curse, that we will eat nothing until we have slain Paul.
15 Now therefore ye with the

---

[s] ἔκραζεν TTrA. [t] Φαρισαίων of Pharisees LTTrAW. [v] εἰπόντος LTrW. [w] — τῶν LTTrAW. [x] + μὲν indeed L. [y] — μὲν L[Tr]. [z] μήτε LTTrAW. [a] τινὲς some LTTrA. [b] τῶν γραμματέων τοῦ μέρους TTrA; — γραμ. τοῦ μέρους L. [c] ; — μὴ θεομαχῶμεν (*leaving the sentence incomplete*) GLTTrAW. [d] στάσεως γινομένης φοβηθεὶς L; γενομένης (γιν. T) στάσεως φοβηθεὶς TTrA. [e] — Παῦλε GLTTrAW. [f] συστροφὴν οἱ Ἰουδαῖοι GLTTrAW. [g] τεσσερακοντα TTrA. [h] ποιησάμενοι LTTrAW. [i] εἶπαν LTTrA. [k] μηθενὸς A.

council signify to the
chief captain that he
bring him down unto
you to morrow, as
though ye would in-
quire something more
perfectly concerning
him: and we, or ever
he come near, are ready
to kill him. 16 And
when Paul's sister's
son heard of their ly-
ing in wait, he went
and entered into the
castle, and told Paul.
17 Then Paul called
one of the centurions
unto *him*, and said,
Bring this young man
unto the chief cap-
tain: for he hath a
certain thing to tell
him. 18 So he took
him, and brought *him*
to the chief captain,
and said, Paul the
prisoner called me un-
to *him*, and prayed me
to bring this young
man unto thee, who
hath something to say
unto thee. 19 Then
the chief captain took
him by the hand, and
went *with him* aside
privately, and asked
him, What is that
thou hast to tell me?
20 And he said, The
Jews have agreed
to desire thee that
thou wouldest bring
down Paul to morrow
into the council, as
though they would
inquire somewhat of
him more perfectly.
21 But do not thou
yield unto them: for
there lie in wait for
him of them more
than forty men, which
have bound themselves
with an oath, that
they will neither eat
nor drink till they
have killed him: and
now are they ready,
looking for a promise
from thee. 22 So the
chief captain *then* let
the young man de-
part, and charged *him*,
See thou tell no man
that thou hast shewed
these things to me.
23 And he called unto
him two centurions,
saying, Make ready
two hundred soldiers
to go to Cæsarea, and

τῷ χιλιάρχῳ σὺν τῷ συνεδρίῳ, ὅπως [l]αὔριον‖ [m]αὐτὸν
to the chief captain with the sanhedrim, so that to-morrow him

καταγάγῃ πρὸς‖ ὑμᾶς, ὡς μέλλοντας διαγινώσκειν ἀκρι-
he may bring down to you, as being about to examine more

βέστερον τὰ περὶ αὐτοῦ· ἡμεῖς.δέ, πρὸ τοῦ ἐγγίσαι
accurately the things concerning him, and we, before [2]drawing [3]near

αὐτὸν ἕτοιμοί ἐσμεν τοῦ ἀνελεῖν αὐτόν. 16 Ἀκούσας.δὲ
[1]his [5]ready [4]are to put to death him. But [8]having [9]heard [10]of

ὁ υἱὸς τῆς ἀδελφῆς Παύλου [n]τὸ ἔνεδρον,‖ παραγενόμενος
[1]the [2]son [3]of [4]the [5]sister [6]of [7]Paul the lying in wait, having come near

καὶ εἰσελθὼν εἰς τὴν παρεμβολὴν ἀπήγγειλεν τῷ Παύλῳ.
and entered into the fortress he reported [it] to Paul.

17 προσκαλεσάμενος.δὲ ὁ Παῦλος ἕνα τῶν ἑκατοντάρχων,
And [2]having [3]called [4]to [[5]him] [1]Paul one of the centurions,

ἔφη, Τὸν.νεανίαν.τοῦτον [o]ἀπάγαγε‖ πρὸς τὸν χιλίαρχον· ἔχει
said, [2]This [3]young [4]man [1]take to the chief captain, [2]he [3]has

γάρ [p]τι ἀπαγγεῖλαι‖ αὐτῷ. 18 Ὁ μὲν οὖν παραλαβὼν
[1]for something to report to him. He indeed therefore having taken

αὐτὸν ἤγαγεν πρὸς τὸν χιλίαρχον, καί φησιν, Ὁ δέσμιος
him brought [him] to the chief captain, and says, The prisoner

Παῦλος προσκαλεσάμενός με ἠρώτησεν τοῦτον τὸν
Paul having called [2]to [[3]him] [1]me asked [me] this

[q]νεανίαν‖ ἀγαγεῖν πρός σε, ἔχοντά τι λαλῆσαί σοι.
young man to lead to thee, having something to say to thee.

19 Ἐπιλαβόμενος.δὲ τῆς.χειρὸς.αὐτοῦ ὁ χιλίαρχος, καὶ
And [4]having [5]taken [6]hold [7]of [8]his [9]hand [1]the [2]chief [3]captain, and

ἀναχωρήσας κατ᾽.ἰδίαν ἐπυνθάνετο, Τί ἐστιν ὃ ἔχεις
having withdrawn apart inquired, What is it which thou hast

ἀπαγγεῖλαί μοι; 20 Εἶπεν.δέ, Ὅτι οἱ Ἰουδαῖοι συνέθεντο
to report to me? And he said, The Jews agreed

τοῦ ἐρωτῆσαί σε, ὅπως αὔριον [r]εἰς τὸ συνέδριον κατα-
to request thee, that to-morrow into the sanhedrim thou mayest

γάγῃς τὸν Παῦλον, ὡς μέλλοντές‖ τι ἀκριβέστερον
bring down Paul, as being about [3]something [4]more [5]accurately

πυνθάνεσθαι περὶ αὐτοῦ. 21 σὺ οὖν μὴ.πεισθῇς αὐτοῖς·
[1]to [2]inquire concerning him. Thou therefore be not persuaded by them,

ἐνεδρεύουσιν.γὰρ αὐτὸν ἐξ αὐτῶν ἄνδρες πλείους [s]τεσσαρά-
for lie in wait for him of them [4]men [1]more [2]than [3]forty

κοντα,‖ οἵτινες ἀνεθεμάτισαν ἑαυτοὺς μήτε φαγεῖν μήτε
who put [2]under [3]a [4]curse [1]themselves neither to eat nor

πιεῖν ἕως.οὗ ἀνέλωσιν αὐτόν· καὶ νῦν [t]ἕτοιμοί εἰσιν‖
to drink till they put to death him; and now ready they are

προσδεχόμενοι τὴν ἀπὸ σοῦ ἐπαγγελίαν. 22 Ὁ μὲν οὖν
waiting the [2]from [3]thee [1]promise. The [3]therefore

χιλίαρχος ἀπέλυσεν τὸν [q]νεανίαν,‖ παραγγείλας μηδενὶ
[1]chief [2]captain dismissed the young man, having charged [him] to no one

ἐκλαλῆσαι ὅτι ταῦτα ἐνεφάνισας πρός [v]με.‖ 23 Καὶ
to utter that these things thou didst represent to me. And

προσκαλεσάμενος [w]δύο τινὰς‖ τῶν ἑκατοντάρχων εἶπεν,
having called to [him] [2]two [1]certain of the centurions he said,

Ἑτοιμάσατε στρατιώτας διακοσίους ὅπως πορευθῶσιν ἕως
Prepare soldiers two hundred, that they may go as far as

---

[l] — αὔριον GLTTrAW. [m] καταγάγῃ αὐτὸν εἰς LTTrAW. [n] τὴν ἐνέδραν EGLTTrA. [o] ἄπαγε TTr. [p] ἀπαγγεῖλαί τι LTrAW. [q] νεανίσκον LTTrA. [r] τὸν Παῦλον καταγάγῃς εἰς τὸ συνέδριον ὡς μέλλων LTTrAW. [s] τεσσεράκοντα TTrA. [t] εἰσὶν ἕτοιμοι LTTrAW. [v] ἐμέ TTr. [w] τινας δυο TTr.

[x]Καισαρείας,‖ καὶ ἱππεῖς ἑβδομήκοντα, καὶ δεξιολάβους δια-
Cæsarea, and horsemen seventy, and spearmen two
κοσίους, ἀπὸ τρίτης ὥρας τῆς νυκτός· 24 κτήνη.τε παραστῆ-
hundred, for the third hour of the night. And [4]beasts [1]to [2]have [3]pro-
σαι, ἵνα ἐπιβιβάσαντες τὸν Παῦλον διασώσωσιν
vided, that having set [2]on [1]Paul they may carry [him] safe through
πρὸς Φήλικα τὸν ἡγεμόνα· 25 γράψας ἐπιστολὴν [y]περι-
to Felix the governor, having written a letter hav-
έχουσαν‖ τὸν.τύπον.τοῦτον· 26 Κλαύδιος Λυσίας τῷ κρατίστῳ
ing this form: Claudius Lysias to the most excellent
ἡγεμόνι Φήλικι χαίρειν. 27 Τὸν.ἄνδρα.τοῦτον [z]συλληφθέντα‖
governor, Felix, greeting. This man, having been seized
ὑπὸ τῶν Ἰουδαίων, καὶ μέλλοντα ἀναιρεῖσθαι ὑπ᾽ αὐτῶν,
by the Jews, and being about to be put to death by them,
ἐπιστὰς σὺν τῷ στρατεύματι [a]ἐξειλόμην‖ [b]αὐτόν,‖ μαθὼν
having come up with the troop I rescued him, having learnt
ὅτι Ῥωμαῖός ἐστιν. 28 βουλόμενος.[c]δὲ γνῶναι‖ τὴν αἰτίαν
that a Roman he is. And desiring to know the charge
δι᾽ ἣν ἐνεκάλουν αὐτῷ κατήγαγον [d]αὐτὸν‖ εἰς τὸ
on account of which they accused him I brought down him to
συνέδριον.αὐτῶν· 29 ὃν εὗρον ἐγκαλούμενον περὶ ζητη-
their sanhedrim: whom I found to be accused concerning ques-
μάτων τοῦ.νόμου.αὐτῶν, μηδὲν.δὲ ἄξιον θανάτου ἢ δεσμῶν
tions of their law, but [2]no [4]worthy [5]of [6]death [7]or [8]of [9]bonds
[e]ἔγκλημα ἔχοντα.‖ 30 μηνυθείσης.δέ μοι ἐπιβουλῆς εἰς
[3]accusation [1]having. And it having been intimated to me of a plot against
τὸν ἄνδρα [f]μέλλειν‖ ἔσεσθαι [g]ὑπὸ τῶν Ἰουδαίων‖
the man about to be [carried out] by the Jews
[h]ἐξαυτῆς‖ ἔπεμψα πρός σε, παραγγείλας καὶ τοῖς κα-
at once I sent [him] to thee, having charged also the ac-
τηγόροις λέγειν [i]τὰ‖ [k]πρὸς αὐτὸν‖ ἐπὶ σοῦ. [l]Ἔρρωσο.‖
cusers to say the things against him before thee. Farewell.
31 Οἱ μὲν οὖν στρατιῶται, κατὰ τὸ διατεταγμένον
The [2]therefore [1]soldiers, according to the orders given
αὐτοῖς, ἀναλαβόντες τὸν Παῦλον ἤγαγον διὰ [m]τῆς‖ νυκτὸς
to them, having taken Paul brought [him] by night
εἰς τὴν Ἀντιπατρίδα. 32 τῇ.δὲ ἐπαύριον ἐάσαντες τοὺς
to Antipatris, and on the morrow having left the
ἱππεῖς [n]πορεύεσθαι‖ σὺν αὐτῷ, ὑπέστρεψαν εἰς τὴν παρεμ-
horsemen to go with him, they returned to the for-
βολήν· 33 οἵτινες εἰσελθόντες εἰς τὴν [o]Καισάρειαν,‖ καὶ
tress. Who having entered into Cæsarea, and
ἀναδόντες τὴν ἐπιστολὴν τῷ ἡγεμόνι, παρέστησαν καὶ τὸν
given up the letter to the governor, presented also
Παῦλον αὐτῷ. 34 ἀναγνοὺς.δὲ [p]ὁ ἡγεμών,‖ καὶ ἐπερω-
Paul to him. And [3]having [4]read [[5]it] [1]the [2]governor, and having
τήσας ἐκ ποίας [q]ἐπαρχίας‖ ἐστίν, καὶ πυθόμενος ὅτι ἀπὸ
asked of what province he is, and having learnt that from
Κιλικίας, 35 Διακούσομαί σου, ἔφη, ὅταν καὶ οἱ κατήγοροί
Cilicia [he is], I will [2]hear [1]fully thee, he said, when also [2]accusers

horsemen threescore and ten, and spearmen two hundred, at the third hour of the night; 24 and provide *them* beasts, that they may set Paul on, and bring *him* safe unto Felix the governor. 25 And he wrote a letter after this manner: 26 Claudius Lysias unto the most excellent governor Felix *sendeth* greeting. 27 This man was taken of the Jews, and should have been killed of them: then came I with an army, and rescued him, having understood that he was a Roman. 28 And when I would have known the cause wherefore they accused him, I brought him forth into their council: 29 whom I perceived to be accused of questions of their law, but to have nothing laid to his charge worthy of death or of bonds. 30 And when it was told me how that the Jews laid wait for the man, I sent straightway to thee, and gave commandment to his accusers also to say before thee what *they had* against him. Farewell. 31 Then the soldiers, as it was commanded them, took Paul, and brought *him* by night to Antipatris. 32 On the morrow they left the horsemen to go with him, and returned to the castle: 33 who, when they came to Cæsarea, and delivered the epistle to the governor, presented Paul also before him. 34 And when the governor had read *the letter*, he asked of what province he was. And when he understood that *he was* of Cilicia; 35 I will hear thee, said he, when thine ac-

---

[x] Καισαρίας T. [y] ἔχουσαν LTTr; [περι]έχουσαν A. [z] συλλημφθέντα LTTrA. [a] ἐξειλάμην LTTrAW. [b] — αὐτόν LTTr[A]W. [c] τε (δὲ W) ἐπιγνῶναι LTTrAW. [d] — αὐτὸν (read [him]) T[Tr]. [e] ἔχοντα ἔγκλημα LTTrAW. [f] — μέλλειν LTTrA. [g] — ὑπὸ τῶν Ἰουδαίων LTTrA. [h] ἐξ αὐτῶν by them LTTr; ἐξ αὐτῆς A. [i] — τὰ LTTr. [k] αὐτοὺς for them (to speak) LT. [l] — Ἔρρωσο LTTrA. [m] — τῆς LTTrAW. [n] ἀπέρχεσθαι to go away LTTrA. [o] Καισαρίαν T. [p] — ὁ ἡγεμών GLTTrAW [q] ἐπαρχείας T.

cusers are also come.
And he commanded
him to be kept in Herod's judgment hall.

XXIV. And after
five days Ananias the
high priest descended
with the elders, and
with a certain orator
named Tertullus, who
informed the governor against Paul.
2 And when he was
called forth, Tertullus
began to accuse *him*,
saying, Seeing that by
thee we enjoy great
quietness, and that
very worthy deeds are
done unto this nation
by thy providence,
3 we accept *it* always,
and in all places, most
noble Felix, with all
thankfulness. 4 Notwithstanding, that I
be not further tedious
unto thee, I pray thee
that thou wouldest
hear us of thy clemency a few words.
5 For we have found
this man *a* pestilent
fellow, and a mover of
sedition among all the
Jews throughout the
world, and a ringleader of the sect of
the Nazarenes: 6 who
also hath gone about
to profane the temple:
whom we took, and
would have judged
according to our law.
7 But the chief captain Lysias came *upon*
us, and with great violence took *him* away
out of our hands,
8 commanding his accusers to come unto
thee: by examining
of whom thyself mayest take knowledge of
all these things, whereof we accuse him.
9 And the Jews also
assented, saying that
these things were so.
10 Then Paul, after
that the governor had
beckoned unto him to
speak, answered, Forasmuch as I know
that thou hast been
of many years a judge
unto this nation, I do
the more cheerfully
answer for myself:
11 because that thou
mayest understand,
that there are yet but
twelve days since I

σου παραγένωνται[r]. Ἐκέλευσέν.τε αὐτὸν[s] ἐν τῷ πραιτωρίῳ
[1]thine may have arrived. And he commanded him in the prætorium
τοῦ Ἡρώδου φυλάσσεσθαι[s].
of Herod to be kept.

24 Μετὰ.δὲ πέντε ἡμέρας κατέβη ὁ ἀρχιερεὺς Ἀνανίας
And after five days came down the high priest Ananias
μετὰ [t]τῶν πρεσβυτέρων[ll] καὶ ῥήτορος Τερτύλλου τινός, οἵτινες
with the elders and an orator [3]Tertullus [1]a [2]certain, who
ἐνεφάνισαν τῷ ἡγεμόνι κατὰ τοῦ Παύλου. 2 κληθέν-
made a representation to the governor against Paul. [3]Having [4]been
τος δὲ αὐτοῦ ἤρξατο κατηγορεῖν ὁ Τέρτυλλος λέγων,
[5]called [1]and [2]he [7]began [8]to [9]accuse [6]Tertullus, saying,
3 Πολλῆς εἰρήνης τυγχάνοντες διὰ σοῦ, καὶ [v]κατορθωμάτων[ll]
[2]Great [3]peace [1]obtaining through thee, and excellent measures
γινομένων τῷ.ἔθνει.τούτῳ διὰ τῆς.σῆς.προνοίας, πάντῃ.τε
being done for this nation through thy forethought, both in every way
καὶ πανταχοῦ ἀποδεχόμεθα, κράτιστε Φῆλιξ, μετὰ πάσης
and everywhere we gladly accept [it], most excellent Felix, with all
εὐχαριστίας. 4 ἵνα.δὲ μὴ ἐπὶ πλεῖόν σε [w]ἐγκόπτω[ll]
thankfulness. But that [3]not [7]to [9]longer [8]thee [1]I [2]may [4]be [5]a [6]hindrance
παρακαλῶ ἀκοῦσαί σε ἡμῶν συντόμως τῇ.σῇ.ἐπιεικείᾳ. 5 εὑ-
I beseech [2]to [3]hear [1]thee us briefly in thy clemency. [2]Having
ρόντες γὰρ τὸν.ἄνδρα.τοῦτον λοιμόν, καὶ κινοῦντα [x]στάσιν[ll]
[3]found [1]for this man a pest, and moving insurrection
πᾶσιν τοῖς Ἰουδαίοις τοῖς κατὰ τὴν οἰκουμένην, πρωτοστάτην
among all the Jews in the habitable world, [2]a [3]leader
τε τῆς τῶν Ναζωραίων αἱρέσεως· 6 ὃς καὶ τὸ ἱερὸν
[1]and of the [2]of [3]the [4]Nazaræans [1]sect; who also the temple
ἐπείρασεν βεβηλῶσαι, ὃν καὶ ἐκρατήσαμεν [y]καὶ κατὰ
attempted to profane, whom also we seized, and according to
τὸν ἡμέτερον νόμον ἠθελήσαμεν [z]κρίνειν.[l] 7 παρελθὼν.δὲ
our law wished to judge; but [5]having [6]come [7]up
Λυσίας ὁ χιλίαρχος μετὰ πολλῆς βίας ἐκ τῶν.χειρῶν.ἡμῶν
[1]Lysias [2]the [3]chief [4]captain with great force out of our hands
ἀπήγαγεν, 8 κελεύσας τοὺς.κατηγόρους.αὐτοῦ ἔρχεσθαι
took away [him], having commanded his accusers to come
[a]ἐπὶ σέ[ll] παρ' οὗ δυνήσῃ αὐτὸς ἀνακρίνας περὶ
to thee, from whom thou wilt be able thyself, having examined concerning
πάντων τούτων ἐπιγνῶναι ὧν ἡμεῖς κατηγοροῦμεν
all these things [6]to [7]know [1]of [2]which [3]we [4]accuse
αὐτοῦ. 9 [b]Συνέθεντο[ll].δὲ καὶ οἱ Ἰουδαῖοι, φάσκοντες ταῦτα
[5]him. And [4]agreed [3]also [1]the [2]Jews, declaring these things
οὕτως ἔχειν. 10 Ἀπεκρίθη.[c]δὲ[ll] ὁ Παῦλος, νεύσαντος
[3]thus [1]to [2]be. But [2]answered [1]Paul, [5]having [6]made [7]a [8]sign
αὐτῷ τοῦ ἡγεμόνος λέγειν, Ἐκ.πολλῶν ἐτῶν ὄντα σε
[9]to [10]him [3]the [4]governor to speak, [5]For [6]many [7]years [3]as [4]being [2]thee
κριτὴν τῷ.ἔθνει.τούτῳ ἐπιστάμενος, [d]εὐθυμότερον[ll] τὰ
[8]judge [9]to [10]this [11]nation [1]knowing, more cheerfully [as to] the things
περὶ ἐμαυτοῦ ἀπολογοῦμαι. 11 δυναμένου σου [e]γνῶναι[ll]
concerning myself I make defence. [2]Being [3]able [1]thou to know
ὅτι οὐ πλείους εἰσίν μοι ἡμέραι [f]ἢ[ll] [g]δεκαδύο[ll] ἀφ'.ἧς
that [3]not [4]more [5]than [1]there [2]are [8]to [9]me [7]days [6]twelve since

---

[r] , κελεύσας having commanded LTTrA. [s] + αὐτόν him LTTrA. [t] πρεσβυτέρων τινῶν certain elders LTTrA. [v] διορθωμάτων reforms LTTrA. [w] ἐνκόπτω T. [x] στάσεις insurrections LTTrW. [y] — καὶ κατὰ . . . . ἐπὶ σέ (verse 8) LTTr[A]. [z] κρῖναι A. [a] πρὸς A. [b] συνεπέθεντο joined in attack GLTTrAW. [c] τε and LTTrA. [d] εὐθύμως cheerfully LTTrA. [e] ἐπιγνῶναι LTTrA. [f] — ἢ GLTTrAW. [g] δώδεκα LTTrA.

ἀνέβην προσκυνήσων [h]ἐν‖ Ἱερουσαλήμ 12 καὶ οὔτε ἐν τῷ
I went up to worship at Jerusalem, and neither in the
ἱερῷ εὗρόν με πρός τινα διαλεγόμενον ἢ [i]ἐπισύστασιν‖
temple did they find me with anyone reasoning, or a tumultuous gathering
ποιοῦντα ὄχλου οὔτε ἐν ταῖς συναγωγαῖς οὔτε κατὰ τὴν
making of a crowd neither in the synagogues nor in the
πόλιν· 13 [k]οὔτε‖ παραστῆσαί [l]με‖ δύνανται [m] περὶ
city; neither [4]to [5]prove [1]are [2]they [3]able [the things] concerning
ὧν [n]νῦν‖ κατηγοροῦσίν μου. 14 ὁμολογῶ.δὲ τοῦτό σοι,
which now they accuse me. But I confess this to thee,
ὅτι κατὰ τὴν ὁδὸν ἣν λέγουσιν αἵρεσιν, οὕτως λατρεύω τῷ
that in the way which they call sect, so I serve the
πατρῴῳ θεῷ, πιστεύων πᾶσιν τοῖς κατὰ τὸν νόμον καὶ [o]
ancestral God, believing all things which throughout the law and
τοῖς προφήταις γεγραμμένοις, 15 ἐλπίδα ἔχων [p]εἰς‖ τὸν θεόν,
the prophets have been written, a hope having in God,
ἣν καὶ αὐτοὶ οὗτοι προσδέχονται, ἀνάστασιν μέλλειν
which also they themselves receive, [that] a resurrection is about
ἔσεσθαι [q]νεκρῶν,‖ δικαίων.τε καὶ ἀδίκων· 16 ἐν.τούτῳ.[r]δὲ‖
to be of [the] dead, both of just and of unjust. And in this
αὐτὸς ἀσκῶ, ἀπρόσκοπον συνείδησιν ἔχειν πρὸς τὸν θεὸν
myself I exercise, [5]without [6]offence [3]a [4]conscience [1]to [2]have towards God
καὶ τοὺς ἀνθρώπους [s]διαπαντός.‖ 17 δι'.ἐτῶν.δὲ πλειόνων
and men continually. And after [2]years [1]many
[t]παρεγενόμην‖ ἐλεημοσύνας ποιήσων εἰς τὸ.ἔθνος.μου [t] καὶ
I arrived [2]alms [1]bringing to my nation and
προσφοράς· 18 ἐν [v]οἷς‖ εὗρόν με ἡγνισμένον ἐν τῷ ἱερῷ,
offerings. Amidst which they found me purified in the temple,
οὐ μετὰ ὄχλου οὐδὲ μετὰ θορύβου, τινὲς.[w]δὲ‖ ἀπὸ τῆς
not with crowd nor with tumult. But [it was] certain [2]from
Ἀσίας Ἰουδαῖοι, 19 οὓς [x]δεῖ‖ ἐπὶ σοῦ παρεῖναι καὶ κατηγορεῖν
[3]Asia [1]Jews, who ought before thee to appear and to accuse
εἴ τι ἔχοιεν πρός [y]με·‖ 20 ἢ αὐτοὶ.οὗτοι εἰπάτωσαν,
if anything they may have against me; or these themselves let them say,
[z]εἴ‖ τι εὗρον [a]ἐν ἐμοὶ‖ ἀδίκημα, στάντος.μου ἐπὶ τοῦ
if any [2]they [3]found [4]in [5]me [1]unrighteousness, when I stood before the
συνεδρίου, 21 ἢ περὶ μιᾶς.ταύτης φωνῆς, ἧς [b]ἔκραξα‖
sanhedrim, [other] than concerning this one voice, which I cried out
[c]ἑστὼς ἐν αὐτοῖς,‖ Ὅτι περὶ ἀναστάσεως νεκρῶν ἐγὼ
standing among them: Concerning a resurrection of [the] dead I
κρίνομαι σήμερον [d]ὑφ'‖ ὑμῶν. 22 [e]Ἀκούσας.δὲ ταῦτα ὁ
am judged this day by you. And [2]having [3]heard [4]these [5]things
Φῆλιξ ἀνεβάλετο αὐτούς,‖ ἀκριβέστερον εἰδὼς τὰ περὶ
[1]Felix he put [2]off [1]them, more accurately knowing the things concerning
τῆς ὁδοῦ, [f]εἰπών,‖ Ὅταν Λυσίας ὁ χιλίαρχος καταβῇ,
the way, saying, When Lysias the chief captain may have come down,
διαγνώσομαι τὰ καθ' ὑμᾶς· 23 διαταξάμενός [g]τε‖ τῷ ἑκα-
I will examine the things as to you; having ordered the
τοντάρχῃ τηρεῖσθαι [ha]τὸν Παῦλον,‖ ἔχειν.τε ἄνεσιν, καὶ
centurion to keep Paul, and to [let him] have ease, and

went up to Jerusalem
for to worship. 12 And
they neither found me
in the temple disputing with any man,
neither raising up the
people, neither in the
synagogues, nor in the
city: 13 neither can
they prove the things
whereof they now accuse me. 14 But this
I confess unto thee,
that after the way
which they call heresy,
so worship I the God
of my fathers, believing all things
which are written in
the law and in the
prophets: 15 and have
hope toward God,
which they themselves
also allow, that there
shall be a resurrection of the dead, both
of the just and unjust. 16 And herein
do I exercise myself,
to have always a conscience void of offence
toward God, and *toward* men. 17 Now
after many years I
came to bring alms to
my nation, and offerings. 18 Whereupon
certain Jews from Asia
found me purified in
the temple, neither
with multitude, nor
with tumult. 19 Who
ought to have been here
before thee, and object, if they had ought
against me. 20 Or else
let these same *here*
say, if they have found
any evil doing in me,
while I stood before
the council, 21 except
it be for this one
voice, that I cried
standing among them,
Touching the resurrection of the dead I
am called in question by you this
day. 22 And when
Felix heard these
things, having more
perfect knowledge of
that way, he deferred
them, and said, When
Lysias the chief captain shall come down,
I will know the uttermost of your matter.
23 And he commanded
a centurion to keep
Paul, and to let *him*
have liberty, and that

---

[h] εἰς LTTrAW. [i] ἐπίστασιν LTTrA. [k] οὐδὲ LT. [l] — με EGLTTrAW. [m] + σοι to thee LTTrAW. [n] νυνὶ LTTrA. [o] + ἐν in ELW; + τοῖς ἐν GTTr[A]. [p] πρὸς towards T. [q] — νεκρῶν LTTrA. [r] καὶ LTTrAW. [s] διὰ παντός LTrA. [t] παρεγενόμην *placed after* μου LTTrA. [v] αἷς LTTrA. [w] — δὲ but E. [x] ἔδει EGLTTrAW. [y] ἐμέ LTTrA. [z] — εἴ (*read* τι what) GLTTrAW. [a] — ἐν ἐμοὶ LT[TrA]. [b] ἐκέκραξα TTrA. [c] ἐν αὐτοῖς ἑστὼς LTTrAW. [d] ἀφ' LTTrAW. [e] Ἀνεβάλετο δὲ αὐτοὺς ὁ Φῆλιξ GLTTrAW. [f] εἴπας LTTrAW. [g] — τε TTrAW. [ha] αὐτὸν him GLTTrAW.

he should forbid none of his acquaintance to minister or come unto him. 24 And after certain days, when Felix came with his wife Drusilla, which was a Jewess, he sent for Paul, and heard him concerning the faith in Christ. 25 And as he reasoned of righteousness, temperance, and judgment to come, Felix trembled, and answered, Go thy way for this time; when I have a convenient season, I will call for thee. 26 He hoped also that money should have been given him of Paul, that he might loose him: wherefore he sent for him the oftener, and communed with him. 27 But after two years Porcius Festus came into Felix' room: and Felix, willing to shew the Jews a pleasure, left Paul bound.

μηδένα κωλύειν τῶν.ἰδίων.αὐτοῦ ὑπηρετεῖν [i]ἢ προσέρχεσθαι‖
[3]none [1]to [2]forbid of his own to minister or to come
αὐτῷ. 24 Μετὰ.δὲ [k]ἡμέρας τινὰς‖ παραγενόμενος ὁ Φῆλιξ
to him. And after [2]days [1]certain [4]having [5]arrived [3]Felix
σὺν Δρουσίλλῃ τῇ[l].γυναικὶ.[m]αὐτοῦ‖ οὔσῃ Ἰουδαίᾳ, μετε-
with Drusilla his wife, who was a Jewess, he
πέμψατο τὸν Παῦλον, καὶ ἤκουσεν αὐτοῦ περὶ τῆς εἰς
sent for Paul, and heard him concerning the [2]in
χριστὸν [n] πίστεως. 25 διαλεγομένου.δὲ αὐτοῦ περὶ δικαιο-
[3]Christ [1]faith. And as [2]reasoned [1]he concerning right-
σύνης καὶ ἐγκρατείας καὶ τοῦ κρίματος τοῦ μέλλοντος [o]ἔσεσθαι,‖
eousness and self-control and the judgment about to be,
ἔμφοβος γενόμενος ὁ Φῆλιξ ἀπεκρίθη, Τὸ.νῦν.ἔχον πορεύου·
[2]afraid [1]becoming Felix answered, For the present go,
καιρὸν.δὲ μεταλαβὼν μετακαλέσομαί σε· 26 ἅμα [p]δὲ‖
and an opportunity having found I will call for thee; withal too
καὶ ἐλπίζων ὅτι χρήματα δοθήσεται αὐτῷ ὑπὸ τοῦ Παύλου,
also hoping that riches will be given him by Paul,
[q]ὅπως λύσῃ αὐτόν·‖ διὸ καὶ πυκνότερον αὐτὸν μετα-
that he might loose him: wherefore also oftener him send-
πεμπόμενος ὡμίλει αὐτῷ. 27 Διετίας.δὲ πληρωθείσης
ing for he conversed with him. But two years being completed
ἔλαβεν διάδοχον ὁ Φῆλιξ Πόρκιον Φῆστον· θέλων.τε
[2]received [[3]as] [4]successor [1]Felix Porcius Festus; and wishing
[r]χάριτας‖ καταθέσθαι τοῖς Ἰουδαίοις ὁ Φῆλιξ κατέλιπεν
favours to acquire for himself with the Jews Felix left
τὸν Παῦλον δεδεμένον.
Paul bound.

XXV. Now when Festus was come into the province, after three days he ascended from Cæsarea to Jerusalem. 2 Then the high priest and the chief of the Jews informed him against Paul, and besought him, 3 and desired favour against him, that he would send for him to Jerusalem, laying wait in the way to kill him. 4 But Festus answered, that Paul should be kept at Cæsarea, and that he himself would depart shortly *thither*. 5 Let them therefore, said he, which among you are able, go down with *me*, and accuse this man, if there be any wickedness in him. 6 And when he had tarried among them more than ten days, he went down

25 Φῆστος οὖν ἐπιβὰς τῇ [s]ἐπαρχίᾳ,‖ μετὰ τρεῖς
Festus therefore being come into the province, after three
ἡμέρας ἀνέβη εἰς Ἱεροσόλυμα ἀπὸ [t]Καισαρείας.‖ 2 ἐνε-
days went up to Jerusalem from Cæsarea. [2]Made [3]a [4]re-
φάνισαν [v]δὲ‖ αὐτῷ [w]ὁ ἀρχιερεὺς‖ καὶ οἱ πρῶτοι τῶν
presentation [5]before [1]and him the high priest and the chief of the
Ἰουδαίων κατὰ τοῦ Παύλου, καὶ παρεκάλουν αὐτόν, 3 αἰτού-
Jews against Paul, and besought him, ask-
μενοι χάριν κατ' αὐτοῦ, ὅπως μεταπέμψηται αὐτὸν εἰς
ing a favour against him, that he would send for him to
Ἱερουσαλήμ, ἐνέδραν ποιοῦντες ἀνελεῖν αὐτὸν κατὰ τὴν
Jerusalem, an ambush forming to put to death him on the
ὁδόν. 4 ὁ.μὲν.οὖν.Φῆστος ἀπεκρίθη, τηρεῖσθαι τὸν Παῦλον
way. Festus therefore answered, [2]should [3]be [4]kept [1]Paul
[x]ἐν Καισαρείᾳ,‖ ἑαυτὸν.δὲ μέλλειν ἐν.τάχει ἐκπορεύεσθαι.
at Cæsarea, and himself was about shortly to set out.
5 Οἱ οὖν [y]δυνατοὶ ἐν ὑμῖν, φησίν,‖ [z]συγκαταβάντες,‖
Those therefore in-power among you, says he, having gone down too,
εἴ τι ἐστὶν ἐν τῷ ἀνδρὶ [a]τούτῳ,‖ κατηγορείτωσαν αὐτοῦ.
if anything is in [2]man [1]this, let them accuse him.
6 Διατρίψας.δὲ ἐν αὐτοῖς ἡμέρας [b]πλείους ἢ‖ δέκα, κατα-
And having spent among them [4]days [1]more [2]than [3]ten, having

---

[i] — ἢ προσέρχεσθαι LTTrAW. [k] τινας ἡμέρας L. [l] + ἰδίᾳ LTTr. [m] — αὐτοῦ GLTTrA. [n] + Ἰησοῦν Jesus LT. [o] — ἔσεσθαι (*read* μέλλοντος coming) GLTTrAW. [p] — δὲ GLTTrAW. [q] — ὅπως λύσῃ αὐτόν LTTrAW. [r] χάριτα a favour LTTrAW. [s] ἐπαρχείῳ T. [t] Καισαρίας T. [v] τε LTTrA. [w] οἱ ἀρχιερεῖς the chief priests LTTrA. [x] εἰς Καισάρειαν LTrAW; εἰς Καισαρίαν T. [y] ἐν ὑμῖν, φησίν, δυνατοὶ GLTTrAW. [z] συν- T. [a] ἄτοπον amiss (in the man) LTTrA; — τούτῳ G. [b] οὐ πλείους ὀκτὼ ἢ not more than eight or GLTTrAW.

βὰς εἰς [c]Καισάρειαν,‖ τῇ ἐπαύριον καθίσας ἐπὶ τοῦ
gone down to Cæsarea, on the morrow having sat on the
βήματος ἐκέλευσεν τὸν Παῦλον ἀχθῆναι. 7 παραγενομένου
judgment seat he commanded Paul to be brought. [3]Being [4]come
δὲ αὐτοῦ, περιέστησαν [d] οἱ ἀπὸ Ἱεροσολύμων καταβε-
[1]and [2]he, stood round the [2]from [3]Jerusalem [4]who [5]had [6]come
βηκότες Ἰουδαῖοι, πολλὰ καὶ βαρέα [e]αἰτιάματα‖ [f]φέροντες
[7]down [1]Jews, many and weighty charges bringing
κατὰ τοῦ Παύλου,‖ ἃ οὐκ.ἴσχυον ἀποδεῖξαι, 8 [g]ἀπο-
against Paul, which they were not able to prove: [2]said [3]in
λογουμένου αὐτοῦ,‖ Ὅτι οὔτε εἰς τὸν νόμον τῶν Ἰουδαίων
[4]defence [1]he, Neither against the law of the Jews
οὔτε εἰς τὸ ἱερὸν οὔτε εἰς Καίσαρά τι ἥμαρτον.
nor against the temple nor against Cæsar [in] anything sinned I.
9 Ὁ.Φῆστος.δὲ [h]τοῖς Ἰουδαίοις θέλων‖ χάριν κατα-
But Festus, [7]with [8]the [9]Jews [1]wishing [6]favour [2]to [3]acquire [4]for
θέσθαι ἀποκριθεὶς τῷ Παύλῳ εἶπεν, Θέλεις εἰς Ἱεροσόλυμα
[5]himself answering Paul said, Art thou willing to Jerusalem
ἀναβάς, ἐκεῖ περὶ τούτων [i]κρίνεσθαι‖ ἐπ' ἐμοῦ;
having gone up there concerning these things to be judged before me?
10 Εἶπεν.δὲ ὁ Παῦλος, [k]Ἐπὶ τοῦ βήματος Καίσαρος [k]ἑ-
But [2]said [1]Paul, Before the judgment seat of Cæsar stand-
στώς‖ εἰμι, οὗ με.δεῖ κρίνεσθαι. Ἰουδαίους οὐδὲν [l]ἠδί-
ing I am, where it behoves me to be judged. To Jews [3]nothing [1]I [2]did
κησα,‖ ὡς καὶ σὺ κάλλιον ἐπιγινώσκεις· 11 εἰ μὲν [m]γὰρ‖
wrong, as also thou very well knowest. [2]If [3]indeed [1]for
ἀδικῶ καὶ ἄξιον θανάτου πέπραχά τι, οὐ.παραιτοῦμαι
I do wrong and worthy of death have done anything, I do not deprecate
τὸ ἀποθανεῖν· εἰ.δὲ οὐδέν ἐστιν ὧν οὗτοι κατηγοροῦσίν
to die; but if nothing there is of which they accuse
μου, οὐδείς με δύναται αὐτοῖς χαρίσασθαι. Καίσαρα ἐπι-
me, no one me can to them give up. To Cæsar I ap-
καλοῦμαι. 12 Τότε ὁ Φῆστος [n]συλλαλήσας‖ μετὰ τοῦ συμ-
peal. Then Festus, having conferred with the coun-
βουλίου, ἀπεκρίθη, Καίσαρα ἐπικέκλησαι, ἐπὶ Καίσαρα
cil, answered, To Cæsar thou hast appealed, to Cæsar
πορεύσῃ.
thou shalt go.

unto Cæsarea; and the next day sitting on the judgment seat commanded Paul to be brought.
7 And when he was come, the Jews which came down from Jerusalem stood round about, and laid many and grievous complaints against Paul, which they could not prove.
8 While he answered for himself, Neither against the law of the Jews, neither against the temple, nor yet against Cæsar, have I offended any thing at all.
9 But Festus, willing to do the Jews a pleasure, answered Paul, and said, Wilt thou go up to Jerusalem, and there be judged of these things before me?
10 Then said Paul, I stand at Cæsar's judgment seat, where I ought to be judged: to the Jews have I done no wrong, as thou very well knowest.
11 For if I be an offender, or have committed any thing worthy of death, I refuse not to die: but if there be none of these things whereof these accuse me, no man may deliver me unto them. I appeal unto Cæsar.
12 Then Festus, when he had conferred with the council, answered, Hast thou appealed unto Cæsar? unto Cæsar shalt thou go.

13 Ἡμερῶν.δὲ διαγενομένων τινῶν, Ἀγρίππας ὁ βασιλεὺς
And [2]days [3]having [4]passed [1]certain, Agrippa the king
καὶ Βερνίκη κατήντησαν εἰς [o]Καισάρειαν,‖ [p]ἀσπασόμενοι‖ τὸν
and Bernice came down to Cæsarea, saluting
Φῆστον. 14 ὡς.δὲ πλείους ἡμέρας διέτριβον ἐκεῖ ὁ Φῆστος
Festus. And when many days they stayed there Festus
τῷ βασιλεῖ ἀνέθετο τὰ κατὰ τὸν Παῦλον λέγων,
[3]the [4]king [1]laid [2]before the things relating to Paul, saying,
Ἀνήρ τις ἐστὶν καταλελειμμένος ὑπὸ Φήλικος δέσμιος,
A [2]man [1]certain there is left by Felix a prisoner,
15 περὶ οὗ, γενομένου μου εἰς Ἱεροσόλυμα, ἐνε-
concerning whom, [3]being [1]on [2]my in Jerusalem, [4]made [5]a [6]re-
φάνισαν οἱ ἀρχιερεῖς καὶ οἱ πρεσβύτεροι τῶν Ἰουδαίων,
presentation [1]the [2]chief [3]priests and the elders of the Jews,

13 And after certain days king Agrippa and Bernice came unto Cæsarea to salute Festus.
14 And when they had been there many days, Festus declared Paul's cause unto the king, saying, There is a certain man left in bonds by Felix:
15 about whom, when I was at Jerusalem, the chief priests and the elders of the Jews informed *me*, desiring *to*

---

[c] Καισαρίαν T. [d] + αὐτὸν him LTTrAW. [e] αἰτιώματα GLTTrAW. [f] καταφέροντες (— κατὰ τοῦ Παύλου) LTTrA. [g] τοῦ Παύλου ἀπολογουμένου Paul said in defence LTTrA. [h] θέλων τοῖς Ἰουδαίοις LTTrAW. [i] κριθῆναι LTTrAW. [k] ἑστὼς *placed before* Ἐπὶ T. [l] ἠδίκηκα I have done wrong TTr. [m] οὖν therefore LTTrAW. [n] συνλαλήσας T. [o] Καισαρίαν T. [p] ἀσπασάμενοι TTrA.

have judgment against
him. 16 To whom I
answered, It is not
the manner of the Ro-
mans to deliver any
man to die, before
that he which is ac-
cused have the ac-
cusers face to face, and
have licence to an-
swer for himself con-
cerning the crime laid
against him. 17 There-
fore, when they were
come hither, without
any delay on the mor-
row I sat on the judg-
ment seat, and com-
manded the man to be
brought forth. 18 A-
gainst whom when the
accusers stood up,
they brought none
accusation of such
things as I supposed:
19 but had certain
questions against him
of their own supersti-
tion, and of one Jesus,
which was dead, whom
Paul affirmed to be
alive. 20 And because
I doubted of such man-
ner of questions, I
asked *him* whether he
would go to Jerusa-
lem, and there be
judged of these mat-
ters. 21 But when Paul
had appealed to be
reserved unto the
hearing of Augustus,
I commanded him to
be kept till I might
send him to Cæsar.
22 Then Agrippa said
unto Festus, I would
also hear the man my-
self. To morrow, said
he, thou shalt hear
him.

23 And on the mor-
row, when Agrippa
was come, and Ber-
nice, with great pomp,
and was entered into
the place of hearing,
with the chief cap-
tains, and principal
men of the city, at
Festus' commandment
Paul was brought
forth. 24 And Festus
said, King Agrippa,
and all men, which
are here present with
us, ye see this man,
about whom all the
multitude of the
Jews have dealt with
me, both at Jerusa-
lem, and *also* here,
crying that he ought

αἰτούμενοι κατ' αὐτοῦ [q]δίκην·‖ 16 πρὸς οὓς ἀπεκρίθην,
asking [2]against [3]him [1]judgment: to whom I answered,
ὅτι οὐκ.ἔστιν ἔθος Ῥωμαίοις χαρίζεσθαί τινα ἄνθρωπον
It is not a custom with Romans to give up any man
[r]εἰς ἀπώλειαν,‖ πρὶν ἢ ὁ κατηγορούμενος κατὰ.πρόσωπον
to destruction, before he being accused face to face
ἔχοι τοὺς κατηγόρους, τόπον.τε ἀπολογίας λάβοι
may have the accusers, and opportunity of defence he may get
περὶ τοῦ ἐγκλήματος. 17 συνελθόντων οὖν [s]αὐτῶν‖
concerning the accusation. [2]Having [3]come [4]together [5]therefore [1]they
ἐνθάδε, ἀναβολὴν μηδεμίαν ποιησάμενος, τῇ ἑξῆς καθίσας
here, delay none having made, the next [day] having sat
ἐπὶ τοῦ βήματος ἐκέλευσα ἀχθῆναι τὸν ἄνδρα· 18 περὶ
on the judgment seat I commanded to be brought the man; concerning
οὗ σταθέντες οἱ κατήγοροι οὐδεμίαν αἰτίαν [t]ἐπέφερον‖ ὧν
whom standing up the accusers [2]no [3]charge [1]brought of which
[v]ὑπενόουν ἐγώ‖ [w]· 19 ζητήματα.δέ τινα περὶ τῆς.ἰδίας
[2]supposed [1]I; but [2]questions [1]certain concerning their own
δεισιδαιμονίας εἶχον πρὸς αὐτόν, καὶ περί τινος Ἰησοῦ
system of religion they had against him, and concerning a certain Jesus
(*lit.* demon-worship)
τεθνηκότος, ὃν ἔφασκεν ὁ Παῦλος ζῆν. 20 ἀπορούμενος.δὲ
who is dead, whom [2]affirmed [1]Paul to be alive. And [2]being [3]perplexed
ἐγὼ [x]εἰς‖ τὴν περὶ [y]τούτου‖ ζήτησιν ἔλεγον, εἰ.βούλοιτο
[1]I as to the [2]concerning [3]this [1]inquiry said, Would he be willing
πορεύεσθαι εἰς [z]Ἱερουσαλήμ,‖ κἀκεῖ κρίνεσθαι περὶ
to go to Jerusalem, and there to be judged concerning
τούτων. 21 τοῦ.δὲ.Παύλου ἐπικαλεσαμένου τηρηθῆναι αὐ-
these things. But Paul having appealed for [2]to [3]be [4]kept [1]him-
τὸν εἰς τὴν τοῦ Σεβαστοῦ διάγνωσιν, ἐκέλευσα τηρεῖσθαι
self for the [2]of [3]Augustus [1]cognizance, I commanded [2]to [3]be [4]kept
αὐτὸν ἕως.οὗ [a]πέμψω‖ αὐτὸν πρὸς Καίσαρα. 22 Ἀγρίππας
[1]him till I might send him to Cæsar. [2]Agrippa
δὲ πρὸς τὸν Φῆστον [b]ἔφη,‖ Ἐβουλόμην καὶ αὐτὸς τοῦ
[1]and to Festus said, I was desiring also myself the
ἀνθρώπου ἀκοῦσαι. [c]Ὁ.δέ,‖ Αὔριον, φησίν, ἀκούσῃ αὐτοῦ.
man to hear. And he [2]To-morrow [1]says, thou shalt hear him.
23 Τῇ οὖν ἐπαύριον ἐλθόντος τοῦ Ἀγρίππα καὶ τῆς
On the [2]therefore [1]morrow [4]having [5]come [3]Agrippa and
Βερνίκης μετὰ πολλῆς φαντασίας, καὶ εἰσελθόντων εἰς τὸ
Bernice, with great pomp, and having entered into the
ἀκροατήριον, σύν τε [d]τοῖς‖ χιλιάρχοις καὶ ἀνδράσιν τοῖς
hall of audience, with both the chief captains and men
κατ'.ἐξοχὴν [e]οὖσιν‖ τῆς πόλεως, καὶ κελεύσαντος τοῦ Φήστου
of eminence being of the city, and [2]having [3]commanded [1]Festus
ἤχθη ὁ Παῦλος. 24 καί φησιν ὁ Φῆστος, Ἀγρίππα βασι-
[5]was [6]brought [4]Paul. And [2]says [1]Festus, [4]Agrippa [3]king
λεῦ, καὶ πάντες οἱ [f]συμπαρόντες‖ ἡμῖν ἄνδρες, θεωρεῖτε τοῦ-
and all the [2]being [3]present [4]with [5]us [1]men, ye see this
τον περὶ οὗ [g]πᾶν‖ τὸ πλῆθος τῶν Ἰουδαίων ἐνέτυχόν
one concerning whom all the multitude of the Jews pleaded
μοι ἔν τε Ἱεροσολύμοις καὶ ἐνθάδε, [h]ἐπιβοῶντες‖ μὴ
with me in both Jerusalem and here, crying out [that]

[q] καταδίκην LTTrAW. [r] — εἰς ἀπώλειαν GLTTrAW. [s] [αὐτῶν] A. [t] ἔφερον LTTrAW.
[v] ἐγὼ ὑπενόουν LTTrAW. [w] + πονηράν (*read* evil charge) LT[A]W; πονηρῶν of evils Tr.
[x] — εἰς TTr[A]. [y] τούτων these things LTTrAW. [z] Ἱεροσόλυμα LTTrAW. [a] ἀναπέμψω
I might send up LTTrAW. [b] — ἔφη (*read* [said]) LTTrA. [c] — Ὁ δέ (*read* φησίν says
he) LTTrA. [d] — τοῖς LTTrA. [e] — οὖσιν LTTrAW. [f] συν- T. [g] ἅπαν LTTrAW.
[h] βοῶντες crying LTTr; [ἐπι]βοῶντες A.

δεῖν [i]ζῆν αὐτὸν" μηκέτι 25 ἐγὼ.δὲ [k]καταλαβόμενος" μηδὲν
[2]ought [3]to [4]live [1]he no longer. But I having perceived nothing
ἄξιον [l]θανάτου αὐτὸν" πεπραχέναι, [m]καὶ" αὐτοῦ δὲ τούτου
worthy of death he had done, [5]also [4]himself [1]and [2]this [3]one
ἐπικαλεσαμένου τὸν Σεβαστόν, ἔκρινα πέμπειν [n]αὐτόν·"
having appealed to Augustus, I determined to send him,
26 περὶ οὗ ἀσφαλές τι γράψαι τῷ.κυρίῳ οὐκ.ἔχω·
concerning whom [2]certain [1]anything to write to [my] lord I have not.
διὸ προήγαγον αὐτὸν ἐφ' ὑμῶν, καὶ μάλιστα ἐπὶ σοῦ,
Wherefore I brought [2]forth [1]him before you, and specially before thee,
βασιλεῦ Ἀγρίππα, ὅπως τῆς ἀνακρίσεως γενομένης
king Agrippa, so that the examination having taken place
σχῶ τι [o]γράψαι." 27 ἄλογον.γάρ μοι δοκεῖ πέμ-
I may have something to write; for irrational to me it seems send-
ποντα δέσμιον, μὴ καὶ τὰς κατ' αὐτοῦ αἰτίας σημᾶναι.
ing a prisoner, not also the [2]against [3]him [1]charges to signify.

26 Ἀγρίππας.δὲ πρὸς τὸν Παῦλον ἔφη, Ἐπιτρέπεταί σοι
And Agrippa to Paul said, It is allowed thee
[p]ὑπὲρ" σεαυτοῦ λέγειν. Τότε ὁ Παῦλος [q]ἀπελογεῖτο," ἐκτείνας
for thyself to speak. Then Paul made a defence, stretching out
τὴν χεῖρα,[q] 2 Περὶ πάντων ὧν ἐγκαλοῦμαι ὑπὸ Ἰου-
the hand: Concerning all of which I am accused by Jews,
δαίων, βασιλεῦ Ἀγρίππα, ἥγημαι ἐμαυτὸν μακάριον [r]μέλλων
king Agrippa, I esteem myself happy being about
ἀπολογεῖσθαι ἐπὶ σοῦ σήμερον·" 3 μάλιστα γνώστην [s]ὄντα
to make defence before thee to-day, especially [3]acquainted [2]being
σε" πάντων τῶν κατὰ Ἰουδαίους ἐθῶν τε καὶ ζητημάτων.
[1]thou of all the [5]among [6]Jews [1]customs [2]and [3]also [4]questions;
διὸ δέομαί [t]σου" μακροθύμως ἀκοῦσαί μου. 4 τὴν μὲν οὖν
wherefore I beseech thee patiently to hear me. The [5]then
βίωσίν μου [v]τὴν" ἐκ νεότητος, τὴν ἀπ' ἀρχῆς
[1]manner [2]of [4]life [3]my from youth, which from [its] commencement
γενομένην ἐν τῷ.ἔθνει.μου ἐν [w]Ἱεροσολύμοις, ἴσασιν πάντες
was among my nation in Jerusalem, know all
[x]οἱ" Ἰουδαῖοι, 5 προγινώσκοντές με ἄνωθεν, ἐὰν θέλωσιν
the Jews, who before knew me from the first, if they would
μαρτυρεῖν, ὅτι κατὰ τὴν ἀκριβεστάτην αἵρεσιν τῆς
bear witness, that according to the strictest sect
ἡμετέρας [y]θρησκείας" ἔζησα Φαρισαῖος· 6 καὶ νῦν ἐπ'
of our religion I lived a Pharisee. And now for [the]
ἐλπίδι τῆς [z]πρὸς" τοὺς πατέρας [a]ἐπαγγελίας γενομένης ὑπὸ
hope of the [3]to [4]the [5]fathers [1]promise [2]made by
τοῦ θεοῦ ἕστηκα κρινόμενος, 7 εἰς ἣν τὸ.δωδεκάφυλον.ἡμῶν
God, I stand being judged, to which our twelve tribes
ἐν.ἐκτενείᾳ νύκτα καὶ ἡμέραν λατρεῦον ἐλπίζει καταντῆσαι·
intently night and day serving hope to arrive;
περὶ ἧς ἐλπίδος ἐγκαλοῦμαι, [b]βασιλεῦ Ἀγρίππα," ὑπὸ
concerning which hope I am accused, O king Agrippa, by
[c]τῶν" Ἰουδαίων[d]. 8 τί ἄπιστον κρίνεται παρ' ὑμῖν εἰ ὁ θεὸς
the Jews. Why incredible is it judged by you if God
νεκροὺς ἐγείρει; 9 ἐγὼ μὲν οὖν ἔδοξα ἐμαυτῷ πρὸς
[the] dead raises? I indeed therefore thought in myself [6]to

not to live any longer. 25 But when I found that he had committed nothing worthy of death, and that he himself hath appealed to Augustus, I have determined to send him. 26 Of whom I have no certain thing to write unto my lord. Wherefore I have brought him forth before you, and specially before thee, O king Agrippa, that, after examination had, I might have somewhat to write. 27 For it seemeth to me unreasonable to send a prisoner, and not withal to signify the crimes *laid* against him.

XXVI. Then Agrippa said unto Paul, Thou art permitted to speak for thyself. Then Paul stretched forth the hand, and answered for himself: 2 I think myself happy, king Agrippa, because I shall answer for myself this day before thee touching all the things whereof I am accused of the Jews: 3 especially *because I know* thee to be expert in all customs and questions which are among the Jews: wherefore I beseech thee to hear me patiently. 4 My manner of life from my youth, which was at the first among mine own nation at Jerusalem, know all the Jews; 5 which knew me from the beginning, if they would testify, that after the most straitest sect of our religion I lived a Pharisee. 6 And now I stand and am judged for the hope of the promise made of God unto our fathers: 7 unto which *promise* our twelve tribes, instantly serving *God* day and night, hope to come. For which hope's sake, king Agrippa, I am accused of the Jews. 8 Why should it be thought a thing incredible with you, that God should raise the dead? 9 I verily thought with

[i] αὐτὸν ζῆν LTTrAW. [k] κατελαβόμην LTTrAW. [l] αὐτὸν θανάτου LTTrAW. [m] — καὶ LTTrAW. [n] — αὐτὸν (*read* [him]) LTTrA. [o] γράψω I shall write LTTrAW. [p] περὶ LTTrA. [q] ἀπελογεῖτο *placed after* χεῖρα LTTrAW. [r] ἐπὶ σοῦ μέλλων σήμερον ἀπολογεῖσθαι GLTTrA. [s] σε ὄντα T. [t] — σου LTTrA. [v] — τὴν Tr[A]. [w] + τε and (in) LTTrAW. [x] — οἱ LTrA. [y] θρησκίας T. [z] εἰς LTTrAW. [a] + ἡμῶν (*read* our fathers) LTTrAW. [b] — βασιλεῦ Ἀγρίππα LTTrA; — Ἀγρίππα W. [c] — τῶν GLTTrAW. [d] + βασιλεῦ O king LTTrA.

myself, that I ought
to do many things
contrary to the name
of Jesus of Nazareth.
10 Which thing I also
did in Jerusalem: and
many of the saints did
I shut up in prison,
having received au-
thority from the chief
priests; and when
they were put to death,
I gave my voice a-
gainst *them*. 11 And
I punished them oft
in every synagogue,
and compelled *them*
to blaspheme; and
being exceedingly mad
against them, I per-
secuted *them* even
unto strange cities.
12 Whereupon as I
went to Damascus
with authority and
commission from the
chief priests, 13 at
midday, O king, I saw
in the way a light
from heaven, above
the brightness of the
sun, shining round
about me and them
which journeyed with
me. 14 And when we
were all fallen to the
earth, I heard a voice
speaking unto me,
and saying in the He-
brew tongue, Saul,
Saul, why persecutest
thou me? *It is* hard
for thee to kick a-
gainst the pricks.
15 And I said, Who
art thou, Lord? And
he said, I am Jesus
whom thou persecut-
est. 16 But rise, and
stand upon thy feet:
for, I have appeared
unto thee for this pur-
pose, to make thee a
minister and a wit-
ness both of these
things which thou
hast seen, and of those
things in the which I
will appear unto thee;
17 delivering thee from
the people, and *from*
the Gentiles, unto
whom now I send
thee, 18 to open their
eyes, *and* to turn
them from darkness
to light, and *from* the
power of Satan unto
God, that they may
receive forgiveness of
sins, and inheritance
among them which
are sanctified by faith
that is in me. 19 Where-
upon, O king Agrippa,

τὸ ὄνομα Ἰησοῦ τοῦ Ναζωραίου δεῖν πολλὰ ἐναντία
[7]the [8]name [9]of [10]Jesus [11]the [12]Nazaræan [1]I [2]ought [3]many [4]things [5]contrary
πρᾶξαι· 10 ὃ καὶ ἐποίησα ἐν Ἱεροσολύμοις, καὶ πολλούς [e]
to do. Which also I did in Jerusalem, and many
τῶν ἁγίων ἐγὼ [f]φυλακαῖς κατέκλεισα, τὴν παρὰ τῶν ἀρχ-
of the saints I in prisons shut up, the [2]from [3]the [4]chief
ιερέων ἐξουσίαν λαβών· ἀναιρουμένων.τε αὐτῶν
[5]priests [1]authority having received; and [2]being [3]put [4]to [5]death [1]they
κατήνεγκα.ψῆφον. 11 καὶ κατὰ πάσας τὰς συναγωγὰς
I gave [my] vote against [them]. And in all the synagogues
πολλάκις τιμωρῶν αὐτούς, ἠνάγκαζον βλασφημεῖν· περισ-
often punishing them, I compelled [them] to blaspheme. [4]Exceed-
σῶς τε ἐμμαινόμενος αὐτοῖς ἐδίωκον ἕως.καὶ εἰς
ingly [1]and [2]being [3]furious against them I persecuted [them] even as far as to
τὰς ἔξω πόλεις. 12 ἐν οἷς [g]καὶ‖ πορευόμενος εἰς τὴν Δα-
foreign cities. During which also journeying to Da-
μασκὸν μετ' ἐξουσίας καὶ ἐπιτροπῆς [h]τῆς παρὰ‖ τῶν ἀρχ-
mascus, with authority and a commission from the chief
ιερέων, 13 ἡμέρας.μέσης κατὰ τὴν ὁδὸν εἶδον, βασιλεῦ,
priests, at mid-day in the way I saw, O king,
οὐρανόθεν ὑπὲρ τὴν λαμπρότητα τοῦ ἡλίου περιλάμψαν
from heaven above the brightness of the sun [3]shining [4]round [5]about
με φῶς καὶ τοὺς σὺν ἐμοὶ πορευομένους. 14 πάντων.[i]δὲ‖
[6]me [1]a [2]light and those with me journeying. And all
καταπεσόντων ἡμῶν εἰς τὴν γῆν ἤκουσα φωνὴν [k]λαλοῦσαν‖
[3]having [4]fallen [5]down [1]of [2]us to the ground I heard a voice speaking
πρός με [l]καὶ λέγουσαν‖ τῇ Ἑβραΐδι διαλέκτῳ, Σαούλ, Σαούλ,
to me and saying in the Hebrew language, Saul, Saul,
τί με διώκεις; σκληρόν σοι πρὸς κέντρα λακτίζειν.
why me persecutest thou? [it is] hard for thee against goads to kick.
15 Ἐγὼ.δὲ [m]εἶπον,‖ Τίς εἶ κύριε; Ὁ.δὲ [n]εἶπεν, Ἐγώ εἰμι
And I said, Who art thou, Lord? And he said, I am
Ἰησοῦς ὃν σὺ διώκεις. 16 ἀλλὰ ἀνάστηθι, καὶ στῆθι ἐπὶ
Jesus whom thou persecutest: but rise up, and stand on
τοὺς.πόδας.σου· εἰς.τοῦτο.γὰρ ὤφθην σοι, προχειρίσασθαί
thy feet; for, for this purpose I appeared to thee, to appoint
σε ὑπηρέτην καὶ μάρτυρα ὧν.τε εἶδες ὧν.τε
thee an attendant and a witness both of what thou didst see and in what
ὀφθήσομαί σοι, 17 ἐξαιρούμενός σε ἐκ τοῦ λαοῦ καὶ [o]
I shall appear to thee, taking out thee from among the people and
τῶν ἐθνῶν, εἰς οὓς [p]νῦν σε ἀποστέλλω,‖ 18 ἀνοῖξαι ὀφθαλμοὺς
the nations, to whom now thee I send, to open [2]eyes
αὐτῶν, τοῦ.ἐπιστρέψαι ἀπὸ σκότους εἰς φῶς καὶ τῆς ἐξουσίας
[1]their, that [they] may turn from darkness to light and the authority
τοῦ σατανᾶ ἐπὶ τὸν θεόν, τοῦ.λαβεῖν αὐτοὺς ἄφεσιν ἁμαρ-
of Satan to God, that [2]may [3]receive [1]they remission of sins
τιῶν καὶ κλῆρον ἐν τοῖς ἡγιασμένοις πίστει τῇ
and inheritance among those that have been sanctified by faith that [is]
εἰς ἐμέ. 19 Ὅθεν, βασιλεῦ Ἀγρίππα, οὐκ.ἐγενόμην ἀπειθὴς
in me. Whereupon, O king Agrippa, I was not disobedient
τῇ οὐρανίῳ ὀπτασίᾳ, 20 ἀλλὰ τοῖς ἐν Δαμασκῷ πρῶτον [q]
to the heavenly vision; but to those in Damascus first

---

[e] + τε also LTTrA. [f] + ἐν in (prisons) GLTTrAW. [g] — καὶ LTTrA. [h] — τῆς παρὰ (*read* τῶν from the) L; — τῆς [Tr]W; — παρὰ TTr. [i] τε LTTrAW. [k] λέγουσαν LTTrA. [l] — καὶ λέγουσαν LTTrA. [m] εἶπα LTTrA. [n] + κύριος (*read* the Lord said) LTTrAW. [o] + ἐκ from among LTTrA. [p] ἐγὼ ἀποστέλλω σε (*omit* now) LTTrA; ἐγὼ σε ἀποστ. GW. [q] + τε (*read* and also) LTTrA.

καὶ [r]Ἱεροσολύμοις, [s]εἰς‖ πᾶσάν τε τὴν χώραν τῆς Ἰουδαίας
and Jerusalem, [2]to [3]all [1]and the region of Judæa
καὶ τοῖς ἔθνεσιν, [t]ἀπαγγέλλων‖ μετανοεῖν καὶ ἐπιστρέφειν
and to the nations declaring [to them] to repent and to turn
ἐπὶ τὸν θεόν, ἄξια τῆς μετανοίας ἔργα πράσσοντας. 21 ἕνεκα
to God, [3]worthy [4]of [5]repentance [2]works [1]doing. On account of
τούτων με [v]οἱ‖ Ἰουδαῖοι συλλαβόμενοι [w] ἐν τῷ ἱερῷ, ἐπει-
these things me the Jews having seized in the temple, at-
ρῶντο διαχειρίσασθαι. 22 ἐπικουρίας οὖν τυχὼν τῆς
tempted to kill. Aid therefore having obtained
[x]παρὰ‖ τοῦ θεοῦ ἄχρι τῆς.ἡμέρας.ταύτης ἕστηκα, [y]μαρτυρού-
from God unto this day I have stood, bearing wit-
μενος‖ μικρῷ.τε καὶ μεγάλῳ, οὐδὲν ἐκτὸς λέγων ὧν τε
ness both to small and to great, nothing else saying than what both
οἱ προφῆται ἐλάλησαν μελλόντων γίνεσθαι καὶ [z]Μωσῆς,‖
the prophets [3]said [4]was [5]about [6]to [7]happen [1]and [2]Moses,
23 εἰ παθητὸς ὁ χριστός, εἰ πρῶτος ἐξ ἀναστά-
whether [2]should [3]suffer [1]Christ; whether [he] first through resurrec-
σεως νεκρῶν φῶς μέλλει καταγγέλλειν τῷ [a] λαῷ καὶ τοῖς
tion of [the] dead [5]light [1]is [2]about [3]to [4]announce to the people and to the
ἔθνεσιν. 24 Ταῦτα.δὲ αὐτοῦ.ἀπολογουμένου, ὁ Φῆστος με-
nations. And [2]these [3]things [1]uttering in his defence, Festus with
γάλῃ τῇ φωνῇ [b]ἔφη,‖ Μαίνῃ Παῦλε· τὰ πολλά σε γράμ-
loud voice said, Thou art mad, Paul; much [3]thee [1]learn-
ματα εἰς μανίαν περιτρέπει. 25 Ὁ.δὲ [c], Οὐ.μαίνομαι, φησίν,
ing [4]to [5]madness [2]turns. But he, [2]I [3]am [4]not [5]mad, [1]says,
κράτιστε Φῆστε, [d]ἀλλ'‖ ἀληθείας καὶ σωφροσύνης ῥήματα
most noble Festus, but of truth and discreetness words
ἀποφθέγγομαι· 26 ἐπίσταται.γὰρ περὶ τούτων ὁ βασι-
I utter; for [3]is [4]informed [5]concerning [6]these [7]things [1]the [2]king
λεύς, πρὸς ὃν καὶ παῤῥησιαζόμενος λαλῶ· λανθάνειν.γὰρ
to whom also using boldness I speak. For hidden from
αὐτόν τι τούτων οὐ πείθομαι [e]οὐδέν·‖ οὐ γάρ
him any of these things [are] not I am persuaded; [6]not [1]for
ἐστιν ἐν γωνίᾳ πεπραγμένον τοῦτο. 27 πιστεύεις βασιλεῦ
[7]in [8]a [9]corner [3]has [5]been [6]done [2]this. Believest thou, king
Ἀγρίππα τοῖς προφήταις; οἶδα ὅτι πιστεύεις. 28 Ὁ δὲ
Agrippa, the prophets? I know that thou believest. And
Ἀγρίππας πρὸς τὸν Παῦλον [f]ἔφη,‖ Ἐν ὀλίγῳ με [g]πείθεις‖
Agrippa to Paul said, In a little [3]me [1]thou [2]persuadest
χριστιανὸν [h]γενέσθαι.‖ 29 Ὁ.δὲ.Παῦλος [i]εἶπεν,‖ [k]Εὐξαίμην‖ ἂν
a Christian to become. And Paul said, I would wish
τῷ θεῷ, καὶ ἐν ὀλίγῳ καὶ ἐν [l]πολλῷ‖ οὐ μόνον σε ἀλλὰ καὶ
to God, both in a little and in much not only thou but also
πάντας τοὺς ἀκούοντάς μου σήμερον γενέσθαι τοιούτους
all those hearing me this day should become such
ὁποῖος κἀγώ εἰμι, παρεκτὸς τῶν.δεσμῶν.τούτων. 30 [m]Καὶ
as I also am, except these bonds. And
ταῦτα εἰπόντος αὐτοῦ,‖ ἀνέστη [n] ὁ βασιλεὺς καὶ ὁ ἡγεμὼν
these things [2]having [3]said [1]he, [6]rose [7]up [4]the [5]king and the governor
ἥ τε Βερνίκη καὶ οἱ [o]συγκαθήμενοι‖ αὐτοῖς· 31 καὶ ἀνα-
also Bernice and those who sat with them, and having

I was not disobedient unto the heavenly vision: 20 but shewed first unto them of Damascus, and at Jerusalem, and throughout all the coasts of Judæa, and *then* to the Gentiles, that they should repent and turn to God, and do works meet for repentance. 21 For these causes the Jews caught me in the temple, and went about to kill *me*. 22 Having therefore obtained help of God, I continue unto this day, witnessing both to small and great, saying none other things than those which the prophets and Moses did say should come: 23 that Christ should suffer, *and* that he should be the first that should rise from the dead, and should shew light unto the people, and to the Gentiles. 24 And as he thus spake for himself, Festus said with a loud voice, Paul, thou art beside thyself; much learning doth make thee mad. 25 But he said, I am not mad, most noble Festus; but speak forth the words of truth and soberness. 26 For the king knoweth of these things, before whom also I speak freely: for I am persuaded that none of these things are hidden from him; for this thing was not done in a corner. 27 King Agrippa, believest thou the prophets? I know that thou believest. 28 Then Agrippa said unto Paul, Almost thou persuadest me to be a Christian. 29 And Paul said, I would to God, that not only thou, but also all that hear me this day, were both almost, and altogether such as I am, except these bonds. 30 And when he had thus spoken, the king rose up, and the governor, and Bernice, and they that sat with them: 31 and when they were gone

[r] + ἐν in L. [s] — εἰς LTTr[A]. [t] ἀπήγγελλον I was declaring EGLTTrAW. [v] — οἱ TTr. [w] + ὄντα being T. [x] ἀπὸ LTTrAW. [y] μαρτυρόμενος LTTrAW. [z] Μωϋσῆς GLTTrAW. [a] + τε (*read* both to the) LTTrA. [b] φησίν says LTTrA. [c] + Παῦλος (*read* Paul says) LTTrW. [d] ἀλλὰ LTTrA. [e] — οὐδέν L; οὐθέν T[Tr]A. [f] — ἔφη (*read* [said]) LTTrAW. [g] πείθῃ thou persuadest thyself A. [h] ποιῆσαι to make (me a Christian) LTTrA. [i] — εἶπεν (*read* [said]) LTTrA. [k] εὐξάμην T. [l] μεγάλῳ LTTrA. [m] — καὶ ταῦτα εἰπόντος αὐτοῦ GLTTrAW. [n] + τε both GLTTrAW. [o] συν- T.

aside, they talked be-
tween themselves, say-
ing, This man doeth
nothing worthy of
death or of bonds.
32 Then said Agrippa
unto Festus, This man
might have been set
at liberty, if he had
not appealed unto Cæ-
sar.

XXVII. And when
it was determined that
we should sail into
Italy, they delivered
Paul and certain other
prisoners unto *one*
named Julius, a cen-
turion of Augustus'
band. 2 And entering
into a ship of Adra-
myttium, we launched,
meaning to sail by the
coasts of Asia; *one*
Aristarchus, a Mace-
donian of Thessalo-
nica, being with us.
3 And the next *day* we
touched at Sidon. And
Julius courteously en-
treated Paul, and gave
him liberty to go unto
his friends to refresh
himself. 4 And when
we had launched from
thence, we sailed un-
der Cyprus, because
the winds were con-
trary. 5 And when
we had sailed over the
sea of Cilicia and
Pamphylia, we came
to Myra, *a city* of Ly-
cia. 6 And there the
centurion found a ship
of Alexandria sailing
into Italy; and he put
us therein. 7 And
when we had sailed
slowly many days, and
scarce were come over
against Cnidus, the
wind not suffering us,
we sailed under Crete,
over against Salmone;
8 and, hardly passing
it, came unto a place
which is called The
fair havens; nigh
whereunto was the
city *of* Lasea. 9 Now
when much time was
spent, and when sail-
ing was now danger-
ous, because the fast
was now already past,
Paul admonished *them*,
10 and said unto them,
Sirs, I perceive that
this voyage will be
with hurt and much
damage, not only of

χωρήσαντες ἐλάλουν πρὸς ἀλλήλους λέγοντες, "Οτι οὐδὲν
withdrawn they spoke to one another saying, Nothing
θανάτου [p]ἄξιον ἢ δεσμῶν" [q] πράσσει ὁ.ἄνθρωπος.οὗτος.
[2]of [3]death [1]worthy or of bonds does this man.
32 Ἀγρίππας.δὲ τῷ Φήστῳ ἔφη, Ἀπολελύσθαι [r]ἐδύνατο" ὁ
And Agrippa to Festus said, [4]Have [5]been [6]let [7]go [3]might
ἄνθρωπος.οὗτος εἰ μὴ.[s]ἐπεκέκλητο" Καίσαρα.
[1]this [2]man if he had not appealed to Cæsar.

27 Ὡς.δὲ ἐκρίθη τοῦ.ἀποπλεῖν ἡμᾶς εἰς τὴν Ἰταλίαν
But when it was decided that [2]should [3]sail [1]we to Italy
παρεδίδουν τόν.τε.Παῦλον καί τινας ἑτέρους δεσμώτας ἑκα-
they delivered up both Paul and certain other prisoners to a
τοντάρχῃ, ὀνόματι Ἰουλίῳ, σπείρης Σεβαστῆς. 2 ἐπιβάν-
centurion, by name Julius, of the band of Augustus. [2]Having [3]gone [4]on
τες δὲ πλοίῳ Ἀδραμυττηνῷ [t]μέλλοντες" πλεῖν [u] τοὺς κατὰ
[5]board [1]and a ship of Adramyttium about to navigate the [2]along
τὴν Ἀσίαν [v]τόπους ἀνήχθημεν, ὄντος σὺν ἡμῖν Ἀριστάρχου
[3]Asia [1]places we set sail, being with us Aristarchus
Μακεδόνος Θεσσαλονικέως. 3 τῇ.τε.ἑτέρᾳ κατήχθημεν εἰς
a Macedonian of Thessalonica. And the next [day] we landed at
Σιδῶνα· φιλανθρώπως.τε ὁ Ἰούλιος τῷ Παύλῳ χρησάμενος
Sidon. And [5]kindly [1]Julius [4]Paul [2]having [3]treated
ἐπέτρεψεν πρὸς [v] φίλους [w]πορευθέντα" ἐπιμελείας
allowed [him] [2]to [[3]his] [4]friends [1]going [[7]their] [6]care
τυχεῖν. 4 κἀκεῖθεν ἀναχθέντες ὑπεπλεύσαμεν τὴν Κύπρον
[5]to [6]receive. And thence setting sail we sailed under Cyprus
διὰ τὸ τοὺς ἀνέμους εἶναι ἐναντίους. 5 τό.τε.πέλαγος τὸ
because the winds were contrary. And the sea
κατὰ τὴν Κιλικίαν καὶ Παμφυλίαν διαπλεύσαντες [x]κατήλθομεν"
along Cilicia and Pamphylia having sailed over we came
εἰς [y]Μύρα" τῆς Λυκίας. 6 Κἀκεῖ εὑρὼν ὁ [z]ἑκατόνταρχος"
to Myra of Lycia. And there [3]having [4]found [1]the [2]centurion
πλοῖον Ἀλεξανδρῖνον πλέον εἰς τὴν Ἰταλίαν ἐνεβίβασεν
a ship of Alexandria sailing to Italy he caused [2]to [3]enter
ἡμᾶς εἰς αὐτό. 7 ἐν.ἱκαναῖς.δὲ ἡμέραις βραδυπλοοῦντες καὶ
[1]us into it. And for many days sailing slowly and
μόλις γενόμενοι κατὰ τὴν Κνίδον, μὴ προσεῶντος ἡμᾶς
hardly having come over against Cnidus, [3]not [4]suffering [5]us
τοῦ ἀνέμου, ὑπεπλεύσαμεν τὴν Κρήτην κατὰ Σαλμώνην·
[1]the [2]wind, we sailed under Crete over against Salmone;
8 μόλις.τε παραλεγόμενοι αὐτὴν ἤλθομεν εἰς τόπον τινὰ
and hardly coasting along it we came to a [2]place [1]certain
καλούμενον Καλοὺς Λιμένας, ᾧ.ἐγγὺς [a]ἦν πόλις" [b]Λασαία."
called Fair Havens, near which was a city of Lasæa.
9 Ἱκανοῦ δὲ χρόνου διαγενομένου καὶ ὄντος ἤδη ἐπισφαλοῦς
And much time having passed and being already dangerous
τοῦ πλοός, διὰ τὸ καὶ τὴν νηστείαν ἤδη παρεληλυθέναι,
the voyage, because also the fast already had past,
παρῄνει ὁ Παῦλος 10 λέγων αὐτοῖς, Ἄνδρες, θεωρῶ ὅτι μετὰ
[2]exhorted [1]Paul [4]saying [3]them, Men, I perceive that with
ὕβρεως καὶ πολλῆς ζημίας οὐ μόνον τοῦ [c]φόρτου" καὶ τοῦ
disaster and much loss not only of the cargo and of the

---

[p] ἢ δεσμῶν ἄξιον LTTr. [q] + τι T. [r] ἠδύνατο LW. [s] ἐπικέκλητο L. [t] μέλλοντι LTTrAW. [u] + εἰς in LTTr[A]. [v] + τοὺς the GLTTrAW. [w] πορευθέντι LTTrA. [x] κατήλθαμεν TTr. [y] Μύῤῥα LTTrA. [z] ἑκατοντάρχης LTTrA. [a] πόλις ἦν T. [b] Ἄλασσα Alassa L; Λασέα Lasea TrA. [c] φορτίου GLTTrAW

πλοίου ἀλλὰ καὶ τῶν.ψυχῶν.ἡμῶν μέλλειν ἔσεσθαι τον πλοῦν.
ship but also of our lives is about to be the voyage.
11 Ὁ.δὲ [d]ἑκατόνταρχος‖ τῷ κυβερνήτῃ καὶ τῷ ναυκλήρῳ
But the centurion by the steersman and the ship-owner
[e]ἐπείθετο μᾶλλον‖ ἢ τοῖς ὑπὸ [f]τοῦ‖ Παύλου λεγο-
was persuaded rather than by the things [2]by [3]Paul [1]spoken.
μένοις. 12 ἀνευθέτου.δὲ τοῦ λιμένος ὑπάρχοντος πρὸς παρα-
And ill-adapted the port being to winter
χειμασίαν, οἱ [g]πλείους‖ ἔθεντο.βουλὴν ἀναχθῆναι [h]κἀκεῖθεν,‖
in, the most counselled to set sail thence also,
[i]εἴπως‖ δύναιντο καταντήσαντες εἰς Φοίνικα παρα-
if by any means they might be able having arrived at Phœnice to
χειμάσαι, λιμένα τῆς Κρήτης βλέποντα κατὰ λίβα
winter [there], a port of Crete looking towards south-west
καὶ κατὰ χῶρον. 13 ὑποπνεύσαντος.δὲ νότου, δόξαν-
and towards north-west. And [4]blowing [5]gently [1]a [2]south [3]wind, think-
τες τῆς προθέσεως κεκρατηκέναι, ἄραντες ἆσσον
ing the purpose to have gained, having weighed [anchor] [4]close [5]by
παρελέγοντο τὴν Κρήτην. 14 μετ' οὐ πολὺ δὲ ἔβαλεν
[1]they [2]coasted [3]along Crete. [4]After [2]not [3]long [1]but there came
κατ' αὐτῆς ἄνεμος τυφωνικός, ὁ καλούμενος [k]εὐροκλύδων.‖
down it a [2]wind [1]tempestuous, called Euroclydon.
15 συναρπασθέντος.δὲ τοῦ πλοίου, καὶ μὴ δυναμένου ἀντ-
And [3]having [4]been [5]caught [1]the [2]ship, and not able to bring
οφθαλμεῖν τῷ ἀνέμῳ, ἐπιδόντες ἐφερόμεθα. 16 νησίον
[her] head to the wind, giving [her] up we were driven along. [6]Small [7]island
δέ τι ὑποδραμόντες καλούμενον [l]Κλαύδην‖ [m]μόλις
[1]but [4]a [5]certain [2]running [3]under called Clauda [2]hardly
ἰσχύσαμεν‖ περικρατεῖς γενέσθαι τῆς σκάφης· 17 ἣν ἄραν-
[1]we were able masters to become of the boat; which having taken
τες βοηθείαις ἐχρῶντο, ὑποζωννύντες τὸ πλοῖον· φοβούμενοί
up helps they used, undergirding the ship; [2]fearing
τε μὴ εἰς τὴν σύρτιν ἐκπέσωσιν, χαλάσαντες τὸ σκεῦος
[1]and lest into the quicksand they should fall, having lowered the gear
οὕτως ἐφέροντο. 18 Σφοδρῶς.δὲ χειμαζομένων ἡμῶν
so they were driven. But [3]violently [2]being [4]tempest-tossed [1]we
τῇ ἑξῆς ἐκβολὴν ἐποιοῦντο· 19 καὶ τῇ
on the next [day] [3]a [4]casting [5]out [[6]of [7]cargo] [1]they [2]made, and on the
τρίτῃ αὐτόχειρες τὴν σκευὴν τοῦ πλοίου [n]ἐῤῥίψαμεν·‖
third [day] with [our] own hands the equipment of the ship we cast away.
20 μήτε.δὲ ἡλίου μήτε ἄστρων ἐπιφαινόντων ἐπὶ πλείονας
And neither sun nor stars appearing for many
ἡμέρας, χειμῶνός.τε οὐκ ὀλίγου ἐπικειμένου, λοιπὸν περιῃ-
days, and [3]tempest [1]no [2]small lying on [us], henceforth was taken
ρεῖτο [o]πᾶσα ἐλπὶς‖ τοῦ.σώζεσθαι.ἡμᾶς. 21 πολλῆς.[p]δὲ‖ ἀσιτίας
away all hope of our being saved. And [3]a [4]long [5]abstinence
ὑπαρχούσης, τότε σταθεὶς ὁ Παῦλος ἐν μέσῳ.αὐτῶν εἶπεν,
[1]there [2]being, then [2]standing [3]up [1]Paul in their midst said,
Ἔδει μέν, ὦ ἄνδρες, πειθαρχήσαντάς μοι μὴ ἀνά-
It behoved [you] indeed, O men, having been obedient to me not to have
γεσθαι ἀπὸ τῆς Κρήτης κερδῆσαί.τε τὴν.ὕβριν.ταύτην καὶ
set sail from Crete and to have gained this disaster and

the lading and ship, but also of our lives. 11 Nevertheless the centurion believed the master and the owner of the ship, more than those things which were spoken by Paul. 12 And because the haven was not commodious to winter in, the more part advised to depart thence also, if by any means they might attain to Phenice, *and there* to winter; *which is* an haven of Crete, and lieth toward the south west and north west. 13 And when the south wind blew softly, supposing that they had obtained *their* purpose, loosing *thence*, they sailed close by Crete. 14 But not long after there arose against it a tempestuous wind, called Euroclydon. 15 And when the ship was caught, and could not bear up into the wind, we let *her* drive. 16 And running under a certain island which is called Clauda, we had much work to come by the boat: 17 which when they had taken up, they used helps, undergirding the ship; and, fearing lest they should fall into the quicksands, strake sail, and so were driven. 18 And we being exceedingly tossed with a tempest, the next *day* they lightened the ship; 19 and the third *day* we cast out with our own hands the tackling of the ship. 20 And when neither sun nor stars in many days appeared, and no small tempest lay on *us*, all hope that we should be saved was then taken away. 21 But after long abstinence Paul stood forth in the midst of them, and said, Sirs, ye should have hearkened unto me, and not have loosed from Crete, and to have gained this harm and loss.

---

[d] ἑκατοντάρχης GLTTrA. [e] μᾶλλον ἐπείθετο LTTrA. [f] — τοῦ LTTr[A]W. [g] πλείονες LTTrA. [h] ἐκεῖθεν thence LTTrA. [i] εἴ πως LTrA. [k] εὐρακύλων Euracylon LTTrAW; εὐρυκλύδων Euryclydon G. [l] Καῦδα Cauda LTr; Κλαῦδα T; K[λ]αῦδα A [m] ἰσχύσαμεν μόλις LTTrAW. [n] ἔῤῥιψαν they cast away GLTrAW; ἔριψαν T. [o] ἐλπὶς πᾶσα LTTrA. [p] τε LTTrAW.

22 And now I exhort
you to be of good
cheer: for there shall
be no loss of *any man's*
life among you, but of
the ship. 23 For there
stood by me this night
the angel of God,
whose I am, and whom
I serve, 24 saying, Fear
not, Paul; thou must
be brought before Cæ-
sar: and, lo, God hath
given thee all them
that sail with thee.
25 Wherefore, sirs, be
of good cheer: for I
believe God, that it
shall be even as it was
told me. 26 Howbeit
we must be cast upon
a certain island. 27 But
when the fourteenth
night was come, as we
were driven up and
down in Adria, about
midnight the shipmen
deemed that they drew
near to some country;
28 and sounded, and
found *it* twenty fa-
thoms: and when they
had gone a little fur-
ther, they sounded
again, and found *it* fifteen fathoms. 29 Then
fearing lest we should
have fallen upon rocks,
they cast four anchors
out of the stern, and
wished for the day.
30 And as the shipmen
were about to flee out
of the ship, when they
had let down the boat
into the sea, under
colour as though they
would have cast an-
chors out of the fore-
ship, 31 Paul said to
the centurion and to
the soldiers, Except
these abide in the ship,
ye cannot be saved.
32 Then the soldiers
cut off the ropes of
the boat, and let her
fall off. 33 And while
the day was coming
on, Paul besought
them all to take meat,
saying, This day is the
fourteenth day that ye
have tarried and con-
tinued fasting, hav-
ing taken nothing.
34 Wherefore I pray
you to take *some* meat:
for this is for your

τὴν ζημίαν. 22 καὶ [q]ταννῦν‖ παραινῶ ὑμᾶς εὐθυμεῖν·
loss: and now I exhort you to be of good cheer,
ἀποβολὴ.γὰρ ψυχῆς οὐδεμία ἔσται ἐξ ὑμῶν, πλὴν τοῦ
for [3]loss [4]of [5]life [1]not [2]any shall be from among you, only of the
πλοίου. 23 παρέστη.γάρ μοι [r]τῇ.νυκτὶ.ταύτῃ‖ [s]ἄγγελος‖ τοῦ
ship. For stood by me this night an angel
θεοῦ, οὗ εἰμι[t] ᾧ.καὶ λατρεύω,[s] 24 λέγων, Μὴ.φοβοῦ Παῦλε,
of God, whose I am and whom I serve, saying, Fear not, Paul;
Καίσαρί σε δεῖ παραστῆναι· καὶ ἰδοὺ κεχάρισταί σοι ὁ θεὸς
Cæsar thou must stand before; and lo [2]has [3]granted [4]to [5]thee [1]God
πάντας τοὺς πλέοντας μετὰ σοῦ. 25 Διὸ εὐθυμεῖτε ἄνδρες·
all those sailing with thee. Wherefore be of good cheer, men,
πιστεύω.γὰρ τῷ θεῷ ὅτι οὕτως ἔσται καθ' ὃν.τρόπον
for I believe God that thus it shall be according to the way
λελάληταί μοι. 26 εἰς.νῆσον.δέ τινα δεῖ.ἡμᾶς ἐκπεσεῖν.
it has been said to me. But on [3]island [1]a [2]certain we must fall.
27 Ὡς.δὲ τεσσαρεσκαιδεκάτη νὺξ ἐγένετο διαφερομένων
And when the fourteenth night was come [2]being [3]driven [4]about
ἡμῶν ἐν τῷ Ἀδρίᾳ, κατὰ μέσον τῆς νυκτὸς ὑπενόουν
[1]we in the Adriatic, towards [the] middle of the night [3]supposed
οἱ ναῦται προσάγειν τινὰ αὐτοῖς χώραν· 28 καὶ βολίσαντες
[1]the [2]sailors [6]neared [4]some [7]them [5]country, and having sounded
εὗρον ὀργυιὰς εἴκοσι· βραχὺ.δὲ διαστήσαντες καὶ πάλιν
they found [2]fathoms [1]twenty, and [3]a [4]little [1]having [2]gone [5]farther and again
βολίσαντες εὗρον ὀργυιὰς δεκαπέντε· 29 φοβούμενοί.τε
having sounded they found [2]fathoms [1]fifteen; and fearing
[v]μήπως‖ [w]εἰς‖ τραχεῖς τόπους [x]ἐκπέσωσιν,‖ ἐκ πρύμνης
lest on rocky places they should fall, out of [the] stern
ῥίψαντες ἀγκύρας τέσσαρας [y]ηὔχοντο‖ ἡμέραν γενέσθαι.
having cast [2]anchors [1]four they wished day to come.
30 τῶν.δὲ ναυτῶν ζητούντων φυγεῖν ἐκ τοῦ πλοίου, καὶ
But the sailors seeking to flee out of the ship, and
χαλασάντων τὴν σκάφην εἰς τὴν θάλασσαν, προφάσει ὡς ἐκ
having let down the boat into the sea, with pretext as from
[z]πρώρας‖ [a]μελλόντων ἀγκύρας‖ ἐκτείνειν, 31 εἶπεν ὁ Παῦ-
[the] prow being about [4]anchors [1]to [2]cast [3]out, [6]said [5]Paul
λος τῷ ἑκατοντάρχῃ καὶ τοῖς στρατιώταις, Ἐὰν.μὴ οὗτοι
to the centurion and to the soldiers, Unless these
μείνωσιν ἐν τῷ πλοίῳ, ὑμεῖς σωθῆναι οὐ.δύνασθε. 32 Τότε [b]οἱ
abide in the ship ye [2]be [3]saved [1]cannot. Then the
στρατιῶται ἀπέκοψαν‖ τὰ σχοινία τῆς σκάφης καὶ εἴασαν
soldiers cut away the ropes of the boat and let
αὐτὴν ἐκπεσεῖν. 33 ἄχρι.δὲ.οὗ [c]ἔμελλεν ἡμέρα‖ γίνεσθαι,
her fall. And until [2]was [3]about [1]day [4]to [5]come,
παρεκάλει ὁ Παῦλος ἅπαντας μεταλαβεῖν τροφῆς, λέγων,
[7]exhorted [6]Paul all to partake of food, saying,
Τεσσαρεσκαιδεκάτην σήμερον ἡμέραν προσδοκῶντες ἄσι-
[4]The [5]fourteenth [1]to-[2]day [[3]is] day watching without
τοι διατελεῖτε, [d]μηδὲν‖ [e]προσλαβόμενοι.‖ 34 διὸ παρα-
taking food ye continue, nothing having taken. Wherefore I ex-
καλῶ ὑμᾶς [f]προσλαβεῖν‖ τροφῆς· τοῦτο.γὰρ πρὸς τῆς
hort you to take food, for this for

---

[q] τὰ νῦν LTTrA. [r] ταύτῃ τῇ νυκτὶ GLTTrAW. [s] ἄγγελος placed after λατρεύω LTTrAW. [t] + ἐγώ LT[A]. [v] μήπω L; μήπου TTr; μή που A. [w] κατὰ against LTTrAW. [x] ἐκπέσωμεν we should fall GLTTrAW. [y] εὔχοντο TTrA. [z] πρῴρης LT. [a] ἀγκύρας μελλόντων LTTrA. [b] ἀπέκοψαν οἱ στρατιῶται LTTrA. [c] ἡμέρα ἤμελλεν (ἔμελλεν T) LTTrA. [d] μηθὲν LTTrA. [e] προσλαμβανόμενοι taking L. [f] μεταλαβεῖν to partake of GLTTrAW.

ὑμετέρας.σωτηρίας ὑπάρχει· [g]οὐδενὸς‖.γὰρ ὑμῶν θρὶξ [h]ἐκ‖
your safety is; for of no one of you a hair of
τῆς κεφαλῆς [i]πεσεῖται.‖ 35 [k]Εἰπὼν‖.δὲ ταῦτα καὶ λαβὼν
the head shall fall. And having said these things and having taken
ἄρτον εὐχαρίστησεν τῷ θεῷ ἐνώπιον πάντων, καὶ κλάσας
a loaf he gave thanks to God before all, and having broken [it]
ἤρξατο ἐσθίειν. 36 εὔθυμοι.δὲ γενόμενοι πάντες καὶ αὐ-
began to eat. And [4]of [5]good [6]cheer [2]having [3]become [1]all also them-
τοὶ προσελάβοντο τροφῆς· 37 [l]ἦμεν‖.δὲ [m]ἐν τῷ πλοίῳ αἱ
selves took food. And we were in the ship [2]the
πᾶσαι ψυχαὶ‖ διακόσιαι [n]ἑβδομηκονταέξ.‖ 38 κορεσθέντες.δὲ
[1]all souls two hundred [and] seventy six. And being satisfied
τροφῆς ἐκούφιζον τὸ πλοῖον, ἐκβαλλόμενοι τὸν σῖτον εἰς τὴν
with food they lightened the ship, casting out the wheat into the
θάλασσαν. 39 Ὅτε.δὲ ἡμέρα ἐγένετο τὴν γῆν οὐκ.ἐπεγίνωσκον·
sea. And when [3]day [1]it [2]was the land they did not recognize;
κόλπον.δέ τινα κατενόουν ἔχοντα αἰγιαλόν, εἰς ὃν [o]ἐβου-
but a [2]bay [1]certain they perceived having a shore, on which they
λεύσαντο‖ εἰ δύναιντο ἐξῶσαι τὸ πλοῖον. 40 καὶ τὰς
purposed if they should be able to drive the ship; and [4]the
ἀγκύρας περιελόντες εἴων εἰς τὴν θάλασσαν, ἅμα
[5]anchors [1]having [2]cut [3]away they left in the sea, at the same time
ἀνέντες τὰς ζευκτηρίας τῶν πηδαλίων· καὶ ἐπάραντες τὸν
having loosened the bands of the rudders, and having hoisted the
[p]ἀρτέμονα‖ τῇ πνεούσῃ κατεῖχον εἰς τὸν αἰγιαλόν. 41 περι-
foresail to the wind they made for the shore. [2]Having
πεσόντες δὲ εἰς τόπον διθάλασσον [q]ἐπώκειλαν‖ τὴν ναῦν·
[3]fallen [1]and into a place where two seas met they ran aground the vessel;
καὶ ἡ μὲν πρῷρα ἐρείσασα ἔμεινεν ἀσάλευτος, ἡ.δὲ
and the prow having stuck fast remained immovable, but the
πρύμνα ἐλύετο ὑπὸ τῆς βίας [r]τῶν κυμάτων.‖ 42 τῶν.δὲ
stern was broken by the violence of the waves. And of the
στρατιωτῶν βουλὴ ἐγένετο ἵνα τοὺς δεσμώτας ἀποκτείνωσιν,
soldiers [the] counsel was that the prisoners they should kill,
μήτις ἐκκολυμβήσας [s]διαφύγοι·‖ 43 ὁ.δὲ [t]ἑκατόνταρχος‖
lest anyone having swum out should escape. But the centurion
βουλόμενος διασῶσαι τὸν Παῦλον ἐκώλυσεν αὐτοὺς τοῦ
desiring to save Paul hindered them of [their]
βουλήματος, ἐκέλευσέν.τε τοὺς δυναμένους κολυμβᾷν, [v]ἀπορ-
purpose, and commanded those being able to swim, having
ῥίψαντας‖ πρώτους, ἐπὶ τὴν γῆν ἐξιέναι, 44 καὶ τοὺς
cast [themselves] off first, on the land to go out; and the
λοιπούς, οὓς μὲν ἐπὶ σανίσιν οὓς.δὲ ἐπί τινων.τῶν ἀπὸ τοῦ
rest, some indeed on boards and others on some things from the
πλοίου· καὶ οὕτως ἐγένετο πάντας διασωθῆναι ἐπὶ τὴν γῆν.
ship; and thus it came to pass all were brought safely to the land.

28 Καὶ διασωθέντες τότε [w]ἐπέγνωσαν‖ ὅτι Μελίτη ἡ
And having been saved then they knew that Melita the
νῆσος καλεῖται. 2 Οἱ.[x]δὲ‖ βάρβαροι [y]παρεῖχον‖ οὐ τὴν
island is called. And the barbarians shewed no
τυχοῦσαν φιλανθρωπίαν ἡμῖν· [z]ἀνάψαντες‖.γὰρ πυράν προσ-
common philanthropy to us; for having kindled a fire they

health: for there shall
not an hair fall from
the head of any of you
35 And when he had
thus spoken, he took
bread, and gave thanks
to God in presence of
them all: and when
he had broken *it*, he began to eat. 36 Then
were they all of good
cheer, and they also
took *some* meat. 37 And
we were in all in
the ship two hundred
threescore and sixteen
souls. 38 And when
they had eaten enough,
they lightened the
ship, and cast out the
wheat into the sea.
39 And when it was
day, they knew not
the land: but they
discovered a certain
creek with a shore,
into the which they
were minded, if it were
possible, to thrust in
the ship. 40 And when
they had taken up the
anchors, they commit-
ted *themselves* unto
the sea, and loosed the
rudder bands, and
hoised up the mainsail
to the wind, and made
toward shore. 41 And
falling into a place
where two seas met,
they ran the ship a-
ground; and the fore-
part stuck fast, and
remained unmoveable,
but the hinder part
was broken with the
violence of the waves.
42 And the soldiers'
counsel was to kill
the prisoners, lest any
of them should swim
out, and escape. 43 But
the centurion, willing
to save Paul, kept
them from *their* pur-
pose; and command-
ed that they which
could swim should
cast *themselves* first
into the sea, and get
to land: 44 and the
rest, some on boards,
and some on *broken*
pieces of the ship. And
so it came to pass,
that they escaped all
safe to land.

XXVIII. And when
they were escaped, then
they knew that the
island was called Me-
lita. 2 And the barbar-
ous people shewed us
no little kindness: for
they kindled a fire,

---

[g] οὐθενὸς L. [h] ἀπὸ LTTrA. [i] ἀπολεῖται shall perish GLTTrAW. [k] εἴπας LTTrA. [l] ἤμεθα LTTrAW. [m] αἱ πᾶσαι ψυχαὶ ἐν τῷ πλοίῳ LTTrAW. [n] ἑβδομήκοντα ἕξ GLTTrW. [o] ἐβουλεύοντο LTTrAW. [p] ἀρτέμωνα LTTrAW. [q] ἐπέκειλαν LTTrA. [r] — τῶν κυμάτων LT[Tr A]. [s] διαφύγῃ GLTTrAW. [t] ἑκατοντάρχης LTTrA. [v] ἀπορίψαντας T. [w] ἐπέγνωμεν we knew LTTrAW. [x] τε LTTrAW. [y] παρεῖχαν LTTrA. [z] ἅψαντες LTTrAW.

and received us every
one, because of the pre-
sent rain, and because
of the cold. 3 And
when Paul had ga-
thered a bundle of
sticks, and laid *them*
on the fire, there
came a viper out of
the heat, and fastened
on his hand. 4 And
when the barbarians
saw the *venomous*
beast hang on his
hand, they said among
themselves, No doubt
this man is a mur-
derer, whom, though
he hath escaped the
sea, yet vengeance
suffereth not to live.
5 And he shook off the
beast into the fire, and
felt no harm. 6 How-
beit they looked when
he should have swol-
len, or fallen down
dead suddenly: but
after they had looked
a great while, and saw
no harm come to him,
they changed their
minds, and said that
he was a god. 7 In the
same quarters were
possessions of the chief
man of the island,
whose name was Pub-
lius; who received us,
and lodged us three
days courteously.
8 And it came to pass,
that the father of Pub-
lius lay sick of a fever
and of a bloody flux: to
whom Paul entered in,
and prayed, and laid
his hands on him, and
healed him. 9 So
when this was done,
others also, which had
diseases in the island,
came, and were healed:
10 who also honoured
us with many hon-
ours; and when we
departed, they laded
us with such things as
were necessary.

11 And after three
months we departed in
a ship of Alexandria,
which had wintered in
the isle, whose sign
was Castor and Pol-
lux. 12 And landing
at Syracuse, we tar-
ried *there* three days.
13 And from thence we
fetched a compass, and
came to Rhegium: and

ελάβοντο πάντας ἡμᾶς, διὰ τὸν ὑετὸν τὸν ἐφεστῶτα καὶ
received all of us, because of the rain that was present and
διὰ τὸ ψύχος. 3 Συστρέψαντος.δὲ τοῦ Παύλου φρυγάνων[a]
because of the cold. And [2]having [3]gathered [1]Paul [6]of [7]sticks
πλῆθος, καὶ ἐπιθέντος ἐπὶ τὴν πυρὰν ἔχιδνα [b]ἐκ‖ τῆς
[4]a [5]quantity, and having laid [them] on the fire a viper out of the
θέρμης [c]ἐξελθοῦσα‖ καθῆψεν τῆς-χειρὸς-αὐτοῦ. 4 ὡς.δὲ [d]εἶδον‖
heat having come wound about his hand. And when [3]saw
οἱ βάρβαροι κρεμάμενον τὸ θηρίον ἐκ τῆς-χειρὸς-αὐτοῦ
[1]the [2]barbarians [6]hanging [4]the [5]beast from his hand
[e]ἔλεγον πρὸς ἀλλήλους,‖ Πάντως φονεύς ἐστιν ὁ ἄνθρωπος
they said to one another, By all means a murderer is [2]man
οὗτος, ὃν διασωθέντα ἐκ τῆς θαλάσσης ἡ δίκη ζῆν οὐκ
[1]this, whom having been saved from the sea justice [3]to [4]live [2]not
εἴασεν. 5 Ὁ μὲν οὖν [f]ἀποτινάξας‖ τὸ θηρίον εἰς τὸ πῦρ
[1]permitted. He indeed then having shaken off the beast into the fire
ἔπαθεν οὐδὲν κακόν. 6 οἱ.δὲ προσεδόκων αὐτὸν μέλλειν
suffered no injury. But they were expecting him to be about
[g]πίμπρασθαι‖ ἢ καταπίπτειν ἄφνω νεκρόν· ἐπὶ.πολὺ.δὲ
to become inflamed or to fall down suddenly dead. But for a long time
αὐτῶν προσδοκώντων καὶ θεωρούντων μηδὲν ἄτοπον εἰς αὐτὸν
they expecting and seeing nothing amiss to him
γινόμενον, [h]μεταβαλλόμενοι‖ ἔλεγον [i]θεὸν αὐτὸν εἶναι.‖
happening, changing their opinion said a god he was.
7 Ἐν.δὲ τοῖς περὶ τὸν.τόπον.ἐκεῖνον ὑπῆρχεν χωρία
Now in the [parts] about that place were lands
τῷ πρώτῳ τῆς νήσου, ὀνόματι Ποπλίῳ, ὃς ἀνα-
belonging to the chief of the island, by name Publius, who having
δεξάμενος ἡμᾶς [k]τρεῖς ἡμέρας‖ φιλοφρόνως ἐξένισεν.
received us three days in a friendly way lodged [us].
8 ἐγένετο.δὲ τὸν πατέρα τοῦ Ποπλίου πυρετοῖς καὶ [l]δυσεν-
And it happened the father of Publius [4]fevers [5]and [6]dysen-
τερίᾳ‖ συνεχόμενον κατακεῖσθαι· πρὸς ὃν ὁ Παῦλος εἰσελ-
tery [2]oppressed [3]with [1]lay, to whom Paul having en-
θὼν καὶ προσευξάμενος, ἐπιθεὶς τὰς χεῖρας αὐτῷ ἰάσατο
tered and having prayed, having laid on [[2]his] [3]hands [1]him cured
αὐτόν. 9 τούτου [m]οὖν‖ γενομένου καὶ οἱ λοιποὶ οἱ [n]ἔχον-
him. This therefore having taken place also the rest who had
τες ἀσθενείας ἐν τῇ νήσῳ‖ προσήρχοντο καὶ ἐθεραπεύοντο
infirmities in the island came and were healed:
10 οἳ καὶ πολλαῖς τιμαῖς ἐτίμησαν ἡμᾶς, καὶ ἀναγομένοις
who also with many honours honoured us, and on setting sail
ἐπέθεντο τὰ πρὸς [o]τὴν χρείαν.‖
they laid on [us] the things for [our] need.

11 Μετὰ.δὲ τρεῖς μῆνας ἀνήχθημεν ἐν πλοίῳ παρακεχει-
And after three months we sailed in a ship which had
μακότι ἐν τῇ νήσῳ, Ἀλεξανδρίνῳ, παρασήμῳ Διοσκούροις·
wintered in the island, an Alexandrian, with an ensign [the] Dioscuri.
12 καὶ καταχθέντες εἰς Συρακούσας ἐπεμείναμεν [p]ἡμέρας
And having been brought to at Syracuse we remained [2]days
τρεῖς·‖ 13 ὅθεν περιελθόντες κατηντήσαμεν εἰς Ῥήγιον, καὶ
[1]three. Whence having gone round we arrived at Rhegium; and

[a] + τι (*read* a certain quantity) LTTrAW. [b] ἀπὸ from LTTrAW. [c] διεξελθοῦσα AW. [d] εἶδαν Tr. [e] πρὸς ἀλλήλους ἔλεγον LTTrA. [f] ἀποτιναξάμενος W. [g] ἐμπιπρᾶσθαι T. [h] μεταβαλόμενοι TrA. [i] αὐτὸν εἶναι θεόν LTTrAW. [k] ἡμέρας τρεῖς A. [l] δυσεντερίῳ LTTrAW. [m] δὲ and (this) LTTrA. [n] ἐν τῇ νήσῳ ἔχοντες ἀσθενείας LTTrA. [o] τὰς χρείας needs LTTrAW. [p] ἡμέραις τρισίν L.

μετὰ μίαν ἡμέραν ἐπιγενομένου νότου δευτεραῖοι
after one day, [4]having [5]come [6]on [1]a [2]south [3]wind. on the second day
ἤλθομεν εἰς Ποτιόλους· 14 οὗ εὑρόντες ἀδελφοὺς παρε-
we came to Puteoli; where having found brethren we were
κλήθημεν [q]ἐπ'‖ αὐτοῖς ἐπιμεῖναι ἡμέρας ἑπτά· καὶ οὕτως [r]εἰς
entreated [3]with [4]them [1]to [2]remain [6]days [5]seven. And thus to
τὴν Ῥώμην ἤλθομεν.‖ 15 κἀκεῖθεν οἱ ἀδελφοὶ ἀκούσαντες
Rome we came. And thence the brethren having heard
τὰ περὶ ἡμῶν [s]ἐξῆλθον‖ εἰς ἀπάντησιν ἡμῖν [t]ἄχρις‖
the things concerning us came out to meet us as far as
Ἀππίου.Φόρου καὶ Τριῶν Ταβερνῶν· οὓς ἰδὼν ὁ Παῦ-
[the] market-place of Appius and Three Taverns; whom [2]seeing [1]Paul,
λος, εὐχαριστήσας τῷ θεῷ ἔλαβεν θάρσος.
having given thanks to God he took courage.

16 "Ὅτε.δὲ [v]ἤλθομεν‖ εἰς [w]Ῥώμην [x]ὁ ἑκατόνταρχος παρέ-
And when we came to Rome the centurion de-
δωκεν τοὺς δεσμίους τῷ στρατοπεδάρχῃ·‖ [y]τῷ.δὲ.Παύλῳ
livered the prisoners to the commander of the camp, but Paul
ἐπετράπη‖ μένειν καθ'.ἑαυτόν, σὺν τῷ φυλάσσοντι αὐτὸν
was allowed to remain by himself, with the [2]who [3]kept [4]him
στρατιώτῃ. 17 Ἐγένετο.δὲ μετὰ ἡμέρας τρεῖς [z]συγκαλέσασ-
[1]soldier. And it came to pass after [2]days [1]three [4]called [5]to-
θαι‖ [a]τὸν Παῦλον‖ τοὺς ὄντας τῶν Ἰουδαίων πρώτους·
gether [3]Paul those who were [3]of [4]the [5]Jews [1]chief [2]ones.
συνελθόντων.δὲ αὐτῶν ἔλεγεν πρὸς αὐτούς, [b]Ἄνδρες
And [2]having [3]come [4]together [1]they he said to them, Men
ἀδελφοί, ἐγὼ‖ οὐδὲν ἐναντίον ποιήσας τῷ λαῷ ἢ τοῖς
brethren, I [3]nothing [4]against [1]having [2]done the people or the
ἔθεσιν τοῖς πατρῴοις δέσμιος ἐξ Ἱεροσολύμων παρεδόθην
[2]customs [1]ancestral a prisoner from Jerusalem was delivered
εἰς τὰς χεῖρας τῶν Ῥωμαίων· 18 οἵτινες ἀνακρίναντές με
into the hands of the Romans, who having examined me
ἐβούλοντο ἀπολῦσαι, διὰ τὸ μηδεμίαν αἰτίαν θανάτου
wished to let [me] go, because not one cause of death
ὑπάρχειν ἐν ἐμοί. 19 ἀντιλεγόντων.δὲ τῶν Ἰουδαίων
was there in me. But [3]speaking [4]against [5it] [1]the [2]Jews
ἠναγκάσθην ἐπικαλέσασθαι Καίσαρα, οὐχ ὡς τοῦ.ἔθνους.μου
I was compelled to appeal to Cæsar, not as [6]my [7]nation
ἔχων τι [c]κατηγορῆσαι.‖ 20 διὰ ταύτην οὖν τὴν αἰτίαν
[1]having [2]anything [3]to [4]lay [5]against. For this [2]therefore [1]cause
παρεκάλεσα ὑμᾶς ἰδεῖν καὶ προσλαλῆσαι· [d]ἕνεκεν‖.γὰρ
I called for you to see and to speak to [you]; for on account of
τῆς ἐλπίδος τοῦ Ἰσραὴλ τὴν.ἅλυσιν.ταύτην περίκειμαι.
the hope of Israel this chain I have around [me].
21 Οἱ.δὲ πρὸς αὐτὸν [e]εἶπον,‖ Ἡμεῖς οὔτε γράμματα [f]περὶ
And they to him said, We neither letters concerning
σοῦ ἐδεξάμεθα‖ ἀπὸ τῆς Ἰουδαίας οὔτε παραγενόμενός τις
thee received from Judæa, nor having arrived any one
τῶν ἀδελφῶν ἀπήγγειλεν ἢ ἐλάλησέν τι περὶ σοῦ
of the brethren reported or said anything [2]concerning [3]thee
πονηρόν. 22 ἀξιοῦμεν.δὲ παρὰ σοῦ ἀκοῦσαι ἃ φρονεῖς·
[1]evil. But we think well from thee to hear what thou thinkest,

after one day the south wind blew, and we came the next day to Puteoli:
14 where we found brethren, and were desired to tarry with them seven days: and so we went toward Rome.
15 And from thence, when the brethren heard of us, they came to meet us as far as Appii forum, and The three taverns: whom when Paul saw, he thanked God, and took courage.

16 And when we came to Rome, the centurion delivered the prisoners to the captain of the guard: but Paul was suffered to dwell by himself with a soldier that kept him.
17 And it came to pass, that after three days Paul called the chief of the Jews together: and when they were come together, he said unto them, Men *and* brethren, though I have committed nothing against the people, or customs of our fathers, yet was I delivered prisoner from Jerusalem into the hands of the Romans.
18 Who, when they had examined me, would have let *me* go, because there was no cause of death in me.
19 But when the Jews spake against *it*, I was constrained to appeal unto Cæsar; not that I had ought to accuse my nation of.
20 For this cause therefore have I called for you, to see *you*, and to speak with *you*: because that for the hope of Israel I am bound with this chain.
21 And they said unto him, We neither received letters out of Judæa concerning thee, neither any of the brethren that came shewed or spake any harm of thee.
22 But we desire to hear of thee what thou thinkest:

[q] παρ' LTTrA. [r] ἤλθαμεν εἰς Ῥώμην L; εἰς τὴν Ῥώμην ἤλθαμεν TTrA. [s] ἦλθαν came TTrA; ἦλθον L. [t] ἄχρι TTrA. [v] εἰσήλθομεν we came in LTA; εἰσήλθαμεν Tr. [w] + τὴν T. [x] — ὁ ἑκατόνταρχος .... στρατοπεδάρχῃ LTTrA. [y] ἐπετράπη τῷ Παύλῳ (*omit* but) LTTrA. [z] συν- T. [a] αὐτὸν he GLTTrAW. [b] Ἐγώ, ἄνδρες ἀδελφοί, LTTrA. [c] κατηγορεῖν LTTrA. [d] εἵνεκεν T. [e] εἶπαν LTTrA. [f] ἐδεξάμεθα περὶ σοῦ L.

for as concerning this sect, we know that every where it is spoken against. 23 And when they had appointed him a day, there came many to him into *his* lodging; to whom he expounded and testified the kingdom of God, persuading them concerning Jesus, both out of the law of Moses, and *out of* the prophets, from morning till evening. 24 And some believed the things which were spoken, and some believed not. 25 And when they agreed not among themselves, they departed, after that Paul had spoken one word, Well spake the Holy Ghost by Esaias the prophet unto our fathers, 26 saying, Go unto this people, and say, Hearing ye shall hear, and shall not understand; and seeing ye shall see, and not perceive: 27 for the heart of this people is waxed gross, and their ears are dull of hearing, and their eyes have they closed; lest they should see with *their* eyes, and hear with *their* ears, and understand with *their* heart, and should be converted, and I should heal them. 28 Be it known therefore unto you, that the salvation of God is sent unto the Gentiles, and *that* they will hear it. 29 And when he had said these words, the Jews departed, and had great reasoning among themselves.

περὶ.μὲν.γὰρ τῆς.αἱρέσεως.ταύτης γνωστόν [g]ἐστιν ἡμῖν‖
for indeed as concerning this sect known it is to us
ὅτι πανταχοῦ ἀντιλέγεται. 23 Ταξάμενοι.δὲ αὐτῷ ἡμέραν
that everywhere it is spoken against. And having appointed him a day
[h]ἧκον‖ πρὸς αὐτὸν εἰς τὴν ξενίαν πλείονες· οἷς ἐξετίθετο
came to him to the lodging many, to whom he expounded,
διαμαρτυρόμενος τὴν βασιλείαν τοῦ θεοῦ, πείθων.τε αὐτοὺς
fully testifying the kingdom of God, and persuading them
[i]τὰ‖ περὶ τοῦ Ἰησοῦ, ἀπό.τε τοῦ νόμου [k]Μωσέως‖
the things concerning Jesus, both from the law of Moses
καὶ τῶν προφητῶν, ἀπὸ πρωῒ ἕως ἑσπέρας. 24 καὶ οἱ
and the prophets, from morning to evening. And some
μὲν ἐπείθοντο τοῖς λεγομένοις, οἱ.δὲ ἠπίστουν.
indeed were persuaded of the things spoken, but some disbelieved.
25 ἀσύμφωνοι.[l]δὲ‖.ὄντες πρὸς ἀλλήλους ἀπελύοντο, εἰπόν-
And disagreeing with one another they departed; [2]having
τος τοῦ Παύλου ῥῆμα ἕν, Ὅτι καλῶς τὸ πνεῦμα τὸ ἅγιον
[3]spoken [1]Paul [5]word [4]one, Well the Spirit the Holy
ἐλάλησεν διὰ Ἡσαΐου τοῦ προφήτου πρὸς τοὺς πατέρας
spoke by Esaias the prophet to [2]fathers
[m]ἡμῶν,‖ 26 [n]λέγον,‖ Πορεύθητι πρὸς τὸν.λαὸν.τοῦτον καὶ
[1]our, saying, Go to this people, and
[o]εἰπέ,‖ Ἀκοῇ ἀκούσετε, καὶ οὐ.μὴ συνῆτε· καὶ βλέποντες
say, In hearing ye shall hear, and in no wise understand, and seeing
βλέψετε, καὶ οὐ.μὴ ἴδητε· 27 ἐπαχύνθη.γὰρ ἡ καρδία
ye shall see, and in no wise perceive. For has grown fat the heart
τοῦ.λαοῦ.τούτου, καὶ τοῖς ὠσὶν βαρέως ἤκουσαν, καὶ
of this people, and with the ears heavily they have heard, and
τοὺς.ὀφθαλμοὺς.αὐτῶν ἐκάμμυσαν· μήποτε ἴδωσιν τοῖς
their eyes they have closed, lest they should see with the
ὀφθαλμοῖς, καὶ τοῖς ὠσὶν ἀκούσωσιν, καὶ τῇ καρδίᾳ
eyes, and with the ears they should hear, and with the heart
συνῶσιν, καὶ ἐπιστρέψωσιν, καὶ [p]ἰάσωμαι‖ αὐτούς.
they should understand, and should be converted, and I should heal them.
28 Γνωστὸν οὖν [q]ἔστω ὑμῖν,‖ ὅτι τοῖς ἔθνεσιν ἀπεστάλη [r]
Known therefore be it to you, that to the nations is sent
τὸ σωτήριον τοῦ θεοῦ, αὐτοὶ.καὶ ἀκούσονται. 29 [s]Καὶ ταῦτα
the salvation of God; and they will hear. And these things
αὐτοῦ εἰπόντος ἀπῆλθον οἱ Ἰουδαῖοι, πολλὴν ἔχοντες ἐν
he having said [3]went [4]away [1]the [2]Jews, [6]much [5]having [8]among
ἑαυτοῖς συζήτησιν.‖
[9]themselves [7]discussion.

30 And Paul dwelt two whole years in his own hired house, and received all that came in unto him, 31 preaching the kingdom of God, and teaching those things which concern the Lord Jesus Christ, with all confidence, no man forbidding him.

30 [t]Ἔμεινεν .δὲ [v]ὁ Παῦλος‖ διετίαν ὅλην ἐν ἰδίῳ μισ-
And [2]abode [1]Paul two [2]years [1]whole in his own hired
θώματι, καὶ ἀπεδέχετο πάντας τοὺς εἰσπορευομένους πρὸς
house, and welcomed all who came in to
αὐτόν, 31 κηρύσσων τὴν βασιλείαν τοῦ θεοῦ, καὶ διδάσκων
him, proclaiming the kingdom of God, and teaching
τὰ περὶ τοῦ κυρίου Ἰησοῦ [w]χριστοῦ,‖ μετὰ πάσης
the things concerning the Lord Jesus Christ, with all
παῤῥησίας ἀκωλύτως. [x]
freedom unhinderedly.

---

g ἡμῖν ἐστιν LTTrA. h ἦλθον LTTrA. i — τὰ LTTrA. k Μωϋσέως GLTTrAW. l τε T. m ὑμῶν your LTTrA. n λέγων TTrA. o εἰπόν GLTTrAW. p ἰάσομαι I shall heal TTrA. q ὑμῖν ἔστω A. r + τοῦτο (*read* this salvation) LTTrA. s — *verse* 29 LTTrA. t Ἐνέμεινεν TTrA. v — ὁ Παῦλος (*read* he abode) GLTTrAW. w — χριστοῦ T. x + Πράξεις Ἀποστόλων TrA.

[a]ΠΑΥΛΟΥ ΤΟΥ ΑΠΟΣΤΟΛΟΥ Η ΠΡΟΣ ΡΩΜΑΙΟΥΣ ΕΠΙΣΤΟΛΗ.[||]

[3]OF [4]PAUL [5]THE [6]APOSTLE [1]THE [7]TO [[8]THE] [9]ROMANS [2]EPISTLE.

ΠΑΥΛΟΣ δοῦλος [b]Ἰησοῦ χριστοῦ,|| κλητὸς ἀπόστολος, ἀφω-
Paul, bondman of Jesus Christ, a called apostle, sepa-
ρισμένος εἰς εὐαγγέλιον θεοῦ, 2 ὃ προεπηγγείλατο διὰ
rated to glad tidings of God, which he before promised through
τῶν.προφητῶν.αὐτοῦ ἐν γραφαῖς ἁγίαις, 3 περὶ τοῦ υἱοῦ
his prophets in [2]writings [1]holy, concerning [2]Son
αὐτοῦ, τοῦ γενομένου ἐκ σπέρματος [c]Δαβὶδ|| κατὰ
[1]his, who came of [the] seed of David according to
σάρκα, 4 τοῦ ὁρισθέντος υἱοῦ θεοῦ ἐν δυνάμει, κατὰ
flesh, who was marked out Son of God in power, according to [the]
πνεῦμα ἁγιωσύνης, ἐξ ἀναστάσεως νεκρῶν, Ἰησοῦ χριστοῦ
Spirit of holiness, by resurrection of [the] dead— Jesus Christ
τοῦ.κυρίου.ἡμῶν, 5 δι' οὗ ἐλάβομεν χάριν καὶ ἀποστολὴν
our Lord; by whom we received grace and apostleship
εἰς ὑπακοὴν πίστεως ἐν πᾶσιν τοῖς ἔθνεσιν, ὑπὲρ τοῦ
unto obedience of faith among all the nations, in behalf of
ὀνόματος.αὐτοῦ, 6 ἐν οἷς ἐστε καὶ ὑμεῖς, κλητοὶ Ἰησοῦ
his name, among whom are also ye, called of Jesus
χριστοῦ· 7 πᾶσιν τοῖς οὖσιν ἐν Ῥώμῃ ἀγαπητοῖς θεοῦ,
Christ: to all those who are in Rome beloved of God,
κλητοῖς ἁγίοις· χάρις ὑμῖν καὶ εἰρήνη ἀπὸ θεοῦ πατρὸς.ἡμῶν
called saints: grace to you and peace from God our Father
καὶ κυρίου Ἰησοῦ χριστοῦ.
and Lord Jesus Christ.

8 Πρῶτον μὲν εὐχαριστῶ τῷ.θεῷ.μου διὰ Ἰησοῦ χριστοῦ
First, I thank my God through Jesus Christ
[d]ὑπὲρ|| πάντων ὑμῶν, ὅτι ἡ.πίστις.ὑμῶν καταγγέλλεται ἐν
for [2]all [1]you, that your faith is announced in
ὅλῳ τῷ κόσμῳ· 9 μάρτυς.γάρ μου ἐστὶν ὁ θεός, ᾧ λατρεύω
[2]whole [1]the world; for [4]witness [3]my [2]is [1]God, whom I serve
ἐν τῷ.πνεύματί.μου ἐν τῷ εὐαγγελίῳ τοῦ.υἱοῦ.αὐτοῦ, ὡς
in my spirit in the glad tidings of his Son, how
ἀδιαλείπτως μνείαν ὑμῶν ποιοῦμαι, 10 πάντοτε ἐπὶ τῶν
unceasingly mention of you I make, always at
προσευχῶν.μου δεόμενος, [e]εἴπως|| ἤδη ποτὲ εὐοδωθήσομαι
my prayers beseeching, if by any means now at length I shall be prospered
ἐν τῷ θελήματι τοῦ θεοῦ ἐλθεῖν πρὸς ὑμᾶς· 11 ἐπιποθῶ.γὰρ
by the will of God to come to you. For I long
ἰδεῖν ὑμᾶς, ἵνα τι μεταδῶ χάρισμα ὑμῖν πνευματικόν,
to see you, that some [3]I [4]may [5]impart [2]gift [6]to [7]you [1]spiritual,
εἰς τὸ στηριχθῆναι ὑμᾶς, 12 τοῦτο.δέ.ἐστιν, [f]συμπαρα-
to the [end] [2]be [3]established [1]ye, that is, to be comforted

PAUL, a servant of Jesus Christ, called *to be* an apostle, separated unto the gospel of God, 2 (which he had promised afore by his prophets in the holy scriptures,) 3 concerning his Son Jesus Christ our Lord, which was made of the seed of David according to the flesh; 4 and declared *to be* the Son of God with power, according to the spirit of holiness, by the resurrection from the dead: 5 by whom we have received grace and apostleship, for obedience to the faith among all nations, for his name: 6 among whom are ye also the called of Jesus Christ: 7 to all that be in Rome, beloved of God, called *to be* saints: Grace to you and peace from God our Father, and the Lord Jesus Christ.

8 First, I thank my God through Jesus Christ for you all, that your faith is spoken of throughout the whole world. 9 For God is my witness, whom I serve with my spirit in the gospel of his Son, that without ceasing I make mention of you always in my prayers; 10 making request, if by any means now at length I might have a prosperous journey by the will of God to come unto you. 11 For I long to see you, that I may impart unto you some spiritual gift, to the end ye may be established; 12 that is, that I may be comforted together with

---

[a] **Παύλου Ἐπιστολὴ πρὸς Ῥωμαίους** G; **Πρὸς Ῥω.** TAW; **Ἐπιστολαὶ Παύλου. Πρὸς Ῥω.** Epistles of Paul. To [the] Romans LTr. [b] χριστοῦ Ἰησοῦ TTr. [c] **Δαυείδ** LTTrA; **Δαυὶδ** GW. [d] **περὶ** LTTrAW. [e] **εἴ πως** LTrA. [f] **συν-** TA.

you by the mutual
faith both of you and
me. 13 Now I would
not have you ignorant,
brethren, that oftentimes
I purposed to
come unto you, (but
was let hitherto,) that
I might have some
fruit among you also,
even as among other
Gentiles. 14 I am
debtor both to the
Greeks, and to the
Barbarians; both to
the wise, and to the
unwise. 15 So, as much
as in me is, I am ready
to preach the gospel to
you that are at Rome
also. 16 For I am not
ashamed of the gospel
of Christ: for it is the
power of God unto
salvation to every one
that believeth; to the
Jew first, and also to
the Greek. 17 For
therein is the righteousness
of God revealed
from faith to
faith: as it is written,
The just shall live by
faith.

18 For the wrath of
God is revealed from
heaven against all
ungodliness and unrighteousness
of men,
who hold the truth
in unrighteousness;
19 because that which
may be known of God
is manifest in them;
for God hath shewed
it unto them. 20 For
the invisible things of
him from the creation
of the world are clearly
seen, being understood
by the things that are
made, *even* his eternal
power and Godhead;
so that they are without
excuse: 21 because
that, when they knew
God, they glorified
him not as God, neither
were thankful;
but became vain in
their imaginations,
and their foolish heart
was darkened. 22 Professing
themselves to
be wise, they became
fools, 23 and changed
the glory of the uncorruptible
God into
an image made like to
corruptible man, and
to birds, and fourfooted
beasts, and creeping
things. 24 Wherefore
God also gave
them up to uncleanness
through the lusts
of their own hearts, to

κληθῆναι‖ ἐν ὑμῖν διὰ τῆς ἐν ἀλλήλοις πίστεως ὑμῶν.τε
together among you, through the [2]in [3]one [4]another [1]faith, both yours
καὶ ἐμοῦ· 13 οὐ.θέλω.δὲ ὑμᾶς ἀγνοεῖν, ἀδελφοί, ὅτι πολ-
and mine. But I do not wish you to be ignorant, brethren, that many
λάκις προεθέμην ἐλθεῖν πρὸς ὑμᾶς, καὶ ἐκωλύθην ἄχρι τοῦ
times I proposed to come to you, and was hindered until the
δεῦρο, ἵνα [g]καρπόν τινα‖ σχῶ καὶ ἐν ὑμῖν, καθὼς
present, that [2]fruit [1]some I might have also among you, according as
καὶ ἐν τοῖς λοιποῖς ἔθνεσιν. 14 Ἕλλησίν.τε καὶ βαρβάροις,
also among the other nations. Both to Greeks and barbarians,
σοφοῖς.τε καὶ ἀνοήτοις, ὀφειλέτης εἰμί· 15 οὕτως τὸ κατ' ἐμὲ
both to wise and unintelligent, a debtor I am: so as to me
πρόθυμον καὶ ὑμῖν τοῖς ἐν Ῥώμῃ εὐαγ-
[there is] readiness [3]also [4]to [5]you [6]who [[7]are] [8]in [9]Rome [1]to [2]announce
γελίσασθαι. 16 οὐ.γὰρ.ἐπαισχύνομαι τὸ εὐαγγέλιον [h]τοῦ
the glad tidings. For I am not ashamed of the glad tidings of the
χριστοῦ·‖ δύναμις.γὰρ θεοῦ ἐστιν εἰς σωτηρίαν παντὶ τῷ
Christ: for power of God it is unto salvation to every one that
πιστεύοντι, Ἰουδαίῳ.τε [i]πρῶτον‖ καὶ Ἕλληνι. 17 δικαιοσύνη
believes, both to Jew first and to Greek: [2]righteousness
γὰρ θεοῦ ἐν αὐτῷ ἀποκαλύπτεται ἐκ πίστεως εἰς πίστιν,
[1]for of God in it is revealed by faith to faith;
καθὼς γέγραπται, Ὁ.δὲ δίκαιος ἐκ πίστεως ζήσεται.
according as it has been written, But the just by faith shall live.

18 Ἀποκαλύπτεται.γὰρ ὀργὴ θεοῦ ἀπ' οὐρανοῦ ἐπὶ πᾶσαν
For there is revealed wrath of God from heaven upon all
ἀσέβειαν καὶ ἀδικίαν ἀνθρώπων τῶν τὴν ἀλήθειαν ἐν
ungodliness and unrighteousness of men who the truth in
ἀδικίᾳ κατεχόντων. 19 διότι τὸ.γνωστὸν τοῦ θεοῦ
unrighteousness hold. Because that which is known of God
φανερόν ἐστιν ἐν αὐτοῖς, ὁ.[k]γὰρ.θεὸς‖ αὐτοῖς ἐφανέρωσεν·
[2]manifest [1]is among them, for God to them manifested [it];
20 τὰ.γὰρ ἀόρατα αὐτοῦ ἀπὸ κτίσεως κόσμου τοῖς
for the invisible things of him from creation of [the] world by the
ποιήμασιν νοούμενα καθορᾶται, ἥ.τε ἀΐδιος αὐτοῦ δύνα-
things made being understood are perceived, both [2]eternal [1]his power
μις καὶ θειότης, εἰς τὸ εἶναι αὐτοὺς ἀναπολογήτους. 21 διότι
and divinity; for [2]to [3]be [1]them without excuse. Because
γνόντες τὸν θεόν, οὐχ ὡς θεὸν ἐδόξασαν ἢ [l]εὐχαρίσ-
having known God, not as God they glorified [him] or were thank-
τησαν,‖ [m]ἀλλ'‖ ἐματαιώθησαν ἐν τοῖς.διαλογισμοῖς.αὐτῶν, καὶ
ful; but became vain in their reasonings, and
ἐσκοτίσθη ἡ ἀσύνετος αὐτῶν καρδία· 22 φάσκοντες
was darkened the [4]without [5]understanding [2]of [3]them [1]heart: professing
εἶναι σοφοὶ ἐμωράνθησαν, 23 καὶ ἤλλαξαν τὴν δόξαν τοῦ
to be wise they became fools, and changed the glory of the
ἀφθάρτου θεοῦ ἐν ὁμοιώματι εἰκόνος φθαρτοῦ ἀνθρώπου
incorruptible God into a likeness of an image of corruptible man
καὶ πετεινῶν καὶ τετραπόδων καὶ ἑρπετῶν. 24 διὸ [n]καὶ‖
and of birds and quadrupeds and creeping things. Wherefore also
παρέδωκεν αὐτοὺς ὁ θεὸς ἐν ταῖς ἐπιθυμίαις τῶν.καρδιῶν.αὐ-
[2]gave [4]up [3]them [1]God in the desires of their hearts
τῶν εἰς ἀκαθαρσίαν, τοῦ ἀτιμάζεσθαι τα.σώματα.αὐτῶν ἐν
to uncleanness, [3]to [4]be [5]dishonoured [1]their [2]bodies between

---

g τινὰ καρπὸν GLTTrAW. h — τοῦ χριστοῦ GLTTrAW. i [πρῶτον] L. k θεὸς γὰρ GLTTrAW. l εὐχαρίστησαν GLTTrA. m ἀλλὰ Tr. n — καὶ LTTr[A].

[o]ἑαυτοῖς·" 25 οἵτινες μετήλλαξαν τὴν ἀλήθειαν τοῦ θεοῦ ἐν
themselves: who changed the truth of God into
τῷ ψεύδει, καὶ ἐσεβάσθησαν καὶ ἐλάτρευσαν τῇ κτίσει
falsehood, and reverenced and served the created thing
παρὰ τὸν κτίσαντα, ὅς ἐστιν εὐλογητὸς εἰς τοὺς αἰῶνας.
beyond him who created [it], who is blessed to the ages.
ἀμήν. 26 διὰ.τοῦτο παρέδωκεν αὐτοὺς ὁ θεὸς εἰς πάθη
Amen. For this reason [2]gave [4]up [3]them [1]God to passions
ἀτιμίας· αἵ τε γὰρ θήλειαι αὐτῶν μετήλλαξαν τὴν φυσικὴν
of dishonour, [2]both [1]for [4]females [3]their changed the natural
χρῆσιν εἰς τὴν παρὰ φύσιν· 27 ὁμοίως.[p]τε" καὶ οἱ [q]ἄῤῥενες"
use into that contrary to nature; and in like manner also the males
ἀφέντες τὴν φυσικὴν χρῆσιν τῆς θηλείας, ἐξεκαύθησαν ἐν τῇ
having left the natural use of the female, were inflamed in
ὀρέξει.αὐτῶν εἰς ἀλλήλους, [r]ἄρσενες" ἐν [s]ἄρσεσιν" τὴν
their lust towards one another, males with males
ἀσχημοσύνην κατεργαζόμενοι, καὶ τὴν ἀντιμισθίαν ἣν ἔδει
[3]shame [1]working [2]out, and the recompense which was fit
τῆς.πλάνης.αὐτῶν ἐν ἑαυτοῖς ἀπολαμβάνοντες. 28 καὶ
of their error in themselves receiving. And
καθὼς οὐκ.ἐδοκίμασαν τὸν θεὸν ἔχειν ἐν ἐπιγνώσει,
according as they did not approve [3]God [1]to [2]have in [their] knowledge,
παρέδωκεν αὐτοὺς ὁ θεὸς εἰς ἀδόκιμον νοῦν, ποιεῖν τὰ μὴ
[2]gave [4]up [3]them [1]God to an unapproving mind, to do things not
καθήκοντα, 29 πεπληρωμένους πάσῃ ἀδικίᾳ, [t]πορνείᾳ,"
fitting; being filled with all unrighteousness, fornication,
[v]πονηρίᾳ, πλεονεξίᾳ, κακίᾳ·" μεστοὺς φθόνου, φόνου, ἔριδος,
wickedness, covetousness, malice; full of envy, murder, strife,
δόλου, κακοηθείας· ψιθυριστάς, 30 καταλάλους, θεοστυγεῖς,
guile, evil dispositions; whisperers, slanderers, hateful to God,
ὑβριστάς, ὑπερηφάνους, ἀλαζόνας, ἐφευρετὰς κακῶν,
insolent, proud, vaunting, inventors of evil things,
γονεῦσιν ἀπειθεῖς, 31 ἀσυνέτους, ἀσυνθέτους, ἀ-
to parents disobedient, without understanding, perfidious, without
στόργους, [w]ἀσπόνδους," ἀνελεήμονας· 32 οἵτινες τὸ
natural affection, implacable, unmerciful; who the
δικαίωμα τοῦ θεοῦ ἐπιγνόντες, ὅτι οἱ τὰ.τοιαῦτα
righteous judgment of God having known, that those such things
πράσσοντες ἄξιοι θανάτου εἰσίν, οὐ μόνον αὐτὰ ποιοῦσιν,
doing worthy of death are, not only [2]them [1]practise,
ἀλλὰ καὶ συνευδοκοῦσιν τοῖς πράσσουσιν.
but also are consenting to those that do [them].

2 Διὸ ἀναπολόγητος εἶ, ὦ ἄνθρωπε, πᾶς ὁ κρίνων·
Wherefore inexcusable thou art, O man, every one who judgest,
ἐν.ᾧ.γὰρ κρίνεις τὸν ἕτερον, σεαυτὸν κατακρίνεις·
for in that in which thou judgest the other, thyself thou condemnest:
τὰ.γὰρ αὐτὰ πράσσεις ὁ κρίνων. 2 οἴδαμεν [x]δὲ" ὅτι τὸ
for the same things thou doest who judgest. [2]We [3]know [1]but that the
κρῖμα τοῦ θεοῦ ἐστιν κατὰ ἀλήθειαν ἐπὶ τοὺς τὰ τοιαῦτα
judgment of God is according to truth upon those that such things
πράσσοντας. 3 λογίζῃ.δὲ τοῦτο, ὦ ἄνθρωπε, ὁ κρίνων
do. And reckonest thou this, O man, who judgest
τοὺς τα.τοιαῦτα πράσσοντας καὶ ποιῶν αὐτά, ὅτι
those that such things do, and practisest them [thyself], that

dishonour their own bodies between themselves: 25 who changed the truth of God into a lie, and worshipped and served the creature more than the Creator, who is blessed for ever. Amen. 26 For this cause God gave them up unto vile affections: for even their women did change the natural use into that which is against nature: 27 and likewise also the men, leaving the natural use of the woman, burned in their lust one toward another; men with men working that which is unseemly, and receiving in themselves that recompence of their error which was meet. 28 And even as they did not like to retain God in *their* knowledge, God gave them over to a reprobate mind, to do those things which are not convenient; 29 being filled with all unrighteousness, fornication, wickedness, covetousness, maliciousness; full of envy, murder, debate, deceit, malignity; whisperers, 30 backbiters, haters of God, despiteful, proud, boasters, inventors of evil things, disobedient to parents, 31 without understanding, covenantbreakers, without natural affection, implacable, unmerciful: 32 who knowing the judgment of God, that they which commit such things are worthy of death, not only do the same, but have pleasure in them that do them.

II. Therefore thou art inexcusable, O man, whosoever thou art that judgest: for wherein thou judgest another, thou condemnest thyself; for thou that judgest doest the same things. 2 But we are sure that the judgment of God is according to truth against them which commit such things. 3 And thinkest thou this, O man, that judgest them which do such things, and doest the same, that thou

[o] αὐτοῖς LTTrA. [p] δὲ L. [q] ἄρσενες ELTrAW. [r] ἄῤῥενες T. [s] ἄῤῥεσιν T. [t] — πορνείᾳ GLTTrAW. [v] κακίᾳ πονηρίᾳ πλεονεξίᾳ, L; πονηρίᾳ κακίᾳ πλε. T. [w] — ἀσπόνδους LTTrAW. [x] γὰρ for T.

shalt escape the judgment of God? 4 or despisest thou the riches of his goodness and forbearance and longsuffering; not knowing that the goodness of God leadeth thee to repentance? 5 But after thy hardness and impenitent heart treasurest up unto thyself wrath against the day of wrath and revelation of the righteous judgment of God; 6 who will render to every man according to his deeds: 7 to them who by patient continuance in well doing seek for glory and honour and immortality, eternal life: 8 but unto them that are contentious, and do not obey the truth, but obey unrighteousness, indignation and wrath, 9 tribulation and anguish, upon every soul of man that doeth evil, of the Jew first, and also of the Gentile; 10 but glory, honour, and peace, to every man that worketh good, to the Jew first, and also to the Gentile: 11 for there is no respect of persons with God. 12 For as many as have sinned without law shall also perish without law: and as many as have sinned in the law shall be judged by the law; 13 (for not the hearers of the law *are* just before God, but the doers of the law shall be justified. 14 For when the Gentiles, which have not the law, do by nature the things contained in the law, these, having not the law, are a law unto themselves: 15 which shew the work of the law written in their hearts, their conscience also bearing witness, and *their* thoughts the mean while accusing or else excusing one another;) 16 in the day when God shall judge the secrets of men by Jesus Christ according to my gospel.

17 Behold, thou art called a Jew, and restest in the law, and

σὺ ἐκφεύξῃ τὸ κρῖμα τοῦ θεοῦ; 4 ἢ τοῦ πλούτου τῆς χρη-
thou shalt escape the judgment of God? or the riches of the kind-
στότητος αὐτοῦ καὶ τῆς ἀνοχῆς καὶ τῆς μακροθυμίας κατα-
ness of him and the forbearance and the long-suffering despisest
φρονεῖς, ἀγνοῶν ὅτι τὸ χρηστὸν τοῦ θεοῦ εἰς μετάνοιάν σε
thou, not knowing that the kindness of God to repentance thee
ἄγει; 5 κατὰ.δὲ τὴν.σκληρότητά.σου καὶ ἀμετανόητον
leads? but according to thy hardness and impenitent
καρδίαν θησαυρίζεις σεαυτῷ ὀργὴν ἐν ἡμέρᾳ ὀργῆς καὶ ἀπο-
heart treasurest up to thyself wrath in a day of wrath and re-
καλύψεως δικαιοκρισίας τοῦ θεοῦ. 6 ὃς ἀποδώσει ἑκάστῳ
velation of righteous judgment of God, who will render to each
κατὰ τὰ.ἔργα.αὐτοῦ. 7 τοῖς μὲν καθ' ὑπομονὴν ἔργου
according to his works: to those that with endurance in [2]work
ἀγαθοῦ, δόξαν καὶ τιμὴν καὶ ἀφθαρσίαν ζητοῦσιν, ζωὴν
[1]good, glory and honour and incorruptibility are seeking— life
αἰώνιον. 8 τοῖς.δὲ ἐξ ἐριθείας, καὶ ἀπειθοῦσιν [y]μὲν‖ τῇ
eternal. But to those of contention, and who disobey the
ἀληθείᾳ, πειθομένοις.δὲ τῇ ἀδικίᾳ, [z]θυμὸς καὶ ὀργή,‖
truth, but obey unrighteousness— indignation and wrath,
9 θλίψις καὶ στενοχωρία, ἐπὶ πᾶσαν ψυχὴν ἀνθρώπου τοῦ
tribulation and strait, on every soul of man that
κατεργαζομένου τὸ κακόν, Ἰουδαίου.τε πρῶτον καὶ Ἕλληνος·
works out evil, both of Jew first and of Greek;
10 δόξα.δὲ καὶ τιμὴ καὶ εἰρήνη παντὶ τῷ ἐργαζομένῳ τὸ
but glory and honour and peace to everyone that works
ἀγαθόν, Ἰουδαίῳ.τε πρῶτον καὶ Ἕλληνι· 11 οὐ.γάρ.ἐστιν
good, both to Jew first, and to Greek: for there is not
[a]προσωποληψία‖ παρὰ τῷ θεῷ. 12 ὅσοι.γὰρ ἀνόμως ἥμαρτον,
respect of persons with God. For as many as without law sinned,
ἀνόμως καὶ ἀπολοῦνται· καὶ ὅσοι ἐν νόμῳ ἥμαρτον, διὰ
without law also shall perish; and as many as in law sinned, by
νόμου κριθήσονται, 13 οὐ.γὰρ οἱ ἀκροαταὶ [b]τοῦ‖ νόμου δίκαιοι
law shall be judged, (for not the hearers of the law [are] just
παρὰ [c]τῷ‖ θεῷ, ἀλλ' οἱ ποιηταὶ [b]τοῦ‖ νόμου δικαιωθήσονται.
with God, but the doers of the law shall be justified.
14 Ὅταν.γὰρ ἔθνη τὰ μὴ νόμον ἔχοντα φύσει τὰ
For when nations which [2]not [3]law [1]have by nature the things
τοῦ νόμου [d]ποιῇ,‖ οὗτοι νόμον μὴ ἔχοντες, ἑαυτοῖς εἰσιν
of the law practise, these, law not having, to themselves are
νόμος· 15 οἵτινες ἐνδείκνυνται τὸ ἔργον τοῦ νόμου γραπτὸν
a law; who shew the work of the law written
ἐν ταῖς.καρδίαις.αὐτῶν, [e]συμμαρτυρούσης‖ αὐτῶν τῆς συνει-
in their hearts, [3]bearing [4]witness [5]with [1]their [2]con-
δήσεως, καὶ μεταξὺ ἀλλήλων τῶν λογισμῶν κατηγορούντων
science, and between one another the reasonings accusing
ἢ καὶ ἀπολογουμένων, 16 ἐν ἡμέρᾳ [f]ὅτε‖ κρινεῖ ὁ θεὸς
or also defending;) in a day when [2]shall [3]judge [1]God
τὰ κρυπτὰ τῶν ἀνθρώπων, κατὰ τὸ.εὐαγγέλιόν.μου, διὰ
the secrets of men, according to my glad tidings, by
[g]Ἰησοῦ χριστοῦ.‖
Jesus Christ.
17 [h]Ἴδε‖ σὺ Ἰουδαῖος ἐπονομάζῃ, καὶ ἐπαναπαύῃ [i]τῷ‖
Lo, thou a Jew art named, and restest in the

[y] — μὲν LTTr. [z] ὀργὴ καὶ θυμός GLTTrAW. [a] προσωπολημψία LTTrA. [b] — τοῦ the LTTrAW. [c] — τῷ [L]Tr. [d] ποιῶσιν LTTrA. [e] συν- T. [f] ᾗ in which LA. [g] χριστοῦ Ἰησοῦ T. [h] εἰ δὲ but if GLTTrAW. [i] — τῷ the LTTrAW.

νόμῳ, καὶ καυχᾶσαι ἐν θεῷ, 18 καὶ γινώσκεις τὸ θέλημα, καὶ
law, and boastest in God, and knowest the will, and
δοκιμάζεις τὰ διαφέροντα, κατηχούμενος ἐκ τοῦ
approvest the things that are more excellent, being instructed out of the
νόμου· 19 πέποιθάς.τε σεαυτὸν ὁδηγὸν εἶναι τυφλῶν,
law; and art persuaded [that] thyself a guide art of [the] blind,
φῶς τῶν ἐν σκότει, 20 παιδευτὴν ἀφρόνων, διδάσκαλον
a light of those in darkness, an instructor of [the] foolish, a teacher
νηπίων, ἔχοντα τὴν μόρφωσιν τῆς γνώσεως καὶ τῆς ἀληθείας
of infants, having the form of knowledge and of the truth
ἐν τῷ νόμῳ· 21 ὁ.οὖν διδάσκων ἕτερον, σεαυτὸν οὐ δι-
in the law: thou then that teachest another, thyself [3]not [1]dost
δάσκεις; ὁ κηρύσσων μὴ κλέπτειν, κλέπτεις; 22 ὁ
[2]thou teach? thou that proclaimest not to steal, dost thou steal? thou that
λέγων μὴ μοιχεύειν, μοιχεύεις; ὁ
sayest not to commit adultery, dost thou commit adultery? thou that
βδελυσσόμενος τὰ εἴδωλα, ἱεροσυλεῖς; 23 ὃς ἐν
abhorrest idols, dost thou commit sacrilege? thou who in
νόμῳ καυχᾶσαι, διὰ τῆς παραβάσεως τοῦ νόμου τὸν θεὸν
law boastest, through the transgression of the law [3]God
ἀτιμάζεις; 24 Τὸ.γὰρ ὄνομα τοῦ θεοῦ δι' ὑμᾶς βλασ-
[4]dishonourest [2]thou? For the name of God through you is blas-
φημεῖται ἐν τοῖς ἔθνεσιν, καθὼς γέγραπται. 25 Περι-
phemed among the nations, according as it has been written. [2]Circum-
τομὴ μὲν.γὰρ ὠφελεῖ ἐὰν νόμον πράσσῃς· ἐὰν.δὲ
cision [3]indeed [1]for profits if [the] law thou doest; but if
παραβάτης νόμου ᾖς, ἡ.περιτομή.σου ἀκροβυστία γέγονεν.
a transgressor of law thou art, thy circumcision uncircumcision has become.
26 ἐὰν οὖν ἡ ἀκροβυστία τὰ δικαιώματα τοῦ νόμου φυλάσ-
If therefore the uncircumcision the requirements of the law keep,
σῃ, [k]οὐχὶ‖ ἡ.ἀκροβυστία.αὐτοῦ εἰς περιτομὴν λογισθήσεται;
[2]not [3]his [4]uncircumcision [5]for [6]circumcision [1]shall be reckoned?
27 καὶ κρινεῖ ἡ ἐκ φύσεως ἀκροβυστία, τὸν νόμον τελοῦσα,
and [8]shall [9]judge [1]the [3]by [4]nature [2]uncircumcision, [6]the [7]law [5]fulfilling,
σὲ τὸν διὰ γράμματος καὶ περιτομῆς παραβάτην νόμου;
thee who with letter and circumcision [art] a transgressor of law?
28 οὐ.γὰρ ὁ ἐν.τῷ.φανερῷ Ἰουδαῖός ἐστιν, οὐδὲ
For not he that [is one] outwardly [2]a [3]Jew [1]is, neither
ἡ ἐν.τῷ.φανερῷ ἐν σαρκὶ περιτομή· 29 [l]ἀλλ'‖ ὁ
that outwardly in flesh [is] circumcision; but he that [is]
ἐν.τῷ.κρυπτῷ Ἰουδαῖος, καὶ περιτομὴ καρδίας ἐν πνεύ-
hiddenly a Jew [is one]; and circumcision [is] of heart, in spi-
ματι, οὐ γράμματι· οὗ ὁ ἔπαινος οὐκ ἐξ ἀνθρώπων,
rit, not in letter; of whom the praise [is] not of men,
[m]ἀλλ'‖ ἐκ τοῦ θεοῦ.
but of God.

3 Τί οὖν τὸ περισσὸν τοῦ Ἰουδαίου, ἢ τίς ἡ ὠφέλεια
What then [is] the superiority of the Jew? or what the profit
τῆς περιτομῆς; 2 πολὺ κατὰ πάντα τρόπον. πρῶτον μὲν
of the circumcision? Much in every way: [2]first
[n]γὰρ‖ ὅτι ἐπιστεύθησαν τὰ λόγια τοῦ θεοῦ. 3 τί.γάρ, εἰ
[1]for that they were entrusted with the oracles of God. For what, if
ἠπίστησάν τινες; μὴ ἡ.ἀπιστία.αὐτῶν τὴν πίστιν τοῦ θεοῦ
[8]not [7]believed [1]some? [5]their [6]unbelief [11]the [12]faith [13]of [14]God

makest thy boast of
God, 18 and knowest
his will, and approv-
est the things that are
more excellent, being
instructed out of the
law; 19 and art con-
fident that thou thy-
self art a guide of the
blind, a light of them
which are in darkness,
20 an instructor of the
foolish, a teacher of
babes, which hast the
form of knowledge
and of the truth in the
law. 21 Thou there-
fore which teachest
another, teachest thou
not thyself? thou that
preachest a man should
not steal, dost thou
steal? 22 thou that
sayest a man should
not commit adultery,
dost thou commit a-
dultery? thou that
abhorrest idols, dost
thou commit sacrilege?
23 thou that makest
thy boast of the law,
through breaking the
law dishonourest thou
God? 24 For the name
of God is blasphemed
among the Gentiles
through you, as it is
written. 25 For circum-
cision verily profiteth,
if thou keep the law:
but if thou be a break-
er of the law, thy cir-
cumcision is made un-
circumcision. 26 There-
fore if the uncircum-
cision keep the right-
eousness of the law,
shall not his uncir-
cumcision be count-
ed for circumcision?
27 And shall not un-
circumcision which is
by nature, if it fulfil
the law, judge thee,
who by the letter
and circumcision dost
transgress the law?
28 For he is not a Jew,
which is one outward-
ly; neither *is that*
circumcision, which is
outward in the flesh:
29 but he *is* a Jew,
which is one inward-
ly; and circumcision
is that of the heart, in
the spirit, *and* not in
the letter; whose
praise *is* not of men,
but of God.

III. What advan-
tage then hath the
Jew? or what profit
is there of circumci-
sion? 2 Much every
way: chiefly, because
that unto them were
committed the oracles

[k] οὐχ LTTr. [l] ἀλλὰ LTr. [m] ἀλλὰ Tr. [n] — γὰρ LTr[A].

καταργήσει; 4 μὴ.γένοιτο· γινέσθω.δὲ ὁ θεὸς ἀληθής,
[4]shall [7]make [8]of [9]no [10]effect? may it not be! but let [2]be [1]God true,
πᾶς.δὲ ἄνθρωπος ψεύστης, [o]καθὼς‖ γέγραπται, "Οπως
and every man false, according as it has been written, That
ἂν.δικαιωθῇς ἐν τοῖς.λόγοις.σου, καὶ [p]νικήσῃς‖ ἐν τῷ
thou shouldest be justified in thy words, and overcome in
κρίνεσθαί.σε. 5 Εἰ.δὲ ἡ.ἀδικία.ἡμῶν θεοῦ δικαιοσύνην συνί-
thy being judged. But if our unrighteousness [2]God's [3]righteousness [1]com-
στησιν, τί ἐροῦμεν; μὴ ἄδικος ὁ θεὸς ὁ ἐπιφέρων τὴν
mend, what shall we say? [is] [2]unrighteous [1]God who inflicts
ὀργήν; κατὰ ἄνθρωπον λέγω. 6 μὴ.γένοιτο· ἐπεὶ πῶς
wrath? According to man I speak. May it not be! since how
κρινεῖ ὁ θεὸς τὸν κόσμον; 7 εἰ [q]γὰρ‖ ἡ ἀλήθεια τοῦ θεοῦ
shall [2]judge [1]God the world? [2]If [1]for the truth of God
ἐν τῷ.ἐμῷ.ψεύσματι ἐπερίσσευσεν εἰς τὴν.δόξαν.αὐτοῦ, τί ἔτι
in my lie abounded to his glory, why yet
κἀγὼ ὡς ἁμαρτωλὸς κρίνομαι; 8 καὶ μὴ καθὼς βλασ-
[3]also [2]I [4]as [5]a [6]sinner [1]am judged? and not, according as we are
φημούμεθα, καὶ καθώς φασίν τινες ἡμᾶς λέγειν, "Οτι
injuriously charged and according as [2]affirm [1]some [that] we say,
ποιήσωμεν τὰ.κακὰ ἵνα ἔλθῃ τὰ.ἀγαθά; ὧν τὸ κρίμα
Let us practise evil things that [3]may [4]come [1]good [2]things? whose judgment
ἔνδικόν ἐστιν.
[2]just [1]is.

9 Τί οὖν; προεχόμεθα; οὐ.πάντως· προῃτιασάμεθα.γὰρ
What then? are we better? not at all: for we before charged
Ἰουδαίους.τε καὶ Ἕλληνας πάντας ὑφ' ἁμαρτίαν εἶναι,
both Jews and Greeks all [3]under [4]sin [[1]with] [2]being:
10 καθὼς γέγραπται, "Οτι οὐκ.ἔστιν δίκαιος οὐδὲ
according as it has been written, There is not a righteous one, not even
εἷς· 11 οὐκ.ἔστιν [r]ὁ‖ συνιῶν, οὐκ.ἔστιν [s]ὁ‖ ἐκζητῶν
one: there is not [one] that understands, there is not [one] that seeks after
τὸν θεόν. 12 πάντες ἐξέκλιναν, ἅμα [t]ἠχρειώθη-
God. All did go out of the way, together they became unprofit-
σαν·‖ οὐκ.ἔστιν [v] ποιῶν χρηστότητα, οὐκ.ἔστιν ἕως
able; there is not [one] practising kindness, there is not so much as
ἑνός. 13 τάφος ἀνεῳγμένος ὁ.λάρυγξ.αὐτῶν, ταῖς γλώσσαις
one; [3]sepulchre [1]an [2]opened [is] their throat, with [2]tongues
αὐτῶν ἐδολιοῦσαν· ἰὸς ἀσπίδων ὑπὸ τὰ.χείλη.αὐτῶν·
[1]their they used deceit: poison of asps [is] under their lips:
14 ὧν τὸ στόμα [w] ἀρᾶς καὶ πικρίας γέμει· 15 ὀξεῖς οἱ
of whom the mouth of cursing and of bitterness is full; swift
πόδες.αὐτῶν ἐκχέαι αἷμα· 16 σύντριμμα καὶ ταλαιπωρία
their feet to shed blood; ruin and misery [are]
ἐν ταῖς.ὁδοῖς.αὐτῶν· 17 καὶ ὁδὸν εἰρήνης οὐκ.ἔγνωσαν.
in their ways; and a way of peace they did not know;
18 οὐκ.ἔστιν φόβος θεοῦ ἀπέναντι τῶν.ὀφθαλμῶν.αὐτῶν.
there is no fear of God before their eyes.
19 Οἴδαμεν.δὲ ὅτι ὅσα ὁ νόμος λέγει, τοῖς ἐν τῷ νόμῳ
Now we know that whatsoever the law says, to those in the law
λαλεῖ· ἵνα πᾶν στόμα φραγῇ, καὶ ὑπόδικος γένηται
it speaks, that every mouth may be stopped, and under judgment be
πᾶς ὁ κόσμος τῷ θεῷ. 20 διότι ἐξ ἔργων νόμου οὐ δικαιω-
all the world to God. Wherefore by works of law [2]not [1]shall be

of God. 3 For what if
some did not believe?
shall their unbelief
make the faith of God
without effect? 4 God
forbid: yea, let God be
true, but every man a
liar; as it is written,
That thou mightest be
justified in thy say-
ings, and mightest
overcome when thou
art judged. 5 But if our
unrighteousness com-
mend the righteous-
ness of God, what shall
we say? *Is* God un-
righteous who taketh
vengeance? (I speak
as a man) 6 God for-
bid: for then how
shall God judge the
world? 7 For if the
truth of God hath more
abounded through my
lie unto his glory;
why yet am I also
judged as a sinner?
8 And not *rather*, (as
we be slanderously re-
ported, and as some af-
firm that we say,) Let
us do evil, that good
may come? whose
damnation is just.

9 What then? are
we better *than they?*
No, in no wise: for
we have before proved
both Jews and Gen-
tiles, that they are all
under sin; 10 as it is
written, There is none
righteous, no, not one:
11 there is none that
understandeth, there
is none that seeketh
after God. 12 They are
all gone out of the
way, they are together
become unprofitable;
there is none that do-
eth good, no, not one.
13 Their throat *is* an
open sepulchre; with
their tongues they
have used deceit; the
poison of asps *is* under
their lips: 14 whose
mouth *is* full of curs-
ing and bitterness:
15 their feet *are* swift
to shed blood: 16 de-
struction and misery
are in their ways:
17 and the way of
peace have they not
known: 18 there is no
fear of God before
their eyes. 19 Now we
know that what things
soever the law saith,
it saith to them who
are under the law: that
every mouth may be
stopped, and all the
world may become
guilty before God.

---

[o] καθάπερ TTr. [p] νικήσεις shalt overcome T. [q] δὲ but T. [r] — ὁ L[Tr]. [s] [ὁ] L.
[t] ἠχρεώθησαν TTr. [v] + ὁ (*read* that practises) T. [w] + [αὐτῶν] (*read* their mouth) L.

θήσεται πᾶσα σὰρξ ἐνώπιον αὐτοῦ· διὰ.γὰρ νόμου ἐπί-
justified any (lit. all) flesh before him; for through law [is] know-
γνωσις ἁμαρτίας.
ledge of sin.

21 Νυνὶ.δὲ χωρὶς νόμου δικαιοσύνη θεοῦ πεφανέρωται,
But now apart from law righteousness of God has been manifested,
μαρτυρουμένη ὑπὸ τοῦ νόμου καὶ τῶν προφητῶν· 22 δι-
being borne witness to by the law and the prophets: [2]right-
καιοσύνη δὲ θεοῦ διὰ πίστεως Ἰησοῦ χριστοῦ, εἰς πάντας
eousness [1]even of God through faith of Jesus Christ, towards all
[x]καὶ ἐπὶ πάντας‖ τοὺς πιστεύοντας· οὐ.γάρ.ἐστιν διαστολή·
and upon all those that believe: for there is no difference:
23 πάντες.γὰρ ἥμαρτον καὶ ὑστεροῦνται τῆς δόξης τοῦ θεοῦ,
for all sinned and come short of the glory of God;
24 δικαιούμενοι δωρεὰν τῇ.αὐτοῦ.χάριτι, διὰ τῆς ἀπολυ-
being justified gratuitously by his grace, through the re-
τρώσεως τῆς ἐν χριστῷ Ἰησοῦ, 25 ὃν προέθετο ὁ θεὸς
demption which [is] in Christ Jesus; whom [2]set [3]forth [1]God
ἱλαστήριον διὰ [y]τῆς‖ πίστεως ἐν τῷ.αὐτοῦ.αἵματι, εἰς ἔν-
a mercy seat through faith in his blood, for a shew-
δειξιν τῆς.δικαιοσύνης.αὐτοῦ, διὰ τὴν πάρεσιν τῶν
ing forth of his righteousness, in respect of the passing by the
προγεγονότων ἁμαρτημάτων 26 ἐν τῇ ἀνοχῇ τοῦ
[2]that [3]had [4]before [5]taken [6]place [1]sins in the forbearance
θεοῦ, πρὸς [z] ἔνδειξιν τῆς.δικαιοσύνης.αὐτοῦ ἐν τῷ νῦν
of God; for [the] shewing forth of his righteousness in the present
καιρῷ, εἰς τὸ εἶναι.αὐτὸν δίκαιον καὶ δικαιοῦντα τὸν ἐκ
time, for his being just and justifying him that [is] of [the]
πίστεως Ἰησοῦ. 27 Ποῦ οὖν ἡ καύχησις; ἐξεκλείσθη.
faith of Jesus. Where then [is] the boasting? It was excluded.
διὰ ποίου νόμου; τῶν ἔργων; οὐχί, ἀλλὰ διὰ νόμου
Through what law? of works? No, but through a law
πίστεως. 28 λογιζόμεθα [a]οὖν‖ [b]πίστει δικαιοῦσθαι‖ ἄνθρω-
of faith. [2]We [3]reckon [1]therefore [8]by [10]faith [6]to [7]be [8]justified [4]a [5]man
πον, χωρὶς ἔργων νόμου. 29 ἢ Ἰουδαίων ὁ θεὸς μόνον;
apart from works of law. Of Jews [is he] the God only?
οὐχὶ.[c]δὲ‖ καὶ ἐθνῶν; ναὶ καὶ ἐθνῶν· 30 [d]ἐπείπερ‖ εἷς
and not also of Gentiles? Yea, also of Gentiles: since indeed one
ὁ θεὸς ὃς δικαιώσει περιτομὴν ἐκ πίστεως, καὶ
God [it is] who will justify [the] circumcision by faith, and
ἀκροβυστίαν διὰ τῆς πίστεως. 31 νόμον οὖν καταργοῦ-
uncircumcision through faith. [5]Law [3]then [1]do [2]we [4]make of no
μεν διὰ τῆς πίστεως; μὴ.γένοιτο· ἀλλὰ νόμον [e]ἱστῶμεν.‖
effect through faith? May it not be! but [3]law [1]we [2]establish.

4 Τί οὖν ἐροῦμεν [f]Ἀβραὰμ τὸν.πατέρα.ἡμῶν εὑρηκέναι‖
What then shall we say Abraham our father has found
κατὰ σάρκα; 2 εἰ.γὰρ Ἀβραὰμ ἐξ ἔργων ἐδικαιώθη, ἔχει
according to flesh? For if Abraham by works was justified, he has
καύχημα, ἀλλ' οὐ πρὸς [g]τὸν‖ θεόν. 3 τί.γὰρ ἡ γραφὴ
ground of boasting, but not towards God. For what [2]the [3]scripture
λέγει; Ἐπίστευσεν.δὲ Ἀβραὰμ τῷ θεῷ, καὶ ἐλογίσθη αὐτῷ
[1]says? And [2]believed [1]Abraham God, and it was reckoned to him

20 Therefore by the deeds of the law there shall no flesh be justified in his sight: for by the law *is* the knowledge of sin.
21 But now the righteousness of God without the law is manifested, being witnessed by the law and the prophets; 22 even the righteousness of God *which is* by faith of Jesus Christ unto all and upon all them that believe: for there is no difference: 23 for all have sinned, and come short of the glory of God; 24 being justified freely by his grace through the redemption that is in Christ Jesus: 25 whom God hath set forth *to be* a propitiation through faith in his blood, to declare his righteousness for the remission of sins that are past, through the forbearance of God; 26 to declare, *I say*, at this time his righteousness: that he might be just, and the justifier of him which believeth in Jesus. 27 Where *is* boasting then? It is excluded. By what law? of works? Nay: but by the law of faith. 28 Therefore we conclude that a man is justified by faith without the deeds of the law. 29 *Is he* the God of the Jews only? *is he* not also of the Gentiles? Yes, of the Gentiles also: 30 seeing *it is* one God, which shall justify the circumcision by faith, and uncircumcision through faith. 31 Do we then make void the law through faith? God forbid: yea, we establish the law.

IV. What shall we say then that Abraham our father, as pertaining to the flesh, hath found? 2 For if Abraham were justified by works, he hath *whereof* to glory; but not before God. 3 For what saith the scripture? Abraham believed God, and it was counted unto him for righteousness. 4 Now to him that worketh is the

[x] — καὶ ἐπὶ πάντας LTTr[A]. [y] — τῆς LTTrA. [z] + τὴν the LTTrA. [a] γὰρ [1]for GLTTrAW. [b] δικαιοῦσθαι πίστει GLTTrA. [c] — δὲ and GLTTrA. [d] εἴ περ LTTrA. [e] ἱστάνομεν LTTrA. [f] εὑρηκέναι ([εὑρηκέναι] A) Ἀβραὰμ τὸν προπάτορα (forefather) ἡμῶν LTTrA. [g] — τὸν LTTrAW.

reward not reckoned of grace, but of debt. 5 But to him that worketh not, but believeth on him that justifieth the ungodly, his faith is counted for righteousness. 6 Even as David also describeth the blessedness of the man, unto whom God imputeth righteousness without works, 7 *saying,* Blessed *are* they whose iniquities are forgiven, and whose sins are covered. 8 Blessed *is* the man to whom the Lord will not impute sin.

9 *Cometh* this blessedness then upon the circumcision *only,* or upon the uncircumcision also? for we say that faith was reckoned to Abraham for righteousness. 10 How was it then reckoned? when he was in circumcision, or in uncircumcision? Not in circumcision, but in uncircumcision. 11 And he received the sign of circumcision, a seal of the righteousness of the faith which *he had yet* being uncircumcised: that he might be the father of all them that believe, though they be not circumcised; that righteousness might be imputed unto them also: 12 and the father of circumcision to them who are not of the circumcision only, but who also walk in the steps of that faith of our father Abraham, which *he had* being *yet* uncircumcised.

13 For the promise, that he should be the heir of the world, *was* not to Abraham, or to his seed, through the law, but through the righteousness of faith. 14 For if they which are of the law *be* heirs, faith is made void, and the promise made of none effect: 15 because the law worketh wrath: for where no law is, *there is* no transgression. 16 Therefore *it is* of faith, that *it might be* by grace; to the end the promise might be sure to all the seed; not to that only which is of the

εἰς δικαιοσύνην. 4 Τῷ.δὲ ἐργαζομένῳ ὁ μισθὸς οὐ.λογίζεται
for righteousness. Now to him that works the reward is not reckoned
κατὰ χάριν, ἀλλὰ κατὰ [i]τὸ‖ ὀφείλημα· 5 τῷ.δὲ
according to grace, but according to debt: but to him that
μὴ.ἐργαζομένῳ, πιστεύοντι.δὲ ἐπὶ τὸν δικαιοῦντα τὸν [k]ἀ-
does not work, but believes on him that justifies the un-
σεβῆ,‖ λογίζεται ἡ.πίστις.αὐτοῦ εἰς δικαιοσύνην. 6 καθάπερ
godly, [3]is [4]reckoned [1]his [2]faith for righteousness. Even as
καὶ [l]Δαβὶδ‖ λέγει τὸν μακαρισμὸν τοῦ ἀνθρώπου ᾧ ὁ θεὸς
also David declares the blessedness of the man to whom God
λογίζεται δικαιοσύνην χωρὶς ἔργων, 7 Μακάριοι ὧν
reckons righteousness apart from works: Blessed [they] of whom
ἀφέθησαν αἱ ἀνομίαι, καὶ ὧν ἐπεκαλύφθησαν αἱ ἁμαρτίαι.
are forgiven the lawlessnesses, and of whom are covered the sins:
8 μακάριος ἀνὴρ [m]ᾧ‖ οὐ.μὴ λογίσηται κύριος ἁμαρτίαν.
blessed [the] man to whom in no wise [3]will [4]reckon [[1]the] [2]Lord sin.

9 Ὁ.μακαρισμὸς.οὖν.οὗτος ἐπὶ τὴν περιτομήν, ἢ καὶ ἐπὶ
[Is] this blessedness then on the circumcision, or also on
τὴν ἀκροβυστίαν; λέγομεν.γὰρ [n]ὅτι‖ ἐλογίσθη τῷ Ἀβραὰμ
the uncircumcision? For we say that was reckoned to Abraham
ἡ πίστις εἰς δικαιοσύνην. 10 πῶς οὖν ἐλογίσθη; ἐν περι-
faith for righteousness. How then was it reckoned? [2]in [3]circum-
τομῇ ὄντι, ἢ ἐν ἀκροβυστίᾳ; οὐκ ἐν περιτομῇ, ἀλλ' ἐν ἀκρο-
cision [1]being, or in uncircumcision? Not in circumcision, but in uncir-
βυστίᾳ· 11 καὶ σημεῖον ἔλαβεν περιτομῆς, σφραγῖδα
cumcision. And [the] sign he received of circumcision, [as] seal
τῆς δικαιοσύνης τῆς πίστεως τῆς ἐν τῇ ἀκροβυστίᾳ,
of the righteousness of the faith which [he had] in the uncircumcision,
εἰς τὸ.εἶναι.αὐτὸν πατέρα πάντων τῶν πιστευόντων [o]δι'‖
for him to be father of all those that believe in
ἀκροβυστίας, εἰς τὸ λογισθῆναι [p]καὶ‖ αὐτοῖς [q]τὴν‖ δικαιο-
uncircumcision, for [4]to [5]be [6]reckoned [3]also [7]to [8]them [1]the [2]righteous-
σύνην· 12 καὶ πατέρα περιτομῆς τοῖς οὐκ ἐκ περιτομῆς
ness; and father of circumcision to those not of circumcision
μόνον, ἀλλὰ καὶ τοῖς στοιχοῦσιν τοῖς ἴχνεσιν τῆς ἐν
only, but also to those that walk in the steps of the [2]during
[r]τῇ ἀκροβυστίᾳ πίστεως τοῦ.πατρὸς.ἡμῶν Ἀβραάμ.
[3]uncircumcision [1]faith of our father Abraham.

13 Οὐ.γὰρ διὰ νόμου ἡ ἐπαγγελία τῷ Ἀβραὰμ ἢ τῷ
For not by law the promise [was] to Abraham or
σπέρματι.αὐτοῦ, τὸ κληρονόμον αὐτὸν εἶναι [s]τοῦ‖ κόσμου,
to his seed, that heir he should be of the world,
ἀλλὰ διὰ δικαιοσύνης πίστεως. 14 εἰ.γὰρ οἱ ἐκ νόμου
but by righteousness of faith. For if those of law [be]
κληρονόμοι, κεκένωται ἡ πίστις, καὶ κατήργηται ἡ ἐ-
heirs, [2]has [3]been [4]made [5]void [1]faith, and [3]made [4]of [5]no [6]effect [1]the [2]pro-
παγγελία· 15 ὁ.γὰρ.νόμος ὀργὴν κατεργάζεται· οὗ [t]γὰρ‖ οὐκ
mise. For the law [3]wrath [1]works [2]out; [5]where [4]for [8]not
ἔστιν νόμος, οὐδὲ παράβασις. 16 διὰ.τοῦτο ἐκ πίστεως,
[7]is [6]law, neither [is] transgression. Wherefore of faith
ἵνα κατὰ χάριν, εἰς τὸ εἶναι βεβαίαν τὴν
[it is], that according to grace [it might be], for [3]to [4]be [5]sure [1]the
ἐπαγγελίαν παντὶ τῷ σπέρματι, οὐ τῷ ἐκ τοῦ νόμου μόνον,
[2]promise to all the seed, not to that of the law only,

i — τὸ GLTTrAW. k ἀσεβῆν T. l Δαυεὶδ LTTrA; Δαυίδ GW. m οὗ whose (sin) TTr. n — ὅτι [L]TTr. o διὰ L. p — καὶ TTr[A]. q — τὴν T. r — τῇ GLTTrAW. s — τοῦ (*read* [the]) GLTTrAW. t δὲ but LTTrAW.

ἀλλὰ καὶ τῷ ἐκ πίστεως Ἀβραάμ, ὅς ἐστιν πατὴρ
but also to that of [the] faith of Abraham, who is father
πάντων.ἡμῶν, 17 καθὼς γέγραπται, Ὅτι πατέρα πολ-
of us all, (according as it has been written, A father of
λῶν ἐθνῶν τέθεικά σε, κατέναντι οὗ ἐπίστευσεν θεοῦ,
many nations I have made thee,) before [2]whom [3]he [4]believed [1]God,
τοῦ ζωοποιοῦντος τοὺς νεκρούς, καὶ καλοῦντος τὰ μὴ
who quickens the dead, and calls the things not
ὄντα ὡς ὄντα. 18 Ὃς παρ' ἐλπίδα [v]ἐπ'‖ ἐλπίδι ἐπίστευσεν,
being as being; who against hope in hope believed,
εἰς τὸ γενέσθαι αὐτὸν πατέρα πολλῶν ἐθνῶν, κατὰ τὸ
for [2]to [3]become [1]him father of many nations, according to that which
εἰρημένον, Οὕτως ἔσται τὸ.σπέρμα.σου· 19 καὶ μὴ ἀσθενήσας
had been said, So shall be thy seed: and not being weak
τῇ πίστει, [w]οὐ‖ κατενόησεν τὸ.ἑαυτοῦ σῶμα [x]ἤδη‖ νενεκρω-
in the faith, [3]not [1]he [2]considered his own body already become
μένον, ἑκατονταέτης που ὑπάρχων, καὶ τὴν νέκρωσιν
dead, [3]a [4]hundred [5]years [6]old [2]about [1]being, and the deadening
τῆς μήτρας Σάῤῥας· 20 εἰς.δὲ τὴν ἐπαγγελίαν τοῦ θεοῦ οὐ
of the womb of Sarah, and at the promise of God [2]not
διεκρίθη τῇ ἀπιστίᾳ, [y]ἀλλ'‖ ἐνεδυναμώθη τῇ πίστει,
[1]doubted through unbelief; but was strengthened in faith,
δοὺς δόξαν τῷ θεῷ, 21 καὶ πληροφορηθεὶς ὅτι ὃ ἐπήγ-
giving glory to God, and being fully assured that what he has
γελται, δυνατός ἐστιν καὶ ποιῆσαι. 22 διὸ [z]καὶ‖ ἐλογίσθη
promised, able he is also to do; wherefore also it was reckoned
αὐτῷ εἰς δικαιοσύνην. 23 Οὐκ.ἐγράφη δὲ δι' αὐτὸν
to him for righteousness. [2]It [3]was [4]not [5]written [1]but on account of him
μόνον, ὅτι ἐλογίσθη αὐτῷ· 24 ἀλλὰ καὶ δι' ἡμᾶς,
only, that it was reckoned to him, but also on account of us,
οἷς μέλλει λογίζεσθαι, τοῖς πιστεύουσιν ἐπὶ τὸν
to whom it is about to be reckoned, to those that believe on him who
ἐγείραντα Ἰησοῦν τὸν.κύριον.ἡμῶν ἐκ νεκρῶν, 25 ὃς
raised Jesus our Lord from among [the] dead, who
παρεδόθη διὰ τὰ.παραπτώματα.ἡμῶν, καὶ ἠγέρθη διὰ τὴν
was delivered for our offences, and was raised for
δικαίωσιν.ἡμῶν.
our justification.

5 Δικαιωθέντες οὖν ἐκ πίστεως, εἰρήνην [a]ἔχομεν‖
Having been justified therefore by faith, peace we have
πρὸς τὸν θεὸν διὰ τοῦ.κυρίου.ἡμῶν Ἰησοῦ χριστοῦ, 2 δι'
toward God through our Lord Jesus Christ, through
οὗ καὶ τὴν προσαγωγὴν ἐσχήκαμεν [b]τῇ πίστει‖ εἰς τὴν χάριν
whom also access we have by faith into [2]grace
ταύτην ἐν ᾗ ἑστήκαμεν· καὶ καυχώμεθα ἐπ' ἐλπίδι τῆς δόξης
[1]this in which we stand, and we boast in hope of the glory
τοῦ θεοῦ. 3 οὐ.μόνον.δέ, ἀλλὰ καὶ [c]καυχώμεθα‖ ἐν ταῖς
of God. And not only [so], but also we boast in
θλίψεσιν, εἰδότες ὅτι ἡ θλῖψις ὑπομονὴν κατεργάζεται,
tribulations, knowing that the tribulation [3]endurance [1]works [2]out;
4 ἡ.δὲ ὑπομονὴ δοκιμήν, ἡ.δὲ δοκιμὴ ἐλπίδα, 5 ἡ.δὲ ἐλπὶς
and the endurance proof; and the proof hope; and the hope
οὐ.καταισχύνει· ὅτι ἡ ἀγάπη τοῦ θεοῦ ἐκκέχυται ἐν
does not make ashamed, because the love of God has been poured out in

law, but to that also which is of the faith of Abraham; who is the father of us all, 17 (as it is written, I have made thee a father of many nations,) before him whom he believed, *even* God, who quickeneth the dead, and calleth those things which be not as though they were. 18 Who against hope believed in hope, that he might become the father of many nations, according to that which was spoken, So shall thy seed be. 19 And being not weak in faith, he considered not his own body now dead, when he was about an hundred years old, neither yet the deadness of Sarah's womb: 20 he staggered not at the promise of God through unbelief; but was strong in faith, giving glory to God; 21 and being fully persuaded that, what he had promised, he was able also to perform. 22 And therefore it was imputed to him for righteousness. 23 Now it was not written for his sake alone, that it was imputed to him; 24 but for us also, to whom it shall be imputed, if we believe on him that raised up Jesus our Lord from the dead; 25 who was delivered for our offences, and was raised again for our justification.

V. Therefore being justified by faith, we have peace with God through our Lord Jesus Christ: 2 by whom also we have access by faith into this grace wherein we stand, and rejoice in hope of the glory of God. 3 And not only *so*, but we glory in tribulations also: knowing that tribulation worketh patience; 4 and patience, experience; and experience, hope: 5 and hope maketh not ashamed; because the love of God is shed abroad in

---

[v] ἐφ' L. [w] — οὐ (*read* εἰς δὲ, *verse* 20, but at) LTTr[A]. [x] — ἤδη [L]T[A]. [y] ἀλλὰ Tr. [z] [καὶ] LTrA. [a] ἔχωμεν we should have TTrA. [b] — τῇ πίστει [LTr]A. [c] καυχώμενοι boasting TrA.

our hearts by the Holy Ghost which is given unto us. 6 For when we were yet without strength, in due time Christ died for the ungodly. 7 For scarcely for a righteous man will one die: yet peradventure for a good man some would even dare to die. 8 But God commendeth his love toward us, in that, while we were yet sinners, Christ died for us. 9 Much more then, being now justified by his blood, we shall be saved from wrath through him. 10 For if, when we were enemies, we were reconciled to God by the death of his Son, much more, being reconciled, we shall be saved by his life. 11 And not only *so*, but we also joy in God through our Lord Jesus Christ, by whom we have now received the atonement.

12 Wherefore, as by one man sin entered into the world, and death by sin; and so death passed upon all men, for that all have sinned: 13 (for until the law sin was in the world: but sin is not imputed when there is no law. 14 Nevertheless death reigned from Adam to Moses, even over them that had not sinned after the similitude of Adam's transgression, who is the figure of him that was to come. 15 But not as the offence, so also *is* the free gift. For if through the offence of one many be dead, much more the grace of God, and the gift by grace, *which is* by one man, Jesus Christ, hath abounded unto many. 16 And not as *it was* by one that sinned, *so is* the gift: for the judgment *was*

ταῖς.καρδίαις.ἡμῶν διὰ πνεύματος ἁγίου τοῦ δοθέντος ἡμῖν.
our hearts by the [2]Spirit [1]Holy which was given to us:
6 [d]Ἔτι.γὰρ‖ χριστὸς ὄντων ἡμῶν ἀσθενῶν [e] κατὰ.καιρὸν
for still [5]Christ [2]being [1]we [3]without [4]strength in due time
ὑπὲρ ἀσεβῶν ἀπέθανεν. 7 μόλις.γὰρ ὑπὲρ δικαίου
for [the] ungodly died. For hardly for a just [man]
τις ἀποθανεῖται· ὑπὲρ.γὰρ τοῦ ἀγαθοῦ τάχα τις
[2]any [3]one [1]will die; for on behalf of the good [man] perhaps some one
καὶ τολμᾷ ἀποθανεῖν· 8 συνίστησιν.δὲ τὴν.ἑαυτοῦ ἀγάπην
even might dare to die; but [2]commends [3]his [4]own [5]love
εἰς ἡμᾶς [f]ὁ θεός,‖ ὅτι ἔτι ἁμαρτωλῶν ὄντων ἡμῶν χριστὸς
[6]to [7]us [1]God, that [2]still [4]sinners [3]being [1]we Christ
ὑπὲρ ἡμῶν ἀπέθανεν. 9 πολλῷ οὖν μᾶλλον, δικαιωθέντες
[2]for [3]us [1]died. Much therefore more, having been justified
νῦν ἐν τῷ.αἵματι.αὐτοῦ, σωθησόμεθα δι' αὐτοῦ ἀπὸ τῆς
now by his blood, we shall be saved by him from
ὀργῆς. 10 εἰ.γὰρ ἐχθροὶ ὄντες κατηλλάγημεν τῷ θεῷ διὰ
wrath. For if, [2]enemies [1]being we were reconciled to God through
τοῦ θανάτου τοῦ.υἱοῦ.αὐτοῦ, πολλῷ μᾶλλον καταλλαγέντες
the death of his Son, much more, having been reconciled
σωθησόμεθα ἐν τῇ.ζωῇ.αὐτοῦ· 11 οὐ.μόνον.δέ, ἀλλὰ καὶ
we shall be saved by his life. And not only [so], but also
καυχώμενοι ἐν τῷ θεῷ διὰ τοῦ.κυρίου.ἡμῶν Ἰησοῦ χριστοῦ,
boasting in God through our Lord Jesus Christ,
δι' οὗ νῦν τὴν καταλλαγὴν ἐλάβομεν.
through whom now the reconciliation we received.

12 Διὰ.τοῦτο ὥσπερ δι' ἑνὸς ἀνθρώπου ἡ ἁμαρτία εἰς τὸν
On this account, as by one man sin into the
κόσμον εἰσῆλθεν, καὶ διὰ τῆς ἁμαρτίας ὁ θάνατος, καὶ οὕτως
world entered, and by sin death, and thus
εἰς πάντας ἀνθρώπους [g]ὁ θάνατος‖ διῆλθεν, ἐφ'.ᾧ πάντες
to all men death passed, for that all
ἥμαρτον. 13 ἄχρι.γὰρ νόμου ἁμαρτία ἦν ἐν κόσμῳ·
sinned: (for until law sin was in [the] world;
ἁμαρτία.δὲ οὐκ.ἐλλογεῖται, μὴ.ὄντος νόμου· 14 [h]ἀλλ'‖
but sin is not put to account, there not being law; but
ἐβασίλευσεν ὁ θάνατος ἀπὸ Ἀδὰμ μέχρι [i]Μωσέως‖ καὶ ἐπὶ
[2]reigned [1]death from Adam until Moses even upon
τοὺς μὴ.ἁμαρτήσαντας ἐπὶ τῷ ὁμοιώματι τῆς παραβάσεως
those who had not sinned in the likeness of the transgression
Ἀδάμ, ὅς ἐστιν τύπος τοῦ μέλλοντος. 15 Ἀλλ' οὐχ
of Adam, who is a figure of the coming [one]. But [shall] not
ὡς τὸ παράπτωμα, οὕτως καὶ τὸ χάρισμα.[k] εἰ.γὰρ τῷ
as the offence, so also [be] the free gift? For if by the
τοῦ ἑνὸς παραπτώματι οἱ πολλοὶ ἀπέθανον, πολλῷ μᾶλλον
[2]of [3]the [4]one [1]offence the many died, much more
ἡ χάρις τοῦ θεοῦ καὶ ἡ δωρεὰ ἐν χάριτι τῇ τοῦ ἑνὸς
the grace of God, and the gift in grace, which [is] of the one
ἀνθρώπου Ἰησοῦ χριστοῦ εἰς τοὺς πολλοὺς ἐπερίσσευσεν.
man Jesus Christ, to the many did abound.
16 καὶ οὐχ ὡς δι' ἑνὸς ἁμαρτήσαντος τὸ δώρημα·[k]
And [shall] not as by one having sinned [be] the gift?

---

[d] εἴ γε if indeed A. [e] + ἔτι still GLTTrAW. [f] — ὁ θεός (*read* συνίστησιν he commends) A. [g] [ὁ θάνατος] A. [h] ἀλλὰ TTrAW. [i] Μωϋσέως GLTTrAW. [k] *The various Editors do not mark this as a question: to read it as pointed in the Greek omit* [shall] *and substitute* [is] *for* [be].

τὸ.μὲν.γὰρ κρῖμα ἐξ ἑνὸς εἰς κατάκριμα, τὸ.δὲ χάρισμα
For the [2]indeed [1]judgment [was] of one to condemnation, but the free gift
ἐκ πολλῶν παραπτωμάτων εἰς δικαίωμα. 17 εἰ.γὰρ τῷ
[is] of many offences to justification. For if by the
τοῦ ἑνὸς παραπτώματι ὁ θάνατος ἐβασίλευσεν διὰ τοῦ ἑνός,
[2]of [3]the [4]one [1]offence death reigned by the one,
πολλῷ μᾶλλον οἱ τὴν περισσείαν τῆς χάριτος καὶ [m]τῆς
much more those the abundance of grace, and of the
δωρεᾶς‖ τῆς δικαιοσύνης λαμβάνοντες, ἐν ζωῇ βασιλεύσουσιν
gift of righteousness receiving, in life shall reign
διὰ τοῦ ἑνὸς Ἰησοῦ χριστοῦ. 18 Ἄρα οὖν ὡς δι' ἑνὸς παρα-
by the one Jesus Christ:) so then as by one of-
πτώματος εἰς πάντας ἀνθρώπους εἰς κατάκριμα,
fence [it was] towards all men to condemnation,
οὕτως καὶ δι' ἑνὸς δικαιώματος εἰς πάντας ἀνθρώ-
so also by one accomplished righteousness towards all men
πους εἰς δικαίωσιν ζωῆς. 19 ὥσπερ.γὰρ διὰ τῆς παρακοῆς
to justification of life. For as by the disobedience
τοῦ ἑνὸς ἀνθρώπου ἁμαρτωλοὶ κατεστάθησαν οἱ πολλοί,
of the one man [5]sinners [3]were [4]constituted [1]the [2]many,
οὕτως καὶ διὰ τῆς ὑπακοῆς τοῦ ἑνὸς δίκαιοι κατασταθήσονται
so also by the obedience of the one [6]righteous [3]shall [4]be [5]constituted
οἱ πολλοί. 20 Νόμος.δὲ παρεισῆλθεν, ἵνα πλεονάσῃ τὸ
[1]the [2]many. But law came in by the bye, that might abound the
παράπτωμα. οὗ.δὲ ἐπλεόνασεν ἡ ἁμαρτία, ὑπερεπερίσσευσεν
offence; but where abounded sin, overabounded
ἡ χάρις· 21 ἵνα ὥσπερ ἐβασίλευσεν ἡ ἁμαρτία ἐν τῷ θανάτῳ,
grace, that as [2]reigned [1]sin in death,
οὕτως καὶ ἡ χάρις βασιλεύσῃ διὰ δικαιοσύνης εἰς ζωὴν
so also grace might reign through righteousness to life
αἰώνιον, διὰ Ἰησοῦ χριστοῦ τοῦ.κυρίου ἡμῶν.
eternal, through Jesus Christ our Lord.

6 Τί οὖν ἐροῦμεν; [n]ἐπιμενοῦμεν‖ τῇ ἁμαρτίᾳ ἵνα ἡ χάρις
What then shall we say? Shall we continue in sin that grace
πλεονάσῃ; 2 μὴ.γένοιτο. οἵτινες.ἀπεθάνομεν τῇ ἁμαρτίᾳ,
may abound? May it not be! We who died to sin,
πῶς ἔτι ζήσομεν ἐν αὐτῇ; 3 ἢ ἀγνοεῖτε ὅτι ὅσοι
how still shall we live in it? Or are ye ignorant that [2]as [3]many [4]as
ἐβαπτίσθημεν εἰς χριστὸν Ἰησοῦν, εἰς τὸν.θάνατον.αὐτοῦ
[1]we were baptized unto Christ Jesus, unto his death
ἐβαπτίσθημεν; 4 συνετάφημεν οὖν αὐτῷ διὰ τοῦ βαπ-
we were baptized? We were buried therefore with him by bap-
τίσματος εἰς τὸν θάνατον· ἵνα ὥσπερ ἠγέρθη χριστὸς
tism unto death, that as [2]was [3]raised [4]up [1]Christ
ἐκ νεκρῶν διὰ τῆς δόξης τοῦ πατρός, οὕτως καὶ
from among [the] dead by the glory of the Father, so also
ἡμεῖς ἐν καινότητι ζωῆς περιπατήσωμεν. 5 Εἰ.γὰρ σύμφυτοι
we in newness of life should walk. For if conjoined
γεγόναμεν τῷ ὁμοιώματι τοῦ.θανάτου.αὐτοῦ, ἀλλὰ.καὶ
we have become in the likeness of his death, so also
τῆς.ἀναστάσεως ἐσόμεθα· 6 τοῦτο γινώσκοντες, ὅτι ὁ παλαιὸς
of [his] resurrection we shall be; this knowing, that [2]old
ἡμῶν ἄνθρωπος συνεσταυρώθη, ἵνα καταργηθῇ τὸ σῶμα
[1]our man was crucified with [him], that might be annulled the body

by one to condemnation, but the free gift *is* of many offences unto justification. 17 For if by one man's offence death reigned by one; much more they which receive abundance of grace and of the gift of righteousness shall reign in life by one, Jesus Christ.) 18 Therefore as by the offence of one *judgment came* upon all men to condemnation; even so by the righteousness of one *the free gift came* upon all men unto justification of life. 19 For as by one man's disobedience many were made sinners, so by the obedience of one shall many be made righteous. 20 Moreover the law entered, that the offence might abound. But where sin abounded, grace did much more abound: 21 that as sin hath reigned unto death, even so might grace reign through righteousness unto eternal life by Jesus Christ our Lord.

VI. What shall we say then? Shall we continue in sin, that grace may abound? 2 God forbid. How shall we, that are dead to sin, live any longer therein? 3 Know ye not, that so many of us as were baptized into Jesus Christ were baptized into his death? 4 Therefore we are buried with him by baptism into death: that like as Christ was raised up from the dead by the glory of the Father, even so we also should walk in newness of life. 5 For if we have been planted together in the likeness of his death, we shall be also *in the likeness* of *his* resurrection: 6 knowing this, that our old man is crucified with *him*, that the body of sin might be destroyed,

---

m [τῆς δωρεᾶς] L. n ἐπιμένωμεν should we continue GLTTrAW.

that henceforth we
should not serve sin.
7 For he that is dead
is freed from sin.
8 Now if we be dead
with Christ, we believe
that we shall also live
with him: 9 knowing
that Christ being raised
from the dead dieth no
more; death hath no
more dominion over
him. 10 For in that
he died, he died unto
sin once: but in that
he liveth, he liveth
unto God. 11 Like-
wise reckon ye also
yourselves to be
dead indeed unto sin,
but alive unto God
through Jesus Christ
our Lord. 12 Let not
sin therefore reign in
your mortal body, that
ye should obey it in
the lusts thereof.
13 Neither yield ye
your members *as* in-
struments of unright-
eousness unto sin: but
yield yourselves unto
God, as those that are
alive from the dead,
and your members *as*
instruments of right-
eousness unto God.
14 For sin shall not
have dominion over
you: for ye are not
under the law, but un-
der grace.
15 What then? shall
we sin, because we are
not under the law, but
under grace? God
forbid. 16 Know ye
not, that to whom ye
yield yourselves ser-
vants to obey, his ser-
vants ye are to whom
ye obey; whether of
sin unto death, or of
obedience unto right-
eousness? 17 But God
be thanked, that ye
were the servants of
sin, but ye have o-
beyed from the heart
that form of doctrine
which was delivered
you. 18 Being then
made free from sin,
ye became the ser-
vants of righteous-
ness. 19 I speak after
the manner of men
because of the infirmi-
ty of your flesh: for
as ye have yielded
your members ser-
vants to uncleanness
and to iniquity unto
iniquity; even so now
yield your members
servants to righteous-
ness unto holiness.
20 For when ye were

τῆς ἁμαρτίας, τοῦ μηκέτι δουλεύειν ἡμᾶς τῇ ἁμαρτίᾳ.
of sin, that [2]no [3]longer [4]be [5]subservient [1]we to sin.
7 ὁ.γὰρ ἀποθανὼν δεδικαίωται ἀπὸ τῆς ἁμαρτίας. 8 Εἰ.δὲ
For he that died has been justified from sin. Now if
ἀπεθάνομεν σὺν χριστῷ, πιστεύομεν ὅτι καὶ [o]συζήσομεν‖
we died with Christ, we believe that also we shall live with
αὐτῷ, 9 εἰδότες ὅτι χριστὸς ἐγερθεὶς ἐκ
him, knowing that Christ having been raised up from among [the]
νεκρῶν, οὐκέτι ἀποθνήσκει· θάνατος αὐτοῦ οὐκέτι κυριεύει.
dead, no more dies: death [5]him [1]no [2]more [3]rules [4]over.
10 [p]ὃ‖.γὰρ ἀπέθανεν, τῇ ἁμαρτίᾳ ἀπέθανεν ἐφάπαξ. [p]ὃ‖.δὲ
For in that he died, to sin he died once for all; but in that
ζῇ, ζῇ τῷ θεῷ. 11 οὕτως καὶ ὑμεῖς λογίζεσθε ἑαυτοὺς [q]
he lives, he lives to God. So also ye reckon yourselves
νεκροὺς μὲν [r]εἶναι‖ τῇ ἁμαρτίᾳ, ζῶντας.δὲ τῷ θεῷ, ἐν χριστῷ
[3]dead [4]indeed [1]to [2]be to sin, but alive to God, in Christ
Ἰησοῦ [s]τῷ.κυρίῳ.ἡμῶν.‖ 12 Μὴ οὖν βασιλευέτω ἡ ἁμαρτία
Jesus our Lord. [2]Not [4]therefore [1]let [5]reign [3]sin
ἐν τῷ.θνητῷ.ὑμῶν σώματι, εἰς τὸ ὑπακούειν [t]αὐτῇ ἐν‖ [v]ταῖς
in your mortal body, for to obey it in
ἐπιθυμίαις.αὐτοῦ·‖ 13 μηδὲ παριστάνετε τὰ.μέλη.ὑμῶν ὅπλα
its desires. Neither be yielding your members instruments
ἀδικίας τῇ ἁμαρτίᾳ· ἀλλὰ παραστήσατε ἑαυτοὺς τῷ
of unrighteousness to sin, but yield yourselves
θεῷ [w]ὡς‖ ἐκ νεκρῶν ζῶντας, καὶ τὰ.μέλη.ὑμῶν
to God as [2]from [3]among [[4]the] [5]dead [1]alive, and your members
ὅπλα δικαιοσύνης τῷ θεῷ. 14 ἁμαρτία.γὰρ ὑμῶν οὐ
instruments of righteousness to God. For sin [5]you [2]not
κυριεύσει· οὐ.γάρ ἐστε ὑπὸ νόμον, [x]ἀλλ'‖ ὑπὸ χάριν.
[1]shall [3]rule [4]over, for [3]not [2]are [1]ye under law, but under grace.
15 Τί οὖν; [y]ἁμαρτήσομεν‖ ὅτι οὐκ.ἐσμὲν ὑπὸ νόμον,
What then? shall we sin because we are not under law
[x]ἀλλ'‖ ὑπὸ χάριν; μὴ.γένοιτο. 16 οὐκ.οἴδατε ὅτι ᾧ
but under grace? May it not be! Know ye not that to whom
παριστάνετε ἑαυτοὺς δούλους εἰς ὑπακοήν, δοῦλοί ἐστε
ye yield yourselves bondmen for obedience, bondmen ye are
ᾧ ὑπακούετε, ἤτοι ἁμαρτίας εἰς θάνατον, ἢ ὑπακοῆς
to him whom ye obey, whether of sin to death, or of obedience
εἰς δικαιοσύνην; 17 χάρις.δὲ τῷ θεῷ, ὅτι ἦτε δοῦλοι τῆς
to righteousness? But thanks [be] to God, that ye were bondmen
ἁμαρτίας, ὑπηκούσατε.δὲ ἐκ καρδίας εἰς ὃν παρεδόθητε
of sin, but ye obeyed from [the] heart [5]to [6]which [7]ye [8]were [9]delivered
τύπον διδαχῆς. 18 ἐλευθερωθέντες.δὲ ἀπὸ τῆς ἁμαρτίας,
[1]a [2]form [3]of [4]teaching. And having been set free from sin,
ἐδουλώθητε τῇ δικαιοσύνῃ. 19 Ἀνθρώπινον λέγω διὰ
ye became bondmen to righteousness. Humanly I speak on account of
τὴν ἀσθένειαν τῆς.σαρκὸς.ὑμῶν. ὥσπερ.γὰρ παρεστήσατε
the weakness of your flesh. For as ye yielded
τὰ.μέλη.ὑμῶν δοῦλα τῇ ἀκαθαρσίᾳ καὶ τῇ ἀνομίᾳ εἰς τὴν
your members in bondage to uncleanness and to lawlessness unto
ἀνομίαν, οὕτως νῦν παραστήσατε τὰ.μέλη.ὑμῶν δοῦλα τῇ
lawlessness, so now yield your members in bondage
δικαιοσύνῃ εἰς ἁγιασμόν. 20 ὅτε.γὰρ δοῦλοι ἦτε τῆς
to righteousness unto sanctification. For when bondmen ye were

---

[o] συνζ- LTTrA. [p] ὃ E. [q] + εἶναι to be T[Tr]. [r] — εἶναι GLTTrAW. [s] — τῷ κυρίῳ ἡμῶν GLTTrAW. [t] — αὐτῇ ἐν GLTTrAW. [v] — ταῖς ἐπιθυμίαις αὐτοῦ G. [w] ὡσεὶ LTTrA. [x] ἀλλὰ LTTrAW. [y] ἁμαρτήσωμεν should we sin LTTrAW.

ἁμαρτίας, ἐλεύθεροι ἦτε τῇ δικαιοσύνῃ. 21 τίνα οὖν
of sin, free ye were as to righteousness. What ^{2}therefore
καρπὸν εἴχετε τότε, [z] ἐφ'.οἷς νῦν ἐπαισχύνεσθε;
^{1}fruit had ye then, in the [things] of which now ye are ashamed?
τὸ[a].γὰρ τέλος ἐκείνων θάνατος. 22 νυνὶ.δὲ ἐλευθερω-
for the end of those things [is] death. But now having been
θέντες ἀπὸ τῆς ἁμαρτίας, δουλωθέντες.δὲ τῷ θεῷ, ἔχετε
set free from sin, and having become bondmen to God, ye have
τὸν.καρπὸν.ὑμῶν εἰς ἁγιασμόν, τὸ.δὲ τέλος ζωὴν αἰώνιον.
your fruit unto sanctification, and the end life eternal.
23 τὰ.γὰρ ὀψώνια τῆς ἁμαρτίας θάνατος· τὸ.δὲ χάρισμα
For the wages of sin [is] death; but the free gift
τοῦ θεοῦ ζωὴ αἰώνιος ἐν χριστῷ Ἰησοῦ τῷ.κυρίῳ.ἡμῶν.
of God life eternal in Christ Jesus our Lord.

7 Ἠ.ἀγνοεῖτε, ἀδελφοί, γινώσκουσιν.γὰρ νόμον λαλῶ, ὅτι
Are ye ignorant, brethren, for to those knowing law I speak, that
ὁ νόμος κυριεύει τοῦ ἀνθρώπου ἐφ' ὅσον χρόνον ζῇ;
the law rules over the man for as long ^{2}as ^{1}time he may live?
2 ἡ.γὰρ ὕπανδρος γυνὴ τῷ ζῶντι ἀνδρὶ δέδεται νόμῳ·
For the married woman to the living husband is bound by law;
ἐὰν.δὲ ἀποθάνῃ ὁ ἀνὴρ κατήργηται ἀπὸ [b]τοῦ νόμου‖ τοῦ
but if should die the husband, she is cleared from the law of the
ἀνδρός. 3 ἄρα.οὖν ζῶντος τοῦ ἀνδρὸς μοιχαλὶς χρηματίσει,
husband: so then, ^{3}living ^{1}the ^{2}husband, an adulteress she shall be called,
ἐὰν γένηται ἀνδρὶ ἑτέρῳ· ἐὰν.δὲ ἀποθάνῃ ὁ ἀνήρ, ἐλευθέρα
if she be to ^{2}man ^{1}another; but if should die the husband, free
ἐστὶν ἀπὸ τοῦ νόμου, τοῦ.μὴ.εἶναι.αὐτὴν μοιχαλίδα, γενο-
she is from the law, so as for her not to be an adulteress, having
μένην ἀνδρὶ ἑτέρῳ. 4 ὥστε, ἀδελφοί.μου, καὶ ὑμεῖς ἐθανατώ-
become to ^{2}man ^{1}another. So that, my brethren, also ye were made
θητε τῷ νόμῳ διὰ τοῦ σώματος τοῦ χριστοῦ, εἰς τὸ γενέσθαι
dead to the law by the body of the Christ, for ^{2}to ^{3}be
ὑμᾶς ἑτέρῳ, τῷ ἐκ νεκρῶν ἐγερθέντι, ἵνα καρπο-
^{1}you to another, who from among [the] dead was raised, that we should
φορήσωμεν τῷ θεῷ. 5 ὅτε.γὰρ ἦμεν ἐν τῇ σαρκί, τὰ παθή-
bring forth fruit to God. For when we were in the flesh, the pas-
ματα τῶν ἁμαρτιῶν τὰ διὰ τοῦ νόμου ἐνηργεῖτο ἐν
sions of sins, which [were] through the law, wrought in
τοῖς.μέλεσιν.ἡμῶν εἰς τὸ καρποφορῆσαι τῷ θανάτῳ· 6 νυνὶ.δὲ
our members to the bringing forth fruit to death; but now
κατηργήθημεν ἀπὸ τοῦ νόμου, [c]ἀποθανόντες‖ ἐν ᾧ κατει-
we were cleared from the law, having died [in that] in which we were
χόμεθα, ὥστε δουλεύειν [d]ἡμᾶς‖ ἐν καινότητι πνεύματος, καὶ
held, so that ^{2}should ^{3}serve ^{1}we in newness of spirit, and
οὐ παλαιότητι γράμματος.
not in oldness of letter.

7 Τί οὖν ἐροῦμεν; ὁ νόμος ἁμαρτία; μὴ.γένοιτο·
What then shall we say? [Is] the law sin? May it not be!
ἀλλὰ τὴν ἁμαρτίαν οὐκ.ἔγνων εἰ.μὴ διὰ νόμου· τήν.τε.γὰρ
But sin I knew not unless by law: for also
ἐπιθυμίαν οὐκ.ᾔδειν εἰ.μὴ ὁ νόμος ἔλεγεν, Οὐκ
lust I had not been conscious of unless the law said, ^{3}Not
ἐπιθυμήσεις· 8 ἀφορμὴν.δὲ λαβοῦσα ἡ ἁμαρτία διὰ τῆς
^{1}thou ^{2}shalt lust; but ^{4}an ^{5}occasion ^{2}having ^{3}taken ^{1}sin by the

the servants of sin, ye
were free from right-
eousness. 21 What
fruit had ye then in
those things whereof
ye are now ashamed?
for the end of those
things *is* death. 22 But
now being made free
from sin, and become
servants to God, ye
have your fruit unto
holiness, and the end
everlasting life. 23 For
the wages of sin *is*
death; but the gift of
God *is* eternal life
through Jesus Christ
our Lord.

VII. Know ye not,
brethren, (for I speak
to them that know
the law,) how that
the law hath domi-
nion over a man as
long as he liveth?
2 For the woman
which hath an hus-
band is bound by the
law to *her* husband so
long as he liveth; but
if the husband be
dead, she is loosed
from the law of *her*
husband. 3 So then
if, while *her* husband
liveth, she be married
to another man, she
shall be called an a-
dulteress: but if her
husband be dead, she
is free from that law;
so that she is no adul-
teress, though she be
married to another
man. 4 Wherefore, my
brethren, ye also are
become dead to the
law by the body of
Christ; that ye should
be married to another,
even to him who is
raised from the dead,
that we should bring
forth fruit unto God.
5 For when we were in
the flesh, the motions
of sins, which were by
the law, did work in
our members to bring
forth fruit unto death.
6 But now we are de-
livered from the law,
that being dead where-
in we were held; that
we should serve in
newness of spirit, and
not *in* the oldness of
the letter.

7 What shall we say
then? *Is* the law sin?
God forbid. Nay, I
had not known sin,
but by the law: for I
had not known lust,
except the law had
said, Thou shalt not
covet. 8 But sin,

---

[z] ; *the question ends at* then LTA. [a] + μὲν indeed LA. [b] — τοῦ νόμου E.
[c] ἀποθανόντος (*read as A.V.*) E. [d] [ἡμᾶς] LTr.

taking occasion by
the commandment,
wrought in me all
manner of concupis-
cence. For without
the law sin *was* dead.
9 For I was alive
without the law once:
but when the com-
mandment came, sin
revived, and I died.
10 And the command-
ment, which *was or-
dained* to life, I found
to be unto death.
11 For sin, taking oc-
casion by the com-
mandment, deceived
me, and by it slew *me*.
12 Wherefore the law
is holy, and the com-
mandment holy, and
just, and good. 13 Was
then that which is
good made death unto
me? God forbid. But
sin, that it might
appear sin, working
death in me by that
which is good; that
sin by the com-
mandment might be-
come exceeding sinful.
14 For we know that
the law is spiritual:
but I am carnal, sold
under sin. 15 For that
which I do I allow
not: for what I would,
that do I not; but
what I hate, that do
I. 16 If then I do
that which I would
not, I consent unto
the law that *it is*
good. 17 Now then it
is no more I that do
it, but sin that dwell-
eth in me. 18 For I know
that in me (that is, in
my flesh,) dwelleth no
good thing: for to will
is present with me; but
how to perform that
which is good I find
not. 19 For the good
that I would I do not:
but the evil which I
would not, that I do.
20 Now if I do that
I would not, it is
no more I that do
it, but sin that dwell-
eth in me. 21 I find
then a law, that, when
I would do good, evil
is present with me.
22 For I delight in the
law of God after the
inward man: 23 but I
see another law in my

ἐντολῆς [e]κατειργάσατο[‖] ἐν ἐμοὶ πᾶσαν ἐπιθυμίαν. χωρὶς.γὰρ
commandment worked out in me every lust; for apart from
νόμου ἁμαρτία νεκρά· 9 ἐγὼ.δὲ ἔζων χωρὶς νόμου
law sin [was] dead. But I was alive apart from law
ποτέ ἐλθούσης.δὲ τῆς ἐντολῆς, ἡ ἁμαρτία ἀνέζησεν, ἐγὼ.δὲ
once; but having come the commandment, sin revived, but I
ἀπέθανον· 10 καὶ εὑρέθη μοι ἡ ἐντολὴ ἡ
died. And was found to me [that] the commandment which [was]
εἰς ζωήν, [f]αὕτη[‖] εἰς θάνατον. 11 ἡ.γὰρ.ἁμαρτία ἀφορμὴν
to life, this [to be] to death: for sin [3]an [4]occasion
λαβοῦσα διὰ τῆς ἐντολῆς ἐξηπάτησέν με, καὶ δι' αὐτῆς
[1]having [2]taken by the commandment, deceived me, and by it
ἀπέκτεινεν. 12 ὥστε ὁ.μὲν.νόμος ἅγιος, καὶ ἡ ἐντολὴ
slew [me]. So that the law indeed [is] holy, and the commandment
ἁγία καὶ δικαία καὶ ἀγαθή. 13 Τὸ οὖν ἀγαθὸν ἐμοὶ
holy and just and good. That which then [is] good, to me
[g]γέγονεν[‖] θάνατος; μὴ.γένοιτο· [h]ἀλλὰ[‖] ἡ ἁμαρτία, ἵνα
has it become death? May it not be! But sin, that
φανῇ ἁμαρτία, διὰ τοῦ ἀγαθοῦ μοι κατεργαζομένη
it might appear sin, by that which [is] good to me working out
θάνατον, ἵνα γένηται καθ'.ὑπερβολὴν ἁμαρτωλὸς ἡ ἁμαρτία
death; that [2]might [3]become [4]excessively [5]sinful [1]sin
διὰ τῆς ἐντολῆς. 14 Οἴδαμεν.γὰρ ὅτι ὁ νόμος πνευματικός
by the commandment. For we know that the law spiritual
ἐστιν· ἐγὼ.δὲ [i]σαρκικός[‖] εἰμι, πεπραμένος ὑπὸ τὴν ἁμαρτίαν.
is; but I [2]fleshly [1]am, having been sold under sin.
15 ὃ.γὰρ κατεργάζομαι, οὐ.γινώσκω· οὐ.γὰρ ὃ θέλω, τοῦτο
For what I work out, I do not own: for not what I will, this
πράσσω· ἀλλ' ὃ μισῶ, τοῦτο ποιῶ. 16 εἰ.δὲ ὃ οὐ.θέλω,
I do; but what I hate, this I practise. But if what I do not will,
τοῦτο ποιῶ, [k]σύμφημι[‖] τῷ νόμῳ ὅτι καλός. 17 νυνὶ.δὲ
this I practise, I consent to the law that [it is] right. Now then
οὐκέτι ἐγὼ κατεργάζομαι αὐτό, [l]ἀλλ'[‖] ἡ [m]οἰκοῦσα[‖] ἐν ἐμοὶ
no longer [2]I [1]am working [2]out [1]it; but the [2]dwelling [3]in [4]me
ἁμαρτία. 18 Οἶδα.γὰρ ὅτι οὐκ.οἰκεῖ ἐν ἐμοί, [n]τουτέστιν[‖] ἐν
[1]sin. For I know that there dwells not in me, that is in
τῇ.σαρκί.μου, ἀγαθόν· τὸ.γὰρ.θέλειν παράκειταί μοι, τὸ δὲ
my flesh, good: for to will is present with me, but
κατεργάζεσθαι τὸ καλὸν [o]οὐχ.εὑρίσκω.[‖] 19 οὐ.γὰρ ὃ θέλω
to work out the right I find not. For not what [2]I [3]will
ποιῶ ἀγαθόν· [p]ἀλλ'[‖] ὃ οὐ.θέλω κακόν, τοῦτο πράσ-
[4]do [5]I [6]practise [1]good; but what [2]I [3]do [4]not [5]will [1]evil, this I do.
σω. 20 εἰ.δὲ ὃ οὐ.θέλω [q]ἐγώ,[‖] τοῦτο ποιῶ, οὐκέτι
But if what [2]do [3]not [4]will [1]I, this I practise, [it is] no longer
ἐγὼ κατεργάζομαι αὐτό, [p]ἀλλ'[‖] ἡ οἰκοῦσα ἐν ἐμοὶ ἁμαρτία.
I [who] work [2]out [1]it, but the [2]dwelling [3]in [4]me [1]sin.
21 Εὑρίσκω ἄρα τὸν νόμον τῷ θέλοντι ἐμοὶ ποιεῖν τὸ καλόν,
I find then the law [3]who [4]will [1]to [2]me to practise the right,
ὅτι ἐμοὶ τὸ κακὸν παράκειται. 22 συνήδομαι.γὰρ τῷ νόμῳ
that me evil is present with. For I delight in the law
τοῦ θεοῦ κατὰ τὸν ἔσω ἄνθρωπον· 23 βλέπω.δὲ ἕτερον
of God according to the inward man: but I see another

[e] κατηργάσατο TTrA. [f] αὐτὴ GW. [g] ἐγένετο did it become LTTrAW. [h] ἀλλ' LA. [i] σάρκινός fleshy GLTTrAW. [k] σύν- T. [l] ἀλλὰ LTTrA. [m] ἐνοικοῦσα T. [n] τοῦτ' ἔστιν GT. [o] οὔ [is] not LTTrA. [p] ἀλλὰ TTrA. [q] — ἐγώ (*read* οὐ θέλω I do not will) LTr[A]W.

νόμον ἐν τοῖς.μέλεσίν.μου ἀντιστρατευόμενον τῷ νόμῳ τοῦ
law in my members warring against the law
νοός.μου, καὶ αἰχμαλωτίζοντά με [r] τῷ νόμῳ τῆς ἁμαρτίας
of my mind, and leading [2]captive [1]me to the law of sin
τῷ ὄντι ἐν τοῖς.μέλεσίν.μου. 24 ταλαίπωρος ἐγὼ ἄνθρωπος·
which is in my members. O wretched [2]I [1]man!
τίς με ῥύσεται ἐκ τοῦ σώματος τοῦ.θανάτου.τούτου;
who [3]me [1]shall [2]deliver out of the body of this death?
25 [s]εὐχαριστῶ‖ τῷ θεῷ διὰ Ἰησοῦ χριστοῦ τοῦ.κυρίου.ἡμῶν·
I thank God through Jesus Christ our Lord.
ἄρα.οὖν αὐτὸς ἐγὼ τῷ [t]μὲν‖ νοῒ δουλεύω νόμῳ θεοῦ·
So then [2]myself [1]I with the [2]indeed [1]mind serve [2]law [1]God's;
τῇ.δὲ σαρκὶ νόμῳ ἁμαρτίας.
but with the flesh [2]law [1]sin's.

8 Οὐδὲν.ἄρα.νῦν κατάκριμα τοῖς ἐν χριστῷ Ἰησοῦ, [u]μὴ
[There is] then now no condemnation to those in Christ Jesus, [3]not
κατὰ σάρκα περιπατοῦσιν, ἀλλὰ κατὰ πνεῦμα.‖ 2 ὁ.γὰρ
[4]according [5]to [6]flesh [1]who [2]walk, but according to Spirit. For the
νόμος τοῦ πνεύματος τῆς ζωῆς ἐν χριστῷ Ἰησοῦ ἠλευθέρωσέν
law of the Spirit of life in Christ Jesus set [2]free
[v]με‖ ἀπὸ τοῦ νόμου τῆς ἁμαρτίας καὶ τοῦ θανάτου. 3 Τὸ γὰρ
[1]me from the law of sin and of death. For
ἀδύνατον τοῦ νόμου, ἐν.ᾧ ἠσθένει διὰ τῆς σαρκός,
[4]powerless [[3]being] [1]the [2]law, in that it was weak through the flesh,
ὁ θεὸς τὸν.ἑαυτοῦ υἱὸν πέμψας ἐν ὁμοιώματι σαρκὸς ἁμαρτίας
God, [3]his [4]own [5]Son [1]having [2]sent, in likeness of flesh of sin,
καὶ περὶ ἁμαρτίας κατέκρινεν τὴν ἁμαρτίαν ἐν τῇ σαρκί, 4 ἵνα
and for sin, condemned sin in the flesh, that
τὸ δικαίωμα τοῦ νόμου πληρωθῇ ἐν ἡμῖν, τοῖς μὴ κατὰ
the requirement of the law should be fulfilled in us, who not according to
σάρκα περιπατοῦσιν, ἀλλὰ κατὰ πνεῦμα. 5 Οἱ.γὰρ
flesh walk, but according to Spirit. For they that
κατὰ σάρκα ὄντες, τὰ τῆς σαρκὸς φρονοῦσιν· οἱ.δὲ
according to flesh are, the things of the flesh mind; and they
κατὰ πνεῦμα, τὰ τοῦ πνεύματος. 6 τὸ.γὰρ φρόνημα
according to Spirit, the things of the Spirit. For the mind
τῆς σαρκὸς θάνατος· τὸ.δὲ φρόνημα τοῦ πνεύματος, ζωὴ
of the flesh [is] death; but the mind of the Spirit, life
καὶ εἰρήνη. 7 Διότι τὸ φρόνημα τῆς σαρκὸς ἔχθρα εἰς
and peace. Because the mind of the flesh [is] enmity towards
θεόν· τῷ.γὰρ νόμῳ τοῦ θεοῦ οὐχ.ὑποτάσσεται, οὐδὲ.γὰρ δύνα-
God: for to the law of God it is not subject; for neither can
ται· 8 οἱ.δὲ ἐν σαρκὶ ὄντες, θεῷ ἀρέσαι οὐ.δύνανται.
it [be]; and they that [2]in [3]flesh [1]are, [6]God [5]please [4]cannot.
9 Ὑμεῖς.δὲ οὐκ ἐστὲ ἐν σαρκί, [w]ἀλλ'‖ ἐν πνεύματι, εἴπερ
But ye [2]not [1]are in flesh, but in Spirit, if indeed [the]
πνεῦμα θεοῦ οἰκεῖ ἐν ὑμῖν. εἰ.δέ τις πνεῦμα χριστοῦ
Spirit of God dwells in you; but if anyone [the] Spirit of Christ
οὐκ.ἔχει, οὗτος οὐκ.ἔστιν αὐτοῦ. 10 εἰ.δὲ χριστὸς ἐν ὑμῖν, τὸ
has not, he is not of him: but if Christ [be] in you, the
μὲν σῶμα νεκρὸν [x]δι'‖ ἁμαρτίαν, τὸ.δὲ πνεῦμα ζωὴ
[2]indeed [1]body [is] dead on account of sin, but the Spirit life
διὰ δικαιοσύνην. 11 εἰ.δὲ τὸ πνεῦμα τοῦ ἐγείραντος [y]
on account of righteousness. But if the Spirit of him who raised up

members, warring against the law of my mind, and bringing me into captivity to the law of sin which is in my members.
24 O wretched man that I am! who shall deliver me from the body of this death?
25 I thank God through Jesus Christ our Lord. So then with the mind I myself serve the law of God; but with the flesh the law of sin.

VIII. *There is* therefore now no condemnation to them which are in Christ Jesus, who walk not after the flesh, but after the Spirit.
2 For the law of the Spirit of life in Christ Jesus hath made me free from the law of sin and death.
3 For what the law could not do, in that it was weak through the flesh, God sending his own Son in the likeness of sinful flesh, and for sin, condemned sin in the flesh:
4 that the righteousness of the law might be fulfilled in us, who walk not after the flesh, but after the Spirit.
5 For they that are after the flesh do mind the things of the flesh; but they that are after the Spirit the things of the Spirit.
6 For to be carnally minded *is* death; but to be spiritually minded *is* life and peace.
7 Because the carnal mind *is* enmity against God: for it is not subject to the law of God, neither indeed can be.
8 So then they that are in the flesh cannot please God.
9 But ye are not in the flesh, but in the Spirit, if so be that the Spirit of God dwell in you. Now if any man have not the Spirit of Christ, he is none of his.
10 And if Christ *be* in you, the body *is* dead because of sin; but the Spirit *is* life because of righteousness.
11 But if the Spirit of him that raised up Jesus from the dead dwell in you, he that raised up Christ from

[r] + ἐν in (the) TTr[A]. [s] χάρις thanks (to God) LTTrA. [t] — μὲν T. [u] — μὴ κατὰ to *end of verse* GLTTrAW. [v] σε thee T. [w] ἀλλὰ TTrA. [x] διὰ LTTrA. [y] + τὸν TTr[A].

the dead shall also
quicken your mortal
bodies by his Spirit
that dwelleth in you.
12 Therefore, brethren,
we are debtors, not to
the flesh, to live after
the flesh. 13 For if ye
live after the flesh, ye
shall die: but if ye
through the Spirit do
mortify the deeds of
the body, ye shall
live. 14 For as many
as are led by the Spirit
of God, they are the
sons of God. 15 For
ye have not received
the spirit of bondage
again to fear; but ye
have received the Spirit
of adoption, whereby
we cry, Abba, Father.
16 The Spirit itself
beareth witness with
our spirit, that we are
the children of God:
17 And if children,
then heirs; heirs of
God, and joint-heirs
with Christ; if so be
that we suffer with
him, that we may be
also glorified together.

18 For I reckon that
the sufferings of this
present time *are* not
worthy *to be compared*
with the glory which
shall be revealed in
us. 19 For the earnest
expectation of the
creature waiteth for
the manifestation of
the sons of God.
20 For the creature
was made subject to
vanity, not willingly,
but by reason of him
who hath subjected
the same in hope,
21 because the crea-
ture itself also shall
be delivered from the
bondage of corruption
into the glorious li-
berty of the children
of God. 22 For we
know that the whole
creation groaneth and
travaileth in pain to-
gether until now.
23 And not only *they*,
but ourselves also,
which have the first-
fruits of the Spirit,
even we ourselves
groan within our-
selves, waiting for the
adoption, *to wit*, the
redemption of our
body. 24 For we are
saved by hope: but
hope that is seen is
not hope: for what a

Ἰησοῦν ἐκ νεκρῶν οἰκεῖ ἐν ὑμῖν, ὁ ἐγείρας [z]τὸν‖
Jesus from among [the] dead dwells in you, he who raised up the
[a]χριστὸν ἐκ νεκρῶν‖ ζωοποιήσει καὶ τὰ θνητὰ σώματα
Christ from among [the] dead will quicken also [2]mortal [3]bodies
ὑμῶν διὰ [b]τὸ ἐνοικοῦν αὐτοῦ πνεῦμα‖ ἐν ὑμῖν.
[1]your on account of [3]that [4]dwells [1]his [2]Spirit in you.
12 Ἄρα
So
οὖν, ἀδελφοί, ὀφειλέται ἐσμὲν οὐ τῇ σαρκί, τοῦ κατὰ σάρκα
then, brethren, debtors we are, not to the flesh, [3]according [4]to [5]flesh
ζῆν· 13 εἰ.γὰρ κατὰ σάρκα ζῆτε, μέλλετε ἀποθνήσκειν·
[1]to [2]live; for if according to flesh ye live, ye are about to die;
εἰ.δὲ πνεύματι τὰς πράξεις τοῦ σώματος θανατοῦτε, ζήσεσθε.
but if by [the] Spirit the deeds of the body ye put to death, ye will live:
14 Ὅσοι.γὰρ πνεύματι θεοῦ ἄγονται, οὗτοί [c]εἰσιν υἱοὶ θεοῦ.‖
for as many as by [the] Spirit of God are led, these are sons of God.
15 οὐ.γὰρ ἐλάβετε πνεῦμα [d]δουλείας‖ πάλιν εἰς φόβον, [e]ἀλλ'‖
For [3]not [1]ye [2]received a spirit of bondage again unto fear, but
ἐλάβετε πνεῦμα υἱοθεσίας, ἐν.ᾧ κράζομεν, Ἀββᾶ, ὁ πατήρ.
ye received a Spirit of adoption, whereby we cry, Abba, Father.
16 Αὐτὸ τὸ πνεῦμα [f]συμμαρτυρεῖ‖ τῷ.πνεύματι.ἡμῶν, ὅτι
[3]Itself [1]the [2]Spirit bears witness with our spirit, that
ἐσμὲν τέκνα θεοῦ. 17 εἰ.δὲ τέκνα, καὶ κληρονόμοι· κληρονόμοι
we are children of God. And if children, also heirs: heirs
μὲν θεοῦ, [f]συγκληρονόμοι‖.δὲ χριστοῦ· εἴπερ [g]συμπάσχομεν,‖
indeed of God, and joint-heirs of Christ; if indeed we suffer together,
ἵνα καὶ συνδοξασθῶμεν.
that also we may be glorified together.

18 Λογίζομαι.γὰρ ὅτι οὐκ ἄξια τὰ παθήματα τοῦ νῦν
For I reckon that not worthy [are] the sufferings of the present
καιροῦ πρὸς τὴν μέλλουσαν δόξαν ἀποκαλυφθῆναι
time [to be compared] with the [2]about [1]glory to be revealed
εἰς ἡμᾶς. 19 Ἡ.γὰρ ἀποκαραδοκία τῆς κτίσεως τὴν ἀποκά-
to us. For the earnest expectation of the creation [2]the [3]reve-
λυψιν τῶν υἱῶν τοῦ θεοῦ ἀπεκδέχεται. 20 τῇ.γὰρ.ματαιότητι
lation [4]of [5]the [6]sons [7]of [8]God [1]awaits; for to vanity
ἡ κτίσις ὑπετάγη, οὐχ ἑκοῦσα, ἀλλὰ διὰ τὸν ὑπο-
the creation was subjected, not willingly, but by reason of him who sub-
τάξαντα, [h]ἐπ'‖ ἐλπίδι 21 [i]ὅτι‖ καὶ αὐτὴ ἡ κτίσις ἐλευθερω-
jected [it], in hope that also [3]itself [1]the [2]creation shall be
θήσεται ἀπὸ τῆς [j]δουλείας‖ τῆς φθορᾶς εἰς τὴν ἐλευθερίαν
freed from the bondage of corruption into the freedom
τῆς δόξης τῶν τέκνων τοῦ θεοῦ. 22 οἴδαμεν.γὰρ ὅτι πᾶσα ἡ
of the glory of the children of God. For we know that all the
κτίσις [g]συστενάζει‖ καὶ συνωδίνει ἄχρι τοῦ νῦν· 23 οὐ
creation groans together and travails together until now. [2]Not
μόνον δέ, ἀλλὰ καὶ αὐτοὶ τὴν ἀπαρχὴν τοῦ πνεύματος
[3]only [1]and [so], but even ourselves the first-fruit of the Spirit
ἔχοντες, [k]καὶ ἡμεῖς‖ αὐτοὶ ἐν ἑαυτοῖς στενάζομεν, υἱοθεσίαν
having, also we ourselves [2]in [3]ourselves [1]groan, [5]adoption
ἀπεκδεχόμενοι, τὴν ἀπολύτρωσιν τοῦ.σώματος.ἡμῶν. 24 τῇ
[4]awaiting— the redemption of our body.
γὰρ.ἐλπίδι ἐσώθημεν· ἐλπὶς.δὲ βλεπομένη οὐκ.ἔστιν ἐλπίς·
For in hope we were saved; but hope seen is not hope;

---

[z] — τὸν LTTrA. [a] χριστὸν ['Ἰησοῦν] (Jesus) ἐκ νεκρῶν L; ἐκ νεκρῶν χριστὸν Ἰησοῦν T. [b] τοῦ ἐνοικοῦντος αὐτοῦ πνεύματος (*read as A.V.*) ET. [c] υἱοί εἰσιν θεοῦ LTTrAW. [d] δουλίας T. [e] ἀλλὰ LTTrA. [f] συν- T. [g] συν- TA. [h] ἐφ' T. [i] διότι T. [j] δουλίας T. [k] ἡμεῖς καὶ TA; [ἡμεῖς] καὶ LTr.

ὃ.γὰρ βλέπει τις τί [m]καὶ[‖] ἐλπίζει; 25 εἰ.δὲ ὃ οὐ
for what [2]sees [1]anyone why also does he hope for? But if what [3]not
βλέπομεν ἐλπίζομεν, δι' ὑπομονῆς ἀπεκδεχόμεθα. 26 Ὡσαύτως
[1]we [2]see we hope for, in endurance we await. [2]In [3]like [4]manner
δὲ καὶ τὸ πνεῦμα συναντιλαμβάνεται [n]ταῖς.ἀσθενείαις[‖].ἡμῶν·
[1]and also the Spirit jointly helps our weaknesses;
τὸ.γὰρ τί προσευξώμεθα καθὸ δεῖ, οὐκ.οἴδαμεν, [o]ἀλλ'[‖]
for that which we should pray for according as it behoves, we know not, but
αὐτὸ τὸ πνεῦμα ὑπερεντυγχάνει [p]ὑπὲρ ἡμῶν[‖] στεναγμοῖς
[3]itself [1]the [2]Spirit makes intercession for us with groanings
ἀλαλήτοις· 27 ὁ.δὲ [q]ἐρευνῶν[‖] τὰς καρδίας οἶδεν τί τὸ
inexpressible But he who searches the hearts knows what [is] the
φρόνημα τοῦ πνεύματος, ὅτι κατὰ θεὸν ἐντυγχάνει ὑπὲρ
mind of the Spirit, because according to God he intercedes for
ἁγίων. 28 Οἴδαμεν.δὲ ὅτι τοῖς ἀγαπῶσιν τὸν θεὸν πάντα
saints. But we know that to those who love God all things
[r]συνεργεῖ[‖] εἰς ἀγαθόν, τοῖς κατὰ πρόθεσιν κλητοῖς
work together for good, to those who according to purpose [2]called
οὖσιν. 29 ὅτι οὓς προέγνω, καὶ προώρισεν συμμόρ-
[1]are. Because whom he foreknew, also he predestinated [to be] conformed
φους τῆς εἰκόνος τοῦ.υἱοῦ.αὐτοῦ, εἰς τὸ εἶναι αὐτὸν πρω-
to the image of his Son, for [2]to [3]be [1]him [the] first-
τότοκον ἐν πολλοῖς ἀδελφοῖς· 30 οὓς.δὲ προώρισεν, τούτους
born among many brethren. But whom he predestinated, these
καὶ ἐκάλεσεν· καὶ οὓς ἐκάλεσεν, τούτους καὶ ἐδικαίωσεν· οὓς
also he called; and whom he called, these also he justified; [2]whom
δὲ ἐδικαίωσεν, τούτους καὶ ἐδόξασεν.
[1]but he justified, these also he glorified.

31 Τί οὖν ἐροῦμεν πρὸς ταῦτα; εἰ ὁ θεὸς ὑπὲρ ἡμῶν,
What then shall we say to these things? If God [be] for us,
τίς καθ' ἡμῶν; 32 ὅς γε τοῦ.ἰδίου.υἱοῦ οὐκ.ἐφείσατο, [s]ἀλλ'[‖]
who against us? Who indeed his own Son spared not, but
ὑπὲρ ἡμῶν πάντων παρέδωκεν αὐτόν, πῶς οὐχὶ καὶ σὺν αὐτῷ
for us all gave up him, how [3]not [4]also [5]with [6]him
τὰ.πάντα ἡμῖν χαρίσεται; 33 τίς ἐγκαλέσει κατὰ
[9]all [10]things [8]us [1]will [2]he [7]grant? Who shall bring an accusation against
ἐκλεκτῶν θεοῦ; θεὸς ὁ δικαιῶν. 34 τίς ὁ κατα-
[the] elect of God? [It is] God who justifies: who he that con-
κρίνων; χριστὸς [t] ὁ ἀποθανών, μᾶλλον.δὲ [v]καὶ[‖] ἐγερθείς,
demns? [It is] Christ who died, but rather also is raised up;
ὃς [w]καὶ[‖] ἔστιν ἐν δεξιᾷ τοῦ θεοῦ, ὃς καὶ ἐντυγχάνει ὑπὲρ
who also is at [the] right hand of God; who also intercedes for
ἡμῶν. 35 τίς ἡμᾶς χωρίσει ἀπὸ τῆς ἀγάπης τοῦ χριστοῦ;
us: who us shall separate from the love of Christ?
θλίψις, ἢ στενοχωρία, ἢ διωγμός, ἢ λιμός, ἢ γυμνότης, ἢ
tribulation, or strait, or persecution, or famine, or nakedness, or
κίνδυνος, ἢ μάχαιρα; 36 καθὼς γέγραπται, Ὅτι [x]ἕνεκά[‖].σου
danger, or sword? According as it has been written, For thy sake
θανατούμεθα ὅλην τὴν ἡμέραν· ἐλογίσθημεν ὡς πρόβατα
we are put to death [2]whole [1]the day; we were reckoned as sheep
σφαγῆς. 37 Ἀλλ' ἐν τούτοις πᾶσιν ὑπερνικῶμεν διὰ
of slaughter. But in [2]these [3]things [1]all we more than overcome through

man seeth, why doth he yet hope for? 25 But if we hope for that we see not, *then* do we with patience wait for *it*. 26 Likewise the Spirit also helpeth our infirmities: for we know not what we should pray for as we ought: but the Spirit itself maketh intercession for us with groanings which cannot be uttered. 27 And he that searcheth the hearts knoweth what *is* the mind of the Spirit, because he maketh intercession for the saints according to *the will of* God. 28 And we know that all things work together for good to them that love God, to them who are the called according to *his* purpose. 29 For whom he did foreknow, he also did predestinate *to be* conformed to the image of his Son, that he might be the firstborn among many brethren. 30 Moreover whom he did predestinate, them he also called: and whom he called, them he also justified: and whom he justified, them he also glorified.

31 What shall we then say to these things? If God *be* for us, who *can be* against us? 32 He that spared not his own Son, but delivered him up for us all, how shall he not with him also freely give us all things? 33 Who shall lay any thing to the charge of God's elect? *It is* God that justifieth. 34 Who *is* he that condemneth? *It is* Christ that died, yea rather, that is risen again, who is even at the right hand of God, who also maketh intercession for us. 35 Who shall separate us from the love of Christ? *shall* tribulation, or distress, or persecution, or famine, or nakedness, or peril, or sword? 36 As it is written, For thy sake we are killed all the day long; we are

---

[m] — καὶ LTr[A]. [n] τῇ ἀσθενείᾳ (*read* our weakness) LTTrAW. [o] ἀλλὰ TTrW. [p] — ὑπὲρ ἡμῶν LTTrAW. [q] ἐραυνῶν TTr. [r] συνεργεῖ ὁ θεὸς God works together L. [s] ἀλλὰ LTTrA. [t] + Ἰησοῦς Jesus [L]T. [v] — καὶ LTTr[A]. [w] — καὶ [L]T. [x] ἕνεκεν GLTTrAW.

accounted as sheep for the slaughter. 37 Nay, in all these things we are more than conquerors through him that loved us. 38 For I am persuaded, that neither death, nor life, nor angels, nor principalities, nor powers, nor things present, nor things to come, 39 nor height, nor depth, nor any other creature, shall be able to separate us from the love of God, which is in Christ Jesus our Lord.

IX. I say the truth in Christ, I lie not, my conscience also bearing me witness in the Holy Ghost, 2 that I have great heaviness and continual sorrow in my heart. 3 For I could wish that myself were accursed from Christ for my brethren, my kinsmen according to the flesh: 4 who are Israelites; to whom *pertaineth* the adoption, and the glory, and the covenants, and the giving of the law, and the service *of God*, and the promises; 5 whose *are* the fathers, and of whom as concerning the flesh Christ *came*, who is over all, God blessed for ever. Amen. 6 Not as though the word of God hath taken none effect. For they *are* not all Israel, which are of Israel: 7 Neither, because they are the seed of Abraham, *are they* all children: but, In Isaac shall thy seed be called. 8 That is, They which are the children of the flesh, these *are* not the children of God: but the children of the promise are counted for the seed. 9 For this *is* the word of promise, At this time will I come, and Sarah shall have a son. 10 And not only *this*; but when Rebecca also had conceived by one, *even* by our father Isaac; 11 (for *the children* being not yet born, neither having done any good or evil, that the purpose of God according to election might stand, not of works, but of him that

τοῦ ἀγαπήσαντος ἡμᾶς. 38 πέπεισμαι.γὰρ ὅτι οὔτε
him who loved us. For I am persuaded that neither
θάνατος, οὔτε ζωή, οὔτε ἄγγελοι, οὔτε ἀρχαί, [y]οὔτε δυ-
death, nor life, nor angels, nor principalities, nor
νάμεις,‖ οὔτε ἐνεστῶτα, οὔτε μέλλοντα,[y] 39 οὔτε ὕψωμα, οὔτε
powers, nor things present, nor things to be, nor height, nor
βάθος, οὔτε τις κτίσις ἑτέρα δυνήσεται ἡμᾶς χωρίσαι
depth, nor any [2]created [3]thing [1]other will be able us to separate
ἀπὸ τῆς ἀγάπης τοῦ θεοῦ, τῆς ἐν χριστῷ Ἰησοῦ τῷ κυρίῳ
from the love of God, which [is] in Christ Jesus [2]Lord
ἡμῶν.
[1]our.

9 Ἀλήθειαν λέγω ἐν χριστῷ, οὐ.ψεύδομαι, [z]συμμαρτυρούσης‖
Truth I say in Christ, I lie not, bearing witness with
μοι τῆς.συνειδήσεώς.μου ἐν πνεύματι ἁγίῳ, 2 ὅτι λύπη
me my conscience in [the] [2]Spirit [1]Holy, that [2]grief
μοι ἐστὶν μεγάλη, καὶ ἀδιάλειπτος ὀδύνη τῇ.καρδίᾳ.μου·
[3]to [4]me [5]is [1]great, and unceasing sorrow in my heart,
3 ηὐχόμην.γὰρ [a]αὐτὸς ἐγὼ ἀνάθεμα εἶναι‖ ἀπὸ τοῦ χριστοῦ
for I was wishing [2]myself [1]I a curse to be from the Christ
ὑπὲρ τῶν.ἀδελφῶν.μου, τῶν.συγγενῶν.μου κατὰ σάρκα·
for my brethren, my kinsmen according to flesh;
4 οἵτινές εἰσιν [b]Ἰσραηλῖται,‖ ὧν ἡ υἱοθεσία καὶ ἡ δόξα,
who are Israelites, whose [is] the adoption and the glory,
καὶ [c]αἱ διαθῆκαι‖ καὶ ἡ νομοθεσία, καὶ ἡ λατρεία καὶ αἱ
and the covenants and the lawgiving, and the service and the
ἐπαγγελίαι, 5 ὧν οἱ πατέρες, καὶ ἐξ ὧν ὁ χριστὸς τὸ
promises; whose [are] the fathers; and of whom [is] the Christ
κατὰ σάρκα, ὁ ὢν ἐπὶ πάντων θεὸς εὐλογητὸς εἰς τοὺς
according to flesh, who is over all God blessed to the
αἰῶνας. ἀμήν. 6 Οὐχ οἷον.δὲ ὅτι ἐκπέπτωκεν ὁ λόγος τοῦ
ages. Amen. Not however that has failed the word
θεοῦ. οὐ.γὰρ πάντες οἱ ἐξ Ἰσραήλ, οὗτοι Ἰσραήλ·
of God; for not all [4]which [[5]are] [6]of [7]Israel [1]those [[2]are] [3]Israel:
7 οὐδ᾽ ὅτι εἰσὶν σπέρμα Ἀβραάμ, πάντες τέκνα, ἀλλ᾽
nor because they are seed of Abraham [are] all children: but,
ἐν Ἰσαὰκ κληθήσεταί σοι σπέρμα. 8 [d]Τουτέστιν,‖ οὐ τὰ
In Isaac shall be called to thee a seed. That is, [8]not [1]the
τέκνα τῆς σαρκός, ταῦτα τέκνα τοῦ θεοῦ· ἀλλὰ τὰ τέκνα
[2]children [3]of [4]the [5]flesh [6]these [[7]are] children of God; but the children
τῆς ἐπαγγελίας λογίζεται εἰς σπέρμα. 9 ἐπαγγελίας.γὰρ
of the promise are reckoned for seed. For of promise
ὁ.λόγος.οὗτος, Κατὰ τὸν.καιρὸν.τοῦτον ἐλεύσομαι, καὶ
this word [is], According to this time I will come, and
ἔσται τῇ Σάρρᾳ υἱός. 10 Οὐ.μόνον.δέ, ἀλλὰ καὶ Ῥε-
there shall be to Sarah a son. And not only [that], but also Re-
βέκκα ἐξ ἑνὸς κοίτην ἔχουσα, Ἰσαὰκ τοῦ.πατρὸς.ἡμῶν·
becca [3]by [4]one [2]conception [1]having, Isaac our father,
11 [e]μήπω‖ γὰρ γεννηθέντων, μηδὲ πραξάντων
[4]not [5]yet [[2]the [3]children] [1]for being born, nor having done
τι ἀγαθὸν ἢ [f]κακόν,‖ ἵνα ἡ κατ᾽ ἐκλογὴν [g]τοῦ θεοῦ
anything good or evil, (that the [4]according [5]to [6]election [2]of [3]God
πρόθεσις‖ μένῃ, οὐκ ἐξ ἔργων, ἀλλ᾽ ἐκ τοῦ καλοῦντος,
[1]purpose might abide, not of works, but of him who calls),

[y] οὔτε δυνάμεις *placed after* μέλλοντα GLTTrAW. [z] συνμ- T. [a] ἀνάθεμα εἶναι αὐτὸς ἐγὼ LTTrAW. [b] Ἰσραηλεῖται T. [c] ἡ διαθήκη the covenant L. [d] τοῦτ᾽ ἔστιν GTTrA. [e] μή πω LTr. [f] φαῦλον LTTrA. [g] πρόθεσις τοῦ θεοῦ GLTTrAW.

12 [h]ἐῤῥήθη‖ αὐτῇ, Ὅτι ὁ μείζων δουλεύσει τῷ ἐλάσσονι·
it was said to her, The greater shall serve the lesser:
13 καθὼς γέγραπται, Τὸν Ἰακὼβ ἠγάπησα, τὸν.δὲ.Ἡσαῦ
according as it has been written, Jacob I loved, and Esau
ἐμίσησα.
I hated.
14 Τί οὖν ἐροῦμεν; μὴ ἀδικία παρὰ τῷ θεῷ;
What then shall we say? Unrighteousness with God [is there]?
μὴ.γένοιτο· 15 τῷ.[i]γὰρ.Μωσῇ‖ λέγει, Ἐλεήσω ὃν.ἂν
May it not be! For to Moses he says, I will shew mercy to whomsoever
ἐλεῶ, καὶ οἰκτειρήσω ὃν.ἂν οἰκτείρω.
I shew mercy, and I will feel compassion on whomsoever I feel compassion.
16 Ἄρα οὖν οὐ τοῦ θέλοντος, οὐδὲ τοῦ τρέχοντος,
So then [it is] not of him that wills, nor of him that runs,
ἀλλὰ τοῦ [k]ἐλεοῦντος‖ θεοῦ. 17 λέγει.γὰρ ἡ γραφὴ τῷ Φαραώ,
but [3]who [4]shews [5]mercy [1]of [2]God. For says the scripture to Pharaoh,
Ὅτι εἰς αὐτὸ.τοῦτο ἐξήγειρά σε, ὅπως ἐνδείξωμαι ἐν σοὶ
For this same thing I raised out thee, so that I might shew in thee
τὴν.δύναμίν.μου, καὶ ὅπως διαγγελῇ τὸ.ὄνομά.μου ἐν πάσῃ
my power, and so that should be declared my name in all
τῇ γῇ. 18 Ἄρα οὖν ὃν θέλει ἐλεεῖ· ὃν.δὲ θέλει
the earth. So then to whom he will he shews mercy, and whom he will
σκληρύνει.
he hardens.
19 Ἐρεῖς [l]οὖν μοι,‖ Τί[m] ἔτι μέμφεται; τῷ.[n]γὰρ‖ βου-
Thou wilt say then to me, Why yet does he find fault? for [4]the [5]pur-
λήματι αὐτοῦ τίς ἀνθέστηκεν; 20 [o]Μενοῦνγε, ὦ ἄνθρωπε,‖
pose [6]of [7]him [1]who [2]has [3]resisted? Yea, rather, O man,
σὺ τίς εἶ ὁ ἀνταποκρινόμενος τῷ θεῷ; μὴ ἐρεῖ τὸ
[3]thou [1]who [2]art that answerest against God? Shall [4]say [1]the
πλάσμα τῷ πλάσαντι, Τί με ἐποίησας οὕτως;
[3]thing [3]formed to him who formed [it], Why me madest thou thus?
21 Ἢ οὐκ.ἔχει ἐξουσίαν ὁ κεραμεὺς τοῦ πηλοῦ, ἐκ τοῦ
Or has not authority the potter over the clay, out of the
αὐτοῦ φυράματος ποιῆσαι ὃ.μὲν εἰς τιμὴν σκεῦος, ὃ.δὲ
same lump to make one [2]to [3]honour [1]vessel, and another
εἰς ἀτιμίαν; 22 εἰ.δὲ θέλων ὁ θεὸς ἐνδείξασθαι τὴν ὀργήν,
to dishonour? And if [2]willing [1]God to shew wrath,
καὶ γνωρίσαι τὸ.δυνατὸν.αὐτοῦ, ἤνεγκεν ἐν πολλῇ μακρο-
and to make known his power, bore in much long-
θυμίᾳ σκεύη ὀργῆς κατηρτισμένα εἰς ἀπώλειαν· 23 καὶ ἵνα
suffering vessels of wrath fitted for destruction; and that
γνωρίσῃ τὸν πλοῦτον τῆς.δόξης.αὐτοῦ ἐπὶ σκεύη
he might make known the riches of his glory upon vessels
ἐλέους, ἃ προητοίμασεν εἰς δόξαν; 24 οὓς καὶ ἐκάλεσεν
of mercy, which he before prepared for glory, [2]whom [3]also [4]he [5]called
ἡμᾶς οὐ μόνον ἐξ Ἰουδαίων, ἀλλὰ καὶ ἐξ
[1]us not only from among [the] Jews, but also from among [the]
ἐθνῶν· 25 ὡς καὶ ἐν τῷ Ὡσηὲ λέγει, Καλέσω τὸν οὐ
nations? As also in Hosea he says, I will call that which [is] not
λαόν.μου, λαόν.μου· καὶ τὴν οὐκ ἠγαπημένην, ἠγαπημένην.
my people, My People; and that not beloved, Beloved.
26 Καὶ ἔσται, ἐν τῷ τόπῳ οὗ [h]ἐῤῥήθη‖ [p]αὐτοῖς,‖ Οὐ λαός
And it shall be, in the place where it was said to them, Not [2]people

calleth;) 12 it was
said unto her, The
elder shall serve the
younger. 13 As it is
written, Jacob have I
loved, but Esau have
I hated.
14 What shall we
say then? *Is there*
unrighteousness with
God? God forbid.
15 For he saith to Mo-
ses, I will have mercy
on whom I will have
mercy, and I will have
compassion on whom
I will have compas-
sion. 16 So then *it is*
not of him that will-
eth, nor of him that
runneth, but of God
that sheweth mercy.
17 For the scripture
saith unto Pharaoh,
Even for this same
purpose have I raised
thee up, that I might
shew my power in
thee, and that my
name might be de-
clared throughout all
the earth. 18 There-
fore hath he mercy on
whom he will *have
mercy*, and whom he
will he hardeneth.
19 Thou wilt say
then unto me, Why
doth he yet find fault?
For who hath resisted
his will? 20 Nay but,
O man, who art thou
that repliest against
God? Shall the thing
formed say to him
that formed *it*, Why
hast thou made me
thus? 21 Hath not the
potter power over the
clay, of the same
lump to make one
vessel unto honour,
and another unto dis-
honour? 22 *What* if
God, willing to shew
his wrath, and to make
his power known, en-
dured with much
longsuffering the ves-
sels of wrath fitted to
destruction: 23 and
that he might make
known the riches of
his glory on the ves-
sels of mercy, which
he had afore prepared
unto glory, 24 even
us, whom he hath
called, not of the Jews
only, but also of the
Gentiles? 25 As he
saith also in Osee, I
will call them my
people, which were
not my people; and
her beloved, which
was not beloved.
26 And it shall come

---

[h] ἐῤῥέθη LTTrA. [i] γὰρ Μωϋσῇ G; Μωσῇ γὰρ LA; Μωϋσεῖ γὰρ TTr; Μωϋσῃ γὰρ W. [k] ἐλεῶντος LTTrA. [l] μοι οὖν LTTrAW. [m] + οὖν then L[A]W. [n] — γὰρ for E. [o] ὦ ἄνθρωπε, μενοῦνγε (μενοῦν γε LTr) LTTrA. [p] — αὐτοῖς [L]Tr.

μου ὑμεῖς, ἐκεῖ κληθήσονται υἱοὶ θεοῦ ζῶντος. 27 Ἡ-
[1]my [are] ye, there they shall be called sons of [3]God [[1]the] [2]living. [2]E-
σαΐας δὲ κράζει· ὑπὲρ τοῦ Ἰσραήλ, Ἐὰν.ᾖ ὁ ἀριθμὸς
saias [1]but cries concerning Israel, If [8]should [9]be [1]the [2]number
τῶν υἱῶν Ἰσραὴλ ὡς ἡ ἄμμος τῆς θαλάσσης, τὸ [r]κατάλειμ-
[3]of [4]the [5]sons [6]of [7]Israel as the sand of the sea, the remnant
μα[‖] σωθήσεται· 28 λόγον γὰρ συντελῶν καὶ συντέμνων
shall be saved: for [the] matter [he is] concluding and cutting short
[s]ἐν δικαιοσύνῃ· ὅτι λόγον συντετμημένον[‖] ποιήσει
in righteousness: because a matter cut short will [3]do [[1]the]
κύριος ἐπὶ τῆς γῆς. 29 Καὶ καθὼς προείρηκεν Ἡσαΐας,
[2]Lord upon the earth. And according as said before Esaias,
Εἰ.μὴ κύριος Σαβαὼθ [t]ἐγκατέλιπεν[‖] ἡμῖν σπέρμα, ὡς Σόδομα
Unless [the] Lord of Hosts had left us a seed, as Sodom
ἂν.ἐγενήθημεν, καὶ ὡς Γόμοῤῥα ἂν.ὡμοιώθημεν.
we should have become, and as Gomorrha we should have been made like.

30 Τί οὖν ἐροῦμεν; ὅτι ἔθνη τὰ μὴ.διώκοντα δικαιο-
What then shall we say? That Gentiles that follow not after right-
σύνην, κατέλαβεν δικαιοσύνην, δικαιοσύνην.δὲ τὴν ἐκ πίστεως·
eousness, attained righteousness, but righteousness that [is] by faith.
31 Ἰσραὴλ.δὲ διώκων νόμον δικαιοσύνης, εἰς νόμον [v]δι-
But Israel, following after a law of righteousness, to a law of
καιοσύνης[‖] οὐκ.ἔφθασεν. 32 [w]διατί;[‖] ὅτι .οὐκ ἐκ πίσ-
righteousness did not attain. Why? Because [it was] not by faith,
τεως, ἀλλ' ὡς ἐξ ἔργων [x]νόμου·[‖] προσέκοψαν.[y]γὰρ[‖] τῷ λίθῳ
but as by works of law. For they stumbled at the stone
τοῦ προσκόμματος, 33 καθὼς γέγραπται, Ἰδοὺ τίθημι ἐν
of stumbling, according as it has been written, Behold I place in
Σιὼν λίθον προσκόμματος καὶ πέτραν σκανδάλου· καὶ [z]πᾶς[‖]
Sion a stone of stumbling and rock of offence: and every one
ὁ πιστεύων ἐπ' αὐτῷ οὐ.καταισχυνθήσεται.
that believes on him shall not be ashamed.

10 Ἀδελφοί, ἡ μὲν εὐδοκία τῆς.ἐμῆς καρδίας, καὶ ἡ
Brethren, the good pleasure of my own heart, and
δέησις [a]ἡ[‖] πρὸς τὸν θεὸν ὑπὲρ [b]τοῦ Ἰσραήλ ἐστιν[‖] εἰς
supplication to God on behalf of Israel is for
σωτηρίαν. 2 μαρτυρῶ.γὰρ αὐτοῖς ὅτι ζῆλον θεοῦ ἔχουσιν,
salvation. For I bear witness to them that zeal for God they have,
ἀλλ' οὐ κατ' ἐπίγνωσιν. 3 ἀγνοοῦντες.γὰρ τὴν τοῦ θεοῦ
but not according to knowledge. For being ignorant of the [2]of [3]God
δικαιοσύνην, καὶ τὴν.ἰδίαν [c]δικαιοσύνην[‖] ζητοῦντες στῆσαι,
[1]righteousness, and their own righteousness seeking to establish,
τῇ δικαιοσύνῃ τοῦ θεοῦ οὐχ.ὑπετάγησαν. 4 τέλος.γὰρ
to the righteousness of God they submitted not. For [[3]the] [4]end
νόμου χριστὸς εἰς δικαιοσύνην παντὶ τῷ πιστεύοντι.
[5]of [6]law [1]Christ [[2]is] for righteousness to every one that believes.

5 [d]Μωσῆς[‖].γὰρ γράφει [e] τὴν δικαιοσύνην τὴν ἐκ [f]τοῦ[‖]
For Moses writes [of] the righteousness which [is] of the
νόμου, [g]Ὅτι[‖] ὁ ποιήσας [h]αὐτὰ[‖] ἄνθρωπος ζήσεται
law, That the [2]having [3]practised [4]those [5]things [1]man shall live
ἐν [i]αὐτοῖς.[‖] 6 Ἡ.δὲ ἐκ πίστεως δικαιοσύνη οὕτως λέγει,
by them. But the [2]of [3]faith [1]righteousness thus speaks:

to pass, *that* in the place where it was said unto them, Ye *are* not my people; there shall they be called the children of the living God. 27 Esaias also crieth concerning Israel, Though the number of the children of Israel be as the sand of the sea, a remnant shall be saved: 28 for he will finish the work, and cut *it* short in righteousness: because a short work will the Lord make upon the earth. 29 And as Esaias said before, Except the Lord of Sabaoth had left us a seed, we had been as Sodoma, and been made like unto Gomorrha.

30 What shall we say then? That the Gentiles, which followed not after righteousness, have attained to righteousness, even the righteousness which is of faith. 31 But Israel, which followed after the law of righteousness, hath not attained to the law of righteousness. 32 Wherefore? Because *they sought it* not by faith, but as it were by the works of the law. For they stumbled at that stumblingstone; 33 as it is written, Behold, I lay in Sion a stumblingstone and rock of offence: and whosoever believeth on him shall not be ashamed.

X. Brethren, my heart's desire and prayer to God for Israel is, that they might be saved. 2 For I bear them record that they have a zeal of God, but not according to knowledge. 3 For they being ignorant of God's righteousness, and going about to establish their own righteousness, have not submitted themselves unto the righteousness of God. 4 For Christ *is* the end of the law for righteousness to every one that believeth.

5 For Moses describ-

[r] ὑπόλειμμα LTTrA. [s] — ἐν δικαιοσύνῃ ὅτι λόγον συντετμημένον LTTr[A]. [t] ἐν- T. [v] — δικαιοσύνης (*read* to [that] law) LTTrAW. [w] διὰ τί LTrA. [x] — νόμου LTTr[A]W. [y] — γὰρ for LTTrA. [z] — πᾶς (*read* ὁ he that) LTTrAW. [a] — ἡ LTTrAW. [b] αὐτῶν them [is] GLTTrAW. [c] — δικαιοσύνην GLTr[A]W. [d] Μωϋσῆς GLTTrAW. [e] + ὅτι that T. [f] — τοῦ TTrA. [g] — ὅτι T. [h] — αὐτὰ [L]T. [i] αὐτῇ it LTTrA.

Μὴ.εἴπῃς ἐν [k]τῇ[ǁ].καρδίᾳ.σου, Τίς ἀναβήσεται εἰς τὸν
Thou mayest not say in thy heart, Who shall ascend to the
οὐρανόν; τοῦτ' ἔστιν χριστὸν καταγαγεῖν· 7 ἤ, Τίς κατα-
heaven? that is, Christ to bring down. Or, Who shall
βήσεται εἰς τὴν ἄβυσσον; τοῦτ' ἔστιν χριστὸν ἐκ
descend into the abyss? that is, Christ from among [the]
νεκρῶν ἀναγαγεῖν. 8 ἀλλὰ τί λέγει; Ἐγγύς σου τὸ ῥῆμά
dead to bring up. But what says it? Near thee the word
ἐστιν, ἐν τῷ.στόματί.σου καὶ ἐν τῇ.καρδίᾳ.σου. τοῦτ' ἔστιν τὸ
is, in thy mouth and in thy heart: that is the
ῥῆμα τῆς πίστεως ὃ κηρύσσομεν· 9 ὅτι ἐὰν ὁμολογήσῃς
word of faith which we proclaim, that if thou confess
ἐν τῷ.στόματί.σου κύριον Ἰησοῦν, καὶ πιστεύσῃς ἐν τῇ
with thy mouth [the] Lord Jesus, and believe in
καρδίᾳ.σου ὅτι ὁ θεὸς αὐτὸν ἤγειρεν ἐκ νεκρῶν,
thy heart that God him raised from among [the] dead,
σωθήσῃ· 10 καρδίᾳ.γὰρ πιστεύεται εἰς δικαιοσύνην.
thou shalt be saved. For with [the] heart is belief to righteousness;
στόματι.δὲ ὁμολογεῖται εἰς σωτηρίαν. 11 Λέγει.γὰρ ἡ
and with [the] mouth is confession to salvation. For says the
γραφή, Πᾶς ὁ πιστεύων ἐπ' αὐτῷ οὐ.καταισχυνθήσεται.
scripture, Everyone that believes on him shall not be ashamed.
12 Οὐ.γάρ.ἐστιν διαστολὴ Ἰουδαίου τε καὶ Ἕλληνος· ὁ.γὰρ
For there is not a difference of Jew and Greek; for the
αὐτὸς κύριος πάντων πλουτῶν εἰς πάντας τοὺς ἐπικαλου-
same Lord of all [is] rich toward all that call
μένους αὐτόν. 13 Πᾶς.γὰρ ὃς.ἂν ἐπικαλέσηται τὸ ὄνομα
upon him. For everyone, whoever may call on the name
κυρίου, σωθήσεται. 14 Πῶς οὖν [l]ἐπικαλέσονται[ǁ] εἰς
of [the] Lord, shall be saved. How then shall they call on [him]
ὃν οὐκ.ἐπίστευσαν; πῶς.δὲ [m]πιστεύσουσιν[ǁ] οὗ
whom they believed not? and how shall they believe on [him] of whom
οὐκ.ἤκουσαν; πῶς.δὲ [n]ἀκούσουσιν[ǁ] χωρὶς κηρύσσοντος;
they heard not? and how shall they hear apart from [one] preaching?
15 πῶς.δὲ [o]κηρύξουσιν,[ǁ] ἐὰν.μὴ ἀποσταλῶσιν; καθὼς
and how shall they preach, unless they be sent? according as
γέγραπται, Ὡς ὡραῖοι οἱ πόδες τῶν [p]εὐαγγελιζο-
it has been written, How beautiful the feet of those announcing the glad
μένων εἰρήνην, τῶν[ǁ] εὐαγγελιζομένων [q]τὰ[ǁ] ἀγαθά.
tidings of peace, of those announcing the glad tidings of good things!
16 Ἀλλ' οὐ πάντες ὑπήκουσαν τῷ εὐαγγελίῳ· Ἡσαΐας.γὰρ
But not all obeyed the glad tidings. For Esaias
λέγει, Κύριε, τίς ἐπίστευσεν τῇ.ἀκοῇ.ἡμῶν; 17 Ἄρα ἡ πίστις
says, Lord, who believed our report? So faith [is]
ἐξ ἀκοῆς, ἡ.δὲ ἀκοὴ διὰ ῥήματος [r]θεοῦ.[ǁ] 18 ἀλλὰ λέγω,
by report, but the report by [the] word of God. But I say,
Μὴ οὐκ.ἤκουσαν; [s]μενοῦνγε[ǁ] εἰς πᾶσαν τὴν γῆν ἐξῆλθεν
Did they not hear? Yea, rather, Into all the earth went out
ὁ.φθόγγος.αὐτῶν, καὶ εἰς τὰ πέρατα τῆς οἰκουμένης τὰ ῥήματα
their voice, and to the ends of the habitable world [2]words
αὐτῶν. 19 Ἀλλὰ λέγω, Μὴ.[t]οὐκ.ἔγνω Ἰσραήλ[ǁ]; πρῶτος
[1]their. But I say, Did not [2]know [1]Israel? First,

eth the righteousness which is of the law, That the man which doeth those things shall live by them.
6 But the righteousness which is of faith speaketh on this wise, Say not in thine heart, Who shall ascend into heaven? (that is, to bring Christ down *from above:*)
7 or, Who shall descend into the deep? (that is, to bring up Christ again from the dead.)
8 But what saith it? The word is nigh thee, *even* in thy mouth, and in thy heart: that is, the word of faith, which we preach;
9 That if thou shalt confess with thy mouth the Lord Jesus, and shalt believe in thine heart that God hath raised him from the dead, thou shalt be saved.
10 For with the heart man believeth unto righteousness; and with the mouth confession is made unto salvation.
11 For the scripture saith, Whosoever believeth on him shall not be ashamed.
12 For there is no difference between the Jew and the Greek: for the same Lord over all is rich unto all that call upon him.
13 For whosoever shall call upon the name of the Lord shall be saved.
14 How then shall they call on him in whom they have not believed? and how shall they believe in him of whom they have not heard? and how shall they hear without a preacher?
15 And how shall they preach, except they be sent? as it is written, How beautiful are the feet of them that preach the gospel of peace, and bring glad tidings of good things!
16 But they have not all obeyed the gospel. For Esaias saith, Lord, who hath believed our report?
17 So then faith *cometh* by hearing, and hearing by the word of God.
18 But I say,

---

[k] — τῇ E. [l] ἐπικαλέσωνται should they call LTTrAW. [m] πιστεύσωσιν should they believe LTTrAW. [n] ἀκούσονται T; ἀκούσωσιν should they hear LTrAW. [o] κηρύξωσιν should they preach LTTrAW. [p] — εὐαγγελιζομένων εἰρήνην τῶν LTTr[A]. [q] — τὰ LTrAW. [r] χριστοῦ of Christ LTTrA. [s] μενοῦν γε LTrW. [t] Ἰσραὴλ οὐκ ἔγνω GLTTrAW.

Have they not heard? Yes verily, their sound went into all the earth, and their words unto the ends of the world. 19 But I say, Did not Israel know? First Moses saith, I will provoke you to jealousy by *them that are* no people, *and* by a foolish nation I will anger you. 20 But Esaias is very bold, and saith, I was found of them that sought me not; I was made manifest unto them that asked not after me. 21 But to Israel he saith, All day long I have stretched forth my hands unto a disobedient and gainsaying people.

XI. I say then, Hath God cast away his people? God forbid. For I also am an Israelite, of the seed of Abraham, *of* the tribe of Benjamin. 2 God hath not cast away his people which he foreknew. Wot ye not what the scripture saith of Elias? how he maketh intercession to God against Israel, saying, 3 Lord, they have killed thy prophets, and digged down thine altars; and I am left alone, and they seek my life. 4 But what saith the answer of God unto him? I have reserved to myself seven thousand men, who have not bowed the knee to *the image of* Baal. 5 Even so then at this present time also there is a remnant according to the election of grace. 6 And if by grace, then *is it* no more of works: otherwise grace is no more grace. But if *it be* of works, then is it no more grace: otherwise work is no more work.

7 What then? Israel hath not obtained that which he seeketh for; but the election hath obtained it, and the rest were blinded 8 (according as it is written, God hath given them the spirit

[u]Μωσῆς‖ λέγει, Ἐγὼ παραζηλώσω ὑμᾶς ἐπ' οὐκ
Moses says, I will provoke to jealousy you through [those] not
ἔθνει, [v]ἐπὶ‖ ἔθνει ἀσυνέτῳ παροργιῶ ὑμᾶς. 20 Ἠ-
a nation, through a nation without understanding I will anger you. [2]E-
σαΐας δὲ ἀποτολμᾷ καὶ λέγει, Εὑρέθην [w] τοῖς ἐμὲ μὴ ζη-
saias [1]but is very bold and says, I was found by those [3]me [1]not [2]seek-
τοῦσιν, ἐμφανὴς ἐγενόμην [x] τοῖς ἐμὲ μὴ ἐπερωτῶσιν. 21 πρὸς
ing; manifested I became to those [4]me [1]not [2]enquiring [3]after. [6]To
δὲ τὸν Ἰσραὴλ λέγει, Ὅλην τὴν ἡμέραν ἐξεπέτασα τὰς
[5]but Israel he says, [2]Whole [1]the day I stretched out
χεῖράς.μου πρὸς λαὸν ἀπειθοῦντα καὶ ἀντιλέγοντα.
my hands to a people disobeying and contradicting.

11 Λέγω οὖν, Μὴ ἀπώσατο ὁ θεὸς τὸν.λαὸν.αὐτοῦ[y];
I say then, Did [2]thrust [3]away [1]God his people?
μὴ.γένοιτο· καὶ.γὰρ ἐγὼ [z]Ἰσραηλίτης‖ εἰμί, ἐκ σπέρματος
May it not be! For also I an Israelite am, of [the] seed
Ἀβραάμ, φυλῆς [a]Βενιαμίν.‖ 2 οὐκ.ἀπώσατο ὁ θεὸς
of Abraham, of [the] tribe of Benjamin. [2]Did [3]not [4]thrust [5]away [1]God
τὸν.λαὸν.αὐτοῦ, ὃν προέγνω. ἢ οὐκ.οἴδατε ἐν
his people, whom he foreknew. Know ye not in [the history of]
[b]Ἠλίᾳ‖ τί λέγει ἡ γραφή; ὡς ἐντυγχάνει τῷ θεῷ κατὰ
Elias what says the scripture? how he pleads with God against
τοῦ Ἰσραήλ, [c]λέγων,‖ 3 Κύριε, τοὺς.προφήτας.σου ἀπέκτειναν,
Israel, saying, Lord, thy prophets they killed,
[d]καὶ‖ τὰ.θυσιαστήριά.σου κατέσκαψαν· κἀγὼ ὑπελείφθην μό-
and thine altars they dug down; and I was left a-
νος, καὶ ζητοῦσιν τὴν.ψυχήν.μου. 4 Ἀλλὰ τί λέγει αὐτῷ ὁ
lone, and they seek my life. But what says to him the
χρηματισμός; Κατέλιπον ἐμαυτῷ ἑπτακισχιλίους ἄνδρας
divine answer? I left to myself seven thousand men
οἵτινες οὐκ.ἔκαμψαν γόνυ τῇ Βάαλ. 5 Οὕτως οὖν καὶ ἐν τῷ
who bowed not a knee to Baal. Thus then also in the
νῦν καιρῷ λεῖμμα κατ' ἐκλογὴν χάριτος γέγονεν.
present time a remnant according to election of grace there has been.
6 εἰ.δὲ χάριτι, οὐκέτι ἐξ ἔργων· ἐπεὶ ἡ χάρις οὐκέτι γίνεται
But if by grace, no longer of works; else grace no longer becomes
χάρις. [e]εἰ.δὲ ἐξ ἔργων, οὐκέτι [f]ἐστὶν[f] χάρις· ἐπεὶ τὸ ἔργον
grace; but if of works, no longer is it grace; else work
οὐκέτι ἐστὶν ἔργον.‖
no longer is work.

7 Τί οὖν; ὃ ἐπιζητεῖ Ἰσραήλ, [g]τούτου‖ οὐκ.ἐπέτυχεν,
What then? What [2]seeks [3]for [1]Israel, this it did not obtain;
ἡ.δὲ ἐκλογὴ ἐπέτυχεν· οἱ.δὲ λοιποὶ ἐπωρώθησαν, 8 [h]καθὼς‖
but the election obtained [it], and the rest were hardened, according as
γέγραπται, Ἔδωκεν αὐτοῖς ὁ θεὸς πνεῦμα κατανύξεως,
it has been written, [2]Gave [3]them [1]God a spirit of slumber,
ὀφθαλμοὺς τοῦ.μὴ βλέπειν, καὶ ὦτα τοῦ.μὴ ἀκούειν, ἕως
eyes so as not to see, and ears so as not to hear, unto
τῆς.σήμερον.ἡμέρας. 9 καὶ [i]Δαβὶδ‖ λέγει, Γενηθήτω ἡ τράπεζα
this day. And David says, Let be [2]table
αὐτῶν εἰς παγίδα, καὶ εἰς θήραν, καὶ εἰς σκάνδαλον, καὶ εἰς
[1]their for a snare, and for a trap, and for cause of offence, and for

---

[u] Μωϋσῆς GLTTrAW. [v] ἐπ' TTr. [w] + [ἐν] by (those) LTrA. [x] + [ἐν] by (those) LTr. [y] + [, ὃν προέγνω] whom he foreknew L. [z] Ἰσραηλείτης T. [a] Βενιαμείν LTTrA. [b] Ἠλείᾳ T. [c] — λέγων GLTTrAW. [d] — καὶ LTTrAW. [e] — εἰ δὲ ἐξ *to end of verse* GLTTr[A]. [f] — ἐστὶν A. [g] τοῦτο GLTTrAW. [h] καθάπερ even as TTr. [i] Δαυείδ LTTrA; Δαυίδ GW.

ἀνταπόδομα αὐτοῖς· 10 σκοτισθήτωσαν οἱ.ὀφθαλμοὶ.αὐτῶν
a recompense to them: let be darkened their eyes
τοῦ.μὴ βλέπειν, καὶ τὸν.νῶτον.αὐτῶν [k]διαπαντὸς" [l]σύγ-
so as not to see, and their back continually bow thou
καμψον."
down.

11 Λέγω οὖν, μὴ ἔπταισαν ἵνα πέσωσιν; μὴ.γένοιτο·
I say then, Did they stumble that they might fall? May it not be!
ἀλλὰ τῷ.αὐτῶν παραπτώματι ἡ σωτηρία τοῖς ἔθνεσιν, εἰς
but by their offence salvation [is] to the nations, for
τὸ παραζηλῶσαι αὐτούς. 12 εἰ.δὲ τὸ.παράπτωμα.αὐτῶν
to provoke to jealousy them. But if their offence [be the]
πλοῦτος κόσμου, καὶ τὸ.ἥττημα.αὐτῶν πλοῦτος ἐθνῶν,
wealth of [the] world, and their default [the] wealth of [the] nations,
πόσῳ μᾶλλον τὸ.πλήρωμα.αὐτῶν; 13 Ὑμῖν [m]γὰρ" λέγω
how much more their fulness? ²To ³you ¹for I speak,
τοῖς ἔθνεσιν· ἐφ'.ὅσον μέν [n] εἰμι ἐγὼ ἐθνῶν ἀπόστολος,
the nations, inasmuch as ²am ¹I ⁴of [⁵the] ⁶nations ³apostle,
τὴν.διακονίαν.μου δοξάζω, 14 εἴ.πως παραζηλώσω
my service I glorify, if by any means I shall provoke to jealousy
μου τὴν σάρκα, καὶ σώσω τινὰς ἐξ αὐτῶν. 15 εἰ.γὰρ
my flesh, and shall save some from among them. For if
ἡ.ἀποβολὴ.αὐτῶν καταλλαγὴ κόσμου, τίς ἡ [o]πρόσ-
their casting away [be the] reconciliation of [the] world, what the recep-
ληψις," εἰ.μὴ ζωὴ ἐκ νεκρῶν;
tion, except life from among [the] dead?

16 εἰ.δὲ ἡ ἀπαρχὴ ἁγία, καὶ τὸ φύραμα· καὶ εἰ ἡ ῥίζα
Now if the first-fruit [be] holy, also the lump; and if the root
ἁγία, καὶ οἱ κλάδοι. 17 εἰ.δέ τινες τῶν κλάδων ἐξεκλάσθη-
[be] holy, also the branches. But if some of the branches were broken
σαν, σὺ.δὲ ἀγριέλαιος ὢν ἐνεκεντρίσθης ἐν αὐτοῖς, καὶ
off, and thou, a wild olive tree being, wast grafted in amongst them, and
[l]συγκοινωνὸς" τῆς ῥίζης [p]καὶ" τῆς πιότητος τῆς ἐλαίας
a fellow-partaker of the root and of the fatness of the olive tree
ἐγένου, 18 μὴ.κατακαυχῶ τῶν κλάδων· εἰ.δὲ κατακαυχᾶσαι,
became, boast not against the branches; but if thou boastest against
οὐ σὺ τὴν ῥίζαν βαστάζεις, [q]ἀλλ'" ἡ ῥίζα σέ. 19 Ἐ-
[them], ³not ¹thou ⁴the ⁵root ²bearest, but the root thee. Thou
ρεῖς οὖν, Ἐξεκλάσθησαν [r]οἱ" κλάδοι, ἵνα ἐγὼ [s]ἐγκεντρισθῶ."
wilt say then, Were broken out the branches, that I might be grafted in.
20 Καλῶς· τῇ ἀπιστίᾳ [t]ἐξεκλάσθησαν," σὺ.δὲ τῇ πίστει
Well; by unbelief they were broken out, and thou by faith
ἕστηκας. μὴ.[v]ὑψηλοφρόνει," ἀλλὰ φοβοῦ· 21 εἰ.γὰρ ὁ θεὸς
standest. Be not high-minded, but fear: for if God
τῶν κατὰ φύσιν κλάδων οὐκ.ἐφείσατο, [w]μήπως" οὐδέ σου
the ²according ³to ⁴nature ¹branches spared not— lest neither thee
[x]φείσηται." 22 Ἴδε οὖν χρηστότητα καὶ ἀποτομίαν θεοῦ·
he should spare. Behold then [the] kindness and severity of God:
ἐπὶ μὲν τοὺς πεσόντας, [y]ἀποτομίαν·" ἐπὶ.δέ σε, [z]χρηστό-
upon those that fell, severity; and upon thee, kind-
τητα," ἐὰν [a]ἐπιμείνῃς" τῇ χρηστότητι· ἐπεὶ καὶ σὺ ἐκ-
ness, if thou continue in [his] kindness, else also thou wilt

of slumber, eyes that they should not see, and ears that they should not hear;) unto this day.
9 And David saith, Let their table be made a snare, and a trap, and a stumblingblock, and a recompence unto them:
10 let their eyes be darkened, that they may not see, and bow down their back alway.
11 I say then, Have they stumbled that they should fall? God forbid: but *rather* through their fall salvation *is come* unto the Gentiles, for to provoke them to jealousy.
12 Now if the fall of them *be* the riches of the world, and the diminishing of them the riches of the Gentiles; how much more their fulness?
13 For I speak to you Gentiles, inasmuch as I am the apostle of the Gentiles, I magnify mine office:
14 if by any means I may provoke to emulation *them which are* my flesh, and might save some of them.
15 For if the casting away of them *be* the reconciling of the world, what *shall* the receiving *of them be*, but life from the dead?
16 For if the firstfruit *be* holy, the lump *is* also *holy*: and if the root *be* holy, so *are* the branches.
17 And if some of the branches be broken off, and thou, being a wild olive tree, wert graffed in among them, and with them partakest of the root and fatness of the olive tree;
18 boast not against the branches. But if thou boast, thou bearest not the root, but the root thee.
19 Thou wilt say then, The branches were broken off, that I might be graffed in.
20 Well; because of unbelief they were broken off, and thou standest by faith. Be not highminded, but fear:
21 for if God spared not the natural

k διὰ παντὸς LTTrA. l συν- T. m δὲ and LTTrA. n + οὖν then LT[Tr]AW. o πρόσλημψις LTTrA. p — καὶ T[Tr]A. q ἀλλὰ TTrA. r — οἱ GLTTrAW. s ἐν- T. t ἐκλάσθησαν broken off LTr. v ὑψηλὰ φρόνει TTr. w — μήπως LTTr[A]. x φείσεται he will spare GLTTrAW. y ἀποτομία LTTrA. z χρηστότης θεοῦ kindness of God LTTrA. a ἐπιμένῃς TTr.

branches, *take heed*
lest he also spare not
thee. 22 Behold there-
fore the goodness and
severity of God: on
them which fell, seve-
rity; but toward thee,
goodness, if thou con-
tinue in *his* goodness:
otherwise thou also
shalt be cut off. 23 And
they also, if they a-
bide not still in un-
belief, shall be graffed
in: for God is able to
graff them in again.
24 For if thou wert
cut out of the olive
tree which is wild by
nature, and wert graff-
ed contrary to nature
into a good olive tree:
how much more shall
these, which be the
natural *branches*, be
graffed into their own
olive tree? 25 For I
would not, brethren,
that ye should be ig-
norant of this mys-
tery, lest ye should be
wise in your own con-
ceits; that blindness
in part is happened to
Israel, until the ful-
ness of the Gentiles be
come in. 26 And so all
Israel shall be saved:
as it is written, There
shall come out of Sion
the Deliverer, and
shall turn away un-
godliness from Jacob:
27 For this *is* my
covenant unto them,
when I shall take away
their sins. 28 As con-
cerning the gospel,
they are enemies for
your sakes: but as
touching the election,
they are beloved for
the fathers' sakes.
29 For the gifts and
calling of God *are*
without repentance.
30 For as ye in times
past have not believed
God, yet have now ob-
tained mercy through
their unbelief: 31 even
so have these also
now not believed, that
through your mercy
they also may obtain
mercy. 32 For God
hath concluded them
all in unbelief, that he
might have mercy up-
on all. 33 O the depth
of the riches both of
the wisdom and know-
ledge of God! how
unsearchable *are* his
judgments, and his
ways past finding out!
34 For who hath known
the mind of the Lord?

κοπήσῃ. 23 [b]καὶ ἐκεῖνοι‖ δέ, ἐὰν μὴ-[c]ἐπιμείνωσιν‖ τῇ ἀπιστίᾳ,
be cut off. [3]Also [2]they [1]and, if they continue not in unbelief,
[d]ἐγκεντρισθήσονται‖ δυνατὸς-γάρ ἐστιν ὁ θεὸς πάλιν [d]ἐγκεν-
shall be grafted in; for able is God again to graft
τρίσαι‖ αὐτούς. 24 εἰ-γὰρ σὺ ἐκ τῆς κατὰ φύσιν ἐξε-
in them. For if thou out of the [4]according [5]to [6]nature [7]wast
κόπης ἀγριελαίου, καὶ παρὰ φύσιν ἐνεκεντρίσθης εἰς
[8]cut [9]off [1]wild [2]olive [3]tree, and, contrary to nature, wast grafted in to
καλλιέλαιον, πόσῳ μᾶλλον οὗτοι οἱ κατὰ φύσιν,
a good olive tree, how much more these who according to nature [are],
[d]ἐγκεντρισθήσονται‖ τῇ-ἰδίᾳ ἐλαίᾳ; 25 Οὐ-γὰρ θέλω ὑμᾶς
shall be grafted into their own olive tree? For [3]not [2]do [1]I wish you
ἀγνοεῖν, ἀδελφοί, τὸ-μυστήριον-τοῦτο, ἵνα μὴ-ἦτε [e]παρ'‖
to be ignorant, brethren, of this mystery, that ye may not be in
ἑαυτοῖς φρόνιμοι, ὅτι πώρωσις ἀπὸ μέρους τῷ Ἰσραὴλ γέ-
yourselves wise, that hardness in part to Israel has
γονεν, ἄχρις-οὗ τὸ πλήρωμα τῶν ἐθνῶν εἰσέλθῃ· 26 καὶ
happened, until the fulness of the nations be come in; and
οὕτως πᾶς Ἰσραὴλ σωθήσεται, καθὼς γέγραπται,
so all Israel shall be saved, according as it has been written,
Ἥξει ἐκ Σιὼν ὁ ῥυόμενος, [f]καὶ‖ ἀποστρέψει ἀσεβείας
Shall come out of Sion the deliverer, and he shall turn away ungodliness
ἀπὸ Ἰακώβ· 27 καὶ αὕτη αὐτοῖς ἡ παρ' ἐμοῦ διαθήκη,
from Jacob. And this [is] [5]to [6]them [1]the [3]from [4]me [2]covenant,
ὅταν ἀφέλωμαι τὰς-ἁμαρτίας-αὐτῶν. 28 Κατὰ μὲν
when I may have taken away their sins. As regards indeed
τὸ εὐαγγέλιον, ἐχθροὶ δι'-ὑμᾶς· κατὰ-δὲ τὴν
the glad tidings, [they are] enemies on your account; but as regards the
ἐκλογήν, ἀγαπητοὶ διὰ τοὺς πατέρας. 29 ἀμεταμέλητα
election, beloved on account of the fathers. [2]Not [3]to [4]be [5]repented [6]of
γὰρ τὰ χαρίσματα καὶ ἡ κλῆσις τοῦ θεοῦ. 30 ὥσπερ-γὰρ
[1]for [are] the gifts and the calling of God. For as
[g]καὶ ὑμεῖς ποτε ἠπειθήσατε τῷ θεῷ, νῦν-δὲ ἠλεήθητε
also ye once were disobedient to God, but now have been shewn mercy
τῇ-τούτων ἀπειθείᾳ· 31 οὕτως καὶ οὗτοι νῦν ἠπείθησαν
through their disobedience; so also these now were disobedient
τῷ-[h]ὑμετέρῳ‖-ἐλέει, ἵνα καὶ αὐτοὶ [i] ἐλεηθῶσιν.
to your mercy, that also they may have mercy shewn [them].
32 συνέκλεισεν-γὰρ ὁ θεὸς τοὺς πάντας εἰς ἀπείθειαν, ἵνα τοὺς
For [2]shut [3]up [4]together [1]God all in disobedience, that
πάντας ἐλεήσῃ. 33 Ὦ βάθος πλούτου καὶ σοφίας
all he might shew mercy to. O depth of riches both of wisdom
καὶ γνώσεως θεοῦ. ὡς [k]ἀνεξερεύνητα‖ τὰ-κρίματα-αὐτοῦ, καὶ
and knowledge of God! How unsearchable his judgments, and
ἀνεξιχνίαστοι αἱ-ὁδοὶ-αὐτοῦ. 34 τίς-γὰρ ἔγνω νοῦν
untraceable his ways! For who did know [the] mind
κυρίου; ἢ τίς σύμβουλος-αὐτοῦ ἐγένετο; 35 ἢ τίς προέ-
of [the] Lord, or who his counsellor became? Or who first
δωκεν αὐτῷ, καὶ ἀνταποδοθήσεται αὐτῷ; 36 ὅτι ἐξ αὐτοῦ
gave to him, and it shall be recompensed to him? For of him
καὶ δι' αὐτοῦ καὶ εἰς αὐτὸν τὰ-πάντα· αὐτῷ ἡ δόξα
and through him and unto him [are] all things: to him [be] the glory
εἰς τοὺς αἰῶνας. ἀμήν.
to the ages. Amen.

---

[b] κἀκεῖνοι GLTTrAW. [c] ἐπιμένωσιν TTr. [d] ἐν- T. [e] ἐν TrA. [f] — καὶ LTTrAW
[g] — καὶ GLTTrAW. [h] ἡμετέρῳ (*read* to our mercy) E. [i] + νῦν now [L]T. [k] ἀνεξεραύνητα TTr.

12 Παρακαλῶ οὖν ὑμᾶς, ἀδελφοί, διὰ τῶν οἰκτιρμῶν τοῦ
I exhort therefore you, brethren, by the compassions
θεοῦ, παραστῆσαι τὰ.σώματα.ὑμῶν θυσίαν ζῶσαν, ἁγίαν,
of God, to present your bodies a [2]sacrifice [1]living, holy,
[l]εὐάρεστον τῷ θεῷ," τὴν λογικὴν λατρείαν ὑμῶν· 2 καὶ μὴ
well-pleasing to God, [2]intelligent [3]service [1]your. And [2]not
[m]συσχηματίζεσθε" τῷ.αἰῶνι.τούτῳ, ἀλλὰ [n]μεταμορφοῦσθε" τῇ
[1]fashion yourselves to this age, but be transformed by the
ἀνακαινώσει τοῦ.νοὸς.[o]ὑμῶν," εἰς τὸ δοκιμάζειν ὑμᾶς τί
renewing of your mind, for to prove by you what [is]
τὸ θέλημα τοῦ θεοῦ τὸ ἀγαθὸν καὶ εὐάρεστον καὶ τέλειον.
[7]will [8]of [9]God [1]the [2]good [3]and [4]well-pleasing [5]and [6]perfect.
3 Λέγω.γὰρ διὰ τῆς χάριτος τῆς δοθείσης μοι, παντὶ
For I say through the grace which is given to me, to everyone
τῷ.ὄντι ἐν ὑμῖν, μὴ ὑπερφρονεῖν παρ' ὃ δεῖ
that is among you, not to be high-minded above what it behoves [you]
φρονεῖν, ἀλλὰ φρονεῖν εἰς.τὸ σωφρονεῖν, ἑκάστῳ ὡς ὁ
to be minded; but to be minded so as to be sober-minded to each as
θεὸς ἐμέρισεν μέτρον πίστεως. 4 Καθάπερ.γὰρ ἐν ἑνὶ σώματι
God divided a measure of faith. For even as in one body
[p]μέλη πολλὰ" ἔχομεν, τὰ.δὲ μέλη πάντα οὐ τὴν αὐτὴν
[2]members [1]many we have, but the members all [2]not [3]the [4]same
ἔχει πρᾶξιν· 5 οὕτως οἱ πολλοὶ ἓν σῶμά ἐσμεν ἐν χριστῷ,
[1]have function; thus [2]the [3]many [5]one [6]body [1]we [4]are in Christ,
[q]ὁ".δὲ.καθ'.εἷς ἀλλήλων μέλη. 6 ἔχοντες.δὲ χαρίσματα
and each one [2]of [3]each [4]other [1]members. But having [2]gifts
κατὰ τὴν χάριν τὴν δοθεῖσαν ἡμῖν διάφορα· εἴτε
[3]according [4]to [5]the [6]grace [7]which [8]is [9]given [10]to [11]us [1]different, whether
προφητείαν, κατὰ τὴν ἀναλογίαν τῆς πίστεως· 7 εἴτε δια-
prophecy— according to the proportion of faith; or ser-
κονίαν, ἐν τῇ διακονίᾳ· εἴτε ὁ διδάσκων, ἐν τῇ διδασκαλίᾳ·
vice— in service; or he that teaches— in teaching;
8 εἴτε ὁ παρακαλῶν, ἐν τῇ παρακλήσει· ὁ μεταδιδούς, ἐν
or that exhorts— in exhortation; he that imparts— in
ἁπλότητι· ὁ προϊστάμενος, ἐν σπουδῇ· ὁ ἐλεῶν,
simplicity, he that takes the lead— with diligence; he that shews mercy—
ἐν ἱλαρότητι. 9 Ἡ ἀγάπη ἀνυπόκριτος· ἀποστυγοῦντες τὸ
with cheerfulness. [Let] love [be] unfeigned; abhorring
πονηρόν, κολλώμενοι τῷ ἀγαθῷ· 10 τῇ φιλαδελφίᾳ εἰς ἀλ-
evil, cleaving to good; in brotherly love towards one
λήλους φιλόστοργοι· τῇ τιμῇ ἀλλήλους προηγούμενοι·
another kindly affectioned; in [giving] honour [3]one [4]another [1]going [2]before;
11 τῇ σπουδῇ μὴ ὀκνηροί, τῷ πνεύματι ζέοντες, [r]τῷ καιρῷ"
in diligence, not slothful; in spirit, fervent; [2]in [3]season
δουλεύοντες· 12 τῇ ἐλπίδι χαίροντες, τῇ θλίψει ὑπομένον-
[1]serving. In hope, rejoicing; in tribulation, endur-
τες, τῇ προσευχῇ προσκαρτεροῦντες· 13 ταῖς χρείαις τῶν
ing; in prayer, stedfastly continuing; to the needs of the
ἁγίων κοινωνοῦντες, τὴν φιλοξενίαν διώκοντες· 14 εὐλογεῖτε
saints communicating; hospitality pursuing. Bless
τοὺς διώκοντας ὑμᾶς· εὐλογεῖτε, καὶ μὴ.καταρᾶσθε. 15 χαί-
those that persecute you; bless, and curse not. Re-
ρειν μετὰ χαιρόντων, [s]καὶ" κλαίειν μετὰ κλαιόντων. 16 τὸ
joice with rejoicing ones, and weep with weeping ones; the

or who hath been his
counseller? 35 or who
hath first given to him,
and it shall be recom-
pensed unto him again?
36 For of him, and
through him, and to
him, *are* all things: to
whom *be* glory for
ever. Amen.

XII. I beseech you
therefore, brethren, by
the mercies of God,
that ye present your
bodies a living sacri-
fice, holy, acceptable
unto God, *which is*
your reasonable ser-
vice. 2 And be not
conformed to this
world: but be ye trans-
formed by the renew-
ing of your mind, that
ye may prove what *is*
that good, and accept-
able, and perfect, will
of God. 3 For I say,
through the grace
given unto me, to
every man that is a-
mong you, not to think
of himself more highly
than he ought to think;
but to think soberly,
according as God hath
dealt to every man the
measure of faith. 4 For
as we have many mem-
bers in one body, and
all members have not
the same office: 5 so we,
being many, are one
body in Christ, and
every one members one
of another. 6 Having
then gifts differing ac-
cording to the grace
that is given to us,
whether prophecy, *let
us prophesy* according
to the proportion of
faith; 7 or ministry,
let us wait on *our*
ministering: or he
that teacheth, on
teaching; 8 or he that
exhorteth, on exhor-
tation: he that giveth,
let him do it with sim-
plicity; he that ruleth,
with diligence; he that
sheweth mercy, with
cheerfulness. 9 *Let*
love be without dissi-
mulation. Abhor that
which is evil; cleave
to that which is good.
10 *Be* kindly affec-
tioned one to another
with brotherly love;
in honour preferring
one another; 11 not
slothful in business;
fervent in spirit; serv-
ing the Lord; 12 re-
joicing in hope; pa-
tient in tribulation;
continuing instant in

---

[l] τῷ θεῷ εὐάρεστον T. [m] συ(συν- A)σχηματίζεσθαι to fashion yourselves) LA; συνσχηματίζεσθε T. [n] μεταμορφοῦσθαι to be transformed LA. [o] — ὑμῶν (*read* the mind) LTTrAW. [p] πολλὰ μέλη LTTrAW. [q] τὸ LTTrAW. [r] τῷ κυρίῳ the Lord ELTTrAW. [s] — καὶ LTTrAW.

prayer; 13 distributing to the necessity of saints; given to hospitality. 14 Bless them which persecute you: bless, and curse not. 15 Rejoice with them that do rejoice, and weep with them that weep. 16 *Be* of the same mind one toward another. Mind not high things, but condescend to men of low estate. Be not wise in your own conceits. 17 Recompense to no man evil for evil. Provide things honest in the sight of all men. 18 If it be possible, as much as lieth in you, live peaceably with all men. 19 Dearly beloved, avenge not yourselves, but *rather* give place unto wrath: for it is written, Vengeance *is* mine; I will repay, saith the Lord. 20 Therefore if thine enemy hunger, feed him; if he thirst, give him drink: for in so doing thou shalt heap coals of fire on his head. 21 Be not overcome of evil, but overcome evil with good.

XIII. Let every soul be subject unto the higher powers. For there is no power but of God: the powers that be are ordained of God. 2 Whosoever therefore resisteth the power, resisteth the ordinance of God: and they that resist shall receive to themselves damnation. 3 For rulers are not a terror to good works, but to the evil. Wilt thou then not be afraid of the power? do that which is good, and thou shalt have praise of the same: 4 for he is the minister of God to thee for good. But if thou do that which is evil, be afraid; for he beareth not the sword in vain: for he is the minister of God, a revenger to *execute* wrath upon him that doeth evil. 5 Wherefore *ye* must needs be subject, not only for wrath, but also for conscience sake. 6 For for this cause pay ye tribute also: for they are God's ministers, attending continually

αὐτὸ εἰς ἀλλήλους φρονοῦντες· μὴ τὰ.ὑψηλὰ φρο-
same thing toward one another minding, not high things mind-
νοῦντες, ἀλλὰ τοῖς ταπεινοῖς συναπαγόμενοι. μὴ.γίνεσθε
ing, but with the lowly going along: be not
φρόνιμοι παρ' ἑαυτοῖς. 17 μηδενὶ κακὸν ἀντὶ κακοῦ ἀποδι-
wise in yourselves: to no one evil for evil ren-
δόντες· προνοούμενοι καλὰ [t] ἐνώπιον [v]πάντων‖ ἀνθρώπων·
dering: providing right [things] before all men:
18 εἰ δυνατόν, τὸ.ἐξ.ὑμῶν, μετὰ πάντων ἀνθρώπων εἰρη-
if possible, as to yourselves, with all men being
νεύοντες. 19 μὴ ἑαυτοὺς ἐκδικοῦντες, ἀγαπητοί, ἀλλὰ δότε
at peace; not yourselves avenging, beloved, but give
τόπον τῇ ὀργῇ· γέγραπται.γάρ, Ἐμοὶ ἐκδίκησις, ἐγὼ ἀντα-
place to wrath; for it has been written, To me vengeance! I will
ποδώσω, λέγει κύριος. 20 [w]Ἐὰν οὖν‖ πεινᾷ ὁ ἐχθρός
recompense, says [the] Lord. If therefore should hunger [2]enemy
σου, ψώμιζε αὐτόν· ἐὰν διψᾷ, πότιζε αὐτόν· τοῦτο
[1]thine, feed him; if he should thirst, give [2]drink [1]him; [4]this
γὰρ ποιῶν, ἄνθρακας πυρὸς σωρεύσεις ἐπὶ τὴν κεφαλὴν
[3]for doing, coals of fire thou wilt heap upon [2]head
αὐτοῦ. 21 μὴ.νικῶ ὑπὸ τοῦ κακοῦ, ἀλλὰ νίκα ἐν τῷ
[1]his. Be not overcome by evil, but overcome [2]with
ἀγαθῷ τὸ κακόν.
[3]good [1]evil.

13 Πᾶσα ψυχὴ ἐξουσίαις ὑπερεχούσαις ὑποτασσέσθω.
[2]Every [3]soul [6]to [7]authorities [8]above [[9]him] [1]let [4]be [5]subject.
οὐ.γάρ.ἐστιν ἐξουσία εἰ.μὴ [x]ἀπὸ‖ θεοῦ· αἱ.δὲ οὖσαι
For there is no authority except from God; and those that are
[y]ἐξουσίαι‖ ὑπὸ [z]τοῦ‖ θεοῦ τεταγμέναι.εἰσίν. 2 ὥστε ὁ
authorities, by God have been appointed. So that he that
ἀντιτασσόμενος τῇ ἐξουσίᾳ, τῇ.τοῦ θεοῦ διαταγῇ ἀνθέστηκεν·
sets himself against the authority, the [2]of [3]God [1]ordinance resists;
οἱ.δὲ ἀνθεστηκότες, ἑαυτοῖς κρίμα [a]λήψονται.‖ 3 οἱ
and they that resist, to themselves judgment shall receive. [2]The
γὰρ ἄρχοντες οὐκ.εἰσὶν φόβος [b]τῶν ἀγαθῶν ἔργων,‖ ἀλλὰ
[1]for rulers are not a terror to good works, but
[c]τῶν κακῶν.‖ θέλεις.δὲ μὴ φοβεῖσθαι τὴν ἐξουσίαν; τὸ
to evil [ones]. Dost thou desire not to be afraid of the authority? [2]the
ἀγαθὸν ποίει, καὶ ἕξεις ἔπαινον ἐξ αὐτῆς· 4 θεοῦ.γὰρ
[3]good [1]practise, and thou shalt have praise from it; for of God
διάκονός ἐστίν σοι εἰς τὸ ἀγαθόν. ἐὰν δὲ τὸ κακὸν ποιῇς,
a servant it is to thee for good. But if evil thou practisest,
φοβοῦ· οὐ.γὰρ εἰκῇ τὴν μάχαιραν φορεῖ· θεοῦ.γὰρ διάκονός
fear; for not in vain the sword it wears; for of God a servant
ἐστιν, ἔκδικος εἰς ὀργὴν τῷ τὸ κακὸν πράσσοντι. 5 διὸ
it is, an avenger for wrath to him that [2]evil [1]does. Wherefore
ἀνάγκη ὑποτάσσεσθαι, οὐ μόνον διὰ τὴν ὀργήν,
necessary [it is] to be subject, not only on account of wrath,
ἀλλὰ καὶ διὰ τὴν συνείδησιν. 6 διὰ.τοῦτο.γὰρ καὶ
but also on account of conscience. For on this account also
φόρους τελεῖτε· λειτουργοὶ.γὰρ θεοῦ εἰσιν, εἰς.αὐτὸ.τοῦτο
tribute pay ye; for ministers of God they are, on this same thing
προσκαρτεροῦντες. 7 ἀπόδοτε [d]οὖν‖ πᾶσιν τὰς ὀφειλάς·
attending continually. Render therefore to all their dues:

---

[t] + [ἐνώπιον τοῦ θεοῦ καὶ] before God and L. [v] τῶν L. [w] ἀλλὰ ἐὰν But if LTTrA. [x] ὑπὸ LTTr. [y] — ἐξουσίαι GLTTrAW. [z] — τοῦ GLTTrAW. [a] λήμψονται LTTrA. [b] τῷ ἀγαθῷ ἔργῳ to a good work LTTrAW. [c] τῷ κακῷ to an evil [one] LTTrAW. [d] — οὖν LTTrAW.

τῷ τὸν φόρον, τὸν φόρον· τῷ τὸ τέλος, τὸ τέλος· τῷ
to whom tribute, tribute; to whom custom, custom; to whom
τὸν φόβον, τὸν φόβον· τῷ τὴν τιμήν, τὴν τιμήν. 8 Μηδενὶ
fear, fear; to whom honour, honour. To no one
μηδὲν ὀφείλετε, εἰ.μὴ τὸ [e]ἀγαπᾷν ἀλλήλους·‖ ὁ.γὰρ
anything owe ye, unless to love one another: for he that
(*lit.* nothing)
ἀγαπῶν τὸν ἕτερον, νόμον πεπλήρωκεν. 9 τὸ γάρ, Οὐ
loves the other, law has fulfilled. For, [3]Not
μοιχεύσεις, οὐ.φονεύσεις, οὐ.κλέψεις,
[1]thou [2]shalt commit adultery, Thou shalt not commit murder, Thou shalt not steal,
[f]οὐ.ψευδομαρτυρήσεις,‖ οὐκ.ἐπιθυμήσεις, καὶ εἴ τις ἑτέρα
Thou shalt not bear false witness, Thou shalt not lust; and if any other com-
ἐντολή, ἐν [g]τούτῳ τῷ λόγῳ‖ ἀνακεφαλαιοῦται, [h]ἐν τῷ,‖ Ἀγα-
mandment, in this word it is summed up, in this, Thou
πήσεις τὸν.πλησίον.σου ὡς [i]ἑαυτόν.‖ 10 Ἡ ἀγάπη τῷ πλη-
shalt love thy neighbour as thyself. Love to the neigh-
σίον κακὸν οὐκ.ἐργάζεται· πλήρωμα οὖν νόμου ἡ ἀγάπη.
bour, evil does not work: [3]fulness [4]therefore [5]of [[6]the] [7]law [1]love [[2]is].
11 Καὶ τοῦτο, εἰδότες τὸν καιρόν, ὅτι ὥρα [k]ἡμᾶς
Also this, knowing the time, that [the] hour [4]we [[1]it [2]is]
ἤδη‖ ἐξ ὕπνου ἐγερθῆναι· νῦν.γὰρ ἐγγύτερον ἡμῶν ἡ
[3]already out of sleep should be roused; for now nearer [is] of us the
σωτηρία, ἢ ὅτε ἐπιστεύσαμεν. 12 ἡ νὺξ προέκοψεν, ἡ.δὲ
salvation, than when we believed. The night is advanced, and the
ἡμέρα ἤγγικεν. ἀποθώμεθα οὖν τὰ ἔργα τοῦ σκότους,
day has drawn near; we should cast off therefore the works of darkness,
[l]καὶ ἐνδυσώμεθα‖ τὰ ὅπλα τοῦ φωτός. 13 ὡς ἐν ἡμέρᾳ,
and should put on the armour of light. As in [the] day,
εὐσχημόνως περιπατήσωμεν, μὴ κώμοις καὶ μέθαις, μὴ κοί-
becomingly we should walk; not in revels and drinking, not in cham-
ταις καὶ ἀσελγείαις, μὴ ἔριδι καὶ ζήλῳ· 14 [m]ἀλλ'‖ ἐνδύσασθε
bering and wantonness, not in strife and emulation. But put on
τὸν κύριον Ἰησοῦν χριστόν, καὶ τῆς σαρκὸς πρόνοιαν μὴ
the Lord Jesus Christ, and [7]of [8]the [9]flesh [4]forethought [2]not
ποιεῖσθε εἰς ἐπιθυμίας.
[1]do [3]take [5]for [6]desire.

14 Τὸν.δὲ ἀσθενοῦντα τῇ πίστει προσλαμβάνεσθε, μὴ εἰς
But him being weak in the faith receive not for
διακρίσεις διαλογισμῶν. 2 Ὃς.μὲν πιστεύει φαγεῖν πάντα,
decisions of reasonings. One believes to eat all things;
ὁ.δὲ ἀσθενῶν λάχανα ἐσθίει. 3 ὁ ἐσθίων, τὸν μὴ
another being weak [2]herbs [1]eats. He that eats, [5]him [6]that [8]not
ἐσθίοντα μὴ.ἐξουθενείτω· [n]καὶ ὁ‖ μὴ.ἐσθίων, τὸν ἐ-
[7]eats [1]let [2]him [3]not [4]despise; and he that eats not, [5]him [6]that
σθίοντα μὴ.κρινέτω· ὁ.θεὸς.γὰρ αὐτὸν προσελάβετο. 4 σὺ
[7]eats [1]let [2]him [3]not [4]judge: for God him received. [3]Thou
τίς εἶ ὁ κρίνων ἀλλότριον οἰκέτην; τῷ.ἰδίῳ κυρίῳ στήκει
[1]who [2]art judging another's servant? to his own master he stands
ἢ πίπτει. σταθήσεται.δέ· [o]δυνατὸς.γάρ ἐστιν ὁ θεὸς‖
or falls. And he shall be made to stand; for able is God
στῆσαι αὐτόν. 5 Ὃς.μὲν [p]κρίνει ἡμέραν παρ' ἡμέραν,
to make [2]stand [1]him. One judges a day [to be] above a day;

upon this very thing. 7 Render therefore to all their dues: tribute to whom tribute *is due*; custom to whom custom; fear to whom fear; honour to whom honour. 8 Owe no man any thing, but to love one another: for he that loveth another hath fulfilled the law. 9 For this, Thou shalt not commit adultery, Thou shalt not kill, Thou shalt not steal, Thou shalt not bear false witness, Thou shalt not covet; and if *there be* any other commandment, it is briefly comprehended in this saying, namely, Thou shalt love thy neighbour as thyself. 10 Love worketh no ill to his neighbour: therefore love *is* the fulfilling of the law.

11 And that, knowing the time, that now *it is* high time to awake out of sleep: for now *is* our salvation nearer than when we believed. 12 The night is far spent, the day is at hand: let us therefore cast off the works of darkness, and let us put on the armour of light. 13 Let us walk honestly, as in the day; not in rioting and drunkenness, not in chambering and wantonness, not in strife and envying. 14 But put ye on the Lord Jesus Christ, and make not provision for the flesh, to *fulfil* the lusts *thereof*.

XIV. Him that is weak in the faith receive ye, *but* not to doubtful disputations. 2 For one believeth that he may eat all things: another, who is weak, eateth herbs. 3 Let not him that eateth despise him that eateth not; and let not him which eateth not judge him that eateth: for God hath received him. 4 Who art thou that judgest another man's servant? to his own master he standeth or falleth. Yea, he shall be holden up: for God is able to make him stand. 5 One man es-

---

[e] ἀλλήλους ἀγαπᾶν GLTTrAW. [f] — οὐ ψευδομαρτυρήσεις GLTTrAW. [g] τῷ λόγῳ τούτῳ LTTrAW. [h] [ἐν τῷ] LTrA. [i] σεαυτόν LTTrA. [k] ἤδη ἡμᾶς LTrW; ἤδη ὑμᾶς already you TA. [l] ἐνδυσώμεθα δὲ LTTrAW. [m] ἀλλὰ TTrAW. [n] ὁ δὲ LTTrA. [o] δυνατεῖ γὰρ ὁ κύριος for able is the Lord LTTrA; δυνατεῖ γὰρ ὁ θεὸς W. [p] + γὰρ for (one) [L]T.

teemeth one day above
another: another es-
teemeth every day *a-*
like. Let every man
be fully persuaded in
his own mind. 6 He
that regardeth the day,
regardeth *it* unto the
Lord; and he that re-
gardeth not the day, to
the Lord he doth not
regard *it.* He that
eateth, eateth to the
Lord, for he giveth
God thanks; and he
that eateth not, to
the Lord he eateth
not, and giveth God
thanks. 7 For none of
us liveth to himself,
and no man dieth to
himself. 8 For whether
we live, we live unto
the Lord; and whether
we die, we die unto
the Lord: whether we
live therefore, or die,
we are the Lord's.
9 For to this end
Christ both died, and
rose, and revived, that
he might be Lord both
of the dead and living.
10 But why dost thou
judge thy brother? or
why dost thou set at
nought thy brother?
for we shall all stand
before the judgment
seat of Christ. 11 For
it is written, *As* I live,
saith the Lord, every
knee shall bow to me,
and every tongue shall
confess to God. 12 So
then every one of us
shall give account of
himself to God. 13 Let
us not therefore judge
one another any more:
but judge this rather,
that no man put a
stumbling block or an
occasion to fall in *his*
brother's way. 14 I
know, and am per-
suaded by the Lord
Jesus, that *there is* nothing unclean of it-
self: but to him that
esteemeth any thing
to be unclean, to him
it is unclean. 15 But
if thy brother be
grieved with *thy* meat,
now walkest thou not
charitably. Destroy
not him with thy
meat, for whom Christ
died. 16 Let not then
your good be evil
spoken of: 17 for the
kingdom of God is
not meat and drink;
but righteousness, and

ὃς.δὲ κρίνει πᾶσαν ἡμέραν. ἕκαστος ἐν τῷ.ἰδίῳ νοῒ
another judges every day [to be alike]. [2]Each [3]in [4]his [5]own [6]mind
πληροφορείσθω. 6 ὁ φρονῶν τὴν ἡμέραν, κυρίῳ φρονεῖ·
[1]let be fully assured. He that regards the day, to [the] Lord regards [it];
[q]καὶ ὁ μὴ.φρονῶν τὴν ἡμέραν, κυρίῳ οὐ.φρονεῖ.‖ [r]ὁ
and he that regards not the day, to [the] Lord regards [it] not. He that
ἐσθίων, κυρίῳ ἐσθίει, εὐχαριστεῖ.γὰρ τῷ θεῷ· καὶ ὁ μὴ
eats, to [the] Lord eats, for he gives thanks to God; and he that [2]not
ἐσθίων, κυρίῳ οὐκ.ἐσθίει, καὶ εὐχαριστεῖ τῷ θεῷ. 7 οὐδεὶς
[1]eats, to [the] Lord he eats not, and gives thanks to God. [2]No [3]one
γὰρ ἡμῶν ἑαυτῷ ζῇ, καὶ οὐδεὶς ἑαυτῷ ἀποθνήσκει. 8 ἐάν.τε
[1]for of us to himself lives, and no one to himself dies. [2]Both [3]if
γὰρ ζῶμεν, τῷ κυρίῳ ζῶμεν· ἐάν.τε [s]ἀποθνήσκωμεν,‖
[1]for we should live, to the Lord we should live; and if we should die,
τῷ κυρίῳ ἀποθνήσκομεν. ἐάν.τε οὖν ζῶμεν, ἐάν.τε [s]ἀπο-
to the Lord we die: both if then we should live, and if we should
θνήσκωμεν,‖ τοῦ κυρίου ἐσμέν. 9 εἰς.τοῦτο.γὰρ χριστὸς [t]καὶ‖
die, the Lord's we are. For, for this Christ both
ἀπέθανεν καὶ [v]ἀνέστη καὶ ἀνέζησεν,‖ ἵνα καὶ νεκρῶν καὶ
died and rose and lived again, that both [the] dead and
ζώντων κυριεύσῃ. 10 Σὺ.δὲ τί κρίνεις τὸν ἀδελφόν
living he might rule over. But thou why judgest thou [2]brother
σου; ἢ καὶ σὺ τί ἐξουθενεῖς τὸν.ἀδελφόν.σου; πάντες.γὰρ
[1]thy? or also thou why dost thou despise thy brother? For [2]all
παραστησόμεθα τῷ βήματι [w]τοῦ χριστοῦ.‖ 11 γέγραπται
[1]we shall stand before the judgment seat of the Christ. [2]It [3]has [4]been [5]written
γάρ, Ζῶ ἐγώ, λέγει κύριος· ὅτι ἐμοὶ κάμψει πᾶν γόνυ,
[1]for, [7]Live [6]I, says [the] Lord, that to me shall bow every knee,
καὶ [x]πᾶσα γλῶσσα ἐξομολογήσεται‖ τῷ θεῷ. 12 Ἄρα [y]οὖν‖
and every tongue shall confess to God. So then
ἕκαστος ἡμῶν περὶ ἑαυτοῦ λόγον [z]δώσει‖ [a]τῷ θεῷ.‖ 13 Μη-
each of us concerning himself account shall give to God. No
κέτι οὖν ἀλλήλους κρίνωμεν· ἀλλὰ τοῦτο κρίνατε μᾶλλον,
longer therefore one another should we judge; but this judge ye rather,
τὸ μὴ.τιθέναι πρόσκομμα τῷ ἀδελφῷ ἢ σκάνδαλον.
not to put an occasion of stumbling to the brother or a cause of offence.
14 οἶδα καὶ πέπεισμαι ἐν κυρίῳ Ἰησοῦ, ὅτι οὐδὲν
I know and am persuaded in [the] Lord Jesus, that nothing [is]
κοινὸν δι' [b]ἑαυτοῦ·‖ εἰ.μὴ τῷ λογιζομένῳ τι κοινὸν
unclean of itself: except to him who reckons anything unclean
εἶναι, ἐκείνῳ κοινόν· 15 εἰ [c]δὲ‖ διὰ βρῶμα ὁ
to be, to that one unclean [it is]. [2]If [1]but on account of meat
ἀδελφός.σου λυπεῖται, οὐκέτι κατὰ ἀγάπην περιπατεῖς.
thy brother is grieved, no longer according to love thou walkest.
μὴ τῷ.βρώματί.σου ἐκεῖνον ἀπόλλυε ὑπὲρ οὗ χριστὸς ἀπέ-
[2]Not [3]with [4]thy [5]meat [6]him [1]destroy for whom Christ died.
θανεν. 16 Μὴ.βλασφημείσθω οὖν ὑμῶν τὸ ἀγαθόν· 17 οὐ
Let not [4]be [5]evil [6]spoken [7]of [1]therefore [2]your [3]good; [9]not
γάρ ἐστιν ἡ βασιλεία τοῦ θεοῦ βρῶσις καὶ πόσις, ἀλλὰ
[8]for is the kingdom of God eating and drinking; but
δικαιοσύνη καὶ εἰρήνη καὶ χαρὰ ἐν πνεύματι ἁγίῳ· 18 ὁ
righteousness and peace and joy in [the] [2]Spirit [1]Holy. [4]He [5]that

---

[q] — καὶ ὁ μὴ φρονῶν τὴν ἡμέραν, κυρίῳ οὐ φρονεῖ LTTr[A]. [r] + καὶ and GLTTrAW. [s] ἀποθνήσκομεν we die L. [t] — καὶ LTTrAW. [v] ἔζησεν lived GLTTrAW. [w] τοῦ θεοῦ of God LTTrAW. [x] ἐξομολογήσεται πᾶσα γλῶσσα LTr. [y] — οὖν LTr[A]. [z] ἀποδώσει LTr; [ἀπο]δώσει A. [a] [τῷ θεῷ] L. [b] αὐτοῦ GLTrW. [c] γὰρ for LTTrAW.

γὰρ ἐν [d]τούτοις‖ δουλεύων [e]τῷ‖ χριστῷ εὐάρεστος τῷ θεῷ,
for in these things serves the Christ [is] well-pleasing to God,
καὶ δόκιμος τοῖς ἀνθρώποις. 19 ἄρα οὖν τὰ τῆς εἰρήνης
and approved by men. So then the things of peace
[f]διώκωμεν,‖ καὶ τὰ τῆς οἰκοδομῆς τῆς.εἰς.ἀλλήλους.
we should pursue, and the things for building up one another.
20 Μὴ ἕνεκεν βρώματος κατάλυε τὸ ἔργον τοῦ θεοῦ.
Not for the sake of meat destroy the work of God.
πάντα μὲν καθαρά, ἀλλὰ κακὸν τῷ ἀνθρώπῳ τῷ
All things indeed [are] pure; but [it is] evil to the man who
διὰ προσκόμματος ἐσθίοντι. 21 καλὸν τὸ μὴ φαγεῖν κρέα,
through stumbling eats. [It is] right not to eat flesh,
μηδὲ πιεῖν οἶνον, μηδὲ ἐν ᾧ ὁ.ἀδελφός.σου προσκόπτει [g]ἢ
nor drink wine, nor in what thy brother stumbles, or
σκανδαλίζεται ἢ ἀσθενεῖ.‖ 22 Σὺ πίστιν [h]ἔχεις; κατὰ‖ [i]σαυτὸν‖
is offended, or is weak. [2]Thou [3]faith [1]hast? To thyself
ἔχε ἐνώπιον τοῦ θεοῦ· μακάριος ὁ μὴ.κρίνων ἑαυτὸν
have [it] before God. Blessed [is] he that judges not himself
ἐν ᾧ δοκιμάζει. 23 ὁ.δὲ διακρινόμενος, ἐὰν φάγῃ, κατα-
in what he approves. But he that doubts, if he eat, has been
κέκριται, ὅτι οὐκ ἐκ πίστεως· πᾶν.δὲ ὃ οὐκ ἐκ
condemned, because [it is] not of faith; and everything which [is] not of
πίστεως, ἁμαρτία ἐστίν. [k]
faith, [2]sin [1]is.

15 Ὀφείλομεν.δὲ ἡμεῖς οἱ δυνατοὶ τὰ ἀσθενήματα τῶν
But we ought, we who [are] strong, the infirmities of the
ἀδυνάτων βαστάζειν, καὶ μὴ ἑαυτοῖς ἀρέσκειν· 2 ἕκαστος.[l]γὰρ‖
weak to bear, and not ourselves to please. For [2]each
ἡμῶν τῷ πλησίον ἀρεσκέτω εἰς τὸ ἀγαθὸν πρὸς οἰκοδομήν.
[3]of [4]us [6]the [7]neighbour [1]let [5]please unto good for building up.
3 καὶ.γὰρ ὁ χριστὸς οὐχ ἑαυτῷ ἤρεσεν, ἀλλά, καθὼς γέ-
For also the Christ [2]not [3]himself [1]pleased; but, according as it has
γραπται, Οἱ ὀνειδισμοὶ τῶν ὀνειδιζόντων σε [m]ἐπέπεσον‖
been written, The reproaches of those reproaching thee fell
ἐπ' ἐμέ. 4 Ὅσα.γὰρ προεγράφη, εἰς τὴν ἡμετέραν
on me. For as many things as were written before for our
διδασκαλίαν [n]προεγράφη,‖ ἵνα διὰ τῆς ὑπομονῆς καὶ [o] τῆς
instruction were written before, that through endurance and
παρακλήσεως τῶν γραφῶν τὴν ἐλπίδα ἔχωμεν. 5 ὁ.δὲ
encouragement of the scriptures hope we might have. Now the
θεὸς τῆς ὑπομονῆς καὶ τῆς παρακλήσεως δῴη ὑμῖν τὸ αὐτὸ
God of endurance and encouragement give you [3]the [4]same [5]thing
φρονεῖν ἐν ἀλλήλοις κατὰ [p]χριστὸν Ἰησοῦν·‖ 6 ἵνα
[1]to [2]mind with one another according to Christ Jesus; that
ὁμοθυμαδὸν ἐν ἑνὶ στόματι δοξάζητε τὸν θεὸν καὶ πατέρα
with one accord with one mouth ye may glorify the God and Father
τοῦ.κυρίου.ἡμῶν Ἰησοῦ χριστοῦ. 7 Διὸ προσλαμβάνεσθε
of our Lord Jesus Christ. Wherefore receive ye
ἀλλήλους, καθὼς καὶ ὁ χριστὸς προσελάβετο [q]ἡμᾶς‖ εἰς
one another, according as also the Christ received us to
δόξαν [r] θεοῦ.
[the] glory of God.

peace, and joy in the Holy Ghost.
18 For he that in these things serveth Christ *is* acceptable to God, and approved of men.
19 Let us therefore follow after the things which make for peace, and things wherewith one may edify another.
20 For meat destroy not the work of God. All things indeed *are* pure; but *it is* evil for that man who eateth with offence.
21 *It is* good neither to eat flesh, nor to drink wine, nor *any thing* whereby thy brother stumbleth, or is offended, or is made weak.
22 Hast thou faith? have *it* to thyself before God. Happy *is* he that condemneth not himself in that thing which he alloweth.
23 And he that doubteth is damned if he eat, because *he eateth* not of faith: for whatsoever *is* not of faith is sin.

XV. We then that are strong ought to bear the infirmities of the weak, and not to please ourselves.
2 Let every one of us please *his* neighbour for *his* good to edification.
3 For even Christ pleased not himself; but, as it is written, The reproaches of them that reproached thee fell on me.
4 For whatsoever things were written aforetime were written for our learning, that we through patience and comfort of the scriptures might have hope.
5 Now the God of patience and consolation grant you to be likeminded one toward another according to Christ Jesus:
6 that ye may with one mind *and* one mouth glorify God, even the Father of our Lord Jesus Christ.
7 Wherefore receive ye one another, as Christ also received us to the glory of God.

---

[d] τούτῳ this GLTTrAW. [e] — τῷ L[Tr]. [f] διώκομεν we pursue T. [g] — ἢ σκανδαλίζεται ἢ ἀσθενεῖ T. [h] ἣν ([ἣν] A) ἔχεις κατὰ (*read* faith which thou hast, to &c.) LTTrA. [i] σεαυτὸν GLTTrAW. [k] *Place here verses* 25—27 *of chapter* XVI. G. [l] — γὰρ for GLTTrAW. [m] ἐπέπεσαν LTTrA. [n] ἐγράφη were written LTTrAW. [o] + διὰ through LTTrAW. [p] Ἰησοῦν χριστόν Tr. [q] ὑμᾶς you GLTTrAW. [r] + τοῦ LTTrA.

8 Now I say that
Jesus Christ was a
minister of the cir-
cumcision for the truth
of God, to confirm the
promises *made* unto
the fathers: 9 and
that the Gentiles
might glorify God for
his mercy; as it is
written, For this cause
I will confess to thee
among the Gentiles,
and sing unto thy
name. 10 And again
he saith, Rejoice, ye
Gentiles, with his peo-
ple. 11 And again,
Praise the Lord, all ye
Gentiles; and laud
him, all ye people.
12 And again, Esaias
saith, There shall be a
root of Jesse, and he
that shall rise to reign
over the Gentiles; in
him shall the Gentiles
trust. 13 Now the God
of hope fill you with
all joy and peace in
believing, that ye
may abound in hope,
through the power of
the Holy Ghost.

14 And I myself al-
so am persuaded of
you, my brethren, that
ye also are full of
goodness, filled with
all knowledge, able
also to admonish one
another. 15 Neverthe-
less, brethren, I have
written the more bold-
ly unto you in some
sort, as putting you
in mind, because of
the grace that is
given to me of God,
16 that I should be
the minister of Jesus
Christ to the Gentiles,
ministering the gospel
of God, that the offer-
ing up of the Gentiles
might be acceptable,
being sanctified by the
Holy Ghost. 17 I have
therefore whereof I
may glory through Je-
sus Christ in those
things which pertain
to God. 18 For I will
not dare to speak of
any of those things
which Christ hath not
wrought by me, to
make the Gentiles o-
bedient, by word and
deed, 19 through migh-
ty signs and wonders,
by the power of the
Spirit of God; so that

8 Λέγω [s]δέ," [t]Ἰησοῦν" χριστὸν διάκονον [v]γεγενῆσθαι" περι-
[2]I [3]say [1]but, Jesus Christ a servant has become of cir-
τομῆς ὑπὲρ ἀληθείας θεοῦ, εἰς τὸ βεβαιῶσαι τὰς ἐπαγ-
cumcision for [the] truth of God, for to confirm the pro-
γελίας τῶν πατέρων· 9 τὰ.δὲ ἔθνη ὑπὲρ ἐλέους δοξάσαι τὸν
mises of the fathers; and the nations for mercy to glorify
θεόν, καθὼς γέγραπται, Διὰ τοῦτο ἐξομολογήσομαί
God; according as it has been written, Because of this I will confess
σοι ἐν ἔθνεσιν, καὶ τῷ.ὀνόματί.σου ψαλῶ. 10 Καὶ
to thee among [the] nations, and thy name will I praise. And
πάλιν λέγει, Εὐφράνθητε, ἔθνη, μετὰ τοῦ.λαοῦ.αὐτοῦ. 11 Καὶ
again it says, Rejoice ye, nations, with his people. And
πάλιν[w], Αἰνεῖτε [x]τὸν κύριον πάντα τὰ ἔθνη," καὶ [y]ἐπαινέσατε"
again, Praise the Lord, all the nations, and praise
αὐτὸν πάντες οἱ λαοί. 12 Καὶ πάλιν, Ἡσαΐας λέγει, Ἔ-
him, all the peoples. And again, Esaias says, There
σται ἡ ῥίζα τοῦ Ἰεσσαί, καὶ ὁ ἀνιστάμενος ἄρχειν
shall be the root of Jesse, and he that arises to rule [the]
ἐθνῶν, ἐπ' αὐτῷ ἔθνη ἐλπιοῦσιν. 13 Ὁ.δὲ θεὸς τῆς
nations: in him [the] nations shall hope. Now [2]the [3]God
ἐλπίδος πληρώσαι ὑμᾶς πάσης χαρᾶς καὶ εἰρήνης ἐν τῷ
[4]of [5]hope [1]may fill you with all joy and peace in
πιστεύειν, εἰς τὸ περισσεύειν ὑμᾶς ἐν τῇ ἐλπίδι, ἐν δυνάμει
believing, for [2]to [3]abound [1]you in hope, in power
πνεύματος ἁγίου.
of [the] [2]Spirit [1]Holy.

14 Πέπεισμαι.δέ, ἀδελφοί.μου, καὶ αὐτὸς ἐγὼ περὶ
But [4]am [5]persuaded, [6]my [7]brethren, [2]also [3]myself [1]I concerning
ὑμῶν, ὅτι καὶ αὐτοὶ μεστοί ἐστε ἀγαθωσύνης, πεπληρωμένοι
you, that also yourselves full are of goodness, being filled
πάσης [z]γνώσεως, δυνάμενοι καὶ ἀλλήλους νουθετεῖν. 15 [a]τολ-
with all knowledge, being able also one another to admonish. [2]More
μηρότερον" δὲ ἔγραψα ὑμῖν, [b]ἀδελφοί," ἀπὸ μέρους, ὡς
[3]boldly [1]but I did write to you, brethren, in part, as
ἐπαναμιμνήσκων ὑμᾶς, διὰ τὴν χάριν τὴν δοθεῖσάν μοι
reminding you, because of the grace which was given to me
[c]ὑπὸ" τοῦ θεοῦ, 16 εἰς τὸ εἶναί με λειτουργὸν [d]Ἰησοῦ χριστοῦ"
by God, for [2]to [3]be [1]me a minister of Jesus Christ
εἰς τὰ ἔθνη, ἱερουργοῦντα τὸ εὐαγγέλιον τοῦ θεοῦ,
to the nations, administering in sacred service the glad tidings of God,
ἵνα γένηται ἡ προσφορὰ τῶν ἐθνῶν εὐπρόσδεκτος, ἡγιασμένη
that might be the offering up of the nations acceptable, sanctified
ἐν πνεύματι ἁγίῳ. 17 ἔχω οὖν [e]καύχησιν ἐν χριστῷ
by [the] [2]Spirit [1]Holy. I have therefore boasting in Christ
Ἰησοῦ τὰ πρὸς [f]θεόν· 18 οὐ.γὰρ τολμήσω [g]λα-
Jesus [as to] the things pertaining to God. For not will I dare to
λεῖν τι" ὧν οὐ κατειργάσατο χριστὸς δι' ἐμοῦ, εἰς
speak anything of what [3]not [2]worked [4]out [1]Christ by me, for [the]
ὑπακοὴν ἐθνῶν, λόγῳ καὶ ἔργῳ, 19 ἐν δυνάμει ση-
obedience of [the] nations, by word and work, in [the] power of
μείων καὶ τεράτων, ἐν δυνάμει πνεύματος [h]θεοῦ·" ὥστε.με
signs and wonders, in [the] power of [the] Spirit of God; so as for me

---

[s] γὰρ for LTTrAW. [t] — Ἰησοῦν LTTrA. [v] γενέσθαι became LTr. [w] + λέγει it says L[A]. [x] πάντα τὰ ἔθνη τὸν κύριον LTTrA. [y] ἐπαινεσάτωσαν LTTrA. [z] + τῆς T[A] [a] τολμηροτέρως Tr. [b] — ἀδελφοί LTTr[A]. [c] ἀπὸ TTr. [d] χριστοῦ Ἰησοῦ LTTrAW. [e] + τὴν LTTrAW. [f] + τὸν GLTTrAW. [g] τι λαλεῖν LTTrAW. [h] ἁγίου Holy (Spirit) GLTr[A]W.

ἀπὸ Ἱερουσαλὴμ καὶ κύκλῳ μέχρι τοῦ Ἰλλυρικοῦ πεπληρω-
from Jerusalem, and in a circuit unto Illyricum, to have fully
κέναι τὸ εὐαγγέλιον τοῦ χριστοῦ· 20 οὕτως.δὲ [i]φιλοτιμού-
preached the glad tidings of the Christ; and so being am-
μενον‖ εὐαγγελίζεσθαι, οὐχ ὅπου ὠνομάσθη χριστός,
bitious to announce the glad tidings, not where [2]was [3]named [1]Christ,
ἵνα μὴ ἐπ' ἀλλότριον θεμέλιον οἰκοδομῶ· 21 ἀλλὰ καθὼς
that not upon another's foundation I might build; but according as
γέγραπται, Οἷς οὐκ.ἀνηγγέλη περὶ αὐτοῦ, ὄψον-
it has been written, To whom it was not announced concerning him, they shall
ται· καὶ οἳ οὐκ.ἀκηκόασιν, συνήσουσιν. 22 Διὸ καὶ ἐνε-
see; and those that have not heard, shall understand. Wherefore also I was
κοπτόμην [k]τὰ.πολλὰ‖ τοῦ.ἐλθεῖν πρὸς ὑμᾶς. 23 νυνὶ.δὲ
hindered many times from coming to you. But now,
μηκέτι τόπον ἔχων ἐν τοῖς.κλίμασιν.τούτοις, ἐπιποθίαν.δὲ
no longer [2]place [1]having in these regions, and [2]a [3]longing
ἔχων [l]τοῦ‖ ἐλθεῖν πρὸς ὑμᾶς ἀπὸ [m]πολλῶν‖ ἐτῶν, 24 ὡς.[n]ἐὰν‖
[1]having to come to you for many years, whenever
πορεύωμαι εἰς τὴν Σπανίαν, [o]ἐλεύσομαι πρὸς ὑμᾶς·‖ ἐλπίζω
I may go to Spain, I will come to you; [2]I [3]hope
γὰρ διαπορευόμενος θεάσασθαι ὑμᾶς, καὶ [p]ὑφ'‖ ὑμῶν προπεμ-
[1]for going through to see you, and by you to be set
φθῆναι ἐκεῖ, ἐὰν ὑμῶν πρῶτον ἀπὸ μέρους ἐμπλησθῶ.
forward thither, if of you first in part I should be filled.
25 Νυνὶ.δὲ πορεύομαι εἰς Ἱερουσαλήμ, διακονῶν τοῖς ἁγίοις.
But now I go to Jerusalem, doing service to the saints;
26 [q]εὐδόκησαν‖.γὰρ Μακεδονία καὶ Ἀχαΐα κοινωνίαν τινὰ
for [4]were [5]pleased [1]Macedonia [2]and [3]Achaia [6]a [8]contribution [7]certain
ποιήσασθαι εἰς τοὺς πτωχοὺς τῶν ἁγίων τῶν ἐν Ἱερουσα-
to make for the poor of the saints who [are] in Jerusa-
λήμ· 27 [q]εὐδόκησαν‖.γὰρ καὶ ὀφειλέται [r]αὐτῶν εἰσιν.‖ εἰ.γὰρ
lem. For they were pleased and [2]debtors [1]their they are; for if
τοῖς.πνευματικοῖς.αὐτῶν ἐκοινώνησαν τὰ ἔθνη, ὀφείλουσιν
in their spiritual things [3]participated [1]the [2]nations, they ought
καὶ ἐν τοῖς σαρκικοῖς λειτουργῆσαι αὐτοῖς. 28 τοῦτο οὖν
also in the fleshly things to minister to them. This therefore
ἐπιτελέσας, καὶ σφραγισάμενος αὐτοῖς τὸν.καρπὸν.τοῦτον,
having finished, and having sealed to them this fruit,
ἀπελεύσομαι δι' ὑμῶν εἰς [s]τὴν‖ Σπανίαν. 29 οἶδα.δὲ ὅτι
I will set off by you into Spain. And I know that
ἐρχόμενος πρὸς ὑμᾶς, ἐν πληρώματι εὐλογίας [t]τοῦ εὐαγγελίου
coming to you, in fulness of blessing of the glad tidings
τοῦ‖ χριστοῦ ἐλεύσομαι. 30 Παρακαλῶ.δὲ ὑμᾶς, [v]ἀδελφοί,‖ διὰ
of Christ I shall come. But I exhort you, brethren, by
τοῦ.κυρίου.ἡμῶν Ἰησοῦ χριστοῦ, καὶ διὰ τῆς ἀγάπης τοῦ
our Lord Jesus Christ, and by the love of the
πνεύματος, συναγωνίσασθαί μοι ἐν ταῖς προσευχαῖς ὑπὲρ
Spirit, to strive together with me in prayers for
ἐμοῦ πρὸς τὸν θεόν· 31 ἵνα ῥυσθῶ ἀπὸ τῶν ἀπει-
me to God, that I may be delivered from those being
θούντων ἐν τῇ Ἰουδαίᾳ, καὶ [w]ἵνα‖ ἡ [x]διακονία‖ μου ἡ
disobedient in Judæa; and that [2]service [1]my which [is]

from Jerusalem, and round about unto Illyricum, I have fully preached the gospel of Christ. 20 Yea, so have I strived to preach the gospel, not where Christ was named, lest I should build upon another man's foundation: 21 but as it is written, To whom he was not spoken of, they shall see: and they that have not heard shall understand. 22 For which cause also I have been much hindered from coming to you. 23 But now having no more place in these parts, and having a great desire these many years to come unto you; 24 whensoever I take my journey into Spain, I will come to you: for I trust to see you in my journey, and to be brought on my way thitherward by you, if first I be somewhat filled with your *company*. 25 But now I go unto Jerusalem to minister unto the saints. 26 For it hath pleased them of Macedonia and Achaia to make a certain contribution for the poor saints which are at Jerusalem. 27 It hath pleased them verily; and their debtors they are. For if the Gentiles have been made partakers of their spiritual things, their duty is also to minister unto them in carnal things. 28 When therefore I have performed this, and have sealed to them this fruit, I will come by you into Spain. 29 And I am sure that, when I come unto you, I shall come in the fulness of the blessing of the gospel of Christ. 30 Now I beseech you, brethren, for the Lord Jesus Christ's sake, and for the love of the Spirit, that ye strive together with me in *your* prayers to God for me; 31 that I may be delivered from them that do not believe in Judæa; and that my service which

[i] φιλοτιμοῦμαι I am ambitious LTr. [k] πολλάκις L. [l] [τοῦ] L. [m] ἱκανῶν TrA.
[n] ἂν LTTrAW. [o] — ἐλεύσομαι πρὸς ὑμᾶς GLTTrAW. [p] ἀφ' LA. [q] ηὐδόκησαν TTr.
[r] εἰσὶν αὐτῶν LTTrAW. [s] — τὴν LTTrA. [t] — τοῦ εὐαγγελίου τοῦ GLTTrAW. [v] [ἀδελφοί] A.
[w] — ἵνα LTTrA. [x] δωροφορία offering of gifts L.

[y]εἰς‖ Ἱερουσαλὴμ εὐπρόσδεκτος [z]γένηται τοῖς ἁγίοις·‖ 32 ἵνα
for Jerusalem acceptable may be to the saints; that
[a]ἐν χαρᾷ ἔλθω‖ πρὸς ὑμᾶς διὰ θελήματος [b]θεοῦ,‖ [c]καὶ
in joy I may come to you by [the] will of God, and
συναναπαύσωμαι ὑμῖν.‖ 33 ὁ.δὲ θεὸς τῆς εἰρήνης μετὰ
I may be refreshed with you. And the God of peace [be] with
πάντων ὑμῶν. [d]ἀμήν.‖
[2]all [1]you. Amen.

16 Συνίστημι.δὲ ὑμῖν Φοίβην τὴν.ἀδελφὴν.ἡμῶν, οὖσαν
But I commend to you Phœbe, our sister, being
διάκονον τῆς ἐκκλησίας τῆς ἐν [e]Κεγχρεαῖς·‖ 2 ἵνα [f]αὐτὴν προσ-
servant of the assembly in Cenchrea; that her ye may
δέξησθε‖ ἐν κυρίῳ ἀξίως τῶν ἁγίων, καὶ παραστῆτε αὐτῇ
receive in [the] Lord worthily of saints, and ye may assist her
ἐν ᾧ.ἂν ὑμῶν χρῄζῃ πράγματι· καὶ.γὰρ [g]αὕτη‖ προ-
in whatever [2]of [3]you [4]she [5]may [6]need [1]matter; for also she a suc-
στάτις πολλῶν ἐγενήθη, καὶ [h]αὐτοῦ ἐμοῦ.‖ 3 Ἀσπάσασθε
courer of many has been, and [3]myself [1]of [2]me. Salute
[i]Πρίσκιλλαν‖ καὶ Ἀκύλαν τοὺς.συνεργούς.μου ἐν χριστῷ Ἰη-
Priscilla and Aquila my fellow-workers in Christ Je-
σοῦ· 4 οἵτινες ὑπὲρ τῆς.ψυχῆς.μου τὸν.ἑαυτῶν τράχηλον
sus, (who for my life their own neck
ὑπέθηκαν, οἷς οὐκ ἐγὼ μόνος εὐχαριστῶ, ἀλλὰ καὶ πᾶσαι αἱ
laid down: whom not [2]I [1]only thank, but also all the
ἐκκλησίαι τῶν ἐθνῶν· 5 καὶ τὴν κατ' οἶκον αὐτῶν ἐκκλησίαν.
assemblies of the nations,) and the [2]at [4]house [3]their [1]assembly.
ἀσπάσασθε Ἐπαίνετον τὸν.ἀγαπητόν.μου, ὅς ἐστιν ἀπαρχὴ
Salute Epænetus my beloved, who is a first-fruit
τῆς [k]Ἀχαΐας‖ εἰς χριστόν. 6 ἀσπάσασθε [l]Μαριάμ,‖ ἥτις πολλὰ
of Achaia for Christ. Salute Mary, who [2]much
ἐκοπίασεν εἰς [m]ἡμᾶς.‖ 7 ἀσπάσασθε Ἀνδρόνικον καὶ Ἰουνίαν
[1]laboured for us. Salute Andronicus and Junias
τοὺς.συγγενεῖς.μου καὶ συναιχμαλώτους μου· οἵτινές εἰσιν
my kinsmen and [2]fellow-prisoners [1]my, who are
ἐπίσημοι ἐν τοῖς ἀποστόλοις, οἳ καὶ πρὸ ἐμοῦ [n]γεγόνασιν‖
of note among the apostles; who also before me were
ἐν χριστῷ. 8 ἀσπάσασθε [o]Ἀμπλίαν‖ τὸν.ἀγαπητόν.μου ἐν
in Christ. Salute Amplias my beloved in [the]
κυρίῳ. 9 ἀσπάσασθε Οὐρβανὸν τὸν.συνεργὸν.ἡμῶν ἐν [p]χριστῷ,‖
Lord. Salute Urbanus our fellow-worker in Christ,
καὶ Στάχυν τὸν.ἀγαπητόν.μου. 10 ἀσπάσασθε Ἀπελλῆν τὸν
and Stachys my beloved. Salute Apelles the
δόκιμον ἐν χριστῷ. ἀσπάσασθε τοὺς ἐκ τῶν Ἀρι-
approved in Christ. Salute those of the [household] of Ari-
στοβούλου. 11 ἀσπάσασθε [q]Ἡροδίωνα‖ τὸν.[r]συγγενῆ‖.μου.
stobulus. Salute Herodion my kinsman.
ἀσπάσασθε τοὺς ἐκ τῶν Ναρκίσσου, τοὺς ὄντας ἐν
Salute those of the [household] of Narcissus, who are in [the
κυρίῳ. 12 ἀσπάσασθε Τρύφαιναν καὶ Τρυφῶσαν τὰς κοπιώσας
Lord. Salute Tryphæna and Tryphosa, who labour
ἐν κυρίῳ. [s]ἀσπάσασθε Περσίδα τὴν ἀγαπητήν, ἥτις πολλὰ
in [the] Lord. Salute Persis the beloved, who much

I have for Jerusalem may be accepted of the saints; 32 that I may come unto you with joy by the will of God, and may with you be refreshed. 33 Now the God of peace *be* with you all. Amen.

XVI. I commend unto you Phebe our sister, which is a servant of the church which is at Cenchrea: 2 that ye receive her in the Lord, as becometh saints, and that ye assist her in whatsoever business she hath need of you: for she hath been a succourer of many, and of myself also. 3 Greet Priscilla and Aquila my helpers in Christ Jesus: 4 who have for my life laid down their own necks: unto whom not only I give thanks, but also all the churches of the Gentiles. 5 Likewise *greet* the church that is in their house. Salute my wellbeloved Epænetus, who is the firstfruits of Achaia unto Christ. 6 Greet Mary, who bestowed much labour on us. 7 Salute Andronicus and Junia my kinsmen, and my fellowprisoners, who are of note among the apostles, who also were in Christ before me. 8 Greet Amplias my beloved in the Lord. 9 Salute Urbane, our helper in Christ, and Stachys my beloved. 10 Salute Apelles approved in Christ. Salute them which are of Aristobulus' *household.* 11 Salute Herodion my kinsman. Greet them that be of the *household* of Narcissus, which are in the Lord. 12 Salute Tryphena and Tryphosa, who labour in the Lord. Salute the beloved Persis, which laboured

[y] ἐν at L, [z] τοῖς ἁγίοις γένηται LTTrA. [a] ἐλθὼν (having come) ἐν χαρᾷ T. [b] κυρίου Ἰησοῦ of [the] Lord Jesus L. [c] — καὶ T; — καὶ συναναπαύσωμαι ὑμῖν L[A]. [d] [ἀμήν] LTr. [e] Κεν- T [f] προσδέξησθε αὐτὴν LTTrA. [g] αὐτὴ GLTAW. [h] ἐμοῦ αὐτοῦ LTTrA. [i] Πρίσκαν Prisca GLTTrAW. [k] Ἀσίας Asia GLTTrAW. [l] Μαρίαν LTrA. [m] ὑμᾶς you LTTrA. [n] γέγοναν LTTrA. [o] Ἀμπλίατον Ampliatus TTrA. [p] κυρίῳ [the] Lord L. [q] Ἡρωδίωνα GLTTrAW. [r] συγγενὴν Tr. [s] [ἀσπάσασθε .... κυρίῳ] L.

ἐκοπίασεν ἐν κυρίῳ.ǁ 13 ἀσπάσασθε Ῥοῦφον τὸν ἐκλεκτὸν
laboured in [the] Lord. Salute Rufus the chosen
ἐν κυρίῳ, καὶ τὴν.μητέρα.αὐτοῦ καὶ ἐμοῦ. 14 ἀσπάσασθε
in [the] Lord, and his mother and mine. Salute
[t]Ἀσύγκριτον,ǁ Φλέγοντα, [v]Ἑρμᾶν,ǁ Πατρόβαν, [w]Ἑρμῆν,ǁ καὶ
Asyncritus, Phlegon, Hermas, Patrobas, Hermes, and
τοὺς σὺν αὐτοῖς ἀδελφούς. 15 ἀσπάσασθε Φιλόλογον καὶ
the [2]with [3]them [1]brethren, Salute Philologus and
Ἰουλίαν, Νηρέα καὶ τὴν.ἀδελφὴν.αὐτοῦ, καὶ Ὀλυμπᾶν, καὶ
Julias, Nereus and his sister, and Olympas, and
τοὺς σὺν αὐτοῖς πάντας ἁγίους. 16 ἀσπάσασθε ἀλλήλους
[2]the [4]with [5]them [1]all [3]saints. Salute one another
ἐν φιλήματι ἁγίῳ. ἀσπάζονται ὑμᾶς αἱ ἐκκλησίαι [x] τοῦ
with a [2]kiss [1]holy. [7]Salute [8]you [3]the [4]assemblies
χριστοῦ.
[5]of [6]Christ.

much in the Lord. 13 Salute Rufus chosen in the Lord, and his mother and mine. 14 Salute Asyncritus, Phlegon, Hermas, Patrobas, Hermes, and the brethren which are with them. 15 Salute Philologus, and Julia, Nereus, and his sister, and Olympas, and all the saints which are with them. 16 Salute one another with an holy kiss. The churches of Christ salute you.

17 Παρακαλῶ.δὲ ὑμᾶς, ἀδελφοί, σκοπεῖν τοὺς τὰς διχο-
But I exhort you, brethren to consider those who [2]divi-
στασίας καὶ τὰ σκάνδαλα, παρὰ τὴν διδαχὴν ἣν ὑμεῖς
sions [3]and [4]causes [5]of [6]offence [7]contrary [8]to [9]the [10]teaching [11]which [12]ye
ἐμάθετε, ποιοῦντας· καὶ [y]ἐκκλίνατεǁ ἀπ' αὐτῶν. 18 οἱ γὰρ
[13]learnt, [1]make, and turn away from them. For
τοιοῦτοι τῷ.κυρίῳ.ἡμῶν [z]Ἰησοῦǁ χριστῷ οὐ.δουλεύουσιν, ἀλλὰ
such [3]our [4]Lord [5]Jesus [6]Christ [1]serve [2]not, but
τῇ.ἑαυτῶν κοιλίᾳ· καὶ διὰ τῆς χρηστολογίας καὶ εὐλογίας
their own belly, and by kind speaking and praise
ἐξαπατῶσιν τὰς καρδίας τῶν ἀκάκων. 19 ἡ.γὰρ ὑμῶν ὑπακοὴ
deceive the hearts of the innocent. For the [2]of [3]you [1]obedience
εἰς πάντας ἀφίκετο· [a]χαίρω οὖν τὸ.ἐφ' ὑμῖν.ǁ θέλω.δὲ
[5]to [6]all [4]reached. I rejoice therefore concerning you; but I wish
ὑμᾶς σοφοὺς [b]μὲνǁ εἶναι εἰς τὸ ἀγαθόν, ἀκεραίους.δὲ εἰς τὸ
you wise to be [as] to good, and simple to
κακόν. 20 ὁ.δὲ θεὸς τῆς εἰρήνης συντρίψει τὸν σατανᾶν ὑπὸ
evil. But the God of peace will bruise Satan under
τοὺς.πόδας.ὑμῶν ἐν τάχει. ἡ χάρις τοῦ.κυρίου.ἡμῶν Ἰησοῦ
your feet shortly. The grace of our Lord Jesus
[c]χριστοῦǁ μεθ' ὑμῶν. [d]
Christ [be] with you.

17 Now I beseech you, brethren, mark them which cause divisions and offences contrary to the doctrine which ye have learned; and avoid them. 18 For they that are such serve not our Lord Jesus Christ, but their own belly; and by good words and fair speeches deceive the hearts of the simple. 19 For your obedience is come abroad unto all *men*. I am glad therefore on your behalf: but yet I would have you wise unto that which is good, and simple concerning evil. 20 And the God of peace shall bruise Satan under your feet shortly. The grace of our Lord Jesus Christ *be* with you. Amen.

21 [e]Ἀσπάζονταιǁ ὑμᾶς Τιμόθεος ὁ.συνεργός.μου καὶ Λούκιος
[12]Salute [13]you [1]Timotheus [2]my [3]fellow-worker [4]and [5]Lucius
καὶ Ἰάσων καὶ Σωσίπατρος οἱ.συγγενεῖς.μου. 22 ἀσπάζομαι
[6]and [7]Jason [8]and [9]Sosipater [10]my [11]kinsmen. [20]Salute
ὑμᾶς ἐγὼ Τέρτιος ὁ γράψας τὴν ἐπιστολὴν ἐν κυρίῳ.
[21]you [14]I [15]Tertius [16]who [17]wrote [18]the [19]epistle in [the] Lord.
23 ἀσπάζεται ὑμᾶς Γάϊος ὁ ξένος μου καὶ [f]τῆς ἐκκλησίας
[2]Salutes [3]you [1]Gaius, the host of me and of the [2]assembly
ὅλης.ǁ ἀσπάζεται ὑμᾶς Ἔραστος ὁ οἰκονόμος τῆς πόλεως,
[1]whole. [13]Salutes [14]you [3]Erastus [4]the [5]steward [6]of [7]the [8]city,
καὶ Κούαρτος ὁ ἀδελφός. 24 [g]Ἡ χάρις τοῦ.κυρίου.ἡμῶν
[9]and [10]Quartus [11]the [12]brother. The grace of our Lord
Ἰησοῦ χριστοῦ μετὰ πάντων ὑμῶν. ἀμήν.ǁ
Jesus Christ [be] with [2]all [1]you. Amen.

21 Timotheus my workfellow, and Lucius, and Jason, and Sosipater, my kinsmen, salute you. 22 I Tertius, who wrote *this* epistle, salute you in the Lord. 23 Gaius mine host, and of the whole church, saluteth you. Erastus the chamberlain of the city saluteth you, and Quartus a brother. 24 The grace of our Lord Jesus Christ *be* with you all. Amen.

---

[t] Ἀσύν- T. [v] Ἑρμῆν LTTrAW. [w] Ἑρμᾶν LTTrAW. [x] + πᾶσαι all (the assemblies) GLTTrAW. [y] ἐκκλίνετε TTr. [z] — Ἰησοῦ GLTTrAW. [a] ἐφ' ὑμῖν οὖν χαίρω LTTrAW. [b] — μὲν LTTrA. [c] — χριστοῦ T[TrA]. [d] + ἀμήν Amen E. [e] Ἀσπάζεται Salutes LTTrAW. [f] ὅλης τῆς ἐκκλησίας LTTrA. [g] — *verse* 24 LTTr[A].

25 Now to him that is of power to stablish you according to my gospel, and the preaching of Jesus Christ, according to the revelation of the mystery, which was kept secret since the world began,
26 but now is made manifest, and by the scriptures of the prophets, according to the commandment of the everlasting God, made known to all nations for the obedience of faith :
27 to God only wise, *be* glory through Jesus Christ for ever. Amen.

25 [h]Τῷ.δὲ δυναμένῳ ὑμᾶς στηρίξαι κατὰ τὸ εὐαγ-
Now to him who is able you to establish according to ²glad
γέλιόν μου καὶ τὸ κήρυγμα Ἰησοῦ χριστοῦ, κατὰ ἀπο-
³tidings ¹my and the proclamation of Jesus Christ, according to a reve-
κάλυψιν μυστηρίου χρόνοις αἰωνίοις σεσιγημένου,
lation of [the] mystery in times of the ages having been kept secret,
26 φανερωθέντος.δὲ νῦν, διά.τε γραφῶν προφητικῶν, κατ'
but made manifest now, and by ²scriptures ¹prophetic, according to
ἐπιταγὴν τοῦ αἰωνίου θεοῦ, εἰς ὑπακοὴν πίστεως εἰς πάντα
commandment of the eternal God, for obedience of faith to all
τὰ ἔθνη γνωρισθέντος, 27 μόνῳ σοφῷ θεῷ, διὰ Ἰη-
the nations having been made known— [the] only wise God, through Je-
σοῦ χριστοῦ, ᾧ ἡ δόξα εἰς τοὺς αἰῶνας[i]· ἀμήν.
sus Christ, to whom be glory to the ages. Amen.

[k]Πρὸς Ῥωμαίους ἐγράφη ἀπὸ Κορίνθου, διὰ Φοίβης τῆς
To [the] Romans written from Corinth, by Phœbe
διακόνου τῆς ἐν Κεγχρεαῖς ἐκκλησίας.‖
servant of the ²in ³Cenchrea ¹assembly.

---

[a]Η ΠΡΟΣ ΤΟΥΣ ΚΟΡΙΝΘΙΟΥΣ ΕΠΙΣΤΟΛΗ ΠΡΩΤΗ.‖

¹THE ⁴TO ⁵THE ⁶CORINTHIANS ³EPISTLE ²FIRST.

PAUL, called *to be* an apostle of Jesus Christ through the will of God, and Sosthenes *our* brother, 2 unto the church of God which is at Corinth, to them that are sanctified in Christ Jesus, called *to be* saints, with all that in every place call upon the name of Jesus Christ our Lord, both theirs and ours:
3 Grace *be* unto you, and peace, from God our Father, and *from* the Lord Jesus Christ.

ΠΑΥΛΟΣ [b]κλητὸς‖ ἀπόστολος [c]Ἰησοῦ χριστοῦ,‖ διὰ θελή-
Paul a called apostle of Jesus Christ, by [the] will
ματος θεοῦ, καὶ Σωσθένης ὁ ἀδελφός, 2 τῇ ἐκκλησίᾳ τοῦ
of God, and Sosthenes the brother, to the assembly
θεοῦ [d]τῇ οὔσῃ ἐν Κορίνθῳ,‖ ἡγιασμένοις ἐν χριστῷ Ἰη-
of God which is in Corinth, having been sanctified in Christ Je-
σοῦ,[d] κλητοῖς ἁγίοις, σὺν πᾶσιν τοῖς ἐπικαλουμένοις τὸ ὄνομα
sus, called saints, with all those ⁴calling ⁵on ⁶the ⁷name
τοῦ.κυρίου.ἡμῶν Ἰησοῦ χριστοῦ ἐν παντὶ τόπῳ, αὐτῶν.[e]τε‖
⁸of ⁹our ¹⁰Lord ¹¹Jesus ¹²Christ ¹in ²every ³place, both theirs
καὶ ἡμῶν· 3 χάρις ὑμῖν καὶ εἰρήνη ἀπὸ θεοῦ πατρὸς.ἡμῶν
and ours: grace to you and peace from God our Father
καὶ κυρίου Ἰησοῦ χριστοῦ.
and [the] Lord Jesus Christ.

4 I thank my God always on your behalf, for the grace of God which is given you by Jesus Christ; 5 that in every thing ye are enriched by him, in all utterance, and *in* all knowledge; 6 even as the testimony of Christ was confirmed in you: 7 so that ye come behind in no gift; waiting for the coming of our Lord Jesus Christ: 8 who

4 Εὐχαριστῶ τῷ.θεῷ.μου πάντοτε περὶ ὑμῶν, ἐπὶ τῇ
I thank my God always concerning you, for the
χάριτι τοῦ θεοῦ τῇ δοθείσῃ ὑμῖν ἐν χριστῷ Ἰησοῦ, 5 ὅτι ἐν
grace of God that was given to you in Christ Jesus, that in
παντὶ ἐπλουτίσθητε ἐν αὐτῷ, ἐν παντὶ λόγῳ καὶ πάσῃ
everything ye were enriched in him, in all discourse and all
γνώσει, 6 καθὼς τὸ μαρτύριον τοῦ χριστοῦ ἐβεβαιώθη ἐν
knowledge, according as the testimony of the Christ was confirmed in
ὑμῖν· 7 ὥστε ὑμᾶς μὴ ὑστερεῖσθαι ἐν μηδενὶ χαρίσματι, ἀπεκ-
you, so that ye are behind in not one gift,
δεχομένους τὴν ἀποκάλυψιν τοῦ.κυρίου.ἡμῶν Ἰησοῦ χριστοῦ·
awaiting the revelation of our Lord Jesus Christ;

---

[h] *Verses* 25–27 *placed at end of chapter* xiv. G. [i] + τῶν αἰώνων of ages LT. [k] — *the subscription* GLTW ; Πρὸς Ῥωμαίους TrA.

[a] + Παύλου τοῦ Ἀποστόλου of Paul the Apostle E ; + Παύλου G ; — τοὺς EG ; Πρὸς Κορινθίους ά LTTrAW. [b] [κλητὸς] LA. [c] χριστοῦ Ἰησοῦ LTTrAW. [d] τῇ οὔσῃ ἐν Κορίνθῳ *placed after* Ἰησοῦ LTrA. [e] — τε both LTTr[A].

8 ὃς καὶ βεβαιώσει ὑμᾶς ἕως τέλους, ἀνεγκλήτους ἐν τῇ
who also will confirm you to [the] end, unimpeachable in the
ἡμέρᾳ τοῦ.κυρίου.ἡμῶν Ἰησοῦ χριστοῦ. 9 πιστὸς ὁ θεός, δι'
day of our Lord Jesus Christ. Faithful [is] God, by
οὗ ἐκλήθητε εἰς κοινωνίαν τοῦ.υἱοῦ.αὐτοῦ Ἰησοῦ χριστοῦ
whom ye were called into fellowship of his Son Jesus Christ
τοῦ.κυρίου.ἡμῶν.
our Lord.

10 Παρακαλῶ.δὲ ὑμᾶς, ἀδελφοί, διὰ τοῦ ὀνόματος τοῦ
Now I exhort you, brethren, by the name
κυρίου.ἡμῶν Ἰησοῦ χριστοῦ, ἵνα τὸ αὐτὸ λέγητε πάντες,
of our Lord Jesus Christ, that [4]the [5]same [6]thing [1]ye [3]say [2]all,
καὶ μὴ ᾖ ἐν ὑμῖν σχίσματα, ἦτε.δὲ κατηρτισμένοι
and [3]no [1]there [2]be [5]among [6]you [4]divisions; but ye be knit together
ἐν τῷ αὐτῷ νοῒ καὶ ἐν τῇ αὐτῇ γνώμῃ. 11 ἐδηλώθη.γάρ
in the same mind and in the same judgment. For it was shewn
μοι περὶ ὑμῶν, ἀδελφοί.μου, ὑπὸ τῶν Χλόης,
to me concerning you, my brethren, by those of [the house of] Chloe,
ὅτι ἔριδες ἐν ὑμῖν εἰσιν· 12 λέγω.δὲ τοῦτο, ὅτι ἕκαστος
that strifes among you there are. But I say this, that each
ὑμῶν λέγει, Ἐγὼ μέν εἰμι Παύλου, ἐγὼ.δὲ Ἀπολλώ, ἐγὼ.δὲ
of you says, I am of Paul, and I of Apollos, and I
Κηφᾶ, ἐγὼ.δὲ χριστοῦ. 13 Μεμέρισται ὁ χριστός; μὴ Παῦ-
of Cephas, and I of Christ. Has [3]been [4]divided [1]the [2]Christ? [5]Paul
λος ἐσταυρώθη [f]ὑπὲρ‖ ὑμῶν; ἢ εἰς τὸ ὄνομα Παύλου ἐβαπ-
[4]was crucified for you? or to the name of Paul were ye
τίσθητε; 14 εὐχαριστῶ [g]τῷ θεῷ‖ ὅτι οὐδένα ὑμῶν ἐβάπτισα,
baptized? I thank God that no one of you I baptized,
εἰ.μὴ Κρίσπον καὶ Γάϊον· 15 ἵνα μή τις εἴπῃ ὅτι εἰς τὸ
except Crispus and Gaius, that not anyone should say that unto
ἐμὸν ὄνομα [h]ἐβάπτισα.‖ 16 ἐβάπτισα.δὲ καὶ τὸν Στεφανᾶ
my name I baptized. And I baptized also the [2]of [3]Stephanas
οἶκον· λοιπὸν οὐκ.οἶδα εἴ τινα ἄλλον ἐβάπτισα. 17 Οὐ.γὰρ
[1]house; as to the rest I know not if any other I baptized. For [4]not
ἀπέστειλέν με [i]χριστὸς βαπτίζειν, [k]ἀλλ'‖ εὐαγγελίζεσθαι·
[2]sent [3]me [1]Christ to baptize, but to announce the glad tidings;
οὐκ ἐν σοφίᾳ λόγου, ἵνα μὴ κενωθῇ ὁ σταυρὸς τοῦ χριστοῦ.
not in wisdom of word, that [2]not [1]be made void the cross of the Christ.
18 ὁ.λόγος.γὰρ ὁ τοῦ σταυροῦ τοῖς μὲν ἀπολλυμένοις μωρία
For the word of the cross to those perishing [2]foolishness
ἐστίν, τοῖς.δὲ σωζομένοις ἡμῖν δύναμις θεοῦ ἐστιν. 19 γέ-
[1]is, but [3]who [4]are [5]being [6]saved [1]to [2]us [9]power [10]of [11]God [7]it [8]is. [13]It [14]has
γραπται γάρ, Ἀπολῶ τὴν σοφίαν τῶν σοφῶν, καὶ τὴν
[15]been [16]written [12]for, I will destroy the wisdom of the wise, and the
σύνεσιν τῶν συνετῶν ἀθετήσω. 20 Ποῦ σοφός;
understanding of the understanding ones I will set aside. Where [is the] wise?
ποῦ γραμματεύς; ποῦ [l]συζητητὴς‖ τοῦ.αἰῶνος.τούτου;
where [the] scribe? where [the] disputer of this age?
οὐχὶ.ἐμώρανεν ὁ θεὸς τὴν σοφίαν τοῦ.κόσμου.[m]τούτου‖;
did not [2]make [3]foolish [1]God the wisdom of this world?
21 Ἐπειδὴ.γὰρ ἐν τῇ σοφίᾳ τοῦ θεοῦ οὐκ.ἔγνω ὁ κόσμος διὰ
For since, in the wisdom of God, [4]knew [5]not [1]the [2]world [3]by
τῆς σοφίας τὸν θεόν, εὐδόκησεν ὁ θεὸς διὰ τῆς μωρίας τοῦ
[4]wisdom God, [2]was [3]pleased [1]God by the foolishness of the

shall also confirm you
unto the end, *that ye
may be* blameless in
the day of our Lord
Jesus Christ. 9 God
is faithful, by whom
ye were called unto
the fellowship of his
Son Jesus Christ our
Lord.

10 Now I beseech
you, brethren, by the
name of our Lord Je-
sus Christ, that ye all
speak the same thing,
and *that* there be no
divisions among you;
but *that* ye be per-
fectly joined together
in the same mind and
in the same judgment.
11 For it hath been
declared unto me of
you, my brethren, by
them *which are of the
house* of Chloe, that
there are contentions
among you. 12 Now
this I say, that every
one of you saith, I am
of Paul; and I of
Apollos; and I of Ce-
phas; and I of Christ.
13 Is Christ divided?
was Paul crucified for
you? or were ye bap-
tized in the name of
Paul? 14 I thank God
that I baptized none
of you, but Crispus
and Gaius; 15 lest any
should say that I had
baptized in mine own
name. 16 And I bap-
tized also the house-
hold of Stephanas;
besides, I know not
whether I baptized any
other. 17 For Christ
sent me not to bap-
tize, but to preach the
gospel: not with wis-
dom of words, lest the
cross of Christ should
be made of none effect.
18 For the preaching
of the cross is to them
that perish foolish-
ness; but unto us
which are saved it is
the power of God.
19 For it is written, I
will destroy the wis-
dom of the wise, and
will bring to nothing
the understanding of
the prudent. 20 Where
is the wise? where *is*
the scribe? where *is*
the disputer of this
world? hath not God
made foolish the wis-
dom of this world?
21 For after that in
the wisdom of God
the world by wisdom
knew not God, it
pleased God by the

[f] περὶ L. [g] — τῷ θεῷ (read εὐχαριστῶ I give thanks) T. [h] ἐβαπτίσθητε ye were baptized LTTrAW. [i] + [ὁ] L. [k] ἀλλὰ TTrA. [l] συνζητητὴς LTTrA. [m] — τούτου (read the world) LTTrAW.

foolishness of preaching to save them
that believe. 22 For
the Jews require a
sign, and the Greeks
seek after wisdom:
23 but we preach
Christ crucified, unto
the Jews a stumblingblock, and unto the
Greeks foolishness;
24 but unto them
which are called, both
Jews and Greeks,
Christ the power of
God, and the wisdom
of God. 25 Because
the foolishness of God
is wiser than men; and
the weakness of God
is stronger than men.
26 For ye see your
calling, brethren, how
that not many wise
men after the flesh,
not many mighty, not
many noble, *are called:* 27 but God hath
chosen the foolish
things of the world
to confound the wise;
and God hath chosen
the weak things of
the world to confound
the things which are
mighty; 28 and base
things of the world,
and things which are
despised, hath God
chosen, *yea,* and things
which are not, to
bring to nought things
that are: 29 that no
flesh should glory in
his presence. 30 But
of him are ye in
Christ Jesus, who of
God is made unto us
wisdom, and righteousness, and sanctification, and redemption: 31 that, according as it is written,
He that glorieth, let
him glory in the
Lord.

II. And I, brethren,
when I came to you,
came not with excellency of speech or of
wisdom, declaring unto you the testimony
of God. 2 For I determined not to know
any thing among you,
save Jesus Christ, and
him crucified. 3 And
I was with you in
weakness, and in fear,
and in much trembling. 4 And my speech
and my preaching *was*
not with enticing
words of man's wisdom, but in demon-

κηρύγματος σῶσαι τοὺς πιστεύοντας· 22 ἐπειδὴ καὶ Ἰου-
proclamation to save those that believe. Since both Jews

δαῖοι [n]σημεῖον[ǁ] αἰτοῦσιν, καὶ Ἕλληνες σοφίαν ζητοῦσιν.
[3]a [4]sign [1]ask [2]for, and Greeks [2]wisdom [1]seek;

23 ἡμεῖς.δὲ κηρύσσομεν χριστὸν ἐσταυρωμένον, Ἰουδαίοις
but we proclaim Christ crucified, to Jews

μὲν σκάνδαλον, [o]Ἕλλησιν[ǁ] δὲ μωρίαν· 24 αὐτοῖς.δὲ τοῖς
indeed a cause of offence, [2]to [3]Greeks [1]and foolishness; but to those the

κλητοῖς, Ἰουδαίοις.τε καὶ Ἕλλησιν, χριστὸν θεοῦ δύναμιν καὶ
called, both Jews and Greeks, Christ God's power and

θεοῦ σοφίαν. 25 ὅτι τὸ μωρὸν τοῦ θεοῦ σοφώτερον τῶν
God's wisdom. Because the foolishness of God wiser

ἀνθρώπων ἐστίν· καὶ τὸ ἀσθενὲς τοῦ θεοῦ ἰσχυρότερον τῶν
than men is, and the weakness of God stronger

ἀνθρώπων [p]ἐστίν.[ǁ] 26 Βλέπετε.γὰρ τὴν.κλῆσιν.ὑμῶν, ἀδελφοί,
than men is. For ye see your calling, brethren,

ὅτι οὐ πολλοὶ σοφοὶ κατὰ σάρκα, οὐ πολλοὶ δυνα-
that not many wise according to flesh [there are], not many power-

τοί, οὐ πολλοὶ εὐγενεῖς· 27 ἀλλὰ τὰ μωρὰ τοῦ κόσμου
ful, not many high-born. But the foolish things of the world

ἐξελέξατο ὁ θεός, [q]ἵνα τοὺς σοφοὺς καταισχύνῃ·[ǁ] [r]καὶ τὰ
[2]chose [1]God, that the wise he might put to shame; and the

ἀσθενῆ τοῦ κόσμου ἐξελέξατο ὁ θεός,[ǁ] ἵνα καταισχύνῃ
weak things of the world [2]chose [1]God, that he might put to shame

τὰ ἰσχυρά· 28 καὶ τὰ ἀγενῆ τοῦ κόσμου καὶ τὰ ἐξουθενη-
the strong things; and the low-born of the world, and the de-

μένα ἐξελέξατο ὁ θεός, [s]καὶ[ǁ] τὰ μὴ.ὄντα, ἵνα τὰ
spised [2]chose [1]God, and the things that are not, that the things that

ὄντα καταργήσῃ· 29 ὅπως μὴ [t]καυχήσηται[ǁ] πᾶσα σὰρξ
are he may annul; so that [4]not [3]might [5]boast [1]all [2]flesh

ἐνώπιον [v]αὐτοῦ.[ǁ] 30 ἐξ.αὐτοῦ.δὲ ὑμεῖς ἐστε ἐν χριστῷ Ἰησοῦ,
before him. But of him ye are in Christ Jesus,

ὃς ἐγενήθη [w]ἡμῖν σοφία[ǁ] ἀπὸ θεοῦ δικαιοσύνη.τε καὶ ἁγιασ-
who was made to us wisdom from God and righteousness and sancti-

μὸς καὶ ἀπολύτρωσις· 31 ἵνα, καθὼς γέγραπται,
fication and redemption; that, according as it has been written,

Ὁ καυχώμενος, ἐν κυρίῳ καυχάσθω.
He that boasts, in [the] Lord let him boast.

2 Κἀγὼ ἐλθὼν πρὸς ὑμᾶς, ἀδελφοί, ἦλθον οὐ καθ'
And I having come to you, brethren, came not according to

ὑπεροχὴν λόγου ἢ σοφίας καταγγέλλων ὑμῖν τὸ μαρτύριον
excellency of word or wisdom, announcing to you the testimony

τοῦ θεοῦ. 2 οὐ.γὰρ ἔκρινα [x]τοῦ[ǁ] [y]εἰδέναι τι[ǁ] ἐν ὑμῖν,
of God. For [3]not [1]I [2]decided to know anything among you,

εἰ.μὴ Ἰησοῦν χριστόν, καὶ τοῦτον ἐσταυρωμένον. 3 [z]καὶ ἐγὼ[ǁ]
except Jesus Christ, and him crucified. And I

ἐν ἀσθενείᾳ καὶ ἐν φόβῳ καὶ ἐν τρόμῳ πολλῷ ἐγενόμην πρὸς
in weakness and in fear and in [2]trembling [1]much was with

ὑμᾶς· 4 καὶ ὁ.λόγος.μου καὶ τὸ.κήρυγμά.μου οὐκ ἐν πειθοῖς
you; and my word and my preaching [was] not in persuasive

[a]ἀνθρωπίνης[ǁ] σοφίας λόγοις, [b]ἀλλ'[ǁ] ἐν ἀποδείξει πνεύματος
[3]human [2]of [4]wisdom [1]words, but in demonstration of [the] Spirit

---

[n] σημεῖα signs GLTTrAW. [o] ἔθνεσιν to nations GLTTrAW. [p] — ἐστίν TTr. [q] ἵνα καταισχύνῃ τοὺς σοφούς [L]TTrA. [r] [καὶ τὰ . . . . ὁ θεός] L. [s] — καὶ LTTrA. [t] καυχήσεται E. [v] τοῦ θεοῦ God GLTTrAW. [w] σοφία ἡμῖν LTTrA. [x] — τοῦ GLTTrAW. [y] τι εἰδέναι GLTrAW. [z] κἀγὼ LTTrA. [a] — ἀνθρωπίνης GLTTrAW. [b] ἀλλὰ Tr.

καὶ δυνάμεως· 5 ἵνα ἡ.πίστις.ὑμῶν μὴ.ᾖ ἐν σοφίᾳ ἀνθρώ-
and of power; that your faith might not be in wisdom of men,
πων, [b]ἀλλ'‖ ἐν δυνάμει θεοῦ.
but in power of God.

6 Σοφίαν.δὲ λαλοῦμεν ἐν τοῖς τελείοις· σοφίαν.δὲ οὐ τοῦ
But wisdom we speak among the perfect; but wisdom, not
αἰῶνος.τούτου, οὐδὲ τῶν ἀρχόντων τοῦ.αἰῶνος.τούτου, τῶν
of this age, nor of the rulers of this age, who
καταργουμένων· 7 ἀλλὰ λαλοῦμεν [c]σοφίαν θεοῦ‖ ἐν μυστηρίῳ,
are coming to nought. But we speak wisdom of God in a mystery,
τὴν ἀποκεκρυμμένην ἣν προώρισεν ὁ θεὸς πρὸ τῶν
the hidden [wisdom] which [2]predetermined [1]God before the
αἰώνων εἰς δόξαν.ἡμῶν, 8 ἣν οὐδεὶς τῶν ἀρχόντων τοῦ
ages for our glory, which no one of the rulers
αἰῶνος.τούτου ἔγνωκεν· εἰ.γὰρ ἔγνωσαν, οὐκ ἂν τὸν κύριον
of this age has known, (for if they had known, [8]not [1]the [2]Lord
τῆς δόξης ἐσταύρωσαν· 9 ἀλλὰ καθὼς γέγραπ-
[3]of [4]the [5]glory [6]they [7]would have crucified,) but according as it has been
ται, Ἃ ὀφθαλμὸς οὐκ.εἶδεν, καὶ οὖς οὐκ.ἤκουσεν, καὶ
written, Things which eye saw not, and ear heard not, and
ἐπὶ καρδίαν ἀνθρώπου οὐκ.ἀνέβη, [d]ἃ‖ ἡτοίμασεν ὁ θεὸς
into heart of man came not, which [2]prepared [1]God
τοῖς ἀγαπῶσιν αὐτόν· 10 ἡμῖν.δὲ [e]ὁ θεὸς ἀπεκάλυψεν‖
for those that love him, but to us God revealed [them]
διὰ τοῦ.πνεύματος.[f]αὐτοῦ·‖ τὸ.γὰρ πνεῦμα πάντα [g]ἐρευνᾷ,‖
by his Spirit; for the Spirit all things searches,
καὶ τὰ βάθη τοῦ θεοῦ. 11 τίς.γὰρ οἶδεν ἀνθρώπων τὰ
even the depths of God. For who [3]knows [1]of [2]men the things
τοῦ ἀνθρώπου, εἰ.μὴ τὸ πνεῦμα τοῦ ἀνθρώπου τὸ ἐν
of man, except the spirit of man which [is] in
αὐτῷ; οὕτως καὶ τὰ τοῦ θεοῦ οὐδεὶς [h]οἶδεν,‖ εἰ.μὴ τὸ
him? so also the things of God no one knows, except the
πνεῦμα τοῦ θεοῦ. 12 ἡμεῖς.δὲ οὐ τὸ πνεῦμα τοῦ κόσμου ἐλά-
Spirit of God. But we not the spirit of the world re-
βομεν, ἀλλὰ τὸ πνεῦμα τὸ ἐκ τοῦ θεοῦ, ἵνα εἰδῶμεν
ceived, but the Spirit which [is] from God, that we might know
τὰ ὑπὸ τοῦ θεοῦ χαρισθέντα ἡμῖν. 13 Ἃ καὶ λαλοῦμεν,
the things by God granted to us: which also we speak,
οὐκ ἐν διδακτοῖς ἀνθρωπίνης σοφίας λόγοις, ἀλλ' ἐν δι-
not in [2]taught [3]of [4]human [5]wisdom [1]words, but in [those]
δακτοῖς πνεύματος [i]ἁγίου,‖ πνευματικοῖς πνευματικὰ
taught of [the] [2]Spirit [1]Holy, [6]by [7]spiritual [[8]means] [4]spiritual [5]things
[k]συγκρίνοντες.‖ 14 ψυχικὸς.δὲ ἄνθρωπος οὐ.δέχεται τὰ
[3]communicating. But [the] natural man receives not the things
τοῦ πνεύματος τοῦ θεοῦ· μωρία.γὰρ αὐτῷ ἐστιν, καὶ
of the Spirit of God, for foolishness to him they are; and
οὐ.δύναται γνῶναι, ὅτι πνευματικῶς ἀνακρίνεται.
he cannot know [them], because spiritually they are discerned;
15 ὁ.δὲ πνευματικὸς ἀνακρίνει [l]μὲν‖ πάντα, αὐτὸς.δὲ ὑπ'
but the spiritual discerns all things, but he by
οὐδενὸς ἀνακρίνεται. 16 τίς.γὰρ ἔγνω νοῦν κυρίου,
no one is discerned. For who did know [the] mind of [the] Lord?
ὃς συμβιβάσει αὐτόν; ἡμεῖς.δὲ νοῦν [m]χριστοῦ‖ ἔχομεν.
who shall instruct him? But we [the] mind of Christ have.

stration of the Spirit and of power: 5 that your faith should not stand in the wisdom of men, but in the power of God.

6 Howbeit we speak wisdom among them that are perfect: yet not the wisdom of this world, nor of the princes of this world, that come to nought:
7 but we speak the wisdom of God in a mystery, *even* the hidden *wisdom*, which God ordained before the world unto our glory:
8 which none of the princes of this world knew: for had they known *it*, they would not have crucified the Lord of glory.
9 But as it is written, Eye hath not seen, nor ear heard, neither have entered into the heart of man, the things which God hath prepared for them that love him.
10 But God hath revealed *them* unto us by his Spirit: for the Spirit searcheth all things, yea, the deep things of God.
11 For what man knoweth the things of a man, save the spirit of man which is in him? even so the things of God knoweth no man, but the Spirit of God.
12 Now we have received, not the spirit of the world, but the spirit which is of God; that we might know the things that are freely given to us of God.
13 Which things also we speak, not in the words which man's wisdom teacheth, but which the Holy Ghost teacheth; comparing spiritual things with spiritual.
14 But the natural man receiveth not the things of the Spirit of God: for they are foolishness unto him: neither can he know *them*, because they are spiritually discerned.
15 But he that is spiritual judgeth all things, yet he himself is judged of no man.
16 For who hath known the mind of the Lord, that he may instruct him? But we have the mind of Christ.

[b] ἀλλὰ Tr. [c] θεοῦ σοφίαν GLTTrAW. [d] ὅσα whatsoever LTrA. [e] ἀπεκάλυψεν ὁ θεὸς LTTrAW. [f] — αὐτοῦ (*read* the Spirit) LTTr[A]. [g] ἐραυνᾷ TTrA. [h] ἔγνωκεν has known LTTrAW. [i] — Ἁγίου GLTTrAW. [k] συν- T. [l] [τὰ] L; — μὲν T[TrA]. [m] κυρίου of [the] Lord L.

III. And I, brethren,
could not speak unto
you as unto spiritual,
but as unto carnal,
even as unto babes in
Christ. 2 I have fed
you with milk, and
not with meat: for
hitherto ye were not
able *to bear it*, neither
yet now are ye able.
3 For ye are yet carnal:
for whereas *there is*
among you envying,
and strife, and divi-
sions, are ye not car-
nal, and walk as men?
4 For while one saith,
I am of Paul; and an-
other, I *am* of Apollos;
are ye not carnal?
5 Who then is Paul,
and who *is* Apollos,
but ministers by whom
ye believed, even as
the Lord gave to every
man? 6 I have planted,
Apollos watered; but
God gave the increase.
7 So then neither is
he that planteth any-
thing, neither he that
watereth; but God
that giveth the in-
crease. 8 Now he that
planteth and he that
watereth are one: and
every man shall re-
ceive his own reward
according to his own
labour. 9 For we are
labourers together
with God: ye are God's
husbandry, *ye are*
God's building. 10 Ac-
cording to the grace of
God which is given
unto me, as a wise
masterbuilder, I have
laid the foundation,
and another buildeth
thereon. But let every
man take heed how
he buildeth thereupon.
11 For other foun-
dation can no man
lay than that is
laid, which is Jesus
Christ. 12 Now if any
man build upon this
foundation gold, sil-
ver, precious stones,
wood, hay, stubble,
13 every man's work
shall be made mani-
fest: for the day shall
declare it, because it
shall be revealed by
fire; and the fire
shall try every man's
work of what sort it
is. 14 If any man's

3 [n]Καὶ ἐγώ,‖ ἀδελφοί, οὐκ.ἠδυνήθην λαλῆσαι ὑμῖν ὡς
And I, brethren, was not able to speak to you as
πνευματικοῖς, ἀλλ' ὡς [o]σαρκικοῖς,‖ ὡς νηπίοις ἐν χριστῷ.
to spiritual, but as to fleshly; as to babes in Christ.
2 γάλα ὑμᾶς ἐπότισα, [p]καὶ‖ οὐ βρῶμα· οὔπω.γὰρ [q]ἠδύνασθε,‖
Milk [3]you [1]I [2]gave to drink; and not meat, for not yet were ye able,
ἀλλ' [r]οὔτε‖ [s]ἔτι‖ νῦν δύνασθε· 3 ἔτι.γὰρ σαρκικοί ἐστε.
but neither yet now are ye able; for yet fleshly ye are.
ὅπου.γὰρ ἐν ὑμῖν ζῆλος καὶ ἔρις [t]καὶ διχοστασίαι,‖
For where among you emulation and strife and divisions [there are],
οὐχὶ σαρκικοί ἐστε. καὶ κατὰ ἄνθρωπον περιπατεῖτε;
[3]not [4]fleshly [1]are [2]ye, and [2]according [3]to [4]man [1]walk?
4 ὅταν.γὰρ λέγῃ τις, Ἐγὼ μέν εἰμι Παύλου, ἕτερος.δέ, Ἐγὼ
For when [2]may [3]say [1]one, I am of Paul, and another, I
Ἀπολλώ, [v]οὐχὶ σαρκικοί‖ ἐστε; 5 [w]Τίς‖ οὖν ἐστιν [x]Παῦλος,‖
of Apollos, [3]not [4]fleshly [1]are [2]ye? Who then is Paul,
[w]τίς‖ δὲ [y] [x]Ἀπολλώς,‖ [z]ἀλλ' ἢ‖ διάκονοι δι' ὧν ἐπιστεύ-
[2]who [1]and Apollos? but servants through whom ye be-
σατε, καὶ ἑκάστῳ ὡς ὁ κύριος ἔδωκεν; 6 ἐγὼ ἐφύτευσα,
lieved, and to each as the Lord gave? I planted,
Ἀπολλὼς ἐπότισεν, [a]ἀλλ'‖ ὁ θεὸς ηὔξανεν· 7 ὥστε οὔτε
Apollos watered; but God gave growth. So that neither
ὁ φυτεύων ἐστίν τι, οὔτε ὁ ποτίζων, ἀλλ' ὁ αὐξά-
he that plants is anything, nor he that waters; but [2]who [3]gives
νων θεός. 8 ὁ.φυτεύων.δὲ καὶ ὁ ποτίζων ἕν εἰσιν· ἕκαστος
[4]growth [1]God. But he that plants and he that waters [2]one [1]are; [4]each
δὲ τὸν.ἴδιον μισθὸν [b]λήψεται‖ κατὰ τὸν.ἴδιον κόπον.
[3]but his own reward shall receive according to his own labour.
9 θεοῦ.γάρ ἐσμεν συνεργοί· θεοῦ γεώργιον, θεοῦ οἰκοδομή
For God's [2]we [3]are [1]fellow-workers; God's husbandry, God's building
ἐστε. 10 Κατὰ τὴν χάριν τοῦ θεοῦ τὴν δοθεῖσάν μοι, ὡς
ye are. According to the grace of God which was given to me, as
σοφὸς ἀρχιτέκτων θεμέλιον [c]τέθεικα,‖ ἄλλος.δὲ ἐποικοδομεῖ·
a wise architect [the] foundation I have laid, and another builds up.
ἕκαστος.δὲ βλεπέτω πῶς ἐποικοδομεῖ· 11 θεμέλιον.γὰρ ἄλλον
But [2]each [1]let take heed how he builds up. For [2]foundation [1]other
οὐδεὶς δύναται θεῖναι παρὰ τὸν κείμενον, ὅς ἐστιν [d]Ἰη-
no one is able to lay besides that which is laid, which is Je-
σοῦς ὁ χριστός.‖ 12 εἰ.δέ τις ἐποικοδομεῖ ἐπὶ τὸν θεμέλιον
sus the Christ. Now if anyone build up on [2]foundation
[e]τοῦτον‖ [f]χρυσόν, ἄργυρον,‖ λίθους τιμίους, ξύλα, χόρτον,
[1]this gold, silver, [2]stones [1]precious, wood, grass,
καλάμην, 13 ἑκάστου τὸ ἔργον φανερὸν γενήσεται· ἡ.γὰρ
straw, of each the work manifest will become; for the
ἡμέρα δηλώσει· ὅτι ἐν πυρὶ ἀποκαλύπτεται· καὶ ἑκάστου
day will declare [it], because in fire it is revealed; and of each
τὸ ἔργον ὁποῖόν ἐστιν, τὸ πῦρ [g] δοκιμάσει. 14 εἴ τινος τὸ
the work what sort it is, the fire will prove. If of anyone the
ἔργον [h]μένει‖ ὃ [i]ἐπῳκοδόμησεν,‖ μισθὸν [k]λήψεται.‖ 15 εἴ
work abides which he built up, a reward he shall receive. If

---

[n] κἀγώ GLTTrAW. [o] σαρκίνοις to fleshy GLTTrAW. [p] — καὶ GLTTrAW. [q] ἐδύνασθε GLTTrA. [r] οὐδὲ GLTTrAW. [s] [ἔτι] L. [t] — καὶ διχοστασίαι LTTrA. [v] οὐκ (οὐχὶ W) ἄνθρωποί not men LTTrAW. [w] τί what LTTr; τί[ς] A. [x] Ἀπολλῶς and Παῦλος *transposed* LTTrAW. [y] + ἐστιν is LTTrA. [z] — ἀλλ' ἢ GLTTrAW. [a] ἀλλὰ LTTrA. [b] λήμψεται LTTrA. [c] ἔθηκα I laid LTTrA. [d] χριστὸς Ἰησοῦς L; — ὁ GTTrAW. [e] — τοῦτον *read* the foundation) LTTr[A]. [f] χρυσίον, ἀργύριον TTr. [g] + αὐτὸ itself LTTrAW. [h] μενεῖ shall abide GLTAW. [i] ἐποικοδόμησεν TTrA. [k] λήμψεται LTTrA.

τινος τὸ ἔργον κατακαήσεται, ζημιωθήσεται· αὐτὸς.δὲ
of anyone the work shall be consumed, he shall suffer loss, but himself
σωθήσεται, οὕτως.δὲ ὡς διὰ πυρός. 16 Οὐκ.οἴδατε ὅτι ναὸς
shall be saved, but so as through fire. Know ye not that [2]temple
θεοῦ ἐστε, καὶ τὸ πνεῦμα τοῦ θεοῦ οἰκεῖ ἐν ὑμῖν; 17 εἴ τις
[1]God's ye are, and the Spirit of God dwells in you? If anyone
τὸν ναὸν τοῦ θεοῦ φθείρει, φθερεῖ [l]τοῦτον‖ ὁ
the temple of God corrupt, [2]shall [4]bring [5]to [6]corruption [1]him
θεός· ὁ.γὰρ ναὸς τοῦ θεοῦ ἅγιός ἐστιν, οἵτινές ἐστε ὑμεῖς.
[3]God; for the temple of God [2]holy [1]is, which [2]are [1]ye.
18 μηδεὶς ἑαυτὸν ἐξαπατάτω· εἴ τις δοκεῖ σοφὸς
[4]No [5]one [7]himself [3]let [6]deceive: if anyone [3]thinks [[4]himself] [7]wise
εἶναι ἐν ὑμῖν ἐν τῷ.αἰῶνι.τούτῳ, μωρὸς γενέσθω, ἵνα
[5]to [6]be, [1]among [2]you in this age, foolish let him become, that
γένηται σοφός. 19 ἡ.γὰρ σοφία τοῦ.κόσμου.τούτου μωρία
he may be wise. For the wisdom of this world foolishness
παρὰ [m]τῷ θεῷ ἐστιν· γέγραπται.γάρ, Ὁ δρασσόμενος τοὺς
with God is; for it has been written, He takes the
σοφοὺς ἐν τῇ.πανουργίᾳ.αὐτῶν. 20 καὶ πάλιν, Κύριος
wise in their craftiness. And again, [The] Lord
γινώσκει τοὺς διαλογισμοὺς τῶν σοφῶν, ὅτι εἰσὶν μάταιοι.
knows the reasonings of the wise, that they are vain.
21 Ὥστε μηδεὶς καυχάσθω ἐν ἀνθρώποις· πάντα.γὰρ ὑμῶν
So that [2]no [3]one [1]let boast in men; for all things [2]yours
ἐστιν, 22 εἴτε Παῦλος, εἴτε Ἀπολλώς, εἴτε Κηφᾶς, εἴτε
[1]are. Whether Paul, or Apollos, or Cephas, or [the]
κόσμος, εἴτε ζωή, εἴτε θάνατος, εἴτε ἐνεστῶτα, εἴτε μέλλοντα·
world, or life, or death, or present things, or coming things,
πάντα ὑμῶν [n]ἐστιν·‖ 23 ὑμεῖς.δὲ χριστοῦ· χριστὸς.δὲ θεοῦ.
all [2]yours [1]are; and ye Christ's, and Christ God's.
4 Οὕτως ἡμᾶς λογιζέσθω ἄνθρωπος ὡς ὑπηρέτας χριστοῦ
So [5]of [6]us [1]let [4]reckon [2]a [3]man as attendants of Christ
καὶ οἰκονόμους μυστηρίων θεοῦ. 2 [o]ὃ δὲ‖ λοιπόν, ζητεῖται
and stewards [3]mysteries [1]of [2]God's. But as to the rest, it is required
ἐν τοῖς οἰκονόμοις ἵνα πιστός τις εὑρεθῇ. 3 ἐμοὶ.δὲ εἰς ἐλά-
in stewards that faithful one be found. But to me the small-
χιστόν ἐστιν ἵνα ὑφ' ὑμῶν ἀνακριθῶ, ἢ ὑπὸ ἀνθρωπίνης
est matter it is that by you I be examined, or by man's
ἡμέρας· ἀλλ' οὐδὲ ἐμαυτὸν ἀνακρίνω. 4 οὐδὲν.γὰρ ἐμαυτῷ
day. But neither myself do I examine. For of nothing in myself
σύνοιδα· ἀλλ' οὐκ ἐν τούτῳ δεδικαίωμαι· ὁ.δὲ ἀνα-
I am conscious; but not by this have I been justified: but he who ex-
κρίνων με κύριός ἐστιν. 5 ὥστε μὴ πρὸ καιροῦ τι
amines me [the] Lord is. So that not before [the] time anything
κρίνετε, ἕως ἂν ἔλθῃ ὁ κύριος, ὃς καὶ φωτίσει τὰ
judge, until may have come the Lord, who both will bring to light the
κρυπτὰ τοῦ σκότους, καὶ φανερώσει τὰς βουλὰς τῶν
hidden things of darkness, and will make manifest the counsels
καρδιῶν· καὶ τότε ὁ ἔπαινος γενήσεται ἑκάστῳ ἀπὸ τοῦ θεοῦ.
of hearts; and then praise shall be to each from God.
6 Ταῦτα.δέ, ἀδελφοί, μετεσχημάτισα εἰς ἐμαυτὸν καὶ [p]Ἀ-
Now these things, brethren, I transferred to myself and A-
πολλὼ‖ δι' ὑμᾶς, ἵνα ἐν ἡμῖν μάθητε τὸ μὴ ὑπὲρ
pollos on account of you, that in us ye may learn not [3]above

work abide which he
hath built thereupon,
he shall receive a re-
ward. 15 If any man's
work shall be burned,
he shall suffer loss:
but he himself shall
be saved; yet so as by
fire. 16 Know ye not
that ye are the temple
of God, and *that* the
Spirit of God dwelleth
in you? 17 If any
man defile the temple
of God, him shall God
destroy; for the tem-
ple of God is holy,
which *temple* ye are.
18 Let no man deceive
himself. If any man
among you seemeth to
be wise in this world,
let him become a fool,
that he may be wise.
19 For the wisdom of
this world is foolish-
ness with God. For
it is written, He taketh
the wise in their own
craftiness. 20 And
again, The Lord know-
eth the thoughts of the
wise, that they are
vain. 21 Therefore let
no man glory in men.
For all things are
yours; 22 whether
Paul, or Apollos, or
Cephas, or the world,
or life, or death, or
things present, or
things to come; all
are yours; 23 and ye
are Christ's; and
Christ *is* God's.
IV. Let a man so
account of us, as of
the ministers of Christ,
and stewards of the
mysteries of God.
2 Moreover it is re-
quired in stewards,
that a man be found
faithful. 3 But with
me it is a very small
thing that I should be
judged of you, or of
man's judgment: yea,
I judge not mine own
self. 4 For I know
nothing by myself;
yet am I not hereby
justified: but he that
judgeth me is the
Lord. 5 Therefore
judge nothing before
the time, until the
Lord come, who both
will bring to light the
hidden things of dark-
ness, and will make
manifest the counsels
of the hearts: and
then shall every man
have praise of God.
6 And these things,
brethren, I have in a
figure transferred to
myself and *to* Apollos
for your sakes; that

[l] αὐτὸν L. [m] — τῷ L[A]. [n] — ἐστιν (*read* [are]) LTTrA. [o] ὧδε here LTTrA.
[p] Ἀπολλῶν TTr.

ye might learn in us
not to think *of men*
above that which is
written, that no one
of you be puffed up
for one against an-
other. 7 For who
maketh thee to differ
from another? and
what hast thou that
thou didst not receive?
now if thou didst re-
ceive *it*, why dost thou
glory, as if thou hadst
not received *it?* 8 Now
ye are full, now ye
are rich, ye have
reigned as kings with-
out us: and I would
to God ye did reign,
that we also might
reign with you. 9 For
I think that God hath
set forth us the apos-
tles last, as it were
appointed to death:
for we are made a
spectacle unto the
world, and to angels,
and to men. 10 We
are fools for Christ's
sake, but ye *are* wise
in Christ; we *are*
weak, but ye *are*
strong; ye *are* ho-
nourable, but we *are*
despised. 11 Even un-
to this present hour
we both hunger, and
thirst, and are naked,
and are buffeted, and
have no certain dwell-
ingplace; 12 and la-
bour, working with
our own hands: being
reviled, we bless; being
persecuted, we suffer
it: 13 being defamed, we
intreat: we are made
as the filth of the
world, *and are* the off-
scouring of all things
unto this day. 14 I
write not these things
to shame you, but as
my beloved sons I
warn *you*. 15 For
though ye have ten
thousand instructors
in Christ, yet *have ye*
not many fathers; for
in Christ Jesus I have
begotten you through
the gospel. 16 Where-
fore I beseech you,
be ye followers of me.

17 For this cause
have I sent unto you
Timotheus, who is my
beloved son, and faith-
ful in the Lord, who
shall bring you into
remembrance of my
ways which be in
Christ, as I teach
every where in every
church. 18 Now some
are puffed up, as

[q]ὅ'' γέγραπται [r]φρονεῖν,'' ἵνα μὴ εἷς ὑπὲρ τοῦ ἑνὸς
[4]what [5]has [6]been [7]written [1]to [2]think, that not one for one
φυσιοῦσθε κατὰ τοῦ ἑτέρου. 7 τίς.γάρ σε διακρίνει;
ye be puffed up against the other. For who thee makes to differ?
τί.δὲ ἔχεις ὃ οὐκ.ἔλαβες; εἰ.δὲ καὶ ἔλαβες,
and what hast thou which thou didst not receive? but if also thou didst receive,
τί καυχᾶσαι ὡς μὴ λαβών; 8 ἤδη κεκορεσμένοι ἐστέ,
why boastest thou as not having received? Already satiated ye are;
ἤδη ἐπλουτήσατε, χωρὶς ἡμῶν ἐβασιλεύσατε· καὶ ὄφελόν
already ye were enriched; apart from us ye reigned; and I would
γε ἐβασιλεύσατε, ἵνα καὶ ἡμεῖς ὑμῖν [s]συμβασιλεύσωμεν.''
surely ye did reign, that also we [4]you [1]might [2]reign [3]with.
9 δοκῶ.γὰρ [t]ὅτι'' ὁ θεὸς ἡμᾶς τοὺς ἀποστόλους ἐσχάτους ἀπέ-
For I think that God us the apostles last set
δειξεν ὡς ἐπιθανατίους· ὅτι θέατρον ἐγενήθημεν τῷ κόσμῳ,
forth as appointed to death. For a spectacle we became to the world,
καὶ ἀγγέλοις καὶ ἀνθρώποις. 10 ἡμεῖς μωροὶ διὰ
both to angels and to men. We [are] fools on account of
χριστόν, ὑμεῖς.δὲ φρόνιμοι ἐν χριστῷ· ἡμεῖς ἀσθενεῖς, ὑμεῖς.δὲ
Christ, but ye prudent in Christ; we weak, but ye
ἰσχυροί· ὑμεῖς ἔνδοξοι, ἡμεῖς.δὲ ἄτιμοι. 11 ἄχρι τῆς ἄρτι
strong; ye glorious, but we without honour. To the present
ὥρας καὶ πεινῶμεν καὶ διψῶμεν, καὶ [v]γυμνητεύομεν,'' καὶ
hour both we hunger and thirst and are naked, and
κολαφιζόμεθα, καὶ ἀστατοῦμεν, 12 καὶ κοπιῶμεν, ἐργα-
are buffeted, and wander without a home, and labour, work-
ζόμενοι ταῖς.ἰδίαις χερσίν· λοιδορούμενοι, εὐλογοῦμεν· διω-
ing with our own hands. Railed at, we bless; per-
κόμενοι, ἀνεχόμεθα· 13 [w]βλασφημούμενοι,'' παρακαλοῦμεν·
secuted, we bear; evilly spoken to, we beseech:
ὡς περικαθάρματα τοῦ κόσμου ἐγενήθημεν, πάντων
as [the] refuse of the world we are become, of all [the]
περίψημα ἕως ἄρτι. 14 Οὐκ ἐντρέπων ὑμᾶς γράφω ταῦτα,
off-scouring until now. Not shaming you do I write these things,
[x]ἀλλ''' ὡς τέκνα μου ἀγαπητὰ [y]νουθετῶ.'' 15 ἐὰν.γὰρ
but as [3]children [1]my [2]beloved I admonish [you]. For if
μυρίους παιδαγωγοὺς ἔχητε ἐν χριστῷ, ἀλλ' οὐ πολ-
ten thousand tutors ye should have in Christ, yet not [1]many
λοὺς πατέρας· ἐν.γὰρ χριστῷ Ἰησοῦ διὰ τοῦ εὐαγγελίου
fathers; for in Christ Jesus through the glad tidings
ἐγὼ ὑμᾶς ἐγέννησα. 16 παρακαλῶ οὖν ὑμᾶς, μιμηταί μου
I you did beget. I exhort therefore you, [2]imitators [3]of [4]me
γίνεσθε.
[1]become.

17 Διὰ τοῦτο [z]ἔπεμψα ὑμῖν Τιμόθεον, ὅς ἐστιν [a]τέκνον
On account of this I sent to you Timotheus, who is [3]child
μου'' ἀγαπητὸν καὶ πιστὸν ἐν κυρίῳ, ὃς ὑμᾶς ἀναμνήσει
[1]my [2]beloved and faithful in [the] Lord, who [3]you [1]will [2]remind of
τὰς.ὁδούς.μου τὰς ἐν χριστῷ,[b] καθὼς πανταχοῦ ἐν πάσῃ
my ways that [are] in Christ, according as everywhere in every
ἐκκλησίᾳ διδάσκω. 18 ὡς μὴ.ἐρχομένου δέ μου πρὸς ὑμᾶς
assembly I teach. [2]As [3]to [5]not [6]coming [1]now [4]my to you
ἐφυσιώθησάν τινες· 19 ἐλεύσομαι.δὲ ταχέως πρὸς ὑμᾶς, ἐὰν
[2]were [3]puffed [4]up [1]some; but I shall come shortly to you, if

---

[q] ἃ LTTrAW. [r] — φρονεῖν (read μὴ nothing) LTTrAW. [s] συν- T. [t] — ὅτι LTTrAW. [v] γυμνιτεύομεν LTTrAW. [w] δυσφημούμενοι defamed TA. [x] ἀλλὰ Tr. [y] νουθετῶν admonishing T. [z] + αὐτὸ very [thing] T. [a] μου τέκνον LTTrA. [b] + Ἰησοῦ Jesus LT.

ὁ κύριος θελήσῃ, καὶ γνώσομαι, οὐ τὸν λόγον τῶν
the Lord will, and I will know, not the word of those who
πεφυσιωμένων, ἀλλὰ τὴν δύναμιν. 20 οὐ.γὰρ ἐν λόγῳ ἡ
are puffed up, but the power. For not in word the
βασιλεία τοῦ θεοῦ, ἀλλ' ἐν δυνάμει. 21 τί θέλετε; ἐν
kingdom of God [is], but in power. What will ye? with
ῥάβδῳ ἔλθω πρὸς ὑμᾶς, ἢ ἐν ἀγάπῃ πνεύματί.τε [c]πραό-
a rod I should come to you, or in love and a spirit of meek-
τητος||;
ness?

5 "Ολως ἀκούεται ἐν ὑμῖν πορνεία, καὶ τοιαύτη πορνεία
Commonly [2]is [3]reported [4]among [5]you [1]fornication, and such fornication
ἥτις οὐδὲ ἐν τοῖς ἔθνεσιν [d]ὀνομάζεται,|| ὥστε γυναῖκά
which not even among the nations is named, so as [6]wife
τινα τοῦ πατρὸς ἔχειν. 2 καὶ ὑμεῖς πεφυσιωμένοι ἐστέ,
[1]one [[4]his] [5]father's [2]to [3]have. And ye [2]puffed [3]up [1]are,
καὶ οὐχὶ μᾶλλον ἐπενθήσατε, ἵνα [e]ἐξαρθῇ|| ἐκ μέσου.ὑμῶν
and not rather did mourn, that might be taken out of your midst
ὁ τὸ.ἔργον.τοῦτο [f]ποιήσας;|| 3 ἐγὼ μὲν.γὰρ [g]ὡς|| ἀπὼν τῷ
he who this deed did! [1]I [1]for as being absent
σώματι, παρὼν.δὲ τῷ πνεύματι, ἤδη κέκρικα ὡς παρών,
in body, but being present in spirit, already have judged as being present,
τὸν οὕτως τοῦτο κατεργασάμενον, 4 ἐν τῷ ὀνόματι τοῦ
him who so [3]this [1]worked [2]out, in the name
κυρίου.[h]ἡμῶν|| Ἰησοῦ [i]χριστοῦ,|| συναχθέντων ὑμῶν καὶ
of our Lord Jesus Christ, being gathered together ye and
τοῦ ἐμοῦ πνεύματος, σὺν τῇ δυνάμει τοῦ.κυρίου.[k]ἡμῶν|| Ἰησοῦ
my spirit, with the power of our Lord Jesus
[l]χριστοῦ,|| 5 παραδοῦναι τὸν.τοιοῦτον τῷ σατανᾷ εἰς ὄλεθρον
Christ— to deliver such a one to Satan for destruction
τῆς σαρκός, ἵνα τὸ πνεῦμα σωθῇ ἐν τῇ ἡμέρᾳ τοῦ κυρίου
of the flesh, that the spirit may be saved in the day of the Lord
[l]Ἰησοῦ.|| 6 Οὐ καλὸν τὸ.καύχημα.ὑμῶν· οὐκ.οἴδατε ὅτι μικρὰ
Jesus. Not good [is] your boasting. Know ye not that a little
ζύμη ὅλον τὸ φύραμα ζυμοῖ; 7 ἐκκαθάρατε [m]οὖν|| τὴν πα-
leaven [3]whole [2]the [4]lump [1]leavens? Purge out therefore the
λαιὰν ζύμην, ἵνα ἦτε νέον φύραμα, καθώς ἐστε ἄζυμοι·
old leaven, that ye may be a new lump, according as ye are unleavened.
καὶ.γὰρ τὸ.πάσχα.ἡμῶν [n]ὑπὲρ ἡμῶν|| [o]ἐτύθη|| χριστός.
For also [2]our [3]passover [6]for [7]us [4]was [5]sacrificed [1]Christ.
8 ὥστε ἑορτάζωμεν, μὴ ἐν ζύμῃ παλαιᾷ, μηδὲ ἐν
So that we should celebrate the feast, not with [2]leaven [1]old, nor with
ζύμῃ κακίας καὶ πονηρίας, ἀλλ' ἐν ἀζύμοις [p]εἰλι-
leaven of malice and wickedness, but with unleavened [bread] of
κρινείας|| καὶ ἀληθείας.
sincerity and of truth.

9 Ἔγραψα ὑμῖν ἐν τῇ ἐπιστολῇ, μὴ συναναμίγνυσθαι
I wrote to you in the epistle, not to associate with
πόρνοις· 10 [q]καὶ|| οὐ πάντως τοῖς πόρνοις τοῦ.κόσμου.τού-
fornicators; and not altogether with the fornicators of this world,
του, ἢ τοῖς πλεονέκταις, [r]ἢ|| ἅρπαξιν, ἢ εἰδωλολάτραις· ἐπεὶ
or with the covetous, or rapacious, or idolaters, since

though I would not come to you. 19 But I will come to you shortly, if the Lord will, and will know not the speech of them which are puffed up, but the power. 20 For the kingdom of God *is* not in word, but in power. 21 What will ye? shall I come unto you with a rod, or in love, and *in* the spirit of meekness?

V. It is reported commonly *that there is* fornication among you, and such fornication as is not so much as named among the Gentiles, that one should have his father's wife. 2 And ye are puffed up, and have not rather mourned, that he that hath done this deed might be taken away from among you. 3 For I verily, as absent in body, but present in spirit, have judged already, as though I were present, *concerning* him that hath so done this deed, 4 in the name of our Lord Jesus Christ, when ye are gathered together, and my spirit, with the power of our Lord Jesus Christ, 5 to deliver such an one unto Satan for the destruction of the flesh, that the spirit may be saved in the day of the Lord Jesus. 6 Your glorying *is* not good. Know ye not that a little leaven leaveneth the whole lump? 7 Purge out therefore the old leaven, that ye may be a new lump, as ye are unleavened. For even Christ our passover is sacrificed for us: 8 therefore let us keep the feast, not with old leaven, neither with the leaven of malice and wickedness; but with the unleavened *bread* of sincerity and truth.

9 I wrote unto you in an epistle not to company with fornicators: 10 yet not altogether with the fornicators of this world, or with the covetous, or extortioners, or

[c] πραΰτητος LTTrA. [d] — ὀνομάζεται (*read* [is]) GLTTrAW. [e] ἀρθῇ GLTTrAW. [f] πράξας; T. [g] — ὡς LTTrAW. [h] — ἡμῶν (*read* the Lord) [L]T. [i] — χριστοῦ LTTrA. [k] [ἡμῶν] L. [l] [ἡμῶν Ἰησοῦ χριστοῦ] (*read* our Lord Jesus Christ) L; — Ἰησοῦ A; ἡμῶν Ἰησοῦ W. [m] — οὖν GLTTrAW. [n] — ὑπὲρ ἡμῶν LTTrAW. [o] ἐθύθη E. [p] εἰλικρινίας T. [q] — καὶ LTTrAW. [r] καὶ and LTTrAW.

with idolaters; for
then must ye needs
go out of the world.
11 But now I have
written unto you not
to keep company, if
any man that is called
a brother be a forni-
cator, or covetous, or
an idolater, or a rail-
er, or a drunkard, or
an extortioner; with
such an one no not to
eat. 12 For what have
I to do to judge them
also that are without?
do not ye judge them
that are within? 13 But
them that are without
God judgeth. There-
fore put away from
among yourselves that
wicked person.
VI. Dare any of you,
having a matter a-
gainst another, go to
law before the un-
just, and not before
the saints? 2 Do ye
not know that the
saints shall judge the
world? and if the
world shall be judg-
ed by you, are ye
unworthy to judge
the smallest matters?
3 Know ye not that
we shall judge an-
gels? how much more
things that pertain
to this life? 4 If then
ye have judgments
of things pertaining
to this life, set them
to judge who are
least esteemed in the
church. 5 I speak to
your shame. Is it so,
that there is not a
wise man among you?
no, not one that shall
be able to judge be-
tween his brethren?
6 But brother goeth
to law with brother,
and that before the
unbelievers. 7 Now
therefore there is ut-
terly a fault among
you, because ye go to
law one with another.
Why do ye not rather
take wrong? why do
ye not rather *suffer
yourselves to* be de-
frauded? 8 Nay, ye
do wrong, and de-
fraud, and that *your*
brethren. 9 Know ye
not that the unright-
eous shall not inherit
the kingdom of God?
Be not deceived: nei-
ther fornicators, nor
idolaters, nor adul-
terers, nor effemin-

[s]ὀφείλετε" ἄρα ἐκ τοῦ κόσμου ἐξελθεῖν. 11 [t]νυνὶ".δὲ ἔγραψα
ye ought then out of the world to go. But now, I wrote
ὑμῖν μὴ συναναμίγνυσθαι, ἐάν τις ἀδελφὸς ὀνομαζόμενος
to you not to associate with [him], if anyone [2]brother [1]designated
[v]ἢ" πόρνος, ἢ πλεονέκτης, ἢ εἰδωλολάτρης, ἢ λοίδορος,
[be] either a fornicator, or covetous, or idolater, or railer,
ἢ μέθυσος, ἢ ἅρπαξ· τῷ.τοιούτῳ· μηδὲ συνεσθίειν. 12 τί
or a drunkard, or rapacious; with such a one not even to eat. [2]What
γάρ μοι [w]καὶ" τοὺς ἔξω κρίνειν; οὐχὶ τοὺς ἔσω ὑμεῖς
[1]for [is it] to me also those outside to judge, [4]not [6]those [7]within [1]ye
κρίνετε; 13 τοὺς.δὲ ἔξω ὁ θεὸς [x]κρίνει." [y]καὶ ἐξαρεῖτε"
[2]do [3]ye [5]judge? But those outside God judges. And ye shall put out
τὸν πονηρὸν ἐξ ὑμῶν.αὐτῶν.
the wicked person from among yourselves.

6 Τολμᾷ τις ὑμῶν, πρᾶγμα ἔχων πρὸς τὸν ἕτερον,
Dare anyone of you, a matter having against the other,
κρίνεσθαι ἐπὶ τῶν ἀδίκων, καὶ οὐχὶ ἐπὶ τῶν ἁγίων; 2 [z]οὐκ
go to law before the unrighteous, and not before the saints? [3]Not
οἴδατε ὅτι οἱ ἅγιοι τὸν κόσμον κρινοῦσιν; καὶ εἰ ἐν ὑμῖν
[1]know [2]ye that the saints [3]the [4]world [1]will [2]judge? and if by you
κρίνεται ὁ κόσμος, ἀνάξιοί ἐστε κριτηρίων ἐλαχίστων; 3 οὐκ
is judged the world, [3]unworthy [1]are [2]ye of judgments the smallest? [3]Not
οἴδατε ὅτι ἀγγέλους κρινοῦμεν; [a]μήτι.γε" βιωτικά;
[1]know [2]ye that angels we shall judge? much more then things of this life?
4 βιωτικὰ μὲν οὖν κριτήρια ἐὰν ἔχητε, τοὺς
[8]Things [9]of [10]this [11]life [4]then [5]judgment [[6]as [7]to] [1]if [2]ye [3]have, who
ἐξουθενημένους ἐν τῇ ἐκκλησίᾳ, τούτους [b]καθίζετε." 5 πρὸς
are least esteemed in the assembly, [4]those [1]set [2]ye [3]up. For
ἐντροπὴν ὑμῖν [c]λέγω." οὕτως οὐκ.[d]ἔστιν" ἐν ὑμῖν [e]σοφὸς
shame to you I speak. Thus is there not among you a wise [man]
οὐδὲ εἷς," ὃς δυνήσεται διακρῖναι ἀνὰ.μέσον τοῦ ἀδελφοῦ
not even one, who shall be able to decide between [2]brother
αὐτοῦ; 6 ἀλλὰ ἀδελφὸς μετὰ ἀδελφοῦ κρίνεται, καὶ
[1]his [and brother]? But brother with brother goes to law, and
τοῦτο ἐπὶ ἀπίστων; 7 ἤδη μὲν [f]οὖν" ὅλως ἥττημα
this before unbelievers! Already indeed therefore altogether a default
[g]ἐν" ὑμῖν ἐστιν, ὅτι κρίματα ἔχετε μεθ' ἑαυτῶν. [h]διατί" οὐχὶ
among you is, that law-suits ye have among yourselves. Why not
μᾶλλον ἀδικεῖσθε; [h]διατί" οὐχὶ μᾶλλον ἀποστερεῖσθε; 8 ἀλλὰ
rather suffer wrong? why not rather be defrauded? But
ὑμεῖς ἀδικεῖτε καὶ ἀποστερεῖτε, καὶ [i]ταῦτα" ἀδελφούς.
ye do wrong and defraud, and these things [to your] brethren.
9 ἢ οὐκ.οἴδατε ὅτι ἄδικοι [k]βασιλείαν θεοῦ" οὐ κληρονο-
Or know ye not that unjust ones [the] kingdom of God [2]not [1]shall in-
μήσουσιν; Μὴ.πλανᾶσθε· οὔτε πόρνοι, οὔτε εἰδωλολάτραι,
herit? Be not misled; neither fornicators, nor idolaters,
οὔτε μοιχοί, οὔτε μαλακοί, οὔτε ἀρσενο-
nor adulterers, nor abusers of themselves as women, nor abusers of them-
κοῖται, 10 οὔτε κλέπται, οὔτε πλεονέκται, [l]οὔτε" μέθυσοι,
selves with men, nor thieves, nor covetous, nor drunkards,
οὐ λοίδοροι, οὐχ ἅρπαγες, βασιλείαν θεοῦ [m]οὐ" κληρονο-
nor railers, nor rapacious, [the] kingdom of God shall

[s] ὠφείλετε LTTrA. [t] νῦν LTrA. [v] ᾖ be EGLTTrAW. [w] — καὶ LTTrA. [x] κρινεῖ (; LTr) will judge GLT. [y] ἐξάρατε put ye out GLTTrAW. [z] + ἢ or GLTTrAW. [a] μήτιγε GT. [b] καθίζετε; (*read* do ye set up those, &c.) GTW. [c] λαλῶ L. [d] ἔνι GLTTrAW. [e] οὐδεὶς σοφός LTTrA. [f] — οὖν T[Tr]. [g] — ἐν (*read* ὑμῖν with you) GLTTrAW. [h] διὰ τί LTrA. [i] τοῦτο this LTTrAW. [k] θεοῦ βασιλείαν GLTTrAW. [l] οὐ TA. [m] — οὐ LTTrA.

μήσουσιν. 11 καὶ ταῦτά τινες.ἦτε· [n]ἀλλὰ‖ ἀπελού-
inherit. And these things some of you were; but ye were
σασθε, ἀλλὰ ἡγιάσθητε, [o]ἀλλ'‖ ἐδικαιώθητε, ἐν τῷ ὀνόματι
washed, but ye were sanctified, but ye were justified, in the name
τοῦ κυρίου [p] Ἰησοῦ, [q] καὶ ἐν τῷ πνεύματι τοῦ.θεοῦ.ἡμῶν.
of the Lord Jesus, and by the Spirit of our God.

12 Πάντα μοι ἔξεστιν, ἀλλ' οὐ πάντα συμφέρει· πάντα
All things to me are lawful, but not all things do profit; all things
μοι ἔξεστιν, ἀλλ' οὐκ ἐγὼ ἐξουσιασθήσομαι ὑπό τινος.
to me are lawful, but [3]not [1]I [2]will be brought under the power of any.
13 Τὰ βρώματα τῇ κοιλίᾳ, καὶ ἡ κοιλία τοῖς βρώμασιν·
Meats for the belly, and the belly for meats;
ὁ.δὲ.θεὸς καὶ ταύτην καὶ ταῦτα καταργήσει. τὸ.δὲ σῶμα
but God both this and these will bring to nought: but the body [is]
οὐ τῇ πορνείᾳ, ἀλλὰ τῷ κυρίῳ, καὶ ὁ κύριος τῷ σώματι·
not for fornication, but for the Lord, and the Lord for the body.
14 ὁ.δὲ.θεὸς καὶ τὸν κύριον ἤγειρεν, καὶ [r]ἡμᾶς‖ [s]ἐξεγερεῖ‖ διὰ
And God both the Lord raised up, and us will raise out by
τῆς.δυνάμεως.αὐτοῦ. 15 οὐκ.οἴδατε ὅτι τὰ.σώματα.ὑμῶν μέλη
his power, Know ye not that your bodies members
χριστοῦ ἐστιν; ἄρας οὖν τὰ μέλη τοῦ χριστοῦ, ποιήσω
of Christ are? Having taken then the members of the Christ, shall I make
πόρνης μέλη; μὴ.γένοιτο. 16 ἢ οὐκ.οἴδατε ὅτι ὁ
[them] [2]of [3]a [4]harlot [1]members? May it not be! Or know ye not that he that
κολλώμενος τῇ πόρνῃ, ἓν σῶμά ἐστιν; Ἔσονται.γάρ, [t]φησίν,‖
is joined to the harlot, [2]one [3]body [1]is? For shall be, he says,
οἱ δύο εἰς σάρκα μίαν· 17 ὁ.δὲ κολλώμενος τῷ κυρίῳ, ἓν
the two for [2]flesh [1]one. But he that is joined to the Lord, [2]one
πνεῦμά ἐστιν. 18 Φεύγετε τὴν πορνείαν. πᾶν ἁμάρτημα ὃ
[3]spirit [1]is. Flee fornication. Every sin which
ἐὰν ποιήσῃ ἄνθρωπος, ἐκτὸς τοῦ σώματός ἐστιν· ὁ.δὲ
[3]may [4]practise [1]a [2]man, without the body is, but he that
πορνεύων, εἰς τὸ.ἴδιον σῶμα ἁμαρτάνει. 19 ἢ οὐκ
commits fornication, against his own body sins. Or [2]not
οἴδατε ὅτι τὸ.σῶμα.ὑμῶν ναὸς τοῦ ἐν ὑμῖν ἁγίου πνεύματός
[1]know [3]ye that your body a temple of the [3]in [4]you [1]Holy [2]Spirit
ἐστιν, οὗ ἔχετε ἀπὸ θεοῦ, καὶ οὐκ ἐστὲ ἑαυτῶν; 20 ἠγοράσθητε
is, which ye have from God; and [3]not [2]are [1]ye your own? [2]ye [3]were
σθητε γὰρ τιμῆς· δοξάσατε δὴ τὸν θεὸν ἐν τῷ σώματι
[4]bought [1]for with a price; glorify [2]indeed [1]God in [2]body
ὑμῶν, [v]καὶ ἐν τῷ.πνεύματι.ὑμῶν, ἅτινά ἐστιν τοῦ θεοῦ.‖
[1]your, and in your spirit, which are God's.

7 Περὶ.δὲ ὧν ἐγράψατέ [w]μοι,‖ καλὸν ἀνθρώπῳ
But concerning what things ye wrote to me: [It is] good for a man
γυναικὸς μὴ ἅπτεσθαι· 2 διὰ.δὲ τὰς πορνείας ἕκαστος
[4]a [5]woman [1]not [2]to [3]touch; but on account of fornication [2]each
τὴν.ἑαυτοῦ.γυναῖκα ἐχέτω, καὶ ἑκάστη τὸν.ἴδιον ἄνδρα ἐχέτω.
[4]his [5]own [6]wife [1]let [3]have, and [2]each [4]her [5]own [6]husband [1]let [3]have.
3 τῇ γυναικὶ ὁ ἀνὴρ τὴν [x]ὀφειλομένην εὔνοιαν‖ ἀπο-
To the wife [2]the [3]husband [5]due [6]benevolence [1]let
διδότω· ὁμοίως.[y]δὲ‖ καὶ ἡ γυνὴ τῷ ἀνδρί. 4 ἡ γυνὴ τοῦ.ἰδίου
[4]render, and likewise also the wife to the husband. The wife her own
σώματος οὐκ.ἐξουσιάζει, [z]ἀλλ'‖ ὁ ἀνήρ· ὁμοίως.δὲ καὶ ὁ
body has not authority over, but the husband; and likewise also the

ate, nor abusers of themselves with mankind, 10 nor thieves, nor covetous, nor drunkards, nor revilers, nor extortioners, shall inherit the kingdom of God. 11 And such were some of you: but ye are washed, but ye are sanctified, but ye are justified in the name of the Lord Jesus, and by the Spirit of our God.

12 All things are lawful unto me, but all things are not expedient: all things are lawful for me, but I will not be brought under the power of any. 13 Meats for the belly, and the belly for meats: but God shall destroy both it and them. Now the body *is* not for fornication, but for the Lord; and the Lord for the body. 14 And God hath both raised up the Lord, and will also raise up us by his own power. 15 Know ye not that your bodies are the members of Christ? shall I then take the members of Christ, and make *them* the members of an harlot? God forbid. 16 What? know ye not that he which is joined to an harlot is one body? for two, saith he, shall be one flesh. 17 But he that is joined unto the Lord is one spirit. 18 Flee fornication. Every sin that a man doeth is without the body; but he that committeth fornication sinneth against his own body. 19 What! know ye not that your body is the temple of the Holy Ghost *which is* in you, which ye have of God, and ye are not your own? 20 For ye are bought with a price: therefore glorify God in your body, and in your spirit, which are God's.

VII. Now concerning the things whereof ye wrote unto me: *It is* good for a man not to touch a woman. 2 Nevertheless, *to avoid* fornication, let every man have

---

[n] ἀλλ' L. [o] ἀλλὰ TTrA. [p] + [ἡμῶν] (*read* our Lord) L. [q] + χριστοῦ Christ LTTr. [r] ὑμᾶς you E. [s] ἐξεγείρει raises out L. [t] [φησιν] L. [v] — καὶ ἐν *to end of verse* GLTTrAW. [w] — μοι T[Tr]A. [x] ὀφειλὴν [her] due GLTTrAW. [y] [δὲ] L. [z] ἀλλὰ LTTrA.

his own wife, and let
every woman have her
own husband. 3 Let
the husband render
unto the wife due be-
nevolence: and like-
wise also the wife un-
to the husband. 4 The
wife hath not power
of her own body, but
the husband: and like-
wise also the husband
hath not power of his
own body, but the wife.
5 Defraud ye not one
the other, except *it*
be with consent for a
time, that ye may give
yourselves to fasting
and prayer; and come
together again, that
Satan tempt you not
for your incontinency.
6 But I speak this by
permission, *and* not of
commandment. 7 For
I would that all men
were even as I myself.
But every man hath
his proper gift of God,
one after this manner,
and another after that.
8 I say therefore to
the unmarried and
widows, It is good for
them if they abide
even as I. 9 But if
they cannot contain,
let them marry: for
it is better to marry
than to burn. 10 And
unto the married I
command, *yet* not I,
but the Lord, Let not
the wife depart from
her husband: 11 but
and if she depart, let
her remain unmar-
ried, or be reconciled
to *her* husband: and
let not the husband
put away *his* wife.
12 But to the rest speak
I, not the Lord: If
any brother hath a
wife that believeth
not, and she be pleased
to dwell with him, let
him not put her away.
13 And the woman
which hath an hus-
band that believeth
not, and if he be
pleased to dwell with
her, let her not leave
him. 14 For the un-
believing husband is
sanctified by the wife,
and the unbelieving
wife is sanctified by
the husband: else
were your children
unclean; but now are
they holy. 15 But if
the unbelieving de-

ἀνὴρ τοῦ.ἰδίου σώματος οὐκ.ἐξουσιάζει, [z]ἀλλ'‖ ἡ γυνή. 5 μὴ
husband his own body has not authority over, but the wife. [2]Not
ἀποστερεῖτε ἀλλήλους, εἰ.μή τι ἂν ἐκ συμφώνου πρὸς καιρόν,
[1]defraud one another, unless by consent for a season,
ἵνα [a]σχολάζητε‖ [b]τῇ νηστείᾳ καὶ‖ τῇ προσευχῇ, καὶ πάλιν
that ye may be at leisure for fasting and for prayer, and again
[c]ἐπὶ.τὸ.αὐτὸ συνέρχησθε,‖ ἵνα μὴ πειράζῃ ὑμᾶς ὁ σατανᾶς
into one place come together, that [3]not [2]may [4]tempt [5]you [1]Satan
διὰ τὴν.ἀκρασίαν.ὑμῶν. 6 τοῦτο.δὲ λέγω κατὰ [d]συγ-
because of your incontinence. But this I say by way of per-
γνώμην,‖ οὐ κατ' ἐπιταγήν. 7 θέλω [e]γὰρ‖ πάντας ἀνθρώ-
mission, not by way of command. [2]I [3]wish [1]but all men
πους εἶναι ὡς.καὶ ἐμαυτόν· [z]ἀλλ'‖ ἕκαστος ἴδιον [f]χάρισμα
to be even as myself: but each his own gift
ἔχει‖ ἐκ θεοῦ, [g]ὃς‖ μὲν οὕτως, [g]ὃς‖.δὲ οὕτως. 8 Λέγω.δὲ
has from God; one so, and another so. But I say
τοῖς ἀγάμοις καὶ ταῖς χήραις, καλὸν αὐτοῖς [h]ἐστιν‖ ἐὰν [i]
to the unmarried and to the widows, good for them it is if
μείνωσιν ὡς κἀγώ. 9 εἰ.δὲ οὐκ.ἐγκρατεύονται, γαμησά-
they should remain as even I. But if they have not self-control, let them
τωσαν· [k]κρεῖσσον‖.γάρ [l]ἐστιν‖ [m]γαμῆσαι‖ ἢ πυροῦσθαι.
marry; for better it is to marry than to burn.
10 Τοῖς.δὲ γεγαμηκόσιν παραγγέλλω, οὐκ ἐγώ, [z]ἀλλ'‖ ὁ
But to the married I charge, not I, but the
κύριος, γυναῖκα ἀπὸ ἀνδρὸς μὴ [n]χωρισθῆναι·‖ 11 ἐὰν.δὲ καὶ
Lord, wife from husband not to be separated; (but if also
χωρισθῇ, μενέτω ἄγαμος, ἢ τῷ ἀνδρὶ καταλλαγήτω·
she be separated, let her remain unmarried, or to the husband be reconciled;)
καὶ ἄνδρα γυναῖκα μὴ ἀφιέναι. 12 Τοῖς.δὲ λοιποῖς [o]ἐγὼ λέγω,‖
and husband [4]wife [1]not [2]to [3]leave. But to the rest I say,
οὐχ ὁ κύριος, εἴ τις ἀδελφὸς γυναῖκα ἔχει ἄπιστον, καὶ
not the Lord, If any brother [4]wife [1]has [2]an [3]unbelieving, and
[p]αὐτὴ‖ συνευδοκεῖ οἰκεῖν μετ' αὐτοῦ, μὴ.ἀφιέτω αὐτήν·
she consents to dwell with him, let him not leave her.
13 καὶ γυνὴ [q]ἥτις‖ ἔχει ἄνδρα ἄπιστον, καὶ [r]αὐτὸς‖
And a woman who has [3]husband [1]an [2]unbelieving, and he
συνευδοκεῖ οἰκεῖν μετ' αὐτῆς, μὴ.ἀφιέτω [s]αὐτόν.‖ 14 ἡγίασται
consents to dwell with her, let her not leave him. [2]Is [3]sanctified
γὰρ ὁ ἀνὴρ ὁ ἄπιστος ἐν τῇ γυναικί, καὶ ἡγίασται ἡ γυνὴ
[1]for the [2]husband [1]unbelieving in the wife, and is sanctified the [2]wife
ἡ ἄπιστος ἐν τῷ [t]ἀνδρί·‖ ἐπεὶ ἄρα τὰ.τέκνα.ὑμῶν ἀκάθαρτά
[1]unbelieving in the husband; else then your children unclean
ἐστιν, νῦν.δὲ ἅγιά ἐστιν. 15 εἰ.δὲ ὁ ἄπιστος χωρίζεται,
are, but now [2]holy [1]are. But if the unbeliever separates himself,
χωριζέσθω. οὐ.δεδούλωται ὁ ἀδελφὸς ἢ ἡ ἀδελφὴ ἐν
let him separate himself; is not under bondage the brother or the sister in
τοῖς τοιούτοις· ἐν.δὲ εἰρήνῃ κέκληκεν [v]ἡμᾶς‖ ὁ θεός. 16 τί
such [cases], but in peace [2]has [3]called [4]us [1]God. [6]What
γὰρ οἶδας, γύναι, εἰ τὸν ἄνδρα σώσεις; ἢ τί οἶδας,
[5]for knowest thou, O wife, if the husband thou shalt save? or what knowest thou,

[z] ἀλλὰ LTTrA. [a] σχολάσητε GLTTrAW. [b] — τῇ νηστείᾳ καὶ GLTTrAW. [c] ἐπὶ τὸ αὐτο συνέρχεσθε E; ἐπὶ τὸ αὐτὸ ἦτε together may be GLTTrAW. [d] συν- T. [e] δὲ but LTTrAW. [f] ἔχει χάρισμα GLTTrAW. [g] ὁ LTTrAW. [h] — ἐστιν (*read* [it is]) GLTTrAW. [i] + [οὕτως] L. [k] κρεῖττον LTTr. [l] — ἐστιν W. [m] γαμεῖν T. [n] χωρίζεσθαι L. [o] λέγω ἐγώ LTTrAW. [p] αὕτη LTAW. [q] εἴ τις if any T. [r] οὗτος LTTrAW. [s] τὸν ἄνδρα the husband LTTrAW. [t] ἀδελφῷ brother LTTrAW. [v] ὑμᾶς you T.

ἄνερ, εἰ τὴν·γυναῖκα σώσεις; 17 εἰ.μὴ· ἑκάστῳ ὡς
O husband, if the wife thou shalt save? Only to each as
[w]ἐμέρισεν‖ [x]ὁ θεός,‖ ἕκαστον ὡς κέκληκεν [x]ὁ κύριος,‖ οὕτως
[2]divided [1]God, each as [3]has [4]called [1]the [2]Lord, so
περιπατείτω· καὶ οὕτως ἐν ταῖς ἐκκλησίαις πάσαις διατάσ-
let him walk; and thus in [2]the [3]assemblies [1]all I order.
σομαι. 18 Περιτετμημένος τις ἐκλήθη; μὴ.ἐπι-
Having been circumcised [2]any [3]one [1]was called? let him not be
σπάσθω. ἐν ἀκροβυστίᾳ [y]τις ἐκλήθη;‖ μὴ.περι-
uncircumcised: in uncircumcision [2]any [3]one [1]was called? let him not be
τεμνέσθω. 19 ἡ περιτομὴ οὐδέν ἐστιν, καὶ ἡ ἀκροβυστία οὐδέν
circumcised. Circumcision [2]nothing [1]is, and uncircumcision [2]nothing
ἐστιν, ἀλλὰ τήρησις ἐντολῶν θεοῦ. 20 ἕκαστος ἐν τῇ κλήσει
[1]is, but keeping [2]commandments [1]God's. Each in the calling
ᾗ ἐκλήθη, ἐν ταύτῃ μενέτω. 21 δοῦλος ἐκλή-
in which he was called, in this let him abide. Bondman [being] wast
θης; μή σοι μελέτω· ἀλλ' εἰ.καὶ δύνασαι ἐλεύθερος
thou called, not to thee let it be a care; but and if thou art able [3]free
γενέσθαι, μᾶλλον χρῆσαι. 22 ὁ.γὰρ ἐν κυρίῳ κληθεὶς
[1]to [2]become, [6]rather [4]use [[5]it]. For he [3]in [[4]the] [5]Lord [1]being [2]called
δοῦλος, ἀπελεύθερος κυρίου ἐστίν· ὁμοίως [z]καὶ‖ ὁ
[being] a bondman, a freedman of [the] Lord is; likewise also he
ἐλεύθερος κληθείς, δοῦλός ἐστιν χριστοῦ. 23 τιμῆς ἠγορά-
free being called, a bondman is of Christ. With a price ye were
σθητε· μὴ.γίνεσθε δοῦλοι ἀνθρώπων. 24 ἕκαστος ἐν.ᾧ ἐκλή-
bought; become not bondmen of men. Each wherein he was
θη, ἀδελφοί, ἐν τούτῳ μενέτω παρὰ [a]τῷ‖ θεῷ.
called, brethren, in that let him abide with God.

25 Περὶ.δὲ τῶν παρθένων ἐπιταγὴν κυρίου οὐκ.ἔχω·
But concerning virgins, commandment of [the] Lord I have not;
γνώμην.δὲ δίδωμι, ὡς ἠλεημένος ὑπὸ κυρίου πιστὸς
but judgment I give, as having received mercy from [the] Lord [3]faithful
εἶναι. 26 νομίζω οὖν τοῦτο καλὸν ὑπάρχειν διὰ τὴν ἐν-
[1]to [2]be. I think then this [2]good [1]is because of the pre-
εστῶσαν ἀνάγκην, ὅτι καλὸν ἀνθρώπῳ τὸ οὕτως εἶναι.
sent necessity, that [it is] good for a man so to be.
27 δέδεσαι γυναικί; μὴ.ζήτει λύσιν. λέλυσαι ἀπὸ
Hast thou been bound to a wife? seek not to be loosed. Hast thou been loosed from
γυναικός; μὴ.ζήτει γυναῖκα. 28 ἐὰν.δὲ καὶ [b]γήμῃς,‖
a wife? seek not a wife. But if also thou mayest have married,
οὐχ.ἥμαρτες· καὶ ἐὰν γήμῃ [c]ἡ‖ παρθένος, οὐχ
thou didst not sin; and if [3]may [4]have [5]married [1]the [2]virgin, [6]not
ἥμαρτεν· θλίψιν.δὲ τῇ σαρκὶ ἕξουσιν οἱ τοιοῦτοι· ἐγὼ.δὲ
[6]she [7]did sin: but tribulation in the flesh [2]shall [3]have [1]such; but I
ὑμῶν φείδομαι. 29 Τοῦτο.δέ φημι, ἀδελφοί, [d] ὁ καιρὸς συν-
[2]you [1]spare. But this I say, brethren, the season strait-
εσταλμένος· [e]τὸ.λοιπόν ἐστιν,‖ ἵνα καὶ [f]οἱ‖ ἔχοντες γυναῖκας,
ened [is]. For the rest is, that even those having wives,
ὡς μὴ ἔχοντες ὦσιν· 30 καὶ οἱ κλαίοντες, ὡς μὴ κλαίοντες· καὶ
[3]as [2]not [4]having [1]be; and those weeping, as not weeping; and
οἱ χαίροντες, ὡς μη χαίροντες· καὶ οἱ ἀγοράζοντες, ὡς μὴ
those rejoicing, as not rejoicing; and those buying, as not

part, let him depart. A brother or a sister is not under bondage in such *cases:* but God hath called us to peace. 16 For what knowest thou, O wife, whether thou shalt save *thy* husband? or how knowest thou, O man, whether thou shalt save *thy* wife? 17 But as God hath distributed to every man, as the Lord hath called every one, so let him walk. And so ordain I in all churches. 18 Is any man called being circumcised? let him not become uncircumcised. Is any called in uncircumcision? let him not be circumcised. 19 Circumcision is nothing, and uncircumcision is nothing, but the keeping of the commandments of God. 20 Let every man abide in the same calling wherein he was called. 21 Art thou called *being* a servant? care not for it: but if thou mayest be made free, use *it* rather. 22 For he that is called in the Lord, *being* a servant, is the Lord's freeman: likewise also he that is called, *being* free, is Christ's servant. 23 Ye are bought with a price; be not ye the servants of men. 24 Brethren, let every man, wherein he is called, therein abide with God.

25 Now concerning virgins I have no commandment of the Lord: yet I give my judgment, as one that hath obtained mercy of the Lord to be faithful. 26 I suppose therefore that this is good for the present distress, *I say,* that *it is* good for a man so to be. 27 Art thou bound unto a wife? seek not to be loosed. Art thou loosed from a wife? seek not a wife. 28 But and if thou marry, thou hast not sinned; and if a virgin marry, she hath not sinned. Nevertheless such shall have trouble in the flesh: but I spare you. 29 But this I say,

[w] μεμέρικεν has divided TTr. [x] ὁ θεός *and* ὁ κύριος *transposed* GLTTrAW. [y] κέκληταί τις has any one been called LTTrAW. [z] — καὶ LTTrAW. [a] — τῷ GLTTrAW. [b] γαμήσῃς LTTrA. [c] [ἡ] LTrA. [d] + ὅτι E. [e] ἐστὶν τὸ λοιπόν, (τὸ λοιπόν ἐστιν· E) (*read* is for the rest *joined to* straitened) ETrAW; ἐστίν· τὸ λοιπὸν LT. [f] — οἱ E.

brethren, the time *is*
short: it remaineth,
that both they that
have wives be as
though they had none;
30 and they that weep,
as though they wept
not; and they that re-
joice, as though they
rejoiced not; and they
that buy, as though
they possessed not;
31 and they that use
this world, as not a-
busing *it*: for the
fashion of this world
passeth away. 32 But
I would have you
without carefulness.
He that is unmarried
careth for the things
that belong to the
Lord, how he may
please the Lord: 33 but
he that is married
careth for the things
that are of the world,
how he may please *his*
wife. 34 There is dif-
ference *also* between a
wife and a virgin. The
unmarried woman car-
eth for the things of
the Lord, that she may
be holy both in body
and in spirit: but she
that is married careth
for the things of the
world, how she may
please *her* husband.
35 And this I speak
for your own profit;
not that I may cast
a snare upon you, but
for that which is
comely, and that ye
may attend upon the
Lord without distrac-
tion. 36 But if any
man think that he
behaveth himself un-
comely toward his vir-
gin, if she pass the
flower of *her* age, and
need so require, let
him do what he will,
he sinneth not: let
them marry. 37 Ne-
vertheless he that
standeth stedfast in
his heart, having no
necessity, but hath
power over his own
will, and hath so de-
creed in his heart that
he will keep his virgin,
doeth well. 38 So then
he that giveth *her* in
marriage doeth well;
but he that giveth *her*

κατέχοντες 31 καὶ οἱ χρώμενοι [g]τῷ.κόσμῳ.τούτῳ,‖ ὡς μὴ
possessing; and those using this world, as not
καταχρώμενοι. παράγει.γὰρ τὸ σχῆμα τοῦ.κόσμου.τούτου.
using [it] as their own; for passes away the fashion of this world.
32 θέλω.δὲ ὑμᾶς ἀμερίμνους εἶναι. ὁ ἄγαμος μεριμνᾷ τὰ
But I wish you without care to be. The unmarried cares for the things
τοῦ κυρίου, πῶς [h]ἀρέσει‖ τῷ κυρίῳ· 33 ὁ.δὲ γαμήσας
of the Lord, how he shall please the Lord; but he that is married
μεριμνᾷ τὰ τοῦ κόσμου, πῶς [h]ἀρέσει‖ τῇ γυναικί.
cares for the things of the world, how he shall please the wife.
34 [i]μεμέρισται‖ ἡ [k]γυνὴ‖ καὶ ἡ παρθένος. [l]ἡ ἄγαμος‖ μεριμνᾷ
Divided are the wife and the virgin. The unmarried cares for
τὰ τοῦ κυρίου, ἵνα ᾖ ἁγία [m]καὶ‖ [n] σώματι καὶ [n]
the things of the Lord, that she may be holy both in body and
πνεύματι· ἡ.δὲ γαμήσασα μεριμνᾷ τὰ τοῦ κόσμου,
spirit; but she that is married cares for the things of the world,
πῶς [o]ἀρέσει‖ τῷ ἀνδρί. 35 τοῦτο.δὲ πρὸς τὸ.ὑμῶν.αὐτῶν
how she shall please the husband. But this for your own
[p]συμφέρον‖ λέγω· οὐχ ἵνα βρόχον ὑμῖν ἐπιβάλω, ἀλλὰ
profit I say; not that a noose [5]you [1]I [2]may [3]cast [4]before, but
πρὸς τὸ εὔσχημον καὶ [q]εὐπρόσεδρον‖ τῷ κυρίῳ ἀπερι-
for what [is] seemly, and waiting on the Lord without
σπάστως. 36 εἰ.δέ τις ἀσχημονεῖν ἐπὶ τὴν παρθένον
distraction. But if anyone [2he] [3]behaves [4]unseemly [5]to [7]virginity
αὐτοῦ νομίζει, ἐὰν ᾖ ὑπέρακμος, καὶ οὕτως ὀφείλει γίνε-
[6]his [1]thinks, if he be beyond [his] prime, and so it ought to
σθαι, ὃ θέλει ποιείτω, οὐχ.ἁμαρτάνει· γαμείτωσαν. 37 ὃς.δὲ
be, what he wills let him do, he does not sin: let them marry. But he who
ἕστηκεν [r]ἑδραῖος ἐν τῇ καρδίᾳ,‖ μὴ ἔχων ἀνάγκην, ἐξουσίαν.δὲ
stands firm in heart, not having necessity, but authority
ἔχει περὶ τοῦ.ἰδίου θελήματος, καὶ τοῦτο κέκρικεν ἐν τῇ [s]
has over his own will, and this has judged in
καρδίᾳ.[t]αὐτοῦ‖ [v]τοῦ‖ τηρεῖν τὴν.ἑαυτοῦ παρθένον, καλῶς
his heart to keep his own virginity, well
[w]ποιεῖ.‖ 38 ὥστε καὶ ὁ [x]ἐκγαμίζων καλῶς ποιεῖ· [y]ὁ.δὲ‖
he does. So that also he that gives in marriage [2]well [1]does; and he that
μὴ [z]ἐκγαμίζων‖ κρεῖσσον [w]ποιεῖ.‖ 39 Γυνὴ δέδεται [a]νόμῳ‖
[2]not [1]gives in marriage [2]better [1]does. A wife is bound by law
ἐφ' ὅσον χρόνον ζῇ ὁ.ἀνὴρ.αὐτῆς· ἐὰν.δὲ κοι-
for as long [2]as [1]time [5]may [6]live [3]her [4]husband; but if may have fallen
μηθῇ ὁ ἀνὴρ [b]αὐτῆς,‖ ἐλευθέρα ἐστὶν ᾧ θέλει γαμη-
asleep the husband of her, free she is to whom she wills to be
θῆναι, μόνον ἐν κυρίῳ. 40 μακαριωτέρα.δέ ἐστιν ἐὰν οὕτως
married, only in [the] Lord. But happier she is if so
μείνῃ, κατὰ τὴν ἐμὴν γνώμην· δοκῶ.δὲ κἀγὼ
she should remain, according to my judgment; and I think I also
πνεῦμα θεοῦ ἔχειν.
[3]Spirit [2]God's [1]have.

---

[g] τὸν κόσμον the world LTTrA. [h] ἀρέσῃ he should please LTTrA. [i] , καὶ μεμέρισται. καὶ and has become divided. Also LTr; καὶ (— καὶ W) μεμέρισται καὶ And divided are also TAW. [k] γυνὴ ἡ ἄγαμος unmarried woman LTr. [l] — . ἡ ἄγαμος (*read* the virgin cares for) Tr. [m] [καὶ] LTr. [n] + τῷ the LTTrA. [o] ἀρέσῃ she should please LTTrA. [p] σύμφορον LTTrA. [q] εὐπάρεδρον GLTTrAW. [r] ἐν τῇ καρδίᾳ αὐτοῦ (in his heart) ἑδραῖος LTTrA. [s] + ἰδίᾳ (*read* his own) TTrA. [t] — αὐτοῦ LTTrA. [v] — τοῦ LTTrA. [w] ποιήσει he shall do LTTrA. [x] γαμίζων τὴν παρθένον ἑαυτοῦ (ἑαυτοῦ παρθένον T) marries his own virginity LTTr; [ἐκ]γαμίζων [τὴν ἑαυτοῦ παρθένον] A. [y] καὶ ὁ GLTTrAW. [z] γαμίζων marries GLTTr; [ἐκ]γαμίζων A. [a] — νόμῳ GLTTrAW. [b] — αὐτῆς LTTrA.

8 Περὶ.δὲ τῶν.εἰδωλοθύτων, οἴδαμεν, ὅτι πάντες γνῶσιν
But concerning things sacrificed to idols, we know, (for [2]all [4]knowledge

ἔχομεν. ἡ γνῶσις φυσιοῖ, ἡ δὲ ἀγάπη οἰκοδομεῖ. 2 εἰ.[c]δέ‖
[1]we [3]have: knowledge puffs up, but love builds up. But if

τις δοκεῖ [d]εἰδέναι‖ τι, [e]οὐδέπω.οὐδὲν ἔγνωκεν‖
anyone thinks to have known anything, nothing yet he has known

καθὼς δεῖ γνῶναι. 3 εἰ.δέ τις ἀγαπᾷ τὸν θεόν,
according as it is necessary to know. But if anyone love God,

οὗτος ἔγνωσται ὑπ' αὐτοῦ. 4 περὶ τῆς βρώσεως οὖν τῶν
he is known by him:) concerning the eating then

εἰδωλοθύτων, οἴδαμεν ὅτι οὐδὲν εἴδωλον ἐν κόσμῳ,
of things sacrificed to idols, we know that nothing an idol [is] in [the] world,

καὶ ὅτι οὐδεὶς θεὸς [f]ἕτερος‖ εἰ.μὴ εἷς. 5 καὶ.γὰρ εἴπερ
and that [there is] no [2]God [1]other except one. For even if indeed

εἰσὶν λεγόμενοι θεοί, εἴτε ἐν οὐρανῷ εἴτε ἐπὶ [g]τῆς‖
there are [those] called gods, whether in heaven or on the

γῆς· ὥσπερ εἰσὶν θεοὶ πολλοὶ καὶ κύριοι πολλοί· 6 [h]ἀλλ'‖
earth, as there are gods many and lords many, but

ἡμῖν εἷς θεὸς ὁ πατήρ, ἐξ οὗ τὰ.πάντα, καὶ ἡμεῖς
to us [there is] one God the Father, of whom [are] all things, and we

εἰς αὐτόν· καὶ εἷς κύριος Ἰησοῦς χριστός, δι' οὗ τὰ.πάντα,
for him; and one Lord Jesus Christ, by whom [are] all things,

καὶ ἡμεῖς δι' αὐτοῦ. 7 ἀλλ' οὐκ ἐν πᾶσιν ἡ γνῶσις· τινὲς
and we by him. But not in all [is] the knowledge: [2]some

δὲ τῇ [i]συνειδήσει‖ [k]τοῦ εἰδώλου ἕως ἄρτι‖ ὡς εἰδωλό-
[1]but with conscience of the idol, until now [2]as [3]of [4]a [5]thing [6]sacrificed

θυτον ἐσθίουσιν, καὶ ἡ.συνείδησις.αὐτῶν ἀσθενὴς οὖσα
[7]to [8]an [9]idol [1]eat, and their conscience, [2]weak [1]being,

μολύνεται. 8 βρῶμα.δὲ ἡμᾶς οὐ.[l]παρίστησιν‖ τῷ θεῷ· οὔτε
is defiled. But meat us does not commend to God; [2]neither

[m]γὰρ‖ ἐὰν [n]φάγωμεν περισσεύομεν· οὔτε ἐὰν μὴ.φάγωμεν
[1]for if we eat have we an advantage; neither if we eat not

ὑστερούμεθα.‖ 9 βλέπετε.δὲ μήπως ἡ ἐξουσία ὑμῶν αὕτη
do we come short. But take heed lest [3]power [2]your [1]this

πρόσκομμα γένηται [o]τοῖς ἀσθενοῦσιν.‖ 10 ἐὰν.γάρ
an occasion of stumbling become to those being weak. For if

τίς ἴδῃ [p]σε,‖ τὸν ἔχοντα γνῶσιν, ἐν [q]εἰδωλείῳ‖ κατακείμενον,
anyone see thee, who hast knowledge, in an idol-temple reclining

οὐχὶ ἡ συνείδησις αὐτοῦ ἀσθενοῦς ὄντος οἰκοδο-
[at table], [2]not [3]the [4]conscience [5]of [6]him [8]weak [7]being [1]will be

μηθήσεται εἰς.τὸ τὰ.εἰδωλόθυτα ἐσθίειν; 11 [r]καὶ ἀπο-
built up so as [3]things [4]sacrificed [5]to [6]idols [1]to [2]eat? and will

λεῖται‖ ὁ ἀσθενῶν [s]ἀδελφὸς ἐπὶ τῇ.σῇ.γνώσει,‖ δι' ὃν χριστὸς
perish the weak brother on thy knowledge, for whom Christ

ἀπέθανεν. [t] 12 οὕτως.δὲ ἁμαρτάνοντες εἰς τοὺς ἀδελφούς,
died. Now thus sinning against the brethren,

καὶ τύπτοντες αὐτῶν τὴν συνείδησιν ἀσθενοῦσαν, εἰς χριστὸν
and wounding their [2]conscience [1]weak, against Christ

ἁμαρτάνετε. 13 [v]διόπερ‖ εἰ βρῶμα σκανδαλίζει τὸν ἀδελφόν
ye sin. Wherefore if meat cause [3]to [4]offend [2]brother

not in marriage doeth better. 39 The wife is bound by the law as long as her husband liveth; but if her husband be dead, she is at liberty to be married to whom she will; only in the Lord. 40 But she is happier if she so abide, after my judgment: and I think also that I have the Spirit of God.

VIII. Now as touching things offered unto idols, we know that we all have knowledge. Knowledge puffeth up, but charity edifieth. 2 And if any man think that he knoweth any thing, he knoweth nothing yet as he ought to know. 3 But if any man love God, the same is known of him. 4 As concerning therefore the eating of those things that are offered in sacrifice unto idols, we know that an idol *is* nothing in the world, and that *there is* none other God but one. 5 For though there be that are called gods, whether in heaven or in earth, (as there be gods many, and lords many,) 6 but to us *there is but* one God, the Father, of whom *are* all things, and we in him; and one Lord Jesus Christ, by whom *are* all things, and we by him. 7 Howbeit *there is* not in every man that knowledge: for some with conscience of the idol unto this hour eat *it* as a thing offered unto an idol; and their conscience being weak is defiled. 8 But meat commendeth us not to God: for neither, if we eat, are we the better; neither, if we eat not, are we the worse. 9 But take heed lest by any means this liberty of yours become a stumblingblock to them that are weak. 10 For if any man see thee which hast knowledge sit at meat in

---

c — δὲ but LTTrAW. d ἐγνωκέναι LTTrAW. e οὔπω ἔγνω not yet did he know LTTrA. f — ἕτερος LTTrA. g — τῆς GLTTrAW. h [ἀλλ'] L. i συνηθείᾳ from custom (with respect to the idol) LTTr. k ἕως ἄρτι τοῦ εἰδώλου LTTrAW. l παραστήσει shall not commend LTTrA. m — γὰρ for LTTrA. n μὴ φάγωμεν ὑστερούμεθα (περισσεύομεν L)· οὔτε ἐὰν φάγωμεν περισσεύομεν (ὑστερούμεθα L περισσευόμεθα Tr) LTrA. o τοῖς ἀσθενέσιν to the weak LTTrAW. p [σὲ] L. q εἰδωλίῳ T. r ἀπόλλυται γὰρ for perishes LTTr; καὶ ἀπόλλυται AW. s ἐν τῇ σῇ γνώσει, ὁ ἀδελφὸς LTTrAW. t ; (*read verse* 11 *as a question*) A. v διό περ Tr.

the idol's temple, shall not the conscience of him which is weak be emboldened to eat those things which are offered to idols; 11 and through thy knowledge shall the weak brother perish, for whom Christ died? 12 But when ye sin so against the brethren, and wound their weak conscience, ye sin against Christ. 13 Wherefore, if meat make my brother to offend, I will eat no flesh while the world standeth, lest I make my brother to offend.

IX. Am I not an apostle? am I not free? have I not seen Jesus Christ our Lord? are not ye my work in the Lord? 2 If I be not an apostle unto others, yet doubtless I am to you: for the seal of mine apostleship are ye in the Lord. 3 Mine answer to them that do examine me is this, 4 Have we not power to eat and to drink? 5 have we not power to lead about a sister, a wife, as well as other apostles, and *as* the brethren of the Lord, and Cephas? 6 or I only and Barnabas, have not we power to forbear working? 7 Who goeth a warfare any time at his own charges? who planteth a vineyard, and eateth not of the fruit thereof? or who feedeth a flock, and eateth not of the milk of the flock? 8 Say I these things as a man? or saith not the law the same also? 9 for it is written in the law of Moses, Thou shalt not muzzle the mouth of the ox that treadeth out the corn. Doth God take care for oxen? 10 or saith he *it* altogether for our sakes? For our sakes, no doubt, *this* is written: that he that ploweth should plow in hope; and that he that thresheth in hope should be partaker of his hope. 11 If we have sown unto you spiritual things, *is it* a great thing if we

μου, οὐ.μὴ φάγω κρέα εἰς.τὸν.αἰῶνα, ἵνα μὴ τὸν ἀδελφόν
[2]my, not at all should I eat flesh for ever, that [3]not [6]brother
μου σκανδαλίσω.
[5]my [1]I [2]may [4]cause to offend.

9 Οὐκ.εἰμὶ [x]ἀπόστολος‖; οὐκ.εἰμὶ [x]ἐλεύθερος‖; οὐχὶ Ἰησοῦν
Am I not an apostle? am I not free? [3]not [5]Jesus
[y]χριστὸν‖ τὸν.κύριον.ἡμῶν [z]ἑώρακα‖; οὐ τὸ.ἔργον.μου ὑμεῖς
[6]Christ [7]our [8]Lord [1]have [2]I [4]seen? [10]not [12]my [13]work [11]ye
ἐστε ἐν κυρίῳ; 2 εἰ ἄλλοις οὐκ.εἰμὶ ἀπόστολος, ἀλλά
[9]are in [the] Lord? If to others I am not an apostle, yet
γε ὑμῖν εἰμι· ἡ.γὰρ σφραγὶς [a]τῆς.ἐμῆς.ἀποστολῆς‖ ὑμεῖς
at any rate to you I am; for the seal of my apostleship ye
ἐστε ἐν κυρίῳ. 3 ἡ.ἐμὴ.ἀπολογία τοῖς ἐμὲ ἀνακρίνουσιν
are in [the] Lord. My defence to those [3]me [1]who [2]examine
[b]αὕτη ἐστίν,‖ 4 Μὴ οὐκ.ἔχομεν ἐξουσίαν φαγεῖν καὶ [c]πιεῖν‖;
[5]this [4]is: Have we not authority to eat and to drink?
5 μὴ οὐκ.ἔχομεν ἐξουσίαν ἀδελφὴν γυναῖκα περιάγειν, ὡς καὶ
have we not authority a sister, a wife, to take about, as also
οἱ λοιποὶ ἀπόστολοι, καὶ οἱ ἀδελφοὶ τοῦ κυρίου, καὶ Κηφᾶς;
the other apostles, and the brethren of the Lord, and Cephas?
6 ἢ μόνος ἐγὼ καὶ Βαρνάβας οὐκ.ἔχομεν ἐξουσίαν [d]τοῦ‖ μὴ
Or only I and Barnabas have we not authority not
ἐργάζεσθαι; 7 Τίς στρατεύεται ἰδίοις ὀψωνίοις ποτέ;
to work? Who serves as a soldier at his own charges at any time?
τίς φυτεύει ἀμπελῶνα, καὶ [e]ἐκ τοῦ καρποῦ‖ αὐτοῦ οὐκ.ἐσθίει;
who plants a vineyard, and of the fruit of it does not eat?
[f]ἢ‖ τίς ποιμαίνει ποίμνην, καὶ ἐκ τοῦ γάλακτος τῆς ποίμνης
or who shepherds a flock, and of the milk of the flock
οὐκ.ἐσθίει; 8 μὴ κατὰ ἄνθρωπον ταῦτα λαλῶ; ἢ [g]οὐχὶ
does not eat? according to a man these things do I speak, or [2]not
καὶ ὁ νόμος ταῦτα‖ λέγει; 9 ἐν.γὰρ τῷ [h]Μωσέως‖ νόμῳ
[3]also [4]the [5]law [6]these [7]things [1]says? For in the [2]of [3]Moses [1]law
γέγραπται, Οὐ.[i]φιμώσεις‖ βοῦν ἀλοῶντα. μὴ τῶν
it has been written, Thou shalt not muzzle an ox treading out corn. [4]For [5]the
βοῶν μέλει τῷ θεῷ; 10 ἢ δι' ἡμᾶς πάντως λέγει;
[6]oxen [1]is [2]there [3]care with God? or because of us altogether says he [it]?
δι'.ἡμᾶς.γὰρ ἐγράφη, ὅτι [j]ἐπ' ἐλπίδι ὀφείλει‖ ὁ ἀροτριῶν
For because of us it was written, that in hope ought he that ploughs
ἀροτριᾷν, καὶ ὁ ἀλοῶν [k]τῆς.ἐλπίδος.αὐτοῦ μετέχειν
to plough, and he that treads out corn, [5]of [6]his [7]hope [3]to [4]partake
ἐπ' ἐλπίδι.‖ 11 Εἰ ἡμεῖς ὑμῖν τὰ πνευματικὰ ἐσπείραμεν,
[1]in [2]hope. If we to you spiritual things did sow, [is it]
μέγα εἰ ἡμεῖς ὑμῶν τὰ σαρκικὰ θερίσομεν; 12 εἰ ἄλλοι
a great thing if we your fleshly things shall reap? If others
τῆς [l]ἐξουσίας ὑμῶν‖ μετέχουσιν, οὐ μᾶλλον ἡμεῖς;
[2]of [3]the [4]authority [5]over [6]you [1]partake, [should] not rather we?
ἀλλ' οὐκ.ἐχρησάμεθα τῇ.ἐξουσίᾳ.ταύτῃ· ἀλλὰ πάντα στέ-
But we did not use this authority; but all things we
γομεν, ἵνα μὴ [m]ἐγκοπήν τινα‖ δῶμεν τῷ εὐαγγελίῳ τοῦ
bear, that not [2]hindrance [1]any we should give to the glad tidings of the
χριστοῦ. 13 οὐκ.οἴδατε ὅτι οἱ τὰ.ἱερὰ ἐργαζόμενοι, [n]
Christ. Know ye not that those [2at] [3]sacred [4]things [1]labouring, [the

---

[x] ἀπόστολος *and* ἐλεύθερος *transposed* GLTTrAW. [y] — χριστὸν LTTrA. [z] ἑόρακα T. [a] μου τῆς ἀποστολῆς LTTrA. [b] ἐστιν αὐτὴ LTTrA. [c] πεῖν TA. [d] — τοῦ LTTr[A]. [e] τὸν καρπὸν the fruit LTTrAW. [f] — ἢ L[Tr]AW. [g] καὶ ὁ νόμος ταῦτα οὐ LTTrAW. [h] Μωϋσέως GLTTrAW. [i] κημώσεις TTrA. [j] ὀφείλει ἐπ' ἐλπίδι LTTrA. [k] ἐπ' ἐλπίδι τοῦ μετέχειν GLTTrAW. [l] ὑμῶν ἐξουσίας GLTTrAW. [m] τινα ἐγκοπὴν (ἐκκ- T) LTTrAW. [n] + τὰ the things TTr[A].

ἐκ τοῦ ἱεροῦ ἐσθίουσιν· οἱ τῷ θυσιαστηρίῳ [o]προσεδ-
things] of the temple eat; those [2]at [3]the [4]altar [1]attend-
ρεύοντες,‖ τῷ θυσιαστηρίῳ συμμερίζονται; 14 οὕτως καὶ ὁ
ing, with the altar partake? So also the
κύριος διέταξεν τοῖς τὸ εὐαγγέλιον καταγγέλλουσιν, ἐκ τοῦ
Lord did order to those the glad tidings announcing, of the
εὐαγγελίου ζῆν. 15 ἐγὼ.δὲ [p]οὐδενὶ ἐχρησάμην‖ τούτων·
glad tidings to live. But I [2]none [1]used of these things.
οὐκ.ἔγραψα.δὲ ταῦτα ἵνα οὕτως γένηται ἐν ἐμοί·
Now I did not write these things that thus it should be with me; [[2]it [3]were]
καλὸν γάρ μοι μᾶλλον ἀποθανεῖν, ἢ τὸ.καύχημά.μου [q]ἵνα
[4]good [1]for for me rather to die, than [3]my [4]boasting [1]that
τις‖ [r]κενώσῃ.‖ 16 ἐὰν.γὰρ εὐαγγελίζωμαι, οὐκ.ἔστιν
[2]anyone should make void. For if I announce the glad tidings, there is not
μοι καύχημα· ἀνάγκη.γάρ μοι ἐπίκειται· οὐαὶ.[s]δέ‖ μοι
[2]to [3]me [1]boasting; for necessity [4]me [1]is [2]laid [3]upon; [6]woe [5]but to me
ἐστὶν ἐὰν μὴ.[t]εὐαγγελίζωμαι.‖ 17 εἰ.γὰρ ἑκὼν τοῦτο
it is if I should not announce the glad tidings. For if willingly this
πράσσω, μισθὸν ἔχω· εἰ.δὲ ἄκων οἰκονομίαν πεπί-
I do, a reward I have; but if unwillingly an administration I am en-
στευμαι. 18 τίς οὖν [v]μοι‖ ἐστὶν ὁ μισθός; ἵνα εὐαγ-
trusted with. What then [2]my [1]is reward? That in announcing
γελιζόμενος ἀδάπανον θήσω τὸ εὐαγγέλιον· [w]τοῦ
the glad tidings [4]without [5]expense [1]I [2]should [3]make [6]the [10]glad [11]tidings [7]of [8]the
χριστοῦ,‖ εἰς.τὸ μὴ καταχρήσασθαι τῇ.ἐξουσίᾳ.μου ἐν τῷ
[9]Christ, so as not using as my own my authority in the
εὐαγγελίῳ. 19 Ἐλεύθερος.γὰρ ὢν ἐκ πάντων, πᾶσιν ἐμαυτὸν
glad tidings. For free being from all, to all myself
ἐδούλωσα, ἵνα τοὺς πλείονας κερδήσω· 20 καὶ ἐγενόμην
I became bondman, that the more I might gain. And I became
τοῖς Ἰουδαίοις ὡς Ἰουδαῖος, ἵνα Ἰουδαίους κερδήσω· τοῖς
to the Jews as a Jew, that Jews I might gain: to those
ὑπὸ νόμον ὡς ὑπὸ νόμον, [x] ἵνα τοὺς ὑπὸ νόμον κερδήσω·
under law as under law, that those under law I might gain:
21 τοῖς ἀνόμοις ὡς ἄνομος, μὴ ὢν ἄνομος [y]θεῷ,‖ ἀλλ'
to those without law as without law, (not being without law to God, but
ἔννομος [z]χριστῷ,‖ ἵνα [a]κερδήσω‖ ἀνόμους. 22 ἐγενόμην
within law to Christ,) that I might gain those without law. I became
τοῖς ἀσθενέσιν [b]ὡς‖ ἀσθενής, ἵνα τοὺς ἀσθενεῖς κερδήσω.
to the weak as weak, that the weak I might gain.
τοῖς.πᾶσιν γέγονα [c]τὰ‖.πάντα, ἵνα πάντως τινὰς σώσω.
To all these I have become all things, that by all means some I might save.
23 [d]τοῦτο‖ δὲ ποιῶ διὰ τὸ εὐαγγέλιον, ἵνα [e]συγκοινωνὸς‖
[2]This [1]and I do on account of the glad tidings, that a fellow-partaker
αὐτοῦ γένωμαι.
with it I might be.

24 Οὐκ.οἴδατε ὅτι οἱ ἐν σταδίῳ τρέχοντες πάντες μὲν
Know ye not that those who in a race-course run all
τρέχουσιν, εἷς.δὲ λαμβάνει τὸ βραβεῖον; οὕτως τρέχετε, ἵνα
run, but one receives the prize? Thus run, that
καταλάβητε. 25 πᾶς.δὲ ὁ ἀγωνιζόμενος, πάντα ἐγκρα-
ye may obtain. But everyone that strives, in all things controls

shall reap your carnal
things? 12 If others
be partakers of *this*
power over you, *are*
not we rather? Never-
theless we have not
used this power; but
suffer all things, lest
we should hinder the
gospel of Christ. 13 Do
ye not know that they
which minister about
holy things live *of the*
things of the temple?
and they which wait
at the altar are par-
takers with the altar?
14 Even so hath the
Lord ordained that
they which preach the
gospel should live of
the gospel. 15 But I
have used none of these
things: neither have I
written these things,
that it should be so
done unto me: for *it*
were better for me to
die, than that any
man should make my
glorying void. 16 For
though I preach the
gospel, I have nothing
to glory of: for ne-
cessity is laid upon me;
yea, woe is unto me, if
I preach not the gos-
pel! 17 For if I do this
thing willingly, I have
a reward: but if a-
gainst my will, a dis-
pensation *of the gospel*
is committed unto me.
18 What is my reward
then? *Verily* that,
when I preach the gos-
pel, I may make the
gospel of Christ with-
out charge, that I a-
buse not my power in
the gospel. 19 For
though I be free from
all *men*, yet have I
made myself servant
unto all, that I might
gain the more. 20 And
unto the Jews I be-
came as a Jew, that I
might gain the Jews;
to them that are under
the law, as under the
law, that I might gain
them that are under
the law; 21 to them
that are without law,
as without law, (being
not without law to
God, but under the
law to Christ,) that I
might gain them that
are without law. 22 To
the weak became I as
weak, that I might
gain the weak: I am
made all things to all
men, that I might by

[o] παρεδρεύοντες LTTrAW. [p] οὐ κέχρημαι οὐδενὶ have not used any GLTTrAW. [q] οὐδεὶς LTTr. [r] κενώσει shall make vain LTTrA. [s] γάρ for GLTTrAW. [t] εὐαγγελίσωμαι LTrAW. [v] μου TTrA. [w] — τοῦ χριστοῦ LTTrAW. [x] + μὴ ὢν αὐτὸς ὑπὸ νόμον not being myself under law GLTTrAW. [y] θεοῦ of God LTTrAW. [z] χριστοῦ of Christ LTTrAW. [a] κερδάνω τοὺς LTTrAW. [b] — ὡς [L]TTrAW. [c] — τὰ LTTrAW. [d] πάντα all things LTTrAW. [e] συν- T.

all means save some.
23 And this I do for
the gospel's sake, that
I might be partaker
thereof with *you*.
24 Know ye not that
they which run in a
race run all, but one
receiveth the prize?
So run, that ye may
obtain. 25 And every
man that striveth for
the mastery is temper-
ate in all things. Now
they *do it* to obtain
a corruptible crown;
but we an incorrupti-
ble. 26 I therefore so
run, not as uncertain-
ly; so fight I, not as
one that beateth the
air: 27 but I keep
under my body, and
bring *it* into subjec-
tion: lest that by any
means, when I have
preached to others, I
myself should be a
castaway.
X. Moreover, breth-
ren, I would not that
ye should be ignorant,
how that all our fa-
thers were under the
cloud, and all passed
through the sea; 2 and
were all baptized unto
Moses in the cloud and
in the sea; 3 and did
all eat the same spi-
ritual meat; 4 and did
all drink the same spi-
ritual drink: for they
drank of that spiritual
Rock that followed
them: and that Rock
was Christ. 5 But with
many of them God
was not well pleased:
for they were over-
thrown in the wilder-
ness. 6 Now these
things were our ex-
amples, to the intent
we should not lust
after evil things, as
they also lusted. 7 Nei-
ther be ye idolaters, as
were some of them;
as it is written, The
people sat down to eat
and drink, and rose up
to play. 8 Neither let
us commit fornication,
as some of them com-
mitted, and fell in one
day three and twenty
thousand. 9 Neither
let us tempt Christ, as
some of them also
tempted, and were de-
stroyed of serpents.
10 Neither murmur ye,
as some of them also
murmured, and were

τεύεται· ἐκεῖνοι μὲν οὖν ἵνα φθαρτὸν στέφανον λάβωσιν,
himself: they indeed then that a corruptible crown they may receive,
ἡμεῖς.δὲ ἄφθαρτον. 26 ἐγὼ τοίνυν οὕτως τρέχω, ὡς οὐκ
but we an incorruptible. I therefore so run, as not
ἀδήλως· οὕτως πυκτεύω, ὡς οὐκ ἀέρα δέρων· 27 [g]ἀλλ'‖
uncertainly; so I combat, as not [the] air beating. But
ὑπωπιάζω μου τὸ σῶμα, καὶ δουλαγωγῶ, μήπως ἄλλοις
I buffet my body, and bring [it] into servitude, lest to others
κηρύξας αὐτὸς ἀδόκιμος γένωμαι.
having preached [2]myself [5]rejected [1]I [3]might [4]be.

10 Οὐ.θέλω [h]δὲ‖ ὑμᾶς ἀγνοεῖν, ἀδελφοί, ὅτι οἱ πατέρες
[2]I [3]wish [4]not [1]now you to be ignorant, brethren, that [2]fathers
ἡμῶν πάντες ὑπὸ τὴν νεφέλην ἦσαν, καὶ πάντες διὰ τῆς
[1]our all under the cloud were, and all through the
θαλάσσης διῆλθον, 2 καὶ πάντες εἰς τὸν [i]Μωσῆν‖ [k]ἐβαπτίσαντο‖
sea passed, and all to Moses were baptized
ἐν τῇ νεφέλῃ καὶ ἐν τῇ θαλάσσῃ, 3 καὶ πάντες τὸ αὐτὸ [l]βρῶμα
in the cloud and in the sea, and all the same [2]meat
πνευματικὸν ἔφαγον,‖ 4 καὶ πάντες τὸ αὐτὸ [m]πόμα πνευ-
[1]spiritual ate, and all the same [2]drink [1]spi-
ματικὸν ἔπιον·‖ ἔπινον.γὰρ ἐκ πνευματικῆς ἀκολουθούσης
ritual drank; for they drank of a spiritual [2]following
πέτρας· ἡ.[n]δὲ πέτρα‖ ἦν ὁ χριστός. 5 ἀλλ' οὐκ ἐν τοῖς
[1]rock, and the rock was the Christ: yet not with the
πλείοσιν αὐτῶν [o]εὐδόκησεν‖ ὁ θεός· κατεστρώθησαν.γὰρ ἐν
most of them was [2]well [3]pleased [1]God; for they were strewed in
τῇ ἐρήμῳ. 6 ταῦτα.δὲ τύποι ἡμῶν ἐγενήθησαν, εἰς τὸ μὴ
the desert. But these things types for us became, for [2]not
εἶναι ἡμᾶς ἐπιθυμητὰς κακῶν, καθὼς κἀκεῖνοι ἐπεθύμη-
[3]to [4]be [1]us desirers of evil things, according as they also desired,
σαν. 7 μηδὲ εἰδωλολάτραι γίνεσθε, καθώς τινες αὐτῶν· [p]ὡς‖
Neither idolaters be ye, according as some of them; as
γέγραπται, Ἐκάθισεν ὁ λαὸς φαγεῖν καὶ [q]πιεῖν,‖ καὶ ἀν-
it has been written, [3]Sat [4]down [1]the [2]people to eat and to drink, and rose
έστησαν παίζειν. 8 μηδὲ πορνεύωμεν, καθώς τινες
up to play. Neither should we commit fornication, according as some
αὐτῶν ἐπόρνευσαν, καὶ [r]ἔπεσον‖ [s]ἐν‖ μιᾷ ἡμέρᾳ εἰκοσιτρεῖς
of them committed fornication, and fell in one day twenty-three
χιλιάδες. 9 μηδὲ ἐκπειράζωμεν τὸν [t]χριστόν,‖ καθὼς [v]καί‖
thousand. Neither should we tempt the Christ, according as also
τινες αὐτῶν [w]ἐπείρασαν,‖ καὶ ὑπὸ τῶν ὄφεων [x]ἀπώλοντο.‖
some of them tempted, and by the serpents perished.
10 μηδὲ γογγύζετε, [y]καθὼς‖ [v]καί‖ τινες αὐτῶν ἐγόγγυσαν,
Neither murmur ye, according as also some of them murmured,
καὶ ἀπώλοντο ὑπὸ τοῦ ὀλοθρευτοῦ. 11 ταῦτα.δὲ [z]πάντα‖
and perished by the destroyer. Now these things all [as]
[a]τύποι‖ [b]συνέβαινον‖ ἐκείνοις· ἐγράφη.δὲ πρὸς νουθεσίαν
types happened to them, and were written for [2]admonition
ἡμῶν εἰς οὓς τὰ τέλη τῶν αἰώνων [c]κατήντησεν.‖ 12 ὥστε
[1]our on whom the ends of the ages are arrived. So that

[g] ἀλλὰ Tr. [h] γὰρ for GLTTrAW. [i] Μωϋσῆν GLTTrAW. [k] ἐβαπτίσθησαν LT. [l] πνευματικὸν ἔφαγον βρῶμα (βρῶμα ἔφαγον TTr) LTTr. [m] πνευματικὸν ἔπιον πόμα LTTrAW. [n] πέτρα δὲ LTTrA. [o] ηὐδόκησεν LTrAW. [p] ὥσπερ LTTrA. [q] πεῖν TA. [r] ἔπεσαν LTTrAW. [s] — ἐν LTTr[A]. [t] κύριον Lord LTTrA. [v] — καὶ LTTrAW. [w] ἐξεπείρασαν T. [x] ἀπώλλυντο TTr. [y] καθάπερ TTr. [z] — πάντα [L]TTr[A]. [a] τυπικῶς typically LTTrAW. [b] συνέβαινεν TTr. [c] κατήντηκεν have come LTTrAW.

ὁ δοκῶν ἑστάναι, βλεπέτω μὴ πέσῃ. 13 Πειρασμὸς
he that thinks to stand, let him take heed lest he fall. Temptation
ὑμᾶς οὐκ.εἴληφεν εἰ.μὴ ἀνθρώπινος· πιστὸς.δὲ ὁ θεός, ὃς
you has not taken except what belongs to man; and faithful [is] God, who
οὐκ.ἐάσει ὑμᾶς πειρασθῆναι ὑπὲρ ὃ δύνασθε, ἀλλὰ ποιήσει
will not suffer you to be tempted above what ye are able, but will make
σὺν τῷ πειρασμῷ καὶ τὴν ἔκβασιν, τοῦ.δύνασθαι [e]ὑμᾶς"
with the temptation also the issue, for 2to 3be 4able 1you
ὑπενεγκεῖν. 14 Διόπερ, ἀγαπητοί.μου, φεύγετε ἀπὸ τῆς
to bear [it]. Wherefore, my beloved, flee from
εἰδωλολατρείας. 15 ὡς φρονίμοις λέγω· κρίνατε ὑμεῖς ὅ
idolatry. As to intelligent ones I speak: judge ye what
φημι. 16 τὸ ποτήριον τῆς εὐλογίας ὃ εὐλογοῦμεν, οὐχὶ
I say. The cup of blessing which we bless, 3not
κοινωνία [f]τοῦ αἵματος τοῦ χριστοῦ ἐστιν;" τὸν ἄρτον ὃν
4fellowship 5of 6the 7blood 8of 9the 10Christ 1is 2it? The bread which
κλῶμεν, οὐχὶ κοινωνία τοῦ σώματος τοῦ χριστοῦ ἐστιν;
we break, 3not 4fellowship 5of 6the 7body 8of 9the 10Christ 1is 2it?
17 ὅτι εἷς ἄρτος, ἓν σῶμα οἱ πολλοί ἐσμεν· οἱ γὰρ πάντες
Because 5one 6loaf, 7one 8body 2the 3many 1we 4are; for 2all
ἐκ τοῦ ἑνὸς ἄρτου μετέχομεν. 18 βλέπετε τὸν Ἰσραὴλ κατὰ
3of 4the 5one 6loaf 1we partake. See Israel according to
σάρκα· [g]οὐχὶ" οἱ ἐσθίοντες τὰς θυσίας, κοινωνοὶ
flesh: 2not 3those 4eating 5the 6sacrifices, 7fellow-partakers
τοῦ θυσιαστηρίου εἰσίν; 19 τί οὖν φημι; ὅτι [h]εἴδωλον" τί
8with 9the 10altar 1are? What then say I? that an idol anything
ἐστιν; ἢ ὅτι [h]εἰδωλόθυτον" τί ἐστιν; 20 ἀλλ' ὅτι
is, or that what is sacrificed to an idol anything is? but that
ἃ [i]θύει" [k]τὰ ἔθνη," δαιμονίοις [l]θύει," καὶ οὐ θεῷ[m]·
what 3sacrifice 1the 2nations, to demons they sacrifice, and not to God.
οὐ.θέλω.δὲ ὑμᾶς κοινωνοὺς τῶν δαιμονίων γίνεσθαι.
But I do not wish you fellow-partakers with demons to be.
21 οὐ.δύνασθε ποτήριον κυρίου πίνειν, καὶ ποτήριον
Ye cannot [the] cup of [the] Lord drink, and [the] cup
δαιμονίων· οὐ.δύνασθε τραπέζης κυρίου μετέχειν καὶ
of demons: ye cannot of [the] table of [the] Lord partake and
τραπέζης δαιμονίων. 22 ἢ παραζηλοῦμεν τὸν κύριον;
of [the] table of demons. Or, do we provoke to jealousy the Lord?
μὴ ἰσχυρότεροι αὐτοῦ ἐσμεν;
stronger than he are we?
23 Πάντα [n]μοι" ἔξεστιν, ἀλλ' οὐ πάντα συμφέρει·
All things for me are lawful, but 4not 1all 2things 3are profitable;
πάντα [n]μοι" ἔξεστιν, ἀλλ' οὐ πάντα οἰκοδομεῖ. 24 μηδεὶς
all things for me are lawful, but 3not 1all 2do build up. 2No 3one
τὸ ἑαυτοῦ ζητείτω, ἀλλὰ τὸ τοῦ ἑτέρου [o]ἕκαστος."
5that 6of 7himself 1let 4seek, but 3that 4of 5the 6other 1each 2one.
25 Πᾶν τὸ ἐν μακέλλῳ πωλούμενον ἐσθίετε, μηδὲν ἀνα-
Everything that in a market is sold eat, nothing in-
κρίνοντες διὰ τὴν συνείδησιν· 26 τοῦ.[p]γὰρ. κυρίου"
quiring on account of conscience. For 4the 5Lord's [3is]
ἡ γῆ καὶ τὸ πλήρωμα αὐτῆς. 27 εἰ.[q]δέ" τις καλεῖ ὑμᾶς
1the 2earth and the fulness of it. But if anyone 4invite 5you

destroyed of the de-
stroyer. 11 Now all
these things happened
unto them for en-
samples: and they are
written for our ad-
monition, upon whom
the ends of the world
are come. 12 Where-
fore let him that think-
eth he standeth take
heed lest he fall.
13 There hath no
temptation taken you
but such as is com-
mon to man: but God
is faithful, who will
not suffer you to be
tempted above that ye
are able; but will with
the temptation also
make a way to escape,
that ye may be able to
bear *it*. 14 Wherefore,
my dearly beloved, flee
from idolatry. 15 I
speak as to wise men;
judge ye what I say.
16 The cup of blessing
which we bless, is it not
the communion of the
blood of Christ? The
bread which we break,
is it not the communion
of the body of Christ?
17 For we *being* many
are one bread, *and* one
body: for we are all
partakers of that one
bread. 18 Behold Israel
after the flesh: are
not they which eat of
the sacrifices parta-
kers of the altar?
19 What say I then?
that the idol is any
thing, or that which is
offered in sacrifice to
idols is any thing?
20 But *I say*, that the
things which the Gen-
tiles sacrifice, they
sacrifice to devils, and
not to God: and I
would not that ye
should have fellow-
ship with devils. 21 Ye
cannot drink the cup
of the Lord, and the
cup of devils: ye can-
not be partakers of
the Lord's table, and
of the table of devils.
22 Do we provoke the
Lord to jealousy? are
we stronger than he?
23 All things are
lawful for me, but all
things are not expe-
dient: all things are
lawful for me, but all
things edify not. 24 Let
no man seek his own,
but every man ano-
ther's *wealth*. 25 What-
soever is sold in the

---

e — ὑμᾶς (*read* [you]) GLTTrAW. f ἐστὶν τοῦ αἵματος τοῦ χριστοῦ Tr. g οὐχ LTAW. h εἴδωλον *and* εἰδωλόθυτον *transposed* LTTrAW. i θύουσιν they sacrifice LTTrAW. k — τὰ ἔθνη LTA. l — θύει LTTrA. m + θύουσιν they sacrifice LTTrA. n — μοι GLTTrAW. o — ἕκαστος GLTTrAW. p κυρίου γὰρ LTTrAW. q — δὲ but LTTrAW.

τῶν ἀπίστων, καὶ θέλετε πορεύεσθαι, πᾶν τὸ παρατιθέμενον
[1]of [2]the [3]unbelieving, and ye wish to go, all that is set before
ὑμῖν ἐσθίετε, μηδὲν ἀνακρίνοντες διὰ τὴν συνείδησιν.
you eat, nothing inquiring on account of conscience.
28 ἐὰν.δέ τις ὑμῖν εἴπῃ, Τοῦτο [r]εἰδωλόθυτόν[ǁ] ἐστιν· μὴ
But if anyone to you say, This [2]offered [3]to [4]an [5]idol [1]is, [7]not
ἐσθίετε, δι' ἐκεῖνον τὸν μηνύσαντα καὶ τὴν συνείδησιν·
[6]do eat, on account of him that shewed [it], and the conscience;
[s]τοῦ.γὰρ κυρίου ἡ γῆ καὶ τὸ πλήρωμα αὐτῆς.[ǁ] 29 συνεί-
for [4]the [5]Lord's [[3]is] [1]the [2]earth and the fulness of it. [2]Con-
δησιν δὲ λέγω, οὐχὶ τὴν ἑαυτοῦ, ἀλλὰ τὴν τοῦ ἑτέρου.
science [1]but, I say, not that of thyself, but that of the other;
ἵνα.τί.γὰρ ἡ.ἐλευθερία.μου κρίνεται ὑπὸ ἄλλης συνειδήσεως;
for why [2]my [3]freedom [1]is judged by another's conscience?
30 εἰ.[t]δὲ[ǁ] ἐγὼ χάριτι μετέχω, τί βλασφημοῦμαι ὑπὲρ οὗ
But if I with thanks partake, why am I evil spoken of for what
ἐγὼ εὐχαριστῶ; 31 Εἴτε οὖν ἐσθίετε, εἴτε πίνετε, εἴτε
I give thanks? Whether therefore ye eat, or ye drink or
τι ποιεῖτε, πάντα εἰς δόξαν θεοῦ ποιεῖτε. 32 ἀπρόσκοποι
anything ye do, all things to [2]glory [1]God's do. Without offence
[v]γίνεσθε καὶ Ἰουδαίοις[ǁ] καὶ Ἕλλησιν καὶ τῇ ἐκκλησίᾳ τοῦ
be ye both to Jews and Greeks and to the assembly
θεοῦ· 33 καθὼς κἀγὼ πάντα πᾶσιν ἀρέσκω, μὴ ζητῶν
of God. According as I also all in all things please; not seeking
τὸ ἐμαυτοῦ [w]συμφέρον,[ǁ] ἀλλὰ τὸ τῶν πολλῶν, ἵνα σωθῶ-
the [2]of [3]myself [1]profit, but that of the many, that they may
σιν. 11 μιμηταί μου γίνεσθε, καθὼς κἀγὼ χριστοῦ.
be saved. Imitators of me be, according as I also [am] of Christ.
2 Ἐπαινῶ.δὲ ὑμᾶς, [x]ἀδελφοί,[ǁ] ὅτι πάντα μου μέ-
Now I praise you, brethren, that in all things me ye have
μνησθε, καὶ καθὼς παρέδωκα ὑμῖν, τὰς παραδόσεις κατ-
remembered; and according as I delivered to you, the traditions ye
έχετε. 3 θέλω.δὲ ὑμᾶς εἰδέναι, ὅτι παντὸς ἀνδρὸς ἡ κεφαλὴ
keep. But I wish you to know, that of every man [4]the [5]head
ὁ χριστός ἐστιν· κεφαλὴ.δὲ γυναικὸς ὁ ἀνήρ· κεφαλὴ.δὲ
[1]the [2]Christ [3]is, but head of [the] woman [is] the man, and head
[y]χριστοῦ, ὁ θεός. 4 πᾶς ἀνὴρ προσευχόμενος ἢ προφητεύων,
of Christ, God. Every man praying or prophesying,
κατὰ κεφαλῆς ἔχων, καταισχύνει τὴν.κεφαλὴν.αὐτοῦ.
[anything] on [his] head having, puts to shame his head.
5 πᾶσα.δὲ γυνὴ προσευχομένη ἢ προφητεύουσα ἀκατακαλύπτῳ
But every woman praying or prophesying [4]uncovered
τῇ κεφαλῇ, καταισχύνει τὴν.κεφαλὴν.[z]ἑαυτῆς·[ǁ] ἓν.γάρ
[1]with [2]the [3]head, puts to shame her head; for one
ἐστιν καὶ τὸ αὐτὸ τῇ.ἐξυρημένῃ. 6 εἰ.γὰρ οὐ.κατακαλύπ-
it is and the same with having been shaven. For if be not covered
τεται γυνή, καὶ κειράσθω· εἰ.δὲ αἰσχρὸν γυναικὶ τὸ
a woman, also let her be shorn. But if [it be] shameful to a woman
κείρασθαι ἢ ξυρᾶσθαι, κατακαλυπτέσθω. 7 ἀνὴρ.μὲν.γὰρ οὐκ
to be shorn or to be shaven, let her be covered. For man indeed [2]not
ὀφείλει κατακαλύπτεσθαι τὴν κεφαλήν, εἰκὼν καὶ δόξα θεοῦ
[1]ought to have [3]covered [1]the [2]head, image and glory of God
ὑπάρχων· [a]γυνὴ.δὲ δόξα ἀνδρός ἐστιν· 8 οὐ.γάρ ἐστιν ἀνὴρ
being; but woman glory of man is. For not is man

shambles, *that* eat,
asking no question
for conscience sake:
26 for the earth *is* the
Lord's, and the ful-
ness thereof. 27 If any
of them that believe
not bid you *to a feast*,
and ye be disposed to
go; whatsoever is set
before you, eat, asking
no question for con-
science sake. 28 But
if any man say unto
you, This is offered in
sacrifice unto idols, eat
not for his sake that
shewed it, and for
conscience sake: for
the earth *is* the Lord's,
and the fulness there-
of: 29 conscience, I
say, not thine own, but
of the other: for why
is my liberty judged
of another *man's* con-
science? 30 For if I by
grace be a partaker,
why am I evil spoken
of for that for which
I give thanks? 31 Whe-
ther therefore ye eat,
or drink, or whatso-
ever ye do, do all to
the glory of God.
32 Give none offence,
neither to the Jews,
nor to the Gentiles,
nor to the church of
God: 33 even as I
please all *men* in all
things, not seeking
mine own profit, but
the *profit* of many, that
they may be saved.
XI. Be ye followers
of me, even as I also
am of Christ.

2 Now I praise you,
brethren, that ye re-
member me in all
things, and keep the
ordinances, as I de-
livered *them* to you.
3 But I would have
you know, that the
head of every man is
Christ; and the head
of the woman *is* the
man; and the head of
Christ *is* God. 4 Every
man praying or pro-
phesying, having *his*
head covered, dis-
honoureth his head.
5 But every woman
that prayeth or pro-
phesieth with *her* head
uncovered dishonour-
eth her head: for that
is even all one as if
she were shaven. 6 For
if the woman be not
covered, let her also
be shorn: but if it be
a shame for a woman
to be shorn or shaven,
let her be covered.

[r] ἱερόθυτόν offered in sacrifice LTTrA. [s] — τοῦ γὰρ *to end of verse* GLTTrAW. [t] — δὲ but GLTTrAW. [v] καὶ Ἰουδαίοις γίνεσθε LTTrA. [w] σύμφορον LTTrA. [x] — ἀδελφοί LTTrAW. [y] + τοῦ (*read* of the Christ) [L]TTrA. [z] αὐτῆς LTTrA. [a] + ἡ the (woman) LTTrAW.

ἐκ γυναικός, ἀλλὰ γυνὴ ἐξ ἀνδρός· 9 καὶ.γὰρ οὐκ ἐκτίσθη
of woman, but woman of man. For also not was created
ἀνὴρ διὰ τὴν γυναῖκα, ἀλλὰ γυνὴ διὰ τὸν ἄνδρα·
man on account of the woman, but woman on account of the man.
10 διὰ τοῦτο ὀφείλει ἡ γυνὴ ἐξουσίαν ἔχειν ἐπὶ τῆς κε-
Because of this ought the woman authority to have on the
φαλῆς, διὰ τοὺς ἀγγέλους. 11 πλὴν οὔτε [b]ἀνὴρ
head, on account of the angels. However neither [is] man
χωρὶς γυναικός, οὔτε γυνὴ χωρὶς ἀνδρός,‖ ἐν κυρίῳ·
apart from woman, nor woman apart from man, in [the] Lord.
12 ὥσπερ.γὰρ ἡ γυνὴ ἐκ τοῦ ἀνδρός, οὕτως καὶ ὁ ἀνὴρ
For as the woman of the man [is], so also the man
διὰ τῆς γυναικός, τὰ.δὲ.πάντα ἐκ τοῦ θεοῦ. 13 ἐν ὑμῖν.αὐτοῖς
by the woman [is]; but all things of God. In yourselves
κρίνατε· πρέπον ἐστὶν γυναῖκα ἀκατακάλυπτον τῷ θεῷ
judge: becoming is it for a woman uncovered to God
προσεύχεσθαι; 14 [c]ἢ‖ οὐδὲ [d]αὐτὴ ἡ φύσις‖ διδάσκει ὑμᾶς,
to pray? Or [2]not [3]even [5]itself [4]nature [1]does teach you,
ὅτι ἀνὴρ μὲν ἐὰν κομᾷ, ἀτιμία αὐτῷ ἐστιν· 15 γυνὴ
that [2]a [3]man [1]if have long hair a dishonour to him it is? [3]A [4]woman
δὲ ἐὰν κομᾷ, δόξα αὐτῇ ἐστιν; ὅτι ἡ κόμη ἀντὶ
[1]but [2]if have long hair, glory to her it is; for the long hair instead
περιβολαίου δέδοται [e]αὐτῇ.‖ 16 εἰ.δέ τις δοκεῖ φιλόνεικος
of a covering is given to her. But if anyone thinks [3]contentious
εἶναι, ἡμεῖς τοιαύτην συνήθειαν οὐκ.ἔχομεν, οὐδὲ αἱ ἐκκλησίαι
[1]to [2]be, we [3]such [4]custom [1]have [2]not, nor the assemblies
τοῦ θεοῦ.
of God.

17 Τοῦτο.δὲ [f]παραγγέλλων οὐκ.ἐπαινῶ,‖ ὅτι οὐκ
But [3]as [4]to] [5]this [1]charging [[2]you] I do not praise [you], that not
εἰς τὸ [g]κρεῖττον,‖ [h]ἀλλ'‖ εἰς τὸ [i]ἧττον‖ συνέρχεσθε. 18 πρῶτον
for the better, but for the worse ye come together. [2]First
μὲν γὰρ συνερχομένων ὑμῶν ἐν [k]τῇ‖ ἐκκλησίᾳ, ἀκούω σχίσ-
[3]indeed [1]for coming together ye in the assembly, I hear di-
ματα ἐν ὑμῖν ὑπάρχειν, καὶ μέρος.τι πιστεύω· 19 δεῖ.γὰρ
visions among you to be, and partly I believe [it]. For there must
καὶ αἱρέσεις ἐν ὑμῖν εἶναι, ἵνα [l] οἱ δόκιμοι φανεροὶ γένωνται
also sects among you be, that the approved manifest may become
ἐν ὑμῖν. 20 συνερχομένων οὖν ὑμῶν ἐπὶ.τὸ.αὐτό, οὐκ
among you. Coming together therefore ye into one place, [3]not
ἔστιν κυριακὸν δεῖπνον φαγεῖν· 21 ἕκαστος.γὰρ τὸ.ἴδιον
[1]it [2]is [the] Lord's supper to eat. For each one his own
δεῖπνον προλαμβάνει ἐν τῷ φαγεῖν, καὶ ὃς.μὲν πεινᾷ ὃς.δὲ
supper takes first in eating, and one is hungry and another
μεθύει. 22 μὴ γὰρ οἰκίας οὐκ.ἔχετε εἰς τὸ ἐσθίειν καὶ πίνειν;
is drunken. For houses have ye not for eating and drinking?
ἢ τῆς ἐκκλησίας τοῦ θεοῦ καταφρονεῖτε, καὶ καταισχύνετε
or the assembly of God do ye despise, and put to shame
τοὺς μὴ.ἔχοντας; τί [m]ὑμῖν εἴπω‖; [n]ἐπαινέσω‖ ὑμᾶς [o]ἐν
them that have not? What to you should I say? shall I praise you in
τούτῳ; οὐκ‖.ἐπαινῶ. 23 Ἐγὼ.γὰρ παρέλαβον ἀπὸ τοῦ κυρίου,
this? I do not praise. For I received from the Lord

7 For a man indeed ought not to cover *his* head, forasmuch as he is the image and glory of God: but the woman is the glory of the man. 8 For the man is not of the woman; but the woman of the man. 9 Neither was the man created for the woman; but the woman for the man. 10 For this cause ought the woman to have power on her head because of the angels. 11 Nevertheless neither is the man without the woman, neither the woman without the man, in the Lord. 12 For as the woman *is* of the man, even so *is* the man also by the woman; but all things of God. 13 Judge in yourselves: is it comely that a woman pray unto God uncovered? 14 Doth not even nature itself teach you, that, if a man have long hair, it is a shame unto him? 15 But if a woman have long hair, it is a glory to her: for *her* hair is given her for a covering. 16 But if any man seem to be contentious, we have no such custom, neither the churches of God.

17 Now in this that I declare *unto you* I praise *you* not, that ye come together not for the better, but for the worse. 18 For first of all, when ye come together in the church, I hear that there be divisions among you; and I partly believe it. 19 For there must be also heresies among you, that they which are approved may be made manifest among you. 20 When ye come together therefore into one place, *this* is not to eat the Lord's supper. 21 For in eating every one taketh before *other* his own supper: and one is hungry, and another is drunken. 22 What? have ye not houses to eat and to drink in? or despise ye the church of God, and shame them that have not? What shall I say to

---

[b] γυνὴ χωρὶς ἀνδρὸς οὔτε ἀνὴρ χωρὶς γυναικὸς GLTTrAW. [c] — ἢ LTTrAW. [d] ἡ φύσις αὐτὴ LTTrAW. [e] [αὐτῇ] A. [f] παραγγέλλω οὐκ ἐπαινῶν LTrAW. [g] κρεῖσσον LTTrA. [h] ἀλλὰ TTrA. [i] ἧσσον LTTrA. [k] — τῇ GLTTrAW. [l] + καὶ also [L]Tr[A]. [m] εἴπω ὑμῖν LTTrAW. [n] ἐπαινῶ praise I L. [o] ; ἐν τούτῳ οὐκ (*read* In this I do not praise) ET.

you? shall I praise you
in this? I praise *you*
not. 23 For I have re-
ceived of the Lord that
which also I delivered
unto you, That the
Lord Jesus the *same*
night in which he was
betrayed took bread:
24 and when he had
given thanks, he brake
it, and said, Take, eat:
this is my body, which
is broken for you: this
do in remembrance of
me. 25 After the same
manner also *he took*
the cup, when he had
supped, saying, This
cup is the new testa-
ment in my blood: this
do ye, as oft as ye drink
it, in remembrance of
me. 26 For as often as
ye eat this bread, and
drink this cup, ye do
shew the Lord's death
till he come. 27 Where-
fore whosoever shall
eat this bread, and
drink *this* cup of the
Lord, unworthily,
shall be guilty of the
body and blood of the
Lord. 28 But let a man
examine himself, and
so let him eat of *that*
bread, and drink of
that cup. 29 For he
that eateth and drink-
eth unworthily, eateth
and drinketh damna-
tion to himself, not
discerning the Lord's
body. 30 For this cause
many *are* weak and
sickly among you, and
many sleep. 31 For if
we would judge our-
selves, we should not
be judged. 32 But when
we are judged, we are
chastened of the Lord,
that we should not be
condemned with the
world. 33 Wherefore,
my brethren, when ye
come together to eat,
tarry one for another.
34 And if any man
hunger, let him eat at
home; that ye come
not together unto con-
demnation. And the
rest will I set in order
when I come.
XII. Now concern-
ing spiritual *gifts*,
brethren, I would not
have you ignorant.
2 Ye know that ye
were Gentiles, carried
away unto these dumb
idols, even as ye were
led. 3 Wherefore I give
you to understand, that

ὃ καὶ παρέδωκα ὑμῖν, ὅτι ὁ κύριος Ἰησοῦς ἐν τῇ νυκτὶ
that which also I delivered to you, that the Lord Jesus in the night
ᾗ [p]παρεδίδοτο,‖ ἔλαβεν ἄρτον, 24 καὶ εὐχαριστήσας
in which he was delivered up took bread, and having given thanks
ἔκλασεν, καὶ εἶπεν, [q]Λάβετε, φάγετε·‖ τοῦτό μου ἐστὶν τὸ
he broke [it], and said, Take, eat, this of me is the
σῶμα τὸ ὑπὲρ ὑμῶν [r]κλώμενον·‖ τοῦτο ποιεῖτε εἰς τὴν
body which for you [is] being broken: this do in
ἐμὴν.ἀνάμνησιν. 25 Ὡσαύτως καὶ τὸ ποτήριον, μετὰ τὸ
remembrance of me. In like manner also the cup, after
δειπνῆσαι, λέγων, Τοῦτο τὸ ποτήριον ἡ καινὴ διαθήκη ἐστὶν
having supped, saying, This cup the new covenant is
ἐν τῷ.ἐμῷ.αἵματι· τοῦτο ποιεῖτε, ὁσάκις [s]ἂν‖ πίνητε,
in my blood: this do, as often as ye may drink [it],
εἰς τὴν.ἐμὴν.ἀνάμνησιν. 26 Ὁσάκις.γὰρ [s]ἂν‖ ἐσθίητε τὸν
in remembrance of me. For as often as ye may eat
ἄρτον.τοῦτον, καὶ τὸ.ποτήριον.[t]τοῦτο‖ πίνητε, τὸν θάνατον
this bread, and this cup may drink, the death
τοῦ κυρίου καταγγέλλετε, [v]ἄχρις‖ οὗ [w]ἂν‖ ἔλθῃ. 27 Ὥστε
of the Lord ye announce, until he may come. So that
ὃς.ἂν ἐσθίῃ τὸν.ἄρτον.[x]τοῦτον‖ ἢ πίνῃ τὸ ποτήριον
whosoever should eat this bread or should drink the cup
τοῦ κυρίου ἀναξίως, ἔνοχος ἔσται τοῦ σώματος καὶ [y] αἵματος
of the Lord unworthily, guilty shall be of the body and blood
τοῦ κυρίου. 28 δοκιμαζέτω.δὲ [z]ἄνθρωπος ἑαυτόν,‖ καὶ οὕτως
of the Lord. But let [3]prove [1]a [2]man himself, and thus
ἐκ τοῦ ἄρτου ἐσθιέτω, καὶ ἐκ τοῦ ποτηρίου πινέτω· 29 ὁ.γὰρ
of the bread let him eat, and of the cup let him drink. For he that
ἐσθίων καὶ πίνων [a]ἀναξίως,‖ κρίμα ἑαυτῷ ἐσθίει καὶ πίνει,
eats and drinks unworthily, judgment to himself eats and drinks,
μὴ διακρίνων τὸ σῶμα [b]τοῦ κυρίου.‖ 30 διὰ τοῦτο ἐν ὑμῖν
not discerning the body of the Lord. Because of this among you
πολλοὶ ἀσθενεῖς καὶ ἄῤῥωστοι, καὶ κοιμῶνται ἱκανοί.
many [are] weak and infirm, and are fallen asleep many.
31 εἰ [c]γὰρ‖ ἑαυτοὺς διεκρίνομεν, οὐκ.ἂν.ἐκρινόμεθα· 32 κρινό-
[2]If [1]for ourselves we scrutinized, we should not be judged. [2]Being
μενοι δέ, ὑπὸ [d] κυρίου παιδευόμεθα, ἵνα μὴ σὺν τῷ
[3]judged [1]but, by [the] Lord we are disciplined, that not with the
κόσμῳ κατακριθῶμεν. 33 Ὥστε, ἀδελφοί.μου, συνερχόμενοι
world we should be condemned. So that, my brethren, coming together
εἰς τὸ φαγεῖν, ἀλλήλους ἐκδέχεσθε· 34 εἰ.[e]δέ‖ τις πεινᾷ,
for to eat, one another wait for. But if anyone be hungry,
ἐν.οἴκῳ ἐσθιέτω· ἵνα μὴ εἰς κρίμα συνέρχησθε. τὰ.δὲ
at home let him eat, that not for judgment ye may come together; and the
λοιπά, ὡς.ἂν ἔλθω, διατάξομαι.
other things whenever I may come, I will set in order.

12 Περὶ.δὲ τῶν πνευματικῶν, ἀδελφοί, οὐ.θέλω ὑμᾶς
But concerning spirituals, brethren, I do not wish you
ἀγνοεῖν. 2 οἴδατε ὅτι [f] ἔθνη ἦτε, πρὸς τὰ εἴδωλα τὰ ἄφωνα
to be ignorant. Ye know that Gentiles ye were, [3]to [5]idols [4]dumb
ὡς ἂν.ἤγεσθε, ἀπαγόμενοι· 3 διὸ γνωρίζω ὑμῖν, ὅτι
[6]as [7]ye [8]might [9]be [10]led, [1]led [2]away. Therefore I give [2]to [3]know [1]you, that

[p] παρεδίδετο LTTrA. [q] — Λάβετε, φάγετε GLTTrAW. [r] — κλώμενον LTTrA. [s] ἐὰν LTTrA. [t] — τοῦτο (*read* the cup) LTTrAW. [v] ἄχρι T. [w] — ἂν GLTTrA. [x] — τοῦτον (*read* the bread) GLTTrAW. [y] + τοῦ of the GLTTrAW. [z] ἑαυτὸν ἄνθρωπος W. [a] — ἀναξίως LTTrA. [b] — τοῦ κυρίου LTTrA. [c] δὲ but LTTrAW. [d] + τοῦ the TTr[A]W. [e] — δὲ but GLTTrAW. [f] + ὅτε when [L]TTrA.

οὐδεὶς ἐν πνεύματι θεοῦ λαλῶν λέγει ἀνάθεμα [h]Ἰησοῦν·‖
no one in [the] Spirit of God speaking says accursed [is] Jesus;
καὶ οὐδεὶς δύναται εἰπεῖν [i]Κύριον Ἰησοῦν,‖ εἰ.μὴ ἐν πνεύ-
and no one can say Lord Jesus, except in [the] [2]Spirit
ματι ἁγίῳ. 4 διαιρέσεις.δὲ χαρισμάτων εἰσίν. τὸ.δὲ αὐτὸ
[1]Holy. But diversities of gifts there are, but the same
πνεῦμα· 5 καὶ διαιρέσεις διακονιῶν εἰσίν, καὶ ὁ αὐτὸς κύριος·
Spirit; and diversities of services there are, and the same Lord;
6 καὶ διαιρέσεις ἐνεργημάτων εἰσίν, [k]ὁ.δὲ‖ αὐτός [l]ἐστιν‖ θεός,
and diversities of operations there are, but the same [2]it [3]is [1]God,
ὁ ἐνεργῶν τὰ.πάντα ἐν πᾶσιν. 7 ἑκάστῳ.δὲ δίδοται ἡ φανέ-
who operates all things in all. But to each is given the mani-
ρωσις τοῦ πνεύματος πρὸς τὸ συμφέρον. 8 ᾧ.μὲν.γὰρ διὰ
festation of the Spirit for profit. For to one by
τοῦ πνεύματος δίδοται λόγος σοφίας, ἄλλῳ.δὲ λόγος
the Spirit is given a word of wisdom; and to another a word
γνώσεως, κατὰ τὸ αὐτὸ πνεῦμα· 9 ἑτέρῳ.[m]δὲ‖ πίστις,
of knowledge, according to the same Spirit; and to a different one faith,
ἐν τῷ αὐτῷ πνεύματι· ἄλλῳ.δὲ χαρίσματα ἰαμάτων, ἐν τῷ
in the same Spirit; and to another gifts of healing, in the
[n]αὐτῷ‖ πνεύματι· 10 ἄλλῳ.δὲ ἐνεργήματα δυνάμεων,
same Spirit; and to another operations of works of power;
ἄλλῳ.[o]δὲ‖ προφητεία, ἄλλῳ.[p]δὲ‖ [q]διακρίσεις‖ πνευμάτων,
and to another prophecy; and to another discerning of spirits;
ἑτέρῳ.[r]δὲ‖ γένη γλωσσῶν, ἄλλῳ.δὲ [s]ἑρμηνεία‖ γλωσ-
and to a different one kinds of tongues; and to another interpretation of
σῶν· 11 πάντα.δὲ ταῦτα ἐνεργεῖ τὸ ἓν καὶ τὸ αὐτὸ πνεῦ-
tongues. But all these things [7]operates [1]the [2]one [3]and [4]the [5]same [6]Spirit,
μα, διαιροῦν ἰδίᾳ ἑκάστῳ καθὼς βούλεται. 12 Καθάπερ
dividing separately to each according as he wills. [2]Even [3]as
γὰρ τὸ σῶμα ἕν ἐστιν καὶ μέλη [t]ἔχει πολλά,‖ πάντα.δὲ τὰ
[1]for the body [2]one [1]is and [3]members [1]has [2]many, but all the
μέλη τοῦ σώματος [v]τοῦ ἑνός,‖ πολλὰ ὄντα, ἕν ἐστιν σῶμα·
members of the [2]body [1]one, [4]many [3]being, [6]one [5]are body:
οὕτως καὶ ὁ χριστός. 13 καὶ.γὰρ ἐν ἑνὶ πνεύματι ἡμεῖς
so also [is] the Christ. For also by one Spirit we
πάντες εἰς ἓν σῶμα ἐβαπτίσθημεν, εἴτε Ἰουδαῖοι εἴτε Ἕλ-
all into one body were baptized, whether Jews or
ληνες, εἴτε δοῦλοι εἴτε ἐλεύθεροι· καὶ πάντες [w]εἰς‖ ἓν πνεῦμα
Greeks, whether bondmen or free and all into one Spirit
ἐποτίσθημεν. 14 Καὶ.γὰρ τὸ σῶμα οὐκ.ἔστιν ἓν μέλος, ἀλλὰ
were made to drink. For also the body is not one member, but
πολλά. 15 ἐὰν εἴπῃ ὁ πούς, Ὅτι οὐκ.εἰμὶ χείρ, οὐκ.εἰμὶ
many. If should say the foot, Because I am not a hand, I am not
ἐκ τοῦ σώματος· οὐ παρὰ τοῦτο οὐκ.ἔστιν ἐκ τοῦ σώματος[x];
of the body: on account of this is it not of the body?
16 καὶ ἐὰν εἴπῃ τὸ οὖς, Ὅτι οὐκ.εἰμὶ ὀφθαλμὸς οὐκ.εἰμὶ ἐκ
And if should say the ear, Because I am not an eye I am not of
τοῦ σώματος· οὐ παρὰ τοῦτο οὐκ.ἔστιν ἐκ τοῦ σώματος[x];
the body: on account of this is it not of the body?
17 εἰ ὅλον τὸ σῶμα ὀφθαλμός, ποῦ ἡ ἀκοή; εἰ ὅλον
If [2]whole [1]the body [were] an eye, where the hearing? if [the] whole

no man speaking by
the Spirit of God call-
eth Jesus accursed:
and *that* no man can
say that Jesus is the
Lord, but by the Holy
Ghost. 4 Now there
are diversities of gifts,
but the same Spirit.
5 And there are differ-
ences of administra-
tions, but the same
Lord. 6 And there are
diversities of opera-
tions, but it is the
same God which work-
eth all in all. 7 But the
manifestation of the
Spirit is given to every
man to profit withal.
8 For to one is given
by the Spirit the word
of wisdom; to another
the word of knowledge
by the same Spirit;
9 to another faith by
the same Spirit; to
another the gifts of
healing by the same
Spirit; 10 to another
the working of mira-
cles; to another pro-
phecy; to another dis-
cerning of spirits; to
another *divers* kinds
of tongues; to another
the interpretation of
tongues: 11 but all
these worketh that one
and the selfsame Spi-
rit, dividing to every
man severally as he
will. 12 For as the body
is one, and hath many
members, and all the
members of that one
body, being many, are
one body: so also *is*
Christ. 13 For by one
Spirit are we all bap-
tized into one body,
whether *we be* Jews or
Gentiles, whether *we*
be bond or free; and
have been all made to
drink into one Spirit.
14 For the body is not
one member, but many.
15 If the foot shall
say, Because I am not
the hand, I am not of
the body; is it there-
fore not of the body?
16 And if the ear shall
say, Because I am not
the eye, I am not of
the body; is it there-
fore not of the body?
17 If the whole body
were an eye, where
were the hearing? If
the whole *were* hear-

---

h Ἰησοῦς LTTrAW. i Κύριος Ἰησοῦς LTTrAW. k καὶ ὁ and the A. l — ἐστιν GLTTrAW. m — δὲ and [L]TTr[A]. n ἑνὶ one LTTrA. o — δὲ and LTr. p — δὲ and LTr. q διάκρισις T. r — δὲ and LTTr. s διερμηνεία L. t πολλὰ ἔχει LTTrA. v — τοῦ ἑνός LTTrAW. w — εἰς LTTrAW. x — ; (*read* it is not on account of this not of the body.) LT.

ing, where *were* the
smelling? 18 But now
hath God set the mem-
bers every one of them
in the body, as it hath
pleased him. 19 And if
they were all one mem-
ber, where *were* the
body? 20 But now *are*
they many members,
yet but one body.
21 And the eye can-
not say unto the
hand, I have no need
of thee: nor again
the head to the feet,
I have no need of
you. 22 Nay, much
more those members
of the body, which
seem to be more feeble,
are necessary: 23 and
those *members* of the
body, which we think
to be less honourable,
upon these we bestow
more abundant hon-
our; and our uncome-
ly *parts* have more
abundant comeliness.
24 For our comely *parts*
have no need: but God
hath tempered the
body together, having
given more abundant
honour to that *part*
which lacked: 25 that
there should be no
schism in the body;
but *that* the members
should have the same
care one for another.
26 And whether one
member suffer, all the
members suffer with
it; or one member be
honoured, all the mem-
bers rejoice with it.
27 Now ye are the body
of Christ, and mem-
bers in particular.
28 And God hath set
some in the church,
first apostles, second-
arily prophets, thirdly
teachers, after that
miracles, then gifts of
healings, helps, go-
vernments, diversities
of tongues. 29 *Are* all
apostles? *are* all pro-
phets? *are* all teach-
ers? *are* all workers
of miracles? 30 have
all the gifts of heal-
ing? do all speak with
tongues? do all inter-
pret? 31 But covet
earnestly the best
gifts: and yet shew I
unto you a more ex-
cellent way.

XIII. Though I speak
with the tongues of

ἀκοή, ποῦ ἡ ὄσφρησις; 18 [y]νυνὶ[ǁ].δὲ ὁ θεὸς ἔθετο τὰ μέλη,
hearing, where the smelling? But now God set the members,
ἓν ἕκαστον αὐτῶν ἐν τῷ σώματι, καθὼς ἠθέλησεν. 19 εἰ.δὲ
[2]one [1]each of them in the body, according as he would. But if
ἦν [z]τὰ[ǁ] πάντα ἓν μέλος, ποῦ τὸ σῶμα; 20 νῦν.δὲ πολλὰ
[2]were [1]all one member, where the body? But now many
[a]μὲν[ǁ] μέλη, ἓν.δὲ σῶμα. 21 οὐ.δύναται.[b]δὲ[ǁ] [c] ὀφ-
[are the] members, but one body. And is not able [the]
θαλμὸς εἰπεῖν τῇ χειρί, Χρείαν σου οὐκ.ἔχω· ἢ πάλιν ἡ
eye to say to the hand, Need of thee I have not; or again the
κεφαλὴ τοῖς ποσίν, Χρείαν ὑμῶν οὐκ.ἔχω. 22 ἀλλὰ πολλῷ
head to the feet, Need of you I have not. But much
μᾶλλον τὰ δοκοῦντα μέλη τοῦ σώματος ἀσθενέστερα ὑπάρ-
rather the [5]which [6]seem [1]members [2]of [3]the [4]body [9]weaker [7]to
χειν, ἀναγκαῖά ἐστιν· 23 καὶ ἃ δοκοῦμεν [d]ἀτιμότερα[ǁ]
[8]be, necessary are; and those which we think more void of honour
εἶναι τοῦ σώματος, τούτοις τιμὴν περισσοτέραν περιτίθεμεν·
to be of the body, [4]these [7]honour [5]more [6]abundant [1]we [2]put [3]about;
καὶ τὰ ἀσχήμονα ἡμῶν εὐσχημοσύνην περισσοτέραν ἔχει·
and the uncomely [parts] of us comeliness more abundant have;
24 τὰ.δὲ εὐσχήμονα ἡμῶν οὐ χρείαν ἔχει. [e]ἀλλ'[ǁ] ὁ θεὸς
but the comely [parts] of us [2]no [3]need [1]have. But God
συνεκέρασεν τὸ σῶμα, τῷ [f]ὑστεροῦντι[ǁ] περισσοτέραν
tempered together the body, to that being deficient more abundant
δοὺς τιμήν, 25 ἵνα μὴ.ᾖ [g]σχίσμα[ǁ] ἐν τῷ
[2]having [3]given [1]honour, that there might not be division in the
σώματι, ἀλλὰ τὸ αὐτὸ ὑπὲρ ἀλλήλων μεριμνῶσιν τὰ
body, but [5]the [6]same [8]for [9]one [10]another [3]might [4]have [7]concern [1]the
μέλη· 26 καὶ [h]εἴτε[ǁ] πάσχει ἓν μέλος, [i]συμπάσχει[ǁ] πάντα
[2]members. And if suffers one member, suffers with [it] all
τὰ μέλη· εἴτε δοξάζεται [k]ἓν[ǁ] μέλος, [l]συγχαίρει[ǁ] πάντα τὰ
the members; if be glorified one member, rejoice with [it] all the
μέλη. 27 ὑμεῖς.δέ ἐστε σῶμα χριστοῦ, καὶ μέλη ἐκ
members. Now ye are [the] body of Christ, and members in
μέρους. 28 Καὶ οὓς μὲν ἔθετο ὁ θεὸς ἐν τῇ ἐκκλησίᾳ πρῶ-
particular. And [4]certain [2]did [3]set [1]God in the assembly: first,
τον ἀποστόλους, δεύτερον προφήτας, τρίτον διδασκάλους,
apostles; secondly, prophets; thirdly, teachers;
ἔπειτα δυνάμεις, [m]εἶτα[ǁ] χαρίσματα ἰαμάτων, [n]ἀντιλήψεις,[ǁ]
then works of power; then gifts of healings; helps;
κυβερνήσεις, γένη γλωσσῶν. 29 μὴ πάντες ἀπόστολοι; μὴ
governments; kinds of tongues. [Are] all apostles?
πάντες προφῆται; μὴ πάντες διδάσκαλοι; μὴ πάντες δυνά-
all prophets? all teachers? [have] all works of
μεις; 30 μὴ πάντες χαρίσματα ἔχουσιν ἰαμάτων; μὴ πάντες
power? [2]all [3]gifts [1]have of healings? [2]all
γλώσσαις λαλοῦσιν; μὴ πάντες διερμηνεύουσιν; 31 Ζηλοῦτε
[1]do speak with tongues? [2]all [1]do interpret? [2]Be [3]emulous [4]of
δὲ τὰ χαρίσματα τὰ [o]κρείττονα·[ǁ] καὶ ἔτι καθ'.ὑπερβολὴν
[1]but the [5]gifts [6]better, and yet [2]more [3]surpassing
ὁδὸν ὑμῖν δείκνυμι.
[1]a [4]way to you I shew.

---

[y] νῦν LTrA. [z] [τὰ] LTrA. [a] [μὲν] LTr. [b] — δὲ and G[L]. [c] + ὁ the GLTTrAW.
[d] ἀτιμώτερα E. [e] ἀλλὰ LTTrA. [f] ὑστερουμένῳ LTTrA. [g] σχίσματα divisions T.
[h] εἴ τι if anything LTr. [i] συν- TA. [k] — ἓν (*read* a member) TTr[A]. [l] συν- T.
[m] ἔπειτα LTTrA. [n] ἀντιλήμψεις LTTrA. [o] μείζονα greater LTTrA.

13 Ἐὰν ταῖς γλώσσαις τῶν ἀνθρώπων λαλῶ καὶ τῶν
If with the tongues of men I speak and
ἀγγέλων, ἀγάπην.δὲ μὴ.ἔχω, γέγονα χαλκὸς ἠχῶν ἢ
of angels, but love have not, I have become ²brass ¹sounding or
κύμβαλον ἀλαλάζον. 2 [p]καὶ ἐὰν[‖] ἔχω προφητείαν, καὶ εἰδῶ
a ²cymbal ¹clanging. And if I have prophecy, and know
τὰ μυστήρια πάντα καὶ πᾶσαν τὴν γνῶσιν, [q]καὶ ἐὰν[‖] ἔχω
²mysteries ¹all and all knowledge, and if I have
πᾶσαν τὴν πίστιν, ὥστε ὄρη [r]μεθιστάνειν,[‖] ἀγάπην.δὲ
all faith, so as mountains to remove, but love
μὴ.ἔχω, [s]οὐθέν[‖] εἰμι. 3 [t]καὶ ἐὰν[‖] [v]ψωμίσω[‖] πάντα τὰ
have not, nothing I am. And if I give away in food all
ὑπάρχοντά.μου, [w]καὶ ἐὰν[‖] παραδῶ τὸ.σῶμά.μου ἵνα [x]καυθή-
my goods, and if I deliver up my body that I may be
σωμαι,[‖] ἀγάπην.δὲ μὴ.ἔχω, [y]οὐδὲν[‖] ὠφελοῦμαι. 4 Ἡ ἀγάπη
burned, but love have not, nothing I am profited. Love
μακροθυμεῖ, χρηστεύεται· ἡ ἀγάπη οὐ.ζηλοῖ· [z]ἡ ἀγάπη[‖] οὐ
has patience, is kind; love is not envious; love ²not
περπερεύεται, οὐ.φυσιοῦται, 5 οὐκ.ἀσχημονεῖ, οὐ.ζητεῖ τὰ
¹is vain-glorious, is not puffed up, acts not unseemly, seeks not the things
ἑαυτῆς, οὐ.παροξύνεται, οὐ.λογίζεται τὸ κακόν, 6 οὐ.χαίρει
of its own, is not quickly provoked, reckons not evil, rejoices not
ἐπὶ τῇ ἀδικίᾳ, [a]συγχαίρει[‖].δὲ τῇ ἀληθείᾳ, 7 πάντα στέγει,
at unrighteousness, but rejoices with the truth; all things covers,
πάντα πιστεύει, πάντα ἐλπίζει, πάντα ὑπομένει. 8 Ἡ ἀγάπη
all things believes, all things hopes, all things endures. Love
οὐδέποτε [b]ἐκπίπτει.[‖] εἴτε.[c]δὲ[‖] προφητεῖαι, καταργηθήσονται·
never fails; but whether prophecies, they shall be done away;
εἴτε γλῶσσαι, παύσονται· εἴτε γνῶσις, καταργηθήσεται.
whether tongues, they shall cease; whether knowledge it shall be done away.
9 ἐκ.μέρους.γὰρ γινώσκομεν, καὶ ἐκ μέρους προφητεύομεν·
For in part we know, and in part we prophesy;
10 ὅταν.δὲ ἔλθῃ τὸ τέλειον, [d]τότε[‖] τὸ ἐκ μέρους κατ-
but when may come that which is perfect, then that in part shall be
αργηθήσεται. 11 ὅτε ἤμην νήπιος, [e]ὡς νήπιος ἐλάλουν,[‖] [f]ὡς
done away. When I was an infant, as an infant I spoke, as
νήπιος ἐφρόνουν, ὡς νήπιος ἐλογιζόμην·[‖] ὅτε.[g]δὲ[‖] γέγονα
an infant I thought, as an infant I reasoned; but when I became
ἀνήρ, κατήργηκα τὰ τοῦ νηπίου. 12 βλέπομεν.γὰρ
a man, I did away with the things of the infant. For we see
ἄρτι δι' ἐσόπτρου ἐν αἰνίγματι, τότε.δὲ πρόσωπον πρὸς
now through a glass obscurely, but then face to
πρόσωπον· ἄρτι γινώσκω ἐκ μέρους, τότε.δὲ ἐπιγνώσομαι
face; now I know in part, but then I shall know
καθὼς καὶ ἐπεγνώσθην. 13 νυνὶ.δὲ μένει πίστις, ἐλπίς,
according as also I have been known. And now abides faith, hope,
ἀγάπη, τὰ.τρία.ταῦτα· μείζων.δὲ τούτων ἡ ἀγάπη.
love; these three things; but the greater of these [is] love.

14 Διώκετε τὴν ἀγάπην· ζηλοῦτε.δὲ τὰ πνευματικά,
Pursue love, and be emulous of spirituals,
μᾶλλον.δὲ ἵνα προφητεύητε. 2 ὁ.γὰρ λαλῶν γλώσσῃ, οὐκ
but rather that ye may prophesy. For he that speaks with a tongue, not

men and of angels, and have not charity, I am become *as* sounding brass, or a tinkling cymbal. 2 And though I have *the gift of* prophecy, and understand all mysteries, and all knowledge; and though I have all faith, so that I could remove mountains, and have not charity, I am nothing. 3 And though I bestow all my goods to feed *the poor*, and though I give my body to be burned, and have not charity, it profiteth me nothing. 4 Charity suffereth long, *and is* kind; charity envieth not; charity vaunteth not itself, is not puffed up, 5 doth not behave itself unseemly, seeketh not her own, is not easily provoked, thinketh no evil; 6 rejoiceth not in iniquity, but rejoiceth in the truth; 7 beareth all things, believeth all things, hopeth all things, endureth all things. 8 Charity never faileth: but whether *there be* prophecies, they shall fail; whether *there be* tongues, they shall cease; whether *there be* knowledge, it shall vanish away. 9 For we know in part, and we prophesy in part. 10 But when that which is perfect is come, then that which is in part shall be done away. 11 When I was a child, I spake as a child, I understood as a child, I thought as a child: but when I became a man, I put away childish things. 12 For now we see through a glass, darkly; but then face to face: now I know in part; but then shall I know even as also I am known. 13 And now abideth faith, hope, charity, these three; but the greatest of these *is* charity.

XIV. Follow after charity, and desire spiritual *gifts*, but rather that ye may prophesy. 2 For he that speaketh in an *unknown* tongue speaketh not unto men, but

---

[p] κἂν LA. [q] κἂν TrA. [r] μεθιστάναι LTTr. [s] οὐδέν EGW. [t] κἂν LTrA. [v] ψωμίζω E. [w] κἂν LA. [x] καυθήσομαι I shall be burned T. [y] οὐθὲν T. [z] [ἡ ἀγάπη] LTrA. [a] συν- T. [b] πίπτει LTTrA. [c] [δὲ] Tr. [d] — τότε LTTrAW. [e] ἐλάλουν ὡς νήπιος LTTrAW. [f] ἐφρόνουν ὡς νήπιος, ἐλογιζόμην ὡς νήπιος LTTrA. [g] — δὲ but LTTrA.

unto God: for no man understandeth *him;* howbeit in the spirit he speaketh mysteries. 3 But he that prophesieth speaketh unto men *to* edification, and exhortation, and comfort. 4 He that speaketh in an *unknown* tongue edifieth himself; but he that prophesieth edifieth the church. 5 I would that ye all spake with tongues, but rather that ye prophesied: for greater *is* he that prophesieth than he that speaketh with tongues, except he interpret, that the church may receive edifying. 6 Now, brethren, if I come unto you speaking with tongues, what shall I profit you, except I shall speak to you either by revelation, or by knowledge, or by prophesying, or by doctrine? 7 And even things without life giving sound, whether pipe or harp, except they give a distinction in the sounds, how shall it be known what is piped or harped? 8 For if the trumpet give an uncertain sound, who shall prepare himself to the battle? 9 So likewise ye, except ye utter by the tongue words easy to be understood, how shall it be known what is spoken? for ye shall speak into the air. 10 There are, it may be, so many kinds of voices in the world, and none of them *is* without signification. 11 Therefore if I know not the meaning of the voice, I shall be unto him that speaketh a barbarian, and he that speaketh *shall be* a barbarian unto me. 12 Even so ye, forasmuch as ye are zealous of spiritual *gifts,* seek that ye may excel to the edifying of the church. 13 Wherefore let him that speaketh in an *unknown* tongue pray that he may interpret. 14 For if I pray in an *unknown* tongue, my spirit prayeth, but my understanding is unfruitful. 15 What is it then? I

ἀνθρώποις λαλεῖ, ἀλλὰ [h]τῷ‖ θεῷ· οὐδεὶς.γὰρ ἀκούει, πνεύματι
to men speaks, but to God: for no one hears; [2]in [3]spirit

δὲ λαλεῖ μυστήρια· 3 ὁ.δὲ προφητεύων, ἀνθρώποις λαλεῖ
[1]but he speaks mysteries. But he that prophesies, to men speaks

οἰκοδομὴν καὶ παράκλησιν καὶ παραμυθίαν. 4 ὁ λαλῶν
[for] building up and encouragement and consolation. He that speaks

γλώσσῃ, ἑαυτὸν οἰκοδομεῖ· ὁ.δὲ προφητεύων, ἐκκλησίαν
with a tongue, himself builds up; but he that prophesies, [the] assembly

οἰκοδομεῖ. 5 θέλω.δὲ πάντας ὑμᾶς λαλεῖν γλώσσαις, μᾶλλον
builds up. Now I desire all you to speak with tongues, [2]rather

δὲ ἵνα προφητεύητε· μείζων [i]γὰρ‖ ὁ προφητεύων ἢ
[1]but that ye should prophesy: [2]greater [1]for [is] he that prophesies than

ὁ λαλῶν γλώσσαις, ἐκτὸς εἰ.μὴ διερμηνεύῃ, ἵνα ἡ ἐκ-
he that speaks with tongues, unless he should interpret, that the as-

κλησία οἰκοδομὴν λάβῃ. 6 [k]Νυνὶ‖.δέ, ἀδελφοί, ἐὰν ἔλθω
sembly building up may receive. And now, brethren, if I come

πρὸς ὑμᾶς γλώσσαις λαλῶν, τί ὑμᾶς ὠφελήσω, ἐὰν.μὴ
to you with tongues speaking, what you shall I profit, unless

ὑμῖν λαλήσω ἢ ἐν ἀποκαλύψει, ἢ ἐν γνώσει, ἢ ἐν προ-
to you I shall speak either in revelation, or in knowledge, or in pro-

φητείᾳ, ἢ [l]ἐν‖ διδαχῇ; 7 ὅμως τὰ ἄψυχα φωνὴν διδόντα,
phecy, or in teaching? Even lifeless things a sound giving,

εἴτε αὐλὸς εἴτε κιθάρα, ἐὰν διαστολὴν [m]τοῖς φθόγγοις‖
whether pipe or harp, if distinction to the sounds

μὴ.δῷ, πῶς γνωσθήσεται τὸ αὐλούμενον ἢ τὸ κιθαρι-
they give not, how shall be known that being piped or being

ζόμενον; 8 καὶ.γὰρ ἐὰν ἄδηλον [n]φωνὴν σάλπιγξ‖ δῷ, τίς
harped? For also if an uncertain sound a trumpet give, who

παρασκευάσεται εἰς πόλεμον; 9 οὕτως καὶ ὑμεῖς διὰ τῆς
shall prepare himself for war? So also ye, by means of the

γλώσσης ἐὰν.μὴ εὔσημον λόγον δῶτε, πῶς γνωσθήσεται τὸ
tongue unless an intelligible speech ye give, how shall be known that

λαλούμενον; ἔσεσθε.γὰρ εἰς ἀέρα λαλοῦντες. 10 Τοσαῦτα,
being spoken? for ye will be [2]into [[3]the] [4]air [1]speaking. So many,

εἰ τύχοι, γένη φωνῶν [o]ἐστιν‖ ἐν κόσμῳ, καὶ οὐδὲν [p]αὐ-
it may be, kinds of sounds there are in [the] world, and none of

τῶν‖ ἄφωνον· 11 ἐὰν οὖν μὴ.εἰδῶ τὴν δύναμιν
them without [distinct] sound. If therefore I know not the power

τῆς φωνῆς, ἔσομαι τῷ λαλοῦντι βάρβαρος· καὶ ὁ
of the sound, I shall be to him that speaks a barbarian; and he that

λαλῶν, ἐν ἐμοὶ βάρβαρος· 12 οὕτως καὶ ὑμεῖς, ἐπεὶ ζηλωταί
speaks, [3]for [4]me [1]a [2]barbarian. So also ye, since emulous

ἐστε πνευμάτων, πρὸς τὴν οἰκοδομὴν τῆς ἐκκλησίας ζητεῖτε
ye are of spirits, for the building up of the assembly seek

ἵνα περισσεύητε. 13 [q]Διόπερ‖ ὁ λαλῶν γλώσσῃ, προσευ-
that ye may abound. Wherefore he that speaks with a tongue, let him

χέσθω ἵνα διερμηνεύῃ. 14 ἐὰν.[r]γὰρ‖ προσεύχωμαι γλώσσῃ,
pray that he may interpret. For if I pray with a tongue,

τὸ.πνεῦμά.μου προσεύχεται, ὁ.δὲ.νοῦς.μου ἄκαρπός ἐστιν.
my spirit prays, but my understanding unfruitful is.

15 τί οὖν ἐστιν; προσεύξομαι τῷ πνεύματι, προσεύξομαι
What then is it? I will pray with the Spirit, [2]I [3]will [4]pray

δὲ καὶ τῷ νοΐ· ψαλῶ τῷ πνεύματι, ψαλῶ
[1]but also with the understanding. I will praise with the Spirit, [2]I [3]will [4]praise

---

[h] — τῷ LTTr[A]. [i] δὲ and LTTrA. [k] νῦν LTTrAW. [l] — ἐν T[Tr]. [m] τοῦ φθόγγου of the sound L. [n] σάλπιγξ φωνὴν T. [o] εἰσὶν LTTrAW. [p] — αὐτῶν LTTrAW. [q] διὸ LTTrA. [r] [γὰρ] LTr.

[s]δὲ‖ καὶ [t]τῷ‖ νοΐ. 16 ἐπεὶ ἐὰν [v]εὐλογήσῃς‖ [w]τῷ‖
[1]but also with the understanding. Else if thou bless with the
πνεύματι, ὁ ἀναπληρῶν τὸν τόπον τοῦ ἰδιώτου πῶς
spirit, he that fills the place of the uninstructed how
ἐρεῖ τὸ ἀμὴν ἐπὶ τῇ.σῇ.εὐχαριστίᾳ, ἐπειδὴ τί λέγεις
shall he say the Amen at thy giving of thanks, since what thou sayest
οὐκ.οἶδεν; 17 σὺ.μὲν.γὰρ καλῶς εὐχαριστεῖς, [x]ἀλλ'‖ ὁ ἕτερος
he knows not? For thou indeed well givest thanks, but the other
οὐκ.οἰκοδομεῖται. 18 εὐχαριστῶ τῷ θεῷ [y]μου,‖ πάντων ὑμῶν
is not built up. I thank [2]God [1]my, [7]than [8]all [9]of [10]you
μᾶλλον [z]γλώσσαις λαλῶν·‖ 19 [a]ἀλλ'‖ ἐν ἐκκλησίᾳ θέλω πέντε
[6]more [4]with [5]tongues [3]speaking; but in [the] assembly I desire five
λόγους [b]διὰ τοῦ νοός‖ μου λαλῆσαι, ἵνα καὶ ἄλλους
words with [2]understanding [1]my to speak, that also others
κατηχήσω, ἢ μυρίους λόγους ἐν γλώσσῃ. 20 Ἀδελφοί, μὴ
I may instruct, than ten thousand words in a tongue. Brethren, [2]not
παιδία γίνεσθε ταῖς.φρεσίν· ἀλλὰ τῇ κακίᾳ νηπιάζετε,
[3]children [1]be in [your] minds, but in malice be babes;
ταῖς.δὲ φρεσὶν τέλειοι γίνεσθε. 21 ἐν τῷ νόμῳ γέγρα-
but in [your] minds [2]full [3]grown [1]be. In the law it has been
πται, Ὅτι ἐν ἑτερογλώσσοις, καὶ ἐν χείλεσιν [c]ἑτέροις,‖ λα-
written, By other tongues, and by [2]lips [1]other I will
λήσω τῷ.λαῷ.τούτῳ, καὶ οὐδ' οὕτως εἰσακούσονταί μου,
speak to this people, and not even thus will they hear me,
λέγει κύριος. 22 Ὥστε αἱ γλῶσσαι εἰς σημεῖόν εἰσιν, οὐ
saith [the] Lord. So that the tongues for a sign are, not
τοῖς πιστεύουσιν, ἀλλὰ τοῖς ἀπίστοις· ἡ.δὲ.προφητεία,
to those that believe, but to the unbelievers; but prophecy,
οὐ τοῖς ἀπίστοις, ἀλλὰ τοῖς πιστεύουσιν. 23 ἐὰν οὖν
not to the unbelievers, but to those that believe. If therefore
[d]συνέλθῃ‖ ἡ ἐκκλησία ὅλη ἐπὶ.τὸ.αὐτό, καὶ πάντες [e]γλώσ-
[4]come [5]together [1]the [3]assembly [2]whole in one place, and all with
σαις λαλῶσιν,‖ εἰσέλθωσιν.δὲ ἰδιῶται ἢ ἄπιστοι,
tongues should speak, and come in uninstructed ones or unbelievers,
οὐκ.ἐροῦσιν ὅτι μαίνεσθε; 24 ἐὰν.δὲ πάντες προφητεύωσιν,
will they not say that ye are mad? But if all prophesy,
εἰσέλθῃ.δέ τις ἄπιστος ἢ ἰδιώτης, ἐλέγχεται ὑπὸ πάν-
and should come in some unbeliever or uninstructed, he is convicted by all,
των, ἀνακρίνεται ὑπὸ πάντων, 25 [f]καὶ οὕτως‖ τὰ κρυπτὰ
he is examined by all; and thus the secrets
τῆς.καρδίας.αὐτοῦ φανερὰ γίνεται· καὶ οὕτως πεσὼν ἐπὶ
of his heart manifest become; and thus, falling upon
πρόσωπον, προσκυνήσει τῷ θεῷ, ἀπαγγέλλων ὅτι [g]ὁ θεὸς
[his] face, he will do homage to God, declaring that God
ὄντως‖ ἐν ὑμῖν ἐστιν.
indeed amongst you is.

26 Τί οὖν ἐστιν, ἀδελφοί; ὅταν συνέρχησθε, ἕκαστος
What then is it, brethren? when ye may come together, each
[h]ὑμῶν‖ ψαλμὸν ἔχει, διδαχὴν ἔχει, [i]γλῶσσαν ἔχει, ἀποκά-
of you a psalm has, a teaching has, a tongue has, a reve-
λυψιν ἔχει,‖ ἑρμηνείαν ἔχει· πάντα πρὸς οἰκοδομὴν [k]γε-
lation has, an interpretation has. All things for building up let be

will pray with the spi-
rit, and I will pray with
the understanding al-
so: I will sing with
the spirit, and I will
sing with the under-
standing also. 16 Else
when thou shalt bless
with the spirit, how
shall he that occupieth
the room of the un-
learned say Amen at
thy giving of thanks,
seeing he understand-
eth not what thou say-
est? 17 For thou verily
givest thanks well, but
the other is not edified.
18 I thank my God, I
speak with tongues
more than ye all:
19 yet in the church I
had rather speak five
words with my under-
standing, that *by my
voice* I might teach
others also, than ten
thousand words in
an *unknown* tongue.
20 Brethren, be not
children in under-
standing: howbeit in
malice be ye children,
but in understanding
be men. 21 In the law
it is written, With
men of other tongues
and other lips will I
speak unto this peo-
ple; and yet for all
that will they not hear
me, saith the Lord.
22 Wherefore tongues
are for a sign, not to
them that believe, but
to them that believe
not: but prophesying
serveth not for them
that believe not, but
for them which be-
lieve. 23 If therefore
the whole church be
come together into one
place, and all speak
with tongues, and
there come in *those
that are* unlearned, or
unbelievers, will they
not say that ye are
mad? 24 But if all
prophesy, and there
come in one that be-
lieveth not, or *one* un-
learned, he is convinc-
ed of all, he is judged
of all: 25 and thus
are the secrets of his
heart made manifest;
and so falling down
on *his* face he will
worship God, and re-
port that God is in you
of a truth.
26 How is it then,
brethren? when ye
come together, every

---

[s] — δὲ L[Tr]. [t] — τῷ the E. [v] εὐλογῇς LTTrA. [w] — τῷ (*read* πνευ. with [the] Spirit) LTTrA. [x] ἀλλὰ Tr. [y] — μου GLTTrAW. [z] γλώσσῃ λαλῶ I speak with a tongue LTTrA. [a] ἀλλὰ LTTrA. [b] τῷ νοΐ LTTrAW. [c] ἑτέρων 'others' LTTrA. [d] ἔλθῃ come L. [e] λαλῶσιν γλώσσαις LTTrA. [f] — καὶ οὕτως GLTTrAW. [g] ὄντως ὁ (— ὁ T) θεὸς LTTrAW. [h] — ὑμῶν LTTr[A]. [i] ἀποκάλυψιν ἔχει, γλῶσσαν ἔχει LTTrAW. [k] γινέσθω GLTTrAW.

one of you hath a
psalm, hath a doctrine,
hath a tongue, hath a
revelation, hath an in-
terpretation. Let all
things be done unto
edifying. 27 If any
man speak in an *un-
known* tongue, *let it be*
by two, or at the most
by three, and *that* by
course; and let one
interpret. 28 But if
there be no interpreter,
let him keep silence in
the church; and let
him speak to himself,
and to God. 29 Let
the prophets speak two
or three, and let the
other judge. 30 If *any
thing* be revealed to
another that sitteth
by, let the first hold
his peace. 31 For ye
may all prophesy one
by one, that all may
learn, and all may be
comforted. 32 And the
spirits of the prophets
are subject to the pro-
phets. 33 For God is
not *the author* of con-
fusion, but of peace, as
in all churches of the
saints.
34 Let your women
keep silence in the
churches: for it is not
permitted unto them
to speak; but *they are
commanded* to be un-
der obedience, as also
saith the law. 35 And
if they will learn any
thing, let them ask
their husbands at
home: for it is a shame
for women to speak
in the church.
36 What? came the
word of God out from
you? or came it unto
you only? 37 If any
man think himself to
be a prophet, or spi-
ritual, let him ac-
knowledge that the
things that I write un-
to you are the com-
mandments of the
Lord. 38 But if any
man be ignorant, let
him be ignorant.
39 Wherefore, breth-
ren, covet to prophesy,
and forbid not to speak
with tongues. 40 Let
all things be done de-
cently and in order.
XV. Moreover, bre-
thren, I declare unto
you the gospel which
I preached unto you,

νέσθω.‖ 27 εἴτε γλώσσῃ τις λαλεῖ, κατὰ δύο ἢ τὸ
done. If with a tongue anyone speak, [let it be] by two or the
πλεῖστον τρεῖς, καὶ ἀνὰ.μέρος, καὶ εἷς διερμηνευέτω. 28 ἐὰν.δὲ
most three, and in succession, and [2]one [1]let interpret; and if
μὴ.ᾖ [l]διερμηνευτής,‖ σιγάτω ἐν ἐκκλησίᾳ· ἑαυτῷ.δὲ
there be not an interpreter, let him be silent in an assembly; and to himself
λαλείτω καὶ τῷ θεῷ. 29 προφῆται.δὲ δύο ἢ τρεῖς λαλεί-
let him speak and to God. And prophets [2]two [3]or [4]three [1]let
τωσαν, καὶ οἱ ἄλλοι διακρινέτωσαν· 30 ἐὰν.δὲ ἄλλῳ
speak, and [2]the [3]others [1]let discern. But if to another
ἀποκαλυφθῇ καθημένῳ, ὁ πρῶτος σιγάτω. 31 δύ-
[3]should [4]be [5]a [6]revelation [1]sitting [2]by, [8]the [9]first [7]let be silent. [2]Ye
νασθε γὰρ καθ'.ἕνα πάντες προφητεύειν, ἵνα πάντες μαν-
[3]can [1]for one by one all prophesy, that all may
θάνωσιν, καὶ πάντες παρακαλῶνται· 32 καὶ πνεύματα
learn, and all may be exhorted. And spirits
προφητῶν προφήταις ὑποτάσσεται· 33 οὐ.γάρ ἐστιν ἀκατα-
of prophets to prophets are subject. For [3]not [1]he [2]is [6]of [7]dis-
στασίας ὁ θεός, [m]ἀλλ'‖ εἰρήνης, ὡς ἐν πάσαις ταῖς ἐκκλησίαις
order [4]the [5]God, but of peace, as in all the assemblies
τῶν [n]ἁγίων.
of the saints.

34 Αἱ‖ γυναῖκες [o]ὑμῶν‖ ἐν ταῖς ἐκκλησίαις σιγάτωσαν·
[2]Women [1]your in the assemblies let them be silent,
οὐ.γὰρ.[p]ἐπιτέτραπται‖ αὐταῖς λαλεῖν, [m]ἀλλ'‖ [q]ὑποτάσσεσθαι,‖
for it is not allowed to them to speak; but to be in subjection,
καθὼς καὶ ὁ νόμος λέγει. 35 εἰ.δέ τι μαθεῖν θέλουσιν,
according as also the law says. But if anything to learn they wish,
ἐν.οἴκῳ τοὺς.ἰδίους ἄνδρας ἐπερωτάτωσαν· αἰσχρὸν.γάρ ἐστιν
at home their own husbands let them ask; for a shame it is
[r]γυναιξὶν ἐν ἐκκλησίᾳ λαλεῖν.‖
for women in assembly to speak.

36 Ἢ ἀφ' ὑμῶν ὁ λόγος τοῦ θεοῦ ἐξῆλθεν; ἢ εἰς ὑμᾶς
Or [3]from [4]you [5]the [6]word [7]of [8]God [1]went [2]out, or to you
μόνους κατήντησεν; 37 εἴ τις δοκεῖ προφήτης εἶναι ἢ
only did it arrive? If anyone thinks a prophet to be or
πνευματικός, ἐπιγινωσκέτω ἃ γράφω ὑμῖν, ὅτι [s]τοῦ‖
spiritual, let him recognize the things I write to you, that of the
κυρίου [t]εἰσὶν‖ [v]ἐντολαί·‖ 38 εἰ.δέ τις ἀγνοεῖ, [w]ἀγνοείτω.‖
Lord they are commands. But if any be ignorant, let him be ignorant.
39 Ὥστε, ἀδελφοί[x], ζηλοῦτε τὸ προφητεύειν, καὶ τὸ λαλεῖν
So that, brethren, be emulous to prophesy, and to speak
[y]γλώσσαις μὴ.κωλύετε.‖ 40 πάντα [z] εὐσχημόνως καὶ κατὰ
with tongues do not forbid. All things becomingly and with
τάξιν γινέσθω.
order let be done.

15 Γνωρίζω.δὲ ὑμῖν, ἀδελφοί, τὸ εὐαγγέλιον ὃ εὐηγ-
But I make known to you, brethren, the glad tidings which I an-
γελισάμην ὑμῖν, ὃ καὶ παρελάβετε, ἐν ᾧ καὶ ἑστήκατε,
nounced to you, which also ye received, in which also ye stand,

---

[l] διερμηνευτής LTr. [m] ἀλλὰ LTTrAW. [n] ἁγίων, αἱ (*read verse* 33 *joined to verse* 34) GLT. [o] — ὑμῶν LTTrA. [p] ἐπιτρέπεται LTTrAW. [q] ὑποτασσέσθωσαν let them be in subjection LTTr. [r] γυναικὶ (a woman) λαλεῖν ἐν ἐκκλησίᾳ LTTrA. [s] — τοῦ (*read* of [the]) GLTTrAW. [t] ἐστὶν it is LTTrAW. [v] ἐντολή a command LTr[A]W; — ἐντολαί T. [w] ἀγνοεῖται he is ignored LT. [x] + μου my (brethren) [L]TTr[A]. [y] μὴ κωλύετε (+ ἐν [L]A) γλώσσαις LTTrA. [z] + δὲ But (all things) GLTTrAW.

2 δι' οὗ καὶ σώζεσθε. τίνι λόγῳ ᵇεὐηγγελισάμην‖ ὑμῖν
by which also ye are being saved, ⁵what ⁶word ⁷I ⁸announced ⁹to ¹⁰you
εἰ κατέχετε, ἐκτὸς εἰ.μὴ εἰκῇ ἐπιστεύσατε. 3 Παρέδωκα.γὰρ
¹if ²ye ³hold ⁴fast, unless in vain ye believed. For I delivered
ὑμῖν ἐν πρώτοις, ὃ καὶ παρέλαβον, ὅτι χριστὸς ἀπέθανεν
to you in the first place, what also I received, that Christ died
ὑπὲρ τῶν.ἁμαρτιῶν.ἡμῶν, κατὰ τὰς γραφάς· 4 καὶ ὅτι
for our sins, according to the scriptures; and that
ἐτάφη, καὶ ὅτι ἐγήγερται τῇ ᶜτρίτῃ ἡμέρᾳ,‖ κατὰ τὰς
he was buried; and that he was raised the third day, according to the
γραφάς· 5 καὶ ὅτι ὤφθη Κηφᾷ, ᵈεἶτα‖ τοῖς δώδεκα. 6 ἔπειτα
scriptures; and that he appeared to Cephas, then to the twelve. Then
ὤφθη ἐπάνω πεντακοσίοις ἀδελφοῖς ἐφάπαξ, ἐξ ὧν οἱ
he appeared to above five hundred brethren at once, of whom the
ᵉπλείους‖ μένουσιν ἕως ἄρτι, τινὲς.δὲ ᶠκαὶ‖ ἐκοιμήθησαν.
greater part remain until now, but some also are fallen asleep.
7 ἔπειτα ὤφθη Ἰακώβῳ, *εἶτα‖ τοῖς ἀποστόλοις πᾶσιν.
Then he appeared to James; then to ²the ³apostles ¹all;
8 ἔσχατον.δὲ πάντων, ὡσπερεὶ τῷ.ἐκτρώματι ὤφθη κἀμοί.
and last of all, as to an abortion, he appeared also to me.
9 ἐγὼ.γάρ εἰμι ὁ ἐλάχιστος τῶν ἀποστόλων, ὃς οὐκ.εἰμὶ
For I am the least of the apostles, who am not
ἱκανὸς καλεῖσθαι ἀπόστολος, διότι ἐδίωξα τὴν ἐκκλησίαν
fit to be called apostle, because I persecuted the assembly
τοῦ θεοῦ. 10 χάριτι.δὲ θεοῦ εἰμι ὅ εἰμι, καὶ ἡ.χάρις.αὐτοῦ
of God. But by grace of God I am what I am, and his grace
ἡ εἰς ἐμὲ οὐ κενὴ ἐγενήθη, ἀλλὰ περισσότερον αὐ-
which [was] towards me not void has been, but more abundantly than
τῶν πάντων ἐκοπίασα· οὐκ.ἐγὼ.δέ, ᵍἀλλ'‖ ἡ χάρις τοῦ θεοῦ
them all I laboured, but not I, but the grace of God
ʰἡ‖ σὺν ἐμοί. 11 εἴτε οὖν ἐγὼ εἴτε ἐκεῖνοι, οὕτως κηρύσ-
with me. Whether therefore I or they, so we
σομεν, καὶ οὕτως ἐπιστεύσατε. 12 Εἰ.δὲ χριστὸς κηρύσσεται,
preach, and so ye believed. Now if Christ is preached,
ⁱὅτι ἐκ νεκρῶν‖ ἐγήγερται, πῶς λέγουσίν ᵏτινες
that from among [the] dead he has been raised, how say some
ἐν ὑμῖν‖ ὅτι ἀνάστασις νεκρῶν οὐκ.ἔστιν; 13 εἰ.δὲ ἀνά-
among you that a resurrection of [the] dead there is not? But if a resur-
στασις νεκρῶν οὐκ.ἔστιν, οὐδὲ χριστὸς ἐγήγερται· 14 εἰ.δὲ
rection of [the] dead there is not, neither Christ has been raised: but if
χριστὸς οὐκ.ἐγήγερται, κενὸν.ἄρα ˡ τὸ.κήρυγμα.ἡμῶν, κενὴ
Christ has not been raised, then void [is] our proclamation, ²void
ᵐδὲ‖ καὶ ἡ.πίστις.ὑμῶν. 15 εὑρισκόμεθα.δὲ καὶ ψευδομάρτυρες
¹and also your faith. And we are found also false witnesses
τοῦ θεοῦ, ὅτι ἐμαρτυρήσαμεν κατὰ τοῦ θεοῦ ὅτι ἤγειρεν
of God; for we witnessed concerning God that he raised up
τὸν χριστόν, ὃν οὐκ.ἤγειρεν εἴπερ ἄρα νεκροὶ οὐκ
the Christ, whom he raised not if then [the] dead ²not
ἐγείρονται· 16 εἰ.γὰρ νεκροὶ οὐκ.ἐγείρονται, οὐδὲ χριστὸς
¹are raised. For if [the] dead are not raised, neither Christ
ἐγήγερται· 17 εἰ.δὲ χριστὸς οὐκ.ἐγήγερται, ματαία ἡ πίστις
has been raised: but if Christ has not been raised, vain ²faith

which also ye have received, and wherein ye stand; 2 by which also ye are saved, if ye keep in memory what I preached unto you, unless ye have believed in vain. 3 For I delivered unto you first of all that which I also received, how that Christ died for our sins according to the scriptures; 4 and that he was buried, and that he rose again the third day according to the scriptures: 5 and that he was seen of Cephas, then of the twelve: 6 after that, he was seen of above five hundred brethren at once; of whom the greater part remain unto this present, but some are fallen asleep. 7 After that, he was seen of James; then of all the apostles. 8 And last of all he was seen of me also, as of one born out of due time. 9 For I am the least of the apostles, that am not meet to be called an apostle, because I persecuted the church of God. 10 But by the grace of God I am what I am: and his grace which *was bestowed* upon me was not in vain; but I laboured more abundantly than they all: yet not I, but the grace of God which was with me. 11 Therefore whether *it were* I or they, so we preach, and so ye believed. 12 Now if Christ be preached that he rose from the dead, how say some among you that there is no resurrection of the dead? 13 But if there be no resurrection of the dead, then is Christ not risen: 14 and if Christ be not risen, then *is* our preaching vain, and your faith *is* also vain. 15 Yea, and we are found false witnesses of God; because we have testified of God that he raised up Christ: whom he raised not up, if so be that the dead rise not. 16 For if the dead rise not, then is not Christ raised: 17 and if Christ

---

ᵇ εὐαγγελισάμην L. ᶜ ἡμέρᾳ τῇ τρίτῃ LTTrAW. ᵈ ἔπειτα T. ᵉ πλείονες LTTrAW. ᶠ — καὶ LTTr[A]. * ἔπειτα TA. ᵍ ἀλλὰ LTTrAW. ʰ — ἡ LTTrA. ⁱ ἐκ νεκρῶν ὅτι A. ᵏ ἐν ὑμῖν τινὲς LTTrAW. ˡ + καὶ also [L]TAW. ᵐ — δὲ LTTrAW.

be not raised, your
faith *is* vain; ye are
yet in your sins.
18 Then they also
which are fallen asleep
in Christ are perished.
19 If in this life only
we have hope in Christ,
we are of all men most
miserable.

20 But now is Christ
risen from the dead,
and become the first-
fruits of them that
slept. 21 For since by
man *came* death, by
man *came* also the re-
surrection of the dead.
22 For as in Adam all
die, even so in Christ
shall all be made a-
live. 23 But every man
in his own order:
Christ the firstfruits;
afterward they that
are Christ's at his
coming. 24 Then *com-*
eth the end, when he
shall have delivered
up the kingdom to
God, even the Father;
when he shall have put
down all rule and all
authority and power.
25 For he must reign,
till he hath put all
enemies under his feet.
26 The last enemy *that*
shall be destroyed *is*
death. 27 For he hath
put all things under
his feet. But when he
saith, all things are put
under *him*, *it is* manifest that he is except-
ed, which did put all
things under him.
28 And when all things
shall be subdued unto
him, then shall the
Son also himself be
subject unto him that
put all things under
him, that God may be
all in all.

29 Else what shall
they do which are
baptized for the dead,
if the dead rise not
at all? why are they
then baptized for the
dead? 30 and why
stand we in jeopardy
every hour? 31 I pro-
test by your rejoicing
which I have in Christ
Jesus our Lord, I die
daily. 32 If after the
manner of men I have

ὑμῶν[o] · ἔτι ἐστὲ ἐν ταῖς.ἁμαρτίαις.ὑμῶν· 18 ἄρα.καὶ οἱ
[1]your [is]; still ye are in your sins. And then those that
κοιμηθέντες ἐν χριστῷ ἀπώλοντο. 19 εἰ ἐν τῇ.ζωῇ.ταύτῃ
fell asleep in Christ perished. If in this life
[p]ἠλπικότες.ἐσμὲν ἐν χριστῷ‖ μόνον, ἐλεεινότεροι πάντων ἀν-
[2]we [3]have [4]hope [5]in [6]Christ [1]only, more miserable than all
θρώπων ἐσμέν.
men we are.

20 Νυνὶ.δὲ χριστὸς ἐγήγερται ἐκ νεκρῶν, ἀπαρχὴ
But now Christ has been raised from among [the] dead, first-fruit
τῶν κεκοιμημένων [q]ἐγένετο.‖ 21 ἐπειδὴ.γὰρ δι' ἀνθρώπου
of those fallen asleep he became. For since by man [is]
[r]ὁ‖ θάνατος, καὶ δι' ἀνθρώπου ἀνάστασις νεκρῶν. 22 ὥσπερ
death, also by man resurrection of [the] dead. [2]As
γὰρ ἐν τῷ Ἀδὰμ πάντες ἀποθνήσκουσιν, οὕτως καὶ ἐν τῷ
[1]for in Adam all die, so also in the
χριστῷ πάντες ζωοποιηθήσονται. 23 ἕκαστος.δὲ ἐν τῷ.ἰδίῳ
Christ all shall be made alive. But each in his own
τάγματι· ἀπαρχὴ χριστός, ἔπειτα οἱ [s] χριστοῦ ἐν τῇ
rank: [[2]the] [3]first-fruit [1]Christ, then those of Christ at
παρουσίᾳ αὐτοῦ· 24 εἶτα τὸ τέλος, ὅταν [t]παραδῷ‖ τὴν
his coming. Then the end, when he shall have given up the
βασιλείαν τῷ θεῷ καὶ πατρί, ὅταν καταργήσῃ
kingdom to him who [is] God and Father; when he shall have annulled
πᾶσαν ἀρχὴν καὶ πᾶσαν ἐξουσίαν καὶ δύναμιν· 25 δεῖ.γὰρ
all rule and all authority and power. For it behoves
αὐτὸν βασιλεύειν, [v]ἄχρις‖ οὗ [w]ἂν‖ θῇ πάντας τοὺς
him to reign, until he shall have put all
ἐχθροὺς [x] ὑπὸ τοὺς.πόδας.αὐτοῦ. 26 ἔσχατος ἐχθρὸς καταρ-
enemies under his feet. [The] last enemy an-
γεῖται ὁ θάνατος. 27 Πάντα.γὰρ ὑπέταξεν ὑπὸ τοὺς
nulled [is] death. For all things he put in subjection under
πόδας.αὐτοῦ· ὅταν.δὲ εἴπῃ [y]ὅτι‖ πάντα ὑποτέτακται,
his feet. But when it be said that all things have been put in subjection,
δῆλον ὅτι ἐκτὸς τοῦ ὑποτάξαντος αὐτῷ τὰ.πάντα·
[it is] manifest that [it is] except him who put in subjection to him all things.
28 ὅταν.δὲ ὑποταγῇ αὐτῷ τὰ.πάντα, τότε
But when shall have been put in subjection to him all things, then
[z]καὶ‖ αὐτὸς ὁ υἱὸς ὑποταγήσεται τῷ ὑποτάξαντι
also [3]himself [1]the [2]Son will be put in subjection to him who put in subjection
αὐτῷ τὰ.πάντα, ἵνα ᾖ ὁ θεὸς [a]τὰ‖ πάντα ἐν πᾶσιν.
to him all things, that [2]may [3]be [1]God all in all.

29 Ἐπεὶ τί ποιήσουσιν οἱ βαπτιζόμενοι ὑπὲρ τῶν νεκρῶν
Since what shall they do who are baptized for the dead
εἰ ὅλως νεκροὶ οὐκ ἐγείρονται; τί καὶ βαπτίζονται ὑπὲρ
if [4]at [5]all [[1]the] [2]dead [3]not are raised? why also are they baptized for
[b]τῶν νεκρῶν‖; 30 τί καὶ ἡμεῖς κινδυνεύομεν πᾶσαν ὥραν;
the dead? Why also [2]we [1]are in danger every hour?
31 καθ'.ἡμέραν ἀποθνήσκω, νὴ τὴν [c]ἡμετέραν‖ καύχησιν, [d]
Daily I die, by our boasting,
ἣν ἔχω ἐν χριστῷ Ἰησοῦ τῷ.κυρίῳ.ἡμῶν. 32 εἰ κατὰ
which I have in Christ Jesus our Lord. If according to

---

[o] + [ἐστίν] is L. [p] ἐν χριστῷ ἠλπικότες ἐσμὲν LTTrAW. [q] — ἐγένετο GLTTrAW. [r] — ὁ LTTr[A]W. [s] + τοῦ (*read* of the Christ) GLTTrAW. [t] παραδιδοῖ he may give up LTTrA. [v] ἄχρι TA. [w] — ἂν LTTrAW. [x] + [αὐτοῦ] his (enemies) L. [y] [ὅτι] L. [z] — καὶ [L]Tr[A]. [a] — τὰ LTrA. [b] αὐτῶν them GLTTrAW. [c] ὑμετέραν your EGLTTrAW. [d] + ἀδελφοί brethren LTTrA.

ἄνθρωπον ἐθηριομάχησα ἐν Ἐφέσῳ, τί μοι τὸ [e]ὄφελος,
man I fought with beasts in Ephesus, what to me the profit,
εἰ νεκροὶ οὐκ.ἐγείρονται ;‖ φάγωμεν καὶ πίωμεν,
if [the] dead are not raised? We may eat and we may drink;
αὔριον.γὰρ ἀποθνήσκομεν. 33 μὴ.πλανᾶσθε· φθείρουσιν ἤθη
for to-morrow we die. Be not misled: [3]corrupt [5]manners
[f]χρήσθ'‖ ὁμιλίαι κακαί. 34 ἐκνήψατε δικαίως, καὶ μὴ
[4]good [2]companionships [1]evil. Awake up righteously, and [2]not
ἁμαρτάνετε· ἀγνωσίαν.γὰρ θεοῦ τινες ἔχουσιν· πρὸς ἐντροπὴν
[1]sin; for ignorance of God some have: to [2]shame
ὑμῖν [g]λέγω.‖
[1]your I speak.

35 [h]Ἀλλ'‖ ἐρεῖ τις, Πῶς ἐγείρονται οἱ νεκροί; ποίῳ
But will say some one, How are raised the dead? [2]with [3]what
δὲ σώματι ἔρχονται; 36 [i]ἄφρον,‖ σὺ ὃ σπείρεις, οὐ
[1]and body do they come? Fool; [2]thou [1]what sowest, [2]not
ζωοποιεῖται ἐὰν.μὴ ἀποθάνῃ· 37 καὶ ὃ σπείρεις, οὐ τὸ σῶμα
[1]is quickened unless it die. And what thou sowest, not the body
τὸ γενησόμενον σπείρεις, ἀλλὰ γυμνὸν κόκκον, εἰ τύχοι,
that shall be thou sowest, but a bare grain, it may be
σίτου ἤ τινος τῶν λοιπῶν· 38 ὁ.δὲ.θεὸς [j]αὐτῷ δίδωσιν‖
of wheat or of some one of the rest; and God to it gives
σῶμα καθὼς ἠθέλησεν, καὶ ἑκάστῳ τῶν σπερμάτων [k]τὸ‖.ἴδιον
a body according as he willed, and to each of the seeds its own
σῶμα. 39 οὐ πᾶσα σὰρξ ἡ αὐτὴ σάρξ· ἀλλὰ ἄλλη μὲν
body. Not every flesh [is] the same flesh, but one
[l]σὰρξ‖ ἀνθρώπων, ἄλλη.δὲ σὰρξ κτηνῶν, ἄλλη.δὲ [m] [n]ἰχθύων,
flesh of men, and another flesh of beasts, and another of fishes,
ἄλλη.δὲ πτηνῶν.‖ 40 καὶ σώματα ἐπουράνια, καὶ
and another of birds. And bodies [there are] heavenly, and
σώματα ἐπίγεια· [o]ἀλλ'‖ ἑτέρα μὲν ἡ τῶν ἐπουρανίων
bodies earthly: but different [is] the [2]of [3]the [4]heavenly
δόξα, ἑτέρα.δὲ ἡ τῶν ἐπιγείων. 41 ἄλλη δόξα ἡλίου,
[1]glory, and different that of the earthly: one glory of [the] sun,
καὶ ἄλλη δόξα σελήνης, καὶ ἄλλη δόξα ἀστέρων ἀστὴρ
and another glory of [the] moon, and another glory of [the] stars; [2]star
γὰρ ἀστέρος διαφέρει ἐν δόξῃ. 42 οὕτως καὶ ἡ ἀνάστασις
[1]for [4]from [5]star [3]differs in glory. So also [is] the resurrection
τῶν νεκρῶν. σπείρεται ἐν φθορᾷ, ἐγείρεται ἐν ἀφθαρσίᾳ·
of the dead. It is sown in corruption, it is raised in incorruptibility.
43 σπείρεται ἐν ἀτιμίᾳ, ἐγείρεται ἐν δόξῃ· σπείρεται ἐν ἀ-
It is sown in dishonour, it is raised in glory. It is sown in weak-
σθενείᾳ, ἐγείρεται ἐν δυνάμει· 44 σπείρεται σῶμα ψυχικόν,
ness, it is raised in power. It is sown a [2]body [1]natural,
ἐγείρεται σῶμα πνευματικόν. [p]ἔστιν σῶμα ψυχικόν, [q]καὶ
it is raised a [2]body [1]spiritual: there is a [2]body [1]natural, and
ἔστιν‖ [r]σῶμα‖ πνευματικόν. 45 οὕτως καὶ γέγραπται,
there is a [2]body [1]spiritual. So also it has been written,
Ἐγένετο ὁ πρῶτος [s]ἄνθρωπος‖ Ἀδὰμ εἰς ψυχὴν ζῶσαν· ὁ
[5]Became [1]the [2]first [3]man [4]Adam a [2]soul [1]living; the
ἔσχατος Ἀδὰμ εἰς πνεῦμα ζωοποιοῦν. 46 ἀλλ' οὐ πρῶτον
last Adam a [2]spirit [1]quickening. But not first [was]

fought with beasts at
Ephesus, what ad-
vantageth it me, if
the dead rise not? let
us eat and drink; for
to morrow we die.
33 Be not deceived:
evil communications
corrupt good manners.
34 Awake to righteous-
ness, and sin not; for
some have not the
knowledge of God: I
speak *this* to your
shame.

35 But some *man*
will say, How are the
dead raised up? and
with what body do
they come? 36 *Thou*
fool, that which thou
sowest is not quicken-
ed, except it die: 37 and
that which thou sow-
est, thou sowest not
that body that shall
be, but bare grain, it
may chance of wheat,
or of some other *grain*:
38 but God giveth it a
body as it hath pleas-
ed him, and to every
seed his own body.
39 All flesh *is* not the
same flesh: but *there*
is one *kind of* flesh
of men, another flesh
of beasts, another of
fishes, *and* another of
birds. 40 *There are* al-
so celestial bodies, and
bodies terrestrial: but
the glory of the celes-
tial *is* one, and the
glory of the terrestrial
is another. 41 *There*
is one glory of the sun,
and another glory of
the moon, and another
glory of the stars: for
one star differeth from
another star in glory.
42 So also *is* the resurrection of the dead. It
is sown in corruption;
it is raised in incor-
ruption: 43 it is sown
in dishonour; it is
raised in glory: it is
sown in weakness; it
is raised in power: 44 it
is sown a natural
body; it is raised a
spiritual body. There
is a natural body, and
there is a spiritual
body. 45 And so it is
written, The first man
Adam was made a liv-
ing soul; the last A-
dam *was made* a quick-
ening spirit. 46 How-
beit that *was* not first
which is spiritual,

[e] ὄφελος; .... ἐγείρονται, (*end the question at* profit) GLTTrA. [f] χρηστὰ GTTrAW. [g] λαλῶ LTTrA. [h] ἀλλὰ TTr. [i] ἄφρων LTTrA. [j] δίδωσιν αὐτῷ LTTrAW. [k] — τὸ LTTrA. [l] — σὰρξ GLTTrAW. [m] + σὰρξ flesh [L]TTrA. [n] πτηνῶν, ἄλλη δὲ ἰχθύων LTTrAW. [o] ἀλλὰ LTTrAW. [p] + εἰ if LTTrAW. [q] ἔστιν καὶ there is also LTTrAW. [r] — σῶμα LTTrAW. [s] [ἄνθρωπος] L.

but that which is natural: and afterward
that which is spiritual.
47 The first man *is* of
the earth, earthy: the
second man *is* the Lord
from heaven. 48 As *is*
the earthy, such *are*
they also that are
earthy: and as *is* the
heavenly, such *are*
they also that are
heavenly. 49 And as we
have borne the image
of the earthy, we shall
also bear the image of
the heavenly. 50 Now
this I say, brethren,
that flesh and blood
cannot inherit the
kingdom of God; neither doth corruption
inherit incorruption.

51 Behold, I shew
you a mystery; We
shall not all sleep, but
we shall all be changed, 52 in a moment, in
the twinkling of an
eye, at the last trump:
for the trumpet shall
sound, and the dead
shall be raised incorruptible, and we shall
be changed. 53 For this
corruptible must put
on incorruption, and
this mortal *must* put
on immortality. 54 So
when this corruptible
shall have put on incorruption, and this
mortal shall have put
on immortality, then
shall be brought to
pass the saying that
is written, Death is
swallowed up in victory. 55 O death, where
is thy sting? O grave,
where *is* thy victory?
56 The sting of death
is sin; and the strength
of sin *is* the law.
57 But thanks *be* to
God, which giveth us
the victory through
our Lord Jesus Christ.
58 Therefore, my beloved brethren, be ye
stedfast, unmoveable,
always abounding in
the work of the Lord,
forasmuch as ye know
that your labour is
not in vain in the
Lord.

XVI. Now concerning the collection for
the saints, as I have

τὸ πνευματικόν, ἀλλὰ τὸ ψυχικόν, ἔπειτα τὸ πνευματικόν.
the spiritual, but the natural, then the spiritual:
47 ὁ πρῶτος ἄνθρωπος ἐκ γῆς, χοϊκός· ὁ δεύτερος ἄν-
the first man out of earth, made of dust; the second
θρωπος, [t]ὁ κύριος" ἐξ οὐρανοῦ. 48 οἷος ὁ χοϊκός, τοιοῦτοι
man, the Lord out of heaven. Such as he made of dust, such
καὶ οἱ χοϊκοί· καὶ οἷος ὁ ἐπουράνιος, τοιοῦτοι καὶ οἱ
also [are] those made of dust; and such as the heavenly [one], such also the
ἐπουράνιοι· 49 καὶ καθὼς ἐφορέσαμεν τὴν εἰκόνα τοῦ
heavenly [ones]. And according as we bore the image of the [one]
χοϊκοῦ, [v]φορέσομεν" καὶ τὴν εἰκόνα τοῦ ἐπουρανίου.
made of dust, we shall bear also the image of the [2one] [1]heavenly.
50 Τοῦτο.δέ φημι, ἀδελφοί, ὅτι σὰρξ καὶ αἷμα βασιλείαν
But this I say, brethren, that flesh and blood [the] kingdom
θεοῦ κληρονομῆσαι οὐ.[w]δύνανται," οὐδὲ ἡ φθορὰ τὴν ἀ-
of God [2]inherit [1]cannot, nor [2]corruption [4]incor-
φθαρσίαν [x]κληρονομεῖ."
ruptibility [1]does [3]inherit.

51 Ἰδοὺ μυστήριον ὑμῖν λέγω· Πάντες [y]μὲν" [z]οὐ κοιμηθη-
Lo a mystery to you I tell: All [3]not [1]we [2]shall
σόμεθα," πάντες.δὲ ἀλλαγησόμεθα, 52 ἐν ἀτόμῳ, ἐν
fall asleep, but all we shall be changed, in an instant, in [the]
ῥιπῇ ὀφθαλμοῦ, ἐν τῇ ἐσχάτῃ σάλπιγγι· σαλπίσει.γάρ,
twinkling of an eye, at the last trumpet; for a trumpet shall sound,
καὶ οἱ νεκροὶ [a]ἐγερθήσονται" ἄφθαρτοι, καὶ ἡμεῖς ἀλλαγησό-
and the dead shall be raised incorruptible, and we shall be
μεθα. 53 δεῖ.γὰρ τὸ.φθαρτὸν.τοῦτο ἐνδύσασθαι ἀφθαρσίαν,
changed. For it behoves this corruption to put on incorruptibility,
καὶ τὸ.θνητὸν.τοῦτο ἐνδύσασθαι ἀθανασίαν. 54 ὅταν.δὲ τὸ
and this mortal to put on immortality. But when
φθαρτὸν.τοῦτο ἐνδύσηται ἀφθαρσίαν, καὶ τὸ.θνητὸν.τοῦτο
this corruptible shall have put on incorruptibility, and this mortal
ἐνδύσηται ἀθανασίαν, τότε γενήσεται ὁ λόγος ὁ γε-
shall have put on immortality, then shall come to pass the word that has
γραμμένος, Κατεπόθη ὁ θάνατος εἰς νῖκος. 55 Ποῦ σου,
been written: [2]Was [3]swallowed [4]up [1]death in victory. Where of thee,
θάνατε, τὸ [b]κέντρον"; ποῦ σου, [c]ᾅδη," τὸ [b]νῖκος"; 56 Τὸ.δὲ
O death, the sting? where of thee, O hades, the victory? Now the
κέντρον τοῦ θανάτου ἡ ἁμαρτία· ἡ.δὲ δύναμις τῆς ἁμαρ-
sting of death [is] sin, and the power of sin
τίας ὁ νόμος· 57 τῷ.δὲ.θεῷ χάρις τῷ διδόντι ἡμῖν τὸ νῖκος
the law; but to God [be] thanks, who gives us the victory
διὰ τοῦ.κυρίου.ἡμῶν Ἰησοῦ χριστοῦ. 58 Ὥστε, ἀδελφοί.μου
by our Lord Jesus Christ. So that, my brethren
ἀγαπητοί, ἑδραῖοι γίνεσθε, ἀμετακίνητοι, περισσεύοντες ἐν τῷ
beloved, [2]firm [1]be, immovable, abounding in the
ἔργῳ τοῦ κυρίου πάντοτε, εἰδότες ὅτι ὁ.κόπος.ὑμῶν οὐκ.ἔστιν
work of the Lord always, knowing that your toil is not
κενὸς ἐν κυρίῳ.
void in [the] Lord.

16 Περὶ.δὲ τῆς λογίας τῆς εἰς τοὺς ἁγίους, ὥσπερ
Now concerning the collection which [is] for the saints, as

---

[t] — ὁ κύριος LTTrA. [v] φορέσωμεν we should bear LTTr. [w] δύναται TTr. [x] κληρονομήσει shall inherit L. [y] — μὲν [L]TTrA. [z] κοιμηθησόμεθα, οὐ (*read* we shall all sleep, but not all &c.) L. [a] ἀναστήσονται L. [b] νῖκος *and* κέντρον *transposed* LTTr. [c] θάνατε O death LTTrA.

διέταξα ταῖς ἐκκλησίαις τῆς Γαλατίας, οὕτως καὶ ὑμεῖς
I directed the assemblies of Galatia, so also ye
ποιήσατε. 2 κατὰ.μίαν [d]σαββάτων[||] ἕκαστος ὑμῶν παρ'
do. Every first [day] of the week [2]each [3]of [4]you [6]by
ἑαυτῷ τιθέτω, θησαυρίζων ὅ.τι [e]ἂν[||] εὐοδῶται· ἵνα μὴ
[7]him [1]let [5]put, treasuring up whatever he may be prospered in, that not
ὅταν ἔλθω τότε λογίαι γίνωνται. 3 ὅταν.δὲ παραγένω-
when I may come then collections there should be. And when I shall have
μαι, οὓς.[f]ἐὰν[||] δοκιμάσητε δι' ἐπιστολῶν τούτους πέμψω
arrived, whomsoever ye may approve by epistles these I will send
ἀπενεγκεῖν τὴν.χάριν.ὑμῶν εἰς Ἱερουσαλήμ· 4 ἐὰν.δὲ [g]ᾖ
to carry your bounty to Jerusalem: and if it be
ἄξιον[||] τοῦ.κἀμὲ πορεύεσθαι, σὺν ἐμοὶ πορεύσονται. 5 Ἐλεύ-
suitable for me also to go, with me they shall go. [2]I [3]will
σομαι δὲ πρὸς ὑμᾶς ὅταν Μακεδονίαν διέλθω·
[4]come [1]but to you when Macedonia I shall have gone through;
Μακεδονίαν.γὰρ διέρχομαι. 6 πρὸς.ὑμᾶς.δὲ τυχὸν παραμενῶ,
for Macedonia I do go through. And with you it may be I shall stay,
ἢ καὶ παραχειμάσω, ἵνα ὑμεῖς με προπέμψητε οὗ.ἐὰν
or even I shall winter, that ye me may set forward wheresoever
πορεύωμαι. 7 οὐ.θέλω.γὰρ ὑμᾶς ἄρτι ἐν παρόδῳ ἰδεῖν· ἐλπίζω
I may go. For I will not [3]you [4]now [5]in [6]passing [1]to [2]see, [8]I [9]hope
[h]δὲ[||] χρόνον τινὰ ἐπιμεῖναι πρὸς ὑμᾶς, ἐὰν ὁ κύριος [i]ἐπι-
[7]but a [2]time [1]certain to remain with you, if the Lord per-
τρέπῃ.[||] 8 ἐπιμενῶ.δὲ ἐν Ἐφέσῳ ἕως τῆς πεντηκοστῆς·
mit. But I shall remain in Ephesus till Pentecost.
9 θύρα.γάρ μοι ἀνέῳγεν μεγάλη καὶ ἐνεργής, καὶ ἀντι-
For a door to me has been opened great and efficient, and op-
κείμενοι πολλοί.
posers [are] many.

10 Ἐὰν.δὲ ἔλθῃ Τιμόθεος, βλέπετε ἵνα ἀφόβως γένηται
Now if [2]come [1]Timotheus, see that without fear he may be
πρὸς ὑμᾶς· τὸ.γὰρ ἔργον κυρίου ἐργάζεται, ὡς [k]καὶ ἐγώ.[||]
with you; for the work of [the] Lord he works, as even I.
11 μή τις οὖν αὐτὸν ἐξουθενήσῃ· προπέμψατε.δὲ αὐτὸν
[2]Not [3]anyone [1]therefore him should despise; but set forward him
ἐν εἰρήνῃ, ἵνα ἔλθῃ πρός [l]με[||] ἐκδέχομαι.γὰρ αὐτὸν μετὰ
in peace, that he may come to me; for I await him with
τῶν ἀδελφῶν. 12 Περὶ.δὲ Ἀπολλὼ τοῦ ἀδελφοῦ, πολλὰ
the brethren. And concerning Apollos the brother, much
παρεκάλεσα αὐτὸν ἵνα ἔλθῃ πρὸς ὑμᾶς μετὰ τῶν
I exhorted him that he should go to you with the
ἀδελφῶν· καὶ πάντως.οὐκ ἦν θέλημα ἵνα νῦν ἔλθῃ,
brethren; and not at all was [his] will that now he should come;
ἐλεύσεται.δὲ ὅταν εὐκαιρήσῃ. 13 Γρηγορεῖτε, στήκετε
but he will come when he shall have opportunity. Watch ye; stand fast
ἐν τῇ πίστει, ἀνδρίζεσθε, [m]κραταιοῦσθε. 14 πάντα
in the faith, quit yourselves like men, be strong. [2]All [4]things
ὑμῶν ἐν ἀγάπῃ γινέσθω.
[3]your [5]in [6]love [1]let be done.

15 Παρακαλῶ.δὲ ὑμᾶς, ἀδελφοί· οἴδατε τὴν οἰκίαν Στεφανᾶ,
But I exhort you, brethren, (ye know the house of Stephanas,
ὅτι ἐστὶν ἀπαρχὴ τῆς Ἀχαΐας, καὶ εἰς διακονίαν τοῖς ἁγίοις
that it is [2]first-fruit [1]Achaia's, and [7]for [8]service [4]to [5]the [6]saints

given order to the churches of Galatia, even so do ye. 2 Upon the first *day* of the week let every one of you lay by him in store, as *God* hath prospered him, that there be no gatherings when I come. 3 And when I come, whomsoever ye shall approve by *your* letters, them will I send to bring your liberality unto Jerusalem. 4 And if it be meet that I go also, they shall go with me. 5 Now I will come unto you, when I shall pass through Macedonia: for I do pass through Macedonia. 6 And it may be that I will abide, yea, and winter with you, that ye may bring me on my journey whithersoever I go. 7 For I will not see you now by the way; but I trust to tarry a while with you, if the Lord permit. 8 But I will tarry at Ephesus until Pentecost. 9 For a great door and effectual is opened unto me, and *there are* many adversaries.

10 Now if Timotheus come, see that he may be with you without fear: for he worketh the work of the Lord, as I also *do*. 11 Let no man therefore despise him: but conduct him forth in peace, that he may come unto me: for I look for him with the brethren. 12 As touching *our* brother Apollos, I greatly desired him to come unto you with the brethren: but his will was not at all to come at this time; but he will come when he shall have convenient time. 13 Watch ye, stand fast in the faith, quit you like men, be strong. 14 Let all your things be done with charity.

15 I beseech you, brethren, (ye know the house of Stephanas, that it is the firstfruits of Achaia, and *that* they have addicted themselves to the ministry of the

---

[d] σαββάτου LTTrAW. [e] ἐὰν Tr. [f] ἂν LTr. [g] ἄξιον ᾖ LTrA. [h] γὰρ for GLTTrAW. [i] ἐπιτρέψῃ LTTrAW. [k] κἀγώ LTTrA. [l] ἐμέ LTr. [m] + [καὶ] and L.

saints,) 16 that ye submit yourselves unto such, and to every one that helpeth with *us*, and laboureth. 17 I am glad of the coming of Stephanas and Fortunatus and Achaicus: for that which was lacking on your part they have supplied. 18 For they have refreshed my spirit and yours: therefore acknowledge ye them that are such. 19 The churches of Asia salute you. Aquila and Priscilla salute you much in the Lord, with the church that is in their house. 20 All the brethren greet you. Greet ye one another with an holy kiss.

ἔταξαν ἑαυτούς· 16 ἵνα καὶ ὑμεῖς ὑποτάσσησθε τοῖς
[1]they [2]appointed [3]themselves,) that also ye be subject
τοιούτοις, καὶ παντὶ τῷ συνεργοῦντι καὶ κοπιῶντι. 17 Χαίρω
to such, and to everyone working with [us] and labouring. [2]I [3]rejoice
δὲ ἐπὶ τῇ παρουσίᾳ Στεφανᾶ καὶ [n]Φουρτουνάτου‖ καὶ Ἀχαϊκοῦ,
[1]but at the coming of Stephanas and Fortunatus and Achaicus;
ὅτι τὸ [o]ὑμῶν‖ ὑστέρημα [p]οὗτοι‖ ἀνεπλήρωσαν· 18 ἀνέπαυ-
because your deficiency these filled up. [2]They [3]re-
σαν γὰρ τὸ ἐμὸν πνεῦμα καὶ τὸ ὑμῶν, ἐπιγινώσκετε οὖν
freshed [1]for my spirit and yours; recognize therefore
τοὺς τοιούτους. 19 Ἀσπάζονται ὑμᾶς αἱ ἐκκλησίαι τῆς Ἀσίας·
such. [5]Salute [6]you [1]the [2]assemblies [3]of [4]Asia.
[q]ἀσπάζονται‖ ὑμᾶς ἐν κυρίῳ πολλὰ Ἀκύλας καὶ [r]Πρίσ-
[10]Salute [11]you [13]in [[14]the] [15]Lord [12]much [7]Aquila [8]and [9]Pris-
κιλλα,‖ σὺν τῇ κατ' οἶκον.αὐτῶν ἐκκλησίᾳ· 20 ἀσπάζονται
cilla, with the [2]in [3]their [4]house [1]assembly. [4]Salute
ὑμᾶς οἱ ἀδελφοὶ πάντες. ἀσπάσασθε ἀλλήλους ἐν φιλήματι
[5]you [2]the [3]brethren [1]all. Salute ye one another with a [2]kiss
ἁγίῳ.
[1]holy.

21 The salutation of *me* Paul with mine own hand. 22 If any man love not the Lord Jesus Christ, let him be Anathema Maranatha. 23 The grace of our Lord Jesus Christ *be* with you. 24 My love *be* with you all in Christ Jesus. Amen.

21 Ὁ ἀσπασμὸς τῇ.ἐμῇ χειρὶ Παύλου· 22 εἴ τις οὐ.φιλεῖ
The salutation [3]by [4]my [[5]own] [6]hand [1]of [2]Paul. If anyone love not
τὸν κύριον [s]Ἰησοῦν χριστόν,‖ ἤτω ἀνάθεμα· μαρὰν ἀθά.
the Lord Jesus Christ, let him be accursed: Maran atha.
23 ἡ χάρις τοῦ κυρίου Ἰησοῦ [t]χριστοῦ‖ μεθ' ὑμῶν. 24 ἡ
The grace of the Lord Jesus Christ [be] with you.
ἀγάπη.μου μετὰ πάντων ὑμῶν ἐν χριστῷ Ἰησοῦ. [v]ἀμήν.‖
My love [be] with [2]all [1]you in Christ Jesus. Amen.
[w]Πρὸς Κορινθίους πρώτη ἐγράφη ἀπὸ Φιλίππων, διὰ
[2]To [[3]the] [4]Corinthians [1]first written from Philippi, by
Στεφανᾶ καὶ Φουρτουνάτου καὶ Ἀχαϊκοῦ καὶ Τιμοθέου.‖
Stephanas and Fortunatus and Achaicus and Timotheus.

---

[a]Η ΠΡΟΣ ΤΟΥΣ ΚΟΡΙΝΘΙΟΥΣ ΕΠΙΣΤΟΛΗ ΔΕΥΤΕΡΑ.‖
THE [3]TO [4]THE [5]CORINTHIANS [2]EPISTLE [1]SECOND.

PAUL, an apostle of Jesus Christ by the will of God, and Timothy *our* brother, unto the church of God which is at Corinth, with all the saints which are in all Achaia: 2 Grace *be* to you and peace from God our Father, and *from* the Lord Jesus Christ.

ΠΑΥΛΟΣ ἀπόστολος [b]Ἰησοῦ χριστοῦ‖ διὰ θελήματος θεοῦ,
Paul, apostle of Jesus Christ by will of God,
καὶ Τιμόθεος ὁ ἀδελφός, τῇ ἐκκλησίᾳ τοῦ θεοῦ τῇ οὔσῃ ἐν
and Timotheus the brother, to the assembly of God which is in
Κορίνθῳ, σὺν τοῖς ἁγίοις πᾶσιν τοῖς οὖσιν ἐν ὅλῃ τῇ Ἀ-
Corinth, with [2]the [3]saints [1]all who are in [2]whole [1]the [of] A-
χαΐᾳ· 2 χάρις ὑμῖν καὶ εἰρήνη ἀπὸ [c]θεοῦ‖ πατρὸς.ἡμῶν καὶ
chaia. Grace to you and peace from God our Father and
κυρίου Ἰησοῦ χριστοῦ.
[the] Lord Jesus Christ.

3 Blessed *be* God, even the Father of our Lord Jesus Christ, the

3 Εὐλογητὸς ὁ θεὸς καὶ πατὴρ τοῦ.κυρίου.ἡμῶν Ἰησοῦ
Blessed [be] the God and Father of our Lord Jesus

---

[n] Φορτουνάτου LTTrAW. [o] ὑμέτερον LTTrAW. [p] αὐτοὶ they LAW. [q] ἀσπάζεται TA. [r] Πρίσκα Prisca TTr. [s] — Ἰησοῦν χριστόν LTTrA. [t] — χριστοῦ TTrA. [v] — ἀμήν [L]TTr[A]. [w] — *the subscription* GLTTrW; Πρὸς Κορινθίους ά A.

[a] + Παύλου τοῦ Ἀποστόλου of Paul the Apostle E; + Παύλου of Paul G; — τοὺς EG; Πρὸς Κορινθίους β' LTTrAW. [b] χριστοῦ Ἰησοῦ TTrA. [c] — θεοῦ W.

χριστοῦ, ὁ πατὴρ τῶν οἰκτιρμῶν καὶ θεὸς πάσης παρακλή-
Christ, the Father of compassions, and God of all encourage-
σεως, 4 ὁ παρακαλῶν ἡμᾶς ἐπὶ πάσῃ τῇ.θλίψει.ἡμῶν, εἰς
ment; who encourages us in all our tribulation, for
τὸ δύνασθαι ἡμᾶς παρακαλεῖν τοὺς ἐν πάσῃ θλίψει, διὰ
²to ³be ⁴able ¹us to encourage those in every tribulation, through
τῆς παρακλήσεως ἧς παρακαλούμεθα αὐτοὶ ὑπὸ τοῦ
the encouragement with which we are encouraged ourselves by
θεοῦ· 5 ὅτι καθὼς περισσεύει τὰ παθήματα τοῦ χριστοῦ
God. Because according as abound the sufferings of the Christ
εἰς ἡμᾶς, οὕτως διὰ [d] χριστοῦ περισσεύει καὶ ἡ.παράκλησις
toward us, so through Christ abounds also ²encouragement
ἡμῶν. 6 εἴτε.δὲ θλιβόμεθα, ὑπὲρ τῆς.ὑμῶν.παρακλήσεως
¹our. But whether we are troubled, [it is] for your encouragement
καὶ σωτηρίας, [e]τῆς ἐνεργουμένης ἐν ὑπομονῇ τῶν αὐτῶν
and salvation, being wrought in [the] endurance of the same
παθημάτων ὧν καὶ ἡμεῖς πάσχομεν·‖ [f]εἴτε παρακαλούμεθα,
sufferings which ²also ¹we suffer, whether we are encouraged,
ὑπὲρ τῆς.ὑμῶν.παρακλήσεως[e] [g]καὶ σωτηρίας·[f]‖ καὶ ἡ ἐλπὶς
[it is] for your encouragement and salvation; (and ²hope
ἡμῶν βεβαία ὑπὲρ ὑμῶν[f]· 7 εἰδότες ὅτι [h]ὥσπερ‖ κοινωνοί
¹our [is] sure for you;) knowing that as partners
ἐστε τῶν παθημάτων, οὕτως καὶ τῆς παρακλήσεως. 8 Οὐ.γὰρ
ye are of the sufferings, so also of the encouragement. For ³not
θέλομεν ὑμᾶς ἀγνοεῖν, ἀδελφοί, [i]ὑπὲρ‖ τῆς.θλίψεως.ἡμῶν
²do ¹we wish you to be ignorant, brethren, as to our tribulation
τῆς γενομένης [k]ἡμῖν‖ ἐν τῇ Ἀσίᾳ, ὅτι καθ'.ὑπερβολὴν [l]ἐβαρή-
which happened to us in Asia, that excessively we were
θημεν ὑπὲρ δύναμιν,‖ ὥστε ἐξαπορηθῆναι.ἡμᾶς καὶ τοῦ.ζῆν·
burdened beyond [our] power, so as for us to despair even of living.
9 [m]ἀλλὰ‖ αὐτοὶ ἐν ἑαυτοῖς τὸ ἀπόκριμα τοῦ θανάτου ἐσχή-
But ourselves in ourselves the sentence of death we have
καμεν, ἵνα μὴ.πεποιθότες.ὦμεν ἐφ' ἑαυτοῖς, ἀλλ' ἐπὶ τῷ
had, that we should not have trust in ourselves, but in
θεῷ τῷ ἐγείροντι τοὺς νεκρούς· 10 ὃς ἐκ τηλικούτου θανάτου
God who raises the dead; who from so great a death
[n]ἐρρύσατο‖ ἡμᾶς [o]καὶ ῥύεται,‖ εἰς ὃν ἠλπίκαμεν [p]ὅτι‖ καὶ
delivered us and does deliver; in whom we have hope that also
ἔτι ῥύσεται, 11 συνυπουργούντων καὶ ὑμῶν ὑπὲρ ἡμῶν
still he will deliver; labouring together ²also ¹ye for us
τῇ δεήσει, ἵνα ἐκ πολλῶν προσώπων τὸ εἰς ἡμᾶς χάρισμα
by supplication, that by many persons the ²towards ³us ¹gift
διὰ πολλῶν εὐχαριστηθῇ ὑπὲρ ἡμῶν. 12 Ἡ
⁹through ¹⁰many ⁴might ⁵be ⁶subject ⁷of ⁸thanksgiving for us.
γὰρ καύχησις.ἡμῶν αὕτη ἐστίν, τὸ μαρτύριον τῆς συνειδήσεως
For our boasting this is, the testimony of ²conscience
ἡμῶν, ὅτι ἐν [q]ἁπλότητι‖ καὶ [r]εἰλικρινείᾳ‖ [s] θεοῦ, οὐκ ἐν σοφίᾳ
¹our, that in simplicity and sincerity of God, (not in ²wisdom
σαρκικῇ, ἀλλ' ἐν χάριτι θεοῦ, ἀνεστράφημεν ἐν τῷ κόσμῳ,
¹fleshly, but in grace of God,) we had our conduct in the world,
περισσοτέρως.δὲ πρὸς ὑμᾶς. 13 οὐ.γὰρ ἄλλα γράφομεν
and more abundantly towards you. For not other things do we write

Father of mercies, and the God of all comfort; 4 who comforteth us in all our tribulation, that we may be able to comfort them which are in any trouble, by the comfort wherewith we ourselves are comforted of God. 5 For as the sufferings of Christ abound in us, so our consolation also aboundeth by Christ.
6 And whether we be afflicted, *it is* for your consolation and salvation, which is effectual in the enduring of the same sufferings which we also suffer: or whether we be comforted, *it is* for your consolation and salvation. 7 And our hope of you *is* stedfast, knowing, that as ye are partakers of the sufferings, so *shall ye be* also of the consolation. 8 For we would not, brethren, have you ignorant of our trouble which came to us in Asia, that we were pressed out of measure, above strength, insomuch that we despaired even of life: 9 but we had the sentence of death in ourselves, that we should not trust in ourselves, but in God which raiseth the dead: 10 who delivered us from so great a death, and doth deliver: in whom we trust that he will yet deliver *us*; 11 ye also helping together by prayer for us, that for the gift *bestowed* upon us by the means of many persons thanks may be given by many on our behalf. 12 For our rejoicing is this, the testimony of our conscience, that in simplicity and godly sincerity, not with fleshly wisdom, but by the grace of God, we have had our conversation in the world, and more abundantly to you-ward. 13 For we write none other things unto you, than

+ τοῦ the GLTTrAW. [e] τῆς ἐνεργουμένης .... πάσχομεν *placed after* παρακλήσεως GT. [f] εἴτε παρακαλούμεθα .... σωτηρίας *placed after* ὑπὲρ ὑμῶν LTrAW. [g] — καὶ σωτηρίας GT. [h] ὡς LTTrAW. [i] περὶ LTTr. [k] — ἡμῖν LTTrAW. [l] ὑπὲρ δύναμιν ἐβαρήθημεν LTTrA. [m] ἀλλ' L [n] ἐρύσατο Tr. [o] καὶ ῥύσεται and will deliver [L]TTrA. [p] [ὅτι] LTr. [q] ἁγιότητι holiness LTTrA. [r] εἰλικρινίᾳ T. [s] + τοῦ LTTrAW.

what ye read or acknowledge: and I trust ye shall acknowledge even to the end; 14 as also ye have acknowledged us in part, that we are your rejoicing, even as ye also *are* ours in the day of the Lord Jesus. 15 And in this confidence I was minded to come unto you before, that ye might have a second benefit; 16 and to pass by you into Macedonia, and to come again out of Macedonia unto you, and of you to be brought on my way toward Judæa. 17 When I therefore was thus minded, did I use lightness? or the things that I purpose, do I purpose according to the flesh, that with me there should be yea yea, and nay nay? 18 But *as* God *is* true, our word toward you was not yea and nay. 19 For the Son of God, Jesus Christ, who was preached among you by us, *even* by me and Silvanus and Timotheus, was not yea and nay, but in him was yea. 20 For all the promises of God in him *are* yea, and in him Amen, unto the glory of God by us. 21 Now he which stablisheth us with you in Christ, and hath anointed us, *is* God; 22 who hath also sealed us, and given the earnest of the Spirit in our hearts.

ὑμῖν [t]ἀλλ'‖ ἢ ἃ ἀναγινώσκετε, ἢ καὶ ἐπιγινώσκετε, ἐλπίζω.δὲ
to you but what ye read, or even recognize; and I hope
ὅτι [v]καὶ‖ ἕως τέλους ἐπιγνώσεσθε, 14 καθὼς καὶ ἐπέ-
that even to [the] end ye will recognize, according as also ye did
γνωτε ἡμᾶς ἀπὸ μέρους, ὅτι καύχημα.ὑμῶν ἐσμεν, καθάπερ
recognize us in part, that [3]your [4]boasting [1]we [2]are, even as
καὶ ὑμεῖς ἡμῶν ἐν τῇ ἡμέρᾳ τοῦ κυρίου [w] Ἰησοῦ. 15 Καὶ
also ye [are] ours in the day of the Lord Jesus. And
ταύτῃ τῇ πεποιθήσει ἐβουλόμην [x]πρὸς ὑμᾶς ἐλθεῖν πρότερον,‖
with this confidence I purposed [3]to [4]you [1]to [2]come previously,
ἵνα δευτέραν χάριν [y]ἔχητε·‖ 16 καὶ δι' ὑμῶν [z]διελθεῖν‖
that a second favour ye might have; and by you to pass through
εἰς Μακεδονίαν, καὶ πάλιν ἀπὸ Μακεδονίας ἐλθεῖν πρὸς ὑμᾶς,
to Macedonia, and again from Macedonia to come to you,
καὶ ὑφ' ὑμῶν προπεμφθῆναι εἰς τὴν Ἰουδαίαν. 17 τοῦτο.οὖν
and by you to be set forward to Judæa. This therefore
[a]βουλευόμενος,‖ μή τι ἄρα τῇ ἐλαφρίᾳ ἐχρησάμην; ἢ ἃ
purposing, [3]indeed [5]lightness [1]did [2]I [4]use? or what
βουλεύομαι, κατὰ σάρκα βουλεύομαι, ἵνα ᾖ παρ'
I purpose, according to flesh do I purpose, that there should be with
ἐμοὶ τὸ ναὶ ναί, καὶ τὸ οὒ οὔ; 18 πιστὸς.δὲ ὁ θεός, ὅτι ὁ
me yea yea, and nay nay? Now faithful God [is], that
λόγος.ἡμῶν ὁ πρὸς ὑμᾶς οὐκ [b]ἐγένετο‖ ναὶ καὶ οὔ· 19 ὁ.[c]γὰρ
our word to you [2]not [1]was yea and nay. For the
τοῦ θεοῦ‖ υἱὸς [d]Ἰησοῦς χριστὸς‖ ὁ ἐν ὑμῖν δι' ἡμῶν κη-
[2]of [3]God [1]Son, Jesus Christ, who among you by us was
ρυχθείς, δι' ἐμοῦ καὶ Σιλουανοῦ καὶ Τιμοθέου, οὐκ.ἐγένετο ναὶ
proclaimed, (by me and Silvanus and Timotheus,) was not yea
καὶ οὔ, ἀλλὰ ναὶ ἐν αὐτῷ γέγονεν· 20 ὅσαι.γὰρ ἐπαγγελίαι
and nay, but yea in him has been. For whatever promises
θεοῦ, ἐν αὐτῷ τὸ ναί, [e]καὶ ἐν αὐτῷ‖ τὸ ἀμήν,
of God [there are], in him [is] the yea, and in him the Amen,
τῷ θεῷ πρὸς δόξαν δι' ἡμῶν. 21 ὁ.δὲ βεβαιῶν ἡμᾶς σὺν
[3]to [4]God [1]for [2]glory by us. Now he who confirms us with
ὑμῖν εἰς χριστόν, καὶ χρίσας ἡμᾶς, θεός· 22 ὁ καὶ σφραγι-
you unto Christ, and anointed us, [is] God, who also sealed
σάμενος ἡμᾶς, καὶ δοὺς τὸν [f]ἀρραβῶνα‖ τοῦ πνεύματος ἐν
us, and gave the earnest of the Spirit in
ταῖς.καρδίαις.ἡμῶν.
our hearts.

23 Moreover I call God for a record upon my soul, that to spare you I came not as yet unto Corinth. 24 Not for that we have dominion over your faith, but are helpers of your joy: for by faith ye stand. II. But I determined this with myself, that I would not come again to you in heaviness. 2 For if I make you sorry, who is he then that maketh me glad, but the same

23 Ἐγὼ.δὲ μάρτυρα τὸν θεὸν ἐπικαλοῦμαι ἐπὶ τὴν ἐμὴν
But I [3]as [4]witness [2]God [1]call upon my
ψυχήν, ὅτι φειδόμενος ὑμῶν οὐκέτι ἦλθον εἰς Κόρινθον·
soul, that sparing you not yet did I come to Corinth.
24 οὐχ ὅτι κυριεύομεν ὑμῶν τῆς πίστεως, ἀλλὰ συνεργοί
Not that we rule over your faith, but fellow-workers
ἐσμεν τῆς.χαρᾶς.ὑμῶν, τῇ.γὰρ.πίστει ἑστήκατε. 2 ἔκρινα.δὲ
are of your joy: for by faith ye stand. But I judged
ἐμαυτῷ τοῦτο, τὸ μὴ πάλιν [g]ἐλθεῖν ἐν λύπῃ πρὸς ὑμᾶς.‖
with myself this, not again to come in grief to you.
2 εἰ.γὰρ ἐγὼ λυπῶ ὑμᾶς, καὶ τίς [h]ἐστιν‖ ὁ εὐφραίνων με, εἰ.μὴ
For if I grieve you, [2]also [1]who is it that gladdens me, except

[t] [ἀλλ'] L; ἀλλὰ W. [v] — καὶ LTTrA. [w] + ἡμῶν (*read* our Lord) [L]TA. [x] πρότερον πρὸς ὑμᾶς ἐλθεῖν LTTrA; πρό. ἐλθ. πρὸς ὑμᾶς W. [y] σχῆτε TTrA. [z] ἀπελθεῖν to pass on L. [a] βουλόμενος LTTrAW. [b] ἔστιν is LTTrAW. [c] τοῦ θεοῦ γὰρ LTTrAW. [d] χριστὸς Ἰησοῦς T. [e] διὸ καὶ δι' αὐτοῦ wherefore also through him LTTrAW. [f] ἀραβῶνα LT. [g] ἐν λύπῃ πρὸς ὑμᾶς ἐλθεῖν GLTTrAW. [h] — ἐστιν LTTrAW.

ὁ λυπούμενος ἐξ ἐμοῦ; 3 καὶ ἔγραψα ⁱὑμῖν" τοῦτο αὐτό,
he who is grieved by me? And I wrote to you this same,
ἵνα.μὴ ἐλθὼν λύπην ᵏἔχω" ἀφ' ὧν ἔδει με
lest having come grief I might have from [those] of whom it behoves me
χαίρειν· πεποιθὼς ἐπὶ πάντας ὑμᾶς, ὅτι ἡ.ἐμὴ.χαρὰ
to rejoice; trusting in ²all ¹you, that my joy [²that]
πάντων ὑμῶν ἐστιν. 4 ἐκ.γὰρ πολλῆς θλίψεως καὶ συνοχῆς
³of ⁵all ⁴you ¹is. For out of much tribulation and distress
καρδίας ἔγραψα ὑμῖν διὰ πολλῶν δακρύων, οὐχ ἵνα λυπη-
of heart I wrote to you through many tears; not that ye might
θῆτε, ἀλλὰ τὴν ἀγάπην ἵνα γνῶτε ἣν ἔχω περισ-
be grieved, but ²the ³love ¹that ye might know which I have more
σοτέρως εἰς ὑμᾶς. 5 Εἰ.δέ τις λελύπηκεν, οὐκ ἐμὲ
abundantly towards you. But if anyone has grieved, ³not ⁵me
λελύπηκεν, ˡἀλλ'" ἀπὸ.μέρους, ἵνα μὴ.ἐπιβαρῶ, πάντας
¹he ²has ⁴grieved, but in part (that I may not overcharge) ²all
ὑμᾶς. 6 ἱκανὸν τῷ.τοιούτῳ ἡ.ἐπιτιμία.αὕτη ἡ ὑπὸ τῶν
¹you. Sufficient to such a one [is] this rebuke which [is] by the
πλειόνων· 7 ὥστε τοὐναντίον ᵐμᾶλλον" ὑμᾶς χαρίσασθαι
greater part; so that on the contrary rather ye should forgive
καὶ παρακαλέσαι, μήπως τῇ.περισσοτέρᾳ λύπῃ κατα-
and encourage, lest with more abundant grief should be swal-
ποθῇ ὁ.τοιοῦτος. 8 διὸ παρακαλῶ ὑμᾶς κυρῶσαι εἰς
lowed up such a one. Wherefore I exhort you to confirm ²towards
αὐτὸν ἀγάπην. 9 εἰς.τοῦτο.γὰρ καὶ ἔγραψα, ἵνα γνῶ
³him ¹love. For, for this also did I write, that I might know
τὴν δοκιμὴν ὑμῶν, εἰ εἰς πάντα ὑπήκοοί ἐστε. 10 ᾧ.δέ
the proof of you, if to everything obedient ye are. But to whom
τι χαρίζεσθε, ⁿκαὶ ἐγώ·" καὶ.γὰρ ἐγὼ ᵒεἴ τι κεχάρισ-
anything ye forgive, also I; for also I if anything I have for-
μαι, ᾧ κεχάρισμαι," δι' ὑμᾶς, ἐν προσώπῳ χριστοῦ,
given, of whom I have forgiven, [is] for sake of you, in [the] person of Christ;
11 ἵνα μὴ.πλεονεκτηθῶμεν ὑπὸ τοῦ σατανᾶ· οὐ.γὰρ αὐτοῦ
that we should not be overreached by Satan, for not of his
τὰ νοήματα ἀγνοοῦμεν.
thoughts are we ignorant.

12 Ἐλθὼν.δὲ εἰς τὴν ᵖΤρωάδα" εἰς τὸ εὐαγγέλιον τοῦ
Now having come to Troas for the glad tidings of the
χριστοῦ, καὶ θύρας μοι ἀνεῳγμένης ἐν κυρίῳ, 13 οὐκ
Christ, also a door to me having been opened in [the] Lord, ³not
ἔσχηκα ἄνεσιν τῷ.πνεύματί.μου τῷ.μὴ.εὑρεῖν.με Τίτον τὸν
¹I ²had ease in my spirit at my not finding Titus
ἀδελφόν.μου· ἀλλὰ ἀποταξάμενος αὐτοῖς, ἐξῆλθον εἰς Μακε-
my brother; but having taken leave of them, I went out to Mace-
δονίαν. 14 Τῷ.δὲ.θεῷ χάρις τῷ πάντοτε θριαμβεύοντι
donia. But to God [be] thanks, who always leads in triumph
ἡμᾶς ἐν τῷ χριστῷ, καὶ τὴν ὀσμὴν τῆς γνώσεως αὐτοῦ
us in the Christ, and the odour of the knowledge of him
φανεροῦντι δι' ἡμῶν ἐν παντὶ τόπῳ. 15 ὅτι χριστοῦ
makes manifest through us in every place. For of Christ
εὐωδία ἐσμὲν τῷ θεῷ ἐν τοῖς σωζομένοις καὶ ἐν τοῖς ἀπολ-
a sweet perfume we are to God in those being saved and in those perish-
λυμένοις· 16 οἷς.μέν, ὀσμὴ ᵠθανάτου εἰς θάνατον· οἷς.δέ,
ing; to the ones, an odour of death to death, but to the others,

which is made sorry
by me? 3 And I wrote
this same unto you,
lest, when I came, I
should have sorrow
from them of whom I
ought to rejoice; hav-
ing confidence in you
all, that my joy is *the*
joy of you all. 4 For
out of much affliction
and anguish of heart
I wrote unto you with
many tears; not that
ye should be grieved,
but that ye might
know the love which
I have more abundant-
ly unto you. 5 But if
any have caused grief,
he hath not grieved
me, but in part: that
I may not overcharge
you all. 6 Sufficient to
such a man *is* this
punishment, which
was inflicted of many.
7 So that contrariwise
ye *ought* rather to for-
give *him*, and comfort
him, lest perhaps such a
one should be swallow-
ed up with overmuch
sorrow. 8 Wherefore I
beseech you that ye
would confirm *your*
love toward him.
9 For to this end also
did I write, that I
might know the proof
of you, whether ye be
obedient in all things.
10 To whom ye forgive
any thing, I *forgive*
also: for if I forgave
any thing, to whom I
forgave *it*, for your
sakes *forgave I it* in
the person of Christ;
11 lest Satan should
get an advantage of
us: for we are not ig-
norant of his devices.

12 Furthermore, when
I came to Troas to
preach Christ's gospel,
and a door was opened
unto me of the Lord,
13 I had no rest in my
spirit, because I found
not Titus my brother:
but taking my leave
of them, I went from
thence into Macedo-
nia. 14 Now thanks
be unto God, which
always causeth us to
triumph in Christ, and
maketh manifest the
savour of his know-
ledge by us in every
place. 15 For we are
unto God a sweet sa-
vour of Christ, in
them that are saved,
and in them that pe-
rish: 16 to the one *we*

ⁱ — ὑμῖν LTTrAW. ᵏ σχῶ TTrA. ˡ ἀλλὰ LTTrAW. ᵐ [μᾶλλον] TrA. ⁿ κἀγώ LTTrAW. ᵒ ὃ κεχάρισμαι, εἴ τι κεχάρισμαι GLTTrAW. ᵖ Τρῳάδα LT. ᵠ + ἐκ (read from death) LTTrA.

are the savour of death
unto death; and to
the other the savour
of life unto life. And
who *is* sufficient for
these things? 17 For
we are not as many,
which corrupt the
word of God: but as
of sincerity, but as of
God, in the sight of
God speak we in
Christ.

III. Do we begin
again to commend
ourselves? or need we,
as some *others*, epis-
tles of commendation
to you, or *letters* of
commendation from
you? 2 Ye are our
epistle written in our
hearts, known and
read of all men: 3 *for-
asmuch as ye are* man-
ifestly declared to be
the epistle of Christ
ministered by us,
written not with ink,
but with the Spirit of
the living God; not
in tables of stone, but
in fleshy tables of the
heart. 4 And such
trust have we through
Christ to God-ward:
5 not that we are
sufficient of our-
selves to think any
thing as of ourselves;
but our sufficiency *is*
of God; 6 who also
hath made us able
ministers of the new
testament; not of the
letter, but of the spi-
rit: for the letter kill-
eth, but the spirit
giveth life. 7 But if
the ministration of
death, written *and* en-
graven in stones, was
glorious, so that the
children of Israel
could not stedfastly
behold the face of Mo-
ses for the glory of his
countenance; which
glory was to be done
away: 8 how shall not
the ministration of
the spirit be rather
glorious? 9 For if
the ministration of
condemnation *be* glo-
ry, much more doth
the ministration of
righteousness exceed
in glory. 10 For even
that which was made
glorious had no glory

ὀσμὴ [q] ζωῆς εἰς ζωήν. καὶ πρὸς ταῦτα τίς ἱκανός;
an odour of life to life; and for these things who [is] competent?
17 οὐ.γάρ ἐσμεν ὡς οἱ πολλοί, καπηλεύοντες τὸν λόγον
For [3]not [1]we [2]are as the many, making gain by corrupting the word
τοῦ θεοῦ, [r]ἀλλ'‖ ὡς ἐξ [s]εἰλικρινείας,‖ ἀλλ' ὡς ἐκ θεοῦ, [t]κατ-
of God, but as of sincerity, but as of God. be-
ενώπιον‖ [u]τοῦ‖ θεοῦ, ἐν χριστῷ λαλοῦμεν.
fore God, in Christ we speak.

3 Ἀρχόμεθα πάλιν ἑαυτοὺς [v]συνιστάνειν‖; [w]εἰ‖.μὴ χρῄ-
Do we begin again ourselves to commend? unless we
ζομεν, ὥς [x] τινες, [y]συστατικῶν‖ ἐπιστολῶν πρὸς ὑμᾶς, ἢ ἐξ
need, as some, commendatory epistles to you, or [3]from
ὑμῶν [z]συστατικῶν‖; 2 ἡ.ἐπιστολὴ.ἡμῶν ὑμεῖς ἐστε, [a]ἐγγεγραμ-
[4]you [1]commendatory [[2]ones]? Our epistle ye are, having been
μένη‖ ἐν ταῖς.καρδίαις.ἡμῶν, γινωσκομένη καὶ ἀναγινω-
inscribed in our hearts, being known and being
σκομένη ὑπὸ πάντων ἀνθρώπων· 3 φανερούμενοι ὅτι ἐστὲ
read by all men, being manifested that ye are
ἐπιστολὴ χριστοῦ διακονηθεῖσα ὑφ' ἡμῶν, [a]ἐγγεγραμμένη‖
[2]epistle [1]Christ's, ministered by us; having been inscribed,
οὐ μέλανι, ἀλλὰ πνεύματι θεοῦ ζῶντος, οὐκ ἐν πλαξὶν
not with ink, but with [the] Spirit of [3]God [[1]the] [2]living; not on tablets
λιθίναις, [b]ἀλλ'‖ ἐν πλαξὶν [c]καρδίας‖ σαρκίναις. 4 Πεποί-
of stone, but on [2]tablets [3]of [[4]the] [5]heart [1]fleshy. [7]Confi-
θησιν δὲ τοιαύτην ἔχομεν διὰ τοῦ χριστοῦ πρὸς τὸν θεόν·
dence [6]and such have we through the Christ towards God:
5 οὐχ ὅτι [d]ἱκανοί ἐσμεν ἀφ' ἑαυτῶν λογίσασθαί τι‖ ὡς ἐξ
not that competent we are from ourselves to reckon anything as of
[e]ἑαυτῶν,‖ ἀλλ' ἡ.ἱκανότης.ἡμῶν ἐκ τοῦ θεοῦ· 6 ὃς καὶ
ourselves, but our competency [is] of God; who also
ἱκάνωσεν ἡμᾶς διακόνους καινῆς διαθήκης, οὐ γράμ-
made [2]competent [1]us [as] servants of a new covenant; not of let-
ματος, ἀλλὰ πνεύματος· τὸ.γὰρ γράμμα [f]ἀποκτείνει,‖ τὸ.δὲ
ter, but of Spirit; for the letter kills, but the
πνεῦμα ζωοποιεῖ. 7 Εἰ.δὲ ἡ διακονία τοῦ θανάτου ἐν [g]γράμ-
Spirit quickens. But if the service of death in let-
μασιν,‖ ἐντετυπωμένη [h]ἐν‖ λίθοις, ἐγενήθη ἐν δόξῃ, ὥστε
ters, having been engraven in stones, was produced with glory, so as
μὴ.δύνασθαι ἀτενίσαι τοὺς υἱοὺς Ἰσραὴλ εἰς τὸ πρόσω-
[5]not [6]to [7]be [8]able [9]to [10]look [11]intently [1]the [2]children [3]of [4]Israel into the face
πον [i]Μωσέως,‖ διὰ τὴν δόξαν τοῦ.προσώπου.αὐτοῦ, τὴν
of Moses, on account of the glory of his face, which
καταργουμένην· 8 πῶς οὐχὶ μᾶλλον ἡ διακονία τοῦ πνεύμα-
is being annulled; how not rather the service of the Spirit
τος ἔσται ἐν δόξῃ; 9 εἰ.γὰρ [k]ἡ διακονία‖ τῆς κατακρίσεως
shall be in glory? For if the service of condemnation [be]
δόξα, πολλῷ μᾶλλον περισσεύει ἡ διακονία τῆς δικαιοσύνης
glory, much rather abounds the service of righteousness
[l]ἐν‖ δόξῃ. 10 καὶ.γὰρ [m]οὐδὲ‖ δεδόξασται τὸ
in glory. For even neither [7]has [8]been [9]made [10]glorious [1]that [2]which

---

[q] + ἐκ (*read* from life) LTTrA. [r] ἀλλὰ Tr. [s] εἰλικρινίας T. [t] κατέναντι LTTrA.
[u] — τοῦ LTT[A]. [v] συνιστᾶν LTr. [w] ἢ (*read* or need we) GLTTrA. [x] + [πέρ] L. [y] συνσ- Tr.
[z] — συστατικῶν LTTrAW. [a] ἐν- T. [b] ἀλλὰ EGW. [c] καρδίαις hearts LTTrA. [d] ἱκανοί ἐσμεν λογίζεσθαί (λογίσασθαί AW) τι ἀφ' ἑαυτῶν LAW; ἀφ' ἑαυτῶν ἱκανοί ἐσμεν λογίσασθαι τι TTr. [e] αὐτῶν them LTr. [f] ἀποκταίνει L; ἀποκτέννει TTrA. [g] γράμματι writing LTrA.
[h] — ἐν (*read* λίθοις on stones) LTTrAW. [i] Μωϋσέως GLTTrAW. [k] τῇ διακονίᾳ with the service LTTr. [l] — ἐν (*read* δόξῃ in glory) LTTrA. [m] οὐ not GLTTrAW.

δεδοξασμένον ἐν τούτῳ τῷ μέρει, [n]ἕνεκεν‖ τῆς ὑπερ-
[3]has [4]been [5]made [6]glorious in this respect, on account of the sur-
βαλλούσης δόξης. 11 εἰ.γὰρ τὸ καταργούμενον διὰ
passing glory. For if that which is being annulled [was] through
δόξης, πολλῷ μᾶλλον τὸ μένον ἐν δόξῃ. 12 Ἔχοντες
glory, much rather that which remains [is] in glory. Having
οὖν τοιαύτην ἐλπίδα, πολλῇ παῤῥησίᾳ χρώμεθα· 13 καὶ
therefore such hope, much boldness we use: and
οὐ καθάπερ [o]Μωσῆς‖ ἐτίθει κάλυμμα ἐπὶ τὸ πρόσωπον [p]ἑαυ-
not according as Moses put a veil on the face of him-
τοῦ,‖ πρὸς τὸ μὴ ἀτενίσαι τοὺς υἱοὺς Ἰσραὴλ εἰς τὸ τέλος
self, for [5]not [6]to [7]look [8]intently [1]the [2]sons [3]of [4]Israel to the end
τοῦ καταργουμένου· 14 [q]ἀλλ'‖ ἐπωρώθη τὰ.νοήματα.αὐτῶν.
of that being annulled. But were hardened their thoughts,
ἄχρι.γὰρ τῆς σήμερον [r]τὸ αὐτὸ κάλυμμα ἐπὶ τῇ ἀναγνώσει
for unto the present the same veil at the reading
τῆς παλαιᾶς διαθήκης μένει, μὴ ἀνακαλυπτόμενον, [s]ὅ τι‖
of the old covenant remains, not uncovered, which
ἐν χριστῷ καταργεῖται· 15 ἀλλ' ἕως σήμερον, ἡνίκα [t]ἀνα-
in Christ is being annulled. But unto this day, when is
γινώσκεται‖ [o]Μωσῆς,‖ κάλυμμα ἐπὶ τὴν.καρδίαν.αὐτῶν κεῖται·
read Moses, a veil upon their heart lies.
16 ἡνίκα.[v]δ' ἂν‖ ἐπιστρέψῃ πρὸς κύριον, περιαιρεῖται τὸ
But when it shall have turned to [the] Lord, is taken away the
κάλυμμα. 17 Ὁ.δὲ κύριος τὸ πνεῦμά ἐστιν· οὗ.δὲ τὸ πνεῦμα
veil. Now the Lord the Spirit is; and where the Spirit
κυρίου, [w]ἐκεῖ‖ ἐλευθερία. 18 ἡμεῖς.δὲ πάντες ἀνακεκα-
of [the] Lord [is], there [is] freedom. But we all with un-
λυμμένῳ προσώπῳ τὴν δόξαν κυρίου κατοπτριζόμενοι,
covered face the glory of [the] Lord beholding as in a mirror, [to]
τὴν αὐτὴν εἰκόνα μεταμορφούμεθα ἀπὸ δόξης εἰς δόξαν,
the same image are being transformed from glory to glory,
καθάπερ ἀπὸ κυρίου πνεύματος.
even as from [the] Lord [the] Spirit.

4 Διὰ.τοῦτο ἔχοντες τὴν.διακονίαν.ταύτην, καθὼς ἠλεή-
Therefore, having this service, according as we re-
θημεν, οὐκ.[x]ἐκκακοῦμεν·‖ 2 [y]ἀλλ'‖ ἀπειπάμεθα τὰ κρυπτὰ
ceived mercy, we faint not. But we renounced the hidden things
τῆς αἰσχύνης, μὴ περιπατοῦντες ἐν πανουργίᾳ μηδὲ δολοῦν-
of shame, not walking in craftiness, nor falsify-
τες τὸν λόγον τοῦ θεοῦ, ἀλλὰ τῇ φανερώσει τῆς ἀληθείας
ing the word of God, but by manifestation of the truth
[z]συνιστῶντες‖ ἑαυτοὺς πρὸς πᾶσαν συνείδησιν ἀνθρώπων
commending ourselves to every conscience of men
ἐνώπιον τοῦ θεοῦ. 3 Εἰ.δὲ καὶ ἔστιν κεκαλυμμένον τὸ εὐαγ-
before God. But if also is covered [2]glad
γέλιον ἡμῶν, ἐν τοῖς ἀπολλυμένοις ἐστὶν κεκαλυμμένον· 4 ἐν
[3]tidings [1]our, in those perishing it is covered; in
οἷς ὁ θεὸς τοῦ.αἰῶνος.τούτου ἐτύφλωσεν τὰ νοήματα τῶν
whom the god of this age blinded the thoughts of the
ἀπίστων, εἰς.τὸ μὴ αὐγάσαι [a]αὐτοῖς‖ τὸν φωτισμὸν τοῦ
unbelieving, so as not to beam forth to them the radiancy of the

in this respect, by rea-
son of the glory that
excelleth. 11 For if
that which is done a-
way *was* glorious,
much more that which
remaineth *is* glorious.
12 Seeing then that we
have such hope, we
use great plainness of
speech: 13 and not as
Moses, *which* put a vail
over his face, that
the children of Israel
could not stedfastly
look to the end of that
which is abolished:
14 but their minds
were blinded: for un-
til this day remaineth
the same vail untaken
away in the reading
of the old testament;
which *vail* is done a-
way in Christ. 15 But
even unto this day,
when Moses is read,
the vail is upon their
heart. 16 Nevertheless
when it shall turn to
the Lord, the vail shall
be taken away. 17 Now
the Lord is that Spirit:
and where the Spirit of
the Lord *is*, there *is*
liberty. 18 But we all,
with open face behold-
ing as in a glass the
glory of the Lord, are
changed into the same
image from glory to
glory, *even* as by the
Spirit of the Lord.

IV. Therefore seeing we have this ministry, as we have re-
ceived mercy, we faint
not; 2 but have re-
nounced the hidden
things of dishonesty,
not walking in crafti-
ness, nor handling the
word of God deceit-
fully; but by mani-
festation of the truth
commending ourselves
to every man's con-
science in the sight of
God. 3 But if our gos-
pel be hid, it is hid to
them that are lost: 4 in
whom the god of this
world hath blinded the
minds of them which
believe not, lest the
light of the glorious
gospel of Christ, who
is the image of
God, should shine

[n] εἵνεκεν LTTrA. [o] Μωϋσῆς GLTTrAW. [p] αὐτοῦ (*read* his face) LTrAW. [q] ἀλλὰ Tr. [r] + ἡμέρας day LTTrAW. [s] ὅτι that [it] GLTTrAW. [t] ἂν ἀναγινώσκηται may be read LTTrA. [v] δὲ ἂν Tr; δὲ ἐὰν T. [w] — ἐκεῖ LTTrAW. [x] ἐγκ- LTTrAW. [y] ἀλλὰ LTTrA. [z] συνιστάντες LTTrAW. [a] — αὐτοῖς GLTTrAW.

unto them. 5 For we preach not ourselves, but Christ Jesus the Lord; and ourselves your servants for Jesus' sake. 6 For God, who commanded the light to shine out of darkness, hath shined in our hearts, to *give* the light of the knowledge of the glory of God in the face of Jesus Christ. 7 But we have this treasure in earthen vessels, that the excellency of the power may be of God, and not of us. 8 *We are* troubled on every side, yet not distressed; *we are* perplexed, but not in despair; 9 persecuted, but not forsaken; cast down, but not destroyed; 10 always bearing about in the body the dying of the Lord Jesus, that the life also of Jesus might be made manifest in our body. 11 For we which live are alway delivered unto death for Jesus' sake, that the life also of Jesus might be made manifest in our mortal flesh. 12 So then death worketh in us, but life in you. 13 We having the same spirit of faith, according as it is written, I believed, and therefore have I spoken; we also believe, and therefore speak; 14 knowing that he which raised up the Lord Jesus shall raise up us also by Jesus, and shall present *us* with you. 15 For all things *are* for your sakes, that the abundant grace might through the thanksgiving of many redound to the glory of God.

εὐαγγελίου [c]τῆς[||] δόξης τοῦ χριστοῦ, ὅς ἐστιν εἰκὼν τοῦ
glad tidings of the glory of the Christ, who is [the] image
θεοῦ. 5 οὐ.γὰρ ἑαυτοὺς κηρύσσομεν, ἀλλὰ [d]χριστὸν Ἰη-
of God. For not ourselves do we proclaim, but Christ Je-
σοῦν[||] κύριον· ἑαυτοὺς.δὲ δούλους.ὑμῶν διὰ Ἰησοῦν.
sus Lord, and ourselves your bondmen for the sake of Jesus.
6 ὅτι ὁ θεὸς ὁ εἰπὼν ἐκ σκότους φῶς [e]λάμψαι,[||] ὃς
Because [it is] God who spoke out of darkness light to shine, who
ἔλαμψεν ἐν ταῖς.καρδίαις.ἡμῶν, πρὸς φωτισμὸν τῆς γνώ-
shone in our hearts, for [the] radiancy of the know-
σεως τῆς δόξης [f]τοῦ θεοῦ[||] ἐν προσώπῳ [g]Ἰησοῦ[||] χριστοῦ.
ledge of the glory of God in [the] face of Jesus Christ.
7 Ἔχομεν.δὲ τὸν.θησαυρὸν.τοῦτον ἐν ὀστρακίνοις σκεύεσιν,
But we have this treasure in earthen vessels,
ἵνα ἡ ὑπερβολὴ τῆς δυνάμεως ᾖ τοῦ θεοῦ, καὶ μὴ ἐξ
that the surpassingness of the power may be of God, and not from
ἡμῶν· 8 ἐν παντὶ θλιβόμενοι, ἀλλ' οὐ στενοχωρούμενοι·
us: in every [way] oppressed, but not straitened;
ἀπορούμενοι, ἀλλ' οὐκ ἐξαπορούμενοι· 9 διωκόμενοι, ἀλλ' οὐκ
perplexed, but not utterly at a loss; persecuted, but not
ἐγκαταλειπόμενοι· καταβαλλόμενοι, ἀλλ' οὐκ ἀπολλύμενοι·
forsaken; cast down, but not destroyed;
10 πάντοτε τὴν νέκρωσιν τοῦ [h]κυρίου[||] Ἰησοῦ ἐν τῷ σώματι
always the dying of the Lord Jesus in the body
περιφέροντες, ἵνα καὶ ἡ ζωὴ τοῦ Ἰησοῦ ἐν [i]τῷ σώματι[||] ἡμῶν
bearing about, that also the life of Jesus in [2]body [1]our
φανερωθῇ. 11 ἀεὶ.γὰρ ἡμεῖς οἱ ζῶντες εἰς θάνατον παρα-
may be manifested; for always we who live to death are de-
διδόμεθα διὰ Ἰησοῦν, ἵνα καὶ ἡ ζωὴ τοῦ Ἰησοῦ φανε-
livered on account of Jesus, that also the life of Jesus may be
ρωθῇ ἐν τῇ θνητῇ σαρκὶ ἡμῶν. 12 Ὥστε ὁ [k]μὲν[||] θάνατος
manifested in [2]mortal [3]flesh [1]our; so that death
ἐν ἡμῖν ἐνεργεῖται, ἡ.δὲ.ζωὴ ἐν ὑμῖν· 13 ἔχοντες.δὲ τὸ αὐτὸ
in us works, and life in you. And having the same
πνεῦμα τῆς πίστεως, κατὰ τὸ γεγραμμένον, Ἐπίστευσα,
spirit of faith, according to what has been written, I believed,
διὸ [l]ἐλάλησα, καὶ ἡμεῖς πιστεύομεν, διὸ καὶ λαλοῦμεν·
therefore I spoke; [2]also [1]we believe, therefore also we speak;
14 εἰδότες ὅτι ὁ ἐγείρας τὸν [m]κύριον[||] Ἰησοῦν, καὶ ἡμᾶς
knowing that he who raised up the Lord Jesus, also us
[n]διὰ[||] Ἰησοῦ ἐγερεῖ, καὶ παραστήσει σὺν ὑμῖν. 15 τὰ
through Jesus will raise up, and will present with you.
γὰρ πάντα δι' ὑμᾶς, ἵνα ἡ χάρις πλεονάσασα
For all things [are] for the sake of you, that the grace, abounding
διὰ τῶν πλειόνων τὴν εὐχαριστίαν περισσεύσῃ εἰς τὴν
through the most, [3]thanksgiving [1]may [2]cause to exceed to the
δόξαν τοῦ θεοῦ.
glory of God.

16 For which cause we faint not; but though our outward man perish, yet the inward *man* is renewed day by day. 17 For

16 Διὸ οὐκ.[o]ἐκκακοῦμεν·[||] ἀλλ' εἰ καὶ ὁ ἔξω ἡμῶν ἄν-
Wherefore we faint not; but if indeed [2]outward [1]our
θρωπος διαφθείρεται, ἀλλ' ὁ [p]ἔσωθεν[||] ἀνακαινοῦται
man is being brought to decay, yet the inward is being renewed

---

[c] τὸν the B. [d] Ἰησοῦν χριστὸν L. [e] λάμψει shall shine LTTrA. [f] αὐτοῦ (*read* his glory) L. [g] — Ἰησοῦ LTTrA. [h] — κυρίου GLTTrAW. [i] τοῖς σώμασιν bodies T. [k] — μὲν GLTTrAW. [l] + καὶ also T. [m] [κύριον] TrA. [n] σὺν with LTTrAW. [o] ἐγκ- LTTrAW. [p] ἔσω ἡμῶν (*read* our inward [man]) LTTr; ἔσω[θεν] ἡμῶν A.

ἡμέρᾳ.καὶ.ἡμέρᾳ. 17 τὸ.γὰρ παραυτίκα ἐλαφρὸν τῆς θλίψεως
day by day. For the momentary lightness of [2]tribulation
ἡμῶν καθ᾽.ὑπερβολὴν.εἰς.ὑπερβολὴν αἰώνιον βάρος δόξης
[1]our [4]excessively [5]surpassing [3]an eternal weight of glory
κατεργάζεται ἡμῖν, 18 μὴ σκοπούντων ἡμῶν τὰ βλεπό-
works out for us; [2]not [3]considering [1]we the things seen,
μενα, ἀλλὰ τὰ μὴ βλεπόμενα· τὰ.γὰρ βλεπόμενα
but the things not seen; for the things seen [are]
πρόσκαιρα· τὰ.δὲ μὴ βλεπόμενα αἰώνια. 5 οἴδαμεν.γὰρ
temporary, but the things not seen eternal. For we know
ὅτι ἐὰν ἡ ἐπίγειος ἡμῶν οἰκία τοῦ σκήνους καταλυθῇ, οἰκο-
that if [2]earthly [1]our house of the tabernacle be destroyed, a build-
δομὴν ἐκ θεοῦ ἔχομεν, οἰκίαν ἀχειροποίητον, αἰώνιον ἐν τοῖς
ing from God we have, a house not made with hands, eternal in the
οὐρανοῖς. 2 καὶ.γὰρ ἐν τούτῳ στενάζομεν, τὸ.οἰκητήριον.ἡμῶν
heavens. For indeed in this we groan, our dwelling
τὸ ἐξ οὐρανοῦ ἐπενδύσασθαι ἐπιποθοῦντες· 3 [q]εἴγε
which [is] from heaven [2]to [3]be [4]clothed [5]with [1]longing; if indeed
καὶ ἐνδυσάμενοι, οὐ γυμνοὶ εὑρεθησόμεθα. 4 καὶ.γὰρ οἱ
also being clothed, not naked we shall be found. For indeed [2]who
ὄντες ἐν τῷ σκήνει στενάζομεν βαρούμενοι· [r]ἐπειδὴ οὐ
[3]are [4]in [5]the [6]tabernacle [1]we groan being burdened; since [3]not
θέλομεν ἐκδύσασθαι, [s]ἀλλ᾽ ἐπενδύσασθαι, ἵνα καταποθῇ
[1]we [2]do wish to be unclothed, but to be clothed upon, that may be swallowed up
τὸ θνητὸν ὑπὸ τῆς ζωῆς. 5 ὁ.δὲ κατεργασάμενος ἡμᾶς εἰς
the mortal by life. Now he who wrought out us for
αὐτὸ.τοῦτο θεός, ὁ [t]καὶ δοὺς ἡμῖν τὸν [v]ἀῤῥαβῶνα τοῦ
this same thing [is] God, who also gave to us the earnest of the
πνεύματος. 6 θαῤῥοῦντες οὖν πάντοτε, καὶ εἰδότες ὅτι
Spirit. Being [2]confident [3]therefore [1]always, and knowing that
ἐνδημοῦντες ἐν τῷ σώματι ἐκδημοῦμεν ἀπὸ τοῦ κυρίου·
being at home in the body we are from home away from the Lord,
7 διὰ.πίστεως.γὰρ περιπατοῦμεν, οὐ διὰ εἴδους· 8 θαῤῥοῦμεν δέ,
(for by faith we walk, not by sight;) we are confident,
καὶ εὐδοκοῦμεν μᾶλλον ἐκδημῆσαι ἐκ τοῦ σώματος καὶ
and are pleased rather to be from home out of the body and
ἐνδημῆσαι πρὸς τὸν κύριον. 9 Διὸ καὶ φιλοτιμούμεθα,
to be at home with the Lord. Wherefore also we are ambitious,
εἴτε ἐνδημοῦντες εἴτε ἐκδημοῦντες, εὐάρεστοι αὐτῷ εἶναι.
whether being at home or being from home, well-pleasing to him to be.
10 τοὺς.γὰρ.πάντας ἡμᾶς φανερωθῆναι δεῖ ἔμπροσθεν τοῦ
For [2]all [1]we [4]be [5]manifested [3]must before the
βήματος τοῦ χριστοῦ, ἵνα κομίσηται ἕκαστος τὰ
judgment seat of the Christ, that [2]may [3]receive [1]each the things [done]
διὰ τοῦ σώματος, πρὸς ἃ ἔπραξεν, εἴτε ἀγαθὸν εἴτε
in the body, according to what he did, whether good or
[w]κακόν. 11 Εἰδότες οὖν τὸν φόβον τοῦ κυρίου, ἀνθρώπους
evil. Knowing therefore the terror of the Lord, [3]men
πείθομεν, θεῷ.δὲ πεφανερώμεθα· ἐλπίζω.δὲ καὶ ἐν ταῖς
[1]we [2]persuade, but to God we have been manifested, and I hope also in
συνειδήσεσιν.ὑμῶν πεφανερῶσθαι. 12 οὐ.[x]γὰρ πάλιν ἑαυτοὺς
your consciences to have been manifested. For not again ourselves
συνιστάνομεν ὑμῖν, ἀλλὰ ἀφορμὴν διδόντες ὑμῖν καυχήματος
do we commend to you, but occasion are giving to you of boasting

our light affliction, which is but for a moment, worketh for us a far more exceeding *and* eternal weight of glory; 18 while we look not at the things which are seen, but at the things which are not seen: for the things which are seen *are* temporal; but the things which are not seen *are* eternal.
V. For we know that if our earthly house of *this* tabernacle were dissolved, we have a building of God, an house not made with hands, eternal in the heavens.
2 For in this we groan, earnestly desiring to be clothed upon with our house which is from heaven: 3 if so be that being clothed we shall not be found naked. 4 For we that are in *this* tabernacle do groan, being burdened: not for that we would be unclothed, but clothed upon, that mortality might be swallowed up of life.
5 Now he that hath wrought us for the selfsame thing *is* God, who also hath given unto us the earnest of the Spirit.
6 Therefore *we are* always confident, knowing that, whilst we are at home in the body, we are absent from the Lord: 7 (for we walk by faith, not by sight:) 8 we are confident, *I say*, and willing rather to be absent from the body, and to be present with the Lord. 9 Wherefore we labour, that, whether present or absent, we may be accepted of him. 10 For we must all appear before the judgment seat of Christ; that every one may receive the things *done* in *his* body, according to that he hath done, whether *it be* good or bad.
11 Knowing therefore the terror of the Lord, we persuade men; but we are made manifest unto God; and I trust also are made manifest in your consciences. 12 For we commend not ourselves again unto you,

---

[q] εἴ περ LTr. [r] ἐφ' ᾧ for that EGLTTrAW. [s] ἀλλὰ Tr. [t] — καὶ LTTrAW.
[v] ἀραβῶνα T. [w] φαῦλον TTr. [x] — γὰρ for LTTrAW.

but give you occasion
to glory on our be-
half, that ye may have
somewhat to *answer*
them which glory in
appearance, and not in
heart. 13 For whe-
ther we be beside our-
selves, *it is* to God:
or whether we be so-
ber, *it is* for your
cause. 14 For the love
of Christ constraineth
us; because we thus
judge, that if one died
for all, then were all
dead: 15 and *that* he
died for all, that they
which live should
not henceforth live
unto themselves, but
unto him which died
for them, and rose a-
gain. 16 Wherefore
henceforth know we
no man after the flesh:
yea, though we have
known Christ after
the flesh, yet now
henceforth know we
him no more. 17 There-
fore if any man *be* in
Christ, *he is* a new creature: old things are
passed away; behold,
all things are become
new. 18 And all things
are of God, who hath
reconciled us to him-
self by Jesus Christ,
and hath given to us
the ministry of recon-
ciliation; 19 to wit,
that God was in
Christ, reconciling the
world unto himself,
not imputing their
trespasses unto them;
and hath committed
unto us the word of
reconciliation. 20 Now
then we are ambassa-
dors for Christ, as
though God did beseech
you by us: we pray *you*
in Christ's stead, be
ye reconciled to God.
21 For he hath made
him *to be* sin for us,
who knew no sin; that
we might be made the
righteousness of God
in him.
VI. We then, *as*
workers together *with*
him, beseech *you* also
that ye receive not the
grace of God in vain.
2 (For he saith, I have
heard thee in a time
accepted, and in the
day of salvation have
I succoured thee: be-
hold, now *is* the ac-
cepted time; behold,
now *is* the day of sal-
vation.) 3 Giving no
offence in anything,
that the ministry be

ὑπὲρ ἡμῶν, ἵνα ἔχητε [z]πρὸς τοὺς ἐν προσώπῳ
in behalf of us, that ye may have [such] towards those [2]in [3]appearance
καυχωμένους καὶ [y]οὐ[||] καρδίᾳ. 13 εἴτε.γὰρ ἐξέστημεν,
[1]boasting and not in heart. For whether we were beside ourselves,
θεῷ· εἴτε σωφρονοῦμεν, ὑμῖν. 14 ἡ.γὰρ ἀγάπη
[it was] to God; or are sober-minded [it is] for you. For the love
τοῦ χριστοῦ συνέχει ἡμᾶς, κρίναντας τοῦτο, ὅτι [z]εἰ[||] εἷς ὑπὲρ
of the Christ constrains us, having judged this, that if one [2]for
πάντων ἀπέθανεν, ἄρα οἱ πάντες ἀπέθανον· 15 καὶ ὑπὲρ
[3]all [1]died, then all died; and for
πάντων ἀπέθανεν, ἵνα οἱ ζῶντες μηκέτι ἑαυτοῖς ζῶ-
all he died, that they who live no longer to themselves should
σιν, ἀλλὰ τῷ ὑπὲρ αὐτῶν ἀποθανόντι καὶ ἐγερθέντι.
live, but to him who for them died and was raised again.
16 ὥστε ἡμεῖς ἀπὸ τοῦ νῦν οὐδένα οἴδαμεν κατὰ σάρκα·
So that we from now no one know according to flesh;
εἰ.[a]δὲ[||] καὶ ἐγνώκαμεν κατὰ σάρκα χριστόν, ἀλλὰ νῦν
but if even we have known according to flesh Christ, yet now
οὐκέτι γινώσκομεν 17 ὥστε εἴ τις ἐν χριστῷ,
no longer we know [him]. So that if anyone [be] in Christ [there is]
καινὴ κτίσις· τὰ ἀρχαῖα παρῆλθεν, ἰδοὺ γέγονεν καινὰ
a new creation: the old things passed away; lo, have become new
[b]τὰ.πάντα.[||] 18 τὰ.δὲ.πάντα ἐκ τοῦ θεοῦ, τοῦ καταλλάξαν-
all things: and all things [are] of God, who reconciled
τος ἡμᾶς ἑαυτῷ διὰ [c]Ἰησοῦ[||] χριστοῦ, καὶ δόντος ἡμῖν τὴν
us to himself by Jesus Christ, and gave to us the
διακονίαν τῆς καταλλαγῆς· 19 ὡς ὅτι θεὸς ἦν ἐν χριστῷ
service of reconciliation: how that God was in Christ [the]
κόσμον καταλλάσσων ἑαυτῷ, μὴ λογιζόμενος αὐτοῖς τὰ
world reconciling to himself, not reckoning to them
παραπτώματα.αὐτῶν, καὶ θέμενος ἐν ἡμῖν τὸν λόγον τῆς
their offences, and having put in us the word
καταλλαγῆς. 20 ὑπὲρ χριστοῦ οὖν πρεσβεύομεν, ὡς
of reconciliation. For Christ therefore we are ambassadors, as it were
τοῦ θεοῦ παρακαλοῦντος δι' ἡμῶν· δεόμεθα ὑπὲρ χριστοῦ,
God exhorting by us, we beseech for Christ,
καταλλάγητε τῷ θεῷ· 21 τὸν.[d]γὰρ[||] μὴ.γνόντα ἁμαρτίαν
Be reconciled to God. For him who knew not sin
ὑπὲρ ἡμῶν ἁμαρτίαν ἐποίησεν, ἵνα ἡμεῖς [e]γινώμεθα[||] δι-
[4]for [5]us [3]sin [1]he [2]made, that we might become right-
καιοσύνη θεοῦ ἐν αὐτῷ.
eousness of God in him.

6 Συνεργοῦντες.δὲ καὶ παρακαλοῦμεν μὴ εἰς κενὸν τὴν
But working together [2]also [1]we exhort [2]not [3]in [4]vain [5]the
χάριν τοῦ θεοῦ δέξασθαι ὑμᾶς· 2 λέγει.γάρ, Καιρῷ δεκτῷ
[6]grace [7]of [8]God [9]to [10]receive [1]you: (for he says, In a time accepted
ἐπήκουσά σου, καὶ ἐν ἡμέρᾳ σωτηρίας ἐβοήθησά σοι· ἰδοὺ νῦν
I listened to thee, and in a day of salvation I helped thee: lo, now
καιρὸς εὐπρόσδεκτος, ἰδοὺ νῦν ἡμέρα σωτηρίας· 3 μηδεμίαν
[the] time well-accepted; behold, now [the] day of salvation:) not one
ἐν μηδενὶ διδόντες προσκοπήν, ἵνα μὴ.μωμηθῇ ἡ διακονία·
[3]in [4]anything [2]giving [1]offence, that be not blamed the service;
(*lit.* nothing)
4 ἀλλ' ἐν παντὶ [f]συνιστῶντες[||] ἑαυτοὺς ὡς θεοῦ διάκονοι,
but in everything commending ourselves as God's servants,

---

[y] μὴ ἐν LTTr. [z] — εἰ LTTrAW. [a] — δὲ but LTTrA. [b] — τὰ πάντα LTTrA. [c] — Ἰησοῦ LTTrAW. [d] — γὰρ for LTTrAW. [e] γενώμεθα LTTrAW. [f] συνιστάντες LTTrAW.

ἐν ὑπομονῇ πολλῇ, ἐν θλίψεσιν, ἐν ἀναγκαις, ἐν στενο-
in [2]endurance [1]much, in tribulations, in necessities, in straits,
χωρίαις, 5 ἐν πληγαῖς, ἐν φυλακαῖς, ἐν ἀκαταστασίαις, ἐν
in stripes, in imprisonments, in commotions, in
κόποις, ἐν ἀγρυπνίαις, ἐν νηστείαις, 6 ἐν ἁγνότητι, ἐν γνώσει,
labours, in watchings, in fastings, in pureness, in knowledge,
ἐν μακροθυμίᾳ, ἐν χρηστότητι, ἐν πνεύματι ἁγίῳ, ἐν ἀγάπῃ
in long-suffering, in kindness, in [the] [2]Spirit [1]Holy, in love
ἀνυποκρίτῳ, 7 ἐν λόγῳ ἀληθείας, ἐν δυνάμει θεοῦ,
unfeigned, in [the] word of truth, in [the] power of God;
διὰ τῶν ὅπλων τῆς δικαιοσύνης τῶν δεξιῶν καὶ ἀριστερῶν,
through the arms of righteousness on the right hand and left,
8 διὰ δόξης καὶ ἀτιμίας, διὰ δυσφημίας καὶ εὐφημίας· ὡς
through glory and dishonour, through evil report and good report: as
πλάνοι, καὶ ἀληθεῖς· 9 ὡς ἀγνοούμενοι, καὶ ἐπιγινωσκόμενοι·
deceivers, and true; as being unknown, and well-known;
ὡς ἀποθνήσκοντες, καὶ ἰδοὺ ζῶμεν· ὡς παιδευόμενοι, καὶ
as dying, and lo we live; as disciplined, and
μὴ θανατούμενοι· 10 ὡς λυπούμενοι, ἀεὶ.δὲ χαίροντες· ὡς
not put to death; as sorrowful, but always rejoicing; as
πτωχοί, πολλοὺς.δὲ πλουτίζοντες· ὡς μηδὲν ἔχοντες, καὶ
poor, but many enriching; as nothing having, and
πάντα κατέχοντες.
all things possessing.

11 Τὸ.στόμα.ἡμῶν ἀνέῳγεν πρὸς ὑμᾶς, Κορίνθιοι, ἡ
Our mouth has been opened to you, Corinthians,
καρδία.ἡμῶν πεπλάτυνται· 12 οὐ.στενοχωρεῖσθε ἐν ἡμῖν,
our heart has been expanded. Ye are not straitened in us,
στενοχωρεῖσθε.δὲ ἐν τοῖς.σπλάγχνοις.ὑμῶν. 13 τὴν.δὲ αὐτὴν
but ye are straitened in your bowels; but the same
ἀντιμισθίαν, ὡς τέκνοις λέγω, πλατύνθητε καὶ ὑμεῖς.
[as] recompense, (as to children I speak,) be expanded also ye.

14 Μὴ.γίνεσθε ἑτεροζυγοῦντες ἀπίστοις· τίς.γὰρ με-
Be not diversely yoked with unbelievers; for what par-
τοχὴ δικαιοσύνῃ καὶ ἀνομίᾳ; [h]τίς.δὲ" κοινωνία φωτὶ
ticipation [has] righteousness and lawlessness? and what fellowship light
πρὸς σκότος; 15 τίς.δὲ συμφώνησις [i]χριστῷ" πρὸς [k]Βελίαρ";
with darkness? and what concord Christ with Beliar,
ἢ τίς μερὶς πιστῷ μετὰ ἀπίστου; 16 τίς.δὲ [l]συγκατά-
or what part to a believer with an unbeliever? and what agree-
θεσις" ναῷ θεοῦ μετὰ εἰδώλων; [m]ὑμεῖς" γὰρ ναὸς θεοῦ
ment a temple of God with idols? [2]ye [1]for a temple of [3]God
[n]ἐστε" ζῶντος, καθὼς εἶπεν ὁ θεός, "Οτι ἐνοικήσω ἐν
[4]are [[1]the] [2]living, according as [2]said [1]God, I will dwell among
αὐτοῖς, καὶ [o]ἐμπεριπατήσω·" καὶ ἔσομαι αὐτῶν θεός, καὶ
them, and walk among [them]; and I will be their God, and
αὐτοὶ ἔσονταί [p]μοι" λαός. 17 διὸ [q]ἐξέλθετε" ἐκ μέσου
they shall be to me a people. Wherefore come out from the midst
αὐτῶν καὶ ἀφορίσθητε, λέγει κύριος, καὶ ἀκαθάρτου
of them and be separated, says [the] Lord, and [the] unclean
μὴ.ἅπτεσθε· κἀγὼ εἰσδέξομαι ὑμᾶς, 18 καὶ ἔσομαι ὑμῖν εἰς
touch not. and I will receive you; and I will be to you for
πατέρα, καὶ ὑμεῖς ἔσεσθέ μοι εἰς υἱοὺς καὶ θυγατέρας, λέγει
a father, and ye shall be to me for sons and daughters, says

not blamed: 4 but in all *things* approving ourselves as the ministers of God, in much patience, in afflictions, in necessities, in distresses, 5 in stripes, in imprisonments, in tumults, in labours, in watchings, in fastings; 6 by pureness, by knowledge, by long-suffering, by kindness, by the Holy Ghost, by love unfeigned, 7 by the word of truth, by the power of God, by the armour of righteousness on the right hand and on the left, 8 by honour and dishonour, by evil report and good report: as deceivers, and *yet* true; 9 as unknown, and *yet* well known; as dying, and, behold, we live; as chastened, and not killed; 10 as sorrowful, yet alway rejoicing; as poor, yet making many rich; as having nothing, and *yet* possessing all things.

11 O *ye* Corinthians, our mouth is open unto you, our heart is enlarged. 12 Ye are not straitened in us, but ye are straitened in your own bowels. 13 Now for a recompence in the same, (I speak as unto *my* children,) be ye also enlarged.

14 Be ye not unequally yoked together with unbelievers: for what fellowship hath righteousness with unrighteousness? and what communion hath light with darkness? 15 and what concord hath Christ with Belial? or what part hath he that believeth with an infidel? 16 and what agreement hath the temple of God with idols? for ye are the temple of the living God; as God hath said, I will dwell in them, and walk in *them;* and I will be their God, and they shall be my people. 17 Wherefore come out from among them, and be ye separate, saith the Lord, and touch not the unclean *thing;* and I will receive you, 18 and will be a

---

[h] ἢ τίς or what LTTrAW. [i] χριστοῦ of Christ LTTrA. [k] Βελίαλ Belial EL. [l] συν- T. [m] ἡμεῖς we LTTr. [n] ἐσμὲν LTTr. [o] ἐν- T. [p] μου of me LTTr. [q] ἐξέλθατε LTTrA.

Father unto you, and
ye shall be my sons
and daughters, saith
the Lord Almighty.
VII. Having therefore
these promises, dearly
beloved, let us cleanse
ourselves from all fil-
thiness of the flesh
and spirit, perfecting
holiness in the fear of
God.
2 Receive us; we
have wronged no man,
we have corrupted no
man, we have defraud-
ed no man. 3 I speak not
this to condemn *you*:
for I have said before,
that ye are in our
hearts to die and live
with *you*. 4 Great *is*
my boldness of speech
toward you, great *is*
my glorying of you: I
am filled with com-
fort, I am exceeding
joyful in all our tri-
bulation. 5 For, when
we were come into Ma-
cedonia, our flesh had
no rest, but we were
troubled on every
side; without *were*
fightings, within *were*
fears. 6 Nevertheless
God, that comforteth
those that are cast
down, comforted us
by the coming of Ti-
tus; 7 and not by his
coming only, but by
the consolation where-
with he was comfort-
ed in you, when he
told us your earnest
desire, your mourn-
ing, your fervent mind
toward me; so that I
rejoiced the more.
8 For though I made
you sorry with a let-
ter, I do not repent,
though I did repent:
for I perceive that the
same epistle hath made
you sorry, though *it*
were but for a season.
9 Now I rejoice, not
that ye were made
sorry, but that ye sor-
rowed to repentance:
for ye were made sor-
ry after a godly man-
ner, that ye might re-
ceive damage by us in
nothing. 10 For godly
sorrow worketh re-
pentance to salvation
not to be repented of:
but the sorrow of the
world worketh death.
11 For behold this
selfsame thing, that
ye sorrowed after a
godly sort, what care-
fulness it wrought in
you, yea, *what* clear-

κύριος παντοκράτωρ. 7 Ταύτας οὖν ἔχοντες τὰς
[the] Lord Almighty. ³These ²therefore ¹having
ἐπαγγελίας, ἀγαπητοί, καθαρίσωμεν ἑαυτοὺς ἀπὸ παντὸς
promises, beloved, we should cleanse ourselves from every
μολυσμοῦ σαρκὸς καὶ πνεύματος, ἐπιτελοῦντες ἁγιωσύνην ἐν
defilement of flesh and spirit, perfecting holiness in
φόβῳ θεοῦ.
fear of God.

2 Χωρήσατε ἡμᾶς· οὐδένα ἠδικήσαμεν, οὐδένα ἐφθείραμεν,
Receive us: no one did we wrong, no one did we corrupt,
οὐδένα ἐπλεονεκτήσαμεν. 3 ʳοὐ πρὸς κατάκρισιν‖ λέγω·
no one did we overreach. Not for condemnation I speak,
προείρηκα.γὰρ ὅτι ἐν ταῖς.καρδίαις.ἡμῶν ἐστε εἰς τὸ συν-
for I have before said that in our hearts ye are, for to die
αποθανεῖν καὶ ˢσυζῆν.‖ 4 πολλή μοι παῤῥησία πρὸς
together and to live together. Great [is] to me boldness towards
ὑμᾶς, πολλή μοι καύχησις ὑπὲρ ὑμῶν· πεπλήρωμαι
you, great to me boasting in respect of you; I have been filled
τῇ παρακλήσει, ὑπερπερισσεύομαι τῇ χαρᾷ ἐπὶ πάσῃ τῇ
with encouragement; I overabound with joy at all
θλίψει.ἡμῶν. 5 Καὶ.γὰρ ἐλθόντων ἡμῶν εἰς Μακεδονίαν,
our tribulation. For indeed, ²having ³come ¹we into Macedonia,
οὐδεμίαν ᵗἔσχηκεν‖ ἄνεσιν ἡ.σὰρξ.ἡμῶν, ἀλλ' ἐν παντὶ
⁴not ⁵any ³had ⁶ease ¹our ²flesh, but in every [way]
θλιβόμενοι· ἔξωθεν μάχαι, ἔσωθεν φόβοι. 6 ἀλλ' ὁ
being oppressed; without contentions, within fears. But he who
παρακαλῶν τοὺς ταπεινοὺς παρεκάλεσεν ἡμᾶς ὁ θεὸς ἐν τῇ
encourages those brought low encouraged us— God—by the
παρουσίᾳ Τίτου· 7 οὐ.μόνον.δὲ ἐν τῇ παρουσίᾳ.αὐτοῦ, ἀλλὰ
coming of Titus; and not only by his coming, but
καὶ ἐν τῇ παρακλήσει ᾗ παρεκλήθη ἐφ' ὑμῖν,
also by the encouragement with which he was encouraged as to you;
ἀναγγέλλων ἡμῖν τὴν.ὑμῶν.ἐπιπόθησιν, τὸν.ὑμῶν.ὀδυρμόν,
relating to us your longing, your mourning,
τὸν.ὑμῶν.ζῆλον ὑπὲρ ἐμοῦ, ὥστε.με μᾶλλον χαρῆναι. 8 Ὅτι
your zeal for me; so as for me the more to be rejoiced. For
εἰ καὶ ἐλύπησα ὑμᾶς ἐν τῇ ἐπιστολῇ, οὐ.μεταμέλομαι, εἰ καὶ
if also I grieved you in the epistle, I do not regret [it], if even
μετεμελόμην· βλέπω.ᵛγὰρ‖ ὅτι ἡ.ἐπιστολὴ.ἐκείνη εἰ καὶ πρὸς
I did regret; for I see that that epistle, if even for
ὥραν ἐλύπησεν ὑμᾶς. 9 νῦν χαίρω, οὐχ ὅτι ἐλυπήθητε, ἀλλ'
an hour, grieved you. Now I rejoice, not that ye were grieved, but
ὅτι ἐλυπήθητε εἰς μετάνοιαν· ἐλυπήθητε.γὰρ κατὰ θεόν,
that ye were grieved to repentance; for ye were grieved according to God,
ἵνα ἐν μηδενὶ ζημιωθῆτε ἐξ ἡμῶν. 10 ἡ.γὰρ κατὰ
that in nothing ye might suffer loss by us. For the ²according ³to
θεὸν λύπη μετάνοιαν εἰς σωτηρίαν ἀμεταμέλητον ʷκατερ-
⁴God ¹grief repentance to salvation not to be regretted works
γάζεται·‖ ἡ.δὲ τοῦ κόσμου λύπη θάνατον κατεργάζεται.
out; but the ²of ³the ⁴world ¹grief death works out.
11 ἰδοὺ.γὰρ αὐτὸ.τοῦτο τὸ κατὰ θεὸν λυπηθῆναι ˣὑμᾶς,‖
For lo, this same thing, according to God ²to ³have ⁴been ⁵grieved ¹you,
πόσην ʸκατειργάσατο‖ ᶻὑμῖν σπουδήν, ἀλλὰ ἀπολογίαν,
how much ²it ³worked ⁴out ⁵in ⁶you ¹diligence, but [what] defence,

---

ʳ πρὸς κατάκρισιν οὐ LTTrA. ˢ συνζῆν LTTrA. ᵗ ἔσχεν LTr. ᵛ — γὰρ for [L]Tr.
ʷ ἐργάζεται WORKS LTTrAW. ˣ — ὑμᾶς LTT[A]. ʸ κατηργάσατο T. ᶻ + [ἐν] L.

ἀλλὰ ἀγανάκτησιν, ἀλλὰ φόβον, ἀλλὰ ἐπιπόθησιν, ἀλλὰ
but indignation, but fear, but longing, but
ζῆλον, [a]ἀλλ'" ἐκδίκησιν; ἐν παντὶ συνεστήσατε ἑαυτοὺς
zeal, but vengeance! in every [way] ye proved yourselves
ἁγνοὺς εἶναι [b]ἐν" τῷ πράγματι. 12 ἄρα εἰ καὶ ἔγραψα ὑμῖν,
[3]pure [1]to [2]be in the matter. Then if also I wrote to you,
οὐχ [c]εἵνεκεν" τοῦ ἀδικήσαντος, οὐδὲ [c]εἵνεκεν" τοῦ
not for the sake of him who did wrong, nor for the sake of him who
ἀδικηθέντος· [d]ἀλλ'" [c]εἵνεκεν" τοῦ φανερωθῆναι τὴν σπουδὴν
suffered wrong, but for the sake of [7]being [8]manifested [2]diligence
[e]ὑμῶν" τὴν ὑπὲρ [f]ἡμῶν" πρὸς ὑμᾶς ἐνώπιον τοῦ θεοῦ.
[1]your [3]which [[4]is] [5]for [6]us to you before God.
13 Διὰ τοῦτο παρακεκλήμεθα ἐπὶ [g] τῇ παρακλήσει
On account of this we have been encouraged in [2]encouragement
[h]ὑμῶν·" περισσοτέρως.[i]δὲ" μᾶλλον ἐχάρημεν ἐπὶ τῇ χαρᾷ
[1]your, and the more abundantly rather we rejoiced at the joy
Τίτου, ὅτι ἀναπέπαυται τὸ.πνεῦμα.αὐτοῦ ἀπὸ πάντων
of Titus, because has been refreshed his spirit by all
ὑμῶν· 14 ὅτι εἴ τι αὐτῷ ὑπὲρ ὑμῶν κεκαύχημαι, οὐ
of you. Because if anything to him about you I have boasted, [3]not
κατῃσχύνθην· ἀλλ' ὡς πάντα ἐν ἀληθείᾳ ἐλαλήσαμεν
[1]I [2]was put to shame; but as all things in truth we spoke
ὑμῖν, οὕτως καὶ ἡ καύχησις [k]ἡμῶν" [l]ἡ" ἐπὶ Τίτου
to you, so also the boasting of us which [was] to Titus
ἀλήθεια ἐγενήθη· 15 καὶ τὰ.σπλάγχνα.αὐτοῦ περισσοτέρως
truth became; and his bowels more abundantly
εἰς ὑμᾶς ἐστιν, ἀναμιμνῃσκομένου τὴν πάντων ὑμῶν
towards you are, remembering the [2]of [3]all [4]of [5]you
ὑπακοήν, ὡς μετὰ φόβου καὶ τρόμου ἐδέξασθε αὐτόν.
[1]obedience, how with fear and trembling ye received him.
16 χαίρω [m] ὅτι ἐν παντὶ θαῤῥῶ ἐν ὑμῖν.
I rejoice that in everything I am confident in you.

ing of yourselves, yea, *what* indignation, yea, *what* fear, yea, *what* vehement desire, yea, *what* zeal, yea, *what* revenge! In all *things* ye have approved yourselves to be clear in this matter. 12 Wherefore, though I wrote unto you, *I did it* not for his cause that had done the wrong, nor for his cause that suffered wrong, but that our care for you in the sight of God might appear unto you. 13 Therefore we were comforted in your comfort: yea, and exceedingly the more joyed we for the joy of Titus, because his spirit was refreshed by you all. 14 For if I have boasted anything to him of you, I am not ashamed; but as we spake all things to you in truth, even so our boasting, which *I made* before Titus, is found a truth. 15 And his inward affection is more abundant toward you, whilst he remembereth the obedience of you all, how with fear and trembling ye received him. 16 I rejoice therefore that I have confidence in you in all *things*.

8 Γνωρίζομεν.δὲ ὑμῖν, ἀδελφοί, τὴν χάριν τοῦ θεοῦ τὴν
But we make known to you, brethren, the grace of God which
δεδομένην ἐν ταῖς ἐκκλησίαις τῆς Μακεδονίας· 2 ὅτι ἐν πολλῇ
has been given in the assemblies of Macedonia; that in much
δοκιμῇ θλίψεως ἡ περισσεία τῆς.χαρᾶς.αὐτῶν καὶ ἡ κατὰ
proof of tribulation the abundance of their joy and
βάθους πτωχεία αὐτῶν ἐπερίσσευσεν εἰς [n]τὸν πλοῦτον" τῆς
[2]deep [3]poverty [1]their abounded to the riches
ἁπλότητος.αὐτῶν· 3 ὅτι κατὰ δύναμιν, μαρτυρῶ,
of their liberality. For according to [their] power, I bear witness,
καὶ [o]ὑπὲρ" δύναμιν αὐθαίρετοι, 4 μετὰ πολ-
and beyond [their] power [they were] willing of themselves, with much
λῆς παρακλήσεως δεόμενοι ἡμῶν τὴν χάριν καὶ τὴν κοινωνίαν
entreaty beseeching of us, [5]the [6]grace [7]and [8]the [9]fellowship
τῆς διακονίας τῆς εἰς τοὺς ἁγίους [p]δέξασθαι.ἡμᾶς·"
[10]of [11]the [12]service [13]which [[14]was] [15]for [16]the [17]saints [1]for [2]us [3]to [4]receive.
5 καὶ οὐ καθὼς ἠλπίσαμεν, [q]ἀλλ'" ἑαυτοὺς ἔδωκαν πρῶ-
And not [only] according as we hoped, but themselves they gave first
τον τῷ κυρίῳ, καὶ ἡμῖν διὰ θελήματος θεοῦ 6 εἰς.τὸ παρα-
to the Lord, and to us by [the] will of God. So that [2]ex-

VIII. Moreover, brethren, we do you to wit of the grace of God bestowed on the churches of Macedonia; 2 how that in a great trial of affliction the abundance of their joy and their deep poverty abounded unto the riches of their liberality. 3 For to *their* power, I bear record, yea, and beyond *their* power *they were* willing of themselves; 4 praying us with much intreaty that we would receive the gift, and *take upon us* the fellowship of the ministering to the saints. 5 And *this they did*, not as we hoped, but first gave their own selves to the Lord, and unto us by the will of God. 6 Insomuch that we desired Titus, that

[a] ἀλλὰ LTTrAW. [b] — ἐν (read τῷ in the) [L]TTrAW. [c] ἕνεκεν LTTrA. [d] ἀλλὰ Tr. [e] ἡμῶν our EG. [f] ὑμῶν you EG. [g] + δὲ and (in) *commencing a sentence at* ἐπὶ LTTrAW. [h] ἡμῶν our LTTrAW. [i] — δὲ and LTTrAW. [k] ὑμῶν of you LA. [l] — ἡ T[Tr]. [m] + οὖν therefore E. [n] τὸ πλοῦτος LTTrA. [o] παρὰ LTTrAW. [p] — δέξασθαι ἡμᾶς GLTTrAW. [q] ἀλλὰ TTr.

as he had begun, so he
would also finish in
you the same grace
also. 7 Therefore, as
ye abound in every
thing, in faith, and utterance, and know-
ledge, and *in* all dili-
gence, and *in* your love
to us, *see* that ye a-
bound in this grace
also. 8 I speak not by
commandment, but by
occasion of the for-
wardness of others,
and to prove the sin-
cerity of your love.
9 For ye know the
grace of our Lord Je-
sus Christ, that, though
he was rich, yet for
your sakes he became
poor, that ye through
his poverty might be
rich. 10 And herein I
give *my* advice: for
this is expedient for
you, who have begun
before, not only to do,
but also to be forward
a year ago. 11 Now
therefore perform the
doing *of it;* that as
there was a readiness
to will, so *there may
be* a performance also
out of that which ye
have. 12 For if there
be first a willing
mind, *it is* accepted according to that a man
hath, *and* not accord-
ing to that he hath
not. 13 For *I mean*
not that other men be
eased, and ye be bur-
dened: 14 but by an
equality, *that* now at
this time your abun-
dance *may be a supply*
for their want, that
their abundance also
may be *a supply* for
your want: that there
may be equality: 15 as
it is written, He that
had gathered much
had nothing over; and
he that *had gathered*
little had no lack.

16 But thanks *be* to
God, which put the
same earnest care into
the heart of Titus for
you. 17 For indeed
he accepted the exhor-
tation; but being
more forward, of his
own accord he went
unto you. 18 And we
have sent with him the
brother, whose praise
is in the gospel
throughout all the
churches; 19 and not
that only, but who
was also chosen of the

καλέσαι ἡμᾶς Τίτον, ἵνα καθὼς προενήρξατο, οὕτως καὶ
horted [1]we Titus, that according as he before began, so also
ἐπιτελέσῃ εἰς ὑμᾶς καὶ τὴν.χάριν.ταύτην. 7 Ἀλλ' ὥσπερ
he might complete with you also this grace. But even as
ἐν παντὶ περισσεύετε, πίστει, καὶ λόγῳ, καὶ γνώσει, καὶ
in every [way] ye abound, in faith, and word, and knowledge, and
πάσῃ σπουδῇ, καὶ τῇ ἐξ ὑμῶν ἐν ἡμῖν ἀγάπῃ, ἵνα καὶ ἐν
all diligence, and in the [2]from [3]you [4]to [5]us [1]love, that also in
ταύτῃ τῇ χάριτι περισσεύητε. 8 οὐ κατ' ἐπιταγὴν λέγω,
this grace ye should abound. Not according to a command do I speak,
ἀλλὰ διὰ τῆς ἑτέρων σπουδῆς καὶ τὸ τῆς [r]ὑμετέρας[ǁ] ἀγάπης
but through the [2]of [3]others [1]diligence and the [2]of [3]your [4]love
γνήσιον δοκιμάζων. 9 γινώσκετε.γὰρ τὴν χάριν τοῦ κυρίου
[1]genuineness proving. For ye know the grace of [2]Lord
ἡμῶν Ἰησοῦ χριστοῦ, ὅτι δι' ὑμᾶς ἐπτώχευσεν
[1]our Jesus Christ, that [2]for [4]the [5]sake [6]of [7]you [8]he [9]became [10]poor,
πλούσιος ὤν, ἵνα ὑμεῖς τῇ.ἐκείνου.πτωχείᾳ πλουτήσητε.
[2]rich [1]being, that ye by his poverty might be enriched.
10 καὶ γνώμην ἐν τούτῳ δίδωμι. τοῦτο.γὰρ ὑμῖν συμφέρει,
And a judgment in this I give, for this for you is profitable,
οἵτινες οὐ μόνον τὸ ποιῆσαι, ἀλλὰ καὶ τὸ θέλειν προενήρ-
who not only the doing, but also the being willing began
ξασθε ἀπὸ.πέρυσι. 11 νυνὶ.δὲ καὶ τὸ ποιῆσαι ἐπιτελέσατε,
before a year ago. But now also [2]the [3]doing [1]complete;
ὅπως καθάπερ ἡ προθυμία τοῦ θέλειν, οὕτως καὶ
so that even as [there was] the readiness of the being willing, so also
τὸ ἐπιτελέσαι ἐκ τοῦ ἔχειν. 12 Εἰ.γὰρ ἡ προθυμία πρό-
the completing out of that [ye] have. For if the readiness is pre-
κειται, καθὸ [s]ἐὰν[ǁ] ἔχῃ [t]τις[ǁ] εὐπρόσδεκτος, οὐ καθὸ
sent, according as [2]may [3]have [1]anyone [he is] accepted, not according as
οὐκ.ἔχει. 13 οὐ.γὰρ ἵνα ἄλλοις ἄνεσις, ὑμῖν.[v]δὲ[ǁ]
he has not. For [it is] not that to others [there may be] ease, but for you
θλίψις. ἀλλ' ἐξ ἰσότητος, ἐν τῷ νῦν καιρῷ τὸ ὑμῶν περίσ-
pressure, but of equality, in the present time your abun-
σευμα εἰς τὸ.ἐκείνων.ὑστέρημα, 14 ἵνα καὶ τὸ ἐκείνων περίσ-
dance for their deficiency, that also their abun-
σευμα γένηται εἰς τὸ.ὑμῶν.ὑστέρημα. ὅπως γένηται
dance may be for your deficiency, so that there should be
ἰσότης. 15 καθὼς γέγραπται, Ὁ τὸ πολὺ οὐκ
equality. According as it has been written, He that [gathered] much [2]not
ἐπλεόνασεν. καὶ ὁ τὸ ὀλίγον οὐκ.ἠλαττόνησεν.
[1]had over, and he that [gathered] little did not lack.

16 Χάρις.δὲ τῷ θεῷ, τῷ [w]διδόντι[ǁ] τὴν αὐτὴν σπουδὴν ὑπὲρ
But thanks to God, who gives the same diligence for
ὑμῶν ἐν τῇ καρδίᾳ Τίτου. 17 ὅτι τὴν μὲν παράκλησιν ἐ-
you in the heart of Titus. For the [2]indeed [1]exhortation he
δέξατο, σπουδαιότερος.δὲ ὑπάρχων, αὐθαίρετος ἐξῆλθεν
received, but more diligent being, of his own accord he went out
πρὸς ὑμᾶς. 18 συνεπέμψαμεν.δὲ [x]μετ' αὐτοῦ τὸν ἀδελφὸν[ǁ]
to you. But we sent with him the brother
οὗ ὁ ἔπαινος ἐν τῷ εὐαγγελίῳ διὰ πασῶν τῶν ἐκ-
of whom the praise [is] in the glad tidings through all the as-
κλησιῶν. 19 οὐ.μόνον.δέ, ἀλλὰ καὶ χειροτονηθεὶς ὑπὸ τῶν
semblies; and not only [so], but also having been chosen by the

---

[r] ἡμετέρας of our E. [s] ἂν T. [t] — τις (read ἔχῃ he may have) LTTrAW. [v] — δὲ but LTTr[A]. [w] δόντι gave W. [x] τὸν ἀδελφὸν μετ' αὐτοῦ T.

ἐκκλησιῶν συνέκδημος.ἡμῶν [y]σὺν‖ τῇ.χάριτι.ταύτῃ τῇ
assemblies [is] our fellow-traveller with this grace, which [is]
διακονουμένῃ ὑφ' ἡμῶν πρὸς τὴν [z]αὐτοῦ‖ τοῦ κυρίου δόξαν
served by us to the [5]himself [2]of [3]the [4]Lord [1]glory
καὶ προθυμίαν [a]ὑμῶν·‖ 20 στελλόμενοι τοῦτο, μή
and [a witness of] [2]readiness [1]your; avoiding this, lest
τις ἡμᾶς μωμήσηται ἐν τῇ.ἁδρότητι.ταύτῃ τῇ διακονου-
anyone us should blame in this abundance which [is] served
μένῃ ὑφ' ἡμῶν· 21 [b]προνοούμενοι‖ καλὰ οὐ μόνον ἐνώπιον
by us; providing things right not only before
κυρίου, ἀλλὰ καὶ ἐνώπιον ἀνθρώπων. 22 Συνεπέμψαμεν.δὲ
[the] Lord, but also before men. And we sent with
αὐτοῖς τὸν.ἀδελφὸν.ἡμῶν ὃν ἐδοκιμάσαμεν ἐν πολλοῖς πολ-
them our brother whom we proved in many things often
λάκις σπουδαῖον ὄντα, νυνὶ.δὲ πολὺ σπουδαιότερον πεποι-
diligent to be, and now much more diligent by the [2]con-
θήσει πολλῇ τῇ εἰς ὑμᾶς. 23 εἴτε ὑπὲρ Τίτου,
fidence [1]great which [is] towards you. Whether as regards Titus,
κοινωνὸς ἐμὸς καὶ εἰς ὑμᾶς συνεργός· εἴτε ἀδελφοὶ
[he is] [2]partner [1]my and for you a fellow-worker; or [2]brethren
ἡμῶν, ἀπόστολοι ἐκκλησιῶν, δόξα χριστοῦ. 24 Τὴν
[1]our, [they are] messengers of assemblies, [2]glory [1]Christ's. The
οὖν ἔνδειξιν τῆς.ἀγάπης.ὑμῶν, καὶ ἡμῶν καυχήσεως ὑπὲρ
[2]therefore [1]proof of your love, and of our boasting about
ὑμῶν, εἰς αὐτοὺς [c]ἐνδείξασθε‖ [d]καὶ‖ εἰς πρόσωπον τῶν ἐκκλησιῶν.
you, [3]to [4]them [1]shew [2]ye and in face of the assemblies.

9 Περὶ.μὲν.γὰρ τῆς διακονίας τῆς εἰς τοὺς ἁγίους
For concerning the service which [is] for the saints
περισσόν μοι ἐστιν τὸ γράφειν ὑμῖν. 2 οἶδα.γὰρ τὴν προθυ-
superfluous for me it is writing to you. For I know [2]readi-
μίαν ὑμῶν ἣν ὑπὲρ ὑμῶν καυχῶμαι Μακεδόσιν, ὅτι
ness [1]your which concerning you I boast of to Macedonians; that
Ἀχαΐα παρεσκεύασται ἀπὸ.πέρυσι· καὶ [e]ὁ‖ [f]ἐξ‖ ὑμῶν ζῆλος
Achaia has been prepared a year ago, and the [2]of [3]you [1]zeal
ἠρέθισεν τοὺς πλείονας. 3 ἔπεμψα.δὲ τοὺς ἀδελφούς, ἵνα.μὴ
provoke the greater number. But I sent the brethren, lest
τὸ.καύχημα.ἡμῶν τὸ ὑπὲρ ὑμῶν κενωθῇ ἐν τῷ
our boasting which [is] about you should be made void in
μέρει.τούτῳ· ἵνα καθὼς ἔλεγον, παρεσκευασμένοι ἦτε,
this respect, that according as I said, prepared ye may be;
4 μήπως ἐὰν ἔλθωσιν σὺν ἐμοὶ Μακεδόνες, καὶ εὕρωσιν ὑμᾶς
lest perhaps if should come with me Macedonians, and find you
ἀπαρασκευάστους, καταισχυνθῶμεν ἡμεῖς, ἵνα μὴ.λέγωμεν
unprepared, [2]should [3]be [4]put [5]to [6]shame [1]we, (that we may not say
ὑμεῖς, ἐν τῇ.ὑποστάσει.ταύτῃ [g]τῆς καυχήσεως.‖ 5 ἀναγκαῖον
ye,) in this confidence of boasting. Necessary
οὖν ἡγησάμην παρακαλέσαι τοὺς ἀδελφοὺς ἵνα προέλ-
therefore I esteemed [it] to exhort the brethren that they should
θωσιν [h]εἰς‖ ὑμᾶς, καὶ προκαταρτίσωσιν τὴν [i]προκατηγ-
go before to you, and should complete beforehand [3]fore-
γελμένην‖ εὐλογίαν ὑμῶν ταύτην ἑτοίμην εἶναι οὕτως ὡς
announced [4]blessing [2]your [1]this [7]ready [5]to [6]be thus as

churches to travel with us with this grace, which is administered by us to the glory of the same Lord, and *declaration of* your ready mind:
20 avoiding this, that no man should blame us in this abundance which is administered by us:
21 providing for honest things, not only in the sight of the Lord, but also in the sight of men.
22 And we have sent with them our brother, whom we have oftentimes proved diligent in many things, but now much more diligent, upon the great confidence which *I have* in you.
23 Whether *any do inquire* of Titus, *he is* my partner and fellowhelper concerning you: or our brethren *be inquired of, they are* the messengers of the churches, *and* the glory of Christ.
24 Wherefore shew ye to them, and before the churches, the proof of your love, and of our boasting on your behalf.

IX. For as touching the ministering to the saints, it is superfluous for me to write to you:
2 for I know the forwardness of your mind, for which I boast of you to them of Macedonia, that Achaia was ready a year ago; and your zeal hath provoked very many.
3 Yet have I sent the brethren, lest our boasting of you should be in vain in this behalf; that, as I said, ye may be ready:
4 lest haply if they of Macedonia come with me, and find you unprepared, we (that we say not, ye) should be ashamed in this same confident boasting.
5 Therefore I thought it necessary to exhort the brethren, that they would go before unto you, and make up beforehand your bounty, whereof ye had notice before, that the same might be ready, as *a matter of*

---

[y] ἐν in LTrAW. [z] — αὐτοῦ LTrAW. [a] ἡμῶν our GLTTrAW. [b] προνοοῦμεν γὰρ for we provide LTTrA; προνοούμενοι γὰρ G. [c] ἐνδεικνύμενοι shewing LTTrA. [d] — καὶ GLTTrAW. [e] τὸ TTr. [f] — ἐξ (read ὑμῶν of you) LTTr[A]. [g] — τῆς καυχήσεως GLTTrAW. [h] πρὸς LTrW. [i] προεπηγγελμένην before promised LTTrAW.

bounty, and not as *of*
covetousness. 6 But
this *I say*, He which
soweth sparingly shall
reap also sparingly;
and he which soweth
bountifully shall reap
also bountifully. 7 E-
very man according as
he purposeth in his
heart, *so let him give*;
not grudgingly, or of
necessity: for God
loveth a cheerful
giver. 8 And God *is*
able to make all grace
abound toward you;
that ye, always having
all sufficiency in all
things, may abound to
every good work: 9 (as
it is written, He hath
dispersed abroad; he
hath given to the poor:
his righteousness re-
maineth for ever.
10 Now he that mi-
nistereth seed to the
sower both minister
bread for *your* food,
and multiply your
seed sown, and in-
crease the fruits of
your righteousness;)
11 being enriched in
every thing to all
bountifulness, which
causeth through us
thanksgiving to God.
12 For the administra-
tion of this service not
only supplieth the
want of the saints, but
is abundant also by
many thanksgivings
unto God; 13 whiles by
the experiment of this
ministration they glo-
rify God for your pro-
fessed subjection unto
the gospel of Christ,
and for *your* libe-
ral distribution unto
them, and unto all
men; 14 and by their
prayer for you, which
long after you for the
exceeding grace of
God in you. 15 Thanks
be unto God for his
unspeakable gift.

X. Now I Paul
myself beseech you
by the meekness and
gentleness of Christ,
who in presence *am*
base among you, but
being absent am bold
toward you: 2 but I
beseech *you*, that I
may not be bold when
I am present with that
confidence, wherewith
I think to be bold a-
gainst some, which

εὐλογίαν, [k]καὶ‖ μὴ [l]ὥσπερ‖ πλεονεξίαν. 6 Τοῦτο.δέ, ὁ
a blessing, and not as [of] covetousness. But this [I say], he that
σπείρων φειδομένως, φειδομένως καὶ θερίσει· καὶ ὁ σπείρων
sows sparingly, sparingly also shall reap; and he that sows
ἐπ' εὐλογίαις, ἐπ' εὐλογίαις καὶ θερίσει. 7 ἕκαστος καθὼς
on blessings, on blessings also shall reap: each according as
[m]προαιρεῖται‖ τῇ καρδίᾳ· μὴ ἐκ.λύπης ἢ ἐξ ἀνάγκης· ἱλαρὸν
he purposes in the heart; not grievingly, or of necessity; [2]a [3]cheerful
γὰρ δότην ἀγαπᾷ ὁ θεός. 8 [n]δυνατὸς.δὲ‖ ὁ θεὸς πᾶσαν χάριν
[1]for giver [2]loves [1]God. For able [is] God every grace
περισσεῦσαι εἰς ὑμᾶς, ἵνα ἐν παντὶ πάντοτε πᾶσαν
to make abound towards you, that in every [way] always all
αὐτάρκειαν ἔχοντες, περισσεύητε εἰς πᾶν ἔργον ἀγαθόν·
sufficiency having, ye may abound to every [2]work [1]good:
9 καθὼς γέγραπται, Ἐσκόρπισεν, ἔδωκεν τοῖς πένησιν·
according as it has been written, He scattered abroad, he gave to the poor,
ἡ.δικαιοσύνη.αὐτοῦ μένει εἰς.τὸν.αἰῶνα. 10 Ὁ.δὲ ἐπιχορηγῶν
his righteousness abides for ever. Now he that supplies
[o]σπέρμα‖ τῷ σπείροντι καὶ ἄρτον εἰς βρῶσιν [p]χορηγήσαι‖
seed to him that sows and bread for eating may he supply
καὶ [q]πληθύναι‖ τὸν.σπόρον.ὑμῶν, καὶ [r]αὐξήσαι‖ τὰ [s]γεννή-
and may he multiply your sowing, and may he increase the fruits
ματα‖ τῆς.δικαιοσύνης.ὑμῶν. 11 ἐν παντὶ πλουτιζόμενοι
of your righteousness: in every [way] being enriched
εἰς πᾶσαν ἁπλότητα, ἥτις κατεργάζεται δι' ἡμῶν εὐχαρισ-
to all liberality, which works out through us thanks-
τίαν [t]τῷ‖ θεῷ· 12 ὅτι ἡ διακονία τῆς.λειτουργίας.ταύτης
giving to God. Because the service of this ministration
οὐ μόνον ἐστὶν προσαναπληροῦσα τὰ ὑστερήματα τῶν ἁγίων,
not only is completely filling up the deficiencies of the saints,
ἀλλὰ καὶ περισσεύουσα διὰ πολλῶν εὐχαριστιῶν τῷ θεῷ·
but also abounding through many thanksgivings to God;
13 διὰ τῆς δοκιμῆς τῆς.διακονίας.ταύτης δοξάζοντες τὸν
through the proof of this service [they] glorifying
θεὸν ἐπὶ τῇ ὑποταγῇ τῆς.ὁμολογίας.ὑμῶν εἰς τὸ εὐαγγέλιον
God at the subjection, by your confession, to the glad tidings
τοῦ χριστοῦ, καὶ ἁπλότητι τῆς κοινωνίας εἰς αὐτοὺς καὶ
of the Christ, and liberality of the communication towards them and
εἰς πάντας, 14 καὶ αὐτῶν.δεήσει ὑπὲρ ὑμῶν, ἐπιποθούν-
towards all; and in their supplication for you, a longing
των ὑμᾶς διὰ τὴν ὑπερβάλλουσαν χάριν τοῦ θεοῦ ἐφ'
for you, on account of the surpassing grace of God upon
ὑμῖν. 15 χάρις.[v]δὲ‖ τῷ θεῷ ἐπὶ τῇ ἀνεκδιηγήτῳ αὐτοῦ δωρεᾷ.
you. Now thanks [be] to God for [2]indescribable [1]his free gift.

10 Αὐτὸς.δὲ ἐγὼ Παῦλος παρακαλῶ ὑμᾶς διὰ τῆς [w]πρᾳό-
Now [2]myself [1]I Paul exhort you by the meek-
τητος‖ καὶ ἐπιεικείας τοῦ χριστοῦ, ὃς κατὰ πρόσωπον μὲν
ness and gentleness of the Christ, who as to appearance [am]
ταπεινὸς ἐν ὑμῖν, ἀπὼν.δὲ θαῤῥῶ εἰς ὑμᾶς· 2 δέομαι.δὲ
mean among you, but absent am bold towards you; but I beseech
τὸ μὴ παρὼν θαῤῥῆσαι τῇ πεποιθήσει ᾗ
that [5]not [1]being [2]present [3]I [4]should be bold with the confidence with which

---

[k] — καὶ T. [l] ὡς GLTTrAW. [m] προῄρηται he has purposed LTTrAW. [n] δυνατεῖ δὲ For is able LTTrA. [o] σπόρον LTr. [p] χορηγήσει will supply GLTTrAW. [q] πληθυνεῖ will multiply GLTAW; πληθύνει multiplies Tr. [r] αὐξήσει will increase GLTTrAW. [s] γενήματα GLTTrAW. [t] [τῷ] L. [v] — δὲ now LTTrA. [w] πραΰτητος LTTrAW.

λογίζομαι τολμῆσαι ἐπί τινας τοὺς λογιζομένους ἡμᾶς ὡς
I reckon to be daring towards some who reckon of us as
κατὰ σάρκα περιπατοῦντας. 3 ἐν.σαρκὶ.γὰρ περιπατοῦντες,
[2]according [3]to [4]flesh [1]walking. For in flesh walking,
οὐ κατὰ σάρκα στρατευόμεθα· 4 τὰ.γὰρ ὅπλα τῆς [x]στρα-
not according to flesh do we war. For the arms of [2]war-
τείας‖ ἡμῶν οὐ σαρκικά, ἀλλὰ δυνατὰ τῷ θεῷ πρὸς
fare [1]our [are] not fleshly, but powerful through God to [the]
καθαίρεσιν ὀχυρωμάτων· 5 λογισμοὺς καθαιροῦντες καὶ πᾶν
overthrow of strong-holds; [2]reasonings [1]overthrowing and every
ὕψωμα ἐπαιρόμενον κατὰ τῆς γνώσεως τοῦ θεοῦ, καὶ αἰχμα-
high thing lifting itself up against the knowledge of God, and leading
λωτίζοντες πᾶν νόημα εἰς τὴν ὑπακοὴν τοῦ χριστοῦ, 6 καὶ
captive every thought into the obedience of the Christ; and
ἐν ἑτοίμῳ ἔχοντες ἐκδικῆσαι πᾶσαν παρακοήν, ὅταν πλη-
[2]in [3]readiness [1]having to avenge all disobedience, when may have
ρωθῇ ὑμῶν ἡ ὑπακοή. 7 Τὰ κατὰ πρόσωπον
been fulfilled your obedience. The things according to appearance
βλέπετε; εἴ τις πέποιθεν ἑαυτῷ χριστοῦ εἶναι, τοῦτο
do ye look at? If anyone is persuaded in himself of Christ to be, this
λογιζέσθω πάλιν [y]ἀφ'‖ ἑαυτοῦ, ὅτι καθὼς αὐτὸς χριστοῦ,
let him reckon again of himself, that according as he [is] of Christ,
οὕτως καὶ ἡμεῖς [z]χριστοῦ.‖ 8 ἐάν.[a]τε‖.γὰρ [b]καὶ‖ περισ-
so also [are] we of Christ. For and if even more a-
σότερόν τι [c]καυχήσωμαι‖ περὶ τῆς.ἐξουσίας.ἡμῶν, ἧς
bundantly somewhat I should boast concerning our authority, which
ἔδωκεν ὁ κύριος [d]ἡμῖν‖ εἰς οἰκοδομὴν καὶ οὐκ εἰς καθαίρεσιν
[3]gave [1]the [2]Lord to us for building up and not for overthrowing
ὑμῶν, οὐκ.αἰσχυνθήσομαι 9 ἵνα μὴ.δόξω ὡς ἂν ἐκφοβεῖν
you, I shall not be put to shame; that I may not seem as if frightening
ὑμᾶς διὰ τῶν ἐπιστολῶν. 10 ὅτι αἱ [e]μὲν ἐπιστολαί,
you by means of epistles: because the epistles,
φησίν,‖ βαρεῖαι καὶ ἰσχυραί· ἡ.δὲ παρουσία τοῦ σώματος
says he, [are] weighty and strong, but the presence of the body
ἀσθενής, καὶ ὁ λόγος [f]ἐξουθενημένος.‖ 11 τοῦτο λογιζέσθω
weak, and the speech naught. This let [4]reckon
ὁ τοιοῦτος, ὅτι οἷοί ἐσμεν τῷ λόγῳ δι' ἐπιστολῶν ἀπόντες,
[1]such [2]a [3]one, that such as we are in word by epistles being absent,
τοιοῦτοι καὶ παρόντες τῷ ἔργῳ. 12 Οὐ.γὰρ τολμῶμεν
such [we are] also being present in deed. For [3]not [2]dare [1]we
[g]ἐγκρῖναι‖ ἢ [h]συγκρῖναι‖ ἑαυτούς τισιν τῶν ἑαυτοὺς συν-
rank among or compare [2]with [1]ourselves some who themselves com-
ιστανόντων, ἀλλὰ αὐτοὶ ἐν ἑαυτοῖς ἑαυτοὺς μετροῦντες, καὶ
mend; but these by themselves themselves measuring, and
[h]συγκρίνοντες‖ ἑαυτοὺς ἑαυτοῖς, οὐ.[i]συνιοῦσιν.‖ 13 ἡμεῖς
comparing themselves with themselves, do not understand. [2]We
δὲ [k]οὐχὶ‖ εἰς τὰ ἄμετρα καυχησόμεθα, ἀλλὰ κατὰ
[1]now not to the things beyond measure will boast, but according to
τὸ μέτρον τοῦ κανόνος οὗ ἐμέρισεν ἡμῖν ὁ θεὸς μέτρου
the measure of the rule which [5]divided [6]to [7]us [1]the [2]God [3]of [4]measure
ἐφικέσθαι ἄχρι καὶ ὑμῶν. 14 [l]οὐ γὰρ ὡς‖ μὴ ἐφικνούμενοι εἰς
to reach [2]to [1]also you. [2]Not [1]for as not reaching to

think of us as if we
walked according to
the flesh. 3 For though
we walk in the flesh,
we do not war after
the flesh: 4 (for the
weapons of our war-
fare *are* not carnal,
but mighty through
God to the pulling
down of strong holds;)
5 casting down imagi-
nations, and every
high thing that exalt-
eth itself against the
knowledge of God, and
bringing into captivi-
ty every thought to the
obedience of Christ;
6 and having in a
readiness to revenge
all disobedience, when
your obedience is ful-
filled. 7 Do ye look
on things after the
outward appearance?
If any man trust to
himself that he is
Christ's, let him of
himself think this a-
gain, that, as he *is*
Christ's, even so *are*
we Christ's. 8 For
though I should boast
somewhat more of our
authority, which the
Lord hath given us for
edification, and not for
your destruction, I
should not be asham-
ed: 9 that I may not
seem as if I would
terrify you by letters.
10 For *his* letters, say
they, *are* weighty and
powerful; but *his* bo-
dily presence *is* weak,
and *his* speech con-
temptible. 11 Let such
an one think this, that,
such as we are in word
by letters when we are
absent, such *will we*
be also in deed when
we are present. 12 For
we dare not make our-
selves of the number,
or compare ourselves
with some that com-
mend themselves: but
they measuring them-
selves by themselves,
and comparing them-
selves among them-
selves, are not wise.
13 But we will not
boast of things with-
out *our* measure, but
according to the mea-
sure of the rule which
God hath distributed
to us, a measure to
reach even unto you.
14 For we stretch not
ourselves beyond *our*
measure, as though we

---

[x] στρατιᾶς T. [y] ἐφ' TTr. [z] — χριστοῦ GLTTrAW. [a] — τε and [L]Tr[A]. [b] — καὶ LTTrA. [c] καυχήσομαι I shall boast T. [d] — ἡμῖν LTTrA. [e] ἐπιστολαὶ μέν φησιν (φασιν say they L) LTTr. [f] ἐξουδενημένος L. [g] ἐν- T. [h] συν- T. [i] συνιᾶσιν LTTrA. [k] οὐκ LTTrAW. [l] ὡς γὰρ (*reading the sentence as a question*) L.

reached not unto you: for we are come as far as to you also in *preaching* the gospel of Christ: 15 not boasting of things without *our* measure, *that is*, of other men's labours; but having hope, when your faith is increased, that we shall be enlarged by you according to our rule abundantly, 16 to preach the gospel in the *regions* beyond you, *and* not to boast in another man's line of things made ready to our hand. 17 But he that glorieth, let him glory in the Lord. 18 For not he that commendeth himself is approved, but whom the Lord commendeth.

XI. Would to God ye could bear with me a little in *my* folly: and indeed bear with me. 2 For I am jealous over you with godly jealousy: for I have espoused you to one husband, that I may present *you as* a chaste virgin to Christ. 3 But I fear, lest by any means, as the serpent beguiled Eve through his subtilty, so your minds should be corrupted from the simplicity that is in Christ. 4 For if he that cometh preacheth another Jesus, whom we have not preached, or *if* ye receive another spirit, which ye have not received, or another gospel, which ye have not accepted, ye might well bear with *him*. 5 For I suppose I was not a whit behind the very chiefest apostles. 6 But though *I be* rude in speech, yet not in knowledge; but we have been throughly made manifest among you in all things. 7 Have I committed an offence in abasing myself that ye might be exalted, because I have preached to you the gospel of God freely? 8 I robbed other churches, taking wages *of them*, to do you service. 9 And

ὑμᾶς ὑπερεκτείνομεν ἑαυτούς· ἄχρι.γὰρ καὶ ὑμῶν ἐφθάσαμεν
you do we overstretch ourselves, (for to [2]also [1]you we came
ἐν τῷ εὐαγγελίῳ τοῦ χριστοῦ· 15 οὐκ εἰς τὰ ἄμετρα
in the glad tidings of the Christ;) not [2]to [3]the [4]things [5]beyond [6]measure
καυχώμενοι ἐν ἀλλοτρίοις κόποις, ἐλπίδα.δὲ ἔχοντες, αὐξανο-
[1]boasting in others' labours, but hope having, [3]increas-
μένης τῆς.πίστεως.ὑμῶν, ἐν ὑμῖν μεγαλυνθῆναι κατὰ
ing [1]your [2]faith, among you to be enlarged according to
τὸν.κανόνα.ἡμῶν εἰς περισσείαν, 16 εἰς τὰ ὑπερέκεινα ὑμῶν
our rule to abundance, to that beyond you
εὐαγγελίσασθαι, οὐκ ἐν ἀλλοτρίῳ κανόνι εἰς τὰ
to announce the glad tidings, not [3]in [4]another's [5]rule [6]as [7]to [8]things
ἕτοιμα καυχήσασθαι. 17 Ὁ.δὲ καυχώμενος, ἐν κυρίῳ
[9]ready [1]to [2]boast. But he that boasts, in [the] Lord
καυχάσθω· 18 οὐ.γὰρ ὁ ἑαυτὸν [n]συνιστῶν,‖ ἐκεῖνός ἐστιν
let him boast, For not he that himself commends, this [one] is
δόκιμος, [o]ἀλλ'‖ ὃν ὁ κύριος συνίστησιν.
approved, but whom the Lord commends.

11 Ὄφελον [p]ἀνείχεσθέ‖ μου μικρὸν [q] [r]τῇ ἀφροσύνῃ·‖
I would ye were bearing with me a little in folly;
ἀλλὰ καὶ ἀνέχεσθέ μου. 2 ζηλῶ.γὰρ ὑμᾶς θεοῦ ζή-
but indeed bear with me. For I am jealous as to you [4]of [5]God [1]with [[2]the]
λῳ· ἡρμοσάμην.γὰρ ὑμᾶς ἑνὶ ἀνδρὶ παρθένον ἁγνὴν
[3]jealousy, for I have espoused you to one man [4]a [6]virgin [5]chaste
παραστῆσαι τῷ χριστῷ· 3 φοβοῦμαι.δὲ μήπως ὡς ὁ
[1]to [2]present [[3]you] to the Christ. But I fear lest by any means as the
ὄφις [s]Εὔαν ἐξηπάτησεν‖ ἐν τῇ.πανουργίᾳ.αὐτοῦ, [t]οὕτως‖
serpent [2]Eve [1]deceived in his craftiness, so
φθαρῇ τὰ.νοήματα.ὑμῶν ἀπὸ τῆς ἁπλότητος [v] τῆς
should be corrupted your thoughts from simplicity which [is]
εἰς [w]τὸν‖ χριστόν. 4 εἰ.μὲν.γὰρ ὁ ἐρχόμενος ἄλλον Ἰησοῦν
as to the Christ. For if indeed he that comes another Jesus
κηρύσσει ὃν οὐκ.ἐκηρύξαμεν, ἢ πνεῦμα ἕτερον λαμβάνετε
proclaims whom we did not proclaim, or a [2]spirit [1]different ye receive
ὃ οὐκ.ἐλάβετε, ἢ εὐαγγέλιον ἕτερον ὃ οὐκ.ἐδέξασθε,
which ye did not receive, or [2]glad [3]tidings [1]different which ye did not accept,
καλῶς [x]ἠνείχεσθε.‖ 5 Λογίζομαι [y]γὰρ‖ μηδὲν ὑστερη-
well were ye bearing with [it]. [2]I [3]reckon [1]for in nothing to have been
κέναι τῶν [z]ὑπὲρ.λίαν‖ ἀποστόλων. 6 εἰ.δὲ καὶ ἰδιώτης
behind those in a surpassing degree apostles. But if even unpolished
τῷ λόγῳ, ἀλλ' οὐ τῇ γνώσει· ἀλλ' ἐν παντὶ [a]φανε-
in speech [I am], yet not in knowledge; but in every [way] made
ρωθέντες‖ ἐν πᾶσιν εἰς ὑμᾶς. 7 ἢ ἁμαρτίαν.ἐποίησα, ἐμαυτὸν
manifest in all things to you. Or did I commit sin, [2]myself
ταπεινῶν ἵνα ὑμεῖς ὑψωθῆτε, ὅτι δωρεὰν τὸ τοῦ θεοῦ
[1]humbling that ye might be exalted, because gratuitously the [3]of [4]God
εὐαγγέλιον εὐηγγελισάμην ὑμῖν; 8 ἄλλας ἐκκλησίας ἐσύλησα,
[1]glad [2]tidings I announced to you? Other assemblies I despoiled,
λαβὼν ὀψώνιον πρὸς τὴν ὑμῶν διακονίαν· 9 καὶ
having received wages for [2]towards [3]you [1]service. And
παρὼν πρὸς ὑμᾶς καὶ ὑστερηθείς, οὐ κατενάρκησα
being present with you and having been deficient, I did lazily burden

---

[n] συνιστάνων LTTrAW. [o] ἀλλὰ LTr. [p] ἠνείχεσθέ E. [q] + τι some (little) ELTTrAW. [r] τῆς E; ἀφροσύνης ELTTrAW. [s] ἐξηπάτησεν Εὔαν LTTrAW. [t] — οὕτως LTTrA. [v] + καὶ τῆς ἁγνότητος and the purity LTrAW. [w] — τὸν T. [x] ἀνείχεσθε GTTrW; ἀνέχεσθε ye bear with LA. [y] δὲ but L. [z] ὑπερλίαν GLTAW. [a] φανερώσαντες having made [it] manifest LTTrA.

[b]οὐδενός·‖ τὸ.γὰρ ὑστέρημά μου προσανεπλήρωσαν οἱ ἀδελ-
no one, (for the deficiency of me [3]completely [4]filled [5]up [1]the [2]breth-
φοὶ ἐλθόντες ἀπὸ Μακεδονίας· καὶ ἐν παντὶ ἀβαρῆ
ren who came from Macedonia,) and in everything not burdensome
[c]ὑμῖν ἐμαυτὸν‖ ἐτήρησα καὶ τηρήσω. 10 ἔστιν ἀλήθεια
to you myself I kept and will keep. [5]Is [[1]the] [2]truth
χριστοῦ ἐν ἐμοὶ ὅτι ἡ.καύχησις.αὕτη [d]οὐ.σφραγίσεται‖ εἰς ἐμὲ
[3]of [4]Christ in me that this boasting shall not be sealed up as to me
ἐν τοῖς κλίμασιν τῆς Ἀχαΐας. 11 [e]διατί‖; ὅτι οὐκ.ἀγαπῶ
in the regions of Achaia. Why? because I do not love
ὑμᾶς; ὁ θεὸς οἶδεν· 12 ὃ.δὲ ποιῶ, καὶ ποιήσω, ἵνα ἐκ-
you? God knows. But what I do, also I will do, that I may
κόψω τὴν ἀφορμὴν τῶν θελόντων ἀφορμήν, ἵνα ἐν.ᾧ καυ-
cut off the occasion of those wishing an occasion, that wherein they
χῶνται εὑρεθῶσιν καθὼς καὶ ἡμεῖς. 13 οἱ.γὰρ.τοιοῦτοι
boast they may be found according as also we. For such [are]
ψευδαπόστολοι, ἐργάται δόλιοι, μετασχηματιζόμενοι εἰς ἀπο-
false apostles, [2]workers [1]deceitful, transforming themselves into apo-
στόλους χριστοῦ· 14 καὶ [f]οὐ θαυμαστόν·‖ αὐτὸς.γὰρ ὁ
stles of Christ. And not wonderful [is it], for [2]himself
σατανᾶς μετασχηματίζεται εἰς ἄγγελον φωτός· 15 οὐ
[1]Satan transforms himself into an angel of light. [It is] not
μέγα οὖν εἰ καὶ οἱ.διάκονοι.αὐτοῦ μετασχηματίζον-
a great thing therefore if also his servants transform themselves
ται ὡς διάκονοι δικαιοσύνης, ὧν τὸ τέλος ἔσται κατὰ
as servants of righteousness; of whom the end shall be according to
τὰ.ἔργα.αὐτῶν.
their works.

16 Πάλιν λέγω, μή τίς με δόξῃ ἄφρονα εἶναι· εἰ.δὲ
Again I say, Not anyone [3]me [1]should [2]think a fool to be; but if
μήγε, κἂν ὡς ἄφρονα δέξασθέ με, ἵνα [g]μικρόν τι κἀγὼ‖
otherwise, even as a fool receive me, that [2]little [1]some I also
καυχήσωμαι. 17 ὃ λαλῶ, οὐ [h]λαλῶ κατὰ κύριον,‖
may boast. What I speak, [2]not [3]do [1]I speak according to [the] Lord,
ἀλλ' ὡς ἐν ἀφροσύνῃ, ἐν ταύτῃ τῇ ὑποστάσει τῆς καυχήσεως.
but as in folly, in this confidence of boasting.
18 ἐπεὶ πολλοὶ καυχῶνται κατὰ [i]τὴν‖ σάρκα, κἀγὼ καυ-
Since many boast according to flesh, I also will
χήσομαι. 19 ἡδέως.γὰρ ἀνέχεσθε τῶν ἀφρόνων, φρόνιμοι
boast. For [4]gladly [1]ye [5]bear [6]with [7]fools [3]intelligent
ὄντες· 20 ἀνέχεσθε.γὰρ εἴ τις ὑμᾶς καταδουλοῖ, εἴ τις
[2]being. For ye bear [it] if anyone [2]you [1]bring into bondage, if anyone
κατεσθίει, εἴ τις λαμβάνει, εἴ τις ἐπαίρεται,
devour [you], if anyone take [from you], if anyone exalt himself,
εἴ τις [k]ὑμᾶς εἰς πρόσωπον‖ δέρει. 21 κατὰ ἀτιμίαν λέγω,
if anyone [2]you [3]on [4]the [5]face [1]beat. As to dishonour I speak,
ὡς ὅτι ἡμεῖς [l]ἠσθενήσαμεν·‖ ἐν.ᾧ.δ' ἄν τις τολμᾷ, ἐν
as that we were weak; but wherein anyone may be daring, (in
ἀφροσύνῃ λέγω, τολμῶ κἀγώ. 22 Ἑβραῖοί εἰσιν; κἀγώ·
folly I speak,) [2]am [3]daring [1]I also. Hebrews are they? I also.
[m]Ἰσραηλῖταί‖ εἰσιν; κἀγώ· σπέρμα Ἀβραάμ εἰσιν; κἀγώ·
Israelites are they? I also. Seed of Abraham are they? I also.

when I was present with you, and wanted, I was chargeable to no man: for that which was lacking to me the brethren which came from Macedonia supplied: and in all *things* I have kept myself from being burdensome unto you, and *so* will I keep *myself*. 10 As the truth of Christ is in me, no man shall stop me of this boasting in the regions of Achaia. 11 Wherefore? because I love you not? God knoweth. 12 But what I do, that I will do, that I may cut off occasion from them which desire occasion; that wherein they glory, they may be found even as we. 13 For such *are* false apostles, deceitful workers, transforming themselves into the apostles of Christ. 14 And no marvel; for Satan himself is transformed into an angel of light. 15 Therefore *it is* no great thing if his ministers also be transformed as the ministers of righteousness; whose end shall be according to their works.

16 I say again, Let no man think me a fool; if otherwise, yet as a fool receive me, that I may boast myself a little. 17 That which I speak, I speak *it* not after the Lord, but as it were foolishly, in this confidence of boasting. 18 Seeing that many glory after the flesh, I will glory also. 19 For ye suffer fools gladly, seeing ye *yourselves* are wise. 20 For ye suffer, if a man bring you into bondage, if a man devour *you*, if a man take *of you*, if a man exalt himself, if a man smite you on the face. 21 I speak as concerning reproach, as though we had been weak. Howbeit whereinsoever any is bold, (I speak foolishly,) I am bold also. 22 Are they Hebrews? so *am* I. Are they Israelites? so *am* I. Are they the seed of

---

[b] οὐθενός LTTrA. [c] ἐμαυτὸν ὑμῖν LTTrA. [d] οὐ φραγήσεται shall not be stopped EGLTTrAW. [e] διὰ τί LTrA. [f] οὐ θαῦμα no wonder LTTrAW. [g] κἀγὼ μικρόν τι GLTTrAW. [h] κατὰ κύριον λαλῶ LTTrAW. [i] — τὴν TTr. [k] εἰς πρόσωπον ὑμᾶς LTTrAW. [l] ἠσθενήκαμεν have been weak LTTr. [m] Ἰσραηλεῖταί T.

Abraham? so *am* I.
23 Are they mini-ters
of Christ? (I speak as
a fool) I *am* more;
in labours more abun-
dant, in stripes above
measure, in prisons
more frequent, in
deaths oft. 24 Of the
Jews five times re-
ceived I forty *stripes*
save one. 25 Thrice
was I beaten with
rods, once was I stoned,
thrice I suffered ship-
wreck, a night and
a day I have been
in the deep; 26 *in*
journeyings often, *in*
perils of waters, *in*
perils of robbers, *in*
perils by *mine own*
countrymen, *in* perils
by the heathen, *in* pe-
rils in the city, *in* perils in the wilderness,
in perils in the sea, *in*
perils among false
brethren; 27 in weari-
ness and painfulness,
in watchings often, in
hunger and thirst, in
fastings often, in cold
and nakedness. 28 Be-
side those things that
are without, that
which cometh upon
me daily, the care
of all the churches.
29 Who is weak, and I
am not weak? who is
offended, and I burn
not? 30 If I must
needs glory, I will
glory of the things
which concern mine
infirmities. 31 The God
and Father of our
Lord Jesus Christ,
which is blessed for
evermore, knoweth
that I lie not. 32 In
Damascus the govern-
or under Aretas the
king kept the city of
the Damascenes with
a garrison, desirous to
apprehend me: 33 and
through a window in a
basket was I let down
by the wall, and escap-
ed his hands.

XII. It is not expe-
dient for me doubt-
less to glory. I will
come to visions and
revelations of the
Lord. 2 I knew a man
in Christ above four-
teen years ago, (whe-
ther in the body, I can-
not tell; or whether
out of the body, I can-
not tell: God know-
eth;) such an one

23 διάκονοι χριστοῦ εἰσιν; παραφρονῶν λαλῶ, [n]ὑπὲρ
Servants of Christ are they? (as being beside myself I speak,) above

ἐγώ·‖ ἐν κόποις περισσοτέρως, [o]ἐν πληγαῖς ὑπερ-
[measure] I [too]; in labours more abundantly, in stripes above

βαλλόντως, ἐν φυλακαῖς περισσοτέρως,‖ ἐν θανάτοις πολ-
measure, in imprisonments more abundantly, in deaths often.

λάκις. 24 ὑπὸ Ἰουδαίων πεντάκις [p]τεσσαράκοντα‖
From Jews five times forty [stripes]

παρὰ μίαν ἔλαβον, 25 τρὶς [q]ἐῤῥαβδίσθην,‖ ἅπαξ ἐλιθάσθην,
except one I received. Thrice I was beaten with rods, once I was stoned,

τρὶς ἐναυάγησα, νυχθήμερον ἐν τῷ βυθῷ πεποίηκα·
three times I was shipwrecked, a night and a day in the deep I have passed:

26 ὁδοιπορίαις πολλάκις· κινδύνοις ποταμῶν, κινδύνοις
in journeyings often, in perils of rivers, in perils

λῃστῶν, κινδύνοις ἐκ γένους, κινδύνοις ἐξ ἐθνῶν,
of robbers, in perils from [my own] race, in perils from [the] nations,

κινδύνοις ἐν πόλει, κινδύνοις ἐν ἐρημίᾳ, κινδύνοις ἐν
in perils in [the] city, in perils in [the] desert, in perils on

θαλάσσῃ, κινδύνοις ἐν ψευδαδέλφοις· 27 [r]ἐν‖ κόπῳ καὶ
[the] sea, in perils among false brethren; in labour and

μόχθῳ, ἐν ἀγρυπνίαις πολλάκις, ἐν λιμῷ καὶ δίψει, ἐν νη-
toil, in watchings often, in hunger and thirst, in fast-

στείαις πολλάκις, ἐν ψύχει καὶ γυμνότητι· 28 χωρὶς τῶν
ings often, in cold and nakedness. Besides the things

παρεκτός, [s]ἡ ἐπισύστασίς μου‖ ἡ καθ᾽.ἡμέραν, ἡ μέριμνα
without, the crowding on me daily, the care

πασῶν τῶν ἐκκλησιῶν. 29 τίς ἀσθενεῖ, καὶ οὐκ.ἀσθενῶ; τίς
concerning all the assemblies. Who is weak, and I am not weak? who

σκανδαλίζεται, καὶ οὐκ ἐγὼ πυροῦμαι; 30 εἰ καυχᾶσθαι
is offended, and [3]not [1]I [2]do burn? If [3]to [4]boast

δεῖ, τὰ τῆς.ἀσθενείας.μου καυχήσομαι. 31 Ὁ
[1]it [2]behoves, [in] the things concerning my infirmity I will boast. The

θεὸς καὶ πατὴρ τοῦ.κυρίου.[t]ἡμῶν‖ Ἰησοῦ [v]χριστοῦ‖ οἶδεν, ὁ
God and Father of our Lord Jesus Christ knows, he who

ὢν εὐλογητὸς εἰς τοὺς αἰῶνας, ὅτι οὐ.ψεύδομαι. 32 ἐν Δα-
is blessed to the ages, that I do not lie. In Da-

μασκῷ ὁ ἐθνάρχης Ἀρέτα τοῦ βασιλέως ἐφρούρει τὴν
mascus the ethnarch of Aretas the king was guarding the

[w]Δαμασκηνῶν πόλιν,‖ πιάσαι με [x]θέλων·‖ 33 καὶ διὰ
[2]of [3]the [4]Damascenes [1]city, [6]to [7]take [8]me [5]wishing. And through

θυρίδος ἐν σαργάνῃ ἐχαλάσθην διὰ τοῦ τείχους, καὶ
a window in a basket I was let down through the wall, and

ἐξέφυγον τὰς.χεῖρας.αὐτοῦ.
escaped his hands.

12 Καυχᾶσθαι [y]δὴ οὐ.συμφέρει μοι· ἐλεύσομαι.γὰρ‖ [z]εἰς
To boast indeed is not profitable to me; for I will come to

ὀπτασίας καὶ ἀποκαλύψεις κυρίου· 2 οἶδα ἄνθρωπον ἐν
visions and revelations of [the] Lord. I know a man in

χριστῷ πρὸ.ἐτῶν δεκατεσσάρων, εἴτε ἐν σώματι οὐκ.οἶδα,
Christ [2]years [3]ago [1]fourteen, (whether in [the] body I know not,

εἴτε ἐκτὸς [a]τοῦ‖ σώματος οὐκ.οἶδα· ὁ θεὸς οἶδεν· ἁρπαγέντα
or out of the body I know not, God knows,) [4]caught [5]away

---

[n] ὑπερεγώ L. [o] ἐν φυλακαῖς περισσοτέρως, ἐν πληγαῖς ὑπερβαλλόντως LTrA; ἐν πλη. περισ. ἐν φυλ. ὑπερβ. T. [p] τεσσεράκοντα LTTrA. [q] ἐραβδίσθην LTTrA. [r] — ἐν LTTrAW. [s] ἡ ἐπίστασίς μοι my anxiety LTTrAW. [t] — ἡμῶν (read the Lord) LTTrAW. [v] — χριστοῦ LTTrA. [w] πόλιν Δαμασκηνῶν LTTrA. [x] — θέλων LTTr[A]W. [y] δεῖ, οὐ συμφέρον μέν, ἐλεύσομαι δὲ it behoves [me], not profitable [is it], but I will come LTTr. [z] + καὶ also L. [a] — τοῦ L.

τὸν.τοιοῦτον ἕως [a] τρίτου οὐρανοῦ. 3 καὶ οἶδα τὸν τοιοῦτον
[1]such [2]a [3]one to [the] third heaven. And I know such
ἄνθρωπον, εἴτε ἐν σώματι εἴτε [b]ἐκτὸς[॥] τοῦ σώματος [c]οὐκ
a man, (whether in [the] body or out of the body [3]not
οἶδα·[॥] ὁ θεὸς οἶδεν· 4 ὅτι ἡρπάγη εἰς τὸν παράδεισον,
[1]I [2]know, God knows:) that he was caught away to Paradise,
καὶ ἤκουσεν ἄῤῥητα ῥήματα, ἃ οὐκ.ἐξὸν ἀνθρώπῳ
and heard unutterable sayings, which it is not permitted to man
λαλῆσαι. 5 ὑπὲρ τοῦ.τοιούτου καυχήσομαι· ὑπὲρ.δὲ ἐμαυτοῦ
to speak. Concerning such a one I will boast, but concerning myself
οὐ.καυχήσομαι, εἰ.μὴ ἐν ταῖς.ἀσθενείαις.[d]μου·[॥] 6 ἐὰν.γὰρ
I will not boast, unless in my weaknesses. For if
θελήσω καυχήσασθαι, οὐκ.ἔσομαι ἄφρων· ἀλήθειαν.γὰρ
I should desire to boast, I shall not be a fool; for truth
ἐρῶ· φείδομαι.δέ, μή τις εἰς ἐμὲ λογίσηται ὑπὲρ ὃ
I will say; but I forbear, lest anyone as to me should reckon above what
βλέπει με, ἢ ἀκούει [e]τι[॥] ἐξ ἐμοῦ. 7 Καὶ τῇ ὑπερβολῇ
he sees me, or hears anything of me. And by the surpassingness
τῶν ἀποκαλύψεων [f]ἵνα μὴ.ὑπεραίρωμαι, ἐδόθη μοι σκόλοψ
of the revelations that I might not be exalted, was given to me a thorn
τῇ σαρκί, ἄγγελος [g]σατᾶν[॥] ἵνα με κολαφίζῃ, [h]ἵνα μὴ
for the flesh, a messenger of Satan, that me he might buffet, that [3]not
ὑπεραίρωμαι.[॥] 8 [i]ὑπὲρ τούτου τρὶς τὸν κύριον παρεκάλεσα,
[1]I [2]might be exalted. For this thrice the Lord I besought
ἵνα ἀποστῇ ἀπ' ἐμοῦ· 9 καὶ εἴρηκέν μοι, Ἀρκεῖ σοι ἡ
that it might depart from me, And he said to me, Suffices thee
χάρις.μου· ἡ.γὰρ δύναμίς [k]μου[॥] ἐν ἀσθενείᾳ [l]τελειοῦται.[॥]
my grace; for the power of me in weakness is perfected.
ἥδιστα οὖν μᾶλλον καυχήσομαι ἐν ταῖς.ἀσθενείαις.[m]μου[॥]
Most gladly therefore rather will I boast in my weaknesses
ἵνα ἐπισκηνώσῃ ἐπ' ἐμὲ ἡ δύναμις τοῦ χριστοῦ. 10 διὸ
that may dwell upon me the power of the Christ. Wherefore
εὐδοκῶ ἐν ἀσθενείαις, ἐν ὕβρεσιν, ἐν ἀνάγκαις, ἐν διωγ-
I take pleasure in weaknesses, in insults, in necessities, in perse-
μοῖς, [n]ἐν[॥] στενοχωρίαις, ὑπὲρ χριστοῦ· ὅταν.γὰρ ἀσθενῶ,
cutions, in straits, for Christ: for when I may be weak,
τότε δυνατός εἰμι.
then powerful I am.

11 Γέγονα ἄφρων [o]καυχώμενος·[॥] ὑμεῖς με ἠναγκάσατε.
I have become a fool boasting; ye me compelled:
ἐγὼ.γὰρ ὤφειλον ὑφ' ὑμῶν συνίστασθαι· οὐδὲν.γὰρ
for I ought by you to have been commended; for nothing
ὑστέρησα τῶν [p]ὑπὲρ.λίαν[॥] ἀποστόλων, εἰ καὶ οὐδέν εἰμι.
I was behind those in a surpassing degree apostles, if also nothing I am.
12 Τὰ μὲν σημεῖα τοῦ ἀποστόλου [q]κατειργάσθη[॥] ἐν ὑμῖν
The [2]indeed [1]signs of the apostle were worked out among you
ἐν πάσῃ ὑπομονῇ, [r]ἐν[॥] σημείοις [s]καὶ[॥] τέρασιν καὶ δυνάμεσιν.
in all endurance, in signs and wonders and works of power.
13 τί.γάρ ἐστιν ὃ [t]ἡττήθητε[॥] ὑπὲρ τὰς λοιπὰς ἐκ-
For in what is it that ye were inferior beyond the rest [of the] as-
κλησίας, εἰ.μὴ ὅτι αὐτὸς ἐγὼ οὐ.κατενάρκησα ὑμῶν; χαρί-
semblies, unless that [2]myself [1]I did not lazily burden you? For-

caught up to the third heaven. 3 And I knew such a man, (whether in the body, or out of the body, I cannot tell: God knoweth;) 4 how that he was caught up into paradise, and heard unspeakable words, which it is not lawful for a man to utter. 5 Of such an one will I glory: yet of myself I will not glory, but in mine infirmities. 6 For though I would desire to glory, I shall not be a fool; for I will say the truth: but *now* I forbear, lest any man should think of me above that which he seeth me *to be*, or *that* he heareth of me. 7 And lest I should be exalted above measure through the abundance of the revelations, there was given to me a thorn in the flesh, the messenger of Satan to buffet me, lest I should be exalted above measure. 8 For this thing I besought the Lord thrice, that it might depart from me. 9 And he said unto me, My grace is sufficient for thee: for my strength is made perfect in weakness. Most gladly therefore will I rather glory in my infirmities, that the power of Christ may rest upon me. 10 Therefore I take pleasure in infirmities, in reproaches, in necessities, in persecutions, in distresses for Christ's sake: for when I am weak, then am I strong.

11 I am become a fool in glorying; ye have compelled me: for I ought to have been commended of you: for in nothing am I behind the very chiefest apostles, though I be nothing. 12 Truly the signs of an apostle were wrought among you in all patience, in signs, and wonders, and mighty deeds. 13 For what is it wherein ye were inferior to other churches,

---

[b] χωρὶς apart from LTTrA. [c] — οὐκ οἶδα L. [d] — μου my LTr[A]. [e] — τι LTTr[A]. [f] + διὸ therefore LTr[A]. [g] σατανᾶ LTTrA. [h] — ἵνα μὴ ὑπεραίρωμαι [L]Tr[A]. [i] + [καὶ] and L. [k] — μου LTTrA. [l] τελεῖται LTTrA. [m] [μου] Tr. [n] καὶ and T. [o] — καυχώμενος GLTTrAW. [p] ὑπερλίαν GLTAW. [q] κατηργάσθη T. [r] — ἐν LTTrAW. [s] τε καὶ and also TA. [t] ἡσσώθητε LTTrA.

except *it be* that I myself was not burdensome to you? forgive me this wrong. 14 Behold, the third time I am ready to come to you; and I will not be burdensome to you: for I seek not yours, but you: for the children ought not to lay up for the parents, but the parents for the children. 15 And I will very gladly spend and be spent for you; though the more abundantly I love you, the less I be loved. 16 But be it so, I did not burden you: nevertheless, being crafty, I caught you with guile. 17 Did I make a gain of you by any of them whom I sent unto you? 18 I desired Titus, and with *him* I sent a brother. Did Titus make a gain of you? walked we not in the same spirit? *walked we* not in the same steps?

19 Again, think ye that we excuse ourselves unto you? we speak before God in Christ: but *we do* all things, dearly beloved, for your edifying. 20 For I fear, lest, when I come, I shall not find you such as I would, and *that* I shall be found unto you such as ye would not: lest *there be* debates, envyings, wraths, strifes, backbitings, whisperings, swellings, tumults: 21 *and* lest, when I come again, my God will humble me among you, and *that* I shall bewail many which have sinned already, and have not repented of the uncleanness and fornication and lasciviousness which they have committed.

XIII. This *is* the third *time* I am coming to you. In the mouth of two or three witnesses shall every word be established. 2 I told you before, and foretell you, as if I were present, the second time; and being absent now I write

σασθέ μοι τὴν.ἀδικίαν.ταύτην. 14 ἰδοὺ τρίτον [u] ἑτοίμως ἔχω
give me this injustice. Lo, a third time ready I am
ἐλθεῖν πρὸς ὑμᾶς, καὶ οὐ καταναρκήσω [v]ὑμῶν·‖ οὐ.γὰρ.ζητῶ
to come to you, and I will not lazily burden you; for I do not seek
τὰ ὑμῶν, [w]ἀλλ'‖ ὑμᾶς. οὐ.γὰρ ὀφείλει τὰ τέκνα τοῖς
the things of you, but you; for [4]not [3]ought [1]the [2]children for the
γονεῦσιν θησαυρίζειν, [x]ἀλλ'‖ οἱ γονεῖς τοῖς τέκνοις. 15 ἐγὼ.δὲ
parents to treasure up, but the parents for the children. Now I
ἥδιστα δαπανήσω καὶ ἐκδαπανηθήσομαι ὑπὲρ τῶν ψυχῶν
most gladly will spend and will be utterly spent for [2]souls
ὑμῶν· εἰ [y]καὶ‖ περισσοτέρως ὑμᾶς [z]ἀγαπῶν,‖ [a]ἧττον‖ [b]ἀγαπῶ-
[1]your, if even more abundantly [2]you [1]loving, less I am loved.
μαι.‖ 16 Ἔστω.δέ, ἐγὼ οὐ.κατεβάρησα ὑμᾶς· [w]ἀλλ'‖ ὑπάρχων
But be it so, I did not burden you; but being
πανοῦργος δόλῳ ὑμᾶς ἔλαβον. 17 μή τινα ὧν ἀπέσταλκα
crafty with guile you I took. Any of whom I have sent
πρὸς ὑμᾶς, δι' αὐτοῦ ἐπλεονέκτησα ὑμᾶς; 18 παρεκάλεσα
to you, by him did I overreach you? I besought
Τίτον, καὶ συναπέστειλα τὸν ἀδελφόν· μή τι ἐπλεονέκτησεν
Titus, and sent with [him] the brother: Did [2]overreach
ὑμᾶς Τίτος; οὐ τῷ αὐτῷ πνεύματι περιεπατήσαμεν; οὐ
[3]you [1]Titus? Not by the same spirit walked we? Not
τοῖς αὐτοῖς ἴχνεσιν;
in the same steps?

19 [c]Πάλιν‖ δοκεῖτε ὅτι ὑμῖν ἀπολογούμεθα;[c] [d]κατενώ-
Again do ye think that to you we are making a defence? be-
πιον‖ [e]τοῦ‖ θεοῦ ἐν χριστῷ λαλοῦμεν· τὰ.δὲ.πάντα, ἀγαπητοί,
fore God in Christ we speak; and all things, beloved,
ὑπὲρ τῆς.ὑμῶν.οἰκοδομῆς. 20 φοβοῦμαι.γάρ, μήπως ἐλθὼν
for your building up. For I fear, lest perhaps having come
οὐχ οἵους θέλω εὕρω ὑμᾶς, κἀγὼ εὑρεθῶ ὑμῖν οἷον
not such as I wish I should find you, and I be found by you such as
οὐ.θέλετε· μήπως [f]ἔρεις,‖ [g]ζῆλοι,‖ θυμοί, ἐριθεῖαι,
ye do not wish: lest perhaps [there be] strifes, jealousies, indignations, contentions,
καταλαλιαί, ψιθυρισμοί, φυσιώσεις, ἀκαταστασίαι· 21 μὴ
evil speakings, whisperings, puffings up, commotions; lest
πάλιν [h]ἐλθόντα με‖ [i]ταπεινώσῃ‖ [k] ὁ θεός μου πρὸς ὑμᾶς,
again having come [5]me [3]should [4]humble [2]God [1]my as to you,
καὶ πενθήσω πολλοὺς τῶν προημαρτηκότων, καὶ
and I should mourn over many of those who have before sinned, and
μὴ.μετανοησάντων ἐπὶ τῇ ἀκαθαρσίᾳ καὶ πορνείᾳ καὶ ἀσελ-
have not repented upon the uncleanness and fornication and licen-
γείᾳ ᾗ ἔπραξαν.
tiousness which they practised.

13 Τρίτον.τοῦτο ἔρχομαι πρὸς ὑμᾶς. ἐπὶ στόματος
This third time I am coming to you. In [the] mouth
δύο μαρτύρων καὶ τριῶν σταθήσεται πᾶν ῥῆμα. 2 προεί-
of two witnesses or of three shall be established every matter. I have be-
ρηκα καὶ προλέγω, ὡς παρὼν τὸ δεύτερον, καὶ
fore declared and I say beforehand, as being present the second time, and
ἀπὼν νῦν [l]γράφω‖ τοῖς προημαρτηκόσιν, καὶ τοῖς
being absent now I write to those who have before sinned, and to [2]the

[u] + τοῦτο this (third time) GLTTr[A]W. [v] — ὑμῶν LTTrA. [w] ἀλλὰ LTTrAW. [x] ἀλλὰ TTr. [y] — καὶ LTTrA. [z] ἀγαπῶ I love T. [a] ἧσσον LTTrA. [b] ἀγαπῶμαι; am I loved? T. [c] Πάλαι and —; (*read* Long ago ye are thinking, &c.) LTTrA. [d] κατέναντι LTTrAW. [e] — τοῦ LTTrAW. [f] ἔρις strife LT. [g] ζῆλος jealousy LTTrAW. [h] ἐλθόντος μου I having come LTTrAW. [i] ταπεινώσει shall humble LTTrA. [k] + με [5]me LTTrAW. [l] — γράφω GLTTrAW.

λοιποῖς πᾶσιν, ὅτι ἐὰν ἔλθω εἰς τὸ πάλιν οὐ.φείσομαι. 3 ἐπεὶ
[2]rest [1]all, that if I come again I will not spare. Since
δοκιμὴν ζητεῖτε τοῦ ἐν ἐμοὶ λαλοῦντος χριστοῦ, ὃς εἰς
a proof ye seek [4]in [5]me [3]speaking [1]of [2]Christ, (who towards
ὑμᾶς οὐκ.ἀσθενεῖ, ἀλλὰ δυνατεῖ ἐν ὑμῖν· 4 καὶ.γὰρ [m]εἰ‖
you is not weak, but is powerful in you, for indeed if
ἐσταυρώθη ἐξ ἀσθενείας, ἀλλὰ ζῇ ἐκ δυνάμεως θεοῦ·
he was crucified in weakness, yet he lives by [2]power [1]God's;
καὶ.γὰρ [n] ἡμεῖς ἀσθενοῦμεν ἐν αὐτῷ, ἀλλὰ [o]ζησόμεθα‖ σὺν
for indeed we are weak in him, but we shall live with
αὐτῷ ἐκ δυνάμεως θεοῦ [p]εἰς ὑμᾶς·‖ 5 ἑαυτοὺς πειράζετε
him by [2]power [1]God's towards you,) yourselves try ye
εἰ ἐστὲ ἐν τῇ πίστει, ἑαυτοὺς δοκιμάζετε. ἢ οὐκ.ἐπιγινώσκετε
if ye are in the faith; yourselves prove: or do ye not recognize
ἑαυτούς, ὅτι [q]Ἰησοῦς χριστὸς‖ ἐν ὑμῖν [r]ἐστιν‖; εἰ.μή τι ἀδό-
yourselves, that Jesus Christ in you is, unless re-
κιμοί ἐστε. 6 ἐλπίζω.δὲ ὅτι γνώσεσθε ὅτι ἡμεῖς οὐκ.ἐσμὲν
jected ye are? Now I hope that ye will know that we are not
ἀδόκιμοι. 7 [s]εὔχομαι‖.δὲ πρὸς τὸν θεὸν μὴ ποιῆσαι ὑμᾶς
rejected. But I pray to God [that] [2]may [3]do [1]ye
κακὸν μηδέν, οὐχ ἵνα ἡμεῖς δόκιμοι φανῶμεν, ἀλλ' ἵνα ὑμεῖς
[5]evil [4]nothing; not that we approved may appear, but that ye
τὸ καλὸν ποιῆτε, ἡμεῖς.δὲ ὡς ἀδόκιμοι ὦμεν. 8 οὐ.γὰρ
what [is] right may do, and we as rejected be. For not
δυνάμεθά τι κατὰ τῆς ἀληθείας, [t]ἀλλ'‖ ὑπὲρ τῆς ἀληθείας.
have we [2]power [1]any against the truth, but for the truth.
9 χαίρομεν.γὰρ ὅταν ἡμεῖς ἀσθενῶμεν, ὑμεῖς.δὲ δυνατοὶ ἦτε·
For we rejoice when we may be weak, and ye powerful may be.
τοῦτο.[v]δὲ‖ καὶ εὐχόμεθα, τὴν.ὑμῶν.κατάρτισιν. 10 διὰ.τοῦτο
But this also we pray for, your perfecting. On this account
ταῦτα ἀπὼν γράφω, ἵνα παρὼν μὴ ἀποτόμως χρή-
these things being absent I write, that being present not with severity I may
σωμαι, κατὰ τὴν ἐξουσίαν ἣν [w]ἔδωκέν μοι ὁ κύριος‖ εἰς
treat [you], according to the authority which [3]gave [4]me [1]the [2]Lord for
οἰκοδομὴν καὶ οὐκ εἰς καθαίρεσιν.
building up and not for overthrowing.

11 Λοιπόν, ἀδελφοί, χαίρετε, καταρτίζεσθε, παρακαλεῖσθε,
For the rest, brethren, rejoice; be perfected; be encouraged;
τὸ.αὐτὸ φρονεῖτε, εἰρηνεύετε· καὶ ὁ θεὸς τῆς ἀγάπης καὶ
[2]the [3]same [4]thing [1]mind; be at peace; and the God of love and
εἰρήνης ἔσται μεθ' ὑμῶν. 12 Ἀσπάσασθε ἀλλήλους ἐν ἁγίῳ
peace shall be with you. Salute one another with a holy
φιλήματι. ἀσπάζονται ὑμᾶς οἱ ἅγιοι πάντες. 13 Ἡ χάρις
kiss. [4]Salute [5]you [2]the [3]saints [1]all. The grace
τοῦ κυρίου Ἰησοῦ χριστοῦ, καὶ ἡ ἀγάπη τοῦ θεου, καὶ ἡ
of the Lord Jesus Christ, and the love of God, and the
κοινωνία τοῦ ἁγίου πνεύματος μετὰ πάντων ὑμῶν. [x]ἀμήν.‖
fellowship of the Holy Spirit [be] with [2]all [1]you. Amen.
[y]Πρὸς Κορινθίους δευτέρα ἐγράφη ἀπὸ Φιλίππων τῆς
[2]To [3]the] [4]Corinthians [1]second written from Philippi
Μακεδονίας, διὰ Τίτου καὶ Λουκᾶ.‖
of Macedonia, by Titus and Lucas.

to them which heretofore have sinned, and to all other, that, if I come again, I will not spare: 3 since ye seek a proof of Christ speaking in me, which to you-ward is not weak, but is mighty in you. 4 For though he was crucified through weakness, yet he liveth by the power of God. For we also are weak in him, but we shall live with him by the power of God toward you. 5 Examine yourselves, whether ye be in the faith; prove your own selves. Know ye not your own selves, how that Jesus Christ is in you, except ye be reprobates? 6 But I trust that ye shall know that we are not reprobates. 7 Now I pray to God that ye do no evil; not that we should appear approved, but that ye should do that which is honest, though we be as reprobates. 8 For we can do nothing against the truth, but for the truth. 9 For we are glad, when we are weak, and ye are strong: and this also we wish, *even* your perfection. 10 Therefore I write these things being absent, lest being present I should use sharpness, according to the power which the Lord hath given me to edification, and not to destruction.

11 Finally, brethren, farewell. Be perfect, be of good comfort, be of one mind, live in peace; and the God of love and peace shall be with you. 12 Greet one another with an holy kiss. 13 All the saints salute you. 14 The grace of the Lord Jesus Christ, and the love of God, and the communion of the Holy Ghost, *be* with you all. Amen.

---

[m] — εἰ [L]TTrA. [n] + καὶ also E. [o] ζήσομεν LTTrAW. [p] [εἰς ὑμᾶς] A. [q] χριστὸς Ἰησοῦς TTr. [r] — ἐστιν (*read* [is]) [L]TTr[A]. [s] εὐχόμεθα we pray LTTrAW. [t] ἀλλὰ TTrA. [v] — δὲ but LTTrAW. [w] ὁ κύριος ἔδωκέν μοι LTTrA. [x] — ἀμήν GLTTrAW. [y] — *the subscription* GLTW; Πρὸς Κορινθίους β' TrA.

[a]Η ΠΡΟΣ ΓΑΛΑΤΑΣ ΕΠΙΣΤΟΛΗ ΠΑΥΛΟΥ.ǁ
THE [4]TO [5THE] [6]GALATIANS [1]EPISTLE [2]OF [3]PAUL.

PAUL, an apostle, (not of men, neither by man, but by Jesus Christ, and God the Father, who raised him from the dead;) 2 and all the brethren which are with me, unto the churches of Galatia: 3 Grace *be* to you and peace from God the Father, and *from* our Lord Jesus Christ, 4 who gave himself for our sins, that he might deliver us from this present evil world, according to the will of God and our Father: 5 to whom *be* glory for ever and ever. Amen.

6 I marvel that ye are so soon removed from him that called you into the grace of Christ unto another gospel: 7 which is not another; but there be some that trouble you, and would pervert the gospel of Christ. 8 But though we, or an angel from heaven, preach any other gospel unto you than that which we have preached unto you, let him be accursed. 9 As we said before, so say I now again, If any *man* preach any other gospel unto you than that ye have received, let him be accursed. 10 For do I now persuade men, or God? or do I seek to please men? for if I yet pleased men, I should not be the servant of Christ.

11 But I certify you, brethren, that the gospel which was preached of me is not after man. 12 For I nei-

ΠΑΥΛΟΣ ἀπόστολος, οὐκ ἀπ' ἀνθρώπων οὐδὲ δι' ἀν-
Paul apostle, not from men nor through
θρώπου, ἀλλὰ διὰ Ἰησοῦ χριστοῦ, καὶ θεοῦ πατρὸς τοῦ
man, but through Jesus Christ, and God [the] Father, who
ἐγείραντος αὐτὸν ἐκ νεκρῶν, 2 καὶ οἱ σὺν ἐμοὶ
raised him from among [the] dead, and [3]the [4]with [5]me
πάντες ἀδελφοί, ταῖς ἐκκλησίαις τῆς Γαλατίας· 3 χάρις ὑμῖν
[1]all [2]brethren, to the assemblies of Galatia. Grace to you
καὶ εἰρήνη ἀπὸ θεοῦ πατρὸς καὶ κυρίου ἡμῶν Ἰησοῦ χρισ-
and peace from God [the] Father and [2]Lord [1]our Jesus Christ,
τοῦ, 4 τοῦ δόντος ἑαυτὸν [b]ὑπὲρǁ τῶν.ἁμαρτιῶν.ἡμῶν, ὅπως
who gave himself for our sins, so that
ἐξέληται ἡμᾶς ἐκ τοῦ [c]ἐνεστῶτος αἰῶνοςǁ πονηροῦ,
he might deliver us out of the present [2]age [1]evil,
κατὰ τὸ θέλημα τοῦ θεοῦ καὶ πατρὸς ἡμῶν, 5 ᾧ
according to the will of [2]God [3]and [4]Father [1]our; to whom [be]
ἡ δόξα εἰς τοὺς αἰῶνας τῶν αἰώνων. ἀμήν.
the glory to the ages of the ages. Amen.

6 Θαυμάζω ὅτι οὕτως ταχέως μετατίθεσθε ἀπὸ τοῦ
I.wonder that thus quickly ye are being changed from him who
καλέσαντος ὑμᾶς ἐν χάριτι χριστοῦ, εἰς ἕτερον εὐαγ-
called you in [2]grace [1]Christ's, to a different glad
γέλιον· 7 ὃ οὐκ.ἔστιν ἄλλο, εἰ.μή τινές εἰσιν οἱ ταράσ-
tidings, which is not another; but [3]some [1]there [2]are who trou-
σοντες ὑμᾶς, καὶ θέλοντες μεταστρέψαι τὸ εὐαγγέλιον τοῦ
ble you, and desire to pervert the glad tidings of the
χριστοῦ. 8 ἀλλὰ καὶ ἐὰν ἡμεῖς ἢ ἄγγελος ἐξ οὐρανοῦ [d]εὐαγ-
Christ: but even if we or an angel out of heaven should an-
γελίζηταιǁ [e]ὑμῖνǁ παρ' ὃ εὐηγγελισάμεθα ὑμῖν, ἀνάθεμα
nounce glad tidings to you contrary to what we announced to you, accursed
ἔστω. 9 ὡς προειρήκαμεν, καὶ ἄρτι πάλιν λέγω, εἴ τις
let him be. As we have said before, [2]also [1]now again I say, If anyone
ὑμᾶς εὐαγγελίζεται παρ' ὃ παρελάβετε, ἀνάθεμα
[to] you announces glad tidings contrary to what ye received, accursed
ἔστω. 10 ἄρτι.γὰρ ἀνθρώπους πείθω ἢ τὸν θεόν; ἢ
let him be. For now men do I persuade or God? or
ζητῶ ἀνθρώποις ἀρέσκειν; εἰ.[f]γὰρǁ ἔτι ἀνθρώποις ἤρεσκον,
do I seek men to please? For if yet men I were pleasing,
χριστοῦ δοῦλος οὐκ.ἂν.ἤμην.
Christ's bondman I should not be.

11 Γνωρίζω [g]δὲǁ ὑμῖν, ἀδελφοί, τὸ εὐαγγέλιον τὸ εὐαγ-
[2]I [3]make [4]known [1]but to you, brethren, the glad tidings which was
γελισθὲν ὑπ' ἐμοῦ, ὅτι οὐκ.ἔστιν κατὰ ἄνθρωπον· 12 οὐδὲ
announced by me, that it is not according to man. [2]Neither

---

[a] + τοῦ ἀποστόλου the apostle E; Πρὸς Γαλάτας LTTrAW. [b] περὶ GLTTrAW. [c] αἰῶνος τοῦ ἐνεστῶτος LTTrA. [d] εὐαγγελίσηται T. [e] — ὑμῖν T. [f] — γὰρ for LTTrAW. [g] γὰρ for TrA.

γὰρ ἐγὼ παρὰ ἀνθρώπου παρέλαβον αὐτό, [h]οὔτε‖ ἐδιδάχθην,
¹for I from man received it, nor was I taught [it],
ἀλλὰ δι' ἀποκαλύψεως Ἰησοῦ χριστοῦ. 13 Ἠκούσατε.γὰρ τὴν
but by a revelation of Jesus Christ. For ye heard of
ἐμὴν.ἀναστροφήν ποτε ἐν τῷ Ἰουδαϊσμῷ, ὅτι καθ'.ὑπερβολὴν
my conduct once in Judaism, that excessively
ἐδίωκον τὴν ἐκκλησίαν τοῦ θεοῦ καὶ ἐπόρθουν αὐτήν·
I was persecuting the assembly of God and was ravaging it;
14 καὶ προέκοπτον ἐν τῷ Ἰουδαϊσμῷ ὑπὲρ πολλοὺς συνηλικιώτας
and was advancing in Judaism beyond many contemporaries
ἐν τῷ.γένει.μου, περισσοτέρως ζηλωτὴς ὑπάρχων τῶν πατρι-
in my [own] race, more abundantly zealous being ⁴of ⁶fathers
κῶν μου παραδόσεων. 15 ὅτε.δὲ εὐδόκησεν [i]ὁ θεὸς‖ ὁ
⁵my ¹for [²the] ³traditions. But when ²was ³pleased ¹God, who
ἀφορίσας με ἐκ κοιλίας μητρός.μου, καὶ καλέσας διὰ τῆς
selected me from ³womb ¹my ²mother's, and called [me] by
χάριτος.αὐτοῦ, 16 ἀποκαλύψαι τὸν.υἱὸν.αὐτοῦ ἐν ἐμοί, ἵνα
his grace, to reveal his Son in me, that
εὐαγγελίζωμαι.αὐτὸν ἐν τοῖς ἔθνεσιν· εὐθέως
I should announce him as the glad tidings among the nations, immediately
οὐ.προσανεθέμην σαρκὶ καὶ αἵματι, 17 οὐδὲ [k]ἀνῆλθον‖ εἰς
I conferred not with flesh and blood, nor went I up to
Ἱεροσόλυμα πρὸς τοὺς πρὸ ἐμοῦ ἀποστόλους, [l]ἀλλ'‖
Jerusalem to those [who were] ²before ³me ¹apostles, but
ἀπῆλθον εἰς Ἀραβίαν, καὶ πάλιν ὑπέστρεψα εἰς Δαμασκόν.
I went away into Arabia, and again returned to Damascus.
18 Ἔπειτα μετὰ [m]ἔτη τρία‖ ἀνῆλθον εἰς Ἱεροσόλυμα ἱσ-
Then after ²years ¹three I went up to Jerusalem to make
τορῆσαι [n]Πέτρον,‖ καὶ ἐπέμεινα πρὸς αὐτὸν ἡμέρας
acquaintance with Peter, and I remained with him ²days
δεκαπέντε· 19 ἕτερον.δὲ τῶν ἀποστόλων οὐκ.εἶδον, εἰ.μὴ
¹fifteen; but other of the apostles I saw not, except
Ἰάκωβον τὸν ἀδελφὸν τοῦ κυρίου. 20 ἃ.δὲ γράφω ὑμῖν,
James the brother of the Lord. Now what [things] I write to you,
ἰδοὺ ἐνώπιον τοῦ θεοῦ, ὅτι οὐ.ψεύδομαι. 21 Ἔπειτα ἦλθον εἰς
lo, before God, I lie not. Then I came into
τὰ κλίματα τῆς Συρίας καὶ τῆς Κιλικίας· 22 ἤμην.δὲ ἀ-
the regions of Syria and Cilicia; but I was un-
γνοούμενος τῷ προσώπῳ ταῖς ἐκκλησίαις τῆς Ἰουδαίας ταῖς
known by face to the assemblies of Judæa which
ἐν χριστῷ· 23 μόνον.δὲ ἀκούοντες ἦσαν, Ὅτι ὁ
[are] in Christ, only ³hearing ¹they ²were, That he who
διώκων ἡμᾶς ποτε, νῦν εὐαγγελίζεται τὴν πίστιν
²persecuted ³us ¹once, now announces the glad tidings— the faith,
ἥν ποτε ἐπόρθει. 24 καὶ ἐδόξαζον ἐν ἐμοὶ τὸν θεόν.
which once he ravaged: and they were glorifying ²in ³me ¹God.
2 Ἔπειτα διὰ δεκατεσσάρων ἐτῶν πάλιν ἀνέβην εἰς Ἱε-
Then after fourteen years again I went up to Je-
ροσόλυμα μετὰ Βαρνάβα, [o]συμπαραλαβὼν‖ καὶ Τίτον·
rusalem with Barnabas, taking with [me] also Titus;
2 ἀνέβην.δὲ κατὰ ἀποκάλυψιν, καὶ ἀνεθέμην αὐτοῖς τὸ
but I went up according to revelation, and laid before them the
εὐαγγέλιον ὃ κηρύσσω ἐν τοῖς ἔθνεσιν, κατ'.ἰδίαν.δὲ τοῖς
glad tidings which I proclaim among the nations, but privately to those

ther received it of
man, neither was I
taught *it*, but by the
revelation of Jesus
Christ. 13 For ye have
heard of my conver-
sation in time past in
the Jews' religion, how
that beyond measure
I persecuted the church
of God, and wasted it:
14 and profited in the
Jews' religion above
many my equals in
mine own nation, be-
ing more exceedingly
zealous of the tradi-
tions of my fathers.
15 But when it pleased
God, who separated
me from my mother's
womb, and called *me*
by his grace, 16 to re-
veal his Son in me,
that I might preach
him among the hea-
then; immediately I
conferred not with
flesh and blood: 17 nei-
ther went I up to Je-
rusalem to them which
were apostles before
me; but I went into
Arabia, and returned
again unto Damascus.
18 Then after three
years I went up to Je-
rusalem to see Peter,
and abode with him
fifteen days. 19 But
other of the apostles
saw I none, save James
the Lord's brother.
20 Now the things
which I write unto
you, behold, before
God, I lie not. 21 Af-
terwards I came into
the regions of Syria
and Cilicia; 22 and
was unknown by face
unto the churches of
Judæa which were in
Christ: 23 but they
had heard only, That
he which persecuted
us in times past now
preacheth the faith
which once he de-
stroyed. 24 And they
glorified God in me.

II. Then fourteen
years after I went up
again to Jerusalem
with Barnabas, and
took Titus with *me*
also. 2 And I went
up by revelation, and
communicated unto
them that gospel
which I preach among
the Gentiles, but pri-
vately to them which
were of reputation,
lest by any means I
should run, or had
run, in vain. 3 But
neither Titus, who

---

[h] οὐδὲ LTr. [i] — ὁ θεὸς (*read* he was pleased) [L]TA. [k] ἀπῆλθον went I away LA.
[l] ἀλλὰ LTTrA. [m] τρία ἔτη T. [n] Κηφᾶν Cephas LTTrAW. [o] συν- TA.

was with me, being a
Greek, was compelled
to be circumcised:
4 and that because of
false brethren una-
wares brought in,
who came in privily to
spy out our liberty
which we have in
Christ Jesus, that they
might bring us into
bondage: 5 to whom
we gave place by sub-
jection, no, not for an
hour; that the truth
of the gospel might
continue with you.
6 But of these who
seemed to be some-
what, (whatsoever
they were, it maketh
no matter to me: God
accepteth no man's
person:) for they who
seemed *to be somewhat*
in conference added
nothing to me: 7 but
contrariwise, when
they saw that the gos-
pel of the uncircumci-
sion was committed
unto me, as *the gospel*
of the circumcision
was unto Peter; 8 (for
he that wrought ef-
fectually in Peter to
the apostleship of the
circumcision, the same
was mighty in me to-
ward the Gentiles:)
9 and when James,
Cephas, and John, who
seemed to be pillars,
perceived the grace
that was given unto
me, they gave to me
and Barnabas the
right hands of fellow-
ship; that we *should*
go unto the heathen
and they unto the cir-
cumcision. 10 Only
they would that we
should remember the
poor; the same which I
also was forward to do.
11 But when Peter
was come to Antioch,
I withstood him to
the face, because he
was to be blamed.
12 For before that cer-
tain came from James,
he did eat with the
Gentiles: but when
they were come, he
withdrew and sepa-
rated himself, fear-
ing them which were
of the circumcision.
13 And the other Jews
dissembled likewise
with him; insomuch
that Barnabas also
was carried away
with their dissimula-
tion. 14 But when I
saw that they walked

δοκοῦσιν, μήπως εἰς κενὸν τρέχω ἢ ἔδραμον· 3 ἀλλ'
of repute, lest somehow in vain I should be running or had run; (but
οὐδὲ Τίτος ὁ σὺν ἐμοί, Ἕλλην ὤν, ἠναγκάσθη περι-
not even Titus who [was] with me, [2]a [3]Greek [1]being, was compelled to be
τμηθῆναι. 4 διὰ.δὲ τοὺς παρεισάκτους ψευδ-
circumcised;) and [this] on account of the [3]brought [4]in [5]stealthily [1]false
ἀδέλφους, οἵτινες παρεισῆλθον κατασκοπῆσαι τὴν ἐλευθερίαν
[2]brethren, who came in by stealth to spy out [2]freedom
ἡμῶν ἣν ἔχομεν ἐν χριστῷ Ἰησοῦ, ἵνα ἡμᾶς [p]καταδουλώ-
[1]our which we have in Christ Jesus, that us they might bring
σωνται·‖ 5 οἷς οὐδὲ πρὸς ὥραν εἴξαμεν τῇ ὑποταγῇ,
into bondage; to whom not even for an hour did we yield in subjection,
ἵνα ἡ ἀλήθεια τοῦ εὐαγγελίου διαμείνῃ πρὸς ὑμᾶς. 6 Ἀπὸ
that the truth of the glad tidings might continue with you. [2]From
δὲ τῶν δοκούντων εἶναί τι, ὁποῖοί.ποτε ἦσαν οὐδέν
[1]but those reputed to be something, whatsoever they were [2]no
μοι διαφέρει· πρόσωπον [q]θεὸς ἀνθρώπου οὐ λαμ-
[4]to [5]me [1]makes [3]difference: [the] person [3]God [1]of [2]man [5]not [4]does
βάνει· ἐμοὶ.γὰρ οἱ δοκοῦντες οὐδὲν προσανέθεντο, 7 ἀλλὰ
accept; for to me those of repute nothing conferred; but
τοὐναντίον, ἰδόντες ὅτι πεπίστευμαι τὸ εὐαγγέλιον
on the contrary, having seen that I have been entrusted with the glad tidings
τῆς ἀκροβυστίας, καθὼς Πέτρος τῆς περιτομῆς· 8 ὁ
of the uncircumcision, according as Peter [that] of the circumcision, ([2]he [3]who
γὰρ ἐνεργήσας Πέτρῳ εἰς ἀποστολὴν τῆς περιτομῆς, ἐνήργη-
[1]for wrought in Peter for apostleship of the circumcision, wrought
σεν [r]καὶ ἐμοὶ‖ εἰς τὰ ἔθνη· 9 καὶ γνόντες τὴν χάριν τὴν
also in me towards the nations,) and having known the grace which
δοθεῖσάν μοι, Ἰάκωβος καὶ Κηφᾶς καὶ [s]Ἰωάννης,‖ οἱ δο-
was given to me, James and Cephas and John, those re-
κοῦντες στῦλοι εἶναι, δεξιὰς ἔδωκαν ἐμοὶ καὶ Βαρνάβᾳ
puted [3]pillars [1]to [2]be, [the] right hands [3]they [4]gave [5]to [6]me [7]and [8]Barnabas
κοινωνίας, ἵνα ἡμεῖς [t] εἰς τὰ ἔθνη, αὐτοὶ.δὲ εἰς τὴν
[1]of [2]fellowship, that we [should go] to the nations, and they to the
περιτομήν· 10 μόνον τῶν πτωχῶν ἵνα μνημονεύωμεν, ὃ
circumcision: only the poor that we should remember, which
καὶ ἐσπούδασα αὐτὸ.τοῦτο ποιῆσαι.
[3]also [4]I [5]was [6]diligent [1]very [2]thing to do.

11 Ὅτε.δὲ ἦλθεν [v]Πέτρος‖ εἰς Ἀντιόχειαν, κατὰ.πρόσωπον
But when [2]came [1]Peter to Antioch, to [the] face
αὐτῷ ἀντέστην, ὅτι κατεγνωσμένος ἦν. 12 πρὸ.τοῦ.γὰρ
him I withstood, because to be condemned he was: for before that
ἐλθεῖν τινας ἀπὸ Ἰακώβου, μετὰ τῶν ἐθνῶν συνήσθιεν· ὅτε.δὲ
[2]came [1]some from James, with the nations he was eating; but when
[w]ἦλθον,‖ ὑπέστελλεν καὶ ἀφώριζεν ἑαυτόν, φοβούμενος
they came, he was drawing back and was separating himself, being afraid of
τοὺς ἐκ περιτομῆς· 13 καὶ συνυπεκρίθησαν αὐτῷ καὶ οἱ
those of [the] circumcision; and conjointly dissembled with him also the
λοιποὶ Ἰουδαῖοι, ὥστε καὶ Βαρνάβας συναπήχθη αὐτῶν
rest of [the] Jews, so that even Barnabas was carried away [2]their
τῇ ὑποκρίσει. 14 Ἀλλ' ὅτε εἶδον ὅτι οὐκ.ὀρθοποδοῦσιν
[1]by dissimulation. But when I saw that they walk not uprightly
πρὸς τὴν ἀλήθειαν τοῦ εὐαγγελίου, εἶπον τῷ [x]Πέτρῳ‖
according to the truth of the glad tidings, I said to Peter

[p] καταδουλώσουσιν they shall bring into bondage LTTrAW. [q] + ὁ T. [r] κἀμοὶ LTrW.
[s] Ἰωάνης Tr. [t] + μὲν G[L]. [v] Κηφᾶς Cephas LTTrAW. [w] ἦλθεν he came LTr.
[x] Κηφᾷ Cephas LTTrAW.

ἔμπροσθεν πάντων, Εἰ σύ, Ἰουδαῖος ὑπάρχων, ἐθνικῶς
before all, If thou, [2]a [3]Jew [1]being, nation-like
[y]ζῇς καὶ οὐκ Ἰουδαϊκῶς,‖ [z]τί‖ τὰ ἔθνη ἀναγκάζεις Ἰου-
livest and not Jewishly, why the nations dost thou compel to ju-
δαΐζειν; 15 Ἡμεῖς φύσει Ἰουδαῖοι, καὶ οὐκ ἐξ ἐθνῶν
daize? We, [2]by [3]nature [1]Jews, and not [2]of [[3]the] [4]nations
ἁμαρτωλοί, 16 εἰδότες [a]ὅτι οὐ.δικαιοῦται ἄνθρωπος ἐξ ἔργων
[1]sinners, knowing that [3]is [4]not [5]justified [1]a [2]man by works
νόμου, ἐὰν.μὴ διὰ πίστεως [b]Ἰησοῦ χριστοῦ,‖ καὶ ἡμεῖς εἰς
of law, but through faith of Jesus Christ, also we on
χριστὸν Ἰησοῦν ἐπιστεύσαμεν, ἵνα δικαιωθῶμεν ἐκ πίστεως
Christ Jesus believed, that we might be justified by faith
χριστοῦ, καὶ οὐκ ἐξ ἔργων νόμου· [c]διότι‖ [d]οὐ.δικαιωθήσεται
of Christ, and not by works of law; because shall not be justified
ἐξ ἔργων νόμου‖ πᾶσα σάρξ. 17 εἰ.δὲ ζητοῦντες δικαιωθῆναι
by works of law any (*lit.* all) flesh. Now if seeking to be justified
ἐν χριστῷ εὑρέθημεν καὶ αὐτοὶ ἁμαρτωλοί, [e]ἄρα‖ χριστὸς
in Christ we [3]were [4]found [2]also [1]ourselves sinners, [is] then Christ
ἁμαρτίας διάκονος; [f] μὴ.γένοιτο. 18 εἰ.γὰρ ἃ κατέλυσα
[2]of [3]sin [1]minister? May it not be! For if what I threw down
ταῦτα πάλιν οἰκοδομῶ, παραβάτην ἐμαυτὸν [g]συνίστημι.‖
these things again I build, a transgressor myself I constitute.
19 Ἐγὼ.γὰρ διὰ νόμου νόμῳ ἀπέθανον, ἵνα θεῷ ζήσω.
For I through law to law died, that to God I may live.
20 χριστῷ συνεσταύρωμαι· ζῶ.δέ, οὐκέτι ἐγώ, ζῇ.δὲ
[6]Christ [1]I [2]have [3]been [4]crucified [5]with, yet I live, no longer I, but [2]lives
ἐν ἐμοὶ χριστός· ὃ.δὲ νῦν ζῶ ἐν σαρκί, ἐν πίστει
[3]in [4]me [1]Christ; but that which now I live in flesh, in faith
ζῶ τῇ [h]τοῦ υἱοῦ τοῦ θεοῦ,‖ τοῦ ἀγαπήσαντός με καὶ παρα-
I live, that of the Son of God, who loved me and gave
δόντος ἑαυτὸν ὑπὲρ ἐμοῦ. 21 οὐκ.ἀθετῶ τὴν χάριν τοῦ θεοῦ·
up himself for me. I do not set aside the grace of God;
εἰ.γὰρ διὰ νόμου δικαιοσύνη, ἄρα χριστὸς δωρεὰν
for if through law righteousness [is], then Christ [2]for [3]nought
ἀπέθανεν.
[1]died.

3 Ὦ ἀνόητοι Γαλάται, τίς ὑμᾶς ἐβάσκανεν [i]τῇ ἀληθείᾳ
O senseless Galatians, who you bewitched, [4]the [5]truth
μὴ πείθεσθαι;‖ οἷς κατ' ὀφθαλμοὺς Ἰησοῦς χριστὸς προε-
[1]not [2]to [3]obey? [7]whose [6]before eyes Jesus Christ was openly
γράφη [j]ἐν ὑμῖν‖ ἐσταυρωμένος; 2 τοῦτο μόνον θέλω μαθεῖν
set forth among you— crucified? This only I wish to learn
ἀφ' ὑμῶν, ἐξ ἔργων νόμου τὸ πνεῦμα ἐλάβετε, ἢ ἐξ ἀκοῆς
from you, by works of law the Spirit receive ye, or by report
πίστεως; 3 οὕτως ἀνόητοί ἐστε; ἐναρξάμενοι πνεύματι, νῦν
of faith? So senseless are ye? Having begun in Spirit, now
σαρκὶ ἐπιτελεῖσθε; 4 τοσαῦτα ἐπάθετε εἰκῆ; εἴγε
in flesh are ye being perfected? So many things did ye suffer in vain? if indeed
καὶ εἰκῆ. 5 ὁ οὖν ἐπιχορηγῶν ὑμῖν τὸ πνεῦμα, καὶ
also in vain. He who therefore supplies to you the Spirit, and
ἐνεργῶν δυνάμεις ἐν ὑμῖν, ἐξ ἔργων νόμου ἢ ἐξ ἀκοῆς
works works of power among you, [is it] by works of law or by report

not uprightly according to the truth of the gospel, I said unto Peter before *them* all, If thou, being a Jew, livest after the manner of Gentiles, and not as do the Jews, why compellest thou the Gentiles to live as do the Jews? 15 We *who are* Jews by nature, and not sinners of the Gentiles, 16 knowing that a man is not justified by the works of the law, but by the faith of Jesus Christ, even we have believed in Jesus Christ, that we might be justified by the faith of Christ, and not by the works of the law: for by the works of the law shall no flesh be justified. 17 But if, while we seek to be justified by Christ, we ourselves also are found sinners, *is* therefore Christ the minister of sin? God forbid. 18 For if I build again the things which I destroyed, I make myself a transgressor. 19 For I through the law am dead to the law, that I might live unto God. 20 I am crucified with Christ: nevertheless I live; yet not I, but Christ liveth in me: and the life which I now live in the flesh I live by the faith of the Son of God, who loved me, and gave himself for me. 21 I do not frustrate the grace of God: for if righteousness *come* by the law, then Christ is dead in vain.

III. O foolish Galatians, who hath bewitched you, that ye should not obey the truth, before whose eyes Jesus Christ hath been evidently set forth, crucified among you? 2 This only would I learn of you, Received ye the Spirit by the works of the law, or by the hearing of faith? 3 Are ye so foolish? having begun in the Spirit, are ye now made perfect by the flesh. 4 Have ye suffered so many things in vain? if it

[y] καὶ οὐχ (οὐκ TrA) Ἰουδαϊκῶς ζῇς LTTrA. [z] πῶς how GLTTrAW. [a] + δὲ but (knowing) GLTTrAW. [b] χριστοῦ Ἰησοῦ TTr. [c] ὅτι LTTrA. [d] ἐξ ἔργων νόμου οὐ δικαιωθήσεται GLTTrAW. [e] ἄρα L. [f] —; (*read* Christ [is] then &c.) L. [g] συνιστάνω GLTTrAW. [h] τοῦ θεοῦ καὶ χριστοῦ of God and Christ LTr. [i] — τῇ ἀληθείᾳ μὴ πείθεσθαι GLTTrAW. — ἐν ὑμῖν LTTrA.

πίστεως; 6 καθὼς Ἀβραὰμ ἐπίστευσεν τῷ θεῷ, καὶ ἐλογίσθη
of faith? Even as Abraham believed God, and it was reckoned
αὐτῷ εἰς δικαιοσύνην. 7 γινώσκετε ἄρα ὅτι οἱ ἐκ πίστεως,
to him for righteousness. Know then that they that of faith
οὗτοί [k]εἰσιν υἱοὶ‖ Ἀβραάμ. 8 προϊδοῦσα.δὲ ἡ γραφὴ
[are], these are sons of Abraham; and [3]foreseeing [1]the [2]scripture
ὅτι ἐκ πίστεως δικαιοῖ τὰ ἔθνη ὁ θεός, προευηγγελί-
that by faith [2]justifies [3]the [4]nations [1]God, before announced glad
σατο τῷ Ἀβραάμ, "Οτι [l]ἐνευλογηθήσονται‖ ἐν σοὶ πάντα τὰ
tidings to Abraham: Shall be blessed in thee all the
ἔθνη. 9 ὥστε οἱ ἐκ πίστεως εὐλογοῦνται σὺν τῷ πιστῷ
nations. So that those of faith are being blessed with the believing
Ἀβραάμ. 10 ὅσοι.γὰρ ἐξ ἔργων νόμου εἰσίν, ὑπὸ κατάραν
Abraham. For as many as of works of law are, under a curse
εἰσίν· γέγραπται.γάρ, [m]Ἐπικατάρατος πᾶς ὃς οὐκ ἐμ-
are. For it has been written, Cursed [is] everyone who [2]not [1]does
μένει [n]ἐν‖ πᾶσιν τοῖς γεγραμμένοις ἐν τῷ βιβλίῳ τοῦ νόμου,
continue in all things which have been written in the book of the law
τοῦ ποιῆσαι αὐτά. 11 "Οτι.δὲ ἐν νόμῳ οὐδεὶς δικαιοῦται
to do them. But that in virtue of law no one is being justified
παρὰ τῷ θεῷ δῆλον· ὅτι ὁ δίκαιος ἐκ πίστεως ζήσεται·
with God [is] manifest; because the just by faith shall live;
12 ὁ.δὲ νόμος οὐκ.ἔστιν ἐκ πίστεως, [o]ἀλλ'‖ ὁ ποιήσας
but the law is not of faith; but, the [2]who [3]did
αὐτὰ [p]ἄνθρωπος‖ ζήσεται ἐν αὐτοῖς. 13 χριστὸς ἡμᾶς
[4]these [5]things [1]man shall live in virtue of them. Christ us
ἐξηγόρασεν ἐκ τῆς κατάρας τοῦ νόμου, γενόμενος ὑπὲρ ἡμῶν
ransomed from the curse of the law, having become for us
κατάρα· [q]γέγραπται.γάρ,‖ Ἐπικατάρατος πᾶς ὁ κρεμά-
a curse, (for it has been written, Cursed [is] everyone who hangs
μενος ἐπὶ ξύλου· 14 ἵνα εἰς τὰ ἔθνη ἡ εὐλογία τοῦ Ἀβραὰμ
on a tree,) that to the nations the blessing of Abraham
γένηται ἐν [r]χριστῷ Ἰησοῦ,‖ ἵνα τὴν ἐπαγγελίαν τοῦ πνεύμα-
might come in Christ Jesus, that the promise of the Spirit
τος λάβωμεν διὰ τῆς πίστεως.
we might receive through faith.

15 Ἀδελφοί, κατὰ ἄνθρωπον λέγω, ὅμως ἀνθρώπου
Brethren, (according to man I am speaking,) even of man
κεκυρωμένην διαθήκην οὐδεὶς ἀθετεῖ ἢ ἐπιδιατάσσεται.
a confirmed covenant no one sets aside, or adds thereto.
16 τῷ.δὲ Ἀβραὰμ [s]ἐῤῥήθησαν‖ αἱ ἐπαγγελίαι, καὶ τῷ σπέρματι
But to Abraham were spoken the promises, and to [2]seed
αὐτοῦ· οὐ.λέγει, Καὶ τοῖς σπέρμασιν, ὡς ἐπὶ πολλῶν, [t]ἀλλ'‖
[1]his: he does not say, And to seeds, as of many; but
ὡς ἐφ' ἑνός, Καὶ τῷ.σπέρματί.σου, ὅς ἐστιν χριστός. 17 τοῦτο
as of one, And to thy seed; which is Christ. [2]This
δὲ λέγω, διαθήκην προκεκυρωμένην ὑπὸ τοῦ θεοῦ [v]εἰς χρισ-
[1]now I say, [the] covenant confirmed beforehand by God to Christ,
τὸν‖ ὁ μετὰ [w]ἔτη τετρακόσια καὶ τριάκοντα‖ γεγονὼς
the [5]after [10]years [6]four [7]hundred [8]and [9]thirty [2]which [3]took [4]place
νόμος οὐκ.ἀκυροῖ, εἰς.τὸ καταργῆσαι τὴν ἐπαγγελίαν. 18 εἰ
[1]law does not annul so as to make of no effect the promise. [2]If

be yet in vain. 5 He
therefore that minis-
tereth to you the Spi-
rit, and worketh mira-
cles among you, *doeth*
he it by the works of
the law, or by the
hearing of faith?
6 Even as Abraham
believed God, and it
was accounted to
him for righteousness.
7 Know ye therefore
that they which are
of faith, the same are
the children of Abra-
ham. 8 And the scrip-
ture, foreseeing that
God would justify the
heathen through faith,
preached before the
gospel unto Abraham,
saying, In thee shall
all nations be blessed.
9 So then they which
be of faith are blessed
with faithful Abra-
ham. 10 For as many
as are of the works of
the law are under the
curse: for it is writ-
ten, Cursed *is* every
one that continueth
not in all things which
are written in the book
of the law to do them.
11 But that no man is
justified by the law
in the sight of God, *it*
is evident: for, The
just shall live by faith.
12 And the law is not
of faith: but, The man
that doeth them shall
live in them. 13 Christ
hath redeemed us from
the curse of the law,
being made a curse for
us: for it is written,
Cursed *is* every one
that hangeth on a
tree: 14 that the
blessing of Abraham
might come on the
Gentiles through Je-
sus Christ; that we
might receive the pro-
mise of the Spirit
through faith.
15 Brethren, I speak
after the manner of
men; Though *it be*
but a man's covenant,
yet *if it be* confirmed,
no man disannulleth,
or addeth thereto.
16 Now to Abraham
and his seed were the
promises made. He
saith not, And to seeds,
as of many; but as
of one, And to thy
seed, which is Christ.
17 And this I say, *that*
the covenant, that was
confirmed before of
God in Christ, the law,
which was four hun-

[k] υἱοί εἰσιν LTTr. [l] εὐλογηθήσονται E. [m] + ὅτι that GLTTrAW. [n] — ἐν (*read* πᾶσιν in all things) TTr. [o] ἀλλὰ TTr. [p] — ἄνθρωπος (*read* ὁ ποιήσας he who did) GLTTrAW. [q] ὅτι γέγραπται LTTrAW. [r] Ἰησοῦ χριστῷ Tr. [s] ἐῤῥέθησαν LTTrA. [t] ἀλλὰ Tr. [v] — εἰς χριστὸν LTTrA. [w] τετρακόσια καὶ τριάκοντα ἔτη GLTTrAW.

γὰρ ἐκ νόμου ἡ κληρονομία, οὐκέτι ἐξ ἐπαγγελίας·
[1]for by law [be] the inheritance, [it is] no longer by promise;
τῷ.δὲ.'Αβραὰμ δι' ἐπαγγελίας κεχάρισται ὁ θεός. 19 Τί
but to Abraham through promise [2]granted [[3]it] [1]God. Why
οὖν ὁ νόμος; τῶν παραβάσεων χάριν [x]πρόσετέθη,‖
then the law? [5]transgressions [1]for [2]the [3]sake [4]of it was added,
ἄχρις οὗ ἔλθῃ τὸ σπέρμα ᾧ ἐπήγγελται,
until should have come the seed to whom promise has been made,
διαταγεὶς δι' ἀγγέλων ἐν χειρὶ μεσίτου. 20 ὁ.δὲ
having been ordained through angels in [3]hand [1]a [2]mediator's. But the
μεσίτης ἑνὸς οὐκ.ἔστιν, ὁ.δὲ.θεὸς εἷς ἐστιν.
mediator [3]of [4]one [1]is [2]not, but God [2]one [1]is.
21 Ὁ.οὖν.νόμος κατὰ τῶν ἐπαγγελιῶν [y]τοῦ θεοῦ‖;
The law then [is it] against the promises of God?
μὴ.γένοιτο· εἰ.γὰρ ἐδόθη νόμος ὁ δυνάμενος ζωοποιῆσαι,
May it not be! For if was given a law which was able to quicken,
ὄντως [z]ἂν ἐκ νόμου ἦν‖ ἡ δικαιοσύνη· 22 ἀλλὰ συνέ-
indeed by law would have been righteousness; but [3]shut
κλεισεν ἡ γραφὴ τὰ.πάντα [a]ὑπὸ‖ ἁμαρτίαν, ἵνα ἡ ἐπαγγελία
[4]up [1]the [2]scripture all things under sin, that the promise
ἐκ πίστεως Ἰησοῦ χριστοῦ δοθῇ τοῖς πιστεύουσιν.
by faith of Jesus Christ might be given to those that believe.
23 Πρὸ.τοῦ.δὲ ἐλθεῖν τὴν πίστιν, ὑπὸ νόμον ἐφρουρούμεθα,
But before [2]came [1]faith, under law we were guarded,
[b]συγκεκλεισμένοι‖ εἰς τὴν μέλλουσαν πίστιν ἀποκαλυφθῆναι·
having been shut up to the [2]being [3]about [1]faith to be revealed.
24 ὥστε ὁ νόμος παιδαγωγὸς ἡμῶν γέγονεν εἰς χριστόν, ἵνα
So that the law [2]tutor [1]our has been [up] to Christ, that
ἐκ πίστεως δικαιωθῶμεν· 25 ἐλθούσης.δὲ τῆς πίστεως,
by faith we might be justified. But [2]having [3]come [1]faith,
οὐκέτι ὑπὸ παιδαγωγόν ἐσμεν. 26 πάντες.γὰρ υἱοὶ θεοῦ
no longer under a tutor we are; for all sons of God
ἐστε διὰ τῆς πίστεως ἐν χριστῷ Ἰησοῦ· 27 ὅσοι.γὰρ εἰς
ye are through faith in Christ Jesus. For as many as to
χριστὸν ἐβαπτίσθητε, χριστὸν ἐνεδύσασθε. 28 οὐκ.ἔνι Ἰου-
Christ were baptized, [5]Christ [1]ye [2]did [3]put [4]on. There is not Jew
δαῖος οὐδὲ Ἕλλην· οὐκ.ἔνι δοῦλος οὐδὲ ἐλεύθερος· οὐκ.ἔνι
nor Greek; there is not bondman nor free; there is not
ἄρσεν καὶ θῆλυ· [c]πάντες‖.γὰρ ὑμεῖς εἷς ἐστε ἐν.χριστῷ Ἰησοῦ·
male and female; for all ye one are in Christ Jesus:
29 εἰ.δὲ ὑμεῖς χριστοῦ, ἄρα τοῦ 'Αβραὰμ σπέρμα ἐστέ,
but if ye [are] Christ's, then Abraham's seed ye are,
[d]καὶ‖ [e]κατ'‖ ἐπαγγελίαν κληρονόμοι.
and according to promise heirs.

4 Λέγω.δέ, ἐφ' ὅσον χρόνον ὁ κληρονόμος νήπιός ἐστιν,
Now I say, for as long [2]as [1]time the heir an infant is,
οὐδὲν διαφέρει δούλου, κύριος πάντων ὤν· 2 ἀλλὰ
nothing he differs from a bondman, [though] [2]lord [3]of [4]all [1]being; but
ὑπὸ ἐπιτρόπους ἐστὶν καὶ οἰκονόμους ἄχρι τῆς προθεσμίας
under guardians he is and stewards until the time before appointed
τοῦ πατρός. 3 οὕτως καὶ ἡμεῖς, ὅτε ἦμεν νήπιοι, ὑπὸ τὰ
of the father. So also we, when we were infants, under the
στοιχεῖα τοῦ κόσμου [f]ἦμεν‖ δεδουλωμένοι· 4 ὅτε.δὲ ἦλθεν τὸ
elements of the world were held in bondage; but when came the

dred and thirty years after, cannot disannul, that it should make the promise of none effect. 18 For if the inheritance *be* of the law, *it is* no more of promise: but God gave *it* to Abraham by promise. 19 Wherefore then *serveth* the law? It was added because of transgressions, till the seed should come to whom the promise was made; *and it was* ordained by angels in the hand of a mediator. 20 Now a mediator is not *a mediator* of one, but God is one.

21 *Is* the law then against the promises of God? God forbid: for if there had been a law given which could have given life, verily righteousness should have been by the law. 22 But the scripture hath concluded all under sin, that the promise by faith of Jesus Christ might be given to them that believe. 23 But before faith came, we were kept under the law, shut up unto the faith which should afterwards be revealed. 24 Wherefore the law was our schoolmaster *to bring us* unto Christ, that we might be justified by faith. 25 But after that faith is come, we are no longer under a schoolmaster. 26 For ye are all the children of God by faith in Christ Jesus. 27 For as many of you as have been baptized into Christ have put on Christ. 28 There is neither Jew nor Greek, there is neither bond nor free, there is neither male nor female: for ye are all one in Christ Jesus. 29 And if ye *be* Christ's, then are ye Abraham's seed, and heirs according to the promise.

IV. Now I say, *That* the heir, as long as he is a child, differeth nothing from a servant, though he be lord of all; 2 but is under tutors and governors until the time appointed of the father. 3 Even so we, when

---

[x] ἐτέθη it was appointed G. [y] [τοῦ θεοῦ] L. [z] ἐκ νόμου ἂν ἦν (ἦν ἂν T) LTTrA. [a] ὑφ' L. [b] συγ(συν- T)κλειόμενοι being shut up LTTrA. [c] ἅπαντες TTrA. [d] — καὶ LTTrA. [e] κατὰ T. [f] ἤμεθα T.

we were children,
were in bondage under
the elements of the
world: 4 but when the
fulness of the time
was come, God sent
forth his Son, made of
a woman, made under
the law, 5 to redeem
them that were under
the law, that we might
receive the adoption
of sons. 6 And because
ye are sons, God hath
sent forth the Spirit
of his Son into your
hearts, crying, Abba,
Father. 7 Wherefore
thou art no more a
servant, but a son;
and if a son, then an
heir of God through
Christ. 8 Howbeit
then, when ye knew
not God, ye did ser-
vice unto them which
by nature are no
gods. 9 But now, after
that ye have known
God, or rather are
known of God, how
turn ye again to the
weak and beggarly
elements, whereunto
ye desire again to be
in bondage? 10 Ye
observe days, and
months, and times, and
years. 11 I am afraid
of you, lest I have be-
stowed upon you la-
bour in vain.
12 Brethren, I be-
seech you, be as I *am;*
for I *am* as ye *are:*
ye have not injured
me at all. 13 Ye know
how through infirmity
of the flesh I preached
the gospel unto you
at the first. 14 And my
temptation which was
in my flesh ye despised
not, nor rejected; but
received me as an an-
gel of God, *even* as
Christ Jesus. 15 Where
is then the blessed-
ness ye spake of? for
I bear you record,
that, if *it had been*
possible, ye would
have plucked out your
own eyes, and have
given them to me.
16 Am I therefore be-
come your enemy, be-
cause I tell you the
truth? 17 They zeal-
ously affect you, *but*
not well; yea, they
would exclude you,
that ye might affect
them. 18 But *it is*
good to be zealously
affected always in *a*
good *thing,* and not
only when I am pre-

πλήρωμα τοῦ.χρόνου, ἐξαπέστειλεν ὁ θεὸς τὸν.υἱὸν.αὐτοῦ,
fulness of the time, ²sent ³forth ¹God his Son,
γενόμενον ἐκ γυναικός, γενόμενον ὑπὸ νόμον, 5 ἵνα τοὺς
come of woman, come under law, that those
ὑπὸ νόμον ἐξαγοράσῃ, ἵνα τὴν υἱοθεσίαν ἀπολάβωμεν.
under law he might ransom, that adoption we might receive.
6 ὅτι.δέ ἐστε υἱοί, ἐξαπέστειλεν ὁ θεὸς τὸ πνεῦμα τοῦ
But because ye are sons, ²sent ³forth ¹God the Spirit
υἱοῦ.αὐτοῦ εἰς τὰς καρδίας [g]ὑμῶν,‖ κρᾶζον, Ἀββᾶ ὁ πατήρ.
of his Son into ²hearts ¹your, crying, Abba, Father.
7 ὥστε οὐκέτι εἶ δοῦλος, [h]ἀλλ'‖ υἱός· εἰ.δὲ υἱός, καὶ
So no longer thou art bondman, but son; and if son, also
κληρονόμος [i]θεοῦ διὰ χριστοῦ.‖ 8 Ἀλλὰ τότε μὲν οὐκ
heir of God through Christ. But then indeed not
εἰδότες θεόν, ἐδουλεύσατε τοῖς [k]μὴ φύσει‖ οὖσιν
knowing God, ye were in bondage to those who not by nature are
θεοῖς· 9 νῦν.δέ, γνόντες θεόν, μᾶλλον.δὲ γνωσθέντες
gods; but now, having known God, but rather having been known
ὑπὸ θεοῦ, πῶς ἐπιστρέφετε πάλιν ἐπὶ τὰ ἀσθενῆ καὶ πτωχὰ
by God, how do ye turn again to the weak and beggarly
στοιχεῖα οἷς πάλιν ἄνωθεν [l]δουλεύειν‖ θέλετε; 10 ἡμέρας
elements to which again anew to be in bondage ye desire? Days
παρατηρεῖσθε, καὶ μῆνας, καὶ καιρούς, καὶ ἐνιαυτούς.[m] 11 φο-
ye observe, and months, and times, and years. I am
βοῦμαι ὑμᾶς, μήπως εἰκῇ κεκοπίακα εἰς ὑμᾶς.
afraid of you, lest somehow in vain I have laboured as to you.

12 Γίνεσθε ὡς ἐγώ, ὅτι.κἀγὼ ὡς ὑμεῖς, ἀδελφοί, δέο-
Be as I [am], for I also [am] as ye, brethren, I be-
μαι ὑμῶν· οὐδέν με ἠδικήσατε. 13 οἴδατε.δὲ ὅτι δι'
seech you: in nothing me ye wronged. But ye know that in
ἀσθένειαν τῆς σαρκὸς εὐηγγελισάμην ὑμῖν τὸ.πρότερον,
weakness of the flesh I announced the glad tidings to you at the first;
14 καὶ τὸν πειρασμόν [n]μου τὸν‖ ἐν τῇ.σαρκί.μου οὐκ ἐξου-
and ²temptation ¹my in my flesh ³not ¹ye ²de-
θενήσατε οὐδὲ ἐξεπτύσατε, [h]ἀλλ'‖ ὡς ἄγγελον θεοῦ ἐ-
spised nor rejected with contempt; but as an angel of God ye
δέξασθέ με, ὡς χριστὸν Ἰησοῦν. 15 [o]τίς‖ οὖν [p]ἦν‖ ὁ μακαρισμὸς
received me, as Christ Jesus. What then was ²blessedness
ὑμῶν; μαρτυρῶ.γὰρ ὑμῖν ὅτι, εἰ δυνατόν, τοὺς ὀφθαλμοὺς
¹your? for I bear ²witness ¹you that, if possible, ²eyes
ὑμῶν ἐξορύξαντες [q]ἂν‖ ἐδώκατέ μοι. 16 ὥστε ἐχθρὸς
¹your having plucked out ye would have given [them] to me. So ²enemy
ὑμῶν γέγονα ἀληθεύων ὑμῖν; 17 Ζηλοῦσιν ὑμᾶς
¹your have I become speaking truth to you? They are zealous after you
οὐ καλῶς, ἀλλὰ ἐκκλεῖσαι [r]ὑμᾶς‖ θέλουσιν, ἵνα αὐτοὺς
not rightly, but to exclude you [from us] they desire, that them
ζηλοῦτε. 18 καλὸν.δὲ [s]τὸ‖ ζηλοῦσθαι ἐν καλῷ
ye may be zealous after. But right [it is] to be zealous in a right [thing]
πάντοτε, καὶ μὴ μόνον ἐν τῷ.παρεῖναί.με πρὸς ὑμᾶς, 19 [t]τεκ-
at all times, and not only in my being present with you— ²little
νία‖ μου, οὓς πάλιν ὠδίνω [v]ἄχρις‖ οὗ μορφωθῇ
³children ¹my, of whom again I travail until shall have been formed

[g] ἡμῶν our GLTTrAW. [h] ἀλλὰ LTTrA. [i] διὰ θεοῦ through God LTTrA. [k] φύσει μὴ (*read* are not &c.) GLTTrAW. [l] δουλεῦσαι TTr. [m] ; (*read* Do ye observe &c.) GLT. [n] ὑμῶν your LTTrA; ὑμῶν τὸν W. [o] ποῦ where LTTrAW. [p] — ἦν LTTrAW. [q] — ἂν (*read* ye had given) LTTrAW. [r] ἡμᾶς us E. [s] — τὸ LTTrA. [t] τέκνα children LTTr. [v] μέχρις TTr.

χριστὸς ἐν ὑμῖν· 20 ἤθελον.δὲ παρεῖναι πρὸς ὑμᾶς ἄρτι, καὶ
Christ in you: and I was wishing to be present with you now, and
ἀλλάξαι τὴν.φωνήν.μου, ὅτι ἀποροῦμαι ἐν ὑμῖν.
to change my voice, for I am perplexed as to you.
21 Λέγετέ μοι, οἱ ὑπὸ νόμον θέλοντες εἶναι, τὸν νόμον
Tell me, ye who under law wish to be, the law
οὐκ.ἀκούετε; 22 γέγραπται.γάρ, ὅτι Ἀβραὰμ δύο υἱοὺς
do ye not hear? For it has been written, that Abraham two sons
ἔσχεν· ἕνα ἐκ τῆς παιδίσκης, καὶ ἕνα ἐκ τῆς ἐλευθέρας·
had; one of the maid-servant, and one of the free [woman].
23 [w]ἀλλ'‖ ὁ [x]μὲν‖ ἐκ τῆς παιδίσκης, κατὰ σάρκα [y]γε-
But he of the maid-servant, according to flesh has
γέννηται·‖ ὁ.δὲ ἐκ τῆς ἐλευθέρας, [z]διὰ τῆς‖ ἐπαγγελίας.
been born, and he of the free [woman], through the promise.
24 ἅτινά ἐστιν ἀλληγορούμενα· αὗται.γάρ εἰσιν [a]αἱ‖ δύο
Which things are allegorized; for these are the two
διαθῆκαι· μία μὲν ἀπὸ ὄρους Σινᾶ, εἰς [b]δουλείαν‖ γεννῶσα,
covenants; one from mount Sina, to bondage bringing forth,
ἥτις ἐστὶν Ἄγαρ. 25 τὸ γὰρ [c]Ἄγαρ‖ Σινᾶ ὄρος ἐστὶν ἐν τῇ
which is Agar. For Agar [3]Sina mount [1]is in
Ἀραβίᾳ, [d]συστοιχεῖ‖.δὲ τῇ νῦν Ἱερουσαλήμ, δουλεύει
Arabia, and corresponds to the now Jerusalem, [2]she [3]is [4]in [5]bondage
[e]δὲ‖ μετὰ τῶν.τέκνων.αὐτῆς. 26 ἡ.δὲ ἄνω Ἱερουσαλήμ, ἐλευ-
[1]and with her children; but the [2]above [1]Jerusalem, [4]free
θέρα ἐστίν, ἥτις ἐστὶν μήτηρ [f]πάντων‖ ἡμῶν. 27 γέγραπται
[3]is, which is mother of all of us. [2]It [3]has [4]been [5]written
γάρ, Εὐφράνθητι στεῖρα ἡ οὐ.τίκτουσα· ῥῆξον καὶ βόησον
[1]for, Rejoice, O barren that bearest not; break forth and cry,
ἡ οὐκ.ὠδίνουσα· ὅτι πολλὰ τὰ τέκνα τῆς ἐρήμου μᾶλλον ἢ
that travailest not; because many the children of the desolate more than
τῆς ἐχούσης τὸν ἄνδρα. 28 [g]Ἡμεῖς‖.δέ, ἀδελφοί, κατὰ Ἰσαάκ,
of her that has the husband. But we, brethren, like Isaac,
ἐπαγγελίας τέκνα [h]ἐσμέν·‖ 29 ἀλλ' ὥσπερ τότε ὁ κατὰ
[3]of [4]promise [2]children [1]are. But as then he who according to
σάρκα γεννηθεὶς ἐδίωκεν τὸν κατὰ πνεῦμα, οὕτως καὶ
flesh was born persecuted him [born] according to Spirit, so also
νῦν. 30 ἀλλὰ τί λέγει ἡ γραφή; Ἔκβαλε τὴν παιδίσκην
now. But what says the scripture? Cast out the maid-servant
καὶ τὸν.υἱὸν.αὐτῆς, οὐ.γὰρ.μὴ [i]κληρονομήσῃ‖ ὁ υἱὸς τῆς
and her son, for in no wise may [6]inherit [1]the [2]son [3]of [4]the
παιδίσκης μετὰ τοῦ υἱοῦ τῆς ἐλευθέρας. 31 [k]Ἄρα,‖ ἀδελ-
[5]maid-servant with the son of the free [woman]. So then, breth-
φοί, οὐκ.ἐσμὲν παιδίσκης τέκνα, ἀλλὰ τῆς ἐλευθέρας.
ren, we are not [2]of [3]a [4]maid-servant [1]children, but of the free [woman].
5 Τῇ ἐλευθερίᾳ [l]οὖν‖ [m]ᾗ‖ [n]χριστὸς ἡμᾶς‖ ἠλευθέρω-
In the freedom therefore wherewith Christ us made free,
σεν, [o]στήκετε,‖ [p]καὶ μὴ πάλιν ζυγῷ [q]δουλείας‖ ἐνέχεσθε. 2 ἴδε
stand fast, and not again in a yoke of bondage be held. Lo,
ἐγὼ Παῦλος λέγω ὑμῖν, ὅτι ἐὰν περιτέμνησθε, χριστὸς ὑμᾶς
I Paul say to you, that if ye be circumcised, Christ [3]you
οὐδὲν ὠφελήσει· 3 μαρτύρομαι.δὲ πάλιν παντὶ ἀνθρώπῳ
[4]nothing [1]shall [2]profit. And I testify again to every man

sent with you. 19 My
little children, of
whom I travail in
birth again until
Christ be formed in
you, 20 I desire to be
present with you now,
and to change my
voice; for I stand in
doubt of you.
21 Tell me, ye that
desire to be under the
law, do ye not hear
the law? 22 For it is
written, that Abra-
ham had two sons, the
one by a bondmaid, the
other by a freewoman.
23 But he *who was* of
the bondwoman was
born after the flesh;
but he of the freewo-
man *was* by promise.
24 Which things are
an allegory: for these
are the two covenants;
the one from the mount
Sinai, which gender-
eth to bondage, which
is Agar. 25 For this
Agar is mount Sinai
in Arabia, and answer-
eth to Jerusalem which
now is, and is in bon-
dage with her child-
ren. 26 But Jerusalem
which is above is free,
which is the mother
of us all. 27 For it is
written, Rejoice, *thou*
barren that bearest
not; break forth and
cry, thou that travail-
est not: for the deso-
late hath many more
children than she
which hath an hus-
band. 28 Now we, bre-
thren, as Isaac was,
are the children of
promise. 29 But as
then he that was born
after the flesh perse-
cuted him *that was*
born after the Spirit,
even so *it is* now.
30 Nevertheless what
saith the scripture?
Cast out the bond-
woman and her son:
for the son of the
bondwoman shall not
be heir with the son
of the freewoman.
31 So then, brethren,
we are not children of
the bondwoman, but
of the free.
V. Stand fast there-
fore in the liberty
wherewith Christ hath
made us free, and be
not entangled again
with the yoke of bon-
dage. 2 Behold, I Paul

[w] ἀλλὰ Tr. [x] [μὲν] L. [y] γεγένηται W. [z] δι' Tr. [a] — αἱ GLTTrAW. [b] δουλίαν T. [c] — Ἄγαρ LT[Tr]. [d] συνσ- T. [e] γὰρ for GLTTrAW. [f] — πάντων G[L]TTrA. [g] ὑμεῖς you LTTrA. [h] ἐστέ LTTrA. [i] κληρονομήσει shall inherit LTTr. [k] διό wherefore LTTrA. [l] — οὖν GLTTrAW. [m] — ᾗ (*read* With freedom &c.) LTTrA. [n] ἡμᾶς χριστὸς GLTTrAW. [o] . στήκετε (*commencing a sentence at* Stand fast) LTTrA. [p] + οὖν therefore LTTrAW. [q] δουλίας T.

say unto you, that if
ye be circumcised,
Christ shall profit you
nothing. 3 For I tes-
tify again to every
man that is circum-
cised, that he is a
debtor to do the whole
law. 4 Christ is be-
come of no effect un-
to you, whosoever of
you are justified by
the law; ye are fallen
from grace. 5 For we
through the Spirit
wait for the hope of
righteousness by faith.
6 For in Jesus Christ
neither circumcision
availeth any thing,
nor uncircumcision;
but faith which work-
eth by love. 7 Ye did
run well; who did
hinder you that ye
should not obey the
truth? 8 This per-
suasion *cometh* not of
him that calleth you.
9 A little leaven
leaveneth the whole
lump. 10 I have con-
fidence in you through
the Lord, that ye will
be none otherwise
minded: but he that
troubleth you shall
bear his judgment,
whosoever he be.

11 And I, brethren,
if I yet preach cir-
cumcision, why do I
yet suffer persecution?
then is the offence of
the cross ceased. 12 I
would they were even
cut off which trouble
you. 13 For, brethren,
ye have been called
unto liberty; only *use*
not liberty for an oc-
casion to the flesh, but
by love serve one an-
other. 14 For all the
law is fulfilled in one
word, *even* in this;
Thou shalt love thy
neighbour as thyself.
15 But if ye bite and
devour one another,
take heed that ye be
not consumed one of
another. 16 *This* I say
then, Walk in the Spi-
rit, and ye shall not
fulfil the lust of the
flesh. 17 For the flesh
lusteth against the
Spirit, and the Spirit
against the flesh: and
these are contrary the
one to the other: so
that ye cannot do the
things that ye would.
18 But if ye be led of
the Spirit, ye are not
under the law. 19 Now

περιτεμνομένῳ, ὅτι ὀφειλέτης ἐστὶν ὅλον τὸν νόμον ποιῆσαι.
being circumcised, that a debtor he is [2]whole [1]the law to do.

4 κατηργήθητε ἀπὸ [r]τοῦ'' χριστοῦ, οἵτινες ἐν νόμῳ δι-
Ye are deprived of all effect from the Christ, whosoever in law are

καιοῦσθε, τῆς χάριτος ἐξεπέσατε· 5 ἡμεῖς.γὰρ πνεύματι
being justified; grace ye fell from. For we, by [the] Spirit

ἐκ πίστεως ἐλπίδα δικαιοσύνης ἀπεκδεχόμεθα. 6 ἐν.γὰρ
by faith [the] hope of righteousness await. For in

χριστῷ Ἰησοῦ οὔτε περιτομή τι ἰσχύει, οὔτε ἀκροβυστία,
Christ Jesus neither circumcision [3]any [1]is [2]of force, nor uncircumcision;

ἀλλὰ πίστις δι' ἀγάπης ἐνεργουμένη. 7 Ἐτρέχετε καλῶς
but faith [2]by [3]love [1]working. Ye were running well:

τίς ὑμᾶς [s]ἀνέκοψεν'' [t]τῇ'' ἀληθείᾳ μὴ πείθεσθαι; 8 ἡ πεισ-
who [2]you [1]hindered [6]the [7]truth [3]not [4]to [5]obey? The persua-

μονὴ οὐκ ἐκ τοῦ καλοῦντος ὑμᾶς. 9 Μικρὰ ζύμη ὅλον
sion [is] not of him who calls you. A little leaven [3]whole

τὸ φύραμα ζυμοῖ. 10 ἐγὼ[v] πέποιθα εἰς ὑμᾶς ἐν κυρίῳ,
[2]the [4]lump [1]leavens. I am persuaded as to you in [the] Lord,

ὅτι οὐδὲν.ἄλλο.φρονήσετε, ὁ.δὲ ταράσσων ὑμᾶς βαστάσει τὸ
that ye will have no other mind, and he troubling you shall bear the

κρίμα, ὅστις [w]ἂν'' ᾖ.
judgment, whosoever he may be.

11 Ἐγὼ.δέ, ἀδελφοί, εἰ περιτομὴν ἔτι κηρύσσω, τί ἔτι διώ-
But I, brethren, if circumcision yet I proclaim, why yet am I

κομαι; ἄρα κατήργηται τὸ σκάνδαλον τοῦ σταυροῦ.
persecuted? Then has been done away the offence of the cross.

12 ὄφελον καὶ ἀποκόψονται οἱ ἀναστατοῦντες
I would [3]even [1]they [2]would cut themselves off who throw [2]into [3]confusion

ὑμᾶς. 13 Ὑμεῖς.γὰρ ἐπ' ἐλευθερίᾳ ἐκλήθητε, ἀδελφοί· μόνον
[1]you. For ye for freedom were called, brethren; only

μὴ τὴν ἐλευθερίαν εἰς ἀφορμὴν τῇ σαρκί, ἀλλὰ διὰ τῆς
[use] not the freedom for an occasion to the flesh, but by

ἀγάπης δουλεύετε ἀλλήλοις. 14 ὁ.γὰρ.πᾶς νόμος ἐν ἑνὶ
love serve ye one another. For the whole law in one

λόγῳ [x]πληροῦται,'' ἐν τῷ, Ἀγαπήσεις τὸν.πλησίον.σου ὡς
word is fulfilled, in Thou shalt love thy neighbour as

[y]ἑαυτόν.'' 15 εἰ.δὲ ἀλλήλους δάκνετε καὶ κατεσθίετε, βλέπετε
thyself; but if one another ye bite and devour, take heed

μὴ [z]ὑπὸ'' ἀλλήλων ἀναλωθῆτε.
[3]not [5]by [6]one [7]another [1]ye [2]be [4]consumed.

16 Λέγω.δέ, Πνεύματι περιπατεῖτε, καὶ ἐπιθυμίαν σαρκὸς
But I say, By [the] Spirit walk ye, and [2]desire [1]flesh's

οὐ.μὴ τελέσητε. 17 ἡ.γὰρ σὰρξ ἐπιθυμεῖ κατὰ τοῦ πνεύ-
in no wise should ye fulfil. For the flesh desires against the Spirit,

ματος, τὸ.δὲ πνεῦμα κατὰ τῆς σαρκός· ταῦτα [a]δὲ'' [b]ἀντί-
and the Spirit against the flesh; [2]these [3]things [1]and are op-

κειται ἀλλήλοις,'' ἵνα μὴ ἃ [c]ἂν'' θέλητε ταῦτα ποιῆτε.
posed to one another, that not whatsoever ye may wish those things ye should do;

18 εἰ.δὲ πνεύματι ἄγεσθε, οὐκ.ἐστὲ ὑπὸ νόμον. 19 φανερὰ
but if by [the] Spirit ye are led, ye are [2]no [1]under law. [2]Manifest

δέ ἐστιν τὰ ἔργα τῆς σαρκός, ἅτινά ἐστιν [d]μοιχεία,'' πορνεία,
[1]now are the works of the flesh, which are adultery, fornication,

ἀκαθαρσία, ἀσέλγεια, 20 εἰδωλολατρεία, φαρμακεία, ἔχθραι,
uncleanness, licentiousness, idolatry, sorcery, enmities,

---

[r] — τοῦ LTTr[A]. [s] ἐνέκοψεν GLTTrAW. [t] — τῇ TTr[A]. [v] + [δὲ] but L. [w] ἐὰν TTrA. [x] πεπλήρωται has been fulfilled LTTrAW. [y] σεαυτόν GLTTrAW. [z] ὑπ' LTTr. [a] γὰρ for LTTrAW. [b] ἀλλήλοις ἀντίκειται GLTTrAW. [c] ἐαν [L]TTrA. [d] — μοιχεία GLTTrAW.

[e]ἔρεις, ζῆλοι,‖ θυμοί, ἐριθεῖαι, διχοστασίαι, αἱρέσεις,
strifes, jealousies, indignations, contentions, divisions, sects,
21 φθόνοι, [f]φόνοι,‖ μέθαι, κῶμοι, καὶ τὰ ὅμοια τούτοις·
envyings, murders, drunkennesses, revels, and things like these;
ἃ προλέγω ὑμῖν, καθὼς [g]καὶ‖ προεῖπον, ὅτι οἱ
as to which I tell [2]beforehand [1]you, even as also I said before, that they who
τὰ.τοιαῦτα πράσσοντες βασιλείαν θεοῦ οὐ.κληρονομήσουσιν.
such things do [2]kingdom [1]God's shall not inherit.
22 ὁ.δὲ καρπὸς τοῦ πνεύματός ἐστιν ἀγάπη, χαρά, εἰρήνη,
But the fruit of the Spirit is love, joy, peace,
μακροθυμία, χρηστότης, ἀγαθωσύνη, πίστις, 23 [h]πρᾳότης,‖
long-suffering, kindness, goodness, faith, meekness,
ἐγκράτεια· κατὰ τῶν.τοιούτων οὐκ.ἔστιν νόμος. 24 οἱ.δὲ
self-control: against such things there is no law. But they that [are]
τοῦ χριστοῦ [i] τὴν σάρκα ἐσταύρωσαν σὺν τοῖς παθήμασιν καὶ
of the Christ [2]the [3]flesh [1]crucified with the passions and
ταῖς ἐπιθυμίαις. 25 εἰ ζῶμεν πνεύματι, πνεύματι καὶ
the desires. If we live by [the] Spirit, by [the] Spirit also
στοιχῶμεν. 26 μὴ.γινώμεθα κενόδοξοι, ἀλλήλους προκα-
we should walk. We should not become vain-glorious, one another provok-
λούμενοι, [k]ἀλλήλοις‖ φθονοῦντες.
ing, one another envying.

6 Ἀδελφοί, ἐὰν καὶ [l]προληφθῇ‖ ἄνθρωπος ἔν τινι παρα-
Brethren, if even be taken a man in some of-
πτώματι, ὑμεῖς οἱ πνευματικοὶ καταρτίζετε τὸν.τοιοῦτον ἐν
fence, ye, the spiritual [ones], restore such a one in
πνεύματι [m]πρᾳότητος,‖ σκοπῶν σεαυτὸν μὴ καὶ σὺ πει-
a spirit of meekness, considering thyself lest also thou be
ρασθῇς. 2 ἀλλήλων τὰ βάρη βαστάζετε, καὶ οὕτως [n]ἀνα-
tempted. One another's burdens bear ye, and thus ful-
πληρώσατε‖ τὸν νόμον τοῦ χριστοῦ. 3 εἰ.γὰρ δοκεῖ τις
fil the law of the Christ. For if [2]thinks [1]anyone
εἶναί τι, μηδὲν ὤν, [o]ἑαυτὸν φρεναπατᾷ.‖ 4 τὸ.δὲ ἔργον
to be something, [2]nothing [1]being, himself he deceives: but the work
ἑαυτοῦ δοκιμαζέτω ἕκαστος, καὶ τότε εἰς ἑαυτὸν μόνον τὸ
of himself let [2]prove [1]each, and then as to himself alone the
καύχημα ἕξει, καὶ οὐκ εἰς τὸν.ἕτερον· 5 ἕκαστος.γὰρ τὸ
boasting he will have, and not as to another. For each
ἴδιον φορτίον βαστάσει.
his own load shall bear.

6 Κοινωνείτω.δὲ ὁ κατηχούμενος τὸν λόγον τῷ
Let [7]share [1]him [2]being [3]taught [4]in [5]the [6]word with him that
κατηχοῦντι ἐν πᾶσιν ἀγαθοῖς. 7 μὴ.πλανᾶσθε, θεὸς οὐ μυκ-
teaches in all good things. Be not misled; God [2]not [1]is
τηρίζεται· ὃ.γὰρ.[p]ἐὰν‖ σπείρῃ ἄνθρωπος, τοῦτο καὶ θερί-
mocked; for whatsoever [3]may [4]sow [1]a [2]man, that also he shall
σει· 8 ὅτι ὁ σπείρων εἰς τὴν.σάρκα.ἑαυτοῦ, ἐκ τῆς σαρκὸς
reap. For he that sows to his own flesh, from the flesh
θερίσει φθοράν· ὁ.δὲ σπείρων εἰς τὸ πνεῦμα, ἐκ τοῦ
shall reap corruption; but he that sows to the Spirit, from the
πνεύματος θερίσει ζωὴν αἰώνιον. 9 τὸ.δὲ καλὸν ποιοῦντες
Spirit shall reap life eternal: but [in] well doing

the works of the flesh
are manifest, which
are *these;* Adultery,
fornication, unclean-
ness, lasciviousness,
20 idolatry, witchcraft,
hatred, variance, emu-
lations, wrath, strife,
seditions, heresies,
21 envyings, murders,
drunkenness, revel-
lings, and such like:
of the which I tell
you before, as I have
also told *you* in time
past, that they which
do such things shall
not inherit the king-
dom of God. 22 But
the fruit of the Spirit
is love, joy, peace,
longsuffering, gentle-
ness, goodness, faith,
23 meekness, temper-
ance: against such
there is no law. 24 And
they that are Christ's
have crucified the flesh
with the affections and
lusts. 25 If we live in
the Spirit, let us also
walk in the Spirit.
26 Let us not be de-
sirous of vain glory,
provoking one another,
envying one another.

VI. Brethren if a
man be overtaken in a
fault, ye which are
spiritual, restore such
an one in the spirit of
meekness; considering
thyself, lest thou also
be tempted. 2 Bear ye
one another's burdens,
and so fulfil the law of
Christ. 3 For if a man
think himself to be
something, when he is
nothing, he deceiveth
himself. 4 But let
every man prove his
own work, and then
shall he have rejoicing
in himself alone, and
not in another. 5 For
every man shall bear
his own burden.

6 Let him that is
taught in the word
communicate unto
him that teacheth in
all good things. 7 Be
not deceived; God is
not mocked: for what-
soever a man soweth,
that shall he also reap.
8 For he that soweth
to his flesh shall of the
flesh reap corruption;
but he that soweth
to the Spirit shall of the
Spirit reap life ever-
lasting. 9 And let us

---

e ἔρις, ζῆλος strife, jealousy LTTrAW. f — φόνοι [L]T[TrA]. g — καὶ [L]TTr. h πραΰτης LTTrAW. i + Ἰησοῦ Jesus [L]TTrA. k ἀλλήλους L. l προλημφθῇ LTTrA. m πραΰτητος TTrAW. n ἀναπληρώσετε ye shall fulfil LT. o φρεναπατᾷ ἑαυτὸν LTTrA. p ἂν LTr.

not be weary in well
doing: for in due sea-
son we shall reap, if
we faint not. 10 As
we have therefore op-
portunity, let us do
good unto all *men*, es-
pecially unto them
who are of the house-
hold of faith.

μὴ.[q]ἐκκακῶμεν·‖ καιρῷ.γὰρ ἰδίῳ θερίσομεν, μὴ ἐκλυόμενοι.
we should not lose heart; for in [2]time [1]due [5]we [6]shall [7]reap [4]not [3]fainting.
10 ἄρα οὖν ὡς καιρὸν [r]ἔχομεν‖ ἐργαζώμεθα τὸ ἀγαθὸν πρὸς
So then as occasion we have we should work good towards
πάντας, μάλιστα.δὲ πρὸς τοὺς οἰκείους τῆς πίστεως.
all, and specially towards those of the household of faith.
11 Ἴδετε πηλίκοις ὑμῖν γράμμασιν ἔγραψα τῇ.ἐμῇ.χειρί.
See in how large [4]to [5]you [1]letters [2]I [3]wrote with my [own] hand.

11 Ye see how large
a letter I have written
unto you with mine
own hand. 12 As many
as desire to make a fair
shew in the flesh, they
constrain you to be
circumcised; only lest
they should suffer per-
secution for the cross
of Christ. 13 For nei-
ther they themselves
who are circumcised
keep the law; but de-
sire to have you cir-
cumcised, that they
may glory in your
flesh. 14 But God for-
bid that I should glory,
save in the cross of
our Lord Jesus Christ,
by whom the world is
crucified unto me, and
I unto the world.
15 For in Christ Jesus
neither circumcision
availeth any thing, nor
uncircumcision, but a
new creature. 16 And
as many as walk ac-
cording to this rule,
peace *be* on them, and
mercy, and upon the
Israel of God.

12 ὅσοι θέλουσιν εὐπροσωπῆσαι ἐν σαρκί, οὗτοι
As many as wish to have a fair appearance in [the] flesh, these
ἀναγκάζουσιν ὑμᾶς περιτέμνεσθαι, μόνον ἵνα [s]μὴ‖ τῷ
compel you to be circumcised, only that not for the
σταυρῷ τοῦ χριστοῦ [s] [t]διώκωνται.‖ 13 οὐδὲ.γὰρ οἱ
cross of the Christ they may be persecuted. For neither they who
[u]περιτεμνόμενοι‖ αὐτοὶ νόμον φυλάσσουσιν· ἀλλὰ θέ-
are being circumcised themselves [the] law keep; but they
λουσιν ὑμᾶς περιτέμνεσθαι, ἵνα ἐν τῇ.ὑμετέρᾳ.σαρκὶ καυ-
wish you to be circumcised, that in your flesh they
χήσωνται. 14 ἐμοὶ.δὲ μὴ.γένοιτο καυχᾶσθαι εἰ.μὴ ἐν τῷ
might boast. But for me may it not be to boast except in the
σταυρῷ τοῦ κυρίου.ἡμῶν Ἰησοῦ χριστοῦ· δι᾽ οὗ ἐμοὶ
cross of our Lord Jesus Christ; through whom to me [the]
κόσμος ἐσταύρωται, κἀγὼ [v]τῷ‖ κόσμῳ. 15 [w]ἐν γὰρ χριστῷ
world has been crucified, and I to the world. [2]In [1]for Christ
Ἰησοῦ οὔτε‖ περιτομή [x]τι ἰσχύει,‖ οὔτε ἀκροβυστία,
Jesus neither circumcision [3]any [1]is [2]of force, nor uncircumcision;
ἀλλὰ καινὴ κτίσις. 16 καὶ ὅσοι τῷ.κανόνι.τούτῳ στοι-
but a new creation. And as many as by this rule shall
χήσουσιν, εἰρήνη ἐπ᾽ αὐτοὺς καὶ ἔλεος, καὶ ἐπὶ τὸν Ἰσραὴλ
walk, peace [be] upon them and mercy, and upon the Israel
τοῦ θεοῦ.
of God.

17 From henceforth
let no man trouble
me: for I bear in my
body the marks of the
Lord Jesus. 18 Bre-
thren, the grace of our
Lord Jesus Christ *be*
with your spirit. A-
men.

17 Τοῦ.λοιποῦ, κόπους μοι μηδεὶς παρεχέτω· ἐγὼ.γὰρ τὰ
For the rest, [6]troubles [6]to [7]me [2]no [3]one [1]let [4]give, for I the
στίγματα τοῦ [y]κυρίου‖ Ἰησοῦ ἐν τῷ.σώματί.μου βαστάζω.
brands of the Lord Jesus in my body bear.
18 Ἡ χάρις τοῦ.κυρίου.ἡμῶν Ἰησοῦ χριστοῦ μετὰ τοῦ πνεύ-
The grace of our Lord Jesus Christ [be] with [2]spi-
ματος ὑμῶν, ἀδελφοί. ἀμήν.
rit [1]your, brethren. Amen.

[z]Πρὸς Γαλάτας ἐγράφη ἀπὸ Ῥώμης.‖
To [the] Galatians written from Rome.

---

[a]ΠΡΟΣ ΕΦΕΣΙΟΥΣ ΕΠΙΣΤΟΛΗ ΠΑΥΛΟΥ.‖
[4]TO [[5]THE] [6]EPHESIANS [1]EPISTLE [2]OF [3]PAUL.

PAUL, an apostle of
Jesus Christ by the
will of God, to the
saints which are at
Ephesus, and to the

ΠΑΥΛΟΣ ἀπόστολος [b]Ἰησοῦ χριστοῦ‖ διὰ θελήματος θεοῦ,
Paul, apostle of Jesus Christ by will of God,
τοῖς ἁγίοις τοῖς οὖσιν [c]ἐν Ἐφέσῳ‖ καὶ πιστοῖς ἐν χριστῷ
to the saints who are at Ephesus and faithful in Christ

---

[q] ἐγ- LTrAW; ἐν- T. [r] ἔχωμεν we may have T. [s] μὴ *placed after* χριστοῦ LTTrA. [t] διώκονται are being persecuted T [u] περιτετμημένοι have been circumcised L. [v] — τῷ (*read* to [the]) LTTrA. [w] οὔτε γὰρ For neither TTrA. [x] τι ἐστὶν is anything GLTTrAW. [y] — κυρίου LTTrAW. [z] — *the subscription* GLTW; Πρὸς Γαλάτας TrA.

[a] + τοῦ Ἀποστόλου of the Apostle E; Πρὸς Ἐφεσίους LTTrAW. [b] χριστοῦ Ἰησοῦ LTTrA. [c] [ἐν Ἐφέσῳ] TA.

Ἰησοῦ· 2 χάρις ὑμῖν καὶ εἰρήνη ἀπὸ θεοῦ πατρὸς.ἡμῶν καὶ
Jesus. Grace to you and peace from God our Father and
κυρίου Ἰησοῦ χριστοῦ.
[the] Lord Jesus Christ.

3 Εὐλογητὸς ὁ θεὸς καὶ πατὴρ τοῦ.κυρίου.ἡμῶν Ἰησοῦ
Blessed [be] the God and Father of our Lord Jesus
χριστοῦ, ὁ εὐλογήσας ἡμᾶς ἐν πάσῃ εὐλογίᾳ πνευματικῇ ἐν
Christ, who blessed us with every [2]blessing [1]spiritual in
τοῖς ἐπουρανίοις [d] χριστῷ, 4 καθὼς ἐξελέξατο ἡμᾶς ἐν αὐτῷ
the heavenlies with Christ; according as he chose us in him
πρὸ καταβολῆς κόσμου, εἶναι.ἡμᾶς ἁγίους καὶ ἀμώ-
before [the] foundation of [the] world, for us to be holy and blame-
μους κατενώπιον αὐτοῦ [e]ἐν ἀγάπῃ,‖ 5 προορίσας ἡμᾶς εἰς
less before him in love; having predestinated us for
υἱοθεσίαν διὰ Ἰησοῦ χριστοῦ εἰς αὐτόν, κατὰ τὴν εὐδο-
adoption through Jesus Christ to himself, according to the good
κίαν τοῦ.θελήματος.αὐτοῦ, 6 εἰς ἔπαινον δόξης τῆς χάρι-
pleasure of his will, to [the] praise of [the] glory of [2]grace
τος αὐτοῦ, [f]ἐν.ᾗ‖ ἐχαρίτωσεν ἡμᾶς ἐν τῷ ἠγαπημένῳ·
[1]his, wherein he made [2]objects [3]of [4]grace [1]us in the Beloved:
7 ἐν ᾧ ἔχομεν τὴν ἀπολύτρωσιν διὰ τοῦ.αἵματος.αὐτοῦ,
in whom we have redemption through his blood,
τὴν ἄφεσιν τῶν παραπτωμάτων, κατὰ [g]τὸν πλοῦτον‖ τῆς
the remission of offences, according to the riches
χάριτος.αὐτοῦ· 8 ἧς ἐπερίσσευσεν εἰς ἡμᾶς ἐν πάσῃ
of his grace; which he caused to abound toward us in all
σοφίᾳ καὶ φρονήσει, 9 γνωρίσας ἡμῖν τὸ μυστήριον τοῦ
wisdom and intelligence, having made known to us the mystery
θελήματος.αὐτοῦ, κατὰ τὴν.εὐδοκίαν.αὐτοῦ, ἣν προέθετο
of his will, according to his good pleasure, which he purposed
ἐν αὐτῷ 10 εἰς οἰκονομίαν τοῦ πληρώματος τῶν καιρῶν,
in himself for [the] administration of the fulness of times;
ἀνακεφαλαιώσασθαι τὰ.πάντα ἐν τῷ χριστῷ, τά.[h]τε‖ [i]ἐν‖
to head up all things in the Christ, both the things in
τοῖς οὐρανοῖς καὶ τὰ ἐπὶ τῆς γῆς· 11 ἐν αὐτῷ, ἐν ᾧ
the heavens and the things upon the earth; in him, in whom
καὶ [k]ἐκληρώθημεν,‖ προορισθέντες κατὰ πρό-
also we obtained an inheritance, being predestinated according to [the] pur-
θεσιν τοῦ τὰ.πάντα ἐνεργοῦντος κατὰ τὴν βουλὴν
pose of him who [2]all [3]things [1]works according to the counsel
τοῦ.θελήματος.αὐτοῦ, 12 εἰς τὸ εἶναι ἡμᾶς εἰς ἔπαινον
of his will, for [2]to [3]be [1]us to [the] praise
[l]τῆς‖.δόξης.αὐτοῦ, τοὺς προηλπικότας ἐν τῷ χριστῷ· 13 ἐν
of his glory; who have fore-trusted in the Christ: in
ᾧ καὶ ὑμεῖς, ἀκούσαντες τὸν λόγον τῆς ἀληθείας, τὸ εὐαγ-
whom also ye, having heard the word of the truth, the glad
γέλιον τῆς.σωτηρίας.ὑμῶν, ἐν ᾧ καὶ πιστεύσαντες ἐσφρα-
tidings of your salvation— in whom also, having believed, ye were
γίσθητε τῷ πνεύματι τῆς ἐπαγγελίας τῷ ἁγίῳ, 14 [m]ὅς‖ ἐστιν
sealed with the Spirit of promise the Holy, who is
ἀῤῥαβὼν τῆς.κληρονομίας.ἡμῶν, εἰς ἀπολύτρωσιν τῆς
[the] earnest of our inheritance, to [the] redemption of the
περιποιήσεως, εἰς ἔπαινον τῆς.δόξης.αὐτοῦ.
acquired possession, to praise of his glory.

faithful in Christ Jesus: 2 Grace *be* to you, and peace, from God our Father, and *from* the Lord Jesus Christ.

3 Blessed *be* the God and Father of our Lord Jesus Christ, who hath blessed us with all spiritual blessings in heavenly *places* in Christ: 4 according as he hath chosen us in him before the foundation of the world, that we should be holy and without blame before him in love: 5 having predestinated us unto the adoption of children by Jesus Christ to himself, according to the good pleasure of his will, 6 to the praise of the glory of his grace, wherein he hath made us accepted in the beloved. 7 In whom we have redemption through his blood, the forgiveness of sins, according to the riches of his grace; 8 wherein he hath abounded toward us in all wisdom and prudence; 9 having made known unto us the mystery of his will, according to his good pleasure which he hath purposed in himself: 10 that in the dispensation of the fulness of times he might gather together in one all things in Christ, both which are in heaven, and which are on earth; *even* in him: 11 in whom also we have obtained an inheritance, being predestinated according to the purpose of him who worketh all things after the counsel of his own will: 12 that we should be to the praise of his glory, who first trusted in Christ. 13 In whom ye also *trusted*, after that ye heard the word of truth, the gospel of your salvation: in whom also after that ye believed, ye were sealed with that holy Spirit of promise, 14 which is the earnest of our inheritance until the redemption of the purchased possession, unto the praise of his glory.

---

[d] + ἐν in (Christ) EGLTTrAW. [e] , ἐν ἀγάπῃ (*read* in love having predestinated us) GLT. [f] ἧς which (*read* ἐχα. he freely bestowed on) LTTrA. [g] τὸ.πλοῦτος LTTrAW. [h] — τε both LTTrAW. [i] ἐπὶ upon LTTrA. [k] ἐκλήθημεν we were called L. [l] — τῆς LTTrAW. [m] ὅ which LA.

15 Wherefore I also, after I heard of your faith in the Lord Jesus, and love unto all the saints, 16 cease not to give thanks for you, making mention of you in my prayers; 17 that the God of our Lord Jesus Christ, the Father of glory, may give unto you the spirit of wisdom and revelation in the knowledge of him: 18 the eyes of your understanding being enlightened; that ye may know what is the hope of his calling, and what the riches of the glory of his inheritance in the saints, 19 and what *is* the exceeding greatness of his power to us-ward who believe, according to the working of his mighty power, 20 which he wrought in Christ, when he raised him from the dead, and set *him* at his own right hand in the heavenly *places*, 21 far above all principality, and power, and might, and dominion, and every name that is named, not only in this world, but also in that which is to come: 22 and hath put all *things* under his feet, and gave him *to be* the head over all *things* to the church, 23 which is his body, the fulness of him that filleth all in all. II. And you *hath he quickened*, who were dead in trespasses and sins; 2 wherein in time past ye walked according to the course of this world, according to the prince of the power of the air, the spirit that now worketh in the children of disobedience: 3 among whom also we all had our conversation in times past in the lusts of our flesh, fulfilling the desires of the flesh and of the mind; and were by nature the children of

15 Διὰ τοῦτο κἀγὼ ἀκούσας [1] τὴν καθ' ὑμᾶς πίστιν ἐν
Because of this I also having heard of the [2]among [3]you [1]faith in
τῷ κυρίῳ Ἰησοῦ, καὶ [n]τὴν ἀγάπην‖ τὴν εἰς πάντας τοὺς
the Lord Jesus, and the love which [is] toward all the
ἁγίους, 16 οὐ-παύομαι εὐχαριστῶν ὑπὲρ ὑμῶν, μνείαν [o]ὑμῶν‖
saints, do not cease giving thanks for you, mention of you
ποιούμενος ἐπὶ τῶν-προσευχῶν-μου· 17 ἵνα ὁ θεὸς τοῦ κυρίου
making in my prayers, that the God of [2]Lord
ἡμῶν Ἰησοῦ χριστοῦ, ὁ πατὴρ τῆς δόξης, δῴη ὑμῖν πνεῦμα
[1]our Jesus Christ, the Father of glory, may give to you [the] spirit
σοφίας καὶ ἀποκαλύψεως ἐν ἐπιγνώσει αὐτοῦ, 18 πεφω-
of wisdom and revelation in [the] knowledge of him, [6]being
τισμένους τοὺς ὀφθαλμοὺς τῆς [p]διανοίας‖ ὑμῶν, εἰς τὸ εἰδέναι
[7]enlightened [1]the [2]eyes [5]mind [3]of [4]your, for [2]to [3]know
ὑμᾶς τίς ἐστιν ἡ ἐλπὶς τῆς-κλήσεως-αὐτοῦ, [q]καὶ‖ τίς ὁ πλοῦ-
[1]you what is the hope of his calling, and what the riches
τος τῆς δόξης τῆς-κληρονομίας-αὐτοῦ ἐν τοῖς ἁγίοις, 19 καὶ
of the glory of his inheritance in the saints, and
τί τὸ ὑπερβάλλον μέγεθος τῆς-δυνάμεως-αὐτοῦ εἰς ἡμᾶς
what the surpassing greatness of his power towards us
τοὺς πιστεύοντας κατὰ τὴν ἐνέργειαν τοῦ κράτους τῆς
who believe according to the working of the might
ἰσχύος-αὐτοῦ, 20 ἣν [r]ἐνήργησεν‖ ἐν τῷ χριστῷ ἐγείρας
of his strength, which he wrought in the Christ, having raised
αὐτὸν ἐκ [s] νεκρῶν, καὶ [t]ἐκάθισεν‖ [v] ἐν δεξιᾷ
him from among [the] dead, and he set [him] at [2]right [3]hand
αὐτοῦ ἐν τοῖς [w]ἐπουρανίοις,‖ 21 ὑπεράνω πάσης ἀρχῆς
[1]his in the heavenlies, above every principality
καὶ ἐξουσίας καὶ δυνάμεως καὶ κυριότητος, καὶ παντὸς ὀνό-
and authority and power and lordship, and every name
ματος ὀνομαζομένου οὐ μόνον ἐν τῷ-αἰῶνι-τούτῳ, ἀλλὰ καὶ
named, not only in this age, but also
ἐν τῷ μέλλοντι· 22 καὶ [x] πάντα ὑπέταξεν ὑπὸ τοὺς πόδας
in the coming [one]; and all things he put under [2]feet
αὐτοῦ· καὶ αὐτὸν ἔδωκεν κεφαλὴν ὑπὲρ πάντα τῇ ἐκ-
[1]his, and [2]him [1]gave [to be] head over all things to the as-
κλησίᾳ, 23 ἥτις ἐστὶν τὸ-σῶμα-αὐτοῦ, τὸ πλήρωμα τοῦ
sembly, which is his body, the fulness of him who
[y]πάντα ἐν πᾶσιν πληρουμένου 2 καὶ ὑμᾶς ὄντας νεκροὺς
all things in all fills— and you being dead
τοῖς παραπτώμασιν καὶ ταῖς ἁμαρτίαις[z], 2 ἐν αἷς ποτε
in offences and sins, in which once
περιεπατήσατε κατὰ τὸν αἰῶνα τοῦ-κόσμου-τούτου, κατὰ
ye walked according to the age of this world, according to
τὸν ἄρχοντα τῆς ἐξουσίας τοῦ ἀέρος, τοῦ πνεύματος τοῦ νῦν
the ruler of the authority of the air, the spirit that now
ἐνεργοῦντος ἐν τοῖς υἱοῖς τῆς ἀπειθείας· 3 ἐν οἷς καὶ ἡμεῖς
works in the sons of disobedience: among whom also we
πάντες ἀνεστράφημέν ποτε ἐν ταῖς ἐπιθυμίαις τῆς σαρκὸς
all had our conduct once in the desires of [2]flesh
ἡμῶν, ποιοῦντες τὰ θελήματα τῆς σαρκὸς καὶ τῶν διανοιῶν,
[1]our, doing the things willed of the flesh and of the thoughts,

---

[n] — τὴν ἀγάπην L[A]. [o] — ὑμῶν LTTrA. [p] καρδίας heart GLTTrAW. [q] — καὶ LTTrA. [r] ἐνήργηκεν he has wrought LTA. [s] + τῶν the W. [t] καθίσας having set LTTrA. [v] + αὐτὸν him T. [w] οὐρανοῖς heavens L. [x] + τὰ W. [y] + τὰ GLTTrAW. [z] + ὑμῶν (*read* your offences and sins) LTTr[A].

καὶ [a]ἦμεν‖ [b]τέκνα φύσει‖ ὀργῆς, ὡς καὶ οἱ λοιποί· 4 ὁ.δὲ.θεός,
and were children, by nature, of wrath, as even the rest: but God,
πλούσιος ὢν ἐν ἐλέει, διὰ τὴν πολλὴν ἀγάπην αὐτοῦ
[2]rich [1]being in mercy, because of [2]great [3]love [1]his
ἣν ἠγάπησεν ἡμᾶς, 5 καὶ ὄντας ἡμᾶς νεκροὺς τοῖς
wherewith he loved us, [2]also [3]being [1]we dead
παραπτώμασιν, συνεζωοποίησεν [c] τῷ χριστῷ· χάριτί ἐστε
in offences, quickened [us] with the Christ, (by grace ye are
σεσωσμένοι· 6 καὶ συνήγειρεν, καὶ συνεκάθισεν ἐν τοῖς
saved,) and raised [us] up together, and seated [us] together in the
ἐπουρανίοις ἐν χριστῷ Ἰησοῦ· 7 ἵνα ἐνδείξηται ἐν τοῖς
heavenlies in Christ Jesus, that he might shew in the
αἰῶσιν τοῖς ἐπερχομένοις [d]τὸν ὑπερβάλλοντα πλοῦτον‖
ages that [are] coming the surpassing riches
τῆς.χάριτος.αὐτοῦ ἐν χρηστότητι ἐφ᾽ ἡμᾶς ἐν χριστῷ Ἰησοῦ·
of his grace in kindness toward us in Christ Jesus.
8 τῇ γὰρ χάριτί ἐστε σεσωσμένοι διὰ [e]τῆς‖ πίστεως· καὶ
For by grace ye are saved through faith; and
τοῦτο οὐκ ἐξ ὑμῶν, θεοῦ τὸ δῶρον· 9 οὐκ ἐξ ἔργων, ἵνα
this not of yourselves; [it is] God's gift: not of works, that
μή τις καυχήσηται. 10 αὐτοῦ.γάρ ἐσμεν ποίημα, κτισθέν-
not anyone might boast. For his [2]we [3]are [1]workmanship, created
τες ἐν χριστῷ Ἰησοῦ ἐπὶ ἔργοις ἀγαθοῖς, οἷς προητοίμασεν ὁ
in Christ Jesus for [2]works [1]good, which [2]before [3]prepared
θεὸς ἵνα ἐν αὐτοῖς περιπατήσωμεν.
[1]God that in them we should walk.

wrath, even as others. 4 But God, who is rich in mercy, for his great love wherewith he loved us, 5 even when we were dead in sins, hath quickened us together with Christ, (by grace ye are saved;) 6 and hath raised *us* up together, and made *us* sit together in heavenly *places* in Christ Jesus: 7 that in the ages to come he might shew the exceeding riches of his grace in *his* kindness toward us through Christ Jesus. 8 For by grace are ye saved through faith; and that not of yourselves: *it is* the gift of God: 9 not of works, lest any man should boast. 10 For we are his workmanship, created in Christ Jesus unto good works, which God hath before ordained that we should walk in them.

11 Διὸ μνημονεύετε ὅτι [f]ὑμεῖς ποτε‖ τὰ ἔθνη ἐν
Wherefore remember that ye once the nations in [the]
σαρκί, οἱ λεγόμενοι ἀκροβυστία ὑπὸ τῆς λεγομένης περιτο-
flesh, who are called uncircumcision by that called circum-
μῆς ἐν σαρκὶ χειροποιήτου, 12 ὅτι ἦτε [g]ἐν‖ τῷ.καιρῷ.ἐκείνῳ
cision in [the] flesh made by hand— that ye were at that time
χωρὶς χριστοῦ, ἀπηλλοτριωμένοι τῆς πολιτείας τοῦ Ἰσραήλ,
apart from Christ, alienated from the commonwealth of Israel,
καὶ ξένοι τῶν διαθηκῶν τῆς ἐπαγγελίας, ἐλπίδα μὴ ἔχον-
and strangers from the covenants of promise, hope not hav-
τες, καὶ ἄθεοι ἐν τῷ κόσμῳ· 13 νυνὶ.δὲ ἐν χριστῷ Ἰησοῦ,
ing, and without God in the world: but now in Christ Jesus,
ὑμεῖς οἱ ποτὲ ὄντες μακρὰν [h]ἐγγὺς ἐγενήθητε‖ ἐν τῷ αἵματι
ye who once were afar off near are become by the blood
τοῦ χριστοῦ. 14 αὐτὸς.γάρ ἐστιν ἡ.εἰρήνη.ἡμῶν, ὁ ποιήσας
of the Christ. For he is our peace, who made
τὰ ἀμφότερα ἕν, καὶ τὸ μεσότοιχον τοῦ φραγμοῦ λύσας·
both one, and the middle wall of the fence broke down,
15 τὴν ἔχθραν ἐν τῇ.σαρκὶ.αὐτοῦ, τὸν νόμον τῶν ἐντολῶν
[6]the [7]enmity [3]in [4]his [5]flesh, [8]the [9]law [10]of [11]commandments
ἐν δόγμασιν καταργήσας· ἵνα τοὺς δύο κτίσῃ ἐν [i]ἑαυ-
[12]in [13]decrees [1]having [2]annulled, that the two he might create in him-
τῷ‖ εἰς ἕνα καινὸν ἄνθρωπον, ποιῶν εἰρήνην· 16 καὶ ἀπο-
self into one new man, making peace; and might
καταλλάξῃ τοὺς ἀμφοτέρους ἐν ἑνὶ σώματι τῷ θεῷ διὰ τοῦ
reconcile both in one body to God through the
σταυροῦ, ἀποκτείνας τὴν ἔχθραν ἐν αὐτῷ· 17 καὶ ἐλθὼν
cross, having slain the enmity by it; and having come

11 Wherefore remember, that ye *being* in time past Gentiles in the flesh, who are called Uncircumcision by that which is called the Circumcision in the flesh made by hands; 12 that at that time ye were without Christ, being aliens from the commonwealth of Israel, and strangers from the covenants of promise, having no hope, and without God in the world: 13 but now in Christ Jesus ye who sometimes were far off are made nigh by the blood of Christ. 14 For he is our peace, who hath made both one, and hath broken down the middle wall of partition *between us;* 15 having abolished in his flesh the enmity, *even* the law of commandments *contained* in ordinances; for to make in himself of twain one new man, *so* making peace; 16 and that he might reconcile both unto God in one body by the cross, having slain the enmity thereby: 17 and came and preached

[a] ἤμεθα TTrA. [b] φύσει τέκνα L. [c] + [ἐν] L. [d] τὸ ὑπερβάλλον πλοῦτος LTTrAW. [e] — τῆς LTTr[A]. [f] ποτὲ ὑμεῖς LTTrA. [g] — ἐν (*read* τῷ κ. ἐκ. at that time) LTTrAW. [h] ἐγενήθητε ἐγγὺς LTTrA. [i] αὐτῷ LTTrA.

peace to you which
were afar off, and to
them that were nigh.
18 For through him
we both have access by
one Spirit unto the Father.
19 Now therefore
ye are no more
strangers and foreigners,
but fellowcitizens
with the saints, and
of the household of
God; 20 and are built
upon the foundation
of the apostles and
prophets, Jesus Christ
himself being the
chief corner *stone;*
21 in whom all the
building fitly framed
together groweth unto
an holy temple in the
Lord: 22 in whom ye
also are builded together
for an habitation
of God through the
Spirit.

III. For this cause
I Paul, the prisoner
of Jesus Christ for you
Gentiles, 2 if ye have
heard of the dispensation
of the grace of
God which is given me
to you-ward: 3 how
that by revelation he
made known unto me
the mystery; (as I
wrote afore in few
words, 4 whereby,
when ye read, ye may
understand my knowledge
in the mystery
of Christ) 5 which in
other ages was not
made known unto the
sons of men, as it is
now revealed unto his
holy apostles and prophets
by the Spirit;
6 that the Gentiles
should be fellowheirs,
and of the same body,
and partakers of his
promise in Christ by
the gospel: 7 whereof
I was made a minister,
according to the gift
of the grace of God
given unto me by the
effectual working of
his power. 8 Unto me,
who am less than the
least of all saints, is
this grace given, that
I should preach among
the Gentiles the unsearchable
riches of

εὐηγγελίσατο εἰρήνην ὑμῖν τοῖς μακρὰν καὶ [k]
he announced the glad tidings— peace to you who [were] afar off and
τοῖς ἐγγύς, 18 ὅτι.δι' αὐτοῦ ἔχομεν τὴν προσαγωγὴν οἱ
to those near. For through him we have access
ἀμφότεροι ἐν ἑνὶ πνεύματι πρὸς τὸν πατέρα. 19 ἄρα οὖν
both by one Spirit to the Father. So then
οὐκέτι ἐστὲ ξένοι καὶ πάροικοι, [l]ἀλλὰ‖ [m] [n]συμπολῖται‖ τῶν
no longer are ye strangers and sojourners, but fellow-citizens of the
ἁγίων καὶ οἰκεῖοι τοῦ θεοῦ, 20 ἐποικοδομηθέντες ἐπὶ τῷ
saints and of the household of God, being built up on the
θεμελίῳ τῶν ἀποστόλων καὶ προφητῶν, ὄντος ἀκρο-
foundation of the apostles and prophets, [4]being [[5]the] [6]corner-
γωνιαίου αὐτοῦ [o]Ἰησοῦ χριστοῦ,‖ 21 ἐν ᾧ πᾶσα [p]ἡ‖ οἰκοδομὴ
stone [3]himself [1]Jesus [2]Christ, in whom all the building
συναρμολογουμένη αὔξει εἰς ναὸν ἅγιον ἐν κυρίῳ, 22 ἐν
fitted together increases to a [2]temple [1]holy in [the] Lord; in
ᾧ καὶ ὑμεῖς συνοικοδομεῖσθε εἰς κατοικητήριον τοῦ θεοῦ
whom also ye are being built together for a habitation of God
ἐν πνεύματι.
in [the] Spirit.

3 Τούτου.χάριν ἐγὼ Παῦλος ὁ δέσμιος τοῦ χριστοῦ [q]Ἰη-
For this cause I Paul prisoner of the Christ Je-
σοῦ‖ ὑπὲρ ὑμῶν τῶν ἐθνῶν· 2 εἴγε ἠκούσατε τὴν οἰκονομίαν
sus for you nations, if indeed ye heard of the administration
τῆς χάριτος τοῦ θεοῦ τῆς δοθείσης μοι εἰς ὑμᾶς, 3 [r]ὅτι‖
of the grace of God which was given to me towards you, that
κατὰ ἀποκάλυψιν [s]ἐγνώρισέν‖ μοι τὸ μυστήριον, καθὼς
by revelation he made known to me the mystery, (according as
προέγραψα ἐν.ὀλίγῳ, 4 πρὸς ὃ δύνασθε ἀναγινώσκοντες
I wrote before briefly, by which ye are able, reading [it],
νοῆσαι τὴν.σύνεσίν.μου ἐν τῷ μυστηρίῳ τοῦ χριστοῦ· 5 ὃ
to perceive my understanding in the mystery of the Christ,) which
[t]ἐν‖ ἑτέραις γενεαῖς οὐκ.ἐγνωρίσθη τοῖς υἱοῖς τῶν ἀνθρώ-
in other generations was not made known to the sons of men,
πων, ὡς νῦν ἀπεκαλύφθη τοῖς ἁγίοις ἀποστόλοις αὐτοῦ καὶ
as now it was revealed to [2]holy [3]apostles [1]his and
προφήταις ἐν πνεύματι· 6 εἶναι τὰ ἔθνη [v]συγκληρονόμα‖
prophets in [the] Spirit, [3]to [4]be [1]the [2]nations joint-heirs
καὶ [w]σύσσωμα‖ καὶ [v]συμμέτοχα‖ τῆς.ἐπαγγελίας.[x]αὐτοῦ‖ ἐν
and a joint-body and joint-partakers of his promise in
[y]τῷ‖ χριστῷ[z], διὰ τοῦ εὐαγγελίου, 7 οὗ [a]ἐγενόμην‖ διάκονος
the Christ through the glad tidings; of which I became servant
κατὰ τὴν δωρεὰν τῆς χάριτος τοῦ θεοῦ [b]τὴν δοθεῖσάν‖
according to the gift of the grace of God given
μοι κατὰ τὴν ἐνέργειαν τῆς.δυνάμεως.αὐτοῦ· 8 ἐμοὶ
to me, according to the working of his power. To me,
τῷ ἐλαχιστοτέρῳ πάντων [c]τῶν‖ ἁγίων ἐδόθη ἡ.χάρις.αὕτη,
the less than the least of all the saints, was given this grace,
[d]ἐν‖ τοῖς ἔθνεσιν εὐαγγελίσασθαι [e]τὸν‖ ἀνεξιχνίαστον
among the nations to announce the glad tidings— the unsearchable

---

[k] + εἰρήνην peace LTTrAW. [l] ἀλλ' L. [m] + ἐστὲ ye are LTTrA. [n] συν- TA. [o] χριστοῦ Ἰησοῦ LTTrA. [p] — ἡ (*read* [the]) LTTrAW. [q] — Ἰησοῦ T[A]. [r] [ὅτι] L. [s] ἐγνωρίσθη was made known GLTTrAW. [t] — ἐν (*read* ἑτέραις to other) GLTTrAW. [v] συν- T. [w] σύν- LTTrA. [x] — αὐτοῦ (*read* of the promise) LTTrA. [y] — τῷ LTTrA. [z] + Ἰησοῦ Jesus LTTrA. [a] ἐγενήθην LTTrAW. [b] τῆς δοθείσης GLTTrA. [c] — τῶν GLTTrAW. [d] — ἐν (*read* τοῖς to the) LTTrA. [e] τὸ LTTrAW.

[f]πλοῦτον‖ τοῦ χριστοῦ, 9 καὶ φωτίσαι [g]πάντας‖ τίς
riches of the Christ, and to enlighten all [as to] what [is]
ἡ [h]κοινωνία‖ τοῦ μυστηρίου τοῦ ἀποκεκρυμμένου ἀπὸ τῶν
the fellowship of the mystery which has been hidden from the
αἰώνων ἐν τῷ θεῷ, τῷ τὰ.πάντα κτίσαντι [i]διὰ Ἰησοῦ χριστοῦ,‖
ages in God, who all things created by Jesus Christ,
10 ἵνα γνωρισθῇ νῦν ταῖς ἀρχαῖς καὶ ταῖς ἐξουσίαις ἐν
that might be known now to the principalities and the authorities in
τοῖς ἐπουρανίοις διὰ τῆς ἐκκλησίας ἡ πολυποίκιλος σοφία
the heavenlies through the assembly the multifarious wisdom
τοῦ θεοῦ, 11 κατὰ πρόθεσιν τῶν αἰώνων, ἣν ἐποίησεν
of God, according to [the] purpose of the ages, which he made
ἐν [k]χριστῷ Ἰησοῦ τῷ.κυρίῳ.ἡμῶν, 12 ἐν ᾧ ἔχομεν τὴν παρ-
in Christ Jesus our Lord, in whom we have bold-
ῥησίαν καὶ [l]τὴν‖ προσαγωγὴν ἐν πεποιθήσει διὰ τῆς πίστεως
ness and access in confidence by the faith
αὐτοῦ. 13 διὸ αἰτοῦμαι μὴ [m]ἐκκακεῖν‖ ἐν ταῖς θλίψεσίν
of him. Wherefore I beseech [you] not to faint at [2]tribulations
μου ὑπὲρ ὑμῶν, ἥτις ἐστὶν δόξα.ὑμῶν. 14 τούτου.χάριν
[1]my for you, which is your glory. For this cause
κάμπτω τὰ.γόνατά.μου πρὸς τὸν πατέρα [n]τοῦ.κυρίου.ἡμῶν
I bow my knees to the Father of our Lord
Ἰησοῦ χριστοῦ,‖ 15 ἐξ οὗ πᾶσα πατριὰ ἐν οὐρανοῖς καὶ
Jesus Christ, of whom every family in [the] heavens and
ἐπὶ γῆς ὀνομάζεται, 16 ἵνα [o]δῴη‖ ὑμῖν κατὰ [p]τὸν
on earth is named, that he may give you according to the
πλοῦτον‖ τῆς.δόξης.αὐτοῦ, δυνάμει κραταιωθῆναι διὰ τοῦ
riches of his glory, with power to be strengthened by
πνεύματος.αὐτοῦ εἰς τὸν ἔσω ἄνθρωπον, 17 κατοικῆσαι τὸν
his Spirit in the inner man; [for] [3]to [4]dwell [1]the
χριστὸν διὰ τῆς πίστεως ἐν ταῖς.καρδίαις.ὑμῶν· 18 ἐν ἀγάπῃ
[2]Christ, through faith, in your hearts, in love
ἐῤῥιζωμένοι καὶ τεθεμελιωμένοι ἵνα ἐξισχύσητε κατα-
being rooted and founded, that ye may be fully able to ap-
λαβέσθαι σὺν πᾶσιν τοῖς ἁγίοις τί τὸ πλάτος καὶ μῆκος
prehend with all the saints what [is] the breadth and length
καὶ [q]βάθος καὶ ὕψος,‖ 19 γνῶναί.τε τὴν ὑπερβάλλουσαν
and depth and height; and to know the surpassing
τῆς γνώσεως ἀγάπην τοῦ χριστοῦ, ἵνα πληρωθῆτε εἰς πᾶν
knowledge love of the Christ; that ye may be filled unto all
τὸ πλήρωμα τοῦ θεοῦ. 20 τῷ.δὲ δυναμένῳ ὑπὲρ πάντα
the fulness of God. But to him who is able above all things
ποιῆσαι [r]ὑπὲρ.ἐκ.περισσοῦ‖ ὧν αἰτούμεθα ἢ νοοῦμεν, κατὰ
to do exceedingly above what we ask or think, according to
τὴν δύναμιν τὴν ἐνεργουμένην ἐν ἡμῖν, 21 αὐτῷ ἡ δόξα
the power which works in us, to him [be] glory
ἐν τῇ ἐκκλησίᾳ [s]ἐν χριστῷ Ἰησοῦ, εἰς πάσας τὰς γενεὰς τοῦ
in the assembly in Christ Jesus, to all the generations of the
αἰῶνος τῶν αἰώνων. ἀμήν. 4 Παρακαλῶ οὖν ὑμᾶς ἐγὼ
age of the ages. Amen. I exhort therefore you, I
ὁ δέσμιος ἐν κυρίῳ, ἀξίως περιπατῆσαι τῆς κλήσεως
the prisoner in [the] Lord, [3]worthily [1]to [2]walk of the calling

Christ; 9 and to make all *men* see what *is* the fellowship of the mystery, which from the beginning of the world hath been hid in God, who created all things by Jesus Christ: 10 to the intent that now unto the principalities and powers in heavenly *places* might be known by the church the manifold wisdom of God, 11 according to the eternal purpose which he purposed in Christ Jesus our Lord: 12 in whom we have boldness and access with confidence by the faith of him. 13 Wherefore I desire that ye faint not at my tribulations for you, which is your glory. 14 For this cause I bow my knees unto the Father of our Lord Jesus Christ, 15 of whom the whole family in heaven and earth is named, 16 that he would grant you, according to the riches of his glory, to be strengthened with might by his Spirit in the inner man; 17 that Christ may dwell in your hearts by faith; that ye, being rooted and grounded in love, 18 may be able to comprehend with all saints what *is* the breadth, and length, and depth, and height; 19 and to know the love of Christ, which passeth knowledge, that ye might be filled with all the fulness of God. 20 Now unto him that is able to do exceeding abundantly above all that we ask or think, according to the power that worketh in us, 21 unto him *be* glory in the church by Christ Jesus throughout all ages, world without end. Amen. IV. I therefore, the prisoner of the Lord, beseech you that ye walk worthy of the vocation wherewith ye are call-

---

[f] πλοῦτος LTTrAW. [g] — πάντας [L]T. [h] οἰκονομία administration GLTTrAW. [i] — διὰ Ἰησοῦ χριστοῦ GLTTrAW. [k] + τῷ LTTrA. [l] — τὴν LTTr[A]. [m] ἐγ- LTrAW; ἐν- T. [n] — τοῦ κυρίου ἡμῶν Ἰησοῦ χριστοῦ LTTrAW. [o] δῷ LTTrA. [p] τὸ πλοῦτος LTTrAW. [q] ὕψος καὶ βάθος LTrA. [r] ὑπερεκπερισσοῦ GLTTrAW. [s] + καὶ and LTTr[A].

ed, 2 with all lowliness and meekness, with longsuffering, forbearing one another in love; 3 endeavouring to keep the unity of the Spirit in the bond of peace. 4 *There is* one body, and one Spirit, even as ye are called in one hope of your calling; 5 one Lord, one faith, one baptism, 6 one God and Father of all, who *is* above all, and through all, and in you all. 7 But unto every one of us is given grace according to the measure of the gift of Christ. 8 Wherefore he saith, When he ascended up on high, he led captivity captive, and gave gifts unto men. 9 (Now that he ascended, what is it but that he also descended first into the lower parts of the earth? 10 He that descended is the same also that ascended up far above all heavens, that he might fill all things.) 11 And he gave some, apostles; and some, prophets; and some, evangelists; and some, pastors and teachers; 12 for the perfecting of the saints, for the work of the ministry, for the edifying of the body of Christ: 13 till we all come in the unity of the faith, and of the knowledge of the Son of God, unto a perfect man, unto the measure of the stature of the fulness of Christ: 14 that we *henceforth* be no more children, tossed to and fro, and carried about with every wind of doctrine, by the sleight of men, *and* cunning craftiness, whereby they lie in wait to deceive; 15 but speaking the truth in love, may grow up into him in all things, which is the head, *even* Christ: 16 from whom the whole body fitly joined together and compacted by that which every joint supplieth, according to the effectual working in the measure of every part,

ἧς ἐκλήθητε, 2 μετὰ πάσης ταπεινοφροσύνης καὶ [t]πρᾳό-
wherewith ye were called, with all humility and meek-
τητος,‖ μετὰ μακροθυμίας, ἀνεχόμενοι ἀλλήλων ἐν ἀγάπῃ,
ness, with longsuffering, bearing with one another in love;
3 σπουδάζοντες τηρεῖν τὴν ἑνότητα τοῦ πνεύματος ἐν τῷ
being diligent to keep the unity of the Spirit in the
συνδέσμῳ τῆς εἰρήνης. 4 Ἓν σῶμα καὶ ἓν πνεῦμα, καθὼς καὶ
bond of peace. One body and one Spirit, even as also
ἐκλήθητε ἐν μιᾷ ἐλπίδι τῆς-κλήσεως-ὑμῶν· 5 εἷς κύριος, μία
ye were called in one hope of your calling; one Lord, one
πίστις, ἓν βάπτισμα· 6 εἷς θεὸς καὶ πατὴρ πάντων, ὁ
faith, one baptism; one God and Father of all, who [is]
ἐπὶ πάντων, καὶ διὰ πάντων, καὶ ἐν πᾶσιν [v]ὑμῖν.‖
over all, and through all, and in [2]all [1]you.
7 ἑνὶ-δὲ-ἑκάστῳ ἡμῶν ἐδόθη [w]ἡ‖ χάρις κατὰ τὸ μέτρον
But to each one of us was given grace according to the measure
τῆς δωρεᾶς τοῦ χριστοῦ. 8 διὸ λέγει, Ἀναβὰς εἰς
of the gift of the Christ. Wherefore he says, Having ascended up on
ὕψος ᾐχμαλώτευσεν αἰχμαλωσίαν, [x]καὶ‖ ἔδωκεν δόματα τοῖς
high he led [2]captive [1]captivity, and gave gifts
ἀνθρώποις. 9 Τὸ-δὲ ἀνέβη, τί ἐστιν εἰ-μὴ ὅτι καὶ κατέβη
to men. But that he ascended, what is it but that also he descended
[y]πρῶτον‖ εἰς τὰ κατώτερα [z]μέρη‖ τῆς γῆς; 10 ὁ καταβὰς
first into the lower parts of the earth? He that descended
αὐτός ἐστιν καὶ ὁ ἀναβὰς ὑπεράνω πάντων τῶν οὐρανῶν,
[2]the [3]same [1]is also who ascended above all the heavens,
ἵνα πληρώσῃ τὰ-πάντα. 11 καὶ αὐτὸς ἔδωκεν τοὺς-μὲν ἀπο-
that he might fill all things; and he gave some apo-
στόλους, τοὺς-δὲ προφήτας, τοὺς-δὲ εὐαγγελιστάς, τοὺς-δὲ
stles, and some prophets, and some evangelists, and some
ποιμένας καὶ διδασκάλους, 12 πρὸς τὸν καταρτισμὸν τῶν
shepherds and teachers, with a view to the perfecting of the
ἁγίων, εἰς ἔργον διακονίας, εἰς οἰκοδομὴν τοῦ σώματος τοῦ
saints; for work of [the] service, for building up of the body of the
χριστοῦ· 13 μέχρι καταντήσωμεν οἱ πάντες εἰς τὴν ἑνότητα
Christ; until we [2]may [3]arrive [1]all at the unity
τῆς πίστεως καὶ τῆς ἐπιγνώσεως τοῦ υἱοῦ τοῦ θεοῦ, εἰς ἄνδρα
of the faith and of the knowledge of the Son of God, at a [2]man
τέλειον, εἰς μέτρον ἡλικίας τοῦ πληρώματος τοῦ
[1]full-grown, at [the] measure of [the] stature of the fulness of the
χριστοῦ· 14 ἵνα μηκέτι ὦμεν νήπιοι, κλυδωνιζόμενοι καὶ
Christ; that no longer we may be infants, being tossed and
περιφερόμενοι παντὶ ἀνέμῳ τῆς διδασκαλίας ἐν τῇ [a]κυβείᾳ‖
carried about by every wind of the teaching in the sleight
τῶν ἀνθρώπων, ἐν πανουργίᾳ πρὸς τὴν [b]μεθοδείαν‖ τῆς
of men, in craftiness with a view to the systematizing
πλάνης· 15 ἀληθεύοντες-δὲ ἐν ἀγάπῃ αὐξήσωμεν εἰς αὐτὸν
of error; but holding the truth in love we may grow up into him
τὰ-πάντα, ὅς ἐστιν ἡ κεφαλή, [c]ὁ‖ χριστός, 16 ἐξ οὗ πᾶν
in all things, who is the head, the Christ: from whom all
τὸ σῶμα συναρμολογούμενον καὶ [d]συμβιβαζόμενον‖ διὰ πάσης
the body, fitted together and compacted by every
ἁφῆς τῆς ἐπιχορηγίας κατ' ἐνέργειαν ἐν μέτρῳ
joint of supply according to [the] working in [its] measure

[t] πραΰτητος TTrA. [v] — ὑμῖν LTTrA; ἡμῖν us GW. [w] — ἡ LTr[A]. [x] — καὶ LTW.
[y] — πρῶτον GLTTrAW. [z] — μέρη (*read* [parts]) W. [a] κυβίᾳ T. [b] μεθοδίαν T.
[c] — ὁ LTTrAW. [d] συν- T.

ἑνὸς.ἑκάστου μέρους, τὴν αὔξησιν τοῦ σώματος ποιεῖται εἰς
of each one part, the increase of the body makes for itself to
οἰκοδομὴν [e]ἑαυτοῦ‖ ἐν ἀγάπῃ.
[the] building up of itself in love.
17 Τοῦτο οὖν λέγω καὶ μαρτύρομαι ἐν κυρίῳ, μηκέτι
This therefore I say, and testify in [the] Lord, [3]no [4]longer
ὑμᾶς.περιπατεῖν, καθὼς καὶ τὰ [f]λοιπὰ‖ ἔθνη περιπατεῖ ἐν
[1]that [2]ye walk even as also the rest, [the] nations, are walking in
ματαιότητι τοῦ.νοὸς.αὐτῶν, 18 [g]ἐσκοτισμένοι‖ τῇ δια-
[the] vanity of their mind, being darkened in the under-
νοίᾳ, ὄντες ἀπηλλοτριωμένοι τῆς ζωῆς τοῦ θεοῦ, διὰ
standing, being alienated from the life of God, on account of
τὴν ἄγνοιαν τὴν οὖσαν ἐν αὐτοῖς, διὰ τὴν πώρωσιν
the ignorance which is in them, on account of the hardness
τῆς.καρδίας.αὐτῶν· 19 οἵτινες ἀπηλγηκότες ἑαυτοὺς
of their heart, who having cast off all feeling, themselves
παρέδωκαν τῇ ἀσελγείᾳ εἰς ἐργασίαν ἀκαθαρσίας πάσης
gave up to licentiousness, for [the] working of [2]uncleanness [1]all
ἐν πλεονεξίᾳ· 20 ὑμεῖς.δὲ οὐχ οὕτως ἐμάθετε τὸν χριστόν,
with craving. But ye [2]not [3]thus [1]learned the Christ,
21 εἴγε αὐτὸν ἠκούσατε καὶ ἐν αὐτῷ ἐδιδάχθητε, καθώς
if indeed him ye heard and in him were taught, according as
ἐστιν ἀλήθεια ἐν τῷ Ἰησοῦ· 22 ἀποθέσθαι.ὑμᾶς κατὰ
is [the] truth in Jesus; for you to have put off according to
τὴν προτέραν ἀναστροφὴν τὸν παλαιὸν ἄνθρωπον, τὸν
the former conduct the old man, which
φθειρόμενον κατὰ τὰς ἐπιθυμίας τῆς ἀπάτης· 23 ἀνα-
is corrupt according to the desires of deceit; [2]to [3]be [4]re-
νεοῦσθαι [h]δὲ‖ τῷ πνεύματι τοῦ.νοὸς ὑμῶν· 24 καὶ ἐνδύσασθαι
newed [1]and in the spirit of your mind; and to have put on
τὸν καινὸν ἄνθρωπον, τὸν κατὰ θεὸν κτισθέντα ἐν δι-
the new man, which according to God was created in right-
καιοσύνῃ καὶ ὁσιότητι τῆς ἀληθείας. 25 Διὸ ἀποθέμενοι τὸ
eousness and holiness of truth. Wherefore having put off
ψεῦδος, λαλεῖτε ἀλήθειαν ἕκαστος μετὰ τοῦ.πλησίον.αὐτοῦ·
falsehood, speak truth each with his neighbour,
ὅτι ἐσμὲν ἀλλήλων μέλη. 26 Ὀργίζεσθε καὶ μὴ ἁμαρ-
because we are of one another members. Be angry, and [2]not [1]sin;
τάνετε· ὁ ἥλιος μὴ.ἐπιδυέτω ἐπὶ [i]τῷ‖.παροργισμῷ.ὑμῶν,
[5]the [6]sun [3]let [4]not set upon your provocation,
27 [k]μήτε‖ δίδοτε τόπον τῷ διαβόλῳ. 28 ὁ κλέπτων μηκέτι
neither give place to the devil. He that steals [4]no [5]more
κλεπτέτω, μᾶλλον.δὲ κοπιάτω, ἐργαζόμενος [l]τὸ ἀγαθὸν
[1]let [2]him [3]steal, but rather let him labour, working what [is] good
ταῖς.χερσίν,‖ ἵνα ἔχῃ μεταδιδόναι τῷ χρείαν ἔχοντι.
with [his] hands, that he may have to impart to him that [2]need [1]has.
29 πᾶς λόγος σαπρὸς ἐκ τοῦ.στόματος.ὑμῶν μὴ ἐκ-
[5]Any [7]word [6]corrupt [10]out [11]of [12]your [13]mouth [4]not [3]let
(*lit.* every)
πορευέσθω, [m]ἀλλ'‖ εἴ τις ἀγαθὸς πρὸς οἰκοδομὴν τῆς.χρείας,
[8]go [9]forth, but if any good for building up in respect of need,
ἵνα δῷ χάριν τοῖς ἀκούουσιν. 30 καὶ μὴ.λυπεῖτε τὸ
that it may give grace to them that hear. And grieve not the
πνεῦμα τὸ ἅγιον τοῦ θεοῦ, ἐν ᾧ ἐσφραγίσθητε εἰς ἡμέραν
Spirit the Holy of God, by which ye were sealed for [the] day

maketh increase of the
body unto the edifying
of itself in love.
17 This I say there-
fore, and testify in the
Lord, that ye hence-
forth walk not as other
Gentiles walk, in the
vanity of their mind,
18 having the under-
standing darkened,
being alienated from
the life of God through
the ignorance that is
in them, because of
the blindness of their
heart: 19 who being
past feeling have given
themselves over unto
lasciviousness, to work
all uncleanness with
greediness. 20 But ye
have not so learned
Christ; 21 if so be that
ye have heard him, and
have been taught by
him, as the truth is in
Jesus: 22 that ye put
off concerning the
former conversation
the old man, which is
corrupt according to
the deceitful lusts;
23 and be renewed in
the spirit of your
mind; 24 and that ye
put on the new man,
which after God is
created in righteous-
ness and true holiness.
25 Wherefore putting
away lying, speak
every man truth with
his neighbour: for we
are members one of
another. 26 Be ye an-
gry, and sin not: let
not the sun go down
upon your wrath:
27 neither give place
to the devil. 28 Let
him that stole steal no
more: but rather let
him labour, working
with *his* hands the
thing which is good,
that he may have to
give to him that need-
eth. 29 Let no corrupt
communication pro-
ceed out of your
mouth, but that which
is good to the use of
edifying, that it may
minister grace unto
the hearers. 30 And
grieve not the holy
Spirit of God, where-
by ye are sealed unto
the day of redemption.

---

[e] αὐτοῦ T. [f] — λοιπὰ LTTrA. [g] ἐσκοτωμένοι LTTrA. [h] [δὲ] L. [i] — τῷ LTTr[A]. [k] μηδὲ LTTrAW. [l] ταῖς ἰδίαις with his own (— ἰδίαις A) χερσὶν τὸ ἀγαθόν LTTrAW. [m] ἀλλὰ LTTr.

31 Let all bitterness,
and wrath, and anger,
and clamour, and evil
speaking, be put away
from you, with all ma-
lice: 32 and be ye kind
one to another, ten-
der-hearted, forgiving
one another, even as
God for Christ's sake
hath forgiven you.
V. Be ye therefore fol-
lowers of God, as dear
children; 2 and walk
in love, as Christ also
hath loved us, and hath
given himself for us
an offering and a sa-
crifice to God for a
sweetsmelling savour.

3 But fornication,
and all uncleanness,
or covetousness, let it
not be once named a-
mong you, as becom-
eth saints; 4 neither
filthiness, nor foolish
talking, nor jesting,
which are not conve-
nient: but rather giv-
ing of thanks. 5 For
this ye know, that no
whoremonger, nor un-
clean person, nor cove-
tous man, who is an
idolater, hath any in-
heritance in the king-
dom of Christ and of
God. 6 Let no man
deceive you with vain
words: for because of
these things cometh
the wrath of God upon
the children of disobe-
dience. 7 Be not ye
therefore partakers
with them. 8 For ye
were sometimes dark-
ness, but now *are ye*
light in the Lord:
walk as children of
light: 9 (for the fruit
of the Spirit *is* in all
goodness and right-
eousness and truth;)
10 proving what is
acceptable unto the
Lord. 11 And have no
fellowship with the
unfruitful works of
darkness, but rather
reprove *them*. 12 For
it is a shame even to
speak of those things
which are done of
them in secret. 13 But
all things that are re-
proved are made mani-
fest by the light: for
whatsoever doth make
manifest is light.
14 Wherefore he saith,
Awake thou that sleep-
est, and arise from the
dead, and Christ shall

ἀπολυτρώσεως. 31 πᾶσα πικρία καὶ θυμὸς καὶ ὀργὴ καὶ
of redemption. All bitterness, and indignation, and wrath, and
κραυγὴ καὶ βλασφημία ἀρθήτω ἀφ' ὑμῶν, σὺν πάσῃ
clamour, and evil speaking let be removed from you, with all
κακίᾳ· 32 γίνεσθε.[n]δὲ‖ εἰς ἀλλήλους χρηστοί, εὔσπλαγχνοι,
malice; and be to one another kind, tender-hearted,
χαριζόμενοι ἑαυτοῖς, καθὼς καὶ ὁ θεὸς ἐν χριστῷ ἐχαρί-
forgiving each other, according as also God in Christ for-
σατο [o]ὑμῖν.‖ 5 Γίνεσθε οὖν μιμηταὶ τοῦ θεοῦ, ὡς τέκνα
gave you. Be ye therefore imitators of God, as children
ἀγαπητά· 2 καὶ περιπατεῖτε ἐν ἀγάπῃ, καθὼς καὶ ὁ χριστὸς
beloved, and walk in love, even as also the Christ
ἠγάπησεν [p]ἡμᾶς,‖ καὶ παρέδωκεν ἑαυτὸν ὑπὲρ [q]ἡμῶν‖ προσ-
loved us, and gave up himself for us, an of-
φορὰν καὶ θυσίαν τῷ θεῷ εἰς ὀσμὴν εὐωδίας.
fering and a sacrifice to God for an odour of a sweet smell.
3 Πορνεία.δὲ καὶ [r]πᾶσα ἀκαθαρσία‖ ἢ πλεονεξία μηδὲ
But fornication and all uncleanness or covetousness not even
ὀνομαζέσθω ἐν ὑμῖν, καθὼς πρέπει ἁγίοις· 4 [s]καὶ‖ αἰσχρό-
let it be named among you, even as is becoming to saints; and filthi-
της [t]καὶ‖ μωρολογία ἢ εὐτραπελία, [v]τὰ οὐκ.ἀνήκοντα,‖ ἀλλὰ
ness and foolish talking or jesting, which are not becoming; but
μᾶλλον εὐχαριστία. 5 τοῦτο.γάρ [w]ἐστε.γινώσκοντες‖ ὅτι πᾶς
rather thanksgiving. For this ye know that any (*lit.* every)
πόρνος, ἢ ἀκάθαρτος, ἢ πλεονέκτης, [x]ὅς‖ ἐστιν εἰδωλολά-
fornicator, or unclean person, or covetous, who is an idolater,
τρης, οὐκ.ἔχει κληρονομίαν ἐν τῇ βασιλείᾳ τοῦ χριστοῦ καὶ
has not inheritance in the kingdom of the Christ and
θεοῦ. 6 μηδεὶς ὑμᾶς ἀπατάτω κενοῖς λόγοις· διὰ
of God. ²No ³one ⁵you ¹let ⁴deceive with empty words; ²on ³account ⁴of
ταῦτα γὰρ ἔρχεται ἡ ὀργὴ τοῦ θεοῦ ἐπὶ τοὺς υἱοὺς τῆς
⁵these ⁶things ¹for comes the wrath of God upon the sons
ἀπειθείας. 7 μὴ οὖν γίνεσθε [y]συμμέτοχοι‖ αὐτῶν. 8 ἦτε
of disobedience. ²Not ³therefore ¹be joint-partakers with them; ²ye ³were
γάρ ποτε σκότος, νῦν.δὲ φῶς ἐν κυρίῳ· ὡς τέκνα φωτὸς
¹for once darkness, but now light in [the] Lord; as children of light
περιπατεῖτε· 9 ὁ.γὰρ καρπὸς τοῦ [z]πνεύματος‖ ἐν πάσῃ
walk, (for the fruit of the Spirit [is] in all
ἀγαθωσύνῃ καὶ δικαιοσύνῃ καὶ ἀληθείᾳ· 10 δοκιμάζοντες τί
goodness and righteousness and truth,) proving what
ἐστιν εὐάρεστον τῷ κυρίῳ. 11 καὶ μὴ.[a]συγκοινωνεῖτε‖ τοῖς
is well-pleasing to the Lord; and have no fellowship with the
ἔργοις τοῖς ἀκάρποις τοῦ σκότους, μᾶλλον.δὲ καὶ ἐλέγχετε·
²works ¹unfruitful of darkness, but rather also reprove;
12 τὰ.γὰρ [b]κρυφῇ‖ γινόμενα ὑπ' αὐτῶν αἰσχρόν ἐστιν καὶ
for the things in secret being done by them shameful it is even
λέγειν. 13 τὰ.δὲ.πάντα ἐλεγχόμενα ὑπὸ τοῦ φωτὸς φανεροῦ-
to say. But all of them being reproved by the light are made mani-
ται· πᾶν.γὰρ τὸ φανερούμενον φῶς ἐστιν· 14 διὸ
fest; for ⁴everything ¹that ²which ³makes ⁵manifest ⁷light ⁶is. Wherefore
λέγει, [c]Ἔγειραι‖ ὁ καθεύδων, καὶ ἀνάστα ἐκ τῶν
he says, Arouse, [thou] that sleepest, and rise up from among the

---

[n] — δὲ and L. [o] ἡμῖν us L. [p] ὑμᾶς you TTrA. [q] ὑμῶν you A. [r] ἀκαθαρσία πᾶσα LTTrA. [s] ἢ or L. [t] ἢ or LT. [v] ἃ οὐκ ἀνῆκεν LTTrA. [w] ἴστε γινώσκοντες ye are aware of, knowing GLTTrAW. [x] ὅ that LTTrA. [y] συν- TA. [z] φωτὸς light GLTTrAW. [a] συν- T. [b] κρυφῆ L. [c] Ἔγειρε GLTTrAW.

νεκρῶν, καὶ ἐπιφαύσει σοι ὁ χριστός. 15 Βλέπετε οὖν
dead, and shall shine upon thee the Christ. Take heed therefore
[d]πῶς ἀκριβῶς‖ περιπατεῖτε, μὴ ὡς ἄσοφοι, ἀλλ' ὡς σοφοί,
how accurately ye walk, not as unwise, but as wise,
16 ἐξαγοραζόμενοι τὸν καιρόν, ὅτι αἱ ἡμέραι πονηραί εἰσιν.
ransoming the time, because the days ²evil ¹are.
17 διὰ.τοῦτο μὴ.γίνεσθε ἄφρονες, ἀλλὰ [e]συνιέντες‖ τί τὸ
On this account be not foolish, but understanding what the
θέλημα τοῦ κυρίου. 18 καὶ μὴ.μεθύσκεσθε οἴνῳ, ἐν ᾧ
will of the Lord [is]. And be not drunk with wine, in which
ἐστιν ἀσωτία· ἀλλὰ πληροῦσθε ἐν πνεύματι, 19 λα-
is dissoluteness; but be filled with [the] Spirit, speak-
λοῦντες ἑαυτοῖς [f] ψαλμοῖς καὶ ὕμνοις καὶ ᾠδαῖς [g]πνευματι-
ing to each other in psalms and hymns and ²songs ¹spiritual,
καῖς,‖ ᾄδοντες καὶ ψάλλοντες [h]ἐν‖ [i]τῇ καρδίᾳ‖ ὑμῶν τῷ κυρίῳ,
singing and praising with ²heart ¹your to the Lord;
20 εὐχαριστοῦντες πάντοτε ὑπὲρ πάντων ἐν ὀνόματι τοῦ
giving thanks at all times for all things in [the] name
κυρίου.ἡμῶν Ἰησοῦ χριστοῦ τῷ θεῷ καὶ πατρί· 21 ὑπο-
of our Lord Jesus Christ to him who [is] God and Father, submit-
τασσόμενοι ἀλλήλοις ἐν φόβῳ [k]θεοῦ.‖
ting yourselves to one another in [the] fear of God.

22 Αἱ γυναῖκες, τοῖς.ἰδίοις ἀνδράσιν [l]ὑποτάσσεσθε,‖ ὡς τῷ
Wives, to your own husbands submit yourselves, as to the
κυρίῳ· 23 ὅτι [m]ὁ‖ ἀνήρ ἐστιν κεφαλὴ τῆς γυναικός, ὡς καὶ
Lord, for the husband is head of the wife, as also
ὁ χριστὸς κεφαλὴ τῆς ἐκκλησίας, [n]καὶ‖ αὐτός [o]ἐστιν‖ σωτὴρ
the Christ [is] head of the assembly, and he is Saviour
τοῦ σώματος· 24 [p]ἀλλ'‖ [q]ὥσπερ‖ ἡ ἐκκλησία ὑποτάσσεται τῷ
of the body. But even as the assembly is subjected to the
χριστῷ, οὕτως καὶ αἱ γυναῖκες τοῖς.[r]ἰδίοις‖ ἀνδράσιν ἐν παντί.
Christ, so also wives to their own husbands in everything.
25 Οἱ ἄνδρες, ἀγαπᾶτε τὰς.γυναῖκας.[s]ἑαυτῶν,‖ καθὼς καὶ ὁ
Husbands, love your own wives, even as also the
χριστὸς ἠγάπησεν τὴν ἐκκλησίαν, καὶ ἑαυτὸν παρέδωκεν ὑπὲρ
Christ loved the assembly, and himself gave up for
αὐτῆς· 26 ἵνα αὐτὴν ἁγιάσῃ, καθαρίσας τῷ λουτρῷ
it, that it he might sanctify, having cleansed [it] by the washing
τοῦ ὕδατος ἐν ῥήματι, 27 ἵνα παραστήσῃ [t]αὐτὴν‖ ἑαυτῷ
of water by [the] word, that he might present it to himself
ἔνδοξον τὴν ἐκκλησίαν μὴ ἔχουσαν σπῖλον ἢ ῥυτίδα ἤ τι
³glorious ¹the ²assembly, not having spot, or wrinkle, or any
τῶν.τοιούτων, ἀλλ' ἵνα ᾖ ἁγία καὶ ἄμωμος. 28 οὕτως
of such things; but that it might be holy and blameless. So
[v]ὀφείλουσιν [w] οἱ ἄνδρες‖ ἀγαπᾷν τὰς.ἑαυτῶν.γυναῖκας ὡς
ought husbands to love their own wives as
τὰ.ἑαυτῶν σώματα· ὁ ἀγαπῶν τὴν ἑαυτοῦ γυναῖκα ἑαυτὸν
their own bodies: he that loves his own wife ²himself
ἀγαπᾷ· 29 οὐδεὶς.γάρ ποτε τὴν.ἑαυτοῦ σάρκα ἐμίσησεν,
¹loves. For no one at any time his own flesh hated,

give thee light. 15 See
then that ye walk circumspectly, not as
fools, but as wise,
16 redeeming the
time, because the days
are evil. 17 Wherefore
be ye not unwise, but
understanding what
the will of the Lord
is. 18 And be not
drunk with wine,
wherein is excess; but
be filled with the Spirit;
19 speaking to
yourselves in psalms
and hymns and spiritual songs, singing and
making melody in
your heart to the Lord;
20 giving thanks always for all things
unto God and the Father in the name of
our Lord Jesus Christ;
21 submitting yourselves one to another
in the fear of God.

22 Wives, submit
yourselves unto your
own husbands, as unto
the Lord. 23 For the
husband is the head
of the wife, even as
Christ is the head of
the church: and he is
the saviour of the body.
24 Therefore as
the church is subject
unto Christ, so *let* the
wives *be* to their own
husbands in every
thing. 25 Husbands,
love your wives, even
as Christ also loved the
church, and gave himself for it;
26 that he
might sanctify and
cleanse it with the
washing of water by
the word, 27 that he
might present it to
himself a glorious
church, not having
spot, or wrinkle, or
any such thing; but
that it should be holy
and without blemish.
28 So ought men to
love their wives as
their own bodies. He
that loveth his wife
loveth himself. 29 For
no man ever yet hated
his own flesh; but

[d] ἀκριβῶς πῶς T. [e] συνίετε understand LTTrA. [f] + [ἐν] LA. [g] [πνευματικαῖς] LA. [h] — ἐν (*read* with your heart) T[TrA]. [i] ταῖς καρδίαις hearts L. [k] χριστοῦ of Christ GLTTrAW. [l] — ὑποτάσσεσθε TA; ὑποτασσέσθωσαν (*read* to their own husbands let them submit themselves) LTr. [m] — ὁ (*read* a husband) GLTTrAW. [n] — καὶ GLTTrAW. [o] — ἐστιν LTTrAW. [p] ἀλλὰ LTTrA. [q] ὡς as LTTrA. [r] — ἰδίοις (*read* to the husbands) LTTrA. [s] — ἑαυτῶν (*read* the wives) LTTrA. [t] αὐτὸς (*read* he might himself present) GLTTrAW. [v] καὶ (also) οἱ ἄνδρες ὀφείλουσιν LTr. [w] + καὶ also TrA.

nourisheth and cherisheth it, even as the Lord the church: 30 for we are members of his body, of his flesh, and of his bones. 31 For this cause shall a man leave his father and mother, and shall be joined unto his wife, and they two shall be one flesh. 32 This is a great mystery: but I speak concerning Christ and the church. 33 Nevertheless let every one of you in particular so love his wife even as himself; and the wife *see* that she reverence *her* husband.

[x]ἀλλ'‖ ἐκτρέφει καὶ θάλπει αὐτήν, καθὼς καὶ ὁ [y]κύριος‖ τὴν
but nourishes and cherishes it, even as also the Lord the
ἐκκλησίαν. 30 ὅτι μέλη ἐσμὲν τοῦ.σώματος.αὐτοῦ, [z]ἐκ τῆς
assembly: for members we are of his body, of
σαρκὸς.αὐτοῦ, καὶ ἐκ τῶν.ὀστέων.αὐτοῦ.‖ 31 Ἀντὶ τούτου
his flesh, and of his bones. Because of this
καταλείψει ἄνθρωπος [a]τὸν‖ πατέρα [b]αὐτοῦ‖ καὶ [c]τὴν‖ μητέρα,
[3]shall [4]leave [1]a [2]man [6]father [5]his and mother,
καὶ προσκολληθήσεται [d]πρὸς τὴν γυναῖκα‖ [e]αὐτοῦ,‖ καὶ ἔσον-
and shall be joined to [2]wife [1]his, and [3]shall
ται οἱ δύο εἰς σάρκα μίαν. 32 Τὸ.μυστήριον.τοῦτο μέγα ἐστίν·
[4]be [1]the [2]two for [2]flesh [1]one. This mystery [2]great [1]is,
ἐγὼ.δὲ λέγω εἰς χριστὸν καὶ [f]εἰς‖ τὴν ἐκκλησίαν. 33 πλὴν
but I speak as to Christ and as to the assembly. However
καὶ ὑμεῖς οἱ.καθ'.ἕνα, ἕκαστος τὴν.ἑαυτοῦ γυναῖκα οὕτως ἀγα-
also ye everyone, [2]each [4]his [5]own [6]wife [7]so [1]let
πάτω ὡς ἑαυτόν· ἡ.δὲ γυνὴ ἵνα φοβῆται τὸν ἄνδρα.
[3]love as himself; and the wife that she may fear the husband.

VI. Children, obey your parents in the Lord: for this is right. 2 Honour thy father and mother; which is the first commandment with promise; 3 that it may be well with thee, and thou mayest live long on the earth. 4 And, ye fathers, provoke not your children to wrath: but bring them up in the nurture and admonition of the Lord.

6 Τὰ τέκνα, ὑπακούετε τοῖς.γονεῦσιν.ὑμῶν [g]ἐν κυρίῳ·‖
Children, obey your parents in [the] Lord,
τοῦτο.γάρ ἐστιν δίκαιον. 2 Τίμα τὸν.πατέρα.σου καὶ τὴν
for this is just. Honour thy father and
μητέρα· ἥτις ἐστὶν ἐντολὴ πρώτη ἐν ἐπαγγελίᾳ· 3 ἵνα
mother, which is [3]commandment [1]the [2]first with a promise, that
εὖ σοι γένηται, καὶ ἔσῃ μακροχρόνιος ἐπὶ τῆς γῆς.
well with thee it may be, and thou mayest be long-lived on the earth.
4 Καὶ οἱ πατέρες, μὴ.παροργίζετε τὰ.τέκνα.ὑμῶν, [x]ἀλλ'‖ ἐκ-
And fathers, do not provoke your children, but bring
τρέφετε αὐτὰ ἐν παιδείᾳ καὶ νουθεσίᾳ κυρίου.
up them in [the] discipline and admonition of [the] Lord.

5 Servants, be obedient to them that are *your* masters according to the flesh, with fear and trembling, in singleness of your heart, as unto Christ; 6 not with eyeservice, as menpleasers; but as the servants of Christ, doing the will of God from the heart; 7 with good will doing service, as to the Lord, and not to men: 8 knowing that whatsoever good thing any man doeth, the same shall he receive of the Lord, whether *he be* bond or free. 9 And, ye masters, do the same things unto them, forbearing threatening: knowing that your Master also is in heaven; neither is there respect of persons with him.

5 Οἱ δοῦλοι, ὑπακούετε τοῖς [h]κυρίοις κατὰ σάρκα‖
Bondmen, obey [your] masters according to flesh
μετὰ φόβου καὶ τρόμου, ἐν ἁπλότητι [i]τῆς‖.καρδίας.ὑμῶν, ὡς
with fear and trembling, in simplicity of your heart, as
τῷ χριστῷ· 6 μὴ κατ' [k]ὀφθαλμοδουλείαν‖ ὡς ἀνθρωπάρεσκοι,
to the Christ; not with eye-service as men-pleasers;
ἀλλ' ὡς δοῦλοι [l]τοῦ‖ χριστοῦ, ποιοῦντες τὸ θέλημα τοῦ θεοῦ
but as bondmen of the Christ, doing the will of God
ἐκ ψυχῆς, 7 μετ' εὐνοίας δουλεύοντες [m]τῷ κυρίῳ καὶ
from [the] soul, with good will doing service to the Lord and
οὐκ ἀνθρώποις· 8 εἰδότες ὅτι [n]ὃ.ἐάν.τι ἕκαστος‖ ποιήσῃ
not to men; knowing that whatsoever [2]each [3]may [4]have [5]done
ἀγαθόν, τοῦτο [o]κομιεῖται‖ παρὰ [p]τοῦ‖ κυρίου, εἴτε δοῦλος
[1]good, this he shall receive from the Lord, whether bondman
εἴτε ἐλεύθερος. 9 Καὶ οἱ κύριοι, τὰ.αὐτὰ ποιεῖτε πρὸς
or free. And masters, the same things do towards
αὐτούς, ἀνιέντες τὴν ἀπειλήν· εἰδότες ὅτι καὶ [q]ὑμῶν.αὐτῶν
them, giving up threatening, knowing that also your own
ὁ‖ κύριός ἐστιν ἐν οὐρανοῖς, καὶ [r]προσωποληψία‖ οὐκ.ἔστιν
master is in [the] heavens, and respect of persons there is not
παρ' αὐτῷ.
with him.

[x] ἀλλὰ LTTrAW. [y] χριστὸς Christ GLTTrAW. [z] — ἐκ τῆς *to end of verse* LTTr[A]. [a] — τὸν LTrA. [b] — αὐτοῦ LTTrA. [c] — τὴν LTrA. [d] τῇ γυναικὶ to the wife LTTr. [e] — αὐτοῦ T. [f] [εἰς] LA. [g] — ἐν κυρίῳ L[TrA]. [h] κατὰ σάρκα κυρίοις LTTr. [i] — τῆς T. [k] ὀφθαλμοδουλίαν T. [l] — τοῦ the LTTrAW. [m] + ὡς as GLTTrAW. [n] ἕκαστος ὃ (— ὃ (*read* if anything) TA) ἐάν (ἂν Tr) τι (— τι LTr) LTTrAW. [o] κομίσεται LTTrA. [p] — τοῦ (*read* [the]) GLTTrAW. [q] αὐτῶν καὶ ὑμῶν ὁ of them and of you the LTTrAW. [r] προσωποληµψία LTTrA.

10 [t]Τὸ.λοιπόν,‖ [v]ἀδελφοί.μου,‖ ἐνδυναμοῦσθε ἐν κυρίῳ,
For the rest, my brethren, be empowered in [the] Lord,
καὶ ἐν τῷ κράτει τῆς.ἰσχύος.αὐτοῦ. 11 ἐνδύσασθε τὴν παν-
and in the might of his strength. Put on the pan-
οπλίαν τοῦ θεοῦ, πρὸς τὸ δύνασθαι ὑμᾶς στῆναι πρὸς τὰς
oply of God, for [2]to [3]be [4]able [1]you to stand against the
[w]μεθοδείας‖ τοῦ διαβόλου· 12 ὅτι οὐκ.ἔστιν [x]ἡμῖν‖ ἡ πάλη
artifices of the devil: because [3]is [4]not [5]to [6]us [1]the [2]wrestling
πρὸς αἷμα καὶ σάρκα, ἀλλὰ πρὸς τὰς ἀρχάς, πρὸς τὰς
against blood and flesh, but against principalities, against
ἐξουσίας, πρὸς τοὺς κοσμοκράτορας τοῦ σκότους [y]τοῦ αἰῶνος‖
authorities, against the world-rulers of the darkness of [a]age
[z]τούτου,‖ πρὸς τὰ πνευματικὰ τῆς πονηρίας ἐν τοῖς ἐπου-
[1]this, against the spiritual [powers] of wickedness in the hea-
ρανίοις. 13 διὰ τοῦτο ἀναλάβετε τὴν πανοπλίαν τοῦ θεοῦ,
venlies. Because of this take up the panoply of God,
ἵνα δυνηθῆτε ἀντιστῆναι ἐν τῇ ἡμέρᾳ τῇ πονηρᾷ, καὶ ἅπαντα
that ye may be able to withstand in the [2]day [1]evil, and all things
κατεργασάμενοι στῆναι. 14 στῆτε οὖν περιζωσάμενοι τὴν
having worked out to stand. Stand therefore, having girt about
ὀσφὺν.ὑμῶν ἐν ἀληθείᾳ, καὶ ἐνδυσάμενοι τὸν θώρακα τῆς
your loins with truth, and having put on the breastplate
δικαιοσύνης, 15 καὶ ὑποδησάμενοι τοὺς πόδας ἐν ἑτοι-
of righteousness, and having shod the feet with [the] pre-
μασίᾳ τοῦ εὐαγγελίου τῆς εἰρήνης· 16 [a]ἐπὶ‖ πᾶσιν ἀναλα-
paration of the glad tidings of peace: besides all having
βόντες τὸν θυρεὸν τῆς πίστεως, ἐν ᾧ δυνήσεσθε πάντα
taken up the shield of faith, with which ye will be able all
τὰ βέλη τοῦ πονηροῦ [b]τὰ‖ πεπυρωμένα σβέσαι· 17 καὶ
the [2]darts [3]of [4]the [5]wicked [6]one [1]burning to quench. Also
τὴν περικεφαλαίαν τοῦ σωτηρίου δέξασθε, καὶ τὴν μάχαιραν
the helmet of salvation receive, and the sword
τοῦ πνεύματος, ὅ ἐστιν ῥῆμα θεοῦ· 18 διὰ πάσης προσευχῆς
of the Spirit, which is [2]word [1]God's; by all prayer
καὶ δεήσεως προσευχόμενοι ἐν παντὶ καιρῷ ἐν πνεύματι,
and supplication praying in every season in [the] Spirit,
καὶ εἰς αὐτὸ [c]τοῦτο‖ ἀγρυπνοῦντες ἐν πάσῃ προσκαρτερήσει
and unto this very thing watching with all perseverance
καὶ δεήσει περὶ πάντων τῶν ἁγίων, 19 καὶ ὑπὲρ ἐμοῦ ἵνα
and supplication for all saints; and for me that
μοι [d]δοθείη‖ λόγος ἐν ἀνοίξει τοῦ.στόματός.μου ἐν
to me may be given utterance in [the] opening of my mouth with
παῤῥησίᾳ, γνωρίσαι τὸ μυστήριον [e]τοῦ εὐαγγελίου,‖ 20 ὑπὲρ
boldness to make known the mystery of the glad tidings, for
οὗ πρεσβεύω ἐν ἁλύσει, ἵνα ἐν αὐτῷ παῤῥησιάσωμαι
which I am an ambassador in a chain, that in it I may be bold
ὡς δεῖ με λαλῆσαι.
as it behoves me to speak.

21 [f]Ἵνα.δὲ εἰδῆτε καὶ ὑμεῖς‖ τὰ κατ' ἐμέ, τί
But that [3]may [4]know [2]also [1]ye the things concerning me, what
πράσσω, πάντα [g]ὑμῖν γνωρίσει‖ Τυχικὸς ὁ ἀγαπητὸς
I am doing, all things to you will make known Tychicus the beloved

10 Finally, my brethren, be strong in the Lord, and in the power of his might.
11 Put on the whole armour of God, that ye may be able to stand against the wiles of the devil.
12 For we wrestle not against flesh and blood, but against principalities, against powers, against the rulers of the darkness of this world, against spiritual wickedness in high *places*.
13 Wherefore take unto you the whole armour of God, that ye may be able to withstand in the evil day, and having done all, to stand. 14 Stand therefore, having your loins girt about with truth, and having on the breastplate of righteousness; 15 and your feet shod with the preparation of the gospel of peace; 16 above all, taking the shield of faith, wherewith ye shall be able to quench all the fiery darts of the wicked.
17 And take the helmet of salvation, and the sword of the Spirit, which is the word of God: 18 praying always with all prayer and supplication in the Spirit, and watching thereunto with all perseverance and supplication for all saints; 19 and for me, that utterance may be given unto me, that I may open my mouth boldly, to make known the mystery of the gospel, 20 for which I am an ambassador in bonds: that therein I may speak boldly, as I ought to speak.

21 But that ye also may know my affairs, *and* how I do, Tychicus, a beloved brother

---

[t] τοῦ λοιποῦ LTTrA. [v] — ἀδελφοί μου LTTrA. [w] μεθοδίας T. [x] ὑμῖν to you L. [y] — τοῦ αἰῶνος (*read* of this darkness) GLTTrAW. [z] — τούτου (*read* of darkness) W. [a] ἐν in LTTr. [b] — τὰ L[TrA]. [c] — τοῦτο very thing LTTrA. [d] δοθῇ GLTTrAW. [e] [τοῦ εὐαγγελίου] L. [f] καὶ ὑμεῖς εἰδῆτε LTTr. [g] γνωρίσει ὑμῖν LTTr.

and faithful minister in the Lord, shall make known to you all things: 22 whom I have sent unto you for the same purpose, that ye might know our affairs, and *that* he might comfort your hearts.

ἀδελφὸς καὶ πιστὸς διάκονος ἐν κυρίῳ· 22 ὃν ἔπεμψα
brother and faithful servant in [the] Lord; whom I sent
πρὸς ὑμᾶς εἰς αὐτὸ.τοῦτο, ἵνα γνῶτε τὰ περὶ
to you for this very thing, that ye might know the things concerning
ἡμῶν καὶ παρακαλέσῃ τὰς.καρδίας.ὑμῶν.
us and he might encourage your hearts.

23 Peace *be* to the brethren, and love with faith, from God the Father and the Lord Jesus Christ. 24 Grace *be* with all them that love our Lord Jesus Christ in sincerity. Amen.

23 Εἰρήνη τοῖς ἀδελφοῖς καὶ ἀγάπη μετὰ πίστεως ἀπὸ
Peace to the brethren, and love with faith from
θεοῦ πατρὸς καὶ κυρίου Ἰησοῦ χριστοῦ. 24 Ἡ.χάρις μετὰ
God [the] Father and Lord Jesus Christ. Grace with
πάντων τῶν ἀγαπώντων τὸν.κύριον.ἡμῶν Ἰησοῦν χριστὸν
all those that love our Lord Jesus Christ
ἐν ἀφθαρσίᾳ. [h]ἀμήν.‖
in incorruption. Amen.

[i]Πρὸς Ἐφεσίους ἐγράφη ἀπὸ Ῥώμης, διὰ Τυχικοῦ.‖
To [the] Ephesians written from Rome, by Tychicus.

---

[k]Η ΠΡΟΣ ΤΟΥΣ ΦΙΛΙΠΠΗΣΙΟΥΣ ΕΠΙΣΤΟΛΗ.‖
THE [2]TO [3]THE [4]PHILIPPIANS [1]EPISTLE.

PAUL and Timotheus, the servants of Jesus Christ, to all the saints in Christ Jesus which are at Philippi, with the bishops and deacons: 2 Grace *be* unto you, and peace, from God our Father, and *from* the Lord Jesus Christ.

ΠΑΥΛΟΣ καὶ Τιμόθεος δοῦλοι [l]Ἰησοῦ χριστοῦ,‖ πᾶσιν τοῖς
Paul and Timotheus, bondmen of Jesus Christ, to all the
ἁγίοις ἐν χριστῷ Ἰησοῦ τοῖς οὖσιν ἐν Φιλίπποις, σὺν
saints in Christ Jesus who are in Philippi, with [the]
ἐπισκόποις καὶ διακόνοις· 2 χάρις ὑμῖν καὶ εἰρήνη ἀπὸ θεοῦ
overseers and those who serve. Grace to you and peace from God
πατρὸς.ἡμῶν καὶ κυρίου [m]Ἰησοῦ χριστοῦ.‖
our Father and [the] Lord Jesus Christ.

3 I thank my God upon every remembrance of you, 4 always in every prayer of mine for you all making request with joy, 5 for your fellowship in the gospel from the first day until now; 6 being confident of this very thing, that he which hath begun a good work in you will perform *it* until the day of Jesus Christ: 7 even as it is meet for me to think this of you all, because I have you in my heart; inasmuch as both in my bonds, and in the defence and confirmation of the gospel, ye all are partakers of my grace. 8 For God is my re-

3 Εὐχαριστῶ τῷ.θεῷ.μου ἐπὶ πάσῃ.τῇ μνείᾳ ὑμῶν,
I thank my God on the whole remembrance of you,
4 πάντοτε ἐν πάσῃ δεήσει μου ὑπὲρ πάντων ὑμῶν μετὰ
always in [2]every [3]supplication [1]my for [2]all [1]you with
χαρᾶς τὴν δέησιν ποιούμενος, 5 ἐπὶ τῇ.κοινωνίᾳ.ὑμῶν εἰς
joy [2]supplication [1]making, for your fellowship in
τὸ εὐαγγέλιον, ἀπὸ [n] πρώτης ἡμέρας ἄχρι τοῦ νῦν· 6 πε-
the glad tidings, from [the] first day until now; being
ποιθὼς αὐτὸ.τοῦτο, ὅτι ὁ ἐναρξάμενος ἐν ὑμῖν ἔργον
persuaded of this very thing, that he who began in you a [2]work
ἀγαθὸν ἐπιτελέσει [o]ἄχρις‖ ἡμέρας [l]Ἰησοῦ χριστοῦ·‖
[1]good will complete [it] until [the] day of Jesus Christ:
7 καθώς ἐστιν δίκαιον ἐμοὶ τοῦτο φρονεῖν ὑπὲρ πάντων ὑμῶν,
as it is righteous for me this to think as to [2]all [1]you,
διὰ τὸ ἔχειν με ἐν τῇ καρδίᾳ ὑμᾶς, ἔν.τε τοῖς.δεσμοῖς.μου
because [2]have [3]me [4]in [5]the [6]heart [1]ye, both in my bonds
καὶ [p] τῇ ἀπολογίᾳ καὶ βεβαιώσει τοῦ εὐαγγελίου, [q]συγ-
and in the defence and confirmation of the glad tidings, fellow-
κοινωνούς‖ μου.τῆς.χάριτος πάντας ὑμᾶς ὄντας. 8 μάρτυς.γάρ
partakers of my grace all ye are. For [1]witness

---

[h] — ἀμήν GLTTrA. [i] — *the subscription* GLTW; Πρὸς Ἐφεσίους TrA.
[k] + Παύλου τοῦ Ἀποστόλου of Paul the Apostle E; + Παύλου G; — τοὺς FG · Πρὸς Φιλιππησίους LTTrAW. [l] χριστοῦ Ἰησοῦ LTTrAW. [m] χριστοῦ Ἰησοῦ W. [n] + τῆς the LTTrA. [o] ἄχρι LTA. [p] + ἐν in (*read* τῇ the) [L]TTrAW. [q] συν- T.

μου [r]ἐστὶν‖ ὁ θεός, ὡς ἐπιποθῶ πάντας ὑμᾶς ἐν σπλάγ-
my [2]is [1]God, how I long after [2]all [1]you in [the] bowels
χνοις [s]Ἰησοῦ χριστοῦ.‖ 9 καὶ τοῦτο προσεύχομαι, ἵνα ἡ ἀγάπη
of Jesus Christ. And this I pray, that [2]love
ὑμῶν ἔτι μᾶλλον καὶ μᾶλλον [t]περισσεύῃ‖ ἐν ἐπιγνώσει καὶ
[1]your yet more and more may abound in knowledge and
πάσῃ αἰσθήσει, 10 εἰς τὸ δοκιμάζειν ὑμᾶς τὰ δια-
all intelligence, for [2]to [3]approve [1]you the things that are
φέροντα, ἵνα ἦτε εἰλικρινεῖς καὶ ἀπρόσκοποι εἰς ἡμέραν
excellent, that ye may be pure and without offence for [the] day
χριστοῦ, 11 πεπληρωμένοι [v]καρπῶν‖ δικαιοσύνης [w]τῶν‖
of Christ, being filled with fruits of righteousness which [are]
διὰ Ἰησοῦ χριστοῦ, εἰς δόξαν καὶ ἔπαινον θεοῦ.
by Jesus Christ, to [2]glory [3]and [4]praise [1]God's.

12 Γινώσκειν.δὲ ὑμᾶς βούλομαι, ἀδελφοί, ὅτι τὰ κατ'
But [4]to [5]know [3]you [1]I [2]wish, brethren, that the things concerning
ἐμὲ μᾶλλον εἰς προκοπὴν τοῦ εὐαγγελίου ἐλήλυθεν·
me rather to [the] advancement of the glad tidings have turned out,
13 ὥστε τοὺς.δεσμούς.μου φανεροὺς ἐν χριστῷ γενέσθαι
so as my bonds [4]manifest [5]in [6]Christ [1]to [2]have [3]become
ἐν ὅλῳ τῷ πραιτωρίῳ καὶ τοῖς λοιποῖς πᾶσιν· 14 καὶ τοὺς
in [2]whole [1]the prætorium and to [2]the [3]rest [1]all; and the
πλείονας τῶν ἀδελφῶν ἐν κυρίῳ πεποιθότας τοῖς δεσμοῖς
most of the brethren [2]in [[3]the] [4]Lord [1]trusting by [2]bonds
μου περισσοτέρως τολμᾶν ἀφόβως τὸν λόγον [x]λαλεῖν. 15 Τινὲς
[1]my [4]more [5]abundantly [3]dare [10]fearlessly [8]the [9]word [6]to [7]speak. Some
μὲν καὶ διὰ φθόνον καὶ ἔριν, τινὲς.δὲ καὶ δι' εὐδοκίαν τὸν
indeed even from envy and strife, but some also from good-will the
χριστὸν κηρύσσουσιν. 16 οἱ μὲν [y]ἐξ ἐριθείας [z]τὸν‖ χριστὸν
Christ are proclaiming. Those indeed out of contention the Christ
καταγγέλλουσιν οὐχ ἁγνῶς, οἰόμενοι θλῖψιν [a]ἐπιφέρειν‖
are announcing, not purely, supposing tribulation to add
τοῖς.δεσμοῖς.μου·‖ 17 οἱ.δὲ [y]ἐξ ἀγάπης, εἰδότες ὅτι εἰς ἀπο-
to my bonds, but those out of love, knowing that for de-
λογίαν τοῦ εὐαγγελίου κεῖμαι.‖ 18 τί.γάρ; πλὴν [b]παντὶ
fence of the glad tidings I am set. What then? nevertheless in every
τρόπῳ, εἴτε προφάσει εἴτε ἀληθείᾳ, χριστὸς καταγγέλλεται·
way, whether in pretext or in truth, Christ is announced;
καὶ ἐν τούτῳ χαίρω, ἀλλὰ καὶ χαρήσομαι. 19 οἶδα.γὰρ ὅτι
and in this I rejoice, yea, also I will rejoice: for I know that
τοῦτό μοι ἀποβήσεται εἰς σωτηρίαν διὰ τῆς.ὑμῶν.δεήσεως,
this for me shall turn out to salvation through your supplication,
καὶ ἐπιχορηγίας τοῦ πνεύματος Ἰησοῦ χριστοῦ, 20 κατὰ
and [the] supply of the Spirit of Jesus Christ: according to
τὴν ἀποκαραδοκίαν καὶ ἐλπίδα μου, ὅτι ἐν οὐδενὶ αἰσχυνθή-
[2]earnest [3]expectation [4]and [5]hope [1]my, that in nothing I shall be
σομαι, ἀλλ' ἐν πάσῃ παῤῥησίᾳ, ὡς πάντοτε, καὶ νῦν μεγα-
ashamed, but in all boldness, as always, also now shall be
λυνθήσεται χριστὸς ἐν τῷ.σώματί.μου εἴτε διὰ ζωῆς εἴτε διὰ
magnified Christ in my body whether by life or by
θανάτου. 21 Ἐμοὶ.γὰρ τὸ ζῆν χριστός, καὶ τὸ ἀποθανεῖν
death. For to me to live [is] Christ, and to die

cord, how greatly I long after you all in the bowels of Jesus
Christ. 9 And this I pray, that your love may abound yet more and more in knowledge and *in* all judgment;
10 that ye may approve things that are excellent; that ye may be sincere and without offence till the day of Christ;
11 being filled with the fruits of righteousness, which are by Jesus Christ, unto the glory and praise of God.

12 But I would ye should understand, brethren, that the things *which happened* unto me have fallen out rather unto the furtherance of the gospel;
13 so that my bonds in Christ are manifest in all the palace, and in all other *places;*
14 and many of the brethren in the Lord, waxing confident by my bonds, are much more bold to speak the word without fear.
15 Some indeed preach Christ even of envy and strife; and some also of good will:
16 the one preach Christ of contention, not sincerely, supposing to add affliction to my bonds:
17 but the other of love, knowing that I am set for the defence of the gospel.
18 What then? notwithstanding, every way, whether in pretence, or in truth, Christ is preached; and I therein do rejoice, yea, and will rejoice.
19 For I know that this shall turn to my salvation through your prayer, and the supply of the Spirit of Jesus Christ,
20 according to my earnest expectation and *my* hope, that in nothing I shall be ashamed, but *that* with all boldness, as always, *so* now also Christ shall be magnified in my body, whether *it be* by life, or by death.
21 For to me to live *is* Christ, and to die *is*

[r] — ἐστὶν (*read* [is]) [L]TTrA. [s] χριστοῦ Ἰησοῦ GLTTrAW. [t] περισσεύσῃ L. [v] καρπὸν (with) fruit GLTTrAW. [w] τὸν (*read* which [is]) G[L]TTrAW. [x] + τοῦ θεοῦ of God LTTrA. [y] *verses* 16 *and* 17 *transposed, except* οἱ μὲν *and* οἱ δὲ GLTTrAW. [z] [τὸν] LTrA. [a] ἐγείρειν to arouse LTTrAW. [b] + ὅτι that (*read* πλὴν except) LTTrA.

gain. 22 But if I live
in the flesh, this *is* the
fruit of my labour:
yet what I shall choose
I wot not. 23 For I am
in a strait betwixt
two, having a desire
to depart, and to be
with Christ; which is
far better: 24 never-
theless to abide in the
flesh *is* more needful
for you. 25 And hav-
ing this confidence, I
know that I shall a-
bide and continue
with you all for your
furtherance and joy
of faith; 26 that your
rejoicing may be more
abundant in Jesus
Christ for me by my
coming to you again.
27 Only let your con-
versation be as it be-
cometh the gospel of
Christ: that whether
I come and see you,
or else be absent, I
may hear of your af-
fairs, that ye stand
fast in one spirit, with
one mind striving to-
gether for the faith of
the gospel; 28 and
in nothing terrified
by your adversaries,
which is to them an
evident token of per-
dition, but to you of
salvation, and that
of God. 29 For unto
you it is given in the
behalf of Christ, not
only to believe on
him, but also to suffer
for his sake; 30 hav-
ing the same conflict
which ye saw in me,
and now hear *to be* in
me.

II. If *there be* there-
fore any consolation
in Christ, if any com-
fort of love, if any
fellowship of the Spi-
rit, if any bowels and
mercies, 2 fulfil ye my
joy, that ye be like-
minded, having the
same love, *being* of one
accord, of one mind.
3 *Let* nothing *be done*
through strife or vain-
glory; but in low-
liness of mind let
each esteem other bet-
ter than themselves.
4 Look not every man
on his own things, but

κέρδος. 22 εἰ.δὲ τὸ ζῆν ἐν σαρκί, τοῦτό μοι καρπὸς ἔργου·
gain; but if to live in flesh, this for me [is] fruit of labour:
καὶ τί αἱρήσομαι οὐ.γνωρίζω· 23 συνέχομαι [c]γὰρ[‖] ἐκ τῶν
and what I shall choose I know not. [2]I [3]am [4]pressed [1]for by the
δύο, τὴν ἐπιθυμίαν ἔχων εἰς τὸ ἀναλῦσαι, καὶ σὺν χριστῷ
two, [2]the [3]desire [1]having for to depart, and with Christ
εἶναι, πολλῷ[d].μᾶλλον κρεῖσσον· 24 τὸ.δὲ.ἐπιμένειν [e]ἐν[‖]
to be, [for it is] very much better; but to remain in
τῇ σαρκὶ ἀναγκαιότερον δι' ὑμᾶς· 25 καὶ τοῦτο
the flesh [is] more necessary for the sake of you; and this
πεποιθὼς οἶδα ὅτι μενῶ καὶ [f]συμπαραμενῶ[‖] πᾶσιν
being persuaded of, I know that I shall abide and continue with [2]all
ὑμῖν εἰς τὴν.ὑμῶν.προκοπὴν καὶ χαρὰν τῆς πίστεως, 26 ἵνα
[1]you; for your advancement and joy of faith; that
τὸ.καύχημα.ὑμῶν περισσεύῃ ἐν χριστῷ Ἰησοῦ ἐν ἐμοὶ διὰ
your boasting may abound in Christ Jesus in me through
τῆς.ἐμῆς.παρουσίας πάλιν πρὸς ὑμᾶς. 27 Μόνον ἀξίως τοῦ
my presence again with you. Only worthily of the
εὐαγγελίου τοῦ χριστοῦ πολιτεύεσθε, ἵνα εἴτε ἐλθὼν καὶ
glad tidings of the Christ conduct yourselves, that whether having come and
ἰδὼν ὑμᾶς, εἴτε ἀπὼν [g]ἀκούσω[‖] τὰ περὶ ὑμῶν,
having seen you, or being absent I might hear the things concerning you,
ὅτι στήκετε ἐν ἑνὶ πνεύματι, μιᾷ ψυχῇ συναθλοῦντες
that ye stand fast in one spirit, with one soul striving together
τῇ πίστει τοῦ εὐαγγελίου, 28 καὶ μὴ πτυρόμενοι ἐν μη-
with the faith of the glad tidings; and being frightened in no-
δενὶ ὑπὸ τῶν ἀντικειμένων· ἥτις [h]αὐτοῖς μέν ἐστιν[‖] ἔν-
thing by those who oppose; which to them is a demon-
δειξις ἀπωλείας, [i]ὑμῖν[‖] δὲ σωτηρίας, καὶ τοῦτο ἀπὸ θεοῦ·
stration of destruction, [2]to [3]you [1]but of salvation, and this from God;
29 ὅτι ὑμῖν ἐχαρίσθη τὸ ὑπὲρ χριστοῦ, οὐ μόνον τὸ
because to you it was granted concerning Christ, not only
εἰς αὐτὸν πιστεύειν, ἀλλὰ καὶ τὸ ὑπὲρ αὐτοῦ πάσχειν·
[3]on [4]him [1]to [2]believe, but also concerning him to suffer,
30 τὸν αὐτὸν ἀγῶνα ἔχοντες οἷον [k]ἴδετε[‖] ἐν ἐμοί, καὶ νῦν
the same conflict having such as ye saw in me, and now
ἀκούετε ἐν ἐμοί.
hear of in me.

2 Εἴ τις οὖν παράκλησις ἐν χριστῷ, εἴ τι παρα-
If [2]any [1]then encouragement [there be] in Christ, if any conso-
μύθιον ἀγάπης, εἴ τις κοινωνία πνεύματος, εἴ [l]τινα[‖] σπλάγ-
lation of love, if any fellowship of [the] Spirit, if any bowels
χνα καὶ οἰκτιρμοί, 2 πληρώσατέ μου τὴν χαράν, ἵνα
and compassions, fulfil my joy, that
τὸ.αὐτὸ.φρονῆτε, τὴν αὐτὴν ἀγάπην ἔχοντες, [m]σύμψυχοι,[‖]
ye may be of the same mind, the same love having, joined in soul,
τὸ ἓν φρονοῦντες· 3 μηδὲν [n]κατὰ[‖] ἐριθείαν [o]ἢ[‖] κενο-
the one thing minding— nothing according to contention or vain-
δοξίαν, ἀλλὰ τῇ ταπεινοφροσύνῃ ἀλλήλους ἡγούμενοι ὑπερ-
glory, but in humility one another esteeming a-
έχοντας ἑαυτῶν. 4 μὴ τὰ ἑαυτῶν [p]ἕκαστος[‖]
bove themselves, [2]not [4]the [5]things [6]of [7]themselves [3]each

---

[c] δὲ but GLTTrAW. [d] + γὰρ for EGLTTrAW. [e] — ἐν (*read* τῇ in the) T. [f] παραμενῶ continue (*read* πᾶσιν with all) LTTrA. [g] ἀκούω LTTr. [h] ἐστὶν αὐτοῖς GLTTrAW. [i] ὑμῶν (*read* but of your salvation) LTTrAW. [k] εἴδετε LTTrAW. [l] τις GLTTrA. [m] συν- T. [n] κατ' TTrAW. [o] μηδὲ κατὰ nor according to LTTrA. [p] ἕκαστοι LTTrA.

[q]σκοπεῖτε,‖ ἀλλὰ καὶ τὰ ἑτέρων [r]ἕκαστος.‖ 5 Τοῦτο
[1]consider, but [2]also [3]the [4]things [5]of [6]others [1]each. [2]This
[s]γὰρ φρονείσθω‖ ἐν ὑμῖν ὃ καὶ ἐν χριστῷ Ἰησοῦ, 6 ὃς
[1]for [3]let mind be in you which also in Christ Jesus [was]; who,
ἐν μορφῇ θεοῦ ὑπάρχων, οὐχ ἁρπαγμὸν ἡγήσατο τὸ εἶναι
in [the] form of God subsisting, [3]not [4]rapine [1]esteemed [2]it to be
[t]ἴσα[t] θεῷ, 7 [v]ἀλλ'‖ ἑαυτὸν ἐκένωσεν, μορφὴν δούλου
equal with God; but [2]himself [1]emptied, [7]form [5]a [6]bondman's
λαβών, ἐν ὁμοιώματι ἀνθρώπων γενόμενος· 8 καὶ σχή-
[3]having [4]taken, in [the] likeness of men having become; and in
ματι εὑρεθεὶς ὡς ἄνθρωπος, ἐταπείνωσεν ἑαυτόν, γενό-
figure having been found as a man, he humbled himself, having
μενος ὑπήκοος μέχρι θανάτου, θανάτου.δὲ σταυροῦ. 9 διὸ
become obedient unto death, even death of [the] cross. Wherefore
καὶ ὁ θεὸς αὐτὸν ὑπερύψωσεν καὶ ἐχαρίσατο αὐτῷ [w] ὄνομα
also God him highly exalted and granted to him a name
τὸ ὑπὲρ πᾶν ὄνομα· 10 ἵνα ἐν τῷ ὀνόματι Ἰησοῦ πᾶν
which [is] above every name, that at the name of Jesus every
γόνυ κάμψῃ ἐπουρανίων καὶ ἐπιγείων καὶ καταχθονίων·
knee should bow of [beings] in heaven and on earth and under the earth,
11 καὶ πᾶσα γλῶσσα [x]ἐξομολογήσηται‖ ὅτι κύριος Ἰησοῦς
and every tongue should confess that [3is] [4]Lord [1]Jesus
χριστὸς εἰς δόξαν θεοῦ πατρός.
[2]Christ to [the] glory of God [the] Father.

12 Ὥστε, ἀγαπητοί.μου, καθὼς πάντοτε ὑπηκούσατε, μὴ
So that, my beloved, even as always ye obeyed, not
ὡς ἐν τῇ.παρουσίᾳ.μου μόνον, ἀλλὰ νῦν πολλῷ μᾶλλον ἐν
as in my presence only, but now much rather in
τῇ.ἀπουσίᾳ.μου, μετὰ φόβου καὶ τρόμου τὴν.ἑαυτῶν σωτηρίαν
my absence, with fear and trembling your own salvation
κατεργάζεσθε· 13 [y]ὁ‖.θεὸς.γάρ ἐστιν ὁ ἐνεργῶν ἐν ὑμῖν καὶ τὸ
work out, for God it is who works in you both
θέλειν καὶ τὸ ἐνεργεῖν ὑπὲρ τῆς εὐδοκίας. 14 πάντα
to will and to work according to [his] good pleasure. [2]All [3]things
ποιεῖτε χωρὶς γογγυσμῶν καὶ διαλογισμῶν, 15 ἵνα [z]γένησθε‖
[1]do apart from murmurings and reasonings, that ye may be
ἄμεμπτοι καὶ ἀκέραιοι, τέκνα θεοῦ [a]ἀμώμητα‖ [b]ἐν μέσῳ‖
faultless and simple, children of God unblamable in [the] midst
γενεᾶς σκολιᾶς καὶ διεστραμμένης, ἐν οἷς φαίνεσθε ὡς
of a generation crooked and perverted; among whom ye appear as
φωστῆρες ἐν κόσμῳ, 16 λόγον ζωῆς ἐπέχοντες, εἰς καύχημα
luminaries in [the] world, [the] word of life holding forth, for a boast
ἐμοὶ εἰς ἡμέραν χριστοῦ, ὅτι οὐκ εἰς κενὸν ἔδραμον οὐδὲ εἰς
to me in [2]day [1]Christ's, that not in vain I ran nor in
κενὸν ἐκοπίασα. 17 [c]ἀλλ'‖ εἰ καὶ σπένδομαι ἐπὶ τῇ θυσίᾳ καὶ
vain laboured. But if also I am poured out on the sacrifice and
λειτουργίᾳ τῆς.πίστεως.ὑμῶν, χαίρω καὶ [d]συγχαίρω‖ πᾶσιν
ministration of your faith, I rejoice, and rejoice with all
ὑμῖν· 18 τὸ.[e]δ'‖.αὐτὸ καὶ ὑμεῖς χαίρετε καὶ [d]συγχαίρετέ‖ μοι.
you. And in the same also [2]ye [1]rejoice and rejoice with me.
19 Ἐλπίζω.δὲ ἐν [f]κυρίῳ‖ Ἰησοῦ Τιμόθεον ταχέως πέμψαι
But I hope in [the] Lord Jesus [3]Timotheus [4]soon [1]to [2]send

every man also on the
things of others. 5 Let
this mind be in you,
which was also in
Christ Jesus: 6 who,
being in the form of
God, thought it not
robbery to be equal
with God: 7 but made
himself of no reputa-
tion, and took upon
him the form of a
servant, and was made
in the likeness of men:
8 and being found in
fashion as a man, he
humbled himself, and
became obedient unto
death, even the death
of the cross. 9 Where-
fore God also hath
highly exalted him,
and given him a name
which is above every
name: 10 that at the
name of Jesus every
knee should bow, of
things in heaven, and
things in earth, and
things under the earth;
11 and *that* every
tongue should confess
that Jesus Christ *is*
Lord, to the glory of
God the Father.

12 Wherefore, my
beloved, as ye have
always obeyed, not as
in my presence only,
but now much more in
my absence, work out
your own salvation
with fear and trem-
bling. 13 For it is God
which worketh in you
both to will and to do
of *his* good pleasure.
14 Do all things with-
out murmurings and
disputings: 15 that ye
may be blameless and
harmless, the sons of
God, without rebuke,
in the midst of a
crooked and perverse
nation, among whom
ye shine as lights in
the world; 16 holding
forth the word of life;
that I may rejoice in
the day of Christ, that
I have not run in vain,
neither laboured in
vain. 17 Yea, and if I
be offered upon the
sacrifice and service of
your faith, I joy, and
rejoice with you all.
18 For the same cause
also do ye joy, and re-
joice with me. 19 But
I trust in the Lord
Jesus to send Timo-
theus shortly unto

---

[q] σκοποῦντες considering GLTTrAW. [r] ἕκαστοι GLTTrAW. [s] φρονεῖτε (*omit* for) LTTrA. [t] ἴσα LTAW. [v] ἀλλὰ LTTrAW. [w] + τὸ the (name) LTTr[A]W. [x] ἐξομολογήσεται shall confess TAW. [y] — ὁ LTTrAW. [z] ἦτε L. [a] ἄμωμα LTTrA. [b] μέσον [in the] midst LTTrAW. [c] ἀλλὰ LTTrAW. [d] συν- T. [e] δὲ TTr. [f] χριστῷ Christ L.

you, that I also may
be of good comfort,
when I know your
state. 20 For I have
no man likeminded,
who will naturally
care for your state.
21 For all seek their
own, not the things
which are Jesus
Christ's. 22 But ye
know the proof of him,
that, as a son with the
father, he hath served
with me in the gospel.
23 Him therefore I
hope to send presently,
so soon as I shall see
how it will go with
me. 24 But I trust in
the Lord that I also
myself shall come
shortly. 25 Yet I sup-
posed it necessary to
send to you Epaphro-
ditus, my brother, and
companion in labour,
and fellowsoldier, but
your messenger, and
he that ministered to
my wants. 26 For he
longed after you all,
and was full of heavi-
ness, because that ye
had heard that he had
been sick. 27 For in-
deed he was sick nigh
unto death: but God
had mercy on him;
and not on him only,
but on me also, lest I
should have sorrow up-
on sorrow. 28 I sent
him therefore the more
carefully, that, when
ye see him again, ye
may rejoice, and that I
may be the less sorrow-
ful. 29 Receive him
therefore in the Lord
with all gladness; and
hold such in reputa-
tion: 30 because for
the work of Christ he
was nigh unto death,
not regarding his life,
to supply your lack of
service toward me.

III. Finally, my
brethren, rejoice in
the Lord. To write the
same things to you, to
me indeed *is* not griev-
ous, but for you *it*
is safe. 2 Beware of
dogs, beware of evil
workers, beware of the
concision. 3 For we are
the circumcision, which
worship God in the
spirit, and rejoice in
Christ Jesus, and have
no confidence in the
flesh. 4 Though I might
also have confidence in

ὑμῖν, ἵνα κἀγὼ εὐψυχῶ, γνοὺς τὰ περὶ
to you, that I also may be of good courage, having known the things concerning
ὑμῶν· 20 οὐδένα.γὰρ ἔχω ἰσόψυχον, ὅστις γνησίως τὰ
you. For no one have I like-minded, who genuinely the things
περὶ ὑμῶν μεριμνήσει· 21 οἱ.πάντες.γὰρ τὰ ἑαυτῶν
relative to you will care for. For all the things of themselves
ζητοῦσιν, οὐ τὰ [h]τοῦ[‖] [i]χριστοῦ Ἰησοῦ·[‖] 22 τὴν.δὲ δοκιμὴν
are seeking, not the things of Christ Jesus. But the proof
αὐτοῦ γινώσκετε, ὅτι ὡς πατρὶ τέκνον, σὺν ἐμοὶ ἐδούλευσεν
of him ye know, that, as [3]to [4]a [5]father [1]a [2]child, with me he served
εἰς τὸ εὐαγγέλιον. 23 τοῦτον μὲν οὖν ἐλπίζω πέμψαι ὡς
for the glad tidings. Him therefore I hope to send [3]when
ἂν [k]ἀπίδω[‖] τὰ περὶ ἐμέ, ἐξαυτῆς· 24 πέ-
[4]I [5]shall [6]have [7]seen [8]the [9]things [10]concerning [11]me [1]at [2]once: [13]I [14]am
ποιθα δὲ ἐν κυρίῳ ὅτι καὶ αὐτὸς ταχέως ἐλεύσομαι.
[15]persuaded [12]but in [the] Lord that also [2]myself [4]soon [1]I [3]shall come:
25 Ἀναγκαῖον.δὲ ἡγησάμην Ἐπαφρόδιτον τὸν ἀδελφὸν καὶ
but necessary I esteemed [it] [5]Epaphroditus, [7]brother [8]and
συνεργὸν καὶ [l]συστρατιώτην[‖] μου, ὑμῶν.δὲ ἀπόστολον καὶ
[9]fellow-worker [10]and [11]fellow-soldier [6]my, [12]but [13]your [14]messenger [15]and
λειτουργὸν τῆς.χρείας.μου, πέμψαι πρὸς ὑμᾶς· 26 ἐπειδὴ
[16]minister [17]of [18]my [19]need, [1]to [2]send [3]to [4]you, since
ἐπιποθῶν ἦν πάντας ὑμᾶς[m], καὶ ἀδημονῶν διότι
[3]longing [4]after [1]he [2]was [6]all [5]you, and [was] deeply depressed because
ἠκούσατε ὅτι ἠσθένησεν· 27 καὶ.γὰρ ἠσθένησεν παραπλήσιον
ye heard that he was sick; for indeed he was sick like
θανάτῳ· [n]ἀλλ'[‖] ὁ θεὸς [o]αὐτὸν ἠλέησεν,[‖] οὐκ.αὐτὸν.δὲ μόνον,
to death, but God him had mercy on, and not him alone,
ἀλλὰ καὶ ἐμέ, ἵνα μὴ λύπην ἐπὶ [p]λύπῃ[‖] σχῶ. 28 σπου-
but also me, that not sorrow upon sorrow I might have. The more
δαιοτέρως οὖν ἔπεμψα αὐτόν, ἵνα ἰδόντες αὐτὸν πάλιν
diligently therefore I sent him, that seeing him again
χαρῆτε, κἀγὼ ἀλυπότερος ὦ. 29 προσδέχεσθε οὖν
ye might rejoice, and I the less sorrowful might be. Receive therefore
αὐτὸν ἐν κυρίῳ μετὰ πάσης χαρᾶς, καὶ τοὺς τοιούτους
him in [the] Lord with all joy, and such
ἐντίμους ἔχετε· 30 ὅτι διὰ τὸ ἔργον [q]τοῦ[‖] [r]χριστοῦ[‖]
in honour hold; because for the sake of the work of the Christ
μέχρι θανάτου ἤγγισεν, [s]παραβουλευσάμενος[‖] τῇ ψυχῇ,
unto death he went near, having disregarded [his] life,
ἵνα ἀναπληρώσῃ τὸ.ὑμῶν.ὑστέρημα τῆς πρός με λειτουργίας.
that he might fill up your deficiency [1]of the [2]towards [3]me [1]ministration.

3 Τὸ.λοιπόν, ἀδελφοί.μου, χαίρετε ἐν κυρίῳ· τὰ αὐτὰ
For the rest, my brethren, rejoice in [the] Lord: the same things
γράφειν ὑμῖν, ἐμοὶ μὲν οὐκ ὀκνηρόν, ὑμῖν.δὲ ἀσφαλές.
to write to you, to me [is] not irksome, and for you safe.
2 βλέπετε τοὺς κύνας, βλέπετε τοὺς κακοὺς ἐργάτας, βλέπετε
See to dogs, see to evil workers, see to
τὴν κατατομήν· 3 ἡμεῖς.γάρ ἐσμεν ἡ περιτομή, οἱ πνεύματι
the concision. For we are the circumcision, who [3]in [4]spirit
[t]θεῷ[‖] λατρεύοντες, καὶ καυχώμενοι ἐν χριστῷ Ἰησοῦ, καὶ οὐκ
[2]God [1]serve, and boast in Christ Jesus, and not

---

[h] — τοῦ GLTTrAW. [i] Ἰησοῦ χριστοῦ GLTrAW. [k] ἀφίδω LTTrA. [l] συνσ- LTTrA.
[m] + [ἰδεῖν] to see L. [n] ἀλλὰ LTTrAW. [o] ἠλέησεν αὐτόν LTTrAW. [p] λύπην GLTTrAW.
[q] — τοῦ the LTTrA. [r] — χριστοῦ A. [s] παραβολευσάμενος having hazarded GLTTrAW.
[t] θεοῦ (*read* serve in [the] Spirit of God) LTTrAW.

ἐν σαρκὶ πεποιθότες,.[v] 4 καίπερ ἐγὼ ἔχων πεποίθησιν καὶ ἐν
in flesh trust. Though I have trust even in
σαρκί· [v] εἴ τις δοκεῖ ἄλλος πεποιθέναι ἐν σαρκί, ἐγὼ μᾶλλον·
flesh; if any [2]thinks [1]other to trust in flesh, I rather:
5 [w]περιτομῇ ὀκταήμερος, ἐκ γένους Ἰσραήλ, φυλῆς
[as to] circumcision, on [the] eighth day; of [the] race of Israel, of [the] tribe
[x]Βενιαμίν," Ἑβραῖος ἐξ Ἑβραίων, κατὰ νόμον Φαρισαῖος,
of Benjamin, Hebrew of Hebrews; according to [the] law a Pharisee;
6 κατὰ [y]ζῆλον" διώκων τὴν ἐκκλησίαν, κατὰ δικαιοσύ-
according to zeal, persecuting the assembly; according to righteous-
νην τὴν ἐν νόμῳ γενόμενος ἄμεμπτος. 7 [z]ἀλλ'" ἅτινα
ness which [is] in [the] law, having become blameless; but what things
[a]ἦν μοι" κέρδη, ταῦτα ἥγημαι διὰ τὸν χριστὸν
were to me gain, these I have esteemed, on account of Christ,
ζημίαν· 8 ἀλλὰ [b]μενοῦνγε" καὶ ἡγοῦμαι πάντα ζημίαν
loss. But yea rather, also I am esteeming all things loss
εἶναι διὰ τὸ ὑπερέχον τῆς γνώσεως [c] χριστοῦ Ἰησοῦ
to be on account of the excellency of the knowledge of Christ Jesus
τοῦ.κυρίου.μου, δι' ὃν τὰ.πάντα ἐζημιώθην, καὶ ἡγοῦ-
my Lord, on account of whom all things I suffered loss of, and esteem
μαι σκύβαλα [d]εἶναι," ἵνα χριστὸν κερδήσω, 9 καὶ εὑρεθῶ
[them] refuse to be, that Christ I may gain; and be found
ἐν αὐτῷ, μὴ ἔχων ἐμὴν.δικαιοσύνην τὴν ἐκ νόμου, ἀλλὰ
in him, not having my righteousness which [is] of law, but
τὴν διὰ πίστεως χριστοῦ, τὴν ἐκ θεοῦ δικαιοσύνην ἐπὶ
that which by faith of Christ [is], the [2]of [3]God [1]righteousness on
τῇ πίστει, 10 τοῦ γνῶναι αὐτὸν καὶ τὴν δύναμιν τῆς ἀνα-
faith, to know him and the power of [2]resur-
στάσεως αὐτοῦ, καὶ [e]τὴν" κοινωνίαν [f]τῶν".παθημάτων.αὐτοῦ,
rection [1]his, and the fellowship of his sufferings,
[g]συμμορφούμενος" τῷ.θανάτῳ.αὐτοῦ, 11 εἴ.πως καταντήσω
being conformed to his death, if by any means I may arrive
εἰς τὴν ἐξανάστασιν [h]τῶν" νεκρῶν. 12 οὐχ ὅτι ἤδη ἔλαβον,
at the resurrection of the dead. Not that [2]already [1]I received,
ἢ ἤδη τετελείωμαι· διώκω.δὲ εἰ [i]καὶ" καταλάβω
or already have been perfected; but I am pursuing, if also I may lay hold,
ἐφ'.ᾧ καὶ [k]κατελήφθην" ὑπὸ [l]τοῦ" χριστοῦ [m]Ἰησοῦ." 13 ἀδελ-
for that also I was laid hold of by the Christ Jesus. Bre-
φοί, ἐγὼ ἐμαυτὸν [n]οὐ" λογίζομαι κατειληφέναι· ἓν.δέ,
thren, I myself [2]not [1]do reckon to have laid hold; but one thing—
τὰ μὲν ὀπίσω ἐπιλανθανόμενος, τοῖς.δὲ ἔμπροσθεν
the things behind forgetting, and to the things before
ἐπεκτεινόμενος, 14 κατὰ σκοπὸν διώκω [o]ἐπὶ" τὸ βραβεῖον
stretching out, towards [the] goal I pursue for the prize
τῆς ἄνω κλήσεως τοῦ θεοῦ ἐν χριστῷ Ἰησοῦ. 15 Ὅσοι
of the [2]on [3]high [1]calling of God in Christ Jesus. As many as
οὖν τέλειοι τοῦτο.φρονῶμεν· καὶ εἴ τι ἑτέρως
therefore [are] perfect should be of this mind; and if [in] anything differently
φρονεῖτε, καὶ τοῦτο ὁ θεὸς ὑμῖν ἀποκαλύψει. 16 πλὴν εἰς.ὃ
ye are minded, [2]also [1]this God to you will reveal. But whereto

the flesh. If any other man thinketh that he hath whereof he might trust in the flesh, I more: 5 circumcised the eighth day, of the stock of Israel, *of* the tribe of Benjamin, an Hebrew of the Hebrews; as touching the law, a Pharisee; 6 concerning zeal, persecuting the church; touching the righteousness which is in the law, blameless. 7 But what things were gain to me, those I counted loss for Christ. 8 Yea doubtless, and I count all things *but* loss for the excellency of the knowledge of Christ Jesus my Lord: for whom I have suffered the loss of all things, and do count them *but* dung, that I may win Christ, 9 and be found in him, not having mine own righteousness, which is of the law, but that which is through the faith of Christ, the righteousness which is of God by faith: 10 that I may know him, and the power of his resurrection, and the fellowship of his sufferings, being made conformable unto his death; 11 if by any means I might attain unto the resurrection of the dead. 12 Not as though I had already attained, either were already perfect: but I follow after, if that I may apprehend that for which also I am apprehended of Christ Jesus. 13 Brethren, I count not myself to have apprehended: but *this* one thing *I do*, forgetting those things which are behind, and reaching forth unto those things which are before, 14 I press toward the mark for the prize of the high calling of God in Christ Jesus. 15 Let us therefore, as many as be perfect, be thus minded: and if in any thing ye be otherwise

---

[v] *To read as pointed in the Greek join* though I have &c. *to what precedes, commencing a sentence at* εἴ τις. [w] περιτομῇ GLTTrAW. [x] Βενιαμείν LTTr. [y] ζῆλος LTTrAW. [z] ἀλλὰ [L]Tr[A]; — ἀλλ' T. [a] μοι ἦν L. [b] μὲν οὖν then indeed GLTrAW. [c] + τοῦ (*read* of the Christ) L. [d] — εἶναι LTTr. [e] — τὴν LTTr[A]. [f] — τῶν TTr. [g] συμμορφιζόμενος (συν- T) LTTrAW. [h] τὴν ἐκ from among [the] LTTrAW. [i] — καὶ T. [k] κατελήμφθην LTTrA. [l] — τοῦ GLTTrAW. [m] — Ἰησοῦ GLTrAW. [n] οὔπω not yet T. [o] εἰς LTTrA.

minded, God shall reveal even this unto you. 16 Nevertheless, whereto we have already attained, let us walk by the same rule, let us mind the same thing. 17 Brethren, be followers together of me, and mark them which walk so as ye have us for an ensample. 18 (For many walk, of whom I have told you often, and now tell you even weeping, *that they are* the enemies of the cross of Christ: 19 whose end *is* destruction, whose God *is their* belly, and *whose* glory *is* in their shame, who mind earthly things.) 20 For our conversation is in heaven; from whence also we look for the Saviour, the Lord Jesus Christ: 21 who shall change our vile body, that it may be fashioned like unto his glorious body, according to the working whereby he is able even to subdue all things unto himself.

IV. Therefore, my brethren dearly beloved and longed for, my joy and crown, so stand fast in the Lord, *my* dearly beloved. 2 I beseech Euodias, and beseech Syntyche, that they be of the same mind in the Lord. 3 And I entreat thee also, true yokefellow, help those women which laboured with me in the gospel, with Clement also, and *with* other my fellowlabourers, whose names *are* in the book of life.

4 Rejoice in the Lord alway: *and* again I say, Rejoice. 5 Let your moderation be known unto all men. The Lord *is* at hand. 6 Be careful for nothing; but in every thing by prayer and supplication with thanksgiving let your requests be made known unto God. 7 And the peace of God, which passeth all understanding, shall keep your hearts and minds through Christ Jesus. 8 Finally, brethren, whatsoever things

ἐφθάσαμεν, τῷ αὐτῷ στοιχεῖν [p]κανόνι, τὸ.αὐτὸ.φρονεῖν.
we attained, by the same [2]to [3]walk [1]rule, to be of the same mind.
17 [q]Συμμιμηταί μου γίνεσθε, ἀδελφοί, καὶ σκοπεῖτε τοὺς
[2]Imitators [3]together [4]of [5]me [1]be, brethren, and consider those
οὕτως περιπατοῦντας καθὼς ἔχετε τύπον ἡμᾶς. 18 πολ-
thus walking as ye have [[2]for] [3]a [4]pattern [1]us; [6]many
λοὶ γὰρ περιπατοῦσιν οὓς πολλάκις ἔλεγον ὑμῖν, νῦν.δὲ
[5]for are walking [of] whom often I told you, and now
καὶ κλαίων λέγω, τοὺς ἐχθροὺς τοῦ σταυροῦ τοῦ
even weeping I tell [you, they are] the enemies of the cross
χριστοῦ· 19 ὧν τὸ τέλος ἀπώλεια, ὧν ὁ θεὸς ἡ κοιλία,
of Christ: whose end [is] destruction, whose God [is] the belly,
καὶ ἡ δόξα ἐν τῇ.αἰσχύνῃ.αὐτῶν, οἱ τὰ.ἐπίγεια φρονοῦντες.
and the glory in their shame, who earthly things mind:
20 ἡμῶν.γὰρ τὸ πολίτευμα ἐν οὐρανοῖς ὑπάρχει, ἐξ οὗ
for of us the commonwealth in [the] heavens exists, from which
καὶ σωτῆρα ἀπεκδεχόμεθα κύριον Ἰησοῦν χριστόν, 21 ὃς
also [as] Saviour we are awaiting [the] Lord Jesus Christ, who
μετασχηματίσει τὸ σῶμα τῆς ταπεινώσεως ἡμῶν, [r]εἰς τὸ γε-
will transform [2]body [3]of [4]humiliation [1]our, for [2]to
νέσθαι αὐτὸ [q]σύμμορφον τῷ σώματι τῆς.δόξης.αὐτοῦ, κατὰ
[3]become [1]it conformed to [2]body [3]of [1]his [4]glory, according to
τὴν ἐνέργειαν τοῦ.δύνασθαι.αὐτὸν καὶ ὑποτάξαι [s]ἑαυτῷ
the working of his power even to subdue to himself
τὰ.πάντα.
all things.

4 Ὥστε, ἀδελφοί.μου ἀγαπητοὶ καὶ ἐπιπόθητοι, χαρὰ καὶ
So that, my brethren beloved and longed for, [2]joy [3]and
στέφανός μου, οὕτως στήκετε ἐν κυρίῳ, ἀγαπητοί. 2 [t]Εὐω-
[4]crown [1]my, thus stand fast in [the] Lord, beloved. Euo-
δίαν παρακαλῶ, καὶ Συντύχην παρακαλῶ, τὸ.αὐτὸ.φρονεῖν
dia I exhort, and Syntyche I exhort, to be of the same mind
ἐν κυρίῳ· 3 [v]καὶ ἐρωτῶ καί σε, [w]σύζυγε γνήσιε, [x]συλ-
in [the] Lord. And I ask also thee, [2]yoke-fellow [1]true, as-
λαμβάνου αὐταῖς, αἵτινες ἐν τῷ εὐαγγελίῳ συνήθλησάν
sist these [women], who in the glad tidings strove together
μοι, μετὰ καὶ Κλήμεντος, καὶ τῶν λοιπῶν συνεργῶν.μου,
with me; with also Clement, and the rest of my fellow-workers,
ὧν τὰ ὀνόματα ἐν βίβλῳ ζωῆς.
whose names [are] in [the] book of life.

4 Χαίρετε ἐν κυρίῳ πάντοτε· πάλιν ἐρῶ, χαίρετε.
Rejoice in [the] Lord always: again I will say, rejoice.
5 τὸ.ἐπιεικὲς.ὑμῶν γνωσθήτω πᾶσιν ἀνθρώποις. ὁ κύριος
[2]Your [3]gentleness [1]let be known to all men. The Lord [is]
ἐγγύς. 6 Μηδὲν μεριμνᾶτε, ἀλλ' ἐν παντὶ τῇ.προσευχῇ
near. Nothing be careful about, but in everything by prayer
καὶ τῇ.δεήσει μετὰ εὐχαριστίας τὰ.αἰτήματα.ὑμῶν γνωρι-
and by supplication with thanksgiving [2]your [3]requests [1]let be made
ζέσθω πρὸς τὸν θεόν· 7 καὶ ἡ εἰρήνη τοῦ θεοῦ ἡ ὑπερέχουσα
known to God; and the peace of God which surpasses
πάντα νοῦν φρουρήσει τὰς.καρδίας.ὑμῶν καὶ τὰ νοήματα
every understanding shall guard your hearts and [2]thoughts
ὑμῶν ἐν χριστῷ Ἰησοῦ. 8 Τὸ.λοιπόν, ἀδελφοί, ὅσα
[1]your in Christ Jesus. For the rest, brethren, whatsoever [things]

p — κανόνι, τὸ αὐτὸ φρονεῖν GLTTrA. q συν- T. r — εἰς τὸ γενέσθαι αὐτὸ GLTTrAW. s αὐτῷ LTTrA. t Εὐοδίαν EGLTTrAW. v ναί yea GLTTrAW. w γνήσιε σύνζυγε LTTrA. x συν- TTrA.

ἐστὶν ἀληθῆ, ὅσα σεμνά, ὅσα δίκαια, ὅσα ἁγνά,
are true, whatsoever venerable, whatsoever just, whatsoever pure,
ὅσα προσφιλῆ, ὅσα εὔφημα, εἴ τις ἀρετὴ καὶ εἴ τις
whatsoever lovely, whatsoever of good report; if any virtue and if any
ἔπαινος, ταῦτα λογίζεσθε· 9 ἃ καὶ ἐμάθετε καὶ παρελάβετε
praise, these things consider. What also ye learned and received
καὶ ἠκούσατε καὶ εἴδετε ἐν ἐμοί, ταῦτα πράσσετε· καὶ ὁ θεὸς
and heard and saw in me, these things do; and the God
τῆς εἰρήνης ἔσται μεθ' ὑμῶν. 10 Ἐχάρην.δὲ ἐν κυρίῳ
of peace shall be with you. But I rejoiced in [the] Lord
μεγάλως, ὅτι ἤδη.ποτὲ ἀνεθάλετε τὸ ὑπὲρ ἐμοῦ φρονεῖν·
greatly, that now at length ye revived [your] [2]of [3]me [1]thinking;
ἐφ'.ᾧ καὶ ἐφρονεῖτε, ἠκαιρεῖσθε.δέ. 11 οὐχ ὅτι
although also ye were thinking, but ye were lacking opportunity. Not that
καθ' ὑστέρησιν λέγω· ἐγὼ.γὰρ ἔμαθον ἐν οἷς εἰμι,
as to destitution I speak; for I learned in what [circumstances] I am,
αὐτάρκης εἶναι. 12 οἶδα.[y]δὲ‖ ταπεινοῦσθαι, οἶδα.καὶ
content to be. And I know [how] to be brought low, and I know [how]
περισσεύειν· ἐν παντὶ καὶ ἐν πᾶσιν μεμύημαι καὶ χορτά-
to abound. In everything and in all things I am initiated both to be
ζεσθαι καὶ πεινᾷν, καὶ περισσεύειν καὶ ὑστερεῖσθαι· 13 πάντα
full and to hunger, both to abound and to be deficient. [5]All [6]things
ἰσχύω ἐν τῷ ἐνδυναμοῦντί με [z]χριστῷ.‖ 14 πλὴν
[1]I [2]am [3]strong [4]for in the [2]who [3]empowers [4]me [1]Christ. But
καλῶς ἐποιήσατε, [a]συγκοινωνήσαντές‖ μου τῇ θλίψει. 15 οἴδατε
well ye did, having fellowship in my tribulation. [2]Know
δὲ καὶ ὑμεῖς, Φιλιππήσιοι, ὅτι ἐν ἀρχῇ τοῦ εὐαγγελίου,
[1]and also ye, O Philippians, that in [the] beginning of the glad tidings,
ὅτε ἐξῆλθον ἀπὸ Μακεδονίας, οὐδεμία μοι ἐκκλησία ἐκοι-
when I came out from Macedonia, not any [4]with [5]me [1]assembly [2]had
νώνησεν εἰς λόγον δόσεως καὶ [b]λήψεως,‖ εἰ.μὴ ὑμεῖς
[3]fellowship with regard to an account of giving and receiving, except ye
μόνοι· 16 ὅτι καὶ ἐν Θεσσαλονίκῃ καὶ ἅπαξ καὶ δὶς [c]εἰς‖ τὴν
alone; because also in Thessalonica both once and twice for
χρείαν.μοι ἐπέμψατε. 17 οὐχ ὅτι ἐπιζητῶ τὸ δόμα, [d]ἀλλ'‖
my need ye sent. Not that I seek after gift, but
ἐπιζητῶ τὸν καρπὸν τὸν πλεονάζοντα εἰς λόγον.ὑμῶν·
I seek after fruit that abounds to your account.
18 ἀπέχω.δὲ πάντα καὶ περισσεύω· πεπλήρωμαι, δεξάμενος
But I have all things and abound; I am full, having received
παρὰ Ἐπαφροδίτου τὰ παρ' ὑμῶν, ὀσμὴν εὐωδίας,
from Epaphroditus the things from you, an odour of a sweet smell,
θυσίαν δεκτήν, εὐάρεστον τῷ θεῷ. 19 ὁ δὲ θεός.μου πληρώσει
a sacrifice acceptable, well-pleasing to God. But my God will fill up
πᾶσαν χρείαν.ὑμῶν κατὰ [e]τὸν.πλοῦτον‖.αὐτοῦ ἐν δόξῃ ἐν
all your need according to his riches in glory in
χριστῷ Ἰησοῦ. 20 τῷ.δὲ θεῷ καὶ πατρὶ ἡμῶν ἡ δόξα εἰς
Christ Jesus. But to the God and Father of us [be] glory to
τοὺς αἰῶνας τῶν αἰώνων. ἀμήν.
the ages of the ages. Amen.

21 Ἀσπάσασθε πάντα ἅγιον ἐν χριστῷ Ἰησοῦ. ἀσπάζον-
Salute every saint in Christ Jesus. [8]Sa-
ται ὑμᾶς οἱ σὺν ἐμοὶ ἀδελφοί. 22 ἀσπάζονται ὑμᾶς πάν-
lute [9]you [1]the [3]with [4]me [2]brethren. [10]Salute [11]you [7]all

are true, whatsoever things *are* honest, whatsoever things *are* just, whatsoever things *are* pure, whatsoever things *are* lovely, whatsoever things *are* of good report; if *there be* any virtue, and if *there be* any praise, think on these things.
9 Those things, which ye have both learned, and received, and heard, and seen in me, do: and the God of peace shall be with you.
10 But I rejoiced in the Lord greatly, that now at the last your care of me hath flourished again; wherein ye were also careful, but ye lacked opportunity.
11 Not that I speak in respect of want: for I have learned, in whatsoever state I am, *therewith* to be content.
12 I know both how to be abased, and I know how to abound: every where and in all things I am instructed both to be full and to be hungry, both to abound and to suffer need.
13 I can do all things through Christ which strengtheneth me.
14 Notwithstanding ye have well done, that ye did communicate with my affliction.
15 Now ye Philippians know also, that in the beginning of the gospel, when I departed from Macedonia, no church communicated with me as concerning giving and receiving, but ye only.
16 For even in Thessalonica ye sent once and again unto my necessity.
17 Not because I desire a gift: but I desire fruit that may abound to your account.
18 But I have all, and abound: I am full, having received of Epaphroditus the things *which were sent* from you, an odour of a sweet smell, a sacrifice acceptable, wellpleasing to God.
19 But my God shall supply all your need according to his riches in glory by Christ Jesus.
20 Now unto God and our Father *be* glory for ever and ever. Amen.
21 Salute every saint

---

[y] καὶ GLTTrAW. [z] — χριστῷ (*read* τῷ him) GLTTrAW. [a] συν- T. [b] λήμψεως LTTrA.
[c] [εἰς] L. [d] ἀλλὰ LTTrAW. [e] τὸ πλοῦτος LTTrAW.

in Christ Jesus. The brethren which are with me greet you. 22 All the saints salute you, chiefly they that are of Cæsar's household. 23 The grace of our Lord Jesus Christ *be* with you all. Amen.

τες οἱ ἅγιοι, μάλιστα.δὲ οἱ ἐκ τῆς Καίσαρος οἰκίας. 23 Ἡ
[8]the [9]saints, and especially those of the [2]of [3]Cæsar [1]household. The
χάρις τοῦ.κυρίου.[f]ἡμῶν‖ Ἰησοῦ χριστοῦ μετὰ [g]πάντων
grace of our Lord Jesus Christ [be] with [2]all
ὑμῶν.‖ [h]ἀμήν.‖
[1]you. Amen.
[i]Πρὸς Φιλιππησίους ἐγράφη ἀπὸ Ῥώμης, δι' Ἐπα-
To [the] Philippians written from Rome, by Epa-
φροδίτου.‖
phroditus.

---

[k]Η ΠΡΟΣ ΚΟΛΑΣΣΑΕΙΣ ΕΠΙΣΤΟΛΗ ΠΑΥΛΟΥ.‖
THE [4]TO [[5]THE] [6]COLOSSIANS [1]EPISTLE [2]OF [3]PAUL.

PAUL, an apostle of Jesus Christ by the will of God, and Timotheus *our* brother, 2 to the saints and faithful brethren in Christ which are at Colosse: Grace *be* unto you, and peace, from God our Father and the Lord Jesus Christ.

ΠΑΥΛΟΣ ἀπόστολος [l]Ἰησοῦ χριστοῦ‖ διὰ θελήματος θεοῦ, καὶ
Paul apostle of Jesus Christ by [2]will [1]God's, and
Τιμόθεος ὁ ἀδελφός, 2 τοῖς ἐν [m]Κολασσαῖς‖ ἁγίοις καὶ πισ-
Timotheus the brother, to the [7]in [8]Colosse [1]saints [2]and [3]faith-
τοῖς ἀδελφοῖς ἐν χριστῷ·[n] χάρις ὑμῖν καὶ εἰρήνη ἀπὸ θεοῦ
ful [4]brethren [5]in [6]Christ. Grace to you and peace from God
πατρὸς.ἡμῶν [o]καὶ κυρίου Ἰησοῦ χριστοῦ.‖
our Father and [the] Lord Jesus Christ.

3 We give thanks to God and the Father of our Lord Jesus Christ, praying always for you, 4 since we heard of your faith in Christ Jesus, and of the love *which ye have* to all the saints, 5 for the hope which is laid up for you in heaven, whereof ye heard before in the word of the truth of the gospel; 6 which is come unto you, as *it is* in all the world; and bringeth forth fruit, as *it doth* also in you, since the day ye heard *of it*, and knew the grace of God in truth: 7 as ye also learned of Epaphras our dear fellowservant, who is for you a faithful minister of Christ; 8 who also declared unto us your love in the Spirit.

3 Εὐχαριστοῦμεν τῷ θεῷ [p]καὶ‖ πατρὶ τοῦ.κυρίου.ἡμῶν Ἰη-
We give thanks to the God and Father of our Lord Je-
σοῦ χριστοῦ, πάντοτε [q]περὶ‖ ὑμῶν προσευχόμενοι· 4 ἀκού-
sus Christ, continually [2]for [3]you [1]praying, having
σαντες τὴν.πίστιν.ὑμῶν ἐν χριστῷ Ἰησοῦ, καὶ τὴν ἀγάπην
heard of your faith in Christ Jesus, and the love
[r]τὴν‖ εἰς πάντας τοὺς ἁγίους, 5 διὰ τὴν ἐλπίδα
which [ye have] towards all the saints, on account of the hope
τὴν ἀποκειμένην ὑμῖν ἐν τοῖς οὐρανοῖς, ἣν προηκούσατε
which [is] laid up for you in the heavens; which ye heard of before
ἐν τῷ λόγῳ τῆς ἀληθείας τοῦ εὐαγγελίου, 6 τοῦ παρόντος εἰς
in the word of the truth of the glad tidings, which are come to
ὑμᾶς, καθὼς καὶ ἐν παντὶ τῷ κόσμῳ, [s]καὶ‖ ἔστιν καρποφορού-
you, even as also in all the world, and are bringing forth
μενον[t], καθὼς καὶ ἐν ὑμῖν, ἀφ' ἧς.ἡμέρας ἠκούσατε καὶ
fruit, even as also among you, from the day in which ye heard and
ἐπέγνωτε τὴν χάριν τοῦ θεοῦ ἐν ἀληθείᾳ· 7 καθὼς [u]καὶ‖
knew the grace of God in truth: even as also
ἐμάθετε ἀπὸ Ἐπαφρᾶ τοῦ ἀγαπητοῦ συνδούλου ἡμῶν, ὅς
ye learned from Epaphras [2]beloved [3]fellow-bondman [1]our, who
ἐστιν πιστὸς ὑπὲρ [v]ὑμῶν‖ διάκονος τοῦ χριστοῦ, 8 ὁ καὶ
is [2]faithful [6]for [7]you [1]a [3]servant [4]of [5]Christ, who also
δηλώσας ἡμῖν τὴν.ὑμῶν.ἀγάπην ἐν πνεύματι.
signified to us your love in [the] Spirit.

---

f — ἡμῶν (*read* of the Lord) LTTrAW. g τοῦ πνεύματος ὑμῶν your spirit LTTrAW. h — ἀμήν [L]TTr[A]. i — *the subscription* GLTW; Πρὸς Φιλιππησίους TrA. k + τοῦ Ἀποστόλου of the Apostle E; Πρὸς Κολοσσαεῖς ET; Παῦλου ἐπιστολὴ πρὸς Κολοσσαεῖς G; Πρὸς Κολασσαεῖς LTrAW. l χριστοῦ Ἰησοῦ LTTrAW. m Κολοσσαῖς EGTW. n + Ἰησοῦ Jesus L. o — καὶ κυρίου Ἰησοῦ χριστοῦ G[L]TTrAW. p — καὶ (*read* to God [the] Father) LA. q ὑπὲρ LTr. r ἣν ἔχετε which ye have LTTrAW. s — καὶ LTTrAW. t + καὶ αὐξανόμενον and growing GLTTrAW. u — καὶ LTTrAW. v ἡμῶν us LTrA.

9 Διὰ τοῦτο καὶ ἡμεῖς ἀφ' ἧς.ἡμέρας ἠκούσαμεν,
On account of this also we from the day in which we heard [of it],
οὐ.παυόμεθα ὑπὲρ ὑμῶν προσευχόμενοι καὶ αἰτούμενοι ἵνα
do not cease [2]for [3]you [1]praying and asking that
πληρωθῆτε τὴν ἐπίγνωσιν τοῦ.θελήματος.αὐτοῦ ἐν πάσῃ
ye may be filled with the knowledge of his will in all
σοφίᾳ καὶ συνέσει πνευματικῇ, 10 περιπατῆσαι [w]ὑμᾶς‖
wisdom and [2]understanding [1]spiritual, [5]to [6]walk [[3]for] [4]you
ἀξίως τοῦ κυρίου εἰς πᾶσαν [x]ἀρέσκειαν‖ ἐν παντὶ ἔργῳ ἀγαθῷ
worthily of the Lord to all pleasing, in every [2]work [1]good
καρποφοροῦντες καὶ αὐξανόμενοι [y]εἰς τὴν ἐπίγνωσιν‖ τοῦ
bringing forth fruit and growing into the knowledge
θεοῦ· 11 ἐν πάσῃ δυνάμει δυναμούμενοι κατὰ τὸ κράτος
of God; with all power being strengthened according to the might
τῆς.δόξης.αὐτοῦ εἰς πᾶσαν ὑπομονὴν καὶ μακροθυμίαν μετὰ
of his glory to all endurance and longsuffering with
χαρᾶς· 12 εὐχαριστοῦντες τῷ πατρί, τῷ [z] ἱκανώσαντι [a]ἡμᾶς‖
joy; giving thanks to the Father, who made [2]competent [1]us
εἰς τὴν μερίδα τοῦ κλήρου τῶν ἁγίων ἐν τῷ φωτί, 13 ὃς
for the share of the inheritance of the saints in the light, who
[b]ἐρρύσατο‖ ἡμᾶς ἐκ τῆς ἐξουσίας τοῦ σκότους, καὶ μετέστη-
delivered us from the authority of darkness, and trans-
σεν εἰς τὴν βασιλείαν τοῦ υἱοῦ τῆς.ἀγάπης.αὐτοῦ, 14 ἐν
lated [us] into the kingdom of the Son of his love: in
ᾧ ἔχομεν τὴν ἀπολύτρωσιν [c]διὰ τοῦ.αἵματος.αὐτοῦ,‖ τὴν
whom we have redemption through his blood, the
ἄφεσιν τῶν ἁμαρτιῶν· 15 ὅς ἐστιν εἰκὼν τοῦ θεοῦ τοῦ
remission of sins; who is [the] image of God the
ἀοράτου, πρωτότοκος πάσης κτίσεως· 16 ὅτι ἐν αὐτῷ ἐ-
invisible, firstborn of all creation; because by him were
κτίσθη τὰ.πάντα, [d]τὰ‖ ἐν τοῖς οὐρανοῖς καὶ [e]τὰ‖ ἐπὶ τῆς
created all things, the things in the heavens and the things upon the
γῆς, τὰ ὁρατὰ καὶ τὰ ἀόρατα, εἴτε θρόνοι εἴτε κυριότητες
earth, the visible and the invisible, whether thrones, or lordships,
εἴτε ἀρχαὶ εἴτε ἐξουσίαι· τὰ.πάντα δι' αὐτοῦ καὶ εἰς αὐτὸν
or principalities, or authorities: all things by him and for him
ἔκτισται· 17 καὶ αὐτός ἐστιν πρὸ πάντων, καὶ τὰ.πάντα
have been created. And he is before all, and all things
ἐν αὐτῷ συνέστηκεν· 18 καὶ αὐτός ἐστιν ἡ κεφαλὴ τοῦ σώμα-
in him subsist. And he is the head of the body,
τος τῆς ἐκκλησίας· ὅς ἐστιν ἀρχή, πρωτότοκος ἐκ
the assembly; who is [the] beginning, firstborn from among
τῶν νεκρῶν, ἵνα γένηται ἐν πᾶσιν αὐτὸς πρωτεύων·
the dead, that [2]might [3]be [4]in [5]all [6]things [1]he holding the first place;
19 ὅτι ἐν αὐτῷ εὐδόκησεν πᾶν τὸ πλήρωμα κατοικῆσαι,
because in him [4]was [5]pleased [1]all [2]the [3]fulness to dwell,
20 καὶ δι' αὐτοῦ ἀποκαταλλάξαι τὰ.πάντα εἰς αὐτόν, εἰρη-
and by him to reconcile all things to itself, having
νοποιήσας διὰ τοῦ αἵματος τοῦ.σταυροῦ.αὐτοῦ, [f]δι' αὐτοῦ,‖
made peace by the blood of his cross, by him,
εἴτε τὰ ἐπὶ τῆς γῆς, εἴτε τὰ ἐν τοῖς οὐρανοῖς. 21 καὶ
whether the things on the earth, or the things in the heavens. And
ὑμᾶς ποτε ὄντας ἀπηλλοτριωμένους καὶ ἐχθροὺς τῇ διανοίᾳ
you once being alienated and enemies in mind

9 For this cause we
also, since the day we
heard *it*, do not cease
to pray for you, and
to desire that ye might
be filled with the
knowledge of his will
in all wisdom and
spiritual understand-
ing; 10 that ye might
walk worthy of the
Lord unto all pleas-
ing, being fruitful in
every good work, and
increasing in the
knowledge of God;
11 strengthened with
all might, according
to his glorious power,
unto all patience and
longsuffering with
joyfulness; 12 giving
thanks unto the Fa-
ther, which hath made
us meet to be par-
takers of the inherit-
ance of the saints in
light: 13 who hath de-
livered us from the
power of darkness,
and hath translated
us into the kingdom of
his dear Son: 14 in
whom we have re-
demption through his
blood, *even* the for-
giveness of sins: 15 who
is the image of the in-
visible God, the first-
born of every crea-
ture: 16 for by him
were all things cre-
ated, that are in hea-
ven, and that are
in earth, visible and
invisible, whether
they be thrones, or
dominions, or princi-
palities, or powers:
all things were cre-
ated by him, and for
him: 17 and he is be-
fore all things, and by
him all things con-
sist. 18 And he is
the head of the body,
the church: who is
the beginning, the
firstborn from the
dead; that in all *things*
he might have the pre-
eminence. 19 For it
pleased *the Father*
that in him should all
fulness dwell; 20 and,
having made peace
through the blood of
his cross, by him to re-
concile all things unto
himself; by him, *I
say*, whether *they be*
things in earth, or
things in heaven.
21 And you, that were
sometime alienated
and enemies in *your*
mind by wicked works,

[w] — ὑμᾶς GLTTrA. [x] ἀρεσκίαν T. [y] τῇ ἐπιγνώσει by the knowledge GLTTrAW. [z] + καλέσαντι καὶ called and L. [a] ὑμᾶς you T. [b] ἐρύσατο TTr. [c] — διὰ τοῦ αἵματος αὐτοῦ GLTTrAW. [d] — τὰ LTTr. [e] — τὰ [L]T[Tr]. [f] — δι' αὐτοῦ LTr.

yet now hath he reconciled 22 in the body of his flesh through death, to present you holy and unblameable and unreproveable in his sight: 23 if ye continue in the faith grounded and settled, and *be* not moved away from the hope of the gospel, which ye have heard, *and* which was preached to every creature which is under heaven; whereof I Paul am made a minister;

24 who now rejoice in my sufferings for you, and fill up that which is behind of the afflictions of Christ in my flesh for his body's sake, which is the church: 25 whereof I am made a minister, according to the dispensation of God which is given to me for you, to fulfil the word of God; 26 *even* the mystery which hath been hid from ages and from generations, but now is made manifest to his saints: 27 to whom God would make known what *is* the riches of the glory of this mystery among the Gentiles; which is Christ in you, the hope of glory: 28 whom we preach, warning every man, and teaching every man in all wisdom; that we may present every man perfect in Christ Jesus: 29 whereunto I also labour, striving according to his working, which worketh in me mightily.

II. For I would that ye knew what great conflict I have for you, and *for* them at Laodicea, and *for* as many as have not seen my face in the flesh; 2 that their hearts might be comforted, being knit

ἐν τοῖς ἔργοις τοῖς πονηροῖς. νυνὶ.δὲ [g]ἀποκατήλλαξεν· 22 ἐν
by ²works ¹wicked, yet now he reconciled in
τῷ σώματι τῆς.σαρκὸς.αὐτοῦ διὰ τοῦ θανάτου[h], παρα-
the body of his flesh through death, to pre-
στῆσαι ὑμᾶς ἁγίους καὶ ἀμώμους καὶ ἀνεγκλήτους κατενώ-
sent you holy and unblamable and unimpeachable before
πιον αὐτοῦ· 23 εἴγε ἐπιμένετε τῇ πίστει τεθεμελιωμένοι
him, if indeed ye continue in the faith founded
καὶ ἑδραῖοι, καὶ μὴ μετακινούμενοι ἀπὸ τῆς ἐλπίδος τοῦ
and firm, and not being moved away from the hope of the
εὐαγγελίου οὗ ἠκούσατε, τοῦ κηρυχθέντος ἐν πάσῃ [i]τῇ[i]
glad tidings, which ye heard, which were proclaimed in all the
κτίσει τῇ ὑπὸ τὸν οὐρανόν, οὗ ἐγενόμην ἐγὼ Παῦλος
creation which [is] under heaven, of which ³became ¹I ²Paul
διάκονος.
servant.

24 Νῦν χαίρω ἐν τοῖς.παθήμασίν.[k]μου[k] ὑπὲρ ὑμῶν, καὶ
Now, I am rejoicing in my sufferings for you, and
ἀνταναπληρῶ τὰ ὑστερήματα τῶν θλίψεων τοῦ χριστοῦ
I am filling up that which is behind of the tribulations of the Christ
ἐν τῇ.σαρκί.μου ὑπὲρ τοῦ.σώματος.αὐτοῦ, ὅ ἐστιν ἡ ἐκ-
in my flesh for his body, which is the as-
κλησία· 25 ἧς ἐγενόμην ἐγὼ διάκονος κατὰ τὴν οἰκονο-
sembly; of which ²became ¹I servant, according to the adminis-
μίαν τοῦ θεοῦ τὴν δοθεῖσάν μοι εἰς ὑμᾶς πληρῶσαι τὸν
tration of God which [is] given me towards you to complete the
λόγον τοῦ θεοῦ, 26 τὸ μυστήριον τὸ ἀποκεκρυμμένον ἀπὸ
word of God, the mystery which has been hidden from
τῶν αἰώνων καὶ ἀπὸ τῶν γενεῶν, [l]νυνὶ[l].δὲ ἐφανερώθη
ages and from generations, but now was made manifest
τοῖς.ἁγίοις.αὐτοῦ· 27 οἷς ἠθέλησεν ὁ θεὸς γνωρίσαι [m]τίς
to his saints; to whom ²did ³will ¹God to make known what
ὁ[m] πλοῦτος τῆς δόξης τοῦ.μυστηρίου.τούτου ἐν τοῖς ἔ-
the riches of the glory of this mystery [are] among the na-
θνεσιν, [n]ὅς[n] ἐστιν χριστὸς ἐν ὑμῖν ἡ ἐλπὶς τῆς δόξης· 28 ὃν
tions, which is Christ in you the hope of glory: whom
ἡμεῖς καταγγέλλομεν, νουθετοῦντες πάντα ἄνθρωπον, καὶ
we announce, admonishing every man, and
διδάσκοντες πάντα ἄνθρωπον ἐν πάσῃ σοφίᾳ, ἵνα παρα-
teaching every man in all wisdom, that we may
στήσωμεν πάντα ἄνθρωπον τέλειον ἐν χριστῷ [o]Ἰησοῦ.[o]
present every man perfect in Christ Jesus.
29 εἰς.ὃ καὶ κοπιῶ, ἀγωνιζόμενος κατὰ τὴν ἐνέργειαν
Whereunto also I labour, striving according to ²working
αὐτοῦ τὴν ἐνεργουμένην ἐν ἐμοὶ ἐν δυνάμει.
¹his which works in me in power.

2 Θέλω.γὰρ ὑμᾶς εἰδέναι ἡλίκον ἀγῶνα ἔχω [p]περὶ[p] ὑμῶν
For I wish you to know how great conflict I have for you,
καὶ τῶν ἐν [q]Λαοδικείᾳ,[q] καὶ ὅσοι οὐχ.[r]ἑωράκασιν[r] τὸ πρόσω-
and those in Laodicea, and as many as have not seen ²face
πόν μου ἐν σαρκί, 2 ἵνα παρακληθῶσιν αἱ.καρδίαι.αὐτῶν,
¹my in flesh; that may be encouraged their hearts,

---

[g] ἀποκατηλλάγητε were ye reconciled L. [h] + [αὐτοῦ] (*read* his death) L. [i] — τῇ LTTrAW. [k] — μου (*read* the sufferings) GLTTrAW. [l] νῦν LTTrA. [m] τί τὸ LTTrAW. [n] ὅ LTrA. [o] — Ἰησοῦ GLTTrAW. [p] ὑπὲρ LTTrA. [q] Λαοδικίᾳ T. [r] ἑώρακαν LTrAW; ἑόρακαν T.

[s]συμβιβασθέντων‖ ἐν ἀγάπῃ, καὶ εἰς [t]πάντα πλοῦτον‖ τῆς
being knit together in love, and to all riches of the
πληροφορίας τῆς συνέσεως, εἰς ἐπίγνωσιν τοῦ μυστηρίου
full assurance of understanding; to [the] knowledge of the mystery
τοῦ θεοῦ [v]καὶ πατρὸς καὶ τοῦ‖ [w]χριστοῦ,‖ 3 ἐν ᾧ εἰσιν
of God and of [the] Father and of the Christ; in which are
πάντες οἱ θησαυροὶ τῆς σοφίας καὶ [x]τῆς‖ γνώσεως ἀπόκρυ-
all the treasures of wisdom and of knowledge hid.
φοι. 4 τοῦτο [y]δὲ‖ λέγω, ἵνα [z]μή τις‖ ὑμᾶς παραλογίζηται ἐν
And this I say, that not anyone you may beguile by
πιθανολογίᾳ· 5 εἰ γὰρ καὶ τῇ σαρκὶ ἄπειμι, ἀλλὰ τῷ
persuasive speech. For if indeed in the flesh I am absent, yet
πνεύματι σὺν ὑμῖν εἰμι, χαίρων καὶ βλέπων ὑμῶν τὴν τάξιν,
in spirit with you I am, rejoicing and seeing your order,
καὶ τὸ στερέωμα τῆς εἰς χριστὸν πίστεως ὑμῶν. 6 ὡς οὖν
and the firmness [4]in [5]Christ [1]of [2]your [3]faith. As therefore
παρελάβετε τὸν χριστὸν Ἰησοῦν τὸν κύριον, ἐν αὐτῷ περιπα-
ye received the Christ, Jesus the Lord, in him walk,
τεῖτε, 7 ἐρριζωμένοι καὶ ἐποικοδομούμενοι ἐν αὐτῷ, καὶ
having been rooted and being built up in him, and
βεβαιούμενοι [a]ἐν‖ τῇ πίστει, καθὼς ἐδιδάχθητε, περισσεύοντες
being confirmed in the faith, even as ye were taught, abounding
[b]ἐν αὐτῇ‖ ἐν εὐχαριστίᾳ.
in it with thanksgiving.

8 Βλέπετε μή τις [c]ὑμᾶς ἔσται‖ ὁ συλαγωγῶν
Take heed lest [4]anyone [10]you [1]there [2]shall [3]be [5]who [6]makes [7]a [8]prey [9]of
διὰ τῆς φιλοσοφίας καὶ κενῆς ἀπάτης, κατὰ τὴν παρά-
through philosophy and empty deceit, according to the tra-
δοσιν τῶν ἀνθρώπων, κατὰ τὰ στοιχεῖα τοῦ κόσμου, καὶ
dition of men, according to the elements of the world, and
οὐ κατὰ χριστόν· 9 ὅτι ἐν αὐτῷ κατοικεῖ πᾶν τὸ πλήρωμα
not according to Christ. For in him dwells all the fulness
τῆς θεότητος σωματικῶς, 10 καί ἐστε ἐν αὐτῷ πεπληρωμένοι·
of the Godhead bodily; and ye are [2]in [3]him [1]complete,
[d]ὅς‖ ἐστιν ἡ κεφαλὴ πάσης ἀρχῆς καὶ ἐξουσίας· 11 ἐν ᾧ
who is the head of all principality and authority, in whom
καὶ περιετμήθητε περιτομῇ ἀχειροποιήτῳ, ἐν τῇ ἀπ-
also ye were circumcised with circumcision not made by hand, in the put-
εκδύσει τοῦ σώματος [e]τῶν ἁμαρτιῶν‖ τῆς σαρκός, ἐν τῇ περι-
ting off of the body of the sins of the flesh, in the circum-
τομῇ τοῦ χριστοῦ, 12 συνταφέντες αὐτῷ ἐν τῷ [f]βαπτίσματι·‖
cision of the Christ; having been buried with him in baptism,
ἐν ᾧ καὶ συνηγέρθητε διὰ τῆς πίστεως τῆς ἐνερ-
in which also ye were raised with [him] through the faith of the work-
γείας τοῦ θεοῦ τοῦ ἐγείραντος αὐτὸν ἐκ [g]τῶν‖ νεκρῶν.
ing of God who raised him from among the dead.
13 καὶ ὑμᾶς νεκροὺς ὄντας [h]ἐν‖ τοῖς παραπτώμασιν καὶ τῇ
And you, [2]dead [1]being in offences and in the
ἀκροβυστίᾳ τῆς σαρκὸς ὑμῶν, [i]συνεζωποίησεν‖ [k]σὺν αὐτῷ,
uncircumcision of your flesh, he quickened together with him,

together in love, and
unto all riches of the
full assurance of un-
derstanding, to the
acknowledgement of
the mystery of God,
and of the Father, and
of Christ; 3 in whom
are hid all the trea-
sures of wisdom and
knowledge. 4 And this
I say, lest any man
should beguile you
with enticing words.
5 For though I be
absent in the flesh, yet
am I with you in the
spirit, joying and be-
holding your order,
and the stedfastness
of your faith in Christ.
6 As ye have there-
fore received Christ
Jesus the Lord, *so* walk
ye in him: 7 rooted
and built up in him,
and stablished in the
faith, as ye have been
taught, abounding
therein with thanks-
giving.

8 Beware lest any
man spoil you through
philosophy and vain
deceit, after the tra-
dition of men, af-
ter the rudiments of
the world, and not
after Christ. 9 For in
him dwelleth all the
fulness of the God-
head bodily. 10 And
ye are complete in
him, which is the head
of all principality and
power: 11 in whom al-
so ye are circumcised
with the circumcision
made without hands,
in putting off the body
of the sins of the flesh
by the circumcision of
Christ: 12 buried with
him in baptism, where-
in also ye are risen
with *him* through the
faith of the operation
of God, who hath rais-
ed him from the dead.
13 And you, being dead
in your sins and
the uncircumcision of
your flesh, hath he
quickened together
with him, having for-

---

[s] συμβιβασθέντες GLTTrAW. [t] πᾶν (+ τὸ the L[Tr]W) πλοῦτος LTTrAW. [v] — καὶ πατρὸς καὶ τοῦ (*read* [even] Christ) GLTTrAW. [w] — χριστοῦ GA. [x] — τῆς LTTrA. [y] — δὲ and T[TrA]. [z] μηδεὶς LTTrAW. [a] — ἐν (*read* τῇ in the) LTTr[A]. [b] — ἐν αὐτῇ TTr[A]. [c] ἔσται ὑμᾶς L. [d] ὅ L. [e] — τῶν ἁμαρτιῶν GLTTrAW. [f] βαπτισμῷ TrA. [g] — τῶν (*read* [the]) LT[A]W. [h] — ἐν (*read* παραπ. in offences) TTr. [i] συνεζωοποίησεν GLTTrAW. [k] + ὑμᾶς you LTTrAW.

given you all trespasses; 14 blotting out the handwriting of ordinances that was against us, which was contrary to us, and took it out of the way, nailing it to his cross; 15 *and* having spoiled principalities and powers, he made a shew of them openly, triumphing over them in it.

χαρισάμενος [l]ἡμῖν[ll] πάντα τὰ παραπτώματα· 14 ἐξαλείψας
having forgiven us all the offences; having blotted out
τὸ καθ' ἡμῶν χειρόγραφον τοῖς δόγμασιν, ὃ ἦν ὑπεναν-
the [5]against [6]us [1]handwriting [2]in [3]the [4]decrees, which was adverse
τίον ἡμῖν, καὶ αὐτὸ ἦρκεν ἐκ τοῦ μέσου, προσηλώσας
to us, also it he has taken out of the midst, having nailed
αὐτὸ τῷ σταυρῷ, 15 ἀπεκδυσάμενος τὰς ἀρχὰς καὶ τὰς
it to the cross; having stripped the principalities and the
ἐξουσίας ἐδειγμάτισεν ἐν-παῤῥησίᾳ, θριαμβεύσας
authorities, he made a show [of them] publicly, leading in triumph
αὐτοὺς ἐν αὐτῷ.
them in it.

16 Let no man therefore judge you in meat, or in drink, or in respect of an holyday, or of the new moon, or of the sabbath *days:* 17 which are a shadow of things to come; but the body *is* of Christ. 18 Let no man beguile you of your reward in a voluntary humility and worshipping of angels, intruding into those things which he hath not seen, vainly puffed up by his fleshly mind, 19 and not holding the Head, from which all the body by joints and bands having nourishment ministered, and knit together, increaseth with the increase of God.

16 Μὴ οὖν τις ὑμᾶς κρινέτω ἐν βρώσει [m]ἢ[ll] ἐν πόσει,
[2]Not [3]therefore [4]anyone [6]you [1]let [5]judge in meat or in drink,
ἢ ἐν μέρει ἑορτῆς ἢ [n]νουμηνίας[ll] ἢ σαββάτων· 17 [o]ἅ[ll] ἐστιν
or in respect of feast, or new moon, or sabbaths, which are
σκιὰ τῶν-μελλόντων, τὸ-δὲ σῶμα [p]τοῦ[ll] χριστοῦ. 18 μη-
a shadow of things to come; but the body [is] of the Christ. [2]No
δεὶς ὑμᾶς καταβραβευέτω θέλων ἐν ταπεινοφροσύνῃ καὶ
[3]one [5]you [1]let [4]defraud of the prize, doing [his] will in humility and
[q]θρησκείᾳ[ll] τῶν ἀγγέλων, ἃ [r]μὴ[ll] [s]ἑώρακεν[ll] ἐμβατεύων,
worship of the angels, [3]things [4]which [7]not [5]he [6]has [8]seen [1]intruding [2]into,
εἰκῆ φυσιούμενος ὑπὸ τοῦ νοὸς τῆς-σαρκὸς-αὐτοῦ, 19 καὶ οὐ
vainly puffed up by the mind of his flesh, and not
κρατῶν τὴν κεφαλήν, ἐξ οὗ πᾶν τὸ σῶμα διὰ τῶν ἁφῶν
holding fast the head, from whom all the body, by the joints
καὶ συνδέσμων ἐπιχορηγούμενον καὶ [t]συμβιβαζόμενον,[ll] αὔξει
and bands being supplied and knit together, increases
τὴν αὔξησιν τοῦ θεοῦ.
[with] the increase of God.

20 Wherefore if ye be dead with Christ from the rudiments of the world, why, as though living in the world, are ye subject to ordinances, 21 (Touch not; taste not; handle not; 22 which all are to perish with the using;) after the commandments and doctrines of men? 23 which things have indeed a shew of wisdom in will worship, and humility, and neglecting of the body; not in any honour to the satisfying of the flesh.

20 Εἰ [v]οὖν[ll] ἀπεθάνετε σὺν [w]τῷ[ll] χριστῷ ἀπὸ τῶν στοιχείων
If then ye died with the Christ from the elements
τοῦ κόσμου, τί ὡς ζῶντες ἐν κόσμῳ δογματί-
of the world, why as if alive in [the] world do ye subject yourselves
ζεσθε; [x] 21 Μὴ-ἅψῃ, μηδὲ-γεύσῃ, μηδὲ-θίγῃς·
to decrees? Thou mayest not handle, Thou mayest not taste, Thou mayest not touch,
22 ἅ ἐστιν πάντα εἰς φθορὰν τῇ ἀποχρήσει· κατὰ
(which things are all unto corruption in the using,) according to
τὰ ἐντάλματα καὶ διδασκαλίας τῶν ἀνθρώπων· [x] 23 ἅτινά
the injunctions and teachings of men, which
ἐστιν λόγον μὲν ἔχοντα σοφίας ἐν [y]ἐθελοθρησκείᾳ[ll]
are [2]an [3]appearance [4]indeed [1]having of wisdom in voluntary worship
καὶ ταπεινοφροσύνῃ [z]καὶ[ll] [a]ἀφειδίᾳ[ll] σώματος, οὐκ ἐν
and humility and unsparing treatment of [the] body, not in
τιμῇ τινι πρὸς πλησμονὴν τῆς σαρκός.[x]
[3]honour [1]a [2]certain for satisfaction of the flesh.

III. If ye then be risen with Christ, seek those things which are above, where Christ sitteth on the right hand of God. 2 Set your affection on things above, not on things on the earth. 3 For ye are dead, and

3 Εἰ οὖν συνηγέρθητε τῷ χριστῷ, τὰ ἄνω ζητεῖτε,
If therefore ye were raised with Christ, [2]the [3]things [4]above [1]seek,
οὗ ὁ χριστός ἐστιν ἐν δεξιᾷ τοῦ θεοῦ καθήμενος·
where the Christ is [2]at [3the] [4]right [5]hand [6]of [7]God [1]sitting:
2 τὰ ἄνω φρονεῖτε, μὴ τὰ ἐπὶ τῆς γῆς. 3 ἀπεθάνετε
[9]the [10]things [11]above [8]mind, not the things on the earth; [2]ye [3]died

---

[l] ὑμῖν you E. [m] καὶ and A. [n] νεομηνίας LTr. [o] ὅ LA. [p] — τοῦ (*read* of Christ) GW. [q] θρησκίᾳ T. [r] — μὴ (*read* ἐμβ. [1]standing [2]on) [L]TTrA. [s] ἑόρακεν TA. [t] συν- TA. [v] — οὖν GLTTrAW. [w] — τῷ GLTTrAW. [x] *Continue question to end of verse* 21 GW; *to end of verse* 22 LT; *to end of verse* 23 A. [y] ἐθελοθρησκίᾳ T. [z] [καὶ] L. [a] ἀφειδείᾳ L.

γάρ, καὶ ἡ.ζωὴ.ὑμῶν κέκρυπται σὺν τῷ χριστῷ ἐν τῷ θεῷ·
[1]for, and your life has been hid with the Christ in God.
4 ὅταν ὁ χριστὸς φανερωθῇ ἡ.ζωὴ.[b]ἡμῶν,‖ τότε καὶ
When the Christ [3]may [4]be [5]manifested [1]our [2]life, then also
ὑμεῖς σὺν αὐτῷ φανερωθήσεσθε ἐν δόξῃ.
ye with him shall be manifested in glory.

5 Νεκρώσατε οὖν τὰ μέλη [c]ὑμῶν‖ τὰ ἐπὶ τῆς γῆς,
Put to death therefore [2]members [1]your which [are] on the earth,
πορνείαν, ἀκαθαρσίαν, πάθος, ἐπιθυμίαν κακήν, καὶ τὴν
fornication, uncleanness, passion, [2]desire [1]evil, and
πλεονεξίαν, ἥτις ἐστὶν εἰδωλολατρεία, 6 δι' [d]ἃ‖
covetousness, which is idolatry. On account of which things
ἔρχεται [e]ἡ‖ ὀργὴ τοῦ θεοῦ [f]ἐπὶ τοὺς υἱοὺς τῆς ἀπειθείας·‖
comes the wrath of God upon the sons of disobedience.
7 ἐν οἷς καὶ ὑμεῖς περιεπατήσατέ ποτε ὅτε ἐζῆτε ἐν
Among whom also ye walked once when ye were living in
[g]αὐτοῖς·‖ 8 νυνὶ.δὲ ἀπόθεσθε καὶ ὑμεῖς τὰ.πάντα, ὀργήν,
these things. But now, put off also ye, all [these] things, wrath,
θυμόν, κακίαν, βλασφημίαν, αἰσχρολογίαν ἐκ τοῦ στόμα-
indignation, malice, blasphemy, foul language out of [2]mouth
τος ὑμῶν. 9 Μὴ.ψεύδεσθε εἰς ἀλλήλους, ἀπεκδυσάμενοι τὸν
[1]your. Do not lie to one another, having put off the
παλαιὸν ἄνθρωπον σὺν ταῖς.πράξεσιν.αὐτοῦ, 10 καὶ ἐνδυσά-
old man with his deeds, and having
μενοι τὸν νέον τὸν ἀνακαινούμενον εἰς ἐπίγνωσιν κατ'
put on the new that [is] being renewed into knowledge according to
εἰκόνα τοῦ κτίσαντος αὐτόν· 11 ὅπου οὐκ.ἔνι
[the] image of him who created him; where there is not
Ἕλλην καὶ Ἰουδαῖος, περιτομὴ καὶ ἀκροβυστία, βάρβαρος,
Greek and Jew, circumcision and uncircumcision, barbarian,
Σκύθης, δοῦλος, [h]ἐλεύθερος· ἀλλὰ [i]τὰ‖.πάντα καὶ ἐν πᾶσιν
Scythian, bondman, free; but [3]all [4]things [5]and [6]in [7]all
χριστός.
[[2]is] [1]Christ.

12 Ἐνδύσασθε οὖν, ὡς ἐκλεκτοὶ [k]τοῦ‖ θεοῦ, ἅγιοι καὶ
Put on therefore, as elect of God, holy and
ἠγαπημένοι, σπλάγχνα [l]οἰκτιρμῶν,‖ χρηστότητα, ταπεινο-
beloved, bowels of compassions, kindness, humi-
φροσύνην, [m]πρᾳότητα,‖ μακροθυμίαν· 13 ἀνεχόμενοι ἀλ-
lity, meekness, long-suffering; bearing with one
λήλων, καὶ χαριζόμενοι ἑαυτοῖς, ἐάν τις πρός τινα ἔχῃ
another, and forgiving each other, if any against any should have
μομφήν· καθὼς καὶ ὁ [n]χριστὸς‖ ἐχαρίσατο ὑμῖν, οὕτως καὶ
a complaint; even as also the Christ forgave you, so also [do]
ὑμεῖς· 14 ἐπὶ.πᾶσιν.δὲ τούτοις τὴν ἀγάπην, [o]ἥτις‖ ἐστὶν
ye. And to all these [add] love, which is [the]
σύνδεσμος τῆς τελειότητος· 15 καὶ ἡ εἰρήνη [p]τοῦ θεοῦ‖ βρα-
bond of perfectness. And the peace of God let
βευέτω ἐν ταῖς.καρδίαις.ὑμῶν, εἰς ἣν καὶ ἐκλήθητε ἐν ἑνὶ σώ-
preside in your hearts, to which also ye were called in one
ματι· καὶ εὐχάριστοι γίνεσθε. 16 ὁ λόγος τοῦ χριστοῦ ἐνοικείτω
body, and thankful be. The word of the Christ let dwell

your life is hid with
Christ in God. 4 When
Christ, *who is* our
life, shall appear, then
shall ye also appear
with him in glory.

5 Mortify therefore
your members which
are upon the earth;
fornication, unclean-
ness, inordinate affec-
tion, evil concupis-
cence, and covetous-
ness, which is idola-
try: 6 for which
things' sake the wrath
of God cometh on the
children of disobedi-
ence: 7 in the which
ye also walked some
time, when ye lived in
them. 8 But now ye
also put off all these;
anger, wrath, malice,
blasphemy, filthy com-
munication out of
your mouth. 9 Lie not
one to another, seeing
that ye have put off
the old man with his
deeds; 10 and have
put on the new *man*,
which is renewed in
knowledge after the
image of him that
created him: 11 where
there is neither Greek
nor Jew, circumcision
nor uncircumcision,
Barbarian, Scythian,
bond *nor* free: but
Christ *is* all, and in all.

12 Put on therefore,
as the elect of God,
holy and beloved,
bowels of mercies,
kindness, humbleness
of mind, meekness,
longsuffering; 13 for-
bearing one another,
and forgiving one
another, if any man
have a quarrel against
any: even as Christ
forgave you, so also
do ye. 14 And above
all these things *put on*
charity, which is the
bond of perfectness.
15 And let the peace
of God rule in your
hearts, to the which
also ye are called in
one body; and be ye
thankful. 16 Let the
word of Christ dwell
in you richly in all

---

[b] ὑμῶν (*read* your life) TTr. [c] — ὑμῶν (*read* the members) TTrA. [d] ὃ which A. [e] [ἡ] L. [f] — ἐπὶ τοὺς υἱοὺς τῆς ἀπειθείας (*read* ἐν οἷς In which things) [L]TTrA. [g] τούτοις LTTrAW. [h] + καὶ and L. [i] — τὰ T. [k] — τοῦ L. [l] οἰκτιρμοῦ of compassion GLTTrAW. [m] πραΰτητα LTTrAW. [n] κύριος Lord LTrA. [o] ὅ LTTrAW. [p] τοῦ χριστοῦ of the Christ GLTTrAW.

wisdom; teaching and
admonishing one an-
other in psalms and
hymns and spiritual
songs, singing with
grace in your hearts
to the Lord. 17 And
whatsoever ye do in
word or deed, *do* all in
the name of the Lord
Jesus, giving thanks
to God and the Father
by him.

18 Wives, submit
yourselves unto your
own husbands, as it is
fit in the Lord. 19 Hus-
bands, love *your*
wives, and be not
bitter against them.
20 Children, obey
your parents in all
things: for this is well
pleasing unto the Lord.
21 Fathers, provoke
not your children *to*
anger, lest they be
discouraged. 22 Ser-
vants, obey in all
things *your* masters
according to the flesh;
not with eyeservice,
as menpleasers; but
in singleness of heart,
fearing God: 23 and
whatsoever ye do, do
it heartily, as to the
Lord, and not unto
men; 24 knowing that
of the Lord ye shall
receive the reward of
the inheritance: for ye
serve the Lord Christ.
25 But he that doeth
wrong shall receive
for the wrong which
he hath done: and
there is no respect of
persons. IV. Masters,
give unto *your* ser-
vants that which is
just and equal; know-
ing that ye also have
a Master in heaven.

2 Continue in prayer,
and watch in the same
with thanksgiving;
3 withal praying also
for us, that God would
open unto us a door of
utterance, to speak
the mystery of Christ,
for which I am also
in bonds: 4 that I
may make it manifest,

ἐν ὑμῖν πλουσίως, ἐν πάσῃ σοφίᾳ· διδάσκοντες καὶ νουθε-
in you richly, in all wisdom; teaching and admon-
τοῦντες ἑαυτοὺς ψαλμοῖς [q]καὶ‖ ὕμνοις [r]καὶ‖ ᾠδαῖς.πνευματι-
ishing each other in psalms and hymns and [2]songs [1]spiritual
καῖς ἐν [s]χάριτι ᾄδοντες ἐν [t]τῇ καρδίᾳ‖ ὑμῶν [v]τῷ κυρίῳ.‖
with grace singing in [2]heart [1]your to the Lord.
17 καὶ πᾶν ὅ.τι.[w]ἂν‖ ποιῆτε ἐν λόγῳ ἢ ἐν ἔργῳ, πάντα
And everything, whatsoever ye may do in word or in work, [do] all
ἐν ὀνόματι [x]κυρίου Ἰησοῦ,‖ εὐχαριστοῦντες τῷ θεῷ [y]καὶ‖
in [the] name of [the] Lord Jesus, giving thanks to God and
πατρὶ δι' αὐτοῦ.
[the] Father by him.

18 Αἱ γυναῖκες, ὑποτάσσεσθε τοῖς.[z]ἰδίοις‖ ἀνδράσιν, ὡς
Wives, subject yourselves to your own husbands, as
ἀνῆκεν ἐν κυρίῳ. 19 Οἱ ἄνδρες, ἀγαπᾶτε τὰς γυναῖκας[a]
is becoming in [the] Lord. Husbands, love the wives,
καὶ μὴ.πικραίνεσθε πρὸς αὐτάς. 20 Τὰ τέκνα, ὑπακούετε
and be not bitter against them. Children, obey
τοῖς γονεῦσιν κατὰ.πάντα· τοῦτο.γὰρ [b]ἐστὶν εὐάρεστον‖ [c]τῷ‖
the parents in all things; for this is well-pleasing to the
κυρίῳ. 21 Οἱ πατέρες, μὴ.[d]ἐρεθίζετε‖ τὰ.τέκνα.ὑμῶν, ἵνα μὴ
Lord. Fathers, do not provoke your children, that [3]not
ἀθυμῶσιν. 22 Οἱ δοῦλοι, ὑπακούετε κατὰ.πάντα τοῖς
[1]they [2]be disheartened. Bondmen, obey in all things the
κατὰ σάρκα κυρίοις, μὴ ἐν [e]ὀφθαλμοδουλείαις‖ ὡς ἀν-
[2]according [3]to [4]flesh [1]masters, not with eye-services, as
θρωπάρεσκοι, [f]ἀλλ'‖ ἐν ἁπλότητι καρδίας, φοβούμενοι [g]τὸν
men-pleasers, but in simplicity of heart, fearing
θεόν.‖ 23 [h]καὶ πᾶν.ὅ.τι‖ ἐὰν ποιῆτε, ἐκ.ψυχῆς ἐργάζεσθε, ὡς
God. And whatsoever ye may do, [2]heartily [1]work, as
τῷ κυρίῳ καὶ οὐκ ἀνθρώποις· 24 εἰδότες ὅτι ἀπὸ κυρίου
to the Lord and not to men; knowing that from [the] Lord
[i]ἀπολήψεσθε‖ τὴν ἀνταπόδοσιν τῆς κληρονομίας· τῷ.[k]γὰρ‖
ye shall receive the recompense of the inheritance, for the
κυρίῳ χριστῷ δουλεύετε. 25 ὁ.[l]δὲ‖ ἀδικῶν [m]κομιεῖται
Lord Christ ye serve. But he that does wrong shall receive [for]
ὃ ἠδίκησεν, καὶ οὐκ.ἔστιν [n]προσωποληψία.‖ 4 Οἱ κύριοι,
what he did wrong, and there is no respect of persons. Masters,
τὸ δίκαιον καὶ τὴν ἰσότητα τοῖς δούλοις
that which [is] just and that which [is] equal to bondmen
παρέχεσθε, εἰδότες ὅτι καὶ ὑμεῖς ἔχετε κύριον ἐν [o]οὐρανοῖς.‖
give, knowing that also ye have a Master in [the] heavens.

2 Τῇ προσευχῇ προσκαρτερεῖτε, γρηγοροῦντες ἐν αὐτῇ ἐν
In prayer stedfastly continue, watching in it with
εὐχαριστίᾳ· 3 προσευχόμενοι ἅμα καὶ περὶ ἡμῶν, ἵνα ὁ θεὸς
thanksgiving; praying withal also for us, that God
ἀνοίξῃ ἡμῖν θύραν τοῦ λόγου λαλῆσαι τὸ μυστήριον τοῦ
may open to us a door of the word to speak the mystery of the
χριστοῦ, δι' [p]ὃ‖ καὶ δέδεμαι, 4 ἵνα φανε-
Christ, on account of which also I have been bound, that I may make

[q] — καὶ LTTrAW. [r] — καὶ LTTrAW. [s] + τῇ LTTrAW. [t] ταῖς καρδίαις hearts GLTTrAW. [v] τῷ θεῷ to God GLTTrAW. [w] ἐὰν LTr. [x] Ἰησοῦ χριστοῦ of Jesus Christ LW. [y] — καὶ LTTrAW. [z] — ἰδίοις (*read* to the husbands) GLTTrAW. [a] + ὑμῶν (*read* your wives) L. [b] εὐάρεστόν ἐστιν LTTrA. [c] ἐν in [the] GLTTrAW. [d] παροργίζετε L. [e] ὀφθαλμοδουλείᾳ eye-service LW; ὀφθαλμοδουλίαις T. [f] ἀλλὰ Tr. [g] τὸν κύριον the Lord GLTTrAW. [h] ὃ (*read* whatever) LTTrAW. [i] ἀπολήμψεσθε LTTrA. [k] — γὰρ for LTTrAW. [l] γὰρ (*read* for he that) LTTrAW. [m] κομίσεται L. [n] προσωπολημψία LTTrA. [o] οὐρανῷ heaven LTTrAW. [p] ὃν whom L.

ρώσω αὐτὸ ὡς δεῖ με λαλῆσαι. 5 Ἐν σοφίᾳ περιπατεῖτε
manifest it as it behoves me to speak. In wisdom walk
πρὸς τοὺς ἔξω, τὸν καιρὸν ἐξαγοραζόμενοι. 6 ὁ λόγος
towards those without, [2]the [3]time [1]ransoming. [Let] [2]word
ὑμῶν πάντοτε ἐν χάριτι, ἅλατι ἠρτυμένος, εἰδέναι πῶς
[1]your [be] always with grace, [2]with [3]salt [1]seasoned, to know how
δεῖ ὑμᾶς ἑνὶ.ἑκάστῳ ἀποκρίνεσθαι.
it behoves you [3]each [4]one [1]to [2]answer.

7 Τὰ κατ' ἐμὲ πάντα γνωρίσει ὑμῖν Τυχικὸς
[2]The [3]things [4]concerning [5]me [1]all [7]will [8]make [9]known [10]to [11]you [6]Tychicus
ὁ ἀγαπητὸς ἀδελφὸς καὶ πιστὸς διάκονος καὶ σύνδουλος
the beloved brother and faithful servant and fellow-bondman
ἐν κυρίῳ, 8 ὃν ἔπεμψα πρὸς ὑμᾶς εἰς αὐτὸ.τοῦτο, ἵνα
in [the] Lord; whom I sent to you for this very thing, that
[q]γνῷ‖ τὰ περὶ [r]ὑμῶν‖ καὶ παρακαλέσῃ τὰς
he might know the things concerning you, and might encourage
καρδίας.ὑμῶν, 9 σὺν Ὀνησίμῳ, τῷ πιστῷ καὶ ἀγαπητῷ
your hearts; with Onesimus, the faithful and beloved
ἀδελφῷ, ὅς ἐστιν ἐξ ὑμῶν· πάντα ὑμῖν [s]γνωριοῦσιν‖
brother, who is of you. All things [2]to [3]you [4]they [5]will [6]make [7]known
τὰ ὧδε.
[1]here.

10 Ἀσπάζεται ὑμᾶς Ἀρίσταρχος ὁ.συναιχμάλωτός.μου, καὶ
[4]Salutes [5]you [1]Aristarchus [2]my [3]fellow-prisoner, and
Μάρκος ὁ ἀνεψιὸς Βαρνάβα, περὶ οὗ ἐλάβετε ἐντολάς·
Mark, the cousin of Barnabas, concerning whom ye received orders,
ἐὰν ἔλθῃ πρὸς ὑμᾶς, δέξασθε αὐτόν· 11 καὶ Ἰησοῦς ὁ λεγό-
(if he come to you, receive him,) and Jesus called
μενος Ἰοῦστος, οἱ ὄντες ἐκ περιτομῆς· [t] οὗτοι μόνοι
Justus, who are of [the] circumcision. These [are the] only
συνεργοὶ εἰς τὴν βασιλείαν τοῦ θεοῦ, οἵτινες ἐγενήθησάν
fellow-workers for the kingdom of God, who were
μοι παρηγορία. 12 ἀσπάζεται ὑμᾶς Ἐπαφρᾶς ὁ ἐξ ὑμῶν
to me a consolation. [2]Salutes [3]you [1]Epaphras who [is] of you,
δοῦλος χριστοῦ[u], πάντοτε ἀγωνιζόμενος ὑπὲρ ὑμῶν ἐν ταῖς
a bondman of Christ, always striving for you in
προσευχαῖς, ἵνα [v]στῆτε‖ τέλειοι καὶ [w]πεπληρωμένοι‖ ἐν
prayers, that ye may stand perfect and complete in
παντὶ θελήματι τοῦ θεοῦ. 13 μαρτυρῶ.γὰρ αὐτῷ ὅτι ἔχει
every will of God. For I bear witness to him that he has
[x]ζῆλον πολὺν‖ ὑπὲρ ὑμῶν καὶ τῶν ἐν [y]Λαοδικείᾳ‖ καὶ τῶν
[2]zeal [1]much for you and them in Laodicea and them
ἐν Ἱεραπόλει. 14 ἀσπάζεται ὑμᾶς Λουκᾶς ὁ ἰατρὸς ὁ ἀγα-
in Hierapolis. [5]Salutes [6]you [1]Luke [2]the [4]physician [3]be-
πητός, καὶ Δημᾶς. 15 ἀσπάσασθε τοὺς ἐν [y]Λαοδικείᾳ‖ ἀδελ-
loved, and Demas. Salute the [2]in [3]Laodicea [1]breth-
φούς, καὶ [z]Νυμφᾶν‖ καὶ τὴν κατ'.οἶκον.[a]αὐτοῦ‖ ἐκκλησίαν·
ren, and Nymphas, and the [2]in [3]his [4]house [1]assembly.
16 καὶ ὅταν ἀναγνωσθῇ παρ' ὑμῖν ἡ ἐπιστολή, ποιήσατε
And when may be read among you the epistle, cause
ἵνα καὶ ἐν τῇ Λαοδικέων ἐκκλησίᾳ ἀναγνωσθῇ, καὶ
that also in the [2]of [[3]the] [4]Laodiceans [1]assembly it may be read, and

as I ought to speak.
5 Walk in wisdom to-
ward them that are
without, redeeming
the time. 6 Let your
speech *be* alway with
grace, seasoned with
salt, that ye may know
how ye ought to an-
swer every man.

7 All my state shall
Tychicus declare unto
you, *who is* a beloved
brother, and a faith-
ful minister and fel-
lowservant in the
Lord: 8 whom I have
sent unto you for the
same purpose, that he
might know your es-
tate, and comfort
your hearts; 9 with
Onesimus, a faithful
and beloved brother,
who is *one* of you.
They shall make
known unto you all
things which *are done*
here.

10 Aristarchus my
fellowprisoner salut-
eth you, and Marcus,
sister's son to Barna-
bas, (touching whom
ye received command-
ments: if he come un-
to you, receive him;)
11 and Jesus, which is
called Justus, who are
of the circumcision.
These only *are my*
fellowworkers unto
the kingdom of God,
which have been a
comfort unto me. 12 E-
paphras, who is *one*
of you, a servant of
Christ, saluteth you,
always labouring fer-
vently for you in
prayers, that ye may
stand perfect and com-
plete in all the will of
God. 13 For I bear
him record, that he
hath a great zeal for
you, and them *that are*
in Laodicea, and them
in Hierapolis. 14 Luke,
the beloved physician,
and Demas, greet you.
15 Salute the brethren
which are in Laodicea,
and Nymphas, and the
church which is in his
house. 16 And when
this epistle is read a-
mong you, cause that
it be read also in the
church of the Laodi-
ceans; and that ye

---

[q] γνῶτε ye might know LTTr. [r] ἡμῶν us LTTr. [s] γνωρίσουσιν L. [t] *Punctuate so as to read* These only who are of the circumcision [are the] &c. LTA. [u] + Ἰησοῦ Jesus LTTrA. [v] σταθῆτε TTr. [w] πεπληροφορημένοι fully assured LTTrAW. [x] πολὺν πόνον much labour GLTTrA; πόνον πολὺν W. [y] Λαοδικίᾳ T. [z] Νύμφαν Nympha L. [a] αὐτῆς (*read* her house) L; αὐτῶν (*read* their house) TTrA.

likewise read the *epistle* from Laodicea.
17 And say to Archippus, Take heed to the ministry which thou hast received in the Lord, that thou fulfil it.
18 The salutation by the hand of me Paul. Remember my bonds. Grace *be* with you. Amen.

τὴν ἐκ [b]Λαοδικείας‖ ἵνα καὶ ὑμεῖς ἀναγνῶτε· 17 καὶ εἴπατε
that from Laodicea that also ye may read. And say
Ἀρχίππῳ, Βλέπε τὴν διακονίαν ἣν παρέλαβες ἐν
to Archippus, Take heed to the service which thou didst receive in [the]
κυρίῳ, ἵνα αὐτὴν πληροῖς. 18 Ὁ ἀσπασμὸς τῇ.ἐμῇ.χειρὶ
Lord, that it thou fulfil. The salutation [3]by [4]my [[5]own] [6]hand
Παύλου. μνημονεύετέ μου τῶν δεσμῶν. ἡ χάρις μεθ'
[1]of [2]Paul. Remember my bonds. Grace [be] with
ὑμῶν. [c]ἀμήν.‖
you. Amen.

[d]Πρὸς Κολασσαεῖς ἐγράφη ἀπὸ Ῥώμης, διὰ Τυχικοῦ καὶ
To [the] Colossians written from Rome, by Tychicus and
Ὀνησίμου.‖
Onesimus.

---

[e]Η ΠΡΟΣ ΘΕΣΣΑΛΟΝΙΚΕΙΣ ΕΠΙΣΤΟΛΗ ΠΑΥΛΟΥ ΠΡΩΤΗ.‖
THE [5]TO [[6]THE] [7]THESSALONIANS [2]EPISTLE [3]OF [4]PAUL [1]FIRST.

PAUL, and Silvanus, and Timotheus, unto the church of the Thessalonians *which is* in God the Father and *in* the Lord Jesus Christ: Grace *be* unto you, and peace, from God our Father, and the Lord Jesus Christ.

ΠΑΥΛΟΣ καὶ Σιλουανὸς καὶ Τιμόθεος, τῇ ἐκκλησίᾳ Θεσ-
Paul and Silvanus and Timotheus, to the assembly of Thes-
σαλονικέων ἐν θεῷ πατρὶ καὶ κυρίῳ Ἰησοῦ χριστῷ·
salonians in God [the] Father and [the] Lord Jesus Christ.
χάρις ὑμῖν καὶ εἰρήνη [f]ἀπὸ θεοῦ πατρὸς.ἡμῶν καὶ κυρίου
Grace to you and peace from God our Father and [the] Lord
Ἰησοῦ χριστοῦ.‖
Jesus Christ.

2 We give thanks to God always for you all, making mention of you in our prayers; 3 remembering without ceasing your work of faith, and labour of love, and patience of hope in our Lord Jesus Christ, in the sight of God and our Father; 4 knowing, brethren beloved, your election of God. 5 For our gospel came not unto you in word only, but also in power, and in the Holy Ghost, and in much assurance; as ye know what manner of men we were among you for your sake. 6 And ye became followers of us,

2 Εὐχαριστοῦμεν τῷ θεῷ πάντοτε περὶ πάντων ὑμῶν,
We give thanks to God always concerning all you,
μνείαν [g]ὑμῶν‖ ποιούμενοι ἐπὶ τῶν.προσευχῶν.ἡμῶν, 3 ἀδια-
[2]mention [3]of [4]you [1]making at our prayers, un-
λείπτως μνημονεύοντες ὑμῶν τοῦ ἔργου τῆς πίστεως καὶ τοῦ
ceasingly remembering your work of faith and
κόπου τῆς ἀγάπης καὶ τῆς ὑπομονῆς τῆς ἐλπίδος τοῦ κυρίου
labour of love and endurance of hope of [2]Lord
ἡμῶν Ἰησοῦ χριστοῦ, ἔμπροσθεν τοῦ θεοῦ καὶ πατρὸς ἡμῶν·
[1]our Jesus Christ, before [2]God [3]and [4]Father [1]our;
4 εἰδότες, ἀδελφοὶ ἠγαπημένοι ὑπὸ [h]θεοῦ, τὴν.ἐκλογὴν.ὑμῶν·
knowing, brethren beloved by God, your election.
5 ὅτι τὸ.εὐαγγέλιον.ἡμῶν οὐκ.ἐγενήθη [i]εἰς‖ ὑμᾶς ἐν λόγῳ
Because our glad tidings came not to you in word
μόνον, ἀλλὰ καὶ ἐν δυνάμει καὶ ἐν πνεύματι ἁγίῳ, καὶ [k]ἐν‖
only, but also in power and in [the] [2]Spirit [1]Holy, and in
πληροφορίᾳ πολλῇ, καθὼς οἴδατε οἷοι ἐγενήθημεν [l]ἐν‖
[2]full [3]assurance [1]much, even as ye know what we were among
ὑμῖν δι' ὑμᾶς. 6 καὶ ὑμεῖς μιμηταὶ ἡμῶν ἐγενήθητε
you for the sake of you: and ye imitators of us became

---

[b] Λαοδικίας T. [c] — ἀμήν GLTTrAW. [d] Πρὸς Κολοσσαεῖς &c. E; — *the subscription* GLTW; Πρὸς Κολασσαεῖς TrA. [e] + τοῦ Ἀποστόλου the apostle E; Πρὸς Θεσσαλονικεις α´ LTTrAW. [f] — ἀπὸ θεοῦ *to end of verse* [L]TTrA. [g] — ὑμῶν LTTr[A]. [h] + τοῦ T. [i] πρὸς L. [k] — ἐν T[Tr]. [l] [ἐν] Tr.

καὶ τοῦ κυρίου, δεξάμενοι τὸν λόγον ἐν θλίψει πολλῇ
and of the Lord, having accepted the word in [2]tribulation [1]much
μετὰ χαρᾶς πνεύματος ἁγίου, 7 ὥστε γενέσθαι ὑμᾶς [m]τύπους‖
with joy of [the] [2]Spirit [1]Holy, so that [2]became [1]ye patterns
πᾶσιν τοῖς πιστεύουσιν ἐν τῇ Μακεδονίᾳ καὶ [n] τῇ Ἀχαΐᾳ.
to all those believing in Macedonia and Achaia:
8 ἀφ᾽ ὑμῶν γὰρ ἐξήχηται ὁ λόγος τοῦ κυρίου οὐ μόνον ἐν
for from you has sounded out the word of the Lord not only in
τῇ Μακεδονίᾳ καὶ [o] Ἀχαΐᾳ, [p]ἀλλὰ‖ [q]καὶ‖ ἐν παντὶ τόπῳ ἡ
Macedonia and Achaia, but also in every place
πίστις ὑμῶν ἡ πρὸς τὸν θεὸν ἐξελήλυθεν, ὥστε μὴ
your faith which [is] towards God has gone abroad, so as [5]no
χρείαν [r]ἡμᾶς ἔχειν‖ λαλεῖν τι· 9 αὐτοὶ γὰρ περὶ
[6]need [1]for [2]us [3]to [4]have to say anything; for themselves concerning
ἡμῶν ἀπαγγέλλουσιν ὁποίαν εἴσοδον [s]ἔχομεν‖ πρὸς ὑμᾶς,
us relate what entrance in we have to you,
καὶ πῶς ἐπεστρέψατε πρὸς τὸν θεὸν ἀπὸ τῶν εἰδώλων, δου-
and how ye turned to God from idols, to
λεύειν θεῷ ζῶντι καὶ ἀληθινῷ, 10 καὶ ἀναμένειν τὸν υἱὸν
serve a [4]God [1]living [2]and [3]true, and to await [2]Son
αὐτοῦ ἐκ τῶν οὐρανῶν, ὃν ἤγειρεν ἐκ [t] νεκρῶν, Ἰη-
[1]his from the heavens, whom he raised from among [the] dead— Je-
σοῦν τὸν ῥυόμενον ἡμᾶς [v]ἀπὸ‖ τῆς ὀργῆς τῆς ἐρχομένης.
sus, who delivers us from the [2]wrath [1]coming.

and of the Lord, having received the word in much affliction, with joy of the Holy Ghost: 7 so that ye were ensamples to all that believe in Macedonia and Achaia. 8 For from you sounded out the word of the Lord not only in Macedonia and Achaia, but also in every place your faith to God-ward is spread abroad; so that we need not to speak any thing. 9 For they themselves shew of us what manner of entering in we had unto you, and how ye turned to God from idols to serve the living and true God; 10 and to wait for his Son from heaven, whom he raised from the dead, *even* Jesus, which delivered us from the wrath to come.

2 Αὐτοὶ γὰρ οἴδατε, ἀδελφοί, τὴν εἴσοδον ἡμῶν τὴν
For [2]yourselves [1]ye know, brethren, our entrance in which [we had]
πρὸς ὑμᾶς, ὅτι οὐ κενὴ γέγονεν. 2 ἀλλὰ [w]καὶ‖ προπαθόν-
to you, that not void it has been; but also having before suf-
τες καὶ ὑβρισθέντες, καθὼς οἴδατε, ἐν Φιλίπποις, ἐπαρ-
fered and having been insulted, even as ye know, at Philippi, we
ῥησιασάμεθα ἐν τῷ θεῷ ἡμῶν λαλῆσαι πρὸς ὑμᾶς τὸ εὐαγγέλιον
were bold in our God to speak to you the glad tidings
τοῦ θεοῦ ἐν πολλῷ ἀγῶνι. 3 Ἡ γὰρ παράκλησις ἡμῶν οὐκ
of God in much conflict. For [2]exhortation [1]our [was] not
ἐκ πλάνης, οὐδὲ ἐξ ἀκαθαρσίας, [x]οὔτε‖ ἐν δόλῳ, 4 ἀλλὰ καθὼς
of error, nor of uncleanness, nor in guile; but even as
δεδοκιμάσμεθα ὑπὸ τοῦ θεοῦ πιστευθῆναι τὸ εὐαγγέλιον,
we have been approved by God to be entrusted with the glad tidings,
οὕτως λαλοῦμεν, οὐχ ὡς ἀνθρώποις ἀρέσκοντες, ἀλλὰ [y]τῷ‖
so we speak; not as [2]men [1]pleasing, but
θεῷ, τῷ δοκιμάζοντι τὰς καρδίας [z]ἡμῶν.‖ 5 Οὔτε γάρ ποτε
God, who proves the hearts of us. For neither at any time
ἐν λόγῳ [a]κολακείας‖ ἐγενήθημεν, καθὼς οἴδατε, οὔτε
with word of flattery were we [with you], even as ye know, nor
ἐν προφάσει πλεονεξίας, θεὸς μάρτυς, 6 οὔτε ζητοῦντες
with a pretext of covetousness, God [is] witness; nor seeking
ἐξ ἀνθρώπων δόξαν, οὔτε ἀφ᾽ ὑμῶν οὔτε ἀπ᾽ ἄλλων,
from men glory, neither from you nor from others, [though]
δυνάμενοι ἐν βάρει εἶναι ὡς χριστοῦ ἀπόστολοι; 7 [b]ἀλλ᾽‖
having power [3]burdensome [1]to [2]be as Christ's apostles; but
ἐγενήθημεν [c]ἤπιοι‖ ἐν μέσῳ ὑμῶν, ὡς [d]ἂν‖ τροφὸς θάλπῃ
we were gentle in your midst, as a nurse would cherish

II. For yourselves, brethren, know our entrance in unto you, that it was not in vain: 2 but even after that we had suffered before, and were shamefully entreated, as ye know, at Philippi, we were bold in our God to speak unto you the gospel of God with much contention. 3 For our exhortation *was* not of deceit, nor of uncleanness, nor in guile: 4 but as we were allowed of God to be put in trust with the gospel, even so we speak; not as pleasing men, but God, which trieth our hearts. 5 For neither at any time used we flattering words, as ye know, nor a cloke of covetousness; God *is* witness: 6 nor of men sought we glory, neither of you, nor *yet* of others, when we might have been burdensome, as the apostles of Christ. 7 But we were gentle among you, even as a nurse cherisheth her chil-

---

[m] τύπον a pattern LTTrAW. [n] + ἐν in LTTrAW. [o] + ἐν (in) τῇ LT. [p] ἀλλ᾽ LA. [q] — καὶ LTTrAW. [r] ἔχειν ἡμᾶς LTTrAW. [s] ἔσχομεν we had GLTTrAW. [t] + τῶν the GLTTrA. [v] ἐκ out of TTr. [w] — καὶ GLTTrAW. [x] οὐδὲ LTTrAW. [y] — τῷ [L]TTrA. [z] ἡμῶν of you W. [a] κολακίας T. [b] ἀλλὰ TTr. [c] νήπιοι simple L. [d] ἐὰν LTTrA.

dren: 8 so being af-
fectionately desirous
of you, we were will-
ing to have imparted
unto you, not the gos-
pel of God only, but
also our own souls,
because ye were dear
unto us. 9 For ye re-
member, brethren, our
labour and travail:
for labouring night
and day, because we
would not be charge-
able unto any of you,
we preached unto you
the gospel of God.
10 Ye *are* witnesses,
and God *also*, how
holily and justly and
unblameably we be-
haved ourselves a-
mong you that be-
lieve: 11 as ye know
how we exhorted and
comforted and charged
every one of you, as a
father *doth* his chil-
dren, 12 that ye would
walk worthy of God,
who hath called you
unto his kingdom and
glory. 13 For this
cause also thank we
God without ceasing,
because, when ye re-
ceived the word of
God which ye heard
of us, ye received *it*
not *as* the word of
men, but as it is in
truth, the word of
God, which effectually
worketh also in you
that believe. 14 For
ye, brethren, became
followers of the
churches of God which
in Judæa are in Christ
Jesus: for ye also
have suffered like
things of your own
countrymen, even as
they *have* of the Jews:
15 who both killed the
Lord Jesus, and their
own prophets, and
have persecuted us;
and they please not
God, and are con-
trary to all men:
16 forbidding us to
speak to the Gentiles
that they might be
saved, to fill up their
sins alway: for the
wrath is come upon
them to the utter-
most.

17 But we, brethren,
being taken from you
for a short time in

τὰ.ἑαυτῆς τέκνα. 8 οὕτως [e]ἱμειρόμενοι‖ ὑμῶν, εὐδοκοῦμεν
her own children. Thus yearning over you, we were pleased
μεταδοῦναι ὑμῖν οὐ μόνον τὸ εὐαγγέλιον τοῦ θεοῦ, ἀλλὰ
to have imparted to you not only the glad tidings of God, but
καὶ τὰς ἑαυτῶν ψυχάς, διότι ἀγαπητοὶ ἡμῖν [f]γεγένησθε.‖
also our own lives, because beloved to us ye have become.
9 μνημονεύετε.γάρ, ἀδελφοί, τὸν.κόπον.ἡμῶν καὶ τὸν μόχθον·
For ye remember, brethren, our labour and the toil,
νυκτὸς.[g]γὰρ‖ καὶ ἡμέρας ἐργαζόμενοι, πρὸς τὸ μὴ ἐπιβαρῆσαί
for night and day working, for not to burden
τινα ὑμῶν, ἐκηρύξαμεν εἰς ὑμᾶς τὸ εὐαγγέλιον τοῦ θεοῦ.
anyone of you, we proclaimed to you the glad tidings of God.
10 ὑμεῖς μάρτυρες καὶ ὁ θεός, ὡς ὁσίως καὶ δικαίως καὶ
Ye [are] witnesses, and God, how holily and righteously and
ἀμέμπτως ὑμῖν τοῖς πιστεύουσιν ἐγενήθημεν, 11 καθάπερ
blamelessly with you that believe we were: even as
οἴδατε, ὡς ἕνα.ἕκαστον ὑμῶν, ὡς πατὴρ τέκνα ἑαυτοῦ, παρα-
ye know, how each one of you, as a father [3]children [1]his [2]own, ex-
καλοῦντες ὑμᾶς καὶ παραμυθούμενοι 12 καὶ [h]μαρτυρούμενοι,‖
horting you and consoling and testifying,
εἰς τὸ [i]περιπατῆσαι‖ ὑμᾶς ἀξίως τοῦ θεοῦ τοῦ καλοῦντος
for [2]to [3]have [4]walked [1]you worthily of God, who calls
ὑμᾶς εἰς τὴν.ἑαυτοῦ βασιλείαν καὶ δόξαν. 13 [k]Διὰ τοῦτο
you to his own kingdom and glory. Because of this
καὶ ἡμεῖς εὐχαριστοῦμεν τῷ θεῷ ἀδιαλείπτως, ὅτι παραλα-
also we give thanks to God unceasingly, that, having re-
βόντες λόγον ἀκοῆς παρ' ἡμῶν τοῦ θεοῦ ἐδέξασθε οὐ
ceived [the] word of [the] report [3]by [4]us [1]of [2]God, ye accepted not
λόγον ἀνθρώπων, ἀλλὰ καθώς ἐστιν ἀληθῶς, λόγον θεοῦ, ὃς
[2]word [1]men's, but even as it is truly, [2]word [1]God's, which
καὶ ἐνεργεῖται ἐν ὑμῖν τοῖς πιστεύουσιν. 14 ὑμεῖς.γὰρ μιμηταὶ
also works in you who believe. For ye imitators
ἐγενήθητε, ἀδελφοί, τῶν ἐκκλησιῶν τοῦ θεοῦ τῶν οὐσῶν ἐν τῇ
became, brethren, of the assemblies of God which are in
Ἰουδαίᾳ ἐν χριστῷ Ἰησοῦ, ὅτι [l]ταὐτὰ‖ ἐπάθετε καὶ ὑμεῖς
Judæa in Christ Jesus; because the same things [3]suffered [2]also [1]ye
ὑπὸ τῶν.ἰδίων συμφυλετῶν καθὼς καὶ αὐτοὶ ὑπὸ τῶν Ἰου-
from your own countrymen as also they from the Jews,
δαίων, 15 τῶν καὶ τὸν κύριον ἀποκτεινάντων Ἰησοῦν καὶ
who [2]both [3]the [4]Lord [1]killed Jesus and
τοὺς.[m]ἰδίους‖ προφήτας, καὶ [n]ὑμᾶς‖ ἐκδιωξάντων, καὶ θεῷ
their own prophets, and [2]you [1]drove out, and [4]God
μὴ.ἀρεσκόντων, καὶ πᾶσιν ἀνθρώποις ἐναντίων, 16 κω-
[1]do [2]not [3]please, and [4]all [3]to [5]men [[1]are] [2]contrary, for-
λυόντων ἡμᾶς τοῖς ἔθνεσιν λαλῆσαι ἵνα σωθῶσιν, εἰς
bidding us to the nations to speak that they may be saved, for
τὸ ἀναπληρῶσαι αὐτῶν τὰς ἁμαρτίας πάντοτε· [o]ἔφθασεν‖.δὲ
to fill up their sins always: but is come
ἐπ' αὐτοὺς ἡ ὀργὴ εἰς.τέλος.
upon them the wrath to the uttermost.

17 Ἡμεῖς.δέ, ἀδελφοί, ἀπορφανισθέντες ἀφ' ὑμῶν πρὸς
But we, brethren, having been bereaved of you for

---

[e] ὁμειρόμενοι GLTTrAW. [f] ἐγενήθητε ye became LTTrAW. [g] — γὰρ for GLTTrAW. [h] μαρτυρόμενοι TTrAW. [i] περιπατεῖν [2]to [3]walk LTTrAW. [k] + καὶ and LTTrA. [l] τὰ αὐτὰ GLTTrAW. [m] — ἰδίους (*read* the prophets) GLTTrAW. [n] ἡμᾶς us EGLTTrAW. [o] ἔφθακεν has come L.

καιρὸν ὥρας προσώπῳ οὐ καρδίᾳ, περισσοτέρως ἐσπου-
time of an hour in face, not in heart, more abundantly were
δάσαμεν τὸ.πρόσωπον.ὑμῶν ἰδεῖν ἐν πολλῇ ἐπιθυμίᾳ· 18 [q]διὸ
diligent your face to see with much desire; wherefore
ἠθελήσαμεν ἐλθεῖν πρὸς ὑμᾶς, ἐγὼ μὲν Παῦλος καὶ ἅπαξ
we wished to come to you, I indeed Paul, both once
καὶ δίς, καὶ ἐνέκοψεν ἡμᾶς ὁ σατανᾶς. 19 τίς.γὰρ ἡμῶν
and twice, and [2]hindered [3]us [1]Satan; for what [is] our
ἐλπὶς ἢ χαρὰ ἢ στέφανος καυχήσεως; ἢ οὐχὶ καὶ ὑμεῖς
hope or joy or crown of boasting? or [are] not even ye
ἔμπροσθεν τοῦ.κυρίου.ἡμῶν Ἰησοῦ [r]χριστοῦ ἐν τῇ αὐτοῦ
before our Lord Jesus Christ at his
παρουσίᾳ; 20 ὑμεῖς.γάρ ἐστε ἡ.δόξα.ἡμῶν καὶ ἡ χαρά.
coming? for ye are our glory and joy.

3 Διὸ μηκέτι στέγοντες, [s]εὐδοκήσαμεν καταλειφθῆναι
Wherefore no longer enduring, we thought good to be left
ἐν Ἀθήναις μόνοι, 2 καὶ ἐπέμψαμεν Τιμόθεον τὸν ἀδελφὸν
in Athens alone, and sent Timotheus [2]brother
ἡμῶν καὶ [t]διάκονον τοῦ θεοῦ [v]καὶ συνεργὸν ἡμῶν ἐν τῷ
[1]our and servant of God and [2]fellow-worker [1]our in the
εὐαγγελίῳ τοῦ χριστοῦ, εἰς τὸ στηρίξαι ὑμᾶς καὶ παρακαλέσαι
glad tidings of the Christ, for to establish you and to encourage
[w]ὑμᾶς [x]περὶ τῆς.πίστεως.ὑμῶν 3 [y]τῷ [z]μηδένα σαίνεσθαι
you concerning your faith that no one be moved
ἐν ταῖς.θλίψεσιν.ταύταις· αὐτοὶ.γὰρ οἴδατε ὅτι εἰς τοῦτο
by these tribulations. (For yourselves know that for this
κείμεθα· 4 καὶ.γὰρ ὅτε πρὸς ὑμᾶς ἦμεν, προελέγομεν ὑμῖν
we are set; for also, when with you we were, we told [2]beforehand [1]you
ὅτι μέλλομεν θλίβεσθαι, καθὼς καὶ ἐγένετο καὶ οἴ-
we are about to suffer tribulation, even as also it came to pass and ye
δατε· 5 διὰ τοῦτο κἀγὼ μηκέτι στέγων, ἔπεμψα εἰς τὸ
know.) Because of this I also no longer enduring, sent for
γνῶναι τὴν.πίστιν.ὑμῶν, μήπως ἐπείρασεν ὑμᾶς ὁ
to know your faith, lest perhaps [4]did [5]tempt [6]you [1]he [2]who
πειράζων, καὶ εἰς κενὸν γένηται ὁ.κόπος.ἡμῶν. 6 ἄρτι.δὲ
[3]tempts, and void should become our labour. But now
ἐλθόντος Τιμοθέου πρὸς ἡμᾶς ἀφ᾽ ὑμῶν, καὶ εὐαγγελισα-
[2]having [3]come [1]Timotheus to us from you, and having announced
μένου ἡμῖν τὴν πίστιν καὶ τὴν ἀγάπην ὑμῶν, καὶ ὅτι
glad tidings to us [of] [2]faith [3]and [4]love [1]your, and that
ἔχετε μνείαν ἡμῶν ἀγαθὴν πάντοτε, ἐπιποθοῦντες ἡμᾶς
ye have [3]remembrance [4]of [5]us [2]good [1]always, longing [3]us
ἰδεῖν, καθάπερ καὶ ἡμεῖς ὑμᾶς, 7 διὰ τοῦτο παρεκλή-
[1]to [2]see, even as also we you: because of this we were encou-
θημεν, ἀδελφοί, ἐφ᾽ ὑμῖν, ἐπὶ πάσῃ τῇ [a]θλίψει καὶ ἀνάγκῃ
raged, brethren, as to you, in all [2]tribulation [3]and [4]necessity
ἡμῶν, διὰ τῆς.ὑμῶν.πίστεως· 8 ὅτι νῦν ζῶμεν ἐὰν ὑμεῖς
[1]our, through your faith, because now we live if ye
[b]στήκητε ἐν κυρίῳ. 9 τίνα.γὰρ εὐχαριστίαν δυνάμεθα
should stand fast in [the] Lord. For what thanksgiving are we able
τῷ θεῷ ἀνταποδοῦναι περὶ ὑμῶν, ἐπὶ πάσῃ τῇ χαρᾷ
[3]to [4]God [1]to [2]render concerning you, for all the joy

presence, not in heart, endeavoured the more abundantly to see your face with great desire.
18 Wherefore we would have come unto you, even I Paul, once and again; but Satan hindered us.
19 For what *is* our hope, or joy, or crown of rejoicing? *Are* not even ye in the presence of our Lord Jesus Christ at his coming?
20 For ye are our glory and joy.

III. Wherefore when we could no longer forbear, we thought it good to be left at Athens alone;
2 and sent Timotheus, our brother, and minister of God, and our fellowlabourer in the gospel of Christ, to establish you, and to comfort you concerning your faith:
3 that no man should be moved by these afflictions: for yourselves know that we are appointed thereunto.
4 For verily, when we were with you, we told you before that we should suffer tribulation; even as it came to pass, and ye know.
5 For this cause, when I could no longer forbear, I sent to know your faith, lest by some means the tempter have tempted you, and our labour be in vain.
6 But now when Timotheus came from you unto us, and brought us good tidings of your faith and charity, and that ye have good remembrance of us always, desiring greatly to see us, as we also *to see* you:
7 therefore, brethren, we were comforted over you in all our affliction and distress by your faith:
8 for now we live, if ye stand fast in the Lord.
9 For what thanks can we render to God again for you, for all the joy where-

---

[q] διότι because LTTrAW. [r] — χριστοῦ LTTrA. [s] ηὐδοκήσαμεν TTr. [t] συνεργὸν fellow-worker (*read* τοῦ θεοῦ under God) GLAW. [v] — καὶ συνεργὸν ἡμῶν GLTTrAW. [w] — ὑμᾶς LTTrAW. [x] ὑπὲρ GLTTrAW. [y] τὸ LTTrAW. [z] μηδὲν (nothing [ye]) ἀσαίνεσθαι L. [a] ἀνάγκῃ καὶ θλίψει LTTrAW. [b] στήκετε stand fast TTrA.

with we joy for your
sakes before our God;
10 night and day pray-
ing exceedingly that
we might see your
face, and might per-
fect that which is
lacking in your faith?
11 Now God himself
and our Father, and
our Lord Jesus Christ,
direct our way unto
you. 12 And the Lord
make you to increase
and abound in love
one toward another,
and toward all *men*,
even as we *do* toward
you: 13 to the end he
may stablish your
hearts unblameable in
holiness before God,
even our Father, at the
coming of our Lord
Jesus Christ with all
his saints.

IV. Furthermore then
we beseech you, bre-
thren, and exhort *you*
by the Lord Jesus, that
as ye have received of
us how ye ought to
walk and to please
God, *so* ye would a-
bound more and more.
2 For ye know what
commandments we
gave you by the Lord
Jesus. 3 For this is
the will of God, *even*
your sanctification,
that ye should abstain
from fornication:
4 that every one of you
should know how to
possess his vessel in
sanctification and ho-
nour; 5 not in the lust
of concupiscence, even
as the Gentiles which
know not God: 6 that
no *man* go beyond and
defraud his brother in
any matter: because
that the Lord *is* the
avenger of all such, as
we also have fore-
warned you and testi-
fied. 7 For God hath
not called us unto un-
cleanness, but unto
holiness. 8 He there-
fore that despiseth, de-
spiseth not man, but
God, who hath also
given unto us his holy
Spirit.

ᾗ χαίρομεν δι' ὑμᾶς ἔμπροσθεν τοῦ.θεοῦ.ἡμῶν,[c]
wherewith we rejoice on account of you before our God,
10 νυκτὸς καὶ ἡμέρας [d]ὑπὲρ.ἐκπερισσοῦ‖ δεόμενοι εἰς τὸ ἰδεῖν
night and day exceedingly beseeching for to see
ὑμῶν τὸ πρόσωπον, καὶ καταρτίσαι τὰ.ὑστερήματα τῆς πίστεως
your face, and to perfect the things lacking in [2]faith
ὑμῶν; 11 Αὐτὸς.δὲ ὁ θεὸς καὶ πατὴρ.ἡμῶν καὶ ὁ.κύριος.ἡμῶν
[1]your? But [6]himself [3]God [4]and [2]our [5]Father [7]and [8]our [9]Lord
Ἰησοῦς [e]χριστὸς‖ κατευθύναι τὴν.ὁδὸν.ἡμῶν πρὸς ὑμᾶς.
[10]Jesus [11]Christ [1]may direct our way to you.
12 ὑμᾶς.δὲ ὁ κύριος πλεονάσαι καὶ περισσεύσαι τῇ
But [5]you [2]the [3]Lord [1]may [4]make to exceed and to abound
ἀγάπῃ εἰς ἀλλήλους καὶ εἰς πάντας, καθάπερ καὶ ἡμεῖς
in love toward one another and toward all, even as also we
εἰς ὑμᾶς, 13 εἰς τὸ στηρίξαι ὑμῶν τὰς καρδίας ἀμέμπτους
toward you, for to establish your hearts blameless
ἐν ἁγιωσύνῃ ἔμπροσθεν τοῦ θεοῦ καὶ πατρὸς ἡμῶν, ἐν τῇ
in holiness before [2]God [3]and [4]Father [1]our, at the
παρουσίᾳ τοῦ.κυρίου.ἡμῶν Ἰησοῦ [f]χριστοῦ‖ μετὰ πάντων τῶν
coming of our Lord Jesus Christ with all
ἁγίων.αὐτοῦ.[g]
his saints.

4 [h]Τὸ‖λοιπὸν οὖν, ἀδελφοί, ἐρωτῶμεν ὑμᾶς καὶ παρα-
For the rest then, brethren, we beseech you and we
καλοῦμεν ἐν κυρίῳ Ἰησοῦ, [i] καθὼς παρελάβετε παρ' ἡμῶν
exhort in [the] Lord Jesus, even as ye received from us
τὸ πῶς δεῖ ὑμᾶς περιπατεῖν καὶ ἀρέσκειν θεῷ, [k]ἵνα περισ-
how it behoves you to walk and please God, that ye should
σεύητε μᾶλλον. 2 οἴδατε.γὰρ τίνας παραγγελίας ἐδώκαμεν
abound more. For ye know what injunctions we gave
ὑμῖν διὰ τοῦ κυρίου Ἰησοῦ. 3 τοῦτο.γάρ ἐστιν [l] θέλημα τοῦ
you through the Lord Jesus. For this is [2]will
θεοῦ, ὁ.ἁγιασμὸς.ὑμῶν, ἀπέχεσθαι ὑμᾶς ἀπὸ τῆς πορνείας,
[1]God's, your sanctification, [3]to [4]abstain [[1]for] [2]you from fornication,
4 εἰδέναι ἕκαστον ὑμῶν τὸ.ἑαυτοῦ σκεῦος κτᾶσθαι ἐν
[4]to [5]know [1]each [2]of [3]you [how] [3]his [4]own [5]vessel [1]to [2]possess in
ἁγιασμῷ καὶ τιμῇ, 5 μὴ ἐν πάθει ἐπιθυμίας καθάπερ καὶ
sanctification and honour, (not in passion of lust even as also
τὰ ἔθνη τὰ μὴ.εἰδότα τὸν θεόν· 6 τὸ μὴ ὑπερβαίνειν καὶ
the nations who know not God,) not to go beyond and
πλεονεκτεῖν ἐν τῷ πράγματι τὸν.ἀδελφὸν.αὐτοῦ, διότι ἔκ-
to overreach in the matter his brother; because [the] a-
δικος [m]ὁ‖ κύριος περὶ πάντων τούτων, καθὼς καὶ
venger [is] the Lord concerning all these things, even as also
[n]προείπαμεν‖ ὑμῖν καὶ διεμαρτυράμεθα. 7 οὐ.γὰρ ἐκάλεσεν
we told [2]before [1]you and fully testified. For [4]not [2]called
ἡμᾶς ὁ θεὸς ἐπὶ ἀκαθαρσίᾳ, [o]ἀλλ'‖ ἐν ἁγιασμῷ. 8 τοιγαροῦν
[3]us [1]God to uncleanness, but in sanctification. So then
ὁ ἀθετῶν, οὐκ ἄνθρωπον ἀθετεῖ, ἀλλὰ τὸν θεόν, τὸν
he that sets aside, [2]not [3]man [1]sets aside, but God, who
[p]καὶ‖ [q]δόντα‖ [r]τὸ.πνεῦμα.αὐτοῦ‖ τὸ ἅγιον εἰς [s]ἡμᾶς.‖
also gave his [2]Spirit [1]Holy to us.

---

c ; (*ending the question at* ἡμῶν) GA. d ὑπερεκπερισσοῦ GLTTrAW. e — χριστὸς LTTrA.
f — χριστοῦ LTTrAW. g + ἀμήν Amen [L]T. h — Τὸ GLTTrAW. i + ἵνα that LTTrA.
k + καθὼς καὶ περιπατεῖτε even as also ye are walking LTTrAW. l + [τὸ] (*read* the will of God) L. m — ὁ (*read* [the]) LTTrA. n προείπομεν G. o ἀλλὰ TTr. p — καὶ LTr[A].
q διδόντα gives LTTr. r αὐτοῦ τὸ πνεῦμα L. s ὑμᾶς you LTTrAW.

9 Περὶ.δὲ τῆς φιλαδελφίας οὐ χρείαν [t]ἔχετε‖ γρά-
Now concerning brotherly love [3]no [4]need [1]ye [2]have [for me] to
φειν ὑμῖν, αὐτοὶ.γὰρ ὑμεῖς θεοδίδακτοί ἐστε εἰς τὸ ἀγαπᾷν
write to you, for [2]yourselves [1]ye [4]taught [5]of [6]God [3]are for to love
ἀλλήλους· 10 καὶ.γὰρ ποιεῖτε αὐτὸ εἰς πάντας τοὺς ἀδελ-
one another. For also ye do this towards all the bre-
φοὺς [v]τοὺς‖ ἐν ὅλῃ.τῇ.Μακεδονίᾳ. παρακαλοῦμεν.δὲ ὑμᾶς,
thren who [are] in the whole of Macedonia; but we exhort you,
ἀδελφοί, περισσεύειν μᾶλλον, 11 καὶ φιλοτιμεῖσθαι ἡσυχάζειν
brethren, to abound more, and endeavour earnestly to be quiet
καὶ πράσσειν τὰ.ἴδια, καὶ ἐργάζεσθαι ταῖς.[w]ἰδίαις‖.χερσὶν
and to do your own things, and to work with [2]own [3]hands
ὑμῶν, καθὼς ὑμῖν παρηγγείλαμεν, 12 ἵνα περιπατῆτε εὐ-
[1]your, even as on you we enjoined, that ye may walk be-
σχημόνως πρὸς τοὺς ἔξω, καὶ μηδενὸς χρείαν ἔχητε.
comingly towards those without, and of no one [3]need [1]may [2]have.

13 Οὐ [x]θέλω‖ δὲ ὑμᾶς ἀγνοεῖν, ἀδελφοί, περὶ
[4]Not [2]I [3]do [5]wish [1]but you to be ignorant, brethren, concerning
τῶν [y]κεκοιμημένων,‖ ἵνα μὴ.λυπῆσθε, καθὼς καὶ οἱ λοιποὶ
those who have fallen asleep, that ye be not grieved, even as also the rest
οἱ μὴ.ἔχοντες ἐλπίδα. 14 εἰ.γὰρ πιστεύομεν ὅτι Ἰησοῦς ἀπέ-
who have no hope. For if we believe that Jesus died
θανεν καὶ ἀνέστη, οὕτως καὶ ὁ θεὸς τοὺς κοιμηθέντας
and rose again, so also God those who are fallen asleep
διὰ τοῦ Ἰησοῦ ἄξει σὺν αὐτῷ. 15 τοῦτο.γὰρ ὑμῖν λέ-
through Jesus will bring with him. For this to you we
γομεν ἐν λόγῳ κυρίου, ὅτι ἡμεῖς οἱ ζῶντες, οἱ περι-
say in [the] word of [the] Lord, that we the living who re-
λειπόμενοι εἰς τὴν παρουσίαν τοῦ κυρίου, οὐ.μὴ φθάσωμεν
main to the coming of the Lord, in no wise may anticipate
τοὺς κοιμηθέντας· 16 ὅτι αὐτὸς ὁ κύριος ἐν κελεύσ-
those who are fallen asleep; because [3]himself [1]the [2]Lord with a shout of com-
ματι, ἐν φωνῇ ἀρχαγγέλου καὶ ἐν σάλπιγγι θεοῦ κατα-
mand, with [2]voice [1]archangel's and with trumpet of God shall
βήσεται ἀπ' οὐρανοῦ, καὶ οἱ νεκροὶ ἐν χριστῷ ἀναστήσονται
descend from heaven, and the dead in Christ shall rise
πρῶτον· 17 ἔπειτα ἡμεῖς οἱ ζῶντες οἱ περιλειπόμενοι, ἅμα
first; then we the living who remain, together
σὺν αὐτοῖς ἁρπαγησόμεθα ἐν νεφέλαις εἰς ἀπάντησιν
with them shall be caught away in [the] clouds for [the] meeting
τοῦ κυρίου εἰς ἀέρα, καὶ οὕτως πάντοτε σὺν κυρίῳ ἐσό-
of the Lord in [the] air; and thus always with [the] Lord we shall
μεθα. 18 ὥστε παρακαλεῖτε ἀλλήλους ἐν τοῖς.λόγοις.τούτοις.
be. So encourage one another with these words.

5 Περὶ.δὲ τῶν χρόνων καὶ τῶν καιρῶν, ἀδελφοί, οὐ χρείαν
But concerning the times and the seasons, brethren, [3]no [4]need
ἔχετε ὑμῖν γράφεσθαι· 2 αὐτοὶ.γὰρ ἀκριβῶς οἴδατε ὅτι
[1]ye [2]have for you to be written [to], for [2]yourselves [4]accurately [1]ye [3]know that
[z]ἡ‖ ἡμέρα κυρίου ὡς κλέπτης ἐν νυκτὶ οὕτως ἔρχεται·
the day of [the] Lord as a thief by night so comes.
3 ὅταν.[a]γὰρ‖ λέγωσιν, Εἰρήνη καὶ ἀσφάλεια, τότε αἰφνί-
For when they may say, Peace and security, then sud-
διος αὐτοῖς [b]ἐφίσταται‖ ὄλεθρος, ὥσπερ ἡ.ὠδὶν τῇ
den [3]upon [4]them [2]comes [1]destruction, as travail to her

9 But as touching
brotherly love ye need
not that I write unto
you: for ye yourselves
are taught of God
to love one another.
10 And indeed ye do
it toward all the bre-
thren which are in all
Macedonia: but we
beseech you, brethren,
that ye increase more
and more; 11 and that
ye study to be quiet, and
to do your own busi-
ness, and to work with
your own hands, as
we commanded you;
12 that ye may walk
honestly toward them
that are without, and
that ye may have lack
of nothing.

13 But I would not
have you to be igno-
rant, brethren, con-
cerning them which
are asleep, that ye sor-
row not, even as others
which have no hope.
14 For if we believe
that Jesus died and
rose again, even so
them also which sleep
in Jesus will God bring
with him. 15 For this
we say unto you by
the word of the Lord,
that we which are a-
live *and* remain unto
the coming of the Lord
shall not prevent them
which are asleep.
16 For the Lord him-
self shall descend from
heaven with a shout,
with the voice of the
archangel, and with
the trump of God:
and the dead in Christ
shall rise first: 17 then
we which are alive *and*
remain shall be caught
up together with them
in the clouds, to meet
the Lord in the air:
and so shall we ever
be with the Lord.
18 Wherefore comfort
one another with these
words.

V. But of the times
and the seasons, bre-
thren, ye have no need
that I write unto you.
2 For yourselves know
perfectly that the day
of the Lord so com-
eth as a thief in the
night. 3 For when
they shall say, Peace
and safety; then sud-
den destruction com-
eth upon them, as
travail upon a woman

---

[t] ἔχομεν we have L. [v] — τοὺς LT[Tr]. [w] — ἰδίαις own LTTrAW. [x] θέλομεν [2]we [3]do [5]wish GLTTrAW. [y] κοιμωμένων are falling asleep LTTrA. [z] — ἡ (*read* [the]) LTTr[A]W. [a] — γὰρ for GTTrA; [δὲ] but L. [b] ἐπίσταται TTr.

with child; and they
shall not escape. 4 But
ye, brethren, are not
in darkness, that that
day should overtake
you as a thief. 5 Ye
are all the children of
light, and the children
of the day: we are
not of the night, nor of
darkness. 6 Therefore
let us not sleep, as *do*
others; but let us
watch and be sober.
7 For they that sleep
sleep in the night;
and they that be
drunken are drunken
in the night. 8 But
let us, who are of the
day, be sober, putting
on the breastplate of
faith and love; and for
an helmet, the hope
of salvation. 9 For
God hath not appointed
us to wrath, but to
obtain salvation by
our Lord Jesus Christ,
10 who died for us,
that, whether we wake
or sleep, we should live
together with him.
11 Wherefore comfort
yourselves together,
and edify one another,
even as also ye do.

ἐν.γαστρὶ.ἐχούσῃ, καὶ οὐ.μὴ ἐκφύγωσιν. 4 ὑμεῖς.δέ, ἀδελ-
that is with child; and in no-wise shall they escape. But ye, bre-
φοί, οὐκ.ἐστὲ ἐν σκότει, ἵνα [c]ἡ ἡμέρα ὑμᾶς" ὡς [d]κλέπτης"
thren, are not in darkness, that the day you as a thief
καταλάβῃ· 5 πάντες [e] ὑμεῖς υἱοὶ φωτός ἐστε καὶ υἱοὶ ἡμέρας·
should overtake: all ye sons of light are and sons of day;
οὐκ.ἐσμὲν νυκτὸς οὐδὲ σκότους. 6 ἄρα οὖν μὴ.καθεύδωμεν
we are not of night nor of darkness. So then we should not sleep
ὡς [f]καὶ" οἱ λοιποί, ἀλλὰ γρηγορῶμεν καὶ νήφωμεν.
as also the rest, but we should watch and we should be sober;
7 οἱ.γὰρ καθεύδοντες νυκτὸς καθεύδουσιν, καὶ οἱ μεθυ-
for they that sleep ²by ³night ¹sleep, and they that are
σκόμενοι νυκτὸς μεθύουσιν· 8 ἡμεῖς.δὲ ἡμέρας ὄντες νήφω-
drunken ³by ⁴night ¹get ²drunk; but we ²of ³day ¹being should be
μεν, ἐνδυσάμενοι θώρακα πίστεως καὶ ἀγάπης, καὶ
sober, having put on [the] breastplate of faith and love, and [as]
περικεφαλαίαν ἐλπίδα σωτηρίας· 9 ὅτι οὐκ ἔθετο ἡμᾶς
helmet ²hope ¹salvation's; because ³not ²has ⁴set ⁵us
ὁ θεὸς εἰς ὀργήν, [g]ἀλλ'" εἰς περιποίησιν σωτηρίας διὰ τοῦ
¹God for wrath, but for obtaining salvation through
κυρίου.ἡμῶν Ἰησοῦ χριστοῦ, 10 τοῦ ἀποθανόντος [h]ὑπὲρ" ἡμῶν,
our Lord Jesus Christ, who died for us,
ἵνα εἴτε γρηγορῶμεν εἴτε καθεύδωμεν, ἅμα σὺν αὐτῷ
that whether we may watch or we may sleep, together with him
ζήσωμεν. 11 διὸ παρακαλεῖτε ἀλλήλους, καὶ οἰκοδομεῖτε εἷς
we may live. Wherefore encourage one another, and build up one
τὸν ἕνα, καθὼς καὶ ποιεῖτε.
the other, even as also ye are doing.

12 And we beseech
you, brethren, to know
them which labour among
you, and are over
you in the Lord, and
admonish you; 13 and
to esteem them very
highly in love for
their work's sake.
And be at peace
among yourselves.
14 Now we exhort you,
brethren, warn them
that are unruly, comfort
the feebleminded,
support the weak, be
patient toward all *men*.
15 See that none render
evil for evil unto any
man; but ever follow
that which is good,
both among yourselves,
and to all *men*.
16 Rejoice evermore.
17 Pray without ceasing.
18 In every thing
give thanks: for this
is the will of God
in Christ Jesus concerning
you. 19 Quench
not the Spirit. 20 Despise
not prophesyings.
21 Prove all
things; hold fast that

12 Ἐρωτῶμεν.δὲ ὑμᾶς, ἀδελφοί, εἰδέναι τοὺς κοπιῶντας
But we beseech you, brethren, to know those who labour
ἐν ὑμῖν, καὶ προϊσταμένους ὑμῶν ἐν κυρίῳ, καὶ νουθε-
among you, and take the lead of you in [the] Lord, and admo-
τοῦντας ὑμᾶς, 13 καὶ ἡγεῖσθαι αὐτοὺς [i]ὑπὲρ.ἐκπερισσοῦ" ἐν
nish you, and to esteem them exceedingly in
ἀγάπῃ διὰ τὸ.ἔργον.αὐτῶν. εἰρηνεύετε ἐν [k]ἑαυτοῖς."
love on account of their work. Be at peace among yourselves.
14 παρακαλοῦμεν.δὲ ὑμᾶς, ἀδελφοί, νουθετεῖτε τοὺς ἀτάκτους,
But we exhort you, brethren, admonish the disorderly,
παραμυθεῖσθε τοὺς ὀλιγοψύχους, ἀντέχεσθε τῶν ἀσθενῶν, μα-
console the faint-hearted, sustain the weak, be
κροθυμεῖτε πρὸς πάντας. 15 ὁρᾶτε μή τις κακὸν ἀντὶ κακοῦ
patient towards all. See that not anyone evil for evil
τινὶ [l]ἀποδῷ·" ἀλλὰ πάντοτε τὸ ἀγαθὸν διώκετε [m]καὶ" εἰς
to anyone render, but always the good pursue both towards
ἀλλήλους καὶ εἰς πάντας. 16 πάντοτε χαίρετε. 17 ἀδια-
one another and towards all; always rejoice; unceas-
λείπτως προσεύχεσθε. 18 ἐν παντὶ εὐχαριστεῖτε· τοῦτο.γὰρ [n]
ingly pray; in everything give thanks, for this
θέλημα θεοῦ ἐν χριστῷ Ἰησοῦ εἰς ὑμᾶς. 19 τὸ πνεῦμα
[is the] will of God in Christ Jesus towards you; the Spirit
μὴ.[o]σβέννυτε." 20 προφητείας μὴ.ἐξουθενεῖτε. 21 πάντα [p]
do not quench; prophecies do not set at naught; all things

---

[c] ὑμᾶς ἡ ἡμέρα LW. [d] κλέπτας thieves L. [e] + γὰρ for (all) GLTTrAW. [f] — καὶ LTTr[A]. [g] ἀλλὰ TTrA. [h] περὶ TTr. [i] ὑπερεκπερισσῶς LTTrA; ὑπερεκπερισσοῦ GW. [k] αὐτοῖς (read with them) TTr. [l] ἀποδοῖ T. [m] — καὶ LTTr. [n] + ἐστιν is L. [o] ζβέννυτε T. [p] + δὲ but (all things) GLTTrAW.

δοκιμάζετε· τὸ καλὸν κατέχετε. 22 ἀπὸ παντὸς εἴδους πονη-
prove, the right hold fast; from every form of wicked-
ροῦ ἀπέχεσθε. 23 Αὐτὸς.δὲ ὁ θεὸς τῆς εἰρήνης ἁγιάσαι
ness abstain. Now [6]himself [2]the [3]God [4]of [5]peace [1]may sanctify
ὑμᾶς ὁλοτελεῖς· καὶ ὁλόκληρον ὑμῶν τὸ πνεῦμα καὶ ἡ ψυχὴ
you wholly; and [3]entire [2]your [4]spirit [5]and [6]soul
καὶ τὸ σῶμα ἀμέμπτως ἐν τῇ παρουσίᾳ τοῦ.κυρίου.ἡμῶν
[7]and [8]body [11]blameless [12]at [13]the [14]coming [15]of [16]our [17]Lord
Ἰησοῦ χριστοῦ τηρηθείη. 24 πιστὸς ὁ καλῶν ὑμᾶς,
[18]Jesus [19]Christ [1]may [9]be [10]preserved. [He is] faithful who calls you,
ὃς καὶ ποιήσει. 25 Ἀδελφοί, προσεύχεσθε [q] περὶ ἡμῶν.
who also will perform [it]. Brethren, pray for us.
26 ἀσπάσασθε τοὺς ἀδελφοὺς πάντας ἐν φιλήματι ἁγίῳ.
Salute [2]the [3]brethren [1]all with a [2]kiss [1]holy.
27 [r]ὁρκίζω‖ ὑμᾶς τὸν κύριον ἀναγνωσθῆναι τὴν ἐπιστο-
I adjure you [by] the Lord [that] be read the epistle
λὴν πᾶσιν τοῖς [s]ἁγίοις‖ ἀδελφοῖς. 28 ἡ χάρις τοῦ.κυρίου.ἡμῶν
to all the holy brethren. The grace of our Lord
Ἰησοῦ χριστοῦ μεθ' ὑμῶν. [t]ἀμήν.‖
Jesus Christ [be] with you. Amen.

[v] Πρὸς Θεσσαλονικεῖς πρώτη ἐγράφη ἀπὸ Ἀθηνῶν.‖
[2]To [[3]the] [4]Thessalonians [1]first written from Athens.

which is good. 22 Abstain from all appearance of evil. 23 And the very God of peace sanctify you wholly; and *I pray God* your whole spirit and soul and body be preserved blameless unto the coming of our Lord Jesus Christ. 24 Faithful *is* he that calleth you, who also will do *it*. 25 Brethren, pray for us. 26 Greet all the brethren with an holy kiss. 27 I charge you by the Lord that this epistle be read unto all the holy brethren. 28 The grace of our Lord Jesus Christ *be* with you. Amen.

---

[a]Η ΠΡΟΣ ΘΕΣΣΑΛΟΝΙΚΕΙΣ ΕΠΙΣΤΟΛΗ ΔΕΥΤΕΡΑ.‖
THE [3]TO [[4]THE] [5]THESSALONIANS [2]EPISTLE [1]SECOND.

ΠΑΥΛΟΣ καὶ Σιλουανὸς καὶ Τιμόθεος, τῇ ἐκκλησίᾳ Θεσ-
Paul and Silvanus and Timotheus, to the assembly of Thes-
σαλονικέων ἐν θεῷ πατρὶ ἡμῶν καὶ κυρίῳ Ἰησοῦ χριστῷ·
salonians in God [2]Father [1]our and Lord Jesus Christ.
2 χάρις ὑμῖν καὶ εἰρήνη ἀπὸ θεοῦ πατρὸς [b]ἡμῶν‖ καὶ κυρίου
Grace to you and peace from God [2]Father [1]our and Lord
Ἰησοῦ χριστοῦ.
Jesus Christ.

PAUL, and Silvanus, and Timotheus, unto the church of the Thessalonians in God our Father and the Lord Jesus Christ: 2 Grace unto you, and peace, from God our Father and the Lord Jesus Christ.

3 Εὐχαριστεῖν ὀφείλομεν τῷ θεῷ πάντοτε περὶ ὑμῶν,
[3]To [4]thank [1]we [2]ought God always concerning you,
ἀδελφοί, καθὼς ἄξιόν ἐστιν, ὅτι ὑπεραυξάνει ἡ πίστις
brethren, even as meet it is, because increases exceedingly [2]faith
ὑμῶν, καὶ πλεονάζει ἡ ἀγάπη ἑνὸς ἑκάστου πάντων ὑμῶν
[1]your, and abounds the love of [2]one [1]each of [2]all [1]you
εἰς ἀλλήλους· 4 ὥστε [c]ἡμᾶς αὐτοὺς‖ ἐν ὑμῖν [d]καυχᾶσθαι‖ ἐν
to one another; so as for us ourselves [3]in [4]you [1]to [2]boast in
ταῖς ἐκκλησίαις τοῦ θεοῦ ὑπὲρ τῆς.ὑπομονῆς.ὑμῶν καὶ πίστεως
the assemblies of God for your endurance and faith
ἐν πᾶσιν τοῖς.διωγμοῖς.ὑμῶν καὶ ταῖς θλίψεσιν αἷς ἀνέ-
in all your persecutions and the tribulations which ye are
χεσθε, 5 ἔνδειγμα τῆς δικαίας κρίσεως τοῦ θεοῦ, εἰς τὸ
bearing; a manifest token of the righteous judgment of God, for

3 We are bound to thank God always for you, brethren, as it is meet, because that your faith groweth exceedingly, and the charity of every one of you all toward each other aboundeth; 4 so that we ourselves glory in you in the churches of God for your patience and faith in all your persecutions and tribulations that ye endure: 5 *which is* a manifest token of the righteous judgment of God, that ye may be

---

q + [καὶ] also L. r ἐνορκίζω LTTrAW. s — ἁγίοις LTTrA. t — ἀμήν GLTTrAW.
v — *the subscription* GLTW; Πρὸς Θεσσαλονικεῖς α΄ TrA.
a + Παύλου τοῦ Ἀποστόλου of the Apostle Paul E; + Παύλου G; Πρὸς Θεσσαλονικεῖς β΄ LTTrAW. b — ἡμῶν (*read* [the]) [LTr]A c αὐτοὺς ἡμᾶς TTrA. d ἐγκαυχᾶσθαι (ἐν- T) LTTrA.

counted worthy of the kingdom of God, for which ye also suffer: 6 seeing *it is* a righteous thing with God to recompense tribulation to them that trouble you; 7 and to you who are troubled rest with us, when the Lord Jesus shall be revealed from heaven with his mighty angels, 8 in flaming fire taking vengeance on them that know not God, and that obey not the gospel of our Lord Jesus Christ: 9 who shall be punished with everlasting destruction from the presence of the Lord, and from the glory of his power; 10 when he shall come to be glorified in his saints, and to be admired in all them that believe (because our testimony among you was believed) in that day. 11 Wherefore also we pray always for you, that our God would count you worthy of *this* calling, and fulfil all the good pleasure of *his* goodness, and the work of faith with power: 12 that the name of our Lord Jesus Christ may be glorified in you, and ye in him, according to the grace of our God and the Lord Jesus Christ.

II. Now we beseech you, brethren, by the coming of our Lord Jesus Christ, and *by* our gathering together unto him, 2 that ye be not soon shaken in mind, or be troubled, neither by spirit, nor by word, nor by letter as from us, as that the day of Christ is at hand. 3 Let no man deceive you by any means: for *that day shall not come*, except there come a falling away first, and that man of sin be revealed, the son of perdition; 4 who opposeth and exalteth himself above all that is called

καταξιωθῆναι ὑμᾶς τῆς βασιλείας τοῦ θεοῦ, ὑπὲρ ἧς

[2]to [3]be [4]accounted [5]worthy [1]you of the kingdom of God, for which

καὶ πάσχετε· 6 εἴπερ δίκαιον παρὰ θεῷ ἀνταποδοῦναι

also ye suffer; if at least righteous [it is] with God to recompense

τοῖς θλίβουσιν ὑμᾶς θλίψιν, 7 καὶ ὑμῖν τοῖς θλιβο-

to those who oppress you tribulation, and to you that are op-

μένοις ἄνεσιν μεθ' ἡμῶν, ἐν τῇ ἀποκαλύψει τοῦ κυρίου Ἰησοῦ

pressed repose with us, at the revelation of the Lord Jesus

ἀπ' οὐρανοῦ μετ' ἀγγέλων δυνάμεως.αὐτοῦ, 8 ἐν [e]πυρὶ φλογός,‖

from heaven with [the] angels of his power, in a fire of flame,

διδόντος ἐκδίκησιν τοῖς μὴ εἰδόσιν θεόν, καὶ τοῖς μὴ

awarding vengeance on those that [2]not [1]know God, and those that [2]not

ὑπακούουσιν τῷ εὐαγγελίῳ τοῦ.κυρίου.ἡμῶν Ἰησοῦ [f]χριστοῦ·‖

[1]obey the glad tidings of our Lord Jesus Christ,

9 οἵτινες δίκην τίσουσιν, [g]ὄλεθρον‖ αἰώνιον, ἀπὸ

who [the] penalty shall suffer, [2]destruction [1]eternal, from [the]

προσώπου τοῦ κυρίου, καὶ ἀπὸ τῆς δόξης τῆς.ἰσχύος.αὐτοῦ,

presence of the Lord, and from the glory of his strength,

10 ὅταν ἔλθῃ ἐνδοξασθῆναι ἐν τοῖς.ἁγίοις.αὐτοῦ καὶ

when he shall have come to be glorified in his saints and

θαυμασθῆναι ἐν πᾶσιν τοῖς [h]πιστεύουσιν,‖ ὅτι ἐπιστεύθη

to be wondered at in all them that believe, (because [5]was [6]believed

τὸ.μαρτύριον.ἡμῶν ἐφ' ὑμᾶς, ἐν τῇ.ἡμέρᾳ.ἐκείνῃ. 11 εἰς ὃ

[1]our [2]testimony [3]to [4]you,) in that day. For which

καὶ προσευχόμεθα πάντοτε περὶ ὑμῶν, ἵνα ὑμᾶς ἀξιώσῃ

also we pray always for you, that [5]you [3]may [4]count [6]worthy

τῆς κλήσεως ὁ.θεὸς.ἡμῶν, καὶ πληρώσῃ πᾶσαν εὐδοκίαν

[7]of [8]the [9]calling [1]our [2]God, and may fulfil every good pleasure

ἀγαθωσύνης καὶ ἔργον πίστεως ἐν δυνάμει· 12 ὅπως ἐν-

of goodness and work of faith with power, so that may

δοξασθῇ τὸ ὄνομα τοῦ.κυρίου.ἡμῶν Ἰησοῦ [i]χριστοῦ‖ ἐν ὑμῖν,

be glorified the name of our Lord Jesus Christ in you,

καὶ ὑμεῖς ἐν αὐτῷ, κατὰ τὴν χάριν τοῦ.θεοῦ.ἡμῶν καὶ

and ye in him, according to the grace of our God and

κυρίου Ἰησοῦ χριστοῦ.

of [the] Lord Jesus Christ.

2 Ἐρωτῶμεν.δὲ ὑμᾶς, ἀδελφοί, ὑπὲρ τῆς παρουσίας τοῦ

Now we beseech you, brethren, by the coming

κυρίου.ἡμῶν Ἰησοῦ χριστοῦ καὶ ἡμῶν ἐπισυναγωγῆς ἐπ'

of our Lord Jesus Christ and our gathering together to

αὐτόν, 2 εἰς τὸ μὴ ταχέως σαλευθῆναι ὑμᾶς ἀπὸ τοῦ νοός,

him, for [2]not [5]quickly [3]to [4]be [6]shaken [1]you in mind,

[k]μήτε‖ θροεῖσθαι, μήτε διὰ πνεύματος, μήτε διὰ λόγου, μήτε

nor to be troubled, neither by spirit, nor by word, nor

δι' ἐπιστολῆς ὡς δι' ἡμῶν, ὡς ὅτι ἐνέστηκεν ἡ ἡμέρα τοῦ

by epistle, as if by us, as that is present the day of the

[l]χριστοῦ.‖ 3 Μή τις ὑμᾶς ἐξαπατήσῃ κατὰ μηδένα τρόπον·

Christ. Not anyone [3]you [1]should [2]deceive in any (*lit.* no) way,

ὅτι ἐὰν.μὴ ἔλθῃ ἡ ἀποστασία πρῶτον

because [it will not be] unless shall have come the apostasy first,

καὶ ἀποκαλυφθῇ ὁ ἄνθρωπος τῆς [m]ἁμαρτίας,‖ ὁ υἱὸς

and shall have been revealed the man of sin, the son

τῆς ἀπωλείας, 4 ὁ ἀντικείμενος καὶ ὑπεραιρόμενος ἐπὶ πάντα

of perdition, he who opposes and exalts himself above all

[e] φλογὶ πυρὸς a flame of fire LTrW. [f] — χριστοῦ [L]TTrA. [g] ὀλέθριον, (*read* fatal, eternal) L. [h] πιστεύσασιν believed GLTTrAW. [i] — χριστοῦ [L]TTrAW. [k] μηδὲ LTTrAW. [l] κυρίου Lord GLTTrAW. [m] ἀνομίας of lawlessness TTr.

λεγόμενον θεὸν ἢ σέβασμα, ὥστε.αὐτὸν εἰς τὸν ναὸν
called God or object of veneration: so as for him in the temple
τοῦ θεοῦ ⁿὡς θεὸν‖ καθίσαι, ἀποδεικνύντα ἑαυτὸν ὅτι ἐστὶν
of God as God to sit down, setting forth himself that he is
θεός. 5 οὐ.μνημονεύετε ὅτι ἔτι ὢν πρὸς ὑμᾶς, ταῦτα
God. Do ye not remember that, yet being with you, these things
ἔλεγον ὑμῖν; 6 καὶ νῦν τὸ κατέχον οἴδατε, εἰς τὸ ἀπο-
I said to you? And now that which restrains ye know, for ²to ³be
καλυφθῆναι αὐτὸν ἐν τῷ.ᵒἑαυτοῦ‖ καιρῷ. 7 τὸ.γὰρ μυστήριον
¹revealed ¹him in his own time. For the mystery
ἤδη ἐνεργεῖται τῆς ἀνομίας, μόνον ὁ κατέχων
³already ⁴is ⁵working ¹of ²lawlessness; only [there is] he who restrains
ἄρτι ἕως ἐκ μέσου γένηται· 8 καὶ τότε ἀποκαλυ-
at present until out of [the] midst he be [gone], and then will be re-
φθήσεται ὁ ἄνομος, ὃν ὁ κύριος ᵖ ᵠἀναλώσει‖ τῷ
vealed the lawless [one], whom the Lord will consume with the
πνεύματι τοῦ.στόματος.αὐτοῦ, καὶ καταργήσει τῇ ἐπιφανείᾳ
breath of his mouth, and annul by the appearing
τῆς.παρουσίας.αὐτοῦ· 9 οὗ ἐστιν ἡ παρουσία κατ'
of his coming; whose ²is ¹coming according to [the]
ἐνέργειαν τοῦ σατανᾶ ἐν πάσῃ δυνάμει καὶ σημείοις.καὶ τέρασιν
working of Satan in every power and signs and wonders
ψεύδους, 10 καὶ ἐν πάσῃ ἀπάτῃ ʳτῆς‖ ἀδικίας ˢἐν‖ τοῖς
of falsehood, and in every deceit of unrighteousness in them that
ἀπολλυμένοις, ἀνθ'.ὧν τὴν ἀγάπην τῆς ἀληθείας οὐκ.ἐδέξαντο
perish, because the love of the truth they received not
εἰς τὸ σωθῆναι αὐτούς· 11 καὶ διὰ τοῦτο ᵗπέμψει‖
for ²to ³be ⁴saved ¹them. And on account of this ²will ³send
αὐτοῖς ὁ θεὸς ἐνέργειαν πλάνης, εἰς τὸ πιστεῦσαι αὐτοὺς
⁴to ⁵them ¹God a working of error, for ²to ³believe ¹them
τῷ ψεύδει· 12 ἵνα κριθῶσιν ᵛπάντες‖ οἱ μὴ.πιστεύσαντες
what [is] false, that may be judged all who believed not
τῇ ἀληθείᾳ, ʷἀλλ'‖ εὐδοκήσαντες ˣἐν‖ τῇ ἀδικίᾳ.
the truth, but delighted in unrighteousness.

13 Ἡμεῖς.δὲ ὀφείλομεν εὐχαριστεῖν τῷ θεῷ πάντοτε περὶ
But we ought to give thanks to God always concerning
ὑμῶν, ἀδελφοὶ ἠγαπημένοι ὑπὸ κυρίου, ὅτι ʸεἵλετο‖ ὑμᾶς
you, brethren beloved by [the] Lord, that ²chose ³you
ὁ θεὸς ᶻἀπ' ἀρχῆς‖ εἰς σωτηρίαν ἐν ἁγιασμῷ πνεύματος
¹God from [the] beginning to salvation in sanctification of [the] Spirit
καὶ πίστει ἀληθείας, 14 εἰς.ὃ ᵃ ἐκάλεσεν ᵇὑμᾶς‖ διὰ τοῦ
and belief of [the] truth; whereto he called you by
εὐαγγελίου.ἡμῶν, εἰς περιποίησιν δόξης τοῦ κυρίου
our glad tidings, to [the] obtaining of [the] glory of ²Lord
ἡμῶν Ἰησοῦ χριστοῦ. 15 ἄρα οὖν, ἀδελφοί, στήκετε, καὶ
¹our Jesus Christ. So then, brethren, stand firm, and
κρατεῖτε τὰς παραδόσεις ἃς ἐδιδάχθητε, εἴτε διὰ λόγου
hold fast the traditions which ye were taught, whether by word
εἴτε δι' ἐπιστολῆς.ἡμῶν. 16 αὐτὸς.δὲ ὁ κύριος ἡμῶν Ἰησοῦς
or by our epistle. But ⁵himself ²Lord ¹our ³Jesus
ᶜ χριστός, καὶ ᵈὁ‖ θεὸς ᵉκαὶ‖ πατὴρ ἡμῶν, ὁ ἀγαπήσας ἡμᾶς
⁴Christ, and ²God ³and ⁴Father ¹our, who loved us,

God, or that is worshipped; so that he as God sitteth in the temple of God, shewing himself that he is God. 5 Remember ye not, that, when I was yet with you, I told you these things? 6 And now ye know what withholdeth that he might be revealed in his time. 7 For the mystery of iniquity doth already work: only he who now letteth *will let*, until he be taken out of the way. 8 And then shall that Wicked be revealed, whom the Lord shall consume with the spirit of his mouth, and shall destroy with the brightness of his coming: 9 *even him*, whose coming is after the working of Satan with all power and signs and lying wonders, 10 and with all deceivableness of unrighteousness in them that perish; because they received not the love of the truth, that they might be saved. 11 And for this cause God shall send them strong delusion, that they should believe a lie: 12 that they all might be damned who believed not the truth, but had pleasure in unrighteousness.

13 But we are bound to give thanks alway to God for you, brethren beloved of the Lord, because God hath from the beginning chosen you to salvation through sanctification of the Spirit and belief of the truth: 14 whereunto he called you by our gospel, to the obtaining of the glory of our Lord Jesus Christ. 15 Therefore, brethren, stand fast, and hold the traditions which ye have been taught, whether by word, or our epistle. 16 Now our Lord Jesus Christ himself, and God, even our Father, which hath loved us, and hath

---

ⁿ — ὡς θεὸν GLTTrAW. ᵒ αὐτοῦ (*read* his time) TTr. ᵖ + Ἰησοῦς Jesus GLTTrAW. ᵠ ἀνελεῖ will slay LTTrA. ʳ — τῆς LTTrAW. ˢ — ἐν (*read* τοῖς to them that) LTTrAW. ᵗ πέμπει sends LTTrAW. ᵛ ἅπαντες TTrA. ʷ ἀλλὰ TTr. ˣ — ἐν (*read* ἀδικίᾳ in unrighteousness) [L]TTr[A]. ʸ εἵλατο GLTTrAW. ᶻ ἀπαρχὴν L. ᵃ + καὶ also T. ᵇ ἡμᾶς us L. ᶜ + ὁ the L. ᵈ — ὁ [L]Tr. ᵉ ὁ LTTrA.

given *us* everlasting consolation and good hope through grace,
17 comfort your hearts, and stablish you in every good word and work.

III. Finally, brethren, pray for us, that the word of the Lord may have *free* course, and be glorified, even as *it is* with you:
2 and that we may be delivered from unreasonable and wicked men: for all *men* have not faith.
3 But the Lord is faithful, who shall stablish you, and keep *you* from evil.
4 And we have confidence in the Lord touching you, that ye both do and will do the things which we command you.
5 And the Lord direct your hearts into the love of God, and into the patient waiting for Christ.

6 Now we command you, brethren, in the name of our Lord Jesus Christ, that ye withdraw yourselves from every brother that walketh disorderly, and not after the tradition which he received of us.
7 For yourselves know how ye ought to follow us: for we behaved not ourselves disorderly among you;
8 neither did we eat any man's bread for nought; but wrought with labour and travail night and day, that we might not be chargeable to any of you:
9 not because we have not power, but to make ourselves an ensample unto you to follow us.
10 For even when we were with you, this we commanded you, that if any would not work, neither should he eat.
11 For we hear that there are some which walk among you disorderly, working not at all, but are busybodies.
12 Now them that are such we command and exhort by our Lord Je-

καὶ δοὺς παράκλησιν αἰωνίαν καὶ ἐλπίδα ἀγαθὴν ἐν χάριτι,
and gave [us] [2]encouragement [1]eternal and [2]hope [1]good by grace,
17 παρακαλέσαι ὑμῶν τὰς καρδίας, καὶ στηρίξαι [f]ὑμᾶς‖
may he encourage your hearts, and may he establish you
ἐν παντὶ [g]λόγῳ καὶ ἔργῳ‖ ἀγαθῷ.
in every [2]word [3]and [4]work [1]good.

3 Τὸ.λοιπόν, προσεύχεσθε, ἀδελφοί, περὶ ἡμῶν, ἵνα ὁ
For the rest, pray, brethren, for us, that the
λόγος τοῦ κυρίου τρέχῃ καὶ δοξάζηται, καθὼς καὶ πρὸς
word of the Lord may run and may be glorified, even as also with
ὑμᾶς, 2 καὶ ἵνα ῥυσθῶμεν ἀπὸ τῶν ἀτόπων καὶ πονηρῶν
you; and that we may be delivered from perverse and wicked
ἀνθρώπων· οὐ.γὰρ πάντων ἡ πίστις. 3 πιστὸς
men, for [3]not [6]of [7]all [[2]is] [1]faith [[4]the [5]portion]. [9]Faithful
δέ ἐστιν [h]ὁ κύριος,‖ ὃς στηρίξει ὑμᾶς καὶ φυλάξει
[8]but is the Lord, who will establish you and will keep [you]
ἀπὸ τοῦ πονηροῦ. 4 πεποίθαμεν.δὲ ἐν κυρίῳ ἐφ' ὑμᾶς,
from evil. But we trust in [the] Lord as to you,
ὅτι ἃ παραγγέλλομεν [i]ὑμῖν,‖ [k] [l]καὶ‖ ποιεῖτε καὶ
that the things which we charge you, both ye are doing and
ποιήσετε. 5 ὁ.δὲ κύριος κατευθύναι ὑμῶν τὰς καρδίας εἰς
will do. But [2]the [3]Lord [1]may direct your hearts into
τὴν ἀγάπην τοῦ θεοῦ, καὶ εἰς [m] ὑπομονὴν τοῦ χριστοῦ.
the love of God, and into [the] endurance of the Christ.

6 Παραγγέλλομεν.δὲ ὑμῖν, ἀδελφοί, ἐν ὀνόματι τοῦ
Now we charge you, brethren, in [the] name
κυρίου.[n]ἡμῶν‖ Ἰησοῦ χριστοῦ, στέλλεσθαι ὑμᾶς ἀπὸ παν-
of our Lord Jesus Christ, [that] [2]withdraw [1]ye from every
τὸς ἀδελφοῦ ἀτάκτως περιπατοῦντος, καὶ μὴ κατὰ τὴν
brother [2]disorderly [1]walking, and not according to the
παράδοσιν ἣν [o]παρέλαβεν‖ παρ' ἡμῶν. 7 αὐτοὶ.γὰρ οἴδατε
tradition which he received from us. For [2]yourselves [1]ye know
πῶς δεῖ μιμεῖσθαι ἡμᾶς· ὅτι οὐκ.ἠτακτήσαμεν
how it behoves [you] to imitate us, because we behaved not disorderly
ἐν ὑμῖν, 8 οὐδὲ δωρεὰν ἄρτον ἐφάγομεν παρά τινος, [p]ἀλλ'‖
among you; nor for nought bread did we eat from anyone; but
ἐν κόπῳ καὶ μόχθῳ, [q]νύκτα καὶ ἡμέραν‖ ἐργαζόμενοι, πρὸς τὸ
in labour and toil, night and day working, for
μὴ ἐπιβαρῆσαί τινα ὑμῶν· 9 οὐχ ὅτι οὐκ.ἔχομεν ἐξουσίαν,
not to be burdensome to anyone of you. Not that we have not authority,
ἀλλ' ἵνα ἑαυτοὺς τύπον δῶμεν ὑμῖν εἰς τὸ μιμεῖσθαι ἡμᾶς.
but that ourselves a pattern we might give to you for to imitate us.
10 καὶ.γὰρ ὅτε ἦμεν πρὸς ὑμᾶς τοῦτο παρηγγέλλομεν ὑμῖν,
For also when we were with you this we charged you,
ὅτι εἴ τις οὐ.θέλει ἐργάζεσθαι, μηδὲ ἐσθιέτω. 11 ἀκούομεν
that if anyone does not wish to work, neither let him eat. [2]We [3]hear
γάρ τινας περιπατοῦντας ἐν ὑμῖν ἀτάκτως, μηδὲν ἐργαζο-
[1]for some are walking among you disorderly, not at all work-
μένους, ἀλλὰ περιεργαζομένους. 12 τοῖς.δὲ.τοιούτοις παραγ-
ing, but being busy bodies. Now such we
γέλλομεν καὶ παρακαλοῦμεν [r]διὰ τοῦ.κυρίου.ἡμῶν Ἰησοῦ
charge and exhort by our Lord Jesus

---

[f] — ὑμᾶς (*read* [you]) LTTrAW. [g] ἔργῳ καὶ λόγῳ LTTrAW. [h] ὁ θεός God L. [i] — ὑμῖν [L]TTrA. [k] + [καὶ ἐποιήσατε] ye did L. [l] — καὶ [L]T[Tr]. [m] + τὴν the GLTTrAW. [n] — ἡμῶν (*read* the Lord) [L]A. [o] παρελάβοσαν they received, GATW; παρελάβετε ye received LTr. [p] ἀλλὰ Tr. [q] νυκτὸς καὶ ἡμέρας LTTr. [r] ἐν κυρίῳ Ἰησοῦ χριστῷ in [the] Lord Jesus Christ LTTrA.

χριστοῦ,ǁ ἵνα μετὰ ἡσυχίας ἐργαζόμενοι, τὸν.ἑαυτῶν ἄρτον
Christ, that with quietness working, their own bread
ἐσθίωσιν. 13 ὑμεῖς.δέ, ἀδελφοί, μὴ.[s]ἐκκακήσητεǁ καλοποιοῦν-
they may eat. But ye, brethren, do not lose heart [in] well-doing.
τες. 14 εἰ.δέ τις οὐχ.ὑπακούει τῷ.λόγῳ.ἡμῶν διὰ τῆς ἐπι-
But if anyone obey not our word by the epis-
στολῆς, τοῦτον σημειοῦσθε [t]καὶǁ [v]μὴ.συναναμίγνυσθεǁ αὐτῷ,
tle, [2]that [[3]man] [1]mark and associate not with him,
ἵνα ἐντραπῇ· 15 καὶ μὴ ὡς ἐχθρὸν ἡγεῖσθε, ἀλλὰ
that he may be ashamed; and not as an enemy esteem [him], but
νουθετεῖτε ὡς ἀδελφόν. 16 αὐτὸς.δὲ ὁ κύριος τῆς εἰρήνης
admonish [him] as a brother. But [6]himself [2]the [3]Lord [4]of [5]peace
δῴη ὑμῖν τὴν εἰρήνην διὰ.παντὸς ἐν παντὶ [w]τρόπῳ.ǁ ὁ
[1]may give you peace continually in every way. The
κύριος μετὰ πάντων ὑμῶν.
Lord [be] with all you.
17 Ὁ ἀσπασμὸς τῇ.ἐμῇ.χειρὶ Παύλου, ὅ ἐστιν σημεῖον
The salutation [3]by [4]my [[5]own] [6]hand [1]of [2]Paul, which is [the] sign
ἐν πάσῃ ἐπιστολῇ· οὕτως γράφω. 18 ἡ χάρις τοῦ.κυρίου.ἡμῶν
in every epistle; so I write. The grace of our Lord
Ἰησοῦ χριστοῦ μετὰ πάντων ὑμῶν. [x]ἀμήν.ǁ
Jesus Christ [be] with [2]all [1]you. Amen.
[y]Πρὸς Θεσσαλονικεῖς δευτέρα ἐγράφη ἀπὸ Ἀθηνῶν.ǁ
[2]To [[3]the] [4]Thessalonians [1]second written from Athens.

sus Christ, that with quietness they work, and eat their own bread. 13 But ye, brethren, be not weary in well doing. 14 And if any man obey not our word by this epistle, note that man, and have no company with him, that he may be ashamed. 15 Yet count *him* not as an enemy, but admonish *him* as a brother. 16 Now the Lord of peace himself give you peace always by all means. The Lord *be* with you all.

17 The salutation of Paul with mine own hand, which is the token in every epistle: so I write. 18 The grace of our Lord Jesus Christ *be* with you all. Amen.

---

[a]Η ΠΡΟΣ ΤΙΜΟΘΕΟΝ ΕΠΙΣΤΟΛΗ ΠΡΩΤΗ.ǁ
THE [3]TO [4]TIMOTHY [2]EPISTLE [1]FIRST.

ΠΑΥΛΟΣ ἀπόστολος [b]Ἰησοῦ χριστοῦǁ κατʼ ἐπιταγὴν
Paul, apostle of Jesus Christ according to [the] command
θεοῦ σωτῆρος.ἡμῶν, καὶ [c]κυρίουǁ [d]Ἰησοῦ χριστοῦǁ τῆς
of God our Saviour, and of [the] Lord Jesus Christ
ἐλπίδος.ἡμῶν, 2 Τιμοθέῳ γνησίῳ τέκνῳ ἐν πίστει· χάρις,
our hope, to Timotheus, [my] true child in faith; grace,
ἔλεος, εἰρήνη ἀπὸ θεοῦ πατρὸς.[e]ἡμῶνǁ καὶ χριστοῦ Ἰησοῦ
mercy, peace, from God our Father and Christ Jesus
τοῦ.κυρίου.ἡμῶν.
our Lord.
3 Καθὼς παρεκάλεσά σε προσμεῖναι ἐν Ἐφέσῳ,
Even as I besought thee to remain in Ephesus, [when I was]
πορευόμενος εἰς Μακεδονίαν, ἵνα παραγγείλῃς τισὶν μὴ
going to Macedonia, that thou mightest charge some not
ἑτεροδιδασκαλεῖν, 4 μηδὲ προσέχειν μύθοις καὶ γενεαλογίαις
to teach other doctrines, nor to give heed to fables and [2]genealogies
ἀπεράντοις, αἵτινες [f]ζητήσειςǁ παρέχουσιν μᾶλλον ἢ [g]οἰκονο-
[1]interminable, which [2]questionings [1]bring rather than [2]adminis-
μίανǁ θεοῦ τὴν ἐν πίστει· 5 τὸ.δὲ τέλος τῆς παραγγελίας
tration [1]God's which [is] in faith. But the end of the charge

PAUL, an apostle of Jesus Christ by the commandment of God our Saviour, and Lord Jesus Christ, *which is* our hope; 2 unto Timothy, *my* own son in the faith: Grace, mercy, *and* peace, from God our Father and Jesus Christ our Lord.

3 As I besought thee to abide still at Ephesus, when I went into Macedonia, that thou mightest charge some that they teach no other doctrine, 4 neither give heed to fables and endless genealogies, which minister questions, rather than godly edifying which is in faith: *so do.* 5 Now the end of the commandment is cha-

---

[s] ἐγ- LTTrAW. [t] — καὶ LTTrA. [v] μὴ συναναμίγνυσθαι not to associate yourselves with LTrA. [w] τόπῳ place L. [x] — ἀμήν TTrA. [y] — *the subscription* GLTW; Πρὸς Θεσσαλονικεῖς β΄ TrA.
[a] + Παύλου τοῦ Ἀποστόλου of the Apostle Paul E; + Παύλου G; Πρὸς Τιμόθεον α΄ LTTrAW. [b] χριστοῦ Ἰησοῦ TTrAW. [c] — κυρίου GLTTrAW. [d] χριστοῦ Ἰησοῦ GLTTrAW. [e] — ἡμῶν (*read* [the]) LTTrAW. [f] ἐκζητήσεις TTr. [g] οἰκοδομίαν building up E.

rity out of a pure
heart, and *of* a good
conscience, and *of*
faith unfeigned: 6 from
which some having
swerved have turned
aside unto vain jang-
ling; 7 desiring to be
teachers of the law;
understanding neither
what they say, nor
whereof they affirm.
8 But we know that
the law *is* good, if a
man use it lawfully;
9 knowing this, that
the law is not made
for a righteous man,
but for the lawless
and disobedient, for
the ungodly and for
sinners, for unholy
and profane, for mur-
derers of fathers and
murderers of mothers,
for manslayers, 10 for
whoremongers, for
them that defile them-
selves with mankind,
for menstealers, for
liars, for perjured
persons, and if there
be any other thing
that is contrary
to sound doctrine;
11 according to the
glorious gospel of the
blessed God, which
was committed to my
trust. 12 And I thank
Christ Jesus our Lord,
who hath enabled me,
for that he counted
me faithful, putting
me into the ministry;
13 who was before a
blasphemer, and a per-
secutor, and injurious:
but I obtained mercy,
because I did *it* igno-
rantly in unbelief.
14 And the grace of
our Lord was exceed-
ing abundant with
faith and love which
is in Christ Jesus.
15 This *is* a faithful
saying, and worthy of
all acceptation, that
Christ Jesus came into
the world to save sin-
ners; of whom I am
chief. 16 Howbeit for
this cause I obtained
mercy, that in me first
Jesus Christ might
shew forth all long-
suffering, for a pat-
tern to them which
should hereafter be-
lieve on him to life
everlasting. 17 Now
unto the King eternal,
immortal, invisible,
the only wise God, *be*
honour and glory for
ever and ever. Amen.
18 This charge I com-

ἐστὶν ἀγάπη ἐκ καθαρᾶς καρδίας καὶ συνειδήσεως ἀγαθῆς
is love out of [2]pure [1]a heart and a [2]conscience [1]good

καὶ πίστεως ἀνυποκρίτου· 6 ὧν τινες ἀστοχήσαντες,
and faith unfeigned; from which some, having missed the mark,

ἐξετράπησαν εἰς ματαιολογίαν, 7 θέλοντες εἶναι νομοδιδάσ-
turned aside to vain talking, wishing to be law-teachers,

καλοι, μὴ νοοῦντες μήτε ἃ λέγουσιν, μήτε περὶ τίνων
understanding neither what they say, nor concerning what

διαβεβαιοῦνται. 8 οἴδαμεν.δὲ ὅτι καλὸς ὁ νόμος, ἐάν τις
they strongly affirm. Now we know that good [is] the law, if anyone

αὐτῷ νομίμως [h]χρῆται,‖ 9 εἰδὼς τοῦτο, ὅτι δικαίῳ
[2]it [3]lawfully [1]use, knowing this, that for a righteous [one]

νόμος οὐ.κεῖται, ἀνόμοις.δὲ καὶ ἀνυποτάκτοις, ἀσεβέσιν
law is not enacted, but for lawless and insubordinate [ones], for [the] ungodly

καὶ ἁμαρτωλοῖς, ἀνοσίοις καὶ βεβήλοις, [i]πατραλῴαις‖
and sinful, for [the] unholy and profane, for smiters of fathers

καὶ [k]μητραλῴαις,‖ ἀνδροφόνοις, 10 πόρνοις, ἀρσενο-
and smiters of mothers; for slayers of man, fornicators, abusers of them-

κοίταις, ἀνδραποδισταῖς, ψεύσταις, ἐπιόρκοις, καὶ εἴ
selves with men, men-stealers, liars, perjurers, and if

τι ἕτερον τῇ ὑγιαινούσῃ διδασκαλίᾳ ἀντίκειται, 11 κατὰ
any [2]thing [1]other to sound teaching is opposed, according to

τὸ εὐαγγέλιον τῆς δόξης τοῦ μακαρίου θεοῦ, ὃ ἐπιστεύ-
the glad tidings of the glory of the blessed God, which [2]was [3]entrusted

θην ἐγώ. 12 [l]καὶ‖ χάριν.ἔχω τῷ ἐνδυναμώσαντί με χριστῷ
[4]with [1]I. And I thank him who strengthened me, Christ

Ἰησοῦ τῷ.κυρίῳ.ἡμῶν, ὅτι πιστόν με ἡγήσατο, θέμενος εἰς
Jesus our Lord, that faithful me he esteemed, appointing [me] to

διακονίαν, 13 [m]τὸν‖ πρότερον ὄντα [n] βλάσφημον καὶ διώκτην
service, [2]previously [1]being a blasphemer and persecutor

καὶ ὑβριστήν· [o]ἀλλ'‖ ἠλεήθην, ὅτι ἀγνοῶν ἐποίησα
and insolent; but I was shewn mercy, because being ignorant I did

ἐν ἀπιστίᾳ· 14 ὑπερεπλεόνασεν.δὲ ἡ χάρις τοῦ.κυρίου.ἡμῶν
[it] in unbelief. But superabounded the grace of our Lord

μετὰ πίστεως καὶ ἀγάπης τῆς ἐν χριστῷ Ἰησοῦ. 15 πιστὸς
with faith and love which [is] in Christ Jesus. Faithful

ὁ λόγος καὶ πάσης ἀποδοχῆς ἄξιος, ὅτι χριστὸς Ἰησοῦς
[is] the word, and of all acceptation worthy, that Christ Jesus

ἦλθεν εἰς τὸν κόσμον ἁμαρτωλοὺς σῶσαι, ὧν πρῶτός
came into the world sinners to save, of whom [the] first

εἰμι ἐγώ. 16 ἀλλὰ διὰ.τοῦτο ἠλεήθην, ἵνα ἐν ἐμοὶ
[2]am [1]I. But for this reason I was shewn mercy, that in me, [the]

πρώτῳ ἐνδείξηται [p]Ἰησοῦς χριστὸς‖ τὴν [q]πᾶσαν‖ μακρο-
first, [3]might [4]shew [5]forth [1]Jesus [2]Christ the whole long-

θυμίαν, πρὸς ὑποτύπωσιν τῶν μελλόντων πιστεύειν ἐπ'
suffering, for a delineation of those being about to believe on

αὐτῷ εἰς ζωὴν αἰώνιον. 17 τῷ.δὲ βασιλεῖ τῶν αἰώνων,
him to life eternal. Now to the King of the ages, [the]

ἀφθάρτῳ, ἀοράτῳ, μόνῳ [r]σοφῷ‖ θεῷ, τιμὴ καὶ δόξα εἰς τοὺς
incorruptible, invisible, only wise God, honour and glory to the

αἰῶνας τῶν αἰώνων. ἀμήν. 18 ταύτην τὴν παραγγελίαν
ages of the ages. Amen. This charge

παρατίθεμαί σοι, τέκνον Τιμόθεε, κατὰ τὰς προ-
I commit to thee, [my] child Timotheus, according to the [5]going

---

[h] χρήσηται L. [i] πατρολῴαις LTTrA. [k] μητρολῴαις LTTrA. [l] — καὶ LTTrA. [m] τὸ LTTrA. [n] + με me (being) L. [o] ἀλλὰ LTTrAW. [p] χριστὸς Ἰησοῦς LTrA. [q] ἅπασαν LTTrAW. [r] — σοφῷ GLTTrAW.

αγούσας ἐπὶ σε προφητείας, ἵνα [s]στρατεύῃ‖ ἐν αὐταῖς τὴν
[6]before [2]as [3]to [4]thee [1]prophecies, that thou mightest war by them the
καλὴν στρατείαν, 19 ἔχων πίστιν καὶ ἀγαθὴν συνείδησιν,
good warfare, holding faith and [2]good [1]a conscience;
ἥν τινες ἀπωσάμενοι, περὶ τὴν πίστιν ἐναυάγησαν·
which [conscience] some, having cast away, as to faith made shipwreck;
20 ὧν ἐστιν Ὑμέναιος καὶ Ἀλέξανδρος, οὓς παρέδωκα τῷ
of whom are Hymenæus and Alexander, whom I delivered up
σατανᾷ, ἵνα παιδευθῶσιν μὴ βλασφημεῖν.
to Satan, that they may be disciplined not to blaspheme.

2 Παρακαλῶ οὖν πρῶτον πάντων ποιεῖσθαι δεήσεις,
I exhort therefore, first of all, to be made supplications,
προσευχάς, ἐντεύξεις, εὐχαριστίας, ὑπὲρ πάντων ἀνθρώ-
prayers, intercessions, thanksgivings, for all men;
πων, 2 ὑπὲρ βασιλέων καὶ πάντων τῶν ἐν ὑπεροχῇ ὄντων,
for kings and all that in dignity are,
ἵνα ἤρεμον καὶ ἡσύχιον βίον διάγωμεν ἐν πάσῃ εὐσεβείᾳ καὶ
that a tranquil and quiet life we may lead in all piety and
σεμνότητι· 3 τοῦτο.[t]γὰρ‖ καλὸν καὶ ἀποδεκτὸν ἐνώπιον τοῦ
gravity; for this [is] good and acceptable before
σωτῆρος.ἡμῶν θεοῦ, 4 ὃς πάντας ἀνθρώπους θέλει σωθῆναι
our Saviour God, who [2]all [3]men [1]wishes to be saved
καὶ εἰς ἐπίγνωσιν ἀληθείας ἐλθεῖν. 5 εἷς.γὰρ θεός, εἷς.καὶ
and [3]to [4]knowledge [5]of [[6]the] [7]truth [1]to [2]come. For [3]one [1]God [[2]is], and one
μεσίτης θεοῦ καὶ ἀνθρώπων, ἄνθρωπος χριστὸς Ἰη-
[the] mediator of God and men, [the] man Christ Je-
σοῦς, 6 ὁ δοὺς ἑαυτὸν ἀντίλυτρον ὑπὲρ πάντων, [v]τὸ μαρ-
sus, who gave himself a ransom for all, the tes-
τύριον‖ καιροῖς ἰδίοις, 7 εἰς ὃ ἐτέθην ἐγὼ
timony [to be rendered] in [3]times [1]its [2]own, to which [2]was [3]appointed [1]I
κήρυξ καὶ ἀπόστολος· ἀλήθειαν λέγω [w]ἐν χριστῷ,‖ οὐ
a herald and apostle, ([the] truth I speak in Christ, [3]not
ψεύδομαι· διδάσκαλος ἐθνῶν, ἐν πίστει καὶ ἀληθείᾳ.
[1]I [2]do lie,) a teacher of [the] nations, in faith and truth.
8 Βούλομαι οὖν προσεύχεσθαι τοὺς ἄνδρας ἐν παντὶ τόπῳ,
I will therefore [3]to [4]pray [1]the [2]men in every place,
ἐπαίροντας ὁσίους χεῖρας χωρὶς ὀργῆς καὶ διαλογισμοῦ·
lifting up holy hands apart from wrath and reasoning.
9 ὡσαύτως [x]καὶ‖ [y]τὰς‖ γυναῖκας ἐν καταστολῇ κοσμίῳ μετὰ
In like manner also the women in [2]guise [1]seemly with
αἰδοῦς καὶ σωφροσύνης κοσμεῖν ἑαυτάς, μὴ ἐν πλέγμασιν,
modesty and discreetness to adorn themselves, not with plaitings,
[z]ἢ [a]χρυσῷ,‖ ἢ μαργαρίταις, ἢ ἱματισμῷ πολυτελεῖ, 10 [b]ἀλλ'‖
or gold, or pearls, or [2]clothing [1]costly, but
ὃ πρέπει γυναιξὶν ἐπαγγελλομέναις θεοσέβειαν, δι'
what is becoming to women professing [the] fear of God, by
ἔργων ἀγαθῶν. 11 Γυνὴ ἐν ἡσυχίᾳ μανθανέτω ἐν πάσῃ
[2]works [1]good. [4]A [5]woman [7]in [8]quietness [3]let [6]learn in all
ὑποταγῇ· 12 [c]γυναικὶ.δὲ διδάσκειν‖ οὐκ.ἐπιτρέπω, οὐδὲ αὐ-
subjection; but a woman to teach I do not allow, nor to exercise
θεντεῖν ἀνδρός, [d]ἀλλ'‖ εἶναι ἐν ἡσυχίᾳ. 13 Ἀδὰμ.γὰρ
authority over man, but to be in quietness; for Adam
πρῶτος ἐπλάσθη, εἶτα Εὔα. 14 καὶ Ἀδὰμ οὐκ.ἠπατήθη· ἡ.δὲ
first was formed, then Eve: and Adam was not deceived; but the

mit unto thee, son Ti-
mothy, according to
the prophecies which
went before on thee,
that thou by them
mightest war a good
warfare; 19 holding
faith, and a good con-
science; which some
having put away con-
cerning faith have
made shipwreck: 20 of
whom is Hymenæus
and Alexander; whom
I have delivered unto
Satan, that they may
learn not to blas-
pheme.

II. I exhort there-
fore, that, first of all,
supplications, prayers,
intercessions, *and* giv-
ing of thanks, be made
for all men; 2 for
kings, and *for* all that
are in authority; that
we may lead a quiet
and peaceable life in
all godliness and ho-
nesty. 3 For this *is*
good and acceptable in
the sight of God our
Saviour; 4 who will
have all men to be
saved, and to come
unto the knowledge
of the truth. 5 For
there is one God, and
one mediator between
God and men, the man
Christ Jesus; 6 who
gave himself a ransom
for all, to be testified
in due time. 7 Where-
unto I am ordained a
preacher, and an apo-
stle, (I speak the truth
in Christ, *and* lie not;)
a teacher of the Gen-
tiles in faith and ve-
rity.
8 I will therefore
that men pray every
where, lifting up holy
hands, without wrath
and doubting. 9 In
like manner also, that
women adorn them-
selves in modest ap-
parel, with shamefac-
edness and sobriety;
not with broided hair,
or gold, or pearls, or
costly array; 10 but
(which becometh wo-
men professing godli-
ness) with good works.
11 Let the woman
learn in silence with
all subjection. 12 But
I suffer not a woman
to teach, nor to usurp
authority over the
man, but to be in si-
lence. 13 For Adam
was first formed, then
Eve. 14 And Adam
was not deceived, but

[s] στρατεύσῃ TTr. [t] — γὰρ for LTTr. [v] — τὸ μαρτύριον L. [w] — ἐν χριστῷ GLTTrAW.
[x] — καὶ LT[Tr]. [y] — τὰς LTTrAW. [z] καὶ and LTTrA. [a] χρυσίῳ L. [b] ἀλλὰ W.
[c] διδάσκειν δὲ γυναικὶ LTTrA. [d] ἀλλὰ LTr.

γυνὴ [e]ἀπατηθεῖσα‖ ἐν παραβάσει γέγονεν· 15 σωθήσεται.δὲ
woman, having been deceived, in transgression has become. But she shall be saved
διὰ τῆς τεκνογονίας, ἐὰν μείνωσιν ἐν πίστει καὶ ἀγάπῃ
through the childbearing, if they abide in faith and love
καὶ ἁγιασμῷ μετὰ σωφροσύνης.
and sanctification with discreetness.

3 Πιστὸς ὁ λόγος· εἴ τις ἐπισκοπῆς ὀρέγεται,
Faithful [is] the word: if any [4]overseership [1]stretches [2]forward [3]to
καλοῦ ἔργου ἐπιθυμεῖ. 2 δεῖ οὖν τὸν ἐπίσκοπον [f]ἀνεπί-
of [2]good [1]a work he is desirous. It behoves then the overseer irreproach-
ληπτον‖ εἶναι, μιᾶς γυναικὸς ἄνδρα, [g]νηφάλεον,‖ σώφρονα,
able to be, [2]of [3]one [4]wife [1]husband, sober, discreet,
κόσμιον, φιλόξενον, διδακτικόν· 3 μὴ πάροινον, μὴ πλήκτην,
decorous, hospitable, apt to teach; not given to wine, not a striker,
[h]μὴ αἰσχροκερδῆ,‖ [i]ἀλλ'‖ ἐπιεικῆ, ἄμαχον, ἀφιλάργυρον·
not greedy of base gain, but gentle, not contentious, not loving money;
4 τοῦ.ἰδίου.οἴκου καλῶς προϊστάμενον, τέκνα ἔχοντα ἐν
his own house well ruling, [his] children having in
ὑποταγῇ μετὰ πάσης σεμνότητος· 5 εἰ.δέ τις τοῦ.ἰδίου.οἴκου
subjection with all gravity; (but if one his own house
προστῆναι οὐκ.οἶδεν, πῶς ἐκκλησίας θεοῦ ἐπιμελήσεται;
[how] to rule knows not, how [the] assembly of God shall he take care of?)
6 μὴ νεόφυτον, ἵνα.μὴ τυφωθεὶς εἰς κρίμα ἐμπέσῃ
not a novice, lest being puffed up, into [the] crime [4]he [5]may [6]fall
τοῦ διαβόλου. 7 δεῖ.δὲ [k]αὐτὸν‖ καὶ μαρτυρίαν καλὴν
[1]of [2]the [3]devil. But it behoves [4]him also a [2]testimony [1]good
ἔχειν ἀπὸ τῶν ἔξωθεν, ἵνα.μὴ εἰς ὀνειδισμὸν ἐμπέσῃ καὶ
to have from those without, lest into reproach he may fall and [the]
παγίδα τοῦ διαβόλου. 8 Διακόνους ὡσαύτως σεμνούς, μὴ
snare of the devil. Those who serve, in like manner, grave, not
διλόγους, μὴ οἴνῳ πολλῷ προσέχοντας, μὴ αἰσχροκερδεῖς,
double-tongued, not to [2]wine [1]much given, not greedy of base gain,
9 ἔχοντας τὸ μυστήριον τῆς πίστεως ἐν καθαρᾷ συνειδήσει.
holding the mystery of the faith in [2]pure [1]a conscience.
10 καὶ.οὗτοι.δὲ δοκιμαζέσθωσαν πρῶτον, εἶτα διακονείτωσαν,
And these also let them be proved first, then let them serve,
ἀνέγκλητοι ὄντες. 11 γυναῖκας ὡσαύτως σεμνάς, μὴ δια-
[2]unimpeachable [1]being. Women in like manner grave, not slan-
βόλους, [l]νηφαλέους,‖ πιστὰς ἐν πᾶσιν. 12 διάκονοι ἔστω-
derers, sober, faithful in all things. [2]Those [3]who [4]serve [1]let
σαν μιᾶς γυναικὸς ἄνδρες, τέκνων καλῶς προϊστάμενοι
[5]be [7]of [8]one [9]wife [6]husbands, [[12]their] [13]children [11]well [10]ruling
καὶ τῶν.ἰδίων οἴκων. 13 οἱ.γὰρ καλῶς διακονήσαντες, βαθμὸν
and their own houses. For those well having served, a [2]degree
ἑαυτοῖς καλὸν περιποιοῦνται, καὶ πολλὴν παῤῥησίαν ἐν
[3]for [4]themselves [1]good acquire, and much boldness in
πίστει τῇ ἐν χριστῷ Ἰησοῦ.
faith which [is] in Christ Jesus.

14 Ταῦτά σοι γράφω, ἐλπίζων ἐλθεῖν πρός σε [m]τάχιον·‖
These things to thee I write, hoping to come to thee more quickly;
15 ἐὰν.δὲ βραδύνω, ἵνα εἰδῇς πῶς δεῖ ἐν
but if I should delay, that thou mayest know how it behoves [one] in [the]
οἴκῳ θεοῦ ἀναστρέφεσθαι, ἥτις ἐστὶν ἐκκλησία θεοῦ
house of God to conduct oneself, which is [the] assembly of [3]God [[1]the]

the woman being deceived was in the transgression. 15 **Notwithstanding she shall be saved in childbearing, if they continue in faith and charity and holiness with sobriety.**

III. This *is* a true saying, If a man desire the office of a bishop, he desireth a good work.
2 A bishop then must be blameless, the husband of one wife, vigilant, sober, of good behaviour, given to hospitality, apt to teach;
3 not given to wine, no striker, not greedy of filthy lucre; but patient, not a brawler, not covetous;
4 one that ruleth well his own house, having his children in subjection with all gravity;
5 (for if a man know not how to rule his own house, how shall he take care of the church of God?)
6 not a novice, lest being lifted up with pride he fall into the condemnation of the devil.
7 Moreover he must have a good report of them which are without; lest he fall into reproach and the snare of the devil.
8 Likewise *must* the deacons *be* grave, not doubletongued, not given to much wine, not greedy of filthy lucre;
9 holding the mystery of the faith in a pure conscience.
10 And let these also first be proved; then let them use the office of a deacon, being *found* blameless.
11 Even so *must their* wives *be* grave, not slanderers, sober, faithful in all things.
12 Let the deacons be the husbands of one wife, ruling their children and their own houses well.
13 For they that have used the office of a deacon well purchase to themselves a good degree, and great boldness in the faith which is in Christ Jesus.

14 These things write I unto thee, hoping to come unto thee shortly:
15 but if I tarry long, that thou mayest

[e] ἐξαπατηθεῖσα LTTrAW. [f] ἀνεπίλημπτον LTTrA. [g] νηφάλιον EGLTTrAW. [h] — μὴ αἰσχροκερδῆ GLTTrAW. [i] ἀλλὰ LTTr. [k] — αὐτὸν (*read* δεῖ it is necessary) LTTrA. [l] νηφαλίους EGLTTrAW. [m] ἐν τάχει quickly LTr.

ζῶντος, στῦλος καὶ ἑδραίωμα τῆς ἀληθείας. 16 καὶ ὁμολο-
[3]living, pillar and base of the truth. And confes-
γουμένως μέγα ἐστὶν τὸ τῆς εὐσεβείας μυστήριον· [n]θεὸς‖
sedly great is the [2]of [3]piety [1]mystery: God
ἐφανερώθη ἐν σαρκί, ἐδικαιώθη ἐν πνεύματι, ὤφθη ἀγ-
was manifested in flesh, was justified in [the] Spirit, was seen by
γέλοις,. ἐκηρύχθη ἐν ἔθνεσιν, ἐπιστεύθη ἐν κόσμῳ,
angels, was proclaimed among [the] nations, was believed on in [the] world,
[o]ἀνελήφθη‖ ἐν δόξῃ.
was received up in glory.

4 Τὸ.δὲ πνεῦμα ῥητῶς λέγει, ὅτι ἐν ὑστέροις καιροῖς ἀπο-
But the Spirit expressly speaks, that in latter times [2]shall
στήσονταί τινες τῆς πίστεως, προσέχοντες πνεύμασιν πλάνοις
[3]depart [4]from [1]some the faith, giving heed to [2]spirits [1]deceiving
καὶ διδασκαλίαις δαιμονίων 2 ἐν ὑποκρίσει ψευδολόγων,
and teachings of demons in hypocrisy of speakers of lies,
[p]κεκαυτηριασμένων‖ τὴν.ἰδίαν συνείδησιν, 3 κωλυόντων
being cauterized [as to] their own conscience, forbidding
γαμεῖν, ἀπέχεσθαι βρωμάτων, ἃ ὁ θεὸς ἔκτισεν εἰς
to marry, [bidding] to abstain from meats, which God created for
[q]μετάληψιν‖ μετὰ εὐχαριστίας τοῖς πιστοῖς καὶ ἐπεγνωκόσιν
reception with thanksgiving for the faithful and who know
τὴν ἀλήθειαν. 4 ὅτι πᾶν κτίσμα θεοῦ καλόν, καὶ οὐδὲν
the truth. Because every creature of God [is] good, and nothing
ἀπόβλητον, μετὰ εὐχαριστίας λαμβανόμενον· 5 ἁγιάζεται
to be rejected, with thanksgiving being received; [2]it [3]is [4]sanctified
γὰρ διὰ λόγου θεοῦ καὶ ἐντεύξεως. 6 Ταῦτα ὑποτι-
[1]for by [2]word [1]God's and intercourse [with him]. These things laying
θέμενος τοῖς ἀδελφοῖς, καλὸς ἔσῃ διάκονος [r]Ἰησοῦ
before the brethren, [2]good [4]thou [5]wilt [6]be [1]a [3]servant of Jesus
χριστοῦ,‖ ἐντρεφόμενος τοῖς λόγοις τῆς πίστεως, καὶ τῆς
Christ, being nourished with the words of the faith, and of the
καλῆς διδασκαλίας ᾗ παρηκολούθηκας. 7 Τοὺς.δὲ βεβήλους
good teaching which thou hast closely followed. But the profane
καὶ .γραώδεις μύθους παραιτοῦ· γύμναζε.δὲ σεαυτὸν πρὸς
and old wives' fables refuse, but exercise thyself to
εὐσέβειαν· 8 ἡ.γὰρ.σωματικὴ γυμνασία πρὸς ὀλίγον ἐστὶν
piety; for bodily exercise for a little is
ὠφέλιμος· ἡ.δὲ.εὐσέβεια πρὸς πάντα ὠφέλιμός ἐστιν, ἐπαγγε-
profitable, but piety for everything [2]profitable [1]is, pro-
λίαν ἔχουσα ζωῆς τῆς .νῦν καὶ τῆς μελλούσης.
mise having of life, of that which [is] now and of that which [is] coming.
9 πιστὸς ὁ λόγος καὶ πάσης ἀποδοχῆς ἄξιος. 10 εἰς.τοῦτο.γὰρ
Faithful [is] the word and of all acceptation worthy; for, for this
[s]καὶ‖ κοπιῶμεν καὶ [t]ὀνειδιζόμεθα,‖ ὅτι ἠλπίκαμεν ἐπὶ θεῷ
both we labour and are reproached, because we have hope in a [2]God
ζῶντι, ὅς ἐστιν σωτὴρ πάντων ἀνθρώπων, μάλιστα πιστῶν.
[1]living, who is Preserver of all men, specially of believers.
11 Παράγγελλε ταῦτα καὶ δίδασκε. 12 μηδείς σου τῆς
Charge these things and teach. [2]No [3]one [5]thy
νεότητος καταφρονείτω, ἀλλὰ τύπος γίνου τῶν πιστῶν ἐν
[6]youth [1]let [4]despise, but a pattern be of the believers in
λόγῳ, ἐν ἀναστροφῇ, ἐν ἀγάπῃ, [v]ἐν πνεύματι,‖ ἐν πίστει,
word, in conduct, in love, in [the] Spirit, in faith,

know how thou oughtest to behave thyself in the house of God, which is the church of the living God, the pillar and ground of the truth. 16 And without controversy great is the mystery of godliness: God was manifest in the flesh, justified in the Spirit, seen of angels, preached unto the Gentiles, believed on in the world, received up into glory.

IV. Now the Spirit speaketh expressly, that in the latter times some shall depart from the faith, giving heed to seducing spirits, and doctrines of devils; 2 speaking lies in hypocrisy; having their conscience seared with a hot iron; 3 forbidding to marry, *and commanding* to abstain from meats, which God hath created to be received with thanksgiving of them which believe and know the truth. 4 For every creature of God *is* good, and nothing to be refused, if it be received with thanksgiving: 5 for it is sanctified by the word of God and prayer. 6 If thou put the brethren in remembrance of these things, thou shalt be a good minister of Jesus Christ, nourished up in the words of faith and of good doctrine, whereunto thou hast attained. 7 But refuse profane and old wives' fables, and exercise thyself *rather* unto godliness. 8 For bodily exercise profiteth little: but godliness is profitable unto all things, having promise of the life that now is, and of that which is to come. 9 This *is* a faithful saying and worthy of all acceptation. 10 For therefore we both labour and suffer reproach, because we trust in the living God, who is the Saviour of all men, specially of those that believe. 11 These things command and teach. 12 Let no man despise thy youth; but be thou an example of the believers, in word, in

[n] ὃς who GLTTrAW. [o] ἀνελήμφθη LTTrA. [p] κεκαυστηριασμένων TTr. [q] μετάλημψιν LTTrA. [r] χριστοῦ Ἰησοῦ LTTrAW. [s] — καὶ LTTr[A]. [t] ἀγωνιζόμεθα we combat LTTr. [v] — ἐν πνεύματι GLTTrAW.

conversation, in cha-
rity, in spirit, in faith,
in purity. 13 Till I
come, give attendance
to reading, to exhor-
tation, to doctrine.
14 Neglect not the gift
that is in thee, which
was given thee by pro-
phecy, with the laying
on of the hands of the
presbytery. 15 Medi-
tate upon these things;
give thyself wholly to
them ; that thy profit-
ing may appear to all.
16 Take heed unto
thyself, and unto the
doctrine ; continue in
them : for in doing
this thou shalt both
save thyself, and them
that hear thee.

V. Rebuke not an
elder, but intreat *him*
as a father; *and* the
younger men as bre-
thren ; 2 the elder
women as mothers ;
the younger as sis-
ters, with all purity.
3 Honour widows that
are widows indeed.
4 But if any widow
have children or ne-
phews, let them learn
first to shew piety at
home, and to requite
their parents : for that
is good and acceptable
before God. 5 Now
she that is a widow
indeed, and desolate,
trusteth in God, and
continueth in suppli-
cations and prayers
night and day. 6 But
she that liveth in
pleasure is dead while
she liveth. 7 And these
things give in charge,
that they may be
blameless. 8 But if
any provide not for
his own, and specially
for those of his own
house, he hath denied
the faith, and is worse
than an infidel. 9 Let
not a widow be taken
into the number under
threescore years old,
having been the wife
of one man, 10 well
reported of for good
works; if she have
brought up child-
ren, if she have
lodged strangers, if
she have washed the
saints' feet, if she have
relieved the afflicted,
if she have diligently
followed every good
work. 11 But the
younger widows re-
fuse : for when they
have begun to wax

ἐν ἁγνείᾳ. 13 ἕως ἔρχομαι, πρόσεχε τῇ ἀναγνώσει, τῇ παρα-
in purity. Till I come, give heed to reading, to exhor-
κλήσει, τῇ διδασκαλίᾳ. 14 μὴ.ἀμέλει τοῦ ἐν σοὶ χαρίσματος,
tation, to teaching. Be not negligent of the ²in ³thee ¹gift,
ὃ ἐδόθη σοι διὰ προφητείας μετὰ ἐπιθέσεως τῶν χει-
which was given to thee through prophecy with laying on of the hands
ρῶν τοῦ πρεσβυτερίου. 15 ταῦτα μελέτα, ἐν τούτοις ἴσθι·
of the elderhood. These things meditate on, in them be,
ἵνα σου ἡ.προκοπὴ φανερὰ ᾖ [w]ἐν[||] πᾶσιν. 16 ἔπεχε
that thy advancement manifest may be among all. Give heed
σεαυτῷ καὶ τῇ διδασκαλίᾳ· ἐπίμενε αὐτοῖς· τοῦτο.γὰρ
to thyself and to the teaching; continue in them; for this
ποιῶν, καὶ σεαυτὸν σώσεις καὶ τοὺς ἀκούοντάς σου.
doing, both thyself thou shalt save and those that hear thee.

5 Πρεσβυτέρῳ μὴ.ἐπιπλήξῃς, ἀλλὰ παρακάλει ὡς
An elder do not sharply rebuke, but exhort [him] as
πατέρα· νεωτέρους ὡς ἀδελφούς· 2 πρεσβυτέρας ὡς
a father; younger [men] as brethren; elder [women] as
μητέρας· νεωτέρας ὡς ἀδελφάς, ἐν πάσῃ ἁγνείᾳ. 3 χήρας
mothers; younger as sisters, with all purity. ²Widows
τίμα τὰς ὄντως χήρας. 4 εἰ.δέ τις χήρα τέκνα ἢ ἔκγονα
¹honour that [are] ³indeed ¹widows; but if any widow ²children ³or ⁴descendants
ἔχει, μανθανέτωσαν πρῶτον τὸν.ἴδιον οἶκον εὐσεβεῖν, καὶ
¹have, let them learn first [as to] their own house to be pious, and
ἀμοιβὰς ἀποδιδόναι τοῖς.προγόνοις· τοῦτο.γάρ ἐστιν [x]καλὸν
³recompense ¹to ²render to [their] parents; for this is good
καὶ[||] ἀποδεκτὸν ἐνώπιον τοῦ θεοῦ. 5 ἡ.δὲ ὄντως χήρα
and acceptable before God. Now she who [is] ³indeed ¹a ²widow,
καὶ μεμονωμένη ἤλπικεν ἐπὶ [y]τὸν[||] θεόν, καὶ προσμένει ταῖς
and left alone, has [her] hope in God, and continues
δεήσεσιν καὶ ταῖς προσευχαῖς νυκτὸς καὶ ἡμέρας· 6 ἡ.δὲ
in supplications and prayers night and day. But she that
σπαταλῶσα, ζῶσα τέθνηκεν. 7 καὶ ταῦτα παράγγελλε,
lives in self-gratification, living is dead. And these things charge,
ἵνα [z]ἀνεπίληπτοι[||] ὦσιν. 8 εἰ.δέ τις τῶν.ἰδίων καὶ μάλιστα
that irreproachable they may be. But if anyone his own and specially
[a]τῶν[||] οἰκείων οὐ.[b]προνοεῖ,[||] τὴν πίστιν ἤρνηται, καὶ
[his] household does not provide for, the faith he has denied, and
ἔστιν ἀπίστου χείρων. 9 Χήρα καταλεγέσθω μὴ
is ²than ³an ⁴unbeliever ¹worse. ⁶A ⁷widow ⁵let be put on the list ²not
ἔλαττον ἐτῶν ἑξήκοντα γεγονυῖα, ἑνὸς ἀνδρὸς γυνή, 10 ἐν
³less ⁴than ⁶years ⁵sixty ¹being, of one man wife, in
ἔργοις καλοῖς μαρτυρουμένη, εἰ ἐτεκνοτρόφησεν, εἰ ἐξενο-
²works ¹good being borne witness to, if she brought up children, if she enter-
δόχησεν, εἰ ἁγίων πόδας ἔνιψεν, εἰ θλιβομένοις ἐπήρ-
tained strangers, if saints' feet she washed, if to the oppressed she impart-
κεσεν, εἰ παντὶ ἔργῳ ἀγαθῷ ἐπηκολούθησεν. 11 Νεωτέρας.δὲ
ed relief, if every ²work ¹good she followed after. But younger
χήρας παραιτοῦ· ὅταν.γὰρ [c]καταστρηνιάσωσιν[||] τοῦ
widows refuse; for when they may have grown wanton against
χριστοῦ, γαμεῖν θέλουσιν, 12 ἔχουσαι κρίμα ὅτι τὴν
Christ, to marry they wish, having judgment because [their]
πρώτην πίστιν ἠθέτησαν. 13 ἅμα.δὲ καὶ ἀργαὶ μανθά-
first faith they cast off. And withal also [to be] idle they

[w] — ἐν (*read* πᾶσιν to all) LTTrAW. [x] — καλὸν καὶ GLTTrAW. [y] — τὸν [L]T.
[z] ἀνεπίλημπτοι LTTrA. [a] — τῶν LTTr[A]. [b] προνοεῖται TTr. [c] καταστρηνιασουσιν they shall grow wanton against A.

νουσιν, περιερχόμεναι τὰς οἰκίας· οὐ.μόνον.δὲ ἀργαί, ἀλλὰ
learn, going about to the houses; and not only idle, but
καὶ φλύαροι καὶ περίεργοι, λαλοῦσαι τὰ μὴ.δέοντα. 14 βού-
also tattlers and busy-bodies, speaking things [they] ought not. I
λομαι οὖν νεωτέρας γαμεῖν, τεκνογονεῖν, οἰκοδεσποτεῖν,
will therefore younger [ones] to marry, to bear children, to rule the house,
μηδεμίαν ἀφορμὴν διδόναι τῷ ἀντικειμένῳ λοιδορίας χάριν.
[3]no [4]occasion [1]to [2]give to the adversary [3]of [4]reproach [1]on [2]account.
15 ἤδη.γάρ τινες ἐξετράπησαν ὀπίσω τοῦ σατανᾶ. 16 Εἴ τις
For already some are turned aside after Satan. If any
[d]πιστὸς ἢ[ll] πιστὴ ἔχει χήρας, [e]ἐπαρκείτω[ll] αὐ-
believing [man] or believing [woman] have widows, let him impart relief to
ταῖς. καὶ μὴ βαρείσθω ἡ ἐκκλησία, ἵνα ταῖς ὄντως χήραις
them, and not let be burdened the assembly, that to the [2]indeed [1]widows
ἐπαρκέσῃ.
it may impart relief.

17 Οἱ καλῶς προεστῶτες πρεσβύτεροι διπλῆς τιμῆς
The [6]well [2]who [3]take [4]the [5]lead [1]elders of double honour
ἀξιούσθωσαν, μάλιστα οἱ κοπιῶντες ἐν λόγῳ καὶ διδασ-
let be counted worthy, specially those labouring in word and teach-
καλίᾳ. 18 λέγει.γὰρ ἡ γραφή, [f]Βοῦν ἀλοῶντα οὐ φι-
ing; for says the scripture, An ox treading out corn [3]not [1]thou
μώσεις·[ll] καί, Ἄξιος ὁ ἐργάτης τοῦ.μισθοῦ.αὐτοῦ. 19 Κατὰ
[2]shalt muzzle, and, Worthy [is] the workman of his hire. Against
πρεσβυτέρου κατηγορίαν μὴ.παραδέχου, ἐκτὸς εἰ.μὴ ἐπὶ
an elder an accusation receive not, unless on [the testi-
δύο ἢ τριῶν μαρτύρων. 20 Τοὺς [g] ἁμαρτάνοντας ἐνώπιον
mony of] two or three witnesses. Those that sin [2]before
πάντων ἔλεγχε, ἵνα καὶ οἱ λοιποὶ φόβον ἔχωσιν. 21 Διαμαρ-
[3]all [1]convict, that also the rest [3]fear [1]may [2]have. I earnestly
τύρομαι ἐνώπιον τοῦ θεοῦ καὶ [h]κυρίου Ἰησοῦ χριστοῦ[ll] καὶ
testify before God and [the] Lord Jesus Christ and
τῶν ἐκλεκτῶν ἀγγέλων, ἵνα ταῦτα φυλάξῃς χωρὶς
the elect angels, that these things thou shouldest keep, apart from
προκρίματος, μηδὲν ποιῶν κατὰ [i]πρόσκλισιν.[ll]
prejudice, nothing doing by partiality.

22 Χεῖρας ταχέως μηδενὶ ἐπιτίθει, μηδὲ κοινώνει ἁμαρτίαις
Hands quickly on no one lay, nor share in sins
ἀλλοτρίαις. σεαυτὸν ἁγνὸν τήρει. 23 μηκέτι ὑδροπότει, [k]ἀλλ'[ll]
of others. Thyself pure keep. No longer drink water, but
οἴνῳ ὀλίγῳ χρῶ διὰ τὸν.στόμαχόν.[l]σου[ll] καὶ τὰς πυκνάς
[4]wine [2]a [3]little [1]use on account of thy stomach and [2]frequent
σου ἀσθενείας. 24 Τινῶν ἀνθρώπων αἱ ἁμαρτίαι πρόδηλοί
[1]thy infirmities. Of some men the sins manifest
εἰσιν, προάγουσαι εἰς κρίσιν· τισὶν.δὲ καὶ ἐπακολουθοῦσιν.
are, going before to judgment; and some also they follow after.
25 ὡσαύτως [m] καὶ τὰ [n]καλὰ ἔργα[ll] πρόδηλά [o]ἐστιν·[ll] καὶ τὰ
In like manner also good works manifest are, and those that
ἄλλως ἔχοντα, κρυβῆναι οὐ.[p]δύναται.[ll]
otherwise are, [2]be [3]hid [1]cannot.

6 Ὅσοι εἰσὶν ὑπὸ ζυγὸν δοῦλοι, τοὺς.ἰδίους δεσπότας
As many [2]as [3]are [4]under [5]yoke [1]bondmen, their own masters

wanton against Christ,
they will marry;
12 having damnation,
because they have cast
off their first faith.
13 And withal they
learn *to be* idle, wan-
dering about from
house to house; and
not only idle, but
tattlers also and busy-
bodies, speaking things
which they ought not.
14 I will therefore
that the younger wo-
men marry, bear chil-
dren, guide the house,
give none occasion to
the adversary to speak
reproachfully. 15 For
some are already turn-
ed aside after Satan.
16 If any man or wo-
man that believeth
have widows, let them
relieve them, and let
not the church be
charged; that it may
relieve them that are
widows indeed.

17 Let the elders
that rule well be
counted worthy of
double honour, espe-
cially they who labour
in the word and doc-
trine. 18 For the scrip-
ture saith, Thou shalt
not muzzle the ox that
treadeth out the corn.
And, The labourer *is*
worthy of his reward.
19 Against an elder
receive not an accusa-
tion, but before two
or three witnesses.
20 Them that sin re-
buke before all, that
others also may fear.
21 I charge *thee* before
God, and the Lord Je-
sus Christ, and the
elect angels, that thou
observe these things
without preferring one
before another, doing
nothing by partiality.

22 Lay hands sud-
denly on no man, nei-
ther be partaker of
other men's sins: keep
thyself pure. 23 Drink
no longer water, but
use a little wine for
thy stomach's sake
and thine often infir-
mities. 24 Some men's
sins are open before-
hand, going before to
judgment; and some
men they follow after.
25 Likewise also the
good works *of some*
are manifest before-

---

[d] — πιστὸς ἢ (*read* ἐπαρ. let her impart relief) LTTr[A]. [e] ἐπαρκείσθω LTTr. [f] οὐ φιμώσεις βοῦν ἀλοῶντα L. [g] + δὲ but (those that) L[A]. [h] χριστοῦ Ἰησοῦ LTTrAW. [i] πρόσκλησιν advocacy L. [k] ἀλλὰ LTTrA. [l] — σοῦ (*read* [thy]) LTTrA. [m] + δὲ but (in like manner) LW. [n] ἔργα τὰ καλὰ LTTrAW. [o] — ἐστιν LTTrA; εἰσιν W. [p] δύνανται LTTrAW.

hand; and they that
are otherwise cannot
be hid.
VI. Let as many
servants as are under
the yoke count their
own masters worthy
of all honour, that the
name of God and *his*
doctrine be not blas-
phemed. 2 And they
that have believing
masters, let them not
despise *them*, because
they are brethren; but
rather do *them* ser-
vice, because they are
faithful and beloved,
partakers of the bene-
fit. These things teach
and exhort. 3 If any
man teach otherwise,
and consent not to
wholesome words, *even*
the words of our Lord
Jesus Christ, and to
the doctrine which is
according to godliness;
4 he is proud, knowing
nothing, but doting
about questions and
strifes of words,
whereof cometh envy,
strife, railings, evil
surmisings, 5 perverse
disputings of men
of corrupt minds,
and destitute of the
truth, supposing that
gain is godliness: from
such withdraw thy-
self. 6 But godliness
with contentment is
great gain. 7 For we
brought nothing into
this world, *and it is*
certain we can carry
nothing out. 8 And
having food and rai-
ment let us be there-
with content. 9 But
they that will be rich
fall into temptation
and a snare, and *into*
many foolish and hurt-
ful lusts, which drown
men in destruction and
perdition. 10 For the
love of money is the
root of all evil: which
while some coveted
after, they have erred
from the faith, and
pierced themselves
through with many
sorrows. 11 But thou,
O man of God, flee
these things; and fol-
low after righteous-
ness, godliness, faith,
love, patience, meek-
ness. 12 Fight the good
fight of faith, lay hold
on eternal life, where-
unto thou art also call-
ed, and hast professed a
good profession before
many witnesses. 13 I

πάσης τιμῆς ἀξίους ἡγείσθωσαν, ἵνα μὴ τὸ ὄνομα τοῦ θεοῦ
of all honour worthy let them esteem, that not the name of God
καὶ ἡ διδασκαλία βλασφημῆται. 2 οἱ.δὲ πιστοὺς ἔχοντες
and the teaching be blasphemed. And they that [2]believing [1]have
δεσπότας, μὴ.καταφρονείτωσαν, ὅτι ἀδελφοί εἰσιν· ἀλλὰ
masters, let them not despise [them], because brethren they are; but
μᾶλλον δουλευέτωσαν, ὅτι πιστοί εἰσιν καὶ ἀγα-
rather let them serve [them], because believing [ones] they are and be-
πητοὶ οἱ τῆς εὐεργεσίας ἀντιλαμβανόμενοι. ταῦτα δίδασκε
loved who [5]the [6]good [7]service [1]are [2]being [3]helped [4]by. These things teach
καὶ παρακάλει. 3 Εἴ τις ἑτεροδιδασκαλεῖ, καὶ [q]μὴ.προσέρχεται‖
and exhort. If anyone teaches other doctrine, and draws not near
ὑγιαίνουσιν λόγοις τοῖς τοῦ.κυρίου.ἡμῶν Ἰησοῦ χριστοῦ, καὶ
[2]sound [1]to words, those of our Lord Jesus Christ, and
τῇ κατ εὐσέβειαν διδασκαλίᾳ, 4 τετύφωται, μηδὲν
the [2]according [3]to [4]piety [1]teaching, he is puffed up, nothing
ἐπιστάμενος, ἀλλὰ νοσῶν περὶ ζητήσεις καὶ λογομαχίας,
knowing, but sick about questions and disputes of words,
ἐξ ὧν γίνεται φθόνος, ἔρις, βλασφημίαι, ὑπόνοιαι πονηραί,
out of which come envy, strife, evil speakings, [2]suspicions [1]wicked,
5 [r]παραδιατριβαὶ‖ διεφθαρμένων ἀνθρώπων τὸν νοῦν, καὶ
vain argumentations [3]corrupted [1]of [2]men in mind, and
ἀπεστερημένων τῆς ἀληθείας, νομιζόντων πορισμὸν εἶναι τὴν
destitute of the truth, holding [4]gain [2]to [3]be
εὐσέβειαν· [s]ἀφίστασο ἀπὸ τῶν τοιούτων.‖ 6 Ἔστιν.δὲ πορισμὸς
[1]piety; withdraw from such. But [4]is [6]gain
μέγας ἡ εὐσέβεια μετὰ αὐταρκείας. 7 οὐδὲν.γὰρ εἰσηνέγκαμεν
[5]great [1]piety [2]with [3]contentment. For nothing we brought
εἰς τὸν κόσμον, [t]δῆλον‖ ὅτι οὐδὲ ἐξενεγκεῖν τι δυνά-
into the world, [it is] manifest that neither to carry out anything are we
μεθα· 8 ἔχοντες.δὲ διατροφὰς καὶ σκεπάσματα, τούτοις ἀρ-
able. But having sustenance and coverings, with these we shall
κεσθησόμεθα. 9 Οἱ.δὲ βουλόμενοι πλουτεῖν, ἐμπίπτουσιν εἰς
be satisfied. But those desiring to be rich, fall into
πειρασμὸν καὶ παγίδα καὶ ἐπιθυμίας πολλὰς ἀνοήτους καὶ
temptation and a snare and [5]desires [1]many [2]unwise [3]and
βλαβεράς, αἵτινες βυθίζουσιν τοὺς ἀνθρώπους εἰς ὄλεθρον
[4]hurtful, which sink men into destruction
καὶ ἀπώλειαν. 10 ῥίζα.γὰρ πάντων τῶν κακῶν ἐστιν ἡ φιλ-
and perdition. For a root of all evils is the love
αργυρία· ἧς τινες ὀρεγόμενοι ἀπεπλανήθησαν ἀπὸ τῆς
of money; which some stretching after were seduced from the
πίστεως, καὶ ἑαυτοὺς περιέπειραν ὀδύναις πολλαῖς. 11 Σὺ
faith, and themselves pierced with [2]sorrows [1]many. [4]Thou
δέ, ὦ ἄνθρωπε [u]τοῦ‖ θεοῦ, ταῦτα φεῦγε· δίωκε.δὲ δικαιο-
[3]but, O man of God, these things flee, and pursue right-
σύνην, εὐσέβειαν, πίστιν, ἀγάπην, ὑπομονήν, [v]πρᾳότητα·‖
eousness, piety, faith, love, endurance, meekness.
12 ἀγωνίζου τὸν καλὸν ἀγῶνα τῆς πίστεως· ἐπιλαβοῦ τῆς
Combat the good combat of the faith. Lay hold
αἰωνίου ζωῆς, εἰς ἣν [w]καὶ‖ ἐκλήθης, καὶ ὡμολόγησας
of eternal life, to which also thou wast called, and didst confess
τὴν καλὴν ὁμολογίαν ἐνώπιον πολλῶν μαρτύρων. 13 Παραγ-
the good confession before many witnesses. I

[q] μὴ προσέχεται cleaves not T. [r] διαπαρατριβαὶ constant quarrellings GLTTrAW. [s] — ἀφίστασο ἀπὸ τῶν τοιούτων LTTrAW. [t] — δῆλον (read ὅτι so that) LTTrA. [u] — τοῦ LTTr[A]. [v] πραϋπάθειαν meekness of spirit LTrAW; πραϋπαθίαν T. [w] — καὶ GLTTrAW.

γέλλω [x]σοι‖ ἐνώπιον [y]τοῦ‖ θεοῦ τοῦ [z]ζωοποιοῦντος‖ τὰ.πάντα,
charge thee before God who quickens all things,
καὶ χριστοῦ Ἰησοῦ τοῦ μαρτυρήσαντος ἐπὶ Ποντίου [a]Πι-
and Christ Jesus who witnessed before Pontius Pi-
λάτου‖ τὴν καλὴν ὁμολογίαν, 14 τηρῆσαί.σε τὴν ἐντολὴν
late the good confession, that thou keep the commandment
ἄσπιλον, [b]ἀνεπίληπτον,‖ μέχρι τῆς ἐπιφανείας τοῦ κυρίου
spotless, irreproachable, until the appearing of [2]Lord
ἡμῶν Ἰησοῦ χριστοῦ, 15 ἣν καιροῖς.ἰδίοις δείξει ὁ
[1]our Jesus Christ; which in its own times [6]shall [7]shew [1]the
μακάριος καὶ μόνος δυνάστης, ὁ βασιλεὺς τῶν βασιλευόν-
[2]blessed [3]and [4]only [5]Ruler, the King of those being kings
των καὶ κύριος τῶν κυριευόντων, 16 ὁ μόνος ἔχων ἀθα-
and Lord of those being lords; who alone has im-
νασίαν, φῶς οἰκῶν ἀπρόσιτον, ὃν εἶδεν οὐδεὶς
mortality, [2]in [4]light [1]dwelling [3]unapproachable, whom [5]did [6]see [1]no [2]one
ἀνθρώπων οὐδὲ ἰδεῖν δύναται, ᾧ τιμὴ καὶ κράτος
[3]of [4]men nor to see is able; to whom honour, and might
αἰώνιον. ἀμήν.
eternal. Amen.

17 Τοῖς πλουσίοις ἐν τῷ νῦν αἰῶνι παράγγελλε, μὴ
To the rich in the present age charge, not
[c]ὑψηλοφρονεῖν,‖ μηδὲ ἠλπικέναι ἐπὶ πλούτου ἀδηλότητι,
to be high-minded, nor to have hope in [3]of [4]riches [[1]the] [2]uncertainty;
ἀλλ' [d]ἐν‖ [e]τῷ‖ θεῷ [f]τῷ ζῶντι,‖ τῷ παρέχοντι ἡμῖν [g] [h]πλου-
but in [3]God [1]the [2]living, who gives us richly
σίως πάντα‖ εἰς ἀπόλαυσιν· 18 ἀγαθοεργεῖν, πλουτεῖν ἐν
all things for enjoyment; to do good, to be rich in
ἔργοις καλοῖς, εὐμεταδότους εἶναι, κοινωνικούς, 19 ἀπο-
[2]works [1]good, liberal in distributing to be, ready to communicate, trea-
θησαυρίζοντας ἑαυτοῖς θεμέλιον καλὸν εἰς τὸ μέλλον, ἵνα
suring up for themselves a [2]foundation [1]good for the future, that
ἐπιλάβωνται τῆς [i]αἰωνίου‖ ζωῆς.
they may lay hold of eternal life.

20 Ὦ Τιμόθεε, τὴν [k]παρακαταθήκην‖ φύλαξον,
O Timotheus, the deposit committed [to thee] keep,
ἐκτρεπόμενος τὰς βεβήλους κενοφωνίας, καὶ ἀντιθέσεις τῆς
avoiding profane empty babblings, and oppositions
ψευδωνύμου.γνώσεως· 21 ἥν τινες ἐπαγγελλόμενοι, περὶ
of falsely-named knowledge, which some professing, in reference to
τὴν πίστιν ἠστόχησαν. Ἡ χάρις [l]μετὰ σοῦ.‖ [m]ἀμήν.‖
the faith missed the mark. Grace [be] with thee. Amen.

[n]Πρὸς Τιμόθεον πρώτη ἐγράφη ἀπὸ Λαοδικείας, ἥτις
[2]To [3]Timothy [1]first written from Laodicæa, which
ἐστὶν μητρόπολις Φρυγίας τῆς Πακατιανῆς.‖
is the chief city of Phrygia Pacatiana.

give thee charge in the sight of God, who quickeneth all things, and *before* Christ Jesus, who before Pontius Pilate witnessed a good confession; 14 that thou keep *this* commandment without spot, unrebukeable, until the appearing of our Lord Jesus Christ: 15 which in his times he shall shew, *who is* the blessed and only Potentate, the King of kings, and Lord of lords; 16 who only hath immortality, dwelling in the light which no man can approach unto; whom no man hath seen, nor can see: to whom *be* honour and power everlasting. Amen.

17 Charge them that are rich in this world, that they be not high-minded, nor trust in uncertain riches, but in the living God, who giveth us richly all things to enjoy; 18 that they do good, that they be rich in good works, ready to distribute, willing to communicate; 19 laying up in store for themselves a good foundation against the time to come, that they may lay hold on eternal life.

20 O Timothy, keep that which is committed to thy trust, avoiding profane *and* vain babblings, and oppositions of science falsely so called: 21 which some professing have erred concerning the faith. Grace *be* with thee. Amen.

---

[x] — σοι (*read* [thee]) T. [y] — τοῦ T. [z] ζωογονοῦντος preserves alive LTTrA. [a] Πειλάτου T. [b] ἀνεπίλημπτον LTTrA. [c] ὑψηλὰ φρονεῖν to mind high things T. [d] ἐπὶ LTTr. [e] — τῷ TTr. [f] — τῷ ζῶντι LTTrA. [g] + τὰ L. [h] πάντα πλουσίως GLTTrAW. [i] ὄντως (*read* of that which [is] truly life) GLTTrAW. [k] παραθήκην GLTTrAW. [l] μεθ' ὑμῶν with you LTTr. [m] — ἀμήν GLTTrAW. [n] — *the subscription* GLTW; Πρὸς Τιμόθεον α' TrA.

[a]Η ΠΡΟΣ ΤΙΜΟΘΕΟΝ ΕΠΙΣΤΟΛΗ ΔΕΥΤΕΡΑ.[a]
THE [3]TO [4]TIMOTHY [2]EPISTLE [1]SECOND

PAUL, an apostle of Jesus Christ by the will of God, according to the promise of life which is in Christ Jesus, 2 to Timothy, *my* dearly beloved son: Grace, mercy, *and* peace, from God the Father and Christ Jesus our Lord.

3 I thank God, whom I serve from *my* forefathers with pure conscience, that without ceasing I have remembrance of thee in my prayers night and day; 4 greatly desiring to see thee, being mindful of thy tears, that I may be filled with joy; 5 when I call to remembrance the unfeigned faith that is in thee, which dwelt first in thy grandmother Lois, and thy mother Eunice; and I am persuaded that in thee also. 6 Wherefore I put thee in remembrance that thou stir up the gift of God, which is in thee by the putting on of my hands. 7 For God hath not given us the spirit of fear; but of power, and of love, and of a sound mind. 8 Be not thou therefore ashamed of the testimony of our Lord, nor of me his prisoner: but be thou partaker of the afflictions of the gospel according to the power of God; 9 who hath saved us, and called *us* with an holy calling, not according to our works, but according to his own purpose and grace, which was given us in Christ Jesus before the world began, 10 but is now made manifest by the appearing of our Saviour Jesus Christ, who hath abolished death, and hath brought life and immortality to light through the gospel: 11 whereunto I am

ΠΑΥΛΟΣ ἀπόστολος [b]Ἰησοῦ χριστοῦ‖ διὰ θελήματος θεοῦ
Paul, apostle of Jesus Christ by [the] will of God
κατ' ἐπαγγελίαν ζωῆς τῆς ἐν χριστῷ Ἰησοῦ, 2 Τι-
according to promise of life which [is] in Christ Jesus, to Ti-
μοθέῳ ἀγαπητῷ τέκνῳ· χάρις, ἔλεος, εἰρήνη ἀπὸ θεοῦ
motheus [my] beloved child: Grace, mercy, peace from God [the]
πατρὸς καὶ χριστοῦ Ἰησοῦ τοῦ.κυρίου.ἡμῶν.
Father and Christ Jesus our Lord.
3 Χάριν.ἔχω τῷ θεῷ, ᾧ λατρεύω ἀπὸ προγόνων ἐν
I am thankful to God, whom I serve from [my] forefathers with
καθαρᾷ συνειδήσει, ὡς ἀδιάλειπτον ἔχω τὴν περὶ σοῦ μνείαν
pure conscience, how unceasingly I have the [2]of [3]thee [1]remembrance
ἐν ταῖς.δεήσεσίν.μου [c]νυκτὸς καὶ ἡμέρας,‖ 4 ἐπιποθῶν σε
in my supplications night and day, longing [3]thee
ἰδεῖν, μεμνημένος σου τῶν δακρύων, ἵνα χαρᾶς πληρωθῶ·
[1]to [2]see, remembering thy tears, that with joy I may be filled;
5 ὑπόμνησιν [d]λαμβάνων‖ τῆς ἐν σοὶ ἀνυποκρίτου πίστεως,
[2]remembrance [1]taking of the [3]in [4]thee [1]unfeigned [2]faith,
ἥτις ἐνῴκησεν πρῶτον ἐν τῇ.μάμμῃ.σου Λωΐδι καὶ τῇ μητρί
which dwelt first in thy grandmother Lois and in [2]mother
σου [e]Εὐνείκῃ,‖ πέπεισμαι.δὲ ὅτι καὶ ἐν σοί. 6 Δι' ἣν αἰτίαν
[1]thy Eunice, and I am persuaded that also in thee. For which cause
ἀναμιμνήσκω σε ἀναζωπυρεῖν τὸ χάρισμα τοῦ θεοῦ, ὅ ἐστιν
I remind thee to kindle up the gift of God which is
ἐν σοὶ διὰ τῆς ἐπιθέσεως τῶν.χειρῶν.μου· 7 οὐ.γὰρ ἔδωκεν
in thee by the laying on of my hands. For [4]not [2]gave
ἡμῖν ὁ θεὸς πνεῦμα δειλίας, ἀλλὰ δυνάμεως καὶ ἀγάπης
[3]us [1]God a spirit of cowardice, but of power, and of love,
καὶ σωφρονισμοῦ. 8 μὴ οὖν ἐπαισχυνθῇς τὸ
and of wise discretion. [4]Not [1]therefore [2]thou [3]shouldest be ashamed of the
μαρτύριον τοῦ.κυρίου.ἡμῶν, μηδὲ ἐμὲ τὸν.δέσμιον.αὐτοῦ· ἀλλὰ
testimony of our Lord, nor me his prisoner; but
[f]συγκακοπάθησον‖ τῷ εὐαγγελίῳ κατὰ δύναμιν θεοῦ, 9 τοῦ
suffer evils along with the glad tidings according to [2]power [1]God's; who
σώσαντος ἡμᾶς καὶ καλέσαντος κλήσει ἁγίᾳ, οὐ κατὰ
saved us and called [us] with a [2]calling [1]holy, not according to
τὰ.ἔργα.ἡμῶν, ἀλλὰ [g]κατ'‖ ἰδίαν πρόθεσιν καὶ χάριν τὴν
our works, but according to his own purpose and grace, which
δοθεῖσαν ἡμῖν ἐν χριστῷ Ἰησοῦ πρὸ χρόνων.αἰωνίων,
[was] given us in Christ Jesus before the ages of time,
10 φανερωθεῖσαν.δὲ νῦν διὰ τῆς ἐπιφανείας τοῦ.σωτῆρος.ἡμῶν
but made manifest now by the appearing of our Saviour
[h]Ἰησοῦ χριστοῦ,‖ καταργήσαντος μὲν τὸν θάνατον, φωτίσαν-
Jesus Christ, who annulled death, [2]brought [3]to
τος δὲ ζωὴν καὶ ἀφθαρσίαν διὰ τοῦ εὐαγγελίου, 11 εἰς ὃ
[4]light [1]and life and incorruptibility by the glad tidings; to which

---

[a] + Παύλου τοῦ Ἀποστόλου of the Apostle Paul E; + Παύλου G; Πρὸς Τιμόθεον β' LTTrAW. [b] χριστοῦ Ἰησοῦ TTrAW. [c], νυκτὸς καὶ ἡμέρας (*read* night and day longing &c. LTr. [d] λαβὼν having taken LTTrA. [e] Εὐνίκῃ EGLTTrAW. [f] συν- T. [g] κατὰ LTTrA. [h] χριστοῦ Ἰησοῦ LTTr.

ἐτέθην ἐγὼ κήρυξ καὶ ἀπόστολος καὶ διδάσκαλος
[2]was [3]appointed [1]I a herald and apostle and teacher
[i]ἐθνῶν·‖ 12 δι᾽ .ἣν αἰτίαν καὶ ταῦτα πάσχω· ἀλλ᾽ οὐκ
of [the] nations. For which cause also these things I suffer; but [3]not
ἐπαισχύνομαι, οἶδα.γὰρ ᾧ πεπίστευκα, καὶ πέπεισμαι ὅτι
[1]I [2]am ashamed; for I know whom I have believed, and am persuaded that
δυνατός ἐστιν τὴν παραθήκην μου φυλάξαι εἰς ἐκείνην
able he is the deposit committed [to him] of me to keep for that
τὴν ἡμέραν. 13 ὑποτύπωσιν ἔχε ὑγιαινόντων λόγων, ὧν
day. [2]A [3]delineation [1]have of sound words, which [words]
παρ᾽ ἐμοῦ ἤκουσας, ἐν πίστει καὶ ἀγάπῃ τῇ ἐν χριστῷ
from me thou didst hear, in faith and love which [are] in Christ
Ἰησοῦ. 14 τὴν καλὴν [j]παρακαταθήκην‖ φύλαξον διὰ
Jesus. The good deposit committed [to thee] keep by [the]
πνεύματος ἁγίου τοῦ ἐνοικοῦντος ἐν ἡμῖν. 15 Οἶδας τοῦτο,
[2]Spirit [1]Holy which dwells in us. Thou knowest this,
ὅτι ἀπεστράφησάν με πάντες οἱ ἐν τῇ Ἀσίᾳ, ὧν ἐστιν
that turned away from me all who [are] in Asia, of whom is
[k]Φύγελλος‖ καὶ [l]Ἑρμογένης.‖ 16 Δῴη ἔλεος ὁ κύριος τῷ
Phygellus and Hermogenes. May [3]grant [4]mercy [1]the [2]Lord to the
Ὀνησιφόρου οἴκῳ· ὅτι πολλάκις με ἀνέψυξεν, καὶ τὴν
[2]of [3]Onesiphorus [1]house, because oft me he refreshed, and
ἅλυσίν.μου οὐκ.[m]ἐπῃσχύνθη,‖ 17 ἀλλὰ γενόμενος ἐν Ῥώμῃ,
my chain was not ashamed of; but having been in Rome,
[n]σπουδαιότερον‖ ἐζήτησέν με καὶ εὗρεν· 18 δῴη αὐτῷ
more diligently he sought out me and found [me]— may [3]grant [4]to [5]him
ὁ κύριος εὑρεῖν ἔλεος παρὰ κυρίου ἐν ἐκείνῃ τῇ ἡμέρᾳ· καὶ
[1]the [2]Lord to find mercy from [the] Lord in that day— and
ὅσα ἐν Ἐφέσῳ διηκόνησεν βέλτιον σὺ γινώσκεις.
how much in Ephesus he served [3]better [[4]than [5]I [6]need [7]say] [1]thou [2]knowest.

2 Σὺ οὖν, τέκνον.μου, ἐνδυναμοῦ ἐν τῇ χάριτι τῇ
Thou therefore, my child, be strong in the grace which [is]
ἐν χριστῷ Ἰησοῦ· 2 καὶ ἃ ἤκουσας παρ᾽ ἐμοῦ
in Christ Jesus. And the things which thou didst hear of me
διὰ πολλῶν μαρτύρων, ταῦτα παράθου πιστοῖς ἀνθρώποις,
with many witnesses, these commit to faithful men,
οἵτινες ἱκανοὶ ἔσονται καὶ ἑτέρους διδάξαι. 3 [o]σὺ οὖν
such as competent shall be also others to teach. Thou therefore
κακοπάθησον‖ ὡς καλὸς στρατιώτης [p]Ἰησοῦ χριστοῦ.‖ 4 οὐδεὶς
suffer hardship as [2]good [1]a soldier of Jesus Christ. No one
στρατευόμενος ἐμπλέκεται ταῖς τοῦ βίου [q]πραγματείαις,‖
serving as a soldier entangles himself with the [2]of [3]life [1]affairs,
ἵνα τῷ στρατολογήσαντι ἀρέσῃ. 5 ἐὰν.δὲ καὶ ἀθλῇ
that him who enrolled him as a soldier he may please. And if also [2]contend
τις, οὐ.στεφανοῦται ἐὰν.μὴ νομίμως ἀ-
[[3]in [4]the [5]games] [1]anyone, he is not crowned unless lawfully he shall
θλήσῃ. 6 τὸν κοπιῶντα γεωργὸν δεῖ πρῶτον τῶν
have contended. The [3]labour [1]husbandman [2]must before of the
καρπῶν μεταλαμβάνειν.
fruits partaking.

7 Νόει [r]ἃ‖ λέγω· [s]δῴη‖ γάρ σοι ὁ κύριος σύνεσιν
Consider the things I say, [2]may [5]give [1]for [6]thee [3]the [4]Lord understanding

appointed a preacher, and an apostle, and a teacher of the Gentiles. 12 For the which cause I also suffer these things: nevertheless I am not ashamed: for I know whom I have believed, and am persuaded that he is able to keep that which I have committed unto him against that day. 13 Hold fast the form of sound words, which thou hast heard of me, in faith and love which is in Christ Jesus. 14 That good thing which was committed unto thee keep by the Holy Ghost which dwelleth in us. 15 This thou knowest, that all they which are in Asia be turned away from me; of whom are Phygellus and Hermogenes. 16 The Lord give mercy unto the house of Onesiphorus; for he oft refreshed me, and was not ashamed of my chain: 17 but, when he was in Rome, he sought me out very diligently, and found *me*. 18 The Lord grant unto him that he may find mercy of the Lord in that day: and in how many things he ministered unto me at Ephesus, thou knowest very well.

II. Thou therefore, my son, be strong in the grace that is in Christ Jesus. 2 And the things that thou hast heard of me among many witnesses, the same commit thou to faithful men, who shall be able to teach others also. 3 Thou therefore endure hardness, as a good soldier of Jesus Christ. 4 No man that warreth entangleth himself with the affairs of *this* life; that he may please him who hath chosen him to be a soldier. 5 And if a man also strive for masteries, *yet* is he not crowned, except he strive lawfully. 6 The husbandman that laboureth must be first partaker of the fruits.

7 Consider what I

---

[i] — ἐθνῶν T. [j] παραθήκην GLTTrAW. [k] Φύγελος Phygelus LTTrAW. [l] Ἑρμογένης Ermogenes T. [m] ἐπαισχύνθη LTTrA. [n] σπουδαίως diligently LTTr. [o] συγκακοπάθησον (συνκ- T) suffer hardship with [me] LTTrAW. [p] χριστοῦ Ἰησοῦ LTTrAW. [q] πραγματίαις T. [r] ὃ what LTTrAW. [s] δώσει will give LTTrAW.

ay; and the Lord give
thee understanding in
all things. 8 Remem-
ber that Jesus Christ
of the seed of David
was raised from the
dead according to my
gospel; 9 wherein I
suffer trouble, as an
evildoer, *even* unto
bonds; but the word
of God is not bound.
10 Therefore I endure
all things for the
elect's sakes, that they
may also obtain the
salvation which is in
Christ Jesus with eter-
nal glory. 11 *It is* a
faithful saying: For
if we be dead with
him, we shall also live
with *him*: 12 if we
suffer, we shall also
reign with *him*: if we
deny *him*, he also will
deny us: 13 if we
believe not, *yet* he a-
bideth faithful: he
cannot deny himself.

14 Of these things put
them in remembrance,
charging *them* before
the Lord that they
strive not about words
to no profit, *but* to
the subverting of the
hearers. 15 Study to
shew thyself approved
unto God, a workman
that needeth not to be
ashamed, rightly di-
viding the word of
truth. 16 But shun pro-
fane *and* vain bab-
blings; for they will
increase unto more un-
godliness. 17 And their
word will eat as doth
a canker: of whom is
Hymenæus and Phile-
tus; 18 who concern-
ing the truth have
erred, saying that the
resurrection is past al-
ready; and overthrow
the faith of some.
19 Nevertheless the
foundation of God
standeth sure, having
this seal, The Lord
knoweth them that are
his. And, Let every
one that nameth the
name of Christ depart
from iniquity. 20 But
in a great house there
are not only vessels of
gold and of silver, but
also of wood and of
earth; and some to
honour, and some to
dishonour. 21 If a man
therefore purge him-
self from these, he

ἐν πᾶσιν. 8 Μνημόνευε Ἰησοῦν χριστὸν ἐγηγερμένον ἐκ
in all things. Remember Jesus Christ raised from among
νεκρῶν, ἐκ σπέρματος [t]Δαβίδ,‖ κατὰ τὸ εὐαγγέλιόν
[the] dead, of [the] seed of David, according to [2]glad [3]tidings
μου· 9 ἐν ᾧ κακοπαθῶ μέχρι δεσμῶν ὡς κακοῦργος· [v]ἀλλ'‖
[1]my, in which I suffer hardship unto bonds as an evil doer: but
ὁ λόγος τοῦ θεοῦ οὐ.δέδεται. 10 διὰ τοῦτο πάντα ὑπο-
the word of God is not bound. Because of this all things I en-
μένω διὰ τοὺς ἐκλεκτούς, ἵνα καὶ αὐτοὶ σωτηρίας τύ-
dure for sake of the elect, that also they [the] salvation may
χωσιν τῆς ἐν χριστῷ Ἰησοῦ μετὰ δόξης αἰωνίου. 11 πιστὸς
obtain which [is] in Christ Jesus with [2]glory [1]eternal. Faithful
ὁ λόγος· εἰ.γὰρ συναπεθάνομεν, καὶ [w]συζήσομεν·‖
[is] the word; for if we died together with [him], also we shall live together;
12 εἰ ὑπομένομεν, καὶ [x]συμβασιλεύσομεν·‖ εἰ [y]ἀρνούμεθα,‖
if we endure, also we shall reign together; if we deny
κἀκεῖνος ἀρνήσεται ἡμᾶς· 13 εἰ ἀπιστοῦμεν, ἐκεῖνος
[him], he also will deny us; if we are unfaithful, he
πιστὸς μένει· ἀρνήσασθαι [z] ἑαυτὸν οὐ.δύναται.
faithful abides; to deny himself he is not able.

14 Ταῦτα ὑπομίμνησκε, διαμαρτυρόμενος ἐνώπιον
[2]These [3]things [4]put [5]in [6]remembrance [1]of, testifying earnestly before
[a]τοῦ κυρίου‖ [b]μὴ λογομαχεῖν‖ [c]εἰς‖ οὐδὲν χρήσιμον, ἐπὶ
the Lord not to dispute about words [2]for [3]nothing [1]profitable, to
καταστροφῇ τῶν ἀκουόντων. 15 σπούδασον σεαυτὸν
subversion of those who hear. Be diligent [3]thyself
δόκιμον παραστῆσαι τῷ θεῷ, ἐργάτην ἀνεπαίσχυντον, ὀρθο-
[4]approved [1]to [2]present to God, a workman not ashamed, straight-
τομοῦντα τὸν λόγον τῆς ἀληθείας· 16 τὰς.δὲ.βεβήλους κενο-
ly cutting the word of truth; but profane empty
φωνίας περιΐστασο· ἐπὶ πλεῖον γὰρ προκόψουσιν ἀσεβείας,
babblings stand aloof from, [2]to [3]more [1]for they will advance of ungodliness,
17 καὶ ὁ.λόγος.αὐτῶν ὡς γάγγραινα νομὴν ἕξει· ὧν ἐστιν
and their word as a gangrene pasture will have; of whom is
Ὑμέναιος καὶ Φιλητός, 18 οἵτινες περὶ τὴν ἀλήθειαν
Hymenæus and Philetus; who concerning the truth
ἠστόχησαν, λέγοντες [d]τὴν‖ ἀνάστασιν ἤδη γεγονέναι,
missed the mark, asserting the resurrection already to have taken place;
καὶ ἀνατρέπουσιν τήν τινων πίστιν. 19 ὁ [e]μέντοι‖ στερεὸς
and are overthrowing the [2]of [3]some [1]faith. Nevertheless [2]firm
θεμέλιος τοῦ θεοῦ ἕστηκεν, ἔχων τὴν.σφραγῖδα.ταύτην, Ἔγνω
[3]foundation [1]God's stands, having this seal, [3]Knows
κύριος τοὺς ὄντας αὐτοῦ, καὶ Ἀποστήτω ἀπὸ ἀδι-
[[1]the] [2]Lord those that are his, and Let depart from unright-
κίας πᾶς ὁ ὀνομάζων τὸ ὄνομα [f]χριστοῦ.‖ 20 ἐν μεγάλῃ
eousness everyone who names the name of Christ. [2]In [4]great
δὲ οἰκίᾳ οὐκ.ἔστιν μόνον σκεύη χρυσᾶ καὶ ἀργυρᾶ, ἀλλὰ
[1]but [3]a house there are not only vessels golden and silver, but
καὶ ξύλινα καὶ ὀστράκινα, καὶ ἃ μὲν εἰς τιμήν, ἃ.δὲ εἰς
also wooden and earthen, and some to honour, others to
ἀτιμίαν. 21 ἐὰν οὖν τις ἐκκαθάρῃ ἑαυτὸν ἀπὸ τούτων,
dishonour. If therefore one shall have purged himself from these,

---

[t] Δαυείδ LTTrA; Δαυΐδ GW. [v] ἀλλὰ LTTrAW. [w] συν- LTTrA. [x] συν- T. [y] ἀρνησόμεθα we shall deny LTTrA. [z] + γὰρ for (to deny) LTTrAW. [a] τοῦ θεοῦ God TTr. [b] . μὴ λογομάχει Dispute thou not about words L. [c] ἐπ' LTTrA. [d] — τὴν (read [the]) TTr[A] [e] μέν τοι Tr. [f] κυρίου of [the] Lord GLTTrAW.

ἔσται σκεῦος εἰς τιμήν, ἡγιασμένον, [g]καὶ[||] εὔχρηστον
he shall be a vessel to honour, having been sanctified, and serviceable
τῷ δεσπότῃ, εἰς πᾶν ἔργον ἀγαθὸν ἡτοιμασμένον.
to the master, for every [2]work [1]good having been prepared.
22 τὰς.δὲ.νεωτερικὰς ἐπιθυμίας φεῦγε· δίωκε.δὲ δικαιοσύνην,
But youthful lusts flee, and pursue righteousness,
πίστιν, ἀγάπην, εἰρήνην μετὰ [h] τῶν ἐπικαλουμένων τὸν
faith, love, peace with those that call on the
κύριον ἐκ καθαρᾶς καρδίας. 23 τὰς.δὲ.μωρὰς καὶ ἀπαι-
Lord out of [2]pure [1]a heart. But foolish and undis-
δεύτους ζητήσεις παραιτοῦ, εἰδὼς ὅτι γεννῶσιν μάχας·
ciplined questionings refuse, knowing that they beget contentions.
24 δοῦλον.δὲ κυρίου οὐ.δεῖ μάχεσθαι, [i]ἀλλ'[||] ἤπιον
And [3]a [4]bondman [5]of [[6]the] [7]Lord [1]it [2]behoves not to contend, but gentle
εἶναι πρὸς πάντας, διδακτικόν, ἀνεξίκακον, 25 ἐν [k]πρᾳότητι[||]
to be towards all; apt to teach; forbearing; in meekness
παιδεύοντα τοὺς ἀντιδιατιθεμένους, μήποτε [l]δῷ[||] αὐτοῖς
disciplining those that oppose, if perhaps [2]may [3]give [4]them
ὁ θεὸς μετάνοιαν εἰς ἐπίγνωσιν ἀληθείας, 26 καὶ ἀνα-
[1]God repentance to acknowledgment of [the] truth, and they may
νήψωσιν ἐκ τῆς τοῦ διαβόλου παγίδος, ἐζωγρημένοι ὑπ'
awake up out of the [2]of [3]the [4]devil [1]snare, having been taken by
αὐτοῦ εἰς τὸ ἐκείνου θέλημα.
him for his will.

3 Τοῦτο.δὲ [m]γίνωσκε,[||] ὅτι ἐν ἐσχάταις ἡμέραις ἐνστή-
But this know thou, that in [the] last days [3]will [4]be
σονται καιροὶ χαλεποί. 2 ἔσονται.γὰρ οἱ ἄνθρωποι φίλαυτοι,
[5]present [2]times [1]difficult; for [2]will [3]be [1]men lovers of self,
φιλάργυροι, ἀλαζόνες, ὑπερήφανοι, βλάσφημοι, γονεῦσιν
lovers of money, vaunting, proud, evil speakers, to parents
ἀπειθεῖς, ἀχάριστοι, ἀνόσιοι, 3 ἄστοργοι, ἄσπονδοι,
disobedient, unthankful, unholy, without natural affection, implacable,
διάβολοι, ἀκρατεῖς, ἀνήμεροι, ἀφιλάγαθοι, 4 προδόται,
slanderers, incontinent, savage, not lovers of good, betrayers,
προπετεῖς, τετυφωμένοι, φιλήδονοι μᾶλλον ἢ φιλόθεοι,
headlong, puffed up, lovers of pleasure rather than lovers of God;
5 ἔχοντες μόρφωσιν εὐσεβείας, τὴν.δὲ δύναμιν αὐτῆς ἠρνη-
having a form of piety, but the power of it deny-
μένοι. καὶ τούτους ἀποτρέπου. 6 ἐκ.τούτων.γάρ εἰσιν οἱ
ing: and these turn away from. For of these are those who
ἐνδύνοντες εἰς τὰς οἰκίας καὶ [n]αἰχμαλωτεύοντες τὰ[||] γυναικάρια
[are] entering into houses and leading captive silly women
σεσωρευμένα ἁμαρτίαις, ἀγόμενα ἐπιθυμίαις ποικίλαις, 7 πάν-
laden with sins, led away by [2]lusts [1]various, al-
τοτε μανθάνοντα καὶ μηδέποτε εἰς ἐπίγνωσιν ἀληθείας
ways learning and never to [the] knowledge of [the] truth
ἐλθεῖν δυνάμενα. 8 ὃν.τρόπον.δὲ Ἰαννῆς καὶ Ἰαμβρῆς ἀντέ-
[2]to [3]come [1]able. Now in the way Jannes and Jambres with-
στησαν Μωϋσεῖ, οὕτως καὶ οὗτοι ἀνθίστανται τῇ ἀληθείᾳ,
stood Moses, thus also these withstand the truth,
ἄνθρωποι κατεφθαρμένοι τὸν.νοῦν, ἀδόκιμοι περὶ
men utterly corrupted in mind, found worthless as regards
τὴν πίστιν. 9 ἀλλ' οὐ.προκόψουσιν ἐπὶ.πλεῖον· ἡ γὰρ ἄνοια
the faith. But they shall not advance farther, [1]for [2]folly

shall be a vessel unto honour, sanctified, and meet for the master's use, *and* prepared unto every good work. 22 Flee also youthful lusts: but follow righteousness, faith, charity, peace, with them that call on the Lord out of a pure heart. 23 But foolish and unlearned questions avoid, knowing that they do gender strifes. 24 And the servant of the Lord must not strive; but be gentle unto all *men*, apt to teach, patient, 25 in meekness instructing those that oppose themselves; if God peradventure will give them repentance to the acknowledging of the truth; 26 and *that* they may recover themselves out of the snare of the devil, who are taken captive by him at his will.

III. This know also, that in the last days perilous times shall come. 2 For men shall be lovers of their own selves, covetous, boasters, proud, blasphemers, disobedient to parents, unthankful, unholy, 3 without natural affection, trucebreakers, false accusers, incontinent, fierce, despisers of those that are good, 4 traitors, heady, highminded, lovers of pleasures more than lovers of God; 5 having a form of godliness, but denying the power thereof: from such turn away. 6 For of this sort are they which creep into houses, and lead captive silly women laden with sins, led away with divers lusts, 7 ever learning, and never able to come to the knowledge of the truth. 8 Now as Jannes and Jambres withstood Moses, so do these also resist the truth: men of corrupt minds, reprobate concerning the faith. 9 But they shall proceed no further: for their folly

---

g — καὶ LTTrA. h + πάντων all L. i ἀλλὰ LTTrA. k πραΰτητι LTTrAW. l δῴη LTTrAW.
m γινώσκετε know ye L. n αἰχμαλωτίζοντες GLTTrAW.

shall be manifest unto
all *men*, as theirs also
was. 10 But thou hast
fully known my doc-
trine, manner of life,
purpose, faith, long-
suffering, charity, pa-
tience, 11 persecutions,
afflictions, which came
unto me at Antioch, at
Iconium, at Lystra;
what persecutions I
endured: but out of
them all the Lord de-
livered me. 12 Yea,
and all that will live
godly in Christ Jesus
shall suffer persecu-
tion. 13 But evil men
and seducers shall wax
worse and worse, de-
ceiving, and being de-
ceived. 14 But con-
tinue thou in the
things which thou hast
learned and hast been
assured of, knowing of
whom thou hast learn-
ed *them*; 15 and that
from a child thou hast
known the holy scrip-
tures, which are able
to make thee wise un-
to salvation through
faith which is in Christ
Jesus. 16 All scrip-
ture *is* given by inspi-
ration of God, and *is*
profitable for doctrine,
for reproof, for correc-
tion, for instruction in
righteousness: 17 that
the man of God may
be perfect, throughly
furnished unto all
good works.

IV. 1 I charge *thee*
therefore before God,
and the Lord Jesus
Christ, who shall judge
the quick and the dead
at his appearing and
his kingdom; 2 preach
the word; be instant
in season, out of
season; reprove, re-
buke, exhort with all
longsuffering and doc-
trine. 3 For the time
will come when they
will not endure sound
doctrine; but after
their own lusts shall
they heap to them-
selves teachers, having
itching ears; 4 and
they shall turn away
their ears from the
truth, and shall be

αὐτῶν ἔκδηλος ἔσται πᾶσιν, ὡς καὶ ἡ ἐκείνων ἐγένετο.
[1]their fully manifest shall be to all, as also that of those became.
10 σὺ.δὲ [o]παρηκολούθηκάς[||] μου τῇ διδασκαλίᾳ, τῇ ἀγωγῇ,
But thou hast closely followed my teaching, conduct,
τῇ προθέσει, τῇ πίστει, τῇ μακροθυμίᾳ, τῇ ἀγάπῃ, τῇ ὑπομονῇ,
purpose, faith, patience, love, endurance,
11 τοῖς διωγμοῖς, τοῖς παθήμασιν, οἷά μοι ἐγένετο ἐν Ἀν-
persecutions, sufferings: such as to me happened in An-
τιοχείᾳ, ἐν Ἰκονίῳ, ἐν Λύστροις· οἵους διωγμοὺς ὑπ-
tioch, in Iconium, in Lystra; what manner of persecutions I en-
ήνεγκα, καὶ ἐκ πάντων με [p]ἐῤῥύσατο[||] ὁ κύριος. 12 καὶ
dured; and out of all [4]me [3]delivered [1]the [2]Lord. And
πάντες δὲ οἱ θέλοντες [q]εὐσεβῶς ζῇν[||] ἐν χριστῷ Ἰησοῦ
all indeed who wish piously to live in Christ Jesus
διωχθήσονται· 13 πονηροὶ.δὲ ἄνθρωποι καὶ γόητες προ-
will be persecuted. But wicked men and impostors shall
κόψουσιν ἐπὶ τὸ χεῖρον, πλανῶντες καὶ πλανώμενοι. 14 σὺ.δὲ
advance to worse, misleading and being misled. But thou
μένε ἐν οἷς ἔμαθες καὶ ἐπιστώθης, εἰδὼς παρὰ
abide in the things thou didst learn, and wast assured of, having known from
[r]τίνος[||] ἔμαθες, 15 καὶ ὅτι ἀπὸ βρέφους [s]τὰ[||] ἱερὰ
whom thou didst learn [them]; and that from a babe the sacred
γράμματα οἶδας, τὰ δυνάμενά σε σοφίσαι εἰς
letters thou hast known, which [are] able [3]thee [1]to [2]make wise to
σωτηρίαν, διὰ πίστεως τῆς ἐν χριστῷ Ἰησοῦ. 16 πᾶσα
salvation, through faith which [is] in Christ Jesus. Every
γραφὴ θεόπνευστος καὶ ὠφέλιμος πρὸς διδασκαλίαν, πρὸς
scripture [is] God-inspired and profitable for teaching, for
[t]ἔλεγχον,[||] πρὸς ἐπανόρθωσιν, πρὸς [v]παιδείαν[||] τὴν ἐν
conviction, for correction, for discipline which [is] in
δικαιοσύνῃ· 17 ἵνα ἄρτιος ᾖ ὁ τοῦ θεοῦ ἄνθρωπος, πρὸς
righteousness; that complete may be the [2]of [3]God [1]man, to
πᾶν ἔργον ἀγαθὸν ἐξηρτισμένος.
every [2]work [1]good fully fitted.

4 Διαμαρτύρομαι [w]οὖν ἐγὼ[||] ἐνώπιον τοῦ θεοῦ καὶ [x]τοῦ
[2]Earnestly [3]testify [4]therefore [1]I before God and the
κυρίου[||] [y]Ἰησοῦ χριστοῦ,[||] τοῦ μέλλοντος κρίνειν ζῶντας καὶ
Lord Jesus Christ, who is about to judge living and
νεκροὺς [z]κατὰ[||] τὴν.ἐπιφάνειαν.αὐτοῦ καὶ τὴν βασιλείαν
dead according to his appearing and [2]kingdom
αὐτοῦ, 2 κήρυξον τὸν λόγον, ἐπίστηθι εὐκαίρως ἀκαίρως,
[1]his, proclaim the word; be urgent in season, out of season,
ἔλεγξον, [a]ἐπιτίμησον, παρακάλεσον,[||] ἐν πάσῃ μακροθυμίᾳ
convict, rebuke, encourage, with all patience
καὶ διδαχῇ. 3 ἔσται.γὰρ καιρὸς ὅτε τῆς ὑγιαινούσης δι-
and teaching. For there will be a time when sound teach-
δασκαλίας οὐκ.ἀνέξονται, ἀλλὰ κατὰ τὰς [b]ἐπιθυμίας
ing they will not bear; but according to [3]desires
τὰς.ἰδίας[||] ἑαυτοῖς ἐπισωρεύσουσιν διδασκάλους, κνηθό-
[1]their [2]own to themselves will heap up teachers,
μενοι.τὴν.ἀκοήν· 4 καὶ ἀπὸ μὲν τῆς ἀληθείας τὴν ἀκοὴν ἀπο-
having an itching ear; and from the truth the ear they will

---

[o] παρηκολούθησάς didst closely follow LTTrA. [p] ἐρύσατο LTTr. [q] ζῇν εὐσεβῶς TTr. [r] τίνων what [persons] LTTrA. [s] — τὰ [L]T[TrA]. [t] ἐλεγμόν LTTrA. [v] παιδίαν T. [w] — οὖν ἐγὼ GLTTrAW. [x] — τοῦ κυρίου GLTTrAW. [y] χριστοῦ Ἰησοῦ LTTrAW. [z], καὶ and [by] GLTTrAW. [a] παρακαλεσον, ἐπιτίμησον T. [b] ἰδίας ἐπιθυμίας GLTTrAW.

στρέψουσιν, ἐπὶ.δὲ τοὺς μύθους ἐκτραπήσονται. 5 σὺ.δὲ
turn away, and to fables will be turned aside. But thou,
νῆφε ἐν πᾶσιν, κακοπάθησον, ἔργον ποίησον εὐαγ-
be sober in all things, suffer hardships, [the] work do of an
γελιστοῦ, τὴν.διακονίαν.σου πληροφόρησον. 6 Ἐγὼ.γὰρ ἤδη
evangelist, thy service fully carry out. For I already
σπένδομαι, καὶ ὁ καιρὸς τῆς.[c]ἐμῆς.ἀναλύσεως‖ ἐφ-
am being poured out, and the time of my release is
έστηκεν. 7 τὸν [d]ἀγῶνα τὸν καλὸν‖ ἠγώνισμαι, τὸν .δρόμον
come. The [2]combat [1]good I have combated, the course
τετέλεκα, τὴν πίστιν τετήρηκα· 8 λοιπὸν ἀπόκειταί μοι
I have finished, the faith I have kept. Henceforth is laid up for me
ὁ τῆς δικαιοσύνης στέφανος, ὃν ἀποδώσει μοι ὁ κύριος
the [2]of [3]righteousness [1]crown, which [6]will [7]render [8]to [9]me [1]the [2]Lord
ἐν ἐκείνῃ τῇ ἡμέρᾳ, ὁ δίκαιος κριτής· οὐ.μόνον.δὲ ἐμοί,
[10]in [11]that [12]day [3]the [4]righteous [5]judge; and not only to me,
ἀλλὰ καὶ πᾶσιν τοῖς ἠγαπηκόσιν τὴν.ἐπιφάνειαν.αὐτοῦ.
but also to all who love his appearing.

9 Σπούδασον ἐλθεῖν πρός με ταχέως. 10 Δημᾶς.γάρ με
Be diligent to come to me quickly; for Demas [2]me
ἐγκατέλιπεν, ἀγαπήσας τὸν νῦν αἰῶνα, καὶ ἐπορεύθη εἰς
[1]forsook, having loved the present age, and is gone to
Θεσσαλονίκην· Κρήσκης εἰς [e]Γαλατίαν,‖ Τίτος εἰς [f]Δαλματίαν·‖
Thessalonica; Crescens to Galatia, Titus to Dalmatia.
11 Λουκᾶς ἐστιν μόνος μετ' ἐμοῦ. Μάρκον ἀναλαβὼν ἄγε
Luke [2]is [1]alone with me. Mark having taken bring
μετὰ σεαυτοῦ· ἔστιν.γάρ μοι εὔχρηστος εἰς διακονίαν. 12 Τυ-
with thyself, for he is [2]to [3]me [1]useful for service. [2]Ty-
χικὸν δὲ ἀπέστειλα εἰς Ἔφεσον. 13 Τὸν [g]φαιλόνην‖ ὃν
chicus [1]but I sent to Ephesus. The cloak which
ἀπέλιπον ἐν [h]Τρωάδι‖ παρὰ Κάρπῳ, ἐρχόμενος φέρε, καὶ τὰ
I left in Troas with Carpus, [when] coming bring, and the
βιβλία, μάλιστα τὰς μεμβράνας. 14 Ἀλέξανδρος ὁ χαλκεὺς
books, especially the parchments. Alexander the smith
πολλά μοι κακὰ ἐνεδείξατο· [i]ἀποδῴη‖ αὐτῷ ὁ
[2]many [5]against [6]me [3]evil [4]things [1]did. May [3]render [4]to [5]him [1]the
κύριος κατὰ τὰ.ἔργα.αὐτοῦ· 15 ὃν καὶ σὺ φυλάσσου,
[2]Lord according to his works. Whom also thou be ware of,
λίαν.γὰρ [k]ἀνθέστηκεν‖ τοῖς ἡμετέροις λόγοις. 16 Ἐν τῇ
for exceedingly he has withstood our words. In
πρώτῃ.μου ἀπολογίᾳ οὐδείς μοι [l]συμπαρεγένετο,‖ ἀλλὰ πάντες
my first defence no one [3]me [1]stood [2]with, but all
με ἐγκατέλιπον· μὴ αὐτοῖς λογισθείη· 17 ὁ.δὲ κύριός
me forsook. Not to them may it be reckoned. But the Lord
μοι παρέστη, καὶ ἐνεδυνάμωσέν με, ἵνα δι' ἐμοῦ τὸ κή-
[3]me [1]stood [2]by, and strengthened me, that through me the pro-
ρυγμα πληροφορηθῇ, καὶ [m]ἀκούσῃ‖ πάντα τὰ ἔθνη· καὶ
clamation might be fully made, and [4]should [5]hear [1]all [2]the [3]nations; and
[n]ἐρρύσθην‖ ἐκ στόματος λέοντος. 18 [o]καὶ‖ ῥύσεταί με
I was delivered out of [the] [2]mouth [1]lion's. And [3]will [4]deliver [5]me
ὁ κύριος ἀπὸ παντὸς ἔργου πονηροῦ, καὶ σώσει εἰς τὴν
[1]the [2]Lord from every [2]work [1]wicked, and will preserve [me] for

turned unto fables. 5 But watch thou in all things, endure afflictions, do the work of an evangelist, make full proof of thy ministry. 6 For I am now ready to be offered, and the time of my departure is at hand. 7 I have fought a good fight, I have finished *my* course, I have kept the faith: 8 henceforth there is laid up for me a crown of righteousness, which the Lord, the righteous judge, shall give me at that day; and not to me only, but unto all them also that love his appearing.

9 Do thy diligence to come shortly unto me: 10 for Demas hath forsaken me, having loved this present world, and is departed unto Thessalonica; Crescens to Galatia, Titus unto Dalmatia. 11 Only Luke is with me. Take Mark, and bring him with thee: for he is profitable to me for the ministry. 12 And Tychicus have I sent to Ephesus. 13 The cloke that I left at Troas with Carpus, when thou comest, bring *with thee*, and the books, *but* especially the parchments. 14 Alexander the coppersmith did me much evil: the Lord reward him according to his works: 15 of whom be thou ware also; for he hath greatly withstood our words. 16 At my first answer no man stood with me, but all *men* forsook me: *I pray God* that it may not be laid to their charge. 17 Notwithstanding the Lord stood with me, and strengthened me; that by me the preaching might be fully known, and *that* all the Gentiles might hear: and I was delivered out of the mouth of the lion. 18 And the Lord shall deliver me from every evil work, and will preserve *me* unto his

---

[c] ἀναλύσεώς μου LTTr. [d] καλὸν ἀγῶνα LTTr. [e] Γαλλίαν Gallia T. [f] Δελματίαν L. [g] φελόνην EGLTTrAW. [h] Τρῳάδι LT. [i] ἀποδώσει shall render LTTrAW. [k] ἀντέστη he withstood LTTrAW. [l] συν- A; παρεγένετο stood by LTTr. [m] ἀκούσωσιν LTTrAW. [n] ἐρύσθην LTTrA. [o] — καὶ LTTrA.

heavenly kingdom: to whom *be* glory for ever and ever. Amen.

βασιλείαν.αὐτοῦ τὴν ἐπουράνιον· ᾧ ἡ δόξα εἰς τοὺς
his kingdom the heavenly; to whom [be] glory unto the
αἰῶνας τῶν αἰώνων. ἀμήν.
ages of the ages. Amen.

19 Salute Prisca and Aquila, and the household of Onesiphorus. 20 Erastus abode at Corinth: but Trophimus have I left at Miletum sick. 21 Do thy diligence to come before winter. Eubulus greeteth thee, and Pudens, and Linus, and Claudia, and all the brethren. 22 The Lord Jesus Christ *be* with thy spirit. Grace *be* with you. Amen.

19 "Ασπασαι Πρίσκαν καὶ Ἀκύλαν, καὶ τὸν Ὀνησιφόρου
Salute Prisca and Aquila, and the [2]of [3]Onesiphorus
οἶκον. 20 "Ἔραστος ἔμεινεν ἐν Κορίνθῳ· Τρόφιμον.δὲ ἀπέλιπον
[1]house. Erastus remained in Corinth, but Trophimus I left
ἐν Μιλήτῳ ἀσθενοῦντα. 21 Σπούδασον πρὸ χειμῶνος ἐλθεῖν.
in Miletus sick. Be diligent before winter to come.
Ἀσπάζεταί σε Εὔβουλος, καὶ Πούδης, καὶ [q]Λῖνος," καὶ
[2]Salutes [3]thee [1]Eubulus, and Pudens, and Linus, and
Κλαυδία, καὶ οἱ ἀδελφοὶ πάντες. 22 Ὁ κύριος [r]Ἰησοῦς"
Claudia, and [2]the [3]brethren [1]all. The Lord Jesus
[s]χριστὸς" μετὰ τοῦ.πνεύματός.σου. ἡ χάρις μεθ' ὑμῶν.
Christ [be] with thy spirit. Grace [be] with you.
[t]ἀμήν."
Amen.

[v]Πρὸς Τιμόθεον δευτέρα, τῆς Ἐφεσίων ἐκκλη-
[2]To [3]Timotheus [1]second, [8]of [9]the [11]of [[12]the] [13]Ephesians [10]assem-
σίας πρῶτον ἐπίσκοπον χειροτονηθέντα, ἐγράφη ἀπὸ
bly [[5]the] [6]first [7]overseer [4]chosen, written from
Ῥώμης, ὅτε ἐκ.δευτέρου παρέστη Παῦλος τῷ Καίσαρι
Rome, when a second time [2]was [3]placed [4]before [1]Paul Cæsar
Νέρωνι."
Nero.

---

[a]Η ΠΡΟΣ ΤΙΤΟΝ ΕΠΙΣΤΟΛΗ ΠΑΥΛΟΥ."
THE [4]TO [5]TITUS [1]EPISTLE [2]OF [3]PAUL.

PAUL, a servant of God, and an apostle of Jesus Christ, according to the faith of God's elect, and the acknowledging of the truth which is after godliness; 2 in hope of eternal life, which God, that cannot lie, promised before the world began; 3 but hath in due times manifested his word through preaching, which is committed unto me according to the commandment of God our Saviour; 4 to Titus, *mine* own son after the common faith: Grace, mercy, *and* peace, from God the Father and the Lord Jesus Christ our Saviour.

ΠΑΥΛΟΣ δοῦλος θεοῦ, ἀπόστολος.δὲ Ἰησοῦ χριστοῦ κατὰ
Paul bondman of God, and apostle of Jesus Christ according to
πίστιν ἐκλεκτῶν θεοῦ καὶ ἐπίγνωσιν ἀληθείας τῆς
[the] faith [3]elect [1]of [2]God's and knowledge of [the] truth which [is]
κατ' εὐσέβειαν, 2 ἐπ' ἐλπίδι ζωῆς αἰωνίου, ἣν ἐπηγ-
according to piety; in [the] hope of life eternal, which [6]pro-
γείλατο ὁ ἀψευδὴς θεὸς πρὸ χρόνων.αἰωνίων, 3 ἐ-
mised [1]the [3]who [4]cannot [5]lie [2]God before the ages of time,
φανέρωσεν.δὲ καιροῖς.ἰδίοις τὸν.λόγον.αὐτοῦ, ἐν κηρύγματι
but manifested in its own seasons his word in [the] proclamation
ὃ ἐπιστεύθην ἐγὼ κατ' ἐπιταγὴν τοῦ σωτῆρος
which [2]was [3]entrusted [4]with [1]I according to [the] commandment of [2]Saviour
ἡμῶν θεοῦ, 4 Τίτῳ γνησίῳ τέκνῳ κατὰ κοινὴν
[1]our God; to Titus [my] true child according to [our] common
πίστιν, χάρις, [b]ἔλεος," εἰρήνη ἀπὸ θεοῦ πατρός, καὶ
faith: Grace, mercy peace. from God [the] Father, and [the]
[c]κυρίου Ἰησοῦ χριστοῦ" τοῦ.σωτῆρος.ἡμῶν
Lord Jesus Christ our Saviour.

5 For this cause left I thee in Crete, that

5 Τούτου.χάριν [d]κατέλιπόν" σε ἐν Κρήτῃ, ἵνα τὰ.λείποντα
For this cause I left thee in Crete, that the things lacking

---

[q] Λίνος LTW. [r] — Ἰησοῦς TTr[A]. [s] — χριστὸς LTTr[A]. [t] — ἀμήν GLTTrAW.
[v] — *the subscription* GLTW; Πρὸς Τιμόθεον β' (— β' A) TrA.
[a] + τοῦ Ἀποστόλου the apostle E; Πρὸς Τίτον LTTrAW. [b] καὶ and TTrAW. [c] χριστοῦ Ἰησοῦ LTTrA. [d] ἀπέλιπόν LTTrAW.

ᵉἐπιδιορθώσῃ,ˡˡ καὶ καταστήσῃς κατὰ.πόλιν πρεσ-
thou mightest go on to set right, and mightest appoint in every city
βυτέρους, ὡς ἐγώ σοι διεταξάμην· 6 εἴ τις ἐστιν ἀνέγ-
elders, as I [2]thee [1]ordered: if anyone is unim-
κλητος, μιᾶς γυναικὸς ἀνήρ, τέκνα ἔχων πιστά, μὴ ἐν
peachable, [2]of [3]one [4]wife [1]husband, [7]children [5]having [6]believing, not under
κατηγορίᾳ ἀσωτίας ἢ ἀνυπότακτα. 7 δεῖ.γὰρ τὸν ἐπί-
accusation of dissoluteness or insubordinate. For it behoves the over-
σκοπον ἀνέγκλητον εἶναι, ὡς θεοῦ οἰκονόμον· μὴ αὐθάδη,
seer unimpeachable to be, as God's steward; not selfwilled,
μὴ ὀργίλον, μὴ πάροινον, μὴ πλήκτην, μὴ αἰσχροκερδῆ,
not passionate, not given to wine, not a striker, not greedy of base gain,
8 ἀλλὰ φιλόξενον, φιλάγαθον, σώφρονα, δίκαιον, ὅσιον, ἐγ-
but hospitable, a lover of good, discreet, just, holy, tem-
κρατῆ, 9 ἀντεχόμενον τοῦ κατὰ τὴν διδαχὴν πιστοῦ
perate, holding to the [3]according [4]to [5]the [6]teaching [1]faithful
λόγου, ἵνα.δυνατὸς ᾖ καὶ παρακαλεῖν ἐν τῇ διδασκαλίᾳ
[2]word, that able he may be both to encourage with [2]teaching
τῇ ὑγιαινούσῃ, καὶ τοὺς ἀντιλέγοντας ἐλέγχειν. 10 εἰσὶν.γὰρ
[1]sound, and those who gainsay to convict. For there are
πολλοὶ ᶠκαὶˡˡ ἀνυπότακτοι ματαιολόγοι καὶ φρεναπάται, μά-
many and insubordinate vain talkers and mind-deceivers, espe-
λιστα ᵍ οἱ ἐκ ʰ περιτομῆς, 11 οὓς δεῖ ἐπιστο-
cially those of [the] circumcision, whom it is necessary to stop the
μίζειν· οἵτινες ὅλους οἴκους ἀνατρέπουσιν, διδάσκοντες
mouths of, who whole houses overthrow, teaching
ἃ μὴ.δεῖ, αἰσχροῦ κέρδους χάριν· 12 εἶπέν
things which [they] ought not, [4]base [5]gain [1]for [2]sake [3]of. [14]Said
τις ἐξ αὐτῶν ἴδιος.αὐτῶν προφήτης, Κρῆτες ἀεὶ
[6]one [7]of [8]themselves [11]of [12]their [13]own [9]a [10]prophet, Cretans always [are]
ψεῦσται, κακὰ θηρία, γαστέρες ἀργαί. 13 ἡ.μαρτυρία.αὕτη
liars, evil wild beasts, [2]gluttons [1]lazy. This testimony
ἐστὶν ἀληθής· δι' ἣν αἰτίαν ἔλεγχε αὐτοὺς ἀποτόμως, ἵνα
is true; for which cause convict them with severity, that
ὑγιαίνωσιν ἐν τῇ πίστει, 14 μὴ προσέχοντες Ἰουδαϊκοῖς
they may be sound in the faith, not giving heed to Jewish
μύθοις καὶ ἐντολαῖς ἀνθρώπων ἀποστρεφομένων τὴν ἀλή-
fables and commandments of men, turning away from the truth.
θειαν. 15 πάντα ⁱμὲνˡˡ καθαρὰ τοῖς καθαροῖς· τοῖς.δὲ
All things [are] pure to the pure; but to those who
ᵏμεμιασμένοιςˡˡ καὶ ἀπίστοις οὐδὲν καθαρόν, ἀλλὰ μεμίαν-
are defiled and unbelieving nothing [is] pure; but are de-
ται αὐτῶν καὶ ὁ νοῦς καὶ ἡ.συνείδησις. 16 θεὸν ὁμολογοῦσιν
filed [2]their [1]both mind and [their] conscience. God they profess
εἰδέναι, τοῖς.δὲ.ἔργοις ἀρνοῦνται, βδελυκτοὶ ὄντες καὶ
to know, but in works deny [him], [2]abominable [1]being and
ἀπειθεῖς, καὶ πρὸς πᾶν ἔργον ἀγαθὸν ἀδόκιμοι.
disobedient, and as to every [2]work [1]good found worthless.
2 Σὺ.δὲ λάλει ἃ πρέπει τῇ ὑγιαινούσῃ διδασ-
But [2]thou [1]speak the things that become sound teach-
καλίᾳ· 2 πρεσβύτας νηφαλίους εἶναι, σεμνούς, σώ-
ing: [the] aged [men] [3]sober [1]to [2]be, grave, dis-
φρονας, ὑγιαίνοντας τῇ πίστει, τῇ ἀγάπῃ, τῇ ὑπομονῇ·
creet, sound in faith, in love, in endurance;

thou shouldest set in
order the things that
are wanting, and or-
dain elders in every
city, as I had appointed
thee: 6 if any be
blameless, the husband
of one wife, having
faithful children not
accused of riot or un-
ruly. 7 For a bishop
must be blameless, as
the steward of God;
not selfwilled, not
soon angry, not given
to wine, no striker,
not given to filthy
lucre; 8 but a lover
of hospitality, a lover
of good men, sober,
just, holy, temperate;
9 holding fast the
faithful word as he
hath been taught, that
he may be able by
sound doctrine both to
exhort and to con-
vince the gainsayers.
10 For there are
many unruly and vain
talkers and deceivers,
specially they of the
circumcision: 11 whose
mouths must be stop-
ped, who subvert whole
houses, teaching things
which they ought not,
for filthy lucre's sake.
12 One of themselves,
even a prophet of their
own, said, The Cre-
tians *are* alway liars,
evil beasts, slow bel-
lies. 13 This witness is
true. Wherefore re-
buke them sharply,
that they may be sound
in the faith; 14 not
giving heed to Jewish
fables, and command-
ments of men, that
turn from the truth.
15 Unto the pure all
things *are* pure: but
unto them that are de-
filed and unbelieving
is nothing pure; but
even their mind and
conscience is defiled.
16 They profess that
they know God; but
in works they deny
him, being abominable,
and disobedient, and
unto every good work
reprobate. II. But
speak thou the things
which become sound
doctrine: 2 that the
aged men be so-
ber, grave, temperate,
sound in faith, in cha-
rity, in patience. 3 The

ᵉ ἐπιδιορθώσῃς L. ᶠ — καὶ LTTr[A]. ᵍ + [δὲ] but (especially) L. ʰ + τῆς the TTr.
ⁱ — μὲν LTTrAW. ᵏ μεμιαμμένοις LTTr; μεμιαμένοις A.

aged women likewise, that *they be* in behaviour as becometh holiness, not false accusers, not given to much wine, teachers of good things; 4 that they may teach the young women to be sober, to love their husbands, to love their children, 5 *to be* discreet, chaste, keepers at home, good, obedient to their own husbands, that the word of God be not blasphemed. 6 Young men likewise exhort to be sober minded. 7 In all things shewing thyself a pattern of good works: in doctrine *shewing* uncorruptness, gravity, sincerity, 8 sound speech, that cannot be condemned; that he that is of the contrary part may be ashamed, having no evil thing to say of you. 9 *Exhort* servants to be obedient unto their own masters, *and* to please *them* well in all *things;* not answering again; 10 not purloining, but shewing all good fidelity; that they may adorn the doctrine of God our Saviour in all things. 11 For the grace of God that bringeth salvation hath appeared to all men, 12 teaching us that, denying ungodliness and worldly lusts, we should live soberly, righteously, and godly, in this present world; 13 looking for that blessed hope, and the glorious appearing of the great God and our Saviour Jesus Christ; 14 who gave himself for us, that he might redeem us from all iniquity, and purify unto himself a peculiar people, zealous of good works. 15 These things speak, and exhort, and rebuke with all authority. Let no man despise thee.

3 πρεσβύτιδας ὡσαύτως ἐν καταστήματι ἱερο-
[the] aged [women] in like manner in deportment as becomes
πρεπεῖς, μὴ διαβόλους, [l]μὴ[ǁ] οἴνῳ πολλῷ δεδουλωμένας,
sacred ones, not slanderers, not [2]to [4]wine [3]much [1]enslaved,
καλοδιδασκάλους, 4 ἵνα [m]σωφρονίζωσιν[ǁ] τὰς νέας
teachers of what is right; that they may school the young [women]
φιλάνδρους εἶναι, φιλοτέκνους, 5 σώφρονας,
lovers of [their] husbands to be, lovers of [their] children, discreet,
ἁγνάς, [n]οἰκουρούς,[ǁ] ἀγαθάς, ὑποτασσομένας τοῖς.ἰδίοις ἀν-
chaste, keepers at home, good, subject to their own hus-
δράσιν, ἵνα μὴ ὁ λόγος τοῦ θεοῦ βλασφημῆται. 6 Τοὺς
bands, that not the word of God may be evil spoken of. The
νεωτέρους ὡσαύτως παρακάλει σωφρονεῖν, [o] 7 περὶ
younger [men] in like manner exhort to be discreet; in
πάντα σεαυτὸν παρεχόμενος τύπον καλῶν ἔργων, ἐν τῇ
all things thyself holding forth a pattern of good works; in
διδασκαλίᾳ [p]ἀδιαφθορίαν,[ǁ] σεμνότητα, [q]ἀφθαρσίαν,[ǁ] 8 λόγον
teaching uncorruptness, gravity, incorruption, [2]speech
ὑγιῆ, ἀκατάγνωστον, ἵνα ὁ.ἐξ.ἐναντίας ἐντραπῇ, μηδὲν
[1]sound, not to be condemned; that he who is opposed may be ashamed, [2]nothing
ἔχων [r]περὶ ὑμῶν λέγειν[ǁ] φαῦλον. 9 Δούλους [s]ἰδίοις
[1]having [6]concerning [7]you [4]to [5]say [3]evil. Bondmen to their own
δεσπόταις[ǁ] ὑποτάσσεσθαι, ἐν πᾶσιν εὐαρέστους εἶναι, μὴ
masters to be subject, in everything well-pleasing to be, not
ἀντιλέγοντας, 10 μὴ νοσφιζομένους, ἀλλὰ [t]πίστιν πᾶσαν[ǁ]
contradicting; not purloining, but [4]fidelity [2]all
ἐνδεικνυμένους ἀγαθήν· ἵνα τὴν διδασκαλίαν [v] τοῦ σωτῆρος
[1]shewing [3]good, that the teaching [3]Saviour
[w]ὑμῶν[ǁ] θεοῦ κοσμῶσιν ἐν πᾶσιν. 11 Ἐπεφάνη.γὰρ ἡ
[1]of [2]your God they may adorn in all things. For [11]appeared [1]the
χάρις τοῦ θεοῦ [x]ἡ[ǁ] σωτήριος πᾶσιν ἀνθρώποις,
[2]grace [3]of [4]God [5]which [6]brings [7]salvation [8]for [9]all [10]men,
12 παιδεύουσα ἡμᾶς ἵνα ἀρνησάμενοι τὴν ἀσέβειαν καὶ τὰς
instructing us that, having denied ungodliness and
κοσμικὰς.ἐπιθυμίας, σωφρόνως καὶ δικαίως καὶ εὐσεβῶς ζή-
worldly desires, discreetly and righteously and piously we
σωμεν ἐν τῷ νῦν αἰῶνι, 13 προσδεχόμενοι τὴν μακαρίαν
should live in the present age, awaiting the blessed
ἐλπίδα καὶ ἐπιφάνειαν τῆς δόξης τοῦ μεγάλου θεοῦ καὶ σωτῆ-
hope and appearing of the glory [3]great [4]God [5]and [6]Sa-
ρος ἡμῶν [y]Ἰησοῦ χριστοῦ,[ǁ] 14 ὃς ἔδωκεν ἑαυτὸν ὑπὲρ ἡμῶν,
viour [1]of [2]our Jesus Christ; who gave himself for us,
ἵνα λυτρώσηται ἡμᾶς ἀπὸ πάσης ἀνομίας, καὶ καθαρίσῃ
that he might redeem us from all lawlessness, and might purify
ἑαυτῷ λαὸν περιούσιον, ζηλωτὴν καλῶν ἔργων. 15 Ταῦτα
to himself a people peculiar, zealous of good works. These things
λάλει, καὶ παρακάλει, καὶ ἔλεγχε μετὰ πάσης ἐπιταγῆς.
speak, and exhort, and convict with all command.
μηδείς σου περιφρονείτω.
[2]No [3]one [5]thee [1]let [4]despise.

III. Put them in mind to be subject to principalities and

3 Ὑπομίμνησκε αὐτοὺς ἀρχαῖς [z]καὶ[ǁ] ἐξουσίαις ὑποτάσ-
Put [2]in [3]remembrance [1]them to rulers and to authorities to be

---

[l] μηδὲ nor TTrA. [m] σωφρονίζουσιν they school TTrA. [n] οἰκουργούς workers at home LTTrA. [o] *Read* to be discreet in all things, T. [p] ἀφθορίαν incorruption LTTrAW. [q] — ἀφθαρσίαν EGLTTrAW. [r] λέγειν περὶ ἡμῶν (us) LTTrA; περὶ ἡμῶν λέγειν GW. [s] δεσπόταις ἰδίοις L. [t] πᾶσαν πίστιν LTTrA. [v] + τὴν which [is] LTTrAW. [w] ἡμῶν of our EGLTTrAW. [x] — ἡ (*read* σωτή. bringing salvation) LTTrA. [y] χριστοῦ Ἰησοῦ TTr. [z] — καὶ LTTrA.

σεσθαι, πειθαρχεῖν, πρὸς πᾶν ἔργον ἀγαθὸν ἑτοίμους εἶναι,
subject, to be obedient, [4]to [5]every [7]work [6]good [3]ready [1]to [2]be,
2 μηδένα βλασφημεῖν, ἀμάχους εἶναι, ἐπιεικεῖς,
no one to speak evil of, not [3]contentious [1]to [2]be, [to be] gentle,
πᾶσαν ἐνδεικνυμένους [a]πρᾳότητα‖ πρὸς πάντας ἀνθρώπους.
[2]all [1]shewing meekness towards all men.
3 ἦμεν.γάρ ποτε καὶ ἡμεῖς ἀνόητοι, ἀπειθεῖς, πλανώ-
For [2]were [3]once [4]also [1]we without intelligence, disobedient, led
μενοι, δουλεύοντες ἐπιθυμίαις καὶ ἡδοναῖς ποικίλαις, ἐν κακίᾳ
astray, serving [2]lusts [3]and [4]pleasures [1]various, in malice
καὶ φθόνῳ διάγοντες, στυγητοί, μισοῦντες ἀλλήλους· 4 ὅτε.δὲ
and envy living, hateful, hating one another. But when
ἡ χρηστότης καὶ ἡ φιλανθρωπία ἐπεφάνη τοῦ.σωτῆρος.ἡμῶν
the kindness and the love to man [5]appeared [1]of [2]our [3]Saviour
θεοῦ, 5 οὐκ ἐξ ἔργων τῶν ἐν δικαιοσύνῃ [b]ὧν‖ ἐποιήσαμεν
[4]God, not by works which [were] in righteousness which [2]practised
ἡμεῖς, ἀλλὰ κατὰ [c]τὸν.αὐτοῦ.ἔλεον‖ ἔσωσεν ἡμᾶς, διὰ
[1]we, but according to his mercy he saved us, through [the]
λουτροῦ [d]παλιγγενεσίας‖ καὶ ἀνακαινώσεως πνεύματος ἁγίου,
washing of regeneration and renewing of [the] [2]Spirit [1]Holy,
6 οὗ ἐξέχεεν ἐφ᾽ ἡμᾶς πλουσίως διὰ Ἰησοῦ χριστοῦ τοῦ
which he poured out on us richly through Jesus Christ
σωτῆρος.ἡμῶν· 7 ἵνα δικαιωθέντες τῇ.ἐκείνου.χάριτι, κληρο-
our Saviour; that having been justified by his grace, heirs
νόμοι [e]γενώμεθα‖ κατ᾽ ἐλπίδα ζωῆς αἰωνίου.
we should become according to [the] hope of life eternal.
8 Πιστὸς ὁ λόγος, καὶ περὶ τούτων βούλομαί σε δια-
Faithful [is] the word, and concerning these things I desire thee to
βεβαιοῦσθαι, ἵνα φροντίζωσιν καλῶν ἔργων προΐστασθαι
affirm strongly, that [6]may [7]take [8]care [13]good [14]works [9]to [10]be [11]forward [12]in
οἱ πεπιστευκότες [f]τῷ‖ θεῷ. ταῦτά ἐστιν [g]τὰ‖ καλὰ καὶ
[1]they [2]who [3]have [4]believed [5]God. These things are good and
ὠφέλιμα τοῖς ἀνθρώποις· 9 μωρὰς.δὲ ζητήσεις καὶ γενεαλο-
profitable to men; but foolish questions and genealo-
γίας καὶ [h]ἔρεις‖ καὶ μάχας νομικὰς περιΐστασο· εἰσὶν
gies and strifes and contentions about [the] law stand aloof from; [2]they [3]are
γὰρ ἀνωφελεῖς καὶ μάταιοι. 10 Αἱρετικὸν ἄνθρωπον μετὰ
[1]for unprofitable and vain. A sectarian man after
μίαν καὶ δευτέραν νουθεσίαν παραιτοῦ, 11 εἰδὼς ὅτι ἐξέ-
one and a second admonition reject, knowing that is
στραπται ὁ τοιοῦτος, καὶ ἁμαρτάνει, ὢν αὐτοκατάκριτος.
perverted such a one, and sins, being self-condemned.

12 Ὅταν πέμψω Ἀρτεμᾶν πρός σε ἢ Τυχικόν, σπούδα-
When I shall send Artemas to thee, or Tychicus, be dili-
σον ἐλθεῖν πρός με εἰς Νικόπολιν· ἐκεῖ.γὰρ κέκρικα
gent to come to me to Nicopolis; for there I have decided
παραχειμάσαι. 13 Ζηνᾶν τὸν νομικὸν καὶ [i]Ἀπολλὼ‖ σπου-
to winter. Zenas the lawyer and Apollos dili-
δαίως πρόπεμψον, ἵνα μηδὲν αὐτοῖς [k]λείπῃ.‖ 14 μαν-
gently set forward, that nothing to them may be lacking; [2]let
θανέτωσαν δὲ καὶ οἱ ἡμέτεροι καλῶν ἔργων προΐστασθαι
[5]learn [1]and [4]also [3]ours [10]good [11]works [6]to [7]be [8]forward [9]in
εἰς τὰς ἀναγκαίας χρείας, ἵνα μὴ.ὦσιν ἄκαρποι. 15 Ἀσ-
for necessary wants, that they may not be unfruitful. [5]Sa-

powers, to obey magis-
trates, to be ready to
every good work, 2 to
speak evil of no man,
to be no brawlers, *but*
gentle, shewing all
meekness unto all men.
3 For we ourselves al-
so were sometimes
foolish, disobedient,
deceived, serving di-
vers lusts and plea-
sures, living in malice
and envy, hateful, *and*
hating one another.
4 But after that the
kindness and love of
God our Saviour to-
ward man appeared,
5 not by works of
righteousness which
we have done, but ac-
cording to his mercy
he saved us, by the
washing of regenera-
tion, and renewing
of the Holy Ghost;
6 which he shed on us
abundantly through
Jesus Christ our Sa-
viour; 7 that being
justified by his grace,
we should be made
heirs according to the
hope of eternal life.
8 *This is* a faithful saying, and these things
I will that thou affirm
constantly, that they
which have believed
in God might be care-
ful to maintain good
works. These things
are good and profitable
unto men. 9 But a-
void foolish questions,
and genealogies, and
contentions, and striv-
ings about the law;
for they are un-
profitable and vain.
10 A man that is an
heretick after the first
and second admonition
reject; 11 knowing
that he that is such is
subverted, and sin-
neth, being condemned
of himself.

12 When I shall send
Artemas unto thee, or
Tychicus, be diligent
to come unto me to
Nicopolis: for I have
determined there to
winter. 13 Bring Ze-
nas the lawyer and
Apollos on their jour-
ney diligently, that
nothing be wanting
unto them. 14 And
let ours also learn to
maintain good works
for necessary uses, that
they be not unfruitful.
15 All that are with

[a] πραΰτητα LTTrA. [b] ἃ LTTrA. [c] τὸ αὐτοῦ ἔλεος LTTrAW. [d] παλινγενεσίας T. [e] γενηθῶμεν LTTrAW. [f] — τῷ LTTrAW. [g] — τὰ LTTrAW. [h] ἔριν strife T. [i] Ἀπολλῶν T. [k] λίπῃ T.

me salute thee. Greet them that love us in the faith. Grace *be* with you all. Amen.

πάζονταί σε οἱ μετ' ἐμοῦ πάντες. ἄσπασαι τοὺς φι-
lute [6]thee [2]those [3]with [4]me [1]all. Salute those who
λοῦντας ἡμᾶς ἐν πίστει. ἡ χάρις μετὰ πάντων ὑμῶν.
love us in [the] faith. Grace [be] with [2]all [1]you.
[l]ἀμήν.‖
Amen.

[m]Πρὸς Τίτον, τῆς Κρητῶν ἐκκλησίας πρῶτον ἐπί-
To Titus [4]of [5]the [7]of [8the] [9]Cretans [6]assembly [2]first [3]over-
σκοπον χειροτονηθέντα, ἐγράφη ἀπὸ Νικοπόλεως τῆς Μακε-
seer [1]chosen. written from Nicopolis of Mace-
δονίας.‖
donia.

---

[a]Η ΠΡΟΣ ΦΙΛΗΜΟΝΑ ΕΠΙΣΤΟΛΗ ΠΑΥΛΟΥ.‖
THE [4]TO [5]PHILEMON [1]EPISTLE [2]OF [3]PAUL.

PAUL, a prisoner of Jesus Christ, and Timothy *our* brother, unto Philemon our dearly beloved, and fellowlabourer, 2 and to *our* beloved Apphia, and Archippus our fellowsoldier, and to the church in thy house: 3 Grace to you, and peace, from God our Father and the Lord Jesus Christ.

4 I thank my God, making mention of thee always in my prayers, 5 hearing of thy love and faith, which thou hast toward the Lord Jesus, and toward all saints; 6 that the communication of thy faith may become effectual by the acknowledging of every good thing which is in you in Christ Jesus. 7 For we have great joy and consolation in thy love, because the bowels of the saints are refreshed by thee, brother.

8 Wherefore, though I might be much bold in Christ to enjoin thee that which is convenient, 9 yet for love's sake I rather beseech *thee*, being such an one as Paul the aged, and now also a prisoner of Jesus Christ. 10 I beseech thee for my son One-

ΠΑΥΛΟΣ δέσμιος χριστοῦ Ἰησοῦ, καὶ Τιμόθεος ὁ ἀδελφός,
Paul, prisoner of Christ Jesus, and Timotheus the brother,
Φιλήμονι τῷ ἀγαπητῷ καὶ συνεργῷ.ἡμῶν, 2 καὶ Ἀπφίᾳ τῇ
to Philemon the beloved and our fellow-worker, and to Apphia the
[b]ἀγαπητῇ,‖ καὶ Ἀρχίππῳ τῷ.[c]συστρατιώτῃ‖.ἡμῶν, καὶ τῇ
beloved, and to Archippus our fellow-soldier, and to the
κατ' οἶκόν.σου ἐκκλησίᾳ· 3 χάρις ὑμῖν καὶ εἰρήνη ἀπὸ θεοῦ
[2]in [3]thy [4]house [1]assembly: Grace to you and peace from God
πατρὸς.ἡμῶν καὶ κυρίου Ἰησοῦ χριστοῦ.
our Father and [the] Lord Jesus Christ.
4 Εὐχαριστῶ τῷ.θεῷ.μου, πάντοτε μνείαν σου ποιούμενος
I thank my God, always mention of thee making
ἐπὶ τῶν.προσευχῶν.μου, 5 ἀκούων σου τὴν ἀγάπην καὶ τὴν
at my prayers, hearing of thy love and
πίστιν ἣν ἔχεις [d]πρὸς‖ τὸν κύριον Ἰησοῦν καὶ εἰς πάν-
faith which thou hast towards the Lord Jesus, and towards all
τας τοὺς ἁγίους, 6 ὅπως ἡ κοινωνία τῆς.πίστεώς.σου ἐνεργὴς
the saints, so that the fellowship of thy faith efficient
γένηται ἐν ἐπιγνώσει παντὸς ἀγαθοῦ [e]τοῦ‖ ἐν
may become in [the] acknowledgment of every good [thing] which [is] in
[f]ὑμῖν‖ εἰς χριστὸν [g]Ἰησοῦν.‖ 7 [h]χάριν‖ γὰρ [i]ἔχομεν πολλὴν‖
you towards Christ Jesus. [5]Thankfulness [1]for [2]we [3]have [4]great
καὶ παράκλησιν ἐπὶ τῇ.ἀγάπῃ.σου, ὅτι τὰ σπλάγχνα
and encouragement by occasion of thy love, because the bowels
τῶν ἁγίων ἀναπέπαυται διὰ σοῦ, ἀδελφέ.
of the saints have been refreshed by thee, brother.
8 Διὸ πολλὴν ἐν χριστῷ παῤῥησίαν ἔχων ἐπιτάσσειν σοι
Wherefore much [2]in [3]Christ [1]boldness having to order thee
τὸ ἀνῆκον, 9 διὰ τὴν ἀγάπην μᾶλλον παρακαλῶ·
what [is] becoming, for the sake of love rather I exhort,
τοιοῦτος ὢν ὡς Παῦλος πρεσβύτης, νυνὶ.δὲ καὶ δέσμιος
such a one being as Paul [the] aged, and now also prisoner
[k]Ἰησοῦ χριστοῦ·‖ 10 παρακαλῶ σε περὶ τοῦ ἐμοῦ τέκνου, ὃν
of Jesus Christ. I exhort thee for my child, whom

---

[l] — ἀμήν G[L]TTrAW. [m] — *the subscription* GLTW; Πρὸς Τίτον TrA.
[a] + τοῦ Ἀποστόλου the Apostle E; Πρὸς Φιλήμονα LTTrAW. [b] ἀδελφῇ sister LTTrA
[c] συνσ- LTTrA. [d] εἰς LTrA. [e] — τοῦ LTr. [f] ἡμῖν us GLTrAW. [g] — Ἰησοῦν LTTr[A].
[h] χαρὰν joy EGLTTrAW. [i] πολλὴν ἔσχον I had great LTTrAW. [k] χριστοῦ Ἰησοῦ LTTrA.

ἐγέννησα ἐν τοῖς δεσμοῖς [l]μου,‖ Ὀνήσιμον, 11 τόν ποτέ σοι
I begot in [2]bonds [1]my, Onesimus, once to thee
ἄχρηστον. νυνὶ.δέ [m] σοὶ καὶ ἐμοὶ εὔχρηστον, ὃν ἀνέπεμ-
unserviceable, but now to thee and to me serviceable: whom I sent
ψα[n]· 12 [o]σὺ.δὲ‖ αὐτόν, [p]τουτέστιν‖ τὰ ἐμὰ σπλάγχνα,
back [to thee]: but thou him, (that is, my bowels,)
[q]προσλαβοῦ·‖ 13 ὃν ἐγὼ ἐβουλόμην πρὸς ἐμαυτὸν κατέχειν,
receive: whom I was desiring with myself to keep,
ἵνα ὑπὲρ σοῦ [r]διακονῇ μοι‖ ἐν τοῖς δεσμοῖς τοῦ εὐαγγελίου·
that for thee he might serve me in the bonds of the glad tidings;
14 χωρὶς.δὲ τῆς.σῆς.γνώμης οὐδὲν ἠθέλησα ποιῆσαι, ἵνα μὴ
but apart from thy mind nothing I wished to do, that not
ὡς κατὰ.ἀνάγκην τὸ.ἀγαθόν.σου ᾖ, ἀλλὰ κατὰ.ἑκούσιον.
as of necessity thy good might be, but of willingness:
15 τάχα.γὰρ διὰ τοῦτο ἐχωρίσθη πρὸς ὥραν,
for perhaps because of this he was separated [from thee] for a time,
ἵνα αἰώνιον αὐτὸν ἀπέχῃς· 16 οὐκέτι ὡς δοῦλον,
that eternally him thou mightest possess; no longer as a bondman,
[s]ἀλλ'‖ ὑπὲρ δοῦλον, ἀδελφὸν ἀγαπητόν, μάλιστα ἐμοί,
but above a bondman, a brother beloved, specially to me,
πόσῳ.δὲ μᾶλλόν σοι καὶ ἐν σαρκὶ καὶ ἐν κυρίῳ;
and how much rather to thee both in [the] flesh and in [the] Lord?
17 εἰ οὖν [t]ἐμὲ‖ ἔχεις κοινωνόν, προσλαβοῦ αὐτὸν ὡς
If therefore me thou holdest a partner, receive him as
ἐμέ· 18 εἰ.δέ τι ἠδίκησέν σε ἢ ὀφείλει, τοῦτο ἐμοὶ.[v]ἐλλόγει.‖
me; but if anything he wronged thee, or owes, this put to my account.
19 ἐγὼ Παῦλος ἔγραψα τῇ.ἐμῇ χειρί, ἐγὼ ἀποτίσω· ἵνα
I Paul wrote [it] with my [own] hand; I will repay; that
μὴ.λέγω σοι ὅτι καὶ σεαυτόν μοι προσοφείλεις. 20 Ναί,
I may not say to thee that even thyself to me thou owest also. Yea,
ἀδελφέ, ἐγώ σου ὀναίμην ἐν κυρίῳ· ἀνάπαυσόν μου
brother, [2]I [3]of [4]thee [1]may have profit in [the] Lord: refresh my
τὰ σπλάγχνα ἐν [w]κυρίῳ.‖ 21 πεποιθὼς τῇ.ὑπακοῇ.σου
bowels in [the] Lord. Being persuaded of thy obedience
ἔγραψά σοι, εἰδὼς ὅτι καὶ ὑπὲρ [x]ὃ‖ λέγω ποιήσεις.
I wrote to thee, knowing that even above what I may say thou wilt do.
22 Ἅμα.δὲ καὶ ἑτοίμαζέ μοι ξενίαν· ἐλπίζω.γὰρ ὅτι διὰ
But withal also prepare me a lodging; for I hope that through
τῶν.προσευχῶν.ὑμῶν χαρισθήσομαι ὑμῖν. 23 [y]Ἀσπάζονταί‖
your prayers I shall be granted to you. [13]Salute
σε Ἐπαφρᾶς ὁ συναιχμάλωτός μου ἐν χριστῷ Ἰησοῦ,
[14]thee [1]Epaphras [3]fellow-prisoner [2]my [4]in [5]Christ [6]Jesus;
24 Μάρκος, Ἀρίσταρχος, Δημᾶς, Λουκᾶς, οἱ.συνεργοί.μου.
[7]Mark, [8]Aristarchus, [9]Demas, [10]Luke, [11]my [12]fellow-workers.
25 ἡ χάρις τοῦ.κυρίου.[z]ἡμῶν‖ Ἰησοῦ χριστοῦ μετὰ τοῦ
The grace of our Lord Jesus Christ [be] with
πνεύματος.ὑμῶν. [a]ἀμήν.‖
your spirit. Amen.

[b]Πρὸς Φιλήμονα ἐγράφη ἀπὸ Ῥώμης, διὰ Ὀνησίμου
To Philemon written from Rome, by Onesimus
οἰκέτου.‖
a servant.

simus, whom I have begotten in my bonds:
11 which in time past was to thee unprofitable, but now profitable to thee and to me:
12 whom I have sent again: thou therefore receive him, that is, mine own bowels:
13 whom I would have retained with me, that in thy stead he might have ministered unto me in the bonds of the gospel:
14 but without thy mind would I do nothing; that thy benefit should not be as it were of necessity, but willingly.
15 For perhaps he therefore departed for a season, that thou shouldest receive him for ever;
16 not now as a servant, but above a servant, a brother beloved, specially to me, but how much more unto thee, both in the flesh, and in the Lord?
17 If thou count me therefore a partner, receive him as myself.
18 If he hath wronged thee, or oweth *thee* ought, put that on mine account;
19 I Paul have written *it* with mine own hand, I will repay *it*: albeit I do not say to thee how thou owest unto me even thine own self besides.
20 Yea, brother, let me have joy of thee in the Lord: refresh my bowels in the Lord.
21 Having confidence in thy obedience I wrote unto thee, knowing that thou wilt also do more than I say.
22 But withal prepare me also a lodging: for I trust that through your prayers I shall be given unto you.
23 There salute thee Epaphras, my fellowprisoner in Christ Jesus;
24 Marcus, Aristarchus, Demas, Lucas, my fellowlabourers.
25 The grace of our Lord Jesus Christ *be* with your spirit. Amen.

---

[l] — μου LTTrA. [m] + καὶ also T. [n] + σοι to thee LTTrAW. [o] — σὺ δὲ LTTrA. [p] τοῦτ' ἔστιν GT. [q] — προσλαβοῦ LTTrA. [r] μοι διακονῇ GLTTrAW. [s] ἀλλὰ TTr. [t] με GLTTrAW. [v] ἐλλόγα LTTrA. [w] χριστῷ Christ GLTTrAW. [x] ἃ the things which LTTrA. [y] ἀσπάζεταί (*read* Epaphras my fellow-prisoner salutes thee) GLTTrAW. [z] — ἡμῶν (*read* of the Lord) T. [a] — ἀμήν GLTTrAW. [b] — *the subscription* GLTW; Πρὸς Φιλήμονα TrA.

[a]Ἡ ΠΡΟΣ ΕΒΡΑΙΟΥΣ ΕΠΙΣΤΟΛΗ ΠΑΥΛΟΥ.‖
THE [4]TO [[5]THE] [6]HEBREWS [1]EPISTLE [2]OF [3]PAUL.

GOD, who at sundry
times and in divers
manners spake in time
past unto the fathers
by the prophets, 2 hath
in these last days
spoken unto us by *his*
Son, whom he hath
appointed heir of all
things, by whom also
he made the worlds;
3 who being the bright-
ness of *his* glory, and
the express image of his
person, and upholding
all things by the word
of his power, when he
had by himself purged
our sins, sat down on
the right hand of
the Majesty on high;
4 being made so much
better than the angels,
as he hath by inherit-
ance obtained a more
excellent name than
they. 5 For unto which
of the angels said he
at any time, Thou art
my Son, this day have
I begotten thee? And
again, I will be to him
a Father, and he shall
be to me a Son? 6 And
again, when he bring-
eth in the firstbegotten
into the world, he
saith, And let all the
angels of God worship
him. 7 And of the
angels he saith, Who
maketh his angels spi-
rits, and his minis-
ters a flame of fire.
8 But unto the Son
he saith, Thy throne,
O God, *is* for ever and
ever: a sceptre of
righteousness *is* the
sceptre of thy king-
dom. 9 Thou hast lov-
ed righteousness, and
hated iniquity; there-
fore God, *even* thy
God, hath anointed
thee with the oil of
gladness above thy
fellows. 10 And, Thou,
Lord, in the beginning
hast laid the founda-
tion of the earth; and
the heavens are the
works of thine hands:
11 they shall perish;

ΠΟΛΥΜΕΡΩΣ καὶ πολυτρόπως πάλαι ὁ θεὸς λαλήσας
In many parts and in many ways of old God having spoken

τοῖς πατράσιν ἐν τοῖς προφήταις, ἐπ' [b]ἐσχάτων‖ τῶν ἡμερῶν
to the fathers in the prophets, in [2]last [3]days

τούτων, ἐλάλησεν ἡμῖν ἐν.υἱῷ, 2 ὃν ἔθηκεν κληρονό-
[1]these spoke to us in Son, whom he appointed heir

μον πάντων, δι' οὗ καὶ [c]τοὺς αἰῶνας ἐποίησεν,‖ 3 ὃς ὢν
of all things, by whom also the worlds he made: who being

ἀπαύγασμα τῆς.δόξης καὶ χαρακτὴρ τῆς ὑποστάσεως
[the] effulgence of [his] glory and [the] exact expression of [2]substance

αὐτοῦ, φέρων.τε τὰ.πάντα τῷ ῥήματι τῆς.δυνάμεως.αὐτοῦ,
[1]his, and upholding all things by the word of his power,

[d]δι' ἑαυτοῦ‖ καθαρισμὸν [e]ποιησάμενος τῶν ἁμαρτιῶν‖
by himself [the] purification having made of [2]sins

[f]ἡμῶν,‖ ἐκάθισεν ἐν δεξιᾷ τῆς μεγαλωσύνης ἐν ὑψηλοῖς,
[1]our, sat down on [the] right hand of the greatness on high,

4 τοσούτῳ κρείττων γενόμενος τῶν ἀγγέλων, ὅσῳ
by so much better having become than the angels, as much as

διαφορώτερον παρ' αὐτοὺς κεκληρονόμηκεν ὄνομα. 5 Τίνι.γὰρ
[3]more [4]excellent [5]beyond [6]them [7]he [8]has [9]inherited [1]a [2]name. For to which

εἶπέν ποτε τῶν ἀγγέλων, Υἱός μου εἶ σύ, ἐγὼ σήμερον
[4]said [5]he [6]ever [1]of [2]the [3]angels, [8]Son [7]my art thou: I to-day

γεγέννηκά σε; καὶ πάλιν, Ἐγὼ ἔσομαι αὐτῷ εἰς πατέρα,
have begotten thee? and again, I will be to him for Father,

καὶ αὐτὸς ἔσται μοι εἰς υἱόν; 6 ὅταν.δὲ πάλιν εἰσαγάγῃ
and he shall be to me for Son? and [2]when [1]again he brings in

τὸν πρωτότοκον εἰς τὴν οἰκουμένην, λέγει, Καὶ προσκυνη-
the first-born into the habitable world, he says, And let wor-

σάτωσαν αὐτῷ πάντες ἄγγελοι θεοῦ. 7 Καὶ πρὸς μὲν
ship him all [the] angels of God. And as to

τοὺς ἀγγέλους λέγει, Ὁ ποιῶν τοὺς.ἀγγέλους.αὐτοῦ πνεύ-
the angels he says, Who makes his angels spi-

ματα, καὶ τοὺς.λειτουργοὺς.αὐτοῦ πυρὸς φλόγα· 8 πρὸς.δὲ
rits, and his ministers [3]of [4]fire [1]a [2]flame; but as to

τὸν υἱόν, Ὁ.θρόνος.σου, ὁ θεός, εἰς τὸν αἰῶνα τοῦ αἰῶνος·
the Son, Thy throne, O God, [is] to the age of the age.

[g]ῥάβδος [h]εὐθύτητος [i]ἡ‖ ῥάβδος τῆς.βασιλείας.σου. 9 ἠγά-
a sceptre of uprightness [is] the sceptre of thy kingdom. Thou

πησας δικαιοσύνην καὶ ἐμίσησας [k]ἀνομίαν.‖ διὰ τοῦτο
didst love righteousness and didst hate lawlessness; because of this

ἔχρισέν σε ὁ θεὸς ὁ.θεός.σου ἔλαιον ἀγαλλιάσεως παρὰ τοὺς
[4]anointed [5]thee [1]God [2]thy [3]God with [the] oil of exultation above

μετόχους.σου. 10 Καί, Σὺ κατ'.ἀρχάς, κύριε, τὴν γῆν ἐθε-
thy companions. And, Thou in the beginning, Lord, the earth didst

μελίωσας, καὶ ἔργα τῶν.χειρῶν.σου εἰσιν οἱ οὐρανοί· 11 αὐτοὶ
found, and works of thy hands are the heavens. They

[a] — Παύλου EG; Πρὸς Ἑβραίους LTTrAW. [b] ἐσχάτου (*read* at the end of these days) GLTTrAW. [c] ἐποίησεν τοὺς αἰῶνας LTTrAW. [d] — δι' ἑαυτοῦ LTTrA. [e] τῶν ἁμαρτιῶν ποιησάμενος LTTrA. [f] — ἡμῶν LTTrAW. [g] + καὶ and L; + καὶ ἡ and the (sceptre) TTrA. [h] + τῆς LTTr. [i] — ἡ (*read* [the]) LTTr. [k] ἀδικίαν unrighteousness T.

ἀπολοῦνται, σὺ.δὲ διαμένεις· καὶ πάντες ὡς ἱμάτιον παλαιω-
shall perish, but thou continuest; and [they] all as a garment shall grow
θήσονται, 12 καὶ ὡσεὶ περιβόλαιον [l]ἑλίξεις‖ αὐτούς[m], καὶ
old, and as a covering thou shalt roll up them, and
ἀλλαγήσονται· σὺ.δὲ ὁ αὐτὸς εἶ, καὶ τὰ.ἔτη.σου οὐκ ἐκλεί-
they shall be changed; but thou the same art, and thy years [2]not [1]shall
ψουσιν. 13 Πρὸς.τίνα.δὲ τῶν ἀγγέλων εἴρηκέν ποτε, Κάθου ἐκ
fail. But as to which of the angels said he ever, Sit at
δεξιῶν.μου, ἕως.ἂν.θῶ τοὺς.ἐχθρούς.σου ὑποπόδιον τῶν
my right hand until I place thine enemies [as] a footstool [1]for
ποδῶν σου; 14 οὐχὶ πάντες εἰσὶν λειτουργικὰ πνεύματα, εἰς
[3]feet [2]thy? [6]Not [7]all [4]are [5]they ministering spirits, for
διακονίαν ἀποστελλόμενα διὰ τοὺς μέλλοντας κληρονο-
service being sent forth on account of those being about to inherit
μεῖν σωτηρίαν;
salvation?

but thou remainest;
and they all shall wax
old as doth a garment;
12 and as a vesture
shalt thou fold them
up, and they shall be
changed: but thou art
the same, and thy years
shall not fail. 13 But
to which of the angels
said he at any time,
Sit on my right hand,
until I make thine
enemies thy footstool?
14 Are they not all
ministering spirits,
sent forth to minister
for them who shall be
heirs of salvation?

2 Διὰ τοῦτο δεῖ περισσοτέρως [n]ἡμᾶς προσέχειν‖
On account of this it behoves more abundantly us to give heed
τοῖς ἀκουσθεῖσιν, μήποτε [o]παραῤῥυῶμεν.‖ 2 εἰ.γὰρ
to the things heard, lest at any time we should slip away. For if
ὁ δι' ἀγγέλων λαληθεὶς λόγος ἐγένετο βέβαιος, καὶ πᾶσα
the [3]by [4]angels [2]spoken [1]word was confirmed, and every
παράβασις καὶ παρακοὴ ἔλαβεν ἔνδικον μισθαποδοσίαν, 3 πῶς
transgression and disobedience received just recompense, how
ἡμεῖς ἐκφευξόμεθα τηλικαύτης ἀμελήσαντες σωτηρίας; ἥτις
[2]we [1]shall escape [5]so [6]great [[1]if [2]we] [3]have [4]neglected a salvation? which
ἀρχὴν λαβοῦσα λαλεῖσθαι διὰ τοῦ κυρίου, ὑπὸ
[3]a [4]commencement [1]having [2]received to be spoken [of] by the Lord, [5]by
τῶν ἀκουσάντων εἰς ἡμᾶς ἐβεβαιώθη, 4 συνεπιμαρτυ-
[6]those [7]that [8]heard [3]to [4]us [1]was [2]confirmed; [10]bearing [11]witness
ροῦντος τοῦ θεοῦ σημείοις τε καὶ τέρασιν, καὶ ποικίλαις
[12]with [[13]them] [9]God [15]by [16]signs [14]both and wonders, and various
δυνάμεσιν, καὶ πνεύματος ἁγίου μερισμοῖς, κατὰ τὴν
acts of power, and [2]of [[3]the] [5]Spirit [4]Holy [1]distributions, according to
αὐτοῦ θέλησιν.
his will.

II. Therefore we
ought to give the more
earnest heed to the
things which we have
heard, lest at any time
we should let *them*
slip. 2 For if the word
spoken by angels was
stedfast, and every
transgression and dis-
obedience received a
just recompence of re-
ward; 3 how shall we
escape, if we neglect
so great salvation;
which at the first be-
gan to be spoken by
the Lord, and was con-
firmed unto us by
them that heard *him*;
4 God also bearing
them witness, both
with signs and won-
ders, and with divers
miracles, and gifts of
the Holy Ghost, ac-
cording to his own
will?

5 Οὐ.γὰρ ἀγγέλοις ὑπέταξεν τὴν οἰκουμένην τὴν μέλ-
For not to angels did he subject the habitable world which is to
λουσαν, περὶ ἧς λαλοῦμεν· 6 διεμαρτύρατο.δέ που τὶς
come, of which we speak; but [2]fully [3]testified [4]somewhere [1]one
λέγων, Τί ἐστιν ἄνθρωπος, ὅτι μιμνήσκῃ αὐτοῦ· ἢ υἱὸς
saying, What is man, that thou art mindful of him, or son
ἀνθρώπου, ὅτι ἐπισκέπτῃ [p]αὐτόν;‖ 7 ἠλάττωσας αὐτὸν
of man, that thou visitest him? Thou didst make [4]lower [1]him
βραχύ τι παρ' ἀγγέλους· δόξῃ καὶ τιμῇ ἐστεφάνωσας
[3]little [2]some than [the] angels; with glory and honour thou didst crown
(or for a little)
αὐτόν, [q]καὶ κατέστησας αὐτὸν ἐπὶ τὰ ἔργα τῶν.χειρῶν.σου·‖
him, and didst set him over the works of thy hands;
8 πάντα ὑπέταξας ὑποκάτω τῶν.ποδῶν.αὐτοῦ. Ἐν.[r]γὰρ
all things thou didst subject under his feet. For in
τῷ‖ ὑποτάξαι [s]αὐτῷ‖ τὰ.πάντα, οὐδὲν ἀφῆκεν αὐτῷ ἀνυπότακ-
subjecting to him all things, nothing he left to him unsubject.
τον· νῦν.δὲ οὔπω ὁρῶμεν αὐτῷ τὰ.πάντα ὑποτεταγμένα·
But now not yet do we see to him all things subjected;

5 For unto the angels
hath he not put in
subjection the world
to come, whereof we
speak. 6 But one in a
certain place testified,
saying, What is man,
that thou art mindful
of him? or the son of
man, that thou visit-
est him? 7 Thou mad-
est him a little lower
than the angels; thou
crownedst him with
glory and honour, and
didst set him over the
works of thy hands:
8 thou hast put all
things in subjection
under his feet. For in
that he put all in sub-
jection under him, he
left nothing *that is*
not put under him.
But now we see not
yet all things put un-

[l] ἀλλάξεις thou shalt change T. [m] + ὡς ἱμάτιον as a garment L[T·]. [n] προσέχειν ἡμᾶς LTTrAW. [o] παραρυῶμεν LTTrA. [p] αὐτοῦ W. [q] — καὶ κατέστησας *to end of verse* G[L]T[Tr]A. [r] τῷ γὰρ LTTrAW. [s] [αὐτῷ] L.

der him. 9 But we see Jesus, who was made a little lower than the angels for the suffering of death, crowned with glory and honour; that he by the grace of God should taste death for every man. 10 For it became him, for whom *are* all things, and by whom *are* all things, in bringing many sons unto glory, to make the captain of their salvation perfect through sufferings. 11 For both he that sanctifieth and they who are sanctified *are* all of one: for which cause he is not ashamed to call them brethren, 12 saying, I will declare thy name unto my brethren, in the midst of the church will I sing praise unto thee. 13 And again, I will put my trust in him. And again, Behold I and the children which God hath given me. 14 Forasmuch then as the children are partakers of flesh and blood, he also himself likewise took part of the same; that through death he might destroy him that had the power of death, that is, the devil; 15 and deliver them who through fear of death were all their lifetime subject to bondage. 16 For verily he took not on *him the nature of* angels; but he took on *him* the seed of Abraham. 17 Wherefore in all things it behoved him to be made like unto *his* brethren, that he might be a merciful and faithful high priest in things *pertaining* to God, to make reconciliation for the sins of the people. 18 For in that he himself hath suffered being tempted, he is able to succour them that are tempted.

III. Wherefore, holy brethren, partakers of the heavenly calling, consider the Apostle and High Priest of our profession, Christ Jesus; 2 who was faithful to him that appointed him, as also Moses *was faithful* in all his house. 3 For

9 τὸν.δὲ βραχύ τι παρ' ἀγγέλους ἠλαττωμένον βλέπομεν
but ^{4}who ^{8}little ^{7}some ^{10}than [^{11}the] ^{12}angels [^{5}was] ^{6}made ^{9}lower ^{1}we ^{2}see
(*or* for a little)
Ἰησοῦν διὰ τὸ πάθημα τοῦ θανάτου δόξῃ καὶ τιμῇ
^{3}Jesus on account of the suffering of death with glory and with honour
ἐστεφανωμένον, ὅπως χάριτι θεοῦ ὑπὲρ παντὸς γεύσηται
crowned; so that by [the] grace of God for every one he might taste
(*or* every thing)
θανάτου. 10 Ἔπρεπεν.γὰρ αὐτῷ, δι' ὃν τὰ.πάντα καὶ δι'
death. For it was becoming to him, for whom [are] all things and by
οὗ τὰ.πάντα, πολλοὺς υἱοὺς εἰς δόξαν ἀγαγόντα, τὸν
whom [are] all things, many sons to glory bringing, the
ἀρχηγὸν τῆς.σωτηρίας.αὐτῶν διὰ παθημάτων τελειῶσαι.
leader of their salvation through sufferings to make perfect.
11 ὅ.τε.γὰρ ἁγιάζων καὶ οἱ ἁγιαζόμενοι, ἐξ ἑνὸς πάντες·
For both he who sanctifies and those sanctified of one [are] all;
δι' ἣν αἰτίαν οὐκ.ἐπαισχύνεται ἀδελφοὺς αὐτοὺς καλεῖν, 12 λέ-
for which cause he is not ashamed ^{4}brethren ^{3}them ^{1}to ^{2}call, say-
γων, Ἀπαγγελῶ τὸ.ὄνομά.σου τοῖς.ἀδελφοῖς.μου, ἐν μέσῳ
ing, I will declare thy name to my brethren; in [the] midst
ἐκκλησίας ὑμνήσω.σε. 13 Καὶ πάλιν, Ἐγὼ ἔσομαι
of [the] assembly I will sing praise to thee. And again, I will be
πεποιθὼς ἐπ' αὐτῷ. Καὶ πάλιν, Ἰδοὺ ἐγὼ καὶ τὰ παιδία ἅ
trusting in him. And again, Behold I and the children which
μοι ἔδωκεν ὁ θεός. 14 Ἐπεὶ οὖν τὰ παιδία κεκοινώνηκεν
^{3}me ^{2}gave ^{1}God. Since therefore the children have partaken
[v]σαρκὸς καὶ αἵματος,‖ καὶ αὐτὸς παραπλησίως μετέσχεν
of flesh and blood, also he in like manner took part in
τῶν.αὐτῶν, ἵνα διὰ τοῦ θανάτου καταργήσῃ τὸν τὸ κράτος
the same, that through death he might annul him who ^{2}the ^{3}might
ἔχοντα τοῦ θανάτου, [w]τουτέστιν‖ τὸν διάβολον, 15 καὶ ἀπαλ-
^{1}has of death, that is, the devil; and might set
λάξῃ τούτους ὅσοι φόβῳ θανάτου διὰ παντὸς τοῦ.ζῆν
free those whosoever by fear of death through all their lifetime
ἔνοχοι ἦσαν [x]δουλείας.‖ 16 οὐ.γὰρ δήπου ἀγγέλων ἐπιλαμ-
^{2}subject ^{1}were to bondage. For not indeed of angels takes he
βάνεται, ἀλλὰ σπέρματος Ἀβραὰμ ἐπιλαμβάνεται. 17 ὅθεν
hold, but of [the] seed of Abraham he takes hold. Wherefore
ὤφειλεν κατὰ πάντα τοῖς.ἀδελφοῖς ὁμοιωθῆναι, ἵνα ἐλεή-
it behoved [him] in all things to [his] brethren to be made like, that a merci-
μων γένηται καὶ πιστὸς ἀρχιερεὺς τὰ πρὸς τὸν θεόν,
ful ^{5}he ^{6}might ^{7}be ^{1}and ^{2}faithful ^{3}high ^{4}priest [in] things relating to God,
εἰς τὸ ἱλάσκεσθαι τὰς ἁμαρτίας τοῦ λαοῦ. 18 ἐν.ᾧ.γὰρ
for to make propitiation for the sins of the people; for in that
πέπονθεν αὐτὸς πειρασθείς, δύναται τοῖς πειραζομένοις
he ^{2}has ^{3}suffered ^{1}himself having been tempted, he is able those being tempted
βοηθῆσαι.
to help.

3 Ὅθεν, ἀδελφοὶ ἅγιοι, κλήσεως ἐπουρανίου μέτοχοι,
Wherefore, ^{2}brethren ^{1}holy, of [the] ^{2}calling ^{1}heavenly partakers,
κατανοήσατε τὸν ἀπόστολον καὶ ἀρχιερέα τῆς.ὁμολογίας.ἡμῶν
consider the apostle and high priest of our confession,
[y]χριστὸν‖ Ἰησοῦν· 2 πιστὸν ὄντα τῷ ποιήσαντι αὐτόν, ὡς
Christ Jesus, ^{2}faithful ^{1}being to him who appointed him, as
καὶ [z]Μωσῆς‖ ἐν ὅλῳ τῷ.οἴκῳ.αὐτοῦ. 3 πλείονος.γὰρ [a]δόξης
also Moses in all his house. For ^{2}of ^{3}more ^{4}glory

[v] αἵματος καὶ σαρκός LTTrAW. [w] τοῦτ' ἔστιν GT. [x] δουλίας T. [y] — χριστὸν GLTTrAW.
[z] Μωϋσῆς GLTTrAW. [a] οὗτος δόξης GLTTrAW.

οὗτος‖ παρὰ [b]Μωσῆν‖ ἠξίωται, καθ'.ὅσον πλείονα τιμὴν
[1]he than Moses has been counted worthy, by how much more honour
ἔχει τοῦ οἴκου ὁ κατασκευάσας αὐτόν· 4 πᾶς.γὰρ οἶκος
has [5]than [6]the [7]house [1]he [2]who [3]built [4]it. For every house
κατασκευάζεται ὑπό τινος· ὁ.δὲ [c]τὰ‖.πάντα κατασκευάσας
is built by some one; but he who all things built [is]
θεός. 5 καὶ [d]Μωσῆς‖ μὲν πιστὸς ἐν ὅλῳ τῷ.οἴκῳ.αὐτοῦ ὡς
God. And Moses indeed [was] faithful in all his house as
θεράπων, εἰς μαρτύριον τῶν λαληθησομένων·
a ministering servant, for a testimony of the things going to be spoken;
6 χριστὸς.δὲ ὡς υἱὸς ἐπὶ τὸν.οἶκον.αὐτοῦ, οὗ οἶκός ἐσμεν
But Christ as Son over his house, whose house are
ἡμεῖς, [e]ἐάνπερ‖ τὴν παῤῥησίαν καὶ τὸ καύχημα τῆς ἐλπίδος
we, if indeed the boldness and the boasting of the hope
[f]μέχρι τέλους βεβαίαν‖ κατάσχωμεν.
unto [the] end firm we should hold.

7 Διό, καθὼς λέγει τὸ πνεῦμα τὸ ἅγιον, Σήμερον ἐὰν τῆς
Wherefore, even as says the Spirit the Holy, To-day if
φωνῆς.αὐτοῦ ἀκούσητε, 8 μὴ.σκληρύνητε τὰς.καρδίας.ὑμῶν,
his voice ye will hear, harden not your hearts,
ὡς ἐν τῷ παραπικρασμῷ, κατὰ τὴν ἡμέραν τοῦ πειρασμοῦ ἐν
as in the provocation, in the day of temptation, in
τῇ ἐρήμῳ, 9 οὗ ἐπείρασάν [g]με‖ οἱ.πατέρες.ὑμῶν, [h]ἐδοκίμασάν
the wilderness, where [3]tempted [4]me [1]your [2]fathers, proved
με,‖ καὶ εἶδον τὰ.ἔργα.μου [i]τεσσαράκοντα‖ ἔτη· 10 διὸ προσ-
me, and saw my works forty years. Wherefore I was
ώχθισα τῇ γενεᾷ [j]ἐκείνῃ,‖ καὶ [k]εἶπον,‖ Ἀεὶ πλανῶνται τῇ
indignant with [2]generation [1]that, and said, Always they err
καρδίᾳ· αὐτοὶ.δὲ οὐκ.ἔγνωσαν τὰς.ὁδούς.μου· 11 ὡς ὤμοσα ἐν
in heart; and they did not know my ways; so I swore in
τῇ.ὀργῇ.μου, Εἰ εἰσελεύσονται εἰς τὴν.κατάπαυσίν.μου. 12 Βλέ-
my wrath, If they shall enter into my rest. Take
πετε, ἀδελφοί, μήποτε ἔσται ἔν τινι ὑμῶν καρδία πονηρὰ
heed, brethren, lest perhaps shall be in anyone of you a [2]heart [1]wicked
ἀπιστίας ἐν τῷ ἀποστῆναι ἀπὸ θεοῦ ζῶντος· 13 ἀλλὰ
of unbelief in departing from [3]God [[1]the] [2]living. But
παρακαλεῖτε ἑαυτοὺς καθ'.ἑκάστην.ἡμέραν, ἄχρις.οὗ τὸ σήμερον
encourage yourselves every day as long as [4]to-day
καλεῖται, ἵνα μὴ σκληρυνθῇ [l]τις ἐξ ὑμῶν‖ ἀπάτῃ τῆς
it is [5]called, that not may be hardened any of you by [the] deceitfulness
ἁμαρτίας· 14 μέτοχοι.γὰρ [m]γεγόναμεν τοῦ χριστοῦ,‖ [n]ἐάνπερ‖
of sin. For companions we have become of the Christ, if indeed
τὴν ἀρχὴν τῆς ὑποστάσεως μέχρι τέλους βεβαίαν κατά-
the beginning of the assurance unto [the] end firm we
σχωμεν· 15 ἐν τῷ.λέγεσθαι, Σήμερον ἐὰν τῆς.φωνῆς.αὐτοῦ
should hold; in its being said, To-day if his voice
ἀκούσητε, μὴ.σκληρύνητε τὰς.καρδίας.ὑμῶν, ὡς ἐν τῷ παραπι-
ye will hear, harden not your hearts, as in the provoca-
κρασμῷ. 16 [o]τινὲς.γὰρ ἀκούσαντες παρεπίκραναν,‖ ἀλλ' οὐ
tion. For some having heard provoked, but not
πάντες οἱ ἐξελθόντες ἐξ Αἰγύπτου διὰ [p]Μωσέως.‖[q] 17 τίσιν.δὲ[r]
all who came out from Egypt by Moses. And with whom

this *man* was counted
worthy of more glory
than Moses, inasmuch
as he who hath build-
ed the house hath more
honour than the house.
4 For every house is
builded by some *man*;
but he that built all
things *is* God. 5 And
Moses verily *was* faith-
ful in all his house, as
a servant, for a testi-
mony of those things
which were to be
spoken after; 6 but
Christ as a son over
his own house; whose
house are we, if we
hold fast the confi-
dence and the rejoic-
ing of the hope firm
unto the end.

7 Wherefore (as the
Holy Ghost saith, To
day if ye will hear his
voice, 8 harden not
your hearts, as in the
provocation, in the
day of temptation in
the wilderness: 9 when
your fathers tempted
me, proved me, and
saw my works forty
years. 10 Wherefore I
was grieved with that
generation, and said,
They do alway err in
their heart; and they
have not known my
ways. 11 So I sware in
my wrath, They shall
not enter into my rest.)
12 Take heed, brethren,
lest there be in any of
you an evil heart of
unbelief, in departing
from the living God.
13 But exhort one an-
other daily, while it is
called To day; lest any
of you be hardened
through the deceitful-
ness of sin. 14 For we
are made partakers of
Christ, if we hold the
beginning of our con-
fidence stedfast unto
the end; 15 while it is
said, To day if ye will
hear his voice, harden
not your hearts, as in
the provocation. 16 For
some, when they had
heard, did provoke:
howbeit not all that
came out of Egypt by
Moses. 17 But with

[b] Μωϋσῆν GLTTrAW. [c] — τὰ LTTrAW. [d] Μωϋσῆς GLTTrAW. [e] ἐάν[περ] L; ἐὰν if TTrA. [f] — μέχρι τέλους βεβαίαν A. [g] — με LTTrAW. [h] ἐν δοκιμασίᾳ by proving [me] LTTrAW. [i] τεσσεράκοντα TTrA. [j] ταύτῃ this LTTrAW. [k] εἶπα L. [l] ἐξ ὑμῶν τις GLAW. [m] τοῦ χριστοῦ γεγόναμεν GLTTrAW. [n] ἐάν περ LTr. [o] τίνες γὰρ ἀκού. παρεπίκραναν; For who, having heard, provoked? GLTTrAW. [p] Μωϋσέως GLTTrAW. [q] ; (*read as a question* but [was it] not all, &c.?) GLTTrAW. [r] + [καὶ] also L.

whom was he grieved
forty years? *was it* not
with them that had
sinned, whose carcases
fell in the wilderness?
18 And to whom sware
he that they should
not enter into his rest,
but to them that be-
lieved not? 19 So we
see that they could not
enter in because of
unbelief. IV. Let us
therefore fear, lest, a
promise being left *us*
of entering into his
rest, any of you should
seem to come short of
it. 2 For unto us was
the gospel preached, as
well as unto them: but
the word preached did
not profit them, not
being mixed with faith
in them that heard *it*.
3 For we which have
believed do enter into
rest, as he said, As I
have sworn in my
wrath, if they shall
enter into my rest:
although the works
were finished from
the foundation of the
world. 4 For he spake
in a certain place of
the seventh *day* on this
wise, And God did rest
the seventh day from
all his works. 5 And
in this *place* again, If
they shall enter into
my rest. 6 Seeing
therefore it remaineth
that some must enter
therein, and they to
whom it was first
preached entered not
in because of unbe-
lief: 7 again, he li-
miteth a certain day,
saying in David, To
day, after so long a
time; as it is said, To
day if ye will hear his
voice, harden not your
hearts. 8 For if Jesus
had given them rest,
then would he not
afterward have spok-
en of another day.
9 There remaineth
therefore a rest to the
people of God. 10 For
he that is entered into
his rest, he also hath
ceased from his own
works, as God *did*
from his. 11 Let us
labour therefore to en-
ter into that rest, lest
any man fall after the
same example of un-

προσώχθισεν [s]τεσσαράκοντα‖ ἔτη; οὐχὶ τοῖς ἁμαρ-
was he indignant forty years? [Was it] not with those who
τήσασιν, ὧν τὰ κῶλα ἔπεσεν ἐν τῇ ἐρήμῳ; 18 τίσιν.δὲ
sinned, of whom the carcases fell in the wilderness? And to whom
ὤμοσεν μὴ.εἰσελεύσεσθαι εἰς τὴν.κατάπαυσιν.αὐτοῦ, εἰ.μὴ
swore he [that they] shall not enter into his rest, except
τοῖς ἀπειθήσασιν; 19 καὶ βλέπομεν ὅτι οὐκ.ἠδυνήθησαν
to those who disobeyed? And we see that they were not able
εἰσελθεῖν δι' ἀπιστίαν. 4 Φοβηθῶμεν οὖν μήποτε
to enter in on account of unbelief. We should fear therefore lest perhaps
καταλειπομένης ἐπαγγελίας εἰσελθεῖν εἰς τὴν.κατάπαυσιν.αὐ-
[3]being [4]left [1]a [2]promise to enter into his rest,
τοῦ, δοκῇ τις ἐξ ὑμῶν ὑστερηκέναι. 2 καὶ.γάρ ἐσμεν.εὐηγ-
[4]might [5]seem [1]any [2]of [3]you to come short. For indeed we have had
γελισμένοι, καθάπερ κἀκεῖνοι· ἀλλ' οὐκ ὠφέλησεν ὁ
glad tidings announced [to us] even as also they; but not did profit [2]the
λόγος τῆς ἀκοῆς ἐκείνους, μὴ [t]συγκεκραμένος‖ τῇ πίστει
[3]word [4]of [5]the [6]report [1]them, not having been mixed with faith
τοῖς ἀκούσασιν. 3 εἰσερχόμεθα.γὰρ εἰς [v]τὴν‖ κατάπαυσιν
in those who heard. For we enter into the rest,
οἱ πιστεύσαντες, καθὼς εἴρηκεν, Ὡς ὤμοσα ἐν τῇ.ὀργῇ.μου,
who believed; as he has said, So I swore in my wrath,
Εἰ εἰσελεύσονται εἰς τὴν.κατάπαυσίν.μου· καίτοι τῶν ἔργων
If they shall enter into my rest; though verily the works
ἀπὸ καταβολῆς κόσμου γενηθέντων. 4 Εἴρηκεν.γάρ που
from [the] foundation of [the] world were done. For he has said somewhere
περὶ τῆς ἑβδόμης οὕτως, Καὶ κατέπαυσεν ὁ θεὸς ἐν τῇ
concerning the seventh [day] thus, And [2]rested [1]God on the
ἡμέρᾳ τῇ ἑβδόμῃ ἀπὸ πάντων τῶν.ἔργων.αὐτοῦ· 5 καὶ ἐν τού-
[2]day [1]seventh from all his works: and in this
τῳ πάλιν, Εἰ εἰσελεύσονται εἰς τὴν.κατάπαυσίν.μου. 6 Ἐπεὶ
[place] again, If they shall enter into my rest. Since
οὖν ἀπολείπεταί τινας εἰσελθεῖν εἰς αὐτήν, καὶ οἱ πρό-
therefore it remains [for] some to enter into it, and those who
τερον εὐαγγελισθέντες οὐκ.εἰσῆλθον [w]δι'‖ ἀπείθειαν, 7 πά-
formerly heard glad tidings did not enter in on account of disobedience, again
λιν τινὰ ὁρίζει ἡμέραν, Σήμερον, ἐν [x]Δαβὶδ‖ λέγων, μετὰ
a certain [2]he [3]determines [1]day, To-day, in David saying, after
τοσοῦτον χρόνον, καθὼς [y]εἴρηται,‖ Σήμερον ἐὰν τῆς φωνῆς
so long a time, (according as it has been said,) To-day, if [2]voice
αὐτοῦ ἀκούσητε, μὴ.σκληρύνητε τὰς.καρδίας.ὑμῶν. 8 Εἰ.γὰρ
[1]his ye will hear, harden not your hearts. For if
αὐτοὺς Ἰησοῦς κατέπαυσεν, οὐκ ἂν περὶ ἄλλης ἐλά-
[3]them [1]Jesus [2]gave [4]rest, not concerning another [2]would [3]he [4]have
(*i.e.* Joshua)
λει μετὰ.ταῦτα ἡμέρας· 9 ἄρα ἀπολείπεται σαββατισμὸς τῷ
[5]spoken [6]afterwards [1]day. Then remains a sabbatism to the
λαῷ τοῦ.θεοῦ. 10 ὁ.γὰρ εἰσελθὼν εἰς τὴν.κατάπαυσιν.αὐτοῦ,
people of God. For he that entered into his rest,
καὶ αὐτὸς κατέπαυσεν ἀπὸ τῶν.ἔργων.αὐτοῦ, ὥσπερ ἀπὸ
also he rested from his works, as [3]from
τῶν.ἰδίων ὁ θεός. 11 Σπουδάσωμεν οὖν εἰσελθεῖν εἰς
[4]his [5]own [1]God [[2]did]. We should be diligent therefore to enter into
ἐκείνην τὴν κατάπαυσιν, ἵνα.μὴ ἐν τῷ αὐτῷ τις ὑποδείγ-
that rest, lest [4]after [5]the [6]same [1]anyone [7]example

[s] τεσσεράκοντα TTrA. [t] συγκεκερασμένους LTTrA, συγκεκραμένους W, (*read* them not united in faith with those, &c.); συνκεκερασμένος T. [v] [τὴν] Tr. [w] διὰ A. [x] Δαυεὶδ LTTrA; Δαυὶδ GW. [y] προείρηται it has been said before LTTrAW.

ματι πέσῃ τῆς ἀπειθείας. 12 Ζῶν-γὰρ ὁ λόγος τοῦ θεοῦ καὶ
[2]may [3]fall of disobedience. For living [is] the word of God and
ἐνεργής, καὶ τομώτερος ὑπὲρ πᾶσαν μάχαιραν δίστομον, καὶ
efficient, and sharper than every [2]sword [1]two-edged, even
διϊκνούμενος ἄχρι μερισμοῦ ψυχῆς [z]τε‖ καὶ πνεύματος, ἁρ-
penetrating to [the] division both of soul and spirit, [2]of
μῶν τε καὶ μυελῶν, καὶ κριτικὸς ἐνθυμήσεων καὶ ἐννοιῶν
[3]joints [1]both and marrows, and [is] a discerner of [the] thoughts and intents
καρδίας· 13 καὶ οὐκ-ἔστιν κτίσις ἀφανὴς ἐνώπιον αὐτοῦ·
of [the] heart. And there is not a created thing unapparent before him;
πάντα-δὲ γυμνὰ καὶ τετραχηλισμένα τοῖς ὀφθαλμοῖς αὐτοῦ,
but all things [are] naked and laid bare to the eyes of him,
πρὸς ὃν ἡμῖν ὁ λόγος.
with whom [is] our account.

14 Ἔχοντες-οὖν ἀρχιερέα μέγαν διεληλυθότα τοὺς
Having therefore a [2]high [3]priest [1]great [who] has passed through the
οὐρανούς, Ἰησοῦν τὸν υἱὸν τοῦ θεοῦ, κρατῶμεν τῆς ὁμο-
heavens, Jesus the Son of God, we should hold fast the con-
λογίας. 15 οὐ-γὰρ ἔχομεν ἀρχιερέα μὴ δυνάμενον [a]συμπα-
fession. For not have we a high priest not able to sym-
θῆσαι‖ ταῖς-ἀσθενείαις-ἡμῶν, [b]πεπειραμένον‖-δὲ κατὰ πάντα
pathise with our infirmities, but [who] has been tempted in all things
καθ'-ὁμοιότητα χωρὶς ἁμαρτίας. 16 προσερχώμεθα οὖν
according to [our] likeness, apart from sin. We should come therefore
μετὰ παῤῥησίας τῷ θρόνῳ τῆς χάριτος, ἵνα λάβωμεν [c]ἔλεον,‖
with boldness to the throne of grace, that we may receive mercy,
καὶ χάριν εὕρωμεν εἰς εὔκαιρον βοήθειαν.
and [3]grace [1]may [2]find for opportune help.

5 Πᾶς-γὰρ ἀρχιερεὺς ἐξ ἀνθρώπων λαμβανόμενος, ὑπὲρ
For every high priest from among men being taken for
ἀνθρώπων καθίσταται τὰ πρὸς τὸν θεόν, ἵνα προσφέρῃ
men is constituted in things relating to God, that he may offer
δῶρά-[d]τε‖ καὶ θυσίας ὑπὲρ ἁμαρτιῶν, 2 μετριοπαθεῖν δυνά-
both gifts, and sacrifices for sins; [3]to [4]exercise [5]forbearance [1]being
μενος τοῖς ἀγνοοῦσιν καὶ πλανωμένοις, ἐπεὶ καὶ αὐτὸς
[2]able with those being ignorant and erring, since also himself
περίκειται ἀσθένειαν· 3 καὶ [e]διὰ ταύτην‖ ὀφείλει,
is encompassed with infirmity; and on account of this [infirmity] he ought,
καθὼς περὶ τοῦ λαοῦ, οὕτως καὶ περὶ [f]ἑαυτοῦ‖ προσφέρειν
even as for the people, so also for himself to offer
[g]ὑπὲρ‖ ἁμαρτιῶν. 4 Καὶ οὐχ ἑαυτῷ τις λαμβάνει τὴν τιμήν,
for sins. And not to himself anyone takes the honour,
ἀλλὰ [h]ὁ‖ καλούμενος ὑπὸ τοῦ θεοῦ, [i]καθάπερ‖ καὶ [h]ὁ‖ Ἀαρών.
but he being called by God, even as also Aaron.
5 οὕτως καὶ ὁ χριστὸς οὐχ ἑαυτὸν ἐδόξασεν γενηθῆναι ἀρχ-
Thus also the Christ not himself did glorify to become a high
ιερέα, ἀλλ' ὁ λαλήσας πρὸς αὐτόν, Υἱός μου εἶ σύ, ἐγὼ σή-
priest; but he who said to him, [2]Son [1]my art thou, I to-
μερον γεγέννηκά σε. 6 καθὼς καὶ ἐν ἑτέρῳ λέγει, Σὺ
day have begotten thee. Even as also in another [place] he says, Thou [art]
ἱερεὺς εἰς-τὸν-αἰῶνα κατὰ τὴν τάξιν Μελχισεδέκ. 7 Ὃς ἐν
a priest for ever according to the order of Melchisedec. Who in

belief. 12 For the word
of God *is* quick, and
powerful, and sharper
than any twoedged
sword, piercing even to
the dividing asunder
of soul and spirit, and
of the joints and mar-
row, and *is* a discerner
of the thoughts and
intents of the heart.
13 Neither is there any
creature that is not
manifest in his sight:
but all things *are* na-
ked and opened unto
the eyes of him with
whom we have to do.

14 Seeing then that
we have a great high
priest, that is passed
into the heavens, Je-
sus the Son of God, let
us hold fast *our* pro-
fession. 15 For we
have not an high
priest which cannot
be touched with the
feeling of our infirm-
ities; but was in all
points tempted like
as *we are*, *yet* without
sin. 16 Let us there-
fore come boldly unto
the throne of grace,
that we may obtain
mercy, and find grace
to help in time of need.

V. For every high
priest taken from a-
mong men is ordained
for men in things *per-
taining* to God, that
he may offer both gifts
and sacrifices for sins:
2 who can have com-
passion on the igno-
rant, and on them that
are out of the way;
for that he himself al-
so is compassed with
infirmity. 3 And by
reason hereof he ought,
as for the people, so
also for himself, to of-
fer for sins. 4 And no
man taketh this ho-
nour unto himself, but
he that is called of
God, as *was* Aaron.
5 So also Christ glori-
fied not himself to be
made an high priest;
but he that said unto
him, Thou art my Son,
to day have I begotten
thee. 6 As he saith al-
so in another *place*,
Thou *art* a priest for
ever after the order of
Melchisedec. 7 Who in

---

z — τε both LTTrAW. a συν- TA. b πεπειρασμένον EGLTTrAW. c ἔλεος LTTrAW.
d — τε both L[Tr]. e δι' αὐτὴν on account of it LTTrAW. f αὐτοῦ L. g περὶ LTTrAW.
h — ὁ GLTTrAW. i καθὼς L; καθώσπερ TA; καθώς περ Tr.

the days of his flesh, when he had offered up prayers and supplications with strong crying and tears unto him that was able to save him from death, and was heard in that he feared; 8 though he were a Son, yet learned he obedience by the things which he suffered; 9 and being made perfect, he became the author of eternal salvation unto all them that obey him; 10 called of God an high priest after the order of Melchisedec. 11 Of whom we have many things to say, and hard to be uttered, seeing ye are dull of hearing. 12 For when for the time ye ought to be teachers, ye have need that one teach you again which *be* the first principles of the oracles of God; and are become such as have need of milk, and not of strong meat. 13 For every one that useth milk *is* unskilful in the word of righteousness: for he is a babe. 14 But strong meat belongeth to them that are of full age, *even* those who by reason of use have their senses exercised to discern both good and evil.

ταῖς ἡμέραις τῆς.σαρκὸς.αὐτοῦ δεήσεις.τε καὶ ἱκετηρίας πρὸς
the days of his flesh both supplications and entreaties [3]to
τὸν δυνάμενον σώζειν αὐτὸν ἐκ θανάτου, μετὰ κραυ-
[4]him [5]who [[6]was] [7]able [8]to [9]save [10]him [11]from [12]death, [13]with [15]cry-
γῆς ἰσχυρᾶς καὶ δακρύων προσενέγκας, καὶ εἰσακουσθεὶς ἀπὸ
ing [14]strong [16]and [17]tears [1]having [2]offered, and having been heard in
τῆς.εὐλαβείας, 8 καίπερ ὢν υἱός, ἔμαθεν ἀφ' ὧν
that [he] feared; though being a son, he learned, from the things which
ἔπαθεν τὴν ὑπακοήν, 9 καὶ τελειωθεὶς ἐγένετο [k]τοῖς
he suffered, obedience; and having been perfected became to [2]those [3]that
ὑπακούουσιν αὐτῷ πᾶσιν‖ αἴτιος σωτηρίας αἰωνίου· 10 προσ-
[4]obey [5]him [1]all, author of [2]salvation [1]eternal; having
αγορευθεὶς ὑπὸ τοῦ θεοῦ ἀρχιερεὺς κατὰ τὴν τάξιν Μελ-
been saluted by God [as] high priest according to the order of Mel-
χισεδέκ. 11 Περὶ οὗ πολὺς ἡμῖν.ὁ.λόγος καὶ δυσερμή-
chisedec. Concerning whom [[3]is] [4]much [1]our [2]discourse and difficult in inter-
νευτος λέγειν, ἐπεὶ νωθροὶ γεγόνατε ταῖς.ἀκοαῖς. 12 καὶ.γὰρ
pretation to speak, since sluggish ye have become in hearing. For truly
ὀφείλοντες εἶναι διδάσκαλοι διὰ τὸν χρόνον, πάλιν
[when ye] ought to be teachers because of the time, again
χρείαν ἔχετε τοῦ.διδάσκειν ὑμᾶς τίνα τὰ στοιχεῖα τῆς
need ye have of [one] to teach you what [are] the elements of the
ἀρχῆς τῶν λογίων τοῦ θεοῦ· καὶ γεγόνατε χρείαν ἔχοντες
beginning of the oracles of God, and have become [2]need [1]having
γάλακτος, [l]καὶ‖ οὐ στερεᾶς τροφῆς. 13 πᾶς.γὰρ ὁ μετέχων
of milk, and not of solid food; for everyone that partakes
γάλακτος ἄπειρος λόγου δικαιοσύνης· νήπιος.γάρ ἐστιν·
of milk [is] unskilled in [the] word of righteousness, for an infant he is;
14 τελείων.δέ ἐστιν ἡ στερεὰ τροφή, τῶν διὰ τὴν
but [4]for [[5]the] [6]fully [7]grown [3]is [1]solid [2]food, who on account of
ἕξιν τὰ αἰσθητήρια γεγυμνασμένα ἐχόντων πρὸς διάκρισιν
habit [2]the [3]senses [4]exercised [1]have for distinguishing
καλοῦ τε καὶ κακοῦ.
[2]good [1]both and evil.

VI. Therefore leaving the principles of the doctrine of Christ, let us go on unto perfection; not laying again the foundation of repentance from dead works, and of faith toward God, 2 of the doctrine of baptisms, and of laying on of hands, and of resurrection of the dead, and of eternal judgment. 3 And this will we do, if God permit. 4 For *it is* impossible for those who were once enlightened, and have tasted of the heavenly gift, and were made partakers of the Holy Ghost, 5 and have tasted the good word of God, and the powers of the world to come, 6 if they shall fall away, to renew them again unto repentance;

6 Διὸ ἀφέντες τὸν τῆς ἀρχῆς τοῦ χριστοῦ λόγον, ἐπὶ
Wherefore, having left the [2]of [3]the [4]beginning [5]of [6]the [7]Christ [1]discourse, to
τὴν τελειότητα φερώμεθα· μὴ πάλιν θεμέλιον καταβαλλόμενοι
the full growth we should go on; not again a foundation laying
μετανοίας ἀπὸ νεκρῶν ἔργων, καὶ πίστεως ἐπὶ θεόν, 2 βαπ-
of repentance from dead works, and faith in God, [4]of [5]wash-
τισμῶν [m]διδαχῆς,‖ ἐπιθέσεώς.τε χειρῶν, ἀναστάσεώς.[n]τε‖ νε-
ings [1]of [[2]the] [3]doctrine, and of laying on of hands, and of resurrection of [the]
κρῶν, καὶ κρίματος αἰωνίου. 3 καὶ τοῦτο ποιήσομεν, [o]ἐάνπερ‖
dead, and of [2]judgment [1]eternal; and this will we do, if indeed
ἐπιτρέπῃ ὁ θεός. 4 ἀδύνατον.γὰρ τοὺς ἅπαξ φωτισθέντας,
[2]permit [1]God. For [it is] impossible, those once enlightened,
γευσαμένους.τε τῆς δωρεᾶς τῆς ἐπουρανίου, καὶ μετόχους
and [who] tasted of the [2]gift [1]heavenly, and partakers
γενηθέντας πνεύματος ἁγίου, 5 καὶ καλὸν γευσαμένους
became of [the] [2]Spirit [1]Holy, and [[2]the] [3]good [1]tasted
θεοῦ ῥῆμα δυνάμεις.τε μέλλοντος αἰῶνος, 6 καὶ
[5]of [6]God [4]word and [the] works of power of [the] [2]to [3]come [1]age, and
παραπεσόντας, πάλιν ἀνακαινίζειν εἰς μετάνοιαν, ἀνασταυ-
[who] fell away, again to renew to repentance, crucify-

---

[k] πᾶσιν τοῖς ὑπακούουσιν αὐτῷ LTTrA   [l] — καὶ T[Tr].   [m] διδαχήν [the] doctrine L.
[n] [τε] Tr.   [o] ἐάν περ LTrW.

ῥοῦντας ἑαυτοῖς τὸν υἱὸν τοῦ θεοῦ καὶ παραδειγ-
ing for themselves [as they do] the Son of God, and exposing
ματίζοντας. 7 γῆ-γὰρ ἡ πιοῦσα τὸν ἐπ' αὐτῆς ᵖπολλάκις
[him] publicly. For ground which drank the ⁴upon ⁵it ³often
ἐρχόμενον‖ ὑετόν, καὶ τίκτουσα βοτάνην εὔθετον ἐκείνοις
²coming ¹rain, and produces ²herbage ¹fit for those
δι' οὓς καὶ γεωργεῖται, μεταλαμβάνει εὐλογίας ἀπὸ τοῦ
for sake of whom also it is tilled, partakes of blessing from
θεοῦ· 8 ἐκφέρουσα.δὲ ἀκάνθας καὶ τριβόλους, ἀδόκιμος καὶ
God; but [that] bringing forth thorns and thistles [is] rejected and
κατάρας ἐγγύς, ἧς τὸ τέλος εἰς καῦσιν. 9 Πεπείσμεθα.δὲ
³a ⁴curse ¹near ²to, of which the end [is] for burning. But we are persuaded
περὶ ὑμῶν, ἀγαπητοί, τὰ.ᑫκρείττονα‖ καὶ ἐχόμενα
concerning you, beloved, better things, and [things] connected with
σωτηρίας, εἰ καὶ οὕτως λαλοῦμεν. 10 οὐ.γὰρ ἄδικος ὁ θεὸς
salvation, ²if ¹even thus we speak. For not unrighteous [is] God
ἐπιλαθέσθαι τοῦ.ἔργου.ὑμῶν καὶ ʳτοῦ κόπου‖ τῆς ἀγάπης ἧς
to forget your work and the labour of love which
ἐνεδείξασθε εἰς τὸ.ὄνομα.αὐτοῦ, διακονήσαντες τοῖς ἁγίοις καὶ
ye did shew to his name, having served to the saints and
διακονοῦντες. 11 ἐπιθυμοῦμεν.δὲ ἕκαστον ὑμῶν τὴν αὐτὴν
[still] serving. But we desire each of you the same
ἐνδείκνυσθαι σπουδὴν πρὸς τὴν πληροφορίαν τῆς ἐλπίδος ἄχρι
²to ³shew ¹diligence to the full assurance of the hope unto
τέλους· 12 ἵνα μὴ νωθροὶ γένησθε, μιμηταὶ.δὲ τῶν διὰ
[the] end; that ³not ⁴sluggish ¹ye ²be, but imitators of those who through
πίστεως καὶ μακροθυμίας κληρονομούντων τὰς ἐπαγγελίας.
faith and long patience inherit the promises.
13 Τῷ.γὰρ.Ἀβραὰμ ἐπαγγειλάμενος ὁ θεός, ἐπεὶ κατ' οὐδενὸς
For ⁴to ⁵Abraham ²having ³promised ¹God, since by no one
εἶχεν μείζονος ὀμόσαι, ὤμοσεν καθ' ἑαυτοῦ, 14 λέγων, ˢἨ‖.μὴν
he had greater to swear, swore by himself, saying, Surely
εὐλογῶν εὐλογήσω σε, καὶ πληθύνων πληθυνῶ σε· 15 καὶ
blessing I will bless thee, and multiplying I will multiply thee; and
οὕτως μακροθυμήσας ἐπέτυχεν τῆς ἐπαγγελίας. 16 ἄνθρω-
thus having had long patience he obtained the promise. ²Men
ποι ᵗμὲν‖ γὰρ κατὰ τοῦ μείζονος ὀμνύουσιν, καὶ πάσης αὐτοῖς
³indeed ¹for ⁵by ⁶the ⁷greater ⁴swear, and of all ²to ³them
ἀντιλογίας πέρας εἰς βεβαίωσιν ὁ ὅρκος· 17 ἐν.ᾧ περισσό-
¹gainsaying an end for confirmation [is] the oath. Wherein ³more ⁴a-
τερον βουλόμενος ὁ θεὸς ἐπιδεῖξαι τοῖς κληρονόμοις τῆς ἐπαγ-
bundantly ²desiring ¹God to shew to the heirs of pro-
γελίας τὸ ἀμετάθετον τῆς.βουλῆς.αὐτοῦ, ἐμεσίτευσεν ὅρκῳ,
mise the unchangeableness of his counsel, interposed by an oath,
18 ἵνα διὰ δύο πραγμάτων ἀμεταθέτων, ἐν οἷς ἀδύνατον
that by two ²things ¹unchangeable, in which [it was] impossible
ψεύσασθαι ᵛθεόν, ἰσχυρὰν παράκλησιν ἔχωμεν οἱ κατα-
³to ⁴lie [¹for] ²God, strong encouragement we might have who fled
φυγόντες κρατῆσαι τῆς προκειμένης ἐλπίδος· 19 ἣν ὡς
for refuge to lay hold on the ²set ³before [⁴us] ¹hope, which as
ἄγκυραν ἔχομεν τῆς ψυχῆς ʷἀσφαλῆ‖.τε καὶ βεβαίαν, καὶ εἰσ-
an anchor we have of the soul both certain and firm, and en-
ερχομένην εἰς τὸ ἐσώτερον τοῦ καταπετάσματος, 20 ὅπου
tering into that within the veil; where

seeing they crucify to themselves the Son of God afresh, and put *him* to an open shame. 7 For the earth which drinketh in the rain that cometh oft upon it, and bringeth forth herbs meet for them by whom it is dressed, receiveth blessing from God: 8 but that which beareth thorns and briers *is* rejected, and *is* nigh unto cursing; whose end *is* to be burned. 9 But, beloved, we are persuaded better things of you, and things that accompany salvation, though we thus speak. 10 For God *is* not unrighteous to forget your work and labour of love, which ye have shewed toward his name, in that ye have ministered to the saints, and do minister. 11 And we desire that every one of you do shew the same diligence to the full assurance of hope unto the end: 12 that ye be not slothful, but followers of them who through faith and patience inherit the promises. 13 For when God made promise to Abraham, because he could sware by no greater, he sware by himself, 14 saying, Surely blessing I will bless thee, and multiplying I will multiply thee. 15 And so, after he had patiently endured, he obtained the promise. 16 For men verily swear by the greater: and an oath for confirmation *is* to them an end of all strife. 17 Wherein God, willing more abundantly to shew unto the heirs of promise the immutability of his counsel, confirmed *it* by an oath: 18 that by two immutable things, in which *it was* impossible for God to lie, we might have a strong consolation, who have fled for refuge to lay hold upon the hope set before us: 19 which *hope* we have as an anchor of the soul, both sure and stedfast, and which entereth into that within the veil; 20 whi-

ᵖ ἐρχόμενον πολλάκις LTTrAW. ᑫ κρείσσονα LTTrAW. ʳ — τοῦ κόπου (read τῆς ἀγ. the love) GLTTrAW. ˢ Εἰ LTTrA. ᵗ — μὲν LTTr[A]. ᵛ + τὸν T. ʷ ἀσφαλὴν LTr.

ther the forerunner is for us entered, *even* Jesus, made an high priest for ever after the order of Melchisedec.

VII. For this Melchisedec, king of Salem, priest of the most high God, who met Abraham returning from the slaughter of the kings, and blessed him; 2 to whom also Abraham gave a tenth part of all; first being by interpretation King of righteousness, and after that also King of Salem, which is, King of peace; 3 without father, without mother, without descent, having neither beginning of days, nor end of life; but made like unto the Son of God; abideth a priest continually. 4 Now consider how great this man *was*, unto whom even the patriarch Abraham gave the tenth of the spoils. 5 And verily they that are of the sons of Levi, who receive the office of the priesthood, have a commandment to take tithes of the people according to the law, that is, of their brethren, though they come out of the loins of Abraham: 6 but he whose descent is not counted from them received tithes of Abraham, and blessed him that had the promises. 7 And without all contradiction the less is blessed of the better. 8 And here men that die receive tithes; but there he *receiveth them*, of whom it is witnessed that he liveth. 9 And as I may so say, Levi also, who receiveth tithes, payed tithes in Abraham. 10 For he was yet in the loins of his father, when Melchisedec met him. 11 If therefore perfection were by the Levitical priesthood, (for under it the people received the law,) what further need *was there* that another priest should rise after the order of Melchisedec, and not be called

πρόδρομος ὑπὲρ ἡμῶν εἰσῆλθεν Ἰησοῦς, κατὰ τὴν τάξιν
[as] forerunner for us [2]entered [1]Jesus, according to the order
Μελχισεδὲκ ἀρχιερεὺς γενόμενος εἰς.τὸν.αἰῶνα.
of Melchisedec a high priest having become for ever.

7 Οὗτος.γὰρ ὁ Μελχισεδέκ, βασιλεὺς Σαλήμ, ἱερεὺς τοῦ θεοῦ
For this Melchisedec, king of Salem, priest of God
[x]τοῦ‖ ὑψίστου, [y]ὁ‖ συναντήσας Ἀβραὰμ ὑποστρέφοντι ἀπὸ τῆς
the most high, who met Abraham returning from the
κοπῆς τῶν βασιλέων, καὶ εὐλογήσας αὐτόν· 2 ᾧ καὶ δεκάτην
smiting of the kings, and having blessed him; to whom also [3]a [4]tenth
ἀπὸ πάντων ἐμέρισεν Ἀβραάμ· πρῶτον μὲν ἑρμηνευόμενος
[5]of [6]all [2]divided [1]Abraham; first being interpreted
βασιλεὺς δικαιοσύνης, ἔπειτα.δὲ καὶ βασιλεὺς Σαλήμ, ὅ ἐστιν
king of righteousness, and then also king of Salem, which is
βασιλεὺς εἰρήνης· 3 ἀπάτωρ, ἀμήτωρ, ἀγενεαλόγητος·
king of peace; without father, without mother, without genealogy;
μήτε ἀρχὴν ἡμερῶν, μήτε ζωῆς τέλος ἔχων· ἀφωμοιωμένος.δὲ
neither beginning of days nor [2]of [3]life [1]end having, but assimilated
τῷ υἱῷ τοῦ θεοῦ, μένει ἱερεὺς εἰς.τὸ.διηνεκές. 4 Θεωρεῖτε.δὲ
to the Son of God, abides a priest in perpetuity. Now consider
πηλίκος οὗτος, ᾧ [z]καὶ‖ δεκάτην Ἀβραὰμ ἔδωκεν ἐκ
how great this [one was], to whom [5]even [6]a [7]tenth [1]Abraham [4]gave [8]out [9]of
τῶν ἀκροθινίων ὁ πατριάρχης. 5 καὶ οἱ μὲν ἐκ τῶν
[10]the [11]spoils [2]the [3]patriarch. And they indeed from among the
[a]υἱῶν‖ [b]Λευῒ‖ τὴν ἱερατείαν λαμβάνοντες, ἐντολὴν ἔχουσιν
sons of Levi, [3]the [4]priesthood [[1]who] [2]receive, commandment have
[c]ἀποδεκατοῦν‖ τὸν λαὸν κατὰ τὸν νόμον, [d]τουτέστιν,‖
to take tithes from the people according to the law, that is [from]
τοὺς.ἀδελφοὺς.αὐτῶν, καίπερ ἐξεληλυθότας ἐκ τῆς ὀσφύος
their brethren though having come out of the loins
Ἀβραάμ· 6 ὁ.δὲ μὴ.γενεαλογούμενος ἐξ αὐτῶν δεδεκάτω-
of Abraham; but he [who] reckons no genealogy from them has tithed
κεν [e]τὸν‖ Ἀβραάμ, καὶ τὸν ἔχοντα τὰς ἐπαγγελίας [f]εὐλό-
Abraham, and [3]him [4]who [5]had [6]the [7]promises, [1]has
γηκεν·‖ 7 χωρὶς.δὲ πάσης ἀντιλογίας τὸ ἔλαττον ὑπὸ τοῦ
[2]blessed. But apart from all gainsaying the inferior by the
κρείττονος εὐλογεῖται. 8 καὶ ὧδε μὲν δεκάτας ἀποθνήσκοντες
superior is blessed. And here [5]tithes [[2]that] [3]die
ἄνθρωποι λαμβάνουσιν· ἐκεῖ.δέ, μαρτυρούμενος ὅτι ζῇ.
[1]men [4]receive; but there [one] witnessed of that he lives;
9 καί, ὡς.ἔπος.εἰπεῖν, [g]διὰ‖ Ἀβραὰμ καὶ [h]Λευῒ‖ ὁ δεκάτας
and, so to speak, through Abraham, also Levi, who [2]tithes
λαμβάνων δεδεκάτωται· 10 ἔτι.γὰρ ἐν τῇ ὀσφύϊ τοῦ.πατρὸς
[1]receives, has been tithed. For yet in the loins of [his] father
ἦν, ὅτε συνήντησεν αὐτῷ [i]ὁ‖ Μελχισεδέκ. 11 Εἰ μὲν οὖν
he was when [2]met [3]him [1]Melchisedec. If indeed then
τελείωσις διὰ τῆς [k]Λευϊτικῆς‖ ἱερωσύνης ἦν, ὁ.λαὸς.γὰρ
perfection by the Levitical priesthood were, for the people [[5]based]
ἐπ' [l]αὐτῇ‖ [m]νενομοθέτητο,‖ τίς ἔτι χρεία κατὰ
[6]upon [7]it [1]had [2]received [[3]the] [4]law, what still need [was there] according to
τὴν τάξιν Μελχισεδὲκ ἕτερον ἀνίστασθαι ἱερέα, καὶ οὐ
the order of Melchisedec [for] another [2]to [3]arise [1]priest; and not

---

[x] — τοῦ E. [y] ὃς (*read* who, having met) LTrA. [z] — καὶ LTr. [a] — υἱῶν (*read* [sons]) L. [b] Λευεὶ TTrA. [c] ἀποδεκατοῖν TTrA. [d] τοῦτ' ἔστιν GT. [e] — τὸν LTTrA. [f] ηὐλόγηκεν L. [g] δι' LTTrA. [h] Λευῒς L; Λευεὶς TTrA. [i] — ὁ LTTrA. [k] Λευειτικῆς TA. [l] αὐτῆς (*read* on the ground of it) LTTrAW. [m] νενομοθέτηται has received [the] law LTTrAW.

κατὰ τὴν τάξιν Ἀαρὼν λέγεσθαι; 12 μετατιθεμένης.γὰρ
according to the order of Aaron to be named? For [3]being [4]changed
τῆς ἱερωσύνης, ἐξ ἀνάγκης καὶ νόμου μετάθεσις γίνεται.
[1]the [2]priesthood, from necessity also of law a change takes place.
13 ἐφ'.ὃν.γὰρ λέγεται ταῦτα, φυλῆς ἑτέρας μετέσχηκεν, ἀφ'.ἧς
For he of whom are said these things, a [2]tribe [1]different has part in, of which
οὐδεὶς προσέσχηκεν τῷ θυσιαστηρίῳ· 14 πρόδηλον.γὰρ ὅτι
no one has given attendance at the altar. For [it is] manifest that
ἐξ Ἰούδα ἀνατέταλκεν ὁ.κύριος.ἡμῶν, εἰς ἣν φυλὴν [n]οὐδὲν
out of Juda has sprung our Lord, as to which tribe [3]nothing
περὶ ἱερωσύνης" [o]Μωσῆς" ἐλάλησεν. 15 Καὶ περισσότερον
[4]concerning [5]priesthood [1]Moses [2]spoke. And more abundantly
ἔτι κατάδηλόν ἐστιν, εἰ κατὰ τὴν ὁμοιότητα Μελχισεδὲκ
yet quite manifest it is, since according to the similitude of Melchisedec
ἀνίσταται ἱερεὺς ἕτερος, 16 ὃς οὐ κατὰ νόμον ἐντο-
arises a [2]priest [1]different, who not according to law of [2]command-
λῆς [p]σαρκικῆς" γέγονεν, ἀλλὰ κατὰ δύναμιν ζωῆς
ment [1]fleshly has been constituted, but according to power of [2]life
ἀκαταλύτου· 17 [q]μαρτυρεῖ".γάρ, Ὅτι σὺ ἱερεὺς εἰς τὸν
[1]indissoluble. For he testifies, Thou [art] a priest for
αἰῶνα κατὰ τὴν τάξιν Μελχισεδέκ. 18 Ἀθέτησις μὲν γὰρ
ever after the order of Melchisedec. [2]A [3]putting [4]away [1]for
γίνεται προαγούσης ἐντολῆς, διὰ τὸ.αὐτῆς.ἀσθενὲς
there is of the [2]going [3]before [1]commandment, because of its weakness
καὶ ἀνωφελές, 19 οὐδὲν.γὰρ ἐτελείωσεν ὁ νόμος, ἐπεισ-
and unprofitableness, (for [4]nothing [3]perfected [1]the [2]law,) [[6]the] [7]intro-
αγωγὴ δὲ κρείττονος ἐλπίδος, δι' ἧς ἐγγίζομεν τῷ θεῷ. 20 Καὶ
duction [5]and of a better hope by which we draw near to God. And
καθ'.ὅσον οὐ χωρὶς ὁρκωμοσίας· οἱ μὲν γάρ,
by how much [it was] not apart from [the] swearing of an oath, ([2]they [1]for
χωρὶς ὁρκωμοσίας εἰσὶν ἱερεῖς γεγονότες, 21 ὁ.δέ,
without [the] swearing of an oath are [2]priests [1]become, but he
[r]μετὰ" ὁρκωμοσίας, διὰ τοῦ λέγοντος πρὸς αὐτόν,
with [the] swearing of an oath, by him who says, as to him,
Ὤμοσεν κύριος καὶ οὐ.μεταμεληθήσεται, Σὺ ἱερεὺς εἰς τὸν
[3]swore [[1]the] [2]Lord, and will not repent, Thou [art] a priest for
αἰῶνα [s]κατὰ τὴν τάξιν Μελχισεδέκ·" 22 κατὰ.[t]τοσοῦτον"[u]
ever according to the order of Melchisedec,) by so much
κρείττονος διαθήκης γέγονεν ἔγγυος Ἰησοῦς. 23 Καὶ οἱ
of a better covenant [2]has [3]become [4]surety [1]Jesus. And they
μὲν πλείονές εἰσιν.[v]γεγονότες ἱερεῖς" διὰ τὸ θανάτῳ κω-
[2]many [1]are priests on account of by death being
λύεσθαι παραμένειν· 24 ὁ.δέ, διὰ τὸ.μένειν.αὐτὸν εἰς
hindered from continuing; but he, because of his abiding for
τὸν αἰῶνα, ἀπαράβατον ἔχει τὴν ἱερωσύνην· 25 ὅθεν καὶ
ever, [4]intransmissible [1]has [2]the [3]priesthood. Whence also
σώζειν εἰς.τὸ.παντελὲς δύναται τοὺς προσερχομένους δι'
to save completely he is able those who approach by
αὐτοῦ τῷ θεῷ, πάντοτε ζῶν εἰς.τὸ.ἐντυγχάνειν ὑπὲρ αὐτῶν.
him to God, always living to intercede for them.
26 τοιοῦτος.γὰρ ἡμῖν [w]ἔπρεπεν ἀρχιερεύς, ὅσιος, ἄκακος,
For such [5]us [4]became [1]a [2]high [3]priest, holy, harmless,

after the order of Aar-
on? 12 For the priest-
hood being changed,
there is made of ne-
cessity a change also
of the law. 13 For
he of whom these
things are spoken per-
taineth to another
tribe, of which no man
gave attendance at the
altar. 14 For *it is* evident that our Lord
sprang out of Juda;
of which tribe Moses
spake nothing con-
cerning priesthood.
15 And it is yet far
more evident: for that
after the similitude of
Melchisedec there a-
riseth another priest,
16 who is made, not
after the law of a car-
nal commandment,
but after the power of
an endless life. 17 For
he testifieth, Thou
art a priest for ever
after the order of
Melchisedec. 18 For
there is verily a dis-
annulling of the com-
mandment going be-
fore for the weakness
and unprofitableness
thereof. 19 For the law
made nothing perfect,
but the bringing in of
a better hope *did*; by
the which we draw
nigh unto God. 20 And
inasmuch as not with-
out an oath *he was*
made priest: 21 (for
those priests were
made without an oath;
but this with an oath
by him that said unto
him, The Lord sware
and will not repent,
Thou *art* a priest for
ever after the order
of Melchisedec:) 22 by
so much was Jesus
made a surety of a bet-
ter testament. 23 And
they truly were many
priests, because they
were not suffered to
continue by reason of
death: 24 but this
man, because he con-
tinueth ever, hath an
unchangeable priest-
hood. 25 Wherefore he
is able also to save
them to the uttermost
that come unto God
by him, seeing he ever
liveth to make in-
tercession for them.
26 For such an high
priest became us, *who*

---

[n] περὶ ἱερέων (priests) οὐδὲν LTTrAW. [o] Μωϋσῆς GLTTrAW. [p] σαρκίνης fleshy LTTrAW. [q] μαρτυρεῖται (*read* for he is testified of) LTTrAW. [r] μεθ' L. [s] - κατὰ τὴν τάξιν Μελχισεδέκ TTrA. [t] τοσοῦτο LTTrAW. [u] + καὶ also TA. [v] ἱερεῖς γεγονότες LAW. [w] + καὶ also [L]TTrAW.

is holy, harmless, un-
defiled, separate from
sinners, and made
higher than the hea-
vens; 27 who needeth
not daily, as those high
priests, to offer up sa-
crifice, first for his own
sins, and then for the
people's: for this he
did once, when he
offered up himself.
28 For the law maketh
men high priests which
have infirmity; but
the word of the oath,
which was since the
law, *maketh* the Son,
who is consecrated for
evermore.

VIII. Now of the
things which we have
spoken *this is* the sum:
We have such an high
priest, who is set on
the right hand of the
throne of the Majesty
in the heavens; 2 a
minister of the sanctu-
ary, and of the true
tabernacle, which the
Lord pitched, and not
man.

3 For every high
priest is ordained to
offer gifts and sacri-
fices: wherefore *it is*
of necessity that this
man have somewhat
also to offer. 4 For if
he were on earth, he
should not be a priest,
seeing that there are
priests that offer gifts
according to the law:
5 who serve unto the
example and shadow
of heavenly things,
as Moses was admo-
nished of God when
he was about to make
the tabernacle: for,
See, saith he, *that*
thou make all things
according to the pat-
tern shewed to thee in
the mount. 6 But now
hath he obtained a
more excellent mini-
stry, by how much al-
so he is the mediator
of a better covenant,
which was established
upon better promises.
7 For if that first *co-
venant* had been fault-
less, then should no
place have been sought
for the second. 8 For
finding fault with

ἀμίαντος, κεχωρισμένος ἀπὸ τῶν.ἁμαρτωλῶν, καὶ ὑψηλότερος
undefiled, separated from sinners, and [2]higher
τῶν οὐρανῶν γενόμενος· 27 ὃς οὐκ.ἔχει καθ'.ἡμέραν ἀνάγ-
[3]than [4]the [5]heavens [1]become: who has not day by day neces-
κην, ὥσπερ οἱ ἀρχιερεῖς, πρότερον ὑπὲρ τῶν.ἰδίων ἁμαρτιῶν
sity, as the high priests, first for his own sins
θυσίας ἀναφέρειν, ἔπειτα τῶν τοῦ λαοῦ· τοῦτο.γὰρ
[4]sacrifices [1]to [2]offer [3]up, then for those of the people; for this
ἐποίησεν [x]ἐφάπαξ, ἑαυτὸν [y]ἀνενέγκας. 28 ὁ.νόμος.γὰρ ἀν-
he did once for all, [4]himself [1]having [2]offered [3]up. For the law
θρώπους καθίστησιν ἀρχιερεῖς, ἔχοντας ἀσθένειαν· ὁ.λόγος.δὲ
[2]men [1]constitutes high priests, [who] have infirmity; but the word
τῆς ὁρκωμοσίας τῆς μετὰ τὸν νόμον, υἱὸν εἰς τὸν
of the swearing of the oath, which [is] after the law, a Son for
αἰῶνα τετελειωμένον.
ever has perfected.

8 Κεφάλαιον.δὲ ἐπὶ τοῖς λεγομένοις, τοιοῦτον
Now a summary of the things being spoken of [is], [3]such
ἔχομεν ἀρχιερέα, ὃς ἐκάθισεν ἐν δεξιᾷ τοῦ θρόνου τῆς
[1]we [2]have a high priest, who sat down on [the] right hand of the throne of the
μεγαλωσύνης ἐν τοῖς οὐρανοῖς, 2 τῶν ἁγίων λειτουργός, καὶ
greatness in the heavens; [2]of [3]the [4]holies [1]minister, and
τῆς σκηνῆς τῆς ἀληθινῆς, ἣν ἔπηξεν ὁ κύριος, [z]καὶ οὐκ
of the [2]tabernacle [1]true which [3]pitched [1]the [2]Lord and not
ἄνθρωπος.
man.

3 Πᾶς.γὰρ ἀρχιερεὺς εἰς τὸ προσφέρειν δῶρά.τε καὶ θυσίας
For every high priest for to offer both gifts and sacrifices
καθίσταται· ὅθεν ἀναγκαῖον ἔχειν τι καὶ τοῦ-
is constituted; whence [it is] necessary [4]to [5]have [6]something [7]also [[1]for] [2]this
τον ὃ προσενέγκῃ. 4 εἰ.μὲν [a]γὰρ ἦν ἐπὶ γῆς, οὐδ'
[3]one which he may offer. [2]If [3]indeed [1]for he were on earth, not even
ἂν.ἦν ἱερεύς, ὄντων [b]τῶν ἱερέων τῶν προσφερόντων
would he be a priest, there being the priests who offer
κατὰ [c]τὸν νόμον τὰ δῶρα, 5 οἵτινες ὑποδείγματι καὶ
according to the law the gifts, who [the] representation and
σκιᾷ λατρεύουσιν τῶν ἐπουρανίων, καθὼς κεχρημάτισ-
shadow serve of the heavenlies, according as [2]was [3]divinely [4]in-
ται [d]Μωσῆς μέλλων ἐπιτελεῖν τὴν σκηνήν, Ὅρα,.γάρ
structed [1]Moses being about to construct the tabernacle; for, see,
φησιν, [e]ποιήσῃς πάντα κατὰ τὸν τύπον τὸν δειχθέντα
says he, thou make all things according to the pattern which was shewn
σοι ἐν τῷ ὄρει. 6 [f]νυνὶ.δὲ διαφορωτέρας [g]τέτευχεν
thee in the mountain. But now a more excellent [2]he [3]has [4]obtained
λειτουργίας, ὅσῳ καὶ κρείττονός ἐστιν διαθήκης μεσίτης,
[1]ministry by so much as also of a better [2]he [3]is [1]covenant mediator,
ἥτις ἐπὶ κρείττοσιν ἐπαγγελίαις νενομοθέτηται. 7 Εἰ.γὰρ
which upon better promises has been established. For if
ἡ.πρώτη.ἐκείνη ἦν ἄμεμπτος, οὐκ ἂν δευτέρας ἐζητεῖτο
that first [one] were faultless, not for a second would [2]be [3]sought
τόπος. 8 μεμφόμενος.γὰρ [h]αὐτοῖς λέγει, Ἰδού, ἡμέραι ἔρ-
[1]place. For finding fault, [3]to [4]them [1]he [2]says, Lo, days are

---

[x] ἐφ' ἅπαξ Tr. [y] προσενέγκας having offered T. [z] — καὶ LTTrAW. [a] οὖν (read if then indeed) LTTrAW. [b] — τῶν ἱερέων (read τῶν those who) LTTrAW. [c] — τὸν LTTrA. [d] Μωϋσῆς GLTTrAW. [e] ποιήσεις thou shalt make LTTrAW. [f] νῦν L. [g] τέτυχεν LTAW. [h] αὐτοὺς (read finding fault with them) LT

χονται, λέγει κύριος, καὶ συντελέσω ἐπὶ τὸν οἶκον
coming, saith [the] Lord, and I will ratify as regards the house
Ἰσραὴλ καὶ ἐπὶ τὸν οἶκον Ἰούδα διαθήκην καινήν· 9 οὐ
of Israel and as regards the house of Juda a [2]covenant [1]new; not
κατὰ τὴν.διαθήκην ἣν ἐποίησα τοῖς.πατράσιν.αὐτῶν,
according to the covenant which I made with their fathers,
ἐν ἡμέρᾳ ἐπιλαβομένου.[i]μου‖ τῆς.χειρὸς.αὐτῶν ἐξαγαγεῖν
in [the] day of my taking hold of their hand to lead
αὐτοὺς ἐκ γῆς Αἰγύπτου· ὅτι αὐτοὶ οὐκ.ἐνέμειναν ἐν
them out of [the] land of Egypt; because they did not continue in
τῇ.διαθήκῃ.μου, κἀγὼ ἠμέλησα αὐτῶν, λέγει κύριος. 10 ὅτι
my covenant, and I disregarded them, saith [the] Lord. Because
αὕτη ἡ διαθήκη [k] ἣν διαθήσομαι τῷ οἴκῳ Ἰσραὴλ μετὰ
this [is] the covenant which I will covenant with the house of Israel after
τὰς.ἡμέρας.ἐκείνας, λέγει κύριος, διδοὺς νόμους.μου εἰς
those days, says [the] Lord, giving my laws into
τὴν.διάνοιαν.αὐτῶν καὶ ἐπὶ [l]καρδίας‖ αὐτῶν ἐπιγράψω αὐτούς·
their mind, also upon [2]hearts [1]their I will inscribe them;
καὶ ἔσομαι αὐτοῖς εἰς θεόν, καὶ αὐτοὶ ἔσονταί μοι εἰς λαόν.
and I will be to them for God, and they shall be to me for people.
11 καὶ οὐ.μὴ διδάξωσιν ἕκαστος τὸν [m]πλησίον‖ αὐτοῦ, καὶ
And not at all shall they teach each [2]neighbour [1]his, and
ἕκαστος τὸν.ἀδελφὸν.αὐτοῦ, λέγων, Γνῶθι τὸν κύριον· ὅτι
each his brother, saying, Know the Lord; because
πάντες εἰδήσουσίν με, ἀπὸ μικροῦ [n]αὐτῶν‖ ἕως
all shall know me, from [the] little [one] of them to [the]
μεγάλου αὐτῶν· 12 ὅτι ἵλεως ἔσομαι ταῖς.ἀδικίαις.αὐτῶν,
great [one] of them. Because merciful I will be to their unrighteousnesses,
καὶ τῶν.ἁμαρτιῶν.αὐτῶν [o]καὶ τῶν.ἀνομιῶν.αὐτῶν‖ οὐ.μὴ
and their sins and their lawlessnesses in no wise
μνησθῶ ἔτι. 13 Ἐν τῷ λέγειν καινήν, πεπαλαίωκεν
will I remember more. In the saying New, he has made old
τὴν πρώτην· τὸ.δὲ παλαιούμενον καὶ γηράσκον ἐγγὺς
the first; but that which grows old and aged [is] near
ἀφανισμοῦ.
disappearing.

them, he saith, Behold, the days come, saith the Lord, when I will make a new covenant with the house of Israel and with the house of Judah: 9 not according to the covenant that I made with their fathers in the day when I took them by the hand to lead them out of the land of Egypt; because they continued not in my covenant, and I regarded them not, saith the Lord. 10 For this *is* the covenant that I will make with the house of Israel after those days, saith the Lord; I will put my laws into their mind, and write them in their hearts: and I will be to them a God, and they shall be to me a people: 11 and they shall not teach every man his neighbour, and every man his brother, saying, Know the Lord: for all shall know me, from the least to the greatest. 12 For I will be merciful to their unrighteousness, and their sins and their iniquities will I remember no more. 13 In that he saith, A new *covenant*, he hath made the first old. Now that which decayeth and waxeth old *is* ready to vanish away.

9 [p]Εἶχεν‖ μὲν οὖν [q]καὶ‖ ἡ πρώτη [r]σκηνὴ‖ δικαιώματα
[4]Had [7]indeed [5]therefore [6]also [1]the [2]first [3]tabernacle ordinances
λατρείας, τό.τε ἅγιον κοσμικόν. 2 σκηνὴ.γὰρ κατε-
of service, and the sanctuary, a worldly [one]. For a tabernacle was
σκευάσθη ἡ πρώτη, ἐν ᾗ ἥ.τε λυχνία καὶ ἡ τρά-
prepared, the first, in which [were] both the lampstand and the ta-
πεζα καὶ ἡ πρόθεσις τῶν ἄρτων, ἥτις λέγεται [s]ἅγια.‖ 3 μετὰ
ble and the presentation of the loaves, which is called holy; [2]after
δὲ τὸ δεύτερον καταπέτασμα σκηνὴ ἡ λεγομένη [t]ἅγια‖
[1]but the second veil a tabernacle which [is] called holy
ἁγίων, 4 χρυσοῦν ἔχουσα θυμιατήριον, καὶ τὴν κιβωτὸν τῆς
of holies, [2]a [3]golden [1]having censer, and the ark of the
διαθήκης περικεκαλυμμένην πάντοθεν χρυσίῳ, ἐν ᾗ
covenant, having been covered round [3]in [4]every [5]part [1]with [2]gold, in which
στάμνος χρυσῆ ἔχουσα τὸ μάννα, καὶ ἡ ῥάβδος Ἀαρὼν
[was the] [2]pot [1]golden having the manna, and the rod of Aaron

IX. Then verily the first *covenant* had also ordinances of divine service, and a worldly sanctuary. 2 For there was a tabernacle made; the first, wherein *was* the candlestick, and the table, and the shewbread; which is called the sanctuary. 3 And after the second veil, the tabernacle which is called the Holiest of all; 4 which had the golden censer, and the ark of the covenant overlaid round about with gold, wherein *was* the golden pot that had manna, and

---

[i] — μου my E. [k] + [μου] (*read* my covenant) L. [l] καρδίαν heart T. [m] πολίτην (*read* his [fellow] citizen) GLTTrAW. [n] — αὐτῶν LTTrA. [o] — καὶ τῶν ἀνομιῶν αὐτῶν TTrA. [p] Εἶχε T. [q] [καὶ] Tr. [r] — σκηνὴ GLTTrAW. [s] ἅγια holy place EGTTrAW; ἅγια ἁγίων holy of holies L. [t] τὰ ἅγια τῶν (*read* the holy of holies) Tr.

Aaron's rod that budded, and the tables of the covenant; 5 and over it the cherubims of glory shadowing the mercyseat; of which we cannot now speak particularly.

6 Now when these things were thus ordained, the priests went always into the first tabernacle, accomplishing the service *of God.* 7 But into the second *went* the high priest alone once every year, not without blood, which he offered for himself, and *for* the errors of the people: 8 the Holy Ghost this signifying, that the way into the holiest of all was not yet made manifest, while as the first tabernacle was yet standing: 9 which *was* a figure for the time then present, in which were offered both gifts and sacrifices, that could not make him that did the service perfect, as pertaining to the conscience; 10 *which stood* only in meats and drinks, and divers washings, and carnal ordinances, imposed *on them* until the time of reformation. 11 But Christ being come an high priest of good things to come, by a greater and more perfect tabernacle, not made with hands, that is to say, not of this building; 12 neither by the blood of goats and calves, but by his own blood he entered in once into the holy place, having obtained eternal redemption *for us.* 13 For if the blood of bulls and of goats, and the ashes of an heifer sprinkling the unclean, sanctifieth to the purifying of the flesh: 14 how much more shall the blood of Christ, who through the eternal Spirit offered himself without spot to God, purge your conscience from dead works to serve the living God? 15 And for this cause he is the mediator of

ἡ βλαστήσασα, καὶ αἱ πλάκες τῆς διαθήκης· 5 ὑπεράνω.δὲ
that sprouted, and the tablets of the covenant; and above
αὐτῆς [t]χερουβὶμ‖ δόξης κατασκιάζοντα τὸ ἱλαστήριον·
it [the] cherubim of glory overshadowing the mercy seat;
περὶ ὧν οὐκ.ἔστιν νῦν λέγειν κατὰ.μέρος.
concerning which it is not now [the time] to speak in detail.
6 Τούτων.δὲ οὕτως κατεσκευασμένων, εἰς μὲν τὴν πρώτην
Now these things thus having been prepared, into the first
σκηνὴν [v]διαπαντὸς‖ εἰσίασιν οἱ ἱερεῖς τὰς λατρείας ἐπιτελοῦν-
tabernacle at all times enter the priests, the services accomplish-
τες· 7 εἰς.δὲ τὴν δευτέραν ἅπαξ τοῦ.ἐνιαυτοῦ μόνος ὁ ἀρχιε-
ing; but into the second once in the year alone the high
ρεύς, οὐ χωρὶς αἵματος, ὃ προσφέρει ὑπὲρ ἑαυτοῦ καὶ
priest, not apart from blood, which he offers for himself and
τῶν τοῦ λαοῦ ἀγνοημάτων· 8 τοῦτο δηλοῦντος τοῦ πνεύ-
the [4]of [5]the [6]people [1]sins [2]of [3]ignorance: [11]this [12]signifying [7]the [8]Spirit
ματος τοῦ ἁγίου, μήπω πεφανερῶσθαι τὴν τῶν ἁγίων
[9]the [10]Holy, [that] not yet has been made manifest the [2]of [3]the [4]holies
ὁδὸν ἔτι τῆς πρώτης σκηνῆς ἐχούσης στάσιν· 9 ἥτις
[1]way, [9]still [5]the [6]first [7]tabernacle [8]having a standing; which [is]
παραβολὴ εἰς τὸν καιρὸν τὸν ἐνεστηκότα, καθ' [w]ὃν‖ δῶρά.τε
a simile for the [2]time [1]present, in which both gifts
καὶ θυσίαι προσφέρονται, μὴ δυνάμεναι κατὰ συνείδησιν τε-
and sacrifices are offered, not being able as to conscience to
λειῶσαι τὸν λατρεύοντα, 10 μόνον ἐπὶ βρώμασιν καὶ
perfect him who serves, [consisting] only in meats and
πόμασιν καὶ διαφόροις βαπτισμοῖς, [x]καὶ‖ [y]δικαιώμασιν‖ σαρκός,
drinks and divers washings, and ordinances of flesh,
μέχρι καιροῦ διορθώσεως ἐπικείμενα. 11 Χριστὸς.δὲ
[2]until [[3]the] [4]time [5]of [6]setting [7]things [8]right [1]imposed. But Christ
παραγενόμενος ἀρχιερεὺς τῶν [z]μελλόντων‖ ἀγαθῶν, διὰ τῆς
being come high priest of the coming good things, by the
μείζονος καὶ τελειοτέρας σκηνῆς, οὐ χειροποιήτου, [a]τουτέστιν‖
greater and more perfect tabernacle, not made by hand, (that is,
οὐ ταύτης τῆς κτίσεως, 12 οὐδὲ δι' αἵματος τράγων καὶ
not of this creation,) nor by blood of goats and
μόσχων, διὰ.δὲ τοῦ.ἰδίου.αἵματος εἰσῆλθεν [b]ἐφάπαξ‖ εἰς
calves, but by his own blood, entered once for all into
τὰ ἅγια, αἰωνίαν λύτρωσιν [c]εὑράμενος.‖ 13 εἰ.γὰρ τὸ αἷμα
the holies, eternal redemption having found. For if the blood
[d]ταύρων καὶ τράγων‖, καὶ σποδὸς δαμάλεως ῥαντίζουσα τοὺς
of bulls and of goats, and ashes of a heifer sprinkling the
κεκοινωμένους, ἁγιάζει πρὸς τὴν τῆς σαρκὸς καθαρότητα,
defiled, sanctifies for the [2]of [3]the [4]flesh [1]purity,
14 πόσῳ μᾶλλον τὸ αἷμα τοῦ χριστοῦ, ὃς διὰ πνεύματος
how much rather the blood of the Christ who through [the] [2]Spirit
αἰωνίου ἑαυτὸν προσήνεγκεν ἄμωμον τῷ θεῷ, καθαριεῖ τὴν
[1]eternal [4]himself [3]offered spotless to God, shall purify
συνείδησιν [e]ὑμῶν‖ ἀπὸ νεκρῶν ἔργων, εἰς τὸ λατρεύειν θεῷ
[2]conscience [1]your from dead works for to serve [3]God [[1]the]
ζῶντι[f]; 15 Καὶ διὰ.τοῦτο διαθήκης καινῆς μεσίτης ἐστίν,
[2]living! And for this reason of a [2]covenant [1]new [5]mediator [3]he [4]is,

---

[t] χερουβεὶν LTTr; χερουβὶν A. [v] διὰ παντὸς LTrA. [w] ἣν (*read* according to which [simile]) LTTrAW. [x] — καὶ GLT[Tr]AW. [y] δικαιώματα LTTrAW. [z] γενομένων L. [a] τουτ' ἔστιν GT. [b] ἐφ' ἅπαξ Tr. [c] εὑρόμενος E. [d] τράγων καὶ ταύρων LTTrAW. [e] ἡμῶν our LAW. [f] + καὶ ἀληθινῷ and true L.

ὅπως θανάτου γενομένου, εἰς ἀπολύτρωσιν τῶν ἐπὶ τῇ
so that, death having taken place for redemption of the [2]under [3]the
πρώτῃ διαθήκῃ παραβάσεων, τὴν ἐπαγγελίαν λάβωσιν
[4]first [5]covenant [1]transgressions, the promise [10]might [11]receive
οἱ κεκλημένοι τῆς αἰωνίου κληρονομίας. 16 ὅπου.γὰρ
[8]they [6]who [7]have [8]been [9]called [1]of [2]the [3]eternal [4]inheritance. (For where
διαθήκη, θάνατον ἀνάγκη φέρεσθαι τοῦ
[there is] a testament, [[4]for [5]the] [6]death [[1]it [2]is] [3]necessary [10]to [11]come [12]in [7]of [8]the
διαθεμένου· 17 διαθήκη.γὰρ ἐπὶ.νεκροῖς βεβαία, ἐπεὶ
[9]testator. For a testament in the case of [the] dead [is] affirmed, since
μήποτε ἰσχύει ὅτε ζῇ ὁ διαθέμενος.[g] 18 ὅθεν [h]οὐδ'
in no way it is of force when [3]is [4]living [1]the [2]testator.) Whence neither
ἡ πρώτη χωρὶς αἵματος [i]ἐγκεκαίνισται. 19 λαληθείσης
the first apart from blood has been inaugurated. [4]Having [5]been [6]spoken
γὰρ πάσης ἐντολῆς κατὰ [k]νόμον ὑπὸ Μωϋσέως παντὶ
[1]for [2]every [3]commandment according to law by Moses to all
τῷ λαῷ, λαβὼν τὸ αἷμα τῶν μόσχων καὶ [l]τράγων, μετὰ
the people, having taken the blood of calves and of goats, with
ὕδατος καὶ ἐρίου κοκκίνου καὶ ὑσσώπου, αὐτό.τε τὸ βιβλίον
water and [2]wool [1]scarlet and hyssop, both [3]itself [1]the [2]book
καὶ πάντα τὸν λαὸν [m]ἐῤῥάντισεν, 20 λέγων, Τοῦτο τὸ
and all the people he sprinkled, saying, This [is] the
αἷμα τῆς διαθήκης ἧς ἐνετείλατο πρὸς ὑμᾶς ὁ θεός. 21 καὶ
blood of the covenant which [2]enjoined [3]to [4]you [1]God. And
τὴν σκηνὴν δὲ καὶ πάντα τὰ σκεύη τῆς λειτουργίας τῷ
the tabernacle too and all the vessels of the ministration with
αἵματι ὁμοίως [m]ἐῤῥάντισεν· 22 καὶ σχεδὸν ἐν αἵματι
blood in like manner he sprinkled; and almost [3]with [4]blood
πάντα καθαρίζεται κατὰ τὸν νόμον, καὶ χωρὶς αἱματ-
[1]all [2]things are purified according to the law, and apart from blood-
εκχυσίας οὐ.γίνεται ἄφεσις. 23 Ἀνάγκη οὖν τὰ μὲν
shedding there is no remission. [It was] necessary then [for] the
ὑποδείγματα τῶν ἐν τοῖς οὐρανοῖς τούτοις καθαρίζεσθαι,
representations of the things in the heavens with these to be purified,
αὐτὰ.δὲ τὰ ἐπουράνια κρείττοσιν θυσίαις παρὰ ταύτας.
but [3]themselves [1]the [2]heavenlies with better sacrifices than these.
24 οὐ.γὰρ εἰς χειροποίητα [n]ἅγια εἰσῆλθεν [o]ὁ χριστός, ἀντί-
For not into [2]made [3]by [4]hands [1]holies entered the Christ, fi-
τυπα τῶν ἀληθινῶν, ἀλλ' εἰς αὐτὸν τὸν οὐρανόν, νῦν ἐμφα-
gures of the true [ones], but into [2]itself [1]heaven, now to
νισθῆναι τῷ.προσώπῳ τοῦ θεοῦ ὑπὲρ ἡμῶν· 25 οὐδ' ἵνα
appear before the face of God for us: nor that
πολλάκις προσφέρῃ ἑαυτόν, ὥσπερ ὁ ἀρχιερεὺς εἰσέρχεται εἰς
often he should offer himself, even as the high priest enters into
τὰ ἅγια κατ'.ἐνιαυτὸν ἐν αἵματι ἀλλοτρίῳ· 26 ἐπεὶ ἔ-
the holies year by year with [2]blood [1]another's; since it was neces-
δει αὐτὸν πολλάκις παθεῖν ἀπὸ καταβολῆς κόσμου·
sary for him often to have suffered from [the] foundation of [the] world.
[p]νῦν .δὲ ἅπαξ ἐπὶ συντελείᾳ τῶν αἰώνων, εἰς ἀθέτη-
But now once in [the] consummation of the ages, for [the] putting
σιν [q]ἁμαρτίας, διὰ τῆς.θυσίας.αὐτοῦ πεφανέρωται. 27 καὶ
away of sin by his sacrifice he has been manifested. And
καθ'.ὅσον ἀπόκειται τοῖς ἀνθρώποις ἅπαξ ἀποθανεῖν, μετὰ
for as much as it is apportioned to men once to die, [2]after

the new testament,
that by means of death,
for the redemption of
the transgressions *that
were* under the first
testament, they which
are called might re-
ceive the promise of
eternal inheritance.
16 For where a testa-
ment *is*, there must al-
so of necessity be the
death of the testator.
17 For a testament *is*
of force after men are
dead: otherwise it is
of no strength at
all while the testator
liveth. 18 Whereupon
neither the first *testa-
ment* was dedicated
without blood. 19 For
when Moses had spok-
en every precept to
all the people ac-
cording to the law,
he took the blood of
calves and of goats,
with water, and scar-
let wool, and hyssop,
and sprinkled both the
book, and all the peo-
ple, 20 saying, This *is*
the blood of the tes-
tament which God
hath enjoined unto
you. 21 Moreover he
sprinkled with blood
both the tabernacle,
and all the vessels of
the ministry. 22 And
almost all things are
by the law purged with
blood; and without
shedding of blood is no
remission. 23 *It was*
therefore necessary
that the patterns of
things in the heavens
should be purified with
these; but the hea-
venly things them-
selves with better sac-
rifices than these.
24 For Christ is not
entered into the holy
places made with
hands, *which are* the
figures of the true;
but into heaven itself,
now to appear in the
presence of God for
us: 25 nor yet that he
should offer himself
often, as the high
priest entereth into
the holy place every
year with blood of
others; 26 for then
must he often have
suffered since the foun-
dation of the world:
but now once in the
end of the world hath
he appeared to put a-
way sin by the sacri-
fice of himself. 27 And
as it is appointed unto

g *Read the sentence as a question* L. h οὐδὲ LTrAW. i ἐν- T. k + τὸν the LTrAW.
l + τῶν LTTrAW. m ἐράντισεν LTTrA. n εἰσῆλθεν ἅγια TTrA. o — ὁ LTTrAW
p νυνὶ LTTrA. q + τῆς LTTr.

men once to die, but after this the judgment: 28 so Christ was once offered to bear the sins of many; and unto them that look for him shall he appear the second time without sin unto salvation.

X. For the law having a shadow of good things to come, *and* not the very image of the things, can never with those sacrifices which they offered year by year continually make the comers thereunto perfect. 2 For then would they not have ceased to be offered? because that the worshippers once purged should have had no more conscience of sins. 3 But in those *sacrifices there is* a remembrance again *made* of sins every year. 4 For *it is* not possible that the blood of bulls and of goats should take away sins. 5 Wherefore when he cometh into the world, he saith, Sacrifice and offering thou wouldest not, but a body hast thou prepared me: 6 in burnt offerings and *sacrifices* for sin thou hast had no pleasure. 7 Then said I, Lo, I come (in the volume of the book it is written of me,) to do thy will, O God. 8 Above when he said, Sacrifice and offering and burnt offerings and *offering* for sin thou wouldest not, neither hadst pleasure *therein*; which are offered by the law; 9 then said he, Lo, I come to do thy will, O God. He taketh away the first, that he may establish the second. 10 By the which will we are sanctified through the offering of the body of Jesus Christ once *for all.* 11 And every priest standeth daily ministering and offering oftentimes the same sacrifices, which can never take away sins:

δὲ τοῦτο κρίσις· 28 οὕτως [r]ὁ χριστὸς ἅπαξ προσενεχθεὶς
[1]and this, judgment; thus the Christ, once having been offered
εἰς τὸ πολλῶν ἀνενεγκεῖν ἁμαρτίας, ἐκ.δευτέρου χωρὶς
for [5]of [6]many [1]to [2]bear [[3]the] [4]sins, a second time [8]apart [9]from
ἁμαρτίας ὀφθήσεται τοῖς αὐτὸν ἀπεκδεχομένοις εἰς
[10]sin [1]shall [2]appear [3]to [4]those [5]that [7]him [6]await for
σωτηρίαν.
salvation.

10 Σκιὰν.γὰρ ἔχων ὁ νόμος τῶν μελλόντων ἀγαθῶν, οὐκ
For [4]a [5]shadow [3]having [1]the [2]law of the coming good things, not
αὐτὴν τὴν εἰκόνα τῶν πραγμάτων, κατ'.ἐνιαυτὸν ταῖς.αὐταῖς
[3]itself [1]the [2]image of the things, year by year with the same
θυσίαις [s]ἃς‖ προσφέρουσιν εἰς.τὸ.διηνεκὲς οὐδέποτε [t]δύναται‖
sacrifices which they offer in perpetuity never is able
τοὺς προσερχομένους τελειῶσαι. 2 ἐπεὶ [v]οὐκ.ἂν.ἐπαύσαντο
[3]those [4]who [5]approach [1]to [2]perfect. Since would they not have ceased
προσφερόμεναι, διὰ τὸ μηδεμίαν ἔχειν ἔτι συνείδησιν
to be offered, on account of [7]no [9]any [6]having [8]longer [10]conscience
ἁμαρτιῶν τοὺς λατρεύοντας, ἅπαξ [w]κεκαθαρμένους‖; 3 ἀλλ'
[11]of [12]sins [1]those [2]who [3]serve [4]once [5]purged? But
ἐν αὐταῖς ἀνάμνησις ἁμαρτιῶν κατ'.ἐνιαυτόν. 4 ἀδύ-
in these a remembrance of sins year by year [there is]. [4]Impos-
νατον γὰρ αἷμα ταύρων καὶ τράγων ἀφαιρεῖν ἁμαρ-
sible [[2]it [3]is] [1]for [for the] blood of bulls and of goats to take away sins.
τίας. 5 Διὸ εἰσερχόμενος εἰς τὸν κόσμον λέγει, [x]Θυσίαν καὶ
Wherefore coming into the world he says, Sacrifice and
προσφορὰν‖ οὐκ.ἠθέλησας, σῶμα.δὲ κατηρτίσω μοι· 6 ὁλο-
offering thou willedst not, but a body thou didst prepare me. Burnt
καυτώματα καὶ περὶ ἁμαρτίας οὐκ.[y]εὐδόκησας.‖
offerings and [sacrifices] for sin thou delightedst not in.
7 τότε εἶπον, Ἰδοὺ ἥκω, ἐν κεφαλίδι βιβλίου γέγραπται
Then I said, Lo, I come, (in [the] roll of [the] book it is written
περὶ ἐμοῦ, τοῦ ποιῆσαι, ὁ θεός, τὸ.θέλημά.σου. 8 Ἀνώτερον
of me,) to do, O God, thy will. Above
λέγων, Ὅτι [z]θυσίαν‖ καὶ [a]προσφορὰν‖ καὶ ὁλοκαυτώματα
saying, Sacrifice and offering and burnt offerings
καὶ περὶ ἁμαρτίας οὐκ.ἠθέλησας, οὐδὲ [b]εὐδόκησας,‖
and [sacrifices] for sin thou willedst not, nor delightedst in,
αἵτινες κατὰ [c]τὸν‖ νόμον προσφέρονται, 9 τότε εἴρηκεν,
(which according to the law are offered); then he said,
Ἰδοὺ ἥκω τοῦ ποιῆσαι, [d]ὁ θεός,‖ τὸ.θέλημά.σου. ἀναιρεῖ τὸ
Lo, I come, to do, O God, thy will. He takes away the
πρῶτον, ἵνα τὸ δεύτερον στήσῃ· 10 ἐν ᾧ θελήματι
first, that the second he may establish; by which will
ἡγιασμένοι ἐσμὲν [e]οἱ διὰ τῆς προσφορᾶς τοῦ σώματος [f]τοῦ‖
[3]sanctified [1]we [2]are through the offering of the body
Ἰησοῦ χριστοῦ [g]ἐφάπαξ.‖ 11 Καὶ πᾶς μὲν [h]ἱερεὺς‖ ἕστηκεν
of Jesus Christ once for all. And every priest stands
καθ'.ἡμέραν λειτουργῶν, καὶ τὰς αὐτὰς πολλάκις προσφέρων
day by day ministering, and the same [2]often [3]offering
θυσίας, αἵτινες οὐδέποτε δύνανται περιελεῖν ἁμαρτίας·
[1]sacrifices, which never are able to take away sins.

[r] + καὶ also GLTTrAW. [s] αἷς TA. [t] δύνανται they are able LTr. [v] — οὐκ not (*read the sentence not as a question*) E. [w] κεκαθερισμένους L; κεκαθαρισμένους TTrAW. [x] προσφορὰν καὶ θυσίαν W. [y] ηὐδόκησας LTTrA. [z] θυσίας sacrifices LTTrAW. [a] προσφορὰς offerings LTTrAW. [b] ηὐδόκησας LTTr. [c] — τὸν LTTr[A]. [d] — ὁ θεός GLTTrAW. [e] — οἱ EGLTTrAW. [f] — τοῦ GLTTrAW. [g] ἐφ' ἅπαξ Tr. [h] ἀρχιερεὺς high priest LA.

12 [i]αὐτὸς[ǁ].δὲ μίαν ὑπὲρ ἁμαρτιῶν προσενέγκας θυσίαν, εἰς
But he, [3]one [5]for [6]sins [1]having [2]offered [4]sacrifice, in
τὸ διηνεκὲς ἐκάθισεν ἐν δεξιᾷ τοῦ θεοῦ, 13 τὸ.λοιπὸν
perpetuity sat down at [the] right hand of God, henceforth
ἐκδεχόμενος ἕως τεθῶσιν οἱ.ἐχθροὶ.αὐτοῦ ὑποπόδιον τῶν
awaiting until be placed his enemies [as] a footstool
ποδῶν αὐτοῦ. 14 μιᾷ.γὰρ προσφορᾷ τετελείωκεν εἰς.τὸ.διη-
for [2]feet [1]his. For by one offering he has perfected in perpe-
νεκὲς τοὺς ἁγιαζομένους. 15 Μαρτυρεῖ.δὲ ἡμῖν καὶ τὸ πνεῦμα
tuity the sanctified. And bears witness to us also the Spirit
τὸ ἅγιον· μετὰ.γὰρ τὸ [k]προειρηκέναι,[ǁ] 16 Αὕτη ἡ δια-
the Holy; for after the having said before, This [is] the cove-
θήκη ἣν διαθήσομαι πρὸς αὐτοὺς μετὰ τὰς.ἡμέρας.ἐκείνας,
nant which I will covenant towards them after those days,
λέγει κύριος, διδοὺς νόμους.μου ἐπὶ καρδίας.αὐτῶν, καὶ ἐπὶ
says [the] Lord: giving my laws into their hearts, also into
[l]τῶν διανοιῶν[ǁ] αὐτῶν ἐπιγράψω αὐτούς· 17 καὶ τῶν ἁμαρτιῶν
[2]minds [1]their I will inscribe them; and [2]sins
αὐτῶν καὶ τῶν.ἀνομιῶν.αὐτῶν οὐ.μὴ [m]μνησθῶ[ǁ] ἔτι.
[1]their and their lawlessnesses in no wise will I remember any more.
18 ὅπου.δὲ ἄφεσις τούτων, οὐκέτι προσφορὰ περὶ
But where remission of these [is], no longer [is there] an offering for
ἁμαρτίας.
sin.

12 but this man, after he had offered one sacrifice for sins for ever, sat down on the right hand of God; 13 from henceforth expecting till his enemies be made his footstool. 14 For by one offering he hath perfected for ever them that are sanctified. 15 *Whereof* the Holy Ghost also is a witness to us: for after that he had said before, 16 This *is* the covenant that I will make with them after those days, saith the Lord, I will put my laws into their hearts, and in their minds will I write them; 17 and their sins and iniquities will I remember no more. 18 Now where remission of these *is, there is* no more offering for sin.

19 Ἔχοντες οὖν, ἀδελφοί, παῤῥησίαν εἰς τὴν.εἴσοδον
Having therefore, brethren, boldness for entrance into
τῶν ἁγίων ἐν τῷ αἵματι Ἰησοῦ, 20 ἣν ἐνεκαίνισεν ἡμῖν
the holies by the blood of Jesus, [7]which [8]he [9]dedicated [10]for [11]us
ὁδὸν πρόσφατον καὶ ζῶσαν διὰ τοῦ καταπετάσματος, [n]τουτ-
[1]a [2]way [3]newly [4]made [5]and [6]living through the veil, that
έστιν[ǀ] τῆς.σαρκὸς.αὐτοῦ, 21 καὶ ἱερέα μέγαν ἐπὶ τὸν οἶκον
is, his flesh; and a [2]priest [1]great over the house
τοῦ θεοῦ, 22 προσερχώμεθα μετὰ ἀληθινῆς καρδίας ἐν
of God [having], we should approach with a true heart, in
πληροφορίᾳ πίστεως, [o]ἐῤῥαντισμένοι[ǁ] τὰς καρδίας ἀπὸ συν-
full assurance of faith, having been sprinkled [as to] the hearts from a [2]con-
ειδήσεως πονηρᾶς, καὶ [p]λελουμένοι[ǁ] τὸ σῶμα ὕδατι
science [1]wicked, and having been washed [as to] the body with [2]water
καθαρῷ· [q] 23 κατέχωμεν τὴν ὁμολογίαν τῆς ἐλπίδος ἀκλινῆ,
[1]pure. We should hold fast the confession of the hope unwavering,
πιστὸς.γὰρ ὁ ἐπαγγειλάμενος· 24 καὶ κατανοῶμεν ἀλ-
for [is] faithful he who promised; and we should consider one
λήλους εἰς παροξυσμὸν ἀγάπης καὶ καλῶν ἔργων, 25 μὴ
another for provoking to love and to good works; not
ἐγκαταλείποντες τὴν ἐπισυναγωγὴν ἑαυτῶν, καθὼς
forsaking the assembling together of ourselves, even as [the]
ἔθος τισίν, ἀλλὰ παρακαλοῦντες· καὶ τοσούτῳ
custom [is] with some; but encouraging [one another], and by so much
μᾶλλον ὅσῳ βλέπετε ἐγγίζουσαν τὴν ἡμέραν. 26 ἑκου-
[the] more as ye see drawing near the day. [[2]Where] [3]will-
σίως γὰρ ἁμαρτανόντων ἡμῶν μετὰ τὸ.λαβεῖν τὴν ἐπίγνωσιν
ingly [1]for [5]sin [4]we after receiving the knowledge
τῆς ἀληθείας, οὐκέτι περὶ ἁμαρτιῶν ἀπολείπεται θυσία·
of the truth, no longer [3]for [4]sins [5]remains [1]a [2]sacrifice,

19 Having therefore, brethren, boldness to enter into the holiest by the blood of Jesus, 20 by a new and living way, which he hath consecrated for us, through the veil, that is to say, his flesh; 21 and *having* an high priest over the house of God; 22 let us draw near with a true heart in full assurance of faith, having our hearts sprinkled from an evil conscience, and our bodies washed with pure water. 23 Let us hold fast the profession of *our* faith without wavering; (for he *is* faithful that promised;) 24 and let us consider one another to provoke unto love and to good works: 25 not forsaking the assembling of ourselves together, as the manner of some *is;* but exhorting *one another:* and so much the more, as ye see the day approaching. 26 For if we sin wilfully after that we have received the knowledge of the truth, there remaineth no more sacrifice for sins, 27 but a certain fearful looking for of

[i] οὗτος (*read* But this one LTTrAW. [k] εἰρηκέναι having said LTTrAW. [l] τὴν διάνοιαν mind LTTrAW. [m] μνησθήσομαι LTTrA. [n] τουτ' ἔστιν GT. [o] ῥεραντισμένοι LTTrA. [p] λελουσμένοι T. [q] *Punctuate so as to join* we should hold fast *with what precedes* GLTTr.

judgment and fiery
indignation, which
shall devour the ad-
versaries. 28 He that
despised Moses' law
died without mercy
under two or three
witnesses: 29 of how
much sorer punish-
ment, suppose ye, shall
he be thought worthy,
who hath trodden un-
der foot the Son of God,
and hath counted the
blood of the covenant,
wherewith he was
sanctified, an unholy
thing, and hath done
despite unto the Spirit
of grace? 30 For we
know him that hath
said, Vengeance *be-
longeth* unto me, I will
recompense, saith the
Lord. And again, The
Lord shall judge his
people. 31 *It is* a fearful thing to fall into
the hands of the living
God.

32 But call to re-
membrance the former
days, in which, after
ye were illuminated,
ye endured a great
fight of afflictions;
33 partly, whilst ye
were made a gazing-
stock both by re-
proaches and afflic-
tions; and partly,
whilst ye became com-
panions of them that
were so used. 34 For
ye had compassion of
me in my bonds, and
took joyfully the
spoiling of your goods,
knowing in yourselves
that ye have in hea-
ven a better and an
enduring substance.
35 Cast not away
therefore your confi-
dence, which hath
great recompence of
reward. 36 For ye have
need of patience, that,
after ye have done the
will of God, ye might
receive the promise.
37 For yet a little
while, and he that
shall come will come,
and will not tarry.
38 Now the just shall
live by faith: but if
any man draw back,
my soul shall have no
pleasure in him. 39 But
we are not of them who
draw back unto per-
dition; but of them
that believe to the
saving of the soul.

27 φοβερὰ.δέ τις ἐκδοχὴ κρίσεως, καὶ πυρὸς ζῆλος ἐσ-
but a [2]fearful [1]certain expectation of judgment, and [2]of [3]fire [1]fervour [5]to
θίειν μέλλοντος τοὺς ὑπεναντίους. 28 ἀθετήσας τις
[6]devour [4]about the adversaries. [3]Having [4]set [5]aside [1]any [2]one
νόμον [r]Μωσέως‖ χωρὶς οἰκτιρμῶν ἐπὶ δυσὶν
[the] law of Moses, [2]without [3]compassions [4]on [[5]the [6]testimony [7]of] [8]two
ἢ τρισὶν μάρτυσιν ἀποθνήσκει· 29 πόσῳ δοκεῖτε χείρονος
[9]or [10]three [11]witnesses [1]dies: how much [3]think [4]ye [1]worse
ἀξιωθήσεται τιμωρίας ὁ τὸν υἱὸν τοῦ θεοῦ
[5]shall [6]he [7]be [8]counted [9]worthy [10]of [2]punishment who the Son of God
καταπατήσας, καὶ τὸ αἷμα τῆς διαθήκης κοινὸν ἡγησά-
trampled upon, and [3]the [4]blood [5]of [6]the [7]covenant [2]common [1]esteem-
μενος ἐν.ᾧ ἡγιάσθη, καὶ τὸ πνεῦμα τῆς χάριτος
ed wherewith he was sanctified, and the Spirit of grace
ἐνυβρίσας; 30 οἴδαμεν.γὰρ τὸν εἰπόντα, Ἐμοὶ ἐκδίκησις,
insulted! For we know him who said, To me [2]vengeance
ἐγὼ ἀνταποδώσω, [s]λέγει κύριος·‖ καὶ πάλιν, [t]Κύριος
[[1]belongs]; I will recompense, says [the] Lord: and again, [The]
Κύριος κρινεῖ‖ τὸν.λαὸν.αὐτοῦ. 31 Φοβερὸν τὸ ἐμπεσεῖν
Lord will judge his people. [It is] a fearful thing to fall
εἰς χεῖρας θεοῦ ζῶντος.
into [the] hands of [3]God [[1]the] [2]living.

32 Ἀναμιμνήσκεσθε.δὲ τὰς πρότερον ἡμέρας, ἐν αἷς φωτισ-
But call to remembrance the former days in which, having
θέντες πολλὴν ἄθλησιν ὑπεμείνατε παθημάτων· 33 τοῦτο
been enlightened, [3]much [4]conflict [1]ye [2]endured of sufferings; partly,
μέν, ὀνειδισμοῖς.τε καὶ θλίψεσιν θεατριζόμενοι· τοῦτο.δέ,
both in reproaches and tribulations being made a spectacle; and partly,
κοινωνοὶ τῶν οὕτως ἀναστρεφομένων γενηθέντες·
[3]partners [4]of [5]those [6]thus [7]passing [8]through [[9]them] [1]having [2]become.
34 καὶ.γὰρ τοῖς.[v]δεσμοῖς.μου‖ συνεπαθήσατε, καὶ τὴν ἁρπαγὴν
For both with my bonds ye sympathized, and the plunder
τῶν.ὑπαρχόντων.ὑμῶν μετὰ χαρᾶς προσεδέξασθε, γινώσκοντες
of your possessions with joy ye received, knowing
ἔχειν [w]ἐν‖ [x]ἑαυτοῖς κρείττονα‖ ὕπαρξιν [y]ἐν οὐρανοῖς‖ καὶ
to have in yourselves a better [3]possession [4]in [[5]the] [6]heavens [1]and
μένουσαν. 35 μὴ.ἀποβάλητε οὖν τὴν.παῤῥησίαν.ὑμῶν,
[2]abiding. Cast not away therefore your boldness
ἥτις ἔχει [z]μισθαποδοσίαν μεγάλην.‖ 36 ὑπομονῆς.γὰρ ἔχετε
which has [2]recompense [1]great. For of endurance ye have
χρείαν, ἵνα τὸ θέλημα τοῦ θεοῦ ποιήσαντες κομίσησθε τὴν
need, that the will of God having done ye may receive the
ἐπαγγελίαν. 37 ἔτι.γὰρ μικρὸν.ὅσον.ὅσον, ὁ ἐρχόμενος
promise. For yet a very little while, he who comes
ἥξει, καὶ οὐ.[a]χρονιεῖ.‖ 38 ὁ.δὲ [b]δίκαιος‖ ἐκ πίστεως ζήσε-
will come, and will not delay. But the just by faith shall
ται· καὶ ἐὰν ὑποστείληται, οὐκ.εὐδοκεῖ ἡ.ψυχή.μου ἐν αὐτῷ.
live; and if he draw back, [3]delights [4]not [1]my [2]soul in him.
39 ἡμεῖς.δὲ οὐκ.ἐσμὲν ὑποστολῆς εἰς ἀπώλειαν, ἀλλὰ
But we are not of [those] drawing back to destruction, but
πίστεως εἰς περιποίησιν ψυχῆς.
of faith to saving [the] soul.

---

[r] Μωϋσέως GLTTrAW. [s] — λέγει κύριος TTr. [t] κρινεῖ κύριος LTTrAW. [v] δεσμίοις (*read* with prisoners) GLTTrAW. [w] — ἐν GLTTrAW. [x] ἑαυτοὺς κρείσσονα LTTr; ἑαυτοῖς (for yourselves) κρείσσονα A. [y] — ἐν οὐρανοῖς LTTrAW. [z] μεγάλην μισθαποδοσίαν LTTrAW. [a] χρονίσει TTr. [b] δίκαιός μου (*read* my just [one]) LTTrA.

11 Ἔστιν.δὲ πίστις ἐλπιζομένων ὑπόστασις, πραγμά-
Now [2]is [1]faith of [things] hoped for [the] assurance, of things
των ἔλεγχος οὐ βλεπομένων. 2 ἐν.ταύτῃ.γὰρ ἐμαρτυ-
[[3]the] [4]conviction [1]not [2]seen. For by this [3]were [4]borne
ρήθησαν οἱ πρεσβύτεροι. 3 Πίστει νοοῦμεν κατηρτίσθαι
[5]witness [6]to [1]the [2]elders. By faith we apprehend to have been framed
τοὺς αἰῶνας ῥήματι θεοῦ, εἰς.τὸ μὴ ἐκ φαινομένων
the worlds by [the] word of God, so that [5]not [7]from [[8]things] [9]appearing
[c]τὰ βλεπόμενα‖ γεγονέναι. 4 Πίστει πλείονα θυσίαν
[1]the [2]things [3]seen [4]have [6]being. By faith [2]a [3]more [4]excellent [5]sacrifice
Ἄβελ παρὰ Κάϊν προσήνεγκεν τῷ θεῷ, δι' ἧς ἐμαρτυ-
[1]Abel than Cain offered to God, by which he was borne wit-
ρήθη εἶναι δίκαιος, μαρτυροῦντος ἐπὶ τοῖς.δώροις.αὐτοῦ [d]τοῦ
ness to as being righteous, [2]bearing [3]witness [4]to [5]his [6]gifts
θεοῦ·‖ καὶ δι' αὐτῆς ἀποθανὼν ἔτι [e]λαλεῖται.‖ 5 Πίστει Ἐνὼχ
[1]God, and through it, having died, yet speaks. By faith Enoch
μετετέθη τοῦ μὴ ἰδεῖν θάνατον, καὶ οὐχ.[f]εὑρίσκετο,‖ διότι
was translated not to see death, and was not found, because
μετέθηκεν αὐτὸν ὁ θεός· πρὸ.γὰρ τῆς.μεταθέσεως.[g]αὐτοῦ‖ με-
[2]translated [3]him [1]God; for before his translation he has
μαρτύρηται [h]εὐηρεστηκέναι‖ τῷ θεῷ. 6 χωρὶς.δὲ πίστεως
been borne witness to to have well pleased God. But apart from faith
ἀδύνατον εὐαρεστῆσαι· πιστεῦσαι.γὰρ δεῖ τὸν
[it is] impossible to well please [him]. For [8]to [9]believe [1]it [2]behoves [3]him [4]who
προσερχόμενον [i]τῷ‖ θεῷ. ὅτι ἐστίν, καὶ τοῖς ἐκζητοῦσιν
[5]approaches [6]to [7]God, that he is, and [that] for those who seek [2]out
αὐτὸν μισθαποδότης γίνεται. 7 Πίστει χρηματισ-
[1]him a rewarder he becomes. By faith [2]having [3]been [4]divinely [5]in-
θεὶς Νῶε περὶ τῶν μηδέπω βλεπομένων, εὐλαβη-
structed [1]Noah concerning the things not yet seen, having been moved
θεὶς κατεσκεύασεν κιβωτὸν εἰς σωτηρίαν τοῦ οἴκου
with fear, prepared an ark for [the] salvation of [2]house
αὐτοῦ· δι' ἧς κατέκρινεν τὸν κόσμον, καὶ τῆς κατὰ πίστιν
[1]his; by which he condemned the world, and of the [2]according [3]to [4]faith
δικαιοσύνης ἐγένετο κληρονόμος. 8 Πίστει [k]καλούμενος Ἀ-
[1]righteousness became heir. By faith being called A-
βραὰμ ὑπήκουσεν ἐξελθεῖν εἰς [l]τὸν‖ τόπον ὃν [m]ἤμελλεν‖
braham obeyed to go out into the place which he was about
λαμβάνειν εἰς κληρονομίαν, καὶ ἐξῆλθεν, μὴ ἐπιστάμενος ποῦ
to receive for an inheritance, and went out, not knowing where
ἔρχεται. 9 Πίστει παρῴκησεν εἰς [n]τὴν‖ γῆν τῆς ἐπαγγελίας,
he is going. By faith he sojourned in the land of the promise,
ὡς ἀλλοτρίαν, ἐν σκηναῖς κατοικήσας μετὰ Ἰσαὰκ καὶ
as [in] a strange [country], in tents having dwelt with Isaac and
Ἰακὼβ τῶν [o]συγκληρονόμων‖ τῆς ἐπαγγελίας τῆς αὐτῆς·
Jacob, the joint-heirs of the [2]promise [1]same;
10 ἐξεδέχετο.γὰρ τὴν τοὺς θεμελίους ἔχουσαν πόλιν, ἧς
for he was waiting for the [3]foundations [2]having [1]city, of which [the]
τεχνίτης καὶ δημιουργὸς ὁ θεός. 11 Πίστει καὶ αὐτὴ Σάῤῥα
artificer and constructor [is] God. By faith also [2]herself [1]Sarah
δύναμιν εἰς καταβολὴν σπέρματος ἔλαβεν, καὶ παρὰ καιρὸν
power for [the] conception of seed received, and beyond [2]age

XI. Now faith is the
substance of things
hoped for, the evi-
dence of things not
seen. 2 For by it the
elders obtained a good
report. 3 Through
faith we understand
that the worlds were
framed by the word of
God, so that things
which are seen were
not made of things
which do appear. 4 By
faith Abel offered un-
to God a more excel-
lent sacrifice than
Cain, by which he ob-
tained witness that he
was righteous, God
testifying of his gifts:
and by it he being dead
yet speaketh. 5 By
faith Enoch was trans-
lated that he should
not see death; and
was not found, be-
cause God had trans-
lated him: for before
his translation he had
this testimony, that
he pleased God. 6 But
without faith *it is* im-
possible to please *him*:
for he that cometh to
God must believe that
he is, and *that* he is a
rewarder of them that
diligently seek him.
7 By faith Noah, be-
ing warned of God of
things not seen as yet,
moved with fear, pre-
pared an ark to the
saving of his house;
by the which he con-
demned the world, and
became heir of the
righteousness which is
by faith. 8 By faith
Abraham, when he was
called to go out into a
place which he should
after receive for an in-
heritance, obeyed; and
he went out, not know-
ing whither he went.
9 By faith he sojourn-
ed in the land of pro-
mise, as *in* a strange
country, dwelling in
tabernacles with Isaac
and Jacob, the heirs
with him of the same
promise: 10 for he
looked for a city
which hath founda-
tions, whose builder
and maker *is* God.
11 Through faith also
Sara herself received
strength to conceive
seed, and was delivered
of a child when she

---

[c] τὸ βλεπόμενον that seen (*read* γεγ. [4]has [5]being) LTTrA. [d] τῷ θεῷ (*read* bearing witness by his gifts to God) LTr. [e] λαλεῖ GLTTrAW. [f] ηὑρίσκετο LTTrAW. [g] — αὐτοῦ (*read* the translation) LTTrA. [h] εὐαρεστηκέναι LA. [i] — τῷ T[Tr]. [k] + ὁ the [one] L[Tr]. [l] — τὸν (*read* a place) LTTrA. [m] ἔμελλεν LA. [n] — τὴν (*read* [the]) LTTrA. [o] συν- T.

was past age, because
she judged him faith-
ful who had promised.
12 Therefore sprang
there even of one, and
him as good as dead,
so many as the stars
of the sky in multi-
tude. and as the sand
which is by the sea
shore innumerable.

13 These all died in
faith, not having re-
ceived the promises,
but having seen them
afar off, and were per-
suaded of *them*, and
embraced *them*, and
confessed that they
were strangers and
pilgrims on the earth.
14 For they that say
such things declare
plainly that they seek
a country. 15 And
truly, if they had been
mindful of that *coun-
try* from whence they
came out, they might
have had opportunity
to have returned.
16 But now they desire
a better *country*, that
is, an heavenly: where-
fore God is not a-
shamed to be called
their God: for he hath
prepared for them a
city.

17 By faith Abra-
ham, when he was
tried, offered up Isaac:
and he that had re-
ceived the promises of-
fered up his only be-
gotten *son*, 18 of whom
it was said, That in
Isaac shall thy seed
be called: 19 account-
ing that God *was*
able to raise *him* up,
even from the dead;
from whence also he
received him in a
figure. 20 By faith
Isaac blessed Jacob
and Esau concerning
things to come. 21 By
faith Jacob, when he
was a dying, blessed
both the sons of Jo-
seph; and worshipped,
leaning upon the top
of his staff. 22 By
faith Joseph, when he
died, made mention of
the departing of the
children of Israel; and
gave commandment
concerning his bones.
23 By faith Moses,
when he was born, was

ἡλικίας [p]ἔτεκεν,‖ ἐπεὶ πιστὸν ἡγήσατο τὸν ἐπαγγειλάμενον.
[1]seasonable gave birth; since faithful she esteemed him who promised.
12 διὸ καὶ ἀφ' ἑνὸς [q]ἐγεννήθησαν,‖ καὶ.ταῦτα νενεκρω-
Wherefore also from one were born, and that too of [one] having
μένου, καθὼς τὰ ἄστρα τοῦ οὐρανοῦ τῷ πλήθει, καὶ [r]ὡσεὶ‖
become dead, even as the stars of the heaven in multitude, and as
ἄμμος ἡ παρὰ τὸ χεῖλος τῆς θαλάσσης ἡ ἀναρίθμητος.
[3]sand [4]which [[5]is] [6]by [7]the [8]shore [9]of [10]the [11]sea [1]the [2]countless.

13 Κατὰ πίστιν ἀπέθανον οὗτοι πάντες, μὴ [s]λαβόντες‖ τὰς
In faith [3]died [2]these [1]all, not having received the
ἐπαγγελίας, ἀλλὰ πόῤῥωθεν αὐτὰς ἰδόντες, [t]καὶ πεισθέν-
promises, but from afar them having seen, and having been per-
τες,‖ καὶ ἀσπασάμενοι, καὶ ὁμολογήσαντες ὅτι ξένοι καὶ
suaded, and having embraced [them], and having confessed that strangers and
παρεπίδημοί εἰσιν ἐπὶ τῆς γῆς. 14 οἱ.γὰρ τοιαῦτα λέ-
sojourners they are on the earth. For they who such things
γοντες, ἐμφανίζουσιν ὅτι πατρίδα ἐπιζητοῦσιν. 15 καὶ.εἰ
say, make manifest that [their] own country they are seeking. And if
μὲν ἐκείνης [v]ἐμνημόνευον‖ ἀφ' ἧς [w]ἐξῆλθον,‖ εἶ-
indeed [4]that [1]they [2]were [3]remembering from whence they came out, they might
χον.ἂν καιρὸν ἀνακάμψαι· 16 [x]νυνὶ‖.δὲ κρείττονος ὀρέ-
have had opportunity to have returned; but now a better they stretch
γονται, [y]τουτέστιν,‖ ἐπουρανίου· διὸ οὐκ.ἐπαισχύνεται
forward to, that is, a heavenly; wherefore [2]is [3]not [4]ashamed [5]of
αὐτοὺς ὁ θεός, θεὸς ἐπικαλεῖσθαι αὐτῶν· ἡτοίμασεν.γὰρ αὐτοῖς
[6]them [1]God. [11]God [7]to [8]be [9]called [10]their; for he prepared for them
πόλιν.
a city.

17 Πίστει προσενήνοχεν Ἀβραὰμ τὸν Ἰσαὰκ πειραζόμενος,
By faith [4]has [5]offered [6]up [1]Abraham [7]Isaac [2]being [3]tried,
καὶ τὸν.μονογενῆ προσέφερεν ὁ τὰς ἐπαγγελίας ἀνα-
and [[9]his] [10]only-begotten [6]was [7]offering [8]up [1]he [2]who [4]the [5]promises [3]ac-
δεξάμενος, 18 πρὸς ὃν ἐλαλήθη, Ὅτι ἐν Ἰσαὰκ κληθήσεταί
cepted, as to whom it was said, In Isaac shall be called
σοι σπέρμα· 19 λογισάμενος ὅτι καὶ ἐκ νεκρῶν
thy seed; reckoning that even from among [the] dead
[z]ἐγείρειν δυνατὸς‖ ὁ θεός, ὅθεν αὐτὸν καὶ ἐν παραβολῇ
[4]to [5]raise [3]able [[2]was] [1]God, whence him also in a simile
ἐκομίσατο. 20 Πίστει [a] περὶ μελλόντων [b]εὐλόγησεν‖ Ἰσαὰκ
he received. By faith concerning things coming [2]blessed [1]Isaac
τὸν Ἰακὼβ καὶ τὸν Ἡσαῦ. 21 Πίστει Ἰακὼβ ἀποθνήσκων
Jacob and Esau. By faith Jacob dying
ἕκαστον τῶν υἱῶν Ἰωσὴφ [b]εὐλόγησεν‖ καὶ προσεκύνησεν
[2]each [3]of [4]the [5]sons [6]of [7]Joseph [1]blessed and worshipped
ἐπὶ τὸ ἄκρον τῆς.ῥάβδου.αὐτοῦ. 22 Πίστει Ἰωσὴφ τελευτῶν
on the top of his staff. By faith Joseph, dying,
περὶ τῆς ἐξόδου τῶν υἱῶν Ἰσραὴλ ἐμνημόνευσεν, καὶ
concerning the going forth of the sons of Israel made mention, and
περὶ τῶν.ὀστέων.αὐτοῦ ἐνετείλατο.
concerning his bones gave command.
23 Πίστει [c]Μωσῆς‖ γεννηθεὶς ἐκρύβη τρίμηνον ὑπὸ
By faith Moses, having been born, was hid three months by

---

p — ἔτεκεν (*read* and [that] beyond a seasonable age) GLTTrA. q ἐγενήθησαν LA. r ὡς ἡ GLTTrAW. s προσδεξάμενοι L; κομισάμενοι TTr. t — καὶ πεισθέντες GLTTrAW. v μνημονεύουσιν they are mindful TTr. w ἐξέβησαν they went out LTTrAW. x νῦν GLTTrAW. y τοῦτ' ἔστιν GT. z ἐγεῖραι δύναται is able to raise L. a + καὶ also L[Tr]AW. b ηὐλόγησεν LA. c Μωϋσῆς GLTTrAW.

τῶν.πατέρων.αὐτοῦ διότι εἶδον ἀστεῖον τὸ παιδίον· καὶ
his parents because they saw [4]beautiful [1]the [2]little [3]child; and
οὐκ.ἐφοβήθησαν τὸ [d]διάταγμα‖ τοῦ βασιλέως. 24 Πίστει
did not fear the injunction of the king. By faith
[e]Μωσῆς‖ μέγας γενόμενος ἠρνήσατο λέγεσθαι υἱὸς θυγατρὸς
Moses, great having become, refused to be called son of [2]daughter
Φαραώ, 25 μᾶλλον ἑλόμενος [f]συγκακουχεῖσθαι‖ τῷ λαῷ
[1]Pharaoh's; [5]rather [3]having [4]chosen to suffer affliction with the people
τοῦ θεοῦ, ἢ πρόσκαιρον ἔχειν ἁμαρτίας ἀπόλαυσιν·
of God, than [[3]the] [4]temporary [1]to [2]have [6]of [7]sin [5]enjoyment;
26 μείζονα πλοῦτον ἡγησάμενος τῶν [g]ἐν‖ [h]Αἰγύπτῳ‖ θη-
greater riches having esteemed [6]than [7]the [9]in [10]Egypt [8]trea-
σαυρῶν τὸν ὀνειδισμὸν τοῦ χριστοῦ· ἀπέβλεπεν.γὰρ εἰς τὴν
sures [1]the [2]reproach [3]of [4]the [5]Christ; for he had respect to the
μισθαποδοσίαν. 27 Πίστει κατέλιπεν Αἴγυπτον, μὴ φοβηθεὶς
recompense. By faith he left Egypt, not having feared
τὸν θυμὸν τοῦ βασιλέως· τὸν.γὰρ ἀόρατον ὡς ὁρῶν
the indignation of the king; for [3]the [4]invisible [[5]one] [1]as [2]seeing
ἐκαρτέρησεν. 28 Πίστει πεποίηκεν τὸ πάσχα καὶ τὴν πρόσ-
he persevered. By faith he has kept the passover and the affu-
χυσιν τοῦ αἵματος, ἵνα.μὴ ὁ.[i]ὀλοθρεύων‖ τὰ πρωτότοκα θί-
sion of the blood, lest the destroyer of the firstborn [ones] might
γῃ αὐτῶν. 29 Πίστει διέβησαν τὴν ἐρυθρὰν θάλασσαν
touch them. By faith they passed through the Red Sea
ὡς διὰ ξηρᾶς[k]. ἧς πεῖραν.λαβόντες οἱ Αἰγύπτιοι
as through dry [land]; of which [3]having [4]made [5]trial [1]the [2]Egyptians
κατεπόθησαν. 30 Πίστει τὰ τείχη [l]Ἱεριχὼ‖ [m]ἔπεσεν‖, κυ-
were swallowed up. By faith the walls of Jericho fell, having
κλωθέντα ἐπὶ ἑπτὰ ἡμέρας. 31 Πίστει Ῥαὰβ ἡ πόρνη οὐ
been encircled for seven days. By faith Rahab the harlot [2]not
συναπώλετο τοῖς ἀπειθήσασιν, δεξαμένη τοὺς κατασκό-
[1]did [3]perish [4]with those who disobeyed, having received the spies
πους μετ' εἰρήνης.
with peace.

32 Καὶ τί ἔτι λέγω; ἐπιλείψει.[n]γάρ με‖ διηγούμενον ὁ
And what more do I say? For [3]will [4]fail [5]me [6]relating [1]the
χρόνος περὶ Γεδεών, [o]Βαράκ [p]τε καὶ‖ Σαμψὼν [q]καὶ‖ Ἰεφθάε,
[2]time of Gedeon, Barak also and Sampson and Jephthae,
[r]Δαβὶδ‖ τε καὶ Σαμουὴλ καὶ τῶν προφητῶν· 33 οἳ διὰ πίστεως
David also and Samuel and of the prophets: who by faith
κατηγωνίσαντο βασιλείας, [s]εἰργάσαντο‖ δικαιοσύνην, ἐπέτυχον
overcame kingdoms, wrought righteousness, obtained
ἐπαγγελιῶν, ἔφραξαν στόματα λεόντων, 34 ἔσβεσαν δύναμιν
promises, stopped mouths of lions, quenched [the] power
πυρός, ἔφυγον στόματα [t]μαχαίρας,‖ [v]ἐνεδυναμώθησαν‖ ἀπὸ
of fire, escaped [the] mouths of [the] sword, acquired strength out of
ἀσθενείας, ἐγενήθησαν ἰσχυροὶ ἐν πολέμῳ, παρεμβολὰς
weakness, became mighty in war, [[2]the] [3]armies
ἔκλιναν ἀλλοτρίων· 35 ἔλαβον [w]γυναῖκες‖ ἐξ ἀνα-
[1]made [6]to [7]give [8]way [4]of [5]strangers. [10]Received [9]women by resur-
στάσεως τοὺς.νεκροὺς.αὐτῶν· ἄλλοι.δὲ ἐτυμπανίσθησαν, οὐ
rection their dead; and others were tortured, not

hid three months of his parents, because they saw *he was* a proper child; and they were not afraid of the king's commandment. 24 By faith Moses, when he was come to years, refused to be called the son of Pharaoh's daughter; 25 choosing rather to suffer affliction with the people of God, than to enjoy the pleasures of sin for a season; 26 esteeming the reproach of Christ greater riches than the treasures in Egypt: for he had respect unto the recompence of the reward. 27 By faith he forsook Egypt, not fearing the wrath of the king: for he endured, as seeing him who is invisible. 28 Through faith he kept the passover, and the sprinkling of blood, lest he that destroyed the firstborn should touch them. 29 By faith they passed through the Red sea as by dry *land*: which the Egyptians assaying to do were drowned. 30 By faith the walls of Jericho fell down, after they were compassed about seven days. 31 By faith the harlot Rahab perished not with them that believed not, when she had received the spies with peace.

32 And what shall I more say? for the time would fail me to tell of Gedeon, and *of* Barak, and *of* Samson, and *of* Jephthae; *of* David also, and Samuel, and *of* the prophets: 33 who through faith subdued kingdoms, wrought righteousness, obtained promises, stopped the mouths of lions, 34 quenched the violence of fire, escaped the edge of the sword, out of weakness were made strong, waxed valiant in fight, turned to flight the armies of the aliens. 35 Women received their dead raised to life a-

[d] δόγμα decree L. [e] Μωϋσῆς GLTTrAW. [f] συν- T. [g] — ἐν GTTrAW. [h] Αἰγύπτου of Egypt GLTTrAW. [i] ὀλεθρεύων LA. [k] + γῆς land LTTrAW. [l] Ἱερειχὼ T. [m] ἔπεσαν LTTrA. [n] με γὰρ LTTrA. [o] + καὶ and W. [p] — τε καὶ LTTrW. [q] — καὶ LTTr. [r] Δαυείδ LTTrA; Δαυὶδ GW. [s] ἠργάσαντο TTr. [t] μαχαίρης LTTrA. [v] ἐδυναμώθησαν were strengthened LTTr. [w] γυναικας (*read* they received by resurrection women [that is] their dead L.

gain: and others were tortured, not accepting deliverance; that they might obtain a better resurrection: 36 and others had trial of *cruel* mockings and scourgings, yea, moreover of bonds and imprisonment: 37 they were stoned, they were sawn asunder, were tempted, were slain with the sword: they wandered about in sheepskins and goatskins; being destitute, afflicted, tormented; 38 (of whom the world was not worthy:) they wandered in deserts, and *in* mountains, and *in* dens and caves of the earth. 39 And these all, having obtained a good report through faith, received not the promise: 40 God having provided some better thing for us, that they without us should not be made perfect.

XII. Wherefore seeing we also are compassed about with so great a cloud of witnesses, let us lay aside every weight, and the sin which doth so easily beset *us*, and let us run with patience the race that is set before us, 2 looking unto Jesus the author and finisher of *our* faith; who for the joy that was set before him endured the cross, despising the shame, and is set down at the right hand of the throne of God. 3 For consider him that endured such contradiction of sinners against himself, lest ye be wearied and faint in your minds. 4 Ye have not yet resisted unto blood, striving against sin. 5 And ye have forgotten the exhortation which speaketh unto you as unto children, My son, despise not thou the chastening of the Lord, nor faint when thou art rebuked of him: 6 for whom the Lord loveth he chasteneth, and scourgeth every son whom he receiveth. 7 If ye endure chastening, God dealeth

προσδεξάμενοι τὴν ἀπολύτρωσιν, ἵνα κρείττονος ἀναστάσεως
having accepted redemption, that a better resurrection
τύχωσιν· 36 ἕτεροι.δὲ ἐμπαιγμῶν καὶ μαστίγων πεῖραν
they might obtain; and others [2]of [3]mockings [4]and [5]of [6]scourgings [1]trial
ἔλαβον, ἔτι.δὲ δεσμῶν καὶ φυλακῆς· 37 ἐλιθάσθησαν,
received, yea, moreover, of bonds and of imprisonment. They were stoned,
[x]ἐπρίσθησαν, ἐπειράσθησαν,‖ ἐν φόνῳ [y]μαχαίρας‖ ἀπέθα-
were sawn asunder, were tempted, by slaughter of [the] sword they
νον· περιῆλθον ἐν μηλωταῖς, ἐν αἰγείοις δέρμασιν, ὑστερού-
died; they wandered in sheep-skins, in goats' skins, being des-
μενοι, θλιβόμενοι, κακουχούμενοι, 38 ὧν οὐκ.ἦν ἄξιος ὁ
titute, being oppressed, being evil treated, (of whom [3]was [4]not [5]worthy [1]the
κόσμος· [z]ἐν‖ ἐρημίαις πλανώμενοι καὶ ὄρεσιν καὶ σπηλαίοις
[2]world,) in deserts wandering and in mountains and in caves
καὶ ταῖς ὀπαῖς τῆς γῆς. 39 Καὶ οὗτοι πάντες μαρτυρη-
and in the holes of the earth. And these all, having been borne
θέντες διὰ τῆς πίστεως, οὐκ.ἐκομίσαντο [a]τὴν ἐπαγγελίαν,‖
witness to through faith, did not receive the promise,
40 τοῦ θεοῦ περὶ ἡμῶν κρεῖττόν τι προβλεψαμένου, ἵνα μὴ
God for us [2]better [1]something having foreseen, that not
χωρὶς ἡμῶν τελειωθῶσιν.
apart from us they should be made perfect.

12 Τοιγαροῦν καὶ ἡμεῖς τοσοῦτον ἔχοντες περικείμενον
Therefore also we [2]so [3]great [1]having [8]encompassing
ἡμῖν νέφος μαρτύρων, ὄγκον ἀποθέμενοι πάντα καὶ
[9]us [4]a [5]cloud [6]of [7]witnesses, [14]weight [10]having [11]laid [12]aside [13]every and
τὴν εὐπερίστατον ἁμαρτίαν, δι' ὑπομονῆς τρέχωμεν τὸν
the easily-surrounding sin, with endurance we should run the
προκείμενον ἡμῖν ἀγῶνα, 2 ἀφορῶντες εἰς τὸν τῆς πίστεως
[2]lying [3]before [4]us [1]race, looking away to [5]the [6]of [7]faith
ἀρχηγὸν καὶ τελειωτὴν Ἰησοῦν, ὃς ἀντὶ τῆς προκει-
[3]leader [4]and [5]completer [1]Jesus: who in view of the [2]ly-
μένης αὐτῷ χαρᾶς ὑπέμεινεν σταυρόν, αἰσχύνης
ing [3]before [4]him [1]joy endured [the] cross, [the] shame
καταφρονήσας, ἐν.δεξιᾷ.τε τοῦ θρόνου τοῦ θεοῦ [b]ἐκάθι-
having despised, and at [the] right hand of the throne of God sat
σεν.‖ 3 ἀναλογίσασθε.γὰρ τὸν τοιαύτην ὑπομεμενηκότα
down. For consider well him who [3]so [4]great [1]has [2]endured
ὑπὸ τῶν ἁμαρτωλῶν εἰς [c]αὐτὸν‖ ἀντιλογίαν, ἵνα μὴ κά-
[6]from [7]sinners [8]against [9]himself [5]gainsaying, that [3]not [1]ye [2]be
μητε, ταῖς.ψυχαῖς.ὑμῶν ἐκλυόμενοι. 4 Οὔπω μέχρις αἵματος
[4]wearied, [6]in [7]your [8]souls [5]fainting. Not yet unto blood
ἀντικατέστητε πρὸς τὴν ἁμαρτίαν ἀνταγωνιζόμενοι, 5 καὶ
resisted ye [2]against [3]sin [1]wrestling, and
ἐκλέλησθε τῆς παρακλήσεως, ἥτις ὑμῖν ὡς υἱοῖς διαλέ-
ye have quite forgotten the exhortation, which to you, as to sons, he ad-
γεται·[d] Υἱέ.μου, μὴ.ὀλιγώρει [e]παιδείας‖ κυρίου, μηδὲ ἐκ-
dresses: My son, despise not [the] discipline of [the] Lord, nor
λύου ὑπ' αὐτοῦ ἐλεγχόμενος. 6 ὃν.γὰρ ἀγαπᾷ κύριος
faint, by him being reproved; for whom [3]loves [1]the [2]Lord
παιδεύει· μαστιγοῖ.δὲ πάντα υἱὸν ὃν παραδέχεται. 7 [f]Εἰ‖
he disciplines, and scourges every son whom he receives. If
[g]παιδείαν‖ ὑπομένετε, ὡς υἱοῖς ὑμῖν προσφέρεται
discipline ye endure, [6]as [7]with [8]sons [4]with [5]you [2]is [3]dealing

[x] ἐπειράσθησαν, ἐπρίσθησαν T. [y] μαχαίρης LTTrA. [z] ἐπὶ LTTrA. [a] τὰς ἐπαγγελίας the promises L. [b] κεκάθικεν has sat down GLTTrAW. [c] ἑαυτὸν LTTrA. [d] *Read the sentence as a question* L. [e] παιδίας T. [f] εἰς (*read* ye endure for discipline) LTTrA. [g] παιδίαν T.

ὁ θεός· τίς.γάρ [h]ἐστιν‖ υἱὸς ὃν οὐ.παιδεύει πατήρ;
[1]God; for who is [the] son whom [3]disciplines [4]not [[1]the] [2]Father?
8 εἰ.δὲ χωρίς ἐστε [i]παιδείας,‖ ἧς μέτοχοι γεγόνασιν πάν-
But if [3]without [1]ye [2]are discipline, of which [4]partakers [2]have [3]become [1]all,
τες, ἄρα νόθοι [j]ἐστὲ καὶ οὐχ υἱοί.‖ 9 εἶτα τοὺς μὲν τῆς σαρκὸς
then bastards ye are and not sons. Moreover the [4]flesh
ἡμῶν πατέρας εἴχομεν παιδευτάς, καὶ [k]ἐνετρε-
[2]of [3]our [1]fathers we have had [as] those who discipline [us], and we respected
πόμεθα·‖ οὐ [l]πολλῷ‖ μᾶλλον ὑποταγησόμεθα τῷ πατρὶ
[them]; [2]not [4]much [5]rather [1]shall [3]we be in subjection to the Father
τῶν πνευμάτων, καὶ ζήσομεν; 10 οἱ.μὲν.γὰρ πρὸς ὀλίγας
of spirits, and shall live? For they indeed for a few
ἡμέρας κατὰ τὸ δοκοῦν αὐτοῖς ἐπαίδευον· ὁ.δὲ ἐπὶ
days according to that which seemed good to them disciplined; but he for
τὸ συμφέρον, εἰς τὸ μεταλαβεῖν τῆς.ἁγιότητος.αὐτοῦ. 11 πᾶσα
profit, for [us] to partake of his holiness. [2]Any
(*lit.* every)
[m]δὲ παιδεία‖ πρὸς μὲν τὸ.παρὸν οὐ.δοκεῖ χαρᾶς εἶναι,
[1]but discipline for the present seems not [[3]matter] [4]of [5]joy [1]to [2]be,
ἀλλὰ λύπης· ὕστερον.δὲ καρπὸν εἰρηνικὸν τοῖς δι' αὐτῆς
but of grief; but afterwards [3]fruit [2]peaceable [6]to [7]those [11]by [12]it
γεγυμνασμένοις ἀποδίδωσιν δικαιοσύνης.
[8]having [9]been [10]exercised [1]renders [4]of [5]righteousness.

12 Διὸ τὰς παρειμένας χεῖρας καὶ τὰ παραλελυμένα γόνατα
Wherefore the [2]hanging [3]down [1]hands and the enfeebled knees
ἀνορθώσατε 13 καὶ τροχιὰς ὀρθὰς [n]ποιήσατε‖ τοῖς.ποσὶν.ὑμῶν,
lift up; and [2]paths [1]straight make for your feet,
ἵνα.μὴ τὸ χωλὸν ἐκτραπῇ, ἰαθῇ.δὲ
lest that which [is] lame be turned aside; but that [2]it [3]may [4]be [5]healed
μᾶλλον. 14 εἰρήνην διώκετε μετὰ πάντων, καὶ τὸν ἁγιασμόν,
[1]rather. Peace pursue with all, and sanctification,
οὗ χωρὶς οὐδεὶς ὄψεται τὸν κύριον· 15 ἐπισκοποῦντες μή
[3]which [1]apart [2]from no one shall see the Lord; looking diligently lest
τις ὑστερῶν ἀπὸ τῆς χάριτος τοῦ θεοῦ· μή τις ῥίζα πικρίας
any lack the grace of God; lest any root of bitterness
ἄνω φύουσα ἐνοχλῇ, καὶ [o]διὰ ταύτης‖ μιανθῶσιν [p]
[2]up [1]springing should trouble [you], and by this be defiled
πολλοί· 16 μή τις πόρνος ἢ βέβηλος, ὡς Ἡσαῦ, ὃς
many; lest [there be] any fornicator or profane person, as Esau, who
ἀντὶ βρώσεως μιᾶς [q]ἀπέδοτο‖ τὰ πρωτοτόκια [r]αὐτοῦ.‖ 17 ἴστε
for [2]meal [1]one sold [2]birthright [1]his; [4]ye [5]know
γὰρ ὅτι καὶ μετέπειτα θέλων κληρονομῆσαι τὴν εὐλογίαν ἀπε-
[3]for that also afterwards, wishing to inherit the blessing, he was
δοκιμάσθη· μετανοίας.γὰρ τόπον οὐχ.εὗρεν, καίπερ μετὰ δακ-
rejected, for [2]of [3]repentance [1]place he found not, although with
ρύων ἐκζητήσας αὐτήν.
tears having earnestly sought it.

18 Οὐ.γὰρ προσεληλύθατε ψηλαφωμένῳ [s]ὄρει,‖ καὶ
For [3]not [1]ye [2]have come to [3]being [4]touched [[1]the] [2]mount and
κεκαυμένῳ πυρί, καὶ γνόφῳ, καὶ [t]σκότῳ,‖ καὶ θυέλλῃ,
having been kindled with fire, and to obscurity, and to darkness, and to tempest,
19 καὶ σάλπιγγος ἤχῳ, καὶ φωνῇ ῥημάτων, ἧς οἱ
and [2]trumpet's [1]to sound, and to voice of words; which [voice] they that

with you as with sons;
for what son is he
whom the father chas-
teneth not? 8 But if
ye be without chastise-
ment, whereof all are
partakers, then are ye
bastards, and not sons.
9 Furthermore we have
had fathers of our
flesh which corrected
us, and we gave *them*
reverence: shall we
not much rather be in
subjection unto the
Father of spirits, and
live? 10 For they ve-
rily for a few days
chastened *us* after
their own pleasure;
but he for *our* profit,
that *we* might be par-
takers of his holiness.
11 Now no chastening
for the present seem-
eth to be joyous, but
grievous: nevertheless
afterward it yieldeth
the peaceable fruit of
righteousness unto
them which are ex-
ercised thereby.

12 Wherefore lift up
the hands which hang
down, and the feeble
knees; 13 and make
straight paths for your
feet, lest that which is
lame be turned out
of the way; but let
it rather be healed.
14 Follow peace with
all *men*, and holiness,
without which no man
shall see the Lord:
15 looking diligently
lest any man fail of
the grace of God; lest
any root of bitterness
springing up trouble
you, and thereby many
be defiled; 16 lest there
be any fornicator, or
profane person, as E-
sau, who for one mor-
sel of meat sold his
birthright. 17 For ye
know how that after-
ward, when he would
have inherited the
blessing, he was re-
jected: for he found
no place of repentance,
though he sought it
carefully with tears.

18 For ye are not
come unto the mount
that might be touched,
and that burned with
fire, nor unto black-
ness, and darkness,
and tempest, 19 and
the sound of a trumpet,
and the voice of words;

---

[h] — ἐστιν LTTr[A]. [i] παιδίας T. [j] καὶ οὐχ υἱοί ἐστε LTTrA. [k] ἐντρεπόμεθα we respect E. [l] πολὺ LTTrA. [m] μὲν παιδία discipline indeed T. [n] ποιεῖτε TTr. [o] δι' αὐτῆς through it L. [p] + οἱ the LTTrAW. [q] ἀπέδετο LA. [r] ἑαυτοῦ his own LTTrA. [s] — ὄρει (*read* [that] being touched) LTTrA. [t] ζόφῳ LTTrAW.

which *voice* they that heard intreated that the word should not be spoken to them any more: 20 (for they could not endure that which was commanded, And if so much as a beast touch the mountain, it shall be stoned, or thrust through with a dart: 21 and so terrible was the sight, *that* Moses said, I exceedingly fear and quake:) 22 but ye are come unto mount Sion, and unto the city of the living God, the heavenly Jerusalem, and to an innumerable company of angels, 23 to the general assembly and church of the firstborn, which are written in heaven, and to God the Judge of all, and to the spirits of just men made perfect, 24 and to Jesus the mediator of the new covenant, and to the blood of sprinkling, that speaketh better things than *that of* Abel. 25 See that ye refuse not him that speaketh. For if they escaped not who refused him that spake on earth, much more *shall not* we *escape*, if we turn away from him that *speaketh* from heaven: 26 whose voice then shook the earth: but now he hath promised, saying, Yet once more I shake not the earth only, but also heaven. 27 And this *word*, Yet once more, signifieth the removing of those things that are shaken, as of things that are made, that those things which cannot be shaken may remain. 28 Wherefore we receiving a kingdom which cannot be moved, let us have grace, whereby we may serve God acceptably with reverence and godly fear: 29 for our God *is* a consuming fire.

XIII. Let brotherly love continue. 2 Be not forgetful to entertain strangers: for thereby some have entertained angels una-

ἀκούσαντες παρῃτήσαντο μὴ προστεθῆναι αὐτοῖς
heard excused themselves [asking] [3]not [4]to [5]be [6]addressed [7]to [8]them [[1]the]

λόγον· 20 οὐκ.ἔφερον.γὰρ τὸ διαστελλόμενον, Κἂν θηρίον
[2]word; (for they could not bear that [which] was commanded: And if a beast

θίγῃ τοῦ ὄρους λιθοβοληθήσεται, [u]ἢ βολίδι κατατοξευ-
should touch the mountain, it shall be stoned, or with a dart shot

θήσεται·‖ 21 καί, οὕτως φοβερὸν ἦν τὸ φανταζόμενον,
through; and, so fearful was the spectacle [that]

[v]Μωσῆς‖ εἶπεν, Ἔκφοβός εἰμι καὶ ἔντρομος· 22 ἀλλὰ προσ-
Moses said, [3]greatly [4]afraid [1]I [2]am and trembling:) but ye have

εληλύθατε Σιὼν ὄρει, καὶ πόλει θεοῦ ζῶντος, Ἱερου-
come to [2]Sion [1]mount; and [the] city of [3]God [[1]the] [2]living, [5]Jeru-

σαλὴμ ἐπουρανίῳ, καὶ μυριάσιν [w]ἀγγέλων 23 πανηγύρει,
salem [4]heavenly; and to myriads of angels, [the] universal gathering;

καὶ ἐκκλησίᾳ πρωτοτόκων [x]ἐν οὐρανοῖς ἀπογεγραμ-
and to [the] assembly of [the] firstborn [ones] in [the] heavens regis-

μένων,‖ καὶ κριτῇ θεῷ πάντων, καὶ πνεύμασιν δικαίων
tered; and to [[2]the] [3]judge [1]God of all; and to [the] spirits of [the] just

τετελειωμένων, 24 καὶ διαθήκης νέας μεσίτῃ Ἰησοῦ, καὶ
[who] have been perfected; and [4]of [5]a [7]covenant [6]fresh [3]mediator [1]to [2]Jesus; and

αἵματι ῥαντισμοῦ [y]κρείττονα‖ λαλοῦντι παρὰ τὸν Ἄβελ.
to [the] blood of sprinkling, [2]better [3]things [1]speaking than Abel.

25 Βλέπετε μὴ.παραιτήσησθε τὸν λαλοῦντα. εἰ.γὰρ ἐκεῖνοι
Take heed ye refuse not him who speaks. For if they

οὐκ.[z]ἔφυγον,‖ [a]τὸν‖ ἐπὶ [b]τῆς‖ γῆς παραιτησάμενοι[a] χρη-
escaped not, [3]him [4]that [5]on [6]the [7]earth [[1]who] [2]refused divine-

ματίζοντα, [c]πολλῷ‖.μᾶλλον ἡμεῖς οἱ τὸν ἀπ' οὐρανῶν
ly instructed [them], much more we who [4]him [5]from [[6]the] [7]heavens

ἀποστρεφόμενοι, 26 οὗ ἡ φωνὴ τὴν γῆν ἐσάλευσεν τότε,
[1]turn [2]away [3]from! whose voice [2]the [3]earth [1]shook then;

νῦν.δὲ ἐπήγγελται, λέγων, Ἔτι ἅπαξ ἐγὼ [d]σείω‖ οὐ μόνον
but now he has promised, saying, Yet once I shake not only

τὴν γῆν, ἀλλὰ καὶ τὸν οὐρανόν. 27 Τὸ.δὲ Ἔτι.ἅπαξ, δηλοῖ
the earth, but also the heaven. But the Yet once, signifies

[e]τῶν σαλευομένων τὴν‖ μετάθεσιν, ὡς πεποιημένων,
[3]of [4]the [[5]things] [6]shaken [1]the [2]removing, as having been made,

ἵνα μείνῃ τὰ μὴ.σαλευόμενα. 28 διὸ βασιλείαν
that [5]may [6]remain [1]the [[2]things] [3]not [4]shaken. Wherefore a kingdom

ἀσάλευτον παραλαμβάνοντες, ἔχωμεν χάριν, δι' ἧς
not to be shaken receiving, may we have grace, by which

λατρεύωμεν εὐαρέστως τῷ θεῷ μετὰ [f]αἰδοῦς καὶ εὐλαβείας.‖
we may serve [2]well [3]pleasingly [1]God with reverence and fear.

29 καὶ.γὰρ ὁ.θεὸς.ἡμῶν πῦρ καταναλίσκον.
For also our God [is] a [2]fire [1]consuming.

13 Ἡ φιλαδελφία μενέτω. 2 τῆς φιλοξενίας μὴ ἐπιλαν-
[2]Brotherly [3]love [1]let abide; of hospitality [2]not [1]be for-

θάνεσθε· διὰ.ταύτης.γὰρ ἔλαθόν τινες ξενίσαντες ἀγγέλους.
getful; for by this unawares some entertained angels.

3 μιμνήσκεσθε τῶν δεσμίων, ὡς συνδεδεμένοι· τῶν κακου-
Be mindful of prisoners, as bound with [them]; those being

χουμένων, ὡς καὶ αὐτοὶ ὄντες ἐν σώματι. 4 τίμιος
evil-treated, as also yourselves being in [the] body. Honourable [let]

---

[u] — ἢ βολίδι κατατοξευθήσεται GLTTrAW. [v] Μωϋσῆς GLTTrAW. [w] *Separate* myriads *from* of angels *by a comma* GLTTrA. [x] ἀπογεγραμμένων ἐν οὐρανοῖς GLTTrAW. [y] κρεῖττον a better thing GLTTrAW. [z] ἐξέφυγον LTTrA. [a] τὸν *placed after* παραιτησάμενοι LTTrA. [b] — τῆς GLTTrAW. [c] πολὺ LTTrA. [d] σείσω will shake LTTrA. [e] τὴν τῶν σαλευομένων LTTrA. [f] εὐλαβείας καὶ δέους fear and awe LTTrA.

ὁ γάμος ἐν πᾶσιν, καὶ ἡ κοίτη ἀμίαντος· πόρ-
marriage [be held] in every [way], and the bed [be] undefiled; [2]for-
νους [g]δὲ‖ καὶ μοιχοὺς κρινεῖ ὁ θεός. 5 ἀφιλάργυρος
nicators [1]but and adulterers [2]will [3]judge [1]God. Without love of money [let
ὁ τρόπος· ἀρκούμενοι τοῖς.παροῦσιν· αὐτὸς
your] manner of life [be], satisfied with present [circumstances]; [2]he
γὰρ εἴρηκεν, Οὐ.μή σε ἀνῶ, οὐδ᾽.οὐ.μή σε [h]ἐγκαταλίπω.‖
[1]for has said, In no wise thee will I leave, nor in any wise thee will I forsake.
6 ὥστε θαῤῥοῦντας.ἡμᾶς.λέγειν, Κύριος ἐμοὶ βοηθός,
So that we may boldly say, [The] Lord [is] to me a helper,
[i]καὶ‖ οὐ.φοβηθήσομαι·[k] τί ποιήσει μοι ἄνθρωπος;
and I will not be afraid: what shall [2]do [3]to [4]me [1]man?
7 Μνημονεύετε τῶν.ἡγουμένων.ὑμῶν, οἵτινες ἐλάλησαν
Remember your leaders, who spoke
ὑμῖν τὸν λόγον τοῦ θεοῦ· ὧν ἀναθεωροῦντες τὴν ἔκβασιν
to you the word of God; of whom, considering the issue
τῆς.ἀναστροφῆς, μιμεῖσθε τὴν.πίστιν. 8 Ἰησοῦς χριστὸς
of [their] conduct, imitate [their] faith. Jesus Christ
[l]χθὲς‖ καὶ σήμερον ὁ αὐτός, καὶ εἰς τοὺς αἰῶνας. 9 διδα-
yesterday and to-day [is] the same, and to the ages. With
χαῖς ποικίλαις καὶ ξέναις μὴ.[m]περιφέρεσθε·‖ καλὸν.γὰρ
[4]teachings [1]various [2]and [3]strange be not carried about; for [it is] good [for]
χάριτι βεβαιοῦσθαι τὴν καρδίαν, οὐ βρώμασιν, ἐν οἷς οὐκ
[6]with [7]grace [3]to [4]be [5]confirmed [1]the [2]heart. not meats; in which [2]not
ὠφελήθησαν οἱ [n]περιπατήσαντες.‖ 10 Ἔχομεν θυσια-
[1]were [3]profited those who walked [therein]. We have an al-
στήριον ἐξ οὗ φαγεῖν οὐκ.ἔχουσιν ἐξουσίαν οἱ τῇ σκηνῇ
tar of which to eat they have not authority who the tabernacle
λατρεύοντες. 11 ὧν.γὰρ εἰσφέρεται ζώων τὸ αἷμα
serve; for of those [2]whose [4]is [5]brought [1]animals [3]blood [as sacri-
[o]περὶ ἁμαρτίας‖ εἰς τὰ ἅγια [p] διὰ τοῦ ἀρχιερέως, τούτων
fices] for sin into the holies by the high priest, of these
τὰ σώματα κατακαίεται ἔξω τῆς παρεμβολῆς· 12 διὸ καὶ
the bodies are burned outside the camp. Wherefore also
Ἰησοῦς, ἵνα ἁγιάσῃ διὰ τοῦ.ἰδίου αἵματος τὸν λαόν,
Jesus, that he might sanctify by his own blood the people,
ἔξω τῆς πύλης ἔπαθεν. 13 τοίνυν ἐξερχώμεθα πρὸς αὐτὸν
outside the gate suffered: therefore we should go forth to him
ἔξω τῆς παρεμβολῆς, τὸν.ὀνειδισμὸν.αὐτοῦ φέροντες· 14 οὐ
outside the camp, his reproach bearing; [4]not
γὰρ ἔχομεν ὧδε μένουσαν πόλιν, ἀλλὰ τὴν μέλλουσαν ἐπι-
[1]for [2]we [3]have here an abiding city, but the coming one we are
ζητοῦμεν. 15 Δι᾽ αὐτοῦ [q]οὖν‖ ἀναφέρωμεν θυσίαν αἰνέσεως
seeking for. By him therefore we should offer [the] sacrifice of praise
[r]διαπαντὸς‖ τῷ θεῷ, [s]τουτέστιν,‖ καρπὸν χειλέων ὁμολογούν-
continually to God, that is, fruit of [the] lips confess-
των τῷ.ὀνόματι.αὐτοῦ. 16 τῆς.δὲ.εὐποιΐας καὶ κοινωνίας
ing to his name. But of doing good and of communicating
μὴ.ἐπιλανθάνεσθε· τοιαύταις.γὰρ θυσίαις εὐαρεστεῖται ὁ θεός.
be not forgetful, for with such sacrifices is [2]well [3]pleased [1]God.
17 Πείθεσθε τοῖς.ἡγουμένοις.ὑμῶν, καὶ ὑπείκετε· αὐτοὶ.γὰρ
Obey your leaders, and be submissive: for they

wares. 3 Remember
them that are in bonds,
as bound with them;
and them which suffer
adversity, as being
yourselves also in the
body. 4 Marriage *is*
honourable in all, and
the bed undefiled: but
whoremongers and a-
dulterers God will
judge. 5 *Let your* con-
versation *be* without
covetousness; *and be*
content with such
things as ye have: for
he hath said, I will
never leave thee, nor
forsake thee. 6 So that
we may boldly say,
The Lord *is* my helper,
and I will not fear
what man shall do un-
to me.
7 Remember them
which have the rule
over you, who have
spoken unto you the
word of God: whose
faith follow, consider-
ing the end of *their*
conversation. 8 Jesus
Christ the same yester-
day, and to day, and
for ever. 9 Be not
carried about with di-
vers and strange doc-
trines. For *it is* a good
thing that the heart
be established with
grace; not with meats,
which have not profit-
ed them that have been
occupied therein. 10 We
have an altar, where-
of they have no right
to eat which serve the
tabernacle. 11 For the
bodies of those beasts,
whose blood is brought
into the sanctuary by
the high priest for sin,
are burned without
the camp. 12 Where-
fore Jesus also, that he
might sanctify the
people with his own
blood, suffered with-
out the gate. 13 Let
us go forth therefore
unto him without the
camp, bearing his re-
proach. 14 For here
have we no continuing
city, but we seek one
to come. 15 By him
therefore let us offer
the sacrifice of praise
to God continually,
that is, the fruit of *our*
lips giving thanks to
his name. 16 But to
do good and to com-
municate forget not:
for with such sacrifices

---

g γὰρ for LTTrA. h ἐγκαταλείπω do I forsake TA. i — καὶ [L]T[TrA]. k *Textus Receptus is punctuated as in Authorized version.* l ἐχθὲς LTTrAW. m παραφέρεσθε carried away GLTTrAW. n περιπατοῦντες walk LTTr. o — περὶ ἁμαρτίας LA. p + περὶ ἁμαρτίας for sin L. q [οὖν] Tr. r διὰ παντὸς LTrA. s τοῦτ᾽ ἔστιν GT.

God is well pleased.
17 Obey them that have
the rule over you, and
submit yourselves:
for they watch for
your souls, as they
that must give ac-
count, that they may
do it with joy, and not
with grief: for that *is*
unprofitable for you.
18 Pray for us: for
we trust we have a
good conscience, in all
things willing to live
honestly. 19 But I be-
seech *you* the rather to
do this, that I may be
restored to you the
sooner. 20 Now the God
of peace, that brought
again from the dead
our Lord Jesus, that
great Shepherd of
the sheep, through
the blood of the
everlasting covenant,
21 make you perfect in
every good work to do
his will, working in
you that which is well-
pleasing in his sight,
through Jesus Christ;
to whom *be* glory for
ever and ever. Amen.
22 And I beseech you,
brethren, suffer the
word of exhortation:
for I have written a
letter unto you in few
words.

23 Know ye that *our*
brother Timothy is set
at liberty; with whom,
if he come shortly, I
will see you. 24 Salute
all them that have the
rule over you, and all
the saints. They of
Italy salute you.
25 Grace *be* with you
all. Amen.

ἀγρυπνοῦσιν ὑπὲρ τῶν.ψυχῶν.ὑμῶν, ὡς λόγον ἀποδώσον-
watch for your souls, as [4]account [1]about [2]to [3]ren-
τες· ἵνα μετὰ χαρᾶς τοῦτο ποιῶσιν, καὶ μὴ στενάζοντες·
der; that with joy this they may do, and not groaning,
ἀλυσιτελὲς.γὰρ ὑμῖν τοῦτο. 18 Προσεύχεσθε περὶ
for unprofitable for you [would be], this. Pray for
ἡμῶν· [t]πεποίθαμεν‖.γάρ, ὅτι καλὴν συνείδησιν ἔχομεν, ἐν
us: for we are persuaded, that a good conscience we have, in
πᾶσιν καλῶς θέλοντες ἀναστρέφεσθαι· 19 περισσοτέρως.δὲ
all things [5]well [1]wishing [2]to [3]conduct [4]ourselves. But more abundantly
παρακαλῶ τοῦτο ποιῆσαι, ἵνα τάχιον ἀποκατασταθῶ
I exhort [you] this to do, that more quickly I may be restored
ὑμῖν. 20 Ὁ.δὲ θεὸς τῆς εἰρήνης, ὁ ἀναγαγὼν ἐκ
to you. And the God of peace, who brought again from among [the]
νεκρῶν τὸν ποιμένα τῶν προβάτων τὸν μέγαν ἐν
dead the Shepherd of the sheep the great [one] in [the power of
αἵματι διαθήκης αἰωνίου, τὸν.κύριον.ἡμῶν Ἰησοῦν,
the] blood of [the] [2]covenant [1]eternal, our Lord Jesus,
21 καταρτίσαι ὑμᾶς ἐν παντὶ [v]ἔργῳ‖ ἀγαθῷ, εἰς τὸ ποιῆσαι
perfect you in every [2]work [1]good, for to do
τὸ.θέλημα.αὐτοῦ, [w]ποιῶν ἐν [x]ὑμῖν‖ τὸ εὐάρεστον ἐνώ-
his will, doing in you that which [is] well pleasing be-
πιον αὐτοῦ, διὰ Ἰησοῦ χριστοῦ· ᾧ ἡ δόξα εἰς τοὺς
fore him, through Jesus Christ; to whom [be] glory to the
αἰῶνας τῶν αἰώνων. ἀμήν. 22 Παρακαλῶ.δὲ ὑμᾶς, ἀδελ-
ages of the ages. Amen. But I exhort you, breth-
φοί, [y]ἀνέχεσθε‖ τοῦ λόγου τῆς παρακλήσεως· καὶ.γὰρ διὰ
ren, bear the word of exhortation, for also in
βραχέων ἐπέστειλα ὑμῖν.
few words I wrote to you.

23 Γινώσκετε τὸν ἀδελφὸν [z] Τιμόθεον ἀπολελυμένον, μεθ'
Know ye the brother Timotheus has been released; with
οὗ, ἐὰν τάχιον ἔρχηται, ὄψομαι ὑμᾶς. 24 Ἀσπάσασθε
whom, if sooner he should come, I will see you. Salute
πάντας τοὺς.ἡγουμένους.ὑμῶν, καὶ πάντας τοὺς ἁγίους.
all your leaders, and all the saints.
ἀσπάζονται ὑμᾶς οἱ ἀπὸ τῆς Ἰταλίας. 25 ἡ χάρις μετὰ
[4]Salute [5]you [1]they [2]from [3]Italy. Grace [be] with
πάντων ὑμῶν. [a]ἀμήν.‖[a]
[2]all [1]you. Amen.

[b]Πρὸς Ἑβραίους ἐγράφη ἀπὸ τῆς Ἰταλίας, διὰ Τιμοθέου.‖
To [the] Hebrews written from Italy, by Timotheus.

---

[c]ΙΑΚΩΒΟΥ ΕΠΙΣΤΟΛΗ ΚΑΘΟΛΙΚΗ.‖
[4]OF [5]JAMES [[1]THE] [3]EPISTLE [2]GENERAL.

JAMES, a servant of God and of the Lord Jesus Christ, to the twelve tribes which are scattered abroad, greeting.

ἸΑΚΩΒΟΣ θεοῦ καὶ κυρίου Ἰησοῦ χριστοῦ δοῦλος, ταῖς
James [2]of [3]God [4]and [5]of [[6]the] [7]Lord [8]Jesus [9]Christ [1]bondman, to the
δώδεκα φυλαῖς ταῖς ἐν τῇ διασπορᾷ χαίρειν.
twelve tribes which [are] in the dispersion, greeting.

---

[t] πειθόμεθα we persuade ourselves LTTrAW. [v] — ἔργῳ T. [w] + αὐτῷ to himself L.
[x] ἡμῖν us T. [y] ἀνέχεσθαι to bear L. [z] + ἡμῶν (*read* our brother) LTTrAW. [a] — ἀμήν T.
[b] — *the subscription* GLTW; Πρὸς Ἑβραίους TrA.
[c] + τοῦ ἀποστόλου the Apostle E; Ἐπιστολαὶ (— Ἐπιστ. L) καθολικαί. Ἰακώβου ἐπιστολή General Epistles. Epistle of James GLW; Ἰακώβου ἐπιστολή TTrA.

2 Πᾶσαν χαρὰν ἡγήσασθε, ἀδελφοί.μου, ὅταν πειρασμοῖς
All joy esteem [it], my brethren, when [6]temptations
περιπέσητε ποικίλοις, 3 γινώσκοντες ὅτι τὸ δοκίμιον ὑμῶν
[1]ye [2]may [3]fall [4]into [5]various, knowing that the proving of your
τῆς πίστεως κατεργάζεται ὑπομονήν· 4 ἡ.δὲ.ὑπομονὴ ἔργον
faith works out endurance. But [2]endurance [[4]its] [6]work
τέλειον ἐχέτω, ἵνα ἦτε τέλειοι καὶ ὁλόκληροι, ἐν μηδενὶ λει-
[5]perfect [1]let [3]have, that ye may be perfect and complete, in nothing lack-
πόμενοι. 5 εἰ.δέ τις ὑμῶν λείπεται σοφίας, αἰτείτω παρὰ τοῦ
ing. But if anyone of you lack wisdom, let him ask from [2]who
διδόντος θεοῦ πᾶσιν ἁπλῶς, καὶ μὴ.ὀνειδίζοντος, καὶ δοθήσε-
[3]gives [1]God to all freely, and reproaches not, and it shall be
ται αὐτῷ. 6 αἰτείτω.δὲ ἐν πίστει, μηδὲν διακρινόμενος· ὁ.γὰρ
given to him: but let him ask in faith, nothing doubting. For he that
διακρινόμενος ἔοικεν κλύδωνι θαλάσσης ἀνεμιζομένῳ καὶ
doubts is like a wave of [the] sea being driven by the wind and
ῥιπιζομένῳ. 7 μὴ.γὰρ οἰέσθω ὁ.ἄνθρωπος.ἐκεῖνος, ὅτι [d]λή-
being tossed; for [2]not [1]let [5]suppose [3]that [4]man that he
ψεταί‖ τι παρὰ τοῦ κυρίου· 8 ἀνὴρ δίψυχος,
shall receive anything from the Lord; [he is] a [2]man [1]double-minded,
ἀκατάστατος ἐν πάσαις ταῖς.ὁδοῖς.αὐτοῦ. 9 Καυχάσθω.δὲ
unstable in all his ways. But let [6]boast
ὁ ἀδελφὸς ὁ ταπεινὸς ἐν τῷ.ὕψει.αὐτοῦ· 10 ὁ.δὲ πλούσιος
[1]the [2]brother [3]of [4]low [5]degree in his elevation, and the rich
ἐν τῇ.ταπεινώσει.αὐτοῦ, ὅτι ὡς ἄνθος χόρτου παρελεύ-
in his humiliation, because as [3]flower [[1]the] [2]grass's he will pass
σεται. 11 ἀνέτειλεν.γὰρ ὁ ἥλιος σὺν τῷ.καύσωνι, καὶ ἐξή-
away. For [3]rose [1]the [2]sun with [its] burning heat, and dried
ρανεν τὸν χόρτον, καὶ τὸ ἄνθος αὐτοῦ ἐξέπεσεν, καὶ ἡ εὐ-
up the grass, and the flower of it fell, and the
πρεπεια τοῦ.προσώπου.αὐτοῦ ἀπώλετο· οὕτως καὶ ὁ πλούσιος
comeliness of its appearance perished: thus also the rich
ἐν ταῖς.πορείαις.αὐτοῦ μαρανθήσεται. 12 Μακάριος ἀνὴρ
in his goings shall wither. Blessed [is the] man
ὃς ὑπομένει πειρασμόν· ὅτι δόκιμος γενόμενος [e]λήψεται‖
who endures temptation; because [3]proved [1]having [2]been he shall receive
τὸν στέφανον τῆς ζωῆς, ὃν ἐπηγγείλατο [f]ὁ κύριος‖ τοῖς
the crown of life, which [3]promised [1]the [2]Lord to those that
ἀγαπῶσιν αὐτόν.
love him.

13 Μηδεὶς πειραζόμενος λεγέτω, Ὅτι ἀπὸ [g]τοῦ‖ θεοῦ πειρά-
[2]No [3]one [4]being [5]tempted [1]let say, From God I am
ζομαι· ὁ.γὰρ.θεὸς ἀπείραστός ἐστιν κακῶν, πειράζει.δὲ αὐτὸς
tempted. For God [2]not [3]to [4]be [5]tempted [1]is by evils, and [2]tempts [1]himself
οὐδένα. 14 ἕκαστος.δὲ πειράζεται, [h]ὑπὸ‖ τῆς.ἰδίας ἐπιθυμίας
no one. But each one is tempted, by his own lust
ἐξελκόμενος καὶ δελεαζόμενος· 15 εἶτα ἡ ἐπιθυμία συλλαβοῦσα
being drawn away and being allured; then lust having conceived
τίκτει ἁμαρτίαν· ἡ.δὲ.ἁμαρτία ἀποτελεσθεῖσα ἀποκύει
gives birth to sin; but sin having been completed brings forth
θάνατον. 16 Μὴ.πλανᾶσθε, ἀδελφοί μου ἀγαπητοί· 17 πᾶσα
death. Be not misled, [3]brethren [1]my [2]beloved. Every
δόσις ἀγαθὴ καὶ πᾶν δώρημα τέλειον ἄνωθέν ἐστιν
[2]act [3]of [4]giving [1]good and every [2]gift [1]perfect [6]from [7]above [5]is

2 My brethren, count it all joy when ye fall into divers temptations; 3 knowing *this*, that the trying of your faith worketh patience. 4 But let patience have *her* perfect work, that ye may be perfect and entire, wanting nothing. 5 If any of you lack wisdom, let him ask of God, that giveth to all *men* liberally, and upbraideth not; and it shall be given him. 6 But let him ask in faith, nothing wavering. For he that wavereth is like a wave of the sea driven with the wind and tossed. 7 For let not that man think that he shall receive any thing of the Lord. 8 A double minded man *is* unstable in all his ways. 9 Let the brother of low degree rejoice in that he is exalted: 10 but the rich, in that he is made low: because as the flower of the grass he shall pass away. 11 For the sun is no sooner risen with a burning heat, but it withereth the grass, and the flower thereof falleth, and the grace of the fashion of it perisheth: so also shall the rich man fade away in his ways. 12 Blessed *is* the man that endureth temptation: for when he is tried, he shall receive the crown of life, which the Lord hath promised to them that love him.

13 Let no man say when he is tempted, I am tempted of God: for God cannot be tempted with evil, neither tempteth he any man: 14 but every man is tempted, when he is drawn away of his own lust, and enticed. 15 Then when lust hath conceived, it bringeth forth sin: and sin, when it is finished, bringeth forth death. 16 Do not err, my beloved brethren. 17 Every good gift and every perfect gift is from above, and cometh down from the Father of lights, with

[d] λήμψεταί LTTrA. [e] λήμψεται LTTrA. [f] — ὁ κύριος (read ἐπηγ. he promised) LTTrA.
[g] — τοῦ GLTTrAW. [h] ἀπὸ A.

whom is no variableness, neither shadow of turning. 18 Of his own will begat he us with the word of truth, that we should be a kind of firstfruits of his creatures.

19 Wherefore, my beloved brethren, let every man be swift to hear, slow to speak, slow to wrath: 20 for the wrath of man worketh not the righteousness of God. 21 Wherefore lay apart all filthiness and superfluity of naughtiness, and receive with meekness the engrafted word, which is able to save your souls. 22 But be ye doers of the word, and not hearers only, deceiving your own selves. 23 For if any be a hearer of the word, and not a doer, he is like unto a man beholding his natural face in a glass: 24 for he beholdeth himself, and goeth his way, and straightway forgetteth what manner of man he was. 25 But whoso looketh into the perfect law of liberty, and continueth *therein*, he being not a forgetful hearer, but a doer of the work, this man shall be blessed in his deed. 26 If any man among you seem to be religious, and bridleth not his tongue, but deceiveth his own heart, this man's religion *is* vain. 27 Pure religion and undefiled before God and the Father is this, To visit the fatherless and widows in their affliction, *and* to keep himself unspotted from the world.

II. My brethren, have not the faith of our Lord Jesus Christ, *the Lord* of glory, with respect of persons. 2 For if there come un-

καταβαῖνον ἀπὸ τοῦ πατρὸς τῶν φώτων, παρ' ᾧ οὐκ.ἔνι
[4]coming [5]down from the Father of lights, with whom there is not
παραλλαγή, ἢ τροπῆς ἀποσκίασμα. 18 βουληθεὶς ἀπε-
variation, or [2]of [3]turning [1]shadow. Having willed [it] he be-
κύησεν ἡμᾶς λόγῳ ἀληθείας, εἰς τὸ εἶναι ἡμᾶς ἀπαρχήν
gat us by [the] word of truth, for [2]to [3]be [1]us [7]first-fruits
τινα τῶν.αὐτοῦ.κτισμάτων.
[4]a [5]sort [6]of of his creatures.

19 [i]"Ωστε," ἀδελφοί μου ἀγαπητοί, ἔστω [k] πᾶς ἄνθρωπος
So that, [3]brethren [1]my [2]beloved, let [3]be [1]every [2]man
ταχὺς εἰς τὸ ἀκοῦσαι, βραδὺς εἰς τὸ λαλῆσαι, βραδὺς εἰς ὀργήν.
swift to hear, slow to speak, slow to wrath;
20 ὀργὴ.γὰρ ἀνδρὸς δικαιοσύνην θεοῦ [l]οὐ.κατεργάζεται."
for [2]wrath [1]man's [7]righteousness [6]God's [3]works [4]not [5]out.
21 Διὸ ἀποθέμενοι πᾶσαν ῥυπαρίαν καὶ περισσείαν κα-
Wherefore, having laid aside all filthiness and abounding of wick-
κίας, ἐν πραΰτητι δέξασθε τὸν ἔμφυτον λόγον, τὸν δυνά-
edness, in meekness accept the implanted word, which [is]
μενον σῶσαι τὰς.ψυχὰς.ὑμῶν. 22 γίνεσθε.δὲ ποιηταὶ λόγου,
able to save your souls. But be ye doers of [the] word,
καὶ μὴ [m]μόνον ἀκροαταί," παραλογιζόμενοι ἑαυτούς. 23 ὅτι
and not only hearers, beguiling yourselves. Because
εἴ τις ἀκροατὴς λόγου ἐστὶν καὶ οὐ ποιητής, οὗτος
if any man a hearer of [the] word is and not a doer, this one
ἔοικεν ἀνδρὶ κατανοοῦντι τὸ πρόσωπον τῆς γενέσεως αὐτοῦ
is like to a man considering [3]face [2]natural [1]his
ἐν ἐσόπτρῳ· 24 κατενόησεν.γὰρ ἑαυτὸν καὶ ἀπελήλυθεν, καὶ
in a mirror: for he considered himself and has gone away, and
εὐθέως ἐπελάθετο ὁποῖος ἦν. 25 ὁ.δὲ παρακύψας εἰς
immediately forgot what [3]like [1]he [2]was. But he that looked into
νόμον τέλειον τὸν τῆς ἐλευθερίας, καὶ παραμείνας,
[the] [2]law [1]perfect, that of freedom, and continued in [it],
[n]οὗτος" οὐκ ἀκροατὴς ἐπιλησμονῆς γενόμενος, ἀλλὰ ποιητὴς
this one not a [2]hearer [1]forgetful having been, but a doer
ἔργου, οὗτος μακάριος ἐν τῇ.ποιήσει.αὐτοῦ ἔσται. 26 Εἴ
of [the] work, this one blessed in his doing shall be. If
[o]τις δοκεῖ θρῆσκος εἶναι [p]ἐν ὑμῖν," μὴ χαλιναγωγῶν
anyone [3]seems [6]religious [4]to [5]be [1]among [2]you, not bridling
γλῶσσαν.αὐτοῦ, [q]ἀλλ'" ἀπατῶν καρδίαν.[r]αὐτοῦ," τούτου
his tongue, but deceiving his heart, of this one
μάταιος ἡ [s]θρησκεία." 27 [s]θρησκεία" καθαρὰ καὶ ἀμίαντος
vain [is] the religion. Religion pure and undefiled
παρὰ [t]τῷ" θεῷ καὶ πατρὶ αὕτη ἐστίν, ἐπισκέπτεσθαι ὀρ-
before God and [the] Father [2]this [1]is: to visit or-
φανοὺς καὶ χήρας ἐν τῇ.θλίψει.αὐτῶν, ἄσπιλον ἑαυτὸν τηρεῖν
phans and widows in their tribulation, unspotted [3]oneself [1]to [2]keep
ἀπὸ τοῦ κόσμου.
from the world.

2 'Αδελφοί.μου, μὴ ἐν [v]προσωποληψίαις" ἔχετε τὴν πίστιν
My brethren, [2]not [4]with [5]respect [6]of [7]persons [1]do [3]have the faith
τοῦ.κυρίου.ἡμῶν Ἰησοῦ χριστοῦ τῆς δόξης· 2 ἐὰν.γὰρ
of our Lord Jesus Christ, [Lord] of glory; for if

---

[i] Ἴστε Ye know [it] LTTrA. [k] + δὲ but (let) LTTrA. [l] οὐκ ἐργάζεται works not LTTrA. [m] ἀκροαταὶ μόνον LTrAW. [n] — οὗτος LTTrA. [o] + δὲ but (if) L. [p] — ἐν ὑμῖν GLTTrAW. [q] ἀλλὰ LTTrAW. [r] ἑαυτοῦ (*read* his own heart) L. [s] θρησκία T. [t] — τῷ TW. [v] προσωπολημψίαις LTTrA.

εἰσέλθῃ εἰς [w]τὴν‖.συναγωγὴν.ὑμῶν ἀνὴρ χρυσοδακτύλιος
may have come into your synagogue a man with gold rings
ἐν ἐσθῆτι λαμπρᾷ, εἰσέλθῃ.δὲ καὶ πτωχὸς ἐν ῥυπαρᾷ
in [2]apparel [1]splendid, and may have come in also a poor [man] in vile
ἐσθῆτι, 3 [x]καὶ ἐπιβλέψητε‖ ἐπὶ τὸν φοροῦντα τὴν ἐσθῆτα
apparel, and ye may have looked upon him who wears the [2]apparel
τὴν λαμπράν, καὶ εἴπητε [y]αὐτῷ,‖ Σὺ κάθου ὧδε καλῶς, καὶ
[1]splendid, and may have said to him, Thou sit thou here well, and
τῷ πτωχῷ εἴπητε, Σὺ στῆθι ἐκεῖ, ἢ κάθου [z]ὧδε‖ ὑπὸ
to the poor may have said, Thou stand thou there, or sit thou here under
τὸ.ὑποπόδιόν.μου· 4 [a]καὶ‖ οὐ διεκρίθητε ἐν ἑαυτοῖς,
my footstool: [4]also [3]not [1]did [2]ye make a difference among yourselves,
καὶ ἐγένεσθε κριταὶ διαλογισμῶν πονηρῶν; 5 Ἀκούσατε,
and became judges [having] [2]reasonings [1]evil? Hear,
ἀδελφοί μου ἀγαπητοί, οὐχ ὁ θεὸς ἐξελέξατο τοὺς πτωχοὺς
[3]brethren [1]my [2]beloved: [5]not [6]God [4]did choose the poor
[b]τοῦ κόσμου‖ [c]τούτου,‖ πλουσίους ἐν πίστει, καὶ κληρονόμους
[3]world [1]of [2]this, rich in faith, and heirs
τῆς βασιλείας ἧς ἐπηγγείλατο τοῖς ἀγαπῶσιν αὐτόν;
of the kingdom which he promised to those that love him?
6 ὑμεῖς.δὲ ἠτιμάσατε τὸν πτωχόν. [d]οὐχ‖ οἱ πλούσιοι
But ye dishonoured the poor [man]. [2]Not [3]the [4]rich
καταδυναστεύουσιν [e]ὑμῶν,‖ καὶ αὐτοὶ ἕλκουσιν ὑμᾶς
[1]do oppress you, and [[2]not] [3]they [1]do drag you
εἰς κριτήρια; 7 οὐκ αὐτοὶ βλασφημοῦσιν τὸ καλὸν
before [the] tribunals? [2]not [3]they [1]do blaspheme the good
ὄνομα τὸ ἐπικληθὲν ἐφ' ὑμᾶς; 8 Εἰ μέντοι νόμον τελεῖτε
name which was called upon you? If indeed [the] [2]law [3]ye [4]keep
βασιλικόν, κατὰ τὴν γραφήν, Ἀγαπήσεις τὸν.πλησίον.σου
[1]royal according to the scripture, Thou shalt love thy neighbour
ὡς σεαυτόν, καλῶς ποιεῖτε· 9 εἰ.δὲ [f]προσωποληπτεῖτε,‖ ἁμαρ-
as thyself, [3]well [1]ye [2]do. But if ye have respect of persons, [3]sin
τίαν ἐργάζεσθε, ἐλεγχόμενοι ὑπὸ τοῦ νόμου ὡς παραβάται.
[1]ye [2]work, being convicted by the law as transgressors.
10 ὅστις.γὰρ ὅλον τὸν νόμον [g]τηρήσει, πταίσει‖ δὲ ἐν ἑνί,
For whosoever [2]whole [1]the law shall keep, [2]shall [3]stumble [1]but in one
γέγονεν πάντων ἔνοχος. 11 ὁ.γὰρ εἰπών, Μὴ μοι-
[point], he has become [2]of [3]all [1]guilty. For he who said, [3]not [1]Thou
χεύσῃς, εἶπεν καί, Μὴ.φονεύσῃς· εἰ.δὲ
[2]mayest commit adultery, said also, Thou mayest not commit murder. Now if
οὐ.[h]μοιχεύσεις, φονεύσεις‖ δέ, γέγονας
thou shalt not commit adultery, [2]shalt [3]commit [4]murder [1]but, thou hast become
παραβάτης νόμου. 12 Οὕτως λαλεῖτε καὶ οὕτως ποιεῖτε, ὡς
a transgressor of [the] law. So speak ye and so do, as
διὰ νόμου ἐλευθερίας μέλλοντες κρίνεσθαι· 13 ἡ.γὰρ.κρίσις
by [the] law of freedom being about to be judged; for judgment
[i]ἀνίλεως‖ τῷ μὴ.ποιήσαντι ἔλεος· [k]καὶ‖ κατα-
[will be] without mercy to him that wrought not mercy. And [2]boasts
καυχᾶται ἔλεος κρίσεως.
[3]over [1]mercy judgment.

14 Τί [l]τὸ‖ ὄφελος, ἀδελφοί.μου, ἐὰν πίστιν [m]λέγῃ τις‖
What [is] the profit, my brethren, if [5]faith [2]say [1]anyone

to your assembly a man with a gold ring, in goodly apparel, and there come in also a poor man in vile raiment; 3 and ye have respect to him that weareth the gay clothing, and say unto him, Sit thou here in a good place; and say to the poor, Stand thou there, or sit here under my footstool: 4 are ye not then partial in yourselves, and are become judges of evil thoughts? 5 Hearken, my beloved brethren, Hath not God chosen the poor of this world rich in faith, and heirs of the kingdom which he hath promised to them that love him? 6 But ye have despised the poor. Do not rich men oppress you, and draw you before the judgment seats? 7 Do not they blaspheme that worthy name by the which ye are called? 8 If ye fulfil the royal law according to the scripture, Thou shalt love thy neighbour as thyself, ye do well: 9 but if ye have respect to persons, ye commit sin, and are convinced of the law as transgressors. 10 For whosoever shall keep the whole law, and yet offend in one *point*, he is guilty of all. 11 For he that said, Do not commit adultery, said also, Do not kill. Now if thou commit no adultery, yet if thou kill, thou art become a transgressor of the law. 12 So speak ye, and so do, as they that shall be judged by the law of liberty. 13 For he shall have judgment without mercy, that hath shewed no mercy; and mercy rejoiceth against judgment.

14 What *doth it* profit, my brethren,

[w] — τὴν LTTrA. [x] ἐπιβλέψητε δὲ A. [y] — αὐτῷ GLTTrA. [z] — ὧδε LTTrA. [a] — καὶ LTTrA. [b] τῷ κόσμῳ (as regards the world) LTTrAW. [c] — τούτου GLTTrAW. [d] οὐχὶ LW. [e] ὑμᾶς T. [f] προσωπολημπτεῖτε LTTrA. [g] τηρήσῃ, πταίσῃ (*read* shall have kept, but shall have stumbled) LTTrAW. [h] μοιχεύεις, φονεύεις (*read* if thou committest not adultery but committest murder) LTTrA. [i] ἀνέλεος pitiless LTTrAW. [k] — καὶ GLTTrAW. [l] — τὸ L. [m] τις λέγῃ L.

though a man say he
hath faith, and have
not works? can faith
save him? 15 If a
brother or sister be
naked, and destitute
of daily food, 16 and
one of you say unto
them, Depart in peace,
be *ye* warmed and fill-
ed; notwithstanding
ye give them not those
things which are need-
ful to the body; what
doth it profit? 17 Even
so faith, if it hath not
works, is dead, being
alone. 18 Yea, a man
may say, Thou hast
faith, and I have
works: shew me thy
faith without thy
works, and I will shew
thee my faith by my
works. 19 Thou be-
lievest that there is
one God; thou doest
well: the devils also
believe, and tremble.
20 But wilt thou know,
O vain man, that faith
without works is dead?
21 Was not Abraham
our father justified by
works, when he had
offered Isaac his son
upon the altar?
22 Seest thou how faith
wrought with his
works, and by works
was faith made per-
fect? 23 And the
scripture was fulfilled
which saith, Abraham
believed God, and it
was imputed unto him
for righteousness: and
he was called the
Friend of God. 24 Ye
see then how that by
works a man is justi-
fied, and not by faith
only. 25 Likewise also
was not Rahab the
harlot justified by
works, when she had
received the messen-
gers, and had sent *them*
out another way?
26 For as the body
without the spirit is
dead, so faith without
works is dead also.

III. My brethren, be
not many masters,
knowing that we shall
receive the greater
condemnation. 2 For
in many things we of-
fend all. If any man

ἔχειν, ἔργα.δὲ μὴ.ἔχῃ; μὴ δύναται ἡ πίστις σῶσαι αὐτόν;
[[3]he] [4]has, but works have not? is [2]able [1]faith to save him?
15 ἐὰν.[n]δὲ‖ ἀδελφὸς ἢ ἀδελφὴ γυμνοὶ ὑπάρχωσιν, καὶ λειπό-
Now if a brother or a sister [2]naked [1]be, and desti-
μενοι [o]ὦσιν‖ τῆς ἐφημέρου τροφῆς, 16 εἴπῃ.δέ τις αὐτοῖς
tute may be of daily food, and [5]say [1]anyone [6]to [7]them
ἐξ ὑμῶν, Ὑπάγετε ἐν εἰρήνῃ, θερμαίνεσθε καὶ χορτά-
[2]from [3]amongst [4]you, Go in peace; be warmed and be fill-
ζεσθε, μὴ.δῶτε.δὲ αὐτοῖς τὰ ἐπιτήδεια τοῦ σώματος, τί
ed; but give not to them the needful things for the body, what [is]
[p]τὸ‖ ὄφελος; 17 οὕτως καὶ ἡ πίστις ἐὰν μὴ [q]ἔργα ἔχῃ‖ νεκρά
the profit? So also faith, if [3]not [4]works [1]it [2]have, [6]dead
ἐστιν καθ' ἑαυτήν. 18 ἀλλ' ἐρεῖ τις Σὺ πίστιν ἔχεις,
[5]is by itself. But [3]will [4]say [1]some [2]one, Thou [2]faith [1]hast
κἀγὼ ἔργα ἔχω· δεῖξόν μοι τὴν.πίστιν.σου [r]ἐκ‖ τῶν ἔργων
and I [2]works [1]have. Shew me thy faith from [2]works
[s]σου,‖ κἀγὼ [t]δείξω σοι‖ ἐκ τῶν.ἔργων.μου τὴν πίστιν [u]μου.‖
[1]thy, and I will shew thee from my works [2]faith [1]my.
19 σὺ πιστεύεις ὅτι [v]ὁ θεὸς εἷς ἐστιν.‖ καλῶς ποιεῖς· καὶ τὰ
Thou believest that God [2]one [1]is. [5]Well [3]thou [4]doest; even the
δαιμόνια πιστεύουσιν, καὶ φρίσσουσιν. 20 θέλεις.δὲ γνῶναι,
demons believe, and shudder. But wilt thou know,
ὦ ἄνθρωπε κενέ, ὅτι ἡ πίστις χωρὶς τῶν ἔργων [w]νεκρά‖ ἐστιν;
O [2]man [1]empty, that faith apart from works dead is?
21 Ἀβραὰμ ὁ.πατὴρ.ἡμῶν οὐκ ἐξ ἔργων ἐδικαιώθη, ἀνε-
[3]Abraham [4]our [5]father [2]not [7]by [8]works [1]was [6]justified, having
νέγκας Ἰσαὰκ τὸν.υἱὸν.αὐτοῦ ἐπὶ τὸ θυσιαστήριον; 22 βλέ-
offered Isaac his son upon the altar? Thou
πεις ὅτι ἡ πίστις [x]συνήργει‖ τοῖς.ἔργοις.αὐτοῦ, καὶ ἐκ τῶν
seest that faith was working with his works, and by
ἔργων ἡ πίστις ἐτελειώθη;[y] 23 καὶ ἐπληρώθη ἡ γραφὴ ἡ
works faith was perfected. And was fulfilled the scripture which
λέγουσα, Ἐπίστευσεν.δὲ Ἀβραὰμ τῷ θεῷ, καὶ ἐλογίσθη
says, Now [2]believed [1]Abraham God, and it was reckoned
αὐτῷ εἰς δικαιοσύνην, καὶ φίλος θεοῦ ἐκλήθη. 24 Ὁρᾶτε
to him for righteousness, and friend of God he was called. Ye see
[z]τοίνυν‖ ὅτι ἐξ ἔργων δικαιοῦται ἄνθρωπος, καὶ οὐκ ἐκ πίστεως
then that by works is justified a man, and not by faith
μόνον.[a] 25 ὁμοίως.δὲ καὶ Ῥαὰβ ἡ πόρνη οὐκ ἐξ ἔργων
only. But in like manner also [3]Rahab [4]the [5]harlot [2]not [7]by [8]works
ἐδικαιώθη, ὑποδεξαμένη τοὺς ἀγγέλους, καὶ ἑτέρᾳ ὁδῷ
[1]was [6]justified, having received the messengers, and by another way
ἐκβαλοῦσα; 26 ὥσπερ.γὰρ τὸ σῶμα χωρὶς πνεύματος
having put [them] forth? For as the body apart from spirit
νεκρόν ἐστιν, οὕτως καὶ ἡ πίστις χωρὶς [b]τῶν‖ ἔργων νεκρά
[2]dead [1]is, so also faith apart from works [2]dead
ἐστιν.
[1]is.

3 Μὴ πολλοὶ διδάσκαλοι γίνεσθε, ἀδελφοί.μου, εἰδότες ὅτι
[2]Not [3]many [4]teachers [1]be, my brethren, knowing that
μεῖζον κρίμα [c]λη ψόμεθα·‖ 2 πολλὰ.γὰρ πταίομεν ἅπαντες.
greater judgment we shall receive. For [3]often [1]we [4]stumble [2]all.

---

[n] — δὲ now TTr. [o] — ὦσιν TTrA. [p] — τὸ L. [q] ἔχῃ ἔργα GLTTrAW. [r] χωρὶς apart from GLTTrAW. [s] — σου LTTrAW. [t] σοι δείξω TTr. [u] — μου TTrAW. [v] εἷς ἐστιν ὁ θεός LTTr; εἷς ὁ θεός ἐστιν AW. [w] ἀργή idle LTTrA. [x] συνεργεῖ works with TTr. [y] *Read verse 22 interrogatively, as pointed in the Greek.* EGLTrW. [z] — τοίνυν GLTTrAW. [a] *Read verse 24 as a question* GLTr. [b] — τῶν T[Tr]. [c] λημψόμεθα LTTrA.

εἴ τις ἐν λόγῳ οὐ.πταίει, οὗτος τέλειος ἀνήρ, δυνατὸς
If anyone in word stumble not, this one [is] a perfect man, able
χαλιναγωγῆσαι καὶ ὅλον τὸ σῶμα. 3 [d]Ἰδοὺ‖ τῶν ἵππων
to bridle also [2]whole [1]the body. Lo, [6]of [7]the [8]horses
τοὺς χαλινοὺς εἰς τὰ στόματα βάλλομεν [e]πρὸς‖ τὸ πείθεσθαι
[1]the [2]bits [3]in [4]the [5]mouths we put, for [2]to [3]obey
αὐτοὺς ἡμῖν,‖ καὶ ὅλον τὸ.σῶμα.αὐτῶν μετάγομεν. 4 Ἰδοὺ
[1]them us, and [2]whole [1]their body we turn about. Lo,
καὶ τὰ πλοῖα τηλικαῦτα ὄντα, καὶ ὑπὸ [g]σκληρῶν ἀνέμων‖
also the ships, [2]so [3]great [1]being, and by violent winds
ἐλαυνόμενα, μετάγεται ὑπὸ ἐλαχίστου πηδαλίου, ὅπου
being driven, are turned about by a very small rudder, wherever
[h]ἂν‖ ἡ ὁρμὴ τοῦ εὐθύνοντος [i]βούληται.‖ 5 οὕτως καὶ
the impulse of him who steers may will. Thus also
ἡ γλῶσσα μικρὸν μέλος ἐστίν, καὶ [k]μεγαλαυχεῖ.‖ Ἰδού,
the tongue a little member is, and boasts great things. Lo,
[l]ὀλίγον‖ πῦρ ἡλίκην ὕλην ἀνάπτει· 6 [m]καὶ‖ ἡ γλῶσσα
a little fire how large a wood it kindles; and the tongue [is]
πῦρ, ὁ κόσμος τῆς ἀδικίας. [n]οὕτως‖ ἡ γλῶσσα καθίσταται
fire, the world of unrighteousness. Thus the tongue is set
ἐν τοῖς.μέλεσιν.ἡμῶν, [o]ἡ‖ σπιλοῦσα ὅλον τὸ σῶμα, καὶ φλο-
in our members, the defiler [of] [2]whole [1]the body, and setting
γίζουσα τὸν τροχὸν τῆς γενέσεως, καὶ φλογιζομένη ὑπὸ τῆς
on fire the course of nature, and being set on fire by
γεέννης· 7 πᾶσα.γὰρ φύσις θηρίων.τε καὶ πετεινῶν, ἑρπε-
gehenna. For every species both of beasts and of birds, [2]of [3]creeping
τῶν τε καὶ ἐναλίων, δαμάζεται καὶ δεδάμασται τῇ
[4]things [1]both and things of the sea, is subdued and has been subdued by
φύσει τῇ ἀνθρωπίνῃ· 8 τὴν.δὲ γλῶσσαν οὐδεὶς [p]δύναται
[3]species [1]the [2]human; but the tongue no one [3]is [4]able
ἀνθρώπων δαμάσαι·‖ [q]ἀκατάσχετον‖ κακόν, μεστὴ ἰοῦ
[1]of [2]men to subdue; [it is] an unrestrainable evil, full of [2]poison
θανατηφόρου. 9 ἐν.αὐτῇ εὐλογοῦμεν [r]τὸν θεὸν‖ καὶ πατέρα,
[1]death-bringing. Therewith we bless God and [the] Father,
καὶ ἐν.αὐτῇ καταρώμεθα τοὺς ἀνθρώπους τοὺς καθ'
and therewith we curse men who according to [the]
ὁμοίωσιν θεοῦ γεγονότας· 10 ἐκ τοῦ αὐτοῦ στόματος ἐξέρ-
likeness of God are made. Out of the same mouth goes
χεται εὐλογία καὶ κατάρα. οὐ χρή, ἀδελφοί.μου, ταῦτα
forth blessing and cursing. [6]Not [5]ought, [1]my [2]brethren, [3]these [4]things
οὕτως γίνεσθαι. 11 μήτι ἡ.πηγὴ ἐκ τῆς αὐτῆς ὀπῆς
thus to be. [3]The [4]fountain [5]out [6]of [7]the [8]same [9]opening
βρύει τὸ γλυκὺ καὶ τὸ πικρόν; 12 μὴ δύναται, ἀδελφοί
[1]pours [2]forth sweet and bitter? Is able, [2]brethren
μου, συκῆ ἐλαίας ποιῆσαι, ἢ ἄμπελος σῦκα; [s]οὕτως‖ [t]οὐδεμία
[1]my, a fig-tree olives to produce, or a vine figs? Thus no
πηγὴ ἁλυκὸν καὶ‖ γλυκὺ ποιῆσαι ὕδωρ.
fountain [is able] salt and sweet [2]to [3]produce [1]water.

13 Τίς σοφὸς καὶ ἐπιστήμων ἐν ὑμῖν; δειξάτω ἐκ τῆς
Who [is] wise and understanding among you; let him shew out of

offend not in word, the same *is* a perfect man, *and* able also to bridle the whole body. 3 Behold, we put bits in the horses' mouths, that they may obey us; and we turn about their whole body. 4 Behold also the ships, which though *they be* so great, and *are* driven of fierce winds, yet are they turned about with a very small helm, whithersoever the governor listeth. 5 Even so the tongue is a little member, and boasteth great things. Behold, how great a matter a little fire kindleth! 6 And the tongue *is* a fire, a world of iniquity: so is the tongue among our members, that it defileth the whole body, and setteth on fire the course of nature; and it is set on fire of hell. 7 For every kind of beasts, and of birds, and of serpents, and of things in the sea, is tamed, and hath been tamed of mankind: 8 but the tongue can no man tame; *it is* an unruly evil, full of deadly poison. 9 Therewith bless we God, even the Father; and therewith curse we men, which are made after the similitude of God. 10 Out of the same mouth proceedeth blessing and cursing. My brethren, these things ought not so to be. 11 Doth a fountain send forth at the same place sweet *water* and bitter? 12 Can the fig tree, my brethren, bear olive berries? either a vine, figs? so *can* no fountain both yield salt water and fresh.

13 Who *is* a wise man and endued with knowledge among you?

---

[d] ἴδε G; εἰ δὲ but if (*read* καὶ also) LTTrAW. [e] εἰς LTTrA. [f] ἡμῖν αὐτούς A. [g] ἀνέμων σκληρῶν LTTrAW. [h] — ἂν (*read* where) TTr. [i] βούλεται wills TTr. [k] μεγάλα αὐχεῖ LTTrA. [l] ἡλίκον *literally* how great (*some translate* how small) LTTrAW. [m] — καὶ (*read* the tongue kindles. A fire, &c.) T. [n] — οὕτως LTTrAW. [o] καὶ (*read* both defiling) T. [p] δαμάσαι δύναται ἀνθρώπων LTrA. [q] ἀκατάστατον an unsettled LTTrAW. [r] τὸν κύριον the Lord LTTrA. [s] — οὕτως LTTrAW. [t] οὔτε ἁλυκὸν neither salt [water is able] GLTTrAW.

let him shew out of a
good conversation his
works with meekness
of wisdom. 14 But if
ye have bitter envying
and strife in your
hearts, glory not, and
lie not against the
truth. 15 This wisdom
descendeth not from
above, but *is* earth-
ly, sensual, devilish.
16 For where envying
and strife *is*, there *is*
confusion and every
evil work. 17 But the
wisdom that is from
above is first pure,
then peaceable, gentle,
and easy to be intreat-
ed, full of mercy and
good fruits, without
partiality, and with-
out hypocrisy. 18 And
the fruit of righteous-
ness is sown in peace of
them that make peace.
IV. From whence *come*
wars and fightings a-
mong you? *come they*
not hence, *even* of your
lusts that war in your
members? 2 Ye lust,
and have not: ye kill,
and desire to have, and
cannot obtain: ye
fight and war, yet ye
have not, because ye
ask not. 3 Ye ask, and
receive not, because ye
ask amiss, that ye may
consume *it* upon your
lusts. 4 Ye adulterers
and adulteresses, know
ye not that the friend-
ship of the world is
enmity with God?
Whosoever therefore
will be a friend of
the world is the
enemy of God. 5 Do
ye think that the
scripture saith in vain,
The spirit that dwell-
eth in us lusteth to
envy? 6 But he giveth
more grace. Wherefore
he saith, God resisteth
the proud, but giveth
grace unto the humble.
7 Submit yourselves
therefore to God. Re-
sist the devil, and he
will flee from you.
8 Draw nigh to God,
and he will draw nigh
to you. Cleanse *your*
hands, *ye* sinners; and
purify *your* hearts, *ye*
double minded. 9 Be
afflicted, and mourn,
and weep: let your

καλῆς ἀναστροφῆς τὰ.ἔργα.αὐτοῦ ἐν πραΰτητι σοφίας. 14 εἰ.δὲ
good conduct his works in meekness of wisdom; but if

ζῆλον πικρὸν ἔχετε καὶ ἐριθείαν ἐν τῇ.καρδίᾳ.ὑμῶν, μὴ κατα-
[2]emulation [1]bitter ye have and contention in your heart, [2]not [1]do

καυχᾶσθε [u]καὶ ψεύδεσθε κατὰ τῆς ἀληθείας.ǁ 15 Οὐκ ἔστιν
boast against and lie against the truth. [3]Not [2]is

αὕτη ἡ σοφία ἄνωθεν κατερχομένη, [v]ἀλλ'ǁ ἐπίγειος, ψυ-
[1]this the wisdom from above coming down, but earthly, na-

χική, δαιμονιώδης. 16 ὅπου.γὰρ ζῆλος καὶ ἐριθεία, ἐκεῖ
tural, devilish. For where emulation and contention [are]; there

ἀκαταστασία καὶ πᾶν φαῦλον πρᾶγμα. 17 ἡ.δὲ ἄνωθεν
[is] commotion and every evil thing. But the [2]from [3]above

σοφία πρῶτον μὲν ἁγνή ἐστιν, ἔπειτα εἰρηνική, ἐπιεικής,
[1]wisdom [5]first [6]pure [4]is, then peaceful, gentle,

εὐπειθής, μεστὴ ἐλέους καὶ καρπῶν ἀγαθῶν, ἀδιάκριτος [w]καὶǁ
yielding, full of mercy and of [2]fruits [1]good, impartial and

ἀνυπόκριτος. 18 καρπὸς.δὲ [x]τῆςǁ δικαιοσύνης ἐν εἰρήνῃ σπεί-
unfeigned. But [the] fruit of righteousness in peace is

ρεται τοῖς ποιοῦσιν εἰρήνην. 4 Πόθεν πόλεμοι καὶ [y]
sown for those that make peace. Whence [come] wars and

μάχαι ἐν ὑμῖν; οὐκ ἐντεῦθεν, ἐκ τῶν.ἡδονῶν.ὑμῶν
fightings among you? [Is it] not thence, from your pleasures,

τῶν στρατευομένων ἐν τοῖς.μέλεσιν.ὑμῶν; 2 ἐπιθυμεῖτε, καὶ
which war in your members? Ye desire, and

οὐκ.ἔχετε· φονεύετε καὶ ζηλοῦτε, καὶ οὐ.δύνασθε ἐπιτυχεῖν.
have not; ye kill and are emulous, and are not able to obtain;

μάχεσθε καὶ πολεμεῖτε, [z]οὐκ.ἔχετε [a]δέ,ǁ διὰ τὸ μὴ αἰτεῖσθαι
ye fight and war, [2]ye [3]have [4]not [1]but because [3]not [2]ask

ὑμᾶς· 3 αἰτεῖτε, καὶ οὐ.λαμβάνετε, διότι κακῶς αἰτεῖσθε ἵνα
[1]you. Ye ask, and receive not, because evilly ye ask, that

ἐν ταῖς.ἡδοναῖς.ὑμῶν δαπανήσητε. 4 [b]Μοιχοὶ καὶǁ μοιχα-
in your pleasures ye may spend [it]. Adulterers and adulte-

λίδες, οὐκ.οἴδατε ὅτι ἡ φιλία τοῦ κόσμου, ἔχθρα [c]τοῦ
resses, know ye not that the friendship of the world enmity [with]

θεοῦ ἐστιν;ǁ ὃς.[d]ἂνǁ οὖν βουληθῇ φίλος εἶναι τοῦ κόσμου,
God is? Whosoever therefore be minded a friend to be of the world,

ἐχθρὸς τοῦ θεοῦ καθίσταται. 5 ἢ δοκεῖτε ὅτι κενῶς ἡ γρα-
an enemy of God is constituted. Or think ye that in vain the scrip-

φὴ λέγει;[e] πρὸς φθόνον ἐπιποθεῖ τὸ πνεῦμα ὃ [f]κατῴκησενǁ
ture speaks? with envy does [3]long [1]the [2]Spirit which took up [his] abode

ἐν ἡμῖν;[g] 6 μείζονα.δὲ δίδωσιν χάριν· διὸ λέγει, Ὁ θεὸς
in us? But [3]greater [1]he [2]gives grace. Wherefore he says, God

ὑπερηφάνοις ἀντιτάσσεται, ταπεινοῖς.δὲ δίδωσιν χάριν.
[[4]the] [5]proud [1]sets [2]himself [3]against, but to [the] lowly he gives grace.

7 Ὑποτάγητε οὖν τῷ θεῷ. ἀντίστητε [h] τῷ διαβόλῳ, καὶ
Subject yourselves therefore to God. Resist the devil, and

φεύξεται ἀφ' ὑμῶν· 8 ἐγγίσατε τῷ θεῷ, καὶ ἐγγιεῖ ὑμῖν.
he will flee from you. Draw near to God, and he will draw near to you.

καθαρίσατε χεῖρας, ἁμαρτωλοί, καὶ ἁγνίσατε καρδίας,
Have cleansed [your] hands, sinners, and have purified [your] hearts,

δίψυχοι. 9 ταλαιπωρήσατε καὶ πενθήσατε [i]καὶǁ κλαύσατε.
ye double minded. Be wretched, and mourn, and weep.

---

[u] τῆς ἀληθείας καὶ ψεύδεσθε T. [v] ἀλλὰ TTr. [w] — καὶ LTTrA. [x] — τῆς GLTTrAW. [y] + πόθεν whence LTTrAW. [z] + καὶ and T. [a] — δέ GLTTrA. [b] — Μοιχοὶ καὶ LTTrAW; *join* adulteresses *to what precedes* T. [c] ἐστὶν τῷ θεῷ is with God T. [d] ἐὰν LT. [e] — ; *Text. Rec. and* LA. [f] κατῴκισεν he made to dwell LTTrA. [g] — ; T. [h] + δὲ but (resist) LTTrA. [i] — καὶ T.

ὁ.γέλως.ὑμῶν εἰς πένθος μεταστραφήτω, καὶ ἡ.χαρὰ εἰς
[2]Your [3]laughter [4]to [5]mourning [1]let be turned, and [your] joy to

κατήφειαν. 10 ταπεινώθητε ἐνώπιον [k]τοῦ[ll] κυρίου, καὶ ὑψώ-
heaviness. Humble yourselves before the Lord, and he will

σει ὑμᾶς.
exalt you.

11 Μὴ.καταλαλεῖτε ἀλλήλων, ἀδελφοί· ὁ καταλαλῶν
Speak not against one another, brethren. He that speaks against

ἀδελφοῦ, [l]καὶ[ll] κρίνων τὸν.ἀδελφὸν.αὐτοῦ, καταλαλεῖ
[his] brother, and judges his brother, speaks against [the]

νόμου, καὶ κρίνει νόμον· εἰ.δὲ νόμον κρίνεις, οὐκ
law, and judges [the] law. But if [the] law thou judgest, [3]not

εἶ ποιητὴς νόμου, ἀλλὰ κριτής. 12 εἷς ἐστιν ὁ νομο-
[1]thou [2]art a doer of [the] law, but a judge. One is the law-

θέτης[m], ὁ δυνάμενος σῶσαι καὶ ἀπολέσαι· σὺ [n]τίς εἶ [o]ὃς
giver, who is able to save and to destroy: [3]thou [1]who [2]art that

κρίνεις[ll] τὸν [p]ἕτερον[ll];
judgest the other?

13 Ἄγε νῦν οἱ λέγοντες, Σήμερον [q]καὶ[ll] αὔριον [r]πορευ-
Go to now, ye who say, To-day and to-morrow we may

σώμεθα[ll] εἰς τήνδε.τὴν.πόλιν, καὶ [s]ποιήσωμεν[ll] ἐκεῖ ἐνιαυτὸν
go into such a city and may spend there [2]year

[t]ἕνα[ll] καὶ [v]ἐμπορευσώμεθα,[ll] καὶ [w]κερδήσωμεν·[ll] 14 οἵτινες οὐκ
[1]one and may traffic, and may make gain, ye who [2]not

ἐπίστασθε [x]τὸ[ll] τῆς αὔριον· ποία.[y]γὰρ[ll] ἡ.ζωὴ.ὑμῶν;
[1]know what on the morrow [will be], (for what [is] your life?

ἀτμὶς [z]γάρ[ll] [a]ἐστιν[ll] ἡ πρὸς ὀλίγον φαινομένη, ἔπειτα
A vapour even it is, which for a little [while] appears, [2]then

[b]δὲ[ll] ἀφανιζομένη· 15 ἀντὶ τοῦ λέγειν.ὑμᾶς, Ἐὰν ὁ κύριος
[1]and disappears,) instead of your saying, If the Lord

θελήσῃ, καὶ [c]ζήσωμεν,[ll] καὶ [d]ποιήσωμεν[ll] τοῦτο ἢ ἐκεῖνο.
should will and we should live, also we may do this or that.

16 νῦν.δὲ καυχᾶσθε ἐν ταῖς.[e]ἀλαζονείαις[ll].ὑμῶν· πᾶσα καύχη-
But now ye boast in your vauntings: all [2]boasting

σις τοιαύτη πονηρά ἐστιν. 17 εἰδότι οὖν καλὸν ποιεῖν,
[1]such evil is. To [him] knowing therefore good to do,

καὶ μὴ ποιοῦντι, ἁμαρτία αὐτῷ ἐστιν.
and not doing [it], sin to him it is.

5 Ἄγε νῦν οἱ.πλούσιοι, κλαύσατε ὀλολύζοντες ἐπὶ ταῖς
Go to now, [ye] rich, weep, howling over

ταλαιπωρίαις ὑμῶν ταῖς ἐπερχομέναις. 2 ὁ πλοῦτος
[2]miseries [1]your that [are] coming upon [you]. [2]Riches

ὑμῶν σέσηπεν, καὶ τὰ.ἱμάτια.ὑμῶν σητόβρωτα γέγονεν·
[1]your have rotted, and your garments moth-eaten have become.

3 ὁ.χρυσὸς.ὑμῶν καὶ ὁ ἄργυρος κατίωται, καὶ ὁ.ἰὸς.αὐτῶν
Your gold and silver has been eaten away, and their canker

εἰς μαρτύριον ὑμῖν ἔσται, καὶ φάγεται τὰς.σάρκας.ὑμῶν ὡς
for a testimony against you shall be, and shall eat your flesh as

πῦρ· ἐθησαυρίσατε ἐν ἐσχάταις ἡμέραις. 4 ἰδού, ὁ μισθὸς
fire. Ye treasured up in [the] last days. Lo, the hire

laughter be turned to mourning, and *your* joy to heaviness.
10 Humble yourselves in the sight of the Lord, and he shall lift you up.

11 Speak not evil one of another, brethren. He that speaketh evil of *his* brother, and judgeth his brother, speaketh evil of the law, and judgeth the law: but if thou judge the law, thou art not a doer of the law, but a judge. 12 There is one lawgiver, who is able to save and to destroy: who art thou that judgest another?

13 Go to now, ye that say, To day or to morrow we will go into such a city, and continue there a year, and buy and sell, and get gain: 14 whereas ye know not what *shall be* on the morrow. For what *is* your life? It is even a vapour, that appeareth for a little time, and then vanisheth away. 15 For that ye *ought* to say, If the Lord will, we shall live, and do this, or that. 16 But now ye rejoice in your boastings: all such rejoicing is evil. 17 Therefore to him that knoweth to do good, and doeth *it* not, to him it is sin.

V. Go to now, *ye* rich men, weep and howl for your miseries that shall come upon *you*. 2 Your riches are corrupted, and your garments are motheaten. 3 Your gold and silver is cankered; and the rust of them shall be a witness against you, and shall eat your flesh as it were fire. Ye have heaped treasure together for the last days. 4 Behold, the

---

[k] — τοῦ (*read* [the]) LTTrA. [l] ἢ or LTTrA. [m] + καὶ κριτής and judge, GLTTrA. [n] + δὲ but (who) GLTTrA. [o] ὁ κρίνων LTTrA. [p] πλησίον (*read* [thy] neighbour) LTTrA. [q] ἢ or ELTTr. [r] πορευσόμεθα we will go ELTTrAW. [s] ποιήσομεν will spend ELTAW. [t] — ἕνα (*read* a year) LTTr. [v] ἐμπορευσόμεθα will traffic ELTTrAW. [w] κερδήσομεν will make gain ELTTrAW. [x] τὰ L. [y] [γὰρ] Tr. [z] — γάρ L. [a] ἐστε ye are LTTrAW. [b] καὶ LTTrA; — δὲ W. [c] ζήσομεν we shall live LTTrAW. [d] ποιήσομεν we shall do ELTTrAW. [e] ἀλαζονίαις T.

hire of the labourers
who have reaped down
your fields, which is
of you kept back by
fraud, crieth: and the
cries of them which
have reaped are en-
tered into the ears of
the Lord of sabaoth.
5 Ye have lived in
pleasure on the earth,
and been wanton; ye
have nourished your
hearts, as in a day of
slaughter. 6 Ye have
condemned *and* killed
the just; *and* he doth
not resist you.

7 Be patient there-
fore, brethren, unto
the coming of the Lord.
Behold, the husband-
man waiteth for the
precious fruit of the
earth, and hath long
patience for it, until
he receive the early
and latter rain. 8 Be
ye also patient; sta-
blish your hearts: for
the coming of the
Lord draweth nigh.
9 Grudge not one a-
gainst another, bre-
thren, lest ye be con-
demned: behold, the
judge standeth before
the door. 10 Take, my
brethren, the prophets,
who have spoken in
the name of the Lord,
for an example of suf-
fering affliction, and
of patience. 11 Be-
hold, we count them
happy which endure.
Ye have heard of the
patience of Job, and
have seen the end of
the Lord; that the
Lord is very pitiful,
and of tender mercy.
12 But above all things,
my brethren, swear
not, neither by hea-
ven, neither by the
earth, neither by any
other oath: but let
your yea be yea;
and *your* nay, nay;
lest ye fall into con-
demnation. 13 Is any
among you afflicted?
let him pray. Is any
merry? let him sing
psalms. 14 Is any sick
among you? let him
call for the elders of
the church; and let
them pray over him,
anointing him with
oil in the name of the

τῶν ἐργατῶν τῶν ἀμησάντων τὰς.χώρας.ὑμῶν, ὁ [f]ἀπεστερη-
of the workmen who harvested your fields, which has been
μένος‖ ἀφ' ὑμῶν κράζει, καὶ αἱ βοαὶ τῶν θερισάντων εἰς
kept back by you, cries out, and the cries of those who reaped, into
τὰ ὦτα κυρίου Σαβαὼθ [g]εἰσεληλύθασιν.‖ 5 ἐτρυφήσατε
the ears of [the] Lord of Hosts have entered. Ye lived in indulgence
ἐπὶ τῆς γῆς, καὶ ἐσπαταλήσατε. ἐθρέψατε τὰς.καρδίας.ὑμῶν
upon the earth, and lived in self-gratification; ye nourished your hearts
[h]ὡς‖ ἐν ἡμέρᾳ σφαγῆς. 6 κατεδικάσατε, ἐφονεύσατε τὸν δί-
as in a day of slaughter; ye condemned, ye killed, the
καιον· οὐκ.ἀντιτάσσεται ὑμῖν.
just; he does not resist you.

7 Μακροθυμήσατε οὖν, ἀδελφοί, ἕως τῆς παρουσίας τοῦ
Be patient therefore, brethren, till the coming of the
κυρίου. ἰδού, ὁ γεωργὸς ἐκδέχεται τὸν τίμιον καρπὸν τῆς
Lord. Lo, the husbandman awaits the precious fruit of the
γῆς, μακροθυμῶν ἐπ' αὐτῷ ἕως [i]ἂν‖ λάβῃ [j]ὑετὸν‖ [k]πρώ-
earth, being patient for it until it receive [the] [4]rain [1]ear-
ϊμον‖ καὶ ὄψιμον· 8 μακροθυμήσατε καὶ ὑμεῖς, στηρίξατε
ly [2]and [3]latter. Be patient also ye: establish
τὰς.καρδίας.ὑμῶν, ὅτι ἡ παρουσία τοῦ κυρίου ἤγγικεν.
your hearts, because the coming of the Lord has drawn near.
9 Μὴ.στενάζετε [l]κατ' ἀλλήλων, ἀδελφοί,‖ ἵνα μὴ [m]κατακρι-
Groan not against one another, brethren, that [3]not [1]ye [2]be con-
θῆτε·‖ ἰδού, [n] κριτὴς πρὸ τῶν θυρῶν ἕστηκεν. 10 Ὑπό-
demned. Lo, [the] judge before the door stands. [As] an ex-
δειγμα λάβετε [o]τῆς κακοπαθείας, ἀδελφοί.μου,‖ καὶ τῆς
ample [9]take [1]of [2]suffering [3]evils, [7]my [8]brethren, [4]and
μακροθυμίας, τοὺς προφήτας οἳ ἐλάλησαν [p] τῷ ὀνόματι κυ-
[5]of [6]patience, the prophets who spoke in the name of [the]
ρίου. 11 ἰδού, μακαρίζομεν τοὺς [q]ὑπομένοντας.‖ τὴν ὑπο-
Lord. Lo, we call blessed those who endure. The en-
μονὴν Ἰὼβ ἠκούσατε, καὶ τὸ τέλος κυρίου [r]εἴδετε,‖ ὅτι
durance of Job ye have heard of, and the end of [the] Lord ye saw; that
πολύσπλαγχνός ἐστιν ὁ κύριος καὶ οἰκτίρμων. 12 Πρὸ
full of tender pity is the Lord and compassionate. [2]Before
πάντων δέ, ἀδελφοί.μου, μὴ.ὀμνύετε, μήτε τὸν οὐρανόν,
[3]all [4]things [1]but my brethren, swear not, neither [by] heaven,
μήτε τὴν γῆν, μήτε ἄλλον.τινὰ ὅρκον· ἤτω.δὲ ὑμῶν τὸ ναί,
nor the earth, nor any other oath; but let be of you the yea,
ναί, καὶ τὸ οὔ, οὔ· ἵνα μὴ [s]εἰς ὑπόκρισιν‖ πέσητε. 13 Κακο-
yea, and the nay, nay, that not into hypocrisy ye may fall. Does [4]suf-
παθεῖ τις ἐν ὑμῖν; προσευχέσθω· εὐθυμεῖ τις;
fer [5]hardships [1]anyone [2]among [3]you? let him pray: is [2]cheerful [1]anyone?
ψαλλέτω. 14 ἀσθενεῖ τις ἐν ὑμῖν; προσκαλεσάσθω
let him praise; is [2]sick [1]anyone among you? let him call to [him]
τοὺς πρεσβυτέρους τῆς ἐκκλησίας, καὶ προσευξάσθωσαν ἐπ'
the elders of the assembly, and let them pray over
αὐτόν, ἀλείψαντες [t]αὐτὸν‖ ἐλαίῳ ἐν τῷ ὀνόματι [v]τοῦ‖ κυρίου·
him, having anointed him with oil in the name of the Lord;

---

[f] ἀφυστερημένος TTr. [g] εἰσελήλυθαν LTTrAW. [h] — ὡς LTTrAW. [i] — ἂν TTrA. [j] — ὑετὸν (*read* [rain]) LTTrA. [k] πρόϊμον TTr. [l] ἀδελφοί, κατ' ἀλλήλων LTrA. [m] κριθῆτε [1]ye [2]be judged GLTTrAW. [n] + ὁ the GLTTrAW. [o] , ἀδελφοί μου, τῆς κακοπαθείας (— μου my LTTrAW) GLTTrAW. [p] + ἐν in (the) LTTr. [q] ὑπομείναντας endured LTTrA. [r] ἴδετε see ye A. [s] ὑπὸ κρίσιν under judgment EGLTTrAW. [t] — αὐτὸν (*read* [him]) T. [v] — τοῦ (*read* of [the]) L[Tr]A.

15 καὶ ἡ εὐχὴ τῆς πίστεως σώσει τὸν κάμνοντα, καὶ ἐγε-
and the prayer of faith shall save the exhausted one, and [3]will
ρεῖ αὐτὸν ὁ κύριος· κἂν ἁμαρτίας ᾖ.πεποιηκώς,
[4]raise [5]up [6]him [1]the [2]Lord; and if [7]sins [1]he [2]be [[3]one [4]who] [5]has [6]committed,
ἀφεθήσεται αὐτῷ. 16 ἐξομολογεῖσθε [w] ἀλλήλοις
it shall be forgiven him. Confess to one another [your]
[x]τὰ παραπτώματα, καὶ [y]εὔχεσθε ὑπὲρ ἀλλήλων, ὅπως ἰαθῆ-
offences, and pray for one another, that ye may be
τε. πολὺ ἰσχύει δέησις δικαίου ἐνεργουμένη.
healed. [9]Much [8]prevails [[1]the] [2]supplication [4]of [5]a [6]righteous [[7]man] [3]operative.
17 [z]Ἠλίας ἄνθρωπος ἦν ὁμοιοπαθὴς ἡμῖν, καὶ προσευχῇ
Elias [2]a [3]man [1]was of like feelings to us, and with prayer
προσηύξατο τοῦ μὴ βρέξαι· καὶ οὐκ.ἔβρεξεν ἐπὶ τῆς γῆς
he prayed [for it] not to rain; and it did not rain upon the earth
ἐνιαυτοὺς τρεῖς καὶ μῆνας ἕξ. 18 καὶ πάλιν προσηύξατο, καὶ
[2]years [1]three and [2]months [1]six; and again he prayed, and
ὁ οὐρανὸς [a]ὑετὸν ἔδωκεν, καὶ ἡ γῆ ἐβλάστησεν τὸν
the heaven [2]rain [1]gave, and the earth caused [3]to [4]sprout
καρπὸν αὐτῆς.
[2]fruit [1]its.

19 Ἀδελφοί, [b] ἐάν τις ἐν ὑμῖν πλανηθῇ ἀπὸ τῆς ἀλη-
Brethren, if anyone among you err from the truth,
θείας, καὶ ἐπιστρέψῃ τις αὐτόν, 20 [c]γινωσκέτω ὅτι ὁ
and [2]bring [3]back [1]anyone him, let him know that he who
ἐπιστρέψας ἁμαρτωλὸν ἐκ πλάνης ὁδοῦ.αὐτοῦ, σώσει
brings back a sinner from [the] error of his way, shall save
ψυχὴν [d] ἐκ θανάτου, καὶ καλύψει πλῆθος ἁμαρτιῶν.
a soul from death, and shall cover a multitude of sins.

[e]Ἰακώβου ἐπιστολή.
[2]Of [3]James [1]epistle.

Lord: 15 and the prayer of faith shall save the sick, and the Lord shall raise him up; and if he have committed sins, they shall be forgiven him. 16 Confess *your* faults one to another, and pray one for another, that ye may be healed. The effectual fervent prayer of a righteous man availeth much. 17 Elias was a man subject to like passions as we are, and he prayed earnestly that it might not rain: and it rained not on the earth by the space of three years and six months. 18 And he prayed again, and the heaven gave rain, and the earth brought forth her fruit.

19 Brethren, if any of you do err from the truth, and one convert him; 20 let him know, that he which converteth the sinner from the error of his way shall save a soul from death, and shall hide a multitude of sins.

---

[f]ΠΕΤΡΟΥ ΚΑΘΟΛΙΚΗ ΕΠΙΣΤΟΛΗ ΠΡΩΤΗ.
[4]OF [5]PETER [2]GENERAL [3]EPISTLE [1]FIRST.

ΠΕΤΡΟΣ ἀπόστολος Ἰησοῦ χριστοῦ, ἐκλεκτοῖς παρεπιδήμοις
Peter, apostle of Jesus Christ, to [the] elect sojourners
διασπορᾶς Πόντου, Γαλατίας, Καππαδοκίας, Ἀσίας, καὶ
of [the] dispersion of Pontus, of Galatia, of Cappadocia, of Asia, and
Βιθυνίας, 2 κατὰ πρόγνωσιν θεοῦ πατρός, ἐν ἁγιασ-
Bithynia, according to [the] foreknowledge of God [the] Father, by sanctifi-
μῷ πνεύματος, εἰς ὑπακοὴν καὶ ῥαντισμὸν αἵματος
cation of [the] Spirit, unto [the] obedience and sprinkling of [the] blood
Ἰησοῦ χριστοῦ· χάρις ὑμῖν καὶ εἰρήνη πληθυνθείη.
of Jesus Christ: Grace to you and peace be multiplied.
3 Εὐλογητὸς ὁ θεὸς καὶ πατὴρ τοῦ.κυρίου.ἡμῶν Ἰησοῦ
Blessed [be] the God and Father of our Lord Jesus
χριστοῦ, ὁ κατὰ τὸ.πολὺ.αὐτοῦ ἔλεος ἀναγεννήσας [g]ἡμᾶς
Christ, who according to his great mercy begat [2]again [1]us

PETER, an apostle of Jesus Christ, to the strangers scattered throughout Pontus, Galatia, Cappadocia, Asia, and Bithynia, 2 elect according to the foreknowledge of God the Father, through sanctification of the Spirit, unto obedience and sprinkling of the blood of Jesus Christ: Grace unto you, and peace, be multiplied.
3 Blessed *be* the God and Father of our Lord Jesus Christ, which according to

---

[w] + οὖν therefore LTTrA. [x] τὰς ἁμαρτίας sins LTTr. [y] προσεύχεσθε L. [z] Ἠλείας T. [a] ἔδωκεν ὑετὸν LTTr. [b] + μου my (brethren) LTTrA. [c] γινώσκετε know ye A. [d] + αὐτοῦ (*read* his soul) LT. [e] — *the subscription* EGLTW; Ἰακώβου TrA. [f] + τοῦ ἀποστόλου the apostle E; — καθολικὴ G; Πέτρου ἐπιστολὴ α΄ Tr; Πέτρου α LTAW. [g] ὑμᾶς you E.

his abundant mercy hath begotten us again unto a lively hope by the resurrection of Jesus Christ from the dead, 4 to an inheritance incorruptible, and undefiled, and that fadeth not away, reserved in heaven for you, 5 who are kept by the power of God through faith unto salvation ready to be revealed in the last time. 6 Wherein ye greatly rejoice, though now for a season, if need be, ye are in heaviness through manifold temptations: 7 that the trial of your faith, being much more precious than of gold that perisheth, though it be tried with fire, might be found unto praise and honour and glory at the appearing of Jesus Christ: 8 whom having not seen, ye love; in whom, though now ye see *him* not, yet believing, ye rejoice with joy unspeakable and full of glory: 9 receiving the end of your faith, *even* the salvation of *your* souls. 10 Of which salvation the prophets have inquired and searched diligently, who prophesied of the grace *that should come* unto you: 11 searching what, or what manner of time the Spirit of Christ which was in them did signify, when it testified beforehand the sufferings of Christ, and the glory that should follow. 12 Unto whom it was revealed, that not unto themselves, but unto us they did minister the things, which are now reported unto you by them that have preached the gospel unto you with the Holy Ghost sent down from heaven; which things the angels desire to look into.

13 Wherefore gird up the loins of your mind, be sober, and hope to the end for the grace that is to be brought unto you at the revelation of Jesus Christ; 14 as obedient children, not fashioning yourselves

εἰς ἐλπίδα ζῶσαν δι' ἀναστάσεως Ἰησοῦ χριστοῦ ἐκ
to a [2]hope [1]living through [the] resurrection of Jesus Christ from among
νεκρῶν, 4 εἰς κληρονομίαν ἄφθαρτον καὶ ἀμίαντον καὶ
[the] dead, to an inheritance incorruptible and undefiled and
ἀμάραντον, τετηρημένην ἐν οὐρανοῖς εἰς [h]ἡμᾶς,‖ 5 τοὺς ἐν
unfading, reserved in [the] heavens for us, who by
δυνάμει θεοῦ φρουρουμένους διὰ πίστεως, εἰς σωτηρίαν
[the] power of God [are] being guarded through faith, for salvation
ἑτοίμην ἀποκαλυφθῆναι ἐν καιρῷ ἐσχάτῳ· 6 ἐν.ᾧ ἀγαλ-
ready to be revealed in [the] [2]time [1]last. Wherein ye ex-
λιᾶσθε, ὀλίγον ἄρτι, εἰ δέον [i]ἐστίν,‖ λυπηθέντες
ult, for a little while at present, if necessary it is, having been put to grief
ἐν ποικίλοις πειρασμοῖς, 7 ἵνα τὸ δοκίμιον ὑμῶν τῆς πίστεως
in various trials, that the proving of your faith,
[k]πολὺ τιμιώτερον‖ χρυσίου τοῦ ἀπολλυμένου, διὰ πυρὸς δὲ
(much more precious than gold that perishes,) [2]by [3]fire [1]though
δοκιμαζομένου, εὑρεθῇ εἰς ἔπαινον καὶ [l]τιμὴν καὶ δόξαν,‖ ἐν
being proved, be found to praise and honour and glory, in
ἀποκαλύψει Ἰησοῦ χριστοῦ· 8 ὃν οὐκ [m]εἰδότες‖ ἀγαπᾶτε,
[the] revelation of Jesus Christ, whom not having seen ye love;
εἰς ὃν ἄρτι μὴ ὁρῶντες, πιστεύοντες.δέ, ἀγαλλιᾶσθε
on whom now [though] not looking, but believing, ye exult
χαρᾷ ἀνεκλαλήτῳ καὶ δεδοξασμένῃ, 9 κομιζόμενοι τὸ τέλος
with joy unspeakable and glorified, receiving the end
τῆς.πίστεως.ὑμῶν, σωτηρίαν ψυχῶν· 10 περὶ ἧς
of your faith, [the] salvation of [your] souls; concerning which
σωτηρίας ἐξεζήτησαν καὶ [n]ἐξηρεύνησαν‖ προφῆται οἱ περὶ
salvation [9]sought [10]out [11]and [12]searched [13]out [1]prophets, [2]who [4]of
τῆς εἰς ὑμᾶς χάριτος προφητεύσαντες, 11 [o]ἐρευνῶντες‖ εἰς
[5]the [7]towards [8]you [6]grace [3]prophesied; searching to
τίνα ἢ ποῖον καιρὸν ἐδήλου τὸ ἐν αὐτοῖς πνεῦμα
what or what manner of time [7]was [8]signifying [1]the [5]in [6]them [2]Spirit
χριστοῦ, προμαρτυρόμενον τὰ εἰς.χριστὸν παθήματα, καὶ
[3]of [4]Christ, testifying beforehand of the [[2]belonging] [3]to [4]Christ [1]sufferings, and
τὰς μετὰ ταῦτα δόξας· 12 οἷς ἀπεκαλύφθη ὅτι οὐχ ἑαυτοῖς,
the [2]after [3]these [1]glories; to whom it was revealed, that not to themselves
[p]ἡμῖν‖ δὲ διηκόνουν αὐτά, ἃ νῦν ἀνηγγέλη ὑμῖν διὰ
[2]to [3]us [1]but were serving those things, which now were announced to you by
τῶν εὐαγγελισαμένων ὑμᾶς [q]ἐν‖ πνεύματι ἁγίῳ ἀπο-
those who announced the glad tidings to you in [the] [2]Spirit [1]Holy
σταλέντι ἀπ' οὐρανοῦ, εἰς ἃ ἐπιθυμοῦσιν ἄγγελοι παρακύψαι.
sent from heaven, into which [2]desire [1]angels to look.

13 Διὸ ἀναζωσάμενοι τὰς ὀσφύας τῆς.διανοίας.ὑμῶν, νή-
Wherefore having girded up the loins of your mind, be-
φοντες, τελείως ἐλπίσατε ἐπὶ τὴν φερομένην ὑμῖν χάριν ἐν
ing sober, perfectly hope in the [2]being [3]brought [4]to [5]you [1]grace at
ἀποκαλύψει Ἰησοῦ χριστοῦ. 14 ὡς τέκνα ὑπακοῆς, μὴ
[the] revelation of Jesus Christ; as children of obedience, not
[r]συσχηματιζόμενοι‖ ταῖς πρότερον ἐν τῇ.ἀγνοίᾳ.ὑμῶν ἐπιθυ-
fashioning yourselves to the former [2]in [3]your [4]ignorance [1]de-
μίαις, 15 ἀλλὰ κατὰ τὸν καλέσαντα ὑμᾶς ἅγιον καὶ
sires; but according as he who called you [is] holy, also
αὐτοὶ ἅγιοι ἐν πάσῃ ἀναστροφῇ γενήθητε· 16 διότι
[3]yourselves [4]holy [5]in [6]all [[7]your] [8]conduct [1]be [2]ye; because

---

[h] ὑμᾶς you GLTTrAW. [i] — ἐστίν TTr. [k] πολυτιμότερον GLTTrA. [l] δόξαν καὶ τιμὴν LTTrAW. [m] ἰδόντες LTTrAW. [n] ἐξηραύνησαν TTrA. [o] ἐραυνῶντες TTrA. [p] ὑμῖν to you GLTTrAW. [q] — ἐν (read ἁγίῳ by [the] Holy) LTrA. [r] συνσ- TrA.

γέγραπται, Ἅγιοι [s]γένεσθε,ǁ [t]ὅτιǁ ἐγὼ ἅγιός [v]εἰμι.ǁ 17 Καὶ
It has been written, [3]Holy [1]be [2]ye, because I [2]holy [1]am. And
εἰ πατέρα ἐπικαλεῖσθε τὸν [w]ἀπροσωπολήπτωςǁ κρίνοντα
if [as] Father ye call on him who without regard of persons judges
κατὰ τὸ ἑκάστου ἔργον, ἐν φόβῳ τὸν τῆς.παροικίας.ὑμῶν
according to the [2]of [3]each [1]work, in fear the [2]of [3]your [4]sojourn
χρόνον ἀναστράφητε· 18 εἰδότες ὅτι οὐ φθαρτοῖς, ἀρ-
[1]time pass ye, knowing that not by corruptible things, by
γυρίῳ ἢ χρυσίῳ, ἐλυτρώθητε ἐκ τῆς.ματαίας.ὑμῶν ἀναστροφῆς
silver or by gold, ye were redeemed from your vain manner of life
πατροπαραδότου, 19 ἀλλὰ τιμίῳ αἵματι ὡς ἀμνοῦ
handed down from [your] fathers, but by precious blood as of a lamb
ἀμώμου καὶ ἀσπίλου χριστοῦ· 20 προεγνωσ-
without blemish and without spot [the blood] of Christ: having been fore-
μένου μὲν πρὸ καταβολῆς κόσμου, φανερωθέντος.δὲ ἐπ'
known indeed before [the] foundation of [the] world, but manifested at
[x]ἐσχάτωνǁ τῶν χρόνων δι' ὑμᾶς, 21 τοὺς δι' αὐτοῦ
[the] last times for the sake of you, who by him
[y]πιστεύονταςǁ εἰς θεόν, τὸν ἐγείραντα αὐτὸν ἐκ νεκρῶν,
believe in God, who raised up him from among [the] dead,
καὶ δόξαν αὐτῷ δόντα, ὥστε τὴν.πίστιν.ὑμῶν καὶ ἐλπίδα εἶναι
and glory to him gave, so as for your faith and hope to be
εἰς θεόν. 22 Τὰς.ψυχὰς.ὑμῶν ἡγνικότες ἐν τῇ ὑπακοῇ τῆς
in God. Your souls having purified by obedience to the
ἀληθείας [z]διὰ πνεύματοςǁ εἰς φιλαδελφίαν ἀνυπόκριτον, ἐκ
truth through [the] Spirit to brotherly love unfeigned, out of
[a]καθαρᾶςǁ καρδίας ἀλλήλους ἀγαπήσατε ἐκτενῶς· 23 ἀναγε-
[2]pure [1]a heart one another love ye fervently. Having been
γεννημένοι οὐκ ἐκ σπορᾶς φθαρτῆς, ἀλλὰ ἀφθάρτου, διὰ
begotten again, not of [2]seed [1]corruptible, but of incorruptible, by
λόγου ζῶντος θεοῦ καὶ μένοντος [b]εἰς.τὸν.αἰῶνα.ǁ 24 διότι
[the] word [3]living [1]of [2]God and abiding for ever. Because
πᾶσα σὰρξ [c]ὡςǁ χόρτος, καὶ πᾶσα δόξα [d]ἀνθρώπουǁ ὡς
all flesh [is] as grass, and all [the] glory of man as [the]
ἄνθος χόρτου. ἐξηράνθη ὁ χόρτος, καὶ τὸ ἄνθος [e]αὐτοῦǁ
flower of grass. [3]Withered [1]the [2]grass, and the flower of it
ἐξέπεσεν· 25 τὸ.δὲ ῥῆμα κυρίου μένει εἰς.τὸν.αἰῶνα. Τοῦτο.δέ
fell away; but the word of [the] Lord abides for ever. But this
ἐστιν τὸ ῥῆμα τὸ εὐαγγελισθὲν εἰς ὑμᾶς.
is the word which was announced to you.

2 Ἀποθέμενοι οὖν πᾶσαν κακίαν καὶ πάντα δόλον καὶ
Having laid aside therefore all malice and all guile and
ὑποκρίσεις καὶ φθόνους καὶ πάσας καταλαλιάς, 2 ὡς ἀρτιγέν-
hypocrisies and envyings and all evil speakings, as new-
νητα βρέφη, τὸ λογικὸν ἄδολον γάλα ἐπιποθήσατε, ἵνα ἐν
born babes, the [2]mental [1]genuine milk long ye after, that by
αὐτῷ αὐξηθῆτε,[f] 3 [g]εἴπερǁ ἐγεύσασθε ὅτι χρηστὸς ὁ κύριος.
it ye may grow, if indeed ye did taste that [3is] [4]good [1]the [2]Lord.
4 πρὸς ὃν προσερχόμενοι, λίθον ζῶντα, ὑπὸ ἀνθρώπων μὲν
To whom coming, a [2]stone [1]living, by men indeed
ἀποδεδοκιμασμένον, παρὰ.δὲ θεῷ ἐκλεκτόν, ἔντιμον, 5 καὶ αὐ-
rejected, but with God chosen, precious, also your-

according to the former lusts in your ignorance: 15 but as he which hath called you is holy, so be ye holy in all manner of conversation; 16 because it is written, Be ye holy; for I am holy.
17 And if ye call on the Father, who without respect of persons judgeth according to every man's work, pass the time of your sojourning *here* in fear:
18 forasmuch as ye know that ye were not redeemed with corruptible things, *as* silver and gold, from your vain conversation *received* by tradition from your fathers;
19 but with the precious blood of Christ, as of a lamb without blemish and without spot:
20 who verily was foreordained before the foundation of the world, but was manifest in these last times for you,
21 who by him do believe in God, that raised him up from the dead, and gave him glory; that your faith and hope might be in God.
22 Seeing ye have purified your souls in obeying the truth through the Spirit unto unfeigned love of the brethren, *see that ye* love one another with a pure heart fervently:
23 being born again, not of corruptible seed, but of incorruptible, by the word of God, which liveth and abideth for ever.
24 For all flesh *is* as grass, and all the glory of man as the flower of grass. The grass withereth, and the flower thereof falleth away:
25 but the word of the Lord endureth for ever. And this is the word which by the gospel is preached unto you.

II. Wherefore laying aside all malice, and all guile, and hypocrisies, and envies, and all evil speakings,
2 as new born babes, desire the sincere milk of the word, that ye may grow thereby:

---

[s] ἔσεσθε ye shall be LTTrAW. [t] διότι T. [v] — εἰμι (*read* [am]) LTTrAW. [w] ἀπροσωπολήμπτως LTTrA. [x] ἐσχάτου (*read* end of the times) LTTrAW. [y] πιστοὺς [are] believers LTTrA. [z] — διὰ πνεύματος LTTrAW. [a] — καθαρᾶς (*read* from [the] heart) LTTrA. [b] — εἰς τὸν αἰῶνα GLTTrAW. [c] — ὡς L. [d] αὐτῆς (*read* its glory) GLTTrAW. [e] — αὐτοῦ LTTr[A]W. [f] + εἰς σωτηρίαν unto salvation GLTTrAW. [g] εἰ if LTTr.

τοὶ ὡς λίθοι ζῶντες [i]οἰκοδομεῖσθε,ǁ οἶκος πνευματικός,[k]
selves, as [2]stones [1]living, are being built up, a [2]house [1]spiritual,
ἱεράτευμα ἅγιον, ἀνενέγκαι πνευματικὰς θυσίας εὐπροσδέκτους
a [2]priesthood [1]holy to offer spiritual sacrifices acceptable
[l]τῷ θεῷ διὰ Ἰησοῦ χριστοῦ. 6 [m]Διὸ καὶǁ περιέχει [n]ἐν τῇ
to God by Jesus Christ. Wherefore also it is contained in the
γραφῇ,ǁ Ἰδοὺ τίθημι ἐν Σιὼν λίθον ἀκρογωνιαῖον, ἐκλεκτόν,
scripture: Behold, I place in Sion a [3]stone [1]corner, chosen,
ἔντιμον· καὶ ὁ πιστεύων ἐπ' αὐτῷ οὐ.μὴ καταισχυνθῇ.
precious: and he that believes on him in no wise should be put to shame.
7 Ὑμῖν οὖν ἡ τιμὴ τοῖς πιστεύουσιν· [o]ἀπει-
To you therefore [[3]is] [4]the [5]preciousness [1]who [2]believe; [7]to [[8]those] [9]dis-
θοῦσινǁ δέ, [p]λίθονǁ ὃν ἀπεδοκίμασαν οἱ οἰκοδομοῦντες,
obeying [6]but, [the] stone which [3]rejected [1]those [2]building,
οὗτος ἐγενήθη εἰς κεφαλὴν γωνίας, 8 καὶ λίθος προσκόμ-
this became head of [the] corner, and a stone of stum-
ματος καὶ πέτρα σκανδάλου· οἳ προσκόπτουσιν τῷ λόγῳ
bling and a rock of offence; who stumble at the word,
ἀπειθοῦντες, εἰς ὃ καὶ ἐτέθησαν· 9 ὑμεῖς.δὲ γένος ἐκ-
being disobedient, to which also they were appointed. But ye [are] a [2]race
λεκτόν, βασίλειον ἱεράτευμα, ἔθνος ἅγιον, λαὸς εἰς περι-
[1]chosen, a kingly priesthood, a [2]nation [1]holy, a people for a pos-
ποίησιν, ὅπως τὰς ἀρετὰς ἐξαγγείλητε τοῦ ἐκ σκότους
session, that the virtues ye might set forth of him who out of darkness
ὑμᾶς καλέσαντος εἰς τὸ.θαυμαστὸν.αὐτοῦ φῶς· 10 οἵ ποτὲ
[2]you [1]called to his wonderful light; who once
οὐ λαός, νῦν.δὲ λαὸς θεοῦ· οἱ οὐκ.ἠλεημένοι,
[were] not a people, but now [are] [2]people [1]God's; who had not received mercy,
νῦν.δὲ ἐλεηθέντες.
but now received mercy

11 Ἀγαπητοί, παρακαλῶ ὡς παροίκους καὶ παρεπιδή-
Beloved, I exhort [you] as strangers and sojourners,
μους, ἀπέχεσθαι[q] τῶν σαρκικῶν ἐπιθυμιῶν, αἵτινες στρατεύον-
to abstain from fleshly desires, which war
ται κατὰ τῆς ψυχῆς· 12 τὴν.ἀναστροφὴν.ὑμῶν ἐν τοῖς
against the soul; [2]your [3]manner [4]of [5]life [7]among [8]the
ἔθνεσιν ἔχοντες καλήν, ἵνα ἐν.ᾧ καταλαλοῦσιν ὑμῶν ὡς
[9]nations [1]having [6]right that wherein they speak against you as
κακοποιῶν, ἐκ τῶν καλῶν ἔργων [r]ἐποπτεύσαντεςǁ δοξά-
evil doers, through [your] good works having witnessed they
σωσιν τὸν θεὸν ἐν ἡμέρᾳ ἐπισκοπῆς.
may glorify God in [the] day of visitation.

13 Ὑποτάγητε [s]οὖνǁ πάσῃ ἀνθρωπίνῃ κτίσει, διὰ
Be in subjection therefore to every human institution for the sake of
τὸν κύριον· εἴτε βασιλεῖ, ὡς ὑπερέχοντι· 14 εἴτε ἡγεμόσιν,
the Lord; whether to [the] king as supreme, or to governors
ὡς δι' αὐτοῦ πεμπομένοις εἰς ἐκδίκησιν [t]μὲνǁ κακοποιῶν,
as by him sent, for vengeance [on] evil doers,
ἔπαινον.δὲ ἀγαθοποιῶν· 15 ὅτι οὕτως ἐστὶν τὸ θέλημα
and praise [to] well doers; (because so is the will
τοῦ θεοῦ, ἀγαθοποιοῦντας φιμοῦν τὴν τῶν ἀφρόνων
of God, [by] well doing to put to silence the [2]of [3]senseless

3 if so be ye have
tasted that the Lord
is gracious. 4 To whom
coming, *as unto* a liv-
ing stone, disallowed
indeed of men, but
chosen of God, *and*
precious, 5 ye also, as
lively stones, are built
up a spiritual house,
an holy priesthood, to
offer up spiritual sac-
rifices, acceptable to
God by Jesus Christ.
6 Wherefore also it is
contained in the scrip-
ture, Behold, I lay in
Sion a chief corner
stone, elect, precious:
and he that believeth
on him shall not be
confounded. 7 Unto
you therefore which
believe *he is* precious:
but unto them which
be disobedient, the
stone which the build-
ers disallowed, the
same is made the head
of the corner, 8 and a
stone of stumbling,
and a rock of offence,
even to them which
stumble at the word,
being disobedient:
whereunto also they
were appointed. 9 But
ye *are* a chosen gene-
ration, a royal priest-
hood, an holy nation,
a peculiar people; that
ye should shew forth
the praises of him who
hath called you out of
darkness into his mar-
vellous light: 10 which
in time past *were* not
a people, but *are* now
the people of God:
which had not ob-
tained mercy, but now
have obtained mercy.
11 Dearly beloved, I
beseech *you* as strang-
ers and pilgrims, ab-
stain from fleshly lusts,
which war against the
soul; 12 having your
conversation honest a-
mong the Gentiles:
that, whereas they
speak against you
as evildoers, they
may by *your* good
works, which they
shall behold, glorify
God in the day of visi-
tation.
13 Submit yourselves
to every ordinance of
man for the Lord's
sake: whether it be to
the king, as supreme;
14 or unto governors,
as unto them that are

---

[i] ἐποικοδομεῖσθε T. [k] + εἰς for LTTrA. [l] — τῷ LTTrA. [m] διότι because GLTTrAW. [n] — τῇ TTrA; ἡ γραφή (*read* the scripture contains) L. [o] ἀπιστοῦσιν (*read* but to [those] unbelieving) TTr. [p] λίθος LTrA. [q] + ὑμᾶς (*read* that ye abstain) L. [r] ἐποπτεύοντες witnessing LTTrAW. [s] — οὖν LTTrA. [t] — μὲν GLTTrAW.

ἀνθρώπων ἀγνωσίαν· 16 ὡς ἐλεύθεροι, καὶ μὴ ὡς ἐπικά-
[4]men [1]ignorance;) as free, and not [3]as [4]a
λυμμα ἔχοντες τῆς κακίας τὴν ἐλευθερίαν, ἀλλ' ὡς [v]δοῦλοι
[5]cloak [1]having [6]of [7]malice [2]freedom, but as bondmen
θεοῦ.‖ 17 πάντας τιμήσατε, τὴν ἀδελφότητα ἀγαπᾶτε, τὸν
of God. [4]All [1]shew [2]honour [3]to, [6]the [7]brotherhood [5]love,
θεὸν φοβεῖσθε, τὸν βασιλέα τιμᾶτε.
[9]God [8]fear, [11]the [12]king [10]honour.

18 Οἱ οἰκέται, ὑποτασσόμενοι ἐν παντὶ φόβῳ τοῖς δεσ-
Servants, being subject with all fear to [your]
πόταις, οὐ μόνον τοῖς ἀγαθοῖς καὶ ἐπιεικέσιν, ἀλλὰ καὶ
masters, not only to the good and gentle, but also
τοῖς σκολιοῖς. 19 τοῦτο γὰρ χάρις, εἰ διὰ συνείδησιν
to the crooked. For this [is] acceptable if for sake of conscience
θεοῦ ὑποφέρει τις λύπας, πάσχων ἀδίκως. 20 ποῖον γὰρ
towards God [2]endures [1]anyone griefs, suffering unjustly. For what
κλέος, εἰ ἁμαρτάνοντες καὶ κολαφιζόμενοι ὑπομενεῖτε;
glory [is it], if sinning and being buffeted ye endure it?
ἀλλ' εἰ ἀγαθοποιοῦντες καὶ πάσχοντες ὑπομενεῖτε, τοῦτο [w]
but if doing good and suffering ye endure [it], this [is]
χάρις παρὰ θεῷ. 21 εἰς τοῦτο γὰρ ἐκλήθητε, ὅτι καὶ
acceptable with God. For to this ye were called; because also
χριστὸς ἔπαθεν ὑπὲρ [x]ἡμῶν,‖ [y]ἡμῖν‖ ὑπολιμπάνων ὑπογραμ-
Christ, suffered for us, [2]us [1]leaving a model
μόν, ἵνα ἐπακολουθήσητε τοῖς ἴχνεσιν αὐτοῦ· 22 ὃς ἁμαρτίαν
that ye should follow after in his steps; who [3]sin
οὐκ ἐποίησεν, οὐδὲ εὑρέθη δόλος ἐν τῷ στόματι αὐτοῦ· 23 ὃς
[1]did [2]no, neither was [2]found [1]guile in his mouth; who,
λοιδορούμενος οὐκ ἀντελοιδόρει, πάσχων οὐκ ἠπείλει,
being railed at, railed not in return; [when] suffering threatened not;
παρεδίδου δὲ τῷ κρίνοντι δικαίως· 24 ὃς τὰς
but gave [himself] over to him who judges righteously; who
ἁμαρτίας ἡμῶν αὐτὸς ἀνήνεγκεν ἐν τῷ σώματι αὐτοῦ ἐπὶ τὸ
our sins himself bore in his body on the
ξύλον, ἵνα ταῖς ἁμαρτίαις ἀπογενόμενοι, τῇ δικαιοσύνῃ ζή-
tree, that, to sins [we] being dead, to righteousness we
σωμεν· οὗ τῷ μώλωπι [z]αὐτοῦ‖ ἰάθητε. 25 ἦτε γὰρ ὡς πρό-
may live; by whose bruise ye were healed. For ye were as
βατα [a]πλανώμενα·‖ ἀλλ' ἐπεστράφητε νῦν ἐπὶ τὸν ποιμένα
sheep going astray, but are returned now to the shepherd
καὶ ἐπίσκοπον τῶν ψυχῶν ὑμῶν.
and overseer of your souls.

3 Ὁμοίως, [b]αἱ‖ γυναῖκες, ὑποτασσόμεναι τοῖς ἰδίοις ἀν-
Likewise, wives, being subject to your own hus-
δράσιν, ἵνα καὶ εἴ τινες ἀπειθοῦσιν τῷ λόγῳ, διὰ τῆς τῶν
bands, that, even if any are disobedient to the word, by the [2]of [3]the
γυναικῶν ἀναστροφῆς ἄνευ λόγου [c]κερδηθήσωνται,‖ 2 ἐπο-
[4]wives [1]conduct without [the] word they may be gained, hav-
πτεύσαντες τὴν ἐν φόβῳ ἁγνὴν ἀναστροφὴν ὑμῶν·
ing witnessed [[4]carried [5]out] [6]in [7]fear [2]chaste [3]conduct [1]your;
3 ὧν ἔστω οὐχ ὁ ἔξωθεν ἐμπλοκῆς [d]τριχῶν,‖ [e]καὶ‖
whose [2]let [3]it [4]not [5]be [6]the [7]outward [[8]one] [9]of [10]braiding [11]of [12]hair, [13]and
περιθέσεως χρυσίων, ἢ ἐνδύσεως ἱματίων κόσμος·
[14]putting [15]around [16]of [17]gold, [18]or [19]putting [20]on [21]of [22]garments [1]adorning;

sent by him for the
punishment of evil-
doers, and for the
praise of them that do
well. 15 For so is the
will of God, that with
well doing ye may put
to silence the ignor-
ance of foolish men:
16 as free, and not
using *your* liberty for
a cloke of malicious-
ness, but as the ser-
vants of God. 17 Ho-
nour all *men*. Love
the brotherhood. Fear
God. Honour the king.
18 Servants, *be* sub-
ject to *your* masters
with all fear; not
only to the good and
gentle, but also to the
froward. 19 For this
is thankworthy, if a
man for conscience to-
ward God endure grief,
suffering wrongfully.
20 For what glory *is it*,
if, when ye be buffeted
for your faults, ye
shall take it patiently?
but if, when ye do
well, and suffer *for it*,
ye take it patient-
ly, this *is* acceptable
with God. 21 For
even hereunto were
ye called: because
Christ also suffered for
us, leaving us an ex-
ample, that ye should
follow his steps: 22 who
did no sin, neither was
guile found in his
mouth: 23 who, when
he was reviled, reviled
not again; when he
suffered, he threatened
not; but committed
himself to him that
judgeth righteously:
24 who his own self
bare our sins in his
own body on the tree,
that we, being dead to
sins, should live un-
to righteousness: by
whose stripes ye were
healed. 25 For ye were
as sheep going astray;
but are now returned
unto the Shepherd and
Bishop of your souls.
III. Likewise, ye
wives, *be* in subjection
to your own husbands;
that, if any obey not
the word, they also
may without the word
be won by the conver-
sation of the wives;
2 while they behold
your chaste conversa-
tion *coupled* with fear.
3 Whose adorning let
it not be that outward
adorning of plaiting
the hair, and of wear-

---

[v] θεοῦ δοῦλοι TTrA. [w] + γὰρ for (this) LA. [x] ὑμῶν you EGLTTrA. [y] ὑμῖν you EGLTTrAW. [z] — αὐτοῦ LTr[A]. [a] πλανώμενοι (*read* ye were going astray as sheep) LTTrA. [b] — αἱ LTTr[A]. [c] κερδηθήσονται they will be gained LTTrA. [d] — τριχῶν L. [e] ἢ or L.

ing of gold, or of put-
ting on of apparel;
4 but *let it be* the hidden man of the heart,
in that which is not
corruptible, *even the*
ornament of a meek
and quiet spirit, which
is in the sight of God
of great price. 5 For
after this manner in
the old time the holy
women also, who trust-
ed in God, adorned
themselves, being in
subjection unto their
own husbands: 6 even
as Sara obeyed Abra-
ham, calling him lord:
whose daughters ye
are, as long as ye do
well, and are not a-
fraid with any amaze-
ment. 7 Likewise, ye
husbands, dwell with
them according to
knowledge, giving ho-
nour unto the wife, as
unto the weaker ves-
sel, and as being heirs
together of the grace
of life; that your
prayers be not hin-
dered.

8 Finally, *be ye* all
of one mind, having
compassion one of an-
other, love as brethren,
be pitiful, *be* court-
eous: 9 not rendering
evil for evil, or railing
for railing: but con-
trariwise blessing;
knowing that ye are
thereunto called, that
ye should inherit a
blessing. 10 For he
that will love life, and
see good days, let him
refrain his tongue
from evil, and his lips
that they speak no
guile: 11 let him es-
chew evil, and do good;
let him seek peace, and
ensue it. 12 For the
eyes of the Lord *are*
over the righteous, and
his ears *are open* unto
their prayers: but the
face of the Lord *is* a-
gainst them that do
evil. 13 And who *is* he
that will harm you,
if *ye* be followers of
that which is good?
14 But and if ye suf-
fer for righteousness'
sake, happy *are ye*:
and be not afraid of
their terror, neither
be troubled; 15 but
sanctify the Lord God
in your hearts: and *be*

4 ἀλλ' ὁ κρυπτὸς τῆς καρδίας ἄνθρωπος, ἐν τῷ ἀφθάρτῳ
but the hidden [2]of [3]the [4]heart [1]man, in the incorruptible
τοῦ [f]πραέος καὶ ἡσυχίου‖ πνεύματος, ὅ ἐστιν ἐνώπιον
[ornament] of the meek and quiet spirit, which is before
τοῦ θεοῦ πολυτελές. 5 οὕτως-γάρ ποτε καὶ αἱ ἅγιαι γυναῖκες
God of great price. For thus formerly also the holy women
αἱ ἐλπίζουσαι [g]ἐπὶ τὸν‖ θεὸν ἐκόσμουν ἑαυτάς, ὑποτασσό-
those hoping in God adorned themselves, being sub-
μεναι τοῖς-ἰδίοις ἀνδράσιν· 6 ὡς Σάῤῥα [h]ὑπήκουσεν‖ τῷ
ject to their own husbands; as Sarah obeyed
'Αβραάμ, κύριον αὐτὸν καλοῦσα, ἧς ἐγενήθητε τέκνα· ἀγα-
Abraham, [3]lord [2]him [1]calling; of whom ye became children, do-
θοποιοῦσαι καὶ μὴ-φοβούμεναι μηδεμίαν πτόησιν. 7 Οἱ
ing good and not fearing [with] any consternation.
(*lit.* no)
ἄνδρες ὁμοίως, συνοικοῦντες κατὰ γνῶσιν, ὡς ἀσθε-
Husbands likewise, dwelling with [them] according to knowledge, as with a
νεστέρῳ σκεύει τῷ γυναικείῳ ἀπονέμοντες τιμήν, ὡς
weaker [even] [4]vessel [1]with [2]the [3]female, rendering [them] honour, as
καὶ [i]συγκληρονόμοι‖ χάριτος ζωῆς, εἰς τὸ μὴ [k]ἐκκόπτεσ-
also [being] joint-heirs of [the] grace of life, so as [3]not [4]to [5]be [6]cut
θαι‖ τὰς-προσευχὰς-ὑμῶν.
[7]off [1]your [2]prayers.

8 Τὸ-δὲ-τέλος, πάντες ὁμόφρονες, συμπαθεῖς, φιλ-
Finally, all [being] of one mind, sympathizing, loving
άδελφοι, εὔσπλαγχνοι, [l]φιλόφρονες·‖ 9 μὴ ἀποδιδόντες
the brethren, tender hearted, friendly, not rendering
κακὸν ἀντὶ κακοῦ, ἢ λοιδορίαν ἀντὶ λοιδορίας· τοὐναντίον-δὲ
evil for evil, or railing for railing; but on the contrary,
εὐλογοῦντες, [m]εἰδότες‖ ὅτι εἰς τοῦτο ἐκλήθητε, ἵνα εὐλογίαν
blessing, knowing that to this ye were called, that blessing
κληρονομήσητε. 10 ὁ-γὰρ θέλων ζωὴν ἀγαπᾷν, καὶ ἰδεῖν
ye should inherit. For he that wills [3]life [1]to [2]love, and to see
ἡμέρας ἀγαθάς, παυσάτω τὴν-γλῶσσαν-[n]αὐτοῦ‖ ἀπὸ
[2]days [1]good, let him cause to cease his tongue from
κακοῦ, καὶ χείλη [n]αὐτοῦ‖ τοῦ μὴ λαλῆσαι δόλον. 11 ἐκκλι-
evil, and [2]lips [1]his not to speak guile. Let him turn
νάτω [o] ἀπὸ κακοῦ, καὶ ποιησάτω ἀγαθόν· ζητησάτω εἰρήνην,
aside from evil, and let him do good. Let him seek peace
καὶ διωξάτω αὐτήν. 12 ὅτι [p]οἱ‖ ὀφθαλμοὶ κυρίου ἐπὶ
and let him pursue it: because the eyes of [the] Lord [are] on
δικαίους, καὶ ὦτα-αὐτοῦ εἰς δέησιν-αὐτῶν· πρόσωπον-δὲ
[the] righteous, and his ears towards their supplication. But [the] face
κυρίου ἐπὶ ποιοῦντας κακά. 13 καὶ τίς ὁ κακώ-
of [the] Lord [is] against those doing evil. And who [is] he that shall in-
σων ὑμᾶς, ἐὰν τοῦ ἀγαθοῦ [q]μιμηταὶ‖ γένησθε;
jure you, if [2]of [3]that [4]which [[5]is] [6]good [1]imitators ye should be?
14 ἀλλ' εἰ καὶ πάσχοιτε διὰ δικαιοσύνην, μακάριοι.
But if also ye should suffer on account of righteousness, blessed [are ye];
τὸν-δὲ-φόβον-αὐτῶν μὴ-φοβηθῆτε, μηδὲ ταραχθῆτε·
but their fear ye should not be afraid of, neither should ye be troubled;
15 κύριον-δὲ τὸν [r]θεὸν‖ ἁγιάσατε ἐν ταῖς-καρδίαις-ὑμῶν·
but [3]Lord [2]the [4]God [1]sanctify in your hearts,

---

[f] ἡσυχίου καὶ πραέος L; πραέως (πραέος A) καὶ ἡσυχίου TTrA. [g] εἰς LTTrAW. [h] ὑπήκουεν L. [i] συνκληρονόμοις T; συγκληρονόμοις to joint-heirs TrA. [k] ἐγκόπτεσθαι to be hindered GLTrAW; ἐν- T. [l] ταπεινόφρονες humble minded GLTTrAW. [m] — εἰδότες (*read* ὅτι because) LTTrA. [n] — αὐτοῦ (*read* [his]) LTTrA. [o] + δὲ and (let him turn aside) LTrA. [p] — οἱ (*read* [the] Lord's eyes) LTTrA. [q] ζηλωταὶ zealous LTTrAW. [r] χριστὸν Christ LTTrAW.

ἕτοιμοι[s]δὲ‖ ἀεὶ πρὸς ἀπολογίαν παντὶ τῷ αἰτοῦντι ὑμᾶς
and ready [be] always for a defence to everyone that asks you
λόγον περὶ τῆς ἐν ὑμῖν ἐλπίδος, [t] μετὰ πραΰτητος καὶ
an account concerning the [2]in [3]you [1]hope, with meekness and
φόβου· 16 συνείδησιν ἔχοντες ἀγαθήν, ἵνα ἐν.ᾧ [v]καταλαλῶ-
fear; [2]a [4]conscience [1]having [3]good, that whereas they may speak
σιν‖ [w]ὑμῶν ὡς κακοποιῶν,‖ καταισχυνθῶσιν οἱ ἐπηρεάζοντες
against you as evil doers, they may be ashamed who calumniate
ὑμῶν τὴν ἀγαθὴν ἐν χριστῷ ἀναστροφήν. 17 κρεῖττον.γὰρ
your good [4]in [5]Christ [1]manner [2]of [3]life. For [it is] better,
ἀγαθοποιοῦντας, εἰ [x]θέλει‖ τὸ θέλημα τοῦ θεοῦ, πάσχειν,
[8]for [9]you] [10]doing [11]good, [1]if [6]wills [[7]it] [2]the [3]will [4]of [5]God, to suffer,
ἢ κακοποιοῦντας· 18 ὅτι καὶ χριστὸς ἅπαξ περὶ ἁμαρ-
than doing evil; because [2]indeed [1]Christ once for sins
τιῶν [y]ἔπαθεν‖ δίκαιος ὑπὲρ ἀδίκων, ἵνα ἡμᾶς προσαγάγῃ
suffered, [the] just for [the] unjust, that us he might bring
[z]τῷ‖ θεῷ, θανατωθεὶς μὲν σαρκί, ζωοποιηθεὶς.δὲ [a]τῷ‖
to God; having been put to death in flesh, but made alive by the
πνεύματι, 19 ἐν ᾧ καὶ τοῖς ἐν φυλακῇ πνεύμασιν πορευθεὶς
Spirit, in which also to the [2]in [3]prison [1]spirits having gone
ἐκήρυξεν, 20 ἀπειθήσασίν ποτε, ὅτε [b]ἅπαξ ἐξεδέχετο‖ ἡ
he preached, [who] disobeyed sometime, when once was waiting the
τοῦ θεοῦ μακροθυμία ἐν ἡμέραις Νῶε, κατασκευα-
[2]of [3]God [1]longsuffering in [the] days of Noe, [while was] being pre-
ζομένης κιβωτοῦ, εἰς ἣν [c]ὀλίγαι,‖ [d]τουτέστιν‖ ὀκτώ, ψυχαὶ
pared [the] ark, into which few, that is eight souls,
διεσώθησαν δι' ὕδατος, 21 [e]ὃ‖ καὶ [f]ἡμᾶς‖ ἀντίτυπον νῦν
were saved through water, which [2]also [5]us [1]figure [3]now
σώζει βάπτισμα, οὐ σαρκὸς ἀπόθεσις ῥύπου, ἀλλὰ
[4]saves [even] baptism, not of flesh a putting away of [the] filth, but
συνειδήσεως ἀγαθῆς ἐπερώτημα εἰς θεόν, δι' ἀνα-
[5]of [6]a [8]conscience [7]good [[1]the] [2]demand [3]towards [4]God, by [the] re-
στάσεως Ἰησοῦ χριστοῦ, 22 ὅς ἐστιν ἐν δεξιᾷ [g]τοῦ‖ θεοῦ,
surrection of Jesus Christ, who is at [the] right hand of God,
πορευθεὶς εἰς οὐρανόν, ὑποταγέντων αὐτῷ ἀγγέλων καὶ
gone into heaven, [6]having [7]been [8]subjected [9]to [10]him [1]angels [2]and
ἐξουσιῶν καὶ δυνάμεων.
[3]authorities [4]and [5]powers.

4 Χριστοῦ οὖν παθόντος [h]ὑπὲρ ἡμῶν‖ σαρκί, καὶ ὑμεῖς τὴν
Christ then having suffered for us in [the] flesh, also ye [4]the
αὐτὴν ἔννοιαν ὁπλίσασθε· ὅτι ὁ παθὼν [i]ἐν‖ σαρκί,
[5]same [6]mind [1]arm [2]yourselves [3]with; for he that suffered in [the] flesh
πέπαυται ἁμαρτίας· 2 εἰς τὸ μηκέτι ἀνθρώπων ἐπιθυμίαις,
has done with sin; no longer [10]men's [9]to [11]lusts,
ἀλλὰ θελήματι θεοῦ τὸν ἐπίλοιπον ἐν σαρκὶ βιῶσαι χρόνον.
[12]but [13]to [15]will [14]God's [3]the [4]remaining [6]in [[7]the] [8]flesh [1]to [2]live [5]time.
3 ἀρκετὸς.γὰρ [k]ἡμῖν‖ ὁ παρεληλυθὼς χρόνος [l]τοῦ βίου,‖ τὸ
For [is] sufficient for us the past time of life the
[m]θέλημα‖ τῶν ἐθνῶν [n]κατεργάσασθαι,‖ πεπορευμένους ἐν
will of the nations to have worked out, having walked in

ready always to *give*
an answer to every
man that asketh you
a reason of the hope
that is in you with
meekness and fear:
16 having a good con-
science; that, where-
as they speak evil of
you, as of evildoers,
they may be ashamed
that falsely accuse
your good conversa-
tion in Christ. 17 For
it is better, if the will
of God be so, that ye
suffer for well doing,
than for evil doing.
18 For Christ also hath
once suffered for sins,
the just for the un-
just, that he might
bring us to God, being
put to death in the
flesh, but quickened by
the Spirit: 19 by which
also he went and
preached unto the spi-
rits in prison; 20 which
sometime were disobe-
dient, when once the
longsuffering of God
waited in the days
of Noah, while the
ark was a preparing,
wherein few, that is,
eight souls were saved
by water. 21 The like
figure whereunto *even*
baptism doth also now
save us (not the put-
ting away of the filth
of the flesh, but the
answer of a good con-
science toward God,)
by the resurrection of
Jesus Christ: 22 who is
gone into heaven, and
is on the right hand of
God; angels and au-
thorities and powers
being made subject un-
to him.

IV. Forasmuch then
as Christ hath suffered
for us in the flesh, arm
yourselves likewise
with the same mind:
for he that hath suf-
fered in the flesh hath
ceased from sin; 2 that
he no longer should
live the rest of *his* time
in the flesh to the lusts
of men, but to the will
of God. 3 For the time
past of *our* life may
suffice us to have
wrought the will of
the Gentiles, when we

---

[s] — δὲ and LTTr[A]. [t] + ἀλλὰ but LTTrAW. [v] καταλαλοῦσιν they speak against LTrW; καταλαλεῖσθε ye are spoken against TA. [w] — ὑμῶν ὡς κακοποιῶν TA. [x] θέλοι may will GLTTrAW. [y] ἀπέθανεν died LTTr. [z] — τῷ W. [a] — τῷ (*read* [in the]) GLTTrAW. [b] ἀπεξεδέχετο (*omit* once) GLTTrAW. [c] ὀλίγοι few [persons] LTTrAW. [d] τοῦτ' ἔστιν GT. [e] ᾧ to which E. [f] ὑμᾶς you LTTrA. [g] — τοῦ TTr[A]. [h] — ὑπὲρ ἡμῶν LTTrA. [i] — ἐν (*read* [in]) LTTrA. [k] — ἡμῖν LTTrA. [l] — τοῦ βίου LTTrAW. [m] βούλημα LTTrAW. [n] κατειργάσθαι LTTrAW.

walked in lascivious-
ness, lusts, excess of
wine, revellings, ban-
quetings, and abo-
minable idolatries :
4 wherein they think it
strange that ye run not
with *them* to the same
excess of riot, speak-
ing evil of *you:* 5 who
shall give account to
him that is ready to
judge the quick and
the dead. 6 For for
this cause was the
gospel preached also to
them that are dead,
that they might be
judged according to
men in the flesh, but
live according to God
in the spirit.
7 But the end of all
things is at hand : be
ye therefore sober, and
watch unto prayer.
8 And above all things
have fervent charity
among yourselves : for
charity shall cover
the multitude of sins.
9 Use hospitality one
to another without
grudging. 10 As every
man hath received the
gift, *even so* minister
the same one to an-
other, as good stewards
of the manifold grace
of God. 11 If any man
speak, *let him speak*
as the oracles of God ;
if any man minister,
let him do it as of the
ability which God giv-
eth : that God in all
things may be glorified
through Jesus Christ,
to whom be praise and
dominion for ever and
ever. Amen.
12 Beloved, think it
not strange concern-
ing the fiery trial
which is to try you, as
though some strange
thing happened unto
you : 13 but rejoice,
inasmuch as ye are par-
takers of Christ's suf-
ferings; that, when his
glory shall be revealed,
ye may be glad also
with exceeding joy.
14 If ye be reproached
for the name of Christ,
happy *are ye;* for the
spirit of glory and of
God resteth upon you:
on their part he is evil
spoken of, but on your
part he is glorified.
15 But let none of you
suffer as a murderer,
or *as* a thief, or *as* an
evildoer, or as a busy-
body in other men's
matters. 16 Yet if *any*

ἀσελγείαις, ἐπιθυμίαις, οἰνοφλυγίαις, κώμοις, πότοις, καὶ
licentiousness, lusts, wine-drinking, revels, drinkings, and
ἀθεμίτοις εἰδωλολατρείαις· 4 ἐν.ᾧ ξενίζονται, μὴ συν-
unhallowed idolatries. Wherein they think it strange [2]not [3]run-
τρεχόντων ὑμῶν εἰς τὴν αὐτὴν τῆς ἀσωτίας ἀνάχυσιν,
ning [4]with [[5]them] [1]your to the same [2]of [3]dissoluteness [1]overflow,
βλασφημοῦντες· 5 οἳ ἀποδώσουσιν λόγον τῷ ἑτοίμως
speaking evil [of you]; who shall render account to him [3]ready
ἔχοντι κρῖναι ζῶντας καὶ νεκρούς. 6 εἰς.τοῦτο.γὰρ καὶ
[1]who [2]is to judge [the] living and [the] dead. For to this [end] also
νεκροῖς εὐηγγελίσθη, ἵνα κριθῶσιν μὲν
to [the] dead were the glad tidings announced, that they might be judged indeed
κατὰ ἀνθρώπους σαρκί, ζῶσιν.δὲ κατὰ θεὸν πνεύματι.
as regards men in [the] flesh; but might live as regards God in [the] Spirit.
7 Πάντων.δὲ τὸ τέλος ἤγγικεν· σωφρονήσατε οὖν
But of all things the end has drawn near: be sober-minded therefore,
καὶ νήψατε εἰς [o]τὰς‖ προσευχάς· 8 πρὸ πάντων [p]δὲ‖ τὴν
and be watchful unto prayers; [2]before [3]all [4]things [1]but
εἰς ἑαυτοὺς ἀγάπην ἐκτενῆ ἔχοντες, ὅτι [q] ἀγάπη [r]καλύψει‖
among yourselves [3]love [2]fervent [1]having, because love will cover
πλῆθος ἁμαρτιῶν. 9 φιλόξενοι εἰς ἀλλήλους ἄνευ [s]γογγυσ-
a multitude of sins; hospitable to one another, without murmur-
μῶν·‖ 10 ἕκαστος καθὼς ἔλαβεν χάρισμα, εἰς ἑαυτοὺς
ings; each according as he received a gift, to each other
αὐτὸ διακονοῦντες, ὡς καλοὶ οἰκονόμοι ποικίλης χάριτος
[2]it [1]serving, as good stewards of [the] various grace
θεοῦ· 11 εἴ τις λαλεῖ, ὡς λόγια θεοῦ· εἴ τις διακονεῖ, ὡς
of God. If anyone speaks— as oracles of God; if anyone serves— as
ἐξ ἰσχύος ἧς χορηγεῖ ὁ θεός· ἵνα ἐν πᾶσιν δοξάζηται ὁ
of strength which [2]supplies [1]God; that in all things may be glorified
θεὸς διὰ Ἰησοῦ χριστοῦ, ᾧ ἐστιν ἡ δόξα καὶ τὸ κράτος
God through Jesus Christ, to whom is the glory and the might
εἰς τοὺς αἰῶνας τῶν αἰώνων. ἀμήν.
to the ages of the ages. Amen.
12 Ἀγαπητοί, μὴ.ξενίζεσθε τῇ ἐν ὑμῖν πυρώσει
Beloved, take not as strange the [4]amongst [5]you [1]fire [[2]of [3]persecution]
πρὸς πειρασμὸν ὑμῖν γινομένῃ, ὡς ξένου ὑμῖν
for trial to you [which is] taking place, as if a strange thing to you
συμβαίνοντος· 13 ἀλλὰ [t]καθὸ‖ κοινωνεῖτε τοῖς τοῦ χρισ-
[is] happening; but according as ye have share in the [2]of
τοῦ παθήμασιν, χαίρετε, ἵνα καὶ ἐν τῇ ἀποκαλύψει τῆς δόξης
[3]Christ [1]sufferings, rejoice, that also in the revelation of [2]glory
αὐτοῦ χαρῆτε ἀγαλλιώμενοι. 14 εἰ ὀνειδίζεσθε ἐν
[1]his ye may rejoice exulting. If ye are reproached in [the]
ὀνόματι χριστοῦ, μακάριοι· ὅτι τὸ τῆς δόξης[v] καὶ
name of Christ, blessed [are ye]; because the [spirit] of glory and
τὸ τοῦ θεοῦ πνεῦμα ἐφ' ὑμᾶς ἀναπαύεται· [w]κατὰ.μὲν.αὐτοὺς
the [2]of [3]God [1]Spirit upon you rests; on their part
βλασφημεῖται, κατὰ.δὲ.ὑμᾶς δοξάζεται.‖ 15 μὴ.γάρ τις
he is blasphemed, but on your part he is glorified. Assuredly [2]not [3]anyone
ὑμῶν πασχέτω ὡς φονεύς, ἢ κλέπτης, ἢ κακοποιός, ἢ ὡς
[4]of [5]you [1]let suffer as a murderer, or thief, or evil doer, or as
[x]ἀλλοτριοεπίσκοπος.‖ 16 εἰ.δὲ ὡς χριστιανός, μὴ αἰσχυ-
overlooker of other people's matters; but if as a christian, [3]not [1]let [2]him

[o] — τὰς LTTrAW. [p] — δὲ TTrA. [q] + ἡ EG. [r] καλύπτει covers LTTrAW. [s] γογγυσμοῦ murmuring LTTrAW. [t] καθὼς E. [v] + καὶ δυνάμεως and of power L. [w] — κατὰ μὲν *to end of verse* LTTrA. [x] ἀλλοτριεπίσκοπος LTTr.

νέσθω, δοξαζέτω.δὲ τὸν θεὸν ἐν τῷ [y]μέρει‖ τούτῳ. 17 ὅτι
be ashamed, but let him glorify God in 2respect 1this. Because

ὁ καιρὸς τοῦ ἄρξασθαι τὸ κρίμα ἀπὸ τοῦ οἴκου τοῦ θεοῦ·
the time [for] 3to 4have 5begun 1the 2judgment from the house of God

εἰ.δὲ πρῶτον ἀφ' ἡμῶν, τί τὸ τέλος τῶν ἀπειθούντων
[is come]; but if first from us, what the end of those disobeying

τῷ τοῦ θεοῦ εὐαγγελίῳ; 18 καὶ εἰ ὁ δίκαιος μόλις σώζεται,
the 3of 4God 1glad 2tidings? And if the righteous with difficulty is saved,

ὁ ἀσεβὴς καὶ [z] ἁμαρτωλὸς ποῦ φανεῖται; 19 ὥστε καὶ
3the 4ungodly 5and 6sinner 1where 2shall appear? Wherefore also

οἱ πάσχοντες κατὰ τὸ θέλημα τοῦ θεοῦ, [a]ὡς‖ πιστῷ
they who suffer according to the will of God as to a faithful

κτίστῃ παρατιθέσθωσαν τὰς.ψυχὰς.[b]ἑαυτῶν‖ ἐν [c]ἀγαθοποιΐᾳ.‖
Creator let them commit their souls in well doing.

5 Πρεσβυτέρους [d] [e]τοὺς‖ ἐν ὑμῖν παρακαλῶ ὁ [f]συμ-
Elders who [are] among you I exhort who [am] a

πρεσβύτερος‖ καὶ μάρτυς τῶν τοῦ χριστοῦ παθημάτων, ὁ
fellow elder and witness of the 2of 3the 4Christ 1sufferings, who

καὶ τῆς μελλούσης ἀποκαλύπτεσθαι δόξης κοινωνός, 2 ποι-
also of the 2about 3to 4be 5revealed 1glory [am] partaker: shep-

μάνατε τὸ ἐν ὑμῖν ποίμνιον τοῦ θεοῦ, [g]ἐπισκοποῦντες‖ μὴ
herd the 4among 5you 1flock 2of 3God, exercising oversight not

ἀναγκαστῶς, [h]ἀλλ'‖ ἑκουσίως[i]· μηδὲ αἰσχροκερδῶς, ἀλλὰ προ-
by constraint, but willingly; not for base gain, but readi-

θύμως· 3 μηδ' ὡς κατακυριεύοντες τῶν κλήρων, ἀλλὰ
ly; not as exercising lordship over [your] possessions, but

τύποι γινόμενοι τοῦ ποιμνίου. 4 καὶ φανερωθέντος
patterns being of the flock. And 4having 5been 6manifested

τοῦ ἀρχιποίμενος, κομιεῖσθε τὸν ἀμαράντινον τῆς δόξης
1the 2chief 3shepherd, ye shall receive the unfading 2of 3glory

στέφανον.
1crown.

5 Ὁμοίως, νεώτεροι, ὑποτάγητε πρεσβυτέροις· πάντες
Likewise, [ye] younger [ones], be subject to [the] elder [ones], 2all

δὲ ἀλλήλοις [k]ὑποτασσόμενοι‖ τὴν ταπεινοφροσύνην ἐγκομβώ-
1and one to another being subject 3humility 1bind

σασθε· ὅτι ὁ θεὸς ὑπερηφάνοις ἀντιτάσσεται, ταπεινοῖς
2on; because God [the] proud sets himself against, 2to [3the] 4humble

δὲ δίδωσιν χάριν. 6 ταπεινώθητε οὖν ὑπὸ τὴν κραταιὰν
1but gives grace. Be humbled therefore under the mighty

[l]χεῖρα‖ τοῦ θεοῦ, ἵνα ὑμᾶς ὑψώσῃ ἐν καιρῷ[m]· 7 πᾶσαν
hand of God, that you he may exalt in [due] time; all

τὴν.μέριμναν.ὑμῶν [n]ἐπιῤῥίψαντες‖ ἐπ' αὐτόν, ὅτι αὐτῷ
your care having cast upon him, because with him

μέλει περὶ ὑμῶν. 8 νήψατε, γρηγορήσατε, [o]ὅτι‖ ὁ ἀντίδικος
there is care about you. Be sober, watch, because 2adversary

ὑμῶν διάβολος, ὡς λέων ὠρυόμενος, περιπατεῖ, ζητῶν [p]τίνα‖
1your [the] devil, as a 2lion 1roaring, goes about, seeking whom

[q]καταπίῃ·‖ 9 ᾧ ἀντίστητε στερεοὶ τῇ πίστει, εἰδότες τὰ
he may swallow up. Whom resist, firm in faith, knowing the

αὐτὰ τῶν παθημάτων τῇ ἐν [r] κόσμῳ ὑμῶν.ἀδελφότητι
same sufferings 7which [8is] 9in [10the] 11world 4in 5your 6brotherhood

man suffer as a Christian, let him not be ashamed; but let him glorify God on this behalf. 17 For the time *is come* that judgment must begin at the house of God: and if *it* first *begin* at us, what shall the end *be* of them that obey not the gospel of God? 18 And if the righteous scarcely be saved, where shall the ungodly and the sinner appear? 19 Wherefore let them that suffer according to the will of God commit the keeping of their souls *to him* in well doing, as unto a faithful Creator.

V. The elders which are among you I exhort, who am also an elder, and a witness of the sufferings of Christ, and also a partaker of the glory that shall be revealed: 2 Feed the flock of God which is among you, taking the oversight *thereof*, not by constraint, but willingly; not for filthy lucre, but of a ready mind; 3 neither as being lords over *God's* heritage, but being ensamples to the flock. 4 And when the chief Shepherd shall appear, ye shall receive a crown of glory that fadeth not away.

5 Likewise, ye younger, submit yourselves unto the elder. Yea, all *of you* be subject one to another, and be clothed with humility: for God resisteth the proud, and giveth grace to the humble. 6 Humble yourselves therefore under the mighty hand of God, that he may exalt you in due time: 7 casting all your care upon him; for he careth for you. 8 Be sober, be vigilant; because your adversary the devil, as a roaring lion, walketh about, seeking whom he may devour: 9 whom resist stedfast in the faith, knowing that the same afflictions are

[y] ὀνόματι name LTTrAW. [z] + ὁ the T. [a] — ὡς LTTrA. [b] αὐτῶν LTTrAW. [c] ἀγαθοποιΐαις LW. [d] + οὖν then LTTrA. [e] — τοὺς LTrA. [f] συν- T. [g] — ἐπισκοποῦντες T[A]. [h] ἀλλὰ TTrA. [i] + κατὰ θεόν according to God LTTr. [k] — ὑποτασσόμενοι LTTrAW. [l] χεῖραν T. [m] + ἐπισκοπῆς (*read* in time of visitation) L. [n] ἐπιρίψαντες LTTrA. [o] — ὅτι GLTTrAW. [p] τινὰ some one L. [q] καταπιεῖν to swallow up LTA; καταπίειν Tr. [r] + τῷ the TTr.

accomplished in your
brethren that are in
the world. 10 But the
God of all grace, who
hath called us unto his
eternal glory by Christ
Jesus, after that ye
have suffered a while,
make you perfect, sta-
blish, strengthen, set-
tle *you*. 11 To him *be*
glory and dominion
for ever and ever. A-
men.

12 By Silvanus, a
faithful brother unto
you, as I suppose, I
have written briefly,
exhorting, and testify-
ing that this is the true
grace of God wherein
ye stand. 13 The *church*
that is at Babylon,
elected together with
you, saluteth you ; and
so doth Marcus my son.
14 Greet ye one an-
other with a kiss of
charity. Peace *be* with
you all that are in
Christ Jesus. Amen.

ἐπιτελεῖσθαι. 10 ὁ.δὲ θεὸς πάσης χάριτος, ὁ καλέσας
[1]are [2]being [3]accomplished. But the God of all grace, who called
[s]ἡμᾶς εἰς τὴν αἰώνιον αὐτοῦ δόξαν ἐν χριστῷ [t]Ἰησοῦ," ὀλίγον
us to [2]eternal [1]his glory in Christ Jesus, a little while
παθόντας, αὐτὸς [v]καταρτίσαι ὑμᾶς," [w]στηρίξαι, σθενώ-
[ye] having suffered, [2]himself [1]may perfect you, may he establish, may he
σαι," [x]θεμελιώσαι." 11 αὐτῷ [y]ἡ δόξα καὶ" τὸ κράτος εἰς
strengthen, may he found [you]: to him [be] the glory and the might, to
τοὺς αἰῶνας τῶν αἰώνων. ἀμήν.
the ages of the ages. Amen.

12 Διὰ Σιλουανοῦ ὑμῖν [z]τοῦ" πιστοῦ ἀδελφοῦ, ὡς λογίζο-
By Silvanus, [4]to [5]you [1]the [2]faithful [3]brother, as I reckon,
μαι, δι᾽.ὀλίγων ἔγραψα, παρακαλῶν καὶ ἐπιμαρτυρῶν ταύτην
briefly I wrote, exhorting and testifying this
εἶναι ἀληθῆ χάριν τοῦ θεοῦ, εἰς ἣν [a]ἑστήκατε." 13 Ἀσπά-
to be [the] true grace of God, in which ye stand. [7]Sa-
ζεται ὑμᾶς ἡ ἐν Βαβυλῶνι συνεκλεκτή, καὶ Μάρκος
lutes [8]you [1]she [5]in [6]Babylon [2]elected [3]with [[4]you], and Mark
ὁ.υἱός.μου. 14 ἀσπάσασθε ἀλλήλους ἐν φιλήματι ἀγάπης
my son. Salute one another with a kiss of love.
εἰρήνη ὑμῖν πᾶσιν τοῖς ἐν χριστῷ [b]Ἰησοῦ." [c]ἀμήν."
Peace [be] with you all who [are] in Christ Jesus. Amen.

[d]Πέτρου ἐπιστολὴ καθολικὴ πρώτη."
[4]Of [5]Peter [3]Epistle [2]General [1]First.

---

[e]ΕΠΙΣΤΟΛΗ ΠΕΤΡΟΥ ΚΑΘΟΛΙΚΗ ΔΕΥΤΕΡΑ."
[3]EPISTLE [4]OF [5]PETER [2]GENERAL [1]SECOND.

SIMON Peter, a ser-
vant and an apostle of
Jesus Christ, to them
that have obtained like
precious faith with us
through the righteous-
ness of God and our
Saviour Jesus Christ :
2 Grace and peace be
multiplied unto you
through the know-
ledge of God, and of
Jesus our Lord,

3 According as his
divine power hath giv-
en unto us all things
that *pertain* unto life
and godliness, through
the knowledge of him
that hath called us
to glory and virtue :
4 whereby are given
unto us exceeding
great and precious
promises: that by these
ye might be partakers
of the divine nature,
having escaped the

[f]ΣΥΜΕΩΝ" Πέτρος δοῦλος καὶ ἀπόστολος Ἰησοῦ χριστοῦ,
Simeon Peter, bondman and apostle of Jesus Christ,
τοῖς ἰσότιμον ἡμῖν λαχοῦσιν πίστιν ἐν δικαιο-
to those who [2]like [3]precious [5]with [6]us [1]obtained [4]faith through [the] right-
σύνῃ τοῦ.θεοῦ.ἡμῶν καὶ σωτῆρος [g] Ἰησοῦ χριστοῦ· 2 χάρις
eousness of our God and Saviour Jesus Christ: Grace
ὑμῖν καὶ εἰρήνη πληθυνθείη ἐν ἐπιγνώσει τοῦ θεοῦ, καὶ
to you and peace be multiplied in [the] knowledge of God, and
Ἰησοῦ τοῦ.κυρίου.ἡμῶν.
of Jesus our Lord.

3 Ὡς[h] πάντα ἡμῖν τῆς θείας.δυνάμεως αὐτοῦ τὰ
As [8]all [9]things [6]to [7]us [2]divine [3]power [1]his [10]which [[11]pertain]
πρὸς ζωὴν καὶ εὐσέβειαν δεδωρημένης, διὰ τῆς ἐπιγνώσεως
[12]to [13]life [14]and [15]piety [4]has [5]given, through the knowledge
τοῦ καλέσαντος ἡμᾶς [i]διὰ δόξης καὶ ἀρετῆς," 4 δι᾽ ὧν
of him who called us by glory and virtue, through which
τὰ [k]μέγιστα ἡμῖν καὶ τίμια" ἐπαγγέλματα δεδώρηται, ἵνα
[6]the [7]greatest [4]to [5]us [8]and [9]precious [10]promises [1]he [2]has [3]given, that
διὰ τούτων γένησθε θείας κοινωνοὶ φύσεως, ἀπο-
through these ye may become [2]of [[3]the] [4]divine [1]partakers nature, hav-

---

[s] ὑμᾶς you LTTrAW. [t] — Ἰησοῦ T[Tr]. [v] καταρτίσει will perfect [you] LTTrAW. [w] στηρίξει, σθενώσει will establish, will strengthen GLTTrAW. [x] θεμελιώσει will found GTAW ; — θεμελιώσαι LTr. [y] — ἡ δόξα καὶ LTTrA. [z] — τοῦ L. [a] στῆτε stand ye LTTrA. [b] — Ἰησοῦ LTTrA. [c] — ἀμήν GLTTrA. [d] — *the subscription* EGLTW ; Πέτρου α΄ TrA.

[e] + τοῦ ἀποστόλου the apostle E ; — καθολικὴ G ; Πέτρου β΄ LTAW ; Πέτρου ἐπιστολὴ β΄ Tr. [f] Σίμων Simon L. [g] + ἡμῶν our (Saviour) E. [h] + τὰ T. [i] ἰδίᾳ δόξῃ καὶ ἀρετῇ by [his] own glory and virtue LTTrAW. [k] μέγιστα καὶ τίμια ἡμῖν LTrA ; τίμια ἡμῖν καὶ μέγιστα T.

φυγόντες τῆς ἐν [l]κόσμῳ ἐν ἐπιθυμίᾳ φθορᾶς. 5 καὶ
ing escaped the [2]in [[3]the] [4]world [5]through [6]lust [1]corruption. [12]also
[m]αὐτὸ.τοῦτο‖ δέ, σπουδὴν πᾶσαν παρεισενέγκαν-
[8]for [9]this [10]very [11]reason [7]but, [18]diligence, [17]all [13]having [14]brought [15]in [16]be-
τες, ἐπιχορηγήσατε ἐν τῇ.πίστει.ὑμῶν τὴν ἀρετήν, ἐν.δὲ τῇ ἀρετῇ
sides, supply ye in your faith virtue, and in virtue
τὴν γνῶσιν, 6 ἐν.δὲ τῇ γνώσει τὴν ἐγκράτειαν, ἐν.δὲ τῇ ἐγκρα-
knowledge, and in knowledge self-control, and in self-con-
τείᾳ τὴν ὑπομονήν, ἐν.δὲ τῇ ὑπομονῇ τὴν εὐσέβειαν, 7 ἐν.δὲ
trol endurance, and in endurance piety, and in
τῇ εὐσεβείᾳ τὴν φιλαδελφίαν, ἐν.δὲ τῇ φιλαδελφίᾳ τὴν ἀγάπην.
piety brotherly love, and in brotherly love love:
8 ταῦτα.γὰρ ὑμῖν [n]ὑπάρχοντα‖ καὶ πλεονάζοντα, οὐκ
for these things [2]in [3]you [1]being and abounding [[3]to [4]be] [5]neither
ἀργοὺς οὐδὲ ἀκάρπους καθίστησιν εἰς τὴν τοῦ.κυρίου.ἡμῶν
[6]idle [7]nor [8]unfruitful [1]make [[2]you] as to the [2]of [3]our [4]Lord
Ἰησοῦ χριστοῦ ἐπίγνωσιν· 9 ᾧ.γὰρ μὴ.πάρεστιν ταῦτα
[5]Jesus [6]Christ [1]knowledge; for with whom are not present these things
τυφλός ἐστιν, μυωπάζων, λήθην.λαβὼν τοῦ καθαρισμοῦ τῶν
blind he is, short sighted, having forgotten the purification
πάλαι αὐτοῦ [o]ἁμαρτιῶν.‖ 10 Διὸ μᾶλλον, ἀδελφοί, σπου-
[4]of [5]old [1]of [2]his [3]sins. Wherefore rather, brethren, be dili-
δάσατε [p] βεβαίαν ὑμῶν τὴν κλῆσιν καὶ ἐκλογὴν [q]ποιεῖσθαι·‖
gent [7]sure [3]your [4]calling [5]and [6]election [1]to [2]make,
ταῦτα.γὰρ ποιοῦντες οὐ.μὴ πταίσητέ ποτε. 11 οὕτως
for these things doing in no wise shall ye stumble at any time. [2]Thus
γὰρ πλουσίως ἐπιχορηγηθήσεται ὑμῖν ἡ εἴσοδος εἰς τὴν αἰώ-
[1]for [5]richly [3]shall [4]be supplied to you the entrance into the eter-
νιον βασιλείαν τοῦ.κυρίου.ἡμῶν καὶ σωτῆρος Ἰησοῦ χριστοῦ.
nal kingdom of our Lord and Saviour Jesus Christ.
12 Διὸ [r]οὐκ.ἀμελήσω‖ [s]ὑμᾶς ἀεὶ‖ ὑπομιμνήσκειν
Wherefore I will not neglect [3]you [4]always [1]to [2]put in remembrance
περὶ τούτων, καίπερ εἰδότας, καὶ ἐστηριγμένους ἐν
concerning these things, although knowing [them] and having been established in
τῇ παρούσῃ ἀληθείᾳ. 13 δίκαιον.δὲ ἡγοῦμαι, ἐφ'.ὅσον εἰμὶ ἐν
the present truth. But right I esteem it, as long as I am in
τούτῳ τῷ σκηνώματι, διεγείρειν ὑμᾶς ἐν ὑπομνήσει·
this tabernacle, to stir up you by putting [you] in remembrance,
14 εἰδὼς ὅτι ταχινή ἐστιν ἡ ἀπόθεσις τοῦ.σκηνώματός.μου,
knowing that speedily is the putting off of my tabernacle
καθὼς καὶ ὁ.κύριος.ἡμῶν Ἰησοῦς χριστὸς ἐδήλωσέν μοι.
[to be], as also our Lord Jesus Christ signified to me;
15 σπουδάσω.δὲ καὶ ἑκάστοτε ἔχειν.ὑμᾶς μετὰ
but I will be diligent also at every time for you to have [it in your power] after
τὴν.ἐμὴν ἔξοδον τὴν τούτων μνήμην.ποιεῖσθαι. 16 οὐ.γὰρ
my departure [5]these [6]things [1]to [2]have [3]in [4]remembrance. For not
σεσοφισμένοις μύθοις ἐξακολουθήσαντες ἐγνωρίσαμεν ὑμῖν τὴν
[4]cleverly-imagined [5]fables [1]having [2]followed [3]out we made known to you the
τοῦ.κυρίου.ἡμῶν Ἰησοῦ χριστοῦ δύναμιν καὶ παρουσίαν, ἀλλ'
[4]of [5]our [6]Lord [7]Jesus [8]Christ [1]power [2]and [3]coming, but
ἐπόπται γενηθέντες τῆς.ἐκείνου μεγαλειότητος. 17 λαβὼν
eye-witnesses having been of his majesty. [2]Having [3]received
γὰρ παρὰ θεοῦ πατρὸς τιμὴν καὶ δόξαν, φωνῆς ἐνεχθεί-
[1]for from God [the] Father honour and glory, [2]a [3]voice [4]having [5]been

corruption that is in
the world through lust.
5 And beside this, giv-
ing all diligence, add
to your faith virtue;
and to virtue know-
ledge; 6 and to know-
ledge temperance; and
to temperance pati-
ence; and to patience
godliness; 7 and to
godliness brotherly
kindness; and to bro-
therly kindness cha-
rity. 8 For if these
things be in you, and
abound, they make
you that ye shall nei-
ther *be* barren nor un-
fruitful in the know-
ledge of our Lord Je-
sus Christ. 9 But he
that lacketh these
things is blind, and
cannot see afar off,
and hath forgotten
that he was purged
from his old sins.
10 Wherefore the ra-
ther, brethren, give
diligence to make your
calling and election
sure: for if ye do these
things, ye shall never
fall: 11 for so an en-
trance shall be mini-
stered unto you abun-
dantly into the ever-
lasting kingdom of our
Lord and Saviour Je-
sus Christ.

12 Wherefore I will
not be negligent to put
you always in remem-
brance of these things,
though ye know *them*,
and be established in
the present truth.
13 Yea, I think it meet,
as long as I am in this
tabernacle, to stir you
up by putting *you* in remembrance; 14 know-
ing that shortly I
must put off *this* my
tabernacle, even as our
Lord Jesus Christ hath
shewed me. 15 More-
over I will endeavour
that ye may be able
after my decease to
have these things al-
ways in remembrance.
16 For we have not
followed cunningly
devised fables, when
we made known unto
you the power and
coming of our Lord
Jesus Christ, but were
eyewitnesses of his
majesty. 17 For he re-
ceived from God the
Father honour and
glory when there came
such a voice to him
from the excellent
glory, This is my be-

[l] + τῷ the LTTr. [m] αὐτοὶ (*read* but ye also) L [n] παρόντα being present L.
[o] ἁμαρτημάτων GTTr. [p] + ἵνα διὰ τῶν καλῶν ὑμῶν ἔργων that by your good works L.
[q] ποιεῖσθε ye make L. [r] μελλήσω I will take care LTTrAW. [s] ἀεὶ ὑμᾶς GTTrAW.

loved Son, in whom I
am well pleased. 18 And
this voice which came
from heaven we heard,
when we were with
him in the holy mount.
19 We have also a more
sure word of prophecy;
whereunto ye do well
that ye take heed, as
unto a light that
shineth in a dark place,
until the day dawn,
and the day star a-
rise in your hearts:
20 knowing this first,
that no prophecy of
the scripture is of any
private interpretation.
21 For the prophecy
came not in old time
by the will of man:
but holy men of God
spake *as they were*
moved by the Holy
Ghost.

II. But there were
false prophets also a-
mong the people, even
as there shall be false
teachers among you,
who privily shall bring
in damnable heresies,
even denying the Lord
that bought them,
and bring upon them-
selves swift destruc-
tion. 2 And many shall
follow their pernicious
ways; by reason of
whom the way of truth
shall be evil spoken
of. 3 And through co-
vetousness shall they
with feigned words
make merchandise of
you: whose judgment
now of a long time
lingereth not, and
their damnation slum-
bereth not. 4 For if
God spared not the
angels that sinned,
but cast *them* down to
hell, and delivered
them into chains of
darkness, to be reserv-
ed unto judgment;
5 and spared not the
old world, but saved
Noah the eighth *per-
son*, a preacher of
righteousness, bring-
ing in the flood upon
the world of the un-
godly; 6 and turning
the cities of Sodom and
Gomorrha into ashes
condemned *them* with
an overthrow, making
them an ensample unto
those that after should
live ungodly; 7 and
delivered just Lot,
vexed with the filthy
conversation of the

σης αὐτῷ τοιᾶσδε ὑπὸ τῆς μεγαλοπρεποῦς δόξης, [t]Οὗτός
[6]brought [7]to [8]him [1]such by the very excellent glory: This
ἐστιν ὁ.υἱός.μου ὁ ἀγαπητός,‖ εἰς ὃν ἐγὼ εὐδόκησα. 18 καὶ
is my Son the beloved, in whom I have found delight. And
ταύτην τὴν φωνὴν ἡμεῖς ἠκούσαμεν ἐξ οὐρανοῦ ἐνεχθεῖσαν,
this voice we heard [2]from [3]heaven [1]brought,
σὺν αὐτῷ ὄντες ἐν τῷ [v]ὄρει τῷ ἁγίῳ.‖ 19 καὶ ἔχομεν βεβαι-
[5]with [6]him [4]being on the [2]mount [1]holy. and we have more
ότερον τὸν προφητικὸν λόγον, ᾧ καλῶς ποιεῖτε προσέχοντες,
sure the prophetic word, to which [3]well [1]ye [2]do taking heed,
ὡς λύχνῳ φαίνοντι ἐν αὐχμηρῷ τόπῳ, ἕως.οὗ ἡμέρα διαυγάσῃ,
as to a lamp shining in an obscure place, until day should dawn,
καὶ φωσφόρος ἀνατείλῃ ἐν ταῖς.καρδίαις.ὑμῶν· 20 τοῦτο
and [the] morning star should arise in your hearts; this
πρῶτον γινώσκοντες, ὅτι πᾶσα προφητεία γραφῆς ἰδίας
first knowing, that [2]any [3]prophecy [4]of [5]scripture [7]of [8]its [9]own
(*lit.* every)
ἐπιλύσεως οὐ.γίνεται. 21 οὐ.γὰρ θελήματι ἀνθρώπου ἠνέχθη
[10]interpretation [6]is [1]not, for not by [the] will of man was [2]brought
[w]ποτὲ προφητεία,‖ [x]ἀλλ'‖ ὑπὸ πνεύματος ἁγίου φερό-
[3]at [4]any [5]time [1]prophecy, but, [3]by [[4]the] [6]Spirit [5]Holy [1]being
μενοι ἐλάλησαν [y]οἱ‖ [z]ἅγιοι‖ [a] θεοῦ ἄνθρωποι.
[2]borne, [12]spoke [7]the [8]holy [10]of [11]God [9]men.

2 Ἐγένοντο.δὲ καὶ ψευδοπροφῆται ἐν τῷ λαῷ, ὡς καὶ
But there were also false prophets among the people, as also
ἐν ὑμῖν ἔσονται ψευδοδιδάσκαλοι, οἵτινες παρεισάξουσιν
among you will be false teachers, who will bring in stealthily
αἱρέσεις ἀπωλείας, καὶ τὸν ἀγοράσαντα αὐτοὺς δεσπότην ἀρ-
[2]sects [1]destructive, and [2]the [4]who [5]bought [6]them [3]Master [1]de-
νούμενοι, ἐπάγοντες ἑαυτοῖς ταχινὴν ἀπώλειαν· 2 καὶ πολλοὶ
nying, bringing upon themselves swift destruction; and many
ἐξακολουθήσουσιν αὐτῶν ταῖς [b]ἀπωλείαις,‖ δι' οὓς ἡ ὁδὸς
will follow out their destructive ways, through whom the way
τῆς ἀληθείας βλασφημηθήσεται· 3 καὶ ἐν πλεονεξίᾳ πλασ-
of the truth will be evil spoken of. And through covetousness with
τοῖς λόγοις ὑμᾶς ἐμπορεύσονται· οἷς τὸ κρίμα ἔκπαλαι
well-turned words you they will make gain of: for whom judgment of old
οὐκ.ἀργεῖ, καὶ ἡ.ἀπώλεια.αὐτῶν οὐ.νυστάζει. 4 Εἰ.γὰρ ὁ θεὸς
is not idle, and their destruction slumbers not. For if God
ἀγγέλων ἁμαρτησάντων οὐκ.ἐφείσατο, ἀλλὰ [c]σειραῖς‖
[the] angels who sinned spared not, but [8]to [9]chains
ζόφου ταρταρώσας παρέδωκεν
[10]of [11]darkness [1]having [2]cast [[3]them] [4]to [5]the [6]deepest [7]abyss delivered [them]
εἰς κρίσιν [d]τετηρημένους·‖ 5 καὶ ἀρχαίου κόσμου οὐκ
for judgment having been kept; and [the] ancient world [2]not
ἐφείσατο, [e]ἀλλ'‖ ὄγδοον Νῶε δικαιοσύνης κήρυκα ἐφύ-
[1]spared, but [[3]the] [4]eighth [2]Noe [7]of [8]righteousness [5]a [6]herald [1]pre-
λαξεν, κατακλυσμὸν κόσμῳ ἀσεβῶν ἐπάξας· 6 καὶ
served, [the] flood upon [the] world of [the] ungodly having brought in; and
πόλεις Σοδόμων καὶ Γομόρρας τεφρώσας κατα-
[the] cities of Sodom and Gomorrha having reduced to ashes with an
στροφῇ κατέκρινεν, ὑπόδειγμα μελλόντων ἀσε-
overthrow condemned [them], [3]an [4]example [[5]to [6]those] [7]being [8]about [9]to [10]live

---

[t] Ὁ υἱός μου ὁ ἀγαπητός μου οὗτός ἐστιν my Son my beloved this is A. [v] ἁγίῳ ὄρει TrA. [w] προφητεία ποτέ TrA. [x] ἀλλὰ TTrAW. [y] — οἱ GLTTrAW. [z] ἀπὸ (read men from God) TA. [a] + τοῦ L. [b] ἀσελγείαις licentiousnesses GLTTrAW. [c] σιροῖς to dens LT; σειροῖς to dens TrA. [d] τηρουμένους to be kept GTTrAW; κολαζομένους τηρεῖν to keep, to be punished L. [e] ἀλλὰ TTrA.

ζειν τεθεικώς· 7 καὶ δίκαιον Λώτ, καταπονούμενον ὑπὸ τῆς
11ungodly 1having 2set; and righteous Lot, oppressed by the
τῶν ἀθέσμων ἐν ἀσελγείᾳ ἀναστροφῆς, [f]ἐῤῥύσατο·‖ 8 βλέμ-
4of 5the 6lawless 2in 3licentiousness 1conduct he delivered, (2through
ματι γὰρ καὶ ἀκοῇ [g]ὁ‖ δίκαιος, [h]ἐγκατοικῶν‖ ἐν αὐτοῖς,
3seeing 1for and hearing, the righteous [man], dwelling among them,
ἡμέραν ἐξ ἡμέρας ψυχὴν δικαίαν ἀνόμοις ἔργοις
day by day [2his] 4soul 3righteous 5with [6their] 7lawless 8works
ἐβασάνιζεν· 9 οἶδεν κύριος εὐσεβεῖς ἐκ [i]πειρασμοῦ‖
1tormented,) 11knows [9the] 10Lord [how the] pious out of temptation
ῥύεσθαι, ἀδίκους.δὲ εἰς ἡμέραν κρίσεως κολαζομένους
to deliver, and [the] unrighteous to a day of judgment 3to 4be 5punished
τηρεῖν· 10 μάλιστα.δὲ τοὺς ὀπίσω σαρκὸς ἐν ἐπιθυμίᾳ
1to 2keep; and specially those who after [the] flesh in [the] lust
μιασμοῦ πορευομένους, καὶ κυριότητος καταφρονοῦντας.
of pollution walk, and lordship despise. [They
Τολμηταί, αὐθάδεις, δόξας οὐ.τρέμουσιν βλασφημοῦντες·
are] daring, self-willed; 7glories 1they 2tremble 3not 4speaking 5evil 6of;
11 ὅπου ἄγγελοι ἰσχύϊ καὶ δυνάμει μείζονες ὄντες, οὐ φέ-
where angels 3in 4strength 5and 6power 2greater 1being, 8not 7do
ρουσιν κατ' αὐτῶν [k]παρὰ κυρίῳ‖ βλάσφημον κρίσιν.
bring against them, before [the] Lord, a railing charge.
12 οὗτοι.δέ, ὡς ἄλογα ζῶα [l]φυσικὰ γεγενημένα‖ εἰς ἅλω-
But these, as 2irrational 3animals 1natural born for cap-
σιν καὶ φθοράν, ἐν οἷς ἀγνοοῦσιν βλασφημοῦντες, ἐν
ture and corruption, 3in 4what 5they 6are 7ignorant 8of 1speaking 2evil, in
τῇ.φθορᾷ.αὐτῶν [m]καταφθαρήσονται,‖ 13 κομιούμενοι
their corruption shall utterly perish, being about to receive [the]
μισθὸν ἀδικίας, ἡδονὴν ἡγούμενοι τὴν ἐν.ἡμέρᾳ τρυφήν,
reward of unrighteousness; 4pleasure 1esteeming 2ephemeral 3indulgence;
σπῖλοι καὶ μῶμοι, ἐντρυφῶντες ἐν ταῖς [n]ἀπάταις‖ αὐτῶν, συν-
spots and blemishes, luxuriating in 2deceits 1their, feast-
ευωχούμενοι ὑμῖν, 14 ὀφθαλμοὺς ἔχοντες μεστοὺς μοιχαλίδος
ing with you; eyes having full of an adulteress,
καὶ [o]ἀκαταπαύστους‖ ἁμαρτίας, δελεάζοντες ψυχὰς ἀστηρίκ-
and that cease not from sin, alluring souls unestablish-
τους, καρδίαν γεγυμνασμένην [p]πλεονεξίαις‖ ἔχοντες, κατάρας
ed; 2a 3heart 4exercised 5in 6craving 1having, 8of 9curse
τέκνα, 15 [q]καταλιπόντες‖ [r]τὴν‖ εὐθεῖαν ὁδόν, ἐπλανήθησαν,
7children; having left the straight way, they went astray,
ἐξακολουθήσαντες τῇ ὁδῷ τοῦ Βαλαὰμ τοῦ Βοσόρ, ὃς
having followed in the way of Balaam, [son] of Bosor, who [the]
μισθὸν ἀδικίας ἠγάπησεν, 16 ἔλεγξιν.δὲ ἔσχεν ἰδίας
reward of unrighteousness loved; but reproof had of his own
παρανομίας· ὑποζύγιον ἄφωνον, ἐν ἀνθρώπου φωνῇ
wickedness, [the] 2beast 3of 4burden 1dumb, in man's voice
φθεγξάμενον, ἐκώλυσεν τὴν τοῦ προφήτου παραφρονίαν.
speaking, forbade the 2of 3the 4prophet 1madness.
17 οὗτοί εἰσιν πηγαὶ ἄνυδροι, [s]νεφέλαι‖ ὑπὸ λαίλαπος ἐλαυ-
These are fountains without water, clouds by storm being
νόμεναι, οἷς ὁ ζόφος τοῦ σκότους [t]εἰς.αἰῶνα‖ τετήρηται.
driven, to whom the gloom of darkness for ever is kept.

wicked: 8 (for that righteous man dwelling among them, in seeing and hearing, vexed *his* righteous soul from day to day with *their* unlawful deeds;) 9 the Lord knoweth how to deliver the godly out of temptations, and to reserve the unjust unto the day of judgment to be punished: 10 but chiefly them that walk after the flesh in the lust of uncleanness, and despise government. Presumptuous *are they*, selfwilled, they are not afraid to speak evil of dignities. 11 Whereas angels, which are greater in power and might, bring not railing accusation against them before the Lord. 12 But these, as natural brute beasts, made to be taken and destroyed, speak evil of the things that they understand not; and shall utterly perish in their own corruption; 13 and shall receive the reward of unrighteousness, *as* they that count it pleasure to riot in the daytime. Spots *they are* and blemishes, sporting themselves with their own deceivings while they feast with you; 14 having eyes full of adultery, and that cannot cease from sin; beguiling unstable souls: an heart they have exercised with covetous practices; cursed children: 15 which have forsaken the right way, and are gone astray, following the way of Balaam *the son* of Bosor, who loved the wages of unrighteousness; 16 but was rebuked for his iniquity: the dumb ass speaking with man's voice forbad the madness of the prophet. 17 These are wells without water, clouds that are carried with a tempest; to whom the mist of darkness is reserved for ever. 18 For when they speak great swelling *words* of vanity, they

---

[f] ἐρύσατο TrA. [g] — ὁ (*read* [the]) L. [h] ἐν- T. [i] πειρασμῶν temptations T. [k] — παρὰ κυρίῳ L[Tr]. [l] φυσικὰ γεγεννημένα EG; γεγεννημ. (γεγενημ. T) φυσικὰ (*read* irrational animals, born naturally) LTTrAW. [m] καὶ φθαρήσονται shall even perish LTTrAW. [n] ἀγάπαις 2love 3feasts LTr. [o] ἀκαταπάστους insatiable (for sin) L. [p] πλεονεξίας GLTTrAW. [q] καταλείποντες leaving T. [r] — τὴν (*read* [the]) GLTTrAW. [s] καὶ ὁμίχλαι and mists GLTTrAW. [t] — εἰς αἰῶνα LTTrA.

allure through the
lusts of the flesh,
through much wanton-
ness, those that were
clean escaped from
them who live in error.
19 While they promise
them liberty, they
themselves are the ser-
vants of corruption:
for of whom a man is
overcome, of the same
is he brought in bon-
dage. 20 For if after
they have escaped the
pollutions of the world
through the know-
ledge of the Lord and
Saviour Jesus Christ,
they are again en-
tangled therein, and
overcome, the latter
end is worse with them
than the beginning.
21 For it had been bet-
ter for them not to
have known the way of
righteousness, than,
after they have known
it, to turn from the
holy commandment
delivered unto them.
22 But it is happened
unto them according
to the true proverb,
The dog *is* turned to
his own vomit again;
and the sow that was
washed to her wallow-
ing in the mire.
III. This second e-
pistle, beloved, I now
write unto you; in
both which I stir up
your pure minds by
way of remembrance:
2 that ye may be mind-
ful of the words which
were spoken before by
the holy prophets, and
of the commandment
of us the apostles of
the Lord and Saviour:
3 knowing this first,
that there shall come
in the last days scof-
fers, walking after
their own lusts, 4 and
saying, Where is the
promise of his coming?
for since the fathers
fell asleep, all things
continue as *they were*
from the beginning of
the creation. 5 For
this they willingly are
ignorant of, that by
the word of God the
heavens were of old,
and the earth standing
out of the water and
in the water: 6 where-
by the world that then
was, being overflowed
with water, perished:

18 ὑπέρογκα.γὰρ ματαιότητος φθεγγόμενοι, δελεάζουσιν
For great swelling [words] of vanity speaking, they allure
ἐν ἐπιθυμίαις σαρκός, [v]ἀσελγείαις, τοὺς [w]ὄντως[x]
with [the] desires of [the] flesh, by licentiousnesses, those who indeed
[x]ἀποφυγόντας‖ τοὺς ἐν πλάνῃ ἀναστρεφομένους, 19 ἐλευ-
escaped from those who [2]in [3]error [1]walk, [6]free-
θερίαν αὐτοῖς ἐπαγγελλόμενοι, αὐτοὶ δοῦλοι ὑπάρχοντες
dom [5]them [4]promising, themselves [2]bondmen [1]being
τῆς φθορᾶς· ᾧ.γάρ τις ἥττηται, τούτῳ [y]καὶ‖ δε-
of corruption; for by whom anyone has been subdued, by him also he is
δούλωται. 20 εἰ.γὰρ ἀποφυγόντες τὰ μιάσματα τοῦ κόσμου
held in bondage. For if having escaped the pollutions of the world
ἐν ἐπιγνώσει τοῦ κυρίου [z] καὶ σωτῆρος Ἰησοῦ χριστοῦ,
through [the] knowledge of the Lord and Saviour Jesus Christ,
τούτοις.δὲ πάλιν ἐμπλακέντες ἡττῶνται, γέγονεν
but [8]by [9]these [1]again [2]having [3]been [4]entangled [5]they [6]are [7]subdued, has become
αὐτοῖς τὰ ἔσχατα χείρονα τῶν πρώτων. 21 [a]κρεῖττον‖
to them the last [state] worse than the first. [2]Better
γὰρ ἦν αὐτοῖς μὴ ἐπεγνωκέναι τὴν ὁδὸν τῆς δικαιοσύνης,
[1]for it were for them not to have known the way of righteousness,
ἢ ἐπιγνοῦσιν [b] [c]ἐπιστρέψαι‖ [d]ἐκ‖ τῆς παραδοθείσης αὐ-
than having known [it] to have turned from the [3]delivered [4]to
τοῖς ἁγίας ἐντολῆς. 22 συμβέβηκεν.[e]δὲ‖ αὐτοῖς τὸ τῆς
[5]them [1]holy [2]commandment. But has happened to them the [word] of the
ἀληθοῦς παροιμίας, Κύων ἐπιστρέψας ἐπὶ τὸ.ἴδιον ἐξέραμα·
true proverb: [The] dog having returned to his own vomit;
καί, [ε]Ὗς λουσαμένη, εἰς [f]κύλισμα‖ βορβόρου.
and, [The] [2]sow [1]washed, to [her] rolling place in [the] mire.
3 Ταύτην ἤδη, ἀγαπητοί, δευτέραν ὑμῖν γράφω ἐπιστολήν,
This now, beloved, a second [2]to [3]you [4]I [5]write [1]epistle,
ἐν αἷς διεγείρω ὑμῶν ἐν ὑπομνήσει τὴν εἰλικρι-
in [both] which I stir up your [3]in [4]putting [[5]you] [6]in [7]remembrance [1]pure
νῆ διάνοιαν, 2 μνησθῆναι τῶν προειρημένων ῥημάτων ὑπὸ τῶν
[2]mind, to be mindful of the [2]spoken [3]before [1]words by the
ἁγίων προφητῶν, καὶ τῆς τῶν ἀποστόλων [g]ἡμῶν‖ ἐντολῆς,
holy prophets, and of the [9]the [10]apostles [7]by [8]us [1]commandment
τοῦ κυρίου καὶ σωτῆρος· 3 τοῦτο πρῶτον γινώσκοντες, ὅτι
[2]of [3]the [4]Lord [5]and [6]Saviour; this first knowing, that
ἐλεύσονται ἐπ'.[h]ἐσχάτου‖ τῶν ἡμερῶν [i] ἐμπαῖκται, κατὰ
will come at the close of the days mockers, according to
τὰς.ἰδίας.[k]αὐτῶν ἐπιθυμίας‖ πορευόμενοι, 4 καὶ λέγοντες, Ποῦ
their own lusts walking, and saying, Where
ἐστιν ἡ ἐπαγγελία τῆς.παρουσίας.αὐτοῦ; ἀφ'.ἧς.γὰρ οἱ πατέ-
is the promise of his coming? for since the fa-
ρες ἐκοιμήθησαν, πάντα οὕτως διαμένει ἀπ' ἀρχῆς κτί-
thers fell asleep, all things thus continue from [the] beginning of [the]
σεως. 5 λανθάνει.γὰρ αὐτοὺς τοῦτο θέλοντας, ὅτι
creation. For [2]is [3]hidden [4]from [5]them [1]this, [they] willing [it], that
οὐρανοὶ ἦσαν ἔκπαλαι, καὶ γῆ ἐξ ὕδατος καὶ δι' ὕδατος
heavens were of old, and an earth out of water and in water
συνεστῶσα, τῷ τοῦ θεοῦ λόγῳ, 6 δι' ὧν ὁ τότε
subsisting, by the [2]of [3]God [1]word, through which [waters] the then

[v] + ἐν E. [w] ὀλίγως scarcely GLTTrAW. [x] ἀποφεύγοντας are escaping from LTTrAW. [y] — καὶ T[Tr]. [z] + ἡμῶν (*read* our Lord) LT. [a] κρεῖσσον T. [b] + εἰς τὰ ὀπίσω to the [things] behind L. [c] ὑποστρέψαι to have turned back LTTrA. [d] ἀπὸ L. [e] — δὲ but LTTrA. [f] κυλισμὸν rolling TTrA. [g] ὑμῶν (*read* by your apostles) LTTrAW. [h] ἐσχάτων (*read* in the last days) LTTrAW. [i] + ἐν ἐμπαιγμονῇ (*read* mockers, with mocking) GLTTrAW. [k] ἐπιθυμίας αὐτῶν GLTrA.

κόσμος ὕδατι κατακλυσθεὶς ἀπώλετο· 7 οἱ.δὲ νῦν οὐρανοὶ
world with water having been deluged perished. But the now heavens
καὶ ἡ γῆ [l]αὐτοῦ[ll] λόγῳ τεθησαυρισμένοι εἰσίν, πυρὶ τηρού-
and the earth by his word [2]treasured [3]up [1]are, for fire being
μενοι εἰς ἡμέραν κρίσεως καὶ ἀπωλείας τῶν ἀσεβῶν ἀνθρώπων.
kept to a day of judgment and destruction of ungodly men.
8 ἓν.δὲ.τοῦτο μὴ.λανθανέτω ὑμᾶς, ἀγαπητοί, ὅτι μία ἡμέρα
But this one thing let not be hidden from you, beloved, that one day
παρὰ κυρίῳ ὡς χίλια ἔτη, καὶ χίλια ἔτη ὡς ἡμέρα
with [the] Lord [is] as a thousand years, and a thousand years as [2]day
μία. 9 οὐ.βραδύνει [m]ὁ[ll] κύριος τῆς ἐπαγγελίας, ὥς τινες βρα-
[1]one. [5]Does [6]not [7]delay [3]the [4]Lord the promise, as some [2]de-
δυτῆτα ἡγοῦνται· ἀλλὰ μακροθυμεῖ [n]εἰς[ll] [o]ἡμᾶς,[ll] μὴ βουλό-
lay [1]esteem, but is longsuffering towards us, not will-
μενός τινας ἀπολέσθαι, ἀλλὰ πάντας εἰς μετάνοιαν χωρῆ-
ing [for] any to perish, but all to repentance to
σαι. 10 ἥξει.δὲ [p]ἡ[ll] ἡμέρα κυρίου ὡς κλέπτης [q]ἐν νυκτί,[ll]
come. But shall come the day of [the] Lord as a thief in [the] night,
ἐν ᾗ [r]οἱ[ll] οὐρανοὶ ῥοιζηδὸν παρελεύσονται, στοιχεῖα.δὲ
in which the heavens with rushing noise shall pass away, and [the] elements
καυσούμενα [s]λυθήσονται,[ll] καὶ γῆ καὶ τὰ ἐν αὐτῇ ἔργα
burning with heat shall be dissolved, and [the] earth and the [2]in [3]it [1]works
[t]κατακαήσεται.[ll]
shall be burnt up.

11 Τούτων [v]οὖν[ll] πάντων λυομένων, ποταποὺς
These things then all being to be dissolved, what kind of [persons]
δεῖ ὑπάρχειν ὑμᾶς ἐν ἁγίαις ἀναστροφαῖς καὶ εὐσεβείαις,
ought [2]to [3]be [1]ye in holy conduct and piety,
12 προσδοκῶντας καὶ σπεύδοντας τὴν παρουσίαν τῆς τοῦ
expecting and hastening the coming of the
θεοῦ ἡμέρας δι' ἣν οὐρανοὶ πυρούμενοι λυθή-
[2]of [3]God [1]day by reason of which [the] heavens, being on fire, shall be dis-
σονται, καὶ στοιχεῖα καυσούμενα [w]τήκεται;[ll] 13 καινοὺς
solved, and [the] elements burning with heat shall melt? [2]New
δὲ οὐρανοὺς καὶ [x]γῆν καινὴν[ll] [y]κατὰ[ll] [z]τὸ ἐπάγγελμα[ll] αὐτοῦ
[1]but heavens and [3]earth [1]a [2]new according to [2]promise [1]his,
προσδοκῶμεν, ἐν οἷς δικαιοσύνη κατοικεῖ. 14 διό, ἀγαπη-
we expect, in which righteousness dwells. Wherefore, belov-
τοί, ταῦτα προσδοκῶντες, σπουδάσατε ἄσπιλοι καὶ ἀμώ-
ed, these things expecting be diligent without spot and unblam-
μητοι αὐτῷ εὑρεθῆναι ἐν εἰρήνῃ, 15 καὶ τὴν τοῦ.κυρίου.ἡμῶν
able by him to be found in peace; and the [2]of [3]our [4]Lord
μακροθυμίαν, σωτηρίαν ἡγεῖσθε· καθὼς καὶ ὁ ἀγαπητὸς
[1]longsuffering, [7]salvation [5]esteem [6]ye; according as also [2]beloved
ἡμῶν ἀδελφὸς Παῦλος κατὰ τὴν [a]αὐτῷ δοθεῖσαν[ll] σοφίαν
[1]our brother Paul according to the [3]to [4]him [2]given [1]wisdom
ἔγραψεν ὑμῖν, 16 ὡς καὶ ἐν πάσαις [b]ταῖς[ll] ἐπιστολαῖς, λαλῶν
wrote to you, as also in all [his] epistles, speaking
ἐν αὐταῖς περὶ τούτων· ἐν [c]οἷς[ll] ἐστιν δυσνόητά
in them concerning these things, among which are [3]hard [4]to [5]be [6]understood

7 but the heavens and the earth, which are now, by the same word are kept in store, reserved unto fire against the day of judgment and perdition of ungodly men. 8 But, beloved, be not ignorant of this one thing, that one day *is* with the Lord as a thousand years, and a thousand years as one day. 9 The Lord is not slack concerning his promise, as some men count slackness; but is longsuffering to us-ward, not willing that any should perish, but that all should come to repentance. 10 But the day of the Lord will come as a thief in the night; in the which the heavens shall pass away with a great noise, and the elements shall melt with fervent heat, the earth also and the works that are therein shall be burned up.

11 *Seeing* then *that* all these things shall be dissolved, what manner *of* persons ought ye to be in *all* holy conversation and godliness, 12 looking for and hasting unto the coming of the day of God, wherein the heavens being on fire shall be dissolved, and the elements shall melt with fervent heat? 13 Nevertheless we, according to his promise, look for new heavens and a new earth, wherein dwelleth righteousness. 14 Wherefore, beloved, seeing that ye look for such things, be diligent that ye may be found of him in peace, without spot, and blameless. 15 And account *that* the longsuffering of our Lord *is* salvation; even as our beloved brother Paul also according to the wisdom given unto him hath written unto you; 16 as also in all *his* epistles, speaking in them of these things; in which are some things hard to be

---

[l] τῷ αὐτῷ (*read* by the same word) ELT; τῷ αὐτοῦ GTrAW. [m] — ὁ (*read* [the]) LTTrAW. [n] δι' because of LT. [o] ὑμᾶς you LTTrA. [p] — ἡ (*read* [the]) LTTrAW. [q] — ἐν νυκτί GLTTrAW. [r] — οἱ (*read* [the]) TA. [s] λυθήσεται LTTr. [t] εὑρεθήσεται shall be detected Tr. [v] οὕτως thus A. [w] τακήσεται L. [x] καινὴν γῆν T. [y] καὶ and L. [z] τὰ ἐπαγγέλματα promises LT. [a] δοθεῖσαν αὐτῷ LTTrAW. [b] — ταῖς LTrAW. [c] αἷς LTTrAW.

understood, which they that are unlearned and unstable wrest, as *they do* also the other scriptures, unto their own destruction.
17 Ye therefore, beloved, seeing ye know *these things* before, beware lest ye also, being led away with the error of the wicked, fall from your own stedfastness. 18 But grow in grace, and *in* the knowledge of our Lord and Saviour Jesus Christ. To him *be* glory both now and for ever. Amen.

τινα, ἃ οἱ ἀμαθεῖς καὶ ἀστήρικτοι στρεβλοῦσιν, ˋὡς
[1]some [2]things, which the untaught and unestablished wrest, as
καὶ τὰς λοιπὰς γραφάς, πρὸς τὴν.ἰδίαν.αὐτῶν ἀπώλειαν.
also the other scriptures, to their own destruction.
17 Ὑμεῖς οὖν, ἀγαπητοί, προγινώσκοντες φυλάσσεσθε,
Ye therefore, beloved, knowing beforehand, beware,
ἵνα.μὴ τῇ τῶν ἀθέσμων πλάνῃ συναπαχθέντες, ἐκπέ-
lest with the [2]of [3]the [4]lawless [[5]ones] [1]error having been led away, ye should
σητε τοῦ.ἰδίου στηριγμοῦ· 18 αὐξάνετε.δὲ ἐν χάριτι καὶ
fall from your own steadfastness: but grow in grace, and
γνώσει τοῦ.κυρίου.ἡμῶν καὶ σωτῆρος Ἰησοῦ χριστοῦ.
in [the] knowledge of our Lord and Saviour Jesus Christ.
αὐτῷ ἡ δόξα καὶ νῦν καὶ εἰς ἡμέραν αἰῶνος. [d]ἀμήν.‖ [e]
To him [be] glory both now and to [the] day of eternity. Amen.

---

[f]ΕΠΙΣΤΟΛΗ ΙΩΑΝΝΟΥ ΚΑΘΟΛΙΚΗ ΠΡΩΤΗ.‖
[3]EPISTLE [4]OF [5]JOHN [2]GENERAL [1]FIRST.

THAT which was from the beginning, which we have heard, which we have seen with our eyes, which we have looked upon, and our hands have handled, of the Word of life; 2 (for the life was manifested, and we have seen *it*, and bear witness, and shew unto you that eternal life, which was with the Father, and was manifested unto us;) 3 that which we have seen and heard declare we unto you, that ye also may have fellowship with us: and truly our fellowship *is* with the Father, and with his Son Jesus Christ. 4 And these things write we unto you, that your joy may be full.

Ὃ ἦν ἀπ' ἀρχῆς, ὃ ἀκηκόαμεν, ὃ ἑω-
That which was from [the] beginning, that which we have heard, that which we
ράκαμεν τοῖς.ὀφθαλμοῖς.ἡμῶν, ὃ ἐθεασάμεθα καὶ αἱ χεῖρες
have seen with our eyes, that which we gazed upon and [2]hands
ἡμῶν ἐψηλάφησαν περὶ τοῦ λόγου τῆς ζωῆς· 2 καὶ ἡ ζωὴ
[1]our handled concerning the Word of life; (and the life
ἐφανερώθη, καὶ ἑωράκαμεν, καὶ μαρτυροῦμεν, καὶ ἀπαγγέλ-
was manifested, and we have seen, and bear witness, and re-
λομεν ὑμῖν τὴν ζωὴν τὴν αἰώνιον, ἥτις ἦν πρὸς τὸν πατέρα,
port to you the [2]life [1]eternal, which was with the Father,
καὶ ἐφανερώθη ἡμῖν· 3 ὃ ἑωράκαμεν καὶ ἀκηκόαμεν,
and was manifested to us:) that which we have seen and have heard
ἀπαγγέλλομεν[g] ὑμῖν, ἵνα καὶ ὑμεῖς κοινωνίαν ἔχητε μεθ'
we report to you, that also ye fellowship may have with
ἡμῶν· καὶ ἡ κοινωνία δὲ ἡ ἡμετέρα μετὰ τοῦ πατρὸς καὶ
us; and [2]fellowship [3]indeed [1]our [is] with the Father, and
μετὰ τοῦ.υἱοῦ.αὐτοῦ Ἰησοῦ χριστοῦ· 4 καὶ ταῦτα [h]γράφο-
with his Son Jesus Christ. And these things we
μεν ὑμῖν,‖ ἵνα ἡ χαρὰ [i]ἡμῶν‖ ᾖ πεπληρωμένη.
write to you that [2]joy [1]our may be full.

5 This then is the message which we have heard of him, and declare unto you, that God is light, and in him is no darkness at all. 6 If we say that we have fellowship with him, and walk in darkness, we lie, and do not the truth: 7 but if we walk in the light, as he is in the light, we have fellowship one

5 Καὶ [k]αὕτη ἐστὶν‖ ἡ [l]ἐπαγγελία‖ ἣν ἀκηκόαμεν ἀπ'
And this is the message which we have heard from
αὐτοῦ, καὶ ἀναγγέλλομεν ὑμῖν, ὅτι ὁ θεὸς φῶς ἐστιν, καὶ
him, and announce to you, that God [2]light [1]is, and
σκοτία [m]ἐν αὐτῷ οὐκ.ἔστιν‖.οὐδεμία. 6 ἐὰν εἴπωμεν ὅτι
darkness in him is not any at all. If we should say that
κοινωνίαν ἔχομεν μετ' αὐτοῦ, καὶ ἐν τῷ σκότει περιπατῶμεν,
fellowship we have with him, and in darkness should walk,
ψευδόμεθα, καὶ οὐ.ποιοῦμεν τὴν ἀλήθειαν· 7 ἐὰν.δὲ ἐν τῷ
we lie, and do not practise the truth. But if in the
φωτὶ περιπατῶμεν, ὡς αὐτός ἐστιν ἐν τῷ φωτί, κοινωνίαν
light we should walk, as he is in the light, fellowship

---

[d] — ἀμήν T[TrA]. [e] + Πέτρου β' 2 Peter TrA.
[f] + τοῦ ἀποστόλου the apostle E; — καθολικὴ G; Ἰωάννου α' LTAW; Ἰωάνου ἐπιστολὴ α' Tr. [g] + καὶ also LTTrAW. [h] γράφομεν ἡμεῖς we write TTrA. [i] ὑμῶν [1]your EGW.
[k] ἔστιν αὕτη TTrAW. [l] ἀγγελια GLTTrAW. [m] οὐκ ἔστιν ἐν αὐτῷ Tr.

ἔχομεν μετ' ἀλλήλων, καὶ τὸ αἷμα Ἰησοῦ [n]χριστοῦ‖ τοῦ υἱοῦ
we have with one another, and the blood of Jesus Christ [2]Son
αὐτοῦ καθαρίζει ἡμᾶς ἀπὸ πάσης ἁμαρτίας. 8 ἐὰν εἴπωμεν
[1]his cleanses us from every sin. If we should say
ὅτι ἁμαρτίαν οὐκ.ἔχομεν, ἑαυτοὺς πλανῶμεν καὶ ἡ ἀλήθεια
that sin we have not, ourselves we deceive, and the truth
[o]οὐκ.ἔστιν ἐν ἡμῖν.‖ 9 ἐὰν ὁμολογῶμεν τὰς.ἁμαρτίας.ἡμῶν,
is not in us. If we should confess our sins,
πιστός ἐστιν καὶ δίκαιος, ἵνα ἀφῇ [p]ἡμῖν‖ τὰς ἁμαρτίας,
faithful he is and righteous, that he may forgive us the sins,
καὶ καθαρίσῃ ἡμᾶς ἀπὸ πάσης ἀδικίας. 10 ἐὰν εἴπωμεν
and may cleanse us from all unrighteousness. If we should say
ὅτι οὐχ.ἡμαρτήκαμεν, ψεύστην ποιοῦμεν αὐτόν, καὶ ὁ λόγος
that we have not sinned, a liar we make him, and [2]word
αὐτοῦ οὐκ.ἔστιν ἐν ἡμῖν.
[1]his is not in us.

2 Τεκνία μου, ταῦτα γράφω ὑμῖν, ἵνα μὴ.ἁμάρτητε·
[2]Little [3]children [1]my, these things I write to you, that ye may not sin;
καὶ ἐάν τις ἁμάρτῃ, παράκλητον ἔχομεν πρὸς τὸν πατέρα,
and if anyone should sin, a Paraclete we have with the Father,
Ἰησοῦν χριστὸν δίκαιον· 2 καὶ αὐτὸς [q]ἱλασμός ἐστιν‖
Jesus Christ [the] righteous; and he [the] propitiation is
περὶ τῶν.ἁμαρτιῶν.ἡμῶν· οὐ περὶ τῶν.ἡμετέρων δὲ μόνον,
for our sins; [2]not [3]for [4]ours [1]but only,
ἀλλὰ καὶ περὶ ὅλου τοῦ κόσμου.
but also for [2]whole [1]the world.

3 Καὶ ἐν τούτῳ γινώσκομεν ὅτι ἐγνώκαμεν αὐτόν, ἐὰν
And by this we know that we have known him, if
τὰς.ἐντολὰς.αὐτοῦ τηρῶμεν. 4 ὁ λέγων, [r] Ἔγνωκα αὐτόν,
his commandments we keep. He that says, I have known him,
καὶ τὰς.ἐντολὰς.αὐτοῦ μὴ.τηρῶν, ψεύστης ἐστίν, καὶ ἐν τούτῳ
and his commandments is not keeping, a liar is, and in him
ἡ ἀλήθεια οὐκ.ἔστιν· 5 ὃς.δ'.ἂν τηρῇ αὐτοῦ τὸν λόγον,
the truth is not; but whoever may keep his word,
ἀληθῶς ἐν τούτῳ ἡ ἀγάπη τοῦ θεοῦ τετελείωται. ἐν τούτῳ
truly in him the love of God has been perfected. By this
γινώσκομεν ὅτι ἐν αὐτῷ ἐσμεν. 6 ὁ λέγων ἐν αὐτῷ
we know that in him we are. He that says in him [he]
μένειν, ὀφείλει, καθὼς ἐκεῖνος περιεπάτησεν, καὶ αὐτὸς [s]οὕτως‖
abides, ought, even as he walked, also himself so
περιπατεῖν. 7 [t]ἀδελφοί,‖ οὐκ ἐντολὴν καινὴν γράφω ὑμῖν,
to walk. Brethren, not a [2]commandment [1]new I write to you,
ἀλλ' ἐντολὴν παλαιάν, ἣν εἴχετε ἀπ' ἀρχῆς· ἡ
but [3]commandment [1]an [2]old, which ye had from [the] beginning: the
ἐντολὴ ἡ παλαιά ἐστιν ὁ λόγος ὃν ἠκούσατε [v]ἀπ'
[2]commandment [1]old is the word which ye heard from [the]
ἀρχῆς.‖ 8 πάλιν ἐντολὴν καινὴν γράφω ὑμῖν, ὅ ἐστιν
beginning. Again a [2]commandment [1]new I write to you, which is
ἀληθὲς ἐν αὐτῷ καὶ ἐν ὑμῖν, ὅτι ἡ σκοτία παράγεται,
true in him and in you, because the darkness is passing away,
καὶ τὸ φῶς τὸ ἀληθινὸν ἤδη φαίνει. 9 ὁ λέγων ἐν τῷ
and the [2]light [1]true already shines. He that says in the
φωτὶ εἶναι, καὶ τὸν.ἀδελφὸν.αὐτοῦ μισῶν, ἐν τῇ σκοτίᾳ ἐστὶν
light [he] is, and [2]his [3]brother [1]hates, in the darkness is

with another, and the
blood of Jesus Christ
his Son cleanseth us
from all sin. 8 If we
say that we have no
sin, we deceive our-
selves, and the truth
is not in us. 9 If we
confess our sins, he is
faithful and just to
forgive us *our* sins,
and to cleanse us from
all unrighteousness.
10 If we say that we
have not sinned, we
make him a liar, and
his word is not in us.

II. My little chil-
dren, these things
write I unto you, that
ye sin not. And if any
man sin, we have an
advocate with the Fa-
ther, Jesus Christ the
righteous: 2 and he is
the propitiation for
our sins: and not for
ours only, but also for
the sins of the whole
world.

3 And hereby we do
know that we know
him, if we keep his
commandments. 4 He
that saith, I know him,
and keepeth not his
commandments, is a
liar, and the truth is
not in him. 5 But who-
so keepeth his word, in
him verily is the love
of God perfected:
hereby know we that
we are in him. 6 He
that saith he abideth
in him ought himself
also so to walk, even
as he walked. 7 Bre-
thren, I write no new
commandment unto
you, but an old com-
mandment which ye
had from the begin-
ning. The old com-
mandment is the word
which ye have heard
from the beginning.
8 Again, a new com-
mandment I write un-
to you, which thing is
true in him and in you:
because the darkness
is past, and the true
light now shineth.
9 He that saith he
is in the light, and
hateth his brother, is
in darkness even until

[n] — χριστοῦ LTTrA. [o] ἐν ἡμῖν οὐκ ἔστιν LTrW. [p] ἡμῶν our (sins) W. [q] ἐστιν ἱλασμὸς L. [r] + ὅτι [L]TTrA. [s] — οὕτως LTr[A]. [t] ἀγαπητοί beloved GLTTrAW. [v] — ἀπ' ἀρχῆς LTTrA.

now. 10 He that lov-
eth his brother abideth
in the light, and there
is none occasion of
stumbling in him.
11 But he that hateth
his brother is in dark-
ness, and walketh in
darkness, and know-
eth not whither he
goeth, because that
darkness hath blinded
his eyes.

12 I write unto you,
little children, because
your sins are forgiven
you for his name's
sake.

13 I write unto you,
fathers, because ye
have known him *that*
is from the beginning.
I write unto you,
young men, because ye
have overcome the
wicked one. I write
unto you, little chil-
dren, because ye have
known the Father.
14 I have written
unto you, fathers, be-
cause ye have known
him *that is* from the
beginning. I have
written unto you,
young men, because
ye are strong, and the
word of God abideth
in you, and ye have
overcome the wicked
one. 15 Love not the
world, neither the
things *that are* in the
world. If any man
love the world, the
love of the Father is
not in him. 16 For all
that *is* in the world,
the lust of the flesh,
and the lust of the
eyes, and the pride of
life, is not of the Fa-
ther, but is of the
world. 17 And the
world passeth away,
and the lust thereof:
but he that doeth the
will of God abideth
for ever. 18 Little
children, it is the last
time: and as ye have
heard that antichrist
shall come, even now
are there many anti-
christs; whereby we
know that it is the
last time. 19 They went
out from us, but they
were not of us; for if
they had been of us,
they would *no doubt*
have continued with
us: but *they went out*,
that they might be
made manifest that
they were not all of

ἕως ἄρτι. 10 ὁ ἀγαπῶν τὸν.ἀδελφὸν αὐτοῦ, ἐν τῷ φωτὶ
until now. He that loves his brother, in the light
μένει, καὶ σκάνδαλον [w]ἐν αὐτῷ οὐκ.ἔστιν.‖ 11 ὁ.δὲ
abides, and [4]cause [5]of [6]offence [7]in [8]him [1]there [2]is [3]not. But he that
μισῶν τὸν.ἀδελφὸν.αὐτοῦ, ἐν τῇ σκοτίᾳ ἐστίν, καὶ ἐν τῇ σκοτίᾳ
hates his brother, in the darkness is, and in the darkness
περιπατεῖ, καὶ οὐκ.οἶδεν ποῦ ὑπάγει, ὅτι ἡ σκοτία ἐτύφ-
walks, and knows not where he goes, because the darkness blind-
λωσεν τοὺς.ὀφθαλμοὺς.αὐτοῦ.
ed his eyes.

12 Γράφω ὑμῖν, τεκνία, ὅτι ἀφέωνται ὑμῖν
I write to you, little children, because have been forgiven you [your]
αἱ ἁμαρτίαι διὰ τὸ.ὄνομα.αὐτοῦ.
sins for the sake of his name.

13 Γράφω ὑμῖν, πατέρες, ὅτι ἐγνώκατε τὸν ἀπ'
I write to you, fathers, because ye have known him who [is] from
ἀρχῆς. Γράφω ὑμῖν, νεανίσκοι, ὅτι νενικήκατε τὸν
[the] beginning. I write to you, young men, because ye have overcome the
πονηρόν. [x]Γράφω‖ ὑμῖν, παιδία, ὅτι ἐγνώκατε τὸν
wicked [one]. I write to you, little children, because ye have known the
πατέρα.
Father.

14 Ἔγραψα ὑμῖν, πατέρες, ὅτι ἐγνώκατε τὸν
I wrote to you, fathers, because ye have known him who [is]
ἀπ' ἀρχῆς. Ἔγραψα ὑμῖν, νεανίσκοι, ὅτι ἰσχυροί ἐστε,
from [the] beginning. I wrote to you, young men, because strong ye are
καὶ ὁ λόγος τοῦ θεοῦ ἐν ὑμῖν μένει, καὶ νενικήκατε τὸν
and the word of God in you abides, and ye have overcome the
πονηρόν. 15 μὴ.ἀγαπᾶτε τὸν κόσμον, μηδὲ τὰ ἐν τῷ
wicked [one]. Love not the world, nor the things in the
κόσμῳ· ἐάν τις ἀγαπᾷ τὸν κόσμον, οὐκ ἔστιν ἡ ἀγάπη
world. If anyone should love the world, [7]not [6]is [1]the [2]love
τοῦ πατρὸς ἐν αὐτῷ· 16 ὅτι πᾶν τὸ ἐν τῷ κόσμῳ,
[3]of [4]the [5]Father in him; because all that which [is] in the world,
ἡ ἐπιθυμία τῆς σαρκός, καὶ ἡ ἐπιθυμία τῶν ὀφθαλμῶν, καὶ
the desire of the flesh, and the desire of the eyes, and
ἡ [y]ἀλαζονεία‖ τοῦ βίου, οὐκ.ἔστιν ἐκ τοῦ πατρός, [z]ἀλλ'‖ ἐκ
the vaunting of life, is not of the Father, but of
τοῦ κόσμου ἐστίν. 17 καὶ ὁ κόσμος παράγεται, καὶ ἡ ἐπι-
the world is; and the world is passing away, and the
θυμία αὐτοῦ· ὁ.δὲ ποιῶν τὸ θέλημα τοῦ θεοῦ μένει εἰς τὸν
lust of it, but he that does the will of God abides for
αἰῶνα. 18 Παιδία, ἐσχάτη ὥρα ἐστίν· καὶ καθὼς
ever. Little children, [the] last hour it is, and according as
ἠκούσατε ὅτι [a]ὁ‖ ἀντίχριστος ἔρχεται, καὶ νῦν ἀντίχριστοι
ye heard that the antichrist is coming, even now [2]antichrists
πολλοὶ γεγόνασιν· ὅθεν γινώσκομεν ὅτι ἐσχάτη ὥρα ἐστίν
[1]many have arisen, whence we know that [the] last hour it is.
19 ἐξ ἡμῶν [b]ἐξῆλθον,‖ ἀλλ' οὐκ.ἦσαν ἐξ ἡμῶν· εἰ.γὰρ
From among us they went out, but they were not of us; for if
[c]ἦσαν ἐξ ἡμῶν,‖ μεμενήκεισαν.ἂν μεθ' ἡμῶν· ἀλλ' ἵνα φανε-
they were of us, they would have remained with us, but that they
ρωθῶσιν ὅτι οὐκ.εἰσὶν πάντες ἐξ ἡμῶν. 20 καὶ ὑμεῖς
might be made manifest that [2]are [3]not [1]all of us. And ye

---

[w] οὐκ ἔστιν ἐν αὐτῷ LTA. [x] ἔγραψα I wrote LTTrAW. [y] ἀλαζονία T. [z] ἀλλὰ TTrW.
[a] — ὁ LTTrAW. [b] ἐξῆλθαν LTTrAW. [c] ἐξ ἡμῶν ἦσαν Tr.

χρῖσμα ἔχετε ἀπὸ τοῦ ἁγίου, καὶ οἴδατε ᵈπάντα.‖
[the] anointing have from the holy [one], and ye know all things.
21 οὐκ.ἔγραψα ὑμῖν ὅτι οὐκ.οἴδατε τὴν ἀλήθειαν, ἀλλ' ὅτι
I wrote not to you because ye know not the truth, but because
οἴδατε αὐτήν, καὶ ὅτι πᾶν ψεῦδος ἐκ τῆς ἀληθείας οὐκ ἔστιν.
ye know it, and that ²any ³lie ⁵of ⁶the ⁷truth ¹not ⁴is.
(lit. every)
22 Τίς ἐστιν ὁ ψεύστης εἰ.μὴ ὁ ἀρνούμενος ὅτι Ἰησοῦς οὐκ
Who is the liar but he that denies that Jesus
ἔστιν ὁ χριστός; οὗτός ἐστιν ὁ ἀντίχριστος ὁ ἀρνούμενος
is the Christ? He is the antichrist who denies
τὸν πατέρα καὶ τὸν υἱόν. 23 πᾶς ὁ ἀρνούμενος τὸν υἱόν,
the Father and the Son. Everyone that denies the Son,
οὐδὲ τὸν πατέρα ἔχει. ᵉ 24 Ὑμεῖς ᶠοὖν‖ ὃ ἠκούσατε ἀπ'
neither ³the ⁴Father ¹has ²he. Ye therefore what ye heard from
ἀρχῆς, ἐν ὑμῖν μενέτω. ἐὰν ἐν ὑμῖν μείνῃ ὃ ἀπ'
[the] beginning, in you let it abide: if in you should abide what from
ἀρχῆς ἠκούσατε, καὶ ὑμεῖς ἐν τῷ υἱῷ καὶ ᵍἐν‖ τῷ πατρὶ
[the] beginning ye heard, also ye in the Son and in the Father
μενεῖτε. 25 καὶ αὕτη ἐστὶν ἡ ἐπαγγελία, ἣν αὐτὸς ἐπηγ-
shall abide. And this is the promise which he pro-
γείλατο ἡμῖν, τὴν ζωὴν τὴν αἰώνιον. 26 Ταῦτα ἔγραψα ὑμῖν
mised us, life eternal. These things I wrote to you
περὶ τῶν πλανώντων ὑμᾶς. 27 καὶ ὑμεῖς τὸ χρῖσμα
concerning those who lead ²astray ¹you: and you the anointing
ὃ ἐλάβετε ἀπ' αὐτοῦ, ʰἐν ὑμῖν μένει,‖ καὶ οὐ χρείαν ἔχετε
which ye received from him, in you abides, and not need ye have
ἵνα τις διδάσκῃ ὑμᾶς· ἀλλ' ὡς τὸ ⁱαὐτὸ‖ χρῖσμα διδάσκει
that anyone should teach you; but as the same anointing teaches
ὑμᾶς περὶ πάντων, καὶ ἀληθές ἐστιν, καὶ οὐκ.ἔστιν ψεῦ-
you concerning all things, and true is, and is not a
δος· καὶ καθὼς ἐδίδαξεν ὑμᾶς, ʲμενεῖτε‖ ἐν αὐτῷ.
lie; and even as it taught you, ye shall abide in him.
28 Καὶ νῦν, τεκνία, μένετε ἐν αὐτῷ· ἵνα ᵏὅταν‖ φανερω-
And now, little children, abide in him, that when he be mani-
θῇ, ˡἔχωμεν‖ παῤῥησίαν, καὶ μὴ αἰσχυνθῶμεν ἀπ'.αὐτοῦ,
fested we may have boldness, and not be put to shame from before him
ἐν τῇ.παρουσίᾳ.αὐτοῦ.
at his coming.
29 Ἐὰν εἰδῆτε ὅτι δίκαιός ἐστιν, γινώσκετε ὅτι ᵐ πᾶς ὁ
If ye know that righteous he is, ye know that everyone who
ποιῶν τὴν δικαιοσύνην, ἐξ αὐτοῦ ⁿγεγέννηται.‖ 3 Ἴδετε πο-
practises righteousness of him has been begotten. See
ταπὴν ἀγάπην δέδωκεν ἡμῖν ὁ πατήρ, ἵνα τέκνα θεοῦ
what love ³has ⁴given ⁵to ⁶us ¹the ²Father, that children of God
κληθῶμενᵒ· διὰ τοῦτο ὁ κόσμος οὐ.γινώσκει ἡμᾶς,
we should be called. On account of this the world knows not us,
ὅτι οὐκ.ἔγνω αὐτόν. 2 ἀγαπητοί, νῦν τέκνα θεοῦ ἐσμεν,
because it knew not him. Beloved, now children of God are we,
καὶ οὔπω ἐφανερώθη τί ἐσόμεθα· οἴδαμεν.ᵖδὲ‖ ὅτι ἐὰν
and not yet was it manifested what we shall be; but we know that if
φανερωθῇ, ὅμοιοι αὐτῷ ἐσόμεθα, ὅτι ὀψόμεθα αὐτὸν καθὼς
he be manifested, like him we shall be, for we shall see him as

us. 20 But ye have an unction from the Holy One, and ye know all things. 21 I have not written unto you because ye know not the truth, but because ye know it, and that no lie is of the truth. 22 Who is a liar but he that denieth that Jesus is the Christ? He is antichrist, that denieth the Father and the Son. 23 Whosoever denieth the Son, the same hath not the Father: [*but*] *he that acknowledgeth the Son hath the Father also.* 24 Let that therefore abide in you, which ye have heard from the beginning. If that which ye have heard from the beginning shall remain in you, ye also shall continue in the Son, and in the Father. 25 And this is the promise that he hath promised us, *even* eternal life. 26 These *things* have I written unto you concerning them that seduce you. 27 But the anointing which ye have received of him abideth in you, and ye need not that any man teach you: but as the same anointing teacheth you of all things, and is truth, and is no lie, and even as it hath taught you, ye shall abide in him.

28 And now, little children, abide in him; that, when he shall appear, we may have confidence, and not be ashamed before him at his coming.

29 If ye know that he is righteous, ye know that every one that doeth righteousness is born of him.

III. Behold, what manner of love the Father hath bestowed upon us, that we should be called the sons of God: therefore the world knoweth us not, because it knew him not. 2 Beloved, now are we the sons of God, and it doth not yet appear what we shall be: but we know that, when he shall appear, we shall be like him; for we shall see him

ᵈ πάντες (*read* ye all know) T. ᵉ + ὁ ὁμολογῶν τὸν υἱὸν καὶ τὸν πατέρα ἔχει he that confesses the Son has the Father also GLTTrAW. ᶠ — οὖν LTTrA. ᵍ — ἐν L. ʰ μένει ἐν ὑμῖν LTTrA. ⁱ αὐτοῦ (*read* as his anointing) TTrA. ʲ μένετε abide LTTrAW. ᵏ ἐὰν if LTTrA. ˡ σχῶμεν LTTrA. ᵐ + καὶ also TTrA. ⁿ γεγένηται *in Stephens.* ᵒ + καὶ ἐσμέν and we are [such] LTTrA. ᵖ — δὲ but LTTrAW.

ἐστιν. 3 καὶ πᾶς ὁ ἔχων τὴν.ἐλπίδα.ταύτην ἐπ' αὐτῷ,
he is. And everyone that has this hope in him,
ἁγνίζει ἑαυτόν, καθὼς ἐκεῖνος ἁγνός ἐστιν.
purifies himself, even as he [2]pure [1]is.

4 Πᾶς ὁ ποιῶν τὴν ἁμαρτίαν, καὶ τὴν ἀνομίαν ποιεῖ·
Everyone that practises sin, also lawlessness practises;
καὶ [q]ἡ[||] ἁμαρτία ἐστὶν ἡ ἀνομία. 5 καὶ οἴδατε ὅτι ἐκεῖνος
and sin is lawlessness. And ye know that he
ἐφανερώθη, ἵνα τὰς ἁμαρτίας [r]ἡμῶν[||] ἄρῃ· καὶ
was manifested, that [2]sins [1]our he might take away; and
ἁμαρτία ἐν αὐτῷ οὐκ.ἔστιν. 6 πᾶς ὁ ἐν αὐτῷ μένων οὐχ
sin in him is not. [2]Anyone [3]that [5]in [6]him [4]abides [1]not
(*lit.* everyone)
ἁμαρτάνει· πᾶς ὁ ἁμαρτάνων οὐχ εώρακεν αὐτόν, οὐδὲ
sins: [2]anyone [3]that [4]sins [1]not has seen him, nor
(*lit.* everyone)
ἔγνωκεν αὐτόν.
has known him.

7 Τεκνία, μηδεὶς πλανάτω ὑμᾶς· ὁ ποιῶν τὴν
Little children, [2]no [3]one [1]let [4]lead [6]astray [5]you; he that practises
δικαιοσύνην, δίκαιός ἐστιν, καθὼς ἐκεῖνος δίκαιός ἐστιν. 8 ὁ
righteousness, righteous is, even as he righteous is. He that
ποιῶν τὴν ἁμαρτίαν, ἐκ τοῦ διαβόλου ἐστίν· ὅτι ἀπ'
practises sin, of the devil is; because from [the]
ἀρχῆς ὁ διάβολος ἁμαρτάνει. εἰς τοῦτο ἐφανερώθη ὁ υἱὸς
beginning the devil sins. For this was manifested the Son
τοῦ θεοῦ, ἵνα λύσῃ τὰ ἔργα τοῦ διαβόλου. 9 πᾶς ὁ
of God, that he might undo the works of the devil. [2]Anyone [3]that
(*lit.* everyone)
γεγεννημένος ἐκ τοῦ θεοῦ ἁμαρτίαν οὐ ποιεῖ, ὅτι σπέρμα
[4]has [5]been [6]begotten [7]of [8]God, [10]sin [1]not [9]practises, because [2]seed
αὐτοῦ ἐν αὐτῷ μένει· καὶ οὐ.δύναται ἁμαρτάνειν, ὅτι ἐκ τοῦ
[1]his in him abides, and he is not able to sin, because of
θεοῦ γεγέννηται. 10 ἐν τούτῳ φανερά ἐστιν τὰ τέκνα τοῦ
God he has been begotten. In this manifest are the children
θεοῦ καὶ τὰ τέκνα τοῦ διαβόλου. πᾶς ὁ μὴ [s]ποιῶν
of God and the children of the devil. [2]Anyone [3]that [5]not [4]practises
(*lit.* everyone)
δικαιοσύνην[||] οὐκ ἔστιν ἐκ τοῦ θεοῦ, καὶ ὁ μὴ.ἀγαπῶν τὸν
[6]righteousness [1]not is of God, and he that loves not
ἀδελφὸν αὐτοῦ. 11 ὅτι αὕτη ἐστὶν ἡ ἀγγελία ἣν ἠκούσατε
[2]brother [1]his. Because this is the message which ye heard
ἀπ' ἀρχῆς, ἵνα ἀγαπῶμεν ἀλλήλους· 12 οὐ καθὼς
from [the] beginning; that we should love one another: not as
Κάϊν ἐκ τοῦ πονηροῦ ἦν, καὶ ἔσφαξεν τὸν ἀδελφὸν
Cain [who] of the wicked [one] was, and slew [2]brother
αὐτοῦ· καὶ χάριν τίνος ἔσφαξεν αὐτόν; ὅτι τὰ.ἔργα.αὐτοῦ
[1]his; and on account of what slew he him? because his works
πονηρὰ ἦν, τὰ.δὲ τοῦ.ἀδελφοῦ.αὐτοῦ δίκαια.
[2]wicked [1]were, and those of his brother righteous.

13 [t]Μὴ.θαυμάζετε, ἀδελφοί [v]μου,[||] εἰ μισεῖ ὑμᾶς ὁ κόσμος.
Wonder not, [2]brethren [1]my, if [3]hates [4]you [1]the [2]world.
14 ἡμεῖς οἴδαμεν ὅτι μεταβεβήκαμεν ἐκ τοῦ θανάτου εἰς τὴν
We know that we have passed from death to
ζωήν, ὅτι ἀγαπῶμεν τοὺς ἀδελφούς· ὁ μὴ.ἀγαπῶν
life, because we love the brethren. He that loves not [his]
[w]τὸν ἀδελφόν,[||] μένει ἐν τῷ θανάτῳ. 15 πᾶς ὁ μισῶν τὸν
brother, abides in death. Everyone that hates

as he is. 3 And every man that hath this hope in him purifieth himself, even as he is pure.

4 Whosoever committeth sin transgresseth also the law: for sin is the transgression of the law. 5 And ye know that he was manifested to take away our sins; and in him is no sin. 6 Whosoever abideth in him sinneth not: whosoever sinneth hath not seen him, neither known him.

7 Little children, let no man deceive you: he that doeth righteousness is righteous, even as he is righteous. 8 He that committeth sin is of the devil; for the devil sinneth from the beginning. For this purpose the Son of God was manifested, that he might destroy the works of the devil. 9 Whosoever is born of God doth not commit sin; for his seed remaineth in him: and he cannot sin, because he is born of God. 10 In this the children of God are manifest, and the children of the devil: whosoever doeth not righteousness is not of God, neither he that loveth not his brother. 11 For this is the message that ye heard from the beginning, that we should love one another. 12 Not as Cain, *who* was of that wicked one, and slew his brother. And wherefore slew he him? Because his own works were evil, and his brother's righteous.

13 Marvel not, my brethren, if the world hate you. 14 We know that we have passed from death unto life, because we love the brethren. He that loveth not *his* brother abideth in death. 15 Whosoever hateth

[q] — ἡ L (*misinformed as to codex* B). [r] — ἡμῶν LTTrA. [s] ὢν δίκαιος (*read* that is not righteous) L. [t] + καὶ And T. [v] — μου LTTrAW. [w] — [illegible] LTTrAW.

ἀδελφὸν αὐτοῦ, ἀνθρωποκτόνος ἐστίν, καὶ οἴδατε ὅτι πᾶς
[2]brother [1]his a murderer is, and ye know that [2]any (*lit.* every)
ἀνθρωποκτόνος οὐκ ἔχει ζωὴν αἰώνιον ἐν [x]αὐτῷ‖ μένουσαν.
[3]murderer [1]not has life eternal [2]in [3]him [1]abiding.
16 Ἐν τούτῳ ἐγνώκαμεν τὴν ἀγάπην, ὅτι ἐκεῖνος ὑπὲρ
By this we have known love, because he for
ἡμῶν τὴν.ψυχὴν.αὐτοῦ ἔθηκεν· καὶ ἡμεῖς ὀφείλομεν ὑπὲρ τῶν
us his life laid down; and we ought for the
ἀδελφῶν τὰς ψυχὰς [y]τιθέναι.‖ 17 ὃς.δ᾽.ἂν ἔχῃ τὸν
brethren [our] lives to lay down. But whoever may have
βίον τοῦ κόσμου, καὶ θεωρῇ τὸν.ἀδελφὸν.αὐτοῦ χρείαν
[3]means [4]of [5]life [1]the [2]world's, and may see his brother [2]need
ἔχοντα, καὶ κλείσῃ τὰ.σπλάγχνα.αὐτοῦ ἀπ᾽ αὐτοῦ, πῶς ἡ
[1]having, and may shut up his bowels from him, how [2]the
ἀγάπη τοῦ θεοῦ μένει ἐν αὐτῷ;
[3]love [4]of [5]God [1]abides in him?
18 Τεκνία [z]μου,‖ μὴ.ἀγαπῶμεν λόγῳ μηδὲ [a] γλώσσῃ,
[2]Little [3]children [1]my, we should not love in word, nor with tongue,
[b]ἀλλ᾽‖ [c] ἔργῳ καὶ ἀληθείᾳ. 19 [d]καὶ‖ ἐν τούτῳ [e]γινώσκομεν‖
but in work and in truth. And by this we know
ὅτι ἐκ τῆς ἀληθείας ἐσμέν, καὶ ἔμπροσθεν αὐτοῦ πείσομεν
that of the truth we are, and before him shall persuade
τὰς.καρδίας.ἡμῶν· 20 [f]ὅτι‖ ἐὰν καταγινώσκῃ ἡμῶν ἡ καρδία,
our hearts, that if [3]should [4]condemn [1]our [2]heart,
ὅτι μείζων ἐστὶν ὁ θεὸς τῆς.καρδίας.ἡμῶν καὶ γινώσκει πάντα.
that greater is God than our heart and knows all things.
21 ἀγαπητοί, ἐὰν ἡ καρδία [g]ἡμῶν‖ μὴ.καταγινώσκῃ ἡμῶν,
Beloved, if [2]heart [1]our should not condemn us,
παῤῥησίαν ἔχομεν πρὸς τὸν θεόν, 22 καὶ ὃ.ἐὰν αἰτῶμεν,
boldness we have towards God, and whatsoever we may ask,
λαμβάνομεν [h]παρ᾽‖ αὐτοῦ, ὅτι τὰς.ἐντολὰς.αὐτοῦ τηροῦμεν,
we receive from him, because his commandments we keep,
καὶ τὰ ἀρεστὰ ἐνώπιον αὐτοῦ ποιοῦμεν. 23 καὶ αὕτη
and the things pleasing before him we practise. And this
ἐστὶν ἡ.ἐντολὴ.αὐτοῦ, ἵνα [i]πιστεύσωμεν‖ τῷ ὀνόματι τοῦ
is his commandment, that we should believe on the name
υἱοῦ.αὐτοῦ Ἰησοῦ χριστοῦ, καὶ ἀγαπῶμεν ἀλλήλους, καθὼς
of his Son Jesus Christ, and should love one another, even as
ἔδωκεν ἐντολὴν ἡμῖν. 24 καὶ ὁ τηρῶν τὰς.ἐντολὰς.αὐτοῦ,
he gave commandment to us. And he that keeps his commandments,
ἐν αὐτῷ μένει, καὶ αὐτὸς ἐν αὐτῷ· καὶ ἐν τούτῳ γινώσκομεν
in him abides, and he in him: and by this we know
ὅτι μένει ἐν ἡμῖν, ἐκ τοῦ πνεύματος οὗ ἡμῖν ἔδωκεν.
that he abides in us, by the Spirit which to us he gave.
4 Ἀγαπητοί, μὴ παντὶ πνεύματι πιστεύετε, ἀλλὰ δοκιμά-
Beloved, [2]not [3]every [4]spirit [1]believe, but prove
ζετε τὰ πνεύματα, εἰ ἐκ τοῦ θεοῦ ἐστιν· ὅτι πολλοὶ ψευδο-
the spirits, if of God they are; because many false
προφῆται ἐξεληλύθασιν εἰς τὸν κόσμον. 2 ἐν τούτῳ γινώσκετε
prophets have gone out into the world. By this ye know
τὸ πνεῦμα τοῦ θεοῦ· πᾶν πνεῦμα ὃ ὁμολογεῖ Ἰησοῦν χριστὸν
the Spirit of God: every spirit which confesses Jesus Christ

his brother is a murderer: and ye know that no murderer hath eternal life abiding in him.

16 Hereby perceive we the love *of God*, because he laid down his life for us: and we ought to lay down *our* lives for the brethren.
17 But whoso hath this world's good, and seeth his brother have need, and shutteth up his bowels *of compassion* from him, how dwelleth the love of God in him?

18 My little children, let us not love in word, neither in tongue; but in deed and in truth.
19 And hereby we know that we are of the truth, and shall assure our hearts before him.
20 For if our heart condemn us, God is greater than our heart, and knoweth all things.
21 Beloved, if our heart condemn us not, *then* have we confidence toward God.
22 And whatsoever we ask, we receive of him, because we keep his commandments, and do those things that are pleasing in his sight.
23 And this is his commandment, That we should believe on the name of his Son Jesus Christ, and love one another, as he gave us commandment.
24 And he that keepeth his commandments dwelleth in him, and he in him. And hereby we know that he abideth in us, by the Spirit which he hath given us.

IV. Beloved, believe not every spirit, but try the spirits whether they are of God: because many false prophets are gone out into the world.
2 Hereby know ye the Spirit of God: Every spirit that confesseth that Jesus Christ is come

---

[x] ἑαυτῷ himself LT. [y] θεῖναι LTTrAW [z] — μου LTTrAW. [a] + τῇ (*read* with the tongue) GLTTrAW. [b] ἀλλὰ TTr. [c] + ἐν in (work) GLTTrAW. [d] — καὶ L[TrA]. [e] γνωσόμεθα we shall know LTTrAW. [f] ὅ τι (*read* whatever our heart) L. [g] — ἡμῶν (*read* the heart) LTr[A]. [h] ἀπ᾽ LTTrA. [i] πιστεύωμεν we believe LTTr; πιστεύ[σ]ωμεν A.

in the flesh is of God:
3 and every spirit that
confesseth not that
Jesus Christ is come in
the flesh is not of God:
and this is that *spirit*
of antichrist, where-
of ye have heard that
it should come; and
even now already is it
in the world. 4 Ye are
of God, little children,
and have overcome
them: because greater
is he that is in you,
than he that is in the
world. 5 They are of
the world: therefore
speak they of the
world, and the world
heareth them. 6 We
are of God: he that
knoweth God heareth
us; he that is not of
God heareth not us.
Hereby know we the
spirit of truth, and the
spirit of error.

7 Beloved, let us
love one another: for
love is of God; and
every one that loveth
is born of God, and
knoweth God. 8 He
that loveth not know-
eth not God; for God
is love. 9 In this was
manifested the love
of God toward us, be-
cause that God sent
his only begotten Son
into the world, that we
might live through
him. 10 Herein is love,
not that we loved God,
but that he loved us,
and sent his Son *to*
be the propitiation for
our sins. 11 Beloved,
if God so loved us, we
ought also to love one
another. 12 No man
hath seen God at
any time. If we love
one another, God
dwelleth in us, and his
love is perfected in us.
13 Hereby know we
that we dwell in him,
and he in us, because
he hath given us of
his Spirit. 14 And we
have seen and do testi-
fy that the Father sent
the Son *to be* the Sa-
viour of the world.

ἐν σαρκὶ ἐληλυθότα, ἐκ τοῦ θεοῦ ἐστιν. 3 καὶ πᾶν πνεῦμα
[2]in [3]flesh [1]come, of God is; and [2]any [3]spirit
(*lit.* every)
ὃ μὴ.ὁμολογεῖ τὸν Ἰησοῦν [k]χριστὸν ἐν σαρκὶ ἐληλυθότα,[ǁ] ἐκ
[4]which [5]confesses [6]not [7]Jesus [8]Christ [10]in [11]flesh [9]come, [13]of
τοῦ θεοῦ οὐκ ἔστιν· καὶ τοῦτό ἐστιν τὸ τοῦ ἀντιχρίστου,
[14]God [1]not [12]is: and this is that [power] of the antichrist,
ὃ ἀκηκόατε ὅτι ἔρχεται, καὶ νῦν ἐν τῷ κόσμῳ ἐστὶν ἤδη.
[of] which ye heard that it comes, and now in the world is it already.
4 Ὑμεῖς ἐκ τοῦ θεοῦ ἐστε, τεκνία, καὶ νενικήκατε αὐτούς·
Ye of God are, little children, and have overcome them,
ὅτι μείζων ἐστὶν ὁ ἐν ὑμῖν ἢ ὁ ἐν τῷ κόσμῳ.
because greater is he who [is] in you than he who [is] in the world.
5 αὐτοὶ ἐκ τοῦ κόσμου εἰσίν, διὰ τοῦτο ἐκ τοῦ κόσμου λα-
They of the world are; because of this of the world they
λοῦσιν, καὶ ὁ κόσμος αὐτῶν ἀκούει. 6 ἡμεῖς ἐκ τοῦ θεοῦ
talk, and the world [2]them [1]hears. We of God
ἐσμεν· ὁ γινώσκων τὸν θεόν, ἀκούει ἡμῶν· ὃς οὐκ.ἔστιν
are; he that knows God, hears us; he that is not
ἐκ τοῦ θεοῦ, οὐκ.ἀκούει ἡμῶν. ἐκ τούτου γινώσκομεν τὸ πνεῦμα
of God, hears not us. By this we know the spirit
τῆς ἀληθείας καὶ τὸ πνεῦμα τῆς πλάνης.
of truth and the spirit of error.

7 Ἀγαπητοί, ἀγαπῶμεν ἀλλήλους· ὅτι ἡ ἀγάπη ἐκ τοῦ
Beloved, we should love one another; because love [2]of
θεοῦ ἐστιν, καὶ πᾶς ὁ ἀγαπῶν, ἐκ τοῦ θεοῦ γεγέννηται,
[3]God [1]is, and everyone that loves, of God has been begotten,
καὶ γινώσκει τὸν θεόν. 8 ὁ μὴ.ἀγαπῶν, οὐκ.ἔγνω τὸν θεόν·
and knows God. He that loves not, knew not God;
ὅτι ὁ θεὸς ἀγάπη ἐστίν. 9 ἐν τούτῳ ἐφανερώθη ἡ ἀγάπη
because God [2]love [1]is. In this was manifested the love
τοῦ θεοῦ ἐν ἡμῖν, ὅτι τὸν.υἱὸν.αὐτοῦ τὸν μονογενῆ ἀπέ-
of God as to us, that his Son the only-begotten [2]has
σταλκεν ὁ θεὸς εἰς τὸν κόσμον, ἵνα ζήσωμεν δι' αὐτοῦ.
[3]sent [1]God into the world, that we might live through him.
10 ἐν τούτῳ ἐστὶν ἡ ἀγάπη, οὐχ ὅτι ἡμεῖς ἠγαπήσαμεν τὸν
In this is love, not that we loved
θεόν, ἀλλ' ὅτι αὐτὸς ἠγάπησεν ἡμᾶς, καὶ ἀπέστειλεν τὸν υἱὸν
God, but that he loved us, and sent [2]Son
αὐτοῦ ἱλασμὸν περὶ τῶν.ἁμαρτιῶν.ἡμῶν. 11 ἀγαπητοί, εἰ
[1]his a propitiation for our sins. Beloved, if
οὕτως ὁ θεὸς ἠγάπησεν ἡμᾶς, καὶ ἡμεῖς ὀφείλομεν ἀλλήλους
[2]so [1]God loved us, also we ought one another
ἀγαπᾷν. 12 θεὸν οὐδεὶς πώποτε τεθέαται· ἐὰν ἀγαπῶμεν
to love. [5]God [1]no [2]one [6]at [7]any [8]time [3]has [4]seen; if we should love
ἀλλήλους, ὁ θεὸς ἐν ἡμῖν μένει, καὶ ἡ.ἀγάπη.αὐτοῦ [l]τετελειω-
one another, God in us abides, and his love [2]perfect-
μένη ἐστὶν ἐν ἡμῖν.[ǁ] 13 ἐν τούτῳ γινώσκομεν ὅτι ἐν αὐτῷ
ed [1]is in us. By this we know that in him
μένομεν, καὶ αὐτὸς ἐν ἡμῖν, ὅτι ἐκ τοῦ.πνεύματος.αὐτοῦ
we abide, and he in us, because of his Spirit
δέδωκεν ἡμῖν. 14 καὶ ἡμεῖς τεθεάμεθα καὶ μαρτυροῦμεν ὅτι
he has given to us. And we have seen and bear witness that
ὁ πατὴρ ἀπέσταλκεν τὸν υἱὸν σωτῆρα τοῦ κόσμου.
the Father has sent the Son [as] Saviour of the world.

---

k — χριστὸν w; — χριστὸν ἐν σαρκὶ ἐληλυθότα (read the Jesus) GLTTrA. l ἐν ἡμῖν τετελειωμένη ἐστίν L; τετελ. ἐν ἡμῖν ἐστίν TTrA.

15 [ʺ]Ὃς.ἂν ὁμολογήσῃ ὅτι Ἰησοῦς ἐστιν ὁ υἱὸς τοῦ θεοῦ, ὁ
Whosoever may confess that Jesus is the Son of God,
θεὸς ἐν αὐτῷ μένει, καὶ αὐτὸς ἐν τῷ θεῷ. 16 καὶ ἡμεῖς ἐγνώ-
God in him abides, and he in God. And we have
καμεν καὶ πεπιστεύκαμεν τὴν ἀγάπην ἣν ἔχει ὁ θεὸς ἐν ἡμῖν.
known and have believed the love which [2]has [1]God as to us.
ὁ θεὸς ἀγάπη ἐστίν, καὶ ὁ μένων ἐν τῇ ἀγάπῃ, ἐν τῷ θεῷ
God [2]love [1]is, and he that abides in love, in God
μένει, καὶ ὁ θεὸς ἐν αὐτῷ[m]. 17 ἐν τούτῳ τετελείωται ἡ ἀγάπη
abides, and God in him. In this has been perfected love
μεθ' ἡμῶν, ἵνα παῤῥησίαν ἔχωμεν ἐν τῇ ἡμέρᾳ τῆς κρίσεως,
with us, that boldness we may have in the day of judgment,
ὅτι καθὼς ἐκεῖνός ἐστιν, καὶ ἡμεῖς ἐσμεν ἐν τῷ.κόσμῳ.τούτῳ.
that even as he is, also we are in this world.
18 φόβος οὐκ.ἔστιν ἐν τῇ ἀγάπῃ, [n]ἀλλ'‖ ἡ τελεία ἀγάπη ἔξω
[4]Fear [1]there [2]is [3]not in love, but perfect love [2]out
βάλλει τὸν φόβον, ὅτι ὁ φόβος κόλασιν ἔχει· ὁ.δὲ φοβού-
[1]casts fear; because fear [2]torment [1]has, and he that fears
μενος οὐ.τετελείωται ἐν τῇ ἀγάπῃ. 19 ἡμεῖς [o] ἀγαπῶμεν
has not been made perfect in love. We love
[p]αὐτὸν‖ ὅτι [q]αὐτὸς‖ πρῶτος ἠγάπησεν ἡμᾶς.
him because he first loved us.

15 Whosoever shall confess that Jesus is the Son of God, God dwelleth in him, and he in God. 16 And we have known and believed the love that God hath to us. God is love; and he that dwelleth in love dwelleth in God, and God in him. 17 Herein is our love made perfect, that we may have boldness in the day of judgment: because as he is, so are we in this world. 18 There is no fear in love; but perfect love casteth out fear: because fear hath torment. He that feareth is not made perfect in love. 19 We love him, because he first loved us.

20 Ἐάν τις εἴπῃ, [ʺ]Ὅτι ἀγαπῶ τὸν θεόν, καὶ τὸν ἀδελ-
If anyone should say, I love God, and [4]bro-
φὸν αὐτοῦ μισῇ, ψεύστης ἐστίν· ὁ.γὰρ μὴ.ἀγαπῶν τὸν
ther [3]his [1]should [2]hate, a liar he is. For he that loves not
ἀδελφὸν.αὐτοῦ ὃν ἑώρακεν, τὸν θεὸν ὃν οὐχ.ἑώρακεν,
his brother whom he has seen, [7]God [8]whom [9]he [10]has [11]not [12]seen,
[r]πῶς‖ δύναται ἀγαπᾶν; 21 καὶ ταύτην τὴν ἐντολὴν ἔχο-
[1]how [2]is [3]he [4]able [5]to [6]love? And this commandment we
μεν ἀπ' αὐτοῦ, ἵνα ὁ ἀγαπῶν τὸν θεὸν ἀγαπᾷ καὶ τὸν
have from him, that he that loves God should love also
ἀδελφὸν αὐτοῦ. 5 Πᾶς ὁ πιστεύων ὅτι Ἰησοῦς ἐστιν ὁ
[2]brother [1]his. Everyone that believes that Jesus is the
χριστὸς ἐκ τοῦ θεοῦ γεγέννηται· καὶ πᾶς ὁ ἀγαπῶν τὸν
Christ, of God has been begotten; and everyone that loves him that
γεννήσαντα ἀγαπᾷ [s]καὶ‖ τὸν γεγεννημένον ἐξ αὐτοῦ. 2 ἐν
begat, loves also him that has been begotten of him. By
τούτῳ γινώσκομεν ὅτι ἀγαπῶμεν τὰ τέκνα τοῦ θεοῦ, ὅταν τὸν
this we know that we love the children of God, when
θεὸν ἀγαπῶμεν καὶ τὰς.ἐντολὰς.αὐτοῦ [t]τηρῶμεν.‖ 3 αὕτη.γάρ
God we love and his commandments keep. For this
ἐστιν ἡ ἀγάπη τοῦ θεοῦ, ἵνα τὰς.ἐντολὰς.αὐτοῦ τηρῶμεν·
is the love of God, that his commandments we should keep;
καὶ αἱ.ἐντολαὶ.αὐτοῦ βαρεῖαι οὐκ.εἰσίν. 4 ὅτι πᾶν τὸ γε-
and his commandments burdensome are not. Because all that has
γεννημένον ἐκ τοῦ θεοῦ νικᾷ τὸν κόσμον· καὶ αὕτη ἐστὶν
been begotten of God overcomes the world; and this is
ἡ νίκη ἡ νικήσασα τὸν κόσμον, ἡ.πίστις.ἡμῶν· 5 τίς [v]
the victory which overcame the world, our faith. Who
ἐστιν ὁ νικῶν τὸν κόσμον, εἰ.μὴ ὁ πιστεύων ὅτι Ἰησοῦς
is he that overcomes the world, but he that believes that Jesus
ἐστιν ὁ υἱὸς τοῦ θεοῦ;
is the Son of God?

20 If a man say, I love God, and hateth his brother, he is a liar: for he that loveth not his brother whom he hath seen, how can he love God whom he hath not seen? 21 And this commandment have we from him, That he who loveth God love his brother also. V. Whosoever believeth that Jesus is the Christ is born of God: and every one that loveth him that begat loveth him also that is begotten of him. 2 By this we know that we love the children of God, when we love God, and keep his commandments. 3 For this is the love of God, that we keep his commandments: and his commandments are not grievous. 4 For whatsoever is born of God overcometh the world: and this is the victory that overcometh the world, *even* our faith. 5 Who is he that overcometh the world, but he that believeth that Jesus is the Son of God?

---

m + μένει abides [L]TA. n ἀλλὰ Tr. o + οὖν therefore L. p — αὐτὸν LTTrAW. q ὁ θεὸς God L. r οὐ (*read* he is not able) LTTrA. s [καὶ] LTr. t ποιῶμεν may do LTTrAW. v + [δέ] but (who) Tr.

6 This is he that came by water and blood, *even* Jesus Christ; not by water only, but by water and blood. And it is the Spirit that beareth witness, because the Spirit is truth. 7 For there are three that bear record in heaven, the Father, the Word, and the Holy Ghost: and these three are one. 8 And there are three that bear witness in earth, the Spirit, and the water, and the blood: and these three agree in one. 9 If we receive the witness of men, the witness of God is greater: for this is the witness of God which he hath testified of his Son. 10 He that believeth on the Son of God hath the witness in himself: he that believeth not God hath made him a liar; because he believeth not the record that God gave of his Son. 11 And this is the record, that God hath given to us eternal life, and this life is in his Son. 12 He that hath the Son hath life; *and* he that hath not the Son of God hath not life.

6 Οὗτός ἐστιν ὁ ἐλθὼν δι' ὕδατος καὶ αἵματος, Ἰησοῦς
This is he who came by water and blood, Jesus
[w]ὁ‖ χριστός· οὐκ ἐν τῷ ὕδατι μόνον, [x]ἀλλ'‖ ἐν τῷ ὕδατι καὶ [y]
the Christ; not by water only, but by water and
τῷ αἵματι· καὶ τὸ πνεῦμά ἐστιν τὸ μαρτυροῦν ὅτι τὸ πνεῦμά
blood. And the Spirit it is that bears witness, because the Spirit
ἐστιν ἡ ἀλήθεια. 7 ὅτι τρεῖς εἰσιν οἱ μαρτυροῦντες [z]ἐν τῷ
is the truth. Because three there are who bear witness in
οὐρανῷ, ὁ πατήρ, ὁ λόγος, καὶ τὸ ἅγιον πνεῦμα· καὶ οὗτοι
heaven, the Father, the Word, and the Holy Ghost; and these
οἱ τρεῖς ἕν εἰσιν. 8 καὶ τρεῖς εἰσιν οἱ μαρτυροῦντες ἐν τῇ
three one are. And three there are who bear witness on
γῇ,‖ τὸ πνεῦμα, καὶ τὸ ὕδωρ, καὶ τὸ αἷμα, καὶ οἱ τρεῖς εἰς τὸ
earth, the Spirit, and the water, and the blood; and the three to the
ἕν εἰσιν. 9 εἰ τὴν μαρτυρίαν τῶν ἀνθρώπων λαμβάνο-
one [point] are. If the witness of men we re-
μεν, ἡ μαρτυρία τοῦ θεοῦ μείζων ἐστίν· ὅτι αὕτη ἐστὶν
ceive, the witness of God [2]greater [1]is. Because this is
ἡ μαρτυρία τοῦ θεοῦ, [a]ἣν‖ μεμαρτύρηκεν περὶ τοῦ.υἱοῦ.αὐτοῦ.
the witness of God which he has witnessed concerning his Son.
10 ὁ πιστεύων εἰς τὸν υἱὸν τοῦ θεοῦ ἔχει τὴν μαρτυρίαν [b] ἐν
He that believes on the Son of God has the witness in
[c]ἑαυτῷ·‖ ὁ μὴ.πιστεύων [d]τῷ θεῷ‖ ψεύστην πεποίηκεν αὐτόν,
himself; he that believes not God [4]a [5]liar [1]has [2]made [3]him.
ὅτι οὐ.πεπίστευκεν εἰς τὴν μαρτυρίαν, ἣν μεμαρτύρηκεν ὁ
because he has not believed in the witness which [2]has [3]witnessed
θεὸς περὶ τοῦ.υἱοῦ.αὐτοῦ. 11 καὶ αὕτη ἐστὶν ἡ μαρτυρία
[1]God concerning his Son. And this is the witness,
ὅτι ζωὴν αἰώνιον ἔδωκεν ἡμῖν ὁ θεός· καὶ αὕτη ἡ ζωὴ ἐν τῷ
that life eternal [2]gave [3]to [4]us [1]God; and this life [2]in
υἱῷ αὐτοῦ ἐστιν. 12 ὁ ἔχων τὸν υἱόν, ἔχει τὴν ζωήν· ὁ
[4]Son [3]his [1]is: he that has the Son, has life: he that
μὴ.ἔχων τὸν υἱὸν τοῦ θεοῦ, τὴν ζωὴν οὐκ.ἔχει.
has not the Son of God, life has not.

13 These things have I written unto you that believe on the name of the Son of God; that ye may know that ye have eternal life, and that ye may believe on the name of the Son of God. 14 And this is the confidence that we have in him, that, if we ask any thing according to his will, he heareth us: 15 and if we know that he hear us, whatsoever we ask, we know that we have the petitions that we desired of him.

13 Ταῦτα ἔγραψα ὑμῖν [e]τοῖς πιστεύουσιν εἰς τὸ ὄνομα
These things I wrote to you who believe on the name
τοῦ υἱοῦ τοῦ θεοῦ,‖ ἵνα εἰδῆτε ὅτι ζωὴν [f]ἔχετε αἰώνιον,‖ [g]καὶ
of the Son of God, that ye may know that [4]life [1]ye [2]have [3]eternal, and
ἵνα πιστεύητε‖ εἰς τὸ ὄνομα τοῦ υἱοῦ τοῦ θεοῦ. 14 καὶ αὕτη
that ye may believe on the name of the Son of God. And this
ἐστὶν ἡ παῤῥησία ἣν ἔχομεν πρὸς αὐτόν, [h]ὅτι ἐάν τι‖
is the boldness which we have towards him, that if anything
αἰτώμεθα κατὰ τὸ.θέλημα.αὐτοῦ, ἀκούει ἡμῶν· 15 καὶ
we may ask according to his will, he hears us. And
[i]ἐὰν‖ οἴδαμεν ὅτι ἀκούει ἡμῶν, ὃ.[k]ἂν‖ αἰτώμεθα, οἴδαμεν ὅτι
if we know that he hears us, whatsoever we may ask, we know that
ἔχομεν τὰ αἰτήματα ἃ ᾐτήκαμεν [l]παρ'‖ αὐτοῦ.
we have the requests which we have asked from him.

16 If any man see his brother sin a sin *which is* not unto death, he shall ask, and he shall give him life for them that

16 Ἐάν τις [m]ἴδῃ‖ τὸν.ἀδελφὸν.αὐτοῦ ἁμαρτάνοντα
If anyone should see his brother sinning
ἁμαρτίαν μὴ πρὸς θάνατον, αἰτήσει, καὶ δώσει αὐτῷ ζωήν,
a sin not to death, he shall ask, and he shall give him life

---

[w] — ὁ TTrAW. [x] ἀλλὰ Tr [y] + ἐν by LTTrAW. [z] — ἐν τῷ οὐρανῷ . . . . τῇ γῇ *verse* 8 GLTTrAW. [a] ὅτι that LTTrAW. [b] + τοῦ θεοῦ of God L. [c] αὐτῷ him TTrA. [d] τῷ υἱῷ the Son L. [e] — τοῖς πιστεύουσιν εἰς τὸ ὄνομα τοῦ υἱοῦ τοῦ θεοῦ GLTTrAW. [f] αἰώνιον ἔχετε G. [g] οἱ πιστεύοντες [ye] believers GLW; τοῖς πιστεύουσιν to [you] who believe TTrA. [h] ὅ τι ἂν whatever L. [i] ἂν L. [k] ἐὰν T. [l] ἀπ' LTTr. [m] εἰδῇ L.

τοῖς ἁμαρτάνουσιν μὴ πρὸς θάνατον. ἔστιν ἁμαρτία
for those that sin not to death. There is a sin
πρὸς θάνατον· οὐ περὶ ἐκείνης λέγω ἵνα ἐρωτήσῃ·
to death; not concerning that do I say that he should beseech.
17 πᾶσα ἀδικία ἁμαρτία ἐστίν, καὶ ἔστιν ἁμαρτία οὐ πρὸς
Every unrighteousness [2]sin [1]is; and there is a sin not to
θάνατον. 18 οἴδαμεν ὅτι πᾶς ὁ γεγεννημένος ἐκ τοῦ θεοῦ
death. We know that [2]anyone [3]that [4]has [5]been [6]begotten [7]of [8]God (*lit.* everyone)
οὐχ ἁμαρτάνει· [n]ἀλλ'‖ ὁ γεννηθεὶς ἐκ τοῦ θεοῦ τηρεῖ [o]ἑαυ-
[1]not sins, but he that was begotten of God keeps him-
τόν,‖ καὶ ὁ πονηρὸς οὐχ.ἅπτεται αὐτοῦ. 19 οἴδαμεν ὅτι
self, and the wicked [one] does not touch him. We know that
ἐκ τοῦ θεοῦ ἐσμεν, καὶ ὁ κόσμος ὅλος ἐν τῷ πονηρῷ κεῖται.
of God we are, and the [2]world [1]whole in the wicked [one] lies.
20 [p]οἴδαμεν.δὲ‖ ὅτι ὁ υἱὸς τοῦ θεοῦ ἥκει, καὶ δέδωκεν ἡμῖν
And we know that the Son of God is come, and has given us
διάνοιαν ἵνα [q]γινώσκωμεν‖ τὸν ἀληθινόν· καί ἐσμεν
an understanding that we might know him that [is] true; and we are
ἐν τῷ ἀληθινῷ, ἐν τῷ.υἱῷ.αὐτοῦ Ἰησοῦ χριστῷ. οὗτός
in him that [is] true, in his Son Jesus Christ. He
ἐστιν ὁ ἀληθινὸς θεός, καὶ [r]ἡ‖ ζωὴ αἰώνιος.
is the true God, and life eternal.

21 Τεκνία, φυλάξατε [s]ἑαυτοὺς‖ ἀπὸ τῶν εἰδώλων. [t]ἀμήν.‖
Little children, keep yourselves from idols. Amen.

[v]Ἰωάννου ἐπιστολὴ καθολικὴ πρώτη.‖
[4]Of [5]John [3]epistle [2]general [1]first.

sin not unto death. There is a sin unto death: I do not say that he shall pray for it. 17 All unrighteousness is sin: and there is a sin not unto death. 18 We know that whosoever is born of God sinneth not; but he that is begotten of God keepeth himself, and that wicked one toucheth him not. 19 *And* we know that we are of God, and the whole world lieth in wickedness. 20 And we know that the Son of God is come, and hath given us an understanding, that we may know him that is true, and we are in him that is true, *even* in his Son Jesus Christ. This is the true God, and eternal life.

21 Little children, keep yourselves from idols. Amen.

---

[a]ΕΠΙΣΤΟΛΗ ΙΩΑΝΝΟΥ ΔΕΥΤΕΡΑ.‖
[2]EPISTLE [3]OF [4]JOHN [1]SECOND.

Ὁ πρεσβύτερος [b]ἐκλεκτῇ‖ [c]κυρίᾳ‖ καὶ τοῖς.τέκνοις.αὐτῆς,
The elder to [the] elect lady and her children,
οὓς ἐγὼ ἀγαπῶ ἐν ἀληθείᾳ, καὶ οὐκ ἐγὼ μόνος, ἀλλὰ καὶ
whom I love in truth, and not I only, but also
πάντες οἱ ἐγνωκότες τὴν ἀλήθειαν, 2 διὰ τὴν ἀλή-
all those who have known the truth, for sake of the
θειαν τὴν μένουσαν ἐν ἡμῖν, καὶ μεθ' ἡμῶν ἔσται εἰς.τὸν.αἰῶνα·
truth which abides in us, and with us shall be for ever.
3 ἔσται μεθ' [d]ἡμῶν‖ χάρις, ἔλεος, εἰρήνη παρὰ θεοῦ πατρὸς
[2]Shall [3]be [4]with [5]us [1]grace, mercy, peace, from God [the] Father,
καὶ παρὰ [e]κυρίου‖ Ἰησοῦ χριστοῦ τοῦ υἱοῦ τοῦ πατρός, ἐν
and from [the] Lord Jesus Christ, the Son of the Father, in
ἀληθείᾳ καὶ ἀγάπῃ.
truth and love.

4 Ἐχάρην λίαν ὅτι εὕρηκα ἐκ τῶν.τέκνων.σου περιπα-
I rejoiced exceedingly that I have found of thy children walk-
τοῦντας ἐν ἀληθείᾳ, καθὼς ἐντολὴν ἐλάβομεν παρὰ τοῦ
ing in truth, as commandment we received from the

THE elder unto the elect lady and her children, whom I love in the truth; and not I only, but also all they that have known the truth; 2 for the truth's sake, which dwelleth in us, and shall be with us for ever. 3 Grace be with you, mercy, *and* peace, from God the Father, and from the Lord Jesus Christ, the Son of the Father, in truth and love.

4 I rejoiced greatly that I found of thy children walking in truth, as we have received a commandment from the Father.

---

[n] ἀλλὰ Tr. [o] αὐτόν him TTrA. [p] καὶ οἴδαμεν GL. [q] γινώσκομεν we know TTrA. [r] — ἡ LTTrA. [s] ἑαυτὰ LTTr. [t] — ἀμήν GLTTrAW. [v] — *the subscription* EGLTW; Ἰωάνου α' Tr; Ἰωάννου α' A.

[a] + τοῦ ἀποστόλου the apostle E; + καθολικὴ general E; Ἰωάννου β' LTAW; Ἰωάνου ἐπιστολὴ β' Tr. [b] *Stephens puts a capital* Ἐ, *reading the word as a proper name.* [c] Κυρίᾳ Cyria (*reading the word as a proper name*) GLT. [d] ὑμῶν you EGLW. [e] — κυρίου LTTrAW.

5 And now I beseech
thee, lady, not as
though I wrote a new
commandment unto
thee, but that which
we had from the be-
ginning, that we love
one another. 6 And
this is love, that we
walk after his com-
mandments. This is
the commandment,
That, as ye have heard
from the beginning,
ye should walk in it.
7 For many deceivers
are entered into the
world, who confess
not that Jesus Christ
is come in the flesh.
This is a deceiver and
an antichrist. 8 Look
to yourselves, that
we lose not those
things which we have
wrought, but that we
receive a full reward.
9 Whosoever trans-
gresseth, and abideth
not in the doctrine of
Christ, hath not God.
He that abideth in the
doctrine of Christ, he
hath both the Father
and the Son. 10 If
there come any unto
you, and bring not
this doctrine, receive
him not into *your*
house, neither bid him
God speed: 11 for he
that biddeth him God
speed is partaker of
his evil deeds.

12 Having many
things to write unto
you, I would not *write*
with paper and ink:
but I trust to come
unto you, and speak
face to face, that our
joy may be full. 13 The
children of thy elect
sister greet thee. A-
men.

πατρός. 5 καὶ νῦν ἐρωτῶ σε, [f]κυρία,‖ οὐχ ὡς ἐντολὴν
Father And now I beseech thee, lady, not as a [2]commandment
[g]γράφω σοι καινήν,‖ ἀλλὰ ἣν [h]εἴχομεν‖ ἀπ' ἀρ-
[3]I [4]write [5]to [6]thee [1]new, but that which we were having from [the] begin-
χῆς, ἵνα ἀγαπῶμεν ἀλλήλους. 6 καὶ αὕτη ἐστὶν ἡ ἀγάπη,
ning, that we should love one another. And this is love,
ἵνα περιπατῶμεν κατὰ τὰς.ἐντολὰς.αὐτοῦ. αὕτη [i]ἐστὶν ἡ
that we should walk according to his commandments. This is the
ἐντολή,‖ [k]καθὼς ἠκούσατε ἀπ' ἀρχῆς, ἵνα ἐν αὐτῇ
commandment, even as ye heard from [the] beginning, that in it
περιπατῆτε· 7 ὅτι πολλοὶ πλάνοι [l]εἰσῆλθον‖ εἰς τὸν
ye might walk. Because many deceivers entered into the
κόσμον, οἱ μὴ.ὁμολογοῦντες Ἰησοῦν χριστὸν ἐρχόμενον ἐν
world, those who do not confess Jesus Christ coming in
σαρκί· οὗτός ἐστιν ὁ πλάνος καὶ ὁ ἀντίχριστος. 8 βλέπετε
flesh— this is the deceiver and the antichrist. See to
ἑαυτούς, ἵνα μὴ [m]ἀπολέσωμεν‖ ἃ [n]εἰργασάμεθα,‖ ἀλλὰ
yourselves, that [3]not [1]we [2]may lose what things we wrought, but
μισθὸν πλήρη [o]ἀπολάβωμεν.‖ 9 πᾶς ὁ [p]παραβαίνων,‖ καὶ
a [2]reward [1]full we may receive. [2]Anyone [3]who [4]transgresses, [5]and
(*lit.* everyone)
μὴ.μένων ἐν τῇ διδαχῇ τοῦ χριστοῦ, θεὸν οὐκ ἔχει· ὁ
[6]abides [7]not [8]in [9]the [10]teaching [11]of [12]the [13]Christ, [15]God [1]not [14]has. He that
μένων ἐν τῇ διδαχῇ [q]τοῦ χριστοῦ,‖ οὗτος καὶ τὸν πατέρα
abides in the teaching of the Christ, this [one] both the Father
καὶ τὸν υἱὸν ἔχει. 10 εἴ τις ἔρχεται πρὸς ὑμᾶς, καὶ ταύτην
and the Son has. If anyone comes to you, and this
τὴν διδαχὴν οὐ.φέρει, μὴ.λαμβάνετε αὐτὸν εἰς οἰκίαν,
teaching does not bring, do not receive him into [the] house,
καὶ χαίρειν αὐτῷ μὴ.λέγετε· 11 ὁ.[r]γὰρ λέγων‖ αὐτῷ χαίρειν,
and [3]Hail! [4]to [5]him [1]say [2]not; for he who says to him Hail!
κοινωνεῖ τοῖς ἔργοις αὐτοῦ τοῖς πονηροῖς.
partakes in [3]works [1]his [2]evil.

12 Πολλὰ ἔχων ὑμῖν γράφειν, οὐκ.[s]ἠβουλήθην‖ διὰ χάρ-
Many things having [3]to [4]you [1]to [2]write, I would not with pa-
του καὶ μέλανος· [t]ἀλλὰ ἐλπίζω· [v]ἐλθεῖν‖ πρὸς ὑμᾶς, καὶ στόμα
per and ink; but hope to come to you, and mouth
πρὸς στόμα λαλῆσαι, ἵνα ἡ χαρὰ [w]ἡμῶν‖ [x]ᾖ.πεπληρωμένη.‖
to mouth to speak, that [2]joy [1]our may be full.
13 ἀσπάζεταί σε τὰ τέκνα τῆς ἀδελφῆς σου τῆς [y]ἐκλεκ-
[7]Salute [8]thee [1]the [2]children [6]sister [3]of [4]thine [5]elect.
τῆς.‖ [z]ἀμήν.‖
Amen.

[a]Ἰωάννου ἐπιστολὴ δευτέρα.‖
[3]Of [4]John [2]epistle [1]second.

---

[f] Κυρία Cyria (*see verse* 1) GLT. [g] γράφων (writing) σοι καινὴν EGAW; καινὴν γράφων σοι LTTr. [h] εἴχαμεν TTr. [i] ἡ ἐντολή ἐστιν LTTrAW. [k] + ἵνα that T. [l] ἐξῆλθαν (-θον TAW) went forth LTr. [m] ἀπολέσητε ye may lose LTTrAW. [n] εἰργάσασθε ye wrought LTTrW. [o] ἀπολάβητε ye may receive LTTrAW. [p] προάγων goes forward LTTrAW. [q] — τοῦ χριστοῦ LTTrAW. [r] λέγων γὰρ LTTrA. [s] ἐβουλήθην LTTrAW. [t] ἐλπίζω γὰρ for I hope GL. [v] γενέσθαι LTTrAW. [w] ὑμῶν your LTrA. [x] πεπληρωμένη ᾖ LT. [y] *See* note b *verse* 1. [z] — ἀμήν GLTTrAW. [a] — *the subscription* EGLTW; Ἰωάνου β' Tr; Ἰωάννου β' A.

[b]ΕΠΙΣΤΟΛΗ ΙΩΑΝΝΟΥ ΤΡΙΤΗ.‖
²EPISTLE ³OF ⁴JOHN ¹THIRD.

Ὁ πρεσβύτερος Γαΐῳ τῷ ἀγαπητῷ, ὃν ἐγὼ ἀγαπῶ ἐν
The elder to Gaius the beloved, whom I love in
ἀληθείᾳ.
truth.
2 Ἀγαπητέ, περὶ πάντων εὔχομαί σε εὐοδοῦσθαι καὶ
Beloved, concerning all things I wish thee to prosper and
ὑγιαίνειν, καθὼς εὐοδοῦταί σου ἡ ψυχή. 3 ἐχάρην.[c]γὰρ‖
be in health, even as prospers thy soul. For I rejoiced
λίαν ἐρχομένων ἀδελφῶν καὶ μαρτυρούντων σου τῇ
exceedingly, ³coming [¹the] ²brethren and bearing witness of thy
ἀληθείᾳ, καθὼς σὺ ἐν ἀληθείᾳ περιπατεῖς. 4 μειζοτέραν τού-
truth, even as thou in truth walkest. ⁵Greater ⁶than
των οὐκ.ἔχω χαράν, ἵνα ἀκούω τὰ.ἐμὰ.τέκνα ἐν [d]
⁷these ⁸things ¹I ²have ³not ⁴joy, that I should hear of my children in
ἀληθείᾳ περιπατοῦντα. 5 Ἀγαπητέ, πιστὸν ποιεῖς ὃ.ἐὰν
truth walking. Beloved, faithfully thou doest whatever
[e]ἐργάσῃ‖ εἰς τοὺς ἀδελφοὺς καὶ [f]εἰς τοὺς‖
thou mayest have wrought towards the brethren and towards
ξένους, 6 οἳ ἐμαρτύρησάν σου τῇ ἀγάπῃ ἐνώπιον ἐκ-
strangers, (who witnessed of thy love before [the] as-
κλησίας· οὓς καλῶς ποιήσεις προπέμψας ἀξίως τοῦ θεοῦ·
sembly) whom ⁹well ⁸thou ⁷wilt ⁸do ¹setting ²forward ³worthily ⁴of ⁵God;
7 ὑπὲρ.γὰρ τοῦ ὀνόματος [g] [h]ἐξῆλθον‖ μηδὲν λαμβάνοντες
for. for the name they went forth, ²nothing ¹taking
ἀπὸ τῶν [i]ἐθνῶν.‖ 8 ἡμεῖς οὖν ὀφείλομεν [k]ἀπολαμβάνειν‖
from the nations. We therefore ought to receive
τοὺς τοιούτους, ἵνα συνεργοὶ γινώμεθα τῇ ἀληθείᾳ. 9 Ἔ-
such, that fellow-workers we may be with the truth. I
γραψα [l] τῇ ἐκκλησίᾳ· ἀλλ' ὁ φιλοπρωτεύων αὐτῶν
wrote to the assembly; but ²who ³loves ⁴to ⁵be ⁶first ⁷among ⁸them
[m]Διοτρεφὴς‖ οὐκ.ἐπιδέχεται ἡμᾶς. 10 διὰ τοῦτο, ἐὰν ἔλθω,
¹Diotrephes, receives not us. On account of this, if I come,
ὑπομνήσω αὐτοῦ τὰ ἔργα ἃ ποιεῖ, λόγοις
I will bring to remembrance of him the works which he does, with ²words
πονηροῖς φλυαρῶν ἡμᾶς· καὶ μὴ ἀρκούμενος ἐπὶ τούτοις,
¹evil prating against us; and not satisfied with these,
οὔτε αὐτὸς ἐπιδέχεται τοὺς ἀδελφούς, καὶ τοὺς βουλομέ-
neither himself receives the brethren, and those who would
νους κωλύει, καὶ [n]ἐκ‖ τῆς ἐκκλησίας ἐκβάλλει. 11 Ἀγα-
he forbids, and from the assembly casts [them] out. Be-
πητέ, μὴ.μιμοῦ τὸ κακόν, ἀλλὰ τὸ ἀγαθόν. ὁ
loved, do not imitate that which [is] evil, but what [is] good. He that
ἀγαθοποιῶν, ἐκ τοῦ θεοῦ ἐστιν· ὁ.[o]δὲ‖ κακοποιῶν οὐχ ἑώ-
does good, of God is; but he that does evil ²not ¹has
ρακεν τὸν θεόν. 12 Δημητρίῳ μεμαρτύρηται ὑπὸ πάντων, καὶ
seen God. To Demetrius witness is borne by all, and

THE elder unto the wellbeloved Gaius, whom I love in the truth.

2 Beloved, I wish above all things that thou mayest prosper and be in health, even as thy soul prospereth.
3 For I rejoiced greatly, when the brethren came and testified of the truth that is in thee, even as thou walkest in the truth.
4 I have no greater joy than to hear that my children walk in truth. 5 Beloved, thou doest faithfully whatsoever thou doest to the brethren, and to strangers; 6 which have borne witness of thy charity before the church: whom if thou bring forward on their journey after a godly sort, thou shalt do well: 7 because that for his name's sake they went forth, taking nothing of the Gentiles. 8 We therefore ought to receive such, that we might be fellowhelpers to the truth. 9 I wrote unto the church: but Diotrephes, who loveth to have the preeminence among them, receiveth us not. 10 Wherefore, if I come, I will remember his deeds which he doeth, prating against us with malicious words: and not content therewith, neither doth he himself receive the brethren, and forbiddeth them that would, and casteth *them* out of the church. 11 Beloved, follow not that which is evil, but that which is good. He that doeth good is of God: but he that doeth evil hath not seen God. 12 Demetrius hath good report of all *men*,

---

[b] + τοῦ ἀποστόλου the apostle E; + καθολικὴ general E; Ἰωάννου γ' LTAW; Ἰωάνου ἐπιστολὴ γ' Tr. [c] — γὰρ T[Tr]. [d] + τῇ the LTTrAW. [e] ἐργάζῃ thou workest L. [f] τοῦτο that LTTrAW. [g] + αὐτοῦ (*read* his name) E. [h] ἐξῆλθαν LTTr. [i] ἐθνικῶν (*read* those of the nations) LTTrAW. [k] ὑπολαμβάνειν to sustain LTTrAW. [l] + τι somewhat LTTrAW. [m] Διοτρέφης LA. [n] — ἐκ (*read* [from]) T. [o] — δὲ but GLTTrAW.

and of the truth itself: yea, and we *also* bear record; and ye know that our record is true.

13 I had many things to write, but I will not with ink and pen write unto thee: 14 but I trust I shall shortly see thee, and we shall speak face to face. Peace *be* to thee. *Our* friends salute thee. Greet the friends by name.

[p]ὑπ'‖ αὐτῆς τῆς ἀληθείας· καὶ ἡμεῖς δὲ μαρτυροῦμεν, καὶ
by [3]itself [1]the [2]truth; and we also bear witness, and
[q]οἴδατε‖ ὅτι ἡ.μαρτυρία.ἡμῶν ἀληθής ἐστιν.
ye know that our witness [2]true [1]is.
13 Πολλὰ εἶχον [r]γράφειν,‖ ἀλλ' οὐ.θέλω διὰ μέλανος καὶ
Many things I had to write, but I will not with ink and
καλάμου [s]σοι γράψαι·‖ 14 ἐλπίζω.δὲ εὐθέως [t]ἰδεῖν σε,‖
pen [3]to [4]thee [1]to [2]write; but I hope immediately to see thee,
καὶ στόμα πρὸς στόμα λαλήσομεν. 15 Εἰρήνη σοι. ἀσπά-
and mouth to mouth we shall speak. Peace to thee. [3]Sa-
ζονταί σε οἱ φίλοι. ἀσπάζου τοὺς φίλους κατ' ὄνομα.
lute [4]thee [1]the [2]friends. Salute the friends by name.
[v]Ἰωάννου ἐπιστολὴ καθολικὴ τρίτη.‖
[4]Of [5]John [3]epistle [2]general [1]third.

---

[a]ΕΠΙΣΤΟΛΗ ΤΟΥ ΙΟΥΔΑ ΚΑΘΟΛΙΚΗ.‖
[2]EPISTLE [3]OF [4]JUDE [1]GENERAL.

JUDE, the servant of Jesus Christ, and brother of James, to them that are sanctified by God the Father, and preserved in Jesus Christ, *and* called: 2 Mercy unto you, and peace, and love, be multiplied.

3 Beloved, when I gave all diligence to write unto you of the common salvation, it was needful for me to write unto you, and exhort *you* that ye should earnestly contend for the faith which was once delivered unto the saints. 4 For there are certain men crept in unawares, who were before of old ordained to this condemnation, ungodly men, turning the grace of our God into lasciviousness, and denying the only Lord God, and our Lord Jesus Christ.

5 I will therefore put you in remembrance, though ye once knew this, how that the Lord, having saved the people out of the land of Egypt, afterward destroyed them that believed

ΙΟΥΔΑΣ Ἰησοῦ χριστοῦ δοῦλος, ἀδελφὸς.δὲ Ἰακώβου, τοῖς
Jude, of Jesus Christ bondman, and brother of James, to the
ἐν θεῷ πατρὶ [b]ἡγιασμένοις‖ καὶ Ἰησοῦ χριστῷ τετηρη-
[4]in [5]God [[6]the] [7]Father [3]sanctified [8]and [10]in [11]Jesus [12]Christ [9]kept
μένοις κλητοῖς· 2 ἔλεος ὑμῖν καὶ εἰρήνη καὶ ἀγάπη
[1]called [[2]ones]. Mercy to you and peace, and love
πληθυνθείη.
be multiplied.
3 Ἀγαπητοί, πᾶσαν σπουδὴν ποιούμενος γράφειν ὑμῖν
Beloved, [2]all [3]diligence [1]using to write to you
περὶ τῆς κοινῆς [c] σωτηρίας, ἀνάγκην ἔσχον γράψαι ὑμῖν,
concerning the common salvation, necessity I had to write to you,
παρακαλῶν ἐπαγωνίζεσθαι τῇ ἅπαξ παραδοθείσῃ τοῖς
exhorting [you] to contend earnestly for the [2]once [3]delivered [4]to [5]the
ἁγίοις πίστει. 4 παρεισέδυσαν.γάρ τινες ἄνθρωποι, οἱ
[6]saints [1]faith. For came in stealthily certain men, they who
πάλαι προγεγραμμένοι εἰς τοῦτο τὸ κρίμα, ἀσεβεῖς
of old have been before marked out to this sentence, ungodly [persons]
τὴν τοῦ.θεοῦ.ἡμῶν [d]χάριν‖ μετατιθέντες εἰς ἀσέλγειαν καὶ τὸν
[2]the [4]of [5]our [6]God [3]grace [1]changing into licentiousness and [2]the
μόνον δεσπότην [e]θεὸν‖ καὶ κύριον.ἡμῶν Ἰησοῦν χριστὸν
[3]only [4]master— [5]God [6]and [7]our [8]Lord [9]Jesus [10]Christ
ἀρνούμενοι.
[1]denying.
5 Ὑπομνῆσαι.δὲ ὑμᾶς βούλομαι, εἰδότας [f]ὑμᾶς‖ ἅπαξ
But [3]put [5]in [6]remembrance [4]you [1]I [2]would, [8]knowing [7]you once
[g]τοῦτο,‖ ὅτι [h]ὁ‖ [i]κύριος‖ λαὸν ἐκ γῆς Αἰγύπτου σώ-
this, that the Lord a people out of [the] land of Egypt having
σας, τὸ.δεύτερον τοὺς μὴ.πιστεύσαντας ἀπώλεσεν. 6 ἀγ-
saved, in the second place those who believed not he destroyed.

---

[p] ὑπὸ T. [q] οἶδας thou knowest LTTrA. [r] γράψαι σοι to write to thee LTTrAW. [s] γράφειν σοι L; σοι γράφειν TTrAW. [t] σε ἰδεῖν LTTrAW. [v] — *the subscription* EGLTW; Ἰωάνου γ' Tr; Ἰωάννου γ' A.

[a] + ἀποστόλου apostle E; Ἰούδα ἐπιστολή GLTrW; Ἰούδα TA. [b] ἠγαπημένοις beloved LTTrAW. [c] + ἡμῶν (*read* our common) LTTrA. [d] χάριτα LTTrAW. [e] — θεὸν GLTTrAW. [f] — ὑμᾶς LTTrAW. [g] πάντα all things LTTrAW. [h] — ὁ TTrA. [i] Ἰησοῦς Jesus LA.

γέλους τε τοὺς μὴ.τηρήσαντας τὴν.ἑαυτῶν ἀρχήν, ἀλλὰ
[2]Angels [1]and who kept not their own first-state, but

ἀπολιπόντας τὸ.ἴδιον οἰκητήριον, εἰς κρίσιν μεγάλης
left their own dwelling, unto [the] judgment of [the] great

ἡμέρας δεσμοῖς ἀϊδίοις ὑπὸ ζόφον τετήρηκεν· 7 ὡς Σόδομα
day in [2]bonds [1]eternal under darkness he keeps; as Sodom

καὶ Γόμοῤῥα, καὶ αἱ περὶ αὐτὰς πόλεις, τὸν ὅμοιον [l]τού-
and Gomorrha, and the [2]around [3]them [1]cities, in like [2]with

τοις τρόπον|| ἐκπορνεύσασαι, καὶ ἀπελθοῦσαι
[3]them [1]manner having given themselves to fornication and having gone

ὀπίσω σαρκὸς ἑτέρας, πρόκεινται δεῖγμα, πυρὸς αἰωνίου
after [2]flesh [1]other, are set forth as an example, [4]of [6]fire [5]eternal

δίκην ὑπέχουσαι. 8 ὁμοίως.μέντοι καὶ οὗτοι ἐνυπνια-
[[2]the] [3]penalty [1]undergoing. Yet in like manner also these dream-

ζόμενοι, σάρκα μὲν μιαίνουσιν, κυριότητα.δὲ ἀθετοῦσιν,
ers [[2]the] [3]flesh [1]defile, and [3]lordship [1]set [2]aside,

δόξας.δὲ βλασφημοῦσιν. 9 [m]ὁ.δὲ||.Μιχαὴλ ὁ ἀρχάγγελος,
and [4]glories [1]speak [2]evil [3]of. But Michael the archangel,

[n]ὅτε|| τῷ διαβόλῳ διακρινόμενος διελέγετο περὶ τοῦ [o]Μω-
when with the devil disputing he reasoned about the [2]of

σέως|| σώματος, οὐκ.ἐτόλμησεν κρίσιν ἐπενεγκεῖν βλασ-
[3]Moses [1]body, did not dare [5]a [7]charge [1]to [2]bring [3]against [[4]him] [6]rail-

φημίας, [p]ἀλλ'|| εἶπεν, Ἐπιτιμήσαι σοι κύριος. 10 οὗτοι.δὲ
ing, but said, [3]Rebuke [4]thee [[1]the] [2]Lord. But these,

ὅσα μὲν οὐκ.οἴδασιν βλασφημοῦσιν· ὅσα.δὲ
whatever things they know not they speak evil of; but whatever things

φυσικῶς, ὡς τὰ ἄλογα ζῶα, ἐπίστανται, ἐν τούτοις
naturally, as the irrational animals, they understand, in these things

φθείρονται. 11 οὐαὶ αὐτοῖς· ὅτι τῇ ὁδῷ τοῦ Κάϊν
they corrupt themselves. Woe to them! because in the way of Cain

ἐπορεύθησαν, καὶ τῇ πλάνῃ τοῦ Βαλαὰμ μισθοῦ ἐξεχύθησαν,
they went, and to the error of Balaam for reward rushed,

καὶ τῇ ἀντιλογίᾳ τοῦ Κορὲ ἀπώλοντο. 12 οὗτοί εἰσιν [q] ἐν
and in the gainsaying of Korah perished. These are in

ταῖς.ἀγάπαις.ὑμῶν σπιλάδες, συνευωχούμενοι [r] ἀφόβως,[r]
your love feasts sunken rocks, feasting together [with you] fearlessly,

ἑαυτοὺς ποιμαίνοντες· νεφέλαι ἄνυδροι, ὑπὸ ἀνέμων
[2]themselves [1]pasturing; clouds without water, by winds

[s]περιφερόμεναι·|| δένδρα φθινοπωρινὰ ἄκαρπα δὶς ἀποθα-
being carried about, [2]trees [1]autumnal, without fruit, twice dead,

νόντα ἐκριζωθέντα· 13 κύματα ἄγρια θαλάσσης ἐπαφρίζοντα
rooted up; [2]waves [1]wild of [the] sea, foaming out

τὰς.ἑαυτῶν αἰσχύνας· ἀστέρες πλανῆται, οἷς ὁ ζόφος τοῦ
their own shames; [2]stars [1]wandering, to whom the gloom

σκότους εἰς.[t]τὸν||.αἰῶνα τετήρηται. 14 [v]προεφήτευσεν||.δὲ καὶ
of darkness for ever has been kept. And [6]prophesied [7]also

τούτοις ἕβδομος ἀπὸ Ἀδὰμ Ἐνώχ, λέγων, Ἰδού,
[8]as [9]to [10]these [[2]the] [3]seventh [4]from [5]Adam, [1]Enoch, saying, Behold,

ἦλθεν κύριος ἐν [w]μυριάσιν ἁγίαις|| αὐτοῦ, 15 ποιῆσαι
[3]came [[1]the] [2]Lord amidst [3]myriads [2]holy [1]his, to execute

κρίσιν κατὰ πάντων, καὶ [x]ἐξελέγξαι|| πάντας τοὺς ἀσεβεῖς
judgment against all, and to convict all the ungodly

not. 6 And the angels
which kept not their
first estate, but left
their own habitation,
he hath reserved in
everlasting chains un-
der darkness unto the
judgment of the great
day. 7 Even as Sodom
and Gomorrha, and
the cities about them
in like manner, giving
themselves over to
fornication, and going
after strange flesh, are
set forth for an ex-
ample, suffering the
vengeance of eternal
fire. 8 Likewise also
these *filthy* dreamers
defile the flesh, despise
dominion, and speak
evil of dignities. 9 Yet
Michael the archangel,
when contending with
the devil he disputed
about the body of Mo-
ses, durst not bring a-
gainst him a railing
accusation, but said,
The Lord rebuke thee.
10 But these speak evil
of those things which
they know not: but
what they know na-
turally, as brute
beasts, in those things
they corrupt them-
selves. 11 Woe unto
them! for they have
gone in the way of
Cain, and ran greedily
after the error of
Balaam for reward,
and perished in the
gainsaying of Core.
12 These are spots in
your feasts of charity,
when they feast with
you, feeding them-
selves without fear:
clouds *they are* with-
out water, carried a-
bout of winds; trees
whose fruit withereth,
without fruit, twice
dead, plucked up by
the roots; 13 raging
waves of the sea, foam-
ing out their own
shame; wandering
stars, to whom is re-
served the blackness
of darkness for ever.
14 And Enoch also,
the seventh from A-
dam, prophesied of
these, saying, Behold,
the Lord cometh with
ten thousands of his
saints, 15 to execute
judgment upon all,
and to convince all

---

[l] τρόπον τούτοις LTTrAW. [m] ὅτε when L. [n] τότε at that time L. [o] Μωϋσέως LTTrAW. [p] ἀλλὰ LTTrAW. [q] + οἱ (*read* the sunken rocks) LTTrA. [r] *Text. Rec. and Tr place the comma after* συνευ-. [s] παραφερόμεναι being carried along GLTTrAW. [t] — τὸν GLTTrAW. [v] ἐπροφήτευσεν TTr. [w] ἁγίαις μυριάσιν GLTTrAW. [x] ἐλέγξαι LTTrA.

that are ungodly among them of all their ungodly deeds which they have ungodly committed, and of all their hard *speeches* which ungodly sinners have spoken against him. 16 These are murmurers, complainers, walking after their own lusts; and their mouth speaketh great swelling *words*, having men's persons in admiration because of advantage. 17 But, beloved, remember ye the words which were spoken before of the apostles of our Lord Jesus Christ; 18 how that they told you there should be mockers in the last time, who should walk after their own ungodly lusts. 19 These be they who separate themselves, sensual, having not the Spirit. 20 But ye, beloved, building up yourselves on your most holy faith, praying in the Holy Ghost, 21 keep yourselves in the love of God, looking for the mercy of our Lord Jesus Christ unto eternal life. 22 And of some have compassion, making a difference: 23 and others save with fear, pulling *them* out of the fire; hating even the garment spotted by the flesh.

24 Now unto him that is able to keep you from falling, and to present *you* faultless before the presence of his glory with exceeding joy, 25 to the only wise God our Saviour, *be* glory and majesty, dominion and power, both now and ever. Amen.

[y]αὐτῶν‖ περὶ πάντων τῶν ἔργων [z]ἀσεβείας‖ αὐτῶν ὧν
of them concerning all [2]works [3]of [4]ungodliness [1]their which

ἠσέβησαν, καὶ περὶ πάντων τῶν σκληρῶν [a] ὧν
they did ungodlily, and concerning all the hard [things] which

ἐλάλησαν κατ' αὐτοῦ ἁμαρτωλοὶ ἀσεβεῖς. 16 οὗτοί εἰσιν
[3]spoke [4]against [5]him [2]sinners [1]ungodly. These are

γογγυσταί, μεμψίμοιροι, κατὰ τὰς.ἐπιθυμίας.αὐτῶν πορευό-
murmurers, complainers, [2]after [3]their [4]lusts [1]walk-

μενοι· καὶ τὸ.στόμα.αὐτῶν λαλεῖ ὑπέρογκα, θαυμάζοντες
ing; and their mouth speaks great swelling [words], admiring

πρόσωπα ὠφελείας χάριν. 17 ὑμεῖς.δέ, ἀγαπητοί, μνή-
persons [5]profit [1]for [2]the [3]sake [4]of. But ye, beloved, re-

σθητε τῶν [b]ῥημάτων τῶν προειρημένων‖ ὑπὸ τῶν ἀπο-
member the words which have been spoken before by the apo-

στόλων τοῦ.κυρίου.ἡμῶν Ἰησοῦ χριστοῦ· 18 ὅτι ἔλεγον ὑμῖν,
stles of our Lord Jesus Christ, that they said to you,

[c]ὅτι‖ [d]ἐν ἐσχάτῳ χρόνῳ‖ ἔσονται ἐμπαῖκται, κατὰ τὰς
that in [the] last time there will be mockers, [2]after

ἑαυτῶν ἐπιθυμίας πορευόμενοι τῶν ἀσεβειῶν. 19 οὗτοί εἰσιν
[3]their [4]own [5]desires [1]walking of ungodlinesses. These are

οἱ ἀποδιορίζοντες[e], ψυχικοί, πνεῦμα μὴ
they who set apart [themselves], natural [men], [3]the] [4]Spirit [1]not

ἔχοντες. 20 ὑμεῖς.δέ, ἀγαπητοί, [f]τῇ.ἁγιωτάτῃ.ὑμῶν πίστει
[2]having. But ye, beloved, on your most holy faith

ἐποικοδομοῦντες ἑαυτούς,‖ ἐν πνεύματι ἁγίῳ προσευχό-
building up yourselves, in [the] [2]Spirit [1]Holy pray-

μενοι, 21 ἑαυτοὺς ἐν ἀγάπῃ θεοῦ τηρήσατε, προσδεχό-
ing, [2]yourselves [3]in [[4]the] [5]love [6]of [7]God [1]keep, await-

μενοι τὸ ἔλεος τοῦ.κυρίου.ἡμῶν Ἰησοῦ χριστοῦ, εἰς ζωὴν
ing the mercy of our Lord Jesus Christ unto life

αἰώνιον. 22 καὶ οὓς μὲν [g]ἐλεεῖτε διακρινόμενοι·‖ 23 [h]οὓς.δὲ
eternal. And [2]some [1]pity, making a difference but others

ἐν φόβῳ σώζετε, ἐκ τοῦ πυρὸς ἁρπάζοντες,‖ μισοῦντες
with fear save, out of the fire snatching [them]; hating

καὶ τὸν ἀπὸ τῆς σαρκὸς ἐσπιλωμένον χιτῶνα.
even the [3]by [4]the [5]flesh [2]spotted [1]garment.

24 Τῷ.δὲ δυναμένῳ φυλάξαι [i]αὐτοὺς‖ ἀπταίστους, καὶ
But to him who is able to keep them without stumbling, and

στῆσαι κατενώπιον τῆς.δόξης.αὐτοῦ ἀμώμους ἐν ἀγαλ-
to set [them] before his glory blameless with exul-

λιάσει, 25 μόνῳ [k]σοφῷ‖ θεῷ σωτῆρι.ἡμῶν, [l] δόξα [m]καὶ‖
tation, to [the] only wise God our Saviour, [be] glory and

μεγαλωσύνη, κράτος καὶ ἐξουσία, [n] καὶ νῦν καὶ εἰς πάντας
greatness, might and authority, both now, and to all

τοὺς αἰῶνας. ἀμήν.
the ages. Amen.

[o]Ἐπιστολὴ Ἰούδα καθολική.‖
[2]Epistle [3]of [4]Jude [1]general.

---

[y] — αὐτῶν LTTrA. [z] [ἀσεβείας] Tr. [a] + λόγων speeches T. [b] προειρημένων ῥημάτων words having been spoken before L. [c] — ὅτι LT[Tr]. [d] ἐπ' ἐσχάτου τοῦ (— τοῦ Tr[A]W) χρόνου at the end of the time LTTrAW. [e] + ἑαυτοὺς themselves EG [f] ἐποικοδομοῦντες ἑαυτοὺς τῇ ἁγιωτάτῃ ὑμῶν πίστει LTTrAW. [g] ἐλέγχετε διακρινομένους [who] dispute, convict LTTrAW. [h] οὓς δὲ σώζετε ἐκ πυρὸς ἁρπάζοντες, οὓς δὲ ἐλεᾶτε (ἐλεεῖτε W) ἐν φόβῳ but others save, from [the] fire snatching [them], and others pity in fear LTTrAW. [i] ὑμᾶς you (*and read* set [you] before) EGLTTrW. [k] — σοφῷ GLTTrAW. [l] + διὰ Ἰησοῦ χριστοῦ τοῦ κυρίου ἡμῶν through Jesus Christ our Lord GLTTrAW. [m] — καὶ LTTrAW. [n] + πρὸ παντὸς τοῦ αἰῶνος before the whole age (*read* καὶ and) LTTrAW. [o] — *the subscription* EGLTW; Ἰούδα TrA.

[a]ΑΠΟΚΑΛΥΨΙΣ ΙΩΑΝΝΟΥ ΤΟΥ ΘΕΟΛΟΓΟΥ.‖
REVELATION OF JOHN THE DIVINE

ΑΠΟΚΑΛΥΨΙΣ Ἰησοῦ χριστοῦ, ἣν ἔδωκεν αὐτῷ ὁ θεός,
Revelation of Jesus Christ, which [2]gave [3]to [4]him [1]God,
δεῖξαι τοῖς-δούλοις-αὐτοῦ ἃ δεῖ γενέσθαι ἐν-τάχει, καὶ
to shew to his bondmen what things must take place shortly: and
ἐσήμανεν ἀποστείλας διὰ τοῦ-ἀγγέλου-αὐτοῦ τῷ-δούλῳ-αὐτοῦ
he signified [it], having sent by his angel to his bondman
[b]Ἰωάννῃ,‖ 2 ὃς ἐμαρτύρησεν τὸν λόγον τοῦ θεοῦ καὶ τὴν
John, who testified the word of God and the
μαρτυρίαν Ἰησοῦ χριστοῦ, ὅσα [c]τε‖ [d]εἶδεν.‖ 3 μακά-
testimony of Jesus Christ, [2]whatsoever [3]things [1]and he saw. Bless-
ριος ὁ ἀναγινώσκων, καὶ οἱ ἀκούοντες [e]τοὺς λόγους‖
ed [is] he that reads, and they that hear the words
τῆς προφητείας, καὶ τηροῦντες τὰ ἐν αὐτῇ γεγραμμένα·
of the prophecy, and keep the things [2]in [3]it [1]written;
ὁ-γὰρ καιρὸς ἐγγύς.
for the time [is] near.

4 [f]Ἰωάννης‖ ταῖς ἑπτὰ ἐκκλησίαις ταῖς ἐν τῇ Ἀσίᾳ·
John to the seven assemblies which [are] in Asia:
χάρις ὑμῖν καὶ εἰρήνη ἀπὸ [g]τοῦ‖ ὁ ὢν καὶ ὁ ἦν καὶ ὁ
Grace to you and peace from him who is and who was and who [is]
ἐρχόμενος· καὶ ἀπὸ τῶν ἑπτὰ πνευμάτων [h]ἃ‖ [i]ἐστιν‖ ἐνώπιον
to come; and from the seven Spirits which are before
τοῦ-θρόνου-αὐτοῦ· 5 καὶ ἀπὸ Ἰησοῦ χριστοῦ, ὁ μάρτυς ὁ
his throne; and from Jesus Christ, the [2]witness
πιστός, ὁ πρωτότοκος [k]ἐκ‖ τῶν νεκρῶν, καὶ ὁ ἄρχων τῶν
[1]faithful, the firstborn from among the dead, and the ruler of the
βασιλέων τῆς γῆς· τῷ [l]ἀγαπήσαντι‖ ἡμᾶς, καὶ [m]λού-
kings of the earth. To him who loved us, and wash-
σαντι‖ ἡμᾶς [n]ἀπὸ‖ τῶν-ἁμαρτιῶν-[o]ἡμῶν‖ ἐν τῷ-αἵματι-αὐτοῦ·
ed us from our sins in his blood,
6 καὶ ἐποίησεν [p]ἡμᾶς‖ [q]βασιλεῖς καὶ‖ ἱερεῖς τῷ θεῷ καὶ πατρὶ
and made us kings and priests to [2]God [3]and [4]Father
αὐτοῦ· αὐτῷ ἡ δόξα καὶ τὸ κράτος εἰς τοὺς αἰῶνας [r]τῶν
[1]his: to him [be] the glory and the might to the ages of the
αἰώνων.‖ ἀμήν.
ages. Amen.

7 Ἰδού, ἔρχεται μετὰ τῶν νεφελῶν, καὶ ὄψεται αὐτὸν πᾶς
Behold, he comes with the clouds, and shall see him every
ὀφθαλμός, καὶ οἵτινες αὐτὸν ἐξεκέντησαν· καὶ κόψονται
eye, and they which [2]him [1]pierced, and [7]shall [8]wail
ἐπ' αὐτὸν πᾶσαι αἱ φυλαὶ τῆς γῆς. ναί, ἀμήν.
[9]on [10]account [11]of [12]him [1]all [2]the [3]tribes [4]of [5]the [6]earth. Yea, amen.
8 Ἐγώ εἰμι τὸ [s]Α‖ καὶ τὸ [t]Ω,‖ [v]ἀρχὴ καὶ τέλος·‖ λέγει
I am the A and the Ω, beginning and ending, says

THE Revelation of Jesus Christ, which God gave unto him, to shew unto his servants things which must shortly come to pass; and he sent and signified *it* by his angel unto his servant John: 2 who bare record of the word of God, and of the testimony of Jesus Christ, and of all things that he saw. 3 Blessed *is* he that readeth, and they that hear the words of this prophecy, and keep those things which are written therein: for the time *is* at hand.

4 JOHN to the seven churches which are in Asia: Grace *be* unto you, and peace, from him which is, and which was, and which is to come; and from the seven Spirits which are before his throne; 5 and from Jesus Christ, *who is* the faithful witness, *and* the firstbegotten of the dead, and the prince of the kings of the earth. Unto him that loved us, and washed us from our sins in his own blood, 6 and hath made us kings and priests unto God and his Father; to him *be* glory and dominion for ever and ever. Amen.

7 Behold, he cometh with clouds; and every eye shall see him, and they *also* which pierced him: and all kindreds of the earth shall wail because of him. Even so, Amen.

8 I am Alpha and Omega, the beginning and the ending, saith

---

[a] Ἀποκάλυψις G; Ἀποκάλυψις Ἰωάννου (Ἰωάνου Tr) LTTrAW. [b] Ἰωάνῃ Tr. [c] — τε GLTTrAW. [d] ἴδεν T. [e] τὸν λόγον the word T. [f] Ἰωάνης Tr. [g] — τοῦ (*read* [him]) GLTTrAW. [h] τῶν Tr. [i] — ἐστιν (*read* [are]) LTTrAW. [k] — ἐκ (*read* τῶν of the) GLTTrAW. [l] ἀγαπῶντι loves GLTTrAW. [m] λύσαντι freed LTTr; λ[ο]ύσαντι A. [n] ἐκ LTTrA. [o] [ἡμῶν] A. [p] ἡμῶν L; ἡμῖν for us Tr. [q] βασιλείαν, a kingdom, GLTTrAW. [r] — τῶν αἰώνων A. [s] ἄλφα Alpha LTTrAW. [t] ὦ LA. [v] — ἀρχὴ καὶ τέλος GLTTrAW.

the Lord, which is,
and which was, and
which is to come, the
Almighty.

9 I John, who also
am your brother, and
companion in tribula-
tion, and in the king-
dom and patience of
Jesus Christ, was in
the isle that is called
Patmos, for the word
of God, and for the
testimony of Jesus
Christ. 10 I was in the
Spirit on the Lord's
day, and heard behind
me a great voice, as of
a trumpet, 11 saying,
I am Alpha and Ome-
ga, the first and the
last: and, What thou
seest, write in a book;
and send *it* unto the
seven churches which
are in Asia; unto Eph-
esus, and unto Smyr-
na, and unto Perga-
mos, and unto Thya-
tira, and unto Sardis,
and unto Philadelphia,
and unto Laodicea.
12 And I turned to see
the voice that spake
with me. And being
turned, I saw seven
golden candlesticks;
13 and in the midst of
the seven candlesticks
one like unto the Son
of man, clothed with
a garment down to
the foot, and girt a-
bout the paps with a
golden girdle. 14 His
head and *his* hairs
were white like wool,
as white as snow; and
his eyes *were* as a
flame of fire; 15 and
his feet like unto fine
brass, as if they burn-
ed in a furnace; and
his voice as the sound
of many waters. 16 And
he had in his right
hand seven stars: and
out of his mouth went
a sharp two-edged
sword: and his coun-
tenance *was* as the
sun shineth in his
strength. 17 And when
I saw him, I fell at his
feet as dead. And he

[w]ὁ κύριος,‖ ὁ ὢν καὶ ὁ ἦν καὶ ὁ ἐρχόμενος, ὁ παντο-
the Lord, who is and who was and who [is] to come, the Al-
κράτωρ.
mighty.

9 Ἐγὼ [x]Ἰωάννης,‖ ὁ [y]καὶ‖ ἀδελφὸς ὑμῶν καὶ [z]συγκοινωνὸς‖
I John, also [2]brother [1]your and fellow-partaker
ἐν τῇ θλίψει καὶ [a]ἐν τῇ‖ βασιλείᾳ καὶ ὑπομονῇ [b] [c]Ἰησοῦ χρισ-
in the tribulation and in the kingdom and endurance of Jesus Christ,
τοῦ,‖ ἐγενόμην ἐν τῇ νήσῳ τῇ καλουμένῃ Πάτμῳ, διὰ
was in the island which [is] called Patmos, because of
τὸν λόγον τοῦ θεοῦ καὶ [d]διὰ‖ τὴν μαρτυρίαν Ἰησοῦ [e]χρισ-
the word of God and because of the testimony of Jesus Christ.
τοῦ.‖ 10 ἐγενόμην ἐν πνεύματι ἐν τῇ κυριακῇ ἡμέρᾳ· καὶ
I became in [the] Spirit on the Lord's day, and
ἤκουσα ὀπίσω μου φωνὴν μεγάλην ὡς σάλπιγγος, 11 λεγού-
I heard behind me a [2]voice [1]loud as of a trumpet, say-
σης, [f]Ἐγώ εἰμι τὸ Α καὶ τὸ Ω, ὁ πρῶτος καὶ ὁ ἔσχατος· καί,‖
ing, I am the Α and the Ω, the first and the last; and,
Ὃ βλέπεις γράψον εἰς βιβλίον, καὶ πέμψον ταῖς [g] ἐκκλησίαις
What thou seest write in a book, and send to the assemblies
[h]ταῖς ἐν Ἀσίᾳ,‖ εἰς Ἔφεσον, καὶ εἰς [i]Σμύρναν,‖ καὶ εἰς
which [are] in Asia: to Ephesus, and to Smyrna, and to
Πέργαμον, καὶ εἰς [k]Θυάτειρα,‖ καὶ εἰς Σάρδεις, καὶ εἰς [l]Φιλα-
Pergamos, and to Thyatira, and to Sardis, and to Phila-
δέλφειαν,‖ καὶ εἰς [m]Λαοδίκειαν.‖ 12 καὶ ἐπέστρεψα βλέπειν
delphia, and to Laodicea. And I turned to see
τὴν φωνὴν ἥτις [n]ἐλάλησεν‖ μετ' ἐμοῦ· καὶ ἐπιστρέψας εἶδον
the voice which spoke with me, and having turned I saw
ἑπτὰ λυχνίας χρυσᾶς, 13 καὶ ἐν μέσῳ τῶν [o]ἑπτὰ‖ λυχ-
seven [2]lampstands [1]golden, and in [the] midst of the seven lamp-
νιῶν ὅμοιον [p]υἱῷ‖ ἀνθρώπου, ἐνδεδυμένον
stands [one] like [the] Son of man, clothed in [a garment]
ποδήρη, καὶ περιεζωσμένον πρὸς τοῖς [q]μαστοῖς‖ ζώνην
reaching to the feet, and [4]girt [5]about [6]with [1]at [2]the [3]breasts [7]a [9]girdle
[r]χρυσῆν·‖ 14 ἡ.δὲ.κεφαλὴ.αὐτοῦ καὶ αἱ τρίχες λευκαὶ [s]ὡσεὶ‖
[8]golden: and his head and hair white as if
ἔριον λευκόν, ὡς χιών· καὶ οἱ.ὀφθαλμοὶ.αὐτοῦ ὡς φλὸξ πυρός·
[2]wool [1]white, as snow; and his eyes as a flame of fire;
15 καὶ οἱ.πόδες.αὐτοῦ ὅμοιοι χαλκολιβάνῳ ὡς ἐν καμίνῳ
and his feet like fine brass, as if [3]in [4]a [5]furnace [[1]they]
[t]πεπυρωμένοι·‖ καὶ ἡ.φωνὴ.αὐτοῦ ὡς φωνὴ ὑδάτων πολλῶν·
[2]glowed; and his voice as [the] voice of [2]waters [1]many,
16 καὶ ἔχων ἐν τῇ δεξιᾷ [v]αὐτοῦ χειρὶ‖ ἀστέρας ἑπτά· καὶ ἐκ
and having in [2]right [1]his hand [2]stars [1]seven, and out of
τοῦ.στόματος.αὐτοῦ ῥομφαία δίστομος ὀξεῖα ἐκπορευομένη· καὶ
his mouth a [3]sword [2]two-edged [1]sharp going forth, and
ἡ.ὄψις.αὐτοῦ ὡς ὁ ἥλιος φαίνει ἐν τῇ.δυνάμει.αὐτοῦ. 17 καὶ
his countenance as the sun shines in its power. And
ὅτε εἶδον αὐτόν, ἔπεσα πρὸς τοὺς.πόδας.αὐτοῦ ὡς νεκρός· καὶ
when I saw him, I fell at his feet as dead: and

---

[w] κυριος ὁ θεός [the] Lord God GLTTrAW. [x] Ἰωάνης Tr. [y] — καὶ GLTTrAW. [z] συν T. [a] — ἐν τῇ GLTTrAW. [b] + ἐν in (Jesus) LTTrAW. [c] χριστῷ Ἰησοῦ W; — χριστοῦ LTTrA. [d] — διὰ LTr[A]. [e] — χριστοῦ LTTrA. [f] — Ἐγώ εἰμι . . . ἔσχατος· καὶ GLTTrAW. [g] + ἑπτὰ seven GLTTrAW. [h] — ταῖς ἐν Ἀσίᾳ GLTTrAW. [i] Ζμύρναν T. [k] Θυάτειραν LAW. [l] Φιλαδελφίαν T. [m] Λαοδικίαν T. [n] ἐλάλει was speaking LTTrAW. [o] — ἑπτὰ LT[Tr A]. [p] υἱὸν T. [q] μαζοῖς L; μασθοῖς T. [r] χρυσᾶν LTTrA. [s] ὡς as GLTTrAW. [t] πεπυρωμένης (-ένῳ T) [it] glowed LTr. [v] χειρὶ αὐτοῦ LTTrA.

[w]ἐπέθηκεν‖ τὴν.δεξιὰν.αὐτοῦ [x]χεῖρα‖ ἐπ' ἐμέ, λέγων [y]μοι,‖
he laid his right hand upon me, saying to me,
Μὴ.φοβοῦ· ἐγώ εἰμι ὁ πρῶτος καὶ ὁ ἔσχατος, 18 καὶ ὁ
Fear not; I am the first and the last, and the
ζῶν, καὶ ἐγενόμην νεκρός, καὶ ἰδοὺ ζῶν εἰμι εἰς.τοὺς
living [one]: and I became dead, and behold [3]alive [1]I [2]am to the
αἰῶνας τῶν αἰώνων· [z]ἀμήν·‖ καὶ ἔχω τὰς κλεῖς τοῦ [a]ᾅδου καὶ
ages of the ages, Amen; and have the keys of hades and
τοῦ θανάτου.‖ 19 γράψον [b] ἃ εἶδες, καὶ ἅ
of death. Write the things which thou sawest and the things
εἰσιν, καὶ ἃ μέλλει [c]γίνεσθαι‖ μετὰ ταῦτα· 20 τὸ
which are, and the things which are about to take place after these. The
μυστήριον τῶν ἑπτὰ ἀστέρων [d]ὧν‖ εἶδες [e]ἐπὶ τῆς δεξιᾶς‖
mystery of the seven stars which thou sawest on [2]right [3]hand
μου, καὶ τὰς ἑπτὰ λυχνίας τὰς χρυσᾶς. οἱ ἑπτὰ ἀστέρες
[1]my. and the seven [2]lampstands [1]golden. The seven stars
ἄγγελοι τῶν ἑπτὰ ἐκκλησιῶν εἰσιν· καὶ [f]αἱ‖ [g]ἑπτὰ λυχνίαι‖
[2]angels [3]of [4]the [5]seven [6]assemblies [1]are; and the seven lampstands
[h]ἃς εἶδες‖ ἑπτὰ ἐκκλησίαι εἰσίν.
which thou sawest [2]seven [3]assemblies [1]are.

laid his right hand upon me, saying unto me, Fear not; I am the first and the last:
18 *I am* he that liveth, and was dead; and, behold, I am alive for evermore, Amen; and have the keys of hell and of death.
19 Write the things which thou hast seen, and the things which are, and the things which shall be hereafter;
20 the mystery of the seven stars which thou sawest in my right hand, and the seven golden candlesticks. The seven stars are the angels of the seven churches: and the seven candlesticks which thou sawest are the seven churches.

2 Τῷ ἀγγέλῳ [i]τῆς‖ [k]Ἐφεσίνης‖ ἐκκλησίας γράψον, Τάδε
To the angel of the Ephesian assembly write: These things
λέγει ὁ κρατῶν τοὺς ἑπτὰ ἀστέρας ἐν τῇ.δεξιᾷ.αὐτοῦ, ὁ
says he who holds the seven stars in his right hand, who
περιπατῶν ἐν μέσῳ τῶν ἑπτὰ λυχνιῶν τῶν [l]χρυσῶν·‖
walks in [the] midst of the seven [2]lampstands [1]golden.
2 Οἶδα τὰ.ἔργα.σου, καὶ τὸν κόπον [m]σου,‖ καὶ τὴν ὑπομονήν
I know thy works, and [2]labour [1]thy, and [2]endurance
σου, καὶ ὅτι οὐ.δύνῃ βαστάσαι κακούς, καὶ [n]ἐπειράσω‖
[1]thy. and that thou canst not bear evil [ones]; and thou didst try
τοὺς [o]φάσκοντας εἶναι ἀποστόλους‖ καὶ οὐκ.εἰσίν,
those who declare [themselves] to be apostles and are not,
καὶ εὗρες αὐτοὺς ψευδεῖς, 3 καὶ [p]ἐβάστασας καὶ ὑπομονὴν
and didst find them liars; and didst bear and [2]endurance
ἔχεις, καὶ‖ διὰ τὸ.ὄνομά.μου [q]κεκοπίακας καὶ οὐ.κέκμηκας.‖
[1]hast, and for the sake of my name hast laboured and hast not wearied:
4 [r]ἀλλ'‖ ἔχω κατὰ σοῦ, ὅτι τὴν.ἀγάπην.σου τὴν πρώτην
but I have against thee, that thy [2]love [1]first
[s]ἀφῆκας.‖ 5 μνημόνευε οὖν πόθεν [t]ἐκπέπτωκας,‖ καὶ
thou didst leave. Remember therefore whence thou hast fallen from, and
μετανόησον, καὶ τὰ πρῶτα ἔργα ποίησον· εἰ.δὲ μή, ἔρχομαι
repent, and the first works do: but if not, I am coming
σοι [v]τάχει,‖ καὶ κινήσω τὴν.λυχνίαν.σου ἐκ τοῦ τόπου
to thee quickly, and I will remove thy lampstand out of [2]place
αὐτῆς, ἐὰν.μὴ μετανοήσῃς. 6 ἀλλὰ τοῦτο ἔχεις, ὅτι
[1]its, except thou shouldest repent. But this thou hast, that
μισεῖς τὰ ἔργα τῶν Νικολαϊτῶν, ἃ κἀγὼ μισῶ. 7 ὁ
thou hatest the works of the Nicolaitanes, which I also hate. He that

II. Unto the angel of the church of Ephesus write; These things saith he that holdeth the seven stars in his right hand, who walketh in the midst of the seven golden candlesticks;
2 I know thy works, and thy labour, and thy patience, and how thou canst not bear them which are evil: and thou hast tried them which say they are apostles, and are not, and hast found them liars:
3 and hast borne, and hast patience, and for my name's sake hast laboured, and hast not fainted.
4 Nevertheless I have *somewhat* against thee, because thou hast left thy first love.
5 Remember therefore from whence thou art fallen, and repent, and do the first works; or else I will come unto thee quickly, and will remove thy candlestick out of his place, except thou repent.
6 But this thou hast, that thou hatest the deeds of the Nicolaitanes, which I also hate.
7 He that hath

---

[w] ἔθηκεν GLTTrAW. [x] — χεῖρα (*read* δεξιὰν right hand) GLTTrAW. [y] — μοι GLTTrAW. [z] — ἀμήν GLTTrAW. [a] θανάτου καὶ τοῦ ᾅδου GLTTrAW. [b] + οὖν therefore GLTTrAW. [c] γενέσθαι TA. [d] οὓς LTTrA. [e] ἐν (in) τῇ δεξιᾷ L. [f] — αἱ W. [g] λυχνίαι αἱ ἑπτὰ GLTTrAW. [h] — ἃς εἶδες GLTTrAW. [i] τῷ (*read* ἐκκλ. of the assembly) LTr. [k] ἐν Ἐφέσῳ in Ephesus GLTTrAW. [l] χρυσέων LTrA. [m] — σου LTTrA [n] ἐπείρασας GLTTrAW. [o] λέγοντας ἑαυτοὺς ἀποστόλους εἶναι declare themselves to be apostles (— εἶναι LTTrA) GLTTrAW. [p] ὑπομονὴν ἔχεις καὶ ἐβάστασας GLTTrAW. [q] καὶ οὐ κεκοπίακες and hast not wearied LTTrA; καὶ οὐκ ἐκοπίασας and didst not weary GW. [r] ἀλλὰ TTrW. [s] ἀφῆκες TTr. [t] πέπτωκας thou hast fallen GLTrAW; πέπτωκες T. [v] ταχὺ EGW; — τάχει LTTrA.

an ear, let him hear
what the Spirit saith
unto the churches ; To
him that overcometh
will I give to eat of
the tree of life, which
is in the midst of the
paradise of God.

8 And unto the an-
gel of the church in
Smyrna write ; These
things saith the first
and the last, which
was dead, and is a-
live ; 9 I know thy
works, and tribula-
tion, and poverty, (but
thou art rich) and *I
know* the blasphemy of
them which say they
are Jews, and are not,
but *are* the synagogue
of Satan. 10 Fear none
of those things which
thou shalt suffer : be-
hold, the devil shall
cast *some* of you into
prison, that ye may be
tried ; and ye shall
have tribulation ten
days: be thou faithful
unto death, and I will
give thee a crown of
life. 11 He that hath
an ear, let him hear
what the Spirit saith
unto the churches ;
He that overcometh
shall not be hurt of
the second death.

12 And to the angel
of the church in Per-
gamos write ; These
things saith he which
hath the sharp sword
with two edges ; 13 I
know thy works, and
where thou dwellest,
even where Satan's
seat *is:* and thou hold-
est fast my name, and
hast not denied my
faith, even in those
days wherein Antipas
was my faithful mar-
tyr, who was slain a-
mong you, where Sa-
tan dwelleth. 14 But I
have a few things a-
gainst thee, because
thou hast there them
that hold the doctrine
of Balaam, who taught
Balac to cast a stum-
blingblock before the
children of Israel, to
eat things sacrificed
unto idols, and to com-
mit fornication. 15 So

ἔχων οὖς ἀκουσάτω τί τὸ πνεῦμα λέγει ταῖς[w] ἐκκλησίαις·
has an ear, let him hear what the Spirit says to the assemblies.
τῷ [x]νικῶντι" δώσω αὐτῷ φαγεῖν ἐκ τοῦ ξύλου τῆς ζωῆς
To him that overcomes, I will give to him to eat of the tree of life
ὅ ἐστιν ἐν [y]μέσῳ τοῦ παραδείσου" τοῦ θεοῦ[z].
which is in [the] midst of the paradise of God.
8 Καὶ τῷ ἀγγέλῳ [a]τῆς" [b]ἐκκλησίας Σμυρναίων" γράψον,
And to the angel of the assembly of Smyrneans write :
Τάδε λέγει ὁ πρῶτος καὶ ὁ ἔσχατος, ὃς ἐγένετο νεκρὸς
These things says the first and the last, who became dead
καὶ ἔζησεν· 9 Οἶδά σου [c]τὰ ἔργα καὶ" τὴν θλίψιν καὶ τὴν
and lived. I know thy works and tribulation and
πτωχείαν· [d]πλούσιος.δὲ" εἶ· καὶ τὴν βλασφημίαν[e] τῶν
poverty ; but rich thou art; and the calumny of those who
λεγόντων Ἰουδαίους εἶναι ἑαυτούς, καὶ οὐκ.εἰσίν, ἀλλὰ συν-
declare [4]Jews [2]to [3]be [1]themselves, and are not, but a syn-
αγωγὴ τοῦ σατανᾶ. 10 [f]μηδὲν" φοβοῦ ἃ μέλλεις
agogue of Satan. [2]Not [3]at [4]all [1]fear the things which thou art about
πάσχειν. ἰδού,[g] μέλλει [h]βαλεῖν" [i]ἐξ ὑμῶν ὁ διάβολος"
to suffer. Lo, [3]is [4]about [5]to [6]cast [[7]some] [8]of [9]you [1]the [2]devil
εἰς φυλακήν, ἵνα πειρασθῆτε· καὶ [k]ἕξετε" θλίψιν ἡμερῶν
into prison, that ye may be tried ; and ye shall have tribulation [2]days
δέκα. γίνου πιστὸς ἄχρι θανάτου, καὶ δώσω σοι τὸν στέ-
[1]ten. Be thou faithful unto death, and I will give to thee the
φανον τῆς ζωῆς. 11 ὁ ἔχων οὖς ἀκουσάτω τί τὸ πνεῦμα
crown of life. He that has an ear, let him hear what the Spirit
λέγει ταῖς ἐκκλησίαις· ὁ νικῶν οὐ.μὴ ἀδικηθῇ ἐκ
says to the assemblies. He that overcomes in no wise shall be injured of
τοῦ θανάτου τοῦ δευτέρου.
the [2]death [1]second.
12 Καὶ τῷ ἀγγέλῳ τῆς ἐν Περγάμῳ ἐκκλησίας γράψον,
And to the angel of the [2]in [3]Pergamos [1]assembly write :
Τάδε λέγει ὁ ἔχων τὴν ῥομφαίαν τὴν δίστομον τὴν
These things says he who has the [3]sword [2]two-edged
ὀξεῖαν· 13 Οἶδα [l]τὰ.ἔργα.σου καὶ" ποῦ κατοικεῖς, ὅπου ὁ
[1]sharp, I know thy works and where thou dwellest, where the
θρόνος τοῦ σατανᾶ, καὶ κρατεῖς τὸ.ὄνομά.μου, καὶ οὐκ
throne of Satan [is]; and thou holdest fast my name, and [2]not
ἠρνήσω τὴν.πίστιν.μου [m]καὶ" ἐν ταῖς ἡμέραις [n]ἐν" [o]αἷς" [p]Ἀν-
[1]didst [3]deny my faith even in the days in which An-
τίπας" ὁ.μάρτυς.μου ὁ πιστός[q], ὃς ἀπεκτάνθη παρ' ὑμῖν,
tipas my [2]witness [1]faithful [was], who was killed among you,
ὅπου [r]κατοικεῖ ὁ σατανᾶς." 14 [s]ἀλλ'" ἔχω κατὰ σοῦ ὀλίγα,
where [2]dwells [1]Satan. But I have against thee a few things;
[t]ὅτι" ἔχεις ἐκεῖ κρατοῦντας τὴν διδαχὴν Βαλαάμ, ὃς
because thou hast there [those] holding the teaching of Balaam, who
ἐδίδασκεν [v]ἐν" [wa]τῷ" Βαλὰκ βαλεῖν σκάνδαλον ἐνώπιον τῶν
taught Balak to cast a snare before the
υἱῶν Ἰσραήλ, φαγεῖν εἰδωλόθυτα καὶ πορνεῦσαι.
sons of Israel, to eat things sacrificed to idols and to commit fornication.

---

[w] + ἑπτὰ seven L. [x] νικοῦντι L. [y] τῷ παραδείσῳ the paradise GLTTrAW. [z] + μου (*read* of my God) G[A]W. [a] τῷ (*read* ἐκκλ. of the assembly) L. [b] ἐν Σμύρνῃ (Ζμύρνῃ T.) ἐκκλησίας assembly in Smyrna GLTTrAW. [c] — τὰ ἔργα καὶ LTTrA. [d] ἀλλὰ πλούσιος GLTTrAW. [e] + ἐκ of (those who) GLTTrAW. [f] μη Not LTrAW. [g] + δὴ indeed [A]W. [h] βάλλειν LTrA. [i] ὁ διάβολος ἐξ ὑμῶν GLTTrAW. [k] ἔχητε ye may have L. [l] — τὰ ἔργα σου καὶ LTTrA. [m] — καὶ T[TrA]. [n] — ἐν LTTrAW. [o] — αἷς (*read* in those days [was] Antipas) LTTr[A]. [p] Ἀντείπας T. [q] + μου (*read* my faithful [one]) LT[TrA]W. [r] ὁ σατανᾶς κατοικεῖ GLTTrAW. [s] ἀλλὰ W. [t] — ὅτι L. [v] — ἐν EGLTTrAW. [wa] τὸν E.

15 οὕτως ἔχεις καὶ σὺ κρατοῦντας τὴν διδαχὴν ˣτῶν‖
So hast also thou [those] holding the teaching of the
Νικολαϊτῶν ʸὃ μισῶ.‖ 16 μετανόησονᶻ· εἰ.δὲ μή, ἔρχομαί
Nicolaitanes, which thing I hate. Repent! but if not, I am coming
σοι ταχύ, καὶ πολεμήσω μετ' αὐτῶν ἐν τῇ ῥομφαίᾳ τοῦ
to thee quickly, and will make war with them with the sword
στόματός.μου. 17 ὁ ἔχων οὖς ἀκουσάτω τί τὸ πνεῦμα
of my mouth. He that has an ear, let him hear what the Spirit
λέγει ταῖς ἐκκλησίαις· τῷ ᵃνικῶντι‖ δώσω αὐτῷ ᵇφαγεῖν
says to the assemblies. To him that overcomes, I will give to him to eat
ἀπὸ‖ τοῦ μάννα τοῦ κεκρυμμένου, καὶ δώσω αὐτῷ ψῆφον
of the ²manna ¹hidden; and I will give to him a ²pebble
λευκήν, καὶ ἐπὶ τὴν ψῆφον ὄνομα καινὸν γεγραμμένον, ὃ
¹white, and on the pebble a ²name ¹new written, which
οὐδεὶς ᶜἔγνω‖ εἰ.μὴ ὁ λαμβάνων.
no one knew except he who receives [it].

18 Καὶ τῷ ἀγγέλῳ ᵈτῆς‖ ἐν Θυατείροις ἐκκλησίας γράψον,
And to the angel of the ²in ³Thyatira ¹assembly write:
Τάδε λέγει ὁ υἱὸς τοῦ θεοῦ, ὁ ἔχων τοὺς ὀφθαλμοὺς
These things says the Son of God, he who has ²eyes
ᵉαὐτοῦ‖ ὡς ᶠφλόγα‖ πυρός, καὶ οἱ.πόδες.αὐτοῦ ὅμοιοι χαλκολι-
¹his as a flame of fire, and his feet like fine
βάνῳ· 19 Οἶδά σου τὰ ἔργα καὶ τὴν ᵍἀγάπην, καὶ τὴν δια-
brass. I know thy works, and love, and ser-
κονίαν, καὶ τὴν πίστιν‖ καὶ ʰτὴν‖ ὑπομονήν ⁱσου,‖ καὶ τὰ ἔργα
vice, and faith, and ²endurance ¹thy, and ²works
σου, ᵏκαὶ‖ τὰ ἔσχατα πλείονα τῶν πρώτων. 20 ˡἀλλ'‖
¹thy, and the last [to be] more than the first. But
ἔχω κατὰ σοῦ ᵐὀλίγα,‖ ὅτι ⁿἐᾷς‖ τὴν γυναῖκαᵒ ᵖ'Ιεζα-
I have against thee a few things that thou sufferest the woman Jeze-
βήλ,‖ ᵠτὴν λέγουσαν‖ ʳἑαυτὴν‖ προφῆτιν, ˢδιδάσκειν καὶ πλα-
bel, her who calls herself a prophetess, to teach and to
νᾶσθαι‖ ἐμοὺς δούλους, πορνεῦσαι καὶ ᵗεἰδωλό-
mislead my bondmen to commit fornication and ³things ⁴sacrificed ⁵to
θυτα φαγεῖν.‖ 21 καὶ ἔδωκα αὐτῇ χρόνον ἵνα μετανοήσῃ ᵛἐκ
⁶idols ¹to ²eat. And I gave her time that she might repent of
τῆς.πορνείας.αὐτῆς, καὶ οὐ.μετενόησεν.‖ 22 ἰδού, ʷἐγὼ‖ βάλλω
her fornication; and she repented not. Lo, I cast
αὐτὴν εἰς κλίνην, καὶ τοὺς μοιχεύοντας μετ' αὐτῆς εἰς
her into a bed, and those who commit adultery with her into
θλίψιν μεγάλην, ἐὰν.μὴ ˣᵃμετανοήσωσιν‖ ἐκ τῶν ἔργων
²tribulation ¹great, except they should repent of ²works
ʸᵃαὐτῶν.‖ 23 καὶ τὰ.τέκνα.αὐτῆς ἀποκτενῶ ἐν θανάτῳ· καὶ
¹their. And her children I will kill with death; and
γνώσονται πᾶσαι αἱ ἐκκλησίαι ὅτι ἐγώ εἰμι ὁ ᶻᵃἐρευνῶν‖
⁴shall ⁵know ¹all ²the ³assemblies that I am he who searches

hast thou also them that hold the doctrine of the Nicolaitanes, which thing I hate. 16 Repent; or else I will come unto thee quickly, and will fight against them with the sword of my mouth. 17 He that hath an ear, let him hear what the Spirit saith unto the churches; To him that overcometh will I give to eat of the hidden manna, and will give him a white stone, and in the stone a new name written, which no man knoweth saving he that receiveth *it.*

18 And unto the angel of the church in Thyatira write; These things saith the Son of God, who hath his eyes like unto a flame of fire, and his feet *are* like fine brass; 19 I know thy works, and charity, and service, and faith, and thy patience, and thy works; and the last *to be* more than the first. 20 Notwithstanding I have a few things against thee, because thou sufferest that woman Jezebel, which calleth herself a prophetess, to teach and to seduce my servants to commit fornication, and to eat things sacrificed unto idols. 21 And I gave her space to repent of her fornication; and she repented not. 22 Behold, I will cast her into a bed, and them that commit adultery with her into great tribulation, except they repent of their deeds. 23 And I will kill her children with death; and all the churches shall know that I am he which searcheth the

---

ˣ — τῶν the L[Tr]AW. ʸ ὁμοίως in like manner GLTTrAW. ᶻ + οὖν therefore GLTr[A]W. ᵃ νικοῦντι LTTr. ᵇ — φαγεῖν ἀπὸ GLTTrAW. ᶜ οἶδεν knows GLTTrAW. ᵈ τῷ (read ἐκκλ. of the assembly) L. ᵉ — αὐτοῦ L. ᶠ φλὸξ T. ᵍ ἀγάπην, καὶ τὴν πίστιν καὶ τὴν διακονίαν GLTA; πίστιν καὶ τὴν ἀγάπην καὶ τὴν διακονίαν Tr. ʰ — τὴν L. ⁱ — σου T. ᵏ — καὶ (read thy last works) GLTTrAW. ˡ ἀλλὰ TrAW. ᵐ — ὀλίγα GLTTrAW. ⁿ ἀφεῖς thou lettest alone GLTTrAW. ᵒ + σου (read thy wife) GL[A]W. ᵖ τὴν 'Ιεζάβελ L; 'Ιεζάβελ GT; 'Ιεζαβὲλ TrAW. ᵠ ἡ λέγουσα she who calls GLTTrAW. ʳ αὐτὴν T. ˢ καὶ διδάσκει καὶ πλανᾷ τοὺς and she teaches and misleads GLTTrAW. ᵗ φαγεῖν εἰδωλόθυτα GLTTrAW. ᵛ καὶ οὐ θέλει μετανοῆσαι ἐκ τῆς πορνείας αὐτῆς and she wills not to repent of her fornication GLTTrAW. ʷ — ἐγὼ (read βάλλω I cast) GLTTrAW. ˣᵃ μετανοήσουσιν they shall repent TTrA. ʸᵃ αὐτῆς her GLTTrAW. ᶻᵃ ἐραυνῶν LTTr.

reins and hearts: and
I will give unto every
one of you according
to your works. 24 But
unto you I say, and
unto the rest in Thya-
tira, as many as have
not this doctrine, and
which have not known
the depths of Satan,
as they speak; I will
put upon you none
other burden. 25 But
that which ye have
already hold fast till
I come. 26 And he that
overcometh, and keep-
eth my works unto the
end, to him will I give
power over the na-
tions: 27 and he shall
rule them with a rod of
iron; as the vessels of
a potter shall they be
broken to shivers:
even as I received of
my Father. 28 And I
will give him the
morning star. 29 He
that hath an ear, let
him hear what the
Spirit saith unto the
churches.

III. And unto the
angel of the church in
Sardis write; These
things saith he that
hath the seven Spirits
of God, and the
seven stars; I know
thy works, that thou
hast a name that
thou livest, and art
dead. 2 Be watch-
ful, and strengthen
the things which re-
main, that are ready
to die: for I have not
found thy works per-
fect before God. 3 Re-
member therefore how
thou hast received and
heard, and hold fast,
and repent. If there-
fore thou shalt not
watch, I will come on
thee as a thief, and
thou shalt not know
what hour I will come
upon thee. 4 Thou
hast a few names even
in Sardis which have
not defiled their gar-
ments; and they shall
walk with me in
white: for they are
worthy. 5 He that
overcometh, the same
shall be clothed in
white raiment; and I
will not blot out his

νεφροὺς καὶ καρδίας· καὶ δώσω ὑμῖν ἑκάστῳ κατὰ τὰ
reins and hearts; and I will give to you each according to
ἔργα ὑμῶν. 24 ὑμῖν.δὲ λέγω [a]καὶ[‖] λοιποῖς τοῖς ἐν
[2]works [1]your. But to you I say, and to [the] rest who [are] in
Θυατείροις, ὅσοι οὐκ.ἔχουσιν τὴν.διδαχὴν.ταύτην, [b]καὶ[‖]
Thyatira, as many as have not this teaching, and
οἵτινες οὐκ.ἔγνωσαν τὰ [c]βάθη[‖] τοῦ σατανᾶ, ὡς λέγουσιν, Οὐ
who knew not the depths of Satan, as they say; [3]not
[d]βαλῶ[‖] ἐφ' ὑμᾶς ἄλλο βάρος· 25 πλὴν ὃ ἔχετε κρατή-
[1]I [2]will [4]cast upon you any other burden; but what ye have hold
σατε, [e]ἄχρις[‖] οὗ.ἂν.ἥξω. 26 καὶ ὁ νικῶν καὶ ὁ
fast till I shall come. And he that overcomes, and he that
τηρῶν ἄχρι τέλους τὰ.ἔργα.μου, δώσω αὐτῷ ἐξουσίαν
keeps until [the] end my works, I will give to him authority
ἐπὶ τῶν ἐθνῶν· 27 καὶ ποιμανεῖ αὐτοὺς ἐν ῥάβδῳ σι-
over the nations, and he shall shepherd them with [3]rod [1]an
δηρᾷ· ὡς τὰ σκεύη τὰ.κεραμικὰ συντρίβεται, ὡς κἀγὼ
[2]iron, as vessels of pottery are broken in pieces; as I also
εἴληφα παρὰ τοῦ.πατρός.μου· 28 καὶ δώσω αὐτῷ τὸν
have received from my Father; and I will give to him the
ἀστέρα τὸν πρωϊνόν. 29 ὁ ἔχων οὖς ἀκουσάτω τί τὸ
[2]star [1]morning. He that has an ear, let him hear what the
πνεῦμα λέγει ταῖς ἐκκλησίαις.
Spirit says to the assemblies.

3 Καὶ τῷ ἀγγέλῳ τῆς ἐν Σάρδεσιν ἐκκλησίας γράψον,
And to the angel of the [2]in [3]Sardis [1]assembly write:
Τάδε λέγει ὁ ἔχων τὰ [f] πνεύματα τοῦ θεοῦ καὶ τοὺς
These things says he who has the Spirits of God and the
ἑπτὰ ἀστέρας· Οἶδά σου τὰ ἔργα, ὅτι [g]τὸ[‖] ὄνομα ἔχεις ὅτι
seven stars. I know thy works, that [3]the [4]name [1]thou [2]hast that
ζῇς, καὶ νεκρὸς εἶ. 2 γίνου γρηγορῶν, καὶ [h]στήριξον[‖]
thou livest, and [2]dead [1]art. Be watchful, and strengthen
τὰ.λοιπὰ ἃ [i]μέλλει[‖] ἀποθανεῖν· οὐ.γὰρ.εὕρηκά
the things that remain, which are about to die, for I have not found
σου [j]τὰ[‖] ἔργα πεπληρωμένα ἐνώπιον τοῦ θεοῦ[k]. 3 μνημόνευε
thy works complete before God. Remember
[l]οὖν[‖] πῶς εἴληφας καὶ ἤκουσας, καὶ τήρει, καὶ
therefore how thou hast received and heard, and keep [it] and
μετανόησον· ἐὰν οὖν μὴ.γρηγορήσῃς, ἥξω [m]ἐπὶ σὲ[‖]
repent. If therefore thou shalt not watch I will come upon thee
ὡς κλέπτης, καὶ οὐ.μὴ [n]γνῷς[‖] ποίαν ὥραν ἥξω
as a thief, and in no wise shalt thou know what hour I shall come
ἐπὶ σέ. 4 [o] [p]ἔχεις ὀλίγα[‖] ὀνόματα [q]καὶ[‖] ἐν Σάρδεσιν, ἃ οὐκ
upon thee. Thou hast a few names also in Sardis which [2]not
ἐμόλυναν τὰ.ἱμάτια.αὐτῶν· καὶ περιπατήσουσιν μετ' ἐμοῦ ἐν
[1]defiled their garments, and they shall walk with me in
λευκοῖς, ὅτι ἄξιοί εἰσιν. 5 ὁ νικῶν, [r]οὗτος[‖] περι-
white, because worthy they are. He that overcomes, he shall
βαλεῖται ἐν ἱματίοις λευκοῖς· καὶ οὐ.μὴ ἐξαλείψω τὸ ὄνομα
be clothed in [2]garments [1]white; and in no wise will I blot out [2]name

---

[a] τοῖς to the (rest) GLTTrAW. [b] — καὶ GLTTrAW. [c] βαθέα GLTTrAW. [d] βάλλω I cast (not) LTTrAW. [e] ἄχρι LTTr. [f] + ἑπτὰ seven EGLTTrAW. [g] — τὸ (read a name) GLTTrAW. [h] στήρισον GLTTrAW. [i] ἔμελλον were about GLTTrAW. [j] — τὰ L[TrA]. [k] + μου (read my God) GLTTrAW. [l] [οὖν] A. [m] — ἐπὶ σὲ LTTrA. [n] γνώσῃ TTr. [o] + ἀλλὰ (ἀλλ' G) But LTTrAW. [p] ὀλίγα ἔχεις T. [q] — καὶ GLTTrAW. [r] οὕτως thus LTTr.

αὐτοῦ ἐκ τῆς βίβλου τῆς ζωῆς, καὶ [s]ἐξομολογήσομαι‖ τὸ ὄνομα
[1]his from the book of life, and will confess [2]name
αὐτοῦ ἐνώπιον τοῦ.πατρός.μου καὶ ἐνώπιον τῶν ἀγγέλων
[1]his before my Father and before [2]angels
αὐτοῦ. 6 ὁ ἔχων οὖς ἀκουσάτω τί τὸ πνεῦμα λέγει
[1]his. He that has an ear, let him hear what the Spirit says
ταῖς ἐκκλησίαις.
to the assemblies.

7 Καὶ τῷ ἀγγέλῳ τῆς ἐν [t]Φιλαδελφείᾳ‖ ἐκκλησίας γράψον,
And to the angel of the [2]in [3]Philadelphia [1]assembly write:
Τάδε λέγει [v]ὁ ἅγιος, ὁ ἀληθινός,‖ ὁ ἔχων τὴν [w]κλεῖδα‖
These things says the Holy, the True; he who has the key
[x]τοῦ‖ [y]Δαβίδ,‖ ὁ ἀνοίγων καὶ οὐδεὶς [z]κλείει,‖ [a]καὶ‖ [b]κλείει‖ καὶ
of David, who opens and no one shuts, and shuts and
οὐδεὶς [c]ἀνοίγει·‖ 8 Οἶδά σου τὰ ἔργα· ἰδού, δέδωκα ἐνώπιόν
no one opens. I know thy works. Lo, I have set before
σου θύραν [d]ἀνεῳγμένην,‖ [e]καὶ‖ οὐδεὶς δύναται κλεῖσαι αὐτήν·
thee [3]door [1]an [2]opened, and no one is able to shut it,
ὅτι μικρὰν ἔχεις δύναμιν, καὶ ἐτήρησάς μου τὸν λόγον,
because [3]a [4]little [1]thou [2]hast power, and didst keep my word,
καὶ οὐκ.ἠρνήσω τὸ.ὄνομά.μου. 9 ἰδού, [f]δίδωμι‖ ἐκ τῆς συνα-
and didst not deny my name. Lo, I give of the syna-
γωγῆς τοῦ σατανᾶ τῶν λεγόντων ἑαυτοὺς Ἰουδαίους εἶναι,
gogue of Satan those that declare themselves [3]Jews [1]to [2]be,
καὶ οὐκ.εἰσίν, ἀλλὰ ψεύδονται· ἰδού, ποιήσω αὐτοὺς ἵνα
and are not, but do lie; lo, I will cause them that
[g]ἥξωσιν‖ καὶ [h]προσκυνήσωσιν‖ ἐνώπιον τῶν.ποδῶν.σου,
they should come and should do homage before thy feet,
καὶ γνῶσιν ὅτι ἐγὼ ἠγάπησά σε. 10 ὅτι ἐτήρησας τὸν
and should know that I loved thee. Because thou didst keep the
λόγον τῆς.ὑπομονῆς.μου, κἀγώ σε τηρήσω ἐκ τῆς ὥρας τοῦ
word of my endurance, I also thee will keep out of the hour
πειρασμοῦ τῆς μελλούσης ἔρχεσθαι ἐπὶ τῆς οἰκουμένης
of trial which [is] about to come upon the [2]habitable [3]world
ὅλης, πειράσαι τοὺς κατοικοῦντας ἐπὶ τῆς γῆς. 11 [i]Ἰδού,‖
[1]whole, to try them that dwell upon the earth. Behold,
ἔρχομαι ταχύ· κράτει ὃ ἔχεις, ἵνα μηδεὶς λάβῃ τὸν
I come quickly: hold fast what thou hast, that no one take
στέφανόν σου. 12 ὁ νικῶν, ποιήσω αὐτὸν στύλον ἐν τῷ
[2]crown [1]thy. He that overcomes, I will make him a pillar in the
ναῷ τοῦ.θεοῦ.μου, καὶ ἔξω οὐ.μὴ ἐξέλθῃ ἔτι, καὶ γράψω
temple of my God, and out not at all shall he go more; and I will write
ἐπ' αὐτὸν τὸ ὄνομα τοῦ.θεοῦ.μου, καὶ τὸ ὄνομα τῆς πόλεως
upon him the name of my God, and the name of the city
τοῦ.θεοῦ.μου, τῆς καινῆς Ἱερουσαλήμ, [k]ἡ καταβαίνουσα‖
of my God, the new Jerusalem, which comes down
ἐκ τοῦ οὐρανοῦ ἀπὸ τοῦ.θεοῦ.μου, καὶ τὸ.ὄνομά.μου τὸ
out of heaven from my God, and my [2]name
καινόν. 13 ὁ ἔχων οὖς ἀκουσάτω τί τὸ πνεῦμα λέγει
[1]new. He that has an ear, let him hear what the Spirit says
ταῖς ἐκκλησίαις.
to the assemblies.

name out of the book
of life, but I will con-
fess his name before
my Father, and before
his angels. 6 He that
hath an ear, let him
hear what the Spi-
rit saith unto the
churches.

7 And to the angel
of the church in Phil-
adelphia write; These
things saith he that is
holy, he that is true,
he that hath the key
of David, he that
openeth, and no man
shutteth; and shut-
teth, and no man
openeth; 8 I know thy
works: behold, I have
set before thee an open
door, and no man can
shut it: for thou hast
a little strength, and
hast kept my word,
and hast not denied
my name. 9 Behold, I
will make them of the
synagogue of Satan,
which say they are
Jews, and are not, but
do lie; behold, I will
make them to come
and worship before
thy feet, and to know
that I have loved thee.
10 Because thou hast
kept the word of my
patience, I also will
keep thee from the
hour of temptation,
which shall come upon
all the world, to try
them that dwell upon
the earth. 11 Behold,
I come quickly: hold
that fast which thou
hast, that no man take
thy crown. 12 Him
that overcometh will
I make a pillar in the
temple of my God, and
he shall go no more
out: and I will write
upon him the name of
my God, and the name
of the city of my God,
which is new Jerusa-
lem, which cometh
down out of heaven
from my God: and *I
will write upon him*
my new name. 13 He
that hath an ear, let
him hear what the
Spirit saith unto the
churches.

---

[s] ὁμολογήσω GLTTrAW. [t] Φιλαδελφίᾳ T. [v] ὁ ἀληθινός, ὁ ἅγιος A. [w] κλεῖν GLTTrAW. [x] — τοῦ LTr[A.] [y] Δαυεὶδ LTTrA; Δαυὶδ GW. [z] κλείσει shall shut LTTrAW. [a] [καὶ] L. [b] κλείων shutting LTTr. [c] ἀνοίξει shall open TTrAW. [d] ἠνεῳγμένην T. [e] ἣν which GLTTrAW. [f] διδῶ I will give LTA; δίδω Tr. [g] ἥξουσιν they shall come LTTrA. [h] προσκυνήσουσιν shall do homage LTTrA. [i] — Ἰδού GLTTrAW. [k] ἡ καταβαίνει B.

14 And unto the angel of the church of
the Laodiceans write;
These things saith the
Amen, the faithful
and true witness, the
beginning of the creation of God; 15 I know
thy works, that thou
art neither cold nor
hot: I would thou wert
cold or hot. 16 So then
because thou art lukewarm, and neither cold
nor hot, I will spue
thee out of my mouth.
17 Because thou sayest, I am rich, and
increased with goods,
and have need of nothing; and knowest
not that thou art
wretched, and miserable, and poor, and
blind, and naked: 18 I
counsel thee to buy of
me gold tried in the
fire, that thou mayest
be rich; and white raiment, that thou mayest be clothed, and
that the shame of thy
nakedness do not appear; and anoint thine
eyes with eyesalve,
that thou mayest see.
19 As many as I love,
I rebuke and chasten:
be zealous therefore,
and repent. 20 Behold,
I stand at the door,
and knock: if any man
hear my voice, and
open the door, I will
come in to him, and
will sup with him, and
he with me. 21 To him
that overcometh will
I grant to sit with me
in my throne, even as
I also overcame, and
am set down with my
Father in his throne.
22 He that hath an ear,
let him hear what the
Spirit saith unto the
churches.

IV. After this I
looked, and, behold, a
door *was* opened in
heaven: and the first
voice which I heard
was as it were of a
trumpet talking with
me; which said, Come
up hither, and I
will shew thee things
which must be hereafter. 2 And imme-

14 Καὶ τῷ ἀγγέλῳ τῆς [l]ἐκκλησίας Λαοδικέων[‖] γράψον,
And to the angel of the assembly of [the] Laodiceans write:

Τάδε λέγει ὁ ἀμήν, ὁ μάρτυς ὁ πιστὸς καὶ ἀληθινός, ἡ
These things says the Amen, the witness faithful and true, the

ἀρχὴ τῆς κτίσεως τοῦ θεοῦ· 15 Οἶδά σου τὰ ἔργα, ὅτι οὔτε
beginning of the creation of God. I know thy works, that neither

ψυχρὸς εἶ, οὔτε ζεστός· ὄφελον ψυχρὸς [m]εἴης,[‖] ἢ ζεστός·
cold thou art, nor hot; I would cold thou wert or hot.

16 οὕτως ὅτι χλιαρὸς εἶ, καὶ οὔτε [n]ψυχρὸς οὔτε ζεστός,[‖]
Thus because lukewarm thou art, and neither cold nor hot,

μέλλω σε ἐμέσαι ἐκ τοῦ-στόματός-μου. 17 ὅτι λέγεις,
I am about [3]thee [1]to [2]spue out of my mouth. Because thou sayest,

[o]Ὅτι[‖] πλούσιός εἰμι καὶ πεπλούτηκα καὶ [p]οὐδενὸς[‖] χρείαν ἔχω,
Rich I am, and have grown rich and [3]of [4]nothing [2]need [1]have,

καὶ οὐκ-οἶδας ὅτι σὺ εἶ [q] ὁ ταλαίπωρος καὶ [r]ἐλεεινός,[‖] καὶ
and knowest not that thou art the wretched, and miserable, and

πτωχὸς καὶ τυφλὸς καὶ γυμνός· 18 συμβουλεύω σοι ἀγοράσαι
poor, and blind, and naked; I counsel thee to buy

παρ' ἐμοῦ χρυσίον πεπυρωμένον ἐκ πυρός, ἵνα πλουτήσῃς,
from me gold purified by fire, that thou mayest be rich;

καὶ ἱμάτια λευκά, ἵνα περιβάλῃ καὶ μὴ-φανερωθῇ
and [2]garments [1]white, that thou mayest be clothed, and may not be made manifest

ἡ αἰσχύνη τῆς-γυμνότητός-σου· καὶ [s]κολλούριον[‖] [t]ἔγχρισον[‖]
the shame of thy nakedness; and [4]eye-salve [1]anoint [2]thou [3]with

τοὺς-ὀφθαλμούς-σου, ἵνα βλέπῃς. 19 ἐγὼ ὅσους ἐὰν φιλῶ,
thine eyes, that thou mayest see. I as many as I love

ἐλέγχω καὶ παιδεύω· [v]ζήλωσον[‖] οὖν καὶ μετανόησον.
I rebuke and discipline; be thou zealous therefore and repent.

20 ἰδού, ἕστηκα ἐπὶ τὴν θύραν καὶ κρούω· ἐάν τις ἀκούσῃ
Behold, I stand at the door and knock; if anyone hear

τῆς-φωνῆς-μου, καὶ ἀνοίξῃ τὴν θύραν, [w] εἰσελεύσομαι πρὸς
my voice and open the door, I will come in to

αὐτόν, καὶ δειπνήσω μετ' αὐτοῦ, καὶ αὐτὸς μετ' ἐμοῦ. 21 ὁ
him, and will sup with him, and he with me. He that

νικῶν, δώσω αὐτῷ καθίσαι μετ' ἐμοῦ ἐν τῷ-θρόνῳ-μου, ὡς
overcomes, I will give to him to sit with me in my throne, as

κἀγὼ ἐνίκησα, καὶ ἐκάθισα μετὰ τοῦ-πατρός-μου ἐν τῷ θρόνῳ
I also overcame, and sat down with my Father in [2]throne

αὐτοῦ. 22 ὁ ἔχων οὖς ἀκουσάτω τί τὸ πνεῦμα λέγει
[1]his. He that has an ear, let him hear what the Spirit says

ταῖς ἐκκλησίαις.
to the assemblies.

4 Μετὰ ταῦτα [x]εἶδον,[‖] καὶ ἰδοὺ θύρα [y]ἠνεῳγμένη[‖] ἐν τῷ
After these things I saw, and behold a door opened in

οὐρανῷ, καὶ ἡ φωνὴ ἡ πρώτη ἣν ἤκουσα ὡς σάλπιγγος
heaven, and the [2]voice [1]first which I heard [was] as of a trumpet

λαλούσης μετ' ἐμοῦ, [z]λέγουσα,[‖] [a]Ἀνάβα[‖] ὧδε, καὶ δείξω
speaking with me, saying, Come up hither, and I will shew

σοι [b]ἃ[‖] δεῖ γενέσθαι μετὰ ταῦτα.[c] 2 [d]καὶ[‖] εὐθέως
to thee what things must take place after these things. And immediately

---

[l] ἐν Λαοδικείᾳ (Λαοδικίᾳ T) ἐκκλησίας assembly in Laodicea GLTTrAW. [m] ἦς GLTTrAW. [n] ζεστὸς οὔτε ψυχρός GTTrAW. [o] — ὅτι [A]W. [p] οὐδὲν [3]in [4]no [5]wise LTTrA. [q] + ὁ the GL[A]. [r] ἐλεινος A. [s] κολλύριον TTrA. [t] ἐγχρίσαι GW; ἐγχρῖσαι to anoint with LA; ἔγχρισαι anoint with TTr. [v] ζήλευε LTTrAW. [w] + καὶ (*read* I will both come in) T[A]W. [x] ἴδον T. [y] ἀνεῳγμένη GLW. [z] λέγων GLTTrAW. [a] Ἀνάβηθι L. [b] ὅσα whatsoever things L. [c] *Punctuate so as to read* Immediately after these things L. [d] — καὶ LTTrAW.

ἐγενόμην ἐν πνεύματι· καὶ ἰδού, θρόνος ἔκειτο ἐν τῷ
I became in [the] Spirit; and behold, a throne was set in the
οὐρανῷ, καὶ ἐπὶ [e]τοῦ θρόνου‖ καθήμενος· 3 καὶ ὁ καθή-
heaven, and upon the throne [one] sitting, and he who [was] sit-
μενος [f]ἦν· ὅμοιος ὁράσει λίθῳ ἰάσπιδι καὶ [g]σαρδίνῳ· καὶ
ting was like in appearance to a [2]stone [1]jasper and a sardius; and
ἶρις κυκλόθεν τοῦ θρόνου [h]ὅμοιος‖ ὁράσει σμαραγ-
a rainbow [was] around the throne like in appearance to an eme-
δίνῳ. 4 καὶ κυκλόθεν τοῦ θρόνου [i]θρόνοι‖ εἴκοσι [k]καὶ [l]τέσ-
rald. And around the throne [4]thrones [1]twenty [2]and
σαρες,‖ καὶ ἐπὶ τοὺς [m]θρόνους εἶδον τοὺς εἴκοσι καὶ τέσσαρας‖
[3]four, and on the thrones I saw twenty and four
πρεσβυτέρους καθημένους, περιβεβλημένους [n]ἐν‖ ἱματίοις
elders sitting, clothed in [2]garments
λευκοῖς· καὶ [o]ἔσχον ἐπὶ τὰς κεφαλὰς αὐτῶν στεφάνους [p]χρυσ-
[1]white; and they had on their heads [2]crowns [1]gold-
οῦς.‖ 5 καὶ ἐκ τοῦ θρόνου ἐκπορεύονται ἀστραπαὶ καὶ
en. And out of the throne go forth lightnings and
[q]βρονταὶ καὶ φωναί·‖ καὶ ἑπτὰ λαμπάδες πυρὸς καιόμεναι
thunders and voices; and seven lamps of fire burning
ἐνώπιον τοῦ θρόνου[r], [s]αἵ‖ [t]εἰσιν‖ [v]τὰ‖ ἑπτὰ πνεύματα τοῦ
before the throne, which are the seven Spirits
θεοῦ· 6 καὶ ἐνώπιον τοῦ θρόνου [w] θάλασσα ὑαλίνη, ὁμοία
of God; and before the throne a [2]sea [1]glass, like
κρυστάλλῳ. καὶ ἐν μέσῳ τοῦ θρόνου καὶ κύκλῳ τοῦ θρόνου
crystal. And in [the] midst of the throne and around the throne
[x]τέσσαρα‖ ζῶα γέμοντα ὀφθαλμῶν [y]ἔμπροσθεν‖ καὶ
four living creatures, full of eyes before and
ὄπισθεν. 7 καὶ τὸ ζῶον τὸ πρῶτον ὅμοιον λέοντι,
behind; and the [2]living [3]creature [1]first [was] like a lion,
καὶ τὸ δεύτερον ζῶον ὅμοιον μόσχῳ, καὶ τὸ τρίτον ζῶ-
and the second living creature like a calf, and the third living
ον [z]ἔχον‖ τὸ πρόσωπον [a]ὡς‖ [b]ἄνθρωπος,‖ καὶ τὸ τέταρτον
creature having the face as a man, and the fourth
ζῶον ὅμοιον ἀετῷ [c]πετωμένῳ.‖ 8 καὶ [d] [ea]τέσσαρα‖
living creature like [3]eagle [1]a [2]flying. And [the] four
ζῶα, ἓν [fa]καθ' ἑαυτό,‖ [ga]εἶχον‖ ἀνὰ πτέρυγας ἕξ,
living creatures, each for itself had respectively [2]wings [1]six;
κυκλόθεν καὶ ἔσωθεν [ha]γέμοντα‖ ὀφθαλμῶν, καὶ ἀνάπαυσιν οὐκ
around and within full of eyes; and [4]cessation [3]not
ἔχουσιν ἡμέρας καὶ νυκτός, [ia]λέγοντα,‖ Ἅγιος, ἅγιος, ἅγιος
[1]they [2]have day and night, saying, Holy, holy, holy,
κύριος ὁ θεὸς ὁ παντοκράτωρ, ὁ ἦν καὶ ὁ ὢν καὶ ὁ
Lord God Almighty, who was, and who is, and who [is]
ἐρχόμενος. 9 καὶ ὅταν δώσουσιν τὰ ζῶα δόξαν καὶ
to come. And when [4]shall [5]give [1]the [2]living [3]creatures glory and
τιμὴν καὶ εὐχαριστίαν τῷ καθημένῳ ἐπὶ [ka]τοῦ θρόνου,‖ τῷ
honour and thanksgiving to him who sits upon the throne, who

diately I was in the
Spirit: and, behold, a
throne was set in hea-
ven, and *one* sat on
the throne. 3 And he
that sat was to look
upon like a jasper and
a sardine stone: and
there was a rain-
bow round about the
throne, in sight like
unto an emerald.
4 And round about the
throne *were* four and
twenty seats: and up-
on the seats I saw four
and twenty elders sit-
ting, clothed in white
raiment; and they had
on their heads crowns
of gold. 5 And out of
the throne proceeded
lightnings and thun-
derings and voices:
and *there were* seven
lamps of fire burning
before the throne,
which are the seven
Spirits of God. 6 And
before the throne *there*
was a sea of glass like
unto crystal: and in
the midst of the
throne, and round a-
bout the throne, *were*
four beasts full of eyes
before and behind.
7 And the first beast
was like a lion, and
the second beast like a
calf, and the third
beast had a face as a
man, and the fourth
beast *was* like a flying
eagle. 8 And the four
beasts had each of
them six wings about
him; and *they were*
full of eyes within:
and they rest not day
and night, saying,
Holy, holy, holy, Lord
God Almighty, which
was, and is, and is to
come. 9 And when
those beasts give glory
and honour and thanks
to him that sat on the

---

[e] τὸν θρόνον LTTrAW. [f] — ἦν GLTTrAW. [g] σαρδίῳ GLTTrAW. [h] ὁμοία E. [i] θρόνους LT. [k] — καὶ GLTTrAW. [l] τέσσερας L; τέσσαρας T. [m] θρόνους τοὺς (— τοὺς GTT) εἴκοσι τέσσαρας GTTrW; εἴκοσι τέσσερας (τέσσαρας A) θρόνους LA. [n] — ἐν (*read* ἱματίοις with garments) L. [o] — ἔσχον GLTTrAW. [p] χρυσέους Tr. [q] φωναὶ καὶ βρονταί GLTTrAW. [r] + [αὐτοῦ] (*read* his throne) A. [s] ἅ LT. [t] ἐστιν L. [v] [τὰ] A. [w] + ὡς as GLTTrAW. [x] τέσσερα LTTr. [y] ἐνπροσθεν T. [z] ἔχων TTrA. [a] — ὡς G[A]W. [b] ἀνθρώπου of a man GLTTrAW. [c] πετομένῳ GLTTrAW. [d] + τὰ the GLTTrAW. [ea] τέσσερα LTTr. [fa] καθ' ἓν αὐτῶν (ἕκαστον αὐτῶν Tr) (*read* each of them) GLTA. [ga] ἔχον (ἔχων TTrA) having GLW. [ha] γέμουσιν are full GLTTrAW. [ia] λέγοντες GLTTrAW. [ka] τῷ θρόνῳ LTTrA.

throne, who liveth for
ever and ever, 10 the
four and twenty elders
fall down before him
that sat on the throne,
and worship him
that liveth for ever
and ever, and cast
their crowns before
the throne, saying,
11 Thou art worthy,
O Lord, to receive
glory and honour and
power: for thou hast
created all things, and
for thy pleasure they
are and were created.

V. And I saw in the
right hand of him that
sat on the throne a
book written within
and on the backside,
sealed with seven
seals. 2 And I saw a
strong angel proclaim-
ing with a loud voice,
Who is worthy to open
the book, and to loose
the seals thereof?
3 And no man in hea-
ven, nor in earth, nei-
ther under the earth,
was able to open the
book, neither to look
thereon. 4 And I wept
much, because no man
was found worthy to
open and to read the
book, neither to look
thereon. 5 And one of
the elders saith unto
me, Weep not: behold,
the Lion of the tribe
of Juda, the Root of
David, hath prevailed
to open the book, and
to loose the seven
seals thereof. 6 And
I beheld, and, lo, in
the midst of the
throne and of the
four beasts, and in the
midst of the elders,
stood a Lamb as it had
been slain, having
seven horns and seven
eyes, which are the
seven Spirits of God
sent forth into all the
earth. 7 And he came
and took the book out
of the right hand of

ζῶντι εἰς τοὺς αἰῶνας τῶν αἰώνων, 10 πεσοῦνται οἱ εἴκοσι [l]καὶ‖
lives to the ages of the ages, shall fall the twenty and
τέσσαρες πρεσβύτεροι ἐνώπιον τοῦ καθημένου ἐπὶ τοῦ
four elders before him who sits upon the
θρόνου, καὶ [m]προσκυνοῦσιν‖ τῷ ζῶντι εἰς τοὺς αἰῶνας τῶν
throne, and they worship him who lives to the ages of the
αἰώνων, καὶ [n]βάλλουσιν‖ τοὺς.στεφάνους.αὐτῶν ἐνώπιον τοῦ
ages; and cast their crowns before the
θρόνου, λέγοντες, 11 Ἄξιος εἶ, [o]κύριε,‖ λαβεῖν τὴν δόξαν
throne, saying, Worthy art thou, O Lord, to receive glory
καὶ τὴν τιμὴν καὶ [p]τὴν‖ δύναμιν· ὅτι σὺ ἔκτισας τὰ
and honour and power: because thou didst create
πάντα, καὶ διὰ τὸ.θέλημά.σου [q]εἰσὶν‖ καὶ.ἐκτίσθησαν.
all things, and for thy will they are, and were created.

5 Καὶ εἶδον ἐπὶ τὴν δεξιὰν τοῦ καθημένου ἐπὶ τοῦ
And I saw on the right hand of him who sits upon the
θρόνου βιβλίον γεγραμμένον ἔσωθεν καὶ ὄπισθεν, κατεσφρα-
throne a book, written within and on [the] back, having been
γισμένον σφραγῖσιν ἑπτά. 2 καὶ εἶδον ἄγγελον ἰσχυρὸν κη-
sealed with ²seals ¹seven. And I saw ³angel ¹a ²strong pro-
ρύσσοντα [r] φωνῇ μεγάλῃ, Τίς [s]ἐστιν‖ ἄξιος ἀνοῖξαι τὸ
claiming with a ²voice ¹loud, Who is worthy to open the
βιβλίον, καὶ λῦσαι τὰς σφραγῖδας αὐτοῦ; 3 καὶ οὐδεὶς [t]ἠδύ-
book, and to loose the seals of it? And no one was
νατο‖ ἐν τῷ οὐρανῷ, [v]οὐδὲ‖ ἐπὶ τῆς γῆς, [v]οὐδὲ‖ ὑποκάτω τῆς
able in the heaven, nor upon the earth, nor under the
γῆς, ἀνοῖξαι τὸ βιβλίον, [w]οὐδὲ‖ βλέπειν αὐτό. 4 καὶ [x]ἐγὼ‖
earth, to open the book, nor to look at it. And I
ἔκλαιον [y]πολλά,‖ ὅτι οὐδεὶς ἄξιος εὑρέθη ἀνοῖξαι [z]καὶ ἀνα-
was weeping much because no one worthy was found to open and to
γνῶναι‖ τὸ βιβλίον, οὔτε βλέπειν αὐτό. 5 καὶ εἷς ἐκ τῶν
read the book, nor to look at it. And one of the
πρεσβυτέρων λέγει μοι, Μὴ.κλαῖε· ἰδού, ἐνίκησεν ὁ λέων
elders says to me, Do not weep. Behold, ³overcame ¹the ²Lion
ὁ [a]ὢν‖ ἐκ τῆς φυλῆς Ἰούδα, ἡ ῥίζα [b]Δαβίδ,‖ ἀνοῖξαι
which is of the tribe of Juda, the root of David, [so as] to open
τὸ βιβλίον, καὶ [c]λῦσαι‖ τὰς ἑπτὰ σφραγῖδας αὐτοῦ. 6 καὶ
the book, and to loose the seven seals of it. And
εἶδον [d]καὶ‖ [e]ἰδού,‖ ἐν μέσῳ τοῦ θρόνου καὶ τῶν τεσσάρων
I saw, and behold, in [the] midst of the throne and of the four
ζώων, καὶ ἐν μέσῳ τῶν πρεσβυτέρων, ἀρνίον [f]ἑστη-
living creatures, and in [the] midst of the elders, a Lamb stand-
κὸς‖ ὡς ἐσφαγμένον, [g]ἔχον‖ κέρατα ἑπτὰ καὶ ὀφθαλμοὺς
ing as having been slain, having ²horns ¹seven and ²eyes
ἑπτά, [h]οἵ‖ εἰσιν τὰ [i]ἑπτὰ‖ [k]τοῦ θεοῦ πνεύματα‖ [la]τὰ‖ [ma]ἀπε-
¹seven, which are the seven ²of ³God ¹Spirits which have
σταλμένα‖ εἰς πᾶσαν τὴν γῆν. 7 καὶ ἦλθεν, καὶ εἴληφεν [na]τὸ
been sent into all the earth: and he came and took the

---

[l] — καὶ GLTTrAW. [m] προσκυνήσουσιν shall worship EGLTTrAW. [n] βαλοῦσιν shall cast EGLTTrAW. [o] ὁ κύριος καὶ ὁ θεὸς ἡμῶν O Lord and our God LTTrAW. [p] — τὴν L. [q] ἦσαν they were GLTTrAW. [r] + ἐν in (a loud voice) GLTTrAW. [s] — ἐστιν (*read* [is]) LTTrAW. [t] ἐδύνατο T. [v] οὔτε T. [w] οὔτε LTTr. [x] — ἐγὼ (*read* ἔκλαιον I was weeping) T[Tr]. [y] πολύ LTTrAW. [z] — καὶ ἀναγνῶναι GLTTrAW. [a] — ὢν (*read* [is]) GLTTrAW. [b] Δαυείδ LTTrA; Δαυῒδ GW. [c] — λῦσαι GLTTrAW. [d] — καὶ GTTrAW. [e] — ἰδού GLTTrAW. [f] ἑστηκὼς TTr. [g] ἔχων TTrA. [h] ἃ W. [i] — ἑπτὰ L. [k] πνεύματα τοῦ θεοῦ GLTTrA. [la] — τὰ (*read* ἀπεστ. having been sent) LTTrA. [ma] ἀπεσταλμένοι LTr; ἀποστελλόμενα [are] being sent W. [na] — τὸ βιβλίον (*read* [it]) LTTrA.

βιβλίον‖ ἐκ τῆς δεξιᾶς τοῦ καθημένου επὶ τοῦ θρόνου.
book out of the right hand of him who sits on the throne.
8 καὶ ὅτε ἔλαβεν τὸ βιβλίον τὰ [o]τέσσαρα‖ ζῶα καὶ οἱ
And when he took the book the four living creatures and the
[p]εἰκοσιτέσσαρες‖ πρεσβύτεροι [q]ἔπεσον‖ ἐνώπιον τοῦ ἀρνίου,
four-and-twenty elders fell before the Lamb,
ἔχοντες ἕκαστος [r]κιθάρας‖ καὶ φιάλας [s]χρυσᾶς‖ γεμούσας θυ-
having each harps and [2]bowls [1]golden full of
μιαμάτων, αἵ εἰσιν αἱ προσευχαὶ τῶν ἁγίων· 9 καὶ ᾄδουσιν
incenses, which are the prayers of the saints. And they sing
ᾠδὴν καινήν, λέγοντες, Ἄξιος εἶ λαβεῖν τὸ βιβλίον, καὶ
a [2]song [1]new, saying, Worthy art thou to take the book, and
ἀνοῖξαι τὰς.σφραγῖδας.αὐτοῦ· ὅτι ἐσφάγης καὶ ἠγόρασας
to open its seals; because thou wast slain, and didst purchase
τῷ θεῷ [t]ἡμᾶς‖ ἐν τῷ.αἵματί.σου, ἐκ πάσης φυλῆς καὶ γλώσ-
[2]to [3]God [1]us by thy blood, out of every tribe and tongue
σης καὶ λαοῦ καὶ ἔθνους, 10 καὶ ἐποίησας [v]ἡμᾶς‖ [w]τῷ.θεῷ.ἡμῶν‖
and people and nation, and didst make us to our God
[x]βασιλεῖς‖ καὶ ἱερεῖς· καὶ [y]βασιλεύσομεν‖ ἐπὶ τῆς γῆς. 11 Καὶ
kings and priests; and we shall reign over the earth. And
εἶδον, καὶ ἤκουσα [z] φωνὴν ἀγγέλων πολλῶν [a]κυκλόθεν‖ τοῦ
I saw, and I heard [the] voice of [2]angels [1]many around the
θρόνου καὶ τῶν ζώων καὶ τῶν πρεσβυτέρων·[b] καὶ χιλι-
throne and of the living creatures and of the elders; and thou-
άδες χιλιάδων, 12 λέγοντες φωνῇ μεγάλῃ, [c]Ἄξιόν‖ ἐστιν
sands of thousands; saying with a [2]voice [1]loud, Worthy is
τὸ ἀρνίον τὸ ἐσφαγμένον λαβεῖν τὴν δύναμιν καὶ [d] πλοῦτον
the Lamb that has been slain to receive power, and riches,
καὶ σοφίαν καὶ ἰσχὺν καὶ τιμὴν καὶ δόξαν καὶ εὐλογίαν.
and wisdom, and strength, and honour, and glory, and blessing.
13 Καὶ πᾶν κτίσμα ὅ [e]ἐστιν‖ ἐν τῷ οὐρανῷ, καὶ [f]ἐν τῇ γῇ,‖
And every creature which is in the heaven and in the earth
καὶ ὑποκάτω τῆς γῆς, καὶ ἐπὶ τῆς θαλάσσης [g]ἅ‖ [h]ἐστιν,‖
and under the earth, and [4]on [5]the [6]sea [1]those [2]that [3]are,
καὶ τὰ ἐν αὐτοῖς [i]πάντα,‖ [k]ἤκουσα [l]λέγοντας,‖ Τῷ
and [2]the [3]things [4]in [5]them [1]all, heard I saying, To him who
καθημένῳ ἐπὶ [m]τοῦ θρόνου‖ καὶ τῷ ἀρνίῳ ἡ εὐλογία καὶ ἡ
sits on the throne, and to the Lamb, Blessing, and
τιμὴ καὶ ἡ δόξα καὶ τὸ κράτος εἰς τοὺς αἰῶνας τῶν αἰώνων.
honour, and glory, and might, to the ages of the ages.
14 Καὶ τὰ [n]τέσσαρα‖ ζῶα ἔλεγον, [oa]Ἀμήν· καὶ οἱ [pa]εἰκοσι-
And the four living creatures said, Amen; and the four-and-
τέσσαρες‖ πρεσβύτεροι ἔπεσαν, καὶ προσεκύνησαν
twenty elders fell down and worshipped [him who]
[qa]ζῶντι εἰς τοὺς αἰῶνας τῶν αἰώνων.‖
lives to the ages of the ages.

6 Καὶ [ra]εἶδον‖ ὅτε ἤνοιξεν τὸ ἀρνίον μίαν ἐκ τῶν [sa] σφρα-
And I saw when [3]opened [1]the [2]Lamb one of the seals,

him that sat upon the throne. 8 And when he had taken the book, the four beasts and four *and* twenty elders fell down before the Lamb, having every one of them harps, and golden vials full of odours, which are the prayers of saints. 9 And they sung a new song, saying, Thou art worthy to take the book, and to open the seals thereof: for thou wast slain, and hast redeemed us to God by thy blood out of every kindred, and tongue, and people, and nation; 10 and hast made us unto our God kings and priests: and we shall reign on the earth. 11 And I beheld, and I heard the voice of many angels round about the throne and the beasts and the elders: and the number of them was ten thousand times ten thousand, and thousands of thousands; 12 saying with a loud voice, Worthy is the Lamb that was slain to receive power, and riches, and wisdom, and strength, and honour, and glory, and blessing. 13 And every creature which is in heaven, and on the earth, and under the earth, and such as are in the sea, and all that are in them, heard I saying, Blessing, and honour, and glory, and power, *be* unto him that sitteth upon the throne, and unto the Lamb for ever and ever. 14 And the four beasts said, Amen. And the four *and* twenty elders fell down and worshipped him that liveth for ever and ever.

VI. And I saw when the Lamb opened one

---

[o] τέσσερα LTTr. [p] εἴκοσι τέσσαρες LTA. [q] ἔπεσαν LTTrAW. [r] κιθάραν a harp LTTrAW. [s] χρυσέας Tr. [t] — ἡμᾶς LTAW. [v] αὐτοὺς them GLTTrAW. [w] — τῷ θεῷ ἡμῶν A. [x] βασιλείαν a kingdom LTTrA. [y] βασιλευουσιν they reign LTrAW; βασιλεύσουσιν they shall reign GT. [z] + ὡς as TTr[A]. [a] κύκλῳ GLTTrAW. [b] + καὶ ἦν ὁ ἀριθμὸς αὐτῶν μυριάδες μυριάδων and the number of them was myriads of myriads EGLTTrAW. [c] Ἄξιός T. [d] + τὸν W. [e] — ἐστιν (*read* [is]) LTTrAW. [f] ἐπὶ τῆς γῆς on the earth GLTTrAW. [g] — ἅ LTTrA. [h] — ἐστιν TTr. [i] , πάντας (*read* I heard all) W. [k] + καὶ also T. [l] λέγοντα L. [m] τῷ θρόνῳ LTA. [n] τέσσερα LTTr. [oa] + τὸ W. [pa] — εἰκοσιτέσσαρες GLTTrAW. [qa] — ζῶντι *to end of verse* GLTTrAW. [ra] ἴδον T. [sa] + ἑπτὰ seven GLTTrAW.

of the seals, and I heard, as it were the noise of thunder, one of the four beasts saying, Come and see. 2 And I saw, and behold a white horse: and he that sat on him had a bow; and a crown was given unto him: and he went forth conquering, and to conquer.

3 And when he had opened the second seal, I heard the second beast say, Come and see. 4 And there went out another horse *that was* red: and *power* was given to him that sat thereon to take peace from the earth, and that they should kill one another: and there was given unto him a great sword.

5 And when he had opened the third seal, I heard the third beast say, Come and see. And I beheld, and lo a black horse; and he that sat on him had a pair of balances in his hand. 6 And I heard a voice in the midst of the four beasts say, A measure of wheat for a penny, and three measures of barley for a penny; and *see* thou hurt not the oil and the wine.

7 And when he had opened the fourth seal, I heard the voice of the fourth beast say, Come and see. 8 And I looked, and behold a pale horse: and his name that sat on him was Death, and Hell followed with him. And power was given unto them over the fourth part of the earth, to kill with sword, and with hunger, and with death, and with the beasts of the earth.

9 And when he had opened the fifth seal,

γίδων. καὶ ἤκουσα ἑνὸς ἐκ τῶν τεσσάρων ζώων λέγον-
and I heard [6]one [7]of [8]the [9]four [10]living [11]creatures [12]say-
τος, ὡς [t]φωνῆς‖ βροντῆς, Ἔρχου [v]καὶ βλέπε.‖ 2 Καὶ [w]εἶδον,‖
ing, [1]as [2]a [3]voice [4]of [5]thunder, Come and see. And I saw,
καὶ ἰδού, ἵππος λευκός, καὶ ὁ καθήμενος ἐπ' [x]αὐτῷ‖ ἔχων
and behold, a [2]horse [1]white, and he sitting on it having
τόξον· καὶ ἐδόθη αὐτῷ στέφανος, καὶ ἐξῆλθεν νικῶν, καὶ
a bow; and was given to him a crown, and he went forth overcoming and
ἵνα νικήσῃ.
that he might overcome.

3 Καὶ ὅτε ἤνοιξεν τὴν [y]δευτέραν σφραγῖδα‖ ἤκουσα τοῦ
And when he opened the second seal I heard the
δευτέρου ζώου λέγοντος, Ἔρχου [z]καὶ βλέπε.‖ 4 Καὶ
second living creature saying, Come and see. And
ἐξῆλθεν ἄλλος ἵππος πυῤῥός· καὶ τῷ καθημένῳ ἐπ' [x]αὐτῷ‖
went forth another horse red; and to him sitting on it
ἐδόθη [a]αὐτῷ‖ λαβεῖν τὴν εἰρήνην [b]ἀπὸ‖ τῆς γῆς, καὶ ἵνα
was given to him to take peace from the earth, and that
ἀλλήλους [c]σφάξωσιν·‖ καὶ ἐδόθη αὐτῷ μάχαιρα μεγάλη.
one another they should slay; and was given to him a [2]sword [1]great.

5 Καὶ ὅτε ἤνοιξεν τὴν [d]τρίτην σφραγῖδα‖ ἤκουσα τοῦ τρίτου
And when he opened the third seal I heard the third
ζώου λέγοντος, Ἔρχου [v]καὶ βλέπε.‖ Καὶ [w]εἶδον,‖ καὶ
living creature saying, Come and see. And I saw, and
ἰδού, ἵππος μέλας, καὶ ὁ καθήμενος ἐπ' [x]αὐτῷ‖ ἔχων ζυγὸν
behold, a [2]horse [1]black, and he sitting on it having a balance
ἐν τῇ χειρὶ αὐτοῦ. 6 καὶ ἤκουσα [e] φωνὴν ἐν μέσῳ τῶν
in his hand. And I heard a voice in [the] midst of the
τεσσάρων ζώων λέγουσαν, Χοῖνιξ σίτου δηναρίου,
four living creatures, saying, A chœnix of wheat for a denarius,
καὶ τρεῖς χοίνικες [f]κριθῆς‖ δηναρίου· καὶ τὸ ἔλαιον καὶ τὸν
and three chœnixes of barley for a denarius: and the oil and the
οἶνον μὴ ἀδικήσῃς.
wine thou mayest not injure.

7 Καὶ ὅτε ἤνοιξεν τὴν σφραγῖδα τὴν τετάρτην, ἤκουσα
And when he opened the [2]seal [1]fourth, I heard [the]
[g]φωνὴν‖ τοῦ τετάρτου ζώου [h]λέγουσαν,‖ Ἔρχου [v]καὶ
voice of the fourth living creature saying, Come and
βλέπε.‖ 8 Καὶ [w]εἶδον,‖ καὶ ἰδού, ἵππος χλωρός, καὶ ὁ καθήμενος
see. And I saw, and behold, a [2]horse [1]pale, and he sitting
ἐπάνω αὐτοῦ, ὄνομα αὐτῷ [i]ὁ‖ Θάνατος, καὶ ὁ ᾅδης [k]ἀκο-
on it, [2]name [1]his [was] Death, and hades fol-
λουθεῖ‖ μετ' αὐτοῦ· καὶ ἐδόθη [l]αὐτοῖς‖ ἐξουσία [m]ἀποκτεῖναι
lows with him; and was given to them authority to kill
ἐπὶ τὸ τέταρτον τῆς γῆς‖ ἐν ῥομφαίᾳ καὶ ἐν λιμῷ καὶ ἐν
over the fourth of the earth with sword and with famine and with
θανάτῳ, καὶ ὑπὸ τῶν θηρίων τῆς γῆς.
death, and by the beasts of the earth.

9 Καὶ ὅτε ἤνοιξεν τὴν πέμπτην σφραγῖδα [w]εἶδον‖ ὑποκάτω
And when he opened the fifth seal I saw under

---

[t] φωνὴ (*read without the numerals*) GLTTrAW. [v] καὶ ἴδε and behold GW; — καὶ βλέπε LTTrA. [w] ἴδον T. [x] αὐτὸν GLTTrAW. [y] σφραγῖδα τὴν δευτέραν GLTTrAW. [z] — καὶ βλέπε GLTTrAW. [a] [αὐτῷ] L. [b] ἐκ GLTTrAW. [c] σφάξουσιν they shall slay LTTrA. [d] σφραγῖδα τὴν τρίτην GLTTrAW. [e] + ὡς as LTTrA. [f] κριθῶν LTTrAW. [g] — φωνὴν (*read* I heard the fourth) G[Tr]W. [h] λέγοντος (*connect* λέγουσαν *with* φωνὴν; λέγοντος *with* ζώου) GLTTrAW. [i] — ὁ T[A]. [k] ἠκολούθει followed GLTTrAW. [l] αὐτῷ to him G. [m] ἐπὶ τὸ τέταρτον τῆς γῆς, ἀποκτεῖναι GLTTrAW.

τοῦ θυσιαστηρίου·τὰς ψυχὰς τῶν ἐσφαγμένων διὰ τὸν
the altar the souls of those having been slain because of the
λόγον τοῦ θεοῦ, καὶ [o]διὰ‖ τὴν μαρτυρίαν ἣν εἶχον, 10 καὶ
word of God, and because of the testimony which they held; and
[p]ἔκραζον‖ φωνῇ μεγάλῃ, λέγοντες, ‖Ἕως πότε, ὁ δεσ-
they were crying with a [2]voice [1]loud, saying, Until when, O Mas-
πότης ὁ ἅγιος καὶ [q]ὁ‖ ἀληθινός, οὐ.κρίνεις καὶ ἐκδικεῖς
ter, the holy and the true, dost thou not judge and avenge
τὸ.αἷμα.ἡμῶν [r]ἀπὸ‖ τῶν κατοικούντων ἐπὶ τῆς γῆς; 11 Καὶ
our blood on those who dwell on the earth? And
[s]ἐδόθησαν‖ [t] [v]ἑκάστοις‖ [w]στολαὶ λευκαί,‖ καὶ ἐῤῥέθη αὐτοῖς ἵνα
were given to each [2]robes [1]white; and it was said to them that
ἀναπαύσωνται [x]ἔτι χρόνον‖ [y]μικρόν,‖ ἕως [z]οὗ‖ [a]πληρώσονται‖
they should rest yet a [2]time [1]little, until shall be fulfilled
καὶ οἱ.σύνδουλοι.αὐτῶν καὶ οἱ.ἀδελφοὶ.αὐτῶν, οἱ μέλλοντες
both their fellow-bondmen and their brethren, those being about
[b]ἀποκτείνεσθαι‖ ὡς καὶ αὐτοί.
to be killed as also they.

12 Καὶ [c]εἶδον‖ ὅτε ἤνοιξεν τὴν σφραγῖδα τὴν ἕκτην· καὶ
And I saw when he opened the [2]seal [1]sixth, and
[d]ἰδού,‖ σεισμὸς μέγας ἐγένετο, καὶ ὁ ἥλιος [e]ἐγένετο μέλας‖
behold, [5]earthquake [3]a [4]great [1]there [2]was, and the sun became black
ὡς σάκκος τρίχινος, καὶ ἡ σελήνη [f] ἐγένετο ὡς αἷμα, 13 καὶ
as [2]sackcloth [1]hair, and the moon became as blood, and
οἱ ἀστέρες τοῦ οὐρανοῦ ἔπεσαν εἰς τὴν γῆν, ὡς συκῆ [g]βάλλει‖
the stars of the heaven fell unto the earth, as a fig-tree casts
τοὺς.ὀλύνθους.αὐτῆς, ὑπὸ [h]μεγάλου ἀνέμου‖ σειομένη· 14 καὶ
its untimely figs, by a great wind being shaken. And
[i] οὐρανὸς ἀπεχωρίσθη ὡς βιβλίον [k]εἱλισσόμενον,‖ καὶ πᾶν
heaven departed as a book being rolled up, and every
ὄρος καὶ νῆσος ἐκ τῶν.τόπων.αὐτῶν ἐκινήθησαν· 15 καὶ
mountain and island out of their places were moved. And
οἱ βασιλεῖς τῆς γῆς, καὶ οἱ μεγιστᾶνες, καὶ οἱ [l]πλούσιοι, καὶ
the kings of the earth, and the great, and the rich, and
οἱ χιλίαρχοι,‖ καὶ οἱ [m]δυνατοί,‖ καὶ πᾶς δοῦλος καὶ [n]πᾶς‖
the chief captains, and the powerful, and every bondman, and every
ἐλεύθερος ἔκρυψαν ἑαυτοὺς εἰς τὰ σπήλαια καὶ εἰς τὰς
free [man] hid themselves in the caves and in the
πέτρας τῶν ὀρέων, 16 καὶ λέγουσιν τοῖς ὄρεσιν καὶ ταῖς
rocks of the mountains; and they say to the mountains and to the
πέτραις, [oa]Πέσετε‖ ἐφ᾽ ἡμᾶς, καὶ κρύψατε ἡμᾶς ἀπὸ προσ-
rocks, Fall on us, and hide us from [the] face
ώπου τοῦ καθημένου ἐπὶ [pa]τοῦ θρόνου,‖ καὶ ἀπὸ τῆς ὀργῆς
of him who sits on the throne, and from the wrath
τοῦ ἀρνίου· 17 ὅτι ἦλθεν ἡ ἡμέρα ἡ μεγάλη τῆς ὀργῆς
of the Lamb; because is come the [2]day [1]great [5]wrath
[qa]αὐτοῦ,‖ καὶ τίς δύναται σταθῆναι;
[3]of [4]his, and who is able to stand?

I saw under the altar the souls of them that were slain for the word of God, and for the testimony which they held: 10 and they cried with a loud voice, saying, How long, O Lord, holy and true, dost thou not judge and avenge our blood on them that dwell on the earth? 11 And white robes were given unto every one of them; and it was said unto them, that they should rest yet for a little season, until their fellowservants also and their brethren, that should be killed as they *were*, should be fulfilled.

12 And I beheld when he had opened the sixth seal, and, lo, there was a great earthquake; and the sun became black as sackcloth of hair, and the moon became as blood; 13 and the stars of heaven fell unto the earth, even as a fig tree casteth her untimely figs, when she is shaken of a mighty wind. 14 And the heaven departed as a scroll when it is rolled together; and every mountain and island were moved out of their places. 15 And the kings of the earth, and the great men, and the rich men, and the chief captains, and the mighty men, and every bondman, and every free man, hid themselves in the dens and in the rocks of the mountains; 16 and said to the mountains and rocks, Fall on us, and hide us from the face of him that sitteth on the throne, and from the wrath of the Lamb: 17 for the great day of his wrath is come; and who shall be able to stand?

---

[o] — διὰ L[A]. [p] ἔκραξαν they cried GLTTrAW. [q] — ὁ GLTTrAW. [r] ἐκ from LTTrAW. [s] ἐδόθη was given GLTTrAW. [t] + αὐτοῖς to them GLTTrAW. [v] — ἑκάστοις GW; ἑκάστῳ each LTTr[A]. [w] στολὴ λευκή a white robe GLTTrAW. [x] χρόνον ἔτι L. [y] — μικρόν G. [z] — οὗ GLTTrAW. [a] πληρωθῶσιν should be fulfilled LW; πληρώσωσιν should fulfil [it] GTTrA. [b] ἀποκτέννεσθαι GLTTrA. [c] ἴδον T. [d] — ἰδού GLTTrAW. [e] μέλας ἐγένετο GT. [f] + ὅλη whole (moon) GLTTrAW. [g] βάλλουσα casting T. [h] ἀνέμου μεγάλου GLTTrAW. [i] + ὁ the GLTTrAW. [k] ἑλισσόμενον LTTrAW. [l] χιλίαρχοι, καὶ οἱ πλούσιοι GLTTrAW. [m] ἰσχυροὶ strong GLTTrAW. [n] — πᾶς LTTrAW. [oa] Πέσατε LAW. [pa] τῷ θρόνῳ TA. [qa] αὐτῶν [3]of [4]their TTr.

7 [r]Καὶ‖ μετὰ [s]ταῦτα‖ [t]εἶδον‖ τέσσαρας ἀγγέλους ἑστῶτας
And after these things I saw four angels standing
ἐπὶ τὰς τέσσαρας γωνίας τῆς γῆς, κρατοῦντας τοὺς τέσσαρας
upon the four corners of the earth, holding the four
ἀνέμους τῆς γῆς, ἵνα μὴ πνέῃ ἄνεμος ἐπὶ τῆς γῆς, μήτε
winds of the earth, that no [2]might [3]blow [1]wind on the earth, nor
ἐπὶ τῆς θαλάσσης, μήτε ἐπὶ [v]πᾶν‖ δένδρον. 2 Καὶ [t]εἶδον‖ ἄλ-
on the sea, nor upon any (*lit.* every) tree. And I saw an-
λον ἄγγελον [w]ἀναβάντα‖ ἀπὸ [x]ἀνατολῆς‖ ἡλίου, ἔχοντα
other angel having ascended from [the] rising of [the] sun, having
σφραγῖδα θεοῦ ζῶντος· καὶ ἔκραξεν φωνῇ μεγάλῃ
[the] seal of [3]God [[1]the] [2]living; and he cried with a [2]voice [1]loud
τοῖς τέσσαρσιν ἀγγέλοις, οἷς ἐδόθη αὐτοῖς ἀδικῆσαι τὴν
to the four angels to whom it was given to them to injure the
γῆν καὶ τὴν θάλασσαν, 3 λέγων, Μὴ ἀδικήσητε τὴν γῆν,
earth and the sea, saying, Injure not the earth,
μήτε τὴν θάλασσαν, μήτε τὰ δένδρα, [y]ἄχρις‖ [z]οὗ‖ [a]σφραγίζω-
nor the sea, nor the trees, until we
μεν‖ τοὺς δούλους τοῦ θεοῦ ἡμῶν ἐπὶ τῶν μετώπων αὐτῶν.
seal the bondmen of our God on their foreheads.
4 Καὶ ἤκουσα τὸν ἀριθμὸν τῶν ἐσφραγισμένων· [b]ρμδ'‖ χιλιάδες,
And I heard the number of the sealed, 144 thousand,
ἐσφραγισμένοι ἐκ πάσης φυλῆς υἱῶν Ἰσραήλ· 5 ἐκ
sealed out of every tribe of [the] sons of Israel; out of [the]
φυλῆς Ἰούδα, [c]ιβ'‖ χιλιάδες ἐσφραγισμένοι· ἐκ φυλῆς
tribe of Judah, 12 thousand sealed; out of [the] tribe
Ῥουβήν, [c]ιβ'‖ χιλιάδες [d]ἐσφραγισμένοι·‖ ἐκ φυλῆς Γάδ,
of Reuben, 12 thousand sealed; out of [the] tribe of Gad,
[c]ιβ'‖ χιλιάδες [d]ἐσφραγισμένοι·‖ 6 ἐκ φυλῆς Ἀσήρ, [c]ιβ'‖
12 thousand sealed; out of [the] tribe of Aser, 12
χιλιάδες [d]ἐσφραγισμένοι·‖ ἐκ φυλῆς [e]Νεφθαλείμ,‖ [c]ιβ'‖
thousand sealed; out of [the] tribe of Nepthalim, 12
χιλιάδες [d]ἐσφραγισμένοι·‖ ἐκ φυλῆς [f]Μανασσῆ,‖ [c]ιβ'‖
thousand sealed; out of [the] tribe of Manasses, 12
χιλιάδες [d]ἐσφραγισμένοι‖ 7 ἐκ φυλῆς Συμεών, [c]ιβ'‖ χιλι-
thousand sealed; out of [the] tribe of Simeon, 12 thou-
άδες [d]ἐσφραγισμένοι·‖ ἐκ φυλῆς [g]Λευΐ,‖ [c]ιβ'‖ χιλιάδες
sand sealed; out of [the] tribe of Levi, 12 thousand
[d]ἐσφραγισμένοι·‖ ἐκ φυλῆς [h]Ἰσαχάρ,‖ [c]ιβ'‖ χιλιάδες [d]ἐσφρα-
sealed; out of [the] tribe of Issachar, 12 thousand seal-
γισμένοι·‖ 8 ἐκ φυλῆς Ζαβουλών, [c]ιβ'‖ χιλιάδες [d]ἐσφρα-
ed; out of [the] tribe of Zabulon, 12 thousand seal-
γισμένοι·‖ ἐκ φυλῆς Ἰωσήφ, [c]ιβ'‖ χιλιάδες [d]ἐσφραγισμένοι·‖
ed; out of [the] tribe of Joseph, 12 thousand sealed;
ἐκ φυλῆς [i]Βενιαμίν,‖ [c]ιβ'‖ χιλιάδες ἐσφραγισμένοι.
out of [the] tribe of Benjamin, 12 thousand sealed.

9 Μετὰ ταῦτα [t]εἶδον,‖ [k]καὶ‖ [l]ἰδού,‖ [m]ὄχλος πολύς,‖ ὃν
After these things I saw, and behold, a [2]crowd [1]great, which
ἀριθμῆσαι αὐτὸν οὐδεὶς [n]ἠδύνατο,‖ ἐκ παντὸς ἔθνους καὶ
[5]to [6]number [7]it [1]no [2]one [3]was [4]able, out of every nation and

VII. And after these things I saw four angels standing on the four corners of the earth, holding the four winds of the earth, that the wind should not blow on the earth, nor on the sea, nor on any tree. 2 And I saw another angel ascending from the east, having the seal of the living God: and he cried with a loud voice to the four angels, to whom it was given to hurt the earth and the sea, 3 saying, Hurt not the earth, neither the sea, nor the trees, till we have sealed the servants of our God in their foreheads. 4 And I heard the number of them which were sealed: *and there were* sealed an hundred *and* forty *and* four thousand of all the tribes of the children of Israel. 5 Of the tribe of Juda *were* sealed twelve thousand. Of the tribe of Reuben *were* sealed twelve thousand. Of the tribe of Gad *were* sealed twelve thousand. 6 Of the tribe of Aser *were* sealed twelve thousand. Of the tribe of Nepthalim *were* sealed twelve thousand. Of the tribe of Manasses *were* sealed twelve thousand. 7 Of the tribe of Simeon *were* sealed twelve thousand. Of the tribe of Levi *were* sealed twelve thousand. Of the tribe of Issachar *were* sealed twelve thousand. 8 Of the tribe of Zabulon *were* sealed twelve thousand. Of the tribe of Joseph *were* sealed twelve thousand. Of the tribe of Benjamin *were* sealed twelve thousand.

9 After this I beheld, and, lo, a great multitude, which no man could number, of all nations, and

---

[r] — καὶ L[TrA]. [s] τοῦτο this LTTrAW. [t] ἴδον T. [v] τι any LTr[A]W. [w] ἀναβαίνοντα ascending GLTTrAW. [x] ἀνατολῶν L. [y] ἄχρι LTA. [z] — οὗ LTTrA. [a] σφραγίσωμεν we may have sealed EGLTTrAW. [b] ἑκατὸν τεσσεράκοντα (τεσσαρ- GW) τέσσαρες a hundred and forty-four GLTTrAW. [c] δώδεκα twelve LTTrAW. [d] — ἐσφραγισμένοι LTTrAW. [e] Νεφθαλὶμ A. [f] Μαννασσῆ Tr. [g] Λευεὶ TTr. [h] Ἰσασχὰρ E; Ἰσσαχὰρ TrA; Ἰσσάχαρ T. [i] Βενιαμεὶν LTTr. [k] — καὶ L. [l] — ἰδού L. [m] ὄχλον πολὺν E. [n] ἐδύνατο LTTrAW.

φυλῶν καὶ λαῶν καὶ γλωσσῶν, [o]ἑστῶτες ἐνώπιον τοῦ θρόνου
tribes, and peoples, and tongues. standing before the throne
καὶ ἐνώπιον τοῦ ἀρνίου, [p]περιβεβλημένοι‖ στολὰς λευκάς, καὶ
and before the Lamb, clothed with [2]robes [1]white, and
[q]φοίνικες‖ ἐν ταῖς.χερσὶν.αὐτῶν· 10 καὶ [r]κράζοντες‖ φωνῇ
palms in their hands; and crying with a [2]voice
μεγάλῃ, λέγοντες, Ἡ σωτηρία [s]τῷ καθημένῳ ἐπὶ τοῦ
[1]loud, saying, Salvation to him who sits on the
θρόνου τοῦ.θεοῦ.ἡμῶν,‖ καὶ τῷ ἀρνίῳ. 11 Καὶ πάντες οἱ ἄγ-
throne of our God, and to the Lamb. And all the an-
γελοι [t]ἑστήκεσαν‖ κύκλῳ τοῦ θρόνου καὶ τῶν πρεσβυτέρων καὶ
gels stood around the throne and the elders and
τῶν τεσσάρων ζώων, καὶ [v]ἔπεσον‖ ἐνώπιον τοῦ θρόνου
the four living creatures, and fell before the throne
ἐπὶ [w]πρόσωπον‖ αὐτῶν, καὶ προσεκύνησαν τῷ θεῷ, 12 λέγον-
upon [2]face [1]their, and worshipped God, say-
τες, Ἀμήν· ἡ εὐλογία καὶ ἡ δόξα καὶ ἡ σοφία καὶ ἡ εὐχαριστία
ing, Amen Blessing, and glory, and wisdom, and thanksgiving,
καὶ ἡ τιμὴ καὶ ἡ δύναμις καὶ ἡ ἰσχὺς τῷ.θεῷ.ἡμῶν εἰς τοὺς
and honour, and power, and strength, to our God to the
αἰῶνας τῶν αἰώνων. [x]ἀμήν.‖
ages of the ages. Amen.

kindreds, and peo-
ple, and tongues, stood
before the throne, and
before the Lamb,
clothed with white
robes, and palms in
their hands; 10 and
cried with a loud voice,
saying, Salvation to
our God which sitteth
upon the throne, and
unto the Lamb. 11 And
all the angels stood
round about the
throne, and *about* the
elders and the four
beasts, and fell before
the throne on their
faces, and worshipped
God, 12 saying, Amen:
Blessing, and glory,
and wisdom, and
thanksgiving, and
honour, and power,
and might, *be* unto
our God for ever and
ever. Amen.

13 Καὶ ἀπεκρίθη εἷς ἐκ τῶν πρεσβυτέρων, λέγων μοι, Οὗτοι
And [5]answered [1]one [2]of [3]the [4]elders, saying to me, These
οἱ περιβεβλημένοι τὰς στολὰς τὰς λευκάς, τίνες εἰσίν, καὶ
who are clothed with the [2]robes [1]white, who are they, and
πόθεν ἦλθον; 14 Καὶ εἴρηκα αὐτῷ, Κύριε[y], σὺ οἶδας. Καὶ
whence came they? And I said to him, [My] lord, thou knowest. And
εἶπέν μοι, Οὗτοί εἰσιν οἱ ἐρχόμενοι [z]ἐκ τῆς θλίψεως τῆς‖
he said to me, These are they who come out of the [2]tribulation
μεγάλης, καὶ ἔπλυναν τὰς.στολὰς.αὐτῶν, καὶ ἐλεύκαναν
[1]great, and they washed their robes, and made white
[a]στολὰς‖ [b]αὐτῶν‖ ἐν τῷ αἵματι τοῦ ἀρνίου. 15 διὰ τοῦτό
[2]robes [1]their in the blood of the Lamb. Because of this
εἰσιν ἐνώπιον τοῦ θρόνου τοῦ θεοῦ, καὶ λατρεύουσιν αὐτῷ
are they before the throne of God, and serve him
ἡμέρας καὶ νυκτὸς ἐν τῷ.ναῷ.αὐτοῦ· καὶ ὁ καθήμενος ἐπὶ
day and night in his temple; and he who sits on
[c]τοῦ θρόνου‖ σκηνώσει ἐπ' αὐτούς. 16 οὐ.πεινάσουσιν
the throne shall tabernacle over them. They shall not hunger
ἔτι, οὐδὲ [d] διψήσουσιν ἔτι, [e]οὐδὲ‖ μὴ πέσῃ ἐπ' αὐ-
any more, neither shall they thirst any more, nor at all shall fall upon
τοὺς ὁ ἥλιος, οὐδὲ πᾶν καῦμα· 17 ὅτι τὸ ἀρνίον τὸ
them the sun, nor any heat; because the Lamb which [is]
[f]ἀνάμεσον‖ τοῦ θρόνου ποιμανεῖ αὐτούς, καὶ ὁδηγήσει αὐτοὺς
in [the] midst of the throne will shepherd them, and will lead them
ἐπὶ [g]ζώσας‖ πηγὰς ὑδάτων, καὶ ἐξαλείψει ὁ θεὸς πᾶν
to living fountains of waters, and [2]will [3]wipe [4]away [1]God every
δάκρυον [h]ἀπὸ‖ τῶν.ὀφθαλμῶν.αὐτῶν.
tear from their eyes.

13 And one of the
elders answered, say-
ing unto me, What
are these which are
arrayed in white robes?
and whence came
they? 14 And I said
unto him, Sir, thou
knowest. And he
said to me, These are
they which came out
of great tribulation,
and have washed their
robes, and made them
white in the blood of
the Lamb. 15 There-
fore are they be-
fore the throne of God,
and serve him day and
night in his temple:
and he that sitteth on
the throne shall dwell
among them. 16 They
shall hunger no more,
neither thirst any
more; neither shall
the sun light on them,
nor any heat. 17 For
the Lamb which is in
the midst of the
throne shall feed them,
and shall lead them
unto living fountains
of waters: and God
shall wipe away all
tears from their eyes.

---

[o] ἑστῶτας AW. [p] περιβεβλημένους GLTTrAW. [q] φοίνικας T. [r] κράζουσιν they cry GLTTrAW. [s] τῷ θεῷ ἡμῶν τῷ καθημένῳ ἐπὶ τῷ θρόνῳ (τοῦ θρόνου EG) to our God who sits on the throne EGLTTrAW. [t] εἱστήκεισαν LTTrA; ἑστήκεισαν W. [v] ἔπεσαν LTTrAW. [w] τὰ πρόσωπα faces GLTTrAW. [x] — ἀμήν L. [y] + μου my (lord) G[L]TTrAW. [z] ἀπὸ θλίψεως from tribulation L. [a] — στολὰς GLTTrAW. [b] αὐτὰς them GLTTr[A]W. [c] τῷ θρόνῳ T. [d] + μὴ (*read* neither at all) L. [e] οὐδ' οὐ A. [f] ἀνὰ μέσον EGLTAW. [g] ζωῆς (*read* to fountains of waters of life) GLTTrAW. [h] ἐκ GLTTrAW.

VIII. And when he
had opened the seventh
seal, there was silence
in heaven about the
space of half an hour.
2 And I saw the seven
angels which stood be-
fore God; and to them
were given seven
trumpets. 3 And ano-
ther angel came and
stood at the altar, hav-
ing a golden censer;
and there was given
unto him much in-
cense, that he should
offer *it* with the
prayers of all saints
upon the golden altar
which was before the
throne. 4 And the
smoke of the incense,
which came with the
prayers of the saints,
ascended up before
God out of the angel's
hand. 5 And the an-
gel took the censer,
and filled it with fire
of the altar, and cast
it into the earth: and
there were voices,
and thunderings, and
lightnings, and an
earthquake.

6 And the seven an-
gels which had the
seven trumpets pre-
pared themselves to
sound.

7 The first angel
sounded, and there
followed hail and fire
mingled with blood,
and they were cast up-
on the earth: and the
third part of trees
was burnt up, and all
green grass was burnt
up.

8 And the second
angel sounded, and as
it were a great moun-
tain burning with fire
was cast into the sea:
and the third part of
the sea became blood;
9 and the third part
of the creatures which
were in the sea, and
had life, died; and the
third part of the ships
were destroyed.

10 And the third an-
gel sounded, and there

8 Καὶ [i]ὅτε‖ ἤνοιξεν τὴν σφραγῖδα τὴν ἑβδόμην, ἐγένετο
And when he opened the [2]seal [1]seventh, [4]was
σιγὴ ἐν τῷ οὐρανῷ ὡς [k]ἡμιώριον.‖ 2 Καὶ [l]εἶδον‖ τοὺς ἑπτὰ
[3]silence in the heaven about half-an-hour. And I saw the seven
ἀγγέλους, οἳ ἐνώπιον τοῦ θεοῦ ἑστήκασιν, καὶ ἐδόθησαν
angels, who [2]before [3]God [1]stand, and were given
αὐτοῖς ἑπτὰ σάλπιγγες. 3 καὶ ἄλλος ἄγγελος ἦλθεν, καὶ
to them seven trumpets. And another angel came and
ἐστάθη ἐπὶ [m]τὸ θυσιαστήριον,‖ ἔχων λιβανωτὸν χρυσοῦν· καὶ
stood at the altar, having a [2]censer [1]golden; and
ἐδόθη αὐτῷ θυμιάματα πολλά, ἵνα [n]δώσῃ‖ ταῖς
[3]was [4]given [5]to [6]him [2]incense [1]much, that he might give [it] to the
προσευχαῖς τῶν ἁγίων πάντων ἐπὶ τὸ θυσιαστήριον τὸ
prayers of [2]the [3]saints [1]all upon the [2]altar
χρυσοῦν τὸ ἐνώπιον τοῦ θρόνου. 4 καὶ ἀνέβη ὁ καπνὸς
[1]golden which [was] before the throne. And went up the smoke
τῶν θυμιαμάτων ταῖς προσευχαῖς τῶν ἁγίων, ἐκ χειρὸς
of the incense with the prayers of the saints, out of [the] hand
τοῦ ἀγγέλου, ἐνώπιον τοῦ θεοῦ. 5 καὶ εἴληφεν ὁ ἄγγελος [o]τὸ‖
of the angel, before God. And [3]took [1]the [2]angel the
λιβανωτόν, καὶ ἐγέμισεν [p]αὐτὸ‖ ἐκ τοῦ πυρὸς τοῦ θυσιαστη-
censer, and filled it from the fire of the altar,
ρίου, καὶ ἔβαλεν εἰς τὴν γῆν· καὶ ἐγένοντο [q]φωναὶ καὶ
and cast [it] into the earth: and there were voices, and
βρονταὶ καὶ ἀστραπαὶ καὶ σεισμός.
thunders, and lightnings, and an earthquake.
6 Καὶ οἱ ἑπτὰ ἄγγελοι [r] ἔχοντες τὰς ἑπτὰ σάλπιγγας ἡτοί-
And the seven angels having the seven trumpets pre-
μασαν [s]ἑαυτοὺς‖ ἵνα σαλπίσωσιν.
pared themselves that they might sound [their] trumpets.
7 Καὶ ὁ πρῶτος [t]ἄγγελος‖ ἐσάλπισεν, καὶ ἐγένετο
And the first angel sounded [his] trumpet; and there was
χάλαζα καὶ πῦρ [v]μεμιγμένα‖ [w] αἵματι, καὶ ἐβλήθη εἰς τὴν
hail and fire mingled with blood, and it was cast upon the
γῆν· [x] καὶ τὸ τρίτον τῶν δένδρων κατεκάη, καὶ πᾶς χόρτος
earth: and the third of the trees was burnt up, and all [2]grass
χλωρὸς κατεκάη.
[1]green was burnt up.
8 Καὶ ὁ δεύτερος ἄγγελος ἐσάλπισεν, καὶ ὡς
And the second angel sounded [his] trumpet; and as [it were]
ὄρος μέγα πυρὶ καιόμενον ἐβλήθη εἰς τὴν θάλασσαν· καὶ
a [2]mountain [1]great [4]with [5]fire [3]burning was cast into the sea, and
ἐγένετο τὸ τρίτον τῆς θαλάσσης αἷμα. 9 καὶ ἀπέθανεν τὸ
[6]became [1]the [2]third [3]of [4]the [5]sea blood; and [14]died [1]the
τρίτον τῶν κτισμάτων τῶν ἐν τῇ θαλάσσῃ τὰ ἔχοντα
[2]third [3]of [4]the [5]creatures [6]which [[7]were] [8]in [9]the [10]sea [11]which [12]have
ψυχάς, καὶ τὸ τρίτον τῶν πλοίων [y]διεφθάρη.‖
[13]life; and the third of the ships was destroyed.
10 Καὶ ὁ τρίτος ἄγγελος ἐσάλπισεν, καὶ ἔπεσεν ἐκ
And the third angel sounded [his] trumpet; and [4]fell [5]out [6]of

---

[i] ὅταν LTTrA. [k] ἡμίωρον LTTrA. [l] ἴδον T. [m] τοῦ θυσιαστηρίου TTrA. [n] δώσει he shall give LTTrA. [o] τὸν EGLTTrAW. [p] αὐτὸν EGLTTrAW. [q] βρονταὶ καὶ ἀστραπαὶ καὶ φωναὶ L; βρονταὶ καὶ φωναὶ καὶ ἀστραπαὶ TTrA. [r] + οἱ (*read* who have) GLTTrAW. [s] αὐτοὺς LTTr. [t] — ἄγγελος GLTTrAW. [v] μεμιγμένον T. [w] + ἐν with (blood) GLTTrAW. [x] + καὶ τὸ τρίτον τῆς γῆς κατεκάη, and the third of the earth was burnt up GLTTrAW. [y] διεφθάρησαν were destroyed LTTrA.

τοῦ οὐρανοῦ ἀστὴρ μέγας καιόμενος ὡς λαμπάς, καὶ ἔπεσεν
[7]the [8]heaven [1]a [3]star [2]great, burning as a lamp, and it fell
ἐπὶ.τὸ τρίτον τῶν ποταμῶν, καὶ ἐπὶ τὰς πηγὰς [z] ὑδάτων.
upon the third of the rivers, and upon the fountains of waters.
11 καὶ τὸ ὄνομα τοῦ ἀστέρος λέγεται [a] "Αψινθος· καὶ [b]γίνεται‖
And the name of the star is called Wormwood; and [3]becomes
τὸ τρίτον [c] εἰς ἄψινθον, καὶ πολλοὶ [d] ἀνθρώπων ἀπέθανον
[1]the [2]third into wormwood, and [3]many [1]of [2]men died
ἐκ τῶν ὑδάτων, ὅτι ἐπικράνθησαν.
of the waters, because they were made bitter.
12 Καὶ ὁ τέταρτος ἄγγελος ἐσάλπισεν, καὶ ἐπλήγη
And the fourth angel sounded [his] trumpet; and was smitten
τὸ τρίτον τοῦ ἡλίου καὶ τὸ τρίτον τῆς σελήνης καὶ τὸ τρίτον
the third of the sun, and the third of the moon, and the third
τῶν ἀστέρων, ἵνα σκοτισθῇ τὸ τρίτον αὐτῶν, καὶ ἡ
of the stars; that should be darkened the third of them, and the
ἡμέρα μὴ [e]φαίνῃ‖ τὸ τρίτον αὐτῆς, καὶ ἡ νὺξ ὁμοίως.
day [2]not [1]should appear [for] the third of it, and the night likewise.
13 Καὶ [f]εἶδον,‖ καὶ ἤκουσα ἑνὸς [g]ἀγγέλου πετωμένου‖ ἐν
And I saw, and heard one angel flying in
μεσουρανήματι, λέγοντος φωνῇ μεγάλῃ, Οὐαί, οὐαί, οὐαί,
mid-heaven, saying with a [2]voice [1]loud, Woe, woe, woe,
[h]τοῖς κατοικοῦσιν‖ ἐπὶ τῆς γῆς, ἐκ τῶν λοιπῶν φωνῶν
to those who dwell on the earth, from the remaining voices
τῆς σάλπιγγος τῶν τριῶν ἀγγέλων τῶν μελλόντων σαλ-
of the trumpet of the three angels who [are] about to sound
πίζειν.
[their] trumpets.
9 Καὶ ὁ πέμπτος ἄγγελος ἐσάλπισεν, καὶ [i]εἶδον‖
And the fifth angel sounded [his] trumpet; and I saw
ἀστέρα ἐκ τοῦ οὐρανοῦ πεπτωκότα εἰς τὴν γῆν, καὶ ἐδό-
a star out of the heaven fallen to the earth, and there was
θη αὐτῷ ἡ κλεὶς τοῦ φρέατος τῆς ἀβύσσου. 2 καὶ ἤνοιξεν
given to it the key of the pit of the abyss. And it opened
τὸ φρέαρ τῆς ἀβύσσου. καὶ ἀνέβη καπνὸς ἐκ τοῦ φρέατος
the pit of the abyss; and there went up smoke out of the pit
ὡς καπνὸς καμίνου μεγάλης, καὶ [k]ἐσκοτίσθη‖ ὁ ἥλιος
as [the] smoke of a [2]furnace [1]great; and [3]was [4]darkened [1]the [2]sun
καὶ ὁ ἀὴρ ἐκ τοῦ καπνοῦ τοῦ φρέατος. 3 καὶ ἐκ τοῦ καπνοῦ
and the air by the smoke of the pit. And out of the smoke
ἐξῆλθον ἀκρίδες εἰς τὴν γῆν, καὶ ἐδόθη [l]αὐταῖς‖ ἐξουσία,
came forth locusts unto the earth, and was given to them power,
ὡς ἔχουσιν ἐξουσίαν οἱ σκορπίοι τῆς γῆς· 4 καὶ ἐῤῥέθη
as [6]have [7]power [1]the [2]scorpions [3]of [4]the [5]earth; and it was said
[l]αὐταῖς‖ ἵνα μὴ [m]ἀδικήσωσιν‖ τὸν χόρτον τῆς γῆς, οὐδὲ πᾶν
to them, that [3]not [1]they [2]should injure the grass of the earth, nor any
χλωρόν, οὐδὲ πᾶν δένδρον, εἰ.μὴ τοὺς ἀνθρώπους [n]μόνους‖
green thing, nor any tree, but the men only
οἵτινες οὐκ.ἔχουσιν τὴν σφραγῖδα τοῦ θεοῦ ἐπὶ τῶν μετώπων
who have not the seal of God on [2]foreheads
[o]αὐτῶν.‖ 5 καὶ ἐδόθη [p]αὐταῖς‖ ἵνα μὴ.ἀποκτείνωσιν αὐτούς,
[1]their. And it was given to them that they should not kill them,

fell a great star from heaven, burning as it were a lamp, and it fell upon the third part of the rivers, and upon the fountains of
waters; 11 and the name of the star is called Wormwood: and the third part of the waters became wormwood; and many men died of the waters, because they were made bitter.
12 And the fourth angel sounded, and the third part of the sun was smitten, and the third part of the moon, and the third part of the stars; so as the third part of them was darkened, and the day shone not for a third part of it, and the night likewise.
13 And I beheld, and heard an angel flying through the midst of heaven, saying with a loud voice, Woe, woe, woe, to the inhabiters of the earth by reason of the other voices of the trumpet of the three angels which are yet to sound!

IX. And the fifth angel sounded, and I saw a star fall from heaven unto the earth: and to him was given the key of the bottomless pit.
2 And he opened the bottomless pit; and there arose a smoke out of the pit, as the smoke of a great furnace; and the sun and the air were darkened by reason of the smoke of the pit.
3 And there came out of the smoke locusts upon the earth: and unto them was given power, as the scorpions of the earth have power.
4 And it was commanded them that they should not hurt the grass of the earth, neither any green thing, neither any tree; but only those men which have not the seal of God in their foreheads.
5 And to them it was given

[z] + τῶν of the (waters) GLTTrAW. [a] + ὁ GLTAW. [b] ἐγένετο became LTTrAW. [c] + τῶν ὑδάτων of the waters EGLTTrAW. [d] + τῶν of the (men) GLTTrAW. [e] φάνῃ LTW; φανῇ TrA. [f] ἴδον T. [g] ἀετοῦ πετομένου eagle flying GLTTrAW. [h] τοὺς κατοικοῦντας TTrA. [i] ἴδον T. [k] ἐσκοτώθη LTA. [l] αὐτοῖς T. [m] ἀδικήσουσιν [1]they [2]shall injure LTA. [n] — μόνους GLTTrAW. [o] — αὐτῶν (*read* on the foreheads) LTTrA. [p] αὐτοῖς LT.

that they should not kill them, but that they should be tormented five months: and their torment *was* as the torment of a scorpion, when he striketh a man. 6 And in those days shall men seek death, and shall not find it; and shall desire to die, and death shall flee from them. 7 And the shapes of the locusts *were* like unto horses prepared unto battle; and on their heads *were* as it were crowns like gold, and their faces *were* as the faces of men. 8 And they had hair as the hair of women, and their teeth were as *the teeth* of lions. 9 And they had breastplates, as it were breastplates of iron; and the sound of their wings *was* as the sound of chariots of many horses running to battle. 10 And they had tails like unto scorpions, and there were stings in their tails: and their power *was* to hurt men five months. 11 And they had a king over them, *which is* the angel of the bottomless pit, whose name in the Hebrew tongue *is* Abaddon, but in the Greek tongue hath *his* name Apollyon.

12 One woe is past; *and*, behold, there come two woes more hereafter.

13 And the sixth angel sounded, and I heard a voice from the four horns of the golden altar which is before God, 14 saying to the sixth angel which had the trumpet, Loose the four angels which are bound in the great river Euphrates. 15 And the four angels were loosed, which were prepared for an hour,

ἀλλ' ἵνα [q]βασανισθῶσιν‖ μῆνας πέντε· καὶ ὁ βασανισμὸς
but that they should be tormented [2]months [1]five; and [2]torment
αὐτῶν ὡς βασανισμὸς σκορπίου, ὅταν παίσῃ ἄν-
[1]their [was] as [the] torment of a scorpion, when it may strike a
θρωπον· 6 καὶ ἐν ταῖς.ἡμέραις.ἐκείναις ζητήσουσιν οἱ ἄνθρω-
man. And in those days [2]shall [3]seek [1]men
ποι τὸν θάνατον, καὶ [r]οὐχ‖ [s]εὑρήσουσιν‖ αὐτόν· καὶ ἐπιθυμή-
death, and [2]not [1]shall find it; and shall
σουσιν ἀποθανεῖν, καὶ [t]φεύξεται‖ [v]ὁ θάνατος ἀπ' αὐτῶν.‖
desire to die, and [2]shall [3]flee [1]death from them.
7 καὶ τὰ ὁμοιώματα τῶν ἀκρίδων [w]ὅμοια‖ ἵπποις ἡτοι-
And the likenesses of the locusts [were] like to horses pre-
μασμένοις εἰς πόλεμον, καὶ ἐπὶ τὰς.κεφαλὰς.αὐτῶν ὡς στέφανοι
pared for war, and upon their heads as crowns
ὅμοιοι [x]χρυσῷ,‖ καὶ τὰ.πρόσωπα.αὐτῶν ὡς πρόσωπα ἀνθρώ-
like gold; and their faces as faces of
πων· 8 καὶ [y]εἶχον‖ τρίχας ὡς τρίχας γυναικῶν· καὶ οἱ ὀδόντες
men; and they had hair as [2]hair [1]women's; and [2]teeth
αὐτῶν ὡς λεόντων ἦσαν· 9 καὶ εἶχον θώρακας ὡς θώρακας
[1]their [4]as [5]of [6]lions [3]were; and they had breastplates as [2]breastplates
σιδηροῦς· καὶ ἡ φωνὴ τῶν.πτερύγων.αὐτῶν ὡς φωνὴ
[1]iron; and the sound of their wings [was] as [the] sound
ἁρμάτων ἵππων πολλῶν τρεχόντων εἰς πόλεμον. 10 καὶ
of chariots of [2]horses [1]many running to war; and
ἔχουσιν οὐρὰς [z]ὁμοίας‖ σκορπίοις, καὶ κέντρα·[a] [b]ἦν‖ ἐν ταῖς
they have tails like scorpions, and stings; [4]was [5]in
οὐραῖς αὐτῶν [c]καὶ‖ ἡ.ἐξουσία.αὐτῶν ἀδικῆσαι τοὺς ἀνθρώπους
[7]tails [6]their [1]and [2]their [3]power to injure men
μῆνας πέντε. 11 [d]καὶ‖ ἔχουσιν [e]ἐφ' αὐτῶν‖ βασιλέα [f]τὸν‖
[2]months [1]five. And they have over them a king, the
ἄγγελον τῆς ἀβύσσου· [g] ὄνομα αὐτῷ Ἑβραϊστὶ Ἀβαδδών, καὶ
angel of the abyss: his name in Hebrew Abaddon, and
ἐν τῇ Ἑλληνικῇ ὄνομα ἔχει Ἀπολλύων.
in the Greek [for] name he has Apollyon.

12 Ἡ οὐαὶ ἡ μία ἀπῆλθεν· ἰδού, [h]ἔρχονται‖ ἔτι δύο οὐαὶ
[3]Woe [1]the [2]first is past. Lo, [4]come [1]yet [2]two [3]woes
μετὰ ταῦτα.
after these things.

13 Καὶ ὁ ἕκτος ἄγγελος ἐσάλπισεν, καὶ ἤκουσα φωνὴν
And the sixth angel sounded [his] trumpet; and I heard [2]voice
μίαν ἐκ τῶν [i]τεσσάρων‖ κεράτων τοῦ θυσιαστηρίου τοῦ χρυσοῦ
[1]one from the four horns of the [2]altar [1]golden
τοῦ ἐνώπιον τοῦ θεοῦ, 14 [k]λέγουσαν‖ τῷ ἕκτῳ ἀγγέλῳ
which [is] before God, saying to the sixth angel
[l]ὃς εἶχε‖ τὴν σάλπιγγα, Λῦσον τοὺς τέσσαρας ἀγγέλους τοὺς
who had the trumpet, Loose the four angels who
δεδεμένους ἐπὶ τῷ ποταμῷ τῷ μεγάλῳ Εὐφράτῃ. 15 Καὶ ἐλύ-
are bound at the [2]river [1]great Euphrates. And were
θησαν οἱ τέσσαρες ἄγγελοι οἱ ἡτοιμασμένοι εἰς τὴν ὥραν καὶ
loosed the four angels who had been prepared for the hour and

---

[q] βασανισθήσονται they shall be tormented LTTrA. [r] οὐ μὴ in no wise GLTTrAW. [s] εὕρωσιν should find L. [t] φεύγει [2]flees LTTrA. [v] ἀπ' αὐτῶν ὁ θάνατος G. [w] ὅμοιοι T. [x] χρυσοῖ golden G. [y] εἶχαν LTTrA. [z] ὁμοίοις Tr. [a] *Punctuate so as to read* and stings were in their tails *Text. Rec. and* G. [b] καὶ and LTTrAW. [c] — καὶ LTTrAW. [d] — καὶ GLTTrAW. [e] ἐπ' αὐτῶν LTTrA. [f] — τὸν (*read* an angel) A. [g] + ᾧ to whom T. [h] ἔρχεται LTTrA. [i] — τεσσάρων LTr[A]. [k] λέγοντα LTTrAW. [l] ὁ ἔχων who has GLTTrAW.

ἡμέραν καὶ μῆνα καὶ ἐνιαυτόν, ἵνα ἀποκτείνωσιν τὸ τρίτον
day and month and year, that they might kill the third
τῶν ἀνθρώπων. 16 καὶ ὁ ἀριθμὸς [n] στρατευμάτων τοῦ ἱππι-
of men; and the number of [the] armies of the caval-
κοῦ [o]δύο μυριάδες‖ μυριάδων· [p]καὶ‖ ἤκουσα τὸν ἀριθμὸν
ry [was] two myriads of myriads, and I heard the number
αὐτῶν. 17 καὶ οὕτως [q]εἶδον‖ τοὺς ἵππους ἐν τῇ ὁράσει, καὶ
of them. And thus I saw the horses in the vision, and
τοὺς καθημένους ἐπ' αὐτῶν, ἔχοντας θώρακας πυρίνους καὶ
those sitting on them, having breastplates fiery, and
ὑακινθίνους καὶ θειώδεις· καὶ αἱ κεφαλαὶ τῶν ἵππων
hyacinthine, and brimstone-like; and the heads of the horses [were]
ὡς κεφαλαὶ λεόντων, καὶ ἐκ τῶν.στομάτων.αὐτῶν ἐκπορεύε-
as heads of lions, and out of their mouths goes
ται πῦρ καὶ καπνὸς καὶ θεῖον. 18 [r]ὑπὸ‖ τῶν τριῶν [s] τούτων
out fire and smoke and brimstone. By [2]three [1]these
ἀπεκτάνθησαν τὸ τρίτον τῶν ἀνθρώπων, ἐκ τοῦ πυρὸς καὶ
were killed the third of the men, by the fire and
[t]ἐκ‖ τοῦ καπνοῦ καὶ [t]ἐκ‖ τοῦ θείου, τοῦ ἐκπορευομένου ἐκ
by the smoke and by the brimstone, which goes forth out of
τῶν.στομάτων.αὐτῶν. 19 [v]αἱ.γὰρ ἐξουσίαι αὐτῶν ἐν τῷ
their mouths. For the powers of them [2]in
στόματι αὐτῶν εἰσιν·‖ αἱ.γὰρ.οὐραὶ.αὐτῶν ὅμοιαι ὄφεσιν,
[4]mouth [3]their [1]are; for their tails [are] like serpents,
ἔχουσαι κεφαλάς, καὶ ἐν αὐταῖς ἀδικοῦσιν. 20 καὶ οἱ λοιποὶ
having heads, and with them they injure. And the rest
τῶν ἀνθρώπων οἳ οὐκ.ἀπεκτάνθησαν ἐν ταῖς.πληγαῖς.ταύταις,
of the men who were not killed by these plagues,
[w]οὔτε‖ μετενόησαν ἐκ τῶν ἔργων τῶν.χειρῶν.αὐτῶν, ἵνα μὴ
[2]not [3]even [1]repented of the works of their hands, that [3]not
[x]προσκυνήσωσιν‖ τὰ δαιμόνια, καὶ [y] εἴδωλα τὰ χρυσᾶ καὶ
[1]they [2]should do homage to the demons, and [2]idols [1]the golden and
τὰ ἀργυρᾶ καὶ τὰ χαλκᾶ καὶ τὰ λίθινα καὶ τὰ ξύλινα,
silver and brazen and stone and wooden,
ἃ οὔτε βλέπειν [z]δύναται,‖ οὔτε ἀκούειν, οὔτε περιπατεῖν·
which neither [3]to [4]see [1]are [2]able, nor to hear, nor to walk.
21 καὶ οὐ.μετενόησαν ἐκ τῶν.φόνων.αὐτῶν, οὔτε ἐκ τῶν
And they repented not of their murders, nor of
[a]φαρμακειῶν‖ αὐτῶν, οὔτε ἐκ τῆς.πορνείας.αὐτῶν, οὔτε ἐκ
[2]sorceries [1]their, nor of their fornications, nor of
τῶν.κλεμμάτων.αὐτῶν.
their thefts.

10 Καὶ εἶδον ἄλλον ἄγγελον ἰσχυρὸν καταβαίνοντα ἐκ τοῦ
And I saw another [2]angel [1]strong coming down out of the
οὐρανοῦ, περιβεβλημένον νεφέλην, καὶ [b] ἶρις ἐπὶ [c]τῆς κεφ-
heaven, clothed with a cloud, and a rainbow on the
αλῆς‖[d], καὶ τὸ.πρόσωπον.αὐτοῦ ὡς ὁ ἥλιος, καὶ οἱ.πόδες.αὐτοῦ
head, and his face as the sun, and his feet
ὡς στῦλοι πυρός· 2 καὶ [e]εἶχεν‖ ἐν τῇ.χειρὶ.αὐτοῦ βιβλαρίδιον
as pillars of fire, and he had in his hand a little book

and a day, and a month, and a year, for to slay the third part of men. 16 And the number of the army of the horsemen *were* two hundred thousand thousand: and I heard the number of them. 17 And thus I saw the horses in the vision, and them that sat on them, having breastplates of fire, and of jacinth, and brimstone: and the heads of the horses *were* as the heads of lions; and out of their mouths issued fire and smoke and brimstone. 18 By these three was the third part of men killed, by the fire, and by the smoke, and by the brimstone, which issued out of their mouths. 19 For their power is in their mouth, and in their tails: for their tails *were* like unto serpents, and had heads, and with them they do hurt. 20 And the rest of the men which were not killed by these plagues yet repented not of the works of their hands, that they should not worship devils, and idols of gold, and silver, and brass, and stone, and of wood: which neither can see, nor hear, nor walk: 21 neither repented they of their murders, nor of their sorceries, nor of their fornication, nor of their thefts.

X. And I saw another mighty angel come down from heaven, clothed with a cloud: and a rainbow *was* upon his head, and his face *was* as it were the sun, and his feet as pillars of fire: 2 and he had in his hand a little book

[n] + τῶν of the (armies) GLTTrAW. [o] δισμυριάδες LTA. [p] — καὶ GLTTrAW. [q] ἴδον T. [r] ἀπὸ from GLTTrAW. [s] + πληγῶν [3]plagues GLTTrAW. [t] — ἐκ GLTTrAW. [v] ἡ γὰρ ἐξουσία τῶν ἵππων For the power of the horses (αὐτῶν *for* τῶν ἵππων W) ἐν τῷ στόματι αὐτῶν ἐστιν καὶ ἐν ταῖς οὐραῖς αὐτῶν· is in their mouth and in their tails GLTTrAW. [w] οὐ not GW; οὐδὲ TA. [x] προσκυνήσουσιν they shall do homage to LTTrAW. [y] + τὰ GLTTrAW. [z] δύνανται LTTrA. [a] φαρμακιῶν T; φαρμάκων A. [b] + ἡ the (rainbow) GLTTrAW. [c] τὴν κεφαλὴν LTTrAW. [d] + αὐτοῦ (*read* his head) GLTTrAW. [e] ἔχων having GLTTrAW.

open: and he set his
right foot upon the
sea, and *his* left *foot*
on the earth, 3 and
cried with a loud voice,
as *when* a lion roar-
eth: and when he had
cried, seven thunders
uttered their voices.
4 And when the seven
thunders had uttered
their voices, I was
about to write: and I
heard a voice from hea-
ven saying unto me,
Seal up those things
which the seven thun-
ders uttered, and write
them not. 5 And the
angel which I saw
stand upon the sea
and upon the earth
lifted up his hand to
heaven, 6 and sware
by him that liveth for
ever and ever, who
created heaven, and
the things that therein
are, and the earth, and
the things that there-
in are, and the sea, and
the things which are
therein, that there
should be time no
longer: 7 but in the
days of the voice of
the seventh angel,
when he shall begin
to sound, the mystery
of God should be
finished, as he hath
declared to his ser-
vants the prophets.

[f]ἀνεῳγμένον·‖ καὶ ἔθηκεν τὸν.πόδα.αὐτοῦ τὸν δεξιὸν ἐπὶ [g]τὴν
open. And he placed his [2]foot [1]right upon the
θάλασσαν,‖ τὸν.δὲ εὐώνυμον ἐπὶ [h]τὴν γῆν,‖ 3 καὶ ἔκραξεν
sea, and the left upon the earth, and cried
φωνῇ μεγάλῃ ὥσπερ λέων μυκᾶται· καὶ ὅτε ἔκραξεν,
with a [2]voice [1]loud as a lion roars. And when he cried,
ἐλάλησαν αἱ ἑπτὰ βρονταὶ τὰς.ἑαυτῶν.φωνάς· 4 καὶ ὅτε
[4]spoke [1]the [2]seven [3]thunders their voices. And when
ἐλάλησαν αἱ ἑπτὰ βρονταὶ [i]τὰς.φωνὰς.ἑαυτῶν,‖ [k]ἔμελλον‖
[4]spoke [1]the [2]seven [3]thunders their voices, I was about
γράφειν· καὶ ἤκουσα φωνὴν ἐκ τοῦ οὐρανοῦ, λέγουσάν [l]μοι,‖
to write: And I heard a voice out of the heaven, saying to me,
Σφράγισον ἃ ἐλάλησαν αἱ ἑπτὰ βρονταί, καὶ μὴ [m]ταῦτα‖
Seal what [things] [4]spoke [1]the [2]seven [3]thunders, and [3]not [2]them
γράψῃς. 5 Καὶ ὁ ἄγγελος, ὃν εἶδον ἑστῶτα ἐπὶ τῆς θαλάσσης
[1]write. And the angel whom I saw standing on the sea
καὶ ἐπὶ τῆς γῆς, ἦρεν τὴν.χεῖρα.αὐτοῦ [n] εἰς τὸν οὐρανόν,
and on the earth, lifted up his hand to the heaven,
6 καὶ ὤμοσεν ἐν τῷ ζῶντι εἰς τοὺς αἰῶνας τῶν αἰώνων, ὃς
and sware by him who lives to the ages of the ages, who
ἔκτισεν τὸν οὐρανὸν καὶ τὰ ἐν αὐτῷ, καὶ τὴν γῆν καὶ
created the heaven and the things in it, and the earth and
τὰ ἐν αὐτῇ, [o]καὶ τὴν θάλασσαν καὶ τὰ ἐν αὐτῇ,‖
the things in it, and the sea and the things in it,
Ὅτι χρόνος [p]οὐκ ἔσται ἔτι·‖ 7 [q]ἀλλὰ‖ ἐν ταῖς ἡμέραις τῆς
Delay [3]no [1]shall [2]be longer; but in the days of the
φωνῆς τοῦ ἑβδόμου ἀγγέλου, ὅταν μέλλῃ σαλπίζειν,
voice of the seventh angel, when he is about to sound [the] trumpet,
καὶ [r]τελεσθῇ‖ τὸ μυστήριον τοῦ θεοῦ, ὡς εὐηγ-
also should be completed the mystery of God, as he did announce
γέλισεν [s]τοῖς.ἑαυτοῦ.δούλοις τοῖς προφήταις.‖
the glad tidings to his bondmen the prophets.

8 And the voice
which I heard from
heaven spake unto me
again, and said, Go
and take the little
book which is open
in the hand of the
angel which standeth
upon the sea and upon
the earth. 9 And I
went unto the angel,
and said unto him,
Give me the little
book. And he said
unto me, Take *it*, and
eat it up; and it shall
make thy belly bitter,
but it shall be in thy
mouth sweet as honey.
10 And I took the
little book out of the
angel's hand, and ate
it up; and it was in
my mouth sweet as
honey: and as soon

8 Καὶ ἡ φωνὴ ἣν ἤκουσα ἐκ τοῦ οὐρανοῦ, πάλιν
And the voice which I heard out of the heaven [was] again
[t]λαλοῦσα‖ μετ' ἐμοῦ, καὶ [v]λέγουσα,‖ Ὕπαγε λάβε τὸ [w]βιβλα-
speaking with me, and saying, Go, take the little
ρίδιον‖ τὸ ἠνεῳγμένον ἐν τῇ χειρὶ [x] ἀγγέλου τοῦ ἑστῶτος
book which is open in the hand of [the] angel who is standing
ἐπὶ τῆς θαλάσσης καὶ ἐπὶ τῆς γῆς. 9 Καὶ [y]ἀπῆλθον‖ πρὸς τὸν
on the sea and on the earth. And I went to the
ἄγγελον, λέγων αὐτῷ, [z]Δός‖ μοι τὸ βιβλαρίδιον. Καὶ λέγει
angel, saying to him, Give me the little book. And he says
μοι, Λάβε καὶ κατάφαγε αὐτό· καὶ πικρανεῖ σου τὴν
to me, Take and eat [2]up [1]it: and it shall make bitter thy
κοιλίαν, ἀλλ' ἐν τῷ.στόματί.σου ἔσται γλυκὺ ὡς μέλι. 10 Καὶ
belly, but in thy mouth it shall be sweet as honey. And
ἔλαβον τὸ βιβλαρίδιον ἐκ τῆς χειρὸς τοῦ ἀγγέλου, καὶ κατέ-
I took the little book out of the hand of the angel, and ate
φαγον αὐτό· καὶ ἦν ἐν τῷ.στόματί.μου ὡς μέλι γλυκύ· καὶ
[2]up [1]it; and it was in my mouth [2]as [3]honey [1]sweet; and

---

[f] ἠνεῳγμένον LTTrA. [g] τῆς θαλάσσης GLTTrAW. [h] τῆς γῆς GLTTrAW. [i] — τὰς φωνὰς ἑαυτῶν GLTTrAW. [k] ἤμελλον LTrAW. [l] — μοι GLTTrAW. [m] αὐτὰ LTTrAW. [n] + τὴν δεξιὰν the right GLTTrAW. [o] [καὶ τὴν θάλασσαν καὶ τὰ ἐν αὐτῇ] L. [p] οὐκέτι ἔσται GLTTrAW. [q] ἀλλ' LTTrA. [r] ἐτελέσθη was completed GLTTrAW. [s] τοὺς ἑαυτοῦ δούλους τοὺς προφήτας GLTTrAW. [t] λαλοῦσαν LTTrAW. [v] λέγουσαν LTTrAW. [w] βιβλίον book LTrA. [x] + τοῦ of the GLTTrAW. [y] ἀπῆλθα LT. [z] δοῦναι (*read* telling him to give) GLTTrAW.

ὅτε ἔφαγον αὐτό, ἐπικράνθη ἡ.κοιλία.μου. 11 καὶ ^c λέγει^‖
when I did eat it, ³was ⁴made ⁵bitter ¹my ²belly. And he says
μοι, Δεῖ.σε πάλιν προφητεῦσαι ἐπὶ λαοῖς καὶ ^d ἔθνεσιν καὶ
to me, Thou must again prophesy as to peoples, and nations, and
γλώσσαις καὶ βασιλεῦσιν πολλοῖς.
tongues, and ²kings ¹many.

11 Καὶ ἐδόθη μοι κάλαμος ὅμοιος ῥάβδῳ, ^e λέγων, ^f "Ἔγει-
And was given to me a reed like a staff, saying, Rise,
ραι,^‖ καὶ μέτρησον τὸν ναὸν τοῦ θεοῦ, καὶ τὸ θυσιαστήριον,
and measure the temple of God, and the altar,
καὶ τοὺς προσκυνοῦντας ἐν αὐτῷ· 2 καὶ. τὴν αὐλὴν τὴν
and those who worship in it. And the court which
^g ἔσωθεν^‖ τοῦ ναοῦ ἔκβαλε ^h ἔξω,^‖ καὶ μὴ αὐτὴν μετρήσῃς,
[is] within the temple cast out, and ³not ²it ¹measure;
ὅτι ἐδόθη τοῖς ἔθνεσιν· καὶ τὴν πόλιν τὴν ἁγίαν
because it was given [up] to the nations, and the ²city ¹holy
πατήσουσιν μῆνας ^i τεσσαράκοντα^‖ ^k δύο. 3 καὶ δώσω
shall they trample upon ³months ¹forty ²two. And I will give
τοῖς.δυσὶν.μάρτυσίν.μου, καὶ προφητεύσουσιν ἡμέρας
[power] to my two witnesses, and they shall prophesy ⁷days
χιλίας διακοσίας ἑξήκοντα, ^l περιβεβλημένοι^‖ σάκ-
¹a ²thousand ³two ⁴hundred [⁵and] ⁶sixty, clothed in sack-
κους. 4 οὗτοί εἰσιν αἱ δύο ἐλαῖαι, καὶ ^m δύο λυχνίαι
cloth. These are the two olive trees, and [the] two lampstands
αἱ ἐνώπιον ^n τοῦ^‖ ^o θεοῦ^‖ τῆς γῆς ^p ἑστῶσαι.^‖ 5 καὶ εἴ τις
which ²before ³the ⁴God ⁵of ⁶the ⁷earth ¹stand. And if anyone
αὐτοὺς ^q θέλῃ^‖ ἀδικῆσαι, πῦρ ἐκπορεύεται ἐκ τοῦ στόματος
⁵them ¹should ²will ³to ⁴injure, fire goes out of ²mouth
αὐτῶν, καὶ κατεσθίει τοὺς.ἐχθροὺς.αὐτῶν· καὶ εἴ τις ^r αὐτοὺς
¹their, and devours their enemies. And if anyone ⁵them
θέλῃ^‖ ἀδικῆσαι, οὕτως δεῖ.αὐτὸν ἀποκτανθῆναι. 6 οὗτοι
¹should ²will ³to ⁴injure, thus must he be killed. These
ἔχουσιν ^s ^t ἐξουσίαν κλεῖσαι τὸν οὐρανόν,^‖ ἵνα μὴ ^v βρέχῃ
have authority to shut the heaven, that no ²may ³fall
ὑετὸς ἐν ἡμέραις αὐτῶν τῆς προφητείας·^‖ καὶ ἐξουσίαν
¹rain in [the] days of their prophecy; and authority
ἔχουσιν ἐπὶ τῶν ὑδάτων, στρέφειν αὐτὰ εἰς αἷμα, καὶ πατά-
they have over the waters, to turn them into blood, and to
ξαι τὴν γῆν ^w ^x πάσῃ πληγῇ, ὁσάκις ἐὰν θελήσωσιν.^‖ 7 καὶ
smite the earth with every plague, as often as they may will. And
ὅταν τελέσωσιν τὴν.μαρτυρίαν.αὐτῶν, τὸ θηρίον τὸ
when they shall have completed their testimony, the beast who
ἀναβαῖνον ἐκ τῆς ἀβύσσου ποιήσει ^y πόλεμον μετ' αὐτῶν,^‖
comes up out of the abyss will make war with them,
καὶ νικήσει αὐτούς, καὶ ἀποκτενεῖ αὐτούς. 8 καὶ ^z τὰ
and will overcome them, and will kill them: and
πτώματα^‖ αὐτῶν ἐπὶ τῆς πλατείας ^aa πόλεως τῆς με-
²bodies ¹their [will be] on the street of ³city ¹the

as I had eaten it, my belly was bitter. 11 And he said unto me, Thou must prophesy again before many peoples, and nations, and tongues, and kings.

XI. And there was given me a reed like unto a rod: and the angel stood, saying, Rise, and measure the temple of God, and the altar, and them that worship therein. 2 But the court which is without the temple leave out, and measure it not; for it is given unto the Gentiles: and the holy city shall they tread under foot forty *and* two months. 3 And I will give *power* unto my two witnesses, and they shall prophesy a thousand two hundred *and* threescore days, clothed in sackcloth. 4 These are the two olive trees, and the two candlesticks standing before the God of the earth. 5 And if any man will hurt them, fire proceedeth out of their mouth, and devoureth their enemies: and if any man will hurt them, he must in this manner be killed. 6 These have power to shut heaven, that it rain not in the days of their prophecy: and have power over waters to turn them to blood, and to smite the earth with all plagues, as often as they will. 7 And when they shall have finished their testimony, the beast that ascendeth out of the bottomless pit shall make war against them, and shall overcome them, and kill them. 8 And their dead bodies *shall lie* in the street of the great city, which

---

^c λέγουσίν they say LTTrA. ^d + ἐπὶ as to T. ^e + καὶ ὁ ἄγγελος εἱστήκει and the angel stood E. ^f Ἔγειρε LTTrAW. ^g ἔξωθεν outside EGLTTrAW. ^h ἔξωθεν outside LTTr. ^i τεσσεράκοντα LTTrA. ^k + καὶ and LAW. ^l περιβεβλημένους Tr. ^m + αἱ the GLTTrAW. ^n — τοῦ L. ^o κυρίου Lord GLTTrAW. ^p ἑστῶτες GLTTrAW. ^q θέλει wills GLTTrAW. ^r αὐτοὺς θέλει them wills G; θέλει αὐτοὺς LAW; θελήσῃ αὐτοὺς should have willed them T; αὐτοὺς θελήσῃ Tr. ^s + τὴν the LTr[A]W. ^t τὸν οὐρανὸν ἐξουσίαν κλεῖσαι G. ^v ὑετὸς βρέχῃ τὰς ἡμέρας τῆς προφητείας αὐτῶν (αὐτῶν τῆς προφ. W) (*read* [during] the days) GLTTrAW. ^w + ἐν with (every) LTTrA. ^x ὁσάκις ἐὰν θελήσωσιν ἐν πάσῃ πληγῇ GW. ^y μετ' αὐτῶν πόλεμον GLTTrAW. ^z τὸ πτῶμα body GLTTrAW. ^aa + τῆς LTTrAW.

spiritually is called
Sodom and Egypt,
where also our Lord
was crucified. 9 And
they of the people and
kindreds and tongues
and nations shall see
their dead bodies three
days and an half, and
shall not suffer their
dead bodies to be put
in graves. 10 And they
that dwell upon the
earth shall rejoice o-
ver them, and make
merry, and shall send
gifts one to another;
because these two pro-
phets tormented them
that dwelt on the
earth. 11 And after
three days and an
half the Spirit of life
from God entered into
them, and they stood
upon their feet; and
great fear fell upon
them which saw them.
12 And they heard a
great voice from hea-
ven saying unto them,
Come up hither. And
they ascended up to
heaven in a cloud; and
their enemies beheld
them. 13 And the
same hour was there a
great earthquake, and
the tenth part of the
city fell, and in the
earthquake were slain
of men seven thou-
sand: and the rem-
nant were affrighted,
and gave glory to the
God of heaven.

14 The second woe
is past; *and*, behold,
the third woe cometh
quickly.

15 And the seventh
angel sounded; and
there were great voices
in heaven, saying, The
kingdoms of this
world are become *the
kingdoms* of our Lord,
and of his Christ; and
he shall reign for ever
and ever. 16 And the
four and twenty el-
ders, which sat before

γάλης, ἥτις καλεῖται πνευματικῶς Σόδομα καὶ Αἴγυπτος,
[1]great, which is called spiritually Sodom and Egypt,
ὅπου καὶ ὁ κύριος [b]ἡμῶν‖ ἐσταυρώθη. 9 καὶ [c]βλέψουσιν‖
where also [2]Lord [1]our was crucified. And [11]shall [12]see [[1]some]
ἐκ τῶν λαῶν καὶ φυλῶν καὶ γλωσσῶν καὶ ἐθνῶν [d]τὰ πτώ-
[2]of [3]the [4]peoples [5]and [6]tribes [7]and [8]tongues [9]and [10]nations [14]bodies
ματα‖ αὐτῶν ἡμέρας τρεῖς [e]καὶ‖ ἥμισυ, καὶ τὰ πτώματα αὐτῶν
[13]their [16]days [15]three and a half, and their bodies
οὐκ [f]ἀφήσουσιν‖ τεθῆναι εἰς [g]μνήματα.‖ 10 καὶ οἱ κατ-
[3]not [1]they [2]will suffer to be put into tombs. And they that
οικοῦντες ἐπὶ τῆς γῆς [h]χαροῦσιν‖ ἐπ' αὐτοῖς, καὶ [i]εὐφρανθή-
dwell on the earth will rejoice over them, and will make
σονται‖ καὶ δῶρα [k]πέμψουσιν‖ ἀλλήλοις, ὅτι οὗτοι οἱ δύο
merry, and gifts will send to one another, because these, the two
προφῆται ἐβασάνισαν τοὺς κατοικοῦντας ἐπὶ τῆς γῆς.
prophets, tormented them that dwell upon the earth.
11 καὶ μετὰ τὰς τρεῖς ἡμέρας καὶ ἥμισυ, πνεῦμα ζωῆς
And after the three days and a half, [the] spirit of life
ἐκ τοῦ θεοῦ εἰσῆλθεν [l]ἐπ' αὐτούς,‖ καὶ ἔστησαν ἐπὶ τοὺς
from God did enter into them, and they stood upon
πόδας αὐτῶν, καὶ φόβος μέγας [m]ἔπεσεν‖ ἐπὶ τοὺς θεωροῦντας
[2]feet [1]their; and [2]fear [1]great fell upon those beholding
αὐτούς. 12 καὶ ἤκουσαν [n]φωνὴν μεγάλην‖ ἐκ τοῦ οὐρανοῦ,
them: and they heard a [2]voice [1]great out of the heaven,
[o]λέγουσαν‖ αὐτοῖς, [p]Ἀνάβητε‖ ὧδε. Καὶ ἀνέβησαν εἰς τὸν
saying to them, Come up hither. And they went up to the
οὐρανὸν ἐν τῇ νεφέλῃ, καὶ ἐθεώρησαν αὐτοὺς οἱ ἐχθροὶ αὐτῶν.
heaven in the cloud; and [3]beheld [4]them [1]their [2]enemies.
13 Καὶ ἐν ἐκείνῃ τῇ ὥρᾳ ἐγένετο σεισμὸς μέγας, καὶ τὸ
And in that hour there was [3]earthquake [1]a [2]great, and the
δέκατον τῆς πόλεως ἔπεσεν, καὶ ἀπεκτάνθησαν ἐν τῷ σεισμῷ
tenth of the city fell, and there were killed in the earthquake
ὀνόματα ἀνθρώπων χιλιάδες ἑπτά· καὶ οἱ λοιποὶ ἔμφοβοι
[3]names [4]of [5]men [2]thousand [1]seven. And the rest [2]afraid
ἐγένοντο, καὶ ἔδωκαν δόξαν τῷ θεῷ τοῦ οὐρανοῦ.
[1]became, and gave glory to the God of the heaven.

14 Ἡ οὐαὶ [q]ἡ‖ δευτέρα ἀπῆλθεν· ἰδού, ἡ οὐαὶ ἡ τρίτη
[3]Woe [1]the [2]second is past: lo, the [2]woe [1]third
ἔρχεται ταχύ.
comes quickly.

15 Καὶ ὁ ἕβδομος ἄγγελος ἐσάλπισεν, καὶ ἐγένοντο
And the seventh angel sounded [his] trumpet; and [3]were
φωναὶ μεγάλαι ἐν τῷ οὐρανῷ, [r]λέγουσαι,‖ [s]Ἐγένοντο αἱ
[2]voices [1]great in the heaven, saying, [6]Are [7]become [1]the
βασιλεῖαι‖ τοῦ κόσμου τοῦ κυρίου ἡμῶν, καὶ τοῦ χριστοῦ αὐτοῦ,
[2]kingdoms [3]of [4]the [5]world our Lord's, and his Christ's,
καὶ βασιλεύσει εἰς τοὺς αἰῶνας τῶν αἰώνων. 16 Καὶ [t]οἱ‖
and he shall reign to the ages of the ages. And the
εἴκοσι [v]καὶ‖ τέσσαρες πρεσβύτεροι [w]οἱ‖ ἐνώπιον τοῦ θεοῦ [x]καθή-
twenty and four elders, who before God sit

---

[b] αὐτῶν their GLTTrAW. [c] βλέπουσιν see GLTTrAW. [d] τὸ πτῶμα body GLTTrAW. [e] [καὶ] A. [f] ἀφίουσιν they suffer LTTrA; ἀφιοῦσιν W. [g] μνῆμα a tomb GLTTrAW. [h] χαίρουσιν rejoice GLTTrAW. [i] εὐφραίνονται make merry LTTrAW. [k] πέμπουσιν send T. [l] ἐν (— ἐν Tr[A]) αὐτοῖς GLTTrAW. [m] ἐπέπεσεν LTTrAW. [n] φωνῆς μεγάλης TrA. [o] λεγούσης TrA. [p] Ἀνάβατε LTTrAW. [q] — ἡ W. [r] λέγοντες GLTAW. [s] Ἐγένετο ἡ βασιλεία [6]is [7]become [1]the [2]kingdom GLTTrAW. [t] — οἱ L[A]. [v] — καὶ GLTTrAW. [w] — οἱ (*read* καθή. sitting) L[A]. [x] οἳ κάθηνται (*read* who [are] before God who sit) TTr.

μενοι‖ ἐπὶ τοὺς.θρόνους.αὐτῶν, ἔπεσαν ἐπὶ τὰ.πρόσωπα.αὐτῶν,
on their thrones, fell upon their faces,
καὶ προσεκύνησαν τῷ θεῷ, 17 λέγοντες, Εὐχαριστοῦμέν σοι,
and worshipped God, saying, We give thanks to thee,
κύριε ὁ θεὸς ὁ παντοκράτωρ, ὁ ὢν καὶ ὁ ἦν [y]καὶ ὁ
Lord God Almighty, [He] who is, and who was, and who [is]
ἐρχόμενος,‖ [z]ὅτι εἴληφας τὴν δύναμίν σου τὴν μεγάλην,
coming, that thou hast taken [3]power [1]thy [2]great,
καὶ ἐβασίλευσας. 18 καὶ τὰ ἔθνη ὠργίσθησαν, καὶ ἦλθεν ἡ
and reigned. And the nations were angry, and is come
ὀργή σου, καὶ ὁ καιρὸς τῶν νεκρῶν, κριθῆναι, καὶ δοῦναι τὸν
[2]wrath [1]thy, and the time of the dead to be judged, and to give the
μισθὸν τοῖς.δούλοις.σου τοῖς προφήταις, καὶ τοῖς ἁγίοις καὶ
reward to thy bondmen the prophets, and to the saints, and
τοῖς φοβουμένοις τὸ.ὄνομά.σου, [a]τοῖς μικροῖς καὶ τοῖς
to those who fear thy name, the small and the
μεγάλοις,‖ καὶ διαφθεῖραι τοὺς [b]διαφθείροντας‖ τὴν γῆν.
great; and to bring to corruption those who corrupt the earth.

19 Καὶ ἠνοίγη ὁ ναὸς τοῦ θεοῦ [c] ἐν τῷ οὐρανῷ, καὶ ὤφ-
And was opened the temple of God in the heaven, and was
θη ἡ κιβωτὸς τῆς.διαθήκης.[d]αὐτοῦ‖ ἐν τῷ.ναῷ.αὐτοῦ· καὶ
seen the ark of his covenant in his temple: and
ἐγένοντο ἀστραπαὶ καὶ φωναὶ καὶ βρονταὶ καὶ σεισμὸς καὶ
there were lightnings and voices and thunders and an earthquake and
χάλαζα μεγάλη.
[2]hail [1]great.

12 Καὶ σημεῖον μέγα ὤφθη ἐν τῷ οὐρανῷ, γυνὴ περι-
And a [2]sign [1]great was seen in the heaven; a woman cloth-
βεβλημένη τὸν ἥλιον, καὶ ἡ σελήνη ὑποκάτω τῶν.ποδῶν.αὐτῆς,
ed with the sun, and the moon under her feet,
καὶ ἐπὶ τῆς.κεφαλῆς.αὐτῆς στέφανος ἀστέρων δώδεκα· 2 καὶ
and on her head a crown of [2]stars [1]twelve; and
ἐν.γαστρὶ.ἔχουσα, [e] [f]κράζει‖ ὠδίνουσα καὶ βασανιζομένη
being with child she cries being in travail, and being in pain
τεκεῖν.
to bring forth.

3 Καὶ ὤφθη ἄλλο σημεῖον ἐν τῷ οὐρανῷ, καὶ ἰδού, δρά-
And was seen another sign in the heaven, and behold, a [3]dra-
κων [g]μέγας πυῤῥός,‖ ἔχων κεφαλὰς ἑπτὰ καὶ κέρατα δέκα· καὶ
gon [1]great [2]red, having [2]heads [1]seven and [2]horns [1]ten, and
ἐπὶ τὰς.κεφαλὰς.αὐτοῦ [h]διαδήματα ἑπτά·‖ 4 καὶ ἡ.οὐρὰ.αὐτοῦ
upon his heads [2]diadems [1]seven; and his tail
σύρει τὸ τρίτον τῶν ἀστέρων τοῦ οὐρανοῦ, καὶ ἔβαλεν αὐτοὺς
drags the third of the stars of the heaven, and he cast them
εἰς τὴν γῆν. καὶ ὁ δράκων ἕστηκεν ἐνώπιον τῆς γυναικὸς τῆς
to the earth. And the dragon stands before the woman who
μελλούσης τεκεῖν, ἵνα ὅταν τέκῃ, τὸ.τέκνον.αὐτῆς
is about to bring forth, that when she should bring forth, her child
καταφάγῃ. 5 καὶ ἔτεκεν υἱὸν [i]ἄῤῥενα,‖ ὃς μέλλει ποι-
he might devour. And she brought forth a [2]son [1]male, who is about to
μαίνειν πάντα τὰ ἔθνη ἐν ῥάβδῳ σιδηρᾷ· καὶ ἡρπάσθη
shepherd all the nations with [3]rod [1]an [2]iron: and was caught away

God on their seats,
fell upon their faces,
and worshipped God,
17 saying, We give
thee thanks, O Lord
God Almighty, which
art, and wast, and art
to come; because thou
hast taken to thee thy
great power, and hast
reigned. 18 And the na-
tions were angry, and
thy wrath is come, and
the time of the dead,
that they should be
judged, and that thou
shouldest give reward
unto thy servants the
prophets, and to the
saints, and them that
fear thy name, small
and great; and should-
est destroy them
which destroy the
earth.

19 And the temple
of God was opened in
heaven, and there was
seen in his temple the
ark of his testament:
and there were light-
nings, and voices, and
thunderings, and an
earthquake, and great
hail.

XII. And there ap-
peared a great wonder
in heaven; a woman
clothed with the sun,
and the moon under
her feet, and upon her
head a crown of
twelve stars: 2 And
she being with child
cried, travailing in
birth, and pained to
be delivered.

3 And there ap-
peared another won-
der in heaven; and
behold a great red
dragon, having seven
heads and ten horns,
and seven crowns upon
his heads. 4 And his
tail drew the third
part of the stars of
heaven, and did cast
them to the earth:
and the dragon stood
before the woman
which was ready to be
delivered, for to de-
vour her child as soon
as it was born. 5 And
she brought forth a
man child, who was to
rule all nations with
a rod of iron: and her

[y] — καὶ ὁ ἐρχόμενος GLTTrAW. [z] + καὶ and T. [a] τοὺς μικροὺς καὶ τοὺς μεγάλους LTTrA. [b] διαφθείραντας corrupted L. [c] + ὁ which [is] LTTr. [d] τοῦ κυρίου (read the covenant of the Lord) G. [e] + καὶ and LT[A]. [f] ἔκραζεν was crying L. [g] πυῤῥὸς μέγας LTTrA. [h] ἑπτὰ διαδήματα GLTTrAW. [i] ἄρσεν LTTrAW.

child was caught up unto God, and *to* his throne. 6 And the woman fled into the wilderness, where she hath a place prepared of God, that they should feed her there a thousand two hundred *and* threescore days.

7 And there was war in heaven: Michael and his angels fought against the dragon; and the dragon fought and his angels, 8 and prevailed not; neither was their place found any more in heaven. 9 And the great dragon was cast out, that old serpent, called the Devil, and Satan, which deceiveth the whole world: he was cast out into the earth, and his angels were cast out with him. 10 And I heard a loud voice saying in heaven, Now is come salvation, and strength, and the kingdom of our God, and the power of his Christ: for the accuser of our brethren is cast down, which accused them before our God day and night. 11 And they overcame him by the blood of the Lamb, and by the word of their testimony; and they loved not their lives unto the death. 12 Therefore rejoice, *ye* heavens, and *ye* that dwell in them. Woe to the inhabiters of the earth and of the sea! for the devil is come down unto you, having great wrath, because he knoweth that he hath but a short time.

13 And when the dragon saw that he was cast unto the earth, he persecuted the woman which brought forth the man *child*. 14 And to

τὸ.τέκνον.αὐτῆς πρὸς τὸν θεὸν καὶ [k] τὸν.θρόνον.αὐτοῦ. 6 καὶ
her child to God and his throne. And

ἡ γυνὴ ἔφυγεν εἰς τὴν ἔρημον, ὅπου ἔχει [l] τόπον ἡτοιμασ-
the woman fled into the wilderness, where she has a place pre-

μένον ἀπὸ τοῦ θεοῦ, ἵνα ἐκεῖ [m]τρέφωσιν" αὐτὴν ἡμέρας
pared of God, that there they should nourish her [7]days

χιλίας διακοσίας ἑξήκοντα.
[1]a [2]thousand [3]two [4]hundred [[5]and] [6]sixty.

7 Καὶ ἐγένετο πόλεμος ἐν τῷ οὐρανῷ· [n]ὁ" Μιχαὴλ καὶ
And there was war in the heaven: Michael and

οἱ.ἄγγελοι.αὐτοῦ [o]ἐπολέμησαν κατὰ" τοῦ δράκοντος, καὶ ὁ
his angels warred against the dragon, and the

δράκων ἐπολέμησεν, καὶ οἱ.ἄγγελοι.αὐτοῦ· 8 καὶ οὐκ [p]ἴσχυ-
dragon warred, and his angels; and [3]not [1]they [2]pre-

σαν," [q]οὔτε" τόπος εὑρέθη αὐτῶν ἔτι ἐν τῷ οὐρανῷ. 9 καὶ
vailed, nor [3]place [1]was [4]found [2]their any more in the heaven. And

ἐβλήθη ὁ δράκων ὁ μέγας, ὁ ὄφις ὁ ἀρχαῖος, ὁ καλού-
was cast [out] the [2]dragon [1]great, the [2]serpent [1]ancient, who is

μενος διάβολος, καὶ ὁ σατανᾶς, ὁ πλανῶν τὴν οἰκουμένην
called Devil, and the Satan, who misleads the [2]habitable

ὅλην, ἐβλήθη εἰς τὴν γῆν, καὶ οἱ.ἄγγελοι.αὐτοῦ
[[3]world] [1]whole, he was cast into the earth, and his angels

μετ᾽ αὐτοῦ ἐβλήθησαν. 10 Καὶ ἤκουσα φωνὴν μεγάλην [r]λέ-
[3]with [4]him [1]were [2]cast. And I heard a [2]voice [1]great

γουσαν ἐν τῷ οὐρανῷ," Ἄρτι ἐγένετο ἡ σωτηρία καὶ ἡ δύνα-
saying in the heaven, Now is come the salvation and the power

μις καὶ ἡ βασιλεία τοῦ.θεοῦ.ἡμῶν, καὶ ἡ ἐξουσία τοῦ χριστοῦ
and the kingdom of our God, and the authority [3]Christ

αὐτοῦ· ὅτι [s]κατεβλήθη" ὁ [t]κατήγορος" τῶν.ἀδελφῶν.ἡμῶν,
[1]of [2]his; because is cast down the accuser of our brethren,

ὁ κατηγορῶν [v]αὐτῶν" ἐνώπιον τοῦ.θεοῦ.ἡμῶν ἡμέρας καὶ
who accuses them before our God day and

νυκτός. 11 καὶ αὐτοὶ ἐνίκησαν αὐτὸν διὰ τὸ αἷμα τοῦ
night. And they overcame him by reason of the blood of the

ἀρνίου, καὶ διὰ τὸν λόγον τῆς.μαρτυρίας.αὐτῶν, καὶ
Lamb, and by reason of the word of their testimony, and

[w]οὐκ" ἠγάπησαν τὴν.ψυχὴν.αὐτῶν ἄχρι θανάτου. 12 διὰ
[2]not [1]loved their life unto death. Because of

τοῦτο εὐφραίνεσθε [x]οἱ" οὐρανοὶ καὶ οἱ ἐν αὐτοῖς σκηνοῦντες.
this rejoice ye heavens and [ye] who in them tabernacle.

οὐαὶ [y]τοῖς κατοικοῦσιν" [z]τὴν γῆν καὶ τὴν θάλασσαν," ὅτι
Woe to those who inhabit the earth and the sea, because

κατέβη ὁ διάβολος πρὸς ὑμᾶς ἔχων θυμὸν μέγαν, εἰ-
is come down the devil to you having [2]fury [1]great, know-

δὼς ὅτι ὀλίγον καιρὸν ἔχει.
ing that a short time he has.

13 Καὶ ὅτε εἶδεν ὁ δράκων ὅτι ἐβλήθη εἰς τὴν γῆν,
And when [3]saw [1]the [2]dragon that he was cast into the earth,

ἐδίωξεν τὴν γυναῖκα ἥτις ἔτεκεν τὸν [a]ἄρρενα." 14 καὶ
he persecuted the woman which brought forth the male [child]. And

---

[k] + πρὸς to GLTTrAW. [l] + ἐκεῖ there GTAW. [m] τρέφουσιν they nourish TTr; ἐκτρέφωσιν W. [n] ὅ τε both L. [o] τοῦ (— τοῦ T[A]) πολεμῆσαι μετὰ warred with GLTTrAW. [p] ἴσχυσεν he prevailed G. [q] οὐδὲ GLTTrAW. [r] ἐν τῷ οὐρανῷ λέγουσαν GLTTrAW. [s] ἐβλήθη is cast [out] LTTrA. [t] κατήγωρ GLTA. [v] αὐτοὺς LTA. [w] οὐχ L. [x] — οἱ TTrA. [y] — τοῖς κατοικοῦσιν GLTTrAW. [z] τῇ γῇ καὶ τῇ θαλάσσῃ GW. [a] ἄρσεναν L; ἄρσενα TTrA.

ἐδόθησαν τῇ γυναικὶ [b] δύο πτέρυγες τοῦ ἀετοῦ τοῦ μεγάλου,
were given to the woman two wings of the [2]eagle [1]great,
ἵνα πέτηται εἰς τὴν ἔρημον εἰς τὸν.τόπον.αὐτῆς, ὅπου τρέ-
that she might fly into the wilderness into her place, where she is
φεται ἐκεῖ καιρόν, καὶ καιρούς, καὶ ἥμισυ καιροῦ, ἀπὸ
nourished there a time, and times, and half a time, from [the]
προσώπου τοῦ ὄφεως. 15 καὶ ἔβαλεν ὁ ὄφις [c]ὀπίσω τῆς
face of the serpent. And [3]cast [1]the [2]serpent [8]after [9]the
γυναικὸς ἐκ τοῦ.στόματος.αὐτοῦ‖ ὕδωρ ὡς ποταμόν, ἵνα
[10]woman [4]out [5]of [6]his [7]mouth water as a river, that
[d]ταύτην‖ ποταμοφόρητον ποιήσῃ. 16 καὶ
[4]her [[5]as [6]one] [7]carried [8]away [9]by [10]a [11]river [1]he [2]might [3]make. And
ἐβοήθησεν ἡ γῆ τῇ γυναικί, καὶ ἤνοιξεν ἡ γῆ τὸ στόμα
[3]helped [1]the [2]earth the woman, and [3]opened [1]the [2]earth [5]mouth
αὐτῆς, καὶ κατέπιεν τὸν ποταμὸν ὃν ἔβαλεν ὁ δράκων
[4]its, and swallowed up the river which [3]cast [1]the [2]dragon
ἐκ τοῦ.στόματος.αὐτοῦ. 17 καὶ ὠργίσθη ὁ δράκων [e]ἐπὶ‖
out of his mouth. And [3]was [4]angry [1]the [2]dragon with
τῇ γυναικί, καὶ ἀπῆλθεν ποιῆσαι πόλεμον μετὰ τῶν λοιπῶν
the woman, and went to make war with the rest
τοῦ.σπέρματος.αὐτῆς, τῶν τηρούντων τὰς ἐντολὰς τοῦ
of her seed, who keep the commandments
θεοῦ, καὶ ἐχόντων τὴν μαρτυρίαν [f]τοῦ‖ Ἰησοῦ [g]χριστοῦ.‖
of God, and have the testimony of Jesus Christ.
18 Καὶ [h]ἐστάθην‖ ἐπὶ τὴν ἄμμον τῆς θαλάσσης· 13 καὶ
And I stood upon the sand of the sea; and
εἶδον ἐκ τῆς θαλάσσης θηρίον ἀναβαῖνον, ἔχον [i]κεφαλὰς
I saw out of the sea a beast rising, having [2]heads
ἑπτὰ καὶ κέρατα δέκα·‖ καὶ ἐπὶ τῶν.κεράτων.αὐτοῦ δέκα δια-
[1]seven and [2]horns [1]ten, and on its horns ten dia-
δήματα, καὶ ἐπὶ τὰς.κεφαλὰς.αὐτοῦ [k]ὄνομα‖ βλασφημίας.
dems, and upon its heads [the] name of blasphemy.
2 καὶ τὸ θηρίον ὃ εἶδον ἦν ὅμοιον παρδάλει, καὶ οἱ πόδες
And the beast which I saw was like to a leopard, and [2]feet
αὐτοῦ ὡς [l]ἄρκτου,‖ καὶ τὸ.στόμα.αὐτοῦ ὡς στόμα [m]λέοντος.‖
[1]its as of a bear, and its mouth as [the] mouth of a lion;
καὶ ἔδωκεν αὐτῷ ὁ δράκων τὴν.δύναμιν.αὐτοῦ, καὶ τὸν θρόνον
and [3]gave [4]to [5]it [1]the [2]dragon his power, and [2]throne
αὐτοῦ, καὶ ἐξουσίαν μεγάλην. 3 καὶ [n]εἶδον‖ μίαν [o] τῶν κεφα-
[1]his, and [2]authority [1]great. And I saw one [3]heads
λῶν αὐτοῦ ὡς ἐσφαγμένην εἰς θάνατον· καὶ ἡ πληγὴ τοῦ
[1]of [2]its as slain to death; and the wound
θανάτου αὐτοῦ ἐθεραπεύθη, καὶ [p]ἐθαυμάσθη‖ [q]ἐν‖ [r]ὅλῃ τῇ
[3]death [1]of [2]its was healed: and there was wonder in [2]whole [1]the
γῇ‖ ὀπίσω τοῦ θηρίου. 4 καὶ προσεκύνησαν [s]τὸν δράκοντα‖
earth after the beast. And they did homage to the dragon,
[t]ὃς‖ ἔδωκεν [v]ἐξουσίαν τῷ θηρίῳ, καὶ προσεκύνησαν [w]τὸ
who gave authority to the beast; and they did homage to the
θηρίον,‖ λέγοντες, Τίς ὅμοιος τῷ θηρίῳ; [x]τίς δύναται
beast, saying, Who [is] like to the beast? who is able

the woman were given two wings of a great eagle, that she might fly into the wilderness, into her place, where she is nourished for a time, and times, and half a time, from the face of the serpent. 15 And the serpent cast out of his mouth water as a flood after the woman, that he might cause her to be carried away of the flood. 16 And the earth helped the woman, and the earth opened her mouth, and swallowed up the flood which the dragon cast out of his mouth. 17 And the dragon was wroth with the woman, and went to make war with the remnant of her seed, which keep the commandments of God, and have the testimony of Jesus Christ.

XIII. And I stood upon the sand of the sea, and saw a beast rise up out of the sea, having seven heads and ten horns, and upon his horns ten crowns, and upon his heads the name of blasphemy. 2 And the beast which I saw was like unto a leopard, and his feet were as *the feet* of a bear, and his mouth as the mouth of a lion: and the dragon gave him his power, and his seat, and great authority. 3 And I saw one of his heads as it were wounded to death; and his deadly wound was healed: and all the world wondered after the beast. 4 And they worshipped the dragon which gave power unto the beast: and they worshipped the beast, saying, Who *is* like unto the beast? who is able

[b] + αἱ the LTTr[A]W. [c] ἐκ τοῦ στόματος αὐτοῦ ὀπίσω τῆς γυναικὸς GLTTrAW. [d] αὐτὴν GLTTrAW. [e] — ἐπὶ (*read* τῇ with the) L. [f] — τοῦ GLTTrAW. [g] — χριστοῦ GLTTrAW. [h] ἐστάθη it stood LTrA. [i] κέρατα δέκα καὶ κεφαλὰς ἑπτά GLTTrAW. [k] ὀνόματα names GLTTrW. [l] ἄρκου GLTTrAW. [m] λεόντων of lions T. [n] — εἶδον GLTTrAW. [o] + ἐκ of (its) GLTTrAW. [p] ἐθαύμασεν (*read* the whole earth wondered) EGTAW. [q] — ἐν EGLTAW. [r] ὅλη ἡ γῆ EGLTAW. [s] τῷ δράκοντι GLTTrAW. [t] ὅτι (*read* because he gave) GLTTrAW. [v] + τὴν the GLTTrAW. [w] τῷ θηρίῳ GLTTrAW. [x] + καὶ and GLTTrAW

to make war with him? 5 And there was given unto him a mouth speaking great things and blasphemies; and power was given unto him to continue forty *and* two months. 6 And he opened his mouth in blasphemy against God, to blaspheme his name, and his tabernacle, and them that dwell in heaven. 7 And it was given unto him to make war with the saints, and to overcome them: and power was given him over all kindreds, and tongues, and nations. 8 And all that dwell upon the earth shall worship him, whose names are not written in the book of life of the Lamb slain from the foundation of the world. 9 If any man have an ear, let him hear. 10 He that leadeth into captivity shall go into captivity: he that killeth with the sword must be killed with the sword. Here is the patience and the faith of the saints.

11 And I beheld another beast coming up out of the earth; and he had two horns like a lamb, and he spake as a dragon. 12 And he exerciseth all the power of the first beast before him, and causeth the earth and them which dwell therein to worship the first beast, whose deadly wound was healed. 13 And he doeth great wonders, so that he maketh fire come down from heaven on the earth in the sight of men, 14 and deceiveth them that dwell on the earth by *the means of* those miracles which

πολεμῆσαι μετ' αὐτοῦ; 5 καὶ ἐδόθη αὐτῷ στόμα λαλοῦν
to make war with it? And was given to it a mouth speaking
μεγάλα καὶ [y]βλασφημίας· καὶ ἐδόθη αὐτῷ ἐξουσία[z] ποιῆ-
great things and blasphemy; and was given to it authority to
σαι μῆνας [a]τεσσαράκοντα [b]δύο· 6 καὶ ἤνοιξεν τὸ.στόμα.αὐτοῦ
act [3]months [1]forty [2]two. And it opened its mouth
εἰς [c]βλασφημίαν πρὸς τὸν θεόν, βλασφημῆσαι τὸ ὄνομα
for blasphemy against God, to blaspheme [2]name
αὐτοῦ, καὶ τὴν.σκηνὴν.αὐτοῦ, [d]καὶ τοὺς ἐν τῷ οὐρανῷ
[1]his, and his tabernacle, and those who [2]in [3]the [4]heaven
σκηνοῦντας. 7 [e]καὶ ἐδόθη αὐτῷ [f]πόλεμον ποιῆσαι μετὰ τῶν
[1]tabernacle. And was given to it [3]war [1]to [2]make with the
ἁγίων, καὶ νικῆσαι αὐτούς· καὶ ἐδόθη αὐτῷ ἐξουσία ἐπὶ
saints, and to overcome them; and was given to it authority over
πᾶσαν φυλὴν [g] καὶ γλῶσσαν καὶ ἔθνος. 8 καὶ προσκυνήσου-
every tribe, and tongue, and nation; and shall do homage
σιν [h]αὐτῷ πάντες οἱ κατοικοῦντες ἐπὶ τῆς γῆς [i]ὧν οὐ
to it all who dwell on the earth of whom [2]not
γέγραπται [k]τὰ ὀνόματα ἐν [l]τῷ βίβλῳ τῆς ζωῆς τοῦ
[1]have been written the names [7]in [8]the [9]book [10]of [11]life [12]of [13]the
ἀρνίου [m] ἐσφαγμένου ἀπὸ καταβολῆς κόσμου. 9 Εἴ
[15]Lamb [14]slain [1]from [[2]the] [3]founding [4]of [[5]the] [6]world. If
τις ἔχει οὖς, ἀκουσάτω. 10 Εἴ τις [n] [o]αἰχμαλωσίαν
anyone has an ear, let him hear. If anyone [[2]into] [3]captivity
[p]συνάγει, εἰς αἰχμαλωσίαν ὑπάγει· εἴ τις ἐν [q]μαχαίρᾳ
[1]gathers, into captivity he goes. If anyone with [the] sword
[r]ἀποκτενεῖ, [s]δεῖ αὐτὸν ἐν [q]μαχαίρᾳ ἀποκτανθῆναι· ὧδέ
will kill, [2]must [1]he with [the] sword be killed. Here
ἐστιν ἡ ὑπομονὴ καὶ ἡ πίστις τῶν ἁγίων.
is the endurance and the faith of the saints.

11 Καὶ εἶδον ἄλλο θηρίον ἀναβαῖνον ἐκ τῆς γῆς, καὶ
And I saw another beast rising out of the earth, and
εἶχεν κέρατα δύο ὅμοια ἀρνίῳ, καὶ ἐλάλει ὡς δράκων. 12 καὶ
it had [2]horns [1]two like to a lamb, and spoke as a dragon; and
τὴν ἐξουσίαν τοῦ πρώτου θηρίου πᾶσαν ποιεῖ ἐνώπιον
[2]the [3]authority [4]of [5]the [6]first [7]beast [1]all it exercises before
αὐτοῦ· καὶ ποιεῖ τὴν γῆν καὶ τοὺς [t]κατοικοῦντας ἐν αὐτῇ
it, and causes the earth and those who dwell in it
ἵνα [v]προσκυνήσωσιν τὸ θηρίον τὸ πρῶτον, οὗ ἐθερα-
that they should do homage to the [2]beast [1]first, of whom was
πεύθη ἡ πληγὴ τοῦ.θανάτου.αὐτοῦ· 13 καὶ ποιεῖ σημεῖα
healed the wound of its death. And it works [2]signs
μεγάλα, [w]ἵνα καὶ πῦρ ποιῇ [x]καταβαίνειν ἐκ τοῦ οὐ-
[1]great, that even fire it should cause to come down out of the hea-
ρανοῦ εἰς τὴν γῆν ἐνώπιον τῶν ἀνθρώπων. 14 καὶ πλανᾷ
ven to the earth before men. And it misleads
τοὺς κατοικοῦντας ἐπὶ τῆς γῆς, διὰ τὰ σημεῖα ἃ
those who dwell on the earth, by reason of the signs which

---

[y] βλάσφημα blasphemous [things] LA. [z] + πόλεμον war (*read* ποιῆ. to make) E. [a] τεσσαρακονταδύο E; τεσσεράκοντα δύο LTTrA. [b] + [καὶ] and L. [c] βλασφημίας LTTrAW. [d] — καὶ LTTrAW. [e] — καὶ ἐδόθη . . . νικῆσαι αὐτούς L. [f] ποιῆσαι πόλεμον TTrA. [g] + καὶ λαὸν and people GLTTrAW. [h] αὐτὸν GLTTrAW. [i] οὗ (*read* [everyone] of whom has not been written) LTTrA. [k] τὸ ὄνομα αὐτοῦ his name LTTrA; τὸ ὄνομα the name GW. [l] τῷ βιβλίῳ GLTTrAW. [m] + τοῦ (*read* which was slain) GLTTrAW. [n] + εἰς [is] for LTAW. [o] — αἰχμαλωσίαν (*read* εἰς for) Tr. [p] — συνάγει LTTrAW. [q] μαχαίρῃ LTTrA. [r] ἀποκταίνει kills L; ἀποκτανθῆναι to be killed A. [s] — δεῖ A. [t] ἐν αὐτῇ κατοικοῦντας GTTrA. [v] προσκυνήσουσιν they shall do homage LTTrA. [w] καὶ πῦρ ἵνα GW. [x] ἐκ τοῦ οὐρανοῦ καταβαίνειν (καταβῇ G; καταβαίνῃ should come down W) GLTrAW

ἐδόθη αὐτῷ ποιῆσαι ἐνώπιον τοῦ θηρίου, λέγων τοῖς
it was given to it to work before the beast, saying to those who
κατοικοῦσιν ἐπὶ τῆς γῆς, ποιῆσαι [z]εἰκόνα‖ τῷ θηρίῳ [a]ὃ‖
dwell on the earth, to make an image to the beast, which
ἔχει τὴν πληγὴν τῆς [b]μαχαίρας‖ καὶ ἔζησεν. 15 καὶ ἐδόθη
has the wound of the sword, and lived. And it was given
[c]αὐτῷ‖ [d]δοῦναι πνεῦμα‖ τῇ εἰκόνι τοῦ θηρίου, ἵνα καὶ λα-
to it to give breath to the image of the beast, that [7]also [6]should
λήσῃ ἡ εἰκὼν τοῦ θηρίου, καὶ ποιήσῃ, [e] ὅσοι [f]ἂν‖ μὴ
[8]speak [1]the [2]image [3]of [4]the [5]beast, and should cause as many as [2]not
[g]προσκυνήσωσιν‖ [h]τὴν εἰκόνα‖ τοῦ θηρίου [i]ἵνα‖ ἀποκτανθῶσιν.
[1]would do homage to the image of the beast that they should be killed.
16 καὶ ποιεῖ πάντας, τοὺς μικροὺς καὶ τοὺς μεγάλους, καὶ
And it causes all, the small and the great, and
τοὺς πλουσίους καὶ τοὺς πτωχούς, καὶ τοὺς ἐλευθέρους καὶ
the rich and the poor, and the free and
τοὺς δούλους, ἵνα [k]δώσῃ‖ αὐτοῖς χάραγμα ἐπὶ τῆς χειρὸς
the bondmen, that it should give them a mark on [3]hand
αὐτῶν τῆς δεξιᾶς, ἢ ἐπὶ [l]τῶν μετώπων‖ αὐτῶν, 17 [m]καὶ‖ ἵνα
[1]their [2]right, or on [2]foreheads [1]their; and that
μή.τις δύνηται ἀγοράσαι ἢ πωλῆσαι, εἰ.μὴ ὁ ἔχων τὸ
no one should be able to buy or to sell, except he who has the
χάραγμα [n]ἢ‖ [o]τὸ ὄνομα‖ τοῦ θηρίου, ἢ τὸν ἀριθμὸν τοῦ
mark or the name of the beast, or the number
ὀνόματος αὐτοῦ. 18 Ὧδε ἡ σοφία ἐστίν. ὁ ἔχων [p]τὸν‖
[3]name [1]of [2]its. Here [2]wisdom [1]is. He who has
νοῦν, ψηφισάτω τὸν ἀριθμὸν τοῦ θηρίου· ἀριθμὸς.γὰρ
understanding let him count the number of the beast: for [2]number
ἀνθρώπου ἐστίν, καὶ ὁ.ἀριθμὸς.αὐτοῦ [q] [r]χξς΄.‖
[1]a [3]man's it is; and its number [is] 666.

14 Καὶ [s]εἶδον,‖ καὶ ἰδού, [t] ἀρνίον [v]ἑστηκὸς‖ ἐπὶ τὸ ὄρος
And I saw, and behold, [the] Lamb standing upon mount
Σιών, καὶ μετ' αὐτοῦ ἑκατὸν [w]τεσσαράκοντα τέσσαρες‖
Sion, and with him a hundred [and] forty four
χιλιάδες, ἔχουσαι τὸ ὄνομα [x] τοῦ.πατρὸς.αὐτοῦ γεγραμμένον
thousand, having the name of his Father written
ἐπὶ τῶν.μετώπων.αὐτῶν. 2 καὶ ἤκουσα φωνὴν ἐκ τοῦ οὐ-
on their foreheads. And I heard a voice out of the hea-
ρανοῦ ὡς φωνὴν ὑδάτων πολλῶν, καὶ ὡς φωνὴν βροντῆς
ven as a voice of [2]waters [1]many, and as a voice of [2]thunder
μεγάλης· καὶ [y]φωνὴν ἤκουσα‖ [z]κιθαρῳδῶν κιθαριζόντων ἐν
[1]great: and a voice I heard of harpers harping with
ταῖς.κιθάραις.αὐτῶν. 3 καὶ ᾄδουσιν [aa]ὡς‖ ᾠδὴν καινὴν ἐνώ-
their harps. And they sing as a [2]song [1]new be-
πιον τοῦ θρόνου, καὶ ἐνώπιον τῶν τεσσάρων ζώων καὶ
fore the throne, and before the four living creatures and
τῶν πρεσβυτέρων· καὶ οὐδεὶς [ba]ἠδύνατο‖ μαθεῖν τὴν ᾠδήν,
the elders. And no one was able to learn the song

he had power to do in the sight of the beast; saying to them that dwell on the earth, that they should make an image to the beast, which had the wound by a sword, and did live.
15 And he had power to give life unto the image of the beast, that the image of the beast should both speak, and cause that as many as would not worship the image of the beast should be killed.
16 And he causeth all, both small and great, rich and poor, free and bond, to receive a mark in their right hand, or in their foreheads:
17 And that no man might buy or sell, save he that had the mark, or the name of the beast, or the number of his name.
18 Here is wisdom. Let him that hath understanding count the number of the beast: for it is the number of a man; and his number *is* Six hundred threescore *and* six.

XIV. And I looked, and, lo, a Lamb stood on the mount Sion, and with him an hundred forty *and* four thousand, having his Father's name written in their foreheads.
2 And I heard a voice from heaven, as the voice of many waters, and as the voice of a great thunder: and I heard the voice of harpers harping with their harps:
3 And they sung as it were a new song before the throne, and before the four beasts, and the elders: and no man could learn that song but the hundred *and*

---

[z] εἰκόναν L. [a] ὃς who LTTrAW. [b] μαχαίρης LTTrA. [c] αὐτῇ (*that is, the image*) L. [d] πνεῦμα δοῦναι W. [e] + ἵνα that LTr[A]W. [f] ἐὰν LTTrA. [g] προσκυνήσουσιν shall do homage T. [h] τῇ εἰκόνι GTTrW. [i] — ἵνα (*omit* that they) LTTrAW. [k] δῶσιν they should give GLTTrAW. [l] τὸ μέτωπον forehead GLTTrAW. [m] — καὶ LT[A]. [n] — ἢ GLTTrAW. [o] τοῦ ὀνόματος of the name L. [p] — τὸν GLTTrAW. [q] + ἐστιν is Tr. [r] ἑξακόσιοι ἑξήκοντα ἕξ six hundred [and] sixty-six LA. [s] ἴδον T. [t] + τὸ the GLTTrAW. [v] ἑστὸς LTTrAW. [w] τεσσαρακοντατέσσαρες EGW; τεσσεράκοντα τέσσαρες LTTrA. [x] + αὐτου καὶ τὸ ὄνομα (*read* his name and the name) GLTTrAW. [y] ἡ φωνὴ ἣν ἤκουσα the voice which I heard [was] GLTTrAW. [z] + ὡς as GLTTrAW. [aa] — ὡς GT[TrA]. [ba] ἐδύνατο LTTrA.

forty *and* four thou-
sand, which were re-
deemed from the earth.
4 These are they which
were not defiled with
women; for they are
virgins. These are they
which follow the Lamb
whithersoever he go-
eth. These were re-
deemed from among
men, *being* the first-
fruits unto God and
to the Lamb. 5 And
in their mouth was
found no guile: for
they are without fault
before the throne of
God.

6 And I saw another
angel fly in the midst
of heaven, having the
everlasting gospel to
preach unto them that
dwell on the earth, and
to every nation, and
kindred, and tongue,
and people, 7 saying
with a loud voice,
Fear God, and give
glory to him; for the
hour of his judgment
is come: and worship
him that made hea-
ven, and earth, and
the sea, and the foun-
tains of waters.

8 And there followed
another angel, saying,
Babylon is fallen, is
fallen, that great city,
because she made all
nations drink of the
wine of the wrath of
her fornication.

9 And the third angel
followed them, saying
with a loud voice, If
any man worship the
beast and his image,
and receive *his* mark
in his forehead, or in
his hand, 10 the same
shall drink of the wine
of the wrath of God,
which is poured out
without mixture into
the cup of his indig-
nation; and he shall
be tormented with fire
and brimstone in the
presence of the holy
angels, and in the pre-
sence of the Lamb:

εἰ.μὴ αἱ ἑκατὸν [c]τεσσαράκοντα τέσσαρες‖ χιλιάδες, οἱ
except the hundred [and] forty four thousand, who
ἠγορασμένοι ἀπὸ τῆς γῆς. 4 οὗτοί εἰσιν οἳ μετὰ
have been purchased from the earth. These are they who with
γυναικῶν οὐκ.ἐμολύνθησαν· παρθένοι.γάρ εἰσιν· οὗτοί [d]εἰσιν‖
women were not defiled, for virgins they are: these are
οἱ ἀκολουθοῦντες τῷ ἀρνίῳ ὅπου ἂν [e]ὑπάγῃ.‖ οὗτοι
they who follow the Lamb wheresoever he may go. These
ἠγοράσθησαν ἀπὸ τῶν ἀνθρώπων, ἀπαρχὴ τῷ θεῷ καὶ
were purchased from among men [as] firstfruits to God and
τῷ ἀρνίῳ. 5 καὶ ἐν τῷ.στόματι.αὐτῶν οὐχ.εὑρέθη [f]δόλος·‖
to the Lamb: and in their mouth was not found guile;
ἄμωμοι.[g]γάρ‖ εἰσιν [h]ἐνώπιον τοῦ θρόνου τοῦ θεοῦ.‖
for blameless they are before the throne of God.

6 Καὶ εἶδον [i]ἄλλον‖ ἄγγελον [j]πετώμενον‖ ἐν μεσου-
And I saw another angel flying in mid-
ρανήματι, ἔχοντα εὐαγγέλιον αἰώνιον εὐαγγελίσαι [k]
heaven, having [the] [2]glad [3]tidings [1]everlasting to announce [to]
τοὺς [l]κατοικοῦντας‖ ἐπὶ τῆς γῆς, καὶ [m] πᾶν ἔθνος καὶ φυλὴν
those who dwell on the earth, and every nation and tribe
καὶ γλῶσσαν καὶ λαόν, 7 [n]λέγοντα‖ [o]ἐν‖ φωνῇ μεγάλῃ,
and tongue and people, saying with a [2]voice [1]loud,
Φοβήθητε τὸν θεόν, καὶ δότε αὐτῷ δόξαν, ὅτι ἦλθεν ἡ ὥρα
Fear God, and give to him glory, because is come the hour
τῆς.κρίσεως.αὐτοῦ· καὶ προσκυνήσατε τῷ ποιήσαντι τὸν
of his judgment; and do homage to him who made the
οὐρανὸν καὶ τὴν γῆν καὶ [p] θάλασσαν καὶ πηγὰς ὑδάτων.
heaven and the earth and sea and fountains of waters.

8 Καὶ ἄλλος [q]ἄγγελος‖ ἠκολούθησεν, λέγων, Ἔπεσεν [r]ἔπε-
And another angel followed, saying, Is fallen, is
σεν‖ [s]Βαβυλὼν‖ [t]ἡ πόλις‖ ἡ μεγάλη· [v]ὅτι‖ ἐκ τοῦ οἴνου τοῦ
fallen Babylon [3]city [1]the [2]great, because of the wine of the
θυμοῦ τῆς.πορνείας.αὐτῆς πεπότικεν πάντα [w] ἔθνη.
fury of her fornication she has given [3]to [4]drink [1]all [2]nations.

9 Καὶ [x] [y]τρίτος ἄγγελος‖ ἠκολούθησεν αὐτοῖς, λέγων ἐν
And a third angel followed them, saying, with
φωνῇ μεγάλῃ, Εἴ τις [z]τὸ θηρίον προσκυνεῖ‖ καὶ τὴν
a [2]voice [1]loud, If anyone [4]the [5]beast [1]does [2]homage [3]to and
εἰκόνα αὐτοῦ, καὶ λαμβάνει χάραγμα ἐπὶ τοῦ.μετώπου.αὐτοῦ,
[2]image [1]its, and receives a mark on his forehead
ἢ ἐπὶ τὴν.χεῖρα.αὐτοῦ, 10 καὶ αὐτὸς πίεται ἐκ τοῦ οἴνου
or upon his hand, also he shall drink of the wine
τοῦ θυμοῦ τοῦ θεοῦ, τοῦ κεκερασμένου ἀκράτου ἐν τῷ
of the fury of God which is mixed undiluted in the
ποτηρίῳ τῆς.ὀργῆς.αὐτοῦ, καὶ βασανισθήσεται ἐν πυρὶ καὶ
cup of his wrath, and he shall be tormented in fire and
θείῳ ἐνώπιον [a]τῶν‖ [b]ἁγίων ἀγγέλων,‖ καὶ ἐνώπιον τοῦ
brimstone, before the holy angels, and before the

---

[c] τεσσαρακοντατέσσαρες EGW; τεσσεράκοντα τέσσαρες LTTrA. [d] — εισιν (*read* [are]) LTTrA. [e] ὑπάγει he goes LTrA. [f] ψεῦδος falsehood GLTTrAW. [g] — γάρ for LA. [h] — ἐνώπιον τοῦ θρόνου τοῦ θεοῦ GLTTrAW. [i] [ἄλλον] A. [j] πετόμενον GLTTrAW. [k] + ἐπὶ unto LTTrAW. [l] καθημένους sit GLTTrAW. [m] + ἐπὶ unto GLTTrAW. [n] λέγων GLTTrAW. [o] — ἐν (*read* φωνῇ with a voice) L. [p] + τὴν the GTW. [q] δεύτερος ἄγγελος a second angel LTrAW; ἄγ. δεύ. T. [r] [ἔπεσεν] A. [s] Βαβουλὼν E. [t] — ἡ πόλις GLTTrAW. [v] ἣ which (*read* πεπ. has given to drink) LTTrAW. [w] + τὰ the LTTrAW. [x] + ἄλλος another GLTTrAW. [y] ἄγγελος τρίτος GLTTrAW. [z] προσκυνεῖ τὸ θηρίον GLTTrAW. [a] — τῶν LTTr. [b] ἀγγέλων ἁγίων LTTr; — ἁγίων A.

ἀρνίου· 11 καὶ ὁ καπνὸς τοῦ.βασανισμοῦ.αὐτῶν [c]ἀναβαίνει
Lamb. And the smoke of their torment goes up
εἰς αἰῶνας αἰώνων·‖ καὶ οὐκ.ἔχουσιν ἀνάπαυσιν ἡμέρας καὶ
to ages of ages, and they have no respite day and
νυκτὸς οἱ προσκυνοῦντες τὸ θηρίον καὶ τὴν.εἰκόνα.αὐτοῦ, καὶ
night who do homage to the beast and its image, and
εἴ τις λαμβάνει τὸ χάραγμα τοῦ.ὀνόματος.αὐτοῦ. 12 Ὧδε [d]
if anyone receives the mark of its name. Here [²the]
ὑπομονὴ τῶν ἁγίων ἐστίν· [e]ὧδε‖ οἱ τηροῦντες τὰς ἐν-
³endurance ⁴of ⁵the ⁶saints ¹is, here they who keep the command-
τολὰς τοῦ θεοῦ καὶ τὴν πίστιν Ἰησοῦ.
ments of God and the faith of Jesus.

13 Καὶ ἤκουσα φωνῆς ἐκ τοῦ οὐρανοῦ, λεγούσης [f]μοι,‖
And I heard a voice out of the heaven, saying to me,
Γράψον, Μακάριοι οἱ νεκροὶ οἱ ἐν κυρίῳ ἀποθνήσκοντες
Write, Blessed the dead who in [the] Lord die
[g]ἀπάρτι.‖ Ναί, λέγει τὸ πνεῦμα, ἵνα [h]ἀναπαύσωνται‖ ἐκ
from henceforth. Yea, saith the Spirit, that they may rest from
τῶν.κόπων.αὐτῶν· τὰ [i]δὲ‖ ἔργα αὐτῶν ἀκολουθεῖ μετ' αὐτῶν.
their labours; and ²works ¹their follow with them.

14 Καὶ [k]εἶδον,‖ καὶ ἰδού, νεφέλη λευκή, καὶ ἐπὶ τὴν νεφέλην
And I saw, and behold, a ²cloud ¹white, and upon the cloud
[l]καθήμενος ὅμοιος‖ [m]υἱῷ‖ ἀνθρώπου, ἔχων ἐπὶ [n]τῆς
[one] sitting like [the] Son of man, having on
κεφαλῆς‖ αὐτοῦ στέφανον χρυσοῦν, καὶ ἐν τῇ.χειρὶ.αὐτοῦ δρέ-
²head ¹his a ²crown ¹golden, and in his hand a
πανον ὀξύ. 15 καὶ ἄλλος ἄγγελος ἐξῆλθεν ἐκ τοῦ ναοῦ,
²sickle ¹sharp. And another angel came out of the temple,
κράζων ἐν [o]μεγάλῃ φωνῇ‖ τῷ καθημένῳ ἐπὶ τῆς νεφέλης,
crying with loud voice to him sitting on the cloud,
Πέμψον τὸ.δρέπανόν.σου, καὶ θέρισον, ὅτι ἦλθέν [p]σοι‖ ἡ
Send thy sickle and reap; because is come to thee the
ὥρα [q]τοῦ‖ θερίσαι, ὅτι ἐξηράνθη ὁ θερισμὸς τῆς γῆς. 16 Καὶ
hour to reap, because is dried the harvest of the earth. And
ἔβαλεν ὁ καθήμενος ἐπὶ [r]τὴν νεφέλην‖ τὸ.δρέπανον.αὐτοῦ
⁶put ⁷forth ¹he ²sitting ³upon ⁴the ⁵cloud his sickle
ἐπὶ τὴν γῆν, καὶ ἐθερίσθη ἡ γῆ.
upon the earth, and was reaped the earth.

17 Καὶ ἄλλος ἄγγελος ἐξῆλθεν ἐκ τοῦ ναοῦ τοῦ ἐν τῷ
And another angel came out of the temple which [is] in the
οὐρανῷ, ἔχων καὶ αὐτὸς δρέπανον ὀξύ. 18 καὶ ἄλλος ἄγ-
heaven, ³having ²also ¹he a ²sickle ¹sharp. And another an-
γελος [s]ἐξῆλθεν‖ ἐκ τοῦ θυσιαστηρίου, [t]ἔχων ἐξουσίαν ἐπὶ τοῦ
gel came out of the altar, having authority over
πυρός, καὶ ἐφώνησεν [v]κραυγῇ‖ μεγάλῃ τῷ ἔχοντι τὸ δρέπανον
fire, and he called with a ²cry ¹loud to him having ³sickle
τὸ ὀξύ, λέγων, Πέμψον σου τὸ δρέπανον τὸ ὀξύ, καὶ τρύγη-
¹the ²sharp, saying, Send thy ²sickle ¹sharp, and gather
σον τοὺς βότρυας [w] τῆς γῆς, ὅτι ἤκμασαν αἱ σταφυλαὶ
the bunches of the earth; because are fully ripe ²grapes

11 and the smoke of their torment ascendeth up for ever and ever: and they have no rest day nor night, who worship the beast and his image, and whosoever receiveth the mark of his name. 12 Here is the patience of the saints: here *are* they that keep the commandments of God, and the faith of Jesus.

13 And I heard a voice from heaven saying unto me, Write, Blessed *are* the dead which die in the Lord from henceforth: Yea, saith the Spirit, that they may rest from their labours; and their works do follow them.

14 And I looked, and behold a white cloud, and upon the cloud *one* sat like unto the Son of man, having on his head a golden crown, and in his hand a sharp sickle. 15 And another angel came out of the temple, crying with a loud voice to him that sat on the cloud, Thrust in thy sickle, and reap: for the time is come for thee to reap; for the harvest of the earth is ripe. 16 And he that sat on the cloud thrust in his sickle on the earth; and the earth was reaped.

17 And another angel came out of the temple which is in heaven, he also having a sharp sickle. 18 And another angel came out from the altar, which had power over fire; and cried with a loud cry to him that had the sharp sickle, saying, Thrust in thy sharp sickle, and gather the clusters of the vine of the earth; for her grapes

---

[c] εἰς αἰῶνας αἰώνων ἀναβαίνει GLTTrAW. [d] + ἡ the LTTrAW. [e] — ὧδε GLTTrAW. [f] — μοι GLTTrAW. [g] ἀπ' ἄρτι GLA. [h] ἀναπαήσονται they shall rest LTTrA; ἀναπαύσονται they shall rest W. [i] γὰρ for LTTrA. [k] ἴδον T. [l] καθήμενον ὅμοιον GLTTrAW. [m] υἱὸν T. [n] τὴν κεφαλὴν LT. [o] φωνῇ μεγάλῃ GLTTrAW. [p] — σοι GLTTrAW. [q] — τοῦ LTTrAW. [r] τῆς νεφέλης LTTrA. [s] — ἐξῆλθεν L. [t] + ὁ who (*read* ἔχων has) LAW. [v] φωνῇ with a ²voice LTTr. [w] + τῆς ἀμπέλου of the vine EGLTTrAW

are fully ripe. 19 And the angel thrust in his sickle into the earth, and gathered the vine of the earth, and cast *it* into the great winepress of the wrath of God. 20 And the winepress was trodden without the city, and blood came out of the winepress, even unto the horse bridles, by the space of a thousand *and* six hundred furlongs.

αὐτῆς. 19 Καὶ ἔβαλεν ὁ ἄγγελος τὸ.δρέπανον.αὐτοῦ εἰς
[1]her. And [3]put [4]forth [1]the [2]angel his sickle to
τὴν γῆν, καὶ ἐτρύγησεν τὴν ἄμπελον τῆς γῆς, καὶ ἔβαλεν
the earth, and gathered the vine of the earth, and cast [the fruit]
εἰς τὴν ληνὸν τοῦ θυμοῦ τοῦ θεοῦ [x]τὴν μεγάλην.‖ 20 καὶ
into [3]winepress [4]of [5]the [6]fury [7]of [8]God [1]the [2]great; and
ἐπατήθη ἡ ληνὸς [y]ἔξω‖ τῆς πόλεως, καὶ ἐξῆλθεν αἷμα
was trodden the winepress outside the city, and [2]came [3]forth [1]blood
ἐκ τῆς ληνοῦ ἄχρι τῶν χαλινῶν τῶν ἵππων, ἀπὸ
out of the winepress as far as the bits of the horses, to the distance of
σταδίων χιλίων ἑξακοσίων.
[5]furlongs [1]a [2]thousand [3]six [4]hundred.

XV. And I saw another sign in heaven, great and marvellous, seven angels having the seven last plagues; for in them is filled up the wrath of God.

15 Καὶ [a]εἶδον‖ ἄλλο σημεῖον ἐν τῷ οὐρανῷ μέγα καὶ θαυ-
And I saw another sign in the heaven, great and won-
μαστόν, ἀγγέλους ἑπτά, ἔχοντας πληγὰς ἑπτὰ τὰς ἐσχάτας,
derful: [2]angels [1]seven, having [2]plagues [1]seven, the last;
ὅτι ἐν αὐταῖς ἐτελέσθη ὁ θυμὸς τοῦ θεοῦ.
because in them was completed the fury of God.

2 And I saw as it were a sea of glass mingled with fire: and them that had gotten the victory over the beast, and over his image, and over his mark, *and* over the number of his name, stand on the sea of glass, having the harps of God. 3 And they sing the song of Moses the servant of God, and the song of the Lamb, saying, Great and marvellous *are* thy works, Lord God Almighty; just and true *are* thy ways, thou King of saints. 4 Who shall not fear thee, O Lord, and glorify thy name? for *thou* only *art* holy: for all nations shall come and worship before thee; for thy judgments are made manifest.

2 Καὶ [a]εἶδον‖ ὡς θάλασσαν ὑαλίνην μεμιγμένην πυρί,
And I saw as a [2]sea [1]glass mingled with fire,
καὶ τοὺς νικῶντας ἐκ τοῦ θηρίου καὶ ἐκ τῆς.εἰκόνος.αὐτοῦ
and the overcomers of the beast, and of its image,
καὶ [b]ἐκ τοῦ.χαράγματος.αὐτοῦ,‖ ἐκ τοῦ ἀριθμοῦ τοῦ ὀνόματος
and of its mark, of the number [2]name
αὐτοῦ, ἑστῶτας ἐπὶ τὴν θάλασσαν τὴν ὑαλίνην, ἔχοντας
[1]of [2]its, standing upon the [2]sea [1]glass, having
κιθάρας τοῦ θεοῦ. 3 καὶ ᾄδουσιν τὴν ᾠδὴν [c]Μωσέως‖ [d]δού-
harps of God. And they sing the song of Moses, bond-
λου τοῦ θεοῦ, καὶ τὴν ᾠδὴν τοῦ ἀρνίου, λέγοντες, Μεγάλα καὶ
man of God, and the song of the Lamb, saying, Great and
θαυμαστὰ τὰ.ἔργα.σου, κύριε ὁ θεὸς ὁ παντοκράτωρ· δί-
wonderful [are] thy works, Lord God Almighty; right-
καιαι καὶ ἀληθιναὶ αἱ.ὁδοί.σου, ὁ βασιλεὺς τῶν [e]ἁγίων.‖
eous and true [are] thy ways, [thou] King of saints.
4 τίς οὐ μὴ φοβηθῇ [f]σε,‖ κύριε, καὶ [g]δοξάσῃ‖ τὸ.ὄνομά.σου;
Who [2]not [1]should fear thee, O Lord, and glorify thy name?
ὅτι μόνος ὅσιος· ὅτι πάντα τὰ ἔθνη ἥξουσιν καὶ
for [thou] only [art] holy; for all the nations shall come and
προσκυνήσουσιν ἐνώπιόν σου· ὅτι τὰ.δικαιώματά.σου
do homage before thee; for thy righteous [acts]
(*lit.* righteousnesses)
ἐφανερώθησαν.
were manifested.

5 And after that I looked, and, behold, the temple of the tabernacle of the testimony in heaven was opened: 6 and the seven angels came out of the temple, having the seven plagues, clothed in pure and white linen, and having their breasts girded with golden girdles. 7 And one of the

5 Καὶ μετὰ ταῦτα [a]εἶδον,‖ καὶ [h]ἰδού,‖ ἠνοίγη ὁ ναὸς
And after these things I saw, and behold, was opened the temple
τῆς σκηνῆς τοῦ μαρτυρίου ἐν τῷ οὐρανῷ· 6 καὶ ἐξῆλθον οἱ
of the tabernacle of the testimony in the heaven; and came forth the
ἑπτὰ ἄγγελοι [i]ἔχοντες τὰς ἑπτὰ πληγάς, ἐκ τοῦ ναοῦ,
seven angels [5]having [6]the [7]seven [8]plagues [1]out [2]of [3]the [4]temple,
ἐνδεδυμένοι [k]λίνον‖ καθαρὸν [l]καὶ‖ λαμπρόν, καὶ περιεζωσμένοι
clothed in linen pure and bright, and girt with
περὶ τὰ στήθη ζώνας χρυσᾶς. 7 καὶ ἓν ἐκ τῶν τεσσάρων
[3]about [4]the [5]breasts [2]girdles [1]golden. And one of the four

---

[x] τὸν μέγαν GLTTrAW. [y] ἔξωθεν GLTTrAW. [a] ἴδον T. [b] — ἐκ τοῦ χαράγματος αὐτοῦ GLTTrAW. [c] Μωϋσέως GLTTrAW. [d] + τοῦ the LTTrA. [e] ἐθνῶν of nations GLTTrAW. [f] — σε LTTrA. [g] δοξάσει shall glorify LTTrAW. [h] — ἰδού GLTTrAW. [i] + οἱ those GLTTr[A]W. [k] λίθον stone LTr. [l] — καὶ GLTTrAW.

ζώων ἔδωκεν τοῖς ἑπτὰ ἀγγέλοις ἑπτὰ φιάλας χρυσᾶς,
living creatures gave to the seven angels seven [2]bowls [1]golden,
γεμούσας τοῦ θυμοῦ τοῦ θεοῦ τοῦ ζῶντος εἰς τοὺς αἰῶνας
full of the fury of God, who lives to the ages
τῶν αἰώνων. 8 καὶ ἐγεμίσθη ὁ ναὸς καπνοῦ ἐκ τῆς δόξης
of the ages. And [3]was [4]filled [1]the [2]temple with smoke from the glory
τοῦ θεοῦ, καὶ ἐκ τῆς.δυνάμεως.αὐτοῦ· καὶ οὐδεὶς [m]ἠδύνατο‖
of God, and from his power: and no one was able
εἰσελθεῖν εἰς τὸν ναόν, ἄχρι τελεσθῶσιν αἱ ἑπτὰ πληγαὶ τῶν
to enter into the temple until were completed the seven plagues of the
ἑπτὰ ἀγγέλων.
seven angels.

16 Καὶ ἤκουσα [n]φωνῆς μεγάλης‖ ἐκ τοῦ ναοῦ, λεγούσης
And I heard a [2]voice [1]loud out of the temple, saying
τοῖς ἑπτὰ ἀγγέλοις, Ὑπάγετε, καὶ [o]ἐκχέατε‖ τὰς [p] φιάλας τοῦ
to the seven angels, Go, and pour out the bowls of the
θυμοῦ τοῦ θεοῦ εἰς τὴν γῆν.
fury of God into the earth.
2 Καὶ ἀπῆλθεν ὁ πρῶτος, καὶ ἐξέχεεν τὴν.φιάλην.αὐτοῦ
And [3]departed [1]the [2]first, and poured out his bowl
[q]ἐπὶ‖ τὴν γῆν· καὶ ἐγένετο ἕλκος κακὸν καὶ πονηρὸν [r]εἰς‖ τοὺς
on to the earth; and came a sore, evil and grievous, upon the
ἀνθρώπους τοὺς ἔχοντας τὸ χάραγμα τοῦ θηρίου, καὶ τοὺς
men who had the mark of the beast, and those
[s]τῇ.εἰκόνι.αὐτοῦ προσκυνοῦντας.‖
[3]to [4]his [5]image [1]doing [2]homage.
3 Καὶ ὁ δεύτερος [t]ἄγγελος‖ ἐξέχεεν τὴν.φιάλην.αὐτοῦ εἰς
And the second angel poured out his bowl into
τὴν θάλασσαν· καὶ ἐγένετο αἷμα ὡς νεκροῦ, καὶ πᾶσα ψυχὴ
the sea; and it became blood, as of [one] dead; and every [2]soul
[v]ζῶσα‖ ἀπέθανεν [w] ἐν τῇ θαλάσσῃ.
[1]living died in the sea.
4 Καὶ ὁ τρίτος [x]ἄγγελος‖ ἐξέχεεν τὴν.φιάλην.αὐτοῦ εἰς
And the third angel poured out his bowl into
τοὺς ποταμοὺς καὶ [y]εἰς‖ τὰς πηγὰς τῶν ὑδάτων· καὶ [z]ἐγένετο‖
the rivers, and into the fountains of waters; and they became
αἷμα. 5 καὶ ἤκουσα τοῦ ἀγγέλου τῶν ὑδάτων λέγοντος,
blood. And I heard the angel of the waters saying,
Δίκαιος, [a]κύριε,‖ εἶ, ὁ ὢν καὶ ὁ ἦν [b]καὶ ὁ‖ ὅσιος, ὅτι
Righteous, O Lord, art thou, who art and who wast and the holy one, that
ταῦτα ἔκρινας· 6 ὅτι [c]αἷμα‖ ἁγίων καὶ προ-
these things thou didst judge; because [the] blood of saints and of pro-
φητῶν ἐξέχεαν, καὶ αἷμα αὐτοῖς [d]ἔδωκας‖ [e]πιεῖν·‖ ἄξιοι
phets they poured out, and blood to them thou didst give to drink; [2]worthy
[f]γάρ‖ εἰσιν. 7 Καὶ ἤκουσα [g]ἄλλου ἐκ‖ τοῦ θυσιαστηρίου λέ-
[1]for they are. And I heard another out of the altar say-
γοντος, Ναί, κύριε ὁ θεὸς ὁ παντοκράτωρ, ἀληθιναὶ καὶ δίκαιαι
ing, Yea, Lord God Almighty, true and righteous
αἱ.κρίσεις.σου.
[are] thy judgments.
8 Καὶ ὁ τέταρτος [x]ἄγγελος‖ ἐξέχεεν τὴν.φιάλην.αὐτοῦ ἐπὶ
And the fourth angel poured out his bowl upon

four beasts gave unto the seven angels seven golden vials full of the wrath of God, who liveth for ever and ever. 8 And the temple was filled with smoke from the glory of God, and from his power; and no man was able to enter into the temple, till the seven plagues of the seven angels were fulfilled.

XVI. And I heard a great voice out of the temple saying to the seven angels, Go your ways, and pour out the vials of the wrath of God upon the earth.

2 And the first went, and poured out his vial upon the earth; and there fell a noisome and grievous sore upon the men which had the mark of the beast, and *upon* them which worshipped his image.

3 And the second angel poured out his vial upon the sea; and it became as the blood of a dead *man:* and every living soul died in the sea.

4 And the third angel poured out his vial upon the rivers and fountains of waters; and they became blood. 5 And I heard the angel of the waters say, Thou art righteous, O Lord, which art, and wast, and shalt be, because thou hast judged thus. 6 For they have shed the blood of saints and prophets, and thou hast given them blood to drink; for they are worthy. 7 And I heard another out of the altar say, Even so, Lord God Almighty, true and righteous *are* thy judgments.

8 And the fourth angel poured out his

---

[m] ἐδύνατο LTTrA. [n] μεγάλης φωνῆς LTAW. [o] ἐκχέετε LTA. [p] + ἑπτὰ seven GLTTrAW. [q] εἰς into LTTrAW. [r] ἐπὶ upon LTTrAW. [s] προσκυνοῦντας τῇ εἰκόνι αὐτοῦ GLTTrAW. [t] — ἄγγελος LTTrAW. [v] ζωῆς (*read* soul of life) GLTTrA. [w] + τὰ the [things] LTTrAW. [x] — ἄγγελος GLTTrAW. [y] — εἰς LTTrA. [z] ἐγένοντο L. [a] — κύριε GLTTrAW. [b] — καὶ GT; — καὶ ὁ (*read* ὅσιος holy) LTrAW. [c] αἵματα bloods T. [d] δέδωκας thou hast given LTrAW. [e] πῖν L; πεῖν TA. [f] — γάρ GLTTrAW. [g] — ἄλλου ἐκ GLTTrAW.

vial upon the sun ;
and power was given
unto him to scorch
men with fire. 9 And
men were scorched
with great heat, and
blasphemed the name
of God, which hath
power over these
plagues : and they
repented not to give
him glory.
10 And the fifth an-
gel poured out his
vial upon the seat of
the beast ; and his
kingdom was full of
darkness ; and they
gnawed their tongues
for pain, 11 and blas-
phemed the God of
heaven because of
their pains and their
sores, and repented
not of their deeds.

12 And the sixth an-
gel poured out his
vial upon the great
river Euphrates ; and
the water thereof was
dried up, that the way
of the kings of the
east might be prepar-
ed. 13 And I saw three
unclean spirits like
frogs *come* out of the
mouth of the dragon,
and out of the mouth
of the beast, and out
of the mouth of the
false prophet. 14 For
they are the spirits of
devils, working mi-
racles, *which* go forth
unto the kings of the
earth and of the
whole world, to ga-
ther them to the bat-
tle of that great day
of God Almighty.
15 Behold, I come as
a thief. Blessed *is* he
that watcheth, and
keepeth his garments,
lest he walk naked,
and they see his
shame. 16 And he ga-
thered them together
into a place called in
the Hebrew tongue
Armageddon.

17 And the seventh
angel poured out his

τὸν ἥλιον· καὶ ἐδόθη αὐτῷ καυματίσαι τοὺς ἀνθρώπους ἐν
the sun ; and it was given to it to scorch men wi

πυρί· 9 καὶ ἐκαυματίσθησαν οἱ ἄνθρωποι καῦμα μέγα, κα
fire. And [2]were [3]scorched [1]men with [2]heat [1]great, an

ἐβλασφήμησαν τὸ ὄνομα τοῦ θεοῦ τοῦ-ἔχοντος [h] ἐξουσίαν ἐπ
they blasphemed the name of God, who has authority over

τὰς-πληγὰς-ταύτας, καὶ οὐ-μετενόησαν δοῦναι αὐτῷ δόξαν.
these plagues, and did not repent to give him glory.

10 Καὶ ὁ πέμπτος [i]ἄγγελος‖ ἐξέχεεν τὴν-φιάλην-αὐτοῦ ἐπὶ
And the fifth angel poured out his bowl upon

τὸν θρόνον τοῦ θηρίου· καὶ ἐγένετο ἡ-βασιλεία-αὐτοῦ ἐσκοτω-
the throne of the beast ; and [3]became [1]its [2]kingdom dark-

μένη· καὶ [k]ἐμασσῶντο‖ τὰς-γλώσσας-αὐτῶν ἐκ τοῦ πόνου,
ened ; and they were gnawing their tongues for the distress,

11 καὶ ἐβλασφήμησαν τὸν θεὸν τοῦ οὐρανοῦ ἐκ τῶν πόνων
and blasphemed the God of the heaven for [2]distresses

αὐτῶν καὶ ἐκ τῶν-ἑλκῶν-αὐτῶν, καὶ οὐ-μετενόησαν ἐκ τῶν
[1]their and for their sores, and did not repent of

ἔργων αὐτῶν.
[2]works [1]their.

12 Καὶ ὁ ἕκτος [i]ἄγγελος‖ ἐξέχεεν τὴν-φιάλην-αὐτοῦ ἐπὶ τὸν
And the sixth angel poured out his bowl upon the

ποταμὸν τὸν μέγαν [l]τὸν‖ Εὐφράτην· καὶ ἐξηράνθη τὸ ὕδωρ
[2]river [1]great, the Euphrates ; and was dried up [2]water

αὐτοῦ, ἵνα ἑτοιμασθῇ ἡ ὁδὸς τῶν βασιλέων τῶν ἀπὸ
[1]its, that might be prepared the way of the kings [2]the [1]from

[m]ἀνατολῶν‖ ἡλίου. 13 Καὶ [n]εἶδον‖ ἐκ τοῦ στόματος τοῦ
rising of [the] sun. And I saw out of the mouth of the

δράκοντος, καὶ ἐκ τοῦ στόματος τοῦ θηρίου, καὶ ἐκ τοῦ
dragon, and out of the mouth of the beast, and out of the

στόματος τοῦ ψευδοπροφήτου, πνεύματα τρία ἀκάθαρτα
mouth of the false prophet, [3]spirits [1]three [2]unclean

[o]ὅμοια βατράχοις·‖ 14 εἰσὶν-γὰρ πνεύματα [p]δαιμόνων‖ ποι-
like frogs ; for they are spirits of demons do-

οῦντα [q]σημεῖα ἐκπορεύεσθαι‖ ἐπὶ τοὺς βασιλεῖς [r]τῆς γῆς καὶ
ing signs, to go forth to the kings of the earth and

τῆς οἰκουμένης ὅλης, συναγαγεῖν αὐτοὺς εἰς [s] πόλεμον
of the [2]habitable [[3]world] [1]whole to gather together them unto battle

τῆς [t]ἡμέρας ἐκείνης τῆς μεγάλης‖ τοῦ θεοῦ τοῦ παντοκράτορος.
of [3]day [1]that [2]great of God the Almighty.

15 Ἰδού, ἔρχομαι ὡς κλέπτης. μακάριος ὁ γρηγορῶν,
Behold, I come as a thief. Blessed [is] he that watches,

καὶ τηρῶν τὰ-ἱμάτια-αὐτοῦ, ἵνα μὴ γυμνὸς περιπατῇ, καὶ
and keeps his garments, that not naked he may walk, and

βλέπωσιν τὴν-ἀσχημοσύνην-αὐτοῦ. 16 καὶ συνήγαγεν
they see his shame. And he gathered together

αὐτοὺς εἰς τὸν τόπον τὸν καλούμενον Ἑβραϊστὶ [v]Ἀρμα-
them to the place which is called in Hebrew Arma-

γεδδών.‖
geddon.

17 Καὶ ὁ ἕβδομος [w]ἄγγελος‖ ἐξέχεεν τὴν-φιάλην-αὐτοῦ
And the seventh angel poured out his bowl

---

[h] + τὴν LTTrW. [i] — ἄγγελος GLTTrAW. [k] ἐμασῶντο LTTrAW. [l] — τὸν GT[Tr]
[m] ἀνατολῆς TTrA. [n] ἴδον T. [o] ὡς (as) βάτραχοι GLTTrAW. [p] δαιμονίων GLTTrAW
[q] σημεῖα ἃ ἐκπορεύεται signs which go forth EGTTrAW ; σημεῖα· ἐκπορεύεται signs : they go
forth L. [r] — τῆς γῆς καὶ GLTTrAW. [s] + τὸν the GLTTrAW. [t] μεγάλης ἡμέρας L.
ἡμέρας τῆς μεγάλης TTrA. [v] Ἁρμαγεδών GLTTrAW. [w] — ἄγγελος GLTTrAW.

[x]εἰς" τὸν ἀέρα· καὶ ἐξῆλθεν φωνὴ [y]μεγάλη" [z]ἀπὸ" τοῦ ναοῦ
into the air; and came out a [2]voice [1]loud from the temple
[a]τοῦ οὐρανοῦ," ἀπὸ τοῦ θρόνου, λέγουσα, Γέγονεν. 18 Καὶ
of the heaven, from the throne, saying, It is done. And
ἐγένοντο [b]φωναὶ καὶ βρονταὶ καὶ ἀστραπαί," καὶ σεισμὸς
there were voices and thunders and lightnings; and [5]earthquake
ἐγένετο μέγας, οἷος οὐκ.ἐγένετο ἀφ᾽ οὗ [c]οἱ ἄνθρωποι ἐγέ-
[1]there [2]was [3]a [4]great, such as was not since men
νοντο" ἐπὶ τῆς γῆς, τηλικοῦτος σεισμὸς οὕτως μέγας. 19 καὶ
were on the earth so mighty an earthquake, so great. And
ἐγένετο ἡ πόλις ἡ μεγάλη εἰς τρία μέρη, καὶ αἱ πόλεις τῶν
[4]became [1]the [3]city [2]great into three parts; and the cities of the
ἐθνῶν [d]ἔπεσον·" καὶ Βαβυλὼν ἡ μεγάλη ἐμνήσθη ἐνώπιον
nations fell; and Babylon the great was remembered before
τοῦ θεοῦ, δοῦναι αὐτῇ τὸ ποτήριον τοῦ οἴνου τοῦ θυμοῦ τῆς
God, to give her the cup of the wine of the fury
ὀργῆς αὐτοῦ. 20 καὶ πᾶσα νῆσος ἔφυγεν, καὶ ὄρη οὐχ
[3]wrath [1]of [2]his. And every island fled; and [2]mountains [1]no
εὑρέθησαν. 21 καὶ χάλαζα μεγάλη ὡς.ταλαντιαία καταβαίνει
were found; and a [2]hail [1]great as of a talent weight comes down
ἐκ τοῦ οὐρανοῦ ἐπὶ τοὺς ἀνθρώπους· καὶ ἐβλασφήμησαν οἱ
out of the heaven upon men; and [2]blasphemed
ἄνθρωποι τὸν θεόν, ἐκ τῆς πληγῆς τῆς χαλάζης· ὅτι με-
[1]men God, because of the plague of the hail, for
γάλη ἐστὶν ἡ.πληγὴ.αὐτῆς σφόδρα.
[6]great [3]is [4]its [5]plague [1]exceeding.

17 Καὶ ἦλθεν εἷς ἐκ τῶν ἑπτὰ ἀγγέλων τῶν ἐχόντων τὰς
And came one of the seven angels of those having the
ἑπτὰ φιάλας, καὶ ἐλάλησεν μετ᾽ ἐμοῦ, λέγων [e]μοι," Δεῦρο,
seven bowls, and spoke with me, saying to me, Come here,
δείξω σοι τὸ κρίμα τῆς πόρνης τῆς μεγάλης, τῆς καθη-
I will shew thee the sentence of the [2]harlot [1]great, who sits
μένης ἐπὶ [f]τῶν" ὑδάτων [f]τῶν" πολλῶν· 2 μεθ᾽ ἧς ἐπόρνευ-
upon the [2]waters [1]many; with whom [6]committed [7]for-
σαν οἱ βασιλεῖς τῆς γῆς, καὶ ἐμεθύσθησαν [g]ἐκ τοῦ οἴνου
nication [1]the [2]kings [3]of [4]the [5]earth; and were made drunk with the wine
τῆς.πορνείας.αὐτῆς οἱ κατοικοῦντες τὴν γῆν." 3 Καὶ
of her fornication those that dwell on the earth. And
ἀπήνεγκέν με εἰς ἔρημον ἐν πνεύματι· καὶ [h]εἶδον" γυναῖκα
he carried away me [4]to [5]a [6]wilderness [1]in [[2]the] [3]Spirit; and I saw a woman
καθημένην ἐπὶ θηρίον κόκκινον, [i]γέμον ὀνομάτων" βλασφημίας,
sitting upon a [2]beast [1]scarlet, full of names of blasphemy,
[k]ἔχον" κεφαλὰς ἑπτὰ καὶ κέρατα δέκα. 4 καὶ ἡ γυνὴ [l]ἡ"
having [2]heads [1]seven and [2]horns [1]ten. And the woman
περιβεβλημένη [m]πορφύρᾳ" καὶ [n]κοκκίνῳ," [o]καὶ" κεχρυσωμένη
clothed in purple and scarlet, and decked (*lit.* gilded)
[p]χρυσῷ" καὶ λίθῳ τιμίῳ καὶ μαργαρίταις, ἔχουσα [q]χρυσοῦν
with gold and [2]stone [1]precious and pearls, having a golden
ποτήριον" ἐν τῇ.χειρὶ.αὐτῆς, [r]γέμον" βδελυγμάτων καὶ [s]ἀκαθ-
cup in her hand, full of abominations and of unclean-

vial into the air; and
there came a great
voice out of the
temple of heaven,
from the throne,
saying, It is done.
18 And there were
voices, and thunders,
and lightnings; and
there was a great
earthquake, such as
was not since men
were upon the earth,
so mighty an earth-
quake, *and* so great.
19 And the great city
was divided into three
parts, and the cities of
the nations fell: and
great Babylon came
in remembrance be-
fore God, to give unto
her the cup of the wine
of the fierceness of his
wrath. 20 And every
island fled away, and
the mountains were
not found. 21 And
there fell upon men a
great hail out of hea-
ven, *every stone* about
the weight of a talent:
and men blasphemed
God because of the
plague of the hail;
for the plague thereof
was exceeding great.

XVII. And there
came one of the seven
angels which had the
seven vials, and talked
with me, saying unto
me, Come hither; I
will shew unto thee the
judgment of the great
whore that sitteth
upon many waters:
2 with whom the kings
of the earth have com-
mitted fornication,
and the inhabitants
of the earth have been
made drunk with the
wine of her fornica-
tion. 3 So he carried
me away in the spirit
into the wilderness:
and I saw a woman
sit upon a scarlet
coloured beast, full of
names of blasphemy,
having seven heads
and ten horns. 4 And
the woman was array-
ed in purple and scar-
let colour, and decked
with gold and pre-
cious stones and
pearls, having a gold-
en cup in her hand full
of abominations and

[x] ἐπὶ upon GLTTrAW. [y] — μεγάλη LA. [z] ἐκ out of LTTrA. [a] — τοῦ οὐρανοῦ LTTrAW. [b] ἀστραπαὶ καὶ φωναὶ καὶ βρονταί GLTTrAW. [c] ἄνθρωπος ἐγένετο man was LTTrAW. [d] ἔπεσαν LTTrAW. [e] — μοι GLTTrAW. [f] — τῶν LTTr[A]. [g] οἱ κατοικοῦντες τὴν γῆν ἐκ τοῦ οἴνου τῆς πορνείας αὐτῆς GLTTrAW. [h] εἶδα L. [i] γέμοντα ὀνόματα LTA; γέμον τὰ (— τα W) ὀνόματα TrW. [k] ἔχοντα TA. [l] ἦν was GLTTrAW. [m] πορφυροῦν GLTTrAW. [n] κόκκινον GLTTrAW. [o] [καὶ] A. [p] χρυσίῳ GLAW. [q] ποτήριον χρυσοῦν LTTrAW. [r] γέμων T. [s] τὰ ἀκάθαρτα τῆς the unclean things GLTTrAW.

filthiness of her fornication: 5 and upon her forehead *was* a name written, MYSTERY, BABYLON THE GREAT, THE MOTHER OF HARLOTS AND ABOMINATIONS OF THE EARTH. 6 And I saw the woman drunken with the blood of the saints, and with the blood of the martyrs of Jesus: and when I saw her, I wondered with great admiration. 7 And the angel said unto me, Wherefore didst thou marvel? I will tell thee the mystery of the woman, and of the beast that carrieth her, which hath the seven heads and ten horns. 8 The beast that thou sawest was, and is not; and shall ascend out of the bottomless pit, and go into perdition: and they that dwell on the earth shall wonder, whose names were not written in the book of life from the foundation of the world, when they behold the beast that was, and is not, and yet is. 9 And here *is* the mind which hath wisdom. The seven heads are seven mountains, on which the woman sitteth. 10 And there are seven kings: five are fallen, and one is, *and* the other is not yet come; and when he cometh, he must continue a short space. 11 And the beast that was, and is not, even he is the eighth, and is of the seven, and goeth into perdition. 12 And the ten horns which thou sawest are ten kings, which have received no kingdom as yet; but receive power as kings one hour with the beast. 13 These have one mind, and shall give their power and strength unto the beast. 14 These shall

ἀρτητος‖ πορνείας.αὐτῆς, 5 καὶ ἐπὶ τὸ.μέτωπον.αὐτῆς
ness of her fornication; and upon her forehead
ὄνομα γεγραμμένον, Μυστήριον, Βαβυλὼν ἡ μεγάλη, ἡ
a name written, Mystery, Babylon the Great, the
μήτηρ τῶν πορνῶν καὶ τῶν βδελυγμάτων τῆς γῆς. 6 Καὶ
mother of the harlots and of the abominations of the earth. And
ᵗεἶδον‖ τὴν γυναῖκα μεθύουσαν ἐκ τοῦ αἵματος τῶν ἁγίων, καὶ
I saw the woman drunk with the blood of the saints, and
ἐκ τοῦ αἵματος τῶν μαρτύρων Ἰησοῦ· καὶ ἐθαύμασα, ἰδὼν
with the blood of the witnesses of Jesus. And I wondered, having seen
αὐτήν, θαῦμα μέγα. 7 Καὶ εἶπέν μοι ὁ ἄγγελος, ᵛΔιατί‖
her, with ²wonder ¹great. And ³said ⁴to ⁵me ¹the ²angel, Why
ἐθαύμασας; ἐγώ ʷσοὶ ἐρῶ‖ τὸ μυστήριον τῆς γυναικός,
didst thou wonder? I thee will tell the mystery of the woman,
καὶ τοῦ θηρίου τοῦ βαστάζοντος αὐτήν, τοῦ ἔχοντος τὰς
and of the beast which carries her, which has the
ἑπτὰ κεφαλὰς καὶ τὰ δέκα κέρατα. 8 ˣ θηρίον ὃ εἶδες,
seven heads and the ten horns. [The] beast which thou sawest
ἦν, καὶ οὐκ.ἔστιν, καὶ μέλλει ἀναβαίνειν ἐκ τῆς ἀβύσσου,
was, and is not, and is about to come up out of the abyss,
καὶ εἰς ἀπώλειαν ʸὑπάγειν·‖ καὶ ᶻθαυμάσονται‖ οἱ κατοι-
and into destruction to go; and shall wonder they who dwell
κοῦντες ἐπὶ τῆς γῆς, ὧν ᵃοὐ.γέγραπται‖ ᵇτὰ ὀνόματα‖ ἐπὶ
on the earth, of whom are not written the names in
τὸ βιβλίον τῆς ζωῆς ἀπὸ καταβολῆς κόσμου, ᶜβλέ-
the book of life from [the] foundation of [the] world, see-
ποντες‖ τὸ θηρίον ᵈὅ τι‖ ἦν, καὶ οὐκ ἔστιν, ᵉκαίπερ ἐστίν.‖
ing the beast which was and ²not ¹is, and yet is.
9 ὧδε ὁ νοῦς ὁ ἔχων σοφίαν. αἱ ἑπτὰ κεφαλαί, ᶠὄρη
Here [is] the mind which has wisdom: The seven heads ³mountains
εἰσὶν ἑπτά,‖ ὅπου ἡ γυνὴ κάθηται ἐπ' αὐτῶν. 10 καὶ βα-
¹are ²seven, where the woman sits on them. And
σιλεῖς ἑπτά εἰσιν· οἱ πέντε ἔπεσαν, ᵍκαὶ‖ ὁ εἷς ἔστιν, ὁ
⁴kings ³seven ¹there ²are: the five are fallen, and the one is, the
ἄλλος οὔπω ἦλθεν· καὶ ὅταν ἔλθῃ, ὀλίγον αὐτὸν.δεῖ
other ²not ³yet ¹is come: and when he shall have come, a little while he must
μεῖναι. 11 καὶ τὸ θηρίον ὃ ἦν, καὶ οὐκ ἔστιν, καὶ ʰαὐτὸς‖
remain. And the beast which was, and ²not ¹is, ⁴also ³he
ὄγδοός ἐστιν, καὶ ἐκ τῶν ἑπτά ἐστιν, καὶ εἰς ἀπώλειαν
⁶an ⁷eighth ⁵is, and of the seven is, and into destruction
ὑπάγει. 12 καὶ τὰ δέκα κέρατα ἃ εἶδες, δέκα βασιλεῖς
goes. And the ten horns which thou sawest ten kings
εἰσιν, οἵτινες βασιλείαν ⁱοὔπω‖ ἔλαβον, ᵏἀλλ'‖ ἐξουσίαν ὡς
are, which ⁴a ⁵kingdom ²not ³yet ¹received, but authority as
βασιλεῖς μίαν ὥραν λαμβάνουσιν μετὰ τοῦ θηρίου. 13 οὗτοι
kings one hour receive with the beast. These
μίαν ˡγνώμην ἔχουσιν,‖ καὶ τὴν δύναμιν καὶ ᵐτὴν‖ ἐξουσίαν
one mind have, and the power and the authority
ⁿἑαυτῶν‖ τῷ θηρίῳ ᵒδιαδιδώσουσιν.‖ 14 οὗτοι μετὰ τοῦ
of themselves to the beast they shall give up. These with the

ᵗ εἶδα LTTrA. ᵛ Διὰ τί LTrA. ʷ ἐρῶ σοι LTrA. ˣ + τὸ The GLTTrAW. ʸ ὑπάγει goes LAW. ᶻ θαυμασθήσονται L. ᵃ οὐκ ἐγέγραπτο was not written L. ᵇ τὸ ὄνομα (*read* the name is not written) LTTrA. ᶜ βλεπόντων GLTTrAW. ᵈ ὅτι (*read* that it was) GLTTrAW. ᵉ καὶ παρέσται and shall be present GLTTrAW. ᶠ ἑπτὰ ὄρη εἰσίν GLTTrA. ᵍ — καὶ GLTTrAW. ʰ οὗτος this Tr. ⁱ οὐκ not L. ᵏ ἀλλὰ LTTrAW. ˡ ἔχουσιν γνώμην G. ᵐ — τὴν LTrA. ⁿ αὐτῶν (*read* their authority) LTTrAW. ᵒ διδόασιν they give GLTTrAW.

ἀρνίου πολεμήσουσιν, καὶ τὸ ἀρνίον νικήσει αὐτούς, ὅτι
Lamb war will make, and the Lamb will overcome them; because
κύριος κυρίων ἐστὶν καὶ βασιλεὺς βασιλέων· καὶ οἱ
Lord of lords he is and King of kings: and those that [are]
μετ' αὐτοῦ, κλητοὶ καὶ ἐκλεκτοὶ καὶ πιστοί. 15 Καὶ [p]λέγει‖
with him, called, and chosen, and faithful. And he says
μοι, Τὰ ὕδατα ἃ εἶδες, οὗ ἡ πόρνη κάθηται, λαοὶ καὶ
to me, The waters which thou sawest, where the harlot sits, [2]peoples [3]and
ὄχλοι εἰσίν, καὶ ἔθνη καὶ γλῶσσαι. 16 καὶ τὰ δέκα κέρατα
[4]multitudes [1]are, and nations and tongues. And the ten horns
ἃ εἶδες [q]ἐπὶ‖ τὸ θηρίον, οὗτοι μισήσουσιν τὴν πόρνην,
which thou sawest upon the beast, these shall hate the harlot,
καὶ ἠρημωμένην ποιήσουσιν αὐτὴν καὶ γυμνήν, καὶ τὰς
and desolate shall make her and naked, and
σάρκας αὐτῆς φάγονται, καὶ αὐτὴν κατακαύσουσιν [r]ἐν‖ πυρί.
[4]flesh [3]her [1]shall [2]eat, and [3]her [1]shall [2]burn with fire;
17 ὁ.γὰρ.θεὸς ἔδωκεν εἰς τὰς.καρδίας.αὐτῶν ποιῆσαι τὴν
for God gave to their hearts to do
γνώμην αὐτοῦ, [s]καὶ ποιῆσαι μίαν γνώμην,‖ καὶ δοῦναι τὴν
[2]mind [1]his, and to do one mind, and to give
βασιλείαν αὐτῶν τῷ θηρίῳ, ἄχρι [t]τελεσθῇ τὰ ῥήματα‖
[2]kingdom [1]their to the beast, until should be fulfilled the sayings
τοῦ θεοῦ. 18 καὶ ἡ γυνὴ ἣν εἶδες, ἔστιν ἡ πόλις ἡ
of God. And the woman whom thou sawest is the [2]city
μεγάλη, ἡ ἔχουσα βασιλείαν ἐπὶ τῶν βασιλέων τῆς γῆς.
[1]great, which has kingship over the kings of the earth.

make war with the Lamb, and the Lamb shall overcome them: for he is Lord of lords, and King of kings: and they that are with him *are* called, and chosen, and faithful.
15 And he saith unto me, The waters which thou sawest, where the whore sitteth, are peoples, and multitudes, and nations, and tongues. 16 And the ten horns which thou sawest upon the beast, these shall hate the whore, and shall make her desolate and naked, and shall eat her flesh, and burn her with fire. 17 For God hath put in their hearts to fulfil his will, and to agree, and give their kingdom unto the beast, until the words of God shall be fulfilled. 18 And the woman which thou sawest is that great city, which reigneth over the kings of the earth.

18 [v]Καὶ‖ μετὰ ταῦτα εἶδον [w]ἄγγελον καταβαίνοντα ἐκ
And after these things I saw an angel descending out of
τοῦ οὐρανοῦ, ἔχοντα ἐξουσίαν μεγάλην· καὶ ἡ γῆ ἐφω-
the heaven, having [2]authority [1]great: and the earth was enlight-
τίσθη ἐκ τῆς.δόξης.αὐτοῦ. 2 καὶ ἔκραξεν [x]ἐν.ἰσχύϊ, φωνῇ
ened with his glory. And he cried mightily with a [2]voice
μεγάλῃ,‖ λέγων, Ἔπεσεν [y]ἔπεσεν‖ Βαβυλὼν ἡ μεγάλη, καὶ
[1]loud, saying, Is fallen, is fallen Babylon the great, and
ἐγένετο κατοικητήριον [z]δαιμόνων,‖ καὶ φυλακὴ παντὸς πνεύ-
is become a habitation of demons, and a hold of every [3]spi-
ματος ἀκαθάρτου[a], καὶ φυλακὴ παντὸς ὀρνέου ἀκαθάρτου καὶ
rit [1]unclean, and a hold of every [4]bird [1]unclean [2]and
μεμισημένου· 3 ὅτι ἐκ [b]τοῦ οἴνου‖ τοῦ θυμοῦ τῆς πορ-
[3]hated: because of the wine of the fury [3]forni-
νείας αὐτῆς [c]πέπωκεν‖ πάντα τὰ ἔθνη, καὶ οἱ βασιλεῖς
cation [1]of [2]her [7]have [8]drunk [4]all [5]the [6]nations; and the kings
τῆς γῆς μετ' αὐτῆς ἐπόρνευσαν, καὶ οἱ ἔμποροι τῆς
of the earth with her did commit fornication, and the merchants of the
γῆς ἐκ τῆς δυνάμεως τοῦ.στρήνους.αὐτῆς ἐπλούτησαν.
earth through the power of her luxury were enriched.
4 Καὶ ἤκουσα ἄλλην φωνὴν ἐκ τοῦ οὐρανοῦ, λέγουσαν,
And I heard another voice out of the heaven, saying,
[d]Ἐξέλθετε‖ [e]ἐξ αὐτῆς ὁ.λαός.μου,‖ ἵνα μὴ.[f]συγκοινωνήσητε‖
Come ye out of her, my people, that ye may not have fellowship

XVIII. And after these things I saw another angel come down from heaven, having great power; and the earth was lightened with his glory. 2 And he cried mightily with a strong voice, saying, Babylon the great is fallen, is fallen, and is become the habitation of devils, and the hold of every foul spirit, and a cage of every unclean and hateful bird. 3 For all nations have drunk of the wine of the wrath of her fornication, and the kings of the earth have committed fornication with her, and the merchants of the earth are waxed rich through the abundance of her delicacies. 4 And I heard another voice from heaven, saying, Come out of her, my people,

---

[p] εἶπεν L. [q] καὶ and GLTTrAW. [r] — ἐν (*read* πυρί with fire) T[A]. [s] — καὶ ποιῆσαι μίαν γνώμην L; καὶ ποιῆσαι γνώμην μίαν G[A]. [t] τελεσθήσονται (shall be fulfilled) οἱ λόγοι GLTTrAW. [v] — καὶ LTTrAW. [w] + ἄλλον (*read* another angel) GLTTrAW. [x] ἐν ([ἐν] A) ἰσχυρᾷ φωνῇ with a strong voice GLTTrAW. [y] — ἔπεσεν Tr[A]. [z] δαιμονίων LTTrA. [a] + καὶ μεμισημένου and hated (spirit) L. [b] — τοῦ οἴνου L[Tr]A. [c] πέπωκαν LTW; πέπτωκαν have fallen (*read* ἐκ by) Tr; πέπ[τ]ωκαν A. [d] Ἐξέλθατε TTrAW; Ἔξελθε Come thou L. [e] ὁ λαός μου ἐξ αὐτῆς T. [f] συν- T.

that ye be not partakers of her sins, and that ye receive not of her plagues. 5 For her sins have reached unto heaven, and God hath remembered her iniquities. 6 Reward her even as she rewarded you, and double unto her double according to her works: in the cup which she hath filled fill to her double. 7 How much she hath glorified herself, and lived deliciously, so much torment and sorrow give her: for she saith in her heart, I sit a queen, and am no widow, and shall see no sorrow. 8 Therefore shall her plagues come in one day, death, and mourning, and famine; and she shall be utterly burned with fire: for strong *is* the Lord God who judgeth her. 9 And the kings of the earth, who have committed fornication and lived deliciously with her, shall bewail her, and lament for her, when they shall see the smoke of her burning, 10 standing afar off for the fear of her torment, saying, Alas, alas that great city Babylon, that mighty city! for in one hour is thy judgment come. 11 And the merchants of the earth shall weep and mourn over her; for no man buyeth their merchandise any more: 12 the merchandise of gold, and silver, and precious stones, and of pearls, and fine linen, and purple, and silk, and scarlet, and all thyine wood, and all manner vessels of ivory, and all manner vessels of most precious wood, and of brass, and iron, and marble, 13 and cinnamon, and odours, and ointments, and frankincense, and wine, and oil, and fine flour,

ταῖς.ἁμαρτίαις.αὐτῆς, καὶ [g]ἵνα μὴ.λάβητε ἐκ τῶν πληγῶν
in her sins, and that ye may not receive of [2]plagues
αὐτῆς·‖ 5 ὅτι [h]ἠκολούθησαν‖ αὐτῆς αἱ ἁμαρτίαι ἄχρι τοῦ
[1]her: for [3]followed [1]her [2]sins as far as the
οὐρανοῦ, καὶ ἐμνημόνευσεν ὁ θεὸς τὰ.ἀδικήματα.αὐτῆς. 6 ἀπό-
heaven, and [2]remembered [1]God her unrighteousnesses. Ren-
δοτε αὐτῇ ὡς καὶ αὐτὴ ἀπέδωκεν [i]ὑμῖν,‖ καὶ διπλώσατε [k]αὐτῇ‖
der to her as also she rendered to you; and double ye to her
[l]διπλᾶ κατὰ τὰ.ἔργα.αὐτῆς· ἐν τῷ ποτηρίῳ ᾧ ἐκέρασεν,
double, according to her works. In the cup which she mixed,
κεράσατε αὐτῇ διπλοῦν. 7 ὅσα ἐδόξασεν [m]ἑαυτὴν‖ καὶ
mix ye to her double. So much as she glorified herself and
ἐστρηνίασεν, τοσοῦτον δότε αὐτῇ βασανισμὸν καὶ πένθος·
lived luxuriously, so much give to her torment and mourning.
ὅτι ἐν τῇ.καρδίᾳ.αὐτῆς λέγει, [n]Κάθημαι βασίλισσα, καὶ
Because in her heart she says, I sit a queen, and
χήρα οὐκ.εἰμί, καὶ πένθος οὐ.μὴ ἴδω. 8 Διὰ τοῦτο
a widow I am not: and mourning in no wise may I see. On account of this
ἐν μιᾷ ἡμέρᾳ ἥξουσιν αἱ.πληγαὶ.αὐτῆς, θάνατος καὶ πένθος
in one day shall come her plagues, death and mourning
καὶ λιμός· καὶ ἐν πυρὶ κατακαυθήσεται· ὅτι ἰσχυρὸς [o]κύριος‖
and famine, and with fire she shall be burnt; for strong [is the] Lord
ὁ θεὸς ὁ [p]κρίνων‖ αὐτήν. 9 καὶ [q]κλαύσονται‖ [r]αὐτήν,‖ καὶ
God who judges her. And shall weep for her, and
κόψονται ἐπ' [s]αὐτῇ‖ οἱ βασιλεῖς τῆς γῆς, οἱ μετ' αὐτῆς πορ-
shall bewail for her, the kings of the earth, who with her commit-
νεύσαντες καὶ στρηνιάσαντες, ὅταν βλέπωσιν τὸν καπνὸν
ted fornication and lived luxuriously, when they see the smoke
τῆς.πυρώσεως.αὐτῆς, 10 ἀπὸ μακρόθεν ἑστηκότες διὰ
of her burning, [2]from [3]afar [1]standing on account of
τὸν φόβον τοῦ.βασανισμοῦ.αὐτῆς, λέγοντες, Οὐαί, οὐαί, ἡ
the fear of her torment, saying, Woe, woe, the
πόλις ἡ μεγάλη Βαβυλών, ἡ πόλις ἡ ἰσχυρά, ὅτι [t]ἐν‖ μιᾷ ὥρᾳ
[2]city [1]great, Babylon, the [2]city [1]strong! for in one hour
ἦλθεν ἡ.κρίσις.σου. 11 Καὶ οἱ ἔμποροι τῆς γῆς κλαίουσιν καὶ
is come thy judgment. And the merchants of the earth weep and
πενθοῦσιν ἐπ' [v]αὐτῇ,‖ ὅτι τὸν.γόμον.αὐτῶν οὐδεὶς ἀγοράζει
mourn for her, because their lading no one buys
οὐκέτι· 12 γόμον χρυσοῦ, καὶ ἀργύρου, καὶ λίθου τιμίου,
any more; lading of gold, and of silver, and of [2]stone [1]precious,
(*lit.* no more)
καὶ [w]μαργαρίτου,‖ καὶ [x]βύσσου,‖ καὶ πορφύρας, καὶ [y]σηρικοῦ,‖
and of pearl, and of fine linen, and of purple, and of silk,
καὶ κοκκίνου· καὶ πᾶν ξύλον θύϊνον, καὶ πᾶν σκεῦος ἐλεφάν-
and of scarlet, and all [2]wood [1]thyine, and every article of
τινον, καὶ πᾶν σκεῦος ἐκ ξύλου τιμιωτάτου, καὶ χαλκοῦ, καὶ
ivory, and every article of [3]wood [1]most [2]precious, and of brass, and
σιδήρου, καὶ μαρμάρου, 13 καὶ [z]κινάμωμον,‖ [a]καὶ θυμιάματα
of iron, and of marble, and cinnamon, and incense,
καὶ μύρον, καὶ λίβανον, καὶ οἶνον, καὶ ἔλαιον, καὶ σεμίδαλιν,
and ointment, and frankincense, and wine, and oil, and finest flour,

---

[g] ἐκ τῶν πληγῶν αὐτῆς ἵνα μὴ λάβητε GLTTrAW. [h] ἐκολλήθησαν were joined together GLTTrAW. [i] — ὑμῖν GLTTrAW. [k] — αὐτῇ LTTrAW. [l] + τὰ the TTr[A]. [m] αὐτὴν LTTrAW. [n] + ὅτι LTTrA. [o] [κύριος] A. [p] κρίνας judged GLTTrAW. [q] κλαύσουσιν TTrAW. [r] — αὐτήν GLTTrAW. [s] αὐτὴν TTrAW. [t] — ἐν (read [in]) GLTTrAW. [v] αὐτὴν TTrA. [w] μαργαρίτας pearls L; μαργαριτῶν of pearls TTrA. [x] βυσσίνου GLTTrAW. [y] σιρικοῦ LT. [z] κιννάμωμον LTTrA. [a] + καὶ ἄμωμον and amomum GLTTrAW.

καὶ σῖτον, καὶ κτήνη, καὶ πρόβατα, καὶ ἵππων, καὶ ῥεδῶν,
and wheat, and cattle, and sheep, and of horses, and of chariots,
καὶ σωμάτων, καὶ ψυχὰς ἀνθρώπων. 14 καὶ ἡ ὀπώρα [c]τῆς
and of slaves, (lit. of bodies) and souls of men. And the ripe fruits of the
ἐπιθυμίας τῆς ψυχῆς-σου‖ [d]ἀπῆλθεν‖ ἀπὸ σοῦ, καὶ πάντα τὰ
desire of thy soul are departed from thee, and all the
λιπαρὰ καὶ [e]τὰ‖ λαμπρὰ [f]ἀπῆλθεν‖ ἀπὸ σοῦ, καὶ [g]οὐκέτι‖
fat things and the bright things are departed from thee, and [4]any [5]more (lit. no more)
[h]οὐ-μὴ εὑρήσῃς αὐτά.‖ 15 οἱ ἔμποροι τούτων οἱ
[1]in [2]no [3]wise shouldst thou find them. The merchants of these things, who
πλουτήσαντες ἀπ' αὐτῆς, ἀπὸ μακρόθεν στήσονται διὰ
were enriched from her, from afar shall stand because of
τὸν φόβον τοῦ-βασανισμοῦ-αὐτῆς, κλαίοντες καὶ πενθοῦντες,
the fear of her torment, weeping and mourning,
16 [i]καὶ‖ λέγοντες, Οὐαί, οὐαί, ἡ πόλις ἡ μεγάλη, ἡ περι-
and saying, Woe, woe, the [2]city [1]great, which [was] cloth-
βεβλημένη [k]βύσσινον‖ καὶ πορφυροῦν καὶ [k]κόκκινον,‖ καὶ
ed with fine linen and purple and scarlet, and
κεχρυσωμένη [l]ἐν‖ [m]χρυσῷ‖ καὶ λίθῳ τιμίῳ καὶ [n]μαργαρί-
decked (lit. gilded) with gold and [2]stone [1]precious and pearls!
ταις·‖ 17 ὅτι μιᾷ ὥρᾳ ἠρημώθη ὁ τοσοῦτος πλοῦτος. Καὶ
for in one hour was made desolate so great wealth. And
πᾶς κυβερνήτης, καὶ [o]πᾶς ἐπὶ τῶν πλοίων ὁ ὅμιλος,‖ καὶ
every steersman, and all [3]in [4]ships [1]the [2]company, and
ναῦται, καὶ ὅσοι τὴν-θάλασσαν-ἐργάζονται, ἀπὸ-μακρόθεν
sailors, and as many as trade by sea, afar off
ἔστησαν, 18 καὶ [p]ἔκραζον,‖ [q]ὁρῶντες‖ τὸν καπνὸν τῆς πυρώ-
stood, and cried, seeing the smoke [3]burn-
σεως αὐτῆς, λέγοντες, Τίς ὁμοία τῇ πόλει [r] τῇ μεγάλῃ;
ing [1]of [2]her, saying, What [city is] like to the [2]city [1]great?
19 Καὶ [s]ἔβαλον‖ χοῦν ἐπὶ τὰς-κεφαλὰς-αὐτῶν, καὶ [t]ἔκραζον‖
And they cast dust upon their heads, and cried,
κλαίοντες καὶ πενθοῦντες, λέγοντες, Οὐαί, οὐαί, ἡ πόλις ἡ
weeping and mourning, saying, Woe, woe, the [2]city
μεγάλη, ἐν ᾗ ἐπλούτησαν πάντες οἱ ἔχοντες [v] πλοῖα ἐν τῇ
[1]great, in which were enriched all who had ships in the
θαλάσσῃ ἐκ τῆς-τιμιότητος-αὐτῆς, ὅτι μιᾷ ὥρᾳ ἠρημώ-
sea through her costliness! for in one hour she was made
θη. 20 Εὐφραίνου ἐπ' [w]αὐτήν,‖ οὐρανέ, καὶ οἱ ἅγιοι [x] ἀπό-
desolate. Rejoice over her, O heaven, and [ye] holy apo-
στολοι καὶ οἱ προφῆται, ὅτι ἔκρινεν ὁ θεὸς τὸ-κρίμα-ὑμῶν ἐξ
stles and [ye] prophets; for [2]did [3]judge [1]God your judgment upon
αὐτῆς. 21 Καὶ ἦρεν εἷς ἄγγελος ἰσχυρὸς λίθον ὡς [y]μύλον‖
her. And [4]took [5]up [1]one [3]angel [2]strong a stone, as a [2]millstone
μέγαν, καὶ ἔβαλεν εἰς τὴν θάλασσαν, λέγων, Οὕτως ὁρμή-
[1]great, and cast [it] into the sea, saying, Thus with
ματι βληθήσεται Βαβυλὼν ἡ μεγάλη πόλις, καὶ οὐ-μὴ
violence shall be cast down Babylon the great city, and not at all

and wheat, and beasts, and sheep, and horses, and chariots, and slaves, and souls of men. 14 And the fruits that thy soul lusted after are departed from thee, and all things which were dainty and goodly are departed from thee, and thou shalt find them no more at all. 15 The merchants of these things, which were made rich by her, shall stand afar off for the fear of her torment, weeping and wailing, 16 and saying, Alas, alas that great city, that was clothed in fine linen, and purple, and scarlet, and decked with gold, and precious stones, and pearls! 17 for in one hour so great riches is come to nought. And every shipmaster, and all the company in ships, and sailors, and as many as trade by sea, stood afar off, 18 and cried when they saw the smoke of her burning, saying, What *city is* like unto this great city! 19 And they cast dust on their heads, and cried, weeping and wailing, saying, Alas, alas that great city, wherein were made rich all that had ships in the sea by reason of her costliness! for in one hour is she made desolate. 20 Rejoice over her, *thou* heaven, and *ye* holy apostles and prophets; for God hath avenged you on her. 21 And a mighty angel took up a stone like a great millstone, and cast *it* into the sea, saying, Thus with violence shall that great city Babylon be thrown down, and shall be found no more

[c] σου τῆς ἐπιθυμίας τῆς ψυχῆς LTTrAW. [d] ἀπώλετο are destroyed W. [e] [τὰ] A. [f] ἀπώλετο (-λοντο T) are destroyed GLTTrAW. [g] — οὐκέτι Tr. [h] αὐτὰ οὐ μὴ εὑρήσουσιν (shall they find) (εὕρῃς W) LAW; οὐ μὴ αὐτὰ εὑρήσουσιν TTr. [i] — καὶ LTTrAW. [k] βύσσινον *and* κόκκινον *transposed* L. [l] — ἐν (*read* [with]) LTr[A]. [m] χρυσίῳ GLTrAW. [n] μαργαρίτῃ pearl LTTrA. [o] πᾶς ὁ ἐπὶ τόπον πλέων every one who sails to [any] place GLTTrAW. [p] ἔκραξαν LTrA. [q] βλέποντες GLTTrAW. [r] + ταύτῃ (*read* this great city) L. [s] ἔβαλαν L; [ἐπ]έβαλον A. [t] ἔκραξαν LA. [v] + τὰ LTTrAW. [w] αὐτῇ GLTTrAW. [x] + καὶ οἱ (*read* [ye] saints and [ye] apostles) GLTTrAW. [y] μύλινον LA.

at all. 22 And the voice of harpers, and musicians, and of pipers, and trumpeters, shall be heard no more at all in thee; and no craftsman, of whatsoever craft *he be*, shall be found any more in thee; and the sound of a millstone shall be heard no more at all in thee; 23 and the light of a candle shall shine no more at all in thee; and the voice of the bridegroom and of the bride shall be heard no more at all in thee: for thy merchants were the great men of the earth; for by thy sorceries were all nations deceived. 24 And in her was found the blood of prophets, and of saints, and of all that were slain upon the earth.

XIX. And after these things I heard a great voice of much people in heaven, saying, Alleluia; Salvation, and glory, and honour, and power, unto the Lord our God: 2 for true and righteous *are* his judgments: for he hath judged the great whore, which did corrupt the earth with her fornication, and hath avenged the blood of his servants at her hand. 3 And again they said, Alleluia. And her smoke rose up for ever and ever. 4 And the four and twenty elders and the four beasts fell down and worshipped God that sat on the throne, saying, Amen; Alleluia. 5 And a voice came out of the throne, saying, Praise our God, all ye his servants, and ye that fear him, both small and great. 6 And I heard as it were the voice of a great multitude, and as the voice of many waters, and as the voice of

εὑρεθῇ ἔτι. 22 καὶ φωνὴ κιθαρῳδῶν καὶ μουσικῶν καὶ
may be found longer: and voice of harpers and musicians and
αὐλητῶν καὶ σαλπιστῶν οὐ.μὴ ἀκουσθῇ ἐν σοὶ ἔτι, καὶ
flute-players and trumpeters not at all may be heard in thee longer, and
πᾶς τεχνίτης πάσης τέχνης οὐ.μὴ εὑρεθῇ ἐν σοὶ ἔτι, καὶ
any artificer of any art not at all may be found in thee longer, and
(*lit.* every) (*lit.* of every)
φωνὴ μύλου οὐ.μὴ ἀκουσθῇ ἐν σοὶ ἔτι, 23 καὶ φῶς
sound of millstone not at all may be heard in thee longer, and light
λύχνου οὐ.μὴ [z]φανῇ‖ [a]ἐν‖ σοὶ ἔτι, καὶ φωνὴ νυμφίου καὶ
of lamp not at all may shine in thee longer, and voice of bridegroom and
νύμφης οὐ.μὴ ἀκουσθῇ ἐν σοὶ ἔτι· ὅτι [b]οἱ‖.ἔμποροί.σου
of bride not at all may be heard in thee longer; for thy merchants
ἦσαν οἱ μεγιστᾶνες τῆς γῆς, ὅτι ἐν τῇ.[c]φαρμακείᾳ‖.σου ἐπλα-
were the great ones of the earth, for by thy sorcery were
νήθησαν πάντα τὰ ἔθνη. 24 καὶ ἐν αὐτῇ [d]αἷμα‖ προφη-
misled all the nations. And in her [the] blood of pro-
τῶν καὶ ἁγίων εὑρέθη, καὶ πάντων τῶν ἐσφαγμένων ἐπὶ τῆς
phets and saints was found, and of all the slain on the
γῆς.
earth.

19 [e]Καὶ‖ μετὰ ταῦτα ἤκουσα [f] φωνὴν [g]ὄχλου
And after these things I heard a ²voice ³of ⁴a ⁶multitude
πολλοῦ μεγάλην‖ ἐν τῷ οὐρανῷ, [h]λέγοντος,‖ Ἀλληλούϊα· ἡ
⁵great ¹loud in the heaven, saying, Hallelujah: the
σωτηρία καὶ ἡ δόξα [i]καὶ ἡ τιμὴ‖ καὶ ἡ δύναμις [k]κυρίῳ
salvation and the glory and the honour and the power to the Lord
τῷ.θεῷ.ἡμῶν·‖ 2. ὅτι ἀληθιναὶ καὶ δίκαιαι αἱ.κρίσεις.αὐτοῦ·
our God: for true and righteous [are] his judgments;
ὅτι ἔκρινεν τὴν πόρνην τὴν μεγάλην, ἥτις ἔφθειρεν τὴν γῆν
for he judged the ²harlot ¹great, who corrupted the earth
ἐν τῇ.πορνείᾳ.αὐτῆς, καὶ ἐξεδίκησεν τὸ αἷμα τῶν δούλων
with her fornication, and he did avenge the blood ³bondmen
αὐτοῦ ἐκ [l]τῆς‖.χειρὸς.αὐτῆς. 3 Καὶ δεύτερον εἴρηκαν, Ἀλλη-
¹of ²his at her hand. And a second time they said, Halle-
λούϊα· Καὶ ὁ.καπνὸς.αὐτῆς ἀναβαίνει εἰς τοὺς αἰῶνας τῶν
lujah. And her smoke goes up to the ages of the
αἰώνων. 4 Καὶ [m]ἔπεσαν‖ οἱ [n]πρεσβύτεροι οἱ εἴκοσι καὶ τέσ-
ages. And fell down the ⁴elders ¹twenty ²and
σαρες,‖ καὶ τὰ [o]τέσσαρα‖ ζῶα, καὶ προσεκύνησαν τῷ
³four, and the four living creatures and worshipped
θεῷ τῷ καθημένῳ ἐπὶ [p]τοῦ θρόνου,‖ λέγοντες, Ἀμήν· Ἀλλη-
God who sits on the throne, saying, Amen, Halle-
λούϊα. 5 Καὶ φωνὴ [q]ἐκ‖ τοῦ θρόνου ἐξῆλθεν λέγουσα, Αἰνεῖτε
lujah. And a voice out of the throne came forth, saying, Praise
[r]τὸν.θεὸν‖.ἡμῶν πάντες οἱ.δοῦλοι.αὐτοῦ, [s]καὶ‖ οἱ.φοβούμενοι
our God all [ye] his bondmen, and [ye] who fear
αὐτὸν [t]καὶ‖ οἱ μικροὶ καὶ οἱ μεγάλοι. 6 Καὶ ἤκουσα ὡς φωνὴν
him, both the small and the great. And I heard as a voice
ὄχλου πολλοῦ, καὶ [v]ὡς‖ φωνὴν ὑδάτων πολλῶν, καὶ ὡς
of a ²multitude ¹great, and as a voice of ²waters ¹many, and as

---

[z] φάνῃ LT. [a] — ἐν (*read* σοι upon thee) L[A]. [b] — οἱ L. [c] φαρμακίᾳ TA. [d] αἵματα bloods GTW. [e] — καὶ GLTTrAW. [f] + ὡς as EGLTTrAW. [g] μεγάλην ὄχλου πολλοῦ GLTTrA. [h] λεγόντων GLTTrAW. [i] — καὶ ἡ τιμὴ GLTTrAW. [k] τοῦ θεοῦ ἡμῶν of our God GLTTrAW. [l] — τῆς GLTTrAW. [m] ἔπεσον EG. [n] — καὶ GTTrAW; εἴκοσι τέσσαρες πρεσβύτεροι L. [o] τέσσερα LTTrA. [p] τῷ θρόνῳ LTTrAW. [q] ἀπὸ from LTrAW. [r] τῷ θεῷ LTTrAW. [s] — καὶ T[TrA]. [t] — καὶ GLTTrAW. [v] — ὡς L

φωνὴν βροντῶν ἰσχυρῶν, [w]λέγοντας,‖ Ἀλληλούϊα· ὅτι ἐβασί-
a voice of [2]thunders [1]strong, saying, Hallelujah, for has
λευσεν κύριος ὁ θεὸς [x] ὁ παντοκράτωρ. 7 χαίρωμεν καὶ
reigned [the] Lord God the Almighty. We should rejoice and
[y]ἀγαλλιώμεθα,‖ καὶ [z]δῶμεν‖ τὴν δόξαν αὐτῷ· ὅτι ἦλθεν ὁ
should exult; and should give glory to him; for is come the
γάμος τοῦ ἀρνίου, καὶ ἡ.γυνὴ.αὐτοῦ ἡτοίμασεν ἑαυτήν. 8 Καὶ
marriage of the Lamb, and his wife did make [2]ready [1]herself. And
ἐδόθη αὐτῇ ἵνα περιβάληται βύσσινον [a]καθαρὸν καὶ
it was given to her that she should be clothed in fine linen, pure and
λαμπρόν·‖ τὸ.γὰρ βύσσινον τὰ δικαιώματά [b]ἐστιν τῶν
bright; for the fine linen [2]the [3]righteousnesses [1]is of the
ἁγίων.‖ 9 Καὶ λέγει μοι, Γράψον, Μακάριοι οἱ εἰς τὸ
saints. And he says to me, Write, Blessed [are] they who to the
δεῖπνον τοῦ γάμου τοῦ ἀρνίου κεκλημένοι. Καὶ λέγει μοι,
supper of the marriage of the Lamb are called. And he says to me,
Οὗτοι οἱ λόγοι [c] ἀληθινοί [d]εἰσιν τοῦ θεοῦ.‖ 10 Καὶ [e]ἔπεσον‖
These [2]the [4]words [3]true [1]are of God. And I fell
ἔμπροσθεν τῶν.ποδῶν.αὐτοῦ προσκυνῆσαι αὐτῷ· καὶ λέγει
before his feet to do homage to him. And he says
μοι, Ὅρα μή· σύνδουλός σου εἰμὶ καὶ τῶν ἀδελ-
to me, See [thou do it] not. Fellow-bondman of thee I am and [3]breth-
φῶν σου τῶν ἐχόντων τὴν μαρτυρίαν [f]τοῦ‖ Ἰησοῦ· τῷ θεῷ
ren [1]of [2]thy who have the testimony of Jesus. To God
προσκύνησον· ἡ.γὰρ μαρτυρία [f]τοῦ‖ Ἰησοῦ ἐστιν τὸ πνεῦμα
do homage. For [6]the [7]testimony [8]of [9]Jesus [5]is [1]the [2]spirit
τῆς προφητείας.
[3]of [4]prophecy.

11 Καὶ εἶδον τὸν οὐρανὸν [g]ἀνεῳγμένον,‖ καὶ ἰδού, ἵππος
And I saw the heaven opened, and behold, a [2]horse
λευκός, καὶ ὁ καθήμενος ἐπ' αὐτόν, [h]καλούμενος πιστὸς‖
[1]white, and he who sits upon it, called Faithful
καὶ ἀληθινός, καὶ ἐν δικαιοσύνῃ κρίνει καὶ πολεμεῖ· 12 οἱ
and True, and in righteousness he judges and makes war.
δὲ ὀφθαλμοὶ αὐτοῦ [i]ὡς‖ φλὸξ πυρός, καὶ ἐπὶ τὴν κεφαλὴν
And [2]eyes [1]his [were] as a flame of fire, and upon [2]head
αὐτοῦ διαδήματα πολλά, ἔχων [k] ὄνομα γεγραμμένον ὃ οὐδεὶς
[1]his [4]diadems [3]many, having a name written which no one
οἶδεν εἰ.μὴ αὐτός· 13 καὶ περιβεβλημένος ἱμάτιον [l]βεβαμ-
knows but himself, and clothed with a garment dip-
μένον‖ αἵματι· καὶ [m]καλεῖται‖ τὸ.ὄνομα.αὐτοῦ, Ὁ λόγος τοῦ
ped in blood; and [3]is [4]called [1]his [2]name, The Word
θεοῦ. 14 Καὶ τὰ στρατεύματα [n] ἐν τῷ οὐρανῷ ἠκολούθει αὐτῷ
of God. And the armies in the heaven were following him
ἐφ' ἵπποις λευκοῖς, ἐνδεδυμένοι βύσσινον λευκὸν [o]καὶ‖ καθαρόν.
upon [2]horses [1]white, clothed in fine linen, white and pure.
15 καὶ ἐκ τοῦ.στόματος.αὐτοῦ ἐκπορεύεται ῥομφαία ὀξεῖα,
And out of his mouth goes forth a [2]sword [1]sharp,
ἵνα ἐν αὐτῇ [p]πατάσσῃ‖ τὰ ἔθνη· καὶ αὐτὸς ποιμανεῖ
that with it he might smite the nations; and he shall shepherd

mighty thunderings, saying, Alleluia: for the Lord God omnipotent reigneth. 7 Let us be glad and rejoice, and give honour to him: for the marriage of the Lamb is come, and his wife hath made herself ready. 8 And to her was granted that she should be arrayed in fine linen, clean and white: for the fine linen is the righteousness of saints. 9 And he saith unto me, Write, Blessed *are* they which are called unto the marriage supper of the Lamb. And he saith unto me, These are the true sayings of God. 10 And I fell at his feet to worship him. And he said unto me, See *thou do it* not: I am thy fellowservant, and of thy brethren that have the testimony of Jesus: worship God: for the testimony of Jesus is the spirit of prophecy.

11 And I saw heaven opened, and behold a white horse; and he that sat upon him *was* called Faithful and True, and in righteousness he doth judge and make war. 12 His eyes *were* as a flame of fire, and on his head *were* many crowns; and he had a name written, that no man knew, but he himself. 13 And he *was* clothed with a vesture dipped in blood: and his name is called The Word of God. 14 And the armies *which were* in heaven followed him upon white horses, clothed in fine linen, white and clean. 15 And out of his mouth goeth a sharp sword, that with it he should

[w] λεγόντων ELTTrW; λέγοντες GA. [x] + ἡμῶν (*read* our God) GTTrW. [y] ἀγαλλιῶμεν LTTrA. [z] δώσομεν shall give LA. [a] λαμπρὸν καὶ (— καὶ LTTrA) καθαρόν GLTTrA. [b] τῶν ἁγίων ἐστίν LTTrA. [c] + οἱ LAW. [d] τοῦ θεοῦ εἰσιν LTTrA. [e] ἔπεσα LTTrAW. [f] — τοῦ LTTrAW. [g] ἠνεῳγμένον LTTrA. [h] πιστὸς καλούμενος Tr; [καλούμενος] πιστὸς A. [i] — ὡς TTr[A]. [k] + [ὀνόματα γεγραμμένα, καὶ] names written and A. [l] περιρεραμμένον sprinkled round T. [m] κέκληται LTTrAW. [n] + τὰ which [are] EGL[A]W. [o] — καὶ LTAW. [p] πατάξῃ GLTTrAW.

smite the nations:
and he shall rule
them with a rod of
iron: and he treadeth
the winepress of the
fierceness and wrath of
Almighty God. 16And
he hath on *his* ves-
ture and on his thigh
a name written, KING
OF KINGS, AND
LORD OF LORDS.

17 And I saw an an-
gel standing in the
sun; and he cried with
a loud voice, saying to
all the fowls that fly
in the midst of hea-
ven, Come and gather
yourselves together
unto the supper of
the great God; 18 that
ye may eat the flesh
of kings, and the flesh
of captains, and the
flesh of mighty men,
and the flesh of horses,
and of them that sit
on them, and the flesh
of all *men, both* free
and bond, both small
and great.

19 And I saw the
beast, and the kings
of the earth, and their
armies, gathered to-
gether to make war
against him that sat
on the horse, and
against his army.
20 And the beast was
taken, and with him
the false prophet that
wrought miracles be-
fore him, with which
he deceived them that
had received the mark
of the beast, and them
that worshipped his
image. These both
were cast alive into a
lake of fire burning
with brimstone. 21And
the remnant were
slain with the sword
of him that sat upon
the horse, which
sword proceeded out
of his mouth: and all
the fowls were filled
with their flesh.

αὐτοὺς ἐν ῥάβδῳ σιδηρᾷ· καὶ αὐτὸς πατεῖ την ληνὸν τοῦ
them with [3]rod [1]an [2]iron; and he treads the press of the
οἴνου τοῦ θυμοῦ [q]καὶ|| τῆς ὀργῆς τοῦ θεοῦ τοῦ παντοκρά-
wine of the fury and of the wrath of God the Almighty.
τορος. 16 καὶ ἔχει ἐπὶ τὸ ἱμάτιον καὶ ἐπὶ τὸν.μηρὸν.αὐτοῦ
And he has upon [his] garment and upon his thigh
[r]τὸ|| ὄνομα γεγραμμένον, Βασιλεὺς βασιλέων καὶ κύριος
the name written, King of kings and Lord
κυρίων.
of lords.

17 Καὶ εἶδον ἕνα ἄγγελον ἑστῶτα ἐν τῷ ἡλίῳ· καὶ
And I saw one angel standing in the sun; and
ἔκραξεν [s] φωνῇ μεγάλῃ λέγων πᾶσιν τοῖς ὀρνέοις τοῖς
he cried with a [2]voice [1]loud, saying to all the birds which
[t]πετωμένοις|| ἐν μεσουρανήματι, Δεῦτε [v]καὶ συνάγεσθε|| εἰς
fly in mid-heaven, Come and gather yourselves to
τὸ δεῖπνον [w]τοῦ μεγάλου|| θεοῦ, 18 ἵνα φάγητε σάρκας βα-
the supper of the great God, that ye may eat flesh of
σιλέων, καὶ σάρκας χιλιάρχων, καὶ σάρκας ἰσχυρῶν,
kings, and flesh of chief captains, and flesh of strong [men],
καὶ σάρκας ἵππων καὶ τῶν καθημένων ἐπ' [x]αὐτῶν,|| καὶ
and flesh of horses and of those who sit on them, and
σάρκας πάντων, ἐλευθέρων [y] καὶ δούλων, καὶ μικρῶν [z] καὶ
flesh of all, free and bond, and small and
μεγάλων.
great.

19 Καὶ [a]εἶδον|| τὸ θηρίον, καὶ τοὺς βασιλεῖς τῆς γῆς,
And I saw the beast, and the kings of the earth,
καὶ τὰ στρατεύματα [b]αὐτῶν|| συνηγμένα ποιῆσαι [c] πόλε-
and [2]armies [1]their gathered together to make
μον μετὰ τοῦ καθημένου ἐπὶ τοῦ ἵππου, καὶ μετὰ τοῦ
war with him who sits on the horse, and with
στρατεύματος αὐτοῦ. 20 καὶ ἐπιάσθη τὸ θηρίον, καὶ [d] [e]μετὰ
[2]army [1]his. And was taken the beast, and with
τούτου ὁ|| ψευδοπροφήτης ὁ ποιήσας τὰ σημεῖα ἐνώπιον
him the false prophet who wrought the signs before
αὐτοῦ, ἐν οἷς ἐπλάνησεν τοὺς λαβόντας τὸ χάραγμα τοῦ
him, by which he misled those who received the mark of the
θηρίου, καὶ τοὺς προσκυνοῦντας τῇ.εἰκόνι.αὐτοῦ· ζῶντες
beast, and those who do homage to his image. Alive
ἐβλήθησαν οἱ δύο εἰς τὴν λίμνην τοῦ πυρὸς [f]τὴν καιομένην||
were cast the two into the lake of fire which burns
ἐν [g]τῷ|| θείῳ. 21 καὶ οἱ λοιποὶ ἀπεκτάνθησαν ἐν τῇ
with brimstone; and the rest were killed with the
ῥομφαίᾳ τοῦ καθημένου ἐπὶ τοῦ ἵππου, τῇ [h]ἐκπο-
sword of him who sits on the horse, [the sword] which goes
ρευομένῃ|| ἐκ τοῦ.στόματος.αὐτοῦ· καὶ πάντα τὰ ὄρνεα ἐχορ-
forth out of his mouth; and all the birds were
τάσθησαν ἐκ τῶν.σαρκῶν.αὐτῶν.
filled with their flesh.

---

[q] — καὶ GLTTrA. [r] — τὸ (*read* a name) GLTTrAW. [s] + ἐν in (a loud voice) T[A]. [t] πετομένοις GLTTrAW. [v] συνάχθητε GLTTrAW. [w] τὸ μέγα τοῦ (*read* the great supper of) GLTTrAW. [x] αὐτούς LTrA. [y] + τε both (free) GLTTrAW. [z] + τε both (small) W. [a] ἴδον T. [b] αὐτοῦ its L. [c] + τὸν LTTrAW. [d] + [οἱ] those A. [e] μετ' αὐτοῦ ὁ LTTrA; ὁ μετ' αὐτοῦ GW. [f] τῆς καιομένης LTTrA. [g] — τῷ GLTTrAW. [h] ἐξελθούσῃ came forth GLTTrAW.

20 Καὶ [i]εἶδον‖ ἄγγελον καταβαίνοντα ἐκ τοῦ οὐρανοῦ,
And I saw an angel descending out of the heaven,
ἔχοντα τὴν [j]κλεῖδα‖ τῆς ἀβύσσου, καὶ ἅλυσιν μεγάλην ἐπὶ
having the key of the abyss, and a [2]chain [1]great in
τὴν.χεῖρα.αὐτοῦ. 2 καὶ ἐκράτησεν τὸν δράκοντα, [k]τὸν ὄφιν
his hand. And he laid hold of the dragon, the [2]serpent
τὸν ἀρχαῖον,‖ [l]ὅς ἐστιν‖ διάβολος καὶ [m] σατανᾶς, καὶ ἔδησεν
[1]ancient, who is [the] devil and Satan, and bound
αὐτὸν χίλια ἔτη, 3 καὶ ἔβαλεν αὐτὸν εἰς τὴν ἄβυσσον, καὶ
him a thousand years, and cast him into the abyss, and
ἔκλεισεν [n]αὐτόν,‖ καὶ ἐσφράγισεν ἐπάνω αὐτοῦ, ἵνα μὴ
shut him [up], and sealed over him, that [3]not
[o]πλανήσῃ‖ [p]τὰ ἔθνη ἔτι,‖ ἄχρι τελεσθῇ τὰ χίλια
[1]he [2]should mislead the nations longer, until were completed the thousand
ἔτη· [q]καὶ‖ μετὰ ταῦτα δεῖ.[r]αὐτὸν λυθῆναι‖ μικρὸν
years; and after these things he must be loosed a little
χρόνον.
time.

4 Καὶ [i]εἶδον‖ θρόνους, καὶ ἐκάθισαν ἐπ' αὐτούς, καὶ κρίμα
And I saw thrones; and they sat upon them, and judgment
ἐδόθη αὐτοῖς· καὶ τὰς ψυχὰς τῶν πεπελεκισμένων διὰ
was given to them; and the souls of those beheaded on account of
τὴν μαρτυρίαν Ἰησοῦ, καὶ διὰ τὸν λόγον τοῦ θεοῦ, καὶ
the testimony of Jesus, and on account of the word of God, and
οἵτινες οὐ.προσεκύνησαν [s]τῷ θηρίῳ,‖ [t]οὔτε‖ [v]τὴν.εἰκόνα‖.αὐτοῦ,
those who did not do homage to the beast, nor his image,
καὶ οὐκ.ἔλαβον τὸ χάραγμα ἐπὶ τὸ.μέτωπον.[w]αὐτῶν,‖ καὶ ἐπὶ
and did not receive the mark upon their forehead, and upon
τὴν.χεῖρα.αὐτῶν· καὶ ἔζησαν, καὶ ἐβασίλευσαν μετὰ [x] χριστοῦ
their hand; and they lived and reigned with Christ
[y]τὰ‖ χίλια ἔτη· 5 [z] οἱ.[a]δὲ‖ λοιποὶ τῶν νεκρῶν οὐκ [b]ἀνέζησαν
the thousand years: but the rest of the dead [2]not [1]lived again
ἕως‖ τελεσθῇ τὰ χίλια ἔτη. αὕτη ἡ ἀνάστασις
till may have been completed the thousand years. This [is] the [2]resurrection
ἡ πρώτη. 6 μακάριος καὶ ἅγιος ὁ ἔχων μέρος ἐν τῇ ἀνα-
[1]first. Blessed and holy he who has part in the [2]resur-
στάσει τῇ.πρώτῃ· ἐπὶ τούτων ὁ [c]θάνατος ὁ δεύτερος‖ οὐκ.ἔχει
rection [1]first: over these the [2]death [1]second has no
ἐξουσίαν, [d]ἀλλ'‖ ἔσονται ἱερεῖς τοῦ θεοῦ καὶ τοῦ χριστοῦ,
authority; but they shall be priests of God and of the Christ,
καὶ [e]βασιλεύσουσιν‖ μετ' αὐτοῦ [f] χίλια ἔτη. 7 Καὶ ὅταν τε-
and shall reign with him a thousand years. And when may
λεσθῇ τὰ χίλια ἔτη, λυθήσεται ὁ σατανᾶς ἐκ τῆς
have been completed the thousand years, will be loosed Satan out of
φυλακῆς αὐτοῦ, 8 καὶ ἐξελεύσεται πλανῆσαι τὰ ἔθνη τὰ
[2]prison [1]his, and will go out to mislead the nations which [are]
ἐν ταῖς τέσσαρσιν γωνίαις τῆς γῆς, τὸν Γὼγ καὶ [g]τὸν‖ Μαγώγ,
in the four corners of the earth, Gog and Magog,

XX. And I saw an
angel come down
from heaven, having
the key of the bot-
tomless pit and a
great chain in his
hand. 2 And he laid
hold on the dragon,
that old serpent,
which is the Devil,
and Satan, and bound
him a thousand years,
3 and cast him
into the bottomless
pit, and shut him up,
and set a seal upon
him, that he should
deceive the nations no
more, till the thou-
sand years should be
fulfilled: and after
that he must be loosed
a little season.

4 And I saw thrones,
and they sat upon
them, and judgment
was given unto them:
and *I saw* the souls of
them that were be-
headed for the wit-
ness of Jesus, and
for the word of God,
and which had not
worshipped the beast,
neither his image,
neither had received
his mark upon their
foreheads, or in their
hands; and they lived
and reigned with
Christ a thousand
years. 5 But the
rest of the dead
lived not again until
the thousand years
were finished. This
is the first resurrec-
tion. 6 Blessed and
holy *is* he that hath
part in the first re-
surrection: on such
the second death hath
no power, but they
shall be priests of
God and of Christ,
and shall reign with
him a thousand years.
7 And when the thou-
sand years are ex-
pired, Satan shall be
loosed out of his pri-
son, 8 and shall go out
to deceive the nations
which are in the four
quarters of the earth,
Gog and Magog, to

[i] ἴδον T. [j] κλεῖν GLTTrAW. [k] ὁ ὄφις ὁ ἀρχαῖος LTTrA. [l] ὅ ἐστιν ὁ which is the T. [m] + ὁ LTTrAW. [n] — αὐτὸν GLTTrAW. [o] πλανᾷ G. [p] ἔτι τὰ ἔθνη GLTTrA. [q] — καὶ LTTrAW. [r] λυθῆναι αὐτὸν LA. [s] τὸ θηρίον GLTTrAW. [t] οὐδὲ LTTrAW. [v] τῇ εἰκόνι EG. [w] — αὐτῶν (*read* [their]) GLTTrAW. [x] + τοῦ the EGLTTrAW. [y] — τὰ (*read* a thousand) LTTrAW. [z] + καὶ (*read* and the rest) Tr. [a] — δὲ but LTTrAW. [b] ἔζησαν ἄχρι lived till GLTTrAW. [c] δεύτερος θάνατος GLTTrA. [d] ἀλλὰ TTrW. [e] βασιλεύ[σ]ουσιν A. [f] + τὰ the (thousand) TTr[A]. [g] — τὸν LT[Tr]A.

gather them together
to battle: the num-
ber of whom *is* as
the sand of the sea.
9 And they went up
on the breadth of the
earth, and compassed
the camp of the saints
about, and the beloved
city: and fire came
down from God out of
heaven, and devoured
them. 10 And the de-
vil that deceived them
was cast into the lake
of fire and brimstone,
where the beast and
the false prophet *are*,
and shall be torment-
ed day and night for
ever and ever.

11 And I saw a great
white throne, and
him that sat on it,
from whose face the
earth and the heaven
fled away; and there
was found no place
for them. 12 And I
saw the dead, small
and great, stand be-
fore God; and the
books were opened:
and another book was
opened, which is *the*
book of life: and
the dead were judged
out of those things
which were written
in the books, accord-
ing to their works.
13 And the sea gave up
the dead which were
in it; and death and
hell delivered up the
dead which were in
them: and they were
judged every man
according to their
works. 14 And death
and hell were cast
into the lake of
fire. This is the se-
cond death. 15 And
whosoever was not
found written in the
book of life was cast
into the lake of fire.

XXI. And I saw a
new heaven and a new
earth: for the first

συναγαγεῖν αὐτοὺς εἰς [h] πόλεμον, ὧν ὁ ἀριθμὸς [i] ὡς
to gather together them unto war, of whom the number [is] as
ἡ ἄμμος τῆς θαλάσσης. 9 καὶ ἀνέβησαν ἐπὶ τὸ πλάτος τῆς
the sand of the sea. And they went up upon the breadth of the
γῆς, καὶ [k]ἐκύκλωσαν‖ τὴν παρεμβολὴν τῶν ἁγίων, καὶ τὴν
earth, and encircled the camp of the saints, and the
πόλιν τὴν ἠγαπημένην· καὶ κατέβη πῦρ [l]ἀπὸ τοῦ θεοῦ ἐκ
²city ¹beloved: and ²came ³down ¹fire from God out of
τοῦ οὐρανοῦ,‖ καὶ κατέφαγεν αὐτούς· 10 καὶ ὁ διάβολος ὁ
the heaven and devoured them: and the devil who
πλανῶν αὐτοὺς ἐβλήθη εἰς τὴν λίμνην τοῦ πυρὸς καὶ [m]
misleads them was cast into the lake of fire and
θείου, ὅπου [n] τὸ θηρίον καὶ ὁ ψευδοπροφήτης· καὶ
of brimstone, where [are] the beast and the false prophet; and
βασανισθήσονται ἡμέρας καὶ νυκτὸς εἰς τοὺς αἰῶνας τῶν
they shall be tormented day and night for the ages of the
αἰώνων.
ages.

11 Καὶ εἶδον θρόνον [o]λευκὸν μέγαν,‖ καὶ τὸν καθήμενον
And I saw a ³throne ²white ¹great and him who sits
[p]ἐπ'‖ [q]αὐτοῦ,‖ οὗ ἀπὸ [r] προσώπου ἔφυγεν ἡ γῆ καὶ ὁ οὐ-
on it, ²whose ¹from face fled the earth and the hea-
ρανός, καὶ τόπος οὐχ.εὑρέθη αὐτοῖς. 12 καὶ εἶδον τοὺς
ven, and place was not found for them. And I saw the
νεκρούς, [s]μικροὺς καὶ μεγάλους.‖ ἑστῶτας ἐνώπιον [t]τοῦ θεοῦ,‖
dead, small and great, standing before God,
καὶ βιβλία [v]ἠνεῴχθησαν·‖ καὶ [w]βιβλίον ἄλλο‖ [x]ἠνεῴχθη,‖
and books were opened; and ²book ¹another was opened,
ὅ ἐστιν τῆς ζωῆς· καὶ.ἐκρίθησαν οἱ νεκροὶ ἐκ τῶν
which is [that] of life. And were judged the dead out of the things
γεγραμμένων ἐν τοῖς βιβλίοις, κατὰ τὰ.ἔργα.αὐτῶν.
written in the books according to their works.
13 καὶ ἔδωκεν ἡ.θάλασσα τοὺς [y]ἐν αὐτῇ νεκρούς,‖ καὶ ὁ
And ³gave ⁴up ¹the ²sea the ²in ³it ¹dead, and
θάνατος καὶ ὁ ᾅδης [z]ἔδωκαν‖ τοὺς [a]ἐν αὐτοῖς νεκρούς·‖ καὶ ἐ-
death and hades gave up the ²in ³them ¹dead; and they
κρίθησαν ἕκαστος κατὰ τὰ.ἔργα.αὐτῶν. 14 καὶ ὁ θάνατος
were judged each according to their works: and death
καὶ ὁ ᾅδης ἐβλήθησαν εἰς τὴν λίμνην τοῦ πυρός· οὗτός [b]ἐστιν
and hades were cast into the lake of fire. This is
ὁ δεύτερος θάνατος.‖ [c] 15 καὶ εἴ τις οὐχ.εὑρέθη ἐν τῇ
the second death. And if anyone was not found in the
βίβλῳ τῆς ζωῆς γεγραμμένος, ἐβλήθη εἰς τὴν λίμνην τοῦ
book of life written, he was cast into the lake
πυρός.
of fire.

21 Καὶ εἶδον οὐρανὸν καινὸν καὶ γῆν καινήν· ὁ.γὰρ
And I saw a ²heaven ¹new and ³earth ¹a ²new; for the

---

[h] + τὸν LTTrAW. [i] + αὐτῶν of them GLTTrAW. [k] ἐκύκλευσαν LTAW. [l] ἐκ τοῦ οὐρανοῦ ἀπὸ τοῦ θεοῦ G; — ἀπὸ τοῦ θεοῦ LTAW. [m] + τοῦ T. [n] + καὶ both GLTTrAW. [o] μέγαν λευκόν GLTTrAW. [p] ἐπάνω Tr. [q] αὐτόν GT. [r] + τοῦ (*read* from the face of whom) LTTrAW. [s] τοὺς μεγάλους καὶ τοὺς μικρούς the great and the small LTTrAW. [t] τοῦ θρόνου the throne GLTTrAW. [v] ἠνοίχθησαν GLTTrAW. [w] ἄλλο βιβλίον GLTTrAW. [x] ἠνοίχθη LTTrAW. [y] νεκροὺς τοὺς ἐν αὐτῇ dead which [were] in it GLTTrAW. [z] ἔδωκεν L. [a] νεκροὺς τοὺς ἐν αὐτοῖς dead which [were] in them GLTTrAW. [b] ὁ θάνατος ὁ δεύτερος ἐστιν GLTAW; ὁ δεύτερος θάνατός ἐστιν Tr. [c] + , ἡ λίμνη τοῦ πυρός the lake of fire LTTrAW.

πρῶτος οὐρανὸς καὶ ἡ πρώτη γῆ [d]παρῆλθεν,‖ καὶ ἡ θά-
first heaven and the first earth were passed away, and the
λασσα οὐκ ἔστιν ἔτι.
sea ²no ¹is longer.

2 Καὶ [e]ἐγὼ Ἰωάννης‖ [f]εἶδον‖ τὴν πόλιν τὴν ἁγίαν[f], Ἱερ-
And I John saw the ²city ¹holy, ⁴Jer-
ουσαλὴμ καινήν[f], καταβαίνουσαν [g]ἀπὸ τοῦ θεοῦ ἐκ τοῦ οὐ-
usalem ³new, coming down from God out of hea-
ρανοῦ,‖ ἡτοιμασμένην ὡς νύμφην κεκοσμημένην τῷ ἀνδρὶ
ven, prepared as a bride adorned for ²husband
αὐτῆς. 3 καὶ ἤκουσα φωνῆς μεγάλης ἐκ τοῦ [h]οὐρανοῦ,‖
¹her. And I heard a ²voice ¹great out of the heaven,
λεγούσης, Ἰδού, ἡ σκηνὴ τοῦ θεοῦ μετὰ τῶν ἀνθρώπων,
saying, Behold, the tabernacle of God [is] with men,
καὶ σκηνώσει μετ' αὐτῶν· καὶ αὐτοὶ [i]λαοὶ‖ αὐτοῦ ἔσονται,
and he shall tabernacle with them, and they ⁴peoples ³his ¹shall ²be,
καὶ αὐτὸς ὁ θεὸς [k]ἔσται μετ' αὐτῶν‖ [l]θεὸς.αὐτῶν.‖ 4 καὶ ἐξα-
and ²himself ¹God shall be with them their God. And ²shall
λείψει [m]ὁ θεὸς‖ πᾶν δάκρυον [n]ἀπὸ‖ τῶν.ὀφθαλμῶν.αὐτῶν,
³wipe ⁴away ¹God every tear from their eyes;
καὶ [o]ὁ‖ θάνατος οὐκ.ἔσται ἔτι· οὔτε πένθος, οὔτε κραυγή,
and death shall be no longer, nor mourning, nor crying,
οὔτε πόνος οὐκ ἔσται ἔτι· [p]ὅτι‖ τὰ πρῶτα [q]ἀπῆλθον.‖
nor distress ³any ¹shall ²be longer, because the former things are passed away.
(*lit.* not)
5 Καὶ εἶπεν ὁ καθήμενος ἐπὶ [r]τοῦ θρόνου,‖ Ἰδού, καινὰ
And said he who sits on the throne, Lo, new
[s]πάντα ποιῶ.‖ Καὶ λέγει [t]μοι,‖ Γράψον· ὅτι οὗτοι οἱ λόγοι
all things I make. And he says to me, Write, because these words
[v]ἀληθινοὶ καὶ πιστοί‖ εἰσιν. 6 Καὶ εἶπέν μοι, [w]Γέγονεν.‖ ἐγώ
true and faithful are. And he said to me, It is done. I
[x]εἰμι‖ τὸ [y]Α‖ καὶ τὸ [z]Ω,‖ ἡ ἀρχὴ καὶ τὸ τέλος. ἐγὼ τῷ
am the Α and the Ω, the beginning and the end. I to him that
διψῶντι δώσω [a] ἐκ τῆς πηγῆς τοῦ ὕδατος τῆς ζωῆς δωρεάν.
thirsts will give of the fountain of the water of life gratuitously.
7 ὁ νικῶν κληρονομήσει [b]πάντα,‖ καὶ ἔσομαι αὐτῷ θεός,
He that overcomes shall inherit all things, and I will be to him God,
καὶ αὐτὸς ἔσται μοι [c]ὁ‖ υἱός. 8 [da]δειλοῖς.δὲ‖ καὶ ἀπίστοις [ea]
and he shall be to me son: but to [the] fearful, and unbelieving,
καὶ ἐβδελυγμένοις καὶ φονεῦσιν καὶ πόρνοις καὶ [fa]φαρμακεῦσιν‖
and abominable, and murderers, and fornicators, and sorcerers,
καὶ εἰδωλολάτραις, καὶ πᾶσιν τοῖς [ga]ψευδέσιν,‖ τὸ.μέρος.αὐτῶν
and idolaters, and all liars, their part
ἐν τῇ λίμνῃ τῇ καιομένῃ πυρὶ καὶ θείῳ, ὅ ἐστιν
[is] in the lake which burns with fire and brimstone; which is [the]
[ha]δεύτερος θάνατος.‖
second death.

heaven and the first earth were passed away; and there was no more sea.

2 And I John saw the holy city, new Jerusalem, coming down from God out of heaven, prepared as a bride adorned for her husband. 3 And I heard a great voice out of heaven saying, Behold, the tabernacle of God *is* with men, and he will dwell with them, and they shall be his people, and God himself shall be with them, *and be* their God. 4 And God shall wipe away all tears from their eyes; and there shall be no more death, neither sorrow, nor crying, neither shall there be any more pain: for the former things are passed away. 5 And he that sat upon the throne said, Behold, I make all things new. And he said unto me, Write: for these words are true and faithful. 6 And he said unto me, It is done. I am Alpha and Omega, the beginning and the end. I will give unto him that is athirst of the fountain of the water of life freely. 7 He that overcometh shall inherit all things; and I will be his God, and he shall be my son. 8 But the fearful, and unbelieving, and the abominable, and murderers, and whoremongers, and sorcerers, and idolaters, and all liars, shall have their part in the lake which burneth with fire and brimstone: which is the second death.

---

[d] ἀπῆλθον GW; ἀπῆλθαν LTTrA. [e] — ἐγὼ Ἰωάννης GLTTrAW. [f] εἶδον I saw *placed after* καινήν GLTTrW; *after* ἁγίαν A. [g] ἐκ τοῦ οὐρανοῦ ἀπὸ τοῦ θεοῦ GLTTrAW. [h] θρόνου throne LTA. [i] λαὸς people GW. [k] μετ' αὐτῶν ἔσται GLTrAW. [l] — θεὸς αὐτῶν TTr; αὐτῶν θεός LAW. [m] — ὁ θεὸς (*read* ἐξαλείψει he shall wipe away) GTTr[A]W. [n] ἐκ LTTrA. [o] — ὁ T. [p] — ὅτι L[TrA]. [q] ἀπῆλθαν LTTrA; ἀπῆλθεν W. [r] τῷ θρόνῳ GLTTrAW. [s] ποιῶ πάντα LTTrAW. [t] — μοι LT[Tr]AW. [v] πιστοὶ καὶ ἀληθινοί GLTTrAW. [w] Γέγοναν They are done LTTrW; Γέγονα[ν] (*read* Γέγονα ἐγώ I am become) A. [x] — εἰμι (*read* [am] T)[A]. [y] ἄλφα Alpha LTTrAW. [z] ὦ L. [a] + αὐτῷ to him T[A]W. [b] ταῦτα these things GLTTrAW. [c] — ὁ LTTrAW. [da] τοῖς (the) δὲ δειλοῖς GLTTrAW. [ea] + καὶ ἁμαρτωλοῖς and sinners W. [fa] φαρμακοῖς GLTTrAW. [ga] ψεύσταις L. [ha] ὁ θάνατος ὁ δεύτερος GLTTrAW.

9 And there came
unto me one of the
seven angels which
had the seven vials
full of the seven last
plagues, and talked
with me, saying, Come
hither, I will shew
thee the bride, the
Lamb's wife. 10 And
he carried me away
in the spirit to a great
and high mountain,
and shewed me that
great city, the holy Je-
rusalem, descending
out of heaven from
God, 11 having the
glory of God: and her
light *was* like unto a
stone most precious,
even like a jasper
stone, clear as crystal;
12 and had a wall
great and high, *and*
had twelve gates, and
at the gates twelve
angels, and names
written thereon, which
are *the names* of the
twelve tribes of the
children of Israel:
13 on the east three
gates; on the north
three gates; on the
south three gates; and
on the west three
gates. 14 And the wall
of the city had twelve
foundations, and in
them the names of the
twelve apostles of the
Lamb. 15 And he that
talked with me had a
golden reed to measure
the city, and the gates
thereof, and the wall
thereof. 16 And the
city lieth foursquare,
and the length is as
large as the breadth:
and he measured the
city with the reed,
twelve thousand fur-
longs. The length and
the breadth and the
height of it are equal.
17 And he measured
the wall thereof, an
hundred *and* forty *and*
four cubits, *according
to* the measure of a
man, that is, of the an-

9 Καὶ ἦλθεν [i]πρός με‖ εἷς [k] τῶν ἑπτὰ ἀγγέλων τῶν ἐχόν-
And came to me one of the seven angels which had
των τὰς ἑπτὰ φιάλας [l]τὰς γεμούσας‖ τῶν ἑπτὰ πληγῶν τῶν
the seven bowls full of the seven [2]plagues
ἐσχάτων, καὶ ἐλάλησεν μετ' ἐμοῦ, λέγων, Δεῦρο, δείξω
[1]last, and spoke with me, saying, Come hither, I will shew
σοι τὴν νύμφην [m]τοῦ ἀρνίου τὴν γυναῖκα.‖ 10 Καὶ ἀπήνεγκέν
thee the bride [2]Lamb's [1]the wife. And he carried away
με ἐν πνεύματι [n]ἐπ'‖ ὄρος μέγα καὶ ὑψηλόν, καὶ ἔδειξέν
me in [the] Spirit to a mountain great and high, and shewed
μοι τὴν πόλιν [o]τὴν μεγάλην,‖ τὴν ἁγίαν Ἱερουσαλήμ, κατα-
me the [2]city [1]great, the holy Jerusalem, de-
βαίνουσαν ἐκ τοῦ οὐρανοῦ ἀπὸ τοῦ θεοῦ, 11 ἔχουσαν τὴν
scending out of the heaven from God, having the
δόξαν τοῦ θεοῦ· [p]καὶ‖ ὁ.φωστὴρ.αὐτῆς ὅμοιος λίθῳ τιμιω-
glory of God, and her radiance [was] like a stone most pre-
(*lit.* her luminary)
τάτῳ, ὡς λίθῳ ἰάσπιδι κρυσταλλίζοντι· 12 [q]ἔχουσάν τε‖
cious, as a [3]stone [2]jasper [1]crystal-like; having also
τεῖχος μέγα καὶ ὑψηλόν, [r]ἔχουσαν‖ πυλῶνας δώδεκα, [s]καὶ ἐπὶ
a wall great and high; having [2]gates [1]twelve, and at
[t]τοῖς πυλῶσιν‖ ἀγγέλους δώδεκα,‖ καὶ ὀνόματα ἐπιγεγραμ-
the gates [2]angels [1]twelve, and names inscrib-
μένα, ἅ ἐστιν [v] τῶν δώδεκα φυλῶν [w]τῶν‖ υἱῶν Ἰσραήλ.
ed, which are [those] of the twelve tribes of the sons of Israel.
13 [x]ἀπ'‖ [y]ἀνατολῆς‖ πυλῶνες τρεῖς· [z] ἀπὸ βοῤῥᾶ
On [the] east [2]gates [1]three; on [the] north
πυλῶνες τρεῖς· [z] ἀπὸ νότου πυλῶνες τρεῖς· [z] ἀπὸ
[2]gates [1]three; on [the] south [2]gates [1]three, on [the]
δυσμῶν πυλῶνες τρεῖς. 14 καὶ τὸ τεῖχος τῆς πόλεως [a]ἔχον‖
west [2]gates [1]three. And the wall of the city having
θεμελίους δώδεκα, καὶ [b]ἐν αὐτοῖς‖ ὀνόματα τῶν δώδεκα
[2]foundations [1]twelve, and in them names of the twelve
ἀποστόλων τοῦ ἀρνίου. 15 καὶ ὁ λαλῶν μετ' ἐμοῦ εἶχεν [c]
apostles of the Lamb. And he speaking with me had
κάλαμον χρυσοῦν, ἵνα μετρήσῃ τὴν πόλιν, καὶ τοὺς πυ-
a [2]reed [1]golden, that he might measure the city, and
λῶνας αὐτῆς, καὶ τὸ.τεῖχος.αὐτῆς. 16 καὶ ἡ πόλις τετράγωνος
[2]gates [1]its, and its wall. And the city [2]four-square
κεῖται, καὶ τὸ.μῆκος.αὐτῆς [d]τοσοῦτόν ἐστιν‖ ὅσον [e]καὶ‖ τὸ
[1]lies, and its length so much is as also the
πλάτος. καὶ ἐμέτρησεν τὴν πόλιν τῷ καλάμῳ ἐπὶ [f]σταδίων‖
breadth. And he measured the city with the reed— [3]furlongs
δώδεκα χιλιάδων· τὸ μῆκος καὶ τὸ πλάτος καὶ τὸ ὕψος αὐτῆς
[1]twelve [2]thousand; the length and the breadth and the height of it
ἴσα ἐστίν. 17 καὶ ἐμέτρησεν τὸ.τεῖχος.αὐτῆς ἑκατὸν
[2]equal [1]are. And he measured its wall, a hundred [and]
[g]τεσσαράκοντα τεσσάρων‖ πηχῶν μέτρον ἀνθρώπου, ὅ ἐστιν
forty four cubits, [3]measure [1]a [2]man's, which is,

---

[i] — πρός με GLTTrAW. [k] + ἐκ of (the) LTTrA. [l] — τὰς W; τῶν γεμόντων which [angels] were full LTTrA. [m] τὴν γυναῖκα τοῦ ἀρνίου LTTrAW. [n] ἐπὶ LTTrAW. [o] — τὴν μεγάλην (*read* the holy city) GLTTrAW. [p] — καὶ GLTTrAW. [q] ἔχουσα (*omit* also) GLTTrAW. [r] ἔχουσα GLTTrA. [s] — καὶ ἐπὶ τοῖς πυλῶσιν ἀγγέλους δώδεκα L. [t] τοὺς πυλῶνας Tr. [v] + τὰ ὀνόματα the names L[TrA]. [w] — τῶν (*read* of [the]) LTTrAW. [x] ἀπὸ GLTTrAW. [y] ἀνατολῶν GW. [z] + καὶ and LTTrAW. [a] ἔχων TTrA. [b] ἐπ' αὐτῶν δώδεκα on them twelve GLTTrAW. [c] + μέτρον a measure GLTTrA. [d] — τοσοῦτόν ἐστιν (*read* [is]) GLTTrAW. [e] — καὶ TTr[A]. [f] σταδίους EGLTrA. [g] τεσσεράκοντα τεσσάρων LT; τεσσαρακοντατεσσάρων (τεσσε- A) EAW.

ἀγγέλου. 18 καὶ [i]ἦν‖ ἡ [k]ἐνδόμησις‖ τοῦ.τείχους.αὐτῆς
[the] angel's. And [6]was [1]the [2]structure [3]of [4]its [5]wall
ἴασπις· καὶ ἡ πόλις χρυσίον καθαρόν, [l]ὁμοία‖ ὑάλῳ καθαρῷ.
jasper; and the city [2]gold [1]pure, like [2]glass [1]pure:
19 [m]καὶ‖ οἱ θεμέλιοι τοῦ τείχους τῆς πόλεως παντὶ λίθῳ
and the foundations of the wall of the city with every [2]stone
τιμίῳ κεκοσμημένοι. ὁ θεμέλιος ὁ πρῶτος ἴασπις· ὁ
[1]precious [were] adorned: the [2]foundation [1]first, jasper; the
δεύτερος σάπφειρος· ὁ τρίτος [n]χαλκηδών·‖ ὁ τέταρτος σμά-
second, sapphire; the third, chalcedony; the fourth, eme-
ραγδος· 20 ὁ πέμπτος [o]σαρδόνυξ·‖ ὁ ἕκτος [p]σάρδιος·‖ ὁ
rald; the fifth, sardonyx; the sixth, sardius; the
ἕβδομος χρυσόλιθος· ὁ ὄγδοος βήρυλλος· ὁ [q]ἔνατος‖ τοπά-
seventh, chrysolite; the eighth, beryl; the ninth, to-
ζιον· ὁ δέκατος [r]χρυσόπρασος·‖ ὁ ἑνδέκατος ὑάκινθος· ὁ
paz; the tenth, chrysoprasus; the eleventh, jacinth; the
δωδέκατος ἀμέθυστος. 21 καὶ οἱ δώδεκα πυλῶνες, δώδεκα
twelfth, amethyst. And the twelve gates, twelve
μαργαρῖται· ἀνὰ εἷς ἕκαστος τῶν πυλώνων ἦν ἐξ ἑνὸς
pearls; [3]respectively [2]one [1]each of the gates was of one
μαργαρίτου· καὶ ἡ πλατεῖα τῆς πόλεως, χρυσίον καθαρόν, ὡς
pearl; and the street of the city [2]gold [1]pure, as
ὕαλος [s]διαφανής.‖ 22 Καὶ ναὸν οὐκ εἶδον ἐν αὐτῇ· ὁ.γὰρ
[2]glass [1]transparent. And [4]temple [3]no [1]I [2]saw in it; for the
κύριος ὁ θεὸς ὁ παντοκράτωρ [t] ναὸς.αὐτῆς ἐστιν, καὶ τὸ
Lord God Almighty its temple is, and the
ἀρνίον. 23 καὶ ἡ πόλις οὐ χρείαν ἔχει τοῦ ἡλίου, οὐδὲ τῆς
Lamb. And the city [2]no [3]need [1]has of the sun, nor of the
σελήνης, ἵνα φαίνωσιν [v]ἐν‖ αὐτῇ· ἡ.γὰρ δόξα τοῦ θεοῦ ἐφώ-
moon, that they should shine in it; for the glory of God en-
τισεν αὐτήν, καὶ ὁ λύχνος αὐτῆς τὸ ἀρνίον. 24 καὶ [w]τὰ
lightened it, and the lamp of it [is] the Lamb. And the
ἔθνη τῶν σωζομένων ἐν τῷ.φωτὶ.αὐτῆς περιπατήσουσιν·‖ καὶ
nations of the saved in its light shall walk; and
οἱ βασιλεῖς τῆς γῆς φέρουσιν τὴν δόξαν [x]καὶ τὴν τιμὴν‖ αὐτῶν
the kings of the earth bring [2]glory [3]and [4]honour [1]their
εἰς αὐτήν. 25 καὶ οἱ.πυλῶνες.αὐτῆς οὐ.μὴ κλεισθῶσιν ἡμέρας·
unto it. And its gates not at all shall be shut by day;
νὺξ γὰρ οὐκ ἔσται ἐκεῖ. 26 καὶ οἴσουσιν τὴν δόξαν καὶ
[3]night [1]for [2]no shall be there. And they shall bring the glory and
τὴν τιμὴν τῶν ἐθνῶν εἰς αὐτήν. 27 καὶ οὐ.μὴ εἰσέλθῃ εἰς
the honour of the nations unto it. And in no wise may enter into
αὐτὴν πᾶν [y]κοινοῦν,‖ καὶ [z]ποιοῦν‖ βδέλυγμα καὶ ψεῦ-
it anything defiling, and practising abomination and a
(*lit.* everything)
δος· εἰ.μὴ οἱ γεγραμμένοι ἐν τῷ βιβλίῳ τῆς ζωῆς τοῦ
lie; but those who are written in the book of life of the
ἀρνίου.
Lamb.

22 Καὶ ἔδειξέν μοι [a]καθαρὸν‖ ποταμὸν ὕδατος ζωῆς,
And he shewed me [2]pure [1]a river of water of life,

gel. 18 And the building of the wall of it
was *of* jasper: and the city *was* pure gold,
like unto clear glass.
19 And the foundations of the wall of the city *were* garnished
with all manner of precious stones. The first foundation *was*
jasper; the second, sapphire; the third, a chalcedony; the
fourth, an emerald;
20 the fifth, sardonyx; the sixth, sardius; the seventh chrysolite;
the eighth, beryl; the ninth, a topaz; the tenth, a chrysoprasus;
the eleventh, a jacinth; the twelfth, an amethyst.
21 And the twelve gates *were* twelve pearls; every several gate was of
one pearl: and the street of the city *was* pure gold, as it were
transparent glass.
22 And I saw no temple therein: for the Lord God Almighty
and the Lamb are the temple of it.
23 And the city had no need of the sun, neither of the moon, to shine in
it: for the glory of God did lighten it, and the Lamb *is* the
light thereof.
24 And the nations of them which are saved shall walk in the light of
it: and the kings of the earth do bring their glory and honour into
it.
25 And the gates of it shall not be shut at all by day: for there shall be no night
there.
26 And they shall bring the glory and honour of the nations into it.
27 And there shall in no wise enter into it any thing that defileth,
neither *whatsoever* worketh abomination, or *maketh* a lie: but
they which are written in the Lamb's book of life.

XXII. And he shewed me a pure river of water of life, clear as

[i] — ἦν (*read* [was]) LTA. [k] ἐνδώμησις TTr. [l] ὅμοιον LTTrAW. [m] — καὶ LTA. [n] χαλκεδών T. [o] σαρδιόνυξ L. [p] σάρδιον LTTrAW. [q] ἔννατος EGW. [r] χρυσόπρασον L. [s] διαυγὴς GLTTrAW. [t] + ὁ L[A]W. [v] — ἐν (*read* αὐτῇ for it) GLTTrAW. [w] περιπατήσουσιν τὰ ἔθνη διὰ τοῦ φωτὸς αὐτῆς the nations shall walk by means of its light GLTTrAW. [x] — τὴν W; — καὶ τὴν τιμὴν LTTrA. [y] κοινὸν common GLTTrAW. [z] (+ ὁ he who TTr) ποιῶν ([he who] LAW) practises LTTrAW. [a] — καθαρὸν GLTTrAW.

crystal, proceeding
out of the throne of
God and of the Lamb.
2 In the midst of the
street of it, and on
either side of the ri-
ver, *was there* the
tree of life, which bare
twelve *manner of*
fruits, *and* yielded her
fruit every month; and
the leaves of the tree
were for the healing
of the nations. 3 And
there shall be no more
curse : but the throne
of God and of the
Lamb shall be in it ;
and his servants shall
serve him : 4 and they
shall see his face ; and
his name *shall be* in
their foreheads. 5 And
there shall be no
night there; and they
need no candle, nei-
ther light of the sun ;
for the Lord God giv-
eth them light : and
they shall reign for
ever and ever.

λαμπρὸν ὡς κρύσταλλον, ἐκπορευόμενον ἐκ τοῦ θρόνου τοῦ
bright as crystal, going forth out of the throne
θεοῦ καὶ τοῦ ἀρνίου. 2 ἐν μέσῳ τῆς.πλατείας.αὐτῆς, καὶ τοῦ
of God and of the Lamb. In the midst of its street, and of the
ποταμοῦ, ἐντεῦθεν καὶ [b]ἐντεῦθεν,ǁ ξύλον ζωῆς, [c]ποιοῦνǁ
river, on this side and on that side, [the] tree of life, producing
καρποὺς δώδεκα, κατὰ [d]μῆναǁ [e]ἕναǁ ἕκαστον [f]ἀποδιδοῦνǁ τὸν
[2]fruits [1]twelve, [4]month [3]each yielding
καρπὸν αὐτοῦ· καὶ τὰ φύλλα τοῦ ξύλου εἰς θεραπείαν τῶν
[2]fruit. [1]its ; and the leaves of the tree for healing of the
ἐθνῶν. 3 Καὶ πᾶν [g]κατ.ανάθεμαǁ οὐκ ἔσται ἔτι· καὶ ὁ θρόνος
nations. And [2]any (*lit.* every) [3]curse [1]not shall be longer; and the throne
τοῦ θεοῦ καὶ τοῦ ἀρνίου ἐν αὐτῇ ἔσται· καὶ οἱ.δοῦλοι.αὐτοῦ
of God and of the Lamb in it shall be ; and his bondmen
λατρεύσουσιν αὐτῷ· 4 καὶ ὄψονται τὸ.πρόσωπον.αὐτοῦ, καὶ
shall serve him, and they shall see his face ; and
τὸ.ὄνομα.αὐτοῦ ἐπὶ τῶν.μετώπων.αὐτῶν. 5 καὶ νὺξ οὐκ ἔσται
his name on their foreheads [is]. And [2]night [1]no shall be
[h]ἐκεῖǁ καὶ [i]χρείαν οὐκ ἔχουσινǁ [k]λύχνου καὶ φωτὸς [l]ἡλίου,ǁ
there, and [4]need [3]no [1]they [2]have of a lamp and of light of [the] sun,
ὅτι κύριος ὁ θεὸς [m]φωτίζειǁ αὐτούς· καὶ βασιλεύσουσιν
because [the] Lord God enlightens them, and they shall reign
εἰς τοὺς αἰῶνας τῶν αἰώνων.
to the ages of the ages.

6 And he said unto
me, These sayings *are*
faithful and true: and
the Lord God of the
holy prophets sent his
angel to shew unto
his servants the things
which must shortly
be done. 7 Behold, I
come quickly : blessed
is he that keepeth the
sayings of the prophe-
cy of this book. 8 And I
John saw these things,
and heard *them*. And
when I had heard and
seen, I fell down to
worship before the
feet of the angel
which shewed me these
things. 9 Then saith
he unto me, See *thou*
do it not : for I am
thy fellowservant,
and of thy brethren
the prophets, and of
them which keep the
sayings of this book :
worship God. 10 And
he saith unto me, Seal
not the sayings of the
prophecy of this book:
for the time is at hand.
11 He that is unjust,

6 Καὶ εἶπέν μοι, Οὗτοι οἱ λόγοι πιστοὶ καὶ ἀληθινοί·
And he said to me, These words [are] faithful and true ;
καὶ [n] κύριος ὁ θεὸς τῶν [o]ἁγίωνǁ προφητῶν ἀπέστειλεν τὸν
and [the] Lord God of the holy prophets sent
ἄγγελον αὐτοῦ δεῖξαι τοῖς.δούλοις.αὐτοῦ ἃ δεῖ γε-
[2]angel [1]his to shew his bondmen the things which must come
νέσθαι ἐν.τάχει. 7 [p]Ἰδού, ἔρχομαι ταχύ. μακάριος ὁ
to pass soon. Behold, I am coming quickly. Blessed [is] he who
τηρῶν τοὺς λόγους τῆς προφητείας τοῦ.βιβλίου.τούτου. 8 [q]Καὶ
keeps the words of the prophecy of this book. And
ἐγὼǁ Ἰωάννης ὁ [r]βλέπων ταῦτα καὶ ἀκούων·ǁ
I John [was] he who [was] seeing [3]these [4]things [1]and [2]hearing.
καὶ ὅτε ἤκουσα καὶ [s]ἔβλεψαǁ [t]ἔπεσαǁ προσκυνῆσαι ἔμπροσθεν
And when I heard and saw I fell down to do homage before
τῶν ποδῶν τοῦ ἀγγέλου τοῦ [u]δεικνύοντόςǁ μοι ταῦτα. 9 καὶ
the feet of the angel who [was] shewing me these things. And
λέγει μοι, Ὅρα μή· σύνδουλός σου [v]γάρǁ εἰμι, καὶ
he says to me, See [thou do it] not : [4]fellowbondman [5]of [6]thee [1]for [2]I [3]am, and
τῶν.ἀδελφῶν.σου τῶν προφητῶν, καὶ τῶν τηρούντων τοὺς
of thy brethren the prophets, and of those who keep the
λόγους τοῦ.βιβλίου.τούτου· τῷ θεῷ προσκύνησον. 10 Καὶ
words of this book : to God do homage. And
λέγει μοι, Μὴ.σφραγίσῃς τοὺς λόγους τῆς προφητείας τοῦ
he says to me, Seal not the words of the prophecy
βιβλίου τούτου· [w]ὅτιǁ ὁ καιρὸς [x]ἐγγύς ἐστιν. 11 ὁ ἀδι-
[3]book [1]of [2]this ; because the time [2]near [1]is. He that is un-

---

[b] ἐκεῖθεν LTTrAW. [c] ποιῶν T. [d] μῆναν L. [e] — ἕνα GLTTrAW. [f] ἀποδιδοὺς TTrA. [g] κατάθεμα GLTTrAW. [h] ἔτι longer GLTTrAW. [i] οὐχ ἕξουσιν they shall have no (οὐκ ἔχουσιν TTr) χρείαν LTTrAW ; οὐ χρεία G. [k] + φωτὸς of light LTTrA. [l] — ἡλίου W. [m] φωτιεῖ (φωτίσει L) ἐπ' shall enlighten GLTTrAW. [n] + ὁ the LTTrA. [o] πνευμάτων τῶν spirits of the GLTTrAW. [p] + καὶ and GLTTrAW. [q] κἀγὼ LTTrAW. [r] ἀκούων καὶ βλέπων ταῦτα GLTrAW ; βλέπων καὶ ἀκούων ταῦτα T. [s] ἔβλεπον W. [t] ἔπεσον EG. [u] δεικνύντος T. [v] — γάρ GLTTrAW. [w] — ὅτι GLTTrAW [x] + γὰρ for (the time) LTTrAW.

κῶν ἀδικησάτω ἔτι· καὶ [y]ὁ ῥυπῶν‖ [z]ῥυπωσάτω‖
righteous let him be unrighteous still; and he that is filthy let him be filthy
ἔτι· καὶ ὁ δίκαιος [a]δικαιωθήτω‖ ἔτι· καὶ ὁ ἅγιος
still; and he that [is] righteous let him be righteous still; and he that [is] holy
ἁγιασθήτω ἔτι. 12 [b]Καὶ‖ ἰδού, ἔρχομαι ταχύ, καὶ ὁ
let him be sanctified still. And, behold, I am coming quickly, and
μισθός μου μετ' ἐμοῦ, ἀποδοῦναι· ἑκάστῳ ὡς τὸ ἔργον [c]αὐτοῦ
[2]reward [1]my with me, to render to each as [2]work [1]his
ἔσται.‖ 13 ἐγώ [d]εἰμι‖ τὸ [e]Α‖ καὶ τὸ [f]Ω,‖ [g]ἀρχὴ καὶ τέλος,
shall be. I am the A and the Ω, [the] beginning and end,
ὁ πρῶτος καὶ ὁ ἔσχατος.‖ 14 Μακάριοι οἱ [h]ποιοῦν-
the first and the last. Blessed [are] they that do
τες τὰς.ἐντολὰς.αὐτοῦ,‖ ἵνα ἔσται ἡ.ἐξουσία.αὐτῶν ἐπὶ τὸ
his commandments, that [3]shall [4]be [1]their [2]authority to the
ξύλον τῆς ζωῆς, καὶ τοῖς πυλῶσιν εἰσέλθωσιν εἰς τὴν πόλιν.
tree of life, and by the gates they should go in to the city.
15 ἔξω.[i]δὲ‖ οἱ κύνες καὶ οἱ φαρμακοὶ καὶ οἱ πόρνοι καὶ
But without [are] the dogs, and the sorcerers, and the fornicators, and
οἱ φονεῖς καὶ οἱ εἰδωλολάτραι, καὶ πᾶς [k]ὁ‖ [l]φιλῶν καὶ
the murderers, and the idolaters, and everyone that loves and
ποιῶν‖ ψεῦδος.
practises a lie.

let him be unjust still: and he which is filthy, let him be filthy still: and he that is righteous, let him be righteous still: and he that is holy, let him be holy still.
12 And, behold, I come quickly; and my reward *is* with me, to give every man according as his work shall be.
13 I am Alpha and Omega, the beginning and the end, the first and the last.
14 Blessed *are* they that do his commandments, that they may have right to the tree of life, and may enter in through the gates into the city.
15 For without *are* dogs, and sorcerers, and whoremongers, and murderers, and idolaters, and whosoever loveth and maketh a lie.

16 Ἐγὼ Ἰησοῦς ἔπεμψα τὸν.ἄγγελόν.μου μαρτυρῆσαι
I Jesus sent mine angel to testify
ὑμῖν ταῦτα [m]ἐπὶ‖ ταῖς ἐκκλησίαις· ἐγώ εἰμι ἡ ῥίζα καὶ
to you these things in the assemblies. I am the root and
τὸ γένος [n]τοῦ‖ [o]Δαβίδ,‖ ὁ ἀστὴρ ὁ λαμπρὸς [p]καὶ‖ [q]ὀρθρι-
the offspring of David, the [4]star [1]bright [2]and [3]morn-
νός.‖ 17 Καὶ τὸ πνεῦμα καὶ ἡ νύμφη λέγουσιν, [r]Ἐλθέ·‖
ing. And the Spirit and the bride say, Come.
καὶ ὁ ἀκούων εἰπάτω, [r]Ἐλθέ.‖ καὶ ὁ διψῶν [s]ἐλθέτω,‖
And he that hears let him say, Come. And he that thirsts let him come;
[t]καὶ‖ ὁ θέλων [v]λαμβανέτω τὸ‖ ὕδωρ ζωῆς δωρεάν.
and he that wills, let him take the water of life gratuitously.

16 I Jesus have sent mine angel to testify unto you these things in the churches. I am the root and the offspring of David, *and* the bright and morning star.
17 And the Spirit and the bride say, Come. And let him that heareth say, Come. And let him that is athirst come. And whosoever will, let him take the water of life freely.

18 [w]Συμμαρτυροῦμαι.γὰρ‖ παντὶ [x] ἀκούοντι τοὺς λόγους
For I jointly testify to everyone hearing the words
τῆς προφητείας τοῦ.βιβλίου.τούτου· ἐάν τις [ya]ἐπιτιθῇ πρὸς
of the prophecy of this book, If anyone should add to
ταῦτα,‖ ἐπιθήσει [za]ὁ θεὸς ἐπ' αὐτὸν‖ τὰς πληγὰς τὰς γε-
these things, [2]shall [3]add [1]God unto him the plagues which are
γραμμένας ἐν [aa] βιβλίῳ.τούτῳ· 19 καὶ ἐάν τις [ba]ἀφαιρῇ‖
written in this book. And if anyone should take
ἀπὸ τῶν λόγων [ca]βίβλου‖ τῆς.προφητείας.ταύτης, [da]ἀφαιρή-
from the words of [the] book of this prophecy, [2]shall [3]take
σει‖ ὁ θεὸς τὸ.μέρος.αὐτοῦ ἀπὸ [ea]βίβλου‖ τῆς ζωῆς, καὶ
[4]away [1]God his part from [the] book of life, and

18 For I testify unto every man that heareth the words of the prophecy of this book, If any man shall add unto these things, God shall add unto him the plagues that are written in this book:
19 and if any man shall take away from the words of the book of this prophecy, God shall take away his part out of the book of life,

---

[y] ὁ ῥυπαρὸς the filthy [one] GLTTrAW. [z] ῥυπανθήτω LTTrA; ῥυπαρευθήτω GW. [a] δικαιοσύνην ποιησάτω let him practise righteousness GLTTrAW. [b] — καὶ GLTTrAW. [c] ἐστὶν αὐτοῦ (*read* his work is) LTTrA. [d] — εἰμι (*read* [am]) GLTTrAW. [e] ἄλφα Alpha LTTrAW. [f] ὦ L. [g] ὁ (— ὁ L[A]) πρῶτος καὶ ὁ (— ὁ L[A]) ἔσχατος, (+ ἡ the GLTA) ἀρχὴ καὶ (+ τὸ the GLTA) τέλος GLTTrA. [h] πλύνοντες τὰς στολὰς αὐτῶν wash their robes LTTrA. [i] — δὲ but GLTTrAW. [k] — ὁ (*read* loving and practising) LTTrAW. [l] ποιῶν καὶ φιλῶν T. [m] — ἐπὶ (*read* ταῖς to the) W; ἐν L. [n] — τοῦ GLTTrAW. [o] Δαυείδ LTTrA; Δαυῒδ GW. [p] — καὶ GTTrAW. [q] ὁ πρωϊνός the morning GLTTrAW. [r] Ἔρχου GLTTrAW. [s] ἐρχέσθω GLTTrAW. [t] — καὶ GLTTrAW. [v] λαβέτω GLTTrAW. [w] Μαρτυρῶ ἐγὼ I testify GLTTrAW. [x] + τῷ who (hears) GLTTrAW. [ya] ἐπιθῇ ἐπ' αὐτά GLTTrAW. [za] ἐπ' αὐτὸν ὁ θεὸς T. [aa] + τῷ GLTTrAW. [ba] ἀφέλῃ GLTTrAW. [ca] τοῦ βιβλίου GLTTrAW. [da] ἀφελεῖ GLTTrAW. [ea] τοῦ ξύλου the tree GLTTrAW.

and out of the holy city, and *from* the things which are written in this book.

[f]ἐκ‖ τῆς πόλεως τῆς ἁγίας, [g]καὶ‖ τῶν γεγραμμένων
out of the [2]city [1]holy, and of those who are written
ἐν [h] βιβλίῳ τούτῳ.
in [2]book [1]this.

20 He which testifieth these things saith, Surely I come quickly. Amen. Even so, come, Lord Jesus.

20 Λέγει ὁ μαρτυρῶν ταῦτα, Ναὶ ἔρχομαι ταχύ.
[6]Says [1]he [2]who [3]testifies [4]these [5]things, Yea, I am coming quickly.
Ἀμήν. [i]Ναί,‖ ἔρχου, κύριε Ἰησοῦ.
Amen; yea, come, Lord Jesus.

21 The grace of our Lord Jesus Christ *be* with you all. Amen.

21 Ἡ χάρις τοῦ.κυρίου.[k]ἡμῶν‖ Ἰησοῦ [l]χριστοῦ‖ μετὰ
The grace of our Lord Jesus Christ [be] with
[m]πάντων‖ [n]ὑμῶν.‖ [o] [p]Ἀμήν.‖ [q]
[2]all [1]you. Amen.

---

[f] — ἐκ L[TrA]. [g] — και (*read* τῶν which) GLTTrAW. [h] + τῷ GLTTrAW. [i] — Ναι GLTTrAW; (*join* Amen *with* quickly ETr). [k] — ἡμῶν (*read* of the Lord) GLTTrAW. [l] — χριστοῦ LTTrA. [m] — πάντων TrA. [n] — ὑμῶν GLTTrAW. [o] + τῶν ἁγίων the saints GTrAW. [p] — Ἀμήν GLTTrA. [q] + ἀποκάλυψις Ἰωάννου Revelation of John A.

ΤΕΛΟΣ.

Greek-English Lexicon

TO THE

New Testament

SUPPLEMENTED BY A CHAPTER ELUCIDATING THE SYNONYMS OF THE NEW TESTAMENT
WITH A COMPLETE INDEX TO THE SYNONYMS

BY

GEORGE RICKER BERRY, PH.D.

OF THE UNIVERSITY OF CHICAGO AND COLGATE UNIVERSITY
DEPARTMENT OF SEMITIC LANGUAGES

EDITOR OF

THE INTERLINEAR HEBREW-ENGLISH OLD TESTAMENT

INTRODUCTION TO NEW TESTAMENT LEXICON.

AS a result of their wide experience as sellers of text-books of all kinds, extending over many years, the publishers have become aware that clergymen, theological students, and New Testament students generally, possess the conviction that none of the smaller New Testament Lexicons is entirely satisfactory. There are several essential and entirely practical features, not embodied in any of the smaller New Testament Lexicons, which should be incorporated in a work intended to fulfill all necessary requirements. It is with the definite intention of supplying this need that the publishers have undertaken the preparation of this new Lexicon. It aims to retain all the desirable features of the best small Lexicons in use, and also to present the several additional points demanded, while keeping within the compass of a volume of convenient size.

This Lexicon endeavors to put into a brief and compact form as much as possible of the material found in the larger New Testament Lexicons. The fact has been remembered that in nine cases out of ten the object in consulting a Lexicon is to refer quickly to the standard meanings of a word, rather than to study an exhaustive treatment of it. Hence, while every clergyman would like to possess one of the larger New Testament Lexicons, he still needs the small one for convenience in ordinary use. So it is assumed that this small New Testament Lexicon will be needed both for use independently, and also by those who have one of the larger Lexicons. It is hoped that in this volume the publishers' intention has been realized of producing a volume that better than any other so far published will serve this purpose quickly and well.

It may be desirable to point out a few features which have been made prominent. It will be at once apparent that some of these are not ordinarily found in the smaller New Testament Lexicons:

The inflection of nouns, adjectives, and verbs has been indicated with all the fullness which was considered practically necessary. In nouns, the ending of the genitive case has regularly been given, being omitted only with indeclinable nouns. The article indicating the gender regularly follows the genitive ending. Other cases have been given only rarely, when they are irregular or peculiar. In adjectives, the endings of the nominative have been given. In verbs, a different form for the present tense, such as a contracted form, has regularly been given, and ordinarily the ending of the future. The endings of the other tenses have only been given in some special cases when they are peculiar, or irregular. Of course the inflection in general has considered only the forms occurring in the New Testament; it is only rarely that classical forms not occurring in the New Testament have been given, since they would be of little practical value in ordinary New Testament study.

The hyphen, to separate the parts of compound words, has been used with considerable freedom, but in general accordance with the following principles. It has been used of course to separate the parts of words which are actually compounded of the two or more portions which appear in the word. Words derived from a compound word would not usually have the hyphen, but sometimes it has been inserted, especially when otherwise the derivation would not be obvious. So, too, the hyphen has been used with derivatives of a compound word, in cases where the original compound word does not occur in the New Testament, as otherwise the character of the word would not appear. The hyphen has also been used in many cases where the compound word is slightly changed in form from the parts of which it is composed, where this variation is not very great. Such a wide use of the hyphen has been for the purpose of increasing the practical value of this feature.

The original plan in reference to Synonyms was to give in the Lexicon itself definitions of a few of the most important ones. After most of the Lexicon was in type, however, it was decided, in view of the importance of the subject, that a very helpful feature would be a special section devoted to Synonyms. This has accordingly been prepared. The result is, of course, that a few words already treated in the Lexicon have here been given a fuller treatment.

The Index to the Synonyms includes all the nouns treated in the Lexicon proper, as well as those in the Synonyms, and this double treatment will always be found to be expressly indicated by its appropriate sign.

Some indications of the history of a word will surely be serviceable to the average student. Consequently, the words whose first known occurrence is in the Septuagint, in the Apocrypha, and in the New Testament, are indicated by the respective abbreviations at the end of the articles. Where the usage is in doubt, no indication has been given. The material for this has been drawn chiefly from Thayer. The other classifications which Thayer gives, it was thought would not be of sufficient practical use to the average student to be incorporated.

In the case of words from foreign languages, the language has been indicated in every instance, except with a part of the proper names, chiefly from the Hebrew, where the origin would be readily inferred. It has been the aim to make this feature accurate and up to date. In this matter, considerable help has been received from E. Kautzsch, *Grammatik des Biblisch-Aramäischen.*

The grammatical references given are to the three grammars which are probably in the most common use, viz.: S. G. Green, *Handbook to the Grammar of the Greek Testament,* Revised and Improved Edition; G. B. Winer, *A Grammar of the Idiom of the New Testament,* Seventh Edition, Translated by J. H. Thayer; and Alexander Buttman, *A Grammar of the New Testament Greek,* Translated by J. H. Thayer. These have been indicated respectively by the abbreviations Gr., Wi., and Bu., the references in the first two being by sections, in the last, for convenience, by pages.

The usual custom has been followed of making the received text, the so-called *Textus Receptus,* the basis of this Lexicon, except that sometimes another accentuation has been adopted, which seemed preferable. All the variations of any importance of the text of Westcott and Hort have been given. This does not include all the minor variations in spelling and accentuation. It was thought that to indicate the variants of other editors would occupy more space than it would be profitable to give. For the same reason no mention has been made of variant readings of the *Textus Receptus* itself.

The asterisk * at the end of many articles indicates that all the passages in which the word occurs in the New Testament have been given.

Besides other works which have already been mentioned, much material has been drawn from R. C. Trench, *Synonyms of the New Testament,* and from the New Testament Lexicons of Thayer and Cremer, as well as from the small ones of Green and Hickie.

The New Testament books have been indicated by the shortest abbreviations that would be easily intelligible. It is thought that they will be understood without explanation. The list of other abbreviations which is here added includes only those which might not be recognized without express indication.

ABBREVIATIONS.

Ap. = Apocrypha (of the Old Testament).
A. V. = Authorized Version.
Bu. = Alexander Buttman (*Grammar of New Testament Greek*).
dim. = diminutive.
fig. = figurative.
Gr. = S. G. Green (*Handbook to the Grammar of the Greek Testament*).
i.e. = that is.
lit. = literally.
met. = metaphorically.
mrg. = margin.
N. T. = New Testament.
orig. = originally.
O. T. = Old Testament.
Rec. = Textus Receptus.
R. V. = Revised Version.
S. = Septuagint.
sc. = namely, to wit.
sq. = following.
W. H. = Westcott and Hort (*The New Testament in the Original Greek*).
Wi. = G. B. Winer (*Grammar of the Idiom of the New Testament*).
- hyphen, see Introduction.
* indicates that all the passages in which a word occurs in the New Testament have been given.

Concerning the abbreviations for the Books of the New Testament, see last paragraph of Introduction.

GREEK-ENGLISH NEW TESTAMENT LEXICON.

Α, α, ἄλφα, *alpha, a,* the first letter. Numerally, α′ = 1; ͵α = 1000. For α in composition, see Gr. § 147*b*, *c*. Fig., τὸ Α, or τὸ Ἄλφα (W. H.), *the first principle of all things;* of the Father, Rev. i. 8, xxi. 6; the Son, i. 11 (W. H. omit), xxii. 13.*

Ἀαρών (Heb.), *Aaron,* Lu. i. 5; Ac. vii. 40; Heb. v. 4, vii. 11, ix. 4.*

Ἀβαδδών, ὁ (Heb. "destruction"), *Abaddon,* Rev. ix. 11. (S.)*

ἀ-βαρής, ές (from βάρος), *without weight;* hence, *not burdensome,* 2 Cor. xi. 9.*

Ἀββᾶ, or Ἀββά (W. H.), (Aram.), *Father!* only as an invocation, Mar. xiv. 36; Ro. viii. 15; Gal. iv. 6. (N. T.)*

Ἄβελ, ὁ (W. H. Ἅβελ), (Heb.), *Abel,* Mat. xxiii. 35; Lu. xi. 51; Heb. xi. 4, xii. 24.*

Ἀβιά, ὁ (Heb.), *Abia* or *Abijah,* the king, Mat. i. 7; the priest, Lu. i. 5.*

Ἀβιάθαρ, ὁ (Heb.), *Abiathar,* Mar. ii. 26.*

Ἀβιληνή, ῆς, ἡ, *Abilene,* a district between Lebanon and Hermon towards Phœnicia, named from Abila, its chief city, Lu. iii. 1.*

Ἀβιούδ, ὁ (Heb.), *Abiud,* Mat. i. 13.*

Ἀβραάμ, ὁ (Heb.), *Abraham,* Mat. i. 1, 2; Ro. iv. 1, 2, 3.

ἄ-βυσσος, ου, ἡ (originally adj. *bottomless*), *abyss,* Lu. viii. 31; Ro. x. 7; Rev. ix. 1, 2, 11, xi. 7, xvii. 8, xx. 1, 3.*

Ἄγαβος, ου, ὁ, *Agabus,* Ac. xi. 28, xxi. 10.*

ἀγαθο-εργέω, ῶ (or ἀγαθουργέω), *to be beneficent,* 1 Tim. vi. 18; Ac. xiv. 17 (W. H.). (N. T.)*

ἀγαθο-ποιέω, ῶ, (1) *to do good to,* acc. of pers., Lu. vi. 33; (2) *to act well,* 1 Pet. ii. 15, 20. (S.)

ἀγαθο-ποιΐα, ας, ἡ, *well-doing,* in sense (2) of preceding, 1 Pet. iv. 19. (N. T.)*

ἀγαθο-ποιός, οῦ, ὁ (originally adj.), *well-doer,* 1 Pet. ii. 14.*

ἀγαθός, ή, όν (κρείσσων, κράτιστος), *good* in general, in various senses, in itself or its effects, physically or morally, used of both persons and things, Mat. vii. 18; Lu. vi. 45; 1 Pet. ii. 18; Phil. i. 6. τὸ ἀγαθόν, *the Good,* Mat. xix. 17 (W. H.); τὰ ἀγαθά, *goods, wealth, blessings,* Lu. i. 53; Ro. x. 15.

ἀγαθωσύνη, ης, ἡ, *goodness,* 2 Th. i. 11. (S.) *Syn.:* ἀγαθωσύνη emphasizes the *zeal for goodness;* χρηστότης, *kindness, benignity.*

ἀγαλλίασις, εως, ἡ, *exultation, gladness,* Lu. i. 14, 44. (S.)

ἀγαλλιάω, ῶ, ασω, *to leap for joy;* hence, *exult, rejoice;* generally deponent. Followed by ἵνα (subj.), Jn. viii. 56; ἐπί (dat.), Lu. i. 47; or ἐν (dat.), Jn. v. 35. (S.)

ἄ-γαμος, ον, adj., *unmarried,* 1 Cor. vii. 8, 11, 32, 34.*

ἀγανακτέω, ῶ, ήσω, *to be indignant, angry.* With περί (gen.), Mat. xx. 24; or ὅτι, Lu. xiii. 14.

ἀγανάκτησις, εως, ἡ, *indignation,* 2 Cor. vii. 11.*

ἀγαπάω, ῶ, ήσω, *to love,* Lu. vii. 47; *to wish well to,* Mat. v. 43, xix. 19; *to take pleasure in,* Heb. i. 9; *to long for,* 2 Tim. iv. 8. *Syn.:* ἀγαπάω denotes the love of the reason, esteem; φιλέω, the love of the feelings, warm instinctive affection.

ἀγάπη, ης, ἡ, *love, benevolence.* Object with εἰς, ἐν, or genitive, Gr. § 269, Wi. § 30*a*, Bu. 329. ἀγάπαι (Ju. 12), *love-feasts.* (S.)

ἀγαπητός, ή, όν, *beloved,* Mat. iii. 17.

Ἄγαρ, ἡ (W. H. Ἁγαρ), (Heb.), *Hagar,* Gal. iv. 24, 25 (W. H.).*

ἀγγαρεύω, σω (from the Persian), *to impress* into the public service; hence, *to compel to perform any service,* Mat. v. 41, xxvii. 32; Mar. xv. 21.*

ἀγγεῖον, ου, τό, *vessel, utensil,* Mat. xiii. 48 (Rec.), xxv. 4.*

ἀγγελία, ας, ἡ, *message,* 1 Jn. i. 5 (W. H.), iii. 11.*

ἄγγελος, ου, ὁ, *messenger,* Mat. xi. 10; spec. of God's messengers to men, *angel,* Mat. iv. 6. So of fallen spirits, Ju. 6. "Angel of a church" (Rev. i. 20, ii., iii.), either *messenger,* or *elder,* or *an angel* who watches over the church.

ἄγγος, εος, τό, *vessel,* Mat. xiii. 48 (W. H.).*

ἄγε, interj. (properly impv. of ἄγω), *come now!* Ja. iv. 13, v. 1.*

ἀγέλη, ης, ἡ, *a flock* or *herd,* Mat. viii. 30.

ἀ-γενεα-λόγητος, ον, adj., *of unrecorded genealogy,* Heb. vii. 3. (N. T.)*

ἀ-γενής, ές (from γένος), *low-born, base,* 1 Cor. i. 28.*

ἁγιάζω, σω (from ἅγιος), *to set apart* from common use. Hence, *to hallow,* or regard with religious reverence, Mat. vi. 9; *to consecrate* to religious service, whether persons or things, Mat. xxiii. 17; Jn. xvii. 19; *to cleanse* for such consecration, Heb. ix. 13; so *to purify, sanctify,* 1 Cor. vi. 11. οἱ ἁγιαζόμενοι, *those who are being sanctified;* οἱ ἡγιασμένοι, *those who are sanctified,* Ac. xx. 32.

ἁγιασμός, οῦ, ὁ, *sanctification, holiness,* 1 Cor. i. 30; 1 Th. iv. 7. (S.)

ἅγιος, α, ον, *hallowed, worthy of veneration, holy, consecrated,* whether persons, places, or things. οἱ ἅγιοι, *"the Saints";* τὸ ἅγιον, *the Temple;* τὰ ἅγια, *the Sanctuary;* ἅγια ἁγίων, *the Holy of Holies;* πνεῦμα ἅγιον, *the Holy Spirit. Syn.:* see Trench, § lxxxviii.

ἁγιότης, τητος, ἡ, *holiness,* Heb. xii. 10; 2 Cor. i. 12 (W. H.). (Ap.)*

ἁγιωσύνη, ης, ἡ, *holiness,* Ro. i. 4; 2 Cor. vii. 1; 1 Th. iii. 13. (S.)*

ἀγκάλη, ης, ἡ, *the* (curve of the) *arm,* Lu. ii. 28.*

ἄγκιστρον, ου, τό, *fishhook,* Mat. xvii. 27.*

ἄγκυρα, ας, ἡ, *an anchor,* Ac. xxvii. 29, 30, 40; Heb. vi. 19.

ἄ-γναφος, ον, adj., *unfulled, undressed,* Mat. ix. 16; Mar. ii. 21. (N. T.)*

ἁγνεία, ας, ἡ, *purity,* 1 Tim. iv. 12, v. 2.*

ἁγνίζω, σω, *to cleanse, purify;* ceremonially, Jn. xi. 55; morally, Ja. iv. 8.

ἁγνισμός, οῦ, ὁ, ceremonial *purification,* Ac. xxi. 26.*

ἀ-γνοέω, ῶ, ήσω (see γιγνώσκω), (1) *not to know, to be ignorant,* 1 Tim. i. 13; ἀγνοῶν, *ignorant;* ἀγνοούμενος, *unknown,* Gal. i. 22; *ignored, disregarded,* 1 Cor. xiv. 38 (W. H.); (2) *not to understand,* Mar. ix. 32; Lu. ix. 45.

ἀγνόημα, ατος, τό, *a sin of ignorance, error,* Heb. ix. 7.* *Syn.:* see Trench, § lxvi.

ἄγνοια, ας, ἡ, *ignorance,* Ac. iii. 17, xvii. 30; Ep. iv. 18; 1 Pet. i. 14.*

ἁγνός, ή, όν, *pure,* 2 Cor. vii. 11; *chaste,* Tit. ii. 5. *Syn.:* see ἅγιος.

ἁγνότης, τητος, ἡ, *purity,* 2 Cor. vi. 6, xi. 3 (W. H.).*

ἁγνῶς, adv., *purely, sincerely,* Phil. i. 17.*

ἀγνωσία, ας, ἡ, *ignorance,* spec. willful ignorance, 1 Cor. xv. 34; 1 Pet. ii. 15.*

ἄγνωστος, ον, *unknown,* Ac. xvii. 23.*

ἀγορά, ᾶς, ἡ (ἀγείρω), *a place of public resort, forum, market place,* Ac. xvii. 17; used for the market, Mar. vii. 4; as the place of public assemblies, trials, etc., Ac. xvi. 19.

ἀγοράζω, σω, *to purchase, buy,* with gen. of price, Mar. vi. 37, or ἐκ, Mat. xxvii. 7, once ἐν, Rev. v. 9; fig., *to redeem, ransom,* Rev. v. 9, xiv. 3.

ἀγοραῖος, ον, *belonging to the forum;* hence (sc. ἡμέραι) *court days,* Ac. xix. 38; (sc. ἄνθρωποι) *idlers,* xvii. 5.*

ἄγρα, ας, ἡ, *a catching,* Lu. v. 4; *the thing caught, a catch* of fish, v. 9.*

ἀ-γράμματος, ον, *unlearned, i.e.,* in Rabbinical lore, Ac. iv. 13.* *Syn.:* ἀγράμματος means *illiterate,* without knowledge gained by study; ἰδιώτης, not a specialist, or without knowledge gained by mingling in public life.

ἀγρ-αυλέω, ῶ, *to live in the fields,* Lu. ii. 8.*

ἀγρεύω, σω (to take in hunting), fig., *to ensnare,* Mar. xii. 13.*

ἀγρι-έλαιος, ου, ἡ, *wild olive,* Ro. xi. 17, 24.*

ἄγριος, ία, ιον, *wild,* of honey, Mat. iii. 4; Mar. i. 6; *fierce,* of waves, Ju. 13.*

Ἀγρίππας, α, ὁ, *Agrippa, i.e.,* Herod Agrippa II. See Ἡρῴδης.

ἀγρός, οῦ, ὁ, *field,* spec. *the country,* Mat. vi. 28; plur., *country districts, hamlets,* Mar. v. 14.

ἀγρυπνέω, ῶ (ὕπνος), *to be sleepless;* hence, met., *to watch, to be vigilant,* Mar. xiii. 33; Lu. xxi. 36; Ep. vi. 18; Heb. xiii. 17.*

ἀγρυπνία, ας, ἡ, *sleeplessness, watching,* 2 Cor. vi. 5, xi. 27.*

ἄγω, ξω, 2 a., ἤγαγον, trans., *to lead, bring;* with πρός (acc.), ἕως, εἰς, of destination; with ἐπί (acc.), of purpose, as Ac. viii. 32; *to bring before,* for trial, Ac. xxv. 17. Also *to spend,* as of time; *to keep,* as a particular day, Mat. xiv. 6 (not W. H.); Lu. xxiv. 21 (impers.). Fig., *to lead the inclination, induce,* Lu. iv. 1. Mid., *to go, depart;* subj., ἄγωμεν, *let us go!* Mat. xxvi. 46.

ἀγωγή, ῆς, ἡ (ἄγω), *a leading, course of life,* 2 Tim. iii. 10.*

ἀγών, ῶνος, ὁ, *contest, conflict;* fig., of the Christian life, as Heb. xii. 1; *solicitude, anxiety,* Col. ii. 1.

ἀγωνία, ας, ἡ, *contest, agony,* Lu. xxii. 44 (not W. H.).*

ἀγωνίζομαι, *to strive,* as in the public games, 1 Cor. ix. 25; *to contend* with an adversary, Jn. xviii. 36; fig., of Christian effort and endurance, Col. i. 29.

Ἀδάμ, ὁ (Heb.), *Adam.*

ἀ-δάπανος, ον, *free of charge, gratuitous,* 1 Cor. ix. 18.*

Ἀδδί, ὁ, *Addi,* Lu. iii. 28 (not mentioned in O. T.).*

ἀδελφή, ῆς, ἡ, *a sister,* (1) lit., Mat. xix. 29; (2) fig. of Christian friendship, 1 Cor. vii. 15.

ἀδελφός, οῦ, ὁ, *a brother,* (1) lit. (see Gr. § 256), Mat. i. 2; (2) of more general relations, *a fellow-countryman,* Mat. v. 47; *a fellow-Christian,* Mat. xxiii. 8; *a fellow-man,* Mat. v. 22–24; also expressing the relation between Christ and believers, Mat. xxv. 40. The "brethren of Jesus" (Mat. xiii. 55; Jn. vii. 3; Ac. i. 14; Gal. i. 19) are probably to be understood literally.

ἀδελφότης, τητος, ἡ, *the brotherhood, i.e.,* the Christian community, 1 Pet. ii. 17, v. 9. (Ap.)*

ἄ-δηλος, ον, *not manifest, uncertain,* Lu. xi. 44; 1 Cor. xiv. 8.*

ἀ-δηλότης, τητος, *uncertainty,* 1 Tim. vi. 17.*

ἀδήλως, adv., *uncertainly,* 1 Cor. ix. 26.*

ἀδημονέω, ῶ, *to be troubled, distressed*, Mar. xiv. 33.

ᾅδης, ου, ὁ (ἀ priv. and ἰδεῖν), *the invisible world, Hades*, Lu. xvi. 23; fig., of deep degradation, Mat. xi. 23. See πύλη.

ἀ-διά-κριτος, ον, *without uncertainty, unambiguous*, Ja. iii. 17.*

ἀ-διά-λειπτος, ον, *without intermission, unceasing*, Ro. ix. 2; 2 Tim. i. 3.*

ἀδιαλείπτως, adv., *without intermission, incessantly*, Ro. i. 9; 1 Th. i. 2, ii. 13, v. 17.*

ἀ-δια-φθορία, ας, ἡ, *incorruptibility, soundness*, Tit. ii. 7 (not W. H.). (N. T.)*

ἀδικέω, ῶ, ήσω (ἄδικος), intrans., *to act unjustly, commit a crime*, Ac. xxv. 11; trans., *to wrong, injure*, Mat. xx. 13; hence, *to hurt*, without any notion of wrong, Lu. x. 19, and Rev. often; pass., *to be wronged*, 2 Cor. vii. 12; mid., *to suffer wrong*, 1 Cor. vi. 7.

ἀδίκημα, ατος, τό, *a wrong, misdeed*, Ac. xviii. 14, xxiv. 20; Rev. xviii. 5.*

ἀδικία, ας, ἡ, *wrong* (towards man or God); hence, *injustice*, Lu. xviii. 6; Ro. ix. 14; *unrighteousness*, Ro. i. 18, 29; *act of unrighteousness*, 1 Jn. v. 17; Heb. viii. 12.

ἄ-δικος, ον, *unjust, unrighteous*, generally, opposed to δίκαιος, as Mat. v. 45, to εὐσεβής, as 2 Pet. ii. 9, or to πιστός, as Lu. xvi. 10.

ἀδίκως, adv., *unjustly, undeservedly*, 1 Pet. ii. 19.*

ἀ-δόκιμος, ον (tested, but not approved), *reprobate, rejected*, Ro. i. 28; 1 Cor. ix. 27; 2 Cor. xiii. 5, 6, 7; 2 Tim. iii. 8; Tit. i. 16; Heb. vi. 8.*

ἄ-δολος, ον, *without fraud, unadulterated*, 1 Pet. ii. 2.* *Syn.:* see Trench, § lvi.

Ἀδραμυττηνός, ή, όν, *of Adramyttium*, a seaport of Mysia, Ac. xxvii. 2.*

Ἀδρίας, ου, ὁ, *the Adriatic*, the sea between Greece and Italy, Ac. xxvii. 27.*

ἁδρότης, τητος, ἡ, *abundance, liberality*, 2 Cor. viii. 20.*

ἀδυνατέω, ῶ, ήσω, *to be impossible*, with dat. of pers., Mat. xvii. 20; or παρά (dat., W. H. gen.), Lu. i. 37.*

ἀ-δύνατος, ον, (1) of persons, act., *powerless*, Ac. xiv. 8; (2) of things, pass., *impossible*, Ro. viii. 3.

ᾄδω, ᾄσω (contr. from ἀείδω), *to sing*, with cognate acc., ᾠδήν, *a song*, Rev. v. 9, xiv. 3, xv. 3; with dat., *to sing* (praise) *to*, Ep. v. 19; Col. iii. 16.*

ἀεί, adv., *always;* of continuous time, *unceasingly*, Ac. vii. 51; of successive intervals, *from time to time, on every occasion*, 1 Pet. iii. 15.

ἀετός, οῦ, ὁ, *an eagle*, Rev. iv. 7; gen. *bird of prey*, as Mat. xxiv. 28.

ἄ-ζυμος, ον, *unleavened*, only in plur., sc. λάγανα, *cakes*, or ἄρτοι, *loaves;* met., *the paschal feast*, Lu. xxii. 1; fig., *uncorrupted, sincere*, 1 Cor. v. 7, 8.

Ἀζώρ, indecl. (Heb.), *Azor*, Mat. i. 13, 14; not mentioned in O. T.*

Ἄζωτος, ου ἡ, *Azotus* or *Ashdod*, Ac. viii. 40.*

ἀήρ, ἀέρος, ὁ, *the air, atmosphere*, Ac. xxii. 23; Ep. ii. 2.

ἀ-θανασία, ας, ἡ (see θάνατος), *immortality*, 1 Cor. xv. 53, 54; 1 Tim. vi. 16.*

ἀ-θέμιτος, ον (θέμις, *law*), *unlawful, criminal*, Ac. x. 28; 1 Pet. iv. 3.*

ἄ-θεος, ον, *without God*, Ep. ii. 12.*

ἄ-θεσμος, ον (θεσμός, *statute*), *lawless*, 2 Pet. ii. 7, iii. 17.*

ἀ-θετέω, ῶ, ήσω (θε- as in τίθημι), *to make void, invalid;* of things, *to nullify*, Lu. vii. 30; chiefly of persons, *to slight, reject*, Lu. x. 16.

ἀ-θέτησις, εως, ἡ, *nullification, abrogation*, Heb. vii. 18, ix. 26.*

Ἀθῆναι, ῶν, αἱ, *Athens*, Ac. xvii. 15.

Ἀθηναῖος, α, ον, *Athenian*, Ac. xvii. 21, 22.*

ἀθλέω, ῶ (ἆθλος, *a contest*), *to contend* in the public games, 2 Tim. ii. 5.*

ἄθλησις, εως, ἡ, *contest*, as in the public games; only fig. Heb. x. 32.*

ἀθροίζω, *to gather together*, Lu. xxiv. 33 (W. H.).*

ἀ-θυμέω, ω, *to lose heart, despond*, Col. iii. 21.*

ἀθῷος, ον, *unpunished, innocent*, Mat. xxvii. 4 (not W. H.); with ἀπό, of the crime, ver. 24.*

αἴγειος, η, ον (αἴξ, *goat*), *of* or *belonging to a goat*, Heb. xi. 37.*

αἰγιαλός, οῦ, ὁ, *the shore, beach;* used of Gennesaret, Mat. xiii. 2, 48; Jn. xxi. 4; of the Mediterranean, Ac. xxi. 5, xxvii. 39, 40.*

Αἰγύπτιος, α, ον, *Egyptian*, Ac. vii. 22.

Αἴγυπτος, ου, ἡ, *Egypt*, Mat. ii. 13.

ἀΐδιος, ον, adj. (ἀεί), *eternal, everlasting*, Ro. i. 20; Ju. 6.*

αἰδώς, οῦς, ἡ, *modesty*, 1 Tim. ii. 9; *reverence*, Heb. xii. 28 (not W. H.).* *Syn.:* see Trench, § xix; Thayer, p. 14.

Αἰθίοψ, οπος, ὁ, *an Ethiopian*, Ac. viii. 27.*

αἷμα, ατος, τό, *blood*, (1) in general, Jn. xix. 34; (2) *natural life*, which was believed to reside in the blood, especially with σάρξ, 1 Cor. xv. 20; so *human nature* generally; hence, (3) *natural relationship*, Jn. i. 13; (4) blood *shed* of sacrificial victims, Heb. ix. 7, 12; (5) hence, *the blood of Christ, his atoning death*, 1 Cor. x. 16; Rev. vii. 14; (6) *violent death, bloodshed, murder*, Lu. xiii. 1; Mat. xxiii. 30, 35; (7) in Ac. ii. 20, etc., the reference is to the *color of blood*.

αἱματ-εκ-χυσία, ας, ἡ, *shedding of blood*, Heb. ix. 22. (N. T.)*

αἱμορροέω, ῶ, *to suffer from a flow of blood*, Mat. ix. 20.*

Αἰνέας, α, ὁ, *Aeneas*, Ac. ix. 33, 34.*

αἴνεσις, εως, ἡ, *praise*, Heb. xiii. 15. (S.)*

αἰνέω, ῶ, έσω and ήσω, *to praise*, only of praise to God, Lu. ii. 13, 20.

αἴνιγμα, ατος, τό, *an enigma, an obscure thing*, 1 Cor. xiii. 12.*

αἶνος, ου, ὁ, *praise* to God, Mat. xxi. 16; Lu. xviii. 43.*

Αἰνών, ἡ (Heb.), *Aenon*, Jn. iii. 23.*

αἵρεσις, εως, ἡ (αἱρέω), *choice*, its act or result; hence, *a* *tenet*, *heresy*, 2 Pet. ii. 1; *a sect*, Ac. v. 17; *dissension*, Gal. v. 20.

αἱρετίζω, σω, *to choose*, Mat. xii. 18.*

αἱρετικός, ή, όν, *schismatic*, *factious*, Tit. iii. 10.*

αἱρέω (irreg., Gr. § 103, 1, Wi. § 15, Bu. 53), *to take*, only in mid. in N. T., *to choose*, *prefer*, Phil. i. 22; 2 Th. ii. 13; Heb. xi. 25.*

αἴρω (Gr. § 92), (1) *to raise*, *lift up*, Mar. xvi. 18; Jn. xi. 41; (2) *to bear*, *carry*, Mat. iv. 6; Lu. ix. 23; (3) *to bear away*, *carry off*, in general, Mat. xxi. 21; Jn. xix. 31; *to take away* sin, of the redeeming work of Christ, Jn. i. 29; 1 Jn. iii. 5; *to remove by death*, Jn. xvii. 15; Mat. xxiv. 39.

αἰσθάνομαι, 2 a. ᾐσθόμην, dep., *to perceive*, *understand*, Lu. ix. 45.*

αἴσθησις, εως, ἡ, *perception*, *discernment*, Phil. i. 9.*

αἰσθητήριον, ου, τό, *organ of perception*, *faculty of judgment*, Heb. v. 14.*

αἰσχρο-κερδής, ές, *eager for base gain*, *sordid*, 1 Tim. iii. 3 (not W. H.), 8; Tit. i. 7.*

αἰσχροκερδῶς, *from eagerness for base gain*, 1 Pet. v. 2. (N. T.)*

αἰσχρο-λογία, ας, ἡ, *foul language*, *scurrility*, Col. iii. 8.*

αἰσχρός, ά, όν, *base*, *disgraceful*, 1 Cor. xi. 6.

αἰσχρότης, τητος, ἡ, *baseness*, *dishonor*, Ep. v. 4.*

αἰσχύνη, ης, ἡ, *shame*, in personal feeling, Lu. xiv. 9; or in the estimation of others, Heb. xii. 2; *a shameful thing*, Ju. 13. *Syn.:* see αἰδώς.

αἰσχύνομαι, οῦμαι, in N. T. only pass., *to be put to shame*, *made ashamed*, 2 Cor. x. 8; Phil. i. 20.

αἰτέω, ῶ, ήσω, *to ask*, *pray*, *require*, Ja. i. 6; usually with two accs., or acc. of thing and ἀπό or παρά (gen.) of person; mid., *to ask for one's self*, *beg*, Jn. xvi. 26. *Syn.:* αἰτέω is to ask a favor, as a suppliant; ἐρωτάω, to ask a question, or as an equal; πυνθάνομαι, to ask for information. But see Thayer, p. 18.

αἴτημα, ατος, τό, *petition*, *request*, Lu. xxiii. 24; Phil. iv. 6; 1 Jn. v. 15. *Syn.:* see Trench, § li.

αἰτία, ας, ἡ, *cause*, (1) as the *reason* or *ground* of anything, Ac. x. 21; (2) in Mat. xix. 10, *the state of the case*; (3) forensically, *a crime*, Ac. xiii. 28; *a charge of crime*, *accusation*, Ac. xxv. 18, 27.

αἰτίαμα, ατος, τό, *accusation*, *charge*, Ac. xxv. 7 (W. H. read αἰτίωμα).*

αἴτιος, ία, ιον, *causative of*, used as subst., in masc., *the cause*, *author*, only Heb. v. 9; in neut., *a cause*, *reason*, espec. of punishment, Ac. xix. 40; *a fault*, *crime*, like αἰτία, Lu. xxiii. 4, 14, 22.*

αἰτίωμα. See αἰτίαμα. (N. T.)*

αἰφνίδιος, ον, *unexpected*, *sudden*, Lu. xxi. 34 (W. H. ἐφνίδιος); 1 Th. v. 3.*

αἰχμ-αλωσία, ας, ἡ, *captivity*, Rev. xiii. 10; abstract for concrete, Ep. iv. 8.*

αἰχμ-αλωτεύω, σω, *to make prisoners of*, *to take captive*, Ep. iv. 8; 2 Tim. iii. 6 (W. H. read the following). (S.)*

αἰχμ-αλωτίζω, σω, *to lead captive*, Lu. xxi. 24.

αἰχμ-άλωτος, ου, ὁ, ἡ, *captive*, Lu. iv. 18 (from Is. lxi. 1).*

αἰών, ῶνος, ὁ (ἀεί), originally *an indefinitely long period of time*, *an age*; hence, (1) *an unbroken age*, *eternity*, past, as Ac. xv. 18; future, 2 Pet. iii. 18, especially in the following phrases: εἰς τὸν αἰῶνα, *for ever*, with negative adv. *never*; εἰς τοὺς αἰῶνας, a stronger expression, *for evermore*; εἰς τοὺς αἰῶνας τῶν αἰώνων, stronger still (see Gr. § 327, ii, Wi. § 36, 2), *for ever and ever*. Phrase slightly varied, Ep. iii. 21; Heb. i. 8; 2 Pet. iii. 18; Ju. 25; Rev. xiv. 11; (2) in plur., *the worlds*, *the universe*, Heb. i. 2, xi. 3; (3) *the present age* (ὁ αἰὼν οὗτος, ὁ ἐνεστὼς αἰών, ὁ νῦν αἰών), Gal. i. 4; 1 Tim. vi. 17, in contrast with the time after the second coming of Christ, *the coming age* (ὁ αἰων ἐκεῖνος, αἰὼν μέλλων, ὁ αἰὼν ὁ ἐρχόμενος, οἱ αἰῶνες οἱ ἐπερχόμενοι), Lu. xx. 35, xviii. 30; Ep. ii. 7; Mat. xii. 32. *Syn.:* αἰών is the world under the aspect of *time*; κόσμος, under that of *space*. See Thayer, p. 19.

αἰώνιος (ία, only in 2 Th. ii. 16; Heb. ix. 12; or ιος), ιον, (1) *without beginning or end*, *eternal*, Ro. xvi. 26; Heb. ix. 14; (2) *without beginning*, Ro. xvi. 25; 2 Tim. i. 9; (3) *without end*, *everlasting*; often with ζωή, *eternal life*, denoting life which in its character is essentially eternal, see Jn. v. 24, vi. 47, xvii. 3. Neut., used as adv., *for ever*, Philem. 15.

ἀ-καθαρσία, ας, ἡ (καθαίρω), *uncleanness*, *impurity*, usually in a moral sense, Ro. i. 24; 2 Cor. xii. 21.

ἀ-καθάρτης, τητος, ἡ, *impurity*, Rev. xvii. 4 (W. H. read the following). (N. T.)*

ἀ-κάθαρτος, ον, *unclean*, *impure*, (1) of ceremonial defilement, Ac. x. 14; 1 Cor. vii. 14; (2) of evil spirits, with πνεῦμα, Gospels, Acts, Rev.; (3) of human beings, *impure*, *lewd*, Ep. v. 5.

ἀ-καιρέομαι, οῦμαι, dep., *to lack opportunity*, Phil. iv. 10.*

ἀ-καίρως, adv., *unseasonably*, 2 Tim. iv. 2, opp. to εὐκαίρως.*

ἄ-κακος, ον, *guileless*, Ro. xvi. 18; Heb. vii. 26.*

ἄκανθα, ης, ἡ, *thorn*, *briar*, Mat. vii. 16.

ἀκάνθινος, ον, *made of thorns*, Mar. xv. 17; Jn. xix. 5.*

ἄ-καρπος, ον, *unfruitful*, *barren*, generally fig., Mat. xiii. 22; Tit. iii. 14.

ἀ-κατά-γνωστος, ον, *not to be condemned*, Tit. ii. 8.*

ἀ-κατα-κάλυπτος, ον, *unveiled*, 1 Cor. xi. 5, 13.*

ἀ-κατά-κριτος, ον, *uncondemned*, Ac. xvi. 37, xxii. 25. (N. T.)*

ἀ-κατά-λυτος, ον, *indissoluble*, Heb. vii. 16.*

ἀ-κατά-παστος, ον, *unfed*, *hungry for* (gen.), 2 Pet. ii. 14 (W. H. for the following). (N. T.)*

ἀ-κατά-παυστος, ον, *not to be restrained*, with gen., 2 Pet. ii. 14 (see preceding).*

ἀ-κατα-στασία, ας, ἡ, *instabil-*

ity; hence, *sedition, tumult, disorder,* Ja. iii. 16, 2 Cor. vi. 5.

ἀ-κατά-στατος, ον, *inconstant, unstable,* Ja. i. 8, iii. 8 (W. H.).*

ἀ-κατά-σχετος, ον, *that cannot be restrained,* Ja. iii. 8 (W. H. read preceding). (S.)*

'Ακελ-δαμά (Aram., *field of blood*), *Aceldama,* Ac. i. 19 (W. H. read 'Ακελδαμάχ). (N. T.)*

ἀ-κέραιος, ον (κεράννυμι), *unmixed;* hence, fig., *simple, innocent, guileless,* Mat. x. 16; Ro. xvi. 19; Phil. ii. 15.*

ἀ-κλινής, ές, *unbending;* hence, *firm, steadfast,* Heb. x. 23.*

ἀκμάζω, σω, *to reach the point of perfection;* so, of fruit, *to be fully ripe,* Rev. xiv. 18.*

ἀκμήν, acc. of ἀκμή as adv., *even now, even yet,* Mat. xv. 16.*

ἀκοή, ῆς, ἡ (ἀκούω), *hearing,* (1) *the sense of hearing,* 2 Pet. ii. 8; (2) *the organ of hearing, the ear,* 2 Tim. iv. 3, 4; (3) *the thing heard, a report, speech, doctrine,* Jn. xii. 38; Mar. i. 28. ἀκοῇ ἀκούειν, "to hear with hearing," *i.e, attentively* (a Hebraism), Mat. xiii. 14.

ἀκολουθέω, ῶ, ήσω, (1) *to accompany, follow,* or *attend,* with dat., or μετά (gen.), or ὀπίσω (gen.), espec. of the disciples of Christ; so, met., *to obey* and *imitate,* Mat. iv. 25; Mar. ix. 38.

ἀκούω, σω or σομαι, pf., ἀκήκοα, *to hear,* (1) without object, Mar. iv. 3, vii. 37; (2) with object (acc. or gen., Gr. § 249*a*, 1, Wi. § 30, 7*c*, Bu. 165 sq., 301), *to hear, listen to, heed, understand,* Mat. xii. 19; Lu. i. 41. οἱ ἀκούοντες, *hearers* or *disciples.* In pass., *to be noised abroad,* Ac. xi. 22.

ἀ-κρασία, ας, ἡ, *intemperance, incontinence,* Mat. xxiii. 25; 1 Cor. vii. 5.*

ἀ-κρατής, ές (κράτος), *powerless, without self-control,* 2 Tim. iii. 3.*

ἄ-κρατος, ον (κεράννυμι), *unmixed, undiluted* (of strong wine), Rev. xiv. 10.*

ἀκρίβεια, ας, ἡ, *exactness, strictness,* Ac. xxii. 3.*

ἀκριβής, ές, *exact, strict,* Ac. xxvi. 5.

ἀκριβόω, ῶ, ώσω, *to inquire closely, learn carefully* (R. V.), Mat. ii. 7, 16.*

ἀκριβῶς, adv., *exactly, diligently,* Ac. xviii. 25.

ἀκρίς, ίδος, ἡ, *a locust,* Mat. iii. 4.

ἀκροατήριον, ίου, τό (ἀκροάομαι, *to hear*), *the place of* (judicial) *hearing,* Ac. xxv. 23.*

ἀκροατής, οῦ, ὁ, *a hearer,* Ro. ii. 13; Ja. i. 22, 23, 25.*

ἀκροβυστία, ας, ἡ, *the foreskin,* Ac. xi. 3; *uncircumcision,* Ro. iv. 10; met., *an uncircumcised Gentile,* Ep. ii. 11. (S.)

ἀκρο-γωνιαῖος, α, ον (with λίθος expressed or understood), *a corner foundation stone,* ref. to Christ, Ep. ii. 20; 1 Pet. ii. 6. (S.)*

ἀκρο-θίνιον, ίου, τό, *first-fruits, i.e.,* the best of the produce, applied (plur.) to spoils taken in battle, Heb. vii. 4.*

ἄκρος, α, ον, *outermost, pointed;* neut., τὸ ἄκρον, *the end, extremity,* Lu. xvi. 24.

'Ακύλας, ου, ὁ (Latin), *Aquila,* Ac. xviii. 2.

ἀ-κυρόω, ῶ, *to deprive of power, set aside* (a law), Mat. xv. 6; Mar. vii. 13; Gal. iii. 17.

ἀ-κωλύτως, adv., *freely, without hindrance,* Ac. xxviii. 31.*

ἄκων, ουσα, ον (ἀ, ἑκών), *unwilling,* 1 Cor. ix. 17.*

ἀλάβαστρον, ου, τό, *a box made of alabaster, a vessel for perfume,* Mat. xxvi. 7; Mar. xiv. 3; Lu. vii. 37.*

ἀλαζονία, ας, ἡ, *boasting, show, ostentation,* Ja. iv. 16; 1 Jn. ii. 16.*

ἀλαζών, όνος, ὁ, *a boaster,* Ro. i. 30; 2 Tim. iii. 2.*

ἀλαλάζω, άσω, *to raise a cry* or loud sound; in mourning, Mar. v. 38; of cymbals, 1 Cor. xiii. 1.*

ἀ-λάλητος, ον, *not to be uttered in words,* Ro. viii. 26.*

ἄ-λαλος, ον, *dumb, making dumb,* Mar. vii. 37, ix. 17, 25.*

ἅλας, ατος, τό, *salt,* lit. and fig., as Mat. v. 13.

ἀλείφω, ψω, *to anoint,* festally, or in homage, also medicinally, or in embalming the dead, Mar. xvi. 1, Lu. vii. 46. *Syn.:* χρίω has always a religious and symbolical force, which is absent in ἀλείφω.

ἀλεκτορο-φωνία, ας, ἡ, *the cock-crowing,* the third watch of the night, between midnight and dawn, Mar. xiii. 35.*

ἀλέκτωρ, ορος, ὁ, *a cock,* Mat. xxvi. 34; Jn. xiii. 38.

'Αλεξανδρεύς, έως, ὁ, *an Alexandrian,* Ac. vi. 9, xviii. 24.*

'Αλεξανδρινός, ή, όν, *Alexandrian,* Ac. xxvii. 6, xxviii. 11.*

'Αλέξανδρος, ου, ὁ, *Alexander.* Four of this name are mentioned, Mar. xv. 21; Ac. iv. 6; Ac. xix. 33; 1 Tim. i. 20; 2 Tim. iv. 14.*

ἄλευρον, ου, τό, *wheaten flour,* Mat. xiii. 33; Lu. xiii. 21.*

ἀλήθεια, ας, ἡ, *truth;* generally, as Mar. v. 33; espec., (1) *freedom from error, exactness,* as (2) the Truth, or *Word of God;* Jesus is called *the Truth,* Jn. xiv. 6; (3) *truthfulness, veracity, sincerity, integrity,* opposed to ἀδικία, Ro. ii. 8; 1 Cor. xiii. 6.

ἀληθεύω, *to speak the truth,* Gal. iv. 16; Ep. iv. 15.*

ἀληθής, ές (ἀ, λαθ- in λανθάνω), *unconcealed, true,* Ac. xii. 9; Jn. iv. 18; *truthful,* Mat. xxii. 16; Mar. xii. 14. *Syn.:* ἀληθής means true *morally,* faithful; ἀληθινός, *genuine,* in contrast either with the *false* or the *imperfect.*

ἀληθινός, ή, όν, *real, genuine,* contrasted with the fictitious, as Lu. xvi. 11; Jn. i. 9; with the typical, as Jn. vi. 32; Heb. viii. 2, ix. 24. *Syn.:* see ἀληθής.

ἀλήθω, ήσω, *to grind* with a handmill, Mat. xxiv. 41; Lu. xvii. 35.*

ἀληθῶς, adv., *truly, really, certainly,* Ac. xii. 11.

ἁλιεύς (W. H. ἁλεεύς), έως, ὁ, *a fisherman,* Mat. iv. 18.

ἁλιεύω, εύσω, *to fish,* Jn. xxi. 3. (S.)*

ἁλίζω, ίσω, *to salt, season with salt,* Mat. v. 13; Mar. ix. 49

ἀλίσγημα, ατος, τό, *pollution* Ac. xv. 20. (N. T.)*

ἀλλά (prop. n. plur. of ἄλλος), *but,* an adversative particle.

See Gr. § 404, Wi. § 53, 7, Bu. 369 sq.

ἀλλάσσω, άξω, *to change*, Ac. vi. 14; *to exchange*, Ro. i. 23; *to transform*, 1 Cor. xv. 51.

ἀλλαχόθεν, adv., *from elsewhere*, Jn. x. 1.*

ἀλλαχοῦ, adv., *elsewhere*, Mar. i. 38 (W. H.).*

ἀλλ-ηγορέω, ῶ, *to speak allegorically;* pass. part., Gal. iv. 24.*

Ἀλληλούϊα (W. H. Ἁλ-), (Heb.), Hallelujah, *Praise ye Jehovah*, Rev. xix, 1, 3, 4, 6. (S.)*

ἀλλήλων, reciprocal pron., gen. plur. (Gr. § 61*c*), *one another, each other*, Ro. i. 12.

ἀλλο-γενής, ές, *of another nation, a foreigner*, Lu. xvii. 18. (S.)*

ἅλλομαι (dep.), ἁλοῦμαι, ἡλάμην, *to leap*, Ac. iii. 8, xiv. 10; *to bubble up*, as water, Jn. iv. 14.*

ἄλλος, η, ο, *other, another*, Mar. vi. 15; ὁ ἄλλος, *the other*, Mat. v. 39; οἱ ἄλλοι, *the others, the rest*. *Syn.:* ἄλλος indicates that which is simply *numerically* distinct; ἕτερος, that which is generically distinct, *different*.

ἀλλοτριο-επίσκοπος, ου, ὁ, *one who looks at* or *busies himself in the things of another, a busybody*, 1 Pet. iv. 15 (W. H. ἀλλοτριεπίσκοπος). (N. T.)*

ἀλλότριος, ία, ιον, *belonging to another*, Heb. ix. 25; *foreign, strange*, Ac. vii. 6; *not of one's own family*, Mat. xvii. 25; *hostile*, Heb. xi. 34.

ἀλλό-φυλος, ου, adj., *foreign, of another tribe* or *race*, Ac. x. 28.*

ἄλλως, adv., *otherwise*, 1 Tim. v. 25.*

ἀλοάω, ῶ, ήσω, *to beat* or *thresh*, as grain, 1 Cor. ix. 9, 10; 1 Tim. v. 18.*

ἄ-λογος, ον, (1) *without speech* or *reason, irrational*, 2 Pet. ii. 12, Ju. 10; (2) *unreasonable, absurd*, Ac. xxv. 27.*

ἀλόη, ης, ἡ, *the aloe*, Jn. xix. 39. (S.)*

ἅλς, ἁλός, ὁ, *salt*. Rec. only in Mar. ix. 49 (dat.), W. H. only in ix. 50 (acc.). See ἅλας.*

ἁλυκός, ή, όν (ἅλς), *salt, brackish*, Ja. iii. 12.*

ἄ-λυπος, ον, *free from sorrow*, Phil. ii. 28.*

ἅλυσις, εως, ἡ, *a chain* or *manacle*, Mar. v. 3; Ac. xxi. 33.

ἀ-λυσιτελής, ές, *without gain, unprofitable*, Heb. xiii. 17.*

ἄλφα, το, see A.

Ἀλφαῖος, ου, ὁ, *Alphæus*. Two of the name are mentioned, Mar. ii. 14, iii. 18 (the latter being called Κλωπᾶς, Jn. xix. 25; another form of the orig. Hebrew name).

ἅλων, ωνος, ὁ, ἡ, *a threshing-floor;* met., *the grain of the threshing-floor*, Mat. iii. 12; Lu. iii. 17.

ἀλώπηξ, εκος, ἡ, *a fox*, Mat. viii. 20; Lu. ix. 58; applied to Herod, Lu. xiii. 32.*

ἅλωσις, εως, ἡ, *a taking* or *catching*, 2 Pet. ii. 12.*

ἅμα, adv., *at the same time*, Ac. xxiv. 26; prep., *with* or *together with* (dat.), Mat. xiii. 29; ἅμα πρωΐ, *with the dawn*, Mat. xx. 1.

ἀ-μαθής, ές, *unlearned, ignorant*, 2 Pet. iii. 16.*

ἀμαράντινος, ου, adj., *composed of amaranth, i.e., everlasting*, 1 Pet. v. 4.*

ἀ-μάραντος, ου, adj. (μαραίνομαι), *unfading*, 1 Pet. i. 4.*

ἁμαρτάνω, τήσω, *to miss a mark, to err, to sin*, Mat. xxvii. 4; Jn. v. 14; with cogn. acc., ἁμαρτίαν, *to sin a sin*, 1 Jn. v. 16; with εἰς, *to sin against*, Lu. xv. 18, 21.

ἁμάρτημα, ατος, τό, *a sin, evil deed*. *Syn.:* see ἀγνόημα.

ἁμαρτία, ας, ἡ, (1) *a sinning* (= τὸ ἁμαρτάνειν), Ro. v. 12, 13; 2 Cor. v. 21; (2) *a sin*, sing., as Ac. vii. 60; plur. (more freq.), spec. in the phrase ἀφιέναι τὰς ἁμαρτίας, *to forgive sins*, Mat. ix. 2, 5, 6. In Heb. x. 6, 8, 18, περὶ ἁμαρτίας is *sin-offering*. *Syn.:* see ἀγνόημα.

ἀ-μάρτυρος, ον, *without witness*, Ac. xiv. 17.*

ἁμαρτωλός, ον, *sinful*, or substantively, *a sinner*, espec. habitually and notoriously, 1 Tim. i. 19; Lu. xv. 2. The Jews used the word for *idolaters, i.e.*, Gentiles, Mar. xiv. 41.

ἄ-μαχος, ον, *not quarrelsome*, 1 Tim. iii. 3; Tit. iii. 2.*

ἀμάω, ῶ, ήσω, *to reap*, Ja. v. 4.*

ἀμέθυστος, ου, ἡ, *an amethyst* (supposed to be an antidote against drunkenness. Hence the name, from ἀ, μεθύω), Rev. xxi. 20.*

ἀμελέω, ῶ, ήσω, *not to care for, to disregard, neglect*, with gen. or inf., Heb. ii. 3; 2 Pet. i. 12 (not W. H.).

ἄ-μεμπτος, ον, *blameless*, Phil. ii. 15; Heb. viii. 7.

ἀ-μέμπτως, adv., *blamelessly*, 1 Th. ii. 10, iii. 13 (W. H. mrg.).

ἀ-μέριμνος, ον, *free from solicitude* or *anxiety*, Mat. xxviii. 14; 1 Cor. vii. 32.*

ἀ-μετά-θετος, ον, *unchangeable*, Heb. vi. 18; τὸ ἀμετάθετον, *immutability*, Heb. vi. 17.*

ἀ-μετα-κίνητος, ου, adj., *immovable, firm*, 1 Cor. xv. 58.*

ἀ-μετα-μέλητος, ον, *not to be regretted* or *repented of*, Ro. xi. 29; hence, *unchangeable*, 2 Cor. vii. 10.*

ἀ-μετα-νόητος, ου, adj., *unrepentant, impenitent*, Ro. ii. 5.*

ἄ-μετρος, ον, *beyond measure, immoderate* 2 Cor. x. 13, 15.*

ἀμήν, Amen, a Hebrew adjective, *true, faithful*, used (1) as an adverb, at the beginning of a sentence, *verily, truly, indeed;* (2) at the end of ascriptions of praise, etc., optatively, as γένοιτο, *so be it;* (3) substantively, 2 Cor. i. 20, as a name of Christ, *the Amen, the faithful witness*, Rev. iii. 14. (S.)

ἀ-μήτωρ, ορος, ὁ, ἡ (μήτηρ), *without mother, i.e.*, in the genealogies, Heb. vii. 3.*

ἀ-μίαντος, ον (μιαίνω), *undefiled, sincere, pure*, Heb. vii. 26, xiii. 4; 1 Pet. i. 4; Ja. i. 27.*

Ἀμιναδάβ, ὁ (Heb.), *Aminadab*, Mat. i. 4; Lu. iii. 33 (not W. H.).*

ἄμμος, ου, ἡ, *sand*, Ro. ix. 27; Heb. xi. 12.

ἀμνός, οῦ, ὁ, *a lamb;* fig., of Christ, Jn. i. 29, 36; Ac. viii 32; 1 Pet. i. 19.*

ἀμοιβή, ῆς, ἡ (ἀμείβω), *requital*, 1 Tim. v. 4.*

ἄμπελος, ου, ἡ, *a vine*, (1) lit., Mat. xxvi. 29; (2) fig., as Jn. xv. 1.

ἀμπελ-ουργός, οῦ, ὁ, ἡ, *a vine-dresser*, Lu. xiii. 7.*

ἀμπελών, ῶνος, ὁ, *a vineyard*, Lu. xx. 9; 1 Cor. ix. 7.

'Αμπλίας, ίου, ὁ, *Amplias*, Ro. xvi. 8.*

ἀμύνω, ῶ, in N. T. only in mid., *to defend from, take vengeance on*, Ac. vii. 24.*

ἀμφιάζω, *to clothe*, Lu. xii. 28 (W. H.).*

ἀμφιβάλλω, *to cast around*, Mar. i. 16 (W. H.).*

ἀμφί-βληστρον, ου, τό, *a fishing net*, Mat. iv. 18; Mar. i. 16 (not W. H.).* *Syn.*: σαγήνη is the *drag-net*, much larger than ἀμφίβληστρον, the *casting net;* δίκτυον is general, a net of any kind.

ἀμφι-έννυμι, έσω, *to put on, to clothe*, Lu. vii. 25.

Ἀμφίπολις, εως, ἡ, *Amphipolis*, a city in the S. of Macedonia, Ac. xvii. 1.*

ἄμφ-οδον, ου, τό, *a street*, Mar. xi. 4.*

ἀμφότεροι, αι, α, *both*, Ac. xxiii. 8.

ἀ-μώμητος, ον, *without blame* or *fault*, Phil. ii. 15 (W. H. ἄμεμπτοι); 2 Pet. iii. 14.*

ἄμωμον, ου, τό, *amomum, a spice plant*, Rev. xviii. 13 (not Rec.).*

ἄ-μωμος, ον, *without blemish*, 1 Pet. i. 19; Heb. ix. 14; fig., *blameless*, Eph. i. 4; Ju. 24.

'Αμών, ὁ (Heb.), *Amon*, Mat. i. 10 (W. H. 'Αμώς).*

'Αμώς, ὁ (Heb.), *Amos*, Lu. iii. 25.*

ἄν, a particle, expressing *possibility, uncertainty*, or *conditionality*. At the beginning of a sentence it is a contraction of ἐάν. See Gr. §§ 378*b*, 380, 383δ, Wi. § 42, Bu. 216 sq.

ἀνά, prep., lit., *upon* (acc.); in composition, *up, again;* used in many phrases. See Gr. §§ 297 and 147*a*, Wi. §§ 49*b*, 52, 4, 2), Bu. 331, 332.

ἀνα-βαθμός, οῦ, ὁ (βαίνω), *means of ascent, steps, stairs*, Ac. xxi. 35, 40.*

ἀνα-βαίνω, βήσομαι, 2 a. ἀνέβην, (1) *to ascend*, espec. to Jerusalem, Mat. xx. 17; on board ship, Mar. vi. 51; to heaven, Ro. x. 6; (2) *to spring up*, as plants, etc., used of a rumor, Ac. xxi. 31; of thoughts coming into mind, Lu. xxiv. 38.

ἀνα-βάλλω, mid., *to postpone, defer*, Ac. xxiv. 22.*

ἀνα-βιβάζω, *to draw up*, as a net to shore, Mat. xiii. 48.*

ἀνα-βλέπω, (1) *to look up*, as Mar. viii. 24; (2) *to look again, to recover sight*, as Mat. xi. 5.

ἀνά-βλεψις, εως, ἡ, *recovery of sight*, Lu. iv. 18.*

ἀνα-βοάω, ῶ, *to exclaim, cry aloud* (not in W. H.), Mat. xxvii. 46, Mar. xv. 8, Lu. ix. 38.*

ἀνα-βολή, ῆς, ἡ, *putting off, delay*, Ac. xxv. 17.*

ἀνάγαιον, ου, τό, *upper room*, W. H. in Mar. xiv. 15; Lu. xxii. 12, for Rec. ἀνώγεον.*

ἀν-αγγέλλω, *to announce, make known*, Ac. xiv. 27, xix. 18; *to report*, 2 Cor. vii. 7.

ἀνα-γεννάω, ῶ, *to beget again*, 1 Pet. i. 3, 23.*

ἀνα-γινώσκω, *to know again, to know well.* N. T., *to read*, Jn. xix. 20; 2 Cor. iii. 15.

ἀναγκάζω, άσω, *to force, to compel* by force or persuasion, Ac. xxvi. 11; 2 Cor. xii. 11.

ἀναγκαῖος, αία, αῖον, *necessary, fit*, Tit. iii. 14; Phil. i. 24; also *close* or *near*, as friends, Ac. x. 24.

ἀναγκαστῶς, adv., *necessarily* or *by constraint*, 1 Pet. v. 2.*

ἀνάγκη, ης, ἡ, (1) *necessity*, Philem. 14; 1 Cor. vii. 37; followed by inf. (with ἐστι understood), *there is need to*, Mat. xviii. 7; (2) *distress*, Lu. xxi. 23.

ἀνα-γνωρίζω, *to make known*, aor. pass., Ac. vii. 13 (Rec.).*

ἀνά-γνωσις, εως, ἡ, *reading*, Ac. xiii. 15; 2 Cor. iii. 14; 1 Tim. iv. 13.*

ἀν-άγω, *to bring, lead*, or *take up*, Lu. ii. 22; Ac. ix. 39; *to offer up*, as sacrifices, Ac. vii. 41; pass., *to put to sea, to set sail*, Lu. viii. 22; Ac. xiii. 13.

ἀνα-δείκνυμι, *to show*, as by uplifting, *to show plainly*, Ac. i. 24; *to appoint, announce*, Lu. x. 1.*

ἀνά-δειξις, εως, ἡ, *a showing* or *public announcing*, Lu. i. 80.*

ἀνα-δέχομαι, dep., *to receive* with a welcome, guests, Ac. xxviii. 7; promises, Heb. xi. 17.*

ἀνα-δίδωμι, *to give up, deliver*, as by messengers, Ac. xxiii. 33.*

ἀνα-ζάω, ῶ, *to live again, revive* (W. H. only in Ro. vii. 9, and doubtfully Lu. xv. 24).

ἀνα-ζητέω, ῶ, *to seek* with diligence, Lu. ii. 44, 45 (W. H.); Ac. xi. 25.*

ἀνα-ζώννυμι, *to gird* or *bind up*, as a loose dress is girded about the loins; mid. fig., 1 Pet. i. 13. (S.)*

ἀνα-ζωπυρέω, ῶ (πῦρ), *to rekindle* or *rouse up;* fig., 2 Tim. i. 6.*

ἀνα-θάλλω, *to thrive* or *flourish again*, Phil. iv. 10.*

ἀνά-θεμα, ατος, τό, *a person* or *thing accursed*, Gal. i. 8; 1 Cor. xvi. 22; *an execration* or *curse*, Ac. xxiii. 14. *Syn.*: ἀνάθημα is a thing *devoted in honor of God, consecrated;* ἀνάθεμα, simply a later form of ἀνάθημα, has come to mean *a thing devoted to destruction.*

ἀναθεματίζω, ίσω, *to bind* (one's self) *by a curse*, Ac. xxiii. 12, 14, 21; *to affirm with curses*, Mar. xiv. 71.*

ἀνα-θεωρέω, ῶ, *to look at attentively, to consider*, Ac. xvi. 23; Heb. xiii. 7.*

ἀνά-θημα, ατος, τό, *anything consecrated and laid by, a votive offering*, Lu. xxi. 5 (W. H.).* *Syn.*: see ἀνάθεμα.

ἀν-αιδεία, ας, ἡ, *shamelessness, impudence*, Lu. xi. 8.*

ἀναίρεσις, εως, ἡ, *a taking away. i.e.*, by a violent death, Ac. viii. 1, xxii. 20 (Rec.).*

ἀν-αίρεω, ῶ (see Gr. § 103, 1, Wi. § 15, Bu. 53), *to take away, to abolish*, Heb. x. 9; *to take off, to kill*, Mat. ii. 16; mid., *to take up*, Ac. vii. 21.

ἀν-αίτιος, ον, *guiltless*, Mat. xii. 5, 7.*

ἀνα-καθίζω, *to sit up* (properly trans. with ἑαυτόν under stood), Lu. vii. 15; Ac. ix. 40.*

ἀνα-καινίζω, *to renew, restore to a former condition*, Heb. vi. 6.*

ἀνα-καινόω, ῶ, *to renew, amend, to change* the life, 2 Cor. iv. 16; Col. iii. 10. (N. T.)*

ἀνα-καίνωσις, εως, ἡ, *a renewal* or *change* of heart and life, Ro. xii. 2: Tit. iii. 5. (N. T.)* *Syn.:* see Trench, § xviii.

ἀνα-καλύπτω, *to unveil, make manifest;* pass., 2 Cor. iii. 14, 18.*

ἀνα-κάμπτω, *to bend* or *turn back, return*, Heb. xi. 15.

ἀνά-κειμαι, dep., *to recline* at a meal, Mat. ix. 10; ὁ ἀνακείμενος, one who reclines at table, *a guest*, Mat. xxii. 10, 11 (W. H. omit in Mar. v. 40).

ἀνα-κεφαλαιόω, ῶ, *to gather together into one, to sum up under one head;* pass., Ro. xiii. 9; mid., Ep. i. 10.*

ἀνα-κλίνω, *to lay down* an infant, Lu. ii. 7; *to make to recline* at table, Mar. vi. 39; pass., *to recline*, as at a feast, like ἀνάκειμαι, Lu. xiii. 29.

ἀνα-κόπτω, *to check* (lit., *beat back*), Gal. v. 7 (W. H. ἐγκόπτω).*

ἀνα-κράζω, *to cry out, to shout aloud*, Mar. i. 23, vi. 49.

ἀνα-κρίνω, *to investigate, inquire, examine* (judicially), *to judge of.* Only in Lu., Ac., and 1 Cor.

ἀνά-κρισις, εως, ἡ, *judicial examination*, Ac. xxv. 26.*

ἀνα-κυλίω, *to roll back*, Mar. xvi. 4 (W. H. for ἀποκ-).*

ἀνα-κύπτω, *to raise one's self up*, Lu. xiii. 11; Jn. viii. 7, 10; fig., *to be elated*, Lu. xxi. 28.*

ἀνα-λαμβάνω, *to take up*, Ac. vii. 43; pass., of Christ's being taken up to heaven, Mar. xvi. 19.

ἀνά-ληψις (W. H. -λημψις), εως, ἡ, *a being taken up, i.e.*, into heaven, Lu. ix. 51.*

ἀν-αλίσκω, λώσω, *to consume, destroy*, Lu. ix. 54; Gal. v. 15; 2 Th. ii. 8 (not W. H.).*

ἀνα-λογία, ας, ἡ, *proportion, analogy*, Ro. xii. 6.*

ἀνα-λογίζομαι, *to think upon, consider attentively*, Heb. xii. 3.*

ἄν-αλος, ον, *without saltness, insipid*, Mar. ix. 50.*

ἀνά-λυσις, εως, ἡ, *a loosening* of a ship from her moorings, *departure*, 2 Tim. iv. 6.*

ἀνα-λύω, *to depart*, Phil. i. 23; *to return*, Lu. xii. 36.*

ἀν-αμάρτητος, ον, *without blame, faultless*, Jn. viii. 7 (W. H. omit).*

ἀνα-μένω, *to await*, 1 Th. i. 10.*

ἀνα-μιμνήσκω, *to remind, admonish*, two accs., or acc. and inf., 1 Cor. iv. 17; pass., *to remember, to call to mind*, gen. or acc., 2 Cor. vii. 15.

ἀνά-μνησις, εως, ἡ, *remembrance, a memorial*, Heb. x. 3.

ἀνα-νεόω, ῶ, *to renew;* mid., *to renew one's self, to be renewed*, Ep. iv. 23.*

ἀνα-νήφω, *to recover soberness*, 2 Tim. ii. 26.*

'Ανανίας, α, ὁ (from Heb.), *Ananias.* Three of the name are mentioned, Ac. v. 1–5, ix. 10, xxiii. 2.

ἀν-αντι-ρρήτος, ον, *indisputable, not to be contradicted*, Ac. xix. 36.*

ἀναντιρρήτως, adv., *without contradiction*, Ac. x. 29.*

ἀν-άξιος, ον, *unworthy, inadequate*, 1 Cor. vi. 2.*

ἀναξίως, adv., *unworthily, unbecomingly*, 1 Cor. xi. 27 (not in ver. 29, W. H.).*

ἀνά-παυσις, εως, ἡ, *rest, cessation from labor, refreshment*, Rev. iv. 8; Mat. xii. 43.

ἀνα-παύω, *to give rest* or *refreshment*, Mat. xi. 28; mid., *to take rest*, Mar. vi. 31 (W. H. read in Rev. xiv. 13, ἀναπαήσονται, 2 fut. pass.).

ἀνα-πείθω, σω, *to persuade*, in a bad sense, *seduce, mislead*, Ac. xviii. 13.*

ἀνα-πέμπω, *to remit, send back*, Lu. xxiii. 11.

ἀνα-πηδάω, *leap up* (W. H., in Mar. x. 50, for Rec. ἀνίστημι).*

ἀνά-πηρος, ον, *maimed, having lost a member*, Lu. xiv. 13, 21 (W. H. ἀνάπειρος).*

ἀνα-πίπτω, *to fall down, lie down*, Mat. xv. 35; N. T., *to recline* at table, Lu. xi. 37, xiv. 10.

ἀνα-πληρόω, ῶ, *to fill up*, 1 Th. ii. 16; *to fulfill*, as a prophecy, Mat. xiii. 14; *to perform*, as a precept, Gal. vi. 2; *to occupy* or *fill* a place, 1 Cor. xiv. 16; *to supply* a deficiency, Phil. ii. 30.

ἀν-απο-λόγητος, ου, adj., *inexcusable*, Ro. i. 20, ii. 1.*

ἀνα-πτύσσω, *to unroll*, as a volume, Lu. iv. 17 (not W. H.).*

ἀν-άπτω, *to kindle, set on fire*, Lu. xii. 49; Ac. xxviii. 2 (not W. H.); Ja. iii. 5.*

ἀν-αρίθμητος, ον, *innumerable*, Heb. xi. 12.*

ἀνα-σείω, *to stir up, move, instigate*, Mar. xv. 11; Lu. xxiii. 5.*

ἀνα-σκευάζω, *to pervert, unsettle, destroy*, Ac. xv. 24.*

ἀνα-σπάω, *to draw up*, Lu. xiv. 5; Ac. xi. 10.*

ἀνά-στασις, εως, ἡ, *a rising up*, as opposed to falling, Lu. ii. 34; *rising*, as from death or the grave, *resurrection, the future state*, Ro. i. 4, vi. 5.

ἀνα-στατόω, ῶ, *to unsettle, put in commotion*, Ac. xvii. 6, xxi. 38; Gal. v. 12.*

ἀνα-σταυρόω, ῶ, *to crucify afresh*, Heb. vi. 6.*

ἀνα-στενάζω, *to groan* or *sigh deeply*, Mar. viii. 12.*

ἀνα-στρέφω, *to turn up, overturn*, Jn. ii. 15; intrans., *to return*, Ac. v. 22; mid. (as Lat. *versari*), *to be* or *to live in* a place or state, *to move among, to pass one's time* or *be conversant with* persons; generally, *to conduct one's self*, 2 Cor. i. 12; 1 Tim. iii. 15.

ἀνα-στροφή, ῆς, ἡ, *behavior, manner of life*, Gal. i. 13; Ep. iv. 22.

ἀνα-τάσσομαι, *to arrange, compose* a narrative, Lu. i. 1.*

ἀνα-τέλλω, *to spring up* or *rise*, as the sun, a star, a cloud, Mat. xiii. 6; Lu. xii. 54; of the Messiah, Heb. vii. 14; trans., *to cause to rise*, Mat v. 45.

ἀνα-τίθημι, mid., *to set forth, declare*, Ac. xxv. 14; Gal. ii. 2.*

ἀνατολή, ῆς, ἡ, *the dawn, dayspring*, Lu. i. 78; generally, *the east*, where the sun rises, Mat. ii. 2, 9; sing. and plur., see Gr. § 240*a*.

ἀνα-τρέπω, *to subvert, overthrow,* 2 Tim. ii. 18; Tit. i. 11.*

ἀνα-τρέφω, *to nurse, bring up, educate,* Lu. iv. 16 (W. H. mrg.); Ac. vii. 20, 21, xxii. 3.*

ἀνα-φαίνω, mid., *to appear,* Lu. xix. 11; pass., *to be shown* a thing (acc.), Ac. xxi. 3 (W. H. read act., in sense *to come in sight of*).*

ἀνα-φέρω, οἴσω, *to bear* or *lead, to offer,* as sacrifice, Heb. vii. 27; *to bear,* as sin, 1 Pet. ii. 24.

ἀνα-φωνέω, ῶ, *to cry out aloud,* Lu. i. 42.*

ἀνά-χυσις, εως, ἡ, *a pouring out;* hence, *excess,* 1 Pet. iv. 4.*

ἀνα-χωρέω, ῶ, *to depart, withdraw,* Mat. ix. 24; Mar. iii. 7.

ἀνά-ψυξις, εως, ἡ, *a refreshing,* Ac. iii. 20.*

ἀνα-ψύχω, *to refresh, to revive,* 2 Tim. i. 16.*

ἀνδραποδιστής, οῦ, ὁ, *a man-stealer,* 1 Tim. i. 10.*

Ἀνδρέας, ου, ὁ, *Andrew,* Jn. i. 40.

ἀνδρίζω, ίσω, mid., *to act like a man, to be brave,* 1 Cor. xvi. 13.*

Ἀνδρόνικος, ου, ὁ, *Andronicus,* Ro. xvi. 7.*

ἀνδρό-φονος, ου, ὁ, *a man-slayer,* 1 Tim. i. 9.*

ἀν-έγκλητος, ον, *not open to accusation, unblamable,* 1 Cor. i. 8; Col. i. 22.

ἀν-εκ-διήγητος, ον, *not to be spoken, inexpressible,* 2 Cor. ix. 15. (N. T.)*

ἀν-εκ-λάλητος, *unspeakable,* 1 Pet. i. 8. (N. T.)*

ἀν-έκ-λειπτος, ον, *unfailing,* Lu. xii. 33.*

ἀνεκτός, ή, όν, *tolerable, supportable;* only in comp., Mat. x. 15, xi. 22, 24.

ἀν-ελεήμων, ον, *without compassion, cruel,* Ro. i. 31.*

ἀνεμίζω, *to agitate* or *drive with wind;* pass., Ja. i. 6. (N. T.)*

ἄνεμος, ου, ὁ, *the wind,* Mat. xi. 7; fig., applied to empty doctrines, Ep. iv. 14.

ἀν-ένδεκτος, ον (ἐνδέχομαι), adj., *impossible,* Lu. xvii. 1. (N. T.)*

ἀν-εξ-ερεύνητος (W. H. -ραύ-), ον, adj., *unsearchable,* Ro. xi. 33.*

ἀνεξί-κακος, ον, *patient of injury,* 2 Tim. ii. 24. (N. T.)*

ἀν-εξ-ιχνίαστος, ον, *that cannot be explored, incomprehensible,* Ro. xi. 33; Ep. iii. 8. (S.)*

ἀν-επ-αίσχυντος, ον, *having no cause to be ashamed,* 2 Tim. ii. 15.*

ἀν-επί-ληπτος (W. H. -λημπ-), ον, adj., *never caught doing wrong, irreproachable,* 1 Tim. iii. 2, v. 7, vi. 14.*

ἀν-έρχομαι, *to come* or *go up,* Jn. vi. 3; Gal. i. 17, 18.*

ἄνεσις, εως, ἡ (ἀνίημι), *relaxation, remission,* as from bonds, burden, etc., Ac. xxiv. 23; 2 Th. i. 7.

ἀν-ετάζω, *to examine judicially,* Ac. xxii. 24, 29. (S.)*

ἄνευ, adv. as prep., with gen., *without,* 1 Pet. iii. 1.

ἀν-εύθετος, ον, *inconvenient,* Ac. xxvii. 12. (N. T.)*

ἀν-ευρίσκω, *to find by searching for,* Lu. ii. 16; Ac. xxi. 4.*

ἀν-έχω, mid., *to bear with, forbear, have patience with, endure,* Mat. xvii. 17; Lu. ix. 41; gen. of pers. or thing.

ἀνεψιός, οῦ, ὁ, *a cousin,* Col. iv. 10.*

ἄνηθον, ου, τό, *anise, dill,* Mat. xxiii. 23.*

ἀνήκει, impers., *it is fit* or *proper;* part., τὸ ἀνῆκον, τὰ ἀνήκοντα, *the becoming,* Philem. 8.

ἀν-ήμερος, ον, adj., *not tame, fierce,* 2 Tim. iii. 3.*

ἀνήρ, ἀνδρός, ὁ, (1) *a man,* in sex and age (Lat. *vir*), Ac. viii. 12; hence, (2) *a husband,* Ro. vii. 2, 3; (3) *a person* generally, Lu. vii. 41; plur. voc., ἄνδρες, Sirs!; often in apposition with adjectives and nouns, as ἀνὴρ ἁμαρτωλός, ἀνὴρ προφήτης, Lu. v. 8, xxiv. 19.

ἀνθ-ίστημι, *to oppose, withstand, resist,* with dat., Ro. ix. 19, Mat. v. 39.

ἀνθ-ομολογέομαι, οῦμαι, *to confess, give thanks to,* dat., Lu. ii. 38.*

ἄνθος, ους, τό, *a flower,* Ja. i. 10, 11; 1 Pet. i. 24.*

ἀνθρακιά, ᾶς, ἡ, *a heap of burning coals,* Jn. xviii. 18, xxi. 9.*

ἄνθραξ, ακος, ὁ, *a coal,* Ro. xii. 20.*

ἀνθρωπ-άρεσκος, ον, *desirous of pleasing men,* Ep. vi. 6; Col. iii. 22. (S.)*

ἀνθρώπινος, ίνη, ινον, *human, belonging to man,* Ja. iii. 7; 1 Cor. x. 13.

ἀνθρωπο-κτόνος, ου, ὁ, ἡ, *a homicide, a manslayer,* Jn. viii. 44; 1 Jn. iii. 15.*

ἄνθρωπος, ου, ὁ, *a man, one of the human race* (Lat. *homo*). Like ἀνήρ, joined in apposition with substantives, as Mat. xviii. 23, xxi. 33.

ἀνθ-υπατεύω, *to be proconsul,* Ac. xviii. 12 (not W. H.).*

ἀνθ-ύπατος, ου, ὁ, *a proconsul,* Ac. xiii. 7, 8, 12.

ἀν-ίημι, *to unloose, let go,* Ac. xvi. 26, xxvii. 40; *to give up,* Ep. vi. 9; *to leave, neglect,* Heb. xiii. 5.*

ἀν-ίλεως, ων, *without mercy,* Ja. ii. 13 (W. H. read ἀνέλεος). (N. T.)*

ἄ-νιπτος, ον, adj., *unwashed,* Mat. xv. 20; Mar. vii. 2, 5 (Rec.).*

ἀν-ίστημι, *to raise up* one lying or dead, Ac. ix. 41; Jn. vi. 39, 40; intrans. (in 2 a., pf. and mid.), *to rise* from a recumbent posture, Mar. i. 35; *to rise again* from the dead, Lu. xvi. 31; aor. part., often combined with other verbs, as "rising (ἀναστάς) he went."

Ἄννα, ας, ἡ, *Anna,* Lu. ii. 36.*

Ἄννας, α, ὁ, *Annas,* Lu. iii. 2; Jn. xviii. 13, 24; Ac. iv. 6.*

ἀ-νόητος, ον, *foolish, thoughtless,* Ro. i. 14; 1 Tim. vi. 9.

ἄνοια, ας, ἡ, *folly, madness,* Lu. vi. 11; 2 Tim. iii. 9.*

ἀνοίγω, ξω, *to open,* Ac. v. 19, xii. 10, 14; intrans. in 2 perf., ἀνέῳγα, *to be open,* 2 Cor. vi. 11; 1 Cor. xvi. 9.

ἀν-οικο-δομέω, ῶ, *to build up again,* Ac. xv. 16.*

ἄνοιξις, εως, ἡ, *opening* (the act of), Ep. vi. 19.*

ἀ-νομία, ας, ἡ, *lawlessness, iniquity,* Mat. xxiii. 28; Tit. ii. 14; αἱ ἀνομίαι, *iniquities, evil deeds,* Ro. iv. 7. *Syn.:* see ἀγνόημα.

ἄ-νομος, ον, (1) *without law,* not subject to the law, used of Gentiles, 1 Cor. ix. 21; (2) *lawless;* as subst., *a male-*

factor; ὁ ἄνομος, *the lawless one*, 2 Th. ii. 8.

ἀνόμως, adv., *without law*, Ro. ii. 12.

ἀν-ορθόω, ῶ, *to make upright* or *straight again*, *to rebuild*, *make strong*, Lu. xiii. 13; Ac. xv. 16; Heb. xii. 12.*

ἀν-όσιος, ον, *unholy*, 1 Tim. i. 9; 2 Tim. iii. 2.*

ἀνοχή, ῆς, ἡ, *forbearance*, *toleration*, Ro. ii. 4, iii. 25.* *Syn.:* ὑπομονή is patience under trials, referring to *things;* μακροθυμία, patience under provocation, referring to *persons;* ἀνοχή is a forbearance *temporary* in its nature.

ἀντ-αγωνίζομαι, *to resist*, *strive against*, Heb. xii. 4.*

ἀντ-άλλαγμα, ατος, τό, *an equivalent*, *price*, Mat. xvi. 26; Mar. viii. 37.*

ἀντ-ανα-πληρόω, ῶ, *to fill up in turn*, Col. i. 24.*

ἀντ-απο-δίδωμι, *to recompense*, *requite*, Lu. xiv. 14; Ro. xii. 19.

ἀντ-από-δομα, ατος, τό, *a recompense*, *requital*, Lu. xiv. 12; Ro. xi. 9. (S.)*

ἀντ-από-δοσις, εως, ἡ, *a reward*, *recompense*, Col. iii. 24.*

ἀντ-απο-κρίνομαι, *to reply against*, *contradict*, Lu. xiv. 6; Ro. ix. 20.*

ἀντ-εῖπον (used as 2 aor. of ἀντιλέγω, see φημί), *to contradict*, *to gainsay*, Lu. xxi. 15; Ac. iv. 14.*

ἀντ-έχω, mid., *to hold fast*, *to adhere to* (gen.), Mat. vi. 24; Lu. xvi. 13; 1 Th. v. 14; Tit. i. 9.*

ἀντί, prep., gen., *instead of*, *for*. See Gr. §§ 291, 147*a*, Wi. §§ 47*a*, 52, 4, 3), Bu. 321.

ἀντι-βάλλω, *to throw in turn*, *exchange words*, Lu. xxiv. 17.*

ἀντι-δια-τίθημι, mid., *to set one's self against*, *oppose*, 2 Tim. ii. 25.*

ἀντί-δικος, ου, ὁ (orig. adj.), *an opponent at law*, Mat. v. 25; Lu. xii. 58, xviii. 3; *an adversary*, 1 Pet. v. 8.*

ἀντι-θεσις, εως, ἡ, *opposition*, 1 Tim. vi. 20.*

ἀντι-καθ-ίστημι, *to resist*, Heb. xii. 4.*

ἀντι-καλέω, *to call* or *invite in turn*, Lu. xiv. 12.*

ἀντί-κειμαι, *to oppose*, *resist* (dat.), Lu. xiii. 17, xxi. 15; ὁ ἀντικείμενος, *an adversary*, 1 Cor. xvi. 9; Phil. i. 28.

ἀντικρύ (W. H. ἄντικρυς), adv., *over against*, Ac. xx. 15.*

ἀντι-λαμβάνω, mid., *to take hold of*, *help*, *share in* (gen.), Lu. i. 54; Ac. xx. 35; 1 Tim. vi. 2.

ἀντι-λέγω, *to speak against*, *contradict* (dat.), Ac. xiii. 45; *to oppose*, *deny*, Jn. xix. 12.

ἀντί-ληψις (W. H. -λημψ-), εως, *help*, *ministration*, 1 Cor. xii. 28.*

ἀντι-λογία, ας, ἡ, *contradiction*, *contention*, *rebellion*, Heb. vi. 16, vii. 7, xii. 3; Ju. 11.*

ἀντι-λοιδορέω, *to revile* or *reproach again*, 1 Pet. ii. 23.*

ἀντί-λυτρον, ου, τό, *a ransom-price*, 1 Tim. ii. 16.*

ἀντι-μετρέω, ῶ, *to measure in return*, Mat. vii. 2 (not W. H.); Lu. vi. 38. (N. T.)*

ἀντι-μισθία, ας, ἡ, *recompense*, Ro. 1. 27; 2 Cor. vi. 13. (N. T.)*

Ἀντιόχεια, ας, ἡ, *Antioch*. Two places of the name are mentioned, Ac. xi. 26, xiii. 14.

Ἀντιοχεύς, έως, ὁ, *a citizen of Antioch*, Ac. vi. 5.*

ἀντι-παρ-έρχομαι, *to pass by opposite to*, Lu. x. 31, 32.*

Ἀντίπας, α, ὁ, *Antipas*, Rev. ii. 13.*

Ἀντιπατρίς, ίδος, ἡ, *Antipatris*, Ac. xxiii. 31.*

ἀντι-πέραν (W. H. ἀντίπερα), adv., *on the opposite side* or *shore*, Lu. viii. 26.*

ἀντι-πίπτω, *to fall against*, *resist*, Ac. vii. 51.*

ἀντι-στρατεύομαι, dep., *to make war against*, Ro. vii. 23.*

ἀντι-τάσσω, mid., *to set one's self against*, *resist* (dat.), Ro. xiii. 2; Ja. iv. 6, v. 6; 1 Pet. v. 5; Ac. xviii. 6.*

ἀντί-τυπος, ον, *like in pattern*, Heb. ix. 24; τὸ ἀντίτυπον, *corresponding in form*, as wax to the seal, *antitype*, 1 Pet. iii. 21.*

Ἀντι-χρίστος, ου, ὁ, *opposer of Christ*, *Antichrist*, 1 Jn. ii. 18, 22, iv. 3; 2 Jn. 7. (N. T.)*

ἀντλέω, ῶ, *to draw* from a vessel, Jn. ii. 8, 9, iv. 7, 15.*

ἄντλημα, ατος, τό, *a bucket*, Jn. iv. 11.*

ἀντ-οφθαλμέω, ῶ, *to look in the face;* so *to meet the wind*, Ac. xxvii. 15.*

ἄν-υδρος, ον, *without water*, *dry*. Mat. xii. 43; Lu. xi. 24.

ἀν-υπό-κριτος, ον, adj., *without hypocrisy*, *unfeigned*, Ro. xii. 9; 2 Cor. vi. 6. (Ap.)

ἀν-υπό-τακτος, ον, *not subject to rule*, of things, Heb. ii. 8; *unruly*, of persons, 1 Tim. i. 9; Tit. i. 6, 10.*

ἄνω, adv. (ἀνά), *up*, *above*, *upwards;* τὰ ἄνω, *heaven* or *heavenly things*, as Jn. viii. 23.

ἀνώγεον, ου, τό, *an upper chamber*. See ἀνάγαιον.*

ἄνωθεν, adv. (ἄνω), (1) of place, *from above*, as Jn. iii. 31, xix. 11; with prepp. ἀπό, ἐκ, *from the top*, as Mar. xv. 38; Jn. xix. 23; (2) of time, *from the first*, only Lu. i. 3; Ac. xxvi. 5. In Jn. iii. 4, 7, *again* (see Gal. iv. 9); or, perhaps here also, *from above*.

ἀνωτερικός, ή, όν, *upper*, *higher*, Ac. xix. 1.*

ἀνώτερος, α, ον (compar. of ἄνω; only neut. as adv.), *higher*, *to a higher place*, Lu. xiv. 10; *above*, *before*, Heb. x. 8.*

ἀν-ωφελής, ές, *unprofitable*, Tit iii. 9; Heb. vii. 18.*

ἀξίνη, ης, ἡ, *an axe*, Mat. iii 10; Lu. iii. 9.*

ἄξιος, ία, ιον, adj., *worthy*, *deserving of*, *suitable to* (gen.), Heb. xi. 38; Lu. xii. 48; Ac. xxvi. 20.

ἀξιόω, ῶ, *to deem worthy* (acc. and gen., or inf.), Lu. vii. 7; 2 Th. i. 11; *think fit*, Ac. xv. 38, xxviii. 22.

ἀξίως, adv., *worthily*, *suitably* (with gen.), Ro. xvi. 2; Phil. i. 27.

ἀ-όρατος, ον, *invisible*, *unseen*, Col. i. 16; 1 Tim. i. 17.

ἀπ-αγγέλλω, *to report*, *relate*, *make known*, *declare*, Ac. iv. 23; 1 Th. i. 9.

ἀπ-άγχω, mid., *to hang* or *strangle one's self*, Mat. xxvii. 5.*

ἀπ-άγω, *to lead*, *carry*, or *take away*, Lu. xiii. 15; *to lead away* to execution, Mat. xxvi. 57; Mar. xiv. 44, 53; *to lead* or *tend*, as a way, Mat. vii. 13, 14.

ἀ-παίδευτος, ον, adj., *uninstructed*, *ignorant*, 2 Tim. ii. 23.*

ἀπ-αίρω, *to take away;* in N.T. only 1 a. pass., Mat. ix. 15; Mar. ii. 20; Lu. v. 35.*

ἀπ-αιτέω, *to ask back, require, reclaim,* Lu. vi. 30, xii. 20.*

ἀπ-αλγέω, *to be past feeling,* Ep. iv. 19.*

ἀπ-αλλάσσω, pass., *to be removed from, to depart,* Ac. xix. 12; pass., *to be set free* (with ἀπό), Lu. xii. 58; *to deliver,* Heb. ii. 15.*

ἀπ-αλλοτριόω, *to estrange, alienate* (gen.), Ep. ii. 12, iv. 18; Col. i. 21.*

ἁπαλός, ή, όν, *tender,* as a shoot of a tree, Mat. xxiv. 32; Mar. xiii. 28.*

ἀπ-αντάω, ῶ, *to meet, to encounter* (dat.), Mar. xiv. 13.

ἀπ-άντησις, εως, ἡ, *a meeting, an encountering;* εἰς ἀπάντησιν (gen. or dat.), *to meet* any one, Ac. xxviii. 15.

ἅπαξ, adv., of time, *once,* 1 Th. ii. 18; *once for all,* Heb. vi. 4, x. 2.

ἀ-παρά-βατος, ον, *inviolable, unchangeable,* Heb. vii. 24.*

ἀ-παρα-σκεύαστος, ου, adj., *unprepared,* 2 Cor. ix. 4.*

ἀπ-αρνέομαι, οῦμαι, *to deny, disown,* Mat. xxvi. 34, 35; *to disregard,* Mar. viii. 34.

ἀπ-άρτι, adv., of time (see ἄρτι), *henceforth,* Rev. xiv. 13. (W. H. read ἀπ' ἄρτι.)*

ἀπ-αρτισμός, οῦ, ὁ, *completion,* Lu. xiv. 28.*

ἀπ-αρχή, ῆς, ἡ, *the first-fruits,* consecrated to God (see W H., 2 Th. ii. 13).

ἅ-πας, ασα, αν (like πᾶς, Gr. § 37), *all, all together, the whole.*

ἀπασπάζομαι, see ἀσπάζομαι. (N. T.)*

ἀπατάω, ῶ, ήσω, *to deceive, lead into error,* Ja. i. 26; Ep. v. 6; 1 Tim. ii. 14 (W. H. ἐξαπ-).* (The stronger form ἐξαπατάω is more freq.)

ἀπάτη, ης, ἡ, *deceit, deceitfulness,* Col. ii. 8; Heb. iii. 13.

ἀ-πάτωρ, ορος, ὁ, ἡ (πατήρ), *without father, i.e.,* in the genealogies, Heb. vii. 3.*

ἀπ-αύγασμα, ατος, τό, *reflected brightness,* Heb. i. 3.*

ἀπ-εῖδον (W H. ἀφεῖδον), 2 aor. of ἀφοράω, which see.

ἀ-πείθεια, ας, ἡ, *willful unbelief, obstinacy, disobedience,* Heb. iv. 6, 11.

ἀ-πειθέω ῶ, *to refuse belief, be disobedient,* Jn. iii. 36; Ro. ii. 8.

ἀ-πειθής, ές, *unbelieving, disobedient,* Lu. i. 17; 2 Tim. iii. 2.

ἀπειλέω, ῶ, ήσω, *to threaten, forbid by threatening,* Ac. iv. 17; 1 Pet. ii. 23.*

ἀπειλή, ῆς, ἡ, *a threatening, threat,* Ac. iv. 17 (W. H. omit), 29, ix. 1; Ep. vi. 9.*

ἄπ-ειμι (εἰμί, *to be*), *to be absent,* as 1 Cor. v. 3.

ἄπ-ειμι (εἶμι, *to go*), *to go away, to depart,* Ac. xvii. 10.*

ἀπ-εῖπον (see εἶπον), mid., *to renounce, disown,* 2 Cor. iv. 2.*

ἀ-πείραστος, ου, adj., *incapable of being tempted,* Ja. i. 13.*

ἄ-πειρος, ου, adj., *inexperienced, unskillful* in (gen.), Heb. v. 13.*

ἀπ-εκ-δέχομαι, *to wait for, expect earnestly* or *patiently,* Ro. viii. 19, 23, 25; Heb. ix. 28. (N. T.)

ἀπ-εκ-δύομαι, *to strip, divest, renounce,* Col. ii. 15, iii. 9.*

ἀπέκδυσις, εως, ἡ, *a putting* or *stripping off, renouncing,* Col. ii. 11. (N. T.)*

ἀπ-ελαύνω, *to drive away,* Ac. xviii. 16.*

ἀπ-ελεγμός, οῦ, ὁ (ἐλέγχω), *repudiation, censure, disrepute,* Ac. xix. 27. (N. T.)*

ἀπ-ελεύθερος, ου, ὁ, ἡ, *a freedman,* 1 Cor. vii. 22.*

Ἀπελλῆς, οῦ, ὁ, *Apelles,* Ro. xvi. 10.*

ἀπ-ελπίζω, σω, *to despair,* Lu. vi. 35; R. V. "never despairing" (see R. V. mrg.).*

ἀπ-έναντι, adv. (gen.), *over against, in the presence of, in opposition to.*

ἀ-πέραντος, ον (περαίνω), *interminable,* 1 Tim. i. 4.*

ἀ-περισπάστως, adv. (περισπάω), *without distraction,* 1 Cor. vii. 35.*

ἀ-περί-τμητος, ον, *uncircumcised;* fig., Ac. vii. 51. (S.)*

ἀπ-έρχομαι, *to go* or *come from* one place to another, *to go away, depart; to go apart; to go back, to return; to go forth,* as a rumor.

ἀπ-έχω, *to have in full,* Mat. vi. 2; *to be far* (abs., or ἀπό), Lu. vii. 6; impers., ἀπέχει, *it is enough,* Mar. xiv. 41; mid., *to abstain from* (gen., or ἀπό), 1 Th. iv. 3.

ἀπιστέω, ῶ, *to disbelieve* (dat.), Mar. xvi. 11; *to be unfaithful,* Ro. iii. 3.

ἀπιστία, ας, ἡ, *unbelief, distrust, a state of unbelief,* 1 Tim. i. 13; Heb. iii. 12, 19; *unfaithfulness,* Ro. iii. 3.

ἄ-πιστος, ον, *not believing, incredulous,* Jn. xx. 27; hence, *an unbeliever* or *infidel,* 2 Cor. iv. 4; *unfaithful,* Lu. xii. 46; Rev. xxi. 8; pass., *incredible,* only Ac. xxvi. 8.

ἁπλόος, οῦς, ῆ, οῦν, *simple, sound,* Mat. vi. 22; Lu. xi. 34.*

ἁπλότης, τητος, ἡ, *simplicity, sincerity, purity,* 2 Cor. i. 12; Col. iii. 22.

ἁπλῶς, adv., *simply, sincerely,* Ja. i. 5.*

ἀπό, prep. gen., *from.* See Gr. § 292, Wi. § 47 *b*, Bu. 321 sq.; and for the force of the prep. in composition, Gr. § 147 *a*, Wi. § 52, 4, Bu. 344.

ἀπο-βαίνω (for βαίνω, see Gr. § 94, I., 6 *d*; fut., -βήσομαι), *to go* or *come out of,* as from a ship, Lu. v. 2; Jn. xxi. 9; *to turn out, result,* Lu. xxi. 13; Phil. i. 19.*

ἀπο-βάλλω, *to throw away,* Mar. x. 50; Heb. x. 35.*

ἀπο-βλέπω, *to look away from* all besides; hence, *to look earnestly at* (εἰς), Heb. xi. 26.*

ἀπό-βλητος, ον, verbal adj., *to be thrown away, rejected,* 1 Tim. iv. 4.*

ἀπο-βολή, ῆς, ἡ, *a casting away. rejection, loss,* Ac. xxvii. 22; Ro. xi. 15.*

ἀπο-γίνομαι, *to die,* 1 Pet. ii. 24.*

ἀπο-γραφή, ῆς, ἡ, *a record, register, enrolment,* Lu. ii. 2; Ac. v. 37.*

ἀπο-γράφω, *to enrol, inscribe in a register,* Lu. ii. 1, 3, 5; Heb. xii. 23.*

ἀπο-δείκνυμι, *to show by proof, demonstrate, set forth,* Ac. ii. 22, xxv. 7; 1 Cor. iv. 9; 2 Th. ii. 4.*

ἀπό-δειξις, εως, ἡ, *demonstration, proof,* 1 Cor. ii. 4.*

ἀπο-δεκατόω, ῶ, (1) *to pay the tenth* or *tithe*, Mat. xxiii. 23; (2) *to levy tithes on*, acc., Heb. vii. 5. (S.)

ἀπό-δεκτος, ον, verbal adj., *acceptable*, 1 Tim. ii. 3, v. 4.*

ἀπο-δέχομαι, *to receive with pleasure, to welcome*, Ac. xviii. 27, xxviii. 30.

ἀπο-δημέω, ῶ, *to go from one's own people, to go into another country;* only in the parables of our Lord, as Mat. xxi. 33; Lu. xv. 13.

ἀπό-δημος, ον, *gone abroad, sojourning in another country* (R. V.), Mar. xiii. 34.*

ἀπο-δίδωμι, *to give from one's self, to deliver*, Mat. xxvii. 58; in mid., *to sell*, Ac. v. 8; *to pay off, discharge* what is due, Mat. v. 26; Lu. xvi. 2; *to restore*, Lu. iv. 20; *to requite, recompense*, Ro. ii. 6; Rev. xviii. 6.

ἀπο-δι-ορίζω, *to separate off, i.e.*, into parties, Ju. 19.*

ἀπο-δοκιμάζω, *to reject*, as disapproved or worthless, Mar. viii. 31; Heb. xii. 17.

ἀπο-δοχή, ῆς, ἡ, *acceptance, approbation*, 1 Tim. i. 15, iv. 9.*

ἀπό-θεσις, εως, ἡ, *a putting away*, 1 Pet. iii. 21; 2 Pet. i. 14.*

ἀπο-θήκη, ης, ἡ, *a repository, granary, storehouse*, Mat. iii. 12; Lu. iii. 17.

ἀπο-θησαυρίζω, *to treasure up, lay by in store*, 1 Tim. vi. 19.*

ἀπο-θλίβω, *to press closely*, Lu. viii. 45.*

ἀπο-θνήσκω (ἀπό, intensive; the simple θνήσκω is rare), *to die*, (1) of natural death, human, animal, or vegetable, Mat. ix. 24; (2) of spiritual death, Ro. vii. 10; Rev. iii. 2; (3) in Epp. of Paul, *to die to* (dat.), as Ro. vi. 2; also in other shades of meaning. For tenses see θνήσκω.

ἀπο-καθ-ίστημι, ἀποκαταστήσω (also -καθιστάω and -άνω, see Mar. ix. 12; Ac. i. 6), *to restore, e.g.*, to health, or as a state or kingdom, Lu. vi. 10, Ac. i. 6.

ἀπο-καλύπτω, *to uncover, bring to light, reveal*, Mat. x. 26; Lu. x. 21; 1 Cor. ii. 10. See Thayer, p. 62.

ἀπο-κάλυψις, εως, ἡ, *revelation, manifestation, enlightenment*, 1 Cor. xiv. 26; Ep. iii. 3; 2 Th. i. 7. (S.) *Syn.:* see Trench, § xciv.

ἀπο-καρα-δοκία, ας, ἡ (κάρα, *head;* ἀπό, intensive), *earnest expectation*, as if looking for with the head outstretched, Ro. viii. 19; Phil. i. 20.*

ἀπο-κατ-αλλάσσω, *to reconcile, change from one state of feeling to another*, Ep. ii. 16; Col. i. 20, 22. (N. T.)*

ἀπο-κατά-στασις, εως, ἡ, *restitution, restoration*, Ac. iii. 21.*

ἀπό-κειμαι, *to be laid away, to be reserved for* (dat.), Lu. xix. 20; Col. i. 5; 2 Tim. iv. 8; Heb. ix. 27.*

ἀπο-κεφαλίζω (κεφαλή), *to behead*, Mat. xiv. 10; Mar. vi. 16, 27; Lu. ix. 9. (S.)*

ἀπο-κλείω, *to shut close*, as a door, Lu. xiii. 25.*

ἀπο-κόπτω, *to smite* or *cut off*, Mar. ix. 43, 45; Jn. xviii 10, 26; Ac. xxvii. 32; mid., Gal. v. 12 (see R. V.).*

ἀπό-κριμα, ατος, τό, *an answer*, 2 Cor. i. 9.*

ἀπο-κρίνομαι (for aor., see Gr. § 100, Wi. § 39, 2), *to answer*, Mar. xii. 28; Col. iv. 6; often used (like the corresponding Hebrew verb) where the "answer" is not to a distinct question, but to some suggestion of the accompanying circumstances; so especially in the phrase ἀποκριθεὶς εἶπεν, *answered and said*, as Mat. xi. 25; Lu. i. 60.

ἀπό-κρισις, εως, ἡ, *an answer, reply*, Lu. ii. 47.

ἀπο-κρύπτω, *to hide, conceal*, 1 Cor. ii. 7; Ep. iii. 9.

ἀπό-κρυφος, ον, *hidden, concealed*, Mar. iv. 22; Lu. viii. 17; *stored up*, Col. ii. 3.

ἀπο-κτείνω, ενῶ, *to put to death, kill*, Mat. xvi. 21; Rev. ii. 13; fig., *to abolish*, Ep. ii. 16.

ἀπο-κυέω, ῶ, *to bring forth;* fig., Ja. i. 15, 18.*

ἀπο-κυλίω, ίσω, *to roll away*, Mat. xxviii. 2; Mar. xvi. 3; Lu. xxiv. 2. (S.)*

ἀπο-λαμβάνω, *to receive from* any one, Gal. iv. 5· *to receive back, recover*, Lu. xv. 27; mid., *to take aside* with one's self, Mar. vii. 33.

ἀπό-λαυσις, εως, ἡ (λαύω, *to enjoy*), *enjoyment*, 1 Tim. vi. 17; Heb. xi. 25.*

ἀπο-λείπω, *to leave, to leave behind*, 2 Tim. iv. 13, 20; *to desert*, Ju. 6; pass., *to be reserved*, Heb. iv. 9.

ἀπο-λείχω, *to lick*, as a dog, Lu. xvi. 21 (W. H. ἐπιλείχω).*

ἀπ-όλλυμι (see Gr. § 116, 2, Wi. § 15, Bu. 64), *to destroy, to bring to nought, to put to death*, Mar. i. 24; Ro. xiv. 15; *to lose*, Mat. x. 42; Jn. vi. 39; mid., pass. (and 2d perf.), *to perish, die*, Mat. viii. 25; *to be lost*, Lu. xxi. 18.

Ἀπολλύων, οντος, ὁ (prop. part of ἀπολλύω, *Destroyer*), *Apollyon*, Rev. ix. 11. (N. T.)*

Ἀπολλωνία, ας, ἡ, *Apollonia*, a city of Macedonia, Ac. xvii. 1.*

Ἀπολλώς, ώ, ὁ, *Apollos*, Ac. xviii. 24.

ἀπο-λογέομαι, οῦμαι (λόγος), *to defend one's self by speech*, Lu. xxi. 14; Ac. xxvi. 24; *to defend, excuse*, Ro. ii. 15.

ἀπο-λογία, ας, ἡ, *a verbal defense*, "apology," Ac. xxv. 16; 1 Cor. ix. 3.

ἀπο-λούω, mid., *to wash away*, as sins, Ac. xxii. 16; 1 Cor. vi. 11.*

ἀπο-λύτρωσις, εως, ἡ, *redemption, deliverance*, Ro. iii. 24; Heb. ix. 15, xi. 35. *Syn.:* see Trench, § lxxvii.

ἀπο-λύω, *to release, let go, to send away*, Ac. xxviii. 18; Mat. xv. 23; spec., *to put away* a wife, *divorce*, Mat. i. 19; Lu. xvi. 18; mid., *to depart*, Ac. xxviii. 25.

ἀπο-μάσσω, ξω, *to wipe off*, as dust from the feet; mid., Lu. x. 11.*

ἀπο-νέμω, *to assign to, apportion*, 1 Pet. iii. 7.*

ἀπο-νίπτω, mid., *to wash one's self*, Mat. xxvii. 24.*

ἀπο-πίπτω, *to fall from*, Ac. ix. 18.*

ἀπο-πλανάω, ῶ, *to lead astray*, Mar. xiii. 22; 1 Tim. vi. 10.*

ἀπο-πλέω, εύσω, *to sail away*, Ac. xiii. 4, xiv. 26, xx. 15, xxvii. 1.*

ἀπο-πλύνω, *to wash* or *rinse*, as nets, Lu. v. 2 (W. H. πλύνω).*

ἀπο-πνίγω, *to suffocate, choke*, Mat. xiii. 7; Lu. viii. 7, 33.*

ἀ-πορέω, ῶ (πόρος, *resource*), except Mar. vi. 20 (W. H.), only mid. in N. T., *to be in doubt, to be perplexed*, Jn. xiii. 22; 2 Cor. iv. 8.

ἀπορία, ας, ἡ, *perplexity, disquiet*, Lu. xxi. 25.*

ἀπο-ρρίπτω, *to throw* or *cast down* or *off*, Ac. xxvii. 43; ἑαυτούς understood.*

ἀπ-ορφανίζω (ὀρφανος), "to make orphans of"; *to bereave*, pass., 1 Th. ii. 17.*

ἀπο-σκευάζομαι, *to pack away, pack up*, Ac. xxi. 15 (W. H. ἐπισκευάζομαι).*

ἀπο-σκίασμα, ατος, τό (σκιάζω), *a shade, a shadow*, Ja. i. 17. (N. T.)*

ἀπο-σπάω, ῶ, άσω, *to draw out, unsheathe*, Mat. xxvi. 51; *to withdraw, to draw away*, Ac. xxi. 1.

ἀπο-στασία, ας, ἡ, *defection, apostasy*, Ac. xxi. 21; 2 Th. ii. 3.*

ἀπο-στάσιον, ου, τό, *repudiation, divorce*, Mat. xix. 7; Mar. x. 4; met., *bill of divorce*, as Mat. v. 31.*

ἀπο-στεγάζω (στέγη), *to unroof*, Mar. ii. 4.*

ἀπο-στέλλω, *to send forth, send*, as a messenger, commission, etc., spoken of prophets, teachers, and other messengers, Mat. x. 40, Lu. vii. 3; Ac. x. 36; *to send away, dismiss*, Lu. iv. 18; Mar. v. 10, viii. 26.

ἀπο-στερέω, ῶ, ήσω, *to defraud*, abs., as Mar. x. 19; *deprive of* by fraud, acc. and gen., 1 Tim. vi. 5.

ἀπο-στολή, ῆς, ἡ, *apostleship*, Ac. i. 25; Ro. i. 5; 1 Cor. ix. 2; Gal. ii. 8.*

ἀπό-στολος, ου, ὁ, (1) *a messenger*, 2 Cor. viii. 23; Heb. iii. 1; (2) *an apostle, i.e.*, a messenger of Christ to the world, Lu. vi. 13; Gal. i. 1; used of others besides Paul and the Twelve, Ac. xiv. 14; 1 Th. ii. 6; 2 Cor. viii. 23.

ἀπο-στοματίζω (στόμα), *to entice to speak off-hand*, Lu. xi. 53.*

ἀπο-στρέφω, *to turn away*, trans. (with ἀπό, as Ac. iii. 26); *restore, replace*, Mat. xxvi. 52; mid., *to desert, reject*, acc., Mat. v. 42.

ἀπο-στυγέω, ῶ, *to detest, to abhor*, Ro. xii. 9.*

ἀπο-συνάγωγος, ον, *excluded from the synagogue, excommunicated*, Jn. ix. 22, xii. 42, xvi. 2. (N. T.)*

ἀπο-τάσσω, ξω, mid., *to separate one's self from, withdraw from* (dat.), Mar. vi. 46; *to take leave of, renounce, send away* (dat.), Lu. xiv. 33.

ἀπο-τελέω, ῶ, έσω, *to perfect*, Ja. i. 15; Lu. xiii. 32 (W. H.).*

ἀπο-τίθημι, mid., *to lay off* or *aside*, Ac. vii. 58; *to renounce*, Ro. xiii. 12.

ἀπο-τίνασσω, *to shake off*, Lu. ix. 5; Ac. xxviii. 5.*

ἀπο-τίνω (or -τίω), τίσω, *to repay*, Philem. 19.*

ἀπο-τολμάω, ῶ, *to assume boldness*, Ro. x. 20.*

ἀπο-τομία, ας, ἡ (τέμνω, *to cut*), *severity*, Ro. xi. 22.*

ἀπο-τόμως, adv., *severely, sharply*, 2 Cor. xiii. 10; Tit. i. 13.*

ἀπο-τρέπω, mid., *to turn away from, shun*, acc., 2 Tim. iii. 5.*

ἀπ-ουσία, ας (ἄπειμι), *absence*, Phil. ii. 12.*

ἀπο-φέρω, *to bear away* from one place to another, Mar. xv. 1; Rev. xvii. 3.

ἀπο-φεύγω, *to escape*, 2 Pet. i. 4, ii. 18, 20.*

ἀπο-φθέγγομαι, *to speak out, declare*, Ac. ii. 4, 14, xxvi. 25. (S.)*

ἀπο-φορτίζομαι (φόρτος, *a burden*), *to unload, discharge*, Ac. xxi. 3.*

ἀπό-χρησις, εως, ἡ (ἀπό, intens.), *abuse, misuse*, Col. ii. 22.*

ἀπο-χωρέω, ῶ, *to go away, depart*, Mat. vii. 23; Lu. ix. 39; Ac. xiii. 13.*

ἀπο-χωρίζω, *to part asunder*, Ac. xv. 39; Rev. vi. 14.*

ἀπο-ψύχω, *to breathe out life, to faint*, Lu. xxi. 26.*

Ἄππιος, ου, ὁ, *Appius*; Ἀππίου φόρον, *the Forum of Appius*, a town in Italy, situated on the Appian Way, Ac. xxviii. 15.*

ἀ-πρόσ-ιτος, ον (προς, εἶμι), *not to be approached*, 1 Tim. vi. 16.*

ἀ-πρόσ-κοπος, ον (κόπτω), act., *not causing to stumble*, 1 Cor. x. 32; pass., *not caused to stumble, blameless, without offense*, Ac. xxiv. 16; Phil. i. 10. (Ap.)*

ἀ-προσωπο-λήπτως (W. H. -λήμπτ-), adv., *without respect of persons, impartially*, 1 Pet. i. 17. (N. T.)*

ἄ-πταιστος, ον (πταίω, *to fall*), *without stumbling* or *falling*, Ju. 24.*

ἅπτω, ψω, *to kindle*, as light or fire, Lu. viii. 16, xi. 33; mid., *to touch*, Mat viii. 3; 1 Cor. vii. 1. *Syn.*: ἅπτομαι is to touch or handle; θιγγάνω, a lighter touch; ψηλαφάω, to feel or feel after.

Ἀπφία, ας, ἡ, *Apphia*, Philem. 2.*

ἀπ-ωθέω, ῶ, ἀπώσω, mid., *to repulse, to reject*, Ac. vii. 27, 39.

ἀπώλεια, ας, ἡ (ἀπόλλυμι), *destroying, waste*, of things, Ro. ix. 22; Mar. xiv. 4; *destruction*, in general, Ac. viii. 20; *perdition*, 2 Th. ii. 3; Rev. xvii. 8, 11.

ἀρά, ᾶς, ἡ, *curse, imprecation*, Ro. iii. 14.*

ἄρα, conj., illative, *therefore, thence, since*. See Gr. § 406, Wi. § 53, 8, Bu. 371.

ἆρα, adv. interrogative, usually where the answer is negative, Lu. xviii. 8; Ac. viii. 30; Gal. ii. 17.*

Ἀραβία, ας, ἡ, *Arabia*, Gal. i. 17, iv. 25.*

Ἀράμ, ὁ (Heb.), *Aram*, Mat. i. 3, 4; Lu. iii. 33 (not W. H.).*

Ἄραψ, αβος, ὁ, *an Arabian*, Ac. ii. 11.*

ἀργέω, ῶ, *to linger, to delay*, 2 Pet. ii. 3.*

ἀργός, όν (ἀ, ἔργον), *idle, lazy*, Mat. xx. 3; Tit. i. 12.

ἀργύρεος, οῦς, ᾶ, οῦν, *made of silver*, Ac. xix. 24; 2 Tim. ii. 20; Rev. ix. 20.*

ἀργύριον, ου, τό, *silver*, Ac. iii. 6; *a piece of silver, a shekel*, Mat. xvi. 15; *money* in general, Mar. xiv. 11.

ἀργυρο-κόπος, ου, ὁ, *a silversmith*, Ac. xix. 24.*

ἄργυρος, ου, ὁ, *silver*, Ac. xvii. 29; Ja. v. 3.

Ἄρειος πάγος, ου, ὁ, *Areopagus*, or *Mars' Hill*, an open space on a hill in Athens, where the supreme court was held, Ac. xvii. 19, 22.* (῎Αρειος is an adj. from ῎Αρης, *Mars.*)

Ἀρεοπαγίτης, ου, ὁ, *a judge of the Areopagite court,* Ac. xvii. 34.*

ἀρέσκεια, ας, ἡ, *a pleasing, a desire of pleasing,* Col. i. 10.*

ἀρέσκω, ἀρέσω, *to be pleasing to,* Mat. xiv. 6; Gal. i. 10; *to seek to please* or *gratify, to accommodate one's self to* (dat.), 1 Cor. x. 33; 1 Th. ii. 4.

ἀρεστός, ή, όν, *acceptable, pleasing to,* Jn. viii. 29; Ac. xii. 3.

Ἀρέτας, α, ὁ, *Aretas,* a king of Arabia Petræa, 2 Cor. xi. 32.*

ἀρετή, ῆς, ἡ, *virtue,* 2 Pet. i. 5; *any moral excellence, perfection,* Phil. iv. 8; 1 Pet. ii. 9; 2 Pet. i. 3.*

(ἄρην), gen. ἀρνός, *a lamb,* Lu. x. 3.*

ἀριθμέω, ῶ, *to number,* Mat. x. 30; Lu. xii. 7; Rev. vii. 9.*

ἀριθμός, οῦ, ὁ, *a number,* Jn. vi. 10; Ac. vi. 7.

Ἀριμαθαία, ας, ἡ, *Arimathæa,* a city of Palestine, Mat. xxvii. 57; Mar. xv. 43.

Ἀρίσταρχος, ου, ὁ, *Aristarchus,* Ac. xix. 29; Col. iv. 10.

ἀριστάω, ῶ, ήσω (ἄριστον), *to breakfast,* Jn. xxi. 12, 15; *to dine,* Lu xi. 37.

ἀριστερός, ά, όν, *left;* ἡ ἀριστερά (χείρ), *the left hand,* Mat. vi. 3; ἐξ ἀριστερῶν, *on the left,* Mar. x. 37 (W. H.); Lu. xxiii. 33, without ἐξ; 2 Cor. vi. 7. (The more common word is εὐώνυμος.)*

Ἀριστόβουλος, ου, ὁ, *Aristobulus,* Ro. xvi. 10.*

ἄριστον, ου, τό, *dinner,* Mat. xxii. 4; Lu. xi. 38, xiv. 12.* See δεῖπνον.

ἀρκετός, ή, όν, *sufficient,* Mat. vi. 34, x. 25; 1 Pet. iv. 3.*

ἀρκέω, ῶ, *to be sufficient for,* Mat. xxv. 9; 2 Cor. xii. 9; pass., *to be satisfied with,* Lu. iii. 14; Heb. xiii. 5.

ἄρκτος (W. H. ἄρκος), ου, ὁ, ἡ, *a bear,* Rev. xiii. 2.*

ἅρμα, ατος, τό, *a chariot,* Ac. viii. 28, 29, 38; Rev. ix. 9.*

Ἁρμαγεδδών (Heb. or Aram., der. disputed), (W. H. ῞Αρ Μαγεδών), *Harmageddon,* **Rev. xvi. 16. (N. T.)***

ἁρμόζω, σω, *to fit together;* mid., *to espouse, to betroth,* 2 Cor. xi. 2.*

ἁρμός, οῦ, ὁ, *a joint, i.e.,* of limbs in a body, Heb. iv. 12.*

ἀρνέομαι, οῦμαι, *to deny,* Mat. xxvi. 70; Jn. i. 20; 2 Tim. ii. 12; *to renounce,* Tit. ii. 12; *to reject,* Ac. iii. 14.*

ἀρνίον, ου, τό (dimin. of ἀρήν), *a little lamb,* Jn. xxi. 15; freq. in Rev., of Christ.

ἀροτριάω, ῶ, άσω, *to plow,* Lu. xvii. 7; 1 Cor. ix. 10.*

ἄροτρον, ου, τό, *a plow,* Lu. ix. 62.*

ἁρπαγή, ῆς, ἡ (ἁρπάζω), *the act of plundering,* Heb. x. 34; *plunder, spoil,* Mat. xxiii. 25; Lu. xi. 39.*

ἁρπαγμός, οῦ, ὁ, *spoil, an object of eager desire, a prize,* Phil. ii. 6.*

ἁρπάζω, άσω (2 aor. pass., ἡρπάγην), *to snatch, seize violently, take by force,* Jn. x. 12; *to carry off suddenly,* Jn. vi. 15; Ac. xxiii. 10.

ἅρπαξ, αγος, adj., *rapacious, ravenous,* Mat. vii. 15; Lu. xviii. 11; *a robber, an extortioner,* 1 Cor. v. 10, 11, vi. 10.*

ἀρραβών, ῶνος, ὁ (from Heb.), *a pledge, an earnest,* ratifying a contract, 2 Cor. i. 22, v. 5; Ep. i. 14.*

ἄρραφος (W. H. ἄραφος), ον, *not seamed* or *sewn,* Jn. xix. 23. (N. T.)*

ἄρρην, εν (W. H. ἄρσην, εν), *of the male sex,* Ro. i. 27; Rev. xii. 5, 13.*

ἄρρητος, ον, adj., *unspoken, unspeakable,* 2 Cor. xii. 4.*

ἄρρωστος, ον, adj. (ῥώννυμι), *infirm, sick,* Mat. xiv. 14; 1 Cor. xi. 30.

ἀρσενο-κοίτης, ου, ὁ (ἄρσην κοίτη), *a sodomite,* 1 Cor. vi. 9; 1 Tim. i. 10.*

ἄρσην, εν, *male,* Mat. xix. 4; Gal. iii. 28.

Ἀρτεμᾶς, ᾶ, ὁ, *Artemas,* Tit. iii. 12.*

῎Αρτεμις, ιδος or ιος, ἡ, *Artemis,* the Persian or Ephesian Artemis, to be distinguished from the Artemis of the Greeks, the sister of Apollo, Ac. xix. 24, 27, 28, 34, 35.*

ἀρτέμων, ονος, ὁ (ἀρτάω, *to suspend*), prob. *the foresail,* Ac. xxvii. 40.*

ἄρτι, adv. of time, *now, just now, at this moment;* with other particles, as ἕως ἄρτι, *till now;* ἀπ' ἄρτι, *from now* or *henceforward.*

ἀρτι-γέννητος, ον, *newly* or *recently born,* 1 Pet. ii. 2. (N. T.)*

ἄρτιος, ου, adj., *perfect, complete,* wanting in nothing, 2 Tim. iii. 17.* *Syn.:* ἄρτιος means fully adapted for its purpose; ὁλόκληρος, entire, having lost nothing; τέλειος, fully developed, complete.

ἄρτος, ου, ὁ, *bread, loaf, food;* fig., *spiritual nutriment;* ἄρτοι τῆς προθέσεως, *show-bread,* Mat. xii. 4; Mar. ii. 26.

ἀρτύω (ἄρω, *to fit*), *to season, to flavor,* as with salt, Mar. ix. 50; Lu. xiv. 34; fig., Col. iv. 6.*

Ἀρφαξάδ, ὁ (Heb.), *Arphaxad,* Lu. iii. 36.*

ἀρχ-άγγελος, ου, ὁ, *an arch-* or *chief-angel,* 1 Th. iv. 16; Ju. 9. (N. T.)*

ἀρχαῖος, α, ον, *old, ancient,* Lu. ix. 8, 19; 2 Pet. ii. 5.

Ἀρχέλαος, ου, ὁ, *Archelaus,* Mat. ii. 22.*

ἀρχή, ῆς, ἡ, (1) *a beginning,* of time, space, or series, Jn. i. 1; 2 Pet. iii. 4; *the outermost point,* Ac. x. 11. Used of Christ, *the leader,* Col. i. 18; Rev. iii. 14, xxi. 6, xxii. 13. Adv. phrases: ἀπ' ἀρχῆς, *from the beginning;* ἐν ἀρχῇ, *in the beginning;* ἐξ ἀρχῆς, *from the beginning* or *from the first;* κατ' ἀρχάς, *at the beginning;* τὴν ἀρχήν, *originally.* (2) *rule, preeminence, principality* (see ἄρχω): espec. in pl., ἀρχαι, *rulers, magistrates,* as Lu. xii. 11; of supramundane powers, *principalities,* as Ep. iii. 10.

ἀρχ-ηγός, οῦ, ὁ (ἀρχή, ἄγω), *the beginner, author, prince,* Ac. iii. 15, v. 31; Heb. ii. 10, xii. 2.*

ἀρχ-ιερατικός, ή, όν, *belonging to the office of the high-priest, pontifical,* Ac. iv. 6.*

ἀρχ-ιερεύς, έως, ὁ, (1) *the high-priest,* Mat. xxvi. 3; Heb. ix. 7, 25; so of Christ only in

Heb., as ii. 17, iii. 1, etc.; (2) in pl. used more widely to include high-priestly families and deposed high-priests, Mat. ii. 4; Lu. xix. 47; Ac. iv. 23.

ἀρχι-ποίμην, *ενος*, ὁ, *the chief shepherd*, a title of Christ, 1 Pet. v. 4. (N. T.)*

Ἄρχιππος, *ου*, ὁ, *Archippus*, Col. iv. 17; Philem. 2.*

ἀρχι-συνάγωγος, *ου*, ὁ, *presiding officer* or *ruler of a synagogue* Lu. viii. 49; Ac. xiii. 15.

ἀρχι-τέκτων, *ονος*, ὁ, *a master-builder, an architect*, 1 Cor. iii. 10.*

ἀρχι-τελώνης, *ου*, ὁ, *a chief collector of taxes, a chief publican*, Lu. xix. 2. (N. T.)*

ἀρχι-τρίκλινος, *ου*, ὁ, *a superintendent of a dining room*, Jn. ii. 8, 9. (N. T.)*

ἄρχω, *to reign, to rule* (gen.), only Mar. x. 42; Ro. xv. 12; mid., *to begin*, often with infin.; *ἀρξάμενος ἀπό*, *beginning from* (see Gr. § 287).

ἄρχων, *οντος*, ὁ, prop. particip., *ruler, prince, leader*, Ac. xvi. 19; Ro. xiii. 3.

ἄρωμα, *ατος*, *τό*, *spice, perfume*, Mar. xvi. 1; Lu. xxiii. 56, xxiv. 1; Jn. xix. 40.*

Ἀσά, ὁ (Heb.), *Asa*, Mat. i. 7, 8.*

ἀ-σάλευτος, *ον*, *unshaken, immovable*, Ac. xxvii. 41; Heb. xii. 28.*

ἄ-σβεστος, *ον*, adj. (*σβέννυμι*), *not to be quenched, inextinguishable*, Mat. iii. 12; Lu. iii. 17; Mar. ix. 43, 45 (W. H. omit).*

ἀσέβεια, *ας*, ἡ, *impiety, ungodliness, wickedness*, Ro. i. 18; Ju. 15, 18. *Syn.*: see *ἀγνόημα*.

ἀσεβέω, *ῶ*, *ήσω*, *to be ungodly, act impiously*, 2 Pet. ii. 6; Ju. 15.*

ἀ-σεβής, *ές* (*σέβομαι*), *impious, ungodly, wicked*, Ro. iv. 5; Ju. 4, 15.

ἀ-σέλγεια, *ας*, ἡ, *excess, wantonness, lasciviousness*, Mar. vii. 22; Ep. iv. 19.

ἄ-σημος, *ον*, *not remarkable, obscure, ignoble*, Ac. xxi. 39.*

Ἀσήρ, ὁ, *Asher*, Lu. ii. 36; Rev. vii. 6.*

ἀσθένεια, *ας*, ἡ, *weakness, bodily infirmity, sickness*, 1 Cor. xv. 43; Heb. xi. 34; fig., *mental weakness, distress*, Ro. vi. 19; Heb. v. 2.

ἀσθενέω, *ῶ*, *to be weak*, Ro. viii. 3; 2 Cor. xiii. 4; *to be sick*, Lu. iv. 40; Ac. ix. 37.

ἀσθένημα, *ατος*, *τό*, *weakness, infirmity*; fig., Ro. xv. 1.*

ἀ-σθενής, *ές* (*σθένος*, *strength*), "without strength," *weak, infirm*, Mat. xxvi. 41; Ro. v. 6; 1 Cor. iv. 10; *sick*, Lu. x. 9; Ac. iv. 9; 1 Cor. xi. 30.

Ἀσία, *ας*, ἡ, *Asia proper* or *Proconsular Asia*, a district in the west of Asia Minor, Ac. vi. 9; 1 Pet. i. 1; Rev. i. 4; *a part of Proconsular Asia*, Ac. ii. 9.

Ἀσιανός, *οῦ*, ὁ, *belonging to Asia*, Ac. xx. 4.*

Ἀσιάρχης, *ου*, ὁ, *an Asiarch, a president of Asia*, a citizen appointed annually to preside over the worship and celebrations in honor of the gods, Ac. xix. 31.*

ἀσιτία, *ας*, ἡ (*σῖτος*, *corn*), *abstinence, a fast*, Ac. xxvii. 21.*

ἄ-σιτος, *ον*, *fasting*, Ac. xxvii. 33.*

ἀσκέω, *ῶ*, *ήσω*, *to exercise one's self, use diligence in*, Ac. xxiv. 16.*

ἀσκός, *οῦ*, ὁ, *a bottle* of skin, Mat. ix. 17; Mar. ii. 22; Lu. v. 37, 38.*

ἀσμένως, adv. (from part. of *ἥδομαι*), *with joy, gladly*, Ac. ii. 41 (W. H. omit); Ac. xxi. 17.*

ἄ-σοφος, *ον*, *not wise*, Ep. v. 15.*

ἀσπάζομαι, dep., *to embrace, salute, to greet* (actually or by letter), Mat. x. 2; 1 Cor. xvi. 19, 20; always of persons, except Heb. xi. 13, "having embraced (R. V. greeted) the promises"; *to take leave of* (only Ac. xx. 1; in xxi. 6, W. H. read *ἀπασπάζομαι*).

ἀσπασμός, *οῦ*, ὁ, *salutation, greeting*, Mat. xxiii. 7; Col. iv. 18.

ἄ-σπιλος, *ον* (*σπῖλος*), *without spot, unblemished*, 1 Tim. vi. 14; 1 Pet. i. 19.

ἀσπίς, *ίδος*, ἡ, *an asp, a venomous serpent*, Ro. iii. 13.*

ἄ-σπονδος, *ον* (*σπονδή*), "not to be bound by truce," *implacable*, 2 Tim. iii. 3; Ro. i. 31 (not W. H.).*

ἀσσάριον, *ίου*, *τό*, *a small coin* equal to the tenth part of a drachma, *an assarium*, Mat. x. 29; Lu. xii. 6. See Gr. § 154*a*.

ἆσσον, adv. (compar. of *ἄγχι*), *nearer, close by*, Ac. xxvii. 13.*

Ἄσσος, *ου*, ἡ, *Assos*, Ac. xx. 13, 14.*

ἀ-στατέω, *ῶ*, *ήσω*, *to be unsettled, to have no fixed abode*, 1 Cor. iv. 11.*

ἀστεῖος, *ον* (*ἄστυ*, *city*, see urbane), *fair, beautiful*, Ac. vii. 20; Heb. xi. 23.*

ἀστήρ, *έρος*, ὁ, *a star*, Mar. xiii. 25; 1 Cor. xv. 41; Rev. vi. 13.

ἀ-στήρικτος, *ον* (*στηρίζω*), *unsettled, unstable*, 2 Pet. ii. 14, iii. 16.*

ἄ-στοργος, *ον* (*στοργή*), *without natural affection*, Ro. i. 31; 2 Tim. iii. 3.*

ἀ-στοχέω, *ῶ* (*στόχος*), *to miss in aim, swerve from*, 1 Tim. i. 6, vi. 21; 2 Tim. ii. 18.*

ἀστραπή, *ῆς*, ἡ, *lightning*, Lu. x. 18; Rev. iv. 5; vivid *brightness, lustre*, Lu. xi. 36.

ἀστράπτω, *to flash*, as lightning, Lu. xvii. 24; *to be lustrous*, xxiv. 4.*

ἄστρον, *ου*, *τό*, *a star* (orig. *constellation*), Lu. xxi. 25; Ac. vii. 43, xxvii. 20; Heb. xi. 12.*

Ἀσύγκριτος, *ου*, ὁ, *Asyncritus*, Ro. xvi. 14.*

ἀ-σύμφωνος, *ον*, *dissonant, discordant*, Ac. xxviii. 25.*

ἀ-σύνετος, *ον*, *without understanding, foolish*, Mat. xv. 16; Ro. x. 19.

ἀ-σύνθετος, *ον*, *covenant-breaking, treacherous*, Ro. i. 31.*

ἀσφάλεια, *ας*, ἡ, *security*, Ac. v. 23; 1 Th. v. 3; *certainty*, Lu. i. 4.*

ἀ-σφαλής, *ές* (*σφάλλω*, *fallo*), *safe*, Phil. iii. 1; *secure, firm*, Heb. vi. 19; *certain*, Ac. xxv. 26; *τὸ ἀσφαλές*, *the certainty*, Ac. xxi. 34, xxii. 30.*

ἀσφαλίζω, *σω* (mid.), *to make fast, to secure*, Mat. xxvii. 65, 66; Ac. xvi. 24; pass., *to be made secure*, Mat. xxvii. 64.*

ἀσφαλῶς, adv., *safely*, Mar. xiv.

44; Ac. xvi. 23; *assuredly*, Ac. ii. 36.*

ἀσχημονέω, ῶ, *to act improperly* or *unseemly*, 1 Cor. vii. 36, xiii. 5.*

ἀσχημοσύνη, ης, ἡ, *unseemliness*, Ro. i. 27; *shame, nakedness*, Rev. xvi. 15.*

ἀ-σχήμων, ον (σχῆμα), *uncomely, unseemly*, 1 Cor. xii. 23.*

ἀ-σωτία, ας, ἡ (σώζω), *an abandoned course, profligacy*, Ep. v. 18; Tit. i. 6; 1 Pet. iv. 4.*

ἀ-σώτως, adv., *profligately, dissolutely*, Lu. xv. 13.*

ἀτακτέω, ῶ, *to behave disorderly*, 2 Th. iii. 7.*

ἄ-τακτος, ον (τάσσω), *irregular, disorderly*, 1 Th. v. 14.*

ἀτάκτως, adv., *disorderly, irregularly*, 2 Th. iii. 6, 11.*

ἄ-τεκνος, ου, ὁ, ἡ (τέκνον), *childless*, Lu. xx. 28, 29.*

ἀτενίζω, σω, *to look intently upon* (dat. or εἰς), Lu. iv. 20; Ac. i. 10; 2 Cor. iii. 7, 13.

ἄτερ, adv., as prep. with gen., *without, in the absence of*, Lu. xxii. 6, 35.*

ἀτιμάζω, σω, *to dishonor, contemn*, whether persons or things, by word or by deed, Lu. xx. 11; Jn. viii. 49; Ja. ii. 6.

ἀτιμία, ας, ἡ, *dishonor, ignominy, disgrace, ignoble use*, 1 Cor. xi. 14; Ro. i. 26, ix. 21.

ἄ-τιμος, ον (τιμή), *without honor, despised*, Mat. xiii. 57; Mar. vi. 4; 1 Cor. iv. 10, xii. 23.*

ἀτιμόω, ῶ, *to dishonor, treat with indignity*, Mar. xii. 4 (not W. H.).*

ἀτμίς, ίδος, ἡ, *a vapor*, Ac. ii. 19; Ja. iv. 14.

ἄ-τομον, ου, τό (τέμνω), *an atom* of time, *moment*, 1 Cor. xv. 52.*

ἄ-τοπος, ον (τόπος), *misplaced, unbecoming, mischievous*, Lu. xxiii. 41; Ac. xxviii. 6.

Ἀττάλεια, ας, ἡ, *Attalia*, Ac. xiv. 25.*

αὐγάζω, *to shine forth*, 2 Cor. iv. 4.*

αὐγή, ῆς, ἡ, *brightness, daylight*, Ac. xx. 11.*

Αὔγουστος, ου, ὁ (Lat.), *Augustus*, Lu. ii. 1.* Compare Σεβαστός.

αὐθάδης, ες (αὐτός, ἥδομαι), *self-pleasing, arrogant*, Tit. i. 7; 2 Pet. ii. 10.*

αὐθαίρετος, ον (αὐτός, αἱρέομαι), *of one's own accord*, 2 Cor. viii. 3, 17.*

αὐθεντέω, ῶ, *to exercise authority over* (gen.), 1 Tim. ii. 12. (N. T.)*

αὐλέω, ῶ, ήσω, *to play on a flute, to pipe*, Mat. xi. 17; Lu. vii. 32; 1 Cor. xiv. 7.

αὐλή, ῆς, ἡ (ἄω, *to blow*), *an open space, uncovered court* or *hall* of a house, as Lu. xi. 21, xxii. 55; *a sheepfold*, Jn. x. 1, 16.

αὐλητής, οῦ, ὁ, *a flute-player*, Mat. ix. 23; Rev. xviii. 22.*

αὐλίζομαι (to lodge in the open air), *to lodge, pass the night*, Mat. xxi. 17; Lu. xxi. 37.*

αὐλός, οῦ, ὁ (ἄω), *a flute, pipe*, 1 Cor. xiv. 7.*

αὐξάνω (also αὔξω), αὐξήσω, trans., *to make to grow*, as 1 Cor. iii. 6, 7; pass., *to grow, increase, become greater*, Mat. xiii. 32; Col. i. 10; generally intrans., *to grow, increase*, as Mat. vi. 28.

αὔξησις, εως, ἡ, *growth, increase*, Ep. iv. 16; Col. ii. 19.*

αὔριον, adv. (αὔρα, *morning breeze*, ἄω), *to-morrow*, Mat. vi. 30; Lu. xiii. 32, 33; ἡ (sc. ἡμέρα) αὔριον, *the morrow*, Mat. vi. 34; Ac. iv. 3.

αὐστηρός, ά, όν (dry), *harsh, austere*, Lu. xix. 21, 22.*

αὐτάρκεια, ας, ἡ, *sufficiency*, 2 Cor. ix. 8; *contentment*, 1 Tim. vi. 6.*

αὐτ-άρκης, ες (ἀρκέω, sufficient for self), *content, satisfied*, Phil. iv. 11.*

αὐτο-κατά-κριτος, ον, *self-condemned*, Tit. iii. 11. (N. T.)*

αὐτόματος, ον, *spontaneous, of its own accord*, Mar. iv. 28; Ac. xii. 10.*

αὐτ-όπτης, ου, ὁ, *an eye-witness*, Lu. i. 2.*

αὐτός, ή, ό, pron., *he, she, it*; in nom. nearly always emphatic. Properly demonstrative, *self, very*; joined with each of the persons of the verb, with or without a pers. pron., *I myself, thou thyself*, etc.; with the article, *the same; the same* with (dat.), 1 Cor. xi. 5; *ἐπὶ τὸ αὐτό, at the same place* or *time, together; κατὰ τὸ αὐτό, together*, only Ac. xiv. 1. See Gr. § 335, Wi. § 22, 3, 4, Bu. 105 sq.

αὐτοῦ, adv. of place, *here, there*, Mat. xxvi. 36; Ac. xviii. 19, xxi. 4.

αὑτοῦ, ῆς, οῦ, pron. reflex. (contr for ἑαυτοῦ), *of himself, herself*, etc. (W. H. in the majority of cases read αὐτοῦ, αὐτῷ, etc., but retain αὑτοῦ, etc., in some, as Mat. vi. 34; Jn. ii. 24; Ac. xiv. 17, etc.).

αὐτό-φωρος, ον (φώρ, *a thief*), *in the very act*, Jn. viii. 4, neut. dat. with ἐπί (W. H. omit).*

αὐτό-χειρ, ρος, ὁ, *with one's own hand*, Ac. xxvii. 19.*

αὐχμηρός, ά, όν, *dark, dismal*, 2 Pet. i. 19.*

ἀφ-αιρέω, *to take away*, as Lu. x. 42; *to take away* sin, only Ro. xi. 27; Heb. x. 4; *to smite off*, as Mat. xxvi. 51, and parallel passages.

ἀ-φανής, ές (φαίνω), *not appearing, hidden*, Heb. iv. 13.*

ἀ-φανίζω, *to put out of sight, destroy*, Mat. vi. 19, 20; *to disfigure*, Mat. vi. 16; pass., *to vanish, perish*, Ac. xiii. 41; Ja. iv. 14.*

ἀ-φανισμός, οῦ, ὁ, *a disappearing, destruction*, Heb. viii. 13.*

ἄ-φαντος, ον, *disappearing, not seen*, Lu. xxiv. 31.*

ἀφεδρών, ῶνος, ὁ, *draught, privy*, Mat. xv. 17; Mar. vii. 19. (N. T.)*

ἀ-φειδία, ας, ἡ (φείδομαι), *severity*, Col. ii. 23.*

ἀφελότης, τητος, *simplicity, sincerity*, Ac. ii. 46. (N. T.)*

ἄφ-εσις, εως, ἡ (ἀφίημι), *deliverance*; lit., only Lu. iv. 18; elsewhere always of *deliverance* from sin, remission, forgiveness, Mat. xxvi. 28; Lu. i. 77; Ep. i. 7. *Syn.*: πάρεσις is a simple *suspension of punishment* for sin, in contrast with ἄφεσις, *complete forgiveness*.

ἁφή, ῆς, ἡ (ἅπτω, *to fit*), *that which connects, a joint*, Ep. iv. 16; Col. ii. 19.*

ἀφθαρσία, ας, ἡ, *incorruption, immortality*, 1 Cor. xv., Ro. ii. 7; 2 Tim. i. 10; Ep. vi. 24, *incorruptness*, Tit. ii. 7 (W. H. ἀφθορία).*

ἄ-φθαρτος, ον (φθείρω), *incorruptible, imperishable*, Ro. i. 23; 1 Cor. ix. 25, xv. 52; 1 Tim. i. 17; 1 Pet. i. 4, 23, iii. 4.*

ἀ-φθορία, ας, ἡ, *incorruptness*, Tit. ii. 7 (W. H.). (N. T.)*

ἀφ-ίημι (see Gr. § 112, Wi. § 14, 3), *to send away*, as (1) *to let go, emit*, Mat. xxvii. 50; Mar. xv. 37; *dismiss*, in senses varying according to the obj.; spec., *to disregard, pass by, send away, divorce*, Mat. xv. 14; Heb. vi. 1; 1 Cor. vii. 11, 12, 13; hence, (2) *to forgive* (dat. pers.), very often, Mat. xviii. 27; Mar. ii. 5, 7; (3) *to permit, concede*, abs., or with inf., as Mar. x. 14; or acc., as Mat. iii. 15 (dat., Mat. v. 40); or ἵνα, subj., Mar. xi. 6; or subj. alone, Lu. vi. 42; (4) *to leave, depart from, abandon, leave behind*, Mat. xxii. 22; Mar. i. 31; Lu. v. 11, xvii. 34, 35.

ἀφικνέομαι, οῦμαι (2 aor., ἀφικόμην), *to arrive at, to reach*, Ro. xvi. 19.*

ἀ-φιλ-άγαθος, ον, *not loving goodness and good men*, 2 Tim. iii. 3. (N. T.)*

ἀ-φιλ-άργυρος, ον, *not loving money, not avaricious*, 1 Tim. iii. 3; Heb. xiii. 5. (N. T.)*

ἄφιξις, εως, ἡ, orig. arrival; *departure*, Ac. xx. 29.*

ἀφ-ίστημι, ἀποστήσω, trans. in pres., imperf., 1 aor., fut., *to lead away, to seduce;* intrans. in perf., plup., 2 aor., *to go away, depart, avoid, withdraw from* (often with ἀπό); mid., *to fail, abstain from, absent one's self*.

ἄφνω, adv., *suddenly*, Ac. ii. 2, xvi. 26, xxviii. 6.*

ἀ-φόβως, adv., *without fear*, Lu. i. 74; Phil. i. 14; 1 Cor. xvi. 10; Ju. 12.*

ἀφ-ομοιόω, ῶ, *to make like*, in pass., Heb. vii. 3.*

ἀφ-οράω, ῶ (2 a., ἀπ- or ἀφ-εῖδον), *to look away from* others *at* (εἰς) one, *to regard earnestly*, Heb. xii. 2; *to see*, Phil. ii. 23.*

ἀφ-ορίζω, fut. ιῶ, trans., *to separate from* (ἐκ or ἀπό), Mat. xiii. 49, xxv. 32; *to separate* for a purpose (εἰς, Ac. xiii. 2; Ro. i. 1; or inf., Gal. i. 15); *to excommunicate*, Lu. vi. 22.

ἀφ-ορμή, ῆς, ἡ, *an occasion, opportunity*, Ro. vii. 8, 11; 2 Cor. v. 12.

ἀφρίζω, *to foam at the mouth*, Mar. ix. 18, 20.*

ἀφρός, οῦ, ὁ, *foam, froth*, Lu. ix. 39.*

ἀ-φροσύνη, ης, ἡ, *foolishness*, Mar. vii. 22; 2 Cor. xi. 1, 17, 22.*

ἄ-φρων, ονος, ὁ, ἡ (φρήν), *inconsiderate, foolish, rash*, Lu. xi. 40; Ro. ii. 20.

ἀφ-υπνόω, ῶ (ἀπό, intensive), *to fall asleep*, Lu. viii. 23.*

ἀφυστερέω, ῶ, *to keep back by fraud*, Ja. v. 4 (W. H.).*

ἄ-φωνος, ον, *dumb, without the faculty of speech:* of animals, Ac. viii. 32; 2 Pet. ii. 16; of idols, 1 Cor. xii. 2. In 1 Cor. xiv. 10 the R. V. mrg. is probably the correct rendering.*

Ἄχαζ, ὁ (Heb.), *Ahaz*, Mat. i. 9.*

Ἀχαΐα, ας, ἡ, *Achaia*, a Roman province including all Greece except Thessaly, Ac. xix. 21; 1 Cor. xvi. 15.

Ἀχαϊκός, οῦ, ὁ, *Achaicus*, 1 Cor. xvi. 17.*

ἀ-χάριστος, ον, *unthankful*, Lu. vi. 35; 2 Tim. iii. 2.*

Ἀχείμ, ὁ (Heb.), *Achim*, Mat. i. 14.*

ἀ-χειρο-ποίητος, ον, *not made with hands*, Mar. xiv. 58; 2 Cor. v. 1; Col. ii. 11. (N. T.)*

ἀχλύς, ύος, ἡ, *a mist, dimness*, Ac. xiii. 11.*

ἀ-χρεῖος, ον, *useless, good for nothing, unprofitable*, Mat. xxv. 30; Lu. xvii. 10.*

ἀ-χρειόω (W. H. ἀχρεόω), pass., *to be made useless*, Ro. iii. 12.*

ἄ-χρηστος, ον, *useless, unprofitable*, Philem. 11.*

ἄχρι and **ἄχρις**, adv. as prep., with gen., *even to, until, as far as*, whether of place, time, or degree; ἄχρις οὗ or ἄχρις alone, with the force of a conjunction, *until*. See μέχρι.

ἄχυρον, ου, τό, *chaff*, Mat. iii. 12; Lu. iii. 17.*

ἀ-ψευδής, ές, *free from falsehood, truthful*, Tit. i. 2.*

ἄψινθος, ου, ὁ and **ἡ**, *wormwood*, Rev. viii. 11.*

ἄ-ψυχος, ον, *without life, inanimate*, 1 Cor. xiv. 7.*

B

B, β, βῆτα, *beta*, *b*, the second letter. Numerally, β′ = 2; ‚β = 2000.

Βαάλ (W. H. Βάαλ), **ὁ, ἡ** (Heb. *Master*), *Baal*, chief deity of the Phœnicians and other Semitic nations, Ro. xi. 4 (fem.), from 1 Kings xix. 18 (S.)*

Βαβυλών, ῶνος, ἡ, *Babylon*, lit., Mat. i. 11, 12, 17; Ac. vii. 43, and prob. 1 Pet. v. 13; mystically, in Rev. xiv. 8, xvi. 19, xvii. 5, xviii. 2, 10, 21.*

βαθμός, οῦ, ὁ (βαίνω, *to step*), *a step* or *degree* in dignity, 1 Tim. iii. 13. (S.)*

βάθος, ους, τό, *depth*, lit. or fig., Mat. xiii. 5; 1 Cor. ii. 10; 2 Cor. viii. 2 (ἡ κατὰ βάθους πτωχεία, *their deep poverty*).

βαθύνω, υνῶ, *to make deep*, Lu. vi. 48.*

βαθύς, εῖα, ύ, *deep*, Jn. iv. 11; in Lu. xxiv. 1, ὄρθρου βαθέος, in the early dawn (W. H. βαθέως, probably a genit. form).

βαΐον, ου, τό (Egyptian), *a palm branch*, Jn. xii. 13.*

Βαλαάμ, ὁ (Heb.), *Balaam*. A name emblematic of seducing teachers, 2 Pet. ii. 15; Ju. 11; Rev. ii. 14.*

Βαλάκ, ὁ (Heb.), *Balak*, Rev. ii. 14.*

βαλάντιον (W. H. -λλ-), **ου, τό**, *a money-bag, purse*, Lu. x. 4, xii. 33, xxii. 35, 36.*

βάλλω, βαλῶ, βέβληκα, ἔβαλον, *to throw, cast, put* (with more or less force, as modified by the context); of liquids, *to pour*. Pass. perf., with intrans. force, as Mat. viii. 6 ("has been cast"), *lies*. The verb is intrans., Ac. xxvii. 14, *rushed*. In Mar. xiv. 65 the true reading is prob. ἔλαβον. Generally trans. with acc. and dat., or ἐπί (acc., sometimes gen.), εἰς, ἀπό, ἐκ, and other prepp. or advv.

βαπτίζω, σω (in form a frequentative of βάπτω, see Gr.

§ 144*b*), (1) mid. or pass., reflex., *to bathe* one's self, only in Mar. vii. 4; Lu. xi. 38; (2) of the Christian ordinance, *to immerse*, *submerge*, *to baptize*. The material (water, fire, the Holy Spirit) is expressed by dat., εἰς or ἐν; the purpose or result by εἰς. Pass. or. mid., *to be baptized*, *to receive baptism;* (3) fig., of overwhelming woe, Mar. x. 38, 39; Lu. xii. 50.

βάπτισμα, ατος, τό, *the rite* or *ceremony of baptism*, Mat. iii. 7; Ep. iv. 5; fig., for overwhelming afflictions, Mar. x. 38, 39; Lu. xii. 50. (N. T.)

βαπτισμός, οῦ, ὁ, *the act of cleansing*, as vessels, Mar. vii. 4, 8 (W. H. omit); of Jewish lustrations, *washings* (pl.), Heb. ix. 10. For Heb. vi. 2, see Gr. § 260*b*, 2 (*b*).*

βαπτιστής, οῦ, ὁ, *one who baptizes;* the surname of John, Christ's forerunner, Mat. iii. 1; Mar. viii. 28.

βάπτω, βάψω, *to dip*, Lu. xvi. 24; Jn. xiii. 26; *to dye, color*, Rev. xix. 13.*

βάρ (Aram.), *son*, only Mat. xvi. 17 (βὰρ Ἰωνᾶ, W. H. βαριωνᾶ). Also prefix to many surnames, meaning *son of*. (N. T.)

Βαρ-αββᾶς, ᾶ, ὁ, *Barabbas*, Mat. xxvii. 16, 17; Jn. xviii. 40.

Βαράκ, ὁ, *Barak*, Heb. xi. 32.*

Βαραχίας, ου, ὁ, *Barachiah*, Mat. xxiii. 35.*

βάρβαρος, ου, ὁ (prob. onomatop., descriptive of unintelligible sounds), properly adj., *a foreigner*, *barbarian*, as 1 Cor. xiv. 11; used of all foreigners not Greeks, Ac. xxviii. 2, 4; Col. iii. 11; Ro. i. 14.*

βαρέω, ῶ (see βάρος), in N. T. only pass. βαρέομαι, οῦμαι, *to be weighed down*, *to be oppressed*, as by sleep, Lu. ix. 32; mental troubles, 2 Cor. i. 8, v. 4.

βαρέως, adv., *heavily*, *with difficulty*, Mat. xiii. 15; Ac. xxviii. 27.*

Βαρ-θολομαῖος, ου, ὁ, *Bartholomew*, surname (prob.) of Nathanael, Mat. x. 3.

Βαρ-ιησοῦς, οῦ, ὁ, *Bar-Jesus*, Ac. xiii. 6.*

Βαρ-ιωνᾶς, ᾶ, ὁ, *Bar-Jonas*, surname of Peter, Mat. xvi. 17 (W. H.).*

Βαρ-νάβας, α, ὁ, *Barnabas* (perhaps "son of comfort," see παράκλησις), Ac. ix. 27; Col. iv. 10.

βάρος, ους, τό, *weight*, *burden*, only fig., Ac. xv. 28; Rev. ii. 24.

Βαρ-σαβᾶς, ᾶ, ὁ, *Barsabas*. Two are mentioned, Ac. i. 23, xv. 22.*

Βαρ-τίμαιος, ου, ὁ, *Bartimæus*, Mar. x. 46.*

βαρύνω, *to weigh down*, Lu. xxi. 34 (Rec.).*

βαρύς, εῖα, ύ (see βάρος), (1) *heavy*, Mat. xxiii. 4; (2) *weighty*, *important*, Mat. xxiii. 23; Ac. xxv. 7; 2 Cor. x. 10; (3) *oppressive* or *grievous*, Ac. xx. 29; 1 Jn. v. 3.*

βαρύ-τιμος, ον, *of great price*, Mat. xxvi. 7.*

βασανίζω (see βάσανος), *to examine*, as by torture; hence, *to torment*, *vex*, Mar. v. 7; Rev. xi. 10, xii. 2; of waves, *to buffet*, Mat. xiv. 24; Mar. vi. 48.

βασανισμός, οῦ, ὁ, *torture*, *torment*, Rev. ix. 5, xiv. 11, xviii. 7, 10, 15.*

βασανιστής, οῦ, ὁ, *one who tortures, a tormentor, jailer*, Mat. xviii. 34.*

βάσανος, ου, ἡ (lit., *a touchstone*), *torture*, *torment*, Mat. iv. 24; Lu. xvi. 23, 28.*

βασιλεία, ας, ἡ, *a kingdom*, *royal power* or *dignity*, *reign;* ἡ βασιλεία τοῦ Θεοῦ, τοῦ χριστοῦ, τῶν οὐρανῶν (the last form only in Mat.), *the divine*, *spiritual kingdom*, or *reign* of Messiah, in the world, in the individual, or in the future state; υἱοὶ τῆς βασιλείας, *sons of the kingdom*, Jews, its original possessors, Mat. viii. 12; true believers, Mat. xiii. 38. In Rev. i. 6, v. 10, for βασιλεῖς καί, W. H. read βασιλείαν, *a kingdom* consisting of priests (R. V.).

βασίλειος, ον, *royal*, *regal*, 1 Pet. ii. 9, from Exod. xix. 6; τὰ βασίλεια, as subst., *a regal mansion*, *palace*, Lu. vii. 25.*

βασιλεύς, έως, ὁ, *a leader*, *ruler*, *king*, sometimes subordinate to higher authority, as the Herods. Applied to God, always with distinguishing epithets, Mat. v. 35; 1 Tim. i. 17, vi. 15; Rev. xv. 3; to Christ, Mat. ii. 2; Jn. i. 49, etc.; to Christians, Rev. i. 6, v. 10 (Rec., but see under βασιλεία).

βασιλεύω, εύσω, *to have authority*, *to reign*, or *to possess* or *exercise dominion; to be* βασιλεύς generally. With gen. or ἐπί (gen.), of the kingdom; ἐπί (acc.), of the persons governed.

βασιλικός, ή, όν, *belonging to a king*, *royal*, Jn. iv. 46, 49; Ac. xii. 20, 21; Ja. ii. 8.*

βασίλισσα, ης, ἡ, *a queen*, Mat. xii. 42; Lu. xi. 31; Ac. viii. 27; Rev. xviii. 7.*

βάσις, εως, ἡ (βαίνω), prop. *a going*, hence, *the foot*, Ac. iii. 7.*

βασκαίνω, ανῶ, *to bewitch*, *bring under malign influence*, Gal. iii. 1.*

βαστάζω, άσω, *to lift*, *lift up;* often with the sense of bearing away. Thus, (1) *to carry*, a burden, as Lu. xiv. 27; tidings, as Ac. ix. 15; (2) *to take on one's self*, as disease or weaknesses, Ro. xv. 1; condemnation, Gal. v. 10; reproach, Gal. vi. 17; (3) *to bear with* or *endure*, Rev. ii. 2; (4) *to take away*, Mat. viii. 17; Jn. xii. 6.

βάτος, ου, ὁ, ἡ, *a thorn-bush* or *bramble*, Lu. vi. 44; Ac. vii. 30, 35. "The Bush," Mar. xii. 26; Lu. xx. 37 denotes the section of the O. T. so called (Exod. iii.).*

βάτος, ου, ὁ (Heb.), *a bath*, or Jewish measure for liquids containing 8 or 9 gallons, Lu. xvi. 6. (Ap.)*

βάτραχος, ου, ὁ, *a frog*, Rev. xvi. 13.*

βαττο-λογέω, ῶ (prob. from βατ, an unmeaning sound; see βάρβαρος), *to babble*, *talk to no purpose*, Mat. vi. 7. (N. T.)*

βδέλυγμα, ατος, τό (see βδελύσσω), *something unclean and abominable*, *an object of moral repugnance*, Lu. xvi. 15; spec. (as often in O.T.) idolatry, Rev. xvii. 4, 5, xxi. 27. "Abomination of desolation," Mat. xxiv. 15; Mar. xiii. 14 (from Dan. ix. 27) refers to the pollution of the temple by some idolatrous symbol. (S.)*

βδελυκτός, ή, όν, *disgusting, abominable*, Tit. i. 16. (S.)*

βδελύσσω, ξω, *to defile*, only mid.; *to loathe*, Ro. ii. 22; and pass. perf. part., *defiled*, Rev. xxi. 8.*

βέβαιος, α, ον, *steadfast, constant, firm*, Heb. vi. 19; Ro. iv. 16.

βεβαιόω, ῶ, *to confirm, to establish*, whether of persons or things, Mar. xvi. 20; Ro. xv. 8; Heb. xiii. 9.

βεβαίωσις, εως, ή, *confirmation*, Phil. i. 7; Heb. vi. 16.*

βέβηλος, ον (βα- in βαίνω, "that on which any one may step"), *common, unsanctified, profane*, of things or persons, 1 Tim. iv. 7; Heb. xii. 16.

βεβηλόω, ῶ, *to make common, to profane*, the Sabbath, Mat. xii. 5; the temple, Ac. xxiv. 6. (S.)*

Βεελ-ζεβούλ (W. H. Βεεζεβούλ), ὁ (Heb.), *Beelzebul*, a name of *Satan*, Mat. x. 25; Lu. xi. 15, 18, 19. (N. T.)

Βελίαλ, ὁ (Heb. *worthlessness*), or Βελίαρ (W. H.), derivation doubtful, a name for *Satan*, 2 Cor. vi. 15. (N. T.)*

βελόνη, ης, ή, *a needle*, Lu. xviii. 25 (W. H.).*

βέλος, ους, τό (βάλλω), *a missile*, such as *a javelin* or *dart*, Ep. vi. 16.*

βελτίων, ον, ονος (a compar. of ἀγαθός), *better;* neut. as adv., 2 Tim. i. 18.*

Βεν-ιαμίν, ὁ (Heb. *Ben* = son), *Benjamin*, Ac. xiii. 21; Rev. vii. 8.

Βερνίκη, ης, ή, *Bernice*, Ac. xxv. 13, 23, xxvi. 30.*

Βέροια, ας, ή, *Berœa*, Ac. xvii. 10, 13.*

Βεροιαῖος, α, ον, *Berœan*, Ac. xx. 4.*

Βηθ-, a Hebrew and Aramaic prefix to many local names, meaning *house* or *abode of*.

Βηθ-αβαρά, ᾶς, ή, *Bethabara*, "house of the ford," Jn. i. 28 (W. H. read Βηθανία).*

Βηθ-ανία, ας, ή, *Bethany*, "house of misery." There were two places of the name: (1) Jn. xi. 1, etc.; (2) on the Jordan, Jn. i. 28 (W. H.). See Βηθαβαρά.

Βηθ-εσδά, ή, *Bethesda*, "house of compassion," Jn. v. 2 (W. H. Βηθζαθά).*

Βηθ-λεέμ, ή, *Bethlehem*, "house of bread," Lu. ii. 4, 15.

Βηθ-σαϊδά, ή, *Bethsaida*, "house of hunting" or "fishing." There were two places of the name: one in Galilee, Jn. xii. 21; the other on the east of the Jordan, Lu. ix. 10.

Βηθ-φαγή, ή, *Bethphage*, "house of figs," Mat. xxi. 1; Mar. xi. 1; Lu. xix. 29.*

βῆμα, ατος, τό (βα- in βαίνω), *a step, a space;* βῆμα ποδός, a space for the foot, Ac. vii. 5; *a raised space* or *bench, tribunal, judgment-seat*, Jn. xix. 13; 2 Cor. v. 10.

βήρυλλος, ου, ὁ, ή, *a beryl*, a gem of greenish hue, Rev. xxi. 20.*

βία, ας, ή, *force, violence*, Ac. v. 26, xxi. 35, xxiv. 7 (W. H. omit), xxvii. 41.*

βιάζω, *to use violence;* mid., *to enter forcibly*, with εἰς, Lu. xvi. 16; pass., *to suffer violence, to be assaulted*, Mat. xi. 12.*

βίαιος, α, ον, *violent*, Ac. ii. 2.*

βιαστής, οῦ, ὁ, *one who employs force, a man of violence*, Mat. xi. 12.*

βιβλαρίδιον, ου, τό, *a little book*, Rev. x. 2, 8 (not W. H.), 9, 10. (N. T.)*

βιβλίον, ου, τό (dim. of following), *a small book, a scroll*, as Lu. iv. 17; Rev. v. 1; βιβλίον ἀποστασίου, a bill of divorcement, Mat. xix. 7; Mar. x. 4.

βίβλος, ου, ὁ, *a written book, roll* or *volume*, Mat. i. 1; Phil. iv. 3. The word means papyrus, from which ancient books were made.

βιβρώσκω (βρο-), perf. βέβρωκα, *to eat*, Jn. vi. 13.*

Βιθυνία, ας, ή, *Bithynia*, Ac. xvi. 7; 1 Pet. i. 1.*

βίος, ου, ὁ, (1) *life*, as Lu. viii. 14; (2) *means of life, livelihood*, as Lu. viii. 43; (3) *goods* or *property*, as Lu. xv. 12; 1 Jn. iii. 17. *Syn.:* ζωή is life in its *principle*, and used for spiritual and immortal life; βίος is life in its *manifestations*, denoting the manner of life.

βιόω, ῶ, *to pass one's life*, 1 Pet. iv. 2.*

βίωσις, εως, ή, *manner* or *habit of life*, Ac. xxvi. 4. (Ap.)*

βιωτικός, ή, όν, *of* or *belonging to* (this) *life*, Lu. xxi. 34; 1 Cor. vi. 3, 4.*

βλαβερός, ά, όν, *hurtful*, 1 Tim. vi. 9.*

βλάπτω (βλαβ-), βλάψω, *to hurt* or *injure*, Mar. xvi. 18 (W. H. omit); Lu. iv. 35.*

βλαστάνω (or βλαστάω, Mar. iv. 27, W. H.), βλαστήσω, intrans., *to sprout, to spring up, to put forth buds*, Mat. xiii. 26; Mar. iv. 27; Heb. ix. 4; trans., *to bring forth* (καρπόν), Ja. v. 18.*

Βλάστος, ου, ὁ, *Blastus*, Ac. xii. 20.*

βλασφημέω, ῶ, *to speak abusively, to rail*, abs., as Ac. xiii. 45; *to calumniate, speak evil of, blaspheme*, with acc., rarely εἰς; often of men or things. Spec. of God, Rev. xvi. 11; the Holy Spirit, Lu. xii. 10; the divine name or doctrine, 1 Tim. vi. 1.

βλασφημία, ας, ή, *evil-speaking, reviling, blasphemy*, Mat. xii. 31; Mar. xiv. 64.

βλάσφημος, ον, *slanderous*, Ac. vi. 11; subst., *a blasphemer*, 1 Tim. i. 13; 2 Tim. iii. 2.

βλέμμα, ατος, τό, *a look, glance*, 2 Pet. ii. 8.*

βλέπω, ψω, *to see, to have the power of seeing, to look at, behold;* with εἰς, *to look to*, Mat. xxii. 16; Mar. xii. 14; with ἵνα or μή, *to take care* (once without, Mar. xiii. 9) with ἀπό, *to beware of;* once with κατά (acc.), geographically, *to look towards*, Ac. xxvii. 12.

βλητέος, έα, έον, a verbal adj. (βάλλω), *that ought to be put*, Mar. ii. 22 (W. H. omit); Lu. v. 38. (N. T.)*

Βοανεργές (W. H. -ηρ-), (Heb.), *Boanerges*, "sons of thunder," Mar. iii. 17. (N. T.)*

βοάω, ῶ (βοή), *to shout* for joy, Gal. iv. 27; *to cry* for grief,

Ac. viii. 7; *to publish openly, to cry aloud*, Mar. xv. 34; Ac. xvii. 6; with πρός (acc.), *to appeal to*, Lu. xviii. 7, 38.

βοή, ῆς, ἡ, *a loud cry*, Ja. v. 4.*

βοήθεια, ας, ἡ, *help*, Ac. xxvii. 17; Heb. iv. 16.*

βοηθέω, ῶ, *to go to the help of, to succor* (dat.), Mat. xv. 25; Rev. xii. 16.

βοηθός, οῦ, ὁ, ἡ (properly adj.), *a helper*, Heb. xiii. 6.*

βόθυνος, ου, ὁ, *a pit, ditch*, Mat. xii. 11, xv. 14; Lu. vi. 39.*

βολή, ῆς, ἡ, *a throwing;* λίθου βολή, *a stone's throw*, Lu. xxii. 41.*

βολίζω, σω, *to heave the lead, take soundings*, Ac. xxvii. 28. (N. T.)*

βολίς, ίδος, ἡ, *a weapon thrown*, as *a dart* or *javelin*, Heb. xii. 20 (W. H. omit).*

Βοόζ, ὁ (Heb.), *Booz* or *Boaz*, Mat. i. 5 (W. H. Βοές); Lu. iii. 32 (W. H. Βοός).*

βόρβορος, ου, ὁ, *mire, filth*, 2 Pet. ii. 22.*

Βορρᾶς, ᾶ, ὁ (*Boreas*, the north wind), *the North*, Lu. xiii. 29; Rev. xxi. 13.*

βόσκω, ήσω, *to feed*, as Mat. viii. 33; Jn. xxi. 15, 17; mid., *to feed, graze*, as Mar. v. 11. *Syn.:* ποιμαίνω is the broader word, to act as shepherd, literally or spiritually; βόσκω, simply to *feed* the flock.

Βοσόρ, ὁ (Heb. *Beor*), *Bosor*, 2 Pet. ii. 15 (W. H. Βεώρ).*

βοτάνη, ης, ἡ (βόσκω), *herbage, pasturage*, Heb. vi. 7.*

βότρυς, υος, ὁ, *a cluster of grapes*, Rev. xiv. 18.*

βουλευτής, οῦ, ὁ, *a councilor, a senator*, Mar. xv. 43; Lu. xxiii. 50.*

βουλεύω, σω, *to advise*, N. T. mid. only; (1) *to consult, to deliberate*, with εἰ, Lu. xiv. 31; (2) *to resolve on* or *purpose*, with inf., Ac. v. 33, xv. 37 (W. H. in both passages read βούλομαι), xxvii. 39; ἵνα, Jn. xi. 53 (W. H.), xii. 10; acc., 2 Cor. i. 17.*

βουλή, ῆς, ἡ, *a design, purpose, plan*, Lu. xxiii. 51; Ac. v. 38; Ep. i. 11.

βούλημα, ατος, τό (βούλομαι), *will, counsel, purpose*, Ac. xxvii. 43; Ro. ix. 19; 1 Pet. iv. 3 (W. H.).*

βούλομαι, 2d pers. sing. βούλει, aug. with ἐ or ἡ, *to will*, as (1) *to be willing, to incline to*, Mar. xv. 15; (2) *to intend*, Mat. i. 19; (3) *to desire*, 1 Tim. vi. 9. Generally with inf., sometimes understood, as Ja. i. 18; with subj., Jn. xviii. 39.

βουνός, οῦ, ὁ, *a hill, rising ground*, Lu. iii. 5; xxiii. 30.*

βοῦς, βοός, ὁ, ἡ, *an animal of the ox kind*, male or female, Lu. xiii. 15; 1 Tim. v. 18.

βραβεῖον, ου, τό, *the prize*, in the games, 1 Cor. ix. 24; Phil. iii. 14.*

βραβεύω (lit., to act as arbiter in the games), *to rule, arbitrate*, Col. iii. 15.*

βραδύνω, νῶ (βραδύς), *to be slow, to linger*, 1 Tim. iii. 15; 2 Pet. iii. 9 (gen.).*

βραδυ-πλοέω, ῶ, *to sail slowly*, Ac. xxvii. 7. (N. T.)*

βραδύς, εῖα, ύ, *slow;* dat. of sphere, Lu. xxiv. 25; εἰς, Ja. i. 19.*

βραδυτής, τῆτος, ἡ, *slowness*, 2 Pet. iii. 9.*

βραχίων, ονος, ὁ, *the arm;* met., *strength*, Lu. i. 51; Jn. xii. 38; Ac. xiii. 17.*

βραχύς, εῖα, ύ, *short, little*, only neut.; of time, Lu. xxii. 58; Ac. v. 34; Heb. ii. 7, 9; place, Ac. xxvii. 28; διὰ βραχέων, Heb. xiii. 22, *in few words;* βραχύ τι, Jn. vi. 7, of quantity, *a little*.*

βρέφος, ους, τό, *a child unborn*, Lu. i. 41, 44; *a babe*, as Lu. ii. 12, 16; 2 Tim. iii. 15.

βρέχω, ξω, *to moisten*, Lu. vii. 38, 44; *to rain, to send rain*, Mat. v. 45; Lu. xvii. 29; impers., Ja. v. 17; intrans., Rev. xi. 6.*

βροντή, ῆς, ἡ, *thunder*, Jn. xii. 29; Rev. iv. 5.

βροχή, ῆς, ἡ (βρέχω), *a heavy rain*, Mat. vii. 25, 27. (S.)*

βρόχος, ου, ὁ, *a noose* or *snare*, 1 Cor. vii. 35.*

βρυγμός, οῦ, ὁ, *a grinding* or *gnashing*, as Mat. viii. 12.

βρύχω, ξω, *to grind* or *gnash*, as the teeth, for rage or pain, Ac. vii. 54.*

βρύω, σω, *to send forth abundantly*, as a fountain, Ja. iii. 11.*

βρῶμα, ατος, τό (see βιβρώσκω), *food* of any kind, Mat. xiv. 15; Jn. iv. 34; 1 Cor. viii. 8, 13.

βρώσιμος, ον, *eatable*, Lu. xxiv 41.*

βρῶσις, εως, ἡ, (1) *the act of eating*, as 1 Cor. viii. 4; (2) *corrosion*, Mat. vi. 19, 20; (3) *food*, Jn. iv. 32; Heb. xii. 16.

βυθίζω, σω, *to cause to sink*, fig., 1 Tim. vi. 9; mid., *to sink*, Lu. v. 7.*

βυθός, οῦ, ὁ, *the deep, the sea*, 2 Cor. xi. 25.*

βυρσεύς, έως, ὁ, *a tanner*, Ac. ix. 43, x. 6, 32.*

βύσσινος, η, ον, *made of byssus, fine linen*, Rev. xviii. 12 (W. H.), 16, xix. 8, 14.*

βύσσος, ου, ἡ, *byssus*, a species of flax, and of linen manufactured from it, highly prized for its softness, whiteness, and delicacy, Lu. xvi. 19; Rev. xviii. 12 (Rec.).*

βωμός, οῦ, ὁ, *an altar*, Ac. xvii. 23.* *Syn.:* βωμός is a heathen altar; θυσιαστήριον, the altar of the true God.

Γ

Γ, γ, γάμμα, *gamma*, *g* hard, the third letter of the Greek alphabet. In numeral value, γ′ = 3; ͵γ = 3000.

Γαββαθᾶ (W. H. -θά), ἡ (Aram.), *Gabbatha; an elevated place* or *tribunal*, Jn. xix. 13. See λιθόστρωτον. (N. T.)*

Γαβριήλ, ὁ (Heb. *man of God*), the archangel *Gabriel*, Lu. i. 19, 26.*

γάγγραινα, ης, ἡ, *a gangrene, mortification*, 2 Tim. ii. 17.*

Γάδ, ὁ (Heb.), *Gad*, Rev. vii. 5.*

Γαδαρηνός, ή, όν, *belonging to Gadara*, Mar. v. 1 (Rec.); Mat. viii. 28 (W. H.). See Γεργεσηνός.

γάζα, ης, ἡ (Persian), *treasure*, as of a government, Ac. viii. 27.*

Γάζα, ης, ἡ (Heb.), *Gaza*, a strong city of the ancient Philistines in the W. of Palestine, Ac. viii. 26. (The adj., ἔρημος, *desert*, refers to ὁδός.)*

γαζο-φυλάκιον, ου, τό, *a place*

for the guardianship of treasure, treasury; a part of the temple so called, Mar. xii. 41, 43; Lu. xxi. 1; Jn. viii. 20. (S.)*

Γάϊος, *ου, ὁ* (Lat.), *Gaius,* or *Caius.* There are four of the name in N. T., Ac. xix. 29, xx. 4; 1 Cor. i. 14, and Ro. xvi. 23; 3 Jn. 1.*

γάλα, *ακτος, τό, milk,* lit., 1 Cor. ix. 7; fig., for the elements of Christian knowledge, 1 Cor. iii. 2; Heb. v. 12, 13; 1 Pet. ii. 2.*

Γαλάτης, *ου, ὁ, a Galatian,* Gal. iii. 1.*

Γαλατία, *ας, ἡ, Galatia,* or *Gallogræcia,* a province of Asia Minor, Gal. i. 2; 1 Cor. xvi. 1; 2 Tim. iv. 10; 1 Pet. i. 1.*

Γαλατικός, *ή, όν, belonging to Galatia,* Ac. xvi. 6, xviii. 23.*

γαλήνη, *ης, ἡ, a calm,* Mat. viii. 26; Mar. iv. 39; Lu. viii. 24.*

Γαλιλαία, *ας, ἡ* (from Heb.), *Galilee,* the N. division of Palestine, Mat. iv. 15.

Γαλιλαῖος, *αία, αῖον, of* or *belonging to Galilee,* Mat. xxvi. 69; Ac. i. 11.

Γαλλίων, *ωνος, ὁ, Gallio,* a proconsul of Achaia, Ac. xviii. 12, 14, 17.*

Γαμαλιήλ, *ὁ* (Heb.), *Gamaliel,* Ac. v. 34, xxii. 3.*

γαμέω, *ῶ, ήσω,* 1st aor. *ἐγάμησα* and *ἔγημα,* abs. or trans. (with acc.), *to marry;* active properly of the man; pass. and mid. of the woman, with dat., 1 Cor. vii. 39; Mar. x. 12 (W. H. *ἄλλον* for Rec. *ἄλλῳ*); but in N. T. the act. also is used of the woman, as 1 Cor. vii. 28, 34.

γαμίζω, *to give in marriage* (a daughter), Rec. only Mar. xii. 25; Lu. xvii. 27, xx. 35; W. H. add Mat. xxii. 30, xxiv. 38; 1 Cor. vii. 38. (N. T.)*

γαμίσκω = *γαμίζω,* Mar. xii. 25 (Rec.); Lu. xx. 34 (W. H.).*

γάμος, *ου, ὁ, marriage,* spec. *a marriage feast,* sing. or plur., Heb. xiii. 4; Rev. xix. 7. See Gr. § 240, Wi. § 27, 3, Bu. 23.

γάρ (*γε ἄρα*), "truly then," a causal postpositive particle or conjunction, *for,* introducing a reason for the thing previously said. Used in questions to intensify the inquiry; often with other particles. For the special uses of *γάρ,* see Gr. § 407, Wi. § 53, 8, Bu. 370.

γαστήρ, *τρός* (sync.), *ἡ,* (1) *the womb,* as Mat. i. 18; (2) *the stomach,* only Tit. i. 12, from Epimenides, "idle bellies," *gluttons.*

γέ, an enclitic particle indicating emphasis, *at least, indeed.* Sometimes used alone, as Ro. viii. 32; 1 Cor. iv. 8; generally in connection with other particles, as *ἀλλά, ἄρα, εἴ; εἰ δὲ μήγε,* stronger than *εἰ δὲ μή, if otherwise indeed; καίγε, and at least, and even; καίτοιγε, though indeed; μενοῦνγε, yea, indeed; μήτιγε,* "*to say nothing of,*" 1 Cor. vi. 3.

Γεδεών, *ὁ* (Heb.), *Gideon,* Heb. xi. 32.*

γέ-εννα, *ης, ἡ* (Heb. *valley of Hinnom*), met., *Gehenna, place of punishment* in the future world, Mat. x. 28, etc. Sometimes with *τοῦ πυρός,* as Mat. v. 22. Compare 2 Kings xxiii. 10. (S.)

Γεθ-σημανῆ, or *-νεί* (W. H.), *ἡ* (Heb. *oil-press*), *Gethsemane,* a small field at the foot of the Mount of Olives, over the brook Kidron, Mat. xxvi. 36; Mar. xiv. 32.*

γείτων, *ονος, ὁ, ἡ, a neighbor,* Lu. xiv. 12, xv. 6, 9; Jn. ix. 8.*

γελάω, *ῶ, άσω, to laugh,* Lu. vi. 21, 25.*

γέλως, *ωτος, ὁ, laughter,* Ja. iv. 9.*

γεμίζω, *σω, to fill,* with acc. and gen. (also *ἀπό* or *ἐκ*), Mar. xv. 36; Rev. viii. 5; pass. abs., *to be full,* Mar. iv. 37; Lu. xiv. 23.

γέμω, *to be full of,* with gen. (*ἐκ,* Mat. xxiii. 25; perhaps acc., Rev. xvii. 3).

γενεά, *ᾶς, ἡ, generation,* as (1) *offspring, race, descent,* Mat. i. 17; Lu. ix. 41; (2) *the people of any given time;* (3) *an age of the world's duration,* Mat. xxiv. 34; Ac. xiii. 36; *εἰς γενεὰς καὶ γενεάς* (W. H.), *unto generations and generations* (R. V.), Lu. i. 50

γενεα-λογέω, *ῶ, to reckon* [illegible] *genealogy* or *pedigree,* pa[illegible] with *ἐκ,* Heb. vii. 6.*

γενεα-λογία, *ας, ἡ, genealogy,* N. T. plur., 1 Tim. i. 4; Tit. iii. 9; prob. of Gnostic speculations on the origin of being.*

γενέσια, *ων, τά, a birthday celebration,* Mat. xiv. 6; Mar. vi. 21.*

γένεσις, *εως, ἡ, birth, lineage,* Mat. i. 1 (W. H. add Mat. i. 18; Lu. i. 14, for Rec. *γέννησις*); Ja. i. 23, *τὸ πρόσωπον τῆς γενέσεως αὐτοῦ, the countenance of his birth,* or, as A. V., R. V., "his natural face"; Ja. iii. 6, *τὸν τροχὸν τῆς γενέσεως, the wheel of nature* (R. V.).*

γενετή, *ῆς, ἡ, birth,* Jn. ix. 1.*

γένημα, *ατος, τό.* See *γέννημα.*

γεννάω, *ῶ, ήσω, to beget, give birth to, produce, effect,* Mat. i. 3, 5, 6; Lu. i. 13, 57; Ac. vii. 8, 29; pass., *to be begotten, born* (often in John, of spiritual renewal), Mat. i. 20; Jn. i. 13; 1 Jn. v. 1.

γέννημα, *ατος, τό,* (1) *progeny, generation,* as Mat. iii. 7; (2) *produce* generally, as Mat. xxvi. 29; fig., *fruit, result,* as 2 Cor. ix. 10. In sense (2) W. H. always read *γένημα,* and sometimes elsewhere.

Γεννησαρέτ (Aram.), *Gennesaret* (*Chinnereth* or Chinneroth, in O. T.), a region of Galilee, with village or town of the same name, Mat. xiv. 34. Used of the adjacent lake, as Lu. v. 1.

γέννησις, *εως, ἡ.* See *γένεσις.**

γεννητός, *ή, όν,* verb. adj., *begotten, born,* Mat. xi. 11; Lu. vii. 28.*

γένος, *ους, τό,* (1) *offspring,* Ac. xvii. 28, 29; (2) *family,* Ac. xiii. 26; (3) *stock, race,* Ac. vii. 19; Gal. i. 14; (4) *natio*[illegible] Mar. vii. 26; (5) *kind* or *species,* Mar. ix. 29; 1 Cor. xiv. 10.

Γεργεσηνός, *ή, όν,* or *Γερασηνός, Gergesene, belonging to Gergesa* or *Gerasa.* The copies vary between these forms and *Γαδαρηνός,* Mat. viii. 28; Mar. v. 1; Lu. viii. 26, 37.*

γερουσία, ας, ἡ (γέρων), *an assembly of elders, senate*, Ac. v. 21.*

γέρων, οντος, ὁ, *an old man*, Jn. iii. 4.*

γεύω, *to make to taste*, only mid. in N. T.; *to taste*, as abs., *to take food*, Ac. x. 10; or with obj. gen., or acc. See Gr. § 249*a*, (2), Wi. §§ 3, p. 33, 30, 7*c*, Bu. 167. Fig., *to experience*, as Mat. xvi. 28; once with ὅτι, 1 Pet. ii. 3.

γεωργέω, ῶ, *to cultivate* or *till the earth*, Heb. vi. 7.*

γεώργιον, ου, τό, *a tilled field*, fig., 1 Cor. iii. 9. (S.)*

γεωργός, οῦ, ὁ, *one who tills the ground, a husbandman*, 2 Tim. ii. 6; Ja. v. 7: *a vine-dresser*, Lu. xx. 9, 10, 14, 16.

γῆ, γῆς, ἡ, contr. for γέα or γαῖα, *land* or *earth*, as (1) *the material soil;* (2) *the producing soil, the ground;* (3) *land*, as opposed to sea; (4) *earth*, as opposed to heaven, often involving suggestions of human weakness and sin; (5) *region* or *territory*.

γῆρας, (αος) ως, τό, *old age*, Lu. i. 36 (dat., Rec. γήρᾳ, W. H. γήρει).*

γηράσκω, or γηράω, άσω, *to become old*, Jn. xxi. 18; Heb. viii. 13.*

γίνομαι, for γίγνομαι. See Gr. § 94, 8*a*. γενήσομαι, ἐγενόμην and ἐγενήθην, γέγονα (with pres. force) and γεγένημαι, *to become*, as (1) *to begin to be*, used of persons, *to be born*, Jn. viii. 58; of the works of creation, *to be made*, Jn. i. 3, 10; and of other works, *to be wrought* or *performed;* so, to pass out of one state into another, *to grow into, to be changed into*, Jn. ii. 9; often with εἰς, Lu. xiii. 19; (2) of ordinary or extraordinary occurrences, *to happen, to take place, to be done;* of the day, the night, Mar. vi. 2; of thunder, earthquake, calm, etc.; of feasts or public solemnities, *to be held* or *celebrated;* frequently in the phrase καὶ ἐγένετο, *and it came to pass* (with καί, or following verb, or inf.); also, μὴ γένοιτο, *let it never happen!* or *God forbid!;* (3) with adj. or predicative subst., *to become*, where quality, character, or condition is specified; often in prohibitions, μὴ γίνου, μὴ γίνεσθε, *become not*, as Mat vi. 16; (4) with the cases of substantives and the prepositions, the verb forms many phrases, to be interpreted according to the meaning of the case or prep.

γινώσκω, or γιγνώσκω (see Gr. § 94, 8*b*, Wi. § 39, 3, note 2, Bu. 55), γνώσομαι, 2d aor. ἔγνων (imper. γνῶθι), perf. ἔγνωκα, (1) *to become aware of, to perceive*, with acc.; (2) *to know, to perceive, understand*, with acc. or ὅτι, or acc. and inf., or τί interrog.; Ἑλληνιστὶ γ., *to understand* Greek, Ac. xxi. 37; *to be conscious of*, by experience, as 2 Cor. v. 21; (3) *to know carnally* (a Hebraistic euphemism), Mat. i. 25; Lu. i. 34; (4) specially of the fellowship between Christians and God or Christ, 1 Cor. viii. 3; Mat. vii. 23 (negatively); Jn. xvii. 3; Heb. viii. 11; Phil. iii. 10, etc.

γλεῦκος, ους, τό, *sweet* or *new wine*, Ac. ii. 13.*

γλυκύς, εῖα, ύ, *sweet*, Ja. iii. 11, 12; Rev. x. 9, 10.*

γλῶσσα, ης, ἡ, (1) *the tongue*, Mar. vii. 33, 35; 1 Jn. iii. 18 (2) *a language*, Ac. ii. 11; (3) *a nation* or *people* distinguished by their language, Rev. v. 9, vii. 9.

γλωσσό-κομον, ου, τό, *a little box* or *case for money*, Jn. xii. 6, xiii. 29 (orig. from holding the "tongue-pieces" of flutes, etc.).*

γναφεύς, έως, ὁ, *a fuller, cloth-dresser*, Mar. ix. 3.*

γνήσιος, α, ον (sync. from γενήσιος), *legitimate, genuine, true*, 1 Tim. i. 2; Tit. i. 4; Phil. iv. 3; τὸ γνήσιον, *sincerity*, 2 Cor. viii. 8.*

γνησίως, adv., *genuinely, sincerely*, Phil. ii. 20.*

γνόφος, ου, ὁ, *darkness, gloom*, Heb. xii. 18.*

γνώμη, ης, ἡ, (γνο- in γινώσκω), *opinion, judgment, intention*, 1 Cor. i. 10; 2 Cor. viii. 10.

γνωρίζω, ίσω, or ιῶ, (1) *to make known, to declare* (with acc. and dat., ὅτι or τί, interrog., Col. i. 27); (2) intrans., *to know*, only Phil. i. 22.

γνῶσις, εως, ἡ, (1) subj., *knowledge*, with gen. of obj. (gen. subj., Ro. xi. 33); (2) obj., *science, doctrine, wisdom*, as Lu. xi. 52. *Syn.:* see Trench, § lxxv.

γνώστης, ου, ὁ, *one who knows, an expert*, Ac. xxvi. 3. (S.)*

γνωστός, ή, όν, verb. adj., *known*, as Ac. ii. 14, iv. 10; *knowable*, Ro. i. 19; *notable*, Ac. iv. 16; οἱ γνωστοί, *one's acquaintance*, Lu. ii. 44.

γογγύζω, ύσω, *to murmur* in a low voice, Jn. vii. 32; discontentedly, *to grumble*, as 1 Cor. x. 10, with acc., or περί, gen., πρός, acc., κατά, gen. (S.)

γογγυσμός, οῦ, ὁ, *muttering*, Jn. vii. 12; *murmuring*, Ac. vi. 1; Phil. ii. 14; 1 Pet. iv. 9. (S.)*

γογγυστής, οῦ, ὁ, *a murmurer, complainer*, Ju. 16. (N. T.)*

γόης, ητος, ὁ (γοάω, *to moan*), *an enchanter, an impostor*, 2 Tim. iii. 13.*

Γολγοθά (W. H., some -θᾶ), (Aram.), *Golgotha*, "the place of a skull" (prob. from its shape), *Calvary*, Mat. xxvii. 33; Mar. xv. 22; Jn. xix. 17. See κρανίον. (N. T.)*

Γόμορρα, ας, ἡ, and ων, τά, *Gomorrha*, Ro. ix. 29.

γόμος, ου, ὁ (γέμω), (1) *a burden, e.g.*, of a ship, Ac. xxi. 3; (2) *wares* or *merchandise*, Rev. xviii. 11, 12.*

γονεύς, έως, ὁ (γεν- in γίγνομαι), *a parent*, only in plural, Lu. ii. 41; Ep. vi. 1.

γόνυ, ατος, τό, *the knee;* often in plur. after τιθέναι or κάμπτειν, *to put* or *bend the knees, to kneel*, in devotion, Lu. xxii. 41; Ro. xi. 4.

γονυ-πετέω, ῶ (πίπτω), *to fall on the knees, to kneel to* (acc.), Mar. x. 17.

γράμμα, ατος, τό (γράφω), (1) *a letter of the alphabet*, Gal. vi. 11, *in what large letters*, perhaps noting emphasis; *letter*, as opposed to spirit, Ro. ii. 29, etc.; (2) *a writing*, such as *a bill* or *an epistle*, as Lu. xvi. 6, 7; Ac. xxviii. 21; **τὰ ἱερὰ γράμματα**, 2 Tim.

iii. 15, *the holy writings*, or *the Scriptures*; (3) plur., *literature, learning* generally, Jn. vii. 15.

γραμματεύς, έως, ὁ, (1) *a clerk, secretary, a scribe*, Ac. xix. 35; (2) one of that class among the Jews who copied and interpreted the O. T. Scriptures (see νομικός), Mat. xxiii. 34; (3) met., *a man of learning generally*, Mat. xiii. 52.

γραπτός, ή, όν, verb. adj., *written*, Ro. ii. 15.*

γραφή, ῆς, ἡ, (1) *a writing;* (2) spec., ἡ γραφή or αἱ γραφαί, *the Scriptures, writings* of the O. T., 2 Pet. iii. 16; (3) a particular *passage*, Mar. xii. 10.

γράφω, ψω, γέγραφα, *to grave, write, inscribe;* ἐγράφη, γέγραπται, or γεγραμμένον ἐστί, a formula of quotation, *It is written;* often with dat. of pers., as Mar. x. 5.

γραώδης, ες (γραῦς, εἶδος), *old-womanish, foolish*, 1 Tim. iv. 7.*

γρηγορέω, ῶ (from ἐγρήγορα, perf. of ἐγείρω), *to keep awake, watch, be vigilant*, Mar. xiii. 35, 37; Rev. xvi. 15.

γυμνάζω (γυμνός), *to exercise, train*, 1 Tim. iv. 7; Heb. v. 14, xii. 11; 2 Pet. ii. 14.*

γυμνασία, ας, ἡ, *exercise, training*, 1 Tim. iv. 8.*

γυμνητεύω, or ιτεύω (W. H.), *to be naked* or *poorly clad*, 1 Cor. iv. 11.*

γυμνός, ή, όν, (1) *naked*, Mar. xiv. 52; Rev. iii. 17; *ill-clad*, Mat. xxv. 36, 48; *having only an inner garment*, Jn. xxi. 7; (2) *bare, i.e., open* or *manifest*, Heb. iv. 13; (3) *mere*, 1 Cor. xv. 37.

γυμνότης, τητος, ἡ, (1) *nakedness*, Rev. iii. 18; (2) *scanty clothing*, Ro. viii. 35; 2 Cor. xi. 27. (N. T.)*

γυναικάριον, ου, τό (dim.), *a silly woman*, 2 Tim. iii. 6.*

γυναικεῖος, α, ον, *womanish, female;* 1 Pet. iii. 7, the *weaker* vessel.*

γυνή, γυναικός, voc. γύναι, ἡ, (1) *a woman*, Mat. ix. 20; Ro. vii. 2; (2) *a wife*, Ac. v. 1, 7; Ep. v. 28. The voc. is the form of ordinary address, often used in reverence and honor; compare Jn. ii. 4 and xix. 26.

Γώγ, ὁ, a proper name, *Gog*. In Ezek. xxxviii. 2, king of Magog, a land of the remote north; hence, in Rev. xx. 8, of a people far remote from Palestine.*

γωνία, ας, ἡ, *a corner*, as Mat. vi. 5, xxi. 42 (from S.); met., *a secret place*, Ac. xxvi. 26.

Δ

Δ, δ, δέλτα, *delta, d*, the fourth letter of the Greek alphabet. As a numeral, δʹ = 4; ͵δ = 4000.

Δαβίδ, also Δαυΐδ, Δαυείδ (W. H.), ὁ (Heb.), *David*, king of Israel; ὁ υἱὸς Δ., *the Son of David*, an appellation of the Messiah; ἐν Δ., *in David, i.e.*, in the Psalms, Heb. iv. 7.

δαιμονίζομαι (see δαίμων), 1st aor. part., δαιμονισθείς, *to be possessed by a demon*, Mat. iv. 24; Mar. i. 32.

δαιμόνιον, ου, τό (orig. adj.), *a deity*, Ac. xvii. 18; *a demon* or *evil spirit;* δαιμόνιον ἔχειν, *to have a demon* or *to be a demoniac*, Lu. iv. 33; Jn. vii. 20.

δαιμονιώδης, ες, *resembling a demon, demoniacal*, Ja. iii. 15. (N. T.)*

δαίμων, ονος, ὁ, ἡ, in classic Greek, any spirit superior to man; hence often of the inferior deities; in N. T., *an evil spirit, a demon* (W. H. have the word only in one passage, Mat. viii. 31); δαιμόνιον is generally used.

δάκνω, *to bite*, met., Gal. v. 15.*

δάκρυ, υος, or δάκρυον, ου, τό, *a tear*, Ac. xx. 19, 31: Heb. v. 7.

δακρύω, σω, *to weep*, Jn. xi. 35.*

δακτύλιος, ου, ὁ (δάκτυλος), *a ring*, Lu. xv. 22.*

δάκτυλος, ου, ὁ, *a finger;* ἐν δακτύλῳ θεοῦ, met., *by the power of God*, Lu. xi. 20, comp. Mat. xii. 28.

Δαλμανουθά, ἡ, *Dalmanutha*, a town or village near Magdala, Mar. viii. 10.*

Δαλματία, ας, ἡ, *Dalmatia*, a part of Illyricum near Macedonia, 2 Tim. iv. 10.*

δαμάζω, σω, *to subdue, tame*, Mar. v. 4; Ja. iii. 7, 8.*

δάμαλις, εως, ἡ, *a heifer*, Heb. ix. 13.*

Δάμαρις, ιδος, ἡ, *Damaris*, Ac. xvii. 34.*

Δαμασκηνός, ή, όν, *belonging to Damascus*, 2 Cor. xi. 32.*

Δαμασκός, οῦ, ἡ, *Damascus*, Ac. ix. 2, 3.

δανείζω, *to lend* money, Lu. vi. 34, 35; mid., *to borrow*, Mat. v. 42.*

δάνειον, ου, τό, *a loan, a debt*, Mat. xviii. 27.*

δανειστής, οῦ, ὁ, *a money-lender, a creditor*, Lu. vii. 41.*

Δανιήλ, ὁ (Heb.), *Daniel*, Mat. xxiv. 15; Mar. xiii. 14 (not W. H.).*

δαπανάω, ῶ, ήσω, *to spend*, Mar. v. 26; trans., *to bear expense* for (ἐπί, dat.), Ac. xxi. 24; (ὑπέρ, gen.), 2 Cor. xii. 15; *to consume in luxury, to waste*, Lu. xv. 14; Ja. iv. 3.*

δαπάνη, ης, ἡ, *expense, cost*, Lu. xiv. 28.*

δέ, an adversative and distinctive particle, *but, now, moreover*, etc. See Gr. § 404, ii, Wi. § 53, 7, Bu. 364 sq., and μέν.

δέησις, εως, ἡ, *supplication, prayer*, Ep. vi. 18; Ja. v. 16. *Syn.:* see αἴτημα.

δεῖ, impers., see Gr. § 101, Wi. § 58, 9*b*, Bu. 147, 164, *it is necessary, one must, it ought, it is right* or *proper*, with inf. (expressed or implied), as Mat. xvi. 21; Ac. iv. 12; Mar. xiii. 14.

δεῖγμα, ατος, τό (δείκνυμι), *an example, a specimen*, Ju. 7.*

δειγματίζω, σω, *to make an example* or *spectacle of* (as disgrace), Col. ii. 15; Mat. i. 19 (W. H.). (N. T.)*

δείκνυμι and δεικνύω (see Gr. § 114, Bu. 45), (1) *to present to sight, to show, to teach* (acc and dat.), Mat. iv. 18; 1 Cor xii. 31; Rev. xvii. 1; (2) *to prove* (acc. and ἐκ), Ja. ii. 18, iii. 13; *to show by words* (ὅτι), Mat. xvi. 21; inf., Ac. x. 28.

δειλία, ας, ἡ, *timidity, cowardice*, 2 Tim. i. 7.* *Syn.:* δειλία is always used in a bad sense; εὐλάβεια, regularly in a good sense, *pious* fear; φόβος is general, denoting either bad or good.

δειλιάω, ῶ, *to be timid, fearful,* Jn. xiv. 27. (S.)*

δειλός, ή, όν, *timid, cowardly,* Mat. viii. 26; Mar. iv. 40; Rev. xxi. 8.*

δεῖνα, ὁ, ἡ, τό, gen. δεῖνος, pron., *a certain person, such a one,* Mat. xxvi. 18.*

δεινῶς, adv. (δεινός, *vehement*), *vehemently, terribly,* Mat. viii. 6; Lu. xi. 53.*

δειπνέω, ῶ, *to take the δεῖπνον, to sup,* Lu. xvii. 8, xxii. 20; 1 Cor. xi. 25; met., of familiar intercourse, Rev. iii. 20.*

δεῖπνον, ου, τό, *the chief or evening meal, supper* (see ἄριστον), Lu. xiv. 17, 24; Jn. xiii. 2, 4; κυριακὸν δεῖπνον, *the Lord's Supper,* 1 Cor. xi. 20.

δεισιδαιμονία, ας, ἡ, *religion,* in general, Ac. xxv. 19.*

δεισι-δαίμων, ον (δείδω, *to fear*), *devoutly disposed, addicted to worship,* Ac. xvii. 22. See Gr. § 323 *c.** *Syn.:* see Trench, § xlviii.

δέκα, οἱ, αἱ, τά, *ten;* in Rev. ii. 10, *a ten days' tribulation, i.e.,* brief.

δεκα-δύο (W. H. δώδεκα), *twelve,* Ac. xix. 7, xxiv. 11. (S.)*

δεκα-πέντε, *fifteen,* Jn. xi. 18; Ac. xxvii. 28, Gal. i. 18.*

Δεκά-πολις, εως, ἡ, *Decapolis,* a district E. of Jordan comprising ten towns. It is uncertain what they all were, but they included Gadara, Hippo, Pella, and Scythopolis, Mat. iv. 25; Mar. v. 20, vii. 31.*

δεκα-τέσσαρες, ων, οἱ, αἱ, -σαρα, τά, *fourteen,* Mat. i. 17; 2 Cor. xii. 2; Gal. ii. 1.*

δεκάτη, ης, ἡ, *a tenth part, a tithe,* Heb. vii. 2, 4, 8, 9.*

δέκατος, η, ον, ordinal, *tenth,* Jn. i. 39; Rev. xxi. 20; τὸ δέκατον, Rev. xi. 13, *the tenth part.**

δεκατόω, ῶ, *to receive tithe of,* acc., Heb. vii. 6; pass., *to pay tithe,* Heb. vii. 9. (S.)*

δεκτός, ή, όν (verbal adj. from δέχομαι), *accepted, acceptable,* Lu. iv. 19, 24; Ac. x. 35; 2 Cor. vi. 2; Phil. iv. 18. (S.)*

δελεάζω (δέλεαρ, *a bait*), *to take or entice,* as with a bait, Ja. i. 14; 2 Pet. ii. 14, 18.*

δένδρον, ου, τό, *a tree,* Mat. vii. 17; Lu. xiii. 19.

δεξιό-λαβος, ου, ὁ, "holding in the right hand"; plur., *spearmen,* Ac. xxiii. 23. (N. T.)*

δεξιός, ά, όν, *the right,* opp. to ἀριστερός, *the left;* ἡ δεξιά, *the right hand;* τὰ δεξιά, *the right-hand side;* ἐκ δεξιῶν, *on the right* (see Gr. § 293, 1, Wi. § 19, 1 *a*); δεξιὰς διδόναι, *to give the right hand, i.e., to receive to friendship* or *fellowship.*

δέομαι, 1st aor. ἐδεήθην, *to have need of* (gen.), as mid. of δέω (see δεῖ); *to make request of* (gen.); *to beseech, pray,* abs., or with εἰ, ἵνα, or ὅπως, of purpose.

δέον, οντος, τό (particip. of δεῖ, as subst.), *the becoming* or *needful;* with ἐστί = δεῖ, 1 Pet. i. 6; Ac. xix. 36; plur., 1 Tim. v. 13.*

δέος, ους, τό (W. H.), *fear, awe,* Heb. xii. 28.*

Δερβαῖος, ου, ὁ, *of Derbe,* Ac. xx. 4.*

Δέρβη, ης, ἡ, *Derbe,* a city of Lycaonia, Ac. xiv. 6, 20, xvi. 1.*

δέρμα, ατος, τό (δέρω), *an animal's skin,* Heb. xi. 37.*

δερμάτινος, η, ον, *made of skin, leathern,* Mat. iii. 4; Mar. i. 6.*

δέρω, 1st aor. ἔδειρα, 2d fut. pass. δαρήσομαι, *to scourge, to beat,* so as to flay off the skin; ἀέρα δέρων, 1 Cor. ix. 26, *beating air.*

δεσμεύω, σω, *to bind, put in chains* as a prisoner, Lu. viii. 29 (W. H.); Ac. xxii. 4; *to bind* as a bundle, Mat. xxiii. 4.*

δεσμέω, ῶ, *to bind,* Lu. viii. 29 (Rec.).*

δέσμη, ης, ἡ, *a bundle,* Mat. xiii. 30.*

δέσμιος, ίου, ὁ, *one bound, a prisoner,* Ac. xvi. 25, 27; Ep. iii. 1.

δεσμός, οῦ, ὁ (δέω), *a bond,* sing. only in Mar. vii. 35, ὁ δεσμὸς τῆς γλώσσης, and Lu. xiii. 16; plur., δεσμοί or (τὰ) δεσμά, *bonds* or *imprisonment,* Lu. viii. 29; Phil. i. 13.

δεσμο-φύλαξ, ακος, ὁ, *a jailer,* Ac. xvi. 23, 27, 36.*

δεσμωτήριον, ίου, τό, *a prison,* Mat. xi. 2; Ac. v. 21, 23, xvi. 26.*

δεσμώτης, ου, ὁ, *a prisoner,* Ac. xxvii. 1, 42.

δεσπότης, ου, ὁ, *a lord* or *prince, a master,* as 1 Tim. vi. 1; applied to God, Lu. ii. 29; Ac. iv. 24; Ju. 4; to Christ, 2 Pet. ii. 1; Rev. vi. 10. *Syn.:* δεσπότης indicates more absolute and unlimited authority than κύριος.

δεῦρο, adv., (1) of place, *here, hither;* used only as an imperative, *come hither,* as Mat. xix. 21; (2) of time, *hitherto,* only Ro. i. 13.

δεῦτε, adv., as if plur. of δεῦρο (or contr. from δεῦρ' ἴτε), *come, come hither,* as Mat iv. 19, xi. 28.

δευτεραῖος, αία, αῖον, *on the second day,* Ac. xxviii. 13. See Gr. § 319.*

δευτερό-πρωτος, ον, *the second-first,* Lu. vi. 1 (W. H. omit). See Gr. § 148, Wi. § 16. 4, and note. (N. T.)*

δεύτερος, α, ον, ordinal, *second* in number, as Mat. xxii. 26; in order, Mat. xxii. 39; τὸ δεύτερον or δεύτερον, adverbially, *the second time, again,* as 2 Cor. xiii. 2; so ἐκ δευτέρου, as Mar. xiv. 72; ἐν τῷ δευτέρῳ, Ac. vii. 13.

δέχομαι, 1st aor. ἐδεξάμην, dep., *to take, receive, accept, to receive* kindly, *to welcome,* persons, as Mar. vi. 11; things (a doctrine, the kingdom of heaven), as Mar. x. 15; 2 Cor. xi. 4.

δέω, *to want.* See δεῖ and δέομαι.

δέω, 1st aor., ἔδησα; perf., δέδεκα; pass., δέδεμαι; 1st aor. pass. inf., δεθῆναι, *to bind together,* bundles, as Ac. x. 11; *to swathe* dead bodies for burial, as Jn. xi. 44; *to bind* persons in bondage, as Mat. xxii. 13; Mar. vi. 17; 2 Tim. ii. 9; fig., Mat. xviii. 18; δεδεμένος τῷ πνεύματι, Ac. xx. 22, *bound in the spirit,* under an irresistible impulse.

δή, a particle indicating *certainty* or *reality,* and so augmenting the vivacity of a clause or sentence; *truly, indeed, by all means, therefore.* Used with other particles, δήποτε, δήπου, which see.

δῆλος, η, ον, *manifest, evident,* Mat. xxvi. 73; neut., sc. ἐστί, *it is evident,* with ὅτι, 1 Cor. xv. 27; Gal. iii. 11; 1 Tim. vi. 7 (W. H., R. V. omit).*

δηλόω, ῶ, *to manifest, to reveal, to bring to light, to imply* or *signify,* 1 Cor. i. 11, iii. 13; Col. i. 8; Heb. ix. 8, xii. 27; 1 Pet. i. 11; 2 Pet. i. 14.*

Δημᾶς, ᾶ, ὁ, *Demas,* Col. iv. 14; Philem. 24; 2 Tim. iv. 10.*

δημ-ηγορέω, ῶ, *to deliver a public oration;* with πρός, Ac. xii. 21.*

Δημήτριος, ου, ὁ, *Demetrius.* Two of the name are mentioned, Ac. xix. 24, 38; 3 Jn. 12.*

δημι-ουργός, οῦ, ὁ ("a public worker"), *an artisan, a builder,* Heb. xi. 10.* *Syn.:* δημιουργός emphasizes more the idea of *power;* τεχνίτης, that of *wisdom.*

δῆμος, ου, ὁ, *the people,* an organized multitude publicly convened, Ac. xii. 22, xvii. 5, xix. 30, 33.*

δημόσιος, α, ον, *belonging to the people, public,* Ac. v. 18; dat. fem., as adv., δημοσίᾳ, *publicly,* Ac. xvi. 37, xviii. 28, xx. 20.*

δηνάριον, ίου, τό, properly a Latin word (see Gr. § 154*a*), *denarius,* Mat. xviii. 28; Rev. vi. 6.

δή-ποτε, adv. with ᾧ, *whatsoever,* giving a generalizing force, Jn. v. 4 (W. H. omit).*

δή-που, adv., *indeed, perhaps, verily,* Heb. ii. 16.*

διά, prep. (cognate with δύο, *two;* δίς, *twice*), *through;* (1) with gen., *through, during, by means of;* (2) with acc., *through, on account of, for the sake of.* See Gr. §§ 147*a*, 299, Wi. § 47*i*, Bu. 182, 183, 187.

δια-βαίνω, *to pass through,* trans., Heb. xi. 29; or intrans., with πρός (person), Lu. xvi. 26; εἰς (place), Ac. xvi. 9.*

δια-βάλλω, *to slander, accuse,* Lu. xvi. 1.*

δια-βεβαιόω, ῶ, in mid., *to affirm, assert strongly,* 1 Tim. i. 7; Tit. iii. 8.*

δια-βλέπω, *to see through, to see clearly,* Mat. vii. 5; Lu. vi. 42; Mar. viii. 25 (W. H.).*

διάβολος, ον (διαβάλλω), *prone to slander, slanderous,* 1 Tim. iii. 11; 2 Tim. iii. 3; Tit. ii. 3; ὁ διάβολος, *the accuser, the devil,* equivalent to the Hebrew *Satan,* Mat. iv. 1, 5; 2 Tim. ii. 26.

δι-αγγέλλω, *to announce everywhere, publish abroad,* Lu. ix. 60; Ac. xxi. 26; Ro. ix. 17.*

διά-γε, or διά γε (W. H.), *yet on account of,* Lu. xi. 8.*

δια-γίνομαι, *to pass, elapse,* of time; in N. T. only 2d aor. part., gen. abs., *having elapsed,* Mar. xvi. 1; Ac. xxv. 13, xxvii. 9.*

δια-γινώσκω, *to distinguish, know accurately,* Ac. xxiii. 15; *to examine, decide,* Ac. xxiv. 22.*

δια-γνωρίζω, *to publish abroad,* Lu. ii. 17 (W. H. γνωρίζω).*

διά-γνωσις, εως, ἡ, *judicial examination, decision,* Ac. xxv. 21.*

δια-γογγύζω, *to murmur greatly,* Lu. xv. 2, xix. 7. (S.)*

δια-γρηγορέω, ῶ, *to remain awake* or *to be fully awake,* Lu. ix. 32. (N. T.)*

δι-άγω, *to lead* or *pass,* as time, life, 1 Tim. ii. 2 (βίον); Tit. iii. 3 (βίον omitted).*

δια-δέχομαι, *to succeed to,* Ac. vii. 45.*

διά-δημα, ατος, τό (δέω), *a diadem, crown,* Rev. xii. 3, xiii. 1, xix. 12.* *Syn.:* διάδημα always indicates the fillet, the symbol of royalty; στέφανος is the festal *garland* of victory.

δια-δίδωμι, *to distribute, divide,* Lu. xi. 22, xviii. 22; Jn. vi. 11; Ac. iv. 35; Rev. xvii. 13 (W. H. δίδωμι).*

διά-δοχος, ου, ὁ, ἡ, *a successor,* Ac. xxiv. 27.*

δια-ζώννυμι, *to gird,* Jn. xiii. 4, 5, xxi. 7.*

δια-θήκη, ης, ἡ (διατίθημι), (1) *a will* or *testament, a disposition,* as of property, Gal. iii. 15; Heb. ix. 16, 17; (2) *a compact* or *covenant* between God and man (see Gen. vi, ix, xv, xvii; Exod. xxiv; Deut. v, xxviii). The two covenants mentioned, Gal. iv. 24; that of the O. T. is termed ἡ πρώτη δ., Heb. ix. 15; that of the N. T., ἡ καινὴ δ., Lu. xxii. 20. The O. T. itself (ἡ παλαιὰ δ., 2 Cor. iii. 14) as containing the first, and the N. T. as containing the second, are each called διαθήκη.

δι-αίρεσις, εως, ἡ, *difference, distinction,* as the result of distribution, 1 Cor. xii. 4, 5, 6.*

δι-αιρέω, ῶ, *to divide, distribute,* Lu. xv. 12; 1 Cor. xii. 11.*

δια-καθαρίζω, ιῶ, *to cleanse thoroughly,* Mat. iii. 12; Lu. iii. 17 (W. H. διακαθαίρω). (N. T.)*

δια-κατ-ελέγχομαι, *to confute entirely,* Ac. xviii. 28. (N. T.)*

διακονέω, ῶ, *to serve* or *wait upon,* especially at table, Jn. xii. 26; Lu. iv. 39; *to supply wants, to administer* or *distribute alms,* etc. (dat., person; acc., thing; occasionally abs.), Mat. xxv. 44; Ro. xv. 25; specially, *to serve as a deacon,* 1 Tim. iii. 10, 13; of prophets and apostles who *ministered* the divine will, 1 Pet. i. 12; 2 Cor. iii. 3.

διακονία, ας, ἡ, *service, ministry,* in various senses, especially for Christ, 2 Cor. iii. 7; Ro. xi. 13; Ac. vi. 4; *relief,* Ac. xi. 29; *a serving,* Lu. x. 40; *the office of deacon,* Ro. xii. 7.

διάκονος, ου, ὁ, ἡ, *a servant,* viewed in relation to his *work,* specially at table, as Mat. xxiii. 11; Mar. x. 43; one in God's service, *a minister,* as Ro. xiii. 4, xv. 8; *one who serves in the church, deacon* or *deaconess,* Phil. i. 1; 1 Tim. iii. 8, 12; Ro. xvi. 1.

διακόσιοι, αι, α, card. num., *two hundred,* Mar. vi. 37; Jn. vi. 7.

δι-ακούω, *to hear thoroughly,* Ac. xxiii. 35.*

δια-κρίνω, *to discern, to distinguish, make a distinction,* as Ac. xv. 9; 1 Cor. xi. 29. Mid. (aor pass.), (1) *to doubt, to* *hesitate*, as Mat. xxi. 21; Ja. i. 6; (2) *to dispute with*, Ac. xi. 2; Ju. 9.

διά-κρισις, εως, ἡ, *the act of distinction, discrimination*, Ro. xiv. 1; 1 Cor. xii. 10; Heb. v. 14.*

δια-κωλύω, *to hinder*, Mat. iii. 14.*

δια-λαλέω, ῶ, *to converse together*, Lu. vi. 11; *to talk of*, Lu. i. 65.*

δια-λέγω, in mid., *to reason, to discuss, to dispute*, as Mar. ix. 34; Ac. xx. 7; Ju. 9.

δια-λείπω, *to leave off, to cease*, Lu. vii. 45.*

διά-λεκτος, ου, ἡ, *speech, dialect, language*, Ac. i. 19, ii. 6, 8, xxi. 40, xxii. 2, xxvi. 14.*

δι-αλλάσσω, *to change*, as the disposition; pass., *to be reconciled to*, Mat. v. 24.*

δια-λογίζομαι, *to reason, to deliberate, to debate*, as Mar. ii. 6, 8, viii. 16, ix. 33.

διαλογισμός, οῦ, ὁ, *reflection, thought*, as Lu. ii. 35; *reasoning, opinion*, as Ro. i. 21; *hesitation, doubt*, Lu. xxiv. 38; *dispute, debate*, as Phil. ii. 14; 1 Tim. ii. 8.

δια-λύω, *to disperse, to break up*, Ac. v. 36.*

δια-μαρτύρομαι, dep. mid., *to testify, solemnly charge*, as Ac. ii. 40; 1 Tim. v. 21; *to testify to, solemnly affirm*, Ac. viii. 25; Heb. ii. 6.

δια-μάχομαι, dep. mid., *to contend* or *dispute fiercely*, Ac. xxiii. 9.*

δια-μένω, *to remain, continue*, Lu. i. 22, xxii. 28; Gal. ii. 5; Heb. i. 11; 2 Pet. iii. 4.*

δια-μερίζω, (1) *to divide* or *separate into parts*, as Mat. xxvii. 35, etc.; *to distribute*, as Lu. xxii. 17; (2) pass. with ἐπί, *to be divided* against, *be at discord* with; acc., Lu. xi. 17; dat., xii. 52.

δια-μερισμός, οῦ, ὁ, *dissension*, Lu. xii. 51.*

δια-νέμω, *to disseminate, to spread abroad*, Ac. iv. 17.*

δια-νεύω, *to make signs*, prob. by nodding, Lu. i. 22.*

δια-νόημα, ατος, τό, *a thought*, Lu. xi. 17.*

διά-νοια, ας, ἡ, *the mind, the intellect*, or *thinking faculty*, as Mar. xii. 30; *the understanding*, 1 Jn. v. 20; *the feelings, disposition, affections*, as Col. i. 21; plur., *the thoughts*, as willful, depraved, Ep. ii. 3 (in Ep. i. 18, A. V., *the eyes of your understanding* (διανοίας), W. H. and R. V. read καρδίας, *the eyes of your heart*).

δι-αν-οίγω, *to open fully, i.e.*, the ears, Mar. vii. 34; the eyes, Lu. xxiv. 31; the heart, Ac. xvi. 14; the Scriptures, Lu. xxiv. 32.

δια-νυκτερεύω, *to pass the whole night*, Lu. vi. 12.*

δι-ανύω, *to perform to the end, complete*, Ac. xxi. 7.*

δια-παντός, adv., *always, continually* (W. H. always read διὰ παντός).

δια-παρα-τριβή, ῆς, ἡ, *contention, incessant wrangling*, 1 Tim. vi. 5 (W. H., Rec. has παραδιατριβή). (N. T.)*

δια-περάω, ῶ, άσω, *to cross over*, as Mat. ix. 1.

δια-πλέω, εύσω, *to sail across*, Ac. xxvii. 5.*

δια-πονέω, ῶ, mid., aor. pass., *to grieve one's self, to be vexed*, Ac. iv. 2, xvi. 18.*

δια-πορεύομαι, pass., *to go* or *pass through*, as Lu. xiii. 22.

δι-απορέω, ῶ, *to be in great doubt* or *perplexity*, Lu. ix. 7, xxiv. 4 (W. H. ἀπορέω); Ac. ii. 12, v. 24, x. 17.*

δια-πραγματεύομαι, *to gain by business* or *trading*, Lu. xix. 15.*

δια-πρίω (πρίω, *to saw*), in pass., *to be sawn through*; fig., *to be greatly moved with anger*, Ac. v. 33, vii. 54.*

δι-αρπάζω, άσω, *to plunder*, Mat. xii. 29; Mar. iii. 27.*

δια-ρρήγνυμι and διαρρήσσω, ξω, *to tear*, as garments, in grief or indignation, Mat. xxvi. 65; Mar. xiv. 63; Ac. xiv. 14; *to break asunder*, as a net, Lu. v. 6; as bonds, Lu. viii. 29.*

δια-σαφέω, ῶ, *to make clear, to declare*, Mat. xiii. 36 (W. H.), xviii. 31.

δια-σείω, *to treat with violence*, so as to extort anything, Lu. iii. 14.*

δια-σκορπίζω, *to scatter, to winnow*, as Mat. xxv. 24; *to disperse* in conquest, as Lu. i. 51; *to waste* or *squander*, Lu. xv. 13, xvi. 1.

δια-σπάω, 1st aor. pass. διεσπάσθην, *to break asunder*, Mar. v. 4; *to tear in pieces*, Ac. xxiii. 10.*

δια-σπείρω, 2d aor. pass. διεσπάρην, *to scatter abroad, disperse*, Ac. viii. 1, 4, xi. 19.*

δια-σπορά, ᾶς, ἡ, *dispersion, state of being dispersed*; used of the Jews as scattered among the Gentiles, Jn. vii. 35; Ja. i. 1; 1 Pet. i. 1. (Ap.)*

δια-στέλλω, in mid., *to give a command* or *injunction*, Mar. viii. 15; Ac. xv. 24; foll. by ἵνα, Mat. xvi. 20 (W. H. mrg.); Mar. v. 43, vii. 36, ix. 9; pass. part., τὸ διαστελλόμενον, Heb. xii. 20, *the command*.*

διά-στημα, ατος, τό, *an interval* of time, Ac. v. 7.*

δια-στολή, ῆς, ἡ, *distinction, difference*, Ro. iii. 22, x. 12; 1 Cor. xiv. 7.*

δια-στρέφω, *to seduce, turn away*, Lu. xxiii. 2; Ac. xiii. 8; *to pervert, oppose*, Ac. xiii. 10; perf. part. pass., διεστραμμένος, *perverse, corrupt*, Mat. xvii. 17; Lu. ix. 41; Ac. xx. 30; Phil. ii. 15.*

διασώζω, σω, *to save, to convey safe through*, Ac. xxiii. 24, xxvii. 43; 1 Pet. iii. 20; pass., *to reach a place in safety*, Ac. xxvii. 44, xxviii. 1, 4; *to heal perfectly*, Mat. xiv. 36; Lu. vii. 3.*

δια-ταγή, ῆς, ἡ, *a disposition, arrangement, ordinance*, Ac. vii. 53; Ro. xiii. 2.*

διά-ταγμα, ατος, τό, *a mandate, a decree*, Heb. xi. 23.*

δια-ταράσσω, *to trouble greatly, to agitate*, Lu. i. 29.*

δια-τάσσω, *to give orders to* (dat.), *arrange, prescribe*, Mat. xi. 1; Lu. viii. 55; 1 Cor. xvi. 1; mid., *to appoint, to ordain*, as 1 Cor. vii. 17 (also with dat. person; acc., thing).

δια-τελέω, ῶ, *to continue*, Ac. xxvii. 33.*

δια-τηρέω, ῶ, *to guard* or *keep with care*, Lu. ii. 51; with ἑαυτόν, etc., *to guard one's self from, to abstain* (ἐκ or ἀπό), Ac. xv. 29.*

δια-τί or διὰ τί (W. H.), *wherefore?*

δια-τίθημι, only mid. in N. T., *to dispose*, as (1) *to assign*, Lu. xxii. 29; (2) with cog. acc., διαθήκην, *make* a covenant with (dat. or πρός, acc.), Ac. iii. 25; Heb. viii. 10, x. 16; *make* a will, Heb. ix. 16, 17. See διαθήκη.*

δια-τρίβω, *to spend* or *pass* (χρόνον or ἡμέρας), as Ac. xiv. 3, 28; abs., *to stay*, as Jn. iii. 22.

δια-τροφή, ῆς, ἡ, *food, nourishment*, 1 Tim. vi. 8.*

δι-αυγάζω, *to shine through*, *to dawn*, 2 Pet. i. 19.*

δια-φανής, ές, *transparent*, Rev. xxi. 21 (W. H. διαυγής in same signif.).*

δια-φέρω, (1) *to carry through*, Mar. xi. 16; (2) *to spread abroad*, Ac. xiii. 49; (3) *to carry hither and thither*, Ac. xxvii. 27; (4) *to differ from* (gen.), 1 Cor. xv. 41; Gal. iv. 1; hence, (5) *to excel, surpass*, as Mat. vi. 26; (6) impers., διαφέρει, with οὐδέν, *it makes no difference* to (dat.), *matters nothing* to, Gal. ii. 6.

δια-φεύγω, *to escape by flight*, Ac. xxvii. 42.*

δια-φημίζω, *to report, publish abroad*, Mat. ix. 31, xxviii. 15; Mar. i. 45.*

δια-φθείρω, *to corrupt*, 1 Tim. vi. 5; Rev. xi. 18; *to destroy utterly*, Lu. xii. 33; Rev. viii. 9, xi. 18; pass., *to decay. to perish*, 2 Cor. iv. 16; opp. to ἀνακαινόω, *to renew*.*

δια-φθορά, ᾶς, ἡ, *decay, corruption, i.e.*, of the grave, Ac. ii. 27, 31, xiii. 34–37 (from S.).*

διά-φορος, ον, (1) *diverse, of different kinds*, Ro. xii. 6; Heb. ix. 10; (2) compar., *more excellent* than, Heb. i. 4, viii. 6.*

δια-φυλάσσω, *to guard carefully, protect, defend*, Lu. iv. 10 (from S.).*

δια-χειρίζω, mid. N. T., *to lay hands on, put to death*, Ac. v. 30, xxvi. 21.*

δια-χλευάζω, see χλευάζω.

δια-χωρίζω, pass. N. T., "to be separated," *to depart from* (ἀπό), Lu. ix. 33.*

διδακτικός, ή, όν, *apt in teaching*, 1 Tim. iii. 2; 2 Tim. ii. 24.*

διδακτός, ή, όν, *taught, instructed*, Jn. vi. 45; 1 Cor. ii. 13.*

διδασκαλία, ας, ἡ, *instruction, teaching*, as Ro. xii. 7; *the doctrine taught, precept, instruction*, as Mat. xv. 9, etc.

διδάσκαλος, ου, ὁ, *a teacher*, especially of the Jewish law, *master, doctor*, as Lu. ii. 46; often in voc. as a title of address to Christ, *Master, Teacher*.

διδάσκω, διδάξω, *to teach, to be a teacher*, abs., Ro. xii. 7; *to teach*, with acc. of person, generally also acc. of thing; also with inf. or ὅτι, Mat. v. 2; Ac. iv. 2.

διδαχή, ῆς, ἡ, *the act of teaching*, Ac. ii. 42; 2 Tim. iv. 2; *that which is taught*, doctrine, Mar. i. 27; Ac. xvii. 19; Rev. ii. 24; with obj. gen., perhaps in Heb. vi. 2, see Gr. § 260*b*, note, Wi. § 30, 1*a*.

δί-δραχμον, ου, τό (prop. adj., sc. νόμισμα, *coin*), *a double drachma*, or silver half-shekel (in S. often *the shekel*), Mat. xvii. 24. (S.)*

Δίδυμος, η, ον, *double*, or *twin;* a surname of *Thomas* the apostle, Jn. xi. 16, xx. 24, xxi. 2.*

δίδωμι, *to give* (acc. and dat.); hence, in various connections, *to yield, deliver, supply, commit*, etc. When used in a general sense, the dat. of person may be omitted, as Mat. xiii. 8. The thing given may be expressed by ἐκ or ἀπό, with gen. in a partitive sense instead of acc.; so Mat. xxv. 8; Lu. xx. 10. The purpose of a gift may be expressed by inf., as Mat. xiv. 16; Jn. iv. 7; Lu. i. 73.

δι-εγείρω, *to wake up thoroughly*, as Lu. viii. 24; *to excite*, Jn. vi. 18; fig., *to stir up, arouse*, 2 Pet. i. 13.

δι-ενθυμέομαι, οῦμαι (W. H.), *to reflect*, Ac. x. 19. (N. T.)*

δι-έξ-οδος, ου, ἡ, *a meeting-place of roads, a public spot* in a city, Mat. xxii. 9.*

δι-ερμηνευτής, οῦ, ὁ, *an interpreter*, 1 Cor. xiv. 28. (N. T.)*

δι-ερμηνεύω, *to interpret*, Lu. xxiv. 27; 1 Cor. xii. 30, xiv. 5, 13, 27; *to translate*, Ac. ix 36.*

δι-έρχομαι, *to pass through*, acc. or διά (gen.), destination expressed by εἰς or ἕως; *to pass over* or *travel*, abs., Ac. viii. 4; *to spread*, as a report, Lu. v. 15.

δι-ερωτάω, ῶ, *to find by inquiry*, Ac. x. 17.*

δι-ετής, ές (δίς), *of two years*, Mat. ii. 16.*

διετία, ας, ἡ, *the space of two years*, Ac. xxiv. 27, xxviii. 30.*

δι-ηγέομαι, οῦμαι, *to relate in full, describe*, Mar. v. 16; Ac. viii. 33, ix. 27.

διήγησις, εως, ἡ, *a narrative*, Lu. i. 1.*

δι-ηνεκής, ές, *continuous; εἰς τὸ διηνεκές, continually*, Heb vii. 3, x. 1, 12, 14.*

δι-θάλασσος, ον (δίς), *lying between two seas*, Ac. xxvii. 41.*

δι-ϊκνέομαι, οῦμαι, *to pass through, pierce*, Heb. iv. 12.*

δι-ΐστημι, *to put apart, proceed*, Ac. xxvii. 28; 2 aor., intrans., Lu. xxii. 59, *one hour having intervened;* xxiv. 51, *he parted* from them.*

δι-ϊσχυρίζομαι, *to affirm confidently*, Lu. xxii. 59; Ac. xii. 15.*

δικαιο-κρισία, ας, ἡ, *just judgment*, Ro. ii. 5. (S.)*

δίκαιος, α, ον, *just, right, upright, righteous, impartial;* applied to things, to persons, to Christ, to God, Mat. i. 19; Heb. xi. 4; Ac. x. 22.

δικαιοσύνη, ης, ἡ, *righteousness, justice, rectitude*, Mat. iii. 15; Jn. xvi. 8, 10; Ro. v. 17, 21.

δικαιόω, ῶ, *to show to be righteous*, 1 Tim. iii. 16; Ro. iii. 4; usually in N. T. in the declarative sense, *to hold guiltless, to justify, to pronounce* or *treat as righteous*, as Mat. xii. 37; 1 Cor. iv. 4.

δικαίωμα, ατος, τό, *a righteous statute, an ordinance*, Lu. i. 6; Ro. i. 32, ii. 26; Heb. ix. 1, 10; especially *a judicial decree, of acquittal* (opp. to κατάκριμα, *condemnation*), Ro. v. 16; *of condemnation*,

Rev. xv. 4; *a righteous act*, Ro. v. 18; Rev. xix. 8.*

δικαίως, adv., *justly*, 1 Pet. ii. 23; Lu. xxiii. 41; *properly*, 1 Cor. xv. 34; *uprightly*, 1 Th. ii. 10; Tit. ii. 12.*

δικαίωσις, εως, ἡ, *acquittal, justification*, Ro. iv. 25, v. 18.*

δικαστής, οῦ, ὁ, *a judge*, Lu. xii. 14 (W. H. κριτής); Ac. vii. 27, 35.*

δίκη, ης, ἡ, *a judicial sentence*, Ac. xxv. 15 (W. H. καταδίκη); τίνω or ὑπέχω δίκην, *to suffer punishment*, 2 Th. i. 9; Ju. 7; *Justice, the name of a heathen deity*, Ac. xxviii. 4.*

δίκτυον, ου, τό, *a fishing-net*, Jn. xxi. 6, 8, 11. *Syn.:* see ἀμφίβληστρον.

δι-λόγος, ον (δίς), *double-tongued, deceitful*, 1 Tim. iii. 8. (N.T.)*

διό, conj. (διά and ὅ), *on which account, wherefore*.

δι-οδεύω, *to journey through*, Ac. xvii. 1; *to go about*, Lu. viii. 1.*

Διονύσιος, ου, ὁ, *Dionysius*, Ac. xvii. 34.*

διό-περ, conj., *for which very reason*, 1 Cor. viii. 13, x. 14, xiv. 13 (W. H. διό).*

Διο-πετής, ές, *fallen from Zeus, i.e.*, from heaven, Ac. xix. 35.*

δι-όρθωμα, see κατόρθωμα.

δι-όρθωσις, εως, ἡ, *reformation*, Heb. ix. 10.*

δι-ορύσσω, ξω, *to dig through*, Mat. vi. 19, 20, xxiv. 43; Lu. xii. 39.*

Διόσ-κουροι, ων, οἱ (children of Zeus), *Castor* and *Pollux*, Ac. xxviii. 11.*

δι-ότι, conj. (= διὰ τοῦτο, ὅτι), *on this account, because, for*.

Διο-τρεφής, οῦς, ὁ, *Diotrephes*, 3 Jn. 9.*

διπλόος, οῦς, ῆ, οῦν, *double, twofold*, 1 Tim. v. 17; Rev. xviii. 6; comp., διπλότερος with gen., *twofold more than*, Mat. xxiii. 15.*

διπλόω, ῶ, *to double*, Rev. xviii. 6.*

δίς, adv., *twice*, Lu. xviii. 12.

(Δίς), obsolete nom. for Ζεύς, gen. Διός, acc. Δία, *Zeus* or *Jupiter*, see Ζεύς.

διστάζω, σω (δίς), *to waver, to doubt*, Mat. xiv. 31, xxviii. 17.*

δί-στομος, ον (δίς), *two-edged*, Heb. iv. 12; Rev. i. 16, ii. 12.*

δισ-χίλιοι, αι, α, num., *two thousand*, Mar. v. 13.

δι-υλίζω, *to strain off, filter through*, Mat. xxiii. 24.*

διχάζω, σω, *to set at variance, divide*, Mat. x. 35.*

διχο-στασία, ας, ἡ, *division, dissension*, Ro. xvi. 17; 1 Cor. iii. 3 (not W. H.); Gal. v. 20.*

διχο-τομέω, ῶ, ήσω, *to cut in two*, perhaps meaning *to scourge severely*, Mat. xxiv. 51; Lu. xii. 46.*

διψάω, ῶ, ήσω, *to thirst for, to desire earnestly*, acc., Mat. v. 6; or abs., *to thirst*, Jn. iv. 15; 1 Cor. iv. 11.

δίψος, ους, τό, *thirst*, 2 Cor. xi. 27.*

δί-ψυχος, ον (δίς), *double-minded*, Ja. i. 8, iv. 8.*

διωγμός, οῦ, ὁ, *persecution*, Mat. xiii. 21; Ro. viii. 35.

διώκτης, ου, ὁ, *a persecutor*, 1 Tim. i. 13. (N. T.)*

διώκω, ξω, *to pursue*, in various senses according to context; *to follow, follow after, press forward, to persecute*.

δόγμα, ατος, τό (δοκέω), *a decree, edict, ordinance*, Lu. ii. 1; Ac. xvi. 4, xvii. 7; Ep. ii. 15; Col. ii. 14.*

δογματίζω, σω, *to impose an ordinance*; mid., *to submit to ordinances*, Col. ii. 20.*

δοκέω, ῶ, δόξω, (1) *to think*, acc. and inf., Lu. viii. 18; 2 Cor. xi. 16; (2) *to seem, appear*, Lu. x. 36; Ac. xvii. 18; (3) δοκεῖ, impers., *it seems*, Mat. xvii. 25; *it seems good to* or *pleases*, dat., Lu. i. 3; Ac. xv. 22. *Syn.:* φαίνομαι means to appear *on the outside*; δοκέω, to appear *to an individual* to be true.

δοκιμάζω, σω, *to try, scrutinize, prove*, as 2 Cor. viii. 22; Lu. xii. 56; *to judge fit, approve*, as 1 Cor. xvi. 3. *Syn.:* δοκιμάζω means to test anything with the expectation of finding it good; πειράζω, either with no expectation, or of finding it bad.

δοκιμασία, ας, ἡ, the act of *proving*, Heb. iii. 9 (W. H.).*

δοκιμή, ῆς, ἡ, *a trial*, 2 Cor. viii. 2; *a proof*, 2 Cor. xiii. 3; *tried, approved character*, Ro. v. 4; 2 Cor. ix. 13. (N. T.)

δοκίμιον, ου, τό, *a test, trial*, 1 Pet. i. 7; Ja. i. 3.*

δόκιμος, ον (δέχομαι), *approved, acceptable*, as Ro. xiv. 18, xvi. 10.

δοκός, οῦ, ἡ, *a beam*, Mat. vii. 3, 4, 5; Lu. vi. 41, 42.*

δόλιος, ία, ιον, *deceitful*, 2 Cor. xi. 13.*

δολιόω, ῶ, *to deceive*, impf., 3d pers. plur., ἐδολιοῦσαν, an Alexandrian form from S., Ro. iii. 13. (S.)*

δόλος, ου, ὁ, *fraud, deceit, craft*, Mat. xxvi. 4; 2 Cor. xii. 16.

δολόω, ῶ, *to adulterate, corrupt*, 2 Cor. iv. 2.*

δόμα, ατος, τό (δίδωμι), *a gift*, Mat. vii. 11; Lu. xi. 13; Ep. iv. 8; Phil. iv. 17.*

δόξα, ης, ἡ, from δοκέω, in two main significations: (1) *favorable recognition* or *estimation, honor, renown*, as Jn. v. 41, 44; 2 Cor. vi. 8; Lu. xvii. 18; and very frequently (2) *the appearance, the manifestation of that which calls forth praise*; so especially in the freq. phrase ἡ δόξα τοῦ θεοῦ, *glory, splendor*. Concrete plur. δόξαι, in 2 Pet. ii. 10; Ju. 8, *dignities*, angelic powers.

δοξάζω, σω, *to ascribe glory to, to honor, glorify*, Ro. xi. 13; 1 Cor. vi. 20.

Δορκάς, άδος, ἡ, *Dorcas*, Ac. ix. 36, 39.*

δόσις, εως, ἡ, *a giving*, Phil. iv. 15; *a gift*, Ja. i. 17.*

δότης, ου, ὁ, *a giver*, 2 Cor. ix. 7. (S.)*

δουλ-αγωγέω, ῶ, *to bring into subjection*, 1 Cor. ix. 27.*

δουλεία, ας, ἡ, *slavery, bondage*, Ro. viii. 15, 21; Heb. ii. 15.

δουλεύω, σω, (1) *to be a slave*, absolutely, Ep. vi. 7; Ro. ix. 12; (2) *to be subject to, to obey*, dat., Ro. vii. 6; Gal. iv. 8.

δοῦλος, η, ον, adj. only Ro. vi. 19; as subst. ἡ δούλη, *a female slave*, Lu. i. 38, 48; ὁ δοῦλος, *a slave, bondman*, the lowest word for this idea (opp. to ἐλεύθερος); *a servant* (opp. to κύριος, δεσπότης), so in the freq. phrases δοῦλος τοῦ θεοῦ, δοῦλος Χριστοῦ.

δουλόω, ῶ, ώσω, *to reduce to*

bondage (acc. and dat.), Ac. vii. 6; 1 Cor. ix. 19; pass., *to be held subject to, be in bondage*, 1 Cor. vii. 15.

δοχή, ῆς, ἡ (δέχομαι), *a receiving* of guests, *a banquet*, Lu. v. 29, xiv. 13.*

δράκων, οντος, ὁ, *a dragon* or *huge serpent;* symb. for Satan, Rev.

δράμω, obs., *to run*, see τρέχω.

δράσσομαι, dep., *to grasp, take;* acc., 1 Cor. iii. 19.*

δραχμή, ῆς, ἡ, *a drachma*, an Attic silver coin nearly equal to the Roman denarius, or worth about sixteen cents of our money, Lu. xv. 8, 9.*

δρέπανον, ου, τό, *a sickle* or *pruning-hook*, Mar. iv. 29; Rev. xiv. 14–19.*

δρόμος, ου, ὁ, *a running;* fig., *course, career*, Ac. xiii. 25, xx. 24; 2 Tim. iv. 7.*

Δρουσίλλα, ης, ἡ, *Drusilla*, Ac. xxiv. 24.*

δύναμαι, dep. (see Gr. § 109*b*, 1), *to be able*, abs., or with inf. (sometimes omitted) or acc.: *to have a capacity for; to be strong*, as 1 Cor. iii. 2; *to have power to do*, whether through ability, disposition, permission, or opportunity.

δύναμις, εως, ἡ, (1) *power, might*, absolutely or as an attribute, Lu. i. 17; Ac. iii. 12; (2) *power* over, expressed by εἰς or ἐπί (acc.), *ability to do;* (3) *exercise of power, mighty work, miracle*, as Mat. xi. 20; (4) *forces*, as of an army, spoken of the heavenly hosts, as Mat. xxiv. 29; (5) *force*, as of a word, *i.e.*, *significance*, 1 Cor. xiv. 11. *Syn.:* τέρας indicates a miracle as a wonderful portent or prodigy; σημεῖον, as a sign, authenticating the divine mission of the doer; δύναμις, as an exhibition of divine power.

δυναμόω, ῶ, *to strengthen, confirm*, Col. i. 11; Heb. xi. 34 (W. H.). (S.)*

δυνάστης, ου, ὁ, (1) *a potentate, prince*, Lu. i. 52; 1 Tim. vi. 15; (2) *one in authority*, Ac. viii. 27.*

δυνατέω, ῶ, *to be powerful, have power*, 2 Cor. xiii. 3; (inf.), Ro. xiv. 4 (W. H.); 2 Cor. ix. 8 (W. H.). (N. T.)*

δυνατός, ή, όν, *able, having power, mighty*, Lu. xiv. 31; 1 Cor. i. 26; ὁ δυνατός, *the Almighty*, Lu. i. 49; δυνατόν, *possible*, Ro. xii. 18; Gal. iv. 15.

δύνω or δύω, 2d aor. ἔδυν, *to sink; to set*, as the sun, Mar. i. 32; Lu. iv. 40.*

δύο, indecl. num., except dat. δυσί, *two*.

δυς-, an inseparable prefix, implying *adverse, difficult*, or *grievous*.

δυσ-βάστακτος, ον, *hard to be borne*, Mat. xxiii. 4 (not W. H.); Lu. xi. 46. (S.)*

δυσ-εντερία, ας, ἡ (W. H. ιον, τό), *dysentery*, Ac. xxviii. 8.*

δυσ-ερμήνευτος, ον, *hard to explain*, Heb. v. 11.*

δύσ-κολος, ον (lit., "difficult about food"), *difficult*, Mar. x. 24.*

δυσκόλως, adv., *with difficulty, hardly*, Mat. xix. 23; Mar. x. 23; Lu. xviii. 24.*

δυσμή, ῆς, ἡ (only plur., δυσμαί), *the setting of the sun, the west*, Rev. xxi. 13; Mat. viii. 11.

δυσ-νόητος, ον, *hard* or *difficult to be understood*, 2 Pet. iii. 16.*

δυσ-φημέω, ῶ, *to speak evil, defame*, 1 Cor. iv. 13 (W. H.).*

δυσ-φημία, ας, ἡ, *evil report, defamation*, 2 Cor. vi. 8.*

δώδεκα, indecl. num., *twelve;* οἱ δώδεκα, *the twelve, i.e., the Apostles.*

δωδέκατος, η, ον, ord. num., *twelfth*, Rev. xxi. 20.*

δωδεκά-φυλον, ου, τό, *the twelve tribes, Israel*, Ac. xxvi. 7.*

δῶμα, ατος, τό, *a house, a housetop*, Mat. xxiv. 17; Ac. x. 9.

δωρεά, ᾶς, ἡ, *a gift*, Jn. iv. 10; Ro. v. 15; Ep. iv. 7.

δωρεάν, accus. of preced., as an adv., *freely*, as 2 Cor. xi. 7; *without cause, groundlessly*, Jn. xv. 25; Gal. ii. 21.

δωρέομαι, οῦμαι, *to present, bestow*, Mar. xv. 45; pass., 2 Pet. i. 3, 4.*

δώρημα, ατος, τό, *a gift, bounty*, Ro. v. 16; Ja. i. 17.*

δῶρον, ου, τό, *a gift, present*, Ep. ii. 8; Rev. xi. 10.

E

E, ε, ἐψῖλον, *epsilon, e*, the fifth letter. As a numeral, ε′ = 5; ͵ε = 5000.

ἔα, interj., expressing surprise or indignation, *ha! ah!* Mar. i. 24 (W. H. omit); Lu. iv. 34.*

ἐάν or ἄν, conj. (for εἰ ἄν), *if*, usually construed with subjunctive verb. See Gr. § 383, Wi. § 41 *b*, 2, Bu. 221 sq. W. H. have the indic. fut. in Lu. xix. 40; Ac. viii. 31; pres. in 1 Th. iii. 8; 1 Jn. v. 15 (Rec. also). Sometimes equivalent to a particle of time, *when*, Jn. xii. 32; after the relative, with an indefinite force, ὃς ἐάν, who*soever*, as Mat. v. 19, viii. 19; 1 Cor. xvi. 6; ἐὰν δὲ καί, *and if also;* ἐὰν μή, *except, unless*, Mat. v. 20; *but that*, Mar. iv. 22; ἐὰν πέρ, *if indeed*, Heb. vi. 3.

ἑαυτοῦ, ῆς, οῦ, pron., reflex., 3d pers., *of one's self;* used also in 1st and 2d persons. See Gr. § 335, Wi. §§ 22, 5, 38, 6, Bu. 111 sq. Genitive often for possess. pron. λέγειν or εἰπεῖν ἐν ἑαυτῷ, *to say within one's self;* γίνεσθαι or ἔρχεσθαι ἐν ἑαυτῷ, *to come to one's self;* πρὸς ἑαυτόν, *to one's home*, Jn. xx. 10, or *privately*, as Lu. xviii. 11; ἐν ἑαυτοῖς, *among yourselves, i.e.*, one with another; καθ' ἑαυτόν, *apart;* παρ' ἑαυτόν, *at home.*

ἐάω, ῶ, ἐάσω; impf., εἴων; 1st aor., εἴασα, (1) *to permit*, inf., or acc. and inf., Mat. xxiv. 33; Lu. iv. 41; (2) *to leave*, Ac. xxvii. 40.

ἑβδομήκοντα, indecl. num., *seventy;* οἱ ἑβδομήκοντα, *the seventy* disciples, Lu. x. 1, 17.

ἑβδομηκοντάκις, num. adv., *seventy times*, Mat. xviii. 22. (S.)*

ἕβδομος, η, ον, ord. num., *seventh*, Jn. iv. 52; Heb. iv. 4.

Ἔβερ, ὁ, *Eber* or *Heber*, Lu. iii. 35.*

Ἑβραϊκός, ή, όν (from Heb.), *Hebrew*, Lu. xxiii. 38 (W. H. omit). (N. T.)*

Ἑβραῖος (W. H. 'E-), αία, αῖον (from Heb.), also subst., ὁ, ἡ, *a Hebrew;* designating (1) any

Jew, 2 Cor. xi. 22; Phil. iii. 5; (2) a Jew of Palestine, in distinction from οἱ Ἑλληνισταί, or Jews born out of Palestine, and using the Greek language, Ac. vi. 1; (3) any Jewish Christian, Heb. (heading). (S.)* *Syn.:* Ἑβραῖος denotes a Jew who spoke Aramaic or Hebrew, in distinction from Ἑλληνιστής, a Greek-speaking Jew; Ἰουδαῖος, a Jew in distinction from other nations; Ἰσραηλίτης, one of the chosen people.

Ἑβραΐς (W. H. Ἐ-), (from Heb.), ίδος, ἡ, *Hebrew, i.e., the Aramaic language*, vernacular in the time of Christ and the Apostles, Ac. xxi. 40, xxii. 2, xxvi. 14. See Gr. § 150, Wi. § 3*a*. (Ap.)*

Ἑβραϊστί (W. H. Ἐ-), (from Heb.), adv., *in the Hebrew language, i.e., in Aramaic*, Jn. v. 2; Rev. ix. 11. (Ap.)

ἐγγίζω, fut. att., ἐγγιῶ; pf., ἤγγικα, *to approach, to draw near, to be near*, abs., or with dat. or εἰς, or ἐπί (acc.), Lu. xviii. 40; Ac. ix. 3; Mar. xi. 1.

ἐγ-γράφω (W. H. ἐνγ-), *to inscribe, engrave*, 2 Cor. iii. 2; Lu. x. 20 (W. H.).*

ἔγγυος, ου, ὁ, ἡ, *a surety*, Heb. vii. 22.*

ἐγγύς, adv., *near;* used of both place and time, with gen. or dat.

ἐγγύτερον, comp. of preceding, *nearer*, Ro. xiii. 11.*

ἐγείρω, ἐγερῶ, pass. perf., ἐγήγερμαι, *to arouse, to awaken*, Ac. xii. 7; *to raise up*, as a Savior, Ac. xiii. 23 (Rec.); *to erect*, as a building, Jn. ii. 19, 20; mid., *to rise up*, as from sleep, or from a recumbent posture, as at table, Jn. xi. 29, xiii. 4; applied to raising the dead, Jn. v. 21; used also of *rising up against*, as an adversary, or in judgment, Mat. xxiv. 7.

ἔγερσις, εως, ἡ, *a rousing up;* of the resurrection, Mat. xxvii. 53.*

ἐγκ-. In words beginning thus, W. H. generally write ἐνκ-.

ἐγ-κάθ-ετος, ου, ὁ, ἡ (ἐγκαθίημι), *a spy*, Lu. xx. 20.*

ἐγκαίνια, ίων, τά, *a dedication*, Jn. x. 22; of the feast commemorating the dedicating or purifying of the temple, after its pollution by Antiochus Epiphanes, 25 Chisleu, answering to mid-December. (S.)*

ἐγ-καινίζω, *to dedicate*, Heb. ix. 18, x. 20. (S.)*

ἐγ-κακέω, ῶ, and ἐνκακέω, *to grow weary, to faint* (W. H. in many passages for Rec. ἐκκακέω).

ἐγ-καλέω, ῶ, έσω, impf., ἐνεκάλουν, *to bring a charge against, accuse*, pers. dat., or κατά (gen.), crime in gen., Ac. xix. 38, 40; Ro. viii. 33.

ἐγ-κατα-λείπω, ψω, (1) *to desert, to abandon*, Mat. xxvii. 46; 2 Tim. iv. 10, 16; (2) *to leave remaining*, Ro. ix. 29.

ἐγ-κατ-οικέω, ῶ, *to dwell among* (ἐν), 2 Pet. ii. 8.*

ἐγ-καυχάομαι, *to boast in*, 2 Th. i. 4 (W. H.).*

ἐγ-κεντρίζω, *to insert*, as a bud or graft, *to graft in;* fig., Ro. xi. 17, 19, 23, 24.*

ἔγ-κλημα, ατος, τό, *a charge* or *accusation*, Ac. xxiii. 29, xxv. 16.*

ἐγ-κομβόομαι, οῦμαι, *to gird on*, as an outer garment, the badge of slavery, 1 Pet. v. 5. (N. T.)*

ἐγ-κοπή, ῆς, ἡ (W. H. ἐνκ-), *a hindrance*, 1 Cor. ix. 12.*

ἐγ-κόπτω, ψω, *to impede, to hinder* (acc., or inf. with τοῦ), Ro. xv. 22; 1 Th. ii. 18.

ἐγκράτεια, ας, ἡ, *self-control, continence*, Ac. xxiv. 25; Gal. v. 23; 2 Pet. i. 6.*

ἐγκρατεύομαι, dep., *to be self-controlled, continent*, especially in sensual pleasures, 1 Cor. vii. 9, ix. 25.*

ἐγ-κρατής, ές, *self-controlled, continent*, Tit. i. 8.*

ἐγ-κρίνω, *to adjudge* or *reckon*, to a particular rank (acc. and dat.), 2 Cor. x. 12.*

ἐγ-κρύπτω, *to hide in, to mix with*, Mat. xiii. 33; Lu. xiii. 21 (W. H. κρύπτω).*

ἔγ-κυος, ον, *pregnant*, Lu. ii. 5.*

ἐγ-χρίω, *to rub in, anoint*, Rev. iii. 18.*

ἐγώ, pers. pron., *I;* plur., ἡμεῖς, *we*. See Gr. § 53.

ἐδαφίζω, fut. (attic), ιῶ, *to throw to the ground, to raze*, Lu. xix. 44.*

ἔδαφος, ους, τό, *the base, the ground*, Ac xxii. 7.*

ἑδραῖος, αία, αῖον, *steadfast, firm*, 1 Cor. vii. 37, xv. 58; Col. i. 23.*

ἑδραίωμα, ατος, τό, *a stay, support*, 1 Tim. iii. 15. (N. T.)*

Ἐζεκίας, ου, ὁ, *Hezekiah*, Mat. i. 9, 10.*

ἐθελο-θρησκεία, ας, ἡ, *voluntary, arbitrary worship*, Col. ii. 23. (N. T.)*

ἐθέλω, see θέλω.

ἐθίζω, *to accustom;* pass., perf. part., neut., τὸ εἰθισμένον, *the custom*, Lu. ii. 27.*

ἐθνάρχης, ου, ὁ, *a prefect, ethnarch*, 2 Cor. xi. 32.*

ἐθνικός, ή, όν, *of Gentile race, heathen*, as subst. ὁ ἐθνικός, *the pagan, the Gentile*, Mat. v. 47 (W. H.), vi. 7, xviii. 17; 3 Jn. 7 (W. H.).*

ἐθνικῶς, adv., *like the Gentiles*, Gal. ii. 14. (N. T.)*

ἔθνος, ους, τό, *a race, a nation*, Lu. xxii. 25; Ac. x. 35; τὰ ἔθνη, *the nations, the heathen world, the Gentiles*, Mat. iv. 15; Ro. iii. 29; by Paul, even *Gentile Christians*, Ro. xi. 13; Gal. ii. 12.

ἔθος, ους, τό, *a usage, custom*, Lu. i. 9; Ac. xxv. 16.

ἔθω, obs., pf. εἴωθα in pres. signif., *to be accustomed*, Mat. xxvii. 15; Mar. x. 1; τὸ εἰωθὸς αὐτῷ, *his custom*, Lu. iv. 16; Ac. xvii. 2.*

εἰ, a conditional conjunction (see Gr. § 383), *if, since, though*. After verbs indicating emotion, εἰ is equivalent to ὅτι, Mar. xv. 44. As an interrogative particle, εἰ occurs in both indirect and direct questions, Mar. xv. 45; Ac. i. 6. In oaths and solemn assertions, it may be rendered by *that ... not*. εἰ μή and εἰ μήτι, *unless, except;* εἰ δὲ μή, *but if not, otherwise*, Jn. xiv. 2; εἴ περ, *if so be;* εἴ πως, *if possibly;* εἴτε ... εἴτε, *whether ... or*.

εἶδον, see ὁράω, οἶδα.

εἶδος, ους, τό, *outward appearance, form*, Lu. iii. 22, ix. 29; Jn. v. 37; 2 Cor. v. 7; *species, kind*, 1 Th. v. 22.*

εἰδωλεῖον, ου, τό, *an idol-temple*, 1 Cor. viii. 10. (Ap.)*

εἰδωλό-θυτος, ον, *sacrificed to idols;* used of meats, as Ac. xv. 29. (Ap.)

εἰδωλο-λατρεία, ας, ἡ, *idolatry*, 1 Cor. x. 14; Gal. v. 20; Col. iii. 5; 1 Pet. iv. 3. (N. T.)*

εἰδωλο-λάτρης, ου, ὁ, *an idolater*, 1 Cor. x. 7; Rev. xxi. 8. (N. T.)

εἴδωλον, ου, τό, *an idol, a false god* worshipped in an image, Ac. vii. 41; Ro. ii. 22.

εἰκῆ or εἰκῇ (W. H.), adv., *without purpose*, as Ro. xiii. 4; *in vain*, 1 Cor. xv. 2 (W. H. and R. V. omit in Mat. v. 22).

εἴκοσι, indecl. num., *twenty*.

εἴκω, *to give way, to yield*, Gal. ii. 5.*

εἴκω, obs., whence 2d perf. ἔοικα, *to be like;* with dat., Ja. i. 6, 23.*

εἰκών, όνος, ἡ, *an image, likeness*, Mar. xii. 16; 1 Cor. xi. 7. *Syn.:* see Trench, § xv.

εἰλικρίνεια, ας, ἡ, *clearness, sincerity*, 1 Cor. v. 8; 2 Cor. i. 12, ii. 17.*

εἰλικρινής, ές (derivation doubtful), *sincere, pure*, Phil. i. 10; 2 Pet. iii. 1.*

εἱλίσσω (W. H. ἑλίσσω), *to roll together*, as a scroll, Rev. vi. 14.*

εἰμί (see Gr. § 110, Wi. § 14, 2, Bu. 49, 50), a verb of existence, (1) used as a predicate, *to be, to exist, to happen, to come to pass;* with an infin. following, ἔστι, *it is convenient, proper*, etc., as Heb. ix. 5; (2) as the copula of subject and predicate, simply *to be*, or in the sense of *to be like, to represent*, Jn. vi. 35; Mat. xxvi. 26; 1 Cor. x. 4. With participles, it is used to form the periphrastic tenses, as Lu. i. 22, iv. 16; Mat. xvi. 19, etc. With gen., as predicate, it marks quality, possession, participation, etc.; with dat., property, possession, destination, etc. The verb, when copula, is often omitted. Participle, ὤν, *being;* τὸ ὄν, *that which is;* οἱ ὄντες, τὰ ὄντα, persons or things *that are*.

εἶμι, *to go*, in some copies for εἰμί, in Jn. vii. 34, 36 (not W. H.).*

εἵνεκα, εν, see ἕνεκα, εν.

εἴπερ, εἴπως, see under εἰ.

εἶπον (see Gr. § 103, 7, Wi. § 15, Bu. 57), (W. H. εἶπα), from obs. ἔπω, or εἴπω, *to say;* in reply, *to answer;* in narration, *to tell;* in authoritative directions, *to bid* or *command*, as Lu. vii. 7.

εἰρηνεύω, *to have peace, to be at peace*, Mar. ix. 50; Ro. xii. 18; 2 Cor. xiii. 11; 1 Th. v. 13.*

εἰρήνη, ης, ἡ, *peace*, the opposite of strife; *peace of mind*, arising from reconciliation with God. In N. T. (like the corresponding Heb. word in O. T.), εἰρήνη generally denotes *a perfect well-being*. Often employed in salutations, as in Hebrew.

εἰρηνικός, ή, όν, *peaceable*, Ja. iii. 17; *peaceful*, Heb. xii. 11.*

εἰρηνο-ποιέω, ῶ, *to make peace, reconcile*, Col. i. 20. (S.)*

εἰρηνο-ποιός, όν, *pacific, loving peace*, Mat. v. 9.*

εἰς, prep. governing acc., *into, to* (the interior). See Gr. §§ 124, 298. In composition, it implies motion into or towards.

εἷς, μία, ἕν, a card. num., *one;* used distributively, as Mat. xx. 21; by way of emphasis, as Mar. ii. 7; and indefinitely, as Mat. viii. 19; Mar. xii. 42. As an ordinal, *the first*, Mat. xxviii. 1, Rev. ix. 12.

εἰσ-άγω, 2d aor. εἰσήγαγον, *to lead in, bring in*, Lu. xxii. 54; Ac. viii. 45.

εἰσ-ακούω, *to listen to, to hear* prayer, Mat. vi. 7; Lu. i. 13; Ac. x. 31; Heb. v. 7; *to hear* so as to obey (gen.), 1 Cor. xiv. 21.*

εἰσ-δέχομαι, ἔξομαι, *to receive with favor* (acc.), 2 Cor. vi. 17, from S.*

εἴσ-ειμι, impf. εἰσῄειν, inf. εἰσιέναι (εἶμι), *to go in, to enter* (with εἰς), Ac. iii. 3, xxi. 18, 26; Heb. ix. 6.*

εἰσ-έρχομαι, 2d aor. εἰσῆλθον, *to come in, to enter* (chiefly with εἰς), Ac. xxiii. 16, 33; εἰσέρχομαι καὶ ἐξέρχομαι, *to come and go in and out*, spoken of daily life and intercourse, Ac. i. 21; fig., of entrance into any state or condition, Mat. xix. 17; Heb. iii. 11, 18.

εἰσ-καλέω, ῶ, only mid. in N.T., *to call* or *invite in*, Ac. x. 23.*

εἴσ-οδος, ου, ἡ, *an entrance, the act of entering*, Heb. x. 19; 2 Pet. i. 11.

εἰσ-πηδάω, ῶ, *to spring in*, Ac. xiv. 14 (W. H. ἐκπ-), xvi. 29.*

εἰσ-πορεύομαι, dep., *to go in, to enter;* spoken of persons, as Mar. i. 21; of things, as Mat. xv. 17; εἰσπορεύομαι καὶ ἐκπορεύομαι, *to go in and out* in daily duties, Ac. ix. 28.

εἰσ-τρέχω, 2d aor. εἰσέδραμον, *to run in*, Ac. xii. 14.*

εἰσ-φέρω (see Gr. § 103, 6, Wi. § 15, Bu. 68), *to lead into* (with εἰς), *e.g.*, temptation, as Lu. xi. 4; *to bring in*, Ac. xvii. 20; 1 Tim. vi. 7.

εἶτα, adv., *then, afterwards*.

εἴτε, conj., see εἰ.

ἐκ, or, before a vowel, **ἐξ,** a prep. gov. gen., *from, out of* (the interior), used of place, time, and source. See Gr. § 293, Wi. § 47 *b*, Bu. 326 sq. In composition, ἐκ implies *egress, removal, origin, publicity, unfolding*, or is of *intensive force*.

ἕκαστος, η, ον, *each, every one* (with partitive gen.); εἷς ἕκαστος, *every one*.

ἑκάστοτε, adv., *at every time, always*, 2 Pet. i. 15.*

ἑκατόν, card. num., *a hundred*, Mat. xiii. 8, xviii. 12.

ἑκατοντα-έτης, ες, *a hundred years old*, Ro. iv. 9.*

ἑκατονταπλασίων, ον, acc. ονα, *a hundredfold*, Mat. xix. 29 (not W. H.); Mar. x. 30; Lu. viii. 8.*

ἑκατοντάρχης, ου, ὁ, *captain over a hundred men, a centurion*, Ac. x. 1, 22, xxiv. 23.

ἑκατόνταρχος, ου, ὁ = preceding, Mat. viii. 5, 8, 13. In many passages a variant for preceding.

ἐκ-βαίνω, 2d aor. ἐξέβην, *to go out*, Heb. xi. 15 (W. H.).*

ἐκ-βάλλω, βαλῶ, *to cast out*, Jn. vi. 37; *to drive out*, Mat. xxi. 12; *to expel*, Gal. iv. 30; *to send away, dismiss, reject,*

Mar. i. 43; Lu. vi. 22; *to extract, draw out,* Lu. vi. 42; Mat. xii. 35.

ἔκ-βασις, εως, ἡ, *a way of escape,* 1 Cor. x. 13; *end, issue,* Heb. xiii. 7.*

ἐκ-βολή, ῆς, ἡ, *a throwing out,* Ac. xxvii. 18.*

ἐκ-γαμίζω (W. H. γαμίζω), *to give in marriage,* Mat. xxiv. 38 (Rec.); 1 Cor. vii. 38 (Rec.). (N. T.)

ἐκ-γαμίσκω = preceding, Lu. xx. 34, 35 (Rec.). (N. T.)*

ἔκ-γονος, ον, *sprung from;* neut. plur., *descendants,* 1 Tim. v. 4.*

ἐκ-δαπανάω, ῶ, *to spend entirely;* pass. reflex., *to expend one's energies* for (ὑπέρ), 2 Cor. xii. 15.*

ἐκ-δέχομαι, *to expect* (ἕως), *to wait for* (acc. or ἕως), Ja. v. 7; Heb. x. 13.

ἔκ-δηλος, ον, *conspicuous, manifest,* 2 Tim. iii. 9.*

ἐκ-δημέω, ῶ, *to go abroad, to be absent,* 2 Cor. v. 6, 8, 9.*

ἐκ-δίδωμι, N. T. mid., *to let out for one's advantage,* Mat. xxi. 33, 41; Mar. xii. 1; Lu. xx. 9.*

ἐκ-δι-ηγέομαι, οῦμαι, dep. mid., *to narrate at length, to declare,* Ac. xiii. 41, xv. 3.*

ἐκ-δικέω, ῶ, *to do justice to, defend, avenge* a person (acc. and ἀπό), Lu. xviii. 3, 5; Ro. xii. 19; *to demand requital for, avenge* a deed (acc.), 2 Cor. x. 6; Rev. vi. 10, xix. 2.*

ἐκ-δίκησις, εως, ἡ, *an avenging, vindication, punishment,* Ac. vii. 24; Ro. xii. 19; 1 Pet. ii. 14.

ἔκ-δικος, ου, ὁ, ἡ, *an avenger, one who adjudges* a culprit (dat.) *to punishment* for (περί) a crime, Ro. xiii. 4; 1 Th. iv. 6.*

ἐκ-διώκω, ώξω, *to persecute, to expel by persecuting,* Lu. xi. 49 (not W. H.); 1 Th. ii. 15.*

ἔκ-δοτος, ον, *delivered up,* Ac. ii. 23.*

ἐκ-δοχή, ῆς, ἡ, *a waiting for, expectation,* Heb. x. 27.*

ἐκ-δύω, *to unclothe, to strip off* (two accs.), Mat. xxvii. 31; 2 Cor. v. 4.

ἐκεῖ, adv., *there, thither.*

ἐκεῖθεν, adv., *from that place, thence.*

ἐκεῖνος, η, ο, pron., demonst., *that, that one there;* used antithetically, Mar. xvi. 20; and by way of emphasis, Mat. xxii. 23. See Gr. §§ 338, 340, Wi. §§ 18, 4, 23, 1, Bu. 104, 120.

ἐκεῖσε, adv., *thither,* Ac. xxi. 3; in const. præg., Ac. xxii. 5.*

ἐκ-ζητέω, ῶ, *to seek out* with diligence, Heb. xii. 17; 1 Pet. i. 10; *to seek after* God, Ac. xv. 17; Ro. iii. 11; Heb. xi. 6; *to require,* judicially, Lu. xi. 50, 51. (S.)*

ἐκ-ζήτησις, εως, ἡ, *a subject of inquiry,* 1 Tim. i. 4 (W. H.).*

ἐκ-θαμβέω, ῶ, N. T. pass., *to be amazed, greatly astonished,* Mar. ix. 15, xiv. 33, xvi. 5, 6.*

ἔκ-θαμβος, ον, *greatly astonished, amazed,* Ac. iii. 11.*

ἐκ-θαυμάζω, *to wonder greatly,* Mar. xii. 17 (W. H.).*

ἔκ-θετος, ον, *cast out, exposed* to perish, Ac. vii. 19.*

ἐκ-καθαίρω, 1st aor. ἐξεκάθαρα, *to cleanse thoroughly,* 1 Cor. v. 7; 2 Tim. ii. 4.*

ἐκ-καίω, N. T. pass., *to burn vehemently,* as with lust, Ro. i. 27.*

ἐκ-κακέω, ῶ, *to faint, to despond through fear* (Rec., for which W. H. have ἐγκ- and ἐνκ-).

ἐκ-κεντέω, ῶ, *to pierce through, to transfix,* Jn. xix. 37; Rev. i. 7.*

ἐκ-κλάω, *to break off,* Ro. xi. 17, 19, 20 (W. H.).*

ἐκ-κλείω, σω, *to shut out,* Gal. iv. 17; *to exclude,* Ro. iii. 27.*

ἐκκλησία, ας, ἡ (ἐκκαλέω), *an assembly,* Ac. xix. 32, 39, 41; usually legally, sometimes tumultuously gathered. Espec. in N. T., *an assembly of Christian believers, a church* in one place, Ac. xi. 26; often plural, as Ac. xv. 41; *the whole body of believers* on earth, 1 Cor. xii. 28; Ep. i. 22; or in heaven, Heb. xii. 23. *Syn.:* see Trench, § 1.

ἐκ-κλίνω, *to turn away from* (ἀπό), Ro. iii. 12, xvi. 17; 1 Pet. iii. 11.*

ἐκ-κολυμβάω, ῶ, *to swim out,* Ac. xxvii. 42.*

ἐκ-κομίζω, *to carry out* for burial, Lu. vii. 12.*

ἐκ-κόπτω, κόψω, *to cut off,* Mat. iii. 10, v. 30; 2 Cor. xi. 12 (in 1 Pet. iii. 7, W. H. read ἐνκόπτω, *to hinder*).

ἐκ-κρέμαμαι (mid. of ἐκκρεμάννυμι), *to hang upon,* of earnest attention, Lu. xix. 48.*

ἐκ-λαλέω, ῶ, *to speak out, to disclose,* Ac. xxiii. 22.*

ἐκ-λάμπω, *to shine forth,* Mat. xiii. 43.*

ἐκ-λανθάνω, in mid., *to forget entirely,* Heb. xii. 5.*

ἐκ-λέγω, mid. in N. T., 1st aor. ἐξελεξάμην, *to choose out* for one's self, *to elect,* Lu. x. 42; Ac. vi. 5, xiii. 17; 1 Cor. i. 27, 28.

ἐκ-λείπω, 2d aor. ἐξέλιπον, *to fail, to cease, to die,* Lu. xvi. 9, xxii. 32, xxiii. 45 (W. H.); Heb. i. 12.*

ἐκλεκτός, ή, όν, (1) *chosen, elect,* Lu. xviii. 7, xxiii. 35; 1 Tim. v. 21; Ro. viii. 33; Rev. xvii. 14; (2) *choice, select,* 2 Jn. i. 13; 1 Pet. ii. 4.

ἐκλογή, ῆς, ἡ, *a choice, selection,* Ro. ix. 11; 1 Th. i. 4; Ac. ix. 15 (*a vessel of choice, i.e., a chosen vessel*); concr., *the chosen ones,* Ro. xi. 7

ἐκ-λύω, in pass., *to become weary* in body, or *despondent* in mind, Mar. viii. 3; Gal. vi. 9; Heb. xii. 5.

ἐκ-μάσσω, ξω, *to wipe, to wipe off,* Lu. vii. 38, 44; Jn. xi. 2, xii. 3, xiii. 5.*

ἐκ-μυκτηρίζω, *to deride, scoff at* (acc.), Lu. xvi. 14, xxiii. 35. (S.)*

ἐκ-νέω (lit., swim out), or ἐκνεύω (lit., turn by a side motion), *to withdraw,* Jn. v. 13.*

ἐκ-νήφω, *to return to soberness* of mind, 1 Cor. xv. 34.*

ἑκούσιος, ον (ἑκών), *voluntary, spontaneous,* Philem. 14.*

ἑκουσίως, adv., *voluntarily, of one's own accord,* Heb. x. 26; 1 Pet. v. 2.*

ἔκ-παλαι, adv., *from of old,* 2 Pet. ii. 3, iii. 5.*

ἐκ-πειράζω, σω, *to put to the test, to make trial of, to tempt,* Mat. iv. 7; Lu. iv. 12, x. 25; 1 Cor. x. 9. (S.)*

ἐκ-πέμπω, *to send forth*, Ac. xiii. 4, xvii. 10.*

ἐκ-περισσῶς, adv., *exceedingly*, Mar. xiv. 31 (W. H.). (N.T.)*

ἐκ-πετάννυμι, 1st aor. ἐξεπέτασα, *to stretch forth*, Ro. x. 21.*

ἐκ-πηδάω, ῶ, 1st aor. ἐξεπήδησα (W. H.), *to spring forth*, Ac. xiv. 14.*

ἐκ-πίπτω, *to fall from* (ἐκ), Ac. xii. 7; abs., *to fall*, Ja. i. 11; of a ship driven from its course, Ac. xxvii. 17; of love, *to fail*, 1 Cor. xiii. 8; of moral lapse, Gal. v. 4.

ἐκ-πλέω, εύσω, *to sail away*, Ac. xv. 39, xviii. 18, xx. 6.*

ἐκ-πληρόω, ῶ, *to fill entirely, fulfill*, Ac. xiii. 32.*

ἐκ-πλήρωσις, εως, ἡ, *fulfillment*, Ac. xxi. 26.*

ἐκ-πλήσσω, 2d aor. pass. ἐξεπλάγην, *to strike with astonishment*, Mat. xiii. 54; Ac. xiii. 12.

ἐκ-πνέω, εύσω, *to breathe out, to expire*, Mar. xv. 37, 39; Lu. xxiii. 46.*

ἐκ-πορεύομαι, dep., *to go out* (ἀπό, ἐκ, παρά, and εἰς, ἐπί, πρός); *to proceed from*, as from the heart; or as a river from its source, etc.

ἐκ-πορνεύω, *to be given up to fornication*, Ju. 7. (S.)*

ἐκ-πτύω, *to reject, to loathe*, Gal. iv. 14.*

ἐκ-ριζόω, ῶ, *to root out, root up*, Mat. xiii. 29, xv. 13; Lu. xvii. 6; Ju. 12.*

ἔκ-στασις, εως, ἡ, *trance*, Ac. x. 10; *amazement*, Mar. v. 42.

ἐκ-στρέφω, perf. pass. ἐξέστραμμαι, *to change for the worse, to corrupt*, Tit. iii. 11.*

ἐκ-ταράσσω, ξω, *to agitate greatly*, Ac. xvi. 20.*

ἐκ-τείνω, νῶ, 1st aor. ἐξέτεινα, *to stretch out* the hand, as Lu. v. 13; *to cast out*, as anchors, Ac. xxvii. 30.

ἐκ-τελέω, ῶ, έσω, *to complete*, Lu. xiv. 29, 30.*

ἐκτένεια, ας, ἡ, *intentness*, Ac. xxvi. 7.*

ἐκ-τενής, ές, *intense, fervent, intent*, 1 Pet. iv. 8; Ac. xii. 5 (W. H. -ῶς); ἐκτενέστερον, comp. as adv., *more earnestly*, Lu. xxii. 44 (W.H. omit).*

ἐκτενῶς, adv., *intently, earnestly*, 1 Pet. i. 22; Ac. xii. 5 (W. H.).*

ἐκ-τίθημι (see Gr. § 107, Wi. § 14, 1 *b*, Bu. 45 sq.), (1) *to put out, expose* an infant, Ac. vii. 21; (2) *to expound*, Ac. xi. 4, xviii. 26, xxviii. 23.*

ἐκ-τινάσσω, ξω, *to shake off*, Mat. x. 14; Mar. vi. 11; Ac. xiii. 51; *to shake out*, Ac. xviii. 6.*

ἕκτος, η, ον, ord. num., *sixth*.

ἐκτός, adv., generally as prep., with gen., *without, besides, except*, 1 Cor. vi. 18; Ac. xxvi. 22; ἐκτὸς εἰ μή, *except*, 1 Cor. xiv. 5; τὸ ἐκτός, *the outside*, Mat. xxiii. 26.

ἐκ-τρέπω, pass. in mid. sense, *to turn from, to forsake*, 1 Tim. i. 6, v. 15, vi. 20; 2 Tim. iv. 4; Heb. xii. 13.*

ἐκ-τρέφω, *to nourish*, Ep. v. 29; *to bring up*, Ep. vi. 4.*

ἔκ-τρωμα, ατος, τό, *an abortive birth, an abortion*, 1 Cor. xv. 8.*

ἐκ-φέρω, ἐξοίσω, *to bring forth, carry out;* espec. to burial, Ac. v. 6, 9; *to produce*, of the earth, Heb. vi. 8.

ἐκ-φεύγω, *to flee out* (abs., or with ἐκ), Ac. xvi. 27, xix. 16; *to escape*, 1 Th. v. 3; Ro. ii. 3.

ἐκ-φοβέω, ῶ, *to terrify greatly*, 2 Cor. x. 9.*

ἔκ-φοβος, ον, *greatly terrified*, Mar. ix. 6; Heb. xii. 21.*

ἐκ-φύω, 2d aor. pass. ἐξεφύην, *to put forth*, as a tree its leaves, Mat. xxiv. 32; Mar. xiii. 28.*

ἐκ-χέω, also ἐκχύνω; fut. ἐκχεῶ, 1st aor. ἐξέχεα (see Gr. § 96 *c*, Wi. § 13, 3 *a*, Bu. 68), *to pour out*, as Rev. xvi. 1–17; money, Jn. ii. 15; *to shed* blood, Lu. xi. 50; fig., *to shed abroad*, love, Ro. v. 5; pass., *to be wholly given up to*, Ju. 11.

ἐκ-χωρέω, ῶ, *to depart from*, Lu. xxi. 21.*

ἐκ-ψύχω, *to expire*, Ac. v. 5, 10, xii. 23.*

ἑκών, οῦσα, όν, *voluntary, willing;* used adverbially, Ro. viii. 20; 1 Cor. ix. 17.*

ἐλαία, ας, ἡ, *an olive tree*, Ro. xi. 17, 24; its fruit, *the olive*, Ja. iii. 12; τὸ ὄρος τῶν ἐλαιῶν, *the Mount of Olives*, Mar. xi. 1.

ἔλαιον, ου, τό, *olive oil*, Mat. xxv. 3; Rev. vi. 6.

ἐλαιών, ῶνος, ὁ, *an olive orchard*, *i.e.*, the Mount of Olives, Ac. i. 12. (S.)*

Ἐλαμίτης, ου, ὁ, *an Elamite*, *i.e.*, inhabitant of the province of Elymais, Ac. ii. 9.*

ἐλάσσων or -ττων, ον, compar. of ἐλαχύς for μικρός, *less;* in excellence, Jn. ii. 10; in age, Ro. ix. 12; in rank, Heb. vii. 7; ἔλαττον, as adv., *less*, 1 Tim. v. 9.*

ἐλαττονέω, ῶ, *to have less, to lack*, 2 Cor. viii. 15.*

ἐλαττόω, ῶ, *to make less* or *inferior*, Heb. ii. 7, 9; pass., *to decrease*, Jn. iii. 30.*

ἐλαύνω, perf. part. ἐληλακώς, *to drive*, Lu. viii. 29; Ja. iii. 4; 2 Pet. ii. 17; *to drive* a ship, *to row*, Mar. vi. 48; Jn. vi. 19.*

ἐλαφρία, ας, ἡ, *levity, inconstancy*, 2 Cor. i. 17.*

ἐλαφρός, ά, όν, *light*, as a burden, Mat. xi. 30; 2 Cor. iv. 17.*

ἐλάχιστος, η, ον (superl. of ἐλαχύς for μικρός), *smallest, least*, in size, amount, or importance, Ja. iii. 4; Lu. xvi. 10; 1 Cor. vi. 2.

ἐλαχιστότερος, α, ον, a double comparison, *less than the least*, Ep. iii. 8. (N. T.)*

ἐλάω, see ἐλαύνω.

Ἐλεάζαρ, ὁ, *Eleazar*, Mat. i. 15.*

ἐλεάω (W. H., Rec. ἐλεέω), Ro. ix. 16; Ju. 22, 23.*

ἐλεγμός, οῦ, ὁ, *reproof*, 2 Tim iii. 16 (W. H.). (S.)*

ἔλεγξις, εως, ἡ, *refutation, rebuke*, 2 Pet. ii. 16. (S.)*

ἔλεγχος, ου, ὁ, *evident demonstration, proof*, Heb. xi. 1; 2 Tim. iii. 16 (not W. H.).*

ἐλέγχω, ξω, *to convict, refute, reprove*, 1 Cor. xiv. 24; Jn. iii. 20; 1 Tim. v. 20.

ἐλεεινός, ή, όν, *pitiable, miserable*, 1 Cor. xv. 19; Rev. iii. 17.*

ἐλεέω, ῶ, *to have mercy on, succor* (acc.), Mat. ix. 27; Lu. xvi. 24; pass., *to obtain mercy*, Mat. v. 7.

ἐλεημοσύνη, ης, ἡ, *mercy, pity;* in N. T., *alms*, sometimes plur., Mat. vi. 4; Lu. xi. 41; Ac. ix. 36.

ἐλεήμων, ον, *full of pity, merciful*, Mat. v. 7; Heb. ii. 17.*

ἔλεος, ους, τό (and ου, ὁ, see Gr. § 32*a*, Wi. § 9, note 2, Bu. 22), *mercy, pity*, especially on account of misery, Tit. iii. 5; Mat. ix. 13.

ἐλευθερία, ας, ἡ, *liberty, freedom*, from the Mosaic yoke, as 1 Cor. x. 29; Gal. ii. 4; from evil, as Ja. ii. 12; Ro. viii. 21; *license*, 2 Pet. ii. 19.

ἐλεύθερος, α, ον, *free*, as opposed to the condition of a slave; *delivered from obligation* (often with ἐκ, ἀπό); *at liberty to* (inf.); once with dat. of reference, Ro. vi. 20.

ἐλευθερόω, ῶ, *to set free* (generally with acc. and ἀπό); with modal dative, Gal. v. 1.

ἔλευσις, εως, ἡ (ἔρχομαι), *a coming, an advent*, Ac. vii. 52.*

ἐλεφάντινος, η, ον, *made of ivory*, Rev. xviii. 12.*

Ἐλιακείμ, ὁ (Heb.), *Eliakim*, Mat. i. 13; Lu. iii. 30.*

ἕλιγμα, ατος, τό, *a roll*, Jn. xix. 39 (W. H. for Rec. μίγμα).*

Ἐλιέζερ, ὁ (Heb.), *Eliezer*, Lu. iii. 29.*

Ἐλιούδ, ὁ (Heb.), *Eliud*, Mat. i. 14, 15.*

Ἐλισάβετ, ἡ (Heb. *Elisheba*), *Elisabeth*, Lu. i. 5, etc.

Ἐλισσαῖος, ου, ὁ, *Elisha*, Lu. iv. 27.*

ἑλίσσω, ίξω, as εἱλίσσω, *to roll up*, Heb. i. 12; Rev. vi. 14 (W. H.).*

ἕλκος, ους, τό, *a wound, an ulcer, a sore*, Lu. xvi. 21; Rev. xvi. 2, 11.*

ἑλκόω, ῶ, *to make a sore*; pass., *to be full of sores*, Lu. xvi. 20.*

ἑλκύω, σω, *to drag*, Ac. xvi. 19; *to draw*, a net, Jn. xxi. 6, 11; a sword, Jn. xviii. 10; *to draw over, to persuade*, Jn. vi. 44, xii. 32.* *Syn.*: σύρω *always* means to drag *by force*; ἑλκύω only *sometimes* involves force, often not.

ἕλκω (old form of foregoing), impf. εἷλκον, Ja. ii. 6; Ac. xxi. 30.*

Ἑλλάς, άδος, ἡ, *Hellas, Greece*, = Ἀχαΐα, Ac. xx. 2.*

Ἕλλην, ηνος, ὁ, *a Greek*, as distinguished (1) from βάρβαρος, *barbarian*, Ro. i. 14, and (2) from Ἰουδαῖος, *Jew*, as Jn. vii. 35. Used for Greek proselytes to Judaism, Jn. xii. 20; Ac. xvii. 4.

Ἑλληνικός, ή, όν, *Grecian*, Lu. xxiii. 38 (W. H. omit); Rev. ix. 11.*

Ἑλληνίς, ίδος, ἡ, *a Greek* or *Gentile woman*, Mar. vii. 26; Ac. xvii. 12.*

Ἑλληνιστής, οῦ, ὁ (ἑλληνίζω, to *Hellenize*, or *adopt Greek manners and language*), *a Hellenist, Grecian Jew* (R. V.); a Jew by parentage and religion, but born in a Gentile country and speaking Greek, Ac. vi. 1, ix. 29, xi. 20.*

Ἑλληνιστί, adv., *in the Greek language*, Jn. xix. 20; Ac. xxi. 37.*

ἐλ-λογέω (ἐν; W. H. -άω), *to charge to, to put to one's account*, Ro. v. 13; Philem. 18. (N. T.)*

Ἐλμωδάμ (W. H. -μα-), ὁ, *Elmodam*, Lu. iii. 28.*

ἐλπίζω, att. fut. ἐλπιῶ, 1st aor. ἤλπισα, *to expect* (acc. or inf., or ὅτι); *to hope for* (acc.); *to trust in* (ἐπί, dat.; ἐν, once dat. only); *to direct hope towards* (εἰς, ἐπί, acc.).

ἐλπίς, ίδος, ἡ, *expectation, hope*; especially of the Christian *hope*. Met., (1) *the author*, as 1 Tim. i. 1; (2) *the object of hope*, as Tit. ii. 13 (in Ro. viii. 20 W. H. read ἐφ' ἐλπίδι).

Ἐλύμας, α, ὁ (from Aram.), *Elymas*, Ac. xiii. 8.*

ἐλωΐ (prob. Aram. = Heb. ἠλί), *my God!* Mar. xv. 34; Mat. xxvii. 46 (W. H.); see ἠλί. (N. T.)*

ἐμαυτοῦ, ῆς, οῦ, *of myself*, a reflexive pron., found only in the gen., dat., and acc. cases; ἀπ' ἐμαυτοῦ, *from myself*, Jn. v. 30.

ἐμ-βαίνω, 2d aor. ἐνέβην, part. ἐμβάς, *to go upon, into* (εἰς), always of entering a ship except Jn. v. 4 (W. H. omit).

ἐμ-βάλλω, *to cast into*, Lu. xii. 5.*

ἐμ-βάπτω, *to dip into*, Mat. xxvi. 23; Mar. xiv. 20; Jn. xiii. 26 (W. H. βάπτω).*

ἐμ-βατεύω, *to enter, to intrude, to pry into*, Col. ii. 18.*

ἐμ-βιβάζω, *to cause to enter, to put on board*, Ac. xxvii. 6.*

ἐμ-βλέπω, *to direct the eyes to anything, to look fixedly, to consider, to know by inspection* (acc., dat., or εἰς), Mar. viii. 25; Mat. xix. 26; Ac. xxii. 11.

ἐμ-βριμάομαι, ῶμαι, dep., *to snort, to be very angry*, Mar. xiv. 5; Jn. xi. 33, 38; *to charge sternly* (dat.), Mat. ix. 30; Mar. i. 43.*

ἐμέω, ῶ, 1st aor. inf. ἐμέσαι, *to vomit forth*, Rev. iii. 16.*

ἐμ-μαίνομαι, *to rage against* (dat.), Ac. xxvi. 11.*

Ἐμμανουήλ, ὁ (Heb. *God with us*), *Immanuel*, a name of Christ, Mat. i. 23. (S.)*

Ἐμμαούς, ἡ, *Emmaus*, a village a short distance from Jerusalem, Lu. xxiv. 13.*

ἐμ-μένω, *to remain* or *persevere in* (dat. or ἐν), Ac. xxviii. 30 (W. H.); Gal. iii. 10.

Ἐμμόρ, ὁ, *Emmor*, or *Hamor*, Ac. vii. 16.*

ἐμός, ή, όν, *mine*, denoting possession, power over, authorship, right, etc. See Gr. § 336, Wi. § 22, 7, Bu. 115 sq.

ἐμπαιγμονή, ῆς, ἡ, *mockery*, 2 Pet. iii. 3 (W. H.). (N. T.)*

ἐμπαιγμός, οῦ, ὁ, *a mocking, scoffing*, Heb. xi. 36. (S.)*

ἐμ-παίζω, ξω, *to mock* (abs. or dat.), Mar. x. 34, xv. 20; *to delude*, Mat. ii. 16.

ἐμπαίκτης, ου, ὁ, *a mocker*, 2 Pet. iii. 13; Ju. 18. (S.)*

ἐμ-περιπατέω, ῶ, ήσω, *to walk about in* (ἐν), 2 Cor. vi. 16. (S.)*

ἐμ-πίπλημι and -πλάω, ἐμπλήσω, ἐνέπλησα, part. pres. ἐμπιπλῶν, *to fill up, to satisfy*, as with food, etc. (gen.), Lu. i. 53; Ro. xv. 24.

ἐμ-πίπτω, *to fall into* or *among* (εἰς), Lu. x. 36; fig., *to incur*, as condemnation or punishment, 1 Tim. iii. 6; Heb. x. 31.

ἐμ-πλέκω, 2d aor. pass. ἐνεπλάκην, *to entangle, involve in*, 2 Tim. ii. 4; 2 Pet. ii. 20 (dat. of thing).*

ἐμ-πλοκή, ῆς, ἡ, *a plaiting, braiding*, of hair, 1 Pet. iii. 3.*

ἐμ-πνέω (W. H. ἐνπ-), *to breathe in, inhale* (gen.), Ac. ix. 1.*

ἐμ-πορεύομαι, dep., *to go about; hence, to trade, to traffic*, abs., Ja. iv. 13; *to use for gain* (acc.), 2 Pet. ii. 3.*

ἐμ-πορία, ας, ἡ, *trade, merchandise*, Mat. xxii. 5.*

ἐμ-πόριον, ου, τό, *emporium, a place for trading*, Jn. ii. 16.*

ἔμ-πορος, ου, ὁ, *a traveler, merchant, trader*, Mat. xiii. 45; Rev. xviii. 3, 11, 15, 23.*

ἐμ-πρήθω, σω, *to set on fire, to burn*, Mat. xxii. 7.*

ἔμ-προσθεν, adv., *before* (ἔμπροσθεν καὶ ὄπισθεν, *in front and behind*, Rev. iv. 6); as prep. (gen.), *before*, in presence of, Mat. x. 32; *before*, in rank, Jn. i. 15, 30.

ἐμ-πτύω, σω, *to spit upon* (dat. or εἰς), Mat. xxvii. 30; Mar. x. 34.

ἐμ-φανής, ές, *manifest* (dat.), Ac. x. 40; Ro. x. 20.*

ἐμφανίζω, ίσω, *to make manifest* (acc. and dat.), Jn. xiv. 22; Heb. ix. 24; *to disclose, make known* (ὅτι, or prepp. πρός, περί, etc.), Heb. xi. 14; Ac. xxv. 15.

ἔμ-φοβος, ον, *terrified, afraid*, Ac. x. 4, xxiv. 25.

ἐμ-φυσάω, ῶ, *to breathe upon*, acc., Jn. xx. 22.*

ἔμ-φυτος, ον, *implanted*, Ja. i. 21.*

ἐν, prep. gov. dat., *in*, generally as being or resting in; *within, among*. See Gr. § 295, Wi. § 48*a*, Bu. 328 sq. ἐν- in composition has the force of *in, upon, into*. It is changed before γ, κ, ξ, and χ, into ἐγ-; before β, π, φ, ψ, and μ, into ἐμ-; and before λ, into ἐλ- (but W. H. prefer the unassimilated forms). The ν is, however, restored before the augment in verbs.

ἐν-αγκαλίζομαι, *to take into the arms*, Mar. ix. 36, x. 16.*

ἐν-άλιος, ον (ἅλς), *marine*, plur., *marine* animals, Ja. iii. 7.*

ἔν-αντι, adv., as prep. with gen., *in the presence of, before*, Lu. i. 8; Ac. viii. 21 (W. H.). (S.)*

ἐν-αντίος, α, ον, *over against, contrary*, of the wind, as Ac. xxvii. 4; *adverse, hostile*, as Ac. xxvi. 9; ἐξ ἐναντίας, *over against*, Mar. xv. 39. Neut., ἐναντίον, adv. as prep. with gen., *in the presence of*, as Lu. xx. 26; Ac. vii. 10.

ἐν-άρχομαι, *to begin*, Gal. iii. 3; Phil. i. 6.*

ἔνατος, see ἔννατος.

ἐν-δεής, ές, *in want, destitute*, Ac. iv. 34.*

ἔν-δειγμα, ατος, τό, *proof, token*, 2 Th. i. 5.*

ἐν-δείκνυμι, N. T. mid., *to show, to manifest*, Ro. ix. 22; 2 Tim. iv. 14.

ἔνδειξις, εως, ἡ, *a proof, manifestation*, Ro. iii. 25, 26; 2 Cor. viii. 24; *a sign, token*, Phil. i. 28.*

ἕν-δεκα, οἱ, αἱ, τά, *eleven; οἱ ἕνδεκα, the eleven, i.e.*, apostles, Mat. xxviii. 16; Ac. i. 26.

ἐν-δέκατος, η, ον, *eleventh*, Mat. xx. 6, 9; Rev. xxi. 20.*

ἐν-δέχομαι, dep., *to allow*; only impersonally, οὐκ ἐνδέχεται, *it is not admissible* or *possible*, Lu. xiii. 33.*

ἐν-δημέω, ῶ, *to be at home*, 2 Cor. v. 6, 8, 9.*

ἐν-διδύσκω, *to put on, clothe*, Mar. xv. 17 (W. H.); mid., *to clothe one's self with* (acc.), Lu. viii. 27 (not W. H.), xvi. 19; Mar. xv. 17 (W. H.); see ἐνδύνω. (S.)*

ἔν-δικος, ον, *righteous, just*, Ro. iii. 8; Heb. ii. 2.*

ἐν-δόμησις, εως, ἡ, *the material of a building, a structure*, Rev. xxi. 18.*

ἐν-δοξάζω, σω, N. T. pass., *to be glorified in*, 2 Th. i. 10, 12. (S.)*

ἔν-δοξος, ον, *highly esteemed*, 1 Cor. iv. 10; *splendid, glorious*, Lu. xiii. 17; of external appearance, *splendid*, Lu. vii. 25; fig., *free from sin*, Ep. v. 27.*

ἔνδυμα, ατος, τό, *a garment, raiment*, Mat. iii. 4, xxviii. 3. (S.)

ἐν-δυναμόω, ῶ, *to strengthen*, Phil. iv. 13; 1 Tim. i. 12; pass., *to acquire strength, be strengthened*, Ac. ix. 22; Ro. iv. 20. (S.)

ἐν-δύνω (2 Tim. iii. 6) and ἐνδύω, *to clothe* or *to invest with* (two accs.); mid., *to enter, insinuate one's self into* (2 Tim. iii. 6), *to put on, clothe one's self with* (acc.); often fig., *to invest with*.

ἔν-δυσις, εως, ἡ, *a putting on of clothing*, 1 Pet. iii. 3.*

ἐν-έδρα, ας, ἡ, *an ambush*, Ac. xxiii. 16 (W. H.), xxv. 3.*

ἐν-εδρεύω, *to lie in ambush for* (acc.), Lu. xi. 54; Ac. xxiii. 21.*

ἐν-ειλέω, ῶ, 1st aor. ἐνείλησα, *to roll up, wrap in* (acc. and dat.), Mar. xv. 46.*

ἔν-ειμι, *to be in*, Lu. xi. 41, τὰ ἐνόντα, *such things as are in* (the platter, ver. 39), or *the things within your power*. For ἔνεστι, impers., see ἔνι.*

ἕνεκα or ἕνεκεν, sometimes εἵνεκεν, prep. with gen., *because of, by reason of, on account of*; οὗ ἕνεκεν, *because*, Lu. iv. 18; τίνος ἕνεκεν, *for what cause?* Ac. xix. 32.

ἐν-έργεια, ας, ἡ, *working, efficiency*, Ep. i. 19, 20, iv. 16; 2 Th. ii. 9.

ἐν-εργέω, ῶ, *to be operative, to work*, as Gal. ii. 8; trans., *to accomplish*, as 1 Cor. xii. 11; mid., *to work, to display activity*, 2 Cor. i. 6; 1 Th. ii. 13; part., ἐνεργουμένη, Ja. v. 16 (see R. V.).

ἐν-έργημα, ατος, τό, *working, effect*; plur., 1 Cor. xii. 6, 10.*

ἐν-εργής, ές, *active, effectual*, 1 Cor. xvi. 9; Heb. iv. 12; Philem. 6.*

ἐν-εστώς, perf. participle of ἐνίστημι.

ἐν-ευ-λογέω, ῶ, *to bless, to confer benefits on*, Ac. iii. 25 (W. H. εὐλ-); Gal. iii. 8. (S.)*

ἐν-έχω, (1) *to hold in, entangle*, only in pass. (dat.), Gal. v. 1; (2) *to set one's self against* (dat.), Mar. vi. 19; Lu. xi. 53.*

ἐνθά-δε, adv., *here*, Lu. xxiv. 41; Ac. xvii. 6; *hither*, Jn. iv. 15; Ac. xxv. 17.

ἐν-θυμέομαι, οῦμαι, dep. pass., *to revolve in mind, to think upon*, Mat. i. 20, ix. 4; Ac. x. 19 (W. H. διεν-).*

ἐν-θύμησις, εως, ἡ, *thought, reflection*, Mat. ix. 4, xii. 25; Ac. xvii. 29; Heb. iv. 12.*

ἔνι, perhaps contracted from ἔνεστι, impers., *there is in, is present*, 1 Cor. vi. 5 (W. H.); Gal. iii. 28; Col. iii. 11; Ja. i. 17.*

ἐνιαυτός, οῦ, ὁ, *a year*, Ac. xi. 26; Ja. iv. 13.

ἐν-ίστημι, *to place in;* in pf., plpf., and 2d aor., *to be at hand, to threaten,* 2 Th. ii. 2; 2 Tim. iii. 1; perf. part. ἐνεστηκώς, sync. ἐνεστώς, *impending,* or *present,* 1 Cor. vii. 26; Gal. i. 4; Heb. ix. 9; τὰ ἐνεστῶτα, *present things,* opp. to τὰ μέλλοντα, *things to come,* Ro. viii. 38; 1 Cor. iii. 22.*

ἐν-ισχύω, *to invigorate, to strengthen,* Lu. xxii. 43 (W. H. omit); Ac. ix. 19 (see W. H.).*

ἔννατος, η, ον (W. H. ἔνατος), *ninth,* Lu. xxiii. 44; Rev. xxi. 20.

ἐννέα, οἱ, αἱ, τά, *nine,* Lu. xvii. 17.*

ἐννενηκοντα-εννέα (W. H. as two words), *ninety-nine,* Mat. xviii. 12, 13; Lu. xv. 4, 7. (N. T.)*

ἐννεός, ά, όν (W. H. ἐνεός), *dumb, speechless,* as with amazement, Ac. ix. 7.*

ἐν-νεύω, *to signify by a nod* or *sign* (dat.), Lu. i. 62.*

ἔν-νοια, ας, ἡ (νοῦς), *way of thinking, purpose,* Heb. iv. 12; 1 Pet. iv. 1.*

ἔν-νομος, ον, *bound by the law,* 1 Cor. ix. 21; *lawful, regular,* Ac. xix. 39.*

ἔν-νυχος, ον (νύξ), *in the night,* neut. as adv., Mar. i. 35 (W. H. ἔννυχα).*

ἐν-οικέω, ῶ, ήσω, *to dwell in* (ἐν), Ro. viii. 11; Col. iii. 16.

ἑνότης, τητος, ἡ (εἷς), *unity, unanimity,* Ep. iv. 3, 13.*

ἐν-οχλέω, ῶ, *to disturb, to occasion tumult,* Heb. xii. 15; Lu. vi. 18 (W. H.).*

ἔν-οχος, ον, *guilty of* (gen. of the crime, or of that which is violated), 1 Cor. xi. 27; Mar. iii. 29; *liable to* (dat. of court, gen. of punishment, εἰς of the place of punishment), Mat. v. 21, 22; Mar. xiv. 64.

ἔν-ταλμα, ατος, τό, *a precept,* Mat. xv. 9; Mar. vii. 7; Col. ii. 22. (S.)*

ἐν-ταφιάζω, *to prepare for burial,* as by washing, swathing, adorning, anointing the body, Mat. xxvi. 12; Jn. xix. 40.*

ἐνταφιασμός, οῦ, ὁ, *preparation of a body for burial,* Mar. xiv. 8; Jn. xii. 7. (N. T.)*

ἐν-τέλλω, in N. T. only mid. and pass.; fut. mid. ἐντελοῦμαι; perf., ἐντέταλμαι, *to command, to enjoin* (dat. of pers., or πρός with acc.), Ac. i. 2; Heb. ix 20.

ἐντεῦθεν, adv., *hence; from this place* or *cause;* repeated Jn. xix. 18, *on this side and that.*

ἔν-τευξις, εως, ἡ, *prayer, intercession,* 1 Tim. ii. 1, iv. 5.* *Syn.:* see αἴτημα.

ἔν-τιμος, ον, *held in honor; precious, highly esteemed,* Lu. vii. 2, xiv. 8; Phil. ii. 29; 1 Pet. ii. 4, 6.*

ἐντολή, ῆς, ἡ, *a command* or *prohibition: of God's commands,* 1 Cor. vii. 19; *Christ's precepts* or *teachings,* 1 Cor. xiv. 37; 1 Tim. vi. 14; *traditions of the Rabbis,* Tit. i. 14; αἱ ἐντολαί, *the commandments, i.e.,* the ten.

ἐν-τόπιος, ου, ὁ (prop. adj.), *a resident,* Ac. xxi. 12.*

ἐντός, adv. as prep., with gen., *within,* Lu. xvii. 21; τὸ ἐντός, *the inside,* Mat. xxiii. 26.*

ἐν-τρέπω, ψω, 2d fut. pass., ἐντραπήσομαι; 2d aor. pass., ἐνετράπην; *to put to shame,* as 1 Cor. iv. 14; Tit. ii. 8; mid., *to reverence,* as Mat. xxi. 37.

ἐν-τρέφω, *to nourish in* (dat.); pass., fig., *to be educated in,* 1 Tim. iv. 6.*

ἔν-τρομος, ον, *trembling through fear,* Ac. vii. 32, xvi. 29; Heb. xii. 21.*

ἐν-τροπή, ῆς, η, *shame,* 1 Cor. vi. 5, xv. 34.* *Syn.:* see αἰδώς.

ἐν-τρυφάω, ῶ, *to live luxuriously, to revel* (with ἐν), 2 Pet. ii. 13.*

ἐν-τυγχάνω, *to meet with, to address,* Ac. xxv. 24; with ὑπέρ (gen.), *to intercede for,* Ro. viii. 27, 34; Heb. vii. 25; with κατά (gen.), *to plead against,* Ro. xi. 2.*

ἐν-τυλίσσω, ξω, *to wrap in, to wrap up,* Mat. xxvii. 59; Lu. xxiii. 53; Jn. xx. 7.*

ἐν-τυπόω, ῶ, *to engrave,* 2 Cor. iii. 7.*

ἐν-υβρίζω, σω, *to treat contemptuously,* Heb. x. 29.*

ἐν-υπνιάζομαι, dep. pass., *to dream* (cognate acc.), Ac. ii. 17; *to conceive impure thoughts,* Ju. 8.*

ἐν-ύπνιον, ου, τό, *a dream,* Ac. ii. 17.*

ἐνώπιον (neut. of ἐνώπιος, from ἐν ὠπί, *in view*), as prep., with gen., *before, in sight* or *presence of,* Lu. i. 17; Rev. iii. 9; ἐνώπιον τοῦ θεοῦ, *in the sight of God,* Ro. xiv. 22; used in adjuration, 1 Tim. v. 21; χάρις ἐνώπιον τοῦ θεοῦ (Ac. vii. 4), *favor with God.*

Ἐνώς, ὁ, *Enos,* Lu. iii. 38.*

ἐν-ωτίζομαι, dep. mid. (ἐν ὠτίοις, *in the ears*), *to listen to,* Ac. ii. 14. (S.)*

Ἐνώχ, ὁ, *Enoch,* Lu. iii. 37; Ju. 14.*

ἐξ, prep., see ἐκ.

ἕξ, οἱ, αἱ, τά, card. num., *six.*

ἐξ-αγγέλλω, *to declare abroad, celebrate,* 1 Pet. ii. 9.*

ἐξ-αγοράζω, *to redeem,* Gal. iii. 13 (ἐκ), iv. 5; τὸν καιρόν, *to buy up, redeem the opportunity from* being lost, Ep. v. 16; Col. iv. 5.*

ἐξ-άγω, 2d aor. ἐξήγαγον, *to lead out* (with ἔξω, ἐκ, εἰς).

ἐξ-αιρέω, ῶ (see Gr. § 103, 1, Wi. § 15, Bu. 53), *to take out, pluck out,* Mat. v. 29, xviii. 9; mid., *to rescue, deliver,* Ac. vii. 10, 34, xii. 11, xxiii. 27, xxvi. 17; Gal. i. 4.*

ἐξ-αίρω (see Gr. § 92), *to lift up; to remove,* 1 Cor. v. 2 (W. H. αἴρω), 13.*

ἐξ-αιτέω, ῶ, N. T., mid., *to demand of; to ask for,* Lu. xxii. 31.*

ἐξ-αίφνης (W. H. ἐξέφ-, except in Ac. xxii. 6), adv., *suddenly, unexpectedly,* Mar. xiii. 36.

ἐξ-ακολουθέω, ῶ, *to follow after, to imitate,* 2 Pet. i. 16, ii. 2, 15.*

ἑξακόσιοι, αι, α, *six hundred,* Rev. xiii. 18, xiv. 20.*

ἐξ-αλείφω, *to wipe out, obliterate,* Rev. iii. 5; Col. ii. 14; Ac. iii. 19; *to wipe away* (ἀπό or ἐκ), Rev. vii. 17, xxi. 4.*

ἐξ-άλλομαι, *to leap up,* Ac. iii. 8.*

ἐξ-ανά-στασις, εως, ἡ, *a resurrection,* Phil. iii. 11 (followed by ἐκ, W. H.).*

ἐξ-ανα-τέλλω, *to spring up,* as plants or corn, Mat. xiii. 5; Mar. iv. 5.*

ἐξ-αν-ίστημι, (1) trans., *to raise*

up offspring, Mar. xii. 19; Lu xx. 28; (2) 2d aor. intrans., *to rise up*, Ac. xv. 5.*

ἐξ-απατάω, ῶ, *to deceive thoroughly*, Ro. vii. 11; 2 Th. ii. 3.

ἐξάπινα, adv. (= ἐξαίφνης), *suddenly*, Mar. ix. 8. (S.)*

ἐξ-απορέομαι, οῦμαι, dep., *to be utterly without resource, to be in despair*, 2 Cor. i. 8, iv. 8.*

ἐξ-απο-στέλλω, *to send forth, send away*, Ac. vii. 12, xi. 12, xvii. 14.

ἐξ-αρτίζω, (1) *to completely furnish* (πρός, acc.), 2 Tim. iii. 17; (2) *to complete*, Ac. xxi. 5.*

ἐξ-αστράπτω, *to shine*, as lightning; of raiment, Lu. ix. 29. (S.)*

ἐξ-αυτῆς, adv. (sc. ὥρας), *from that very time, instantly*, as Mar. vi. 25; Ac. x. 33.

ἐξ-εγείρω, *to raise up*, Ro. ix. 17; 1 Cor. vi. 14.*

ἔξ-ειμι (εἶμι, see Gr. § 111, Bu. 50), *to go out*, Ac. xiii. 42, xvii 15, xx. 7, xxvii. 43.*

ἔξ-ειμι (εἰμί), see ἔξεστι.

ἐξ-ελέγχω, *to convict, to rebuke sternly, to punish*, Ju. 15 (W. H. ἐλέγχω).*

ἐξ-έλκω, *to draw out* from the right way, Ja. i. 14.*

ἐξ-έραμα, ατος, τό, *vomit*, 2 Pet. ii. 22.*

ἐξερευνάω (W. H. -ραυ-), ῶ, *to search diligently*, 1 Pet. i. 10.*

ἐξ-έρχομαι (see Gr. § 103, 2, Wi. p. 33, § 15, Bu. 58), *to go* or *to come out of* (with gen. or ἐκ, ἀπό, ἔξω, παρά); *to go away, to depart, to issue* or *to spring from; to go forth*; of a rumor, *to be divulged* or *spread abroad; to emanate*, as thoughts from the heart, healing power from the Savior; *to go out, i.e.*, vanish, as expiring hope, Ac. xvi. 19.

ἔξ-εστι, part. neut. ἐξόν (impers. from ἔξειμι), *it is lawful*, as Mat. xiv. 4; *it is becoming*, as Ac. xvi. 21; *it is possible*, as Mat. xx. 15. The part. is used in the same sense, with or without subst. verb, Mat. xii. 4; 2 Cor. xii. 4 (dat. and inf.).

ἐξ-ετάζω, *to search out, to examine strictly*, Mat. ii. 8, x. 11; Jn. xxi. 12.*

ἐξ-ηγέομαι, οῦμαι, dep. mid., *to narrate fully*, as Lu. xxiv. 35; *to declare*, as a teacher, as Jn. i. 18.

ἐξήκοντα, οἱ, αἱ, τά, *sixty*.

ἑξῆς, adv. (ἔχω), *next in order*, only in the phrase τῇ ἑξῆς (sc. ἡμέρᾳ), *on the next day* (ἡμέρᾳ is expressed, Lu. ix. 37).

ἐξ-ηχέω, ῶ, N. T. only in pass., *to be sounded forth, promulgated widely*, 1 Th. i. 8.*

ἕξις, εως, ἡ (ἔχω), *habit, use*, Heb. v. 14.*

ἐξ-ίστημι, -ιστάω and -ιστάνω (see Gr. § 107, Wi. § 14, 1, Bu. 44 sq.), *to displace;* (1) trans., *to astonish*, Lu. xxiv. 22; Ac. viii. 9, 11; (2) 2d aor., perf. and mid., intrans., *to be astonished*, Mat. xii. 23; *to be insane*, 2 Cor. v. 13.

ἐξ-ισχύω, *to be perfectly able*, Ep. iii. 18.*

ἔξ-οδος, ου, ἡ, *an exit, departure*, Heb. xi. 22; *departure*, as from life, Lu. ix. 31; 2 Pet. i. 15.*

ἐξ-ολοθρεύω, *to destroy utterly*, Ac. iii. 23. (S.)*

ἐξ-ομολογέω, ῶ, *to confess fully, to make acknowledgment of*, as of sins, etc.; in mid., *to acknowledge benefits conferred, to praise* (with dat.). Once, *to promise*, Lu. xxii. 6. (S.)

ἐξ-ορκίζω, *to adjure, put to oath*, Mat. xxvi. 63.*

ἐξ-ορκιστής, οῦ, ὁ, *an exorcist*, one who expels demons by conjuration, Ac. xix. 13.*

ἐξ-ορύσσω, ξω, *to dig out*, Gal. iv. 15; *to dig through*, Mar. ii. 4.*

ἐξ-ουδενέω = ἐξουθενέω, ῶ (οὐδείς), Mar. ix. 12 (W. H.).*

ἐξ-ουδενόω, ῶ = preceding, Mar. ix. 12 (Rec.).*

ἐξουθενέω, ῶ, *to make of no account, to despise utterly*, Lu. xviii. 9; Gal. iv. 14; perf. pass. part. ἐξουθενημένος, *contemned, despised*, 1 Cor. i. 28, vi. 4. (S.)

ἐξ-ουσία, ας, ἡ (ἔξεστι), (1) *power, ability*, as Jn. xix. 11; (2) *liberty, license, privilege, right*, as Ro. ix. 21; (3) *commission, authority*, as Mat. xxi. 23; (4) αἱ ἐξουσίαι, *the powers, i.e., rulers, magistrates*, Lu. xii. 11; *angels*, good and bad, Ep. i. 21, vi. 12. In 1 Cor. xi. 10, ἐξουσίαν, *a sign of the authority of a husband over his wife, i.e., the veil.*

ἐξ-ουσιάζω, *to exercise authority over* (gen.), Lu. xxii. 25; 1 Cor. vii. 4; pass., *to be under the power of* (ὑπό), 1 Cor. vi. 12.*

ἐξ-οχή, ῆς, ἡ, *eminence, distinction;* only in the phrase κατ' ἐξοχήν, *by way of distinction*, Ac. xxv. 23 (Gr. § 300β, 5).*

ἐξ-υπνίζω, σω, *to wake from sleep*, Jn. xi. 11. (S.)*

ἔξ-υπνος, ον, *roused out of sleep*, Ac. xvi. 27.*

ἔξω, adv., abs., or as prep. with gen., *without, outside;* οἱ ἔξω, *those without*, as Mar. iv. 11; 1 Cor. v. 12, 13. Used often after verbs of motion compounded with ἐκ.

ἔξωθεν, adv. of place, *from without;* τὸ ἔξωθεν, *the outside*, as Lu. xi. 39; οἱ ἔξωθεν, *those from without*, as 1 Tim. iii. 7; as prep. gen., Mar. vii. 15; Rev. xi. 2.

ἐξ-ωθέω, ῶ, *to drive out, expel*, Ac. vii. 45; *to propel*, as a vessel, Ac. xxvii. 39 (not W. H. text).*

ἐξώτερος, α, ον (comp. of ἔξω), *outer*, in the phrase "outer darkness," Mat. viii. 12, xxii. 13, xxv. 30. (S.)*

ἔοικα, see εἴκω.

ἑορτάζω, *to keep* or *celebrate a feast*, 1 Cor. v. 8.*

ἑορτή, ῆς, ἡ, *a feast, a festival;* used of Jewish feasts, especially of the Passover, as Lu. ii. 41, xxii. 1.

ἐπ-αγγελία, ας, ἡ, (1) *a promise*, as 2 Cor. i. 20; Ac. xxiii. 21, generally plur.; *the promises*, specially, *e.g.*, to Abraham, or those of the Gospel, as 2 Tim. i. 1; (2) met., *the thing promised*, as Ac. ii. 33; Heb. xi. 13, 33, 39.

ἐπ-αγγέλλω, mid. in N. T., except pass., Gal. iii. 19, (1) *to promise*, with dat., or acc. and dat., or inf., once cognate acc., 1 Jn. ii. 25; (2) *to make profession* or *avowal of* (acc.), 1 Tim. ii. 10, vi. 21.

ἐπ-άγγελμα, ατος, τό, *a promise*, 2 Pet. i. 4, iii. 13.*

ἐπ-άγω, *to bring upon*, Ac. v. 28; 2 Pet. ii. 1, 5.*

ἐπ-αγωνίζομαι, *to contend earnestly for* (dat.), Ju. 3.*

ἐπ-αθροίζω, pass., *to gather together*, Lu. xi. 29.*

Ἐπ-αίνετος, ου, ὁ, *Epænetus*, Ro. xvi. 5.*

ἐπ-αινέω, ῶ, έσω, 1st aor. ἐπῄνεσα, *to commend, to praise*, Lu. xvi. 8; Ro. xv. 11; 1 Cor. xi. 2, 17, 22.*

ἔπ-αινος, ου, ὁ, *commendation, praise*, Ro. ii. 29; Ep. i. 6, 12, 14; Phil. i. 11.

ἐπ-αίρω (see Gr. § 92), *to raise up*, as hoisting a sail, Ac. xxvii. 40; *to lift up*, as the eyes, the hands in prayer, the head in courage, the heel against, or in opposition; pass., *to be lifted up* 2 Cor. xi. 20, of the ascen sion of Christ, Ac. i. 9.

ἐπ-αισχύνομαι, *to be ashamed*, abs., 2 Tim. i. 12; *to be ashamed of* (acc. or ἐπί, dat.), Mar. viii. 38; Ro. vi. 21.

ἐπ-αιτέω, ῶ, *to beg, to ask alms*, Lu. xvi. 3, xviii. 35 (W. H.).*

ἐπ-ακολουθέω, ῶ, *to follow after* (dat.); fig., 1 Tim. v. 10, 24; 1 Pet. ii. 21; Mar. xvi. 20 (see W. H.).*

ἐπ-ακούω, *to hearken to favorably* (gen. pers.), 2 Cor. vi. 2.*

ἐπ-ακροάομαι, ῶμαι, *to hear, listen to* (gen. pers.), Ac. xvi. 25.*

ἐπάν, conj. (ἐπεὶ ἄν), *after, when* (subj.), Mat. ii. 8; Lu. xi. 22, 34.*

ἐπ-άναγκες, adv., *necessarily* (with art.), Ac. xv. 28.*

ἐπ-αν-άγω, trans., *to put* a vessel *out to sea*, Lu. v. 3, 4; intrans., *to return*, Mat. xxi. 18.*

ἐν-ανα-μιμνήσκω, *to remind* one *again* (acc.), Ro. xv. 15.*

ἐπ-ανα-παύομαι, *to rest upon* (ἐπί, acc.), Lu. x. 6; *to rely, to trust in* (dat.), Ro. ii. 17. (S.)*

ἐπ-αν-έρχομαι, *to come back again*, Lu. x. 35, xix. 15.*

ἐπ-αν-ίστημι, N. T. mid., *to rise up against* (ἐπί, acc.), Mat. x. 21; Mar. xiii. 12.*

ἐπ-αν-όρθωσις, εως, ἡ, *correction, reformation*, 2 Tim. iii. 16.*

ἐπ-άνω, adv., also used as prep. gen., *above, upon; more than*, in price or number; *superior to*, in authority.

ἐπ-άρατος, ον, *accursed*, Jn. vii. 49 (W. H.).*

ἐπ-αρκέω, ῶ, έσω, *to aid, to relieve* (dat.), 1 Tim. v. 10, 16.*

ἐπ-αρχία, ας, ἡ, *a province*, a region subject to a prefect, Ac. xxiii. 34, xxv. 1.*

ἔπ-αυλις, εως, ἡ, *a dwelling*, Ac. i. 20.*

ἐπ-αύριον, adv., *on the morrow*, τῇ ἐπαύριον (ἡμέρᾳ), *on the next day*, Mar. xi. 12. (S.)

ἐπ-αυτο-φώρῳ = ἐπ' αὐτό-φώρῳ.

Ἐπαφρᾶς, ᾶ, ὁ, *Epaphras* of Colossæ, Col. i. 7, iv. 12; Philem. 23.*

ἐπ-αφρίζω, *to foam up* or *out* (acc.), Ju. 13.*

Ἐπαφρόδιτος, ου, ὁ, *Epaphroditus*, a Macedonian, Phil. ii. 25, iv. 18.*

ἐπ-εγείρω, *to raise up, to excite against* (ἐπί, acc., or κατά, gen.), Ac. xiii. 50, xiv. 2.*

ἐπεί, conj., (1) of time, *after*, only Lu. vii. 1 (W. H. ἐπειδή); (2) of reason, *since, because, seeing that*, Lu. i. 34; Jn. xiii. 29.

ἐπει-δή, conj., *since, inasmuch as*, Lu. xi. 6; Phil. ii. 26; of time, *after that*, only Lu. vii. 1 (W. H.).

ἐπει-δή-περ, conj., *since verily, forasmuch as*, Lu. i. 1.*

ἐπ-εῖδον, see ἐφοράω.

ἔπ-ειμι (εἶμι, Gr. § 111, Bu. 50), *to come after, to follow*; only in part., ἐπιών, οῦσα, όν, *following*, Ac. vii. 26, xxiii. 11; τῇ ἐπιούσῃ (sc. ἡμέρᾳ), *on the following day*, Ac. xvi. 11, xx. 15, xxi. 18.*

ἐπεί-περ, conj., *since indeed*, Ro. iii. 30 (W. H. εἴπερ).*

ἐπ-εισ-αγωγή, ῆς, ἡ, *a bringing in besides*, Heb. vii. 19.*

ἔπ-ειτα, adv., *thereupon, thereafter*; marking succession of time, as Gal. i. 18; also of order, as 1 Cor. xv. 46; 1 Th. iv. 17.

ἐπ-έκεινα (sc. μέρη), adv. with gen., *beyond*, Ac. vii. 43.*

ἐπ-εκ-τείνω, in mid., *to stretch forward to* (dat.), Phil. iii. 14.*

ἐπενδύτης, ου, ὁ, *an upper garment*, Jn. xxi. 7.*

ἐπ-εν-δύω, in mid., *to put on over*, as an upper garment, 2 Cor. v. 2, 4.*

ἐπ-έρχομαι, *to come on, approach, overtake, impend*, Ep. ii. 7; Ac. viii. 24; *to attack*, Lu. xi. 22; τὰ ἐπερχομένα, *the things that are coming on* (dat.), Lu. xxi. 26.

ἐπ-ερωτάω, ῶ, (1) *to interrogate, to question* (two accs., or acc. and περί, gen., or with εἰ, τίς, etc.), Mat. xii. 10; Lu. ii. 46; Ac. xxiii. 34; *to inquire after* God, Ro. x. 20; (2) *to demand of* (acc. and inf.), Mat. xvi. 1.

ἐπ-ερώτημα, ατος, τό, probably *inquiry*, or *earnest desire*, 1 Pet. iii. 21; see R. V.*

ἐπ-έχω, (1) *to apply* (the mind) *to* (dat.), *give attention to*, Lu. xiv. 7; Ac. iii. 5; 1 Tim. iv. 16; (2) *to hold out, to exhibit*, Phil. ii. 16; (3) *to delay, tarry*, Ac. xix. 22.*

ἐπηρεάζω, *to insult, to treat abusively*, Mat. v. 44 (not W. H.); Lu. vi. 28; *to accuse falsely* (acc. of charge), 1 Pet. iii. 16.*

ἐπί, a preposition governing gen., dat., or acc.; general signification, *upon*. For its various applications, see Gr. § 305, Wi. §§ 47*g*, 48*c*, 49*l*, 52, 4, 7), Bu. 336 sq. ἐπί-, in composition, signifies *motion upon, towards*, or *against; rest on, over*, or *at; addition, succession, repetition, renewal;* and it is often intensive.

ἐπι-βαίνω, *to go upon* a ship, *to mount* a horse or ass, *to come to* or *into* a country (ἐπί, acc., εἰς, or simple dat.), Mat. xxi. 5; Ac. xx. 18, xxi. 2, 4 (W. H.), 6 (W. H. ἐμβ-), xxv. 1, xxvii. 2.*

ἐπι-βάλλω, (1) trans., *to cast upon*, as Mar. xi. 7; *to put on*, as a patch on a garment, Lu. v. 36; *to lay upon*, Lu. xx. 19; Jn. vii. 30; (2) intrans., *to rush upon*, Mar. iv. 37; *to fix the mind steadfastly on* (dat.), Mar. xiv. 72; (3) part., ἐπιβάλλων, *falling to* his share, Lu. xv. 12.

ἐπι-βαρέω, ῶ, *to burden*; fig., 2

Cor. ii. 5; 1 Th. ii. 9; 2 Th. iii. 8.*

ἐπι-βιβάζω, *to cause to mount, to place upon,* Lu. x. 34, xix. 35; Ac. xxiii. 24.*

ἐπι-βλέπω, *to look upon* with favor (with ἐπί), Lu. i. 48, ix. 38; Ja. ii. 3.*

ἐπί-βλημα, ατος, τό, *a patch* on a garment, Mat. ix. 16; Mar. ii. 21; Lu. v. 36.*

ἐπι-βοάω, ῶ, *to cry out,* Ac. xxv. 24 (W. H. βοάω).*

ἐπι-βουλή, ῆς, ἡ, *a design against, a plot,* Ac. ix. 24, xx. 3, 19 (plur.), xxiii. 30.*

ἐπι-γαμβρεύω, *to marry a deceased brother's wife* (acc.), Mat. xxii. 24. (S.)*

ἐπί-γειος, ον, *earthly, belonging to the earth,* 2 Cor. v. 1; Phil. ii. 10; τὰ ἐπίγεια, *earthly things,* Phil. iii. 19.

ἐπι-γίνομαι, *to arise, spring up,* as a wind, Ac. xxviii. 13.*

ἐπι-γινώσκω, (1) *to know clearly, understand, discern;* (2) *to acknowledge;* (3) *to recognize;* (4) *to learn* (ὅτι), *become acquainted with* (acc.).

ἐπί-γνωσις, εως, ἡ, *accurate knowledge,* Ro. x. 2; Ep. i. 17; Heb. x. 26. *Syn.:* see γνῶσις.

ἐπι-γραφή, ῆς, ἡ, *an inscription, a title,* as Lu. xx. 24, xxiii. 38.

ἐπι-γράφω, ψω, *to inscribe, write upon,* as Mar. xv. 26; Rev. xxi. 12.

ἐπι-δείκνυμι (see Gr. § 114, Bu. 45), (1) *to show, exhibit,* Mat. xxiv. 1; Lu. xvii. 14; (2) *to demonstrate, prove* by argument, Ac. xviii. 28; Heb. vi. 17.

ἐπι-δέχομαι, *to receive hospitably,* 3 Jn. 10; *to accept, admit,* 3 Jn. 9.*

ἐπι-δημέω, ῶ, *to sojourn,* as foreigners in a country, Ac. ii. 10, xvii. 21.*

ἐπι-δια-τάσσομαι, *to ordain besides,* Gal. iii. 15. (N. T.)*

ἐπι-δίδωμι, *to deliver, to give up* (acc. and dat.), as Mat. vii. 9; Ac. xv. 30; *to give way* to the wind, Ac. xxvii. 15.

ἐπι-δι-ορθόω, *to set in order besides,* Tit. i. 5.*

ἐπι-δύω, *to set,* as the sun, Ep. iv. 26.*

ἐπιείκεια, ας, ἡ, *clemency, gentleness,* Ac. xxiv. 4; 2 Cor. x. 1.*

ἐπι-εικής, ές, *gentle, mild,* Phil. iv. 5; 1 Tim. iii. 3; Tit. iii. 2; Ja. iii. 17; 1 Pet. ii. 18.*

ἐπι-ζητέω, ῶ, *to seek for, search for,* Ac. xii. 19; *to desire,* Mat. vi. 32; Ac. xiii. 7; *to demand,* Mat. xii. 39, xvi. 4.

ἐπι-θανάτιος, ον, *condemned to death,* 1 Cor. iv. 9.*

ἐπί-θεσις, εως, ἡ, *a laying on* of hands, Ac. viii. 18; 1 Tim. iv. 14; 2 Tim. i. 6; Heb. vi. 2.*

ἐπι-θυμέω, ῶ, *to long for, to covet, to lust after,* Ja. iv. 2; Ro. vii. 7; Ac. xx. 33. (On Lu. xxii. 15, see Gr. § 280*b*, Wi. § 54, 3, Bu. 184.)

ἐπι-θυμητής, οῦ, ὁ, *an eager desirer of,* 1 Cor. x. 6.*

ἐπι-θυμία, ας, ἡ, *desire, eagerness for,* 1 Th. ii. 17; generally in a bad sense, *inordinate desire, lust, cupidity,* Ja. i. 14, 15; 2 Pet. ii. 10.

ἐπι-καθίζω, *to sit upon,* Mat. xxi. 7.*

ἐπι-καλέω, ῶ, έσω, *to call upon, to call by name, to invoke* in prayer, Ac. vii. 59 (abs.); Ro. x. 12, 14 (acc.); mid., *to appeal to* (acc.), Ac. xxv. 11; pass., *to be called* or *surnamed,* Lu. xxii. 3; Ac. xv. 17.

ἐπι-κάλυμμα, ατος, τό, *a covering, a cloak, a pretext,* 1 Pet. ii. 16.*

ἐπι-καλύπτω, *to cover over,* of sins, *i.e.,* to pardon, Ro. iv. 7 (from S.).*

ἐπι-κατ-άρατος, ον, *accursed, doomed to punishment* or *destruction,* Jn. vii. 49 (W. H. ἐπάρατος); Gal. iii. 10, 13 (from S.).*

ἐπί-κειμαι, *to lie upon* (dat.), Jn. xi. 38, xxi. 9; so *to press upon,* as the multitude upon Christ, Lu. v. 1; as a tempest on a ship, Ac. xxvii. 20; fig., *to be laid on,* as necessity, 1 Cor. ix. 16; *to be laid* or *imposed upon,* as by a law, Heb. ix. 10; *to be urgent with entreaties,* Lu. xxiii. 23.*

Ἐπικούρειος, ου, ὁ, *an Epicurean,* a follower of Epicurus, Ac. xvii. 18.*

ἐπι-κουρία, ας, ἡ (κοῦρος, *help*), *help, aid,* Ac. xxvi. 22.*

ἐπι-κρίνω, *to decree, to give sentence* (acc. and inf.), Lu. xxiii. 24.*

ἐπι-λαμβάνω, N. T. mid., *to take hold of* (gen.), in kindness, as Lu. ix. 47; Ac. ix. 27; Heb. ii. 16; *to seize,* as a prisoner, Ac. xxi. 30, 33; met., *to lay hold of,* so as to possess, 1 Tim. vi. 12, 19.

ἐπι-λανθάνομαι, dep., *to forget, neglect* (inf., gen. or acc.), Mat. xvi. 5; Heb. vi. 10; part. perf. pass., ἐπιλελησμένος, *forgotten,* Lu. xii. 6.

ἐπι-λέγω, in pass., *to be named,* Jn. v. 2; mid., *to choose,* Ac. xv. 40.*

ἐπι-λείπω, λείψω, *not to suffice, to fail,* Heb. xi. 32.*

ἐπι-λείχω, *to lick over,* Lu. xvi. 21 (W. H.). (N. T.)*

ἐπι-λησμονή, ῆς, ἡ, *forgetfulness,* Ja. i. 25; see Gr. § 257. (Ap.)*

ἐπί-λοιπος, ον, *remaining over,* 1 Pet. iv. 2.*

ἐπί-λυσις, εως, ἡ, *an unloosing, interpretation,* 2 Pet. i. 20. (See ἴδιος.)*

ἐπι-λύω, *to explain, interpret,* Mar. iv. 34; *to decide,* as a debated question, Ac. xix. 39.*

ἐπι-μαρτυρέω, ῶ, *to testify earnestly,* 1 Pet. v. 12.*

ἐπι-μέλεια, ας, ἡ, *care, attention,* Ac. xxvii. 3.*

ἐπι-μέλομαι and έομαι, οῦμαι, fut. ήσομαι, *to take care of* (gen.), Lu. x. 34, 35; 1 Tim. iii. 5.*

ἐπι-μελῶς, adv., *carefully, diligently,* Lu. xv. 8.*

ἐπι-μένω, μενῶ, (1) *to remain, continue,* 1 Cor. xvi. 8; Gal. i. 18; (2) met., *to be constant, to persevere* (dat.), Ro. vi. 1; 1 Tim. iv. 16.

ἐπι-νεύω, *to nod to, to assent,* Ac. xviii. 20.*

ἐπί-νοια, ας, ἡ, *thought, purpose,* Ac. viii. 22.*

ἐπι-ορκέω, ῶ, ήσω, *to swear falsely,* Mat. v. 33.*

ἐπί-ορκος, ον, *perjured,* 1 Tim. i. 10.*

ἐπιούσιος, ον, probably from ἐπιοῦσα (ἔπειμι), *for the morrow, i.e., necessary* or *sufficient,* Mat. vi. 11; Lu. xi. 3. (N. T.)*

ἐπι-πίπτω, *to fall upon* (ἐπί, acc.), *rush upon*, Mar. iii. 10 (dat.); fig., *to come upon* (dat., or ἐπί, acc. or dat.), as an emotion, etc., Lu. i. 12; Ac. viii. 16.

ἐπι-πλήσσω, *to rebuke, to chide*, 1 Tim. v. 1.*

ἐπι-ποθέω, ῶ, *to desire earnestly, to long for* or *after* (inf. or acc.), as 2 Cor v. 2; *to lust*, abs., Ja. iv. 5.

ἐπι-πόθησις, εως, ἡ, *longing*, 2 Cor. vii. 7, 11. (N. T.)*

ἐπι-πόθητος, ον, *longed for*, Phil. iv. 1. (N. T.)*

ἐπι-ποθία, ας, ἡ, like ἐπιπόθησις, *longing*, Ro. xv. 23. (N. T.)*

ἐπι-πορεύομαι, dep., mid., *to journey to* (πρός), Lu. viii. 4.*

ἐπι-ρράπτω, *to sew to*, or *upon*, Mar. ii. 21 (ἐπί, dat.). (N. T.)*

ἐπι-ρρίπτω, *to cast*, or *throw upon*, Lu. xix. 35; of care *cast upon* God, 1 Pet. v. 7 (ἐπί, acc.).*

ἐπί-σημος, ον, *remarkable, distinguished*, in either a bad or good sense, Mat. xxvii. 16; Ro. xvi. 7.*

ἐπι-σιτισμός, οῦ, ὁ, *food, provisions*, Lu. ix. 12.*

ἐπι-σκέπτομαι, σκέψομαι, dep., *to look upon, to visit*, as Ac. vii. 23; Mat. xxv. 36, 43; of God, Ac. xv. 14; *to look out, to select*, Ac. vi. 3.

ἐπι-σκευάζομαι, see ἀποσκ-.

ἐπι-σκηνόω, ῶ, *to fix a tent upon, to dwell*, or *remain on* (ἐπί, acc.), 2 Cor. xii. 9.*

ἐπι-σκιάζω, άσω, *to overshadow* (acc. or dat.), Mat. xvii. 5; Mar. ix. 7; Lu. i. 35, ix. 34; Ac. v. 15.*

ἐπι-σκοπέω, ῶ, to act as ἐπίσκοπος, *to oversee, to care for*, 1 Pet. v. 2 (W. H. omit); μή, *lest*, Heb. xii. 15.*

ἐπι-σκοπή, ῆς, ἡ, (1) *visitation* for kind and gracious purposes, Lu. xix. 44; 1 Pet. ii. 12; (2) *office, charge*, Ac. i. 20 (from S.); (3) *the office of a bishop*, 1 Tim. iii. 1. (S.)*

ἐπί-σκοπος, ου, ὁ, (1) *one who inspects*, or *superintends*, of Christ, 1 Pet. ii. 25; (2) *an overseer of a church*, bishop, Ac. xx. 28; Phil. i. 1; 1 Tim. iii. 2; Tit. i. 7.*

ἐπι-σπάω, ῶ, *to become uncircumcised*, 1 Cor. vii. 18.*

ἐπι-σπείρω, *to sow in addition*, Mat. xiii. 25 (W. H.).*

ἐπ-ίσταμαι, dep., *to know well, to understand* (acc.), *to know*, with ὅτι, ὡς, etc.

ἐπί-στασις, εως, ἡ (W. H.), *approach, onset*, Ac. xxiv. 12; 2 Cor. xi. 28.*

ἐπι-στάτης, ου, ὁ, *superintendent, master*; only in Lu., in voc., ἐπιστάτα, addressed to Jesus, *Master*, v. 5, viii. 24, 45, ix. 33, 49, xvii. 13.*

ἐπι-στέλλω, *to send by letter to, to write*, Ac. xv. 20, xxi. 25 (W. H. ἀποστ-); Heb. xiii. 22.*

ἐπι-στήμων, ον, *skillful, experienced*, Ja. iii. 13.*

ἐπι-στηρίζω, *to establish besides, confirm*, Ac. xiv. 22, xv. 32, 41, xviii. 23 (not W. H.).*

ἐπι-στολή, ῆς, ἡ, *an epistle, a letter*, Ac. xv. 30; 2 Cor. x. 10.

ἐπι-στομίζω, *to stop the mouth of*, Tit. i. 11.*

ἐπι-στρέφω, ψω, (1) trans., *to cause to turn* (acc. and ἐπί), as to God, or to the worship of God, Ac. ix. 35; (2) intrans., *to return, to turn back*, either to good or evil, Ac. xxvi. 18; 2 Pet. ii. 21; *to return upon*, as a refused salutation, Mat. x. 13 (ἐπί, εἰς, πρός).

ἐπι-στροφή, ῆς, ἡ, *a turning, conversion*, Ac. xv. 3.*

ἐπι-συν-άγω, άξω, *to gather together*, into one place, as Mat. xxiii. 37.

ἐπι-συν-αγωγή, ῆς, ἡ, *a gathering together*, in one place, 2 Th. ii. 1; Heb. x. 25. (Ap.)*

ἐπι-συν-τρέχω, *to run together besides*, Mar. ix. 25. (N. T.)*

ἐπι-σύ-στασις, εως, ἡ (W H. ἐπίστασις), (1) *a seditious concourse*, Ac. xxiv. 12; (2) a troublesome *throng*, 2 Cor. xi. 28. (S.)*

ἐπι-σφαλής, ές, *likely to fall, dangerous*, Ac. xxvii. 9.*

ἐπ-ισχύω, *to be more urgent*, Lu. xxiii. 5.*

ἐπι-σωρεύω, εύσω, *to heap up, to obtain a multitude of*, 2 Tim. iv. 3.*

ἐπι-ταγή, ῆς, ἡ, *a command, an injunction*, 2 Cor. viii. 8; Tit. ii. 15.

ἐπι-τάσσω, ξω, *to command* (abs.), Lu. xiv. 22; *enjoin upon* (dat. of pers., thing in acc. or inf.), Mar. ix. 25.

ἐπι-τελέω, ῶ, έσω, *to bring to an end, to perform*, as a service, Heb. ix. 6; mid., *to come to an end, to leave off*, Gal. iii. 3; pass., of sufferings, *to be imposed upon*, 1 Pet. v. 9.

ἐπιτήδειος, α, ον, *fit, needful*, Ja. ii. 16.*

ἐπι-τίθημι, θήσω, *to put, place*, or *lay upon* (with acc. and dat., or ἐπί, acc. or gen.), as the hands (to heal), as stripes, etc.; of gifts, *to load with*, Ac. xxviii. 10; mid., *to rush upon in hostility, to oppose*, Ac. xviii. 10.

ἐπι-τιμάω, ῶ, *to rebuke* (dat.), Lu. xvii. 3; *to admonish* (ἵνα), Mat. xii. 16.

ἐπι-τιμία, ας, ἡ, *punishment*, 2 Cor. ii. 6.*

ἐπι-τρέπω, *to allow, permit*, Mat. viii. 21; Heb. vi. 3.

ἐπι-τροπή, ῆς, ἡ, *commission, full power*, Ac. xxvi. 12.*

ἐπί-τροπος, ου, ὁ, *one who is intrusted with*; (1) *a steward*, Mat. xx. 8; Lu. viii. 3; (2) *a tutor*, Gal. iv. 2.*

ἐπι-τυγχάνω, *to attain, acquire*, (gen. or acc.), Ro. xi. 7; Heb. vi. 15, xi. 33; Ja. iv. 2.*

ἐπι-φαίνω, 1st aor. inf. ἐπιφᾶναι, 2d aor. pass. ἐπεφάνην, (1) *to appear*, as stars, Ac. xxvii. 20; (2) *to shine upon* (dat.), Lu. i. 79; (3) met., *to be clearly known*, Tit. ii. 11, iii. 4.*

ἐπιφάνεια, ας, ἡ, *appearance, the advent* of Christ, past and future, 1 Tim. vi. 14; 2 Tim. i. 10, iv. 1, 8; Tit. ii. 13; *manifestation*, 2 Th. ii. 8.* *Syn.*: see ἀποκάλυψις.

ἐπιφανής, ές, *glorious, illustrious*, Ac. ii. 20.*

ἐπι-φαύω, or -φαύσκω, fut. σω, *to shine upon, give light to* (dat.), Ep. v. 14. (S.)*

ἐπι-φέρω (see Gr. § 103, 6), *to bring to* (ἐπί, acc.), Ac. xix. 12 (not W. H.); *to superadd*, Phil. i. 16; *to bring upon, inflict*, as punishment, Ro. iii. 5; *to bring against*, as an accusation, Ac. xxv. 18 (not W. H.); Ju. 9.*

ἐπι-φωνέω, ῶ, *to cry out, to shout*, Lu. xxiii. 21; Ac. xii. 22, xxi. 34, xxii. 24 (W. H.).*

ἐπι-φώσκω, *to grow light, to dawn*, Mat. xxviii. 1; Lu. xxiii. 54.*

ἐπι-χειρέω, ῶ, *to take in hand, undertake*, Lu. i. 1; Ac. ix. 29, xix. 13.*

ἐπι-χέω, *to pour upon*, Lu. x. 34.*

ἐπι-χορηγέω, ῶ, *to supply*, 2 Pet. i. 5; 2 Cor. ix. 10; Gal. iii. 5; pass., *to be furnished* or *supplied*, Col. ii. 19; 2 Pet. i. 11.*

ἐπι-χορηγία, ας, ἡ, *a supply*, Phil. i. 19; Ep. iv. 16. (N. T.)*

ἐπι-χρίω, *to spread on, anoint* (ἐπί, acc.), Jn. ix. 6 (not W. H.), 11.*

ἐπ-οικοδομέω, ῶ, *to build upon* (ἐπί, acc. or dat.), fig., 1 Cor. iii. 10–14; Ep. ii. 20; *to build up, edify*, Ac. xx. 32 (not W. H.); Col. ii. 7; Ju. 20.*

ἐπ-οκέλλω, *to force forward, to run* (a ship) *aground*, Ac. xxvii. 41 (ἐπικέλλω, W. H.).*

ἐπ-ονομάζω, *to name*, or *call by a name of honor*, pass. only, Ro. ii. 17.*

ἐπ-οπτεύω, *to look upon, view attentively*, 1 Pet. ii. 12, iii. 2.*

ἐπ-όπτης, ου, ὁ, *an eye-witness*, 2 Pet. i. 16.*

ἔπος, ους, τό, *a word; ὡς ἔπος εἰπεῖν, so to speak*, Heb. vii. 9.*

ἐπ-ουράνιος, ον, *heavenly, celestial*, of God, Mat. xviii. 35 (W. H. οὐράνιος); of intelligent beings, Phil. ii. 10; of the starry bodies, 1 Cor. xv. 40; so of kingdom, country, etc.; neut. plur., τὰ ἐπουράνια, *heavenly things*, or *places*, Jn. iii. 12; Ep. i. 3, 20, ii. 6, iii. 10; Heb. viii. 5, ix. 23.

ἑπτά, οἱ, αἱ, τά, card. num., *seven*, Lu. ii. 36; Ac. vi. 3; often symbol. in Revelation; οἱ ἑπτά, *the seven* deacons, Ac. xxi. 8.

ἑπτάκις, num. adv., *seven times*, Mat. xviii. 21, 22; Lu. xvii. 4.*

ἑπτακισ-χίλιοι, αι, α, card. num., *seven thousand*, Ro. xi. 4.*

ἔπω, see εἶπον.

Ἔραστος, ου, ὁ, *Erastus*, (1) Ac. xix. 22; (2) Ro. xvi. 23. Which is meant in 2 Tim. iv. 20 is uncertain.*

ἐργάζομαι, σομαι, dep., perf. in pass. sense, εἴργασμαι; (1) abs., *to work, to trade*, Lu. xiii. 14; Mat. xxv. 16; (2) *to perform, do*, Col. iii. 23; Jn. vi. 28; (3) *to practice*, as virtues, *to commit*, as sin, Ac. x. 35; Ja. ii. 9; (4) *to acquire by labor*, Jn. vi. 27.

ἐργασία, ας, ἡ, (1) *a working, performing*, Ep. iv. 9; (2) *effort, diligent labor*, Lu. xii. 58; (3) *work, gain by work*, Ac. xvi. 16, 19; Ac. xix. 24; (4) *occupation, business*, Ac. xix. 25.*

ἐργάτης, ου, ὁ, *a worker, laborer*, Mat. ix. 37; applied to workers in the church, 2 Tim. ii. 15; *a doer*, of iniquity, Lu. xiii. 27.

ἔργον, ου, τό, *work, employment*, Mat. xiii. 34; Jn. xvii. 4; 1 Cor. xv. 58; *anything accomplished*, Ac. vii. 41; Heb. i. 10; *an act, deed*, in various senses, Jn. ix. 3; Rev. ii. 6; Ja. ii. 14; 1 Pet. i. 17.

ἐρεθίζω, *to stimulate, to provoke*, 2 Cor. ix. 2; Col. iii. 21.*

ἐρείδω, σω, *to stick fast*, Ac. xxvii. 41.*

ἐρεύγομαι, ξομαι, *to utter*, Mat. xiii. 35.*

ἐρευνάω, ῶ, ήσω (W. H. ἐραυνάω), *to search diligently*, Jn. v. 39; Ro. viii. 27; Rev. ii. 23.

ἐρέω, obsolete, see φημί and εἶπον.

ἐρημία, ας, ἡ, *a solitude, a wilderness*, Mat. xv. 33; Mar. viii. 4; Heb. xi. 38; 2 Cor. xi. 26.*

ἔρημος, ον, *deserted, desolate, waste*, Ac. i. 20; Gal. iv. 27; used in the fem., as a subst., for a *wilderness*, Lu. i. 80; ἔρημος τῆς Ἰουδαίας, *the wilderness of Judæa*, the tract west of the Dead Sea, Mat. iii. 1; ἡ ἔρημος, the wilderness in which the Israelites wandered, Ac. vii. 30, 36, 38.

ἐρημόω, ῶ, *to make desolate*, Mat. xii. 25; Lu. xi. 17; *to reduce to naught*, Rev. xvii. 16, xviii. 17, 19.*

ἐρήμωσις, εως, ἡ, *desolation*, Mat. xxiv. 15; Lu. xxi. 20; Mar. xiii. 14. (S.)*

ἐρίζω, ίσω (ἔρις), *to contend, dispute*, Mat. xii. 19.*

ἐριθεία, ας, ἡ (W. H. ἐριθία), *self-seeking, a partisan and factious spirit*, Ro. ii. 8; Phil. i. 16, ii. 3; Ja. iii. 14, 16; plur. in 2 Cor. xii. 20; Gal. v. 20.*

ἔριον, ου, τό, *wool*, Heb. ix. 19; Rev. i. 14.*

ἔρις, ιδος, ἡ, *contention, strife*, Ro. i. 29; Gal. v. 20.

ἐρίφιον, ου, τό, and ἔριφος, ου, ὁ, *a goat, kid*, Mat. xxv. 32, 33; Lu. xv. 29.*

Ἑρμᾶς, ᾶ, ὁ, Doric for Ἑρμῆς, *Hermas*, Ro. xvi. 14.*

ἑρμηνεία, ας, ἡ, *interpretation* 1 Cor. xii. 10, xiv. 26.*

ἑρμηνεύω, *to interpret, translate*, Jn. i. 38 (not W. H.), 42, ix. 7; Heb. vii. 2.*

Ἑρμῆς, οῦ, ὁ, (1) the Greek deity *Hermes* (in Latin, *Mercury*), Ac. xiv. 12; (2) *Hermes*, Ro. xvi. 14.*

Ἑρμογένης, ους, ὁ, *Hermogenes*, 2 Tim. i. 15.*

ἑρπετόν, οῦ, τό, *a creeping creature, a reptile*, Ac. x. 12, xi. 6; Ro. i. 23; Ja. iii. 7.

ἐρυθρός, ά, όν, *red; ἡ ἐρυθρὰ θάλασσα, the Red Sea*, Ac. vii. 36; Heb. xi. 29.*

ἔρχομαι, ἐλεύσομαι (see Gr. § 103, 2, Wi. § 15, Bu. 58), *to come, to go*, of persons or of things; ὁ ἐρχόμενος, *the coming one, i.e.*, the Messiah, Mat. xi. 3; Heb. x. 37; Rev. i. 4, 8, iv. 8; *to come*, after, before, to, against, etc., as determined by the preposition which follows; *to come forth*, as from the grave, 1 Cor. xv. 35; *to come back*, as the prodigal, Lu. xv. 30.

ἐρωτάω, ῶ, ήσω, *to question*, Mat. xxi. 24; *to ask, to beseech*, Lu. vii. 36; Phil. iv. 3. *Syn.*: see αἰτέω.

ἐσθής, ῆτος, ἡ (ἕννυμι, 1st aor. ἕσθην), *clothing, raiment*, Lu. xxiii. 11; Ac. xii. 21.

ἔσθησις, εως, ἡ, *clothing*, Lu. xxiv. 4 (ἐσθῆς, W. H.).*

ἐσθίω, 2d aor., ἔφαγον (see Gr. § 103, 3, Wi. § 15, Bu. 58), *to eat, to partake of food*, used abs. or with acc. of food, or ἐκ, a word like *some* being understood; with μετά, gen., *to eat with;* with dat. (as Ro. xiv. 6), *to eat to the honor of;* met., *to devour, to consume*, as rust does, Ja. v. 3; or fire, Heb. x. 27.

ἔσθω (W. H.) = ἐσθίω, Mar. i. 6; Lu. xxii. 30.

Ἐσλί (W. H. -εί), ὁ, *Esli*, Lu. iii. 25.*

ἔσ-οπτρον, ου, τό, *a mirror* (of polished metal), Ja. i. 23; 1 Cor. xiii. 12.*

ἑσπέρα, ας, ἡ (prop. adj. with ὥρα), *evening*, Lu. xxiv. 29; Ac. iv. 3, xxviii. 23.*

Ἐσρώμ, ὁ, *Esrom*, Mat. i. 3; Lu. iii. 33.*

ἔσχατος, η, ον, (1) *the last, remotest*, in situation, dignity, or time, τὸ ἔσχατον, τὰ ἔσχατα, as subst., *the extremity, last state;* (2) used predicatively as an adverb, Mar. xii. 6, 22; absolutely, 1 Cor. xv. 8; (3) *the end* of what is spoken of, *e.g.*, the feast, Jn. vii. 37; the world, Jn. vi. 39, 40; (4) spec. of the Christian dispensation as *the last*, or *latter* (days), Heb. i. 2; (5) the *last* (day), *i.e.*, the day of judgment; (6) the phrase ὁ πρῶτος καὶ ὁ ἔσχατος, Rev. i. 11, 17, ii. 8, *the first and the last*, describes the *eternity* of God.

ἐσχάτως, adv., *extremely*, ἐσχάτως ἔχει, *is at the last extremity*, Mar. v. 23.*

ἔσω, adv. of place, *within*, abs., Mat. xxvi. 58; with gen., Mar. xv. 16; with an article preced., *the inner*, Ro. vii. 22; οἱ ἔσω, *those within* the Christian fold, opp. to οἱ ἔξω, 1 Cor. v. 12.

ἔσωθεν, adv. of place, *from within, within*, Lu. xi. 7; Rev. iv. 8; τὸ ἔσωθεν, *the interior, i.e.*, the mind or soul, Lu. xi. 39.

ἐσώτερος, α, ον (comp. of ἔσω), *inner*, Ac. xvi. 24; Heb. vi. 19.*

ἑταῖρος, ου, ὁ, *a companion, comrade*, Mat. xi. 16 (ἕτερος, W. H.); ἑταῖρε, voc., *friend*, Mat. xx. 13, xxii. 12, xxvi. 50.*

ἑτερό-γλωσσος, ου, ὁ, *one of another tongue* or *language*, 1 Cor. xiv. 21.*

ἑτερο-διδασκαλέω, ῶ, *to teach a different doctrine*, 1 Tim. i. 3, vi. 3. (N. T.)*

ἑτερο-ζυγέω, ῶ, *to be unequally yoked*, fig., 2 Cor. vi. 14. (N. T.)*

ἕτερος, α, ον, *other, another;* indefinitely, *any other;* definitely, *the other; diverse, different from. Syn.:* see ἄλλος.

ἑτέρως, adv., *otherwise, differently*, Phil. iii. 15.*

ἔτι, adv., *yet, still, even*, Lu. i. 15; *also*, Heb. xi. 36; implying accession or addition, *besides.*

ἑτοιμάζω, άσω, *to prepare, make ready*, Lu. xii. 47; Rev. xix. 7.

ἑτοιμασία, ας, ἡ, *preparation, readiness*, Ep. vi. 15.*

ἕτοιμος, η, ον, and -ος, ον, *prepared, ready*, of things or persons, Mat. xxii. 4, 8; Lu. xii. 40; ἐν ἑτοίμῳ ἔχειν, *to be in readiness*, 2 Cor. x. 6.

ἑτοίμως, adv., *readily, in readiness*, usually with ἔχω, Ac. xxi. 13; 2 Cor. xii. 14; 1 Pet. iv. 5.*

ἔτος, ους, τό, *a year*, Lu. iv. 25; κατ' ἔτος, *yearly*, Lu. ii. 41.

εὖ, adv. (old neuter from ἐΰς), *well*, Ep. vi. 3; εὖ ποιεῖν (acc.), Mar. xiv. 7, *to do good to;* εὖ πράσσειν, *to fare well, to prosper*, Ac. xv. 29; used in commendation, *well! well done!* Mat. xxv. 21, 23; Lu. xix. 17.*

Εὕα, ας, ἡ, *Eve*, 2 Cor. xi. 3; 1 Tim. ii. 13.*

εὐ-αγγελίζω, σω, εὐηγγέλισα, εὐηγγέλισμαι, (1) act., *to bring glad tidings to* (acc. or dat.), Rev. x. 7, xiv. 6; (2) mid., *to announce, to publish* (acc. of message), *to announce the gospel* (abs.), *to preach to, evangelize* (acc. pers.); pass., *to be announced, to have glad tidings announced to* one. See Mat. xi. 5; Heb. iv. 2.

εὐαγγέλιον, ου, τό, *good tidings, the gospel*, Mar. i. 15; Ac. xv. 7; Ep. i. 13.

εὐαγγελιστής, οῦ, ὁ, *a messenger of good tidings, an evangelist*, Ac. xxi. 8; Ep. iv. 11; 2 Tim. iv. 5. (N. T.)*

εὐ-αρεστέω, ῶ, *to be well-pleasing to* (dat.), Heb. xi. 5, 6; pass., *to be pleased with*, Heb. xiii. 16.*

εὐ-άρεστος, ον, *acceptable, well-pleasing*, Ro. xii. 12. (Ap.)

εὐαρέστως, adv., *acceptably*, Heb. xii. 28.*

Εὔβουλος, ου, ὁ, *Eubulus*, 2 Tim. iv. 21.*

εὖ-γε, *well done!* Lu. xix. 17 (W. H.).*

εὐγενής, ές, *well-born, noble, noble-minded*, Lu. xix. 12; Ac. xvii. 11; 1 Cor. i. 26.*

εὐδία, ας, ἡ (from εὖ and Ζεύς, gen. Διός), *fair weather*, Mat. xvi. 2.*

εὐ-δοκέω, ῶ, ήσω, εὐδόκησα and ηὐδόκησα, *to think it good, decide*, Lu. xii. 32; 1 Th. iii. 1; *to be well pleased with*, Mat. xvii. 5; 2 Pet. i. 17.

εὐδοκία, ας, ἡ, *pleasure, good-will*, Phil. ii. 13; 2 Th. i. 11; Mat. xi. 26.

εὐεργεσία, ας, ἡ, *a good deed to* (gen.), *a benefit*, Ac. iv. 9; 1 Tim. vi. 2.*

εὐεργετέω, ῶ, *to do good, to bestow benefits*, Ac. x. 38.*

εὐ-εργέτης, ου, ὁ, *a benefactor*, Lu. xxii. 25.*

εὔ-θετος, ον, *well-placed, fit, useful*, Lu. ix. 62, xiv. 35; Heb. vi. 7.*

εὐθέως, adv., *immediately, soon*, Mat. iv. 20; Gal. i. 16; 3 Jn. 14.

εὐθυ-δρομέω, ῶ, *to run in a straight course*, Ac. xvi. 11, xxi. 1.*

εὐ-θυμέω, ῶ, *to be cheerful*, Ac. xxvii. 22, 25; Ja. v. 13.*

εὔ-θυμος, ον, *cheerful, having good courage*, Ac. xxiv. 10 (Rec.), xxvii. 36.*

εὐθύμως, *cheerfully*, Ac. xxiv. 10 (W. H.).*

εὐθύνω, *to make straight*, Jn. i. 23; *to guide, to steer*, as a ship, Ja. iii. 4.*

εὐθύς, εῖα, ύ, *straight;* met., *right, true;* also adv., of time, *straight, i.e., immediately, forthwith*, as εὐθέως (W. H. often εὐθύς for Rec. εὐθέως).

εὐθύτης, τητος, ἡ, *rectitude, uprightness*, Heb. i. 8 (from S.).*

εὐ-καιρέω, ῶ, *to have leisure* or *opportunity*, Mar. vi. 31; Ac. xvii. 21; 1 Cor. xvi. 12.*

εὐκαιρία, ας, ἡ, *convenient time, opportunity*, Mat. xxvi. 16; Lu. xxii. 6.*

εὔ-καιρος, ον, *well-timed, opportune*, Mar. vi. 21; Heb. iv. 16.*

εὐκαίρως, adv., *opportunely*, Mar. xiv. 11; opposed to ἀκαίρως, 2 Tim. iv. 2.*

εὔ-κοπος, ον, *easy*, neut. comp. only, εὐκοπώτερον, *easier*, as Mat. ix. 5. (N. T.)

εὐ-λάβεια, ας, ἡ, *reverence, fear of God, piety*, Heb. v. 7, xii. 28.* *Syn.:* see δειλία.

εὐ-λαβέομαι, οῦμαι, dep. pass., *to fear*, Ac. xxiii. 10 (W. H. φοβέω); with μή, *to take precaution*, Heb. xi. 7.*

εὐ-λαβής, ές, *cautious, God-fearing, religious*, Lu. ii. 25; Ac. ii. 5, viii. 2, xxii. 12 (W. H.).* *Syn.:* see δεισιδαίμων.

εὐ-λογέω, ῶ, ήσω, *to praise, i.e.*, God, Lu. i. 64; *to invoke blessings on, i.e.*, men, Ro. xii. 14; *to bless* or *to ask blessing on, i.e.*, food, Lu. ix. 16; so of the Lord's Supper, Mat. xxvi. 26; 1 Cor. x. 16; used of what God does, *to bless, to cause to prosper*, Ac. iii. 26; hence, perf. pass. part. εὐλογημένος, *blessed, favored of God*, Mat. xxv. 34.

εὐλογητός, όν (verbal adj. from preced.), *worthy of praise, of blessing*, used only of God, Mar. xiv. 61; Lu. i. 68; Ro. i. 25, ix. 5; 2 Cor. i. 3, xi. 31; Ep. i. 3; 1 Pet. i. 3. (S.)*

εὐ-λογία, ας, ἡ, *adulation, flattery*, Ro. xvi. 18; *blessing, praise*, to God, Rev. vii. 12; *an invocation of blessings, benediction*, Heb. xii. 17; *blessing, benefit*, 2 Cor. ix. 5; 1 Pet. iii. 9.

εὐ-μετά-δοτος, ον, *ready to give, liberal*, 1 Tim. vi. 18. (N.T.)*

Εὐνίκη, ης, ἡ, *Eunice*, 2 Tim. i. 5.*

εὐ-νοέω, ῶ, *to be well disposed to*, Mat. v. 25.*

εὔ-νοια, ας, ἡ, *good-will*, 1 Cor. vii. 3 (not W. H.); Ep. vi. 7.*

εὐνουχίζω, σω, εὐνουχίσθην, *to emasculate, make a eunuch*, pass., Mat. xix. 12.*

εὐνοῦχος, ου, ὁ, *a eunuch*, Mat. xix. 12; Ac. viii. 27–39.*

Εὐοδία, ας, ἡ, *Euodia*, Phil. iv. 2.*

εὐ-οδόω, ῶ, in N. T. pass. only, *to be led in a good way, to prosper*, Ro. i. 10; 1 Cor. xvi. 2; 3 Jn. 2.*

εὐ-πάρεδρος, ον, see εὐπρόσεδρος. (N. T.)

εὐ-πειθής, ές, *easily obeying, compliant*, Ja. iii. 17.*

εὐ-περί-στατος, ον, *skillfully surrounding, i.e., besetting*, Heb. xii. 1.*

εὐ-ποιΐα, ας, ἡ, *well-doing, beneficence*, Heb. xiii. 16.*

εὐ-πορέω, ῶ, mid., *to have means, to be prosperous*, Ac. xi. 29.*

εὐ-πορία, ας, ἡ, *wealth*, Ac. xix. 25.*

εὐ-πρέπεια, ας, ἡ, *beauty, gracefulness*, Ja. i. 11.*

εὐ-πρόσ-δεκτος, ον, *acceptable*, Ro. xv. 16, 31; 2 Cor. vi. 2, viii. 12; 1 Pet. ii. 5.*

εὐ-πρόσ-εδρος, ον, *assiduous, constantly attending on*, 1 Cor. vii. 35 (εὐπάρεδρος, W. H.). (N. T.)*

εὐ-προσωπέω, ῶ, *to make a fair appearance*, Gal. vi. 12. (N. T.)*

εὐρ-ακύλων, ωνος, ὁ, *the Euraquilo, a N.E. wind*, Ac. xxvii. 14 (W. H.). (N. T.)*

εὑρίσκω, εὑρήσω, εὕρηκα, εὗρον, εὑρέθην, (1) *to find, to discover*, Lu. ii. 45; (2) *to ascertain, to find by computation*, or by *examination*, as a judge, Ac. xiii. 28; (3) *to obtain*, Heb. ix. 12; (4) *to contrive, find out how*, Lu. xix. 48.

εὐρο-κλύδων, ωνος, ὁ (from εὖρος, *the S.E. wind*, and κλύδων, *wave*), *Euroclydon, a stormy wind, a hurricane*, Ac. xxvii. 14. (N. T.)*

εὐρύ-χωρος, ον, *broad, spacious*, Mat. vii. 13.*

εὐσέβεια, ας, ἡ, *piety, godliness*, Ac. iii. 12; 2 Tim. iii. 5.

εὐσεβέω, ῶ, *to show piety, to worship*, Ac. xvii. 23; 1 Tim. v. 4.*

εὐ-σεβής, ές, *religious, pious*, Ac. x. 2, 7, xxii. 12 (W. H. εὐλαβής); 2 Pet. ii. 9.* *Syn.:* see δεισιδαίμων.

εὐσεβῶς, adv., *piously, religiously*, 2 Tim. iii. 12; Tit. ii. 12.*

εὔ-σημος, ον, *distinct, intelligible*, 1 Cor. xiv. 9.*

εὔ-σπλαγχνος, ον, *full of pity, tender-hearted*, Ep. iv. 32; 1 Pet. iii. 8.*

εὐ-σχημόνως, adv., *in a seemly manner, decently*, Ro. xiii. 13; 1 Cor. xiv. 40; 1 Th. iv. 12.*

εὐ-σχημοσύνη, ης, ἡ, *decorum, becomingness*, 1 Cor. ii. 23.*

εὐ-σχήμων, ον, *reputable, decorous*, Mar. xv. 43; Ac. xiii. 50, xvii. 12; τὸ εὔσχημον, *seemliness*, 1 Cor. vii. 35, xii. 24.*

εὐ-τόνως, adv., *vehemently, forcibly*, Lu. xxiii. 10; Ac. xviii. 28.*

εὐ-τραπελία, ας, ἡ, *low jesting, ribaldry*, Ep. v. 4.*

Εὔτυχος, ου, ὁ, *Eutychus*, Ac. xx. 9.*

εὐ-φημία, ας, ἡ, *commendation, good report*, 2 Cor. vi. 8.*

εὔ-φημος, ον, *sounding well, spoken in a kindly spirit*, Phil. iv. 8.*

εὐ-φορέω, ῶ, *to bear plentifully*, Lu. xii. 16.*

εὐ-φραίνω, νῶ, εὐφράνθην and ηὐφράνθην, act., *to make glad*, 2 Cor. ii. 2; pass., *to be glad, to rejoice*, Lu. xii. 19; Ac. ii. 26; Rev. xviii. 20.

Εὐφράτης, ου, ὁ, *the Euphrates*, Rev. ix. 14, xvi. 12.*

εὐφροσύνη, ης, ἡ, *joy, gladness*, Ac. ii. 28, xiv. 17.*

εὐ-χαριστέω, ῶ, *to thank, give thanks*, Ac. xxvii. 35; Ro. i. 8.

εὐχαριστία, ας, ἡ, *gratitude, thanksgiving*, as 2 Cor. ix. 11, 12. *Syn.:* see αἴτημα.

εὐ-χάριστος, ον, *thankful, grateful*, Col. iii. 15.*

εὐχή, ῆς, ἡ, (1) *prayer*, Ja. v. 15; (2) *a vow*, Ac. xviii. 18, xxi. 23.* *Syn.:* see αἴτημα.

εὔχομαι, *to pray*, Ac. xxvi. 29; 2 Cor. xiii. 7; Ja. v. 16 (*for* with ὑπέρ or περί, gen.); *to wish*, Ac. xxvii. 29; Ro. ix. 3; 2 Cor. xiii. 9; 3 Jn. 2.*

εὔ-χρηστος, ον, *useful*, 2 Tim. ii. 21, iv. 11; Philem. 11.*

εὐ-ψυχέω, ῶ, *to be in good spirits, to be cheerful*, Phil. ii. 19.*

εὐ-ωδία, ας, ἡ, *fragrance, good odor*, 2 Cor. ii. 15; Ep. v. 2; Phil. iv. 18.*

εὐώνυμος, ον, *left*, hand, Ac. xxi. 3; foot, Rev. x. 2; ἐξ εὐωνύμων (neut. plur.), *on the left*, Mat. xx. 21, 23.

ἐφ-άλλομαι, *to leap upon*, ἐπί, acc., Ac. xix. 16.*

ἐφ-άπαξ, adv., *once for all*, Ro. vi. 10; Heb. vii. 27, ix. 12, x. 10; *at once*, 1 Cor. xv. 6.*

Ἐφεσῖνος, η, ον, *Ephesian*, *i.e.*, church, Rev. ii. 1 (not W. H.).*

Ἐφέσιος, α, ον, *Ephesian*, *belonging to Ephesus*, Ac. xix. 28, 34, 35, xxi. 29.*

Ἔφεσος, ου, ἡ, *Ephesus*, Ac. xviii. 19, 21, 24.

ἐφ-ευρετής, οῦ, ὁ, *an inventor, contriver*, Ro. i. 30.*

ἐφ-ημερία, ας, ἡ, *a course*, a division of priests foı interchange of service, Lu. i. 5, 8. (S.)*

ἐφ-ήμερος, ον, *daily*, Ja. ii. 15.*

ἐφ-ικνέομαι, dep., 2d aor. inf. ἐφικέσθαι, *to come to, reach*, ἄχρι or εἰς, 2 Cor. x. 13, 14.*

ἐφ-ίστημι, 2d aor. ἐπέστην; perf. part. ἐφεστώς; always intrans. or mid. in N. T.; (1) *to stand by*, Lu. ii. 38; Ac. xii. 7; (2) *to be urgent*, 2 Tim. iv. 2; (3) *to befall one*, as evil, Lu. xxi. 34; (4) *to be at hand, to impend*, 2 Tim. iv. 6.

ἐφνίδιος, see αἰφνίδιος.

ἐφ-οράω, ῶ, 2d aor. ἐπεῖδον, *to look upon*, Lu. i. 25; Ac. iv. 29.*

Ἐφραΐμ, ὁ, *Ephraim*, a city, Jn. xi. 54.*

ἐφφαθά, an Aramaic verb, imperative, *be thou opened*, Mar. vii. 34. (N. T.)*

ἐχθές, see χθές.

ἔχθρα, ας, ἡ, *enmity*, Gal. v. 20; Ep. ii. 15, 16.

ἐχθρός, ά, όν, *hated*, Ro. xi. 28; *hostile*, 1 Cor. xv. 25; used as subst., *an enemy*, Mat. x. 36; ὁ ἐχθρός, Lu. x. 19, *the enemy*, *i.e.*, Satan.

ἔχιδνα, ης, ἡ, *a viper*, lit., Ac. xxviii. 3; fig., as Mat. iii. 7.

ἔχω, ἕξω, impf. εἶχον, 2d aor. ἔσχον, perf. ἔσχηκα; (1) *to have* or *possess*, in general, physically or mentally, temporarily or permanently; μὴ ἔχειν, *to lack, to be poor*, Lu. viii. 6; 1 Cor. xi. 22; (2) *to be able*, Mar. xiv. 8; Heb. vi. 13; 2 Pet. i. 15; (3) with adverbs, or adverbial phrases, elliptically, "to have (one's self) in any manner," *to be*, as κακῶς ἔχειν, *to be ill*; ἐσχάτως ἔχειν, *to be at the last extremity*; (4) *to hold*, 1 Tim. iii. 9; 2 Tim. i. 13; *to esteem*, Mat. xiv. 5; Phil. ii. 29; (5) mid., ἔχομαι, *to be near* or *next to*, Mar. i. 38; used of time, Ac. xxi. 26, *the day coming, the next day*; τὰ ἐχόμενα σωτηρίας, *things joined to* or *pertaining to salvation*, Heb. vi. 9.

ἕως, conj. and adv., (1) of time, *till, until*, used also as prep. with gen. ἕως οὗ, or ἕως ὅτου, *until when*, Lu. xiii. 8; (2) of place, *up to*, or *as far as*, also with gen., sometimes with εἰς or πρός (acc.), Mat. xxvi. 58; Lu. xxiv. 50; Ac. xxvi. 11; (3) spoken of a limit or term to anything, *up to the point of*, Mat. xxvi. 38; Lu. xxii. 51; Ro. ii. 12; (4) with particles, ἕως ἄρτι, ἕως τοῦ νῦν, *until now*; ἕως ὧδε, *to this place*; ἕως πότε; *how long?*; ἕως ἑπτάκις, *until seven times*; ἕως ἄνω, *up to the brim*, etc.

Z

Z, ζ, ζῆτα, *zeta*, *z*, the sixth letter, orig. of a mixed or compound sound, as if δs, now generally pronounced *z* or *ts*. As a numeral, ζʹ = 7; ͵ζ = 7000.

Ζαβουλών, ὁ (Heb.), *Zebulon*, Mat. iv. 13, 15; Rev. vii. 8.*

Ζακχαῖος, ου, ὁ, *Zacchæus*, Lu. xix. 2, 5, 8.*

Ζαρά, ὁ (Heb.), *Zara* or *Zerah*, Mat. i. 3.*

Ζαχαρίας, ου, ὁ, *Zacharias* or *Zachariah*, (1) the father of John the Baptist, Lu. i.; (2) the son of Barachiah, slain in the temple, Mat. xxiii. 35; Lu. xi. 51 (in 2 Chron. xxiv. 20 the son of Jehoiada).*

ζάω, ῶ, ζῇς, ζῇ, inf. ζῆν (W. H. ζῆν), fut. ζήσω or -ομαι, 1st aor. ἔζησα, *to live*, as (1) *to be alive*; part. ὁ ζῶν, *the Living One*, a description of God, as Mat. xvi. 16; (2) *to receive* or *regain life*, Jn. iv. 50; Mar. xvi. 11; (3) *to spend life* in any way, Gal. ii. 14; 2 Tim. iii. 12; (4) *to live*, in the highest sense, to possess spiritual and eternal life, Lu. x. 28; Heb. x. 38; (5) met., as of water, *living* or *fresh*, opposed to stagnant, as Jn. iv. 10.

Ζεβεδαῖος, ου, ὁ, *Zebedee*, Mat. iv. 21, x. 2.

ζεστός, ή, όν (ζέω), *boiling, hot*, fig., Rev. iii. 15, 16.*

ζεῦγος, ους, τό, (1) *a yoke* (ζεύγνυμι, *to join*), Lu. xiv. 19; (2) *a pair*, Lu. ii. 24.*

ζευκτηρία, ας, ἡ, *a band, a fastening*, Ac. xxvii. 40. (N.T.)*

Ζεύς, Διός, acc. Δία, *Zeus* (Lat. *Jupiter*), the chief of the heathen deities, Ac. xiv. 12, 13.*

ζέω, part. ζέων, *to boil*; fig., *to be fervent*, Ac. xviii. 25; Ro xii. 11.*

ζηλεύω, *to be zealous*, Rev. iii. 19 (W. H.).*

ζῆλος, ου, ὁ, (1) *fervor, zeal*, Jn. ii. 17; (2) *rivalry, jealousy*, Ac. v. 17, xiii. 45; *fierceness*, Heb. x. 27.

ζηλόω, ῶ, ώσω, (1) *to have zeal for, to desire earnestly* (acc.), 1 Cor. xii. 31; 2 Cor. xi. 2; Gal. iv. 17; (2) *to be envious* or *jealous*, Ac. vii. 9; 1 Cor. xiii. 4; Ja. iv. 2.

ζηλωτής, οῦ, ὁ, (1) *one very zealous for* (gen.), Ac. xxi. 20; (2) *a Zealot*, one of a class of Jews very zealous for the Mosaic law, only Lu. vi. 15; Ac. i. 13. See Κανανίτης.

ζημία, ας, ἡ, *damage, loss*, Ac. xxvii. 10, 21; Phil. iii. 7, 8.*

ζημιόω, ῶ, pass., *to be damaged, to suffer loss of* (acc.), Mat. xvi. 26; Phil. iii. 8.

Ζηνᾶς, ᾶ, ὁ, *Zenas*, Tit. iii. 13.*

ζητέω, ῶ, ήσω, (1) *to seek*, absolutely, as Mat. vii. 7; (2) *to seek for* (acc.), Mat. vi. 33; Jn. v. 30; (3) *to desire, to wish for*, Mat. xii. 46; Col. iii. 1; *to inquire into*, Lu. xii. 29; Jn. xvi. 19.

ζήτημα, ατος, τό, *a question, dispute* (gen., or περί, gen.); Ac. xv. 2, xviii. 15, xxiii. 29, xxv. 19, xxvi. 3.*

ζήτησις, εως, ἡ, *question, debate, controversy*, Jn. iii. 25; Ac. xxv. 20.

ζιζάνιον, ου, τό (perh. Syriac), *zizanium, darnel*, a kind of bastard wheat, Mat. xiii. 25–40. (N. T.)*

Ζοροβάβελ, ὁ (Heb.), *Zerubbabel*, Mat. i. 12, 13; Lu. iii. 27.*

ζόφος, ου, ὁ, *darkness*, *thick gloom*, 2 Pet. ii. 4, 17; Ju. 6, 13; Heb. xii. 18 (W. H.).*

ζυγός, οῦ, ὁ, *a yoke*, (1) met., of servitude, 1 Tim. vi. 1; (2) fig., of any imposition by authority, Mat. xi. 29, 30; Ac. xv. 10; Gal. v. 1; (3) *a balance*, *pair of scales*, Rev. vi. 5.*

ζύμη, ης, ἡ, *leaven*, Mat. xvi. 6; fig., *corruptness*, 1 Cor. v. 6, 7, 8.

ζυμόω, ῶ, *to ferment*, *to leaven*, Mat. xiii. 33; Lu. xiii. 21; 1 Cor. v. 6; Gal. v. 9.*

ζωγρέω, ῶ (ζωός, ἀγρέω), *to take alive*, *to catch*, *capture*, Lu. v. 10; 2 Tim. ii. 26.*

ζωή, ῆς, ἡ (ζάω), *life*, literal, spiritual, eternal; ζωὴ αἰώνιος, *eternal life*, used of Christ, as *the source of life*, Jn. v. 26. *Syn.*: see βίος.

ζώνη, ης, ἡ, *a girdle*, Ac. xxi. 11; used as *a purse*, Mar. vi. 8.

ζώννυμι or -νύω, see Gr. § 114, Bu. 45, *to gird*, Jn. xxi. 18; Ac. xii. 8 (W. H.).*

ζωο-γονέω, ῶ, ήσω, *to preserve alive*, Lu. xvii. 33; Ac. vii. 19; *to give life to*, 1 Tim. vi. 13 (W. H.).*

ζῷον, ου, τό, *a living creature*, *animal*, Heb. xiii. 11; 2 Pet. ii. 12.

ζωο-ποιέω, ῶ, ήσω, *to make alive*, *to give life to*, Jn. v. 21, vi. 63; 1 Cor. xv. 22, 36, 45; 2 Cor. iii. 6; Gal. iii. 21; Ro. iv. 17, viii. 11; 1 Pet. iii. 18.*

H

H, η, ἦτα, *eta*, *e*, the seventh letter. As a numeral, η′ = 8; ‚η = 8000.

ἤ, a particle, disjunctive, *or;* interrogative, *whether* (see Gr. § 405, Wi. § 57, 1 *b*, Bu. 249); or comparative, *than* (see Gr. § 320, Wi. § 35, 1, 2, Bu. 360). With other particles, ἀλλ᾽ ἤ, *except;* ἢ καί, *or else;* ἤπερ, *than at all*, Jn. xii. 43; ἤτοι . . . ἤ, *whether* . . . *or* (excluding any other alternative), Ro. vi. 16.

ἦ, affirmative particle with μήν, *surely*, Heb. vi. 14 (W. H. εἰ).*

ἡγεμονεύω, *to be governor*, as proconsul, Lu. ii. 2; procurator, Lu. iii. 1.*

ἡγεμονία, ας, ἡ, *rule*, as of an emperor, Lu. iii. 1.*

ἡγεμών, όνος, ὁ, *governor*, as the head of a district, Mat. x. 18; especially the procurator of Judæa, as Pilate, Felix, Festus, Lu. xx. 20; *a chief town*, Mat. ii. 6.

ἡγέομαι, οῦμαι, dep. mid., (1) *to be leader*, in N. T. only part., ὁ ἡγούμενος, *the leader* or *chief* (gen.), as Ac. xiv. 12; Heb. xiii. 7, 17, 24; (2) *to consider*, *reckon*, *count*, as Phil. iii. 7, 8.

ἡδέως, adv. (ἡδύς, *sweet*), *gladly*, Mar. vi. 20, xii. 37; 2 Cor. xi. 19.*

ἤδη, adv. of time, *now*, *already*, as Mat. iii. 10; of the immediate future, Ro. i. 10.

ἥδιστα, adv., *most gladly*, 2 Cor. xii. 9, 15.*

ἡδονή, ῆς, ἡ, *pleasure*, *i.e.*, sensual, *lust*, *strong desire*, Lu. viii. 14; Tit. iii. 3; Ja. iv. 3; 2 Pet. ii. 13; *lust*, Ja. iv. 1.*

ἡδύ-οσμον, ου, τό (ἡδύς, ὀσμή), *mint*, Mat. xxiii. 23; Lu. xi. 42.*

ἦθος, ους, τό, as ἔθος, *manner*, *custom;* plur. ἤθη, *morals*, 1 Cor. xv. 33.*

ἥκω, ξω (perf. ἧκα, only Mar. viii. 3), *to have come*, *to be present* (see Gr. § 361 *d*, note, Wi. § 40, 4 *b*, Bu. 203).

Ἡλί, ὁ (Heb.), *Heli*, Lu. iii. 23.*

ἠλί (W. H. ἐλωί), (Heb.), *my God*, Mat. xxvii. 46 (from Ps. xxii. 2). (N. T.)*

Ἡλίας, ου, ὁ, *Elias*, *i.e.*, *Elijah*, Mat. xi. 14, xvi. 14.

ἡλικία, ας, ἡ, (1) *age*, *adult age;* ἡλικίαν ἔχει, *he is of age*, Jn. ix. 21; so, prob., Mat. vi. 27 (R. V. mrg.); (2) *stature*, *size*, Lu. xix. 3.

ἡλίκος, η, ον, *how great*, *how small*, Col. ii. 1; Ja. iii. 5.*

ἥλιος, ου, ὁ, *the sun*, *the light of the sun*, Mat. v. 45; Ac. xiii. 11.

ἧλος, ου, ὁ, *a nail*, Jn. xx. 25.*

ἡμεῖς, gen. ἡμῶν, dat. ἡμῖν, acc. ἡμᾶς, plur. of ἐγώ.

ἡμέρα, ας, ἡ, *a day*, *i.e.*, from sunrise to sunset, Lu. xviii. 7; Ac. ix. 24; *a day* of twenty-four hours, Mat. vi. 34; fig. in various senses.

ἡμέτερος, α, ον, *our*, *our own*, Ac. ii. 11, xxvi. 5.

ἡμιθανής, ές, *half dead*, Lu. x. 30.*

ἥμισυς, εια, υ, gen., ἡμίσους, *half;* in neut. only, *half* of, (gen.) plur. (ἡμίση, W. H. ἡμίσια), Lu. xix. 8; sing., Mar. vi. 23; Rev. xi. 9, 11, xii. 14.*

ἡμιώριον, ου, τό, *a half-hour*, Rev. viii. 1.*

ἡνίκα, adv., *when*, *whenever*, 2 Cor. iii. 15, 16.*

ἤπερ, see ἤ.

ἤπιος, α, ον, *placid*, *gentle*, 1 Th. ii. 7 (W. H. νήπιος); 2 Tim. ii. 24.*

Ἤρ, ὁ (Heb.), *Er*, Lu. iii. 28.*

ἤρεμος, ον, *quiet*, *tranquil*, 1 Tim. ii. 2.*

Ἡρώδης (W. H. -ῴ-), ου, ὁ, *Herod*. Four of the name are mentioned: (1) *Herod the Great*, Mat. ii. 1; (2) *Herod Antipas*, or *H. the tetrarch*, Mat. xiv. 1, 3, 6; Lu. xxiii.; (3) *H. Agrippa*, Ac. xii.; (4) *H. Agrippa* the younger, called only *Agrippa*, Ac. xxv.

Ἡρωδιανοί (W. H. -ῳ-), ῶν, οἱ, *Herodians*, partisans of Herod Antipas, Mat. xxii. 16; Mar. iii. 6, xii. 13.*

Ἡρωδιάς (W. H. -ῳ-), άδος, ἡ, *Herodias*, Mat. xiv. 3, 6.

Ἡρωδίων (W. H. -ῳ-), ωνος, ὁ, *Herodion*, Ro. xvi. 11.*

Ἡσαΐας, ου, ὁ, *Esaias*, *i.e.*, *Isaiah*, Mat. iii. 3, iv. 14.

Ἡσαῦ, ὁ, *Esau*, Ro. ix. 13; Heb. xi. 20, xii. 16.*

ἡσυχάζω, σω, (1) *to rest from work*, Lu. xxiii. 56; (2) *to cease from altercation*, *to be silent*, Lu. xiv. 4; Ac. xi. 18, xxi. 4; (3) *to live quietly*, 1 Th. iv. 11.*

ἡσυχία, ας, ἡ, (1) *silence*, Ac. xxii. 2; 1 Tim. ii. 11; (2) *tranquillity*, *quietness*, 2 Th. iii. 12.*

ἡσύχιος, α, ον, *quiet*, *tranquil* 1 Tim. ii. 2; 1 Pet. iii. 4.*

ἤτοι, see ἤ.

ἡττάομαι, pass., (1) *to be made inferior* (abs.), 2 Cor. xii. 13; (2) *to be overcome by* (dat.), 2 Pet. ii. 19, 20.*

ἥττημα, ατος, τό, *inferiority, diminution*, Ro. xi. 12; *loss*, 1 Cor. vi. 7. (S.)* *Syn.*: see ἀγνόημα.

ἥττων or ἥσσων (W. H.), ον, compar. of κακός, *inferior*, neut. as adv., 2 Cor. xii. 15; τὸ ἧττον, as subst., *the worse*, 1 Cor. xi. 17.*

ἠχέω, ῶ, *to sound*, as the sea, Lu. xxi. 25 (not W. H.); as brass, 1 Cor. xiii. 1.*

ἦχος, ου, ὁ, and ους, τό, *sound, noise*, Lu. xxi. 25 (W. H.); Heb. xii. 19; Ac. ii. 2; *rumor, report*, Lu. iv. 37.*

Θ

Θ, θ, θῆτα, *theta, th*, the eighth letter. As a numeral, θ' = 9; ,θ = 9000.

Θαδδαῖος, ου, ὁ, *Thaddæus*, a surname of the apostle Jude (also called *Lebbæus*), Mat. x. 3; Mar. iii. 18.*

θάλασσα, ης, ἡ, (1) *the sea*, Ro. ix. 27; (2) *sea*, as the Mediterranean, the Red Sea, Ac. vii. 36, x. 6, 32; (3) Hebraistically, for the *lake* Gennesaret, Mat. viii. 24.

θάλπω, *to cherish, nourish*, Ep. v. 29; 1 Th. ii. 7.*

Θάμαρ, ἡ, *Tamar*, Mat. i. 3.*

θαμβέω, ῶ, *to be astonished, amazed*, Ac. ix. 6 (W. H. omit); so pass., Mar. i. 27, x. 32; with ἐπί (dat.), Mar. x. 24.*

θάμβος, ους, τό, *amazement*, Lu. iv. 36, v. 9; Ac. iii. 10.*

θανάσιμος, ον, *deadly, mortal*, Mar. xvi. 18.*

θανατη-φόρος, ον, *death-bringing*, Ja. iii. 8.*

θάνατος, ου, ὁ, *death*, lit. or fig., Jn. xi. 4; 2 Cor. iii. 7; Ro. i. 32; *the cause of death*, Ro. vii. 13.

θανατόω, ῶ, ώσω, *to put to death*, pass., *to be in danger of death*, Ro. viii. 36; fig., *to destroy, subdue*, as evil passions, Ro. viii. 13; pass., *to become dead to* (dat.), Ro. vii. 4.

θάπτω, ψω, 2d aor. ἔταφον, *to bury*, Mat. viii. 21, 22.

Θάρα, ὁ, *Terah*, Lu. iii. 34.*

θαρρέω, ῶ, ήσω, *to be of good courage, to have confidence*, εἰς or ἐν, 2 Cor. v. 6, 8, x. 1. In imperative, forms from θαρσέω are used, θάρσει, θαρσεῖτε, *take courage*.

θάρσος, ους, τό, *courage*, Ac. xxviii. 15.*

θαῦμα, ατος, τό, *a wonder*, 2 Cor. xi. 14 (W. H.); *wonder, amazement*, Rev. xvii. 6.*

θαυμάζω, σω, or σομαι, *to wonder*, abs., with διά, acc., ἐπί, dat., περί, gen., or ὅτι, εἰ; *to wonder at, admire*, acc.; pass., *to be admired* or *honored*.

θαυμάσιος, α, ον, *wonderful*, Mat. xxi. 15.*

θαυμαστός, ή, όν, *wonderful, marvelous*, Mat. xxi. 42; Mar. xii. 11; Jn. ix. 30; 2 Cor. xi. 14 (Rec.); 1 Pet. ii. 9; Rev. xv. 1, 3.*

θεά, ᾶς, ἡ, *a goddess*, Ac. xix. 27, and Rec. in 35, 37.*

θεάομαι, ῶμαι, dep., 1st aor. ἐθεασάμην, pass. ἐθεάθην, *to behold, to contemplate, to visit*, Mat. xi. 7; Ro. xv. 24.

θεατρίζω, *to make a spectacle of, expose to contempt*, Heb. x. 33. (N. T.)*

θέατρον, ου, τό, (1) *a place for public shows, a theatre*, Ac. xix. 29, 31; (2) *a spectacle*, 1 Cor. iv. 9.*

θεῖον, ου, τό, *sulphur* (from the following, *a divine incense*), Rev. ix. 17, 18.

θεῖος, εία, εῖον, *divine*, 2 Pet. i. 3, 4; τὸ θεῖον, *the deity*, Ac. xvii. 29.*

θειότης, τητος, ἡ, *deity, divine nature*, Ro. i. 20.* *Syn.*: θειότης is deity, *abstractly*; θεότης, *personally*.

θειώδης, ες, *sulphurous*, Rev. ix. 17. (N. T.)*

θέλημα, ατος, τό, *will*, Lu. xii. 47; Ep. i. 9; plur., *commands*, Ac. xiii. 22; *desire*, Ep. ii. 3.

θέλησις, εως, ἡ, *a willing, will*, Heb. ii. 4. (S.)*

θέλω, impf. ἤθελον, 1st aor. ἠθέλησα (ἐθέλω is not found in N. T.), *to wish, delight in, prefer, to will*, in the sense of assent, determination, or requirement.

θεμέλιος, ον, *belonging to a foundation*; hence, masc. (sc. λίθος), *a foundation*, or τὸ θεμέλιον (Lu.), in the same sense, 2 Tim. ii. 9; Lu. vi. 49; fig., for the elements of doctrine or life, 1 Cor. iii. 10, 12; Heb. vi. 1.

θεμελιόω, ῶ, ώσω, *to lay a foundation, to found*, Heb. i. 10; fig., *to make stable*, Col. i. 23.

θεο-δίδακτος, ον, *taught of God*, 1 Th. iv. 9. (N. T.)*

θεο-λόγος, ου, ὁ, *one who treats of divine things*, of the apostle John in the title to Rev. (W. H. omit).*

θεο-μαχέω, ῶ, *to fight against God*, Ac. xxiii. 9 (W. H. omit).*

θεο-μάχος, ου, ὁ, *a fighter against God*, Ac. v. 39.*

θεό-πνευστος, ον (πνέω), *God-breathed, inspired by God*, 2 Tim. iii. 16.*

θεός, οῦ, ὁ, voc. once θεέ, Mat. xxvii. 46; (1) *a god*, generically, Ac. vii. 43, xii. 22; 2 Cor. iv. 4; Phil. iii. 19; Jn. x. 34 (quoted from S.); (2) *God*; ὁ θεός, *the revealed God*, Jn. i. 1; Ac. xvii. 24, etc.; (3) applied to Christ, Jn. i. 1, xx. 28.

θεο-σέβεια, ας, ἡ, *fear of God, piety*, 1 Tim. ii. 10.*

θεο-σεβής, ές, *God-worshipping, pious*, Jn. ix. 31.* *Syn.*: see δεισιδαίμων.

θεο-στυγής, ές, *hateful to God*, Ro. i. 30.*

θεότης, τητος, ἡ, *deity, Godhead*, Col. ii. 9.* *Syn.*: see θειότης.

Θεό-φιλος, ου, ὁ, *Theophilus*, Lu. i. 3; Ac. i. 1.*

θεραπεία, ας, ἡ, (1) *service*; hence (abs. for concrete), *servants, household*, Lu. xii. 42; Mat. xxiv. 45 (not W. H.); (2) *medical service, healing*, Lu. ix. 11; Rev. xxii. 2.*

θεραπεύω, εύσω, (1) *to serve, minister to*, only Ac. xvii. 25; (2) *to heal*, acc. of pers., and ἀπό or acc. of disease, Mat. xii. 10; Mar. vi. 5.

θεράπων, οντος, ὁ, *a servant, an attendant*, Heb. iii. 5.*

θερίζω, ίσω, *to reap* or *gather*, as grain, lit. or fig., Mat. vi. 26; Jn. iv. 37, 38.

θερισμός, οῦ, ὁ, *harvest*, lit. or fig., Jn. iv. 35; Lu. x. 2.

θεριστής, οῦ, ὁ, *a reaper*, Mat. xiii. 30, 39.*

θερμαίνω, ανῶ, only mid. in N. T., *to warm one's self*, Mar.

xiv. 54, 67; Jn. xviii. 18, 25; Ja. ii. 16.*
θέρμη, ης, ἡ, *heat,* Ac. xxviii. 3.*
θέρος, ους, τό, *summer,* Mat. xxiv. 32; Mar. xiii. 28; Lu. xxi. 30.*
Θεσσαλονικεύς, έως, ὁ, *a Thessalonian,* Ac. xx. 4.
Θεσσαλονίκη, ης, ἡ, *Thessalonica,* Ac. xvii. 1, 11, 13.
Θευδᾶς, ᾶ, ὁ, *Theudas,* Ac. v. 36.*
θεωρέω, ῶ, *to be a spectator of, to behold, to see, to know by seeing, to experience;* abs., or with acc. or obj. clause.
θεωρία, ας, ἡ, *a sight, a spectacle,* Lu. xxiii. 48.*
θήκη, ης, ἡ (τίθημι), *a receptacle,* as a scabbard, Jn. xviii. 11.*
θηλάζω, (1) *to give suck,* Mat. xxiv. 19; (2) *to suck,* Mat. xxi. 16.
θῆλυς, εια, υ, *female,* fem., Ro. i. 26, 27; neut., Mat. xix. 4; Mar. x. 6; Gal. iii. 28.*
θήρα, ας, ἡ, *hunting,* hence, *a trap,* Ro. xi. 9.*
θηρεύω, σω, *to hunt, to catch,* Lu. xi. 54.*
θηριο-μαχέω, ῶ, *to fight with wild beasts,* 1 Cor. xv. 32.*
θηρίον, ου, τό (prop. *a little beast*), *a wild beast,* as Ac. xi. 6; freq. in Rev.
θησαυρίζω, σω, *to store up, reserve,* lit. and fig., Lu. xii. 21; 2 Pet. iii. 7.
θησαυρός, οῦ, ὁ, *a treasure receptacle, treasure,* Lu. xii. 33, 34.
θιγγάνω, 2d aor. ἔθιγον, *to touch, handle,* abs., Col. ii. 21; with gen., Heb. xii. 20; *to injure,* Heb. xi. 28.* *Syn.:* see ἅπτω.
θλίβω, ψω, *to press upon,* Mar. iii. 9; fig., *to afflict,* 2 Cor. i. 6; pass. perf. part. τεθλιμμένος, *contracted, narrow,* Mat. vii. 14.
θλῖψις, εως, ἡ, *pressure, affliction, tribulation,* Ac. vii. 11; 2 Th. i. 6.
θνήσκω, 2d aor. ἔθανον, *to die;* in N. T. only perf. τέθνηκα, *to be dead,* Lu. viii. 49; 1 Tim. v. 6.
θνητός, ή, όν, *liable to death, mortal,* Ro. vi. 12, viii. 11; 1 Cor. xv. 53, 54; 2 Cor. iv. 11, v. 4.*
θορυβάζω, *to disturb, trouble,* Lu. x. 41 (W. H.). (N. T.)*
θορυβέω, ῶ, *to disturb,* Ac. xvii. 5; pass., *to be troubled, to wail,* Mat. ix. 23; Mar. v. 39; Ac. xx. 10.*
θόρυβος, ου, ὁ, *noise, uproar,* Mar. v. 38; Ac. xx. 1.
θραύω, σω, *to break, shatter,* Lu. iv. 18.*
θρέμμα, ατος, το (τρέφω), *the young of cattle, sheep,* etc., Jn. iv. 12.*
θρηνέω, ῶ, ήσω, abs., *to wail, lament,* Mat. xi. 17; Lu. vii. 32; Jn. xvi. 20; *to bewail,* acc., Lu. xxiii. 27.*
θρῆνος, ου, ὁ, *a wailing,* Mat. ii. 18 (not W. H.).*
θρησκεία, ας, ἡ, *external worship, religious worship,* Ac. xxvi. 5; Col. ii. 18; Ja. i. 26, 27.*
θρῆσκος, ου, ὁ (prop. adj.), *a devotee, religious person,* Ja. i. 26. (N. T.)* *Syn.:* see δεισιδαίμων.
θριαμβεύω, σω, *to triumph over, to lead in triumph,* 2 Cor. ii. 14; Col. ii. 15.*
θρίξ, τριχός, dat. plur. θριξί, ἡ, *a hair,* human or animal, Jn. xi. 2; Rev. ix. 8.
θροέω, ῶ, *to disturb, terrify by clamor;* only pass. in N. T., Mat. xxiv. 6; Mar. xiii. 7; 2 Th. ii. 2.*
θρόμβος, ου, ὁ, *a clot, large drop,* as of blood, Lu. xxii. 44.*
θρόνος, ου, ὁ, *a seat,* as of judgment, Mat. xix. 28; *a throne,* or seat of power, Rev. iii. 21; met., of *kingly power,* Rev. xiii. 2; concrete, of *the ruler,* or occupant of the throne, Col. i. 16.
Θυάτειρα, ων, τά, *Thyatira,* Ac. xvi. 14; Rev. i. 11, ii. 18, 24.*
θυγάτηρ, τρός, ἡ, *a daughter,* Mat. ix. 18; *a female descendant,* Lu. xiii. 16; met., of the inhabitants of a place, collectively, Mat. xxi. 5.
θυγάτριον, ου, τὸ (dim. of θυγάτηρ), *a little daughter,* Mar. v. 23, vii. 25.*
θύελλα, ης, ἡ, *a tempest,* Heb. xii. 18.*
θύϊνος, η, ον, *made of the citrus tree,* a strongly aromatic tree of Africa, Rev. xviii. 12.*
θυμίαμα, ατος, τό, *incense,* Lu. i. 10, 11; Rev. v. 8, viii. 3, 4, xviii. 13.*
θυμιατήριον, ου, τό, *a censer,* or *an altar of incense,* Heb. ix. 4.*
θυμιάω, ῶ, *to burn incense,* Lu. i. 9.*
θυμομαχέω, ῶ, *to be very angry with* (dat.), Ac. xii. 20.*
θυμός, οῦ, ὁ, *passion, great anger, wrath,* Lu. iv 28; Rev. xiv. 19. *Syn.:* θυμός is *impulsive, turbulent* anger; ὀργή is anger as a *settled habit,* both may be right or wrong; παροργισμός is the bitterness of anger, always wrong.
θυμόω, ῶ, *to provoke to great anger;* pass., *to be very angry with,* Mat. ii. 16.*
θύρα, ας, ἡ, *a door,* Lu. xi. 7; Mat. xxvii. 60; met., Jn. x. 7, 9.
θυρεός, οῦ, ὁ, *a large* (door shaped) *shield,* Ep. vi. 16.*
θυρίς, ίδος, ἡ (prop. *a little door*), *a window,* Ac. xx. 9; 2 Cor. xi. 33.*
θυρωρός, οῦ, ὁ, ἡ, *a door-keeper, porter,* Mar. xiii. 34; Jn. x. 3, xviii. 16, 17.*
θυσία, ας, ἡ, *a sacrifice,* lit. and fig., Ep. v. 2; 1 Pet. ii. 5.
θυσιαστήριον, ου, τό, *an altar,* for sacrifices, Lu. i. 11, ii. 51; Ja. ii. 21. (S.) *Syn.:* see βωμός.
θύω, σω, (1) *to slay in sacrifice,* Ac. xiv. 13; (2) *to kill animals,* for feasting, Mat. xxii. 4; (3) *to slay,* generally, Jn. x. 10.
Θωμᾶς, ᾶ, ὁ (from Heb. = δίδυμος), *Thomas,* Mat. x. 3.
θώραξ, ακος, ὁ, *a breast-plate,* Ep. vi. 14; 1 Th. v. 8; Rev. ix. 9, 17.*

I

I, ι, ἰῶτα, *iota, i,* the ninth letter. As a numeral, ι′ = 10; ͵ι = 10,000.
Ἰάειρος, ου, ὁ, *Jairus,* Mar. v. 22; Lu. viii. 41.*
Ἰακώβ, ὁ (Heb.), *Jacob,* (1) the patriarch, Ac. vii. 8; (2) the father-in-law of Mary, Mat. i. 15.
Ἰάκωβος, ου, ὁ, Greek form of preced., *James,* (1) the son of Zebedee, Mat. iv. 21; (2)

the son of Alphæus, Mat. x. 3; (3) the Lord's brother, Mat. xiii. 55. Some identify (2) and (3).

ἴαμα, ατος, τό, *healing, cure*, plur., 1 Cor. xii. 9, 28, 30.*

Ἰαμβρῆς, ὁ, *Jambres*, 2 Tim. iii. 8.*

Ἰαννά, ὁ (W. H. -αί), (Heb.), *Jannai*, Lu. iii. 24.*

Ἰαννῆς, ὁ, *Jannes*, 2 Tim. iii. 8.*

ἰάομαι, ῶμαι, ἰάσομαι, dep., mid. aor., but passive in aor., perf. and fut., *to heal, to restore to health*, of body or mind; with ἀπό, of malady, Mar. v. 29; Jn. xii. 40.

Ἰαρέδ, ὁ (Heb.), *Jared*, Lu. iii. 37.*

ἴασις, εως, ἡ, *a cure, healing*, Lu. xiii. 32; Ac. iv. 22, 30.*

ἴασπις, ιδος, ἡ, *jasper*, a precious stone, Rev. iv. 3, xxi. 11, 18, 19.*

Ἰάσων, ονος, ὁ, *Jason*, Ac. xvii. 5, 6, 7, 9; Ro. xvi. 21; perhaps two persons.*

ἰατρός, οῦ, ὁ, *a physician*, Lu. iv. 23; Col. iv. 14.

ἴδε, or ἰδέ (εἶδον), imper. act. as interj., *behold!* often followed by nominative.

ἰδέα (W. H. ει-), ας, ἡ, *form, outward appearance*, Mat. xxviii. 3.* *Syn.*: see Trench, § lxx.

ἴδιος, α, ον, (1) *one's own*, denoting ownership, Mat. xxii. 5; Jn. x. 12; also what is peculiar to, Ac. i. 19 (W. H. omit); hence, τὰ ἴδια, *one's own things, home, nation* or *people, business* or *duty; οἱ ἴδιοι, one's own people, friends, companions*, neut. and masc. contrasted in Jn. i. 11; (2) *that which specially pertains to, and is proper for*, as 1 Cor. iii. 8; Gal. vi. 9; (3) adverbially, κατ' ἰδίαν, *privately; ἰδίᾳ, individually*.

ἰδιώτης, ου, ὁ, *a private person, one unskilled in anything*, Ac. iv. 13; 1 Cor. xiv. 16, 23, 24; 2 Cor. xi. 6.* *Syn.*: see ἀγράμματος.

ἰδού (see ἴδε), imper. mid. as interj., *lo! behold!* used to call attention not only to that which may be seen, but also heard, or apprehended in any way.

Ἰδουμαία, ας, ἡ, *Idumæa*, the O. T. Edom, Mar. iii. 8.*

ἱδρώς, ῶτος, ὁ, *sweat*, Lu. xxii. 44.*

Ἰεζαβήλ, ἡ (Heb.), *Jezebel*, symbolically used, Rev. ii. 20.*

Ἱερά-πολις, -εως, ἡ, *Hierapolis*, in Phrygia, Col. iv. 13.*

ἱερατεία (W. H. -τία), ας, ἡ, *the office of a priest, priesthood*, Lu. i. 9; Heb. vii. 5.*

ἱεράτευμα, ατος, τό, *the order of priests, priesthood*, applied to Christians, 1 Pet. ii. 5, 9. (S.)*

ἱερατεύω, σω, *to officiate as a priest*, Lu. i. 8.*

Ἱερεμίας, ου, ὁ, *Jeremiah*, Mat. ii. 17, xvi. 14, xxvii. 9 (this quotation is from *Zechariah*).*

ἱερεύς, έως, ὁ, *a priest*, Mat. viii. 4; sometimes *the High Priest*, Ac. v. 24 (not W. H.); of Christ, Heb. v. 6 (Ps. cx. 4); of Christians generally, Rev. i. 6, v. 10.

Ἱεριχώ, ἡ (Heb.), *Jericho*, Lu. x. 30.

ἱερόθυτος, ον, *offered in sacrifice*, 1 Cor. x. 28 (W. H.).*

ἱερόν, οῦ, τό (prop. neut. of ἱερός), *a temple*, used of a heathen temple, as Ac. xix. 27; of the temple at Jerusalem, as Mat. xxiv. 1; and of parts of the temple, as Mat. xii. 5. *Syn.*: ἱερόν is the whole sacred enclosure; ναός, the *shrine* itself, the holy place and the holy of holies.

ἱερο-πρεπής, ές, *suitable to a sacred character* (*reverent*, R. V.), Tit. ii. 3.*

ἱερός, ά, όν, *sacred, holy*, of the Scriptures, 2 Tim. iii. 15; τὰ ἱερά, *sacred things*, 1 Cor. ix. 13.* *Syn.*: see ἅγιος.

Ἱεροσόλυμα (W. H. Ἰ-), ων, τά, the usual form in Mat., Mar., and Jn.; see Ἱερουσαλήμ.

Ἱεροσολυμίτης, ου, ὁ, *one of Jerusalem*, Mar. i. 5; Jn. vii. 25.*

ἱερο-συλέω, ῶ, *to commit sacrilege*, Ro. ii. 22.*

ἱερό-συλος, ον, *robbing temples, sacrilegious*, Ac. xix. 37.*

ἱερουργέω, ῶ (ἱερός, ἔργον), *to minister in holy things*, Ro. xv. 16.*

Ἱερουσαλήμ (W. H. Ἰ-), ἡ (Heb.), (for form, see Gr. § 156, Wi. § 10, 2, Bu. 6, 16, 18, 21), *Jerusalem*, (1) the city; (2) the inhabitants. In Gal. iv. 25, 26, ἡ νῦν Ἰ. is the *Jewish dispensation*, and is contrasted with ἡ ἄνω Ἰ., the ideal *Christian community;* also called Ἰ. ἐπουράνιος, Heb. xii. 22; ἡ καινὴ Ἰ., Rev. iii. 12, xxi. 2.

ἱερωσύνη, ης, ἡ, *the priestly office*, Heb. vii. 11, 12, 14 (not W. H.), 24.*

Ἰεσσαί, ὁ (Heb.), *Jesse*, Mat. i. 5, 6.

Ἰεφθάε, ὁ (Heb.), *Jephthah*, Heb. xi. 32.*

Ἰεχονίας, ου, ὁ, *Jechoniah*, or *Jehoiachin*, Mat. i. 11, 12.*

Ἰησοῦς, οῦ, ὁ (Heb.), (see Gr. § 25, Wi. § 10, 1, Bu. 21), (1) *Jesus*, the Savior, Mat. i. 21, 25; (2) *Joshua*, Ac. vii. 45; Heb. iv. 8; (3) *a fellow-laborer of Paul*, so named, Col. iv. 11; (4) *Barabbas* is so named in some early MSS., Mat. xxvii. 16; (5) *an ancestor of Joseph*, Lu. iii. 29 (W. H.).

ἱκανός, ή, όν, (1) *sufficient, competent* to, inf., πρός (acc.) or ἵνα; (2) *many, much*, of number or time.

ἱκανότης, τητος, ἡ, *sufficiency, ability*, 2 Cor. iii. 5.*

ἱκανόω, ῶ, *to make competent*, 2 Cor. iii. 6; Col. i. 12. (S.)*

ἱκετηρία, ας, ἡ, *supplication*, Heb. v. 7.* *Syn.*: see αἴτημα.

ἰκμάς, άδος, ἡ, *moisture*, Lu. viii. 6.*

Ἰκόνιον, ου, τό, *Iconium*, Ac. xiv. 1, 19, 21.

ἱλαρός, ά, όν, *joyous, cheerful*, 2 Cor. ix. 7.*

ἱλαρότης, τητος, ἡ, *cheerfulness*, Ro. xii. 8. (S.)*

ἱλάσκομαι, άσομαι, 1st aor. ἱλάσθην, (1) *to be propitious to*, dat., Lu. xviii. 13; (2) *to make atonement for, expiate*, acc., Heb. ii. 17.*

ἱλασμός, οῦ, ὁ, *a propitiation, atoning sacrifice*, 1 Jn. ii. 2, iv. 10. (S.)* *Syn.*: see ἀπολύτρωσις.

ἱλαστήριος, α, ον, *atoning*, neut., *propitiation*, Ro. iii. 25; (sc. ἐπίθεμα, *covering*), *the mercy seat*, Heb. ix. 5. (S.)*

ἵλεως, ων (Attic for ἵλαος), *propitious, merciful,* Heb. viii. 12; ἵλεώς σοι, (God be) merciful to thee! *God forbid!* Mat. xvi. 22.*

Ἰλλυρικόν, οὐ, τό, *Illyricum,* Ro. xv. 19.*

ἱμάς, άντος, ὁ, *a thong* for scourging, Ac. xxii. 25; *thong, latchet* of a shoe, Mar. i. 7; Lu. iii. 16; Jn. i. 27.*

ἱματίζω, perf. pass. part. ἱματισμένος, *to clothe,* Mar. v. 15; Lu. viii. 35. (N. T.)*

ἱμάτιον, ου, τό (dim. of ἶμα = εἶμα, from ἕννυμι), (1) *clothing,* Mat. ix. 16; (2) *the outer garment,* worn over the χιτών, Jn. xix. 2. *Syn.*: see Trench, § l.

ἱματισμός, οῦ, ὁ, *clothing, raiment,* Lu. vii. 25. *Syn.*: see ἱμάτιον.

ἱμείρομαι, *to long for, to love earnestly,* 1 Th. ii. 8 (W. H. ὁμείρομαι).*

ἵνα, conj., *that, to the end that; ἵνα μή, that not, lest.* See Gr. § 384, Wi. § 53, 9, Bu. 229 sq.

ἱνα-τί, or ἵνα τί (W. H.), conj., *in order that what* (may happen? sc. γένηται), *to what end?*

Ἰόππη, ης, ἡ, *Joppa,* Ac. xi. 5, 13.

Ἰορδάνης, ου, ὁ, *the Jordan,* Mar. i. 5, 9.

ἰός, οῦ, ὁ, (1) *poison,* Ro. iii. 13; Ja. iii. 8; (2) *rust,* Ja. v. 3.*

Ἰουδαία, ας, ἡ (really adj., fem., sc. γῆ), *Judæa,* Mat. ii. 1; including all Palestine, Lu. vii. 17.

Ἰουδαΐζω (from Heb.), *to conform to Jewish practice,* to "Judaize," in life or ritual, Gal. ii. 14. (S.)*

Ἰουδαϊκός, ή, όν (from Heb.), *Jewish,* or *Judaical,* Tit. i. 14.*

Ἰουδαϊκῶς, adv., *Jewishly,* in Jewish style, Gal. ii. 14.*

Ἰουδαῖος, αία, αῖον, *Jewish,* Jn. iv. 9; Ac. x. 28. Often in plur., with subst. understood, οἱ Ἰουδαῖοι, *the Jews.* *Syn.*: see Ἑβραῖος.

Ἰουδαισμός, οῦ, ὁ (from Heb.), *Judaism, the religion of the Jews,* Gal. i. 13, 14. (Ap.)*

Ἰούδας, α, ὁ, and Ἰούδα, ὁ, indecl., *Judah,* (1) son of Jacob; (2, 3) other unknown ancestors of Christ, Lu. iii. 26, 30; (4) *Jude,* an apostle; (5) *Judas* Iscariot; (6) *Judas* Barsabas, Ac. xv. 22; (7) *Judas,* a Jew living in Damascus, Ac. ix. 11; (8) *Judas,* a leader of sedition, Ac. v. 37; (9) *Judas,* a brother of our Lord, Mat. xiii. 55. See Ἰάκωβος.

Ἰουλία, ας, ἡ, *Julia,* Ro. xvi. 15.*

Ἰούλιος, ου, ὁ, *Julius,* Ac. xxvii. 1, 3.*

Ἰουνίας, α, ὁ, *Junias,* Ro. xvi. 7.*

Ἰοῦστος, ου, ὁ, *Justus.* Three of the name are mentioned, Ac. i. 23, xviii. 7; Col. iv. 11.*

ἱππεύς, έως, ὁ, *a horseman,* Ac. xxiii. 23, 32.*

ἱππικόν (prop. neut. adj.), οῦ, τό, *cavalry,* Rev. ix. 16.*

ἵππος, ου, ὁ, *a horse,* Ja. iii. 3.

ἶρις, ιδος, ἡ, *a rainbow,* Rev. iv. 3, x. 1.*

Ἰσαάκ, ὁ (Heb.), *Isaac,* Ro. ix. 7, 10.

ἰσ-άγγελος, ον, *like angels,* Lu. xx. 36. (N. T.)*

ἴσασι, see οἶδα.

Ἰσαχάρ, or Ἰσασχάρ, or Ἰσσαχάρ (W.H.), (Heb.), *Issachar,* Rev. vii. 7.*

Ἰσκαριώτης, ου, ὁ, a man *of Kerioth,* Mat. xxvi. 14, 25. See Josh. xv. 25.

ἴσος, η, ον (or ἶσος), *equal* (dat.), Mat. xx. 12; Lu. vi. 34; Jn. v. 18; Ac. xi. 17; *alike, consistent,* as truthful witnesses, Mar. xiv. 56, 59; ἴσα, adverbially, *on an equality* Phil. ii. 6; Rev. xxi. 16.*

ἰσότης, τητος, ἡ, *equality,* 2 Cor. viii. 13, 14; *equity,* Col. iv. 1.*

ἰσό-τιμος, ον, *equally precious,* 2 Pet. i. 1.*

ἰσό-ψυχος, ον *like-minded,* Phil. ii. 20.*

Ἰσραήλ, ὁ (Heb.), *Israel,* Ac. vii. 42, met., for the whole nation of the Israelites, Ro. xi. 2, 7, 26.

Ἰσραηλίτης, ου, ὁ, *an Israelite,* Ro. ix. 4. *Syn.*: see Ἑβραῖος.

ἴστε, see οἶδα.

ἵστημι (in Ro. iii. 31, Rec. has ἱστάω, W. H. ἱστάνω, see Gr. § 107, Wi. § 15, Bu. 44), trans. in pres., imperf., fut., 1st aor.; *to cause to stand, to set up, to place, to fix* a time, *to confirm, to establish, to put in the balance, to weigh;* intrans. in perf., plup., and 2d aor., *to stand, to stand still* or *firm, to endure, to be confirmed* or *established, to come to a stand, to cease.*

ἱστορέω, ῶ, *to become personally acquainted with,* Gal. i. 18.*

ἰσχυρός, ά, όν, *strong, mighty, powerful, vehement,* Mar. iii. 27; 1 Cor. i. 25; Rev. xix. 6.

ἰσχύς, ύος, ἡ, *strength, power,* 2 Pet. ii. 11; Ep. i. 19.

ἰσχύω, ύσω, *to be strong, sound to prevail, to be able* (inf.), *to have ability* for (acc.), Mar. ii. 17; Rev. xii. 8.

ἴσως (ἶσος), adv., *perhaps,* Lu. xx. 13.*

Ἰταλία, ας, ἡ, *Italy,* Ac. xviii. 2

Ἰταλικός, ή, όν, *Italian,* Ac. x. 1.*

Ἰτουραία, ας, ἡ, *Ituræa,* Lu. iii. 1.*

ἰχθύδιον, ου, τό (dim. of ἰχθύς), *a little fish,* Mat. xv. 34; Mar. viii. 7.*

ἰχθύς, ύος, ὁ, *a fish,* Lu. v. 6; Jn. xxi. 11.

ἴχνος, ους, τό, *a footstep,* fig., Ro. iv. 12; 2 Cor. xii. 18; 1 Pet. ii. 21.*

Ἰωάθαμ, ὁ (Heb.), *Jotham,* Mat. i. 9.*

Ἰωάννα, ης, ἡ, *Joanna,* Lu. viii. 3, xxiv. 10.*

Ἰωαννᾶς, ᾶ, ὁ, *Joannas,* Lu. iii. 27.*

Ἰωάννης, ου, ὁ, *John,* (1) the Baptist; (2) the apostle; (3) a member of the Sanhedrin, Ac. iv. 6; (4) John Mark, Ac. xii. 12.

Ἰώβ, ὁ (Heb.), *Job,* Ja. v. 11.*

Ἰωβήδ, see Ὠβήδ.

Ἰωήλ, ὁ (Heb.), *Joel,* the prophet, Ac. ii. 16.*

Ἰωνάν, ὁ (Heb.), *Jonan,* Lu. iii. 30.*

Ἰωνᾶς, ᾶ, ὁ, *Jonas,* or *Jonah,* (1) the prophet, Mat. xii. 39–41; (2) the father of Peter, Jn. i. 42.

Ἰωράμ, ὁ (Heb.), *Joram,* or *Jehoram,* son of Jehoshaphat, Mat. i. 8.*

Ἰωρείμ, ὁ (Heb.), *Jorim,* Lu. iii. 29.*

Ἰωσαφάτ, ὁ (Heb.), *Jehoshaphat*, Mat. i. 8.*

Ἰωσῆς, ῆ (or ῆτος, W. H.), ὁ, *Joses*. Four are mentioned: (1) Lu. iii. 29 (W. H. Ἰησοῦ); (2) Mar. vi. 3; Mat. xiii. 55 (W. H. Ἰωσήφ); (3) Mat. xxvii. 56 (W. H. mrg.), Mar. xv. 40, 47; (4) Ac. iv. 36 (W. H. Ἰωσήφ). Some think (2) and (3) identical.*

Ἰωσήφ, ὁ (Heb.), *Joseph*, (1) the patriarch, Jn. iv. 5; (2, 3, 4) three among the ancestors of Jesus, Lu. iii. 24, 26 (W. H. Ἰωσήχ), 30; (5) the husband of Mary, the mother of Jesus, Mat. ii. 13, 19; (6) Joseph of Arimathæa, Mar. xv. 43, 45; (7) Joseph, called also Barsabas, Ac. i. 23. See also under Ἰωσῆς.

Ἰωσίας, ου, ὁ, *Josiah*, Mat. i. 10, 11.*

ἰῶτα, τό, *iota*, *yod*, the smallest letter of the Hebrew alphabet, Mat. v. 18.*

K

K, κ, κάππα, *kappa*, *k*, the tenth letter. As a numeral, κ′ = 20; ͵κ = 20,000.

κἀγώ (κἀμοί, κἀμέ), contr. for καὶ ἐγώ (καὶ ἐμοί, καὶ ἐμέ), *and I*, *I also*, *even I*.

καθά, adv., contr. from καθ' ἅ, *according as*, Mat. xxvii. 10.*

καθ-αίρεσις, εως, ἡ, *demolition*, *destruction* (opp. to οἰκοδομή, which see), 2 Cor. x. 4, 8, xiii. 10.*

καθ-αιρέω, καθελῶ, καθεῖλον, (1) *to take down*, Ac. xiii. 29; (2) *to demolish*, *destroy*, lit., Lu. xii. 18, or fig., 2 Cor. x. 5.

καθαίρω, αρῶ, *to cleanse*, *to prune*, Jn. xv. 2; Heb. x. 2 (W. H. καθαρίζω).*

καθ-άπερ, adv., *even as*, *just as*, 1 Th. ii. 11.

καθ-άπτω, άψω, *to fasten on*, intrans., Ac. xxviii. 3 (gen.).*

καθαρίζω, att. fut. καθαριῶ, *to cleanse*, lit., Lu. xi. 39; a leper, by healing his disease, Mat. viii. 2, 3; from moral pollution, Heb. ix. 22, 23; *to declare clean*, *i.e.*, from ceremonial pollution, Ac. x. 15.

καθαρισμός, οῦ, ὁ, *cleansing*, physical, moral, or ceremonial, Mar. i. 44; Lu. ii. 22, v. 14; Jn. ii. 6, iii. 25; Heb. i. 3; 2 Pet. i. 9. (S.)*

καθαρός, ά, όν, *clean*, *pure*, physically, morally, or ceremonially, Mat. xxiii. 26; Tit. i. 15; Ro. xiv. 20.

καθαρότης, τητος, ἡ, *purity*, *i.e.*, ceremonial, Heb. ix. 13.*

καθ-έδρα, ας, ἡ, *a seat*, lit., Mat. xxi. 12; Mar. xi. 15; met., *a chair* of authority, Mat. xxiii. 2.*

καθ-έζομαι, *to sit down*, ἐν or ἐπί, dat., Lu. ii. 46; Jn. iv. 6.

καθ-εῖς (W. H. καθ' εἷς), adv. (see Gr. § 300β, 4, Wi. § 37, 3, Bu. 30), *one by one*, Jn. viii. 9.

καθ-εξῆς, adv. (see Gr. § 126*d*), *in orderly succession*, Lu. i. 3; Ac. xi. 4, xviii. 23. With art., Lu. viii. 1, ἐν τῷ κ., *soon afterwards*; Ac. iii. 24, οἱ κ., *those that come after*.*

καθ-εύδω, *to sleep*, lit., Mat. viii. 24; fig., 1 Th. v. 6.

καθηγητής, οῦ, ὁ, *a guide*, *master*, Mat. xxiii. 8 (not W. H.), 10.*

καθ-ήκω, used only impers., *it is fit*, *it is becoming* (acc., inf.), Ac. xxii. 22; τὸ καθῆκον, *the becoming*, Ro. i. 28.*

κάθ-ημαι, 2d pers. κάθῃ for κάθησαι, imper., κάθου (see Gr. § 367, Wi. § 15, 4, Bu. 49), *to be seated*, *to sit down*, *to sit*, *to be settled*, *to abide*; with εἰς, ἐν, ἐπί (gen., dat., acc.).

καθ-ημερινός, ή, όν, *daily*, Ac. vi. 1.*

καθ-ίζω, ίσω, (1) trans., *to cause to sit down*, *to set*; (2) intrans., *to seat one's self*, preps. as κάθημαι; *to sit down*, *to be sitting*, *to tarry*; mid. in Mat. xix. 28; Lu. xxii. 30.

καθ-ίημι, 1st aor. καθῆκα (see Gr. § 112, Bu. 46), *to send* or *let down*, Lu. v. 19; Ac. ix. 25, x. 11, xi. 5.*

καθ-ίστημι (and καθιστάω or -ανω), *to appoint*, *constitute*, *make*, *ordain*, *to conduct*, Ac. xvii. 15; *to appoint as ruler* over (ἐπί, gen., dat., acc.).

καθ-ό, adv. (for καθ' ὅ), *as*, *according as*, Ro. viii. 26; 2 Cor. viii. 12; 1 Pet. iv. 13.*

καθολικός, ή, όν, *general*, *universal* (found in the inscriptions of the seven Epistles of James, Peter, John and Jude, but omitted by W. H.).*

καθ-όλου, adv., *entirely*; καθόλου μή, Ac. iv. 18, *not at all*.*

καθ-οπλίζω, *to arm fully*, pass., Lu. xi. 21.*

καθ-οράω, ῶ, *to see clearly*, pass., Ro. i. 20.*

καθ-ότι, adv., *as*, *according as*, Ac. ii. 45, iv. 35; *because that*, *for*, Lu. i. 7, xix. 9; Ac. ii. 24, xvii. 31 (W. H.).*

καθ-ώς, adv., *according as*, *even as*.

καθώσ-περ, adv., *just as*, Heb. v. 4 (W. H.).*

καί, conj., *and*, *also*, *even*. For the various uses of this conjunction, see Gr. § 403, Wi. § 53, 1–4, Bu. 360 sq.

Καϊάφας, α, ὁ, *Caiaphas*, Jn. xi. 49.

Κάϊν, ὁ (Heb.), *Cain*, Heb. xi. 4.

Καϊνάν, ὁ (Heb.), *Cainan*. Two are mentioned, Lu. iii. 36, 37.*

καινός, ή, όν, *new*, Lu. v. 38; Ac. xvii. 19. *Syn.*: νέος is new under the aspect of *time*; καινός, new in quality, of different character.

καινότης, τητος, ἡ, *newness* (moral and spiritual), Ro. vi. 4, vii. 6.*

καί-περ, conj., *although*, Phil. iii. 4; Heb. v. 8.

καιρός, οῦ, ὁ, *a fixed time*, *season*, *opportunity*, Lu. viii. 13; Heb. xi. 15; Ac. xiv. 17; Ro. viii. 18. *Syn.*: χρόνος is time in general, viewed simply as such; καιρός, definite, suitable time, the time of some decisive event, *crisis*, *opportunity*.

Καῖσαρ, αρος, ὁ, *Cæsar*, a title assumed by Roman emperors, after Julius Cæsar, as Lu. ii. 1, xx. 22; Ac. xvii. 7; Phil. iv. 22.

Καισάρεια, ας, ἡ, *Cæsarea*. Two cities of Palestine, one in Galilee (*Cæsarea Philippi*), Mat. xvi. 13; the other on the coast of the Mediterranean, Ac. viii. 40.

καί-τοι, conj., *and yet, although,* Heb. iv. 3; so *καίτοιγε.*

καίω, perf. pass. *κέκαυμαι, to kindle, light,* Mat. v. 15; pass., *to burn,* Lu. xii. 35; *to burn, consume,* Jn. xv. 6; fig., Lu. xxiv. 32.

κἀκεῖ (*καὶ ἐκεῖ*), *and there,* Ac. xiv. 7.

κἀκεῖθεν (*καὶ ἐκεῖθεν*), *and thence,* Ac. vii. 4, xx. 15.

κἀκεῖνος, *η, ο* (*καὶ ἐκεῖνος*), *and he, she, it,* Lu. xi. 7; Ac. xv. 11.

κακία, *ας, ἡ, badness,* (1) of character, *wickedness,* Ac. viii. 22; (2) of disposition, *malice, ill-will,* Col. iii. 8; (3) of condition, *affliction, evil,* Mat. vi. 34.

κακο-ήθεια, *ας, ἡ, malignity,* Ro. i. 29.*

κακο-λογέω, *ῶ, to speak evil of* (acc.), Mar. ix. 39; Ac. xix. 9; *to curse,* Mat. xv. 4; Mar. vii. 10.*

κακο-πάθεια, *ας, ἡ, a suffering of evil, affliction,* Ja. v. 10.*

κακο-παθέω, *ῶ, to suffer evil, to endure affliction,* 2 Tim. ii. 3 (W. H. *συνκακ-*), 9, iv. 5; Ja. v. 13.*

κακοποιέω, *ῶ,* abs., *to do harm,* Mar. iii. 4; Lu. vi. 9; *to do wrong,* 1 Pet. iii. 17; 3 Jn. 11.*

κακο-ποιός, *όν,* as subst., *an evil-doer,* Jn. xviii. 30 (not W. H.); 1 Pet. ii. 12, 14, iii. 16 (W. H. omit), iv. 15.*

κακός, *ἡ, όν, evil, wicked; τὸ κακόν, wickedness,* Mat. xxvii. 23: also *affliction,* Lu. xvi. 35.

κακ-οῦργος, *ον,* as subst., *a malefactor,* Lu. xxiii. 32, 33, 39; 2 Tim. ii. 9.*

κακ-ουχέω, *ῶ,* only in pass., part., *treated ill, harassed,* Heb. xi. 37, xiii. 3.*

κακόω, *ῶ, ώσω, to ill-treat, oppress,* Ac. vii. 6, 19, xii. 1, xviii. 10; 1 Pet. iii. 13; *to embitter,* Ac. xiv. 2.*

κακῶς, adv., *badly, wickedly,* Jn. xviii. 23; *κακῶς ἔχειν, to be sick,* or *in trouble,* Mat. iv. 24; Lu. v. 31.

κάκωσις, *εως, ἡ, affliction, ill-treatment,* Ac. vii. 34.*

καλάμη, *ης, ἡ, stubble,* 1 Cor. iii. 12.*

κάλαμος, *ου, ὁ, a stalk,* as (1) *a reed,* growing, Mat. xi. 7; (2) *a reed,* as a mock sceptre, Mat. xxvii. 29; (3) *a pen,* 3 Jn. 13; (4) *a measuring-rod,* Rev. xxi. 15.

καλέω, *ῶ, έσω, κέκληκα, to call;* hence, (1) *to summon,* Lu. xix. 13; (2) *to name,* Mat. i. 21, x. 25; (3) *to invite,* Jn. ii. 2; (4) *to appoint,* or *select,* for an office, Heb. v. 4; (5) pass., *to be called,* or *accounted, i.e., to be,* Mat. v. 9, 19; Ja. ii. 23.

καλλι-έλαιος, *ου, ἡ, a cultivated olive tree,* Ro. xi. 24.*

καλλίων (compar. of *καλός*), *better;* adv., *κάλλιον,* Ac. xxv. 10.*

καλο-διδάσκαλος, *ου, ὁ, ἡ, a teacher of what is good,* Tit. ii. 3. (N. T.)*

Καλοὶ Λιμένες, *Fair Havens,* a harbor in the island of Crete, Ac. xxvii. 8.*

καλο-ποιέω, *ῶ, to act uprightly,* 2 Th. iii. 13. (S.)*

καλός, *ἡ, όν, beautiful;* (1) physically, Lu. xxi. 25; (2) morally beautiful, *good, noble,* Mat. v. 16; Heb. xiii. 18; (3) *excellent, advantageous,* Lu. vi. 43; 1 Cor. vii. 1.

κάλυμμα, *ατος, τό, a covering, veil,* 2 Cor. iii. 13–16.*

καλύπτω, *ψω, to cover, veil,* Lu. xxiii. 30; 2 Cor. iv. 3.

καλῶς, adv., *well, rightly, nobly,* Jn. iv. 17; 1 Cor. xiv. 17.

κἀμέ, see *κἀγώ.*

κάμηλος, *ου, ὁ, ἡ, a camel,* Mar. i. 6, x. 25.

κάμινος, *ου, ἡ, a furnace,* Mat. xiii. 42, 50; Rev. i. 15, ix. 2.*

καμ-μύω (*κατά* and *μύω*), *to shut, close* the eyes, Mat. xiii. 15; Ac. xxviii. 27.*

κάμνω, *καμῶ,* perf. *κέκμηκα, to be weary, to be sick,* Heb. xii. 3; Ja. v. 15; Rev. ii. 3 (W. H. omit).*

κἀμοί, see *κἀγώ.*

κάμπτω, *ψω, to bend* the knee, *bow,* Ro. xi. 4, xiv. 11; Ep. iii. 14; Phil. ii. 10.*

κἄν (*καὶ ἐάν*), *and if,* Lu. xiii. 9; *even if, though,* Mat. xxvi. 35; *if even,* Heb. xii. 20; elliptically, *if only,* Mar. v. 28; Ac. v. 15.

Κανᾶ, *ἡ, Cana,* Jn. ii. 1, 11.

Κανανίτης, *ου, ὁ, a Zealot* (from the Aramaic, meaning the same as *ζηλωτής*), Mat. x. 4; Mar. iii. 18 (W. H. read *Καναναῖος,* which has the same meaning). (N. T.)*

Κανδάκη, *ης, ἡ, Candace,* Ac. viii. 27.*

κανών, *όνος, ὁ,* prop. *a rod;* hence, (1) *a rule of conduct,* Gal. vi. 16; Phil. iii. 16 (W. H. omit); (2) *a limit* or *sphere of duty, province* (R. V.), 2 Cor. x. 13, 15, 16.*

Καπερ-ναούμ, or *Καφαρ-ναούμ* (W. H.), *ἡ* (Heb.), *Capernaum,* Jn. vi. 17, 24.

καπηλεύω, *to be a petty trader;* hence (with acc.), *to make merchandise of,* or *adulterate, corrupt,* 2 Cor. ii. 17.*

καπνός, *οῦ, ὁ, smoke,* Ac. ii. 19; Rev. viii. 4.

Καππαδοκία, *ας, ἡ, Cappadocia,* Ac. ii. 9; 1 Pet. i. 1.*

καρδία, *ας, ἡ, the heart,* met., as the seat of the affections, but chiefly of the understanding; fig., *the heart* of the earth, Mat. xii. 40.

καρδιο-γνώστης, *ου, ὁ, a knower of hearts,* Ac. i. 24, xv. 8. (N. T.)*

καρπός, *οῦ, ὁ, fruit, produce,* Lu. xii. 17; met., for *children,* Ac. ii. 30; *deeds, conduct,* the fruit of the hands, Mat. iii. 8; *effect, result,* Ro. vi. 21. Praise is called *the fruit of the lips,* Heb. xiii. 15.

Κάρπος, *ου, ὁ, Carpus,* 2 Tim. iv. 13.*

καρποφορέω, *ῶ, ήσω, to bring forth fruit,* Mar. iv. 28; mid., *to bear fruit of one's self,* Col. i. 6.

καρπο-φόρος, *ον, fruitful,* Ac. xiv. 17.*

καρτερέω, *ῶ, ήσω, to be strong, steadfast,* Heb. xi. 27.*

κάρφος, *ους, τό, a dry twig, a straw,* Mat. vii. 3, 4, 5; Lu. vi. 41, 42.*

κατά, prep., gov. the gen. and acc. cases, *down;* hence, gen., *down from, against,* etc.; acc., *according to, against,* etc. (see Gr. §§ 124, 147*a*, Wi. §§ 47*k*, 49*d*, Bu. 334 sq.). In composition, *κατά* may import *descent, subjection, opposition, distribution,* and with certain verbs (as of destruction, diminution, and the like) is *intensive* = "utterly."

κατα-βαίνω, *βήσομαι, βέβηκα,* 2d aor. *κατέβην, to go* or *come down, descend,* used of persons and of things, as gifts from heaven, of the clouds, storms, lightnings; also of anything that falls, Lu. xxii. 44; Rev. xvi. 21.

κατα-βάλλω, 1st aor. pass. *κατεβλήθην, to cast down,* Rev. xii. 10 (W. H. *βάλλω*); 2 Cor. iv. 9 mid., *to lay,* as a foundation, Heb. vi. 1.*

κατα-βαρέω, ῶ, *to weigh down, to burden,* 2 Cor. xii. 16.*

κατα-βαρύνω=*καταβαρέω,*Mar. xiv. 40 (W. H.).*

κατά-βασις, *εως, ἡ, descent, place of descent,* Lu. xix. 37.*

κατα-βιβάζω, *to bring down, cast down,* Mat. xi. 23 (W. H. *καταβαίνω*), Lu. x. 15 (Rec., W. H. mrg.).*

κατα-βολή, *ῆς, ἡ, a founding, laying the foundation of,* Mat. xiii. 35; Heb. xi. 11.

κατα-βραβεύω, *to give judgment against as umpire of the games, to deprive of reward,* Col. ii. 18.*

κατ-αγγελεύς, *έως, ὁ, a proclaimer, a herald,* Ac. xvii. 18. (N. T.)*

κατ-αγγέλλω, *to declare openly, to proclaim, to preach,* Ac. xiii. 5, xv. 36.

κατα-γελάω, ῶ, *to laugh at, deride,* gen., Mat. ix. 24; Mar. v. 40; Lu. viii. 53.*

κατα-γινώσκω, *to condemn, blame,* gen. of persons, Gal. ii. 11; 1 Jn. iii. 20, 21.*

κατ-άγνυμι, fut. *κατεάξω, to break down, to break in pieces,* Mat. xii. 20; Jn. xix. 31–33.*

κατ-άγω, *to bring down,* as Ac. ix. 30; Ro. x. 6; as a nautical term, *to bring to land,* Lu. v. 11; pass., *to come to land,* Ac. xxvii. 3, xxviii. 12.

κατ-αγωνίζομαι, dep., *to contend against, subdue* (acc.), Heb. xi. 33.*

κατα-δέω, ῶ, *to bind up,* as wounds, Lu. x. 34.*

κατά-δηλος, *ον, thoroughly evident,* Heb. vii. 15.*

κατα-δικάζω, *to condemn, to pronounce sentence against,* Mat. xii. 7, 37; Lu. vi. 37; Ja. v. 6.*

κατα-δίκη, *ης, ἡ, a sentence of condemnation,* Ac. xxv. 15 (W. H.).*

κατα-διώκω, *to follow closely,* Mar. i. 36.*

κατα-δουλόω, ῶ, *ώσω, to enslave,* 2 Cor. xi. 20; Gal. ii. 4.*

κατα-δυναστεύω, *to exercise power over, to oppress,* Ac. x. 38; Ja. ii. 6.*

κατά-θεμα, W. H. for *κατανάθεμα,* Rev. xxii. 3. (N T.)*

κατα-θεματίζω, W. H. for *καταναθ-,* Mat. xxvi. 74. (N. T.)*

κατ-αισχύνω, *to make ashamed,* 1 Cor. i. 27; *to dishonor,* 1 Cor. xi. 4, 5; *to shame,* as with disappointed expectation, 1 Pet. ii. 6; pass., *to be ashamed,* as Lu. xiii. 17.

κατα-καίω, *αύσω, to burn up, to consume entirely,* as Mat. iii. 12; Heb. xiii. 11.

κατα-καλύπτω, in mid., *to wear a veil,* 1 Cor. xi. 6, 7.*

κατα-καυχάομαι, *ῶμαι, to rejoice against, to glory over* (gen.), Ro. xi. 18; Ja. ii. 13, iii. 14. (S.)*

κατά-κειμαι, *to lie down,* as the sick, Mar. i. 30; *to recline* at table, Mar. xiv. 3.

κατα-κλάω, ῶ, *to break in pieces,* Mar. vi. 41; Lu. ix. 16.*

κατα-κλείω, *to shut up, confine,* Lu. iii. 20; Ac. xxvi. 10.*

κατα-κληρο-δοτέω, ῶ, *to distribute by lot,* Ac. xiii. 19 (W. H. read the following). (S.)*

κατα-κληρο-νομέω, ῶ, *to distribute by lot,* Ac. xiii. 19 (W. H.). (S.)*

κατα-κλίνω, *νῶ, to cause to recline* at table, Lu. ix. 14, 15 (W. H.); mid., *to recline* at table, Lu. vii. 36 (W. H.), xiv. 8, xxiv. 30.*

κατα-κλύζω, *σω, to inundate, deluge,* pass., 2 Pet. iii. 6.*

κατα-κλυσμός, *οῦ, ὁ, a deluge, flood,* Mat. xxiv. 38, 39; Lu. xvii. 27; 2 Pet. ii. 5.*

κατ-ακολουθέω, ῶ, *to follow after* (abs. or dat.), Lu. xxiii. 55; Ac. xvi. 17.*

κατα-κόπτω, *ψω, to wound,* Mar. v. 5.*

κατα-κρημνίζω, *σω, to cast down headlong,* Lu. iv. 29.*

κατά-κριμα, *ατος, τό, condemnation,* Ro. v. 16, 18, viii. 1.*

κατα-κρίνω, *νῶ, to judge worthy of punishment* (gen. and dat.), *to condemn,* as Mat. xx. 18; Ro. ii. 1, viii. 3; in a more general sense, Lu. xi. 31, 32.

κατά-κρισις, *εως, ἡ, the act of condemnation,* 2 Cor. iii. 9, vii. 3. (N. T.)*

κατα-κυριεύω, *to exercise authority over,* Mat. xx. 25; Mar. x. 42; 1 Pet. v. 3; *to get the mastery of,* Ac. xix. 16 (gen.).

κατα-λαλέω, ῶ, *to speak against* (gen.), Ja. iv. 11; 1 Pet. ii. 12, iii. 16.*

κατα-λαλιά, *ᾶς, ἡ, evil-speaking, defamation,* 2 Cor. xii. 20, 1 Pet. ii. 1. (N. T.)*

κατά-λαλος, *ου, ὁ, ἡ, an evil-speaker, a defamer,* Ro. i. 30. (N. T.)*

κατα-λαμβάνω, *λήψομαι, to seize* or *lay hold of,* as Mar. ix. 18; *to grasp, to obtain,* as the prize in public games, Phil. iii. 12, 13; *to overtake,* 1 Th. v. 4; mid., *to comprehend, to perceive, ὅτι,* or acc. and inf., Ep. iii. 18.

κατα-λέγω, *to register, to enrol,* pass., 1 Tim. v. 9.*

κατά-λειμμα, *ατος, τό, a remnant, a residue,* Ro. ix. 27 (W. H. *ὑπόλιμμα*). (S.)*

κατα-λείπω, *ψω, to leave utterly, to forsake,* Mar. x. 7; *to depart from,* Heb. xi. 27; *to leave remaining, to reserve,* Ro. xi. 4.

κατα-λιθάζω, *σω, to stone, to destroy by stoning,* Lu. xx. 6. (N. T.)*

καταλλαγή, *ῆς, ἡ, reconciliation,* Ro. v. 11, xi. 15; 2 Cor. v. 18, 19.* *Syn.:* see ἀπολύτρωσις.

κατ-αλλάσσω, *ξω, to reconcile* (acc. and dat.), Ro. v. 10; 1 Cor. vii. 11; 2 Cor. v. 18, 19, 20.*

κατά-λοιπος, *ον,* plur., *the rest, the residue,* Ac. xv. 17.*

κατάλυμα, *ατος, τό, a lodging-place, an inn,* Lu. ii. 7; *a guest-chamber,* Mar. xiv. 14 Lu. xxii. 11.*

κατα-λύω, *ύσω, to unloose,* (1) lit., of a building, *to destroy,* Mar. xiv. 58; (2) fig., of law or command, *to render* *void*, Mat. v. 17; (3) *to pass the night*, *to lodge*, Lu. ix. 12, xix. 7.

κατα-μανθάνω, 2d aor. κατέμαθον, *to consider carefully*, Mat. vi. 28.*

κατα-μαρτυρέω, ῶ, *to bear testimony against* (acc. of thing, gen. of pers.), Mat. xxvi. 62, xxvii. 13; Mar. xiv. 60, xv. 4 (not W. H.).*

κατα-μένω, *to remain*, *abide*, Ac. i. 13.*

κατα-μόνας (W. H. κατὰ μόνας), adv., *privately*, *alone*, Mar. iv. 10; Lu. ix. 18.*

κατ-ανά-θεμα, ατος, τό, *a curse*, Rev. xxii. 3; see κατάθεμα. (N. T.)*

κατ-ανα-θεματίζω, *to curse*, *devote to destruction*, Mat. xxvi. 74; see καταθεματίζω. (N. T.)*

κατ-αν-αλίσκω, *to consume*, as fire, Heb. xii. 29.*

κατα-ναρκάω, ῶ, ήσω, *to be burdensome to* (gen.), 2 Cor. xi. 9, xii. 13, 14.*

κατα-νεύω, *to nod*, *to make signs to*, dat., Lu. v. 7.*

κατα-νοέω, ῶ, (1) *to observe carefully*, *perceive*, Lu. vi. 41; (2) *to consider* (acc.), Ac. xi. 6.

κατ-αντάω, ῶ, *to come to*, *to arrive at*, with εἰς, as Ac. xvi. 1; once with ἀντικρύ, Ac. xx. 15; met., *to attain to*, Phil. iii. 11.

κατάνυξις, εως, ἡ, *stupor*, Ro. xi. 8. (S.)*

κατα-νύσσω, ξω, 2d aor., pass. κατενύγην, *to prick through*, *to agitate greatly*, pass., Ac. ii. 37. (S.)*

κατ-αξιόω, ῶ, ώσω, *to judge worthy of* (gen.), pass., Lu. xx. 35, xxi. 36; Ac. v. 41; 2 Th. i. 5.*

κατα-πατέω, ῶ, *to trample on*, *to tread under foot* (acc.), as Lu. viii. 5.

κατάπαυσις, εως, ἡ, *a resting*, *rest*, Ac. vii. 49; Heb. iii. 11, 18, iv. 1, 3, 5, 10, 11.*

κατα-παύω, (1) trans., *to restrain*, acc. (also τοῦ μή, and inf.), Ac. xiv. 18; *to give rest*, Heb. iv. 8; (2) intrans., *to rest*, ἀπό, Heb. iv. 4, 10.*

κατα-πέτασμα (πετάννυμι), ατος, τό, *a veil*, *curtain*, separating the holy place and the holy of holies, as Lu. xxiii. 45. (S.)

κατα-πίνω, 2d aor. κατέπιον, 1st aor. pass. κατεπόθην, *to drink down*, *swallow*, Mat. xxiii. 24; Rev. xii. 16; fig., *to devour*, *destroy*, 1 Cor. xv. 54; 2 Cor. ii. 7, v. 4; Heb. xi. 29; 1 Pet. v. 8.*

κατα-πίπτω, 2d aor. κατέπεσον, *to fall down*, Lu. viii. 6 (W. H.); Ac. xxvi. 14, xxviii. 6.*

κατα-πλέω, εύσομαι, 1st aor. κατέπλευσα, *to sail* to land, Lu. viii. 26.*

κατα-πονέω, ῶ, in pass., *to be oppressed*, *distressed*, Ac. vii. 24; 2 Pet. ii. 7.*

κατα-ποντίζω, pass., *to sink down*, Mat. xiv. 30; *to be drowned*, Mat. xviii. 6.*

κατ-άρα, ας, ἡ, *a curse*, *cursing*, Gal. iii. 10, 13; Heb. vi. 8; 2 Pet. ii. 14; Ja. iii. 10.*

κατ-αράομαι, ῶμαι, *to curse*, Mat. v. 44 (W. H. omit); Mar. xi. 21; Lu. vi. 28; Ro. xii. 14; Ja. iii. 9; pass., perf. part., *accursed*, Mat. xxv. 41.*

κατ-αργέω, ῶ, ήσω, *to render useless*, Lu. xiii. 7; *to cause to cease*, *abolish*, as Ro. iii. 3, 31, and frequently in Paul; *to sever* from (ἀπό), Ro. vii. 2; Gal. v. 4.

κατ-αριθμέω, ῶ, *to number among*, Ac. i. 17.*

κατ-αρτίζω, ίσω, *to refit*, *to repair*, Mat. iv. 21; *to restore* from error or sin, Gal. vi. 1; *to perfect*, *to complete*, 1 Th. iii. 10; 1 Pet. v. 10; pass., *to be restored* to harmony, 1 Cor. i. 10.

κατάρτισις, εως, ἡ, *a perfecting*, 2 Cor. xiii. 9.*

καταρτισμός, οῦ, ὁ, *a perfecting*, Ep. iv. 12. (N. T.)*

κατα-σείω, σω, *to shake* the hand, *to beckon*, Ac. xii. 17, xiii. 16, xix. 33, xxi. 40.*

κατα-σκάπτω, ψω, *to dig under*, *to demolish*, Ro. xi. 3; perf. part., pass., *ruins*, Ac. xv. 16 (not W. H.).*

κατα-σκευάζω, άσω, *to prepare*, *to build*, *to equip*, as Mat. xi. 10; Lu. i. 17; Heb. iii. 3, 4.

κατα-σκηνόω, ῶ, ώσω, *to pitch one's tent*, *to dwell*, Mat. xiii. 32; Mar. iv. 32; Lu. xiii. 19; Ac. ii. 26.*

κατα-σκήνωσις, εως, ἡ, *a dwelling-place*, *a haunt*, as of birds, Mat. viii. 20; Lu. ix. 58.*

κατα-σκιάζω, σω, *to overshadow*, Heb. ix. 5.*

κατα-σκοπέω, ῶ, *to spy out*, *to plot against*, Gal. ii. 4.*

κατά-σκοπος, ου, ὁ, *a spy*, Heb. xi. 31.*

κατα-σοφίζομαι, σομαι, *to deal deceitfully with*, Ac. vii. 19.*

κατα-στέλλω, λῶ, 1st aor. κατέστειλα, *to appease*, *restrain*, Ac. xix. 35, 36.*

κατά-στημα, ατος, τό, *behavior*, *conduct*, Tit. ii. 3.*

κατα-στολή, ῆς, ἡ, *dress*, *attire*, 1 Tim. ii. 9.*

κατα-στρέφω, ψω, *to overthrow*, Mat. xxi. 12; Mar. xi. 15; Ac. xv. 16 (W. H.).*

κατα-στρηνιάω, ῶ, άσω, *to grow wanton* to the loss of (gen.), 1 Tim. v. 11. (N. T.)*

κατα-στροφή, ῆς, ἡ, *overthrow*, *destruction*, 2 Tim. ii. 14; 2 Pet. ii. 6 (W. H. omit).*

κατα-στρώννυμι, στρώσω, *to prostrate*, *slay*, 1 Cor. x. 5.*

κατα-σύρω, *to drag along* by force, Lu. xii. 58.*

κατα-σφάζω, ξω, *to slay*, Lu. xix. 27.*

κατα-σφραγίζω, σω, *to seal up*, as a book, Rev. v. 1.*

κατά-σχεσις, εως, ἡ, *a possession*, Ac. vii. 5, 45. (S.)*

κατα-τίθημι, θήσω, 1st aor. κατέθηκα, *to deposit*, as a body in a tomb, Mar. xv. 46 (W. H. τίθημι); mid. κατατίθεσθαι χάριν, *to gain favor* with (dat.), Ac. xxiv. 27, xxv. 9.*

κατα-τομή, ῆς, ἡ, *mutilation*, paronomasia with περιτομή, Phil. iii. 2.*

κατα-τοξεύω, *to transfix*, Heb xii. 20 (W. H. omit).*

κατα-τρέχω, 2d aor. κατέδραμον, *to run down* (ἐπί, acc.), Ac. xxi. 32.*

κατα-φάγω, see κατεσθίω.

κατα-φέρω, κατοίσω, 1st aor. κατήνεγκα, pass. κατηνέχθην, *to cast down*, as an adverse vote, Ac. xxv. 7, xxvi. 10 (W. H.); pass., *to be borne down*, *to be overcome*, Ac. xx. 9.*

κατα-φεύγω, 2d aor. *κατέφυγον, to flee for refuge,* with *εἰς,* Ac. xiv. 6; with inf., Heb. vi. 18.*

κατα-φθείρω, pass., perf. *κατέφθαρμαι,* 2d aor. *κατεφθάρην, to corrupt,* 2 Tim. iii. 8; *to destroy,* 2 Pet. ii. 12 (W. H. *φθείρω*).*

κατα-φιλέω, ῶ, *to kiss affectionately,* or *repeatedly* (acc.), as Mat. xxvi. 49; Lu. xv. 20.

κατα-φρονέω, ῶ, *ήσω, to despise* (gen.), as Mat. vi. 24.

καταφρονητής, οῦ, ὁ, *a despiser,* Ac. xiii. 41. (S.)*

κατα-χέω, *εύσω,* 1st aor. *κατέχεα, to pour down upon,* Mat. xxvi. 7; Mar. xiv. 3.*

κατα-χθόνιος, *ον, subterranean,* Phil. ii. 10.*

κατα-χράομαι, *ῶμαι, to use fully,* 1 Cor. vii. 31, ix. 18 (dat.).*

κατα-ψύχω, *to cool, to refresh,* Lu. xvi. 24.*

κατ-είδωλος, *ον, full of idols* (R. V.), Ac. xvii. 16. (N. T.)*

κατ-έναντι, adv., or as prep. with gen., *over against, before, in presence* or *in sight of.*

κατ-ενώπιον, adv., *in the presence of* (gen.). (S.)

κατ-εξουσιάζω, *to exercise authority over* (gen.), Mat. xx. 25; Mar. x. 42. (N. T.)*

κατ-εργάζομαι, *άσομαι,* with mid. and pass. aor. (augm. *ει-*), *to accomplish, achieve,* Ro. xv. 18; Ep. vi. 13; *to work out, result in,* Ro. iv. 15, vii. 8.

κατ-έρχομαι, 2d aor. *κατῆλθον, to come down,* Lu. iv. 31, ix. 37.

κατ-εσθίω and *-έσθω* (Mar. xii. 40, W. H.), fut. *καταφάγομαι* (Jn. ii. 17, W. H.), 2d aor. *κατέφαγον, to eat up, to devour entirely,* lit. or fig., Mat. xiii. 4; Jn. ii. 17; Gal. v. 15.

κατ-ευθύνω, *νῶ, to direct, to guide,* Lu. i. 79; 1 Th. iii. 11; 2 Th. iii. 5.*

κατ-ευλογέω, *to bless greatly,* Mar. x. 16 (W. H.).*

κατ-εφ-ίστημι, 2d aor. *κατεπέστην, to rise up against,* Ac. xviii. 12. (N. T.)*

κατ-έχω, *κατασχήσω, to seize on, to hold fast, to retain, possess, to prevent* from doing a thing (*τοῦ μή,* with inf.), *to repress,* Ro. i. 18; *τὸ κατέχον, the hindrance,* 2 Th. ii. 6; *κατεῖχον εἰς τὸν αἰγιαλόν, they held for the shore,* Ac. xxvii. 40.

κατ-ηγορέω, ῶ, *ήσω, to accuse, to speak against,* abs., or with person in gen.; charge in gen. alone or after *περί* or *κατά*; pass., *to be accused;* with *ὑπό* or *παρά,* of the accuser.

κατηγορία, *ας, ἡ, an accusation, a charge,* pers. in gen. alone, or after *κατά*; charge also in gen., 1 Tim. v. 19; Tit. i. 6.

κατήγορος, *ου, ὁ, an accuser,* Ac. xxiii. 30, 35.

κατήγωρ, ὁ (Heb.?), *an accuser,* Rev. xii. 10 (W. H.). (N. T.)*

κατήφεια, *ας, ἡ, dejection, gloom,* Ja. iv. 9.*

κατ-ηχέω, ῶ, *ήσω,* perf., pass. *κατήχημαι* (*ἦχος*), *to instruct orally, to teach, inform,* Lu. i. 4; Ac. xviii. 25, xxi. 21, 24; Ro. ii. 18; 1 Cor. xiv. 19; Gal. vi. 6.*

κατ' ἰδίαν, *separately, privately, by one's self* (see *ἴδιος*).

κατ-ιόω, ῶ (*ἰός*), *to cover with rust,* Ja. v. 3. (Ap.)*

κατ-ισχύω, *to prevail against, overpower* (gen.), Mat. xvi. 18; Lu. xxi. 36 (W. H.), xxiii. 23.*

κατ-οικέω, ῶ, (1) intrans., *to dwell,* with *ἐν, εἰς* (const. præg.), *ἐπί,* gen., or adverbs of place, Ac. i. 20, vii. 4; fig., of qualities or attributes, *to abide,* Col. ii. 9; (2) trans., *to dwell in, to inhabit* (acc.), Mat. xxiii. 21; Ac. i. 19.

κατοίκησις, *εως, ἡ, a dwelling, habitation,* Mar. v. 3.*

κατοικητήριον, *ου, τό, a dwelling-place,* Ep. ii. 22; Rev. xviii. 2. (S.)*

κατοικία, *ας, ἡ, a dwelling, habitation,* Ac. xvii. 26.*

κατ-οικίζω, *to cause to dwell,* Ja. iv. 5 (W. H.).*

κατοπτρίζω, mid., *to behold,* as in a mirror, 2 Cor. iii. 18.*

κατ-όρθωμα, *ατος, τό, an honorable* or *successful achievement,* Ac. xxiv. 2 (W. H. *διόρθωμα*).*

κάτω, adv., *downwards, down,* Mat. iv. 6, *beneath,* Mar. xiv. 66; of age, comp., *κατωτέρω, under,* Mat. ii. 16.

κατώτερος, *α, ον* (*κάτω*), *lower,* Ep. iv. 9 (on which see Gr. § 259, Wi. § 11, 2*c*, Bu. 28).*

καῦμα, *ατος, τό* (*καίω*), *heat, scorching heat,* Rev. vii. 16, xvi. 9.*

καυματίζω, *σω, to scorch, burn,* Mat. xiii. 6; Mar. iv. 6; Rev. xvi. 8, 9.*

καῦσις, *εως, ἡ, a burning, burning up,* Heb. vi. 8.*

καυσόω, ῶ, *to burn up,* pass., 2 Pet. iii. 10, 12. (N. T.)*

καύσων, *ωνος, ὁ, scorching heat;* perhaps *a hot wind* from the E., Mat. xx. 12; Lu. xii. 55; Ja. i. 11 (see Hos. xii. 1, etc.). (S.)*

καυτηριάζω (W. H. *καυστ-*), *to brand,* as with a hot iron; fig., pass., 1 Tim. iv. 2.*

καυχάομαι, *ῶμαι,* 2d pers. *καυχᾶσαι,* fut. *ήσομαι, to glory, to boast,* both in a good sense and in a bad, 1 Cor. i. 29; Ep. ii. 9; followed with prep., *ἐν, περί,* gen.; *ὑπέρ,* gen.; *ἐπί,* dat.

καύχημα, *ατος, τό, the ground of glorying,* as Ro. iv. 2; *a glorying,* 1 Cor. v. 6.

καύχησις, *εως, ἡ, the act of boasting, glorying,* Ro. xv. 17; Ja. iv. 16. (S.)

Καφαρναούμ (see *Καπερναούμ*), *Capernaum.*

Κεγχρεαί, ῶν, *αἱ, Cenchreæ,* a port of Corinth, Ac. xviii. 18; Ro. xvi. 1.*

κέδρος, *ου, ἡ, a cedar,* Jn. xviii. 1; perhaps a mistaken reading for following.*

Κεδρών, ὁ (Heb. *dark* or *turbid*), *Cedron,* a turbid brook between the Mount of Olives and Jerusalem, a variant reading in Jn. xviii. 1.*

κεῖμαι, *σαι, ται*; impf. *ἐκείμην, σο, το*; *to lie, to recline, to be laid,* Lu. xxiii. 53; 1 Jn. v. 19; met., *to be enacted,* as laws, 1 Tim. i. 9.

κειρία, *ας, ἡ, a band* or *bandage* of linen, Jn. xi. 44.*

κείρω, *κερῶ, to shear,* as sheep, Ac. viii. 32; mid., *to have the head shorn,* Ac. xviii. 18; 1 Cor. xi. 6.*

κέλευσμα, *ατος, τό, a command, a loud cry,* 1 Th. iv. 16.*

κελεύω, *σω, to command, to order*, Ac. iv. 15, v. 34.

κενοδοξία, *ας, ἡ, vainglory, empty pride*, Phil. ii. 3.*

κενό-δοξος, *ον, vainglorious*, Gal. v. 26.*

κενός, *ἡ, όν, empty, vain*, Ep. v. 6; Col. ii. 8; *empty-handed*, Lu. i. 53; Ja. ii. 20; *fruitless, ineffectual*, 1 Cor. xv. 10, 58. *Syn.: κενός, empty*, refers to the contents; *μάταιος, aimless, purposeless*, to the result.

κενο-φωνία, *ας, ἡ, empty disputing, useless babbling*, 1 Tim. vi. 20; 2 Tim. ii. 16. (N. T.)*

κενόω, *ῶ, ώσω*, with *ἑαυτόν, to empty* one's self, *divest* one's self *of rightful dignity*, Phil. ii. 7; *to make useless* or *false*, Ro. iv. 14; 1 Cor. i. 17, ix. 15; 2 Cor. ix. 3.*

κέντρον, *ου, τό, a sting*, Rev. ix. 10; 1 Cor. xv. 55, 56; *a goad*, Ac. ix. 5 (W. H. omit), xxvi. 14.*

κεντυρίων, *ωνος, ὁ*, Latin (see Gr. § 154*c*), *a centurion*, the commander of a hundred foot-soldiers, Mar. xv. 39, 44, 45.*

κενῶς, adv., *in vain*, Ja. iv. 5.*

κεραία, or *κερέα* (W. H.), *ας, ἡ, a little horn* (the small projecting stroke by which certain similar Hebrew letters are distinguished, as ר and ד); met., *the minutest part*, Mat. v. 18; Lu. xvi. 17.*

κεραμεύς, *έως, ὁ, a potter*, Mat. xxvii. 7, 10; Ro. ix. 21.*

κεραμικός, *ἡ, όν, made of clay, earthen*, Rev ii. 27.*

κεράμιον, *ου, τό, an earthen vessel, a pitcher*, Mar. xiv. 13; Lu. xxii. 10.*

κέραμος, *ου, ὁ, a roofing tile*, Lu. v. 19.*

κεράννυμι (see Gr. §§ 113, 114, Wi. § 15, Bu. 60), *to mix, to pour out for drinking*, Rev. xiv. 10, xviii. 6.*

κέρας, *ατος, τό, a horn*, as Rev. v. 6; fig., for *strength*, only Lu. i. 69; *a projecting point, horn* of the altar, only Rev. ix. 13.

κεράτιον, *ου, τό, a little horn*, the name of the fruit of the *carob tree*, Lu. xv. 16.*

κερδαίνω, *ανῶ*, 1st aor. *ἐκέρδησα, to gain, acquire*, Mat. xxv. 16 (W. H.), 22; Ja. iv. 13; *to gain, win*, Phil. iii. 8; *to gain over* to a cause, 1 Cor. ix. 19–22.

κέρδος, *ους, τό, gain, advantage*, Phil. i. 21, iii. 7; Tit. i. 11.*

κέρμα, *ατος, τό* (*κείρω*), *a small piece of money*, Jn. ii. 15.*

κερματιστής, *οῦ, ὁ, a money-changer*, Jn. ii. 14.*

κεφάλαιον, *ου, τό, a sum of money*, Ac. xxii. 28; *the sum, main point* of an argument, Heb. viii. 1 (see R. V. and mrg.).*

κεφαλαιόω (W. H. -λιόω), *ῶ, ώσω, to smite on the head*, Mar. xii. 4.*

κεφαλή, *ῆς, ἡ, the head*, of human beings or animals; for the whole person, Ac. xviii. 6; *the head* of a corner (with *γωνία*), *corner-stone*, Lu. xx. 17; met., implying authority, *head, lord*, 1 Cor. xi. 3; Ep. i. 22; Col. i. 18.

κεφαλίς, *ίδος, ἡ* (prop. *top*), *a roll, a volume*, Heb. x. 7.*

κημόω, *to muzzle*, 1 Cor. ix. 9 (W. H. mrg.).*

κῆνσος, *ου, ὁ*, Latin (Gr. § 154*d*, Bu. 16), *a tax, a poll-tax*, Mat. xvii. 25, xxii. 17, 19; Mar. xii. 14.*

κῆπος, *ου, ὁ, a garden*, Lu. xiii. 19; Jn. xviii. 1, 26, xix. 41.*

κηπ-ουρός, *οῦ, ὁ, a gardener*, Jn. xx. 15.*

κηρίον, *ου, τό, a honeycomb*, Lu. xxiv. 42 (W. H. omit).*

κήρυγμα, *ατος, τό, a proclaiming, preaching*, as Mat. xii. 41; 1 Cor. i. 21; 2 Tim. iv. 17.

κήρυξ, *υκος, ὁ, a herald, a preacher*, 1 Tim. ii. 7; 2 Tim. i. 11; 2 Pet. ii. 5.*

κηρύσσω, *ξω*, (1) *to proclaim, to publish*, Mar. vii. 36; (2) specially, *to preach* the Gospel, abs., or acc. and dat., Mar. i. 38; Lu. xii. 3; 1 Pet. iii. 19.

κῆτος, *ους, τό, a sea monster, a whale*, Mat. xii. 40.*

Κηφᾶς, *ᾶ, ὁ* (Aramaic, *a rock*), *Cephas, i.e.*, Peter, 1 Cor. i. 12, iii. 22.

κιβωτός, *οῦ, ἡ, a wooden chest*, used of the ark of the covenant, Heb. ix. 4; Rev. xi. 19; of Noah's ark, Lu. xvii. 27; Heb. xi. 7.

κιθάρα, *ας, ἡ, a harp*, 1 Cor. xiv. 7; Rev. xv. 2.

κιθαρίζω, *to play upon a harp*, 1 Cor. xiv. 7; Rev. xiv. 2.*

κιθαρ-ῳδός, *οῦ, ὁ, a harper, singer to the harp*, Rev. xiv. 2, xviii. 22.*

Κιλικία, *ας, ἡ, Cilicia*, Ac. vi. 9, xxi. 39.

κινάμωμον (W. H. *κιννά-*), *ου, τό, cinnamon*, Rev. xviii. 13.*

κινδυνεύω, *σω, to be in danger*, Lu. viii. 23; Ac. xix. 27, 40; 1 Cor. xv. 30.*

κίνδυνος, *ου, ὁ, danger, peril*, Ro. viii. 35; 2 Cor. xi. 26.*

κινέω, *ῶ, ήσω, to move, to stir*, Mat. xxiii. 4; Ac. xvii. 28; *to shake* the head in mockery, Mat. xxvii. 39; Mar. xv. 29; *to remove*, Rev. ii. 5, vi. 14; *to excite*, Ac. xvii. 28, xxi. 30, xxiv. 5.*

κίνησις, *εως, ἡ, a moving, agitation*, Jn. v. 3 (W. H. omit).*

Κίς (W. H. *Κείς*), *ὁ* (Heb.), *Kish*, father of Saul, Ac. xiii. 21.*

κίχρημι, *to lend*, Lu. xi. 5.*

κλάδος, *ου, ὁ, a branch*, as Mat. xiii. 32; met., Ro. xi. 16–19.

κλαίω, *αύσω*, (1) abs., *to wail, to lament*, Lu. xix. 41; (2) trans., *to weep for* (acc.), Mat. ii. 18.

κλάσις, *εως, ἡ, a breaking*, Lu. xxiv. 35; Ac. ii. 42.*

κλάσμα, *ατος, τό, a broken piece, a fragment*, as Mat. xiv. 20

Κλαύδη (W. H. *Καῦδα*), *ης, ἡ, Clauda* or *Cauda*, a small island near Crete, Ac. xxvii. 16.*

Κλαυδία, *ας, ἡ, Claudia*, 2 Tim. iv. 21.*

Κλαύδιος, *ου, ὁ, Claudius*, the Roman emperor, Ac. xi. 28, xviii. 2; a military tribune (Lysias), Ac. xxiii. 26.*

κλαυθμός, *οῦ, ὁ* (*κλαίω*), *weeping, lamentation*, as Mat. ii. 18.

κλάω, *άσω*, only with *ἄρτον, to break* bread, in the ordinary meal, Mat. xiv. 19; or in the Lord's Supper, xxvi. 26; fig., of the body of Christ, 1 Cor. xi. 24 (W. H. omit).

κλείς, *κλειδός*, acc. sing. *κλεῖδα*

or κλεῖν, acc. plur. κλεῖδας or κλεῖς, ἡ, *a key*, as a symbol of power and authority, Mat. xvi. 19; Rev. i. 18, iii. 7, ix. 1, xx. 1; met., Lu. xi. 52.*

κλείω, σω, *to shut, shut up*, Mat. vi. 6; Lu. iv. 25.

κλέμμα, ατος, τό (κλέπτω), *theft*, Rev. xi. 21.*

Κλεόπας, α, ὁ, *Cleopas*, Lu. xxiv. 18.*

κλέος, ους, τό, *glory, praise*, 1 Pet. ii. 20.*

κλέπτης, ου, ὁ, *a thief*, as Mat. vi. 19; met., of false teachers, Jn. x. 8. *Syn.*: κλέπτης, a thief, who steals *secretly*; λῃστής, a robber, who plunders *openly, by violence*.

κλέπτω, ψω, *to steal*, abs., Mat. xix. 18; or trans. (acc.), Mat. xxvii. 64.

κλῆμα, ατος, τό (κλάω), *a tender branch, a shoot*, of a vine, etc., Jn. xv. 2, 4, 5, 6.*

Κλήμης, εντος, ὁ, *Clement*, Phil. iv. 3.*

κληρονομέω, ῶ, ήσω, *to inherit*, Gal. iv. 30; *to obtain*, generally, Lu. x. 25.

κληρονομία, ας, ἡ, *an inheritance*, Lu. xii. 13; *a possession*, Gal. iii. 18.

κληρο-νόμος, ου, ὁ, *an heir*, Mat. xxi. 38; applied to Christ, Heb. i. 2; in general, *one who obtains a possession*, Heb. vi. 17.

κλῆρος, ου, ὁ, (1) *a lot*, Mat. xxvii. 35; hence, (2) that which is allotted, *a portion*, Ac. i. 17, 25, viii. 21, xxvi. 18; Col. i. 12; plur., *persons assigned to one's care*, 1 Pet. v. 3.*

κληρόω, ῶ, *to make a heritage*, Ep. i. 11.*

κλῆσις, εως, ἡ, *a calling, invitation*, in N. T. always of the divine *call*, as Ro. xi. 29; Ep. iv. 4.

κλητός, ή, όν, verb. adj. (καλέω), *called, invited*, Mat. xxii. 14; of Christians, *the called*, Ro. i. 6, 7, viii. 28; *called* to an office, Ro. i. 1; 1 Cor. i. 1.

κλίβανος, ου, ὁ, *an oven, a furnace*, Mat. vi. 30; Lu. xii. 28.*

κλίμα, ατος, τό, *a tract of country, a region*, Ro. xv. 23; 2 Cor. xi. 10; Gal. i. 21.*

κλινάριον, ου, τό, *a small bed*, Ac. v. 15 (W. H.).*

κλίνη, ης, ἡ, *a bed*, Mar. vii. 30; *a portable bed*, Mat. ix. 2, 6; *a couch for reclining at meals*, Mar. iv. 21.

κλινίδιον, ου, τό (dim.), *a small bed, a couch*, Lu. v. 19, 24.*

κλίνω, νῶ, perf. κέκλικα, (1) trans., *to bow*, in reverence, Lu. xxiv. 5; in death, Jn. xix. 30; *to recline* the head for rest, Mat. viii. 20; *to turn to flight*, Heb. xi. 34; (2) intrans., *to decline*, as the day, Lu. ix. 12.

κλισία, ας, ἡ, *a company reclining* at a meal, Lu. ix. 14.*

κλοπή, ῆς, ἡ, *theft*, Mat. xv. 19; Mar. vii. 21.*

κλύδων, ωνος, ὁ, *a violent agitation* of the sea, *a wave*, Lu. viii. 24; Ja. i. 6.*

κλυδωνίζομαι, *to be agitated*, as waves by the wind, Ep. iv. 14. (S.)*

Κλωπᾶς, ᾶ, ὁ, *Clopas*, Jn. xix. 25.*

κνήθω, *to tickle*; pass., *to be tickled, to itch*, 2 Tim. iv. 3.*

Κνίδος, ου, ἡ, *Cnidus*, Ac. xxvii. 7.*

κοδράντης, ου, ὁ, Lat. (see Gr. § 154*a*, Bu. 17), *a quadrans, farthing*, the fourth part of the Roman *as*, Mat. v. 26; Mar. xii. 42. (N. T.)*

κοιλία, ας, ἡ, (1) *the belly*, Mat. xv. 17; (2) *the womb*, Mat. xix. 12; (3) fig., *the inner man, the heart*, Jn. vii. 38.

κοιμάω, ῶ, pass., *to fall asleep*, Lu. xxii. 45; met., *to die*, Jn. xi. 12.

κοίμησις, εως, ἡ, *repose, taking rest*, Jn. xi. 13.*

κοινός, ή, όν, *common, i.e.*, shared by many, Ac. iv. 32; *unclean*, ceremonially, Ac. x. 15; Heb. x. 29.

κοινόω, ῶ, ώσω, *to make common* or *unclean, to profane*, Mat. xv. 11; Ac. xxi. 28.

κοινωνέω, ῶ, ήσω, *to have common share in, to partake in*, Ro. xv. 27; *to be associated in*, Gal. vi. 6.

κοινωνία, ας, ἡ, *participation, communion, fellowship*, as 1 Cor. x. 16; 2 Cor. xiii. 13; 1 Jn. i. 3, 6, 7; *a contribution*, Ro. xv. 26; Heb. xiii. 16.

κοινωνικός, ή, όν, *ready to communicate, liberal*, 1 Tim. vi. 18.*

κοινωνός, ή, όν, as subst., *a partner*, Lu. v. 10; *a sharer with*, gen. obj., 2 Cor. i. 7.

κοίτη, ης, ἡ, *a bed*, Lu. xi. 7; met., *marriage bed*, Heb. xiii. 4; *sexual intercourse* (as illicit), Ro. xiii. 13; κοίτην ἔχειν, *to conceive*, Ro. ix. 10.*

κοιτών, ῶνος, ὁ, *a bed-chamber*, Ac. xii. 20.*

κόκκινος, η, ον, *dyed from the* κόκκος, *crimson*, Heb. ix. 19; Rev. xvii. 4. (S.)

κόκκος, ου, ὁ, *a kernel, a grain*, Lu. xiii. 19, xvii. 6.

κολάζω, σω, mid., *to chastise, to punish*, Ac. iv. 21; pass., 2 Pet. ii. 9.*

κολακεία (W. H. -κία), ας, ἡ, *flattery*, 1 Th. ii. 5.*

κόλασις, εως, ἡ, *chastisement, punishment*, Mat. xxv. 46; 1 Jn. iv. 18.*

Κολασσαί, ῶν, αἱ, see Κολοσσαί.

κολαφίζω, σω, *to strike with the fist, to maltreat*, Mar. xiv. 65. (N. T.)

κολλάω, ῶ, ήσω, pass., *to cleave to, to join one's self to*, Lu. x. 11; Ac. viii. 29.

κολλούριον, or κολλύριον, ου, τό, *collyrium, eye-salve*, Rev. iii. 18.*

κολλυβιστής, οῦ, ὁ (κόλλυβος, *small coin*), *a money-changer*, Mat. xxi. 12; Mar. xi. 15; Jn. ii. 15.*

κολοβόω, ῶ, ώσω, *to cut off, to shorten*, Mat. xxiv. 22; Mar. xiii. 20.*

Κολοσσαεύς, έως, ὁ, plur. Κολοσσαεῖς (W. H. Κολασσαεῖς), *Colossians*, only in the heading and subscription (Rec.) to the Epistle.

Κολοσσαί, or Κολασσαί, ῶν, αἱ, *Colossæ*, Col. i. 2.*

κόλπος, ου, ὁ, *the bosom, the chest*, (1) of the body; ἐν τῷ κόλπῳ (or τοῖς κόλποις) εἶναι, ἀνακεῖσθαι, *to be in the bosom of, i.e.*, recline next to, at table; Lu. xvi. 22, 23 (of the heavenly banquet); Jn. xiii. 23; the phrase in Jn. i. 18 implies a still closer fellowship; (2) of the dress, used as a bag or pocket, Lu. vi.

38; (3) *a bay, a gulf of the sea*, Ac. xxvii. 39.*

κολυμβάω, ῶ, *ήσω*, *to swim*, Ac. xxvii. 43.*

κολυμβήθρα, *ας*, *ἡ*, *a swimming-place, a pool*, Jn. v. 2, 4 (Rec.), 7, ix. 7, 11 (Rec.).*

κολώνια, or *κολωνία* (W. H.), *ας*, *ἡ* (Lat.), *a colony;* Philippi is so called, Ac. xvi. 12. (N. T.)*

κομάω, ῶ, *to wear the hair long*, 1 Cor. xi. 14, 15.*

κόμη, *ης*, *ἡ*, *hair* of the head, 1 Cor. xi. 15.*

κομίζω, *σω*, mid. fut. *κομίσομαι* or *κομιοῦμαι*, *to bear, to bring*, Lu. vii. 37; mid., *to bring for one's self, i.e., to obtain*, Heb. x. 36; *to receive again, to recover*, Heb. xi. 19.

κομψότερον (comp. of *κομψός*), *better*, of convalescence, adverbially with ἔχω, Jn. iv. 52.*

κονιάω, ῶ, *to whitewash*, Mat. xxiii. 27; pass., Ac. xxiii. 3.*

κονι-ορτός, *οῦ*, *ὁ* (*ὄρνυμι*), *dust*, Mat. x. 14.

κοπάζω, *σω*, *to grow weary, to cease*, of the wind, Mat. xiv. 32; Mar. iv. 39, vi. 51.*

κοπετός, *οῦ*, *ὁ* (*κόπτω*), *vehement lamentation*, Ac. viii. 2.*

κοπή, *ῆς*, *ἡ*, *cutting, slaughter*, Heb. vii. 1.*

κοπιάω, ῶ, *άσω*, *to be weary*, Mat. xi. 28; *to labor, to toil*, Lu. v. 5; in the Gospel, Ro. xvi. 6, 12; 1 Cor. xv. 10.

κόπος, *ου*, *ὁ*, *labor, toil, trouble*, Lu. xi. 7; 2 Th. iii. 8.

κοπρία, *ας*, *ἡ*, *dung, manure*, Lu. xiii. 8 (not W. H.), xiv. 35.*

κόπριον, *ου*, *τό*, *dung*, Lu. xiii. 8 (W. H.).*

κόπτω, mid. fut. *κόψομαι*, *to cut off*, as branches, trees, etc., Mat. xxi. 8; mid., *to beat* or *cut one's self in grief, to bewail*, as Mat. xi. 17.

κόραξ, *ακος*, *ὁ*, *a raven*, Lu. xii. 24.*

κοράσιον, *ου*, *τό* (prop. dim. from *κόρη*), *a girl*, as Mar. vi. 22, 28.

κορβᾶν (W. H. *κορβάν*), (indecl.), and *κορβανᾶς*, *ᾶ*, *ὁ* (from Heb.), (1) *a gift, an offering* to God, Mar. vii. 11; (2) *the sacred treasury*, Mat. xxvii. 6.*

Κορέ, *ὁ* (Heb.), *Korah*, Ju. 11.*

κορέννυμι, *έσω*, pass. perf. *κεκόρεσμαι*, *to satiate, satisfy*, Ac. xxvii. 38; 1 Cor. iv. 8.*

Κορίνθιος, *ου*, *ὁ*, *a Corinthian*, Ac. xviii. 8; 2 Cor. vi. 11.*

Κόρινθος, *ου*, *ἡ*, *Corinth*, Ac. xviii. 1, xix. 1.

Κορνήλιος, *ου*, *ὁ*, *Cornelius*, Ac. x.*

κόρος, *ου*, *ὁ* (from Heb.), *a cor*, the largest dry measure, equal to ten *βάτοι*, or ten Attic medimni, Lu. xvi. 7. (S.)*

κοσμέω, ῶ, *ήσω*, *to put in order, to prepare*, Mat. xxv. 7; *to adorn*, Mat. xxiii. 29; 1 Tim. ii. 9; met., with honor, Tit. ii. 10; 1 Pet. iii. 5.

κοσμικός, *ή*, *όν*, (1) *earthly*, opp. to *ἐπουράνιος*, Heb. ix. 1; (2) *worldly, i.e., corrupt*, Tit. ii. 12.*

κόσμιος, *ον*, *orderly, modest*, 1 Tim. ii. 9, iii. 2.*

κοσμο-κράτωρ, *ορος*, *ὁ*, *lord of this world, world-ruler* (R. V.), Ep. vi. 12.*

κόσμος, *ου*, *ὁ*, (1) *ornament, decoration*, only 1 Pet. iii. 3; hence, (2) *the material universe*, Lu. xi. 50, as well ordered and beautiful; (3) *the world*, Jn. xi. 9; *worldly affairs*, Gal. vi. 14; (4) *the inhabitants of the world*, 1 Cor. iv. 9; as opposed to God, Jn. viii. 23; (5) *a vast collection*, of anything, Ja. iii. 6. *Syn.:* see *αἰών*.

Κούαρτος, *ου*, *ὁ* (Latin, see Gr. § 159), *Quartus*, Ro. xvi. 23.*

κοῦμι (a Hebrew imperative fem.), *arise*, Mar. v. 41 (W. H. read *κούμ*, the masculine form). (N. T.)*

κουστωδία, *ας*, *ἡ* (Latin, see Gr. § 154*c*, Bu. 17), *a guard*, Mat. xxvii. 65, 66, xxviii. 11. (N. T.)*

κουφίζω, *to lighten*, as a ship, Ac. xxvii. 38.*

κόφινος, *ου*, *ὁ*, *a basket*, as Mat. xiv. 20.

κράββατος (W. H. *κράβαττος*), *ου*, *ὁ*, *a couch, a light bed*, as Mar. ii. 12.

κράζω, *ξω*, *to cry out*, hoarsely, or urgently, or in anguish, Mar. v. 5; Ac. xix. 32.

κραιπάλη, *ης*, *ἡ*, *surfeiting*, caused by excessive drinking, Lu. xxi. 34.*

κρανίον, *ου*, *τό*, *a skull*, Lu. xxiii. 33; *Κρανίου Τόπος*, Greek for *Γολγοθά*, which see, Mat. xxvii. 33; Mar. xv. 22; Jn. xix. 17.*

κράσπεδον, *ου*, *τό*, *the fringe, tassel*, of a garment, as Mat. xxiii. 5.

κραταιός, *ά*, *όν*, *strong, mighty*, 1 Pet. v. 6.*

κραταιόω, ῶ, in pass. only, *to be strong, to grow strong*, Lu. i. 80, ii. 40; 1 Cor. xvi. 13; Ep. iii. 16. (S.)*

κρατέω, ῶ, *ήσω*, with acc., or gen., or acc. and gen. (see Gr. § 264, Wi. § 30, 8*d*, Bu. 161), *to get possession of, obtain*, Ac. xxvii. 13; *to take hold of*, Mar. i. 31; Ac. iii. 11; *to seize*, Mat. xiv. 3; *to hold*, Rev. ii. 1; *to hold fast*, Rev. ii. 25, iii. 11; *to retain*, of sins, Jn. xx. 23.

κράτιστος, *η*, *ον* (prop. superlative of *κρατύς*, see *κράτος*), *most excellent, most noble*, a title of honor, Lu. i. 3; Ac. xxiii. 26, xxiv. 3, xxvi. 25.*

κράτος, *ους*, *τό*, *strength, power, dominion*, Ep. i. 19; 1 Pet. iv. 11; Heb. ii. 14; *κατὰ κράτος*, Ac. xix. 20, *greatly, mightily*.

κραυγάζω, *σω*, *to cry out, to shout*, as Mat. xii. 19.

κραυγή, *ῆς*, *ἡ*, *a crying, outcry*, as Heb. v. 7.

κρέας (*ατος*, *αος*, contr. *κρέως*), *τό*, plur. *κρέατα*, *κρέα*, *flesh, flesh-meat*, Ro. xiv. 21; 1 Cor. viii. 13.*

κρείσσων (or *-ττ-*), *ον* (prop. compar. of *κρατύς*, see *κράτος*), *stronger, more excellent*, as Heb. vii. 7, xii. 24.

κρεμάννυμι, or *κρεμάω*, ῶ, fut. *άσω*, *to hang up*, trans., Ac. v. 30; mid., *to be suspended, to hang*, Mat. xxii. 40; Ac. xxviii. 4.

κρημνός, *οῦ*, *ὁ* (*κρεμάννυμι*), *a precipice*, from its overhanging, Mat. viii. 32; Mar. v. 13; Lu. viii. 33.*

Κρής, *ητός*, *ὁ*, *a Cretan*, Ac. ii. 11; Tit. i. 12.*

Κρήσκης, *ὁ* (Latin), *Crescens*, 2 Tim. iv. 10.*

Κρήτη, *ης*, *ἡ*, *Crete*, now Candia, Ac. xxvii. 7.

κριθή, ῆς, ἡ, *barley*, Rev. vi. 6.*

κρίθινος, η, ον, *made of barley; ἄρτοι κρίθινοι, barley loaves*, Jn. vi. 9, 13.*

κρίμα, ατος, τό, *a judgment, a sentence, condemnation*, as 1 Cor. xi. 29.

κρίνον, ου, τό, *a lily*, Mat. vi. 28; Lu. xii. 27.*

κρίνω, νῶ, κέκρικα, 1st aor. pass. ἐκρίθην, (1) *to have an opinion, to think*, Ac. xiii. 46, xv. 19; (2) *to approve, prefer*, Ro. xiv. 5; (3) *to resolve, determine*, 1 Cor. vii. 37; Tit. iii. 12; (4) *to try, to sit in judgment on*, Jn. xviii. 31; pass. and mid., *to appeal to trial, i.e., to have a lawsuit*, 1 Cor. vi. 6.

κρίσις, εως, ἡ, (1) *opinion*, formed and expressed, Jn. viii. 16; Ju. 9; (2) *judgment*, the act or result of, Ja. ii. 13; Lu. x. 14; (3) *condemnation and punishment*, Heb. x. 27; Rev. xviii. 10; (4) *a tribunal*, Mat. v. 21, 22; (5) *justice*, Mat. xxiii. 23.

Κρίσπος, ου, ὁ, *Crispus*, Ac. xviii. 8; 1 Cor. i. 14.*

κριτήριον, ου, τό, (1) *a tribunal, a court of justice*, 1 Cor. vi. 2, 4 (see R. V.); Ja. ii. 6.*

κριτής, οῦ, ὁ, *a judge*, Mat. v. 25; Ac. xviii. 15; of the O. T. "Judges," Ac. xiii. 20.

κριτικός, ή, όν, *skilled in judging*, gen. obj., Heb. iv. 12.*

κρούω, σω, *to knock* at a door, Lu. xiii. 25.

κρύπτη, ης, ἡ, *a cellar, a vault*, Lu. xi. 33.*

κρυπτός, ή, όν, verbal adj. (κρύπτω), *hidden, secret*, Mat. x. 26; Ro. ii. 16.

κρύπτω, ψω, 2d aor. pass. ἐκρύβην, *to hide, conceal, to lay up*, as Col. iii. 3.

κρυσταλλίζω, *to be clear*, like crystal, Rev. xxi. 11. (N.T.)*

κρύσταλλος, ου, ὁ, *crystal*, Rev. iv. 6, xxii. 1.*

κρυφαῖος, α, ον, *hidden, secret*, Mat. vi. 18 (W. H.).*

κρυφῆ (W. H. -ῇ), adv., *in secret, secretly*, Ep. v. 12.*

κτάομαι, ῶμαι, fut. ήσομαι, ἐκτησάμην, dep., *to acquire, procure* (price, gen., or ἐκ), (see Gr. § 273, Wi. §§ 38, 7, 40, 4*b*), Mat. x. 9; Lu. xviii. 12, xxi. 19; Ac. i. 18, viii. 20, xxii. 28; 1 Th. iv. 4.*

κτῆμα, ατος, τό, *anything acquired, a possession*, Mat. xix. 22; Mar. x. 22; Ac. ii. 45, v. 1.

κτῆνος, ους, τό, *a beast of burden* (as representing property), Lu. x. 34; Ac. xxiii. 24; 1 Cor. xv. 39; Rev. xviii. 13.*

κτήτωρ, ορος, ὁ, *a possessor*, Ac. iv. 34.*

κτίζω, σω, perf. pass. ἔκτισμαι, *to create, form, shape*, physically or spiritually, as Ro. i. 25; Ep. ii. 10.

κτίσις, εως, ἡ, *creation*, (1) the act, Ro. i. 20; (2) the thing created, *creature*, Ro. i. 25; *creation*, generally, Ro. viii. 19–22; (3) met., *an ordinance*, 1 Pet. ii. 13.

κτίσμα, ατος, τό, *a thing created, a creature*, 1 Tim. iv. 4; Ja. i. 18; Rev. v. 13, viii. 9.*

κτίστης, ου, ὁ, *a founder; a creator*, 1 Pet. iv. 19.*

κυβεία, ας, ἡ, *dice-playing, fraud*, Ep. iv. 14.*

κυβέρνησις, εως, ἡ, *governing, direction*, 1 Cor. xii. 28.*

κυβερνήτης, ου, ὁ, *a steersman, a pilot*, Ac. xxvii. 11; Rev. xviii. 17.*

κυκλεύω, *to encircle, surround*, Rev. xx. 9 (W. H.).*

κυκλόθεν, adv. (κύκλος), *round about*, gen., Rev. iv. 3, 4, 8, v. 11 (not W. H.).*

κύκλος, ου, ὁ, *a circle*; only in dat., κύκλῳ, as adv., abs., or with gen., *round about, around*, Mar. iii. 34; vi. 6.

κυκλόω, ῶ, *to encircle, surround, besiege*, Lu. xxi. 20; Jn. x. 24; Ac. xiv. 20; Heb. xi. 30; Rev. xx. 9 (Rec.).*

κύλισμα, ατος, τό, *a place for wallowing*, 2 Pet. ii. 22 (not W. H.). (N. T.)*

κυλισμός, οῦ, ὁ, *a rolling, wallowing*, 2 Pet. ii. 22 (W. H.).*

κυλίω (for κυλίνδω), pass., *to be rolled, to wallow*, Mar. ix. 20.*

κυλλός, ή, όν, *crippled, lame*, especially in the hands, Mat. xv. 30 (not W. H.), 31 (not W. H.), xviii. 8; Mar. ix. 43.*

κῦμα, ατος, τό, *a wave*, as Mat. viii. 24; Mar. iv. 37; Ju. 13.

κύμβαλον, ου, τό (κύμβος, *hollow*), *a cymbal*, 1 Cor. xiii. 1.*

κύμινον, ου, τό (from Heb.), *cumin*, Mat. xxiii. 23.*

κυνάριον, ου, τό (dim. of κύων), *a little dog*, Mat. xv. 26, 27; Mar. vii. 27, 28.*

Κύπριος, ου, ὁ, *a Cyprian* or *Cypriote*, Ac. iv. 36.

Κύπρος, ου, ἡ, *Cyprus*, Ac. xi. 19, xiii. 4.

κύπτω, ψω, *to bend, to stoop down*, Mar. i. 7; Jn. viii. 6, 8 (W. H. omit).

Κυρηναῖος, ου, ὁ, *a Cyrenæan*, Ac. vi. 9, xi. 20.

Κυρήνη, ης, ἡ, *Cyrene*, a city of Africa, Ac. ii. 10.*

Κυρήνιος, ου, ὁ, *Cyrenius* or *Quirinius*, Lu. ii. 2.*

κυρία, ας, ἡ, *a lady*, 2 Jn. i. 5 (some read Κυρία, *Cyria*, a proper name).*

κυριακός, ή, όν, *of* or *pertaining to the Lord*, as the supper, 1 Cor. xi. 20; the day, Rev. i. 10.*

κυριεύω, εύσω, *to have authority*, abs., 1 Tim. vi. 15; *to rule over* (gen.), Lu. xxii. 25.

κύριος, ου, ὁ, (1) *lord, master*, Lu. xx. 15; Ac. xvi. 16; a title of honor, Mat. xiii. 27, xvi. 22; (2) *the Lord*, applied to God, Mar. v. 19; Ac. vii. 33; (3) *the Lord*, employed in the Epp. constantly of Christ (see Gr. § 217*b*, Wi. § 19, 1*a*, p. 124, Bu. 89), Ac. ix. 1; Ro. xiv. 8. *Syn.*: see δεσπότης.

κυριότης, τητος, ἡ, *lordship, dominion*; collective concr., *lords*, Ep. i. 21; Col. i. 16; 2 Pet. ii. 10; Ju. 8. (N. T.)*

κυρόω, ῶ, *to confirm, ratify*, 2 Cor. ii. 8; Gal. iii. 15.*

κύων, κυνός, ὁ, ἡ, *a dog*, Lu. xvi. 21; fig., of *shameless persons*, Phil. iii. 2.

κῶλον, ου, τό, *a limb, a carcase*, N T. plur. only, Heb. iii. 17.*

κωλύω, σω, *to restrain, forbid, hinder*, Mar. ix. 38.

κώμη, ης, ἡ, *a village*, unwalled, Mat. ix. 35.

κωμό-πολις, εως, ἡ, *a large, city-like village*, without walls, Mar. i. 38.*

κῶμος, ου, ὁ, *a feasting, revel-*

ing, Ro. xiii. 13; Gal. v. 21; 1 Pet. iv. 3.*

κώνωψ, ωπος, ὁ, *a gnat*, Mat. xxiii. 24.*

Κῶς, ῶ, ἡ, *Cos*, Ac. xxi. 1.*

Κωσάμ, ὁ (Heb.), *Cosam*, Lu. iii. 28.*

κωφός, ή, όν (κόπτω, lit., *blunted*), *dumb*, Mat. ix. 32, 33; *deaf*, Mat. xi. 5.

Λ

Λ, λ, λάμβδα, *lambda, l*, the eleventh letter. As a numeral, λ' = 30; ,λ = 30,000.

λαγχάνω, 2d aor. ἔλαχον, trans., *to obtain by lot, to obtain*, acc. or gen., Lu. i. 9; Ac. i. 17; 2 Pet. i. 1; abs., *to cast lots*, περί, gen., Jn. xix. 24.*

Λάζαρος, ου, ὁ, *Lazarus*, (1) of Bethany, Jn. xi. 1, 2; (2) in the parable, Lu. xvi. 20–25.

λάθρα (W. H. λάθρᾳ), (λανθάνω), adv., *secretly*, Jn. xi. 28.

λαῖλαψ, απος, ἡ, *a whirlwind, a violent storm*, Mar. iv. 37; Lu. viii. 23; 2 Pet. ii. 17.*

λακτίζω (λάξ, adv., *with the heel*), *to kick*, Ac. ix. 5 (W. H. omit), xxvi. 14.*

λαλέω, ῶ, ήσω, (1) *to utter a sound, to speak*, absolutely, Rev. x. 4; Heb. xii. 24; Ja. ii. 12; (2) *to speak, to talk*, with acc. of thing spoken, also with modal dat. and dat. of person addressed. Hence, according to the nature of the case, met., *to declare*, by other methods than *vivâ voce*, as Ro. vii. 1; *to preach, to publish, to announce*. *Syn.:* λέγω has reference to the *thought* uttered; λαλέω simply to the *fact* of utterance.

λαλιά, ᾶς, ἡ, (1) *speech, report*, Jn. iv. 42; (2) *manner of speech, dialect*, Mat. xxvi. 73; Mar. xiv. 70 (W. H. omit); Jn. viii. 43.*

λαμά, or λαμμᾶ (perh. Heb.), and λεμά (Aram.), *why*, Mat. xxvii. 46; Mar. xv. 34 (Ps. xxii. 1). (N. T.)*

λαμβάνω, λήψομαι (W. H. λήμψομαι), εἴληφα, ἔλαβον, (1) *to take*, as in the hand, Mat. xiv. 19; hence, (2) *to claim, procure*, Lu. xix. 12; (3) *to take by force, seize*, Mat. xxi. 35; (4) *to take away*, by violence or fraud, Mat. v. 40; (5) *to choose*, Ac. xv. 14; (6) *to receive, accept, obtain*, Jn. xvi. 24; Ja. iii. 1; Rev. xviii. 4; (7) in certain periphrastic expressions — λαμβάνειν ἀρχήν, *to begin*; λ. λήθην, *to forget*; λ. ὑπόμνησιν, *to remember*; λ. πεῖραν, *to experience*; λ. πρόσωπον, "to accept the person," *i.e.*, *to be partial*. The preposition "from," after this verb, is expressed by ἐκ, ἀπό, παρά (ὑπό, 2 Cor. xi. 24).

Λάμεχ, ὁ (Heb.), *Lamech*, Lu. iii. 36.*

λαμπάς, άδος, ἡ, prop. *a torch*, Rev. iv. 5, viii. 10; also *a lamp*, Jn. xviii. 3. *Syn.:* φῶς is light in general; φέγγος, radiance; φωστήρ, a heavenly body, luminary; λαμπάς, a torch; λύχνος, a lamp.

λαμπρός, ά, όν, *shining, magnificent*, Rev. xxii. 16; Lu. xxiii. 11.

λαμπρότης, τητος, ἡ, *splendor, brightness*, Ac. xxvi. 13.*

λαμπρῶς, adv., *magnificently*, Lu. xvi. 19.*

λάμπω, ψω, *to shine*, Mat. v. 15, 16, xvii. 2.

λανθάνω, 2d aor. ἔλαθον, (1) *to be hidden*, abs., Mar. vii. 24; Lu. viii. 47; (2) *to be hidden from* (acc.), Ac. xxvi. 26; 2 Pet. iii. 5, 8; (3) for part. constr., see Gr. § 394, 2, Wi. § 54, 4, Bu. 299; Heb. xiii. 2.*

λαξευτός, ή, όν, *hewn out of a rock*, Lu. xxiii. 53. (S.)*

Λαοδικεία, ας, ἡ, *Laodicea*, Col. ii. 1, iv. 13.

Λαοδικεύς, έως, ὁ, *a Laodicean*, Col. iv. 16; Rev. iii. 14 (not W. H.).*

λαός, οῦ, ὁ, (1) *a people*, spec. of *the people* of God, Lu. ii. 31; Ac. iv. 10; (2) *the common people*, Mat. xxvi. 5.

λάρυγξ, υγγος, ὁ, *the throat*, Ro. iii. 13.*

Λασαία (W. H. Λασέα), ας, ἡ, *Lasæa*, Ac. xxvii. 8.*

λάσκω, 1st aor. ἐλάκησα, *to burst asunder*, Ac. i. 18.*

λατομέω, ῶ, *to hew stones, to cut stones*, Mat. xxvii. 60; Mar. xv. 46. (S.)*

λατρεία, ας, ἡ, *worship, service rendered to God*, Jn. xvi. 2; Ro. ix. 4, xii. 1; Heb. ix. 1, 6.*

λατρεύω, σω, (1) *to worship, to serve*, Ac. vii. 7; (2) *to officiate as a priest*, Heb. xiii. 10. *Syn.:* λατρεύω is to worship God, as any one may do; λειτουργέω, to serve him in a special office or ministry.

λάχανον, ου, τό, *an herb, a garden plant*, Mat. xiii. 32.

Λεββαῖος, ου, ὁ, *Lebbæus*, Mat. x. 3 (not W. H.). See Θαδδαῖος.*

λεγεών (W. H. λεγιών), ῶνος, ὁ (Lat., see Gr. § 154*c*, Bu. 16), *a legion*, Mat. xxvi. 53; Mar. v. 9, 15; Lu. viii. 30; in N.T. times containing probably 6826 men. (N. T.)*

λέγω, only pres. and impf. in N. T., (1) *to speak, to say*, Ac. xiii. 15; Jn. i. 29; used also of writings, as Jn. xix. 37; (2) *to relate, to tell*, Lu. ix. 31, xviii. 1; (3) *to call*, pass., *to be called* or *named*; (4) pass., *to be chosen* or *appointed*. Dat. of person addressed. *Syn.:* see λαλέω.

λεῖμμα, ατος, τό (λείπω), *a remnant*, Ro. xi. 5.*

λεῖος, εία, εῖον, *smooth, level*, Lu. iii. 5 (from S.).*

λείπω, ψω, *to leave, to be wanting*, Lu. xviii. 22; Tit. i. 5, iii. 13; pass., *to be lacking, to be destitute of*, Ja. i. 4, 5, ii. 15.*

λειτουργέω, ῶ, (1) *to serve publicly in sacred things*, Ac. xiii. 2; Heb. x. 11; (2) *to minister to charitably*, Ro. xv. 27.* *Syn.:* see λατρεύω.

λειτουργία, ας, ἡ, (1) *a public ministration* or *service*, Lu. i. 23; Phil. ii. 17; Heb. viii. 6, ix. 21; (2) *a charitable gift*, Phil. ii. 30; 2 Cor. ix. 12.*

λειτουργικός, ή, όν, *employed in ministering*, Heb. i. 14 (S.)*

λειτουργός, οῦ, ὁ, *a minister* or *servant* to, gen. obj., Ro. xiii. 6, xv. 16; Phil. ii. 25; Heb. i. 7, viii. 2.*

λέντιον, ου, τό (Lat., see Gr. § 154*e*), *a towel, apron*, Jn. xiii. 4, 5. (N. T.)*

λεπίς, ίδος, ἡ, *a scale*, Ac. ix. 18.*

λέπρα, ας, ἡ, *the leprosy*, Mat. viii. 3; Mar. i. 42; Lu. v. 12, 13.*

λεπρός, οῦ, ὁ, *a leper*, Lu. iv. 27, vii. 22.

λεπτόν, οῦ, τό, prop. verb. adj. (sc. *νόμισμα*), from *λέπω* (*to strip off, pare down*), *a mite*, a small brass coin, one eighth of an *as*, the smallest Jewish coin, Mar. xii. 42; Lu. xii. 59, xxi. 2.*

Λευΐ, or *Λευΐς* (W. H. *Λευείς*), gen. *Λευΐ*, ὁ, *Levi*. Four are mentioned: (1) son of Jacob, ancestor of the priestly tribe; (2, 3) ancestors of Jesus, Lu. iii. 24, 29; (4) the apostle, also called *Matthew*, Lu. v. 27, 29.

Λευΐτης, ου, ὁ, *a Levite*, Lu. x. 32; Jn. i. 19; Ac. iv. 36.*

Λευϊτικός, ή, όν, *Levitical*, Heb. vii. 11.*

λευκαίνω, *ανῶ*, 1st aor. *ἐλεύκανα*, *to make white*, Mar. ix. 3; Rev. vii. 14.*

λευκός, ή, όν, (1) *white*, as Mat. v. 36; Jn. iv. 35; (2) *bright*, as Mat. xvii. 2.

λέων, οντος, ὁ, *a lion*, Heb. xi. 33; fig., 2 Tim. iv. 17; of Christ, Rev. v. 5.

λήθη, ης, ἡ, *forgetfulness*, 2 Pet. i. 9.*

ληνός, οῦ, ὁ, ἡ, *a wine-press*, Mat. xxi. 33; fig. in Rev. xiv. 19, 20, xix. 15.*

λῆρος, ου, ὁ, *idle talk*, Lu. xxiv. 11.*

λῃστής, οῦ, ὁ, *a robber*, Mar. xi. 17; Jn. x. 1, 8. *Syn.*: see *κλέπτης*.

λῆψις (W. H. *λῆμψις*), εως, ἡ (*λαμβάνω*), *a receiving*, Phil. iv. 15.*

λίαν, adv., *very much*; with adj. or adv., *very*, Mat. iv. 8; Mar. xvi. 2.

λίβανος, ου, ὁ, *frankincense*, Mat. ii. 11; Rev. xviii. 13.*

λιβανωτός, οῦ, ὁ, *a censer for burning frankincense*, Rev. viii. 3, 5.*

λιβερτῖνος, ου, ὁ (Lat. *libertinus*), *a freedman*, Ac. vi. 9. Probably Jews who had been slaves at Rome under Pompey, and afterwards freed.*

Λιβύη, ης, ἡ, *Libya*, Ac. ii. 10.*

λιθάζω, *σω*, *to stone*, Jn. xi. 8; Ac. xiv. 19.

λίθινος, η, ον, *made of stone*, Jn. ii. 6; 2 Cor. iii. 3; Rev. ix. 20.*

λιθο-βολέω, ῶ, *ήσω*, *to throw stones at, to stone*, Mat. xxiii. 37; Mar. xii. 4 (W. H. omit). (S.)

λίθος, ου, ὁ, *a stone, i.e.*, (1) loose and lying about, Mat. iv. 3, 6; (2) built into a wall, etc., Mar. xiii. 2; (3) *a precious stone*, Rev. iv. 3, xvii. 4; (4) *a statue* or *idol of stone*, Ac. xvii. 29.

λιθό-στρωτον, ου, τό (prop. adj., *spread with stones*), *a mosaic pavement*, as name of a place near the prætorium or palace at Jerusalem, Jn. xix. 13.*

λικμάω, ῶ, *ήσω*, *to scatter*, as grain in winnowing, *to grind to powder* that may be scattered, Mat. xxi. 44; Lu. xx. 18.*

λιμήν, *ένος*, ὁ, *a harbor*, Ac. xxvii. 8, 12.*

λίμνη, ης, ἡ, *a lake, e.g.*, Gennesaret, Lu. v. 1.

λιμός, οῦ, ὁ, (1) *hunger*, 2 Cor. xi. 27; (2) *a famine*, Mat. xxiv. 7.

λίνον, ου, τό, *flax, linen made of flax*, Rev. xv. 6 (W. H. *λίθος*); *a lamp-wick*, Mat. xii. 20.*

Λῖνος (W. H. *Λίνος*), ου, ὁ, *Linus*, 2 Tim. iv. 21.*

λιπαρός, ά, όν, *fat, dainty*, Rev. xviii. 14.*

λίτρα, ας, ἡ, *a pound*, a weight of twelve ounces, Jn. xii. 3, xix. 39.*

λίψ, *λιβός*, ὁ, *the S.W. wind*; used for the S.W. quarter of the heavens, Ac. xxvii. 12.*

λογία, ας, ἡ, *a collection, i.e.*, of money, 1 Cor. xvi. 1, 2. (N. T.)*

λογίζομαι, *σομαι*, dep. with mid. and pass., (1) *to reckon*; (2) *to place to the account of, to charge with*, acc. and dat., or with *εἰς* (see Gr. § 298, 6, Wi. § 32, 4*b*, Bu. 151); (3) *to reason, argue, to infer, conclude*, from reasoning; (4) *to think, suppose*.

λογικός, ή, όν, *rational, i.e.*, belonging to the sphere of the reason, Ro. xii. 1; 1 Pet. ii. 2.*

λόγιον, ου, τό, *something spoken*, in N. T., *a divine communication, e.g.*, the Old Testament, Ac. vii. 38; Ro. iii. 2; and the doctrines of Christ, Heb. v. 12; 1 Pet. iv. 11.*

λόγιος, ον, *eloquent*, Ac. xviii. 24.*

λογισμός, οῦ, ὁ, *a reasoning, decision*, Ro. ii. 15; 2 Cor. x. 5.*

λογο-μαχέω, ῶ, *to contend about words*, 2 Tim. ii. 14. (N.T.)*

λογομαχία, ας, ἡ, *contention about words*, 1 Tim. vi 4. (N. T.)*

λόγος, ου, ὁ, (1) *a speaking, a saying, a word*, as the expression of thought (whereas *ἔπος, ὄνομα, ῥῆμα* refer to words in their outward form, as parts of speech), Mat. viii. 8; (2) the thing spoken, Mat. vii. 24, 26 — whether *doctrine*, 1 Tim. iv. 6; *prophecy*, 2 Pet. i. 19; *question*, Mat. xxi. 24; *a common saying* or *proverb*, Jn. iv. 37; *a precept, a command*, Jn. viii. 55; *the truth*, Mar. viii. 38; *conversation*, Lu. xxiv. 17; *teaching*, 1 Cor. ii. 4; *a narrative*, Ac. i. 1; *a public rumor*, Mat. xxviii. 15; *an argument*, Ac. ii. 40; *a charge* or *accusation*, Ac. xix. 38; (3) *reason*, Ac. xviii. 14; (4) *account, reckoning*, Heb. iv. 13; Ac. xx. 24; Mat. xviii. 23; Ac. x. 29; *λόγος* is used by John as a name of Christ, the Word of God, *i.e.*, the expression or manifestation of his thoughts to man, Jn. i. 1, etc.

λόγχη, ης, ἡ, *a lance, a spear*, Jn. xix. 34.*

λοιδορέω, ῶ, *to rail at, revile*, Jn. ix. 28; Ac. xxiii. 4; 1 Cor. iv. 12; 1 Pet. ii. 23.*

λοιδορία, ας, ἡ, *reviling*, 1 Tim. v. 14; 1 Pet. iii. 9.*

λοίδορος, ου, ὁ, *a reviler*, 1 Cor. v. 11, vi. 10.*

λοιμός, οῦ, ὁ, *a pestilence*, Mat. xxiv. 7 (W. H. omit), Lu. xxi. 11; Paul so called, Ac. xxiv. 5.*

λοιπός, ή, όν, *remaining, the rest*, Mat. xxv. 11; adv. *τὸ λοιπόν*, *as for the rest, more-*

over, finally, henceforth, 1 Cor. i. 16; Heb. x. 13; τοῦ λοιποῦ, *from henceforth*, Gal. vi. 17.

Λουκᾶς, ᾶ, ὁ (from Λουκανός, see Gr. § 159*d*, Wi. § 16, 4, note 1, Bu. 20), *Luke*, Ac. xvi. 10, xx. 5.

Λούκιος, ου, ὁ (Lat.), *Lucius*, Ac. xiii. 1; Ro. xvi. 21.*

λουτρόν, οῦ, τό, *a bath;* in N.T. *baptism*, Ep. v. 26; Tit. iii. 5.*

λούω, σω, *to bathe, to wash*, Ac. ix. 37, xvi. 33; *to cleanse, to purify*, Rev. i. 5 (W. H. λύω). *Syn.:* πλύνω is to wash *inanimate things;* λούω, to bathe *the whole body;* νίπτω, to wash a *part* of the body.

Λύδδα, ης, ἡ, also Λύδδα, ων, τά (W. H.), *Lydda*, Ac. ix. 32, 35, 38.*

Λυδία, ας, ἡ, *Lydia*, Ac. xvi. 14, 40.*

Λυκαονία, ας, ἡ, *Lycaonia*, Ac. xiv. 6.*

Λυκαονιστί, adv., *in the speech of Lycaonia*, Ac. xiv. 11.*

Λυκία, ας, ἡ, *Lycia*, Ac. xxvii. 5.*

λύκος, ου, ὁ, *a wolf*, Jn. x. 12; fig., Ac. xx. 29.

λυμαίνομαι, *to ravage, to devastate*, Ac. viii. 3.*

λυπέω, ῶ, *to grieve*, a general word, 2 Cor. ii. 2, 5; pass., *to be grieved, saddened*, Mat. xxvi. 22, 37; 1 Pet. i. 6; *to aggrieve* or *offend*, Ro. xiv. 15; Ep. iv. 30.

λύπη, ης, ἡ, *grief, sorrow*, 2 Cor. ix. 7; *cause of grief, annoyance*, 1 Pet. ii. 19.

Λυσανίας, ου, ὁ, *Lysanias*, Lu. iii. 1.*

Λυσίας, ου, ὁ, *Lysias*, Ac. xxiii. 26.

λύσις, εως, ἡ, *a loosing, divorce*, 1 Cor. vii. 27.*

λυσι-τελέω, ῶ (lit., *to pay taxes*), impers., -εῖ, *it is profitable* or *preferable* (dat. and ἤ), Lu. xvii. 2.*

Λύστρα, ας, ἡ, or ων, τά, *Lystra*, Ac. xiv. 6, 8.

λύτρον, ου, τό, *a ransom*. Mat. xx. 28; Mar. x. 45.*

λυτρόω, ῶ, ώσω, in N. T. only mid. and pass., *to ransom, to deliver* by paying a ransom, Lu. xxiv. 21; Tit. ii. 14; 1 Pet. i. 18 (acc., pers.; dat., price, and ἀπό or ἐκ).*

λύτρωσις, εως, ἡ, *deliverance, redemption*, Lu. i. 68, ii. 38; Heb. ix. 12.*

λυτρωτής, οῦ, ὁ, *a redeemer, a deliverer*, Ac. vii. 35.*

λυχνία, ας, ἡ, *a lampstand*, Mat. v. 15; fig., of a church, Rev. ii. 1, 5; of a Christian teacher, Rev. xi. 4.

λύχνος, ου, ὁ, *a lamp*, Mat. v. 15, vi. 22; used of John the Baptist, Jn. v. 35; of Christ, Rev. xxi. 23. *Syn.:* see λαμπάς.

λύω, σω, *to loose*, as (1) lit., *to unbind*, Mar. i. 7; Rev. v. 2; (2) *to set at liberty*, Jn. xi. 44; Ac. xxii. 30; (3) *to pronounce not binding*, *e.g.*, a law, Mat. xviii. 18; (4) *to disobey* or *nullify* the divine word, Jn. vii. 23, x. 35; (5) *to destroy*, *e.g.*, the temple, Jn. ii. 19; (6) *to dismiss*, *i.e.*, an assembly, Ac. xiii. 43.

Λωΐς, ΐδος, ἡ, *Lois*, 2 Tim. i. 5.*

Λώτ, ὁ (Heb.), *Lot*, Lu. xvii. 28–32; 2 Pet. ii. 7.*

M

M, μ, μῦ, *mu*, *m*, the twelfth letter. As a numeral, μ′ = 40; ͵μ = 40,000.

Μαάθ, ὁ (Heb.), *Maath*, Lu. iii. 26.*

Μαγδαλά, ἡ (Heb.), *Magdala*, Mat. xv. 39 (W. H. and R.V. Μαγαδάν).*

Μαγδαληνή, ῆς, ἡ, *Magdalene*, *i.e.*, a woman of Magdala, as Mat. xxvii. 56, 61.

μαγεία (W. H. μαγία), ας, ἡ, *magic*, plur., *magical arts*, Ac. viii. 11.*

μαγεύω, σω, *to practice magical arts*, Ac. viii. 9.*

μάγος, ου, ὁ, (1) *a magus*, a Persian astrologer, Mat. ii. 1, 7, 16; (2) *a sorcerer*, Ac. xiii. 6, 8.*

Μαγώγ, ὁ (Heb.), *Magog*, Rev. xx. 8; see Γώγ.*

Μαδιάμ, ἡ (Heb.), *Midian*, Ac. vii. 29.*

μαθητεύω, σω, (1) trans., *to make a disciple of* (acc.), *to instruct*, Mat. xiii. 52, xxviii. 19; Ac. xiv. 21; (2) intrans., *to be a disciple*, Mat. xxvii. 57 (Rec., W. H. read pass., W. H. with active in mrg.).*

μαθητής, οῦ, ὁ (μανθάνω), *a disciple*, Mat. ix. 14, x. 24, xxii. 16; οἱ μαθηταί, specially, *the twelve*, Mat. ix. 19.

μαθήτρια, ας, ἡ, *a female disciple*, Ac. ix. 36.*

Μαθουσάλα, ὁ (Heb.), *Methuselah*, Lu. iii. 37.*

Μαϊνάν, ὁ (W. H. Μεννά) (Heb.), *Mainan* or *Menna*, Lu. iii. 31.*

μαίνομαι, dep., *to be mad, to rave*, Jn. x. 20; Ac. xii. 15, xxvi. 24, 25; 1 Cor. xiv. 23.*

μακαρίζω, fut. ιῶ, *to pronounce happy* or *blessed*, Lu. i. 48; Ja. v. 11.*

μακάριος, α, ον, *happy, blessed*, Mat. v. 3–11; Lu. i. 45, vi. 20; 1 Cor. vii. 40.

μακαρισμός, οῦ, ὁ, *a declaring blessed, a pronouncing happy*, Ro. iv. 6, 9; Gal. iv. 15.*

Μακεδονία, ας, ἡ, *Macedonia*, Ac. xvi. 9, 10, 12.

Μακεδών, όνος, ὁ, *a Macedonian*, Ac. xix. 29, xxvii. 2.

μάκελλον, ου, τό (Lat.), *a meat-market*, 1 Cor. x. 25.*

μακράν, adv. (acc. of μακρός, sc. ὁδόν), *afar, afar off*, Lu. xv. 20; εἰς preceding, Ac. ii. 39; ἀπό following, Ac. xvii. 27.

μακρόθεν, adv., *from afar*, Mar. viii. 3; with ἀπό, as Mat. xxvii. 55.

μακρο-θυμέω, ῶ, ήσω, *to suffer long, to have patience, to be forbearing*, 1 Cor. xiii. 4; *to delay*, Lu. xviii. 7; *to wait patiently*, Heb. vi. 15. (S.)

μακρο-θυμία, ας, ἡ, *forbearance, long-suffering, patience*, Ro. ii. 4, ix. 22. *Syn.:* see ἀνοχή.

μακρο-θύμως, adv., *patiently*, Ac. xxvi. 3. (N. T.)*

μακρός, ά, όν, *long;* of place, *distant*, Lu. xv. 13, xix. 12; of time, *long*, only in the phrase μακρὰ προσεύχεσθαι, *to make long prayers*, Mat. xxiii. 14 (W. H. omit); Mar. xii. 40; Lu. xx. 47.*

μακρο-χρόνιος, ον, *long-lived*, Ep. vi. 3.*

μαλακία, ας, ἡ, *weakness, infirmity*, Mat. iv. 23, ix. 35 x. 1.*

μαλακός, ή, όν, *soft*, of garments, Mat. xi. 8; Lu. vii

25; *disgracefully effeminate*, 1 Cor. vi. 9.*

Μαλελεήλ, ὁ (Heb.), *Maleleel* or *Mahalaleel*, Lu. iii. 37.*

μάλιστα, adv. (superl. of μάλα, *very*), *most of all, especially*, Gal. vi. 10; 2 Tim. iv. 13.

μᾶλλον, adv. (comp. of μάλα), *more, rather*; πολλῷ μᾶλλον, *much more*, Mat. vi. 30; πόσῳ μᾶλλον, *how much more*, Mat. vii. 11; μᾶλλον ἤ, *more than*, Mat. xviii. 13; μᾶλλον is often of intensive force, *e.g.*, Mat. xxvii. 24; Ro. viii. 34. See Gr. § 321, Wi. §§ 35, 1, 65, 2, Bu. 83.

Μάλχος, ου, ὁ (Heb.), *Malchus*, Jn. xviii. 10.*

μάμμη, ης, ἡ, *a grandmother*, 2 Tim. i. 5.*

μαμμωνᾶς (W. H. μαμωνᾶς), ᾶ, ὁ (Aram.), *mammon, gain, wealth*, Mat. vi. 24; Lu. xvi. 9, 11, 13. (N. T.)*

Μαναήν, ὁ (Heb.), *Manaen*, Ac. xiii. 1.*

Μανασσῆς, gen. and acc. ῆ, ὁ, *Manasseh*, (1) son of Joseph, Rev. vii. 6; (2) Mat. i. 10.*

μανθάνω, μαθήσομαι, 2d aor. ἔμαθον, perf. μεμάθηκα, *to learn, to understand, to know, to be informed, to comprehend*. Used abs., or with acc. (ἀπό or παρά with gen. of the teacher, ἐν with example, 1 Cor. iv. 6).

μανία, ας, ἡ, *madness*, Ac. xxvi. 24.*

μάννα, τό (Heb., deriv. uncertain), *manna*, the food of the Israelites in the desert, Jn. vi. 31, 49; Heb. ix. 4. (S.)

μαντεύομαι, dep., *to utter responses, practice divination*, Ac. xvi. 16.*

μαραίνω, ανῶ, fut. pass. μαρανθήσομαι, *to wither, to fade away*, Ja. i. 11.*

μαρὰν ἀθά (two Aram. words), *our Lord cometh* (R.V. mrg.), 1 Cor. xvi. 22. (N. T.)*

μαργαρίτης, ου, ὁ, *a pearl*, Mat. xiii. 45, 46.

Μάρθα, ας, ἡ, *Martha*, Lu. x. 38, 40, 41.

Μαρία, ας, or Μαριάμ, indecl. (Heb. *Miriam*), ἡ, *Mary*. Six of the name are mentioned: (1) the mother of Jesus, Lu. i. 27; (2) the Magdalene, Mar. xv. 40, 47; (3) the sister of Martha and Lazarus, Lu. x. 39, 42; (4) the wife of Cleopas, Mat. xxvii. 56, 61; (5) the mother of John Mark, Ac. xii. 12; (6) a Christian woman in Rome, Ro. xvi. 6.

Μάρκος, ου, ὁ, *Mark*, Ac. xii. 12, 25.

μάρμαρος, ου, ὁ, ἡ, *marble*, Rev. xviii. 12.*

μαρτυρέω, ῶ, ήσω, *to be a witness*, abs., *to testify* (περί, gen.), *to give testimony* (*to*, dat. of pers. or thing), *to commend*; pass., *to be attested, i.e.*, honorably, *to be of good report*.

μαρτυρία, ας, ἡ, *testimony, i.e.*, legal, Mar. xiv. 56, 59; or general, Jn. v. 34; with obj. gen., as Rev. xix. 10.

μαρτύριον, ου, τό, *testimony*, Mat. viii. 4 (*to*, dat.; *against*, ἐπί, acc.).

μαρτύρομαι, dep., *to call to witness*, Ac. xx. 26; Gal. v. 3; *to exhort solemnly*, Ac. xxvi. 22 (W. H.); Ep. iv. 17; 1 Th. ii. 11 (W. H.).*

μάρτυς, υρος, dat. plur. μάρτυσι, ὁ, *a witness, i.e.*, judicially, Mat. xviii. 16; *one who testifies* from what he has seen or experienced, 1 Th. ii. 10, Lu. xxiv. 48; *a martyr*, witnessing by his death, Ac. xxii. 20; Rev. ii. 13, xvii. 6.

μασσάομαι (W. H. -ασά-), ῶμαι, *to bite, to gnaw*, Rev. xvi. 10.*

μαστιγόω, ῶ, ώσω, *to scourge*, Mat. x. 17; fig., Heb. xii. 6.

μαστίζω, *to scourge*, Ac. xxii. 25.*

μάστιξ, ιγος, ἡ, *a whip, a scourge*, Ac. xxii. 24; Heb. xi. 36; fig., *calamity, disease*, Mar. iii. 10, v. 29, 34; Lu. vii. 21.*

μαστός, οῦ, ὁ, *the breast*, pl., Lu. xi. 27, xxiii. 29; Rev. i. 13.*

ματαιολογία, ας, ἡ, *vain, fruitless talk*, 1 Tim. i. 6.*

ματαιο-λόγος, ου, ὁ, *a vain, empty talker*, Tit. i. 10.*

μάταιος (αία), αιον, *vain, useless, empty*, 1 Cor. xv. 17; Ja. i. 26; τὰ μάταια, *vanities*, spec. of heathen deities, Ac. xiv. 15 (and O. T.). *Syn.*: see κενός.

ματαιότης, τητος, ἡ, (1) *vanity*, 2 Pet. ii. 18; (2) *perverseness*, Ep. iv. 17; (3) *frailty*, Ro. viii. 20.*

ματαιόω, ῶ, *to make vain* or *foolish*; pass., Ro. i. 21. (S.)*

μάτην, adv., *in vain, fruitlessly*, Mat. xv. 9; Mar. vii. 7.*

Ματθαῖος (W. H. Μαθθαῖος), ου, ὁ, *Matthew*, the apostle and evangelist, Mat. ix. 9, 10; also called Λευΐ.

Ματθάν (W. H. Μαθθάν), ὁ (Heb.), *Matthan*, Mat. i. 15.*

Ματθάτ, ὁ (Heb.), *Matthat*, Lu. iii. 24, 29 (W. H. Μαθθάτ).*

Ματθίας (W. H. Μαθθίας), α, ὁ, *Matthias*, Ac. i. 23, 26.*

Ματταθά, ὁ (Heb.), *Mattatha*, Lu. iii. 31.*

Ματταθίας, ου, ὁ, *Mattathias*, Lu. iii. 25, 26.*

μάχαιρα, ας and ης, ἡ, *a sword*, Jn. xviii. 10, 11; met., for strife, Mat. x. 34; fig., of spiritual weapons, Ep. vi. 17.

μάχη, ης, ἡ, *battle; contention, strife*, 2 Cor. vii. 5; 2 Tim. ii. 23; Tit. iii. 9; Ja. iv. 1.*

μάχομαι, *to fight, contend, dispute*, Jn. vi. 52; Ac. vii. 26; 2 Tim. ii. 24; Ja. iv. 2.*

μεγαλ-αυχέω, ῶ, *to boast great things, to be arrogant*, Ja. iii. 5 (W. H. μεγάλα αὐχεῖ).*

μεγαλεῖος, εία, εῖον, *grand, magnificent*, Lu. i. 49 (W. H. μεγάλα); Ac. ii. 11.*

μεγαλειότης, τητος, ἡ, *majesty, magnificence*, Lu. ix. 43; Ac. xix. 27; 2 Pet. i. 16.*

μεγαλο-πρεπής, ές, gen. οῦς, *fitting for a great man, magnificent, majestic*, 2 Pet. i. 17.*

μεγαλύνω, νῶ, (1) *to make great*, Mat. xxiii. 5; (2) *to magnify, extol, celebrate with praise*, Lu. i. 46; Ac. v. 13.

μεγάλως, adv., *greatly*, Phil. iv. 10.*

μεγαλωσύνη, ης, ἡ, *majesty*, Heb. i. 3, viii. 1; Ju. 25. (S.)*

μέγας, μεγάλη, μέγα (see Gr. § 39), comp. μείζων, sup. μέγιστος, *great*, in size, *full-grown, intense*, Mat. ii. 10, xxviii. 8; *wonderful*, 2 Cor. xi. 15; *noble, of high rank*, Rev. xi. 18, xiii. 16; applied to age, ὁ μείζων, *the elder*, Ro. ix. 12; μέγας indicates the *size* of things, their *meas-*

ure, number, cost, and estimation; μεγάλη ἡμέρα, a solemn, sacred day, Jn. xix. 31.

μέγεθος, ους, τό, greatness, Ep. i. 19.*

μεγιστᾶνες, άνων, οἱ (sing. μεγιστάν, only in Ap., Sirach iv. 7), princes, great men, nobles, Mar. vi. 21; Rev. vi. 15, xviii. 23. (S.)*

μεθ-ερμηνεύω, to translate, to interpret, pass. only, Mar. v. 41; Jn. i. 41.

μέθη, ης, ἡ, drunkenness, Lu. xxi. 34; Ro. xiii. 13; Gal. v. 21.*

μεθ-ίστημι (and μεθιστάνω, 1 Cor. xiii. 2), μεταστήσω, 1st aor., pass., μετεστάθην, lit., to change the place of; hence, to remove, 1 Cor. xiii. 2; Col. i. 13; to lead astray, Ac. xix. 26; to remove from life, Ac. xiii. 22; to remove from office, Lu. xvi. 4.*

μεθ-οδεία (-οδία, W. H.), ας, ἡ, a fraudulent artifice, a trick, Ep. iv. 14, vi. 11. (N. T.)*

μεθ-όριος, α, ον, bordering on; τὰ μεθόρια, borders, frontiers, Mar. vii. 24 (W. H. ὅρια).*

μεθύσκω, to make drunk; pass., to be drunk, Lu. xii. 45; Jn. ii. 10; Ep. v. 18; 1 Th. v. 7.*

μέθυσος, ου, ὁ (prop. adj.), a drunkard, 1 Cor. v. 11, vi. 10.*

μεθύω, to be drunken, Mat. xxiv. 49; Ac. ii. 15; met., Rev. xvii. 6.

μείζων, comp. of μέγας, which see. It has itself a comparative, μειζότερος, 3 Jn. 4 (see Gr. § 47, Wi. § 11, 2b, Bu. 28).

μέλαν, ανος, τό (μέλας), ink, 2 Cor. iii. 3; 2 Jn. 12; 3 Jn. 13.*

μέλας, αινα, αν, black, Mat. v. 36; Rev. vi. 5, 12.*

Μελεᾶς, ᾶ, ὁ, Melea, Lu. iii. 31.*

μέλει, impers. (see Gr. § 101, Wi. § 30, 10d, Bu. 164), it concerns, dat. of pers., with gen. of object, as 1 Cor. ix. 9; or περί, as Jn. x. 13; or ὅτι, as Mar. iv. 38.

μελετάω, ῶ, ήσω, to practice, 1 Tim. iv. 15; to devise, Ac. iv. 25; to meditate, Mar. xiii. 11 (not W. H.).*

μέλι, ιτος, τό, honey, Mat. iii. 4; Mar. i. 6; Rev. x. 9, 10.*

μελίσσιος, α, ον, made by bees, Lu. xxiv. 42 (W. H. omit). (N. T.)*

Μελίτη, ης, ἡ, Melita, now Malta, Ac. xxviii. 1 (W. H. Μελιτήνη).*

μέλλω, ήσω, to be about to do, to be on the point of doing, with infin., generally the present infin., rarely aor.; the fut. infin. (the regular classical use) occurs only in the phrase μέλλειν ἔσεσθαι (only in Ac.); the verb may often be adequately rendered by our auxiliaries, will, shall, must; to delay, only Ac. xxii. 16. The participle is used absolutely: τὸ μέλλον, the future, Lu. xiii. 9; τὰ μέλλοντα, things to come, Ro. viii. 38. See Gr. § 363f, Wi. § 44, 7c, Bu. 259.

μέλος, ους, τό, a member of the body, a limb, as Mat. v. 29, 30; Ro. xii. 4; fig., 1 Cor. vi. 15.

Μελχί (W. H. -εί), ὁ (Heb.), Melchi. Two are mentioned, Lu. iii. 24, 28.*

Μελχισεδέκ, ὁ (Heb. king of righteousness), Melchizedek, Heb. v., vi., vii.*

μεμβράνα, ης, ἡ (Lat.), parchment, 2 Tim. iv. 13. (N.T.)*

μέμφομαι, ψομαι, dep., to blame, to censure, abs., Mar. vii. 2 (W. H. omit); Ro. ix. 19; abs. or dat., Heb. viii. 8 (W. H. acc., with dat. mrg.).*

μεμψί-μοιρος, ον, discontented, complaining, Ju. 16.*

μέν, antithetic particle, truly, indeed (see Gr. § 136, Wi. § 53, 7b), Bu. 364 sq.).

μεν-οῦν, conj., moreover, therefore, but.

μεν-οῦν-γε, conj., nay rather, nay truly, Lu. xi. 28 (W. H. μενοῦν); Ro. ix. 20, x. 18; Phil. iii. 8 (W. H. μὲν οὖν γε). See Gr. § 406, Wi. § 61, 6, Bu. 370 sq.*

μέν-τοι, conj., yet truly, nevertheless, however, Jn. iv. 27.

μένω, μενῶ, ἔμεινα, (1) intrans., to remain, to abide; so (a) of place, to dwell, Mat. x. 11; to lodge, Lu. xix. 5; (b) of state, as Ac. v. 4; to continue firm and constant in, Jn. xv. 4; to endure, to last, to be permanent, 1 Cor. iii. 14; (2) trans., to await, wait for, only Ac. xx. 5, 23.

μερίζω, σω, (1) to divide, separate, mid., to share (μετά, gen.), Lu. xii. 13; pass., to be divided, to be at variance, Mat. xii. 25, 26; 1 Cor. i. 13; (2) to distribute, Mar. vi. 41, acc. and dat.

μέριμνα, ης, ἡ, care, anxiety, as dividing, distracting the mind, Mat. xiii. 22; Lu. viii. 14.

μεριμνάω, ῶ, ήσω, to be anxious, distracted, to care for; abs., with dat., περί (gen.), acc. The various constructions may be illustrated from Mat. vi.: abs., vers. 27, 31; acc., ver. 34 (Rec.; see also 1 Cor. vii. 32–34); gen., ver. 34 (W. H.); dat., ver. 25; εἰς, ver. 34; περί, ver. 28.

μερίς, ίδος, ἡ, a part or division of a country, Ac. xvi. 12; a share, portion, Lu. x. 42; Ac. viii. 21, 2 Cor. vi. 15; Col. i. 12.*

μερισμός, οῦ, ὁ, a dividing or division, Heb. iv. 12; distribution, gifts distributed, Heb. ii. 4.*

μεριστής, οῦ, ὁ, a divider, Lu. xii. 14. (N. T.)*

μέρος, ους, τό, a part; hence, (1) a share, Rev. xxii. 19; fellowship, Jn. xiii. 8; a business or calling, Ac. xix. 27; (2) a part, as the result of division, Jn. xix. 23. In adverbial phrases, μέρος τι, partly, in some part; ἀνὰ μέρος, alternately; ἀπὸ μέρους, partly; ἐκ μέρους, individually, of persons, partially, imperfectly, of things; κατὰ μέρος, particularly, in detail, Heb. ix. 5.

μεσημβρία, ας, ἡ, midday, noon, Ac. xxii. 6; the south, Ac. viii. 26.

μεσιτεύω, σω, to mediate, to give surety, Heb. vi. 17.*

μεσίτης, ου, ὁ, a mediator, i.e., one who interposes between parties and reconciles them, Gal. iii. 19, 20; 1 Tim. ii. 5; in the phrase μεσίτης διαθήκης, mediator of a covenant, Heb. viii. 6, ix. 15, xii. 24.*

μεσο-νύκτιον, ου, τό, *midnight*, as Lu. xi. 5.

Μεσο-ποταμία, ας, ἡ, *Mesopotamia*, the region between the Euphrates and the Tigris, Ac. ii. 9, vii. 2.*

μέσος, η, ον, *middle*, of time or place, *in the midst* of (gen.), as Mat. xxv. 6; Jn. i. 26, xix. 18; Ac. i. 18, xxvi. 13; neut., τὸ μέσον, *the middle part*, used chiefly in adverbial phrases, with prepositions (art. generally omit.), ἐκ μέσου, *from among, away;* ἐν μέσῳ, *among;* ἀνὰ μέσον, *through the midst, among, between;* also with διά and εἰς.

μεσό-τοιχον, ου, τό, *a partition-wall*, Ep. ii. 14. (N. T.)*

μεσ-ουράνημα, ατος, τό, *mid-heaven*, Rev. viii. 13, xiv. 6, xix. 17.*

μεσόω, ῶ, *to be in the middle*, Jn. vii. 14.*

Μεσσίας, ου, ὁ (from Heb. *anointed*), *Messiah*, the same as Greek Χριστός, Jn. i. 41, iv. 25. (N. T.)*

μεστός, ή, όν, *full*, gen., Jn. xix. 29; Ro. i. 29.

μεστόω, ῶ, *to fill*, gen., Ac. ii. 13.*

μετά (akin to μέσος), prep., gov. the gen. and acc.; gen., *with, among;* acc., *after* (see Gr. § 301, Wi. §§ 47 *h*, 49 *f*, 52, 4, 10), Bu. 338 sq.). In composition, μετά denotes *participation, nearness, change*, or *succession* (often like the Latin prefix *trans-*, as in the words *transfer, translate*).

μετα-βαίνω, βήσομαι, *to pass over, to depart*, Lu. x. 7; Mat. xi. 1.

μετα-βάλλω, in mid., *to change one's mind*, Ac. xxviii. 6.*

μετ-άγω, *to turn about, to direct*, as horses, ships, Ja. iii. 3, 4.*

μετα-δίδωμι, *to share with, to impart*, Lu. iii. 11; Ro. i. 11; 1 Th. ii. 8; Ep. iv. 28; ὁ μεταδιδούς, *a distributor* of alms, Ro. xii. 8.*

μετά-θεσις, εως, ἡ, (1) *a transfer, a translation*, Heb. xi. 5; *a removal*, Heb. xii. 27; (2) *a change*, Heb. vii. 12.*

μετ-αίρω, *to remove*, intrans., *to depart*, Mat. xiii. 53, xix. 1.*

μετα-καλέω, ῶ, in mid., *to call to one's self, to send for*, Ac. vii. 14, x. 32, xx. 17, xxiv. 25.*

μετα-κινέω, ῶ, *to move away*, pass., *to be moved away*, Col. i. 23.*

μετα-λαμβάνω, *to take a share of*, Ac. ii. 46; *partake*, gen., 2 Tim. ii. 6; *to obtain* (acc.), Ac. xxiv. 25.

μετά-ληψις (W. H. -λημψις), εως, ἡ, *participation;* εἰς μ., *to be received*, 1 Tim. iv. 3.*

μετ-αλλάσσω, *to change* one thing (acc.) for (ἐν, εἰς) another, Ro. i. 25, 26.*

μετα-μέλομαι, μελήσομαι, 1st aor. μετεμελήθην, dep., pass., *to change one's mind*, Mat. xxi. 30, 32; Heb. vii. 21; *to repent, to feel sorrow for, regret*, Mat. xxvii. 3, 2 Cor. vii. 8. *Syn.:* μετανοέω is the nobler word, the regular expression for thorough repentance; μεταμέλομαι is more loosely used, generally expressing sorrow, regret or remorse.

μετα-μορφόω, ῶ, *to change the form, to transform*, Mat. xvii. 2; Mar. ix. 2; 2 Cor. iii. 18; Ro. xii. 2.*

μετα-νοέω, ῶ, ήσω, *to change one's views* and *purpose, to repent*, as Mat. iii. 2; Ac. viii. 22. *Syn.:* see μεταμέλομαι.

μετάνοια, ας, ἡ, *change of mind, repentance*, as Mat. iii. 8, 11.

μετα-ξύ (σύν or ξύν), adv. of time, *meanwhile*, Jn. iv. 31; *afterwards*, perh., Ac. xiii. 42 (see Gr. § 298, 7 *b*); as prep. with gen., *between*, of place, Mat. xxiii. 35.

μετα-πέμπω, in mid., *to send for to one's self, to summon*, Ac. x. 5, 22, 29, xi. 13, xxiv. 24, 26, xxv. 3; pass., x. 29.*

μετα-στρέφω (with 2d fut. and 2d aor. pass.), *to turn about, to change*, Ja. iv. 9; Ac. ii. 20; *to pervert, to corrupt*, Gal. i. 7.*

μετα-σχηματίζω, ίσω, *to change the figure of, transfigure*, Phil. iii. 21; mid., *to assume the appearance of any one*, 2 Cor. xi. 13, 14, 15; fig., *to transfer, i.e., to speak by way of illustration*, 1 Cor. iv. 6.*

μετα-τίθημι, *to transpose, to transfer*, Ac. vii. 16; Heb. xi. 5; *to change*, Heb. vii. 12; mid., *to transfer one's self, i.e., to fall away, to desert*, Gal. i. 6; *to pervert*, Ju. 4.*

μετ-έπειτα, adv., *afterwards*, Heb. xii. 17.*

μετ-έχω, μετασχήσω, 2d aor. μετέσχον, *to be partaker of, to share in*, 1 Cor. ix. 10, 12, x. 17, 21, 30; Heb. ii. 14, v. 13, vii. 13.*

μετεωρίζω, in pass., *to be troubled with anxiety, to be in suspense*, Lu. xii. 29.*

μετ-οικεσία, ας, ἡ, *change of abode, migration* (of the Babylonian exile), Mat. i. 11, 12, 17.*

μετ-οικίζω, ιῶ, *to cause to change one's habitation, to cause to migrate*, Ac. vii. 4, 43.*

μετοχή, ῆς, ἡ, *a sharing, a fellowship*, 2 Cor. vi. 14.*

μέτοχος, ου, ὁ (prop. adj.), *a partaker*, Heb. iii. 1, 14, vi. 4, xii. 8; *a partner, an associate*, Heb. i. 9; Lu. v. 7.*

μετρέω, ῶ, *to measure*, Rev. xi. 2; Lu. vi. 38; met., *to estimate, to judge of*, 2 Cor. x. 12.

μετρητής, οῦ, ὁ, prop. *a measurer; an amphora*, a liquid measure containing 72 sextarii, or somewhat less than 9 English gallons, Jn. ii. 6.*

μετριο-παθέω, ῶ, *to treat with moderation, bear gently with* (R. V.), Heb. v. 2.*

μετρίως, adv., *moderately*, Ac. xx. 12.*

μέτρον, ου, τό, *a measure*, Mat. xxiii. 32; Mar. iv. 24; *a measuring-rod*, Rev. xxi. 15; *a definite portion* or *measure*, Ro. xii. 3; Ep. iv. 16; adv. phrases, ἐκ μέτρου, *by measure, sparingly*, Jn. iii. 34; ἐν μέτρῳ, *in due measure*, Ep. iv. 16.

μέτωπον, ου, τό (ὤψ), *the forehead*, Rev. vii. 3, ix. 4 (only in Rev.).

μέχρι, or μέχρις, adv., as prep. with gen., *unto*, time, Mat. xiii 30; Mar. xiii. 30; place, Ro. xv. 19; degree, 2 Tim. ii 9; Heb. xii. 4; as conj., *until*, Ep. iv. 13.

μή, a negative particle, *not;* for

distinction between μή and οὐ, see Gr. § 401, Wi. § 55, 1, Bu. 351; elliptically, *lest*, see Gr. § 384, Wi. § 56, 2*b*, Bu. 241 sq.; interrogatively, see Gr. § 369, Wi. § 57, 3*b*, Bu. 248; for the combination οὐ μή, see Gr. § 377, Wi. § 57, 3*b*, Bu. 211 sq.

μή-γε, in the phrase εἰ δὲ μήγε, *but if not*, emphatic.

μηδαμῶς, adv., *by no means*, Ac. x. 14, xi. 8.*

μηδέ, compare οὐδέ, and see Gr. § 401, Wi. § 55, 6, Bu. 366 sq.; *not even*, Mar. ii. 2; 1 Cor. v. 11; generally used after a preceding μή, *and not, neither, but not, nor yet*, as Mat. vi. 25, vii. 6.

μηδείς, μηδεμία, μηδέν (εἷς), differing from οὐδείς as μή from οὐ (see Gr. § 401, Wi. § 55, 1, Bu. 351); *not one, no one, no person* or *thing, nothing*, Mat. viii. 4; Mar. v. 26; Gal. vi. 3.

μηδέ-ποτε, adv., *never*, 2 Tim. iii. 7.*

μηδέ-πω, adv., *not yet*, Heb. xi. 7.*

Μῆδος, ου, ὁ, *a Mede*, Ac. ii. 9.*

μηκέτι, adv. (ἔτι) *no more, no longer*, Mar. ix. 25, xi. 14; Ac. iv. 17.

μῆκος, ους, τό, *length*, Ep. iii. 18; Rev. xxi. 16.*

μηκύνω, *to make long*; pass., *to grow up*, as plants, Mar. iv. 27.*

μηλωτή, ῆς, ἡ, *a sheepskin*, Heb. xi. 37.*

μήν, a part. of strong affirmation, N. T. only in the combination ἦ μήν, *assuredly, certainly*, Heb. vi. 14 (W. H. εἰ μήν).*

μήν, μηνός, ὁ, (1) *a month*, as Ac. vii. 20; (2) *the new moon*, as a festival, Gal. iv. 10.

μηνύω, *to show, declare*, Lu. xx. 37; Jn. xi. 57; Ac. xxiii. 30; 1 Cor. x. 28.*

μὴ οὐκ, an interrogative formula, expecting the answer "yes," Ro. x. 18, 19; 1 Cor. ix. 4, 5.

μή-ποτε, adv., *never*, Heb. ix. 17; as conj., *lest ever, lest perhaps, lest at any time*, Lu. xii. 58; Ac. v. 39; interrog. part., *whether indeed*, Jn. vii. 26; Lu. iii. 15.

μή που, *lest anywhere*, Ac. xxvii. 29 (W. H., for Rec. μήπως).

μή-πω, adv., *not yet*, Ro. ix. 11; Heb. ix. 8.*

μή-πως, conj., *lest in any way, lest perhaps*, as Ac. xxvii. 29 (W. H. μή που), 1 Th. iii. 5.

μηρός, οῦ, ὁ, *the thigh*, Rev. xix. 16.*

μήτε, conj., differing from οὔτε as μή from οὐ (see Gr. § 401); *and not*, used after a preceding μή or μήτε, *neither ... nor*; in Mar. iii. 20, *not even*, W. H. read μηδέ.

μήτηρ, τρός, ἡ, *a mother*, Mat. i. 18, ii. 11; met., *a mother city*, Gal. iv. 26.

μήτι, adv., interrogatively used, *is it? whether at all?* generally expecting a negative answer; μήτιγε (W. H., Rec. μήτι γε), *not to say then?* 1 Cor. vi. 3.

μήτις (W. H. μή τις), pron. interrog., *has* or *is any one? whether any one?* Jn. iv. 33.*

μήτρα, ας, ἡ, *the womb*, Lu. ii. 23; Ro. iv. 19.*

μητρ-αλῴας (W. H. -ολῴας), ου, ὁ, *a matricide*, 1 Tim. i. 9.*

μία, fem. of εἷς, *one*.

μιαίνω, ανῶ, perf. pass. μεμίασμαι, *to stain, pollute, defile*, Jn. xviii. 28; Tit. i. 15, Heb. xii. 15; Ju. 8.*

μίασμα, ατος, τό, *pollution, defilement*, 2 Pet. ii. 20.*

μιασμός, οῦ, ὁ, *the act of defilement, pollution*, 2 Pet. ii. 10.*

μίγμα, ατος, τό, *a mixture*, Jn. xix. 39 (W. H. text ἕλιγμα).*

μίγνυμι, μίξω, ἔμιξα, perf. pass. μέμιγμαι, *to mix, to mingle*, Mat. xxvii. 34; Lu. xiii. 1; Rev. viii. 7, xv. 2.*

μικρός, ά, όν, *little, small, i.e.*, in size, Mat. xiii. 32; quantity, 1 Cor. v. 6; number, Lu. xii. 32; time, Jn. vii. 33; dignity, Mat x. 42; age, Mat. xviii. 6, 10, 14.

Μίλητος, ου, ἡ, *Miletus*, Ac. xx. 15, 17; 2 Tim. iv. 20.*

μίλιον, ου, τό (Lat. *miliarium*), *a mile* (somewhat less than our mile), Mat. v. 41.*

μιμέομαι, οῦμαι, dep. mid., *to imitate*, 2 Th. iii. 7, 9; Heb. xiii. 7; 3 Jn. 11.*

μιμητής, οῦ, ὁ, *an imitator*, as 1 Cor. iv. 16.

μιμνήσκω (μνα-), mid., with fut. in pass. form μνησθήσομαι, 1st aor. ἐμνήσθην, perf. μέμνημαι, *to call to mind, to remember*, gen. pers. or thing, Mat. xxvi. 75; Lu. xxiii. 42; pass., *to be remembered, to be had in mind*, only Ac. x. 31; Rev. xvi. 16.

μισέω, ῶ, ήσω, *to hate, to detest*, Mat. v. 43; Jn. vii. 7; Ro. ix. 13.

μισθ-απο-δοσία, ας, ἡ, *recompense*, as (1) *reward*, Heb. x. 35, xi. 26; (2) *punishment*, Heb. ii. 2. (N. T.)*

μισθ-απο-δότης, ου, ὁ, *a rewarder*, Heb. xi. 6. (N. T.)*

μίσθιος, α, ον, *hired*, as subst., *a hired servant*, Lu. xv. 17, 19, 21 (W. H. in br.).*

μισθός, οῦ, ὁ, *hire, wages, recompense*, Mat. xx. 8; used of *reward*, Mat. v. 12, 46; of *punishment*, 2 Pet. ii. 13.

μισθόω, ῶ, ώσω, mid., *to hire*, Mat. xx. 1, 7.*

μίσθωμα, ατος, τό, *hire, rent; anything rented*, as a house, Ac. xxviii. 30.*

μισθωτός, οῦ, ὁ, *a hired servant*, Mar. i. 20; Jn. x. 12, 13.*

Μιτυλήνη, ης, ἡ, *Mitylene*, the capital of Lesbos, Ac. xx. 14.*

Μιχαήλ, ὁ (Heb. *who is like God?*), *Michael*, an archangel, Ju. 9; Rev. xii. 7.*

μνᾶ, ᾶς, ἡ, *a mina*, silver money = 100 δραχμαί, or about sixteen or seventeen dollars, Lu. xix. 13–25.*

μνάομαι, see μιμνήσκω.

Μνάσων, ωνος, ὁ, *Mnason*, Ac. xxi. 16.*

μνεία, ας, ἡ, *remembrance, recollection*, Phil. i. 3; 1 Th. iii. 6; μνείαν ποιεῖσθαι, *to mention*, Ro. i. 9.

μνῆμα, ατος, τό, *a monument, a tomb*, Mar. v. 5; Lu. xxiii. 53; less frequent than the following.

μνημεῖον, ου, τό, *a tomb, a sepulchre*, Mat. viii. 28; Jn. xi. 31.

μνήμη, ης, ἡ, *remembrance, mention*; μνήμην ποιεῖσθαι, *to make mention*, 2 Pet. i. 15.*

μνημονεύω, *to remember* (ὅτι),

recollect, call to mind (gen. or acc.), Mat. xvi. 9; Ac. xx. 31; *to be mindful of*, Heb. xi. 15; *to make mention of* (περί, gen.), Heb. xi. 22.

μνημόσυνον, ου, τό, *a memorial, honorable remembrance*, Mat. xxvi. 13; Mar. xiv. 9; Ac. x. 4.*

μνηστεύω, *to ask in marriage;* pass., *to be betrothed*, Mat. i. 18; Lu. i. 27, ii. 5.*

μογι-λάλος, ου, ὁ (prop. adj.), *one speaking with difficulty, a stammerer*, Mar. vii. 32.*

μόγις, adv., *with difficulty, hardly*, Lu. ix. 39 (W. H. μόλις).*

μόδιος, ου, ὁ (Lat.), *a dry measure* (16 sextarii), containing about a peck; *a modius*, Mat. v. 15; Mar. iv. 21; Lu. xi. 33. (N. T.)*

μοιχαλίς, ίδος, ἡ, *an adulteress*, Ro. vii. 3; fig., for departure from God, Mat. xvi. 4; Ja. iv. 4. (S.)

μοιχάομαι, ῶμαι, *to commit adultery*, Mat. v. 32.

μοιχεία, ας, ἡ, *adultery*, Mat. xv. 19.

μοιχεύω, σω, *to commit adultery*, abs. (acc., Mat. v. 28); fig., of forsaking God, Rev. ii. 22.

μοιχός, οῦ, ὁ, *an adulterer*, Lu. xviii. 11; 1 Cor. vi. 9; Heb. xiii. 4; Ja. iv. 4 (not W. H.).*

μόλις, adv., *with difficulty, hardly*, Lu. ix. 39 (W. H.); Ac. xiv. 18, xxvii. 7, 8, 16; Ro. v. 7; 1 Pet. iv. 18.*

Μολόχ, ὁ (Heb.), *Moloch*, Ac. vii. 43 (from S.).*

μολύνω, υνῶ, *to pollute, to defile*, 1 Cor. viii. 7; Rev. iii. 4, xiv. 4.*

μολυσμός, οῦ, ὁ, *pollution, defilement*, 2 Cor. vii. 1. (S.)*

μομφή, ῆς, ἡ, *complaint, ground of complaint*, Col. iii. 13.*

μονή, ῆς, ἡ, *an abode, a dwelling-place*, Jn. xiv. 2, 23.*

μονο-γενής, ές, gen. οῦς, *only begotten*, Lu. vii. 12, viii. 42, ix. 38; Heb. xi. 17; of Christ, Jn. i. 14, 18, iii. 16, 18; 1 Jn. iv. 9.*

μόνος, η, ον, *only, alone, single*, Lu. xxiv. 18; *solitary, without company*, Mar. vi. 47; *forsaken, desolate*, Jn. viii. 29; adv., μόνον, *only*.

μον-όφθαλμος, ον, *having but one eye*, Mat. xviii. 9; Mar. ix. 47.*

μονόω, ῶ, *to leave alone;* pass., *to be left alone* or *desolate*, 1 Tim. v. 5.*

μορφή, ῆς, ἡ, *outward appearance, form, shape*, Mar. xvi. 12; Phil. ii. 6, 7.* *Syn.:* see ἰδέα.

μορφόω, ῶ, ώσω, *to form, to fashion*, Gal. iv. 19.*

μόρφωσις, εως, ἡ, *form, semblance*, 2 Tim. iii. 5; *form, system*, Ro. ii. 20.*

μοσχο-ποιέω, ῶ, *to make an image of a calf*, Ac. vii. 41. (N. T.)*

μόσχος, ου, ὁ, ἡ, *a calf, a young bullock*, Lu. xv. 23, 27, 30; Heb. ix. 12, 19; Rev. iv. 7.*

μουσικός, ή, όν, *skilled in music, a musician*, Rev. xviii. 22.*

μόχθος, ου, ὁ, *wearisome labor, toil*, 2 Cor. xi. 27; 1 Th. ii. 9; 2 Th. iii. 8.*

μυελός, οῦ, ὁ, *marrow*, Heb. iv. 12.*

μυέω, ῶ, *to initiate into, to instruct*, Phil. iv. 12.*

μῦθος, ου, ὁ, *a word;* hence, *a fiction, a fable, a falsehood*, 1 Tim. i. 4, iv. 7; 2 Tim. iv. 4; Tit. i. 14; 2 Pet. i. 16.*

μυκάομαι, ῶμαι, *to bellow, to roar*, as a lion, Rev. x. 3.*

μυκτηρίζω, *to turn up the nose; to mock, deride*, Gal. vi. 7.*

μυλικός, ή, όν, *pertaining to a mill;* with λίθος, *millstone*, Mar. ix. 42 (not W. H.); Lu. xvii. 2 (W. H.). (N. T.)*

μύλινος, η, ον, in sense of foregoing, Rev. xviii. 21 (W. H.).*

μύλος, ου, ὁ, *a millstone*, as Mat. xviii. 6.

μυλών, ῶνος, ὁ, *a mill-house*, the place where grain was ground, Mat. xxiv. 41 (W. H. μύλος).*

Μύρα (W. H. Μύρρα), ων, τά, *Myra*, a city near the coast of Lycia, Ac. xxvii. 5.*

μυριάς, άδος, ἡ, *a myriad, ten thousand*, Ac. xix. 19; *a vast multitude*, Lu. xii. 1; Ac. xxi. 20; Heb. xii. 22; Ju. 14; Rev. v. 11, ix. 16.*

μυρίζω, σω, *to anoint*, Mar. xiv. 8.*

μυρίοι, ίαι, ία, *innumerable*, 1 Cor. iv. 15, xiv. 19; μύριοι, ιαι, ια, *ten thousand*, Mat. xviii. 24.*

μύρον, ου, τό, *ointment*, Mat. xxvi. 7.

Μυσία, ας, ἡ, *Mysia*, Ac. xvi. 7, 8.*

μυστήριον, ου, τό, *a mystery, anything hidden, a secret*, Mat. xiii. 11; Ro. xi. 25. In classical Greek, τὰ μυστήρια are *hidden religious rites and knowledge*, revealed only to the initiated; hence, the word is used in N. T. of the truths of the Gospel as *mysteries* partly hidden, partly revealed, Ep. iii. 9; Col. i. 26, iv. 3; 1 Tim. iii. 16; *a hidden meaning*, Ep. v. 32; Rev. i. 20.

μυωπάζω, *to see dimly*, 2 Pet. i. 9.*

μώλωψ, ωπος, ὁ, *a bruise, a stripe*, 1 Pet. ii. 24.*

μωμάομαι, ῶμαι, dep., aor. mid. and pass., *to blame, to find fault with*, 2 Cor. vi. 3, viii. 20.*

μῶμος, ου, ὁ, *a blemish;* met., *disgrace*, 2 Pet. ii. 13.*

μωραίνω, ανῶ, *to make foolish*, 1 Cor. i. 20; pass., *to become foolish*, Ro. i. 22; *to become insipid, tasteless*, like spoiled salt, Mat. v. 13; Lu. xiv. 34.*

μωρία, ας, ἡ, *folly, absurdity*, 1 Cor. i. 18, 21, 23, ii. 14, iii. 19.*

μωρο-λογία, ας, ἡ, *foolish talking*, Ep. v. 4.*

μωρός, ά, όν, *stupid, foolish*, Mat. vii. 26, xxiii. 17, 19, (on Mat. v. 22, see Gr. § 153, ii.); τὸ μωρὸν, *foolishness*, 1 Cor. i. 25, 27.

Μωσῆς (W. H. Μωυσῆς), έως, dat. εἶ or ῇ; acc. ῆν (once έα, Lu. xvi. 29), ὁ, *Moses*, met., the books of Moses, *the Pentateuch*, Lu. xvi. 29; 2 Cor. iii. 15.

N

N, ν, νῦ, *nu, n*, the thirteenth letter. As a numeral, ν′ = 50; ͵ν = 50,000.

Ναασσών, ὁ (Heb.), *Naasson*, Mat. i. 4; Lu. iii. 32.*

Ναγγαί, ὁ (Heb.), *Naggai*, Lu. iii. 25.*

Ναζαρέτ, -ρέθ or -ρά (W. H.

have all the forms), ἡ, *Nazareth*, Mat. ii. 23; Lu. ii. 4, 39, 51.

Ναζαρηνός, οῦ, ὁ, *a Nazarene*, as Mar. i. 24.

Ναζωραῖος, ου, ὁ, *a Nazarene*, an appellation of Christ, Mat. ii. 23, xxvi. 71; Christians are called οἱ Ναζωραῖοι, Ac. xxiv. 5.

Ναθάν (W. H. -άμ), ὁ (Heb.), *Nathan*, Lu. iii. 31.*

Ναθαναήλ, ὁ, *Nathanael*, perhaps the same as *Bartholomew*, Jn. i. 45–49, xxi. 2.*

ναί, adv., affirming, *yes*, Mat. ix. 28; *even so*, Mat. xi. 26; Lu. x. 21; Rev. xxii. 20; *yea*, strongly affirming, Lu. vii. 26.

Ναΐν, ἡ, *Nain*, Lu. vii. 11.*

ναός, οῦ, ὁ (ναίω), *a temple, a shrine*, in general, Ac. xix. 24; *the temple*, Mat. xxiii. 16; met., used of Jesus Christ, Jn. ii. 19, 20; of Christians generally, 1 Cor. iii. 16; 2 Cor. vi. 16. *Syn.*: see ἱερόν.

Ναούμ, ὁ (Heb.), *Nahum*, Lu. iii. 25 (not the prophet).*

νάρδος, ου, ἡ, *nard, oil* or *ointment*, Mar. xiv. 3; Jn. xii. 3.*

Νάρκισσος, ου, ὁ, *Narcissus*, Ro. xvi. 11.*

ναυαγέω, ῶ (ἄγνυμι), *to suffer shipwreck*, 2 Cor. xi. 25; fig., 1 Tim. i. 19.*

ναύ-κληρος, ου, ὁ, *a ship-master*, or *owner*, Ac. xxvii. 11.*

ναῦς, acc. ναῦν, ἡ, *a ship*, Ac. xxvii. 41.*

ναύτης, ου, ὁ, *a sailor*, Ac. xxvii. 27, 30; Rev. xviii. 17.*

Ναχώρ, ὁ (Heb.), *Nachor*, Lu. iii. 34.*

νεανίας, ου, ὁ, *a young man, a youth*, Ac. vii. 58, xx. 9, xxiii. 17, 18, 22 (not W. H.).*

νεανίσκος, ου, ὁ, *a young man*, Mat. xix. 20; plur., of soldiers, Mar. xiv. 51; 1 Jn. ii. 13, 14; *an attendant*, Ac. v. 10.

Νεάπολις, εως, ἡ, *Neapolis*, Ac. xvi. 11.*

Νεεμάν (W. H. Ναιμάν), ὁ (Heb.), *Naaman*, Lu. iv. 27.*

νεκρός, ά, όν, *dead*, (1) lit., as Mat. xi. 5; οἱ νεκροί, *the dead*, generally, 1 Pet. iv. 6; (2) fig., *dead*, spiritually, Ep. ii. 1; *dead* to (dat.), Ro. vi. 11; *inactive, inoperative*, Ro. vii. 8.

νεκρόω, ῶ, *to put to death*; fig., *to deprive of power, to render weak* and *impotent*, Ro. iv. 19; Col. iii. 5; Heb. xi. 12.*

νέκρωσις, εως, ἡ, *death, a being put to death*, 2 Cor. iv. 10; *deadness, impotency*, Ro. iv. 19.*

νεο-μηνία, see νουμηνία.

νέος, α, ον, (1) *new, fresh*, Mat. ix. 17; 1 Cor. v. 7; Col. iii. 10; (2) *young*, of persons, Tit. ii. 4. *Syn.*: see καινός.

νεοσσός (W. H. νοσσός), οῦ, ὁ, *a young bird*, Lu. ii. 24.*

νεότης, τητος, ἡ, *youth*, Lu. xviii. 21; 1 Tim. iv. 12.

νεό-φυτος, ον, *newly planted*; fig., *a recent convert*, 1 Tim. iii. 6.*

Νέρων, ωνος, ὁ, *Nero*, the Roman emperor, 2 Tim. iv. 23 (Rec.).*

νεύω, σω, *to nod*; so, *to beckon, to signify*, Jn. xiii. 24; Ac. xxiv. 10.*

νεφέλη, ης, ἡ, *a cloud*, Mar. ix. 7, xiii. 26.

Νεφθαλείμ, ὁ (Heb.), *Naphtali*, Mat. iv. 13, 15; Rev. vii. 6.*

νέφος, ους, τό, *a cloud*; met., *a multitude, a great company*, Heb. xii. 1.*

νεφρός, οῦ, ὁ, *a kidney*, plur., *the kidneys, the loins*, used (as Heb.) for the secret thoughts, desires, and purposes, Rev. ii. 23.*

νεω-κόρος, ου, ὁ, ἡ (ναός and κορέω, *to sweep*), *a temple-keeper*, a designation of the people of Ephesus, Ac. xix. 35.*

νεωτερικός, ή, όν, *youthful, juvenile*, 2 Tim. ii. 22.*

νεώτερος, α, ον (comp. of νέος, which see), *younger, inferior in rank*, Lu. xv. 12, 13, xxii. 26; 1 Tim. v. 11, 14.

νή, adv., of affirmative swearing, *by*, with acc., 1 Cor. xv. 31.*

νήθω, *to spin*, Mat. vi. 28; Lu. xii. 27.*

νηπιάζω, *to be an infant*, 1 Cor. xiv. 20.*

νήπιος, α, ον, *infantile*; as subst., *an infant, a babe*, Mat. xxi. 16; 1 Cor. xiii. 11; used of an age below manhood, Gal. iv. 1; fig., of *unlearned, unenlightened* persons, Mat. xi. 25; Ro. ii. 20; 1 Th. ii. 7 (W. H.).

Νηρεύς, έως, ὁ, *Nereus*, Ro. xvi. 15.*

Νηρί, ὁ (Heb.), *Neri*, Lu. iii. 27.*

νησίον, ου, τό (dim. of νῆσος), *a small island*, Ac. xxvii. 16.*

νῆσος, ου, ἡ (νέω, *to swim*), *an island*, Ac. xiii. 6, xxvii. 26.

νηστεία, ας, ἡ, *a fasting, a fast*, Mat. xvii. 21 (W. H. omit); Ac. xiv. 23; *the day of atonement, the chief Jewish fast-day*, Ac. xxvii. 9; *want of food*, 2 Cor. vi. 5, xi. 27.

νηστεύω, σω, *to abstain from food, to fast*, Mat. iv. 2, vi. 16–18.

νῆστις, ιος, plur. νήστεις, ὁ, ἡ, *fasting*, Mat. xv. 32; Mar. viii. 3.*

νηφάλιος or -λεος, ον, *sober, temperate*, 1 Tim. iii. 2, 11; Tit. ii. 2.*

νήφω, ψω, *to be sober, temperate*, fig., 1 Th. v. 6, 8.

Νίγερ, ὁ (Lat.), *Niger*, Ac. xiii. 1.*

Νικάνωρ, ορος, ὁ, *Nicanor*, Ac. vi. 5.*

νικάω, ῶ, ήσω, *to be victorious*, abs., Rev. iii. 21; *to conquer, overcome* (acc.), Lu. xi. 22; Jn. xvi. 33.

νίκη, ης, ἡ, *victory*, 1 Jn. v. 4.*

Νικό-δημος, ου, ὁ, *Nicodemus*, Jn. iii. 1.

Νικολαΐτης, ου, ὁ, *a follower of Nicolaus* (probably a Greek equivalent for *Balaam*), *a Nicolaitan*, Rev. ii. 6, 15.*

Νικό-λαος, ου, ὁ, *Nicolaus*, Ac. vi. 5 (not to be confounded with preced.).*

Νικό-πολις, εως, ἡ, *Nicopolis*, Tit. iii. 12. Several cities of the name existed; this was probably on the promontory of Epirus.*

νῖκος, ους, τό, *victory*, 1 Cor. xv. 55, 57; εἰς νῖκος, from S., *to a victorious consummation, utterly*, Mat. xii. 20; 1 Cor. xv. 54.*

Νινευΐ, ἡ (Heb.), *Nineveh*, Lu. xi. 32 (W. H. read following).*

Νινευίτης (W. H. -είτης), ου, ὁ, *a Ninevite*, Mat. xii. 41; Lu. xi. 30, 32 (W. H.).*

νιπτήρ, ῆρος, ὁ, *a basin*, for washing hands and feet, Jn. xiii. 5. (N. T.)*

νίπτω, ψω, *to wash* (acc.), Jn. xiii. 8; mid., *to wash one's self*, acc. of part, as Mar. vii. 3. *Syn.:* see λούω.

νοέω, ῶ, ήσω, *to understand*, *to consider*, abs., or with acc., or ὅτι, Jn. xii. 40; Ep. iii. 4; Mar xiii. 14.

νόημα, ατος, τό, (1) *a thought*, *purpose*, *device*, 2 Cor. ii. 11, x. 5; Phil. iv. 7; (2) *the mind*, *i.e.*, *the understanding* or *intellect*, 2 Cor. iii. 14, iv. 4, xi. 3.*

νόθος, η, ον, *illegitimate*, *bastard*, Heb. xii. 8.*

νομή, ῆς, ἡ (νέμω, *to pasture*), (1) *pasturage*, Jn. x. 9; (2) met., *growth*, *increase*, as of a gangrene, 2 Tim. ii. 17.*

νομίζω, σω (νόμος), (1) *to think*, *to suppose*, *to expect*, as the result of thinking, Mat. v. 17, xx. 10; (2) pass., *to be customary*, only Ac. xvi. 13 (but see W. H. and R. V.).

νομικός, ή, όν, *pertaining to* (the) *law*, Tit. iii. 9; as subst., *a person learned in* or *teacher of the Mosaic law*, Mat. xxii. 35; Tit. iii. 13.

νομίμως, adv., *lawfully*, 1 Tim. i. 8; 2 Tim. ii. 5.*

νόμισμα, ατος, τό, (lawful) *money*, *coin*, Mat. xxii. 19.*

νομο-διδάσκαλος, ου, ὁ, *a teacher and interpreter of the* Mosaic *law*, Lu v. 17; Ac. v. 34; 1 Tim. i. 7. (N. T.)*

νομο-θεσία, ας, ἡ, *lawgiving*, *legislation*, Ro. ix. 4.*

νομο-θετέω, ῶ, *to enact laws*; pass., *to be enacted*, Heb. viii. 6; *to be furnished with laws*, Heb. vii. 11.*

νομο-θέτης, ου, ὁ (τίθημι), *a lawgiver*, *legislator*, Ja. iv. 12.*

νόμος, ου, ὁ (νέμω, *to apportion*), *a law*, *an edict*, *a statute*, Lu. ii. 22; *a standard of acting* or *judging*, Ro. iii. 27; *a written law*, Ro. ii. 14; *the Mosaic economy*, Mat. v. 18; Ro. x. 4; *the Christian dispensation* or *doctrines*, Gal. vi. 2; Ro. xiii. 8; met., for the books containing the Mosaic law, *i.e.*, the five books of Moses, Mat. xii. 5; and for the Old Testament generally, Jn. x. 34. On the article with νόμος, see Gr. § 234, Wi. § 19, 1 *a*, Bu. 89.

νόος, see νοῦς.

νοσέω, ῶ, *to be sick*; fig., *to have a diseased appetite* or *craving for*, περί (acc.), 1 Tim. vi. 4.*

νόσημα, ατος, τό, *disease*, *sickness*, Jn. v. 4 (W. H. omit).*

νόσος, ου, ἡ, *disease*, *sickness*, Mat. iv. 23, 24.

νοσσιά, ᾶς, ἡ, *a brood of young birds*, Lu. xiii. 34. (S.)*

νοσσίον, ου, τό, *a brood of young birds*, Mat. xxiii. 37.*

νοσσός, see νεοσσός.

νοσφίζω, in mid., *to remove for one's self*, *to purloin*, Ac. v. 2, 3; Tit. ii. 10.*

νότος, ου, ὁ, *the south wind*, Lu. xii. 55; *the South*, Lu. xi. 31.

νου-θεσία, ας, ἡ, *admonition*, *counsel*, 1 Cor. x. 11; Ep. vi. 4; Tit. iii. 10.*

νου-θετέω, ῶ, *to admonish*, *to counsel*, Ac. xx. 31.

νου-μηνία (W. H. νεο-), ας, ἡ, *the new moon*, as a festival, Col. ii. 16.*

νουν-εχῶς, adv., *wisely*, *judiciously*, Mar. xii. 34.*

νοῦς (orig. νόος), νοός, νοΐ, νοῦν, ὁ, *the mind*, *i.e.*, *the understanding* or *intellect*, Lu. xxiv. 45; Phil. iv. 7; *the reason*, Ro. vii. 25, xii. 2; hence, *any affection of the mind* — as modes of thought — *inclinations* or *dispositions*, Ro. xiv. 5; 1 Cor. i. 10.

Νυμφᾶς, ᾶ, ὁ, *Nymphas*, Col. iv. 15.*

νύμφη, ης, ἡ, *a betrothed woman*, *a bride*, Rev. xviii. 23; *a daughter-in-law*, Mat. x. 35.

νυμφίος, ου, ὁ, *a bridegroom*, Jn. iii. 29.

νυμφών, ῶνος, ὁ, *a bridal chamber*; οἱ υἱοὶ τοῦ νυμφῶνος, *the sons of the bridal chamber*, friends of the bridegroom, Mat. ix. 15; Mar. ii. 19; Lu. v. 34; *a room in which the marriage ceremonies were held*, Mat. xxii. 10 (W. H.). (Ap.)*

νῦν and **νυνί,** adv., (1) of time, *now*, *i.e.*, the actually present; *now*, in relation to time just past, *just now*, *even now*; *now*, in relation to future time, *just at hand*, *even now*, *immediately*; ὁ, ἡ, τὸ νῦν, *the present*, with subst. or (neut.) without; (2) of logical connection, *now*, 2 Cor. vii. 9; *now then*, *i.e.*, implying the rise of one thing from another, 1 Cor. xiv. 6; (3) in commands and appeals, νῦν is emphatic, *at this instant*, Mat. xxvii. 42; Ja. iv. 13.

νύξ, νυκτός, ἡ, *the night*, *nighttime*, lit., Ac. xvi. 33; often fig., *a time of darkness and ignorance*, Ro. xiii. 12; 1 Th. v. 5; *death*, Jn. ix. 4.

νύσσω, ξω, *to stab*, *to pierce*, Jn xix. 34.*

νυστάζω, ξω, *to nod* in sleep, *to be drowsy*, Mat. xxv. 5; fig., *to delay*, 2 Pet. ii. 3.*

νυχθ-ήμερον, ου, τό, *a night and a day*, *twenty-four hours*, 2 Cor. xi. 25.*

Νῶε, ὁ (Heb.), *Noah*, Lu. iii. 36, xvii. 26, 27.

νωθρός, ά, όν, *sluggish*, *dull*, *stupid*, Heb. v. 11, vi. 12.*

νῶτος, ου, ὁ, *the back* of men or animals, Ro. xi. 10.*

Ξ

Ξ, ξ, ξῖ, *xi*, the double letter *x* (= γs, κs, or χs), the fourteenth letter of the alphabet. As numeral, ξ′ = 60; ͵ξ = 60,000.

ξενία, ας, ἡ, *hospitality*; *a lodging*, Ac. xxviii. 23; Philem. 22.*

ξενίζω, σω, (1) *to receive as a guest* (acc.), Ac. x. 23, xxviii. 7; Heb. xiii. 2; pass., *to be entertained*, *to lodge*, Ac. x. 6, 18, 32, xxi. 16; (2) *to astonish by strangeness*, Ac. xvii. 20; pass., *to think strangely of*, *to be surprised at* (dat.), 1 Pet. iv. 4, 12.*

ξενο-δοχέω, ῶ, *to entertain guests*, *to practice hospitality*, 1 Tim. v. 10.*

ξένος, η, ον, masc., *a guest-friend*; as subst.. *a stranger*, *foreigner*, Mat. xxv. 35, 38, 43, 44; *a host*, Ro. xvi. 23; *alien*, Ep. ii. 12; *new*, *novel*, Heb. xiii. 9; 1 Pet. iv. 12.

ξέστης, ου, ὁ (the Latin *sextarius*), *a sextarius*, a vessel for measuring liquids, holding about a pint; *a pitcher*, of any size, Mar. vii. 4, 8 (W. H. omit).*

ξηραίνω, ανῶ, 1st aor., act., ἐξήρανα, 1st aor., pass., ἐξηράνθην, perf., pass., ἐξήραμμαι (3 s., ἐξήρανται, Mar. xi. 21), *to make dry, to wither*, Ja. i. 11; pass., *to become dry, be withered*, Mat. xiii. 6; *to be dried up*, Rev. xvi. 12; *to be ripened*, as corn, Rev. xiv. 15; *to pine away*, Mar. ix. 18.

ξηρός, ά, όν, *dry, withered*, of a tree, Lu. xxiii. 31; of a useless limb, Mat. xii. 10; Mar. iii. 3 (W. H.); Lu. vi. 6, 8; Jn. v. 3; of land, Heb. xi. 29; ἡ ξηρά (sc. γῆ), *dry land*, Mat. xxiii. 15.*

ξύλινος, ίνη, ινον, *wooden*, 2 Tim. ii. 20; Rev. ix. 20.*

ξύλον, ου, τό, *wood, e.g., timber* in building, 1 Cor. iii. 12; *anything made of wood, e.g., the stocks*, Ac. xvi. 24; *a staff*, Mat. xxvi. 47, 55; *a cross*, Ac. xiii. 29; Gal. iii. 13; *a living tree*, Rev. ii. 7.

ξυράω, ῶ, ήσω, perf. pass. ἐξύρημαι, *to shave*, Ac. xxi. 24; 1 Cor. xi. 5, 6.*

O

Ο, ο, ὂ μικρόν, *omicron*, short *o*, the fifteenth letter. As a numeral, ο′ = 70; ͵ο = 70,000.

ὁ, ἡ, τό, the definite article, *the*, originally demonstrative. For its uses, see Gr. §§ 193–234, Wi. §§ 17–20, Bu. 85–103.

ὀγδοήκοντα, num., indeclin., *eighty*, Lu. ii. 37, xvi. 7.*

ὄγδοος, η, ον, ord., *eighth*; on 2 Pet. ii. 5, see Gr. § 331, Wi. § 37, 2, Bu. 30.

ὄγκος, ου, ὁ, *a weight, an encumbrance*, Heb. xii. 1.*

ὅδε, ἥδε, τόδε, demon. pron., *this, that* (here). See Gr. § 339, Wi. § 23, 5, Bu. 103.

ὁδεύω, *to pass along a way, to journey*, Lu. x. 33.*

ὁδηγέω, ῶ, ήσω, *to lead along a way, to conduct, to guide*, Mat. xv. 14; Lu. vi. 39; Jn. xvi. 13; Ac. viii. 31; Rev. vii. 17.*

ὁδ-ηγός, οῦ, ὁ, *a leader, a guide*, Ac. i. 16; fig., of instructors, Mat. xv. 14, xxiii. 16, 24; Ro. ii. 19.*

ὁδοι-πορέω, ῶ, *to travel, to pursue a way*, Ac. x. 9.*

ὁδοι-πορία, ας, ἡ, *a journey, a journeying*, Jn. iv. 6; 2 Cor. xi. 26.*

ὁδός, οῦ, ἡ, (1) *a way, a road*, Mat. ii. 12; (2) *a going, a progress*, Mar. vi. 8; (3) *a journey*, a day's or a Sabbath day's, Lu. ii. 44; Ac. i. 12; (4) fig., *manner of action, method of proceeding*, Ac. xiii. 10; Mat. xxi. 32; especially (5) *the Christian way*, Ac. ix. 2; 2 Pet. ii. 2; (6) used of Christ himself, *the Way*, Jn. xiv. 6.

ὀδούς, ὀδόντος, ὁ, *a tooth*, Mat. v. 38.

ὀδυνάω, ῶ, in mid. and pass., *to be tormented, to be greatly distressed*, Lu. ii. 48, xvi. 24, 25; Ac. xx. 38.*

ὀδύνη, ης, ἡ, *pain, distress*, of body or mind, Ro. ix. 2; 1 Tim. vi. 10.*

ὀδυρμός, οῦ, ὁ, *lamentation, wailing*, Mat. ii. 18; 2 Cor. vii. 7.*

Ὀζίας, ου, ὁ, *Uzziah*, Mat. i. 8, 9.*

ὄζω, *to stink, be offensive*, Jn. xi. 39.*

ὅθεν, adv., *whence*, of place, source, or cause, Mat. xii. 44; 1 Jn. ii. 18; Heb. ii. 17.

ὀθόνη, ης, ἡ, *a linen cloth*; hence, *a sheet*, Ac. x. 11, xi. 5.*

ὀθόνιον, ου, τό (dim. of ὀθόνη), *a linen bandage*, Jn. xix. 40.

οἶδα, plur. οἴδαμεν (for Attic ἴσμεν), οἴδατε (and Attic ἴστε, Heb. xii. 17), οἴδασι (and Attic ἴσασι, only Ac. xxvi. 4), *I know* (see Gr. § 103, 4, Wi. § 40, 4*b*).

οἰκειακός, ή, όν, see οἰκιακός.

οἰκεῖος, α, ον, *domestic, belonging to a household*, Gal. vi. 10; Ep. ii. 19; 1 Tim. v. 8.*

οἰκέτεια, ας, ἡ, *household, body of servants*, Mat. xxiv. 45 (W. H.).*

οἰκέτης, ου, ὁ, *a domestic, a household servant*, Lu. xvi. 13; Ac. x. 7; Ro. xiv. 4; 1 Pet. ii. 18.

οἰκέω, ῶ, ήσω, trans., *to inhabit*, 1 Tim. vi. 16; intrans., *to dwell*, Ro. viii. 9; 1 Cor. vii. 12, 13.

οἴκημα, ατος, τό, *a dwelling*, used of *a prison*, Ac xii. 7.*

οἰκητήριον, ου, τό, *a dwelling-place, a habitation*, 2 Cor. v. 2; Ju. 6.*

οἰκία, ας, ἡ, (1) *a house*, Lu. xv. 8; (2) met., *a household, a family, goods, i.e.*, a house and all that is in it, Jn. iv. 53; Mar. xii. 40.

οἰκιακός, οῦ, ὁ, *one of a family*, whether child, or servant, Mat. x. 25, 36.*

οἰκοδεσποτέω, ῶ, *to manage a household*, 1 Tim. v. 14.*

οἰκο-δεσπότης, ου, ὁ, *a householder, a master of a house*, Mat. x. 25.

οἰκοδομέω, ῶ, *to erect a building, build*, Lu. xiv. 30; fig., of the building up of character, *to build up, edify*, 1 Cor. x. 23; *to encourage*, 1 Cor. viii. 10.

οἰκο-δομή, ῆς, ἡ (δέμω), *the act of building*; *a building*, lit., Mat. xxiv. 1; of the spiritual body, 2 Cor. v. 1; of the church, Ep. ii. 21; met., *edification, spiritual advancement*, Ro. xiv. 19, xv. 2.

οἰκοδομία, ας, ἡ, *edification*, 1 Tim. i. 4 (W. H. οἰκονομία).*

οἰκο-δόμος, ου, ὁ, *a builder*, Ac. iv. 11 (W. H.).*

οἰκονομέω, ῶ, *to be a steward*, Lu. xvi. 2.*

οἰκονομία, ας, ἡ, *management of household affairs, stewardship*, Lu. xvi. 2–4; *a dispensation*, 1 Cor. x. 17.

οἰκο-νόμος, ου, ὁ (νέμω), *a house-manager, a steward*, Lu. xvi. 1, 3, 8; of the Christian stewardship, 1 Cor. iv. 1; 1 Pet. iv. 10; Tit. i. 7.

οἶκος, ου, ὁ, *a house, a building*, for any purpose (gen.); met., *a family* resident in one house, *a family* perpetuated by succession; *the house* of God, *i.e.*, the temple; *the family* of God, *i.e.*, the church.

οἰκουμένη, ης, ἡ, pres. part. pass. fem. of οἰκέω (sc. γῆ); *the inhabited land*, or *world*; (1) *the Roman empire*, Lu. ii. 1; (2) *the world at large*, Lu. iv. 5, xxi. 26; (3) met., *the inhabitants of the world*

Ac. xvii. 6, 31; (4) *the universe*, Heb. ii. 5.

οἰκ-ουρός, οῦ, ὁ, ἡ (οὖρος, *keeper*), *attending to household affairs, domestic*, Tit. ii. 5 (W. H. οἰκουργός, with same meaning).*

οἰκτείρω, ήσω, *to pity, to have compassion on*, Ro. ix. 15 (from S.).*

οἰκτιρμός, οῦ, ὁ, *compassion, pity*, Ro. xii. 1; 2 Cor. i. 3; Phil. ii. 1; Col. iii. 12; Heb. x. 28.*

οἰκτίρμων, ον, *pitiful, merciful*, Lu. vi. 36; Ja. v. 11.*

οἶμαι, see οἴομαι.

οἰνο-πότης, ου, ὁ, *one given to wine-drinking*, Mat. xi. 19; Lu. vii. 34.*

οἶνος, ου, ὁ, *wine*, Mar. ii. 22; met., *a vine*, Rev. vi. 6; fig., of that which excites or inflames, Rev. xiv. 10, xvii. 2.

οἰνο-φλυγία, ας, ἡ (φλύω, *to overflow*), *drunkenness*, 1 Pet. iv. 3.*

οἴομαι and οἶμαι, *to think, to suppose*, acc. and inf., or ὅτι, Jn. xxi. 25; Phil. i. 16; Ja. i. 7.*

οἷος, α, ον, rel. pron., correl. to τοιοῦτος, *of what kind, such as*.

οἴσω, see φέρω.

ὀκνέω, ῶ, ήσω, *to be slothful, to delay, to hesitate*, Ac. ix. 38.*

ὀκνηρός, ά, όν, *slothful, backward*, Mat. xxv. 26; Ro. xii. 11; Phil. iii. 1.*

ὀκτα-ήμερος, ον, *of* or *belonging to the eighth day*, Phil. iii. 5.*

ὀκτώ, num., indecl., *eight*, Lu. ii. 21.

ὄλεθρος, ου, ὁ, *destruction, perdition*, 1 Cor. v. 5; 1 Th. v. 3; 2 Th. i. 9; 1 Tim. vi. 9.*

ὀλιγο-πιστία, ας, ἡ, *little faith*, Mat. xvii. 20 (W. H.). (N. T.)*

ὀλιγό-πιστος, ον, *of little faith*, Mat. vi. 30. (N. T.)

ὀλίγος, η, ον, (1) *little, small, brief*, Lu. x. 2; Ac. xiv. 28; (2) in plur., *few*, sometimes with gen., Mat. vii. 14; Ac. xvii. 4; (3) neut. as adv., ὀλίγον, of time, *soon*, Lu. v. 3; of space, *a little way*, Mar. vi. 31; (4) with prepositions preced. in various phrases, as ἐν ὀλίγῳ, *with little trouble*, Ac. xxvi. 28.

ὀλιγό-ψυχος, ον, *faint-hearted*, 1 Th. v. 14. (S.)*

ὀλιγωρέω, ῶ, *to care little for, to despise* (gen.), Heb. xii. 5 (from S.).*

ὀλίγως, adv., *a little, scarcely*, 2 Pet. ii. 18 (W. H.).*

ὀλοθρευτής, οῦ, ὁ, *a destroyer*, 1 Cor. x. 10. (N. T.)*

ὀλοθρεύω, *to destroy*, Heb. xi. 28.*

ὁλο-καύτωμα, ατος, τό (καίω), *a whole burnt-offering*, the whole being consumed, Mar. xii. 33; Heb. x. 6, 8. (S.)*

ὁλοκληρία, ας, ἡ, *perfect soundness*, Ac. iii. 16. (S.)*

ὁλό-κληρος, ον, *complete in every part, sound, perfect*, 1 Th. v. 23; Ja. i. 4. *Syn.*: see ἄρτιος.

ὀλολύζω, as from the cry ολ-ολ, *to howl, to lament aloud*, Ja. v. 1.*

ὅλος, η, ον, *all, the whole* (see Gr. § 225, Wi. § 20, 1 *b*, *a*, Bu. 94), Jn. vii. 23; Ja. iii. 2; 1 Jn. v. 19.

ὁλο-τελής, ές, *perfect, complete*, 1 Th. v. 23.*

Ὀλυμπᾶς, ᾶ, ὁ, *Olympas*, Ro. xvi. 15.*

ὄλυνθος, ου, ὁ, *an unripe fig*, one which, not ripening in due time, grows through the winter and falls off in the spring, Rev. vi. 13.*

ὅλως (ὅλος), adv., *wholly, altogether*, 1 Cor. v. 1, vi. 7; with neg., *not at all*, Mat. v. 34; 1 Cor. xv. 29.*

ὄμβρος, ου, ὁ, *a violent rain*, Lu. xii. 54.*

ὁμείρομαι, *to long for*, 1 Th. ii. 8 (W. H., Rec. ἱμείρομαι).*

ὁμιλέω, ῶ, ήσω, *to associate with* (dat.), *to talk with* (πρός, acc.), Lu. xxiv. 14, 15; Ac. xx. 11, xxiv. 26.*

ὁμιλία, ας, ἡ, *intercourse, companionship*, 1 Cor. xv. 33.*

ὅμιλος, ου, ὁ, *a crowd, company*, Rev. xviii. 17 (not W. H.).*

ὁμίχλη, ης, ἡ, *a mist*, 2 Pet. ii. 17 (W. H.).*

ὄμμα, ατος, τό, *an eye*, Mat. xx. 34 (W. H.); Mar. viii. 23.*

ὄμνυμι and ὀμνύω, ὀμόσω (see Gr. § 116, 3, Wi. § 15, Bu. 45), *to swear, to take an oath*, Mar. xiv. 71; *to promise with an oath*, Mar. vi. 23.

ὁμο-θυμαδόν, adv., *with one mind, unanimously*, only in Ac. and Ro. xv. 6.

ὁμοιάζω, σω, *to be like*, Mat. xxiii. 27 (W. H. mrg.); Mar. xiv. 70 (not W. H.). (N. T.)*

ὁμοιο-παθής, ές, *being affected like another* (dat.), *having like passions* or *feelings*, Ac. xiv. 15; Ja. v. 17.*

ὅμοιος, οία, οιον, *like, similar to, resembling* (dat.), Jn. ix. 9; Rev. iv. 3; *of equal rank*, Mat. xxii. 39.

ὁμοιότης, τητος, ἡ, *likeness*, Heb. iv. 15, vii. 15.*

ὁμοιόω, ῶ, ώσω, (1) *to make like*; pass., *to be like*, or *to resemble*, Mat. vi. 8, xiii. 24; Ac. xiv. 11; (2) *to liken, to compare*, Mat. vii. 24; Mar. iv. 30; with acc. and dat.

ὁμοίωμα, ατος, τό, *likeness, similitude*, Ro. i. 23, v. 14, vi. 5, viii. 3; Phil. ii. 7; Rev. ix. 7.* *Syn.*: see εἰκών.

ὁμοίως, adv., *in like manner*, Lu. iii. 11; Jn. v. 19.

ὁμοίωσις, εως, ἡ, *likeness*, Ja. iii. 9.* *Syn.*: see εἰκών.

ὁμο-λογέω, ῶ, ήσω, 1st aor. ὡμολόγησα, *to speak the same thing*; hence, (1) *to confess*, in the sense of conceding or admitting, generally with ὅτι, Mat. xiv. 7; Heb. xi. 13; (2) *to profess*, or *acknowledge openly*, acc., or with ἐν, Mat. x. 32; Lu. xii. 8; Jn. ix. 22; (3) as ἐξομολογέω, *to praise* (dat.), Heb. xiii. 15.

ὁμολογία, ας, ἡ, *a profession*, or *a confession*, 2 Cor. ix. 13; 1 Tim. vi. 12, 13; Heb. iii. 1, iv. 14, x. 23.*

ὁμολογουμένως, adv., *confessedly, by assent of all*, 1 Tim. iii. 16.*

ὁμό-τεχνος, ον, *of the same trade* or *craft*, Ac. xviii. 3.*

ὁμοῦ, adv., *together, at the same place* or *time*, Jn. iv. 36.

ὁμό-φρων, ον (φρήν), *of one mind*, 1 Pet. iii. 8.*

ὀμόω, see ὄμνυμι.

ὅμως, adv., *yet*, 1 Cor. xiv. 7; Gal. iii. 15; with μέντοι, *nevertheless*, Jn. xii. 42.*

ὄναρ, τό, indecl., *a dream*; κατ' ὄναρ, *in a dream*, Mat. i. 20, ii. 12, 13, 19, 22, xxvii. 19.*

ὀνάριον, ου, τό (dim. of ὄνος), *a young ass*, Jn. xii. 14.*

ὀνειδίζω, σω, *to reproach*, *revile*, *upbraid*, Mat. xi. 20; Mar. xvi. 14; Lu. vi. 22.

ὀνειδισμός, οῦ, ὁ, *reproach*, *reviling*, Ro. xv. 3; 1 Tim. iii. 7; Heb. x. 33, xi. 26, xiii. 13. (S.)*

ὄνειδος, ους, τό, *reproach*, *disgrace*, Lu. i. 25.*

'Ονήσιμος, ου, ὁ (*profitable*), *Onesimus*, Col. iv. 9; Philem. 10.*

'Ονησί-φορος, ου, ὁ, *Onesiphorus*, 2 Tim. i. 16, iv. 19.*

ὀνικός, ή, όν, *pertaining to an ass*; μύλος ὀνικός, *a millstone turned by an ass*, *i.e.*, the large upper millstone, Mat. xviii. 6; Lu. xvii. 2 (not W. H.); Mar. ix. 42 (W. H.). (N. T.)*

ὀνίνημι, *to be useful*, *to help*; mid. aor., opt., ὀναίμην, *may I have help* or *joy from*, Philem. 20.*

ὄνομα, ατος, τό, *a name*, almost always of persons; in N. T., as in O. T., the *name* of a person is a mark of what he himself is, the name expresses the character, Mat. i. 21; Mar. iii. 16, v. 9; Lu. i. 31; hence the expressions ποιεῖν τι ἐπὶ τῷ ὀνόματι, ἐν τῷ ὀνόματι, διὰ τοῦ ὀνόματος; the name is often introduced by ὀνόματι, *by name*, once by τοὔνομα (τὸ ὄνομα), Mat. xxvii. 57; *fame*, *reputation*, Ep. i. 21; Phil. ii. 9.

ὀνομάζω, σω, *to give a name to*, Lu. vi. 13, 14; *to mention*, Ep. v. 3; *to call upon the name of*, 2 Tim. ii. 19.

ὄνος, ου, ὁ, ἡ, *an ass*, Mat. xxi. 2, 7; Lu. xiii. 15.

ὄντως, adv. (ὄν, neut. part. of εἰμί), *really*, *truly*, 1 Cor. xiv. 25; 1 Tim. v. 3, 5.

ὄξος, ους, τό, *vinegar*; in N. T., *sour wine*, mixed with water, a common drink of Roman soldiers, Jn. xix. 29, 30.

ὀξύς, εῖα, ύ, (1) *sharp*, as a weapon, Rev. i. 16, ii. 12; (2) *swift*, *eager*, Ro. iii. 15.

ὀπή, ῆς, ἡ, *an opening*, *a cavern*, Ja. iii. 11; Heb. xi. 38.*

ὄπισθεν, adv. of place, *from behind*, *after*, Mat. ix. 20, xv. 23.

ὀπίσω, adv., *behind*, *after*, of place, Lu. vii. 38; of time, Mat. iii. 11; abs., or with gen.; τὰ ὀπίσω, *those things that are behind*, Phil. iii. 14; εἰς τὰ ὀπίσω, *backward*, Jn. xviii. 6.

ὁπλίζω, σω, N. T., mid., *to arm one's self* with, acc., fig., 1 Pet. iv. 1.*

ὅπλον, ου, τό, *an instrument*, Ro. vi. 13; hence, plur., *arms*, *weapons*, Jn. xviii. 3; Ro. xiii. 12; 2 Cor. vi. 7, x. 4.*

ὁποῖος, οία, οῖον, relat. pron., *of what kind* or *manner*, correl. to τοιοῦτος, Ac. xxvi. 29; 1 Cor. iii. 13; Gal. ii. 6; 1 Th. i. 9; Ja. i. 24.*

ὁπότε, adv. of time, *when*, Lu. vi. 3 (W. H. ὅτε).*

ὅπου, adv. of place, *where*, *whither*; *where*, referring to state, Col. iii. 11; *in case that*, 1 Cor. iii. 3.

ὀπτάνω, *to behold*; in pass., *to appear*, Ac. i. 3; see ὁράω. (S.)*

ὀπτασία, ας, ἡ, *a vision*, *a supernatural appearance*, Lu. i. 22, xxiv. 23; Ac. xxvi. 19; 2 Cor. xii. 1.*

ὀπτός, ή, όν, *roasted*, *broiled*, Lu. xxiv. 42.*

ὄπτω, ὄπτομαι, see ὁράω.

ὀπώρα, ας, ἡ, *autumn*, *autumnal fruits*, Rev. xviii. 14.*

ὅπως, rel. adv., *how*, Lu. xxiv. 20; as conj., *in order that*, *so that*; with ἄν, Ac. iii. 19 (see Gr. § 384, 2, Wi. § 42, 6, Bu. 234); after verbs of *beseeching*, and the like, *that*, Mat. ix. 38; Mar. iii. 6.

ὅραμα, ατος, τό, (1) *a spectacle*, Ac. vii. 31; (2) *a vision*, Ac. ix. 10, 12.

ὅρασις, εως, ἡ, *appearance*, Rev. iv. 3; *a vision*, Ac. ii. 17; Rev. ix. 17.

ὁρατός, ή, όν, *visible*, plur., neut., Col. i. 16.*

ὁράω, ῶ, ὄψομαι, ἑώρακα, εἶδον (see Gr. § 103, 4, Wi. § 15, Bu. 64), (1) *to see*, generally; (2) *to look upon* or *contemplate*; (3) *to see*, and so *to participate in*, Lu. xvii. 22; Jn. iii. 36; (4) *to take heed*, Heb. viii. 5; Mat. viii. 4; with μή or equiv., *to beware*, Mat. xvi. 6; (5) pass., *to be seen*, *to appear to*, *to present one's self to* (dat.).

ὀργή, ῆς, ἡ, *anger*, *indignation*, Ep. iv. 31; often of the *wrath* of God, and its manifestation, Ro. i. 18. *Syn.*: see θυμός.

ὀργίζω, σω, *to irritate*, *to provoke*; pass., *to be angry*, abs., Mat. xviii. 34; *to be enraged with*, dat., or ἐπί, dat., Mat. v. 22; Rev. xii. 17.

ὀργίλος, η, ον, *prone to anger*, Tit. i. 7.*

ὀργυιά, ᾶς, ἡ, *a fathom*, about five or six feet, Ac. xxvii. 28.*

ὀρέγω, *to stretch forth*; mid., *to reach after*, *to desire* or *long eagerly for*, gen., 1 Tim. iii. 1, vi. 10; Heb. xi. 16.*

ὀρεινός, ή, όν, *mountainous*, *hilly* (sc. χώρα), Lu. i. 39, 65.*

ὄρεξις, εως, ἡ, *strong desire*, *lust*, Ro. i. 27.*

ὀρθο-ποδέω, ῶ, *to walk in a straight course*, fig., *to act uprightly*, Gal. ii. 14. (N.T.)*

ὀρθός, ή, όν, *upright*, Ac. xiv. 10; *straight*, Heb. xii. 13.*

ὀρθο-τομέω, ῶ (τέμνω), *to cut straight*; met., *to handle rightly*, *i.e.*, *to teach correctly*, 2 Tim. ii. 15. (S.)*

ὀρθρίζω, *to rise early in the morning*, *to come early in the morning*, Lu. xxi. 38. (S.)*

ὀρθρινός, ή, όν, *early in the morning*, Lu. xxiv. 22 (W. H.); Rev. xxii. 16 (not W. H.).*

ὄρθριος, α, ον, *early in the morning*, Lu. xxiv. 22 (W. H. read preceding).*

ὄρθρος, ου, ὁ, *early dawn*, *daybreak*, Lu. xxiv. 1; Jn. viii. 2 (W. H. omit); Ac. v. 21.*

ὀρθῶς, adv., *rightly*, Mar. vii. 35; Lu. vii. 43, x. 28, xx. 21.*

ὁρίζω, σω, *to define*; *to determine*, Ac. xvii. 26; Heb. iv. 7; *to appoint*, *to decree*, Ac. x. 42, xi. 29; pass., perf. part., ὡρισμένος, *decreed*, Ac. ii. 23; neut., *decree*, Lu. xxii. 22.

ὅριον, ου, τό, plur., *the bound-*

aries of a place; hence, *districts, territory*, Mat. ii. 6, iv. 13.

ὁρκίζω, *to adjure by, to charge solemnly by*, with double acc., Mar. v. 7; Ac. xix. 13; 1 Th. v. 27 (W. H. ἐνορκίζω).*

ὅρκος, ου, ὁ, *an oath*, Mat. xiv. 7, 9; *a promise with an oath, a vow*, Mat. v. 33.

ὁρκ-ωμοσία, ας, ἡ, *the taking of an oath, an oath*, Heb. vii. 20, 21, 28. (S.)*

ὁρμάω, ῶ, ήσω, N. T., intrans., *to rush*, Mat. viii. 32; Ac. vii. 57 (εἰς, or ἐπί, acc.).

ὁρμή, ῆς, ἡ, *a rush, a violent assault*, Ac. xiv. 5; Ja. iii. 4.*

ὅρμημα, ατος, τό, *a rushing on, impulse*, Rev. xviii. 21.*

ὄρνεον, ου, τό, *a bird*, Rev. xviii. 2, xix. 17, 21.*

ὄρνις, ιθος, ὁ, ἡ, *a bird, a hen*, Mat. xxiii. 37; Lu. xiii. 34.*

ὁρο-θεσία, ας, ἡ, *a setting of boundaries, a definite limit*, Ac. xvii. 26. (N. T.)*

ὄρος, ους, τό, *a mountain*, Lu. iii. 5, ix. 28.

ὀρύσσω, ξω, *to dig, to dig out*, Mat. xxi. 33, xxv. 18; Mar. xii. 1.*

ὀρφανός, ή, όν, *bereaved, an orphan*, Jn. xiv. 18; as subst., Ja. i. 27.*

ὀρχέομαι, οῦμαι, ήσομαι, dep., mid., *to dance*, Mat. xi. 17, xiv. 6; Mar. vi. 22; Lu. vii. 32.*

ὅς, ἥ, ὅ, relative pronoun, *who, which* (see Gr. §§ 58, 343–348, Wi. § 24, Bu. 281 sq.; for ὃς ἄν, ὃς ἐάν, *whoever*, see Gr. § 380, Wi. § 42, 3, Bu. 288); as demonst. in the phrase, ὃς μέν ... ὃς δέ, *that one ... this one*, as 2 Cor. ii. 16.

ὁσάκις, rel. adv., *as often as*, always with ἄν or ἐάν, 1 Cor. xi. 25, 26; Rev. xi. 6.*

ὅσιος (α), ον, *holy, pious*, of human beings, of Christ, and of God; τὰ ὅσια, *the holy promises*, Ac. xiii. 34. *Syn.*: see ἅγιος.

ὁσιότης, τητος, ἡ, *holiness, godliness*, Lu. i. 75; Ep. iv. 24.*

ὁσίως, adv., *holily*, 1 Th. ii. 10.*

ὀσμή, ῆς, ἡ, *a smell, an odor*, lit., Jn. xii. 3; fig., 2 Cor. ii. 14, 16; Ep. v. 2; Phil. iv. 18.*

ὅσος, η, ον, relat. pron., *how much, how great*, (1) of time, *how long, as long as*, Ro. vii. 1; repeated, the meaning is intensified, Heb. x. 37: ἔτι μικρὸν ὅσον ὅσον, *yet a little, a very, very little*; (2) of quantity, of number, *how much*, plur., *how many*, Mar. iii. 8; Jn. vi. 11; Ac. ix. 13; *as many as*, Mat. xiv. 36; with ἄν, ἐάν, *as many as, whatsoever*, Mat. vii. 12, xxi. 22; (3) of measure, degree, Heb. vii. 20.

ὅσ-περ, ἥ-περ, ὅ-περ, *the very one who*, Mar. xv. 6 (not W. H.).*

ὀστέον, contr. ὀστοῦν, οῦ, τό, *a bone*, Jn. xix. 36.

ὅσ-τις, ἥ-τις, ὅ, τι, compound relat., *whosoever, whichsoever, whatsoever* (see Gr. §§ 58*c*, 349, Wi. § 42, 3, Bu. 115); the addition of ἄν, ἐάν, gives indefiniteness.

ὀστράκινος, η, ον, *made of earth, earthen*, 2 Cor. iv. 7; 2 Tim. ii. 20.*

ὄσφρησις, εως, ἡ, *the sense of smell, smelling*, 1 Cor. xii. 17.*

ὀσφύς, ύος, ἡ, *the loins*, Mat. iii. 4; Lu. xii. 35; Ac. ii. 30; 1 Pet. i. 13.

ὅταν (ὅτε, ἄν), rel. adv., *when, whensoever*; always with subj. except Mar. iii. 11, xi. 19 (W. H.), 25 (W. H.); Rev. iv. 9, viii. 1 (W. H.).

ὅτε, rel. adv., *when*, Mar. xiv. 12.

ὅτι, conj., (1) *that*, after verbs of declaring, etc., introducing the object-sentence; sometimes as a mere quotation mark, Mat. ii. 23; (2) *because* (see Gr. § 136, 6, Wi. § 53, 8*b*, Bu. 357 sq.).

ὅτου (gen. of ὅστις), ἕως ὅτου, *until*, Lu. xxii. 16.

οὗ, adv. (gen. of ὅς), *where, whither*; οὗ ἐάν, *whithersoever*; also used of time, *when*, in the phrases, ἀφ' οὗ, *since*, ἄχρις, ἕως, μέχρις οὗ, *until*.

οὐ (οὐκ before a vowel, οὐχ if the vowel is aspirated), *no, not* (see Gr. §§ 134, 401, Wi. §§ 55, 56, Bu. 344 sq.).

οὐά, interj., *ah! aha!* derisive, Mar. xv. 29. (N. T.)*

οὐαί, interj., *woe! alas!* uttered in grief or denunciation, Mat. xi. 21; 1 Cor. ix. 16; ἡ οὐαί, as subst., Rev. ix. 12, *the woe, the calamity*. (S.)

οὐδαμῶς, adv., *by no means*, Mat. ii. 6.*

οὐ-δέ, conj., disj. neg., *but not, nor yet* (cf. μηδέ), *neither, nor, not even* (see Gr. § 401, Wi. § 55, 6, Bu. 366 sq.).

οὐδ-είς, οὐδεμία, οὐδέν (οὐδὲ εἷς), neg. adj., *not one, no one, none, nothing, of no moment, of no value, vain*.

οὐδέ-ποτε, adv., *never*, 1 Cor. xiii. 8; Mat. vii. 23.

οὐδέ-πω, adv., *not yet, never*, Jn. xix. 41.

οὐθείς, οὐθέν (οὔτε εἷς), *no one, nothing*, Ac. xxvi. 26 (W. H.); 1 Cor. xiii. 2, 2 Cor. xi. 8 (W. H.).*

οὐκ-έτι, adv., *no further, no more, no longer*.

οὐκ-οῦν, adv., *not therefore*; hence, in ordinary classic usage, an affirmative adverb, *therefore* (whereas οὔκουν retains its negative force, *not therefore*), Jn. xviii. 37.*

οὐ μή, an emphatic negative (see Gr. § 377, Wi. § 56, 3, Bu. 211 sq.).

οὖν, conj., *therefore, then*, Mat. xii. 12; employed espec. (1) in arguing, 1 Cor. iv. 16; (2) in exhortation, Mat. xxii. 9, 17, 21; (3) in interrogation, Mat. xiii. 27; Gal. iii. 19, 21; (4) to resume an interrupted subject, Mar. iii. 31; Jn. xi. 6; (5) to indicate mere transition from one point to another, most frequently in John, as viii. 13.

οὔ-πω, adv., *not yet*.

οὐρά, ᾶς, ἡ, *a tail* of an animal, Rev. ix. 10, 19, xii. 4.*

οὐράνιος, ον, *heavenly, in* or *pertaining to heaven*, as Lu. ii. 13; Ac. xxvi. 19.

οὐρανόθεν, adv., *from heaven*, Ac. xiv. 17, xxvi. 13.*

οὐρανός, οῦ, ὁ, *heaven*, (1) *the visible heavens* (both sing. and plural), through their whole extent, *the atmosphere, the sky, the starry heavens*:

(2) *the spiritual heavens*, the abode of God and holy beings, Mat. vi. 10; 2 Cor. xii. 2; "the third heaven," above the atmospheric and the sidereal; met., for the inhabitants of heaven, Rev. xviii. 20; especially for God, Lu. xv. 18.

Οὐρβανός, οῦ, ὁ, *Urbanus*, Ro. xvi. 9.*

Οὐρίας, ου, ὁ, *Uriah*, Mat. i. 6.*

οὖς, ὠτός, τό, (1) *the ear*, Mat. x. 27; (2) met., *the faculty of perception*, Mat. xi. 15.

οὐσία, ας, ἡ (ὤν, part. εἰμί), *property*, *wealth*, Lu. xv. 12, 13.*

οὔ-τε, conj., *and not; neither, nor*, with a negative preced.; οὔτε ... οὔτε, *neither ... nor.* (The readings often vary between οὔτε and οὐδέ.)

οὗτος, αὕτη, τοῦτο, demonstr. pron., *this* (near), appl. to persons and things, sometimes emphatic, Mat. v. 19; sometimes comtemptuous, *this fellow*, Mat. xiii. 55 (see Gr. §§ 338–342, Wi. § 23, Bu. 103 sq.; also ἐκεῖνος and ὅδε).

οὕτως (and before a consonant sometimes οὕτω), adv., *thus, in this wise, so*, (1) in reference to antecedent or following statement; (2) correlative with ὡς or καθώς, *so ... as*; (3) qualifying adjectives, adverbs, or verbs, *so*, Heb. xii. 21; Mat. ix. 33; οὕτως ... οὕτως, 1 Cor. vii. 7, *in this manner ... in that.*

οὐχί, adv., (1) an intensive form of οὐ, Jn. xiii. 10, *by no means, not at all*, (2) mostly interrog., as Mat. v. 46, expecting an affirmative answer.

ὀφειλέτης, ου, ὁ, *a debtor*, Mat. xviii. 24; *one bound to some duty, e.g.*, obedience to the law, Gal. v. 3; *a delinquent, sinner*, Lu. xiii. 4.

ὀφειλή, ῆς, ἡ, *a debt, a duty*, Mat. xviii. 32; Ro. xiii. 7; 1 Cor. vii. 3 (W. H.). (N. T.)*

ὀφείλημα, ατος, τό, *a debt, what is justly due*, Ro. iv. 4; fig., *an offense, a sin*, Mat. vi. 12.*

ὀφείλω, (1) *to owe* money (acc. and dat.), Mat. xviii. 28; τὸ ὀφειλόμενον, *the due*, Mat. xviii. 30; (2) *to be under obligation*, Mat. xxiii. 16; *to sin against*, Lu. xi. 4.

ὄφελον (see Gr. § 378, Wi. § 41 *b*, 5, note 2, Bu. 214 sq.), interjection, *O that! I wish! would that!* followed by indicative, 1 Cor. iv. 8; 2 Cor. xi. 1; Gal. v. 12; Rev. iii. 15.*

ὄφελος, ους, τό (ὀφέλλω, *to increase*), *profit, advantage*, 1 Cor. xv. 32; Ja. ii. 14, 16.*

ὀφθαλμο-δουλεία, ας, ἡ, *eye-service*, Ep. vi. 6; Col. iii. 22. (N. T.)*

ὀφθαλμός, οῦ, ὁ, *an eye;* fig., of the eye as the receptive channel into mind and heart, Mat. vi. 23 (see Mar. vii. 22; Mat. xx. 15); fig., *the eye of the mind, i.e., the understanding*, Ac. xxvi. 18.

ὄφις, εως, ὁ, *a serpent*, Mat. vii. 10; an emblem of wisdom, Mat. x. 16; of cunning, Mat. xxiii. 33; used symbol. for Satan, Rev. xii. 9, 14.

ὀφρύς, ύος, ἡ, *the eyebrow; the brow* of a mountain or hill, Lu. iv. 29.*

ὀχλέω, ῶ, *to disturb, to vex*, only in pass., Lu. vi. 18 (W. H. ἐνοχλέω), Ac. v. 16.*

ὀχλο-ποιέω, ῶ, *to gather a crowd*, Ac. xvii. 5. (N. T.)*

ὄχλος, ου, ὁ, *a crowd, an unorganized multitude*, Mat. ix. 23, 25; *the multitude, the common people*, Mar. xii. 12.

ὀχύρωμα, ατος, τό, *a fortress, a strong defense*, 2 Cor. x. 4.*

ὀψάριον, ου, τό (a relish with bread), *a little fish*, Jn. vi. 9, 11, xxi. 9, 10, 13. (N. T.)*

ὀψέ, adv., *late, in the evening*, Mar. xi. 11 (W. H.), 19, xiii. 35; *late in*, gen., Mat. xxviii. 1.*

ὄψιμος, ον, *latter*, of the rain, Ja. v. 7.*

ὄψιος, α, ον, *late*, Mar. xi. 11 (not W. H., see mrg.); as subst., ἡ ὀψία, *evening*, either the former of the two evenings reckoned among the Jews, Mat. viii. 16; or the latter, Mat. xiv. 23; see ver. 15.

ὄψις, εως, ἡ, *sight; the countenance*, Jn. xi. 44; Rev. i. 16; *external appearance*, Jn vii. 24.*

ὀψώνιον, ου, τό, lit., *relish, sauce*, like ὀψάριον, (1) plur., the *rations* of soldiers, their *wages*, Lu. iii. 14; 1 Cor. ix. 7; hence, (2) *wages*, generally, Ro. vi. 23; 2 Cor. xi. 8.*

Π

Π, π, πῖ, *pi, p*, the sixteenth letter. As a numeral, π′ = 80; ,π = 80,000.

παγιδεύω, σω, *to ensnare, to entrap*, fig., Mat. xxii. 15. (S.)*

παγίς, ίδος, ἡ, *a snare, a trap*, Lu. xxi. 35; fig., Ro. xi. 9; 1 Tim. iii. 7, vi. 9; 2 Tim. ii. 26.*

πάγος, ου, ὁ, *a hill;* only with the adj. Ἄρειος, *Mars' Hill, Areopagus*, Ac. xvii. 19, 22.*

πάθημα, ατος, τό, (1) *suffering, affliction*, Ro. viii. 18; (2) *affection of mind, passion*, Ro. vii. 5; Gal. v. 24; (3) *an undergoing, an enduring*, Heb. ii. 9.

παθητός, ἡ, όν, *destined to suffer*, Ac. xxvi. 23.*

πάθος, ους, τό, *suffering, emotion*, in N.T., of an evil kind, *depraved passion, lust*, Ro. i. 26; 1 Th. iv. 5; Col. iii. 5.*

παιδ-αγωγός, οῦ, ὁ, *a boys' guardian* or *tutor*, "pædagogue," a slave who had the charge of the life and morals of the boys of a family, not strictly a teacher, 1 Cor. iv. 15; Gal. iii. 24, 25.*

παιδάριον, ου, τό (dim. of παῖς), *a little boy, a lad*, Mat. xi. 16 (W. H. παιδίον); Jn. vi. 9.*

παιδεία, ας, ἡ, *training and education* of children, Ep. vi. 4; hence, *instruction*, 2 Tim. iii. 16; *chastisement, correction*, Heb. xii. 5–11.*

παιδευτής, οῦ, ὁ, (1) *an instructor*, Ro. ii. 20; (2) *a chastiser*, Heb. xii. 9.*

παιδεύω, σω, *to train a child*, Ac. xxii. 3; hence, (1) *to instruct*, 1 Tim. i. 20, (2) *to correct, to chasten*, 2 Tim. ii. 25; Heb. xii. 7.

παιδιόθεν, adv., *from childhood*, Mar. ix. 21. (N. T.)*

παιδίον, ου, τό (dim. of παῖς),

a little child, an infant, Mat. ii. 8; *a child* more advanced, Mat. xiv. 21; fig., 1 Cor. xiv. 20.

παιδίσκη, ης, ἡ (fem. dim. of παῖς), *a young girl; a young female slave*, Lu. xii. 45, xxii. 56.

παίζω, *to play*, as a child, *to sport, to jest*, 1 Cor. x. 7.*

παῖς, παιδός, ὁ, ἡ, (1) *a child, a boy* or *girl*, Lu. ii. 43, viii. 51, 54; (2) *a servant, a slave*, as Mat. viii. 6, 8; ὁ παῖς τοῦ θεοῦ, *the servant of God*, used of any servant, Lu. i. 69; *of the Messiah*, Mat. xii. 18.

παίω, σω, *to strike, to smite*, with the fist, Mat. xxvi. 68; Lu. xxii. 64; with a sword, Mar. xiv. 47; Jn. xviii. 10; as a scorpion with its sting, Rev. ix. 5.*

Πακατιανή, ῆς, ἡ, *Pacatiana*, a part of Phrygia, 1 Tim. vi. 22 (Rec.).*

πάλαι, adv., *of old*, Heb. i. 1; *long ago*, Mat. xi. 21.

παλαιός, ά, όν, (1) *old, ancient*, 2 Cor. iii. 14; ὁ παλαιὸς ἄνθρωπος, *the old* or *former man, i.e.*, man in his old, unrenewed nature, Ro. vi. 6; (2) *worn out*, as a garment, Mat. ix. 16.

παλαιότης, τητος, ἡ, *oldness, obsoleteness*, Ro. vii. 6.*

παλαιόω, ῶ, *to make old, to declare obsolete*, Heb. viii. 13; pass., *to grow old, to become obsolete*, Lu. xii. 33; Heb. i. 11, viii. 13.*

πάλη, ης, ἡ, *a wrestling*, Ep. vi. 12.*

παλιγ-γενεσία (W. H. παλινγ-), ας, ἡ, *a new birth, regeneration*, Tit. iii. 5; *a renovation* of all things, Mat. xix. 28.* *Syn.*: see ἀνακαίνωσις.

πάλιν, adv., *again, back*, used of place or of time; a particle of continuation, *again, once more, further;* and of antithesis, as 2 Cor. x. 7, *on the other hand.*

παμ-πληθεί, adv., *all at once, all together*, Lu. xxiii. 18. (N. T.)*

πάμ-πολυς, παμπόλλη, πάμπολυ, *very great*, Mar. viii. 1 (not W. H.).*

Παμφυλία, ας, ἡ, *Pamphylia*, Ac. xiii. 13.

παν-δοχεῖον, ου, τό, *a khan*, or Eastern *inn*, Lu. x. 34.*

παν-δοχεύς, έως, ὁ (δέχομαι), *the keeper of a khan, a host*, Lu. x. 35.*

παν-ήγυρις, εως, ἡ (ἀγείρω), *a general festal assembly*, Heb. xii. 23.* *Syn.*: see ἐκκλησία.

παν-οικί, adv., *with one's whole household* or *family*, Ac. xvi. 34.*

παν-οπλία, ας, ἡ, *complete armor*, Lu. xi. 22; Ep. vi. 11, 13.*

πανουργία, ας, ἡ, *shrewdness, skill;* hence, *cunning, craftiness*, Lu. xx. 23, 1 Cor. iii. 19; 2 Cor. iv. 2, xi. 3; Ep. iv. 14.*

παν-οῦργος, ον (ἔργον), *doing everything; cunning, crafty*, 2 Cor. xii. 16.*

πανταχῇ, adv., *everywhere*, Ac. xxi. 28 (W. H.).*

πανταχόθεν, adv., *from all sides*, Mar. i. 45 (W. H. πάντοθεν).*

πανταχοῦ, adv., *everywhere*, Mar. xvi. 20; Lu. ix. 6.

παντελής, ές, *complete;* εἰς τὸ παντελές, *completely, perfectly*, Heb. vii. 25; the same phrase, with μή, *not at all*, Lu. xiii. 11.*

πάντῃ, adv., *in every way*, Ac. xxiv. 3.*

πάντοθεν, adv., *from all sides*, Mar. i. 45 (W. H.); Lu. xix. 43; Heb. ix. 4.*

παντο-κράτωρ, ορος, ὁ, *the almighty*, used of God, Rev. i. 8, iv. 8.

πάντοτε, adv., *always, at all times*, Mat. xxvi. 11.

πάντως, adv., *wholly, entirely*, 1 Cor. v. 10; *in every way, by all means*, Ro. iii. 9; *assuredly, certainly*, Ac. xxi. 22.

παρά, prep., gov. the gen., the dat., and accus., *beside;* with a gen. (of person), it indicates *source* or *origin;* with a dat., it denotes *presence with;* with an accus., it indicates motion *towards*, or *alongside*, and is employed in comparisons, *beyond;* for details see Gr. § 306, Wi. §§ 47 *b*, 48 *d*, 49 *g*, Bu. 339 sq. In composition, παρά retains its general meaning, *besides*, sometimes denoting *nearness*, sometimes *motion by* or *past*, so as to miss or fail; occasionally also stealthiness (*by the way*), as in παρεισάγω.

παρα-βαίνω, 2d aor. παρέβην, *to transgress*, Mat. xv. 2, 3; 2 Jn. 9 (W. H. προάγω); *to depart, desert*, Ac. i. 25.*

παρα-βάλλω, (1) *to compare*, Mar. iv. 30 (not W. H.); (2) *to betake one's self, arrive*, Ac. xx. 15.*

παρά-βασις, εως, ἡ, *a transgression*, Ro. ii. 23. *Syn.*: see ἀγνόημα.

παρα-βάτης, ου, ὁ, *a transgressor*, Ro. ii. 25, 27; Gal. ii. 18; Ja. ii. 9, 11.*

παρα-βιάζομαι, *to constrain by entreaties*, Lu. xxiv. 29; Ac. xvi. 15.*

παρα-βολεύομαι, *to expose one's self to peril, to be venturesome*, Phil. ii. 30 (W. H.). (N. T.)*

παρα-βολή, ῆς, ἡ, (1) *a comparison*, Heb. ix. 9; (2) *a parable*, often of those uttered by our Lord, Mar. iv. 2, 10; (3) *a proverb, an adage*, Lu. iv. 23; (4) perhaps in Heb. xi. 19, *a venture, a risk* (see παραβολεύομαι).

παραβουλεύομαι, *to consult amiss, be reckless*, Phil. ii. 30 (Rec.). (N. T.)*

παραγγελία, ας, ἡ, *a command, a charge*, Ac. v. 28, xvi. 24; 1 Th. iv. 2; 1 Tim. i. 5, 18.*

παρ-αγγέλλω, *to notify, to command, to charge*, Lu. viii. 29; 2 Th. iii. 4; dat. of person, acc. of thing, or ὅτι, ἵνα or inf., 1 Tim. vi. 13.

παρα-γίνομαι, *to come near, come forth, come against* (ἐπί, πρός), Lu. xii. 51, xxii. 52; Jn. iii. 23; Heb. ix. 11.

παρ-άγω, *to pass by*, Mat. xx. 30; *to depart*, Mat. ix. 27; *to pass away*, act., 1 Cor. vii. 31; pass., only 1 Jn. ii. 8, 17.

παρα-δειγματίζω, *to make a public example of, to expose to disgrace*, Mat. i. 19 (W. H. δειγματίζω); Heb. vi. 6.*

παράδεισος, ου, ὁ (probably a Persian word, "garden," "park"), *Paradise*, Lu. xxiii. 43; 2 Cor. xii. 4; Rev. ii. 7.*

παρα-δέχομαι, dep., mid., *to receive, accept, acknowledge*, Mar. iv. 20; Ac. xv. 4 (W

H.), xvi. 21, xxii. 18; 1 Tim. v. 19; Heb. xii. 6.*

παρα-δια-τριβή, ῆς, ἡ, *useless occupation*, 1 Tim. vi. 5 (W. H. διαπαρατριβή). (N. T.)*

παρα-δίδωμι, acc. and dat., (1) *to deliver over*, as to prison, judgment, or punishment, Mat. iv. 12; *to betray*, spec. of the betrayal by Judas; (2) *to surrender, abandon* one's self, Ep. iv. 19; (3) *to hand over, entrust, commit, deliver*, as Mat. xxv. 14; Lu. i. 2; Ac. vi. 14; (4) *to commend* to kindness, Ac. xiv. 26; (5) *to give* or *prescribe*, as laws, etc., Ac. vi. 14; (6) prob. *to permit*, in Mar. iv. 29, *when the fruit permits* or *allows*.

παρά-δοξος, ον, *strange, wonderful*, Lu. v. 26.*

παρά-δοσις, εως, ἡ, *an instruction*, or *tradition*, Mat. xv. 2; 1 Cor. xi. 2; 2 Th. ii. 15, iii. 6.

παρα-ζηλόω, ῶ, ώσω, *to provoke to rivalry*, Ro. xi. 11, 14; *to jealousy*, Ro. x. 19; *to anger*, 1 Cor. x. 22. (S.)*

παρα-θαλάσσιος, α, ον, *by the sea*, Mat. iv. 13.*

παρα-θεωρέω, ῶ, *to overlook, neglect*, Ac. vi. 1.*

παρα-θήκη, ης, ἡ, *a deposit, anything committed to one's charge*, 1 Tim. vi. 20 (W. H.); 2 Tim. i. 12, 14 (W. H.).*

παρ-αινέω, ῶ, *to exhort, admonish*, Ac. xxvii. 9, 22.*

παρ-αιτέομαι, οῦμαι, dep., mid., *to entreat for, to beg off, make excuse, refuse, reject*, Mar. xv. 6 (W. H.); Lu. xiv. 18, 19; Ac. xxv. 11; 1 Tim. iv. 7, v. 11; 2 Tim. ii. 23; Tit. iii. 10; Heb. xii. 19, 25.*

παρα-καθέζομαι, *to seat one's self*, Lu. x. 39 (W. H.).*

παρα-καθίζω, intrans., *to sit down beside*, Lu. x. 39 (Rec.).*

παρα-καλέω, ῶ, έσω, (1) *to send for, summon*, Ac. xxviii. 20; (2) *to beseech, entreat*, Mar. i. 40; (3) *to exhort, admonish*, Ac. xv. 32; 1 Tim. vi. 2; (4) *to comfort*, 2 Cor. i. 4; pass., *to be comforted*, Lu. xvi. 25.

παρα-καλύπτω, *to hide, to conceal*, Lu. ix. 45.*

παρα-κατα-θήκη, ης, ἡ, *a trust, a deposit*, 1 Tim. vi. 20; 2 Tim. i. 14 (in both passages W. H. read παραθήκη).*

παρά-κειμαι, *to be at hand, be present with* (dat.), Ro. vii. 18, 21.*

παρά-κλησις, εως, ἡ, *a calling for, a summons*; hence, (1) *exhortation*, Heb. xii. 5; (2) *entreaty*, 2 Cor. viii. 4; (3) *encouragement*, Phil. ii. 1; (4) *consolation, comfort*, Ro. xv. 4; met., of the Consoler, Lu. ii. 25; (5) generally, of the power of imparting all these, Ac. iv. 36.

παρά-κλητος, ου, ὁ, (1) *an advocate, intercessor*, 1 Jn. ii. 1; (2) *a consoler, comforter, helper*, of the Holy Spirit, Jn. xiv. 16, 26, xv. 26, xvi. 7.*

παρ-ακοή, ῆς, ἡ, *disobedience*, Ro. v. 19; 2 Cor. x. 6; Heb. ii. 2.* *Syn.*: see ἀγνόημα.

παρ-ακολουθέω, ῶ, ήσω, *to follow closely, to accompany* (dat.), Mar. xvi. 17 (not W. H., see mrg.); *to follow so as to trace out, to examine*, Lu. i. 3; *to follow* teaching, 1 Tim. iv. 6; 2 Tim. iii. 10.*

παρ-ακούω, *to hear negligently, to disregard*, Mat. xviii. 17; Mar. v. 36 (W. H.).*

παρα-κύπτω, ψω, *to stoop*, Lu. xxiv. 12; Jn. xx. 5, 11; fig., with εἰς, *to search into*, Ja. i. 25; 1 Pet. i. 12.*

παρα-λαμβάνω, λήψομαι (W. H. -λήμψ-), (1) *to take to one's self, to take with one*, Lu. ix. 10, 28, xi. 26; *to lead off* a prisoner, Jn. xix. 16; Ac. xxiii. 18; (2) *to receive by transmission*, Col. iv. 17; Heb. xii. 28; fig., *to receive by instruction*, Mar. vii. 4.

παρα-λέγω, N.T. in mid., *to lay one's course near*, in sailing, *to coast along*, Ac. xxvii. 8, 13.*

παρ-άλιος, ον, *adjacent to the sea, on the coast*, Lu. vi. 17.*

παρ-αλλαγή, ῆς, ἡ, *change, variation*, Ja. i. 17.*

παρα-λογίζομαι, dep., *to impose upon, to delude*, acc., Col. ii. 4; Ja. i. 22.*

παρα-λυτικός, ή, όν, *afflicted with paralysis*, in the whole or a part of the body, Mat. iv. 24, viii. 6. (N. T.)

παρα-λύω, *to relax, to enfeeble*, only perf. part., pass., παραλελυμένος, *paralyzed, enfeebled*.

παρα-μένω, μενῶ, *to remain by* (dat., or πρός, acc.), *to abide with*, 1 Cor. xvi. 6 (W. H. καταμένω); Phil. i. 25 (W. H.); *to continue*, Ja. i. 25; Heb. vii. 23.*

παρα-μυθέομαι, οῦμαι, *to speak to, to cheer, to comfort*, Jn. xi. 19, 31; 1 Th. ii. 11, v. 14.*

παρα-μυθία, ας, ἡ, *encouragement, comfort*, 1 Cor. xiv. 3.*

παρα-μύθιον, ου, τό, *comfort*, Phil. ii. 1.*

παρα-νομέω, ῶ, *to act contrary to law*, Ac. xxiii. 3.*

παρα-νομία, ας, ἡ, *violation of law, transgression*, 2 Pet. ii. 16.* *Syn.*: see ἀγνόημα.

παρα-πικραίνω, ανῶ, 1st aor. παρεπίκρανα, *to provoke* God *to anger*, Heb. iii. 16. (S.)*

παρα-πικρασμός, οῦ, ὁ, *provocation* of God, Heb. iii. 8, 15. (S.)*

παρα-πίπτω, 2d aor. παρέπεσον, *to fall away*, Heb. vi. 6.*

παρα-πλέω, ῶ, εὔσομαι, *to sail past*, acc., Ac. xx. 16.*

παρα-πλήσιον, adv., *near to* (gen.), Phil. ii. 27.*

παραπλησίως, adv., *similarly, in like manner*, Heb. ii. 14.*

παρα-πορεύομαι, dep., mid., *to pass by, to pass along by*, Mar. xi. 20, xv. 29.

παρά-πτωμα, ατος, τό (παραπίπτω), *a falling away* or *aside, a sin*, Ep. i. 7, ii. 1, 5. *Syn.*: see ἀγνόημα.

παρα-ρρέω, 2d aor., pass., παρερρύην, pass., *to be carried past, to lose*, Heb. ii. 1.*

παρά-σημος, ον, *marked with* (dat.), Ac. xxviii. 11.*

παρα-σκευάζω, σω, *to prepare*, Ac. x. 10; mid., *to prepare one's self*, 1 Cor. xiv. 8; pass., *to be in readiness*, 2 Cor. ix. 2, 3.*

παρα-σκευή, ῆς, ἡ, *a preparation, i.e.*, the day immediately before a sabbath or other festival, Mat. xxvii. 62; Mar. xv. 42; Lu. xxiii 54; Jn. xix. 14, 31, 42.*

παρα-τείνω, *to extend, to prolong,* Ac. xx. 7.*

παρα-τηρέω, ῶ, ήσω, (1) *to watch,* Mar. iii. 2; (2) *to observe scrupulously,* Gal. iv. 10.

παρα-τήρησις, εως, ἡ, *observation,* Lu. xvii. 20.*

παρα-τίθημι, θήσω (see Gr. § 107), (1) *to place near* or *by the side of,* as food, Lu. xi. 6; (2) *to set* or *lay before,* as instruction, used of a parable, Mat. xiii. 24; mid., *to give in charge to, to entrust,* Lu. xii. 48; *to commend, to recommend* (acc. and dat., or εἰς), Ac. xiv. 23.

παρα-τυγχάνω, *to fall in with, chance to meet,* Ac. xvii. 17.*

παρ-αυτίκα, adv., *for the moment,* 2 Cor. iv. 17.*

παρα-φέρω (see Gr. § 103, 6, Wi. § 52, 4, 11)), *to remove* (acc. and ἀπό), Mar. xiv. 36; Lu. xxii. 42; pass., *to be led aside, carried away,* Heb. xiii. 9 (W. H.); Ju. 12 (W. H.).*

παρα-φρονέω, ῶ, *to be beside one's self,* 2 Cor. xi. 23.*

παρα-φρονία, ας, ἡ, *being beside one's self, madness, folly,* 2 Pet. ii. 16. (N. T.)*

παρα-χειμάζω, άσω, *to pass the winter,* Ac. xxvii. 12, xxviii. 11; 1 Cor. xvi. 6; Tit. iii. 12.*

παρα-χειμασία, ας, ἡ, *a passing the winter,* Ac. xxvii. 12.*

παρα-χρῆμα, adv., *instantly, immediately,* Lu. i. 64, iv. 39.

πάρδαλις, εως, ἡ, *a leopard, a panther,* Rev. xiii. 2.*

παρ-εδρεύω, *to wait upon, to attend to* (dat.), 1 Cor. ix. 13 (W. H.).*

πάρ-ειμι (εἰμί), *to be near, to be present;* part., παρών, *present;* τὸ παρόν, *the present time;* τὰ παρόντα, *possessions.*

παρ-εισ-άγω, ξω, *to bring in secretly,* 2 Pet. ii. 1.*

παρ-είσ-ακτος, ον, *brought in secretly, surreptitious,* Gal. ii. 4.*

παρ-εισ-δύω, or -ύνω, ύσω, *to come in by stealth, to enter secretly,* Ju. 4.*

παρ-εισ-έρχομαι (see Gr. § 103, 2), (1) *to enter secretly,* Gal. ii. 4; (2) *to enter in addition,* Ro. v. 20.*

παρ-εισ-φέρω, *to contribute besides,* 2 Pet. i. 5.*

παρ-εκτός, adv., *besides;* τὰ παρεκτός, *the things that occur besides,* 2 Cor. xi. 28 (see R.V. mrg.); prep. with gen., *except,* Mat. v. 32; Ac. xxvi. 29; also Mat. xix. 9, W. H. mrg.*

παρ-εμ-βάλλω, βαλῶ, *to cast up* a bank about a city, Lu. xix. 43 (W. H.).*

παρ-εμ-βολή, ῆς, ἡ, (1) *a camp,* Heb. xiii. 11, 13; (2) *soldiers' barracks,* Ac. xxi. 34, 37; (3) *an army in battle array,* Heb. xi. 34.

παρ-εν-οχλέω, ῶ, *to cause disturbance to, to disquiet* (dat.), Ac. xv. 19.*

παρ-επί-δημος, ον, *residing in a strange country;* as subst., *a stranger, foreigner,* Heb. xi. 13; 1 Pet. i. 1, ii. 11.*

παρ-έρχομαι, ελεύσομαι (see Gr. § 103, 2, Wi. § 52, 4, 11)), (1) *to pass by,* with acc. of person or place; (2) *to pass, elapse,* as time; (3) *to pass away* or *perish;* (4) *to pass from* any one; (5) *to pass carelessly, i.e., to disregard, neglect.*

πάρ-εσις, εως, ἡ (ἵημι), *passing over, prætermission,* Ro. iii. 25.* *Syn.:* see ἄφεσις.

παρ-έχω, έξω, 2d aor. παρέσχον (dat. and acc.), (1) *to offer, to supply,* Lu. vi. 29; Ac. xxii. 2; espec. the phrase παρέχω κόπους, *to cause* trouble, Mat. xxvi. 10; (2) in mid., *to present, manifest,* Tit. ii. 7; *to bestow,* Col. iv. 1.

παρ-ηγορία, ας, ἡ, *solace,* Col. iv. 11.*

παρθενία, ας, ἡ, *virginity,* Lu. ii. 36.*

παρθένος, ου, ἡ, *a virgin, a maid,* Mat. xxv. 1, 7, 11; hence one who is *chaste,* Rev. xiv. 4, applied to the male sex.

Πάρθος, ου, ὁ, *a Parthian,* Ac. ii. 9.*

παρ-ίημι, *to pass by* or *over, to relax;* pass., perf. part., παρειμένος, *weary,* Heb. xii. 12.*

παρ-ίστημι, or παριστάνω (Ro. vi. 13, 16; see Gr. § 107), στήσω, (1) trans. in act., pres., imp., fut., and 1st aor., *to place near* or *at hand, to provide,* Ac. xxiii. 24; *to present, to offer,* Ro. vi. 13, 16; specially, *to dedicate, to consecrate,* Lu. ii. 22; *to cause to appear, to demonstrate,* Ac. xxiv. 13; (2) intrans., perf., plup., 2d aor., and mid., *to stand by,* Mar. xiv. 47, 69, 70; Lu. xix. 24; *to have come,* Mar. iv. 29; *to stand by, i.e.,* for aid or support, Ro. xvi. 2; *to stand in hostile array,* Ac. iv. 26.

Παρμενᾶς, acc. ᾶν, ὁ, *Parmenas,* Ac. vi. 5.*

πάρ-οδος, ου, ἡ, *a passing by* or *through,* 1 Cor. xvi. 7.*

παρ-οικέω, ῶ, *to dwell in* (ἐν or εἰς, const. præg.) *as a stranger,* Lu. xxiv. 18; Heb. xi. 9.*

παρ-οικία, ας, ἡ, *a sojourning, a dwelling in a strange land,* Ac. xiii. 17; 1 Pet. i. 17. (S.)*

πάρ-οικος, ον, generally as substantive, *a stranger, a foreigner,* Ac. vii. 6, 29; Ep. ii. 19; 1 Pet. ii. 11.*

παρ-οιμία, ας, ἡ (οἶμος, *a way*), (1) *a current* or *trite saying, a proverb,* 2 Pet. ii. 22; (2) *an obscure saying, a symbolic saying,* Jn. xvi. 25, 29; (3) *a comparative discourse, an allegory,* Jn. x. 6.

πάρ-οινος, ον, *given to wine, drunken,* 1 Tim. iii. 3; Tit. i. 7.*

παρ-οίχομαι, *to pass away,* of time, Ac. xiv. 16.*

παρ-ομοιάζω, *to resemble,* Mat. xxiii. 27. (N. T.)*

παρ-όμοιος, ον, *similar,* Mar. vii. 8 (W. H. omit), 13.*

παρ-οξύνω, *to provoke, to irritate,* in pass., Ac. xvii. 16; 1 Cor. xiii. 5.*

παρ-οξυσμός, οῦ, ὁ, (1) *incitement,* Heb. x. 24; (2) *contention, irritation,* Ac. xv. 39.*

παρ-οργίζω, ιῶ, *to provoke greatly, exasperate,* Ro. x. 19; Ep. vi. 4.*

παρ-οργισμός, οῦ, ὁ, *exasperation, wrath,* Ep. iv. 26. (S.)* *Syn.:* see θυμός.

παρ-οτρύνω, *to stir up, to incite,* Ac. xiii. 50.*

παρ-ουσία, ας, ἡ (εἰμί), (1) *presence*, 2 Cor. x. 10; Phil. ii. 20; (2) *a coming, an arrival, advent*, often of the second coming of Christ, 2 Cor. vii. 6, 7; 1 Th. iii. 13.

παρ-οψίς, ίδος, ἡ, *a dish for delicacies*, Mat. xxiii. 25, 26.*

παρρησία, ας, ἡ, *freedom, openness*, especially in speaking, *boldness, confidence*, Ac. iv. 13; Heb. x. 19; παρρησίᾳ, ἐν παρρησίᾳ, or μετὰ παρρησίας, *boldly, openly*.

παρρησιάζομαι, dep., mid., 1st aor. ἐπαρρησιασάμην, *to speak freely, boldly, to be confident*, Ac. xviii. 26, xxvi. 26.

πᾶς, πᾶσα, πᾶν (see Gr. § 37), *all, the whole, every kind of* (see Gr. § 224, Wi. § 18, 4, Bu. 119 sq., and for negative in phrases, Gr. § 328, iii., Wi. § 26, 1, Bu. 121 sq.); adverbial phrases are διαπαντός (which see), *always; ἐν παντί, ἐν πᾶσιν, in everything;* and πάντα (neut. plur. acc.), *altogether*.

πάσχα, τό (Aram.), *the paschal lamb*, Mar. xiv. 12; applied to Christ, 1 Cor. v. 7; *the paschal supper*, Mar. xiv. 16; *the passover feast*, Mat. xxvi. 2. (S.)

πάσχω (παθ-, see Gr. § 94, i. 7), *to be affected with* anything, good or bad; so, *to enjoy good*, Gal. iii. 4; more commonly, *to endure suffering*, Mat. xvii. 15; *to suffer* (acc. of that suffered, ἀπό or ὑπό, gen., of person inflicting).

Πάταρα, άρων, τά, *Patara*, Ac. xxi. 1.*

πατάσσω, ξω, *to smite, to strike, to smite to death, to afflict*, Mat. xxvi. 31; Ac. xii. 23.

πατέω, ῶ, ήσω, *to tread upon*, Lu. x. 19; *to press by treading*, as grapes, Rev. xiv. 20, xix. 15; fig., *to tread down, to trample upon*, Lu. xxi. 24; Rev. xi. 2.*

πατήρ, τρός, ὁ (see Gr. § 30, ii., Wi. §§ 19, 1 *a*, 30, 3, Bu. 94), *a father;* often of God as the father of men, Mat. v. 16, 45; as the father of the Lord Jesus Christ, Mat. vii. 21; as the first person in the Trinity, Mat. xxviii. 19; as the source of manifold blessings, 2 Cor. i. 3. Secondary meanings are: (1) *a founder of a race, an ancestor;* (2) *a senior, a father in age*, 1 Jn. ii. 13, 14; (3) *the author*, or *cause*, or *source of anything*, Jn. viii. 44; Heb. xii. 9; (4) *a spiritual father*, or means of converting any one to Christ, 1 Cor. iv. 15; (5) *one to whom resemblance is borne*, Jn. viii. 38, 41, 44.

Πάτμος, ου, ἡ, *Patmos*, Rev. i. 9.*

πατρ-αλῴας (W. H. -ολῴας), ου, ὁ, *a parricide*, 1 Tim. i. 9.*

πατριά, ᾶς, ἡ, *a family* (in O. T. a division between the tribe and the household), Lu. ii. 4; Ac. iii. 25; Ep. iii. 15 (on which see Gr. § 224).*

πατρι-άρχης, ου, ὁ, *head* or *founder of a family, a patriarch*, Ac. ii. 29, vii. 8, 9; Heb. vii. 4. (S.)*

πατρικός, ή, όν, *paternal, ancestral*, Gal. i. 14.*

πατρίς, ίδος, ἡ, *one's native place, fatherland*, Heb. xi. 14; *one's native place, i.e., city*, Mat. xiii. 54, 57.

Πατρόβας, acc. αν, ὁ, *Patrobas*, Ro. xvi. 14.*

πατρο-παρά-δοτος, ον, *handed down from ancestors*, 1 Pet. i. 18.*

πατρῷος, α, ον, *received from the fathers, hereditary*, Ac. xxii. 3, xxiv. 14, xxviii. 17.*

Παῦλος, ου, ὁ, *Paul*, (1) Sergius Paulus, Ac. xiii. 7; (2) the apostle of the Gentiles, Ac. xxi. 40 (see Gr. § 159*c*, Wi. § 18, 6).

παύω, σω, *to cause to cease, to restrain*, 1 Pet. iii. 10; generally mid., *to cease, desist*, Lu. v. 4, viii. 24.

Πάφος, ου, ἡ, *Paphos*, Ac. xiii. 6, 13.*

παχύνω (παχύς), *to make fat, to fatten;* pass., fig., *to become stupid*, Mat. xiii. 15; Ac. xxviii. 27.*

πέδη, ης, ἡ, *a shackle, a fetter for the feet*, Mar. v. 4; Lu. viii. 29.*

πεδινός, ή, όν, *level*, Lu. vi. 17.*

πεζεύω (πεζός), *to travel on foot* or *by land*, Ac. xx. 13.*

πεζῇ, adv., *on foot*, or *by land*, Mat. xiv. 13; Mar. vi. 33.*

πειθ-αρχέω, ῶ, (1) *to obey a ruler* or *one in authority*, Ac. v. 29, 32; Tit. iii. 1; (2) *to obey*, or *conform to advice*, Ac. xxvii. 21.*

πειθός (W. H. πιθός), ή, όν, *persuasive*, 1 Cor. ii. 4. (N.T.)*

πείθω, πείσω, *to persuade*, Ac. xviii. 4; *to influence by persuasion*, Mat. xxvii. 20; *to seek to please, to conciliate*, Ac. xiv. 29; 2 Cor. v. 11; *to appease, to render tranquil*, 1 Jn. iii. 19; *to conciliate, to aspire to the favor of*, Gal. i. 10; pass., *to yield to persuasion, to assent, to listen to, to obey*, Ac. v. 36, 37; the 2d perf., πέποιθα, is intrans., *to trust, to rely on, to have confidence in*, Mat. xxvii. 43; Ro. ii. 19.

πεινάω, ῶ, inf. πεινᾶν, άσω, (1) *to be hungry*, Mat. iv. 2, xii. 1, 3; hence, (2) *to be needy*, Lu. i. 53; (3) *to desire earnestly, to long for*, acc., Mat. v. 6.

πεῖρα, ας, ἡ, *trial, experiment;* with λαμβάνω, *to make trial of, to experience*, Heb. xi. 29, 36.*

πειράζω, σω, (1) *to attempt* (inf.), Ac. xvi. 7; (2) *to make trial of, to test* (acc.), Jn. vi. 6; (3) *to tempt to sin*, Ja. i. 13, 14; ὁ πειράζων, *the tempter, i.e., the devil*, Mat. iv. 3. *Syn.:* see δοκιμάζω.

πειρασμός, οῦ, ὁ, *a trying, proving*, 1 Pet. iv. 12; Heb. iii. 8; *a tempting to sin*, Mat. vi. 13; *calamity, adversity*, as trying men, Ac. xx. 19. (S.)

πειράω, ῶ, only in mid., *to attempt*, Ac. ix. 26 (W. H. πειράζω), xxvi. 21.*

πεισμονή, ῆς, ἡ, *persuasion, conviction*, Gal. v. 8. (N.T.)*

πέλαγος, ους, τό, *the sea, the deep*, Mat. xviii. 6; Ac. xxvii. 5.*

πελεκίζω (πέλεκυς, *an axe*), *to behead*, Rev. xx. 4.*

πέμπτος, η, ον, ord. num., *the fifth*, Rev. vi. 9.

πέμπω, ψω, (1) *to send*, of persons, *to send forth*, spoken of teachers, as John Baptist, Jn. i. 33; of Jesus, Jn. iv. 34; of the Spirit, Jn. xiv. 26; of apostles, Jn. xiii. 20; (2) *to send*, of things, *to* *transmit*, Rev. xi. 10; *to send among* or *upon*, 2 Th. ii. 11; *to thrust in* the sickle, Rev. xiv. 15, 18.

πένης, ητος, ὁ, *poor*, 2 Cor. ix. 9.* *Syn.*: πτωχός implies utter destitution, usually beggary; πένης, simply poverty, scanty livelihood.

πενθερά, ᾶς, ἡ, *a mother-in-law*, a wife's mother, Mar. i. 30.

πενθερός, οῦ, ὁ, *a father-in-law*, a wife's father, Jn. xviii. 13.*

πενθέω, ῶ, ήσω, (1) *to mourn*, intrans., Ja. iv. 9; (2) *to mourn passionately for, to lament*, trans., 2 Cor. xii. 21.

πένθος, ους, τό, *mourning*, Ja. iv. 9; Rev. xviii. 7, 8, xxi. 4.*

πενιχρός, ά, όν, *poor, needy*, Lu. xxi. 2.*

πεντάκις, num. adv., *five times*, 2 Cor. xi. 24.*

πεντακισ-χίλιοι, αι, α, num., *five thousand*, Mat. xiv. 21.

πεντακόσιοι, αι, α, num., *five hundred*, Lu. vii. 41; 1 Cor. xv. 6.*

πέντε, οἱ, αἱ, τά, num. indecl., *five*, Mat. xiv. 17.

πεντε-και-δέκατος, η, ον, ord. num., *fifteenth*, Lu. iii. 1. (S.)*

πεντήκοντα, οἱ, αἱ, τά, num. indecl., *fifty*, Lu. vii. 41.

πεντηκοστή, ῆς, ἡ (lit. *fiftieth*), *Pentecost*, the feast beginning the fiftieth day after the second day of the Passover, *i.e.*, from the sixteenth day of the month Nisan, Ac. ii. 1, xx. 16; 1 Cor. xvi. 8.*

πέποιθα, see πείθω.

πεποίθησις, εως, ἡ, *trust, confidence*, with εἰς or ἐν, 2 Cor. viii. 22; Phil. iii. 4. (S.)

πέρ, an enclitic particle, cognate with περί, only found joined to pronouns or particles for intensity of meaning, as ἐάνπερ, εἴπερ, *if indeed; ἐπείπερ, since indeed;* καίπερ, *and really;* ὅσπερ, *the very one who.*

περαιτέρω (πέρα), adv., *further, besides*, Ac. xix. 39 (W. H.).*

πέραν, adv., *over, on the other side, beyond*, with article prefixed or genitive following, Mat. viii. 18, 28, xix. 1.

πέρας, ατος, τό, *a limit, the extremity*, in space, as Mat. xii. 42; or time, Heb. vi. 16.

Πέργαμος, ου, ἡ, *Pergamus* or *Pergamum*, Rev. i. 11, ii. 12.*

Πέργη, ης, ἡ, *Perga*, Ac. xiii. 13.

περί, a prep., governing the gen. and acc.; with gen., *about, i.e.*, concerning or respecting a thing; with acc., *about, around*, in reference to (see Gr. § 302, Wi. §§ 47 *e*, 49 *i*, Bu. 335). In composition, περί denotes *round about, on account of, above, beyond.*

περι-άγω, trans., *to lead* or *take about*, 1 Cor. ix. 5; intrans., *to go about* (acc. of place), Mat. iv. 23, ix. 35, xxiii. 15; Mar. vi. 6; Ac. xiii. 11.*

περι-αιρέω, ῶ (see Gr. § 103, 2, Wi. § 15, Bu. 53), *to take from around, take entirely away*, lit., Ac. xxvii. 40 (*to cast off* anchors, R. V.); fig., of the removal of sin, Heb. x. 11.

περι-άπτω, *to kindle*, Lu. xxii. 55 (W. H.).*

περι-αστράπτω, *to lighten around, to flash around* (acc., or περί, acc.), Ac. ix. 3, xxii. 6. (Ap.)*

περι-βάλλω, βαλῶ, βέβληκα, *to cast around* (acc. and dat.), Lu. xix. 43; *to clothe*, Mat. xxv. 36; for const., see Gr. § 284, Wi. § 53, 4, 12), Bu. 149; mid., *to clothe one's self, to be clothed*, Mat. vi. 29.

περι-βλέπω, N. T., in mid., *to look around*, abs., Mar. v. 32, ix. 8, x. 23; *to look round upon*, acc., Mar. iii. 5, 34, xi. 11; Lu. vi. 10.*

περι-βόλαιον, ου, τό, (1) *a mantle*, Heb. i. 12; (2) *a veil*, 1 Cor. xi. 15.*

περι-δέω, *to bind round about*, pass., plup., Jn. xi. 44.*

περι-δρέμω, see περιτρέχω.

περι-εργάζομαι, *to overdo, to be a busybody*, 2 Th. iii. 11.*

περί-εργος, ον, act., *overdoing, intermeddling*, 1 Tim. v. 13; pass., τὰ περίεργα, *superfluous arts, sorcery*, Ac. xix. 19.*

περι-έρχομαι (see Gr. § 103, 2, Wi. § 53, 4, 12)), *to go about*, Ac. xix. 13; 1 Tim. v. 13; Heb. xi. 37; *to tack*, as a ship, Ac. xxviii. 13 (not W. H.).*

περι-έχω, *to encompass;* so, *to contain*, as a writing, Ac. xxiii. 25 (W. H. ἔχω); intrans., *to be contained*, 1 Pet. ii. 6; *to seize*, as astonishment, Lu. v. 9.*

περι-ζώννυμι, or -ζωννύω (see Gr. § 114, Wi. § 53, 4, 12), Bu. 191), *to gird one's self around*, mid. or pass., Ep. vi. 14; Lu. xii. 35, 37.

περί-θεσις, εως, ἡ, *a putting around*, as ornaments, 1 Pet. iii. 3. (N. T.)*

περι-ΐστημι (see Gr. § 107, Wi. § 14, 1), in intrans. tenses of act., *to stand around*, Jn. xi. 42; Ac. xxv. 7; mid., *to avoid, shun* (acc.), 2 Tim. ii. 16; Tit. iii. 9.*

περι-κάθαρμα, ατος, τό, *refuse, offscouring*, 1 Cor. iv. 13. (S.)*

περι-καλύπτω, *to cover round about, to cover up*, as the face, Mar. xiv. 65; Lu. xxii. 64; Heb. ix. 4.*

περί-κειμαι, *to lie about, surround*, dat., or περί, acc., Mar. ix. 42; Lu. xvii. 2; Heb. xii. 1; *to be encompassed* or *surrounded with*, acc., Ac. xxviii. 20; Heb. v. 2.*

περι-κεφαλαία, ας, ἡ, *a helmet*, Ep. vi. 17; 1 Th. v. 8.*

περι-κρατής, ές, *having full power over* (gen.), Ac. xxvii. 16. (Ap.)*

περι-κρύπτω, *to hide entirely*, Lu. i. 24. (N. T.)*

περι-κυκλόω, ῶ, ώσω, *to encircle, surround*, Lu. xix. 43.*

περι-λάμπω, *to shine around*, Lu. ii. 9; Ac. xxvi. 13.*

περι-λείπω, *to leave remaining;* pass., *to be left*, 1 Th. iv. 15, 17.*

περί-λυπος, ον, *very sorrowful*, Mat. xxvi. 38; Mar. vi. 26, xiv. 34; Lu. xviii. 23, 24 (W. H. omit).*

περι-μένω, *to wait for* (acc.), Ac. i. 4.*

πέριξ, adv., *round about*, Ac. v. 16.*

περι-οικέω, ῶ, *to dwell around, to be neighboring to* (acc.), Lu. i. 65.*

περί-οικος, ον, *dwelling around, a neighbor*, Lu. i. 58.*

περι-ούσιος, ον, *costly, treasured, select;* hence, *specially chosen*, Tit. ii. 14 (S.). (S.)*

περι-οχή, ῆς, ἡ (περιέχω), *a section* or *passage* of Scripture, Ac. viii. 32.*

περι-πατέω, ῶ, ήσω, *to walk, to walk about;* fig., as Hebrew, *to pass one's life, to conduct one's self* (adv. or nom. pred.), *to live according to* (ἐν, dat.; κατά, acc.).

περι-πείρω, *to pierce through*, fig., 1 Tim. vi. 10.*

περι-πίπτω, *to fall into the midst of* (dat.), robbers, Lu. x. 30; temptations, Ja. i. 2; *to happen upon* a place, Ac. xxvii. 41.*

περι-ποιέω, ῶ, N. T. in mid., *to preserve for one's self*, Lu. xvii. 33 (W. H.); *to get for one's self, purchase*, Ac. xx. 28; 1 Tim. iii. 13.*

περι-ποίησις, εως, ἡ, (1) *a preserving*, Heb. x. 39; (2) *an obtaining, a possessing*, 1 Th. v. 9; 2 Th. ii. 14; (3) *a possession*, Ep. i. 14; 1 Pet. ii. 9.

περι-ρρήγνυμι, *to tear off*, as garments, Ac. xvi. 22.*

περι-σπάω, ῶ, *to drag around;* hence, fig., pass., *to be distracted in mind*, Lu. x. 40.*

περισσεία, ας, ἡ, *abundance, superfluity*, Ro. v. 17; 2 Cor. viii. 2; Ja. i. 21; εἰς περισσείαν, as adv., *abundantly*, 2 Cor. x. 15.*

περίσσευμα, ατος, τό, *abundance*, Mat. xii. 34; Lu. vi. 45; 2 Cor. viii. 14; pl. *a residue*, Mar. viii. 8.*

περισσεύω, εύσω, *to be more than enough, to remain over, to be in abundance*, Lu. xii. 15; Jn. vi. 12; τὸ περισσεῦον, *the residue*, Mat. xiv. 20; *to redound to*, εἰς, 2 Cor. viii. 2; *to make to abound*, Mat. xiii. 12; 2 Cor. iv. 15.

περισσός, ή, όν, *abundant, more than is necessary*, Mat. v. 37; Mar. vii. 36; *superior*, Mat. v. 47; τὸ περισσόν, *excellence, pre-eminence*, Ro. iii. 1.

περισσοτέρως, adv. (compar. of περισσῶς), *more abundantly, more earnestly*, 2 Cor. vii. 13, 15.

περισσῶς, adv., *greatly, exceedingly*, Mar. x. 26.

περιστερά, ᾶς, ἡ, *a dove*, Mat. iii. 16, x. 16.

περι-τέμνω, *to cut around, to circumcise*, Lu. i. 59: pass. and mid., *to undergo circumcision, to cause one's self to be circumcised*, 1 Cor. vii. 18.

περι-τίθημι, *to place*, or *put about* or *around* (dat. and acc.), Mat. xxi. 33; fig., *to bestow, to confer*, 1 Cor. xii. 23.

περι-τομή, ῆς, ἡ, *circumcision*, the act, the custom, or state, Jn. v. 22, 23; Gal. v. 6; with art., *the circumcision, i.e.*, the Jews, Ro. iii. 30, iv. 9, 12; fig., for *spiritual purity*, Ro. ii. 29; Col. ii. 11. (S.)

περι-τρέπω, *to turn about, to turn* into (εἰς) madness, Ac. xxvi. 24.*

περι-τρέχω, 2d aor. περιέδραμον, *to run around* (acc.), Mar. vi. 55.*

περι-φέρω, *to bear* or *carry around*, Mar. vi. 55; 2 Cor. iv. 10; pass., fig., *to be carried about, carried away* by false teaching, Ep. iv. 14; Heb. xiii. 9; Ju. 12 (W. H., in last two, παραφέρω).*

περι-φρονέω, ῶ, *to look down upon, to despise*, Tit. ii. 15.*

περί-χωρος, ον, *lying round about;* only as subst., ἡ περίχωρος (sc. γῆ), *the region round about*, Lu. iii. 3, iv. 14; *the inhabitants of such a region*, Mat. iii. 5.

περί-ψημα, ατος, τό, *scrapings, offscourings*, 1 Cor. iv. 13.*

περπερεύομαι, dep., intrans., *to boast*, 1 Cor. xiii. 4.*

Περσίς, ίδος, ἡ, *Persis*, Ro. xvi. 12.*

πέρυσι, adv., *last year;* ἀπὸ πέρυσι, *a year ago*, 2 Cor. viii. 10, ix. 2.*

πετάομαι, ῶμαι, or πέτομαι (W. H.), *to fly*, as a bird, Rev.*

πετεινόν, οῦ, τό, *a bird;* only in plur., *birds*, Mat. vi. 26, xiii. 4.

πέτομαι, see πετάομαι.

πέτρα, ας, ἡ, *a rock, a ledge, cliff*, Mat. vii. 24, 25, xxvii. 51; with art., *the rock, i.e.*, the rocky substratum of the soil, Lu. viii. 6, 13; *a large* detached *rock*, fig., Ro. ix. 33; see also Mat. xvi. 18.

Πέτρος, ου, ὁ, *Peter* (prop., a rock = Κηφᾶς), Lu. iv. 38; Jn. i. 42.

πετρώδης, ες, *rocky, stony*, Mat. xiii. 5, 20; Mar. iv. 5, 16.*

πήγανον, ου, τό, *rue*, Lu. xi. 42.*

πηγή, ῆς, ἡ, *a fountain, spring*, Jn. iv. 14; Ja. iii. 11; fig., Rev. vii. 17; *a flow* of blood, Mar. v. 29.

πήγνυμι, πήξω, *to fasten, to pitch* a tent, Heb. viii. 2.*

πηδάλιον, ου, τό, *the rudder* of a ship, Ac. xxvii. 40; Ja. iii. 4.*

πηλίκος, η, ον, *how large*, Gal. vi. 11 (see γράμμα); *how distinguished*, Heb. vii. 4.*

πηλός, οῦ, ὁ, *clay, mud*, Jn. ix. 6–15; Ro. ix. 21.*

πήρα, ας, ἡ, *a sack, a wallet*, for carrying provisions, Mat. x. 10; Mar. vi. 8; Lu. ix. 3, x. 4, xxii. 35, 36.*

πῆχυς, εως, ὁ, *a cubit*, the length from the elbow to the tip of the middle finger, *about a foot and a half*, Mat. vi. 27; Lu. xii. 25; Jn. xxi. 8; Rev. xxi. 17.*

πιάζω, σω, *to lay hold of*, Ac. iii. 7; *to take*, as in fishing or in hunting, Jn. xxi. 3, 10; Rev. xix. 20; *to arrest*, Jn. vii. 30.

πιέζω, *to press together*, as in a measure, Lu. vi. 38.*

πιθανο-λογία, ας, ἡ, *persuasive* or *plausible speech*, Col. ii. 4.*

πικραίνω, ανῶ, *to render bitter*, lit., Rev. viii. 11, x. 9, 10; *to embitter*, fig., Col. iii. 19.*

πικρία, ας, ἡ, *bitterness*, fig., Ac. viii. 23; Ro. iii. 14; Ep. iv. 31; Heb. xii. 15.*

πικρός, ά, όν, *bitter, acrid, malignant*, Ja. iii. 11, 14.*

πικρῶς, adv., *bitterly*, of weeping, Mat. xxvi. 75; Lu. xxii. 62.*

Πιλάτος, or Πιλᾶτος (W. H. Πειλᾶτος), ου, ὁ (Lat. *pilatus*, "armed with a javelin"), *Pilate*, Mar. xv. 1, 2.

πίμπλημι, πλήσω, 1st aorist pass., ἐπλήσθην, (1) *to fill* with (gen.), Mat. xxvii. 48; fig., of emotions, Lu. iv. 28; or of the Holy Spirit, Ac. ii

4; (2) pass., *to be fulfilled* or *completed*, of time, Lu. i. 23, 57.

πίμπρημι (πρα-), and πιμπράω, pass., inf., *πίμπρασθαι*, *to be inflamed*, *to swell*, Ac. xxviii. 6.*

πινακίδιον, ου, τό (dim. of πίναξ), *a tablet for writing*, Lu. i. 63.*

πίναξ, ακος, ὁ, *a plate*, *platter*, Lu. xi. 39.

πίνω, fut. πίομαι, perf. πέπωκα, 2d aor. ἔπιον (inf. πεῖν, W. H.), *to drink*, abs., or with acc. of thing drunk (sometimes ἐκ or ἀπό), Lu. xii. 19, 29; *to imbibe*, as the earth imbibes rain, Heb. vi. 7; fig., *to receive into the soul*, *to partake of*, Jn. vii. 37.

πιότης, τητος, ἡ, *fatness*, as of the olive, Ro. xi. 17.*

πιπράσκω (πρα-), perf. πέπρακα, 1st aor. pass. ἐπράθην, perf. pass. πέπραμαι, *to sell*, Mat. xiii. 46; pass., with ὑπό, *to be sold under*, *to be a slave to*, Ro. vii. 14.

πίπτω (πετ-, see Gr. § 94, i. 8*d*, Wi. § 13, 1*a*, Bu. 167), πεσοῦμαι, (1) *to fall* (whence, by ἀπό or ἐκ; whither, by ἐπί or εἰς, acc.), Mat. xv. 27; Mar. iv. 5, 7, 8; hence, (2) *to fall prostrate*, as of persons, *to die*, *to perish*, Jn. xviii. 6; Rev. i. 17; of structures, *to fall in ruins*, Mat. vii. 25, 27; of institutions, *to fail;* (3) *to fall to*, as a lot, Ac. i. 26; (4) *to fall into* or *under*, as condemnation.

Πισιδία, ας, ἡ, *Pisidia*, Ac. xiv. 24, xiii. 14, where W. H. have adj. form.*

πιστεύω (see Gr. § 74, Wi. §§ 31, 5, 32, 5, 33*d*, 39, 1*a*, Bu. 173 sq., 337), εύσω, *to believe*, *be persuaded* of a thing (acc. or ὅτι); *to give credit to*, dat.; *to have confidence in*, *to trust*, *believe*, dat., εἰς, ἐν, ἐπί (dat.) or ἐπί (acc.), often of Christian faith, in God, in Christ; *to entrust* something (acc.) to any one (dat.); pass., *to be entrusted with* (acc.).

πιστικός, ή, όν, *genuine*, *pure*, of ointment, Mar. xiv. 3; Jn. xii. 3.*

πίστις, εως, ἡ, (1) *faith*, generally, as 2 Th. ii. 13; Heb. xi. 1; the object of the faith is expressed by obj. gen., or by εἰς, ἐν, πρός (acc.); (2) *fidelity*, *good faith*, Ro. iii. 3; 2 Tim. ii. 22; (3) *a pledge*, *a promise given*, 2 Tim. iv. 7; (4) met., for the whole of the *Christian character*, and (generally with art.) for the *Christian religion*.

πιστός, ή, όν, (1) *trustworthy*, *faithful*, in any relation or to any promise, of things or (generally) persons; (2) *believing*, abs., as οἱ πιστοί, *the followers of Christ*, or with dat.

πιστόω, ῶ, *to make faithful;* N. T., only in pass., *to be assured of*, 2 Tim. iii. 14.*

πλανάω, ῶ, ήσω, *to lead astray*, *to cause to wander*, Heb. xi. 38; fig., *to deceive*, Jn. vii. 12; pass., *to be misled*, *to err*, Mar. xii. 24, 27; Lu. xxi. 8.

πλάνη, ης, ἡ, *a wandering;* only fig., *deceit*, *delusion*, *error*, Mat. xxvii. 64; Ep. iv. 14.

πλανήτης, ου, ὁ, *a wanderer;* ἀστὴρ πλανήτης, *a wandering star*, Ju. 13.*

πλάνος, ον, *causing to wander*, *misleading*, 1 Tim. iv. 1; as subst., *a deceiver*, Mat. xxvii. 63; 2 Cor. vi. 8; 2 Jn. 7.*

πλάξ, ακός, ἡ, *a tablet* to write on, 2 Cor. iii. 3; Heb. ix. 4.*

πλάσμα, ατος, τό, *a thing formed* or *fashioned*, Ro. ix. 20.*

πλάσσω, άσω, *to form*, *mould*, as a potter his clay, Ro. ix. 20; 1 Tim. ii. 13.*

πλαστός, ή, όν, *formed*, *moulded;* fig., *feigned*, 2 Pet. ii. 3.*

πλατεῖα, ας, ἡ (fem. of πλατύς, *broad*, sc. ὁδός), *a street*, Mat. vi. 5, xii. 19.

πλάτος, ους, τό, *breadth*, Ep. iii. 18; Rev. xx. 9, xxi. 16.*

πλατύνω, *to make broad*, *to enlarge*, Mat. xxiii. 5; pass., fig., *to be enlarged*, in mind or heart, 2 Cor. vi. 11, 13.*

πλατύς, εῖα, ύ, *broad*, Mat. vii. 13.*

πλέγμα, ατος, τό (πλέκω), *anything interwoven*, *braided hair*, 1 Tim. ii. 9.*

πλεῖστος, η, ον, superl. of πολύς, *the greatest*, *the most*, *very great;* τὸ πλεῖστον, adv., *mostly*, *at most*, 1 Cor. xiv. 27.

πλείων, εῖον (for declension see Gr. § 44, Bu. 127), compar. of πολύς, *more*, *greater*, in number, magnitude, comparison; οἱ πλείονες, οἱ πλείους, *the more*, *the most*, *the many*, majority, 2 Cor. ii. 6; πλεῖον or πλέον, as adv., *more*, Jn. xxi. 15; ἐπὶ πλεῖον, *further*, *longer*, Ac. iv. 17.

πλέκω, ξω, *to weave together*, *to plait*, Mat. xxvii. 29; Mar. xv. 17; Jn. xix. 2.*

πλέον, see πλείων.

πλεονάζω, σω, intrans., *to have more than enough*, 2 Cor. viii. 15; *to abound*, *to increase*, Ro. v. 20; 2 Cor. iv. 15; trans., *to cause to increase*, 1 Th. iii. 12.

πλεονεκτέω, ῶ, *to have more than another;* hence, *to overreach*, *take advantage of* (R. V.), 2 Cor. vii. 2, xii. 17, 18; 1 Th. iv. 6; pass., 2 Cor. ii. 11.*

πλεον-έκτης, ου, ὁ, *a covetous* or *avaricious person*, 1 Cor. v. 10, 11, vi. 10; Ep. v. 5.*

πλεονεξία, ας, ἡ, *covetousness*, *avarice*, Lu. xii. 15; 2 Pet. ii. 3. *Syn.:* πλεονεξία is more active, seeking to grasp the things it has not; φιλαργυρία, more passive, seeking to retain and multiply what it has.

πλευρά, ᾶς, ἡ, *the side* of the body, Jn. xix. 34.

πλέω, see πίμπλημι.

πλέω, impf. ἔπλεον, *to sail*, Lu. viii. 23; Ac. xxi. 3, xxvii. 6, 24; Rev. xviii. 17 (W. H.); with acc. of direction, Ac. xxvii. 2 (but W. H. read εἰς).*

πληγή, ῆς, ἡ (πλήσσω), *a blow*, *a stripe*, *a wound*, Ac. xvi. 33; Rev. xiii. 14; *an affliction*, Rev. ix. 20.

πλῆθος, ους, τό, *a multitude*, *a great number*, Mar. iii. 7, 8; Heb. xi. 12; with art., *the multitude*, *the whole number*, *the assemblage*, Ac. xiv. 4; *a quantity*, Ac. xxviii. 3.

πληθύνω, νῶ, (1) intrans., *to increase*, Ac. vi. 1; (2) trans., *to multiply*, *augment*, 2 Cor.

ix. 10; pass., *to be increased*, Mat. xxiv. 12.

πλήθω, see πίμπλημι.

πλήκτης, ου, ὁ, *a striker, a contentious person*, 1 Tim. iii. 3; Tit. i. 7.*

πλημμύρα, ας (W. H. ης), ἡ, *a flood*, Lu. vi. 48.*

πλήν, adv. (akin to πλέον, hence it *adds* a thought, generally adversative, sometimes partly confirmatory), *besides, but, nevertheless, of a truth*, Mat. xi. 22, xviii. 7, xxvi. 39, 64; πλὴν ὅτι, *except that*, Ac. xx. 23; as prep. with gen., *besides, excepting*, Mar. xii. 32; Ac. viii. 1.

πλήρης, ες, (1) *full*, abs., Mar. iv. 28; (2) *full of* (gen.), *abounding in*, Mar. viii. 19; Lu. iv. 1.

πληρο-φορέω, ῶ (φέρω), *to bring to the full, to fulfill*, 2 Tim. iv. 5, 17; pass., of things, *to be fully accomplished*, Lu. i. 1; of persons, *to be fully convinced*, Ro. iv. 21, xiv. 5; Col. iv. 12 (W. H.).*

πληρο-φορία, ας, ἡ, *fullness, entire possession, full assurance*, Col. ii. 2; 1 Th. i. 5; Heb. vi. 11, x. 22. (N. T.)*

πληρόω, ῶ, ώσω, *to fill* with (gen.), *to fill up, to pervade, to complete*, either time or number; *to bestow abundantly, to furnish liberally*, Phil. iv. 18; Ep. iii. 19; *to accomplish, to perform fully*, as prophecies, etc.; pass., *to be full of*, 2 Cor. vii. 4; Ep. v. 18; *to be made full, complete*, or *perfect*, Jn. iii. 29; Col. iv. 12 (W. H. read πληροφορέω).

πλήρωμα, ατος, τό, *fullness, plenitude, i.e.*, that which fills, 1 Cor. x. 26, 28; so, *the full number*, Ro. xi. 25; *the completion, i.e.*, that which makes full, *the fulfillment*, Mat. ix. 16; Ro. xiii. 10; *the fullness of time*, Gal. iv. 4, is the completion of an era; *the fullness of Christ*, Ep. i. 23, that which is filled by Christ, *i.e.*, the Church; *the fullness of the Godhead*, Col. ii. 9, all divine attributes.

πλησίον, adv., *near, near by*, with gen., Jn. iv. 5; with the art., ὁ πλησίον, *a neighbor*, Ac. vii. 27.

πλησμονή, ῆς, ἡ, *full satisfying, indulgence*, Col. ii. 23.*

πλήσσω, 2d aor. pass. ἐπλήγην, *to smite*, Rev. viii. 12.*

πλοιάριον, ου, τό (dim. of πλοῖον), *a small vessel, a boat*, Mar. iii. 9; Jn. xxi. 8.

πλοῖον, ου, τό, *a ship, a vessel*, Mat. iv. 21, 22; Mar. i. 19.

πλόος, οῦς, gen. οῦ or οός, ὁ, *a voyage*, Ac. xxi. 7, xxvii. 9, 10.*

πλούσιος, α, ον, *rich, abounding in* (ἐν), Lu. xii. 16; Ep. ii. 4.

πλουσίως, adv., *richly, abundantly*, Col. iii. 16.

πλουτέω, ῶ, ήσω, *to become rich, to be rich, to abound in*, Lu. i. 53; Ro. x. 12; Rev. xviii. 15.

πλουτίζω, *to make rich, to cause to abound in*, 1 Cor. i. 5; 2 Cor. vi. 10, ix. 11.*

πλοῦτος, ου, ὁ (see Gr. § 32*a*, Wi. § 9*e*, note 2, Bu. 22), *riches, wealth, abundance*, Ja. v. 2; Col. i. 27; spiritually, *enrichment*, Ro. xi. 12.

πλύνω, νῶ, *to wash*, Lu. v. 2 (W. H.); Rev. vii. 14, xxii. 14 (W. H.). *Syn.*: see λούω.

πνεῦμα, ατος, τό, (1) properly, *the wind*, or *the air in motion*, Jn. iii. 8; hence, (2) *the human spirit*, dist. from σῶμα and ψυχή, 1 Th. v. 23; (3) *a temper* or *disposition* of the soul, Lu. ix. 55; Ro. viii. 15; (4) *any intelligent, incorporeal being*, as (*a*) *the human spirit*, separated from the body, *the undying soul*; (*b*) *angels*, good and bad; (*c*) *God*, Jn. iv. 24; (*d*) *the Holy Spirit*, the third person of the Trinity (see Gr. § 217*f*, Wi. § 19, 1*a*, Bu. 89), in relation to Jesus, Lu. iv. 1; Ac. x. 38; in relation to prophets and apostles, Ac. xxi. 11; Jn. xx. 22; and in relation to saints generally, Gal. iii. 2.

πνευματικός, ή, όν, *spiritual*, relating to the human spirit, or belonging to a spirit, or imparted by the divine Spirit, 1 Cor. ii. 13 (see Gr. § 316, Wi. § 64, 5), 15, xv. 44; τὰ πνευματικά, *spiritual things*, Ro. xv. 27; *spiritual gifts*, 1 Cor. xii. 1.

πνευματικῶς, adv., *spiritually, i.e.*, by the aid of the Holy Spirit, 1 Cor. ii. 14; in a mystical sense, Rev. xi. 8. (N. T.)*

πνέω, εύσω, *to blow*, as the wind, Mat. vii. 25, 27.

πνίγω, *to choke, to seize by the throat*, Mat. xviii. 28; Mar. v. 13.*

πνικτός, ή, όν, *strangled*, Ac. xv. 20, 29; xxi. 25.

πνοή, ῆς, ἡ, (1) *breath*, Ac. xvii. 25; (2) *wind*, Ac. ii. 2.*

ποδήρης, ες, *reaching to the feet*; as subst. (sc. χιτών or ἐσθής), *a long robe*, Rev. i. 13.* *Syn.*: see ἱμάτιον.

πόθεν, adv., interrog., *whence?* of place, Mat. xv. 33; *from what source?* Mat. xiii. 27; of cause, *how?* Lu. i. 43; Mar. xii. 37.

ποία, ας, ἡ, *grass, herbage*, according to some, in Ja. iv. 14; but more probably the word here is the fem. of ποῖος, *of what sort?* *

ποιέω, ῶ, ήσω, (1) *to make, i.e., to form, to bring about, to cause*; spoken of religious festivals, etc., *to observe, to celebrate*; of trees and plants, *to germinate, to produce*; *to cause to be* or *to become*, Mat. xxi. 13; *to declare to be*, Jn. viii. 53; *to assume*, Mat. xii. 33; (2) *to do*, generally; *to do, i.e.*, habitually, *to perform, to execute, to exercise, to practice, i.e., to pursue a course of action, to be active, to work, to spend, to pass, i.e.*, time or life, Ac. xv. 33. *Syn.*: see Trench, § xcvi.

ποίημα, ατος, τό, *a thing made, a work*, Ro. i. 20; Ep. ii. 10.*

ποίησις, εως, ἡ, *a doing*, Ja. i. 25.*

ποιητής, οῦ, ὁ, (1) *a doer, performer*, Ro. ii. 13; Ja. i. 22, 23, 25, iv. 11; (2) *a poet*, Ac. xvii. 28.*

ποικίλος, η, ον, *various, of different colors, diverse*, Lu. iv. 40.

ποιμαίνω, ανῶ, (1) *to feed a flock*, Lu. xvii. 7; 1 Cor. ix. 7; hence, fig., (2) *to be shepherd of, to tend, to cherish*. Mat. ii. 6; Jn. xxi. 16; Ac. xx. 28; 1 Pet. v. 2; Ju. 12;

Rev. vii. 17; (3) *to rule, govern*, Rev. ii. 27, xii. 5, xix. 15.* *Syn.*: see βόσκω.

ποιμήν, ένος, ὁ, (1) *a shepherd*, Mat. ix. 36, xxv. 32; (2) fig., of Christ as the *Shepherd*, Heb. xiii. 20; 1 Pet. ii. 25; and of his ministers as *pastors*, Ep. iv. 11

ποίμνη, ης, ἡ, (1) *a flock* of sheep or goats, Lu. ii. 8; 1 Cor. ix. 7; (2) fig., of Christ's followers, Mat. xxvi. 31; Jn. x. 16.*

ποίμνιον, ου, τό (= ποίμνη), *a flock*; only fig., Lu. xii. 32; Ac. xx. 28, 29; 1 Pet. v. 2, 3.*

ποῖος, ποία, ποῖον, an interrog. pronoun corresponding to οἷος and τοῖος, *of what kind, sort, species? what? what one?* In Lu. v. 19, sc. ὁδοῦ.

πολεμέω, ῶ, ήσω, *to make war, to contend* with (μετά, gen.), Rev. ii. 16, xiii. 4.

πόλεμος, ου, ὁ, (1) *war, a war*, Lu. xiv. 31; (2) *a battle*, Rev. ix. 7, 9; (3) *strife*, Ja. iv. 1.

πόλις, εως, ἡ, *a city*, Ac. v. 16; met., *the inhabitants of a city*, Mar. i. 33; with art., *the city Jerusalem, the heavenly city*, of which Jerusalem was a symbol, Heb. xiii. 14; Rev. iii. 12.

πολιτ-άρχης, ου, ὁ, *a ruler of a city, a city magistrate*, Ac. xvii. 6, 8.*

πολιτεία, ας, ἡ, (1) *citizenship*, Ac. xxii. 28; (2) *a state, commonwealth*, Ep. ii. 12.*

πολίτευμα, ατος, τό, *a state, a commonwealth*, Phil. iii. 20.*

πολιτεύω, in mid., *to behave as a citizen*; hence, *to live, i.e., to order one's life*, Ac. xxiii. 1; Phil. i. 27.*

πολίτης, ου, ὁ, *a citizen*, Lu. xv. 15; Ac. xxi. 39; with gen., αὐτοῦ, *a fellow-citizen*, Lu. xix. 14; Heb. viii. 11 (W. H.).*

πολλάκις, adv., *many times, often*, Mar. v. 4, ix. 22.

πολλα-πλασίων, ον, gen. ονος, *manifold, many times more*, Mat. xix. 29 (W. H.); Lu. xviii. 30.*

πολυ-λογία, ας, ἡ, *much speaking*, Mat. vi. 7.*

πολυ-μερῶς, adv., *in many parts, by many portions*, Heb. i. 1.*

πολυ-ποίκιλος, ον, *much varied, manifold*, Ep. iii. 10.*

πολύς, πολλή, πολύ (see Gr. § 39, 2), *many, numerous*; πολύ, *much, greatly*, as adv.; πολλοί, *many*, often with partitive genitive, or ἐκ; οἱ πολλοί, *the many* (see Gr. § 227, Wi. § 18, 3); πολλά, in like manner, *much, very much, often, many times*; πολλῷ, *by much*, joined with comparatives; ἐπὶ πολύ, *for a great while*, Ac. xxviii. 6; ἐν πολλῷ, *altogether*, Ac. xxvi. 29 (not W. H.).

πολύ-σπλαγχνος, ον, *very compassionate, of great mercy*, Ja. v. 11. (N. T.)*

πολυ-τελής, ές, *very costly, very precious*, Mar. xiv. 3; 1 Tim. ii. 9; 1 Pet. iii. 4.*

πολύ-τιμος, ον, *of great value, very costly*, Mat. xiii. 46; Jn. xii. 3; compar., 1 Pet. i. 7 (W. H.).*

πολυ-τρόπως, adv., *in many ways*, Heb. i. 1.*

πόμα, ατος, τό, *drink*, 1 Cor. x. 4; Heb. ix. 10.*

πονηρία, ας, ἡ, *evil disposition, wickedness*, Mat. xxii. 18; Lu. xi. 39; Ro. i. 29; 1 Cor. v. 8; Ep. vi. 12; plur., *malignant passions, iniquities*, Mar. vii. 22; Ac. iii. 26.*

πονηρός, ά, όν (πόνος), *evil, bad*, actively, of things or persons; *wicked, depraved*, spec. *malignant*, opp. to ἀγαθός; ὁ πονηρός, *the wicked one, i.e., Satan*; τὸ πονηρόν, *evil*.

πόνος, ου, ὁ, (1) *labor*, Col. iv. 13 (W. H.); (2) *pain, anguish*, Rev. xvi. 10, 11, xxi. 4.*

Ποντικός, ή, όν, *belonging to Pontus*, Ac. xviii. 2.*

Πόντιος, ου, ὁ, *Pontius*, the prænomen of Pilate, Lu. iii. 1.

Πόντος, ου, ὁ, *Pontus*, Ac. ii. 9; 1 Pet. i. 1.*

Πόπλιος, ου, ὁ, *Publius*, Ac. xxviii. 7, 8.*

πορεία, ας, ἡ, *a journey*, Lu. xiii. 22; *a pursuit, undertaking*, Ja. i. 11.*

πορεύομαι, σομαι, dep., with pass. aor., ἐπορεύθην, *to go, to go away, to depart, to journey, to travel*, often (as Hebrew) *to take a course in life*.

πορθέω, ήσω, *to lay waste, to destroy*, Ac. ix. 21; Gal. i. 13, 23.*

πορισμός, οῦ, ὁ, *a source of gain*, 1 Tim. vi. 5, 6.*

Πόρκιος, ου, ὁ, *Porcius*, the prænomen of *Festus*, Ac. xxiv. 27.*

πορνεία, ας, ἡ, *fornication*, Ac. xv. 20, 29; fig. in Rev., *idolatry*, xiv. 8, xvii. 2, 4.

πορνεύω, σω, *to commit fornication*, 1 Cor. vi. 18; fig. in Rev., *to worship idols*, xviii. 3, 9.

πόρνη, ης, ἡ, *a harlot, a prostitute*, Mat. xxi. 31, 32; fig. in Rev., *an idolatrous community*, xvii. 1, 5.

πόρνος, ου, ὁ, *a man who prostitutes himself; a fornicator*, Ep. v. 5.

πόρρω, adv., *far, far off*, Mat. xv. 8; Mar. vii. 6; Lu. xiv. 32; comp., πορρωτέρω (or -τερον, W. H.), Lu. xxiv. 28.*

πόρρωθεν, adv., *from afar, far off*, Lu. xvii. 12; Heb. xi. 13.*

πορφύρα, ας, ἡ, *a purple garment*, indicating wealth or rank, Mar. xv. 17, 20; Lu. xvi. 19; Rev. xvii. 4 (W. H. read following), xviii. 12.*

πορφύρεος, οῦς, ᾶ, οῦν, *purple*, Jn. xix. 2, 5; Rev. xvii. 4 (W. H.), xviii. 16.*

πορφυρό-πωλις, ιδος, ἡ, *a female seller of purple cloth*, Ac. xvi. 14. (N. T.)*

ποσάκις, interrog. adv., *how often?* Mat. xviii. 21, xxiii. 37; Lu. xiii. 34.*

πόσις, εως, ἡ, *drink*, Jn. vi. 55; Ro. xiv. 17; Col. ii. 16.*

πόσος, η, ον, *how much? how great?* plur., *how many?* πόσῳ, as adv. with comparatives, *by how much?*

ποταμός, οῦ, ὁ, *a river, a torrent*, Mar. i. 5; Lu. vi. 48, 49.

ποταμο-φόρητος, ον, *carried away by a stream*, Rev. xii. 15. (N. T.)*

ποταπός, ή, όν, interrog. adj., *of what kind? of what manner?* Lu. i. 29, vii. 39.

πότε, interrog. adv., *when? at what time?* with ἕως, *how long?*

ποτέ, enclitic particle, *at some*

time, at one time or other (see Gr. § 129, Wi. § 57, 2).

πότερος, α, ον, *which of two?* N. T. neut. as adv., *whether*, correlating with ἤ, *or*, Jn. vii. 17.*

ποτήριον, ου, τό, *a drinking-cup*, Mar. vii. 4, xiv. 23; *the contents of the cup*, 1 Cor. xi. 25; fig., *the portion which God allots*, whether of good or ill, commonly of the latter, Mat. xx. 22, 23, xxvi. 39.

ποτίζω, σω, *to cause to drink* (two accs.); *to give drink to* (acc.); fig., 1 Cor. iii. 2; *to water* or *irrigate*, as plants, 1 Cor. iii. 6–8.

Ποτίολοι, ων, οἱ, *Puteoli*, Ac. xxviii. 13.*

πότος, ου, ὁ (πίνω), *a drinking, carousing*, 1 Pet. iv. 3.*

ποῦ, interrog. adv., *where? whither?* Mat. ii. 4; Jn. vii. 35.

πού, an enclitic particle of place or degree, *somewhere, somewhere about*, Heb. ii. 6, 16 (W. H., see δήπου), iv. 4; Ro. iv. 19 (see Gr. § 129, Bu. 71).*

Πούδης, δεντος, ὁ, *Pudens*, 2 Tim. iv. 21.*

πούς, ποδός, ὁ, *the foot*, Lu. i. 79; ὑπὸ τοὺς πόδας, *under the feet, i.e., entirely subdued*, as Ro. xvi. 20.

πρᾶγμα, ατος, τό, *a thing done, a fact, a thing, a business, a suit*, as at law, Lu. i. 1; 1 Th. iv. 6; Ro. xvi. 2; Heb. x. 1.

πραγματεία (W. H. -τία), ας, ἡ, *a business, occupation*, 2 Tim. ii. 4.*

πραγματεύομαι, σομαι, dep., *to transact business, to trade*, Lu. xix. 13.*

πραιτώριον, ου, τό (Lat. *prætorium*), *the palace* at Jerusalem occupied by the Roman governor, Mat. xxvii. 27; Mar. xv. 16; Jn. xviii. 28, 33, xix. 9; so at Cæsarea, Ac. xxiii. 35; *the quarters of the prætorian army* in Rome, Phil. i. 13.*

πράκτωρ, ορος, ὁ, *an officer employed to execute judicial sentences*, Lu. xii. 58.*

πρᾶξις, εως, ἡ, (1) *a doing, action, mode of action*, Mat. xvi. 27; Lu. xxiii. 51; plur., *deeds, acts*, Ac. xix. 18; Ro. viii. 13; Col. iii. 9; and in inscription to the Acts of the Apostles; (2) *function, business*, Ro. xii. 4.*

πρᾷος, α, ον, Rec. in Mat. xi. 29 for πραΰς (W. H.).*

πρᾳότης, τητος, ἡ, Rec. for πραΰτης (W. H.) in 1 Cor. iv. 21; 2 Cor. x. 1; Gal. v. 23, vi. 1; Ep. iv. 2; Col. iii. 12; 1 Tim. vi. 11 (W. H. πραϋπάθια); 2 Tim. ii. 25; Tit. iii. 2.*

πρασιά, ᾶς, ἡ, *a company formed into divisions* like garden-beds, Mar. vi. 40.* For constr., see Gr. § 242, Wi. § 37, 3, Bu. 30, 139.

πράσσω, or πράττω, ξω, pf. πέπραχα, πέπραγμαι, (1) *to do, perform, accomplish*, with acc., 1 Th. iv. 11; 2 Cor. v. 10; (2) with advs., *to be in any condition, i.e., to fare*, Ac. xv. 29; Ep. vi. 21; (3) *to exact, to require*, Lu. iii. 13. *Syn.*: see ποιέω.

πραϋ-πάθεια (or ία), ας, ἡ (W. H.), *mildness*, 1 Tim. vi. 11.*

πραΰς, εῖα, ΰ, gen. έος or έως (W. H.), pl. εῖς, *mild, gentle*, Mat. v. 5, xi. 29 (see πρᾷος), xxi. 5; 1 Pet. iii. 4.*

πρᾳΰτης, τητος, ἡ, *mildness, gentleness*, Ja. i. 21, iii. 13; 1 Pet. iii. 15; and W. H. (πραΰτης) in the passages quoted under πρᾳότης.*

πρέπω, *to become, be fitting to* (dat.), 1 Tim. ii. 10; Tit. ii. 1; Heb. vii. 26; impers. (see Gr. § 101, Bu. 278), *it becomes, it is fitting to*, Mat. iii. 15; 1 Cor. xi. 13; Ep. v. 3; Heb. ii. 10.*

πρεσβεία, ας, ἡ, *an embassy, ambassadors*, Lu. xiv. 32, xix. 14.*

πρεσβεύω, from πρέσβυς (lit., *to be aged*, old men being usually chosen for the office), *to act as ambassador*, 2 Cor. v. 20; Ep. vi. 20.*

πρεσβυτέριον, ου, τό, *an assembly of elders, the Sanhedrin*, Lu. xxii. 66; Ac. xxii. 5; *officers of the church assembled, presbytery*, 1 Tim. iv. 14.*

πρεσβύτερος, τέρα, τερον (compar. of πρέσβυς, *old*), generally used as subst., *elder*, (1) in age, Ac. ii. 17; 1 Tim. v. 1; plur., often, *ancestors*, as Heb. xi. 2; (2) as subst., *an elder*, in dignity and office, *a member of the Jewish Sanhedrin*, Mat. xvi. 21; *an elder* of a Christian church, Ac. xx. 17, 28; in Rev., of the twenty-four *members of the heavenly Sanhedrin*, iv. 4, 10.

πρεσβύτης, ου, ὁ, *an old man*, Lu. i. 18; Tit. ii. 2; Philem. 9.*

πρεσβῦτις, ιδος, ἡ, *an old woman*, Tit. ii. 3.*

πρηνής, ές, *falling headlong*, Ac i. 18.*

πρίζω, or πρίω, 1st aor. pass. ἐπρίσθην, *to saw, to saw asunder*, Heb. xi. 37.*

πρίν, adv., of time, *formerly*; as conj. in N. T., with or without ἤ, *before that*; generally with acc. and inf., Mat. xxvi. 34; but after a negative we find πρὶν ἄν with subj. where the principal verb is in a primary tense, Lu. ii. 26; πρίν with opt. where it is in a historical tense, Ac. xxv. 16.

Πρίσκα, ης, ἡ, and dim. Πρίσκιλλα, ης, ἡ, a proper name, *Prisca* or *Priscilla*, Ro. xvi. 3; 2 Tim. iv. 19.

πρό, prep. with gen., *before, i.e.*, of place, time, or superiority (see Gr. § 294, Wi. § 47 *d*, Bu. 153). In composition, it retains the same meanings.

προ-άγω, άξω, *to bring out*, Ac. xvi. 30; gen. intrans., *to go before, to lead the way, to precede*, in place, Mat. ii. 9; in time, Mar. vi. 45; part. προάγων, *preceding, previous*, 1 Tim. i. 18; Heb. vii. 18.

προ-αιρέω, ῶ, N. T., in mid., *to propose to one's self, to purpose*, 2 Cor. ix. 7.*

προ-αιτιάομαι, ῶμαι, *to lay to one's charge beforehand*, Ro. iii. 9. (N. T.)*

προ-ακούω, *to hear before*, Col i. 5.*

προ-αμαρτάνω, *to sin before*, 2 Cor xii. 21, xiii. 2. (N. T.)*

προ-αύλιον, ου, τό, *a court before a building, a porch*, Mar. xiv. 68.*

προ-βαίνω, *to go forward*, Mat. iv. 21; Mar. i. 19; pf. part προβεβηκὼς ἐν ἡμέραις, *advanced in age*, Lu. i. 7, 18, ii. 36.*

προ-βάλλω, *to put forth*, as trees their leaves, Lu. xxi. 30; *to thrust forward*, Ac. xix. 33.*

προβατικός, ή, όν, *pertaining to sheep*, Jn. v. 2.*

προβάτιον, ου, τό, dim. of following, *a little sheep, a lamb*, Jn. xxi. 16, 17 (W. H.).*

πρόβατον, ου, τό (προβαίνω), *a sheep*, Mat. vii. 15; fig., *a follower of Christ*, Jn. x. 7, 8.

προ-βιβάζω, σω, *to drag forward, to urge forward*, Mat. xiv. 8; Ac. xix. 33 (not W. H.).*

προ-βλέπω, N. T., in mid., *to foresee* or *provide*, Heb. xi. 40. (S.)*

προ-γίνομαι, *to happen before*, Ro. iii. 25.*

προ-γινώσκω, *to know beforehand*, Ac. xxvi. 5; 2 Pet. iii. 17; of the divine foreknowledge, Ro. viii. 29, xi. 2; 1 Pet. i. 20.*

πρόγνωσις, εως, ἡ, *foreknowledge*, Ac. ii. 23; 1 Pet. i. 2.*

πρό-γονος, ου, ὁ, *a progenitor*, plur., *ancestors*, 1 Tim. v. 4; 2 Tim. i. 3.*

προ-γράφω, ψω, *to write before*, in time, Ro. xv. 4; Ep. iii. 3; *to depict* or *portray openly*, Gal. iii. 1; *to designate beforehand*, Ju. 4.*

πρό-δηλος, ον, *manifest to all, evident*, 1 Tim. v. 24, 25; Heb. vii. 14.*

προ-δίδωμι, (1) *to give before*, Ro. xi. 35; (2) *to give forth, betray*; see following word.*

προδότης, ου, ὁ, *a betrayer*, Lu. vi. 16; Ac. vii. 52; 2 Tim. iii. 4.*

πρό-δρομος, ου, ὁ, ἡ (προτρέχω), *a precursor, a forerunner*, Heb. vi. 20.*

προ-εῖδον, 2d aor. of προοράω.

προ-εῖπον, 2d aor. of πρόφημι, perf. προείρηκα.

προ-ελπίζω, *to hope before*, Ep. i. 12.*

προ-εν-άρχομαι, *to begin before*, 2 Cor. viii. 6, 10. (N. T.)*

προ-επ-αγγέλλω, in mid., *to promise before*, Ro. i. 2; 2 Cor. ix. 5 (W. H.). (N. T.)*

προ-έρχομαι (see Gr. § 103, 2, Bu. 144), (1) *to go forward, advance*, Ac. xii. 10; (2) *to go before, precede*, in time or place (gen. or acc.), Lu. xxii. 47; 2 Cor. ix. 5.

προ-ετοιμάζω, σω, *to prepare beforehand, to predestine*, Ro. ix. 23; Ep. ii. 10.*

προ-ευ-αγγελίζομαι, *to foretell good tidings, preach the gospel beforehand*, Gal. iii. 8.*

προ-έχω, in mid., *to hold one's self before, to be superior*, Ro. iii. 9 (see Gr. § 358, Wi. § 39, 3, note 3).*

προ-ηγέομαι, οῦμαι, *to lead onward by example*, Ro. xii. 10.*

πρόθεσις, εως, ἡ (προτίθημι), (1) *a setting forth*; οἱ ἄρτοι τῆς προθέσεως, *the loaves of the presentation*, or *the showbread*, Mat. xii. 4, compare Heb. ix. 2; (2) *a predetermination, purpose*, Ac. xi. 23.

προ-θέσμιος, α, ον, *set beforehand, appointed before*, Gal. iv. 2.*

προ-θυμία, ας, ἡ, *inclination, readiness*, Ac. xvii. 11; 2 Cor. viii. 11, 12, 19, ix. 2.*

πρό-θυμος, ον, *eager, ready, willing*, Mat. xxvi. 41; Mar. xiv. 38; τὸ πρόθυμον, *readiness*, Ro. i. 15.*

προθύμως, adv., *readily, with alacrity*, 1 Pet. v. 2.*

πρόϊμος, W. H., for πρώϊμος.

προ-ΐστημι, N.T. only intrans., act., 2d aor. and perf., and mid., (1) *to preside over, to rule*, gen., Ro. xii. 8; 1 Th. v. 12; 1 Tim. iii. 4, 5, 12, v. 17; (2) *to give attention to*, gen., Tit. iii. 8.*

προ-καλέω, ῶ, in mid., *to provoke, stimulate*, Gal. v. 26.*

προ-κατ-αγγέλλω, *to announce beforehand, to promise*, Ac. iii. 18, 24 (not W. H.), vii. 52; 2 Cor. ix. 5 (not W. H.).*

προ-κατ-αρτίζω, *to prepare beforehand*, 2 Cor. ix. 5.*

πρό-κειμαι, *to lie* or *be placed before, to be appointed*, as duty, example, reward, etc., Heb. vi. 18, xii. 1, 2; Ju. 7; *to be at hand, to be present*, 2 Cor. viii. 12.*

προ-κηρύσσω, ξω, *to announce* or *preach beforehand*, Ac. iii. 20 (not W. H.), xiii. 24.*

προ-κοπή, ῆς, ἡ, *progress, advancement*, Phil. i. 12, 25; 1 Tim. iv. 15.*

προ-κόπτω, *to make progress in* (dat. or ἐν), Lu. ii. 52; *to advance to* (ἐπί, acc.), 2 Tim. iii. 9; of time, *to be advanced* or *far spent*, Ro. xiii. 12.

πρό-κριμα, ατος, τό, *a prejudgment, a prejudice*, 1 Tim. v 21. (N. T.)*

προ-κυρόω, ῶ, *to establish* or *ratify before*, Gal. iii. 17. (N. T.)*

προ-λαμβάνω, *to take before, anticipate*, Mar. xiv. 8 ("she hath anticipated the anointing," *i.e.*, hath anointed beforehand); 1 Cor. xi. 21; pass., *to be overtaken* or *caught*, Gal. vi. 1.*

προ-λέγω, *to tell beforehand, forewarn*, 2 Cor. xiii. 2; Gal. v. 21; 1 Th. iii. 4.*

προ-μαρτύρομαι, *to testify beforehand, to predict*, 1 Pet. i. 11. (N. T.)*

προ-μελετάω, ῶ, *to meditate beforehand*, Lu. xxi. 14.*

προ-μεριμνάω, ῶ, *to be anxious beforehand*, Mar. xiii. 11. (N. T.)*

προ-νοέω, ῶ, *to perceive beforehand, to provide for*, gen., 1 Tim. v. 8; in mid., *to take thought for*, acc., Ro. xii. 17; 2 Cor. viii. 21.*

πρό-νοια, ας, ἡ, *forethought*, Ac. xxiv. 3; *provision for* (gen.), Ro. xiii. 14.*

προ-οράω, ῶ, 2d aor. προεῖδον, *to see beforehand*, Ac. ii. 31, xxi. 29; Gal. iii. 8; mid., *to have before one's eyes*, Ac. ii. 25 (S.).*

προ-ορίζω, *to predetermine, to foreordain*, Ac. iv. 28; Ro. viii. 29, 30; 1 Cor. ii. 7; Ep. i. 5, 11. (N. T.)*

προ-πάσχω, *to suffer beforehand*, 1 Th. ii. 2.*

προ-πάτωρ, ορος, ὁ, *a forefather*, Ro. iv. 1 (W. H.).*

προ-πέμπω, *to send forward, to accompany*, Ro. xv. 24; *to equip for a journey*, Tit. iii. 13.

προ-πετής, ές (πίπτω), *precipitate, rash*, Ac. xix. 36; 2 Tim. iii. 4.*

προ-πορεύομαι, σομαι, in mid., *to precede, to pass on before* (gen.), Lu. i. 76; Ac. vii. 40.*

πρός (see Gr. § 307, Wi. §§ 47*f*,

48*e*, 49*h*, Bu. 340), prep., gov. gen., dat., and accus. cases, general signif., *towards*. In composition, it denotes motion, direction, reference, nearness, addition.

προ-σάββατον, ου, τό, *the day before the sabbath*, Mar. xv. 42. (S.)*

προσ-αγορεύω, *to address by name, to designate*, Heb. v. 10.*

προσ-άγω, (1) trans., *to bring to, to bring near*, Mat. xviii. 24 (W. H.); Lu. ix. 41; Ac. xii 6 (W. H.), xvi. 20; 1 Pet. iii. 18; (2) intrans., *to come to* or *towards, to approach*, Ac. xxvii. 27.*

προσ-αγωγή, ῆς, ἡ, *approach, access* (εἰς, πρός, acc.), Ro. v. 2; Ep. ii. 18, iii. 12.*

προσ-αιτέω, ῶ, *to beg, to ask earnestly*, Mar. x. 46 (not W. H.); Lu. xviii. 35 (not W. H.); Jn. ix. 8.*

προσαίτης, ου, ὁ, *a beggar*, Mar. x. 46 (W. H.); Jn. ix. 8 (W. H.).*

προσ-ανα-βαίνω, *to go up farther*, Lu. xiv. 10.*

προσ-αναλίσκω, *to spend in addition*, Lu. viii. 43 (W. H. omit).*

προσ-ανα-πληρόω, ῶ, *to fill up by adding to, to supply*, 2 Cor. ix. 12, xi. 9.*

προσ-ανα-τίθημι, *to lay up in addition*; in mid., (1) *to communicate* or *impart* (acc. and dat.), Gal. ii. 6; (2) *to consult with* (dat.), Gal. i. 16.*

προσ-απειλέω, ῶ, *to utter additional threats*, Ac. iv. 21.*

προσ-δαπανάω, ῶ, ήσω, *to spend in addition*, Lu. x. 35.*

προσ-δέομαι, *to want more, to need in addition* (gen.), Ac. xvii. 25.*

προσ-δέχομαι, dep. mid., (1) *to receive to companionship*, Lu. xv. 2; (2) *to admit, accept*, Heb. xi. 35; (3) *to await, to expect* (acc.), Mar. xv. 43.

προσ-δοκάω, ῶ, *to look for, expect, anticipate*, whether with hope or fear, Lu. iii. 15, vii. 19, 20.

προσδοκία, ας, ἡ, *a looking for, expectation*, Lu. xxi. 26; Ac. xii. 11.*

προσ-εάω, ῶ, *to permit* one *to approach*, Ac. xxvii. 7. (N. T.)*

προσ-εγγίζω, *to approach, to come near to* (dat.), Mar. ii. 4 (not W. H.).*

προσεδρεύω, *to wait upon, to minister to* (dat.), 1 Cor. ix. 13 (W. H. παρεδρεύω).*

προσ-εργάζομαι, dep. mid., *to gain by labor in addition*, Lu. xix. 16.*

προσ-έρχομαι (see Gr. § 103, 2, Wi. § 52, 3, 4, 14)), (1) generally, *to come* or *to go to, to approach*, abs., or dat. of place or person, Mat. iv. 11, ix. 20, xxiv. 1; (2) specially, *to approach, to draw near to*, God or Christ, Heb. vii. 25; (3) *to assent to, concur in*, 1 Tim. vi. 3.

προσ-ευχή, ῆς, ἡ, (1) *prayer* to God, 1 Cor. vii. 5; Col. iv. 2; (2) *a place where prayer is offered*, only Ac. xvi. 13, 16 (see Gr. § 268, note). *Syn.*: see αἴτημα.

προσ-εύχομαι, dep. mid., *to pray* to God (dat.), *to offer prayer, to pray for* (acc. of thing, ὑπέρ or περί, of person, ἵνα or ὅπως, of object, occasionally inf.).

προσ-έχω, *to apply*, with νοῦν expressed or understood, *to apply the mind, to attend to*, dat.; with ἀπό, *to beware of*; also, *to give heed to*, inf. with μή.

προσ-ηλόω, ῶ, *to fasten with nails, nail to*, Col. ii. 14.*

προσ-ήλυτος, ου, ὁ (from προσέρχομαι, orig. adj.), *a newcomer; a convert to Judaism, a proselyte*, Mat. xxiii. 15; Ac. ii. 10, vi. 5, xiii. 43. (S.)*

πρόσ-καιρος, ον, *for a season, temporary*, Mat. xiii. 21; Mar. iv. 17; 2 Cor. iv. 18; Heb. xi. 25.*

προσ-καλέω, ῶ, N. T., mid., *to call to one's self, to call for, to summon*, Mar. iii. 13, 23, vi. 7; fig., *to call to an office, to call to the Christian faith*, Ac. ii. 39, xiii. 2.

προσ-καρτερέω, ῶ, ήσω, *to persevere in, to continue steadfast in* (dat.), Ac. i. 14, ii. 42; *to wait upon* (dat.), Mar. iii. 9; Ac. x. 7.

προσ-καρτέρησις, εως, ἡ, *perseverance*, Ep. vi. 18. (N. T.)*

προσ-κεφάλαιον, ου, τό, *a cushion for the head, a pillow*, Mar. iv. 38.*

προσ-κληρόω, ῶ, *to assign by lot, to allot*; pass. (dat.), Ac. xvii. 4.*

προσ-κλίνω, *to incline towards*, Ac. v. 36 (W. H.).*

πρόσκλισις, εως, ἡ, *an inclination towards, partiality*, 1 Tim. v. 21.*

προσ-κολλάω, ῶ, pass., *to join one's self to* (dat.), as a companion, Ac. v. 36 (W. H. προσκλίνω); *to cleave to* (πρός, acc.), as husband to wife, Mat. xix. 5 (W. H. κολλάω); Mar. x. 7; Ep. v. 31.*

πρόσ-κομμα, ατος, τό, *a stumbling-block, an occasion of falling*, Ro. xiv. 13, 20; 1 Cor. viii. 9; with λίθος, *a stone of stumbling* (R. V.), 1 Pet. ii. 8; Ro. ix. 32, 33 (S.)*

προσ-κοπή, ῆς, ἡ, *an occasion of stumbling*, 2 Cor. vi. 3.*

προσ-κόπτω, *to strike* the foot *against*, Mat. iv. 6; so, *to stumble*, 1 Pet. ii. 8.

προσ-κυλίω, *to roll to* (dat., or ἐπί, acc.), Mat. xxvii. 60; Mar. xv. 46.*

προσ-κυνέω, ῶ, *to bow down, to prostrate one's self to, to worship*, God or inferior beings, *to adore* (dat. or acc.).

προσ-κυνητής, οῦ, ὁ, *a worshipper*, Jn. iv. 23.*

προσ-λαλέω, ῶ, *to speak to* (dat.), Ac. xiii. 43, xxviii. 20.*

προσ-λαμβάνω, N. T., mid., *to take to one's self, i.e.*, food, companions, Ac. xxvii. 33, xxviii. 2; *to receive to fellowship*, Ro. xiv. 1.

πρόσ-ληψις (W. H. -λημψις), εως, ἡ, *a taking to one's self, a receiving*, Ro. xi. 15.*

προσ-μένω, *to continue with* or *in, to adhere to* (dat.), *to stay in* (ἐν) *a place*, Mat. xv. 32; 1 Tim. i. 3, v. 5.

προσ-ορμίζω (ὅρμος), mid., *to come to anchor*, Mar. vi. 53.*

προσ-οφείλω, *to owe besides*, Philem. 19.*

προσ-οχθίζω (ὀχθέω or ὀχθίζω), *to be displeased* or *offended* *with* (dat.), Heb. iii. 10, 17 (S.).*

πρόσ-πεινος, ον (πεῖνα), *very hungry*, Ac. x. 10. (N. T.)*

προσ-πήγνυμι, *to fasten to*, applied to Christ's being fastened to the cross, Ac. ii. 23.*

προσ-πίπτω, (1) *to fall down before* (dat., or πρός, acc.), Mar. vii. 25; Lu. v. 8; (2) *to beat against* (dat.), Mat. vii. 25.

προσ-ποιέω, ῶ, in mid., *to conform one's self to; hence, to pretend* (inf.), Lu. xxiv. 28; in Jn. viii. 6, perhaps, *to regard* (W. H. omit).*

προσ-πορεύομαι, *to come to, approach* (dat.), Mar. x. 35.*

προσ-ρήγνυμι, *to dash against*, as waves, Lu. vi. 48, 49.*

προσ-τάσσω, ξω, abs., or acc. and inf., *to enjoin* (acc.) *upon* (dat.), Lu. v. 14; Ac. x. 33.

προ-στάτις, ιδος, ἡ, *a female guardian, a protector*, Ro. xvi. 2.*

προσ-τίθημι, *to place near* or *by the side of, to add to* (dat., or ἐπί, dat. or acc.), Lu. iii. 20; Ac. xi. 24; mid., with inf., *to go on to do* a thing, *i.e.*, *to do again*, Ac. xii. 3; Lu. xx. 11, 12; so 1st aor. pass., part., Lu. xix. 11, προσθεὶς εἶπεν, *he spoke again* (see Gr. § 399*d*, Wi. § 54, 5, Bu. 299 sq.).

προσ-τρέχω, 2d aor. προσέδραμον, *to run to*, Mar. ix. 15, x. 17; Ac. viii. 30.*

προσ-φάγιον, ου, τό, *anything eaten with bread*, as fish, meat, etc., Jn. xxi. 5.*

πρό-σφατος, ον (from σφάζω, *to slaughter, just slaughtered*), *recent, new*, Heb. x. 20.*

προσφάτως, adv., *recently*, Ac. xviii. 2.*

προσ-φέρω, *to bring to*, dat., Mat. iv. 24, viii. 16; *to offer, to present*, as money, Ac. viii. 18; specially, *to offer sacrifice*, Ac. vii. 42; pass., *to bear one's self towards, to deal with*, Heb. xii. 7.

προσ-φιλής, ές, *pleasing, acceptable*, Phil. iv. 8.*

προσ-φορά, ᾶς, ἡ, *an offering, a sacrifice*, Ac. xxi. 26; Heb. x. 18.

προσ-φωνέω, ῶ, *to call to* (dat.), Mat. xi. 16; *to call to one's self* (acc.), Lu. vi. 13.

πρόσ-χυσις, εως, ἡ (προσχέω), *an affusion, a sprinkling*, Heb. xi. 28. (N. T.)*

προσ-ψαύω, *to touch lightly*, Lu. xi. 46.*

προσωποληπτέω (W. H. προσωπολημπτέω), ῶ, *to respect the person of any one, to show partiality*, Ja. ii. 9. (N. T.)*

προσωπο-λήπτης (W. H. προσωπολήμπτης), ου, ὁ, *a respecter of persons, a partial one*, Ac. x. 34. (N. T.)*

προσωποληψία (W. H. -λημψ-), ας, ἡ, *respect of persons, partiality*, Ro. ii. 11; Ep. vi. 9; Col. iii. 25; Ja. ii. 1. (N. T.)*

πρόσωπον, ου, τό (ὤψ), (1) *the face, the countenance*, Ja. i. 23; in antithesis with καρδία, *mere appearance*, 2 Cor. v. 12; (2) *the surface*, as of the earth, Lu. xxi. 35; of the heaven, Lu. xii. 56.

προ-τάσσω, *to appoint before*, Ac. xvii. 26 (W. H. προστάσσω).*

προ-τείνω, *to stretch out, to tie up* for scourging, Ac. xxii. 25.*

πρότερος, έρα, ερον (comparative of πρό), *former*, Ep. iv. 22; πρότερον or τὸ πρότερον, as adv., *before, formerly*, Heb. iv. 6.

προ-τίθημι, N. T. mid., *to set forth*, Ro. iii. 25; *to purpose, to design beforehand*, Ro. i. 13; Ep. i. 9.*

προ-τρέπω, in mid., *to exhort*, Ac. xviii. 27.*

προ-τρέχω, 2d aor. προέδραμον, *to run before, to outrun*, Lu. xix. 4; Jn. xx. 4.*

προ-ϋπ-άρχω, *to be previously*, with participle, Lu. xxiii. 12; Ac. viii. 9.*

πρό-φασις, εως, ἡ, *a pretext, an excuse*, 1 Th. ii. 5; dat. adverbially, *in appearance, ostensibly*, Mar. xii. 40.

προ-φέρω, *to bring forth*, Lu. vi. 45.*

πρό-φημι, fut. προερῶ, perf. προείρηκα, 2d aor. προεῖπον, *to say before, i.e.*, at an earlier time, Gal. i. 9; in an earlier part of the discourse, 2 Cor. vii. 3; or prophetically, Mar. xiii. 23.

προ-φητεία, ας, ἡ, *prophecy*, as a gift, or in exercise, Ro. xii. 6; Rev. xix. 10; plur., *prophecies*, 1 Cor. xiii. 8.

προ-φητεύω, σω, *to be a prophet, to prophesy, to forth-tell*, or speak of divine things (the meaning *foretell* is secondary and incidental), Lu. i. 67; Ac. ii. 17, 18; of false prophets, Mat. vii. 22; *to divine*, used in mockery, Mat. xxvi. 68.

προ-φήτης, ου, ὁ, (1) *a prophet, i.e.*, one who has insight into divine things and speaks them forth to others, Mat. v. 12, xxi. 46; plur., *the prophetic books of the O. T.*, Lu. xxiv. 27, 44; (2) *a poet*, Tit. i. 12.

προ-φητικός, ή, όν, *prophetic, uttered by a prophet*, Ro. xvi. 26; 2 Pet. i. 19.*

προ-φῆτις, ιδος, ἡ, *a prophetess*, Lu. ii. 36; Rev. ii. 20.*

προ-φθάνω, *to anticipate, to be beforehand*, with participle, Mat. xvii. 25.*

προ-χειρίζομαι, *to appoint, to choose*, Ac. iii. 20 (W. H.), xxii. 14, xxvi. 16.*

προ-χειρο-τονέω, ῶ, *to designate beforehand*, Ac. x. 41.*

Πρόχορος, ου, ὁ, *Prochorus*, Ac. vi. 5.*

πρύμνα, ης, ἡ, *the hindmost part of a ship, the stern*, Mar. iv. 38; Ac. xxvii. 29, 41.*

πρωΐ, adv., *early in the morning, at dawn*, Mar. i. 35, xi. 20; with advs., ἅμα πρωΐ, λίαν πρωΐ, *very early in the morning*, Mat. xx. 1; Mar. xvi. 2.

πρώϊμος (W. H. πρό-), η, ον, *early*, of the early rain, Ja. v. 7.*

πρωϊνός, ή, όν, *belonging to the morning*, of the morning star, Rev. ii. 28, xxii. 16. (S.)*

πρώϊος, α, ον, *of the morning*; fem. (sc. ὥρα), *morning*, Mat. xxi. 18 (W. H. πρωΐ), xxvii. 1; Jn. xviii. 28 (W. H. πρωΐ), xxi. 4.*

πρώρα, ας, ἡ, *the forward part of a ship, the prow*, Ac. xxvii. 30, 41.*

πρωτεύω, *to have pre-eminence, to be chief*, Col. i. 18.*

πρωτο-καθεδρία, ας, ἡ, *a chief seat*, Lu. xi. 43. (N. T.)
πρωτο-κλισία, ας, ἡ, *the chief place at a banquet*, Mar. xii. 39. (Ap.)
πρῶτος, η, ον (superlative of πρό), *first*, in place, time, or order; like πρότερος with following gen., *before*, only Jn. i. 15, 30; πρῶτον, as adverb, *first*, Mar. iv. 28; with gen., *before*, Jn. xv. 18; τὸ πρῶτον, *at the first*, Jn. x. 40.
πρωτο-στάτης, ου, ὁ, *a leader, a chief*, Ac. xxiv. 5.*
πρωτοτόκια, ων, τά, *the right of the first-born, the birthright*, Heb. xii. 16. (S.)*
πρωτό-τοκος, ον, *first-born; ὁ πρωτότοκος*, specially a title of Christ, Lu. ii. 7; plur., *the first-born*, Heb. xii. 23, of saints already dead.
πρώτως, adv., *first*, Ac. xi. 26 (W. H.).*
πταίω, σω, *to stumble, to fall, to sin*, Ro. xi. 11; 2 Pet. i. 10; Ja. ii. 10, iii. 2.*
πτέρνα, ης, ἡ, *the heel*, Jn. xiii. 18.*
πτερύγιον, ου, τό (dim. of πτέρυξ), *an extremity*, as a *battlement* or *parapet*, Mat. iv. 5; Lu. iv. 9.*
πτέρυξ, υγος, ἡ, *a wing*, Rev. iv. 8, xii. 14.
πτηνός, ἡ, όν (πέτομαι), *winged*, τὰ πτηνά, *birds*, 1 Cor. xv. 39.*
πτοέω, ῶ, *to terrify*, Lu. xxi. 9, xxiv. 37.*
πτόησις, εως, ἡ, *terror, consternation*, 1 Pet. iii. 6.*
Πτολεμαΐς, ΐδος, ἡ, *Ptolemais*, Ac. xxi. 7.*
πτύον, ου, τό, *a winnowing-shovel*, Mat. iii. 12; Lu. iii. 17.*
πτύρω, *to frighten*, Phil. i. 28.*
πτύσμα, ατος, τό, *spittle*, Jn. ix. 6.*
πτύσσω, ξω, *to fold, to roll up*, as a scroll, Lu. iv. 20.*
πτύω, σω, *to spit*, Mar. vii. 33, viii. 23; Jn. ix. 6.*
πτῶμα, ατος, τό (πίπτω), *a body fallen in death, a carcase*, Mat. xxiv. 28.
πτῶσις, εως, ἡ, *a falling, a fall*, lit. or fig., Mat. vii. 27; Lu. ii. 34.*
πτωχεία, ας, ἡ, *beggary, poverty*, 2 Cor. viii. 2, 9; Rev. ii. 9.*
πτωχεύω, σω, *to be in poverty*, 2 Cor. viii. 9.*
πτωχός, ἡ, όν, *reduced to beggary, poor, destitute*, Lu. xiv. 13, 21, xviii. 22; Ja. ii. 5; *spiritually poor*, in a good sense, Mat. v. 3; in a bad sense, Rev. iii. 17. *Syn.*: see πένης.
πυγμή, ῆς, ἡ (πύξ), *the fist*, Mar. vii. 3 (see R. V. and mrg.).*
Πύθων, ωνος, ὁ, *Python;* in N.T. *a divining spirit;* called after the Pythian serpent said to have guarded the oracle at Delphi and been slain by Apollo, Ac. xvi. 16 (see R. V.).*
πυκνός, ἡ, όν, *frequent*, 1 Tim. v. 23; neut. plur. πυκνά, as adverb, *often*, Lu. v. 33; so πυκνότερον, *more frequently*, Ac. xxiv. 26.*
πυκτεύω (πύκτης), *to be a boxer, to box*, 1 Cor. ix. 26.*
πύλη, ης, ἡ, *a door* or *gate; πύλαι ᾅδου, the gates of Hades, i.e.*, the powers of the unseen world, Mat. xvi. 18.
πυλών, ῶνος, ὁ, *a* large *gate*, Ac. x. 17; *a gateway, porch*, Mat. xxvi. 71.
πυνθάνομαι, 2d aor. ἐπυθόμην, (1) *to ask, ask* from (παρά, gen.), *to inquire*, Mat. ii. 4; Lu. xv. 26; (2) *to ascertain by inquiry*, only Ac. xxiii. 34.
πῦρ, πυρός, τό, *fire* generally; of *the heat of the sun*, Rev. xvi. 8; of *lightning*, Lu. ix. 54; God is so called, Heb. xii. 29; fig. for *strife*, Lu. xii. 49; *trials*, 1 Cor. iii. 13; of *the eternal fire*, or future punishment, Mat. xviii. 8.
πυρά, ᾶς, ἡ, *a fire*, a pile of burning fuel, Ac. xxviii. 2, 3.*
πύργος, ου, ὁ, *a tower, fortified structure*, Lu. xiii. 4, xiv. 28.
πυρέσσω, *to be sick with a fever*, Mat. viii. 14; Mar. i. 30.*
πυρετός, οῦ, ὁ, *a fever*, Lu. iv. 38, 39.
πύρινος, η, ον, *fiery, glittering*, Rev. ix. 17.*
πυρόω, ῶ, N. T., pass., *to be set on fire, to burn, to be inflamed*, 2 Pet. iii. 12; 1 Cor. vii. 9; *to glow with heat*, as metal in a furnace, *to be purified by fire*, Rev. iii. 18.
πυρράζω, *to be fire-colored, to be red*, Mat. xvi. 2, 3 (W. H. omit both). (S. πυρρίζω.)*
πυρρός, ά, όν, *fire-colored, red*, Rev. vi. 4, xii. 3.*
Πύρρος, ου, ὁ, *Pyrrhus*, Ac. xx. 4 (W. H.).*
πύρωσις, εως, ἡ, *a burning, a conflagration*, Rev. xviii. 9, 18; *severe trial*, as by fire, 1 Pet. iv. 12.*
πώ, an enclitic particle, *even, yet*, used only in composition; see μήπω, μηδέπω, οὔπω, οὐδέπω.
πωλέω, ῶ, ήσω, *to sell*, Mat. xxi. 12.
πῶλος, ου, ὁ, *a colt, a young ass*, as Mat. xxi. 2.
πώ-ποτε, adv., *at any time*, used only after a negative, *not at any time, never*, Jn. i. 18, v. 37.
πωρόω, ῶ, *to harden, to render callous*, fig., Jn. xii. 40; Ro. xi. 7.
πώρωσις, εως, ἡ, *hardness* of heart, *obtuseness*, Mar. iii. 5; Ro. xi. 25; Ep. iv. 18.*
πῶς, adv., interrog., *how? in what manner? by what means?* Also in exclamations, as Lu. xii. 50; Jn. xi. 36; with subj. or opt. (ἄν), implying a strong negative, Mat. xxvi. 54; Ac. viii. 31; often (N. T.) in indirect interrogations (classical ὅπως), Mat. vi. 28, etc.
πώς, an enclitic particle, *in a manner, by any means.*

Ρ

Ρ, ρ, ῥῶ, *rho, r*, and as an initial always ῥ, *rh*, the seventeenth letter. As a numeral, ρʹ = 100; ͵ρ = 100,000.
'Ραάβ, or 'Ραχάβ, ἡ (Heb.), *Rahab*, Heb. xi. 31.
ῥαββί (W. H. ῥαββεί), (Heb.), *Rabbi, my master*, a title of respect in Jewish schools of learning, often applied to Christ, Jn. iii. 26, iv. 31. (N. T.)
ῥαββονί, or ῥαββουνί (W. H. ῥαββουνεί), (Aram.), similar to ῥαββί, *my master*, Mar. x. 51; Jn. xx. 16. (N. T.)*
ῥαβδίζω, ίσω, *to scourge, to beat*

with rods, Ac. xvi. 22; 2 Cor. xi. 25.*

ῥάβδος, ου, ἡ, *a rod, staff*, Mat. x. 10; 1 Cor. iv. 21; Rev. xi. 1; *a rod of authority, a sceptre*, Heb. i. 8.

ῥαβδ-οῦχος, ου, ὁ (ἔχω), *a holder of the rods, a lictor*, a Roman officer, Ac. xvi. 35, 38.*

Ῥαγαῦ, ὁ (Heb.), *Ragau*, Lu. iii. 35.*

ῥᾳδι-ούργημα, ατος, τό, *a careless action, an act of villainy*, Ac. xviii. 14.*

ῥᾳδι-ουργία, ας, ἡ, *craftiness, villainy*, Ac. xiii. 10.*

ῥακά (Aram.), *an empty, i.e., senseless man*, Mat. v. 22 (see Gr. § 153, ii.). (N. T.)*

ῥάκος, ους, τό (ῥήγνυμι), *a remnant torn off, a piece of cloth*, Mat. ix. 16; Mar. ii. 21.*

Ῥαμᾶ, ἡ (Heb.), *Ramah*, Mat. ii. 18.*

ῥαντίζω, ίσω, *to sprinkle, to cleanse ceremonially* (acc.) *by sprinkling, to purify from* (ἀπό), Mar. vii. 4 (W. H.); Heb. ix. 13, 19, 21, x. 22. (S.)*

ῥαντισμός, οῦ, ὁ, *sprinkling, purification*, Heb. xii. 24; 1 Pet. i. 2. (S.)*

ῥαπίζω, ίσω, *to smite with the hand*, Mat. v. 39, xxvi. 67.*

ῥάπισμα, ατος, τό, *a blow with the open hand*, Mar. xiv. 65; Jn. xviii. 22, xix. 3.*

ῥαφίς, ίδος, ἡ, *a needle*, Mat. xix. 24; Mar. x. 25; Lu. xviii. 25 (W. H. βελόνη).*

Ῥαχάβ, see Ῥαάβ.

Ῥαχήλ, ἡ (Heb.), *Rachel*, Mat. ii. 18.*

Ῥεβέκκα, ης, ἡ, *Rebecca*, Ro. ix. 10.*

ῥέδα, or ῥέδη, ης, ἡ (Gallic), *a chariot*, Rev. xviii. 13. (N. T.)*

Ῥεμφάν, or Ῥεφάν (W. H. Ῥομφά), ὁ (prob. Coptic), *Remphan*, the *Saturn* of later mythology, Ac. vii. 43 (Heb., *Chiun*, Amos v. 26).*

ῥέω, ῥεύσω, *to flow*, Jn. vii. 38.*

ῥέω (see φημί, εἶπον). From this obs. root, *to say*, are derived: act. perf., εἴρηκα; pass., εἴρημαι; 1st aor. pass., ἐρρέθην or ἐρρήθην; part., ῥηθείς; espec. the neut. τὸ ῥηθέν, *that which was spoken* by (ὑπό, gen.).

Ῥήγιον, ου, τό, *Rhegium*, now Reggio, Ac. xxviii. 13.*

ῥῆγμα, ατος, τό (ῥήγνυμι), *what is broken, a ruin*, Lu. vi. 49.*

ῥήγνυμι (or ῥήσσω, as Mar. ix. 18), ῥήξω, *to break, to rend, to burst, to dash down, to break forth*, as into praise, Mat. vii. 6, ix. 17; Mar. ii. 22, ix. 18; Lu. v. 37, ix. 42; Gal. iv. 27.*

ῥῆμα, ατος, τό, *a thing spoken;* (1) *a word* or *saying* of any kind, as *command, report, promise*, Lu. vii. 1, ix. 45; Ro. x. 8; (2) *a thing, a matter, a business*, Lu. ii. 15; 2 Cor. xiii. 1.

Ῥησά, ὁ (Heb.), *Rhesa*, Lu. iii. 27.*

ῥήσσω, see ῥήγνυμι.

ῥήτωρ, ορος, ὁ, *an orator*, Ac. xxiv. 1.*

ῥητῶς, adv., *expressly, in so many words*, 1 Tim. iv. 1.*

ῥίζα, ης, ἡ, (1) *a root of a tree* or *a plant*, Mar. xi. 20; met., *the origin* or *source of anything*, 1 Tim. vi. 10; fig., *constancy, perseverance*, Mat. xiii. 21; (2) that which comes from the root, *a descendant*, Ro. xv. 12; Rev. v. 5.

ῥιζόω, ῶ, *to root;* perf. pass., participle, ἐρριζωμένος, *firmly rooted*, fig., Ep. iii. 17; Col. ii. 7.*

ῥιπή, ῆς, ἡ (ῥίπτω), *a stroke, a twinkle*, as of the eye, 1 Cor. xv. 52.*

ῥιπίζω, *to toss to and fro*, as waves by the wind, Ja. i. 6.*

ῥιπτέω, ῶ, *to throw off* or *away*, Ac. xxii. 23.*

ῥίπτω, ψω, 1st aor. ἔρριψα; part ῥίψας; *to throw, throw down, throw out, prostrate*, Mat. ix. 36, xv. 30, xxvii. 5; Lu. iv. 35, xvii. 2; Ac. xxvii. 19, 29.*

Ῥοβοάμ, ὁ (Heb.), *Rehoboam*, Mat. i. 7.*

Ῥόδη, ης, ἡ (*rose*), *Rhoda*, Ac. xii. 13.*

Ῥόδος, ου, ἡ, *Rhodes*, Ac. xxi. 1.*

ῥοιζηδόν, adv. (ῥοιζέω), *with a great noise*, 2 Pet. iii. 10.*

ῥομφαία, ας, ἡ, *a large sword*, as Rev. i. 16; fig., *piercing grief*, Lu. ii. 35.

Ῥουβήν, ὁ (Heb.), *Reuben*, Rev. vii. 5.*

Ῥούθ, ἡ (Heb.), *Ruth*, Mat. i. 5.*

Ῥοῦφος, ου, ὁ (Lat.), *Rufus*, Mar. xv. 21; Ro. xvi. 13.*

ῥύμη, ης, ἡ, *a street, a lane*, Mat. vi. 2; Lu. xiv. 21; Ac. ix. 11, xii. 10.*

ῥύομαι, σομαι, dep. mid., 1st aor., pass., ἐρρύσθην, *to draw* or *snatch from danger, to deliver*, 2 Pet. ii. 7; ὁ ῥυόμενος, *the deliverer*, Ro. xi. 26.

ῥυπαίνω, *to defile*, Rev. xxii. 11 (W. H.).*

ῥυπαρεύομαι, *to be filthy*, Rev. xxii. 11 (W. H. mrg.). (N. T.)*

ῥυπαρία, ας, ἡ, *filth, pollution*, Ja. i. 21.*

ῥυπαρός, ά, όν, *filthy, defiled*, Ja. ii. 2; Rev. xxii. 11 (W. H.).*

ῥύπος, ου, ὁ, *filth, filthiness*, 1 Pet. iii. 21.*

ῥυπόω, ῶ, *to be filthy*, Rev. xxii. 11 (not W. H.).*

ῥύσις, εως, ἡ (ῥέω), *a flowing, an issue*, Mar. v. 25; Lu. viii. 43, 44.*

ῥυτίς, ίδος, ἡ, *a wrinkle;* fig., *a spiritual defect*, Ep. v. 27.*

Ῥωμαϊκός, ή, όν, *Roman*, Lu. xxiii. 38 (W. H. omit).*

Ῥωμαῖος, ου, ὁ, *a Roman*, Jn. xi. 48.

Ῥωμαϊστί, adv., *in the Latin language*, Jn. xix. 10.*

Ῥώμη, ης, ἡ, *Rome*, Ac. xviii. 2; 2 Tim. i. 17.

ῥώννυμι, *to strengthen;* only perf., pass., impv., ἔρρωσο, ἔρρωσθε, *farewell*, Ac. xv. 29, xxiii. 30 (W. H. omit).*

Σ

Σ, σ, final **ς**, *sigma, s*, the eighteenth letter. As a numeral, σ′=200; ͵σ=200,000.

σαβαχθανί (W. H. -εί), (Aram.), *sabachthani, thou hast forsaken me*, Mat. xxvii. 46; Mar. xv. 34; from the Aramaic rendering of Ps. xxii. 1. (N. T.)*

σαβαώθ (Heb.), *sabaoth, hosts, armies*, Ro. ix. 29; Ja. v. 4. (S.)*

σαββατισμός, οῦ, ὁ, *a keeping of sabbath, a sabbath rest* (R. V.), Heb. iv. 9.*

σάββατον, ου, τό (from Heb.),

dat. plur. σάββασι(ν), (1) *the sabbath*, Mat. xii. 8, xxviii. 1; (2) *a period of seven days, a week*, Mar. xvi. 2, 9; in both senses the plural is also used. (S.)

σαγήνη, ης, ἡ, *a drag-net*, Mat. xiii. 47. (S.)* *Syn.:* see ἀμφίβληστρον.

Σαδδουκαῖος, ου, ὁ, *a Sadducee;* plur., of the sect in general; prob. derived from the Heb. name Zadok.

Σαδώκ, ὁ (Heb.), *Sadok*, Mat. i. 13.*

σαίνω, *to move, disturb*, pass., 1 Th. iii. 3.*

σάκκος, ου, ὁ, *hair-cloth, sack-cloth*, a sign of mourning, Mat. xi. 21; Lu. x. 13; Rev. vi. 12, xi. 3.*

Σαλά, ὁ (Heb.), *Sala*, Lu. iii. 35.*

Σαλαθιήλ, ὁ (Heb.), *Salathiel*, Mat. i. 12; Lu. iii. 27.*

Σαλαμίς, ῖνος, ἡ, *Salamis*, Ac. xiii. 5.*

Σαλείμ, τό, *Salim*, Jn. iii. 23.*

σαλεύω, σω, *to shake, to cause to shake*, as Mat. xi. 7; Heb. xii. 27; so, *to excite*, as the populace, Ac. xvii. 13; *to disturb in mind*, 2 Th. ii. 2.

Σαλήμ, ἡ (Heb.), *Salem*, Heb. vii. 1.*

Σαλμών, ὁ (Heb.), *Salmon*, Mat. i. 4, 5, Lu. iii. 32 (W. H. Σαλά).*

Σαλμώνη, ης, ἡ, *Salmone*, Ac. xxvii. 7.*

σάλος, ου, ὁ, *the tossing of the sea in a tempest*, Lu. xxi. 25.*

σάλπιγξ, ιγγος, ἡ, *a trumpet*, 1 Cor. xiv. 8; 1 Th. iv. 16.

σαλπίζω, ίσω (class. ίγξω), *to sound a trumpet*, Rev. ix. 1, 13; for impers. use, 1 Cor. xv. 52 (see Gr. § 171, Wi. § 58, 9*b*, β), Bu. 134).

σαλπιστής, οῦ, ὁ (class. -ιγκτής), *a trumpeter*, Rev. xviii. 22.*

Σαλώμη, ης, ἡ, *Salome*, wife of Zebedee, Mar. xv. 40, xvi. 1.*

Σαμάρεια, ας, ἡ, *Samaria*, either (1) *the district*, Lu. xvii. 11; Jn. iv. 4; or (2) *the city*, afterwards called *Sebaste*, only Ac. viii. 5 (W. H.).

Σαμαρείτης, ου, ὁ, *a Samaritan*, Mat. x. 5; Lu. ix. 52.

Σαμαρεῖτις, ιδος, ἡ, *a Samaritan woman*, Jn. iv. 9.*

Σαμο-θρᾴκη, ης, ἡ, *Samothrace*, Ac. xvi. 11.*

Σάμος, ου, ἡ, *Samos*, Ac. xx. 15.*

Σαμουήλ, ὁ (Heb.), *Samuel*, Ac. iii. 24.

Σαμψών, ὁ (Heb.), *Samson*, Heb. xi. 32.*

σανδάλιον, ου, τό, *a sandal*, Mar. vi. 9; Ac. xii. 8.*

σανίς, ίδος, ἡ, *a plank, a board*, Ac. xxvii. 44.*

Σαούλ, ὁ (Heb.), *Saul*, (1) the king of Israel, Ac. xiii. 21; (2) the apostle, only in direct address (elsewhere Σαῦλος), Ac. ix. 4, 17.

σαπρός, ά, όν, *rotten*, hence, *useless*, Mat. vii. 17, 18; fig., *corrupt*, Ep. iv. 29.

Σαπφείρη, ης, ἡ, *Sapphira*, Ac. v. 1.*

σάπφειρος, ου, ἡ, *a sapphire*, Rev. xxi. 19.*

σαργάνη, ης, ἡ, *a basket*, generally of twisted cords, 2 Cor. xi. 33.*

Σάρδεις, ων, dat. εσι(ν), αἱ, *Sardis*, Rev. i. 11, iii. 1, 4.*

σάρδινος, ου, ὁ (Rec. in Rev. iv. 3 for following). (N. T.)*

σάρδιον, ου, τό, a precious stone, *sardius* or *carnelian*, Rev. iv. 3 (W. H.), xxi. 20.*

σαρδ-όνυξ, υχος, ὁ, *a sardonyx*, a precious stone, white streaked with red, Rev. xxi. 20.*

Σάρεπτα, ων, τά, *Sarepta*, Lu. iv. 26.*

σαρκικός, ή, όν, *fleshly, carnal*, whether (1) belonging to human nature in its bodily manifestation, or (2) belonging to human nature as sinful, Ro. xv. 27; 1 Cor. iii. 3, ix. 11; 2 Cor. i. 12, x. 4; 1 Pet. ii. 11; for Rec. σαρκικός, W. H. substitute σάρκινος, in Ro. vii. 14; 1 Cor. iii. 1; Heb. vii. 16; and ἄνθρωπος in 1 Cor. iii. 4.*

σάρκινος, η, ον, (1) *fleshy, consisting of flesh*, opp. to λίθινος, 2 Cor. iii. 3; (2) *fleshy, carnal* (W.H. in the passages quoted under σαρκικός).*

σάρξ, σαρκός, ἡ, *flesh*, sing., Lu. xxiv. 39; plur., Ja. v. 3; *the human body, man;* the *human nature* of man as distinguished from his divine nature (πνεῦμα); *human nature*, as sinful; πᾶσα σάρξ, *every man. all men;* κατὰ σάρκα, *as a man;* σὰρξ καὶ αἷμα, *flesh and blood, i.e*, man as frail and fallible; ζῆν, περιπατεῖν κατὰ σάρκα, *to live, to walk after flesh*, cf a carnal, unspiritual life. The word also denotes *kinship*, Ro. xi. 14.

Σαρούχ, ὁ (Heb.), (W. H. Σερούχ), *Saruch* or *Serug*, Lu iii. 35.*

σαρόω, ῶ, *to sweep, to cleanse by sweeping*, Mat. xii. 44, Lu. xi. 25, xv. 8.*

Σάρρα, ας, ἡ, *Sarah*, Ro. iv. 19, ix. 9.

Σάρων, ωνος, ὁ, *Sharon*, Ac. ix. 35.*

σατᾶν, ὁ (Heb.), and σατανᾶς, ᾶ, ὁ, *an adversary, i.e., Satan*, the Heb. proper name for the devil, διάβολος, Mat. iv 10, 15; Ac. xxvi. 18; met., for one who does the work of Satan, Mat. xvi. 23; Mar. viii. 33. (S.)

σάτον, ου, τό (Aram.), *a seah*, a measure equal to about a peck and a half, Mat. xiii. 33; Lu. xiii. 21. (S.)*

Σαῦλος, ου, ὁ, *Saul*, the apostle, generally in this form (see Σαούλ), Ac. vii. 58, viii. 1, 3.

σβέννυμι, σβέσω, (1) *to extinguish, to quench*, Ep. vi. 16; (2) fig., *to suppress*, 1 Th. v. 19.

σεατοῦ, ῆς, οῦ (only masc. in N. T.), a reflex. pron., *of thyself;* dat., σεαυτῷ, *to thyself;* acc., σεαυτόν, *thyself*.

σεβάζομαι, dep., pass., *to stand in awe of, to worship*, Ro. i. 25.*

σέβασμα, ατος, τό, *an object of religious worship*, Ac. xvii. 23; 2 Th. ii. 4.*

σεβαστός, ή, όν, *venerated, august*, a title of the Roman emperors (= Lat. *augustus*), Ac. xxv. 21, 25. Hence, secondarily, *Augustan, imperial*, Ac. xxvii. 1.*

σέβομαι, dep., *to reverence, to worship* God, Mar. vii. 7; οἱ σεβόμενοι, *the devout, i.e.*, proselytes of the gate, Ac xvii. 17.

σειρά, ᾶς, ἡ, *a chain*, 2 Pet. ii. 4 (W. H. read following).*

σειρός, οῦ, ὁ, *a pit*, 2 Pet. ii. 4 (W. H.).*

σεισμός, οῦ, ὁ, *a shaking*, as *an earthquake*, Mat. xxiv. 7; *a storm* at sea, Mat. viii. 24.

σείω, σω, *to shake*, Heb. xii. 26; fig., *to agitate*, Mat. xxi. 10.

Σεκοῦνδος, ου, ὁ (Lat.), *Secundus*, Ac. xx. 4.*

Σελεύκεια, ας, ἡ, *Seleucia*, Ac. xiii. 4.*

σελήνη, ης, ἡ, *the moon*, Mar. xiii. 24.

σεληνιάζομαι, *to be epileptic*, Mat. iv. 24, xvii. 15. (N. T.)*

Σεμεΐ, ὁ (Heb.), (W. H. Σεμεείν), *Semei* or *Semein*, Lu. iii. 26.*

σεμίδαλις, acc. ιν, ἡ, *the finest wheaten flour*, Rev. xviii. 13.*

σεμνός, ή, όν, *venerable, honorable*, of men, 1 Tim. iii. 8, 11; Tit. ii. 2; of acts, Phil. iv. 8.*

σεμνότης, τητος, ἡ, *dignity, honor*, 1 Tim. ii. 2, iii. 4; Tit. ii. 7.*

Σέργιος, ου, ὁ, *Sergius*, Ac. xiii. 7.*

Σήθ, ὁ (Heb.), *Seth*, Lu. iii. 38.*

Σήμ, ὁ (Heb.), *Shem*, Lu. iii. 36.*

σημαίνω, 1st aor. ἐσήμανα, *to signify, indicate*, Jn. xii. 33; Ac. xxv. 27.

σημεῖον, ου, τό, *a sign, that by which a thing is known, a token, an indication*, of divine presence and power, 1 Cor. xiv. 22; Lu. xxi. 7, 11; hence, especially, *a miracle*, whether real or unreal, Lu. xi. 16, 29; 2 Th. ii. 9. *Syn.:* see δύναμις.

σημειόω, ῶ, in mid., *to mark for one's self, to note*, 2 Th. iii. 14.*

σήμερον, adv., *to-day, at this time, now*, Mat. vi. 11; Lu. ii. 11; ἡ σήμερον (ἡμέρα), *this very day*, Ac. xix. 40.

σήπω, *to make rotten*; 2d perf. σέσηπα, *to become rotten, perish*, Ja. v. 2.*

σηρικός, ή, όν (W. H. σιρικός), *silken*; neut. as subst., *silk*, Rev. xviii. 12.*

σής, σητός, ὁ, *a moth*, Mat. vi. 19, 20; Lu. xii. 33.*

σητό-βρωτος, ον, *moth-eaten*, Ja. v. 2.*

σθενόω, ῶ, *to strengthen*, 1 Pet. v. 10. (N. T.)*

σιαγών, όνος, ἡ, *the jawbone*, Mat. v. 39; Lu. vi. 29.*

σιγάω, ῶ, *to keep silence*, Lu. ix. 36; pass., *to be concealed*, Ro. xvi. 25.

σιγή, ῆς, ἡ, *silence*, Ac. xxi. 40; Rev. viii. 1.*

σιδήρεος, έα, εον, contr., οῦς, ᾶ, οῦν, *made of iron*, Ac. xii. 10; Rev. ii. 27.

σίδηρος, ου, ὁ, *iron*, Rev. xviii. 12.*

Σιδών, ῶνος, ἡ, *Sidon*, Mat. xi. 21, 22.

Σιδώνιος, α, ον, *Sidonian, inhabitant of Sidon*, Lu. iv. 26 (W. H.); Ac. xii. 20.

σικάριος, ου, ὁ (Lat.), *an assassin*, Ac. xxi. 38.*

σίκερα, τό (Aram.), *intoxicating drink*, Lu. i. 15. (S.)*

Σίλας, dat. ᾳ, acc. αν, ὁ, *Silas*, contr. from Σιλουανός, Ac. xv. 22, 27.

Σιλουανός, οῦ, ὁ, *Silvanus*, 2 Cor. i. 9.

Σιλωάμ, ὁ, *Siloam*, Lu. xiii. 4; Jn. ix. 7, 11.*

σιμικίνθιον, ου, τό (Lat. *semicinctium*), *an apron*, worn by artisans, Ac. xix. 12. (N. T.)*

Σίμων, ωνος, ὁ, *Simon*; nine persons of the name are mentioned: (1) *Peter*, the apostle, Mat. xvii. 25; (2) the Zealot, an apostle, Lu. vi. 15; (3) a brother of Jesus, Mar. vi. 3; (4) a certain Cyrenian, Mar. xv. 21; (5) the father of Judas Iscariot, Jn. vi. 71; (6) a certain Pharisee, Lu. vii. 40; (7) a leper, Mat. xxvi. 6; (8) *Simon Magus*, Ac. viii. 9; (9) a certain tanner, Ac. ix. 43.

Σινᾶ, τό (Heb.), *Sinai*, Ac. vii. 30, 38; Gal. iv. 24, 25.*

σίναπι, εως, τό, *mustard*, Lu. xiii. 19, xvii. 6.

σινδών, όνος, ἡ, *fine linen, a linen cloth*, Mar. xiv. 51, 52, xv. 46.

σινιάζω, *to sift*, as grain, *to prove by trials*, Lu. xxii. 31. (N. T.)*

σιρικός, see σηρικός.

σιτευτός, ή, όν, *fattened, fatted*, Lu. xv. 23, 27, 30.*

σιτίον, ου, τό, *grain*, Ac. vii. 12 (W. H.).*

σιτιστός, ή, όν, *fattened*; τὰ σιτιστά, *fatlings*, Mat. xxii. 4.*

σιτο-μέτριον, ου, τό, *a measured portion of grain* or *food*, Lu. xii. 42. (N. T.)*

σῖτος, ου, ὁ, *wheat, grain*, Jn. xii. 24; 1 Cor. xv. 37.

Σιχάρ, see Συχάρ.

Σιών, ἡ, τό, *Zion*, the hill; used for the city of Jerusalem, Ro. xi. 26; fig., for *heaven*, the spiritual Jerusalem, Heb. xii. 22; Rev. xiv. 1.

σιωπάω, ῶ, ήσω, *to be silent*, whether voluntarily or from dumbness, Mar. iii. 4; Lu. i. 20; *to become still*, as the sea, Mar. iv. 39.

σκανδαλίζω, ίσω, *to cause to stumble*; met., *to entice to sin*, Mat. xviii. 6, 8, 9; *to cause to fall away*, Jn. vi. 61; pass., *to be indignant*, Mat. xv. 12.

σκάνδαλον, ου, τό, *a snare, a stumbling-block*; fig., *a cause of error* or *sin*, Mat. xiii. 41; Ro. xiv. 13. (S.)

σκάπτω, ψω, *to dig*, Lu. vi. 48, xiii. 8, xvi. 3.*

σκάφη, ης, ἡ, *any hollow vessel*; *a boat*, Ac. xxvii. 16, 30, 32.*

σκέλος, ους, τό, *the leg*, Jn. xix. 31, 32, 33.*

σκέπασμα, ατος, τό, *clothing*, 1 Tim. vi. 8.*

Σκευᾶς, ᾶ, ὁ, *Sceva*, Ac. xix. 14.*

σκευή, ῆς, ἡ, *furniture, fittings*, Ac. xxvii. 19.*

σκεῦος, ους, τό, (1) *a vessel*, to contain a liquid, or for any other purpose, Heb. ix. 21; 2 Tim. ii. 20; fig., of recipients generally, *a vessel* of mercy, of wrath, Ro. ix. 22, 23; *an instrument* by which anything is done; *household utensils*, plur., Mat. xii. 29; of a ship, *the tackling*, Ac. xxvii. 17; fig., of God's servants, Ac. ix. 15; 2 Cor. iv. 7.

σκηνή, ῆς, ἡ, *a tent, a tabernacle, an abode* or *dwelling*, Mat. xvii. 4; Ac. vii. 43, xv. 16; Heb. viii. 5, xiii. 10.

σκηνο-πηγία, ας, ἡ, *the feast of tabernacles*, Jn. vii. 2.*

σκηνο-ποιός, οῦ, ὁ, *a tent-maker*, Ac. xviii. 3. (N. T.)*

σκῆνος, ους, τό, *a tent*; fig., of

the human body, 2 Cor. v. 1, 4.*

σκηνόω, ῶ, ώσω, *to spread a tent,* Rev. vii. 15; met., *to dwell,* Jn. i. 14; Rev. xii. 12, xiii. 6, xxi. 3.*

σκήνωμα, ατος, τό, *a tent pitched, a dwelling,* Ac. vii. 46; fig., of the body, 2 Pet. i. 13, 14.*

σκιά, ᾶς, ἡ, (1) *a shadow, a thick darkness,* Mat. iv. 16 (S.); (2) *a shadow, an outline,* Col. ii. 17.

σκιρτάω, ῶ, ήσω, *to leap* for joy, Lu. i. 41, 44, vi. 23.*

σκληρο-καρδία, ας, ἡ, *hardness of heart, perverseness,* Mat. xix. 8; Mar. x. 5, xvi. 14. (S.)*

σκληρός, ά, όν, *hard, violent,* as the wind, Ja. iii. 4; fig., *grievous, painful,* Ac. ix. 5 (W. H. omit), xxvi. 14; Ju. 15; *harsh, stern,* Mat. xxv. 24; Jn. vi. 60.*

σκληρότης, τητος, ἡ, fig., *hardness* of heart, *obstinacy,* Ro. ii. 5.*

σκληρο-τράχηλος, ον, *stiff-necked;* fig., *obstinate,* Ac. vii. 51. (S.)*

σκληρύνω, fig., *to make hard, to harden,* as the heart, Ro. ix. 18; Heb. iii. 8, 15, iv. 7; pass., *to be hardened, to become obstinate,* Ac. xix. 9; Heb. iii. 13.*

σκολιός, ά, όν, *crooked,* Lu. iii. 5; fig., *perverse,* Ac. ii. 40; Phil. ii. 15; *unfair,* 1 Pet. ii. 18.*

σκόλοψ, οπος, ὁ, *a stake* or *thorn;* fig., *a sharp infliction,* 2 Cor. xii. 7.*

σκοπέω, ῶ, (1) *to look at, to regard attentively,* Ro. xvi. 17; (2) *to take heed* (acc.), *beware* (μή), Gal. vi. 1.

σκοπός, οῦ, ὁ, *a mark aimed at, a goal;* κατὰ σκοπόν, *towards the goal, i.e.,* aiming straight at it, Phil. iii. 14.*

σκορπίζω, σω, *to disperse, to scatter abroad,* as frightened sheep, Jn. x. 12; *to distribute alms,* 2 Cor. ix. 9.

σκορπίος, ου, ὁ, *a scorpion,* Lu. x. 19.

σκοτεινός, ή, όν, *full of darkness, dark,* Mar. vi. 23; Lu. xi. 34, 36.*

σκοτία, ας, ἡ, *darkness,* Mat. x. 27; fig., *spiritual darkness,* Jn. i. 5, vi. 17.

σκοτίζω, σω, in pass., *to be darkened,* as the sun, Mar. xiii. 24; fig., as the mind, Ro. i. 21.

σκότος, ους, τό (σκότος, ου, ὁ, only in Heb. xii. 18, where W. H. read ζόφος), *darkness,* physical, Mat. xxvii. 45; moral, Jn. iii. 19.

σκοτόω, ῶ, pass. only, *to be darkened,* Ep. iv. 18 (W.H.); Rev. ix. 2 (W. H.), xvi. 10.*

σκύβαλον, ου, τό, *refuse, dregs,* Phil. iii. 8.*

Σκύθης, ου, ὁ, *a Scythian,* as typical of the uncivilized, Col. iii. 11.*

σκυθρ-ωπός, όν, *sad-countenanced, gloomy,* Mat. vi. 16; Lu. xxiv. 17.*

σκύλλω, pass. perf. part. ἐσκυλμένος, *to flay; to trouble, annoy,* Mat. ix. 36 (W. H.); Mar. v. 35; Lu. vii. 6, viii. 29.*

σκῦλον, ου, τό, *spoil taken from a foe,* Lu. xi. 22.*

σκωληκό-βρωτος, ον, *eaten by worms,* Ac. xii. 23.*

σκώληξ, ηκος, ὁ, *a* gnawing *worm,* Mar. ix. 44 (W. H. omit), 46 (W. H. omit), 48.*

σμαράγδινος, η, ον, *made of emerald,* Rev. iv. 3. (N.T.)*

σμάραγδος, ου, ὁ, *an emerald,* Rev. xxi. 19.*

σμύρνα, ης, ἡ, *myrrh,* Mat. ii. 11; Jn. xix. 39.*

Σμύρνα, ης, ἡ, *Smyrna.* Rev. i. 11, ii. 8 (W. H.).*

Σμυρναῖος, ου, ὁ, ἡ, *one of Smyrna, a Smyrnæan,* Rev. ii. 8 (not W. H.).*

σμυρνίζω, *to mingle with myrrh,* Mar. xv. 23. (N. T.)*

Σόδομα, ων, τά, *Sodom,* Mat. x. 15, xi. 23, 24.

Σολομών or -μῶν, ῶντος or ῶνος, ὁ, *Solomon,* Mat. vi. 29, xii. 42.

σορός, οῦ, ἡ, *a bier, an open coffin,* Lu. vii. 14.*

σός, σή, σόν, poss. pron., *thy, thine* (see Gr. §§ 56, 255, Bu. 115).

σουδάριον, ου, τό (Lat.), *a handkerchief,* Lu. xix. 20; Jn. xi. 44. (N. T.)

Σουσάννα, ης, ἡ, *Susanna,* Lu. viii. 3.*

σοφία, ας, ἡ, *wisdom, insight, skill,* human, Lu. xi. 31; or divine, 1 Cor. i. 21, 24. *Syn.:* see γνῶσις.

σοφίζω, *to make wise,* 2 Tim. iii. 15; pass., *to be devised skillfully,* 2 Pet. i. 16.*

σοφός, ή, όν, *wise,* either (1) in action, *expert,* Ro. xvi. 19; (2) in acquirement, *learned, cultivated,* 1 Cor. i. 19, 20; (3) philosophically, *profound,* Ju. 25; (4) practically, Ep. v. 15.

Σπανία, ας, ἡ, *Spain,* Ro. xv. 24, 28.*

σπαράσσω, ξω, *to convulse, to throw into spasms,* Mar. i. 26, ix. 20 (not W. H.), 26; Lu. ix. 39.*

σπαργανόω, ῶ, perf. pass. part. ἐσπαργανωμένος, *to swathe, to wrap in swaddling clothes,* Lu. ii. 7, 12.*

σπαταλάω, ῶ, ήσω, *to live extravagantly* or *luxuriously,* 1 Tim. v. 6; Ja. v. 5.* *Syn.:* The fundamental thought of στρηνιάω is of insolence and voluptuousness which spring from abundance; of τρυφάω, *effeminate* self-indulgence; of σπαταλάω, is effeminacy and wasteful extravagance.

σπάω, ῶ, mid., *to draw,* as a sword, Mar. xiv. 47; Ac. xvi. 27.*

σπεῖρα, ης, ἡ, (1) *a cohort* of soldiers, the tenth part of a legion, Ac. x. 1; (2) *a military guard,* Jn. xviii. 3, 12.

σπείρω, σπερῶ, 1st aor. ἔσπειρα, perf. pass. part. ἐσπαρμένος, 2d aor. pass. ἐσπάρην, *to sow* or *scatter,* as seed, Lu. xii. 24; *to spread* or *scatter,* as the word of God, Mat. xiii. 19; applied to giving alms, 2 Cor. ix. 6; to burial, 1 Cor. xv. 42, 43; and to spiritual effort generally, Gal. vi. 8.

σπεκουλάτωρ, ορος, ὁ (Lat.), *a body-guardsman, a soldier in attendance upon royalty,* Mar. vi. 27 (see Gr. § 154*c*). (N. T.)*

σπένδω, *to pour out,* as a libation, fig., Phil. ii. 17; 2 Tim. iv. 6.*

σπέρμα, ατος, τό, *seed, produce,* Mat. xiii. 24–38; *children, offspring, posterity,* Jn. vii. 42; *a remnant,* Ro. ix. 29.

σπερμο-λόγος, *ου, ὁ, a babbler, i.e.,* one who picks up trifles, as birds do seed, Ac. xvii. 18.*

σπεύδω, *σω,* (1) *to hasten,* intrans., usually adding to another verb the notion of speed, Lu. xix. 5, 6; (2) *to desire earnestly* (acc.), 2 Pet. iii. 12.

σπήλαιον, *ου, τό, a cave, a den,* Heb. xi. 38.*

σπιλάς, *άδος, ἡ, a rock in the sea, a reef;* fig., of false teachers, *a hidden rock* (R. V.), Ju. 12.*

σπίλος, *ου, ὁ, a spot;* fig., *a fault,* Ep. v. 27; 2 Pet. ii. 13.*

σπιλόω, *ῶ, to defile, to spot,* Ja. iii. 6; Ju. 23.*

σπλάγχνα, *ων, τά, bowels,* only Ac. i. 18; elsewhere, fig., *the affections, compassion, the heart,* as Col. iii. 12; 1 Jn. iii. 17.

σπλαγχνίζομαι, dep., with 1st aor. pass. *ἐσπλαγχνίσθην, to feel compassion, to have pity* on (gen., or *ἐπί,* dat. or acc., once *περί,* Mat. ix. 36).

σπόγγος, *ου, ὁ, a sponge,* Mat. xxvii. 48; Mar. xv. 36; Jn. xix. 29.*

σποδός, *οῦ, ἡ, ashes,* Mat. xi. 21; Lu. x. 13; Heb. ix. 13.*

σπορά, *ᾶς, ἡ, seed,* 1 Pet. i. 23.*

σπόριμος, *όν, sown;* neut. plur. *τὰ σπόριμα, sown fields,* Mat. xii. 1; Mar. ii. 23; Lu. vi. 1.*

σπόρος, *ου, ὁ, seed,* for sowing, Lu. viii. 5, 11.

σπουδάζω, *άσω, to hasten, to give diligence* (with inf.), Heb. iv. 11; 2 Tim. iv. 9, 21.

σπουδαῖος, *αία, αῖον, diligent, earnest,* 2 Cor. viii. 17, 22; compar. neut. as adv., *σπουδαιότερον,* 2 Tim. i. 17 (not W. H.).*

σπουδαίως, adv., *diligently, earnestly,* Lu. vii. 4; 2 Tim. i. 17 (W. H.); Tit. iii. 13; *hastily,* compar., Phil. ii. 28.*

σπουδή, *ῆς, ἡ,* (1) *speed, haste,* Mar. vi. 25; (2) *diligence, earnestness,* Ro. xii. 11.

σπυρίς (W. H. *σφυρίς*), *ίδος, ἡ, a plaited basket,* Mar. viii. 8, 20.

στάδιον, *ου, τό,* plur. *οἱ στάδιοι,* (1) *a stadium,* one eighth of a Roman mile, Jn. xi. 18; (2) *a race-course,* for public games, 1 Cor. ix. 24.

στάμνος, *ου, ὁ, ἡ, a jar* or *vase,* for the manna, Heb. ix. 4.*

στασιαστής, *οῦ, ὁ, an insurgent,* Mar. xv. 7 (W. H.).*

στάσις, *εως, ἡ* (*ἵστημι*), *a standing,* lit. only Heb. ix. 8; *an insurrection,* Mar. xv. 7; *dissension,* Ac. xv. 2.

στατήρ, *ῆρος, ὁ, a stater,* a silver coin equal to two of the *δίδραχμον* (which see), a Jewish shekel, Mat. xvii. 27.*

σταυρός, *οῦ, ὁ, a cross,* Mat. xxvii. 32, 40; met., often of Christ's death, Gal. vi. 14; Ep. ii. 16.

σταυρόω, *ῶ, ώσω, to fix to the cross, to crucify,* Lu. xxiii. 21, 23; fig., *to destroy,* the corrupt nature, Gal. v. 24.

σταφυλή, *ῆς, ἡ, a grape, a cluster of grapes,* Mat. vii. 16; Lu. vi. 44; Rev. xiv. 18.*

στάχυς, *υος, ὁ, an ear of corn,* Mat. xii. 1; Mar. ii. 23, iv. 28; Lu. vi. 1.*

Στάχυς, *υος, ὁ, Stachys,* Ro. xvi. 9.*

στέγη, *ης, ἡ* (lit. *a cover*), *a* flat *roof* of a house, Mat. viii. 8; Mar. ii. 4; Lu. vii. 6.*

στέγω, *to cover, to conceal, to bear with,* 1 Cor. ix. 12, xiii. 7; 1 Th. iii. 1, 5.*

στεῖρος, *α, ον, barren,* Lu. i. 7, 36, xxiii. 29; Gal. iv. 27.*

στέλλω, *to set, arrange;* in mid., *to provide for, take care,* 2 Cor. viii. 20; *to withdraw from* (*ἀπό*), 2 Th. iii. 6.*

στέμμα, *ατος, τό, a garland,* Ac. xiv. 13.*

στεναγμός, *οῦ, ὁ, a groaning,* Ac. vii. 34; Ro. viii. 26.*

στενάζω, *ξω, to groan,* expressing grief, anger, or desire, Mar. vii. 34; Heb. xiii. 17.

στενός, *ή, όν, narrow,* Mat. vii. 13, 14; Lu. xiii. 24.*

στενο-χωρέω, *ῶ, to be narrow;* in pass., *to be distressed,* 2 Cor. iv. 8, vi. 12.*

στενο-χωρία, *ας, ἡ, a narrow space; great distress,* Ro. ii. 9, viii. 35; 2 Cor. vi. 4, xii. 10.*

στερεός, *ά, όν, solid,* as food, Heb. v. 12, 14; fig., *firm, steadfast,* 1 Pet. v. 9; 2 Tim. ii. 19.*

στερεόω, *ῶ, ώσω, to strengthen, confirm, establish,* Ac. iii. 7, 16, xvi. 5.*

στερέωμα, *ατος, τό, firmness, steadfastness,* Col. ii. 5.*

Στεφανᾶς, *ᾶ, ὁ, Stephanas,* 1 Cor. i. 16, xvi. 15, 17.

στέφανος, *ου, ὁ, a crown, a garland,* of royalty, of victory in the games, of festal joy, Jn. xix. 2, 5; 1 Cor. ix. 25; often used fig., 2 Tim. iv. 8; Rev. ii. 10. *Syn.:* see *διάδημα.*

Στέφανος, *ου, ὁ, Stephen,* Ac. vi., vii.

στεφανόω, *ῶ, ώσω, to crown, to adorn,* 2 Tim. ii. 5; Heb. ii. 7, 9.*

στῆθος, *ους, τό, the breast,* Lu. xviii. 13.

στήκω (*ἵστημι, ἕστηκα*), *to stand,* in the attitude of prayer, Mar. xi. 25; generally, *to stand firm, persevere,* as Ro. xiv. 4; 1 Cor. xvi. 13; Gal. v. 1. (S.)

στηριγμός, *οῦ, ὁ, firmness, steadfastness,* 2 Pet. iii. 17.*

στηρίζω, *ίξω* or *ίσω,* pass. perf. *ἐστήριγμαι,* (1) *to fix, to set firmly,* Lu. ix. 51, xvi. 26; (2) *to strengthen, to confirm, to support,* as Lu. xxii. 32; Ro. i. 11.

στιβάς, see *στοιβάς.*

στίγμα, *ατος, τό, a mark* or *brand,* used of the traces of the apostle's sufferings for Christ, Gal. vi. 17.*

στιγμή, *ῆς, ἡ, a point of time, an instant,* Lu. iv. 5.*

στίλβω, *to shine, to glisten,* Mar. ix. 3.*

στοά, *ᾶς, ἡ, a colonnade, a portico,* Jn. v. 2, x. 23; Ac. iii. 11, v. 12.*

στοιβάς, *άδος, ἡ* (W. H. *στιβάς*), *a bough, a branch of a tree,* Mar. xi. 8.*

στοιχεῖα, *ων, τά, elements, rudiments,* Gal. iv. 3, 9; Col. ii. 8, 20; Heb. v. 12; 2 Pet. iii. 10, 12.*

στοιχέω, *ῶ, ήσω, to walk,* always fig. of conduct; *to walk* in (local dat.), Ac. xxi. 24; Ro. iv. 12; Gal. v. 25, vi. 16; Phil. iii. 16.*

στολή, *ῆς, ἡ, a robe, i.e.,* the

long outer garment which was a mark of distinction, Lu. xv. 22. *Syn.:* see ἱμάτιον.

στόμα, ατος, τό, (1) *the mouth,* generally; hence, (2) *speech, speaking;* used of *testimony,* Mat. xviii. 16; *eloquence* or *power in speaking,* Lu. xxi. 15; (3) applied to an opening in the earth, Rev. xii. 16; (4) *the edge* or *point* of a sword, Lu. xxi. 24.

στόμαχος, ου, ὁ, *the stomach,* 1 Tim. v. 23.*

στρατεία, ας, ἡ, *warfare, military service;* of Christian warfare, 2 Cor. x. 4; 1 Tim. i. 18.*

στράτευμα, ατος, τό, (1) *an army,* Rev. ix. 16; (2) *a detachment of troops,* Ac. xxiii. 10, 27; plur., Lu. xxiii. 11.

στρατεύομαι, dep. mid., *to wage war, to fight,* Lu. iii. 14; fig., of the warring of lusts against the soul, Ja. iv. 1; *to serve as a soldier,* of Christian work, 1 Tim. i. 18; 2 Cor. x. 3.

στρατ-ηγός, οῦ, ὁ (ἄγω), (1) *a leader of an army, a general;* (2) *a magistrate* or *governor,* Ac. xvi. 20–38; (3) *the captain* of the temple, Lu. xxii. 4, 52; Ac. iv. 1, v. 24, 26.*

στρατιά, ᾶς, ἡ, *an army;* met., *a host* of angels, Lu. ii. 13; *the host* of heaven, *i.e., the stars,* Ac. vii. 42.*

στρατιώτης, ου, ὁ, *a soldier,* as Mat. viii. 9; fig., of a Christian, 2 Tim. ii. 3.

στρατο-λογέω, ῶ, ήσω, *to collect an army, to enlist troops,* 2 Tim. ii. 4.*

στρατοπεδ-άρχης, ου, ὁ, *the prætorian prefect, i.e.,* commander of the Roman emperor's body-guard, Ac. xxviii. 16 (W. H. omit).*

στρατό-πεδον, ου, τό, *an encamped army,* Lu. xxi. 20.*

στρεβλόω, ῶ, *to rack, to pervert, to twist,* as words from their proper meaning, 2 Pet. iii. 16.*

στρέφω, ψω, 2d aor. pass. ἐστράφην, *to turn,* trans., Mat. v. 39; Rev. xi. 6 (*to change* into, εἰς); intrans., Ac. vii. 42; mostly in pass., *to turn one's self,* Jn. xx. 14; *to be converted, to be changed* in mind and conduct, Mat. xviii. 3.

στρηνιάω, ῶ, άσω, *to live voluptuously,* Rev. xviii. 7, 9.* *Syn.:* see σπαταλάω.

στρῆνος, ους, τό, *profligate luxury, voluptuousness,* Rev. xviii. 3.*

στρουθίον, ου, τό (dim. of στρουθός), *a small bird, a sparrow,* Mat. x. 29, 31; Lu. xii. 6, 7.*

στρωννύω, or -ώννυμι, στρώσω, pass. perf. part. ἐστρωμένος ἔστρωμαι, *to spread,* Mat. xxi. 8; *to make a bed,* Ac. ix. 34; pass., *to be spread with couches,* ἀνάγαιον ἐστρωμένον, *an upper room furnished,* Mar. xiv. 15; Lu. xxii. 12.

στυγητός, όν, *hateful, detestable,* Tit. iii. 3.*

στυγνάζω, άσω, *to be gloomy,* Mar. x. 22; of the sky, Mat. xvi. 3.*

στῦλος, ου, ὁ, *a pillar,* Gal. ii. 9; 1 Tim. iii. 15; Rev. iii. 12, x. 1.*

Στωϊκός, ή, όν (στοά, *portico*), *Stoic,* Ac. xvii. 18.*

σύ, σοῦ, σοί, σέ, plur. ὑμεῖς, *thou, ye,* the pers. pron. of second person (see Gr. § 53).

συγγ-. In some words commencing thus, W. H. prefer the unassimilated form συνγ-.

συγ-γένεια, ας, ἡ, *kindred, family,* Lu. i. 61; Ac. vii. 3, 14.*

συγ-γενής, ές, *akin,* as subst., *a relative,* Mar. vi. 4; Lu. xiv. 12; *a fellow-countryman,* Ro. ix. 3.

συγ-γενίς, ίδος, ἡ, *a kinswoman,* Lu. i. 36 (W. H.).*

συγ-γνώμη, ης, ἡ, *permission, indulgence,* 1 Cor. vii. 6.*

συγκ-. In words commencing thus, W. H. prefer the unassimilated form συνκ-.

συγ-κάθημαι, *to sit with* (dat. or μετά, gen.), Mar. xiv. 54; Ac. xxvi. 30.*

συγ-καθίζω, σω, (1) *to cause to sit down with,* Ep. ii. 6; (2) *to sit down together,* Lu. xxii. 55.*

συγ-κακο-παθέω, ῶ, *to suffer hardships together with,* 2 Tim. i. 8, ii. 3 (W. H.). (N. T.)*

συγ-κακουχέω, ῶ, pass., *to suffer ill-treatment with,* Heb. xi. 25. (N. T.)*

συγ-καλέω, ῶ, έσω, *to call together,* Lu. xv. 6; mid., *to call together to one's self,* Lu. ix. 1.

συγ-καλύπτω, *to conceal closely, to cover up wholly,* Lu. xii. 2.*

συγ-κάμπτω, ψω, *to bend together; to oppress,* Ro. xi. 10 (S.)*

συγ-κατα-βαίνω, *to go down with* any one, Ac. xxv. 5.*

συγ-κατά-θεσις, εως, ἡ, *assent, agreement,* 2 Cor. vi. 16.*

συγ-κατα-τίθημι, in mid., *to give a vote with, to assent to* (dat.), Lu. xxiii. 51.*

συγ-κατα-ψηφίζω, in pass., *to be voted* or *classed with* (μετά), Ac. i. 26.*

συγ-κεράννυμι, 1st aor. συνεκέρασα, pass. perf. συγκέκραμαι, *to mix with, to unite,* 1 Cor. xii. 24; pass., *to be united with,* Heb. iv. 2.*

συγ-κινέω, ῶ, ήσω, *to move together, stir up,* Ac. vi. 12.*

συγ-κλείω, σω, *to inclose, to shut in,* as fishes in a net, Lu. v. 6; *to shut* one *up* into (εἰς) or under (ὑπό, acc.) something, *to make subject to,* Ro. xi. 32; Gal. iii. 22, 23.*

συγ-κληρο-νόμος, ου, ὁ, ἡ, *a joint heir, a joint participant,* Ro. viii. 17; Ep. iii. 6; Heb. xi. 9; 1 Pet. iii. 7.*

συγ-κοινωνέω, ῶ, *to be a partaker with, have fellowship with,* Ep. v. 11; Phil. iv. 14; Rev. xviii. 4.*

συγ-κοινωνός, ου, ὁ, ἡ, *a partaker with, a co-partner,* Ro. xi. 17. (N. T.)

συγ-κομίζω, *to bear away together,* as in burying a corpse, Ac. viii. 2.*

συγ-κρίνω, *to join together, to combine,* 1 Cor. ii. 13; *to compare* (acc., dat.), 2 Cor. x. 12.*

συγ-κύπτω, *to be bowed together* or *bent double,* Lu. xiii. 11.*

συγ-κυρία, ας, ἡ, *a coincidence, an accident; κατὰ συγκυρίαν, by chance,* Lu. x. 31.*

συγ-χαίρω, 2d aor. in pass. form συνεχάρην, *to rejoice with* (dat.), Lu. i. 58, xv. 6, 9; 1 Cor. xii. 26, xiii. 6; Phil. ii. 17, 18.*

συγ-χέω, also συγχύνω and

συγχύννω, perf. pass. *συγκέχυμαι*, *to mingle together;* (1) *to bewilder*, Ac. ii. 6, ix. 22; (2) *to stir up, to throw into confusion*, Ac. xix. 32, xxi. 27, 31.*

συγ-χράομαι, ῶμαι, *to have dealings with* (dat.), Jn. iv. 9.*

σύγ-χυσις, εως, ἡ, *confusion, disturbance*, Ac. xix. 29.*

συ-ζάω (W. H. *συνζ-*), ῶ, ήσω, *to live together with* (dat.), Ro. vi. 8; 2 Cor. vii. 3; 2 Tim. ii. 11.*

συ-ζεύγνυμι, 1st aor. *συνέζευξα*, *to yoke together; to unite* (acc.), as man and wife, Mat. xix. 6; Mar. x. 9.*

συ-ζητέω, ῶ, *to seek together, to discuss, dispute*, with dat., or πρός, acc., Mar. viii. 11, ix. 16.

συ-ζήτησις, εως, ἡ, *mutual questioning, disputation*, Ac. xv. 2 (W. H. *ζήτησις*), 7 (W. H. *ζήτησις*), xxviii. 29 (W. H. omit).*

συ-ζητητής, οῦ, ὁ, *a disputer*, as the Greek sophists, 1 Cor. i. 20. (N. T.)*

σύ-ζυγος, ου, ὁ, *a yoke-fellow, a colleague*, Phil. iv. 3 (prob. a proper name, *Syzygus*).*

συ-ζωο-ποιέω, ῶ, 1st aor. *συνεζωοποίησα*, *to make alive together with*, Ep. ii. 5; Col. ii. 13. (N. T.)*

συκάμινος, ου, ἡ, *a sycamine-tree*, Lu. xvii. 6.*

συκῆ, ῆς, ἡ (contr. from -έα), *a fig-tree*, Mar. xi. 13, 20, 21.

συκο-μωραία, ας, ἡ (W. H. *-μορέα*), *a sycamore-tree*, Lu. xix. 4.*

σῦκον, ου, τό, *a fig*, Ja. iii. 12.

συκο-φαντέω, ῶ, ήσω, *to accuse falsely, to defraud*, Lu. iii. 14, xix. 8 (gen. person, acc. thing).*

συλ-αγωγέω, ῶ, *to plunder*, Col. ii. 8. (N. T.)*

συλάω, ῶ, *to rob, to plunder*, 2 Cor. xi. 8.*

συλλ-. In words commencing thus, W. H. prefer the unassimilated form *συνλ-*.

συλ-λαλέω, 1st aor. *συνελάλησα*, *to talk with* (dat.), μετά (gen.), πρός (acc.), Mat. xvii. 3; Mar. ix. 4; Lu. iv. 36, ix. 30, xxii. 4; Ac. xxv. 12.*

συλ-λαμβάνω, *συλλήψομαι*, *συνείληφα*, *συνέλαβον*, (1) *to take together, to seize*, Mat. xxvi. 55; (2) *to conceive*, of a woman, Lu. i. 24, 31; (3) mid., *to apprehend* (acc.), *to help* (dat.), Ac. xxvi. 21; Phil. iv. 3.

συλ-λέγω, ξω, *to collect, to gather*, Mat. xiii. 28, 29, 30.

συλ-λογίζομαι, σομαι, *to reckon with one's self, to reason*, Lu. xx. 5.*

συλ-λυπέομαι, οῦμαι, pass., *to be grieved* (ἐπί, dat.), Mar. iii. 5.*

συμβ-, συμμ-, συμπ-, συμφ-. In some words commencing thus, W. H. prefer the unassimilated form *συνβ-*, *συνμ-*, *συνπ-*, *συνφ-*.

συμ-βαίνω, 2d aor. *συνέβην*, *to happen, to occur*, Mar. x. 32; Ac. xx. 19; perf. part. τὸ συμβεβηκός, *an event*, Lu. xxiv. 14.

συμ-βάλλω, 2d aor. *συνέβαλον*, *to throw together*, hence, *to ponder*, Lu. ii. 19; *to come up with, to encounter*, with or without hostile intent (dat.), Lu. xiv. 31; Ac. xx. 14; *to dispute with*, Ac. xvii. 18; mid., *to confer, consult with*, Ac. iv. 15; *to contribute* (dat.), Ac. xviii. 27.*

συμ-βασιλεύω, σω, *to reign together with*, 1 Cor. iv. 8; 2 Tim. ii. 12.*

συμ-βιβάζω, άσω, (1) *to unite*, or *knit together*, Col. ii. 2, 19; (2) *to put together in reasoning*, and so, *to conclude, prove*, Ac. ix. 22; (3) *to teach, instruct*, 1 Cor. ii. 16.

συμ-βουλεύω, *to give advice* (dat.), Jn. xviii. 14; Rev. iii. 18; mid., *to take counsel together* (ἵνα or inf.), Mat. xxvi. 4; Jn. xi. 53 (W. H. *βουλεύομαι*); Ac. ix. 23.*

συμ-βούλιον, ου, τό, (1) *mutual consultation, counsel;* λαμβάνω, ποιέω συμβούλιον, *to take counsel together*, Mat. xii. 14, xxii. 15, xxvii. 1, 7, xxviii. 12; Mar. iii. 6, xv. 1; (2) *a council, a gathering of counselors*, Ac. xxv. 12.*

σύμ-βουλος, ου, ὁ, *an adviser, a counselor*, Ro. xi. 34.*

Συμεών, ὁ (Heb.), *Simeon* or *Simon* (see Σίμων); the apostle Peter is so called, Ac. xv. 14; 2 Pet. i. 1; and four others are mentioned: (1) Lu. ii. 25, 34; (2) Lu. iii. 30; (3) Ac. xiii. 1; (4) Rev. vii. 7.*

συμ-μαθητής, οῦ, ὁ, *a fellow-disciple*, Jn. xi. 16.*

συμ-μαρτυρέω, ῶ, *to bear witness together with*, Ro. ii. 15, viii. 16, ix. 1; Rev. xxii. 18 (not W. H.).*

συμ-μερίζω, in mid., *to divide together with, partake with* (dat.), 1 Cor. ix. 13.*

συμ-μέτοχος, ον, *jointly partaking*, Ep. iii. 6, v. 7.*

συμ-μιμητής, οῦ, ὁ, *a joint-imitator*, Phil. iii. 17. (N. T.)*

συμ-μορφίζω, see *συμμορφόω*. (N. T.)

σύμ-μορφος, ον, *similar, conformed to*, gen., Ro. viii. 29; dat., Phil. iii. 21.*

συμ-μορφόω, ῶ, *to bring to the same form with* (dat.), Phil. iii. 10 (W. H. *συμμορφίζω*, in same sense). (N. T.)*

συμ-παθέω, ῶ, *to sympathize with, to have compassion on* (dat.), Heb. iv. 15, x. 34.*

συμ-παθής, ές, *sympathizing, compassionate*, 1 Pet. iii. 8.*

συμ-παρα-γίνομαι, *to come together to* (ἐπί, acc.), Lu. xxiii. 48; *to stand by one, to help* (dat.), 2 Tim. iv. 16 (W. H. *παραγίνομαι*).*

συμ-παρα-καλέω, ῶ, in pass., *to be strengthened together*, Ro. i. 12.*

συμ-παρα-λαμβάνω, 2d aor. *συμπαρέλαβον*, *to take with one's self*, as companion, Ac. xii. 25, xv. 37, 38; Gal. ii. 1.*

συμ-παρα-μένω, μενῶ, *to remain* or *continue together with* (dat.), Phil. i. 25 (W. H. *παραμένω*).*

συμ-πάρειμι, *to be present together with*, Ac. xxv. 24.*

συμ-πάσχω, *to suffer together with*, Ro. viii. 17; 1 Cor. xii. 26.*

συμ-πέμπω, *to send together with*, 2 Cor. viii. 18, 22.*

συμ-περι-λαμβάνω, *to embrace* completely, Ac. xx. 10.*

συμ-πίνω, 2d aor. *συνέπιον*, *to drink together with*, Ac. x. 41.*

συμ-πίπτω, *to fall together*, Lu. vi. 49 (W. H.).*

συμ-πληρόω, ῶ, *to fill completely*, Lu. viii. 23; pass., *to be completed, to be fully come*, Lu. ix. 51; Ac. ii. 1.*

συμ-πνίγω, *to choke utterly*, as weeds do plants, Mat. xiii. 22; Mar. iv. 7, 19; Lu. viii. 14; *to crowd upon* (acc.), Lu. viii. 42.*

συμ-πολίτης, ου, ὁ, *a fellow-citizen*, Ep. ii. 19.*

συμ-πορεύομαι, (1) *to journey together with* (dat.), Lu. vii. 11, xiv. 25, xxiv. 15; (2) intrans., *to come together, to assemble*, Mar. x. 1.*

συμπόσιον, ου, τό (συμπίνω), *a drinking party, a festive company*, συμπόσια συμπόσια, *by companies*, Mar. vi. 39.*

συμ-πρεσβύτερος, ου, ὁ, *a fellow-elder*, 1 Pet. v. 1. (N. T.)*

συμ-φάγω, see συνεσθίω.

συμ-φέρω, 1st aor. συνήνεγκα, *to bring together, to collect*, only Ac. xix. 19; generally intrans., and often impers., *to conduce to, to be profitable to*, 1 Cor. x. 23; 2 Cor. xii. 1; part. τὸ συμφέρον, *profit, advantage*, 1 Cor. vii. 35.

σύμ-φημι, *to assent to*, Ro. vii. 16.*

σύμ-φορος, ον, *profitable*, 1 Cor. vii. 35, x. 33 (W. H. for Rec. συμφέρον).*

συμ-φυλέτης, ου, ὁ, *one of the same tribe, a fellow-countryman*, 1 Th. ii. 14. (N. T.)*

σύμ-φυτος, ον, *grown together, united with* (R. V.), Ro. vi. 5.*

συμ-φύω, 2d aor. pass. part. συμφυείς, pass., *to grow at the same time*, Lu. viii. 7.*

συμ-φωνέω, ῶ, ήσω, *to agree with, agree together, arrange with* (dat., or μετά, gen.), of persons, Mat. xviii. 19, xx. 2, 13; Ac. v. 9; of things, *to be in accord with*, Lu. v. 36; Ac. xv. 15.*

συμ-φώνησις, εως, ἡ, *concord, agreement*, 2 Cor. vi. 15. (N. T.)*

συμ-φωνία, ας, ἡ, *harmony*, of instruments, *music*, Lu. xv. 25.*

σύμ-φωνος, ον, *harmonious, agreeing with*; ἐκ συμφώνου, *by agreement*, 1 Cor. vii. 5.*

συμ-ψηφίζω, *to compute, reckon up*, Ac. xix. 19.*

σύμ-ψυχος, ον, *of one accord*, Phil. ii. 2. (N. T.)*

σύν, a prep. gov. dative, *with* (see Gr. § 296, Wi. § 48*b*, Bu. 331). In composition, σύν denotes association with, or is intensive. The final ν changes to γ, λ, or μ, or is dropped, according to the initial letter of the word with which it is compounded (see Gr. § 4*d*, 5, Bu. 8); but W. H. usually prefer the unassimilated forms.

συν-άγω, άξω, (1) *to bring together, to gather, to assemble*, Lu. xv. 13; Jn. xi. 47; pass., *to be assembled, to come together*, Ac. iv. 5, xiii. 44; (2) *to receive hospitably*, only Mat. xxv. 35, 38, 43.

συναγωγή, ῆς, ἡ, *an assembly, a congregation, synagogue*, either the place, or the people gathered in the place, Lu. xii. 11, xxi. 12. *Syn.*: see ἐκκλησία.

συν-αγωνίζομαι, *to strive together with* another, *to aid* (dat.), Ro. xv. 30.*

συν-αθλέω, ῶ, ήσω, *to strive together for* (dat. of thing), Phil. i. 27; or *with*. (dat. of person), Phil. iv. 3.*

συν-αθροίζω, σω, *to gather* or *collect together*, Ac. xix. 25; pass., *to be assembled together*, Lu. xxiv. 33 (W. H. ἀθροίζω); Ac. xii. 12.*

συν-αίρω, *to reckon together, to make a reckoning with*, Mat. xviii. 23, 24, xxv. 19.*

συν-αιχμάλωτος, ου, ὁ, *a fellow-captive* or *prisoner*, Ro. xvi. 7; Col. iv. 10; Philem. 23. (N. T.)*

συν-ακολουθέω, ῶ, ήσω, *to follow together with, to accompany*, Mar. v. 37, xiv. 51 (W. H.); Lu. xxiii. 49.*

συν-αλίζω, in pass., *to be assembled together with* (dat.), Ac. i. 4.*

συν-αλλάσσω, *to reconcile*, see συνελαύνω.

συν-ανα-βαίνω, *to go up together with* (dat.), Mar. xv. 41; Ac. xiii. 31.*

συν-ανά-κειμαι, *to recline together with*, as at a meal, *to feast with* (dat.), Mat. ix. 10; part. οἱ συνανακείμενοι, *the guests*, Mar. vi. 22, 26. (Ap.)

συν-ανα-μίγνυμι, pass., *to mingle together with, to keep company with* (dat.), 1 Cor. v. 9, 11; 2 Th. iii. 14.*

συν-ανα-παύομαι, σομαι, *to find rest* or *refreshment together with* (dat.), Ro. xv. 32. (S.)*

συν-αντάω, ῶ, ήσω, (1) *to meet with* (dat.), Lu. ix. 37, xxii. 10; Ac. x. 25; Heb. vii. 1, 10; (2) of things, *to happen to, to befall*; τὰ συναντήσοντα, *the things that shall happen*, Ac. xx. 22.*

συν-άντησις, εως, ἡ, *a meeting with*, Mat. viii. 34 (W. H. ὑπάντησις).*

συν-αντι-λαμβάνω, mid., lit., *to take hold together with*; *to assist, help* (dat.), Lu. x. 40; Ro. viii. 26.*

συν-απ-άγω, *to lead away along with*; in pass., *to be led* or *carried away in mind*, Ro. xii. 16 (see R. V. mrg.); Gal. ii. 13; 2 Pet. iii. 17.*

συν-απο-θνήσκω, *to die together with* (dat.), Mar. xiv. 31; 2 Cor. vii. 3; 2 Tim. ii. 11.*

συν-απ-όλλυμι, in mid., *to perish together with* (dat.), Heb. xi. 31.*

συν-απο-στέλλω, *to send together with* (acc.), 2 Cor. xii. 18.*

συν-αρμολογέω, ῶ, in pass., *to be framed together*, Ep. ii. 21, iv. 16. (N. T.)*

συν-αρπάζω, σω, *to seize*, or *drag by force* (dat.), Lu. viii. 29; Ac. vi. 12, xix. 29, xxvii. 15.*

συν-αυξάνω, in pass., *to grow together*, Mat. xiii. 30.*

σύν-δεσμος, ου, ὁ, *that which binds together, a band, a bond*, Ac. viii. 23; Ep. iv. 3; Col. ii. 19, iii. 14.*

συν-δέω, in pass., *to be bound together with* any one, as fellow-prisoners, Heb. xiii. 3.*

συν-δοξάζω, *to glorify together with* (σύν), pass., Ro. viii. 17.*

σύν-δουλος, ου, ὁ, *a fellow-slave, a fellow-servant*, Mat. xviii. 28–33; of Christians, *a fellow-worker, a colleague*, Col. i. 7.

συν-δρομή, ῆς, ἡ, *a running together*, *a concourse*, Ac. xxi. 30.*

συν-εγείρω, 1st aor. συνήγειρα, pass. συνηγέρθην; *to raise together*, *to raise with*, Ep. ii. 6; Col. ii. 12, iii. 1. (S.)*

συνέδριον, ου, τό, *a council*, *a tribunal*, Mat. x. 17; specially, *the Sanhedrin*, the Jewish council of seventy-one members, usually presided over by the high priest, Mat. v. 22, xxvi. 59; *the council-hall*, where the Sanhedrin met, Ac. iv. 15.

συν-είδησις, εως, ἡ, *consciousness*, Heb. x. 2; *the conscience*, Ro. ii. 15; 2 Cor. iv. 2, v. 11; 1 Pet. ii. 19.

συν-εῖδον, 2d aor. of obs. pres., *to be conscious* or *aware of*, *to understand*, Ac. xii. 12, xiv. 6; perf. σύνοιδα, part. συνειδώς, *to be privy to* a design, Ac. v. 2; *to be conscious* to one's self (dat.) of guilt (acc.), 1 Cor. iv. 4.*

σύν-ειμι, *to be with* (dat.), Lu. ix. 18; Ac. xxii. 11.*

σύν-ειμι (εἶμι), part. συνιών, *to go* or *come with*, *to assemble*, Lu. viii. 4.*

συν-εισ-έρχομαι, *to enter together with* (dat.), Jn. vi. 22, xviii. 15.*

συν-έκδημος, ου, ὁ, ἡ, *a fellow-traveler*, Ac. xix. 29; 2 Cor. viii. 19.*

συν-εκλεκτός, ή, όν, *elected together with*, 1 Pet. v. 13. (N. T.)*

συν-ελαύνω, ελάσω, *to compel*, *to urge* (acc. and εἰς), Ac. vii. 26 (W. H. συναλλάσσω).*

συν-επι-μαρτυρέω, ῶ, *to unite in bearing witness*, Heb. ii. 4.*

συν-επι-τίθημι, mid., *to join in assailing*, Ac. xxiv. 9 (W. H. for συντίθημι).*

συν-έπομαι, *to follow with*, *to accompany* (dat.), Ac. xx. 4.*

συν-εργέω, ῶ, *to co-operate with* (dat.), *to work together*, 1 Cor. xvi. 16; Ro. viii. 28.

συν-εργός, όν, *co-working*, *helping*; as a subst., *a companion in work*, *a fellow-worker*, gen. of person, obj. with εἰς, or dat., or (met.) gen., 2 Cor. i. 24.

συν-έρχομαι (see Gr. § 103, 2, Wi. § 15, Bu. 58), *to come* or *go with*, *to accompany*, Ac. i. 21; *to come together*, *to assemble*, Ac. i. 6, v. 16; used also of conjugal intercourse, *to come* or *live together*, Mat. i. 18.

συν-εσθίω, 2d aor. συνέφαγον, *to eat with* (dat., or μετά, gen.), Lu. xv. 2; Ac. x. 41, xi. 3; 1 Cor. v. 11; Gal. ii. 12.*

σύνεσις, εως, ἡ (συνίημι), *a putting together*, in mind; hence, *understanding*, Lu. ii. 47; *the understanding*, the source of discernment, Mar. xii. 33.

συνετός, ή, όν (συνίημι), *intelligent*, *prudent*, *wise*, Mat. xi. 25; Lu. x. 21; Ac. xiii. 7; 1 Cor. i. 19.*

συν-ευδοκέω, ῶ, *to be pleased together with*, *to approve together* (dat.), Lu. xi. 48; Ac. viii. 1, xxii. 20; *to be of one mind with* (dat.), Ro. i. 32; *to consent*, *agree to* (inf.), 1 Cor. vii. 12, 13.*

συν-ευωχέω, ῶ, in pass., *to feast sumptuously with*, 2 Pet. ii. 13; Ju. 12.*

συν-εφ-ίστημι, *to rise up together against* (κατά), Ac. xvi. 22.*

συν-έχω, ξω, (1) *to press together*, *to close*, Ac. vii. 57; (2) *to press on every side*, *to confine*, Lu. viii. 45; (3) *to hold fast*, Lu. xxii. 63; (4) *to urge*, *impel*, Lu. xii. 50; 2 Cor. v. 14; (5) in pass., *to be afflicted with* sickness, Lu. iv. 38.

συν-ήδομαι, *to delight inwardly in* (dat.), Ro. vii. 22.*

συν-ήθεια, ας, ἡ, *a custom*, Jn. xviii. 39; 1 Cor. viii. 7 (W. H.), xi. 16.*

συν-ηλικιώτης, ου, ὁ, *one of the same age*, Gal. i. 14.*

συν-θάπτω, 2d aor. pass. συνετάφην, in pass., *to be buried together with*, Ro. vi. 4; Col. ii. 12.*

συν-θλάω, ῶ, fut. pass. συνθλασθήσομαι, *to break*, *to break in pieces*, Mat. xxi. 44; Lu. xx. 18.*

συν-θλίβω, *to press on all sides*, *to crowd upon*, Mar. v. 24, 31.*

συν-θρύπτω, *to break in pieces*, *to crush*, fig., Ac. xxi. 13. (N. T.)*

συν-ίημι, inf. συνιέναι, part. συνιῶν or συνιείς, fut. συνήσω, 1st aor. συνῆκα, *to put together*, in mind; hence, *to consider*, *understand* (acc.), *to be aware* (ὅτι), *to attend to* (ἐπί, dat.), Mat. xiii. 23, 51, xvi. 12; Mar. vi. 52.

συν-ίστημι, also συνιστάνω and συνιστάω, *to place together*; *to commend*, 2 Cor. iii. 1, vi. 4; *to prove*, *exhibit*, Gal. ii. 18; Ro. iii. 5, v. 8; perf. and 2d aor., intrans., *to stand with*, Lu. ix. 32; *to be composed of*, *to cohere*, Col. i. 17; 2 Pet. iii. 5.

συν-οδεύω, *to journey with*, *to accompany* (dat.), Ac. ix. 7.*

συν-οδία, ας, ἡ, *a company traveling together*, *a caravan*, Lu. ii. 44.*

συν-οικέω, ῶ, *to dwell together*, as in marriage, 1 Pet. iii. 7.*

συν-οικοδομέω, ῶ, in pass., *to be built up together*, Ep. ii. 22.*

συν-ομιλέω, ῶ, *to talk with* (dat.), Ac. x. 27.*

συν-ομορέω, ῶ, *to be contiguous to* (dat.), Ac. xviii. 7. (N. T.)*

συν-οχή, ῆς, ἡ, *constraint* of mind; hence, *distress*, *anguish*, Lu. xxi. 25; 2 Cor. ii. 4.*

συν-τάσσω, ξω, *to arrange with*, *prescribe*, *appoint*, Mat. xxi. 6 (W. H.), xxvi. 19, xxvii. 10.*

συν-τέλεια, ας, ἡ, *a completion*, *a consummation*, *an end*, Mat. xiii. 39, 40, 49, xxiv. 3, xxviii. 20; Heb. ix. 26.*

συν-τελέω, ῶ, έσω, (1) *to bring completely to an end*, Mat. vii. 28 (W. H. τελέω); Lu. iv. 2, 13; Ac. xxi. 27; (2) *to fulfill*, *to accomplish*, Ro. ix. 28; Mar. xiii. 4; *to make*, *to conclude*, Heb. viii. 8.*

συν-τέμνω, *to cut short*, *to bring to swift accomplishment*, Ro. ix. 28.*

συν-τηρέω, ῶ, (1) *to preserve*, *to keep safe*, Mat. ix. 17; Mar. vi. 20; Lu. v. 38 (W. H. omit); (2) *to keep in mind*, Lu. ii. 19.*

συν-τίθημι, in mid., *to place together*, *to make an agreement*, Lu. xxii. 5; Jn. ix. 22; Ac. xxiii. 20; *to assent*, Ac.

xxiv. 9 (W. H. συνεπιτίθημι).*

συν-τόμως, adv., *concisely, briefly*, Ac. xxiv. 4.*

συν-τρέχω, 2d aor. συνέδραμον, *to run together*, as a multitude, Mar. vi. 33; Ac. iii. 11; *to run with* (fig.), 1 Pet. iv. 4.*

συν-τρίβω, ψω, *to break by crushing, to break in pieces*, Lu. ix. 39; Ro. xvi. 20; perf. pass. part. συντετριμμένος, *bruised*, Mat. xii. 20.

σύν-τριμμα, ατος, τό, *crushing*; fig., *destruction*, Ro. iii. 16. (S.)*

σύν-τροφος, ου, ὁ, *one brought up with, a foster-brother*, Ac. xiii. 1.*

συν-τυγχάνω, 2d aor. inf. συντυχεῖν, *to meet with, come to* (dat.), Lu. viii. 19.*

Συντύχη, acc. ην, ἡ, *Syntyche*, Phil. iv. 2.*

συν-υπο-κρίνομαι, dep. pass., 1st aorist συνυπεκρίθην, *to dissemble with*, Gal. ii. 13.*

συν-υπουργέω, ῶ, *to help together*, 2 Cor. i. 11.*

συν-ωδίνω, *to be in travail together*, Ro. viii. 22.*

συν-ωμοσία, ας, ἡ, *a swearing together, a conspiracy*, Ac. xxiii. 13.*

Συράκουσαι, ῶν, αἱ, *Syracuse*, Ac. xxviii. 12.*

Συρία, ας, ἡ, *Syria*, Lu. ii. 2.

Σύρος, ου, ὁ, *a Syrian*, Lu. iv. 27.*

Συρο-φοίνισσα (W. H. Συροφοινίκισσα, mrg., Σύρα Φοινίκισσα), ης, ἡ, an appellative, *a Syrophenician woman*, Mar. vii. 26.*

Σύρτις, εως, acc. ιν, ἡ, (*a quicksand*), *the Syrtis major*, Ac. xxvii. 17.*

σύρω, *to draw, to drag*, Jn. xxi. 8; Ac. viii. 3, xiv. 19, xvii. 6; Rev. xii. 4.* *Syn.*: see ἕλκω.

συσ-. In some words commencing thus, W. H. prefer the uncontracted form συνσ-.

συ-σπαράσσω, ξω, *to convulse completely* (acc.), Mar. ix. 20 (W. H.); Lu. ix. 42.*

σύσ-σημον, ου, τό, *a concerted signal, a sign agreed upon*, Mar. xiv. 44.*

σύσ-σωμος (W. H. σύνσωμος), ον, *belonging to the same body*; fig., of Jews and Gentiles, in one church, Ep. iii. 6. (N. T.)*

συ-στασιαστής, οῦ, ὁ, *a fellow-insurgent* (W. H. στασιαστής), Mar. xv. 7.*

συ-στατικός, ή, όν, *commendatory*, 2 Cor. iii. 1.*

συ-σταυρόω, ῶ, *to crucify together with* (acc. and dat.); lit., Mat. xxvii. 44; fig., Gal. ii. 19. (N. T.)

συ-στέλλω, (1) *to contract*, perf. pass. part., *contracted, shortened*, 1 Cor. vii. 29; (2) *to wrap round, to swathe*, as a dead body, Ac. v. 6.*

συ-στενάζω, *to groan together*, Ro. viii. 22.*

συ-στοιχέω, ῶ, *to be in the same rank with; to answer to, to correspond to* (dat.), Gal. iv. 25.*

συ-στρατιώτης, ου, ὁ, *a fellow-soldier, i.e.*, in the Christian service, Phil. ii. 25; Philem. 2.*

συ-στρέφω, ψω, *to roll* or *gather together*, Mat. xvii. 22 (W. H.); Ac. xxviii. 3.*

συ-στροφή, ῆς, ἡ, *a gathering together, a riotous concourse*, Ac. xix. 40; *a conspiracy*, Ac. xxiii. 12.*

συ-σχηματίζω, in pass., *to conform one's self, to be assimilated to* (dat.), Ro. xii. 2; 1 Pet. i. 14.*

Συχάρ (W. H.), or Σιχάρ, ἡ, *Sychar*, Jn. iv. 5.*

Συχέμ, *Shechem*, (1) ὁ, the prince, Ac. vii. 16 (Rec., W. H. the city); (2) ἡ, the city, Ac. vii. 16.*

σφαγή, ῆς, ἡ, (1) *slaughter*, Ac. viii. 32; Ro. viii. 36 (S.); Ja. v. 5.*

σφάγιον, ου, τό, *a slaughtered victim*, Ac. vii. 42.*

σφάζω, ξω, pass., perf. part. ἐσφαγμένος, 2d aor. ἐσφάγην, *to kill by violence, to slay*, 1 Jn. iii. 12; Rev. v. 9, vi. 4.

σφόδρα, adv., *exceedingly, greatly*, Mat. ii. 10.

σφοδρῶς, adv., *exceedingly*, Ac. xxvii. 18.*

σφραγίζω, ίσω, *to seal, to set a seal upon*, (1) for security, Mat. xxvii. 66; (2) for secrecy, Rev. xxii. 10; (3) for designation, Ep. i. 13; or (4) for authentication, Ro. xv. 28.

σφραγίς, ῖδος, ἡ, (1) *a seal, a signet-ring*, Rev. vii. 2; (2) *the impression of a seal* whether for security and secrecy, as Rev. v. 1; or for designation, Rev. ix. 4; (3) *that which the seal attests, the proof*, 1 Cor. ix. 2.

σφυρίς, see σπυρίς.

σφυρόν (W. H. σφυδρόν), οῦ, τό, *the ankle-bone*, Ac. iii. 7.*

σχεδόν, adv., *nearly, almost*, Ac. xiii. 44, xix. 26; Heb. ix. 22.*

σχῆμα, ατος, τό, *fashion, habit*, 1 Cor. vii. 31; *form, appearance*, Phil. ii. 7.* *Syn.*: see ἰδέα.

σχίζω, ίσω, *to rend, to divide asunder*, Mat. xxvii. 51; pass., *to be divided into factions*, Ac. xiv. 4.

σχίσμα, ατος, τό, *a rent*, as in a garment, Mar. ii. 21; *a division, a dissension*, 1 Cor. i. 10.

σχοινίον, ου, τό (dim. of σχοῖνος, *a rush*), *a cord, a rope*, Jn. ii. 15; Ac. xxvii. 32.*

σχολάζω, άσω, *to be at leisure; to be empty* or *unoccupied*, Mat. xii. 44; *to have leisure for* (dat.), *give one's self to*, 1 Cor. vii. 5.*

σχολή, ῆς, ἡ, *leisure; a place where there is leisure for anything, a school*, Ac. xix. 9.*

σώζω, σώσω, perf. σέσωκα, pass. σέσωσμαι, 1st aor. pass. ἐσώθην; (1) *to save*, from evil or danger, Mat. viii. 25, xvi. 25; (2) *to heal*, Mat. ix. 21, 22; Jn. xi. 12; (3) *to save, i.e.*, from eternal death, 1 Tim. i. 15; part. pass. οἱ σωζόμενοι, *those who are being saved, i.e.*, who are in the way of salvation, Ac. ii. 47.

σῶμα, ατος, τό, *a body, i.e.*, (1) *the living body* of an animal, Ja. iii. 3; or of a man, as 1 Cor. xii. 12, espec. as the medium of human life, and of human life as sinful; the *body* of Christ, as the medium and witness of his humanity; σώματα, Rev. xviii. 13, *slaves*; (2) *a dead body, a corpse*, Ac. ix. 40; (3) fig., *a community*, the church, *the mystic body of Christ*, Col. i. 24; (4) *any material body*, plants, sun, moon, etc., 1 Cor. xv. 37, 38, 40; (5) *substance*, opp. to shadow, Col. ii. 17.

σωματικός, ή, όν, *of* or *pertaining to the body*, 1 Tim. iv. 8; *bodily*, *corporeal*, Lu. iii. 22.*

σωματικῶς, adv., *bodily*, *corporeally*, Col. ii. 9.*

Σώπατρος, ου, ὁ, *Sopater*, Ac. xx. 4; (perh. = Σωσίπατρος, see Ro. xvi. 21).*

σωρεύω, σω, *to heap up*, *to load*, Ro. xii. 20; 2 Tim. iii. 16.*

Σωσθένης, ου, ὁ, *Sosthenes*, (1) Ac. xviii. 17; (2) 1 Cor. i. 1.*

Σωσίπατρος, ου, ὁ, *Sosipater*, Ro. xvi. 21 (see Ac. xx. 4).*

σωτήρ, ῆρος, ὁ, *a savior*, *deliverer*, *preserver;* a name given to God, Lu. i. 47; 1 Tim. i. 1, ii. 3, iv. 10; Tit. i. 3, ii. 10, iii. 4; Ju. 25; elsewhere always of Christ, Lu. ii. 11; Jn. iv. 42.

σωτηρία, ας, ἡ, *welfare*, *prosperity*, *deliverance*, *preservation*, from temporal evils, Ac. vii. 25, xxvii. 34; Heb. xi. 7; 2 Pet. iii. 15; specially *salvation*, *i.e.*, deliverance from eternal death, viewed either as present or future, 2 Cor. i. 6; 1 Th. v. 9.

σωτήριος, ον, *saving*, *bringing salvation*, Tit. ii. 11; neut. τὸ σωτήριον, *salvation*, Lu. ii. 30, iii. 6; Ac. xxviii. 28; Ep. vi. 17.*

σωφρονέω, ῶ, ήσω, (1) *to be of sound mind*, Mar. v. 15; (2) *to be sober-minded*, Ro. xii. 3; (3) *to exercise self-control*, Tit. ii. 6.

σωφρονίζω, *to make sober-minded*, *to admonish*, Tit. ii. 4.*

σωφρονισμός, οῦ, ὁ, *self-control*, or *discipline*, 2 Tim. i. 7.*

σωφρόνως, adv., *soberly*, *with moderation*, Tit. ii. 12.*

σωφροσύνη, ης, ἡ, *soundness of mind*, *sanity*, Ac. xxvi. 25; *self-control*, *sobriety*, 1 Tim. ii. 9, 15.*

σώ-φρων, ον (σάος, σῶς, *sound*, and φρήν), *of sound mind*, *self-controlled*, *temperate*, 1 Tim. iii. 2; Tit. i. 8, ii. 2, 5.*

T

Τ, τ, ταῦ, *tau*, *t*, the nineteenth letter. As a numeral, τʹ = 300; ͵τ = 300,000.

ταβέρναι, ῶν, αἱ (Lat.), *taverns;* Ac. xxviii. 15, Τρεῖς Ταβέρναι, *Three Taverns*, a place on the Appian Way. (N. T.)*

Ταβιθά, ἡ (Aram.), *Tabitha*, Ac. ix. 36, 40.*

τάγμα, ατος, τό, *an order* or *series*, *a class*, 1 Cor. xv. 23.*

τακτός, ή, όν, *appointed*, *fixed*, Ac. xii. 21.*

ταλαιπωρέω, ῶ, ήσω, *to be distressed*, *to be miserable*, Ja. iv. 9.*

ταλαιπωρία, ας, ἡ, *hardship*, *misery*, Ro. iii. 16; Ja. v. 1.*

ταλαί-πωρος, ον, *afflicted*, *miserable*, Ro. vii. 24; Rev. iii. 17.*

ταλαντιαῖος, αία, αῖον, *of the weight of a talent*, Rev. xvi. 21.*

τάλαντον, ου, τό, *a talent*, of silver or gold, Mat. xviii. 24. The N. T. talent is probably the Syrian silver talent, worth about 237 dollars, rather than the Attic, worth about 1000 dollars.

ταλιθά, ἡ (Aram.), *a damsel*, Mar. v. 41. (N. T.)*

ταμεῖον (or -μιεῖ-), ου, τό, *a store-chamber*, Lu. xii. 24; *a secret chamber*, Mat. vi. 6, xxiv. 26; Lu. xii. 3.*

τανῦν, adv. (τὰ νῦν, *the things that now are*), *as respects the present*, *at present*, *now*, only in Ac. (W. H. always write τὰ νῦν).

τάξις, εως, ἡ, *order*, *i.e.*, (1) *regular arrangement*, Col. ii. 5; (2) *appointed succession*, Lu. i. 8; (3) *position*, *rank*, Heb. v. 6.

ταπεινός, ή, όν, *humble*, *lowly*, in condition or in spirit; in N. T. in a good sense, Ja. i. 9, iv. 6.

ταπεινοφροσύνη, ης, ἡ, *lowliness of mind*, *humility*, real, as Phil. ii. 3; or affected, as Col. ii. 18.

ταπεινό-φρων, ον, *humble*, 1 Pet. iii. 8 (W. H. for φιλόφρων). (S.)*

ταπεινόω, ῶ, ώσω, *to make* or *bring low*, Lu. iii. 5; *to humble*, *humiliate*, 2 Cor. xii. 21; pass., *to be humbled*, Lu. xviii. 14; pass., in mid. sense, *to humble one's self*, Ja. iv. 10.

ταπείνωσις, εως, ἡ, *low condition*, in circumstances, Lu. i. 48; *abasement*, in spirit, Ja. i. 10.

ταράσσω, ξω, *to agitate*, as water in a pool, Jn. v. 4 (W. H. omit), 7; *to stir up*, *to disturb in mind*, with fear, grief, anxiety, doubt, Ac. xviii. 8; 1 Pet. iii. 14.

ταραχή, ῆς, ἡ, *a disturbance*, Jn. v. 4 (W. H. omit); *a tumult*, *sedition*, Mar. xiii. 8 (W. H. omit).*

τάραχος, ου, ὁ, *a disturbance*, Ac. xix. 23; *commotion*, Ac. xii. 18.*

Ταρσεύς, έως, ὁ, *one of Tarsus*, Ac. ix. 11, xxi. 39.*

Ταρσός, οῦ, ἡ, *Tarsus*, Ac. ix. 30.

ταρταρόω, ῶ, ώσω, *to thrust down to Tartarus* (*Gehenna*), 2 Pet. ii. 4. (N. T.)*

τάσσω, ξω, (1) *to assign*, *arrange*, Ro. xiii. 1; (2) *to determine;* mid., *to appoint*, Mat. xxviii. 16.

ταῦρος, ου, ὁ, *a bull*, Ac. xiv. 13.

ταὐτά, by crasis for τὰ αὐτά, *the same things*.

ταῦτα, see οὗτος.

ταφή, ῆς, ἡ (θάπτω), *a burial*, Mat. xxvii. 7.*

τάφος, ου, ὁ, *a burial-place*, *a sepulchre*, as Mat. xxiii. 27.

τάχα, adv., *quickly; perhaps*, Ro. v. 7; Philem. 15.*

ταχέως, adv. (ταχύς), *soon*, *quickly*, Gal. i. 6; *hastily*, 2 Th. ii. 2; 1 Tim. v. 22.

ταχινός, ή, όν, *swift*, *quick*, 2 Pet. i. 14; ii. 1.*

τάχος, ους, τό, *quickness*, *speed*, only in the phrase ἐν τάχει, *quickly*, *speedily*, Lu. xviii. 8.

ταχύς, εῖα, ύ, *quick*, *swift*, only Ja. i. 19; ταχύ, compar. τάχιον (W. H. τάχειον), superl. τάχιστα, adverbially, *swiftly; more*, *most quickly*.

τέ, conj. of annexation, *and*, *both* (see Gr. § 403, Wi. § 53, 2, Bu. 360 sq.).

τεῖχος, ους, τό, *a wall* of a city, Ac. ix. 25.

τεκμήριον, ου, τό, *a sign, a certain proof*, Ac. i. 3.*

τεκνίον, ου, τό (dim. of τέκνον), *a little child*, Jn. xiii. 33; Gal. iv. 19; 1 Jn. ii. 1, 12, 28, iii. 7, 18, iv. 4, v. 21.*

τεκνο-γονέω, ῶ, *to bear children*, 1 Tim. v. 14.*

τεκνο-γονία, ας, ἡ, *child-bearing*, 1 Tim. ii. 15.*

τέκνον, ου, τό (τίκτω), *a child, a descendant; an inhabitant*, Lu. xiii. 34; fig. of various forms of intimate union and relationship, *a disciple, a follower*, Philem. 10; hence, such phrases as τέκνα τῆς σοφίας, τέκνα ὑπακοῆς, τέκνα τοῦ φωτός, *children of wisdom, obedience, the light*, and espec. τέκνα τοῦ θεοῦ, *children of God*, Ro. viii. 16, 17, 21; 1 Jn.

τεκνο-τροφέω, ῶ, *to bring up children*, 1 Tim. v. 10.*

τέκτων, ονος, ὁ, *a carpenter*, Mat. xiii. 55; Mar. vi. 3.*

τέλειος, α, ον, *perfect*, as (1) *complete* in all its parts, Ja. i. 4; (2) *full grown of full age*, Heb. v. 14; (3) specially of the completeness of Christian character, *perfect*, Mat. v. 48. *Syn.:* see ἄρτιος.

τελειότης, τητος, ἡ, *perfectness, perfection*, Col. iii. 14; Heb. vi. 1.*

τελειόω, ῶ, ώσω, (1) *to complete, to finish*, as a course, a race, or the like, Jn. iv. 34; (2) *to accomplish*, as time, or prediction, Lu. ii. 43; Jn. xix. 28; (3) *to make perfect*, Heb. vii. 19; pass., *to be perfected*, Lu. xiii. 32.

τελείως (τέλειος), adv., *perfectly*, 1 Pet. i. 13.*

τελείωσις, εως, ἡ, *completion, fulfillment*, Lu. i. 45; *perfection*, Heb. vii. 11.*

τελειωτής, οῦ, ὁ, *a perfecter*, Heb. xii. 2. (N. T.)*

τελεσ-φορέω, ῶ, *to bring to maturity*, Lu. viii. 14.*

τελευτάω, ῶ, *to end, to finish*, *e.g.*, life; so, *to die*, Mat. ix. 18; Mar. vii. 10.

τελευτή, ῆς, ἡ, *end* of life, *death*, Mat. ii. 15.*

τελέω, ῶ, έσω, τετέλεκα, τετέλεσμαι, ἐτελέσθην, (1) *to end, to finish*, Rev. xx. 3, 5, 7; (2) *to fulfill, to accomplish*, Lu. ii. 39; Ja. ii. 8; (3) *to pay*, Mat. xvii. 24.

τέλος, ους, τό, (1) *an end*, Lu. i. 33; (2) *event* or *issue*, Mat. xxvi. 58; (3) *the principal end, aim, purpose*, 1 Tim. i. 5; (4) *a tax*, Mat. xvii. 25; Ro. xiii. 7.

τελώνης, ου, ὁ, *a collector of taxes*, Lu. iii. 12, v. 27.

τελώνιον, ου, τό, *a toll-house, a tax-collector's office*, Mat. ix. 9; Mar. ii. 14; Lu. v. 27.*

τέρας, ατος, τό, *a wonder, a portent;* in N. T. only in plur., and joined with σημεῖα, *signs and wonders*, Ac. vii. 36; Jn. iv. 48. *Syn.:* see δύναμις.

Τέρτιος, ου, ὁ (Lat.), *Tertius*, Ro. xvi. 22.*

Τέρτυλλος, ου, ὁ, *Tertullus*, Ac. xxiv. 1, 2.*

τεσσαράκοντα, *forty*, Mat. iv. 2; Mar. i. 13.

τεσσαρακοντα-ετής, ές, *of forty years*, age or time, Ac. vii. 23, xiii. 18.*

τέσσαρες, τέσσαρα, gen. ων, *four*, Lu. ii. 37; Jn. xi. 17.

τεσσαρες-και-δέκατος, η, ον, ord. num., *fourteenth*, Ac. xxvii. 27, 33.*

τεταρταῖος, αία, αῖον, *of the fourth* (day); τεταρταῖος ἐστιν, *he has been dead four days*, Jn. xi. 39.*

τέταρτος, η, ον, ord. num., *fourth*, Mat. xiv. 25.

τετρά-γωνος, ον, *four-cornered, square*, Rev. xxi. 16.*

τετράδιον, ου, τό, *a quaternion*, or *guard of four soldiers*, Ac. xii. 4.*

τετρακισ-χίλιοι, αι, α, *four thousand*, Mar. viii. 9, 20.

τετρακόσιοι, αι, α, *four hundred*, Ac. v. 36.

τετρά-μηνος, ον, *of four months;* sc. χρόνος, *a period of four months*, Jn. iv. 35.*

τετρα-πλόος, οῦς, ῆ, οῦν, *four-fold*, Lu. xix. 8.*

τετρά-πους, ουν, gen. οδος, *four-footed*, Ac. x. 12, xi. 6; Ro. i. 23.*

τετρ-αρχέω (W.H. τετρααρχέω), ῶ, *to rule over as a tetrarch* (gen.), Lu. iii. 1.*

τετρ-άρχης (W.H. τετραάρχης), ου, ὁ, *a ruler over a fourth part of a region, a tetrarch*, applied also to rulers over any small dominion, Mat. xiv. 1.

τεύχω, see τυγχάνω.

τεφρόω, ῶ, ώσω (τέφρα, *ashes*), *to reduce to ashes*, 2 Pet. ii. 6.*

τέχνη, ης, ἡ, (1) *art, skill*, Ac. xvii. 29; (2) *an art, a trade*, Ac. xviii. 3; Rev. xviii. 22.*

τεχνίτης, ου, ὁ, *an artificer, craftsman*, Ac. xix. 24, 38; Rev. xviii. 22; used of God, Heb. xi. 10.* *Syn.:* see δημιουργός.

τήκω, *to make liquid;* pass., *to melt*, 2 Pet. iii. 12.*

τηλ-αυγῶς, adv. (τῆλε, *afar*, αὐγή, *radiance*), *clearly, distinctly*, Mar. viii. 25.*

τηλικ-οῦτος, αὕτη, οῦτο, *so great*, 2 Cor. i. 10; Heb. ii. 3; Ja. iii. 4; Rev. xvi. 18.*

τηρέω, ῶ, ήσω, *to watch carefully*, with good or evil design; (1) *to guard*, Mat. xxvii. 36, 54; (2) *to keep* or *reserve*, 1 Cor. vii. 37; (3) *to observe, keep*, enactments or ordinances, Jn. xiv. 15, 21.

τήρησις, εως, ἡ, (1) *a prison*, Ac. iv. 3, v. 18; (2) *observance*, as of precepts, 1 Cor. vii. 19.*

Τιβεριάς, άδος, ἡ, *Tiberias*, Jn. vi. 1, 23, xxi. 1.*

Τιβέριος, ου, ὁ, *Tiberius*, Lu. iii. 1.*

τίθημι, θήσω (see Gr. § 107, Wi. § 14, 1, Bu. 45 sq.), (1) *to place, set, lay, put forth, put down, put away, put aside;* mid., *to cause to put*, or *to put for one's self;* (2) *to constitute, to make, to render;* mid., *to assign, determine*.

τίκτω, τέξομαι, 2d aor. ἔτεκον, 1st aor. pass. ἐτέχθην, *to bear, to bring forth*, of women, Lu. i. 57, ii. 6, 7; *to produce*, of the earth, Heb. vi. 7.

τίλλω, *to pluck, to pluck off*, Mat. xii. 1; Mar. ii. 23; Lu. vi. 1.*

Τιμαῖος, ου, ὁ, *Timæus*, Mar. x. 46.*

τιμάω, ῶ, ήσω, (1) *to estimate, to value at a price*, Mat. xxvii. 9; (2) *to honor, to reverence*, Mar. vii. 6, 10.

τιμή, ῆς, ἡ, (1) *a price*, Mat. xxvii. 6, 9; (2) *honor*, Ro. ix. 21; Heb. v. 4; 2 Tim. ii. 20, 21; 1 Pet. ii. 7.

τίμιος, α, ον, *of great price, precious, honored*, Rev. xvii. 4; Heb. xiii. 4.

τιμιότης, τητος, ἡ, *preciousness, costliness*, Rev. xviii. 19.*

Τιμό-θεος, ου, ὁ, *Timothy*, Ac. xvii. 14, 15.

Τίμων, ωνος, ὁ, *Timon*, Ac. vi. 5.*

τιμωρέω, ῶ, *to punish* (acc.), Ac. xxii. 5, xxvi. 11.*

τιμωρία, ας, ἡ, *punishment, penalty*, Heb. x. 29.*

τίνω, τίσω, *to pay;* with **δίκην**, *to pay penalty, suffer punishment*, 2 Th. i. 9.*

τὶς, τὶ, gen. τινός (enclitic), indef. pron., *any one, some one* (see Gr. § 352, Wi. § 25, 2, Bu. 85, 93).

τίς, τί, gen. τίνος; interrogative pron., *who? which? what?* (see Gr. § 350, Wi. § 25, 1, Bu. 115, 138).

Τίτιος, ου, ὁ, *Titius*, Ac. xviii. 7 (W. H.).*

τίτλος, ου, ὁ (Lat.), *a title, an inscription*, Jn. xix. 19, 20.*

Τίτος, ου, ὁ, *Titus*, 2 Cor. vii. 6, 13, 14.

τοι, an enclitic part., *truly, indeed;* see καιτοίγε, μέντοι, τοιγαροῦν, τοίνυν.

τοι-γαρ-οῦν, *consequently, therefore*, 1 Th. iv. 8; Heb. xii. 1.*

τοί-γε, *although* (in καιτοίγε).

τοί-νυν, *indeed now, therefore*, Lu. xx. 25; 1 Cor. ix. 26; Heb. xiii. 13; Ja. ii. 24 (not W. H.).*

τοιόσ-δε, τοιάδε, τοιόνδε, demonst. pron., *of this kind, such*, 2 Pet. i. 17.*

τοιοῦτος, τοιαύτη, τοιοῦτο, demonst. denoting quality (as τοσοῦτος denotes quantity, and οὗτος simply determines), *of such a kind, such, so*, used either with or without a noun, the corresponding relative is οἷος, *as*, only Mar. xiii. 19; 1 Cor. xv. 48; 2 Cor. x. 11; once ὁποῖος, Ac. xxvi. 29. For τοιοῦτος with the article, see Gr. § 220, Wi. § 18, 4, Bu. 87.

τοῖχος, ου, ὁ, *a wall* of a house, Ac. xxiii. 3; disting. from τεῖχος, *a wall of a city*.*

τόκος, ου, ὁ (*a bringing forth*), *interest, usury*, Mat. xxv. 27; Lu. xix. 23.*

τολμάω, ῶ, ήσω, (1) *to dare* (inf.), Mar. xi. 34; (2) *to endure*, Ro. v. 7; (3) *to be bold*, 2 Cor. xi. 21.

τολμηρότερον (τολμηρός), neut. compar. as adv., *more boldly*, Ro. xv. 15 (W. H. τολμηροτέρως).*

τολμητής, οῦ, ὁ, *a daring, presumptuous man*, 2 Pet. ii. 10.*

τομός, ή, όν, *sharp, keen*, comp. τομώτερος, Heb. iv. 12.*

τόξον, ου, τό, *a bow*, Rev. vi. 2.*

τοπάζιον, ου, τό, *topaz*, Rev. xxi. 20. (N. T.)*

τόπος, ου, ὁ, (1) *a place, i.e., a district* or *region*, or *a particular spot in a region;* (2) *the place one occupies, the room, an abode, a seat, a sheath for a sword;* (3) *a passage in a book;* (4) *state, condition;* (5) *opportunity.*

τοσοῦτος, τοσαύτη, τοσοῦτο, demonst. pron. denoting quantity (see τοιοῦτος), *so great, so much, so long;* plur., *so many.*

τότε, demonst. adv., *then.*

τοὐναντίον, for τὸ ἐναντίον, *on the contrary*, 2 Cor. ii. 7; Gal. ii. 7; 1 Pet. iii. 9.*

τοὔνομα, for τὸ ὄνομα, acc. absol., *by name*, Mat. xxvii. 57.*

τουτέστι, for τοῦτ' ἔστι (W. H. prefer the uncontracted form), *that is*, Ac. i. 19; Ro. x. 6, 7, 8.

τοῦτο, neut. of οὗτος, which see.

τράγος, ου, ὁ, *a he-goat*, Heb. ix. 12, 13, 19, x. 4.*

τράπεζα, ης, ἡ, *a table*, (1) *for food and banqueting*, Mat. xv. 27; met., *food*, Ac. xvi. 34; (2) *for money-changing* or *business*, Mar. xi. 15.

τραπεζίτης, ου, ὁ, *a money-changer, a banker*, Mat. xxv. 27.*

τραῦμα, ατος, τό, *a wound*, Lu. x. 34.*

τραυματίζω, ίσω, *to wound*, Lu. xx. 12; Ac. xix. 16.*

τραχηλίζω, in pass., *to be laid bare, to be laid open*, Heb. iv. 13.*

τράχηλος, ου, ὁ, *the neck*, Lu. xv. 20; Ro. xvi. 4.

τραχύς, εῖα, ύ, *rough*, as ways, Lu. iii. 5; as rocks in the sea, Ac. xxvii. 29.*

Τραχωνῖτις, ιδος, ἡ, *Trachonitis*, the N.E. of the territory beyond Jordan, Lu. iii. 1.*

τρεῖς, τρία, *three*, Mat. xii. 40.

τρέμω, *to tremble*, Mar. v. 33; Lu. viii. 47; Ac. ix. 6 (W. H. omit); *to be afraid*, 2 Pet. ii. 10.*

τρέφω, θρέψω, perf. pass. part. τεθραμμένος, *to feed, to nourish*, Mat. vi. 26; Ac. xii. 20; Ja. v. 5; *to bring up, rear*, Lu. iv. 16.

τρέχω, 2d aor. ἔδραμον, (1) *to run*, in general, Lu. xv. 20; (2) *to exert one's self*, Ro. ix. 16; (3) *to make progress*, as doctrine, 2 Th. iii. 1.

τρῆμα, ατος, τό, *a perforation, the eye* of a needle, Mat. xix. 24 (W. H.); Lu. xviii. 25 (W. H.).*

τριάκοντα, οἱ, αἱ, τά, indecl., *thirty*, Mat. xiii. 8.

τριακόσιοι, αι, α, *three hundred*, Mar. xiv. 5; Jn. xii. 5.*

τρίβολος, ου, ὁ, *a thistle*, Mat. vii. 16; Heb. vi. 8.*

τρίβος, ου, ἡ, *a worn path, a beaten way*, Mat. iii. 3; Mar. i. 3; Lu. iii. 4.*

τρι-ετία, ας, ἡ, *a space of three years*, Ac. xx. 31.*

τρίζω, *to grate, to gnash*, as the teeth, Mar. ix. 18.*

τρί-μηνος, ον, *of three months*, neut. as subst., Heb. xi. 23.*

τρίς, num. adv., *thrice*, Mat. xxvi. 34, 75.

τρί-στεγος, ον, *having three stories;* neut., *the third story*, Ac. xx. 9.*

τρισ-χίλιοι, αι, α, *three thousand*, Ac. ii. 41.*

τρίτος, η, ον, ord. num., *third;* neut. τὸ τρίτον, *the third part*, Rev. viii. 7; *the third time*, Mar. xiv. 41; ἐκ τρίτου, *the third time*, Mat. xxvi. 44; τῇ τρίτῃ (sc. ἡμέρᾳ), *on the third day*, Lu. xiii. 32.

τρίχες, plur. of θρίξ, which see.

τρίχινος, η, ον, *made of hair*, Rev. vi. 12.*

τρομος, ου, ὁ, *a trembling*, from fear, Mar. xvi. 8.

τροπή, ῆς, ἡ, *a turning*, Ja. i. 17 (see R.V.).*

τρόπος, ου, ὁ, (1) *way, manner; ὃν τρόπον, in like manner as, as*, Mat. xxiii. 37; (2) *manner of life, character*, Heb. xiii. 5.

τροπο-φορέω, ῶ, ήσω, *to bear with the disposition* or *character* of others, Ac. xiii. 18 (Rec. W. H., some read ἐτροφοφόρησεν, *he bore them as a nurse*). (S.)*

τροφή, ῆς, ἡ, *food, nourishment*, Mat. iii. 4, vi. 25.

Τρόφιμος, ου, ὁ, *Trophimus*, Ac. xx. 4, xxi. 29; 2 Tim. iv. 20.*

τροφός, οῦ, ἡ, *a nurse*, 1 Th. ii. 7.*

τροφο-φορέω, ῶ, see τροποφορέω.

τροχιά, ᾶς, ἡ, *a track of a wheel, a path*, fig., Heb. xii. 13.*

τροχός, οῦ, ὁ, *a wheel*, Ja. iii. 6.*

τρύβλιον, ου, τό, *a deep dish, a platter*, Mat. xxvi. 23; Mar. xiv. 20.*

τρυγάω, ῶ, ήσω, *to gather*, as the vintage, Lu. vi. 44; Rev. xiv. 18, 19.*

τρυγών, όνος, ἡ (τρύζω), *a turtle-dove*, Lu. ii. 24.*

τρυμαλιά, ᾶς, ἡ, *the eye* of a needle, Mar. x. 25; Lu. xviii. 25 (W. H. τρῆμα).*

τρύπημα, ατος, τό, *a hole, the eye* of a needle, Mat. xix. 24 (W. H. text τρῆμα).*

Τρύφαινα, ης, ἡ, *Tryphæna*, Ro. xvi. 12.*

τρυφάω, ῶ, ήσω, *to live luxuriously and effeminately*, Ja. v. 5.* *Syn.*: see σπαταλάω.

τρυφή, ῆς, ἡ, *effeminate luxury*, Lu. vii. 25; 2 Pet. ii. 13.*

Τρυφῶσα, ης, ἡ, *Tryphosa*, Ro. xvi. 12.*

Τρωάς, άδος, ἡ, *Troas*, a city of Mysia, properly *Alexandria Troas*, Ac. xvi. 8, 11.

Τρωγύλλιον, ου, τό, *Trogyllium*, Ac. xx. 15 (W. H. omit).*

τρώγω, *to eat*, Mat. xxiv. 38; Jn. vi. 54–58, xiii. 18.*

τυγχάνω, 2d aor. ἔτυχον, perf. τέτυχα, (1) *to obtain, to get possession of* (gen.), Lu. xx. 35; Ac. xxiv. 2; (2) *to fall out, to happen, to happen to be; εἰ τύχοι, if it should chance, it may be, perhaps*, 1 Cor. xiv. 10; 2d aor., part., τυχών, *ordinary, commonplace*, Ac. xix. 11; neut. τυχόν, *it may be, perhaps*, 1 Cor. xvi. 6.

τυμπανίζω, *to beat to death when stretched on a wheel*, Heb. xi. 35.*

τυπικῶς, adv., *typically, by way of example*, 1 Cor. x. 11 (W. H.). (N. T.)*

τύπος, ου, ὁ, (1) *a mark, an impression*, produced by a blow, Jn. xx. 25; (2) *the figure of a thing, a pattern*, Ac. vii. 44; Heb. viii. 5; (3) *an emblem, an example*, 1 Cor. x. 6; Phil. iii. 17; (4) *the form* or *contents* of a letter, Ac. xxiii. 25; (5) *a type*, Ro. v. 14.

τύπτω, ψω, *to beat, to strike*, as the breast in grief, Lu. xviii. 13; *to inflict punishment*, Ac. xxiii. 3; *to wound* or *disquiet* the conscience, 1 Cor. viii. 12.

Τύραννος, ου, ὁ, *Tyrannus*, Ac. xix. 9.*

τυρβάζω, *to agitate* or *disturb in mind*, Lu. x. 41 (W. H. θορυβάζω).*

Τύριος, ου, ὁ, ἡ (prop. adj.), *a Tyrian*, an inhabitant of Tyre, Ac. xii. 20.*

Τύρος, ου, ἡ, *Tyre*, a city of Phœnicia, Mat. xi. 21, 22.

τυφλός, ή, όν, *blind*, (1) physically, Lu. xiv. 13, 21; (2) mentally, *i.e., stupid, dull of apprehension*, Ro. ii. 19; 2 Pet. i. 9.

τυφλόω, ῶ, ώσω, fig., *to make blind* or *dull of apprehension*, Jn. xii. 40; 2 Cor. iv. 4; 1 Jn. ii. 11.*

τυφόω, ῶ, *to raise a smoke*; pass., fig., *to be proud, to be arrogant* and *conceited*, 1 Tim. iii. 6, vi. 4; 2 Tim. iii. 4.*

τύφω, pres. pass. part. τυφόμενος, *smoking*, Mat. xii. 20.*

τυφωνικός, ή, όν, *violent, tempestuous*, Ac. xxvii. 14.*

Τυχικός, or Τύχικος (W. H.), ου, ὁ, *Tychichus*, 2 Tim. iv. 12.

τυχόν, see τυγχάνω.

Υ

Υ, υ, ὖψῖλον, *upsilon, u*, the twentieth letter. As a numeral, υ′ = 400; ͵υ = 400,000. At the commencement of a word, υ is always aspirated.

ὑακίνθινος, η, ον, *of the color of hyacinth, dark purple*, Rev. ix. 17.*

ὑάκινθος, ου, ὁ, a precious stone of the color of hyacinth, *jacinth*, Rev. xxi. 20.*

ὑάλινος, η, ον, *glassy, transparent*, Rev. iv. 6, xv. 2.*

ὕαλος, ου, ὁ, *glass*, Rev. xxi. 18, 21.*

ὑβρίζω, σω, *to treat with insolence, to insult*, Mat. xxii. 6; Lu. xi. 45.

ὕβρις, εως, ἡ, (1) *insolence, insult*, 2 Cor. xii. 10; (2) *damage, loss*, Ac. xxvii. 10, 21.*

ὑβριστής, οῦ, ὁ, *an insolent, insulting man*, Ro. i. 30; 1 Tim. i. 13.*

ὑγιαίνω, *to be well, to be in health*, Lu. v. 31, xv. 27; fig., *to be sound*, in (ἐν) faith, doctrine, etc., Tit. i. 13; part. ὑγιαίνων, *healthful, wholesome*, of instruction, 1 Tim. i. 10.

ὑγιής, ές, (1) *sound, whole*, in health, Mat. xii. 13; Jn. v. 11, 15; (2) fig., *wholesome*, of teaching, Tit. ii. 8.

ὑγρός, ά, όν, *moist, green, i.e.*, full of sap, Lu. xxiii. 31.*

ὑδρία, ας, ἡ, *a water-pot*, Jn. ii. 6, 7, iv. 28.*

ὑδρο-ποτέω, ῶ, *to be a water-drinker*, 1 Tim. v. 23.*

ὑδρωπικός, ή, όν, *dropsical*, Lu. xiv. 2.*

ὕδωρ, ὕδατος, τό, *water; ὕδατα, waters, streams*, Jn. iii. 23; also *a body of water*, as Mat. xiv. 28; ὕδωρ ζῶν, *living* or *running water*; fig., of spiritual truth, Jn. iv. 14.

ὑετός, οῦ, ὁ (ὕω, *to rain*), *rain*, Heb. vi. 7.

υἱο-θεσία, ας, ἡ, *adoption* as a son, into the divine family, Ro. viii. 15, 23, ix. 4; Gal. iv. 5; Ep. i. 5.*

υἱός, οῦ, ὁ, *a son*, Mat. x. 37; *a descendant*, Lu. xx. 41, 44; *the offspring* or *young* of an animal, Mat. xxi. 5; *an adopted son*, Heb. xi. 24; of various forms of close union and relationship (see τέκνον); *a disciple* or *follower*, Mat. xii. 27; *one who resembles* (gen.), Mat. v. 45; *one who partakes of any quality* or *character*, Lu. x. 6; Jn. xii. 36; ὁ υἱὸς τοῦ ἀνθρώπου, *son of man* (once only without art., Jn. v. 27), very often used by our Lord of himself (only once by another of him, Ac. vii. 56); *sons of men* denote *men* generally, Mar. iii. 28; Ep. iii. 5; υἱὸς τοῦ θεοῦ, *son of God*, used of men, Lu. xx. 36; Heb. ii. 10; usually of Christ, Mat. viii. 29; Jn. ix. 35; see also Gr. § 217 *c*.

ὕλη, ης, ἡ, *wood*, *fuel*, Ja. iii. 5.*

ὑμεῖς, plur. of σύ, which see.

Ὑμέναιος, ου, ὁ, *Hymenæus*, 1 Tim. i. 20; 2 Tim. ii. 17.*

ὑμέτερος, α, ον, possess. pron., *your*, as belonging to, or as proceeding from; for the use of the article with the word, see Gr. § 223.

ὑμνέω, ῶ, ήσω, *to sing hymns to* (acc.), Ac. xvi. 25; Heb. ii. 12; *to sing*, Mat. xxvi. 30; Mar. xiv. 26.*

ὕμνος, ου, ὁ, *a hymn*, *a sacred song*, Ep. v. 19; Col. iii. 16.* *Syn.*: ψαλμός is used of the Psalms of the O. T.; ὕμνος designates a song of *praise to God*; ᾠδή is a general expression for a song.

ὑπ-άγω, *to go away*, *to depart*, Mar. vi. 31; Jn. vi. 67; imperat., sometimes an expression of aversion, *begone*, Mat. iv. 10; sometimes a farewell only, Mat. viii. 13, 32; *to die*, Mat. xxvi. 24.

ὑπ-ακοή, ῆς, ἡ, *obedience*, Ro. vi. 16. (S.)

ὑπ-ακούω, σω, (1) *to listen*, as at a door, to find who seeks admission, only Ac. xii. 13; (2) *to hearken to*; hence, *to obey* (dat.), Mat. viii. 27; Heb. xi. 8.

ὕπ-ανδρος, ον, *subject to a husband*, *married*, Ro. vii. 2.*

ὑπ-αντάω, ῶ, ήσω, *to meet* (dat.), Mat. viii. 28.

ὑπ-άντησις, εως, ἡ, *a meeting*, Mat. viii. 34 (W. H.), xxv. 1 (W. H.); Jn. xii. 13. (S.)*

ὕπαρξις, εως, ἡ, *goods*, *substance*, *property*, Ac. ii. 45; Heb. x. 34.*

ὑπ-άρχω, *to begin to be*; *to be originally*, *to subsist*; hence generally, *to be*, Lu. viii. 41; Ac. xxi. 20; with dat. of pers., *to have*, *to possess*, Ac. iii. 6, iv. 37; part., neut. pl., τὰ ὑπάρχοντα, *things which one possesses*, *goods*, *property*, Mat. xix. 21.

ὑπ-είκω, *to yield*, *to submit to authority*, Heb. xiii. 17.*

ὑπ-εναντίος, α, ον, *opposite to*, *adverse*, Col. ii. 14; as subst., *an adversary*, Heb. x. 27.*

ὑπέρ, prep., gov. gen. and acc.: with gen., *over*, *for*, *on behalf of*; with acc., *above*, *superior to* (see Gr. § 303, Wi. § 47 *l*, Bu. 335); adverbially, *above*, *more*, 2 Cor. xi. 23. In composition, ὑπέρ denotes *superiority* (above), or *aid* (on behalf of).

ὑπερ-αίρω, in mid., *to lift up one's self*, *to exalt one's self*, *to be arrogant*, 2 Cor. xii. 7; 2 Th. ii. 4.*

ὑπέρ-ακμος, ον, *past the bloom of youth*, 1 Cor. vii. 36.*

ὑπερ-άνω, adv. (gen.), *above*, Ep. i. 21, iv. 10; Heb. ix. 5.*

ὑπερ-αυξάνω, *to increase exceedingly*, 2 Th. i. 3.*

ὑπερ-βαίνω, *to go beyond*, *to overreach*, *defraud*, 1 Th. iv. 6.*

ὑπερ-βαλλόντως, adv., *beyond measure*, 2 Cor. xi. 23.*

ὑπερ-βάλλω, intrans., *to surpass*; N.T., only pres. part. ὑπερβάλλων, *surpassing*, *excelling*, 2 Cor. iii. 10, ix. 14; Ep. i. 19, ii. 7, iii. 19.*

ὑπερ-βολή, ῆς, ἡ, *excess*, *surpassing excellence*, *pre-eminence*, 2 Cor. iv. 7, xii. 7; καθ' ὑπερβολήν, as adv., *exceedingly*, Ro. vii. 13; 1 Cor. xii. 31; 2 Cor. i. 8; Gal. i. 13; καθ' ὑπερβολὴν εἰς ὑπερβολήν, *more and more exceedingly* (R. V.), 2 Cor. iv. 17.*

ὑπερ-εῖδον, *to overlook*, *to take no notice of*, Ac. xvii. 30.*

ὑπερ-έκεινα, adv., *beyond*, 2 Cor. x. 16. (N. T.)*

ὑπερ-εκ-περισσοῦ, adv., *beyond all measure*, *in the highest degree*, Ep. iii. 20; 1 Th. iii. 10, v. 13.*

ὑπερ-εκ-τείνω, *to stretch out beyond measure*, 2 Cor. x. 14.*

ὑπερ-εκ-χύνω, pass., *to be poured out*, *to overflow*, Lu. vi. 38.*

ὑπερ-εν-τυγχάνω, *to intercede for*, Ro. viii. 26. (N. T.)*

ὑπερ-έχω, *to excel*, *to surpass* (gen.), *to be supreme*; N. T. only pres. part., Ro. xiii. 1; Phil. ii. 3, iv. 7; 1 Pet. ii. 13; part. neut. τὸ ὑπερέχον, *excellency*, *super-eminence*, Phil. iii. 8.*

ὑπερηφανία, ας, ἡ, *pride*, *arrogance*, Mar. vii. 22.*

ὑπερ-ήφανος, ον, *proud*, *arrogant*, Ja. iv. 6.

ὑπερ-λίαν, adv., *very much*, *pre-eminently*, 2 Cor. xi. 5, xii. 11.*

ὑπερ-νικάω, ῶ, *to be more than conqueror*, Ro. viii. 37. (N. T.)*

ὑπέρ-ογκος, ον, *immoderate*, *boastful*, of language, 2 Pet. ii. 18; Ju. 16.*

ὑπερ-οχή, ῆς, ἡ, *superiority*, *excellence*, 1 Cor. ii. 1; 1 Tim. ii. 2.*

ὑπερ-περισσεύω, *to superabound*, Ro. v. 20; pass., *to be very abundant in* (dat.), 2 Cor. vii. 4. (N. T.)*

ὑπερ-περισσῶς, adv., *superabundantly*, *beyond measure*, Mar. vii. 37. (N. T.)*

ὑπερ-πλεονάζω, *to be exceedingly abundant*, 1 Tim. i. 14.*

ὑπερ-υψόω, ῶ, *to highly exalt*, Phil. ii. 9. (S.)*

ὑπερ-φρονέω, ῶ, *to think too highly of one's self*, Ro. xii. 3.*

ὑπερῷον, ου, τό, *the upper part of a house*, *an upper chamber*, Ac. i. 13, ix. 37, 39, xx. 8.*

ὑπ-έχω, *to submit to*, *to undergo* (acc.), Ju. 7.*

ὑπ-ήκοος, ον, *listening to*, *obedient*, Ac. vii. 39; 2 Cor. ii. 9; Phil. ii. 8.*

ὑπηρετέω, ῶ, *to minister to*, *to serve* (dat.), Ac. xiii. 36, xx. 34, xxiv. 23.*

ὑπ-ηρέτης, ου, ὁ (ἐρέτης, *a rower*), *a servant*, *attendant*, specially (1) *an officer*, *a lictor*, Mat. v. 25; (2) *an attendant in a synagogue*, Lu. iv. 20; (3) *a minister of the gospel*, Ac. xxvi. 16.

ὕπνος, ου, ὁ, *sleep*, Lu. ix. 32;

fig., *spiritual sleep*, Ro. xiii. 11.

ὑπό, prep., gov. gen. and acc., *under:* with gen., *by*, generally signifying the agent; with acc., *under, beneath*, of place, of time, or of subjection to authority (see Gr. § 304, Wi. §§ 47*b*, 49*k*, Bu. 340 sq.). In composition, ὑπό denotes *subjection, diminution, concealment.*

ὑπο-βάλλω, *to suborn, to instruct privately*, Ac. vi. 11.*

ὑπο-γραμμός, οῦ, ὁ, *a writing-copy; an example*, 1 Pet. ii. 21.*

ὑπό-δειγμα, ατος, τό, (1) *a figure, copy*, Heb. viii. 5, ix. 23; (2) *an example* for imitation, or for warning, Jn. xiii. 15; Heb. iv. 11; 2 Pet. ii. 6; Ja. v. 10.*

ὑπο-δείκνυμι, δείξω, *to show plainly, to teach, to warn*, Mat. iii. 7; Lu. iii. 7, vi. 47, xii. 5; Ac. ix. 16, xx. 35.*

ὑπο-δέχομαι, *to receive as a guest* (acc.), Lu. x. 38, xix. 6; Ac. xvii. 7, Ja. ii. 25.*

ὑπο-δέω, ῶ, ήσω, in mid., *to bind on one's sandals, be shod with* (acc.), Mar. vi. 9; Ac. xii. 8; Ep. vi. 15 (lit., *shod as to your feet*).*

ὑπόδημα, ατος, τό, *a sandal*, Mat. iii. 11, x. 10.

ὑπό-δικος, ον, *subject to judgment, under penalty to* (dat.), Ro. iii. 19.*

ὑπο-ζύγιον, ου, τό, *an animal under yoke, an ass*, Mat. xxi. 5; 2 Pet. ii. 16.*

ὑπο-ζώννυμι, *to under-gird*, as a ship for strength against the waves, Ac. xxvii. 17.*

ὑπο-κάτω, adv., *underneath* (as prep. with gen.), Rev. v. 3, 13.

ὑπο-κρίνομαι, dep., *to act under a mask, to personate, to feign* (acc., inf.), Lu. xx. 20.*

ὑπό-κρισις, εως, ἡ, lit., *stage playing; hypocrisy, dissembling*, 1 Tim. iv. 2.

ὑπο-κριτής, οῦ, ὁ, lit., *a stage player; a hypocrite, a dissembler*, Mat. vi. 2, 5, 16.

ὑπο-λαμβάνω, 2d aor. ὑπέλαβον, (1) *to take from under, to receive up*, Ac. i. 9; (2) *to take up a discourse, to answer*, Lu. x. 30; (3) *to think, to suppose*, Lu. vii. 43; Ac. ii. 15; (4) *to receive, welcome*, 3 Jn. 8 (W. H.).*

ὑπό-λειμμα (or -λιμμα), ατος, τό, *a remnant*, Ro. ix. 27 (W. H.).*

ὑπο-λείπω, *to leave behind*, pass., Ro. xi. 3.*

ὑπο-λήνιον, ου, τό (ληνός), *a wine-vat, a pit under the wine-press*, dug in the ground, Mar. xii. 1. (S.)*

ὑπο-λιμπάνω, *to leave behind*, 1 Pet. ii. 21.*

ὑπο-μένω, μενῶ, (1) *to remain, tarry behind*, Lu. ii. 43; (2) *to bear up under, to endure* (acc.), 1 Pet. ii. 20; (3) *to persevere, to remain constant*, Mat. x. 22.

ὑπο-μιμνήσκω, ὑπομνήσω, 1st aor. pass. ὑπεμνήσθην, *to remind* (acc. of pers.), Jn. xiv. 26; mid., *to be reminded, to remember*, only Lu. xxii. 61.

ὑπό-μνησις, εως, ἡ, (1) *remembrance, recollection*, 2 Tim. i. 5; (2) *a putting in mind*, 2 Pet. i. 13, iii. 1.*

ὑπο-μονή, ῆς, ἡ, *a bearing up under, endurance, steadfastness, patient waiting for* (gen.), Lu. viii. 15; 2 Th. iii. 5. *Syn.:* see ἀνοχή.

ὑπο-νοέω, ῶ, *to conjecture, to suppose*, Ac. xiii. 25, xxv. 18, xxvii. 27.*

ὑπό-νοια, ας, ἡ, *a surmising, suspicion*, 1 Tim. vi. 4.*

ὑπο-πλέω, 1st aor. ὑπέπλευσα, *to sail under, i.e.*, to leeward of (acc.), Ac. xxvii. 4, 7.*

ὑπο-πνέω, 1st aor. ὑπέπνευσα, *to blow gently*, of the wind, Ac. xxvii. 13.*

ὑπο-πόδιον, ου, τό, *a footstool*, Lu. xx. 43; Ac. ii. 35.

ὑπό-στασις, εως, ἡ, *that which underlies;* hence, (1) *the substance, the reality* underlying mere appearance, Heb. i. 3; (2) *confidence, assurance*, 2 Cor. ix. 4, xi. 17; Heb. iii. 14, xi. 1.*

ὑπο-στέλλω, 1st aor. ὑπέστειλα, *to draw back*, Gal. ii. 12; mid., *to shrink, to draw one's self back*, Ac. xx. 27; Heb. x. 38; *to withhold, conceal* (acc.), Ac. xx. 20.*

ὑπο-στολή, ῆς, ἡ, *a shrinking, a drawing back*, Heb. x. 39.*

ὑπο-στρέφω, ψω, *to turn back, to return*, intrans., Lu. ii. 43, viii. 37, 40.

ὑπο-στρώννυμι, or -ωννύω, *to spread under*, Lu. xix. 36. (S.)*

ὑπο-ταγή, ῆς, ἡ, *subjection, submission*, 2 Cor. ix. 13; Gal. ii. 5; 1 Tim. ii. 11, iii. 4.*

ὑπο-τάσσω, ξω, 2d aor. pass. ὑπετάγην, *to place under, to subject*, 1 Cor. xv. 27; mid., *to submit one's self, to be obedient*, Ro. xiii. 5; Ep. v. 21.

ὑπο-τίθημι, *to set* or *put under, to lay down*, Ro. xvi. 4; mid., *to suggest to, put in mind*, 1 Tim. iv. 6.*

ὑπο-τρέχω, 2d aor. ὑπέδραμον, *to run under* lee or shelter of, Ac. xxvii. 16.*

ὑπο-τύπωσις, εως, ἡ, *pattern, example*, 1 Tim. i. 16; 2 Tim. i. 13.*

ὑπο-φέρω, 1st aor. ὑπήνεγκα, *to bear up under, to sustain, to endure*, 1 Cor. x. 13; 2 Tim. iii. 11; 1 Pet. ii. 19.*

ὑπο-χωρέω, ῶ, ήσω, *to withdraw, to retire*, Lu. v. 16, ix. 10.*

ὑπωπιάζω, *to strike under the eye;* hence, (1) *to bruise;* fig., *to buffet*, 1 Cor. ix. 27; (2) *to weary out*, by repeated application, Lu. xviii. 5.*

ὗς, ὑός, ὁ, ἡ, *a hog, boar* or *sow*, 2 Pet. ii. 22.*

ὕσσωπος, ου, ἡ (from Heb.), *hyssop, a stalk* or *stem of hyssop*, Jn. xix. 29; *a bunch of hyssop* for sprinkling, Heb. ix. 19. (S.)*

ὑστερέω, ῶ, ήσω, *to be behind;* abs., *to be lacking, to fall short*, Jn. ii. 3; with obj., *to be lacking* in, acc., Mat. xix. 20; gen., Lu. xxii. 35; ἀπό, Heb. xii. 15; *to be lacking*, Mar. x. 21; pass., *to lack, to come short*, 1 Cor i. 7, viii. 8; *to suffer need*, Lu. xv. 14.

ὑστέρημα, ατος, τό, (1) *that which is lacking* from (gen.), Col. i. 24; 1 Th. iii. 10; (2) *poverty, destitution*, Lu. xxi. 4. (S.)

ὑστέρησις, εως, ἡ, *poverty, penury*, Mar. xii. 44; Phil. iv. 11. (N. T.)*

ὕστερος, α, ον, compar., *later*, only 1 Tim. iv. 1 and Mat. xxi. 31 (W. H.); neut. as an adv., *lastly, afterward*, with gen., Mat. xxii. 27; Lu. xx. 32.

ὑφαντός, ή, όν (ὑφαίνω, *to weave*), *woven*, Jn. xix. 23.*

ὑψηλός, ή, όν, *high*, *lofty*, lit. or fig., τὰ ὑψηλά, *things that are high*, Ro. xii. 16; ἐν ὑψηλοῖς, *on high*, Heb. i. 3.

ὑψηλο-φρονέω, ῶ, *to be high-minded*, *proud*, Ro. xi. 20 (W. H. ὑψηλὰ φρόνει); 1 Tim. vi. 17. (N. T.)*

ὕψιστος, η, ον (superlat. of ὕψι, *highly*), *highest*, *most high*; neut., plur., *the highest places*, *the heights*, *i.e.*, heaven, Lu. ii. 14; ὁ ὕψιστος, *the Most High*, *i.e.*, *God*, Ac. vii. 48, xvi. 17; Lu. i. 32, 35, 76.

ὕψος, ους, τό, *height*, opp. to βάθος, Ep. iii. 18; Rev. xxi. 16; ἐξ ὕψους, *from on high*, *i.e.*, from heaven, Lu. i. 78, xxiv. 49; so εἰς ὕψος, *to heaven*, Ep. iv. 8; fig., *high station*, Ja. i. 9.*

ὑψόω, ῶ, ώσω, (1) *to raise on high*, *to lift up*, as the brazen serpent, and Jesus on the cross, Jn. iii. 14, viii. 28; (2) *to exalt*, *to set on high*, Ac. ii. 33; Mat. xxiii. 12.

ὕψωμα, ατος, τό, *height*, Ro. viii. 39; *barrier*, *bulwark* (fig.), 2 Cor. x. 5.*

Φ

Φ, φ, φῖ, *phi*, *ph*, the twenty-first letter. As a numeral, φ' = 500; ,φ = 500,000.

φάγος, ου, ὁ, *a glutton*, Mat. xi. 19; Lu. vii. 34 (N. T.)*

φάγω, only used in fut. φάγομαι, and 2d aor. ἔφαγον; see ἐσθίω.

φαιλόνης, ου, ὁ (W. H. φελόνης), (Lat. *pænula*), *a traveling-cloak*, 2 Tim. iv. 13. (N. T.)*

φαίνω, φανῶ, 2d aor. pass. ἐφάνην, (1) trans., *to show*, in N.T. only mid. or pass., *to appear*, *to be seen*, *to seem*; τὰ φαινόμενα, *things which can be seen*, Heb. xi. 3; (2) intrans., *to shine*, *to give light*, Jn. i. 5, v. 35. *Syn.*: see δοκέω.

Φάλεκ, ὁ (Heb.), *Peleg*, Lu. iii. 35.*

φανερός, ά, όν, *apparent*, *manifest*, Ac. iv. 16; Gal. v. 19; ἐν τῷ φανερῷ, as adv., *manifestly*, *openly*, Ro. ii. 28.

φανερόω, ῶ, ώσω, *to make apparent*, *to manifest*, *to disclose*, Jn. vii. 4, xxi. 11; pass., *to be manifested*, *made manifest*, 1 Tim. iii. 16; 2 Cor. v. 11.

φανερῶς, adv., *clearly*, Ac. x. 3; *openly*, Mar. i. 45; Jn. vii. 10.*

φανέρωσις, εως, ἡ, *a manifestation* (gen. obj.), 1 Cor. xii. 7; 2 Cor. iv. 2.* *Syn.*: see ἀποκάλυψις.

φανός, οῦ, ὁ, *a torch*, *a lantern*, Jn. xviii. 3.*

Φανουήλ, ὁ (Heb.), *Phanuel*, Lu. ii. 36.*

φαντάζω, *to cause to appear*; pass. part. τὸ φανταζόμενον, *the appearance*, Heb. xii. 21.*

φαντασία, ας, ἡ, *display*, *pomp*, Ac. xxv. 23.*

φάντασμα, ατος, τό, *an apparition*, *a spectre*, Mat. xiv. 26; Mar. vi. 49.*

φάραγξ, αγγος, ἡ, *a valley*, *ravine*, Lu. iii. 5.*

Φαραώ, ὁ, *Pharaoh*, the title of ancient Egyptian kings, Ac. vii. 13, 21.

Φαρές, ὁ (Heb.), *Phares*, Mat. i. 3; Lu. iii. 33.*

Φαρισαῖος, ου, ὁ (from the Heb. verb, *to separate*), *a Pharisee*, one of the Jewish sect so called, Mar. ii. 16, 18, 24. (N. T.)

φαρμακεία (W. H. -κία), ας, ἡ, *magic*, *sorcery*, *enchantment*, Gal. v. 20; Rev. ix. 21 (W. H. φάρμακον), xviii. 23.*

φαρμακεύς, έως, ὁ, *a magician*, *sorcerer*, Rev. xxi. 8 (W. H. read following).*

φάρμακον, ου, τό, *a drug*; *an enchantment*, Rev. ix. 21 (W. H.).*

φαρμακός, οῦ, ὁ (prop. adj.), *a magician*, *sorcerer*, Rev. xxi. 8 (W. H.), xxii. 15.*

φάσις, εως, ἡ, *report*, *tidings*, Ac. xxi. 31.*

φάσκω (freq. of φημί), *to assert*, *to affirm*, *to profess*, Ac. xxiv. 9, xxv. 19; Ro. i. 22; Rev. ii. 2 (W. H. omit).*

φάτνη, ης, ἡ, *a manger*, *a crib*, Lu. ii. 7, 12, 16, xiii. 15.*

φαῦλος, η, ον, *good for nothing*, *wicked*, *base*, Jn. iii. 20, v. 29; Ro. ix. 11 (W. H.); 2 Cor. v. 10 (W. H.); Tit. ii. 8; Ja. iii. 16.*

φέγγος, ους, τό, *brightness*, *light*, Mat. xxiv. 29; Mar. xiii. 24; Lu. xi. 33 (W. H. φῶς). *Syn.*: see λαμπάς.

φείδομαι, φείσομαι, dep., (1) *to spare* (gen.), Ac. xx. 29; (2) *to abstain* (inf.), 2 Cor. xii. 6.

φειδομένως, adv., *sparingly*, 2 Cor. ix. 6.*

φελόνης, see φαιλόνης.

φέρω, οἴσω, ἤνεγκα, ἠνέχθην (see Gr. § 103, Wi. § 15, Bu. 68), *to bear*, as (1) *to carry*, as a burden, Lu. xxiii. 26; (2) *to produce* fruit, Jn. xii. 24; (3) *to bring*, Ac. v. 16; (4) *to endure*, *to bear with*, Ro. ix. 22; (5) *to bring forward*, as charges, Jn. xviii. 29; (6) *to uphold*, Heb. i. 3; (7) pass., as nautical term, *to be borne along*, Ac. xxvii. 15, 17; (8) mid., *to rush* (bear itself on), Ac. ii. 2; *to go on* or *advance*, in learning, Heb. vi. 1. *Syn.*: φορέω means to bear something habitually and continuously, while in φέρω it is temporary bearing, and on special occasions.

φεύγω, ξομαι, ἔφυγον, *to flee*, *to escape*, *to shun* (acc. or ἀπό), Mat. viii. 33; 1 Cor. vi. 18; Heb. xii. 34; Rev. xvi. 20.

Φῆλιξ, ικος, ὁ, *Felix*, Ac. xxv. 14.

φήμη, ης, ἡ, *a report*, *fame*, Mat. ix. 26; Lu. iv. 14.*

φημί, impf. ἔφην (for other tenses, see εἶπον), *to say*, with ὅτι, dat. of pers., πρός (acc.), with pers., acc. of thing (once acc., inf., Ro. iii. 8).

Φῆστος, ου, ὁ, *Festus*, Ac. xxv. 1, 4, 9.

φθάνω, φθάσω, perf. ἔφθακα, (1) *to be before*, *to precede*, 1 Th. iv. 15; (2) *to arrive*, *attain to* (εἰς, ἄχρι, ἐπί), Mat. xii. 28; Lu. xi. 20; Ro. ix. 31; 2 Cor. x. 14; Phil. iii. 16; 1 Th. ii. 16.*

φθαρτός, ή, όν (φθείρω), *corruptible*, *perishable*, Ro. i. 23; 1 Cor. ix. 25, xv. 53, 54; 1 Pet. i. 18, 23.*

φθέγγομαι, γξομαι, dep., *to speak aloud*, *to utter*, Ac. iv. 18; 2 Pet. ii. 16, 18.*

φθείρω, *φθερῶ*, 2d aor. pass. *ἐφθάρην*, *to corrupt*, physically or morally, *to spoil*, *to destroy*, 2 Cor. vii. 2; Rev. xix. 2.

φθιν-οπωρινός, *ή, όν*, *autumnal*, Ju. 12.*

φθόγγος, *ου, ὁ* (*φθέγγομαι*), *a sound*, Ro. x. 18; 1 Cor. xiv. 7.*

φθονέω, *ῶ*, *to envy* (dat.), Gal. v. 26.*

φθόνος, *ου, ὁ*, *envy*, Phil. i. 15; Tit. iii. 3.

φθορά, *ᾶς, ἡ* (*φθείρω*), *corruption*, *destruction*, physical or moral, 1 Cor. xv. 42, 2 Pet. i. 4.

φιάλη, *ης, ἡ*, *a bowl*, broad and flat, Rev. v. 8, xv. 7.

φιλ-άγαθος, *ον*, *loving goodness*, Tit. i. 8.*

Φιλαδέλφεια, *ας, ἡ*, *Philadelphia*, Rev. i. 11, iii. 7.*

φιλαδελφία, *ας, ἡ*, *brotherly love*, *love of Christian brethren*, Ro. xii. 10; 1 Th. iv. 9; Heb. xiii. 1; 1 Pet. i. 22; 2 Pet. i. 7.*

φιλ-άδελφος, *ον*, *loving the brethren*, 1 Pet. iii. 8.*

φίλ-ανδρος, *ον*, *loving one's husband*, Tit. ii. 4.*

φιλ-ανθρωπία, *ας, ἡ*, *love of mankind*, *benevolence*, Ac. xxviii. 2; Tit. iii. 4.*

φιλ-ανθρώπως, adv., *humanely*, *kindly*, Ac. xxvii. 3.*

φιλαργυρία, *ας, ἡ*, *love of money*, *avarice*, 1 Tim. vi. 10.* *Syn.*: see *πλεονεξία*.

φιλ-άργυρος, *ον*, *money-loving*, *avaricious*, Lu. xvi. 14; 2 Tim. iii. 2.*

φίλ-αυτος, *ον*, *self-loving*, *selfish*, 2 Tim. iii. 2.*

φιλέω, *ῶ, ήσω*, (1) *to love*, Mat. vi. 5, x. 37; Lu. xx. 46; (2) *to kiss*, Mat. xxvi. 48. *Syn.*: see *ἀγαπάω*.

φίλη, *ἡ*, see *φίλος*.

φιλ-ήδονος, *ον*, *pleasure-loving*, 2 Tim. iii. 4.*

φίλημα, *ατος, τό*, *a kiss*, Lu. vii. 45; Ro. xvi. 16.

Φιλήμων, *ονος, ὁ*, *Philemon*, Philem. 1.*

Φίλητος, or *Φιλητός*, *ου, ὁ*, *Philetus*, 2 Tim. ii. 17.*

φιλία, *ας, ἡ*, *friendship*, Ja. iv. 4 (gen. obj.).*

Φιλιππήσιος, *ου, ὁ*, *a Philippian*, Phil. iv. 15.*

Φίλιπποι, *ων, οἱ*, *Philippi*, Ac. xvi. 12, xx. 6.

Φίλιππος, *ου, ὁ*, *Philip*. Four of the name are mentioned: (1) Jn. i. 44–47; (2) Ac. vi. 5; (3) Lu. iii. 1; (4) Mat. xiv. 3.

Φιλό-θεος, *ον*, *loving God*, 2 Tim. iii. 4.*

Φιλό-λογος, *ου, ὁ*, *Philologus*, Ro. xvi. 15.*

φιλονεικία, *ας, ἡ*, *love of dispute*, *contention*, Lu. xxii. 24.*

φιλό-νεικος, *ον*, *strife-loving*, *contentious*, 1 Cor. xi. 16.*

φιλοξενία, *ας, ἡ*, *love to strangers*, *hospitality*, Ro. xii. 13; Heb. xiii. 2.*

φιλό-ξενος, *ον*, *hospitable*, 1 Tim. iii. 2; Tit. i. 8; 1 Pet. iv. 9.*

φιλο-πρωτεύω, *to love the first place*, *to desire pre-eminence*, 3 Jn. 9. (N. T.)*

φίλος, *η, ον*, *friendly*; *ὁ φίλος*, as subst., *a friend*, Lu. vii. 6, xi. 5; *an associate*, Mat. xi. 19; *ἡ φίλη*, *a female friend*, only Lu. xv. 9.

φιλοσοφία, *ας, ἡ*, *love of wisdom*, *philosophy*, in N. T. of the Jewish traditional theology, Col. ii. 8.*

φιλό-σοφος, *ου, ὁ* (prop. adj., *wisdom-loving*), *a philosopher*, in N. T. of Greek philosophers, Ac. xvii. 18.*

φιλό-στοργος, *ον*, *tenderly loving*, *kindly affectionate to* (*εἰς*), Ro. xii. 10.*

φιλό-τεκνος, *ον*, *loving one's children*, Tit. ii. 4.*

φιλο-τιμέομαι, *οῦμαι*, dep., *to make a thing one's ambition*, *to desire very strongly* (inf.), Ro. xv. 20; 2 Cor. v. 9; 1 Th. iv. 11.*

φιλοφρόνως, adv., *in a friendly manner*, *kindly*, Ac. xxviii. 7.*

φιλό-φρων, *ον*, *friendly*, *kindly*, 1 Pet. iii. 8 (W. H. *ταπεινόφρων*).*

φιμόω, *ῶ, ώσω*, *to muzzle*, 1 Cor. ix. 9; *to reduce to silence*, Mat. xxii. 34; pass., *to be reduced to silence*, *to be silent*, Mat. xxii. 12; of a storm, Mar. iv. 39.

Φλέγων, *οντος, ὁ*, *Phlegon*, Ro. xvi. 14.*

φλογίζω, *to inflame*, *to fire with passion*, Ja. iii. 6.*

φλόξ, *φλογός, ἡ*, *a flame*, Lu. xvi. 24.

φλυαρέω, *ῶ*, *to talk idly*, *to make empty charges* against any one (acc.), 3 Jn. 10.*

φλύαρος, *ον*, *prating*; *talking foolishly*, 1 Tim. v. 13.*

φοβερός, *ά, όν*, *fearful*, *dreadful*, Heb. x. 27, 31, xii. 21.*

φοβέω, *ῶ, ήσω*, *to make afraid*, *to terrify*; in N.T. only passive, *to be afraid*, *to be terrified*, sometimes with cognate acc., Mar. iv. 41; *to fear* (acc.), Mat. x. 26; *to reverence*, Mar. vi. 20; Lu. i. 50.

φόβητρον (W. H. *-θρον*), *ου, τό*, *a terrible sight*, *a cause of terror*, Lu. xxi 11.*

φόβος, *ου, ὁ*, (1) *fear*, *terror*, *alarm*, Mat. xiv. 26; (2) *the object* or *cause of fear*, Ro. xiii. 3; (3) *reverence*, *respect*, 1 Pet. ii. 18; towards God, Ro. iii. 18; 1 Pet. i. 17. *Syn.*: see *δειλία*.

Φοίβη, *ης, ἡ*, *Phœbe*, Ro. xvi. 1.*

Φοινίκη, *ης, ἡ*, *Phœnice* or *Phœnicia*, Ac. xi. 19, xv. 3, xxi. 2.

φοίνιξ, *ικος, ὁ*, *a palm-tree*, *a palm branch*, Jn. xii. 13; Rev. vii. 9.*

Φοίνιξ, *ικος, ὁ*, a proper name, *Phœnice*, a city of Crete, Ac. xxvii. 12.*

φονεύς, *έως, ὁ*, *a murderer*, Ac. vii. 52, xxviii. 4.

φονεύω, *σω*, *to murder*, Mat. xxiii. 31, 35; Ja. iv. 2.

φόνος, *ου, ὁ*, *murder*, *slaughter*, Heb. xi. 37; Rev. ix. 21.

φορέω, *ῶ, έσω*, *to bear about*, *to wear*, Mat. xi. 8; Jn. xix. 5; Ro. xiii. 4; 1 Cor. xv. 49; Ja. ii. 3.* *Syn.*: see *φέρω*.

φόρον, *ου, τό* (Lat.), *forum* (see *Ἄππιος*), Ac. xxviii. 15. (N. T.)*

φόρος, *ου, ὁ* (*φέρω*), *a tax*, especially on persons, Lu. xx. 22, xxiii. 2; Ro. xiii. 6, 7.*

φορτίζω, perf. pass. part. *πεφορτισμένος*, *to load*, *to burden*, Mat. xi. 28; Lu. xi. 46.*

φορτίον, *ου, τό*, *a burden*, Mat. xi. 30; *the freight* of a ship, Ac. xxvii. 10 (W. H.); *the burden* of ceremonial observances, Mat. xxiii. 4; Lu. xi. 46; *the burden* of faults, Gal. vi. 5.*

φόρτος, *ου, ὁ*, *load*, *a ship's cargo*, Ac. xxvii. 10 (W. H. read *φορτίον*).*

Φορτουνάτος, ου, ὁ (Lat.), *Fortunatus*, 1 Cor. xvi. 17.*

φραγέλλιον, ου, τό (Lat.), *a scourge*, Jn. ii. 15. (N. T.)*

φραγελλόω, ῶ (Lat.), *to flagellate, to scourge*, Mat. xxvii. 26; Mar. xv. 15. (N. T.)*

φραγμός, οῦ, ὁ, *a hedge*, Mat. xxi. 33; Mar. xii. 1; Lu. xiv. 23; fig., *partition*, Ep. ii. 14.*

φράζω, άσω, *to declare, explain, interpret*, Mat. xiii. 36 (not W. H.), xv. 15.*

φράσσω, ξω, *to stop, to close up*, Ro. iii. 19; 2 Cor. xi. 10; Heb. xi. 33.*

φρέαρ, φρέατος, τό, *a pit, a well*, Jn. iv. 11, 12.

φρεναπατάω, ῶ, *to deceive the mind, to impose upon* (acc.), Gal. vi. 3. (N. T.)*

φρεν-απάτης, ου, ὁ, *a mind-deceiver*, Tit. i. 10. (N. T.)*

φρήν, φρενός, ἡ (lit. *diaphragm*), plur. αἱ φρένες, *the mind, the intellect*, 1 Cor. xiv. 20.

φρίσσω, *to shudder*, Ja. ii. 19.*

φρονέω, ῶ, ήσω (φρήν), (1) *to think* (abs.), 1 Cor. xiii. 11; (2) *to think, judge* (acc.), Gal. v. 10; (3) *to direct the mind to, to seek for* (acc.), Ro. viii. 5; (4) *to observe*, a time as sacred, Ro. xiv. 6; (5) with ὑπέρ, *to care for*, Phil. iv. 10.

φρόνημα, ατος, τό, *thought, purpose*, Ro. viii. 6, 7, 27.*

φρόνησις, εως, ἡ, *understanding*, Lu. i. 17; Ep. i. 8.* *Syn.*: see γνῶσις.

φρόνιμος, ον, *intelligent, prudent*, Lu. xii. 42; 1 Cor. x. 15.

φρονίμως, adv., *prudently*, Lu. xvi. 8.*

φροντίζω, *to be thoughtful, to be careful*, inf., Tit. iii. 8.*

φρουρέω, ῶ, *to guard, to keep*, as by a military guard, lit., 2 Cor. xi. 32; fig., Gal. iii. 23 (as if in custody); Phil. iv. 7 (in security); 1 Pet. i. 5 (in reserve).*

φρυάσσω, ξω, *to rage*, Ac. iv. 25. (S.)*

φρύγανον, ου, τό, *a dry stick*, for burning, Ac. xxviii. 3.*

Φρυγία, ας, ἡ, *Phrygia*, Ac. ii. 10, xvi. 6, xviii. 23.

Φύγελλος (W. H. -ελος), ου, ὁ, *Phygellus*, 2 Tim. i. 15.*

φυγή, ῆς, ἡ, *flight*, Mat. xxiv. 20; Mar. xiii. 18 (W. H. omit).*

φυλακή, ῆς, ἡ, (1) *a keeping guard, a watching*, Lu. ii. 8; espec. of the four *watches* into which the night was divided, Mat. xiv. 25, Lu. xii. 38; (2) *a guard, i.e.*, men on guard, *a watch*, Ac. xii. 10; (3) *a prison*, Mat. v. 25; (4) *an imprisonment*, 2 Cor. vi. 5.

φυλακίζω, *to imprison*, Ac. xxii. 19. (S.)*

φυλακτήρια, ων, τά (plur. of adj.), *a safeguard, an amulet, a phylactery*, a slip of parchment, with Scripture words thereon, worn by the Jews, Mat. xxiii. 5.*

φύλαξ, ακος, ὁ, *a keeper, sentinel*, Ac. v. 23, xii. 6, 19.*

φυλάσσω, ξω, (1) *to keep guard*, or *watch over*, Ac. xii. 4; (2) *to keep in safety*, Lu. xi. 21; (3) *to observe*, as a precept, Gal. vi. 13; (4) mid., *to keep one's self from* (acc. or ἀπό), Lu. xii. 15; Ac. xxi. 25.

φυλή, ῆς, ἡ, (1) *a tribe*, of Israel, Heb. vii. 13, 14; (2) *a race*, or *people*, Rev. xiii. 7, xiv. 6.

φύλλον, ου, τό, *a leaf*, Mar. xi. 13.

φύραμα, ατος, τό, *a mass kneaded, a lump*, as of dough or clay, Ro. ix. 21, xi. 16; 1 Cor. v. 6, 7; Gal. v. 9.*

φυσικός, ή, όν, *natural*, as (1) *according to nature*, Ro. i. 26, 27; (2) *merely animal*, 2 Pet. ii. 12.*

φυσικῶς, adv., *by nature*, Ju. 10.*

φυσιόω, ῶ, *to inflate, to puff up*, 1 Cor. viii. 1; pass., *to be inflated, arrogant*, 1 Cor. iv. 6, 18, 19, v. 2, xiii. 4; Col. ii. 18.*

φύσις, εως, ἡ, generally, *nature*; specially, (1) *natural birth*, Gal. ii. 15; (2) *natural disposition, propensity*, Ep. ii. 3; (3) *native qualities*, or *properties*, Ja. iii. 7; 2 Pet. i. 4.

φυσίωσις, εως, ἡ, *a puffing up, pride*, 2 Cor. xii. 20. (N. T.)*

φυτεία, ας, ἡ, *a plant*, Mat. xv. 13.*

φυτεύω, σω, *to plant*, abs., or with acc., Mat. xxi. 33; 1 Cor. iii. 6, 8.

φύω, σω, 2d aor. pass. ἐφύην, part. φυείς, *to produce*; pass., *to grow*, Lu. viii. 6, 8; intrans., *to spring up*, Heb. xii. 15.*

φωλεός, οῦ, ὁ, *a burrow, a hole*, Mat. viii. 20; Lu. ix. 58.*

φωνέω, ῶ, ήσω, (1) *to sound, to utter a sound* or *cry*, Lu. viii. 8; espec. of cocks, *to crow*, Mar. xiv. 30; (2) *to call to, to invite* (acc.), Mat. xx. 32; Lu. xiv. 12; (3) *to address, to name*, acc. (nom. of title), Jn. xiii. 13.

φωνή, ῆς, ἡ, (1) *a sound*, musical or otherwise, 1 Cor. xiv. 7, 8; Rev. vi. 1, xiv. 2, xix. 1, 6; (2) *an articulate sound, a voice, a cry*, Lu. xvii. 13; Ac. iv. 24; (3) *a language*, 1 Cor. xiv. 10.

φῶς, φωτός, τό (contr. from φάος, from φάω, *to shine*), (1) lit., *light*, Mat. xvii. 2; Jn. xi. 9; *a source of light*, Lu. xxii. 56; Ja. i. 17; *brightness*, Rev. xxii. 5; ἐν τῷ φωτί, *publicly*, Mat. x. 27; (2) fig., *light*, as an appellation of God, 1 Jn. i. 5; as a symbol of truth and purity, espec. the truth of Christ, Jn. iii. 19, 20, 21; used of Christ, Jn. i. 7, 8. *Syn.*: see λαμπάς.

φωστήρ, ῆρος, ὁ, (1) *a luminary*, Phil. ii. 15; (2) *brightness, splendor*, Rev. xxi. 11.* *Syn.*: see λαμπάς.

φωσ-φόρος, ον, *light-bearing, radiant*; the name of the morning star (Lat. *Lucifer*), the planet Venus, 2 Pet. i. 19.*

φωτεινός (W. H. -τινός), ή, όν, *bright, luminous, full of light*, lit., Mat. xvii. 5; fig., Mat. vi. 22; Lu. xi. 34, 36.*

φωτίζω, ίσω, pass. perf. πεφώτισμαι, 1st aor. ἐφωτίσθην; (1) *to light up, illumine*, lit. or fig. (acc., but ἐπί in Rev. xxii. 5), Lu. xi. 36; (2) *to bring to light, make evident*, 1 Cor. iv. 5.

φωτισμός, οῦ, ὁ, *light, lustre, illumination*, 2 Cor. iv. 4, 6. (S.)*

X

Χ, χ, χῖ, *chi, ch,* guttural, the twenty-second letter. As a numeral, χ′ = 600; ,χ = 600,000.

χαίρω, χαρήσομαι, 2d aor. pass. as act. ἐχάρην, *to rejoice, to be glad,* Lu. xv. 5, 32; Jn. iii. 29; impv. χαῖρε, χαίρετε, *hail!* Mat. xxvi. 49; inf. χαίρειν, *greeting,* Ac. xv. 23.

χάλαζα, ης, ἡ, *hail,* Rev. viii. 7, xi. 19, xvi. 21.*

χαλάω, ῶ, άσω, 1st aor. pass. ἐχαλάσθην, *to let down, to lower,* Mar. ii. 4; Lu. v. 4, 5; Ac. ix. 25, xxvii. 17, 30; 2 Cor. xi. 33.*

Χαλδαῖος, ου, ὁ, *a Chaldæan,* Ac. vii. 4.*

χαλεπός, ή, όν, (1) *hard, troublesome,* 2 Tim. iii. 1; (2) *harsh, fierce,* Mat. viii. 28.*

χαλιν-αγωγέω, ῶ, *to bridle, to curb,* Ja. i. 26, iii. 2. (N.T.)*

χαλινός, οῦ, ὁ, *a bridle, a curb,* Ja. iii. 3; Rev. xiv. 20.*

χάλκεος, οῦς, ῆ, οῦν, *brazen,* Rev. ix. 20.*

χαλκεύς, έως, ὁ, *a worker in brass* or *copper,* 2 Tim. iv. 14.*

χαλκηδών, όνος, ὁ, *chalcedony,* a precious stone, Rev. xxi. 19.*

χαλκίον, ου, τό, *a brazen vessel,* Mar. vii. 4.*

χαλκο-λίβανον, ου, τό (or -νος, ου, ἡ), meaning uncertain, either *some precious metal,* or *frankincense* (λίβανος) *of a yellow color,* Rev. i. 15, ii. 8. (N. T.)*

χαλκός, οῦ, ὁ, *copper, brass, money,* Mar. vi. 8, 1 Cor. xiii. 1.

χαμαί, adv., *on* or *to the ground,* Jn. ix. 6, xviii. 6.*

Χαναάν, ἡ, *Canaan,* Ac. vii. 11, xiii. 19.*

Χαναναῖος, αία, αῖον, *Canaanite, i.e.,* Phœnician, Mat. xv. 22.*

χαρά, ᾶς, ἡ, *joy, gladness,* Gal. v. 22; Col. i. 11; *a source of joy,* 1 Th. ii. 19, 20.

χάραγμα, ατος, τό, *sculpture,* Ac. xvii. 29; *engraving, a stamp, a sign,* Rev. xiv. 9, 11, xvi. 2.

χαρακτήρ, ῆρος, ὁ, *an impression, an exact reproduction,* Heb. i. 3.*

χάραξ, ακος, ὁ, *a palisade, a mound for besieging,* Lu. xix. 43.*

χαρίζομαι, ίσομαι, dep. mid., fut. pass. χαρισθήσομαι, (1) *to show favor to* (dat.), Gal. iii. 18; (2) *to forgive* (dat. pers., acc. thing), 2 Cor. xii. 10; Ep. iv. 32; Col. ii. 13; (3) *to give freely, bestow,* Lu. vii. 21; 1 Cor. ii. 12.

χάρις, ιτος, acc. χάριν and χάριτα (W. H. in Ac. xxiv. 27; Ju. 4), ἡ, (1) objectively, *agreeableness, charm,* Lu. iv. 22; (2) subjectively, *inclination towards, favor, kindness, liberality, thanks,* Lu. i. 30, ii. 40, 52; Ac. ii. 47, xxiv. 27; χάριν ἔχειν, *to thank;* χάριν ἔχειν πρός, *to be in favor with;* especially of the undeserved favor of God or Christ, 2 Cor. iv. 15, xii. 9; χάριν, used as prep. with gen. (lit., *with inclination towards*), *for the sake of, on account of,* Ep. iii. 14; 1 Tim. v. 14; Tit. i. 11.

χάρισμα, ατος, τό, *a gift of grace, an undeserved favor* from God to man, Ro. i. 11, v. 15, 16, vi. 23, xi. 29, xii. 6; 1 Cor. i. 7, vii. 7, xii. 4, 9, 28, 30, 31; 2 Cor. i. 11; 1 Tim. iv. 14; 2 Tim. i. 6; 1 Pet. iv. 10.*

χαριτόω, ῶ, *to favor, bestow freely on* (acc.), Ep. i. 6; pass., *to be favored,* Lu. i. 28. (Ap.)*

Χαρράν, ἡ (Heb.), *Charran* or *Haran,* Ac. vii. 2, 4.*

χάρτης, ου, ὁ, *paper,* 2 Jn. 12.*

χάσμα, ατος, τό, *a gap, a gulf,* Lu. xvi. 26.*

χεῖλος, ους, τό, *a lip;* plur., *mouth,* Mat. xv. 8; 1 Cor. xiv. 21; fig., *shore,* Heb. xi. 12.

χειμάζω, in pass., *to be storm-beaten,* or *tempest-tossed,* Ac. xxvii. 18.*

χείμαρρος, ου, ὁ, *a storm-brook, a wintry torrent,* Jn. xviii. 1.*

χειμών, ῶνος, ὁ, (1) *a storm, a tempest,* Ac. xxvii. 20; (2) *winter, the rainy season,* Mat. xxiv. 20.

χείρ, χειρός, ἡ, *a hand,* Lu. vi. 6; 1 Tim. ii. 8; met., for any exertion of *power,* Mat. xvii. 22; Lu. ix. 44; espec. in the phrases *the hand* of God, *the hand* of the Lord, for help, Ac. iv. 30, xi. 21; for punishment, Heb. x. 31.

χειραγωγέω, ῶ, *to lead by the hand,* Ac. ix. 8, xxii. 11.*

χειρ-αγωγός, όν, *leading* one *by the hand,* Ac. xiii. 11.*

χειρό-γραφον, ου, τό, *a handwriting, a bond;* fig., of the Mosaic law, Col. ii. 14.*

χειρο-ποίητος, ον, *done* or *made with hands,* Mar. xiv. 58; Ac. vii. 48, xvii. 24; Ep. ii. 11; Heb. ix. 11, 24.*

χειρο-τονέω, ῶ, *to vote by stretching out the hand, to choose by vote,* 2 Cor. viii. 19; *to appoint,* Ac. xiv. 23.*

χείρων, ον, compar. of κακός (which see), *worse,* Mat. xii. 45; *worse, more severe,* Heb. x. 29; εἰς τὸ χεῖρον, *worse,* Mar. v. 26; ἐπὶ τὸ χεῖρον, *worse and worse,* 2 Tim. iii. 13.

χερουβίμ (W. H. Χερουβείν), τά, *cherubim,* the Heb. plural of cherub, the golden figures on the mercy-seat, Heb. ix. 5. (S.)*

χήρα, ας, ἡ, *a widow,* Ac. vi. 1, ix. 39, 41; Ja. i. 27.

χθές (W. H. ἐχθές), adv., *yesterday,* Jn. iv. 52; Ac. vii. 28; Heb. xiii. 8.*

χιλί-αρχος, ου, ὁ, *a commander of a thousand men, a military tribune,* Ac. xxi–xxv.

χιλιάς, άδος, ἡ, *a thousand,* Lu. xiv. 31; 1 Cor. x. 8.

χίλιοι, αι, α, *a thousand,* 2 Pet. iii. 8; Rev. xi. 3.

Χίος, ου, ἡ, *Chios,* Ac. xx. 15.*

χιτών, ῶνος, ὁ, *a tunic,* an under-garment, Lu. iii. 11, vi. 29; *a garment,* Mar. xiv. 63. *Syn.:* see ἱμάτιον.

χιών, όνος, ἡ, *snow,* Mat. xxviii. 3; Mar. ix. 3 (W. H. omit); Rev. i. 14.*

χλαμύς, ύδος, ἡ, *a short cloak* worn by Roman officers and magistrates, Mat. xxvii. 28, 31.* *Syn.:* see ἱμάτιον.

χλευάζω, *to mock, scoff* (abs.), Ac. ii. 13 (W. H. διαχλευάζω), xvii. 32.*

χλιαρός, ά, όν, *lukewarm*, Rev. iii. 16.*

Χλόη, ης, ἡ, *Chloe*, 1 Cor. i. 11.*

χλωρός, ά, όν, (1) *green*, Mar. vi. 39; Rev. viii. 7, ix. 4; (2) *pale*, Rev. vi. 8.*

χξϛʹ, *six hundred and sixty-six*, Rev. xiii. 18 (W. H. write the numbers in full).*

χοϊκός, ή, όν, *earthy, made of earth*, 1 Cor. xv. 47–49. (N. T.)*

χοῖνιξ, ικος, ἡ, *a chœnix*, a measure containing two sextarii (see ξέστης), Rev. vi. 6.*

χοῖρος, ου, ὁ, plur., *swine*, Lu. viii. 32, 33, xv. 15, 16.

χολάω, ῶ, *to be angry* (dat.), Jn. vii. 23.*

χολή, ῆς, ἡ, (1) *gall*, fig., Ac. viii. 23; (2) perh. *bitter herbs*, such as wormwood, Mat. xxvii. 34.*

χόος, see χοῦς.

Χοραζίν (W. H. Χοραζείν), ἡ, *Chorazin*, Mat. xi. 21; Lu. x. 13.*

χορ-ηγέω, ῶ, *to lead* or *furnish a chorus*; hence, *to furnish abundantly, to supply*, 2 Cor. ix. 10; 1 Pet. iv. 11.*

χορός, οῦ, ὁ, *a dance, dancing*, plur., Lu. xv. 25.*

χορτάζω, *to feed, to satisfy* with (gen. or ἀπό), Mat. v. 6, xv. 33; Mar. viii. 4; Lu. xvi. 21.

χόρτασμα, ατος, τό, *food, sustenance*, Ac. vii. 11.*

χόρτος, ου, ὁ, *grass, herbage*, Mat. vi. 30; *growing grain*, Mat. xiii. 26; *hay*, 1 Cor. iii. 12.

Χουζᾶς, ᾶ, ὁ, *Chuzas*, Lu. viii. 3.*

χοῦς, οός, acc. οῦν, ὁ, *dust*, Mar. vi. 11; Rev. xviii. 19.*

χράομαι, ῶμαι, dep. (prop. mid. of χράω), *to use* (dat.), *to make use of*, 1 Cor. ix. 12, 15; 2 Cor. xiii. 10 (dat. om.); *to deal with*, Ac. xxvii. 3.

χράω, see κίχρημι.

χρεία, ας, ἡ, (1) *need, necessity*, plur., *necessities*, Mar. xi. 3; Tit. iii. 14; ἔχω χρείαν, *to need*, Jn. xiii. 10; (2) *business*, Ac. vi. 3.

χρεωφειλέτης (W. H. χρεοφιλέτης), ου, ὁ, *a debtor*, Lu. vii. 41, xvi. 5.*

χρή, impers. (from χράω), *it is necessary, it is proper* (acc. and inf.), Ja. iii. 10.*

χρῄζω, *to have need of, to need* (gen.), Lu. xi. 8, xii. 30.

χρῆμα, ατος, τό, *a thing* of use; *money*, sing., only Ac. iv. 37; plur., *riches, money*, Mar. x. 23; Ac. viii. 18, 20.

χρηματίζω, ίσω, *to transact business*; hence, (1) *to utter an oracle, to give a divine warning*, Lu. ii. 26; Heb. xii. 25; pass., *to receive a divine response, be warned of God*, Mat. ii. 12, 22; Ac. x. 22; Heb. viii. 5, xi. 7; (2) *to receive a name, to be called*, Ac. xi. 26; Ro. vii. 3.*

χρηματισμός, οῦ, ὁ, *an oracle*, Ro. xi. 4.*

χρήσιμος, η, ον, *useful, profitable*, 2 Tim. ii. 14.*

χρῆσις, εως, ἡ, *use*, Ro. i. 26, 27.*

χρηστεύομαι, dep., *to be kind*, 1 Cor. xiii. 4. (N. T.)*

χρηστο-λογία, ας, ἡ, *a kind address*; in a bad sense, *plausible speaking*, Ro. xvi. 18. (N. T.)*

χρηστός, ή, όν, *useful, good*, 1 Cor. xv. 33; *gentle, pleasant*, Lu. v. 39; *kind*, 1 Pet. ii. 3; τὸ χρηστόν, *kindness*, Ro. ii. 4.

χρηστότης, τητος, ἡ, (1) *goodness*, generally, Ro. iii. 12; (2) specially, *benignity, kindness*, Col. iii. 12. *Syn.*: see ἀγαθωσύνη.

χρίσμα, ατος, τό, *an anointing*, 1 Jn. ii. 20, 27.*

Χριστιανός, οῦ, ὁ, *a Christian*, Ac. xi. 26, xxvi. 28; 1 Pet. iv. 16.*

χριστός, οῦ, ὁ (verbal adj. from χρίω), *anointed*; as a proper name, *the Messiah, the Christ* (see Gr. § 217*e*, Wi. § 18, 9, note 1, Bu. 89), Mat. xxiii. 10, etc.

χρίω, σω, *to anoint, to consecrate by anointing*, as Jesus, the Christ, Lu. iv. 18; Ac. iv. 27, x. 38; Heb. i. 9; applied also to Christians, 2 Cor. i. 21. *Syn.*: see ἀλείφω.

χρονίζω, *to delay, to tarry*, Mat. xxiv. 48, xxv. 5; Lu. i. 21, xii. 45; Heb. x. 37.*

χρόνος, ου, ὁ, (1) *time*, generally, Lu. iv. 5; Gal. iv. 4; (2) *a particular time*, or *season*, Mat. ii. 7; Ac. i. 7. *Syn.*: see καιρός.

χρονο-τριβέω, ῶ, *to wear away time, to spend time*, Ac. xx. 16.*

χρύσεος, οῦς, ῆ, οῦν, *golden*, 2 Tim. ii. 20; Heb. ix. 4.

χρυσίον, ου, τό (dim. of χρυσός), *a piece of gold, a golden ornament*, Ac. iii. 6; 1 Pet. iii. 3.

χρυσο-δακτύλιος, ον, *adorned with a gold ring*, Ja. ii. 2. (N. T.)*

χρυσό-λιθος, ου, ὁ (*a golden stone*), a gem of a bright yellow color, *a topaz*, Rev. xxi. 20. (S.)*

χρυσό-πρασος, ου, ὁ, a gem of a greenish-golden color, *a chrysoprase*, Rev. xxi. 20. (N. T.)*

χρυσός, οῦ, ὁ, *gold, anything made of gold, gold coin*, Mat. ii. 11, x. 9; Ja. v. 3.

χρυσόω, ῶ, *to adorn with gold, to gild*, Rev. xvii. 4, xviii. 16.*

χρώς, χρωτός, ὁ, *the skin*, Ac. xix. 12.*

χωλός, ή, όν, *lame*, Ac. iii. 2; *deprived of a foot*, Mar. ix. 45.

χώρα, ας, ἡ, (1) *a country*, or *region*, Jn. xi. 54; (2) *the land*, opposed to the sea, Ac. xxvii. 27; (3) *the country*, dist. from town, Lu. ii. 8; (4) plur., *fields*, Jn. iv. 35.

χωρέω, ῶ, ήσω, lit., *to make room*; hence, (1) *to have room for, receive, contain*, Mat. xix. 11, 12; Jn. ii. 6, xxi. 25; 2 Cor. vii. 2; impers., *to be room for*, Mar. ii. 2; (2) *to make room by departing, to go*, Mat. xv. 17; *to make progress*, Jn. viii. 37; *to turn one's self*, 2 Pet. iii. 9.*

χωρίζω, ίσω, *to put apart, to separate*, Mat. xix. 6; mid. (1st aor. pass.), *to separate one's self*, of divorce, 1 Cor. vii. 11, 15; *to depart, to go away* (ἀπό or ἐκ), Ac. i. 4, xviii. 1.

χωρίον, ου, τό, *a place, a field*

Mar. xiv. 32; plur., *lands*, Ac. iv. 34; *a farm, estate*, Ac. xxviii. 7.

χωρίς, adv., *separately, by itself*, only Jn. xx. 7; as prep. gov. gen., *apart from, without*, Jn. xv. 5; Ro. iii. 21; *besides, exclusive of*, Mat. xiv. 21.

χῶρος, ου, ὁ (Lat. *Caurus*), *the N.W. wind;* used for the N.W. quarter of the heavens, Ac. xxvii. 12. (N. T.)*

Ψ

Ψ, ψ, ψῖ, *psi, ps*, the twenty-third letter. As a numeral, ψ' = 700; ,ψ = 700,000.

ψάλλω, ψαλῶ, *to sing*, accompanied with instruments, *to sing psalms*, Ro. xv. 9; 1 Cor. xiv. 15; Ep. v. 19; Ja. v. 13.*

ψαλμός, οῦ, ὁ, *a psalm, a song of praise*, Ep. v. 19; Col. iii. 16; plur., *the book of Psalms* in the O. T., Lu. xxiv. 44. *Syn.:* see ὕμνος.

ψευδ-άδελφος, ου, ὁ, *a false brother, a pretended Christian*, 2 Cor. xi. 26; Gal. ii. 4. (N. T.)*

ψευδ-απόστολος, ου, ὁ, *a false* or *pretended apostle*, 2 Cor. xi. 13. (N. T.)*

ψευδής, ές, *false, deceitful, lying*, Ac. vi. 13; Rev. ii. 2, xxi. 8.*

ψευδο-διδάσκαλος, ου, ὁ, *a false teacher, a teacher of false doctrines*, 2 Pet. ii. 1. (N. T.)*

ψευδο-λόγος, ον, *false-speaking, speaking lies*, 1 Tim. iv. 2.*

ψεύδομαι, dep., 1st aor. ἐψευσάμην, *to deceive, to lie, to speak falsely*, Heb. vi. 18; Rev. iii. 9; *to lie to* (acc.), Ac. v. 3.

ψευδο-μάρτυρ, or -υς, υρος, ὁ, *a false witness*, Mat. xxvi. 60; 1 Cor. xv. 15.*

ψευδο-μαρτυρέω, ῶ, ήσω, *to testify falsely*, Lu. xviii. 20.

ψευδο-μαρτυρία, ας, ἡ, *false testimony*, Mat. xv. 19, xxvi. 59.*

ψευδο-προφήτης, ου, ὁ, *a false prophet*, one who in God's name teaches what is false, Mar. xiii. 22; 2 Pet. ii. 1. (S.)

ψεῦδος, ους, τό, *a falsehood, a lie*, Jn. viii. 44; 2 Th. ii. 11.

ψευδό-χριστος, ου, ὁ, *a false Christ, a pretended Messiah*, Mat. xxiv. 24; Mar. xiii. 22. (N. T.)*

ψευδ-ώνυμος, ον, *falsely named*, 1 Tim. vi. 20.*

ψεῦσμα, ατος, τό, *falsehood, perfidy*, Ro. iii. 7.*

ψεύστης, ου, ὁ, *a liar, a deceiver*, Jn. viii. 44, 55; Ro. iii. 4.

ψηλαφάω, ῶ, *to feel, to touch, to handle* (acc.), Lu. xxiv. 39; Heb. xii. 18; 1 Jn. i. 1; *to feel after, grope for*, fig., Ac. xvii. 27.* *Syn.:* see ἅπτω.

ψηφίζω, ίσω, *to reckon, to compute*, Lu. xiv. 28; Rev. xiii. 18.*

ψῆφος, ου, ἡ, *a small stone, a pebble*, Rev. ii. 17; used for voting, hence, *a vote*, Ac. xxvi. 10.*

ψιθυρισμός, οῦ, ὁ, *a whispering, a secret slandering*, 2 Cor. xii. 20. (S.)*

ψιθυριστής, οῦ, ὁ, *a whisperer, a secret slanderer*, Ro. i. 30.*

ψιχίον, ου, τό, *a crumb*, Mat. xv. 27; Mar. vii. 28; Lu. xvi. 21 (W. H. omit). (N. T.)*

ψυχή, ῆς, ἡ, (1) *the vital breath, the animal life*, of animals, Rev. viii. 9, xvi. 3, elsewhere only of man, Mat. vi. 25; (2) *the human soul*, as distinguished from the body, Mat. x. 28; (3) *the soul* as the seat of the affections, the will, etc., Ac. xiv. 2, 22; (4) *the self* (like Heb.), Mat. x. 39; (5) *a human person, an individual*, Ro. xiii. 1.

ψυχικός, ή, όν, *animal, natural, sensuous*, 1 Cor. ii. 14, xv. 44, 46; Ja. iii. 15; Ju. 19.*

ψῦχος, ους, τό, *cold*, Jn. xviii. 18.

ψυχρός, ά, όν, *cold*, Mat. x. 42 (sc. ὕδατος); fig., *cold-hearted*, Rev. iii. 15, 16.*

ψύχω, 2d fut. pass. ψυγήσομαι, *to cool;* pass., fig., *to be cooled, to grow cold*, Mat. xxiv. 12.*

ψωμίζω, *to feed*, Ro. xii. 20; *to spend in feeding*, 1 Cor. xiii. 3.*

ψωμίον, ου, τό, *a bit, a morsel*, Jn. xiii. 26, 27, 30. (S.)*

ψώχω, *to rub, to rub to pieces*, as ears of corn, Lu. vi. 1.*

Ω

Ω, ω, ὦ μέγα, *omega, o*, the twenty-fourth letter. As a numeral, ω' = 800; ,ω = 800,000. τὸ Ὦ, a name of God and Christ (see under A), Rev. i. 8, 11 (W. H. omit), xxi. 6, xxii. 13.*

ὦ, interj., *O*, used before the vocative in address, Ac. i. 1, xviii. 14; in exclamation, of admiration, Mat. xv. 28; Ro. xi. 33; or of reproof, Lu. xxiv. 25.

Ὠβήδ, ὁ, *Obed*, Mat. i. 5 (W. H. Ἰωβήδ); Lu. iii. 32 (W. H. Ἰωβήλ).*

ὧδε, adv., of place, *hither, here;* so, *in this life*, Heb. xiii. 14; *herein, in this matter*, Rev. xiii. 10; ὧδε ἢ ὧδε, *here or there*, Mat. xxiv. 23.

ᾠδή, ῆς, ἡ, *an ode, a song*, Rev. v. 9, xv. 3. *Syn.:* see ὕμνος.

ὠδίν, ῖνος, ἡ, *the pain of childbirth, acute pain, severe anguish*, Mat. xxiv. 8; Mar xiii. 8; Ac. ii. 24; 1 Th. v. 3.*

ὠδίνω, *to feel the pains of childbirth, to travail*, Gal. iv. 27; Rev. xii. 2; fig., Gal. iv. 19.*

ὦμος, ου, ὁ, *a shoulder*, Mat. xxiii. 4; Lu. xv. 5.*

ὠνέομαι, οῦμαι, ήσομαι, *to buy* (gen. of price), Ac. vii. 16.*

ὠόν (W. H. ᾠόν), οῦ, τό, *an egg*, Lu. xii. 12.*

ὥρα, ας, ἡ, (1) *a definite space of time, a season;* (2) *an hour*, Mar. xiii. 32; Ac. xvi. 33; (3) *the particular time for anything*, Lu. xiv. 17; Mat. xxvi. 45.

ὡραῖος, αία, αῖον, *fair, beautiful*, Mat. xxiii. 27; Ac. iii. 2, 10; Ro. x. 15.*

ὠρύομαι, dep. mid., *to roar, to howl*, as a beast, 1 Pet. v. 8.*

ὡς, an adv. of comparison, *as, like as, about, as it were, according as*, 2 Pet. i. 3; *how*, Lu. viii. 47; *how!* Ro. x. 15; as particle of time, *when, while, as soon as,* Lu. i. 23, xx. 37; Ro. xv. 24; as consecutive particle, *so that* (inf.), Ac. xx. 24; *ὡς ἔπος εἰπεῖν, so to speak,* Heb. vii. 9.

ὡσαννά, interj., *hosanna!* (Heb., Ps. cxviii. 25, *save now!*), Mat. xxi. 9, 15; Mar. xi. 9, 10; Jn. xii. 13. (N. T.)*

ὡσ-αύτως, adv., *in like manner, likewise,* Mat. xx. 5, 1 Tim. ii. 9.

ὡσ-εί, adv., *as if, as though, like as,* with numerals, *about,* Ac. ii. 3, 41.

Ὡσηέ, ὁ, *Hosea,* Ro. ix. 25.*

ὥσ-περ, adv., *just as, as,* Mat. xii. 40; 1 Cor. viii. 5.

ὡσ-περ-εί, adv., *just as if, as it were,* 1 Cor. xv. 8.*

ὥσ-τε, conj., *so that* (inf., see Gr. § 391, Wi. §§ 41 *b,* 5, note 1, 44, 1, Bu. 244), *therefore,* Mat. viii. 24; Gal. iii. 9, 24.

ὠτάριον, ου, τό (dim. of *οὖς,* see *παιδάριον*), *an ear,* Mar. xiv. 47 (W. H.); Jn. xviii. 10 (W. H.).*

ὠτίον, ου, τό (dim. of *οὖς, an ear*), *an ear,* Mat. xxvi. 51; Lu. xxii. 51; Jn. xviii. 26; also in the passages under *ὠτάριον* (Rec.).*

ὠφέλεια, ας, ἡ, *usefulness, profit, advantage,* Ro. iii. 1; Ju. 16.*

ὠφελέω, ῶ, ήσω, *to be useful, to profit, to benefit, to help* (acc., also acc. of definition), Ro. ii. 25; 1 Cor. xiv. 6; pass., *to be profited, to be helped,* Mat. xvi. 26.

ὠφέλιμος, ον, *profitable, beneficial,* dat. of pers., Tit. iii. 8; *πρός* (acc.), of obj., 1 Tim. iv. 8; 2 Tim. iii. 16.*

NEW TESTAMENT SYNONYMS.

INTRODUCTION.

A *careful* discrimination between synonyms in the study of any language is a matter of the utmost importance, and also consequently of considerable difficulty. But there are some considerations which make a treatment of the synonyms of the New Testament especially difficult and especially necessary. The Greek language in classical times was one which was admirably adapted for expressing fine shades of meaning, and therefore one which abounded in synonyms. In later Greek, outside of the New Testament, some of these distinctions were changed or modified. The writers of the New Testament were men of Semitic habits of thought and expression. They also had theological and ethical teachings to impart which were far more profound and spiritual than had been conveyed by the Greek language previous to that time. These and other facts affecting the New Testament Greek necessarily modify the meaning of many of the synonyms there used, in some cases effecting a complete transformation.

The object in the present treatment is to consider the New Testament usage. Hence, the distinctions of classical Greek are stated only so far as they are also found in New Testament usage, or are of importance for determining the latter. For a discrimination of the distinctive meanings of New Testament synonyms, three things must usually be considered:

First, the etymological meaning of the words;
Second, the relations in which the words are found in classical Greek;
Third, the relations in which they are found in New Testament Greek, the last being often the chief factor.

The use of the words in the Septuagint is also important, for their connection with the Hebrew words which they are used to translate often throws light on their meaning.

The discussions here given aim to be brief, but yet to outline clearly the important and fundamental differences of meaning. Some words which are often given in works on this subject have been omitted, for the reason that the definitions as given in the Lexicon sufficiently indicate the important distinctions. There has been added, however, a consideration of some other words which are not so commonly included.

The chief works from which material and suggestions have been drawn are mentioned in the Introduction to the Lexicon.

The reason is stated in the Introduction to the Lexicon why in some cases the same word is treated both in the synonyms of the Lexicon itself, and also in this place. In every such instance the treatment here is to be regarded as supplementary to that in the Lexicon proper.

The synonyms here discussed do not belong exclusively nor chiefly to any one class of words. Both theological and non-theological terms are included. The aim has been to consider all the synonyms most likely to be confounded with one another, *i.e.*, all those most important, for practical use, to the average student of the New Testament.

INDEX TO SYNONYMS.

This Index includes all the synonyms discussed in any way, even those indicated by simply giving references to literature concerning them, both in the Lexicon itself and in this separate chapter. Where the same word is discussed in both, the treatment in this separate chapter, as previously stated, is to be considered as supplementary to that in the Lexicon proper.

The references BY PAGES *are in every case to the Lexicon itself;* BY SECTIONS, *to this separate chapter.*

§ 1. Holy, sacred, pure.

ἱερός, ὅσιος, ἅγιος, ἁγνός, σεμνός.

None of these words in classical Greek has necessarily any moral significance. Those which now have such a meaning have developed it in Biblical Greek. **ἱερός** means *sacred*, implying some special relation to God, so that it may not be violated. It refers, however, to formal relation rather than to character. It designates an external relation, which ordinarily is not an internal relation as well. It is used to describe persons or things. This is the commonest word for *holy* in classical Greek, and expresses their usual conception of holiness, but it is rare in the N.T. because it fails to express the fullness of the N.T. conception. **ὅσιος**, used of persons or things, describes that which is in harmony with the divine constitution of the moral universe. Hence, it is that which is in accordance with the general and instinctively felt idea of right, "what is consecrated and sanctioned by universal law and consent" (Passow), rather than what is in accordance with any system of revealed truth. As contrary to *ὅσιος*, *i.e.*, as *ἀνοσία*, the Greeks regarded, *e.g.*, a marriage between brother and sister such as was common in Egypt, or the omission of the rites of sepulture in connection with a relative. **ἅγιος** has probably as its fundamental meaning *separation*, *i.e.*, from the world to God's service. If not the original meaning, this at any rate is a meaning early in use. This separation, however, is not chiefly external, it is rather a separation from evil and defilement. The moral signification of the word is therefore the prominent one. This word, rare and of neutral meaning in classical Greek, has been developed in meaning, so that it expresses the full N.T. conception of holiness as no other does. **ἁγνός** is probably related to *ἅγιος*. It means specifically *pure*. But this may be only in a ceremonial sense, or it may have a moral signification. It sometimes describes freedom from impurities of the flesh. **σεμνός** is that which inspires *reverence* or *awe*. In classical Greek it was often applied to the gods. But frequently it has the lower idea of that which is humanly venerable, or even refers simply to externals, as to that which is magnificent, grand, or impressive.

§ 2. Sin.

ἁμαρτία, ἁμάρτημα, ἀσέβεια, παρακοή, ἀνομία, παρανομία, παράβασις, παράπτωμα, ἀγνόημα, ἥττημα.

ἁμαρτία meant originally *the missing of a mark.* When applied to moral things the idea is similar, it is missing the true end of life, and so it is used as a general term for *sin*. It means both the act of sinning and the result, the sin itself. **ἁμάρτημα** means only the sin itself, not the act, in its particular manifestations as separate deeds of disobedience to a divine law. **ἀσέβεια** is *ungodliness*, positive and active irreligion, a condition of direct opposition to God. **παρακοή** is strictly *failing to hear*, or hearing carelessly and inattentively. The sin is in this failure to hear when God speaks, and also in the active disobedience which ordinarily follows. **ἀνομία** is *lawlessness*, contempt of law, a condition or action not simply without law, as the etymology might indicate, but contrary to law. The law is usually by implication the Mosaic law. **παρανομία** occurs only once, 2 Pet. ii. 16, and is practically equivalent to *ἀνομία*. **παράβασις** is *transgression*, the passing beyond some assigned limit. It is the breaking of a distinctly recognized commandment. It consequently means more than *ἁμαρτία*. **παράπτωμα** is used in different senses, sometimes in a milder sense, denoting an error, a mistake, a fault; and sometimes meaning a trespass, a willful sin. **ἀγνόημα** occurs only once, Heb. ix. 7. It indicates *error*, sin which to a certain extent is the result of ignorance. **ἥττημα** denotes *being worsted, defeated*. In an ethical sense it means *a failure in duty, a fault*. — All these different words may occasionally but not usually be used simply to describe the same act from different points of view. The fundamental meanings of these words may well be summed up in the language of Trench: Sin "may be regarded as the missing of a mark or aim: it is then *ἁμαρτία* or *ἁμάρτημα*; the overpassing or transgressing of a line: it is then *παράβασις*; the disobedience to a voice: in which case it is *παρακοή*; the falling where one should have stood upright: this will be *παράπτωμα*; ignorance of what one ought to have known: this will be *ἀγνόημα*; diminishing of that which should have been rendered in full measure, which is *ἥττημα*; non-observance of a law, which is *ἀνομία* or *παρανομία*."

§ 3. Sincere.

ἁπλοῦς, ἀκέραιος, ἄκακος, ἄδολος.

ἁπλοῦς is literally *spread out without folds*, and hence means single, simple, without complexity of character and motive. In the N.T. this idea of simplicity is always favorable; in classical Greek the word is also occasionally used in an unfavorable sense, denoting foolish simplicity. **ἀκέραιος** also means *simple*, literally *free from any foreign admixture, unadulterated, free from disturbing elements*. **ἄκακος** in Heb. vii. 26 means one in whom exists absence of all evil, and so by implication the presence of all good. It passes also through the merely negative meaning of absence of evil, found in S., to the unfavorable meaning of simple, easily deceived, credulous, which is found in Ro. xvi. 18. **ἄδολος**, occurring only in 1 Pet. ii. 2, means *sincere, unmixed, without guile.*

§ 4. Sins of the tongue.

μωρολογία, αἰσχρολογία, εὐτραπελία.

μωρολογία, used only once in the N.T., is *foolish talking*, but this in the Biblical sense of the word foolish, which implies that it is also sinful. It is conversation which is first insipid, then corrupt. It is random talk, which naturally reveals the vanity and sin of the heart. **αἰσχρολογία**, also used once, means any kind of disgraceful language, especially abuse of others. In classical Greek it sometimes means distinctively language which leads to lewdness. **εὐτραπελία**, occurring once, originally meant *versatility in conversation.* It acquires, however, an unfavorable meaning, since polished, refined conversation has a tendency to become evil in many ways. The word denotes, then, a subtle form of evil-speaking, sinful conversation without the coarseness which frequently accompanies it, but not without its malignity.

§ 5. Shame, disgrace.

αἰδώς, αἰσχύνη, ἐντροπή, (σωφροσύνη).

αἰδώς is the feeling of *innate moral repugnance* to doing a dishonorable act. This moral repugnance is not found in **αἰσχύνη**, which is rather the feeling of *disgrace* which results from doing an unworthy thing, or the fear of such disgrace which serves to prevent its being done. *αἰδώς* is thus the nobler word, *αἰσχύνη* having regard chiefly to the opinions of others. *αἰδώς* is the fear of doing a shameful thing, *αἰσχύνη* is chiefly the fear of being found out. "*αἰδώς* would always restrain a good man from an unworthy act, while *αἰσχύνη* might sometimes restrain a bad one" (Trench). **ἐντροπή** stands somewhat between the other two words in meaning, but in the N.T. leans to the nobler side, indicating that *wholesome shame* which leads a man to consideration of his condition if it is unworthy, and to a change of conduct for the better. **σωφροσύνη**, *self-command*, may not seem to have much in common with these three words. As a matter of fact, however, it expresses positively that which *αἰδώς* expresses negatively.

§ 6. Prayer.

εὐχή, προσευχή, δέησις, ἔντευξις, εὐχαριστία, αἴτημα, ἱκετηρία.

εὐχή, when it means *prayer*, has apparently a general signification. **προσευχή** and **δέησις** are often used together. *προσευχή* is restricted to prayer to God, while *δέησις* has no such restriction. *δέησις* also refers chiefly to prayer *for particular benefits*, while *προσευχή* is more general. The prominent thought in **ἔντευξις** is that of boldness and freedom in approach to God. **εὐχαριστία** is *thanksgiving*, the grateful acknowledgment of God's mercies, chiefly in prayer. **αἴτημα**, much like *δέησις*, denotes a specific petition for a particular thing. In **ἱκετηρία** the attitude of humility and deprecation in prayer is specially emphasized. All these words may indicate at times not different kinds of prayer, but the same prayer viewed from different stand-points.

§ 7. To rebuke; rebuke, accusation.

ἐπιτιμάω, ἐλέγχω; αἰτία, ἔλεγχος.

ἐπιτιμάω means simply *to rebuke*, in any sense. It may be justly or unjustly, and, if justly, the rebuke may be heeded or it may not. **ἐλέγχω**, on the other hand, means to rebuke with sufficient cause, and also effectually, so as to bring the one rebuked to a confession or at least a conviction of sin. In other words, it means *to convince*. A similar distinction exists between the nouns **αἰτία** and **ἔλεγχος**. *αἰτία* is an accusation, whether false or true. *ἔλεγχος* is a charge which is shown to be true, and often is so confessed by the accused. It has both a judicial and a moral meaning.

§ 8. Boaster, proud, insolent.

ἀλαζών, ὑπερήφανος, ὑβριστής.

ἀλαζών is properly *a boaster*, who tells great things concerning his own prowess and achievements, with the implied idea that many of his claims are false. This word naturally describes a trait which manifests itself in contact with one's fellow-men, not one which exists simply within the heart. **ὑπερήφανος** describes one who thinks too highly of himself, describing a trait which is simply internal, not referring primarily to external manifestation, although this is implied. It means one who is *proud*, the external manifestation when it appears being in the form of *arrogance* in dealing with others. **ὑβριστής** describes one who delights in *insolent wrong-doing* toward others, finds pleasure in such acts. Cruelty and lust are two of the many forms which this quality assumes. These three words occur together in Ro. i. 30. They are never used in a good sense. They may be said to move in a certain sense in an ascending scale of guilt, designating respectively "the boastful *in words*, the proud and overbearing *in thoughts*, the insolent and injurious *in acts*" (Cremer).

§ 9. Incorruptible, unfading.

ἄφθαρτος, ἀμάραντος, ἀμαράντινος.

ἄφθαρτος is properly *incorruptible*, unaffected by corruption and decay. It is applied to God, and to that which is connected with him. **ἀμάραντος** expresses the same idea in another way. It means *unfading*, the root idea being that it is unaffected by the withering which is common in the case of flowers. **ἀμαράντινος,** derived from *ἀμάραντος*, means *composed of amaranths*, *i.e.*, of unfading flowers.

§ 10. Faultless, unblamed.

ἄμωμος, ἄμεμπτος, ἀνέγκλητος, ἀνεπίληπτος.

ἄμωμος is *faultless, without blemish, free from imperfections.* It refers especially to character. **ἄμεμπτος** is strictly *unblamed*, one with whom no fault is found. This of course refers particularly to the verdict of others upon one. **ἀνέγκλητος** designates one against whom there is no accusation, implying not acquittal of a charge, but that no charge has been made. **ἀνεπίληπτος** means *irreprehensible*, designating one who affords nothing upon which an adversary might seize, in order to make a charge against him.

§ 11. Regeneration, renovation.

παλιγγενεσία, ἀνακαίνωσις.

παλιγγενεσία means *new birth.* In classical Greek it was used in a weakened sense to denote a recovery, restoration, revival. In the N.T. it is used only twice, but in a higher sense. In Tit. iii. 5 it means *new birth, regeneration,* referring to God's act of causing the sinner to pass from the death of sin into spiritual life in Christ. It has a wider meaning in Mat. xix. 28, where it is used of the change which is ultimately to take place in all the universe, its regeneration, which is the full working out of the change involved in the regeneration of the individual. **ἀνακαίνωσις** is *renewal* or *renovation*, denoting a continuous process through which man becomes more fully Christ-like, in which process he is a worker together with God. Some, as *e.g.* Cremer, without sufficient reason, have thought that the early use of *παλιγγενεσία* as a somewhat technical term, to denote the Pythagorean doctrine of transmigration, gave to the word a permanent eschatological coloring, so that in the N.T. it has the meaning *resurrection*, especially in Mat. xix. 28.

§ 12. Murderer.

φονεύς, ἀνθρωποκτόνος, σικάριος.

Both in derivation and usage, **φονεύς** and **ἀνθρωποκτόνος** are distinguished from each other just as the English *murderer* from *manslayer* or *homicide.* **σικάριος,** used only in Ac. xxi. 38, is the Latin *sicarius*, and means *an assassin*, usually hired for the work, who furtively stabbed his enemy with a short sword, the Latin *sica.* *φονεύς* is a generic word and may denote a murderer of any kind, *σικάριος* being one of the specific varieties which it includes.

§ 13. Anti-Christ, false Christ.

ψευδόχριστος, ἀντίχριστος.

ψευδόχριστος means *a false Christ, a pretended Messiah*, who sets himself up instead of Christ, proclaiming that he is Christ. Some have given about the same meaning to **ἀντίχριστος.** But it is much more probable that it means one diametrically opposed to Christ, one who sets himself up against Christ, proclaiming that there is no Christ.

§ 14. Profligacy.

ἀσωτία, ἀσέλγεια.

The fundamental idea of **ἀσωτία** is "wastefulness and riotous excess; of **ἀσέλγεια,** lawless insolence and wanton caprice" (Trench). *ἀσωτία* means reckless and extravagant expenditure, chiefly for the gratification of one's sensual desires. It denotes a dissolute, profligate course of life. In *ἀσέλγεια* also there is included the idea of profligacy, often of lasciviousness, but the fundamental thought is the acknowledging of no restraints, the insolent doing of whatever one's caprice may suggest.

§ 15. Covenant-breaker, implacable.

ἀσύνθετος, ἄσπονδος.

These words are quite similar in their effects, but opposite in their conception. **ἀσύνθετος,** occurring only in Ro. i. 31, is *covenant-breaker,* one who interrupts a state of peace and brings on war by disregarding an agreement by which peace is maintained. **ἄσπονδος** is *implacable,* one who refuses to agree to any terms or suggestions of peace. It implies a state of war, and a refusal of covenant or even of armistice to end it permanently or temporarily. In the N.T. use both words probably refer not to war in the strict sense so much as to discord and strife.

§ 16. Beautiful, graceful.

ἀστεῖος, ὡραῖος, καλός.

ἀστεῖος is properly one living in a city, urban. It soon acquires the meaning *urbane, polite, elegant.* Then it obtains to a limited extent the meaning *beautiful,* although never in the highest degree. **ὡραῖος,** from *ὥρα,* hour, period, means properly *timely.* From that comes the idea of being beautiful, since nearly everything is beautiful in its hour of fullest perfection. **καλός** is a much higher word. It means *beautiful,* physically or morally. It is, however, distinctly the beauty which comes from harmony, the beauty which arises from a symmetrical adjustment in right proportion, in other words, from the harmonious completeness of the object concerned.

§ 17. Wisdom, knowledge.

σοφία, φρόνησις, γνῶσις, ἐπίγνωσις.

σοφία is certainly the highest word of all these. It is properly *wisdom.* It denotes mental excellence in the highest and fullest sense, expressing an *attitude* as well as an *act* of the mind. It comprehends knowledge and implies goodness, including the striving after the highest ends, as well as the using of the best means for their attainment. It is never ascribed to any one but God and good men, except in a plainly ironical sense. **φρόνησις** is a middle term, sometimes having a meaning nearly as high as *σοφία,* sometimes much lower. It means *prudence, intelligence,* a skillful adaptation of the means to the end desired, the end, however, not being necessarily a good one. **γνῶσις** is ***knowledge, cognition,*** the understanding of facts or truths, or else *insight, discernment.* **ἐπίγνωσις** has an intensive meaning as compared with *γνῶσις*, it is a fuller, clearer, more thorough knowledge. The verb *ἐπιγινώσκω* has the same intensive force as compared with *γινώσκω.*

§ 18. Religious.

θεοσεβής, εὐσεβής, εὐλαβής, θρῆσκος, δεισιδαίμων.

θεοσεβής, according to derivation and usage, means *worship of God* (or of the gods), a fulfillment of one's duty towards God. It is a general term, meaning *religious* in a good sense. **εὐσεβής** is distinguished from *θεοσεβής* in two ways. It is used to include the fulfillment of obligations of all kinds, both towards God and man. It is thus applied to the fulfillment of the duties involved in human relations, as towards one's parents. Furthermore, when used in the higher sense, it means not any kind of worship, but, as the etymology indicates, the worshipping of God *aright.* **εὐλαβής,** meaning originally *careful in handling*, in its religious application means careful in handling divine things. It characterizes the anxious and scrupulous worshipper, careful not to change anything that should be observed in worship, and fearful of offending. It means *devout,* and may be applied to an adherent of any religion, being especially appropriate to describe the best of the Jewish worshippers. **θρῆσκος** is one who is diligent in the performance of the *outward* service of God. It applies especially to ceremonial worship. **δεισιδαίμων,** in accordance with its derivation, makes prominent the element of *fear.* It emphasizes strongly the ideas of dependence and of anxiety for divine favor. It may be used as practically equivalent to *θεοσεβής*. Often, however, it implies that the fear which it makes prominent is an unworthy fear, so that it comes to have the meaning *superstitious.* In the N.T. it is used, as is also the noun *δεισιδαιμονία,* in a purposely neutral sense, meaning simply *religious,* neither conveying the highest meaning, nor plainly implying a lower meaning.

§ 19. Pure.

εἰλικρινής, καθαρός, ἀμίαντος.

εἰλικρινής denotes chiefly that which is pure as being *sincere,* free from foreign admixture. **καθαρός** is that which is pure as being *clean,* free from soil or stain. The meaning of both in the N.T. is distinctly ethical. **ἀμίαντος** is *unspotted,* describing that which is far removed from every kind of contamination.

§ 20. Assembly, church.

συναγωγή, ἐκκλησία, πανήγυρις.

According to their derivation, **συναγωγή** is simply *an assembly*, a mass of people gathered together; **ἐκκλησία** is a narrower word, also *an assembly*, but including only those specially *called together out of* a larger multitude, for the transaction of business. *ἐκκλησία* usually denotes a somewhat more select company than *συναγωγή*. A significant use of *ἐκκλησία* in strict harmony with its derivation was common among the Greeks. It was their common word for the lawful assembly in a free Greek city of all those possessing the rights of citizenship, for the transaction of public affairs. They were *summoned out of* the whole population, "a select portion of it, including neither the populace, nor strangers, nor yet those who had forfeited their civic rights" (Trench). *συναγωγή* had been, before N.T. times, appropriated to designate *a synagogue*, a Jewish assembly for worship, distinct from the Temple, in which sense it is used in the N.T. Probably for that reason, and also for its greater inherent etymological fitness, *ἐκκλησία* is the word taken to designate *a Christian church*, a company of believers who meet for worship. Both these words, however, are sometimes used in the N.T. in a non-technical sense. **πανήγυρις**, occurring only in Heb. xii. 23, differs from both, denoting a solemn assembly for festal rejoicing.

§ 21. Humility, gentleness.

ταπεινοφροσύνη, πρᾳότης.

ταπεινοφροσύνη is *humility*, not the making of one's self small when he is really great, but thinking little of one's self, because this is in a sense the right estimate for any human being, however great. **πρᾳότης** is founded upon this idea, and goes beyond it. It is the attitude of mind and behavior which, arising from humility, disposes one to receive with *gentleness* and *meekness* whatever may come to him from others or from God.

§ 22. Gentleness.

πρᾳότης, ἐπιείκεια.

Both words may be translated *gentleness*, yet there are marked differences in meaning. **πρᾳότης** is rather passive, denoting, as has been said above, see § 21, one's attitude toward others in view of their acts, bad or good. **ἐπιείκεια** is distinctly active, it is seen in one's deeds toward others, and it usually implies the relation of superior to inferior. It is fundamentally a relaxing of strict legal requirements concerning others, yet doing this in order more fully to carry out the real spirit of the law. It is *clemency* in which there is no element of weakness or injustice.

§ 23. Desire, lust.

ἐπιθυμία, πάθος, ὁρμή, ὄρεξις.

ἐπιθυμία is the broadest of these words. Its meaning may be good, but it is usually bad. It denotes any natural desire or appetite, usually with the implication that it is a depraved desire. **πάθος** has not as broad a meaning as in classical Greek, but denotes evil desire, chiefly, however, as a condition of the soul rather than in active operation. **ὁρμή** indicates *hostile* motion toward an object, either for seizing or repelling. **ὄρεξις** is a desire or appetite, especially seeking the object of gratification in order to make it one's own.

§ 24. Affliction.

θλῖψις, στενοχωρία.

θλῖψις according to its derivation means *pressure.* In its figurative sense it is that which presses upon the spirit, *affliction.* **στενοχωρία** meant originally *a narrow, confined space.* It denotes affliction as arising from cramping circumstances. In use it cannot always be distinguished from *θλῖψις*, but it is ordinarily a stronger word.

§ 25. Bad, evil.

κακός, πονηρός, φαῦλος.

These words may be used with very little distinction of meaning, but often the difference is marked. **κακός** frequently means *evil* rather negatively, referring to the absence of the qualities which constitute a person or thing what it should be or what it claims to be. It is also used meaning *evil* in a moral sense. It is a general antithesis to *ἀγαθός*. **πονηρός** is a word at once stronger and more active, it means *mischief-making*, delighting in injury, doing evil to others, dangerous, destructive. *κακός* describes the quality according to its nature, *πονηρός*, according to its effects. **φαῦλος** is the bad chiefly as the *worthless*, the good for nothing.

§ 26. Punishment.

τιμωρία, κόλασις.

τιμωρία in classical and N.T. usage denotes especially the vindicative character of punishment, it is the punishment in relation to the *punisher*. **κόλασις** in classical Greek meant usually punishment which aimed at the reformation of the offender. But sometimes in later Greek, and always in the N.T., the idea of reformation seems to disappear, so that there remains simply the idea of punishment, but viewed in relation to the *punished*.

§ 27. To pollute.

μιαίνω, μολύνω.

μιαίνω meant originally *to stain*, as with color. **μολύνω** meant originally *to smear over*, as with mud or filth, always having a bad meaning, while the meaning of *μιαίνω* might be either good or bad. According to classical Greek, *μιαίνω* has a religious meaning, *to profane*, while *μολύνω* is simply *to spoil, disgrace*. As ethically applied in the N.T. they have both practically the same meaning, *to pollute, defile*. It is, however, true that *μιαίνω*, to judge from classical usage, refers chiefly to the effect of the act not on the individual, but on others, on the community.

§ 28. To do.

ποιέω, πράσσω.

These words are often used interchangeably, but in many cases a distinction can be drawn. **ποιέω** refers more to the object and end of an act, **πράσσω** rather to the means by which the object is attained. Hence, while *ποιέω* means *to accomplish*, *πράσσω* may mean nothing more than merely *to busy one's self about*. *ποιέω* often means to do a thing once for all, *πράσσω*, to do continually or repeatedly. From these distinctions it follows that *ποιέω*, being on the whole the higher word, is more often used of doing good, *πράσσω* more frequently of doing evil.

§ 29. Fleshly, fleshy, sensual.

σαρκικός, σάρκινος, ψυχικός.

σαρκικός means *fleshly*, that which is controlled by the wrong desires which rule in the flesh, flesh often being understood in its broad sense, see *σάρξ*. It describes a man who gives the flesh the dominion in his life, a place which does not belong to it by right. It means distinctly opposed to the Spirit of God, anti-spiritual. **σάρκινος** properly means *fleshy*, made of flesh, flesh being the material of which it is composed. When given a bad meaning, however, it is plainly similar to *σαρκικός*, but according to Trench not so strong, denoting one as unspiritual, undeveloped, rather than anti-spiritual. Others, as Cremer and Thayer, with more probability make *σάρκινος* the stronger, it describes one who is flesh, wholly given up to the flesh, rooted in the flesh, rather than one who simply acts according to the flesh (*σαρκικός*). There is much confusion between the two in the N.T. manuscripts. **ψυχικός** has a meaning somewhat similar to *σαρκικός*. Both are used in contrast with *πνευματικός*. But *ψυχικός* has really a distinct meaning, describing the life which is controlled by the *ψυχή*. It denotes, therefore, that which belongs to the animal life, or that which is controlled simply by the appetites and passions of the sensuous nature.

§ 30. Mercy, compassion.

ἔλεος, οἰκτιρμός.

Both words denote sympathy, fellow-feeling with misery, mercy, compassion. **ἔλεος,** however, manifests itself chiefly in acts rather than words, while **οἰκτιρμός** is used rather of the inward feeling of compassion which abides in the heart. A criminal might ask for *ἔλεος*, *mercy*, from his judge; but hopeless suffering may be the object of *οἰκτιρμός*, *compassion*.

§ 31. To love.

ἀγαπάω, φιλέω.

ἀγαπάω, and not **φιλέω,** is the word used of God's love to men, *φιλανθροπία* is, however, once used with this meaning, Tit. iii. 4. *ἀγαπάω* is also the word ordinarily used of men's love to God, but *φιλέω* is once so used, 1 Cor. xvi. 22. *ἀγαπάω* is the word used of love to one's enemies. The interchange of the words in Jn. xxi. 15–17 is very interesting and instructive.

§ 32. To will, to wish.

βούλομαι, θέλω.

In many cases these two words are used without appreciable distinction, meaning *conscious willing, purpose*. But frequently it is evident that a difference is intended, although there is much difference of opinion as to the exact distinction. Thayer says that **βούλομαι** "seems to designate the will which follows deliberation," **θέλω,** "the will which proceeds from inclination." Grimm, on the other hand, says that *θέλω* gives prominence to the emotive element, *βούλομαι* to the rational and volitive; *θέλω* signifies the choice, while *βούλομαι* marks the choice as deliberate and intelligent. The view of Cremer on the whole seems preferable to any other. According to this view, *βούλομαι* has the wider range of meaning, but *θέλω* is the stronger word, *θέλω* denotes the active resolution, the will urging on to action, see Ro. vii. 15, while *βούλομαι* is rather to have in thought, to intend, to be determined. *βούλομαι* sometimes means no more than to have an inclination, see Ac. xxiii. 15. Instructive examples of the use of the two words in close proximity are found in Mar. xv. 9, 15, and especially Mat. i. 19.

§ 33. Schism.

σχίσμα, αἵρεσις.

σχίσμα is *actual division, separation.* **αἵρεσις** is rather *the separating tendency,* so it is really more fundamental than *σχίσμα.*

§ 34. Mind, understanding.

νοῦς, διάνοια.

νοῦς is distinctly *the reflective consciousness,* "the organ of moral thinking and knowing, the intellectual organ of moral sentiment" (Cremer). **διάνοια** meant originally *activity of thinking,* but has borrowed from *νοῦς* its common meaning of *faculty of thought.* It is more common than *νοῦς*, and has largely replaced it in its usual meanings.

§ 35. Law.

νόμος, θεσμός, ἐντολή, δόγμα.

νόμος is the common word meaning *law.* It may mean law in general. In the N.T., however, it usually means the law of God, and most frequently the Mosaic law. **θεσμός** is law considered with special reference to the authority on which it rests. **ἐντολή** is more specific, being used of a particular command. **δόγμα** is an authoritative conclusion, a proposition which it is expected that all will recognize as universally binding.

§ 36. Type, image.

τύπος, ἀντίτυπος.

τύπος has many meanings, among the most common being *image*, *pattern* or *model*, and *type*. In the last sense it means a person or thing prefiguring a future person or thing, *e.g.*, Adam as a type of Christ, Ro. v. 14. **ἀντί-τυπος**, as used in 1 Pet. iii. 21, is by Thayer and many others thought to correspond to *τύπος* as its counterpart, in the sense which the English word antitype suggests. By Cremer it is rather given the meaning *image*.

§ 37. To ask.

αἰτέω, ἐρωτάω.

Thayer, as opposed to Trench and others, would make the distinction between these two words to be this: "**αἰτέω** signifies to ask for something to be given, not done, giving prominence to the thing asked for rather than the person, and hence is rarely used in exhortation. **ἐρωτάω**, on the other hand, is to request a person to do (rarely to give) something; referring more directly to the person, it is naturally used in exhortation, etc."

§ 38. World, age.

αἰών, κόσμος.

It is only in a part of their meanings that these two words are in any real sense synonymous, and it is that part which is here considered. Both A. V. and R. V. often translate **αἰών** by *world*, thus obscuring the distinction between it and **κόσμος**. *αἰών* is usually better expressed by *age*, it is the world at a given time, a particular period in the world's history. *κόσμος* has very frequently an unfavorable meaning, denoting the inhabitants of the world, mankind in general, as opposed to God. A similar meaning is often attached to *αἰών*, it means the spirit of the age, often in an unfavorable sense. See Ep. ii. 2, where both words occur together. An exceptional meaning for the plural of *αἰών* is found in Heb. i. 2 and xi. 3, where it denotes the worlds, apparently in reference to space rather than time.

§ 39. Rest.

ἀνάπαυσις, ἄνεσις.

Both words in a certain sense mean *rest*, but from different standpoints. **ἀνάπαυσις** is rest which comes by cessation from labor, which may be simply temporary. **ἄνεσις** means literally the relaxation of strings which have been drawn tight. Hence, it is used to designate ease, especially that which comes by relaxation of unfavorable conditions of any kind, such as affliction.

§ 40. Wind.

πνεῦμα, πνοή, ἄνεμος, λαῖλαψ, θύελλα.

πνεῦμα when used in its lower meaning to denote wind means simply *an ordinary wind,* a regularly blowing current of air of considerable force. **πνοή** is distinguished from it as being a gentler motion of the air. **ἄνεμος,** on the other hand, is more forcible than *πνεῦμα,* it is the strong, often the tempestuous, wind. **λαῖλαψ** is the violent fitful wind which accompanies a heavy shower. **θύελλα** is more violent than any of the others, and often implies a conflict of opposing winds.

§ 41. Old.

παλαιός, ἀρχαῖος.

According to their derivation, **παλαιός** is that which has been in existence for a long time, **ἀρχαῖος** that which has been from the beginning. In use, at times no distinction can be drawn. Often, however, *ἀρχαῖος* does denote distinctively that which has been from the beginning, and so it reaches back to a point of time beyond *παλαιός.* *παλαιός* has often the secondary meaning of that which is old and so worn out, having suffered more or less from the injuries and ravages of time, its opposite in this sense being *καινός.*

§ 42. Harsh, austere.

αὐστηρός, σκληρός.

αὐστηρός has not necessarily an unfavorable meaning. It is well represented by the word *austere,* it means one who is earnest and severe, strict in his ways, opposed to all levity. By implication it may have the unfavorable meaning of harshness or moroseness. **σκληρός** has always an unfavorable meaning. It indicates one who is uncivil, intractable, rough and harsh. There is in it the implication of inhumanity.

§ 43. Darkness.

σκότος, γνόφος, ζόφος, ἀχλύς.

σκότος is a general word, meaning *darkness* in any sense. **γνόφος** usually refers to darkness that accompanies a storm. **ζόφος** meant originally *the gloom* of twilight. It was then applied in classical Greek to the darkness of the underworld, the gloom of a sunless region. The latter meaning seems to be practically the one which the word has in the N.T. **ἀχλύς** is specifically a misty darkness.

§ 44. People, nation.

λαός, ἔθνος, δῆμος, ὄχλος.

λαός is a word which is usually limited in use to the chosen people, Israel. **ἔθνος** in the singular is a general term for nation, applied to any nation, even to the Jews. In the plural it ordinarily denotes all mankind aside from the Jews and in contrast with them, the Gentiles. **δῆμος** is a people, especially organized and convened together, and exercising their rights as citizens. **ὄχλος** is *a crowd*, an unorganized multitude, especially composed of those who have not the rights and privileges of free citizens.

§ 45. Servant, slave.

δοῦλος, θεράπων, διάκονος, οἰκέτης, ὑπηρέτης.

δοῦλος is the usual word for *slave*, one who is permanently in servitude, in subjection to a master. **θεράπων** is simply one who renders service at a particular time, sometimes as a slave, more often as a freeman, who renders voluntary service prompted by duty or love. It denotes one who serves, *in his relation to a person*. **διάκονος** also may designate either a slave or a freeman, it denotes a servant viewed *in relation to his work*. **οἰκέτης** designates a slave, sometimes being practically equivalent to *δοῦλος*. Usually, however, as the etymology of the term indicates, it means a slave as a member of the household, not emphasizing the servile idea, but rather the relation which would tend to mitigate the severity of his condition. **ὑπηρέτης** means literally *an under-rower*, and was used to describe an ordinary rower on a war-galley. It is then used, as in the N.T., to indicate any man, not a slave, who served in a subordinate position under a superior.

§ 46. To adulterate.

καπηλεύω, δολόω.

Both these words mean *to adulterate*, and some maintain that they are practically identical. But it is more probable that **δολόω** means simply to adulterate, while **κατηλεύω** conveys the idea of adulterating for the sake of making an unjust profit by the process.

§ 47. Animal.

ζῶον, θηρίον.

ζῶον is a general term, meaning *living creature*, which may include all living beings, in classical Greek even including man. In the N.T. it means ordinarily *animal*. **θηρίον** is *beast*, usually wild beast. It implies perhaps not necessarily wildness and ferocity, but at least a certain amount of brutality which is wanting in *ζῶον*. *ζῶον* emphasizes the qualities in which animals are akin to man, *θηρίον*, those in which they are inferior.

§ 48. Sea.

θάλασσα, πέλαγος.

θάλασσα is the more general word, indicating *the sea* or *ocean* as contrasted with the land or shore. It may be applied to small bodies of water. **πέλαγος** is *the open sea*, the uninterrupted expanse of water, in contrast with the portions broken by islands or with partly inclosed bays. The prominent thought is said by Trench to be breadth rather than depth. Noteworthy is the distinction between the two words in Mat. xviii. 6.

§ 49. To grieve.

λυπέομαι, πενθέω, θρηνέω, κόπτομαι.

λυπέομαι is the most general word, meaning simply *to grieve*, outwardly or inwardly. **πενθέω** means properly *to lament for the dead*. It is also applied to passionate lamentation of any kind, so great that it cannot be hid. **θρηνέω** is *to give utterance to a dirge* over the dead, either in unstudied words, or in a more elaborate poem. This word is used by S. in describing David's lament over Saul and Jonathan. **κόπτομαι** is *to beat the breast in grief*, ordinarily for the dead.

§ 50. Form, appearance.

ἰδέα, μορφή, σχῆμα.

ἰδέα denotes merely *outward appearance*. Both **μορφή** and **σχῆμα** express something more than that. They too denote outward form, but as including one's habits, activities and modes of action in general. In *μορφή* it is also implied that the outward form expresses the inner essence, an idea which is absent from *σχῆμα*. *μορφή* expresses the form as that which is intrinsic and essential, *σχῆμα* signifies the figure, shape, as that which is more outward and accidental. Both *σχῆμα* and *ἰδέα* therefore deal with externals, *σχῆμα* being more comprehensive than *ἰδέα*, while *μορφή* deals with externals as expressing that which is internal.

§ 51. Clothing.

ἱμάτιον, χιτών, ἱματισμός, χλαμύς, στολή, ποδήρης.

ἱμάτιον is used in a general sense to mean *clothing*, and may thus be applied to any garment when it is not desired to express its exact nature. In a more specific use, however, it denotes the large loose outer garment, *a cloak*, which ordinarily was worn, but in working was laid aside. **χιτών** is best expressed by the word *tunic*. It was a closely fitting under-garment, usually worn next the skin. At times, especially in working, it was the only garment worn. A person clothed only in the *χιτών* was often called *γυμνός* (Jn. xxi. 7). *ἱμάτιον* and *χιτών* are often found associated as the upper and under garment respectively. **ἱματισμός** does not denote a specific garment, but means *clothing*, being used, however, ordinarily only of garments more or less stately or costly. **χλαμύς** is *a robe* or *cloak*, it is a technical expression for a garment of dignity or office. **στολή** is any stately robe, ordinarily long, reaching to the feet or sweeping the ground, often worn by women. **ποδήρης** was originally an adjective meaning *reaching to the feet*. It can hardly be distinguished in use from *στολή*. It occurs only in Rev. i. 13.

§ 52. New.

νέος, καινός.

νέος is *the new* as contemplated under the aspect of time, that which has recently come into existence. **καινός** is *the new* under the aspect of quality, that which has not seen service. *καινός* therefore often means new as contrasted with that which has decayed with age, or is worn out, its opposite then being *παλαιός*. It sometimes suggests that which is unusual. It often implies praise, the new as superior to the old. Occasionally, on the other hand, it implies the opposite, the new as inferior to that which is old, because the old is familiar or because it has improved with age. Of course it is evident that both *νέος* and *καινός* may sometimes be applied to the same object, but from different points of view.

§ 53. Labor.

μόχθος, πόνος, κόπος.

μόχθος is *labor*, hard and often painful. It is the ordinary word for common labor which is the usual lot of humanity. **πόνος** is *labor* which demands one's whole strength. It is therefore applied to labors of an unusual kind, specially wearing or painful. In classical Greek it was the usual word employed to describe the labors of Hercules. **κόπος** denotes *the weariness* which results from labor, or labor considered from the stand-point of the resulting weariness.

§ 54. Drunkenness, drinking.

μέθη, πότος, οἰνοφλυγία, κῶμος, κραιπάλη.

μέθη is the ordinary word for *drunkenness*. **πότος** is rather concrete, *a drinking, carousing*. **οἰνοφλυγία** is a prolonged condition of drunkenness, *a debauch*. **κῶμος** includes *riot* and *revelry*, usually as arising from drunkenness. **κραιπάλη** denotes *the sickness* and *discomfort* resulting from drunkenness.

§ 55. War, battle.

πόλεμος, μάχη.

πόλεμος ordinarily means *war*, *i.e.*, the whole course of hostilities; **μάχη**, *battle*, a single engagement. It is also true that *μάχη* has often the weaker force of *strife* or *contention*, which is very seldom found in *πόλεμος*.

§ 56. Basket.

σπυρίς, κόφινος.

These words in the N.T. are used with an evident purpose to discriminate between them. The distinction, however, does not seem to have been chiefly one of size, as some have thought, but of use. **σπυρίς** is usually a basket for food, *a lunch-basket, a hamper,* while **κόφινος** is a more general term for *basket.* The descriptions of the two miracles of feeding the multitude use always different words in the two cases, see *e.g.* Mar. viii. 19, 20.

§ 57. It is necessary.

δεῖ, ὀφείλει.

δεῖ, the third person of *δέω*, is commonly used impersonally in classical Greek. This usage is less common, but frequent, in the N.T. *δεῖ* indicates a necessity in the nature of things rather than a personal obligation, it describes that which *must* be done. **ὀφείλει** indicates rather the personal obligation, it is that which is proper, something that *ought* to be done.

§ 58. Tax.

φόρος, τέλος, κῆνσος, δίδραχμον.

φόρος indicates *a direct tax* which was levied annually on houses, lands, and persons, and paid usually in produce. **τέλος** is *an indirect tax* on merchandise, which was collected at piers, harbors, and gates of cities. It was similar to modern import duties. **κῆνσος,** originally an enrollment of property and persons, came to mean *a poll-tax,* levied annually on individuals by the Roman government. **δίδραχμον** was the coin used to pay an annual tax levied by the religious leaders of Israel for the purpose of defraying the general expenses of the Temple.

§ 59. Tax-collector.

τελώνης, ἀρχιτελώνης.

The Roman system of collecting taxes, especially the *τέλοι,* in their provinces, included ordinarily three grades of officials. There was the highest, called in Latin *publicanus,* who paid a sum of money for the taxes of a certain province, and then exacted that and as much more as he could from the province. This man lived in Rome. Then there were the *sub-magistri,* who had charge each of a certain portion of territory, and who lived in the provinces. Then there were the *portitores,* the actual custom-house officers, who did the real work of collecting the taxes. The N.T. word **τελώνης** is used to describe one of the *portitores,* it is the lowest of these three grades. It does not correspond to the Latin *publicanus*, and the word *publican* used to translate it in A. V. and R. V. is apt to be misleading, *tax-collector* would be better. **ἀρχιτελώνης**, only occurring in Lu. xix. 2, evidently describes a higher official than *τελώνης*, and is probably one of the *submagistri*, the next higher grade.

§ 60. Child.

τέκνον, υἱός, παῖς, παιδίον, παιδάριον, παιδίσκη.

τέκνον and **υἱός** both point to parentage. *τέκνον*, however, emphasizes the idea of descent, giving prominence to the physical and outward aspects; while *υἱός* emphasizes the idea of relationship, and considers especially the inward, ethical, and legal aspects. **παῖς** as well as *τέκνον* emphasizes the idea of descent, but gives especial prominence to age, denoting a child as one who is young. *παῖς* is also often used of a servant. The number of years covered by the term *παῖς* is quite indefinite. Its diminutives **παιδίον** and **παιδάριον** are used without appreciable difference to denote a young child. (*παιδίσκος* in classical Greek and) **παιδίσκη**, in which the diminutive force is largely lost, cover the years of late childhood and early youth.

§ 61. Tribe, family, household.

φυλή, πατριά, οἶκος.

These words form a series. **φυλή** is sometimes *a race, nation*, but usually *a tribe*, such as one of the twelve tribes of Israel, descended from the twelve sons of Jacob. **πατριά** is a smaller division within the tribe, it is an association of families closely related, in the N.T. generally used of those descended from a particular one of the sons of Jacob's sons. **οἶκος** is yet narrower, *household*, including all the inmates of a single house, being the unit of organization.